Clue. 1-055

- Cambridge

Oct. 1958

CONCISE

ETYMOLOGICAL DICTIONARY

OF THE

ENGLISH LANGUAGE

SKEAT

Oxford University Press, Amen House, London E.C. 4

GLASGOW NEW YORK TORONTO MELBOURNE WELLINGTON
BOMBAY CALCUTTA MADRAS KARACHI CAPE TOWN IBADAN

Geoffrey Cumberlege, Publisher to the University

A CONCISE

ETYMOLOGICAL DICTIONARY

OF THE

ENGLISH LANGUAGE

BY THE REV.

WALTER W. SKEAT

LITT.D., LL.D., D.C.L., PH.D., F.B.A,

ELRINGTON AND BOSWORTH PROFESSOR OF ANGLO-SAXON IN THE UNIVERSITY OF
CAMBRIDGE, AND FELLOW OF CHRIST'S COLLEGE

NEW AND CORRECTED IMPRESSION

'Were man to live co-eval with the sun,
The patriarch-pupil would be learning still.'
YOUNG, *Night Thoughts*, vii. 86

OXFORD
AT THE CLARENDON PRESS

IMPRESSION OF 1956
FIRST EDITION 1882

PRINTED IN GREAT BRITAIN
AT THE UNIVERSITY PRESS, OXFORD
BY CHARLES BATEY, PRINTER TO THE UNIVERSITY

CONTENTS

PREFACE

TO THE EDITION OF 1911

'A Concise Etymological Dictionary of the English Language' was first published in 1882, and, after passing through several editions, appeared in 1901 in a new form, so largely re-arranged and re-written as to become, practically, a new book.

The edition of 1901 has now been again revised, and numerous corrections have been made, chiefly due to the new light which has been thrown upon some words by the advance of the publication of the New English Dictionary, and by the appearance of new works upon etymology. Among the latter I may especially instance the *Lateinisches Etymologisches Wörterbuch* by Dr. Alois Walde, published at Heidelberg in 1906.

Cambridge, *Dec.*, 1910.

INTRODUCTION

THE first edition of my 'Concise Etymological Dictionary of the English Language' was published in 1882, and it has since passed through several editions.

Each successive edition contained several corrections and additions, in order that the work might be, to some extent, brought up to date.

Meanwhile, numerous and important contributions have been made, by many writers, to the study of Indo-germanic philology; more exact methods of analysing phonetic changes have been adopted, and important advances have been made at many points. Such works as Kluge's Etymological Dictionary of German, Franck's Etymological Dictionary of Dutch, Godefroy's Dictionary of Old French, the Modern French Dictionary by Hatzfeld and Darmesteter, in addition to other highly important books such as the Comparative Grammar of the Indo-germanic languages by Brugmann, have all contributed to a much clearer and more exact view of the science of comparative philology. Hence the time has come when partial emendations of my Concise Dictionary, however diligently made, have (as I fear) failed to keep pace with the requirements of the present day; and I have accordingly rewritten the book from beginning to end, making improvements in nearly every article, whilst at the same time introducing into the body of the work words which have hitherto necessarily been relegated to a continually increasing Supplement. The result is less a new edition than a new book.

Since the year 1882 above-mentioned, a great advance has been made in English lexicography. An entirely new edition of Webster appeared in 1890, and The Century Dictionary, of which the publication was begun in 1889, was completed in 1891. In both of these works my name appears in the 'List of Authorities cited'; though it is seldom expressly mentioned except in cases of considerable difficulty, where the writer preferred not to risk an opinion of his own. But the chief event during this period has been the publication of The New English Dictionary on Historical Principles, the unique value of which is even now too little understood and respected by the general public. The first part of this great national work appeared in 1884.

The chief difference between the second and later editions of my Concise Etymological Dictionary and the present one can now be readily explained. The former editions were mainly reproduced from the first edition, at a time when, from the nature of the case, little help could be had from the works above-mentioned, owing to the fact that they either did not exist or could not be much utilised. But in the present work, I have endeavoured to glean from them all their most important results. The work has been collated with the Century Dictionary throughout, and with the New English Dictionary from A to H (excepting a small portion of G). I have endeavoured to make good use of Kluge, Franck, Brugmann, and other authorities; and have gladly adopted a large number of corrections. In particular, I have now marked the quantities of all the vowels in Latin words, as this often throws much light upon Romance phonology. And in many cases where the result is tolerably certain I have given the primitive types of Teutonic and even of Indo-germanic words.

In all former editions, I endeavoured, by help of cross-references, to arrange derivative words under a more primitive form. Thus *ex-cite*, *in-cite*, *re-cite* and *resus-cit-ate* were all given under *Cite*. But experience has shewn that this endeavour was more ambitious than practical, often causing needless delay and trouble. Hence the only truly practical order, viz. an alphabetical one, has been here adopted, so that the required word can now be found at once. But in order to retain the chief advantages of the old plan, I have prepared two lists, one of Latin and one of Greek words, which account for a large number of derivatives. These will be found in the Appendix, § III, at pp. 632 and 644.

I have much pleasure in mentioning two more circumstances by which I have been greatly assisted and encouraged. Some few years ago, my friend the Rev. A. L. Mayhew was so good as to go patiently through every word of the Concise Etymological Dictionary, making hundreds of suggestions for improvement; and finally sent me the copy in which all these suggestions were entered. They have all been carefully considered, and in a very large number of instances have been fully adopted. Again, while the revises were passing through the press, they were read over by Mr. H. M. Chadwick, M.A., Fellow of Clare College, Cambridge, author of 'Studies in Old English' published by the Cambridge Philological Society in 1899; and his exact knowledge of Indo-germanic phonology has been suggestive of many improvements. I have only to add, in justice to these scholars, that they are not responsible for all the results here given. In some few cases I have held to my own preconceived opinion; perhaps not always wisely. Still it was best that the final form of each article should be left to the author's decision; for the reader is then sure as to where he must lay any blame.

Many articles which, in former editions, appeared only in the Supplement have now been incorporated with the rest, so that the number of words now explained (in alphabetical order) amounts to more than 12,750.

Considerable pains have been taken to ensure accuracy in the printing of the forms cited; and I have received much help from the care exercised by the press-reader. At the same time, I shall be thankful to any reader who will kindly send me a note of any error which he may detect. I have myself discovered, for example, that under the word *Cemetery* the 'Skt. *çi*' is an error for the 'Skt. *çī*.' A few belated corrections appear at pp. 662–3.

As I frequently allude to the ordinary vowel-changes in the course of the work, I may note here those which are the most elementary and common. They deserve to be learnt by heart at once.

ANGLO-SAXON. The most usual vowel-change is that produced by the occurrence of an *i* or *j* (which often disappears by a subsequent contraction of the word) in the following syllable. Owing to this, we frequently find that the vowels, as arranged in row (1) below, are changed into the corresponding vowels in row (2).

(1) *a, u* (*o*), *ea,*   *eo,*   *ā, ō, ū,*   *ēa,*   *ēo.*
(2) *e,   y,   ie*(*y*), *ie*(*y*), *ǣ, ē, ȳ, īe*(*ȳ*, O. Merc. *ē*), *īe*(*ȳ*).

Example:—*fyllan*, to fill, for **fulljan*; from *full*, full.

Moreover, substantives and secondary verbs are often formed from bases seen in the past tense singular, past tense plural, or past participle of a strong verb, rather than from the infinitive mood. Thus *band* and *bend* are from the base seen in the A. S. *band*, pt. t. of *bindan*, to bind; whilst *bundle* is derived from that which appears in the pp. *bund-en*. By way of distinction, I refer to *bind-* as the 'prime grade,' to *band-* as the 'second grade,' and to *bund-* as the 'weak grade.'

Lastly, our modern words of native origin belong rather to the Midland (or Old Mercian) dialect than to the 'Anglo-Saxon' or Wessex; and Old Mercian employs *a* (mutated to *e*) where the A. S. has *ea*, and sometimes *e* for A. S. *eo*.

ICELANDIC. This language abounds in somewhat similar vowel-changes, but very few of these appear *in English*. But we must not pass over the frequent formation of derivatives from the past tenses (singular or plural) and the past participles of strong verbs. Thus *bait*, Icel. *beita*, lit. 'to cause to bite,' is the causal of *bīta*, to bite; its form may be explained by the fact that the pt. t. of *bīta* is *beit*.

Again, as regards the Romance languages, especially French, it must be borne in mind that they are also subject to phonetic laws. These laws are sufficiently illustrated in Mr. Paget Toynbee's translation of Brachet's Historical French Grammar. In particular, I may note that most French substantives are derived from Latin *accusatives*; and that to derive *bounty* from *bonitās* (nom.), or *honour* from Lat. *honor* (nom.), is simply impossible.

For fuller information, the reader is referred to my Principles of English Etymology, First and Second Series; the former deals chiefly with the native, and the latter with the foreign elements of the language. My Primer of English Etymology contains some of the more important facts.

I subjoin a key to the plan of the work, and a list of abbreviations.

KEY TO THE GENERAL PLAN OF THE DICTIONARY.

§ 1. Order of Words. Words are given in their alphabetical order; but a few secondary derivatives are explained under some more important form. Thus *campaign* is given under *Camp*, and *cannon* under *Cane*.

§ 2. The Words selected. The word-list contains nearly all primary words of most frequent occurrence, with a few others that are remarkably prominent in literature, such as *unaneled*. Homonymous forms, such as *bay* (used in *five* senses), are numbered.

§ 3. Definitions. Definitions are omitted in the case of common words; but explanations of original forms are added wherever they seemed to me to be necessary.

§ 4. Language. The language to which each word belongs is distinctly marked, in every case, by means of letters within marks of parenthesis. Here the symbol — or ‑ is to be read as 'derived from.' Thus *Abbey* is (F.—L.—Gk.—Syriac); i. e. a French word derived from Latin; the Latin word being, in its turn, from Greek, whilst the Greek word is of Syriac origin.

The order of derivation is always upward or backward, from late to early, and from early to earlier forms.

The symbol + is employed to distinguish forms which are merely *cognate*, and are adduced merely by way of illustrating and confirming the etymology. Thus, *bite* is a purely *English* word, derived from the Anglo-Saxon *bitan*. The other Teutonic forms, viz. the Du. *bijten*, Icel. *bīta*, Swed. *bita*, Dan. *bide*, G. *beissen*, and the other Indo-germanic forms, viz. Lat. *findere* (base *fid-*) and Skt. *bhid*, to cleave, are merely cognate and illustrative. On this point, there commonly exists the most singular confusion of ideas; and there are many Englishmen who are accustomed to derive English, of all things, from *Modern High German!* I therefore introduce this symbol + by way of warning. It has its usual algebraical value of *plus* or *additional*; and indicates 'additional information to be obtained from the comparison of cognate forms.'

The symbol > means 'older than,' or 'more primitive than'; the symbol < means 'younger than,' or 'derived from.'

§ 5. **Symbols of Languages.** The symbols, such as F.=French, are not used in their usual vague sense, so as to baffle the enquirer who wishes to find the words referred to. Every symbol has a *special sense*, and has reference to certain books, in one at least of which the word cited may be found, as I have ascertained for myself by looking them all out. I have purposely used, as far as was practicable, the most easily accessible authorities. The exact sense of each symbol is given in the list below.

§ 6. **Roots.** In some cases, a word is traced back to its original Indo-germanic root. The root is denoted by the symbol √, to be read as 'root.' Thus *bear*, to carry, is from √BHER. Some of these roots are illustrated by the lists in § III of the Appendix.

§ 7. **Derivatives.** The symbol **Der.**, i. e. Derivatives, is used to introduce forms related to the primary word. Thus, under *Act*, I note such derivatives as *act-ion*, *act-ive*, &c., which cause no difficulty.

LIST OF ABBREVIATIONS.

Arab.—Arabic; as in Richardson's Persian and Arabic Dict., ed. F. Johnson; 1829. See also Devic's Supplement to Littré's F. Dict.

A. S.—Anglo-Saxon; as in the dictionaries by Bosworth and Toller, Ettmüller, and Grein; in the Vocabularies edited by T. Wright and Prof. Wülker; and in Sweet's Oldest English Texts.

Bavar. — Bavarian; as in Schmeller's Bayerisches Wörterbuch; 1827–1837.

Bret.—Breton; as in Legonidec's Bret. Dict., ed. 1821.

Brugm.—Brugmann, Grundriss der vergleichenden Grammatik, &c.; vol. i. (2nd ed.), 1897; vol. ii. 1889–90.

C.—Celtic; used as a general term for Irish, Gaelic, Welsh, Breton, Cornish, &c.

Corn.—Cornish; as in Williams' Dict.; 1865.

Dan.—Danish; as in Ferrall and Repp; 1861.

Dan. dial.—Danish dialects; as in Molbech, 1841.

Du.—Dutch; as in Calisch and in the Tauchnitz Dutch Dict. Middle Dutch words are from Oudemans, Hexham (1658), or Sewel (1754).

E.—Modern English; as in N. E. D. (New English Dictionary); and in the Century Dictionary.

M.E.—Middle English (English from the thirteenth to the fifteenth centuries inclusive); as in Stratmann's Old English Dict., new edition, 1891.

F.—French. Most of the forms cited are not precisely *modern* French, but from Cot. = Cotgrave's Dictionary, ed. 1660. This accounts for citation of forms, such as F. *recreation*, without accents; the F. accents being mostly modern. Such words are usually marked M. F. (Middle French). See also the dictionaries by Hatzfeld and Littré.

O. F.—Old French; as in the dictionaries by Godefroy, Burguy, or Roquefort.

Fries.—Friesic; as in Richthofen, 1840.

Gael. — Gaelic; as in Macleod and Dewar, 1839; or Macbain, 1896.

G.—German; as in Flügel, 1883.

Low G.—Low German; as in the Bremen Wörterbuch, 1767.

M. H. G.—Middle High German; as in Schade, Altdeutsches Wörterbuch, 1882.

O. H. G.—Old High German; as in the same volume.

Gk.—Greek; as in Liddell and Scott's Lexicon.

Goth. — Mœso-Gothic; as in Balg's Glossary, 1887-9.

Heb.—Hebrew; as in Gesenius' Dict., 1893.

Hind.—Hindustani; as in Forbes, Bate, or Wilson's Glossary of Indian Terms.

Icel.—Icelandic; as in Cleasby and Vigfusson, 1874.

Idg. — Indo-germanic; the family of languages which includes Sanskrit, Greek, Latin, English, &c.

Irish.—Irish; as in O'Reilly, 1864.

Ital.—Italian; as in Meadows, 1857; Torriano, 1688; and Florio, 1598.

L.—Latin; as in Lewis and Short, 1880.

Late L.—Late Latin; as in the latest edition of Ducange; by L. Favre, 1884-7. (Low L. = Late L. words of non-Latin origin.)

Lith.—Lithuanian; as in Nesselmann's Dict., 1851.

Low G.—Low German; see under G. above.

Malay.—As in Marsden's Dict., 1812; cf. Notes by C. P. G. Scott.

Mex. — Mexican; as in the Dict. by Siméon, Paris, 1885.

M. E.—Middle English; see under E. above.

M. H. G.—Middle High German; see under G. above.

Norw.—Norwegian; as in Aasen's Norsk Ordbog, 1873.

O. F.—Old French; see under F. above.

O. H. G.—Old High German; see under G. above.

O. Sax.—Old Saxon; as in the Heliand, &c., ed. Heyne.

O. Slav.— Old Slavonic; as in Miklosich, Etym. Dict., Vienna, 1886.

Pers.—Persian; as in Richardson's Arab. and Pers. Dict.; or in Palmer's Pers. Dict., 1876; cf. Horn, Neupersische Etymologie, 1893.

Peruv.—Peruvian; as in the Dict. by Gonçales, Lima, 1608.

Port.—Portuguese; as in Vieyra, 1857.

Prov.—Provençal; as in Raynouard's Lexique Roman, and Bartsch's Chrestomathie Provençale.

Russ.—Russian; as in Reiff's Dict., 1876.

Scand.—Scandinavian; used as a general term for Icelandic, Swedish, Danish, and Norwegian.

Skt.—Sanskrit; as in Benfey's Dict., 1866.

Span.—Spanish; as in Neumann, ed. Seaone, 1862; Pineda, 1740; or Minsheu, 1623.

Swed.—Swedish; as in the Tauchnitz Dict., or in Widegren, or in Öman.

Swed. dial. — Swedish dialects; as in Rietz (1867).

Teut. — Teutonic; a general term for English, Dutch, German, Gothic, and Scandinavian.

Turk.—Turkish; as in Zenker's Dict., 1866-1876.

W.—Welsh; as in Spurrell, 1861.

OTHER ABBREVIATIONS.

acc.—accusative case.
adj.—adjective.
adv.—adverb.
A.V.—Authorised Version of the Bible, 1611.
cf.—confer, i. e. compare.
Ch.—Chaucer.
comp.—comparative.
conj.—conjunction.
dat.—dative case.
decl.—declensional.
Der.—Derivative.
dimin.—diminutive.
f. or fem.—feminine.
frequent.—frequentative.
gen.—genitive case.
i. e.—id est, that is.
inf.—infinitive mood.
interj.—interjection.
lit.—literally.
m. or masc.—masculine.
n. or neut.—neuter.

nom.—nominative case.
obs.—obsolete.
orig.—original or originally.
pl.—plural.
pp.—past participle.
prep.—preposition.
pres. part.—present participle.
pres. t.—present tense.
prob.—probably.
pron.—pronoun.
prov.—provincial.
pt. t.—past tense.
q. v.—quod vide = which see.
s. v.—sub verbo = under the word.
sb.—substantive.
Shak.—Shakespeare.
sing.—singular.
str. vb.—strong verb.
superl.—superlative.
tr.—translated, or translation.
trans.—transitive.
vb.—verb.

Some of the longer articles are marked off into sections by the use of the Greek letters β, γ. This is merely intended to make matters clearer, by separating the various statements from each other.

Notes at the end of an article are marked off by beginning with the symbol ¶. XIV, XV, XVI, mean that the word was introduced in the 14th, 15th, or 16th century, respectively. Hyphens are freely introduced to shew the *etymological* division of a word. Thus the word *concede* is derived from Lat. *con-cēdere*; meaning that *concēdere* can be resolved into *con-* and *cedere*. This etymological division is often very different from that usually adopted in printed books when words have to be divided; thus *capacious* can only be divided, etymologically, as *cap-ac-i-ous*, because *cap-* is the root-syllable; whereas, when divided according to the pronunciation, it becomes *ca-pa-ci-ous*.

Theoretical forms are marked by an asterisk preceding them. Thus, under *Barrow* (1), the Teutonic type **bergoz*, a hill, is the primitive Teutonic form whence the A.S. *beorg* and the G. *berg* are alike descended; and under *Beetle* (2), the A.S. form *bȳtel* must have been **bētel* in Old Mercian.

The symbols ð and þ are both written for *th*. In Icelandic, þ has the sound of *th* in *thin*, and ð that of *th* in *that*; but the M.E. and A.S. symbols are confused. The M.E. symbol ȝ commonly represents *y* at the beginning of a word, and *gh* in the middle. A.S. short and long vowels, such as *a* and *ā*, are as distinct from each other as ε and η, or *o* and ω in Greek.

The distinction between the two values of A.S. long *æ* (as made by Dr. Sweet in his A.S. Dict.) has been carefully observed. Thus the A.S. *ǣ* invariably represents the mutation of A.S. *ā* (as usual), and corresponds to Goth. *ai*; but A.S. *ê* represents the Wessex sound corresponding to the Anglian and Kentish *ē*, and to Goth. *ē*. For example, *heal* is from A.S. *hǣlan*, cognate with Goth. *hailjan*, G. *heilen*; but *deed* is from O. Merc. *dēd* (Wessex *dêd*), cognate with Goth. *dēds*, G. *that*.

ADDENDA ET EMENDANDA

IN the course of revision, the following Errata have been observed. This list is added for the sake of completeness, as the errors are not serious.

Adieu, l. 1. *For* (F.) *read* (F.—L.)

Adulation. Read *adūlātiōnem, adūlātio, adūlātus, adūlārī.*

Allegory. Read (F.—L.—Gk.) XIV cent.

Audience, l. 5. Read ἀϝισθέσθαι.

Chicken, l. 5. Read *kjūklingr.*

Choose, l. 3. *Read* Du. *kiezen,* G. *kiesen.*

Cost, *vb.* Prob. (Du.—F.—L.) Du. *kosten* ; from O. F. *coster.*

Curl, l. 4. For *krulla* read *krulle.*

Cypress (2), l. 2. *For* (F.—L.) *read* (F.—L.—Gk.).

Diphthong, l. 4. *For* G. *read* Gk.

Engage. *For* (F.—L.) *read* (F.—L. *and* Teut.)

Erotic, l. 2. *For* crude form *read* decl. stem.

Exponent, l. 1. Read *expōnent-.*

Falcon. Some take *falco* to be of Teutonic origin.

Fern, last line. The Gk. πτέρις, πτερόν, are merely given by way of illustration. They are not allied words.

Fusil (1). The L. *focīle* is not found ; but Ital. has this very form.

Gunny, ll. 2, 3. Read *gōṇ, gōṇi.*

Hare, ll. 4, 5. Read *sasnis,* **kasnis.* N.B. The Skt. *çasa* is *not* from *çaç,* to jump ; but perhaps meant ' gray' ; cf. A. S. *hasu,* gray.

History, l. 5. *For* base *read* weak grade.

Holly, ll. 5, 6. For G. *hülst* read Low G. *hulse.*

Hone, l. 4. *For* stem *read* type.

Hyson, l. 6. *For* Chin. *read* Amoy.

Indigent, l. 6. Not allied to ἀχήν.

Mist, l. 9. *Read* √MEIGHw, to darken ; distinct from, &c.

Nasturtium, l. 3. *Read* —also spelt *nasturcium* ; both forms are for *nāstorctiom (Walde).

Notorious, l. 3. *Read* — voucher, witness ; cf. L. pp. *nōtus,* &c.

Pier, l. 2. *Read* — M. E. *pere* ; A. F. *pere,* the Norman equivalent of O. F. *piere.*

Plait, l. 3. Read **plictum.*

Scraggy, l. 5. For *skragga* read *skragger.* (Ross gives Norw. *skragg,* a poor weak creature, *skraggen,* scraggy.)

Shaddock, l. 4. *Read* late in the seventeenth.

Shah, l. 2. Read *khsāyathiya.*

Smith, l. 8. *Read* pp. **smidanoz.*

Throstle, l. 5. *Read* Icel. *þröstr.*

Vernal, last line. For *dir* read *fáir.*

Wheel, l. 8. For QEL read QwEL.

P. 652. The lists given in this Section VI are somewhat uncertain, and are only given tentatively. Several will hereafter require slight readjustment.

A

CONCISE ETYMOLOGICAL DICTIONARY

OF THE

ENGLISH LANGUAGE

—◆◆—

A, indef. art. (E.) See **An.**

A- (1), as in *a-down* = A.S. *ofdūne.* (E.) Here *a-* = A. S. *of*; see **Of, Off.**

A- (2), as in *a-foot.* (E.) For *on foot*; see **On.** ¶ This is the commonest value of the prefix *a-.*

A- (3), as in *a-long.* (E.) Here *a-* = A. S. *and-*; see **Along.**

A- (4), as in *a-rise.* (E.) Here *a-* = A. S. *ā-*; see **Arise.**

A- (5), as in *a-chieve, a-stringent.* (F. —L.; *or* L.) Here *a* = F. prefix *a* = L. *ad,* to; see **Ad-.**

A- (6), as in *a-vert.* (L.) Here *a-* = L. *ā*; see **Ab-** (1).

A- (7), as in *a-mend.* (L.) Here *a-mend* is for *e-mend*; and *e-* = L. *ē* or *ex*; see **Ex-.**

A- (8), as in *a-las.* (F.) See **Alas.**

A- (9), as in *a-byss.* (Gk.) Here *a-* = Gk. *ἀ-* or *ἀν-*; see **Un-, Abyss.**

A- (10), as in *a-do.* (E.) For *at do*; see **At, Ado.**

A- (11), as in *a-ware.* (E.) Here *a-* is for M. E. *y-, i-,* A. S. *ge-*; see **Aware.**

A- (12), as in *a-vast.* (Du.) For Du. *houd vast*; see **Avast.**

Ab- (1), *prefix.* (L.) L. *ab,* from; cognate with E. *of*; see **Of.** In F., it becomes *a-* or *av-*; see **Advantage.**

Ab- (2), *prefix.* (L.) For L. *ad,* to, by assimilation; see **Abbreviate.**

Aback. (E.) For *on back.* A. S. *onbæc*; see **A-** (2) and **Back.**

Abaft. (E.) From the prefix *a-* (2), and *b-aft,* short for *bi-aft,* by aft. Thus *a-b-aft* = on by aft, i.e. at the part which lies to the aft. Cf. M. E. *biaften,* Gen. and Exod. 3377; A.S. *beæftan.* See **A-** (2), **By,** and **Aft.**

Abandon. (F.—Low L.—O. H. G.) M. E. *abandounen,* vb.—F. *abandonner.*— F. *à bandon,* at liberty; orig. in the power (of).—L. *ad,* at; Low L. *bandum, bannum,* an order, decree; from O. H. G. *ban,* summons, ban; see **Ban.**

Abase. (F.—L.) M. E. *abasen,* from **A-** (5) and **Base**; imitating O.F. *abaissier,* to lower.

Abash. (F.) M. E. *abaschen, abaischen, abasen.* — O. F. *esbaiss-,* stem of pres. part. of *esbair* (F. *ébahir*), to astonish.—O. F. *es-* (= L. *ex,* out, very much); and *bair, bahir,* to cause astonishment, a word of imitative origin from the interj. *bah!* of astonishment. ¶ Sometimes confused with *abase* in M. E. See **Bashful.**

Abate. (F.—L.) M. E. *abaten.*— O. F. *abatre.* — Late L. **abbattere,* to beat down (as in Ital.).—L. *ad,* to; and *batere,* for *batuere,* to beat. See **Batter.** ¶ Hence *bate,* for *a-bate.* Cf. **Ab-** (2).

Abbot. (L.—Gk.—Syriac.) M. E. *abbot, abbod,* A.S. *abbod.*—L. *abbāt-* (nom. *abbas*), an abbot, lit. a father.—Gk. *ἀββᾶς.* —Syriac *abbā,* a father; Rom. viii. 15.

abbess. (F. — L. — Gk. — Syriac.) M. E. *abbesse.*—O. F. *abesse, abaesse.* — Late L. *abbāt-issa.*—L. *abbāt-* (as above); and *-issa* = Gk. *-ισσα,* fem. suffix.

abbey. (F. — L. — Gk. — Syriac.) M. E. *abbeye.* — O. F. *abeie.* — Late L. *abbāt-ia.*—L. *abbāt-* (above).

Abbreviate. (L.) From pp. of L. *abbreuiāre*, to shorten. — L. *ab-*, for *ad*, to, by assimilation; and *breuis*, short. See **Ab-** (2) and **Brief.**

Abdicate. (L.) From pp. of L. *ab-dicāre*, to renounce. — L. *ab*, from; *dicāre*, to proclaim. Allied to **Diction.**

Abdomen. (L.) L. *abdōmen* (stem *abdōmin-*), lower part of the belly.

Abduction. (L.) L. *abductiōnem*, acc. of *abductio*, a leading away. — L. *ab-dūcere*, to lead away. — L. *ab*, from; *dūcere*, to lead. Cf. **Duke.**

Abed. (E.) For *on bed*; see **A-** (2) and **Bed.**

Aberration. (L.) From acc. of L. *aberrātio*, a wandering from; from pp. of L. *ab-errāre*. — L. *ab*, from; *errāre*, to wander, err. See **Err.**

Abet, to incite. (F. — Scand.) O.F. *abeter*, to excite, set on (Godefroy). — F. *a-* (Lat. *ad-*); and O.F. *beter*, to bait (a bear), to set on, from Icel. *beita*, to make to bite, causal of *bíta*, to bite. See **Bait, Bite.** Der. *bet*, short for *abet*, sb.

Abeyance, expectation, suspension. (F. — L.) A.F. *abeiance*, suspension, waiting (Roq.). — F. *a*; and *beant*, pres. pt. of O.F. *beer* (F. *bayer*), to gape, expect anxiously. — L. *ad*, at; and *badāre*, to gape.

Abhor. (L.) L. *ab-horrēre*, to shrink from in terror. — L. *ab*, from; *horrēre*, to dread. Cf. **Horrid.**

Abide (1), to wait for. (E.) A.S. *ā-bīdan*; from *ā-*, prefix, and *bīdan*, to bide. See **A-** (4) and **Bide.**

Abide (2), to suffer for, pay for. (E.) In Sh.; corrupted from M.E. *abyen*, to pay for, lit. to buy up, redeem. — A.S. *ābycgan*, to pay for. See **A-** (4) and **Buy.**

Abject, mean, lit. cast away. (L.) L. *ab-iectus*, cast away, pp. of *ab-icere*, to cast away. — L. *ab*, away; *iacere*, to cast. Cf. **Jet** (1).

Abjure. (L.) L. *ab-iūrāre*, to deny; lit. to swear away from. — L. *ab*, from; *iūrāre*, to swear. — L. *iūr-*, from nom. *iūs*, law, right. Cf. **Jury.**

Ablative. (L.) L. *ablātīuus*, lit. taking away. — L. *ab*, from; and *lātum* (= *tlātum*), to bear, take; allied to *tollere*, to take. See **Tolerate.**

Ablaze. (E.) For *on blaze*; see **A-** (2) and **Blaze.**

Able, powerful, skilful. (F. — L.) M.E. *able, hable.* — O.F. *habile, able*, able. — L. *habilis*, easy to handle, active. — L.

habēre, to have. Cf. **Habit.** Der. *ability* from L. acc. *habilitātem.*

Ablution. (F. — L.) F.; from L. acc. *ab-lūtiōnem*, a washing away. — L. *ablūtus*, pp. of *ab-luere*, to wash away. — L. *ab*, from; *luere*, to wash.

Abnegate. (L.) From pp. of L. *ab-negāre*, to deny. — L. *ab*, from; *negāre*, to say no. Cf. **Negation.**

Aboard. (E.) For *on board*; see **A-** (2) and **Board.**

Abode, sb. (E.) M.E. *abood*, delay, abiding. Formed as if from A.S. *ābād*, 2nd stem of *ābīdan*, to abide. See **Abide.**

Abolish. (F. — L.) F. *aboliss-*, stem of pres. pt. of *abolir*. — L. *abolēre*, to abolish.

Abominate. (L.) From pp. of L. *ab-ōminārī*, to turn away from that which is of ill omen. — L. *ab*, away; *ōmin-*, for *ōmen*, an omen.

Aborigines, original inhabitants. (L.) L. *aborīgines*, the nations which, previous to historical record, drove out the Siculi (Lewis and Short). Formed from L. *ab origine*, from the beginning; where *orīgine* is the abl. of *orīgo* (Vergil, Æn. i. 642).

Abortion. (L.) From acc. of L. *abortio*, an untimely birth. — L. *abortus*, pp. of *ab-orīrī*, to fail. — L. *ab*, away; *orīrī*, to arise, begin. Cf. **Orient.**

Abound. (F. — L.) A.F. *abunder*, O.F. *abonder*. — L. *ab-undāre*, to overflow. — L. *ab*, away; *unda*, a wave.

About. (E.) M.E. *abuten, abouten.* A.S. *ābūtan, onbūtan*; short for *on-be-ūtan*; where *be* answers to E. *by*, and *ūtan*, outward, is related to *ūt*, out. See **A-** (2), **By** and **Out.**

Above. (E.) M.E. *aboven, abufen.* A.S. *ābufan*, for *on-be-ufan*; where *be* answers to E. *by*, and *ufan*, upward, is extended from Goth. *uf*, up. See **A-** (2), **By, Up.** (A.S. *ufan* = G. *oben.* A.S. *be-ufan* = Du. *boven.*)

Abrade, to scrape off. (L.) L. *ab-rādere*, to scrape off. — L. *ab*, off; *rādere*, to scrape. Der. *abrasion* (from L. pp. *abrāsus*).

Abreast. (E.) Put for *on breast*; see **A-** (2) and **Breast.**

Abridge. (F. — L.) M.E. *abreggen.* A.F. *abregger*, O.F. *abreger, abregier*, to shorten. — L. *abbreuiāre*, to shorten. — L. *ab-*, put for *ad-*, to; and *breuis*, short. Cf. **Brief. Doublet,** *abbreviate.*

Abroach, to set. (E. *and* F.) Put for *to set on broach*; see **A-** (2) and **Broach.**

Abroad. (E.) M. E. *abrood*; put for *on brood*; lit. on broad; see **A-** (2) and **Broad.**

Abrogate. (L.) From pp. of L. *abrogāre*, to repeal a law.—L. *ab*, away; *rogāre*, to ask, propose a law.

Abrupt. (L.) L. *abruptus*, pp. of *ab-rumpere*, to break off.—L. *ab*, off; *rumpere*, to break.

Abscess. (L.) A gathering of humours into one place; lit. a going away.—L. *abscessus*, a going away; abscess (Celsus). — L. *abscessus*, pp. of *abs-cēdere*, to go away.—L. *abs*, away; *cēdere*, to go, cede.

Abscind. (L.) From L. *ab-scindere*, to cut off.—L. *ab*, off; *scindere*, to cut. **Der.** *abscissa*, from fem. of L. *abscissus*, pp. of *abscindere*.

Abscond, to go into hiding. (L.) L. *abscondere*, to hide. — L. *abs*, away; *condere*, to hide. *Condere* is from *con-* (*cum*), together, and *-dere*, to put, allied to Skt. *dhā*, to put. (√DHE, to place; Brugm. i. § 589.) See **Do.**

Absent, adj. (F.—L.) XIV cent. O. F. *absent*, adj.—L. *absent-*, stem of *absens*, being away.—L. *ab-*, away; *-sens*, being, occurring also in *præ-sens*. Cf. Skt. *sant*, pres. pt. of *as*, to be; from √ES, to be. Cf. **Present, Sooth.** **Der.** *absence*, F. *absence*, L. *absentia*.

Absolute, unrestrained, complete. (L.) L. *absolūtus*, pp. of *ab-soluere*, to set free.—L. *ab*, from; *soluere*, to loosen.

absolve. (L.) L. *ab-soluere*, to set free (above). **Der.** *absolut-ion*, from the pp. above.

Absorb. (L.) L. *absorbēre*, to swallow.—L. *ab*, away; *sorbēre*, to sup up.+ Gk. ῥοφέειν, to sup up. (Brugm. ii. § 801.) **Der.** *absorpt-ion*, from pp. *absorptus*.

Abstain. (F.—L.) F. *abstenir* (O.F. *astenir*).—L. *abs-tinēre*, to refrain from.—L. *abs*, from; *tenēre*, to hold. **Der.** *abstinence*, F. *abstinence*, from L. *abstinentia*, sb.; *abstent-ion*, from the pp.

Abstemious. (L.) L. *abstēmius*, refraining from strong drink. — L. *abs*, from; *tēmētum*, strong drink, whence *tēmu-lentus*, drunken.

Abstract. (L.) L. *abstractus*, pp. of *abs-trahere*, to draw away.—L. *abs*, away; *trahere*, to draw.

Abstruse. (L.) L. *abstrūsus*, diffi-

cult, concealed; pp. of *abs-trūdere*, to thrust away.—L. *abs*, away; *trūdere*, to thrust. See **Intrude.**

Absurd. (L.) L. *absurdus*, inharmonious, foolish.—L. *ab*, from; *surdus*, deaf, inaudible, harsh. Cf. **Surd.**

Abundance. (F.—L.) F. *abondance*. —L. *abundantia*. See **Abound.**

Abuse, vb. (F.—L.) F. *abuser*, to use amiss.—L. *abūsus*, pp. of *ab-ūtī*, to use amiss.—L. *ab*, away (amiss); *ūtī*, to use.

Abut, to project towards. (F.—L. *and* G.) O. F. *abouter*, to thrust towards. — L. *ad*, to; O. F. *bouter*, *boter*, to thrust. See **A-** (5) and **Butt** (1).

Abyss, a bottomless gulf. (L.—Gk.) Milton. L. *abyssus*.—Gk. ἄβυσσος, bottomless.—Gk. ἀ-, short for ἀν-, neg. prefix; and βυσσός, depth. See **A-** (9), **Un-** (1).

Acacia, a tree. (L.—Gk.) L. *acacia*. —Gk. ἀκακία, the thorny Egyptian acacia. —Gk. ἀκίς, a point, thorn. (√AK.) See Brugm. ii. § 52 (4).

Academy. (F. — L. — Gk.) F. *académie*.—L. *acadēmīa*.—Gk. ἀκαδήμεια, a grove where Plato taught, named from the hero *Akademus*.

Accede. (L.) L. *ac-cēdere*, to come towards, assent to.—L. *ac-* (for *ad*), to; *cēdere*, to come, cede.

Accelerate. (L.) From pp. of L. *accelerāre*, to quicken.—L. *ac-* (for *ad*), to; *celer*, quick. Cf. **Celerity.**

Accent. (F.—L.) F. *accent*, sb.—L. acc. *accentum*, a tone.—L. *ac-* (for *ad*); *cantus*, a singing, from *canere*, to sing.

Accept. (F.—L.) F. *accepter*.—L. *acceptāre*, frequentative of *ac-cipere*, to receive.—L. *ac-* (for *ad*), to; *capere*, to take.

Access. (L.) L. *accessus*, a coming unto.—L. *accessus*, pp. of *ac-cēdere*, to accede.—L. *ac-* (for *ad*), to; *cēdere*, to come, cede.

Accident. (F.—L.) F. *accident*, a chance event (Cot.).—L. *accident-*, base of pres. pt. of *ac-cidere*, to happen.—L. *ac-* (for *ad*), to; *cadere*, to fall. **Der.** *accidence*, F. *accidence*, L. *accidentia*.

Acclaim. (L.) Formed from L. *ac-clāmāre*, to cry out at.—L. *ac-* (for *ad*), at; *clāmāre*, to cry out. For the spelling, cf. **Claim.**

Acclivity. (L.) XVII cent. From L. *acclīuitātem*, acc. of *acclīuitas*.—L. *ac-* (for *ad*); and *clīu-us*, sloping, a slope; see **Lean** (1). (√KLEI; Brugm. i. § 463.)

Accolade, the dubbing of a knight. (F. — Ital. — L.) F. *accollade*, in Cotgrave, ed. 1660; lit. an embrace round the neck, then a salutation, light tap with a sword in dubbing a knight. — Ital. *accollata*, fem. of pp. of *accollare*, to embrace about the neck (Florio). — L. *ac-* (for *ad*), to, about; *collum*, the neck.

Accommodate. (L.) From pp. of L. *accommodāre*, to fit, adapt. — L. *ac-* (for *ad*), to; and *commodus*, fit. — L. *com-* (= *cum*), with; and *modus*, measure, mode.

Accompany. (F. — L.) F. *accompagner*, to accompany. — F. *a* (L. *ad*), to; and O. F. *compaing*, companion; see **Company.**

Accomplice. (F. — L.) Put for *a complice*; *a* is the indef. art. — F. *complice*, 'a complice, confederate;' Cot. — L. acc. *complicem*, from *complex*, confederate, lit. 'interwoven.' — L. *com-* (*cum*), together; and stem *plic-*, allied to *plicāre*, to weave. Cf. **Ply.**

Accomplish. (F. — L.) M. E. *acomplisen.* — O. F. *acomplis-*, stem of pres. part. of *acomplir*, to complete. — L. *ad*, to; *complēre*, to fulfil. — L. *com-* (*cum*), together; *plēre*, to fill.

Accord. (F. — L.) A. F. *acorder*, to agree. — Late L. *accordāre*. — L. *ac-* (for *ad*), to; and *cord-*, stem of *cor*, heart. Cf. **Concord.**

Accordion, a musical instrument. (Ital. — L.) From Ital. *accord-are*, to accord, to tune an instrument; with suffix *-ion* (as in *clar-ion*). — Late L. *accordāre*, to agree. See above.

Accost, to address. (F. — L.) F. *accoster*, lit. 'to go to the side of.' — Late L. *accostāre* (same). — L. *ac-* (for *ad*), to; *costa*, rib, side. See **Coast.**

Account, vb. (F. — L.) A. F. *acounter*, *acunter.* — O. F. *a*, to; *conter*, *compter*, to count. — L. *ad*; and *com-putāre*, to compute, from *com-* (*cum*), and *putāre*, to think.

Accoutre. (F. — L. ?) F. *accoutrer*, formerly also *accoustrer*, to dress, array. Etym. quite uncertain; perhaps from O. F. *coustre*, *coutre*, a sacristan who had charge of sacred vestments, from Late L. *custor* = L. *custos*, a custodian, keeper.

Accretion, increase. (L.) From acc. of L. *accrētio*, increase. — L. *accrētus*, pp. of *ac-crescere*, to increase. — L. *ac-* (for *ad*); *crescere*, to grow, inchoative form from *cre-āre*, to make. Cf. **Create.**

Accrue, to come to by way of increase. (F. — L.) From A. F. *acru*, O. F. *acreu*, pp. of *acroistre* (F. *accroître*), to increase. — L. *accrescere*; see above.

Accumulate. (L.) From pp. of L. *ac-cumulāre*, to amass. — L. *ac-* (*ad*), to; *cumulāre*, to heap up, from *cumulus*, a heap.

Accurate. (L.) From pp. of L. *accūrāre*, to take pains with. — L. *ac-* (*ad*), to; *cūrāre*, to care for, from *cūra*, care. See **Cure.**

Accursed, cursed. (E.) Pp. of M. E. *acursien.* A. S. *ā-*, prefix; and *cursian*, to curse; see **A-** (4) and **Curse.**

Accuse. (F. — L.) A. F. *acuser.* — L. *accūsāre*, to lay to one's charge. — L. *ac-* (*ad*), to; and *causa*, *caussa*, a suit at law, a cause.

Accustom. (F. — L.) A. F. *acustumer* (F. *accoutumer*), to make usual. — F. *a* (from L. *ad*, to); and A. F. *custume*, custom. See **Custom.**

Ace, the 'one' on dice. (F. — L. — Gk. ?) M. E. *as.* — O. F. *as.* — L. *as.* [Said to be the Tarentine *ás*, for Gk. *εἷς*, one.]

Acephalous, headless. (Gk.) Gk. *ἀκέφαλ-ος*, headless; with suffix *-ous.* — Gk. *ἀ-*, un- ; and *κεφαλή*, head. See **A-** (9).

Acerbity. (F. — L.) XVI cent. F. *acerbité.* — L. acc. *acerbitātem* (nom. *acerbitas*), bitterness. — L. *acer-b-us*, bitter; cf. *āc-er*, sharp, lit. piercing. — L. *acēre*, to be sour.

Ache, verb. (E.) M. E. *aken*, vb. ; pt. t. *ook.* A. S. *acan.* (√AG, to drive.) ¶ Spelt *ache* by confusion with M. E. *ache*, sb., from A. S. *æce*, a pain. The verb survives, spelt as the obs. sb.

Achieve. (F. — L.) M. E. *acheven.* — A. F. *achever*, to achieve; lit. to come to a head. — O. F. *a chef*, to a head. — L. *ad*, to; *caput*, a head. Cf. **Chief.**

Achromatic, colourless. (Gk.) See **A-** (9) and **Chromatic.**

Acid, sour, sharp. (F. — L.; *or* L.) F. *acide.* — L. *ac-idus*, lit. piercing. (√AK, to pierce.) Der. *acid-i-ty*; *acid-ul-at-ed* (from L. *acid-ul-us*, dimin. of *acid-us*).

Acknowledge. (E.) XVI cent. M. E. *knowlechen* ; from the sb. *knowleche*, mod. E. *knowledge*; see **Knowledge.** The prefix is due to M. E. *aknowen* (=A.S. *oncnāwan*), with the same sense; hence the prefix is **A-** (2).

Acme, top. (Gk.) Gk. *ἀκ-μή*, top, sharp edge. (√AK, to pierce.)

Acolyte, a servitor. (F. – Low L. – Gk.) F. *acolyte,* Cot. – Late L. *acolythus.* – Gk. ἀκόλουθος, a follower. – Gk. ἀ-, with (akin to Skt. *sa-,* with); κέλευθος, a path; so that ἀκόλουθος – a travelling companion.

Aconite, monk's-hood. (F. – L. – Gk.) F. *aconit.* – L. *aconītum.* – Gk. ἀκόνῑτον, a plant; perhaps so called from growing ἐν ἀκόναις, on steep sharp rocks. – Gk. ἀκ-όνη, a whetstone, sharp stone.

Acorn. (E.) M. E. *acorn.* A. S. *æcern,* fruit; properly 'fruit of the field,' from A. S. *æcer,* a field; see **Acre.**+Icel. *akarn,* Dan. *agern,* Goth. *akran,* fruit; from Icel. *akr,* Dan. *ager,* Goth. *akrs,* a field. ¶ Not from *oak.*

Acoustic. (Gk.) Gk. ἀκουστικός, relating to hearing (or sound). – Gk. ἀκούειν, to hear.

Acquaint. (F. – L.) M. E. *acqueynten,* earlier *acointen.* – O. F. *acointer, acointier,* to acquaint with. – Late L. *adcognitāre,* to make known (Brachet). – L. *ad,* to; and **cognitāre,* formed from *cognitus,* pp. of *cognoscere,* to know. See **Quaint.**

Acquiesce. (L.) L. *acquiescere,* to rest in. – L. *ac-* (for *ad*), to; *quiescere,* to rest. See **Quiet.**

Acquire. (L.) L. *acquīrere,* to get, obtain. – L. *ac-* (for *ad*), to; *quærere,* to seek. **Der.** *acquisit-ion;* from pp. *acquīsītus.*

Acquit. (F. – L.) M. E. *aquiten.* – O. F. *aquiter,* to settle a claim; Late L. *acquiētāre.* – L. *ac-* (for *ad*), to; *quiētāre,* vb., formed from *quiētus,* discharged, free, orig. at rest. See **Quiet.**

Acre. (E.) M. E. *aker.* A. S. *æcer.*+ Du. *akker,* Icel. *akr,* Swed. *åker,* Dan. *ager,* Goth. *akrs,* G. *acker;* L. *ager,* Gk. ἀγρός, Skt. *ajra.* Teut. type **akroz;* Idg. type, **agros.* The orig. sense was 'pasture.' (√AG.) **Der.** *acor-n,* q. v.

Acrid, tart. (L.) Coined by adding *-d* to L. *ācri-,* stem of *ācer,* sharp; on the analogy of *ac-id.*

Acrimony. (F. – L.) F. *acrimoine.* – L. *ācri-mōn-ia.* – L. *ācri-,* stem of *ācer* (above).

Acrobat, a tumbler. (F. – Gk.) F. *acrobate.* – Gk. ἀκρόβατος, lit. walking on tiptoe. – Gk. ἄκρο-ν, a point, neut. of ἄκ-ρος, pointed; and βατός, verbal adj. of βαίνειν, to walk; see **Come.**

Acropolis, a citadel. (Gk.) Lit.

'upper city.' – Gk. ἄκρο-s, pointed, upper; and πόλις, a city.

Across. (E. *and* Scand.) For *on cross;* see **A-** (2) and **Cross.**

Acrostic, a short poem in which the initial letters spell a word. (Gk.) Gk. ἀκροστιχίς. – Gk. ἄκρο-s, pointed, also first; and στίχος, a row, line, from weak grade of στείχειν, to go. (√STEIGH.)

Act, sb. (F. – L.) F. *acte.* – L. *actus,* m., and *actum,* n. – L. *actus,* done; pp. of *agere,* to do, drive. See **Agent. Der.** *action;* *act-ive* (F. *actif*); *act-or;* *act-u-al* (L. *actuālis*); *act-uary* (L. *actuārius*); *act-u-ate* (from pp. of Late L. *actuāre,* to perform, put in action).

Acumen. (L.) L. *ac-ū-men,* sharpness, acuteness. Cf. *acuere,* to sharpen.

Acute. (L.) L. *acūtus,* sharp; pp. of *ac-u-ere,* to sharpen. (√AK, to pierce.)

Ad-, *prefix.* (L.) L. *ad,* to, cognate with E. **At.** ¶ L. *ad* becomes *ac-* before *c; af-* bef. *f; ag-* bef. *g; al-* bef. *l;* an- bef. *n; ap-* bef. *p; ar-* bef. *r; as-* bef. *s; at-* bef. *t.*

Adage, a saying. (F. – L.) F. *adage.* – L. *adagium.* – L. *ad;* and *agi-,* as in **agio,* orig. form of *āio,* I say.

Adamant. (F. – L. – Gk.) M. E. *adamaunt,* a diamond, a magnet. – O. F. *adamant.* – L. *adamanta,* acc. of *adamas.* – Gk. ἀδάμας, a very hard metal or stone; lit. 'unconquerable.' – Gk. ἀ- (= E. *un-*); and δαμάω, I conquer, tame. See **Tame.**

Adapt. (F. – L.) Early XVII cent. – F. *adapter.* – L. *ad-aptāre,* to fit to. – L. *ad,* to; *aptāre,* to fit, from *aptus,* fit, apt.

Add. (L.) M. E. *adden.* – L. *addere,* lit. to put to. – L. *ad;* and *-dere,* to put. See **Abscond.**

Adder, a viper. (E.) M. E. *addere;* also *naddere, neddere.* [*An adder* resulted from a *nadder,* by mistake.] A. S. *nædre, næddre,* a snake.+G. *natter,* a snake; also cf. Icel. *naðr,* Goth. *nadrs* (with short *a*).

Addict. (L.) From L. *addict-us,* pp. of *ad-dīcere,* to adjudge, assign. – L. *ad,* to; *dīcere,* to say, appoint. Cf. **Diction.**

Addled, corrupt, unproductive. (E.) Due to an attributive use of the M. E. sb. *adel,* filth, used in the compound *adel-ey,* urine-egg; mistaken form of L. *ōvum ūrīnæ,* wind-egg; due to Gk. οὔριον ᾠόν, wind-egg. Orig. 'mud,' from A.S. *adela,* mud (Grein). Cf. Low G. *adel,* a puddle.

Address, vb. (F. – L.) F. *adresser.*

– F. *a*, to; *dresser*, to direct, dress; see **Dress.**

Adduce. (L.) L. *ad-dūcere*, to lead to, bring forward. – L. *ad*, to; *dūcere*, to lead, bring.

Adept, a proficient. (L.) L. *adeptus*, one who has obtained proficiency; pp. of *adipisci*, to obtain. – L. *ad*, to; *apisci*, to obtain, perhaps related to *aptus*, fit. Cf. **Apt.**

Adequate. (L.) L. *adæquātus*, pp. of *adæquāre*, to make equal to. – L. *ad*, to; *æquāre*, to make equal, from *æquus*, equal.

Adhere. (L.) L. *ad-hærēre*, to stick to. – L. *ad*, to; *hærēre*, to stick.

Adieu, farewell. (F.) M. E. *a dieu.* – F. *à dieu*, (I commit you) to God. – L. *ad Deum*, to God. See **Deity.**

Adipose, fatty. (L.) Late L. *adipōsus*, fatty. – L. *adip*-, stem of *adeps*, sb., fat. Connection with Gk. ἄλειφα, fat, is doubtful.

Adit, access to a mine. (L.) L. *adit-us*, approach, entrance. – L. *adit-um*, supine of *ad-īre*, to go to. – L. *ad*, to; *īre*, to go.

Adjacent, near to. (L.) From base of pres. pt. of L. *ad-iacēre*, to lie near. – L. *ad*, near; *iacēre*, to lie.

Adjective. (F.–L.) F. *adjectif* (fem. *-ive*). – L. *ad-iectīuus*, lit. put near to. – L. *ad-iectus*, pp. of *ad-icere*, to put near. – L. *ad*, to; *iacere*, to cast, throw.

Adjoin, to lie next to. (F.–L.) O.F. *adjoindre*. – L. *ad-iungere* (pp. *adiunctus*), to join to. – L. *ad*, to; *iungere*, to join.

Adjourn, to put off till another day. (F.–L.) O.F. *ajorner*, properly to draw near to day, to dawn; also, to appoint a day for one. – Late L. *adjurnāre*, ' diem dicere alicui ; ' Ducange. – L. *ad*, to; and Late L. *jurnus* (Ital. *giorno*), a day, from L. adj. *diurnus*, daily. – L. *diēs*, a day.

Adjudge. (F.–L.) M. E. *adiugen*; also *aiugen* (=*ajugen*). – O. F. *ajuger*, to decide. – L. *adiūdicāre*, to award. – L. *ad*, to; *iūdicāre*, to judge, from *iūdic*-, base of *iūdex*, a judge. See **Judge.**

Adjudicate. (L.) From pp. of L. *adiūdicāre* (above).

Adjure. (L.) L. *ad-iūrāre*, to swear to; in late L., to put to an oath. – L. *ad*, to; *iūrāre*, to swear. See **Jury.**

Adjust, to fit exactly. (F.–L.) From F. *adjuster*, to adjust, place justly; ' Cot. L. *ad*, to; *iustus*, just, exact; see **Just.** ¶ A new F. formation, due to misunder-

standing the sense of O. F. *ajoster*, to put side by side, arrange. – L. *ad*, to; and *iuxtā*, near; see **Joust.**

Adjutant, lit. assistant. (L.) From L. *adiūtant-em*, acc. of pres. part. of *adiūtāre*, to assist, frequent. of *ad-iuuāre*, to aid. – L. *ad*, to; *iuuāre*, to help. Cf. **Aid.**

Administer. (F.–L.) M. E. *aministren*. – O. F. *aministrer*. – L. *ad-ministrāre*, to minister (to). – L. *ad*, to; *ministrāre*, to serve, from *minister*, a servant. See **Minister.**

Admiral. (F.–Arab.) M. E. *admiral*, more often *amiral*. – O. F. *amiral*, *amirail*, also *amire*; cf. Low L. *admiraldus*, a prince, chief. – Arab. *amīr*, a prince; see **Emir.** The suffix is due to Arab. *al* in *amīr-al-bahr*, prince of the sea.

Admire. (F.–L.) F. *admirer* (O. F. *amirer*). – L. *admīrāri*, to wonder at. – L. *ad*, at; *mīrāri*, to wonder.

Admit. (L.) L. *ad-mittere*, to let to, send to. – L. *ad*, to; *mittere*, to send. Der. *admiss-ion*; from pp. *admiss-us.*

Admonish. (F.–L.) M. E. *amonesten*; so that *admonish* has taken the place of *amonest*, with changed suffix due to verbs in *-ish.* ' I amoneste or warne '; Wyclif, 1 Cor. iv. 14. – O. F. *amonester.* – Late L. *admonestāre*, new formation from L. *admonēre*, to advise. – L. *ad*, to; *monēre*, to advise. Cf. **Monition.**

A-do, to-do, trouble. (E.) M. E. *at do*, to do; a Northern idiom, whereby *at* was used as the sign of the infin. mood, as in Icel., Swedish, &c. See **Do** (1).

Adolescent, growing up. (L.) L. *adolescent-em*, acc. of pres. pt. of *ad-olescere*, to grow up. See **Adult.**

Adopt. (L.) L. *ad-optāre*, to adopt, choose. – L. *ad*, to; *optāre*, to wish.

Adore. (L.) L. *ad-ōrāre*, to pray to. – L. *ad*, to; *ōrāre*, to pray, from *ōs* (gen. *ōr-is*), the mouth. Cf. **Oral.**

Adorn. (L.) L. *ad-ornāre*, to deck. – L. *ad*, to; *ornāre*, to adorn.

Adown, downwards. (E.) M. E. *adune.* A.S. *of-dūne*, lit. from a down or hill. – A.S. *of*, off, from ; and *dūne*, dat. of *dūn*, a hill; see **A-** (1) and **Down** (2).

Adrift. (E.) For *on drift*; see **A-** (2) and **Drift.**

Adroit. (F.–L.) F. *adroit*, dexterous. – F. *à droit*, rightfully. – F. *à* (L. *ad*), to; Late L. *dīrectum*, right, justice, neut. of L. *dīrectus*, pp. of *dī-rigere*, to direct, from L. *dī-* (for *dis-*), apart, and *regere*, to rule.

Adulation, flattery. (F. – L.) F. *adulation.* – L. acc. *adulātiōnem,* from *adulātio,* flattery. – L. *adulātus,* pp. of *adulārī,* to flatter.

Adult. (L.) L. *adultus,* grown up; pp. of *ad-olescere,* to grow up. – L. *ad,* to; **olescere,* inceptive form related to *alere,* to nourish; see **Aliment.**

Adulterate, to corrupt. (L.) XVI cent. – L. *adulterātus,* pp. of *adulterāre,* to corrupt. – L. *adulter,* an adulterer, a debaser of money.

Adultery. (F. – L.) M. E. *avoutrie*; but a later form was *adulterie,* in imitation of Latin. Cf. O.F. *avoutrie, avouterie,* adultery; from *avoutre,* an adulterer, which represented L. *adulter* (see above); so that *avoutrie* was equivalent in sense to L. *adulterium,* adultery.

Adumbrate. (L.) From pp. of L. *ad-umbrāre,* to shadow forth. – L. *ad,* to; *umbra,* a shadow.

Advance, to go forward. (F. – L.) XVI cent. A mistaken form; for M. E. *auancen, avancen.* – F. *avancer,* to go forward or before. – F. *avant,* before. – L. *ab, from; ante,* before. See **Ante-, Van.**

Advantage, profit. (F. – L.) A mistaken form for M. E. *avantage.* – F. *avantage*; formed with suffix *-age* from *avant,* before; see above.

Advent, approach. (L.) L. *aduentus,* approach. – L. *aduentus,* pp. of *ad-uenīre,* to approach. – L. *ad,* to; *uenīre,* to come. Cf. **Venture.**

Adventure. (F. – L.) M.E. *aventure*; with F. *a-* replaced by L. *ad-.* – F. *aventure,* a chance, occurrence. – L. *aduentūra,* fem. of *aduentūrus,* about to happen, fut. part. of *aduenīre,* to approach; see above.

Adverb. (F. – L.) Used to qualify a verb. F. *adverbe.* – L. *aduerbium.* – L. *ad,* to; *uerbum,* a word, a verb.

Adverse. (F. – L.) M.F. *advers* (O.F. *avers*). – L. *aduersus,* turned towards, also opposed to; pp. of L. *aduertere,* to turn to (see below). Der. *advers-ary, adversity.*

Advert. (L.) L. *ad-uertere,* to turn to, regard, heed. – L. *ad,* to; *uertere,* to turn; see **Verse.** Der. *in-advert-ent,* not regarding.

Advertise. (F. – L.) M. E. *avertisen,* later *advertise.* From the base of *avertiss-ant,* pres. pt. of *avertir,* to inform,

warn. – Late L. *aduertēre,* put for L. *aduertere,* to turn to, heed; see above.

Advice. (F. – L.) M. E. *auis* (*avis*), without *d.* – O. F. *avis,* an opinion; orig. a compound word, put for *a vis,* i. e. according to my opinion. – L. *ad,* according to; *uīsum,* that which has seemed good to one, orig. neut. of *uīsus,* pp. of *uidēre,* to see.

Advise. (F. – L.) M. E. *aduisen,* also *auisen* (*avisen*), without *d.* – O. F. *aviser,* to be of opinion. – O. F. *avis* (above).

Advocate, sb. (F. – L.) M. F. *advocat,* 'an advocate;' Cot. – L. *aduocātus,* an advocate, one 'called upon' to plead. – L. *aduocātus,* pp. of *ad-uocāre,* to call to, call upon. – L. *ad,* to; *uocāre,* to call.

Advowson. (F. – L.) A. F. *avoeson,* also *advouson,* patronage; hence the right of presentation to a benefice (Roquefort). – Late L. *aduocātiōnem,* acc. of *aduocātio,* patronage. – Late L. *aduocātus,* a patron; the same as L. *aduocātus,* an advocate.

Adze, a cooper's axe. (E.) M. E. *adse, adese.* A.S. *adesa,* an adze.

Aerial. (L. – Gk.) Formed with suffix *-al* from L. *aëri-us,* dwelling in the air. – L. *aër,* air. – Gk. ἀήρ, air; see **Air.**

Aerolite, a meteoric stone. (Gk.) Also *aerolith,* which is a better form. – Gk. ἀερο-, from ἀήρ, air; λίθ-ος, a stone.

Aeronaut, a balloonist. (F. – Gk.) F. *aéronaute.* – Gk. ἀερο-, from ἀήρ, air; ναύτ-ης, a sailor, from ναῦς, a ship.

Aery, an eagle's nest, brood of eagles or hawks. (F. – Late L.) – F. *aire,* 'an airie or nest of hawkes;' Cot. – Late L. *ārea,* a nest of a bird of prey; of uncertain origin. ¶ Sometimes misspelt *eyry,* by confusion with M. E. *ey,* an egg; see **Egg.**

Æsthetic, refined. (Gk.) Gk. αἰσθη-τικός, perceptive. – Gk. αἰσθέσθαι, to perceive. (√AW; see Brugm. ii. § 841.)

anæsthetic, relieving pain, dulling sensation. – Gk. ἀν-, not; and αἰσθητικός.

Afar. (E.) For *on far.*

Affable. (F. – L.) F. *affable.* – L. *affā-bilis,* easy to be spoken to. – L. *af- = ad,* to; *fārī,* to speak.

Affair. (F. – L.) M. E. *affere.* – O. F. *afeire, afaire,* a business; orig. *a faire,* i. e. (something) to do. – L. *ad,* to; *facere,* to do.

Affect. (L.) L. *affectāre,* to apply oneself to (hence, to act upon); frequent. of *afficere,* to aim at, treat. – L. *af- = ad,* to; *facere,* to do, act. **Der.** *dis-affect.*

Affeer, to assess, confirm. (F.−L.) O. F. *afeurer*, to fix the price of a thing (officially).−Late L. *afforāre*, to fix a price. −L. *af-* (for *ad*); and *forum*, market, price.

Affiance. (F.−L.) O.F. *afiance*, trust; cf. *affier, afier*, to trust (whence E. *affy*).− O. F. *a* (L. *ad*), to; and *fīdant-*, stem of pres. pt. of Late L. *fīdāre*, to trust, from L. *fīdere*, to trust. Cf. Late L. *fīdantia*, a pledge.

Affidavit, an oath. (L.) Late L. *affīdāuit*, 3 p. s. pt. t. of *affidāre*, to pledge.− L. *af-* = *ad*, to; Late L. *fīdāre*, for L. *fīdere*, to trust.

Affiliation. (F.−L.) F. *affiliation*, an adoption as a son.−Late L. acc. *affiliātiōnem.*−L. *af-* = *ad*, to; *filius*, a son.

Affinity. (F.−L) F. *affinité.*−L. *affinitātem*, acc. of *affinitas*, nearness.−L. *affinis*, near, bordering on.−L. *af-* (for *ad*), to, near; *finis*, boundary, end.

Affirm. (F.−L.) M. E. *affermen.*− O. F. *afermer*, to fix.−L. *affirmāre.*−L. *af-* (for *ad*), to; *firmāre*, to make firm, from *firmus*, strong; see **Firm.**

Affix. (L.) Late L. *affixāre* (Ducange), frequent. of L. *affigere* (pp. *affix-us*), to fasten to.−L. *af-* (for *ad*), to; *figere*, to fix.

Afflict, to harass. (L.) XVI cent.−L. *afflictus*, pp. of *affligere*, to strike to the ground.−L. *af-* (for *ad*), to; and *flīgere*, to dash. So also *conflict*, from pp. *con-flictus*; *inflict*; and cf. *pro-flig-ate.*

Affluence. (F.−L.) F. *affluence.*− L. *affluentia*, abundance.−L. *affluent-em* (acc.), flowing towards, pres. part. of *affluere*, to flow to, abound.−L. *af-* (for *ad*), to; *fluere*, to flow.

Afford. (E.) Altered from *aforth*, M.E. *aforthen*, to provide, P. Pl. B. vi. 201.− A. S. *geforðian, forðian*, to further, promote, provide.−A.S. *ge-*, prefix; and *forð*, forth, forward; see **Forth.**

Affray, to frighten. (F.−L. *and* Teut.) XIV cent. M. E. *affrayen.*−O. F. *effraier, esfreër*, to frighten.−Low L. *exfridāre*, to break the king's peace, cause an affray or fray; hence, to disturb, frighten.−L. *ex*; and O. H. G. *friđu* (G. *friede*), peace. (See Romania, 1878, vii. 121.) Der. *affray*, sb., also spelt *fray*; and *afraid*, q.v.

Affreightment, the hiring of a vessel to convey cargo. (F.−L. *and* G.) An E. spelling of F. *affretement*, now written *affrétement*, the hiring of a ship.−F. *affreter* (now *affréter*), to hire a ship.−F.

af-, for L. *ad-*, prefix; and F. *fret*, the freight of a ship. See **Fraught, Freight.**

Affright, to frighten. (E.) The double *f* is late. From M. E. *afright*, used as a pp., affrighted. −A. S. *āfyrht, āfyrhted*, pp. affrighted; from infin. *āfyrhtan* (not used).−A. S. *ā-*, intensive; and *fyrhtan*, to terrify, from *fyrhto*, fright; see **Fright.**

Affront. (F.−L.) M. E. *afronten.*− O. F. *afronter*, to confront, oppose face to face.−Late L. *affrontāre.*−L. *af-* (for *ad*), to; *front-em*, acc. of *frons*, forehead, brow.

Afloat. (E.) For *on float*.

Afoot. (E.) For *on foot*.

Afore. (E.) For *on fore*; A. S. *on-foran*, afore.

Afraid. (F.−L. *and* Teut.) Orig. *affrayed*, i. e. 'frightened.' Pp. of **Affray,** q. v.

Afresh. (E.) For *on fresh* or *of fresh*; see **Anew.**

Aft, After. (E.) A. S. *æftan*, behind; *æfter*, after, both prep. and adv.+Icel. *aptan*, behind, *aptr, aftr*, backwards; Dan. and Swed. *efter*, Du. *achter*, O. H. G. *aftar*, prep. and adv. behind. β. *Aftan* is extended from Goth. *af*, off; see **Of.** *Af-ter* is a comp. form, like Gk. ἀπω-τέρ-ω, further off; it means more off, further off, hence behind. Der. *ab-aft*, q. v.; *after-ward* (see **Toward**).

Aftermath, a second crop of mown grass. (E.) Here *after* is an adj.; and *math* means ' a mowing,' unaccented form of A. S. *mǽþ.* Allied to **Mead, Mow.** Cf. G. *mahd*, a mowing; *nachmahd*, aftermath.

Aftermost, hindmost. (E.) A. S. *æftemest*, Goth. *aftumists*; but affected by *after* and *most.* The Goth. *af-tu-m-ists* is a treble superl. form. See **Aft.**

Aga, Agha, a chief officer. (Turk.) Turk. *aghā*, master.

Again. (North E.) Cf. M. E. *ayein*, A. S. *ongegn* (*ongēan*).−A. S. *on*; and *gegn*, of which the primary meaning seems to have been ' direct,' or ' straight.' (N. E. D.)+Dan. *igien*, Swed. *igen*, again.

against. (North E.) The *t* is added. Cf. M. E. *ayeines*, against; extended from M. E. *ayein*, against, with adv. suffix *-es.* −A. S. *ongēan*, against; the same as A. S. *ongēan, ongegn*, again; see above.+Icel. *ī gegn*, G. *entgegen*, against.

Agate. (F.−It.−L.−Gk.) O.F. *agate, agathe.* −Ital. *agata, agatha*, an agate (Florio).−L. *achātem*, acc. of *achātes.*−

8

Gk. ἀχάτης, an agate; so named from being found near the river *Achates* (Sicily).

Age. (F.–L.) O. F. *aage, edage.*–Late L. *ætāticum.*–L. *ætāti-*, stem of *ætās* (from **æui-tās*), age.–L. *æuum*, life, period.+ Gk. αἰών; Goth. *aiws*; Skt. *āyus*, life. Brugm. ii. § 112.

Agent. (L.) XVI cent. L. *agent-*, stem of pres. pt. of *agere* (pp. *actus*), to do, drive, conduct.+Gk. ἄγειν; Icel. *aka*; Skt. *aj*, to drive. (✓ AG.)

Agglomerate, to mass together. (L.) From pp. of L. *agglomerāre*, to form into a mass.–L. *ag-* (= *ad*); and *glomer-*, stem of *glomus*, a mass, ball, clue of thread, allied to *globus*, a globe; see **Globe.**

Agglutinate. (L.) From pp. of *agglutināre*, to glue together.–L. *ag-* (= *ad*), to; *glutin-*, for *glūten*, glue.

Aggrandise. (F.–L.) M. F. *aggrandis-*, stem of pres. pt. of *aggrandir*, to enlarge. Also *agrandir* (with one *g*).–F. *a* (for L. *ad*); and *grandir*, to increase, from L. *grandīre*, to enlarge, which is from L. *grandis*, great.

Aggravate. (L.) From pp. of L. *aggrauāre*, to add to a load.–L. *ag-* (= *ad*), to; *grauāre*, to load, from *grauis*, heavy.

Aggregate. (L.) From pp. of L. *aggregāre*, to collect into a flock.–L. *ag-* (for *ad*), to; *greg-*, stem of *grex*, a flock.

Aggress, to attack. (F.–L.) M.F. *aggresser.*–L. *aggressus*, pp. of *aggredī*, to assail.–L. *ag-* (for *ad*), to; *gradī*, to advance.

Aggrieve. (F.–L.) M. E. *agreven.*–O. F. *agrever*, to overwhelm.–O. F. *a*, to; *grever*, to burden.–L. *ad*, to; *grauāre*, to weigh down, from *grauis*, heavy, grave. See **Grave** (2).

Aghast, horror-struck. (E.) Misspelt for *agast*, which is short for *agasted*, pp. of M. E. *agasten*, to terrify; Ch. C. T. 2341; Leg. of Good Women, Dido, 248.–A. S. *ā-*, prefix; and *gǣstan*, to terrify, torment. β. A. S. *gǣstan* is from the base *gǣs-* = Goth. *gais-* in *us-gais-jan*, to terrify. (✓ GHwAIS.) Brugm. ii. § 802.

Agile. (F.–L.) XVI cent. F. *agile.* –L. *agilis*, nimble; lit. easily driven about.–L. *agere*, to drive.

Agistment, the pasturage of cattle by agreement. (F.–L.) From the F. vb. *agister*, to assign a resting-place.–F. *a* (=L.*ad*),to; and O.F.*giste*, a couch,lodging, verbal sb. from O. F. *gesir* (F. *gésir*), to lie, from L. *iacēre*, to lie.

Agitate. (L.) L. *agitātus*, pp. of *agitāre*, to keep driving about, frequent. of *agere*, to drive; see **Agent.** (✓ AG.)

Aglet, a tag of a lace. (F.–L.) Also *aygulet*, Spenser, F. Q. ii. 3. 26.–F. *aiguillette*, dimin. of *aiguille*, a needle.–Late L. *acūcula*, dimin. of *ac-us*, a needle, pointed thing. Cf. **Acme.** (✓AK.)

Agnail, (1) a corn on the foot, (2) a sore beside the nail. (E.) The sense has been confused or perverted. From A. S. *angnægl*, a corn on the foot (see A. S. Leechdoms, ii. 81, § 34); with which cf. O. Friesic *ogneil, ongneil*, apparently used in a similar sense. From a prefix *ang-*, signifying afflicting, paining, and A. S. *nægl*, a nail (as of iron), hence a hard round-headed excrescence or wart fixed in the flesh; see **Anger and Nail.** β Soon misunderstood as referring to the *nails* of the toes or fingers, and so made to mean 'a sore beside the nail'; prob. by comparing (wrongly) the Gk. παρονυχία, a whitlow (lit. beside the nail), or by confusion with F. *angonaille*, a sore (Cot.). See N. E. D.

Agnate, allied. (L.) L. *agnātus*, allied; pp. of *agnascī* = *ad-gnascī*.–L. *ad*, to; *nascī*, earlier form *gnascī*, to be born.

Ago, Agone, gone away, past. (E.) M. E. *ago, agon, agoon*, pp. of the verb *agon*, to pass by, pass away. A. S. *āgān*, pp. of *āgān*, to pass away. See **A-** (4) and **Go.**

Agog, in eagerness. (F.) For *a-gog*, in activity, in eagerness, where *a-* is the prefix **A-** (2). Adapted from O. F. *en gogues* (Littré), or *a gogue* (Godefroy), in mirth. Cot. has *estre en ses gogues*, 'to be frolicke, . . . in a veine of mirth.' The origin of O. F. *gogue*, fun, diversion, is unknown.

Agony. (F.–L.–Gk.) M. E. *agonie.* –F.*agonie.*–L. *agōnia.*–Gk. ἀγωνία, orig. a contest.–Gk. ἀγών, contest.–Gk. ἄγειν, to drive. (✓ AG.)

Agouti, a rodent animal, of the guinea-pig family. (F.–Sp.–Brazil.) F. *agouti.* –Sp. *aguti.*–Brazil. *aguti, acuti.*

Agraffe, a kind of clasp. (F.–O.H.G.) F. *agrafe*; also *agraphe* (in Cotgrave), a hook, clasp; *agrafer*, to clasp. The verb is from F. *a* (= L. *ad*), to; and M. H. G. *krapfe*, O. H. G. *crapo, chrapfo*, a hook, which is allied to E. *cramp*.

Agree, to accord. (F.–L.) O. F. *agreer*, to receive favourably.–O. F. *a gre*,

9   B 3

favourably. — O. F. *a* (= L. *ad*), according to ; *gre, gret*, pleasure, from L. *grātum*, neut. of *grātus*, dear, pleasing. Cf. **Grace.** Der. *dis-agree.*

Agriculture. (L.) L. *agrī cultūra*, culture of a field. — L. *agrī*, gen. of *ager*, a field ; and *cultūra*. See **Acre** and **Culture.**

Agrimony, a plant. (F. — L. — Gk.) M. E. *agremoine, egremoine*. — M. F. *aigrimoine*. — L. *argemōnia, argemōnē*. — Gk. ἀργεμώνη. (Lewis and Short, L. Dict.)

Aground. (E.) For *on ground.*

Ague, a fever-fit. (F. — L.) Lit. 'acute' attack. — O. F. *ague*, fem. of *agu* (F. *aigu*), acute. — L. *acūta* (*febris*), acute (fever) ; fem. of *acūtus* ; see **Acute.**

Ah! (F. — L.) M. E. *a!* — O. F. *a!* — L. *ah!*

Ahead. (E.) For *on head*, i. e. in a forward direction. See **A-** (2).

Ai, a sloth. (Brazil.) From Brazil. *ai.*

Aid. (F. — L.) M. E. *aiden*. — O. F. *aider*. — L. *adiūtāre*, frequent. of *adiuuāre*, to assist. — L. *ad* ; and *iuuāre*, to help, pp. *iūtus*. Cf. Brugm. ii. § 583.

Ail, v. (E.) M. E. *eilen*. A. S. *eglan*, to pain ; cognate with Goth. *agljan*. — A. S. *egle*, troublesome (allied to Goth. *aglus*, hard). Cf. A. S. *ege*, terror, orig. pain ; see **Awe.**

Aim, to endeavour after. (F. — L.) M. E. *eimen*. From confusion of (1) A. F. *esmer*, from L. *æstimāre*, to estimate, aim at, intend ; and (2) O. F. *aësmer*, from L. *ad-æstimāre*, comp. with prefix *ad-*, to. See **Esteem.**

Air (1). (F. — L. — Gk.) M. E. *air, eir*. — F. *air*. — L. *āer*. — Gk. ἀήρ, air.

air (2), mien, affected manner ; tune. (F. — It. — L. — Gk.) F. *air*, look, tune. — Ital. *aria*, 'a looke, . . a tune ;' Florio. — Folk-L. neut. pl. *aëra*, treated as a fem. sing. (Diez). — L. *āër*. — Gk. ἀήρ (above).

Airt, a point of the compass. (Gael.) Gael. *aird*, a quarter or point of the compass. Cf. O. Irish *aird*, a point, limit.

Aisle, the wing of a church. (F. — L.) Better spelt *aile*. — F. *aile*. — L. *āla*, a wing. Prob. for *axla, dimin. of **Axis.**

Ait. (E.) See **Eyot.**

Aitch-bone, the rump-bone. (Hyb.) F. — L. *and* E.) Orig. spelt *nache-bone*. — O. F. *nache*, sing. of *naches*, the buttocks ; and E. *bone*. *Naches* = Late L. *naticās*, acc. of *naticæ*, dimin. of L. *natēs*, the buttocks.

Ajar. (E.) From *a char, on char*, on the turn (G. Douglas, tr. of Virgil, b. vii, prol.). — A.S. *on cierre*, on the turn ; cf. A.S. *cyrran, cierran*, to turn. See **Char** (2).

Akimbo, in a bent position. (Scand.) M. E. *in kenebowe*, Beryn, 1838. Perhaps from Icel. *ī keng*, into a crook ; with E. *bow*, i. e. bend, superfluously added. Here *keng* is the acc. of *kengr*, a crook, twist, kink. Cf. also Icel. *kengboginn*, bent into a crook, from *kengr*, a crook, twist, kink, and *boginn*, bowed, pp. of lost verb *bjūga*, to bow. See **Kink** and **Bow** (1). (Very doubtful ; a guess.)

Akin, of kin. (E.) For *of kin.*

Alabaster. (F. — L. — Gk.) M.E. *alabastre*. — O. F. *alabastre* (F. *albâtre*). — L. *alabaster, alabastrum*. — Gk. ἀλάβαστρον, ἀλάβαστος. Said to be derived from *Alabastron*, a town in Egypt. (Pliny.)

Alack. (E.) Prob. a corruption of M.E. *a! lack!* alas ! a shame ! lit. 'lack.' (It cannot be the same as *alas*.)

Alacrity. (L.) Formed by analogy with *celerity*, from L. *alacritātem*, acc. of *alacritās*, briskness. — L. *alacer*, brisk.

Alarm, a call to arms. (F. — Ital. — L.) M. E. *alarme*. — F. *alarme*. — Ital. *all'arme*, to arms ! for *alle arme*. — Late L. *ad illas armas*, for L. *ad illa arma*, to those arms ! to your arms !

alarum. (F. — Ital. — L.) The same word, with an old pronunciation, in which the *r* was strongly trilled.

Alas! (F. — L.) M. E. *alas*. — O. F. *alas* (cf. F. *hélas*). — O. F. *a*, ah ! and *las*, wretched that I am ! — L. *ah* ! and *lassus*, tired, wretched. (Allied to **Late.**)

Alb, a white vestment. (F. — L.) M. E. *albe*. — O. F. *albe*. — Late L. *alba*, sb. ; orig. fem. of L. *albus*, white.

Albacore, a kind of tunny. (Port. — Arab.) Port. *albacor, albacora*. Said to be of Arab. origin.

Albatross, a large sea-bird. (Port. — Span. — Arab. — Gk.) Formerly also *algatross*. — Port. *alcatraz*, a cormorant, albatross ; Span. *alcatraz*, a pelican. — Port. *alcatruz*, a bucket, Span. *arcaduz*, M. Span. *alcaduz* (Minsheu), a bucket on a waterwheel. — Arab. *al-qādūs*, the same (Dozy). Similarly Arab. *saqqā*, a water-carrier, a pelican, because it carries water in its pouch. (Devic ; supp. to Littré.)

Album, lit. that which is white. (L.) L. *album*, a tablet, orig. neut. of *albus*, white.

albumen, white of egg. (L.) L. *albū-men ōuī* (also *album ōuī*), white of egg.—L. *albus*, white.

Alcayde, a judge; see **Cadi.**

Alchemy. (F.—Arab.—Gk.) O. F. *alchemie.*—Arab. *al,* the; and *kīmīā,* alchemy.—Late Gk. χημεία, chemistry; probably confused with χύμεία, a mingling, from Gk. χέειν, to pour out, mix.

Alcohol. (Med. L.—Arab.) Med. L. *alcohol,* applied to pure spirit, though the orig. sense was a fine impalpable powder. —Arab. *al,* the; and *kohl* or *kuhl,* a collyrium, very fine powder of antimony, used to paint the eyelids with.

Alcoran; see **Koran.**

Alcove, a vaulted recess. (F.—Span.—Arab.) F. *alcôve.*—Span. *alcoba,* a recess in a room.—Arab. *al,* the; and *qobbah,* a vault, dome, cupola; hence a vaulted space.

Alder, a tree. (E.) M. E. *alder, aller* (*d* being excrescent).—A. S. *alor* (*aler, alr*).+Du. *els*; Icel. *ölr* (for *ǫlr*); Swed. *al*; Dan. *elle, el*; G. *erle*; O. H. G. *erila,* earlier *elira*; Span. *aliso* (from Gothic). Teut. stems **aluz-, *aliz-, *alis-.* Allied to Lith. *alksnis,* L. *alnus* (for **alsnos*); Russ. *olěkha*; and perhaps to **Elm.**

Alder-, prefix, of all. In *alder-liefest* (Sh.); here *alder* is for *aller,* O. Merc. *alra,* A. S. *ealra,* gen. pl. of *al, eal,* all. See **All.**

Alderman. (E.) Merc. *aldorman,* A. S. *caldorman.*—Merc. *aldor* (*ealdor*), a chief; and *man,* man. Allied to O. Fries. *alder,* a parent; G. *eltern,* pl. parents; and to L. *al-tor,* a bringer up, from *alere,* to nourish. Cf. **Old.**

Ale. (E.) M. E. *ale.*—A. S. *ealu,* gen. *aloþ* (stem **alut*).+Icel., Swed., and Dan. *öl*; Lithuan. *alus*; Russ. *olovina.*

Alembic, a vessel for distilling. (F.—Span.—Arab.—Gk.) M. E. *alembyk.*—F. *alambique* (Cot.).—Span. *alambique.*—Arab. *al,* the; and *anbīq* (pronounced *ambīq*), a still.—Gk. ἄμβιξ, a cup, goblet; cap of a still. Cf. **Limbeck.**

Alert. (F.—Ital.—L.) F. *alerte* formerly *allerte,* and (in Rabelais) *a l'herte,* i. e. on the watch.—Ital. *all'erta,* on the watch; from the phr. *stare all'erta,* to stand erect, be on one's guard.—Ital. *alla* (for *a la*), at the, on the; *erta,* fem. of *erto,* erect.—L. *ad,* to, at; *illam,* fem. acc. of *ille,* he; *ērectam,* fem. acc. of *ērectus,* erect; see **Erect.**

Algebra. (Late L.—Arab.) Late L.

algebra, computation.—Arab. *al,* the; and *jabr,* setting, repairing; also, the reduction of fractions to integers in arithmetic; hence, algebra.—Arab. root *jabara,* to set, consolidate.

Alguazil, a police-officer. (Span.—Arab.) Span. *alguazil.*—Arab. *al,* the; *wazīr,* a vizier, officer; see **Vizier.**

Algum, sandal-wood. (Heb.—Skt.) In 2 Chron. ii. 8, ix. 10; spelt *almug,* 1 Kings x. 11.—Heb. *algūmmīm,* or (transposed) *almugīm*; a borrowed word. Supposed by Max Müller (*Sci. Lang.* i. 232) to be from Skt. *valgu-ka,* sandal-wood; where *-ka* is a suffix.

Alias. (L.) L. *aliās,* otherwise.—L. *alius,* another; see **Alien.**

alibi. (L.) L. *alibi,* in another place. —L. *ali-,* as in *alius*; and suffix *-bi* as in *i-bi,* there, *u-bi,* where. See below.

alien. (F.—L.) M. E. *aliene.*—O. F. *alien.*—L. *aliēnus,* strange; a stranger.—L. *alius,* another. + Gk. ἄλλος, another; O. Irish *aile,* W. *aill,* all; Goth. *aljis* (stem *aljo-*), other; see **Else.**

Alight (1), to descend from. (E.) M. E. *alihten,* to alight from horseback; A. S. *ālīhtan,* the prefix *a-* being = A. S. *ā-.* The simple form *līhtan* also occurs in A. S., meaning to make light, relieve of weight, alight (from a horse); from *līht,* light, adj. See **Light** (3).

alight (2), to light upon. (E.) M. E. *alihten,* with reference to the *completion* of the action of alighting. See above.

Align; see **Aline.**

Alike, similar. (E.) M. E. *alike, olike.* A. S. *onlīc,* like; from *līc,* like, with prefix *on-* = on, prep.

Aliment, food. (F.—L.) F. *aliment.* —L. *alimentum,* food; formed with suffix *-mentum* from *alere,* to nourish. (✓AL.)

alimony, money allowed for a wife's support upon her separation from her husband. (L.) L. *alimōnia,* nourishment. —L. *alere,* to nourish; see above.

Aline, Align, to range in a line. (F.—L.) Adapted from mod. F. *aligner,* to range in a line. From the phr. *à ligne,* into line.—L. *ad,* to; *līnea,* a line. See **Line.** (*Aline* is the better spelling for the E. word.)

Aliquot. (L.) L. *aliquot,* some, several (hence, proportionate).—L. *ali-us,* other; and *quot,* how many.

Alive, in life. (E.) From A.S. *on līfe,*

in life; where *līfe* is dat. of *līf*, life; see Life.

Alkali, a salt. (Arab.) Arab. *al*, the; and *qalī*, ashes of salt-wort, which abounds in soda.

All. (E.) M. E. *al*, sing.; *alle*, pl. — O. Merc. *al*, *all*; A. S. *eal*, pl. *ealle*.＋Icel. *allr*; Swed. *all*; Dan. *al*; Du. *al*; O. H. G. *al*; Goth. *alls*, pl. *allai*. Teut. type **alnoz*; allied to Irish *uile*, all, from Idg. type **oljos*.

all, adv., utterly. In the phr. *all-to brake* (correctly *all to-brake*), Judges ix. 53. Here the incorrect *all-to*, for 'utterly,' came up about A.D. 1500, in place of the old idiom which linked *to* to the verb; cf. '*Al* is *tobrosten* thilke regioun,' Chaucer, C. T. 2757. See **To-**, *prefix*.

almost. (E.) A. S. *eal-mǣst*, i. e. quite the greatest part, nearly all; affected by mod. E. *most*. See **Most**.

alway, always. (E.) (1) A. S. *ealne weg*, every way, an accus. case. (2) M. E. *alles weis*, in every way, a gen. case.

Allay. (E.) M. E. *aleyen*, *alaien*, the stem of which is due to A. S. *āleg-es*, *ālegeð*, 2 and 3 pres. t. sing. of A.S. *ālecgan*, to lay down, put down, which produced also M. E. *aleggen*, to lay or set aside.—A. S. *ā-*, prefix; and *lecgan*, to lay, place; see **A-** (4) and **Lay** (1). β. But much confused with other forms, especially with M. E. *aleggen*, to alleviate, from O. F. *aleger*, *alegier*, L. *alleuiāre*; and with old forms of *alloy*. See N. E. D.

Allege. (F.—L.) M. E. *alegen*, *aleggen*. In form, the word answers to A. F. *alegier*, *aligier*＝O. F. *esligier* (see Godefroy); from A. F. *a-*＝O. F. *es-*, and *ligier*.—L. *ex-*; and *lītigāre*, to contend (Ducange), from L. *lis* (gen. *līt-is*), strife. Latinised as *adlēgiāre* (Ducange), and treated as if allied to L. *allēgāre* (F. *alléguer*); hence the sense usually answers to that of L. *allēgāre*, to adduce.—L. *al-* (for *ad*), to; *lēgāre*, to dispatch, to tell, from *lēg-*, base of *lex*, law.

Allegiance, the duty of a subject to his lord. (F.—O. H. G.) M. E. *alegeaunce*. Formed from F. *a* (＝L. *ad*), to; O. F. *ligance*, *ligeance*, homage, from O. F. *lige*, *liege*, liege. See **Liege**. ¶ The form *ligance* (Godefroy) was due to a supposed connexion with L. *ligāre*, to bind.

Allegory. (L.—Gk.) XVI cent. L. *allēgoria*.—Gk. ἀλληγορία, a description of one thing under the image of another.—

Gk. ἀλληγορεῖν, to speak so as to imply something else; Galat. iv. 24.—Gk. ἄλλο-, stem of ἄλλος, other; and ἀγορεύειν, to speak, from ἀγορά, a place of assembly; cf. ἀγείρειν, to assemble. Gk. ἄλλος＝L. *alius*; see **Alien**.

Allegro, lively. (Ital.—L.) Ital. *allegro*.—L. *alacrem*, acc. of *alacer*, brisk.

Alleluia. (Heb.) See **Hallelujah**.

Alleviate. (L.) From pp. of Late L. *alleuiāre*, used for L. *alleuāre*, to lighten. L. *al-* (for *ad*), to; *leuāre*, to lift, lighten, from *leuis*, light.

Alley, a walk. (F.—L.?) M. E. *aley*.—O. F. *alee*, a gallery; a participial sb.—O. F. *aler*, to go; F. *aller*. β. The etymology of *aller*, much and long discussed, is not yet settled; the Prov. equivalent is *anar*, allied to Ital. *andare*, to go.

Alliance; see **Ally**.

Alligator. (Span.—L.) Lit. 'the lizard.'—Span. *el lagarto*, the lizard, i. e. the great lizard.—L. *ille*, he, that; *lacerta*, a lizard. See **Lizard**.

Alliteration, repetition of initial letters. (L.) Coined from L. *al-* (for *ad*), to; and *lītera*, a letter; see **Letter**.

Allocate, to set aside. (L.) From pp. of Late L. *allocāre*, to allot.—L. *al-* (＝*ad*), to; *locāre*, to place, from *locus*, a place. Cf. **Allow** (1).

Allocution, an address. (L.) From L. *allocūtiō*, an address.—L. *al-* (for *ad*), to; *locūtiō*, a speaking, from *locūtus*, pp. of *loquī*, to speak.

Allodial. (Late L.—O. Frankish.) Late L. *allōdiālis*, from *allōdium*, *alōdium*, a derivative of *alōdis*, a free inheritance (Lex Salica). It means 'entirely (one's) property,' from O. Frank. *alōd*; where *al-* is related to E. *all*, and *ōd* signifies 'property' or 'wealth.' This O. Frank. *ōd* is cognate with O. H. G. *ōt*, A. S. *ēad*, Icel. *auðr*, wealth. Cf. Goth. *audags*, blessed.

Allopathy, a treatment by medicines which produce an opposite effect to that of disease. (Gk.) Opposed to *homœopathy*, q. v.—Gk. ἄλλο-, for ἄλλος, other; and παθ-εῖν, to suffer; see **Alien** and **Pathos**.

Allot, to assign a portion to. (F.—L. *and* E.) A. F. *aloter*.—A. F. *a*, from L. *ad*, to; and M. E. *lot*, A. S. *hlot*; see **Lot**.

Allow (1), to assign, grant. (F.—L.) F. *allouer*, to let out for hire, assign for an expense.—Late L. *allocāre*, to allot.—L. *al-* (for *ad*), to; and *locāre*, to place, from *locus*, a place.

Allow (2), to approve of. (F. — L.) M. E. *alouen.* — O. F. *alouer,* later *allouer,* to approve of. — L. *allaudāre.* — L. *al-* (for *ad*), to; *laudāre,* to praise, from *laud-,* stem of *laus,* praise.

Alloy, a due proportion in mixing metals. (F. — L.) Formerly *allay*; M. E. *alay.* — O. F. *alay, aley, alloy.* — O.F. *aleier, aleyer,* to combine. — L. *alligāre,* to bind together; see **Ally.** The O. F. *alei,* sb., became *aloi,* which was misunderstood as being *à loi* = L. *ad lēgem,* according to rule or law (Littré).

Allude. (L.) L. *allūdere,* to laugh at, allude to (pp. *allūsus*). — L. *al-* (= *ad*), at; *lūdere,* to sport. **Der.** *allus-ion.*

Allure, to tempt by a bait. (F. — L. and G.) A. F. *alurer*; from F. *a leurre* = to the bait or lure. — L. *ad,* to; M. H. G. *luoder* (G. *luder*), a bait. See **Lure.**

Alluvial, washed down, applied to soil. (L.) L. *alluui-us,* alluvial. — L. *al-* (= *ad*), to, in addition; *luere,* to wash.

Ally, to bind together. (F. — L.) M. E. *alien.* — O. F. *alier,* to bind up. — L. *ad,* to; *ligāre,* to bind. **Der.** *alli-ance,* M. E. *aliaunce.*

Almanac, Almanack. (Late L.) Late L. *almanach.* ¶ Origin unknown; *not* of Arab. origin (Dozy).

Almighty. (E.) O. Merc. *almæhtig,* A. S. *ælmihtig.* The prefix is O. Merc. *al-,* O. Sax. *alo-,* O. H. G. *ala-,* related to **All.** And see **Might.**

Almond. (F. — L. — Gk.) M. E. *almaund.* — O. F. *almandre,* more correctly, *amandre*; the *al* being due to Span. and Arab. influence; mod. F. *amande.* — L. *amygdala, amygdalum,* an almond; whence the forms *amygd'la, amyd'la, amynd'la, amyndra* (see Brachet). — Gk. ἀμυγδάλη, ἀμύγδαλον, an almond.

Almoner; see **Alms.**

Almost. (E.) A. S. *ealmǣst*; see **All.**

Alms. (L. — Gk.) M. E. *almesse,* later *almes.* A. S. *ælmæsse.* — Folk-L. **alimosina* (whence O. F. *almosne,* F. *aumône,* Ital. *limosina*); Late L. *eleëmosyna.* — Gk. ἐλεημοσύνη, pity; hence alms. — Gk. ἐλεήμων, pitiful. — Gk. ἐλεεῖν, to pity. — Gk. ἔλεος, pity. ¶ Thus *alms* is a *singular* form.

almoner. (F. — L. — Gk.) O.F. *almosnier,* a distributor of alms. — O. F. *almosne,* alms; F. *aumône.* — Folk-L. **alimosina* (above).

Almug, the same as **Algum,** q. v.

Aloe, a plant. (L. — Gk.) L. *aloë* (Pliny). — Gk. ἀλόη; John xix. 39.

Aloft. (Scand.) Icel. *ā lopt* (pron. *loft*), aloft, in the air. — Icel. *ā* (= A. S. *on*), in; *lopt,* air. See **Loft.**

Alone. (E.) M. E. *al one, al oon,* written apart; here *al,* adv., means 'entirely,' and *oon* is the M. E. form of *one.* Cf. Du. *alleen,* G. *allein.* See **All** and One.

Along (1), lengthwise of. (E.) M. E. *along.* A. S. *andlang,* along, prep. with gen.; orig. (like O. Sax. *antlang*) an adj., meaning complete (from end to end). — A.S. *and-,* prefix (allied to Gk. ἀντί, Skt. *anti,* over against); *lang,* long. The sense is 'over against in length,' or 'long from end to end.' + G. *entlang,* along. See **A-** (3) and **Long** (1); and see **Anti-.**

Along (2); in phr. *all along of you, &c.* (E.) Equivalent to M. E. *ilong,* Layamon, 15502. — A. S. *gelang,* 'depending on,' as in *on ðām gelang,* along of that. — A. S. *ge-,* prefix; *lang,* long.

Aloof, away. (E. *and* Du.) For *on loof*; answering to Du. *te loef,* to windward. Cf. Du. *loef houden,* to keep the luff or weather-gage, Dan. *holde luven,* to keep to the windward; which suggested our phrase 'to hold aloof,' i. e. to keep away (from the leeward shore or rock). See **Luff.**

Aloud, loudly. (E.) From *a-,* prefix, due to A. S. *on,* prep.; and A. S. *hlūd,* loud. See **A-** (2) and **Loud.**

Alp, (L.) L. *Alpes,* the Alps; of Celtic origin. Connected with L. *albus,* white (Stokes). **Der.** *trans-alp-ine,* i. e. beyond the Alps.

Alpaca. (Span. — Peruvian.) Span. *alpaca*; from *paco,* the Peruvian name, with the Arab. def. art. *al* prefixed.

Alphabet. (Late L. — Gk. — Phœnician.) Late L. *alphabētum.* — Gk. ἄλφα, βῆτα, the names of α and β, the first two letters of the alphabet; Heb. *āleph,* an ox, the name of the first letter; and *bēth,* a house, the name of the second letter.

Already. (E.) M. E. *al redy,* quite ready; from *al,* quite, representing the neut. of O. Merc. *al,* all, used adverbially; and **Ready.**

Also. (E.) M. E. *al so,* quite so; A. S. *ealswā*; see above.

Altar. (L.) A. S. *altāre,* Matt. v. 24. — L. *altāre,* an altar, high place. — L. *altus,* high.

Alter. (L.) Late L. *alterāre,* to alter.

–L. *alter*, other.**–L.** *al-* (as in *al-ius*); with comparative suffix *-tero-*.

altercation, a dispute. (F. – L.) M. E. *altercation.*–O.F. *altercation.*–L. *altercātiōnem,* acc. of *altercātiō.*–L. *altercātus,* pp. of *altercārī,* to dispute, speak in turns.–L. *alter,* other, another.

alternate. (L.) L. *alternātus,* pp. of *alternāre,* to do by turns.–L. *alternus,* reciprocal. – L. *alter* (with suffix *-no-*).

Although. (E.) M. E. *al thogh* ; see **Already** and **Though.**

Altitude. (F.–L.) XIV cent. – F. *altitude.* – L. *altitūdo,* height.–L. *altus,* high.

alto, high voice. (Ital.–L.) Ital. *alto.* –L. *altus,* high.

Altogether. (E.) M. E. *al together,* quite together. See **Already.**

Altruism, regard for others. (F.– L.; *with* Gk. *suffix.*) Coined from Ital. *altrui,* another, others, a form of *altro,* another, when preceded by a preposition. Orig. a dat. case.–L. *alteri huic,* to this other ; datives of *alter,* other, and *hīc,* this.

Alum. (F.–L.) M. E. *alum.*–O. F. *alum;* F. *alun.*–L. *alūmen,* alum.

Alway, Always. (E.) See **All.**

Am. (E.) See **Are.**

Amain. (E.) For *on main,* in strength, with strength ; see **A-** (2) and **Main,** sb.

Amalgam. (F. *or* Late L.–Gk. ?) F. *amalgame,* Late L. *amalgama,* a mixture, esp. of quicksilver with other metals. Origin unknown ; said by some to be a corruption or an alchemist's anagram of *malagma,* a mollifying application ; perhaps with Arab. *al* (=the) prefixed.–Gk. μάλαγμα, an emollient.–Gk. μαλάσσειν (for *μαλάκ-γειν), to soften.–Gk. μαλακός, soft.

Amanuensis, one who writes to dictation. (L.) L. *āmanuensis.*–L. *ā manū,* by hand ; with suffix *-ensis.*

Amaranth, an unfading flower. (L.– Gk.) Properly *amarant,* as in Milton ; but *-anth* is due to confusion with Greek ἄνθος, a flower. – L. *amarantus.* – Gk. ἀμάραντος, unfading, or as sb. unfading flower.–Gk. ἀ-, not ; and μαραίνειν, to fade. (√MER.)

Amass, to heap up. (F. – L.–Gk.) F. *amasser,* to heap up.–F. *à masse,* into a mass.–L. *ad,* to ; *massa,* a mass.–Gk. μᾶζα, a barley-cake. See **Mass** (1).

Amatory. (L.) L. *amatōrius,* loving. –L. *amātor,* a lover.–L. *amāre,* to love ; with suffix *-tōr-, -tor,* of agent.

Amaze, to astound. (E.) M. E. *amasen.* A. S. *āmasian,* pp. *āmasod;* Wulfstan's Hom. p. 137, l. 23. From A.S. *ā-* (prefix) ; and **masian,* to perplex. See **Maze.**

Amazon, a female warrior. (Gk.) Gk. ἀμαζών, one of a warlike nation of women in Scythia. ¶ To account for the name, the Greeks said that these women cut off the right breast to shoot better ; from Gk. ἀ-, not ; and μαζός, the breast. Obviously an invention.

Ambassador, Embassador. (F. –Late L.–C.) F. *ambassadeur.* – F. *ambassade,* an embassy ; prob. borrowed from Ital. *ambasciata.*–Late L. *ambascia* (Lex Salica) ; more correctly **ambactia;* a mission, service.–L. *ambactus,* a servant, emissary ; Cæsar, de Bell. Gall. vi. 15. The L. word is borrowed from an O. Gaulish (Celtic) word (*ambactos?*) a slave, lit. one driven about, a pp. form from *ambi-,* prefix, about, and the verb *ag-,* cognate with L. *agere;* cf. O. Irish *immagim,* I drive about, send about. (Fick, 1894, ii. 34; Brugm. ii. § 79.) Cf. W. *amaeth,* a husbandman.

Amber. (F. – Span.–Arab.) M. E. *aumbre.* – F. *ambre.* – Span. *ambar.* – Arab. *ʿanbar* (pronounced *ʿambar*), ambergris, a rich perfume. ¶ The resinous amber was so called from a resemblance to ambergris, which is really quite a different substance.

ambergris, i. e. gray amber. Called *gris amber* in Milton, P. R. ii. 344. The F. *gris,* gray, is from O. H. G. *grīs,* gray ; cf. G. *greis,* hoary.

Ambi-, Amb-, prefix. (L.) L. *ambi-,* about ; cf. Gk. ἀμφί, on both sides, whence E. prefix *amphi-.* Related to L. *ambo,* Gk. ἄμφω, both. Cf. A. S. *ymb,* Irish *im,* about.

Ambient, going about. (L.) L. *ambient-,* stem of pres. part. of *amb-īre,* to go about, from *īre,* to go.

Ambiguous, doubtful. (L.) L. *ambiguus,* doubtful, lit. driving about (with *-ous* (=L. *-ōsus*) in place of L. *-us*).–L. *amb-,* about ; and *agere,* to drive.

Ambition. (F.–L.) F. *ambition.*–L. *ambitiōnem,* acc. of *ambitiō,* a going round, esp. used of going round to solicit votes ; hence, a seeking for preferment.–L. *amb-*

ĭtum, supine of *amb-īre,* to go about (but note that *ambĭtio* retains the short *i* of *ĭtum,* the supine of *īre,* the simple verb).

Amble. (F.–L.) M. E. *amblen.*–O.F. *ambler,* to go at an easy pace.–L. *ambulāre,* to walk.

ambulance, a moveable hospital. (F. –L.) F. *ambulance.* – L. *ambulant-,* stem of pres. part. of *ambulāre,* to walk.

ambulation, a walking about. (L.) From L. *ambulātio,* a walking about.–L. *ambulātus,* pp. of *ambulāre.*

Ambrosia, food of the gods. (Gk.) Gk. ἀμβροσία; fem. of ἀμβρόσιος, lengthened form of ἄμβροτος, immortal.–Gk. ἀ-, not (E. *un-*); and *μβροτός, for *μροτός (Gk. βροτός), mortal; see **Mortal.** Cf. Skt. *a-mṛta,* immortal. See **Amaranth.**

Ambry, Aumbry, a cupboard. (F.– L.) M. E. *awmebry, awmery,* Prompt. Parv.; the *b* is excrescent.–O. F. *aumaire, almaire, armarie,* a repository; properly, for arms; but also a cupboard.–Late L. *armāria,* a cupboard; *armārium,* a repository for arms.–L. *arma,* arms.

Ambulance, -ation; see **Amble.**

Ambuscade. (Span.–Late L.) From Span. *emboscada,* an ambush. Orig. pp. of *emboscar,* to set in ambush.–Late Lat. *imboscāre,* lit. to set in a bush or thicket.–L. *im-* (for *in*), in; and Late L. *boscum,* a bush. See **Bush.**

ambush. (F.–Late L.) Formerly *embush.*–O.F. *embuscher, embuissier,* to set in ambush. – Late L. *imboscāre;* as above.

Ameer, the same as **Emir,** q. v.

Ameliorate. (F.–L.; *with* L. *suffix.*) Formed with suffix *-ate* (=L. *-ātus*) from F. *améliorer,* to better, improve.–F. *à* (=L. *ad*), in addition; *-meliorer* (=Late L. *meliōrāre*), to make better.–L. *meliōr-,* from *melior,* better.

Amen. (L.–Gk.–Heb.) L. *āmēn.*– Gk. ἀμήν, verily.–Heb. *āmēn,* verily, so be it.–Heb. *āmēn,* firm, true.–Heb. *āman,* to confirm; orig. 'to be firm.'

Amenable, easy to lead.' (F.–L.) From F. *amener,* to lead to, bring to.– F. *à,* to; *mener,* to conduct, drive.–L. *ad,* to; Late L. *mināre,* to conduct, lead about, also to drive out, chase away; L. *minārī,* to threaten.–L. *minæ,* threats.

Amend. (F.–L.) M. E. *amenden.*– F. *amender.*–L. *ēmendāre,* to free from fault. –L. *ē,* from; *mendum,* a fault.

amends. (F.–L.) M. E. *amendes.*

sb. pl.–O. F. *amende,* reparation.–O.F. *amender* (above).

Amenity, pleasantness. (F.–L.) M F. and F. *amenité.*–L. *amænitātem,* acc. of *amænitās.*–L. *amænus,* pleasant. Cf. L. *amāre,* to love.

Amerce, to fine. (F.–L.) A. F. (not O. F.) *amercier,* to fine.–O. F. *a* (=L. *ad*), to; *mercier,* to pay, acquit, but usually to thank; cf. Late L. *merciāre,* to fix a fine. Cf. O. F. *mercit* (F. *merci*), thanks, pardon. –L. *mercēdem,* acc. of *mercēs,* reward, wages, also pity, indulgence, thanks (passing into the sense of 'fine').–L. *merc-,* stem of *merx,* merchandise, traffic.

Amethyst, a gem. (L.–Gk.) L. *amethystus.*–Gk. ἀμέθυστος, an amethyst; so called because supposed to prevent drunkenness.–Gk. ἀμέθυστος, not drunken.–Gk. ἀ-, not; and μεθύειν, to be drunken, from μέθυ, strong drink; see **Mead.**

Amiable. (F.–L.) O.F. *amiable,* friendly; also loveable, by confusion with *aimable* (from L. *amābilis*).–L. *amīcābilis,* friendly.–L. *amīcus,* a friend.–L. *amāre,* to love.

amicable. (L.) L. *amīcābilis,* friendly; as above.

Amice (1), an oblong piece of linen, variously worn by priests. (F.–L.) M. E. *amyse,* and (earlier) *amit.*–O. F. *amis, amit* (Burguy).–L. *amict-us,* a covering. –L. *amictus,* pp. of *amicīre,* to throw round.–L. *am-* (*amb-*), around; *iacere,* to cast.

Amice (2), a pilgrim's hood. (O. F.– Span.?–Teut.?) 'In *amice* gray;' Milton, P.R. iv. 427.–O. F. *aumuce* (F. *aumusse*); Late L. *almucia.*–Span. *almucio* (Pineda); where *al* seems to be the Arab. def. art. (cf. Port. *murça*).–G. *mütze,* a cap (cf. Lowl. Sc. *mutch*). But G. *mütze* may be from Late L.

Amid, Amidst, in the middle of. (E.) *Amids-t* is lengthened from M. E. *amiddes.* Again, *amidde-s* was due to adding the adv. suffix *-s* to *amidde*=A. S. *on middan,* in the middle; where *middan* is the dat. of *midde,* sb., the middle.–A. S. *mid, midd,* adj., middle. *Amid*=A. S. *on middan* (as before). See **Mid.**

Amiss, adv. wrongly. (E. *or* Scand.) M. E. *on misse,* i. e. in error.–Icel. *ā miss,* amiss.–Icel. *ā* (=A. S. *on*), in; *mis,* adv., wrongly (due to an older lost pp.). See **Miss** (1).

Amity. (F.–L.) O. F. *amiste, amisted,*

amistet. ─ Late L.**amīcitātem*, acc. of **amīcitās*, friendship. ─ L. *amīcus*, friendly. ─ L. *amāre*, to love.

Ammonia, an alkali. (L. ─ Gk. ─ Egyptian.) Suggested by L. *sal ammōniacum*, rock-salt. ─ Gk. ἀμμωνιακόν, sal ammoniac, rock-salt. ─ Gk. ἀμμωνιάς, Libyan. ─ Gk. ἄμμων, the Libyan Zeus-Ammon; a word of Egyptian origin; Herod. ii. 42. ¶ It is said that *sal ammoniac* was first obtained near the temple of Ammon.

ammonite, a fossil shell. (Gk.) Coined with suffix -*ite* (Gk. -ιτης) from the name Ammon; because the shell resembles the twisted ram's horn on the head of the image of Jupiter Ammon.

Ammunition, store for defence. (F. ─ L.) From Mid. F. *amunition,* a soldier's corruption of *munition,* due to substituting *l'amunition* for *la munition* (Littré). ─ L. acc. *mūnītiōnem,* a defending. ─ L. *mūnītus,* pp. of *mūnīre,* to defend.

Amnesty, lit. a forgetting of offences. (F. ─ L. ─ Gk.) F. *amnestie.* ─ L. *amnēstia.* ─ Gk. ἀμνηστία, forgetfulness, esp. of wrong. ─ Gk. ἄμνηστος, forgotten. ─ Gk. ἀ-, not; and μνάομαι, I remember. (√MEN.)

Among, Amongst. (E.) The earliest M.E. form is *amonge,* whence *amonges* with added *s* (a common adverbial suffix); and hence *amongs-t* with excrescent *t.* ─ A.S. *onmang,* prep., among. ─ A.S. *on,* in ; *mang,* a mixture, crowd. Cf. **Mingle.**

Amorous. (F. ─ L.) O. F. *amoros;* F. *amoureux.* ─ L. *amōrōsus.* ─ L. *amor,* love.

Amorphous, formless. (Gk.) From Gk. ἀ-, not; and μορφ-ή, shape, form.

Amount, to mount up to. (F. ─ L.) O. F. *amonter,* to amount to. ─ O.F. *a mont,* towards a mountain or large heap. ─ L. *ad,* to; *montem,* acc. of *mons,* a mountain.

Amour. (F. ─ L.) F. *amour.* ─ L. *amōrem,* acc. of *amor,* love.

Amphi-, *prefix.* (Gk.) Gk. ἀμφί, on both sides, around; see **Ambi-.**

Amphibious. (Gk.) Gk. ἀμφίβιος, living a double life, on land and water. ─ Gk. ἀμφί, on both sides; βίος, life.

Amphibrach, a foot in prosody. (Gk.) The foot composed of a short syllable on each side of a long one (◡–◡). Gk. ἀμφίβραχυς. ─ Gk. ἀμφί, on both sides; and βραχύς, short; see **Amphi-** and **Brief.**

Amphitheatre. (Gk.) Gk. ἀμφιθέα-τρον, a theatre with seats all round the arena. ─ Gk. ἀμφί, around; θέατρον, a theatre.

Ample, full. (F. ─ L.) F. *ample.* ─ L. *amplus,* spacious.

Amputate. (L.) From pp. of L. *amputāre,* to cut off round about. ─ L. *am-,* short for *amb-,* *ambi-,* round about; *putāre,* to cleanse, also to lop or prune trees. ─ L. *putus,* clean.

Amulet. (F. ─ L.) F. *amulette.* ─ L. *amulētum,* a talisman hung round the neck. [Once thought to be of Arabic origin; but now given up.]

Amuse, to divert. (F. ─ L.) F. *amuser,* ' to amuse, make to muse or think of, to gaze at;' Cot. ─ F. *à* (=L. *ad*), to, at; *Muse,* to gaze at, stare at, muse; see **Muse** (1).

An, A, *indefinite article.* (E.) *A* is short for *an;* and *an* is an unaccented form of A.S. *ān,* one; see **One.**

An-, A-, *neg. prefix.* (Gk.) Gk. ἀν-, ἀ-, cognate with L. *in-,* and E. *un-;* see **Un-, In-, A-** (9).

An, if. See **And.**

Ana-, An-, *prefix.* (Gk.) Gk. ἀνα-, ἀν-; from Gk. ἀνά, upon, on, up, back, again; cognate with E. *on;* see **On.**

Ana, Anna, a sixteenth of a rupee. (Hind.) Hind. *āna,* a sixteenth part, esp. of a rupee. (H. H. Wilson.)

Anabaptist. (Gk.) One who baptizes again. Coined from Gk. ἀνά, again; and *baptist.* See **Baptize.**

Anachronism, error in chronology. (Gk.) Gk. ἀναχρονισμός. ─ Gk. ἀναχρονί-ζειν, to refer to a wrong time. ─ Gk. ἀνά, up, back (wrong); χρόνος, time.

Anaconda, a large serpent. (Ceylon.) Now a S. American boa; at first applied to a large snake in Ceylon. But wrongly; it was really a swift whipsnake; Cingh. *henakandayā,* lit. ' lightning stem.'

Anæmia, bloodlessness. (L. ─ Gk.) A Latinised form of Gk. ἀναιμία, want of blood. ─ Gk. ἀν-, not; αἷμα, blood.

Anæsthetic, rendering insensible to pain. (Gk.) Coined from Gk. ἀν-, not; and αἰσθητικός, full of perception; see **An-** and **Æsthetic.**

Anagram, a change in a word due to transposition of letters. (F. ─ L. ─ Gk.) F. *anagramme.* ─ L. *anagramma.* ─ Gk. ἀνά-γραμμα. ─ Gk. ἀνά, up, here used distributively; γράμμα, a letter of the alphabet. ─ Gk. γράφειν, to write.

Analogy, proportion. (F. – L. – Gk.) F. *analogie*. – L. *analogia*. – Gk. ἀναλογία, equality of ratios. – Gk. ἀνά, upon, throughout; -λογία, from λόγ-ος, a word, statement, from λέγειν, to speak.

Analysis. (Gk.) Gk.ἀνάλυσις,a resolving into parts, loosening. – Gk. ἀναλύειν, to undo, resolve. – Gk. ἀνά, back; and λύειν, to loosen. (√LEU.) Der. *analyse*, verb, a coined word.

Ananas, the pine-apple plant. (Span. – Braz.) Span. *ananas* (Pineda); mod. Span. *anana*. – Brazil. *nanas* or *nana*. ¶ The Peruv. name is *achupalla*.

Anapæst, Anapest, a foot in prosody. (Gk.) L. *anapæstus*. – Gk. ἀνάπαιστος, struck back, rebounding; because it is the *reverse* of a dactyl. – Gk. ἀναπαίειν, to strike back. – Gk. ἀνά, back; and παίειν, to strike.

Anarchy. (F. – L. – Gk.) XVI cent. F. *anarchie*. – L. *anarchia*. – Gk. ἀναρχία, lack of government. – Gk. ἄναρχος, without a ruler. – Gk. ἀν-, neg. prefix; ἄρχος, a ruler, from ἄρχειν, to rule, to be first.

Anathema, a curse. (L. – Gk.) L. *anathema*. – Gk. ἀνάθεμα, a thing devoted or accursed. – Gk. ἀνατίθημι, I devote. – Gk. ἀνά, up; τίθημι, I place, set. Cf. **Theme.**

Anatomy. (F. – L. – Gk.) F. *anatomie*. – L. *anatomia*. – Gk. ἀνατομία, the same as ἀνατομή, dissection. – Gk. ἀνατέμνειν, to cut up. – Gk. ἀνά, up; τέμνειν, to cut. Cf. **Tome.**

Ancestor. (F. – L.) M. E. (1) *ancestre*, O. F. *ancestre*, from L. *antecessor*, nom., a predecessor, foregoer; and M. E. (2) *ancessour*, O. F. *ancessour*, from L. *antecessōrem*, acc. – L. *ante*, before; *cess-us*, pp. of *cēdere*, to go.

Anchor. (L. – Gk.) The current spelling imitates the false L. form, *anchora*. A. S. *ancor*. – L. *ancora* (wrongly *anchora*). – Gk. ἄγκυρα, an anchor, lit. a bent hook; cf. Gk. ἀγκών, a bend. (√ANQ.)

Anchoret, Anchorite, a recluse. (F. – Late L. – Gk.) F. *anachorete* (Cot.). – Late L. *anachōrēta*. – Gk. ἀναχωρητής, one who retires from the world. – Gk. ἀναχωρεῖν, to retire. – Gk. ἀνά, back; and χωρεῖν, to withdraw, from χῶρος, space, room. (√GHĒ, GHŌ.)

Anchovy, a fish. (Span. – Basque?) Span. *anchova*; cf. Basque *anchoa, anchua*, an anchovy. Perhaps 'dried fish'; from Basque *antzua*, dry.

Ancient (1), old. (F. – L.) With excrescent *t*. M. E. *auncien*. – F. *ancien*. – Late L. *antiānus*, old, belonging to former time. Formed with suffix -*ānus* from *ante*, before.

Ancient (2), a banner, standard-bearer. (F. – L.) Confused with *ancient* (1); but from O. F. *enseigne*, m. 'ensigne, auncient, standard-bearer;' Cot.; also for O. F. *enseigne*, f., 'a banner;' Cot. See **Ensign.**

And. (E.) A. S. *and, end*. **+** O. Fries. *anda, ende*; O. H. G. *anti, unta*, G. *und*. Prob. related to L. *ante*, before, Gk. ἀντί, over against.

an, if. (E.) Formerly also *and*; Havelok, 2861, &c; the same word as the above. *An if* = if if, a reduplication. *But and if* = but if if; Matt. xxiv. 48.

Andante, slowly. (Ital.) Ital.*andante*, moving slowly, pres. pt. of *andare*, to go.

Andiron, a fire-dog. (F. – L.) Not connected with *iron*, but corrupted from M. E. *anderne, aunderne, aundire*. – O. F. *andier*; mod. F. *landier*, put for *l'andier*, where *l'* is the def. art. Cf. Late L. *anderius, andena*, a fire-dog.

Anecdote. (F. – L. – Gk.) F. *anecdote*. – Late L. *anecdota*, orig. a neut. pl. – Gk. ἀνέκδοτα, neut. pl. of ἀνέκδοτος, unpublished; hence an unpublished story, story in private life. – Gk. ἀν-, not; ἐκ, out; and δοτός, given, allied to δίδωμι, I give.

Anemone, a flower. (Gk.) Gk. ἀνεμώνη, lit. wind-flower. – Gk. ἄνεμος, wind.

Anent, regarding, with reference to. (E.) M. E. *anent, anentis*; older form *onefent*, where the *t* is excrescent. A. S. *anefen, onefen*, near; later form *onemn*. – A. S. *on*, on; *efen*, even. Hence *onefn* – even with, on an equality with. Cf. G. *neben*, near (for *in eben*). See **Even.**

Aneroid, dry, applied to a barometer having no liquid mercury in it. (Gk.) Coined from Gk. ἀ-, not; νηρό-s, wet; εἶδ-os, form, kind.

Aneurysm, a tumour due to dilatation. (Gk.) Gk. ἀνεύρυσμα, a widening. – Gk. ἀν-, for ἀνά, up; and εὐρύνειν, to widen, from εὐρύς, wide. Also *aneurism*.

Anew. (E.) M. E. *of-newe*. A. S.*of-niowe*, John iii. 7 (Rushworth). From **Of** and **New.**

Angel. (F. – L. – Gk.) O. F. *angele*. – L. *angelus*. – Gk. ἄγγελος, a messenger. Cf. Gk. ἄγγαρος, a mounted courier, from

O. Persian. **Der.** *arch-angel*, q. v., *ev-angel-ist*, q. v. ¶ The A. S. form was *engel*, directly from L. *angelus*.

Anger. (Scand.) M. E. *anger*, often with the sense of vexation, trouble. ─ Icel. *angr*, grief; Dan. *anger*, Swed. *ånger*, regret. ╋ L. *angor*, a strangling, anguish. (✓ANGH.) See below.

Angina, acute pain. (L.) L. *angina*, quinsy, lit. choking. ─ L. *angere*, to choke.

Angle (1), a corner. (F. ─ L.) M. E. *angle*. ─ F. *angle*. ─ L. *angulus*, an angle. Cf. Gk. ἀγκύλος, bent.

Angle (2), a hook, fish-hook. (E.) A. S. *angel*, a fish-hook; dimin. of *anga*, *onga*, a sting, prickle; cf. Icel. *angi*, a prickle, Gk. ἄγκυρα, a bent hook; Skt. *aṅka(s)*, a hook.╋Dan. *angel*; G. *angel*, dimin. of O. H. G. *ango*, a prickle, fish-hook. Allied to **Anchor**. **Der.** *angle*, verb, to fish.

Anguish. (F.─L.) M. E. *anguise*, *angoise*. ─ O. F. *anguisse*; F. *angoisse*. ─ L. *angustia*, narrowness, poverty, perplexity. ─ L. *angustus*, narrow. ─ L. *angere*, to choke. (✓ANGH.)

Aniline, a substance which furnishes a number of dyes. (F. ─ Span. ─ Arab. ─ Pers. ─ Skt.) Formed, with suffix -*ine*, from *anil*, a dye-stuff. ─ F. *anil*. ─ Span. *añil*, azure. ─ Arab. *an-nīl*; for *al-nīl*, where *al* is the def. art., and *nil* is borrowed from Pers. *nīl*, blue, or the indigo-plant. ─ Skt. *nīla*, blue; *nīlī*, the indigo-plant.

Animal. (L.) L. *animal*, a living creature. ─ L. *anima*, breath, life. (✓AN.)

animadvert, to censure. (L.) L. *animaduertere*, to turn the mind to, hence, to criticise. ─ L. *anim-*, for *animus*, the mind (allied to *anima*, breath); *ad*, to; and *uertere*, to turn (see **Verse**).

animate. (L.) L. *animātus*, pp. of *animāre*, to endue with life. ─ L. *anima*, life. **Der.** *in-animate*, *re-animate*.

animosity. (F.─L.) F. *animosité*. ─ L. *animōsitātem*, acc. of *animōsitās*, vehemence. ─ L. *animōsus*, vehement, full of mind or courage. ─ L. *animus*, mind, courage, passion.

Anise, a herb. (F. ─ L. ─ Gk.) M. E. *anese*, *anys*. ─ F. *anis* (Cot.). ─ L. *anīsum*; also *anēthum*. ─ Gk. ἄνισον, ἄνησον, orig. ἄνηθον, anise.

Anker, a liquid measure. (Du. ─ Late L.) Du. *anker*, the same. ─ Late L. *anceria*, the same. ╋ Swed. *ankare*; G. *anker*; from the same.

Ankle. (E.) M. E. *ancle*; also *an-*

clowe. ─ O. Fries. *ankel*; also A.S. *ancleow*, with a longer suffix (cf. O. Fries. *onklef*).╋ Dan. and Swed. *ankel*; Icel. *ökkla* (for *önkla* = **ankula*); Du. and G. *enkel*. Perhaps allied to Skt. *aṅguli*, a finger, *aṅga*, a limb.

Anna, a small coin; see **Ana**.

Annals. (F.─L.) F. *annales*, pl. sb. ─ L. *annālēs*, pl. adj., for *librī annālēs*, yearly books, chronicles; from *annālis*, yearly. ─ L. *annus*, a year.

Anneal, to temper by heat. ((1) E.; (2) F.─L.) Two distinct words have been confused. 1. M. E. *anelen*, to inflame, kindle, heat, melt, burn. A. S. *onǣlan*, to burn, kindle; from *on*, prefix, and *ǣlan*, to burn. Cf. A. S. *ǣled*, fire. 2. M. E. *anelen*, to enamel glass. ─ Prefix *a-* (perhaps = F. *à*, L. *ad*); and O. F. *neeler*, *nieler*, to enamel, orig. to paint in black on gold or silver. ─ Late L. *nigellare*, to blacken. ─ L. *nigellus*, blackish; from *niger*, black.

Annex. (F.─L.) F. *annexer*. ─ L. *annexus*, pp. of *annectere*, to knit or bind to. ─ L. *an-* (for *ad*), to; and *nectere*, to bind.

Annihilate. (L.) L. *annihilātus*, pp. of *annihilāre*, to reduce to nothing. ─ L. *an-* (for *ad*), to; and *nihil*, nothing.

Anniversary. (L.) For 'anniversary memorial.' ─ L. *anniuersārius*, returning yearly. ─ L. *anni-* (from *anno-*), from *annus*, a year; and *uersus*, pp. of *uertere*, to turn (see **Verse**).

Annotate, to make notes on. (L.) From pp. of L. *annotāre*, to make notes on. ─ L. *an-* (for *ad*), to, on; *notāre*, mark, from *nota*, a mark. See **Note**.

Announce. (F.─L.) F. *annoncer*. ─ L. *annuntiāre*, to announce. ─ L. *an-* (= *ad*), to; *nuntiāre*, to bring tidings, from *nuntius*, a messenger. See **Nuncio**.

Annoy, to vex. (F.─L.) M. E. *anoien*, *anuien*. ─ O.F. *anoier*, *anuier*, to annoy. ─ O. F. *anoi*, *anui* (F. *ennui*), vexation. Cf. Span. *enojo*, O. Venetian *inodio*, vexation. ─ L. *in odiō*, lit. in hatred, common in the Late L. phr. *in odiō habui*, lit. I had in hatred, I was annoyed with; cf. L. *in odiō esse*, to be hated by (Cicero). ─ L. *in*, in; *odiō*, abl. of *odium*, hatred.

Annual, yearly. (F.─L.) M. E. *annuel*. ─ F. *annuel*. ─ L. *annuālis*, yearly. ─ L. *annus*, a year.

annuity. (A. F.─L.) A. F. *annuité*; A. D. 1304. ─ Late L. *annuitātem*, acc. of *annuitās*. ─ L. *annus*, a year.

Annul. (L.) L. *annullāre*, to bring to

nothing. – L. *an-* (for *ad*), to ; *nullus*, no one ; see **Null**.

Annular, like a ring. (L.) L. *annulāris*, adj. ; from *annulus*, a ring, earlier spelling *ānulus* ; dimin. of L. *ānus*, a rounding, a circular form (Lewis).

Anodyne, a drug to allay pain. (L. – Gk.) XVI cent. Late L. *anōdynus*, a drug relieving pain. – Gk. *ἀνώδυνος*, free from pain. – Gk. *ἀν-*, not ; and *ὀδύνη*, pain.

Anoint. (F. – L.) M. E. *anoint*, used as a pp. = anointed. – O. F. *enoint*, pp. of *enoindre*, to anoint. – O. F. *en*, upon ; *oindre*, to smear. – L. *in*, upon ; *ungere*, to anoint. See **Unguent**.

Anomaly. (Gk.) Gk. *ἀνωμαλία*, deviation from rule. – Gk. *ἀνώμαλος*, uneven. – Gk. *ἀν-*, not ; and *ὁμαλός*, even, related to *ὁμός*, one and the same.

Anon, immediately. (E.) M. E. *anon*, *anoon* ; also *onan*. – A. S. *on ān*, lit. ' in one moment.' – A. S. *on*, on, in ; *ān*, one.

Anonymous, nameless. (Gk.) Gk. *ἀνώννμ-ος*, nameless ; with *-ous* added. – Gk. *ἀν-*, neg. prefix ; and *ὄνομα*, name.

Another. (E.) For *an other*, one other.

Answer, to reply. (E.) Λ. S. *andswerian, andswarian*, to answer, speak in reply ; a weak verb. – A. S. *andswaru*, a reply. – A. S. *and-*, against, in reply ; *swerian*, to speak, to swear. The A. S. *and-* = G. *ant-* (in *ant-worten*) = Gk. *ἀντί* ; see **Anti** and **Swear**.

Ant. (E.) M. E. *amte*, short for *amete*. A. S. *ǣmette*, an emmet, ant. **Doublet**, *emmet*, q. v.

Antagonist, an opponent. (L. – Gk.) Late L. *antagōnista*. – Gk. *ἀνταγωνιστής*, an opponent. – Gk. *ἀντ-*, for *ἀντί*, against ; and *ἀγωνίζομαι*, I struggle, from *ἀγών*, a contest. (√AG.)

Antarctic. (L. – Gk.) L. *antarcticus*. – Gk. *ἀνταρκτικός*, southern, opposite to arctic. – Gk. *ἀντ-*, for *ἀντί*, opposite to ; and *ἀρκτικός*, arctic. See **Arctic**.

Ante-, prefix, before. (L.) L. *ante*, before. Allied to **Anti-**, q. v.

Antecedent. (L.) L. *antecēdent-*, stem of pres. part. of *antecēdere*, to go before. – L. *ante*, before ; *cēdere*, to go.

Antediluvian, before the flood. (L.) L. *ante*, before ; *diluuium*, deluge, a washing away. – L. *dīluere*, to wash away. – L. *dī-*, apart ; *luere*, to wash.

Antelope. (F. – L. – Gk.) In Spenser,

F. Q. i. 6. 26. – O. F. *antelop*. – Late L. *antalopus*. – Late Gk. *ἀνθολοπ-*, the stem of *ἀνθόλοψ*, used by Eustathius of Antioch to signify some uncertain quadruped. Of unknown origin.

Antennae, feelers of insects. (L.) L. *antennæ*, pl. of *antenna*, properly the yard of a sail.

Antepenultima, the last syllable but two in a word. (L.) L. *ante*, before ; *pænultima*, fem. adj., last but one, from *pæn-e*, almost, *ultima*, last.

Anterior. (L.) L. *anterior*, former, more in front, compar. adj. from *ante*, before.

Anthem. (L. – Gk.) Formerly *antem*. A. S. *antefn*. – Late L. *antiphōna*, an anthem. – Gk. *ἀντίφωνα*, considered as fem. sing., but really neut. pl. of *ἀντίφωνος*, sounding in response to ; from the alternate singing of the half-choirs. – Gk. *ἀντί*, over against ; *φωνή*, voice, sound.

Anther, the summit of the stamen of a flower. (Gk.) From Gk. *ἀνθηρός*, blooming. – Gk. *ἀνθεῖν*, to bloom ; *ἄνθος*, a young bud or sprout.

anthology, a collection of choice poems. (Gk.) Lit. a collection of flowers. – Gk. *ἀνθολογία*, a gathering of flowers. – Gk. *ἀνθολόγος*, flower-gathering. – Gk. *ἀνθο-*, for *ἄνθος*, a flower ; and *λέγειν*, to cull.

Anthracite, a kind of hard coal. (Gk.) Gk. *ἀνθρακίτης*, resembling coals. – Gk. *ἀνθρακ-*, stem of *ἄνθραξ*, coal.

Anthropophagi, cannibals. (Gk.) Lit. ' men-eaters.' – Gk. *ἀνθρωποφάγος*, man-eating. – Gk. *ἄνθρωπος*, a man ; and *φαγεῖν*, to eat. (√BHAGw ; Brugm. i. § 641.)

Anti-, Ant-, *prefix*, against. (Gk.) Gk. *ἀντί*, against ; allied to L. *ante*, before. Cf. Skt. *anti*, over against, allied to *anta*, end ; see **End**. ¶ In *anti-cipate*, the prefix is for L. *ante*.

Antic, fanciful, odd ; as sb. a trick. (Ital. – L.) Orig. an adj. Adopted in the XVI cent. from Ital. *antico*, with the sense of ' grotesque' ; lit. antique, old. – L. *antīquus*, old. See **Antique**.

Antichrist. (F. – L. – Gk.) O. F. *Antecrist*. – L. *Antichrīstus* (Vulgate). – Gk. *ἀντιχρίστος* (1 John ii. 18). – Gk. *ἀντί*, against ; *χρίστος*, Christ.

Anticipate. (L.) From the pp. of L. *anticipāre*, to take beforehand. – L. *anti-*, before ; and *capere*, to take.

Anticlimax. (Gk.) From Anti- and Climax.

Antidote. (F.–L.–Gk.) F. *antidote.*–L. *antidotum,* a remedy.–Gk. ἀντίδοτον, a remedy; a thing given as a remedy.–Gk. ἀντί, against; δοτόν, neut. of δοτός, given, from δίδωμι, I give.

Antimony, a metal. (Late L.) Late L. *antimōnium.* (XI cent.) Origin unknown.

Antipathy. (Gk.) From Gk. ἀντιπάθεια, antipathy, lit. 'a suffering (feeling strongly) against.' – Gk. ἀντί, against; παθεῖν, to suffer. See **Pathos.**

Antiphon. (L.–Gk.) Late L. *antiphōna,* an anthem; see **Anthem.**

Antiphrasis. (Gk.) See Anti- and Phrase.

Antipodes. (Gk.) Gk. ἀντίποδες, pl., men with feet opposite to ours, from nom. sing. ἀντίπους.–Gk. ἀντί, opposite to; and πούς, foot, cognate with **Foot.**

Antique, old. (F.–L.) F. *antique.*– L. *antīquus,* also *antīcus,* formed with suffix -*īcus* from *ante,* before; as *postīcus* is from *post,* behind. Doublet, *antic.*

Antiseptic, counteracting putrefaction. (Gk.) Gk. ἀντί, against; and σηπτικός, putrefying, σηπτ-ός, rotten, from σήπειν, to rot.

Antistrophe. (Gk.) From Anti- and Strophe.

Antithesis. (Gk.) From Anti- and Thesis.

Antitype. (Gk.) From Anti- and Type.

Antler. (F.) M. E. *auntelere,* for *auntolier* (?).–O. F. *antoillier,* said to have been once in use (Littré). In this case the O. F. word is supposed to be equivalent to a Late L. **antoculārem,* acc., i. e. the branch (of the horn) in front of the eyes; cf. G. *augen-sprosse,* a browantler (lit. eye-sprout). See *Romania,* iv. 349. From *ante,* before, and *oculus,* the eye.

Anus, the lower orifice of the bowels. (L.) L. *ānus.*

Anvil. (E.) M. E. *anvelt, anfeld, anfelt.* A.S. *anfilte, onfilti.*–A. S. *an, on,* on, upon; and a verb *fieltan (see below), causal of **fealtan,* to infix, redupl. verb cognate with O. H. G. **falzan,* M. H. G. *valzen,* whence G. *falz,* a groove. ¶ Some derive it from *on* and *fealdan,* to fold; however, the O. H. G. *anafalz,* an anvil, is not derived from *ana,* on, and *faldan,*

to fold up, but from M. H. G. *valzen,* as above. Cf. L. *incūs,* an anvil, from *in,* on, and *cūdere,* to strike; and note the A. S. gloss: '*Cudo, percutio,* anfilte;' Voc. 217. 5.

Anxious. (L.) L. *anxi-us,* distressed; with suffix -*ous.*–L. *angere,* to choke, distress.

Any. (E.) A. S. *ǣnig,* any; from *ān,* one, with suffix -*ig* (E. -*y*). + Du. *eenig,* from *een,* one; G. *einiger,* from *ein,* one. See **One.**

Aorta. (L.–Gk.) Late L. *aorta.*– Gk. ἀορτή, the great artery 'rising' from the heart.–Gk. ἀείρεσθαι, to rise up; ἀείρειν, to raise.

Apace. (E. *and* F.) For *a pace,* i. e. at a (good) pace; where *a* is put for *on* (cf. *a-foot*); see A- (2). *Pace,* M. E. *pas,* is from F. *pas* (L. *passus*). See **Pace.**

Apart, aside. (F.–L.) F. *à part,* apart, alone, singly; Cot.–L. *ad partem,* lit. to the one part or side, apart.–L. *ad,* to; *partem,* acc. of *pars,* a part.

apartment, a separate room. (F.– Ital.–L.) F. *appartement.*–Ital. *appartamento,* an apartment, a partition, lit. separation. – Ital. *appartare,* to separate. – Ital. *a parte,* apart.–L. *ad partem*; see above.

Apathy. (Gk.) From Gk. ἀπάθεια, want of feeling.–Gk. ἀ-, not; παθεῖν, to suffer. See **Pathos.**

Ape. (E.) M. E. *ape*; A. S. *apa.*+Du. *aap*; Icel. *api*; Swed. *apa*; G. *affe*; Irish *apa* (from E.); O. Bohem. *op.*

Aperient. (L.) XVII cent. Lit. ' opening.' – L. *aperient-,* stem of pres. pt. of *aperīre,* to open. Perhaps from *ap-,* old form of *ab,* from, away, and -*uer-* = Lith. *wer-* in *werti,* to move (to and fro), whence Lith. *at-werti,* to open. Brugm. i. § 361.

Apex. (L.) L. *apex,* summit.

Aph-, *prefix.* (Gk.) See **Apo-.**

Aphæresis, the taking away of a letter or syllable from the beginning of a word. (L.–Gk.) Late L. *aphæresis.*– Gk. ἀφαίρεσις, a taking away.–Gk. ἀφ-, for ἀπό, away; αἵρεσις, a taking, from αἱρεῖν, to take. See **Heresy.**

Aphelion, the point in a planet's orbit farthest from the sun. (Gk.) Coined from Gk. ἀφ-, for ἀπό, from; ἥλιος, the sun.

Aphorism, a definition. (Gk.) Gk. ἀφορισμός, a definition.–Gk. ἀφορίζειν, to

define, limit. — Gk. ἀφ-, for ἀπό, off;
ὁρίζειν, to limit, from ὅρος, a boundary.

Apiary, a place for bees. (L.) L. *api-
ārium,* neut. of *apiārius,* belonging to
bees. — L. *api-,* stem of *apis,* a bee.

Apiece. (E. *and* F.) Orig. (at so
much) *a piece,* where *a* is the indef. article.

Apo-, *prefix,* off. (Gk.) Gk. ἀπό, off,
from; cognate with E. *of, off*; see **Of.** It
becomes *aph-* before an aspirate.

Apocalypse. (L. — Gk.) M. E. *apo-
calips* (Wyclif). — L. *apocalypsis.* — Gk.
ἀποκάλυψις, a revelation. — Gk. ἀποκαλύπ-
τειν, to uncover, reveal. — Gk. ἀπό, off;
and καλύπτειν, to cover. Cf. καλιά, a cot.

Apocope. (L. — Gk.) L. *apocopē.* — Gk.
ἀποκοπή, a cutting off (of a letter). —
Gk. ἀπό, off; and κόπτειν, to hew, cut.

Apocrypha. (Gk.) Lit. ' hidden
things;' hence, uncanonical books of the
Old Testament. — Gk. ἀπόκρυφα, neut. pl.
of ἀπόκρυφος, hidden. — Gk. ἀποκρύπτειν,
to hide away. — Gk. ἀπό, from, away;
κρύπτειν, to hide.

Apogee, the point of the moon's orbit
furthest from the earth. (F. — L. — Gk.) F.
apogée (Cot.). — L. *apogæum.* — Gk. ἀπόγαιον, neut. of ἀπόγαιος, away from earth.
— Gk. ἀπό, away from; γῆ, earth.

Apologue, a fable, story. (F. — L. —
Gk.) F. *apologue.* — L. *apologus.* — Gk.
ἀπόλογος, a fable. — Gk. ἀπό, off; λόγος,
speech, from λέγειν, to say.

apology, a defence. (L. — Gk.) L.
apologia. — Gk. ἀπολογία, a speech made in
defence. — Gk. ἀπό, off; λόγος, a speech
(above).

Apophthegm, Apothegm. (Gk.)
Gk. ἀπόφθεγμα, a thing uttered, a terse
saying. — Gk. ἀπό, off, out; and φθέγγομαι,
I cry aloud, utter.

Apoplexy. (F. — Late L. — Gk.) F.
apoplexie. — Late L. *apoplēxia.* — Gk. ἀπο-
πληξία, stupor, apoplexy. — Gk. ἀποπλήσ-
σειν, to cripple by a stroke. — Gk. ἀπό, off;
πλήσσειν, to strike.

Apostasy. (F. — Late L. — Gk.) F.
apostasie. — Late L. *apostasia.* — Gk. ἀπο-
στασία, late form for ἀπόστασις, revolt, lit.
' a standing away from.' — Gk. ἀπό, off,
away; στάσις, a standing, from στα-,
base allied to ἵστημι, I place. Cf. **Statics.**

apostate. (Late L. — Gk.) M. E.
apostata. — Late L. *apostata.* — Gk. ἀπο-
στάτης, a deserter, apostate. — Gk. ἀπό, off;
στάτης, standing, from στα- (see above).

Apostle. (L. — Gk.) A. S. *apostol.* —

L. *apostolus.* — Gk. ἀπόστολος, one who is
sent off. — Gk. ἀπό, off; στέλλειν, to send.

Apostrophe. (L. — Gk.) L. *apo-
strophē.* — Gk. ἀποστροφή, a turning away;
in rhetoric, a turning away to address
some one else. — Gk. ἀπό, away; στρέφειν,
to turn. ¶ In the sense of a mark used to
denote an omission, it should be *apostroph*
(L. *apostrophus,* Gk. ἀπόστροφος).

Apothecary. (F. — Late L. — Gk.)
M. E. *apotecary, potecary.* — O. F. *apote-
caire.* — Late L. *apothēcārius,* lit. a store-
keeper. — Late L. *apothēca,* a store-house
(esp. for drugs). — Gk. ἀποθήκη, a store-
house. — Gk. ἀπό, away; τί-θη-μι, I put.

Apotheosis, deification. (L. — Gk.)
L. *apotheōsis.* — Gk. ἀποθέωσις, deification.
— Gk. ἀποθεόω, I deify, set aside as a god.
— Gk. ἀπό, away, fully; θεός, a god.

Appal, to terrify. (F. — L.) The present
sense is late; the M. E. *apalled* meant
' rendered pale'; cf. Chaucer, C. T., 10679
(F 365). — O. F. *apallir, apalir, appalir,*
to wax pale, also to make pale (Cot.). —
O. F. *a-,* prefix; O. F. *pale, palle,* pale. —
L. *ad,* to; *pallidus,* pale. Cf. **Pale.**

Appanage, Apanage, provision for
a dependent, &c. (F. — L.) O. F. *apanage*
(also *appanage*), properly, a provision for
maintenance. — O. F. *apaner,* lit. to supply
with bread (Late L. *appānāre*). — L. *ap-
(for *ad*), to, for; *pān-is,* bread.

Apparatus, gear. (L.) L. *apparātus,*
preparation. — L. *apparātus,* pp. of *appa-
rāre,* to prepare for. — L. *ad,* for; *parāre,*
to get ready.

Apparel, to clothe. (F. — L.) M. E.
aparailen. — O. F. *apareiller,* to dress,
apparel. — O. F. *a,* to; *pareiller, parailler,*
to assort, put like things with like, to
arrange, from *pareil,* like, similar. — L.
ad, to; Med. L. *pariculus* (Ducange
has *paricla, paricula*), similar, from L.
pari-, stem of *par,* equal. Cf. **Par. Der.**
apparel, s.

Apparition. (F. — L.) F. *apparition.*
— L. acc. *appāritiōnem.* — L. *appārēre,* to
appear. See **Appear.**

apparitor, an officer who attends
magistrates to execute their orders; an
officer who serves the process of a spiritual
court. (L.) L. *appāritor,* an attendant,
lictor. — L. *appārēre,* to appear as attendant, wait on. See **Appear.**

Appeal, v. (F. — L.) M. E. *apelen.* —
O. F. *apeler,* to call. — L. *appellāre,* to
address, call upon, speak to; from L. *ap-*

(for *ad*), to; and *pellāre, to speak, allied to A. S. *spell*, a tale.

Appear, to become visible. (F.—L.) M. E. *aperen.* — O. F. *aper-*, tonic stem (as in pres. subj. *apere*) of O. F. *apareir*, *aparoir*, to appear. — L. *appārēre.* — L. *ap-* (for *ad*), to, forth ; *pārēre*, to come in sight, also spelt *parrēre*. Cf. **Apparition.**

Appease. (F. — L.) M. E. *apesen*, *apaisen.* — A. F. *apeser*, *apeiser*, O. F. *apeser* (F. *apaiser*), to bring to a peace. — O. F. *a peis*, *a pais*, to a peace. — L. *ad pācem*, to a peace. See **Peace.**

Appellant. (F.—L.) F. *appellant*, pres. pt. of *appeller*, O. F. *apeler*, to appeal ; see **Appeal.**

Append, to attach. (F.—L.) Formerly also M. E. *apenden*, to pertain to. — O. F. *apendre*, to depend on. — L. *appendēre*, for L. *appendĕre*, to hang to or upon. — L. *ap-* (for *ad*), to ; *pendĕre*, to hang.

appendix, an addition. (L.) L. *appendix.* — L. *appendĕre*, to suspend upon. — L. *ap-* (for *ad*), to ; *pendĕre*, to weigh.

Appertain. (F.—L.) M. E. *apertenen.* — O F. *apartenir* (F. *appartenir*), to belong to. — L. *ap-* (for *ad*), to ; *per-tinēre*, to belong. See **Pertain.**

Appetite. (F.—L.) O. F. *appetit.* — L. *appetītus*, an appetite ; lit. ' assault upon.' — L. *appetere*, to attack. — L. *ap-* (for *ad*), to ; *petere*, to seek, attack.

Applaud. (L.) L. *applaudere*, to applaud. — L. *ap-* (for *ad*), at ; *plaudere*, to applaud, clap (hands). **Der.** *applause*, from pp. *applausus.*

Apple. (E.) M. E. *appel.* A. S. *æppel*, *æpl.*+Du. *appel* ; Icel. *epli* ; Swed. *äple* ; Dan. *æble* ; G. *apfel* ; Irish *abhal* ; Gael. *ubhal* ; W. *afal* ; Russ. *iabloko* ; Lithuan. *obolys.* Origin unknown. Some connect it with Abella in Campania ; cf. Verg. Æn. vii. 740.

Apply. (F.—L.) M. E. *aplyen.* — O. F. *aplier.* — L. *applicāre*, to join to, turn or apply to. — L. *ap-* (for *ad*), to ; *plicāre*, to fold, twine. **Der.** *appli-ance* ; also *appli-cation* (F. *application*).

Appoggiatura, a grace-note or passing tone prefixed, as a support, to an essential note of a melody. (Ital.—L. *and* Gk.) Ital. *appoggiatura*, lit. a support.—Ital. *appoggiare*, to lean upon. — Ital. *ap-* (for *ad*), to, upon ; *poggio*, a place to stand or lean on, &c. — L. *ad*, to ; *podium*, an elevated place, a balcony, from Gk. πόδιον. See **Pew.**

Appoint. (F.—L.) M. E. *apointen.* — O. F. *apointer*, to prepare, arrange, settle. — Late L. *appunctāre*, to repair, appoint, settle a dispute ; Ducange. — L. *ap-* (for *ad*); Late L. *punctāre*, to mark by a point, from Late L. *puncta*, a prick, fem. of *punctus*, pp. ; see **Point.** Der. *disappoint.*

Apportion. (F.—L.) F. *apportioner*, to portion out to. — F. *ap-* (put for *a* before *p*, in imitation of L. *ap-*=*ad*), to ; *portion*, a portion ; see **Portion.**

Appose. (F.—L.) F. *apposer* ; formed to represent L. *appōnere*, on the analogy of *composer*, *exposer*, and other presumed representatives of compounds of L. *pōnere* ; but really formed on F. *poser* (from L. *pausāre*). See **Pose.**

Apposite. (L.) L. *appositus*, suitable ; pp. of *appōnere*, to put near. — L. *ap-* (for *ad*), to ; *pōnere*, to put. See **Position.**

Appraise. (F.—L.) M. E. *apraisen*, to value. — O. F. *apreiser (cf. O. F. *apretier* in Roquefort). — O. F. *a-*, prefix ; *preiser*, to value, from *preis*, value, price. — L. *ad*, at ; *pretium*, a price.

appreciate. (L.) From pp. of L. *appretiāre*, to value at a price. — L. *ap-* (for *ad*), at ; *pretium*, a price.

Apprehend. (F.—L.) F. *apprehendre* (Cot.). — L. *apprehendere*, orig. to lay hold of. — L. *ap-* (for *ad*), to, at ; *prehendere*, to grasp. See **Prehensile.**

apprentice. (F.—L.) O. F. *aprentis*, nom. of *aprentif* (see Godefroy, s. v. *aprentic*). The O. F. *aprentis*, *aprentif*, represent Late L. *apprenditīvus, nom., and *apprenditīvum, acc., from a Late L. *apprenditus, used as a pp. of L. *apprendere*, to learn, short for L. *apprehendere*, to lay hold of (above).

apprise, to inform. (F.—L.) From the M. E. sb. *aprise*, information, teaching. — O. F. *aprise*, instruction. — O. F. *appris*, *apris*, pp. of *aprendre*, to learn. — L. *apprendere* (above).

Approach. (F.—L.) M. E. *approchen*, *aprochen.* — O. F. *aprochier*, to approach. — L. *appropiāre*, to draw near to (Exod. iii. 5). — L. *ap-* (for *ad*), to ; *prope*, near.

Approbation. (F.—L.) F. *approba-tion.* — L. acc. *approbātiōnem*, approval. — L. *approbātus*, pp. of *approbāre*, to approve. See **Approve.**

Appropriate. (L.) From pp. of L. *appropriāre*, to make one's own. — L. *ap-* (for *ad*), to ; *proprius*, one's own. See **Proper.**

Approve. (F.—L.) O. F. *approver.* —
L. *approbāre*, to approve. — L. *ap-* (for *ad*),
to ; *probāre*, to test, try, esteem as good.
Der. *appro-val*; *dis-approve*.

Approximate. (L.) From pp. of L.
approximāre, to draw near to. — L. *ap-*
(for *ad*), to ; *proximus*, very near, superl.
adj. from *prope*, near.

Appurtenance. (F.—L.) A. F. *apur-
tenaunce* (O. F. *apartenance*), that which
belongs to. — O. F. *apartenir*, to belong to.
See **Appertain.**

Apricot. (F.—Port. — Arab. — Gk. —
L.) Formerly also *apricock*, from Port.
albricoque directly. Also *abricot.* — F.
abricot, ' the abricot, or apricock plum ; '
Cot. — Port. *albricoque.* — Arab. *al barqūq*,
where *al* is the def. art. — Mid. Gk. πραικό-
κιον (Dioscorides) ; pl. πραικόκια. The
pl. πραικόκια was borrowed from L. *præ-
coqua*, apricots, neut. pl. of *præcoquus*,
another form of *præcox*, precocious, early
ripe (Pliny ; Martial, 13. 46). — L. *præ*,
beforehand ; and *coquere*, to cook, ripen.
See **Precocious** and **Cook.** ¶ Thus the
word reached us in a very indirect manner.

April. (L.) L. *Aprīlis* ; said to be so
named because the earth then opens to
produce new fruit. — L. *aperīre*, to open ;
see **Aperient.**

Apron. (F.—L.) Formerly *napron.* —
O. F. *naperon*, a large cloth ; augmentative
form of O. F. *nape*, a cloth (F. *nappe*). —
L. *mappa*, a napkin, cloth (with change of
m to *n*, as in F. *natte*, a mat). See
Map.

Apse. (L.—Gk.) Now used of a recess
at the end of a church ; formerly *apse*,
apsis, a turning-point of a planet's orbit. —
L. *apsis*, pl. *apsīdes*, a bow, turn. — Gk.
ἁψίς, a tying, fastening, felloe of a wheel,
curve, bow, arch. — Gk. ἅπτειν, to tie, bind.

Apt, fit. (L.) XIV cent. L. *aptus*,
used as pp. of *apiscī*, to reach, get, but
really pp. of O. Lat. *apere*, to fit or join
together.

Aquatic. (L.) L. *aquāticus*, pertaining to water. — L. *aqua*, water.

aqua-fortis. — L. *aqua fortis*, strong
water.

aquarium. — L. *aquārium*, a water-
vessel. — L. *aqua*, water.

aquarius. — L. *aquārius*, a water-
bearer. — L. *aqua*, water.

aqueduct. — L. *aquæductus*, a conduit ; from *aquæ*, gen. of *aqua*, water, and
ductus, a duct ; see **Duct.**

aqueous. As if from L. *aqueus, adj.,
a form not used. — L. *aqua*, water.

Aquiline, like an eagle. (F.—L.) F.
aquilin ; hence *nez aquilin*, ' a nose like
an eagle ; ' Cot — L. *aquilīnus*, adj. from
aquila, an eagle. Cf. **Eagle.**

Arabesque. (F.—Ital.—Arab.) XVII
cent. F. *Arabesque*, Arabian-like ; also
full of flourishes, like fine Arabian work.
— Ital. *Arabesco* ; where *-esco* = E. *-ish.* —
Arab. *'arab*, Arabia.

Arable. (F.—L.) F. *arable.* — L.
arābilis, that can be ploughed. — L. *arāre*,
to plough. (√AR.) See **Ear** (3).

Arbiter. (L.) In Milton. — L. *arbiter*,
a witness, judge, umpire.

arbitrary. (L.) In Milton. — L.
arbitrārius, orig. like the decision of an
umpire. — L. *arbitrāre*, to act as umpire.
— L. *arbiter* (above).

arbitrate. (L.) From pp. of L.
arbitrāre, to act as umpire (above).

Arboreous, belonging to trees. (L.)
L. *arbore-us*, adj. from *arbor*, a tree ; with
suffix *-ous*.

Arbour, a bower. (F.—L.) The word
seems to be really due to M. E. *herbere*,
also *erbere*, from O. F. *herbier*, L. *her-
bārium*, a herb-garden, also an orchard. —
L. *herba*, grass, herb. The special sense
was due to confusion with L. *arbor*, a
tree.

Arc. (F.—L.) XIV cent. F. *arc.* —
L. *arcum*, acc. of *arcus*, a bow, arch, arc.

arcade. (F. Ital.—L.) F. *arcade*.
— Ital. *arcata*, an arched place ; fem. of
pp. of *arcare*, to arch. — Ital. *arco*, a bow,
— L. acc. *arcum* (above).

Arcana. (L.) L. *arcāna*, things kept
secret, secrets. — L. *arcēre*, to keep.

Arch (1), a vault, &c. (F.—L.) O. F.
arche, a chest, box (L. *arca*, see **Ark**) ;
also, by confusion, an arch, owing to the
use of Med. Lat. *arca* with the sense of
L. *arcus*, a bow, arch. See **Arc.**

Arch (2), roguish, waggish. (L.—Gk.)
' So *arch* a leer ; ' Tatler, no. 193. The
examples in the New E. Dictionary prove
that it is nothing but the prefix **Arch-**,
chief (for which see below), used separately
and peculiarly. Cf. ' The most *arch* act '
in Shak. Rich. III. iv. 3. 2 ; ' An heretic,
an *arch* one ; ' Hen. VIII. iii. 2. 102.
Also ' Byends . . . a very *arch* fellow, a
downright hypocrite ; ' Bunyan's Pilgrim's
Progress. A. S. *arce*, — O. F. *arche-*, L.
archi-, Gk. ἀρχι- (prefix). See below.

Arch-, *prefix,* chief. (L.−Gk.) The form *arch-* is due to A.S. *arce-,* as in *arcebisceop,* an archbishop, and to O.F. *arche-,* as in *arche-diacre,* an archdeacon. This form was borrowed from L. *archi-* = Gk. ἀρχι-, as in ἀρχι-επίσκοπος, an archbishop. **−**Gk. ἄρχειν, to be first, to rule; cf. Gk. ἀρχή, beginning. **Der.** *arch-bishop, arch-deacon,* &c.; but, in *arch-angel,* the *ch* remained hard (as *k*) in the Romance languages, on account of the following *a.* Cf. Ital. *arcangelo,* Span. *arcangel.*

archæology. (Gk.) Gk. ἀρχαιολογία. **−**Gk. ἀρχαῖος, ancient, which is from ἀρχή, the beginning; and the suffix *-logy,* Gk. -λογία, due to λόγος, discourse, from λέγειν, to speak.

archaic. (Gk.) Gk. ἀρχαϊκός, antique, primitive. **−**Gk. ἀρχαῖος, old. **−**Gk. ἀρχή, a beginning.

archaism. (Gk.) Gk. ἀρχαϊσμός, an antiquated phrase. **−** Gk. ἀρχαΐζειν, to speak antiquatedly. **−** Gk. ἀρχαῖος, old (above).

Archer. (F.−L.) M.E. *archer.* **−** A.F. *archer*; O.F. *archier,* a bow-man. **−**Late L. *arcārius,* a bow-man; from *arcus,* a bow.

Archetype, the original type. (F.− L. − Gk.) F. *archetype,* 'a principall type;' Cot. **−** L. *archetypum,* the original pattern. **−** Gk. ἀρχέτυπον, a model; neut. of ἀρχέτυπος, stamped as a model. **−**Gk. ἀρχε- = ἀρχι-, prefix (see **Archi-**); τύπος, a type.

Archi-, *prefix,* chief. (L.−Gk.) L. *archi-,* for Gk. ἀρχι- ; see **Arch-**.

archimandrite. (L.−Gk.) L. *archimandrīta,* a chief or principal of monks, an abbot. **−**Late Gk. ἀρχιμανδρίτης, the same. **−**Gk. ἀρχι-; chief; μάνδρα, an enclosure, fold, afterwards a monastery. See **Arch-**.

archipelago, chief sea, i. e. Aegean sea. (Ital.−Gk.) Ital. *arcipelago,* modified to *archipelago.* **−** Gk. ἀρχι-, chief; and πέλαγος, sea.

architect. (F.−L.−Gk.) F. *architecte.* **−**L. *architectus,* the same as *architectōn.* **−**Gk. ἀρχιτέκτων, a chief builder or artificer. **−**Gk. ἀρχι-, chief (see **Archi-**); τέκτων, a carpenter, builder.

architrave. (F.−Ital.−L. *and* Gk.) In Milton. **−**F. *architrave.* **−**Ital. *architrave,* the part of an entablature resting immediately on the column. A barbarous compound; from Gk. ἀρχι-, prefix, chief,

principal, and Lat. *trabem,* acc. of *trabs,* a beam. See **Trave.**

Archives, s. pl., public records; but properly an *archive* is a place where records are kept. (F.−L.−Gk.) F. *archif,* pl. *archives*; Cot. **−**L. *archīuum, archīum.* **−** Gk. ἀρχεῖον, a public building, residence of magistrates. **−**Gk. ἀρχή, a beginning, a magistracy.

Arctic. (F.−L.−Gk.) M.E. *artik.* **−** O.F. *artique*; F. *arctique.* **−**L. *arcticus.* **−**Gk. ἀρκτικός, near the constellation of the Bear, northern. **−**Gk. ἄρκτος, a bear. Cognate with L. *ursus*; see **Ursine.** **Der.** *ant-arctic.*

Ardent. (F.−L.) XIV cent. M.E. *ardaunt.* **−**O.F. *ardant,* pres. part. of *ardre,* to burn. **−**L. *ardent-em,* acc. of pres. pt. of *ardēre,* to burn.

ardour. (F.−L.) O.F. *ardour, ardor,* heat. **−** L. *ardōrem,* acc. of *ardor,* a burning, fervour. **−**L. *ardēre,* to burn.

Arduous. (L.) L. *ardu-us,* steep, difficult, high; with suffix *-ous.*+Irish *ard,* high; Gk. ὀρθός, upright.

Are, pres. pl. of the verb substantive. (E.) O. Northumbrian *aron,* O. Merc. *earun,* as distinguished from A.S.(Wessex) *sint, sind, sindon.* Cf. Icel. *er-u,* they are. From the Idg. √ES, to be; from whence also are Skt. *s-anti,* Gk. εἰσ-ίν, L. *s-unt,* G. *s-ind,* Icel. *er-u* (for **es-u*), they are.

am. O. Northumb. *am,* O. Merc. *eam,* A.S. *eom.*+Skt. *as-mi,* Gk. εἰ-μί, Goth. *i-m,* Icel. *e-m*; &c.

art. O. Northumb. *arð,* O. Merc. *earð*; A.S. *eart* (with *t* due to *-t* in *sceal-t,* shalt, &c.). Icel. *est, ert.*

is. A.S. *is.*+Icel. *es,* later *er.* Cf. also Goth. and G. *is-t,* Skt. *as-ti,* Gk. ἐσ-τί, L. *es-t.* See also **Be, Was.**

Area. (L.) XVI cent. L. *ārea,* an open space.

Areca, a genus of palms. (Port.− Canarese.) Port. *areca.* **−**Canarese *adiki, adike,* areca-nut; *r* being substituted for the cerebral *d* (H. H. Wilson). Accented on the first syllable.

Arefaction; see **Arid** (below).

Arena. (L.) L. *arēna,* sand; the sanded space in which gladiators fought. Orig. *harēna*; cf. Sabine *fasēna,* sand.

Argent. (F.−L.) White; in heraldry. **−**F. *argent.* **−**L. *argentum,* silver; from its brightness. Cf. Gk. ἄργυρος, silver, Skt. *arjuna(s),* white. (√ARG, to shine.) Brugm. i. §§ 529, 604. See below.

Argillaceous, clayey. (L.) L. *argillāceus*, adj. from *argilla*, clay, esp. white clay. Cf. Gk. ἀργός, white.

Argonaut. (L.–Gk.) L. *argonauta*. –Gk. ἀργοναύτης, one who sailed in the ship Argo. –Gk. ἀργώ, the name of Jason's ship (lit. swift, from ἀργός, swift); and ναύτης, a sailor; see **Nautical.**

Argosy, a merchant-vessel. (Dalmatian.) Formerly spelt *arguze* and *ragusy* (see N. and Q. 6 S. iv. 490; Arber's Eng. Garner, ii. 67). The orig. sense was 'a ship of Ragusa,' which is the name of a port in Dalmatia. Ragusa appears in XVI cent. E. as *Aragouse.*

Argue. (F.–L.) M. E. *arguen.* – O. F. *arguer.* –Late L. *argūtāre* (L. *argūtārī*), frequent. of *arguere*, to prove by argument, lit. to make clear; cf. *argūtus*, clear.

Arid, dry. (L.) XVII cent. L. *āridus*, dry. –L. *ārēre*, to be dry.

arefaction. (L.) XVI cent. Coined from L. *ārefacere*, to make dry. –L. *ārē-re*, to be dry; and *facere*, to make.

Aright. (E.) For *on right*, in the right way.

Arise. (E.) M. E. *arisen.* A. S. *ārīsan.* – A. S. *ā-*, prefix; *rīsan*, to rise. See **Rise.**

Aristocracy. (Gk.) Modified from Gk. ἀριστοκρατία, government by the nobles or 'best' men. –Gk. ἄριστο-, for ἄριστος, best; and κρατεῖν, to be strong, govern, from κρατύς, strong. The form ἄρ-ιστος is a superlative from the base ἀρ- seen in ἀρ-ετή, excellence. **Der.** *aristocratic*; whence *aristocrat*, for 'aristocratic person.'

Arithmetic. (F.–L.–Gk.) In Sh. –F. *arithmétique*; Cot. –L. *arithmētica*. –Gk. ἀριθμητική, the science of numbers; fem. of ἀριθμητικός, adj., from ἀριθμέ-ειν, to number. –Gk. ἀριθμός, number, reckoning.

Ark, a chest, box; hence a large floating vessel. (L.) A. S. *arc*. –L. *arca*, a chest, box; cf. L. *arcēre*, to keep.

Arm (1), part of the body. (E.) M. E. *arm.* A. S. *earm.* +Du. *arm*; Icel. *armr*; Dan., Swed., and G. *arm*; Goth. *arms*; L. *armus*, the shoulder; Russ. *ramo*, shoulder. See Brugm. i. § 524.

Arm (2), to furnish with weapons. (F. –L.) F. *armer.* – L. *armāre*, to furnish with arms. –L. *arma*, arms.

armada, a fleet. (Span.–L.) Span.

armada, an armed fleet; fem. of *armado*, pp. of *armar*, to arm. –L. *armāre*, to arm (above). **Doublet,** *army.*

armadillo, an animal. (Span.–L.) Span. *armadillo*, lit. 'the little armed one,' because of its hard shell. Dimin. of *armado*, pp. of *armar*, to arm; as above.

armament. (L.) L. *armāmentum*, an equipment. –L. *armāre*, to arm, equip. –L. *arma*, arms.

armature, doublet of armour.

armistice. (F.–L.) F. *armistice.* – Mod. L. **armistitium*, coined on the analogy of *sōl-stitium*, i. e. solstice. –L. *armi-*, for *arma*, arms; and *-stitium*, for *-statium* (through atonic position), from *statum*, supine of *stāre*, to stand. (Cf. **Solstice.**)

armour. (F.–L.) M. E. *armour*, *armure.* –O. F. *armure*, *armeüre.* –L. *armātūra*, armour. – L. *armātus*, pp. of *armāre*, to arm. –L. *arma*, arms. **Doublet,** *armature.*

arms, s. pl. weapons. (F.–L.) M. E. *armes.* –O. F. *armes*, pl. –L. *arma*, neut. pl., arms, lit. 'fittings.' (√AR, to fit.)

army. (F.–L.) O. F. *armee*, fem. of pp. of *armer*, to arm. –L. *armāta*, fem. of pp. of *armāre*, to arm. – L. *arma*, arms.

Aroint thee! begone! Origin unknown. The usual reference to *ryntye* in Ray does not help us.

Aroma, a sweet smell. (L.–Gk.) Late L. *arōma.* –Gk. ἄρωμα, a spice, sweet herb. **Der.** *aromat-ic*, from the Gk. stem ἀρωματ-.

Around, prep. and adv. (E. and F. –L.) M. E. *around*; for *on round*; see A- (2) and **Round.**

Arouse. (E. and Scand.) From A- (4) and **Rouse.**

Arquebus, a kind of gun. (F.–Du.) F. *arquebuse*, 'an harquebuse, or hand-gun,' Cot.; Walloon *harkibuse*, dialectal variation of Mid. Du. *haeckbusse*, Du. *haakbus*, lit. 'a gun with a hook.' This refers to the hook whereby it was attached to a point of support. –Mid. Du. *haeck*, Du. *haak*, a hook; and Mid. Du. *busse*, Du. *bus*, a hand-barrel, a gun. See **Hackbut.**

Arrack, an ardent spirit. (Arab.) Arab. *'araq*, sweat, juice, essence, distilled spirit. – Arab. root *'araqa*, to sweat. ¶ Sometimes shortened to *Rack*; cf. Span. *raque*, arrack.

Arraign. (F.—L.) M. E. *arainen.*— O. F. *areisnier*, to speak to, discourse with, cite, arraign.—O. F. *a* (L. *ad*), to ; *reisner*, *reisoner*, to reason, from O. F. *reson*, *raison*, reason, advice, from L. acc. *ratiōnem* ; see **Reason.**

Arrange. (F. — L. *and* O. H. G.) M. E. *arayngen*, *arengen.*—O. F. *arengier*, to put into a rank.—O. F. *a* (L. *ad*), to ; *rangier*, *rengier*, to range, from O. F. *rang*, *reng*, a rank. See **Rank.**

Arrant, knavish, notoriously bad. (F. —L.) This word is now ascertained to be a mere variant of *errant* (cf. *parson* for *person*). Chaucer has *theef erraunt*, arrant thief, C. T. 17173 ; and see Piers Plowman, C. vii. 307. See **Errant.**

Arras, tapestry. (F.) So named from Arras, in Artois, north of France.

Array, verb. (F.—L. *and* O. Low G.) O. F. *arraier*, to array. — O. F. *arrai*, *arroi*, preparation.—L. *ad* (becoming *ar-* before *r*), to, for ; O. Low G. and O. Fries. *rēde* (cf. Goth. *garaid-s*), ready, A. S. *rǣde*, ready ; so that to *array* is 'to get ready.' See **Ready.**

Arrears, sb. pl. (F.—L.) From M. E. *arere*, adv., in the rear.—O. F. *arere* (F. *arrière*), behind.—Late L. *ad retro*, backward.—L. *ad*, to ; *retro*, behind. ¶ What we now call *arrears* answers to M. E. *arerages*, s. pl. formed from M. E. *arere* with F. suffix *-age*.

Arrest, to stop. (F.—L.) O. F. *arester* (F. *arrêter*), to stay.—O. F. *a* (= L. *ad*), to ; L. *restāre*, to stay, remain, from *re-*, back, and *stāre*, to stand ; see **Rest** (2).

Arrive. (F.—L.) F. *arriver.*—Late L. *arrīpāre*, *adrīpāre*, to come to shore, land.—L. *ad*, to ; *rīpa*, shore, bank. **Der.** *arriv-al.*

Arrogate. (L.) From pp. of L. *arrogāre*, to ask, adopt, attribute to, add to. — L. *ar-* (for *ad*), to ; *rogāre*, to ask. **Der.** *arrogant*, from the pres. pt.

Arrow. (E.) M. E. *arewe*, *arwe*. A.S. *arwe*, and *earh* (rare).╇ Icel. *ör*, an arrow (gen. *örvar*) ; allied to Goth. *arhwazna*, an arrow. From Teut. base *arhw-* ; cognate with L. *arc-us*, a bow.

arrow-root. (E.) So called, it is said, because the tubers of the *Maranta* were used as an antidote against poisoned arrows.

Arse. (E.) M. E. *ars*, *ers*. A. S. *ærs*. ╇Gk. ὄρρος, the rump. Idg. type *orsos*.

Arsenal. (Span.—Arab.) Span. *arsenal*, a magazine, dock-yard, arsenal ; longer forms, *atarazanal*, *atarazana*, where the *a-* answers to Arab. *al*, def. article. Cf. Ital. *darsena*, a wet dock.—Arab. *dār aç-çinā'ah*, a house of construction, place for making things, dock-yard. — Arab. *dār*, a house ; *al*, the ; and *çinā'ah*, art, trade, construction.

Arsenic. (L. — Gk. — Arab. — Pers.) Late L. *arsenicum.*— Gk. ἀρσενικόν, arsenic ; seeming to mean a male principle(the alchemists had a strange fancy that metals were of different sexes). But really borrowed from Arab. *az-zernīkh* ; where *az* is for *al*, the, def. art., and *zernīkh*, orpiment, is from Pers. *zernī*, orpiment, yellow arsenic (from *zar*, gold). See Devic, p. 4.

Arson, incendiarism. (F.—L.) O. F. *arson*, incendiarism.— Late L. acc. *arsiōnem*, a burning.—L. *ars-us*, pp. of *ardēre*, to burn. See **Ardent.**

Art (1), 2 p. s. pres. of verb. (E.) See **Are.**

Art (2), skill. (F.—L.) M. E. *art.*— O. F. *art.*—L. *artem*, acc. of *ars*, skill.

Artery. (L.—Gk.) L. *artēria*, properly the wind-pipe ; also, an artery.—Gk. ἀρτηρία, wind-pipe, artery.

Artesian, adj. (F.) *Artesian wells* are named from F. *Artésien*, adj. formed from *Artois*, a province in the north of France, where these wells were early in use.

Artichoke. (Ital.—Arab.) Ital. *articiocco*, a corrupt form ; Florio also gives the spellings *archiciocco*, *archicioffo* ; also (without the *ar*, which answers to the Arab. def. art. *al*, the) the forms *carciocco*, *carcioffo*. Cf. Span. *alcachofa*, an artichoke.—Arab. *al kharshūf*, or *harshaf*, an artichoke. ¶ Not Arab. *ar'dī shaukī* (Diez), which is a modern corrupt form borrowed from Italian.

Article, a small item, part of speech. (F.—L.) F. *article.*—L. *articulus*, a joint, knuckle, article in grammar ; lit. 'a small joint.' Dimin. of *artus*, a joint, limb.

articulate. (L.) L. *articulātus*, distinct ; pp. of *articulāre*, to supply with joints, divide by joints.—L. *articulus*, a joint (above).

Artifice. (F.—L.) In Milton.—F. *artifice.*—L. *artificium*, a trade, handicraft ; hence skill.—L. *arti-*, stem of *ars*, art ; and *-fic-*, for *facere*, to make. **Der.** *artific-er*, a skilled workman.

artillery. (F.—L.) O. F. *artillerie*,

equipment of war, machines of war, including cross-bows, &c., in early times. — O. F. *artiller*, to equip. — Late L. *artillāre*, to make machines; a verb inferred from the sb. *artillātor*, a maker of machines. Extended from *arti-*, stem of *ars*, art. We also find *artilliātor*, answering to an older *articulātor*; also Late L. *articulum*, artifice; *articula*, art.

artisan, a workman. (F. — Ital. — L.) F. *artisan*. — Ital. *artigiano*, a workman. — Late L. *artītiānus*, not found, but formed from L. *artītus*, cunning, artful. — L. *arti-*, stem of *ars*, art.

As, conj. (E.) M. E. *as, als, alse, also, al so. As* is a contraction of *also*. (Proved by Sir F. Madden.) See **Also**.

Asafœtida, Assafœtida, a gum. (Med. L. — Pers. *and* L.) From Pers. *āzā*, mastic; the L. *fœtida*, fetid, refers to its offensive smell. See **Fetid**.

Asbestos, a mineral. (Gk.) Gk. ἄσβεστος, unquenchable; because it is incombustible. — Gk. ἀ-, neg. prefix; and -σβεστος, quenchable, from σβέννυμι, I quench, extinguish. See Brugm. i. § 653.

Ascend. (L.) L. *ascendere*, to climb up. — L. *ad*, to ; *scandere*, to climb. See **Scan**. Der. *ascens-ion*, from pp. *ascensus*.

Ascertain. (F. — L.) From O. F. *acertainer, acertener*, to make certain (with *s* inserted). — F. *a* (= L. *ad*, to); and *certain*, certain. See **Certain**.

Ascetic. (Gk.) Gk. ἀσκητικός, given to exercise, industrious ; applied to hermits, who strictly exercised themselves in religious devotion. — Gk. ἀσκητής, one who practises an art, an athlete. — Gk. ἀσκεῖν, to work, exercise ; also, to mortify the body, as an ascetic.

Ascititious, incidental. (L.) Coined, as if from L. *ascītīcius*, from *ascītus*, pp. of *asciscere*, or *adsciscere*, to receive, learn. — L. *ad*, to; *sciscere*, to learn, inceptive form of *scīre*, to know.

Ascribe. (L.) L. *ascrībere*, to write down to one's account. — L. *a-* (for *ad*), to ; *scrībere*, to write.

Ash, a tree. (E.) M. E. *asch*. A. S. *æsc*. +Du. *esch*; Icel. *askr*; Dan. and Swed. *ask* ; G. *esche*. Teut. type *askiz*. Cf. Russ. *iasene*, Lith. *ŭsis*, ash.

Ashamed. (E.) A. S. *āscamod*, pp. of *āscamian*, to put to shame. — A. S. *ā-*, extremely; *scamian*, to shame, from *scamu*, shame. β. Or for A. S. *ofscamod*, with the same sense (with prefix *of-*, off, very).

Ashes. (E.) The pl. of *ash*, which is little used. M. E. *asche, axe*, sing.; the pl. is commonly *aschen, axen*, but in Northern E. it is *asches, askes*. A. S. *æsce*, pl. *æscan, æxan, ascan.*+Du. *asch* ; Icel. and Swed. *aska* ; Dan. *aske*; Goth. *azgō*, pl. *azgōn* ; G. *asche*. Teut. stems *askōn-, *azgōn-*.

Ashlar, Ashler, a facing made of squared stones. (F. — L.) It consists of thin slabs of stone for facing a building ; formerly applied to a square hewn stone ; and, probably, so called because it took the place of the *wooden* beams used for the same purpose. — O. F. *aiseler* (Livre des Rois), extended from O. F. *aiselle, aisiele*, a little board, dimin. of *ais*, a plank. — L. *axilla*, dimin. of L. *axis* an axis, also, a board, a plank.

Ashore. (E.) For *on shore*.

Aside. (E.) For *on side*.

Ask. (E.) M. E. *asken, axien*. A. S. *āscian, āhsian, ācsian* ; the last answers to prov. E. *ax*. + Du. *eischen* ; Swed. *äska* ; Dan. *æske* ; G. *heischen*, O. H. G. *eiscōn*. Teut. types *aiskōn, *aiskōjan*. Cf. Russ. *iskate*, Lith. *jëskóti*, to seek ; Skt. *ichchhā*, a wish, desire, *esh*, to search.

Askance, obliquely. (Friesic). Spelt *a-scance* by Sir T. Wyat ; *ascanche* by Palsgrave, who gives *de trauers, en lorgnant*, as the F. equivalent. Hardly from Ital. *scansare*, 'to go a-slope or *a-sconce*, or a-skew, to go sidelin;' Florio. Rather from Friesic *aa Skands*, obliquely, to one side (Outzen) ; from *skän*, oblique. Cf. E. Fries. *schün*, oblique, *schüns*, obliquely ; Low G. *schüns* ; Du. *schuin*, oblique (whence Dan. *paa sköns*). O. Fries. *ā*=Teut. *au*.

Askew, awry. (O. Low G.) For *on skew*; Hexham gives M. Du. *scheef*, 'askew, awry ;' see **Skew**.

Aslant. (Scand.) For *on slant*.

Asleep. (E.) For *on sleep*; Acts xiii. 36.

Aslope. (E.) For *on slope*.

Asp, Aspic, a serpent. (F. — L. — Gk.) F. *aspe, aspic*. — L. *aspidem*, acc. of *aspis*. — Gk. ἀσπίς (gen. ἀσπίδος), an asp.

Asparagus, a vegetable. (L. — Gk. — Pers.?) L. *asparagus*. — Gk. ἀσπάραγος. Supposed to be of Pers. origin ; cf. Zend *çparegha*, a shoot, a prong; Lithuan. *spurgas*, a shoot (Fick, Prellwitz).

Aspect. (L.) L. *aspectus*, look. — L. *aspectus*, pp. of *aspicere*, to look. — L. *a-* (for *ad*), to, at ; *specere*, to look.

Aspen, Asp, a tree. (E.) M. E. *asp*, Chaucer, C. T. 2923 ; *aspen* is an adj. (like *golden*), and is used for *aspen-tree* ; cf. Ch. C. T. 7249. A. S. *æspe, æps.* + Du. *esp* ; Icel. *ösp,* Dan. and Swed. *asp* ; G. *espe, äspe.* Cf. Lithuan. *apuszis* ; Russ. *osina.*

Asperity. (F.—L.) F. *aspérité.*—L. *asperitātem,* acc. of *asperitās,* roughness —L. *asper,* rough.

Asperse, to cast calumny upon. (L.) From L. *aspersus,* pp. of *aspergere,* to besprinkle.—L. *as-* (for *ad*) ; *spargere,* to scatter.

Asphalt. (Gk.) Gk. ἄσφαλτος, ἄσφαλτον, asphalt, bitumen. A foreign word.

Asphodel. (Gk.) Gk. ἀσφόδελος, a plant of the lily kind. **Der.** *daffodil,* q. v.

Asphyxia, suffocation. (Gk.) Gk. ἀ-σφυξία, a stopping of the pulse ; cf. ἄ-σφυκτος, without pulsation.—Gk. ἀ-, not ; and σφύξις, the pulse, from σφύζειν, to pulsate ; cf. σφυγμός, pulsation.

Aspire. (F.—L.) F. *aspirer,* to breathe, covet, aspire to.—L. *aspīrāre,* lit. to breathe towards.—L. *a-* (for *ad*), to ; *spīrāre,* to breathe. **Der.** *aspir-ate,* v. to pronounce with a full breathing.

Ass. (C.—L.) M. E. *asse.* A. S. *assa.* —Irish *assan.*—L. *asinus* ; whence also W. *asyn,* Swed. *åsna,* Icel. *asni.* Hence also (or from L. dimin. *asellus*) came Irish *asal,* Du. *ezel,* Dan. and G. *esel,* Goth. *asilus.* Prob. of Semitic origin ; cf. Arab. *atān,* Heb. *āthōn,* a she-ass.

Assail. (F.—L.) M. E. *asailen.*—O. F. *asaillir,* to attack.—Late L. *assalīre* ; L. *assilīre.*—L. *ad,* to ; *salīre,* to leap, rush forth. See Salient.

Assart, the offence of grubbing up trees and destroying the coverts of a forest. (F. —L.) From A. F. *assarter,* F. *essarter,* to grub up, clear ground of shrubs.—L. *ex,* out, thoroughly ; Late L. *sartāre,* frequent. of L. *sarrīre, sarīre,* to grub up weeds.

Assassin, a secret murderer. (F.— Arab.) F. *assassin.* From Arab. *ḥashāshīn,* pl., eaters of ' hashish,' the name of a sect in the 13th century ; the ' Old Man of the Mountain ' roused his followers' spirits by help of this preparation, and sent them to stab his enemies, esp. the leading crusaders.—Arab. *ḥashīsh,* an intoxicating preparation from the *dried* leaves of *Cannabis indica,* a kind of hemp. Cf. Arab. *ḥashīy,* dry.

Assault. (F.—L.) O. F. *assalt.*—L.

ad, to ; *saltus,* a leap, attack, from *saltus,* pp. of *salīre,* to leap. See Assail.

Assay, s. ; the same as **Essay,** q. v.

Assemble. (F.—L.) O. F. *assembler.* —Late L. *assimulāre,* to collect (different from L. *assimulāre,* to feign).—L. *as-* (for *ad*), to ; *simul,* together.

Assent. (F.—L.) O. F. *assentir.*—L. *assentīre,* to assent, agree to.—L. *as-* (for *ad*), to ; *sentīre,* to feel, perceive.

Assert. (L.) From L. *assertus,* pp. of *asserere,* to add to, claim, assert.—L. *as-* (for *ad*), to ; *serere,* to join, connect.

Assess, to fix a tax. (F.—L.) O.F. *assesser.*—Late L. *assessāre,* to sit as assessor, to assess ; cf. L. sb. *assessor,* one who adjusted taxes ; orig. a judge's assistant, one who sat by him.—L. *assessus,* pp. of *assidēre,* to sit near. See Assize (1).

Assets, sufficient effects of a deceased debtor. (F.—L.) O. F. *assez* (pron. *assets*), sufficient (to pay with) ; properly an adv., but, in E. mistaken to be a pl. sb.—L. *ad satis,* up to what is enough.

Asseverate. (L.) L. *asseuērātus,* pp. of *asseuērāre,* to speak in earnest.—L. *as-* (for *ad*), to ; *seuērus,* earnest.

Assiduous. (L.) L. *assidu-us,* sitting down to, applying closely to ; with suffix *-ous.*—L. *assidēre,* to sit near.—L. *as-* (for *ad*), at, near ; *sedēre,* to sit. See Sit.

Assign. (F.—L.) O. F. *assigner.*—L. *assignāre,* to assign, mark out to.—L. *as-* (for *ad*), to ; *signāre,* to mark, from *signum,* a mark, sign.

Assimilate. (L.) From pp. of L. *assimilāre,* to make like to.—L. *as-* (for *ad*), to ; *similis,* like. See Similar.

Assist. (F.—L.) F. *assister.*—L. *as-sistere,* to step to, approach, assist.—L. *as-* (for *ad*), to ; *sistere,* to place, stand, from *stāre,* to stand.

Assize (1), a session of a court of justice. (F.—L.) M. E. *assise.*—O. F. *assise,* an assembly of judges ; also a tax, an impost. Probably fem. pp. of O. F. *asseoir,* to sit near, assist a judge.—L. *assidēre,* to sit near ; see Assiduous, Assess.

assize (2), a fixed quantity or dimension. (F.—L.) O. F. *assise,* a tax, impost ; the Late L. *assīsa* was also used in the sense of a fixed allowance of provisions. The same word as the above. Another form is Size, q. v.

Associate. (L.) From pp. of L. *as-sociāre,* to join to.—L. *as-* (for *ad-*), to ; *sociāre,* to join, associate.—L. *socius,* a companion, lit. follower. — L. *sequī*, to follow. See Sequence.

Assoil, to absolve, acquit. (F. — L.) M. E. *assoilen.* — O. F. *as(s)oille*, pres. subj. of *assoudre, asoldre*, to absolve. — L. *absoluere*, to absolve. — L. *ab*, from ; *soluere*, to loosen. See Solve. Doublet, *absolve.*

Assonant. (L.) L. *assonant-*, stem of *assonans*, sounding like ; pres. pt. of *assonāre*, to respond to. — L. *as-* (for *ad-*), to ; *sonāre*, to sound, from *sonus*, sound.

Assort. (F. — L.) O. F. *assortir*, to sort, assort, match (15th century). — O. F. *as-* (= L. *as-*, for L. *ad*), to ; *sort-*, stem of L. *sors*, lot. See Sort.

Assuage. (F. — L.) O. F. *asouagier, asoagier*, to soften, appease ; (Prov. *asuaviar*). — F. *a* (= L. *ad*), to ; and L. *suāuis*, sweet. See Suave.

Assume. (L.) L. *assūmere* (pp. *assumptus*), to take to oneself. — L. *as-* (for *ad*), to ; *sūmere*, to take, which is from *emere*, to take, with a prefix of doubtful origin. Der. *assumpt-ion* (from the pp.).

Assure. (F. — L.) M. E. *assuren.* — O. F. *aseürer*, to make secure. — O. F. *a* (= L. *ad*), to ; *seür*, sure, from L. *sēcūrus*, secure, sure. See Sure.

Aster, a flower. (Gk.) Gk. ἀστήρ, a star. See Star.

asterisk. (Gk.) Gk. ἀστερίσκος, a little star, also an asterisk *, used for distinguishing fine passages in MSS. — Gk. ἀστερ-, stem of ἀστήρ, a star.

asteroid, a minor planet. (Gk.) Properly an adj., signifying ' star-like.' — Gk. ἀστερο-ειδής, star-like. — Gk. ἀστερο-, for ἀστήρ, a star ; and εἶδ-ος, form, figure.

Asthma, difficulty in breathing. (Gk.) Gk. ἄσθμα, panting. — Gk. ἀάζειν, to breathe hard. Cf. Gk. ἄημι, I blow. See Air.

Astir. (E.) For *on stir* ; Barbour's Bruce, xix. 577.

Astonish, Astound. (F. — L.) The addition of *-ish*, as in *extingu-ish*, is due to analogy with other verbs in *-ish*. M. E. *astonien, astunien, astonen* ; whence later *astony*, afterwards lengthened to *astonish* ; also *astound*, by the addition of excrescent *d* after *n*, as in *sound*, from F. *son*. All from O. F. *estoner* (mod. F. *étonner*), to amaze. — Late L. **extonāre*, to thunder out, from *ex*, out, and *tonāre*, to thunder. Cf. L. *attonāre*, to thunder at, astound (with prefix *at-* for L. *ad*, at).

Astray. For *on stray* ; Barbour's Bruce, xiii. 195. See Stray.

Astriction. (L.) From L. acc. *astrictiōnem*, a drawing together. — L. *astrictus*, pp. of *astringere* ; see Astringent.

Astride. (E.) For *on (the) stride.*

Astringent. (L.) From stem of pres. pt. of *astringere*, to bind or draw closely together. — L. *a-* (for *ad*), to ; *stringere*, to draw tight.

Astrology. (F. — L. — Gk.) F. *astrologie.* — L. *astrologia*, (1) astronomy ; (2) astrology, or science of the stars. — Gk. ἀστρολογία, astronomy. — Gk. ἀστρο-, for ἄστρον, a star ; and -λογία, allied to λόγος, a discourse, from λέγειν, to speak.

Astronomy. (F. — L. — Gk.) F. *astronomie.* — L. *astronomia.* — Gk. ἀστρονομία. — Gk. ἄστρο-ν, a star ; and -νομία, allied to νόμος, law, from νέμειν, to distribute.

Astute. (L.) L. *astūtus*, crafty, cunning. — L. *astus*, craft.

Asunder. (E.) For *on sunder.* A. S. *on-sundran*, apart. See Sunder.

Asylum. (L. — Gk.) L. *asȳlum.* — Gk. ἄσυλον, an asylum ; neut. of ἄσυλος, adj. unharmed, safe from violence. — Gk. ἀ-, not ; and σύλη, a right of seizure ; cf. συλάω, I despoil an enemy.

Asymptote, a line which, indefinitely produced, does not meet the curve which it continually approaches. (Gk.) Gk. ἀσύμπτωτος, not falling together, not coincident. — Gk. ἀ-, not ; σύμ, for σύν, together ; and πτωτός, falling, from πίπτειν (pt. t. πέπτωκα), to fall. (✓PET.)

At. (E.) M. E. *at*, A. S. *æt.* + Icel. *at* ; Goth. *at* ; Dan. *ad* ; Swed. *åt* ; L. *ad.*

Atabal, a kettle-drum. (Span. — Arab.) Span. *atabal.* — Arab. *at* (for *al*, def. article) ; *tabl*, a drum.

Ataghan ; see Yataghan.

Atheism. (Gk.) Coined from Gk. ἄθε-ος, denying the gods, without a god ; with suffix *-ism.* — Gk. ἀ-, negative prefix ; θεός, a god.

Athirst. (E.) M. E. *ofthurst, athurst*, very thirsty ; orig. pp. of a verb. A. S. *ofþyrsted*, very thirsty ; pp. of *ofþyrstan*, to be very thirsty. — A. S. *of*, very (prefix) ; and *þyrstan*, to thirst ; see Thirst.

Athlete. (L. — Gk.) L. *athlēta.* — Gk. ἀθλητής, a combatant, contender in games. — Gk. ἀθλέ-ειν, to contend for a prize. — Gk. ἆθλος (for ἀϝεθλος), a contest ; ἆθλον (for ἀϝεθλον), a prize. See Wed.

Athwart, across. For *on thwart*, on the transverse, across ; see Thwart.

Atlas. (Gk.) Named after Atlas, the demi-god who was said to bear the world on his shoulders; his figure used often to appear on the title-page of atlases. — Gk. Ἄτλας (gen. Ἄτλαντος), prob. 'the sustainer' or bearer, from √TEL, to bear.

atlantic, an ocean, named after Mt. Atlas, in the N.W. of Africa. (Gk.) From Ἀτλαντι-, stem of Ἄτλας; with suffix -κος.

Atmosphere. (Gk.) Lit. 'a sphere of air round the earth.' Coined from ἀτμό-, stem of ἀτμός, vapour, air; and Sphere.

Atoll, a group of coral islands forming a ring. (Maldive Islands.) 'We derive the expression from the Maldive islands . . . where the form of the word is *atolu.* It is prob. connected with the Singhalese prep. *ätul,* inside.' (Yule.)

Atom. (F. — L. — Gk.) F. *atome* (Cot.). — L. *atomus.* — Gk. ἄτομος, sb., an indivisible particle; allied to ἄτομος, adj., indivisible. — Gk. ἀ-, not; τομ-, o-grade of τεμ-, as seen in τέμ-νειν, to cut, divide.

Atone, to set at one, to reconcile. (E.) Made up from the words *at* and *one,* and due to the frequent use of the phrase *at oon,* at one (i. e. reconciled) in Middle English. *Al at on* = all agreed.; Rob. of Glouc. p. 113. Tyndall has *atonemaker,* i. e. reconciler, Works, p. 158. Der. *atonement,* i. e. *at-one-ment*; we actually find the word *onement,* reconciliation, in old authors; see Hall, Satires, iii. 7. 69.

Atrocity. (F. — L.) F. *atrocité,* Cot. — L. *atrōcitātem,* acc. of *atrōcitās,* cruelty. — L. *atrōci-,* from *atrox,* cruel.

Atrophy. (Gk.) Gk. ἀτροφία, want of nourishment or food, hunger, wasting away of the body, atrophy. — Gk. ἀ-, not; and τρέφειν (pt. t. τέ-τροφ-α), to nourish.

Attach. (F. — Teut.?) O. F. *attacher,* to attach, fasten. — O. F. *a,* for L. *ad,* to; and (perhaps) a Low G. word with the sense of E. *tack,* a nail. See **Tack.** Cf. Picard *attaker,* to attach; Bret. *tacha,* to fasten, from *tach,* a tack, nail; and see **Detach, Attack.** Der. *attach-ment.*

attack. (F. — Ital. — Teut.?) F. *attaquer* — Ital. *attaccare,* to fasten, attach; *attaccare battaglia,* 'to ioyne battell,' Florio. Cognate with F. *attacher*; so that *attack* is a doublet of *attach.*

Attain. (F. — L.) M. E. *ateinen.* — O. F. *ateign-,* pres. stem of *ateindre,* *ataindre,* to reach to. — L. *attingere,* to

attain. — L. *at-* (for *ad*), to; *tangere,* to touch.

attainder. (F. — L.) From the O. F. *ateindre,* verb, to convict; used substantively; see above.

attaint, to convict. (F. — L.) From M. E. *atteynt, ateynt,* convicted, whence the verb has been evolved; orig. pp. of O. F. *ateindre* (above). ¶ Confused with L. *attinctus*; whence E. *taint.*

Attar of Roses. (Arab.) Also, less correctly, *otto of roses,* i.e. perfume. — Arab. *'itr,* perfume. — Arab. root *'atara,* to smell sweetly.

Attemper. (F. — L.) O. F. *atemprer* to modify. — O.F. *a* (= L. *ad*), to; *temprer, temperer,* to temper. — L. *temperāre,* to apportion, regulate, qualify. See **Temper.**

Attempt. (F. — L.) O. F. *atempter,* to undertake. — L. *attentāre,* to attempt. — L. *at-* (for *ad*), to; *tentāre,* to try; see **Tempt.**

Attend. (F. — L.) O. F. *atendre,* to wait. — L. *attendere* (pp. *attentus*), to stretch towards, give heed to. — L. *at-* (for *ad*), to; *tendere,* to stretch. Der. *attention* (from the pp.); *attent,* adj., 2 Chron. vi. 40, vii. 15.

Attenuate. (L.) From pp. of L. *attenuāre,* to make thin. — L. *at-* (for *ad*), to; *tenu-is,* thin. See **Thin.**

Attest. (L.) L. *attestārī,* to be witness to. — L. *at-* (= *ad*), to; *testārī,* to be witness, from L. *testis,* a witness.

Attic, a small upper room. (L. — Gk.) It orig. meant the whole of a parapet wall, terminating the upper façade of an edifice. Named from the *Attic* order of architecture; see Phillips, ed. 1706. — L. *Atticus.* — Gk. Ἀττικός, Attic, Athenian. Cf. F. *attique,* an attic; *Attique,* Attic.

Attire. (F. — Teut.?) M. E. *atir, atyr,* sb.; *atiren, atyren,* verb. — O. F. *atirier,* to adorn (Roquefort). — O. F. *a* (= L. *ad,* prefix); and O. F. *tire, tiere,* a row, file; so that *atirier* is properly 'to arrange.' Cf. O. Prov. *tiera,* a row (Bartsch). See **Tier.**

Attitude. (Ital. — L.) Orig. a painter's term, from Italy. — Ital. *attitudine,* aptness, skill, attitude. — L. *aptitūdinem,* acc. of *aptitūdo,* aptitude. — L. *aptus,* apt.

Attorney. (F. — L.) M. E. *attourne.* — O. F. *atorne* [i. e. *atorné*], lit. 'one appointed or constituted;' pp. of *atorner,* to direct, prepare, constitute. — F. *a* (= L. *ad*), to; O. F. *torner,* to turn, from L. *tornāre.* See **Turn.**

Attract. (L.) From L. *attractus*, pp. of *attrahere*, to attract. — L. *at-* (= *ad*), to ; *trahere*, to draw.

Attribute. (L.) From *attribūtus*, pp. of L. *attribuere*, to assign. — L. *at-* (− *ad*), to ; *tribuere*, to assign ; see **Tribute.**

Attrition. (L.) From L. acc. *attrītiōnem*, a rubbing or wearing away. — L. *attrītus*, pp. of *atterere*, to rub away. — L. *at-* (= *ad*), at ; *terere*, to rub. See **Trite.**

Attune, to bring to a like tune. (L. and L. − Gk.) From L. *at-* (= *ad*), to ; and E. **Tune**, q. v.

Auburn. (F. − L.) M. E. *aborne*, *auburne*, orig. citron-coloured or light yellow. − O. F. *alborne*, *auborne*, blond (Godefroy). − Late L. *alburnus*, whitish, light-coloured. Torriano explains Ital. *alburno* by ' that whitish colour of women's hair called an *aburn* colour.' Cf. L. *alburnum*, the sap-wood or inner bark of trees (Pliny). − L. *albus*, white.

Auction. (L.) L. *auctiōnem*, acc. of *auctio*, a sale by auction, lit. ' an increase,' because the sale is to the highest bidder. − L. *auctus*, pp. of *augēre*, to increase. See **Eke.**

Audacious. (F. − L.) F. *audacieux*, bold, audacious. − L. **audāciōsus*, not found ; extended from L. *audāci-*, from *audax*, bold. − L. *audēre*, to dare.

Audience. (F. − L.) F. *audience*, ' an audience or hearing ; ' Cot. − L. *audientia*, a hearing. − L. *audient-*, stem of pres. pt. of *audīre*, to hear. For **auisdīre* ; cf. Gk. αἰσθέσθαι, to perceive, for ἀϝισθεσθαι. Brugm. i. § 240.

audible. (L.) Late L. *audībilis*, that can be heard. − L. *audīre*, to hear.

audit. (L.) From L. *audĭtus*, a hearing. − L. *audīre*, to hear ; whence also *audi-tor*.

Auger. (E.) For *nauger*. M.E. *nauegar* (= *navegar*), *nauger*, a tool for boring holes. − A. S. *nafogār*, an auger, lit. nave-piercer, for boring holes in the nave of a wheel. − A. S. *nafu*, a nave ; *gār*, a piercer, that which gores ; see **Nave** (1) and **Gore** (3). + Du. *avegaar* (for *navegaar*) ; Icel. *nafarr* ; Dan. *naver* ; Swed. *nafvare* ; O. H. G. *nabagēr*.

Aught. (E.) M. E. *aht*, *aght*, *aught*. A. S. *āht*, earlier *āwiht* ; from *ā*, ever, and *wiht*, a creature, wight, whit ; lit. ' e'er a whit.' See **Whit.**

Augment. (F. − L.) F. *augmenter*. − L. *augmentāre*, to enlarge. − L. *augmentum*,

an increase. − L. *augēre*, to increase. See **Auction.**

Augur. (L.) M. E. *augur*. − L. *augur*, a sooth-sayer ; said to mean a diviner by the flight and cries of birds. Hence a supposed etymology (not certain) from *auis*, a bird, and *-gur*, telling, allied to *garrīre*, to shout. Cf. L. *au-ceps*, a bird-catcher.

August. (L.) L. *augustus*, venerable ; whence E. *august*, venerable, and *August*, the month named after Augustus Caesar. Cf. Skt. *ōjas*, strength. Brugm. i. § 213.

Auk, a sea-bird. (Scand.) Swed. *alka* ; Dan. *alke* ; Icel. *alka*, *ālka*, an auk.

Aunt. (F. − L.) M. E. *aunte*. − A. F. *aunte* ; O. F. *ante* (mod. F. *t-ante*). − L. *amita*, a father's sister. Cf. G. *amme*, nurse.

Aureate. (L.) Late L. *aureātus*, gilt, from *aureus*, golden ; in place of L. *aurātus*, gilded, pp. of *aurāre*, to gild. − L. *aurum*, gold ; O. L. *ausum*. Der. *aurelia*, a gold-coloured chrysalis ; *aur-e-ol-a*, *aur-e-ole*, the halo of golden glory in paintings ; *auriferous*, gold-producing ; from *ferre*, to bear.

Auricula, a plant. (L.) L. *auricula*, the lobe of the ear ; used to mean the ' bear's ear,' a kind of primrose ; see below.

auricular, told in the ear, secret. (L.) Late L. *auriculāris*, in the phr. *auriculāris confessio*, auricular confession. − L. *auricula*, the lobe of the ear ; double dimin. from *auri-s*, the ear. See **Ear.**

Aurora, the dawn. (L.) L. *aurōra*, the dawn ; from prehistoric **ausōsa*. + Gk. Æolic αὔως, Ion, ἠώς, dawn, from prehistoric **αὔσως*. See **East.**

Auscultation, a listening. (L.) L. *auscultātiōnem*, acc. of *auscultātio*, a listening ; from the pp. of *auscultāre*, to listen. − L. **aus-*, base of *auris*, the ear. See **Ear.**

Auspice, favour, patronage. (F. − L.) F. *auspice*, a token of things by the flight of birds, an omen, good fortune. − L. *auspicium*, a watching of birds for the purpose of augury. Short for **auispicium*. − L. *aui-*, for *auis*, a bird ; and *spicere*, *specere*, to spy, look into.

Austere. (F. − L. − Gk.) M. E. *austere*. − O. F. *austere*. − L. *austērus*, harsh, severe. − Gk. αὐστηρός, making the tongue dry, harsh. − Gk. αὔειν, to dry. See **Sere.**

Austral. (F. − L. ; or L.) We find F. *australe*, 'southerly ;' Cot. − L. *Austrālis*, southerly. − L. *Auster*, the South wind.

Authentic. (F.−L.−Gk.) M. E. *au-tentike, autentik.*−O. F. *autentique,* later *authentique* (Cot.). − L. *authenticus,* original, written with the author's own hand. − Gk. αὐθεντικός, vouched for, warranted. − Gk. αὐθέντης, also αὐτο-έντης, one who does things with his own hand, a 'self-worker'; see **Auto-.** β. Gk. ἔντης (for *σέντης) is prob. allied to L. *sons* (gen. *sontis*), guilty, responsible.

Author. (F. − L.) M. E. *autour, autor;* later *author* (with *th* once sounded as *t,* but now as *th* in thin).−O. F. *autor* (Bartsch).−L. *auctōrem,* acc. of *auctor,* an originator, lit. 'increaser, grower.'−L. *augēre,* to increase. Cf. **Auction.**

Auto-, prefix. (Gk.) Gk. αὐτο-, stem of αὐτός, self. **Der.** *auto-biography,* a biography written by oneself (see **Biography**); *autograph,* something in one's own handwriting, from Gk. γράφειν, to write (see **Graphic**).

autocracy. (Gk.) Adapted (with suffix -*cy* for Gk. -τεια) from Gk. αὐτο-κράτεια, absolute power.− Gk. αὐτο-, self; -κράτεια (in compounds), power, from κρατέειν, to rule. − Gk. κρατύς, strong; cognate with E. **Hard.**

automaton, a self-moving machine. (G.) Gk. αὐτόματον, neut. of αὐτόματος, self-moving.−Gk. αὐτό-, for αὐτός, self; and -ματός, cognate with Skt. *matás,* thought, considered, known, pp. of *man,* to think. (✓MEN.)

autonomy, self-government. (Gk.) Gk. αὐτονομία, independence. − Gk. αὐτό-νομος, free, living by one's own laws. − Gk. αὐτό-, self; and νόμος, law, from νέμομαι, I sway, νέμειν, to distribute.

autopsy, personal inspection. (Gk.) Gk. αὐτοψία, a seeing with one's own eyes. −Gk. αὐτο-, self; ὄψις, sight (see **Optic**).

Auto-da-fe. (Port. − L.) Lit. ' decree of faith ; ' a judgment of the Inquisition, also, the execution of such judgment, when the decree or sentence is read to the victims. − Port. *auto,* action, decree ; *da,* short for *de a,* of the ; *fé,* faith. [The Span. form is *auto de fé,* without the article *la* = Port. *a.*] − L. *actum,* acc. of *actus,* act, deed ; *dē,* prep. ; *illa,* fem. of *ille,* he ; *fidem,* acc. of *fidēs,* faith.

Autumn. (F.−L.) M. E. *autumpne.* −O.F. *autompne.*−L. *autumnus, auctumnus,* autumn. (Perhaps allied to *augēre,* to increase.)

Auxiliary. (L.) L. *auxiliārius,*

helping, assisting.−L. *auxilium,* help.− L. *augēre,* to increase.

Avadavat, a finch-like E. Indian bird. (Arab. *and* Pers.) Formerly *amadavat* (N. E. D.) ; or *amudavad,* N. and Q. 6 S. ii. 198. Named from the city of *Ahmed-ābād,* whence they were imported.−Arab. *Ahmed,* a proper name ; Pers. *ābād,* a city.

Avail. (F.−L.) M. E. *auailen* (= *availen*). Compounded of O. F. *a,* to ; and *vail-,* tonic stem of O. F. *valoir* (*valer*), to be of use.−L. *ad,* to ; *ualēre,* to be strong.

Avalanche. (F.−L.) F. *avalanche,* the descent of snow into a valley.−F. *avaler,* to swallow ; but the old sense was ' to let fall down.'−F. *aval,* downward, lit. ' to the valley.'− F. *a* (= L. *ad*), to ; *val,* vale, from L. *uallem,* acc. of *uallis,* a valley.

Avarice. (F. − L.) M. E. *auarice* (with *u* for *v*).−F. *avarice.*−L. *auāritia,* greediness.−L. *auārus,* greedy ; cf. L. *auidus,* greedy.−L. *auēre,* to wish, desire.

Avast, stop, hold fast. (Du.) Du. *hou vast, houd vast,* hold fast.−Du. *hou,* short form of *houd,* imper. of *houden,* to hold (see **Hold**) ; and *vast,* fast (see **Fast**).

Avatar. (Skt.) Skt. *avatāra,* descent ; hence, the descent of a Hindu deity in incarnate form.−Skt. *ava,* down ; and *tr̄ī,* to pass over, pass.

Avaunt, begone ! (F. − L.) A. F. *avaunt ;* O.F. *avant,* forward ! See **Advance.**

Ave, hail. (L.) Short for *Auē Maria,* hail, Mary (Luke i. 28).−L. *auē,* hail ! imper. sing. of *auēre,* to fare well.

Avenge. (F.−L.) O. F. *avengier,* to avenge. − F. *a* (L. *ad*), to ; *vengier,* to avenge, from L. *uindicāre,* to lay claim to, also, to avenge. See **Vindicate.**

Aventail, the mouth-piece of a visor. (F. − L.) A. F. *aventaille ;* O.F. *esventail,* air-hole. − O.F. *esventer,* to expose to air. − L. *ex,* out ; *uentus,* wind. See **Ventail.**

Avenue. (F.−L.) F. *avenue, advenue,* access ; hence an approach to a house (esp. one shaded by trees) ; fem. of *avenu,* pp. of F. *avenir,* to come to.−L. *ad,* to ; *uenīre,* to come.

Aver. (F.−L.) A. F. and O. F. *averer.* −Late L. *auērāre, aduērāre,* to affirm to be true.−L. *ad,* to ; *uērus,* true.

Average, an equalised estimate. (F.) Formerly a duty, tax, impost ; then, an extra charge on goods, the incidence of such a charge, the general estimate or apportionment of loss of goods, &c. Formed, with suffix -*age*, from F. *avar-ie*, now usually ' damage' (cf. Span. *averia*, *haberia*, ' the custom paid for goods that are exported' (Pineda), Port. and Ital. *avaria*, Late L. *avaria*, *averia*). A Mediterranean maritime term, orig. signifying ' duty charged on goods' (G. P. Marsh, in N. E. D.). Origin unknown ; perhaps from Ital. *avere*, *havere*, goods, chattels (F. *avoir*), a sb. use of *havere*, *haver* (L. *habēre*), to possess. ¶ Or from Arab. '*avār*, damage, the relationship of which is obscure.

Avert. (L.) L. *ā-uertere*, to turn away. — L. *ā* (=*ab*), off, away ; *uertere*, to turn. Der. *averse*, from L. pp. *āuersus*.

Aviary. (L.) L. *auiārium*, a place for birds ; neut. of adj. *auiārius*, belonging to birds. — L. *aui-*, stem of *auis*, a bird.

Avidity. (F. — L.) F. *avidité*, greediness, eagerness. — L. *auiditātem*, acc. of *auiditās*, eagerness. — L. *auidus*, greedy, desirous. — L. *auēre*, to crave.

Avocation. (L.) From L. *āuocātiōnem*, acc. of *āuocātio*, a calling away of the attention, hence a diversion, amusement ; afterwards used in the sense of employment. — L. *āuocātus*, pp. of *ā-uocāre*, to call away. — L. *ā* (=*ab*), from, away ; *uocāre*, to call. See **Vocation.**

Avoid, to shun. (F. — L.) M. E. *auoiden* (=*avoiden*), to empty, empty out, get rid of ; later, to keep away from, shun. — O. F. *esvuidier*, to empty out, get quit of. — O. F. *es-*, prefix (L. *ex*, out) ; and O. F. *vuit*, *vuide* (F. *vide*), empty, void. See **Void.**

Avoirdupois. (F. — L.) Formerly *avoir de pois* (Anglo-F. *aveir de peis*), goods of weight, i. e. heavy articles. — F. *avoir*, goods, orig. ' to have ;' *de*, of ; O. F. *pois*, A. F. *peis*, weight. — L. *habēre*, to have ; *dē*, of ; *pensum*, that which is weighed out, neut. of *pensus*, pp. of *pendere*, to weigh. ¶ The F. *pois* is now misspelt *poids*. See **Poise.**

Avouch. (F. — L.) M. E. *avouchen*. — O. F. *avochier*, to call upon as guarantor (Godefroy). — L. *aduocāre*, to call to or summon (a witness) — L. *ad*, to ; *uocāre*, to call. Cf. **Vouch.**

avow, to confess, to declare openly. (F.—L.) M. E. *avowen*.—O. F. *avouer*, *avoer*. — L. *aduocāre*, to call upon ; Med. L. to call on as patron or client, to acknow-

ledge, recognise. — L. *ad*, to : *uocāre*, to call. ¶ Another M. E. *avowen*, to bind with a vow, to vow, is obsolete ; see **Vow.** Doublet, *avouch* (above).

Await. (F. L. *and* O. H. G.) O. F. *awaitier*, *agaitier*, to wait for. — O. F. *a* (=L. *ad*), for; *waitier*, to wait, from O. H. G. *wahtēn*, to watch, from the sb. *wahta* (G. *wacht*), a watching. See **Wait.**

Awake, Awaken. (E.) M. E. *awakien*, *awaken* ; and *awaknen*, *awakenen* ; both orig. intransitive. Two A. S. verbs are confused ; *āwacian*, wk. vb.; and *onwæcnan*, with wk. pres. t., but strong pt. t. *onwōc*, pp. *onwacen*. The prefix is either A- (2) or A- (4). See **Wake, Waken.**

Award, vb. (F. — L. *and* O. Low G.) M. E. *awarden*. — A. F. *awarder* ; O. F. *eswarder*, *esgarder*, to examine, adjudge. — O. F. *es-* (= L. *ex*), out ; O. F. *warder*, to ward, guard, from O. Low G., as in O. Sax. *wardōn* (cf. G. *warten*), to watch, guard. See **Ward, Guard.**

Aware. (E.) A corruption of M. E. *iwar*, *ywar*, aware (common) ; from A. S. *gewær*, aware. — A. S. *ge-*, a common prefix, not altering the sense ; *wær*, ware, wary ; see **Wary.**

Away. (E.) For *on way*, i. e. on one's way, so as to depart. A. S. *onweg*, away. See **Way.**

Awe. (Scand.) M. E. *aȝe*, *aghe*, *awe*. [Also *eȝe*, *eghe*, *eye* ; all orig. dissyllabic. The latter set are from A. S. *egu*, awe.] — Icel. *agi*, awe, fear; Dan. *ave.* **+** A. S. *ege* ; Goth. *agis*, fear, anguish ; Irish *eagal*, fear, terror ; Gk. ἄχος, anguish, affliction. (✓AGH.) Der. *aw-ful*.

Awkward, clumsy. (Scand. *and* E.) Orig. an adv., signifying ' transversely,' or ' in a backhanded manner.' M. E. *awkward*, *awkwart* ; ' *aukwart* he couth him ta ' = he gave him a backhanded stroke, Wallace, iii. 175. β. The suffix -*ward* is E., as in *for-ward*, *on-ward*, &c. The prefix is M. E. *auk*, *awk*, contrary, perverse, wrong ; this is a contraction of Icel. *öfug* [Swed. *afvug*, in Widegren], like *hawk* from A. S. *hafoc*. — Icel. *öfugr*, often contracted to *öfgu*, adj., turning the wrong way, back foremost, contrary. γ. Here *öf-* is for *af-*, off, from, away ; and -*ug-* is a suffix. Cf. O. H. G. *ap-uh*, M. H. G. *eb-ich*, turned away, perverse ; from *apa* = G. *ab*, off, away, and the suffix -*h*. δ. Thus the sense of *awk* is ' turned away ' ·

from Icel. *af-*, cognate with E. *of*, *off*, Gk. *ἄπο*.

Awl. (E.) *Aule* in Shak.; M. E. *alle*, *al*, Wyclif, Exod. xxi. 6. A. S. *æl*, *al*; Exod. xxi. 6; Levit. xxv. 10.+Icel. *alr*; O. H. G. *ala*, G. *ahle*; Du. *aal*. Teut. types **aloz*, **alā*. ¶ Distinct from M. E. *aule*, flesh-hook, A. S. *awel*, grappling-hook. (Phil. Soc. Trans. 1906; p. 261.)

Awn. (Scand.) M. E. *agune* (13th cent.), *awene*, *awne*. A. S. pl. *ægnan*, Corp. Gl. — Icel. *ögn*, chaff, a husk; Dan. *avne*, chaff; Swed. *agn*, only in pl. *agnar*, husks.+Goth. *ahana*; O. H. G. *agana*, chaff. Cf. Gk. pl. *ἄχναι*, chaff; O. L. *agna*, a straw.

Awning. (O. F.?) In Sir T. Herbert's Travels, ed. 1665, p. 8; the proper sense seems to be 'a sail or tarpauling spread above a ship's deck, to keep off the sun's heat.' Perhaps from O. F. *auvan*, *auvant*, mod. F. *auvent*, 'a pent-house of cloth before a shop-window;' Cot. Cf. Prov. *anvan*, Late L. *antevanna*, *auvanna*, *avanna*. Perhaps from L. *ante*, before; *uannus*, a fan (fem. sb.).

Awry. (E.) For *on wry*, on the twist; Barbour, Bruce, iv. 705. See **Wry**.

Axe, Ax. (E.) M. E. *ax*, *ex*. A. S. *æx*, older forms *acus*, *æcus*.+Du. *aaks*; Icel. *öx*, *öxi*; Swed. *yxa*; Dan. *öxe*; Goth. *akwizi*; O. H. G. *acchus*; G. *axt*; L. *ascia* (if for **acsia*); Gk. *ἀξίνη*.

Axiom. (Gk.) XV cent. — Gk. *ἀξίωμα* (gen. *ἀξιώματος*), worth, quality; in science, an assumption. — Gk. *ἀξιόω*, I deem worthy. — Gk. *ἄξιος*, worthy, worth, lit. 'weighing as much as.' — Gk. *ἄγειν*, to drive; also, to weigh. (√AG.)

Axis, axle. (L.) L. *axis*, an axis, axle-tree. + Gk. *ἄξων*; Skt. *aksha*, an axle, wheel, cart. Cf. also A. S. *eax*, an axle; Du. *as*; G. *achse*; Russ. *os'*; Lith. *aszis*. (√AG, to drive.) See below.

axle. (Scand.) M. E. *axel*. [A. S. has *eaxl*, but only with the sense of shoulder.] — Icel. *öxull*, axis; whence *öxul-trē*, an axle-tree; Swed. and Dan. *axel*, axle. β. It is a dimin. of the form appearing in L. *axis*; see **Axis**. Cf. W. *echel*, axle. **Der.** *axle-tree*, where *tree* is a block of wood.

Ay! interj. (E.) M. E. *ey!* A natural interjection. ¶ The phr. *ay me* is French; O. F. *aymi*, alas for me! Cf. Ital. *ahimé*, Span. *ay di me*, Gk. *οἴμοι*. See **Ah**.

Ay, Aye, yea, yes. (E.?) Spelt *I* in

old edd. of Shak., &c. Origin uncertain; perhaps a variant of **Yea**.

Ayah, a native waiting-maid, in India. (Port. — L.) Port. *aia*, a nurse, governess (fem. of *aio*, a tutor). Prob. from L. *auia*, a grandmother. — L. *auus*, a grandfather.

Aye, adv., ever. (Scand.) M. E. *ay*.— Icel. *ei*, ever.+A. S. *ā*, ever, also *āwa*; Goth. *aiw*, ever, case-forms from Teut. **aiwoz* (Goth. *aiws*), an age, which is allied to L. *æuum*, Gk. *αἰών*, an age. Cf. Gk. *αἰεί*, *ἀεί*, ever.

Aye-Aye, a kind of lemur. (F. — Mada-gascar.) F. *aye-aye*, supp. to Littré. From the native name *ai-ay* in Madagas-car; said to be named from its cry.

Azimuth. (Arab.) *Azimuthal* circles are great circles on the sphere that pass through the *zenith*. Properly, *azimuth* is a pl. form, answering to Arab. *as-samūt*, ways, or points (or quarters) of the horizon; from *al samt*, sing., the way, or point (or quarter) of the horizon. — Arab. *al*, the; and *samt*, a way, quarter, direction; whence also E. *zenith*. See **Zenith**.

Azote, nitrogen. (F. — Gk.) So called because destructive to animal life. — F. *azote*. — Gk. *ἀ-*, negative prefix; *ζωτικός*, preserving life, from *ζω-ή*, life, *ζάειν*, to live.

Azure, blue. (F. — Arab. — Pers.) M. E. *asur*, *azure*. — O. F. *azur*, azure; a cor-rupted form, standing for *lazur*, which was mistaken for *l'azur*, as if the initial *l* indicated the def. article; Low L. *lazur*, an azure-coloured stone, also called *lapis lazuli*. — Arab. *lāzward* (see Devic). — Pers. *lājuward*, lapis lazuli, a blue colour. So called from the mines of Lajwurd, where the lapis lazuli was found (Marco Polo, ed. Yule).

B

Baa, to bleat. (E.) In Shak.; an imita-tive word.

Babble. (E.) M. E. *babelen*, to prate, mumble, chatter. The suffix *-le* is fre-quentative; the word means 'to keep on saying *ba*, *ba*,' syllables imitative of a child's attempts to speak.+Du. *babbelen*; Dan. *bable*; Icel. *babbla*; G. *bappeln*; and cf. F. *babiller*.

Babe. (E.) M. E. *bab*, earliest form *baban*. Probably due to infantile utterance; cf. **Babble**.

Babirusa, Babiroussa, a kind of wild hog. (Malay.) Malay *bābī rūsa*, lit. 'deer-hog,' or 'hog like a deer'; from *rūsa*, deer, and *bābī*, hog.

Baboon. (F. or Low L.) O. F. *babuin*, F. *babouin*; we also find M. E. *babion*, *babian*, *babewine*; Low L. *babewynus*, a baboon (A.D. 1295). Origin uncertain. Cf. O. F. *babou*, a grimace (Godefroy). Prob. from the motion of the lips. Cf. Babble.

Bacchanal. (L. – Gk.) L. *Bacchānālis*, a worshipper of *Bacchus*, god of wine. – Gk. Βάκχος, god of wine.

Bachelor. (F. – L.) M. E. *bacheler.* – O. F. *bacheler.* – Late L. **baccalāris*, but only found as *baccalārius*, a holder of a small farm or estate, called in Late L. *baccalāria*. Remoter origin unknown, and much disputed. Hardly from Late L. *bacca*, for L. *uacca*, a cow.

Back. (E.) M. E. *bak.* A.S. *bæc.*+ Icel. *bak*; O. Sax. *bak*; O. Fries. *bek*. Der. *a-back*, q. v.; *back-bite*, M. E. *bak-biten* (P. Pl. B. ii. 80); *back-ward*, M. E. *bacward* (Cursor Mundi, 2042).

backgammon, a game. (E.) In Butler's Hudibras, pt. iii. c. 2. The sense is 'back-game,' because the pieces, when taken, are put back. See **gammon** (2).

Bacon. (F. – Teut.) M. E. *bacon.* – O.F. *bacon*; Low L. *baco.* – O. H. G. *bacho*, M. H. G. *bache*, buttock, ham, a flitch of bacon. Cf. G. *bache*, a wild sow; M. Du. *bak*, a pig; M. Dan. *bakke*, a pig.

Bad. (E.) M. E. *badde*. Formed from A.S. *bæddel*, s., a hermaphrodite; and allied to A.S. *bædling*, an effeminate man.

Badge. (Unknown.) M.E. *bage*; Prompt. Parv. Low L. *bagia, bagea*, 'signum, insigne quoddam;' Ducange; apparently, a Latin version of the E. word. Origin unknown.

badger. (Unknown.) Spelt *bageard* in Sir T. More; a nickname for the *brock*. Dr. Murray shews that *badger* = animal with a *badge* or stripe. See above.

Badinage, jesting talk. (F. – Prov. – L.) F. *badinage.* – F. *badiner*, to jest. – F. *badin*, adj., jesting. – Prov. *bader* (= F. *bayer*), lit. to gape; hence, to be silly. – Late L. *badāre*, to gape; prob. of imitative origin, from *ba*, expressive of opening the mouth. Cf. Babble.

Baffle, to foil, disgrace. (F. ? – G. ?) A Scotch word, as explained in Hall's Chron. Hen. VIII, an. 5. *To baffull* is 'a great reproach among the Scottes'; it means to disgrace, vilify. Cf. Lowland Sc. *bauchle* (XV cent. *bachle*), to vilify. Origin doubtful, but cf. F. *beffler*, to deceive, mock (Cot.), *bafouer* (Cot. *baffouer*, to baffle, revile, disgrace); allied to Ital. *beffare*, to flout, scoffe (Florio), from *beffa*, a scoff; Norman F. *baffer*, to slap in the face; Prov. *bafa*, a scoff. Prob. from M. H. G. *beffen*, to scold; cf. G. *bäffen*, Du. *baffen*, to bark, yelp; of imitative origin, like Du. *paf*, a pop, a box on the ear.

Bag. (Scand.) M. E. *bagge.* – Icel. *baggi*, O. Swed. *bagge*, a bag, pack, bundle. Not found elsewhere in Teutonic. (Gael. *bag* is from E.)

bagatelle, a trifle, a game. (F. – Ital. – Teut.) F. *bagatelle*, a trifle. – Ital. *bagat-tella*, a trifle, dimin. of Parmesan *bagata*, a little property; from Lombard *baga*, a wine-skin, of Teut. origin; see **Bag**, **baggage** (1).

baggage (1), luggage. (F. – Scand.) M.E. *baggage, bagage.* – O.F. *bagage*, a collection of bundles. – O. F. *bague*, a bundle.

baggage (2), a worthless woman. (F. – Scand.) The same as **Baggage** (1), in a depraved sense. Perhaps influenced by F. *bagasse*, 'a baggage, quean,' Cot.; Ital. *bagascia*, 'a baggage-wench;' Florio.

Bail (1), security; as verb, to secure. (F. – L.) O. F. *bail*, s. custody; from *bailler*, a law term, to secure, to keep in custody. – L. *baiulare*, to carry a child about, to take charge of a child. – L. *baiulus*, a porter, carrier.

bailiff. (F. – L.) M. E. *bailif.* – O. F. *baillif*, Cot. – Late L. *bājulīvum*, acc. of *bajulīvus*, a custodian, &c. – L. *baiulare* (above).

bailiwick. (F. – L.; *and* E.) From M. E. *baili*, short for *bailif* (above); and M. E. *wik*, A.S. *wīc*, a district; hence, 'district of a bailiff;' later, 'office' of the same.

Bail (2), a bucket. See **Bale** (3).

Bail (3), at cricket. (F. – L. ?) O. F. *bail*, an iron-pointed stake; Godefroy adds that 'in the arrondissements of Vervins and Avesnes, *bail* is the name of a horizontal piece of wood fixed upon two stakes.' Perhaps from L. *baculum*, a stick. (Doubtful.)

Bairn, a child. (E.) M. E. *barn*. A.S. *bearn*. + Icel., Swed., Dan., and Goth. *barn*. Lit. 'that which is born;' Teut.

type *barnom, neut. sb., from bar, 2nd grade of ber-an, to bear ; with suffix -no-. See Bear (1).

Bait, to feed. (Scand.) Lit. ' to make to bite ;' a bait is ' an enticement to bite.' M. E. baiten, beiten. — Icel. beita, to make to bite, causal of bīta, to bite ; Swed. beta, to pasture ; Swed. bete, Dan. bed, a bait. See Bite.

Baize, coarse woollen stuff. (F. — L.) An error for bayes, pl. of F. baye, ' the cloth called bayes ;' Cot. — O. F. bai, bay-coloured. — L. badius, bay. From the orig. colour. Cf. Span. bayo, bay, bayeta, baize ; &c. See Bay (1).

Bake. (E.) M. E. baken. A. S. bacan, pt. t. bōc, pp. bacen. + Icel. and Swed. baka ; Dan. bage ; Du. bakken ; G. backen ; cf. Gk. φώγειν, to roast. (√ BHOG.)

Bakshish, Backsheesh, a present, small gratuity. (Pers.) Pers. bakhshīsh, a gratuity ; from bakhshīdan, to give ; baksh, a share, portion. Cf. Zend. baksh, to distribute ; Skt. bhaj, to divide.

Balance. (F. — L.) M. E. balance. — F. balance, ' a ballance, pair of weights or ballances ;' Cot. Cf. Ital. bilancia. — L. bilancem, acc. of bilanx, having two scales. — L. bi-, for bis, double, twice ; and lanx, a dish, platter, scale of a balance.

Balas-ruby, a variety of ruby, of a pale rose-red or orange colour. (F. — Low L. — Arab. — Pers.) Formerly balais. — F. balais ; Med. L. balascus, balascius. — Arab. balakhsh, a ruby (Devic). — Pers. badakhshī, a ruby ; named from Badakh-shān, N. of the river Amoo (Oxus).

Balcony. (Ital. — Teut.) Ital. balcone, palcone, orig. a stage. — O. H. G. balcho, a beam. + O. Sax. balko, a beam. See Balk(1).

Bald. (C.) M. E. balled ; the orig. sense was ' shining, white,' as in ' bald-faced stag,' a stag with a white streak on its face ; cf. prov. E. ball, a white-faced horse. — Gael. and Irish bal, ball, a spot, mark, speckle (properly a white spot or streak) ; Bret. bal, a white streak on an animal's face ; W. bali, whiteness in a horse's forehead. Cf. Gk. φάλιος, white. φαλακρός, bald-headed ; Lith. baltas, white.

Baldachin (pronounced baoldakin or bældakin), a canopy over an altar, throne, &c. (F. or Ital. — Arab.) F. baldaquin ; Ital. baldacchino, a canopy, tester, orig hangings or tapestry made at Bagdad. — Ital. Baldacco, Bagdad. — Arab. Baghdād, Bagdad.

Balderdash, poor stuff. (Scand. ?) It formerly meant a jumbled mixture of liquors. Cf. Dan. balder, noise, clatter ; and daske, to slap, flap. Hence it appears (like slap-dash) to have meant a confused noise ; secondarily a hodge-podge (Halli-well) ; and generally, any mixture. (Un-certain.)

Baldric, a girdle. (F. — M. H. G. — L.) O. F. *baldric (not recorded), older form of O. F. baldret, baldrei ; Low L. baldringus. — M. H. G. balderich, a girdle ; extended from O. H. G. balz, a belt. — L. balteus, a belt. See Belt.

Bale (1), a package ; see Ball (2).

Bale (2), evil. (E.) M. E. bale. A.S. bealu, balu, evil. + O. Fries. and O.S. balu ; Icel. böl, misfortune ; O. H. G. balo, destruction. Teut. *balwom, neut. of *balwoz, adj. evil ; cf. Goth. balwawesei, wickedness. Der. bale-ful.

Bale (3), to empty water out of a ship. (F. — Teut.) XVII cent. It means to empty a ship by means of bails, i. e. buckets. — F. baille, a bucket. Cf. Du. balie, a tub ; Swed. balja, Dan. ballie, G. balje, a tub. — Late Lat. *bacula (Diez), dimin. from Du. bak, M.Du. back, a trough.

Balk (1), a beam, ridge of land. (E.) M. E. balke. A. S. balca, a ridge, heap ; which explains balked = laid in heaps, 1 Hen. IV, i. i. 69. + O. Sax. balko, a beam ; Du. balk, a beam, bar ; Swed. balk, a beam, partition ; G. balken. Teut. stem *balkon-, a bar. Cf. Phalanx.

balk (2), **baulk**, to hinder. (E.) M. E. balken. To put a balk or bar in a man's way.

Ball (1), a spherical body. (F. — O. H. G.) M. E. bal, balle. — F. balle. — M. H. G. balle, O. H. G. ballo (G. ball), a ball, sphere. + Icel. böllr.

bale (1), a package. (F. — O. H. G.) M. E. bale. — F. bale, a ball, also a pack, as of merchandise ; Cot. The same as F. balle, a ball ; hence, a round package.

Ball (2), a dance. (F. — Late L.) F. bal. — F. baller, to dance. — Late L. ballāre, to dance. + Gk. βαλλίζειν, to dance.

ballad. (F. — Prov. — Late L.) M. E. balade. — O. F. balade ; F. ballade. — Prov. balada, a song for dancing to. — Late L. ballāre, to dance.

Ballast, a load to steady a ship. (Scand. or O. Low G.) Three forms are found : (1) O. Dan. barlast, i.e. bare load, mere weight, Swed. barlast ; (2) O. Low G.

ballast, i.e. ' bale last,' useless load, Du., Dan., E. Fries. *ballast* ; (3) Dan. *bag-last*, i.e. back load. Of these, (3) seems due to popular etymology ; and (2) arose out of (1). See **Last** (4) ; also **Bare**, **Dale** (2), **Back**. Cf. M. Du. *bal-daedt*, evil deed (Hexham).

Ballet. (F. – Late L.) F. *ballet*, dimin. of *bal*, a dance. See **Ball** (2).

Balloon, a large ball. (F.—O. H. G.) Formerly *baloon*, a ball used in a game like football ; (also *ballone*, from Ital. *ballone*, in Florio). – O. F. *balon*, 'a little ball, or pack ; a football or baloon ;' Cot. Mod. F. *ballon* ; Span. *balon* ; Ital. *pallone* ; augmentative form of F. *balle*, &c., a ball. See **Ball** (1).

ballot. (Ital. – O. H. G.) Ital. *ballottare*, ' to cast lots with bullets, as they vse in Venice ;' Florio. – Ital. *ballotta*, a little ball used for voting ; dimin. of Ital. *balla*, a ball. See **Ball** (1).

Balm. (F. – L. – Gk.)   A modified spelling ; M. E. *basme*, *bame*, *baume*. – O. F. *basme*. – L. *balsamum*. – Gk. βάλσαμον, fragrant resin of the βάλσαμος, or balsam-tree.   Prob. Semitic ; cf. Heb. *bāsām*, balsam.

balsam. (L. – Gk.) L. *balsamum* ; as above.

Baluster, a rail of a staircase, small column. (F. – Ital. – L. – Gk.) F. *balustre* ; *balustres*, 'ballisters, little, round, and short pillars, ranked on the outsides of cloisters, terraces,' &c. ; Cot. – Ital. *balaustro*, a baluster ; so called from a fancied resemblance to the flower of the wild pomegranate. – Ital. *balausto*, *balaustra*, the flower of the pomegranate. – L. *balaustium*. – Gk. βαλαύστιον, the flower of the wild pomegranate.   Der. *balustr-ade*, F. *balustrade*, from Ital. *balaustrata*, furnished with balusters.

Bamboo. (Port. – Malay.) Spelt *mambu* (1662). – O. Port. *mambu* (Garcia). – Malay *sĕmámbū*, a rattan like bamboo.

Bamboozle, to hoax. (Unknown.)

Ban, a proclamation. (E.) Chiefly in the pl. *banns* (of marriage). M. E. *ban*. A. S. *gebann*, a proclamation (the prefix *ge-* making no difference). Cf. A. S. *ābannan*, to summon, order out. Influenced by O. F. *ban*, of G. origin (as below).+ Du. *ban*, excommunication ; Icel. and Swed. *bann*, Dan. *band*, O. H. G. *ban*, a ban. All from Teut. strong vb. **bannan-*, to proclaim ; as in O. H. G. *bannan*. Cf.

L. *fāma*, a rumour.   (√BHA.)   Brugm. i. § 559.

Banana, the plantain-tree.   (Span.) Span. *banana*, fruit of the *banano* ; said to be of African origin (from Guinea).

Band (1), **Bond.** (Scand.)   M. E. *band* ; variant, *bond*. – Icel. *band* ; Swed. *band* ; Dan. *baand* ; cf. Du. and G. *band*. Teut. **bandom*, n. ; from *band-*, 2nd grade of *bind-an*, to bind ; see **Bind**.   Allied to A. S. *bend*, Goth. *bandi*, a band.   Cf. Skt. *bandha*, a binding.   Der. *band-age* (F. *bandage*) ; *band-box* ; *bandog*, q. v.

band (2), a company of men. (F. – Teut.) F. *bande* ; Cot. ; whence G. *bande*, a gang, set. – Low Lat. *banda*, a gang ; allied to Low L. *bandum*, a banner.   See **Banner** and **Bind**.

Bandanna, a silk handkerchief with white spots. (Hind.)   Hind. *bāndhnū*, 'a mode of dyeing in which the cloth is tied in different places, to prevent the parts tied from receiving the dye . . . a kind of silk cloth ;' Shakespear's Hind. Dict.

Bandicoot, a large Indian rat. (Telugu.) Telugu *pandi-kokku*, lit. pig-rat (Yule). – Tel. *pandi*, a pig ; *kokku*, a rat.

Bandit. (Ital. – O. H. G.) In Sh. Ital. *bandito*, outlawed, pp. of *bandire*, to proscribe. – Low L. *bannīre*, to proclaim. – O. H. G. *bannan* to summon ; whence O. H. G. *ban*, cognate with E. *ban*.

Bandog, a large dog. (E.)   Orig. *banddog*, a dog that is tied up.   See Prompt. Parv. p. 43.   See **Dand** (1).

Bandy, to beat to and fro, contend. (F. – Teut.)   Orig. to *band* (Turbervile). – F. *bander*, ' to bind ; also, to bandie, at tennis ;' Cot.   Se *bander*, to league against. – F. *bande*, a band ; see **Dand** (2).

bandy-legged, bow-legged. (F. – Teut. *and* Scand.)   Prob. from *bandy*, formerly the name of a bent stick for playing a game called *bandy*, in which a ball was *bandied* about.   See above.

Bane, harm. (E.)   A. S. *bana*, a murderer, bane.+O. Sax. and O. H. G. *bano* ; Icel. *bani*, Dan. and Swed. *bane*, death, murder. Teut. stem **banon-*, m.   Cf. Goth. *banja*, a wound.   Der. *bane-ful*.

Bang (1), to beat. (Scand.)   In Sh. – Icel. *banga*, Dan. *banke*, to beat ; O. Swed. *bǎng*, Icel. *bang*, a hammering.   Cf. G. *bengel*, a cudgel.

Bang (2), a narcotic drug. (Pers.) – Skt.) Pers. *bang*. – Skt. *bhangā*, hemp ; the drug being made from the wild hemp.

Bangle, a kind of bracelet. (Hind.) Hind. *bangrī*, a bracelet, bangle. (H. H. Wilson.)

Banian; see Banyan.

Banish. (F. – O. H. G.) M. E. *banisshen*. – O. F. *banis-*, stem of pres. part. of *banir*, *bannir*, to proscribe. – Low L. *bannīre*, to proclaim; see Bandit.

Banisters; a corruption of Balusters.

Banjo, a six-stringed musical instrument. (Ital. – Gk.) A negro corruption of *bandore*, *bandora*, or *pandore*. – Ital. *pandora*, a musical instrument, usually with three strings. – Gk. πανδοῦρα, the same. Perhaps of Egypt. orig.

Bank (1), a mound of earth. (Scand.) M. E. *banke*. – O. Scand. **banke*, orig. form of Icel. *bakki*, ridge, eminence, bank of a river; cf. Dan. *bakke*, Swed. *backe*, bank; whence also Norman F. *banque*, a bank. Teut. stem **bankon-*. Cf. O. Sax. and Du. *bank*, O. H. G. *banch*, A. S. *benc*, a bench (see Bench).

bank (2), for money. (F. – Teut.) F. *banque*, a money-changer's table or bench. – M. Du. *banck*, M. H. G. *banc*, a bench, table. See above.

bankrupt. (F. – Ital. – Teut. *and* L.) Modified from F. *banqueroute*, bankruptcy, by a knowledge of the relation of the word to L. *ruptus*, broken. – Ital. *banca rotta*, a broken bank, due to the money-changer's failure. – M. H. G. *banc*, a bench (see above); and L. *rupta*, fem. of *ruptus*, pp. of *rumpere*, to break.

Banner. (F. – Teut.) M. E. *banere*. – O. F. *banere* (supp. to Godefroy, s. v. *baniere*), also *baniere*. – Low L. **bandāria* (Ducange gives *bandēria*), a banner. – Low L. *bandum*, *bannum*, a standard. From a Teut. (Langobardic) source; cf. Goth. *bandwa*, a sign, token. 'Uexillum, quod *bandum* appellant;' Paulus, *de Gestis Langob.* i. 20. Prob. allied to Ban; see Skt. *bhanati* in Uhlenbeck.

banneret, orig. a knight who had men under his own banner. (F. – Teut.) M. E. *baneret*. – O. F. *baneret* (F. *banneret*); lit. 'bannered.' – O. F. *banere* (above); with suffix *-et* = L. pp. *-ātus*.

Bannock, a cake. (C. – L. ?) Gael. *bannach*, a cake. Perhaps from L. *pānicium*, a thing baked; from *pāni-s*, bread.

Banns, pl. of Ban, q. v.

Banquet. (F. – Ital. – Teut.) F. *banquet*. – Ital. *banchetto* (Torriano), a feast; also a bench; dimin. of *banco*, a bench. –

M. H. G. *banc*, a bench, table; see **bank** (2).

Banshee, a female spirit supposed to warn families of a death. (C.) Gael. *beanshith*, a banshee, from Gael. *bean*, a woman; *sith*, a fairy; O. Irish *ban-side*, fairies (Windisch, s. v. *side*), from O. Ir. *ben* (= E. *quean*), a woman, *side*, fairies.

Bantam. (Java.) A fowl from *Bantam*, in Java.

Banter, raillery. (Unknown.)

Bantling, an infant. (G. ?) Prob. considered as *band-ling*, one wrapped in swaddling bands; with double dimin. suffix *-l-ing*; but really an adaptation of G. *bänkling* (with the same sense as *bank-art*), an illegitimate child; from *bank*, a bench; i. e. 'a child begotten on a bench,' not in the marriage-bed (Mahn). Cf. **bank** (2).

Banyan, a tree. (Port. – Skt.) An English, not a native name for the tree. So called because used as a market-place for merchants or 'bannyans,' as we termed them; see Sir T. Herbert, Travels, ed. 1665, pp. 51, 123. – Port. *banian*, an Indian merchant. – Skt. *banij*, a merchant.

Baobab, a tree. (African.) The native name in Senegal (Adanson).

Baptise, Baptize. (F. – L. – Gk.) Formerly *baptise*; M. E. *baptisen*. – O. F. *baptiser*. – L. *baptizāre*. – Gk. βαπτίζειν; from βάπτειν, to dip. **Der.** *baptist*, Gk. βαπτιστής, a dipper; *baptism*, Gk. βάπτισμα, βάπτισμος, a dipping.

Bar, a rail. (F. – Late L.) M. E. *barre*. – O. F. *barre*. – Late L. *barra*, a bar.

Barb (1), hook on an arrow. (F. – L.) F. *barbe*. – L. *barba*, a beard. Hence O. F. *flesche barbelée*, 'a bearded or barbed arrow;' Cot. See Beard.

barbel, a fish. (F. – L.) M. E. *barbelle*. – O. F. *barbel*. – F. *barbeau*. – L. *barbellus*, dimin. of *barbus*, a barbel. – L. *barba*, a beard. ¶ Named from four beard-like appendages near the mouth.

barber. (F. – L.) M. E. *barbour*. – A. F. *barbour*, with suffix *-our* = Lat. acc. *-ātorem*; cf. O. F. *barbier*, a barber. – F. *barbe*, a beard; from L. *barba*, beard.

Barb (2), a horse. (F. – Barbary.) F. *barbe*, a Barbary horse; named from the country.

Barbarous. (L. – Gk.) L. *barbar-us*; with suffix *-ous*. – Gk. βάρβαρος, foreign; lit. stammering; a name given by Greeks to express the strange sound of foreign languages. Cf. L. *balbus*, stammering.

Barbed, accoutred, armed; said of horses. (F.—Scand.?) Also (more correctly), *barded.*—F. *bardé*, 'barbed as a horse,' Cot.—F. *barde*, horse-armour.— Icel. *barð*, a brim, edge; also, a beak or armed prow of a warship (cf. *barði*, a shield); whence it may have been applied to horses (Diez).

Barbel, Barber; see Barb (1).

Barberry, Berberry, a shrub. (Med. L.) From Med. L. *barbaris*, a barberry-tree; of unknown origin. Hence also M. F. *berberis*, Sp. *berberis*, and even mod. Arab. *barbārīs*. ¶ The spelling should be *berbery* or *barbary*; no connexion with *berry*.

Barbican. (F.) M. E. *barbican.*—F. *barbacane*, a barbican or outwork of a castle; also, a loop-hole; also, an outlet for water. Prob. from Eastern *bāb-khānah*, gate-house (Yule).

Bard. (C.) W. *bardd*, Irish and Gael. *bard*, a poet. Cf. Gk. φράζειν, to speak.

Bare. (E.) M. E. *bar.* A. S. *bær.* + Icel. *berr*; G. *bar, baar.* Teut. type *baxox; cf. Lith. *basas*, O. Slav. *bosŭ*, barefooted.

Bargain. (F.– Late L.) M. E. *bargayn*, sb.—O. F. *bargaignier, bargenir*, to chaffer.—Late L. *barcāniāre*, to change about. Remoter origin unknown.

Barge. (F.– Late L.– C.?) M.E. *barge.* —F. *barge.*—Late L. *barga*, variant of *barca*; see Bark (1).

bark (1), **barque.** (F.– Late L.– C.?) *Bark* is an E. spelling of F. *barque*, a little ship.—Late L. *barca*, a sort of ship or large boat, a lighter. Perhaps of Celtic origin (Thurneysen). – O. Irish *barc* (fem. *a*-stem), a bark.

Bark (2), the rind of a tree. (Scand.) M. E. *bark.*—Swed. *bark*; Dan. *bark*; Icel. *börkr.* Teut. type *barkuz*.

Bark (3), to yelp as a dog. (E.) M. E. *berken.*—A. S. *beorcan*, to bark. Cf. Icel. *berkja*, A. S. *borcian*, to bark. Perhaps of imitative origin.

Barley. (E.) M.E. *barli.*—A.S. *bærlic.* Cf. A. S. *bere*, barley (Lowl. Sc. *bear*); and *-lic*, for *līc*, like. Cf. also Goth. *barizeins*, made of barley; L. *far*, corn.

barn. (E.) M. E. *berne.* A. S. *bern*, contr. form of *ber-ern* (Luke iii. 17).— A.S. *bere*, barley; and *ern, ærn*, a place

for storing. A.S. *ærn* is for **ran(n)*, cognate with Icel. *rann*; see Ransack.

Barm (1), yeast. (E.) M. E. *berme.* A. S. *beorma.* + Low G. *barm*; Swed. *bärma*; G. *bärme.* Teut. stem **bermon-*; perhaps allied to Ferment.

Barm (2), the lap. (E.) M. E. *barm.* A. S. *bearm*, lap, bosom.+O. Sax., Swed., Dan. *barm*; Icel. *barmr*; Goth. *barms.* Teut. type **barmoz*; from *bar-*, 2nd grade of *ber-an*, to bear; see Bear (1).

Barn. (E.) See Barley.

Barnacle (1), a kind of goose. (F.— Med. L.) Dimin. from F. *bernaque* (Cot.); Med. L. *bernaca.* '*Bernacæ*, aues aucis palustribus similes;' Ducange. Used by Giraldus Cambrensis. Cf. Port. *bernaca, bernacha*; Span. *bernicla* (Neuman). (See Max Müller, Lectures, 2nd Series.)

barnacle (2), a sort of shell-fish. (F. – Med. L.) The same as Barnacle (1). See N. E. D.; and Max Müller, Lect. on Science of Language, ed. 7, ii. 583.

Barnacles, spectacles, orig. irons put on the noses of horses to keep them quiet. (F.) The sense of 'spectacles' is late, and due to a humorous allusion. M. E. *bernak*, dimin. *bernakill.* '*Bernak* for hors, *bernakill,* Chamus' (i.e. L. *camus*), Prompt. Parv. We find *bernac* in A. F. (in an Eng. MS.); Wright's Vocab. i. 100, l. 3. Origin unknown.

Barometer, an instrument for measuring the weight of the air. (Gk.) Gk. βαρο-, for βάρος, weight; and μέτρον, a measure; see Metre.

Baron, a title. (F.– Late L.) M. E. *baron.*—F. *baron*; older form *ber*, nom. (Prov. *bar*), the suffix *-on* marking the acc. case (Diez). Cf. Ital. *barone*, Sp. *varon*, Port. *varão.*—Late L. *baro*, acc. *-ōnem*, a man, a male. Origin unknown.

Barouche, a carriage. (G.– Ital.–L.) G. *barutsche.*—Ital. *baroccio, biroccio*, a chariot, orig. a two-wheeled car.—L. *birotus*, two-wheeled; with suffix *-occio* assimilated to that of *carr-occio*, a chariot (Diez).—L. *bi-*, double; and *rota*, a wheel.

Barracks. (F.– Ital.) F. *baraque.* —Ital. *baracca*, a tent for soldiers; cf. Sp. *barraca.* Prob. connected with Late L. *barra*, a bar, pale.

Barrator, one who incites to quarrels and lawsuits. (F.) Formerly *barratour, baratour*; from M. E. *barat*, deceit, strife. —F. *barat*, 'cheating, deceit, guile, also a barter,' Cotgrave. Allied to Barter.

¶ Influenced by Icel. *barátta*, a fight, a turmoil.

Barrel. (F.) M. E. *barel.*—O. F. (and F.) *baril.* Perhaps from Late L. *barra*, a bar, pale ; from the staves of it.

Barren. (F.) M. E. *barain.*—A. F. *barain, -e* ; O. F. *brehaing*, fem. *brehaingne, baraigne* ; F. *bréhaigne*, sterile. Of unknown origin.

Barricade. (F.—Span.) F. *barricade.*—Span. *barricada*, a barricade, lit. one made with barrels full of earth.—Span. *barrica*, a barrel. Perhaps from Span. *barra*, a bar ; see **Barrel**.

Barrier. (F.) M. E. *barrere.*—O. F. *barrere* (Godefroy, s. v. *bassein*) ; F. *barrière.*—F. *barrer*, to bar up.—F. *barre*, a bar. See **Bar**.

barrister. (Low L.) A barbarous word ; formed with suffix -*ister* (= Low L. -*istārius*) from the sb. *bar*. Spelman gives the Low L. form as *barrastērius*.

Barrow (1), a burial-mound. (E.) For *berrow* (like *parson* for *person*, &c.). M. E. *bergh, berw*, a hill, mound. O. Merc. *berg* ; A. S. *beorg, beorh*, a mountain, hill, mound. **+**O. Sax., Du., G. *berg.* Teut. type *bergoz, a hill. Cf. O. Irish *brí*, a mountain ; Skt. *brhant*, large.

Barrow (2), a wheel-barrow. (E.) M.E. *barewe.*—A. S. *bar-*, 2nd grade of *ber-an*, to bear, carry. Cf. M. H. G. *rade-ber*, wheel-barrow, from *rad*, wheel.

Barter, to traffic. (F.) M. E. *bartryn.* —O. F. *bareter, barater*, 'to cheat, beguile, also to barter ;' Cot. O. F. *barat*, 'cheating, also a barter ;' Cot. **β**. Of doubtful origin ; perhaps Celtic (Littré). Cf. Bret. *barad*, treachery, Irish *brath*, W. *brad*, treachery, Gael. *brath*, advantage by unfair means ; Irish *bradach*, Gael. *bradach*, thievish, roguish ; W. *bradu*, to plot.

Barton, a court-yard, manor. (E.) O. Northumb. *bere-tūn* (Matt. iii. 12).—A. S. *bere*, barley ; and *tūn*, an enclosure ; see **Barley** and **Town**.

Barytes, in chemistry. (Gk.) Named from its weight.—Gk. βαρύτης, weight.— Gk. βαρύς, heavy. See **Grave** (2).

barytone. (Ital.—Gk.) Better *baritone* ; a musical term for a deep voice.— Ital. *baritono*, a baritone.—Gk. βαρύ-s, heavy, deep ; and τόνος, a tone ; see **Tone**.

Basalt. (L.) Also *basaltes.* L. *basaltes*, a hard kind of marble in Æthiopia. An African word (Pliny).

Base (1), low. (F.—L.) M. E. *bass*,

base.—F. *bas*, m., *basse*, fem. —Late L. *bassus*, low ; the same word as L. *Bassus*, proper name, which seems to have meant ' stout, fat,' rather than merely ' low.'

Base (2), a foundation. (F.—L.—Gk.) M. E. *bas.*—F. *base.*—L. *basis.*—Gk. βάσις, a step, a pedestal, base.—Gk. base βα-, to go (as in βαίνειν, to go) ; with suffix -σι- (for -τι-) ; cf. Skt. *ga-ti(s)*, a going, from *gam*, to go. See **Come**.

Basement, lowest floor of a building. (F.—Ital.—L.) Appears in F. as *soubassement*, the basement of a building ; formed from *sous*, under, and -*bassement*, borrowed from Ital. *bassamento*, lit. an abasement.— Ital. *bassare*, to lower.—Ital. *basso*, low.— Late L. *bassus* ; see **Base** (1).

Basenet, Basnet ; see **Basinet**.

Bashaw ; the old form of **Pasha**.

Bashful. (F. *and* E.) For *abash-ful*; see **Abash**. Prob. by confusion with *abase* and *base*.

Basil (1), a plant. (F.—L.—Gk.) O.F. *basile* (Supp. to Godefroy) ; short for *basilic* ; cf. F. *basilic*, ' herb basill ;' Cot. —L. *basilicum*, neut. of *basilicus*, royal.— Gr. βασιλικόν, basil ; neut. of βασιλικός, royal.—Gk. βασιλεύς, a king.

  basilica, a large hall. (L.—Gk.) L. *basilica*, fem. of *basilicus*, royal.

  basilisk, a fabled serpent. (L.—Gk.) L. *basiliscus.*—Gk. βασιλίσκος, lit. royal ; also a lizard or serpent, named from a spot on the head like a crown (Pliny, viii. 21). —Gk. βασιλεύς, a king.

Basil (2), the hide of a sheep tanned. (F.—Span.—Arab.) A. F. *baseyne* (Liber Albus, 225).—F. *basane*, M. F. *bassane.*— Span. *badana*, a dressed sheep-skin.—Arab. *bitānah*, the [inner] lining of a garment, for which basil-leather was used. Cf. Arab. *batn*, the inside.

Basin. (F.—Late L.) M. E. *bacin, basin.*—O. F. *bacin, bachin* ; F. *bassin.*— Late L. *bachīnus, bacchīnus*, a basin (Duc.). Supposed to be from Late L. *bacca*, water-vessel (Isidore). Cf. Du. *bak*, a bowl, trough.

  basinet, basenet, basnet, a light helmet. (F.—Late L.) In Spenser ; F. Q. vi. 1. 31.—O. F. *bacinet*, dimin. of *bacin*, a basin ; from its shape.

Basis. (L.—Gk.) L. *basis.*—Gk. βάσις ; see **Base** (2).

Bask. (Scand.) M. E. *baske*, to bathe oneself, Palsgrave ; and cf. *bathe hire*, to bask herself, Ch. C. T. Nonnes Prestes

Tale, 447. — Icel. *baðask (later baðast), for baða sik, to bathe oneself. Cf. also Swed. dial. at basa sig i solen, to bask in the sun, badfisk, fishes basking in the sun (Wedgwood). See Bathe. ¶ Formed like Busk.

Basket. (F. ?) M. E. basket. Mod. Norman F. basquette (Moisy). Origin unknown.

Basnet; see Basinet.

Bass (1), the lowest part, in music. (F. — L.) The same word as Base (1); but so spelt in imitation of Ital. basso, base.

Bass (2), **Barse,** a fish. (E.) M. E. barse; also base, bace (with loss of r). A. S. bærs, a perch. +Du. baars; G. bars, barsch, a perch. Named from its prickles. From *bars-, 2nd grade of Teut. root *bers, whence also Bristle, q. v. Cf. Skt. bhrshti, pointed.

Bassoon, a base instrument. (F. — L.) F. basson, augmentative from F. basse, base (in music), fem. of bas, base. See Base (1).

Bast. (E.) M. E. bast; bast-tre, a lime-tree. A. S. bæst, inner bark of a lime-tree; whence bast is made.+Icel., Swed., Dan., G. bast. Often spelt bass.

Bastard, an illegitimate child. (F.) M. E. bastard, applied to Will. I. — O. F. bastard, the same as fils de bast, lit. 'the son of a pack-saddle,' not of a bed. [The expression a bast ibore, illegitimate, occurs in Rob. of Glouc. p. 516.] — O. F. bast, a pack-saddle (F. bât); with suffix -ard, from O. H. G. hart, hard, first used as a suffix in proper names and then generally.

Baste (1), to beat. (Scand. ?) The form bas it occurs as a pp. in 1553. Cf. Swed. basa, to strike, beat, whip.

Baste (2), to pour fat over meat. (Unknown.) In Sh. ' To baste, linire;' Levins, ed. 1570.

Baste (3), to sew slightly. (F. — M. H. G.) M. E. basten. — O. F. bastir, F. bâtir, to sew slightly; a tailor's term. — M. H. G. besten (for *bastjan), to bind; orig. to tie with bast. — G. bast, bast. See Bast.

Bastile, a fortress. (F.) O.F. bastille, a building. — O. F. bastir (F. bâtir), to build. Origin uncertain; perhaps allied to Baton.

Bastinado. (Span.) From Span. bastonada, a beating. — Span. baston, a stick. — Late L. bastōnem, acc.; see Baton.

Bastion. (F. — Ital.) F. bastion. — Ital. bastione, part of a fortification. — Ital. bastire, to build; allied to O. F. bastir, to build. See Bastile.

Bat (1), a cudgel. (E.) M. E. batte. — A. S. batt (Eng. Studien, xi. 65). Cf. Irish bata, bat, a staff. Der. bat-let, with double dimin. suffix -l-et.

Bat (2), a winged mammal. (Scand.) Bat has taken the place of M. E. bakke. — Dan. bakke, now only in comp. aften-bakke, evening-bat. Cf. O. Swed. natt-backa, 'night-bat' (Ihre); for which we find Swed. dial. natt-batta (Rietz).

Batch. (E.) A batch is as much as is baked at once; hence, a quantity. M. E. bacche, a baking; from A.S. bacan, to bake. See Bake.

Bate (1), to beat down, diminish. (F. — L.) Short for Abate, by loss of a.

Bate (2), strife. (F. — L.) M. E. bate; a clipt form of Debate, in the sense of strife. ¶ So also fence for de-fence.

Bath. (E.) M. E. baþ. A.S. bæð.+ Icel. bað; O. H. G. bad; Swed., Dan., Du., G. bad. Teut. *ba-þom, neuter. The orig. sense was a place of warmth; cf. O. H. G. bâjan (G. bähen), to foment.

bathe. (E.) A.S. baðian, to bathe. — A. S. bæð, a bath. And see Bask.

Bathos. (Gk.) Lit. depth, sinking. — Gk. βάθος, depth; cf. βαθύς, deep.

Baton, Batoon, a cudgel. (F.) F. bâton, O. F. baston. — Late L. bastōnem, acc. of basto, a cudgel. Origin doubtful; connected by Diez with Gk. βαστάζειν, to support.

Battalion. (F. — Ital. — L.) F. bataillon. — Ital. battaglione, a battalion. — Ital. battaglia, a battle ; see Battle below.

Batten (1), to grow fat; to fatten. (Scand.) Orig. intransitive. — Icel. batna, to grow better, improve, recover. Cf. Goth. ga-batnan, to be bettered ; Icel. bat-i, s., improvement, E. Better, q. v., and Boot (2). Cf. also Du. baten, to yield profit ; baat, profit.

Batten (2), a wooden rod. (F.) To batten down is to fasten with battens. Batten is merely another spelling of Baton.

Batter (1), to beat. (F. — L.) M. E. bat-er-en; with frequentative suffix -er-. — F. battre. — L. battere, popular form of battuere, to beat.

batter (2), a compound of eggs, flour, and milk. (F. — L.) M. E. batour, bature. — O. F. bature, a beating. — F. battre, to beat (above). So called because beaten up.

battery. (F.—L.) F. *baterie, batterie,* 'beating, battery;' Cot. —F. *battre,* to beat.

battle. (F.—L.) M.E. *bataille, bataile.* —O. F. *bataille,* (1) a fight, (2) a battalion. —Folk-L. *battālia,* neut. pl. (turned into a fem. sing.), fights; Late L. *battuālia,* neut. pl. of adj. *battuālis,* fighting. —Late L. *battuere,* to beat.

battledoor. (Prov.—L.) M.E. *batyldoure,* Prompt. Parv. —Prov. *batedor,* Span. *batidor,* a washing-beetle, which was also at first the sense of the E. word. [The corruption to *battledoor* was due to confusion with *battle,* vb. to fight.] —Prov. *batre,* Span. *batir,* the same as F. *battre,* to beat; with suffix *-dor,* which in Prov. and Span.=L. suffix *-tōrem,* acc. form from nom. *-tor,* expressing the agent.

Battlement. (F.) M.E. *batelment, batilment,***bateillement,* from O.F. *bateillier,* to fortify; formed from *bataille,* battle, fight, but confused with O.F. *bastiller,* to fortify, derivative of O.F. *bastir,* to build. See **Battle** and **Bastile.**

Bauble (1), a fool's mace; (2) a plaything. (F.) (1) M.E. *babyll, bable, babel,* Gower, C.A. i. 224; (2) M.E. *babel,* Tudor E. *bauble.* From O.F. *baubel, babel,* a child's plaything (Godefroy). Perhaps connected with M. Ital. *babbola,* a toy (Florio); and with L. *babulus,* a fool. Cf. E. **Babble.**

Bavin, a faggot. (F.) Prov. E. (Wilts.) *bavin,* a faggot; hence, as adj., soon kindled and burnt out, 1 Hen. IV. iii. 2. 61. —O. F. *baffe,* a faggot, bundle (Godefroy, Roquefort). Remoter origin unknown.

Bawd, a procurer or procuress, go-between. (F.—O. H.G.) The full M.E. form is *bawdstrot,* P. Plowm. A. iii. 40 (another MS. has *bawde*).—O.F. *baldestrot (found only in the later form *baudetrot*), equivalent to Lat. *pronuba,* a bridewoman. —O. H. G. *bald,* bold, gay, lively (cognate with E. *bold*); and M. H. G. *strotzen,* vb. (E. *strut*).

Bawl. (Scand.) Icel. *baula,* to low as a cow; Swed. *böla,* to bellow: see **Bull, Bellow.**

Bay (1), reddish brown. (F.—L.) M. E. *bay.*—O. F. *bai.*—L. *badius,* bay-coloured.

bayard. (F.—L.) A bay horse; from the colour; also, any horse. The suffix *-ard* is Teutonic; see **Bastard.**

Bay (2), a kind of laurel; properly, a berry-tree. (F.—L.) M. E. *bay,* a berry —F. *baie,* a berry.—L. *bāca,* a berry.

Bay (3), inlet of the sea. (F.—L.) F. *baie,* an inlet.—Late L. *baia,* a harbour (Isidore). β. Confused with *bay,* a recess in a wall.—O. F. *baee,* a gap.—Late L. *badāta,* fem. of pp. of *badāre,* to gape.

Bay (4), to bark as a dog. (F.—L.) M. E. *bayen.*—O. F. *baier,* to yelp (Godefroy). Cf. Ital. *baiare,* 'to barke,' Florio. From the sound.

Bay (5), in phr. *at bay.* (F.—L.) For *at abay.* —F. *abois, abbois; être aux abois,* to be at bay, lit. 'to be at the baying of the dogs.' Pl. of F. *aboi,* the bark of a dog; verbal sb. from F. *aboyer,* O. F. *abaier,* to yelp, bay.—O. F. *a* (for L. *ad*); and *baier* (above).

Bay-window; from **Bay** (3, sect. β) and **Window.**

Bayonet. (F.) XVII cent. F. *baïonnette; bayonette,* a knife; Cot. Probably named from *Bayonne* (France), where first made or used.

Bazaar. (Pers.) Pers. *bāzār,* a market.

Bdellium. (L.—Gk.—Heb.) A precious substance.—L. *bdellium.*—Gk. βδέλλιον.—Heb. *bedōlakh* (Gen. ii. 12).

Be-, prefix. (E.) A.S. *be-,* prefix; often causative, as in *be-numb,* to make numb. Note also *be-head,* to deprive of the head; *be-set,* to set upon, set round; *be-mire,* to cover with mire; &c.

Be, to exist. (E.) M.E. *been.* A.S. *bēon,* to be.+W. *bod,* to be; Russ. *buite;* L. *fore* (pt. t. *fui*); Gk. φύειν; Skt. *bhū.* (√BHEU.)

Beach. (E.?) XVI cent. Orig. ' shingle.' Prob. E., and the same as prov. E. *bache,* a valley; also, a sandbank near a river. A.S. *bæc,* a valley; Kemble, Cod. Dipl. iii. 386.

Beacon. (E.) M.E. *beken.* A.S. *bēacn, bēcn.* +O. Sax. *bōkan;* O. H.G. *bouhhan.* Teut. type **bauknom,* neut.

Bead. (E.) Orig. 'a prayer;' hence a perforated ball, for counting prayers. M. E. *bede,* a prayer, a bead. A.S. *bed, gebed,* a prayer.—A. S. *biddan* (=*bidjan), to pray. +Du. *bede;* G. *bitte;* Goth. *bida,* a prayer. See **Bid** (1).

Beadle. (F.—Teut.) M.E. *bedel.*—O. F. *bedel,* F. *bedeau,* a beadle; lit. 'proclaimer,' or 'messenger.'—M. H. G. *bütel,* O. H. G. *butil.* —O. H. G. *but-,* weak grade of *biotan*, G. *bieten*; cognate with A. S. *bēodan*, to bid. Cf. A. S. *bydel*, a beadle, from *bēodan*. See **Bid** (2).

Beagle, a dog. (Unknown.) M. E. *begle*, Squire of Low Degree, l. 771.

Beak. (F. – C.) M. E. *bec.* – F. *bec.* – Late L. *beccus*, of Gaulish origin. Cf. Irish *bacc*, W. *bach*, a crook, a hook.

Beaker. (Scand. – L. – Gk.) M. E. *biker, byker.* – Icel. *bikarr*, a cup. + O. Sax. *bikeri*; Du. *beker*; G. *becher*; Ital. *bicchiere*. β. Perhaps from Late L. *bicārium*, a wine-cup. – Gk. βῖκος, an earthen wine-vessel; a word of Eastern origin.

Beam (1), a piece of timber. (E.) M. E. *beem*. A. S. *bēam*, a tree. + Du. *boom*; G. *baum*. Cf. also Iccl. *baðmr*, a tree; Goth. *bagms*.

Beam (2), a ray. (E.) [Usually identified with **Beam** (1), specially used to signify a column of light; cf. A. S. *byrnende bēam*, ' the pillar of fire.'] But A. S. *bēam*, a beam (as in *sunne-bēam*, a sunbeam) answers to a Teut. type *bau-moz*, prob. cognate with Gk. φαῦ-σις, light, φάος (for φάϝος), also φῶς, light. See **Phosphorus**.

Bean. (E.) M. E. *bene*. A. S. *bēan*. + Du. *boon*; Icel. *baun*; O. H. G. *pōna*, *bōna* (G. *bohne*). Teut. type *baunā*, f.

Bear (1), to carry. (E.) M. E. *beren*. A. S. *beran.* + Iccl. *bera*; O. H. G. *beran*; Goth. *bairan*; also L. *ferre*; Gk. φέρειν; Skt. *bhr̥*; O. Ir. *berim*, I bear; Russ. *brate*, to take, carry; Pers. *burdan*, to bear. (√BHER.) **Der.** *upbear*.

Bear (2), an animal. (E.) M. E. *bere*. A. S. *bera.*+Icel. *bera* (*björn*); O. H. G. *bero*, *pero*, G. *bär*; Du. *beer*. Cf. Lith. *bēras*, brown (Kluge). Teut. type *beron-*.

Beard. (E.) M. E. *berd*. A. S. *beard.* + Du. *baard*; G. *bart*. Teut. type *bardoz*. Allied to Russ. *boroda*; Lith. *barzda*; L. *barba*, beard; from Idg. type *bhardhā*.

Beast. (F. – L.) M. E. *beste.* – O. F. *beste* (F. *bête*). – L. *bestia*, a beast.

Beat. (E.) M. E. *beten*. A. S. *bēatan.* +Icel. *bauta*; O. H. G. *pōzan*, M. H. G. *bōzen*. Teut. type *bautan-*.

Beatify. (F. – L.) F. *béatifier.* – L. *beātificāre*, to make happy. – L. *beāti-*, for *beātus*, pp. of *beāre*, to bless, make happy; and *-fic-*, for *facere*, to make.

beatitude. (F. – L.) F. *béatitude.* – L. *beātitūdinem*, acc. from nom. *beātitūdo*, blessedness. – L. *beāti-*, for *beatus*, blessed; with suffix *-tūdo*.

Beau, a dressy man. (F. – L.) F. *beau*; O. F. *bel.* – L. *bellus*, fair. For **ben-lus*; from *ben-* (as in *ben-e*), variant of *bon-*, as in *bon-us*, good. Brugm. ii. § 67.

beauty. (F. – L.) M. E. *beute.* – A. F. *beute*, O. F. *beaute*, *beltet.* – L. *bellitātem*, acc. of *bellitās*, fairness. – L. *bellus*, fair (above). **Der.** *beauti-ful*, *beaute-ous*.

Beaver (1), an animal. (E.) M. E. *bever*. A. S. *befer*, *beofor*. + Du. *bever*; Icel. *björr*; Dan. *bæver*; Swed. *bäfver*; G. *biber*; Russ. *bobr'*; Lith. *bebrus*; L. *fiber*. Skt. *babhrus* (1) brown; (2) a large ichneumon. Teut. type **bebruz*; Idg. type **bhebhrus*, reduplicated deriv. of *bhru-*, brown, tawny. Brugm. i. § 566. See **Brown**.

Beaver (2), **Bever,** lower part of a helmet. (F.) Altered by confusion with *beaver-hat.* – M. E. *baviere.* – O. F. *bavière*, a child's bib; also, the bever (beaver) of a helmet. – F. *baver*, to slaver. – F. *bave*, foam, slaver. Perhaps from the movement of the lips; cf. Bret. *babouz*, slaver.

Beaver (3), **Bever,** a short immediate repast. (F. – L.) M. E. *beuer* (= *bever*). – A. F. *beivre*, a drink; substantival use of O. F. *bevre*, *beivre*, to drink. – L. *bibere*, to drink.

Becalm, to make calm. See **Be-** and **Calm.**

Because. (E. *and* F. – L.) See **Cause.**

Bechance. (E. *and* F. – L.) See **Chance.**

Beck (1), to nod, give a sign. (E.) M. E. *bek-yn*, the same as *bek-nyn*, to beckon (Prompt. Parv.). See **Beckon.**

Beck (2), a stream. (Scand.) M. E. *bek.* – Icel. *bekkr*; Swed. *bäck*; Dan. *bæk*; a stream. Teut. type **bakkiz*. Also Teut. type **bakiz*; whence Du. *beek*, a beck; G. *bach*.

Beckon. (E.) M. E. *beknen*. A. S. *bēcnan*, *bēacnian* (also *bīecnan*), to make signs. – A. S. *bēacn*, a sign. See **Beacon.**

Become. (E.) A. S. *becuman*, to arrive, happen, turn out, befall. + Goth. *bi-kwiman*; cf. G. *be-quem*, suitable, becoming. From **Be-** and **Come.**

Bed. (E.) M. E. *bed*. A. S. *bed*, *bedd.* +Du. *bed*; Goth. *badi*; G. *bett*. Teut. type **badjom*, n.

bedrid, bedridden. (E.) M. E. *bedrede* (Ch. C. T. 7351); *bedreden* (P. Pl. B. viii. 85). A. S. *bedrida*, *bedreda*, lit. ' a bedrider ;' one who can only ride on a bed, not on a horse. – A. S. *bed*, a bed ; and

43

*rid-a, one who rides, from the weak grade of *rīdan*, to ride.

bedstead. (E.) M. E. *bedstede*. — A. S. *bed*, a bed; and *stede*, a stand, station; see Stead.

Bedabble, Bedaub, Bedazzle, Bedew, Bedim, Bedizen. See Dabble, Daub, &c.

Bedell. (Low L. — Teut.) From the Latinised form (*bedellus*), of O. F. and M. E. *bedel*; see Beadle.

Bedlam. (Palestine.) M. E. *bedlem*, corruption of Bethlehem, in Palestine. Now applied to the hospital of St. Mary of Bethlehem, for lunatics.

Bedouin. (F. — Arab.) O. F. *bedouin*, a wandering Arab; orig. pl. — Arab. *badawin*, pl. of Arab. *badawiy*, wandering in the desert. — Arab. *badw*, a desert.

Bedridden, Bedstead; see Bed.

Bee. (E.) M. E. *bee*. A. S. *bēo*, earlier *bīo*.+Du. *bij*; O. H. G. *bīa*. Cf. G. *bie-ne*; Lith. *bi-tte*; Ir. *bea-ch*. Perhaps 'flutterer'; cf. Skt. *bhī*, to fear; O. H. G. *bi-bēn*, to tremble.

Beech. (E.) A. S. *bōēce, bēce*, a beech; *bēcen*, adj., beechen; both derivatives (by mutation) from the older form *bōc*. See Book.

Beef. (F. — L.) M. E. *beef*. — A. F. *bēf*; O. F. *boef* (F. *bœuf*). — L. *bouem*, acc. of *bōs*, an ox.+Gk. βοῦς, ox; Ir. *bó*, Gael. *bò*, W. *buw*, Skt. *go*, A. S. *cū*, a cow; see Cow.

beef-eater, a yeoman of the guard. (Hyb.) Lit. 'an eater of beef;' hence, an attendant. Cf. A. S. *hlāf-ǣta*, a loaf-eater, a servant. ¶ The usual derivation (from Mr. Steevens' imaginary *beaufetier*, later spelt *buffetier*) is historically baseless.

Beer. (E.) M. E. *bere*. A. S. *bēor.* + Du. and G. *bier*; Icel. *bjórr*.

Beestings; see Biestings.

Beet. (L.) M. E. *bete*. A. S. *bēte*. — L. *bēta*, beet (Pliny).

Beetle (1), an insect. (E.) Prov. E. *bittle*. A. S. *bitela*, lit. 'biting one.' — A. S. *bit-*, weak grade of *bītan*, to bite; with adj. suffix *-ol*; cf. *wac-ol*, wakeful. See Bite.

Beetle (2), a large mallet. (E.) M. E. *betel*. A. S. *bȳtel* (= O. Wes. *bīetel, O. Merc. *bētel); cf. Low G. *bötel.* Teut. type *baut-iloz, 'a beater;' from **baut-an-*, to beat; see Beat.

Beetle (3), to overhang. (E.) From the M. E. adj. *bitel-brouwed*, 'beetle-browed;' P. Plowm. A. v. 109. Orig. sense doubtful; either from M. E. *bitel,*

sharp, or from M. E. *bitil*, a beetle. In either case from *bit-*, weak grade of *bītan*, to bite.

Befall, Befool, Before; see Fall, &c.

Beg. (F.) M. E. *beggen*. A. F. *begger*, Langtoft, i. 248; used as equiv. to *be-guigner*, Britton, I. 22. § 15. Formed from the sb. *beggar*; see below.

Beget, Begin; see Get, Gin (1).

Beggar. (F.) M. E. *beggare*; cf. *Begger* = a Beguin or Beghard, Rom. Rose, 7256 (F. text, *Beguin*). — O. F. *begard, be-gart*, Flemish *beggaert*, Late L. *Beghardus.* Formed, with suffix *-ard* (G. *-hart*), from *Bègue*, a man's name. See Beguine.

Begone, Beguile; see Go, Guile.

Beguine, one of a class of religious devotees. (F.) Chiefly used in the fem.; F. *béguine*, Low L. *beghīna*, one of a religious order, first established at Liège, about A. D. 1207. Named after Lambert Le Bègue, priest of Liège (12th c.); whence also Beguin, Beghard, masc. Le Bègue means 'stammerer,' from the verb *bègui*, to stammer, in the dialect of Namur; allied to Picard *béguer*, F. *bégayer*.

Begum, in the E. Indies, a lady of the highest rank. (Pers. — Turk.) Pers. *be-gum*, a queen, lady of rank. — Turk. *beg, bey*, a bey, governor. See Bey.

Behalf, interest. (E.) Formerly in the M. E. phrase *on my behalue* = on my behalf, on my side; substituted for the A. S. phr. *on (mīn) healfe*, on the side of (me), by confusion with *be healfe (mē)*, used in the same sense. From A. S. *be*, by; and *healf*, sb., side. See Half.

Behave. (E.) I. e. to *be-have* oneself, or control oneself; from *have* with prefix *be-*, the same as prep. *by*.

behaviour. (E.; with F. *suffix.*) Formed abnormally from the verb to *behave*; confused with F. sb. *avoir*, (1) wealth, (2) ability. Cf. Lowl. Sc. *havings*, (1) wealth, (2) behaviour.

Behead. (E.) From Be- and Head.

Behemoth. (Heb. — Egypt.) Heb. *behēmōth*, said to be pl. of *behēmāh*, a beast; but probably of Egypt. origin.

Behest, Behind, Behold. (E.) See Hest, Hind, Hold (1).

Behoof, advantage. (E.) M. E. *to bi-houe*, for the advantage of. A. S. *behōf*, advantage.+O. Fries. *bihōf*, Du. *behoef*, advantage; G. *behuf*; Swed. *behof*; Dan. *behov*, need. β. The prefix *be* is A. S. *be,*

E. *by.* The simple sb. appears in Icel. *hôf*, moderation, measure; cf. Goth. *ga-hobains*, temperance, self-restraint. From A. S. *hôf*, 2nd stem of the vb. Heave.

behove, to befit. (E.) A. S. *behôfian*, verb formed from the sb. *behôf* above. + Du. *behoeven*, from sb. *behoef*; Swed. *be-hôfva*; Dan. *behöve.*

Belabour, Belay; see Labour, Lay.

Belch. (E.) M. E. *belken.* A. S. *bealcian, bælcan,* to utter; translating L. *ēructāre*, used figuratively. Cf. *bælc,* sb. + Du. *balken,* to bray. See Bellow and Bell.

Beldam. (F.−L.) Ironically for *bel-dame,* i. e. fine lady. − F. *belle dame.* − L. *bella,* fem. of *bellus,* fair; and *domina,* lady, fem. of *dominus,* lord. See Beau.

Beleaguer. (Du.) See Leaguer.

Belemnite, a fossil. (Gk.) Gk. βελεμνίτης, a stone shaped like the head of a dart. − Gk. βέλεμνον, a dart. − Gk. βάλλειν, to cast. (√GwEL.)

Belfry. (F.−G.) Orig. 'a watch-tower.' Corrupted (partly by influence of *bell*) from M. E. *berfray, berfrey,* a watch-tower. − O. F. *berfrei, berfroi, belfroi* (F. *beffroi*). − M. H. G. *bercfrit,* a watch-tower. − M. H. G. *berc-,* for *berg-,* base of *bergen,* to protect; and M. H. G. *frit, fride,* a place of security, a tower, the same word as G. *friede,* peace; hence the lit. sense is ' a protecting shelter,' watch-tower. Allied to Borough and Free.

Belie. (E.) A. S. *beleogan,* to tell lies about. From *be-,* by, prefix; and *lēogan,* to lie. See Lie (2).

Believe. (E.) M. E. *beleuen (beleven).* The prefix *be-* was substituted for older *ge-.* − O. Merc. *gelēfan,* A.S. *gelīefan, ge-lýfan,* to believe; lit. to hold dear. + Du. *gelooven;* O. H. G. *gilouban,* G. *g-lauben;* Goth. *ga-laubjan.* Teut. type *laubian,* with A. S. *ge-,* prefix; from *laub,* 2nd stem of Teut. root *leub* = Idg. √LEUBH, to like. See Lief.

Bell. (E.) M. E. *belle.* A. S. *belle,* a bell. + Du. *bel.* Perhaps named from its loud sound; cf. A. S. *bellan,* to roar, bellow. See Bellow.

Belle, a fair lady. (F.−L.) F. *belle,* fem. of F. *beau,* O. F. *bel,* fair. − L. *bellus,* fair, fine. See Beau.

belladonna. (Ital.−L.) Ital. *bella donna,* fair lady. − L. *bella domina*; see Beldam. A name given to the nightshade, from the use of it by ladies to give ex-

pression to the eyes, the pupils of which it expands.

Belligerent. (L.) More correctly, *belligerant.* − L. *belligerant-,* stem of pres. pt. of *belligerāre,* to carry on war. − L. *belli-,* for *bello-,* stem of *bellum,* war; *gerere,* to carry on (war). *Bellum* is for O. Lat. *duellum*; see Duel.

Bellow. (E.) M. E. *belwen* (c. 1300). Not fully explained. It may have resulted from confusion of A. S. *bellan,* to roar, bellow, with the str. verb *belgan,* to be angry, or with the rare verb *bylgian,* to bellow (which would have given *billow*). See Bell. Cf. Bull.

Bellows. (Scand.) M. E. *beli, bely, below,* a bag, but also used in the special sense of ' bellows.' *Bellows* is the pl. of M. E. *below,* a bag, from Icel. *belgr*; and M. E. *beli* (from A. S.) also means *belly.* Cf. G. *blase-balg,* a ' blow-bag,' a pair of bellows; A.S. *blǣst-belg,* bellows, lit. ' blast-bag.' See below.

belly. (E.) M. E. *bely.* A. S. *bælg, belg,* a bag, skin (for holding things); hence (later), belly. + Icel. *belgr,* bag; Du. *balg,* skin, belly; Swed. *bälg,* belly, bellows; Dan. *bælg,* husk, belly; G. *balg*; Goth. *balgs,* bag. Teut. type *balgiz.* From *balg-,* 2nd stem of Teut. root *belg* (= Idg. √BHELGH), to swell. Cf. Irish *bolg,* bag, belly; *bolgaim,* I swell; W. *bol,* belly. Der. *bellows,* q. v.

Belong, Beloved, Below; see Long, Love, Low.

Belt, a girdle. (L.) M. E. *belt.* A.S. *belt.* + Icel. *belti*; Irish and Gael. *balt,* a belt, border; O. H. G. *balz*; Swed. *bälte*; Dan. *bælte.* All borrowed from L. *balteus,* a belt.

Beltane, Old May-day. (C.) O. Irish *bel-tene* (Windisch); lit. ' fire-kindling,' from an old custom. Celtic type *belo-te(p)niā*; where *belo-* is cognate with A.S. *bǣl,* a blaze, and *-tepniā* is from *tepnos,* type of O. Irish *ten,* fire; cf. L. *tep-ēre,* to be warm (Fick. ii. 125, 164).

Bemoan. (E.) From Be- and Moan.

Bench. (E.) M. E. *benche.* − A. S. *benc.* + Du. *bank,* a bench, table, bank for money; Swed. *bänk*; Dan. *bænk*; Icel. *bekkr*; G. *bank.* Teut. type *bankiz.* Doublet, *bank.*

Bend (1), to bow, curve. (E.) M. E. *benden.* A. S. *bendan,* orig. to string a bow, fasten a band or string to it; cf. A. S.

bend, a band (= Teut.*bandiz) ; from *band*, 2nd stem of *bind-an*, to bind. See **Bind**. So also Icel. *benda*, to bend a bow ; allied to *band*, a cord.

bend (2), an oblique band, in heraldry. (F. – G.) O. F. *bende*, also *bande*, a band ; see Cotgrave. The same word as F. *bande*, a band of men ; see Band (2).

Beneath. (E.) M. E. *benethe*. A.S. *beneoðan*, prep. below. – A. S. *be-*, by ; *neoðan*, adv. below, from the base *neoð-* in *neoð-era*, nether ; with adv. suffix *-an*. Cf. G. *nied-en*, *nied-er* ; see **Nether**.

Benediction. (F. – L.) F. *bénédic-tion*. – L. *benedictiōnem*, acc. of *benedictio*, a blessing. – L. *benedictus*, pp. of *bene-dīcere*, to speak well, bless. – L. *bene*, well ; and *dīcere*, to speak (see **Diction**).

benison. (F. – L.) M. E. *beneysun*. – O. F. *beneison*. – L. acc. *benedictiōnem*.

Benefactor. (L.) L. *benefactor*, a doer of good. – L. *bene*, well ; and *factor*, a doer, from *facere*, to do.

benefice. (F. – L.) M. E. *benefice*. – F. *bénéfice* (Cot.). – Late L. *beneficium*, a grant of an estate ; L. *beneficium*, a well-doing, a kindness. – L. *bene*, well ; and *facere*, to do.

benefit. (F. – L.) Modified (badly) from M. E. *benfet*. – O. F. *bienfet* (F. *bienfait*). – L. *benefactum*, a kindness conferred ; neut. of pp. of *benefacere*, to do well, be kind.

Benevolence. (F. – L.) F. *bénévo-lence* (Cot.). – L. *beneuolentia*, kindness. – L. acc. *bene uolentem*, kind, lit. well-wishing. – L. *bene*, well ; and *uolentem*, acc. of *uolens*, wishing, from *uolo*, I wish (see **Voluntary**).

Benighted. (E.) See **Night**.

Benign. (F. – L.) O. F. *benigne* (F. *bénin*). – L. *benignus*, kind ; short for *benigenus. – L. *beni-*, for *benus, variant of *bonus*, good ; and *-genus*, born (as in *indigenus*), from *genere*, old form of *gignere*, to beget.

Benison, blessing ; see **Benedic-tion**.

Bent-grass. (E.) M. E. *bent*. A.S. *beonet*, for earlier *binut, bent-grass (in place-names). + O. H. G. *binuz*, G. *binse*, bent-grass.

Benumb. From **Be-** and **Numb**.

Benzoin, a resinous substance. (F. – Ital. – Arab.) F. *benjoin*, ' gum benzoin or gum benjamin ;' Cot. – Ital. *ben-zoino*, *bengivi* (Torriano). The Ital. *lo*

bengivi seems to have been substituted for the Arab. name, *lubān jāwī*, lit. frankincense of Java. (Further corrupted to *gum benjamin*.)

Bequeath. (E.) A. S. *becweðan* to assert, bequeath. – A. S. *be-*, prefix ; and *cweðan*, to say, assert. See **Quoth**.

bequest. (E.) M. E. *biqueste*, *bi-quiste*. Formed, with added *-te* (cf. M. E. *requeste*), from A. S. *bicwiss, *becwiss (not found), sb. due to *becweðan*, to bequeath, assert, say. The components of this form occur ; viz. *be-*, *bi-*, prefix, and *cwiss* (in *ge-cwiss*), a saying. *Cwiss* is from Teut. *kwessiz, Idg.**g(w)ettis*, formed (with suffix *-ti-*) from Idg. base **g(w)et-*, whence *cweðan*, to say (Sievers, A. S. Gr. § 232) ; and *becwiss* is thus a regular deriv. of *becweðan*, to bequeath.

Bereave. (E.) A.S. *beréafian*, to dispossess ; see **Reave**.

Bergamot (1), an essence. (Ital.) Ital. *bergamotta*, the essence called bergamot. – Ital. *Bergamo*, a town in Lombardy.

Bergamot (2), a kind of pear. (F. – Ital. – Turk.) F. *bergamotte* (Cot.). – Ital. *bergamott-a* (pl. *-e*), ' a kind of excellent pears, come out of Turky ;' Torriano. – Turk. *beg armūdi*, ' prince's pear.' – Turk. *beg*, prince ; *armūd*, pear.

Berry. (E.) M. E. *berie*. A. S. *berie*. +Du. *bes*, *bezie* ; Icel. *ber* ; Swed. *bär* ; Dan. *bær* ; G. *beere* ; Goth. *basi*. All from a base *bas-*. Lit. ' edible fruit ;' cf. Skt. *bhas*, to eat. **Der.** *goose-berry*, &c.

Berth. (E.) Formerly ' convenient sea-room.' A 'suitable position.' From A. S. *byr-* (as in *ge-byr-ian*, to suit) with suffix *-th*. Cf. Du. *beurt*, a turn ; Low G. *bört*, good position.

Beryl. (L. – Gk. – Skt.) M. E. *beril*. – O. F. *beril*. – L. *bēryllus*. – Gk. βήρυλ-λος ; cf. Arab. *billaur*, crystal, beryl. – Skt. *vaidūrya* (Prakrit *velūriya*), orig. beryl, brought from Vidûra in S. India (Yule ; Böhtlingk).

Besant, Bezant, a gold circle, in heraldry. (F. – L. – Gk.) Intended to represent a gold coin of Byzantium. – O. F. *besant*, 'an ancient gold coin ;' Cot. – L. *Byzantium*. – Gk. Βυζάντιον, the name of Constantinople.

Beseech. (E.) M. E. *besechen*. From *be-*, prefix ; and *sechen*, Southern form corresponding to Northern *seken*, to seek. See **Seek**.

Beseem, Beset, Beshrew, Beside, Besiege; see Seem, Sit, Shrew, &c.

Besom, a broom. (E.) M. E. *besum*, *besme*. A. S. *besma*.+Du. *bezem*; G. *besen*. Teut. type **besmon-*, m.

Besot, Bespeak; see Sot, Speak.

Best; see Better.

Bestead; from Be- and Stead.

Bestial. (F.–L.) F. *bestial*. – L. *bestiālis*, beast-like.–L. *bestia*, a beast. See Beast.

Bestow, Bestrew, Bestride; see Stow, &c.

Bet, to wager. (F.–Scand.) Short for *abet*, in the sense to maintain, or 'back,' as *abet* is explained in Phillips, ed. 1706. See Abet. Der. *bet*, sb.

Betake. (E. *and* Scand.) See Take.

Betel, a species of pepper. (Port.–Malayalim.) Port. *betel*, *betele*.–Malayalim *vettila*, i. e. *veru ila*, mere leaf (Yule).

Bethink, Betide, Betimes, Betoken; see Think, &c.

Betray. (F.–L.; *with* E. *prefix*.) From *be-*, prefix; and O. F. *traïr* (F. *trahir*), to deliver up, from L. *trādere*. ¶ The prefix *be-* was due to confusion with *bewray*. See Tradition.

Betroth. (E.) See Troth.

Better, Best. (E.) 1. From the Teut. base **bat*, good, was formed the Teut. comp. stem **batizon-*, as in Goth. *batiza*, better, A. S. *betera* (with mutation from *a* to *e*), M. E. *better*. The A. S. *bet*, M. E. *bet*, is adverbial and comparative. 2. From the same base was formed Goth. *batista*, best, A. S. *betst* (for *bet-ist*), M. E. *best*. Similarly Du. *beter*, *best*; Icel. *betri*, *beztr*; Dan. *bedre*, *bedst*; Swed. *bättre*, *bäst*; G. *besser*, *best*. **Der.** (from the same base) *batten*, *boot* (2).

Between. (E.) A. S. *betwēonan*, between; earlier *betwēonum*. – A. S. *be*, by; *twēonum*, dat. pl. of *twēone*, double, allied to *twā*, two; see Two. Here *twēonum* (also *twīnum*) answers to Goth. *tweihnaim*, dat. pl. of *tweihnai*, 'two each.' Cf. L. *bīnī*.

betwixt. (E.) (M. E. *betwix*; to which *t* was afterwards added. – A. S. *betwix*, *betwux*, *betweox*, *betweohs*, apparently extended from A. S. *betwīh*, between. From A. S. *be*, by; and **twīh*, answering to *tweih-* in Goth. *tweih-nai*, two each. See above.

Bevel, sloping; to slope, slant. (F.)

In Sh. Sonn. 121.–O. F. **bivel*, **buvel*, only found in mod. F. *biveau*, and in F. *buveau*, 'a kind of square [carpenter's rule], having moveable and compasse branches, or the one branch compasse and the other straight; some call it a *bevell*;' Cot. Cf. Span. *baivel*. Origin unknown.

Bever, a potation ; see Beaver (3).

beverage. (F.–L.) O. F. *bevrage* (Supp. to Godefroy), drink.–O. F. *bevre*, *boivre*, to drink.–L. *bibere*, to drink.

bevy. (F.–L.) It answers to O. F. *bevee*, a drink ; from O. F. *bevre*, to drink (above). Cf. Ital. *beva*, a bevy (Florio) ; also, a drink (Torriano).

Bewail, Beware, Bewilder, Bewitch; see Wail, Ware, Wild, Witch.

Bewray, to disclose. (E.) Properly to accuse. M. E. *bewraien*, *biwreyen*, to disclose. A. S. *be-*, prefix (see Be-) ; and *wrēgan*, to accuse (for older **wrōgian*, with mutation from *ō* to *ē*). Cf. Icel. *rægja* (for *vrægja*), to slander, Swed. *röja* to discover ; O. Fries. *biwrōgia*, to accuse ; Goth. *wrōhjan*, to accuse ; G. *rügen*, to censure. β. These are causal verbs, from the base *wrōh-* seen in Goth. *wrōhs*, accusation, Icel. *rōg*, a slander.

Bey, a governor. (Turk.) Turk. *beg* (pron. nearly as *bay*), a lord, prince.

Beyond. (E.) M. E. *beyonde*. A. S. *begeondan*, beyond.–A. S. *be-*, for *be* or *bi* by ; and *geond*, prep. across, beyond, from *geon*, yon. Cf. Goth. *jaindrē*, thither, *jaind*, there ; from *jains*, that, yon. See Yon.

Bezel, the part of a ring in which the stone is set. (F.) Also spelt *basil*; also means a sloping edge.–O. F. *bisel* (Roquefort) ; mod. F. *biseau*, a bezel, basil, slant, sloped edge. Cf. Span. *bisel*, slanting edge of a looking-glass. Perhaps from L. *bis*, double.

Bezique, a game at cards. (F.–Pers.) F. *besigue* (with *g*) ; also *bésy* (Littré). β. The first form=Pers. *bāzīchah*, sport, a game ; the second=Pers. *bāzī*, play.–Pers. *bāzīdan*, to play. [A guess.]

Bezoar, a stone. (F.–Span.–Arab. –Pers.) O. F. *bezoar*, F. *bézoard*.–Span. *bezoar*.–Arab. *bādizahr*.–Pers. *pād-zahr*, bezoar ; lit. 'counter-poison,' from its supposed virtue.–Pers. *pād*, expelling ; and *zahr*, poison.

Bezonian, a beggarly fellow. (F.) In 2 Hen. IV. v. 3. 118. Formerly *bisonian*; made by adding E. *-ian* to F. *bisogne*, spelt *bisongne*, in Cotgrave, 'a filthe knave ... bisonian.' Or from Ital. *bisogno*, need, want; whence *bisogni*, pl. 'new-levied souldiers, such as come ... needy to the wars'; Torriano (not in Florio). Origin unknown.

Bi-, prefix. (L.) L. *bi-*, for **dui-*, twice. ‒ L. *duo*, two. So also Gk. δι-, Skt. *dvi*. See Two.

Bias. (F. ‒ L.) F. *biais*, a slant, slope; hence, inclination to one side. Cf. Ital. *s-biesco*, *s-biescio*, oblique. Origin unknown.

Bib. (L.) A cloth under a child's chin; from M. E. *bibben*, to drink. ‒ L. *bibere*, to drink. Hence *wine-bibber* (Luke vii. 34); L. *bibens uīnum* (Vulg.).

Bible. (F. ‒ L. ‒ Gk.) M. E. *bible*. ‒ F. *bible*. ‒ Late L. *biblia*, fem. sing.; for L. *biblia*, neut. pl. ‒ Gk. βιβλία, collection of writings, pl. of βιβλίον, little book, dimin. of βίβλος, a book. ‒ Gk. βύβλος, Egyptian papyrus; hence, a book.

bibliography. (Gk.) Gk. βιβλίο-, for βιβλίον; and γράφειν, to write.

bibliomania. (Gk.) Gk. βιβλίο-, for βιβλίον; and Mania.

Bice. (F.) Properly 'grayish'; hence *blew byce*, grayish blue. ‒ F. *bis*, dusky. Cf. Ital. *bigio*, gray. Origin unknown.

Bicker, to skirmish. (Uncertain.) M. E. *biker*, a fight; *bikeren*, to skirmish. Cf. M. E. *beken*, to peck; *biken*, to thrust with a pointed weapon. Apparently from O. F. *bequer*, to strike with the beak (see Beak); or from A.S. *becca*, a pick-axe. Cf. Du. *bikken*, to notch a mill-stone; also E. Fries. *bikkern*, to hack, gnaw, from *bikken*, to hack, *bikke*, a pickaxe (G. *bicke*).

Bicycle. (Hybrid.) In use since 1868. Coined from Bi- and Cycle.

Bid (1), to pray. (E.) Nearly obsolete; preserved in *bidding-prayer*, and in to *bid beads* (pray prayers). M. E. *bidden*. A.S. *biddan* + Du. *bidden*; G. *bitten*; Icel. *biðja*; Goth. *bidjan*. Teut. type **bidjan-*, allied to L. *fīdo*, I trust; Gk. πείθω, I prevail upon; from √BHEIDH. See Brugm. i. § 589; ii. § 890.

Bid (2), to command. (E.) M. E. *beden*. ‒ A.S. *bēodan*, to command. + Du. *bieden*, to offer; Icel. *bjōða*; G. *bieten*; Goth. *ana-biudan*; Gk. πεύθομαι, I enquire; Skt. *budh*, to understand. Teut. type **beudan-*. (√BHEUDH.) Confused with Bid (1),

the forms of which have taken the place of those of Bid (2).

Bide, to await, wait. (E.) M. E. *biden*. A. S. *bīdan*. + Du. *beiden*; Icel. *bīða*; Swed. *bida*; Dan. *bie*; Goth. *beidan*; O. H. G. *bītan*. Teut. type **bīdan-*.

Biennial, lasting two years. (L.) Formed as if from *bienni-um*, a space of two years; the true L. word is *biennālis*. ‒ L. *bi-* two; and *annālis*, lasting a year, yearly. ‒ L. *annus*. So also *tri-ennial*, from *tri-* (for *tres*), three; *quadr-ennial*, more correctly *quadri-ennial*, from *quadri-* (for *quadrus*), belonging to four; *quinqui-ennial*, from *quinqui-* (for *quinque*), five; *dec-ennial*, from *dec-em*, ten; *cent-ennial* from *centum*, a hundred; *mill-ennial*, from *mille*, a thousand, &c.

Bier, a frame on which a corpse is borne. (E.) M. E. *beere*, *bære*. A. S. *bǣr*, *bēr*. ‒ A. S. *bǣr-*, 3rd stem of *beran*, to carry. + Du. *baar*; O. H. G. *bāra* (G. *bahre*); allied to Icel. *barar*, fem. pl.; L. *feretrum*; Gk. φέρετρον.

Biestings, Beestings, the first milk given by a cow after calving. (E.) A. S. *bȳsting*, *bȳst* (for **bīest*), thick milk. From A. S. *bēost*, first milk after calving. + Du. *biest*; G. *biest-milch*.

Bifurcated, two-pronged. (L.) Late L. *bifurcātus*, pp. of *bifurcārī*, to part in two directions. ‒ L. *bi-furcus*, two-pronged; from *bi-(s)*, double; *furca*, a fork.

Big. (Scand. ?) M. E. *big*; also *bigg*, rich (Hampole). Not A. S. Cf. prov. E. *bug*, big, *bog*, boastful. Prob. of Scand. origin. Cf. Norw. *bugge*, a strong man.

Bigamy, a double marriage. (F. ‒ L. and Gk.) F. *bigamie*. ‒ Late L. *bigamia*; a clumsy compound from L. *bi-*, double (see Bi-), and Gk. *-γαμία*, from γάμος, marriage. It should rather have been *digamy* (Gk. διγαμία).

Biggen, a night-cap. (F.) M. F. *beguin*, 'a biggin for a child;' Cot. Named from the caps worn by beguines; see Beguine.

Bight, a coil of rope, a bay. (E.) M. E. *bight*. A. S. *byht*, as in *wæteres byht*, a bight (bay) of water (see Grein). ‒ A.S. *bug-*, weak grade of *būgan*, to bow, bend; with mutation of *u* to *y*. + G. *bucht*. Teut. type **buhtiz*. See Bow (1).

Bigot, an obstinate devotee to a creed. (F.) F. *bigot*, 'an hypocrite, superstitious fellow;' Cot. Applied by the

French to the Normans as a term of reproach (Wace). Of unknown origin. It is an older word than *beguine*, with which it seems to have been somewhat confused at a later period.

Bijou, a trinket. (F.—C.?) F. *bijou*. Perhaps from Bret. *bizou*, a ring with a stone, a finger-ring, from *biz*, a finger. Cf. Corn. *bisou* (the same), from *bis, bes*, a finger; W. *byson*, ring, from *bys*, finger.

Bilberry, a whortle-berry. (Scand.) Dan. *böllebær*, a bilberry; where *bær* is E. *berry*. In M. Dan., *bölle* had the sense of Dan. *bugle*, i. e. boss (Kalkar). Cf. Norw. *bola*, a swelling, tumour. ¶ North Eng. *blea-berry* = *blue-berry*; see **Blaeberry.** In both cases, *-berry* takes the E. form; see **Berry.**

Bilbo, a sword; **Bilboes,** fetters. (Span.) Both named from Bilboa or Bilbao in Spain, famous for iron and steel.

Bile (1), secretion from the liver. (F. —L.) F. *bile.*—L. *bĭlis*. L. *bīlis* is for **bislis*, Brugm. i. § 877; cf. W. *bustl*, Bret. *bestl*, bile (Fick, ed. 4. ii. 175). Der. *bili-ous*.

Bile (2), a boil. (E.) See **Boil** (2).

Bilge. (F.—C.) A variant of *bulge*, which orig. meant the bottom of a ship's hull; whence *bilge-water* (N. E. D.). See **Bulge.**

Bill (1), a chopper, sword. (E.) M. E. *bil*, sword, axe. A. S. *bill*, sword, axe. + O. Sax. *bil*, O. H. G. *bill*, n.; (cf. G. *bille*, axe, f.). Teut. type **biljom*, n.

bill (2), a bird's beak. (E.) M. E. *bile*. A. S. *bile* (Teut. type **biliz?*). Allied to **Bill** (1).

Bill (3), a writing, account. (F.—L.) A. F. *bille.*— Late L. *billa*, a writing; the dimin. is *billēta, bullēta*, shewing that *billa* is a corruption of L. *bulla*, a papal bull, &c.; see **Bull** (2).

billet (1), a note. (F.—L.) A. F. *billette.*— Late L. *billetta, billēta*, dimin. of *billa*, a writing; see **Bill** (3) above.

Billet (2), a log of wood. (F.) F. *billette, billot*, a billet of wood. Dimin. of *bille*, a log, stump. Origin unknown.

billiards. (F.) F. *billard*, 'a billard, or the stick wherewith we touch the ball at billyards;' Cot. Formed with suffix *-ard* (G. *-hart*) from *bille*, a log, stick, as above.

Billion; see **Million.**

Billow, a wave. (Scand.) Icel. *bylgja*, a billow; Swed. *bölja*; Dan. *bölge.*+M. H. G. *bulge*, a billow, a bag. Lit. 'a swell' or surge; cf. Icel. *belgja*, to inflate, puff out. The Icel. *bylgja* has mutation of *u* to *y*, and, like M. H. G. *bulg-e*, is from *bulg-*, 3rd stem of *belgan*, to swell with anger.

Bin. (E.) M. E. *binne*. A. S. *binn*, a manger; Lu. ii. 7.+Du. *ben*, G. *benne*, a sort of basket. Perhaps of Celtic origin; cf. Gaulish Lat. *benna*, body of a cart; W. *ben*, a cart.

Binary, twofold. (L.) L. *bīnārius*, consisting of two things.—L. *bīnus*, two-fold.—L. *bī-*, double; see **Bi-.**

Bind. (E.) M. E. *binden*. A. S. *bindan.* + Du. and G. *binden*; Icel. and Swed. *binda*; Dan. *binde*; Goth. *bindan*; Skt. *bandh*, to bind. (√BHENDH.)

Bing, a heap of corn; *obs.* (Scand.) In Surrey's Poems.—Icel. *bingr*, Swed. *binge*, a heap.+M. H. G. *bīge*, a heap of corn; whence Ital. *bica*. ¶ Distinct from *bin*, though perhaps confused with it.

Binnacle, a box for a ship's compass. (Port.—L.) A singular corruption of the older word *bittacle*, by confusion with *bin*, a chest.—Port. *bitacola*, a bittacle (i. e. binnacle); Vieyra. Cf. Span. *bitacora*, F. *habitacle*, the same. The Port. *bitacola* stands for **habitacola*, the first syllable being lost.—L. *habitāculum*, a little dwelling, i. e. the ' frame of timber in the steerage of a ship where the compass stands ' (Bailey).—L. *habitare*, to dwell; frequent. of *habēre*, to have.

Binocular, having two eyes. (L.) From Late L. *bĭn-ī*, two each; *ocul-us*, eye; with suffix *-āris*.

Binomial, having two terms. (L.) From Late L. *binōmi-us*, equiv. to L. *binōminis*, adj. having two names; with suffix *-ālis*. From L. *bi-*, two; *nōmin-*, for *nōmen*, a name.

Biography. (Gk.) A written account of a life; from βίο-, for βίος, life; and γράφειν, to write. The sb. βίος is allied to **Quick.**

biology. (Gk.) Science of life; from Gk. βίο-, for βίος, life; and -λογία, a discoursing, from λόγος, a discourse.

Biped. (L.) L. *biped-*, stem of *bipēs*, two-footed; from *bi-*, two; *pēs*, foot.

Birch, a tree. (E.) M E. *birche*. A. S. *birce*, f.+G. *birke*, f.<Teut. **birkjōn-*. β. Also A. S. *berc, beorc.* + Du.

berk; Icel. *björk*, Swed. *björk*, Dan. *birk*
(cf. North E. *birk*).<Teut. *berkā, f. Cf.
also O. Slav. *brĕza*, Russ. *berĕza*; Lith.
beržas. Also Skt. *bhūrja*, a kind of birch.

Bird. (E.) M.E. *brid* (the *r* being
shifted); A.S. *bridd*, a bird, esp. the
young of birds.

Biretta, a clerical cap. (Ital.—L.—
Gk.) Ital. *beretta* (Torriano); cf. Late
L. *birrĕtum*, orig. a scarlet cap.—Late L.
birrus, *burrus*, reddish. See Bureau.

Birth. (Scand.) M.E. *burthe*, *birthe*.
Cf. Icel. *burðr*, m.; Swed. *börd*, Dan.
byrd, f. (= O. Icel. *byrð*, f.). **+** A.S.
gebyrd, f.; O.H.G. *giburt* (G. *geburt*);
Goth. *gabaurths*, f.<Teut. *burðiz=Idg.
**bhr̥tis* (Skt. *bhr̥tis*, f. nourishment). All
from the weak grade of √BHER, to
bear. See Bear (1).

Biscuit, a kind of cake. (F.—L.) F.
biscuit, lit. twice cooked.—F. *bis* (L. *bis*),
twice; and *cuit*, cooked, from L. *coctum*,
acc. of *coctus*, pp. of *coquere*, to cook.

Bisect. (L.) From L. *bi-*, short for
bis, twice; and *sect-um*, supine of *secāre*,
to cut.

Bishop. (L.—Gk.) A.S. *biscop*.—L.
episcopus.—Gk. ἐπίσκοπος, a bishop; lit.
'overseer.'—Gk. ἐπί, upon; σκοπός, one
that watches, from σκοπ-, *o*-grade of σκεπ-,
as in σκέπ-τομαι, I spy, overlook. See
Species.

Bismuth, a metal. (G.) G. *bismuth*;
also spelt *wismut*, *wissmut*, *wissmuth*.
Origin unknown.

Bison, a quadruped. (L.—Teut.) L.
bison (Pliny); Late Gk. βίσων. Not a L.
word, but borrowed from Teutonic;
O.H.G. *wisunt*, G. *wisent*, a bison;
A.S. *weosend*, a wild ox; Icel. *vīsundr*.
See O.H.G. *wisunt* in Schade.

Bissextile, name for leap-year.
(L.) Late L. *bissextīlis annus*, bissextile
year.—L. *bissextus*, an intercalary day; so
called because the intercalated day (formerly Feb. 24) was called the *sixth* of
the calends of March; there being thus
two days with the same name.—L. *bis*,
twice; *sextus*, sixth, from *sex*, six.

Bisson, purblind. (E.) In Sh. M.E.
bisen. O. Northumb. *bisen*, blind (Matt.
ix. 28). Origin unknown.

Bistre, a dark brown. (F.—G.?) F.
bistre, a dark brown. Perhaps from prov.
G. *biester*, dark, gloomy, also bistre (Flügel).

Bit (1), a mouthful, small piece. (E.)

M.E. *bite* (2 syll.). A.S. *bita*, a morsel.
From A.S. *bit-*, weak grade of *bītan*, to
bite.**+**Du. *beet*; Icel. *biti*; Swed. *bit*;
Dan. *bid*.<Teut. type **biton-*, m.

bit (2), a curb for a horse. (E.) M.E.
bitt. A.S. *bite*, m. a bite, a biting.<Teut.
type *bitiz, a bite; cf. *bitol*, a curb.**+**Du.
gebit; Icel. *bitill* (dimin.); Swed. *bett*;
Dan. *bid*; G. *gebiss*.

Bitch. (E.) M.E. *biche*, *bicche*. A.S.
bicce.**+**Icel. *bikkja*; also *grey-baka*.

Bite. (E.) M.E. *biten*. A.S. *bītan*.
+Du. *bijten*; Icel. *bīta*; Swed. *bita*;
Dan. *bide*; G. *beissen*. Teut. type **bītan-*.
Allied to L. *findere* (pt. t. *fīdi*), to cleave;
Skt. *bhid*, to cleave. (√BHEID.)

bitter. (E.) M.E. *biter*. A.S. *biter*,
bitor, lit. 'biting.'—A.S. *bit-*, weak grade
of *bītan*, to bite.**+**Du. *bitter*; Icel. *bitr*;
Swed., Dan., G. *bitter*.

Bittern, a bird. (F.—Late L.) The
n is added. M.E. *botor*, *bitoure*.—F.
butor, 'a bittor [bittern];' Cot. Prob.
named from its cry; cf. L. *būtīre*, *bubere*,
to cry like a bittern; whence also L. *būtio*,
said to mean 'bittern,' though the same
word as *būteo*, i.e. buzzard.

Bitts, naval term. (Scand.?) The
bitts are two strong posts on deck to
which cables are fastened. Prob. from
Icel. *biti*, a bit, mouthful (see Bit (1));
also, a cross-beam in a house; a thwart
(L. *transtrum*) in a ship. [F. *bites*, bitts
(see Cot.), Span. *bitas*, may have been
borrowed from E.] Cf. also A.S. *bæting*,
a cable for holding a ship, from *bætan*,
to restrain, curb, equivalent (in form) to
Icel. *beita*; see Bait. Also Swed. *beting*,
a bitt, whence *betingbult*, a bitt-bolt, bitt-
pin; Dan. *beding*: used also on land for
tethering horses, as in Swed. *betingbult*, a
peg for tethering, from *beta*, to pasture, bait.

Bitumen. (L.) L. *bitūmen*, mineral
pitch. Cf. Brugm. i. § 663.

Bivalve. (F.—L.) From Bi- and
Valve.

Bivouac. (F.—G.) F. *bivouac*, orig.
bivac.—Swiss G. *beiwacht*, an additional
watch at night (Stalder); cf. *bei-geben*,
to add.—G. *bei*, in addition; *wacht*, a
watch, from *wachen*, to wake. See Wake
(1). Cf. G. *beiwache*.

Bizarre, odd. (F.—Span.) F. *bizarre*, strange, capricious; orig. 'valiant.'
—Span. *bizarro*, valiant, gallant. Perhaps
of Basque origin; cf. Basque *bizarra*, a
beard. Cf. Span. *hombre de bigote*, a man

of spirit; where *bigote* means 'moustache.'

Blab, to tell tales. (E.) M. E. *blabbe*, a tell-tale; *blaberen*, to babble. Cf. Dan. *blabbre*, to babble; Dan. dial. *blaffra*, G. *plappern*, to babble, prate. Of imitative origin; cf. Gael. *plab*, a soft noise; *plabair*, a babbler; *blabaran*, a stammerer, *blabhdach*, babbling, garrulous.

Black. (E.) M. E. *blak*. A. S. *blac*, *blæc* [which editors have often confused with *blēc*, bright, shining]. Cf. Icel. *blakkr*, dark; also A. S. *blæc*, Low G. *blak*, O. H. G. *blach*, Icel. *blek*, Swed. *bleck*, Dan. *blæk*, all meaning 'ink.' Connexion with Du. *blaken*, to scorch, is doubtful.

blackguard, a term of reproach. (E. *and* F.) From *black* and *guard*. A name given to scullions, turnspits, and kitchen menials, from the dirty work done by them. See Trench, Select Glossary.

Bladder. (E.) M. E. *bladdre*. A. S. *blêddre*, *blêdre*, a blister, bladder (lit. blowing out).+Du. *blaar* [Icel. *blaðra*?]; O. H. G. *blâtara* (G. *blatter*). Teut. type *blêdrōn-*, wk. fem. From Teut. stem *blê-*, to blow (see Blow (1)); with suffix *-drōn* similar to Gk. -τρᾱ (cf. χύτρα, a pot).

Blade, a leaf, flat of a sword. (E.) M. E. *blade*. A. S. *blæd*, a leaf.+Icel. *blað*, Swed., Dan., Du. *blad*, a leaf, blade; G. *blatt*. Teut. type *bla-dom*, neut., with sense of 'blown,' i. e. 'flourishing;' pp. form (with suffix *-do-* = Idg. *-tō-*) from √BHLÔ. See Blow (2).

Blaeberry, Bleaberry, a bilberry. (Scand. and E.) From North E. *blae*, livid, dark; and *berry*. The form *blae* is from Icel. *blâ-r*, livid; see under Blue.

Blain, a pustule. (E.) M. E. *blein*. A. S. *blegen*, a boil.+Du. *blein*; Dan. *blegn*.

Blame, vb. (F. — L. — Gk.) M. E. *blamen*.—O. F. *blasmer*, to blame.—L. *blasphēmāre*, to speak ill, also to blame. —Gk. βλασφημεῖν; see Blaspheme.

Blanch (1), to whiten. (F.—O. H. G.) From F. *blanchir*, to whiten.—F. *blanc*, white; see Blank below.

Blanch (2), the same as Blench.

Bland. (L.) L. *blandus*, mild.

blandish, to flatter. (F.—L.) M. E. *blandisen*.—O. F. *blandis-*, stem of pres. part of *blandir*, to flatter.—L. *blandīrī*, to caress.—L. *blandus*, bland.

Blank, white. (F. — O. H. G.) In Milton, P. L. x. 656.—F. *blanc*.—O. H. G.

blanch, white. Nasalised form from O. H. G. *blah*, shining; cf. Gk. φλόγ-εος, flaming, shining, from φλέγ-ειν, to shine.

blanket. (F.—O. H. G.) Orig. of a white colour. M. E. *blanket*.—A. F. *blanket* (F. *blanchet*), dimin. from *blanc*, white; see above.

Blare, to make a loud noise. (E.) M. E. *blaren*. Cf. Du. *blaren*, Low G. *blarren*, to bleat; M. H. G. *blēren*, *blerren* (G. *plärren*), to bleat, blubber. Prob. imitative, like *bleat*; but cf. Blaze (2).

Blason; see Blazon.

Blaspheme, to speak injuriously. (L. —Gk.) L. *blasphēmāre*.—Gk. βλασφημεῖν, to speak ill of.—Gk. βλάσφημος, adj., speaking evil.—Gk. βλασ-, for *βλαβεσ-, i. e. hurtful (cf. βλάβ-η, hurt); and φημί, I say: see Fame. Brugm. i. § 744.

Blast, a blowing. (E.) M. E. *blast*. A. S. *blêst*, a blowing; cf. Icel. *blāstr*, a breath, blast of a trumpet; O. H. G. *blāst*. Formed with Idg. suffix *-to-* from the old base of Blaze (2).

Blatant, noisy, roaring. (E.) Spenser has 'blatant beast'; F. Q. vi. 12 (heading); also *blattant*, id. vi. 1. 7. Prob. imitative. Cf. Lowl. Sc. *blad*, to abuse; *blatter*, a rattling noise; G. *platz*, a crash.

Blay, a bleak (fish). (E.) A.S. *blæge*. +Dn. *blei*; G. *bleihe*.

Blaze (1), a flame. (E.) M. E. *blase*. A. S. *blæse*, a flame, in comp. *bāl blæse*, a bright light; *blæse*, f. a torch; < Teut. type *blasōn*. Cf. M. H. G. *blas*, a torch; also G. *blässe*, Icel. *blesi*, a 'blaze' or white mark on a horse, Swed. *blās*, the same.

Blaze (2), to proclaim, noise abroad. (Scand.) Mark i. 45. M. E. *blasen*. — Icel. *blāsa*, to blow, blow a trumpet, sound an alarm; Swed. *blåsa*, to sound; Dan. *blæse*, Du. *blazen*, to blow a trumpet; G. *blasen*. Also Goth. *uf-blēsan*, to puff up. < Teut. type *blês-an-*, to blow; whence A.S. *blêst*, E. *blast*. Much confused with *blazon*.

Blazon (1), **Blason**, a proclamation. Hamlet, i. 5. 21; Shak. Son. 106. A corruption from Blaze (2), M. E. *blasen*, to proclaim; due to confusion with Blazon (2) below.

Blazon (2), to pourtray armorial bearings. (F.) M. E. *blason, blasoun*, a shield; whence *blazon*, verb, to describe a shield. — F. *blason*, a coat of arms, orig. a shield (Brachet). Cf. Span. *blason*, heraldry, blazonry, glory, *hacer blason*, to blazon, *blasonar*, to blazon, brag, boast; suggesting a (very doubtful) connexion with G. *blasen*, to blow the trumpet, as done by heralds, to proclaim a victor's fame; see Blaze (2) above. (See Scheler.) Or if the orig. sense was a bright mark on a shield, it is allied to Blaze (1).

Bleaberry; see Blaeberry.

Bleach. (E.) Orig.'to whiten;' M. E. *blechen*, Ancren Riwle, p. 324, l. 1. A.S. *blǣcan*. ━ A.S. *blāc*, shining, bright, pale. See bleak below. + Icel. *bleikja*; Du. *bleeken*; G. *bleichen*; < Teut. **blaikjan-*.

bleak (1), orig. pale. (Scand.) M. E. *bleik*. ━ Icel. *bleikr*, pale; Swed. *blek*; Dan. *bleg*.+A.S. *blāc*; Du. *bleek*; G. *bleich*. Teut. type **blaikoz*, strong grade of Teut. **bleikan-* (A. S. *blīcan*), to shine.

bleak (2), a fish. (Scand.) From its pale colour.

Blear-eyed, having watery, inflamed, or dim eyes. (E.) M. E. *bleer-eyed*. Cognate with Low G. *blarr-oged*, bleareyed; cf. *blarr-oge*, an eye wet with tears, from *blarren*, to howl, weep; which seems to be allied to E. *blare*.

Bleat. (E.) M. E. *bleten*. A.S. *blǣtan*, *blētan*, to bleat as a sheep.+Du. *blaten*; O.H.G. *plāzan*. Cf. Russ. *blejate*, to bleat; L. *flēre*, to weep.

Bleb, Blob, a small bubble or blister. (E.) Cf. M. E. *blober*, a bubble on water; *blubber*, a bubble. By comparing *blobber*, *blubber*, with *bubble*, having much the same meaning, we see the probability that they are imitative, from the action of forming a bubble with the lips.

Bleed. (E.) M. E. *bleden*. A. S. *blēdan*, formed (by mutation of *ō* to *ē*) from A. S. *blōd*, blood.< Teut. type **blōdjan-*, to lose blood>Icel. *blæða*.

Blemish, to stain. (F.) M. E. *blemisshen*. ━ O. F. *blemis-*, stem of pres. part. of *blemir*, *blesmir*, to wound, stain, make pale. ━ O. F. *bleme*, *blesme*, wan, pale. Of unknown origin.

Blench, to shrink from. (E.) M. E. *blenchen*, to avoid, elude. A.S. *blencan*, to deceive; as if from a Teut. type **blankjan-*, causal of **blinkan-*, to blink. But proof is wanting.

Blend, to mix together. (Scand.) M. E. *blenden*. Due to *blend-*, base of the pres. indic. of Icel. *blanda* (Swed. *blanda*, Dan. *blande*), to blend; cognate with

A. S. and Goth. *blandan*, str. redupl. vb., O. H. G. *blantan*, to mix.

Bless, to consecrate, &c. (E.) The orig. sense may have been 'to consecrate by blood,' i. e. either by sacrifice or by the sprinkling of blood, as the word can be clearly traced back to *blood*. M. E. *blessen*, A. S. *blētsian*, O. Northumb. *blēdsia*, *bloedsia* (Matt. xxv. 34, xxvi. 26), which can be explained from *blōd*, blood, with the usual vowel-change from *o* to *oe* or *ē*. Teut. type **blōdisōn*. Cf. *bleed*. (Suggested by Sweet; Anglia, iii. 156.)

Blight. (E.) XVII cent. Of unknown origin; perhaps from A. S. **bliht*, O. Merc. **bleht*, exactly answering to Icel. *blettr*, a spot, stain.

Blind. (E.) A. S. *blind*.+Du. *blind*; Icel. *blindr*; Sw., Dan., G. *blind*;< Teut. type **blindoz* (Idg. base **bhlendh-*). Cf. Lith. *blęsti-s* (3 pr. s. *blendzia-s*), to become dim (of the sun).

blindfold, vb. (E.) M. E. *blindfolden*, verb (Tyndale); corruption of *blindfelden* (Palsgrave), where the *d* is excrescent. The true word is *blindfellen*, to 'fell' or strike blind, Ancren Riwle, p. 106.━A.S. *blind*, blind; and *fellan*, to strike; see Fell.

Blindman's buff; see Buff.

Blink, to wink, to glance. (E.) M. E. *blenken*, to shine, to glance; whence mod. E. *blink*, by change of *en* to *in*, as in many words. Allied to A.S. *blanc*, white (as in *blanc-a*, a white horse), cognate with O.H.G. *blanch*, M.H.G. *blanc*; see Blank. Cf. Du., G. *blinken*, Swed. *blinka*, Dan. *blinke*, all late forms; and A.S. *blīcan*, to shine.

Bliss. (E.) See Blithe.

Blister. (F.━Teut.) M. E. *blester*, *blister*. (Not found before 1300.)━O. F. *blestre*, 'tumeur,' Godefroy. Of Teut. origin; cf. Icel. *blāstr* (dat. *blǣstri*), a blast, also a swelling, allied to E. Blast. From the notion of blowing out.

Blithe. (E.) M. E. *blithe*. A. S. *blīðe*, sweet, happy.+O. Sax. *blīði*, bright, glad; Du. *blijde*, *blij*; Icel. *blīðr*; Swed., Dan. *blid*; O.H.G. *blīdi*, glad; Goth. *bleiths*, merciful, kind.

bliss. (E.) M. E. *blis*. A.S. *blis*, *bliss*; contr. from A.S. *blīðs*, happiness, lit. blitheness. ━ A.S. *blīðe* (above). + O. Sax. *blīzza*, *blīðsea*, happiness. Teut. stem **blīðsiā*, with *s* < *t*, the suffix being *-tiā*, as in L. *laeti-tia*.

Bloat, to swell. (Scand.) We now generally use *bloated* to mean 'puffed out' or 'swollen,' as if allied to *blow.* But the M. E. form was *blout,* soft; connected with Icel. *blautr,* soft, effeminate, imbecile, *blotna,* to become soft, lose courage. Cf. Swed. *blöt,* Dan. *blöd,* soft, pulpy, mellow. Allied to Icel. *blauðr,* soft; A. S. *blēaþ,* G. *blöde,* weak.

bloater, a prepared herring. (Scand.) A *bloater* is a cured fish, cured by smoke; but formerly a 'soaked' fish. — Icel. *blautr,* soft. Cf. Swed. *blötfisk,* soaked fish; from *blöta,* to soak, steep; from *blöt,* soft (above).

Blob, a bubble. (E.) See **Bleb.**

Block, a large piece of wood. (F. — M. H. G.) M. E. *blok.* — O. F. *bloc.* — M. H. G. *bloch,* a block; cf. Du. *blok,* Dan. *blok,* Swed. *block.* **Der.** *block-ade.*

Blond. (F.) XV cent. F. *blond,* m. *blonde,* fem. 'light yellow;' Cot. Referred by Diez to Icel. *blandinn,* mixed; cf. A. S. *blonden-feax,* having hair of mingled colour, gray-haired. See **Blend.** ¶ But the Low L. form is *blundus,* pointing to a Teut. type **blundo-,* answering to Skt. *bradhna-s,* reddish, pale yellow (Kluge). Cf. O. Slav. *bron',* white; Brugm. i. § 814.

Blood. (E.) M. E. *blod, blood.* A. S. *blōd.* + Du. *bloed,* Icel. *blōð,* Swed. *blod,* Goth. *blōth;* G. *blut;* < Teut. type **blōdom,* n. Hence *bleed.*

Bloom, a flower. (Scand.) M. E. *blome;* not in A. S. — Icel. *blōm, blōmi,* a flower; Swed. *blomma;* Dan. *blomme.* + Du. *bloem;* Goth. *blōma;* allied to O. Ir. *blāth,* L. *flōs;* see **Flower.** And see below.

blossom. (E.) M. E. *blosme,* also *blostme.* A. S. *blōstma,* a blossom; from base *blō-* of A. S. *blō-wan,* with suffixes *-st* and *-ma* (Teut. *-mon*). + Du. *bloesem;* M. H. G. *bluost* (with suffix *-st*). See above.

Blot (1), a spot. (F. — Teut.) M. E. *blot;* from *blotten,* vb. — M. F. *blotter,* 'to blot;' Cot. — O. F. *blotte, bloste,* a clot of earth. (Prob. Teutonic.)

Blot (2), at backgammon. (Scand.) A *blot* is an 'exposed' piece. — Dan. *blot,* bare, naked; whence *give sig blot,* to lay oneself open, expose oneself; Swed. *blott,* naked; *blotta,* to lay oneself open. + Du. *bloot,* naked, *blootstellen,* to expose; G. *bloss,* naked. Allied to Icel. *blautr,* soft; see **Bloat.**

Blotch, a large blot. (F.) From O. F. *bloche,* 'tumeur'; (Godefroy, s. v. *bloste*).

Blouse, a loose outer frock. (F.) From F. *blouse,* a frock much used by workmen (XVIII cent.). Origin unknown.

Blow (1), to puff. (E.) M. E. *blowen.* A. S. *blāwan.* + G. *blähen,* O. H. G. *blā-han;* allied to L. *flāre.*

Blow (2), to bloom, flourish as a flower. (E.) M. E. *blowen.* A. S. *blōwan.* + Du. *bloeijen;* G. *blühen,* O. H. G. *bluojan.* Allied to L. *flōrēre;* see **Flourish.**

Blow (3), a stroke, hit. (E.) M. E. *blowe.* Not in A. S.; but we find M. Du. strong verb *blouwen* (pt. t. *blau*), to strike, dress flax by beating; O. H. G. *bliuwan,* whence G. *bläuen,* to beat; Goth. *bliggwan,* to strike; all from Teut. **bliwwan-,* to strike. (History obscure.)

Blubber. (E.) M. E. *blober,* a bubble; *bloberen,* to bubble up, to weep copiously. Of imitative origin; cf. **Blob.** The *blubber* of the whale consists of bladder-like cells filled with oil. *Blubber-lipped,* with swollen lips. Cf. E. Fries. *blubber,* a bubble, a blob of fat; *blubbern,* to bubble.

Bludgeon. (F. — Teut.) A. F. *bolzon,* a cross-bow bolt. — O. H. G. *bolz;* see **Bolt.**

Blue, a colour. (F. — O. H. G.) M. E. *blew, bleu.* — A. F. *blu, blew,* O. F. *bleu,* blue. — O. H. G. *blāo,* blue, livid, G. *blau.* + Icel. *blār,* livid; Swed. *blå,* Dan. *blaa;* A. S. *blāw* (O. E. Texts, p. 588); < Teut. type **blǣwuz.* Cognate with Lat. *flāuus,* yellow.

Bluff, downright, rude. (Du.?) A *bluff* is a steep headland. It appears to be Dutch. M. Du. *blaf,* flat, broad; *blaffaert,* one having a broad flat face, also, a boaster (Oudemans); *blaf van het voorhooft,* 'the flat of a forehead' (Hexham); *blaffen, bleffen,* to mock (id.). Cf. E. Fries. *bluffen,* to make a noise, bluster, impose on.

Blunder, to flounder about, err. (Scand.) M. E. *blondren,* to confuse, to move blindly or stupidly. Formed (as a frequentative) from Icel. *blunda,* to doze, slumber; Swed. *blunda,* to shut the eyes; Dan. *blunde,* to nap. Cf. Icel. *blundr,* Dan. and Swed. *blund,* a doze, a nap. From the sense of 'confusion.' Allied to **Blend** and **Blind.**

Blunderbuss, a short gun. (Hyb.) In Pope. Formerly spelt *blanterbusse, plantierbusse* (Palmer, Folk-Etymology);

i. e. 'a gun on a rest.' Apparently from L. *plantāre*, to plant (see **Plant**); and Du. *bus*, a gun, orig. a box, barrel; see **Box** (1). But the corresponding Du. word is *donderbus*, i. e. thunder-gun.

Blunt, dull. (Scand. ?) M. E. *blunt*, *blont*, dull, dulled. Origin unknown; perhaps allied to Icel. *blunda*, Dan. *blunde*, to sleep, doze ; see **Blunder**.

Blur, to stain ; a stain. (Scand. ?) Properly 'to dim'; metaphorically, 'to deceive.' We find: '*A blirre*, deceptio ; *to blirre*, fallere ;' Levins (1570). Of uncertain origin. Cf. Swed. dial. *blura*, to blink, partially close the eyes; Swed. *plira*, Swed. dial. *blira*, to blink ; *blirra fojr augu*, to quiver (be dim) before the eyes, said of a haze caused by heat; Bavarian *plerr*, a mist before the eyes.

Blurt, to utter impulsively. (E.) Lowl. Sc. *blirt*, to make a noise in weeping; cf. M. E. *bleren*, to make a loud noise, to *blare*. Of imitative origin.

Blush. (E.) M. E. *bluschen*, *blusshen*, to glow. A. S. *blyscan*, used to translate L. *rutilāre*, to shine (Mone, Quellen, 355); cf. *āblysian*, *āblisian*, to blush ; from A. S. *blys* in *bǣl-blys*, lit. 'a fire-blaze.'+Du. *blozen*, to blush, from *blos*, a blush ; Dan. *blusse*, to flame, glow, from *blus*, a torch ; Swed. *blossa*, to blaze, from *bloss*, a torch. From Teut. root **bleus*, to glow.

Bluster, to be boisterous. (E.) Doubtless associated in idea with *blast* (Icel. *blāstr*, Swed. *blåst*). Cf. E. Fries. *blüstern*, to be tempestuous (esp. of wind) ; *blüster*, *blüser*, a breeze ; *blüsen*, to blow strongly ; *blüse*, wind.

Boa, a large snake. (L.) L. *boa* (Pliny) ; perhaps allied to *bos*, an ox ; from its size.

Boar, an animal. (E.) M. E. *bore*, *boor*. A. S. *bār*. + Du. *beer*; M. H. G. *bēr*. Teut. type **bairoz*, m.

Board (1). (E.) M. E. *bord*. A. S. *bord*, board, side of a ship, shield.+Du. *boord* ; Icel. *borð*, plank, side of a ship; G. *bord* ; Goth. *-baurd* in *fotu-baurd*, a footstool. Cf. Irish, Gael., W., and Corn. *bord*, a board (from E.). Teut. type **bordom*, n. ¶ The sense 'side of a ship' explains *star-board*, *lar-board*, *on board*, *over-board*. Der. *board*, to have meals as a lodger ; from *board*, a table.

board (2), to go on board a ship, to accost. (F. – Teut.) The sb. *board* is E., but the verb, formerly spelt *borde*, *bord*, is short for *aborde*, used by Palsgrave. – F. *aborder*, 'to approach, accost, abboord, or lay aboord ;' Cot. – F. *a*, to (L. *ad*); *bord*, edge, brim, side of a ship, from Icel. *borð*, Du. *boord*, side of a ship. See **Board** (1).

Boast. (F.) M. E. *bost*. [W. *bost*, Corn. *bost*, Irish and Gael. *bosd*, are all borrowed from E.] From A. F. *bost*, a boast. Prob. from Norw. *bausta*, to act with violence, *baust*, boastfully (Ross). Cf. E. Fries. *būsen*, to be boisterous.

Boat. (E.) M. E. *boot*. A. S. *bāt*. Cf. Icel. *bātr* ; Swed. *båt* ; Du. *boot* ; Russ. *bot'* ; W. *bad*; Gael. *bàta*, a boat. β. The Icel. word is borrowed from A. S. ; and the other forms either from E. or Icel. Teut. type **baitoz*, m.

boat-swain. (E.) Lit. 'boat-lad;' Icel. *sveinn*, a lad (= A. S. *swān*).

Bob, to jerk. (E.) Perhaps imitative.

Bobbin, a wooden pin on which thread is wound ; round tape. (F.) Formerly *bobin*. – F. *bobine*, 'a quil for a spinning wheele, a skane ;' Cot. Orig. unknown.

Bode, to foreshew. (E.) M. E. *boden*, *bodian*. – A. S. *bodian*, to announce. – A. S. *boda*, a messenger ; *bod*, a message. From *bod-*, weak grade of *bēodan*, to command, announce. See **Bid** (2).

Bodice, stays. (E.) A corruption of *bodies* (pl. of *body*), which was the old spelling. (Cf. F. *corset*, from *corps*.)

Bodkin, orig. a small dagger. (?) M. E. *boydekin*, Ch. Origin unknown.

Body, the frame of an animal. (E.) M. E. *bodi* ; A. S. *bodig*.+O. H. G. *potach*.

Boer ; the same as **Boor.**

Bog. (C.) Irish *bogach*, a bog, from *bog*, soft; cf. Irish *bogaim*, I shake ; a *bog* being a soft quagmire. So also Gael. *bogan*, a quagmire ; *bog*, soft, moist ; *bog*, to soften, also to agitate. Cf. O. Irish *bocc*, soft.

Boggard, Boggart, a spectre. (C. ; with F. suffix.) From *bog*, variant of **Bug** (1) ; with suffix *-ard*, *-art* (F. *-ard* as in *bast-ard*). See below.

Boggle, to start aside, swerve for fear. (C.?) Prob. coined from prov. E. *boggle*, *bogle*, a spectre. Cf. W. *bwg*, a goblin ; *bygel*, a scarecrow ; *bwgwl*, a threat, *bygylu*, to threaten ; *bwgwth*, to scare. See **Bug** (1).

Bohea, a kind of tea. (Chinese.) So named from the *Bohea* hills ; the mountain called *Bou-y* (or *Wu-i*) is situated in the province of *Fokien* or *Fukian*, on the S. E. coast of China.

Boil (1), to bubble up. (F. – L.) O. F. *boillir*, to boil (F. *bouillir*). – L. *bullīre*, to bubble up, boil. – L. *bulla*, a bubble; see **Bull** (2). Cf. Norman F. *boillir*, to boil.

Boil (2), a small tumour. (E.) Prov. E. *bile*; prob. affected by *boil* (1). M. E. *byle*. – A. S. *bȳl*, a boil, swelling. +Du. *buil*; G. *beule*. Cf. Goth. *ufbauljan*, to puff up; Icel. *beyla*, a hump (with mutation). See **Bowl** (2).

Boisterous. (F.) Lengthened from M. E. *boistous*, Ch.; lit. 'noisy.' *Boistous* is formed, with O. F. suffix *-ous*, from Norw. *baust-a*, to act with violence; like *cloister* from L. *claustrum*. Cf. Norw. *baust*, boastfully; *baus*, blustering. See **Boast**.

Bold. (E.) M. E. *bold*, *bald*; A. S. *beald*, *bald*, *balþ*. +Icel. *ballr*; Du. *boud*; O. H. G. *bald*; cf. Goth. *balthaba*, adv., boldly. Teut. type **balþoz*.

Bole, stem of a tree. (Scand.) M. E. *bole*. – Icel. *bolr*, *bulr*, the trunk of a tree, stem; Swed. *bål*; Dan. *bul*. Cf. Gk. φάλ-αγξ, a log, trunk. Cf. **Balk** (1).

Bolled, swollen. (Scand.) Earlier forms are M. E. *bollen*, pp., and *bolned*, pp. The latter is the pp. of M. E. *bolnen*, to swell. – Dan. *bulne*, Swed. *bulna*, Icel. *bólgna*, to swell, inchoative forms from wk. grade of *belg-* (cf. Icel. *belgja*, to inflate). Cf. A. S. *belgan* (pp. *bolgen*), to swell with anger. See **Bellows**, **Billow**.

Bolster. (E.) A. S. *bolster*, with suffix *-ster* as in *hol-ster*. From its round shape. +Du. *bolster*, *bulster*; Icel. *bolstr*; O. H. G. *bolstar* (G. *polster*). Teut. type **bul-stroz*; from Teut. **bul*, weak grade of **beul*, to puff up. See **Boil** (2). (See Franck.)

Bolt (1), a stout pin of iron, an arrow. (E.) A. S. *bolt*. +Du. *bout*, formerly *bolt*; Dan. *bolt*; G. *bolz*, *bolzen*. Root unknown.

Bolt (2), **Boult**, to sift meal. (F. – L. – Gk.) Spelt *boulte* in Palsgrave. – O. F. *bulter*; mod. F. *bluter*; oldest form *buleter*, a corruption of **bureter*, to sift through coarse cloth; cf. M. Ital. *burattare*, to boult (Florio). – O. F. and F. *bure*, coarse woollen cloth. – Late Lat. *bura*, *burra*, coarse red cloth. – Lat. *burrus*, reddish. – Gk. πυρρός, reddish. – Gk. πῦρ, fire. See **Bureau** and **Fire**.

Bolus, a large pill. (L. – Gk.) Late L. *bōlus* (not L. *bŏlus*), a Latinised form of Gk. βῶλος, a clod, lump.

Bomb, a shell for cannon. (F. *or* Span. – L. – Gk.) F. *bombe*; Span. *bomba*. – L. *bombus*, a humming noise. – Gk. βόμβος, the same. See **Boom** (1).

bombard. (F. – L. – Gk.) The verb is from E. *bombard*, a great gun; Sh. – F. *bombarde*, a cannon; extended from F. *bombe*; see **Bomb**. Der. *bombard-ier*, F. *bombardier* (Cot.).

Bombast, orig. cotton wadding; hence padding, affected language. (F. – L. – Gk.) From O. F. *bombace* (with added *t*), cotton wadding. – Late L. *bombācem*, acc. of *bombax*, cotton; for L. *bombyx*. – Gk. βόμβυξ, silk, cotton; orig. a silkworm. Cf. ' to talk *fustian*.'

bombazine, **bombasine**, a fabric of silk and worsted. (F. – L. – Gk.) F. *bombasin*. – Late L. *bombācinum*. – L. *bombȳcinus*, adj. silken; from *bombyx*, silk; see above.

Bond. (E.) See **Band** (1).

Bondage, servitude. (F. – Scand.) M. E. and A. F. *bondage*, servitude; the sense being due to confusion with the verb *to bind*. But it orig. meant the condition of a *bondman*, called in A. S. *bōnda*, a word borrowed from Icel. *bóndi*, a husbandman. And *bōndi* = *būandi*, a tiller; from Icel. *būa*, to till, prepare, cognate with A. S. *būan*, to dwell, and G. *bauen*. Thus A. S. *bōnda* is allied in sense and origin to E. *boor*, q. v.

Bone. (E.) M. E. *boon*; A. S. *bān*. +Du. *been*; Icel. *bein*; Swed. *ben*; Dan. *been*; O. H. G. *bein*. Teut. type **bainom*.

bonfire. (E.) Orig. a bone-fire. '*Bane-fire*, ignis ossium;' Catholicon Anglicanum, A. D. 1483; where *bane* is the Northern form of *bone*. Cf. Picard *fu d'os*, a bonfire.

Bonito, a kind of tunny. (Span. – Arab.) Span. *bonito*. – Arab. *baynīth*, a bonito.

Bonnet. (F.) F. *bonnet*; O. F. *bonet* (A. D. 1047), the name of a stuff of which bonnets or caps were made. Origin unknown.

Bonny, fair. (F. – L.) From F. *bonne*, fair, fem. of *bon*, good. – L. *bonus*, good; O. L. *duonus*.

Bonze, a priest. (Port. – Japanese.) Port. *bonzo*. – Jap. *bonzo*, a religious man.

Booby. (Span. – L.) Span. *bobo*, a blockhead, booby (related to F. *baube*, stammering). – L. *balbus*, stammering; hence, stupid.

Book. (E.) M. E. *book*; A. S. *bōc*, a book; also, a beech-tree. The orig. 'books' were pieces of writing scratched on a beechen board.+Du. *boek*; Icel. *bōk*; Swed. *bok*; Dan. *bog*; G. *buch*; all in the sense of 'book'; Goth. *bōka*, a letter, pl. *bōkōs*, writings. β. With A.S. *bōc*, beech, cf. L. *fāgus*, a beech, Gk. φηγός, a tree with edible fruit.

Boom (1), to hum. (E.) M. E. *bommen*; not found in A. S.+Du. *bommen*, to boom, to give out a hollow sound like an empty barrel. An imitative word; like L. *bombus*, Gk. βόμβος, a humming.

Boom (2), a pole. (Du.) Du. *boom*; the Du. form of **Beam** (1).

Boomerang, a wooden missile weapon. (Australian.) From the native Australian name.

Boon (1), a petition. (Scand.) M. E. *bone*, Ch. – Icel. *bōn*; Dan. and Swed. *bön*, a petition.+A.S. *bōen*, *bēn* (whence *bene* in Wordsworth). The sense of 'favour' arose from confusion with **Boon** (2).

Boon (2), good. (F. – L.) In the phr. '*boon* companion.' – F. *bon*, good. – L. *bonus*. See **Bonny**.

Boor, a peasant. (Du.) Du. *boer*, a peasant, lit. 'tiller of the soil.' – Du. *bouwen*, to till. + A. S. *būan*, to dwell in, whence *gebūr*, s., a peasant (only preserved in *neigh-bour*). So also G. *bauen*, to till, whence *bauer*, a peasant; Icel. *būa*, Goth. *bauan*, to dwell. Teut. stem **bū-*, related to **Be**. (Streitberg, § 90.)

Boot (1), advantage, profit. (E.) M. E. *bote*, *boot*. A. S. *bōt*, profit.+Du. *boete*; Icel. *bōt* (cf. *bati*), advantage, cure; Dan. *bod*, Swed. *bot*, remedy; G. *busse*, atonement; Goth. *bōta*. Teut. type **bōtā*, f. From *bōt-*, strong grade of *bat-*; see **Better**. **Der.** *boot-less*, profitless.

Boot (2), a covering for the foot. (F.) M. E. *bote*. – O. F. *bote* (F. *botte*); cf. Span., Port., Late L. *bota*. Origin unknown.

Booth. (Scand.) M. E. *bothe*. – M. Dan. *bōth* (Kalkar), Dan. *bod*; Swed. *bod* (cf. Icel. *būð*, a dwelling, booth). – Dan. *boe*, Swed. *bo*, Icel. *būa*, to dwell; see **Boor**. + G. *bude*, a stall. Teut. type **būþā*, f. Cf. also Irish *both*, a hut, W. *bôd*, a residence; Lith. *buta*, *buttas*, a house. See **Build**.

Booty. (F. – Low G.) Formerly spelt *butin*. – F. *butin*, 'a booty, prey;' Cot.

– M. Du. *büte*, Du. *buit*; cf. Icel. *bӯti*, Dan. *bytte*, Swed. *byte*, exchange, barter, also booty, spoil; G. *beute*, spoil.

Borage. (F. – Span. – Arab.) Formerly *bourage*. – F. *bourrache*. – Span. *borraja*. – Arab. *abū rashh*, lit. 'father of sweat;' because it is a sudorific.

Borax. (Low L. – Arab. – Pers.) Low L. *borax*; also *boracum*. – Arab. *būrāq*. – Pers. *būrah*, borax (Vullers).

Border, an edge. (F. – Low L. – Teut.) M. E. *bordure*, *bordeure*. – O. F. *bordeüre* (Span. *bordadura*), an edging. – Low L. *bordātūra*, edging. – Low L. *bordāre* (Ital. *bordare*, Span. *bordar*, F. *border*), to edge. – Low L. *bordus* (F. *bord*). – Teut. (O. Low G.) *bord*, side; see **Board**.

Bore (1), to perforate. (E.) M. E. *borien*, A. S. *borian*. + Du. *boren*; Icel. *bora*; Swed. *borra*; Dan. *bore*; G. *bohren*. Also L. *forāre*, to bore; Gk. φαράειν, to plough. Brugm. i. § 510. (√BHER, to cut.)

bore (2), to worry. (E.) Possibly a metaph. use of the verb above; Hen. VIII, i. 1. 128.

Bore (3), a tidal surge in a river. (Scand.?) Perhaps from Icel. *bāra*, a billow caused by wind; Norw. *baara*, a billow, swell in the sea.

Boreas, the north wind. (L. – Gk.) L. *Boreas*. – Gk. Βορέας, Βορρᾶς, the N. wind.

Borough. (E.) M. E. *burgh*, *borgh*; also *borwe*. A. S. *burh*, *burg* (gen. and dat. *byrig*), a fort. Perhaps from Teut. *burg-*, weak grade of **bergan-*, to protect; whence Goth. *bairgan*, to hide, keep; see **Barrow**. + Du. *burg*; Icel. *borg*; Swed. and Dan. *borg*; G. *burg*; Goth. *baurgs*. See below. Brugm. i. § 566; ii. § 160.

borrow. (E.) M. E. *borwen*; A. S. *borgian*, lit. to give a pledge. – A. S. *borg*, *borh*, a pledge. – A.S. *borg-*, weak grade of *beorgan*, to keep, protect; see **Barrow** and **Borough**.

Bosom. (E.) M. E. *bosom*. A. S. *bōsm*.+Du. *boezem*; G. *busen*.

Boss, a knob. (F. – O. H. G.) M. E. *boce*, *bos*. – O. F. *boce* (F. *bosse*); cf. Ital. *bozza*, a swelling; M. Ital. *bozzare*, to rough-hew, to bungle. Prob. from O. H. G. *bōzan*, to beat; a bump being the effect of a blow. Cf. *botch*, *beat*.

Botany. (F. – Gk.) F. *botanique*,

orig. an adj. — Gk. βοτανικός, belonging to plants. — Gk. βοτάνη, grass. — Gk. βόσκειν, to pasture; cf. βοτόν, a grazing animal.

Botargo, a cake made of the roe of the sea-mullet. (Ital. — Arab.) M. Ital. *botargo,* pl. *botarghe* ; see Florio and Torriano. — Arab. *butarkha,* botargo ; given by Devic. Supposed to be composed of *bu,* Coptic def. article, and Gk. τάριχος, dried fish (Journ. des Savants, Jan. 1848, p. 45).

Botch (1), to patch. (E.) Origin unknown. Similar is M. Du. *butsen,* to strike, beat, also to patch up; cf. Du. *botsen,* to beat.

Botch (2), a swelling. (F. — G.) M. E. *boche.* — O. North F. *boche* ; Picard *boche* ; O. F. *boce* (F. *bosse*), a swelling; see Boss.

Both. (Scand.) M. E. *bāþe,* Scot. *baith.* — Icel. *bāðir,* both, dual adj. ; Dan. *baade* ; Swed. *båda.*+G. *beide.* And cf. A. S. *bā,* both ; Lat. *-bo* in *ambo* ; Gk. *-φω* in ἄμ-φω ; Skt. *-bha* in *u-bha,* both. Icel. *-ðir* is for *ðeir,* they, the; so that *bo-th* was orig. *two* words ; cf. Goth. *ba þō shipa,* both the ships (Luke v. 7).

Bother, vb. and sb. (E.) In Swift. Cf. *pother* ; prov. E. *pudder,* confusion ; M. E. *putheren,* to bestir oneself. Origin unknown.

Bots, small worms. (E.) Lowl. Sc. *bats.* Of unknown origin.

Bottle (1), a hollow vessel. (F. — Late L. — Gk.) M. E. *botel.* — F. *bouteille.* — Late Lat. *buticula,* double dimin. of Late L. *butis, buttis,* a cask, a butt; see Butt (2).

Bottle (2), a bundle of hay. (F. — O. H. G.) M. E. *botel.* — O. F. *botel, hotelle,* a small bundle, dimin. of *botte,* a bundle, as of hay. — O. H. G. *bōzo,* a bundle of straw or flax; allied to O. H. G. *bōzan,* to beat (see Beat); perhaps from the beating of flax.

Bottom. (E.) M. E. *botum, bothom.* A. S. *botm.*+Du. *bodem* ; Icel. *botn* ; Swed. *botten* ; Dan. *bund*; G. *boden* ; Lat. *fundus*; Gk. πυθμήν ; Vedic Skt. *budhna,* depth, ground. Allied to Irish *bonn,* sole of the foot; Gael. *bonn,* sole, bottom ; W. *bon,* base, stock. See Fundament. Brugm. i. §§ 103, 704.

Boudoir. (F.) F. *boudoir,* a private room for a lady ; lit. a place to sulk in. — F. *bouder,* to sulk. Cf. E. *pout.*

Bough. (E.) M. E. *bough.* A. S. *bōg,*

bōh ; of which the orig. sense was 'an arm.'+Icel. *bōgr,* Swed. *bog,* Dan. *bov,* the shoulder of an animal, hence the bow (shoulder) of a ship ; G. *bug* ; Gk. πῆχυς, the fore-arm ; Skt. *bāhus,* the arm. Teut. type **bōguz*; Idg. type **bhāghus.* See Bow (4). Brugm. i. § 184.

Bought, a bend, turn, fold. (Low G.) In Spenser, F. Q. i. 1. 15. Low G. *bugt,* a bend; Du. *bogt, bocht*; Dan. *bugt.* Cf. G. *bucht.* The E. form is Bight. And see Bout.

Boulder, a large stone. (E. ?) Etym. obscure; cf. Swed. dial. *bullersteen,* a large rolling stone ; so called from its rolling down stream with a crash. — Swed. *bullra,* to thunder, roar; and *steen,* a stone. Danish has *buldre,* to roar, *bulder,* a crash.

Boult, to sift meal ; see Bolt (2).

Bounce, to jump up quickly. (E.) M. E. *bunsen,* to beat. Cf. Low G. *bunsen,* to beat, knock at a door; Du. *bonzen,* to bounce, throw, from Du. *bons,* a bounce, thump; G. *bumps,* bounce ; Icel. *bops,* bump! Prob. imitative.

Bound (1), to leap. (F. — L. — Gk.) F. *bondir,* to bound ; but orig. to resound. — L. *bombitāre,* to resound. — L. *bombus,* a humming sound. — Gk. βόμβος, the same. Der. *re-bound* (F. *rebondir*).

Bound (2), a boundary. (F. — C. ?) M. E. *bounde,* Ch. ; with excrescent *d,* as in *soun-d.* A. F. *bounde, bunde* ; O. F. *bonne,* a boundary; also spelt *bodne* (Burguy); Late Lat. *bodina* (contr. form *bonna*), a bound, limit. Perhaps of Celtic origin ; Thurneysen, 91. Der. *bound-ary.*

Bound (3), ready to go. (Scand.) In 'the ship is *bound* for Spain,' &c. Formed, with excrescent *d,* from M. E. *boun,* ready, Ch. C. T. 11807. — Icel. *buinn,* prepared; pp. of *būa,* to till, prepare.+A. S. *būan* ; see Boor.

Bounden, the old pp. of Bind. (E.) As in '*bounden* duty.'

Bounty, orig. goodness. (F. — L.) M. E. *bountee.* — O. F. *bontet.* — L. acc. *bonitātem,* from *bonitās,* goodness. — L. *bonus,* good. See Bonny.

Bouquet. (F. — Late L.) F. *bouquet* ; O. F. *bosquet,* orig. 'a little wood,' dimin. of O. F. *bos* (F. *bois*), a wood. — Late L. *boscum, buscum,* acc. of *boscus, buscus,* a wood ; of unknown origin. Cf. Bush.

Bourd, a jest; to jest. (F.) M. E. *bourde,* sb. ; *bourden,* v. — F. *bourde,* a game; *bourder*, to play. Of unknown origin. (Not as in Diez.)

Bourn (1), a boundary. (F.) In Sh. — F. *borne*, a bound; for O. F. *bodne*, variant of O. F. *bonne*, a boundary; see Bound (2).

Bourn (2), **Burn,** a stream. (E.) M. E. *bourne*. A. S. *burna*, a fountain, stream, well.+Icel. *brunnr*; Swed. *brunn*; Dan. *brönd*; G. *brunnen*; Goth. *brunna*, a spring, well.

Bouse, Bouze, Boose, to drink deeply. (Du.) M. E. *bousen* (ab. 1300). — M. Du. **būsen*, later *buyzen*, to drink deeply. — M. Du. *būse* (Latinised as *būsa* by Erasmus), *buyse*, a large cup, also a tap, a conduit (Kilian); Du. *buis*, a conduit, pipe. Cf. O. F. *buse*, a conduit; G. *bausen*, to bouse.

Bout, a turn, a round, occasion. (Low G.) The same as **Bought** (above); prob. influenced by *about*.

Bow (1), to bend. (E.) M. E. *bowen*, *bogen*, *bugen*. A. S. *būgan*.+Du. *buigen*; O. H. G. *biogan*; Goth. *biugan*; Teut. type **beugan-* or **būgan-*. Cf. Skt. *bhuj*, to bend; Lat. *fugere*, to take to flight, give way; Gk. φεύγειν, to flee. Brugm. i. §§ 658, 701.

bow (2), a bend. (E.) From the verb.

bow (3), a weapon to shoot with. (E.) M. E. *bowe*. A. S. *boga*, a bow; because it is bent or *bowed*.+Du. *boog*; Icel. *bogi*; Swed. *båge*; Dan. *bue*; O. H. G. *bogo*; G. *bogen*. From A. S. *bog-*; cf. *bog-en*, pp. of *būgan*, to bend.

bow-window. (E.) A window of semi-circular form; not the same as *bay-window*.

Bow (4), the 'shoulder' of a ship. (Scand.) From Icel. *bógr*, shoulder; see **Bough.**+Du. *boeg*, bow of a ship.

Bowel. (F. — L.) M. E. *bouel.*—O. F. *boël*; (mod. F. *boyau*). — Lat. acc. *botellum*, a sausage; in Late L., an intestine; dimin. of *botulus*, a sausage.

Bower, an abode, chamber, arbour. (E.) M. E. *bour*. A. S. *būr*, a chamber. — A. S. *būan*, to dwell. + Icel. *búr*, a chamber; Dan. *buur*, Swed. *bur*; O. Sax. *būr*; O. H. G. *būr*. Teut. types **būrom*, n., **būroz*, m. ; see **Boor.** Cf. Booth.

Bowl (1), a round wooden ball. (F.—L.) M. E. *boule.*—F. *boule.*—L. *bulla*, a bubble; hence, a round thing, a ball.

Bowl (2), a drinking-vessel. (E.)

M. E. *bolle*. A. S. *bolla*; from its round form.+Du. *bol*, ball; Icel. *bolli*, O. H. G. *bolla*, bowl (G. *bolle*). From Teut. **bul-*, weak grade of **beul-*, to swell; cf. Goth. *uf-bauljan*, to puff up. See Boil (2).

Bow-line. (Scand.) *Not* so called because it keeps a sail *bowed* (for it rather keeps it straight), but because fastened to the ship's *bow*. — Norw. and Swed. *boglina*, bow-line, from *bog*, bow of a ship; Du. *boeglijn*, from *boeg*, bow. For the pronunciation, cf. *bow-sprit*. See Bow (4) and Line.

Bow-window; see Bow (1).

Box (1), the name of a tree. (L.—Gk.) M. E. *box*; A. S. *box.*—Lat. *buxus*, the box-tree.—Gk. πύξος, the box-tree.

box (2), a chest or case to put things in. (L.—Gk.) M. E. *box*; A. S. *box.*—L. *buxum*, anything made of box-wood; hence, a box.—Lat. *buxus*, the box-tree. (Hence a *box* at a theatre; a shooting-*box*; a Christmas *box* or present; &c.) Cf. Pyx.

Box (3), to fight with fists; a blow. (E.) The verb is from M. E. *box*, sb., a blow. Cf. N. Fries. *bakke*, Silt *bokke*, a blow (Outsen); M. H. G. *buc*, a blow; Du. *beuken*, G. *pochen*, to beat.

Box (4), in phr. 'to box the compass.' Apparently one of the numerous uses of the vb. formed from **box** (2). See N. E. D.

Boy. (E.) M. E. *boi*, *boy*. Preserved in E. Friesic *boi*, *boy* (Koolman); allied to M. Du. *boeve*, a boy, Du. *boef*, a knave. + Icel. *bófi*, a knave; G. *bube*, Bavarian *bueb*, *bua*, *bui*, a boy. Cf. A. S. *Bófa*, personal name.

Boycott, to combine with others in refusing to have dealings with any one. (E.) From the treatment accorded to Capt. *Boycott*, of Lough Mask House, co. Mayo, Ireland, in Dec. 1880.

Brabble, to quarrel. (E.) Cf. Du. *brabbelen*, to stammer, confound; whence *brabbeltaal*, foolish talk. See Blab, Babble.

Brace, orig. a firm hold. (F.—L.) From the notion of embracing.—O. F. *brace*, the two arms (Bartsch); hence a measure of 5 feet, formed with extended arms (Cot.); and hence, a grasp.—Lat. *brāchia*, pl. of *brāchium*, the arm.+Irish *brac*, W. *braich*, the arm; Gk. βραχίων.

bracelet. (F. — L.) F. *bracelet*; dimin. of O. F. *bracel*, an armlet (Bartsch).

−L. *brāchiāle*, an armlet.**−**L. *brāchium*, an arm.

Brach, a kind of hunting-dog. (F.−G.) M. E. *brache*, pl. *braches*. **−** A. F. *brachez*, pl. of *brachet*, dimin. of O. F. *brac* (F. *braque*).**−**O. H. G. *bracco* (G. *brack*), a dog that hunts by the scent.

Bracken, fern. (E.) M. E. *braken*. A. S. *braccan*, pl. ; Kemble, C. D. v. 277. Cf. Swed. *bräken*, Dan. *bregne*, fern ; cf. Icel. *burkni*, fern.

Bracket, a corbel, &c. (F.−C. ?) Formerly spelt *bragget*, as in Minsheu, ed. 1627. So named from the resemblance to the front part of a pair of breeches, as formerly made. **−** F. *braguette*, 'a cod-piece,' Cot. (the front part of a pair of breeches); the allied Span. *bragueta* also meant a projecting mould in architecture, a bracket or corbel. Dimin. of O. F. *brague*, 'a kind of mortaise,' Cot. ; from *bragues*, breeches; so also Span. *bragueta* is the dimin. of Span *bragas*, breeches.**−** L. *brācæ*, breeches ; said to be of Celtic (or Teutonic ?) origin. See **Breeches**.

Brackish. (Du.) Du. *brak*, briny, nauseous; older form *wrack*, brackish (Hexham) ; allied to M. Du. *wracke*, a wreck, Du. *wraken*, to reject, blame, dis-approve.**−**Du. *wrak*, orig. 2nd grade of *wraken*, to wreak ; orig. to drive. See **Wreck**. [So also *wrang*, sour, is allied to *wringen*, to wring. See Franck.]

Bract. (L.) Lat. *bractea*, a thin plate or leaf of metal.

Brad. (Scand.) M. E. *brod*.**−**Icel. *broddr*, a spike ; Swed. *brodd*, Dan. *brodde*, a frost-nail.**+**A. S. *brord*, a spike. Teut. type **brozdoz*. Cf. O. Irish *brot*, Ir. *brod*, W. *brath*, a sting.

Brae, brow of a hill, steep bank, slope. (Scand.) M. E. *brā*, *brō* (North).**−**Icel. *brā*, brow ; hence, brow of a hill ; see **Brow**.

Brag, to boast. (Scand.) M. E. *braggen*, to sound loudly, to vaunt. Prob. from M. Dan. *brage*, to crack, **to** brag. Cf. A. S. *gebrǣc*, a breaking, crash, noise ; Icel. *brak*, a creaking, *braka*, to creak ; cognate with L. *fragor*, noise. Also (late) M. F. *braguer*, 'to flaunt, brag,' Cot. ; M. F. *bragard*, 'gay, gallant, braggard,' whence E. *braggart*. We find also W. *bragal*, to vociferate (from E.) ; Bret. *braga*, to brag (from F.). Cf. **Bray**.

Bragget. (W.) M. E. *bragot*.**−**W. *bragot*, a kind of mead ; allied to Irish

bracat, malt liquor.**−**W. *brag*, malt ; Irish and Gael. *braich*, malt, fermented grain. Cf. Gael. *brach*, to ferment.

Brahman, Brahmin. (Skt.) Skt. *hrāhmana*, a brahman, holy man.**−**Skt. *brahman*, prayer ; also devotion, lit. 'a greatness' of the soul ; cf. *brhant*, great. (√BHERGH, to be great.)

Braid (1), to weave. (E.) M.E. *breiden*. A.S. *bregdan*, *brēdan*, to brandish, weave, braid. **+** Icel. *bregða*, to brandish, turn about, change, start, braid, &c. ; whence *bragð*, a sudden movement.

braid (2), full of deceit. (E.) In All's Well, iv. 2. 73, *braid* is short for *braided*, i. e. full of *braids* or tricks. M.E. *braid*, trick, deceit.**−**A.S. *brægd*, deceit ; from A. S. *brægd*, 2nd grade of *bregdan*, to draw out, weave, knit, braid.

Brail, a kind of ligature or fastening. (F.−C. ?) O. F. *braiel*, a cincture ; orig. for fastening up breeches. **−** F. *braie*, breeches. **−**L. *brācæ*, breeches.

Brain. (E.) M.E.*brayne*. A.S.*brægn*, *brægen*, the brain. **+** Du. *brein*. Cf. Gk. βρεχμός, the top of the head.

Brake (1), a machine for breaking hemp ; a name for various mechanical contrivances. (O. Low G.) M. E. *brake*.**−**Low G. *brake*, a flax-brake ; M. Du. *braecke*, 'a brake to beat flax ;' Hexham ; Du. *braak*.**−**Du. *brak*, 2nd grade of *breken*, to break ; see **Break**.

Brake (2), bush. (E.) M.E. *brake*. **+**Low G. *brake*, willow-bush (Bremen) ; also stumps of broken trees, rough growth. From A. S. *brecan*, (pt. t. *bræc*), to break. ¶ In the sense of 'fern,' modified from **Bracken**.

Bramble. (E.) M. E. *brembil*. A. S. *brēmel*, *brembel*. Allied to Du. *braam*, a blackberry ; Swed. *brom-bär*, Dan. *brom-bær*, G. *brombeere*, a blackberry. Here Du. *braam*, G. *brōm* (O. H. G. *brāma*) answer to A. S. *brōm* (see **Broom**) ; of which A.S. *brēm-el* (for Teut.**brǣmiloz*) is the diminu-tive).

Bran. (F.) M. E. *bran*.**−**O. F. *bran*, *bren*. Cf. W. *bran*, Irish *bran*, husks, chaff(from E.) ; Bret. *brenn*, bran.

Branch. (F.−L.) F. *branche*.**−**Late L. *branca*, the paw of an animal.

Brand, a burning piece of wood, scar of fire, a sword. (E.) M. E. *brond*, A.S. *brand*, a burning, a sword : from *brann*, 2nd stem of Teut. **brennan-*, to burn ; see **Burn**. **+** Icel. *brandr*, a fire-brand, sword-blade (from its flashing) ; Swed. and Dan. *brand*, fire-brand, fire ; M. H. G. *brant*, a brand, sword.

brandish. (F. — Scand.) M.E. *braundisen.* — F. *brandiss-ant*, pres. pt. of *brandir*, to brandish a sword. — A. F. *brand*, a sword. — Icel. *brandr* ; see Brand above.

brandy. (Du.) Formerly *brandwine, brandy-wine* ; whence *brandy.* — Du. *brande-wijn*, M. Du. *brandwijn*, brandy ; lit. 'burnt' (i. e. distilled) wine (or, acc. to Kilian, because it easily burns). — Du. *branden*, to burn ; and *wijn*, wine ; see Burn.

Branks, a punishment for scolds. (F.) See Jamieson. Hence were borrowed Gael. *brangas* (O. Gael. *brancas*), a sort of pillory ; Gael. *brang*, Irish *brancas*, a halter. — North F. *branques*, pl. of *branque*, Norman form of F. *branche*, branch, 'also, the cheeke of a bit,' Cot. See Branch.

Bran-new. (E.) Short for *brand-new*, i. e. new from the fire. See Brand.

Brant-fox, Brant-goose or **brent-goose.** The prefix is Scand., as in Swed. *brandräf*, a brant-fox, *brandgås*, a brent-goose. The orig. sense is 'burnt,' with the notion of redness or blackness.

Brasier, Brazier, a pan to hold coals. (F. — Scand.) F. *brasier.* — F. *braise*, live coals. — Swed. *brasa*, fire (below).

Brass. (E.) M. E. *bras.* A. S. *bræs.* Perhaps allied to the verb seen in Icel. *brasa*, to harden by fire ; Dan. *brase*, to fry ; cf. Swed. *brasa*, fire. Der. *braz-en*, A. S. *bræsen.*

braze (1), to harden. (E.) K. Lear, i. 1. 11. It means to harden like *brass* ; see below.

braze (2), to ornament with brass. (E.) In Chapman, tr. of Homer, Od. xv. 113 ; from *brass*, sb. 'Aero, *ic brasige* ;' Ælfric, Gram. p. 215.

Brassart, the piece of armour which protected the upper part of the arm. (F. — L.) F. *brassart* (Cot.), *brassard* (Littré) ; also *brassal.* Formed with suffix *-ard* from F. *bras*, arm. — L. *brāchium*, arm.

Brat (1), a cloak, rough mantle. (C.) It also meant a rag, clout, or pinafore. — Gael. and Irish *brat*, a cloak, rag ; O. Irish *brat*, a rough cloak ; W. *brethyn*, woollen cloth. (W. *brat* is from E.)

Brat (2), a child ; esp. 'a beggar's *brat.*' Perhaps 'a rag,' the same as Brat (1).

Brattice, a fence of boards in a mine.

(F. — Teut. ?) M. E. *bretasche, bretasce, brutaske*, a parapet, battlement. — O. F. *bretesche*, a small wooden outwork, battlement ; cf. Prov. *bertresca*, Ital. *bertesca*, the same. A difficult word ; prob. formed from G. *brett*, a plank.

Bravado. (Span.) See Brave.

Brave. (F. — Ital.) F. *brave*, 'brave, gay, fine, proud, braggard, valiant ;' Cot. — Ital. *bravo* ; the same as Span. and Port. *bravo* ; Prov. *brau.* Etym. unknown ; none of the explanations are satisfactory ; the Bret. *brav*, O. Swed. *braf*, appear to be borrowed from F.

bravado. (Span.) Altered from Span. *bravada*, 'a bravado ;' Minsheu's Span. Dict. — Span. *bravo*, brave.

bravo, a daring villain. (Ital.) Ital. *bravo*, brave ; as a sb., a cut-throat, villain.

bravo! well done! (Ital.) Ital. *bravo*, brave ; used in the voc. case masc.

Brawl (1), to quarrel. (E. ?) M. E. *brawlen.* Perhaps E. Cf. Du. *brallen*, to brag, boast ; Dan. *bralle*, to prate, chatter ; G. *prahlen*, to brag.

Brawl (2), a sort of dance. (F. — Scand. or O. H. G.) 'A French *brawl*,' L. L. L. iii. 9. — F. *bransle*, 'a totter, swing, . . . brawl or dance ;' Cot. — F. *bransler*, to reel ; mod. F. *branler.* Allied to O. F. *brandeler* (Littré), *brandiller*, to shake (Cot.), frequent. forms of F. *brandir*, to brandish. See Brandish.

Brawn, muscle. (F. — O. H. G.) M. E. *braun*, muscle, boar's flesh. — O. F. *braon*, a slice of flesh ; cf. Prov. *bradon*, the same. — O. H. G. *brāton*, acc. of *brāto*, a slice of flesh for roasting. — O. H. G. *brātan* (G. *braten*), to roast. + A. S. *brǣdan.*

Bray (1), to bruise, pound. (F. — G.) M. E. *brayen.* — O. F. *breier* (F. *broyer*). — O. Sax. *brekan* (G. *brechen*), to break ; see Break.

Bray (2), to make a roaring noise. (F. — C.) A. F. *braier* ; F. *braire* (Med. Lat. *bragīre*). Of Celtic origin ; cf. Gael. *bragh*, a burst, explosion, *braigh*, to crackle (Thurneysen) ; and cf. L. *frag-or*, noise.

Braze ; see Brass.

Brazier ; see Brasier.

Breach. (E.) M. E. *breche*, a fracture — A. S. *brece*, as in *hláf-gebrece*, a piece of bread (more commonly *brice*, a breaking) ; O. Fries. *breke.* — A. S. *brecan*, to break. ¶ M. E. *breche* is also partly from O. F. *breche* (F. *brèche*), a fracture. — G. *brechen* to break.

Bread. (E.) M. E. *breed.* A. S. *brēad.* +Du. *brood*; Icel. *brauð*; Swed. and Dan. *brōd*; G. *brot.* Teut. type **braudom*, n.; or **braudoz*, neut. form in *-oz.* It sometimes means 'bit' or 'piece'; cf. A. S. '*brēadru*, frusta *pānis*,' Blickling Glosses; O. Northumb. *brēad*, a bit, morsel; John xiii. 27.

Breadth. (E.) The final *-th* is late; from M. E. *brede*, breadth; Ch.—A. S. *brǣdu.*+Icel. *breidd*; O. H. G. *breitī* (G. *breite*); Goth. *braidei*, f. From Teut. **braidoz*, broad; see **Broad.**

Break. (E.) M. E. *breken*; pt. t. *brak*; pp. *broken.* A. S. *brecan*, pt. t. *bræc*, pp. *brocen.*+Du. *breken*; Goth. *brikan*; G. *brechen.* Cf. Icel. *braka*, to creak; Swed. *braka*, to crack; Dan. *brække*; Lat. *frangere.* to break; Gael. *bragh*, an explosion. (√BHREG.) The orig. sense is to break with a noise, to crack.

Bream, a fish. (F.—Teut.) M. E. *breem.* —O. F. *bresme* (F. *brème*).—M. H. G. *brahsem* (G. *brassen*); O. H. G. *brahsina* (Kluge). Cf. Du. *brasem.*

Breast. (E.) M. E. *brest, breest.* A. S. *brēost.* + Icel. *brjōst* (Swed. *brōst*, Dan. *bryst*) : Teut. type **breustom*, n. Also G. *brust*, Du. *borst*, Goth. *brusts* : Teut. stem **brust-* (with weak grade).

Breath. (E.) M. E. *breeth, breth.* A. S. *brǣð.*+O. H. G. *brādam*, G. *brodem, broden, brodel*, steam, vapour, exhalation.

Breech. (E.) See **Breeches.**

Breeches. (E.) Really a double plural, the form *breech* being, in itself, a pl. form. A. S. *brēc*, breeches; pl. of *brōc*, with the same sense.+Du. *broek*, a pair of breeches; Icel. *brōk* (pl. *brækr*); M.H.G. *bruoch.* Cf. L. *brācæ*, said to be a word of Celtic (but rather of Teutonic) origin. See **Brogues.**

breech. (E.) M. E. *breech*; A. S. *brēc*, the breech; A. S. Leechdoms. ii. 146. Cf. A. S. *brēc*, breeches, pl. of *brōc*; see above.

Breed. (E.) A. S. *brēdan*, to produce or cherish a brood.—A. S. *brōd*, a brood (with mutation from *ō* to *ē*).+G. *brüten*; from *brut.* See **Brood.**

Breeks, breeches. (Scand.) Northern E. From Icel. *brækr*, pl. of *brōk*; see **Breeches.**

Breeze (1), a gadfly. (E.) M. E. *brese.* A. S. *brīosa.*

Breeze (2), a strong wind. (F.) Formerly *brize.*—O. F. *brise*, used by Rabelais in the

same sense as F. *bise*, the N. wind; cf. Span. *brisa*, Port. *briza*, the N.E. wind; Ital. *brezza*, a cold wind. Orig. unknown.

Breeze (3), cinders. (F.—Scand.) O. F. *brese* (*breze* in Cot.), F. *braise*, live coals. See **Brasier.**

Breve. (Ital.—L.) Orig. a *short* note; now the longest in use.—Ital. *breve*, brief. —L. *breuis*, short. **Der.** *semi-breve.*

brevet. (F.—L.) F. *brevet*, ' a brief, breviate, little writing;' Cot. Dimin. from F. *bref*, brief.—L. *breuis*, short.

breviary. (F.—L.) F. *bréviaire.*— L. *breuiārium*, a summary.—L. *breuis.*

brevity. (F.—L.) F. *brièveté.*—L. acc. *breuitātem*, shortness.—L. *breuis*, short.

Brew. (E.) M. E. *brewen.* A. S. *brēowan*, pt. t. *brēaw*, pp. *gebrowen.*+Du. *brouwen*; G. *brauen*; Icel. *brugga*; Swed. *brygga*; Dan. *brygge.* Cf. L. *dē-fru-tum*, new wine boiled down; Thracian βρῦτον, beer. (√BHREU, to decoct.)

Brewis, Browis, pottage. (F.— O. H. G.) M. E. *brewes, browes.*—O. F. *brouez, broez*, nom. of *brouet, broet*, soup made with broth of meat; dimin. of *breu*, pottage (Roquefort).—O. H. G. *brod, brot*, broth; see **Broth.** Also spelt *brose.*

Briar, Brier. (E.) M. E. *brere.* A. S. *brǣr*, O. Merc. *brēr.*

Bribe. (F.) M. E. *bribe.*—O. F. *bribe*, a piece of bread given to a beggar. Cf. *briber*, to beg; Span. *briba*, idleness; *bribar*, to loiter about; Ital. *birba*, fraud; *birbante*, an idle beggar. Origin unknown; not Celtic.

Brick. (F.—M. Du.) F. *brique*, a brick; also a fragment, bit.—M. Du. *bricke*, a brick; cf. Walloon *briquet*, a large slice of bread.—Du. *breken*, to break. **Der.** *brick-bat* (see **Bat**).

Bride. (E.) M. E. *bride*; also *birde, brude, burde.* A. S. *brȳd*, a bride. + Du. *bruid*; Icel. *brūðr*; Swed. and Dan. *brud*; O.H.G. *brūt*; G. *braut*; Goth. *brūths.* Teut. type **brūdiz*, f.

bridal. (E.) Formerly *bride-ale*, a bride-feast. A. S. *brȳd-ealo*, a bride-ale, bride-feast.—A. S. *brȳd*, bride; and *ealo*, ale, also a feast; see **Ale.**

bridegroom. (E.) For *bridegoom*; the second *r* is intrusive; by confusion with *groom.* A. S. *brȳd-guma*, lit. bride-man; where *guma* is cognate with L. *homo*, a man; see **Homage.**+Du. *bruide-gom*; Icel. *brūðgumi*; Swed. *brudgum*;

Dan. *brudgom*; G. *bräutigam*, O. H. G. *brūtigomo*.

Bridge. (E.) M. E. *brigge, brugge*. A. S. *brycg.*+Icel. *bryggja*; Swed. *brygga*; Dan. *brygge*, a pier; Du. *brug*; G. *brücke*. Teut. type **brugjā*, f. Allied to Icel. *brū*, Dan. *bro*, a bridge, pavement; O. Swed. *bro*, a paved way.

Bridle. (E.) M. E. *bridel*. A. S. *brīdel.* + Du. *breidel*; O. H. G. *brīdel, brittil* (whence F. *bride*). A. S. *brīdel* represents an earlier **brigdel* (cf. *brigdils*, a bridle, O. E. Texts, p. 44, l. 127).—A. S. *bregd-an*, to pull, twitch (with change of *e* to *i*). See Braid.

Brief (1), short. (F.—L.) M. E. *bref*. —F. *bref.*—L. *breuis*, short.+Gk. βραχύς, short.

brief (2), a writ, &c. (F.—L.) F. *brief*, a brief; Cot. The same as F. *bref* above; from its being in a short form.

Brig, Brigade; see Brigand.

Brigand. (F.—Ital.) F. *brigand*, a robber.—Ital. *brigante*, an intriguer, robber; orig. pres. part. of *brigare*, to strive after.—Ital. *briga*, strife, quarrel, trouble. Orig. uncertain.

brig; short for **brigantine**.

brigade; (F.—Ital.) F. *brigade*, a crew, troop.—Ital. *brigata*, a troop; orig. fem. of pp. of *brigare*, to strive, fight, as above.

brigandine, a kind of armour. (F. —Ital.) F. *brigandine*, a kind of armour, worn by brigands.—F. *brigand*, a robber; see above.

brigantine, brig, a ship. (F.— Ital.) *Brig* is merely short for *brigantine*. —F. *brigantin*, a kind of ship.—Ital. *brigantino*, a pirate-ship.—Ital. *brigante*, a robber. See Brigand.

Bright. (E.) M. E. *bright*. A. S. *beorht, berht.* + Icel. *bjartr*; M. H. G. *berht*; Goth. *bairhts*, shining. Teut. type **berhtoz*, shining. Cf. Gk. φορκός, white.

Brill, a fish. (E.) Origin unknown.

Brilliant, shining. (F.—L.—Gk.— Skt.) F. *brillant*, pres. part. of *briller*, to glitter; cf. Ital. *brillare*, to sparkle. The orig. sense was to sparkle as a beryl. —L. *beryllus*, a beryl; see Beryl.

Brim. (E.) M. E. *brim*. (Not in A. S.) Cf. Icel. *barmr*, brim; Swed. *bräm*, border, edge; Dan. *bræmme*; M. Du. *breme*; G. *gebräme*, border.

Brimstone, sulphur. (E.) M. E. *brimston, bremstoon*, also *brenstoon* (Wy-

clif).—M. E. *brenn-en*, to burn, and *stoon*, stone. So also Icel. *brennisteinn*, brimstone. See Burn.

Brindled, Brinded, streaked. (Scand.) Icel. *brönd-*, as in *bröndöttr*, brinded, said of a cow.—Icel. *brandr*, a brand, flame, sword. Thus *brinded* = *branded*.

Brine. (E.) M. E. *brine*. A. S. *brȳne* (for *brine*), brine, salt liquor.+M. Du. *brijne*; Du. *brijn*, pickle.

Bring. (E.) A. S. *bringan*, also *brengan*, pt. t. *bröhte.*+Du. *brengen*; G. *bringen*; Goth. *briggan* (written for *bringan*), pt. t. *brāhta*.

Brink. (Scand.) M. E. *brink.*—Dan. *brink*, verge; Swed. *brink*, descent or slope of a hill; Icel. *brekka* (for *brinka*), a slope, crest of a hill; allied to Icel. *bringa*, a grassy slope, orig. the breast.

Brisk. (F.—Ital.) Spelt *bruisk* in Lowl. Sc. (1560).—F. *brusque*, 'brisk, lively, quicke, rash, harsh;' Cot.—Ital. *brusco*, tart, harsh; see Brusque.

Brisket. (F.) O. F. *brischet* (Brachet), s. v. *brechet*), also *bruschet* (Ducange); *brichet*, 'the brisket, or breast-piece,' *bruchet*, 'the craw-bone of a bird;' Cot. Guernsey *brûquet* (for **brusket*).—Dan. *brusk*, Icel. *brjösk*, gristle; cf. Norw. *brjoskutt*, gristly.

Bristle. (E.) M. E. *bristle, berstle, birstle*; dimin. of A. S. *byrst*, a bristle.+ Du. *borstel*; Icel. *burst*; Swed. *borst*; G. *borste*. From Teut. **burs-*, weak grade of **bers*= Idg. **bhers*, to bristle; cf. Skt. *sahasra-bhṛshti*, having a thousand points. See Burr.

Brittle. (E.) M. E. *britel, brotel, brutel*. For A. S. **brytel* = Teut. **brutiloz*, from *brut-*, weak grade of A. S. *brēotan*, to break. It means 'fragile.' Cf. Icel. *brjóta*, Swed. *bryta*, Dan. *bryde*, to break.

Broach. (F.—L.) M. E. *setten on broche* = to set a-broach, tap liquor.—F. *mettre en broche*, to tap, by piercing a barrel.—F. *brocher*, to pierce; *broche*, 'a broach, spit,' Cot.; see Brooch.

Broad. (E.) M. E. *brood*. A. S. *brād*. + Du. *breed*; Icel. *breiðr*; Swed. and Dan. *bred*; Goth. *braids*; G. *breit*.

Brocade. (Span.—L.) Span. *brocado*, brocade; orig. embroidered, the pp. of a verb **brocar* (not used) answering to F. *brocher*, 'to broach, also, to stitch . . . with great stitches;' Cot.—F. *broche.*—Late L. *brocca*, L. *broccus*; see Brooch.

broccoli. (Ital.—L.) Ital. *broccoli*, sprouts; pl. of *broccolo*, a sprout. Dimin. of *brocco*, a skewer, a shoot, stalk.—L. *broccus*, projecting, like teeth.

brochure, a pamphlet. (F.—L.) F. *brochure*, a few leaves stitched together.— F. *brocher*, to stitch; see Brocade.

Brock, a badger. (C.) A. S. *broc.*— W., Corn., and Bret. *broch*; Irish, Gael., and Manx *broc*, a badger. Named from his white-streaked face; cf. Gael. *brocach*, speckled, grayish, as a badger; Gk. φορκός, white, gray. (Cf. E. *gray*, a badger.)

Brocket, a red deer two years old. (F.—L.) F. *brocart*, the same; so called because he has but one tine to his horn.— F. *broche*, a spit, also, a tine of a stag's horn; see Brooch.

Brogues, coarse shoes, leggings. (C. —E.) Gael. and Irish *brōg*, shoe; M. Irish *brōcc*, shoe.—A. S. *brōc*, breeches; *or* Icel. *brōk.* See Breeches.

Broided, braided. (E.) The wk. pp. *broided* took the place of the str. pp. *broiden*, woven, itself due to confusion of *browden* with *broider* (below). *Browden* represents A. S. *brogden*, pp. of *bregdan*, to braid. See Braid.

Broider, to adorn with needlework. (F.) [In 1 Tim. ii. 9, *broidered* (as in some edd.) is an error for *broided*; see above.] Used as the equivalent of F. *broder*, 'to imbroyder,' Cot. The *oi* is due to confusion with *broided.*—O. F. *brouder*, also *brosder* (Supp. to Godefroy); cf. Late L. *brusdus, brosdus*, embroidered work (Ducange). Of unknown origin; perhaps from Teut. **brozd-*, whence A. S. *brord*, Icel. *broddr*, a spike; see Brad.

Broil (1), to fry, grill. (F.) M. E. *broilen.* — A. F. *broiller* (Bozon), O. F. *bruiller*, to boil, roast (Roquefort). Origin unknown; cf. O.F. *bruir*, to roast; perhaps from M.H.G. *brüejen*, to scald; see Brood.

Broil (2), a tumult. (F.) F. *brouiller*, to jumble, confuse, confound. Cf. Ital. *brogliare*, to disturb, *broglio*, confusion (whence E. *im-broglio*). Origin unknown.

Broker. (F.—L.) M. E. *brocour*, an agent, witness of a transaction.—A. F. *brocour*, an agent; orig. a 'broacher' or seller of wine.—Late L. *broccātor*, one who broaches.—Late L. *brocca*, i. e. spike; see Brooch.

Bromine, a chemical element. (Gk.)

Named from its ill odour. Formed, with suffix *-ine*, from Gk. βρῶμ-ος, a stink.

Bronchial. (Gk.) Gk. βρόγχια, neut. pl., the ramifications of the windpipe.— Gk. βρόγχος, the windpipe; cf. βράγχος, a gill. Der. *bronch-itis*; from βρόγχος.

Bronze. (F.—Ital.—L.) F. *bronze.* —Ital. *bronzo*; *bronzino*, made of bronze (*z* = *ds*).—L. *æs Brundusīnum.*—L. *Brundusium*, Brindisi (in Italy); where bronze mirrors were made (Pliny, xxxiii. 9).

Brooch. (F.—L.) Named from the pin which fastens it. M. E. *broche*, a pin, peg, brooch.—F. *broche*, a spit, point.— Late L. *brocca*, a pointed stick; *broca*, a spike; L. *broccus*, projecting, like teeth.

Brood. (E.) M. E. *brod.* A. S. *brōd* (rare); 'hi *brēdað* heora *brōd*' = they nourish their brood; Ælfric's Hom. ii. 10. +Du. *broed*; G. *brut.* Teut. stem **brō-ð-*, from a verbal base **brō-*, preserved in G. *brü-hen*, to scald (orig. to heat), Du. *broe-ien*, to brood, hatch; from the idea of 'heat' or 'warmth.' Der. *breed.*

Brook (1), to endure, put up with. (E.) M. E. *broken, brouken.* A. S. *brū-can*, to use, enjoy; which was the orig. sense. + Du. *gebruiken*, Icel. *brūka*, G. *brauchen*, Goth. *brukjan*, to use; cf. L. *frui*, to enjoy. See Fruit. (√BHREUG.) Brugm. i. § 111.

Brook (2), a small stream. (E.) M. E. *brook.* A. S. *brōc.*+Du. *broek*, G. *bruch*, a marsh.

brook-lime, a plant. (E.) M. E. *brok-lemke, brok-lemok.* From A. S. *brōc*, a brook, and *hleomoc*, brook-lime.

Broom. (E.) M. E. *brome, broom.* A. S. *brōm*, the plant broom; hence, a besom made from twigs of it.+Du. *brem*; Low G. *braam*, broom. Teut. type **brǣmoz.* Allied to Bramble, q. v.

Brose, a later form of *browis* or *brewis*; see Brewis.

Broth. (E.) A. S. *broþ.*+Icel. *broð*; O. H. G. *brod.* Teut. type **broþom*, n.; from *bro-, bru-*, weak grade of *breu-*, as in A. S. *brēowan*, to brew. Lit. 'brewed.'

Brothel. (E.; *confused with* F.— Teut.) 1. M. E. *brothel*, a lewd person, base wretch. — A.S. *broð-en*, pp. of *brēoðan*, to perish, become vile; whence also *ābroðen*, degenerate, base. Hence was made *brothel-house*, a house for vile people (Much Ado, i. 1. 256), afterwards contracted to *brothel.* 2. Orig. distinct from M. E. *bordel*, which was used, how-

ever, in much the same sense. – O. F. *bordel*, a hut, orig. of boards. – Du. *bord*, a
plank, board; see Board.

Brother. (E.) M. E. *brother*. A. S.
brōðor.+Du. *broeder*; Icel. *brōðir*; Goth.
brothar; Swed. and Dan. *broder*; G.
bruder; Gael. and Ir. *brathair*; W.
brawd; Russ. *brat* '; Lat. *fräter*; Gk.
φράτηρ; Skt. *bhrātṛ*. Teut. stem *brōther-*;
Idg. stem *bhrāter-*.

Brougham, a kind of carriage. (Personal name.) Date 1839. Named after
the first Lord Brougham.

Brow. (E.) M. E. *browe*. A. S. *brū*.
+Icel. *brūn*, eyebrow; Lith. *bruwis*;
Russ. *brove*; Gk. ὀφρύς; Pers. *abrū*; Skt.
bhrū. Brugm. i. § 554.

Brown. (E.) M. E. *broun*. A. S.
brūn.+Du. *bruin*; Icel. *brūnn*; Swed.
brun; Dan.*bruun*; G.*braun*; Lith. *brunas*.
Cf. Gk. φρῦνος, a toad; Skt. *ba-bhru(s)*,
tawny.

Browse. (F. – M. H. G.) For *broust*;
lit. 'to feed on young shoots.' – M. F.
brouster (F. *brouter*), to nibble off young
shoots. – M. F. *broust* (F. *brout*), a sprig,
shoot, bud. – M. H. G. *broz*, a bud; Bavar.
brosst, *bross*, a bud. From the weak grade
of O. H. G. *briozan*, to break, also, to
break into bud; which is cognate with
A. S. *brēotan*. See Brittle.

Bruin. (Du.) In Reynard the Fox,
the bear is called *bruin*, i. e. brown. – Du.
bruin, brown. See Brown.

Bruise. (E.; *partly* F.) A. S. *(tō)-
brȳsan*, to bruise. Influenced by O. F.
bruiser, *briser*, to break, perhaps of Celtic
origin; cf. Gael. *bris*, to break, Irish *bris-
im*, I break. (The spelling *ui*, from A. S.
ȳ, occurs in S. Eng. Legendary, 295. 58.)

Bruit, a rumour. (F. – L.?) F. *bruit*,
a noise. – F. *bruire*, to make a noise.
Scheler derives F. *bruire* from L. *rugire*,
to roar, with prefixed *b*. F. *bruit* = Late
L. *brugitus*, a clamour (Ducange); cf. L.
rugitus, a roaring. Partly imitative; cf.
G. *brüllen*, to roar.

Brunette. (F. – G.) F. *brunette*, fem.
of *brunet*, brownish. – M. H. G. *brūn*,
brown; see Brown.

Brunt. (E.) Prob. imitative; cf. *dint*
(*dunt*), a blow; influenced by North E.
brunt, i. e. 'burnt,' as if the 'hot' part of
the fight.

Brush. (F. – Teut. ?) M. E. *brusche*,
a brush; also brush-wood, which is the
older sense, the orig. brush being made of

twigs. – O. F. *broce*, F. *brosse*, brushwood;
also, later, a brush. – Low L. *bruscia*, a
thicket. Derived by Diez from O. H. G.
bursta, G. *borste*, a bristle; but perhaps
Celtic (Thurneysen).

Brusque, rough in manner. (F. – Ital.)
F. *brusque*. – Ital. *brusco*, sharp, tart, sour,
applied to fruits and wine. Origin uncertain.

Brute. (F. – L.) F. *brut*, fem. *brute*.
– L. *brūtus*, stupid.

Bryony. (L. – Gk.) L. *bryōnia*. –
Gk. βρυωνία, βρυώνη, bryony. – Gk. βρύειν,
to teem, grow luxuriantly.

Bubble. (E.) Cf. Swed. *bubbla*, Dan.
boble, a bubble; also Du. *bobbel*, a bubble,
bobbelen, to bubble. Of imitative origin.

Buccanier. (F. – West Indian.) F.
boucanier, a pirate. – F. *boucaner*, to broil
on a sort of wooden frame. – F. *boucan*,
a wooden frame, used by hunters for
smoking and drying flesh. The word
boucan is said to be a F. spelling of a
Tupi (Brazilian) word, and to mean 'a
frame on which meat is smoke-dried.'

Buck (1), a male deer, goat. (E.)
M. E. *bukke*. A. S. *buc*, male deer, *bucca*,
a he-goat.+Du. *bok*, Icel. *bukkr*, Swed.
bock, a he-goat; Dan. *buk*, a he-goat, ram,
buck; G. *bock*; also W. *bwch*, Gael. *boc*,
Irish *boc*. Brugm. i. § 800.

Buck (2), to steep clothes in lye. (E.)
M. E. *bouken*. As if from A. S. *būcian*,
not found. Prob. from A. S. *būc*, a pitcher
(prov. E. *bouk*, a pail, tub); but M. E.
bouken has the specific sense of 'steep in
lye,' like M. H. G. *büchen*, Swed. *byka*,
Dan. *byge*, Low G. *büken*, *büken* (whence
Ital. *bucare*, F. *buer*).

bucket. (E.) A. F. *boket* (Bozon).
Formed with A. F. dimin. suffix *-et* from
A. S. *būc*, a pitcher. Cf. Gael. *bucaid*,
Irish *buicead*, a bucket (from E.).

Buckle. (F. – L.) M. E. *bokel*. – O. F.
bucle (F. *boucle*), the boss of a shield, a
ring, a buckle. – Late L. *bucula*, the boss
of a shield; *buccula*, beaver of a helm, boss
of a shield, buckle. – Lat. *buccula*, the
cheek, dimin. of *bucca*, the cheek.

buckler. (F. – L.) M. E. *bokeler*. –
O. F. *bucler* (F. *bouclier*), a shield; so
named from the boss on it; see above.

Buckram, a coarse cloth. (F. –
Ital.) M. E. *bokeram*. – O. F. *boquerant*
(F. *bougran*), a coarse kind of cloth; Low
L. *boquerannus* or (in Italy) *būchirānus*
(for Ital. *buchirano*), late Ital. *bucherame*.

Origin uncertain; perhaps from Bokhara (Tartary).

Buckwheat. (E.) Lit. beech-wheat; from the resemblance of its seeds to the mast of the beech-tree. The form *buck* is from A. S. *bōc*, as in *buck-mast*, beech-mast. So also Du. *boekweit*, buckwheat; G. *buchweizen*. See Beech.

Bucolic, pastoral. (L. – Gk.) L. *būco-licus.* – Gk. βουκολικός, pastoral. – Gk. βουκόλος, a cowherd. – Gk. βοῦ-s, an ox; and κέλλειν, to drive.

Bud. (E. ?) M. E. *bodde, budde,* a bud; *budden,* to bud. Not found in A. S. Cf. Du. *bot,* a bud; *botten,* to bud, sprout.

Budge (1), to stir. (F. – L.) F. *bouger,* to stir; answering to Ital. *bulicare,* to bubble up (Diez). – L. *bullīre;* see Boil (1) above. Cf. Span. *bullir,* (1) to boil, (2) to stir.

Budge (2), a kind of fur. (F. ?) Perhaps related to O. F. *bochet, bouchet,* a young kid.

Budget, a leathern bag. (F. – C.) F. *bougette,* dimin. of *bouge,* a bag. – L. *bulga,* a leathern bag (Gaulish). – O. Irish *bolg, bolc,* a sack.

Buff (1), the colour of dressed buffalo-skin. (F. – L. – Gk.) F. *buffle,* a buffalo. – L. *būfalus;* see Buffalo.

Buff (2), in Blindman's buff. (F.) Formerly *blindman-buff,* a game; in which game boys used to *buffet* one (who was blinded) on the back, without being caught, if possible. From O. F. *bufe,* F. *buffe,* a buffet, blow; cf. Low G. *buff, puf,* a blow (Lübben). See Buffet (1).

Buffalo. (Port. *or* Ital. – L. – Gk.) Port. *bufalo,* Ital. *buffalo,* orig. a kind of wild ox. – L. *būfalus,* also *būbalus.* – Gk. βούβαλος, a buffalo; a kind of deer or antelope. (Not a true Gk. word.)

Buffer (1), and (2); see Buffet (1).

Buffet (1), a blow; to strike. (F.) M. E. *boffet, buffet,* a blow, esp. on the cheek. – O. F. *bufet, a* blow, dimin. of *bufe,* a blow, esp. on the cheek; cf. *bufer, buffer,* to puff out the cheeks, also to buffet; mod. F. *bouffer.* Prob. of imitative origin, allied to *pouffer,* to puff; see Buff (2), Puff.

buffer (1), a foolish fellow. (F.) Orig. a stammerer; hence, a foolish fellow. M. E. *buffen,* to stammer. – O. F. *bufer,* to puff out the cheeks (hence, to puff or blow in talking).

buffer (2), a cushion, to deaden concussion. (F.) Lit. 'a striker;' from M. E.

buffen, to strike, orig. to buffet on the cheek; see Buffet (1).

buffoon. (F.) F. *bouffon,* a buffoon, jester, one who makes grimaces. – F. *bouffer,* to puff.

Buffet (2), a side-board. (F.) F. *buffet,* a side-board. Origin unknown.

Bug (1), a spectre. (C.) In Sh. – W. *bwg,* a hobgoblin, spectre; Gael. and Ir. *bocan,* a spectre. + Lithuan. *baugus,* terrific, from *bugti,* to terrify, allied to Skt. *bhuj,* to turn aside; see Bow (1). Brugm. i. § 701.

Bug (2), an insect. (C.?) Said to be so named because an object of terror, exciting disgust; see Bug (1). But cf. A. S. *scearn-budda,* dung-beetle (Voc.), prov. E. *shorn-bug* (Kent).

Bug-bear. (C. *and* E.) A supposed spectre in the shape of a bear; see Bug (1).

Bugle (1), a wild ox; a horn. (F. – L.) *Bugle,* a horn, is short for *bugle-horn;* a *bugle* is a wild ox. – O. F. *bugle,* a wild ox. – L. acc. *būculum,* a young ox; double dimin. of *bōs,* an ox.

Bugle (2), a kind of ornament. (F. – L.) Little black pipes, likened to horns. 'Bugle, a little black horne;' Cockeram. See above.

Bugle (3), a plant. (F.) F. *bugle;* Cot.; cf. Span. and Late L. *bugula.* Cf. L. *bugillo,* (perhaps) bugle.

Bugloss, a plant. (F. – L. – Gk.) Lit. ' ox-tongue.' – F. *buglosse.* – L. *būglōssa;* also *būglōssus.* – Gk. βούγλωσσος, ox-tongue; from the shape of the leaves. – Gk. βοῦ-s, ox; γλῶσσ-α, tongue.

Build. (E.) M. E. *bulden.* Late A. S. *byldan,* to build. – A. S. *bold,* a house, variant of *botl,* a dwelling, n. = Teut. **bu-plom,* from *bu-,* related to *bū-an,* to dwell; see Bower. Cf. A. S. *bytlian,* to build, from *botl* (above). [Cf. O. Swed. *bylja,* to build (Ihre). – O. Swed. *bol,* a house, dwelling; Icel. *bōl,* a house, Dan. *bol,* a small farm.]

Bulb. (F. – L. – Gk.) F. *bulbe.* – L. *bulbus,* a bulb. – Gk. βολβός, a bulbous root, onion.

Bulbul, a nightingale. (Pers.) Pers. *bulbul,* a bird with a melodious voice, resembling the nightingale. Of imitative origin.

Bulge, to swell out. (F. – C.) Formed from M. E. *bulge,* a wallet, pouch. – O. F. *boulge* (*bouge*), a bag. – L. *bulga,* a bag (Gaulish). See Budget. Doublet, *bilge.*

Bulk (1), size. (Scand.) M. E. *bolke,* a heap. — Icel. *būlki,* a heap; O. Swed. *bolk;* Dan. *bulk,* a lump. Cf. Swed. *bulna,* to swell.

Bulk (2), the trunk of the body. (Du.) In Sh. — M. Du. *bulcke,* thorax (Kilian). (Prob. confused with Du. *buik,* Icel. *būkr,* the trunk; Swed. *buk,* Dan. *bug,* G. *bauch,* the belly.)

Bulk (3), a stall of a shop. (Scand.) Perhaps related to **Balk.** Cf. Dan. dial. *bulk,* a half-wall; Icel. *bālkr,* a beam, also, a partition; Linc. *bulker,* a beam, a wooden hutch in a workshop. Der. *bulk-head,* a partition.

Bull (1), male of the cow. (E.) M. E. *bole, bule.* Not found in A. S., but the dimin. *bulluc,* a bullock, occurs. Prob. ' the bellower;' cf. M. H. G. *bullen,* to roar; and see **Bellow.** + Du. *bul;* Icel. *boli;* G. *bulle;* Lithuan. *bullus.* **Der.** *bull-ock,* A. S. *bulluc,* as above.

Bull (2), a papal edict. (L.) M. E. *bulle.* — Lat. *bulla,* a bubble, boss, knob, leaden seal on an edict; a bull (in late Latin).

bullet. (F. — L.) M. F. *boulet,* dimin. of F. *boule,* a ball. — L. *bulla,* a boss, knob, &c.

bulletin. (F. — Ital. — L.) F. *bulletin,* a ticket. — Ital. *bullettino,* a safe-conduct, pass, ticket. Dimin. of *bulletta,* a passport, lottery ticket, dimin. of *bulla,* a seal, bull. — L. *bulla,* a boss, &c.

Bullace, wild plum. (F. — L.) M. E. *bolas.* — O. F. *beloce,* a bullace; M. F. *pelosse,* Cot. — L. type **pilottea,* pellet-like. — Late L. *pilota,* a pellet. — L. *pila,* a ball.

Bullet, Bulletin; see Bull (2).

Bullion. (F. — L.) The A. F. *bullion* meant a mint, and Late L. *bulliōna, bullio* meant a mass of metal, apparently, from its being melted; cf. F. *bouillon,* a boiling. — Late L. *bulliōnem,* acc. of *bullio,* a boiling. — L. *bullīre,* to bubble up, boil. — L. *bulla,* a bubble.

Bully, a noisy rough fellow. (O. Low G.) In Sh. The oldest sense, in E., is ' dear one, lover.' — M. Du. *boel,* a lover (of either sex); borrowed from M. H. G. *buole* (G. *buhle*), lover.

Bulrush. (E.) M.E. *bulrysche,*Prompt. Parv., p. 244, col. 2. Perhaps ' stem-rush'; from its stout stem; cf. Shetl. *bulwand,* a bulrush. — Dan. *bul,* stem, trunk; see

Bole. Or *bull* may mean ' large,' with ref. to a *bull.* Cf. *bull-daisy,* &c. (Britten).

Bulwark. (Scand.) Dan. *bulværk,* Swed. *bolverk* (Ihre); cf. Du. *bolwerk,* G. *boll-werk* (whence F. *boulevard*). Compounded of Dan. *bul,* Swed. *bol,* trunk of a tree, log, Icel. *bulr, bolr,* the stem of a tree; and Dan. *værk,* Swed. *verk,* a work. Lit. ' log-work,' or ' bole-work'; see Bole.

Bum-bailiff, under-bailiff. (E. *and* F.) A slang term. Todd quotes passages to shew that it arose from the pursuer catching at a man by the hinder part of his garment.

Bumble-bee, a bee that booms or hums. See Boom (1).

Bumboat. (E.) From *bum* and *boat.* Orig. a scavenger's boat on the Thames (A. D. 1685); afterwards used to supply vegetables to ships.

Bump (1), to thump; a blow. (E.) Of imitative origin; cf. M. Dan. *bumpe,* to strike with the fist; W. *pwmpio,* to thump; *pwmp,* a lump; Corn. *bom, bum,* a blow. The senses are : (1) to strike, (2) a blow, (3) its effect. See Bunch.

Bump (2), to boom. (E.) Imitative; cf. Boom (1), and Bumble-bee.

Bumper, a full glass. (E.) From *bump;* with the notion of a *bumping* or full glass; cf. *thumping,* i. e. great.

Bumpkin, a thick-headed fellow. (Du.) M. Du. *boomken,* a little tree (Hexham); dimin. of *boom,* a tree, a beam, bar ; see Beam (1). The E. *bumkin* also meant a luff-block, a thick piece of wood (Cot-grave, s. v. *Chicambault,* and see *bumkin* in the E. index) ; hence, readily applied to a block-head, thick-skulled fellow.

Bun. (F.) Cf. prov. F. *bugne,* a kind of fritters ; perhaps the same as O. F. *bugne,* a swelling or bump due to a blow (Burguy), also spelt *bigne,* ' a bump, knob;' Cot. O. F. *bugnete,* a fritter (Godefroy) ; also *bugnet* (id., Supp. p. 393). ' *Bignets,* little round loaves, buns,' &c.; Cot. Minsheu has Span. *buñuelos,* ' pancakes, cobloaves, buns.' See Bunion. (Doubtful.)

Bunch. (E. ?) M. E. *bunche.* Cf. M. E. *bunchen,* to beat. Prob. imitative, like *bump, bounce.* And see Bunk.

Bundle. (E.) M. E. *bundel.* Dimin. of O. Northumb. *bund,* a bundle (Matt. xiii. 30). — A. S. *bund-,* weak grade of *bindan,* to bind.+Du. *bondel;* G. *bündel.*

Bung, a stopple. (Du.—L.) M. Du. *bonge* (Du. *bom*), a bung; dialectal form of **bonde*, as preserved in F. *bonde*, a bung. Cognate with Swiss *punt* (Weigand, s. v. *Spund*).—L. *puncta*, an orifice; orig. fem. pp. of *pungere*, to prick. Cf. W. *bwng*, an orifice, also, a bung.

Bungalow, a Bengal thatched house. (Hind.) Hind. *bangalah*, of or belonging to Bengal, a bungalow; Rich. Dict. p. 293. From the name *Bengal*.

Bungle. (Scand.?) Of imitative origin. Cf. Swed. dial. *bangla*, to work ineffectually; O. Swed. *bunga*, to strike (Rietz, Ihre.) And cf. **Bang.**

Bunion. (F.—G.) O. F. *buignon*, only in the sense of a fritter (Godefroy); but really an augmentative of O. F. *buigne* (F. *bigne*, 'a bump, swelling,' Cot.).—O. H. G. *bungo*, a lump (Graff, in Schmeller); cf. Icel. *bunga*, convexity. So also Ital. *bugnone*, augment. of *bugno*, a boil, a swelling. See **Bun.**

Bunk, a wooden case or box, berth. (Scand.) Cf. O. Swed. *bunke*, the planking of a ship forming a shelter for merchandise, &c. (Ihre); the usual sense of Swed. *bunke* is a heap, pile, something prominent; M. Dan. *bunke*, room for cargo.

Bunt, the belly of a sail. (Scand.) It answers in form to Dan. *bundt*, Swed. *bunt*, a bundle, a bunch; from the weak stem of the verb to **Bind.** ¶ But the right words for 'bunt' are Dan. *bug*, Swed. *buk*, Du. *buik*, G. *bauch*; see **Bulk** (2).

Bunting (1), a bird. (E.?) M. E. *bunting*; also *buntyle* (= *buntel*), Lowl. Sc. *buntlin*. Origin unknown.

Bunting (2), a thin woollen stuff for flags. (E.) Perhaps 'sifting-cloth'; from M. E. *bonten*, prov. E. *bunt*, to sift. Cf. F. *étamine*, in the same senses.

Buoy. (Du.—F.—L.) Du. *boei*, a buoy; also a shackle, a fetter.—O. F. *buie*, a fetter, F. *bouée*, a buoy.—Late L. *boia*, a fetter, clog.—L. *boiæ*, pl. a collar for the neck, orig. of leather.

Bur, Burdock; see **Burr.**

Burbot, a fish. (F.) F. *bourbotte* (also *barbote*).—F. *bourbetter*, 'to wallow in mud,' Cot.—F. *bourbe*, mud.—Late L. *borba*, mud.—Gk. βόρβορος, mud.

Burden (1), **Burthen,** a load carried. (E.) A. S. *byrðen*, a load. From Teut. **bur-*, weak grade of **beran-*, to bear; see **Bear** (1). ✛ Icel. *byrðr*, *byrði*; Swed. *börda*; Dan. *byrde*; Goth. *baurthei*; G. *bürde*; from the same root, with varying suffixes. For the form *burden*, see below.

Burden (2), the refrain of a song. (F.—Late L.) F. *bourdon*, a drone-bee, humming of bees, drone of a bagpipe; see Cot.—Late L. *burdōnem*, acc. of *burdo*, a drone. Prob. of imitative origin; cf. Lowland Sc. *birr*, to make a whizzing noise, E. *buzz.* ¶ Confused with **Burden** (1).

Bureau. (F.—L.) F. *bureau*, a desk, writing-table; so called because covered with brown baize.—F. *bureau*, O. F. *burel*, coarse woollen stuff, russet-coloured.—O. F. *buire*, M. F. *bure*, dark brown; F. *bure*, coarse cloth.—L. *burrus*, reddish.—Gk. πυρρός, reddish.—Gk. πῦρ, fire.

Burgeon, a bud. (F.—Teut.) F. *bourgeon*, a young bud. Lengthened from Languedoc *boure*, a bud, eye of a shoot (Diez).—M. H. G. *buren*, O. H. G. *purjan*, to raise, push up, push out.—M. H. G. *bor*, *por*, an elevation; whence G. *empor* (= *in por*), upwards.

Burgess. (F.—M. H. G.) M. E. *burgeys.*—O. F. *burgeis.*—Low Lat. *burgensis*, belonging to a fort or city.—Low Lat. *burgus*, a fort.—M. H. G. *burc* (G. *burg*); cognate with A. S. *burg*; see **Borough.**

burgher. (Du.) Formerly *burger.*—Du. *burger*, a citizen.—Du. *burg*, a city; cognate with E. **Borough.**

burglar. (A. F.—E.) A. F. *burgler*, *burglour*; Law L. *burgulātor.*—Law L. *burgulāre*, to break into a house.—A. S. *burh*, *burg*; see **Borough.**

burgomaster. (Du. *and* F.) Du. *burge-meester*, a town-master.—Du. *burg*, cognate with E. **Borough**; and *meester*, a master, from O. F. *meistre*; see **Master.**

Burgonet, a helmet. (F.) F. *bourguignote*, 'a burganet,' Cot. So called because first used by the Burgundians.—F. *Bourgogne*, Burgundy.

Burial. (E.) M. E. *buriel*, *biriel*, a tomb; also spelt *beriels*, *biriels.*—A. S. *byrgels*, a tomb.—A. S. *byrgan*, to bury; see **Bury.** The spelling with *-al* is due to association with *funer-al*, &c.

Burin, an engraver's tool. (F.—G.) F. *burin*; Ital. *borino.* Prob. from M. H. G. *boren* (G. *bohren*), to bore; see **Bore** (1).

Burke, to murder by suffocation; to murder, stifle. (Personal name.) From the name of *Burke*, an Irishman who committed murders by suffocation; executed at Edinburgh, Jan. 28, 1829.

Burl, to pick knots and loose threads from cloth. (F.−L.) To *burl* is to pick off *burls*. M. E. *burle,* a knot in cloth. −O. F. *bourle*; dimin. of F. *bourre,* a flock or lock of wool or hair. − Late L. *burra,* a woollen pad; allied to L. *burræ,* trifles, trash, Late L. *reburrus,* rough.

burlesque, comic. (F.−Ital.−L.) F. *burlesque.*−Ital. *burlesco,* ludicrous.− Ital. *burla,* waggery, a trick. A dimin. from L. *burræ,* trifles, nonsense (Ausonius). See Burl.

Burly. (E.) M. E. *burli, burliche, borli*; prov. E. *bowerly*; Shetland *boorly.* Formed by adding the suffix *-ly* (A. S. *-līc*) to A. S. *būr,* a bower, a lady's chamber; hence, the old senses of ' fit for a bower,' stately, excellent, large, great; and, finally, stout, big. E. g. 'a *burly* bed.'

Burn (1), verb. (E.) M. E. *bernen*; also *brennen.* There are two forms. α. intrans. A.S. *beornan, byrnan,* strong verb, pt. t. *bearn, bran,* pp. *bornen.*+O. Icel. *brinna*; Goth. *brinnan*; Teut. type **brennan-*; cf. A. S. *bryne,* flame. β. trans. A. S. *bærnan,* wk. vb.+Icel. *brenna,* Dan. *brænde,* Swed. *bränna*; G. *brennen*; Goth. *brannjan*; Teut. type **brannjan-,* causal to the former.

Burn (2), a brook; see Bourn (2).

Burnet, a plant. (F. − O. H. G.) Low L. *burneta.*−O. F. *brunete,* the name of a flower: *burnette, brunette,* a kind of dark brown cloth, also a brunette. See Brunette. Named from the dark brown colour of the flowers.

burnish, to polish. (F. − O. H. G.) M. E. *burnishen*; also *burnen.* − O. F. *burnir, brunir* (pres. part. *burnis-ant*), to embrown, to polish. − O. H. G. *brūnen* (<**brūnjan*). − O. H. G. *brūn,* brown; see Brown.

Burnouse, Burnoose, an upper cloak worn by the Arabs. (F. − Arab.) F. *burnous, bournous.*−Arab. *burnus,* a kind of high-crowned cap, worn formerly in Barbary and Spain; whence Span. *al-bornoz,* a kind of cloak with a hood.

Burr, Bur. (E.) M. E. *burre,* knob on a burdock; *borre,* roughness in the throat. Not in A.S. N. Fries. *burre, borre,* a burr, burdock.+Swed. *borre,* a sea-urchin; *kardborre,* a burdock; Dan. *borre,* burdock. From Teut. base **burz-*<**burs-,* weak grade of Teut. root **bers,* to bristle. See Bristle. Der. *bur-dock.*

Burrow, a shelter for rabbits. (E.) M. E. *borwgh,* a cave, shelter; merely a varied spelling of *borough.* **Der.** *burrow,* verb.

Bursar. (Med. L. − Gk.) Med. L. *bursārius,* a purse-bearer.− Med. L. *bursa,* a purse.− Gk. βύρσα, a hide, wine-skin.

Burst. (E.) M. E. *bersten, bresten,* pt. t. *brast.* A. S. *berstan,* to burst asunder; break; str. vb.+Du. *bersten*; G. *bersten*; Icel. *bresta*; Swed. *brista*; Dan. *briste*; also O. Irish *briss-im* (for **brest-im*), I break.

Bury (1), vb. (E.) M. E. *burien.* A.S. *byrigan, byrgan,* to hide in the ground, bury. From *burg-,* weak grade of *beorg-an,* to hide; see Borough.

Bury (2), a town. (E.) As in Canterbury.− A. S. *byrig,* dat. of *burh,* a borough. See Borough.

Bus, a shortened form of *omnibus.* (L.) See Omnibus.

Bush (1), a thicket. (Scand.−L.) M. E. *busch, busk.* − Dan. *busk,* Swed. *buske,* a bush, shrub.+Du. *bosch*; O. H. G. *busc*; G. *busch.* All from Late L. *boscus,* a bush; a word of unknown origin.

Bush (2), the metal box in which an axle works. (Du.−L.−Gk.) M. E. *busse.* − Du. *bus, bos,* barrel (of a gun); G. *büchse.*− Late L. *buxis,* a box. − Gk. πύξις, a box. − Gk. πύξος, box-wood, box-tree. See Pyx.

bushel, a measure. (F.−L.−Gk.) M. E. *bushel.*−A. F. *bousselle,* O. F. *boissel*; Late L. *bustellus,* a small box; for **boistel,* dimin. of O. F. *boiste,* a box.− Late L. *buxida,* acc. of *buxis,* a box (above).

Busk (1), to get oneself ready. (Scand.) Icel. *būask,* to get oneself ready.−Icel. *būa,* to prepare; and *-sk,* for *sik,* oneself. See Bound (3); and cf. Bask.

Busk (2), a support for a woman's stays. (F.) M. F. *busque,* ' a buske, or buste;' Cot. Mod. F. *busc.* Of uncertain origin. Cf. M. F. *buc,* ' a busque;' Cot.

Buskin. (F.−Ital.−L.−Gk.) O.F. *bousequin* (1483); also *brousequin.*− M. Ital. *borzachino,* buskin, fine boot.− L. *borsa.*−Gk. βύρσα, a hide. The M. Du. *broseken* was borrowed from F.

Buss, to kiss. (E.) [The old word was *bass.*− F. *baiser,* to kiss.− Lat. *basium,* a kiss.] The modern *buss,* of imitative origin, may have been partly suggested by it. Cf. prov. G. (Bavarian) *bussen,* to kiss ; Lith. *buczoti*, to kiss ; also Gael. and W. *bus*, mouth, lip.

Bust. (F. — Ital.) F. *buste*. — Ital. *busto*, the bust, trunk of human body, stays ; Late L. *bustum*, the trunk of the body. Etym. uncertain.

Bustard, a bird. (F. — L.) Formerly also *bistard* (Sherwood). — O. F. *bistarde*, ' a bustard ; ' Cot. (Mod. F. *outarde*.) — L. *auis tarda*, a slow bird (Pliny, N. H. x. 22). Cf. Port. *abetarda*, also *betarda*, a bustard. ¶ Both O. F. *bistarde* and F. *outarde* are from *auis tarda* ; in the former case, initial *a* is dropped ; in the latter, *outarde* stands for an older *oustarde*, where *ous* = L. *auis*. See Diez. *Auis tarda*, lit. ' slow bird,' is far from being truly descriptive ; so that it is prob. a substitution for some form foreign to Latin.

Bustle. (Scand.) A frequentative of Norw. *busta*, to be violent ; Swed. *bösta*, to bustle, work. Cf. Icel. *bustla*, to splash about as a fish ; E. Fries. *büsen*, to be violent. See **Boast** and **Boisterous.**

Busy. (E.) M. E. *bisy*. A. S. *bisig* (*bysig*), active ; whence *bisgu*, exertion. **+** Du. *bezig*, busy.

But (1), prep. and conj., except. (E.) A. S. *be-ūtan*, *būtan*, *būta*, lit. ' without.' — A. S. *be*, by ; *ūtan*, adv. without, from *ūt*, out. **+** Du. *buiten*.

But (2) ; see **Butt** (1), **Butt** (2).

Butcher. (F. — G.) M. E. *bocher*. — O. F. *bochier*, orig. one who kills goats. — O. F. *boc* (F. *bouc*), a goat. — G. *bock*, a goat. See **Buck.**

Butler. (F. — Late L. — Gk.) M. E. *boteler*, one who attends to bottles ; from M. E. *botel*, a bottle ; see **Bottle.**

Butt (1), a push, thrust ; to thrust. (F. — O. Low G.) [The senses of the sb. may be referred to the verb ; just as F. *botte*, a thrust, depends on *bouter*, to strike.] M. E. *butten*, to push, strike. — O. F. *boter*, to push, butt, strike. — O. Frank. **bōtan*, corresponding to M. Du. *booten*, to beat, M. H. G. *bōzen*, O. H. G. *bōzan*, to beat. Der. *butt* (mound to shoot at), from M. F. *butte*, the same, allied to F. *but*, a mark, from *buter*, O. F. *boter*, to hit. Der. *a-but*. See **Beat.**

Butt (2), a large barrel. (F. — L.) We find A. S. *bytt* ; but our mod. word is really F. — O. F. *boute*, F. *botte*, ' the vessel which we call a *butt* ; ' Cot. — Late Lat. *butta, buttis*, a cask.

Butt (3), a thick end. (E.) M. E. *but*, *butte*. Cognate with Icel. *buttr*, short ; see **Buttock.** Der. *butt-end*.

Butt (4), a kind of flat fish. (E.) Allied to Swed. *butta*, a turbot, M. Dan. *butte*, Low G. *but*, Du. *bot*, a butt. Prob. from *but*, stumpy ; see **Buttock.**

Butter. (L. — Gk.) M. E. *botere* ; A. S. *butere*. — L. *būtyrum*. — Gk. βούτυρον, butter. Probably of Scythian origin.

butterfly. (E.) A. S. *buttor-flēoge*, lit. butter-fly. So called from its excrement resembling butter, as shewn by the M. Du. *boter-schijte*, a butter-fly, lit. butter-voider (Kilian). **+** Du. *botervlieg* ; G. *butter-fliege*.

Buttery, a place for provisions, esp. liquids. (F. — Late L.) A corruption of M. E. *botelerie*, a butlery, properly a place for a butler ; from M. E. *boteler*, a butler ; see **Butler.** (Thus *buttery = bottlery*.) Confused with the word *butter*.

Buttock. (E.) M. E. *buttok*. Formed, with dimin. suffix *-ok* (A. S. *-uc*), from *butt*, a thick end, a stump. Cf. Icel. *buttr*, short, *būtr*, a log ; Dan. *but*, Swed. *butt*, stumpy, surly ; Du. *bot*, blunt, dull. See **Butt** (3).

Button. (F. — O. Low G.) M. E. *boton*, also, a bud. — O. F. *boton* (F. *bouton*), a bud, a button ; properly a round knob pushed out. — O. F. *boter*, to push, push out ; see **Butt** (1).

buttress, a support, in architecture. (F. — O. Low G.) M. E. *boteras* ; Palsgrave has *bottras, butteras*. Orig. a plural form, as if for **butterets*. — O. F. *bouterez*, pl. of *bouteret*, a prop. — F. *bouter*, to thrust, prop. Cotgrave also has *boutant*, a buttress, from the same verb ; see **Butt** (1).

Butty, a companion or partner in a work. (F. — Low G.) Shortened from *boty-felowe* or *booty-fellow*, one who shares booty with others. From *boty*, old spelling of *booty* = F. *butin*, booty. Of Low G. origin ; see **Booty.**

Buxom. (E.) M. E. *boxom, buhsum* ; the old sense was obedient, obliging, good-humoured. Lit. ' bow-some.' — A. S. *būgan*, to bow, bend, obey ; and *-sum*, suffix, as in *win-some*. **+** Du. *buigzaam* ; G. *biegsam*. See **Bow** (1).

Buy. (E.) From A. S. *byg-*, as in *byg-est, byg-eð*, 2 and 3 p. sing. pres. of A. S. *bycgan*, to purchase, whence M. E. *buggen, biggen*. **+** Goth. *bugjan*. Der. *abide* (2), q. v. See Sweet, N. E. G. § 1293.

Buzz. (E.) An imitative word ; cf.

Lowl. Sc. *bizz*, to hiss ; Ital. *buzzicare*, to hum, whisper.

Buzzard. (F. – L.) M. E. *bosard*, *busard*, an inferior kind of falcon. – F. *busard.* – F. *buse*, a buzzard ; with suffix -*ard* (from O.H.G. *hart*). – Late L. *busio* = L. *buteo*, a sparrow-hawk.

By, prep. (E.) M. E. *bi*. A. S. *bī*, *big*. + Du. *bij* ; G. *bei* ; Goth. *bi*. Cf. Skt. *a-bhi*, Gk. ἀμ-φί.

By-law, a law affecting a township. (Scand.) Formerly also *birlaw*. – Icel. *bǣ-r*, *bȳ-r*, a village (gen. *bæjar*, whence *bir-*) ; *lög*, a law. So also Dan. *by-lov*, a town-law. Icel. *bēr* is allied to *būa*, to dwell. See Boor.

Byre, a cow-house. (E.) A Northern E. deriv. of *bower*. A. S. *bȳre*, a shed, hut. – A. S. *būr*, a bower ; cf. Icel. *būr*, a pantry. See Bower.

C.

Cab (1) ; see Cabriolet.

Cab (2), a Heb. measure. (Heb.) Heb. *qab*, the 18th part of an ephah. The literal sense is 'hollow' ; cf. Heb *qābab*, to form in the shape of a vault ; see Alcove.

Cabal. (F. – Heb.) Orig. 'a secret.' F. *cabale*, 'the Jewes Caball, a hidden science ;' Cot. – Heb. *qabbālāh*, reception, mysterious doctrine. – Heb. *qābal*, to receive ; *qibbēl*, to adopt a doctrine.

Cabbage (1), a vegetable. (F. – L.) M. E. *cabache*, *caboche.* – F. (Picard) *caboche*, lit. 'great head ;' cf. Picard *cabus*, F. *choux cabus*, large-headed cabbage. – L. *cap-ut*, head ; with augmentative suffix ; cf. Ital. *capocchia*, head of a nail.

Cabbage (2), to steal. (F.) From F. *cabasser*, to put into a basket ; Norman *cabasser*, to cabbage (and see Supp. to Godefroy). – F. *cabas*, a basket ; Norman *cabas*, tailor's cabbage ; of unknown origin.

Caber, a pole. (C. – L.) Gael. *cabar*, a rafter. – L. type **caprio*, a rafter ; see Chevron.

Cabin. (F.) M.E *cabane*. – F. *cabane*. – Prov. *cabana*. – Late L. *capanna*, a hut (Isidore).

cabinet. (F.) F. *cabinet*, dimin. of F. *cabane*, a cabin (above).

Cable. (F. – L.) M. E. *cable*. – O. F. *cable*. – Late L. *capulum*, *caplum*, a strong (holding) rope. – L. *capere*, to hold.

Caboose, the cook's cabin on board ship. (Du.) Formerly *camboose*. – Du. *kombuis*,

a cook's cabin ; also 'the chimney in a ship,' Sewel. (Hence also Dan. *kabys*, Swed. *kabysa*, caboose.)

Cabriolet. (F. – Ital. – L.) *Cab* is short for *cabriolet*. – F. *cabriolet*, a cab ; from its supposed lightness. – F. *cabriole*, a caper, leap of a goat ; formerly *capriole*. – Ital. *capriola*, a caper, a kid. – Ital. *caprio*, wild goat ; *capra*, a she-goat. – L. *caper*, goat ; fem. *capra*.

Cacao, a tree. (Span. – Mexican.) Span. *cacao* ; from the Mexican name (*cacauatl*) of the tree whence chocolate is made. ¶ Not the same as *cocoa*.

Cachinnation. (L.) L. acc. *cachinnātiōnem*, loud laughter. – L. *cachinnāre*, to laugh. Cf. Cackle.

Cachucha, a dance. (Span.) Span. *cachucha*.

Cacique, a W. Indian chief. (Span. – W. Indian.) Span. *cacique*, an Indian prince. From the old language of Hayti.

Cack, to go to stool. (L.) M. E. *cakken.* – L. *cacāre*.

Cackle. (E.) M.E. *kakelen*, a frequentative form. Not in A. S. + Du. *kakelen* ; Swed. *kackla* ; Dan. *kagle* ; G. *gackeln*. The sense is 'to keep on saying *kak* ;' cf. *gabb-le*, *gobb-le*, *gagg-le*.

Cacophony, a harsh sound. (Gk.) Gk. κακοφωνία, a harsh sound. – Gk. κακό-φωνος, harsh ; – Gk. κακό-s, bad ; and φων-ή, sound. **Der.** *cacophonous* (Gk. κακό-φωνος).

Cad, a low fellow. (F. – L.) Short for Lowl. Sc. *cadie*, an errand-boy ; see Jamieson. – F. *cadet* ; see Cadet.

Cadaverous, corpse-like. (L.) L. *cadāverōsus.* – L. *cadāuer*, a corpse. – Lat. *cad-ere*, to fall, fall dead.

Caddis, a kind of worsted lace or tape. (F.) In Wint. Tale, iv. 4. 208. M. E. *cadas*, explained by *bombicinium* in Prompt. Parv. ; (hence Irish *cadas*, caddis). Though also used to denote 'worsted,' it was orig. coarse silk. – F. *cadarce*, 'the coursest part of silke, whereof sleave is made ;' Cot. Cf. Span. *cadarzo*, coarse, entangled silk, that cannot be spun on a reel ; Port. *cadarço*, a coarse silk. Origin unknown ; probably Eastern. **Der.** *caddis-worm*, from the caddis-like shape of the case of the larva.

Caddy, a small box for tea. (Malay.) Better spelt *catty*. A small package of tea, less than a half-chest, is called in the tea-trade a *caddy* or *catty*. – Malay *kātī*, a weight equal to 1⅓ lb. avoirdupois. This weight is also used in China and Japan, and tea is often made up in packages containing one catty.

Cade, a barrel, cask. (F. L. Gk. Heb.) F. *cade.* — L. *cadus,* a barrel, cask. — Gk. κάδος, a cask, jar. — Heb. *kad,* a pail.

Cadence, a fall of the voice. (F.— Ital.—L.) M. E. *cadence.* — F. *cadence,* 'a cadence, just falling of words;' Cot.— Ital. *cadenza.* — Late L. *cadentia,* a falling. — L. *cadent-,* stem of pres. pt. of *cadere,* to fall. +Skt. *çad,* to fall.

Cadet, orig. a younger son. (F.—L.) F. *cadet,* a younger brother; Prov. *capdel. Capdet* is a Gascon form = Late L. *capitellum* (the substitution of *t* for *ll* being regular in Gascon; P. Meyer); lit. a little (younger) head, dimin. from L. *caput,* a head.

Cadi, a judge.˙ (Arab.)   Arab. *qādī, qāzī,* a cadi or cazi, a judge. Hence Span. *alcalde,* the judge (E. *alcayde*); where *al* is the Arab. def. article.

Caducous, falling. (L.) L. *cadūc-us,* falling; with suffix *-ous.* — L. *cadere,* to fall. See Cadence.

Cæsura. (L.) L. *cæsūra,* a cutting; a pause in a verse. — L. *cæs-us,* pp. of *cædere,* to cut.

Caftan, a Turkish garment. (Turk.) Turk. *qaftān,* a dress.

Cage. (F. — L.)   F. *cage.* — Late L. *cavea,* L. *cauea,* a cave, den, cage.— L. *cauus,* hollow.   See Cave.

Caïque, a boat. (F.—Turk.) F. *caïque.* — Turk. *kaik,* a boat.

Cairn, a pile of stones. (C.)   Gael., Irish, W., Bret. *carn,* a crag, rock; also a pile of stones.

Caitiff. (F. — L.)   M. E. *caitif.* — A. F. *caitif,* a captive, a wretch (F. *chétif*). — L. *captīuum,* acc. of *captīuus;* see Captive.

Cajole. (F.)   F. *cajoler,* to cajole; formerly, to chatter like a jay. Perhaps of imitative origin; cf. *cackle.*

Cajuput, Cajeput (with *j* as *y*), a tree yielding an oil. (Malay.)   Malay *kāyu pūtih,* lit. 'white wood.' — Malay *kāyu,* wood; *pūtih,* white.

Cake. (E. *or* Scand.)   M. E. *cake.* N. Fries. *kāk, kāg,* late Icel. and Swed. *kaka;* Dan. *kage.* Teut. stem **kakōn-,* fem.; from Teut. root **kak-,* of which the strong grade is **kōk-* (whence prov. E. *cookie,* Du. *koek,* G. *kuchen,* a cake).

Calabash, the shell of a gourd. (F. — Span. — Arab. — Pers.)   F. *calebasse.* — Span. *calabaza* (Port. *calabaça*). — Arab. — Pers. *kharbuz,* a melon; lit. 'ass-gourd,' i. e. large gourd — Pers. *khar,* ass (hence, coarse); *buzah,* odoriferous fruit. Cf. Skt. *khara,* an ass.

Calamint, a herb. (F. — L. — Gk.) M. F. *calament,* Cot.— Late L. *calamintha.* — Gk. καλαμίνθη.

Calamity. (F.—L.)   F. *calamité.* — L. acc. *calamitātem,* a misfortune.

Calash, a sort of carriage. (F.—G.— Slavonic.)   F. *calèche.* — G. *kalesche.* — Pol. *kolaska,* a small carriage, dimin. of *kolasa,* a carriage; Russ. *koliaska,* a carriage.— Pol. *koło,* a wheel; O. Slav. *kolo.* (√QEL.)

Calcareous. (L.)   Should be *calcarious.* — L. *calcārius,* pertaining to lime. — L. *calc-,* stem of *calx,* lime.

calcine. (F. — L.)   F. *calciner.* — Mod. L. *calcināre,* to reduce to a calx. — L. *calc-,* stem of *calx,* lime.

calculate. (L.)   L. *calculāt-us,* pp. of *calculāre,* to reckon by help of small pebbles. — L. *calculus,* pebble · dimin. of *calx,* a stone.

Caldron, Cauldron. (F.—L.) M. E. *cauderon,* A. F. *caudrun.* — O. North F. (Picard) *cauderon,* for O.F. *chauderon,* mod. F. *chaudron* (Ital. *calderone,* Span. *calderon*), a vessel for hot water. Extended from L. *caldār-ia,* a hot bath. — L. *caldus,* contr. form of *calidus,* hot. — L. *calēre,* to be hot.

Calendar. (L.)   L. *calendarium,* an account-book kept by money-changers; so called because interest was due on the *calends* (1st day) of each month; also, a calendar. — L. *calendæ,* calends.

Calender (1), a machine for pressing cloth. (F. — L. — Gk.)   F. *calandre.* — Med. L. **calendra, celendra,* a calender; an adaptation of L. *cylindrus,* a cylinder; see Cylinder. Der. *calender,* a smoother of linen, a mistaken form for *calendrer.*

Calender (2), a kind of wandering monk. (F. — Pers.)   F. *calender.* — Pers. *qalandar,* a kind of wandering Muhammadan monk, who abandons everything and retires from the world.

Calends. (L.)   L. *calendæ,* s. pl., the first day of the (Roman) month. Orig. obscure; but certainly from the base *cal-,* as in O. Lat. *calāre,* to proclaim. +Gk. καλεῖν, to summon. Allied to Hale (2).

Calenture, a feverous madness. (F.

71

—Span. —L.) F. *calenture.* —Span. *calentura.* —L. *calent-,* stem of pres. pt. of *calēre,* to be hot.

Calf (1). (E.) M.E. *kalf.* O. Merc. *calf;* A.S. *cealf.* +Du. *kalf;* Icel. *kālfr;* Swed. *kalf;* Dan. *kalv;* Goth. *kalbō;* G. *kalb.* **Der.** *calve,* vb., A. S. *cealfian.* Perhaps allied to Skt. *garbha,* womb, a fœtus. Brugm. i. § 656.

Calf (2), the thick hind part of the shank. (E.) Perhaps the same as the above; cf. Gaulish L. *galba,* great-bellied; Icel. *kālfi,* calf of the leg. See **Cave in.**

Caliber, Calibre, bore of a gun. (F.) F. *calibre,* size of a bore; Span. *calibre* (1623). Etym. unknown. Perhaps from Arab. *qālib,* a form, mould, model, Rich. Dict. p. 1111 (Diez). Mahn suggests L. *quā librā,* with what measure.

Calico, cotton - cloth. (E. Indian.) Named from *Calicut,* on the Malabar coast, whence it was first imported.

Calif, Caliph. (F.—Arab.) F. *calife,* a successor of the prophet. —Arab. *khalīfah,* successor. —Arab. *khalafa,* to succeed. Doublet, *khalifa.*

Caligraphy, Calligraphy, good writing. (Gk.) Gk. καλλιγραφία. —Gk. καλλι-, prefix (for κάλλος, beauty, from καλός, good, fair); and γράφειν, to write.

calisthenics, callisthenics, graceful exercises. (Gk.) From Gk. καλλισθεν-ής, adorned with strength. —Gk. καλλι- (for κάλλος, beauty, from καλός, fair); and σθέν-ος, strength.

Calipers, compasses. (F.) For *caliber-compasses,* i. e. compasses for measuring diameters; see **Caliber.**

Calisthenics; see **Caligraphy.**

Caliver, a sort of musket. (F.) Named from its *caliber* or bore; see Kersey's Dict. See **Caliber.**

Calk; usually **Caulk,** q. v.

Call. (Scand.) Late A.S. *ceallian;* cf. *hildecalla,* a herald. E. Fries. *kallen.* — Icel. and Swed. *kalla;* Dan. *kalde.* +Du. *kallen;* O. H. G. *challōn.* Teut. type **kallōn-* or **kallōjan-,* weak verb; cf. W. *galw,* to call, Russ. *golos',* voice, sound.

Callet, Callat, a worthless woman. (F.—Low L.—Low G.) In Oth. iv. 2. 121. —F. *caillette,* a gossip, chatterer; lit. a little quail; dimin. of *caille,* a quail, also a woman. Littré gives *caille coiffée,* femme galante. See **Quail.** (Doubtful.)

Callous, hard. (F.—L.) F. *calleux.* —

L. *callōsus,* thick-skinned. —L. *callus, callum,* hard skin.

Callow, unfledged, bald. (L.) M. E. *calu, calewe.* A. S. *calu,* bald. +Du. *kaal,* bald; Swed. *kal;* G. *kahl.* Teut. **kalwoz,* early borrowed from L. *caluus,* bald.

Calm. (F.—L.—Gk.) F. *calme,* adj. Allied to Prov. *chaume,* the time when the flocks rest; F. *chômer* (formerly *chaumer),* to rest from work; Ital. *calma,* rest. —Late L. *cauma,* the heat of the sun (whence, time for rest); Job xxx. 30. [It is suggested that the change from *au* to *al* was due to association with L. *cal-ēre,* to be hot.] —Gk. καῦμα, heat. —Gk. καίειν, to burn. **Der.** *be-calm.*

Calomel, a preparation of mercury. (Gk.) Coined to express a *white* product from a *black* substance. —Gk. καλό-s, fair; and μέλ-as, black.

Caloric. (F.—L.) F. *calorique.* —L. *calor,* heat. —L. *calēre,* to be hot.

calorific, making hot. (L.) L. *calōrificus,* making hot. —L. *calōri-,* stem of *calor,* heat; and *-fic-,* for *facere,* to make.

Calthrop, Caltrap, a star-thistle, a ball with spikes for annoying cavalry. (L. *and* Teut.) M. E. *kalketrappe,* A. S. *calcetreppe,* a star-thistle. Coined from L. *calci-,* stem of *calx,* the heel; and the Teutonic word *trap.* Lit. 'heel-trap'; see **Trap.** So also F. *chaussetrappe,* the same.

Calumet, a kind of pipe for tobacco. (F.—L.—Gk.) Norman F. *calumet,* a pipe; parallel form to O. F. *chalemel,* F. *chalumeau,* a pipe. —L. *calamus,* a reed. —Gk. κάλαμος, a reed. See **Shawm.**

Calumny. (F.—L.) F. *calomnie.* —L. *calumnia,* false accusation. —L. *caluī,* *caluere,* to deceive.

Calve; see **Calf.**

Calx. (L.) L. *calx,* stone, lime (stem *calc-);* in Late L., a calx.

Calyx. (L. — Gk.) L. *calyx.* — Gk. κάλυξ, a covering, calyx (or cup) of a flower. Allied to **Helm** (2).

Cam, a projection on a wheel. (Du.) Du. *kamm,* a comb (see Kilian); Low G. *kamm;* cf. Dan. *kam,* comb, also a ridge on a wheel, cam, or cog. See **Comb.**

Cambric. (Flanders.) Named from *Kamerijk,* also called *Cambray,* a town in Flanders, where it was first made.

Camel. (F.—L.—Gk.—Heb.) M. E. *camel, camail, chamel.* —O. North F. *camel,* O. F. *chamel.* —L. *camēlus.* —Gk. κάμηλος. —Heb. *gāmāl.* Cf. Arab. *jamal.*

camelopard, a giraffe. (L. – Heb. and Gk.) Formerly *camelopardalis*. – L. *camēlopardālis*. – Gk. καμηλοπάρδαλις, giraffe; partly like a camel, partly like a pard. – Gk. κάμηλο-ς, a camel (Heb. *gāmāl*); and πάρδαλις, a pard; see **Pard**.

Camellia. (Personal name.) A plant named (by Linnæus) after Geo. Jos. Kamel, a Moravian Jesuit (17th cent.), who described the plants in the island of Luzon.

Camelopard; see **Camel**.

Cameo. (Ital.) Ital. *cammeo*, a cameo, precious stone carved in relief. Origin unknown.

Camera. (L.) L. *camera*, a chamber; hence *camera obscūra*, a dark chamber, box for photography; see **Chamber**.

Camlet, a stuff. (F. – Arab.) Formerly *camelot*. – M. F. *camelot*, Cot.; supposed to be named from containing *camel's* hair. Really from Arab. *khamlat*, *khamalat*, camlet; Rich. Dict. p. 628.

Camomile; see **Chamomile**.

Camp. (F. – Ital. – L.) F. *camp* (Cot.). – Ital. *campo*, a field, camp. – L. *campum*, acc. of *campus*, a field, ground held by an army. Brugm. i. § 563.

campaign, orig. a large field. (F. – Ital. – L.) F. *campaigne*, *campagne*, an open field. – Ital. *campagna*, a field; also a campaign. – L. *campānia*, open field. – L. *campus*, a field. (Also spelt *champaign*, and even *champion* in old authors.)

campestral, growing in fields. (L.) From L. *campestr-is*, growing in fields; with suffix -*al*. – L. *campus*, a field.

Campanula. (L.) Lit. 'a little bell;' dimin. of L. *campāna*, a bell. Hence also *campani-form*.

Camphor. (F. – Arab. – Malay.) Formerly spelt *camphire* (with an inserted *i*). – F. *camphre*, 'camphire;' Cot. – Low L. *camphora* (whence the form *camphor*). – Arab. *kāfūr*, camphor; cf. Skt. *karpūra*, camphor. – Malay *kāpūr*, lit. chalk; *kāpūr Bārūs*, chalk of Barous, a name for camphor. *Barous* is in Sumatra.

Can (1), I am able. (E.) A.S. *can*, *cann*, 1st and 3rd persons sing. pres. of *cunnan*, to know. The pres. t. *can* is really an old perf. t.; the same peculiarity occurs in Du. *kunnen*, Icel. and Swed. *kunna*, Dan. *kunde*, to know, to be able; G. *können*, to know. β. The pt. t. is *could*, with intrusive *l*; M. E. *coude*, A. S. *cūðe*; cf. Goth. *kuntha*, Du. *konde*, G. *konnte*; shewing that A. S. *cūðe* (for

cunðe) has lost an *n*. γ. The pp. *couth*, A. S. *cūð*, known, only survives in *uncouth*, which see. Allied to **Ken** and **Know**. (√ GEN.)

Can (2), a drinking-vessel. (E.) A. S. *canne*, a can. + Du. *kan*; Icel. *kanna*; Swed. *kanna*; Dan. *kande*; G. *kanne*, a tankard, mug. (Apparently a true Teut. word.)

Canal. (F. – L.) F. *canal* (whence also Du. *kanaal*). – L. *canālis*, a channel, trench.

Canary, a bird, a wine, a dance. (Canary Islands.) All named from the *Canary* Islands.

Cancel. (F. – L.) F. *canceller*. – Law L. *cancellāre*, to cancel a deed by drawing lines across it. – L. *cancellus*, a grating, pl. *cancellī*, lattice-work, crossed lines; dimin. of pl. *cancrī*, lattice-work.

Cancer. (L.) L. *cancer*, a crab; also an 'eating' tumour. Cf. Gk. καρκίνος, Skt. *karkata*, a crab; cf. Skt. *karkara*, hard. Named from its hard shell. Brugm. i. § 464.

Candelabrum. (L.) L. *candēlābrum*, a candle-holder; from *candēla*, a candle.

Candid. (F. – L.) F. *candide*, white, fair, sincere. – L. *candidus*, white, shining. – L. *candēre*, to shine. – L. *candēre, to set on fire (in comp. *in-cendere*). + Skt. *chand* (for *çchand*), to shine. (√ SQEND.) Brugm. i. §§ 456, 818 (2).

candidate. (L.) L. *candidātus*, white-robed; because candidates for office wore white. – L. *candidus*, white.

candle. (L.) A. S. *candel*. – L. *candēla*, a candle. – L. *candēre*, to glow.

candour. (F. – L.) F. *candeur*. – L. acc. *candōrem*, brightness (hence, sincerity).

Candy, crystallised sugar. (F. – Ital. – Skt.) F. *sucre candi*, sugar-candy; whence F. *se candir*, 'to candie;' Cot. – Ital. *candire*, to candy; *candi*, candy; *zucchero candi*, sugar-candy. – Arab. *qand*, sugar; whence Arab. *qandī*, made of sugar. The word is Aryan; cf. Skt. *khāndava*, sweetmeats, *khanda*, a broken piece, from *khand*, to break. Der. *sugar-candy*, Ital. *zucchero candi*.

Candytuft, a plant. (Hyb.) From *Candy*, i. e. Candia (Crete); and *tuft*.

Cane. (F. – L. – Gk.) M. E. *cane*, *canne*. – F. *canne*. – L. *canna*. – Gk. κάννα, a reed. Cf. Heb. *qāneh*, reed; Arab. *qanāh*, cane.

canister. (L. – Gk.) L. *canistrum*, a light basket. – Gk. κάναστρον, the same. – Gk. κάνη = κάννα, a reed.

cannon. (F. – Ital. – L. – Gk.) F. *canon.* – Ital. *cannone*, a cannon, orig. a great tube, a gun-barrel. – L. *canna*, a reed; see **Cane.** ¶ The Span. *cañon*, a tube, a deep gorge, is cognate.

canon (1), a rule. (L. – Gk.) A. S. *canon.* – L. *canon*, a rule. – Gk. κανών, a rod, rule. – Gk. κάνη = κάννα, a (straight) cane.

canon (2), a dignitary of the church. (F. – L. – Gk.) M. E. *canun, canoun.* – O. F. *canogne*, now *chanoine.* – Lat. *canonicum*, acc. of *canonicus*, adj., one on the church-roll or list. – L. *canon*, the church-roll; also, a rule. See **canon** (1).

Canine. (L.) L. *caninus*, belonging to a dog. – L. *canis*, a dog; see **Hound.**

Canister; see **Cane.**

Canker. (F. – L.) North F. *cancre.* (F. *chancre*). – L. *cancrum*, acc. of *cancer*, a crab, a canker. See **Cancer.** ¶ The G. *kanker* may be Teutonic (Kluge); so perhaps E. *canker* in the sense of 'disease of trees'; cf. Gk. γόγγρος, an excrescence on trees.

Cannel-coal. (L. *and* E.) Lit. a 'candle-coal,' because it burns brightly. Prov. E. *cannel*, a candle. See **Candle.**

Cannibal. (Span. – W. Indian.) Formerly *canibal.* – Span. *canibal*; for *Caribal*, a Carib, native of the Caribbean Islands. The W. Indian (Hayti) word *carib* means 'brave.' Hence also *Caliban.*

Cannon (1); see **Cane.**

Cannon (2), at billiards. (F. – Span.) A corruption of *carrom*, shortened form of F. *caramboler*, v., to make a cannon at billiards, to touch two other balls with one's own; see Hoyle's Games. Orig. sense, to touch the red ball; whence *caramboler*, to cannon (as above) and *carambolage*, sb , a cannon. – Span. *carambola*, a manner of playing at billiards, a device, trick, cheat. Origin unknown.

Canoe. (Span. – W. Ind.) Span. *canoa*; orig. a Haytian word for 'boat.'

Canon (1) and (2); see **Cane.**

Canopy. (F. – Ital. – L. – Gk.) Should be *conopy*; but we find F. *canopé*, borrowed from Ital. *canopè*. (Also F. *conopée*.) – L. *cōnōpēum*, Judith xiii. 9. – Gk. κωνωπεῖον, an Egyptian bed with mosquito curtains (hence, any sort of hangings). – Gk. κωνωπ-, stem of κώνωψ, a mosquito, gnat; lit. 'cone-faced' or 'cone-headed,' from the shape of its head. – Gk. κῶνο-s, a cone; and ὤψ, face, appearance, from Gk. base ΟΠ, to see (see **Optics**).

Canorous, tuneful. (L.) L. *canōr-us*; with suffix -*ous.* – L. *canere*, to sing. Brugm. i. § 181.

cant (1), to sing in a whining way, whine. (L.) L. *cantāre* (whence Picard and Walloon *canter*, to sing); frequent. of *canere*, to sing. *Cant* was at first a beggar's whine; hence, hypocrisy; see **Recant.**

canticle. (L.) L. *canticulum*, a little song; dimin. of *canticum*, a song; dimin. of *cantus*, a song; cf. *cantus*, pp. of *canere*, to sing.

canto. (Ital. – L.) Ital. *canto*, a singing, section of a poem. – L. acc. *cantum*, a singing, song (above).

canzonet. (Ital. – L.) Ital. *canzonetta*, dimin. of *canzone*, a hymn, song. – L. *cantiōnem*, acc. of *cantio*, a song. – L. *cantus*, pp. of *canere*, to sing.

Cant (2), an edge; as verb, to tilt. (Du. – L.) Du. *kant*, an edge, corner. + Dan. and Swed. *kant*, edge; G. *kante*, a corner. β. All from Late L. *cantus*, a corner; which is prob. from L. *canthus* = Gk. κάνθος, the corner of the eye, felloe of a wheel.

Canteen. (F. – Ital.) F. *cantine.* – Ital. *cantina*, a cellar, cool cave (hence the sense of vessel for liquids). Origin doubtful. Perhaps from Late L. *cantus*, a corner.

Canter, an easy gallop. (Proper name.) Short for *Canterbury* gallop, the pace at which pilgrims rode thither.

Canticle, Canto; see **Cant** (1).

Cantle, a small piece. (F. – L. ?) O.F. *cantel*, a small piece (F. *chanteau*), dimin. of Picard *cant* (F. *chant*), a corner; Late L. *cantus.* Prob. from L. *canthus*, corner of the eye; see **Cant** (2).

Canton, a region. (F. – Ital.) F. *canton.* – Ital. *cantone*, a nook, angle; also, a corporation, township (Torriano); Late L. *cantōnum*, *canto*, a region, province. Origin doubtful. ¶ *Canton* (in heraldry), a corner of a shield, is from F. *canton*, a corner, Ital. *cantone*, from Ital. *canto*, an edge; see **Cant** (2).

Canvas. (F. – L. – Gk.) M. E. *canevas.* North F. *canevas.* – Late L. *canabācius*, hempen cloth. – L. *cannabis*, hemp. – Gk. κάνναβις, hemp. Cf. Skt. *çana*, hemp; see **Hemp.**

canvass. (F. – L. – Gk.) Orig. to toss in a *canvas* sheet, to criticize or discuss thoroughly. From *canvas*, sb.

Canzonet; see **Cant** (1).

Caoutchouc. (F.—Carib.) F. *caoutchouc*; orig. a Caribbean word, *cahuchu*.

Cap, a head-covering. (Late L.) A. S. *cæppe.*—Late L. *cappa*, a cap (Isidore).

Capable. (F.—L.) F. *capable.*—Late L. *capābilis*, comprehensible; afterwards, able to hold.—L. *capere*, to hold (below).

capacious, able to contain. (L.) Coined from L. *capāci-*, stem of *capax*, able to hold.—L. *capere*, to hold, contain; see **Heave.** Brugm. i. § 635. (✓QAP.)

Caparison, trappings of a horse. (F. —Span.—Late L.) O. F. *caparasson.*— Span. *caparazon*, cover for a saddle; augmentative from Med. L. *caparo*, a cowl; from Span. *capa*, a cloak, cover.—Late L. *cāpa*, a cape; as below.

Cape (1), a covering for the shoulders. (F.—Late L.) O. North F. *cape.*—Late L. *cāpa*, a cape (Isidore of Seville); whence also Prov., Span., Port. *capa*, Icel. *kāpa*, &c. Allied to *cap*. Doublet, *cope*.

Cape (2), a headland. (F.—Ital.—L.) F. *cap.*—Ital. *capo*, head, headland.—L. *caput*, head.

Caper (1), to dance about. (Ital.—L.) Abbreviated from *capreole* (Sir P. Sidney). —Ital. *capriolare*, to skip as a goat.—Ital. *capriola*, 'a caper in dancing,' Florio; also, a kid; dimin. of *capra*, a she-goat. —L. *capra*, a she-goat; cf. *caper*, he-goat. +Gk. *κάπρος*, a boar; Λ.S. *hæfer*, Icel. *hafr*.

Caper (2), the flower-bud of a certain plant. (F.—L.—Gk.) M. F. *capre* (F. *câpre*).—L. *capparis.*—Gk. *κάππαρις*, caperplant; its fruit; cf. Pers. *kabar*, capers.

Capercailzie. (Gael.) Here *z* represents M. E. *ʒ*, pron. as *y*.—Gael. *capull-coille*, great cock of the wood; lit. horse of the wood.—Gael. *capull*, a horse (see **Cavalier**); *coille*, gen. of *coill*, a wood, cognate with E. **Holt.**

Capillary, like hair. (L.) L. *capil-lāris*, adj.; from *capillus*, hair. Perhaps allied to *cap-ut*, the head.

Capital (1), chief. (F.—L.) F. *capital.* —L. *capitālis*, belonging to the head.—L. *capit-*, stem of *caput*, the head.+Skt. *kapāla(m)*, skull; A.S. *hafela*, head. Brugm. i. § 641.

capital (2), stock of money. (F.— L.) F. *capital.*—Late L. *capitāle*, wealth; neut. of *capitālis*, chief; see **Capital** (1).

capital (3), head of a pillar. (L.; *or* F.—L.) L. *capitellum*, head of a pillar; dimin. from L. *caput*, head. Or from O.

North F. *capitel* (F. *chapiteau*); from L. *capitellum* (above).

capitation, poll-tax. (F.—L.) F. *capitation.*—Late L. acc. *capitātiōnem*, poll-tax.—L. *capit-*, stem of *caput*, poll, head.

capitol. (L.) The temple of Jupiter, at Rome, called *Capitōlium.*—L. *capit-*, stem of *caput*, a head; but the reason for the name is obscure; see Smith, Class. Dict.

capitular, relating to a chapter. (L.) Med. L. *capitulāris*, adj. of *capitulum*, a chapter of a cathedral, or a chapter of a book; see **Chapter.**

capitulate. (L.) Late L. *capitulātus*, pp. of *capitulāre*, to divide into chapters, also to propose terms (for surrender).— Late L. *capitulum*, a chapter; see **Chapter.** Der. *re-capitulate.*

Capon. (L.—Gk.) A. S. *capun.*—L. acc. *cāpōnem*, from nom. *cāpo.*—Gk. *κάπων*, a capon.

Caprice. (F.—Ital.—L.?) F. *caprice.* —Ital. *capriccio*, a whim. Perhaps from Ital. *capro*, a he-goat; so that *capriccio* might mean a frisk like a goat's; see **Caper** (1).

capricorn. (L.) L. *capricornus*, horned like a goat.—L. *capri-*, for *capro-*, stem of *caper*, goat; and *corn-u*, horn.

capriole, a peculiar frisk of a horse. (F.—Ital.—L.) F. *capriole* (see Cot.).— Ital. *capriola*, the leap of a kid; see **Caper** (1).

Capsize, to upset. (Span.?—L.) Perhaps from Span. *capuzar*, to sink (a ship) by the head; apparently a derivative of L. *caput*, the head. (A guess.)

Capstan. (F.—Span.—L.?) F. *cabestan*; Prov. *cabestan.*—Span. *cabestrante*, *cabrestante*, a capstan. Of these forms, *cabestrante* is the better, and is allied to Span. *cabestrage*, a halter, or a haltering, and to *cabestrar*, to halter.—L. *capistrant-*, stem of pres. pt. of *capistrāre*, to halter. —L. *capistrum* (Span. *cabestro*), a halter. —L. *cap-ere*, to hold; with double suffix *-is-tro.*

Capsule, seed-vessel. (F.—L.) F. *capsule*, a small case.—L. *capsula*, dimin. of *capsa*, a case; see **Case** (2).

Captain. (F.—L.) M. E. *capitain.*— O. F. *capitain.*—Late L. *capitāneus*, *capitānus*, a leader of soldiers.—L. *capit-*, stem of *caput*, head.

Captious. (F.—L.) F. *captieux*, cavilling. – L. *captiōsus.* – L. *captio*, a taking, a sophistical argument. – L. *captus*, pp. of *capere*, to hold. See **Capacious.**

captive. (F. – L.) F. *captif* (fem. *captive*). – L. *captīuus*, a captive. – L. *captus*, pp. of *capere*, to take. + W. *caeth*, a captive; O. Irish *cacht*, a female captive.

captor. (L.) L. *captor*, a taker. – L. *cap-*, as in *capere*, to take; with suffix *-tor.*

capture. (F. – L.) F. *capture.* – L. *captūra*, a taking. – L. *cap-*, as in *capere*, to take; with fem. suffix *-tūra.*

Capuchin, hooded friar, hood. (F. – Ital. – Late L.) M. F. *capuchin*; F. *capucin.* – Ital. *cappucino*, a small hood, hence a hooded friar; dimin. of *cappuccio*, a cowl. – Ital. *cappa*, a cape; see **Cap** and **Cape** (1).

Car. (F. – C.) M. E. *carre.* – O. North F. *carre*, a car (Ducange, s. v. *Marcellum*). – Late L. *carra*, f.; allied to L. *carrus*, a car; of Gaulish origin. – Bret. *karr*, a chariot; W. *car*, O. Gael. *cár*, Irish *carr.* Allied to L. *currus*, a chariot; Brugm. i. § 516.

Caracole. (F. – Span.) F. *caracol*, *caracole*, a snail; whence *faire le caracole*, applied to a manœuvre by soldiers, and to turns made by a horse. – Span. *caracol*, a snail, winding staircase, turning about (from the snail-shell's spiral form). Perhaps of Celtic origin; cf. Gael. *carach*, circling, winding; *car*, a turn, twist.

Carafe, a glass water-bottle. (F. – Span. – Arab.) F. *carafe.* – Span. *garrafa*, a cooler, vessel to cool wines in. – Arab. *ghiráf*, draughts of water; Arab. root *gharafa*, to draw water. (Dozy, Devic.) ¶ Or from Pers. *qarábah*, a large flagon; but see **Carboy.**

Carat. (F. – Ital. – Arab. – Gk.) F. *carat*, a very light weight. – Ital. *carato.* – Arab. *qirrát*, a pod, husk, carat, 24th part of an ounce. – Gk. κεράτιον, fruit of the locust-tree; also, a carat; lit. 'a small horn.' – Gk. κερατ-, stem of κέρας, a horn; see **Horn.**

Caravan. (F. – Pers.) F. *caravane.* – Pers. *kārwān*, a caravan, convoy.

caravansary. (Pers.) Pers. *kārwānsarāy*, an inn for caravans. – Pers. *kārwān*, caravan; *sarāy*, public building, inn.

Caraway, Carraway. (Span. – Arab.) Span. *al-carahueya*, a caraway; where *al* is merely the Arab. def. art.; also written *carvi.* – Arab. *karwiyā-a*,

karawīyā-a, caraway-seeds or plant. Cf. Gk. κάρος, κάρον, cumin.

Carbine. (F. – Gk.) Formerly *carabine*, a musket, the weapon of a *carabin*, or musketeer. – F. *carabin*, 'an arquebuzier;' Cot. Perhaps from O. F. *calabrin*, a light-armed soldier; of uncertain origin.

Carbon. (F. – L.) F. *carbone.* – L. acc. *carbōnem*, a coal.

carbonado, broiled meat. (Span. – L.) Span. *carbonada*, meat broiled over coals. – Span. *carbon*, coal; see above.

carbuncle. L. *carbunculus*, (1) a small coal, (2) a carbuncle, gem, from its glowing, (3) a red tumour. Double dimin. of L. *carbo*, coal.

Carboy, a large glass bottle, protected by wicker-work. (Pers.) Pers. *qarábah*, a large flagon; which is prob. of Arab. origin. Cf. Arab. *qirbah*, a water-skin, water-bottle.

Carcanet. (F. – Teut.) Dimin. of F. *carcan*, a collar of jewels, or of gold. – O. H. G. *querca*, the throat; cf. Icel. *kverkr*, pl. the throat; Lith. *gerkle*, throat, *gerti*, to drink. Brugm. i. § 653.

Carcase, Carcass. (F. – Ital.) From M. F. *carquasse*, a dead body. – Ital. *carcassa*, a kind of bomb-shell, a shell; also, a skeleton, frame; cf. Port. *carcassa*, a carcase, a very old woman. Of unknown origin.

Card (1), piece of pasteboard. (F. – Ital. – Gk.) Corruption of F. *carte*, 'a card,' Cot. – Ital. *carta*; L. *charta.* – Gk. χάρτη, χάρτης, a leaf of papyrus. Der. *cardboard.* **Doublet,** *chart.*

Card (2), an instrument for combing wool. (F. – L.) F. *carde.* – Med. L. *cardus*, L. *carduus*, a thistle; for wool-combing.

Cardinal. (L.) L. *cardinālis*, principal, chief; orig. relating to the hinge of a door. – L. *cardin-*, stem of *cardo*, a hinge.

Cardoon, a plant. (F. – Prov. – L.) F. *cardon*, Cot. – Prov. *cardon*; with augment. suffix from Med. L. *card-us*, a thistle. See **Card** (2).

Care. (E.) M. E. *care.* A. S. *caru*, *cearu*, anxiety. + O. Sax. *kara*, sorrow; O. H. G. *chara*, a lament; Goth. *kara*; Teut. type *karā, f. Hence, *care*, vb.; A. S. *carian.* ¶ Not allied to L. *cūra.*

Careen. (F. – L.) Lit. 'to clean the keel;' hence to lay a ship on its side. – F. *carine*, *carène*, keel. – L. *carīna*, keel.

Career. (F. – C.) F. *carrière*, a racecourse. ▬ Late L. *carrāria uia*), a road for cars. ▬ Late L. *carra*, L. *carrus*, a car ; of Celtic origin ; see **Car.**

Caress. (F. ▬ Ital. ▬ L.) F. *caresse*, a fondling. ▬ Ital. *carezza*, a caress, fondling. ▬ Late L. *cāritia*, dearness. ▬ L. *cārus*, dear. Brugm. i. § 637.

Carfax. (F. ▬ L.) M. E. *carfoukes*, a place where four roads meet. ▬ O. F. pl. *carrefourgs*, the same ; from sing. *carrefourg*. ▬ Late L. *quadrifurcus*, four-forked. ▬ L. *quadri-* (from *quatuor*), four ; and *furca*, a fork. See **Fork.**

Cargo. (Span. ▬ C.) Span. *cargo*, freight, load ; cf. *cargar*, to load. ▬ Late L. *carricāre*, to load a car ; see **Charge.**

caricature. (Ital. ▬ C.) Ital. *caricatura*, a satirical picture ; so called because exaggerated or ' overloaded.' ▬ Ital. *caricare*, to load, burden. ▬ Late L. *carricāre*, to load a car ; see **Charge.**

Caries. (L.) L. *cariēs*, rottenness.

Cark, burden, anxiety. (F. ▬ C.) A. F. *karke*, North. F. form of F. *charge*, i. e. load ; see **Charge.** Cf. M. E. *karke*, a load ; as in ' a *karke of pepper*.'

Carkanet ; see Carcanet.

Carminative, expelling wind from the body. (F. ▬ L.) F. *carminatif*, ' wind-voiding ; ' Cot. ▬ L. *carmināt-us*, pp. of *carmināre*, to card wool (hence, in old medicine, to cleanse from gross humours) ; with suffix *-īuus*. ▬ L. *carmin-*, from *carmen*, a card for wool. ▬ L. *cārere*, to card.

Carmine. (Span. ▬ Arab. ▬ Skt.) Span. *carmin*, short form of *carmesin*, adj. ; from *carmesi*, crimson. ▬ Arab. *qirmizī*, crimson ; from *qirmiz*, cochineal. ▬ Skt. *kṛmi*, a worm, the cochineal insect.

Carnage ; see below.

Carnal. (L.) L. *carnālis*, fleshly. ▬ L. *carn-*, stem of *caro*, flesh. Brugm. i. § 515.

carnage. (F. ▬ L.) F. *carnage*, flesh-time, slaughter of animals. ▬ Late L. *carnāticum*, a tribute of flesh-meat ; cf. *carnātum*, time for eating flesh. ▬ L. *carn-*, stem of *caro*, flesh.

carnation. (F. ▬ L.) F. *carnation*, flesh colour (Littré). ▬ L. acc. *carnātiōnem*, fleshiness. ▬ L. *carn-*, stem of *caro*, flesh.

carnival. (F. ▬ Ital. ▬ L.) F. *carnaval*, Shrovetide. ▬ Ital. *carnevale*, *carnovale*, the last three days before Lent. ▬ Med. L. *carnelevāle*, *carnelevāmen*, removal of flesh. Shrovetide. ▬ L. *carne-m*, acc. of *caro*, flesh ;

and *leuāre*, to lift, remove, take away, from *leuis*, light.

carnivorous. (L.) L. *carniuorus*, flesh-eating. ▬ L. *carni-*, decl. stem of *caro*, flesh ; and *uor-āre*, to devour.

Carob-tree, the locust-tree. (F. ▬ Arab.) M. F. *carobe*, *caroube*. ▬ Arab. *kharrūb*, bean-pods.

Caroche, Carroche, a kind of coach. (F. ▬ Ital. ▬ C.) Nearly obsolete ; but the present sense of *carriage* is due to it. ▬ F. *carroche*, variant of *carrosse*, ' a carosse or caroach ; ' Cot. ▬ Ital. *carroccia*, *carrozza*, a chariot. Extended from Ital. *carro*, a car. See **Car.**

Carol, a song. (F. ▬ L. ▬ Gk. ?) Formerly, a kind of dance. ▬ O. F. *carole*, a (singing) dance. Godefroy (s. v. *carole*) cites Swiss Rom. *coraula*, a round-dance, also a dance-song. Prob. from L. *choraulēs*, a flute-player to a chorus. ▬ Gk. χοραύλης, the same. ▬ Gk. χορ-ός, a chorus, round-dance ; and αὐλός, a flute.

Carotid, adj. (Gk.) Gk. καρωτίδες, s. pl., the two great arteries of the neck ; it was thought that an alteration in the flow of blood through them caused stupor. ▬ Gk. καρόω, I stupefy ; κάρος, stupor.

Carousal, (1) a drinking-bout ; (2), a pageant. (1. F. ▬ G. ; 2. F. ▬ Ital.) **1.** Sometimes used as if from the verb *carouse* below. **2.** But, in old authors, *cárousél* (also *carousal*) means a sort of pageant, of which some kind of chariot-race formed a principal part ; Dryden, Virgil, Æn. v. 777. ▬ F. *carrousel*, a tilting-match. ▬ Ital. *carosello*, also spelt *garosello*, a tournament ; of uncertain origin.

Carouse. (F. ▬ G.) F. *carous*, ' a carousse of drinke,' Cot. ▬ G. *garaus*, right out ; used of emptying a bumper. ▬ G. *gar*, quite ; and *aus*, out. (Raleigh even writes *garouse* ; directly from G. *garaus*.) **Der.** *carous-al*, but only in one sense of that word ; see above.

Carp (1), a fish. (F.) M. E. *carpe*. XV cent. ▬ O. F. *carpe* (Span. Port. *carpa*, Ital. *carpa*, Florio) ; also Du. *karper* ; Icel. *karfi* ; Dan. *karpe* ; Swed. *karp* ; G. *karpfen* ; O. H. G. *charpho* ; Russ. *karp'* ; Lith. *karpa*.

Carp (2), to cavil at. (Scand.) M. E. *carpen*, which often merely means to talk, say. ▬ Icel. *karpa*, to boast ; Swed. dial. *karpa*, to boast, talk much. ¶ The present sinister sense is due to confusion with L. *carpere*, to pluck.

Carpenter. (F.—C.) A. F. *carpenter*; O. North F. *carpentier* (F. *charpentier*).— Late L. *carpentārius*, sb.; *carpentāre*, to work in timber.—L. *carpentum*, a carriage; a word of Celtic origin.—O. Irish *carpat*, Gael. and Irish *carbad*, W. *cerbyd*, a carriage, chariot, litter.

Carpet. (F.—L.) O.F. *carpite*.—Late L. *carpīta*, *carpeta*, a kind of thick cloth; also *carpia* (F. *charpie*), lint.—L. *carpere*, to pluck, pull to pieces (lint being made of rags pulled to pieces, and carpet, probably, from shreds).

Carrack. (F.) O.F. *carraque*, a ship of burden; Late Lat. *carraca*, the same. Of unknown origin.

Carriage. (F.—C.) M.E. *cariage*, that which is carried about (as in Bible, A.V.). —O.F. *cariage*; from *carier*, to carry; see **Carry.** ¶ Its modern use is due to confusion with *caroch*, a vehicle (Massinger, Renegado, i. 2); see **Caroche.**

Carrion. (F.—L.) M.E. *caroigne*, a carcase.—O. North F. *caroigne*; Late L. *carōnia*, a carcase.—L. *caro*, flesh.

Carronade, a sort of cannon. (Scotland.) So named because made at *Carron*, in Stirlingshire.

Carrot. (F.—L.—Gk.) F. *carote*, *carotte*.—L. *carōta*.—Gk. καρωτόν, a carrot.

Carry. (F.—C.) O.F. *carier*.—Late L. *carricāre*.—L. *carrus*, a car; see **Car.**

Cart. (E.) A.S. *cræt*, *crat*; cf. Du. *krat*. Or from Icel. *kartr*, a cart; whence, probably, Picard *carti*, a cart.

Carte, a bill of fare. (F.—Gk.) Chiefly in the F. phr. *carte blanche*, lit. white paper.—Late L. *carta*; see **Card** (1).

cartel. (F.—Ital.—Gk.) F. *cartel.*— Ital. *cartello*, lit. a small paper; dimin. of *carta*, paper, bill; see **Card** (1).

Cartilage. (F.—L.) F. *cartilage*, gristle.—L. *cartilāginem*, acc. of *cartilāgo*. Der. *cartilagin-ous*.

Cartoon. (F.—Ital.—Gk.) F. *carton.*— Ital. *cartone*, lit. a large paper; from *carta*, a card; see **Card** (1).

cartouche, cartridge. (F.—Ital. —Gk.) *Cartridge* (with intrusive *r*) is for *cartidge*, corrupt form of *cartouche*.—F. *cartouche*, a roll of paper.—Ital. *cartoccio*, a roll of paper, cartridge.—Ital. *carta*, paper; Late L. *carta*; see **Card** (1). ¶ The *cartridge* took its name from the paper in which it was rolled up.

cartulary, a register. (Late L.—Gk.) Late L. *cartulārium*, *chartulārium*, a register.—Late L. *chartula*, a document; dimin. of *charta*, a paper; see **Card** (1).

Carve. (E.) M.E. *keruen*. A.S. *ceorfan*; pt. t. *cearf*, pl. *curfon*, pp. *corfen*. [The A.S. *ceorfan* would have given **charve*; *c* was retained from the pt. pl. and pp.] + Du. *kerven*; G. *kerben*, to notch, cut; also Dan. *karve*, Swed. *karfva*, to notch, from the 2nd stem. Gk. γράφειν. Brugm. i. § 791.

Cascade. (F.—Ital.—L.) F. *cascade.*— Ital. *cascata*, a waterfall; orig. fem. pp. of *cascare*, to fall. For **casicare.*—L. *cāsāre*, to totter.—L. *cāsum*, sup. of *cadere*, to fall.

Case (1), an event. (F.—L.) M.E. *cas.*—F. *cas.*—L. acc. *cāsum*, a fall, a case.—L. *cāsus*, pp. of *cadere*, to fall.

Case (2), a receptacle. (F.—L.) O.F. *casse.*—L. *capsa*, a box, cover.—L. *capere*, to hold.

Casemate. (F.—Ital.) F. *casemate*, a loop-hole in a fortified wall.—Ital. *casamatta*, a chamber built under a wall or bulwark, to hinder those who enter the ditch to scale the wall of a fort. It seems to mean 'dark chamber.'—Ital. and L. *casa*, house, cottage, room; and Ital. *matta*, fem. of *matto*, orig. mad, but the Sicilian *mattu* means 'dim.'

Casement, frame of a window. (F.— L.) Coined with the sense of *encasement*, that which encases or encloses. From *case*, verb; with suffix -*ment*.

Cash, coin. (F.—L.) Orig. a till or box to keep money in.—F. *casse*, a case; see **Case** (2) above. Der. *cash-ier*, sb., one who keeps a money-box or cash.

Cashew-nut, the nut of a W. and E. Indian tree. (F.—Brazilian.) *Cashew* is a corruption of F. *acajou.*—Brazil. *acaiu*, the fruit of the tree named *acajaba* or *acajaiba*. (Mahn, Littré.)

Cashier, to dismiss from service. (Du.—F.—L.) Du. *casseren*, to cashier; merely borrowed from F. *casser*, 'to breake, burst, .. also to casseere, discharge;' Cot. [Du. words, borrowed from F., end in -*eren*.]—L. *quassāre*, to shatter, frequent. of *quatere*, to shake; which annexed the senses of L. *cassāre*, to annul, discharge, from L. *cassus*, void, null.

Cashmere, a soft wool. (India.) So called from the vale of *Cashmere*, in India. Also spelt *cassimere*, *kerseymere*.

Casino, a room for dancing. (Ital.—L.) Ital. *casino*, dimin. of *casa*, a cottage, house.—L. *casa*, a cottage.

Cask. (Span.—L.) Span. *casco*, a skull, sherd, coat of an onion; also a cask of wine, a casque or helmet. The orig. sense is 'husk'; cf. Span. *cascara*, peel, rind, shell, Port. *casca*, rind.—Span. *cascar*, to burst open; formed (as if from Lat. **quas-sicāre*) from an extension of L. *quassāre*, to break, burst; see **Quash**.

casque, a helmet. (F.—Span.—L.) F. *casque*.—Span. *casco*, a helmet, head-piece; see above.

Casket, a small box. (Span.—L.) Apparently confused with F. *cassette*, 'a small casket;' Cot. Formally, it is a dimin. of **Cask**.

Casque; see **Cask**.

Cassava, a plant. (Span. — Hayti.) Span. *cazabe*; also *cazavi*, 'the bread made in the W. Indies of the fruit called the *yuca*;' Pineda. It properly means the plant, which is also called manioc; said to be from the Hayti *casabbi*, with the same sense. See R. Eden's works, ed. Arber, p. 175. See **Tapioca**.

Cassia, a species of laurel. (L.—Gk.—Heb.) L. *casia, cassia*.—Gk. κασία, a spice like cinnamon.—Heb. *qetsīʿōth*, in Ps. xlv. 8, a pl. form from *qetsīʿōh*, cassia-bark.—Heb. root *qātsaʿ*, to cut away; because the bark is cut off.

Cassimere; see **Cashmere**.

Cassock, a vestment. (F.—Ital.) F. *casaque*.—Ital. *casacca*, an outer coat. Of uncertain origin.

Cassowary, a bird. (Malay.) First brought from Java. Malay *kasuwāri*.

Cast. (Scand.) Icel. *kasta*, to throw; Swed. *kasta*; Dan. *kaste*. **Der.** *re-cast*.

Castanets, instruments used for making a snapping noise. (F.—Span.—L.—Gk.) F. *castagnettes*, 'finger-knackers, wherewith players make a pretty noise in some dances;' Cot.—Span. *castañetas*, castanets; pl. of *castañeta*, a snapping noise resembling the cracking of roasted chestnuts.—Span. *castaña*, a chestnut.—Lat. *castanea*, the chestnut-tree.—Gk. κάστανον; see **Chestnut**.

Caste, a breed, race. (Port.—L.) Port. *casta*, a race, orig. a 'pure' breed; a name given by the Port. to classes of men in India.—Port. *casta*, fem. of *casto*, pure.—L. *castus*, pure, chaste.

castigate. (L.) L. *castīgātus*, pp. of *castīgāre*, to chasten; lit. 'to keep pure.'—L. *castus*, chaste. **Doublet**, *chastise*.

Castle. (L.) A. S. *castel*.—L. *cas-*

tellum, dimin. of *castrum*, a fortified place. **Der.** *castell-an*, O. North F. *caste-lain*, O. F. *chastelain*, the keeper of a *chastel*, or castle; also *châtelaine* (fem. of F. *châtelain* = O. F. *chastelain*), now applied to a lady's chain or 'keeper' of keys, &c.

Castor. (L.—Gk.) L. *castor*.—Gk. κάστωρ, a beaver. But of Eastern origin; cf. Malay *kastūri*, Skt. *kastūrī*, musk; Pers. *khaz*, beaver.

castor-oil. Named from some confusion with *castoreum*, 'a medicine made of the liquor contained in the little bags that are next the beaver's groin;' Kersey. But is really a vegetable production.

Castrate. (L.) L. *castrātus*, pp. of *castrāre*, to cut.

Casual. (F.—L.) F. *casuel*.—L. *cāsuālis*, happening by chance.—L. *cāsu-*, stem of *cāsus*, chance. See **Case** (1).

Cat. (E.) A. S. *cat*.+Du., Dan. *kat*, Icel. *köttr*, Sw. *katt*, G. *kater, katze*; L. *cātus*, W. *cath*, Ir. Gael. *cat*, Russ. *kot'*, *koshka*, Arab. *qitt*, Turk. *kedī*. (Prob. Eastern.)

Cata-, prefix. (Gk.) Gk. κατά, down, thoroughly.

Cataclysm, deluge. (Gk.) Gk. κατα-κλυσμός, a dashing over, flood.—Gk. κατά, down; κλύζειν, to dash, wash, as waves.

Catacomb. (Ital.—L.) Late L. *cata-comba*, a sepulchral vault.—Late L. *cata-cumbas*; of which the sense and origin are unknown.

Catafalque, a stage or platform, chiefly used at funerals. (F.—Ital.) F. *catafalque*.—Ital. *catafalco*; of unknown origin. See **Scaffold**.

Catalepsy, a sudden seizure. (Gk.) Formerly *catalepsis*.—Gk. κατάληψις, a grasping, seizing.—Gk. κατά, down; λαμβάνειν, to seize.

Catalogue. (F.—Gk.) F. *catalogue*.—Late Lat. acc. *catalogum*.—Gk. κατάλογος, a counting up, enrolment.—Gk. κατά, fully; λέγειν, to say, tell; see **Logic**.

Catamaran, a sort of raft. (Tamil.) In Forbes, Hindustani Dict., ed. 1859, p. 289, we have '*katmaran*, a raft . . ; the word is orig. Tamil, and means *tied logs*.'—Tamil *kattu*, binding; *maram*, wood (Yule).

Cataplasm, a poultice. (F.—L.—Gk.) F. *cataplasme*.—L. *cataplasma*.—Gk. κατάπλασμα, a plaster, poultice.—Gk. καταπλάσσειν, to spread over.—Gk. κατά, fully; and πλάσσειν, to mould; see Plaster.

Catapult. (Late L.—Gk.) Late L. *catapulta*, an engine for throwing stones. — Gk. καταπέλτης, the same. — Gk. κατά, down; πάλλειν, to swing, hurl.

Cataract. (L.—Gk.) L. *cataracta*, Gen. vii. 11. — Gk. καταρράκτης, as sb., a waterfall; as adj., broken, rushing down. Prob. allied to καταρρήγνυμι, I break down; the 2 aor. κατερράγην was used of the rushing down of waterfalls and storms. — Gk. κατά, down; ρήγνυμι, I break.

Catarrh. (F. — Late L. — Gk.) F. *catarrhe*. — Late L. *catarrhus*. — Gk. κατάρροος, a flowing down (of rheum), a cold in the head. — Gk. κατά, down; and ρέειν, to flow.

Catastrophe. (Gk.) Gk. καταστροφή, an overturning, sudden turn. — Gk. κατά, down; στρέφειν, to turn.

Catch. (F.—L.) O. Picard *cachier*, variant of O. F. *chacier*, to hunt, chase; hence, to catch. It answers to Ital. *cacciare*, Late L. **captiāre*, extended form of L. *captāre*, to catch. — L. *captus*, pp. of *capere*, to seize. ¶ We even find M. Du. *kaetsen*, to catch, borrowed from Picard *cachier*. The M. E. pt. t. *cauȝte* imitated *lauȝte*, pt. t. of M. E. *lacchen*, to catch. Doublet, *chase* (1).

Catechise. (L.—Gk.) Late L. *catēchizāre*. — Gk. κατηχίζειν, to catechise, instruct; lengthened form of κατηχέειν, to din into one's ears, lit. 'to din down.' — Gk. κατ-ά, down; ἠχεῖν, to sound; cf. ἦχος, a ringing in the ears; see **Echo.**

Category, a class. (Gk.) Gk. κατηγορία, an accusation; but in logic, a predicament or class. — Gk. κατηγορεῖν, to accuse. — Gk. κατ-ά, down, against; **ἀγορεῖν*, with the sense of ἀγορεύειν, to declaim, address an assembly, from ἀγορά, an assembly.

Catenary, belonging to a chain; used of the curve in which a chain hangs. (L.) From L. *catēna*, a chain; see **Chain.**

Cater, to buy provisions. (F. — L.) Formed as a verb from M. E. *catour*, a buyer of provisions (whom we should now call a *cater-er*). *Catour* is short for *acatour*, formed from *acat*, a buying, purchase, Ch. prol. 571. — O. F. *acat* (mod. F. *achat*), a buying. — Folk-L. *acaptum*, a purchase; for *accaptum*. — Folk-L. *accaptāre*, to purchase (A. D. 1060), frequent. of

accipere, to receive, also to buy; see **Accept** and **Cates.**

Cateran, a Highland robber. (Gael.) Low L. *cateranus*, answering to Gael. *ceathairne*, lit. 'common people;' cf. *ceathairne-choille*, s. pl., freebooters, outlaws. From Irish *cethern*, *ceithern*, a troop, band; cf. L. *caterua*, a band of men. See **Kern.**

Catercousin. (F.—L.) Nares (ed. 1876) has : 'Cater-cousins, friends so familiar that they eat together.' If so, the word is from *cater*, vb., and *cousin.*

Caterpillar. (F.—L.) Adapted from O. F. *chatepelose*, a caterpillar (Godefroy); the latter half of the word was assimilated to *piller*, one who *pills*, or robs or spoils. O. F. *chatepelose* is lit. 'hairy she-cat.' O. F. *chate*, fem. of *chat*, cat; *pelose*, hairy. — L. *cātus*, cat; *pilōsus*, hairy, from *pilus*, a hair.

Caterwaul. (E.) M. E. *caterwawen*; coined from *cat*, and *wawen*, to make a wailing noise.

Cates, provisions. (F. — L.) So called because provided by the *catour*, mod. E. *cater-er*; see **Cater.** 'Cater, a steward, a provider of *cates*;' Baret (1580).

Cathartic, purging. (Gk.) Gk. καθαρτικός, purgative. — Gk. καθαίρειν, to cleanse, purge. — Gk. καθαρός, pure.

Cathedral. (L. — Gk.) L. *cathedrālis ecclesia* = a cathedral church, or one which has a bishop's throne. — Late L. *cathedra*, a throne. — Gk. καθέδρα, a seat. — Gk. καθ-, for κατά, down; and ἕδρα, a seat, chair, from ἕζομαι (= ἑδ-γομαι), I sit; see **Sit.**

Catholic. (L. — Gk.) L. *catholicus* (Tertullian). — Gk. καθολικός, universal. — Gk. καθόλ-ου, adv., on the whole, in general. — Gk. καθ-, for κατά, according to; and ὅλου, gen. of ὅλος, whole.

Catkin. (Du.) A loose spike of flowers, named from its soft downy appearance. — M. Du. *katteken*, 'a kitling;' Hexham. (It also meant 'catkin'; cf. F. *chattons* in Cot.) Dimin. of Du. *kat*, a cat (M. Du. *katte*).

Catoptric, relating to optical reflection. (Gk.) Gk. κατοπτρικός, reflexive. — Gk. κάτοπτρον, a mirror. — Gk. κατ-ά, down, inward; ὄπ-τομαι, I see, with suffix -τρον, of the instrument.

Cattle. (F.—L.) M.E. *catel*, property; hence, live stock, cattle. — O. North F.

catel. ─ Late L. *capitāle*, capital, property ; see **Capital** (2) and **Chattels**.

Caucus, a name applied to certain political meetings. (American Indian?) Said to be from an Algonkin word meaning to speak, to counsel, whence *kaw-kaw-asu*, a counsellor. ' Their elders, called *cawcawwassoughes*;' Capt. Smith's Works, ed. Arber, p. 347. ' *Caucorouse*, which is captaine;' id. p. 377. ¶ This is more likely than the entirely unsupported story about *caulkers'* meetings.

Caudal, belonging to the tail. (L.) L. *cauda*, the tail.

Caudle, a warm drink. (F.─L.) O. North F. *caudel*, O. F. *chaudel*, a sort of warm drink.─O. F. *chaud, chald*, hot.─ L. *caldus*, for *calidus*, hot.

Caul, a net, covering, esp. for the head. (F.) O. F. *cale*, 'a kind of little cap ;' Cot. Origin unknown.

Cauldron; see **Caldron**.

Cauliflower. (F. ─ L.) Formerly *colyflory*. From M. E. *col* (O. F. *col*), a cabbage ; and *flory*, from O. F. *flori, fleuri*, pp. of *fleurir*, to flourish. The O. F. *col* is from L. acc. *caulem*, from *caulis*, a cabbage ; and *fleurir* is from L. *flōrēre*, to flourish. See **Cole** and **Flourish**.

Caulk, Calk. (F. ─ L.) M. E. *cauken*, to tread ; hence, to squeeze in (as oakum into a ship's seams).─O. F. *cauquer*, to tread ; to tent a wound with lint. ─ L. *calcāre*, to tread, force down by pressure.─L. *calc-*, stem of *calx*, the heel.

Cause. (F.─L.) F. *cause*.─L. *causa, caussa*, a cause. Der. *cause*, vb.

Causeway, a paved way, raised way. (F.─L.; *and* E.) Formerly *caus-ey-way* ; by adding *way* to M. E. *causè, causie, causey*.─O. North F. *caucie* (mod. F. *chaussée*, Prov. *causada*, Span. *calzada*).─ Late L. *calciāta*, for *calciāta uia*, a paved way.─Late L. *calciātus*, pp. of *calciāre*, to make a roadway by treading it down ; from L. *calcāre*, to tread.─L. *calc-*, stem of *calx*, heel ; see **Caulk**.

Caustic. (L.─Gk.) L. *causticus*. ─ Gk. καυστικός, burning. ─ Gk. καυστός, burnt.─Gk. καίειν (fut. καύσω), to burn.

cauterise. (F.─Late L.─Gk.) F. *cauteriser*.─Late L. *cautērizāre*, to sear. ─Gk. καυτηριάζειν, to sear.─Gk. καυτήριον, a branding-iron. ─ Gk. καίειν, to burn (above).

Caution. (F.─L.) F. *caution*. ─ L. acc. *cautiōnem*, heed.─L. *cautus*, pp. of

cauēre, to beware. Cf. Skt. *kavi(s)*, wise. Brugm. i. § 635. Der. *pre-caution*.

Cavalier. (F.─Ital.─L.) F. *cavalier*, a horseman. ─ Ital. *cavaliere*, the same.─L. *caballārium*, acc. of *caballārius*, the same.─L. *caballus*, a horse. See **Chevalier**.

cavalcade. (F. ─ Ital. ─ L.) F. *cavalcade*. ─ Ital. *cavalcata*, a troop of horsemen ; orig. fem. of pp. of *cavalcare*, to ride.─Ital. *cavallo*, a horse.─L. *caballum*, acc. of *caballus*, a horse.

cavalry. (F. ─ Ital. ─ L.) O. F. *cavallerie*. ─ Ital. *cavalleria*, cavalry. ─ Ital. *cavaliere*, a knight ; see **Cavalier**.

Cave. (F.─L.) M. E. *caue*.─O. F. *cave*, a cave.─Folk-L. *cava*, a cave.─L. *cauus*, hollow. (√KEU.) Der. *cav-ity*; *cav-ern* (F. *caverne*, L. *cauerna*).

Cave in. (M. Du.) Properly to *calve in*, a phrase introduced by Du. navvies. Cf. W. Flanders *inkalven*, to cave in ; E. Friesic *kalfen*, to calve as a cow, whence *kalfen in*, to cave in. The falling portion of earth is compared to a calf dropped by a cow. Confused with *cave*, a hollow.

Caveat, a caution. (L.) L. *caueat*, lit. let him beware. ─ L. *cauēre*, to beware.

Caviare, roe of the sturgeon. (F.─ Ital.) F. *caviar*.─Ital. *caviaro* ; whence also Turk. *khāvyār*, caviare.

Cavil. (F.─L.) O. F. *caviller*.─L. *cauillārī*, to banter ; hence, to wrangle, object to.─L. *cauilla*, a jeering, cavilling.

Caw. (E.) An imitation of the cry of the crow or daw. Cf. Du. *kaauw*, Dan. *kaa*, a jackdaw : which are imitative.

Cayman, an American alligator. (Caribbean.) Also *caiman*. The spelling *cayman* is Spanish.─Caribbean *acayūman* (Littré).

Cease. (F.─L.) F. *cesser*.─L. *cessāre*, to loiter, go slowly, cease ; frequent. of *cēdere* (pp. *cessus*), to yield, go away, go.

Cedar, a tree. (F.─L.─Gk.) O. F. *cedre*.─L. *cedrus*.─Gk. κέδρος.

Cede. (L.) A late word (A. D. 1633).─ L. *cēdere*, to go, to come, to yield.

Ceil, Ciel, to line the inner roof or walls of a room. (F.─L.) Hence the sb. *ceil-ing* or *ciel-ing*. M. E. *ceelen*, to ceil ; from the sb. *syle* or *cyll*, a canopy.─ F. *ciel*, a canopy ; the same word as *ciel*, heaven. [Cf. Ital. *cielo*, heaven, a canopy, a cieling.] — L. *cælum*, heaven. ¶ Not to be confused with E. *sill*, nor with *seal*; nor with *seel* (F. *siller*); nor with L. *cēlāre*, to hide. The L. *cēlāre*, to emboss, seems to have had some influence on the word, but did not originate it; cf. M. E. *celure*, a canopy. Late L. *cēlātūra*.

Celandine, a plant. (F. — Gk.) O. F. *celidoine.* — Late L. *celidonia.* — L. *chelidonia.* — Gk. χελιδόνιον, swallow-wort. — Gk. χελιδον-, stem of χελιδών, a swallow. (The *n* is intrusive.)

Celebrate. (L.) L. *celebrātus*, pp. of *celebrāre*, to frequent, to solemnise, honour. — L. *celeber*, frequented, populous.

Celerity. (F. — L.) F. *célérité*. — L. acc. *celeritātem*, speed. — L. *celer*, quick. Cf. Gk. κέλης, a runner; Brugm. i. § 633.

Celery. (F. — L. — Gk.) F. *céleri*, introduced from the Piedmontese Ital. *selleri*; for Ital. *selini*, pl. of *selino*, parsley. — L. *selinon*, parsley. — Gk. σέλινον, a kind of parsley.

Celestial. (F. — L.) O. F. *celestiel*. — L. *cælesti-s*, heavenly. — L. *cælum*, heaven.

Celibate. (L.) The orig. sense was 'a single life'; it was afterwards an adj., and again a sb., meaning 'one who is single.' — L. *cælibātus*, sb. celibacy, single life. — L. *cælib-*, stem of *cælebs*, single, unmarried. **Der.** *celibacy* (for **cælibātia*).

Cell. (L.) M. E. *celle*. — L. *cella*, small room, hut. Cf. *cēlāre*, to hide. See **Helm** (2). (√KEL.)

cellar. (F. — L.) M. F. *celer*. A. F. *celer*; O. F. *celier.* — L. *cellārium*, a cellar. — L. *cella* (above).

Celt (1), a name originally given to the Gauls. (C.) From L. pl. *Celtæ*, the Celts; the word probably meant 'warriors'; cf. A.S. *hild*, Icel. *hildr*, war; Lith. *kalti*, to strike; L. *per-cellere*, to strike through, beat down (Rhys).

Celt (2), a primitive chisel or axe. (Late L.) Late L. *celtis*, assumed nom. of the abl. *celte* (=with a chisel), in the Vulgate Version of Job xix. 24. But this reading is due to some error, and there seems to be no such word in Latin.

Cement. (F. — L.) O. F. *ciment*. — L. *cæmentum*, rubble, chippings of stone; hence, cement. Perhaps for **cædmentum*, from *cædere*, to cut (Brugm. i. § 587).

Cemetery. (L. — Gk.) Late L. *cæmētērium*. — Gk. κοιμητήριον, a sleeping-place, cemetery. — Gk. κοιμάω, I lull to sleep; in

pass., to fall asleep. Allied to κεῖμαι, I lie down; Skt. *çi*, to lie down.

Cenobite. (L. — Gk.) L. *cænobīta*, a member of a (social) fraternity (Jerome). — L. *cænobium*, a convent. — Gk. κοινόβιον, a convent. — Gk. κοινόβιος, living socially. — Gk. κοινό-s, common; βίος, life.

Cenotaph. (F. — L. — Gk.) O. F. *cenotaphe*. — L. *cenotaphium*. — Gk. κενοτάφιον, an empty tomb. — Gk. κενό-s, empty; τάφ-os, a tomb.

Censer. (F. — L.) M. E. *censer*. — O. F. *censier*, *senser* (Godefroy); shortened from O. F. *encensier*. — Late L. *incensārium*, also *incensōrium* (whence mod. F. *encensoir*). — L. *incensum*, incense; from pp. of *incendere*, to kindle. See **Incense**.

Censor. (L.) L. *censor*, a taxer, valuer, assessor, critic. — L. *censēre*, to give an opinion, appraise. +Skt. *çaṁs*, to praise.

censure. (F. — L.) F. *censure*. — L. *censūra*, orig. opinion. — L. *censēre* (above).

census. (L.) L. *census*, a registering. — L. *censēre* (above).

Cent, a hundred, as in *per cent*. (L.) In America, the hundredth part of a dollar. — L. *centum*, a hundred; see **Hundred**.

centenary. (L.) L. *centēnārius*, relating to a hundred. — L. *centēnus*, a hundred (usu. distributively). — L. *centum*.

centennial. (L.) Coined to mean relating to a century. — L. *cent-um*, hundred; *ann-us*, a year.

centesimal. (L.) L. *centēsim-us*, hundredth. — L. *cent-um*, hundred.

centigrade. (L.) Divided into a hundred degrees. — L. *centi-*, for *centum*, hundred; *grad-us*, a degree; see **Grade**.

centipede, centiped. (F. — L.) F. *centipède*. — L. *centipeda*, a many-footed (lit. hundred-footed) insect. — L. *centi-*, for *centum*, hundred; and *ped-*, stem of *pēs*, foot.

centuple. (L.) L. *centuplex* (stem *centuplic-*), a hundredfold. — L. *centu-m*, hundred; *plic-āre*, to fold.

centurion. (L.) L. acc. *centuriōnem*, a captain of a hundred. — L. *centuria* (below).

century. (F. — L.) F. *centurie*. — L. *centuria*, a body of a hundred men; number of one hundred. — L. *centu-m*, hundred.

Centaur. (L. — Gk.) L. *Centaurus*.

− Gk. κένταυρος, a centaur, a creature half man and half horse; which some have compared with Skt. *gandharvas*, a demi-god.

centaury, a plant. (L.−Gk.) L. *centaurēa.*−Gk. κενταύρειον, centaury; a plant named from the *Centaur* Chiron.

Centenary, Centennial, Centuple, Centurion, &c.; see Cent.

Centre, Center. (F.−L.−Gk.) F. *centre.* − L. *centrum.* − Gk. κέντρον, a spike, goad, prick, centre. − Gk. κεντέω, I goad on. Cf. W. *cethr*, a spike.

centrifugal, flying from a centre. (L.) L. *centri-*, for *centro-*, stem of *centrum*; and *fug-ere*, to fly.

centripetal, tending towards a centre. (L.) L. *centri-* (above); *pet-ere*, to seek.

Ceramic, relating to pottery. (Gk.) Gk. κεραμικ-ός, adj. − Gk. κέραμ-ος, potter's earth. Cf. κεράννυμι (fut. κερασω), I mix.

Cere, to coat with wax. (L.) L. *cērāre*, to wax. − L. *cēra*, wax. + Gk. κηρός, wax.

cerecloth. (L. *and* E.) Lit. a waxed cloth.

cerement. (L.) From *cere*; with suffix *-ment* (L. *-mentum*).

ceruse, white lead. (F.−L.) O. F. *ceruse.*−L. *cērussa*, white lead. − L. *cēra*, wax.

Cereal, relating to corn. (L.) L. *cerealis.*−L. *ceres*, corn.

Cerebral, relating to the brain. (L.) From L. *cerebr-um*, the brain. Cf. Gk. κάρα, the head. Brugm. i. § 619.

Cerecloth, Cerement; see Cere.

Ceremony. (F.−L.) M. E. *ceremonie.*−F. *cérémonie.*−L. *cærimōnia*, a ceremony, rite.

Certain. (F. − L.) O. F. *certein*, *certain.* − L. *cert-us*, sure; with suffix *-ānus.* Allied to L. *cernere*, to discriminate; Gk. κρίνειν, to separate, decide.

certify. (F.−L.) M. E. *certifien.* − F. *certifier.*−Late L. *certificāre*, to make sure.−L. *certi-*, for *certo-*, stem of *certus* (above); and *-fic-*, for *fac-ere*, to make.

Cerulean, azure. (L.) L. *cæruleus*, *cærulus.* blue; for *cæluleus*, *cælulus*, from *cælum*, sky. Brugm. i. § 483.

Ceruse, white-lead; see Cere.

Cervical, belonging to the neck. (L.) From L. *ceruic-*, stem of *ceruix*, neck.

Cervine, relating to a hart. (L.) L. *ceruin-us.*−L. *ceru-us*, a hart; see Hart.

Cess, limit, measure. (F. − L.) In

1 Hen. IV. ii. 1. 8. Orig. a tax, rate, rating, assessment; see Spenser, State of Ireland, Globe ed., p. 643, col. 2. For *sess*; from *sess*, verb, to rate; which is short for **Assess.**

Cessation. (F.−L.) F. *cessation.*− L. acc. *cessātiōnem*, a ceasing.−L. *cessātus*, pp. of *cessāre*, to cease.−L. *cessus* (below).

cession. (F. − L.) F. *cession.* − L. acc. *cessiōnem*, a yielding.−L. *cessus*, pp. of *cēdere*, to yield, to cede.

Cess-pool. (Hybrid.) Most probably equiv. to (*se*)*cess-pool*; see N. E. D. Cf. Ital. *cesso*, a privy (Torriano); which is a shortened form of *secesso*, a retreat.− L. *sēcessus*, 'the draught;' Matt. xv. 17 (Vulgate).

Cetaceous, of the whale kind. (L.− Gk.) L. *cētus.*−Gk. κῆτος, a sea-monster.

Ch.

Chablis, a white wine. (F.) From *Chablis*, 12 mi. E. of Auxerre, in the department of Yonne, France.

Chafe, to warm by friction, vex. (F.− L.) M. E. *chaufen*, to warm. − O. F. *chaufer* (F. *chauffer*), to warm; cf. Prov. *calfar*, to warm.−Late L. **calefāre*, to warm; for L. *calefacere*, to warm, make to glow.− L. *cale-re*, to glow; *facere*, to make.

Chafer, Cockchafer. (E.) A.S. *cefer* (also *ceafor*), a kind of beetle. + Du. *kever*; G. *käfer*.

Chaff. (E.) A. S. *ceaf*, later *chief*, husk of grain. + Du. *kaf*; Low G. *kaff*. ¶ The verb *to chaff = to chafe*, i. e. vex. So also *chaff-wax*, for *chafe-wax.*

chaffinch, a bird. (E.) I.e. *chaff-finch*; it frequents barn-doors.

Chaffer. (E.) The verb is from the M. E. sb. *chapfare*, also *chaffare*, a bargaining.−A. S. *céap*, a bargain, and *faru*, a journey, also business; see Cheap and Fare.

Chaffinch; see Chaff.

Chagrin. (F.) F. *chagrin*, melancholy. [Diez identifies it with F. *chagrin*, shagreen; but wrongly.]

Chain. (F.−L.) O. F. *chaine*, *chaëne.* − L. *catēna*, a chain.

Chair. (F.−L.−Gk.) M. E. *chaire*, *chaere.*−O. F. *chaiere*, *chaere.*−L. *cathedra*, a throne, raised seat, chair.−Gk. καθέδρα, a seat.−Gk. καθ-, for κατά, down;

ἕδρα, a seat, from ἕζομαι (= ἕδ-yoμαι), I sit; see **Cathedral, Sit.**

chaise, a light carriage. (F.—L.—Gk.) F. *chaise,* a chair, also, a chaise; a Parisian modification of F. *chaire,* a pulpit, orig. a seat.

Chalcedony, a kind of quartz. (L.—Gk.) L. *chalcēdōnius,* Rev. xxi. 19.—Gk. χαλκηδών, Rev. xxi. 19.

Chaldron, a coal-measure. (F.—L.) O. F. *chaldron,* orig. a caldron; see **Caldron.**

Chalice, a cup. (F.—L.) A.F. *chalice;* O. F. *calice.*—L. *calicem,* acc. of *calix,* a cup. Allied to *calyx,* but not the same word.

Chalk. (L.) M. E. *chalk.*—A. S. *cealc* (Southern).—L. *calc-,* stem of *calx,* lime.

Challenge. (F.—L.) M. E. *chalenge, calenge,* often in the sense 'a claim.'—A. F. *chalenge,* O. F. *chalonge, calenge,* a dispute, claim; an accusation.—L. *calumnia,* false accusation; see **Calumny.**

Chalybeate. (L.—Gk.) Used of water containing iron. Coined from L. *chalyb-s,* steel.—Gk. χάλυψ (stem χαλυβ-), steel; named from the *Chalybes,* a people of Pontus, who made it.

Chamber. (F.—L.—Gk.) F. *chambre;* Prov. *cambra.*—L. *camera, camara,* a vault, vaulted room, room.—Gk. καμάρα, a vaulted place.

chamberlain. (F.—O.H.G.—L.—Gk.) F. *chamberlain,* O.F. *chambrelenc.*—O. H. G. *chamerlinc,* M. H. G. *kamerlinc,* one who has the care of rooms; formed with suffix *-l-inc* (the same as E. *-l-ing*), from L. *camera* (above).

Chameleon. (L.—Gk.) L. *chamæleōn.*—Gk. χαμαι-λέων, lit. a ground-lion, dwarf-lion; a kind of lizard.—Gk. χαμαί, on the ground (also dwarf, in comp.); and λέων, lion. Cf. L. *humī,* on the ground.

chamomile. (Late L.—Gk.) Late L. *camomilla* (*chamomilla*).—Gk. χαμαί-μηλον, lit. ground-apple, from the apple-like smell of the flower.—Gk. χαμαί-, on the ground (see above); μῆλον, apple.

Chamois. (F.—G.) F. *chamois;* borrowed from some Swiss dialectal form; cf. Piedmontese *camossa.*—M. H. G. *gamz* (for **gamuz*), a chamois (G. *gemse*).

Champ, to eat noisily. (E.) Formerly *cham* or *chamm;* of imitative origin, like *jam,* to crush. Cf. Swed. dial. *kämsa,* to chew with difficulty.

Champagne. (F.—L.) A wine named from *Champagne* in France, which means 'a plain'; see below.

champaign, open country. (F.—L.) In Sh. F. *champaigne,* of which the Picard form was *campaigne;* see **Campaign.**

Champak, a tree. (Skt.) Skt. *champaka,* the champak.

Champion. (F.—L.) O. F. *champion.*—L. *campiōnem,* acc. of *campio,* a combatant (Isidore).—L. *campus,* a place for military exercise; a peculiar use of *campus,* a field. See **Camp.**

Chance, hap. (F.—L.) M. E. *cheaunce.*—O. F. *cheance, chaance.*—Late L. *cadentia,* a falling, a chance.—L. *cadere,* to fall, happen; see **Cadence.**

Chancel. (F.—L.) So called because orig. fenced off by a latticed screen.—O. F. *chancel,* an enclosure fenced off with an open screen.—Late L. *cancellus,* a chancel, screen; L. *cancellī,* pl., a grating; see **Cancel.**

chancellor. (F.—L.) O. F. *chancelier.*—Late L. acc. *cancellārium,* a chancellor; orig. an officer who stood near the screen before the judgment-seat.—L. *cancellī,* a grating; see **Chancel, Cancel.**

chancery. (F.—L.) For *chancelry.* M. E. *chancelerie.*—O. F. *chancellerie.*—Late L. *cancellāria,* the record-room of a *cancellārius;* see **Chancellor.**

Chandelier. (F.—L.) O. F. *chandelier,* a candle-holder.—Late L. *candēlārius;* cf. *candēlāria,* a candle-stick.—L. *candēla;* see **Candle.**

chandler. (F.—L.) O.F. *chandelier,* a chandler.—Late L. *candēlārius,* a candle-seller.—L. *candēla;* see **Candle.** Der. *corn-chandler,* where *chandler* merely means seller, dealer.

Change, vb. (F.—L.) O. F. *changer, changier.*—Late L. *cambiāre,* to change (Lex Salica).—L. *cambīre,* to exchange. Cf. Late L. *cambium,* exchange; whence F. *change,* E. *change,* sb.

Channel. (F.—L.) M. E. *chanel, canel.*—O. F. *chanel, canel,* a canal.—L. acc. *canālem;* see **Canal.**

Chant. (F.—L.) F. *chanter,* vb.—L. *cantāre,* to sing; frequent. of *canere,* to sing. Der. *chant-ry,* M. E. *chaunterie,* Late L. *cantāria;* *chanti-cleer,* M. E. *chaunte-cleer,* clear-singing.

Chaos. (Gk.) L. *chaos,* Lat. spelling of Gk. χάος, chaos, abyss, lit. a cleft.—Gk. χάσκειν, to gape. See **Chasm.**

Chap (1), to cleave, crack. (E.) M. E.

chappen, to cut; hence, to gape open like a wound made by a cut. E. Fries. *kappen*, to cut; not found in A. S.+M. Du. *kappen*, to cut; Swed. *kappa*, Dan. *kappe*, to cut; G. *kuppen*, to cut, lop. See **Chop** (1).

Chap (2); see **Chapman**.

Chapel. (F.—L.) O. F. *chapele*.— Late L. *cappella*, orig. a shrine in which was preserved the *cāpa* or cope of St. Martin (Brachet).—Late L. *cāpa, cappa*, cape, hooded cloak; see **Cape** (1).

chaperon. (F.—L.) F. *chaperon*, a protector; orig. a kind of hood.—F. *chape*, a cope.—Late L. *cāpa*; as above.

Chapiter, the capital of a column. (F.—L.) O. F. *chapitre*, usually a chapter of a book, but representing L. *capitulum*, which meant 'chapiter' as well as 'chapter.' See **Chapter**.

Chaplet. (F.—L.) M. E. *chapelet*.— O. F. *chapelet*, a head-dress, wreath. — O. F. *chapel*, head-dress. — O. F. *chape*, a cope; see **Chaperon**.

Chapman, a merchant. (E.) The familiar *chap* is merely short for *chapman*.—A. S. *cēapman*, a merchant.—A. S. *cēap*, price, barter (see **Cheap**); and *man*, man.

Chaps, Chops, the jaws. (E.) A late word, of unknown origin; possibly from **Chap** (1). ¶ Perhaps suggested by North E. *chafts* or *chaffs*, jaws (Cleveland Gloss.).—Icel. *kjaptr* (*pt* pron. as *ft*), the jaw; Swed. *käft*, Dan. *kiæft*, jaw.

Chapter, a division of a book, synod of clergy. (F.—L.) M. E. *chapitre*, in both senses.—F. *chapitre*, variant of an older form *chapitle*. — L. *capitulum*, a chapter of a book (little head); also, in Late L., a synod; dimin. of *caput*, a head.

Char (1), a turn of work. (E.) Also *chare, chore, chewre*; M. E. *cher, char*, orig. a turn, hence, a space of time, turn of work, &c.—A. S. *cerr* (below). Hence, *char-woman*, a woman who does a turn of work. See **Ajar**.

char (2), usually **chare**, to do a turn of work. (E.) M. E. *cherren, char-ren*, to turn. A. S. *cerran*, to turn.—A. S. *cerr* (*cierr, cyrr*), a turn. ¶ The sense 'burn' is later than the appearance of the sb. *char-coal*.

Char (3), a fish. (C.?) Of unknown origin; perhaps named from its red belly [the W. name is *torgoch*, red-bellied, from *tor*, belly, and *coch*, red].—O. Gael. *ceara*, red, from *cear*, blood; Irish *cear*, red, also blood.

Character. (L.—Gk.) L. *charactēr*. —Gk. χαρακτήρ, an engraved or stamped mark.—Gk. χαράσσειν, to furrow, scratch, engrave.

Charade. (F. Prov.) F. *charade*, introduced from Provençal *charrada*, a long talk, from *charrà*, to chatter (Supp. to Littré); cf. Languedoc *charrade*, idle talk. Cf. also Span. *charrada*, speech or action of a clown, from Span. *charro*, a clown, peasant.

Charcoal. (E.) From *char* and *coal*; but the sense of *char* remains unknown; some refer it to M. E. *cherren*, to turn (as if to turn to coal), but there is no proof of this. See **char** (2).

Charge. (F.—C.) F. *charger*, to load.—Late L. *carricāre*, to load a car. — L. *carrus*, a car, a Gaulish word; see **Cark, Car**. Der. *charg-er*, a dish or horse, because carrying a burden.

chariot. (F.—C.) F. *chariot*, augmentative of F. *char*, a car.—L. *carrus*, a car; see **Car**.

Charity. (F.—L.) O. F. *charitet*.— L. acc. *cāritatem*, love.—L. *cārus*, dear. Brugm. i. § 637. ¶ Not allied to Gk. χάρις.

Charlatan. (F.—Ital.) F. *charlatan*. —Ital. *ciarlatano*, a mountebank, great talker, prattler.—Ital. *ciarlare*, to prattle;— *ciarla*, prattle; prob. of imitative origin.

Charlock, a kind of wild mustard. (E.) Prov. E. *carlock*. — A. S. *cerlic*; origin unknown.

Charm. (F.—L.) M. E. *charme*, sb. — O. F. *charme*, an enchantment.—L. *carmen*, a song, enchantment.

Charnel. (F.—L.) Properly an adj.; containing carcases, as in *charnel-house*.— O. F. *charnel*, adj. carnal; as sb. a cemetery.—Late L. *carnāle*, glossed by *flǣschūs* (flesh-house); Wright-Wülker, Voc. 184. 37.—L. *carnālis*; see **Carnal**.

Chart. (F.—L.—Gk.) O. F. *charte*. — L. *charta*, a paper.—Gk. χάρτη, a leaf of paper. **Doublet**, *card* (1).

charter. (F. — L. — Gk.) M. E. *chartre*.—O. F. *chartre*.—Late L. *cartula*, a small paper or document.—L. *charta*, a paper; see above.

Chary, careful, cautious. (E.) M. E. *chari*. A.S. *cearig*, full of care, sad.— A. S. *cearu, caru*, care.+Du. *karig*, G. *karg*, sparing. *Chary* meant (1) sorrowful, (2) heedful. See **Care**.

Chase (1), to hunt after. (F.—L.)

O. F. *chacier, chacer,* to pursue; see **Catch**.

Chase (2), to enchase; short for *enchase,* which see.

Chase (3), a printer's frame. (F.–L.) F. *châsse,* a shrine. – L. *capsa,* a box; see **Case** (2).

Chasm. (L. – Gk.) L. *chasma,* a gulf. – Gk. χάσμα, a yawning cleft. Allied to χάσκειν, to gape; see **Chaos**.

Chaste. (F.–L.) O. F. *chaste.* – L. *castus,* chaste; see **Caste**.

chasten. (F.–L.) Used in place of M. E. *chasty* or *chastien;* see below.

chastise. (F.–L.) M. E. *chastisen;* shorter form *chastien.* – O. F. *chastier.* – L. *castīgāre,* lit. ' to make pure.'–L. *castus,* chaste; see **Castigate**.

Chasuble, a vestment. (F.–L.) F. *chasuble.* – Late L. *casubula,* with the same sense as Late L. *casula,* a little house; hence, a mantle.– L. *casa,* a cottage.

Chat, Chatter. (E.) M. E. *chateren,* also *chiteren,* to chatter, twitter; frequentative form of *chat.* An imitative word; cf. Du. *kwetteren,* to warble, chatter, Swed. *kvittra,* to chirp.

Chateau. (F.–L.) F. *château,* O. F. *chastel.* – L. *castellum,* dimin. of *castrum,* a fortified place. Der. *castell-an;* also *châtelaine;* for which see **Castle**.

Chattels. (F.–L.) Pl. of M. E. *chatel,* property, also cattle. – O. F. *chatel,* O. North F. *catel,* property; see **Cattle**.

Chatter; see **Chat**.

Chaudron, entrails. (F.) Macb. iv. 1. 33. The *r* is inserted by confusion with F. *chaudron,* a caldron. – O. F. *chaudun,* older forms *caudun, caldun,* entrails (Godefroy). [Cf. G. *kaldaunen,* entrails; from Mid. Low G. *kaldūne,* the same.] Thought to be from Late L. *caldūna,* a dish containing entrails (Ducange). Perhaps from L. *calidus,* warm (F. *chaud*).

Chaw; see **Chew**.

Chaws, by-form of **Jaws;** see **Jaw**.

Cheap, at a low price; orig. a sb. (E.) M. E. *chep, cheep,* barter, price; always a sb. Hence, *good cheap,* in a good market (F. *bon marché*) ; whence E. *cheap,* used as an adj. A. S. *cēap,* price; whence the verb *cēapian,* to cheapen, buy. So also Du. *koop,* a bargain, *koopen,* to buy; G. *kauf,* purchase, *kaufen,* to buy; Icel. *kaup,* Swed. *köp,* Dan. *kiöb,* a purchase; Goth. *kaupon* (weak vb.), to traffic. ¶ Some say that these words are borrowed from L.; in particular, that O. H. G. *choufo,* a huckster, is from L. *caupo,* a huckster. But this is now held to be unlikely (Kluge, Franck).

Cheat, to defraud. (F.–L.) *Cheat* is merely short for *escheat;* cf. M. E. *chete,* an escheat (Prompt. Parv.). The *escheaters* were often *cheaters;* hence the verb. See **Escheat**.

Check, a sudden stop, repulse. (F.– Pers.) M. E. *chek,* a stop; also check ! in playing chess. The word is due to the game, which is very old. The orig. sense of *check* was ' king!' i. e. mind the king, the king is in danger. – O. F. *eschec,* 'a check at chess-play,' Cot. – Pers. *shāh,* a king, king at chess; whence *shāh-māt,* check-mate, lit. ' the king is dead,' from Arab. *māt,* he is dead. Similarly we have F. *échec,* a check, repulse, defeat, pl. *échecs,* chess; Ital. *scacco,* a square of a chess-board, also a check, defeat. See **chess** below. ¶ Devic shews that O. F. *eschec* represents Arab. *esh-shāg;* where *esh* is for *al,* the def. art., and *shāg* is the Arab. pron. of Pers. *shāh.*

checker, chequer, to mark with squares. (F. – Pers.) To mark with squares like those on a chess-board. M. E. *chekker, chekere,* a chess-board. (Hence *The Checkers,* an inn-sign.) – O. F. *eschequier,* a chess-board, also, an exchequer. – Low L. *scaccārium,* a chess-board. – Low L. *scaccī,* chess, pl. of *scaccus,* from the Arab. form of Pers. *shāh,* king.

checkers, chequers, an old name for the game at draughts; from the *checker* or chess-board; see above.

check-mate. (F. – Pers. *and* Arab.) From Arab. **shāg-māt,* for *shāh-māt,* the king is dead; see **Check**.

cheque. (F. – Pers.) A pedantic spelling of *check,* from confusion with *exchequer;* it is really a name given to a draft for money, of which one keeps a memorandum or *counter-check.*

chess, the game of the kings. (F.– Pers.) Equivalent to *checks,* i. e. kings; see **Check** above. – O. F. *esches,* chess; really the pl. of *eschec,* check, orig. ' king.' ¶ From Pers. *shāh,* a king, were formed O. F. *eschec,* F. *échec,* E. *check,* Ital. *scacco,* Span. *xaque, jaque,* Port. *xaque,* G. *schach,* Du. *schaak,* Dan. *skak,* Swed. *schack,* Low Lat. *lūdus scaccōrum* = game of checks, or of kings.

Cheek. (E.) M. E. *cheke, cheoke.* O.

Merc. *cēce*, A. S. *ceāce*, cheek. **+** Du. *kaak*, jaw, cheek ; Swed. *käk*, jaw.

Cheer. (F.—L.) M. E. *chere*, orig. the mien ; hence, 'to be of good *cheer*.' **—** O. F. *chere*, the face. — Late L. *cara*, face. (Relationship to Gk. *κάρα*, the head, is doubtful.) Der. *cheer-ful*.

Cheese. (L.) M. E. *chese*. O. Merc. *cēse* (A. S. *cȳse*, for earlier **cīese<*cēasi*), with *i*-mutation ; prehistoric A. S. **cēsi* < **cāsioz*. **—** L. *cāseus*, cheese ; whence other forms (G. *käse*, Du. *kaas*) are borrowed. Sievers, 2nd ed. § 75. 2.

Cheeta, Cheetah, the hunting leopard, a leopard used for the chase. (Hind. — Skt.)   Hind. *chītā*. **—** Skt. *chitraka*, a cheeta ; from *chitra*, spotted, also visible, clear. — Skt. *chit*, to perceive.   See **Chintz.**

Chemise. (F.—L.)   F. *chemise*. — Late L. *camisia*, a shirt, thin dress ; whence O. Irish *caimmse*, shirt (Stokes).

Chemist, Chymist; short for *al-chemist* ; see **Alchemy.**

Cheque, Chequer; see **Check.**

Cherish. (F. — L.)   O. F. *cheris-*, stem of pres. pt. of *cherir*, to hold dear. **—** F. *cher*, dear. — L. *cārus*, dear.

Cheroot, a cigar. (Tamil.)   Tamil *shuruṭṭu*, a roll ; hence, a roll of tobacco (Yule).

Cherry. (F.—L.—Gk.) M. E. *cheri*, a mistake for *cheris*, the final *s* being mistaken for the pl. inflexion. — O. North F. *cherise*, O. F. *cerise* ; representing Folk-L. **ceresia, *ceresea*. — L. *cerasus*, a cherrytree. — Gk. *κέρασος*, a cherry-tree ; usually said to come from *Cerasos*, in Pontus ; a story which Curtius doubts.

Chert, a kind of quartz. (?) Unknown. Cf. Irish *ceart*, a pebble.

Cherub. (Heb.) The true pl. is *cherub-im*. — Heb. *k'rūv* (pl. *k'rūvīm*), a mystic figure.

Chervil, a plant. (L.—Gk.) A.S. *cer-fille*. — L. *chærephylla*, pl. of *chærephyllum*. — Gk. *χαιρέφυλλον*, chervil, lit. pleasant leaf. — Gk. *χαίρ-ειν*, to rejoice ; *φύλλον*, leaf.

Chess; see **Check.**

Chest. (L. — Gk.) M. E. *cheste, chiste*. A.S. *cist*. — L. *cista*. — Gk. *κίστη*, a chest, box (whence G. *kiste*, &c.).

Chestnut, Chesnut. (F.—L.—Gk.) *Chesnut* is short for *chestnut*, which is short for *chesten-nut*, nut of the *chesten*, which is the old name of the tree, called

in M. E. *chestein.* **—** O.F. *chastaigne* (F. *châtaigne*). **—** L. *castanea*, chestnut-tree. **—** Gk. *κάστανον*, a chestnut. Chestnuts are said to have been called *κάστανα*, or *κάρυα* Κασταναῖα, from Κάστανα, Castana, the name of a city in Pontus where they abounded ; but more probably from Armen. *kaskeni*, a chestnut-tree, from *kask*, a chestnut (Kluge).

Cheval-de-frise, an obstruction with spikes. (F.)   Lit. 'horse of Friesland,' a jocular name ; the pl. *chevaux-de-Frise* is commoner.   See below.

chevalier. (F.—L.)   F. *chevalier*, a horseman. — F. *cheval*, a horse. — L. *caballum*, acc. of *caballus*, a horse.

Cheveril, kid leather. (F.—L.)   O. F. *chevrele*, fem., a little kid.   Dimin. of O.F. *chevre*, F. *chèvre*, a goat, kid. — L. *capram*, acc. of *capra*, a she-goat.

chevron, an ordinary, in heraldry, resembling two rafters of a house. (F.—L.) (Most likely meant to represent the saddlepeak.) — F. *chevron*, ' a kid, a chevron in building, a rafter;' Cot.   Augmentative form of *chevre*, a she-goat. — L. *capra*, a she-goat ; see **Caper** (1).   Cf. L. *capreolus*, which likewise means a prop.

Chew, Chaw. (E.)   M. E. *chewen*. A. S. *cēowan*, to chew, eat. **+** Du. *kaauwen*; G. *kauen* ; O. H. G. *kiuwan* ; Russ. *jevate*. Cf. also Icel. *tyggja, tyggva*, to chew (Streitberg).

Chibouk, a Turkish pipe. (Turk.) Turk. *chibūk, chybūk*, a stick, tube, pipe (Zenker, p. 349).

Chicanery. (F.—Pers.?)   F. *chicanerie*, wrangling, pettifogging ; Cot. — F. *chicaner*, to wrangle ; orig. to dispute in the game of the mall or *chicane* (Brachet). Perhaps from the medieval Gk. *τζυκάνιον*, a word of Byzantine origin (id.) ; from Pers. *chaugān*, a club, bat.

Chicken. (E.)   Sometimes shortened to *chick*; but the M. E. word is *chiken*. A.S. *cicen*, earlier **ciucin*. **+** Du. *kieken*, *kuiken*, a chicken, Low G. *küken*; cf. G. *küchlein*, a chicken, Icel. *kjúklíng*, Swed. *kyckling*; related to **Cock**, which shews the weak grade **cuc-* ; see **Cock** (1).   Sievers, 2nd ed. § 165.

Chicory, a plant, succory. (F.—L.— Gk.)   F. *chicorée*. — L. *cichorium*. — Gk. *κιχορία*, neut. pl. ; also *κιχώριον, κιχώρη*, succory.   **β**. *Succory* is a corrupter form of the word, apparently for *siccory* or *cichory*, from L. *cichorium*.

Chide. (E.) M.E. *chiden.* A.S. *cídan*, to chide, brawl; pt. t. *cídde.*

Chief. (F.—L.) M.E. *chef, chief.*— O. F. *chef, chief,* the head. — L. type **capum* (Ital. *capo*). — L. *caput,* head. Der. *ker-chief,* q. v.

Chieftain. (F.—L.) O.F. *chevetaine.* —Late L. *capitáneus, capitánus,* a captain. —L. *capit-,* from *caput,* a head.

Chiffonier, a cupboard. (F.) Lit. a place to put rags in.—F. *chiffonier,* a rag-picker, also a cupboard.—F. *chiffon,* augment. of *chiffe,* a rag. Orig. unknown.

Chignon. (F.—L.) Hair twisted; another spelling of F. *chaînon,* a link.— F. *chaîne,* O.F. *chaine,* a chain.—L. *caténa,* a chain.

Chilblain. (E.) A *blain* caused by a *chill.*

Child. (E.) M.E. *child.* A.S. *cild.* Teut. type **kilþom,* neut.; cf. Goth. *kil-thei,* the womb.

Chill, cold. (E.) Orig. a sb. A.S. *cele, ciele,* chilliness. Teut. type **kaliz,* sb.; from **kal-an,* to be cold, as in A.S. *calan,* to be cold, Icel. *kala,* to freeze. + Du. *kil,* a chill; cf. L. *gelu,* frost.

Chime, sb. (F. — L. — Gk.) M.E. *chimbe,* of which the orig. sense was cymbal; hence the chime or ringing of a cymbal. Shortened from O.F. *chimbale,* dialectal form of O.F. *cimbale,* a cymbal.— L. *cymbalum.* — Gk. κύμβαλον; see **Cymbal.** N.B. We find M.E. *chyme-belle,* which looks like a popular form for *cymbal.* Der. *chime,* verb.

Chimera, Chimæra. (L.—Gk.) L. *chimæra.* — Gk. χίμαιρα, a she-goat; also, a fabulous monster, with a goat's body. — Gk. χίμαρος, he-goat.

Chimney. (F.—L.—Gk.) F. *cheminée,* 'a chimney;' Cot.—Late L. *camináta,* provided with a chimney; hence, a chimney. —L. *camínus,* an oven, a fire-place.—Gk. κάμινος, oven, furnace.

Chimpanzee, an ape. (African.) I am informed that the name is *tsimpanzee* in the neighbourhood of the gulf of Guinea.

Chin. (E.) M.E. *chin.* A.S. *cin.*+ Du. *kin,* Icel. *kinn,* Dan. *kind,* Swed. *kind*; Goth. *kinnus,* the cheek; G. *kinn,* chin; L. *gena,* cheek; Gk. γένυς, chin; cf. Skt. *hanus,* jaw.

China. (China.) Short for *china-ware,* or ware from *China.* The name of the people was formerly *Chineses*; we have dropped the final *s,* and use *Chinese* as a pl.; hence *Chinee* in the singular, by a second dropping of *se.*

Chinchilla, a small rodent animal. (Span.—L.) Span. *chinchilla,* lit. 'a little bug,' as if from its smell; but undeservedly so named.—Span. *chinche,* a bug.—L. *cimicem,* acc. of *cimex,* a bug.

Chinchona; the same as **Cinchona.**

Chincough, whooping-cough. (E.) For *chink-cough*; cf. Scotch *kink-cough, kink-host* (*host* means *cough*). A *kink* is a catch in the breath, nasalised form of a base **kik,* to gasp. + Du. *kinkhoest*; M. Du. *kieckhoest*; Swed. *kikhosta,* chincough, *kikna,* to gasp; G. *keichen,* to gasp.

Chine. (F.—O.H.G.) O.F. *eschine* (F. *échine*), the back-bone. — O.H.G. *skina,* a needle, prickle (G. *schiene,* a splint). For the sense, cf. L. *spína,* a thorn, spine, backbone.

Chink (1), a cleft. (E.) Formed with suffixed *k,* from the base of M.E. *chine,* a cleft, rift.—A.S. *cinu,* a chink.—A.S. *cin-,* weak grade of *cínan,* to split (strong vb.). +Du. *keen,* a chink, also a germ, *kenen,* to bud; cf. G. *keimen,* Goth. *keinan,* to bud. (Germinating seeds make a crack in the ground.)

Chink (2), to jingle. (E.) An imitative word; cf. *clink, clank*; and see **Chincough.** E. Fries. *kinken* (a strong vb.); M. Dan. *kinke.*

Chintz. (Hindustani—Skt.) For *chints,* pl. of *chint.* Hind. *chhínt,* spotted cotton cloth, named from the variegated patterns on it; *chhít,* chintz, also a spot.—Skt. *chitra,* variegated, spotted. See **Cheeta.**

Chip, vb. (E.) Related (with a lighter vowel) to *chap* (1) or *chop*; as if to cut a little at a time. Cf. A.S. *for-cyppod,* gloss to *praecisus* (Lye); E. Fries. *kippen,* to cut.

Chirography, handwriting. (Gk.) From Gk. χειρογραφεῖν, to write with the hand. — Gk. χειρο-, from χείρ, the hand; γράφειν, to write. Cf. *chiro-mancy,* fortune-telling by the hand; *chiro-pod-ist,* one who handles (and cures) the feet.

Chirp. (E.) Also *chirrup.* M.E. *chirpen.* Also M.E. *chirken, chirmen,* to chirp. The forms *chir-p, chir-k, chir-m* are from an imitative base; cf. Du. *kirren,* to coo.

Chirurgeon, the old spelling of *surgeon.* (F. — L. — Gk.) F. *chirurgien,* 'a surgeon;' Cot. — F. *chirurgie,* surgery.—L. *chírurgia.*—Gk. χειρουργία, a working with the hands, skill with the hands, art, surgery. ━ Gk. χειρο-, from χείρ, the hand ; and ἔργειν, to work.

Chisel. (F. ─ L.) M. E. *chisel.* ━ A. F. *chisel*, O. F. *cisel* (F. *ciseau*). Cf. Late L. *cīsellus*, scissors (A. D. 1352). O. F. *cisel* answers to Late L. *cīsellum*, with the sense of L. *cīsōrium*, a cutting instrument (Vegetius) ; see Scheler's note to Diez. ━ L. *cīsum, for *cœs-um*, supine of *cædere*, to cut ; whence also Late L. *incīsor*, a carver, cutter ; see **Cæsura.**

Chit (1), a pert child. (E.) M. E. *chit*, a whelp, cub, kitten. Allied to *kit-ling* (Icel. *ketlingr*), and to *kit-ten*; cf. G. *kitze*, a female cat.

Chit (2), a shoot, sprout. (E.) In Holland's Pliny, xiii. 4. Perhaps allied to M. E. *chithe*, a sprout (N. E. D.). ━ A. S. *cīð*, a germ, sprout. Cf. Goth. *keinan*, to produce a shoot ; G. *keim*, a germ.

Chivalry. (F. ─ L.) M. E. *chivalrie.* ━ O. F. *chevalerie*, horsemanship, knighthood. ━ F. *cheval*, a horse. ━ Late L. *caballum*, acc. of *caballus*, a horse.

Chlorine, a pale green gas. (Gk.) Named from its colour. ━ Gk. χλωρ-ός, pale green.

chloroform. (Gk. *and* L.) The latter element relates to *formyl* and *formic* acid, an acid formerly obtained from red ants. ━ L. *formīca*, an ant.

Chocolate, a paste made from cacao. (Span. ─ Mex.) Span. *chocolate.* ━ Mex. *chocolatl*, chocolate ; Clavigero, Hist. Mex. i. 433. ¶ Not allied to *cacao*.

Choice. (F. ─ Teut.) Not E. M. E. *chois.* ━ O. F. *chois* (F. *choix*). ━ O. F. *choisir*, O. North F. *coisir*, to choose. Of Teut. origin. ━ Goth. *kausjan*, to try, test; causal of *kiusan*, to choose. See **Choose.**

Choir. (F. ─ L. ─ Gk.) The *choir* of a church is the part where the *choir* sit. Also spelt *quire* ; M. E. *queir*, *quer.* ━ O. F. *cuer*, later *choeur*, 'the quire of a church, a troop of singers ;' Cot. ━ L. *chorum*, acc. of *chorus*, a choir. ━ Gk. χορός, a dance, a band of dancers or singers. See **Chorus.**

Choke. (E.) M. E. *choken, cheken, cheoken.* A. S. *cēocian* ; only in the derivative *ācēocung*, to translate L. *ruminatio*, which the glossator hardly seems to have understood, and in the pp. *ācēocod*, Ælfric, Hom. i. 216 : with change from *ēo* to *eō*, shortening of *ō* to *o* in M. E., and subse-

quent lengthening. Cf. Icel. *koka*, to gulp ; *kok*, the gullet.

Choler, the bile, anger. (F. ─ L. ─ Gk.) Anger was supposed to be due to excess of bile. M. E. *coler.* ━ O. F. *colere.* ━ L. *cholera*, bile ; also cholera, bilious complaint. ━ Gk. χολέρα, cholera ; χολή, bile ; χόλος, bile, wrath. See **Gall.**

cholera. (L. ─ Gk.) L. *cholera*, as above. And see **Melancholy.**

Choose. (E.) M. E. *chesen, chusen.* A. S. *cēosan* (also *cēosan*), to choose (pt. t. *cēas, ceás*). ╋ Du. and G. *kiesen*, Icel. *kjōsa*, Goth. *kiusan*; Teut. type **keus-an-.* Allied to L. *gus-tare*, to taste, Gk. γεύομαι, I taste, Skt. *jush*, to relish. (√GEUS.) See **Gust.** Brugm. i. § 602.

Chop (1), to cut ; a later form of **Chap** (1).

Chop (2), to barter. (E.) Probably a variant of *chap*, a verb which seems to have been evolved from the sb. *chapman.*

Chopine, a high-heeled shoe. (F. ─ Span.) In Hamlet, ii. 2. 447 ; for *chapine.* ━ O. F. *chapin*; later *chappin* (Cotgrave). ━ Span. *chapin*, a clog with a cork sole, woman's shoe, high cork shoe. Perhaps from Span. *chapa*, a thin plate (of metal), used to strengthen the work it covers.

Chops ; see **Chaps.**

Chord. (L. ─ Gk.) L. *chorda.* ━ Gk. χορδή, the string of a musical instrument, orig. a string of gut. Brugm. i. § 605. ¶ The same word as **Cord.**

Chorus. (L. ─ Gk.) L. *chorus*, a band of singers. ━ Gk. χορός, a dance, a band of dancers or singers. See **Choir. Der.** *chor-al, chor-i-ster.*

Chough, a bird. (E.) M. E. *choȝe, chough.* Not found in A. S., which has (however) the forms *cēo, cīo*, and the early forms *ciae, chyae.* Somewhat similar forms are seen in Du. *kaauw*, Dan. *kaa*, Swed. *kaja*, a jackdaw.

Chouse, to cheat. (Turk. ?) To act as a *chouse* or cheat. Ben Jonson has *chiaus* in the sense of 'a Turk,' with the implied sense of 'cheat'; Alchemist, i. 1. The allusion is *alleged* to be to a Turkish *chiaus* or interpreter, who committed a notorious fraud in 1609. ━ Turk. *chā'ush*, a sergeant, mace-bearer, Palmer's Pers. Dict. ; *chāwush*, a sergeant, herald, messenger, Rich. Dict. p. 534. Or (mediately) from M. Ital. *ciaus.*

Chrism ; see below.

Christ, the anointed one. (L. ─ Gk.)

A. S. *Crist.* – L. *Chrīstus.* – Gk. χριστός, anointed. – Gk. χρίω, I rub, anoint. **Der.** *Christ-ian, Christ-en-dom,* &c. ; *Christ-mas* (see **Mass**) ; *anti-christ,* opponent of Christ (from Gk. ἀντί, against ; see 1 John ii. 18).

chrism, holy unction. (L. – Gk.) Also spelt *chrisome,* whence *chrisome-child,* a child wearing a *chrisome-cloth,* or cloth which a child wore after holy unction ; cf. O. F. *cresme,* ' the crisome, or oyle ; ' Cot. – Late L. *chrisma,* holy oil. – Gk. χρῖσμα, an unguent. – Gk. χρίω (as above).

Chromatic, relating to colours. (Gk.) Gk. χρωματικός, adj. – Gk. χρωματ-, stem of χρῶμα, colour ; allied to χρώς, skin.

chrome, chromium. (Gk.) A metal ; its compounds exhibit beautiful colours. – Gk. χρῶμ-α, colour.

Chronicle. (F. – Late L. – Gk.) M. E. *cronicle,* with inserted *l* ; also *cronike, cronique.* – A. F. *cronicle* ; O. F. *cronique,* pl. *croniques,* chronicles, annals. – Late L. *chronica,* fem. sing. ; for neut. pl. – Gk. χρονικά, pl., annals. – Gk. χρονικός, adj. from χρόνος, time. **Der.** *chron-ic* (= χρονικός).

chronology, science of dates. (Gk.) From χρόνο-s, time ; -λογία, from λόγ-os, discourse ; see **Logic.**

chronometer, time-measurer. (Gk.) From χρόνο-s, time ; μέτρον, measure ; see **Metre.**

Chrysalis, the form taken by some insects. (Gk.) Gk. χρυσαλλίς, the gold-coloured sheath of butterflies, chrysalis. – Gk. χρυσ-ός, gold.

chrysanthemum, a flower. (L. – Gk.) L. *chrȳsanthemum.* – Gk. χρυσάν-θεμον, a marigold. – Gk. χρυσ-ός, gold ; ἄνθεμον, a bloom, from ἀνθεῖν, to bloom, related to ἄνθος, a flower, a bud.

chrysolite, a yellow stone. (F. – L. – Gk.) O. F. *crisolite.* – L. *chrȳsolithus,* Rev. xxi. 20. – Gk. χρυσόλιθος. – Gk. χρυσό-s, gold ; λίθος, stone.

chrysoprase. (L. – Gk.) L. *chrȳsoprasus,* Rev. xxi. 20. – Gk. χρυσόπρασος, a yellow-green stone. – Gk. χρυσό-s, gold ; πράσον, a (green) leek.

Chub, a fish. (E.) Etym. unknown. Cf. Dan. *kobbe,* a seal, prov. Swed. *kubbug,* chubby, fat ; Norw. *kubben,* stumpy ; Swed. *kubb,* a block, log. This does not explain the *ch* ; but see **Chump.**

chubby, fat. (E.) Lit. 'like a chub ; ' cf. prov. Swed. *kubbug* (above).

Chuck (1), to strike gently, toss. (F. – Teut.) Formerly written *chock* (Turberville). – F. *choquer,* to give a shock, jolt. – Du. *schokken,* to jolt, shake ; allied to E. *shock* and *shake.*

Chuck (2), to chuck as a hen. (E.) An imitative word ; Ch. has *chuk* to express the noise made by a cock ; C. T. 15180 (B. 3464). Cf. *cluck.* **Der.** *chuck-le,* in the sense 'to cluck.'

Chuck (3), a chicken. A variety of *chick,* for *chicken.* See above.

Chuckle. (E.) To *chuckle* is to laugh in a suppressed way ; cf. **Chuck** (2).

Chump, a log. (E.) Cf. Swed. dial. *kumpa,* to chop into logs ; *kumping,* a log, round stick ; also Icel. *kumbr, trē-kumbr,* a log of wood, from Icel. *kumbr,* nasalised form of *kubbr,* a chopping ; Icel. *kubba,* to chop. **Der.** *chump-end,* i. e. thick end.

Church. (Gk.) M. E. *chirche, chireche.* A. S. *cirice,* later *circe* ; (cf. Icel. *kirkja* ; G. *kirche,* Du. *kerk*). – Gk. κυριακόν, a church, neut. of κυριακός, belonging to the Lord ; or (possibly) from Gk. κυριακά, pl., treated as a fem. sing. – Gk. κύριος, a lord, orig. mighty. – Gk. κῦρος, strength. Cf. Skt. *çūra,* a hero.

Churl. (E.) M. E. *cherl, cheorl.* A.S. *ceorl,* a man. + Du. *kerel,* G. *kerl* ; Dan. Sw. Icel. *karl.* Teut. types, **kerloz, *karloz.*

Churn, sb. (E.) A. S. *cyrin* ; older form *cirin* (printed *cirm*), Corp. gloss. 1866. + Icel. *kirna,* Swed. *kärna,* Dan. *kierne,* a churn ; cf. O. Swed. *kerna.* – Swed. *kärna,* Dan. *kierne,* to churn, Du. *kernen,* to churn.

Chutney, Chutny, a kind of hot relish. (Hind.) Hind. *chatnī* (Yule).

Chyle, milky fluid. (F. – L. – Gk.) F. *chyle.* – L. *chȳlus.* – Gk. χυλός, juice. – Gk. χέω (= χέϝ-ω), I pour. (√GHEU.)

chyme, liquid pulp. (L. – Gk.) Formerly *chymus.* – L. *chȳmus.* – Gk. χυμός, juice. – Gk. χέ-ω ; as above.

Chymist ; see **Alchemist.**

Ci—Cz.

Cicatrice, scar. (F. – L.) F. *cicatrice.* – L. *cicātrīcem,* acc. of *cicātrix,* a scar.

Cicerone. (Ital. – L.) Ital. *cicerone,* a guide ; orig. a Cicero. – L. acc. *Cicerōnem,* proper name.

Cid, lit. a chief or commander. (Span.

—Arab.) Usually a title of Ruy Diaz, the national hero of Spain. — Arab. *sayyid*, a lord; Richardson's Dict. p. 864.

Cider. (F. — L. — Gk. — Heb.) It merely means strong drink. M. E. *sicer*, *cyder*. — F. *cidre*; O. F. *cisdre* (for **cisre*). — L. *sicera*. — Gk. σίκερα, strong drink. — Heb. *shēkār*, strong drink. — Heb. *shākar*, to be intoxicated.

Cieling; see Ceil.

Cigar, Segar. (Span.) Span. *cigarro*; whence also F. *cigare*.

Cinchona, Peruvian bark. (Span.) Named after the Countess of *Chinchon*, wife of the governor of Peru, cured by it A.D. 1638. Chinchon is S.E. of Madrid. (Should be *chinchona*.)

Cincture. (L.) L. *cinctūra*, a girdle. — L. *cinctus*, pp. of *cingere*, to gird.

Cinder. (E.) Misspelt for *sinder* (by confusion with F. *cendre* = L. *cinerem*; see Cinerary). A.S. *sinder*, 'scoria,' slag. +Icel. *sindr*; Swed. *sinder*; G. *sinter*, dross, whence Du. *sintels*, cinders. ¶ The A. S. *sinder* occurs in the 8th century.

Cinerary, relating to the ashes of the dead. (L.) L. *cinerārius*. — L. *ciner-*, stem of *cinis*, dust, ashes of the dead.+ Gk. κόνις, dust. **Der.** *cineraria*, a flower; named from the ash-coloured down on the leaves. Brugm. i § 84.

Cinnabar, Cinoper. (L. — Gk. — Pers.) L. *cinnabaris*. — Gk. κιννάβαρι, vermilion. From Pers. *zinjifrah*, *zinjarf*, red lead, vermilion, cinnabar.

Cinnamon, a spice. (L. — Gk. — Heb.) L. *cinnamōmum*. — Gk. κιννάμωμον. — Heb. *qinnāmōn*; said to be of Malay origin (Gesenius). Cf. Malay *kāyu-mānis*, cinnamon; from *kāyu*, wood, *mānis*, sweet.

Cipher. (F. — Span. — Arab.) O. F. *cifre* (F. *chiffre*), a cipher, zero. — Span. *cifra*. — Arab. *sifr*, a cipher; lit. 'empty thing;' from *sifr*, adj. empty; Rich. Dict. p. 937. (A translation of Skt. *çūnya*, (1) empty; (2) a cipher.) **Der.** *de-cipher*, from L. *dē*, in the verbal sense of *un-*, and *cipher*; cf. M. F. *dechiffrer*, 'to decypher;' Cot.

Circle. (F. — L.) A.S. *circul*; but M.E. *cercle*. — F. *cercle*. — L. *circulus*, dimin. of *circus*, a ring, circle; see Ring (1). **Der.** *encircle*, *semi-circle*; and see *circum-*.

    circus, a ring. (L.) L. *circus* (above).

Circuit. (F. — L.) F. *circuit*. — L. acc. *circuitum*, a going round. — L. *circuitus*, also *circumitus*, pp. of *circumīre*

(also *circuīre*), to go round. — L. *circum*, round; *īre*, to go.

Circum-, *prefix*, round. (L.) L. *circum*, around, round; orig. acc of *circus*, a circle; see Circle. Der *circum-ambient* (see Ambient); *circum-ambulate* (see Amble); and see below.

    circumcise. (L.) L. *circumcīs-us*, pp. of *circumcīdere*, to cut round. — L. *circum*, round; and *cædere*, to cut.

    circumference. (L.) L. *circumferentia*, boundary of a circle. — L. *circumferent-*, stem of pres. pt. of *circum-ferre*, to carry round; from *ferre*, to bear.

    circumflex. (L.) L. *syllaba circumflexa*, a syllable marked with a circumflex (∧) or 'bent' mark. — L. *circumflexus*, pp. of *circum-flectere*, to bend round; from *flectere*, to bend.

    circumjacent, lying near. (L.) From stem of pres. part. of *circum-iacēre*, to lie around; from *iacēre*, to lie.

    circumlocution. (L.) L. *circumlocūtio*, a periphrasis. — L. *circumlocūtus*, pp. of *circum-loquī*, to speak in a round-about way; from *loquī*, to speak.

    circumscribe. (L.) L. *circumscribere*, to write or draw around, to limit; from *scrībere*, to write.

    circumspect, prudent. (L.) L. *circumspectus*, prudent; orig. pp. of *circumspicere*, to look around; from *specere*, to look.

    circumstance. (F. — L.) Adapted from O. F. *circonstance*. — L. *circumstantia*, lit. a standing around, also an attribute, circumstance (influenced by F. *circonstance*). — L. *circumstant-*, stem of pres. pt. of *circum-stāre*, to stand round; from *stāre*, to stand.

    Circus; see Circle.

Cirrus, a fleecy cloud, tendril. (L.) L. *cirrus*, a curl, curled hair.

Cist, a sort of tomb. (L. — Gk.) L. *cista*, a chest. — Gk. κίστη, a box, chest.

    cistern. (F. — L. — Gk.) F. *cisterne*. — L. *cisterna*, a reservoir for water. — L. *cista*, as above.

    cistvaen, a British monument. (L. and W.) W. *cistfaen*, a stone chest, monument made with four upright stones, and a fifth on the top. — W. *cist*, a chest (from L. *cista*); and *maen*, a stone.

Cit, Citadel; see Civil (below).

Cite, to summon, quote. (F. — L.) F. *citer*. — L. *citāre*, frequent. of *ciēre*, to rouse, excite, call. + Gk. κίω, I go.

(✔KI.) See **Hie.** Der. *ex-cite, in-cite, re-cite.*

Cithern, Cittern, a kind of guitar. (L. — Gk.) [Also M. E. *giterne*; from O. F. *guiterne*, a guitar.] The *n* is excrescent, as in *bitter-n*, in imitation of M. E. *giterne.* — L. *cithara.* — Gk. κιθάρα, a kind of lyre or lute.

Citizen; see **Civil** (below).

Citron. (F. — L. — Gk.) F. *citron.* — Late L. acc. *citrōnem.* — L. *citrus*, orange-tree; orig. a tree with fragrant wood. — Gk. κέδρος, a cedar. Brugm. i. § 764.

City; see **Civil** (below).

Civet. (F. — Arab.) F. *civette*, civet; also the civet-cat; Ital. *zibetto*; borrowed from medieval Gk. ζαπέτιον (Brachet). — Arab. *zabād*, civet; Rich. Dict. p. 767.

Civil. (F. — L.) F. *civil.* — L. *cīuīlis*, belonging to citizens. — L. *cīuis*, a citizen. Allied to A. S. *hīwan*, members of a household. Der. *civil-ise, civil-i-an.*

cit; short for **citizen** (below).

citadel. (F. — Ital. — L.) F. *citadelle.* — Ital. *cittadella*, a small town, fort; dimin. of *cittade = cittate* (*città*), a city. — L. *cīuitātem*, acc. of *cīuitās*, a city. — L. *cīuis*, a citizen (above).

citizen. (F. — L.) M. E. *citesein*, from A. F. *citisein*, in which *s* was an insertion. — O. F. *citeain* (F. *citoyen*); formed from O. F. *cite* (*cité*) city, by help of the suffix *-ain* — L. *-ānus*; see below.

city. (F. — L.) M. E. *cite, citee.* — O. F. *cite* (F. *cité*). — Late L. type *civ'tātem*, for *cīuitātem*, acc. of *cīuitās*; see **citadel.**

Clachan, a small village with a church. (Gael.) Gael. *clachan*, (1) a circle of stones, (2) a small rude church, (3) a small village with a church. — Gael. *clach*, a stone. So also Irish *clachán*, a hamlet; *clach*, O. Ir. *cloch*, a stone.

Clack. (E.) M. E. *clacken.* Imitative; allied to **Crack.** E. Fries. *klakken.*✦ Icel. *klaka*, to chatter; Du. *klakken*, to clack, crack; Irish *clag*, the clapper of a mill.

Claim, to demand, call out for. (F. — L.) O. F. *claimer, clamer.* — L. *clāmāre*, to call out; cf. O. L. *calāre*, to proclaim; Gk. καλεῖν, to summon. Der. *ac-claim, de-claim, ex-claim, pro-claim, re-claim*; also (from pp. *clamātus*) *ac-clamat-ion, de-clamat-ion, ex-clamat-ion, pro-clamat-ion, re-clamat-ion.*

clamour. (F. — L.) M. E. *clamour.* — O. F. *clamour.* — L. acc. *clāmōrem*, an

outcry. — L. *clāmāre* (above). Der. *clamor-ous.*

Clamber, to climb by grasping tightly. (E.; *perhaps* Scand.) XV. cent. M. E. *clameren, clambren.* Cf. Icel. *klambra*, to pinch closely together; Dan. *klamre*, to grip firmly; see **Clamp.** Affected by **Climb,** of which the M. E. pt. t. was *clamb, clam.*

Clammy, viscous. (E.) Earliest form *claymy*, perhaps·from A. S. *clām*, clay (see **Clay**); but confused with an adj. *clam*, sticky; with which cf. E. Fries. and Du. *klam*, Dan. *klam*, clammy, moist. See **Clamp.**

Clamour; see **Claim.**

Clamp. (Du.) XV. cent. Du. *klampe*, a holdfast; whence *klampen*, to clamp, grapple, also to board a ship. ✦ Dan. *klamme*, a cramp-iron; Swed. *klamp*, the same; Icel. *klömbr*, a smith's vice; Teut. base ✦*klamp*, answering to the 2nd grade of M. H. G. *klimpfen*, to press tightly together. Cf. **Clump.**

Clan. (Gael.) Gael. *clann*, offspring, children; Irish *cland, clann*, descendants, a tribe; W. *plant*, pl. offspring, children. Cf. Skt. *kula(m)*, a herd, family. Brugm. i. § 669.

Clandestine. (L.) L. *clandestīnus*, secret, close. Allied to *clam*, secretly.

Clang, to resound. (L.) L. *clangere*, to resound; whence *clangor*, a loud noise. ✦ Gk. κλαγγή, a clang; allied to κλάζειν, to clash (fut. κλάγξω). Der. *clang-or.* See below.

Clank, a heavy ringing sound. (Du.) XVII cent. — Du. *klank*, 'a ringing;' Hexham. Cf. Du. *klonk*, pt. t. of *klinken*, to clink. See **Clink.** Der. *clank*, vb.

Clap. (E.) M. E. *clappen.* [We only find A.S. *clæppetan*, to palpitate; Voc. 473.] E. Fries. *klappen*, to clap hands. The orig. sense is to make a noise by striking. ✦ Icel. *klappa*, Swed. *klappa*, Dan. *klappe*, Du. *klappen*, M. H. G. *klaffen*, to pat, clap, prate, make a noise. Allied to **Clack, Clatter.**

Claret. (F. — L.) Orig. a light red wine. M. E. *claret.* — O. F. *claret, clairet* (F. *clairet*), adj.; dimin. of *clair*, clear. — L. *clārus*, clear. See **Clear.**

clarify. (F. — L.) O. F. *clarifier.* — L. *clārificāre*, to make clear. — L. *clāri-*, from *clārus*, clear; and *-fic-*, for *facere*, to make.

clarion. (F. — L.) M. E. *clarioun.* —

O. F. *clarion, claron (F. clairon), a clear-sounding horn. — Late L. acc. clāriōnem. — L. clāri- (as above).

Clash. (E.) An imitative word; suggested by clack and crash, dash, &c. Cf. E. Fries. klatsen, to crack a whip.

Clasp. (E.) M. E. claspe, clapse, sb.; claspen, clapsen, vb. The base seems to be klap-s-, extended from klap- (see Clap), and influenced by M. E. clippen, to embrace. Cf. G. klafter, a fathom; Lith. glēbys, an armful; and cf. Grasp.

Class. (F. — L.) F. classe, a rank. — L. acc. classem, a class, assembly, fleet.

Clatter. (E.) A frequentative of clat, which is a by-form of Clack. A. S. clatrung, a clattering; E. Fries. klattern, to clatter. + Du. klateren, to clatter. Of imitative origin.

Clause. (F. — L.) F. clause. — Late L. clausa, a passage from a book, a clause. — L. clausus, pp. of claudere, to shut. + O. Fries. slūta, to shut. See Slot (1). (√SKLEU.) Brugm. i. § 795.

Clavicle, the collar-bone. (F. — L.) F. clavicule, the collar-bone. — L. clāuicula, lit. a small key; dimin. of clāuis, a key. Allied to claudere; see Clause.

Claw. (E.) M. E. clau, clee. A. S. clawu (also clēa), a claw. + Du. klaauw; G. klaue; Icel. klō, Dan. Swed. klo. Allied to Clew; from a Teut. base *klau-, 2nd grade of *kleu-, to draw together; cf. O. H. G. kluwi, forceps.

Clay. (E.) M. E. clai, cley. A. S. clǣg. + Du. and Low G. klei, Dan. klæg. Teut. type *klai-jā, fem.; from *klai-, 2nd grade of Teut. root *klei-; cf. A. S. clām (for *klai-moz), earthenware; Gk. γλοι-ός, sticky matter. See Cleave (2) and Glue.

Claymore, a Scottish broadsword. (Gael.) Gael. claidheamh mor, a great sword. Here claidheamh is cognate with W. cleddyf, O. Ir. claideb, sword; and Gael. mor, great, is allied to W. mawr, great. Cf. W. cledd, a sword.

Clean. (E.) M. E. clene. A. S. clǣne, clear, pure. + O. Sax. clēni, cleini; O. Fries. klēn; Du. klein, small; G. klein, O. H. G. chleini, pure, bright, fine, small. All from Teut. *klaini-, orig. ' clear, pure.'

cleanse. (E.) A. S. clǣnsian, to make clean. — A. S. clǣne, clean.

Clear. (F. — L.) M. E. cleer, cler. — O. F. cler, clair. — L. clārus, bright, clear, loud.

Cleat, a piece of iron for strengthening the soles of shoes; a piece of wood or

iron to fasten ropes to. (E.) M. E. clete, a wedge (as if from A. S. *clēat), also clite, clote, a lump; cognate with Du. kloot, a ball, G. kloss, a clot, lump. Allied to Clot; and see Clout.

Cleave (1), to split. (E.) Strong verb. A. S. clēofan, pt. t. clēaf, pp. clofen (= E. cloven). + Du. klieven, Icel. kljūfa (pt. t. klauf), Swed. klyfva, Dan. klöve, G. klieben. Teut. base *kleub; cf. Gk. γλύφειν, to hollow out.

cleft, clift. (Scand.) The old spelling is clift. — Icel. kluft, Swed. klyft, Dan. klöft, a cleft, chink, cave. — Icel. kluf-, weak grade of kljūfa (above); cf. Swed. klyfva, to cleave.

Cleave (2), to stick. (E.) Weak verb. The correct pt. t. is cleaved, not clave, which belongs to the verb above. A. S. clīfian, cleofian, pt. t. clifode. + Du. kleven, Swed. klibba sig, G. kleben, to adhere, cleave to. All from Teut. base *klib-, weak grade of Teut. root *kleib-, found in A. S. clīfan (pt. t. clāf), Du. be-klijven, to cleave to. Allied to Clay, Climb.

Clef, a key, in music. (F. — L.) F. clef. — L. clāuem, acc. of clāuis, a key.

Cleft; see Cleave (1).

Clematis, a plant. (Gk.) Gk. κληματίς, a creeping plant. — Gk. κληματ-, stem of κλῆμα, a shoot, twig. — Gk. κλάειν, to break off, prune (Brugm. ii. § 661).

Clement. (F. — L.) F. clement. — L. clementem, acc. of clēmens, mild.

Clench; see Clinch.

Clerestory, an upper story in a church, furnished with windows. (F. — L.) Old spelling of clear-story. The triforium below is sometimes called the blind-story. See Story (2).

Clerk. (F. — L. — Gk.) A. S. and O. F. clerc. — L. clēricus. — Gk. κληρικός, one of the clergy. — Gk. κλῆρος, a lot; in late Gk., the clergy, whose portion is the Lord, Deut. xviii. 2, 1 Pet. v. 3; cf. Acts i. 17. (St. Jerome.)

clergy. (F. — L.) M. E. clergie, often also (2) ' learning.' — (1) O. F. clergie, as if from L. *clēricia; (2) mod. F. clergé, from Late L. clēricātus, clerkship. — Late L. clēricus, a clerk (above).

Clever. (E.) Cleverly is in Butler's Hudibras, i. 1. 398 (1663). For M. E. cliver, adj., meaning ready to seize, allied to M. E. cliver, a claw, and to Cleave (2). So also E. Fries. klüfer, clever, Dan. dial. klöver, klever (Molbech). ¶ It took the place of M. E. *deliver*, quick, nimble, Ch. prol. 84. – O. F. *delivre*, free, prompt, alert ; compounded of L. *dē*, prefix, and *līber*, free ; see Deliver.

Clew, Clue, a ball of thread. (E.) M. E. *clewe*. A. S. *clīwen*, a clew ; also *clēowe* (Epinal gl. *cleouuae*). + Du. *kluwen* whence *kluwenen*, to wind on clews (E. *clew* up a sail); M. Low G. *kluwen* ; and cf. G. *knäuel* (for **kläuel*), a clew. Perhaps allied to L. *gluere*, to draw together. Cf. Claw.

Click. (E.) An imitative word, expressing a lighter and thinner sound than Clack. E. Fries. *klikken*. Cf. Du. *klik-klakken* to clash.

Client. (F. – L.) F. *client*, a suitor. – L. *clientem*, acc. of *cliens = cluens*, orig. a hearer, one who listens to advice ; pres. pt. of *cluere*, to hear. (√KLEU.)

Cliff, a steep rock, headland. (E.) A. S. *clif*, a rock, cliff. + Du. and Icel. *klif* ; O. H. G. *klep*. Cf. G. and Dan. *klippe*, Swed. *klippa*, a crag ; and Icel. *kleif*, a ridge of cliffs.

Climate. (F. – L. – Gk.) M. E. *climat*. – F. *climat*. Late L. *climat-*, stem of *clima*. – Gk. *κλιματ-*, stem of *κλίμα*, a slope, zone, region of the earth, climate. – Gk. *κλίνειν*, to lean, slope ; see Lean.

climacter, a critical time of life. (F. – Gk.) M. F. *climactere*, adj.; whence *l'an climactere*, ' the climatericall (*sic*) year ; every 7th, or 9th, or the 63 yeare of a man's life, all very dangerous, but the last, most ;' Cot. – Gk. *κλιμακτήρ*, a step of a ladder, a dangerous period of life. – Gk. *κλῖμακ-*, stem of *κλῖμαξ*, a ladder, climax, with suffix -*τηρ* of the agent ; see below.

climax, the highest degree. (Gk.) Gk. *κλῖμαξ*, a ladder, staircase, highest pitch of expression (in rhetoric). – Gk. *κλίνειν*, to slope. Der. *anti-climax*.

clime. (L. – Gk.) L. *clima*, a climate. – Gk. *κλίμα* ; see Climate.

Climb. (E.) M. E. *climben*, pt. t. *clomb*. A. S. *climban*, pt. t. *clamb*, pl. *clumbon*. + Du. *klimmen*, M. H. G. *klimmen*. Teut. type **klimban-*. The *m* was orig. inserted in the present stem, and did not belong to the root ; as is shewn by Icel. *klīfa*, to climb. Hence it is allied to Cleave (2).

Clime ; see Climate.

Clinch, Clench, to rivet. (E.) M.E. *clenchen*, *klenken*, to strike smartly, to make to clink ; causal of *klinken*, to clink.

Cf. Du. *klink*, a latch, rivet ; also, a blow ; and O. H. G. *klenkan*, to knot or bind together.

Cling. (E.) M. E. *clingen*, to become stiff, be matted together. A.S. *clingan* (pt. t. *clang*, pp. *clungen*), to dry up, shrivel up. + Dan. *klynge*, to cluster. Allied to Swed. *klänga*, to climb ; O. H. G. *clunga*, a clew.

Clinical. (F. – L. – Gk.) F. *clinique*, ' one that is bedrid ;' Cot. – L. *clīnicus*, the same. – Gk. *κλινικός*, belonging to a bed, a physician ; *ἡ κλινική*, his art. – Gk. *κλίνη*, a bed. – Gk. *κλίνειν*, to lean ; see Lean (1).

Clink. (E.) E. Fries. *klinken*. Nasalised form of Click. + Du. *klinken*, to sound, pt. t. *klonk*, pp. *geklonken* ; Swed. *klinka*, to jingle. Cf. Clank.

clinker, a hard cinder. (Du.) Du. *klinker*, a clinker, named from the tinkling sound which they make when they strike each other. – Du. *klinken*, to clink ; cognate with E. *clink*.

clinquant, glittering. (F. – Du.) In Shak. Lit. ' tinkling.' – F. *clinquant*, pres. pt. of O. F. *clinquer*, to clink. – Du. *klinken* (above).

Clip, to cut. (Scand.) M. E. *klippen*. – Icel. *klippa*, Swed. *klippa*, Dan. *klippe*, to clip, shear hair. Cf. Snip.

Clip (2), to embrace. (E.) A. S. *clyppan*.

Clique, a gang. (F. – Du.) F. *clique*, a gang, noisy set. – O. F. *cliquer*, to click, make a noise. – Du. *klikken*, to click, clash ; also to inform, tell ; cf. Du. *klikker*, a tell-tale. See Click.

Cloak, Cloke. (F. – C.) M. E. *cloke*. – O. North F. *cloque*, O. F. *cloche*. – Late L. *cloca*, a bell ; also a horseman's cape, which resembled a bell in shape : see below.

clock. (C.) The orig. sense was ' bell ' ; bells preceded clocks for notifying times. Either from M. Du. *clocke* (Du. *klok*), a bell ; or from O. North F. *cloque*, a bell. – Late L. *cloc(c)a*, a bell ; of Celtic origin. – Irish *clog*, a bell, clock ; *clogaim*, I ring or sound as a bell ; O. Irish *cloc*, a bell. Cf. W. *cloch*, a bell, &c. The G. *glocke* is a borrowed word ; so also Du. *klok*, &c.

Clod. (E.) M.E. *clod*, *clodde*. A. S. *clod* (in compounds), a lump of earth. Teut. type **klu-do-*, from the weak grade of Teut. root **kleu-*, to stick together. See Clew, Cloud. Cf. Clot.

Clog, a hindrance ; a wooden sole of a shoe ; wooden shoe. (E.) M. E. *clog*, a log, clump. Not found in A. S. A late word; cf. Norw. *klugu*, a hard log.

Cloister. (F.−L.) M. E. *cloister.* − O. F. *cloistre* (F. *cloître*). − L. *claustrum*, lit. enclosure. − L. *claus-us*, pp. of *claudere*, to shut. See **Clause**.

close (1), to shut in. (F.−L.) M. E. *closen.* − O. F. *clos*, 1 pr. s. of O. F. *clore*, to shut in. − L. *claudere* (above). Der. *close*, a field; *dis-close*, *en-close*, *in-close*.

close (2), shut up. (F.−L.) M. E. *clos*, *cloos.* − O. F. *clos*, pp. of *clore* (above).

closet. (F.−L.) O. F. *closet*, dimin. of *clos*, an enclosed space. − O. F. *clos*, pp.; see **close** (2).

Clot. (E.) M. E. *clot*, *clotte*, a ball, esp. of earth. A. S. *clott*, *clot*, a lump. + G. *klotz*, a lump. Teut. type **klut-to-*, from the weak grade of Teut. base **kleut*; see **Cleat**, **Clout**, **Cluster**.

Cloth. (E.) M. E. *cloth*, *clath*. A. S. *clāð*. + Du. *kleed*, G. *kleid*, a dress. Der. *clothes*, A. S. *clāðas*, pl. of *clāð*.

clothe, to cover with a cloth. (E.) M. E. *clothen*, *clathen*, pt. t. *clothede* (or *cladde*), pp. *clothed* (or *clad*). Formed from A. S. *clāð*. + Du. *kleeden*, from *kleed*; so also G. *kleiden*, from *kleid*. ¶ But the pt. t. and pp. *clad* are of Scand. origin: cf. Icel. *klædd-r*, pp. of *klæða*, to clothe; Swed. *klädd*, pp. of *kläda*.

Cloud. (E.) M. E. *cloud*, orig. a mass of vapours; the same word as M. E. *clūd*, a mass of rock. A. S. *clūd*, a round mass, mass of rock, hill. From Teut. root **kleu*, to stick together; see **Clew**, **Clod**.

Clough, a hollow in a hill-side. (E.) M. E. *clough*, *cloȝe*. Answering to A. S. **clōh*, not found; cognate with O. H. G. *klāh*. The A. S. **clōh* (= O.H.G. *klāh*, as in *Klah-uelde*, Förstemann) represents a Teut. type **klanχo-*, 2nd grade of **klanχ*; cf. G. *klinge*, O. H. G. *chlinga*, a clough (Acad., Aug. and Sept. 1889).

Clout, a patch. (E.) M. E. *clout*. A. S. *clūt*, a patch; whence W. *clwt*, Corn. *clut*, a patch, clout; Ir. and Gael. *clud*, the same. Orig. sense 'mass, piece of stuff'; orig. Teut. type **klūt-oz*, from Teut. root **klūt-*, **kleut-*, as seen in **Clot**. Closely allied to **Cleat** (which is from the 2nd grade of the same root).

Clove (1), a kind of spice. (F.−L.) M. E. *clow*; the change to *clove*, in the XVIth cent., was due to the influence of Ital. *chiovo*. − F. *clou*, a nail; *clou de girofle*, 'a clove,' Cot.; from the semblance to a nail. Cf. Span. *clavo*, a nail, also a clove. − L. *clāuum*, acc. of *clāuus*, a nail. + O. Irish *clo*, a nail.

Clove (2), a bulb, or spherical shell of a bulb of garlic, &c. (E.) A. S. *clufu*, f. ; cf. *cluf-wyrt*, a buttercup (lit. clove-wort). Named from its cleavage into shells. − A. S. *cluf-*, weak grade of *clēofan*, to split; see **Cleave** (1). Cf. Icel. *klofi*, a cleft.

Clove (3), a weight. (F.−L.) A. F. *clou* ; the same word as **Clove** (1). − Late L. *clāvus*, a weight (for wool).

Clover. (E.) M. E. *claver.* A. S. *clāfre*, *clǣfre*, trefoil. + Du. *klaver*, whence Swed. *klöfver*, Dan. *klöver*; Low G. *klever*; cf. G. *klee*. ¶ The supposed connexion with *cleave* (1) is impossible.

Clown. (Scand.) Icel. *klunni*, a clumsy, boorish fellow : Swed. dial. *klunn*, a log, *kluns*, a clownish fellow; Dan. *klunt*, a log; cf. Dan. *kluntet*, clumsy. Allied to **Clump**. Orig. sense 'log' or 'clod.'

Cloy. (F.−L.) Orig. to stop up, hence, to sate. M. F. *cloyer*, 'to cloy, stop up,' Cot.; a by-form of F. *clouer* (O. F. *cloer*), to nail, fasten up. [A horse pricked with a nail, in shoeing, was said to be *cloyed*.] − O. F. *clo*, F. *clou*, a nail; see **Clove** (1). ¶ *Cloy* (in E.) is usually short for *ac-cloy* or *a-cloy*, where the prefix *a-* represents F. *en-*; see F. *enclouer*, *encloyer* in Cotgrave.

Club (1), a heavy stick. (Scand.) M.E. *clubbe*. − Icel. *klubba*, *klumba*, a club; Swed. *klubb*, a club, log, lump; Dan. *klub*, club, *klump*, lump. A mere variant of **Clump** below. See **Golf**.

club (2), an association. (Scand.) XVII cent. Lit. 'a clump of people.' Cf. Swed. dial. *klubb*, a clump, lump, also a knot of people (Rietz). See above.

Cluck. (E.) M. E. *clokken*, to cluck as a hen; a mere variant of **Clack**. + Du. *klokken*, Dan. *klukke*, G. *glucken*; L. *glocīre*. An imitative word.

Clue; see **Clew**.

Clump, a mass, block. (E.) XVI cent. Not in A.S., except as in *clymp-re*, a clump. Cf. Dan. *klump*, Swed. *klump*; Du. *klomp*, Low G. *klump*, a clump, lump, log ; (Icel. *klumba*, a club, with *b* for *p*). From *klump-*, weak grade of Teut. **klemp-*, as in M.H.G. *klimpfen*, to press tightly together. Cf. **Clamp**.

Clumsy. (Scand.) Cf. M. E. *clumsed*, *clomsed*, benumbed; benumbed fingers are clumsy. This is the pp. of *clomsen*, to benumb, or to feel benumbed. Cf. Swed. dial. *klummsen*, benumbed (Rietz) ; Icel. *klumsa*, lock-jawed. Cf. Du. *klemmen*, to pinch; *kleumen*, to be benumbed, *kleumsch*, numb with cold ; also A.S. *clom*, *clam*, a bond, clasp. See **Clammy**.

Cluster, a bunch. (E.) A.S. *cluster*, *clyster*, a bunch.+Low G. *kluster*. Suggests a Teut. type **klut-tro-*, a cluster ; formed with suffix *-tro* from **klut-*, weak grade of Teut. root **kleut-*, to mass together ; for which see **Clot, Cleat, Clout.**

Clutch, to seize. (E.) M. E. *clucchen*, *clicchen*. A.S. *clyccan* (whence pp. *ge-cliht*, Somner). We find also M. E. *cloke*, a claw; which was superseded by the verbal form.

Clutter, a clotted mass; also *clutter*, vb., to clot. (E.) *Clutter*, vb., is a variant of *clotter*, to run into clots; see **Clot**, and cf. E. Fries. *klutern*, to become clotted. *Clutter* also meant confusion, a confused heap, turmoil, din ; by association with **Clatter.** Cf. E. Fries. *klöter*, a rattle.

Clyster. (L. — Gk.) L. *clyster*, an injection into the bowels.—Gk. κλυστήρ, a clyster, syringe.—Gk. κλύζειν, to wash.+ L. *cluere*, to wash. (√KLEU.)

Co-, prefix. (L.) L. *co-*, together ; used for *con-* (*=cum*), together, before a vowel. Hence, *co-efficient*, *co-equal*, *co-operate*, *co-ordinate*. See others below ; and see **Con-.**

Coach. (F. — Hung.) F. *coche*, 'a coach ;' Cot. Etym. disputed. Said, as early as A.D. 1553, to be a Hungarian word ; from Hung. *kocsi*, a coach, so called because first made at a Hung. village called *Kocsi* or *Kocs*, near Raab ; see Littré, and Beckmann, Hist. of Inventions.

Coadjutor. (F. — L.) XV cent. A.F. *coadjutour*.—L. *co-*, for *con-* = *cum*, together; and *adiūtor*, an assistant, from vb. *adiu-uāre*, to assist.—L. *ad-*, to ; *iuuāre*, to help.

Coagulate, to curdle. (L.) L. *coāgu-lātus*, pp. of *coāgulāre*, to curdle. — L. *coāgulum*, rennet, which causes milk to run together. — L. *co-* (*cum*), together ; *ag-ere*, to drive.

Coal. (E.) M. E. *col*. A.S. *col*.+ Du. *kool*, Icel. Swed. *kol*, Dan. *kul*, G. *kohle*. Cf. Skt. *jval*, to blaze.

Coalesce, to grow together. (L.) L. *coalescere*. — L. *co-*, for *con-* = *cum*, together ; and *alescere*, to grow, inceptive of *alere*, to nourish.

Coarse, rough. (F. — L.) Formerly *course*, an adj. which arose from the phrase *in course* to denote anything of an ordinary character; cf. mod. E. *of course*. See **Course.**

Coast. (F. — L.) M. E. *coste*.—O. F. *coste* (F. *côte*), a rib, slope of a hill, shore. — L. *costa*, a rib.

Coat. (F. — G.) M. E. *cote*. — O. F. *cote* (F. *cotte*) ; Low L. *cota*, *cotta*, a coat. — M. H. G. *kotte*, *kutte*, a coarse mantle; O. Sax. *cot*, the same.

Coax, (E.?) Formerly *cokes*, vb., from *cokes*, sb., a simpleton, dupe. Perhaps allied to **Cocker** or to **Cockney.**

Cob (1), a round lump, knob. (E.) As applied to a pony, it means short and stout. M. E. *cob*, a great person (Hoccleve). In some senses, it seems to be allied to A. S. *copp*, a top, summit.

cobble (1), a small round lump. (E.) M. E. *cobylstone*, a cobble-stone. Dimin. of *cob* (above).

Cob (2), to beat. (E.) Cf. W. *cobio*, to thump; *cob*, a bunch ; prov. E. *cop*, to strike, esp. on the *cop* or head. See **Cob** (1).

Cobalt, a mineral. (G.) G. *kobalt*, cobalt ; a nickname given by the miners, because considered poisonous ; better spelt *kobold*, meaning (1) a demon, (2) cobalt. Of G. origin (Kluge).

Cobble (1); see **Cob** (1).

Cobble (2), to patch up. (E.) Origin unknown ; cf. **Cob** (2), of which it seems to be the frequentative.

Cobra, a hooded snake. (Port.—L.) Port. *cobra*, also *cobra de capello*, i. e. snake with a hood.—L. *colubra*, snake ; *dē*, of; *capellum*, acc. of *capellus*, hat, hood, dimin. of *cāpa*, a cape. See Notes and Queries, 7 S. ii. 205.

Cobweb. (E.) M. E. *copweb*, *coppe-web* ; from M. E. *coppe*, a spider, and *web*. Cf. M. Du. *kop*, *koppe*, 'a spider, or a cob,' Hexham. From A.S. *coppa*, as in *āttor-coppa*, a spider ; lit. poison-bunch ; from A.S. *āttor*, *ātor*, poison, and *cop*, a head.

Coca, a Peruvian plant. (Span. — Peruv.) Span. *coca*.—Peruv. *cuca* ; Garcilasso, Peru, bk. 8. c. 15. Distinct both from *cocoa* (or *coco*) and *cacao*. **Der.** *coca-ine*.

Cochineal. (F. — Span. — L. — Gk.) F. *cochenille*.—Span. *cochinilla*, cochineal (made from insects which look like berries). —L. *coccinus*, of a scarlet colour; see Isaiah i. 18 (Vulgate).—L. *coccum*, a berry;

also kermes, supposed to be a berry. — Gk. κόκκος, a berry, cochineal.

Cock (1), a male bird. (E.) M. E. *cok.* A. S. *cocc*; from the bird's cry. ' Cryde anon *cok! cok!* ' Ch. C. T. Nun's Priest's Tale, 457. Cf. Skt. *kukkuṭa*, a cock; Malay *kukuk*, crowing of cocks. And cf. **Cuckoo.**

cock, the stop-cock of a barrel, is the same word. So also G. *hahn*, (1) a cock, (2) a stop-cock.

cock, part of the lock of a gun. From its original shape; cf. G. *den Hahn spannen,* to cock a gun.

cockade, a knot of ribbon on a hat. (F.) F. *coquarde*, fem. of *coquard*, saucy; also *coquarde, bonnet à la coquarde,* ' any bonnet or cap worn proudly;' Cot. Formed with suffix -*ard* from F. *coq*, a cock (from the bird's cry).

cockerel, a young cock. (E.) Double dimin. of Cock (1). Cf. *pik-erel.*

cockloft, upper loft. (E. *and* Scand.) From *cock* and *loft.* So also G. *hahnbalken,* a roost, cockloft; Dan. *loftkammer,* a loft-chamber, room up in the rafters.

Cock (2), a pile of hay. (Scand.) Dan. *kok*, a heap; prov. Dan. *kok*, a hay-cock, *at kokke höet,* to cock hay; Icel. *kökkr*, lump, ball; Swed. *koka*, clod of earth.

Cock (3), to stick up abruptly. (E.) Apparently with reference to the posture of a *cock's* head when crowing; or to that of his crest or tail. Cf. Gael. *coc*, to cock; as in *coc do bhoineid*, cock your bonnet; *coc-shronach*, cock-nosed. And see **Cockade.**

Cock (4), **Cockboat,** a small boat. (F. — L. — Gk.) O. F. *coque*, a kind of boat, orig. a shell. Cf. Span. *coca*, Ital. *cocca*, a small ship. Derived (by Diez) from L. *concha*, a shell; from Gk. κόγκη, a cockle; see **Cockle** (1).

Cockade; see Cock (1).

Cockatoo, a kind of parrot. (Malay.) Malay *kakatūa*; from the bird's cry. Cf. Malay *kukuk*, crowing of cocks. Skt. *kukkuṭa*, a cock. See Cock (1).

Cockatrice. (F. — Late L. — L.) By confusion with *cock*, it was said to be a monster hatched from a cock's egg. — O. F. *cocatrice.* — Late L. *cōcātrīcem,* acc. of *cōcātrix, caucātrix,* answering to a Latin type **calcātrix,* i. e. ' the treader or tracker,' used to render the Gk. ἰχνεύμων, and afterwards transferred to mean ' crocodile ' (see account in N. E. D.). — L. *calcā-re,* to

tread; with fem. suffix -*trix*, of the agent.

Cocker, to pamper. (E. ?) M. E. *cokeren* (whence W. *cocri*, to fondle, indulge). Cf. M. Du. *kokelen, keukelen,* ' to cocker, to foster,' Hexham; M. F. *coqueliner,* ' to dandle, cocker, pamper (a child);' Cot. Norw. *kokra*, to call as a cock; also, to cocker.

Cockerel; see Cock (1).

Cockle (1), a sort of bivalve. (F. — L. — Gk.) M. E. *cokel.* [Cf. *cock*, a cockle (P. Plowman, C. x. 95); A. S. *sǣ-cocca*; (where *sǣ* =sea).] — F. *coquille*, a cockleshell; cf. Ital. *cochiglia.* — Lat. type **cochylium,* for *conchylium,* a cockle, shell-fish. — Gk. κογχύλιον, a cockle, dimin. of κογκύλη, from κόγκη, a cockle or mussel.

Cockle (2), a weed among corn. (E.) A. S. *coccel*, tares; whence Gael. *cogall,* tares, husks, cockle; *cogull*, corn-cockle; Irish *cogall*, corn-cockle.

Cockle (3), to be uneven, pucker up. (Scand.) Of Scand. origin; cf. Norw. *koklutt*, lumpy, uneven, ' cockled up;' from Norw. *kokle*, a little lump, dimin. of *kok*, a lump; see Cock (2). Cf. Swed. *kokkel*, dimin. of *koka*, a clod.

Cockloft; see Cock (1).

Cockney, orig. an effeminate person. (E.) Florio has: ' *Caccherelli*, cacklings of hens; also egs, as we say *cockanegs.*' From M. E. *cokenay*, a foolish person, Ch. C. T. 4208. Lit. ' cocks' egg;' i.e. yolk-less egg. From M. E. *coken*, gen. pl. of *cok*, a cock; and *ay, ey,* A. S. *æg*, egg. See C. S. Burne, Shropshire Folk-lore, p. 229.

Cockroach. (Span.) From Span. *cucaracha*, a wood-louse, cockroach; from *cuca* (also *cuco*), a kind of caterpillar. Origin uncertain.

Cocoa (1), **Coco,** the cocoa-nut palm. (Port.) Port. and Span. *coco*, a bugbear, an ugly mask to frighten children; hence applied to the cocoa-nut on account of the monkey-like face at the base of the nut. Cf. Span. *cocar*, to make grimaces.

Cocoa (2), a corrupt form of Cacao.

Cocoon, case of a chrysalis. (F. — L. — Gk.) F. *cocon*, a cocoon; from *coque*, a shell. See Cock (4).

Cod (1), a fish. (E. ?) Spelt *codde* in Palsgrave. Perhaps named from its rounded shape; cf. M. Du. *kodde*, a club (Hexham); and see below. **Der.** *cod-ling,* a young cod; M. E. *codlyng.*

Cod (2), a husk, bag, bolster. (E.) Hence, *peas-cod*, husk of a pea. A. S. *codd*, a bag.+Icel. *koddi*, pillow, *koðri*, scrotum; Swed. *kudde*, a cushion.

Coddle, to pamper, render effeminate. (F. – L.?) Perhaps for *caudle*, vb. (in Shak.), to treat with *caudle* ; see Caudle. Cf. prov. E. *coddle*, to parboil, stew.

Code, a digest of laws. (F. – L.) F. *code*. – L. *cōdicem*, acc. of *cōdex*, a tablet, book; older form *caudex*, a trunk of a tree.

codicil. (L.) L. *cōdicillus*, a codicil to a will; dimin. of *cōdex* (stem *cōdic*-).

Codling (1), **Codlin**, a kind of apple. (C. ?) Earlier spellings *querdling*, *quadling*, *quodling*. Apparently formed, with E. suffix -*ling*, from Irish *cueirt*, an apple-tree.

Codling (2); see Cod (1).

Coerce. (L.) L. *coercēre*, to compel. – L. *co-*(*cum*), together ; *arcēre*, to en-close, confine, allied to *arca*, a chest ; see Ark.

Coffee. (Turk. – Arab.) Turk. *qah-veh.* – Arab. *qahwah*, coffee.

Coffer. (F. – L. – Gk.) M. E. *cofre*. – O. F. *cofre*, also *cofin*, a chest. – L. acc. *cophinum*. – Gk. κόφινος, a basket.

coffin. (F. – L. – Gk.) Orig. a case, chest. – O. F. *cofin*, as above. (Doublet of *coffer*.)

Cog (1), a tooth on a wheel-rim. (Scand.) M. E. *cogge* [whence Gael. and Irish *cog*, a mill-cog ; W. *cocos*, *cocs*, cogs of a wheel]. Not in A. S. – M. Dan. *kogge*, a cog, *kogge-hjul*, a cog-wheel (Kalkar) ; Swed. *kugge*, a cog ; M. Swed. *kugg* (Ihre).

Cog (2), to trick. (Scand.) Prob. to catch as with a *cog* ; to *cog* a die, to check it so as to make it fall as desired. Cf. Swed. dial. *kugg*, Norw. *kogga*, to dupe; Swed. *kugga*, 'to cheat, to cog ;' Öman.

Cogent. (L.) L. *cōgent*-, stem of pres. part. of *cōgere*, to compel ; for *co-agere* (=*con-agere*), lit. to drive to-gether. Brugm. i. § 968.

Cogitate. (L.) L. *cōgitātus*, pp. of *cōgitāre*, to think ; for *co-agitāre*, from *co-*, *con-*, together, and *agitāre*, to agitate, frequent. of *agere*, to drive.

Cognate. (L.) L. *co-gnātus*, allied by birth. – L. *co-* (for *cum*), together ; *gnātus*, born, old form of *nātus*, pp. of *nasci*, to be born; see Natal.

Cognisance, knowledge, a badge. (F. – L.) Formerly *conisaunce.* – O. F. *con-noissance*, knowledge ; M. F. *cognoissance*. – O. F. *conoissant*, pres. pt. of O. F. *conoistre*, to know. – L. *cognoscere*, to know. – L. *co-* (*cum*), together, fully; *gnoscere*, to know ; see Know.

cognition, perception. (L.) From acc. of L. *cognitio.* – L. *cognitus*, pp. of *cognoscere* (above).

cognomen, a surname. (L.) L. *co-gnōmen*, a surname. – L. *co-* (*cum*), with ; *nōmen*, a name, altered to *gnōmen* by con-fusion with *gnoscere*, *noscere*, to know. See Noun, Name.

Cohabit. (L.) L. *co-habitāre*, to dwell together with. – L. *co-* (*cum*-), to-gether ; *habitāre*, to dwell. See Habi-tation.

Cohere. (L.) L. *co-hærēre*, to stick together (pp. *cohæsus*). – L. *co-*, together ; *hærēre*, to stick. **Der.** *cohes-ion*, *cohes-ive*, from the pp.

Cohort, a band of soldiers. (F. – L.) F. *cohorte.* – L. acc. *cohortem*, from *cohors*, a court, also a band of soldiers. See Court, of which it is a doublet.

Coif, Quoif, a cap. (F. – G. – L.) O. F. *coife*, *coiffe* ; Low L. *cofea*, a cap. – M. H. G. *kuffe*, *kupfe*, a cap worn under the helmet ; O. H. G. *chuppha* ; stem *kupp-jōn-.* – O. H. G. *chuph* (G. *kopf*), a cup; also, the head. – L. *cuppa* ; see Cup.

Coign ; see Coin.

Coil (1), to gather together. (F. – L.) 'Coiled up in a cable ;' Beaumont and Fletcher. – O. F. *coillir*, to collect. – L. *colligere* ; see Collect.

Coil (2), a noise, bustle. (F. – L.?) Orig. a colloquial or slang expression ; prob. from Coil (1). We find 'a *coil* of hay,' a heap; and *coil*, to twist.

Coin. (F. – L.) M. E. *coin.* – O. F. *coin*, a wedge, stamp on a coin, a coin (stamped by means of a wedge). – L. *cuneum*, acc. of *cuneus*, a wedge. ¶ Not allied to Cone.

coign. (F. – L.) F. *coing*, *coin*, a corner ; lit. a wedge (as above).

Coincide, to agree with. (L.) L. *co-* (for *con-*=*cum*, with) ; and *incidere*, to fall upon, from *in*, upon, and *cadere*, to fall.

Coistrel, a mean fellow. (F. – L.) For *coustrel*, the older form (Palsgrave). An E. adaptation of M. F. *coustillier*, an armour-bearer, lackey ; lit. 'one who carries a poinard.' — M. F. *coustille*, a poniard; variant of O. F. *coustel*, better *coutel*, a knife. — L. *cultellum*, acc. of *cultellus*, a knife; dimin. of *culter*. See Coulter.

Coit; see Quoit.

Coke, charred coal. (E. ?) ' *Coke*, pit-coal or sea-coal charred;' Ray, 1674. Etym. unknown; cf. M. E. *colk*, the core (of an apple).

Colander, Cullender, a strainer. (Prov. — L.) M. E. *colyndore*. — O. Prov. *colador*, orig. form of Prov. *couladou*, a strainer. — Late L. *cōlātōrem*, acc.; for L. *cōlātōrium*, a strainer. — L. *cōlāre*, to strain. — L. *cōlum*, a sieve. Cf. Span. *colador*, a strainer from L. *cōlāre*).

Cold. (E.) M. E. *cold*, *kald*, adj.; O. Merc. *cald*, A. S. *ceald*, adj. + Icel. *kaldr*, Swed. *kall*, Dan. *kold*, Du. *koud*, Goth. *kalds*, G. *kalt*. Teut. **kal-doz*, cold; from Teut. **kal*, to be cold (as in Icel. *kala*, to freeze), with suffix -*doz* = Gk. -*τόs*. Cf. Lat. *gel-idus*, cold; see Congeal, Chill, Cool.

Cole, Colewort, cabbage. (L.) For -*wort*, see Wort. M. E. *col*, *caul*. A. S. *caul*, *cāwel* (or Icel. *kāl*). — L. *caulis*, a stalk, cabbage. + Gk. καυλόs, a stalk.

Coleoptera, sheath - winged insects. (Gk.) Gk. κολεό-s, a sheath; πτερ-όν, a wing.

Colic. (F. — L. — Gk.) Short for *colic pain*. — F. *colique*, adj. — L. *cōlicus*. — Gk. κωλικόs, for κολικόs, suffering in the colon. — Gk. κόλον. See Colon (2).

Coliseum. (Med. L. — Gk.) The same as *colosseum*, a large amphitheatre at Rome, so named from its magnitude (Gibbon). The Ital. word is *coliseo*. See Colossus.

Collapse, to shrink together, fall in. (L.) First used in the pp. *collapsed* Englished from L. *collapsus*, pp. of *collābī*, to fall together. — L. *col-* (for *con-*, i. e. *cum*), together; *lābī*, to slip. See Lapse.

Collar. (F. — L.) M. E. and A. F. *coler*. — O. F. *colier*, a collar. — L. *collāre*, a band for the neck. — L. *collum*, the neck. + A. S. *heals*, G. *hals*, the neck.

collet, the part of the ring in which the stone is set. (F. — L.) F. *collet*, a collar. — F. *col*, neck. — L. *collum*, neck.

Collateral. (L.) Late L. *collaterālis*, side by side. — L. *col-* (for *com-* = *cum*), with; *laterālis*, lateral, from *later-*, for **lates-*, stem of *latus*, side.

Collation, a comparison; formerly, a conference. (F. — L.) O. F. *collation*, a conference. — L. acc. *collātiōnem*, a bringing together, a conferring. — L. *collātum*, supine in use with the verb *conferre*, to bring together (but from a different root). — L. *col-* (for *con-* = *cum*), together; *lātum*, supine of *tollere*, to take, bear. See Tolerate.

Colleague (1), a partner. (F. — L.) M. F. *collegue*. — L. *collēga*, a partner in office. — F. *col-* (for *con-*, *cum*), with; *legere*, to choose; see Legend.

Colleague (2), to join in an alliance. (F. — L.) O. F. *colliguer*, *colleguer*, to colleague with. — L. *colligāre*, to bind together. — L. *col-* (for *con-*, *cum*), together; *ligāre*, to bind. See League (1).

Collect, vb. (F. — L.) O. F. *collecter*, to collect money (Roquefort). — Late L. *collectāre* (the same), from *collecta*, a collection, orig. fem. of pp. of *colligere*, to collect. — L. *col-* (for *con-*, *cum*), with; *legere*, to gather; see Legend.

collect, sb. (L.) Late L. *collecta*, a collection in money, an assembly for prayer, hence a short prayer; see above.

Colleen, a girl. (Irish.) Irish *cailin*, a girl; dimin. of *caile*, a country-woman. Gael. *cailin*, dimin. of *caile*.

College, an assembly, seminary. (F. — L.) O. F. *college*. — L. *collēgium*, society of colleagues or companions. — L. *collēga*, a colleague; see Colleague (1).

Collet; see Collar.

Collide. (L.) L. *collīdere*, to dash together. — L. *col-* (for *con-*, *cum*), together; *lædere*, to strike, hurt. Der. *collis-ion* (from pp. *collīs-us*).

Collie, Colly, a kind of shepherd's dog. (E.) Formerly, *coally*, *coley*; prob. the same as *coal-y*, coal-coloured, black. Cf. obs. *colly*, adj., coal-black; *collied* in Shak. M. N. D. i. 1. 145.

Collier. (E.) M. E. *colier*; from M.E. *col*, coal. Cf. *bow-yer*, *saw-yer*.

Collocate, to place together. (L.) From pp. of L. *col-locāre*, to place together. — L. *col-* (for *con-*, *cum*), together; *locāre*, to place, from *locus*, a place.

Collodion, a solution of gun-cotton. (Gk.) From Gk. κολλώδ-ηs, glue-like. — Gk. κόλλ-a, glue; -ειδηs, like, εἶδοs, appearance.

Collop, a slice of meat. (E. ?) M. E. *coloppe*, *col-hoppe*; pl. *col-hoppes* (P. Plowman), whence M. Swed. *kollops*, Swed. *kalops*. Here *col-* = coal (see Coal); cf.

Swed. dial. *glö(d)hoppa*, a cake baked over gledes or hot coals. (E. Björkman).

Colloquy. (L.) From L. *colloquium*, conversation. — L. *col-loquī*, to converse with, lit. to speak together. — L. *col-* (for *con-*, *cum*), together; *loquī*, to speak.

Collude, to act with others in a fraud. (L.) L. *collūdere* (pp. *collūsus*), to play with, act in collusion with. — L. *col-* (for *con-*, *cum*), with; *lūdere*, to play. Der. *collus-ion*, from the pp.

Colocynth, Coloquintida, pith of the fruit of a kind of cucumber. (Gk.) From the nom. and acc. cases of Gk. κολοκυνθίς (acc. κολοκυνθίδα), a kind of round gourd or pumpkin.

Colon (1), a mark (:) in writing and printing. (Gk.) Gk. κῶλον, a limb, clause; hence, a stop marking off a clause.

Colon (2), part of the intestines. (Gk.) Gk. κόλον, the same.

Colonel. (F.—Ital.—L.) Sometimes *coronel*, which is the Span. spelling; whence the pronunciation as *kurnel.* — F. *colonel, colonnel.* — Ital. *colonello*, a colonel; lit. a little column, as being 'the upholder of the regiment;' Torriano. The colonel was he who led the company at the head of the regiment. Dimin. of Ital. *colonna*, a column. — L. *columna*, a column. See **Column.**

colonnade. (F. — Ital. — L.) F. *colonnade.* — Ital. *colonnata*, a range of columns. — Ital. *colonna*, a column (above).

Colony. (F. — L.) F. *colonie.* — L. *colōnia*, a colony, band of husbandmen. — L. *colōnus*, a husbandman. — L. *colere*, to till. *Colere* is for **quelere*; cf. L. *inquilīnus*, a sojourner. Brugm. i. § 121.

Colophon, an inscription at the end of a book, with title, and (sometimes) name and date. (Gk.) Late L. *colophōn.* — Gk. κολοφών, a summit; hence, a finishing-stroke. Allied to **Column.**

Coloquintida; see **Colocynth.**

Colossus. (L.—Gk.) L. *colossus.* — Gk. κολοσσός, a large statue. Der. *coloss-al*, i.e. large; *coliseum*, q. v.

Colour. (F.—L.) M.E. *colour.* — O.F. *colour* (F. *couleur*). — L. acc. *colōrem*, from *color*, a tint.

Colporteur, a hawker of wares. (F.—L.) Lit. 'one who carries wares on his neck;' F. *colporteur.* — F. *colporter*, to carry on the neck. — F. *col*, neck; *porter*, to carry. — L. *collum*, neck; *portāre*, to carry.

Colt. (E.) A.S. *colt*, a young camel, young ass, &c.+Swed. dial. *kullt*, a boy; Swed. *kull*, Dan. *kuld*, a brood; cf. Dan. dial. *koltring*, a lad.

Columbine, a plant. (F.—L.) M.F. *colombin.* — Late L. *columbīna*, a columbine; L. *columbīnus*, dove-like; from a supposed resemblance. — L. *columba*, a dove. See **Culver.**

Column, a pillar, body of troops. (F. — L.) L. *columna*, a pillar; cf. *columen, culmen,* a summit, *collis,* a hill; Gk. κολωνός, a hill. See **Hill.** (√QEL.)

Colure, one of two great circles on the celestial sphere, at right angles to the equator. (L. — Gk.) So called because a part of them is always beneath the horizon. The word means docked, clipped. — L. *colūrus*, curtailed; a colure. — Gk. κόλουρος, dock-tailed, truncated; a colure. — Gk. κόλ-os, docked, clipped; and οὐρά, a tail.

Colza oil, a lamp-oil made from the seeds of a variety of cabbage. (F.—L. *and* Du.) F. *colza*, better *colzat.* — Du. *koolzaad*, rape-seed, cabbage-seed. — Du. *kool* (borrowed from L. *caulis*), cole, cabbage; and Du. *zaad* = E. *seed*.

Com-, prefix. (L.) For L. *cum*, with, together; when followed by *b, f, m, p.* See **Con-.**

Coma. (Gk.) Gk. κῶμα, a deep sleep.

Comb. (E.) A.S. *camb*, a comb, crest, ridge.+Du. *kam*, Icel. *kambr*, Dan. Swed. *kam*; G. *kamm*. Teut. type **kamboz*; Idg. type **gombhos*; cf. Gk. γόμφος, a pin, peg; Skt. *jambha-s*, a tooth.

Comb, Coomb, a dry measure. (E.) A.S. *cumb*, a cup.+Du. *kom*, a bowl; G. *kumpf, kumme*, a bowl.

Combat. (F.—L.) Orig. a verb. — F. *combattre*, O.F. *combatre*, to fight with. — F. *com-* (for L. *cum*), with; and F. *battre*, O.F. *batre*, to fight, from **battere*, for L. *battuere*, to beat. Der. *combat-ant*, from the F. pres. pt.

Combe, a hollow in a hill-side. (C.) W. *cwm*, Corn. *cum*, a hollow, dale; Celtic type **kumbā*, a valley; cf. Irish *cumar*, a valley.

Combine. (L.) L. *combīnāre*, to unite, join two things together. — L. *com-* (*cum*), together; and *bīnus*, twofold. See **Binary.**

Combustion. (F.—L.) F. *combustion.* — L. acc. *combustiōnem*, a burning up. — L. *combust-us*, pp. of *com-būrere*, to burn up. — L. *com-* (for *cum*), together; and (perhaps) *ūrere*, to burn, with *b* inserted by association with *amb-ūrere*.

Come. (E.) A. S. *cuman*, pt. t. *c(w)ōm*, pp. *cumen.*+Du. *komen*, Icel. *koma*, Dan. *komme*, Sw. *komma*, Goth. *kwiman*, G. *kommen*; L. *uen-īre*, (**guen-īre*), Gk. βαίνειν, Skt. *gam*, to go. (✓GwEM.)

Comedy. (F.−L.−Gk.) O.F. *comedie*, ' a play ; ' Cot.−L. *cōmædia.*−Gk. κωμῳδία, a comedy. − Gk. κωμῳδός, a comic actor. − Gk. κῶμο-s, a banquet, revel, festal procession ; ἀοιδός, a singer, from ἀείδειν, to sing. A comedy was a festive spectacle, with singing, &c. See **Ode**.

    comic. (L.−Gk.) L. *cōmicus.*−Gk. κωμικός, belonging to a κῶμος, as above.

Comely. (E.) M. E. *comli, kumli.* A. S. *cymlic*, earlier form *cȳmlic*, beautiful, fair. The A. S. *cȳme*, exquisite, is closely allied to O. H. G. *cūmig*, weak, tender, and to O. H. G. *kūm*, with difficulty (G. *kaum*). The A. S *ȳ* was shortened before *ml*, and the M. E. *comli* was associated with M. E. *comen*, to come, and so gained the sense of 'becoming.' pleasing, decorous. Cf. M. E. *kime*, a weak person.

Comet. (L.−Gk.) Late A. S. *cometa.* −L. *comēta.*−Gk. κομήτης, long-haired ; a tailed star, comet. − Gk. κόμη, hair.+L. *coma*, hair. ¶ Also O. F. *comete*.

Comfit, sb., a sweatmeat. (F.−L.) Formerly *confit, confite.*−O. F. *confit*, lit. confected, prepared ; pp. of *confire.*−L. *confectum*, pp. of *conficere*, to prepare, put together.−L. *con-* (*cum*), together ; *facere*, to make. See **Confect**.

Comfort, vb. (F. − L.) M. E. *conforten*, later *comforten.*−O. F. *conforter*, to comfort.−Late L. *confortāre*, to strengthen. − L. *con-* (*cum*), together ; and *fort-is*, strong ; see **Force** (1).

Comfrey, a plant. (F. − L.) O. F. *confire, cumfirie* ; Late L. *cumfiria* ; probably for Lat. *conferua* (Pliny), comfrey, a name given to the plant from its supposed healing powers.−L. *conferuēre*, to grow together, heal up (Celsus).−L. *con-* (*cum*), together ; *feruēre*, (orig.) to boil. ¶ It was also called *confirma* (from L. *firmāre*, to make firm), and *consolida* (from L. *solidāre*, to make solid).

Comic ; see **Comedy**.

Comity, urbanity. (L.) L. *cōmitātem*, acc. of *cōmitās*, urbanity. − L. *cōmis*, friendly, courteous.

Comma. (L.−Gk.) L. *comma.*−Gk. κόμμα, that which is struck, a stamp, a clause of a sentence, a comma (that marks the clause).−Gk. κόπ-τειν, to hew, strike.

Command. (F. − L.) O. F. *commander, comander.* − L. *commendāre*, to entrust to ; confused with Late L. *commandāre*, as if an intensive form of *mandāre*, to command. Both forms are from L. *com-* (*cum*), together ; and *mandāre*, to put into the hands of, entrust to, command. See **Mandate**.

Commemorate. (L.) From the pp. of L. *commemorāre*, to call to mind.−L. *com-* (for *cum*), together ; *memorāre*, to mention, from *memor*, mindful.

Commence. (F. − L.) F. *commencer* ; O. F. *comencer* (with one *m* ; cf. Ital. *cominciare*). − L. *com-* (*cum*), together ; *initiāre*, to begin ; see **Initiate**.

Commend. (L.) L. *commendāre*, to entrust or commit to ; see **Command**.

Commensurate. (L.) From L. *commensūrātus*, as if from **commensūrāre*, to measure in comparison with ; a coined word.−L. *com-* (*cum*), with ; *mensūra*, measure ; see **Measure**.

Comment, vb. (F.−L.) F. *commenter.* −Late L. *commentāre*, for L. *commentārī*, to consider, make a note on.−L. *com-mentus*, pp. of *comminiscī*, to devise.−L. *com-* (*cum*), with ; *-min-* for **men*, to think, as in *me-min-ī* (=**me-men-ī*), I remember, and *men-s*, mind. See **Mental**.

Commerce, traffic. (F.−L.) F. *commerce.*−L. *commercium*, trade.−L. *com-* (=*cum*), with ; *merc*, stem of *merx*, merchandise, with suffix -*i-um*.

Commination, a threatening, denouncing. (F.−L.) F. *commination.*− L. acc. *comminātiōnem*, a threatening.− L. *comminātus*, pp. of *com-minari*, to threaten. − L. *com-* (*cum*), intensive prefix ; and *minārī*, to threaten. See **Menace**.

Commingle. (L. and E.) From **Com-** and **Mingle**.

Comminution, a reduction to small fragments. (L.) Formed from L. *com-minūt-us*, pp. of *com-minuere*, to break into small pieces ; see **Minute**.

Commiseration. (F.−L.) M. F. *commiseration.*−L. acc. *commiserātiōnem*, part of an oration intended to excite pity. −L. *commiserārī*, to excite pity (pp. -*āt-us*). − L. *com-* (*cum*), with ; *miserārī*, to pity, from L. *miser*, wretched, pitiable.

Commissary, an officer to whom something is entrusted. (L.) Med. L. *commissārius*, a commissary. − L. *com-*

missus, pp. of *committere*, to commit ; see below.

commit, to entrust to. (L.) L. *committere*, to send out, begin, entrust, consign ; pp. *commissus.* — L. *com-* (*cum*), with ; *mittere*, to send, put forth. **Der.** *commiss-ion*, F. *commission*, from L. acc. *commissiōnem*, perpetration.

Commodious. (F.–L.) O. F. *commodieux* ; Med. L. *commodiōsus*, useful. — L. *commodus*, fit, suitable. — L. *com-* (*cum*), with ; *modus*, measure.

Commodore, the commander of a squadron. (Du. — F. – L.) Formerly spelt *commandore* (1695) ; also *commandeur*, as in Dutch ; Hexham has : ' *den Commandeur van een Stadt*, The Commandeur of a Towne.' — F. *commandeur*, a commander. — L. acc. type *commandātōrem, from Late L. *commandāre* ; see **Command**.

Common. (F.–L.) M. E. *commun*, *comoun*. — O. F. *comun*. — L. *commūnis*, common, general. — L. *com-* (*cum*), together with ; and *mūnis*, ready to serve (Plautus) ; cf. *mūnus*, service. (As if ' helping each other.') Cf. Lith. *mainas*, Russ. *miena*, barter. Brugm. i. § 208. **Der.** *commun-ion*, *commun-ity*.

commune, verb. (F. – L.) M. E. *comunen.* — O. F. *communer*, to commune with ; Late L. *commūnāre.* — L. *commūnis*, common (above).

communicate. (L.) L. *commūnicātus*, pp. of *commūnicāre.* — L. *commūnis*, common. **Der.** *excommunicate*.

Commotion. (F.–L.) F. *commotion.* — L. *commōtiōnem*, acc. of *commōtio.* — L. *commōt-us*, pp. of *commouēre*, to disturb. — L. *com-* (*cum*), intensive ; and *mouēre*, to move. See **Move**.

Commute, to exchange. (L.) L. *commūtāre*, to exchange with. — L. *com-* (*cum*), with ; *mūtāre*, to change.

Compact (1), adj., fastened together, fitted, close, firm. (F.–L.) M. F. *compacte.* — L. *compactus*, fitted together, pp. of *compingere.* — L. *com-* (*cum*), together ; *pangere*, to fasten. See **Pact**.

Compact (2), sb., a bargain, agreement. (L.) L. *compactum*, sb. — L. *compactus*, pp. of *compaciscī*, to agree with. — L. *com-* (*cum*), with ; *paciscī*, to make a bargain, inceptive form of O. Lat. *pacere*, to agree. See **Pact**.

Company. (F.–L.) M. E. *companye.* — O. F. *companie*. [Cf. also O. F. *compain*,

a companion, O. F. *companion* (F. *compagnon*), a companion.] — Med. L. *compāniem*, acc. of *compāniēs*, a taking of meals together. — L. *com-* (*cum*), together ; and *pānis*, bread ; see **Pantry**. **Der.** *companion*, from O. F. *companion*. Also *accompany*, O. F. *accompaignier*, from F. *a* (for L. *ad*) and O. F. *compaignier*, to associate with, from *compaignie*, company.

Compare, to set together, so as to examine likeness or difference. (F.–L.) F. *comparer.* — L. *comparāre*, to adjust, set together. — L. *compar*, co-equal. — L. *com-* (*cum*), together ; *par*, equal.

Compartment. (F.–Ital.–L.) F. *compartiment*, ' a partition ;' Cot. — Ital. *compartimento.* — Ital. *compartire* ; Late L. *compartīre*, to share. — L. *com-* (*cum*), together ; *partīre*, to share, to part, from *parti-*, decl. stem of *pars*, a part.

Compass. (F. – L.) F. *compas*, a circuit, circle, limit ; also, a pair of compasses. — Late L. *compassus*, a circuit. — L. *com-* (*cum*), with ; *passus*, a pace, step, passage, track ; so that *compassus* = a track that joins together, circuit. See **Pace**. **Der.** *compass*, verb ; *compasses*, s. pl., an instrument for drawing circles.

Compassion. (F. – L.) F. *compassion.* — L. *compassiōnem*, acc. of *compassio*, sympathy. — L. *com-* (*cum*), with ; *passio*, suffering, from *patī*, to endure.

compatible. (F.–L.) F. *compatible*, ' compatible, concurrable ;' Cot. — Late L. *compatibilis*, adj., used of a benefice which could be held together with another. — L. *compatī*, to endure together with. — L. *com-* (*cum*), with ; *patī*, to endure.

Compeer, an associate. (F. – L.) M. E. *comper.* — F. *com-*, together ; O. F. *per*, a peer, equal. — L. *com-* (*cum*), together ; *parem*, acc. of *par*, equal ; see **Peer**.

Compel. (L.) L. *com-pellere*, to compel, lit. to drive together. — L. *com-* (*cum*), together ; *pellere*, to drive. **Der.** *compulsion*, from pp. *compuls-us*.

Compendious, brief. (F. – L.) F. *compendieux.* — L. *compendiōsus*, adj., from *compendium*, an abridgment, lit. a saving, sparing of expense. — L. *compendere*, to weigh together. — L. *com-* (*cum*), with ; *pendere*, to weigh.

compensate. (L.) From pp. of L. *compensāre*, to weigh one thing against another. — L. *com-* (*cum*), together ; *pen-*

sāre, to weigh, frequent. of *pendere*, to weigh (pp. *pensus*).

Compete. (L.) L. *competere*. – L. *com-* (*cum*), together; *petere*, to strive after.

competent. (F.–L.) M. F. *competent*; orig. pres. part. of *competer*, to be sufficient for. – L. *competere*, to be sufficient for. – L. *com-* (*cum*), with; *petere*, to seek.

competitor. (L.) L. *competītor*, a rival candidate. – L. *com-* (*cum*), with; *petītor*, a seeker, from *petītus*, pp. of *petere*, to seek.

Compile. (F.–L.) O. F. *compiler*. – L. *compīlāre*, lit. to press together. – L. *com-* (for *cum*), together; and *pīlāre*, to press down, from *pīlum*, a pestle. Cf. L. *pinsere*, to pound. See **Pile** (3).

Complacent. (L.) From stem of pres. pt. of *complacēre*, to please. – L. *com-* (*cum*), intensive; *placēre*, to please.

complaisant. (F. – L.) F. *complaisant*, obsequious, pres. part. of *complaire*, to please. – L. *complacēre*, to please (above).

Complain. (F. – L.) O. F. *complaign-*, a stem of *complaindre*. – Late L. *complangere*, to bewail. – L. *com-* (*cum*), with; *plangere*, to bewail, lit. to strike, beat the breast.

Complement. (L.) L. *complēmentum*, that which completes. – L. *complēre* (below). **Doublet,** *compliment*.

complete, perfect, (L.) L. *complētus*, pp. of *complēre*, to fulfil. – L. *com-* (*cum*), together; *plēre*, to fill. Allied to *plē-nus*, full. See **Plenary.**

Complex. (L.) L. *complexus*, entwined round; hence, intricate; pp. of *complectī*, to embrace. – L. *com* (*cum*), together; and *plectere*, to plait, allied to *plic-āre*, to twine. See **Pleach.**

complexion. (F. – L.) F. *complexion*, appearance. – L. *complexiōnem*, acc. of *complexio*, a comprehending, compass, habit of body, complexion. – L. *complexus*, pp. of *complectī*, to surround, entwine. – L. *com-* (*cum*), together; *plectere*, to plait.

complicate. (L.) From pp. of L. *complicāre*, to fold together. – L. *com-* (*cum*), together; *plicāre*, to fold.

complicity. (F.–L.) F. *complicité*, ' a bad confederacy; ' Cot. – F. *complice*, a confederate. – L. *complicem*, acc. of *complex*, interwoven, confederate with; see **Complex.**

Compliance, Compliant; formed with F. suffixes *-ance, -ant*, from the verb to *comply*, which, however, is not of F. origin; see **Comply.**

Compliment. (F. – Ital. – L.) F. *compliment*. – Ital. *complimento*, compliment, civility. – Ital. *complire*, to fill up, to suit. – L. *complēre*, to fill up; see **Complete. Doublet,** *complement*.

compline. (F.–L.) M. E. *complin*, the last church-service of the day; it was orig. an adj. (like *gold-en* from *gold*), and stands for *complin song*; the sb. is *complie* (Ancren Riwle). – O. F. *complie* (mod. F. *complies*, which is pl.), compline. – Late L. *complēta* (sc. *hōra*), fem. of *complētus*, complete; because it completed the 'hours' of the day's service; see **Complete.**

comply, to yield, accord with. (Ital. –L.) It has no doubt been supposed to be allied to *ply* (whence *compliant*, by analogy with *pliant*), but is quite distinct, and of Ital. origin. – Ital. *complire*, to fill up, fulfil, to suit, 'also to use compliments, ceremonies, or kind offices and offers;' Torriano. Cf. Span. *complir*, to fulfil, satisfy. – L. *complēre*, to fill up; see **Complete.** Cf. *supply.*

Complot, a conspiracy; see **Plot** (1).

Component, composing. (L.) L. *compōnent-*, stem of pres. pt. of *compōnere*, to compose. – L. *com-* (*cum*), together; *pōnere*, to put. See **Compound.**

Comport, to behave, suit. (F.–L.) F. *se comporter*, to behave. – L. *comportāre*, to carry together. – L. *com-* (*cum*), together; *portāre*, to carry.

Compose. (F. – L. and Gk.) F. *composer*, to compound, make; Cot. – F. *com-* (L. *cum*), together; and F. *poser*, to put, of Gk. origin, as shewn under **Pose,** q.v. ¶ Distinct from *compound.*

Composition. (F.–L.) F. *composition*. – L. acc. *compositiōnem*, acc. of *compositio*, a putting together. – L. *compositus*, pp. of L. *compōnere*; see **compound.**

compost, a mixture. (F.–L.) O. F. *compost*, a mixture. – L. *compositum*, neut. of *compositus*, pp. of *compōnere* (below).

compound. (F.–L.) The *d* is excrescent; M. E. *compounen*. – O. F. *com-ponre* (Bartsch). – L. *compōnere*, to compound, put together. – L. *com-* (*cum*), together; *pōnere*, to put. See **Component.**

Comprehend. (L.) L. *com-prehendere*, to grasp. – L. *com-* (*cum*), together, and *prehendere*, to seize; see **Prehensile.**

Compress. (L.) L. *compressāre*, to oppress. — L. *com-* (*cum*), together; *pressāre*, frequent. of *premere*, to press.

Comprise. (F. — L.) From O. F. *compris*, comprised, comprehended; pp. of *comprendre*, to comprehend. — L. *comprehendere*; see Comprehend.

Compromise, a settlement by concessions. (F. — L.) F. *compromis*, 'a compromise, mutual promise;' Cot. Orig. pp. of F. *compromettre*, 'to put unto compromise;' Cot. — L. *comprōmittere*, to make a mutual promise. — L. *com-* (*cum*), mutually; *prōmittere*, to promise; see Promise.

Comptroller, another spelling of *controller*; see Control.

Compulsion. (F. — L.) See Compel.

Compunction, remorse. (F. — L.) O. F. *compunction.* — Late L. acc. *compunctiōnem.* — L. *compunctus*, pp. of *compungī*, to feel remorse, pass. of *compungere*, to prick. — L. *com-* (*cum*); *pungere*, to prick.

Compute. (L.) L. *computāre*, to reckon. — L. *com-* (*cum*), together; *putāre*, to clear up, reckon. Doublet, *count* (2).

Comrade. (F. — Span. — L.) F. *camarade.* — Span. *camarada*, a company; also an associate, comrade. — Span. *camara*, a chamber, cabin. — L. *camera*, a chamber.

Con (1), to study, peruse, scan. (E.) M. E. *cunnen*; A. S. *cunnian*, to test. Allied to A. S. *cunnan*, to know; see Can (1). Der. *ale-conner*, i. e. ale-tester.

Con (2), short for *contra*, against. (L.) In the phrase ' pro and *con*.'

Con-, *prefix.* (L.) For *com-* (*cum*), with, when the following letter is *c, d, g, j, n, q, s, t,* or *v*. Before *b, m, p*, it is *com-*; before *l, col-*; before *r, cor-*; before *f, com-* or *con-*.

Concatenate. (L.) L. *concatēnātus*, pp. of *concatēnāre*, to link together. — L. *con-* (*cum*), together; *catēna*, a chain.

Concave. (F. — L.) F. *concave.* — L. *concauus*, hollow. — L. *con-* (*cum*), with, together; *cauus*, hollow.

Conceal. (F. — L.) O. F. *conceler.* — L. *concēlāre*, to hide. — L. *con-* (*cum*), completely; *cēlāre*, to hide. See Helm (2).

Concede. (L.) L. *concēdere*, to retire, yield. — L. *con-* (*cum*), together; *cēdere*, to yield. Der. *concess-ion* (from pp. *concessus*).

Conceit. (F. — L.) M. E. *conceit, conceite*. Formed as if from the pp. of O. F. *concevoir*, to conceive, though the real pp. was *conceu* (F. *conçu*); by analogy with *deceit*, q.v. See below.

conceive. (F. — L.) M. E. *conceven, conceiven.* — A. F. *conceiv-*, a stem of O. F. *concever, concevoir*, to conceive. — L. *cipere*, to conceive. — L. *con-* (*cum*), altogether; *capere*, to take.

conception. (F. — L.) F. *conception.* — L. *conceptiōnem.* — L. *concept-us*, pp. of *concipere*, to conceive (above).

Concentre, to draw to a centre. (F. — L. *and* Gk.) F. *concentrer.* — L. *con-* (*cum*), together; and *centr-um*, a centre, from Gk. κέντρον; see Centre. Der. *concentr-ic*, *concentr-ate* (modern).

Concern, vb. (F. — L.) F. *concerner.* — L. *concernere*, to mix; in Late Lat., to refer to, regard. — L. *con-* (*cum*), with; and *cernere*, to separate, decree, observe. ✛ Gk. κρίνειν, to separate, decide; Lith. *skir-ti*, to separate, distinguish. Brugm. ii. § 612. (✓SKER.)

concert. (F. — Ital. — L.) Often confused with *consort* in old writers. — F. *concerter*, 'to consort, or agree together;' Cot. — Ital. *concertare*, 'to agree or tune together, sing in consort,' Florio; cf. *concerto*, sb., agreement. The Ital. forms shew that it was derived from L. *concertāre*, to contend, struggle together; indeed, we find also Span. *concertar*, to settle or adjust, covenant, bargain; which also points to the same origin. [It would seem that the L. vb. took up the sense of to settle by debate, and so, to agree.] — L. *con-* (*cum*), together; *certāre*, to contend, vie with; orig. ' to decide by contest;' frequent. of *cernere*, to decide. See Concern. Der. *concert*, sb., *concert-ina*.

Concession. (F. — L.) F. *concession.* — L. acc. *concessiōnem.* — L. *concessus*, pp. of *concēdere*, to concede; see Concede.

Conch, a marine shell. (L. — Gk.) L. *concha.* — Gk. κόγχη (also κόγχος), a cockleshell. ✛ Skt. *çankha*, a conch. Der. *conchology* (from κόγχο-ς).

Conciliate. (L.) From the pp. of L. *conciliāre*, to bring together, conciliate. — L. *concilium*, a council; see Council.

Concise. (F. — L. ; *or* L.) F. *concis.* — L. *concīsus*, brief, cut short; pp. of *concīdere.* — L. *con-* (*cum*), intensive; *cædere*, to cut. Der. *concis-ion*.

Conclave. (F. — L.) F. *conclave*, a small room (to meet in). — L. *conclāue*, a room; later, a place of assembly of cardinals, assembly. Orig. a locked up place. — L. *con-* (*cum*), together; *clāuis*, a key.

Conclude. (L.) L. *conclūdere*, to shut up, close, end. — L. *con-* (*cum*), together; and *-clūdere* = *claudere*, to shut. Der. *conclus-ion*. Similarly *ex-clude*, *in-clude*, *pre-clude*, *se-clude*; whence *in-clus-ive*, *pre-clus-ion*, *se-clus-ion* (from pp. *-clūsus* = *clausus*).

Concoct. (L.) From L. *concoctus*, pp. of *concoquere*, to cook together, digest. — L. *con-* (*cum*); *coquere*, to cook.

Concomitant, accompanying. (L.) From L. *con-* (*cum*), together; and *comitant-em*, acc. of pres. pt. of *comitārī*, to accompany, from *comit-*, stem of *comes*, a companion; see Count (1).

Concord. (F. — L.) F. *concorde.* — L. *concordia*, agreement. — L. *concord-*, stem of *con-cors*, agreeing. — L. *con-* (*cum*); *cor* (stem *cord-*), the heart.

concordant. (F. — L.) F. *concord-ant*, pres. pt. of *concorder*, to agree. — L. *concordāre*, to agree. — L. *concord-* (above).

concordat. (F. — L.) F. *concordat*, an agreement. — Late L. *concordātum*, a convention, thing agreed on, esp. between the pope and F. kings; pp. of *concordāre*, to agree (above).

Concourse. (F. — L.) F. *concours.* — L. acc. *concursum*, a running together. — L. *concursus*, pp. of *con-currere*, to run together. — L. *con-* (*cum*), together; and *currere*, to run. See Concur.

Concrete, formed into one mass. (L.) L. *concrēt-us*, pp. of *concrescere*, to grow together. — L. *con-* (*cum*), together; *crescere*, to grow.

Concubine. (F. — L.) O. F. *concubine.* — L. *concubīna.* — L. *con-* (*cum*), together; *cubāre*, to lie.

Concupiscence. (F. — L.) F. *concupiscence.* — L. *concupiscentia*, desire. — L. *concupiscere*, to desire; inceptive form of *concupere*. — L. *con-* (*cum*), intensive; and *cupere*, to long for.

Concur. (L.) L. *concurrere*, to run together, agree. — L. *con-* (*cum*), together; *currere*, to run. Der. *concourse*.

Concussion. (F. — L.) F. *concussion.* — L. *concussiōnem*, acc. of *concussio*, a violent shaking. — L. *concussus*, pp. of *concutere*, to shake together. — L. *con-* (*cum*), together; *quatere*, to shake.

Condemn. (F. — L.) O. F. *condemner.* — L. *condemnāre*, to condemn wholly, pro-

nounce to be guilty. — L. *con-* (*cum*), wholly; *damnāre*, to condemn.

Condense. (F. — L.) F. *condenser.* — L. *condensāre.* — L. *condensus*, very thick. — L. *con-* (*cum*), very; *densus*, thick, dense.

Condescend. (F. — L.) F. *conde-scendre.* — Late L. *condēscendere*, to grant (lit. to descend with). — L. *con-* (*cum*), with; *dēscendere*, to descend; see Descend. Der. *condescens-ion*, from the pp.

Condign, well merited. (F. — L.) O. F. *condigne.* — L. *condignus*, very worthy. — L. *con-* (*cum*), very; *dignus*, worthy.

Condiment. (L.) L. *condīmentum*, seasoning, sauce. — L. *condīre*, to season, spice, preserve (as fruit).

Condition. (F. — L.) F. *condition.* — L. *conditiōnem*, acc. of *conditio*, a late spelling of *condicio*, a covenant, condition. — L. *condīcere*, to talk over together, agree upon. — L. *con-* (*cum*), together; *dīcere*, to speak.

Condole. (L.) L. *condolēre*, to grieve with. — L. *con-* (*cum*), with; *dolēre*, to grieve.

Condone. (L.) L. *condōnāre*, to remit, pardon. — L. *con-* (*cum*), wholly; *dōnāre*, to give; see Donation.

Condor, a large bird. (Span. — Peruvian.) Span. *condor.* — Peruv. *cuntur*, a condor.

Conduce. (L.) L. *condūcere*, to draw together towards, lead to. — L. *con-* (*cum*), together; *dūcere*, to lead.

conduct, sb. (L.) Late L. *conductus*, defence, protection, guard, escort. — L. *conductus*, pp. of *con-dūcere* (above).

conduit. (F. — L.) M. E. *conduit.* — O. F. *conduit*, a conduit. — Late L. *conductus*, a defence, escort; also, a canal, tube; see above.

Cone. (F. — L. — Gk.) M. F. *cone.* — L. *cōnus.* — Gk. κῶνος, a cone, peak, peg. + Skt. *çāṇa-s*, a whetstone; cf. L. *cōs*, the same. See Hone. Brugm. i. § 401.

Coney; see Cony.

Confabulate. (L.) From pp. of L. *confābulāri*, to talk together. — L. *con-* (*cum*), with; *fābulāri*, to converse, from *fābula*, a discourse; see Fable.

Confect, to make up into sweetmeats. (L.) L. *confectus*, pp. of *conficere*, to put together, make up. — L. *con-* (*cum*), together; *facere*, to put. Der. *confect-ion*, *confection-er*. See Comfit.

Confederate. (L.) L. *confœderātus*, united by a covenant, pp. of *confœderāre*.

— L. *con-* (*cum*), together; *fœder-*, for *fœdes*, stem of *fœdus*, a treaty. See Federal.

Confer. (L.) From L. *conferre*, to bring together, collect, bestow. — L. *con-* (*cum*), together; *ferre*, to bring, bear. ¶ Not from F.

Confess. (F. — L.) O. F. *confesser*. — Late L. *confessāre*. — L. *confessus*, pp. of *confitēri*, to confess. — L. *con-* (*cum*), fully; *fatēri*, to acknowledge, allied to *fāri*, to speak. Cf. Gk. φάτις, a speech. Brugm. i. § 195.

Confide. (L.) L. *confīdere*, to trust fully. — L. *con-* (*cum*), fully; *fīdere*, to trust, allied to *fides*, faith; see Faith.

Configuration. (F. — L.) F. *configuration*. — L. *configurātiōnem*, a conformation. — L. *configūrātus*, pp. of *configūrāre*, to put together. — L. *con-* (*cum*); *figūrāre*, to fashion, from *figūra*, a figure. See Figure.

Confine, to limit. (F. — L.) F. *confiner*, to keep within limits. — M. F. *confin*, near; Cot. — L. *confinis*, bordering on. — L. *con-* (*cum*), with; *finis*, boundary. See Final. ¶ Mod. F. has only *confins*, sb. pl., confines; representing O. F. *confines*, L. *confinia*, pl.; whence E. *confines*, pl.

Confirm. (F. — L.) M. E. *confermen*. — O. F. *confermer*. — L. *confirmāre*, to make firm, strengthen. — L. *con-* (*cum*), fully: *firmāre*, to strengthen, from *firmus*, firm.

Confiscate, to adjudge to be forfeit. (L.) L. *confiscātus*, pp. of *confiscāre*, to lay by in a coffer, to confiscate, transfer to the treasury. — L. *con-* (*cum*); *fiscus*, a purse.

Conflagration. (F. — L.) F. *conflagration*. — L. acc. *conflāgrātiōnem*, a great burning. — L. *con-* (*cum*), together; *flāgrāre*, to burn. See Flagrant.

Conflict, an encounter. (L.) L. *conflictus*, a striking together; from the pp. of *conflīgere*, to strike together. — L. *con-* (*cum*), together; *flīgere*, to strike.

Confluent. (L.) From stem. of pres. pt. of *con-fluere*, to flow together; see Fluent. So also *conflux*, sb., from the pp. *confluxus*.

Conform. (F. — L.) F. *conformer*. — L. *conformāre*, to fashion like. — L. *con-*, together; *formāre*, to form, from *forma*, form.

Confound. (F. — L.) F. *confondre*. —

L. *confundere*, to pour together, confound. — L. *con-* (*cum*), together; *fundere*, to pour. See Fuse (1).

Confraternity. (F. — L.) From L. *con-* (*cum*), with; and Fraternity, q.v.

Confront. (F. — L.) F. *confronter*, to bring face to face. — Med. L. *confrontāri*, to be near to. — L. *con-* (*cum*), together; *front-*, stem of *frons*, forehead, front.

Confuse. (L.) M. E. *confus*, used as a pp. in Chaucer. — L. *confūsus*, pp. of *confundere*, to confound; see Confound.

Confute. (F. — L.) F. *confuter*. — L. *confūtāre*, to repress, also to confute. — L. *con-* (*cum*), together; *futāre*, to repress, beat back; probably from the same root as A. S. *bēatan*, to beat (Walde). If so, it is not allied to L. *fūtilis*.

Congeal. (F. — L.) F. *congeler*. — L. *congelāre*, to cause to freeze together. — L. *con-*, together; *gelāre*, to freeze, from *gelu*, frost. See Gelid.

Congee, Congé, leave to depart. (F. — L.) F. *congé*, 'leave, dismission;' Cot. O. F. *congie*, *cunge*, *congiet* (Burguy); the same as Prov. *comjat*. — Late L. *comiātus*, leave, permission (VIII cent.); the same as L. *commeātus*, a travelling together, also leave of absence. — L. *com-* (*cum*), together; *meātus*, a course, from pp. of *meāre*, to go.

Congenial, kindred. (L.) Coined from L. *con-* (*cum*), with; and *genial*, adj. from L. *genius*; see Genial.

Congenital. (L.) Coined by adding *-al* to the obs. word *congenite* (XVII cent.). — L. *congenitus*, born with. — L. *con-* (*cum*), with; *genitus*, born, pp. of *gignere*, to produce. See Genital.

Conger, a sea-eel. (F. — L. — Gk.) M. E. *congre*. — O. F. *congre*. — L. *congrum*, acc. of *congrus*, by-form of *conger*, a sea-eel. — Gk. γόγγρος, the same.

Congeries, a mass of particles. (L.) L. *congeriēs*, a heap. — L. *congerere*, to bring together. — L. *con-* (*cum*), together; *gerere*, to carry.

congestion, accumulation. (L.) From L. acc. *congestiōnem*. — L. *congestus*, pp. of *congerere* (above).

Conglobe, to form into a globe. (L.) L. *con-globāre*. — L. *con-* (*cum*), together; *globus*, a globe.

Conglomerate. (L.) From pp. of *conglomerāre*, to wind into a ball, heap together. — L. *con-* (*cum*), together; and *glomer-*, for **glomes-*, stem of *glomus*, a ball, clew of yarn.

Conglutinate. (L.) From pp. of L. *conglūtināre*, to glue together. — L. *con-* (*cum*), together; *glūtināre*, to glue, from *glūtin-*, stem of *glūten*, glue.

Congou, a kind of tea. (Chinese.) In the Amoy dialect, called *kang-hu tê*, where *kang-hu* is lit. 'work, labour;' i. e. tea on which labour has been expended (Douglas). The true Chinese is *kung-fu ch'a*, with the same sense.

Congratulate. (L.) From pp. of L. *congrātulārī*, to wish much joy. — L. *con-* (*cum*), fully; *grātulārī*, to wish joy, from adj. *grātus*, pleasing. See **Grace**.

Congregate. (L.) From pp. of L. *congregāre*, to collect into a flock. — L. *con-* (*cum*), together; *gregāre*, to assemble a flock, from *greg-*, stem of *grex*, a flock.

Congress, a meeting together. (L.) L. *congressus*. — L. *congressus*, pp. of *congredī*, to meet together. — L. *con-*, together; *gradī*, to advance, walk.

Congrue, to agree, suit. (L.) L. *congruere*, to suit. (Root uncertain.) **Der.** *congru-ous*, from L. *congruus*, suitable; *congru-ity*.

Conjecture. (F.—L.) F. *conjecture*. — L. *coniectūra*, a casting together, a guess. — L. *coniectus*, pp. of *conicere*, to throw or put together. — L. *con-* (*cum*), together; *iacere*, to throw.

Conjoin. (F.—L.) O. F. *conjoindre*. L. *coniungere* (pp. *coniunctus*), to join together. — L. *con-* (*cum*), together; *iungere*, to join. See **Join**. **Der.** *conjunction*, *conjunct-ive*, from the pp.

conjugal, relating to marriage. (F. L.) F. *conjugal*. — L. *coniugālis*, adj. — L. *coniugem*, acc. of *coniux*, a spouse. — L. *con-*, together; *iug-*, allied to *iungere*, to join, *iugum*, a yoke; see **Join**.

conjugation. (L.) From L. *coniugātio*, a conjugation (Priscian); lit. a yoking together. — L. *coniugātus*, pp. of *coniugāre*, to yoke together. — L. *con-* (*cum*), together; *iug-um*, a yoke.

Conjure. (F.—L.) M. E. *coniuren*. — F. *conjurer*. — L. *coniūrāre*, to swear together, combine by oath. — L. *con-*, together; *iūrāre*, to swear; see **Jury**.

Connect. (L.) L. *connectere*, to tie together. — L. *con-* (*cum*), together; and *nectere*, to bind (pp. *nexus*). **Der.** *connex-ion* [not *connection*], from the pp.

Connive. (F.—L.) F. *conniver*. — L. *connīuēre*, to close the eyes at, overlook. — L. *con-* (*cum*), together; and *nīguere, to wink; cf. *nic-tāre*, to wink. + Goth. *hneiwan*, to bow; Brugm. i. § 664.

Connoisseur, a critical judge. (F.— L.) F. *connaisseur*, formerly *connoisseur*, a knowing one. — O. F. *connoiss-ant*, pres. pt. of O. F. *conoistre*; see **Cognisance**.

Connubial. (L.) L. *connūbiālis*, relating to marriage. — L. *co*(*n*)*nūbium*, marriage. — L. *con-* (*cum*), with; *nūbere*, to marry. See **Nuptial**.

Conquer. (F.—L.) M. E. *conqueren*. — O. F. *conquerre*. — L. *conquīrere*, to seek after, go in quest of; in Late L., to conquer. — L. *con-* (*cum*), with; *quaerere*, to seek. **Der.** *conquest*, M. E. *conqueste*, from Late L. *conquesta*, L. *conquīsīta*, fem. of *conquīsītus*, pp. of *conquīrere*.

Consanguineous. (L.) From L. *consanguine-us*, related by blood, with suffix *-ous*. — L. *con-* (*cum*), together; *sanguin-*, stem of *sanguis*, blood.

Conscience. (F.—L.) F. *conscience*. L. *conscientia*, consciousness. — L. *conscient-*, stem of pres. pt. of *conscīre*, to know along with. — L. *con-* (*cum*), with; *scīre*, to know. See **Science**. **Der.** *conscionable*, an ill-contrived word, used as a contraction of *conscien*(*ce*)-*able*.

conscious. (L.) From L. *consci-us*, aware, with suffix *-ous*. — L. *conscīre*, to be aware of (above).

Conscript. (L.) L. *conscriptus*, enrolled, pp. of *conscrībere*, to write down together. — L. *con-* (*cum*), together; *scrībere*, to write.

Consecrate. (L.) From pp. of L. *consecrāre*, to render sacred. — L. *con-* (*cum*), with, wholly; *sacrāre*, to consecrate; see **Sacred**.

Consecutive. (F.—L.) M.F. *consecutif*, Cot. Formed with suffix *-if* (L. *-īuus*) from L. *consecūt-us*, pp. of *consequī*, to follow together. — L. *con-* (*cum*), together; *sequī*, to follow. See **Sequence**.

consequent. (L.) L. *consequent-*, stem of pres. pt. of *consequī* (above).

Consent, vb. (F.—L.) F. *consentir*. — L. *consentīre*, to agree to. — L. *con-* (*cum*), with; *sentīre*, to feel. See **Sense**.

Conserve, vb. (F.—L.) F. *conserver*. — L. *conseruāre*, to preserve. — L. *con-* (*cum*), fully; *seruāre*, to keep. **Der.** *conserve*, vb.; *conserv-atory*. See **Serve**.

Consider. (F.—L.) O. F. *considerer*.

—L. *consīderāre*, to consider, orig. to contemplate the stars (Festus). — L. *con-* (*cum*), together; *sīder-*, for **sīdes-*, stem of *sīdus*, a star.

Consign. (F. — L.) F. *consigner.* — L. *consignāre*, to attest, register, record. — L. *con-* (*cum*), together; *signāre*, to mark; see **Sign**.

Consist. (F. — L.) F. *consister*, to consist, rest, abide, &c. — L. *consistere*, to stand together, consist. — L. *con-* (*cum*), together; *sistere*, causal form from *stāre*, to stand; see **State**. **Der.** *consistory*.

Console. (F. — L.) F. *consoler.* — L. *consōlārī*, to comfort. — L. *con-* (*cum*), with; *sōlārī*, to comfort; see **Solace**.

Consolidate. (L.) From pp. of L. *consolidāre*, to render solid. — L. *con-* (*cum*), together; *solidāre*, to make solid, from *solidus*, solid. **Der.** *consols*, a familiar abbreviation for *consolidated annuities*.

Consonant, agreeing with. (F. — L.) F. *consonant*, accordant; Cot. — L. *consonant-*, stem of pres. pt. of *consonāre*, to sound together. — L. *con-* (*cum*), together; *sonāre*, to sound; see **Sound** (3).

Consort, sb. (F. — L.) F. *consort.* — L. *consort-*, stem of *consors*, one who shares property with another, a partner. — L. *con-* (*cum*), together; *sort-*, stem of *sors*, a lot, share. See **Sort**.

Conspicuous. (L.) L. *conspicu-us*, visible, with suffix *-ous*. — L. *conspicere*, to see thoroughly. — L. *con-*, fully; *specere*, to see. See **Species**.

Conspire. (F. — L.) F. *conspirer.* — L. *conspīrāre*, to breathe together, combine, plot. — L. *con-* (*cum*), together; *spīrāre*, to breathe.

Constable, a peace-officer. (F. — L.) O. F. *conestable* (F. *connétable*). — L. *comes stabulī*, lit. ' count of the stable,' the title of a dignitary of the Roman empire and afterwards in use among the Franks. See **Count** (1) and **Stable**.

Constant, firm. (F. — L.) F. *constant*. — L. *constant-*, stem of *constans*, firm; orig. pres. pt. of *constāre*, to stand together. — L. *con-* (*cum*), together; *stāre*, to stand; see **State**.

Constellation. (F. — L.) F. *constellation.* — L. acc. *constellātiōnem*, cluster of stars. — L. *con-* (*cum*), together; *stellāt-us*, pp. of *stellāre*, to set with stars, from *stella*, a star. See **Star**.

Consternation. (F. — L.) F. *con-*

sternation. — L. acc. *consternātiōnem*, fright. — L. *consternātus*, pp. of *consternāre*, to frighten. — L. *con-* (for *cum*), together; and **sternāre*, prob. allied to Gk. πτύρειν, to frighten (Walde). See Brugmann, i. § 499.

Constipate. (L.) From pp. of L. *constīpāre*, to join closely, press together. — L. *con-* (*cum*), together; *stīpāre*, to press, cram.

Constitute. (L.) L. *constitūtus*, pp. of *constituere*, to cause to stand together, establish. — L. *con-* (*cum*), together; *statuere*, to set up, denom. vb. from *status*, a position; see **Statute**.

Constrain, to compel. (F. — L.) O. F. *constraign-*, a stem of *constraindre*, later *contraindre*. — L. *constringere*, to bind together, fetter. — L. *con-* (*cum*), together; *stringere*, to draw tight.

Construct. (L.) From L. *constructus*, pp. of *construere* (below).

construe. (L.) L. *construere*, to heap together, build, construct; in Late L., to construe a passage. — L. *con-* (*cum*), together; *struere*, to pile, build. **Der.** *mis-construe*.

Consul. (L.) L. *consul*, a consul. Etym. doubtful; but allied to *consulere*, to consult: see below.

consult. (F. — L.) F. *consulter.* — L. *consultāre*, to consult; frequent. form of *con-sulere*, to consult. Root uncertain; prob. allied to *sedēre*, to sit; cf. *solium*, a seat.

Consume. (L.) L. *consūmere*, lit. to take up wholly. — L. *con-* (*cum*), together, wholly; *sūmere*, to take up, from **sups-*, allied to *sub*, under, up, and *emere*, to take, buy. Brugm. i. § 240. **Der.** *consumption*, from the pp.

Consummate. (L.) From pp. of L. *consummāre*, to bring into one sum, to perfect. — L. *con-* (*cum*), together; *summāre*, to sum, from *summa*, a sum; see **Sum**.

Consumption; see **Consume**.

Contact, sb. (L.) L. *contactus*, a touching. — L. *contactus*, pp. of *contingere*, to touch closely; see **Contingent**.

contagion. (F. — L.) F. *contagion*. — L. *contāgiōnem*, acc. of *contāgio*, a touching, hence contagion. — L. *còn-* (*cum*), with; *tāg-*, 2nd grade of *tag-*, as in **tag-tus* (>*tac-tus*), pp. of *tangere*, to touch.

Contain. (F. — L.) From a tonic stem of O. F. *contenir*. — L. *continēre*, to hold together, contain; pp. *contentus.*—L. *con-* (*cum*), together; *tenēre*, to hold.

Contaminate. (L.) From pp. of L. *contāmināre*, to defile. — L. *contāmin-*, stem of *contāmen*, contagion; which stands for *contagmen. — L. *con-* (*cum*); *tag-*, as in *tactus*, for *tag-tus, pp. of *tangere*, to touch. Brugm. i. § 768.

Contemn. (F.—L.) M. F. *contemner.* —L. *contemnere*, to despise. — L. *con-* (*cum*), with, wholly; *temnere*, to despise.

contempt. (F.—L.) M. F. *contempt*; Cot. — L. *contemptus*, scorn. — L. *contemptus*, pp. of *contemnere* (above).

Contemplate. (L.) From pp. of *contemplāri*, to observe, consider; used at first of augurs.—L. *con-* (*cum*); *templum*, an open space for observation (by augurs); see Temple.

Contemporaneous. (L.) L. *contemporāne-us*, adj., at the same time; with suffix *-ous.*—L. *con-* (*cum*), with; *tempor-*, for *tempos-, stem of *tempus*, time.

contemporary. (L.) L. *con-*, with; and L. *temporārius*, temporary, adj., from *tempor-* (above).

Contend. (F.—L.) O. F. *contendre.* — L. *contendere*, to stretch out, exert, fight. — L. *con-* (*cum*), fully; *tendere*, to strive. Der. *content-ion* (from the pp. *contentus*).

Content, adj. (F.—L.) F. *content*, satisfied.—L. *contentus*, content; pp. of *continēre*; see Contain. Der. *dis-content*.

Contest, vb. (F.—L.) F. *contester.* — L. *contestāri*, to call to witness, to bring an action.—L. *con-* (*cum*), together; *testāri*, to witness, from *testis*, a witness. Der. *contest*, sb.

Context. (L.) L. *contextus*, a joining together, order (hence, context of a book). —L. *contextus*, pp. of *contexere*, to weave together. — L. *con-* (*cum*), together; *texere*, to weave.

Contiguous. (L.) L. *contigu-us*, that may be touched, near; with suffix *-ous.* — L. *con-* (*cum*), with; and *tag-*, as in *tac-tus* (for *tag-tus), pp. of *tangere*, to touch; see Contingent.

Continent. (F.—L.) F. *continent*, adj., moderate.—L. *continent-*, stem of pres. pt. of *continēre*; see Contain.

Contingent, dependent on. (L.) From stem of pres. pt. of *contingere*, to touch, relate to.—L. *con-* (*cum*); *tangere*, to touch. See Tangent.

Continue. (F.—L.) F. *continuer.* — L. *continuāre*, to continue.—L. *continuus* (below). Der. *dis-continue*.

continuous. (L.) L. *continu-us*, lit. holding together; with suffix *-ous.* — L. *continēre*, to hold together, contain. See Contain.

Contort. (L.) L. *contortus*, pp. of *contorquēre*, to twist together. — L. *con-* (*cum*), together; *torquēre*, to twist.

Contour, an outline. (F.—Ital.—L.) F. *contour*, esp. in an artistic sense. — Ital. *contorno*, a circuit; *contornare*, 'to encircle;' Florio.—L. *con-* (*cum*), together; *tornāre*, to round off, to turn; see Turn.

Contra-, *prefix.* (L.) L. *contrā*, against; orig. the abl. fem. of an obs. adj. *con-t(e)r-us, a comparative form from *con-*, prep. together; cf. *extrā* from *exterus*.

Contraband. (Span.—Ital.—L. *and* Teut.) Span. *contrabando*, prohibited goods. — Ital. *contrabbando*, prohibited goods. — Ital. *contra* (= L. *contrā*), against; *bando*, a ban, from Late L. *bannum*, a word of Teut. origin, viz. from O. H. G. *ban*, a command. See Ban.

Contract (1), to draw together. (L.) L. *contractus*, pp. of *contrahere*, to draw together.—L. *con-* (*cum*), together; *trahere*, to draw.

contract (2), a bargain. (F.—L.) M. F. *contract*; Cot. — L. *contractum*, acc. of *contractus*, sb., a drawing together, a bargain.—L. *contractus*, pp. (above).

Contradict. (L.) L. *contrādictus*, pp. of *contrādīcere*, to speak against.—L. *contrā*, against; *dīcere*, to speak.

Contralto. (Ital.—L.) Ital. *contralto*, counter-tenor.—Ital. *contra*, opposite to, and *alto*, high.—L. *contra*, against; *altus*, high.

Contrary. (F.—L.) A. F. *contrarie*; F. *contraire.* — L. *contrārius*, contrary; from *contrā*, against; see Contra-.

Contrast, vb. (F.—L.) F. *contraster*, to strive, contend against (hence to be in opposition to, &c.).—Late L. *contrāstāre*, to stand against. — L. *contrā*, against; *stāre*, to stand.

Contravene, to hinder. (F.—L.) F. *contrevenir*, 'to thwart;' Cot. — Late L. *contrāvenīre*, to oppose; to break a law. —L. *contrā*, against; *uenīre*, to come.

Contribute. (L.) From pp. of L. *contribuere*, to contribute, lit. pay together. — L. *con-* (*cum*), together; *tribuere*, to bestow; see Tribute.

Contrite. (F.—L.)   F. *contrit.*—L. *contrītus,* thoroughly bruised, hence, penitent; pp. of L. *conterere,* to rub together, bruise.—L. *con-* (*cum*), together; *terere,* to rub. See **Trite.**

Contrive. (F. — L. *and* Gk.) An altered spelling; M. E. *controuen, contreuen* (= *controven, contreven*).—O. F. *controver,* to find, find out (Bartsch).—O. F. *con-* (L. *con-,* for *cum*); O. F. *trover,* to find; see **Trover.** ¶ *Contrive* (cf. *retrieve*) is from M. E. *contreve,* answering to O. F. *contréuv-,* stressed stem of *cóntrovér.*

Control, sb. (F.—L.) *Control* is short for *contre-roll,* old form of *counter-roll.*—O. F. *contre-rol(l)e,* a duplicate register, used to verify the official or first-made roll.—O. F. *contre,* over against; *rol(l)e,* a roll.—L. *contrā,* against; *rotulum,* acc. of *rotulus,* a roll; see **Roll.**

Controversy. (F.—L.) A. F. *controversie* (1307).—L. *contrōuersia,* a quarrel. — L. *contrōuersus,* opposed. — L. *contrō-,* masc. or neut. form corresponding to fem. *contrā,* against; *uersus,* pp. of *uertere,* to turn. See **Contra-.**

Contumacy. (F.—L.) A. F. *contumacie* (1303).—L. *contumācia,* obstinacy.—L. *contumāci-,* stem of *contumax,* stubborn.—L. *con-* (*cum*), very; and **tum-ax,* prob. from *tum-ēre,* to swell with pride; see **Tumid.**

Contumely. (F.—L.) M. F. *contumelie.*— L. *contumēlia,* insult, reproach; prob. allied to *contumācia;* see **Contumacy.**

Contuse, to bruise severely. (L.) L. *contūsus,* pp. of *contundere,* to bruise severely.—L. *con-* (*cum*), with, much; and *tundere,* to strike.+Skt. *tud,* to strike; Goth. *stautan,* to strike. (√STEUD.) Brugm. i. § 818.

Conundrum. (Unknown.) Formerly used in the sense of whim, crotchet, or hoax. Also *quonundrum;* orig. in univ. slang; prob. of L. origin.

Convalesce. (L.) L. *conualescere,* to begin to grow well; an inceptive form. —L. *con-* (=*cum*), fully; *ualēre,* to be strong.

Convene, to assemble. (F.—L.) F. *convenir,* to assemble.—L. *conuenīre,* to come together.—L. *con-* (*cum*), together; *uenīre,* to come.

convenient, suitable. (F. — L.) From stem of L. *conueniens,* suitable;

orig. pres. pt. of *conuenīre,* to come together, suit (above).

convent. (L.) L. *conuentus,* an assembly.—L. *conuentus,* pp. of *con-uenīre.*

convention. (F.—L.) F. *convention,* 'a compact;' Cot.—L. acc. *conuentiōnem,* a meeting, compact.—L. *conuentus,* pp. of *con-uenīre,* to meet.

Converge. (L.) Late L. *conuergere,* to incline together (Isidore). — L. *con-* (*cum*), together; *uergere,* to bend, incline.

Converse, vb. (F.—L.) F. *converser,* to associate with; Cot.—L. *conuersārī,* to live with.—L. *con-* (*cum*), with; *uersārī,* to dwell (lit. turn oneself about), orig. pass. of the frequent. of *uertere,* to turn.

convert, vb. (F.—L.) O. F. *convertir.*—Folk-L. **convertīre,* for L. *conuertere,* to turn wholly, change.—L. *con-* (*cum*), wholly; *uertere,* to turn.

Convex. (L.) L. *conuexus,* arched, vaulted.—L. *con-* (*cum*), together; and **uaxus* = **uac-sus,* bent, from **uac-* (**uaq-*), to bend, as in *uac-illāre,* to reel, go crookedly. See **Vacillate.** Cf. A.S. *wōh,* crooked.

Convey, Convoy, vb. (F. — L.) M. E. *conueien, conuoien* (*conveien, convoien*), to convey, also to convoy.—A. F. *conveier,* O. F. *convoier,* to convey, convoy, accompany on the way.—Late L. *conuiāre,* to accompany.—L. *con-* (*cum*), with; *uia,* way. ¶ *Convey* is the A. F. or Norman form; *convoy* is Parisian.

Convince. (L.) L. *conuincere,* to overcome by proof. — L. *con-* (*cum*), wholly; *uincere,* to conquer. **Der.** *convict,* verb and sb., from A. F. *convict*<L. *conuictus,* pp. of *conuincere.*

Convivial. (L.) Coined as adj. from L. *conuīui-um,* a feast.—L. *con-* (*cum*), together; *uīuere,* to live (hence, eat).

Convoke. (F.—L.) F. *convoquer.*—L. *conuocāre,* to call together.—L. *con-,* together; *uocāre,* to call.

Convolve. (L.) L. *conuoluere,* to roll together, writhe about.—L. *con-* (*cum*), together; *uoluere,* to roll. **Der.** *convolution,* from pp. *conuolūtus; convolv-ul-us,* L. *conuoluulus,* a twining plant.

Convoy; see **Convey.**

Convulse, to agitate violently. (L.) L. *conuulsus,* pp. of *conuellere,* to pluck up, convulse. — L. *con-* (*cum*), with, severely; *uellere,* to pluck.

Cony, Coney, a rabbit. (F. — L.) M. E. *coni;* also *conyng.* Anglo-F. *conil,* *conin* ; O. F. *connil.* — L. *cunīculus*, a rabbit ; a word of uncertain origin.

Coo. (E.) A purely imitative word ; also spelt *croo*. Cf. *cuckoo*, *cock*.

Cook. (L.) M. E. *coken*, to cook ; A. S. *cōc*, a cook. — L. *coquus*, a cook ; *co-quere*, to cook.+Gk. πέσσειν ; Skt. *pach*, to cook ; Russ. *pech(e)*, to bake. (√PEQ ; whence Lat. *pequere, becoming *quequere by assimilation, and then *coquere* ; Gk. *πέq-ιειν, whence πέσσειν.) Brugm. i. § 661. A.S. *cōc* = Late L. *cŏcus*, for *coquus*.

Cookie, a cake ; see **Cake.**

Cool. (E.) A.S. *cōl*, cool.+Du. *koel* ; Teut. type *kōl-uz ; also, with mutation, Dan. *köl*, G. *kühl* ; from *kōl-*, 2nd grade of *kal-*, as in A.S. *calan*, Icel. *kala*, to freeze (pt. t. *kōl*) ; see **Cold.**

Coolie, Cooly, an East Indian porter. (Hind. *or* Tamil.) Hind. *kūlī*, a labourer, porter, cooley (Forbes) ; prob. from *Kolī*, a tribal name (Yule). Or from Tamil *kūli*, daily hire or wages ; hence, a day-labourer (Wilson).

Coomb ; see **Comb.**

Coop. (L.) M. E. *cupe*, a basket ; answering to A.S. *cūpe, not found, though *cȳpe* (with *i*-mutation) occurs as a gloss to *dolium.* — L. *cūpa*, a tub, whence also Du. *kuip*, Icel. *kūpa*, a bowl ; also Late L. *cōpa*, whence G. *kufe*, tub, vat, coop ; O. Sax. *cōpa*, a tub. Cf. Skt. *kūpa*, a pit, hollow. Der. *coop-er*, tub-maker.

Co-operate. (L.) From pp. of L. *co-operārī*, to work with ; from *co-* (*cum*), with ; and *operārī*, to work ; see **Operate.**

Co-ordinate. (L.) From L. *co-* (*cum*), with ; and the pp. of *ordināre*, to order. See **Ordinate.**

Coot. (E.) M. E. *cote*, *coote*, a waterfowl.+Du. *koet*, a coot. Origin unknown.

Copal. (Span. – Mexican.) Span. *copal.* — Mex. *copalli*, resin.

Co-parcener, a co-partner. (F. – L.) *Parcener* is the true old spelling of *partner* ; see **Partner.**

Cope (1), orig. a cape. (Late L.) M. E. *cope*, earlier *cape* ; A. S. *cāpa, not found ; but Icel. *kāpa* occurs. – Late L. *cāpa*, a cape ; see **Cape** (1). [Cf. *pope*, from A. S. *pāpa*.] Der. *coping-stone.*

Cope (2), to vie with. (F. – L. – Gk.) M. E. *copen*, *coupen*, to fight. – O. F. *coper*, *couper*, *colper*, to strike (F. *couper*, to cut). – O. F. *cop*, *coup*, *colp*, a blow. – Late L. *colpus*, L. *colaphus*, a blow. – Gk. κόλαφος, a blow on the ear. See **Coupon.**

Copeck, a small Russian coin, worth less than ½*d.* ; a hundredth part of a rouble. (Russ.) Russ. *kopieika*, a copeck ; dimin. of Russ. *kopeĕ*, a lance. So called from the figure of Ivan IV, holding a *lance* (1535). See **Rouble.**

Copious, ample. (F. – L.) O. F. *copieux.* – L. *cōpiōsus*, plentiful. – L. *cōpia*, plenty ; for **co-opia.* – L. *co-* (for *cum*), together ; *op-*, base of *op-ēs*, wealth. Cf. *in-opia*, want.

Copper, a metal. (Cyprus.) M.E. *coper.* A. S. *copor.* – Late L. *cuper*, L. *cuprum*, a contraction for *Cuprium æs*, Cyprian brass. – Gk. Κύπριος, Cyprian ; Κύπρος, Cyprus, whence the Romans got copper.

copperas, sulphate of iron. (F. – L.) M. E. *coperose.* – O.F. *coperose* (*couperose*) ; cf. Ital. *copparosa*. According to Diez, from L. *cuprī rosa*, rose of copper, a translation of Gk. χάλκ-ανθος, brass - flower, copperas. But this is prob. only a popular etymology ; and the Late L. *cuprōsa* seems to be merely an adj. form from *cuprum*. See N. E. D.

Coppice, Coppy, Copse, a small wood. (F. – L. – Gk.) *Coppy* is short for *coppice*, and *copse* is contracted. – O. F. *copeis* [Low L. *copecia*], underwood frequently cut, brushwood. – O. F. *coper* (F. *couper*), to cut. – O. F. *cop* (F. *coup*), a stroke. – Low L. *colpus*, L. *colaphus*, stroke, blow. – Gk. κόλαφος, a blow. ¶ O. F. *copeiz* answers to a Late L. type *colpati-cium, from *colpāre*, to strike. *Coppy* arose from *coppice* being taken as *coppies*, pl. ; and *copse* (*cops*) from reducing a supposed pl. *coppis to *cops*.

Coprolite. (Gk.) Lit. ' dung-stone.' Made from Gk. κόπρο-s, dung ; and λίθ-os, a stone. For *-lite*, cf. **Aerolite.**

Copulate. (L.) From pp. of L. *cōpu-lāre*, to join. – L. *cōpula*, a band ; see **Couple.**

Copy. (F. – L.) M. E. *copy*, abundance ; the mod. sense is due to the multiplication of an original by means of *copies*. – O. F. *copie*, abundance ; also a copy. – L. *cōpia*, plenty ; see **Copious.**

Coquette. (F.) F. *coquette*, 'a pratling or proud gossip,' Cot. ; fem. of *coquet*, a little cock, dimin. of *coq*, a cock. Cf. prov. E. *cocky*, i. e. strutting as a cock.

Coracle, a light wicker boat. (W.) W. *corwgl*, *cwrwgl*, coracle ; dimin. of *corwg*, a carcase, *cwrwg*, a boat, frame. So Gael. *curachan*, coracle, from *curach*, boat of wicker-work; cf. Ir. *corrach*, O. Ir. *curach*, a boat.

Coral. (F. – L. – Gk.) O. F. *coral.* – L. *corallum*, *corālium*. – Gk. κοράλλιον, coral. See Schade, p. 1374.

Corban, a gift. (Heb.) Heb. *qorbān*, an offering to God, in fulfilment of a vow; from *qārab*, to draw near. Cf. Arab. *qurbān*, a sacrifice.

Corbel. (F. – L.) O. F. *corbel*, a raven, a corbel (in architecture), from the notion of a projecting beak. – Folk-L. *corbellum*, for *corvellum*, acc. of *corvellus*, dimin. of L. *coruus*, a raven. ¶ Distinct from *corbeil*, a basket full of earth (F. *corbeille*, L. *corbicula*, dimin. of *corbis*, a basket).

Cord. (F. – L. – Gk.) M. E. *corde.* – F. *corde.* – Late L. *corda*, a thin rope; the same as L. *chorda.* – Gk. χορδή, the string of a musical instrument. **Der.** *cord-age* (F. *cordage*); *cord-on* (F. *cordon*); *cord--elier* (F. *cordelier*, a twist of rope, also a Gray Friar, who used such a twist; from *cordeler*, to twist ropes). See **Chord**.

Cordial. (F. – L.) F. *cordial*, hearty. – L. *cordi-*, decl. stem of *cor*, heart; with suffix *-ālis*; see **Heart**.

Corduroy, a thick-ribbed or corded stuff. (F. – L.) F. *corde du roi*, a trade-name, invented in England; lit. 'king's cord.' See **Cord** and **Royal**.

Cordwainer, shoemaker. (F. – Span.) M. E. *cordewaner*, a worker in *cordewane*, i.e. leather of Cordova. – O. F. *cordouan*, Cordovan leather. – Late L. *Cordoa*, Cordova in Spain (L. *Corduba*).

Core, hard centre in fruit, &c. (F. – L.?) Etym. doubtful. Perhaps from F. *cor*, a horn, also, a corn on the foot, callosity. – L. *cornu*, a horn, a horny excrescence.

Coriander. (F. – L. – Gk.) F. *coriandre.* – L. *coriandrum* (whence A. S. *cellendre*). – Gk. κορίαννον, κόριον, coriander.

Cork. (Span. – L.) Apparently from O. Span. *alcorque*, a cork shoe, which seems to be an Arab. form allied to Span. *al-cornoque*, the cork-tree, where *al* is the Arab. def. art., and *corn-oque* is formed from L. *quern-us* (for **quercnus*), oaken, adj. from L. *quercus*, an oak. ¶ But the *bark* of the tree was called, in Span., *corche*, *corcho.* – L. *corticem*, acc. of *cortex*, bark. Hence *cork* is often derived from Span. *corcho*, though *k* for *ch* seems improbable.

Cormorant, a bird. (F. – L.) The *t* is excrescent. – F. *cormoran*; O. F. *corma-* *rant*, *cormaran* (Littré). – O. F. *corp*, a crow; and O. F. **marenc*, belonging to the sea, deriv. of L. *mare*, sea, with G. suffix *-ing*; cf. F. *flamant*, flamingo. – L. *coruum*, acc. of *coruus*, a crow; &c. Cf. Port. *corvomarinho*, a cormorant; lit. 'marine crow;' from L. *coruus marīnus*. But probably *-moran* was due to, or confused with, Bret. *morvran*, a cormorant (from *mor*, sea, and *bran*, a crow).

Corn (1), grain. (E.) A. S. *corn.*+Du. *koren*, Icel. Dan. Swed. G. *korn*, Goth. *kaurn*. Teut. type **kurnom*, Idg. type **g̑r̥nom*, corn; whence O. Slav. *zrŭno*, Russ. *zerno*, corn. Cf. Lat. *grānum*, grain; Skt. *jīrṇa-*, worn down, pp. of *jrī*. **Doublet**, *grain*. See **Grain**. Brugm. i. § 628. (√GER.)

Corn (2), a hard excrescence on the foot. (F. – L.) O. F. *corn* (F. *cor*), a horn, horny swelling. – L. *cornū*, a horn; see **Horn**.

cornea, horny membrane in the eye. (L.) L. *cornea*, fem. of *corneus*, horny. – L. *cornū*, a horn.

cornel, a shrub. (Du. – L.) M. Du. *kornelle*, 'the fruit of the cornelle-tree,' Hexham; cf. M. H. G. *cornelbaum*, cornel-tree; Weigand. [Cf. M. F. *cornille*, a cornel-berry; *cornillier*, cornel-tree.] – Late L. *cornolium*, cornel-tree. – L. *cornus*, a cornel-tree; from the hard, horny nature of the wood. – L. *cornū*, a horn.

cornelian, a kind of chalcedony. (F. – L.) Formerly *cornaline.* – F. *cornaline*, 'the cornix or cornaline, a flesh-coloured stone;' Cot. Cf. Port. *cornelina*; also Ital. *corniola*, (1) a cornel-tree, (2) a cornelian, prob. so named because its colour resembles that of the fruit of the cornel-tree (Schade). – Late L. *corniola*, cornel-berry; *cornolium*, cornel. – L. *corneus*, adj. of *cornus*, a cornel. ¶ Altered to *carneolus* in Late L. (Schade, p. 1379), *carnelian* in E., and *carneol* in G., from a popular etymology which connected it with L. *carn-*, stem of *caro*, flesh. Cf. *onyx* = Gk. ὄνυξ, finger-nail.

corner. (F. – L.) A. F. *cornere*; O. F. *corniere.* – Med. L. *cornēria*, corner, angle. – Med. L. *corna*, angle. – L. *cornua*, pl. of *cornū*, horn, projection; taken as a fem. sing.

cornet. (F. – L.) M. E. *cornet*, a horn; later, a troop of horse (who carried a *cornette* or standard); also an officer of such a troop. – F. *cornet*, *cornette*, dimin. of F.

corne, a horn. — Med. L. *corna*, a horn (above).

Cornice. (F. — Ital.) M. F. and Picard *cornice* ; F. *corniche*. — Ital. *cornice*, a ledge for hanging tapestry (Florio) ; usually, a crow (from L. acc. *cornīcem*, a crow). Origin uncertain ; by some identified with *corōnix*, a square frame. — Gk. κορωνίς, curved ; as sb., a wreath.

Corolla. (L.) L. *corolla*, dimin. of *corōna*, a crown. See **Crown**.

corollary. (L.) L. *corollārium*, a present of a garland, a gratuity ; also, an additional inference. — L. *corolla* (above).

coronal, a crown. (F. — L.) Properly an adj. — F. *coronal*, adj. — L. *corōnālis*, belonging to a crown. — L. *corōna*, a crown.

coronation. (L.) Late L. acc. *corōnātiōnem*, from pp. of *corōnāre*, to crown. — L. *corōna*, a crown.

coroner. (F. — L.) Also *crowner* ; both forms represent A. F. *coruner*, *coroner*, Latinised as *corōnārius*, a crown-officer, a coroner (afterwards Latinised as *corōnātor*). — O. F. *corone*, a crown. — L. *corōna*, a crown.

coronet. (F. — L.) Dimin. of O. F. *corone*, a crown. — L. *corōna*, a crown.

Coronach, a dirge. (Gael.) Gael. *corranach*, a dirge, lit. ' a howling together.' — Gael. *comh*- (= L. *cum*), together ; *rànaich*, a howling, from the verb *ràn*, to howl, cry, roar, which is from *ràn*, sb., an outcry. So also Irish *coranach*, a dirge.

Corporal (1), a subordinate officer. (F. — L.) O. F. *corporal*. — Late L. *corporalis*, a captain ; a leader of a body of troops. — L. *corpor*-, for *corpos-, stem of *corpus*, body. ¶ F. has now the form *caporal*, from Ital. *caporale*, a chief of a band ; as if from Ital. *capo*, head (L. *caput*) ; but this does not explain the -*or*-.

corporal (2), belonging to the body. (F. — L.) O. F. *corporal, corporel*. — L. *corporālis*, bodily. — L. *corpor*-, for *corpos-, stem of *corpus*, the body. **Der.** (from L. *corpor*-) *corpor-ate, corpor-e-al* (L. *corpore-us*), &c. Brugm. i. § 555.

corps, corpse, corse, a body. (F. — L.) [Here *corps* is F. ; *corse* is from the O. F. *cors*.] M. E. *cors, corps*. — O. F. *cors*, M. F. *corps*, the body. — L. *corpus*, body.

corpulent. (F. — L.) F. *corpulent*. — L. *corpulentus*, fat. — L. *corpus*, body.

corpuscle. (L.) L. *corpus-cu-lum*, double dimin. of *corpus*, body.

Corral, an enclosure for animals, pen.

(Span. — L.) Span. *corral*, a court, yard, enclosure. — Span. *corro*, a circle, a ring of people met to see a show. From the phrase *correr toros*, to hold a bull-fight, lit. to run bulls. — L. *currere*, to run (Diez). See **Kraal.**

Correct, adj. (L.) L. *correctus*, pp. of *corrigere*, to correct. — L. *cor*- (for *con*- = *cum*), together ; *regere*, to rule.

corregidor, a Spanish magistrate. (Span. — L.) Span. *corregidor*, lit. ' corrector.' — Span. *corregir*, to correct. — L. *corrigere* (above).

Correlate, to relate or refer mutually. (L.) Coined from L. *cor*- (= *cum*), together ; and **Relate**, q. v.

Correspond. (F. — L.) F. *correspondre*. — L. *cor*- (for *con*-, *cum*), together ; and **Respond,** q. v.

Corridor. (F. — Ital. — L.) F. *corridor*. — Ital. *corridore*, a swift horse ; also, a long (running along) gallery. — Ital. *correre*, to run. — L. *currere*, to run.

Corrie. (Gael.) Gael. *coire*, a circular hollow surrounded with hills, a mountain dell ; also, a cauldron. [Cf. G. *kessel*, a kettle, a ravine.] + O. Irish *coire, core*, a kettle ; W. *pair*, A. S. *hwer*, a cauldron. Brugm. i. § 123.

Corroborate. (L.) From pp. of L. *corrōborāre*, to strengthen. — L. *cor*- (for *con*- = *cum*), wholly ; *rōbor*-, stem of *rōbur*, strength.

Corrode. (F. — L.) F. *corroder*. — L. *corrōdere*, to gnaw to pieces. — L. *cor*- (for *con*- = *cum*), wholly ; *rōdere*, to gnaw. **Der.** *corrosive*, from pp. *corrōs-us*.

Corrody, Corody, allowance, pension. (Low Lat. — Teut.) A. F. *corodie*. — Low L. *corrōdium*, earlier *corrēdium*, L. form of A. F. *conrei*, preparation, provision, allowance. See **Curry** (1).

Corrugate. (L.) From pp. of L. *corrūgāre*, to wrinkle. — L. *cor*- (*cum*), wholly ; and *rūgāre*, to wrinkle, from *rūga*, a wrinkle.

Corrupt, adj. (F. — L.) A. F. *corupt*. — L. *corruptus*, pp. of *corrumpere*, to break wholly, corrupt. — L. *cor*- (for *con*- = *cum*), wholly ; *rumpere*, to break.

Corsair. (F. — Ital. — L.) F. *corsaire* (Prov. *corsari*, one who makes the course, *corsa*). — Ital. *corsare*, earlier *corsaro*, a pirate. — Med. L. *cursārius*, a pirate. — L. *cursus*, a course. See **Course.**

Corse, a body. (F. — L.) M. E. *cors*. — O. F. *cors*. — L. *corpus*, a body.

corset. (F.–L.) F. *corset*, a pair of stays; dimin. of O. F. *cors*, body.

corslet. (F.–L.) F. *corselet*, 'a little body,' Cot.; hence, body-armour. Double dimin. of O. F. *cors*, body (above).

Cortège. (F.–Ital.–L.) F. *cortège*, a train, retinue. – Ital. *corteggio*, a retinue. – Ital. *corte*, a court. – L. *cŏrtem*, *cohortem*, acc. of *cohors*, a court; see Court (1).

cortes, the Span. national assembly. (Span.–L.) Span. *cortes*, pl. of *corte*, a court.–L. *cŏrtem* (above).

Cortex, bark. (L.) L. *cortex* (gen. *corticis*), bark. **Der.** *cortical*.

Coruscate. (L.) From pp. of L. *coruscāre*, to glitter.

Corvette, a small frigate. (F.–Port.–L.) F. *corvette*. – Port. *corveta*; Span. *corbeta*, a corvette.–L. *corbīta*, a slow-sailing ship of burden. – L. *corbis*, a basket.

Cosmic, relating to the world. (Gk.) Gk. κοσμικός, adj., from κόσμος, order, also the world, universe. **Der.** *cosmo-gony*, *cosmo-graphy*, *cosmo-logy*, *cosmo-polite* (citizen of the world, Gk. πολίτης, a citizen).

cosmetic, that which beautifies. (Gk.) Gk. κοσμητικός, skilled in adorning; whence also F. *cosmétique*. – Gk. κοσμέω, I adorn.–Gk. κόσμος, order, ornament.

Cossack, a light-armed S. Russian soldier. (Russ.–Tatar.) Russ. *kozak'*, *kazak'*; of Tatar (Tartar) origin. – Turkī *quzzāq*, a vagabond; a predatory horse-man (Yule).

Cosset, to pet. (E.) From 16th cent. *cosset*, a pet-lamb, a pet. Prob. the same as A. F. *coscet*, *cozet*, a cottar; A. S. *cot-sǣta*, a dweller in a cot, 'cot-sitter.' From A. S. *cot*, cot; *sǣta*, dweller, from *sittan*, to sit. Cf. prov. G. *kossat*, a cottager. [So Ital. *casiccio*, pet lamb (Florio); from *casa*, a cottage.]

Cost, vb. (F.–L.) M. E. *costen.* – O. F. *coster* (F. *coûter*), to cost. – L. *constāre*, to stand together, last; also to cost. – L. *con-* (*cum*), together; and *stāre*, to stand.

Costal, relating to the ribs. (L.) From L. *costa*, a rib. See Coast.

Costermonger. (F. *and* E.) Formerly *costerd-monger*, or *costard-monger*, a seller of *costards* or apples. [The suffix *-monger* is E.; see **Monger**.] M. E. *costard*, an apple, where the suffix *-ard* is F.; prob. from O. F. *coste*, F. *côte*, a rib; cf. F. *fruit côtelé*, ribbed fruit (Hamilton).

Costive. (F.–L.) From O. F. *costevé.* – L. *constipātus*, constipated. See *constiper* in Littré; and **Constipate**.

Costume. (F.–Ital.–L.) O. F. *costume*, a costume. – Ital. *costume*; Low L. *costūma*; see **Custom**. Doublet of *custom*.

Cosy, Cozy, comfortable, snugly sheltered. (Scand.) Lowl. Scotch *cosie*, *cozie* (Burns). Etym. unknown; perhaps cf. Norw. *kosa*, to refresh; *kosa seg*, to enjoy oneself; *koseleg*, snug, cosy; *kosing*, recreation.

Cot, a small dwelling; **Cote,** an enclosure. (E.) M. E. *cote*. A. S. *cot*, *cote*, a cot, den; Northumbrian *cot*.+Du. *kot*, Icel. *kot*, cot, hut; prov. G. *koth*, cot. **Der.** *cott-age* (with F. suffix); *cott-ar* or *cott-er*; *sheep-cote*.

coterie, a set of people. (F.–Teut.) F. *coterie*, a set of people, company; allied to O. F. *coterie*, servile tenure (Littré); Low L. *coteria*, a tenure by cottars who clubbed together.–Low L. *cota*, a cot. – Du. *kot* (above).

Cotillon, Cotillion, a dance for 4 or 8 persons. (F.–M.H.G.) F. *cotillon*, lit. a petticoat; see Cotgrave. Formed, with suffix *-ill-on*, from O. F. *cote*, a coat, frock; see **Coat**.

Cotton (1), a downy substance. (F.–Span.–Arab.) M. E. and A. F. *cotoun.* – F. *coton.* – Span. *coton*, *algodon*, cotton (where *al* is the Arab. art.). – Arab. *qutn*, *qutun*, cotton.

cotton (2), to agree. From a technical use of *cotton*, to form a down upon; from Cotton (1); see Nares.

Cotyledon, seed-lobe. (Gk.) Gk. κοτυληδών, a cup-shaped hollow. – Gk. κοτύλη, a hollow vessel, cup.

Couch, to lay down, place, set. (F.–L.) M. E. *couchen*, to set, arrange. – O. F. *coucher*, *colcher*, to place. – L. *collocāre*, to put together. – L. *col-* (*cum*), together; and *locāre*, to place, from *locus*, a place. **Der.** *couch*, sb., a place on which one is *couched* or laid.

Couch-grass, a grass which is troublesome as a weed. (E.) Here *couch* is a variant of *quitch*, palatalised form of *quick*, i. e. tenacious of life; see **Quick**.

Cough. (E.) M. E. *coughen*, *cowhen.* A. S. **cohhian*, only found in the deriv. *cohhetan*, to make a noise. [The usual A. S. word is *hwōstan*.] Cf. Du. *kuchen*, to cough; M. H. G. *kūchen*, G. *keuchen*, to gasp. From an imitative base *keuh, *kuh, to gasp; see **Chincough.**

Could; see **Can** (1).

Coulter, part of a plough. (L.) M. E. *colter.* A. S. *culter* = L. *culter,* a coulter, knife. Cf. *per-cellere,* to strike.

Council. (F. – L.) F. *concile.* – L. *concilium,* an assembly called together. – L. *con-* (*cum*), together; and *calāre,* to summon. ¶ Often confused with *counsel.*

Counsel. (F. – L.) M. E. *conseil.* – O. F. *conseil.* – L. *consilium,* deliberation. – L. *consulere,* to consult; see **Consult.** ¶ Often confused with *council.*

Count (1), a title of rank. (F. – L.) The orig. sense was ‘ companion.’ A. F. *counte* (not in M. E.). – O. F. *conte*; also *comte.* – L. *comitem,* acc. of *comes,* a companion (stem *com-it-*). – L. *com-* (for *cum-*), together; and *it-um,* supine of *īre,* to go. Der. *count-ess*; also *count-y* (below).

Count (2), to reckon. (F. – L.) F. *conter,* formerly also *compter.* – L. *computāre,* to compute; see **Compute.**

Countenance. (F. – L.) O. F. *contenance,* gesture, demeanour; also look, visage. – L. *continentia,* continence, which in Late L. meant ‘ gesture, demeanour.’ – L. *continent-,* stem of pres. pt. of *continēre*; see **Continent.** Der. *dis-countenance,* vb.

Counter, a piece to count with, a bureau. (F. – L.) M. E. *countour.* – O. F. *conteour, countour.* From O. F. *conter*; see **Count** (2).

Counter-, *prefix.* (F. – L.) F. *contre,* against. – L. *contrā,* against.

Counteract. (F. – L.) See **Counter-,** *prefix,* and **Act.**

Counterfeit, imitated. (F. – L.) M. E. *counterfeit.* – O. F. *controfait,* pp. of *controfaire,* to imitate. – F. *contre,* over against, like; *faire,* to make. – L. *contrā,* against; *facere,* to make.

Countermand, to revoke an order. (F. – L.) F. *contremander,* to recall a command. – F. *contre* (L. *contrā*), against; *mander* (L. *mandāre*), to command.

Counterpane (1), a coverlet for a bed. (F. – L.) An altered form, in place of *counterpoint,* as in Shak. – M. F. *contre-poinct,* the back-stitch or quilting-stitch, also a quilt; Cot. β. Thus named, by a popular etymology, from a fancied connection with M. F. *contrepoincter,* to work the back-stitch (from *contre* = L. *contrā*). But really connected with M. F. *coutrepointer,* to quilt (also in Cotgrave). In fact, *contre-*

poinct is a corruption of O. F. *coutepointe,* a counterpane (see *courtepointe* in Littré). – L. *culcita puncta,* a counterpane, a stitched quilt (see Ducange). – L. *culcita,* a quilt; *puncta,* fem. of *punctus,* pp. of *pungere,* to prick. See **Quilt.**

Counterpane (2), counterpart of a deed. (F. – L.) M. F. *contrepan, contrepant*; Cot. – F. *contre* (L. *contrā*), over against; *pan,* a piece, part; see **Pane.**

Counterpoint, the composing of music in parts. (F. – L.) M. F. *contre-poinct,* ‘ a ground or plain song, in music;’ Cot. The lit. sense is *point against point,* from the *points* or dots which represented musical notes, and were placed on staves over or against each other in compositions in two or more parts. – F. *contre* (L. *con-trā*), against; *point,* a point; see **Point.**

Counterpoise. (F. – L.) From *counter* and *poise*; see **Poise.**

Counterscarp, exterior slope of a ditch. (F. – Ital. – L. *and* Teut.) F. *contrescarpe*; Cot. – Ital. *contrascarpa.* – Ital. *contra,* over against; *scarpa,* a scarp. See **Counter-** and **Scarp.**

Countersign, to attest by signing in addition. (F. – L.) F. *contresigner,* ‘ to subsigne;’ Cot. – F. *contre,* over against; *signer,* to sign; see **Counter-** and **Sign.**

Countertenor. (F. – Ital. – L.) M. F. *contreteneur*; Cot. – Ital. *contratenore,* a countertenor, the highest adult male voice. – Ital. *contra,* against, over against; *tenore,* a tenor; see **Tenor.**

Countervail. (F. – L.) M. E. *con-trevailen.* – O. F. *contrevail-,* a stem of *contrevaloir,* to avail against. O. F. *con-tre,* against; *valoir,* to avail. – L. *contrā,* against; *ualēre,* to be strong.

Country. (F. – L.) M. E. *contree.* – O. F. *contree* (= Ital. *contrada*). – Late L. *contrāda, contrāta,* a region, lit. that which lies opposite; cf. G. *gegend,* country, lit. opposite, from *gegen,* opposite. – L. *contrā,* opposite; see **Contra-.**

Country-dance. (F.) From *country* and *dance.* (The F. *contredanse* was borrowed from this E. form.)

County, orig. a province governed by a count. (F. – L.) M. E. *countee.* – O. F. *counte* (i. e. *coun-té*), F. *comté,* a province. – Late L. *comitātum,* acc. of *comitātus,* a county (though the old meaning was a company or suite). – L. *comit-,* stem of *comes,* a count; see **Count** (1).

Couple. (F. – L.) O. F. *cople,* later

couple. — L. *cōpula*, a bond, band, that which joins; short for **co-ap-ula*. — L. *co-* (*cum*), together; and O. L. *apere*, to join, preserved in the pp. *aptus*; see **Apt.**

Coupon, one of a series of conjoined tickets or certificates. (F. — L. — Gk.) F. *coupon*, a piece cut off, a coupon. — F. *couper*, to cut, slash. — F. *coup*, a blow. — Late L. *colpus*, short for *colaphus*, a blow. — Gk. κόλαφος, a blow on the ear.

Courage. (F. — L.) F. *courage*, O. F. *corage*; formed with suffix -*age* (L. -*āticum*) from O. F. *cor*, heart. — L. *cor*, heart. Der. *encourage.*

Courier. (F. — Ital. — L.) M.F. *courier*, a runner; F. *courrier*. — Ital. *corriere*, lit. ' runner.' — Ital. *correre*, to run. — L. *currere*, to run.

course. (F. — L.) F. *course*. — L. *cursum*, acc. of *cursus*, a course; from pp. of *currere*. Der. *cours-er*, a swift horse.

Court (1), a yard; royal retinue, judicial assembly. (F. — L.) M. E. *cort*, *curt*. — O. F. *cort*, *curt* (F. *court*), a court, a yard, also a tribunal. — L. acc. *cŏrtem*, *cohortem* (nom. *cohors*), a pen, enclosure, cattle-yard, court, also a cohort, or band of soldiers. — L. *co-* (*cum*), together; and *hort-*, as in *hort-us*, a garden, yard, cognate with *yard.* (√GHER.)

court (2), to seek favour. (F. — L.) From the sb. *court*; hence, to practise arts in vogue at court.

courteous, of courtly manners. (F. — L.) M. E. *corteis*, later *corteous*. — O. F. *corteis*, courteous. — O. F. *cort*, a court; with suffix -*eis* (L. -*ensis*).

courtesan. (F. — Ital. — L.) Fem. of F. *courtisan*, a courtier. — Ital. *cortigiano* (in Florio *cortegiano*), a courtier. For **cortesiano*, an extension of *cortese*, courteous; from Ital. *corte*, court. — L. acc. *cŏrtem*; see **Court** (1).

courtesy. (F. — L.) M. E. *cortesie*. — O. F. *cortesie*, courtesy. — O. F. *corteis*, courteous; see **courteous.**

courtier. (F. — L.) M. E. *courteour*. From A. F. **cortei-er* (O. F. *cortoi-er*), to live at court; with suffix -*our* (L. -*ātōrem*). — O. F. *cort*, a court.

Court cards; a corruption of *coat cards*, pictured cards, the old name.

Courteous, &c.; see **Court.**

Cousin. (F. — L.) M. E. *cosin*. — O. F. *cosin* (F. *cousin*; Late L. *cosīnus*, Ital. *cugino*, Romaunsch *cusrin*, *cusdrin*). — L. *consobrīnus*, the child of a mother's sister,

a cousin. — L. *con-* (*cum*), together; *sobrīnus*, for **swesr-īnus*, belonging to a sister; from L. *soror* (for **swesōr*), a sister; cf. Skt. *svasṛ*, a sister. See **Sister.** (Cf. Brugm. i. § 319.)

Cove, a nook. (E.) A.S. *cofa*, a chamber, a cave. + Icel. *kofi*, a hut; Swed. *kofva*; G. *koben*, a cabin. ¶ Distinct from *cave*, *coop*, *alcove*. Brugm. i. § 658.

Covenant, agreement. (F. — L.) O.F. *covenant*, also *convenant*, agreement. — O. F. *co(n)venant*, pres. pt. of *co(n)venir*, to assemble, agree. — L. *conuenīre*, to assemble, come together; see **Convene.**

Cover, to hide. (F. — L.) O. F. *covrir* (*couvrir*). — L. *coöperīre*, to cover. — L. *co-* (*cum*), wholly; *operīre*, to shut, hide. For **op-uerīre*; cf. Lith. * až-weriu*, I shut, *wartai*, doors, Oscan acc. *veru*, a door. Brugm. i. § 350.

coverlet. (F. — L.) M. E. *coverlite*. — A. F. *coverlet*, *coverlit* (not in O. F.), a bed-cover. — O. F. *covrir*, to cover; *lit*, a bed, from L. *lectum*, acc. of *lectus*, a bed.

covert. (F. — L.) O. F. *covert*, pp. of *covrir*, to cover (above).

Covet. (F. — L.) M. E. *coueiten* (*coveiten*). — A. F. *coveiter* (F. *convoiter*). Cf. Ital. *cubitare* (for *cupitare*), to covet. Formed, as if from L. **cupiditāre*, from *cupiditā-tem*, acc., eager desire, which is from *cupidus*, desirous of. — L. *cupere*, to desire. See **Cupid.**

Covey. (F. — L.) O. F. *covee* (F. *couvée*), a brood of partridges; fem. of pp. of *cover* (F. *couver*), to hatch, sit. — L. *cubāre*, to lie down, sit. Cf. Gk. κυφός, bent.

Covin, secret agreement, fraud; a lawterm. (F. — L.) M. E. *covine*. — O. F. *covine*, agreement. — O. F. *covenir*, to assemble, agree. — L. *conuenīre*, to come together. See **Convene, Covenant.** (The O. F. *covine* answers to Late L. *convenia*, pl. of *convenium*, an agreement.)

Cow (1), female of the bull. (E.) A.S. *cū*; pl. *cȳ*, whence M. E. *ky*, and the pl. *kine*; see below. Teut. stem **kū-*, whence also Icel. *kȳr*. + Du. *koe*, Swed. Dan. *ko*, G. *kuh*; Teut. stem **kō-*. Also Irish and Gael. *bō*, W. *buw*, L. *bōs* (gen. *bou-is*), Gk. βοῦς, Pers. *gāw*, Skt. *go-* (nom. *gāus*); cf. Russ. *goviado*, oxen. Idg. stems **g(w)ōu-*, **g(w)ow-*. See **Beef.**

kine, cows. (E.) A new pl.; due to A. S. *cȳna*, gen. pl., ' of cows.' Cf. M. E. *ky*, A. S. *cȳ*, cows. The A. S. *cȳ*, pl. of *cū*, a cow, is formed by vowel-change from *ū* to *ȳ*.

Cow (2), to dishearten. (Scand.) Icel. *kūga*, to tyrannise over; Dan. *kue*, to coerce, subdue; Swed. *kufva*, to suppress.

Coward. (F.—L.) A.F. *couard*, a hare, a coward, F. *couard*, a coward; cf. Ital. *codardo*, a coward. Probably named from the 'bob-tailed' hare.—O.F. *coe* (Ital. *coda*), a tail; with F. suffix *-ard*, from Teut. *-hart*, orig. hard. — L. *cauda*, a tail.

Cower. (Scand.) M.E. *couren*.—Icel. *kūra*, Dan. *kure*, to doze, lie quiet; Swed. *kura*, to cower, lie quiet; Swed. dial. *kura*, to sit hunched up. Cf. G. *kauern*, to cower.

Cowl (1), a monk's hood. (L.) M.E. *cūle, coule.* A.S. *cugele, cugle.*—L. *cuculla*, a cowl; cf. also *cucullus.*

Cowl (2), a vessel carried on a pole. (F.—L.) M.E. *couel.*—O.F. *cuvel* (*cuveau*), a little tub; dimin. of *cuve*, a vat, tub.— L. *cūpa*, a tub. **Der.** *cowl-staff.*

Cowry, a small shell used for money. (Hind.—Skt.) Hind. *kaurī*, a small shell (*Cypræa moneta*) used as coin in the lower provinces of India.—Skt. *kaparda.*

Cowslip, a flower. (E.) M.E. *cou-sloppe.* A.S. *cū-sloppe, cū-slyppe*, lit. cow-slop, i. e. a piece of dung. (Other A.S. names of plants are of a very homely character.) Cf. *oxlip*, q. v.; and prov. E. *bull-slop*, a large kind of oxlip (Britten).

Coxcomb. (E.) A fool, named from his *cock's comb*, or fool's cap, cap with a cock's crest.

Coxswain. (F. *and* Scand.) For *cock-swain*; from *cock* (4), a boat, and *swain.*

Coy. (F.—L.) O.F. *coi*, older form *quei*, quiet, still; spelt *coy, quoy*, in Cotgrave.—Folk-L. **quētum*, acc. of **quētus*, for L. *quiētus*, still. See **Quiet.**

Coyote, a prairie-wolf. (Mexican.) From *coyote*, Span. pron. of Mex. *coyotl.*

Cozen. (F.—L.) To *cozen* is to act as *cousin* or kinsman, to sponge upon, beguile. — F. *cousiner*, to call cousin, to sponge, live on other people; see Hamilton and Cotgrave.—F. *cousin*, a cousin; see **Cousin.**

Crab (1), a shell-fish. (E.) A.S. *crabba.*+Icel. *krabbi*, Swed. *krabba*, Dan. *krabbe*, Du. *krab*, G. *krabbe.* Allied to E. Fries. and Du. *krabben*, to scratch,

claw; G. *krebs* (O. H. G. *crebiz*), a crab, Du. *kreeft*, a crab. See **Crayfish.**

crabbed, peevish, cramped. (E.) From *crab*, sb.; i. e. crab-like, snappish or awkward. Cf. Du. *krabben*, to scratch, *kribben*, to be peevish.

Crab (2), a kind of apple. (E.) Cf. Swed. *krabbäple*, crab-apple. Perhaps allied to **crabbed** (above).

Crabbed; see **Crab** (1).

Crack. (E.) A. S. *cracian*, to crack. +Du. *kraken*, to crack, creak; G. *krachen.* Cf. Gael. *crac*, a fissure, *cnac*, a crack, to crack (from E.). Imitative, like *crake, creak, croak, crash, gnash, knock.*

cracknel. (F.—Du.) Formerly *crakenel*, corruption of F. *craquelin*, a cracknel. — Du. *krakeling*, a cracknel. Named from its crispness. — Du. *kraken*, to crack.

crake, corncrake, a bird. (E.) From its cry; M. E. *craken*, to cry out. Allied to *crack, croak.*

Cradle. (E.) A.S. *cradol.* Cf. O.H.G. *cratto*, a basket; also O. H. G. *crezzo*, prov. G. *krätze*, a basket.

Craft, skill. (E.) A. S. *cræft.*+Du. *kracht*, Icel. *kraptr, kraftr*, Swed. Dan. G. *kraft*, force. Cf. A.S. *crafian*, to crave, demand. **Der.** *handi-craft.*

Crag. (C.) W. *craig*, Gael. *creag*, crag, rock; Irish *creag*, a rock; cf. W. *careg*, Gael. *carraig*, rock, cliff, Bret. *karrek*, O. Irish *carric*, a rock.

Crake; see **Crack.**

Cram. (E.) A. S. *crammian*, to stuff. + Icel. *kremja*, Swed. *krama*, Dan. *kramme*, to squeeze. From *cramm-*, 2nd grade of the str. vb. *crimm-an*, to crumble. And cf. **Cramp.**

Cramp. (F.—Teut.) F. *crampe*, 'the crampe,' Cot.; cf. *crampon*, 'a cramp-iron.'—Du. *kramp*, a cramp, spasm. From the 2nd grade of Teut. **krempan-, *krimpan-*, to draw together, as in O.H.G. *krimphan*, to draw together, str. vb. Cf. E. *crimp, cramp, crumple*; Icel. *krappr*, cramped; *kreppa*, to pinch. And compare **Crank.**

Crane, a bird. (E.) A. S. *cran.*+Du. *kraan*, Icel. *trani* (for *krani*), Swed. *trana*, Dan. *trane*, G. *kran-ich*; W. and Bret. *garan*, Gk. γέρανος, a crane, also a crane for raising weights. Cf. L. *grus*, a crane, Lith. *garnys*, a stork. From √GER, to cry out; cf. Gk. γῆρυς, voice (Prellwitz).

cranberry. (Low G.) Modern; from

Low G. *kraanbere* (Berghaus), G. *kran-beere*, lit. craneberry; cf. Dan. *tranebær* (from *trane* = *krane*, as above); Swed. *tranbär*.

Cranium. (L. – Gk.) Med. L. *crā-nium*. – Gk. κρᾱνίον, skull; allied to κάρα, head.

Crank (1), a bend. (E.) M. E. *cranke*. Allied to E. Fries. *krunken*, pp., bent. Cf. Du. *kronkel*, a wrinkle, *kronkelen*, to wrinkle, turn, wind. Teut. base *krenk-, variant of *kreng-. Cf. **Cringe**, **Crinkle**.

crank (2), easily upset, as a boat. (E.) I. e. easily bent or twisted aside. Cf. Du. *krank*, ill, poor; also *krengen*, to careen a boat; Swed. *kränga*, Dan. *krænge*, to heel over; see **Cringe**.

crank (3), lively. (E.) The same word, from the idea of turning quickly. Cf. Norw. *kring*, active, brisk; Dan. dial. *kræng*, dexterous.

Cranny. (F. – L.?) M. E. *crany*. – F. *cran*, a notch; with E. suffix *-y*. Allied to Ital. *crena*, a notch (Florio). Cf. Late L. *crēna*, a notch (a word of doubt-ful authority). See **Crenellate**.

Crants, a garland. (M. Du. – G.) M. Du. *krants*, Du. *krans*, a garland, wreath (whence Dan. *krands*, Sw. *krans*). All from G. *kranz*, a wreath.

Crape. (F. – L.) F. *crêpe*, formerly *crespe*, 'frizzled, crisped, crisp;' Cot. From its wrinkled surface. – L. *crispus*, curled. See **Crisp**.

Crare, a small ship. (F.) In Cymb. iv. 2. 205. M.E. *crayer*. – O.F. *craier*, *creer*, a war-vessel. Of unknown origin.

Crash, vb. (E.) Of imitative origin; closely allied to *crack*. Cf. *clash*, *dash*; and see **Craze**.

Crasis. (Gk.) Gk. κρᾶσις, a mixing; hence, contraction. – Gk. κεράννῡμι, I mix.

Crass. (L.) L. *crassus*, thick, dense.

Cratch, a crib, manger. (F. – O.H.G.) M. E. *crecche*. – O. F. *creche* (*crèche*); Prov. *crepcha*. – O. H. G. *crippea* (whence G. *krippe*), a crib. See **Crib**.

Crate. (L.) L. *crātes*, a hurdle; hence, a wicker-case, &c.

Crater. (L. – Gk.) L. *crātēr*, a bowl, a crater. – Gk. κρᾱτήρ, a large bowl in which things were mixed. – Gk. κεράννῡμι, I mix.

Cravat. (F. – Slavonic.) F. *cravate*, (1) a Croatian, (2) a cravat. *Cravats* were introduced into France in 1636, as

worn by the *Croatians*, who were called in F. *Croates* or *Crovates* or *Cravates*. *Croat* is a name of Slavonic origin; cf. Russ. *Kroat*, a Croatian.

Crave. (E.) A. S. *crafian*, to crave, ask. Cf. Icel. *krefja*, Swed. *kräfva*, Dan. *kræve*, to demand; Icel. *krafa*, a de-mand.

Craven. (F. – L.?) The oldest form is M. E. *cravant*, with the sense of beaten, foiled, or overcome. 1. Mr. Nicol sug-gested that it is a clipped form of O. F. *cravanté*, pp. explained by Cotgrave by 'oppressed, foiled'; this is the pp. of O. F. *cravanter*, to break, oppress = Late L. *crepantāre, formed from *crepant*-, stem of pres. pt. of *crepāre*, to crack, break. Cf. Span. *quebrantar*, to crack, break. 2. But it seems rather to be due simply to the O. F. *cravant*, pres. participle of the O. F. *craver*, *crever*, to burst, break; hence, to fail, to be overcome, to yield. – L. *crepantem*, acc. of the pres. part. of *crepāre*, to burst. Cf. O. F. *crevé*, dead; Span. *quebrar*, to fail; *quebrants*, want of strength, great loss. See Phil. Soc. Trans. 1902; p. 659. See **Decrepit**.

Craw, crop of fowls. (E.?) M. E. *crawe*. As if from A. S. *craga, the neck; not found; N. Fries. *krage*, neck, craw. Allied to Du. *kraag*, G. *kragen*, neck, collar (whence Late Icel. *kragi*, Swed. *krage*, Dan. *krave*, a collar). Note also Dan. *kro*, the craw of a bird; Swed. *kräfva*.

Crawfish, the same as **Crayfish**.

Crawl. (Scand.) Prov. E. *craffle*, *croffle*, to crawl. – Icel. *krafla*, to paw, crawl; Swed. *krafla*, to grope; Dan. *kravle*, to crawl. Cf. N. Fries. *krabli*, *krawli*, to crawl; Low G. *kraueln*. Fre-quentative from Teut. base *krab-, to scratch, claw; see **Crab**.

Crayfish. (F. – O.H.G.) Altered from M. E. *crevise*. – O. F. *crevisse*, *es-crevisse* (*écrevisse*). – O. H. G. *crebiz*, G. *krebs*, a crab; allied to G. *krabbe*, a crab; see **Crab** (1).

Crayon. (F. – L.) F. *crayon*; extended from F. *craie*, chalk. – L. *crēta*, chalk.

Craze. (Scand.) M. E. *crased*, i. e. cracked. – Swed. *krasa*, Dan. *krase*, to crackle; whence also F. *écraser*, to break in pieces. Cf. Swed. *slå in kras*, Dan. *slaae i kras*, to break in shivers.

Creak. (E.) M. E. *kreken*. Allied to *crake*, *crack*. Cf. Du. *kriek*, a cricket,

M. F. *criquer*, to creak, allied to *craquer*, to crack. Of imitative origin.

Cream. (F.—L.—Gk.) O. F. *cresme* (F. *crème*); really the same word as O. F. *cresme* (F. *chrême*), chrism (though confused with L. *cremor*, thick juice).— Late L. *chrisma*, consecrated oil.— Gk. χρῖσμα, an unguent; see **Chrism**.

Crease (1), a wrinkle, as in folding paper, &c. (F.—L.) Earliest spelling *creast*, a ridge (later, a furrow). Variant of *crest*, ridge (as of a roof). Cf. Walloon *cress*, a crest, ridge of a roof, *kretlé*, wrinkled (Remacle); Prov. *crest*, *creis*, a ridge; and prov. E. *crease*, a ridge-tile of a roof. (*Athen*. Sept. 18, 1897.)

Crease (2), **Creese**, a dagger. (Malay.) Malay *krīs*, 'a dagger, kris, or creese;' Marsden.

Create. (L.) From pp. of L. *creāre*, to make.+Skt. *kṛ*, to make. Der. *creature*, O. F. *creature*, L. *creatūra*. And see **Crescent**. Brugm. i. § 641.

Creed. (L.) M. E. *crede*; A. S. *crēda*.—L. *crēdo*, I believe: the first word of the creed.+O. Irish *cretim*, I believe; Skt. *çrad-dadhāmi*, I believe. Der. *credence* (O. F. *credence*, L. *crēdentia*); *credible*; *credit* (L. pp. *crēditus*); *cred-ulous* (L. *crēdulus*), &c. Brugm. i. § 539.

Creek. (E.?) M. E. *creke*, a creek.+Du. *kreek*, M. Du. *krēke*; cf. Icel. *kriki*, a crack, nook (whence F. *crique*). The orig. sense is 'a bend,' as in Swed. dial. *armkrik*, bend of the arm; *krik*, an angle, nook.

Creel, an angler's osier basket. (F.—L.) O. F. *creil*, wicker-work (Ducange, s.v. *cleia*).—L. type *crāticulum*, for *crāticula*, wicker-work, double dimin. of *crates*, a hurdle. See **Crate** and **Grill**.

Creep. (E.) M. E. *crepen*; A. S. *crēopan*.+Du. *kruipen*, Icel. *krjúpa*, Swed. *krypa*, Dan. *krybe*, to crawl. Teut. type **kreupan-*, str. vb.

Creese; see **Crease** (2).

Cremation, burning. (L.) L. *cremā-tiōnem*, acc. of *cremātio*; from pp. of *cremāre*, to burn.

Crenate, notched. (L.) From Late L. *crēna*, M. Ital. *crena*, a notch.

crenellate. (Late L.—F.—L.) From pp. of Late L. *crēnellāre*, to furnish with battlements.—O. F. *crenel*, a battlement; dimin. of O. F. *cren*, F. *cran*, a notch, from Late L. *crēna* (above).

Creole, one born in the W. Indies, but

of European blood. (F.—Span.—L.) F. *créole*.—Span. *criollo*, a negro corruption of **criadillo*, dimin. of *criado*, one educated, instructed, or brought up; hence, a child of European blood. *Criado* is pp. of *criare*, to create, also, to educate.—L. *creāre*, to create, make. ¶ Cf. Span. *criadilla*, dimin. of *criada*, a servant-maid.

Creosote, a liquid distilled from tar. (Gk.) Lit. 'flesh-preserver.'— Gk. κρεο-, for κρέας, flesh; and σωτ-, short for σωτ-ήρ, preserver, from σώζειν, to preserve. (Ill-formed.)

Crescent. (L.) The 'increasing' moon.—L. *crescent-*, stem of pres. pt. of *crescere*, to grow, increase (pp. *crē-tus*), inchoative form allied to *cre-āre*, to make; see **Create**.

Cress. (E.) M. E. *cres*, also *kerse* (by shifting of *r*). A. S. *cærse*, *cerse*, *cressæ*.+Du. *kers*, M. Du. and Low G. *kerse*, G. *kresse*, O. H. G. *cressa*.

Cresset. (F.—L.) M. E. *cresset*, a light in a cup at the top of a pole.—O. F. *cresset*, *craisset*, a cresset (with grease in an iron cup).—O. F. *craisse* (F. *graisse*), grease; Littré.—Folk-L. **crassia*, grease, from L. *crassus*, thick, dense. So also Walloon *craché*, a cresset, from *crache*, grease.

Crest. (F.—L.) O. F. *creste* (F. *crête*.)—L. *crista*, a comb or tuft on a bird's head, crest.

Cretaceous, chalky. (L.) L. *crē-tāce-us*, adj. from *crēta*, chalk; with suffix *ous*.

Crevice, Crevasse. (F.—L.) M. E. *crevice*, *crevase*, *crevasse*.—O. F. *crevasse*, a rift (Late L. *crepātia*).—O. F. *crever*, to burst asunder.—L. *crepāre*, to crackle, burst.

Crew. (F.—L.) Formerly *crue*, short for *accrue*, a re-inforcement.—O. F. *acreue*, increase; orig. fem. of pp. of *ac-croistre*, to increase.—L. *accrescere*, to grow to.—L. *ac-* (for *ad*), to; *crescere*, to grow.

Crewel, a thin worsted yarn. Origin unknown.

Crib, a manger. (E.) A. S. *crib*.+O. Sax. *kribbia*, Du. *krib*, G. *krippe*; allied to Icel. Swed. *krubba*, Dan. *krybbe*. Allied perhaps to M. H. G. *krebe*, a basket; but not to Du. *korf*, G. *korb*, if these are from L. *corbis*. Der. *crib*, verb, to put by in a crib, purloin; *cribb-age*, where *crib* is the secret store of cards

Crick, a spasm or twist in the neck, (E.) M. E. *crykke*; also used in the sense of wrench. Prob. allied to **Crinkle.**

Cricket (1), an insect. (F. — Teut.) M. E. *criket.* — O. F. *crequet, criquet,* cricket. — O. F. *criquer,* to creak, rattle, chirp. — Du. *kriek,* a cricket; *krikkrakken,* to rattle. From the imitative base *krik*; cf. prov. E. *cracket, creaker,* a cricket. Hexham has M. Du. *kricken,* ' to creake.'

Cricket (2), a game. (F. — Du.) The game was once played with a hooked stick (Cot., s. v. *crosse*). — O. F. *criquet,* ' bâton servant de but au jeu de boule ;' Godefroy. — M. Du. *krick, kricke,* a crutch; Hexham. Cf. A. S. *cricc, crycc,* a crutch, staff.

Crime. (F. — L.) F. *crime.* — L. *crīmen,* an accusation, fault (stem *crīmin-*); allied to *cernere,* to decide. + Gk. κρῖμα, κρίμα, a decision; κρίνειν, to judge. Der. *crimin-al, crimin-ate*; hence, *recriminate*

Crimp, to wrinkle. (E.) In late use; answering to an A.S. **crempan,* E. Fries. *krempen,* causal deriv. of **Cramp.** The orig. str. vb. occurs as E. Fries. and Du. *krimpen,* O.H.G. *krimfan*; Teut. type **krempan-* (*krimpan-*), to draw oneself together, shrink up; pt. t. **kramp,* pp. **krumpano-.* See **Cramp** and **Crumple.**

Crimson. (F. — Arab. — Skt.) M. E. *cremosin.* — O. F. *cramoisin, cramoisyne* (see *cramoisi* in Littré); Low L. *cramesīnus,* also *carmesīnus,* crimson (Span. *carmesi,* Ital. *chermisi*). — Arab. *qirmizī,* crimson; from *qirmiz,* the cochineal insect. — Skt. *krmi(s),* a worm. Brugm. i. § 418.

Cringe. (E.) M. E. *crengen*; causal derivative of A. S. *cringan, crincan,* to sink in battle, fall beneath the foe. *Crincan* is a strong verb; see **Crank, Crinkle.**

Cringle, an iron ring. (Low G.) Low G. *kringel,* a ring (Lübben); E. Fries. *kringel*; allied to Icel. *kringla,* a circle (cf. *kringar,* pl., the pullies of a drag-net). Dimin. of E. Fries. *kring,* a ring, Du. *kring,* a circle; allied to **Crinkle, Crank** (1), and **Cringe.**

Crinkle. (E.) M. E. *crinkled, crencled,* twisted. A frequent. form of the causal deriv. of *crink,* which occurs in the A. S. str. vb. *crincan,* to sink in a heap; see **Cringe.**

Crinoline, a lady's stiff skirt. (F. — L.) F. *crinoline,* (1) hair-cloth, (2) crino-

line. — F. *crin* (L. acc. *crīnem*), hair; and *lin,* flax, hence thread, from L. *līnum,* flax, also, a thread.

Cripple. (E.) M. E. *crepel, crupel*; O. Northumb. *crypel,* Luke v. 24. Lit. ' a creeper.' — A. S. *crup-,* weak grade of *crēopan* (pt. t. *crēap*), to creep; with suffix *-el* (for *-ilo-*) of the agent. + Du. *kreupel,* Icel. *kryppill,* G. *krüppel.* Cf. Dan. *kröbling* (from *krybe,* to creep). See **Creep.**

Crisis ; see **Critic.**

Crisp, wrinkled, curled. (L.) A. S. *crisp.* — L. *crispus,* curled. Brugm. i. § 565.

Critic. (L. — Gk.) L. *criticus.* — Gk. κριτικός, able to discern; cf. κριτής, a judge. — Gk. κρί-νειν, to judge. Der. *criterion,* Gk. κριτήριον, a test; *dia-critic,* from Gk. διακριτικός, fit for distinguishing between.

crisis. (Gk.) Gk. κρίσις, a discerning, a crisis. — Gk. κρί-νειν, to judge.

Croak. (E.) Cf. A. S. *crācetung,* croaking. Of imitative origin. Allied to *crake, creak.*

Crochet. (F. — Late L.) F. *crochet,* a little hook ; dimin. of *croc,* a crook. — Late L. *croccum,* acc. of *croccus,* a hook.

Crock, a pitcher. (C.) A. S. *crocca.* Of Celtic origin. Cf. E. Irish *crocan,* Gael. *crog,* Irish *crogan,* W. *crochan,* a pitcher, pot. + Gk. κρωσσός (for κρωκγός), a pitcher. So also Du. *kruik,* Icel. *krukka,* Swed. *kruka,* Dan. *krukke,* G. *krug.*

Crocodile. (F. — L. — Gk.) F. *crocodile.* — L. *crocodīlus.* — Gk. κροκόδειλος, a lizard, a crocodile.

Crocus. (L. — Gk.) L. *crocus.* — Gk. κρόκος, crocus, saffron. Perhaps Semitic; cf. Arab. *karkam,* Heb. *karkōm,* saffron.

Croft. (E.) A. S. *croft,* a field. + Du. *krocht, kroft,* a field on the downs.

Cromlech. (W.) W. *cromlech,* a flagstone laid across others. — W. *crom,* fem. of *crwm,* crooked, bent; *llech,* flat stone.

Crone, an old woman. (F. — L.) Tusser has *crone,* an old ewe. Prob. from Picard *carone,* carrion; whence M. Du. *karonie, kronie,* an old sheep. See **Carrion.**

Crony, an old chum. (Gk. ?) Pepys has *chrony* (N. E. D.). Perhaps for Gk. χρόνιος, a 'long-lasting' friend ; as it arose in college slang (Skinner). Butler rimes *cronies* with *monies.*

Crook, a hook, bend. (Scand.) M. E. *crok* (Ancren Riwle). — Icel. *krōkr,* Swed. *krok,* Dan. *krog,* hook, bend, angle.

Crop. (E.) A. S. *cropp,* the top of a

plant, the craw of a bird; orig. a bunch. [Hence the verb to *crop*, to cut off the tops; and hence *crop*, a harvest.]+Du. *krop*, G. *kropf*, bird's crop; Icel. *kroppr*, a hunch; Swed. *kropp*, Dan. *krop*, trunk of the body. Cf. W. *cropa*, Gael. and Ir. *sgroban*, bird's crop. [To *crop out* is to bunch out.]

croup (2), hinder part of a horse. (F. —Teut.) F. *croupe*, crupper; orig. protuberance.—Icel. *kroppr*, a hunch (above).

crupper. (F.—Teut.) F. *croupière* (O. F. *cropiere*).—F. *croupe* (O. F. *crope*, above).

Croquet, a game. (F.—Late L.) From N. French *croquet*, a little hook, bent stick; the same as F. *crochet*. See **Crochet.**

Crosier. (F.—Late L.) M. E. *crocer*, *croser*, &c. Formed, with suffix *-er*, from M. E. *croce*, in the same sense of 'bishop's staff.'—O. F. *croce*, 'a crosier,' Cot.; mod. F. *crosse*; Late L. *crocia*.—O. F. *croc*, a hook; see **Crochet.** ¶ Not from *cross*, though early confused with M. E. *croisier*, a coinage from O. F. *crois*, a cross.

Cross. (L.) M. E. *cros*; from Icel. *kross*, adopted from O. Irish *cros*.—L. *cruc-em*, acc. of *crux*, a cross. Der. *a-cross*.

cross, adj. (L.) Orig. transverse, from the shape of a cross; hence, peevish.

Crotchet, in music. (F.—Late L.) F. *crochet*, 'a small hook, a quaver in music;' Cot. (The *hooked* mark now called a quaver was called *crochet* in French.) See **Crochet.**

Croton, plant. (Gk.) Gk. κρότων, a tick, which the castor-berry resembles.

Crouch. (F.—Late L.) M. E. *crouchen*, to stoop, bend. — O. F. *crochir*, to grow crooked (Godefroy). — O. F. *croche*, a crook; also *croc*.—Late L. *croccum*, acc. of *croccus*, a hook.

Croup (1), a disease. (E.) From Lowland Sc. *croupe*, *crope*, to croak, make a harsh noise. Of imitative origin; associated with *crow*, *croak*, and with North E. *roup*, *rope*, to call, shout hoarsely, from Icel. *hrōpa*, weak vb., to cry out. Cf. A. S. *hrōpan* (pt. t. *hrēop*), to cry out; G. *rufen* (pt. t. *rief*).

Croup (2), of a horse; see **Crop.**

Crow (1), vb. (E.) A.S. *crāwan* (pt. t. *crēow*), to crow.+Du. *kraaijen*, G. *krähen*, weak verbs; and cf. O. Slav. *grajati*, Lith. *groti*, to crow. Of imitative origin.

crow (2), a bird. (E.) A.S. *crāwe* (see above).+O. S. *krāia*, Du. *kraai*, G. *krähe.* Der. *crow-bar*, bar with a crow-like beak.

Crowd (1), to push, throng. (E.) A.S. *crūdan* (pr. s. *crȳdeþ*, pt. t. *crēad*), to push; whence *croda*, *gecrod*, a crowd, throng. + M. Du. *kruyden*, *kruyen*, Du. *kruien*, to push along; E. Fries. *krōden*, *krūden.* Teut. type *krūdan-*, str. vb.

Crowd (2), a fiddle. (W.) M. E. *croude.*—W. *crwth*, a trunk, belly, crowd, violin, fiddle; Gael. *cruit*, harp; O. Irish *crot*, harp.

Crown. (F.—L.—Gk.) M. E. *corone*, *coroune* (whence *croune*).— O. F. *corone* (F. *couronne*).—L. *corōna*, a wreath.—Gk. κορώνη, end, tip; κορωνίς, a wreath, garland.—Gk. κορωνός, bent, curved. Cf. Gk. κυρτός, L. *curuus*, bent.

Crucial. (F.—L.) F. *crucial*, 'cross-like;' Cot.—L. *cruci-*, decl. stem of *crux*, a cross; with suffix *-ālis.*

crucify. (F.—L.) O. F. *crucifier.*—Late L. *crucificāre*, for L. *crucifigere* (pp. *crucifixus*), to fix on a cross.—L. *cruci*, dative of *crux*; *figere*, to fix; see **Fix.** Der. *crucifix, -ion.*

Crucible. (L.) From Late L. *crucibolum*, (1) a night-lamp, (2) a vessel for melting metals. The lamp may have been so named from having four nozzles with wicks, forming a cross (still a common Ital. pattern); as if from *cruci-*, decl. stem of *crux*, a cross; with suffix *-bolum* =*-bulum*, as in *tūribulum*, a censer.

Crude. (L.) L. *crūdus*, raw. Allied to **Raw.**

cruel. (F.—L.) O. F. *cruel.* — L. *crūdēlis*, cruel; allied to *crūdus*, raw (above).

Cruet. (F.—Teut.) A. F. *cruet*, a small vessel (Godefroy); dimin. of O. F. *cruie*, *crue*, pot. — Low L. *crūga*, a pitcher. —O.H.G. *kruog*, G. *krug*, a pitcher; allied to **Crock.**

Cruise. (Du.—L.) Du. *kruisen*, to cruise, cross the sea. — Du. *kruis*, a cross. —L. acc. *crūc-em*, from *crux*, a cross; with lengthening of *ŭ.*

Crumb. (E.) Prov. E. *croom.* A. S. *crūma.* (The final *b* is excrescent.)+Du. *kruim*, Dan. *krumme*, G. *krume*, a crumb. Cf. Ital. *grumo*, a clot. Der. *crumb-le*, verb; cf. Du. *kruimelen*, G. *krümeln*, to crumble.

Crumpet, a kind of cake. (E.) Wyclif

has *crompid cake* to render Lat. *laganum* (Ex. xxix. 23); cf. prov. E. *crumpy cake*, crisp cake. For *crump-ed*, pp. of M. E. *crumpen*, to curl up (whence E. *crumple*). Cf. G. *krümpen, krumpen*, to crumple, curl up; *krumm*, curved; Du. *krommen*, to crook, curve. See below.

Crumple, vb. (E.) Frequentative of obs. *crump*, to curl up. From *crump-*, weak grade of A. S. **crimpan*, str. vb.; see **Cramp** and **Crimp**.

Crunch. (E.) An imitative word. Cf. prov. E. *crinch, cranch*, to crunch.

Crupper; see **Crop**.

Crural. (L.) L. *crūrālis*, belonging to the leg. — L. *crūr-*, stem of *crūs*, the leg.

Crusade. (F. *and* Span. — L.) The form is due to confusion of F. *croisade* with Span. *cruzada*. — Late L. *cruciāta*, sb. fem., a marking with the cross, pp. f. of *cruciāre*, to cross. — L. *cruci-*, decl. stem of *crux*, a cross.

Cruse, a small pot. (E.) M. E. *cruse*. W. Fries. *krôss*, E. Fries. *krôs*. + Icel. *krûs*, a pot; Swed. *krus*, Dan. *kruus*, a mug; Du. *kroes*, cup, pot, crucible; M. H. G. *krûse*, G. *krause*, mug.

Crush. (F. — Teut.) O. F. *crusir, cruisir, croissir*, to crack, break; (Span. *cruxir*, Ital. *crosciare*). From a Teut. type **kraustjan-* (see Diez), causal form from Goth. *kriustan*, to gnash with the teeth.

Crust. (F. — L.) O. F. *crouste* (F. *croûte*). — L. *crusta*, crust of bread. Cf. Gk. κρύος, frost; see **Crystal**. Der. *crust-y*, hard like a crust, stubborn, harshly curt (of people).

Crutch. (E.) M. E. *crucche*; from A. S. *crycc*, a crutch, staff. + Du. *kruk*, Swed. *krycka*, Dan. *krykke*, G. *krücke*.

Cry. (F. — L.) M. E. *crien.* — F. *crier*. (Fuller forms occur in Ital. *gridare*, Span. *gritar*, Port. *gritar*.) — L. *quirītāre*, to shriek, cry, lament (Brachet); lit. 'to implore the aid of the *Quirītes*' or Roman citizens (Varro).

Crypt. (L. — Gk.) L. *crypta*. — Gk. κρυπτή, a vault, hidden cave; orig. fem. of κρυπτός, hidden. — Gk. κρύπτειν, to hide.

Crystal. (F. — L. — Gk.) Formerly *cristal*. — O. F. *cristal*. — L. *crystallum*, crystal. — Gk. κρύσταλλος, ice, crystal. — Gk. κρυσταίνειν, to freeze. — Gk. κρύος, frost.

Cub. (E.?) Etym. unknown. Cf.

Shetl. *coob*, to bring forth young, applied only to a seal; Icel. *kobbi, kōpr*, a young seal.

Cube. (F. — L. — Gk.) F. *cube*. — L. acc. *cubum*. — Gk. κύβος, a cube, die.

Cubeb, a spicy berry. (F. — Span. — Arab.) F. *cubebe*, in Cotgrave. — Span. *cubeba*. — Arab. *kabāba(t)*, pl. *kabābah*, cubeb, an aromatic.

Cubit. (L.) L. *cubitus*, an elbow, bend; the length from the elbow to the middle finger's end. Allied to L. *cubāre*, to lie down, recline; see **Covey**.

Cuckold. (F.; *with* G. *suffix*.) M. E. *kokewold, kokeweld, cokold*. — O. F. *cucuault, coucual* (Godefroy), a cuckold. — O. F. *cucu* (F. *coucou*), a cuckoo; with depreciatory suffix *-ault, -al*, from G. *-wald* (Diez, *Gram.* ii. 346). Cf. O. F. *cucu* (F. *coucou*), a cuckoo; secondly, a man whose wife is unfaithful. (There are endless allusions to the comparison between a cuckoo and a cuckold; see Shak. L. L. L. v. 2. 920, &c.)

Cuckoo. (F.) F. *coucou*; from the bird's cry. Cf. L. *cuculus*, a cuckoo; Gk. κόκκυξ, a cuckoo; κόκκυ, its cry; Skt. *kokila-*, a cuckoo; Irish *cuach*, W. *côg*. Cf. *cock, cockatoo*. And see **Coo**.

Cucumber. (L.) The *b* is excrescent; M. E. *cucumer.* — L. *cucumerem*, acc. of *cucumis*, a cucumber.

Cud. (E.) M. E. *cude, code, quide*. A. S. *cwidu, cweodu, cudu*. Teut. type **kwedwom*, neut. Cf. Skt. *jatu-*, resin; also Icel. *kwāδa*, resin. Orig. sense, 'glutinous substance.'

Cuddle. (E.) Perhaps for **couthle*, to be familiar, to fondle; from *couth*, adj. familiar, well known; A. S. *cūδ*, known, pp. of *cunnan*, to know. See **Can** (1). Cf. prov. E. *couth*, loving; *cootle*, to fondle.

Cudgel. (E.) M. E. *kuggel*. A. S. *cycgel*; in Gregory's Pastoral Care, ed. Sweet, p. 297. Cf. **Cog**.

Cudweed. (E.) From *cud* and *weed*; 'the plant being administered to cattle that had lost their cud.' So also *cudwort*.

Cue, for an actor. (L.?) Sometimes written *q* or *qu* in the 16th cent., and supposed to be for L. *quando*, when.

Cuff (1), to strike. (Scand.?) Cf. Swed. *kuffa*, to thrust, push, M. Swed. *kuffa*, to strike, to cuff (Ihre).

Cuff (2), part of the sleeve. (L.?) M. E. *cuffe, coffe*. Cf. Late A. S. *cuffie*, a kind of cap (Leo); M. H. G. *kupfe*, *kuppe*, *kuffe*, a coif; see **Coif**. [Very doubtful.]

Cuirass. (F.—Ital.—L.) Formerly *curace.*—O. F. *cuirace* (F. *cuirasse*).—Ital. *corazza*, a cuirass. Formed from L. *coriāceus*, leathern.—L. *corium*, leather (whence F. *cuir*, leather).

Cuisses, pl. (F.—L.) O. F. *cuissaux*, armour for the thighs.—F. *cuisse*, thigh.—L. *coxa*, hip. Brugm. i. § 609.

Culdee. (C.) Irish *ceilede*, a Culdee, a servant of God.—Ir. *ceile* (O. Irish *cēle*), servant; and *dē*, gen. of *dīa*, God.

Culinary. (L.) L. *culīnārius*, belonging to the kitchen. — L. *culīna*, kitchen.

Cull, to collect, select. (F.—L.) M. E. *cullen.*—O. F. *coillir*, *cuillir*, to collect.— L. *colligere*, to collect. See **Coil** (1) and **Collect**.

Cullender; see **Colander**.

Cullion, a wretch. (F.—L.) A coarse word. F. *couillon* (Ital. *coglione*).—L. *cōleus*.

Cullis, a strong broth, boiled and strained. (F.—L.) Formerly *colys*, *coleys*. — O. F. *coleïs*, *couleïs*, later *coulis*, 'a cullis,' Cot.; substantival use of *coleïs*, later *coulis*, 'gliding,' Cot.—L. type *cōlā-tīcius*; from *cōlāre*, to strain. Cf. **Portcullis**.

Culm, a stem. (L.) L. *culmus*, a stalk; allied to *calamus*, a stalk. See **Haulm**.

Culminate. (L.) From pp. of L. *culmināre*, to come to a top.—L. *culmin-*, stem of *culmen* (= *columen*), a top. See **Column**.

Culpable. (F.—L.) M. E. *coupable*. O. F. *culpable*, *colpable*, *coupable* (F. *coupable*). — L. *culpābilis*, blameworthy.—L. *culpāre*, to blame.—L. *culpa*, a fault.

culprit. (F.—L.) In Dryden. Not orig. a single word, but due to a fusion of A. F. *cul-* (for *culpable*, i. e. guilty) and *prist* or *prest* (i. e. ready to prove it); signifying that the clerk of the crown was ready to prove the indictment (N. E. D.).

Culter; see **Coulter**.

Cultivate. (L.) Late L. *cultīvātus*, pp. of *cultīvāre*, to till.—Late L. *cultīvus*, fit for tilling.—L. *cultus*, pp. of *colere*, to till. Brugm. i. § 121.

culture. (F.—L.) F. *culture.*—L. *cultūra*; allied to *cult-us*, pp. of *colere*, to till.

Culver. (E.) A. S. *culfre*, a dove.

Culverin. (F.—L.) Corrupt form, for **culvrin.*—F. *coulevrine*, a culverin; a piece of ordnance named from its long shape, like a snake.—O. F. *couleuvrin*, adder-like; from *couleuvre*, an adder.—L. *colubra*, *coluber*, an adder.

Culvert, an arched drain. (F.—L.) Of doubtful origin; perhaps formed, with added *t*, from O. F. *coulouère*, 'a channel, gutter,' Cot.—F. *couler*, to trickle.—L. *cōlāre*, to strain, drain. Compare **Portcullis** and **Cullis**.

Cumber. (F.—Late L.) M. E. *combren.*—O. F. *combrer*, to hinder (rare); usual form *en-combrer.*—Late L. *cumbrus*, a heap, a barrier; of doubtful origin. [Cf. L. *cumulus*, a heap; but also G. *kummer*, grief, oppression, prov. G. *kummer*, rubbish. Thus *cumber* = to put a heap in the way.] **Der.** *en-cumber*, from O. F. *encombrer*, to encumber, load.

Cumin, Cummin, a plant. (L.— Gk.—Heb.) M. E. *comin*. A. S. *cumin*, *cymen.*—L. *cumīnum*, Matt. xxiii. 23.— Gk. κύμινον.—Heb. *kammōn*, cumin.

Cumulate. (L.) From pp. of L. *cumulāre*, to heap up.—L. *cumulus*, a heap.

Cuneate, wedge-shaped. (L.) Formed, with suffix *-ate*, from L. *cune-us*, a wedge. Allied to **Coin**. **Der.** *cunei-form*; i. e. wedge-shaped.

Cunning, adj. (E.) Orig. pres. pt. of M. E. *cunnen*, to know; hence, 'knowing.' From A. S. *cunnan*, to know; see **Can** (1).

cunning, sb. (E.) M. E. *cunninge*. From A. S. *cunnan*, to know. Perhaps suggested by Icel. *kunnandi*, knowledge; from Icel. *kunna*, to know.

Cup. (L.) A. S. *cuppe*, a cup.—Late L. *cuppa*, variant of L. *cūpa*, a tub, in Late L., a drinking-vessel; whence also Du. Dan. *kop*, F. *coupe*, &c. See **Coop**.

cupboard. (L. *and* E.) M. E. *cupborde*, orig. a side-board for holding cups; Allit. Poems, B. 1440; Morte Arth. 206.

Cupid, god of love. (L.) L. *cupīdo*, desire.—L. *cupere*, to desire. + Skt. *kup*, to become excited. **Der.** *cupid-i-ty*, F. *cupidité*, from L. acc. *cupiditātem*.

Cupola. (Ital.—L.) Ital. *cupola*, a dome; from its shape.—L. *cūpula*, a small cask, a little vault; dimin. of L. *cūpa*, a cask.

Cupreous, coppery. (L.) L. *cupre-us*,

of copper; with suffix *-ous.*—L. *cuprum,*
copper.

Cur. (E.) M. E. *kur-dogge* (ab. 1225).
+M. Du. *korre,* a house-dog; cf. Swed.
dial. *kurre,* a dog. Named from growling.
Cf. prov. E. *curr,* to purr; Low G.
kurren, to snarl (Lübben); Icel. *kurra,*
to murmur, grumble; Swed. *kurra,* to
rumble.

Curate; see Cure.

Curb. (F. − L.) M. E. *courben,* to
bend.—F. *courber,* to bend, bow. − L.
curuāre, to bend; from *curuus,* bent.

Curd. (E.) M. E. *curd, crud.* Prob.
from A. S. *crud-,* related to *crūdan,*
to crowd, press together. Cf. Ir. *gruth,*
Gael. *gruth,* curds. (Fick, ii. 119.)

Cure. (F.−L.) O. F. *cure.*—L. *cūra,*
attention (prim. Ital. **koizā*). Brugm. i.
§ 874. ¶ Not allied to *care.*

curate. (L.) Med. L. *cūrātus,* a
priest, curate; cf. *cūrātum beneficium,*
a benefice with cure of souls.—L. *cūra,*
cure.

curious. (F.−L.) O. F. *curios.*−L.
cūriōsus, attentive.—L. *cūra,* attention.

Curfew. (F.−L.) A. F. *coeverfu,*
covrefeu, curfeu; O. F. *covrefeu* (F. *couvre-*
feu), a fire-cover, covering of fires, time
for putting out fires.—O. F. *covrir,* to
cover; *feu,* fire (<L. *focum,* acc. of *focus,*
hearth, fire); see Cover and Focus.

Curious; see Cure.

Curl, sb. (E.) M. E. *crul* (with shifting of *r*); from M. E. *crul,* adj., curly
(A. D. 1300). Not in A. S. E. Fries.
krulla, krull, krul, a curl.+Du. *krul,* a
curl, *krullen,* to curl; Dan. *krölle,* a curl,
Swed. *krullig,* curly; G. *krolle,* a curl,
M. H. G. *krülle.* Cf. Norw. *krull,* a curl,
something rolled together; *krulla,* to curl,
bend or bow together. Allied to E. Fries.
krillen, to bend, turn, wind; Low G.
krellen, to turn; N. Fries. *krall,* close-
twisted; suggesting Teut. base **krellan-,*
to wind, str. vb. (Franck, Koolman).

Curlew, a bird. (F.) M. F. *corlieu,*
'a curlue;' Cot. Cf. Ital. *chiurlo,* a curlew, *chiurlare,* to howl, Swed. *kurla,* to
coo; so that it is named from its cry.

Curmudgeon. (E.?) Origin unknown.
In one instance spelt *corn-mudgin* (Phil.
Holland), as if a hoarder of corn, hence,
a stingy fellow; where *mudgin* is for
mudging, pres. pt. of *mudge,* to hoard,
also spelt *mooch* (M. E. *muchen*), to skulk;
from O. F. *mucer,* to hide. But this is a

forced spelling, giving a wrong clue. In
1596, we find *cormullion,* with the same
sense. The first syllable seems to be *cur,*
a whelp; and we find Lowl. Sc. *murgeon,*
to mock, to grumble; *mudgeon,* a grimace.

Currant. (F.−L.−Gk.) Formerly
raysyns of coraunt.−F. *raisins de Corinthe,*
'currants;' Cot. Hence, *currant* is a corruption of *Corinth* (L. *Corinthus,* Gk.
Κόρινθος).

Current, running, flowing. (F.−L.)
M. E. *currant,* O. F. *curant,* pres. pt. of
curre, corre (F. *courir*), to run.—L. *cur-*
rere, to run. Prob. for **cursere.* Brugm.
i. §§ 499, 516. Perhaps allied to Horse.

curricle. (L.) L. *curriculum,* a
running; also, a light car.—L. *currere,*
to run.

Curry (1), to dress leather. (F.−L.
and Teut.) O. F. *correier* (Godefroy),
earlier forms *conreder, conreër,* later *con-*
royer, courroier, to curry, dress leather,
orig. to prepare.—O. F. *conrei,* older form
cunreid, gear, preparation. A hybrid
word; made by prefixing *con-* (=L. *con,*
cum) to O. F. *rei,* order (Ital. *-redo* in
arredo, array). β. This O. F. *rei* is of
Scand. origin; from Dan. *rede,* order (also
to set in order), Icel. *reiði,* tackle. Precisely the same O. F. *rei* helps to form E.
ar-ray; see Array. ¶ To *curry favour*
is a corruption of M. E. *to curry favel,* to
rub down a horse; *Favel* was a common
old name for a horse.

Curry (2), a seasoned dish. (Tamil.)
From Tamil *kari,* sauce, relish for rice
(Yule).

Curse. (E.) A. S. *cursian,* verb; *curs,*
sb., an imprecation. Cf. O. Ir. *cūrsaigim,*
'I reprehend' (Windisch). Der. *ac-cursed,*
from M. E. *acorsien,* to curse extremely,
where the prefix *a-*=A. S. *ā-,* very; see
A- (4).

Cursive. (L.) Med. L. *cursīvus,* flowing; said of handwriting.—L. *curs-us,* pp.
of *currere,* to run. See Current.

cursory. (L.) Late L. *cursōrius,*
hasty.—L. *cursōri-,* decl. stem of *cursor,*
a runner.—L. *curs-us* (above).

Curt. (L.) L. *curtus,* short, cut short.

curtail. (F.−L.) It has nothing to
do with *tail,* but is an alteration of the
older form *curtal,* verb, to dock; from the
adj. *curtal,* having a docked tail (All's
Well, ii. 3. 65). − O. F. *courtault,* later
courtaut, 'curtall, being curtalled;' Cot.
The same as Ital. *cortaldo,* 'a curtall, a

horse without a taile,' Florio. Formed, with suffix *-ault* (=Ital. *-aldo*, Low L. *-aldus*, < G. *wald*, power), from O. F. *court*, short. ─ L. *curtus*, short.

Curtain. (F. L.) M. E. *cortin*. ─ O. F. *cortine*. ─ Late L. *cortīna*, a curtain (Exod. xxvi. 1, Vulgate), a screen, plain wall of a fort, orig. a small yard. ─ L. *cŏrt-em*, acc. of *cŏrs*, a court. See **Court.**

Curtleaxe. (F. ─ L.) A perversion of *cuttleax*, which was a perversion of *cuttleax*, an old spelling of *cutlass*. See **Cutlass.**

Curtsey. (F. ─ L.) The same word as *courtesy*, i. e. a courtly act.

Curve, a bent line. (L.) Late L. *curvus*, L. *curuus*, bent. ✝ Gk. κύρτος, bent. **Der.** *curv-ature*, L. *curuātūra*, from pp. of *curuāre*, to bend; from *curuus*.

curvet. (Ital. ─ L.) Ital. *corvetta*, a curvet, leap, bound; dimin. from M. Ital. *corv-o* (Ital. *curvo*), bent. ─ L. *curuus* (above).

Cushat, the ring-dove. (E.) A.S. *cū-sceote*, a wild pigeon; also *cuscote*. Here *sceote* probably means 'shooter, darter,' from *scēotan*, to shoot (cf. A. S. *scēota*, a kind of trout); and perhaps *cū* refers to the ' coo' of the bird. Cf. Lowl. Sc. *cowshot*, a cushat.

Cushion. (F.─L.) M.E. *quisshin*, *cusshin*. ─ O. F. *coissin*, *coussin*, a cushion. [It is supposed that O. F. *coissin* was the true form, altered to *coussin* (perhaps) by the influence of O. F. *coute*, a quilt.] ─ L. type **coxinum*, a support for the hip, from *coxa*, hip, thigh (like L. *cubital*, elbow-cushion, from *cubitus*, elbow). Cf. Ital. *cuscino*, cushion, *coscia*, hip; Span. *cojin*, cushion, *cuja*, hip. (*Romania*, 1892, p. 87.)

Cusp. (L.) L. *cuspis*, a point.

Custard. (F. ─ Ital. ─ L.) For M. E. *crustade*, by shifting of *r*. Formerly *custade*, *crustade*, and orig. used with the sense of ' pasty.' ─ F. *croustade*, a pasty. ─ Ital. *crostata*, ' a kinde of daintie pye ;' Florio. ─ L. *crustāta*, fem. pp. of *crustāre*, to encrust. ─ L. *crusta*, a crust.

Custody. (L.) L. *custōdia*, a keeping guard. ─ L. *custōd(i)-*, stem of *custos*, a guardian; lit. ' hider.' Cf. Gk. κεύθειν, to hide. See **Hide.** (√KEUDH.) Brugm. i. § 699.

Custom. (F.─L.) M. E. *custume*. ─ O. F. *custume*, *costume* (F. *coutume*).

From a L. type **costumne*, for **costudne*, shortened form of *consuētudinem*, acc. of *consuētudo*, custom. ─ L. *consuētus*, pp. of *consuescere*, to accustom, inchoative form of **consuēre*, to be accustomed. ─ L. *con-* (*cum*), together, very; *suescere* (pp. *suētus*), to be accustomed; possibly from *suus*, own; so that *suescere* = to have it one's own way.

Cut. (Scand.) M. E. *cutten*, a weak verb. Of Scand. origin, but the traces of it are not many. Cf. Mid. Swed. *kotta*, to cut (Ihre); Swed. dial. *kuta*, *kåta*, to cut small with a knife, also spelt *kvðta*, *köta*, *käta*; *kuta*, or *kytti*, a knife (Rietz); Icel. *kuti*, a little knife; Norw. *kyttel*, *kytel*, *kjutul*, a knife for barking trees.

Cuticle. (L.) L. *cutīcula*, double dimin. of *cutis*, hide, skin. See **Hide.** Der. *cut-an-e-ous*, from *cut-is*.

Cutlass. (F.─L.) F. *coutelas*, ' a cuttelas, or courtelas, or short sword ;' Cot. (Cf. Ital. *coltellaccio*, ' a curtleax,' Florio ; which is the same word.) ─ O. F. *coutel*, *cultel* (F. *couteau*), a knife; cf. Ital. *coltello*, knife; with acc. suffix *-āceum*. ─ L. acc. *cultellum*, a knife; dimin. of *culter*, a coulter. ¶ The F. *-as*, Ital. *-accio* = L. *-āceum*; but F. *coutelas* was actually turned into E. *curtleaxe*. Yet a *curtleaxe* was a sort of sword!

cutler. (F.─L.) M. E. *coteler*. ─ O. F. *cotelier*. ─ Late L. *cultellārius*, knife-maker. ─ L. *cultellus*, a knife (above).

Cutlet. (F.─L.) F. *côtelette*, a cutlet; formerly *costelette*, a little rib; dimin. of O. F. *coste*, rib. ─ L. *costa*, a rib; see **Coast.**

Cuttle, a fish. (E.) Formerly *cudele*. A.S. *cudele*, a cuttle-fish. Cf. G. *kuttelfisch* (perhaps from E.).

Cycle. (F.─L.─Gk.) F. *cycle*. ─ L. *cyclum*, acc. of *cyclus*. ─ Gk. κύκλος, a circle, cycle. ✝ Skt. *chakra-*, a wheel, circle. Allied to **Wheel.** Der. *cyclone* = Gk. κυκλῶν, whirling round, pres. pt. of κυκλόω, I whirl round; *epi-cycle*; *bi-cycle*.

Cygnet, a young swan. (F.─L.─Gk.) Dimin. of O. F. *cigne*, a swan. Strangely enough, this O. F. word is *not* immediately from L. *cycnus*, a swan; but the oldest O. F. spelling was *cisne* (as in Spanish), from Late L. *cicinus*, a swan, variant of *cycnus*. ─ Gk. κύκνος, a swan. Cf. L. *ciconia*, a stork. See Diez; 4th ed. p. 714.

Cylinder. (F.—L.—Gk.) O. F. *cilindre*, later *cylindre*.—L. *cylindrus*.—Gk. κύλινδρος, a roller, cylinder.—Gk. κυλίνδειν, to roll; from κυλίειν, to roll. Cf. O. Slav. *kolo*, a wheel. (✓QEL.)

Cymbal. (F.—L.—Gk.) M.E. *cimbale.* —O. F. *cimbale.*— L. *cymbalum.* — Gk. κύμβαλον, a cymbal; named from its cup-like shape. — Gk. κύμβη, a cup. ✦ Skt. *kumbha-*, a jar. Allied to **Cup**; and see **Comb** (2). (✓KEUBH.)

Cynic, lit. dog-like. (L.—Gk.) L. *cynicus.*— Gk. κυνικός, dog-like, a Cynic.— Gk. κυν-, as in κυν-ός, gen. of κύων, a dog (E. *hound*).

cynosure. (L.—Gk.) L. *cynosūra*, the stars in the tail of the constellation of the Lesser Bear; one of these is the Pole-star (hence, a centre of attraction).— Gk. κυνόσουρα, the Cynosure, tail of the Lesser Bear; lit. ' dog's tail.'— Gk. κύνος, gen. of κύων, a dog; οὐρά, a tail.

Cypress (1), a tree. (F.—L.—Gk.) M. E. *cipres.*—O. F. *cypres*, later *cyprès.*— L. *cupressus*, *cyparissus.*— Gk. κυπάρισσος, cypress-tree. Cf. Heb. *gōpher*.

Cypress (2), a cloth of gold, a kind of satin, a kind of crape. (F.—L.) Pals-grave explains F. *crespe* by ' a cypres for a womans neck'; Cotgrave has ' *crespe*, cipres, cobweb lawn'; which suggests some confusion of *cypress* with *crape*. The origin of *cypress* is doubtful; but it occurs as *cipres*, *cypirs* in Piers Plow-man, and as *cyprus* in Sir Degrevant. It seems to have been imported from the isle of *Cyprus*.

Cyst, a pouch (in animals) containing morbid matter. (L. — Gk.) Formerly written *cystis.*— Late L. *cystis.* — Gk. κύστις, a bag. pouch.

Czar, the emperor of Russia. (Russ.— Teut.—L.) Russ. *tsare* (with *e* mute), a king. O. Slav. *cěsarĭ.*—Goth. *kaisar.*— L. *Cæsar.* ¶ This has been disputed; but see Matt. xiii. 24 in Schleicher, Indogermanische Chrestomathie, p. 275, where O.Slav. *cesarstvo* occurs for Russ. *tsarstvo*, kingdom; &c. **Der.** *czarowitz*, from Russ. *tsarevich'*, czar's son; *czaritsa*, from Russ. *tsaritsa*, empress; *czar-ina*, with Ital. suffix -*ina*, from G. fem. suffix -*in*.

D.

Dab (1), to strike gently. (E.) M. E. *dabben*; also *dabbe*, a blow. Not in A. S.

Cf. M. Du. *dabben*, to pinch, fumble, dabble; G. *tappen*, to grope, prov. G. *tappe*, fist, blow. See **Dub**, **Tap**.

dabble. (E.) To keep on dabbing; frequent. of *dab.* ✦ M. Du. *dabbelen*, to fumble, dabble; frequent. of M. Du. *dabben* (above).

Dab (2), expert. (E.?) Prob. from *dab* (1); perhaps influenced by *dapper* or by *adept*.

Dab (3), a fish. (E.) M. E. *dabbe*. Prob. allied to *dab*, a light blow, a soft mass dabbed down. See **Dab** (1), **dabble.**

Dabble; see **Dab** (1).

Dab-chick. (E.) Formerly *dap-chick*, *dop-chick*. Cf. A. S. *dop-enid*, a moorhen, lit. ' dipping duck;' *doppettan*, to dip often, immerse; Du. *dobber*, a float. See **Dip.**

Dace. (F. — O. Low G.) Formerly *darce*.—O. F. *dars*, nom. case of the word also spelt *dart*, meaning (1) a dart, (2) a dace. The fish is also called a *dart* or a *dare*, from its swift motion. See **Dare** (2), **Dart.**

Dacoit, a robber. (Hind.) Hind. *ḍākāit*, a robber belonging to an armed gang; from *ḍākā*, robbery by a gang (Wilson). **Der.** *dacoit-y*, robbery.

Dactyl. (L.—Gk.) L. *dactylus*, the metrical foot marked –◡◡.— Gk. δάκτυλος, a finger, a dactyl.

Dad. (E.) A child's word for ' father.' So also W. *tad*, Irish *daid*, Bret. *tat*, *tad*, father; Gk. τάτα, Skt. *tata*, dad.

Dado. (Ital.—L.) Formerly used of the die, or square part in the middle of the pedestal of a column; afterwards applied to the part of an apartment between the plinth and the impost moulding.— Ital. *dado*, a die, cube, pedestal. (Cf. Prov. *dat-z*, a die.)—Folk-L. *datum*, assumed to mean ' a die'; lit. ' a thing given, a lot.'— L. *datum*, neut. of pp. of *dare*, to give. See **Die** (2).

Daffodil. (F.—L.—Gk.) The *d* is a later addition; perhaps from M. F. *fleur d'affrodille*, translated ' daffodil-flower.' M. F. *affodille* ; Prompt. Parv.—M. F. *asphodile*, also *affrodille*, ' th'affodill, or asphodill flower;' Cot.— L. *asphodelus.*— Gk. ἀσφόδελος, a kind of lily. See **As-phodel.**

Daft, foolish ; the same as **Deft.**

Dagger. (F.) M. E. *daggere* ; allied to *daggen*, to pierce.— F. *dague*, a dagger ; of unknown origin (not Celtic). Cf. Ital. Span. *daga*, Port. *adaga*, dagger. The

Port. form suggests an Eastern origin ; cf. Heb. *dākhāh*, to strike.

Daggle, to moisten, wet with dew or spray. (Scand.) Frequentative verb from Swed. *dagg*, Icel. *dögg* (gen. *daggar*), dew. Cf. Icel. *döggva*, to bedew. See **Dew**.

Daguerreotype. (F. *and* Gk.) Formed by adding -*o-type* to F. *Daguerre*, a personal name, the inventor (A. D. 1838).

Dahlia. (Swed.) Named after *Dahl*, a Swedish botanist (A. D. 1791).

Dainty, a delicacy. (F. — L.) M. E. *deintee*, orig. a sb., a pleasant thing ; cf. A. F. *deyntee*, greediness (Bozon). — O. F. *daintie* (i. e. *daintié*), agreeableness. — L. acc. *dignitātem* ; see **Dignity**. ¶ The O. F. *daintie* is the true popular O. F. form ; *digniteit* is a pedantic form ; cf. O. F. *dain*, old spelling of *digne*, worthy.

Dairy. (Scand.) M. E. *deyerye*, a room for a *deye*, i. e. a milk-woman, farm-servant. — O. Norw. *deigja*, Swed. *deja*, a maid, dairy-maid, who was also the bread-maker ; the orig. sense is 'kneader of dough.' — Teut. type **daig-jōn-*, sb. f., as if from (Goth.) *deigan* (pt. t. *daig*), to mould ; whence also Goth. *daigs*, Icel. *deig*, Swed. *deg*, dough ; see **Dough**. ¶ The cognate or borrowed A. S. *dǣge* occurs once only ; see Thorpe, *Dipl.* p. 641.

Dais, a raised floor in a hall. (F. — L. — Gk.) Now used of the raised platform on which the high table in a hall stands. Properly, it was the table *itself* ; but was also used of a canopy over a seat of state, or of the seat of state. M. E. *deis*, *deys*. — A. F. *deis*, O. F. *dois*, a high table (Supp. to Godefroy). — L. *discum*, acc. of *discus*, a quoit, platter ; in Late L. a table. — Gk. δίσκος, a quoit, disc. See **Disc**.

Daisy. (E.) M. E. *dayēsyē* (4 syllables). A. S. *dæges ēage*, eye of day, i. e. the sun, which it resembles.

Dale, a valley. (E.) M. E. *dale*. — A. S. *dæl* (pl. *dal-u*). + Icel. *dalr*, Dan. Swed. *dal*, a dale ; Du. *dal* ; Goth. *dal* ; G. *thal* ; also O. Slav. *dolŭ* (Russ. *dol'*) ; cf. Gk. θόλος, a vault. **Der.** *dell*.

Dally, to trifle. (F. — Teut.) M. E. *dalien*, to play, trifle. — A. F. *and* O. F. *dalier*, to converse, chat, pass the time in light converse (Bozon). Of Teut. origin ; cf. Bavarian *dalen*, to speak and act as children (Schmeller) ; mod. G. (vulgar) *dahlen*, to trifle.

Dalmatic, a vestment. (F. — Dal-matia.) F. *dalmatique*. — L. *dalmatica* (*uestis*) ; fem. of *Dalmaticus*, belonging to Dalmatia.

Dam (1), a mound, bank against water. (E.) A. S. *damm*, only in the derived verb *for-demman*, to dam up ; O. Fries. *dam* ; North. Fries. *dām*. + Du. *dam*, Icel. *dammr*, Dan. *dam*, Swed. *damm*, M. H. G. *tam*, G. *damm*, a dam, dike. Cf. Goth. *faurdammjan*, to dam up.

Dam (2), a mother, applied to animals. (F — L.) The same word as **Dame**.

Damage. (F. — L.) M. E. *damage*. — A. F. *damage* (F. *dommage*) ; cf. Prov. *damnatje*, answering to Late L. **damnāti-cum*, harm ; we find Late L. *damnāticus*, condemned to the mines. — L. *damnātus*, pp. of *damnāre* ; see **Damn**.

Damask. (Ital. — Syria.) M. E. *da-maske*, cloth of Damascus. — Ital. *damasco*. — Heb. *dmeseq*, damask, *Dammeseq*, Damascus (Gen. xiv. 15). **Der.** *damask-rose* ; *damask-ine*, to inlay with gold (F. *damasquiner*, from *damasqu-in*, adj.).

Dame. (F. — L.) M. E. *dame*. — O. F. *dame*, a lady. — L. *domina* ; fem. of *dominus*, a lord. See **Don** (2).

Damn, to condemn. (F. — L.) M. E. *damnen*, *dampnen*. — F. *damner*. — L. *damnāre*, to condemn, fine. — L. *damnum*, loss, fine, penalty. Brug. i. § 762.

Damp. (E.) Cf. A. S. *dampen*, to suffocate ; E. Fries. *damp*, vapour. + Du. *damp*, vapour, steam ; Dan. *damp*, G. *dampf*, vapour ; Swed. *damb*, dust. From the 2nd grade of Teut. **dempan-*, pt. t. **damp*, pp. **dumpano-*, as in M. H. G. *dimpfen*, *timpfen*, str. vb., to reek ; cf. Swed. dial. *dimba*, str. vb., to reek. See **Dumps**.

Damsel. (F. — L.) M. E. *damosel*. — O. F. *dameisele*, a girl, fem. of *dameisel*, a young man, squire, page. — Late L. *domi-cellus*, a page, short for **dominicellus*, double dimin. of *dominus*, a lord. (Pages were often of high birth.)

Damson. (L. — Syria.) M. E. *dama-scene*. — L. *Damascēnum* (*prūnum*), plum of Damascus. See **Damask**.

Dance. (F. — O. H. G.) M. E. *daun-cen*. — O. F. *danser*. — O. H. G. *dansōn*, to drag along (as in a round dance). — O. H. G. *dans*, 2nd grade of *dinsen*, to pull, draw ; allied to E. **Thin**. Cf. Goth. *at-thinsan*, to draw towards one.

Dandelion, a flower. (F. — L.) F. *dent de lion*, tooth of a lion ; named from the jagged leaves.— L. *dent-em*, acc. of *dens*, tooth ; *dē*, prep. ; *leōnem*, acc. of *leo*, lion.

Dandle. (E.) Prob. of imitative origin ; cf. M. F. *dodiner, dodeliner*, 'to rock, dandle, lull,' Cot. ; M. Ital. *dandolare, dondolare*, 'to dandle or play the baby,' Florio ; *dandola, dondola*, a toy. Godefroy gives M. F. *dandiner*, to balance or sway the body. Cf. E. Fries. *dindannen*, to walk unsteadily, sway from side to side.

Dandriff, scurf on the head. (E.) Formerly also *dandruffe*. Of unknown origin ; but cf. prov. E. *dan*, scurf, *dander*, a slight scurf on the skin ; and prov. E. *hurf, urf*, scurf, from Icel. *hrufa*, a scab. ¶ The W. *marw-don*, dandriff, is from *marw*, dead, and *ton*, skin.

Dandy, a beau (E. ?). Origin unknown. Prov. E. *dandy*, gay, fine. Note M. Dan. *dande*, brave, excellent. *Dandy* is also a form of *Andrew*. [F. *danlin*, ' a meacock, noddy, ninny,' Cot., is unsuitable.]

Danger. (F.—L.) M. E. *daungere*, power, esp. power to harm. — O. F. *dangier* (F. *danger*), also *dongier* (XIII cent.), absolute power, irresponsible authority. This answers to a Late L. type *dominiārium, *dominiārium*, not found, but regularly formed from Late L. *dom(i)nium*, power, authority. — Late L. *domnus*, L. *dominus*, a lord.

Dangle, to swing about. (Scand.) Dan. *dangle*, Swed. dial. *dangla*, to swing about ; cf. Swed. and Icel. *dingla*, Dan. *dingle*, to swing about ; frequentative forms from *ding* (pt. t. *dang*), to throw about. See **Ding**.

Dank, moist. (Scand.) M. E. *dank*, wet (esp. with ref. to dew). — Swed. dial. *dank*, marshy ground ; Icel. *dökk* (stem *dankwō-*), a pool. Cf. Swed. dial. *dänka*, to moisten, Dan. dial. *dönke, dynke*, Norw. *dynka*, to wet ; also Dan. dial. *dunkel*, moist, Swed. dial. *dunkelhet*, moisture ; North. E. *danker*, a dark cloud ; Swed. dial. and M. Dan. *dunken*, musty ; G. *dunkel*, dark.

Dapper. (Du.) Orig. good, valiant ; hence brave, fine, spruce. XV cent. — Du. *dapper*, brave.+O. H. G. *taphar*, weighty, valiant, G. *tapfer*, brave ; Russ. *dobrui*, good. Brugm. i. § 563.

Dapple, a spot on an animal. (Scand.) Icel. *depill*, a spot, dot ; a dog with spots over the eyes is also called *depill*. The orig. sense is ' a little pool,' from Norweg.

dape, a pool, a wet splotch ; whence the idea of ' splash ' or ' blot.'

Dare (1), to venture. (E.) M. E. *dar*, I dare ; pt. t. *dorste, durste*. A. S. *ic dearr*, I dare ; *he dearr*, he dare ; pt. t. *dorste* ; *-daursta*, I durst, infin. *-daursan* ; O. H. G. *tar*, I dare, infin. *turran*. Also Gk. θαρ-σεῖν, to be bold, θρασύς, bold ; Skt. *dṛsh*, to dare. (√DHERS.) Brugm. i. § 502.

Dare (2), a dace. (F.—O. Low G.) A new form, made by taking *darce* (old form of *dace*) as a pl. form (=*dars*), and thence making a singular *dar*, now *dare*. See **Dace**.

Dark. (E.) M. E. *derk*. A. S. *deorc*, with a broken vowel ; for older **derc*. The O. H. G. *tarchanjan*, to hide (answering to W. Germ. **dark-n-jan*) is from the 2nd grade **dark* of the same base. Cf. also O. Sax. *der-ni*, A. S. *derne*, O. H. G. *tar-ni*, secret, dark ; see **Tarnish**.

darkling, in the dark. (E.) Formed with adv. suffix *-ling*, as in *flat-ling*, M. E. *hedling* (headlong), A. S. *bæc-ling*, backwards.

Darling. (E.) M. E. *derling*. A. S. *dēorling*, a favourite. — A. S. *dēor-e* (in comp. *dēor-*), dear ; with double dimin. suffix *-l-ing*. See **Dear**.

Darn. (E.) XVII cent. Prob. from M. E. *dernen*, to conceal, from *derne*, adj., secret, hidden ; cf. prov. E. *dern, darn*, to hide, to stop up a hole.—A. S. *derne, dyrne*, secret, hidden. + O. Sax. *derni*, O. H. G. *tarni*, secret. See **Dark**.

Darnel. (F.) M. E. *darnel, dernel*. From an O. F. word, now only preserved in Walloon (Rouchi), *darnelle*, darnel (Hécart). Hitherto unexplained ; but cf. Swed. *dår-*, as in *dår-repe*, or *repe*, darnel (Lowl. Sc. *dornel*) ; and O. F. *nielle, nelle* (Late L. *nigella*), darnel (Godefroy). The Swed. *dåra* means to stupefy (as with *lolium temulentum*) ; cf. Dan. *daare*, a fool ; Walloon *darnise, daurnise*, drunken (Grandgagnage).

Dart. (F.—O. Low G.) M. E. *dart*.— O. F. *dart* (F. *dard*). Of Teut. origin ; cf. A. S. *daroð*, a dart, Swed. *dart*, a dagger, Icel. *darraðr*, a dart, O. H. G. *tart*, a dart.

Dash. (E.) M. E. *daschen*. Cf. Low G. *daschen*, to thrash (Berghaus) ; Dan. *daske*, to slap, Swed. *daska*, to beat ; we speak of water *dashing* against rocks.

Dastard. (Scand. ; *with* F. *suffix*.)

M. E. *dastard*; where *-ard* is a F. suffix, as in *dull-ard*, *slugg-ard*. *Dast* appears to be for *dazed*; cf. Icel. *dæstr*, exhausted, pp. of *dæsa*, to be out of breath; *dasaðr*, exhausted, weary, pp. of *dasask*, to be weary; see **Daze**. Cf. Icel. *dasi*, a lazy fellow, M. Du. *dasaert*, a fool (whence M. E. *das-art* (i. e. *daz(e)ard*), a dullard, in N. E. D.); Low G. *däskopp*, a blockhead (Berghaus). The orig. sense is 'sluggard.'

Date (1), a given point of time. (F.— L.) M. E. *date*.— F. *date*, date.— Late L. *data*, a date; L. *data*, neut. pl. of *datus*, given, dated.— L. *dare*, to give.+Gk. δίδωμι, I give; δοτός, given; Skt. *dadāmi*, I give; Russ. *date*, to give. (√DŌ.) Brugm. i. §§ 167, 168.

Date (2), fruit of the palm. (F.—L.— Gk.) M. E. *date*.— O. F. *date* (F. *datte*), also *datele*, a date.— L. *dactylum*, acc. of *dactylus*.— Gk. δάκτυλος, a finger; also a date (somewhat like a finger). But it is probable that δάκτυλος, a date, was a word of Semitic origin, assimilated to the word for 'finger.' Cf. Aramaic *diqlā*, a palm-tree (see Gen. x. 27); Arab. *daqal*.

Daub. (F.—L.) M. E. *dauben*.—O. F. *dauber*, to plaster; answering to an older form *dalber*. — L. *dealbāre*, to whiten, plaster.— L. *dē*, down, very; *albāre*, to whiten, from *albus*, white; see **Alb.** Cf. Span. *jalbegar* (=*dealbicāre*), to plaster. **Der.** *be-daub*.

Daughter. (E.) M. E. *doghter*, *dohter*. A. S. *dohtor*.+Du. *dochter*, Dan. *datter*, *dotter*, Swed. *dotter*, Icel. *dóttir*, Goth. *dauhtar*, Gk. θυγάτηρ, Pers. *dukhte*, Gk. θυγάτηρ, Pers. *dukhtar*, Skt. *duhitṛ*. Orig. sense doubtful.

Daunt. (F.—L.) M. E. *daunten*.— O. F. *danter*; also *donter*.—L. *domitāre*, to tame, subdue; frequent. of *domāre*, to tame; see **Tame**.

Dauphin. (F.—L.—Gk.) F. *dauphin*, a dolphin; see **Dolphin**. A title of the eldest son of the king of France, who took it from the province of *Dauphiny* (A. D. 1349); and the province had formerly had several lords named *Dauphin*.

Davit, a support for ship's boats. (Heb.?) Formerly spelt *David*, as if from a proper name (A. D. 1626). Also called *daviot* in A. F., a dimin. of O. F. *Davi*, David.

Daw. (E.) From the noise made by the bird; cf. *caw*.+O. H. G. *tāha*, a daw;

dimin. *tāhele* (now G. *dohle*), a daw; whence Ital. *taccola*, a daw (Florio). **Der.** *jack-daw*.

Dawk, transport by relays of men and horses. (Hindi.) Hindi *ḍāk*, post, transport, &c. (Yule).

Dawn; see **Day**.

Day. (E.) M. E. *day*, *dai*, *dæi*. A. S. *dæg*, pl. *dagas*.+Du. Dan. Swed. *dag*, Icel. *dagr*, G. *tag*, Goth. *dags*. Allied to Lith. *dagas*, hot time, autumn; *dègti*, to burn. Teut. type *dagoz*; Idg. type *dhoghos*; from √DHEGH, to burn; Skt. *dah*, to burn, *ni-dāgha-*, hot season. *Day* is the hot, bright time; as opposed to *night*. ¶ In no way allied to L. *diēs*.

dawn, vb. (Scand.) M. E. *dawnen*; from the older sb. *dawning*.— Swed. Dan. *dagning*, a dawning, dawn; as if from a verb *dag-na*, to become day, from Swed. Dan. *dag*, day. **2.** We also find M. E. *dawen*, to dawn; from A. S. *dagian*, to become day, dawn.—A. S. *dag-*, base of *dæg*, day. (Cf. *fawn*, vb.)

Daywoman, dairy-woman. (Scand. and E.) In Shak. L. L. L. i. 2. 137. The addition of *woman* is needless. *Day* = M. E. *deye*.= O. Norw. *deigja*, a maid; esp. a dairymaid; see **Dairy**.

Daze. (Scand.) M. E. *dasen*, to stupefy. — Swed. *dasa*, to lie idle; Icel. *dasask*, to be wearied, lit. to daze oneself, where *-sk* is the reflexive suffix; *dasi*, a lazy man; *dasinn*, lazy; Dan. dial. *dase*, to be idle; Low G. *däsen*, *dösen*, to be listless; *in 'n däs' sein*, to be in a 'daze' (Berghaus).

dazzle, to confuse. (Scand.) From *daze*; with frequent. suffix *-le*. **Der.** *be-dazzle*.

De- (1), *prefix*. (L.; *or* F.—L.) L. *dē*, down, away, from, very; hence sometimes F. *dé-*, *de-*, O. F. *de-*.

De- (2), *prefix*. (F.—L.) F. *dé-*, O. F. *des-*; from L. *dis-*; see **Dis-**.

Deacon. (L. — Gk.) M. E. *deken*. A. S. *diacon*.— L. *diāconus*.— Gk. διάκονος, a servant, a deacon. Cf. ἐγ-κονέω, I am quick, ἐγ-κονίς, a maid-servant.

Dead. (E.) M. E. *deed* A. S. *dēad*, dead.+Du. *dood*, Dan. *död*, Swed. *död*, Icel. *dauðr*, Goth. *dauths*. Teut. type *dau-ðoz*, orig. a pp. with Idg. suffix *-to-* (Teut. *-ðo-*) from the vb. *dau-jan-* (Icel. *deyja*), to die. See **Die** (1).

Deaf. (E.) M. E. *deef*. A. S. *dēaf*.+ Du. *doof*, Dan. *döv*, Swed. *döf*, Icel. *daufr*, Goth. *daubs*, G. *taub*. Orig. ' obfuscated;'

allied to Gk. τῦφος, smoke, darkness, stupor. τύφ-λος, blind. (√DHEUBH.)

Deal (1), a share. (E.) M. E. *deel*. A. S. *dǣl*, a share.✛Du. *deel*, Dan. *deel*, Swed. *del*, Goth. *dails*, G. *theil*. Cf. O. Slav. *dělŭ*, a part. Brugm. i. § 279 (2).

deal (2), to divide, distribute. (E.) M. E. *delen*. A.S. *dǣlan*.–A.S. *dǣl*, a share (above). ✛ Du. *deelen*, Dan. *dele*, Swed. *dela*, Icel. *deila*, Goth. *dailjan*, G. *theilen* ; cf. the respective sbs. (above).

Deal (3), a thin board. (Du.) Du. *deel*, a plank.✛G. *diele*; see **Thill**.

Dean. (F.–L.) M. E. *dene*.–O. F. *deien* (F. *doyen*).–L. *decānum*, acc. of *decānus*. one set over ten soldiers or over ten monks, a dean.–L. *decem*, ten.

Dear. (E.) M. E. *dere*. A.S. *dēore*, *dȳre*, dear, precious.✛Dan. and Swed. *dyr*, dear, costly, Icel. *dȳrr*, dear, precious; O. Sax. *diuri* ; G. *theuer*.

dearth, scarcity. (E.) M. E. *derthe*, dearness; hence, dearth. Not in A. S.; but formed as *heal th*, *warm-th*, &c.✛ Icel. *dȳrð*, value, from *dȳrr* (above) ; O. Sax. *diuritha*, value, from *diuri*, dear, precious; O. H. G. *tiurida*, from *tiuri* (G. *theuer*).

Death. (E.) M. E. *deeth*. A.S. *dēað*. ✛Du. *dood*, Dan. Swed.*död*, Goth. *dauthus*, G *tod*; cf. Icel. *dauði*. Teut. type **dauðuz*, formed with Idg. suffix *-tu-*, Teut. *-ðu-*, from the base **dau-* ; see **Dead**.

Debar (F.) F. *débarrer*; O. F. *desbarrer*. From **De-** (2) and **Bar**.

Debase. (L., *and* F. - L.) Formed from *base* by prefixing L. *dē*, down.

Debate. (F.–L.) M. E. *debaten*.– O. F. *debatre*, to debate, argue.–L. *dē*, down ; *battere*, to beat. See **Batter** (1).

Debauch. (F.–L. *and* Teut.) O. F. *desbaucher*, (F. *débaucher*), 'to debosh, mar, seduce, mislead ;' Cot. Diez supposes that the orig. sense was 'to entice away from a workshop' ; it is certainly derived from the O. F. prefix *des-* (L. *dis-*), away and O. F. *bauche*, explained by Roquefort as 'a little house,' and by Cotgrave as 'a course of stones or bricks in building.' Cf. M. F. *embaucher*, to use in business, employ, *esbaucher*, to rough-hew, frame. Godefroy gives *desbaucher* only in the sense of 'rough-hew,' but his Supp. adds—'detach from one's service, turn aside, distract.' The orig. sense of *bauche* was prob. 'balk,' i. e. beam, hence frame of a building, course in building,

small building, &c.; of Teut. origin; see **Balk**.

Debenture, acknowledgment of a debt. (L.) Formerly *debentur* (Bacon). –L. *dēbentur*, lit. 'they are due,' because such receipts began with the words *dēbentur mihi* (Webster); pr. pl. pass. of *dēbeo*, I owe; see **Debt**.

Debilitate. (L.) From pp. of L. *dēbilitāre*, to weaken.–L. *dēbilis*, weak.– L. *dē*, away, not ; *-bilis*, prob. allied to Skt. *bala-*, strength; cf. *dur-bala-* (for *dus-bala-*), feeble. Brugm. i. § 553.

Debonair. (F.) M. E. *debonere*, *debonaire* ; A. F. *debonaire* for *de bon aire*, lit. of a good stock. – L.*dē*, of; *bon-us*, good; and O. F. *aire*, place, stock, race, a word of uncertain origin. Diez suggests that it represents Lat. acc. *agrum*, field.

Debouch. (F.–L.) F. *déboucher*, to uncork, to emerge from; hence, to march out of a narrow pass.–F. *dé* (= O. F. *des-* <L. *dis-*), away; and *bouche*, mouth, opening, from L. *bucca*, mouth.

Debris, broken pieces. (F. – L. *and* Teut.) F. *débris*, fragments.–O. F. *debrisier*, to break to pieces.–O. F. *de-*, from L. *dē*. down ; and *brisier* (F. *briser*), to break; see **Bruise**.

Debt. (F. – L.) A bad spelling of *dett*, M. E *dette*.–O. F. *dette* (but in M. F. misspelt *debte*).–L. *dēbita*, a sum due; fem. of *dēbitus*, owed, pp. of *dēbēre*, to owe. *Dēbēre = de-hibēre* (Plautus), i.e. to have away, have on loan.–L. *dē-*, down, away ; *habēre*, to have. Der. *debt-or*, M. E. *det-tur*, from O. F. *deteur*, L. acc. *dēbitōrem*.

Debut. (F.–L. *and* O. H. G.) A first appearance in a play.–F. *début*, a first stroke, first cast or throw at dice first play in the game of bowls ; verbal sb. of *débuter*, M. F. *desbuter*, 'to put from the mark he aimed at' (at bowls), Cot. ; hence, to come in first, be entitled to lead From L. *dis-*, from, and F. *but*,mark. See **Butt** (1).

Decade. (F.–L.–Gk.) F. *decade*, 'a decade.' Cot. ; i.e. an aggregate of ten.– L. *decadem*, acc. of *decas*.– Gk. δεκάδα, acc. of δεκάς, a company of ten.–Gk. δέκα, ten ; see **Ten**.

decagon. (Gk.) Named from its ten angles.–Gk. δέκα, ten ; γων-ία, a corner, angle, allied to γόνυ, knee ; see **Knee**. Der. *hendeca-gon* (ἕνδεκα, eleven); *dodeca-gon* (δώδεκα, twelve).

decahedron. (Gk.) Named from its ten sides or bases. — Gk. δέκα, ten: ἕδ-ρα, a base, lit. 'seat,' from ἕζομαι for ἕδυομαι), I sit; see Sit. **Der.** *do-deca-hedron* (Gk. δώδεκα, twelve).

decalogue. (F. — L. — Gk.) F. *décalogue.* — L. *decalogum,* acc. of *decalogus.* — Gk. δεκάλογος, the ten commandments. — Gk. δέκα, ten; λόγος, a speech, saying; see Logic.

decasyllabic, having ten syllables. (Gk.) Gk. δέκα, ten; συλλαβή, a syllable. **Der.** *hendecasyllabic* (Gk. ἕνδεκα, eleven).

Decadence, decay. (F. — L.) F. *décadence.* — Med. L. *dēcadentia.* — L. *dē,* down; *cadentia,* a falling; see Cadence.

Decamp, to depart. (F. — L.) L. *dē-camper*; O. F. *descamper,* orig. to remove a camp. — L. *dis-,* away; and *campus,* a field, later, a camp. See De- (2) and Camp.

Decanal. (L.) Belonging to a dean. — L. *decān-us,* a dean; with suffix *-al* (L. *-ālis*): see Dean.

Decant. (F. — L. and Gk.) F. *décanter* Span. *decantar).* — Med. L. *dēcanthāre* (a word of the alchemists), to pour out. — L. *dē,* from; *canthus,* the 'lip' of a cup, a peculiar use of Gk. κάνθος, corner of the eye (Hatzfeld). **Der.** *decant-er,* a winevessel.

Decapitate. (L.) From pp. of Late L. *dēcapitāre,* to behead. — L. *dē,* off; and *capit-,* stem of *caput,* head.

Decay, to fall into ruin. (F. — L.) O. North F. *decair* (Span. *decaer*); variant of O. F. *dechair, decheoir.* — O. F. *de-*; and *cheoir* (F. *choir*), to fall. — L. *dē,* down; and Folk-L. *cadīre, cadēre,* to fall, variants of L. *cadere,* to fall.

Decease. (F. — L.) M. E. *deces.* — O F. *deces* (F. *décès*), death. — L. acc. *dēcessum,* departure, death. — L. *dēcessus,* pp. of *dēcēdere,* to depart. — L. *dē,* from; *cēdere* to go away.

Deceive. (F. — L.) A. F. *deceivre*; O. F. *deceveir, decevoir,* pres. subj *deceive.* — L. *dēcipere,* to take away, deceive. — L. *dē,* away; and *capere,* to take. **Der.** *deceit* from O. F. *deceit,* pp. of *deceveir.*

December. (L.; *or* F. — L.) O.F. *Decembre.* — L. *December.* — L. *decem,* ten; as it was the tenth month of the Roman year.

Decemvir, one of ten magistrates. (L.) L. *decemuir,* one of the *decemuirī,* or ten men joined in a commission. — L.

decem, ten (see Ten); and *uir,* a man (see Virile).

Decennial, belonging to ten years. (L.) For L *decenn-ālis,* of ten years; cf *bi-ennial.* — L. *dec-em,* ten; *annus,* a year.

Decent. (F. — L.) O. F. *decent.* — L. *decentem,* acc. of pres. pt. of *decēre,* to b come, befit; cf. *decus,* honour.

Deception. (F. — L.) O. F *deception.* — L. acc *deceptiōnem.* — L. *deceptus,* pp. of *decipere,* to deceive; see Deceive.

Decide. (F. — L.) F. *décider.* — L. *dēcīdere,* pp. *dēcīsus,* to cut off, decide. — L. *dē,* down; and *cædere,* to cut. **Der.** *decis-ion* (from pp. *dēcīsus*).

Deciduous, falling off. (L.) L. *dēcidu-us,* that falls down; with suffix *-ous.* — L. *dēcidere,* to fall down. — L. *dē,* down; and *cadere,* to fall. See Decay.

Decimal. (F — L.) O. F. *decimal.* — Late L *decimālis,* belonging to tithes. — L. *decima.* a tithe; fem. of *decimus,* tenth. Cf. L. *decem,* ten.

decimate. (L.) From pp. of L. *decimāre,* to select every tenth man, for punishment. — L. *decem,* ten.

Decipher. (F. *and* Arab.) Formed after F *déchiffrer,* to decipher. — F. *dé-,* O F. *des-,* L. *dis-,* apart; Cipher, q. v.

Deck, to cover. (Du.) Du. *dekken,* to cover; *dek,* a cover, a ship's deck. Cognate with E. Thatch, q.v.

Declaim. (L.) Formerly *declame.* — L. *dēclāmāre,* to cry aloud. — L. *dē,* down, fully; *clāmāre,* to cry; see Claim.

Declare. (F. — L.) O. F. *declarer.* — L. *dēclārāre,* to make clear, declare. — L. *dē,* fully; *clārus,* clear.

Declension. (F. — L.) O.F. *declinaison,* used for the 'declension' of a noun. — L. *dēclīnātiōnem,* acc. of *dēclīnātio,* declination, declension. — L. *dēclīnātus,* pp. of *dēclīnāre* (below).

decline. (F. — L.) O. F. *decliner.* — L. *dēclīnare,* to lean or bend aside from. — L. *dē-,* from; *-clīnāre* (only in comp.), to lean; see Incline, Lean (1).

Declivity. (F. — L.) F. *déclivité.* — L. *dēclīuitātem,* acc. of *dēclīuitās,* a downward slope. — L. *dēclīuis,* sloping downward. — L. *dē,* down; *clīuus,* a slope, hill. See Lean (1).

Decoct. (L.) L. *dēcoctus,* pp. of *dēcoquere,* to boil down. — L. *dē,* down, away; *coquere* to cook.

Decollation, a beheading. (F. — L.)

O. F. *decollation.*—Late L. acc. *dēcollā-tiōnem.* From pp. of *dēcollāre,* to behead. —L. *dē,* off ; *collum,* the neck.

Decompose. (F.—L. *and* Gk.) F. *décomposer* (XVI c.) ; from *de-,* prefix, and *composer,* to compose. See **Compose.**

Decorate. (L.) From pp. of *decorāre,* to adorn.—L. *decŏr-* (for **decos-*), stem of *decus,* honour, ornament ; cf. L. *decēre,* to be fit.

 decorum. (L.) L. *decŏrum,* seemliness ; neut. of *decŏrus,* seemly.—L. *decŏr-,* stem of *decor,* seemliness, allied to *decus* (above). Der. *in-decōrum.*

Decoy, a contrivance for catching wild-ducks. (F. *and* Du.) Coined from prov. E. *coy,* a decoy, by prefixing the E. *de-* (F. *dé-,* L. *dē*). E. *coy* is from Du. *kooi,* a cage, decoy, M. Du. *koye,* older form *kouwe* (Hexham) ; from L. *cauea,* whence also F. and E. *cage ;* see **Cage.** ¶ The prefixing of *de-* was probably due to confusion with M. E. *coyen,* to quiet ; so that *de-coy* seemed to mean a 'quieting down.'

Decrease. (F.—L.) A. F. *descrees, descreis,* O. F. *descrois,* sb., a decrease ; from *descroistre,* vb., to decrease.—Late L. *discrescere,* used for L. *dēcrescere,* to diminish (pp. *dēcrētus*).—L. *dē,* down, away ; *crescere,* to grow.

 decrement. (L.) L. *dēcrēmentum,* a decrease.—L. *dēcrē-tus,* pp. of *dēcres-cere.*

Decree. (F.—L.) M. E. *decree.*—O. F. *decret.*—L. *dēcrētum.*—L. *dēcrētus,* pp. of *dēcernere,* to decree, lit. to separate. —L. *dē,* away ; *cernere,* to distinguish.

 decretal. (F.—L.) O. F. *decretal.* —Late L. *dēcrētāle,* a decree.—L. *dēcrētus.*

Decrepit. (L.) L. *dēcrepitus,* noise-less, creeping about like an old man, aged. —L. *dē,* away ; *crepitus,* noise, allied to *crepitus,* pp. of *crepāre,* to crackle, make a noise.

Decry, to condemn. (F.—L.) O. F. *descrier,* to cry down, disparage.—O. F. *des-* (L. *dis-*), implying the reversal of an act, and here opposed to ' cry up ' ; *crier,* to cry. See **Cry.**

Decussate, to cross at an acute angle. (L.) From pp. of L. *decussāre,* to cross, to put into the form of an X.—L. *decussis,* a coin worth ten asses (as-es), and there-fore marked with X, i. e. ten.—L. *decem,* ten ; *assi-,* stem of *as,* an ace ; see **Ace.**

Dedicate, to devote. (L.) L. *dēdicā-tus,* pp. of *dēdicāre,* to devote.—L. *dē,*

down ; *dicāre,* to proclaim ; from *dic-,* weak grade of *dīc-,* as in *dīcere,* to say.

Deduce. (L.) L. *dēdūcere,* to bring down (hence, to infer).—L. *dē,* down ; *dūcere,* to bring. See **Duke.**

 deduct. (L.) Orig. to derive from. —L. *dēduct-us,* pp. of *dēdūcere,* to bring down (above).

Deed. (E.) M. E. *deed.* O. Merc. *dēd,* A. S. *dǣd.*+Du. *daad,* Icel. *dáð,* Swed. *dåd,* Dan. *daad,* Goth. *dēds,* G. *that,* O. H. G. *tāt.* Teut. type **dǣdis ;* Idg. type **dhētis ;* from √DHĒ, to place, put, do. See **Do.**

Deem. (E.) M. E. *demen.* A. S. *dē-man,* to judge, give a doom.—A. S. *dōm,* a doom ; see **Doom.** Cf. Du. *doemen,* Icel. *dǽma* (for *dœma*), Swed. *döma,* Dan. *dömme,* Goth. *dōmjan,* O. H. G. *tuomian.* Teut. type **dōmjan-,* from **dōmoz,* doom.

Deep, profound. (E.) M. E. *deep.* A. S. *dēop.*+Du. *diep,* Dan. *dyb,* Swed. *djup,* Icel. *djúpr,* G. *tief,* Goth. *diups.* Teut. type **deupoz ;* see **Dip.**

 depth, deepness. (E.) From *deep ;* cf. Icel. *dýpð,* depth, from *djúpr,* deep.+ Du. *diepte ;* Goth. *diupitha.*

Deer. (E.) M. E. *deer,* an animal. A. S. *dēor,* a wild animal.+Du. *dier,* Dan. *dyr,* Swed. *djur,* Icel. *dýr,* Goth. *dius,* G. *thier.* Teut. type **deuzom ;* Idg. type **dheusom,* prob. ' animal ' ; from **dheus-,* to breathe (Kluge). Brugm. i. § 539 (2). Der. *wilder-ness,* q. v.

Deface. (F.—L.) M. E. *defacen.*—O. F. *desfacier,* to deface, disfigure. — O. F. *des-* (<L. *dis-*), apart ; *face,* face ; see **Face.**

Defalcate, to abate, deduct. (L.) From pp. of Late L. *diffalcāre* or *dēfal-cāre,* to abate, deduct, take away.—L. *dif-* (=*dis-*), apart, or else *dē,* away ; Late L. *falcāre,* to cut with a sickle, from L. *falx* (stem *falc-*), a sickle.

Defame. (F.—L.) M. E. *defamen, diffamen.*—O. F. *diffamer,* to take away a man's character.—L. *diffāmāre,* to spread a bad report.—L. *dif-* (for *dis-*), apart ; *fāma,* a report. See **Fame.**

Default. (F.—L.) M. E. *defaute.*—O. F. *defaute,* a default, from *defaillir,* to fail ; imitating *faute* from *faillir.* See **De-** (1) and **Fault.**

Defeasance, a rendering null. (F.—L.) A. F. law-term *defesance,* a rendering void.—O. F. *defesant, defeisant,* pres. part. of *defaire, desfaire,* to render void.—O. F.

des- (L. *dis-*), apart; *faire* (L. *facere*), to make.

defeat. (F. — L.) M. E. *defaiten*, to defeat. — A. F. *defeter*, formed from O. F. *defait, desfait,* pp. of *defaire, desfaire,* to render void (above).

Defecate. (L.) From pp. of *defaecāre,* to free from dregs. — L. *dē,* out; *faec-,* stem of *faex,* pl. *faecēs,* dregs.

Defect. (L.) L. *dēfectus,* a want. — L. *dēfectus,* pp. of *dēficere,* to fail, orig. to undo. — L. *dē,* away; *facere,* to make. Der. *defect-ion, -ive.*

Defend. (F. — L.) M. E. *defenden.* — O. F. *defendre.* — L. *dēfendere,* to defend, lit. strike down or away. — L. *dē,* down; **fendere,* to strike, only in comp. *dē-fendere, of-fendere.* Cf. G. θείνειν, to strike; Skt. *han.* (√GHwEN.) Brugm. i. § 654.

defence. (F. — L.) M. E. *defence.* — O. F. *defense.* — L. *dēfensa,* a defending (Tertullian). — L. *dēfens-us,* pp. of *dēfendere* (above). Also M. E. *defens,* O. F. *defens,* from L. *dēfensum,* neut.

Defer (1), to delay. (F. — L.) M. E. *differren.* — O. F. *differer,* to delay. — L. *differre,* to bear different ways, delay. — L. *dif-* (for *dis-*), apart; *ferre,* to bear.

defer (2), to lay before, submit oneself. (F. — L.) O. F. *deferer,* to admit or give way to an appeal. — L. *dēferre,* to bring down, bring before one. — L. *dē,* down; *ferre,* to bear, carry.

Deficient. (L.) From stem of pres. pt. of *dēficere,* to fail; see Defect.

deficit, lack. (L.) L. *dēficit,* it fails; 3 p. s. pres. of *dēficere* (above).

Defile (1), to pollute. (F. — L.; confused with I.. and E.) M. E. *defoulen,* to trample under foot; later spelling *defoyle*; see Foil (1). This word is obsolete, but it suggested a hybrid compound made by prefixing L. *dē,* down, to the old word *file,* to defile (Macb. iii. 1. 65) = A. S. *fylan* (for **fūljan*), to defile, make foul, formed (by vowel-change of *ū* to *ȳ*) from A. S. *fūl,* foul; see Foul.

Defile (2), to march in a file. (F. — L.) F. *dēfiler,* to defile. — F. *dē-* = O. F. *des-* (L. *dis-*), apart; *filer,* to spin threads, from L. *fīlum,* thread. Der. *defile,* sb., F. *dēfilé,* a narrow passage; orig. pp. of *defiler.*

Define. (F. — L.) O. F. *definer,* to define, conclude. — L. *dēfīnīre,* to limit. — L. *dē* down; *fīnīre,* to end, from *fīnis,* end.

Deflect. (L.) L. *dēflectere,* to bend

down or aside. — L. *dē,* down; *flectere,* to bend. Der. *deflex-ion,* from *deflex-us,* pp.

Deflour, Deflower. (F. — L.) M. E. *deflouren.* — O. F. *defleurer,* Cotg. — Late L. *dēflōrāre,* to gather flowers. — L. *dē,* away; *flōr-,* for *flōs,* a flower.

Defluxion. (L.) From acc. of L. *dēfluxio,* a flowing down. — L. *dē,* down; *flux-us,* pp. of *fluere,* to flow.

Deforce, to dispossess. (F. — L.) Legal. — A. F. *deforcer,* to dispossess (Med. L. *difforciāre*). — O. F. *de-*=*des-* (L. *dis-*), away; and F. *force.* See Force.

Deform. (F. — L.) M. E. *deformen,* chiefly in pp. *deformed.* — O. F. *difformer,* to deform; Godefroy. — O. F. *difforme,* adj., deformed, ugly; Cot. — L. *dēformis,* ugly. — L. *dē,* away; *forma,* shape, beauty.

Defraud. (F. — L.) O. F. *defrauder.* — L. *dēfraudāre,* to deprive by fraud. — L. *dē,* away; *fraud-,* stem of *fraus,* fraud.

Defray. (F. — L. and O. H. G.) O. F. *desfrayer,* to pay expenses; Littré. — O. F. *des-* (L. *dis-*); *fraier,* to spend. *Fraier* is from O. F. **frai, *fre,* later *frait,* mostly used in the pl. *frais, fres* (F. *frais*), expenses; cf. Low L. *fredum,* a fine, composition. — O. H. G. *fridu* (G. *friede*), peace; also, a fine for a breach of the peace. See **Affray.**

Deft, neat, dexterous. (E.) M. E. *deft, daft.* A. S. *dæfte,* as seen in *ge-dæfte,* mild, gentle, meek; *ge-dæftlīce,* fitly, seasonably; *dæftan,* to prepare. Cf. A. S. *ge-daf-en,* fit, pp. of a lost strong vb. **dafan*; Goth. *gadaban,* to befit, *gadōbs,* fitting.

Defunct, dead. (L.) L. *dēfunctus,* i. e. having fully performed the course of life, pp. of *dēfungī,* to perform fully. — L. *dē,* fully; and *fungī,* to perform; see Function.

Defy. (F. — L.) M. E. *defyen.* — O. F. *defier, deffier, desfier,* orig. to renounce one's faith. — Late L. *diffīdāre,* to renounce faith. — L. *dif-* (for *dis-*), apart; *-fīdāre* (from *fīdus,* faithful), to trust; cf. L. *fīdere,* to trust. See **Faith.**

Degenerate. (L.) From pp. of L. *dēgenerāre,* to become base. — L. *dēgener,* adj., base. — L. *dē,* down; *gener-* (for **genes-*), stem of *genus,* race. See **Genus.**

Deglutition, swallowing. (F. — L.) F. *dēglutition.* — L. *dē,* down; *glūtītus,* pp. of *glūtīre,* to swallow.

Degrade. (F. — L.) O. F. *degrader,* to deprive of rank or office. — Late L. *dē-*

gradāre, the same. — L. *dē*, from ; *gradus*, rank. See **Grade**.

degree. (F.—L.) O.F. *degre, degret*, a step, rank ; orig. a step *down* (used of stairs). — L. *dē*, down ; *gradus* a step.

Dehiscent, gaping. (L.) L. *dēhi-scent-*, stem of pres. pt. of *dēhiscere*, to gape open. — L. *dē*, down ; *hiscere*, to gape, inceptive of *hiāre*, to yawn ; see **Hiatus.**

Deify, Deist ; see Deity.

Deign. (F. — L.) M. E. *deignen.* — A. F. *deign-*, a stem of O. F. *dign'i er*, to deign. — L. *dignāre*, by-form ot *dignāri* to deem worthy. — L. *dignus*, worthy. Brugm. ii. § (6.

Deity. (F.—L.) M. E. *deite.* — O. F. *deite.* — L. *deitātem*, acc. of *deitās*, deity, Godhead. — L. *dei-*, for *deus*, God ; cf. *dīuus*, godlike. Cf. W. *duw*, Gael. and Ir. *dia*, Skt. *dēva-*, a god ; Gk. δῖος, Skt. *daiva-*, divine. See **Tuesday.**

deify. (F. — L.) M. E. *deifyen.* — O. F. *deifier*, ' to deifie ;' Cot. — Late L. *deificāre.* — L *deificus*, accounting as gods. — L. *dei-*, for *deus*, a god ; and *-fic-*, for *facere*, to make. Der. *deificat-ion*, due to pp. of *deificāre.*

deist. (F.—L.) F. *déiste*. From L. *de-us* ; with suffix *-ist.*

Deject, to ca t down. (L.) From L. *dēiectus*, pp. of *dēicere* (*dēiicere*). to cast down. — L. *dē*, down ; *iacere*, to throw.

Delay, vb. (F. — L.) O F *delayer*, *dilaier*; also *deleer* (Godefroy). It answers in sense to L. *dīlātāre*, to defer, delay, put off ; which would properly give O. F. *dileer*. *Dīlātāre* is from *dīlātus*, deferred, put off ; from L. *dī-* (*dis-*), apart ; *lātus*, borne, pp. of *tollere*, to lift, sustain, bear. ¶ The O. F. spelling with *ai* causes a difficulty. Der. *delay*, sb. ; O. F. *delai*.

Delectable. (F.—L.) Late M. E. *delectable.* — F. *délectable* — L *dēlectābilis*, delightiul. — L. *dēlectāre*, to delight ; frequent. of *dēlicere*, to allure. See **Delicious.**

Delegate, a chosen deputy. (L.) L. *dēlēgātus*, pp. of *dēlēgāre*, to depute, appoint. — L. *dē*, away ; *lēgāre*, to depute. See **Legate.**

Delete, to erase. (L) L. *dēlētus*, pp. of *dēlēre*. to destroy. See below.

Deleterious. (Gk.) Late L. *dēlē-tēri-us*, with suffix *-ous*. For Gk. δηλη-τήριος, noxious. — Gk. δηληγήρ, a destroyer. — Gk. δηλέομαι, I harm, injure.

Delf. (Du.) Earthenware first made at *Delft*, formerly *Delf*, a town in S. Holland, about A. D. 1310 (Haydn). The town was named from its *delf* or canal ; cf. **Delve.**

Deliberate, carefully weighed and considered. (L) L. *dēlīberātus*, pp. of *dē-l berāre*, to consult. — L. *dē*, thoroughly ; *librāre*, to weigh, from *libra*, a balance.

Delicate, dainty, refined. (L.) L. *dēlicātus*, luxurious ; probably allied to *dēlicia* (or *dēliciæ*, pl.), pleasure, delight, and to L. *dēlicere*, to amuse (below).

delicious. (F.—L.) M E. *delicious*. — O. F. *delicious*. — Late L. *dēliciōsus*, pleasant. — L. *dēlicia*, pleasure. — L. *dē-licere*, to amuse, allure. — L. *dē*, away ; *lacere*, to entice.

delight. (F. — L.) Misspelt for *delite*. M. E. *deliten*. verb. — O. F. *deliter, delei-ter.* — L. *dēlectāre* ; see **Delectable.**

Delineate. (L.) From pp. of L. *dēlīneāre*, to sketch in outline. — L. *dē*, down ; *lineāre*, to mark out, from *līnea*, a line See **Line.**

Delinquent, failing in duty. (L.) L. *dēlinquent-*, stem of pres. pt. of *dēlinquere*, to fail, to omit one's duty. — L. *dē*, away, from ; *linquere*, to leave.

Deliquesce, to become liquid. (L.) L. *dēlīquescere*, to become liquid. — L. *dē*, away ; *līquescere*, inceptive form of *līquēre*, to be wet. See **Liquid.**

Delirious. (L.) A coined word (with suffix *-ous*), from L. *dēliri-um*, madness, which is also adopted into English. — L. *dēlīrus*, mad : lit. ' going out of the furrow.' — L. *dē*, from ; and *līra*, a furrow. Cf. O. H. G. *leisa*, G. *g-leise*, a track.

Deliver. (F. — L.) O. F. *delivrer*, to set free. — Late L. *dēlīberāre*, to set tree. — L. *dē*, from ; *līberāre*, to free, from *līber*, free.

Dell, a dale. (E.) M. E. *delle*. A. S. *dell*, neut. ; Cart. Sax. i. 547 ; ii. 71. Teut. type **daljom* ; see **Dale.**

Delta. (Gk.) Gk. δέλτα, the letter Δ ; answering to Heb. *daleth*, the name of the 4th letter of the alphabet ; orig. ' a door of a tent.' Orig. Phœnician.) Der. *deltoid.*

Delude. (L.) L. *dēlūdere* (pp. *dēlūsus*), to mock at, cajole. — L. *dē*, down ; *lūdere*, to play. Der. *delus-ion*, from the pp.

Deluge. (F.—L.) O F. *deluge.* — L. *dīluuium*, a washing away. — L diluere, to wash away. — L. *dī-* (*dis-*), apart ; *luere*, to wash, allied to **Lave.**

Delve, to dig. (E.) M. E. *deluen.*

A. S. *delfan*, pt. t. *dealf*, pp. *dolfen*.+Du. *delven*; M. H. G. *telben*. Cf. Russ. *dol-bite*, to hollow out. Brugm. i. § 521 (2).

Demagogue. (F.—Gk.) F. *déma-gogue.* — Gk. δημαγωγός, a popular leader. —Gk. δῆμ-ος, people; ἀγωγός, leading, from ἄγ-ειν, to lead.

Demand. (F.—L.) F. *demander*, to demand, require.—L. *dēmandāre*, to entrust; in late L., to demand.—L. *dē*, away; *mandāre*, to commission, order.

Demarcation. (Span. — L. and M. H. G.) From Span. *demarcacion* (see N. E. D.); whence also F. *démarcation*. — L. *dē*, down; and Span. *marcar*, to mark, a word of German origin; see **Marque.**

Demean (1), to conduct; *reflex.*, to behave. (F.—L.) M. E. *demenen*.—O. F. *demener*, to conduct, guide, manage. — O. F. *de* (=L. *dē*), down, fully; *mener*, to conduct, from Late L. *mināre*, to drive cattle, conduct, from L. *minārī*, to threaten. See **Menace.**

demeanour. (F.—L.) M. E. *demen-ure* (XV cent.); a coined word, from M. E. *demenen*, to demean, behave; see **Demean** (1).

Demean (2), to debase, lower. (Hybrid; L. *and* E.) Made, like *debase*, from the prefix **De-** (1), and the adj. *mean*. See **Mean** (2).

Demented, mad. (L.) Pp. of the old verb to *dement*,—F. *démenter*, to drive out of one's mind.—L. *dē*, from; *ment-*, stem of *mens*, mind.

Demerit, ill desert. (F.—L.) Also merit, in a *good* sense; Cor. i. 1. 276.— O. F. *demerite*, desert; also a fault, demerit.—Late L. *dēmeritum*, a fault; from pp. of L. *dēmerēre*, *dēmerērī*, to deserve (in a *good* sense).—L. *dē*, fully; *merēre*, *merērī*, to deserve. See **Merit.**

Demesne. (F.—L.) A. F. *demeine*, *demene*, also *demesne* (with silent *s*); other spellings of **Domain**, q. v.

Demi-, half. (F. — L.) O. F. *demi*, half.—L. acc. *dīmidium*, half.—L. *dī-* = *dis-*, apart : *medius*, middle; see **Medium.**

Demijohn, a kind of large bottle. (F.) From F. *dame-jeanne*; cf. Span. *damajuana*. Much disputed, but *not* of Eastern origin. The F. form is right as it stands, though often much perverted. From F. *dame* (Sp. *dama*), lady; and *Jeanne* (Sp. *Juana*), Jane, Joan. See N. E. D.

Demise, transference, decease. (F.—L.) O. F. *demise*, *desmise*, fem. of pp. of *desmettre*, to displace, dismiss. —L. *dīmit-tere*; see **Dismiss.**

Democracy. (F.—Gk.) Formerly *de-mocraty* (Milton). —M. F. *democratie*; Cot. — Gk. δημοκρατία, popular government, rule by the people.— Gk. δημο-, for δῆμος, a country-district, also the people; and κρατεῖν, to rule. Cf. O. Ir. *dām*, a retinue.

Demolish. (F.—L.) O. F. *demoliss-*, inchoative stem of *demolir*, to demolish.— L. *dēmōlīrī*, *dēmōlīre*, to pull down.—L. *dē*, from; *mōles*, heap, mass.

Demon. (L.—Gk.) Formerly *dæmon*. —L. *dæmon*.—Gk. δαίμων, a god, genius, spirit. Cf. δαίομαι, I impart.

Demonstrate. (L.) From pp. of L. *dēmonstrāre*, to show fully.—L. *dē*, down, fully; *monstrāre*, to show, from *monstrum*, a portent. See **Monster.**

Demoralise, to corrupt in morals. (F.—L.) Mod. F. *démoraliser*.—F. *dé-*, O. F. *des* (L. *dis-*), apart; *moral*, moral; with suffix *-ise* (=F. *-iser*, for Gk. *-ιζειν*). See **Moral.**

Demur, vb. (F.—L.) O. F. *demourer*, *demeurer*, to tarry; hence, to hesitate.— L. *dēmorārī*, to delay fully.—L. *dē*, fully; *morārī*, to delay, from *mora*, delay.

Demure. (F.—L.) XIV cent. Coined by prefixing *de-* (see **De-** (1)), to M. E. *mure*, mature, calm, demure.—O. F. *meur* (F. *mûr*), mature. — L. *mātūrus*; see **Mature.**

Demy; a spelling of *demi-*.

Den. (E.) M. E. *den*; A. S. *denn*, a cave, allied to *denu*, a valley.+ M. Du. *denne*, a cave (Kilian).

Denary, relating to tens. (L.) L. *dēnārius*, containing ten.—L. *dēnī* (=*dec-nī*), pl. ten by ten.—L. *dec-em*, ten. Hence *denier*, L. *dēnārius*, piece of ten (as *es*).

Dendroid. (Gk.) Gk. δένδρο-ν, a tree; *-ειδης*, like, from εἶδος, form, shape.

Denizen, a naturalised citizen, inhabitant. (F.—L.) Formerly *deynsein*.— A. F. *and* O. F. *deinzein* (also *denzein*), used in the Liber Albus to denote a trader *within* the privilege of the city franchise, as opposed to *forein*. Formed by adding the suffix *-ein* (=L. *-āneus*) to O. F. *deinz*, now spelt *dans*, within.—L. *dē intus*, from within.—L. *dē*, from; *intus*, within, allied to **Interior.**

Denominate. (L.) From pp. of L. *dēnōmināre*, to name.—L. *dē*, down, fully;

nōmināre, to name, from *nōmin-*, stem of *nōmen*, a name; see **Noun**.

Denote. (F.–L.) F. *dénoter.*–L. *dē-notāre*, to mark out. – L. *dē*, down; *notāre*, to mark, from *nota*, a mark. See **Note**.

Denouement, the undoing of a knot. (F.–L.) F. *dénouement*, sb., from *dénouer*, to undo a knot.–L. *dis-*, apart; *nōdāre*, to knot, from *nōdus*, a knot. See **Node**.

Denounce. (F.–L.) O. F. *denoncer.*–L. *dēnuntiāre*, to declare.–L. *dē*, down, fully; *nuntiāre*, to tell, from *nuntius*, a messenger. See **Nuncio**. Der. *denunciation*, from L. pp. *dēnunciātus*.

Dense. (L.) L. *densus*, thick.+Gk. δασύς, thick. Brugm. i. § 851. Der. *condense*.

Dent; see **Dint**.

Dental. (L.) Formed with suffix *-al* (F. *-al*, L. *-ālis*) from L. *dent-*, stem of *dens*, a tooth, cognate with E. **Tooth**.

dentated, furnished with teeth. (L.) L. *dentātus*, toothed.–L. *dent-*, stem of *dens*, a tooth.

denticle, a little tooth. (L.) L. *denticulus*. double dimin. of *dens*, a tooth.

dentifrice, tooth-powder. (F.–L.) F. *dentifrice.*–L. *dentifricium* (Pliny).– L. *denti-*, decl. stem of *dens*, a tooth; *fric-āre*, to rub.

dentist. (F.–L.) F.*dentiste*. Coined from L. *dent-*, stem of *dens*, a tooth.

dentition. (L.) L. *dentītiōnem*, acc. of *dentītio*, cutting of teeth.–L. *dentītus*, pp. of *dentīre*, to cut teeth.–L. *denti-*, decl. stem of *dens*, a tooth.

Denude, to lay bare. (L.) L. *dēnū-dāre*, to make fully bare.–L. *dē*, fully; *nūdāre*, to lay bare, from *nūdus*, bare. See **Nude**.

Denunciation; see **Denounce**.

Deny. (F.–L.) M. E. *denien.*–M. F. *denier*, earlier form *deneier.*–L. *dēnegāre*, to deny fully.–L. *dē*, fully; *negāre*, to deny. See **Negation**.

Deodand, lit. a thing to be given to God. (L.) From L. *deō*, dat. of *deus*, God; *dandum*, neut. of *dandus*, to be given, from *dare*, to give.

Depart. (F.–L.) O. F. *departir, despartir*, to divide, to part from.–L. *dis-*, away from; *partīre*, to part; see **Part**. Cf. L. *dispertīre*.

Depend. (F.–L.) O. F. *dependre*, to depend, hang on; Cot.– L. *dēpendēre*, to

hang down or from.–L. *dē*, down, from; *pendēre*, to hang. See **Pendant**.

Depict. (L.) Formerly used as a pp. – L. *dēpictus*, pp. of *dēpingere*, to depict, lit. paint fully.–L. *dē*, fully; *pingere*, to paint. Cf. **Picture**.

Depilatory, removing hair. (L.) Formed, in imitation of M. F. *depilatoire* (Cot.), from a L. adj. **dēpilātōrius*, not found.–L. *dēpilā-re*, to pluck out hair. – L. *dē*, away; *pilāre*, to pluck away hair, from *pilus*, hair.

Depletion. (L.) '*Depletion*, an emptying;' Blount. Formed, in imitation of *repletion*, from L. *dēplētus*, pp. of *dēplēre*, to empty.–L. *dē*, away; *plēre*, to fill. See **Plenary**.

Deplore. (F.–L.; *or* L.) O. F. *de-plorer.*–L. *dēplōrāre*, to lament over. – L. *dē*, fully; *plōrāre*, to cry out, wail, weep. Brugm. i. § 154.

Deploy, to open out, extend. (F.–L.) F. *déployer*, to unroll, unfold; O. F. *des-ploier*, to unfold. – L. *dis-*, apart; *plicāre*, to fold. A doublet of **Display**.

Deponent, one who testifies. (L.) L. *dēpōnent-*, stem of the pres. pt. of *dēpōnere*, to lay down, also (in late L.) to testify.– L. *dē*, down; *pōnere*, to lay. See **Position**.

Depopulate. (L.) From pp. of L. *dē-populāre*, to lay waste; in Late L. to deprive of people or inhabitants. Orig. to ravage by means of multitudes.–L. *dē*, fully; *populāre*, to populate, fill with people, from *populus*, people; see **People**.

Deport. (F.–L.) M. F. *deporter*, to bear, endure; *se deporter*, to forbear, quiet oneself.–L. *dēportāre*, to carry down, remove; with extended senses in Late Latin. Der. *deportment*, O. F. *deportement*, behaviour. ¶ For the varying senses, see F. *déporter*.

Depose. (F.–L. *and* Gk.) O. F. *de-poser*, to displace. – O. F. *de-* (L. *dē*), from; and F. *poser*, to place, of Gk. origin, as shown under **Pose**. ¶ Much confused with derivatives from L. *pōnere*, to place. See below.

Deposit, vb. (F.–L.) Obs. F. *depositer*, to entrust.–Med. L. *dēpositāre*, to lay down.–L. *dēpositum*, a thing laid down, neut. of pp. of *dēpōnere*; see **Deponent**.

deposition. (F.–L.) O. F. *deposi-tion.*–L. acc. *dēpositiōnem*, a depositing. –L. *dēpositus*, pp. of *dēpōnere*, to lay down (above).

depot, a store. (F.–L.) F. *dépôt*; O. F. *depost*. – L. *dēpositum*, a thing laid down (hence, stored); neut. of *dēpositus*, pp. of *dēponere*; see **Deponent.**

Deprave. (F.–L.) M.E. *deprauen*. – O. F. *depraver*. – L. *dēprāuāre*, to make crooked, distort, vitiate. – L. *dē*, fully; *prāuus*, crooked, depraved.

Deprecate. (L.) From pp. of L. *dēprecārī*, to pray against, pray to remove. – L. *dē*, away; *precārī*, to pray. See **Precarious.**

Depreciate. (L.) From pp. of L. *dēpretiāre*, to lower the price of. – L. *dē*, down; *pretium*, price. See **Precious.**

Depredate. (L.) From pp. of L. *dēprædārī*, to plunder. – L. *dē*, fully; *prædārī*, to rob, from *præda*, prey; see **Prey.**

Depress. (F.–L.) O. F. *depresser* (Godefroy). – L. type **dēpressāre*; from L. *dēpressus*, pp. of *dēprimere*, to press down. – L. *dē*, down; *premere*, to press.

Deprive. (F.–L.) O. F. *depriver* (Godefroy). – Late L. *dēprīvāre*, to deprive of office, degrade. – L. *dē*, fully; *prīuāre*, to deprive. See **Private.**

Depth; see **Deep.**

Depute. (F.–L.) M. F. *deputer*; Cot. – L. *dēputāre*, to cut off, also to impute, destine. – L. *dē*, down; *putāre*, to cut off, orig. to cleanse. Der. *deput-y*, M. F. *deputé*, one deputed, pp. of *deputer*.

Derange. (F.–L. *and* O. H. G.) F. *déranger*, to disarrange; formerly *desrangier*. – L. *dis-*, apart; O. F. *rangier*, *rengier*, to range; see **Range.**

Dereliction, complete abandonment. (L.) L. acc. *dērelictiōnem*, complete neglect. – L. *dērelictus*, pp. of *dērelinquere*, to forsake. – L. *dē*, from; *relinquere*, to leave behind, from *re-*, back, and *linquere*, to leave. See **Relinquish.**

Deride. (L.) L. *dērīdēre*, to laugh down, laugh at; from *dē*, down, and *rīdēre*, to laugh. Der. *deris-ive*, from pp. *dērīsus*.

Derive. (F.–L.) O. F. *deriver*, to derive, also to drain. – L. *dērīuāre*, to drain off water. – L. *dē*, from; *rīuus*, a stream. See **Rivulet.**

Derm, skin. (Gk.) Gk. δέρμα, skin. – Gk. δέρειν, to flay; cognate with E. **Tear,** vb., to rend.

Derogate. (L.) From pp. of L. *dērogāre*, to repeal a law, detract from. – L. *dē*, away; *rogāre*, to ask, propose a law. See **Rogation.**

Derrick, a kind of crane. (Du.) Orig. the gallows; and named from a Dutch hangman; see T. Dekker, Seven Deadly Sins of London, ed. Arber, p. 17. – Du. *Dierryk, Dirk, Diederik*; answering to G. *Dietrich*, A. S. *Þēodrīc*, 'ruler of the people.'

Dervis, Dervish, a Persian monk, ascetic. (Pers.) Pers. *darvīsh*, poor; a dervish, who professed poverty. Cf. Zend *driγu-*, poor (Horn).

Descant. (F.–L.) Orig. a variation in a song. – O. North F. *descant* (O. F. *deschant*), a kind of song. – Late L. *discantus*, a refrain, kind of singing. – L. *dis-*, apart; and *cantus*, a song. See **Cant** (1).

Descend. (F.–L.) M. F. *descendre*; Cot. – L. *dēscendere*, lit. to climb down. – L. *dē*, down; *scandere*, to climb; see **Scan.**

Describe. (L.) L. *dēscrībere*, to write down, describe fully; pp. *dēscriptus* (whence *description*). – L. *dē*, down; *scrībere*, to write. See **Scribe.**

descry. (F.–L.) M. E. *descryen*, to discern. – O. F. *descrire*, short form of O. F. *descrivre*, to describe. – L. *dēscrībere*. ¶ Sense affected by O. F. *descrier*, to proclaim, publish; from O. F. *des-* (L. *dis-*), and *crier*, to cry.

Desecrate. (L.) From pp. of L. *dēsecrāre* or *dēsacrāre*, to consecrate; (with change of sense due to O. F. *dessacrer*, to profane, from L. *dis-*, apart). – L. *dē*, fully; *sacrāre*, to appoint as sacred; see **Sacred.**

Desert (1), a waste. (F.–L.) O. F. *desert*, a wilderness. – L. *dēsertum*, neut. of *dēsertus*, waste; pp. of *dēserere*, to desert, abandon. – L. *dē*, away (negative); *serere*, to join.

Desert (2), merit. (F.–L.) O. F. *desert*, fem. *deserte*, lit. a thing deserved, pp. of *deservir*, to deserve; see below.

deserve. (F.–L.) O. F. *deservir*. – L. *dēseruīre*, to serve fully; in Late L., to deserve. – L. *dē*, fully; *seruīre*, to serve. See **Serve.**

Deshabille, careless dress. (F.–L.) F. *déshabille*, undress. – F. *déshabiller*, to undress. – F. *dés* (L. *dis-*), apart, away, un-; *habiller*, to dress; see **Habiliment.**

Desiccate, to dry up. (L.) From pp. of L. *dēsiccāre*, to drain dry. – L. *dē*, away; *siccāre*, to dry, from *siccus*, dry.

Desiderate; see **Desire.**

Design, vb. (F.–L.) O. F. *designer*, to denote, to design. – L. *dēsignāre*, to denote, mark down. — L. *dē*, down ; *signāre*, to mark, from *signum*, sign. Der. *design-ate*.

Desire, to long for. (F. — L.) O. F. *desirer, desirrer.* — L. *dēsīderāre*, to long for, regret, miss. Perhaps (like *consīderāre*) allied to *sīdus*, a star, as if to turn the eyes from the stars, to regret, miss.

desiderate. (L.) L. *dēsīderātus*, pp. of *dēsīderāre* (above).

Desist. (F. — L.) O. F. *desister*, to cease. — L. *dēsistere*, to put away, also to desist. — L. *dē*, away ; *sistere*, to put, also to stand still, from *stāre*, to stand.

Desk, a sloping table. (L. — Gk.) M. E. *deske, desk*; in Chaucer, C. T., F. 1128. — Med. L. *desca*, a desk; cf. Ital. *desco*, 'a desk ;' Florio. — L. *discum*, acc. of *discus*, a disc, table. See **Disc, Dish.**

Desolate, solitary. (L.) L. *dēsōlātus*, forsaken ; pp. of *dēsōlāre*, to forsake. — L. *dē*, fully ; *sōlāre*, to make lonely, from *sōlus*, alone.

Despair; see **Desperate.**

Despatch; see **Dispatch.**

Desperate, hopeless. (L.) L. *dēspērātus*, pp. of *dēspērāre*, to lose all hope. — L. *dē*, from ; *spērāre*, to hope; from *spēr-*, as in *spēr-es*, O. Lat. pl. of *spēs*, hope.

despair, vb. (F. — L.) M. E. *despeiren, desperen.* — O. F. *despeir-*, tonic stem of *desperer*, to despair. — L. *dēspērāre* (above).

desperado, a desperate man. (Span. — L.) M. Span. *desperado.* — L. *dēspērātus*, pp. of *dēspērāre* (above).

Despise, to contemn. (F. — L.) M. E. *despisen.* — O. F. *despis-*, stem of the pres. part., &c., of *despire*, to despise. — L. *dēspicere*, to look down, look down on (below). Der. *despic-able*, from L. *dēspicārī*, to look down on, allied to *dēspicere*.

despite, spite, hatred. (F. — L.) M.E. *despit.* — O. F. *despit*, 'despight, spight ;' Cot. — L. *dēspectum*, acc. of *dēspectus*, contempt. — L. *dēspectus*, pp. of *dēspicere*, to despise. — L. *dē*, down ; *specere*, to look ; see **Species.**

Despoil. (F. — L.) O. F. *despoiller* (F. *dépouiller*), to despoil. — L. *dēspoliare*, to plunder. — L. *dē*, fully ; *spoliāre*, to strip of clothing, from *spolium*, spoil ; see **Spoil.**

Despond. (L.) L. *dēspondēre*, (1) to promise fully, (2) to give up, yield (hence,

to despair). — L. *dē*, (1) fully, (2) away ; *spondēre*, to promise.

Despot, a tyrant. (F. — L. — Gk.) O.F. *despot.* — Med. L. *despotus.* — Gk. δεσπότης, a master ; lit. ' master of the house.' The syllable δεσ- = Idg. *dems, '* of a house ;' cf. Skt. *dam-pati-*, master of the house. The syllable πατ- is allied to Gk. πόσις, husband, Skt. *pati-*, lord, and to **Potent.** Brugm. i. § 408.

Desquamation, a scaling off. (L.) From pp. of L. *dēsquāmāre*, to remove scales. — L. *dē*, off; *squāma*, a scale.

Dessert. (F. — L.) O. F. *dessert*, the last course at dinner. — O. F. *desservir*, to do ill service to ; also, to take away the courses at dinner. — O. F. *des-*, from L. *dis-*, away ; *servir*, from *seruīre*, to serve.

Destine. (F. — L.) O. F. *destiner*, to ordain. — L. *dēstināre*, to destine, ordain ; allied to L. *dēstina*, a prop, support. — L. *dē*, down ; and **stanāre*, to cause to stand, derivative of *stāre*, to stand. Cf. Cretic στανύω, I set. Brugm. ii. § 603.

Destitute. (L.) L. *dēstitūtus*, left alone ; pp. of *dēstituere*, to place alone. — L. *dē*, away ; *statuere*, to place, causal of *stāre*, to stand.

Destroy. (F. — L.) M. E. *destroien, destruien.* — O. F. *destruire* (F. *détruire ;* Ital. *distruggere*). — L type **dēstrugere*, for L. *dēstruere*, to pull down, unbuild, overthrow (pp. *dēstructus*). — L. *dē*, down; *struere*. to pile up.

destruction. (F. — L.) O. F. *destruction.* — L. acc. *dēstructiōnem ;* from *dēstruct-us*, pp. of *dēstruere* (above).

Desuetude, disuse. (L.) L. *dēsuētūdo*, disuse. — L. *dēsuētus*, pp. of *dēsuescere*, to grow out of use, opposed to *con-suescere ;* see **Custom.**

Desultory, jumping from one thing to another. (L.) L. *dēsultōrius*, orig. belonging to a *dēsultor ;* hence, inconstant. — L. *dēsultor*, one who leaps down, or from horse to horse. — L. *dēsultus*, pp. of *dēsilīre*, to leap down. — L. *de*, down ; *salīre*, to leap.

Detach. (F. — L. *and* G.) F. *détacher*, to unfasten. — F. *dé-* = O. F. *des-* (L. *dis-*), apart ; F. *tache*, a nail, tack ; see **Tack.** Der. *detachment.* Cf. **Attach.**

Detail, a small part. (F. — L.) O. F. *detail*, ' a peece-mealing, also retaile, or a selling by parcels ;' Cot. — O. F. *detailler*, to cut into pieces. — O. F. *de-* (L. *dē-*), down fully; *tailler*, to cut ; see **Tailor.**

Der. *detail,* verb (which is from the sb. in E., though in F. it is the other way).

Detain. (F. – L.) From a tonic stem of O. F. *detenir.* – L. *dētinēre,* to hold back; pp. *dētontus.* – L. *dē,* down; *tenēre,* to hold. Der. *detention* (from the pp.)

Detect. (L.) From L. *dētectus,* pp. of *dētegere,* to uncover, expose. – L. *dē,* away; *tegere,* to cover. See Tegument.

Detention; see Detain.

Deter. (L.) L. *dēterrēre,* to frighten from. – L. *dē,* from; *terrēre,* to frighten. See Terror.

Deterge, to wipe off. (L.) L. *dētergēre,* to wipe off. – L. *dē,* off; *tergēre,* to wipe. Der. *deterg-ent,* from the pres. pt.

Deteriorate. (L.) L. *dēteriōrātus,* pp. of *dēteriōrāre,* to make worse. – L. *dēterior,* worse. Formed from *dē,* away, from; with comp. suffixes *-ter-ior.* (So also *in-ter-ior* from *in.*)

Determine. (F. – L.) O. F. *determiner.* – L. *dētermināre,* to bound, end. – L. *dē,* down, fully; *termināre,* to bound, from *terminus,* a boundary; see Term. Der. *pre-determine.*

Detest. (F. – L.) M. F. *detester,* to loathe. – L. *dētestārī,* to execrate, imprecate evil by calling down the gods to witness. – L. *dē,* down; *testārī,* to witness, from *testis,* a witness.

Dethrone. (F. – L. and Gk.) M. F. *desthroner,* 'to unthrone;' Cot. – O. F. *des-* (L. *dis-*), apart; L. *thronus,* from Gk. θρόνος, a throne. See Throne.

Detonate, to explode. (L.) L. *dētonātus,* pp. of *dētonāre,* to explode. – L. *dē,* fully; *tonāre,* to thunder.

Detour, a winding way. (F. – L.) F. *détour,* a circuit; verbal sb. from F. *détourner,* to turn aside. – F. *dé-* (L. *dis-*), aside, apart; *tourner,* to turn. See Turn.

Detraction. (F. – L.) O. F. *detraction.* – L. *dētractiōnem,* acc. of *dētractio,* a withdrawal; hence a taking away of one's credit. – L. *dētractus,* pp. of *dētrahere,* to take away, also to disparage. – L. *dē,* away; *trahere,* to draw. See Trace (1).

Detriment. (F. – L.) O. F. *detriment.* – L. *dētrīmentum,* loss; lit. ' a rubbing away.' – L. *dētrī-tus,* pp. of *dēterere,* to rub down; with suffix *-mentum.* – L. *dē,* down; *terere,* to rub. See Trite.

Detrude. (L.) L. *dētrūdere,* to thrust down. – L. *dē,* down; *trūdere,* to thrust.

Deuce (1), a two, at cards. (F. – L.)

O. F. *deus* (F. *deux*), also *dous,* two. – L. *duōs,* acc. of *duō,* two.

deuce (2), the devil. (Low G. – F. – L.) Low G. *de duus!* the deuce! (Bremen Wörterbuch); G. *der daus!* Orig. an exclamation on throwing the *deuce* or two at dice, as it was a losing throw. – O. F. *dous,* two (above).

Deuteronomy. (L. – Gk.) Late L. *deuteronomium.* – Gk. δευτερονόμιον, a second giving of the law. – Gk. δεύτερο-s, second; νόμ-ος, law.

Devastate. (L.) From pp. of L. *dēuastāre,* to lay waste. – L. *dē,* down; *uastāre,* to lay waste, from adj. *uastus,* waste.

Develop, to unfold, open out. (F. – L. and Teut.) F. *développer,* O. F. *desveloper, desvoluper.* – O. F. *des-* (L. *dis-*), apart; and the base *velop-* or *volup-,* which appears also in *envelope.* This base represents Teut. *wlap-,* as in M. E. *wlappen,* to wrap up; see Lap (3), Wrap.

Devest, to unclothe. (F. – L.) From M. F. *desvestir,* to devest. – L. *dis-,* off; and *uestire,* to clothe. Doublet, *divest.*

Deviate. (L.) From pp. of L. *dēuiāre,* to go out of the way. – L. *dē,* from; *uia,* way.

devious. (L.) L *dīui-us,* going out of the way; with suffix *-ous.* – L. *dē,* from; *uia,* way.

Device, a plan. (F. – L.) M. E. *deuys, deuise (devys, devise).* – O. F *devis, devise,* a device, also a division. – Late L. *dīuisum, dīuīsa,* a division; also a judgment, device; orig. neut. and fem. of pp of *dīuīdere,* to divide; see Divide.

devise, to plan. (F. – L.) M. E. *deuisen (devisen).* – O. F. *deviser.* – O. F. *devis* or *devise,* sb. (above).

Devil. (L. – Gk.) A. S. *dēoful, dēofol.* – L. *diabolus* – Gk. διάβολος, the slanderer, the devil. – Gk. διαβάλλειν, to throw across, traduce, slander. – Gk. διά, through, across; βάλλειν, to throw; see Belemnite.

Devious; see Deviate.

Devise; see Device.

Devoid, quite void (F. – L.) M. E. *deuoid;* due to *deuoided,* pp. of *deuoiden (devoiden),* to empty. – O. F. *desvuidier, desvoidier,* to empty out. – O. F. *des-* (L. *dis-*); *voidier,* to empty, from *voide, vuide,* adj. empty; see Void.

Devoir, duty. (F. – L.) M.E. *deuoir.* – M F. *devoir,* O. F. *deveir,* to owe; used as a sb. – L. *dēbēre,* to owe; see Debt.

Devolve. (L.) L. *dēuoluere*, to roll down, bring or transfer to. − L. *dē*, down ; *uoluere*, to roll. ¶ A frequent old sense of *devolve* was 'to transfer.' Der. *devolution*, from the pp. *dēvolūtus*.

Devote, vb. (L.) L. *dēuōtus*, pp. of *dēuouēre*, to devote, vow fully. − L. *dē*, fully ; *uouēre*, to vow. See **Vote**.

Devour. (F. − L.) O. F. *devorer* (1 p. s. pr. *devoure*). − L. *dēuorāre*, to consume, eat up. − L. *dē*, fully ; *uorāre*, to gulp down. See **Voracity**.

Devout. (F. − L.) M. E. *deuot* (*devot*), also spelt *devoute*. − O. F. *devot*, devoted. − L. *dēuōtus*, pp. of *dēuouēre* ; see **Devote**.

Dew. (E.) M. E. *deu*, *dew*. A. S. *dēaw*, dew.+Du. *dauw*, Icel. *dögg* (gen. *döggvar*), Dan. *dug*, Swed. *dagg*, G. *thau*. Teut. type **dauwo-*. Perhaps allied to Skt. *dhāv*, to run, flow ; Gk. θέειν, to run.

Dexter. (L.) L. *dexter*, on the right hand side, right.+Gk. δεξιός, right, Skt. *dakshina-*, on the right or south, Goth. *taihswa*, right hand, W. *deheu*, right, southern, Gael. and Irish *deas* (the same). The Skt. *dakshina-* is orig. ' clever ' ; cf. Skt. *daksha-*, able, *daksh*, to be strong.

Dey, a governor of Algiers. (F. − Turk.) F. *dey*. − Turk. *dāi*, a maternal uncle ; afterwards, in Algiers, an officer, chieftain.

Dhow, a slave ship (?). Mod. Arab. *dāo*, but not an Arab. word (Yule). Orig. language unknown.

Di- (1), prefix ; apart. (L.) L. *dī-*, shorter form of *dis-* ; see **Dis-**.

Di- (2), prefix ; twice, double. (Gk.) Gk. δι- (for δίς), twice.+L. *bis*, *bi-* ; Skt. *dvis*, *dvi-*. Allied to **Two**.

Dia-, prefix. (Gk.) Gk. διά, through, between, apart ; allied to **Di-** (2), and to **Two**. ¶ In nearly all words beginning with *dia-*, except *dial*, *diamond*, *diary*.

Diabetes, a disease accompanied with excessive discharge of urine. (Gk.) Gk. διαβήτης, a pair of compasses, a siphon, diabetes. − Gk. διαβαίνειν, to stand with the legs apart (like compasses or a siphon). − Gk. διά, apart ; βαίνειν, to go ; see **Come**.

Diabolical. (L. − Gk.) L. *diabolic-us*, devilish. − Gk. διαβολικός, devilish. − Gk. διάβολος, the devil ; see **Devil**.

Diaconal, belonging to a deacon. (F. − L. − Gk.) F. *diaconal*. − Late L. *diāconālis*, from L. *diāconus*, a deacon ; see **Deacon**.

Diacritic. (Gk.) Gk. διακριτικός, dis-tinctive. − Gk. διακρίνειν, to separate. − Gk. διά, apart ; κρίνειν, to judge.

Diadem, a fillet, crown. (F. − L. − Gk.) M. E. and O. F. *diademe*. − L. *diadēma*. − Gk. διάδημα, a fillet. − Gk. διά, apart, across ; δέ-ω, I bind, allied to Skt. *dā*, to bind (whence *dāman*, a garland). (√DĒ.) Brugm. ii. § 707.

Diæresis, a mark (¨) of separation. (L. − Gk.) L. *diæresis*. − Gk. διαίρεσις, a dividing. − Gk. δι-ά, apart ; αἵρεσις, a taking, from αἱρεῖν, to take.

Diagnosis, scientific determination of a disease. (Gk.) Gk. διάγνωσις, a dis-tinguishing. − Gk. διά, between ; γνῶσις, enquiry, from γνῶναι, to know.

Diagonal. (F. − L. − Gk.) F. *diagonal*. − L. *diagōnālis*, running from corner to corner. − Gk. διαγώνιος (the same). − Gk. διά, through, between ; γωνία, an angle, bend, allied to γόνυ, knee ; see **Knee**.

Diagram. (L. − Gk.) L. *diagramma*, a scale, gamut (hence, sketch, plan). − Gk. διάγραμμα, a figure, plan, gamut. − Gk. διαγράφειν, to mark out by lines, describe. − Gk. διά, through ; γράφειν, to write.

Dial. (L.) M. E. *dial*. − Med. L. *diālis*, relating to a day ; hence a plate for shew-ing the time of day. − L. *diēs*, day. Brugm. i. § 223.

Dialect, a variety of a language. (F. − L. − Gk.) F. *dialecte*. − L. *dialectus*, f. − Gk. διάλεκτος, f., discourse, language, dialect. − Gk. διαλέγομαι, I discourse. − Gk. διά, between ; λέγειν, to speak.

dialogue, a discourse. (F. − L. − Gk.) F. *dialogue*. − L. *dialogum*, acc. of *dialogus*. − Gk. διάλογος, a conversation. − Gk. δια-λέγομαι, I discourse (above).

Diameter, the line measuring the breadth across or thickness through. (F. − L. − Gk.) Mid. F. *diametre*, ' a dia-meter ;' Cot. − L. *diametros*. − Gk. διά-μετρος, f. − Gk. διά, through ; μέτρον, a measure ; cf. μετρεῖν, to measure.

Diamond. (F. − L. − Gk.) M. E. *dia-mant*. − O. F. *diamant*, altered form of *adamant* ; so also Ital. Span. *diamante*, G. *diamant*, *demant*. See **Adamant**.

Diapason, a whole octave, harmony. (L. − Gk.) L. *diapāsōn*, an octave, con-cord of a note with its octave. − Gk. δια-πᾱσῶν, concord of first and last notes of an octave, lit. 'through all' the notes. − Gk. διά, through ; πᾱσῶν, gen. pl. fem. of πᾶς, all (χορδῶν being understood) ; see **Pan-**, prefix.

Diaper, figured linen cloth. (F. – L. – Gk.) Cf. O. F. *diapré*, diapered; from the verb *diaprer*, to diaper, or ' diversifie with flourishings;' Cot. The verb is formed from O. F. *diaspre*, later *diapre*, a fine cloth, often described as *blanc* (white). – Late L. *diasprus*, adj., also used as a sb. (tunica de *diaspra alba*). – Late Byzantine Gk. δίασπρος, adj., pure white; from δι-ά, wholly, ἄσπρος, white (see N. E. D.). ¶ Not the same as Ital. *diaspro*, a jasper; but cf. Prov. *diaspes, diaspres,* diaper, costly cloth (Bartsch); also Late L. *asperī,* white money (Ducange).

Diaphanous, transparent. (Gk.) Gk. διαφαν-ής, transparent; with suffix *-ous.* – Gk. διά, through; φαν-, allied to φαίνειν, to shew. Brugm. i. § 195.

Diaphoretic, causing perspiration. (L. – Gk.) L. *diaphorēticus,* sudorific. – Gk. διαφορητικός (the same). – Gk. διαφόρησις, perspiration. – Gk. διαφορεῖν, to carry off (by perspiration). – Gk. διά, through; φορεῖν, to carry, allied to φέρειν, to bear ; see **Bear.**

Diaphragm, a dividing membrane. (F. – L. – Gk.) F. *diaphragme.* – L. *diaphragma.* – Gk. διάφραγμα, partition, midriff. – Gk. διά, between; φράσσω (fut. φράξω), I fence in, enclose.

Diarrhœa. (L. – Gk.) L. *diarrhœa.* – Gk. διάρροια, lit. 'a flowing through.' – Gk. διαρρέειν, to flow through. – Gk. διά, through; ῥέειν, to flow.

Diary. (L.) L. *diārium,* a daily allowance, also a diary. – L. *diēs,* a day. See **Dial.**

Diastole, dilatation of the heart. (Gk.) Gk. διαστολή, a drawing asunder, dilatation. – Gk. διαστέλλειν, to put aside or apart. – Gk. διά, apart ; στέλλειν, to put.

Diatonic, proceeding by tones. (Gk.) Gk. διατονικός, from διάτονος (lit. stretched out), diatonic. – Gk. διατείνειν, to stretch out. – Gk. διά, fully; τείνειν, to stretch.

Diatribe. (F. – L. – Gk.) F. *diatribe.* – L. *diatriba,* a learned disputation. – Gk. διατριβή, a wearing away of time, waste of time, discussion. – Gk. διατρίβειν, to waste time, to discuss. – Gk. διά, thoroughly; τρίβειν, to rub, waste away (with long ι).

Dib, to dab lightly. (E.) A lighter form of *dab.* Hence *dibber,* a dibble; see below.

dibble, an instrument for setting plants, by making holes. (E.) M. E. *debil, de-*

bylle; apparently formed from **Dab**; see above.

Dice, pl. of **Die** (2), q. v.

Dicker, half a score. (L.) M. E. *diker* (cf. Icel. *dekr*). – L. *decuria,* a set of ten. – L. *dec-em,* ten.

Dicotyledon, a plant with two seed-lobes. (Gk.) From Gk. δι-, double; κοτυληδών, a cup-shaped hollow, from κοτύλη, a cup.

Dictate. (L.) L. *dictātus,* pp. of *dictāre,* to dictate, frequentative of *dīcere,* to say (below). Der. *dictat-or.*

diction, talk. (F. – L.) F. *diction.* – L. *dictiōnem,* acc. of *dictio,* a saying. – L. *dictus,* pp. of *dīcere,* to say, appoint; allied to *dicāre,* to tell, publish. + Gk. δείκνυμι, I shew; Skt. *diç,* to shew; Goth. *gateihan,* to announce, G. *zeigen,* to accuse, point out. Brugm. i. § 207. (√DEIK.)

dictionary. (L.) Late L. *dictionārium,* formed from *diction-,* stem of *dictio,* a saying, word (above).

Didactic, instructive. (Gk.) Gk. διδακτικός, instructive. – Gk. διδάσκειν, to teach (= *διδακ-σκειν*); allied to δοκεῖν, to think, δέκομαι, Ionic for δέχομαι, I accept ; cf. L. *discere,* to learn, *docēre,* to teach. Brugm. i. § 707. (√DEK.)

Didapper, Divedapper, a bird; see **Dive.**

Die (1), to lose life. (Scand.) M. E. *dyen, deyen*; Late A. S. *dēჳan.* – Icel. *deyja*; Swed. *dö,* Dan. *döe,* to die. + M. H. G. *touwen*; cf. Russ. *davit(e),* to strangle. The Teut. base is **dau,* whence **dau-jan* (Icel. *dey-ja*). Cf. **Dead, Death.**

Die (2), a small cube for gaming. (F. – L.) Used as sing. of M. E. *dys,* more usually *dees,* dice. – O. F. *dez,* dice, pl. of *det,* a die (F. *dé*). Cf. Prov. *dat,* Ital. Span. *dado,* a die. – Late L. *datum,* lit. a thing given or decreed; hence applied to a die for casting lots. – L. *datus,* pp. of *dare,* to give. See **Date** (1).

Diet (1), regimen. (F. – L. – Gk.) M. E. *diete.* – O. F. *diete,* daily fare. – Late L. *diēta, diæta,* a ration of food. – Gk. δίαιτα, mode of life, diet. Brugm. i. § 650.

Diet (2), an assembly. (F. – L. – Gk.) M. F. *diete,* ' a diete, parliament;' Cot. – Med. L. *diæta,* a public assembly ; also a ration of food, diet. – Gk. δίαιτα, a mode of life, diet; see **Diet** (1). ¶ The peculiar use of the word was due to a popular etymology which connected *diæta* (often spelt *diēta*) with *diēs,* a day ; we even find *diæta* used to mean ' a day's journey'; and *diēta* for ' a day's work ' and ' a daily office or duty'; Ducange.

Differ. (F.—L.) M. F. *differer.*—L. *differre*, to carry apart, to differ —L. *dif-* (for *dis-*), apart; *ferre*, to bear. Cf. **Defer.**

Difficulty. (F.—L.) M E. *difficultee.* —O. F. *difficulte.*—L. *difficultātem*, acc. of *difficultas* (for **difficilitas*, like *facultas* for *facilitas*), difficulty.—L. *difficilis*, hard. —L. *dif-* (for *dis-*), apart; *facilis*, easy; see **Facile.**

Diffident. (L.) L. *diffīdent-*, stem of *diffīdens*, pres. pt. of *diffīdere*, to distrust. —L. *dif-*(*dis-*), apart; *fīdere*, to trust, allied to *fidēs*, faith. See **Faith.**

Diffuse. (L.) L. *diffūsus*, pp. of *diffundere*, to shed abroad.—L. *dif-* (=*dis-*), apart; *fundere*, to pour; see **Fuse** (1).

Dig. (F.—Du.) F. *diguer*, to make a dike.—F. *digue*, a dike.—Flem. *and* Du. *dijk*, a dike; see **Dike.**

Digest, to assimilate food. (L.) M. E. *digest*, used as a pp. ; digested.—L. *dīgestus*, pp. of *dīgerere*, to carry apart, separate, dissolve, digest.—L. *dī-* (for *dis-*), apart; *gerere*, to carry.

Dight, adorned. (L.) *Dight* as a pp. is short for *dighted*, from the obs. verb *dight*, to arrange, prepare, M. E. *dihten*, to prepare. A.S. *dihtan*, to set in order, arrange ; borrowed from L. *dictāre*, to dictate, prescribe : see **Dictate.**

Digit, a finger, figure. (L.) L. *digitus*, a finger; hence a figure, from counting on the fingers.

Dignity. (F.—L.) M. E. *dignitee.*— O. F. *digneté.* — L. *dignitātem*, acc. of *dignitās*, worthiness.—L. *dignus*, worthy. Brugm. i. § 762 (3).

dignify. (F.—L.) O. F. *dignifier.*— Med. L. *dignificāre*, to make worthy.—L. *dig ni-*, for *dignus*, worthy; *-ficāre*, for *facere*, to make.

Digress, lit. to step aside. (L.) L. *dıgressus*, pp. of *dīgredī*, to go aside.—L. *dī-* (for *dis-*), apart; *gradī*, to go. See **Grade.**

Like, a trench, trench and embankment, bank. (E.) M. E. *dik*. A. S. *dīc*, masc. +Du. *dijk*, Icel. *dıki*, Dan. *dige*, Swed. *dike*, G. *teich*, pond, tank. Der. *dig*, q. v. See **Ditch**

Dilacerate. (L.) From pp. of L. *dīlacerāre*, to tear apart.—L. *dī-* (for *dıs-*), apart; *lacerāre*, to tear. See **Lacerate.**

Dilapidate, to pull down stone build-

ings, to ruin. (L.) From pp. of L. *dīlapidāre*, to scatter like stones.—L. *dī-* (for *dis-*), apart; *lapid-*, stem of *lapis*, a stone.

Dilate. (F.—L.) O. F. *dilater*, to widen.—L. *dīlātāre*, to widen.—L. *dī-* (for *dis-*), apart; *lātus*, broad. See **Latitude.** Der. *dilat-ory*, A. F. *dilatorie.*

Dilemma, a perplexity. (L.—Gk.) L. *dilemma.*—Gk. δίλημμα. a double proposition, or argument in which one is caught between two difficulties.—Gk. δι-, twice, double; λῆμμα, an assumption, premiss. See **Lemma.**

Dilettante, a lover of the fine arts. (Ital.—L.) Ital. *dilettante*, lit. 'delighting in.'—Ital. *dilettare*, to delight.—L. *dēlectāre*, to delight; see **Delectable.**

Diligent, industrious. (F.—L.) O. F. *diligent.*—L. *dīligent-*, stem of *dīligens*, careful, diligent, lit. loving (fond); pres. pt. of *dīligere*, to love, select, lit. choose between.—L. *dī-* (= *dis-*), apart; *legere*, to choose. See **Legend.**

Dill, a plant. (E.) M. E. *dille.* A. S. *dile.*+ Du. *dille*, Da n. *dild*, Swed. *dill*, G. *dill*, *dille*, O. H. G. *tilli.*

Dilute. (L.) L. *dīlūtus*, pp. of *dīluere*, to wash away, also to mix with water.—L. *dī-* (for *dis-*), apart; *luere*, to wash.

Dim. (E.) M. E. *dim.* A.S. *dim*, dark. + Icel. *dimmr*, dim ; M. Dan. *dim.* Cf. M. H. G. *timmer*, dim ; Swed. *dimma*, a fog, haze ; O. Irish *deim*, dark.

Dime, the tenth part of a dollar. (F.— L.) F. *dîme*, O. F *disme*, tenth. — L. *decima*, a tithe ; fem. of L. *decimus*, tenth, allied to *decem*, ten. See **Ten.**

Dimension. F.—L.) O. F. *dimension.*—L. acc. *dīmensiōnem*, a measuring. —L. *dīmensus*, pp. of *dīmetīrī*, to measure off.—L. *dī* (for *dis-*), apart; *metīrī*, to measure. See **Measure.**

Diminish, to lessen. (F.—L.) Coined from L. *dī* (=*dis*), a art, and E. *minish*; in imitation of . *dīminuere*, to diminish (below). See **Minish.**

diminution. (F.—L.) F. *diminution.*—L. acc. *dīminūtiōnem*, diminution. — L. *dīminūtus*, pp. of *dīminuere*, to lessen.—L. *dī-* (=*dis-*), apart; *minuere*, to lessen. See **Minute.**

Dimissory, giving leave to depart. (L.) L. *dımissōrius*, giving leave to go before another judge.—L. *dīmissus*, pp. of *dīmittere* to send away.—L. *dī-* (for *dis-*), away ; *mi'tere*, to send.

Dimity, a white stuff. (Ital.—L.—Gk.)

Ital. *dimito* (pl. *dimiti*), 'a kind of course cotton or flanell;' Florio. — Late L. *dimitum* (pl. *dimita*), silk woven with two threads. — Gk. δίμιτος, made with a double thread. — Gk. δι-, double; μίτος, a thread of the woof.

Dimple, a small hollow. (E.?) M. E. *dympull*. Perhaps from a base **dump-*, allied to *dip*. Cf. Dan. dial. *dump*, a hollow in a field; *dybbel*, a pool, a hollow in the upper lip (Molbech); Du. *dompelen*, to dive; G. *dümpfel*, M. H. G. *tümpfel*. O. H. G. *tumphilo*, a deep pool. Also Lith. *dùbus*, hollow; *dùbti*, to be hollow (pres. t. *dumb-u*).

Din, clamour. (E.) M. E. *dine, dune*. A. S. *dyne, dyn*; *dynnan*, to resound. **+** Icel. *dynr*, Swed. *dån*, Dan. *dön*, noise; Skt. *dhuni-*, roaring, *dhvani-*, a din, *dhvan*, to resound.

Dine. (F. – L.) M. E. *dinen*. — O. F. *disner*, F. *dîner*, to dine. — Late L. **disiūnāre*, short for **disieiūnāre*, to break one's fast. — L. *dis-*; *ieiūnāre*, to fast, from *ieiūnus*, fasting. (Romania, viii. 95.)

dinner. (F. – L.) M. E. *diner*; from O. F. *disner*, to dine; the infinitive mood being used as a sb.

Ding, to throw violently, beat. (E.?) M. E. *dingen*, pt. t. *dang*, pp. *dungen*; as a strong verb; though not found in A. S. Cf. Icel. *dengia*, to bang; Dan. *dænge*, Swed. *dänga*, to bang; all weak verbs. Cf. M. Dan. *dinge*, to blunt an edge by beating on it; O. H. G. *tangvl*, a hammer. From a Teut. type **dengan-*.

Dingle, a deep dell. (E. *or* Scand.) M. E. *dingle*. Cf. *dimble*, in a similar sense. Of uncertain origin. Cf. **Dimple.**

Dingo, the native dog of Australia. (New S. Wales.) New S. Wales *dingo*, written *teingo* in 1798 (Morris).

Dingy, dirty. (E.) Orig. soiled with dung. Cf. A. S. *dingiung* (for **dyng(i'ung*, with *g* as *j*), a dunging; from *dung*, dung; so also Swed. *dyngig*, dungy, from *dyng*, dung; see **Dung.** For the pronunciation, cf. *stingy* (allied to *sting*).

Dingy (with hard *g*), **Dingey,** a small boat. (Bengali.) Beng. *dingy*, a small boat; 'it has become legitimately incorporated in the vocabulary of the British Navy, as the name of the smallest ship's boat' (Yule).

Dinner; see Dine.

Dint, a blow, force. (E.) M. E. *dint*, *dunt*; also *dent*. A. S. *dynt*, a blow.**+**

Icel. *dyntr*, a dint, *dynta*, to dint; Swed. dial. *dunt*, a stroke, *dunta*, to strike.

Diocese. (F. – L. – Gk.) M. E. *diocise.* — O. F. *diocise* (F. *diocèse*). — L. *diœcēsis.* — Gk. διοίκησις, administration, a province, diocese. — Gk. διοικέω, I keep house, govern. — Gk. δι- (for διά), throughout; οἰκέω, I dwell, occupy, from οἶκος, a house; see **Wick,** a town.

Dioptrics, the science of the refraction of light. (Gk.) Gk. τὰ διοπτρικά, dioptrics. — Gk. διοπτρικός, relating to the δίοπτρα, an optical instrument for taking heights, &c. — Gk. δι-ά, through; base **oπ-* (fut. ὄψομαι), to see; -τρα, fem. instrumental suffix. See **Optics.**

Diorama, a scene seen through a small opening. (Gk.) Gk. δι- (for διά), through; ὅραμα, a sight, from ὁράω, I see.

Dip, to plunge, immerge. (E.) M. E. *dippen*. A. S. *dyppan*, later *dippan*; for **dup-jan*, causal form from the base *dup-*, weak grade of *deup-*, as seen in A. S. *dēop*, deep; see **Deep.** Cf. Dan. *dyppe*, to dip.

Diphtheria. (Gk.) From Gk. διφθέρα, leather; from the leathery nature of the false membrane formed in the disease. Cf. Gk. δεψεῖν, to make supple.

Diphthong, a union of two vowel-sounds in one syllable. (F. – L. – Gk.) Formerly *dipthong* (Ben Jonson). — M. F. *dipthongue.* — L. acc. *diphthongum*, f. – G. δίφθογγύς, with two sounds. — Gk. δι- (for δίς), double; φθόγγος, sound, from φθέγγομαι, I cry out.

Diploma. (L. – Gk.) L. *diplōma*, a document conferring a privilege. — Gk. δίπλωμα, a thing folded double; also, a licence, diploma (prob. orig. folded double). — Gk. διπλόος, double. — Gk. δι- (δίς), double; -πλόος, folded. **Der.** *diplomat-ic*, from διπλωματ-, stem of δίπλωμα.

Diptera, two-winged insects. (Gk.) From Gk. δι- (δίς), double; πτερόν, a wing, from the weak grade of πέτομαι, I fly.

Diptych, a double-folding tablet. (L. – Gk.) Late L. pl. *diptycha.* — Gk. δί-πτυχα, a pair of tablets; neut. pl. of δίπτυχος, folded in two. — Gk. δι- (δίς), double; πτυχή, a fold, πτύσσειν, to fold.

Dire. (L.) L. *dīrus*, fearful.

Direct, adj. (L.) L. *dīrectus*, pp. of *dīrigere*, to direct. — L. *dī-* (for *dis-*), apart; *regere*, to rule.

dirge. (L.) Formerly *dīrige*; from the first word of the anthem '*dīrige*, Dominus meus,' in the office for the dead. — L.

dīrige, direct thou (cf. Ps. v. 8); 2 p. imper. sing. of *dīrigere* (above).

Dirk, a dagger. (Du. ?) Spelt *dork* (A. D. 1602); also *durk*. Perhaps from Du. *dolk*, a dagger; a word of Slavonic origin. Cf. Polish *tulich*, a dagger. ¶ Irish *duirc*, a poniard, is borrowed from E.

Dirt. (Scand.) From M. E. *drit* (with shifted *r*). – Icel. *drit*, dirt, excrement of birds. Cf. Icel. *drīta*, to void excrement.+ M. Du. *drete*, Du. *dreet*, sb., *drijten*, vb.

Dis-, *prefix*. (L.) L. *dis-*, apart; cf. Gk. δι-, apart; see **Di-**. Hence O. F. *des-*, which sometimes becomes *dis-* in E., and sometimes *de-*, as in *de-feat*. The prefix *dis-* commonly expresses the reversal of an act, somewhat like the E. verbal prefix *un-*. For most words beginning with this prefix, see the simpler forms. For example, for *dis-abuse*, see *abuse*; and so on.

Disaster. (F.–L.) M. F. *desastre*, 'a disaster, misfortune;' Cot. Lit. 'ill-fortune.' – O. F. *des-*, for L. *dis-*, with a sinister or bad sense; and M. F. *astre*, a star, planet, also destiny, fortune, from L. *astrum*, a star.

Disburse. (F.–L. *and* Gk.) O. F. *desbourser*, to take out of a purse. – O. F. *des-* (L. *dis-*), away; F. *bourse*, a purse, from Late L. *bursa*, Gk. βύρσα, a skin (hence, a bag). See **Bursar**.

Disc, Disk, a round plate. (L. – Gk.) L. *discus*, a quoit, a plate. – Gk. δίσκος, a quoit. – Gk. δικεῖν, to cast, throw. Brugm. i. § 744. See **Dish, Desk, Dais**.

Discern. (F.–L.) F. *discerner*. – L. *discernere*, to separate, determine. – L. *dis-*, apart; *cernere*, to separate. Cf. **Concern**.

Disciple. (F.–L.) F. *disciple*. – L. *discipulum*, acc. of *discipulus*, a learner. – L. *discere*, to learn; allied to *docēre*, to teach; see **Docile**. Der. *discipl-ine*, O. F. *discipline*, L. *disciplīna*, learning.

Disclose. (F.–L.) M. E. *disclosen*. – O. F. *desclos-*, pres. stem of *desclorre*, to unclose, open. – L. *disclaudere*, to unclose. – L. *dis-*, apart; *claudere*, to close. See **Clause**.

Discomfit. (F.–L.) M. E. *discomfit* (Bruce). – O. F. *disconfit*, discomfited, pp. of *desconfire*, ' to discomfit, vanquish,' Cot. – O. F. *des-*; and *confire*, to preserve, make ready. – L. *dis-*, apart; and *conficere*, to preserve, complete, from L. *con-* (*cum*), together, *facere*, to put, make. See **Fact**.

Disconsolate. (L.) Late L. *disconsōlātus*, comfortless. – L. *dis-*, apart; *consōlātus*, pp. of *consōlārī*, to console; from *con-* (*cum*), with, *sōlārī*, to comfort. See **Solace**.

Discord, sb. (F.–L.) O. F. *descord*, *discord*, variance; formed from O. F. *descorder*, vb., to be at variance. – L. *discordāre* (the same). – L. *discord-*, stem of *discors*, adj. discordant. – L. *dis-*, apart; *cord-*, stem of *cor*, heart.

Discount, verb. (F.–L.) Formerly *discompt*. – O. F. *descompter*, to reckon back or off. – O. F. *des-* (L. *dis-*), away; *compter*, to count; see **Count** (2).

Discourse. (F.–L.) O. F. *discours*, sb. – L. *discursum*, acc. of *discursus*, a running about; also, conversation. – L. *discursus*, pp. of *discurrere*, to run about. – L. *dis-*, apart; *currere*, to run.

Discover. (F.–L.) M. E. *discoueren* (*discoveren*). – O. F. *descouvrir*, to uncover, disclose. – O. F. *des-* (L. *dis-*), apart; *couvrir*, to cover. See **Cover**.

Discreet, prudent. (F. – L.) O. F. *discret*. – L. *discrētus*, pp. of *dis-cernere*, to discern; see **Discern**. Der. *discretion*.

Discrepant, differing. (F.–L.) M. F. *discrepant*. – L. *discrepant-*, stem of pres. part. of *discrepāre*, to differ (in sound). – L. *dis-*, apart; *crepāre*, to crackle, sound.

Discriminate. (L.) L. *discrīminātus*, pp. of *discrīmināre*, to separate. – L. *discrīmin-*, stem of *discrīmen*, a separation. – L. *discernere* (pt. t. *discrē-uī*), to distinguish. – L. *dis-*, apart; *cernere*, to separate.

Discursive. (L.) From L. *discursus*, pp. of *discurrere*, to run about; with suffix *-ive*. See **Discourse**.

Discuss. (L.) M. E. *discussed*, pp. driven away. – L. *discussus*, pp. of *discutere*, to shake asunder; in Late L., to discuss. – L. *dis-*, apart; *quatere*, to shake.

Disdain, sb. (F.–L.) M. E. *disdeyn*. – O. F. *desdein*, sb. – O. F. *desdegnier*, to disdain. – O. F. *des-* (L. *dis-*), apart; *degnier* (L. *dignārī*), to think worthy, from *dignus*, worthy. ¶ O. F. *desdegnier* seems to have been substituted for L. *dēdignārī*, to disdain (with prefix *dē-*, down).

Disease. (F.) O. F. *desaise*, want of ease. – O. F. *des-* (L. *dis-*); *aise*, ease.

Disembark. (F.) M. F. *desembarquer*. – O. F. *des-* (L. *dis-*), away; *embarquer*, to embark; see **Embark**.

Disembogue, to flow into the sea, as a river. (Span.—L.) Span. *desembocar,* to disembogue. — Span. *des-* (L. *dis-*), apart ; *embocar,* to enter the mouth, from *em-* (L. *in*), into, and *boca* (L. *bucca*), mouth.

Disgorge. (F.—L.) O. F. *desgorger.* —O. F. *des-* (L. *dis-*), away ; *gorge,* the throat ; see **Gorge.**

Disgrace. (F.—Ital.—L.) M. F. *disgrace.* — Ital. *disgrazia.*—L. *dis-,* apart ; *grātia,* grace. See **Grace.**

Disguise, vb. (F.—L. and O. H. G.) O. F. *desguiser,* to disguise. — O. F. *des-* (L. *dis-*), apart ; and *guise,* guise ; see **Guise.** Lit. ' to change the guise of.'

Disgust, vb. (F.—L.) M. F. *desgouster,* ' to distaste, loath ;' Cot.—O. F. *des-*(L.*dis-*), apart ; *gouster,* to taste, from L. *gustāre,* to taste ; see **Gust** (2).

Dish, a platter. (L. — Gk.) M. E. *disch.* A.S. *disc,* a dish.—L. *discus,* a quoit, platter ; see **Disc.**

Dishabille ; see **Deshabille.**

Dishevil. (F.—L.) M. F. *discheveler* (Cot.), ' to dischevell,' i. e. to disorder the hair.—O F. *des-* (L. *dis-*), apart ; *chevel* (F. *cheveu*), a hair, from L. *capillum,* acc. of *capillus,* hair.

Disinterested. (F. — L.) From **Dis-** (2) and *interested* ; see **Interest** (2).

Disk ; see **Disc.**

Dislocate, to put out of joint. (L.) From pp. of Late L. *dislocāre,* to put out of place.—L. *dis-,* apart ; *locāre,* to place, from *locus,* place.

Dismal. (F. — L.) Orig. A. F. *dis mal,* unlucky days (A. D. 1256). [The phrase was misunderstood, and *dismal* was treated as an adj., with the addition of *days* ; and later, of other sbs.]—L. *diēs malī,* evil days. Cf. F. *Lun-di* = Mon-day.

Dismantle. (F.—L.) M. F. *desmanteller,* ' to take a mans cloake off his backe; also, to raze walls ;' Cot.—O. F. *des-* (L. *dis-*), apart ; *manteler,* to cloak, from *mantel,* sb. ; see **Mantle.**

Dismay, to discourage. (F.—L. and O. H. G.) O. F. **desmayer,* not found (except *dismayé,* pp., in Palsgrave, p. 519), but exactly the same as Span. *desmayar* (Port. *desmaier,* Ital. *smagare*), to dismay, terrify. The O. F. **desmayer* was early supplanted by *esmayer* in the same sense, which only differed in substituting the prefix *es-* (L. *ex-*) for *des-* (L. *dis-*). The latter part (*-mayer*) of these words is from

O. H. G. *magan* (G. *mögen*), to have power, be able. Hence **desmayer* and *esmayer,* at first used in the intrans. sense, to lack power, faint, be discouraged, but afterwards, actively, to discourage. Cf. Ital. *smagare* (for **dis-magare*), orig. to lose courage, also to dismay (Florio). See **May** (1).

Dismiss, to send away. (F. — L.) A coined word ; suggested by F. *desmettre,* pp. *desmis,* ' to displace, dismiss ;' Cot. The true L. form is *dīmittere,* to send away.— L. *dī-* (for *dis-*), apart, away ; *mittere,* to send.

Disparage, to offer indignity, to lower in rank or esteem. (F.—L.) M. E. *desparagen.*—O. F. *desparager.*—O. F. *des-,* apart ; *parage,* rank. — L. *dis-,* apart ; Late L. *parāticum,* society, rank, equality of rank, from L. *par,* equal (Diez). See **Par.**

disparity. (F. — L.) F. *disparité* (Montaigne). From L. *dis-,* apart ; and F. *parité,* equality ; see **Parity.** Suggested by L. *dispar,* unequal.

Dispatch, Despatch. (Span.—L.) Formerly spelt *dis-,* not *des-.*—Span. *despachar,* to dispatch, expedite.—L. *dis-,* away ; and L. type **pactāre,* to fasten, fix, from *pactus,* pp. of *pangere,* to fasten. (See N. E. D.) Cf. Ital. *spacciare,* to dispatch (Florio), answering to a L. type **dispactiāre.*

Dispel. (L.) L. *dispellere,* to drive asunder.—L. *dis-,* apart ; *pellere,* to drive.

Dispense. (F. — L.) O. F. *dispenser,* to dispense with.—L. *dispensāre,* to weigh out, frequent. form of *dispendere,* to weigh out.—L. *dis-,* apart ; *pendere,* to weigh.

Disperse, to scatter abroad. (F.—L.) M. F. *disperser.* From L. pp. *dispersus,* pp. of *dispergere,* to scatter abroad.—L. *dī-* (for *dis-*), apart ; *spargere,* to scatter.

Display. (F.—L.) A. F. *desplayer,* O. F. *desploier,* to unfold, shew.—L. *dis-,* apart ; *plicāre,* to fold. **Doublet,** *deploy.*

Disport. (F. — L.) M. E. *disporten,* to amuse.—O. F. *se desporter,* to amuse oneself, orig. to cease from labour ; later *deporter,* and confused with **Deport.**—L. *dis-,* away, *portāre,* to carry (hence, to remove oneself from or cease from labour). Hence *sport,* q. v.

Dispose. (F.—L. and Gk.) O. F. *disposer,* to arrange.—O. F. *dis-* (L. *dis-*), apart ; F. *poser,* to place ; see **Pose.**

Disposition. (F.—L.) F. *disposi-*

tion.—L. acc. *dispositiōnem*, a setting in order.—L. *dispositus*, pp. of *dispōnere*, to set in various places, to arrange.—L. *dis-*, apart; *pōnere*, to place, put.

Dispute. (F.—L.) F. *disputer.*—L. *disputāre*, to argue.—L. *dis-*, apart; *putāre*, to think. See **Putative.**

Disquisition, an investigation. (L.) From L. *disquīsītiō*, a search into.—L. *disquīsītus*, pp. of *disquīrere*, to examine. L. *dis-*, apart; *quærere*, to seek.

Disruption. (L.) From L. *disruptio, dīruptio*, a breaking asunder.—L. *disruptus, dīruptus*, pp. of *disrumpere, dīrumpere*, to break apart.—L. *dis-*, *dī-*, apart; *rumpere*, to burst.

Dissect. (L.) From L. *dissect-us*, pp. of *dissecāre*, to cut apart.—L. *dis-*, apart; *secāre*, to cut.

Dissemble. (F. — L.) O. F. *dis-* (L. *dis-*), apart; *sembler*, to seem, appear; cf. O. F. *dissimuler*, to dissemble.—L. *dis-*, apart, away; *simulare*, to pretend; cf. L. *dissimulāre*, to pretend that a thing is not. See **Simulate.**

Disseminate. (L.) From pp. of L. *dissēmināre*, to scatter seed.—L. *dis-*, apart; *sēmināre*, to sow, from *sēmin-*, for *sēmen*, seed.

Dissent, vb. (L.) L. *dissentīre* (pp. *dissensus*), to differ in opinion.—L. *dis-*, apart; *sentīre*, to feel, think. Der. *dissens-ion*, from the pp. *dissensus*.

Dissertation, a treatise. (L.) From L. *dissertātio*, a debate.—L. *dissertātus*, pp. of *dissertāre*, to debate; frequent of *disserere*, to disjoin, discuss.—L. *dis-*, apart : *serere*, to join.

Dissever. (F.—L.) O. F. *dessevrer*.—Late L. *dissēparāre*.—L. *dis-*, apart; *sēparāre*, to separate.

Dissident. (L.) L. *dissident-*, stem of pres. pt. of *dissidēre*, to sit apart, to disagree.—L. *dis-*, apart: *sedēre*, to sit.

Dissimilar, unlike. (F—L.) M. F. *dissimilaire.*—O. F. *dis-* (L. *dis-*). apart; and *similaire*, like : see **Similar.**

dissimilitude, dissimulation; from L. *dis-*, apart, and similitude, simulation.

Dissipate. (L.) From pp. of L. *dissipāre*, to disperse.—L. *dis-*, apart; and O. L. *supāre*, to throw; we find also *insipāre*, to throw into. Cf. Skt. *kship*, to throw. Brugm. i. § 761.

Dissociate. (L.) From the pp. of L. *dissociāre*, to separate from.—L. *dis-*,

apart; *sociāre*, to associate, from *socius*, a companion. See **Sociable.**

Dissolute. (L.) L. *dissolūtus*, licentious ; pp. of L. *dissoluere* (below).

dissolve. (L.) L. *dissoluere*, to dissolve, loosen, relax.—L. *dis-*, apart; *soluere*, to loosen. See **Solve.** Der. *dissolut-ion* (from pp. *dissolūtus*).

Dissonant. (F. — L.) M. F. *dissonant* ; Cot.—L. *dissonant-*, stem of pres. pt. of *dissonāre*, to be unlike in sound.—L. *dis-*, apart; *sonāre*, to sound, from *sonus*, sound.

Dissuade. (F.—L.) F. *dissuader* ; Cot.—L. *dissuādēre*, to persuade from.—L. *dis-*, apart; *suādēre*, to persuade ; see **Suasion.**

Distaff. (E.) A distaff is a *staff bedizened* with flax, ready to be spun off. ' I *dysyn* a *dystaffe*, I put the flaxe upon it to spynne ; ' Palsgrave. M. E. *distaf, dysestaf*. A. S. *dīstæf*. The A. S. *dīstæf* stands for **dīse-stæf*, where *stæf* = E. *staff*, and **dīse* = Low G. *diesse*, the bunch of flax on a distaff (Bremen); also spelt *dise, disene* (Lübben); E. Fries. *dīssen*. See **Dizen.**

Distain. (F.—L.) M. E. *disteinen.*—O. F. *desteign-*, a stem of *desteindre*, to distain, take away colour.—O. F. *des-* (L. *dis-*), away; and *teindre*, from L. *tingere*, to dye

Distant. (F.—L.) O. F. *distant.*—L. *distantem*, acc. of *distans*, pres. pt. of *distāre*, to stand apart.—L. *dī-*, apart; *stāre*, to stand.

Distemper (1), to derange the temperament of body or mind (F.—L.) M.E. *distemperen.*—O. F *destemprer*, to mix; whence pp. *destempré*. immoderate. excessive.—O. F *des-* (L. *dis-*), apart; *tremprer* (mod. F. *tremper*), from L. *temperāre*, to regulate. See **Temper.**

distemper (2), a kind of painting. (F—L.) O. F. *destemprer*, later *destremper*, ' to soake, steepe moisten, make fluid, liquid, or thin,' Cot. ; the same verb as above.

Distend. (L.) L. *distendere*, to stretch apart.—L. *dis-* apart; *tendere*, to stretch; see **Tend.** Der. *distent-ion* (from the pp. *distent-us*).

Distich, a couplet. (L.—Gk.) L. *distichus, distichon.*—Gk. δίστιχον, a couplet (in verse) ; neut. of δίστιχος, having two rows.—Gk. δι- (δίς), double; στίχος, a row, allied to στείχειν, to go. (√STEIGH.)

Distil. (F. – L.) O. F. *distiller.* – L. *distillāre, dēstillāre,* to drop or trickle down. – L. *dē,* down; *stillāre,* to drop, from *stilla,* a drop. See Still (2).

Distinguish, to mark off. (F. L.) O. F. *distinguer,* to distinguish; the suffix *-ish* has been added by analogy, and cannot be accounted for in the usual way. – L. *distinguere,* to mark with a prick, distinguish (pp. *distinctus*). – L. *dī-* (for *dis-*), apart; **stinguere* (not in use), to prick, allied to Gk. στίζειν, to prick, and E. *stick,* vb. See Instigate. Brugm. i. § 666.

distinct. (F. – L.) O.F. *distinct.* – L. *distinctus,* distinguished; pp. of *distinguere.*

Distort. (L.) L. *distortus,* pp. of *distorquēre,* to twist aside. – L. *dis-,* apart; *torquēre,* to twist; see Torture.

Distract, vb. (L.) From L. *distractus,* pp. of *distrahere,* to draw apart. – L. *dis-,* apart; *trahere,* to draw; see Trace (1).

Distrain. (F. – L.) O. F. *destreign-,* a stem of *destraindre,* to strain, press, vex extremely, constrain (hence to seize goods for debt). – L. *distringere,* to pull asunder (see below). – L. *dī-* (*dis-*), apart; *stringere,* to draw tight; see Stringent.

distress, calamity. (F. – L.) O.F. *destresse,* oldest form *destrece;* from a Folk-L. **districtia* (not used), regularly formed from L. *districtus,* pp. of *distringere,* to pull asunder (in Late L. to punish, afflict); see Distrain.

Distraught. (L.) A modification of *distract* (= distracted); from L. *distract-us;* see Distract.

Distribute, to allot, deal out. (L.) From *distribūt-us,* pp. of L. *distribuere,* to deal out, allot separately. – L. *dis-,* apart; *tribuere,* to assign; see Tribute.

District, a region. (F. – L.) M.F. *district.* – Late L. *districtus,* territory wherein a lord has power to enforce justice. – L. *districtus,* pp. of *distringere;* see Distrain.

Disturb. (F. – L.) M.E. *destorben, distourben.* – O.F. *destorber,* to vex. – L. *disturbāre,* to disturb. – L. *dis-,* apart; *turbāre,* to disorder, from *turba,* a tumult, crowd. See Turbid.

Ditch. (E.) M.E. *diche;* cf. A.S. *dīce* d..t. of *dīc,* fem. [also masc.], a dike; see Dike.

Dithyramb, a kind of hymn. (L. – Gk.) L. *dīthyrambus.* – Gk. διθύραμβος, a hymn in honour of Bacchus.

Dittany, a plant. (F. – L. – Gk.) M.E. *dytane.* – O. F. *ditan, dictam.* – L. *dictamnum,* acc. of *dictamnus.* – Gk. δίκταμνος, δίκταμνον, dittany; named from Mount *Dictè* in Crete, where it grew.

Ditto. (Ital. – L.) Ital. *ditto, detto,* that which has been said. – L. *dictum,* neut. of pp. of *dīcere,* to say.

Ditty. (F. – L.) M. E. *ditee.* – O. F. *dité,* a kind of poem. – L. *dictātum,* a thing dictated; neut. of *dictātus,* pp. of *dictāre,* frequent. of *dīcere;* see Dictate.

Diuretic, provoking discharge of urine. (F. – L. – Gk.) M.F. *diuretique;* Cot. – L. *diūrēticus.* – Gk. διουρητικός. – Gk. διουρέειν, to pass urine. – Gk. δι-ά, through; οὖρον, urine; see Urine.

Diurnal. (L.) L. *diurnālis,* daily. – L. *diurnus,* daily. – L. *diēs,* a day.

Divan, a council-chamber, sofa. (Pers.) Pers. *dīvān,* a tribunal; Arab. *daywān,* a royal court, tribunal, council of state.

Divaricate, to fork, diverge. (L.) From pp. of L. *dīuāricāre,* to spread apart. – L. *dī-* (for *dis-*), apart; *uāricus,* straddling, from *uārus,* crooked.

Dive. (E.) M.E. *diuen, duuen* (*u = v*). A. S. *dȳfan,* to immerse, weak verb; confused with *dūfan,* strong verb (pt. t. *deaf,* pp. *dofen*), to dive. ✚ Icel. *dȳfa,* to dip. Allied to Dove, Deep, Dip.

didapper, a bird. (E.) Short for *divedapper.* Cf. A.S. *dūfedoppa,* a pelican. Here *dapper* (= A.S. *doppa*) means a dipper or diver; and *dive-dapper* = divedipper, a reduplicated word.

Diverge. (L.) Coined from L. *dī-* (for *dis-*), apart; and *verge,* vb. See Verge (2).

Divers, Diverse, various. (F. – L.) O. F. *divers,* masc., *diverse,* fem., 'divers, differing;' Cot. – L. *dīuersus,* various; orig. pp. of *dīuertere,* to turn asunder, separate, divert (below).

divert. (F. – L.) M. F. *divertir,* 'to divert, alter;' Cot. – L. *dīuertere,* to turn aside. – L. *dī-* (*dis-*), apart; *uertere,* to turn. Der. *divers-ion,* from pp. *dīuersus.*

Divest. (L.) Late L. *dīuestīre,* in place of L. *dēuestīre,* to strip off clothes. – L. *dī-* (for *dis-*), apart, substituted for L. *dē-,* down, away; *uestīre,* to clothe, from *uestis,* clothing. See Vest.

Divide. (L.) L. *dīuidere,* to divide, separate (pp. *dīuīsus*). – L. *dī-* (*dis-*), apart; and **uidere,* a lost verb, prob.

meaning 'to separate'; see **Widow.**
(√WIDH.) Brugm. i. § 589, ii. 528.
Der. *divis-ion* (from the pp.).

Divine. (F.–L.) M.E. *devin.*–O.F.
devin. – L. *dīuīnus,* divine, god-like;
allied to *dīuus,* godlike, *deus,* god; see
Deity.

Divorce, sb. (F.–L.) O.F. *divorce.* –
L. *dīuortium,* a separation. – L. *dīuortere,*
the same as *dīuertere,* to turn aside, separate; see **Divert.**

Divulge. (F.–L.) F. *divulguer,* 'to
divulge, reveal;' Cot. – L. *dīuulgāre,* to
publish abroad. – L. *dī-,* for *dis-,* apart;
uulgāre, to publish, from *uulgus,* the
people, a crowd; see **Vulgar.**

Dizen, to deck out. (E.) To *dizen* was
orig. to furnish a distaff with flax, hence
to deck out. See **Distaff.** Der. *be-dizen.*

Dizzy. (E.) M.E. *dysy, dusi.* A.S.
dysig, foolish, stupid. ✚ E. Fries. *dusig,*
dizzy, foolish; O. H. G. *tusīc.* From
Teut. **dus-,* as in Low G. *dusen,* to loiter
(Lübben); allied to Teut. **dūs-,* as in Du.
duizelen, to be dizzy. Perhaps further
allied to A.S. *dwǣs,* Du. *dwaas,* foolish
(Franck), from Teut. stem **dwǣs-.*

Do, to perform. (E.) M.E. *doon.* A.S.
dōn, pt. t. *dyde,* pp. *gedōn*; the orig. sense
is 'put' or 'place.'✚Du. *doen,* O.H.G.
tuon, G. *thun.* Teut. stem **dō-.* Allied
to Gk. *τί-θη-μι,* I put, Skt. *dhā,* to place.
(√DHĒ.) Brugm. i. § 129.

Docile. (F.–L.) F. *docile.* – L. *docilis,*
teachable. – L. *docēre,* to teach. Allied to
Disciple and **Didactic.**

doctor. (F.–L.) M. E. *doctour.* –
O. F. *doctour.* – L. *doctōrem,* acc. of *doctor,*
a teacher – L. *docēre,* to teach.

doctrine. (F.–L.) F. *doctrine.* – L.
doctrīna, lore, learning. – L. *doctor,* a
teacher. – L. *docēre,* to teach.

document. (F.–L.) F. *document.*
– L. *documentum,* a proof. – L. *docēre,* to
teach, shew.

Dock (1), to curtail. (E.?) From
dock, sb., the stump of a tail, stump, cut
end. Cf. E. Fries. *dokke, dok,* a bundle,
bunch (as of straw); Du. *dok,* a little
bunch (of straw); Dan. *dukke,* a skein,
short column, baluster; G. *docke,* a skein,
rail, plug, peg; Low G. *dokke,* a bunch,
stump, peg (Berghaus).

Dock (2), a plant. (E.) A.S. *docce.*✚
M. Du. *docke* (as in *docken bladeren,* dock-
leaves, Hexham); M. Dan. *å-dokka,* water-
dock (Kalkar). So also Gael. *dogha,* a

burdock; Irish *meacan-dogha,* a great burdock, where *meacan* means a tap-rooted
plant, as a carrot. Der. *bur-dock.*

Dock (3), a basin for ships. (Du.?)
M. Du. *docke,* a harbour (whence Dan.
dokke, Swed. *docka,* G. *docke*); Du. *dok.*
¶ History obscure.

Docket, a label, ticket. (E.?) Orig. an
abstract; apparently allied to **Dock** (1).
¶ History obscure.

Doctor, Doctrine, Document;
see **Docile.**

Dodecagon. (Gk.) Named from its
12 angles. Formed like *decagon,* with
Gk. *δώδεκα,* twelve, instead of *δέκα,* ten.
See **Decagon.**

Dodecahedron. (Gk.) Formed with
Gk. *δώδεκα,* twelve, in place of *δέκα,* ten;
see **Decahedron.**

Dodge, to go hither and thither, to
quibble. (E.) XVI cent. Orig. to walk
unsteadily, hence to go from side to side
as if to escape; perhaps allied to prov. E.
dade, to walk unsteadily, Scotch *daddle,*
doddle, to waddle, *dod,* to jog, *dodge,* to
jog along, *dodgel,* to hobble, North E.
dodder, to shake, totter, *dadge, dodge,* to
walk clumsily. (Very doubtful.)

Dodo, an extinct bird. (Port.) Port.
doudo, silly, foolish; the bird being of a
clumsy make. Said to be borrowed from
Devonsh. *dold,* stupid, the same as E. *dolt*
(Diez). See **Dolt.**

Doe. (E.) M.E. *doo.* A.S. *dā.*✚Dan.
daa. Swed. *dof-,* in *dofhjort,* a buck, may
be allied to G. *damhirsch,* a buck, wherein
the syllable *dam-* is thought to be borrowed
from L. *dāma,* a deer; or Celtic; cf. Corn.
da, a deer, Gael. *damh,* ox, stag.

Doff, to put off clothes. (E.) Short for
do off, i. e. put off. Cf. *don, dup.*

Dog. (E.) M. E. *dogge.* A.S. *docga.*
(Du. *dog,* Swed. *dogg,* a mastiff; Dan.
dogge, a bull-dog; Low G. *dogge,* F. *dogue;*
all borrowed from E.) Der. *dog,* verb, to
track, follow as a dog; *dogg-ed,* sullen;
dog-cheap, very cheap (see N. E. D.);
dog-wood.

Doge, a duke of Venice. (Ital.–L.)
Ital. *doge,* prov. form of **doce,* a duke.–L.
duc-em, acc. of *dux,* a leader. See **Duke.**

Doggerel, wretched poetry. (E.?)
M.E. *dogerel,* Ch. C. T. 13853. Origin
uncertain; but prob. formed from *dog.*
Cf. *dog-rime,* poor verses (N. E. D.).

Dogma, a definite tenet. (Gk.) Gk.
δόγμα, an opinion (stem *δογματ-*). – Gk.

δοκέω, I am of opinion. Allied to **Docile**. Der. *dogmat-ic, dogmat-ise.*

Doily, a small napkin. (Personal name.) Formerly we read of '*doily* stuff,' and '*doily* petticoats.' Said to be named after 'the famous *Doily*'; Spectator, no. 283, Jan. 24, 1712. Mentioned in Dryden's Kind Keeper, iv. 1 (1679).

Doit, a small coin. (Du.–Scand.) Du. *duit*, a doit. – Icel. *þveit*, a piece, bit, small coin, doit. – Icel. **þvíta* (pt. t. **þveit*), to cut, a lost verb, but the same as A. S. *þwitan* ; see Thwite.

Dole, a portion. (E.) M. E. *dol, dale.* A. S. *dǽl*, a division (Exod. viii. 23). A variant of Deal (1), q. v.

Doleful, sad. (Hybrid; F. – L. *and* E.) The suffix *-ful* is E. M. E. *doel, duel, dol* (Scotch *dool*), sorrow, grief. – O. F. *doel, dol* (F. *deuil*), grief; verbal sb. of O. F. *doloir*, to grieve. – L. *dolium*, in *cor-dolium*, grief of heart. – L. *dolēre*, to grieve.

dolour. (F. – L.) M. E. *dolour.* – O. F. *dolour.* – L. *dolōrem*, acc. of *dolor*, grief. – L. *dolēre*, to grieve.

Doll. (Gk.) From *Doll*, for *Dorothy*; a familiar name, of Gk. origin (see N. E. D.). Cf. Lowl. Sc. *doroty*, a doll.

Dollar. (Low G. – G.) Low G. *daler*; Du. *daalder*, a dollar. Adapted and borrowed from G. *thaler*, a dollar. The G. *thaler* is short for *Joachimsthaler*, a coin made from silver found in *Joachimsthal* (Joachim's dale) in Bohemia, ab. A. D. 1519.

Dolman, a kind of loose jacket. (F. – G. – Hung. – Turk.) F. *dolman.* – G. *dolman, dollman.* – Hung. *dolmany.* – Turk. *dōlāmān, dōlāmah,* a kind of long robe.

Dolmen, a monument of two upright stones, with a third across them. (F. – C.) F. *dolmen.* – Bret. *dolmen*, lit. ' stone-table;' Legonidec. – Bret. *tōl, taol,* a table (from L. *tābula*) ; and *men*, a stone ; according to Legonidec. But (see N. E. D.) this is due to some mistake; the F. *dolmen* seems to represent the Cornish *tolmēn*, stone with a hole beneath; from Corn. *toll*, a hole (W. *twll*), and *mēn* (W. *maen*), a stone.

Dolomite, a kind of rock. (F.) Named in 1794 from M. *Dolomieu*, a French geologist (1750–1801).

Dolour; see Doleful.

Dolphin, a fish. (F. – L. – Gk.) M. E. *dolphine.* – O. F. *daulphin* (now *dauphin*). – Folk-L. *dalfinum,* for L. *delphīnum,*

acc. of *delphīnus*, a dolphin. – Gk. δελφῖν-, stem of δελφίς, a dolphin.

Dolt. (E.) Cf. Devonsh. *dold*, a dolt. M. E. *dult* (=*dulled*) ; from M. E. *dul*, dull ; see Dull.

Domain. (F. – L.) F. *domaine*, sb. ; from O. F. *demaine*, adj., belonging to as one's own. – L. *dominicus*, adj., belonging to a lord (the neut. *dominicum* was used for L. *dominium*, lordship). – L. *dominus*, a lord ; allied to L. *domāre*, to tame, subdue ; see Tame. Doublet, *demesne*.

Dome. (F. – Ital. – L.) F. *dôme.* – Ital. *duomo, domo,* a cathedral church (house of God). – L. *domum*, acc. of *domus*, a house, a building. (✓DEM.) See Timber. Brugm. i. § 138.

domestic. (F. – L.) F. *domestique.* – L. *domesticus*, belonging to a household. – L. *dom-us*, a house (above).

domicile. (F. – L.) O. F. *domicile,* a mansion. – L. *domicilium*, a habitation. – L. *domi-*, for *domus*, a house; and *-cilium*, possibly allied to Cell.

Domesday; see Doom.

Dominate. (L.) From pp. of *dominari*, to be lord over. – L. *dominus*, a lord.

domineer. (Du. – F. – L.) M. Du. *domineren*, to feast luxuriously (Oudemans) ; borrowed from O. F. *dominer*, to govern, rule. – L. *dominārī*, to be lord over (above).

dominical. (F. – L.) O. F. *dominical.* – Late L. *dominicālis*, belonging to the Lord's day, or to the Lord. – L. *dominicus*, belonging to a lord. – L. *dominus*, a lord.

dominion. (F. – Late L.) O. F. *dominion.* – Late L. *dominiōnem*, acc. of *dominio*, lordship; allied to L. *dominium*, lordship. – L. *dominus* (above).

domino. (F. – L.) F. *domino*, a masquerade-dress ; orig. a master's hood. – L. *dominus*, a master (above). Der. *dominoes*, sb. pl., a game.

Don (1), to put on clothes. (E.) Short for *do on*, i. e. put on. Cf. *doff, dout, dup.*

Don (2), a Spanish title. (Span. – L.) Span. *don*, sir. – L. *dominum*, acc. of *dominus*, a lord.

Donation. (F. – L.) F. *donation.* – L. acc. *dōnātiōnem*, a gift, from the stem of the pp. of *dōnāre*, to give. – L. *dōnum*, a gift. Cf. Gk. δῶρον, a gift.

Donjon; see Dungeon.

Donkey. (C. *and* E.) Double dimin. with suffix *-k-ey* (= Lowl. Sc. *-ick-ie*, as in *hors-ickie*, a little-little horse, Banffsh.), from *dun*, familiar name for a horse, from its colour (Romeo, i. 4. 41); see Dun (1). ¶ So also M. E. *don-ek*, prov. E. *dunnock*, a hedge-sparrow, from its colour. *Donkey* (first found in 1785) was a prov. E. word, which seems to have rimed with *monkey* (whence the spelling). Cf. Somersets. *duungkee*, pron. of *donkey*.

Donna. (Ital.– L.) Ital. *donna.*– L. *domina*, mistress, fem. of *dominus*, a master. Doublet, *duenna*.

Doom, a judgment, decision. (E.) M E. *dōm*. A.S. *dōm*, lit. a thing set or decided on; from *dōn*, to set, do; see Do. + Swed. Dan. *dom*, Icel. *dōmr*, Goth. *dōms*, O. H. G. *tuom*. Teut. type **dōmoz*, a statute. Cf. Gk. θέμις, law (from τίθημι, I set). Der. *deem*.

doomsday, domesday. (E.) A.S. *dōmes dæg*, day of doom or judgment.

Door, a gate. (E.) M. E. *dore, dure.* A.S. *dor*, n.; *duru*, f.+O. Sax *dor*, Goth. *daur* G. *thor*, n.; and Icel. *dyrr*, f. pl.; Dan. *dör*, Swed. *dörr*, Du. *deur*, G. *thür*, f. sing. Teut. types **durom*, n.; **dures*, f. pl. Cf. L. *fores*, Lith. *dùrys*, f. pl.; O. Irish *dorus*, n., W. *drws*, m.; Russ. *dver(e)*, Gk. θύρα. Skt. *dvār*, f. Brugm. i. § 462.

Dormant, sleeping. (F.– L.) F. *dormant*, pres. pt. of *dormir*, to sleep.– L. *dormīre*, to sleep. + Skt. *drā*, to sleep; Gk. δᾰρθάνειν.

dormer-window. (F. *and* Scand.) A *dormer* was a sleeping-room. – O. F. *dormeor.* – L. *dormītōrium* (below).

dormitory. (L.) L. *dormītōrium*, a sleeping-chamber; neut. of *dormītōrius*, adj., belonging to sleeping.– L. *dormītor*, a sleeper.– L. *dormīre*, to sleep.

Dormouse. (F. *and* E.) M. E. *dormous*. The prefix is perhaps short for North E. *dorm*, to doze (whence *dorm-mouse*). Cf. Icel., Norw., and Swed. dial. *dorma*, to doze; all apparently from F. *dormir*, to sleep; see **Dormant.** We find also prov. E. *dorrer*, a sleeper, as if from *dor*, to sleep.

Dornick, a kind of cloth; *obsolete.* (Flemish.) Named from Flem. *Dornick*, better known by the F. name of *Tournay* (Lat. *Tornacus*).

Dorsal. (F.– L.) F. *dorsal*, belonging to the back.– Late L. *dorsālis*.– L. *dorsum*, the back.

Dory, a fish; see John Dory.

Dose. (F.– L.– Gk.) O. F. *dose*, a quantity of medicine given at once. – Med. L. *dosis.*– Gk. δόσις, a giving.– Gk. δίδωμι (stems δω-, δο-), I give. Brugm. i. § 167.

Dot. (E.) A. S. *dott*, only in the sense 'head of a boil.' Cf. Du. *dot*, a little bundle of spoilt wool, &c., good for nothing (Sewel); Swed. dial. *dott*, a little heap, small lump; M. Dan. *dot*, a bunch; E. Fries. *dot, dotte*, a heap, bunch, lump. Cf. Norw. *dotten*, pp. of *detta*, to fall, to fall to pieces.

Dote. (E.) M. E. *dotien, doten*, to be foolish (Layamon).+ M. Du. *doten*, to dote, mope; Du. *dutten*, to doze; Icel. *dotta*, to nod with sleep, M. H. G. *getotzen*, to doze, *tūzen*, to mope.

dotage. (E.; *with* F. *suffix*.) M. E. *dotage*; from M. E. *dot-en*; with F. suffix *-age* (L. *-āticum*). Cf. F. *radotage*, from *radoter*, to dote.

dotard. (E. *with* F. *suffix*.) From *dote*, with F. suffix *-ard* (O. H. G. *hart*).

dotterel, a kind of plover. (E.) A bird easily caught; from *dote*, vb., with suffix as in *cock-erel*.

Double. (F.– L.) O. F. *doble*, later *double.*– L. *duplus*, lit. two-fold.– L. *du-o*, two; *-plus*, i. e. 'folded.'

doublet. (F.– L.) M. E. *dobbelet.*– O. F. *doublet*, an inner (double) garment. – F. *double*, double; with suffix *-et*.

doubloon. (F.– Span.– L.) F. *doublon.*– Span. *doblon*, a coin, the *double* of a pistole. – Span. *doblo*, double.– L. *duplus* (above).

doubt. (F.– L.) M. E. *douten.*– O. F. *douter.*– L. *dubitāre*, to be of two minds; allied to *dubius*, doubtful; see **Dubious.**

Douceur. (F.– L.) F. *douceur*, lit. sweetness (hence, pleasant gift).– L. *dulcōrem*, acc. of *dulcor*, sweetness.– L. *dulcis*, sweet. See **Dulcet.**

Douche, a shower-bath. (F.– Ital.– L.) F. *douche*, a shower-bath. – Ital. *doccia*, a conduit, water-pipe.– Ital. *docciare*, to pour; equivalent to Late Lat. **ductiāre*, derivative of L. *ductus*, a duct; see **Duct.**

Dough. (E.) M. E. *dah, dogh.* A.S. *dāh* (stem *dāg-*).+ Du. *deeg*, Dan. *deig*, Swed. *deg*, Icel. *deig*, Goth. *daigs*, a kneaded lump, G. *teig*. The Goth. *daigs* is from *daig*, 2nd stem of *deigan*, to knead; see Dike. (√DHEIGH.) Brugm. i. § 604.

Doughty. (E.) M. E. *dohti, duhti,* valiant. A. S. *dohtig,* earlier form *dyhtig,* valiant. – A. S. *dugan,* to be worth, be strong. +Dan. *dygtig,* Swed. *dugtig,* Icel. *dygδugr,* G. *tüchtig*; variously formed from the Teut. verb **dugan-.*

Douse, to immerse. (E.?) Allied to M. Du. *doesen,* 'to smite with violence' (Hexham). See **Dowse** (1).

Dout, to extinguish. (E.) Short for *do out,* i. e. put out.

Dove, a bird. (E.) A. S. *dúfe,* only in comp. *dúfe-doppa,* lit. a diver. – A. S. *dúfan,* to plunge into + O. Sax. *dúva,* Goth. *dubo,* G. *taube,* a dove, lit. diver. [So also L. *columba,* a dove, is allied to Gk. *κολυμβίς,* a diver, sea-bird. First applied to sea-gulls, &c.]

dovetail, to fasten boards together. (E.) From *dove* and *tail*; from the shape of the fitted ends of the board (◁).

Dowager, a widow with a jointure. (F. – L.) O. F. *douagere*; from *douage,* an endowment. Again *douage* is coined (with suffix *-age*) from F. *dou-er,* to endow. – L. *dōtāre,* to endow. – L. *dōt-,* stem of *dōs,* a gift, dowry. Allied to *dō-num,* a gift, *dare,* to give. **Der.** *en-dow,* from F. *en* and *douer.* Brugm. i. § 167.

dower, an endowment. (F. – L.) M. E. *dowere.* – O. F. *doaire,* later *douaire.* – Late L. *dōtārium.* – L. *dōtāre,* to endow (above). **Der.** *dowr-y,* short for *dower-y.*

Dowdy; see **Duds.**

Dowlas, a coarse linen. (Bret.) From *Davulas,* S. E. of Brest, in Brittany.

Down (1), soft plumage. (Scand.) M. E. *down.* – Icel. *dúnn,* Swed. *dun,* Dan. *duun,* down; whence Du. *dons.*

Down (2), a hill. (C.) A. S. *dún,* a hill. – Irish *dún,* a fortified hill, fort; Gael. *dun,* W. *din,* a hill-fort. + A. S. *tún*; see **Town.**

down (3), prep. and adv. (E. *and* C.) A corruption of *adown* = A. S. *ofdūne* = off the hill, downwards. – A. S. *of,* off; *dūne,* dat. of *dún,* a hill; see **Down** (2).

dune, a low sand-hill. (C.) XVIII cent. – F. *dune.* – M. Du. *dune* (Du. *duin*); of Celt. origin. See **Down** (2).

Dowse (1), to strike in the face. (E.?) Apparently the same as **Douse** (above). Cf. Norw. *dūs,* a push, blow; M. Du. *doesen,* to strike, E. Fries. *dössen,* to strike.

Dowse (2), to immerse; see **Douse.** Prob. the same as **Dowse** (1).

Dowse (3), to extinguish. The same as **Dowse** (1); sense perhaps suggested by *dout,* q. v.

Doxology. (L. – Gk.) L. *doxologia.* – Gk. *δοξυλογία,* an ascription of praise. – Gk. *δοξο-,* for *δόξα,* glory, orig. a notion; *-λογια,* from *λέγειν,* to speak.

Doxy. (M. Du.) A cant term. Cf. E. Fries. *doktje,* dimin. of *dokke,* a doll. Prob. introduced from the Netherlands. – M. Du. *docke,* a doll. Cf. O. H. G. *tocchā,* a doll, also a term of endearment (G. *docke*).

Doze. (Scand.) Swed. dial. *dusa,* Dan. *dōse,* to doze, mope; Icel. *dúsa,* to doze; M. Dan. *dåse,* to be torpid. Allied to **Dizzy.**

Dozen, twelve. (F. – L.) O. F. *dosaine* (F. *douzaine*), a dozen. – O. F. *doze* (F. *douze*), twelve; with suffix *-aine* (L. *-ēna,* as in *cent-ēna*). – L. *duodecim,* twelve. – L. *duo,* two; *decem,* ten. See **Two** and **Ten.**

Drab (1), a slut. (E.) Cf. Irish *drabog,* Gael. *drabag,* a slut; Gael. *drabach,* dirty; Irish *drab,* a spot, stain (all from E.). E. Fries. *drabbe,* puddle-water. Also Du. *drabbe,* f. dregs, draff; allied to **Draff.**

Drab (2), dull light brown. (F. – L.) The colour of undyed cloth. – F. *drap,* cloth. See **Drape.**

Drachm; see **Dram.**

Draff, dregs. (E.) M. E. *draf* (Layamon). + Du. *draf,* hogswash, *drabbe,* draff; Icel. *draf,* Swed. *draf,* Dan. *drav,* dregs; G. *träber,* pl. [Cf. Gael. and Irish *drabh,* draff, from E.]

Draft; see **Draught.**

Drag, vb. (Scand.) M. E. *draggen*; a Northern form allied to Icel. *draga,* to draw. Cf. Swed. *dragg,* a drag, grapnel; *dragga,* to drag. See **Draw.**

Dragoman, an interpreter. (Span. – Arab.) Span. *dragoman*; [Late Gk. *δραγούμανος*], an interpreter. – Arab. *tarjumān,* an interpreter, translator; see **Targum.**

Dragon. (F. – L. – Gk.) F. *dragon.* – L. acc. *dracōnem,* from nom. *draco.* – Gk. *δράκων,* a dragon, lit. 'seeing'; from his supposed sharp sight. – Gk. *δρακ-,* weak grade of *δέρκομαι,* I see. ¶ Such is the usual account.

dragoon. (F. – L. – Gk.) F. *dragon,* a dragoon; so called because the dragoons orig. had a *dragon* on their standard; or rather, because they were armed with a short carbine called (in F.) *dragon.*

Drain. (E.) A.S. *drēhnigean, drēh-nian,* to drain away, strain off, Matt. xxiii. 24, also spelt *drēahnian*; orig. 'to become dry.' — A.S. **drēag-* = Teut. **draug-,* second grade of Teut. **dreug-an-,* to be dry. Cf. Icel. *draugr,* a dry log. See **Dry.**

Drake, male of the duck. (L. – Gk.?) M. E. *drake.* Not found in A.S.; cf. *drake,* a drake, in Low G. (Bremen); M. Swed. *drake,* (1) a dragon, (2) a drake, (3) a boy's kite. Supposed to correspond to the latter part of Swed. *and-drake,* a drake (a form thought to be borrowed from Low G.). Cf. Swed. *and,* duck, *anddrake,* drake; Low G. *anderik,* drake (Lübben); G. *ente,* duck; *enterich,* drake; O. H. G. *antrahho,* a drake. β. The Swed. *and,* A.S. *ened,* a duck, is cognate with L. *anas* (stem *anat-*), a duck. The M. E. *drake* was suggested by A. S. *draca,* a dragon, borrowed from L. *draco*; see **Dragon.**

Dram, Drachm. (F. – L. – Gk.) M. F. *drame, drachme,* 'a dram, eighth part of an ounce;' Cot. – L. *drachma.* – Gk. δραχμή, a handful, a drachma, used both as weight and coin; cf. δράγμα, as much as one can grasp. – Gk. δράσσομαι, grasp. Brugm. i. § 509.

Drama. (L. – Gk.) L. *drāma.* – Gk. δρᾶμα (stem δράματ-), an act, a drama. – Gk. δράω, I perform; cf. Lith. *darau,* I make. (√DAR.) **Der.** *dramat-ic* (from δραματ-); &c.

drastic, effective. (Gk.) Gk. δραστικός, effective; allied to δραστέος, verbal adj. of δράω, I perform.

Drape, to cover with cloth. (F.–L.) F. *draper,* to make cloth. – F. *drap,* cloth; Late L. *drappus.* Of unknown origin. **Der.** *drap-er, drap-er-y*; and see *drab* (2).

Drastic; see **Drama.**

Draw. (E.) M. E. *drawen.* A. S. *dragan* (A. S. *-aga-* becoming M.E. *-awe-*). + Du. *dragen,* Icel. Swed. *draga,* Dan. *drage,* Goth. *dragan,* G. *tragen,* to pull along, carry. Teut. type **dragan-,* pt. t. **drōg.*

draught, draft. (E.) *Draft* is a phonetic spelling. M. E. *draught, draht.* From A.S. *drag-an*; with suffixed *t.* + Du. *dragt,* a load, from *dragen,* to carry; Dan. *dræt*; Icel. *drāttr,* a draught of fishes; G. *tracht,* a load, from *tragen.*

drawl. (Du.) Frequentative of *draw*; parallel to *draggle* from *drag.* Introduced from Du. *drālen,* to be slow; from *dragen,*

to draw. + E. Fries. *draulen*; Low G. *draueln.*

dray. (E.) A.S. *dræge,* that which is drawn; as in *dræge, dræg-net,* a draw-net. + Swed. *drög,* a sledge, dray.

Dread, vb. (E.) A.S. **drēdan,* in comp. *on-drēdan,* to dread, fear. + O. Sax. *ant-drādan*; O. H. G. *in-trātan.* Teut. type **drēdan-.*

Dream, a vision. (E.) M. E. *dreem.* A. S. **drēam,* a dream; not found. [Quite distinct from A.S. *drēam,* a sweet sound, harmony, also joy, glee, happiness.] + O. Sax. *drōm,* dream; Du. *droom,* Icel. *draumr,* Dan. Swed. *dröm,* G. *traum.* Kluge suggests comparison with G. *trug-bild,* a phantom; if correct, the Teut. sb. was **draugmoz,* m.; from Teut. **draug,* strong grade of Teut. **dreugan-* (O. H. G. *triogan,* G. *trügen*), to deceive. From the Idg. root **dhreugh,* whence also Skt. *drōgha(s),* a crafty wounding; O. Pers. *drauga* (Pers. *durūgh*), a deceit, lie; Icel. *draugr,* a ghost. Brugm. i. §§ 681, 689.

Dreary, Drear. (E.) *Drear* is short for *dreary.* M.E. *drery.* A.S. *drēorig,* sad; orig. 'gory;' formed with suffix *-ig* from A.S. *drēor,* gore. – A. S. *drēosan,* to drip. + Icel. *dreyrigr,* gory, from *dreyri,* gore; G. *traurig,* sad, orig. gory, from O. H. G. *trōr,* gore. From Teut. **dreusan-,* vb.

Dredge (1), a drag-net. (E.) North E. *dreg.* Answering to A. S. **drecg, *drecge* (not found), for **drag-jo-*; from A.S. *dragan*; see **Draw.** And see **Dregs.**

Dredge (2), to sprinkle flour on meat. (F. – Late L. – Gk.) To *dredge* is to sprinkle, as in sowing *dredge* (M. E. *drage*) or mixed corn. – O. F. *dragée,* mixed corn; also a sweetmeat, sugar-plum. [Prov. *dragea*; Ital. *treggea,* a sugar-plum.] – Late L. *dragāta, drageia,* a sugar-plum; altered form of *tragēmata,* pl. of *tragēma.* – Gk. τράγημα, something nice to eat. – Gk. τρώγειν (2 aor. ἔτραγον), to gnaw.

Dregs, lees. (Scand.) Pl. of M. E. *dreg,* mire; we also find M. E. *dregges,* dregs. – Icel. *dregg,* pl. *dreggjar,* dregs; Swed. *drägg,* pl. dregs, lees. Cf. Gk. θράσσειν, to disturb. Distinct from L. *fracēs,* dregs of oil; Brugm. i. § 417.

Drench, vb. (E.) M. E. *drenchen.* A. S. *drencan,* causal of *drincan*; hence 'to make drink.' + Du. *drenken,* Icel. *drekkja,* Swed. *dränka,* Goth. *dragkjan,* G. *tränken.* See **Drink.**

Dress. (F. – L.) O.F. *dresser, drescer,*

to erect, set up, dress; answering to a Late L. form *dīrectiāre.—L. dīrectus, pp. of dīrigere, to direct; see **Direct**.

Dribble. (E.) Frequentative of obs. E. *drib*, to drip slightly; which is a weakened form of *drip*. Cf. *drib-let*. See **Drip**. So also Dan. dial. *drible*.

Drift; see **Drive**.

Drill (1), to pierce, to train soldiers. (Du.) Borrowed from Du. *drillen*, to drill, to bore, to turn round, shake, brandish, drill soldiers, form to arms. Allied to M. H. G. *drellen*, to turn round (pp. *ge-drollen*), Low G. *drall*, twisted tight. Teut. type *threllan-* (pt. t. *thrall*), to twist; cf. A. S. *þearl*, strict. ¶ Perhaps allied to **Thrill**.

Drill (2), to sow corn in rows. (E.) The same as *drill*, to trickle, which seems to be a variant of *trill*, to trickle.

Drilling, a coarse cloth used for trousers. (G.—L.) Corrupted from G. *drillich*, ticking, huckaback.—L. *trilīc-*, stem of *trilix*, having three threads.—L. *tri-*, from *tres*, three; *līcium*, a thread. See **Three**.

Drink. (E.) A.S. *drincan*, pt. t. *dranc*, pp. *druncen.*+Du. *drinken*, Icel. *drekka*, Swed. *dricka*, Dan. *drikke*, Goth. *drigkan* (=*drinkan*), G. *trinken*. Teut. *drenkan-*.

Drip. (Scand.) M. E. *dryppen.*—Dan. *dryppe*, to drip (= Teut. *drup-jan-*). From Teut. *drup-*, weak grade of *dreu-pan-*, as seen in Icel. *drjúpa*, to drip, A. S. *drēopan* (obs. E. *dreep*), G. *triefen*. Cf. O. Ir. *trucht*, a dew-drop. See **Drop**.

Drive. (E.) M. E. *driuen*. A.S. *drīfan* (pt. t. *drāf*, pp. *drifen*).+Du. *drijven*; Icel. *drīfa*, Swed. *drifva*, Dan. *drive*, Goth. *dreiban*, G. *treiben*. Teut. *dreiban-*.

drift. (E.) M. E. *drift*. Formed from *drif-*, weak grade of *drīfan*; with suffix *-t*. + Du. *drift*, Icel. *drift*, Swed. Dan. *drift*, G. *trift*. Der. *a-drift* = on the drift; see **A-** (2).

drove. (E.) M. E. *drof*. A. S. *drāf*, a drove. From *drāf*, 2nd grade of *drīfan*.

Drivel, vb. (E.) M.E. *drevelen*. A.S. *dreflian*, to dribble or run at the nose. Cf. M. E. *dravelen*, to drivel. From the base *draf-*, as in M. E. *draf*, draff. See **Draff**.

Drizzle, to rain slightly. (E.) Formerly *drisel* or *drisle*, to keep on dripping. Frequent. form of M. E. *dresen*, A. S. *drēosan*, to drip; see **Dreary**. Cf. Dan. *drysse*, to fall in drops; Swed. dial. *drösla*.

Droll. (F.—Du.) M. F. *drole*, 'a pleasant wag;' Cot.—Du. *drollig*, odd, strange; M. Du. *drol*, 'a juglar;' Hexham. Perhaps from Du. *droll-*, pp. stem of *drillen*, to turn, wheel, whirl about; see **Drill** (1).

Dromedary. (F.—L.—Gk.) M. E. *dromedarie.*—O. F. *dromedaire* (older form *dromedarie*).—Late L. *dromadārius.*—L. *dromad-*, stem of *dromas*, a dromedary.— Gk. δρομαδ-, stem of δρομάς, fast running. —Gk. δραμεῖν, to run.+Skt. *dram*, to run.

Drone (1), to hum. (E.) M.E. *dronen* (also *drounen*). Not in A. S. Cf. Icel. *drynja*, Swed. *dröna*, Dan. *dröne*, to drone, roar, rumble, &c. Cf. Goth. *drunjus*, a sound, Gk. θρῆνος, a dirge; Skt. *dhran*, to sound.

Drone (2), a non-working bee. (Low G.) M. E. *dran*. A. S. *drān*; which (like E. Fries. *dräne*) was prob. borrowed from O. Sax. *drān*. Cf. M. H. G. *treno* (G. *drohne* being borrowed from Low G.). Teut. stems *drân-*, *dren-*; cf. Gk. ἀνθρήνη, a wild-bee, θρῶναξ (Hesychius). ¶ With the parallel stems *drân-*, *dren-*, cf. the stems of **Queen** and **Quean**.

Droop; see below.

Drop, sb. (E.) M.E. *droþe*, sb.; hence *dropien*, *droppen*, vb. — A. S. *dropa*, sb.; *dropian*, vb. These are from the weak grade *drup-* (A. S. *drop-*) of the Teut. vb. *dreupan-* (A. S. *drēopan*), to drop, drip.+Du. *drop*, sb., Icel. *dropi*, Swed. *droppe*, Dan. *draabe*, G. *tropfen*. See also **Drip**.

droop, to sink, fail. (Scand.) M. E. *droupen.*—Icel. *drūpa*, to droop; weak vb., allied to *drjūpa*, strong vb., to drip= Teut. *dreupan-* (whence also G. *triefen*); see above. Cf. 'I am ready to *drop*,' i. e. I *droop*.

Dropsy; see **Hydropsy**.

Droshky, Drosky, a kind of carriage. (Russ.) Russ. *drozhki*, *drojki*, a low four-wheeled carriage (the *j* sounded as in French). Dimin. of *drogi*, a waggon; which was orig. pl. of *droga*, a perch (of a carriage).

Dross. (E.) M. E. *dros*. A. S. *drōs*, dross, dregs; cf. also obs. E. *drosen*, A. S. *drōsna*, pl., lees, dregs. + M. Du. *droes*, lees (Kilian); Du. *droesem*, dregs, lees, G. *drusen*, pl. dregs; O. H. G. *trusana*, *truosana*, husks of pressed grapes.

Drought, Drouth; see **Dry**.

Drove; see **Drive**.

Drown. (Scand.) M. E. *drounen*, *dru-*

nen. ▬ M. Dan. *drukne, drougne, drovne, drone,* to sink, be drowned (Kalkar); Icel. *drukna.* The *-nkn-* was preserved in Swed. *drunkna,* A. S. *druncnian,* to be drunk, also to sink, to be drowned. See Drunken. (E. Björkman.)

Drowse, Drowze, to be sluggish. (E.) Formerly *drouse.* A.S. *drūsian,* to be sluggish; allied to A. S. *drēosan,* to fail; also to drip, to fall. See Dreary. Der. *drowz-y.*

Drub, to beat. (Arab.?) '*Drub,* to beat the soles of the feet with a stick, a punishment used in Turkey;' (Phillips). Apparently a travellers' word. Perhaps from Arab. *ḍarb* (*zarb*), a beating with a stick; from Arab. root *ḍaraba* (*zaraba*), he beat; Rich. Dict. p. 952. (N. E. D.)

Drudge, vb. (E.) M. E. *druggen.* A. S. **drycgean,* not found; but regularly formed from *drug-,* weak grade of *drēogan,* to work, perform, endure (= Teut. **dreugan-,* Goth. *driugan,* Lowl. Sc. *dree*). Cf Icel. *drjūg-virkr,* one who works slowly but surely. The Gael. *drugair,* a drudge, is from E.

Drug. (F.) M. E. *drogge, drugge.* ▬ O. F *drogue,* a drug. Also Ital. and Span. *droga.* Origin unknown; perhaps Oriental. Der. *drugg-ist*

Drugget. (F.) M. F *droguet,* 'a kind of stuff that's half silk, half wool;' Cot. Dimin. of *drogue,* used in the sense of rubbish, poor stuff; from the coarseness of the material; cf. E. 'a *drug* in the market.' ¶ Probably not the same word as F. *drogue,* a drug

Druid, a priest of the ancient Britons. (F. – L. – C.) F. *Druide.* ▬ L. (Gaulish) pl. *Druides, Druidae* (Lewis and Short). Cf. O. Irish *druid* dat. and acc. of *drui,* a magician, sorcerer; Ir. *draoi, druidh,* Gael. *druidh* (whence also A. S. *drȳ,* a magicia).

Drum. (Du.) XVI cent. Imperfectly adapted from M. Du. *tromme, trommel.* a drum; Low G. *trumme*; Du. *trom.*+ O. H. G. *trumbā, trumpā,* M. H. G. *trumme,* a pipe, trumpet: Icel. *trumba,* a pipe, trumpet. [So also Ital. *tromba,* Span. *trompa.*] Of imitative origin.

Drunkard. (E.; *with* F. *suffix.*) From A. S. *drunc-,* base of pp. of *drincan,* to drink; with F suffix *-ard* (G. *hart*).

drunken, drunk. (E.) A.S *druncen,* pp. of *drincan,* to drink.

Drupe, a fleshy fruit containing a stone.

(F. – L. – Gk.) F. *drupe.* ▬ L. *drūpa,* an over-ripe olive. ▬ Gk. δρύππα, the same.

Dry. (E.) M. E. *druȝe.* A. S. *drȳge.* Cf. Du. *droog,* dry; G. *trocken,* dry; Icel. *draugr,* a dry log.

drought. (E.) M E. *droȝte, drouȝte*; also *drouthe* (P. Plowman). A.S. *drūgað,* drought. ▬ A. S. *drūgian,* to be dry; *drȳge,* dry. + Du. *droogte,* drought; from *droog,* dry. Doublet, *drouth* (Milton).

Dryad, a nymph of the woods. (L. – Gk.) L. *Dryad-,* stem of *Dryas,* a wood-nymph. ▬ Gk. δρυαδ-, stem of δρυάς, the same. ▬ Gk. δρῦ-s, a tree; see Tree.

Dual, consisting of two. (L.) L. *duālis,* dual. ▬ L. *duo,* two; see Two.

Dub, to confer knighthood by a stroke. (F.) M. E. *dubben.* A. S. *dubban*; A. S. Chron. an. 1086. [So also Swed. *dubba.*] Usually derived from O F. *aduber, adouber, adober,* to dub a knight; a Romanic word of unknown origin (Ital. *addobbare,* O. Span. and Prov. *adobar,* O. Port. *adubar*). ¶ Diez derives *adouber,* conversely, from *dubban*; rather, from the cognate E. Fries. (Low G.) *dubben.*

Dubious. (L.) From L. *dubiōsus,* doubtful. ▬ L. *dubium,* doubt; neuter of L. *dubius,* doubtful, moving in two directions ▬ L. *du-o,* two. See Two.

Ducal. (F. – L.) F. *ducal,* adj.; from *duc,* a duke; see Duke.

ducat, a coin. (F. – Ital. – L.) O.F. *ducat* ▬ Ital. *ducato,* a ducat, also a duchy; named from L. *ducātus* (duchy of Apulia) alluded to in the legend upon it; see duchy below.

duchess. (F. – L.) O. F. *duchesse* (Late L. *ducissa*), fem. of *duc,* duke; see Duke.

duchy. (F. – L.) F. *duché.* ▬ Late L. *ducātum,* acc. of *ducātus,* a dukedom. ▬ L. *duc-* stem of *dux,* a duke. ¶ Also O. F *duchée,* fem., as if from Late L. **ducitātem.*

Duck (1), to dive, bob the head. (E.) M. E. *duken, douken* Not in A.S.+Du. *duiken,* to stoop. dive: G. *tauchen,* to plunge, dive. Teut. type **deukan-,* pt. t. **dauk* (whence G. *tauch-en*), pp. **duk-ano-.* From the weak grade *duk-* we have Dan. *dukke.* Swed. *dyka*: to which the shortening of the vowel in mod. E. *duck* may have been partly due.

duck (2), bird. (E.) M. E. *doke, duke.* Lit. 'diver;' the suffix *-e* represents the A. S. f. suffix of the agent. A. S.

dūce, a duck. From the verb above. Cf. Dan *dukand*, lit. 'diving duck;' Swed. *dykfågel*, 'diving fowl.' **Der.** *duck-l-ing*, with double dimin. suffix.

Duck (3), a pet, darling. (E.) Apparently the same as Duck (2).

Duck (4), light canvas. (Du.) A nautical word. **—** Du. *doek*, linen cloth, canvas. **+** Dan. *dug*, Swed. *duk*, Icel. *dūkr*, G. *tuch*, O. H. G. *tuoh*.

Duct, a conduit-pipe. (L.) L. *ductus*, a leading (hence, a duct). **—** L. *ductus*, pp. of *dūcere*, to lead. See **Duke.**

ductile. (F. **—** L.) F. *ductile*, malleable. **—** L. *ductilis*, easily led. **—** L. *duct-us*, pp. of *dūcere* (above).

Dude, an exquisite, a dandy. (G.) From G. *dude*; see Supplement.

Dudgeon (1), resentment. Of unknown origin.

Dudgeon (2), haft of a dagger. (Unknown.) M. E. *dogeon*, a kind of wood used for the handles of daggers. Etym. unknown.

Duds, clothes. (Scand.) Jamieson has *dudis* as well as *duds*; the *u* was prob. once long. **—** Icel. *dūði*, swaddling clothes; *dūða*, to wrap up. Cf. E. *dowd*, a woman's cap, a slut; *dowd-y*, ill-dressed.

Due. (F. **—** L.) M. E. *dew*, *dewe*. **—** O. F. *deu*, masc., *deue*, fem.; pp. of *devoir*, to owe. **—** L. *debēre*. See **Devoir.**

Duel. (Ital. **—** L.) Ital. *duello*, a duel. **—** L. *duellum*, a fight between two men (archaic form of L. *bellum*, war) **—** L. *du-o*, two.

duet. (Ital. **—** L.) Ital. *duetto*, music for two. **—** Ital. *due*, two. **—** L. *duo*, two.

Duenna. (Span. **—** L.) Span. *dueña*, a married lady, duenna. **—** L. *domina*, fem. of *dominus*, a lord. See **Donna.**

Duet; see Duel.

Duffel, coarse woollen cloth. (Du.) Du. *duffel*; so called from *Duffel*, a place near Antwerp.

Duffer, a stupid person. (Scand.) Lowl Sc. *dowfart*, formed with suffix *-art* from the adj. *dowf*, stupid, dull; lit. 'deaf.' **—** Icel. *dauf-r*, deaf; see **Deaf.**

Dug, a teat. (Scand.) Perhaps allied to Swed. *dägga*, Dan *dægge*, to suckle. Cf. Goth. *daddjan*, O. H. G. *tāan*, to suckle ¶ But cf. Skt. *duh*, to milk.

Dugong, a sea-cow. (Malay.) Malay *dūyong*, *dūyōng*, a sea-cow.

Duke, a leader. (F. **—** L.) M. E. *duk*. **—** O. F. *duc*, acc. formed from O. F. nom.

dux. **—** L. *dux*, a leader. **—** L. *dūcere*, to lead. (√DEUK.) ¶ The L. acc. *ducem* would have given O. F. *dois*, F. *doix*; like F. *noix* from *nucem*, *croix* from *crucem*. (N. E. D.) Brugm. i. § 592.

Dulcet, sweet. (F. **—** L.) M. F. *doucet* (Cot.), refashioned after L. *dulcis* (cf. Ital. *dolcetto*). **—** O. F. *dols* (F. *doux*), sweet. **—** L. *dulcis*, sweet.

dulcimer. (F. **—** Span. **—** L.) Roquefort has F. *doulcemer* (undated); cf. O. F. *doulcemele* (Godefroy). **—** Span. *dulcemele*, a dulcimer; named from its sweet sound. **—** L. *dulce melos*, sweet sound; see **Melody.**

Dull, stupid. (E.) M. E. *dul*; cognate with Low G. *dull*; answering to Teut. **dul-joz*. Closely allied to A. S. *dol*, foolish, cognate with Du. *dol*, mad, G. *toll*, mad, answering to Teut. **dul-oz*. Both are from Teut. **dul-* (< **dwul*), weak grade of **dwel-an*, as seen in A. S. *dwelan*, to err, to be stupid; see **Dwell.** Cf. A.S. *gedwol-god*, a false god, idol; Irish and W. *dall*, blind. Brugm. i. § 375 (6).

Dulse, an edible seaweed. (C.) Irish *duileasg*, Gael. *duileasg*, dulse. According to Macleod, it means 'water-leaf,' from Ir. and Gael. *duille*, leaf, and *uisg(e)*, water.

Dumb. (E.) M. E. *domb*. A.S. *dumb*, mute. **+** Du. *dom*, Icel. *dumbr*, Swed. *dumb*, Dan. *dum*, Goth. *dumbs*, G. *dumm*, O. H. G. *tumb*, *tump*, stupid. The orig. sense seems to have been 'stupid,' and perhaps Goth. *dumbs* is allied to Goth. *daubs*, deaf; see **Deaf. Der.** *dumm-y* (= *dumb-y*).

Dump (1), an ill-shapen piece. (E. ?) Prov. E. *dump*, a clumsy lump, a bit; *dumpy*, short and thick. Probably 'a thing thrown down in a mass'; see **Dump** (2).

dumpling, a kind of pudding. (E. ?) A small solid ball of pudding; *dump-l-ing* is a double dimin. of *dump* (1).

Dump (2), to strike, fling down. (Scand. ?) Cf. Lowl. Sc. *dump*, to beat. Dan. *dumpe*, to plump. plunge; Norw. *dumpa*; Swed. dial. *dompa*. **—** Swed. dial. *dump-*, as in *dump-iδ*, supine of str. vb. *dimpa*, to fall down plump.

Dumps, melancholy. (Scand.) Swed. dial. *dumpin*, melancholy, orig. pp. of *dimba*, to steam. reek; Dan. *dump*, dull, low. **+** Du. *domp*, damp, hazy, G. *dumpf*; damp, dull. Allied to **Damp**; cf. 'to *damp* one's spirits.'

Dun (1), brown. (C.) A. S. *dunn*, dark. —Irish and Gael. *donn*, brown; W. *dwn*, dun, dusky. Celtic type **donnos*.

Dun (2), to urge for payment. (Scand.) Said (in 1708) to be derived from the name of *Joe Dun*, a famous bailiff in the time of Henry VII. But perhaps from the notion of noisiness. Cf. M. E. *dunning*, a loud noise.—Icel. *duna*, to thunder; *koma einum dyn fyrir dyrr*, to make a din before one's door; Swed. *dåna*, to make a noise. Allied to Din.

Dunce, a stupid person. (Scotland.) From the phr. ' a *Duns* man,' i.e. a native of *Dunse*, in Berwickshire. In ridicule of the disciples of John *Duns* Scotus, school-man, died A. D. 1308. ¶ Not to be confused with John Scotus Erigena, died A. D. 875.

Dune, a low sand-hill. (F.—Du.—C.) F. *dune*.—M. Du. *dūne* (Du. *duin*); cognate with A.S. *dūn*, a down; see Down (2). Brugm. i. § 112.

Dung. (E.) A. S. *dung*.+Swed. *dynga*, dung; Dan. *dynge*, a heap, mass; G. *dung*. Root uncertain; it answers, in form, to the pp. of Ding; as if it were ' what is thrown down or away.' Cf. Swed. dial. *dong*, (1) heap, (2) dung.

Dungeon, Donjon. (F.—L.) M. E. *dongeon*.—O. F. *donjon*, the chief tower of a castle —Late L. *domniōnem*, acc. of *domnio*, a dungeon-tower, chief-tower; shortened from *dominio*, properly domi-nion, feudal power; see Dominion.

Duniwassal, a Highland gentleman, yeoman. (C.) In Sir W. Scott's *Bonny Dundee*. —Gael. *duine uasal*, gentleman. — Gael. *duine*, a man (W. *dyn*); *uasal*, noble, gently born (W. *uchel*), orig. ' exalted ;' see Brugm. i. § 219 (4).

Duodecimo. (L.) *In duodecimo* = with 12 leaves to the sheet.—L. *duodecimō*, abl. of *duodecimus*, twelfth; cf. L. *duodecim*, twelve; see Dozen.

Duodenum, the first of the small intestines. (L.) Late L. *duodēnum*, so called because about 12 finger-breadths long.—L. *duodēnī*, twelve apiece, distribu-tive form of *duodecim*, twelve; see Dozen.

Dup. (E.) Short for *do up*, i.e. lift up (a latch) ; to open a door.

Dupe, a person easily deceived. (F.) F. *dupe*, a dupe. The M. F. *dupe* meant a hoopoe; whence *dupe*, a dupe, because the bird was easily caught. (So also Bret. *houperik*, a hoopoe, a dupe.) Perhaps of imitative origin.

Duplicate, two-fold. (L.) L. *dupli-cātus*, pp. of *duplicāre*, to double.—L. *duplic-*, stem of *duplex*, two-fold (below).

duplicity. (F.—L.) Lit. doubleness. —F. *duplicité*.—L. acc. *duplicitātem*.—L. *duplici-*, decl. stem of *duplex*, two-fold.— L. *du-o*, two ; *plic-āre*, to fold.

Durance, Duration ; see Dure.

Durbar, a hall of audience, levee. (Pers.) Pers. *darbār*, a prince's court, levee ; lit. 'door of admittance.'—Pers. *dar*, door (= E. *door*) ; and *bār*, admit-tance, court.

Dure, to last. (F.—L.) F. *durer*.— L. *dūrāre*, to last.—L. *dūrus*, hard, lasting. +Irish and Gael. *dur*, firm ; W. *dur*, steel. Cf. Gk. δύναμις, force. Der. *dur-ing*, orig. pres. pt. of *dure* ; *dur-able*, &c.

durance, captivity. (F.—L.) The orig. sense was long endurance of hardship. O. F. *durance*, duration. — F. *durer*, to last ; with suffix *-ance* ; see above.

duration. (F.—L.) O. F. *duration*. —Late L. *dūrātiōnem*, acc. of *dūrātio*. A coined word ; from the pp. of L. *dūrāre*, to last.

duress, hardship. (F.—L.) M. E. *duresse*.—O. F. *duresce*.—L. *dūritia*, harsh-ness.—L. *dūrus*, hard, severe.

Durian, a fruit. (Malay.) Malay *du-rian*, a fruit with a prickly rind. —Malay *dūrī*, a thorn, prickle.

Dusk, dim. (Scand.) Properly an adj. M. E. *dosk*, dark, dim ; *deosc*, the same. Prob. a Northern form (as the *sk* did not become *sh*). Cf. A.S. *dox* (for **dosc*), translating L. *flāuus* ; Vocab. 239. 36.— Swed. dial. *duska*, to drizzle ; *duskug*, misty, dim ; Norw. *dusk*, mist, *duskregn*, fine rain. Der. *dusk*, sb. ; whence *dusk-y*, adj.

Dust. (E.) A. S. *dūst*. + Du. *duist*, Icel. *dust*, dust, Dan. *dyst*, meal ; G. *dunst*, vapour, fine dust. All from a Teut. base **dunst-* (for **dwuns-t-*), the *n* being lost except in G. Cf. Skt. *dhvams*, to fall to pieces (pp. *dhvas-ta-*).

Dutch, belonging to Holland. (G.) Formerly applied to the Germans.—G. *Deutsch*, German ; lit. belonging to the people ; M. H. G. *diut-isk*, where the suffix *-isk* = E. *-ish*, and *diut* is cognate with A. S. *þēod*, Goth. *thiuda*, a people, nation ; Ir. *tuath*, a people ; cf. Oscan *touto*, a city. Brugm. i. § 218.

Duty. (A. F.—L.) M. E. *duete(e)*. — A. F. *dueté*, duty (O. F. has only *devoir*).

A coined word; from A. F. *deu, du*, due, and the suffix -*té* (L. -*tātem*). See Due.

Dwale; see Dwell.

Dwarf. (E.) M.E. *dwerȝ, dwergh*; the *f* represents the guttural. O. Merc. *dwerg*, A.S. *dweorg*, a dwarf.+Du. *dwerg*, Icel. *dvergr*, Swed. Dan. *dverg*, G. *zwerg*. Teut. type **dwerg-oz*.

Dwell. (E.) M. E. *dwellen*, to linger. A. S. *dwellan*, in the active sense to retard, also to seduce ; also *dwelian*, to go astray, err, tarry, dwell. Causal of A.S. **dwelan* (pt. t. **dwæl*, pp. *dwolen*), to be torpid or dull, to err.+Icel. *dvelja*, to dwell, delay, orig. to hinder; Swed. *dväljas*, to dwell (reflexive) ; Dan. *dvæle*, to linger; M.H.G. *twellen*, to hinder, delay. Teut. type **dwaljan*, causal of the str. vb. **dwelan-* (pt. t. **dwal*, pp. **dwulano-*), to be torpid, to cease, to err (A.S. **dwelan*, O.H.G. *gi-twelan*). Cf. Skt. *dhvṛ*, to bend aside, *dhūr-ta-*, fraudulent. (√DHWEL.) And see Dull.

dwale, deadly nightshade. (Scand.) Named from its soporific effects. Dan. *dvale*, stupor, *dvaledrik*, a soporific, ' dwale-drink;' Swed. *dvala*, a trance. Cf. A.S. *dwala*, an error, stupefaction, from the 2nd grade of A. S. **dwelan* (above).

Dwindle. (E.) The frequent. form of M. E. *dwinen*, to dwindle, A.S. *dwīnan* (pt. t. *dwān*), to dwindle, languish.+ Icel. *dvīna* ; Swed. *tvina*, to dwindle, pine away ; Du. *ver-dwijnen*, to vanish.

Dye, to colour ; a colour. (E.) M. E. *deyen*, vb. ; *deh*, sb. A. S. *dēagian*, vb., to dye ; from *dēah*, sb., dye, colour. A.S. *dēah* (gen. *dēag-e*), sb. f., answers to Teut. type **daug-ā*. ¶ Not allied to L. *fūcus*, which is from Gk. φῦκος.

Dyke; see Dike.

Dynamic, relating to force. (Gk.) Gk. δυναμικός, powerful. — Gk. δύναμις, power.—Gk. δύναμαι, I am strong; see Dure. (√DEU.)

dynasty, lordship. (F. – L. – Gk.) F. *dynastie*.—Late L. *dynastīa*.—Gk. δυναστεία, lordship.—Gk. δυνάστης, a lord. —Gk. δύναμαι, I am strong.

Dysentery, disease of the entrails. (L. – Gk.) L. *dysenteria*. — Gk. δυσεντερία.—Gk. δυσ-, prefix, with a bad sense; ἔντερα, pl., the inwards, bowels, from ἔντος, within, ἐν, in ; see Interior.

Dyspepsy, indigestion. (L. – Gk.) L. *dyspepsia*. — Gk. δυσπεψία. — Gk. δύσπεπτος,

hard to digest. = Gk. δυσ-, prefix, with a bad sense ; πέπτειν, to cook, digest ; see Cook. Der. *dyspeptic* (from δύσπεπτ-ος).

E.

E-, prefix; see Ex-.

Each, every one. (E.) M. E. *eche, elch*. A. S. *ǣlc*, each, short for *ā-gi-līc*, i. e. aye-like (ever -like or ever alike).+Du. *elk*, each; O. H. G. *eogalīh*, M. H. G. *iegelīch*, G. *jeglicher*. See Aye.

Eager. (F.—L.) M. E. *egre.*—A.F. *egre* (F. *aigre*). – L. *ācrem*, acc. of *āc-er*, sharp. See Acid. Der. *vin-egar*.

Eagle. (F.—L.) M. E. *egle.*—A.F. *egle*, O. F. *aigle* (F. *aigle*).—L. *aquila*. See Aquiline.

Eagre, tidal wave in a river. (F. – L.) O. F. *aiguere*, a flood (Godefroy).—Late L. *aquāria*, a conduit; cf. *aquāre*, to irrigate.—L. *aqua*, water. See Ewer.

Eanling, a lamb. (E.) *Eanling* is from the verb *ean*, which is *y-ean* without the prefix *y-* (=A.S. *ge-*). See Yean.

Ear (1), organ of hearing. (E.) M. E. *ere*. A. S. *ēare*.+Du. *oor*, Icel. *eyra*, Swed. *öra*, Dan. *öre*, G. *ohr*, Goth. *auso*. Teut. type **auzon-*. Cf. also Russ. *ucho*, L. *auris*, Lith. *ausis*, Gk. οὖς, O. Irish *ō*.

earwig, an insect. (E.) A.S. *ēar-wicga*, from its being supposed to creep into the ear. Cf. A.S. *wicga*, a kind of insect ; prov. E. *wiggle*, to wriggle.

Ear (2), spike of corn. (E.) M.E. *er*. A.S. *ēar* (pl.) ; Northumb. *eher*.+Du. *aar*, Icel. Dan. Swed. *ax* (for *ahs*), Goth. *ahs*, G. *ähre*. Teut. type **ahoz*, **ahiz-*, cognate with L. *acus* (gen. *aceris*). Brugm. i. § 182. Allied to Awn. (√AK.)

Ear (3), to plough. (E.) M.E. *eren*. A.S. *erian*, to plough.+Icel. *erja*, Goth. *arjan*, L. *arāre*, Lith. *arti*, Russ. *orat(e)* ; also Irish *araim*, I plough, Gk. ἀρόω, I plough. (√AR.)

Earl. (E.) M.E. *erl*. A.S. *eorl*. + Icel. *jarl*, O. Sax. *erl*, a man. O. Norse (runic) type *erilaR*.

Early, soon. (E.) M.E. *erly*. A.S. *ǣrlīce*, adv. ; from **ǣrlīc*, adj., not used. – A.S. *ǣr*, soon ; *līc*, like. See Ere.

Earn. (E.) M.E. *ernien*. A.S. *earnian*. +O. H. G. *arnōn* (cf. also G. *ernten*, to reap, from *ernte*, harvest). Teut. type **az(a)nōjan*, to get the profit of labour ; from the sb. **az(a)nā* (Icel. *önn*), labour ;

cf. O. H. G. *aran*, Goth. *asans*, a harvest. (√AS.) ¶ Others connect it with Gk. ἄρνυμαι, I earn.

Earnest (1), seriousness. (E.) Properly a sb., as in 'in earnest.' M. E. *ernest*, sb. A. S. *eornost*, sb.+Du. *ernst*, sb.; G. *ernst*, O. H. G. *ernust*. Teut. type **ernustiz*.

Earnest (2), a pledge. (F.−L.−Gk. −Heb.) The *t* is added. M. E. *ernes*; also spelt *erles*, *arles*. Dimin. of O. F. *erres*, *arres* (F. *arrhes*), f. pl.−L. *arrha*, *arrhabo*. − Gk. ἀρραβών, a pledge. − Heb. '*ērābōn*, security; from '*ārab*, to give security.

Earth. (E.) M. E. *erthe*. A. S. *eorðe*. +Du. *aarde*, Icel. *jörð*, Dan. Swed. *jord*, Goth. *airtha*, G. *erde*. Teut. types **erthā*, **erthōn-*, f. Cf. Gk. ἔρα, earth.

Earwig ; see Ear (1).

Ease. (F.) M. E. *ese*. − O. F. *aise*, ease. Cf. Ital. *agio*, ease, Port. *azo*, occasion. Orig. unknown. Der. *dis-ease*.

Easel. (Du.−L.) Du. *ezel*, an ass ; also a support, a painter's easel. [G. *esel*; Goth. *asilus*.]−L. *asellus*, dimin. of L. *asinus*, ass.

East, the quarter of sun-rise. (E.) M.E. *est*. A. S. *ēast*, adv., in the east ; *ēastan*, from the east.+Du. *oost*, G. *ost*, Dan.*öst*; Swed. *östan*, G. *osten* ; Du. *ooster-*, G. *oster-*, Dan. Swed. *öster*, Icel. *austr* (gen. *austr-s*). Teut. types **aus-to-*, **aus-to-no-*; also **aust-ro-*,for Idg.**aus-ro-* (see **easter**). Cf. L. *aur-ōra*, dawn, Gk. ἠώς, ἔως, αὔως, dawn, Skt. *ushās*, dawn. Brugm. i. § 218 (4).

easter. (E.) M. E. *ester*. A.S. *ēastor-*, in comp.; *ēastre*, Lu. xxii. 1, Easter.− A.S. *ēastre*, a goddess whose festivities were at the vernal equinox ; see Beda, De Temporum Ratione, c. 15. Cf. Lith. *auszra*, f. dawn; Skt. *usra-*, m. a ray.

Eat. (E.) M. E. *eten*. A. S. *etan*.+ Du *eten*, Icel. *eta*, Swed. *äta*, Dan. *æde*, Goth. *itan*, G. *essen*. Teut type **etan-*. Cf. L. *edere*, Gk. ἔδειν, Skt. *ad*, to eat. (√ED.)

Eaves, the clipped edge of a thatched roof. (E.) Also E. dial. (Essex) *oavis*. M. E. *euese*; pl. *eueses* (= *eaveses*); also *ouese*. A.S. *efes*, a (clipped) edge of thatch, whence *efesian*, to shear, also **oefes*, whence *oefsung*, Corp. gl. 474.+ Icel. *ups*, Swed. dial. *uffs*; Goth. *ubizwa*, a porch, from the projection of the eaves : O. H. G. *opasa*. Teut. type **obeswā*. Prob. allied to **Over**. Der. *eavesdropper*,

one who stands under droppings from the eaves, a secret listener.

Ebb. (E.) M. E. *ebbe*. A. S. *ebba*, ebb of the tide.+ Du. *eb*, *ebbe*, sb. [whence Dan. *ebbe*, sb. and vb., Swed. *ebb*, sb.]. Perhaps the Teut. type is **affon-*, with the sense of going off ; see **Off**.

Ebony, a hard wood. (F.−L.−Gk.− Heb.) Formerly *ebene*.− M.F. *ebene*, ebony. −L. *hebenus*, *ebenus*.− Gk. ἔβενος, ἐβένη. − Heb. *hovnīm*, pl. ebony wood; prob. a non-Semitic word.

Ebriety, drunkenness. (F.−L.) F. *ébriété*.− L. acc. *ēbrietātem*.−L. *ēbrius*, drunken. Der. *in ebriate*, to make drunken.

Ebullition, a boiling over. (F.−L.) O. F. *ebullition*.−L. acc. *ēbullītiōnem* ; a rare word, from *ēbullīre*, pp. of *ēbullīre*, to bubble up.−L. *ē*, out ; *bullīre*, to bubble ; see **Boil** (1).

Écarté, a game at cards. (F.−L. *and* Gk.) In this game, cards may be *discarded* and exchanged; hence the name.− F.*écarté*, discarded, pp. of *écarter*, to discard.−L. *ex*, out, away ; F. *carte*, from Late L. *carta*, from Gk. χάρτη, a leaf of paper, hence a card.

Eccentric, departing from a centre, odd. (F.−L.−Gk.) F. *excentrique*.− Late L. *eccentricus*.− Gk. ἔκκεντρος, out of the centre ; with suffix *-icus*.− Gk. ἐκ, out ; κέντρον, centre. See **Centre**.

Ecclesiastic. (L.−Gk.) Late L. *ecclē-siasticus*.− Gk. ἐκκλησιαστικός, belonging to the ἐκκλησία, i. e. assembly, church.− Gk.ἔκκλητος, summoned.− Gk. ἐκκαλέω, I call forth.− Gk. ἐκ, out ; καλέω, I call.

Echelon. (F.−L.) F. *échelon*, an arrangement of troops in parallel divisions ; orig. a round of a ladder −F. *échelle*, a ladder (O. F. *eschiele*).−L. *scāla*, a ladder; see **Scale** (3).

Echo. (L.−Gk.) M. E. *ecco*.−L. *ēchō*. − Gk. ἠχώ, a sound, echo; cf. ἦχος, ἠχή, a ringing noise. Der. *cat-ech ise*, q. v.

Eclat. (F.−Teut.) F. *éclat*, splendour ; lit. ' a bursting forth.' − F. *éclater*, to burst forth ; O. F. *s'esclater*, to burst. Origin doubtful ; perhaps from L. type **exclappitare*, formed from Low G. *klap-pen*, to clap, make a noise ; see **Clap**.

Eclectic, choosing out; hence, a philosopher who selected doctrines from various sects. (Gk.) Gk. ἐκλεκτικός, selecting ; as sb. an Eclectic.− Gk. ἐκ-λέγειν, to select.− Gk. ἐκ, out ; λέγειν, to choose.

Eclipse. (F.—L.—Gk.) M. E. *eclips, clips.*—O. F. *eclipse.*—L. *eclīpsis.*—Gk. ἔκλειψις, a failure, esp. of light of the sun. — Gk. ἐκλείπειν, to leave out, fail, suffer eclipse.—Gk. ἐκ, out; λείπειν, to leave.

Eclogue, a pastoral poem. (L.—Gk.) L. *ecloga* (the F. word was *églogue*).—Gk. ἐκλογή, a selection, esp. of poems.—Gk. ἐκλέγειν, to choose out; see Eclectic.

Economy. (F.—L.—Gk.) Formerly *œconomy.*—M. F. *œconomie.*—L. *œconomia.* — Gk. οἰκονομία, management of a household.— Gk. οἰκονόμος, a steward. — Gk. οἰκο-, for οἶκος, a house; and νέμειν, to deal out.

Ecstasy. (F.—L.—Gk.) O. F. *ex tasie* (H.).—Late L. *ecstasis,* a trance.— Gk. ἔκστασις, displacement; also, a trance. — Gk. ἐκ, out; στάσις, a standing, allied to ἵσταμαι, I stand.

Ecumenical, general. (L. — Gk.) Late L. *œcūmenicus;* with suffix -*al.*—Gk. οἰκουμενικός, universal. — Gk. οἰκουμένη (sc. γῆ), the inhabited world, fem. of οἰκούμενος, pres. pt. pass. of οἰκέω, I inhabit. —Gk. οἶκος, a house. Brugm. i. § 611.

Eczema, a breaking out of pustules on the skin. (Gk.) Gk. ἔκζεμα, a pustule.— Gk. ἐκζέειν, to boil over.—Gk. ἐκ, out; ζέειν, to boil. See Yeast.

Eddy. (Scand.) M. E. *ydy* (= *idy*). Icel. *iða,* an eddy, whirlpool; cf. *iða,* to whirl about; Swed. dial. *iða, idå,* Dan. dial. *ide,* an eddy. Perhaps formed from Icel. *ið-,* A. S. *ed-,* Goth. *id-* (prefix), backwards. Cf. Brugm. i. § 574.

Edge. (E.) M. E. *egge.* A. S *ecg,* an edge, border.+Du. *egge,* Icel. Swed. *egg,* Dan. *eg,* G *ecke.* Teut. type **agja.* Cf. L. *acies,* Gk. ἀκίς, a point, Skt. *açri-,* edge, corner. (√AK.)

Edible, eatable. (L.) Late L. *edibilis.* —L. *edere,* to eat; see Eat.

Edict. (L.) L. *ēdictum,* neut. of pp. of *ēdicere,* to proclaim.—L. *ē,* out; *dīcere,* to speak.

Edify. (F.—L.) O. F. *edifier.* — L. *ædificāre,* to build (hence, instruct).—L. *ædi-,* stem of *ædēs,* a building, orig. a hearth; -*fic-,* for *facere,* to make. **Der.** *edifice,* F. *édifice,* L. *ædificium,* a building; *edile,* L. *ædīlis,* a magistrate who had the care of public buildings. Brugm. i. § 202.

Edition. (F.—L.) O. F. *edicion* (H.).— L. *ēditiōnem,* acc. of *ēditio,* a publishing.— L. *ēditus,* pp. of *ēdere,* to give out, publish. —L. *ē,* out; *dare,* to give. **Der.** *edit,* a coined word, from the sb. *editor* (L. *ēditor*).

Educate. (L.) From L. *ēducātus,* pp. of *ēducāre,* to educate; allied to L. *ēdūcere,* to bring out.—L. *ē,* out; *dūcere,* to bring.

educe. (L.) L. *ēdūcere,* to bring out. **Der.** *eduction* (from pp. *ēduct-us*).

Eel. (E.) M. E. *ēl.* A. S. *ǣl.*+Du. *aal,* Icel. *áll,* Dan. *aal,* Swed. *ål,* G. *aal.* Teut. type **ǣloz.*

Eery, timid, affected by fears, melancholy, strange. (E) See Jamieson. M. E. *ar3, arh, are3, ar3e, er3e,* timid; spelt *eri* in Cursor Mundi, 17685.—A. S. *earg, earh,* timid, cowardly. Cf. Icel. *argr, ragr;* G. *arg;* Du. *erg,* bad.

Efface. (F.—L.) F. *effacer.*—F. *ef-* (L. *ef-,* for *ex,* out); and *face,* from Folk-L. **facia* (for L. *faciem,* acc. of *faciēs*), face. See Face.

Effect. (F.—L.) A F. *effect* (F. *effet*). —L. *effectum,* acc. of *effectus,* an effect.— L. *effectus,* pp. of *efficere,* to work out.— L. *ef-,* for *ex,* thoroughly; *facere,* to do.

Effeminate. (L.) From pp. of L. *effēmināre,* to make womanish.—L. *ef-,* for *ex,* thoroughly; *fēmina,* a woman. See Feminine.

Effendi, sir, master. (Turkish—Gk.) Turk. *ĕfendi,* sir. — Mod. Gk. ἀφέντης, for Gk. αὐθέντης, a despotic master, ruler; see Authentic.

Effervesce. (L.) L. *efferuescere.*—L. *ef-,* for *ex,* out; *feruescere,* to begin to boil, inceptive of *feruēre,* to boil.

Effete, exhausted. (L.) L. *effētus,* weakened by having brought forth young. — L. *ef-,* for *ex,* out; *fētus,* that has brought forth; allied to L. *fuī,* I was (Brugm. i. § 361; ii. § 587).

Efficacy, force, virtue. (L.) L. *efficācia,* effective power.—L. *efficāc-,* stem of *efficax,* efficacious.—L. *efficere,* to effect (below).

efficient. (L.) From stem of pres. pt. of *efficere,* to effect; see Effect.

Effigy. (F.—L.) F. *effigie.*—L. *effigiem,* acc. of *effigiēs,* an image.—L. *effig-,* base of *effingere,* to form.—L. *ef-,* for *ex,* out; *fingere,* to form. See Figure.

Efflorescence. (F.—L.) F. *efflorescence,* lit. 'a flowering.' From L. *efflōrescere,* inceptive form of *efflōrēre,* to blossom out.—L. *ef-* = *ex,* out; *flōrēre,* to blossom. See Floral.

Effluence, a flowing. (L.) From the

pres. pt. of *effluere*, to flow out. – L. *ef-*, for *ex*, out ; *fluere*, to flow. See **Fluent**.

Effort. (F. – L.) F. *effort*, an effort ; verbal sb. from F. *s'efforcer*, to endeavour. – Med. L. *exfortiāre*, to use force. – L. *ex*, out ; *forti-s*, strong. See **Force**.

Effrontery. (F. – L.) XVIII cent. – F. *effronterie*, 'impudency ;' Cot. – O. F. *effronté*, shameless. – O. F. *ef-* (L. *ef-*, for *ex*), out ; *front*, face, forehead (as if putting forward the forehead). Cf. F. *af-fronter*, to oppose face to face. See **Front**.

Effulgent, bright. (L.) From stem of pres. pt. of L. *effulgēre*, to shine forth. – L. *ef-*, for *ex*, out ; *fulgēre*, to shine.

Effuse. (L.) L. *effūsus*, pp. of *effundere*, to pour out. – L. *ef-*, for *ex*, out; *fundere*, to pour.

Egg (1), the oval body whence chickens, &c. are hatched. (Scand.) M. E. *eg*, pl. *egges*. – Icel. *egg*, Dan. *æg*, Swed. *ägg*.+ A. S. *ǣg* (= M. E. *ey*) ; Du. *ei*, G. *ei*. Prob. allied to Irish *ugh*, Gael. *ubh*, W. *wy*, L. *ōuum*, Gk. *ᾠόν*, egg. Brugm. i. § 309 (2).

Egg (2), to instigate. (Scand.) M. E. *eggen*. – Icel. *eggja*, to goad on. – Icel. *egg*, an edge (point). See **Edge**.

Eglantine. (F. – L.) F. *églantine*, M. F. *aiglantine*, *aiglantier*, sweet-briar. – O. F. *aiglant*, the same. – L. type **aculent-us*, prickly (not found). – L. *acu-s*, a needle ; *-lentus* (as in *uiru-lentus*). Cf. L. *aculeus*, a prickle, dimin. of *acus*. See **Aglet**. (√AK.)

Egotist, Egoist, a self-opinionated person. (L.) Coined from L. *ego*, I ; see I. Cf. F. *égoïste* (A. D. 1755).

Egregious, excellent. (L.) L. *ēgregi-us*, chosen out of a flock, excellent ; with suffix *-ous*. – L. *ē*, out ; *greg-*, stem of *grex*, a flock.

Egress, a going out. (L.) L. *ēgressus*. – L. *ēgressus*, pp. of *ēgredi*, to go out. – L. *ē*, out ; *gradi*, to go.

Egret, the lesser white heron. (F. – O. H. G.) M. F. *egrette*, *aigrette*, dimin. of a form **aigre* (whence also Prov. *aigron*, O. F. *hair-on*, E. *her-on*). – O. H. G. *heigir*, *heiger*, a heron. See **Heron**.

Eh ! interj. (E.) M. E. *ey*. Cf. A. S. *ēa* ; Du. *he !* G. *ei !* F. *eh !*

Eider-duck. (Swed. *and* E.) The E. *duck* is here added to the Swed. spelling of Icel. *æðr*, an eider-duck (*æ* pronounced like *i* in *time*) ; whence Dan. *ederfugl*

(eider-fowl), Swed. *ejder* ; and cf. Swed. dial. *ǟd*. Der. *eider-down*, Icel. *æðardūn*.

Eight. (E.) M. E. *eightè*. A. S. *eahta*. + Du. *acht*, Icel. *ātta*, Dan. *otte*, Swed. *åtta*, Goth. *ahtau*, G. *acht* ; Irish *ocht*, Gael. *ochd*, W. *wyth*, L. *octo*, Gk. *ὀκτώ*, Pers. *hasht*, Zend *ashta*, Skt. *ashṭau*. Idg. type **oktō(u)*. Der. *eigh-teen*, A. S. *eahtatēne*, *eahtatȳne* ; *eigh-ty*, A. S. (*hund*)-*eahtatig* ; *eigh-th*, A. S. *eahtoða*.

Eisel, vinegar. (F. – L.) In Shak. M. E. *eisel*, *eisil*, *aisil*. – O. F. *aisil*, *eisil*, also *aisi*, vinegar (Godefroy). *Aisil* appears to be a dimin. form of *aisi*. – Late L. *acītus*, bitter ; closely related to L. *acētum*, vinegar. The Goth. *akeit*, vinegar, A. S. *ecid*, G. *essig*, is due to Late L. *acītum* or L. *acētum*.

Eisteddfod, a congress of (Welsh) bards. (W.) W. *eisteddfod*, a sitting, congress. – W. *eistedd*, to sit.

Either. (E.) M. E. *either*, *aither*. A. S. *ǣgþer*, contracted form of *ǣghwæþer*. Comp. of *ā-gi-hwæþer* ; where *ā* = aye, *gi* (for *ge-*) is a prefix, and *hwæþer* = whether. +Du. *ieder*, G. *jeder*, O. H. G. *ēohwedar*.

Ejaculate, to jerk out an utterance. (L.) From pp. of L. *ēiaculārī*, to cast out. – L. *ē*, out ; *iaculum*, a missile, from *iacere*, to cast.

eject. (L.) L. *ēiectāre*, frequentative of L. *ēicere*, to cast out. – L. *ē*, out ; *iacere*, to cast.

Eke (1), to augment. (E.) M. E. *eken*. O. Merc. *ēcan*, A. S. *īecan*, weak vb. Teut. type **aukjan-*, weak vb. ; allied to Icel. *auka*, Goth. *aukan* (neuter), str. vb. ; cf. L. *augēre*. (√AUGW.) Brugm. i. § 635.

eke (2), also. (E.) M. E. *eek*, *eke*. A. S. *ēac*.+Du. *ook*, Icel. *auk*, Swed. *och* (and), Dan. *og* (and), G. *auch*. All from the Teut. base *auk-* above.

Elaborate. (L.) L. *ēlabōrātus*, pp. of *ēlabōrāre*, to labour greatly. – L. *ē*, out, greatly ; *labōrāre*, to work, from *labōr-*, stem of *labor*, labour.

Eland, a S. African antelope. (Du. – G. – Lith.) Du. *eland*, an elk. – G. *elend*. – Lithuan. *élnis*, an elk. Cf. W. *elain*, a hind, Russ. *olene*, a stag. See **Elk**.

Elapse, to glide away. (L.) From L. *ēlapsūs*, pp. of *ēlābī*, to glide away. – L. *ē*, away ; *lābī*, to glide.

Elastic. (Gk.) Formerly *elastick*. Gk. **ἐλαστικός*, propulsive, coined from Gk. *ἐλάω* = *ἐλαίνω*, I drive (fut. *ἐλάσ-ω*). Cf. Gk. *ἐλαστής*, also *ἐλατήρ*, a driver.

Elate, lifted up, proud. (L.) L. *ēlātus*, lifted up. — L. *ē*, out ; *lātus*, used as pp. of *ferre*, but allied to *tollere*, to lift.

Elbow, the bend of the arm. (E.) M. E. *elbowe*. A. S. *elboga*, also *eln-boga.* — A. S. *eln*, signifying ' ell,' orig. ' arm ; ' and *boga*, a bow, a bending (see **Bow**). A. S. *eln* is allied to Goth. *aleina*, a cubit, W. *elin*, Irish *uile*, L. *ulna*, Gk. *ὠλένη*, Skt. *aratni-*, the elbow. See **Ell.**+Du. *elle-boog*, Icel. *öln-bogi*, Dan. *al-bue*, G. *ellen-bogen*.

Eld, old age. (E.) M. E. *elde*, old age ; O. Merc. *ældo*, old age ; from *ald*, old. Cf. A. S. *ieldu*, *yldu* ; from *eald*, old. +Icel. *elli* ; Dan. *ælde*. See **Old.**

elder (1), older. (E.) Both as adj. and sb. O. Merc. *ældra* (A. S. *yldra*), elder, adj. ; comparative of *ald* (A. S. *eald*), old.

eldest. (E.) O. Merc. *ældesta* (A. S. *yldesta*), superl. of *ald* (A. S. *eald*), old.

Elder (2), a tree. (E.) The *d* is excrescent. M. E. *eller.* A. S. *ellen*, *ellærn.*+ Low G. *elloorn.* ¶ Distinct from *alder*.

Elecampane, a plant. (L.) A. S. *eolone*, *elene*, perverted from L. *inula* ; and M.F.*enule-campane* (Cot.). — L. *inula campāna*, elecampane. Here *campāna* prob. means wild, growing in the fields ; from L. *campus*, a field.

Elect, chosen. (L.) L. *ēlectus*, pp. of *ēligere*, to choose out. — L. *ē*, out ; *legere*, to choose.

Electric. (L. — Gk.) Coined from L. *ēlectrum*, amber, which has electric properties. — Gk. *ἤλεκτρον*, amber, also shining metal ; allied to *ἠλέκτωρ*, gleaming.

Electuary, a kind of confection. (F. — L. — Gk.) M. E. *letuarie.* — O. F. *lectuaire*, M. F. *electuaire.* — Late L. *electuārium*, *ēlectārium*, a medicine that dissolves in the mouth. Perhaps for *ē(c)lict-ārium*, from Gk. *ἐκλεικτόν*, an electuary, from *ἐκλείχειν*, to lick out. — Gk. *ἐκ*, out ; *λείχειν*, to lick.

Eleemosynary, relating to alms. (Late L. — Gk.) Late L. *eleēmosynārius*, an almoner ; from *eleēmosyna*, alms. — Gk. *ἐλεημοσύνη*, pity, alms. See **Alms.**

Elegant, choice, neat. (F. — L.) M. F. *elegant.* — L. *ēlegant-*, stem of *ēlegans*, tasteful, neat. — L. *ē*, out ; *leg-*, base of *legere*, to choose.

Elegy, a funeral ode. (F. — L. — Gk.) M. F. *elegie.* — L. *elegīa.* — Gk. *ἐλεγεία*, fem. sing., an elegy ; orig. neut. pl. of

ἐλεγεῖον, a distich (of lament). — Gk. *ἔλεγος*, a lament. Der. *elegi-ac*.

Element. (F. — L.) O. F. *element.* — L. *elementum*, a first principle.

Elephant. (F. — L. — Gk.) M. E. *elyphaunt*, *olifaunt.* — O. F. *olifant*, *elefant.* — L. *elephantem*, acc. of *elephas.* — Gk. *ἐλέφας*, an elephant. Origin unknown ; some compare Heb. *eleph*, an ox.

Elevate. (L.) From pp. of L. *ēleuāre*, to lift up. — L. *ē*, out ; *leuāre*, to lighten, lift, from *leuis*, light. See **Levity.**

Eleven. (E.) M. E. *enleuen.* A. S. *en(d)leofan*, *endlufon* ; O. Northumb. *ællefne.*+Du. *elf*, Icel. *ellifu*, Dan. *elleve*, Swed. *elfva*, Goth. *ainlif*, G. *elf*, O. H. G. *einlif.* β. A compound of Teut. **ain-*, one ; and *-lif* = Lithuan. *-lika* (in *vēnolika*, eleven). Lith. *-lika* perhaps means 'remaining' ; cf. L. *linquere*, to leave. Brugm. ii. § 175.

Elf. (E.) M. E. *elf.* O. Merc. *ælf.*+ Icel. *álfr*, Dan. *alf* ; also G. *alp*, a nightmare. Der. *elf-in*, adj., for **elf-en* ; but prob. suggested by the M. E. gen. pl. *elvene*, of elves (in the Southern dialect).

Elicit, to coax out. (L.) From pp. of L. *ēlicere*, to draw out by coaxing. — L. *ē*, out ; *lacere*, to entice. And see **Lace.**

Elide. (L.) L. *ēlīdere*, to strike out. — L. *ē*, out ; *lædere*, to dash. Der. *elis-ion* (from pp. *ēlīs-us*).

Eligible. (F. — L.) F. *éligible.* — Med. L. *ēligibilis*, fit to be chosen. — L. *ēligere*, to choose out ; see **Elect.**

Eliminate. (L.) From pp. of L. *ēlīmināre*, to thrust out of. — L. *ē*, forth ; *līmin-*, stem of *līmen*, a threshold. See **Limit.**

Elision; see **Elide.**

Elixir. (Ar. — Gk.) Med. L. *elixir* ; for Arab. *el iksīr*, the philosopher's stone, esp. a sort of powder (Devic) ; where *el* is the definite article. — Gk. *ξήριον*, dry powder, or *ξηρόν*, dry (residuum).

Elk, a kind of deer. (G.) Prob. adapted from M. H. G. *elch*, an elk ; O. H. G. *elaho.* Cf. Icel. *elgr*, Swed. *elg*, an elk ; Russ. *olene*, a stag ; L. *alces*, Gk. *ἄλκη.* (History obscure.) Found in A. S. as *elch*, *elh.*

Ell. (E.) M. E. *elle*, *elne.* A. S. *el(i)n*, a cubit.+Du. *elle*, *el* ; Icel. *alin*, the arm from the elbow to the tip of the middle finger ; Swed. *aln*, Dan. *alen*, Goth. *aleina*, G. *elle*, ell ; L. *ulna*, elbow, cubit ; Gk. *ὠλένη*, elbow. *Ell* = *el-* in *el-bow.*

Ellipse. (L.—Gk.) Formerly *ellipsis*. —L. *ellipsis*.—Gk. ἔλλειψις, a defect, an ellipse of a word; also, an oval figure, because its plane forms with the base of the cone a less angle than that of a parabola. — Gk. ἐλλείπειν, to leave in, leave behind.—Gk. ἐλ-, for ἐν, in; λείπειν, to leave. cognate with L. *linquere*. Der. *elliptic*, adj., Gk. ἐλλειπτικός.

Elm, a tree. (E.) A.S. *elm*.+O. H.G. *elm*; cf. Icel. *ālmr*, Dan. *alm*, Swed. *alm*; also L. *ulmus* (whence G. *ulme*, Du. *olm*).

Elocution. (L.) From L. *ēlocūtiōnem*, acc. of *ēlocūtio*, clear utterance.—L. *ēlocūtus*, pp. of *ēloquī*, to speak out.—L. *ē*, out; *loquī*, to speak. Cf. **Eloquent.**

Eloign, Eloin, to remove and keep at a distance, to withdraw. (F. — L.) O. F. *esloigner*, to remove, keep away (Law L. *exlongāre*). — O. F. *es*, away; *loing* (F. *loin*), far off.—L. *ex*, away; *longē*, adv. far off. See **Long.**

Elope. (A.F.—Scand.) A. F. *aloper*, to run away (from a husband; see N. E. D.). —A. F. *a-* prefix (perhaps for O. F. *es-*, away, as in E. *a-bash*); and M. E. *lopen*, to run (Cath. Anglicum), from Icel. *hlaupa*, cognate with E. **Leap.** β. Or from M. E. *alop-en*, pp. of *alēpen*, to escape; from A. S. *ā-*, away, and *hlēapan*, to run, to leap.

Eloquent. (F.—L.) M. E. *eloquent*. — O. F. *eloquent*.—L. *ēloquent-*, stem of pres. pt. of *ēloquī*, to speak out or clearly. —L. *ē*, out; *loquī*, to speak.

Else, otherwise. (E.) A.S. *elles*, adv.; stem **aljo-*, signifying ' other,' as in Goth. *aljis*, other.+Swed. *eljest*; allied to L. *alias*, and to **Alien.** The suffix *-es* marks the gen. case, neuter.

Elucidate. (L.) From pp. of Late L. *ēlūcidāre*, to make clear.—L. *ē*, out, very; *lūcid-us*, lucid. clear. See **Lucid.**

Elude, to avoid slily. (L.) L. *ēlūdere* (pp. *ēlūsus*), to mock, deceive.—L. *ē*, out; *lūdere*, to play. Der. *elus-ory*, from the pp.

Elysium, a heaven. (L.—Gk.) L. *ēlysium*. - Gk. ἠλύσιον, short for ἠλύσιον πεδίον, the Elysian field (Od. 4. 563).

Em-, *prefix.* (F.—L.) F. *em-*<L. *im-* (for *in*), in, before *b* and *p*. Hence *embalm*, to anoint with balm; *em-bank*, to enclose with a bank, cast up a bank; *embody*, to invest with a body, &c.

Emaciate. (L.) From pp. of L. *ēmaciāre*, to make thin. — L. *ē*, very;

maci-, base of *maciēs*, leanness; cf. *macer*, lean.

Emanate. (L.) From L. *ēmānātus*, pp. of *ēmānāre*, to flow out.—L. *ē*, out; *mānāre*, to flow.

Emancipate. (L.) From pp. of L. *ēmancipāre*, to set free.—L. *ē*, out; *mancipāre*, to transfer property.—L. *mancip-*, stem of *man-ceps*, lit. one who takes property in hand or receives it.—L. *man-us*, hand; *capere*, to take.

Emasculate, to deprive of virility. (L.) From pp. of L. *ēmasculāre*.—L. *ē*, away from; *masculus*, male. See **Masculine.**

Embargo. (Span.) Span. *embargo*, an arrest, a stoppage of ships; lit. a putting a bar in the way.—Late L. type **imbarricāre*, to bar in. Formed with prefix *em-* (=Lat. *in*) from Span. *barra*, a bar. See **Bar, Barricade.**

Embark. (F.—Late L.) F. *embarquer*.—Late L. *imbarcāre*, to put in a bark.—L. *im-* (for *in*), in; *barca*, a bark; see **Bark** (1).

Embarrass. (F.—Span.) F. *embarrasser*, to perplex; lit. to hinder, put a bar in one's way.—Span. *embarazar*, the same. — Span. *em-* (L. *im-*, for *in*), in; *barra*, a bar. Cf. **Embargo**; and **Bar.**

Embassy, a mission. (F.—Late L.— C.) A modification of O. F. *ambassee*; cf. M. F. *embassade*, Ital. *imbasciata*, weakened form of *ambasciata*. All from Late L. *ambasciāta*, sb., orig. fem. of pp. of *ambasciāre*, to send on a mission, from *ambascia*, a mission. See **Ambassador.**

Embattle, to furnish with battlements. (F.) M. E. *embattelen*. — O. F. *em-* (L. *im-*, for *in-*, prefix); and O. F. *bastiller*, to fortify. See **Battlement.**

Embellish. (F.—L.) M. E. *embelissen*.—O. F. *embeliss-*, stem of pres. pt. of *embellir*, to beautify.—O. F. *em-* (L. *in*); and *bel*, fair. See **Belle.**

Ember-days. (E.) M. E. *ymber*, as in *ymber-weke*. A. S. *ymbren-*. prob. from *ymbryne*, a circuit, or period; the ember-days are days that *recur* at each of the four seasons of the year. The A.S. *ymb-ryne* is lit. ' a running round.'—A. S. *ymb*, round (=G. *um*, Gk. ἀμφί); and *ryne*, a run, course; see **Run.** Prob. confused with L. *quatuor tempora*, four seasons: whence G. *quatember*.

Embers, ashes. (E.) M. E. *emeres*. A. S. *ǣmyrgean*, embers; A. S. Leechdoms, iii. 30 (rare). **+** Icel. *eimyrja*, Dan. *emmer*, Swed. *mörja*, O. H. G. *eimurja*, sb. ember. Cf. Icel. *eim-r*, vapour; prov. E. *ome* (= A. S. *ām*), vapour.

Embezzle, to filch. (F.) A. F. *en-besiler*, to make away with (A. D. 1404). — O. F. *en-* (for L. *in-*, prefix) ; and O. F. *besillier*, to maltreat, destroy, apparently from O. F. *bes-* (Late L. *bis-*, used as a pejorative prefix). Cf. O. F. *besil*, ill-treatment, torture ; and see **Bezzle** in the N. E. D. **¶** Certainly influenced, in the 16th cent., by a supposed etymology from *imbécill*, to weaken, an obsolete verb formed from the adj. *imbecile*, q v.

Emblem. (F. — L. — Gk.) M. F. *embleme.* — L. *emblēma.* — Gk. ἔμβλημα, a thing put on, an ornament. — Gk. ἐμ-, for ἐν, in, on ; βάλλειν, to throw, to put. See **Belemnite**.

Emblements, the produce of sown lands, crops which a tenant may cut after the determination of his tenancy. (F. — L.) O. F. *emblaement*, harvest. — O. F. *em-blaër, emblader* (F. *emblaver*), to sow with corn. — Late Lat. *imblādāre*, to sow. — L. *im-* (for *in*), in ; Late L. *blādum* = L. *ablātum*, a crop, corn, lit. ' what is carried away' (F. *blé*).

Embolism. (F. — L. — Gk.) O. F. *embolisme.* — L. *embolismus.* — Gk. ἐμβο-λισμός, an intercalation or insertion of days, to complete a period. — Gk. ἐμ, for ἐν, in ; βάλλειν, to cast ; cf. ἐμβολή, an insertion.

Embonpoint, plumpness of person. (F. — L.) F. *embonpoint*, plumpness. For *en bon point*, in good case. — L. *in*, in ; *bonum*, neut. of *bonus*, good ; *punctum*, point.

Emboss (1), to adorn with bosses or raised work. (F. — L. *and* G.) From Em-, prefix ; and **Boss**.

Emboss (2), to take shelter, or drive to shelter in a wood, &c. (F. — Late L.) O F. *embosquer*, to shroud in a wood. — O. F. *em-* (L. *in*), in ; O. F. *bosc*, a wood ; see **Bouquet**.

Embouchure. (F. — L.) F. *embou-chure*, the mouth or opening (of a river). — F. *emboucher*, to put in or to the mouth. — L. *in*, in , F. *bouche*, from *bucca*, the mouth.

Embrace. (F. — L.) O. F. *embracer*, to grasp in the arms. — O. F. *em-*, for *en* (L. *in*) ; and *brace*, the grasp of the arms ; see **Brace**.

Embrasure. (F.) F. *embrasure*, an aperture with slant sides. — M. F. *embraser*, to slope the sides of a window. — O. F. *em-* (L. *in*), in ; M. F. *braser*, ' to skue, or chamfret ; ' Cot. (Of unknown origin.)

Embrocation, a fomenting. (F. — Late L. — Gk.) O. F. *embrocation.* — Med. L. *embrocātus*, pp. of *embrocāre*, to foment. — Gk. ἐμβροχή, a fomentation. — Gk. ἐμ-βρέχειν, to soak in. — Gk. ἐμ-= ἐν, in ; βρέχειν, to wet, soak.

Embroider. (F.) From Em- and Broider. Cf. O. F. *embroder*, to embroider.

Embroil. (F.) From F. *embrouiller*, to confuse. — F. *em-* (L. *im-*, for *in*) ; *brouiller*, to confuse. See **Broil** (2) ; and cf. **Imbroglio**.

Embryo. (F. — Gk.) Formerly *embryon.* — M. F. *embryon.* — Gk. ἔμβρυον, the embryo, fœtus. — Gk. ἐμ-= ἐν, within ; βρύον, neut. of pres. pt. of βρύειν, to be full of, swell out.

Emendation. (L.) Coined from the pp. of L. *ēmendāre*, to free from fault. — L. *ē*, free from ; *mendum menda*, a fault.

Emerald, a green gem. (F. — L. — Gk.) M. E. *emeraude.* — O. F. *esmeraude* (Span. *esmeralda*) ; also *esmeragde.* — L. *sma-ragdum*, acc. of *smaragdus.* — Gk. σμά-ραγδος, an emerald. Cf. Skt. *marakata-*, an emerald.

Emerge, to rise from the sea, appear. (L.) L. *ēmergere*, to rise out of water. — L. *ē*, out ; *mergere*, to dip ; see **Merge**.

Emerods ; see Hemorrhoids.

Emery, a hard mineral. (F. — Ital. — Gk.) Formerly *emeril* ; XVII cent. — F. *émeri* ; M. F. *emeril, esmeril.* — Ital. *smeriglio.* — Gk. σμήρις, σμύρις, emery.

Emetic. (L. — Gk.) L. *emeticus.* — Gk. ἐμετικός, causing sickness. — Gk. ἐμέω, I vomit ; see **Vomit**.

Emigrate. (L.) From pp. of L. *ē-migrāre*, to wander forth. — L. *ē*, out ; *migrāre*, to wander ; see **Migrate**.

Eminent, excellent. (L.) L. *ēminent-*, stem of pres. pt. of *ēminēre*, to project, excel. — L. *ē*, out ; *minēre*, to project ; for which cf. *im-minent, pro-minent.*

Emir, a commander. (Arab.) Arab. *amir*, a nobleman, prince. — Arab. root *amara*, he commanded. **Der.** *admir-al.*

Emit, to send forth. (L.) L. *ēmittere*, to send forth ; pp. *ēmissus.* — L. *ē*, out ; *mittere*, to send. **Der.** *emiss-ion, emiss-ary*, from the pp.

Emmet, an ant. (E.) M. E. *emete*, *amote*. A. S. *ǣmette*, or *ǣmette*, an ant.+ G. *ameise*, O. H. G. *āmeiza*, or *ameiza*, an ant. Doublet, *ant*.

Emmew; see **Enew**.

Emollient, softening. (F.−L.) M.F. *emollient*.−L. *ēmollient*-, stem of pres. pt. of *ēmollīre*, to soften.−L. *ē*, out, very; *mollīre*, to soften, from *molli-s*, soft.

Emolument, gain. (F.−L.) O. F. *emolument*.−L. *ēmolumentum*, what is gained by labour.−L. *ēmōlīrī*, to work out, accomplish.−L. *ē*, out, greatly; *mōlīrī*, to work, from *mōles*, heap, also effort. ¶ So usually explained; but the short vowels in -*mŏlŭ*- suggest a derivation from *ēmŏlĕlere*, to grind thoroughly.

Emotion. (L.) Coined from L. *ēmōtus*, pp. of *ēmouēre*, to move away or much.− L. *ē*, out, much; *mouēre*, to move.

Emperor, a ruler. (F.−L.) O.F. *empereor*.−L. *imperātōrem*, acc. of *imperātor*, a ruler.−L. *imperāre*, to rule.− L. *im*- (for *in*-), upon, over; *parāre*, to make ready, order. Der. *empr-ess*.

Emphasis, stress of voice. (L.−Gk.) L. *emphasis*.−Gk. ἔμφασις, a declaration, emphasis; orig. appearance.−Gk. ἐμφαίνομαι, I appear.−Gk. ἐμ- (ἐν), in; φαίνομαι, I appear, whence φάσις, an appearance; see **Phase**. Der. *emphatic*, from Gk. ἐμφατικός, significant.

Empire. (F.−L.) F. *empire*.−L. *imperium*, command.−L. *im*- (*in*-), upon, over; *parāre*, to make ready, order.

Empiric, a quack doctor. (F.−L.− Gk.) M. F. *empirique*.−L. *empīricus*.− Gk. ἐμπειρικός, experienced; also one of a certain set of physicians.−Gk. ἐμ-=ἐν, in; πεῖρα (=*πέρια), a trial, experience, allied to πόρος, a way, and to E. **Fare**. Brugm. i. § 293.

Employ. (F.−L.) M. F. *employer*, to employ.−L. *implicāre*, to implicate (in Late L., to use for, employ).−L. *im*- (for *in*-), in; *plicāre*, to fold; see **Implicate**, **Imply**.

Emporium, a mart. (L.−Gk.) L. *emporium*.−Gk. ἐμπόριον, a mart; neut. of ἐμπόριος, commercial.−Gk. ἐμπορία, commerce, ἔμπορος, a traveller, merchant.− Gk. ἐμ-=ἐν, in; πόρος, a way; see **Fare**.

Emprise, enterprise. (F.−L.) M. E. *emprise*.−O. F. *emprise*; orig. fem. of *empris*, pp. of O. F. *emprendre*, to take in hand.−L. *im*- (*in*-), in; *prehendere*, to take. See **Comprehend**.

Empty, void. (E.) M.E. *empti*. A.S. *ǣmtig*, *ǣmetig*, lit. full of leisure.−A. S. *ǣmta*, *ǣmetta*, leisure, older form *ǣmota* (Epin. Glos. 680). Perhaps *ǣmetta* is for *ǣmōtjon*-, from *ǣ*-, prefix, privative, and *mōt*, a meeting for business.

Empyrean, Empyreal, pertaining to elemental fire. (L.−Gk.) Adjectives coined from L. *empȳræ-us*, Gk. *ἐμπύραιος*, extended from ἔμ-πυρος, exposed to fire.−Gk. ἐμ-=ἐν, in; πῦρ, fire; see **Fire**.

Emu, Emeu, a bird. (Port.) Port. *ema*, an ostrich.

Emulate. (L.) From pp. of L. *æmulārī*, to try to equal.−L. *æmulus*, striving to equal.

Emulsion, a milk-like mixture. (F.− L.) M. F. *emulsion*; formed from L. *ēmuls-us*, pp. of *ēmulgēre*, to milk out.− L. *ē*, out; *mulgēre*, to milk; see **Milk**.

En-, *prefix*. (F.−L.) F. *en*-.−L. *in*-, in; sometimes used with a causal force, as *en-case*, *en-chain*, &c. See **Em-**.

Enact. (F.−L.) In Shak.−F. *en*, in (L. *in*); and **Act**. Lit. 'to put in act.'

Enamel, vb. (F.−O. H. G.) M. E. *enamaile*, sb., *enamelen*, vb.−A. F. *enameller*, *enamailler*, vb.−F. *en* (L. *in*), on; *amaile*, for O. F. *esmail*, enamel (= Ital. *smalto*), from O. Low G. *smalt* (Lübben). See **Smalt**.

Enamour. (F.−L.) O. F. *enamorer*, to inflame with love.−F. *en amour*, in love; where F. *en* is from L. *in*, in, and *amour* from L. acc. *amōrem*, love.

Encamp. (F.−L.) Coined from *en*- (F. *en*, L. *in*) and *camp*; hence 'to form into a camp.' See **Camp**.

Encase. (F.−L.) Cf. F. *encaisser*, 'to put into a case;' Cot.−F. *en*, in (L. *in*); and M.F. *caisse*, *casse*, a case; see **Case** (2).

Encaustic, relating to designs burnt in. (F.−L.−Gk.) F. *encaustique*.−L. *encausticus*.−Gk. ἐγκαυστικός, relating to burning in.−Gk. ἐν, in; καίω, I burn. See **Calm**.

Enceinte, pregnant. (F.−L.) F. *enceinte*.−Late L. *incincta*, ungirt, said of a pregnant woman, fem. of pp. of *cingere*, to gird, with neg. prefix *in*-. ¶ Isidore explains Late L. *incincta* as meaning 'ungirt'; so also Ital. *incinta* (Florio).

Enchant. (F.−L.) F. *enchanter*, to charm.−L. *incantāre*, to repeat a chant.− L. *in*-, upon; and *cantāre*, to sing; see **Cant** (1).

Enchase. (F.—L.) M. F. *enchasser*, 'to enchace or set in gold ;' Cot. Hence to emboss.—F. *en*, in (L. *in*) ; and *chasse* (F. *châsse*), the same as *casse*, a case ; see Case (2).

Encircle. (F.—L.) From En- and Circle.

Encline. (F.—L.) M. E. *enclinen.*— O.F. *encliner.*—L. *inclīnāre*; see Incline.

Enclitic. (Gk.) Gk. ἐγκλιτικός, enclining, dependent ; used of a word which 'leans' its accent upon another.—Gk. ἐγκλίνειν, to lean upon, encline.—Gk. ἐν, on; κλίνειν, to lean; see Lean (1).

Enclose. (F.—L.) From En- and Close (1). Cf. A.F. *enclos*, pp. of *enclorre*, to shut in.

Encomium, commendation. (L.—Gk.) Latinised from Gk. ἐγκώμιον, neut. of ἐγκώμιος, laudatory, full of revelry.—Gk. ἐν, in ; κῶμος, revelry.

Encore, again. (F.—L.) F. *encore* (= Ital. *ancora*), still, again.—L. *hanc hōram*, for *in hanc hōram*, to this hour ; see Hour. ¶ Somewhat disputed.

Encounter, vb. (F.—L.) O.F. *encontrer*, to meet in combat.—F. *en*, in ; *contre*, against.—L. *in*, in ; *contrā*, against.

Encourage. (F.—L.) F. *encourager*; from F. *en* (L. *in*) and *courage* ; see Courage.

Encrinite, the 'stone lily'; a fossil. (Gk.) Coined from Gk. ἐν, in; κρίνον, a lily ; with suffix -*ιτης*.

Encroach. (F.—L. *and* Teut.) Lit. to hook away, catch in a hook.—O.F. *encrochier*, to seize upon.—F. *en*, in ; *croc*, a hook ; cf. F. *accrocher*, to hook up.—L. *in*, in; and M. Du. *kroke*, Icel. *krokr*, &c.; see Crook.

Encumber. (F.—L. ?) O.F. *encombrer*, to block up (a way).—Late L. *incombrāre*, to obstruct.—L. *in-*, in ; and Late L. *combrus*, an obstacle. See Cumber.

Encyclical, circular, said of a letter sent round (ecclesiastical). From Gk. ἐγκύκλι-ος, circular (said of a letter) ; with suffix -*c-al*.—Gk. ἐν, in ; κύκλο-s, a circle.

encyclopædia. (L.—Gk.) Latinised from a (coined) Gk. *ἐγκυκλοπαιδεία, for ἐγκύκλιος παιδεία, circular (or complete) instruction ; from ἐγκύκλιος (above), and παιδεία, instruction.

End, sb. (E.) M.E. *ende*. A.S. *ende*, sb.+Du. *einde*, Icel. *endir*, Sw. *ände*, Dan. *ende*, Goth. *andeis*, G. *ende*. Teut. type

and-joz. Cf. O. Irish *ind*, Skt. *anta-*, end, limit. ¶ Hence the prefixes *ante-*, *anti-*, *an-* in *an-swer*.

Endeavour, to attempt. (F.—L.) Coined from the M. E. sb. *dever*, *devoir*, duty, with F. prefix *en-* (= L. *in*). Compare the old phrase 'to do his *dever*' = to do his duty (Ch. C. T. 2598) ; see Devoir.

Endemic, peculiar to a district. (Gk.) Gk. ἔνδημ-ος, belonging to a people.—Gk. ἐν, in ; δῆμος, a people ; see Democracy.

Endive, a plant. (F.—L.) F. *endive* (Ital. *endivia*).—Lat. type *intibea*, adj.; from L. *intibus, intubus*, endive.

Endogen, a plant that grows from within. (F.—Gk.) F. *endogène* (1813). From Gk. ἔνδο-ν, within ; γεν-, base of γίγνομαι, I am born, allied to γένος, race.

Endorse. (F.—L.) Formerly *endosse*. O. F. *endosser*, to put on the back of.—F. *en*, on; *dos*, the back, from L. *dorsum*, the back (whence the spelling with *rs*).

Endow. (F.—L.) A.F. *endower*. From F. *en-* and *douer*.—L. *in-*, in, and *dōtāre*, to give a dowry, from *dōt-*, stem of *dōs*, a dowry ; cf. *dare*, to give.

Endue (1), to endow. (F.—L.) Another spelling of *endow*; XV cent.—O. F. *endoer* (later *endouer*), to endow (Burguy). —L. *in*, in ; and *dōtare*, to endow; see above. ¶ Confused both with O.F. *enduire*, to introduce (from L. *indūcere*), and with Endue (2) below.

Endue (2), to clothe. (L.) A corruption of *indue* ; as in 'endue thy ministers with righteousness.'—L. *induere*, to clothe. See Indue (2) ; and see above.

Endure. (F.—L.) M. E. *enduren.*— F. *endurer.*—F. *en* (L. *in*) ; and *durer* (L. *dūrāre*), to last. See Dure.

Enemy. (F.—L.) M. E. *enemi.*— O. F. *enemi.*—L. *inimīcus*, unfriendly.— L. *in*, not ; *amīcus*, friendly, from L. *amāre*, to love.

Energy. (F.—L.—Gk.) O.F. *energie*. —Late L. *energīa.*—Gk. ἐνέργεια, vigour, action.—Gk. ἐνεργός, at work.—Gk. ἐν, in ; ἔργον, work ; see Work.

Enervate. (L.) From pp. of L. *ēneruāre*, to deprive of nerve or strength. —L. *ē*, out of ; *neruus*, a nerve ; see Nerve.

Enew. (F.—L.) Misspelt *emmew* in Shak.; read *enew*, to drive into the water. —F. *en*, in ; A.F. *ewe* (F. *eau*), water, from L. *aqua.* Cf. O. F. *enewer,* to soak in water (Godefroy).

Enfeoff, to endue with a fief. (F.–L. and O. H. G.) The spelling is Norman F.; formed from F. *en* (L. *in*), in ; and *fief,* a fief. See **Fief.**

Enfilade, a straight line or passage. (F.–I..) F. *enfilade,* a long string (of things).–F. *enfiler,* to thread.–F. *en-* (L. *in*), in; *fil,* a thread, from L. *filum,* a thread. See **File** (1).

Engage. (F.–L.) O. F. *engager,* to bind by a pledge.–F. *en* (L. *in*), in ; *gage,* a pledge; see **Gage. Der.** *dis-engage.*

Engender, to breed. (F.–L.) M. E. *engendren.* – O. F. *engendrer.*–L. *ingenerāre,* to produce.–L. *in,* in ; *generāre,* to breed, from *gener-* (for **genes-*), stem of *genus,* a race, See **Genus.**

Engine. (F.–L.) O. F. *engin,* a tool.– L. *ingenium,* natural capacity, also, an invention.–L. *in,* in ; *geni-,* as in *genius* ; see **Genius.**

English, belonging to the Angles. (E.) A.S. *Englisc, Ænglisc.* – A. S. *Engl-e, Ængl-e,* pl., the Angles ; with suffix *-isc,* -ish. Cf. A. S. *Angel-cynn,* Angle kin (*gens Anglōrum*).

Engrailed, indented with curved lines; in heraldry. (F.–L. and Teut.) O. F. *engresle,* pp. of *engresler,* to engrail (indent as with hailstones).– O. F. *en,* in ; *gresle* (F. *grêle*), hail.–L. *in,* in ; and (perhaps) G. *gries,* grit. See **Grail** (3).

Engrain, Ingrain, to dye of a fast colour. (F. – L.) M.E. *engreynen,* to dye *in grain,* i.e. of a fast colour. Coined from F. *en* (L. *in*) ; and O. F. *graine,* 'the seed of herbs, also grain, wherewith cloth is died *in grain,* scarlet die, scarlet in graine ;' Cot. From Late L. *grāna,* the cochineal ' berry ' or insect ; a fem. sb. formed from the pl. (*grāna*) of *grānum,* a grain.

Engrave. (F. *and* E.) From En- and Grave (1) ; imitating O. F. *engraver* (from L. *in* and O. H. G. *graban,* Low G. *graven,* cognate with E. *grave*).

Engross, to write in large letters, to occupy wholly. (F. – L.) The former (legal) sense is the older. A. F. *engrosser.* From F. *en grosse,* i. e. in large characters. –L. *in,* in ; Late L. *grossa,* large writing, from L. *grossus,* thick.

Enhance, to raise, exalt, increase. (F.–L.) A. F. *enhauncer,* a form of O. F.

enhaucer, enhaucier, to lift (Ital. *innalzare*).–L. *in* ; and Late L. *altiāre,* to lift, from *altus,* high.

Enigma. (L.–Gk.) L. *ænigma.* – Gk. αἴνιγμα (stem αἰνίγματ-), a riddle, dark saying. – Gk. αἰνίσσομαι, I speak in riddles. –Gk. αἶνος, a tale, story. **Der.** *enigmat-ic* (from the stem).

Enjoin, to bid. (F.–L.) O. F. *enjoindre* (1 p. pres. *enjoin-s*). – L. *iniungere,* to bid, ordain, orig. to join into. – L. *in,* in ; *iungere,* to join. See **Join.**

Enjoy, to joy in. (F.–L.) M. E. *enioien* (=*enjoyen*) ; A. F. *enioier.*–F. *en* (L. *in*) ; O. F. *ioie,* F. *joie* ; see **Joy.**

Enlighten, vb. (E. ; *with* F. *prefix.*) Coined with F. prefix *en-* (L. *in*), from *lighten,* vb.; see **Lighten.**

Enlist, to enter on a list. (F.–G. ; *with* F.–L. *prefix.*) Coined by prefixing F. *en* (L. *in*) to List (2).

Enmity. (F.–L.) M. E. *enmite.*– A. F. *enemite* ; O. F. *enamistie*(*t*). –O. F. *en-* (L. *in-*), neg. prefix ; and *amistie*(*t*), amity ; see **Amity.**

Ennui. (F.–L.) Mod. F. *ennui,* annoyance ; O. F. *anoi.* See **Annoy.**

Enormous, great beyond measure. (F. – L.) Formed from *enorm* (obsolete) ; with suffix *-ous.*–M. F. *enorme,* huge.–L. *ēnormis,* out of rule, huge.–L. *ē,* out of ; *norma,* rule. See **Normal.**

Enough. (E.) M. E. *inoh, enogh* ; pl. *inohe, enoghe.* A.S. *genōh, genōg,* pl. *genōge,* sufficient ; allied to A.S. *geneah,* it suffices.+Icel. *gnōgr,* Dan. *nok,* Swed. *nog,* Du. *genoeg,* G. *genug,* Goth. *ganōhs.* The *ge-* is a prefix. Cf. L. *nanciscī,* to obtain (pp. *nac-tus*) ; Skt. *naç,* to attain.

Enquire. (F.–L.) M. E. *enqueren,* altered from *enquere* to *enquire,* and later to *inquire,* under the influence of the L. form. –O. F. *enquerre, enquerir.*–L. *inquīrere,* to search into.–L. *in,* in ; *quærere,* to seek. **Der.** *enquir-y,* often turned into *inquiry* ; *enquest* (now *inquest*), from O. F. *enqueste,* L. *inquīsīta* (*rēs*), a thing enquired into.

Ensample. (F.–L.) M. E. *ensample.* –A. F. *ensample,* corrupt form of *essample, exemple.*–L. *exemplum,* a sample, pattern. –L. *eximere,* to select a sample.–L. *ex,* out ; *emere,* to take. **Der.** *sample.*

Ensign. (F. – L.) O. F. *ensigne,* more correctly *enseigne,* 'a sign, ensigne, standard ;' Cot.–Late L. *insignia,* pl. of L. *insigne,* a standard.–L. *insignis,* remarkable. – L. *in*, upon; *signum*, a mark; i. e. 'with a mark on it.' See Sign.

Ensilage, the storing of grain, &c., underground. (F. – Span. – L. *and* Gk.) F. *ensilage.* – Span. *ensilar*, to store up underground. – Span. *en*, in; *silo*, a pit for storing grain. – L. *in*, in; *sīrus*, borrowed from Gk. σιρός, a pit for storing grain.

Ensue. (F. – L.) O. F. *ensu-*, a stem of *ensivre*, to follow after. – Late L. *insequere*, for L. *insequī*, to follow upon. – L. *in*, on; *sequī*, to follow.

Ensure, to make sure. (F. – L.) A. F. *enseurer.* – F. *en* (L. *in*), in; and O. F. *seür*, sure; see Sure.

Entablature. (F. – L.) Obs. F. *entablature*, 'an intablature;' Cot. [Cf. Ital. *intavolatura*, 'a planking,' Torriano; from *intavolare*, 'to board,' Florio.] Properly 'something laid flat,' and, though now applied to the part of a building surmounting the columns, orig. applied to a panel or flooring. – L. *in*, upon; **tabulāre*, a verb formed from the sb. *tabulātum*, boardwork, a flooring, from *tabula*, a plank; see Table.

Entail, to bestow as a heritage. (F. – L.) Orig. to convert an estate into *fee-tail* (*feodum talliātum*, where *talliātum* means 'limited' in a certain way). From F. *en-* (L. *in*) and *tailler* (*talliāre*). In another sense we find M. F. *entailen*, to cut, carve. – O. F. *entailler*, to carve, grave. – F. *en-* (L. *in*), in; and *tailler*, to cut; see Tailor, Tail (2), Tally.

Entangle; from En- and Tangle, q. v.

Enter. (F. – L.) M. E. *entren*. – O. F. *entrer.* – L. *intrāre*, to go into. – L. *in*, in; and **trāre*, to go through (cf. *pene-trāre* and *trans*); allied to Skt. *tara-*, a passage. See Brugm. ii. § 579. Der. *entr-ance.*

Enterprise. (F. – L.) O. F. *entreprise*, *enterprinse*, an enterprise. – O. F. *enterpris*, pp. of *enterprendre*, to undertake. – Late L. *interprendere.* – L. *inter*, among; *prendere*, short for *prehendere*, to lay hold of. See Prehensile.

Entertain. (F. – L.) O. F. *entretenir.* – Late L. *intertenēre*, to entertain, lit. 'to hold or keep among.' – L. *inter*, among; *tenēre*, to hold.

Enthusiasm, inspiration. (L. – Gk.) Late L. *enthūsiasmus.* – Gk. ἐνθουσιασμός, inspiration. – Gk. ἐνθουσιάζω, I am inspired.

– Gk. ἔνθεος, full of the god, having a god within, inspired. – Gk. ἐν, in; θεός, a god.

Entice. (F. – L.) M. E. *enticen.* – O. F. *enticier*, *enticher*, to excite. – Lat. type **intitiāre*, to kindle, set on fire. – L. *in*; and **titius*, for *titio*, a firebrand. Cf. F. *attiser*, Ital. *attizzare*, to set on fire.

Entire. (F. – L.) O. F. *entier*, whole. – L. *integrum*, acc. of *integer*, whole. See Integer.

Entity, being. (L.) A coined word, with suffix *-ty*, from L. *enti-*, decl. stem of **ens*, a thing, a being; see Essence.

Entomology. (F. – Gk.) F. *entomologie* (A. D. 1764). From Gk. ἔντομο-ν, an insect; neut. of ἔντομο-ς, cut into, so called from the very thin middle part (see Insect). – Gk. ἐν, in; τέμνειν, to cut; with suffix -λογια, discourse, from λέγειν, to speak.

Entrails, the inward parts. (F. – L.) O. F. *entraille*, intestines. – Late L. *intrālia*, also (more correctly) *intrānea*, entrails. – L. *interānea*, entrails, neut. pl. of *interāneus*, inward, adj., from *inter*, within. ¶ The O. F. *entraille* was a fem. sing. made from a neut. pl.

Entreat. (F. – L.) Orig. to treat; then to treat with, beseech. O. F. *entraiter*, to treat of. – F. *en* (< L. *in*), in, concerning; F. *traiter* < L. *tractāre*, to handle, treat; see Treat.

Enumerate. (L.) From pp. of L. *enumerāre*, to reckon up. – L. *ē*, out, fully; *numerāre*, vb., from *numerus*, number.

Enunciate. (L.) From pp. of L. *ēnunciāre*, better spelt *ēnuntiāre*, to utter, declare fully. – L. *ē*, fully; *nuntiāre*, to tell, from *nuntius*, a messenger.

Envelop. (F. – Teut.) M. E. *envolupen*. O. F. *envoluper*, later *enveloper*, to wrap in, wrap round, enfold. – F. *en* (L. *in*), in; and O. F. *voluper*, *voloper*, *vloper*, to wrap, from a base *vlop-*, to wrap. This base resembles M. E. *wlappen*, to wrap; which, however, is not known outside English. See Lap (3). Note Walloon *ewalpé*, to envelop (Remacle); M. Ital. *goluppare*, to wrap (Florio). Cf. Develop.

Environ, to surround. (F. – L.) O.F. *environner*, to surround. – F. *environ*, round about. – F. *en* (L. *in*), in; O. F. *viron*, a circuit, from *virer*, to turn, veer; see Veer.

Envoy. (F. – L.) O. F. *envoy*, a sending. – O. F. *envoier*, to send. – F. *en voie*, on the way.—L. *in uiam*, on the way. Cf. Ital. *inviare*, to send.

Envy, sb. (F.—L.) M. E. *enuie* (*envie*).—O. F. *envie*.—L. *inuidia*, envy; see Invidious.

Epact. (F.—Late L.—Gk.) O. F. (and F.) *epacte*, an addition, the epact (a term in astronomy).—Late L. *epacta*.—Gk. ἐπακτή (for ἐπακτός ἡμέρα), late fem. of ἐπακτός, added.—Gk. ἐπάγειν, to bring in, add.—Gk. ἐπ-, for ἐπί, to; and ἄγειν, to lead, bring. (√AG.)

Epaulet, a shoulder-knot. (F.—L.—Gk.) F. *épaulette*; dimin. from *épaule* (O. F. *espaule*), a shoulder. — Late L. *spatula*, shoulder-blade; L. *spatula*, a broad blade; see Spatula.

Epergne, an ornamental stand for the centre of a table. (F.—O. H. G.) F. *épergne*, commonly spelt *épargne*, lit. thriftiness, sparingness. So called from the method of ornamentation; the F. *taille d'épargne* is applied to a sort of ornamentation in which certain parts are cut away and filled in with enamel, leaving the design *in relief*, i. e. *spared* or left uncut. See Littré, and Cotgrave (s. v. *espargne*).—F. *épargner*; O. F. *espargner, espergner*, to spare.—O. H. G. *sparōn*, G. *sparen*, to spare; see Spare.

Ephah, a Hebrew measure. (Heb.—Egypt.) Heb. *ēphāh*, a measure; of Egyptian origin; cf. Coptic *ōpi*, measure.

Ephemera, sing.; orig. pl., flies that live for a day. (Gk.) XVII cent.—Gk. ἐφήμερα, neut. pl. of ἐφήμερος, lasting for a day.—Gk. ἐφ-=ἐπί, for; ἡμέρα, a day. Der. *ephemer-al*, adj.; *ephemer-is* (Gk. ἐφημερίς, a diary).

Ephod, part of the priest's habit. (Heb.) Heb. *ēphōd*, a vestment.—Heb. *āphad*, to put on.

Epi-, *prefix.* (Gk.) Gk. ἐπί, upon, to, besides; spelt *eph-* in *eph-emeral*, *ep-* in *ep-isode*, *ep-och*, *ep-ode*.

Epic, narrative. (L.—Gk.) L. *epicus*. —Gk. ἐπικός, narrative.—Gk. ἔπος, word, narrative, song; see Voice.

Epicene, of common gender. (L.—Gk.) L. *epicænus*.—Gk. ἐπίκοινος, common.—Gk. ἐπί, among; κοινός, common.

Epicure, a follower of Epicurus. (L. —Gk.) L. *Epicūrus*.—Gk. Ἐπίκουρος, a proper name; lit. 'assistant.'

Epicycle, a small circle, with its centre on the circumference of a larger one. (L.—Gk.) L. *epicyclus*.—Gk. ἐπίκυκλος.

—Gk. ἐπί, upon; κύκλος, a circle; see Cycle.

Epidemic, affecting a people. (L.—Gk.) Formed from L. *epidēmus*, epidemic.—Gk. ἐπίδημος, among the people, general.—Gk. ἐπί, among; δῆμος, people. See Endemic.

Epidermis, cuticle. (L.—Gk.) L. *epidermis*.—Gk. ἐπιδερμίς, upper skin.—Gk. ἐπί, upon; δέρμ-α, skin. See Derm.

Epiglottis, the cartilage forming a lid over the glottis. (Gk.) Gk. ἐπιγλωττίς. —Gk. ἐπί, upon; γλωττίς, glottis; see Glottis.

Epigram, a short and pithy poem or saying. (F.—L.—Gk.) F. *épigramme*. —L. *epigramma*.—Gk. ἐπίγραμμα, an inscription, epigram.—Gk. ἐπιγράφειν, to inscribe. — Gk. ἐπί, upon; γράφειν, to write. See Grammar.

Epilepsy. (F.—L.—Gk.) M. F. *epilepsie*, 'the falling sickness;' Cot.—L. *epilēpsia*.—Gk. ἐπιληψία, ἐπίληψις, a seizure. —Gk. ἐπιλαμβάνειν, to seize upon.—Gk. ἐπί, on; λαμβάνειν, to seize. Der. *epileptic* (Gk. ἐπιληπτικός).

Epilogue. (F.—L.—Gk.) F. *épilogue*. —L. *epilogus*.—Gk. ἐπίλογος, a concluding speech.—Gk. ἐπί, upon; λόγος, a speech.

Epiphany, Twelfth Day. (F.—L.—Gk.) O. F. *epiphanie*.—L. *epiphania*.—Gk. ἐπιφάνια, manifestation; orig. neut. pl. of ἐπιφάνιος, manifest, but used as equivalent to ἐπιφάνεια, sb.—Gk. ἐπιφαίνειν, to shew forth.—Gk. ἐπί, to, forth; φαίνειν, to shew. See Phantom.

Episcopal. (F. — L. — Gk.) O. F. *episcopal*.—L. *episcopālis*, belonging to a bishop.—L. *episcopus*, a bishop. —Gk. ἐπίσκοπος, an over-seer, bishop.—Gk. ἐπί, upon; σκοπός, one that watches. See Scope.

Episode, a story introduced into another. (Gk.) Gk. ἐπεισόδιον, orig. neut. of ἐπεισόδιος, coming in besides.—Gk. ἐπ-(ἐπί), besides; εἰσόδιος, coming in, from εἰς, in, ὀδός, a way.

Epistle, a letter. (F. — L. — Gk.) O. F. *epistle*, also *epistre*.—L. *epistola*.— Gk. ἐπιστολή, message, letter.—Gk. ἐπιστέλλειν, to send to.—Gk. ἐπί, to; στέλλειν, to equip, send.

Epitaph. (F.—L.—Gk.) F. *épitaphe*. —L. *epitaphium*.—Gk. ἐπιτάφιος, upon a tomb.—Gk. ἐπί, on; τάφος, a tomb.

Epithalamium, a marriage-song. (L.—Gk.) L. *epithalamium*.—Gk. ἐπιθαλάμιον, bridal song. — Gk. ἐπί, upon, for ; θάλαμος, bride-chamber.

Epithet. (L. — Gk.) L. *epitheton*. — Gk. ἐπίθετον, an epithet; neut. of ἐπίθετος, attributed. — Gk. ἐπί, besides; θε-τός, placed, from θε-, weak grade of τίθημι, I place.

Epitome. (L. — Gk.) L. *epitomē*. — Gk. ἐπιτομή, a surface-incision, also an abridgment. — Gk. ἐπί, upon ; τέμνειν, to cut.

Epoch. (L. — Gk.) Late L. *epocha*. — Gk. ἐποχή, a stop, pause, fixed date. — Gk. ἐπ- (ἐπί), upon ; ἔχειν, to hold, check. (√SEGH.) Brugm. i. § 602.

Epode. (F. — L. — Gk.) O. F. *epode*. — L. *epōdos*. — Gk. ἐπῳδός, an epode, something sung after. — Gk. ἐπ-ί, upon, after ; ἀείδειν, to sing.

Equal. (L.) L. *æquālis*, equal. — L. *æquus*, just, exact.

equanimity, evenness of mind. (L.) From L. *æquanimitas*, the same. — L. *æquanimis*, of even temper, kind. — L. *æqu-us*, equal ; *animus*, mind.

equation, a statement of equality. (L.) I. acc. *æquātionem*, an equalising ; from pp. of *æquāre*, to make equal. — L. *æquus*, equal. So also *equator* < L. *æquātor*.

equilibrium, even balancing. (L.) L. *æquilībrium*. — L. *æquilibris*, evenly balanced. — L. *æqui-*, for *æquus*, even ; *lībra*, a balance ; see **Librate**.

equinox. (F. — L.) F. *équinoxe*. — L. *æquinoctium*, time of equal day and night. — L. *æqui-*, for *æquus* ; *nocti-*, decl. stem of *nox*, a night ; see **Night**.

equipollent, equally potent. (F. — L.) O. F. *equipollent*. — L. *æquipollent-*, stem of *æquipollens*, of equal power. — L. *æqui-*, for *æquus* : *pollens*, pres. pt. of *pollēre*, to be strong.

equity. (F. — L.) O. F. *equité*. — L. *æquitātem*, acc. of *æquitas*, equity. — L. *æquus*, equal.

equivalent. (F. — L.) M. F. *equivalent*. — L. *æquiualent-*, stem of pres. pt. of *æquiualēre*, to be of equal force. — L. *æqui-*, for *æquus* ; *ualēre*, to be worth ; see **Value**.

equivocal. (L.) Formed from L. *æquiuoc-us*, of doubtful sense. — L. *æqui-*, *æquus*; *uoc-*, stem of *uocāre*, to call; see **Voice**. Der. *equivoc-ate*, to speak doubtfully. ¶ So also *equi-angular*, *equi-multiple*, &c.

Equerry, an officer who has charge of horses and stables. (F. — O. H. G.) Properly *equerry* means a stable, and mod. E. *equerry* stands for *squire of the equerry*. — F. *écurie*, O. F. *escurie*, a stable ; Low L. *scūria*, a stable. — O. H. G. *skūra*, *skiura* (G. *scheuer*), a shelter, stable; allied to O. H. G. *skūr*, a shelter. Brugm. i. § 109. (√SQEU.) ¶ Altered to *equerry* by confusion with *equus*, a horse.

Equestrian ; see **Equine**.

Equilibrium ; see **Equal**.

Equine. (L.) L. *equīnus*, relating to horses. — L. *equus*, a horse. + Gk. ἵππος, (ἵκκος) ; Skt. *açva* ; Pers. *asp* ; O. Irish *ech* ; A. S. *eoh*. Brugm. i. § 116.

equestrian. (L.) Formed from L. *equestri-*, stem of *equester*, belonging to horsemen. — L. *eques*, a horseman. — L. *equus*, a horse.

Equinox ; see **Equal**.

Equip, to furnish, fit out. (F. — Scand.) M. F. *equiper*, O. North F. *esquiper*, to fit out ; A. F. *eskipper*. — Icel. *skipa*, to set in order, perhaps allied to *skip*, a ship. Der. *equip-age*, *-ment*.

Equipollent, Equity ; see **Equal**.

Equivalent, Equivocal ; see **Equal**.

Era. (L.) L. *æra*, an era, fixed date. From a particular sense of *æra*, counters (for calculation), pl. of *æs*, brass, money.

Eradicate. (L.) From pp. of L. *erādicāre*, to root out. — L. *ē*, out ; *rādicāre*, to root, from *rādic-*, stem of *rādix*, root. See **Radix**.

Erase. (L.) L. *ērāsus*, pp. of *ērādere*, to scratch out. — L. *ē*, out ; *rādere*, to scrape.

Ere, before. (E.) M. E. *er*. A. S. *ǣr*, soon, before ; adv. prep. and conj. + Du. *eer*, O. H. G. *ēr*, G. *eher* ; Goth. *airis*, sooner, comp. of *air*, Icel. *ār*, adv., early, soon. ¶ The two last are positive, not comparative, forms. Cf. Gk. ἦρι, early.

early, soon. (E.) M. E. *erly*. A. S. *ǣrlīce*, adv. ; from *ærlīc*, adj., not used. — A. S. *ǣr*, soon ; *līc*, like.

erst, soonest. (E.) M. E. *erst*. A. S. *ǣrest*, superlative of *ǣr*, soon.

Erect, adj. (L.) L. *ērectus*, upright ; pp. of *ērigere*, to set up straight. — L. *ē*, out, up ; *regere*, to make straight, rule.

Ermine, a beast. (F. — O. H. G.) M. E. *ermine*. — O. F. *ermine* (F. *hermine*). — O. H. G. *harmīn*, ermine-fur (G.

hermelin). **—** O. H. G. *harmo*, an ermine. **+**A.S.*hearma*; Lithuan. *szarmŭ*, a weasel. ¶But Hatzfeld supports the derivation from *Armenius mūs*, an Armenian mouse; cf. *Ponticus mūs*, supposed to be an ermine.

Erode. (F. **—**L.) F. *éroder.* **—** L. *ērōdere*, to eat away. **—** L. *ē*, out ; *rōdere*, to gnaw. **Der.** *eros-ion* (from pp. *ērōs-us*).

Erotic. (Gk.) Gk. *ἐρωτικός*, relating to love. **—**Gk. *ἐρωτι-*, crude form of *ἔρως*, love ; allied to *ἔραμαι*, I love.

Err, to stray. (F.**—**L.) M. E. *erren.* **—** O. F. *errer.* **—**L. *errāre*, to wander (for **ers-āre*).**+**G. *irren*, to stray, Goth. *airzjan*, to make to stray. Brugm. i. § 878.

erratum, an error. (L.) L. *errātum*, neut. of pp. of *errāre*, to make a mistake.

erroneous, faulty. (L.) Put for L. *errōne-us*, wandering ; with suffix *-ous.* **—** L. *errāre* (above).

error. (F. **—** L.) M. E. *errour.* **—** O. F. *errour.* **—**L. *errōrem*, acc. of *error*, a mistake. **—**L. *errāre* (above).

Errand. (E.) M. E. *erende.* A. S. *ǽrende*, a message, business.**+**O. Sax. *ārundi*, O. H. G. *ārunti*, a message ; cf. Icel. *eyrendi*, *örendi*, Swed. *ärende*, Dan. *ærende.* Usually connected with A. S. *ār*, Icel. *árr*, Goth. *airus*, a messenger; which is hardly possible.

Errant, wandering. (F.**—**L.) F. *errant*, pres. pt. of O. F. *errer*, *eirer*, to wander. **—**Late L. *iterāre*, to travel. **—**L. *iter*, a journey. ¶ It sometimes represents the pres. pt. of *errāre*, to wander. **Doublet,** *arrant.*

Erratum, Erroneous, Error ; see Err.

Erst ; see Ere.

Erubescent. (L.) L. *ērubescent-*, stem of pres. pt. of *ērubescere*, to grow red. **—**L. *ē*, out, much; *rubescere*, to grow red, inceptive form of *rubēre*, to be red. See **Red.**

Eructate. (L.) From pp. of L. *ēructāre*, to belch out. **—**L. *ē*, out ; *ructāre*, to belch ; allied to *ē-rūgere*, to belch ; cf. Gk. *ἐρεύγεσθαι.* Brugm. i. § 221.

Erudite, learned. (L.) L. *ērudītus*, pp. of *ērudīre*, to free from rudeness, to teach. **—**L. *ē*, from; *rudis*, rude.

Eruption. (L.) From L. *ēruptiōnem*, acc. of *ēruptio*, a breaking out. **—**L.*ēruptus*, pp. of *ērumpere*, to break out. **—**L. *ē*, out; *rumpere*, to break. See **Rupture.**

Erysipelas, a redness on the skin.

(L. **—** Gk.) L. *erysipelas.* **—** Gk. *ἐρυσίπελας*, redness on the skin. **—**Gk. *ἐρυσι-*, allied to *ἐρυθ-ρός*, red ; *πέλλα*, skin. Cf. *ἐρυσίβη*, red blight on corn.

Escalade, a scaling of walls. (F. **—** Span. **—** L.) F. *escalade.* **—**Span. *escalado*, *escalada*, a scaling ; from *escalar*, to scale. **—** Span. *escala*, a ladder. **—** L. *scāla*, a ladder ; see **Scale** (3). Cf. Ital. *scalata*, an escalade ; Florio also has ' *Scalada*, an escalado,' from Spanish.

Escape. (F.**—**L.) M. E. *escapen.* **—** O. North F.*escaper* (F. *échapper*),to escape, lit. to slip out of one's cape ; Picard *écaper.* **—**L. *ex cappā*, out of one's cape ; see **Cape** (1).

Escarpment. (F. **—** Ital. **—** Teut.) F. *escarpement.* Formed from F. *escarpe*, a scarp ; with suffix *-ment* (L. *-mentum*); see **Scarp.**

Escheat. (F. **—** L.) M. E. *eschete* (also *chete*), a forfeit to the lord of the fee. **—** O. F. *eschete*, rent, that which falls to one, orig. fem. pp. of *escheoir* (F. *échoir*). **—**Late L. *excadere*, to fall to one's share. **—**L. *ex*, out ; and *cadere*, to fall. Hence *cheat.*

Eschew, to shun. (F. **—** O. H. G.) M. E. *eschewen.* **—**O. F. *eschiver*, *eschever*, to shun. **—**O. H. G. *sciuhan*, to frighten; also to fear. **—**O. H. G. **scioh*, M. H. G. *schiech*, shy, timid. See **Shy.**

Escort, a guide, guard. (F.**—**Ital.**—**L.) M. F. *escorte.* **—**Ital. *scorta*, a guide; fem. of pp. of *scorgere*, to see, perceive, guide (orig. to set right). **—** L. *ex*, entirely ; *corrigere*, to correct; see **Correct.**

Escrow, a deed delivered on condition. (F.**—**Teut.) A. F. *escrouwe*, M. E. *scroue*, *scrowe* ; the orig. word of which *scro-ll* is the diminutive. **—**O. F. *escroe*, a slip of parchment. **—**M. Du. *schroode*, a shred, slip of paper (Kilian) ; cf. O. H. G. *scrōt*, a shred. See **Shred** and **Scroll.**

Escuage, a pecuniary satisfaction in lieu of feudal service. (F.**—**L.) O. F. *escuage* < Late L. *scūtāgium.* Formed with suffix *-age* from O. F. *escu*, a shield ; because *escuage* was first paid in lieu of service in the field. **—**L. *scūtum*, a shield.

Esculent, eatable. (L.) L. *esculentus*, fit for eating. **—**L. *ēsca*, food. For **ed-sca.* **—**L. *edere*, to eat. Brugm. i. § 753.

Escutcheon, Scutcheon, a painted shield. (F. **—** L.) Formerly *escochon* ; XV cent.; A. F. *escuchon.* **—**O. North F. *escuchon*, O. F. *escusson*, the same; answering to a Late L. acc. *scūtiōnem, extended from L. scūtum, a shield.

Esophagus, gullet. (L. – Gk.) Late L. æsophagus. – Gk. οἰσωφάγος, the gullet, lit. conveyer of food. – Gk. οἰσο- (of doubtful origin) ; φαγ-, base of φαγεῖν, to eat.

Esoteric. (Gk.) Gk. ἐσωτερικός, inner; hence, secret. – Gk. ἐσώτερος, inner, comp. of ἔσω, adv., within ; from ἐς = εἰς, into, prep. Opposed to exoteric.

Espalier, frame-work for training trees. (F. – Ital. – L. – Gk.) M.F. espallier ; Cot. – Ital. spalliera, back of a chair, support, espalier. – Ital. spalla, shoulder. – L. spatula ; see Epaulet.

Especial. (F. – L.) O. F. especial. – L. speciālis, belong to a special kind. – L. speciēs, a kind. Doublet, special.

Espionage; see Espy.

Esplanade, a level space. (F. – Ital. – L.) M. F. esplanade, 'a planing, levelling, evenning of ways ;' Cot. Formed from O. F. esplaner, to level ; the suffix being due to an imitation of Ital. spianata, an esplanade, a levelled way ; from spianare, to level. – L. explānāre, to level. – L. ex, out ; plānāre, to level, from plānus, flat. See Plain.

Espouse. (F. – L.) O. F. espouser, to espouse, wed. – L. sponsāre, to betroth. – L. sponsus, pp. of spondēre, to promise. See Spouse, Sponsor.

Espy, to spy, see. (F. – O.H.G.) M. E. espyen. – O. F. espier. – O. H. G. spehōn (G. spähen), to spy ; see Species. **Der.** espi-on-age, F. espionnage, from M. F. espion, a spy, borrowed from Ital. spione, a spy, from O. H. G. spehon, to spy.

Esquire, a shield-bearer. (F. – L.) M. E. squyer. – O. F. escuyer, escuier, a squire. – Late L. scūtārius, a shield-bearer. – L. scūt-um, a shield, cover (F. écu). (√SQEU.) Brugm. i. § 109. Doublet, squire.

Essay, Assay, an attempt, trial. (F. – L.) O. F. essai, a trial. – L. exagium, a trial of weight ; cf. exāmen, a weighing, a swarm. – L. ex, out ; ag-ere, to drive, impel, move. (√AG.)

Essence, a quality, being. (F. – L.) F. essence – L. essentia, a being. – L. *essent-, fictitious stem of pres. pt. of esse, to be. Der. essenti-al ; and see entity.

Essoin, an excuse for not appearing in court. (F. – L. and Teut.) O. F. essoine, M. F. exoine, 'an essoine, or excuse ;' Cot. – O. F. essonier, to excuse (Godefroy). –

O. F. es- (L. ex), away ; and Low L. sunnia, O. H. G. sunne (for *sundjā, Braune, xiv. 9), lawful excuse. Cf. Goth. sunjōn sik, to excuse oneself, ga-sunjōn, to justify, from sunja, truth ; Skt. satja-, true. Brugm. i. § 287.

Establish. (F. – L.) M. E. establissen. – O. F. establiss-, base of pres. pt. of establir, to establish. – L. stabilīre, to establish. – L. stabilis, firm ; see Stable (2).

Estate. (F. – L.) O. F. estat. – L. statum, acc. of status, state ; see State.

Esteem, to value. (F. – L.) O. F. estimer. – L. æstimāre, O. L. æstumāre, to value. Allied to Goth. aistan, to regard. Brugm. ii. § 692.

  estimate. (L.) From pp. of L. æstimāre, to value (above).

Estop, to bar. (F. – L.) The same as Stop.

Estovers, supplies of various necessaries. (F. – L.) A. F. estovers, M. E. stovers, pl. of stover ; see Stover.

Estrange, to make strange. (F. – L.) O. F. estranger, to make strange. – O. F. estrange, strange. – L. extrāneum, acc. of extrāneus, foreign, on the outside. – L. extrā, without ; see Extra.

Estreat, a true copy, in law. (F. – L.) Lit. 'extract.' A. F. estrete, fem. of pp. of estraire, to extract. – L. extracta, fem. of pp. of extrahere ; see Extract.

Estuary, mouth of a tidal river. (L.) L. æstuārium, the same. – L. æstuāre, to surge, foam as the tide. – L. æstus, heat, surge, tide. Allied to Ether.

Etch, to engrave with acids. (Du. – G.) Du etsen, to etch. – G. ätzen, to corrode, etch ; orig. 'to make to eat ;' causal of G. essen, to eat. See Eat.

Eternal. (F. – L.) M. E. eternel. – O. F. eternel. – L. æternālis, eternal. – L. æternus, lit. lasting for an age ; for æui-ternus. – L. æui-, for æuum, an age. See Age.

Ether, pure upper air. (L. – Gk.) L. æther. – Gk. αἰθήρ, upper air ; from its brightness. – Gk. αἴθειν, to glow. (√AIDH.) Brugm. i. § 202.

Ethic, relating to morals. (L. – Gk.) L. ēthicus, moral. – Gk. ἠθικός, moral. – Gk. ἦθος, custom, moral nature ; cf. ἔθος, manner, custom. + Skt. svadhā-, self-will, strength, from sva, self, dhā, to place ; cf. Goth. sidus, G. sitte, custom.

Ethnic, relating to a nation. (L. – Gk.)

L. *ethnicus.* — Gk. ἐθνικός, national. — Gk. ἔθνος, a nation.

Etiolate, to blanch plants. (F. — L.) F. *étioler*; with suffix *-ate.* From a dialectal form answering to *s'éteuler*, to grow into haulm or stalk, like etiolated plants. — F. *éteule*, O. F. *esteule*, a stalk. — Late L. *stupula*, for L. *stipula*, straw. See **Stubble.**

Etiquette, ceremony. (F. — G.) F. *étiquette*, a label, ticket, also a form of introduction; cf. M. F. *etiquet* (O. F. *estiquet*), 'a little note, such as is *stuck up* on the gate of a court,' &c.; Cot. — G. *stecken*, to stick, put, set, fix; causal of G. *stechen*, to stick, pierce. See **Stick** (1). Doublet, *ticket.*

Etymon, the true source of a word. (L. — Gk.) L. *etymon.* — Gk. ἔτυμον; neut. of ἔτυμος, real, true.

etymology. (F. — L. — Gk.) F. *etymologie.* — L. *etymologia.* — Gk. ἐτυμολογία, etymology. — Gk. ἔτυμο-ς, true; -λογία, account, from λέγειν, to speak.

Eu-, prefix, well. (Gk.) Gk. εὖ, well; neut. of ἐύς, good. Cf. Skt. *vasu*, wealth.

Eucalyptus, a genus of trees, including the blue gum-tree. (Gk.) Latinised from Gk. εὖ, well; καλυπτός, covered, surrounded. The reference is to the hood protecting the stamens.

Eucharist, the Lord's Supper, lit. thanksgiving. (L. — Gk.) L. *eucharistia.* — Gk. εὐχαριστία, a giving of thanks. — Gk. εὖ, well; χαρίζομαι, I show favour, from χάρις, favour. Cf. **Yearn.**

Eulogy, praise. (L. — Gk.) From L. *eulogium.* — Gk. εὐλογία, praise, lit. good speaking; with suffix suggested by L. *elogium*, an inscription. — Gk. εὖ, well; λέγειν, to speak.

Eunuch, one who is castrated. (L. — Gk.) L. *eunūchus.* — Gk. εὐνοῦχος, a chamberlain; one who had charge of sleeping apartments. — Gk. εὐνή, a couch; ἔχειν, to keep, have in charge.

Euphemism, a softened expression. (Gk.) Gk. εὐφημισμός, the same as εὐφημία, the use of words of good omen. — Gk. εὖ, well; φημί, I speak. (√BHĀ.)

Euphony. (Gk.) Gk. εὐφωνία, a pleasing sound. — Gk. εὔφωνος, sweet-voiced. — Gk. εὖ, well; φωνή, voice. (√BHĀ.)

Euphrasy, the plant eye-bright. (Gk.) Supposed to be beneficial to the eyes; lit. 'delight.' — Gk. εὐφρασία, delight. — Gk.

εὐφραίνειν, to delight, cheer; cf. εὔφρων, cheerful. Allied to Gk. εὖ, well; φρεν-, stem of φρήν, midriff, heart, mind.

Euphuism, affectation in speaking. (Gk.) So named from a book *Euphues* by J. Lyly (1579). — Gk. εὐφυής, well-grown, excellent. — Gk. εὖ, well; φυή, growth, from φύομαι, I grow. (√BHEU.)

Euroclydon, a tempestuous wind. (Gk.) Gk. εὐροκλύδων, supposed to mean 'a storm from the east.' — Gk. εὖρο-ς, S.E. wind; κλύδων, surge, from κλύζειν, to surge, dash as waves. ¶ Only in Acts xxvii. 14; where some read εὐρακύλων, i. e. *Eur-aquilo*; from L. *Eur-us*, E. wind, and *Aquilo*, N. wind.

Euthanasia, easy death. (Gk.) Gk. εὐθανασία, easy death: cf. εὐθάνατος, dying well. — Gk. εὖ, well; θανεῖν, to die.

Evacuate. (L.) From pp. of L. *ēuacuāre*, to empty. — L. *ē*, out; *uacuus*, empty.

Evade, to shun. (F. — L.) F. *évader.* — L. *ēuādere* (pp. *ēuāsus*), to escape. — L. *ē*, away; *uādere*, to go. Der. *evas-ion* (from the pp.).

Evanescent. (L.) From stem of pres. pt. of L. *ēuānescere*, to vanish away. — L. *ē*, away; *uānescere*, to vanish, from *uānus*, empty, vain.

Evangelist, writer of a gospel. (F. — L. — Gk.) O. F. *evangeliste.* — L. *euangelista.* — Gk. εὐαγγελιστής. — Gk. εὐαγγελίζομαι, I bring good news. — Gk. εὖ, well; ἀγγελία, tidings, from ἄγγελος, a messenger; see **Angel.**

Evaporate. (L.) From pp. of L. *ēuaporāre*, to pass off in vapour. — L. *ē*, out; *uapor*, vapour.

Evasion; see **Evade.**

Eve, Even, the latter part of the day. (E.) *Eve* is short for *even.* (For *evening*, see below.) M. E. *eue, euen.* A. S. *ǣfen*, *ēfen.*+O. Sax. *āband*, Du. *avond*, G. *abend.* Of doubtful origin. Der. *even-tide*, A. S. *ǣfentīd.* Brugm. i. § 980.

evening, even. (E.) M. E. *euening.* A. S. *ǣfnung*; formed from *ǣfnian*, to grow towards evening, with suffix *-ung*; from *ǣfen*, even (above).

Even, level. (E.) M. E. *euen* (*even*). A. S. *efen*, *efn.*+Du. *even*, Icel. *jafn*, Dan. *jævn*, Swed. *jämn*, Goth. *ibns*, G. *eben.*

Event, result. (L.) L. *ēuentus*, *ēuentum*, sb. — L. *ēuentus*, pp. of *ēuenīre*, to come out, result. — L. *ē*, out; *uenīre*, to come, allied to **Come.**

Ever. (E.) M. E. *euer* (*ever*). A. S. *ǽfre*, ever. Related to A.S. *ā*, Goth. *aiw*, ever. Der. *ever-lasting, ever-more*.

every, each one. (E.) M. E. *eueri, euerich.* – A. S. *ǽfre*, ever; and *ǽlc*, each. *Ever-y* = *ever-each*; see Each.

everywhere. (E.) M. E. *euerihwar.* – A. S. *ǽfre*, ever; *gehwǽr*, where. The word really stands for *ever-ywhere*, i. e. ever-where; *y-* is a prefix (= *ge-*).

Evict. (L.) From L. *ēuict-us*, pp. of *ēuincere*, to evince; also, to expel. See Evince.

Evident. (F. – L.) O. F. *evident.* – L. *ēuident-*, stem of *ēuidens*, visible, pres. pt. of *ēuidēre*, to see clearly. – L. *ē*, out, clearly; *uidēre*, to see.

Evil. (E.) M. E. *euel*. A. S. *yfel*, adj. and sb. +Du. *euvel*, G. *übel*, Goth. *ubils*. Teut. type *ubiloz*. Prob. allied to *over* (G. *über*), as meaning ‘ excessive.’

Evince. (L.) L. *ēuincere*, to conquer, to prove beyond doubt. – L. *ē*, out, extremely; *uincere*, to conquer.

Eviscerate, to gut. (L.) From pp. of L. *ēuiscerāre*, to gut. – L. *ē*, out; *uiscera*, entrails.

Evoke. (F. – L.) F. *évoquer.* – L. *ēuocāre*, to call forth. – L. *ē*, forth; *uocāre*, to call. See Vocal.

Evolve. (L.) L. *ēuoluere*, to unroll, disclose – L. *ē*, out; *uoluere*, to roll. Der. *evolut-ion*, from pp. *ēuolūtus*.

Ewe. (E.) M. E. *ewe*. A. S. *ewe*, Laws of Ine, 55 ; *eowu*, a female sheep.+ Du. *ooi*, Icel. *ǽr*, M. H. G. *ouwe*; Lithuan. *avis*, a sheep, Russ. *ovtsa*, L. *ouis*, Gk. *ŏïs*, O. Irish *oi*; Skt. *avi-*, a sheep. Cf. Goth. *awi-str*, a sheep-fold.

Ewer. (F. – L.) M. E. *ewer.* – A. F. *ewer*, **eweire*; spelt *ewer*, Royal Wills, pp. 24, 27. – L. *aquārium*, a vessel for water ; cf. A. F. *ewe*, water; mod. F. *eau*. – L. *aqua*, water.

Ex-, E-, prefix. (L.) L. *ex*, *ē*, out. + Gk. *ἐκ*, *ἐξ* out: Russ. *iz'*, Lith. *isz*.

Exacerbate, to embitter. (L.) From pp. of *exacerbāre*, to irritate. – L. *ex*, very; *acerbus*, bitter; see Acerbity.

Exact (1), precise. (L.) From L. *exactus*, pp. of *exigere*, to drive out, weigh out. – L. *ex*, out; and *agere*, to drive.

exact (2), to demand. (F. – L.) From M. F. *exacter*; Cot. (obsolete). – Late L. *exactāre.* – L. *ex*, out; and *actus*, pp. of *agere* (above).

Exaggerate. (L.) From pp. of L.

exaggerāre, to heap up, amplify. – L. *ex*, very ; *agger*, a heap, from *ag-* = *ad*, to ; *gerere*, to bring.

Exalt. (F. – L.) F. *exalter.* – L. *exaltāre*, to lift out, exalt – L. *ex*, out ; *altus*, high.

Examine, to test. (F. – L.) F. *examiner.* – L. *exāmināre*, to weigh carefully. – L. *exāmin-*, stem of *exāmen*, the tongue of a balance, for **exāgmen*; cf. *exigere*, to weigh out. – L. *ex*, out ; *agere*, to drive, move. Brugm. i. § 768.

Example. (F. – L.) O. F. *example* ; F. *exemple.* – L. *exemplum*, a sample. – L. *exim-ere*, to take out ; with suffix *-lum* ; for the inserted *p* cf. the pp. *exem-p-tus.* – L. *ex*, out ; *emere*, to take, procure.

Exasperate, to provoke. (L.) From the pp. of *exasperāre*, to roughen, provoke. – L. *ex*, very ; *asper*, rough.

Excavation. (F. – L.) F. *excavation.* – L. acc. *excauātiōnem*, a hollowing out. – L. *excauātus*, pp. of *excauāre*, to hollow out. – L. *ex*, out ; *cauāre*, to hollow, from *cauus*, hollow.

Exceed. (F. – L.) O. F. *exceder.* – L. *excēdere*, lit. to go out. – L. *ex*, out ; *cēdere*, to go.

Excel, to surpass. (F. – L.) O. F. *exceller.* – L. *excellere*, to rise up, surpass. – L. *ex*, out ; **cellere*, to rise, only in comp. *ante-*, *ex-*, *præ-cellere*, and in *cel-sus*, high, orig. ‘ raised.’ Cf. Lithuan. *kélti*, to raise ; see Hill. Brugm. i. § 633.

Except, to exclude. (F. – L.) F. *excepter*, to except ; Cot. – L. *exceptāre*, frequent. of *excipere*, to take out. – L. *ex*, out ; *capere*, to take. Der. *except*, prep. ; *except-ion*.

Excerpt, a selected passage. (L.) L. *excerptum*, an extract ; neut. of pp. of *excerpere*, to select. – L. *ex*, out ; *carpere*, to cull. See Harvest.

Excess. (F. – L.) O. F. *exces.* – L. acc. *excessum*, lit. a going out or beyond. – L. *excess-*, as in *excessus*, pp. of *excēdere* ; see Exceed.

Exchange. (F. – L.) O. F. *eschange*, sb. ; *eschangier*, vb., to exchange. – O. F. *es-* (< L. *ex*) ; and O. F. *change*, sb., *changier*, to change. See Change.

Exchequer, a court of revenue. (F. – Pers.) M. E. *eschekere.* – O. F. *eschequier*, a chess-board ; hence, a checkered cloth on which accounts were reckoned by means of counters (Low L. *scaccārium*). – O. F. *eschec*, check ; see Check.

Excise, a duty, tax. (Du.–F.–L.) A misspelling of M. Du. *aksiis* or *aksys,* excise. (Cf. G. *accise,* excise.) – O. F. *acceis,* a tax, given in the N. E. D.; allied to Low L. *accīsia* (Ducange); also spelt *exsīsa* (id.). – Late L. *accensus,* a payment, rent; cf. *accensāre,* to tax. – L. *ac-* (for *ad*), to; and *census,* a tax. ¶ For the sound-change, cf. Du. *spijs,* food, from Late L. *spensa* (for *dispensa*), a larder, a spence.

Excision. (F.–L.) F. *excision,* ‘a destroying;’ Cot. – L. acc. *excīsiōnem,* a cutting out, a destroying. – L. *excīsus,* pp. of *excīdere,* to cut out. – L. *ex,* out; and *cædere,* to cut.

Exclaim. (F.–L.) F. *exclamer,* – L. *exclāmāre,* to call out. – L. *ex,* out; *clāmāre,* to call. See **Claim.**

Exclude. (L.) L. *exclūdere,* to shut out. – L. *ex,* out; *claudere,* to shut. See **Clause.**

Excommunicate. (L.) From pp. of L. *excommūnicāre,* to put out of the community. – L. *ex,* out of; *commūnis,* common. See **Communicate.**

Excoriate. (L.) From pp. of L. *excoriāre,* to strip off skin. – L. *ex,* off; *corium,* hide, skin. See **Cuirass.**

Excrement (1). (L.) L. *excrēmentum,* refuse, ordure. – L. *excrētus,* pp. of *excernere,* to separate, sift out. – L. *ex,* out; *cernere,* to sift.

Excrement (2), out-growth. (L.) In Shak. From L. *excrēmentum.* – L. *excrētus,* pp. of *excrescere,* to grow out (below).

excrescence. (F.–L.) O. F. *excrescence.* – L. *excrescentia,* an outgrowth. – L. *excrescent-,* stem of pres. pt. of *excrescere,* to grow out. – L. *ex,* out; *crescere,* to grow. See **Crescent.**

Excretion. (F.–L.) M. F. *excretion;* formed (with suffix *-ion*), from L. *excrētus,* pp. of *excernere;* see **Excrement** (1).

Excruciate, to torture. (L.) From pp. of L. *excruciāre,* to torment greatly. – L. *ex,* very; *cruciāre,* to torture on a gibbet, from *cruci-,* decl. stem of *crux,* a cross.

Exculpate. (L.) From pp. of Late L. *exculpāre,* to clear of blame. – L. *ex,* out of, *culpa,* blame.

Excursion. (L.) L. *excursiōnem,* acc. of *excursio,* a running out. – L. *excursus,* pp. of *excurrere,* to run out. – L. *ex,* out; *currere,* to run.

Excuse. (F.–L.) F. *excuser.* – L.

excūsāre, to release from a charge. – L. *ex,* out; and *causa,* a charge, a cause.

Execrate. (L.) From pp. of L. *execrārī,* for *exsecrārī,* to curse greatly. – L. *ex,* greatly; *sacrāre,* to consecrate, also to declare accursed. – L. *sacr-um,* neut. of *sacer,* sacred; also, accursed.

Execute. (F.–L.) O. F. *executer.* – L. *execūtus, exsecūtus,* pp. of *exsequī,* to follow out, pursue, perform. – L. *ex,* out; *sequī,* to follow.

Exegesis, exposition. (Gk.) Gk. ἐξήγησις, interpretation. – Gk. ἐξηγεῖσθαι, to explain. – Gk. ἐξ, out; ἡγεῖσθαι, to guide, perhaps allied to **Seek.** Brugm. i. § 187.

Exemplar. (F.–L.) M. E. *exemplaire.* – O. F. *exemplaire.* – L. *exemplārium,* late form of *exemplar,* a copy (to which the mod. E. word is now conformed). – L. *exemplāris,* adj., serving as a copy. – L. *exemplum;* see **Example. Der.** *exemplar-y,* from L. *exemplāris.*

exemplify, to shew by example. (F. – L.) A coined word; as if from F. **exemplifier.* – Late L. *exemplificāre,* properly ‘to copy out.’ – L. *exempli-,* for *exemplum,* a copy; *fic-,* for *facere,* to make.

Exempt, freed. (F.–L.) O. F. *exempt;* whence *exempter,* to exempt, free. – L. *exemptus,* pp. of *eximere,* to take out, deliver, free. – L. *ex,* out; *emere,* to take. Cf. Lith. *im-ti,* to take.

Exequies. (F.–L.) O. F. *exeques, exequies,* ‘funerals;’ Cot. – L. *exsequiās,* acc. pl. of *exsequiæ,* funeral obsequies, lit. ‘followings.’ – L. *exsequī,* to follow out. – L. *ex,* out; *sequī,* to follow.

Exercise, sb. (F.–L.) M. E. *exercise.* – O. F. *exercice.* – L. *exercitium,* exercise. – L. *exercitus,* pp. of *exercēre,* to drive out of an enclosure, drive on, set at work. – L. *ex,* out; *arcēre,* to enclose; see **Ark. Der.** *exercise,* vb.

Exergue, the small space left beneath the base-line of a subject engraved on a coin. (F.–Gk.) The final *-ue* is not pronounced; cf. *prologue,* &c. – F. *exergue,* so called because lying ‘out of the work.’ – Gk. ἐξ, out of; ἔργον, work.

Exert. (L.) Lit. to ‘put forth.’ L. *exertus,* also better spelt *exsertus,* thrust forth; pp. of *exserere,* to thrust out. – L. *ex,* out; *serere,* to join, to put.

Exfoliate. (L.) From pp. of L. *exfoliāre,* to strip off leaves; from *ex,* off, and *folium,* a leaf.

Exhale. (F.–L.) F. *exhaler.* – L. *ex-*

hălāre, to breathe out. — L. *ex*, out; *hālāre*, to breathe.

Exhaust. (L.) From L. *exhaustus*, pp. of *exhaurīre*, to draw out, drink up. — L. *ex*, out; *haurīre*, to draw water.

Exhibit, to show. (L.) From L. *exhibit-us*, pp. of *exhibēre*, to hold forth. — L. *ex*, out; *habēre*, to have.

Exhilarate, to cheer. (L. – Gk.; *with* L. *prefix*.) From pp. of L. *exhilarāre*, to gladden greatly. — L. *ex*, very; *hilaris*, *hilarus*, glad, cheerful, from Gk. *ἱλαρός*, cheerful. See Hilarity.

Exhort. (F. – L.) O. F. *ex(h)orter*. — L. *exhortārī*, to encourage greatly. — L. *ex*, out, very; *hortārī*, to encourage ; see Hortatory.

Exhume, to disinter. (F. – L.) F. *exhumer*. – Late L. *exhumāre*. – L. *ex*, out of ; *humus*, the ground.

Exigent, exacting. (L.) From the stem of pres. pt. of *exigere*, to exact. – L. *ex* ; and *agere*, to drive.

Exile, banishment. (F. – L.) O. F. *essil* ; later *exil*, 'an exile, banishment ;' Cot. – L. *exilium*, better *exsilium*, banishment ; cf. *exsul*, a banished man. – L. *ex*, out of; and (perhaps) *sed-ēre*, to sit, abide. Cf. Consul. Der. *exile*, verb; hence, *exile*, sb. (=one who is *exiled*).

Exist, to continue to be. (L.) L. *existere*, better *exsistere*, to stand forth, arise, be. – L. *ex*, out ; *sistere*, to set, stand, from *stāre*, to stand.

Exit. (L.) L. *exit*, i. e. 'he goes out,' used as a stage direction ; 3rd pers. s. pres. of *exīre*, to go out. – L. *ex*, out ; *īre*, to go. ¶ *Exit*, departure, is from L. *exit-us*, sb.

Exodus, departure. (L. – Gk.) L. *exodus*. – Gk. *ἔξοδος*, a going out. – Gk. *ἐξ*, out ; *ὁδός*, a way, a march. (√SED.)

Exogen, a plant that increases outwardly. (F. – Gk.) F. *exogène* (1813). From Gk. *ἐξ-ω*, outside, from *ἐξ*, out ; and *γεν-*, base of *γίγνεσθαι*, to be born.

Exonerate. (L.) From pp. of L. *ex-onerāre*, to free from a burden. – L. *ex*, away ; *onerāre*, to burden, from *oner-* (for *ones-*), stem of *onus*, a burden.

Exorbitant, extravagant. (F. – L.) F. *exorbitant*. – L. *exorbitant-*, stem of pres. pt. of *exorbitāre*, to fly out of a track. – L. *ex*, out ; *orbita*, a track of a wheel, from *orbi-*, stem of *orbis*, a wheel, with suffix *-ta*.

Exorcise. (L. – Gk.) Late L. *exor-*

cīzāre. – Gk. *ἐξορκίζειν*, to drive away by adjuration. – Gk. *ἐξ*, away ; *ὁρκίζειν*, to adjure, from *ὅρκος*, an oath.

Exordium. (L.) L. *exordium*, a beginning. – L. *exordīrī*, to begin, to weave. – L. *ex* ; and *ordīrī*, to begin, weave.

Exoteric, external. (Gk.) Gk. *ἐξωτερικός*, external. – Gk. *ἐξωτέρω*, more outward, comp. of adv. *ἔξω*, outward, from *ἐξ*, out.

exotic, foreign. (L. – Gk.) L. *exōticus*. – Gk. *ἐξωτικός*, outward, foreign. – Gk. *ἔξω*, adv., outward, from *ἐξ*, out.

Expand. (L.) L. *expandere* (pp. *expansus*), to spread out. – L. *ex*, out; *pandere*, to spread out; causal from *patēre*, to lie open. Cf. Gk. *πίτνημι*, I spread out. Der. *expanse*, from the pp.

Expatiate. (L.) From pp. of L. *expatiārī*, better *exspatiārī*, to wander. – L. *ex*, out; *spatiārī*, to roam, from *spatium*, space.

Expatriate. (L.) From pp. of Late L. *expatriāre*, to banish. – L. *ex*, out of; *patria*, native country, from *pater*, father.

Expect. (L.) L. *expectāre*, better *exspectāre*, to look for anxiously. – L. *ex*, thoroughly ; *spectāre*, to look, frequentative of *specere*, to see.

Expectorate. (L.) From pp. of L. *expectorāre*, to expel from the breast. – L. *ex*, out of ; *pector-* (for **pectos*), stem of *pectus*, the breast.

Expedite. (L.) From pp. of L. *expedīre*, to extricate the foot, release, get ready. – L. *ex*, out; *ped-*, stem of *pēs*, foot. Der. *expedient*, from the stem of the pres. pt.

Expel. (L.) L. *expellere*, to drive out. – L. *ex*, out ; *pellere*, to drive. Der. *expulsion*, O. F. *expulsion*, L. acc. *expulsiōnem*, from pp. *expuls-us*.

Expend, to spend. (L.) L. *expendere*, to weigh out, lay out. – L. *ex*, out ; *pendere*, to weigh. Der. *expense*, from A. F. *expense*, L. *expensa*, money spent, fem. of pp. *expensus* ; *expendit-ure*, from Late L. *expenditus*, a mistaken form of the pp. *expensus*.

Experience, knowledge due to trial. (F. – L.) O.F. *experience*. – L. *experientia*, a proof, trial. – L. *experient-*, stem of pres. pt. of *experīrī*, to make a thorough trial of (below). Der. *experi-ment*, M. F. *experiment*, L. *experīmentum*, a trial.

expert, experienced. (F. – L.) O. F. *expert*. – L. *expertus*, pp. of *experīrī*, to make full trial of. —L. *ex*, thoroughly ; and **perīrī*, an obs. vb. of which the pp. *perītus* is common. See **Peril**.

Expiate. (L.) From pp. of L. *expiāre*, to atone for fully. —L. *ex*, fully ; *piāre*, to propitiate, from *pius*, devout.

Expire. (F.—L.) O. F. *expirer*. —L. *expīrāre*, *exspīrāre*, to breathe out, die. — L. *ex*, out ; *spīrāre*, to breathe.

Explain. (F.—L.) M. F. *explaner*, Cot. —L. *explānāre*, to make plain. —L. *ex*, thoroughly ; *plānāre*, to make plain, lit. to flatten, from *plānus*, flat. See **Plain**.

Expletive. (L.) L. *explētīuus*, filling up. —L. *explētus*, pp. of *explēre*, to fill up. —L. *ex*, fully ; *plēre*, to fill. See **Plenary**.

Explicate, to explain. (L.) From pp. of L. *explicāre*, to unfold, explain. — L. *ex*, out ; *plicāre*, to fold.

explicit. (L.) L. *explicitus*, old pp. of *explicāre*, to unfold, make plain (above). Cf. F. *explicite*.

Explode, to drive away noisily, burst. (F.—L.) M. F. *exploder*, ' to explode, publicly to disgrace or drive out ;' Cot. — L. *explōdere* (pp. *explōsus*), to drive off the stage by noise (the old sense in E.). —L. *ex*, away ; *plōdere*, *plaudere*, to clap hands. Der. *explos-ive*, *-ion*, from the pp.

Exploit. (F.—L.) M. E. *esploit*, success, Gower, C. A. ii. 258. —O. F. *esploit*, revenue, profit ; later, an exploit, act. —L. *explicitum*, a thing settled, ended, or displayed ; neut. of *explicitus*; see **explicit**. Cf. Late L. *explicta*, revenue.

Explore. (F.—L.) F. *explorer*. —L. *explōrāre*, to search out, lit.to make to flow out. —L. *ex*, out ; *plōrāre*, to make to flow. Cf. *de-plore*, *im-plore*. Brugm. i. § 154.

Exponent. (L.) L. *exponent-*, stem of pres. pt. of *expōnere*, to expound, indicate. —L. *ex*, out ; *pōnere*, to put.

Export. (L.) L. *exportāre*, to carry away. —L. *ex*, away ; *portāre*, to carry.

Expose. (F.—L. *and* Gk.) O. F. *exposer*, to lay out. —O. F. *ex-* (L. *ex*), out ; F. *poser*, to place, lay. See **Pose** (1).

Exposition. (F.—L.) F. *exposition*. —L. acc. *expositiōnem*. —L. *expositus*, pp. of *expōnere*, to set forth, expound. See **Expound**.

Expostulate. (L.) From pp. of L. *expostulāre*, to demand earnestly. —L. *ex*, fully ; *postulāre*, to ask.

Expound. (L.) The *d* is excrescent,

but was suggested by the form of the O. F. infinitive. M. E. *expounen*. — O. F. *espondre*, to explain. —L. *expōnere*, to set forth, explain. —L. *ex*, out ; *pōnere*, to put. See **Exposition**.

Express, adj., exactly stated. (F.—L.) O. F. *expres*. —L. *expressus*, distinct ; pp. of *exprimere*, to press out. —L. *ex*, out ; *premere*, to press ; see **Press**.

Expulsion ; see **Expel**.

Expunge. (L.) L. *expungere*, to prick out, blot out. [In MSS., *expunction* of a word is denoted by *dots under it.*] —L. *ex*, out ; *pungere*, to prick. Der. *expunct-ion*, from the pp. *expunctus*.

Expurgate. (L.) From pp. of L. *expurgāre*, to purify thoroughly. —L. *ex*, thoroughly ; *purgāre*, to purge, purify ; see **Purge**.

Exquisite, sought out, excellent. (L.) L. *exquīsītus*, pp. of *exquīrere*, to seek out. — L. *ex*, out ; *quærere*, to seek.

Exsequies; see **Exequies**.

Extant, existing. (L.) Late L. *extant-*, stem of *extans*, for *exstans*, pres. pt. of *exstāre*, to stand forth, exist. —L. *ex*, out ; *stāre*, to stand.

Extasy ; see **Ecstasy**.

Extempore. (L.) From L. *ex tempore*, at the moment. —L. *ex*, from, out of ; *tempore*, abl. of *tempus*, time.

Extend. (L.) M. E. *extenden*. —L. *extendere*, to stretch out ; pp. *extentus*, *extensus*. —L. *ex*, out ; *tendere*, to stretch. Der. *extens-ion*, *-ive* (from the pp.).

extent. (F.—L.) O. F. *extente*, commonly *estente*, extent. —Late L. *extenta*, fem. of *extentus*, pp. of *extendere* (above).

Extenuate. (L.) From pp. of L. *extenuāre*, to thin, reduce, palliate. —L. *ex*, out, very ; *tenu-is*, thin. See **Thin**.

Exterior, outward. (F.—L.) Formerly *exteriour*. —M. F. *exterieur*. —L. *exteriōrem*, acc. of *exterior*, outward, comparative of *exterus* or *exter*, outward. —L. *ex*, out ; with compar. suffix *-tero-*.

Exterminate. (L.) From pp. of L. *extermināre*, to put or drive beyond bounds. —L. *ex*, out ; *terminus*, boundary.

External, outward. (L.) From L. *extern-us*, outward, extended form from *exterus*, outward. See **Exterior**.

Extinguish. (L.) Coined, with suffix *-ish*, from L. *extinguere*, better *exstinguere* (pp. *extinctus*, *exstinctus*), to quench. — L. *ex*, out ; **stinguere*, to prick, also to

quench. Der. *extinct* (from pp. *extinctus*).
Cf. Distinguish.

Extirpate. (L.) From pp. of L. *extirpāre*, to root out, better spelt *exstirpāre*, to pluck up by the stem. — L. *ex*, out; *stirp-s*, *stirp-es*, the stem of a tree.

Extol. (L.) L. *extollere*, to lift or raise up. — L. *ex*, out, up; *tollere*, to lift.

Extort. (L.) L. *extort-us*, pp. of *extorquēre*, to twist out, wring out. — L. *ex*, out; *torquēre*, to twist.

Extra. (L.) L. *extrā*, beyond, beyond what is necessary; O. L. *extrād*, allied to L. *exter*; see **Exterior**.

extraneous. (L.) L. *extrāne-us*, external, with suffix *-ous*; extended from *extrā* (above). Cf. **Strange**.

Extract, vb. (L.) L. *extract-us*, pp. of *extrahere*, to draw out. — L. *ex*, out; *trahere*, to draw.

Extraordinary. (L.) L. *extrā-ordinārius*, beyond what is ordinary, rare. — L. *extrā*, beyond; *ordinārius*, ordinary. See **Ordinary**.

Extravagant. (F. — L.) F. *extravagant*. — Late L. *extrāvagant-*, stem of *extrāvagans*, extravagant, lit. wandering beyond. — L. *extrā*, beyond; *uagans*, pres. pt. of *uagārī*, to wander.

Extravasate, to force (blood) out of its (proper) vessel. (L.) Coined from *extrā*, beyond; *uās*, a vessel; with suffix *-ate*.

Extreme. (F. — L.) O. F. *extreme*. — L. *extrēmus*, superl. of *exterus*, outward; see **Exterior**.

Extricate. (L.) From pp. of L. *extrīcāre*, to disentangle. — L. *ex*, out of; *trīcæ*, impediments, perplexities.

Extrinsic, external. (F. — L.) It should rather be *extrinsec*. — O. F. *extrinseque*, outward. — Late L. acc. *extrinsecum*, adj.; allied to L. *extrinsecus*, adv., from without. — L. *extrin* (= *extrim*), adverbial form from *exter*, outward; and *secus*, beside; so that *extrin-secus* = on the outside; cf. *interim*. *Secus* is allied to *secundum*, according to, from *sequī*, to follow; see **Sequence**.

Extrude. (L.) L. *extrūdere*, to thrust out. — L. *ex*, out; *trūdere*, to thrust. Cf. **Intrude**.

Exuberant. (L.) From stem of pres. pt. of L. *exūberāre*, to be fruitful or luxuriant. — L. *ex*, very; and *ūberāre*, to be fruitful, from *ūber*, fertile, allied to *ūber*, an udder, fertility; see **Udder**.

Exude. (L.) From L. *exūdāre*, better *exsūdāre*, to sweat out, distil. — L. *ex*, out; *sūdāre*, to sweat. See **Sweat**.

Exult, to leap for joy. (F. — L.) F. *exulter*. — L. *exultāre*, better spelt *exsultāre*, to leap up, exult. — L. *exsultus*, pp. of *exsilīre*, to leap out. — L. *ex*, out; *salīre*, to leap. See **Salient**.

Exuviæ, cast skins of animals. (L.) L. *exuuiæ*, things stripped off. — L. *exuere*, to strip off. Cf. *induuiæ*, clothes.

Eyas, a nestling. (F. — L.) For *nias*; by substituting *an eyas* for *a nias*. — F. *niais*, a nestling; Cot. He also gives *niard*, whence *faulcon niard*, 'a nias faulcon.' Cp. Ital. *nidiace*, or *nidaso falcone*, ' an eyase-hawk, a young hawk taken out of her nest;' Torriano. Formed as if from Late L. **nīdācem*, acc. of **nīdax*, adj. from L. *nīdus*, a nest. See **Nest**.

Eye. (E.) M.E. *eye*, *eighe*; pl. *eyes*, *eyen* (whence *eyne*). O. Merc. *ēge*; A.S. *ēage*, pl. *ēagan*. + Du. *oog*, Icel. *auga*, Dan. *oie*, Swed. *öga*, Goth. *augō*, G. *auge*. Perhaps allied to Russ. *oko*, L. *oculus* (dimin. of **ocus*); Gk. ὄσσε (dual); Lith. *akis*, Skt. *akshi*. Brugm. i. § 681. Der. *dais-y*, q. v.; *window*, q. v.

Eyelet-hole. (F. — L.; *and* E.) *Eyelet* is for M. E. *oilet*, from M. F. *oeillet*, 'a little eye, an oilet hole,' Cot.; dimin. of O. F. *oeil*, from L. *oculum*, acc. of *oculus*, eye.

Eyot, a little island. (E.) Also spelt *ait*, *eyel*, *eyght*. Late A. S. *ȳget* (Kemble, Cod. Dipl. v. 17, l. 30); for A. S. *igoð*, *īgeoð*, a dimin. from *īg*, *īeg*, an island; see **Island**.

Eyre, a circuit. (F. — L.) M.E. *eire*, circuit, esp. of a judge. — O. F. *eire*, journey, way. — O. F. *eirer*, to journey, wander about. — Late L. *iterāre*, to journey (for L. *itinerāre*); from L. *iter*, a journey. See **Errant**.

Eyry, a nest: see **Aery**.

F.

Fable, a story. (F. — L.) F. *fable*. — L. *fābula*, a narrative. — L. *fā-ri*, to speak, tell. See **Fate**.

Fabric. (F. — L.) F. *fabrique*. — L. *fabrica*, workshop, fabric. — L. *fabri-*, for *faber*, a workman. From L. base **fab-*, to be skilful; cf. Lith. *dab-inù*, I adorn, clean ; Goth. *ga-dab-ith*, it is fit ; Russ. *dob-ruii*, good. See **Deft. Der.** *fabricate*, from pp. of L. *fabricārī*, to construct ; from *fabrica* (above). Brugm. i. § 563.

Façade, face of a building. (F. — Ital. — L.) M. F. *facade* (Cot.). — Ital. *facciata*, face of a building. — Ital. *faccia*, face. — Folk-L. *facia*, for L. *faciēs* (below).

face. (F. — L.) F. *face.* — Folk-L. *facia*, for L. *faciēs*, the face, appearance.

Facetious. (F. — L.) F. *facétieux* (Cot.). — M. F. *facetie*, ' witty mirth,' id. — L. *facētia*, wit ; common in pl. — L. *facētus*, witty, courteous ; orig. ' fine.'

Facile, easy to do. (F. — L.) F. *facile.* — L. *facilis*, i. e. do-able. — L. *facere*, to do. **Der.** *facility* ; *faculty*.

fac-simile. (L.) For *fac simile*, make thou like. — L. *fac*, imp. s. of *facere*, to make ; *simile*, neut. of *similis*, like ; see **Similar.** ¶ We also find *factum simile*, i. e. made like.

fact, a deed, reality. (L.) L. *factum*, a deed ; orig. neut. of *factus*, pp. of *facere*, to make, do.

faction. (F. — L.) F. *faction*, a sect. — L. *factiōnem*, acc. of *factio*, a doing, taking part, faction. — L. *factus*, pp. of *facere*, to do.

factitious. (L.) L. *factīti-us*, artificial ; with suffix *-ous*. — L. *factus*, pp. of *facere*, to make.

factotum. (L.) A general agent. — L. *fac*(*ere*) *tōtum*, to do everything.

faculty, facility to act. (F. — L.) M. E. *facultee.* — F. *faculté.* — L. *facultātem*, acc. of *facultas* (= *facilitas*), facility. — L. *facilis*, easy ; see **Facile.**

Fad, a folly. (F. — Prov. — L.) Apparently shortened from F. *fadaise*, fiddle-faddle ; cf. ' *fadeses*, follies, toyes, fooleries ;' Cot. — Prov. *fadeza*, folly (Hatzfeld). — Prov. *fat* (Gascon *fad*), foolish. — L. *fatuus*, foolish.

Fade, vb. (F. — L.) O. F. *fader* ; from F. *fade*, adj., tasteless, weak, faint. — L. *uapidum*, acc. of *uapidus*, vapid. See **Vapid.** ¶ *Vade*, for *fade*, is from M. Du. *vadden* ; from O. F. *fader*.

Fadge, to fit, suit, be content with, succeed. (E.) Formed, in some unexplained way, from the Teut. base *fag-*, to suit, whence also O. Sax. *fōgian*, A. S. *fēgan*, to join, suit, M. E. *fēʒen*, to adapt, fit, G. *fügen*, Du. *voegen* (see Kluge and Franck). Cf. Goth. *fulla-fah jan*, to satisfy, O. H. G. *gifag*, content, Du. *vage-*

fuur, cleansing fire, purgatory. See Fair.

Fæces. (L.) L. *fæcēs*, dregs ; pl. of *fæx*, the same. **Der.** *fec-ulent*, L. *fæc-ulentus*, adj. from *fæx*.

Fag, to drudge. (E. ?) ' To *fag*, deficere ;' Levins (1570). The orig. sense was ' to droop.' Perhaps a corruption of *flag* ; see **Flag** (1) ; and see below.

Fag-end, remnant. (E. ?) In Massinger, Virg. Mart. ii. 3. Perhaps for *flag-end* = loose end ; see above. Cf. ' the *flagg* or the *fagg federis*' (feathers) ; Book of St. Albans, fol. B 1 *a*.

Faggot, Fagot. (F. — Ital. — L. ?) F. *fagot*, ' a fagot, a bundle of sticks ;' Cot. Of doubtful origin ; perhaps borrowed from Ital. *fagotto* (a faggot,' Florio ; or (like *fagotto*) from Norw. *fagg*, a bundle (Ross).

Fail. (F. — L.) F. *faillir* ; cf. Ital. *fallire.* — Folk-L. **fallīre*, for L. *fallere*, to beguile, also, to be defective ; *fallī*, to err. Brugm. i. § 757.

Fain. (E.) M. E. *fayn.* A. S. *fægen*, glad. ╪ O. Sax. *fagan*, Icel. *feginn*, glad. Cf. A. S. *gefēon* (pt. t. *gefeah*), to rejoice. Teut. root **feh-*, as in A. S. *ge-fēon* (for **-feh-an*) ; cf. Goth. *fah-ēths*, joy.

Faint. (F. — L.) M. E. *feint.* — O. F. *feint*, weak, pretended ; orig. pp. of *feindre*, to feign. — L. *fingere*, to form, feign. See **Figure.**

Fair (1), pleasing, beautiful. (E.) M. E. *fayr*, A. S. *fæger*, fair. ╪ Icel. *fagr* ; Dan. Swed. *fager*, Goth. *fagrs*, fit, O. H. G. *fagar*. Teut. type **fagroz.* Cf. Gk. πήγ-νυμι, I fasten. Brugm. i. §§ 200, 701.

Fair (2), a holiday. (F. — L.) M. E. *feire.* — A. F. *feire* (F. *foire*). — L. *fēria*, a holiday, later, a fair ; commoner as pl. *fēriæ*, for **fēs-iæ*, feast-days ; allied to Feast. Brugm. ii. § 66.

Fairy. (F. — L.) M. E. *faerie*, *fayrye*, enchantment. [The mod. use of the word is new ; *fairy* = enchantment, the old word for ' elf' being *fay*.] — O. F. *faerie*, enchantment. — O. F. *fae*, a fay ; see **Fay.**

Faith. (F. — L.) M. E. *feith* ; also *fey.* Slightly altered from O. F. *feid*, *fei*, faith. — L. *fidem*, acc. of *fides*, faith ; allied to *fīdere*, to trust. Cf. Gk. πίστις, faith. (√BHEIDH.) Allied to **Bide.** Brugm. i. § 202.

Falchion, a sword. (F. — Ital. — L.) M. E. *fauchon.* — O. F. *fauchon.* — Ital. *falcione* (*ci* pron. as *ch*). — Late L. *falciō-*

nem, acc. of *falcio*, a bent sword. — L. *falci-*, decl. stem of *falx*, a sickle. Allied to *flectere*, to bend.

falcon. (F. – L.) M. E. *faucon.* – O. F. *faucon, faulcon.* – Late L. *falōnem*, acc. of *falco*, a falcon, so named from its hooked claws. – L. *falc-*, stem of *falx*, a sickle.

Faldstool, a folding-stool. (Low L. – O. H. G.) Low L. *faldistolium.* – O.H.G. *fald-an*, to fold ; *stuol* (G. *stuhl*), a stool. Cf. F. *fauteuil*. See **Fold**.

Fall, to drop down. (E.) M. E. *fallen.* O. Merc. *fallan* ; A. S. *feallan.*+Du. *vallen*, Icel. *falla*, Dan. *falde* (for *falle*), Swed. *falla*, G. *fallen*. Teut. **fallan-*. Cf. Lith. *pùlti*, to fall ; and perhaps L. *fallere*, to deceive, *fallī*, to err. Brugm. i. § 757. Der. *be-fall*, from A. S. *be-feallan*, to fall out, happen ; *fell* (1).

Fallacy. (F. – L.) Formed by adding *-y* to M. E. *fallace*, a fallacy, deceit. – F. *fallace.* – L. *fallācia*, deceit. – L. *fallāc-*, stem of *fallax*, deceitful. – L. *fallere*, to deceive. See above.

fallible. (L.) L. *fallibilis*, liable to err. – L. *fallī*, to err ; *fallere*, to deceive.

Fallow (1), orig. ' harrowed ;' of land. (E.) A. S. *fælging*, fallow-land. – A. S. *fealh*, a harrow. Cf. E. Fries. *falgen*, to fallow land ; O. H. G. *felgā*, a harrow.

Fallow (2), used with reference to colour. (E.) O. Merc. *falu*; A. S. *fealu*, *fealo*, pale red, yellowish.+Du. *vaal*, Icel. *folr*, pale, G. *fahl*, pale, also *falb*; Lith. *palvas* ; cf. also L. *pallidus*, Gk. πολιός, gray, Skt. *palita-*, gray. See **Pale**.

False. (F. – L.) M. E. *fals.* – O. F. *fals* (F. *faux*). – L. *falsus*, false ; pp. of *fallere*, to deceive.

Falter, to totter, stammer. (E. ?) M. E. *faltren*, to totter ; frequentative from a base *falt-*. Of obscure origin. Perhaps connected with Icel. refl. vb. *faltra-sk*, to be cumbered, to be puzzled.

Fame, report. (F. – L.) F. *fame.* – L. *fāma*, report. – L. *fārī*, to speak ; see **Fate**.

Family. (F. – L.) F. *famille.* – L. *familia*, a household. – L. *famulus*, a servant, Oscan *famel* ; cf. Oscan *faamat*, he dwells. Der. *famili-ar* (L. *familiāris*).

Famine. (F. – L.) F. *famine.* – Late L. **famīna*, unrecorded, but plainly an extension from L. *famēs*, hunger. Der. *fam-ish*, formed (by analogy with *lan-*

guish, &c.) from L. *fam-ēs*, hunger ; cf. O. F. *afamer*, to die of hunger.

Fan, an instrument for blowing. (L.) A. S. *fann.* – Late L. *vannus*, L. *uannus*, a fan (whence also F. *van*) ; see **Van** (2). Brugm. i. § 357.

Fanatic, religiously insane. (F. – L.) F. *fanatique.* – L. *fānāticus*, (1) belonging to a temple, (2) inspired by a divinity, enthusiastic. – L. *fānum*, a temple ; see **Fane**.

Fancy. (F. – L. – Gk.) Short for M.E. *fantasie.* – O. F. *fantasie.* – Late L. *phantasia.* – Gk. φαντασία, a making visible (hence, imagination). – Gk. φαντάζειν, to display ; see **Phantom**.

Fandango, a Spanish dance. (Span.) Span. *fandango*, ' a dance used in the W. Indies ;' Pineda (1740).

Fane, a temple. (L.) L. *fānum*, a temple ; shortened from an earlier form **fasnom* ; cf. Oscan *fīsnam*, a temple ; allied to L. *fēstus, fēria*. Brugm. ii. § 66.

Fanfare, a flourish of trumpets. (F. – Span. ?) F. *fanfare*. Prob. of imitative origin, or borrowed from Span. *fanfarria*, bluster, vaunting, which is of similar formation. Der. *fanfarr-on-ade*, bluster.

Fang, a talon, claw. (E.) A. S. *fang*; lit. a seizing. – A. S. **fōhan*, to seize, only used in the contracted form *fōn*, pt. t. *fēng*, pp. *gefangen* ; the pp. form having alone survived, evolving a infin. mood in dialects.+Du. *vangen*, to catch ; Icel. *fā* (cf. *fang*, sb., a catch of fish), Dan. *faae*, Swed. *få*, Goth. *fāhan*, G. *fangon*, to catch, *fang*, sb., a catch, also a fang. Allied to L. *pangere* ; Brugm. i. § 421.

Fantastic. (Gk.) Gk. φανταστικός, able to represent or shew. – Gk. φαντάζειν, to display. See **Fancy**.

Fantasy, older form of **Fancy**, q. v.

Faquir, Fakir, an Oriental religious mendicant. (F. – Arab.) F. *faquir, fakir.* – Arab. *faqīr*, one of a religious order of mendicants ; lit. ' poor, indigent ;' Richardson's Dict. p. 1096.

Far. (E.) M. E. *fer.* A. S. *feor.*+Du. *ver*, Icel. *fjarri*, Swed. *fjerran*, adv., Dan. *fjern*, G. *fern* ; Goth. *fairra*, adv. Allied to Gk. πέραν, beyond ; Skt. *paras*, beyond, *para-*, far. (✓PER.) The comp. *farther* [for M. E. *ferrer* (i. e. *far-er*)] is due to confusion with *further*, comp. of **Forth**.

Farce. (F. – L.) The orig. sense is ' stuffing '; hence, a jest inserted into a comedy. – F. *farce*, stuffing, a farce. – F.

farcir, to stuff. − L. *farcīre*, to stuff. + Gk. φράσσειν (for *φράκ-yειν), to shut in.

Fardel, a pack, bundle. (F. − Arab.) M. E. *fardel*. − O. F. *fardel* (F *fardeau*). Dimin. of O. F. *farde*, a burden. Prob. from Arab. *fardah*, a package (Devic). Perhaps borrowed through Spanish; cf. Span. *fardel, fardo*, a bundle.

Fare, to travel, speed. (E.) A.S. *faran*, to go, travel. + Du. *varen*, Icel. Swed. *fara*, Dan. *fare*, G. *fahren*, Goth. *faran*, to go; Teut. *faran-* (pt. t. *fōr). Cf. Gk. πορεύομαι, I travel; L. *experior*, I pass through, Skt. *pr*, to bring over. (√PER.) **Der.** *fare-well*, i. e. may you speed well; *thorough-fare*, a passage through; *wel-fare*, successful practice or journey.

Farina, ground corn. (L.) L. *farīna*, meal. − L. *far*, a kind of grain; allied to Barley. **Der.** *farinaceous*, from L. *farīnāceus*. Brugm. i. § 180.

farrago. (L.) L. *farrāgo*, mixed food for cattle, a medley. − L. *far* (gen. *farr-is*), grain (above).

Farm. (F. − L.) [A. S. *feorm*]. A. F. and O. F. *ferme*, a farm. − Late L. *firma*, a feast, farm, tribute; fem. of L. *firmus*, durable. (From the *fixed* rent; also food, from its *support*.) See **Firm**.

Farrier. (F. − L.) Formerly *ferrier*, a worker in iron. − O. F. *ferrier* (the same). − L. *ferrārius*, a blacksmith. − L. *ferrum*, iron.

Farrow, to litter pigs. (E.) From the sb. *farrow*, a litter of pigs. − A. S. *fearh*, a pig; pl. *fearas*. + M. H. G. *varch*, a pig; G. *ferk-el*; L. *porcus*; see **Pork**.

Farther; see **Far**.

Farthing, fourth part of a penny. (E.) M. E. *ferthing*. A. S. *fērþing, feorðing*, older form *feorþling*. − A. S. *fēorð-a*, fourth; with dimin. suffix *-ing* or *-l-ing*. Allied to A. S. *fēower*, four.

Farthingale, Fardingale, a hooped petticoat. (F. − Span. − L.) M. F. *verdugalle*, 'a vardingall;' Cot. − Span. *verdugado*, a farthingale, lit. 'provided with hoops.' − Span. *verdugo*, young shoot of a tree, rod, hoop. − Span. *verde*, green. − L. *uiridis*, green. See **Verdant**.

Fascinate. (L.) From pp. of L. *fascināre*, to enchant. − L. *fascinum*, a spell.

Fascine, a bundle of rods. (F. − L.) F. *fascine*. − L. *fascīna*, a bundle of twigs. − L. *fascis*, a bundle.

Fashion. (F. − L.) O. F. *faceon, fachon*, make, shape. − L. *factiōnem*, acc. of *factio*, a making; see **Faction**.

Fast (1), firm. (E.) A.S. *fæst*. + Du. *vast*, Dan. Swed. *fast*, Icel. *fastr*, G. *fest*; Armen. *hast*. **Der.** *fast* (2), *fast* (3). Brugm. ii. § 79.

fast (2), to abstain from food. (E.) A. S. *fæstan*, orig. to make fast, observe, be strict; from *fæst* (above). + Du. *vasten*, Dan. *faste*, Swed. and Icel. *fasta*, G. *fasten*; Goth. *fastan*, to observe, fast.

fast (3), quick. (Scand.) A peculiar use of *fast* (1) above; this use is Scand. Cf. Icel. *drekka fast*, to drink hard, *sofa fast*, to be fast asleep, *fastr ī verkum*, hard at work, *fylgja fast*, to follow fast, &c. It means firm, close, urgent, quick.

fasten. (E.) A. S. *fæstnian*, to make fast or firm. − A. S. *fæst*, firm.

fastness. (E.) M.E. *festnes, fastness*, orig. 'strength.' − A. S. *fæstness*, the firmament, a fastness; orig. that which is firm. − A. S. *fest*, firm.

Fastidious. (L.) L. *fastīdiōsus*, disdainful. − L. *fastīdium*, loathing; perhaps for *fastutīdium* (Vaniček). − L. *fastu-s*, arrogance; *tædium*, disgust; so that *fastīdium* = arrogant disgust.

Fastness; see **Fast**.

Fat (1), gross. (E.) M. E. *fatt, fet, fat*. A. S. *fætt*, orig. a pp., contr. from *fēted*, fattened, enriched. + O. H. G. *feizit* (G. *feist*), pp. of a Teut. vb. *faitjan-*, formed from Teut. adj. *faitoz*, which is represented by Icel. *feitr* (Swed. *fet*, Dan. *fed*), fat. Cf. Gk. πίων, Skt. *pīvan*, fat.

Fat (2), a vat; see **Vat**.

Fate, destiny. (F. − L.) M. E. *fate*. − O. F. *fat, fate* (not common). − L. *fātum*, what is spoken; neut. of pp. of *fāri*, to speak. + Gk. φημί, I say. Perhaps allied to **Boon** (1). Brugm. i. § 187. (√BHĀ.)

Father. (E.) M. E. *fader*. A. S. *fæder*. The pron. with *th* is due to dialectal influences. + Icel. *faðir*, Du. *vader*, Dan. Swed. *fader*, Goth. *fadar*, G. *vater*, L. *pater*, Gk. πατήρ, O. Irish *athir*, Pers. *pidar*, Skt. *pitṛ*. Idg. type *pater-*.

Fathom. (E.) M. E. *fadme*. A. S. *fæðm*, the space reached by the extended arms, a grasp, embrace. + Du. *vadem*, Icel. *faðmr*, a fathom, Dan. *favn*, Swed. *famn*, an embrace, G. *faden*. Allied to **Patent**.

Fatigue, sb. (F. − L.) O. F. *fatigue*; from *fatiguer*, to weary. − L. *fatīgāre*, to weary.

Fatuous. (L.) L. *fatu-us*, silly, feeble; with suffix *-ous*. Der. *in-fatuate*, from pp. of L. *infatuāre*, to make a fool of.

Fauces. (L.) L. *faucēs*, pl., the upper part of the throat.

Faucet, a spigot, vent. (F. — L.?) F. *fausset*, a faucet; *faulset*, Cot. Origin unknown; but cf. M. F. *faulser*, to falsify, forge; also *faulser un escu*, to pierce a shield; hence, to pierce. — L. *falsāre*, to falsify. — L. *falsus*, false.

Fault. (F. — L.) Formerly *faut*. M. E. *faute*. — O. F. *faute*, a fault. (Span. and Ital. *falta*, a defect.) — Folk-L. **fallita*, a defect, fem. of **fallitus*, new pp. of *fallere*, to deceive; cf. F. *faillir*. See **Fail, Fallible, False.** Hence also O. F. *fauter*, Span. *faltar*, Ital. *faltare*, to be lacking.

Faun, a rural (Roman) deity. (L.) L. *faunus*. — L. *fauēre*, to be propitious (?)

Fauteuil, an arm-chair. (F. — Low L. — O. H. G.) F. *fauteuil*, O. F. *fauldetueil* (Cot.). — Low L. *faldistōlium*, a faldstool; see **Faldstool.**

Favour, sb. (F. — L.) O. F. *favour*. — L. *fauōrem*, acc. of *fauor*, favour. — L. *fauēre*, to befriend, orig. ' to venerate.'

favourite. (F. — Ital. — L.) M. F. *favorit*; cf. F. *favori*, pp. of O. F. *favorir*, to favour. But the final *t* is really due to borrowing from Ital. *favorito*, pp. and sb.; orig. pp. of *favorire*, to favour. — Ital. *favore*, favour. — L. *fauōrem* (above).

Fawn (1), to cringe to, rejoice servilely over. (E.) A. S. *fahnian, fagnian*, to rejoice; variants of *fægenian*, to fawn, from *fægen*, fain, glad. + Icel. *fagna*, to rejoice, welcome one; allied to *feginn*, fain. See **Fain.**

Fawn (2), a young deer. (F. — L.) O. F. *fan, faon*, earlier *feön*, a fawn; answering to a Late L. form **fētōnem* (not found), acc. of **fētō*, a young one. — L. *fētus, fœtus*, offspring. See **Fetus.**

Fay, a fairy. (F. — L.) F. *fée*, O. F. *fae*, a fay. Cf. Port. *fada*, Ital. *fata*, a fay. — Late L. *fāta*, a fate, goddess of destiny, a fay. — L. *fāta*, pl. of L. *fātum*, fate. See **Fate.** Der. *fai-ry*.

Fealty, true service. (F. — L.) O. F. *fealte, feelteit*, fidelity. — L. *fidēlitātem*, acc. of *fidēlitās*, fidelity. — L. *fidēlis*, faithful; from *fidēs*, faith.

Fear. (E.) M. E. *feer*. A. S. *fǣr*, a sudden peril, danger, fear. Orig. used of

the peril of travelling. — A. S. *fǣr-*, 3rd stem of *faran*, to go, travel. + Icel. *fār*, harm, G. *gefahr*, Du. *gevaar*, danger. Cf. L. *perīculum*, danger.

Feasible, easy to be done. (F. — L.) [Also *feisable*.] — M. F. *faisible, faisable*, 'feasible, doable;' Cot. — O. F. *fais-*, as in *fais-ant*, pres. pt. of *faire*, to do. — L. *facere*, to do. See **Fact.**

Feast. (F. — L.) M. E. *feste*. — O. F. *feste* (F. *fête*). — Late L. *festa*, fem. sb. — L. *festa*, lit. festivals, pl. of *festum*. See **Festal.**

Feat, a deed well done. (F. — L.) M.E. *feet, fete*. — A. F. *fet*; O. F. *fait*. — L. *factum*, a deed; see **Fact.**

Feather. (E.) M. E. *fether*. A. S. *feðer*. + Du. *veder*, Dan. *fjæder*, Swed. *fjäder*, Icel. *fjöðr*, G. *feder*; L. *penna* (for **pet-sna*), Skt. *patra-*, Gk. πτερόν, a wing. See **Pen.** (✓PET.)

Feature, make, form. (F. — L.) M. E. *feture*. — A. F. *feture*; O. F. *faiture*, fashion. — L. *factūra*, work, formation. — L. *factus*, pp. of *facere*, to make.

Febrile, relating to fever. (F. — L.) F. *fébrile*. — L. *febrīlis*. — L. *febri-s*, fever.

February. (L.) L. *februārius*, the month of expiation. — L. *februa*, neut. pl., a festival of expiation on Feb. 15. — L. *februum*, purification; *februāre*, to expiate. Of Sabine origin.

Feckless, ineffective. Also *factless*; short for *effect-less*; see **Effect.**

Fœculent, foul. (F. — L.) F. *féculent*. — L. *fæculentus*, full of dregs. — L. *fæces*, dregs. See **Fæces.**

Fecundity. (F. — L.) M. F. *fecondité* (Cot.). — L. acc. *fēcunditātem*, fruitfulness. — L. *fēcundus*, fruitful; allied to *fētus*, offspring. See **Fetus.**

Federal. (F. — L.) F. *fédéral*. Formed, with suffix *-al*, from L. *fœder-* (for **fœdes-*), stem of *fœdus*, a treaty. Akin to *fides*, faith.

Fee, a lordship, a payment. (F. — O. H. G.?) A. F. *fee*, O. F. *fiu* (F. *fief*), a fee, fief. — Late L. *fevum*, a fief (Ducange). Prob. from O. H. G. *fehu*, property. + Du. *vee*, Icel. *fé*, Dan. *fæ*, Swed. *fä*, Goth. *faihu*, L. *pecus*; Skt. *paçu-*, cattle. (✓PEK.) So also A. S. *feoh*, cattle, whence M. E. *fee*, cattle, property, now obsolete. ¶ We also find Late L. *feudum*; see **Feudal.**

Feeble. (F. — L.) M. E. *feble*. — A. F. *feble*, M. F. *foible*, O. F. *fleble* (Godefroy):

cf. Ital. *fievole* (< *flevole*), feeble [since Ital. *fi* < *fl*]. — L. *flēbilis*, doleful; hence, weak. — L. *flēre*, to weep. Brugm. ii. § 590.

Feed, to take food, give food. (E.) M. E. *feden*. A. S. *fēdan*; for **fōdian*; with vowel-change from *ō* to *ē*. — A. S. *fōda*, food. + Du. *voeden*, Icel. *fœða*, Swed. *föda*, Dan. *föde*, O. H. G. *fuotan*, Goth. *fōdjan*; Teut. type **fōdjan-*. See **Food**.

Feel. (E.) M. E. *felen*. A. S. *fēlan*. + Du. *voelen*, G. *fühlen*. Teut. **fōljan-*; from Teut. base *fal-* (2nd grade, *fōl-*), whence also Icel. *falma*, to grope, A. S. *folm*, palm of the hand (L. *palma*). Allied to **Palm** (1).

Feeze, Feaze, Pheeze. (E.) Properly 'to put to flight, drive away, chase away, harass, worry'; often misexplained by 'whip.' M. E. *fesen*; O. Merc. *fēsian*, A. S. *fȳsian*, to drive away quickly, chase. Cf. Norw. *føysa* (= Icel. **feysa*), Swed. *fösa*, to drive. From Teut. base **faus-* (sense unknown). ¶ Distinct from A. S. *fȳsan*, to hurry, from *fūs*, prompt.

Feign. (F. — L.) M. E. *feinen*. — O. F. *feign-*, as in *feign-ant*, pres. pt. of *feindre*. — L. *fingere*, to form, feign. See **Figure**. Der. *feint* (from F. pp. *feint*).

Feldspar, a kind of mineral. (G.) Corrupted from G. *feldspath*, lit. field-spar.

Felicity. (F. — L.) O. F. *felicité*. — L. acc. *fēlicitātem*. — L. *fēlici-*, decl. stem of *fēlix*, happy, fruitful; allied to **Feline**.

Feline. (L.) L. *fēlīnus*, belonging to cats. — L. *fēles*, a cat; perhaps allied to Gk. θῆλυς, female.

Fell (1), to cause to fall. (E.) O. Merc. *fællan*, A. S. *fyllan*, causal of O. Merc. *fallan*, A. S. *feallan*, to fall. So also Du. *vellen*, Dan. *fælde*, Swed. *fälla*, Icel. *fella*, G. *fällen*; all causal forms. Teut. type **falljan-*, causal of *fallan-*, to fall. See **Fall**.

Fell (2), a skin. (E.) M. E. *fel*. A. S. *fel*, *fell*. + Du. *vel*, Icel. *fell*, Goth. *-fill*, M. H. G. *vel*; L. *pellis*, Gk. πέλλα, skin. Doublet, *pell*; cf. *fil-m*.

Fell (3), cruel, dire. (F. — Late L. — L. ?) M. E. *fel*. — O. F. *fel*, cruel (cf. Ital. *fello*, cruel). — Late L. *fello*, *felo*, a malefactor, felon, traitor. Perhaps from L. *fel*, gall (N. E. D.); cf. Du. dial. *fel*, sharp, biting, acrid (Molema). See **Felon**.

Fell (4), a hill. (Scand.) M. E. *fel*. — Icel. *fjall*, *fell*, a hill; Dan. *field*, Swed.

fjäll, a fell. Allied to G. *fels*, a rock (Kluge).

Fellah, a peasant. (Arab.) Pl. *fellahīn*. — Arab. *fellāḥ*, *fallāḥ*, a farmer, peasant. — Arab. root *falaḥa*, to plough, till.

Felloe; see **Felly**.

Fellow, a partner. (Scand.) M. E. *felawe*. — Icel. *fēlagi*, a partner in a 'félag.' — Icel. *fēlag*, companionship; lit. a laying together of property. — Icel. *fē*, property; *lag*, a laying together, a law; see **Law**. The Icel. *fē* is cognate with A. S. *feoh*, cattle, property, L. *pecus*, cattle.

Felly, Felloe, part of a wheel-rim. (E.) M. E. *felwe*. A. S. *felg*, *felge*, a felly. + Du. *velg*, Dan. *fælge*, G. *felge*.

Felon, a wicked person. (F. — Late L. — L. ?) M. E. *felun*. — O. F. *felon*, a traitor. — Late L. *felōnem*, acc. of *felo*, *fello*, a traitor, rebel. See **Fell** (3).

Felt. (E.) M. E. *felt*. A. S. *felt*. + Du. *vilt*, Low G., Swed., Dan. *filt*, G. *filz*. Teut. type **feltoz*, n.; allied to G. *falzen*, to groove, join together. Der. *filter*, *feuter*.

Felucca, a ship. (Ital. — Arab.) Ital. *feluca*. — Arab. *fulk*, a ship. (See Devic.)

Female. (F. — L.) For *femell*, by confusion with *male*. M. E. *femelle*. — O. F. *femelle*. — L. *fēmella*, a young woman; dimin. of *fēmina*, a woman (below).

feminine. (F. — L.) O. F. *feminin*. — L. *fēminīnus*, womanly. — L. *fēmina*, a woman. Cf. *fēlare*, to suckle; Gk. θῆλυς, female, θηλή, the breast; Skt. *dhātrī*, a nurse.

Femoral, belonging to the thigh. (L.) L. *femorālis*; adj. from *femor-*, stem of *femur*, thigh.

Fen, a bog. (E.) M. E. *fen*. A. S. *fenn*. + Du. *veen*, Icel. *fen*, Goth. *fani*, mud. Teut. type **fanjom*, n.

Fence; short for *defence*; see **Defend**.

Fend; short for **Defend**, q. v.

Fender; short for *defender*.

Fennel, a plant. (L.) M. E. *fenel*. A. S. *finol*, *finugle*. — L. *faeniculum*, fennel; double dimin. of *faenum*, hay.

Fenugreek, a plant. (F. — L.) F. *fenugrec*. — L. *faenum Graecum*, lit. Greek hay.

Feoff; see **Fief**.

Ferment. (L.) L. *fermentum* (short for **ferui-mentum*), leaven. — L. *feruēre*, to boil. See **Fervent**.

Fern. (E.) A. S. *fearn*. + Du. *varen*; G. *farn*(*kraut*); Skt. *parṇa-*, a wing, feather, leaf, plant, the orig. sense being 'feather.' Brugm. i. § 973. Cf. also Lith. *papartis*, Russ. *paporot(e)*, Irish *raith*, W. *rhedyn*, fern; Gk. πτέρις, fern, πτερόν, a wing, feather.

Ferocity. (F.–L.) M.F. *ferocité.*– L. acc. *ferōcitātem*, fierceness.–L. *ferōci-*, decl. stem of *ferox*, fierce.–L. *ferus*, fierce, wild. Brugm. i. § 319.

Ferreous. (L.) L. *ferreus*, made of iron; with suffix *-ous.*–L. *ferrum*, iron.

ferruginous. (L.) L. *ferrūgin-us*, same as *ferrūgineus*, rusty; with suffix *-ous.*–L. *ferrūgin-*, stem of *ferrūgo*, rust of iron.–L. *ferrum*, iron.

Ferret (1), an animal. (F.–Low L.– L.?) O. F. *furet*, a ferret.–Late L. *fūrē-tus*, *fūrectus*, a ferret. Also *fūrō*; said to be the same as Late L. *fūrō*, a thief, from L. *fūr*, a thief. Cf. Gk. φώρ, a thief; from the strong ō-grade of φέρειν, to bear, carry off.

Ferret (2), a kind of silk tape. (Ital. –L.) From Ital. *fioretti*, 'little flowers, flourishings; also foret or ferret silke,' Florio. Pl. of *fioretto*, dimin. of *fiore*, a flower.–L. *flōrem*, acc. of *flōs*, a flower; see **Flower.** Cf. F. *fleuret*, ferret; from *fleur*, flower.

Ferruginous; see **Ferreous.**

Ferrule, a metal ring at the end of a stick. (F.–L.) Corrupted spelling (due to confusion with *ferrum*, iron) of the older form *virrol*; XVI cent.–O.F. *virol* (F. *virole*), a ferrule; Late L. *virola*, the same. From L. *uiriola*, a little bracelet; dimin. of **uiria*, an armlet, only found in pl. *uiriae*. (Diez.) Doubtful.

Ferry, vb. (E.) M.E. *ferien.* A.S. *ferian*, to convey across; causal of A.S. *faran*, to go. + Icel. *ferja*, to carry; causal of *fara*, to go; Goth. *farjan*, to travel by ship. See **Fare.** (N.E.D.)

Fertile. (F.–L.) F. *fertile.*–L. *fer-tilis*, fertile. – L. *ferre*, to bear. See **Bear** (1).

Ferule, a rod or bat for punishing children. (L.) Formerly *ferula.*–L. *ferula*, a rod; orig. the plant 'giant-fennel.'

Fervent, hot, zealous. (F.–L.) O.F. *fervent.*–L. *feruent-*, stem of pres. pt. of *feruēre*, to boil. Allied to O. Irish *berb-aim*, I boil. **Der.** *fervour*, from O.F. *fervour*<L. acc. *feruōrem*, heat; *fervid*, from L. *feruidus.*

Fess, a horizontal band in heraldry.

(F.–L.) O.F. *fesse* (Roquefort); mod. F. *fasce*, a fess.–L. *fascia*, a girth; allied to *fascis*, a bundle; see **Fascine.**

Festal. (F.–L.) O.F. *festal.* Formed (with F. suffix *-al*<L. *-ālis*) from L. *fest-um*, a feast, orig. neut. of *festus*, festive, joyful. Allied to **Fair** (2) and **Fane.**

festival. (F.–Late L.–L.) Pro-perly an adj.–O. F. *festival*, festive.– Late L. *festīvālis.*–L. *festīuus* (below).

festive. (L.) L. *festīuus*, belonging to a feast.–L. *festum*, a feast.

Fester, a sore. (F.–L.) O. F. *festre*, also spelt *fistle*, an ulcer; whence *festrir*, to fester (Godefroy).–L. *fistula*, a running sore. See **Fistula.**

Festival, Festive; see **Festal.**

Festoon. (F.–Ital.–L.) F. *feston*, a garland, festoon.–Ital. *festone*, a garland. Usually derived from L. *festum*, a feast.

Fetch. (E.) M. E. *fecchen*, pt. t. *fehte*, *fœhte*. A.S. *feccan*, to fetch, Gen. xviii. 4; Luke xii. 20. Prob. that *fecc(e)an* is a later form of *fetian*, to fetch (Anglia, vi. 177). Allied to A.S. *fæt*, a pace, step, journey; Icel. *fet*, a step, foot-measure; and to L. *pēs* (gen. *ped-is*), a foot. ¶ Cf. A.S. *gefeccan*, O. E. T., p. 178. **Der.** *fetch*, sb., a stratagem.

Fête. (F.–L.) Mod. F. *fête*, the same as O.F. *feste*; see **Feast.**

Fetich, Fetish, an object of super-stitious dread. (F.–Port.–L.) F. *fétiche.*–Port. *feitiço*, sorcery, lit. artificial; also, a name given by the Port. to the roughly made idols of Africa.–L. *factītius*, artificial.–L. *fact-us*, pp. of *facere*, to make.

Fetid. (F.–L.) O. F. *fetide.*–L. *fœtidus*, *fœtidus*, stinking.–L. *fetere*, to stink.

Fetlock. (Scand.) As if the 'lock' or tuft of hair behind a horse's pas-tern-joint. Cf. Low G. *fitlock* (Lübben); M. H. G. *vizzeloch* (Kluge). The syllable *-l-ock* is due to a double suffix, but was thought to refer to Icel. *lokkr*, A.S. *locc*, a lock of hair. *Fet-* is prob. allied to Icel. *fet*, a pace, step, *feti*, a pacer (used of horses); and to Icel. *fōtr*, a foot; cf. G. *fessel*, pastern; and see **Fetch, Foot.** (Kluge, s.v. *Fuss.*)

Fetter, a shackle. (E.) M.E. *feter.* A.S. *fetor*, a shackle for the foot; from **fet-*, ε̆-grade of *fōt*, foot.+Du. *veter*, Icel. *fjöturr*; cf. L. *ped-ica* and *com-pēs*, Gk. πέδη, a fetter. **Der.** *fetter*, vb.

Fetus, offspring. (L.) L. *fētus,* a bringing forth, offspring. — L. **fuēre,* an obsolete verb, to generate, produce; allied to *fu-i,* I was; see **Future,** Be. Brugm. i. § 361, ii. § 587.

Feu, a fief; a variant of **Fee.**

Feud (1), hatred, perpetual hostility. (F. — O. H. G.) M. E. *fede, feid.* Modified in spelling in some unexplained way, perhaps by the influence of *foe.* — O. F. *feide, faide, fede,* perpetual hostility. — O. H. G. *fēhida* (G. *fehde*), enmity; cognate with A. S. *fǣhð,* enmity, from A. S. *fāh,* hostile. See **Foe.**

Feud (2), a fief. (Low L. — F. — O. H. G.) Low L. *feudum,* a Latinised form allied to O. F. *fiu,* also spelt *fief*; see **Fee, Fief.** (The intrusive *d* is unexplained.) Der. *feud-al,* adj.

Feuter, to lay spear in rest. (F. — Teut.) From M. E. *feuter,* a rest for a spear. — O. F. *feutre,* older *feltre,* a piece of felt, also a rest (prob. at first felted) for the lance. Cp. Ital. *feltro,* felt. Of Teut. origin; from Low G. *filt,* felt. See **Felt.**

Feuterer, a dog-keeper. (F. — Low L. — C.) In Ben Jonson, Every Man out of his Humour, ii. 1; see Nares. Older spelling *vewter,* for *veutr-er.* — O. F. *veutre,* mod. F. *vautre,* a mongrel between a hound and a mastiff. — Low Lat. acc. *veltrum*; for L. *vertagus, vertagra, vertraga,* a greyhound. Said to be Celtic. Perhaps from Celtic *ver-,* intensive prefix, and *trag-,* to run; see Fick, ii. 136, 283.

Fever, a kind of disease. (L.) M. E. *feuer (fever).* A. S. *fēfer, fēfor*; see Matt. viii. 15; A. F. *fevre.* — L. *febris,* fever.

feverfew, a plant. (L.) A. S. *fēferfuge*; A. F. *feverfue.* — Late L. *febrifuga,* for L. *febrifugia,* 'fever-dispelling.' — L. *febri-s,* fever; *fugāre,* to put to flight.

Few. (E.) M. E. *fewe.* A. S. pl. *fēawe.* +Icel. *fār,* Dan. *faa,* Swed. *få*; Goth. *fawai,* pl.; cf. L. *paucus,* Gk. παῦρος, small.

Fey, doomed to die. (E.) A. S. *fǣge,* doomed to die.+Icel. *feigr,* Du. *veeg*; G. *feige,* cowardly; Swed. *feg,* Dan. *feig,* cowardly.

Fez, a red Turkish cap, without a brim. (F. — Morocco.) F. and Turk. *fez,* a cap; so called because made at Fez, in Morocco.

Fiasco, lit. 'a bottle.' (Ital.) Ital. *far fiasco,* to make a bottle, also, to fail,

break down. See **Flask.** (Origin of phrase unknown.)

Fiat, a decree. (L.) L. *fīat,* let it be done. — L. *fīo,* I become; used as pass. of *facere,* to do, but really allied to *fui,* I was. Cf. A. S. *bēo,* I am. Brugm. i. § 282.

Fib. (Low G.) Allied to *fob, fub off,* to delude (Shak.); cf. G. *foppen,* to banter (formerly, to lie); Westphal. *fip-ken,* a small lie, fib (Woeste).

Fibre. (F. — L.) F. *fibre.* — L. *fibra,* a thread.

Fickle. (E.) M. E. *fikel.* A. S. *ficol*; from **fician,* to deceive, in comp. *be-fician,* to deceive; cf. *fic,* sb., fraud, *fǣcne,* deceitful; *fācen,* fraud.

Fiction. (F. — L.) F. *fiction.* — L. *fictiōnem,* acc. of *fictio,* a feigning. — L. *fictus,* pp. of *fingere,* to feign. See **Figure.**

Fiddle, a violin. (L.) M. E. *fithel*; A. S. *fiðele*; cf. Icel. *fiðla,* Dan. *fiddel,* Du. *vedel,* G. *fiedel.* Apparently borrowed from Late L. *uitula, uidula,* a viol; see **Viol.**

Fidelity. (F. — L.) M. F. *fidelité.* — L. *fidēlitātem,* acc. of *fidēlitās,* faithfulness. — L. *fidēli-,* stem of *fidēlis,* faithful. — L. *fidēs,* faith. See **Faith.**

Fidget. (Scand.) A dimin. form of *fidge,* to be continually moving up and down, like *fike* in North of England, M. E. *fiken,* to fidget, to hasten. Cf. Icel. *fika,* to climb up nimbly, as a spider; Swed. *fika,* to hunt after, Norw. *fika,* to take trouble, *fika etter,* to hasten after, pursue.

Fiducial, shewing trust. (L.) From Late L. *fidūciālis,* adj. — L. *fidūcia,* trust. — L. *fīdere,* to trust.

Fie. (F. — L.) M. E. *fy.* — F. *fi.* — L. *fī.* Cf. Icel. *fȳ,* Dan. *fy,* Swed. *fy,* G. *pfui,* Lat. *phu, phy,* Skt. *phut,* expressions of disgust.

Fief, land held of a superior. (F. — O. H. G.) O. F. *fief,* formerly spelt *fiu* (Roland). See **Fee.** Der. *feoff,* vb., to put in legal possession; from A. F. *feoffer,* to endow with a *feof* or *fief.* Also *feoffee,* A. F. *feoffé,* pp. of *feoffer.*

Field. (E.) M. E. *feld.* A. S. *feld.*+Du. *veld.* G. *feld* (whence Dan. *felt,* Swed. *fält.*) Allied to A. S. *folde,* earth, land. Teut. type **felthuz.* Cf. Russ. *polé,* a field; Skt. *pṛthivī,* earth. Brugm. i. § 502.

fieldfare, a bird. (E.) A. S. *feldefare* [miswritten *feldeware*], lit. 'field-traveller;' see **Fare.**

Fiend. (E.) M. E. *fend.* A. S. *fīond, fēond,* lit. ' a hating one,' an enemy, the enemy; orig. pres. pt. of *fēog(e)an,* to hate. + Du. *vijand,* Dan. Swed. *fiende;* Icel. *fjāndi,* pres. pt. of *fjā,* to hate; Goth. *fijands,* from *fijan,* to hate; G. *feind.* Cf. Skt. *pīy,* to hate (Fick). See **Foe.**

Fierce. (F. – L.) M. E. *fers.* – O. F. *fers, fiers,* old nom. of O. F. *fer, fier, fier,* fierce (F. *fier,* proud). – L. *ferus,* wild.

Fife. (F. – O. H. G. – L.) F. *fifre.* – O. H. G. *pfīfa,* G. *pfeife,* a pipe. – O. H. G. *pfīfen,* to blow, whistle. – Late L. *pīpāre,* to pipe; L. *pīpāre,* to chirp (as a bird). See **Pipe.**

Fig. (F. – Prov. – L.) F. *figue.* – Prov. *figa.* – Folk-L. **fīca,* used for L. *ficus,* a fig. (Cf. O. F. *fie,* a fig; immediately from *fīca.*)

Fight. (E.) M. E. *fihten, fehten,* vb. O. Merc. *fehtan,* to fight; *fehte,* a fight. + Du. *vechten,* G. *fechten,* to fight (whence Dan. *fegte,* Swed. *fäkta*). Teut. **fehtan-.*

Figment. (L.) L. *figmentum,* an invention. – L. *fig-,* base of *fingere,* to feign (pp. *fic-tus,* for **fig-tus*).

figure. (F. – L.) F. *figure.* – L. *figūra,* a thing made. – L. *fingere* (base *fig-*), to make, fashion, feign. + Goth. *deigan,* to knead, Skt. *dih,* to smear. (√DHEIGH.) Brugm. i. § 589. **Der.** *dis-figure, pre-figure, trans-figure.*

Filament. (F. – L.) F. *filament.* – Late L. *fīlāmentum,* thin thread. – Late L. *fīlāre,* to wind thread. – L. *fīlum,* thread; see **File** (1).

Filbert, fruit of hazel. (F. – O. H. G.) Formerly *philiberd* (Gower); short for *Philiberd* or *Philibert nut,* from the proper name *Philibert;* (S. Philibert's day is Aug. 22); North F. *noix de filbert* (Moisy). – O. H. G. *filu-berht,* very bright; from *filu* (G. *viel*), greatly, *berht,* bright. ¶ Called in Germany *Lambertsnuss,* i. e. nut from Lombardy (Weigand).

Filch. (E.) Etym. unknown; possibly related to M. E. *felen,* to conceal. Cf. Icel. *fela,* to hide, bury; Goth. *filhan,* to hide.

File (1), string, line, order. (F. – L.) Partly from O. F. *file,* a file, from *filer,* to thread; from Late L. *fīlāre* (see **Filament**); partly from F. *fil,* thread, from L. *fīlum,* a thread.

File (2), a steel rasp. (E.) O. Merc. *fil;* A. S. *feol.* + Du. *vijl,* O. H. G. *fīhala,* G. *feile;* as if from a base **fenh-.* The Icel. form is *þēl,* as if from a base **thenh-.*

File (3), to defile. (E.) A. S. *fȳlan,* to make foul; for **fūlian.* – A. S. *fūl,* foul. See **Defile** (1) and **Foul.**

Filial. (L.) From L. *fīli-us,* a son, *filia,* daughter; orig. infant: cf. L. *fēlāre,* to suck. Cf. **Feminine.** (√DHE.)

Filibuster, a freebooter. (Span. – Du.) Span. *filibuster,* a mere corruption of Du. *vrijbuiter,* a freebooter. – Du. *vrijbuiten,* to rob, plunder. – Du. *vrij,* free; *buit,* booty, plunder. See **Booty.**

Filigree. (F. – Ital. – L.) Formerly *filigrane;* XVII cent. – F. *filigrane.* – Ital. *filigrana,* filigree-work, fine wrought work. – Ital. *filo,* a thread or row, *filare,* to spin; *grano,* grain or texture; so called because the chief texture of it was wrought in silver wire. From L. *filum,* thread; *grānum,* grain. ¶ The Span. *filigrana* is merely borrowed from Italian (Monlau).

Fill, vb. (E.) A. S. *fyllan;* formed from *ful,* i. e. full, by vowel-change from *u* to *y.* + Du. *vullen,* Icel. *fylla,* Dan. *fylde,* Swed. *fylla,* Goth. *fulljan,* G. *füllen.*

Fillet. (F. – L.) M. E. *filet.* – O. F. *filet,* dimin. of *fil,* a thread. – L. *filum,* a thread. See **File** (1).

Fillibeg, Philibeg, a kilt. (Gaelic.) Gael. *feileadh-beag,* the modern kilt. – Gael. *feileadh, feile,* a kilt, prob. from L. *uēlum,* a veil (Macbain); and *beag,* little, small. Cf. W. *bach,* little.

Fillip, to strike with the finger-nail, when jerked from the thumb. (E.) Another form of *flip;* see **Flippant.**

Fills, used for *thills.* (E.) See **Thill.**

Filly, a female foal. (Scand.) Icel. *fylja,* a filly, allied to *foli,* a foal, cf. Dan. Swed. *föl,* G. *füllen.* See **Foal.**

Film, a thin skin. (E.) A. S. *filmen* (*fylmen*), neut., membrane (O. Fries. *filmene,* f., skin). For W. Teut. **filmin-jo-,* from **felmen, -mon-,* as in A. S. *ǣgerfelma,* skin of an egg. Extended from the base *fel-* in A. S. *fel,* skin, Goth. *fill,* skin. See **Fell** (2).

Filter, to strain. (F. – O. Low G.) F. *filtrer,* orig. to strain through felt. – F. *filtre,* a strainer, orig. felt (Littré). – Low G. *filt,* felt; see **Felt.**

Filth, foul matter. (E.) A. S. *fȳlð.* – A. S. *fūl,* foul (by vowel-change of *ū* to *ȳ*). So also O. Sax. *fūlithā,* filth, from *fūl,* foul. See **Foul.**

Fin. (E.) A. S. *finn,* a fin. + Du. *vin,* Swed. *fena,* Dan. *finne;* L. *pinna.* See **Pin.**

Final. (F. – L.) O. F. *final.* – L. *finālis,* final. – L. *finis,* end.

Finance, revenue. (F. – L.) O. F. *finance.* – Late L. *finantia,* payment. – Late L. *fināre,* to pay a fine. – Late L. *finis,* a settled payment, a *finish* or end, i. e. final arrangement ; L. *finis,* end.

Finch, a bird. (E.) M. E. *finch.* A. S. *finc.*+Du. *vink,* Dan. *finke,* Swed. and G. *fink.* Cf. W. *pinc,* a chaffinch ; Gk. σπίγγος, σπίζα, a finch ; prov. E. *spink.* Der. *chaf-finch,* q. v., *bull-finch,* &c.

Find. (E.) A. S. *findan.*+Du. *vinden,* Dan. *finde,* Swed. and Icel. *finna* (= *finþa*), Goth. *finthan,* G. *finden.* Teut. **fenth-an-* ; Idg. base **pent-,* whence O. Irish *ēt-aim,* I find. Perhaps allied to L. *petere,* to seek after ; see **Petition.** Brugm. ii. § 634.

Fine (1), exquisite, thin. (F. – L.) O. F. *fin,* witty, perfect. – Late L. *finus,* fine ; used in place of L. *finītus,* well rounded or ended, said of a sentence (Brachet), orig. pp. of *finire,* to end. – L. *finis,* end. ¶ *Finus* is a back-formation from *finire.*

fine (2), a tax. (Law L.) Law L. *finis,* a fine, a final arrangement ; L. *finis,* end. See **Finance** (above).

Finger. (E.) A. S. *finger.*+Du. *vinger,* Icel. *fingr,* Dan. Swed. G. *finger,* Goth. *figgrs* (= *fingrs*). Teut. type **fin-groz* ; orig. sense unknown.

Finial. (L.) A coined word ; from L. *finis,* end. Cf. *final.*

finical. (F. – L.) A coined word ; extended from **Fine** (1) above.

finish, vb. (F. – L.) M. E. *finischen.* – O. F. *finiss-,* base of pres. pt. of *finir,* to finish. – L. *finire,* to end. – L. *finis,* end.

finite, limited. (L.) L. *finītus,* pp. of *finire* (above).

Fiord, a sea-loch, deep inlet of the sea. (Scand.) Norw. *fjord,* Dan. *fiord, fjord* ; Icel. *fjörðr.* See **Frith.**

Fir, a tree. (Scand.) M. E. *fir* ; answering to a mutated form due to A. S. *furh,* which occurs in *furhwudu,* a pine-tree ; but prob. of Scand. origin. Cf. Icel. *fyri-skógr,* a fir-wood (written *fȳriskógr*) ; from Icel. *fura,* a fir ; cf. Dan. *fyr,* Swed. *fura.*+G. *föhre,* W. *pyr.* Cognate with L. *quercus,* an oak ; and O. Lombardic *fereha,* ' æsculus.'

Fire. (E.) A. S. *fȳr.*+Du. *vuur,* Icel. *fȳri,* Dan. and Swed. *fyr,* G. *feuer,* M.H.G.

viur, O. H. G. *fuir.* Teut. type **fū-ir.* Cognate with Gk. πῦρ. Cf. Skt. *pāvaka-* (from *pū*), purifying, also fire. (√PŪ.)

Firk, to conduct, drive, beat. (E.) A. S. *fercian,* to conduct, support. Prob. from A. S. *fær,* a journey ; allied to **Fare.**

Firkin, the fourth part of a barrel. (M. Du.) M. E. *ferdekin.* From Du. *vierde,* fourth ; with suffix *-kin* (as in *kil-der-kin*) answering to the M. Du. double dimin. suffix *-k-in* (G. *-ch-en* in *mädchen*). *Vierde* is from Du. *vier,* four ; see **Four.**

Firm (1), adj. (F. – L.) M. E. *ferme.* – O. F. and F. *ferme.* – L. *firmus,* steadfast. Der. *farm.*

firm (2), a partnership. (Span. – L.) The older sense was ' signature ' of the house or (as we call it) the firm. – Span. *firma,* a signature. – Span. *firmar,* to confirm, sign. – L. *firmāre,* to make firm. – L. *firmus,* firm (above).

firmament, celestial sphere. (F. – L.) O. F. *firmament.* – L. *firmāmentum,* a support ; also, expanse of the sky (Vulgate). – L. *firmāre,* to strengthen ; from *firmus,* firm.

Firman, a mandate. (Pers.) Pers. *fermān,* a mandate, order ; O. Pers. *framāna* (Horn) ; cf. Skt. *pramāṇa-,* a decision, from *pra,* before (Gk. πρό) and *mā,* to measure.

First. (E.) A. S. *fyrst,* the superl. of *fore,* with vowel-change of *u* (A. S. *o*) to *y.*+Icel. *fyrstr* ; Dan. *förste* ; Swed. *första.* Teut. type **furistoz,* superl. from the base **fur-* ; see **Fore.**

Firth ; see **Frith.**

Fiscal, pertaining to the revenue. (F. – L.) O. F. *fiscal.* – Late L. *fiscālis.* – L. *fiscus,* a basket of rushes, also a purse.

Fish. (E.) A. S. *fisc.*+Du. *visch,* Icel. *fiskr,* Dan. and Swed. *fisk,* G. *fisch* ; Goth. *fisks.* Teut. type **fiskoz.* Cognate with L. *piscis,* Irish and Gael. *iasg,* O. Ir. *iasc* (with loss of initial *p*).

Fissure. (F. – L.) O. F. *fissure.* – L. *fissūra.* – L. *fissus,* pp. of *findere,* to cleave.+Skt. *bhid,* to cleave ; A. S. *bītan,* to bite. (√BHEID.) And see **Vent** (1). Brugm. i. § 567.

Fist. (E.) M. E. *fist, fest, fust.* A. S. *fȳst.*+Du. *vuist,* G. *faust,* O. H. G. *fūst.* Teut. **fūstiz.* ¶ If the orig. Teut. form was **funhstiz,* it may be identified with Russ. *piaste,* fist, O. Slav. *pęsti* ; from an Idg. base **pṇksti-,* which is allied to **Five.**

Fistula, a deep, narrow abscess. (L.) From the shape; L. *fistula,* a pipe.

Fit (1), to suit; as adj., apt. (Scand.) M. E. *fitten,* to arrange. — Icel. and Norw. *fitja,* to knit together; Swed. dial. *fittja,* to bind together; cf. G. *fitzen,* to bind into skeins, from *fitze,* a skein. From Icel. *fit,* a hem, also 'web' of a bird's foot; cf. M. Dan. *fidde,* to knit; Dan. *fid,* a skein. Perhaps allied to **Fit** (2). ¶ Influenced as to sense by M. E. *fete,* well done; from O. F. *fait,* Lat. *factus;* see **Feat.**

Fit (2), a part of a poem, attack of illness. (E.) M. E. *fit.* A. S. *fitt,* (1) a song, (2) a struggle; which perhaps are the same word. Cf. **Fit** (1).

Fitch, the same as **Vetch,** q. v.

Fitchet, Fitchew, a pole-cat. (F. — M. Du.) *Fitchew* is from Picard *ficheux,* M. F. *fissau,* a polecat; older form, *fissel.* — M. Du. *fisse,* a polecat; from the smell. Cf. Icel. *fisa,* to make a smell.

Fitz, son. (A. F. — L.) Formerly *fiz* (with *z* as *ts*). — A. F. *fiz* (with *z* as *ts*); also O. F. *filz, fils.* — L. *filius,* a son.

Five. (E.) A. S. *fif;* sometimes *fiue,* as a plural. A. S. *fif* (for **fimf*). + Du. *vijf,* Dan. Swed. *fem,* Icel. *fimm,* Goth. *fimf,* G. *fünf;* W. *pump,* O. Ir. *coic,* L. *quinque,* Lith. *penki,* Gk. *πέντε* (Æol. *πέμπε*), Skt. *pañcha.* Idg. type **penqe.* Der. *fif-th,* A. S. *fifta;* *fifteen,* A. S. *fiftēne;* *fif-ty,* A. S. *fiftig.*

Fix. (F. — L.) O. F. *fix,* fixed. — L. *fixus,* fixed; pp. of *figere,* to fix.

Fizz. (Scand.) Imitative; cf. Icel. *fisa,* Dan. *fise,* with the sense of L. *pedere.*

Flabby; weakened form of *flappy;* see **Flap.** Cf. Low G. *flubbe,* a hanging lip; *flabbsig,* flabby (Danneil).

Flaccid. (F. — L.) F. *flaccide.* — L. *flaccidus,* limp. — L. *flaccus,* flabby.

Flag (1), to droop, grow weary. (E.) Weakened form of *flack,* to hang loosely; M. E. *flakken,* to flap about. From the base *flac-* of A. S. *flac-or,* flying, roving. +Icel. *flakka,* to rove, *flaka,* to flap; *flökra, flögra,* Dan. *flagre,* to flutter; G. *flackern,* to flutter. All from the imitative base *flak-,* allied to *flap, flicker.* And partly from O. F. *flaquir,* to be limp; from O. F. *flaque,* limp, L. *flaccus.*

flag (2), an ensign. (Scand.?) Dan. *flag,* Swed. *flagg,* a flag; from base of Icel. *flögra,* to flutter (above).

flag (3), a reed; the same word as *flag* (2); from its waving in the wind.

Flag (4), **Flagstone,** a paving-stone. (Scand.) Icel. *flaga,* a flag or slab of stone. This might give E. dial. *flaw* (see **Flaw**), but cf. Icel. *flagna,* to flake off, Dan. dial. *flag-törv,* Sc. *flag,* a cut turf. A weakened form of **Flake.**

Flagellate. (L.) From pp. of L. *flagellāre,* to scourge. — L. *flagellum,* dimin. of *flagrum,* a scourge. See **Flail.**

Flageolet, a sort of flute. (F. — Prov.) M. F. *flageolet,* dimin. of *flageol,* with the same sense. — Prov. *flajols, flaujols,* a flageolet; which cannot represent a Late L. **flautiolus,* a little flute, as suggested by Diez.

Flagitious. (L.) L. *flāgitiōs-us,* shameful; with suffix -*ous.* — L. *flāgitium,* a disgraceful act; cf. L. *flāgitāre,* to act with violence. Perhaps allied to **Flagrant.**

Flagon. (F. — Late L.) O. F. *flacon,* another form of *flascon.* — Late L. *flascōnem,* acc. of *flasco,* a flask. — Late L. *flasca,* a flask. See **Flask.**

Flagrant, glaring, as a fault. (F. — L.) O. F. *flagrant,* properly burning. — L. *flagrant-,* stem of pres. pt. of *flagrāre,* to burn.+Gk. *φλέγειν,* to burn; Sk. *bhrāj.* (√BHLEG.) Brugm. i. § 539 (2).

Flail. (L.) M. E. *fliзel, fleзil, fleil.* [Later, *fluyel* (from O. F. *fluël* > F. *fléau*).] From L. *flagellum,* a whip, in Late L., a flail; dimin. of *flagrum,* a scourge. See **Flagellate.**

Flake, a thin slice. (Scand.) Norw. *flak,* a slice, an ice-floe; cf. Icel. *flakna,* *flagna,* to flake off, Swed. *flaga,* a flake. Perhaps allied to **Flay.**

Flambeau. (F. — L.) F. *flambeau,* a torch; dimin. of O. F. *flambe* (below).

flame, sb. (F. — L.) O. F. *flame, flamme;* also *flambe.* — L. *flamma* (**flagma?*), a flame; perhaps from the base *flag-,* to burn. See **Flagrant.**

Flamen. (L.) L. *flāmen,* a priest of Rome. Prob. for **flag-men,* he who burns the sacrifice; cf. *flagrare,* to burn. Or else allied to Goth. *blōtan,* to sacrifice.

Flamingo. (Span. — Prov. — L.) Span. *flamenco,* a flamingo; but said to be a Provençal word; the Prov. form is *flamenc,* where the suffix -*enc* is supposed to be an adaptation of the Teut. suffix -*ing.* The F. form is *flamant,* lit. 'flaming,' but it seems to have been confused with F. *Flamand,* a Fleming, whence the peculiar form of the Prov. form may have arisen; Palsgrave has 'Flemmyng, *flammant.*'

Still, the etymology is certainly from L. *flamma*, a flame; from the flame-like colour of the bird.

Flange, a projecting rim. (F. — Teut.) The same as prov. E. *flanch*, a projection; cf. *flanch* in heraldry, an ordinary on each side (or *flank*) of the shield. ═ O. F. *flanche* (A. F. *flanke*), fem. sb. allied to F. *flanc*, side. See below.

flank, the side. (F. — Teut.) M. E. *flanc.* ═ F. *flanc*, side. ═ O. H. G. *hlancha*, *lanka*, hip, bend, loin; cf. Mid. Du. '*de Lancke*, the flancks;' Hexham. Allied to A. S. *hlanc*, slender; see **Lank**. (Disputed; but probable; see Kluge, s. v. *Gelenk*.)

Flannel. (W.) Prov. E. *flannen*, a better form. ═ W. *gwlanen*, flannel, from *gwlan*, wool. Allied to **Wool**.

Flap, to beat with the wings. (E.) M. E. *flappen*, to beat; not in A. S. E. Fries. *flappen*. Imitative; like *flack*, to beat; see **Flag** (1). ╋ Du. *flappen*, to flap. Der. *flabby* (flappy); *flap*, sb.

Flare; see below.

Flash, to blaze. (E.) M. E. *flaschen*, to dash; cf. Swed. dial. *flasa*, to burn violently; Icel. *flasa*, to rush, *flas*, a swift rushing.

flare. (Scand.) Norweg. *flara*. to blaze; apparently a variant of Swed. dial. *flasa* (above).

Flask. (Late L.?) A. S. *flasce*, *flaxe*; we also find Icel. *flaska*, Dan. *flaske*, Swed. *flaska*, G. *flasche*; but it is hardly a Teut. word. ═ Late L. *flasca*, a flask; cf. also W. *fflasg*, Gael. *flasg* (from E.). Remoter origin uncertain. See **Flagon**.

Flat. (Scand.) M. E. *flat.* ═ Icel. *flatr*, Swed. *flat*, Dan. *flad*.

Flatter. (F. — Teut.; *or* E.) M. E. *flateren*, a frequentative form. Either, with suffix -*er*-, from O. F. *flat-er*, mod. F. *flatter*, to flatter; or formed from an E. base *flat*-, of imitative origin; cf. M. Du. *flattéren*, to flatter (Hexham) from O. F. *flater*, which is from Icel. *flat-r*, flat; from the notion of making smooth. Cf. the base *flak*-, seen in M. Swed. *fleckra*, to flatter, Swed. dial. *fleka*, to caress; also M. E. *flakken*, to move to and fro, and G. *flach*, flat; see **Flag** (1). The sb. *flattery* is plainly adapted from O. F. *flaterie*, F. *flatterie*.

Flatulent, windy. (F. — L.) M. F. *flatulent.* ═ Late L. *flātulentus.* ═ L. *flātus*, breath. ═ L. *flāre*, to blow; see **Blow** (1).

Flaunt, to display ostentatiously. (Scand.) It seems to have been particularly used of the display of fluttering plumes, &c. Norw. *flanta*, to gad about; Dan. *flane*, to flirt. Somewhat similar is Swed. dial. *flankt*, flutteringly, loosely, from *flanka*, to waver; perhaps allied to *flakka*, to waver, answering to M. E. *flakken*; see **Flag** (1).

Flavour. (F. — L.) The form seems to have been influenced by that of the word *savour*. O. Lowl. Sc. *flewoure*, *flewer*. ═ O. F. *flëur*, *fleiur*, *flaur*, smell. Cf. Ital. *fiatore*, a bad odour; answering to Late L. acc. **flātorem*. ═ L. *flātus*, pp. of *flāre*, to blow. (Körting, § 3316.)

Flaw, a crack. (Scand.) M. E. *flawe.* ═ Swed. *flaga*, a crack, flaw, also a flake; see **Flake**. Cf. prov. E. *flaw*, a flake (as of snow); also, a gust of wind, like Du. *vlaag*.

Flawn, a kind of custard. (F. — O.H.G.) M. E. *flaun.* ═ F. *flan*, O. F. *flaon*, a flawn; (cf. Span. *flaon*, Ital. *fiadone*). ═ O. H. G. *flado*, a broad flat cake; G. *fladen*. Allied to Gr. πλατύς, broad.

Flax, a plant. (E.) A. S. *fleax.* ╋ Du. *vlas*, G. *flachs*. Perhaps allied to Goth. *flah-ta*, a plaiting, Gk. πλέκ-ειν, to weave.

Flay, to strip off skin. (E.) M. E. *flean*. A. S. *flēan*, to flay. ╋ Icel. *flā*, pt. t. *flō*, pp. *fleginn*. Teut. type **flahan-* (pt. t. **flōh*), to strike. Cognate with Lith. *plakù*, I strike; cf. Lat. *plāga*, a stroke. See **Plague**. Brugm. i. § 569.

Flea. (E.) M. E. *flee*, pl. *fleen*. A. S. *flēah*, a flea. ╋ Du. *vloo*, Icel. *flō*, G. *floh*. Teut. base **flauh*-, or perhaps **plauh*-, allied to the verb *to flee*. See **Flee**.

Fleam, a kind of lancet. (F. — L. — Gk.) O. F. *flieme*, F. *flamme*, a fleam; Hamilton. ═ Late L. *flētoma*, a lancet (Vocab. 400. 11); shortened from Late L. *flevotomum*, *phlebotomum*, a lancet. ═ Gk. φλεβοτόμον, a lancet. ═ Gk. φλεβο-, decl. stem of φλέψ, a vein; τομ-, o-grade of τέμνειν, to cut. Hence also M. H. G. *fliedeme*, G. *fliete*, Du. *vlijm*, a fleam.

Fleck, a spot. (Scand.) M. E. *flek.* ═ Icel. *flekkr*, a spot; *flekka*, to stain; Swed. *fläck*, a spot. ╋ Du. *vlek*, G. *fleck*.

Flection; see **Flexible**.

Fledge, to be furnished with feathers. (E.) The pp. *fledged* is now used in the place of M. E. *flegge*, adj., ready to fly. *Flegge* is a Kentish form of M. E. *flygge*, ready to fly. From A. S. **flycge*; found in the compound *unflycge*, as in '*inplumes*, unfligge,' Academy, 2 June, 1894 (Napier). E. Fries. *flügge*. **+** Du. *vlug* (M. Du. *vlugge*); O. H. G. *flucchi*. Teut. type *flugjoz*, adj.; from **flug-*, weak grade of **fleugan-*, to fly. See **Fly**.

Flee, to escape. (E.) M. E. *fleen*, pt. t. *fleh, fleih*. [The M. E. pt. t. also appears as *fledde*, whence mod. E. *fled*, of Scand. origin.] A. S. *fléon* (pt. t. *fléah*).**+**O. Sax. *fliohan*, G. *fliehen*; also Icel. *flŷja* (pt. t. *flō*, also *flŷða*); Swed. *fly* (pt. t. *flydde*); Goth. *thliuhan*. Teut. type **thleuhan-* (pt. t. *thlauh*); so that *fl* was orig. *thl*, and there was *no* orig. connexion with the verb *to fly*, which has from an early date been confused with it.

Fleece. (E.) M. E. *flees*. A. S. *fléos*, earlier *flíus*; also *flŷs*.**+**Du. *vlies*, M.H.G. *vlius*; cf. G. *fliess*; also G. *flaus*, a woollen coat, M. H. G. *vlûs*, a sheep-skin. Teut. stems **fleusi-, *fleuso-, flûso-*; possibly allied to L. *plū-ma*. See **Plume**.

Fleer, to mock. (Scand.) M. E. *flerien*. **–** Norw. *flira*, to titter, giggle; also spelt *flisa*; Dan. dial. *flire*, to jeer; Swed *flissa*, to titter.

Fleet (1), a number of ships. (E.) M. E. *flete, fleote*. A. S. *fléot*, a ship; or (collectively) a number of ships. **–** A. S. *fléotan*, to float. **+** O. Sax. *fliotan*, Du. *vlieten*, to flow; O. H. G. *fliozzan*, to float, flow, G. *fliessen*, to flow; Icel. *fljóta*, Swed. *flyta*, Dan. *flyde*. Teut. **fleutan-* (pt. t. *flaut*, pp. *flutanoz*); Idg. base **pleud*, as in Lith. *plūdis*, a float of a fishing-net. (√PLEU.) Cf. Gk. πλέειν, to sail, Skt. *plu, pru*, to swim, float, flow.

fleet (2), a creek. (E.) A. S. *fléot*, a creek, a place where water flows; *fléote*, a stream.**–**A. S. *fléotan*, to float, swim; see **Fleet** (1). Cf. O. Fries. *flét*, stream.

fleet (3), swift. (E.) Cf. A. S. *fléotig*, swift; Icel. *fljótr*, swift. From the verb; see **Fleet** (1).

fleet (4), vb., to move swiftly. (E.) From A. S. *fléotan*; see **Fleet** (1).

Flesh. (E.) M. E. *flesch*. A. S. *flǽsc*, flesh. **+** Icel. *flesk*, bacon; Dan. *flesk*, Swed. *fläsk*, bacon; Du. *vleesch*; G. *fleisch*. Teut. type **flaiskoz*, n.

Fleur-de-lis, flower of the lily. (F. – L.) O. F. *fleur de lis*. Here *lis* = Late L. *lîlius*, corrupt form of L. *lîlium*, a lily; see **Flower** and **Lily**.

Flexible. (F. – L.) M. F. *flexible*. – L. *flexibilis*, easily bent. **–** L. *flexus*, pp. of *flectere*, to bend. Der. *in-flexible*.

flection, a bending. (L.) Better *flexion*; from L. acc. *flexiōnem*, a bending. – L. *flexus*, pp. of *flectere*. So also *flex-or, flex-ure*. (Cf. F. *flexion*.)

Flick, a light blow. (E.) Imitative; cf. *flip*. E. Fries. *flik*, a flick; *flik-flakken*, to strike lightly.

Flicker, to flutter. (E.) M.E *flikeren*. **–**A. S. *flicorian*, to flutter. Imitative; a weakened form of *flacker*, frequent. of M. E. *flakken*, to flap about. Cf. A. S. *flacor*, adj., flying; G. *flackern*, to flutter. See **Flag** (1).

Flight, act of flying. (E.) A. S. *flyht*, allied to *flyge*, flight.**+**Swed. *flykt*, G. *flucht*, Du. *vlucht*. Teut. **fluhti-*; from *flug-*, weak grade of **fleugan-*, to fly. See **Fly**.

Flimsy, weak, slight. (E.) Modern; first recorded in 1702 (Kersey). Prob. imitative, and suggested by *film*; note E. Fries. *flêm, flîm*, a film; Dan. dial. *flems, flims*, a skim on milk. 'For the ending, cf. *tipsy, bumpsy*; also *limpsy*, given by Webster as a U. S. synonym of *flimsy*'; N. E. D.

Flinch. (F. – Teut. ?) XVI cent. **–** O. F. *flenchir, flainchir, flechir*, to turn aside, bend. Of unknown origin; perhaps from O. H. G. **hlencan*, answering to G. *lenken*, to turn, bend. The G. *lenken* is from O. H. G. *hlanca*, the side (Kluge); see **Flank, Flange**. ¶ The initial *fl* would then be accounted for precisely as in the case of *flank*, viz. from O. H. G. *hl*. Cf. **Link** (1).

Fling. (Scand.) Cf. Swed. *flänga*, to use violent action, romp, race about; *i fläng*, at full speed (taking one's fling); M. Swed. *flenga*, to strike; Icel. *flengja*, to whip; Dan. *flenge*, to slash; *i fleng*, indiscriminately. These forms presuppose a strong verb **flinga*, which the E. form perhaps represents.

Flint. (E.) A. S. *flint*.**+**Dan. *flint*; Swed. *flinta*. Perhaps cognate with Gk. πλίνθος, a brick. Brugm. i. §§ 575, 704.

Flip (1), vb., to fillip, jerk lightly. (E.) Of imitative origin, like *flick*. Cf. **Flap**.

Flip (2), a mixture of beer and spirit with sugar, heated. (E.) Prob. from *flip*, to beat up. Moisy (Dict. of Norman patois) spells it *phlippe*, as if from F. *Philippe*; but wrongly.

Flippant. (Scand.) *Flippant* is for

flippand, the North. M. E. pres. pt. ; *flip-pand* = prattling, saucy. Or else, the suffix *-ant* imitates the French (heraldic) suffix in *ramp-ant*, &c. Cf. prov. E. *flip*, nimble, flippant ; from the base *flip-*, as in Icel. *fleipa*, to prattle ; Swed. dial. *flepa*, to talk nonsense ; cf. Swed. dial. *flip*, the lip.

Flirt. (E.) Often written *flurt*, meaning to mock, gibe, scorn ; the oldest sense of *flirt* was to jerk lightly away. Of imitative origin ; cf. *flip*, *flick*. So also E. Fries. *flirr*, *flirt*, a light blow ; *flirtje*, a giddy girl.

Flit, to remove from place to place. (Scand.) M E. *flitten*. — Icel. *flytja*, to cause to flit ; Swed. *flytta*, to flit, remove ; Dan. *flytte* ; causal of Icel. *fljóta*, Swed. *flyta*, Dan. *flyde*, to float. See **Fleet** (1), **Float**.

Flitch, side of bacon. (E.) M E. *flicche*. A. S. *flicce*.+Icel. *flikki*, a flitch ; *flík*, a flap, tatter. Perhaps allied to G. *flick-*, a patch ; and to E. **Fleck**.

Float, to swim on a liquid surface. (E.) M. E. *floten*, *flotien*. A. S. *flotian*. +Icel. *flota*, Du. *vlotten* Teut. *flutōjan-*, wk. vb. ; from *flut-*, weak grade of *fleutan-*, to float, whence mod. E. *fleet*. See **Fleet** (1). ¶ Confused with F. *flotter* (O. F. *floter*), to float, from the same Teut. base *flut-*.

Flock (1), a company of sheep, &c. (E.) M E. *flok*. A. S. *flocc*.+Icel. *flokkr*, Dan. *flok*, Swed *flock*.

Flock (2), a lock of wool. (F. — L.) O. F. *floc*. — L. *floccus*, a lock of wool.

Floe, a flake of ice. (Dan.) Dan. *flage* ; as in *iis-flage*, an ice-floe, lit 'ice flake ' Cf. Norw. *isflak*, *isflōk*, the same. See **Flake**.

Flog, to beat. (L. ?) A late word ; and (in 1676) a cant term. Cf. *flack* ; or probably suggested by *flagellate*, q v. Cf. Low G. *flogger*, a flail, variant of G *flegel*, a flail, from Late L. *flagellum*, a flail ; see **Flail**.

Flood. (E.) A. S *flōd*, a flood ; from *flōwan*, to flow.+Du. *vloed*, Icel. *flōð*, Swed. Dan. *flod*, Goth. *flōdus*, a river, G. *fluth*. Teut. *flō-ðuz*, act of flowing. also a flood ; from Teut base *flō-* ; see **Flow**.

Floor. (E.) A.S *flōr* +Du. *vloer*, G. *flur*. Teut. *flōruz* ; cognate with W. *llawr*, Bret. *leur*. Irish *lār*. Idg. *plārus*, a floor · from *plā-*, to spread out, whence also L. *plā-nus*, plain. See **Plain**.

Floral, pertaining to flowers. (L.) L.

flōrālis, belonging to *Flōra*, goddess of flowers. — L. *flōr-*, as the stem of *flōs*, a flower ; cf. *flōrēre*, to flourish, allied to **Blow** (2) and **Bloom**.

florid. (L.) L. *flōridus*, lit. abounding with flowers ; hence, rosy. — L. *flōri-*, decl. stem of *flōs*, a flower (above).

florin, a coin. (F. — Ital. — L.) M. E. *floren* (about A. D. 1303). — O. F. *florin*, a florin. — Ital. *fiorino* (= *florino*), a coin of Florence, so called because it bore a lily, the symbol of that town. — Ital. *fiore*, a flower. — L. *flōrem*, acc. of *flōs*, a flower.

floscule. (L.) L. *flōsculus*, a little flower ; double dimin. of *flōs*.

Floss, rough silk ; as in *floss-silk*. (F. — L.) From M. F *flosche* ; Cot. has : ' *soye flosche*, sleave silke.' [So also Ital. *floscio*, Venetian *flosso*, soft, weak ; *floscia seta*, floss-silk.] An adj. formation from O. F. *flocher*, to form into ' flocks ' or tufts. — F. *floc* ; see **Flock** (2).

Flotilla. (Span. — Teut.) Span. *flo-tilla*, a little fleet ; dimin. of *flota*, a fleet, cognate with O. F. *flote*, a fleet of ships, a crowd of people. This O. F. *flote* (fem.), F. *flotte* (whence G. *flotte*) is from a Teut. source ; cf. Du. *vloot*, Icel. *floti*, a fleet, A. S *flota*, a ship. From the base *flut-* ; see **Float**. Cf. M. E. *flote*, a fleet. (Körting, § 3349.)

flotsam, goods lost in shipwreck, and floating on the waves. (Law F. — E) An A. F. law-term, formerly *flotson* (Blount). A.F. *floteson* ; O. F. *flotaison*, a flooding of fields (Godefroy). — Low L. type *flot-tātiōnem*, from *flottāre*, to float, to flood (F. *flotter*). From the Teut. base *flut-* (as above). Cf. **Jetsam**.

Flounce (1), to plunge about. (E.) Cf. Swed. dial. and M Swed. *flunsa*, to plunge. Of imitative origin.

Flounce (2), a plaited border on a dress. (F. — L. ?) Changed from M. E. *frounce*, a plait — O. F. *fronser*. *froncer*, to gather, plait, wrinkle ; *fronser le front*, to knit or wrinkle the forehead. Prob. from Late L. *frontiāre*, not found, but regularly formed from *fronti-*, decl. stem of *frons* forehead ; see **Front**. (Körting, § 3477.)

Flounder (1), to flounce about. (E or Scand.) XVI cent. Imitative. Perhaps from Norw. *flundra*, to sprawl. Cf. Du. *flodderen*, to dangle, flap, splash through mire ; Swed. *fladdra*, to flutter.

Flounder (2), a fish. (F. — Scand.)

A.F. *floundre.* – O. F. *flondre* (in Normandy). – Swed. *flundra*, Dan. *flynder*, Icel. *flyðra* ; E. Fries. *flunder.*

Flour, finer part of meal. (F. – L.) Short for ' flower of wheat.' – F. *fleur*, short for *fleur de farine*, flour; see **Flower** below (which is a doublet).

flourish, vb. (F. – L.) M. E. *florisshen* – O. F. *floriss-*, stem of pres. pt. of *florir*, to flourish. – Folk-L. *flōrīre*, for L. *flōrēre*, to blossom; cf. L. *flōrescere*, inceptive form of *flōrēre*. See **Floral.**

Flout, to mock. (F.) Prob. from M. E. *flouten*, to play the flute. Similarly, M. Du. *fluyten* (Du. *fluiten*), to play the flute, also had once the meaning 'to mock, jeer'; Oudemans. See **Flute.**

Flow, to stream. (E.) M. E. *flowen*; A. S. *flōwan*, pt. t. *flēow*; cf. Du. *vloeijen*, to flow; Icel. *flōa*, to flood. Teut. base **flō-* ; cognate with Gk. πλώειν, to float. See **Flood.**

Flower, sb. (F. – L.) M E. *flour.* – O. F. *flour* (F. *fleur*). – L. *flōrem*, acc. of *flōs*, a flower. See **Floral.**

Fluctuate, to waver. (L.) From pp. of *fluctuāre*, to float about. – L. *fluctus*, a wave. – L. *fluctus*, old pp. of *fluere*, to flow.

Flue (1), a chimney-pipe. (F. – L. ?) Of doubtful origin. [*Flue*, in Phaer's Virgil, x. 209, is prob. a misprint for *flute*.] Prob. from M. E. *fluen*, to flow, as the pipe conducts the flow of the smoke; ' To flue, *fluere*,' Cath. Angl. – F, *fluer*, ' to flow, glide;' Cot. – L. *fluere*, to flow.

Flue (2), light, floating down. (E.?) Cf. prov. E. *fluff*, flue. Perhaps a derivative of the verb **Fly** (cf. A. S. pt. t. pl. *flug-on*). We find Low G. *flog*, E. Fries. *flug, flog*, flue; cf. G. *flug*, flight.

Fluent. (L.) From stem of pres. pt. of L. *fluere*, to flow.

fluid. (F. – L.) O. F. *fluide.* – L. *fluidus*, flowing. – L. *fluere*, to flow.

Fluke (1), a fish. (E.) M. E. *floke*, *fluke*. A.S. *flōc*, a kind of plaice. + Icel. *flōki*, a kind of halibut. Lit. 'flat' fish. The base **flōc-* is the strong grade of Teut. **flac-*, as seen in G. *flach*, flat.

Fluke (2), part of an anchor. (E. ?) Also spelt *flook*. Perhaps ' the flat ' end ; and the same word as *fluke* (1). Apparently distinct from G. *flunke*, the hook of an anchor.

Flummery, a light food. (W.) W. *llymru*, *llymruwd*, flummery, sour oat-

meal boiled and jellied. Cf. W. *llymus*, sharp, tart.

Flunkey, a footman. (F. – O. H. G.) Modern. Lowl. Sc. *flunkie*, a servant in livery. Apparently from F. *flanqueur*, a scout (see *Flanker* in N. E. D.). – F. *flanquer*, ' to flank, to be at one's elbow for a help at need ; ' Cot. – F. *flanc*, side; see **Flank.**

Fluor, Fluor-spar, a mineral. (L.) The L. *fluor* (lit. a flowing) was formerly in use as a term in alchemy and chemistry. – L. *fluere*, to flow.

Flurry, hurry. (E.) Swift has *flurry*, a gust of wind. From *flurr*, to whirr (N. E. D.). Imitative ; cf. Swed. dial. *flurig*, disordered (as hair) ; *flur*, disordered hair, whim ; Norweg. *flurutt*, shaggy, disordered. And cf. E. *flutter.*

Flush (1), to inundate. (E.) Apparently of imitative origin; cf. *flush*, to fly up quickly (N. E. D.). Perhaps influenced by F. *flux*, 'a flowing, a flux ; also, a *flush* at cards;' Cot. See **Flux.** Cf *flusch*, a pool of water (G. Douglas) ; M. Du. *fluysen*, to gush or break out violently (Hexham) ; Dan. dial. *fluse*, to gush out.

Flush (2), to blush, to redden. (E.) XVIII cent. Perhaps the same as **Flush** (1), but much influenced by **Flash.** Cf. Swed. dial. *flossa*, to burn, flare ; Norweg. *flosa*, passion, vehemence. And see **Fluster.**

Flush (3), level. (E ?) This is a derived sense; it meant in full flow, abundantly full, hence, level. From **Flush** (1).

Fluster, to heat with drinking, confuse. (Scand.) Icel. *flaustra*, to be flustered ; *flaustr*, fluster, hurry; cf. E. Fries. *flöstern, flustern*, to rustle (as wind). Cf. **Flush** (2) and **Flash.**

Flute, a musical pipe. (F.) M. E. *flowte, floite.* – O. F. *flaute, fleute, flahute, flehute*, a flute (mod. F. *flûte*). Prov. *flauta.* Of uncertain origin. The *fl* may have been suggested by L *flāre*, to blow.

Flutter, to flap the wings. (E.) M. E. *floteren*, to fluctuate. A.S. *flotorian*, to float about; cf. A. S. *flot*, the sea; *flota*, a ship. – A.S. *flot-*, stem of *flot-en*, pp. of *flēotan*, to float. Cf. E. Fries. *fluttern.*

Flux. (F. – L.) O. F. *flux*, a flux. – L. *flūxum*, acc. of *flūxus*, a flowing ; from the pp. of *fluere*, to flow.

Fly (1), to float in air. (E.) M. E. *fleƷen, fliƷen.* A. S. *flēogan* ; pt. t *flēah* ; pp. *flogen.* + Du. *vliegen*, Icel. *fljūga*, Dan.

flyve, Swed. *flyga*, G. *fliegen*. Teut. type **fleugan-*. Cf. L. *plūma*, a feather. (√PLEUGH.) Not allied to **Flee. Der.** *fly*, an insect, A.S. *fléoge*, *flýge* ; G. *fliege*.

Fly (2), a vehicle. (E.) A name given to a kind of four-wheeled vehicle drawn by men at Brighton, in 1816. Called *fly-coach* in 1818 (Scott, Heart Midl. ch. 1). From *fly*, vb. See above.

Foal. (E.) M.E. *fole*, A.S. *fola.*+Du. *veulen*, Icel. *foli*, Dan. *fole*, Swed. *fåle*, Goth. *fula*, G. *fohlen*. Teut. **fulon-*. Cognate with L. *pullus*, young of an animal ; Gk. πῶλος.

Foam. (E.) M.E. *fome*. A.S. *fám.* +Prov. G. *faim* ; O.H.G. *feim*. Teut. **faimo-*. Cognate with Russ. *piena*, foam ; Skt. *phēna*, foam ; and prob. with Lat. *spūma* (for **spoima*), foam, and Lat. *pūmex*, pumice. Allied to **Spume.**

Fob, watch-pocket. (O. Low G.) An O. Low G. word, only preserved in the cognate H. G. (Prussian) *fuppe*, a pocket ; for which see Bremen Wört. i. 437.

Focus, a point where light-rays meet. (L.) L. *focus*, a hearth ; hence, a centre of fire.

Fodder, food for cattle. (E). M.E. *fodder*. A.S. *fódor*, *fóddor* ; extended form of *fóda*, food.+Du. *voeder*, Icel. *fóðr*, Dan. Swed. *foder*, G. *futter*. Teut. type **fódrom*, neut. Allied to **Food**, q. v.

Foe. (E.) M.E. *foo*. A.S. *fáh*, adj. hostile. Teut. type **faihoz*; Idg. **poiqos* (whence Irish *oech*, a foe, with loss of *p*). From the weak grade **piq-* we have Gk. πικρός, bitter, Lith. *piktas*, unkind. Brugm. i. § 646.

Fœtus ; see **Fetus.**

Fog. (E.) In several senses ; M.E. *fogge* is 'coarse grass'; hence *foggy*, mossy, boggy, murky (whence perhaps the sb. *fog*, a mist). Cf. Norw. *fogg*, long-strawed, weak, scattered grass in a moist hollow (Ross). Perhaps allied to A. S. *fúht*, damp, moist.

Foible, a weak point in character. (F.−L.) O.F. *foible*, F. *faible*, weak, feeble ; see **Feeble.**

Foil (1), to defeat. (F.−L.) M.E. *foylen*, to trample under foot.−O.F. *fouler*, to trample on, also to oppress, foil, over-charge extremely (Cot.).−Late L. *fullāre*, *folāre*, to full cloth ; see **Full** (3). **Der.** *foil*, a blunt sword, for practice in *foiling*, i. e. parrying ; *foil*, a defeat.

Foil (2), a set-off, as in setting a gem.

(F.−L.) M. F. *feuille*, a leaf, 'also the foyle of precious stones,' Cot.; Norman *foille*, fem. ; cf. Ital. *foglia*, Span. *hoja*, a leaf.−L. *folia*, pl. of *folium*, a leaf ; afterwards used as a fem. sing. See **Foliage.** Also O. F. *fueil*, *foil*, m. ; from L. *folium*.

Foin, to thrust with a sword. (F.−L.) Obsolete. Lit. 'to thrust with an eel-spear or trident.'−O. F. *foine*, *foisne*, an eel-spear.−L. *fuscina*, a trident, the weapon used by a *retiārius*, or gladiator with a net.

Foison, plenty. (F.−L.) O.F. *foison*, abundance. − Folk-L. *fūsiōnem*, for L. *fūsiōnem*, acc. of *fūsio*, a pouring out, hence profusion.−L. *fūsus*, pp. of *fundere*, to pour. See **Fuse.**

Foist, to palm or put off, to intrude surreptitiously. (Du.) XVI cent. − Du. *vuisten*, to take in the fist or hand; see N. E. D. (Low G. *vūsten*, to take in the hand); hence, to 'palm' a die, to cheat. − Du. *vuist*, fist ; see **Fist.**

Fold (1), to double together. (E.) M.E. *folden*, O. Merc. *faldan*, A. S. *fealdan* (pt. t. *féold*), to fold. − Dan. *folde*, Swed. *fålla* (=*falda*), Icel. *falda*, Goth. *falthan*, G. *falten*. Teut. type **falthan-*. Allied to Gk. δι-πλάσιος, doubled ; πλάσσειν, to form, mould. See **Plaster. Der.** *fold*, sb., a plait ; *-fold*, suffix, as in *two-fold*, &c.

Fold (2), a pen for sheep. (E.) A.S. *fald*, also *falod*, *falud*. Not connected with *fold* (1), but with Dan. *fold*, a sheep-pen ; Du. *vaalt*, a dung-pit ; Low G. *faal*. Low G. *faal.*

Foliage, a cluster of leaves. (F.−L.) Modified from M. F. *fueillage*, from M. F. *fueille*, a leaf.−L. *folia*, pl. of *folium*, a leaf ; used as fem. sing. + Gk. φύλλον, leaf. Cf. **Foil** (2).

folio. (L.) From the L. phr. *in folió*, where *folió* is the abl. of *folium*, a leaf, sheet.

Folk, a crowd of people. (E.) A.S. *folc.*+Icel. *folk*, Dan. Swed. *folk* ; Du. G. *volk.* Teut. type **folkom*, neut. ¶ Lithuan. *pulkas*, a crowd, Russ. *polk′*, an army, were probably borrowed (at an early date) from Teutonic.

Follicle, seed-vessel. (F. − L.) O.F. *follicule*, little bag.−L. *folliculus*, double dimin. of *follis*, a bag.

Follow. (E.) M.E. *folwen*. A.S. *folgian*, also *fylgan*, weak verb, to follow. +O. Fries. *folgia*, *fulia*, O. Sax. *folgōn*, Du. *volgen* ; Icel. *fylgja*, Dan. *fölge*, Swed.

folja; G. *folgen*. We also find A. S. *ful-gangan*, (pt. t. *ful-ēode*), with the same sense, but derived from A. S. *ful*, full, and *gangan*, to go; and, in like manner, O. H. G. *follegān*. Hence the orig. sense was, perhaps, 'to go in full numbers,' to go in a crowd, to accompany; and it is a derivative of Teut. **fulloz*, full. See **Full**. Cf. A.S. *fylstan*, to assist, *fultum*, assistance; also from A.S. *full*.

Folly. (F.−L.) M. E. *folye*.−O. F. *folie*, folly.−O.F. *fol*, foolish. See **Fool** (1).

Foment. (F.−L.) M. F. *fomenter*.− L. *fōmentāre*.−L. *fōmentum*, short for **fouimentum*, a warm application, lotion. −L. *fouēre*, to warm.

Fond, foolish. (E.) M. E. *fond*, more commonly *fonn-ed*, pp. of *fonnen*, to be weak, to act as a fool; from the M. E. sb. *fon*, *fonne*, a fool. The sb. answers to O. Fries. *famne*, *fomne*, Fries. *fone* (see Hettema), E. Fries. *fone*, *fōn*, a maid, girl, weakling, simpleton (see Koolman). All allied to A.S. *fǣmne*, a virgin. **Der.** *fond-le*, vb.

Font (1), basin of water. (L.) A.S. *font*.−L. *fontem*, acc. of *fons*, a fount. See **Fount**.

Font (2), **Fount,** an assortment of types. (F.−L.) F. *fonte*, a casting of metals.− F. *fondre*, to melt. See **Found** (2).

Food. (E.) M. E. *fode*. A.S. *fōda*, what one eats. The A.S. *fōd-* is the strong grade of the base **fad*, corresponding to Gk. πατ- in πατ-έεσθαι, to feed. From the Idg. root *pā-*, to feed, whence L. *pā-nis*, bread, *pā-bulum*, food, and *pā-scere*, to feed. See **Pasture**. **Der.** *fodder*; *feed*.

Fool (1), a jester. (F.−L.) M. E. *fōl*, sb. and adj. O. F. *fol* (F. *fou*), a fool.−L. *follem*, acc. of *follis*, a wind-bag; pl. *follēs*, puffed cheeks, whence the term was easily transferred to a vain or foolish person; as in Late L. *follis*, a fool. **Der.** *be-fool*.

fool (2), a dish of crushed fruit, &c. (F.−L.) From **Fool** (1); named like *trifle*. Florio has: '*Mantiglia*, a kind of clouted creame, called a *foole* or a *trifle* in English.'

fools-cap, paper so called from the water-mark on it.

Foot. (E.) M. E. *fot*, *foot*, pl. *fet*, *feet*. A.S. *fōt*, pl. *fēt*.+Du. *voet*, Icel. *fōtr*, Dan. *fod*, Swed. *fot*, Goth. *fōtus*, G. *fuss*. Teut. type **fōt* (consonant-stem), corre-sponding to Idg. type **pōd*, with the variants **ped*, **pod*. Cf. L. *pēs*, foot (gen.

ped-is); Gk. πούς (Æolic πώς), foot (gen. ποδ-ός), πεζός (=πεδγός), on foot; Skt. *pād*, a foot (gen. *pad-as*). Cf. **Fetter**, **Fetlock**, **Fetch**. Brugm. i. § 578.

Footy, paltry, mean. (E.) A variant of *foughty*, musty (N. E. D.). Orig. 'damp;' from A.S. *fūht*, damp, with suffix *-y*.+Du. *vochtig*, damp; Swed. *fuktig*, Dan. *fugtig*. Cf. G. *feucht*, O. H. G. *fūhti*, *fūht*. From a Teut. type **fūhtuz*, damp; from Teut. base **feuk*, as in Icel. *fjūka*, to drift as snow or dust, whence also Norw. *fuk*, vapour (Franck).

Fop, a coxcomb. (E.) M. E. *fop*, a fool. Cf. Du. *foppen*, to prate, cheat; *fopper*, a wag; *fopperij*, cheating (=E. *foppery*). Cf. *fob off*, to delude (Johnson).

For (1), prep. and conj. (E.) Orig. a prep. A.S. *for*, *fore*, before, for; see **Fore**.+Du. *voor*, Icel. *fyrir*, Dan. *for*, Swed. *för*, G. *für*. Cf. L. *prō*, for; Gk. πρό, before, παρά, near.

For- (2), *prefix*. (E.) *For-* has usually an intensive force, or preserves something of the sense of *from*, to which it is related. (Quite distinct from *fore-*, though ulti-mately allied to it.) A.S. *for-*; Icel. *for-*, Dan. *for-*, Swed. *för-*, Du. *ver-*, G. *ver-*, Goth. *fra-*, *fair-*, Skt. *parā-*. The Skt. *parā* is an old instrumental sing. of *para-*, far; perhaps the orig. sense was 'away' or 'forth.' **Der.** *for-bear*, *for bid*, *for-fend*, *for-go* (misspelt *fore-go*), *for-get*, *for-give*, *for-lorn*, *for-sake*, *for-swear*; see **Bear**, **Bid**, &c.

For- (3), *prefix*. (F.−L.) Only in *for-close* (misspelt *foreclose*), *for-feit*, which see.

Forage, fodder, chiefly obtained by pil-lage. (F.−Low L.−Teut.) M. E. *forage*, *fourage*.−O. F. *fourage*.−O. F. *forrer*, to forage.−O. F. *forre* (F. *feurre*), fodder.− Low L. *fōdrum*, fodder. − Teut. type **fōdrom*, fodder; see **Fodder**.

Foraminate, perforated. (L.) From L. *forāmin-*, stem of *forāmen*, a small hole.−L. *forāre*, to bore; see **Bore**.

Foray, Forray, a raid for foraging. (F.−Low L.−Teut.) *Foray*, *forray* are old Lowl. Scotch spellings, with the sense of 'foraging expedition.' Apparently coined from the M. E. *forrier*, *forreyer*, a forager. − O. F. *forrier*, a forager; from O. F. *forrer*, to forage; see **Forage**.

Forbear (1), vb. (E.) From **For-** (2) and **Bear**. A.S. *forberan*.

Forbear (2), sb., an ancestor. (E.)

M. E. *forbear* (Wallace). For *fore-be-er,* one who is before. See Fore and Be.

Forbid. (E.) From For- (2) and Bid (2). A. S. *forbēodan.*+Du. *verbieden,* Goth. *faurbiudan,* G. *verbieten.*

Force (1). strength. (F.—L.) M. E. *force, fors.*—O. F. *force.*—Late L. *fortia,* strength.—L. *forti-,* decl. stem of *fortis,* strong; O. L. *forctis.* Allied to Borough. Brugm. i. §§ 566, 756. Cf. Fort.

Force (2), to stuff fowls; see Farce.

Force (3), **Foss,** waterfall. (Scand.) Dan. *fos,* Swed. *fors,* Icel. *fors, foss,* a waterfall.

Forceps, pincers. (L.) L. *forceps,* orig. used for holding hot iron; for **formiceps* (Vaniček).— L. *formus,* hot; *capere,* to hold.

Ford. (E.) M. E. *ford*; also *forth.* A. S. *ford,* a ford, passage.+G. *furt.* Teut. type **furduz.* From Idg **por,* weak grade of √PER, to go; see Fare. Allied to L. *portus,* a harbour, O. Welsh (*p*)*rit,* Welsh *rhyd,* a ford, and to *frith*; see Frith and Pore. Brugm. ii. § 108.

Fore, in front, coming first. (E.) A.S. *fore,* for, before, prep.; *fore, foran,* before, adv.+Du. *voor,* G. *vor,* Goth. *faura* : cf. Icel. *fyrir,* Dan. *för,* Swed. *for.* Allied to Gk. πάρος, before; Skt. *puras,* before, in front, Skt. *purā,* formerly. Also to For- (1), prefix, q. v. Der. *fore-arm, -bode, -cast, -castle, -date, -father, -finger, -foot, -front, -go* (in the sense 'to go before' only), *-ground, -hand, -head, -judge, -know, -land, -lock, -man, -noon, -ordain, -part, -rank, -run, -see, -ship, -shorten, -show, -sight, -stall* (A. S. *foresteall.* sb. lit. 'a position in front'), *-taste, -tell, -thought, -token, -tooth, -top, -warn* ; all easily understood.

Foreclose, to preclude, exclude. (F.—L.) Better spelt *forclose.*—O. F. *forclos,* pp. of *forclorre,* to exclude, shut out.— O. F. *for-,* from L. *forīs,* outside; and *clorre* to shut, from L. *claudere.* See Forfeit and Close.

Forego, to relinquish; see Forgo.

Foreign. (F.—L.) The *g* is wrongly inserted. M. E. *foraine, foreyne.*—O. F. *forain,* alien, strange. — Folk-L. **forānus* : for Late L. *forāneus,* adj., from L. *forās,* out of doors, adv. with acc. pl. form, allied to L. *forēs,* doors; cf. L. *forum,* a market-place, and E. *door.*

Forejudge (1), to prejudge. From Fore and Judge.

Forejudge (2); see Forjudge.

Foremost, most in front. (E.) A double superl., the old superl. form being misunderstood. For M.E. *formest,* through secondary influence of *most.*—A.S. *formest,* by-form of the regular *fyrmest* (<**furmistoz*), through the influence of A. S. *forma,* which is cognate with Goth. *fruma,* first, Gk. πράμος, πρόμος, first. Further allied to Gk. πρό, before. Brugm. i. § 518.

Forensic, belonging to law-courts. (L.) Coined from L. *forens-is,* belonging to the forum.—L. *forum,* market-place, meeting-place; orig. a vestibule or doorway. Allied to L. *forēs,* doors, and E. *door.*

forest. (F.—L.) O. F. *forest.*—Late L. *forestis,* free space of hunting-ground; *foresta,* a wood (medieval writers oppose the *forestis,* open hunting-ground, to the *parcus,* enclosed park).—L. *forīs,* out of doors; adv. allied to L. *forēs,* doors. Der. *forest-er,* also *forster, foster.*

Forfeit, a thing forfeited or lost by misdeed. (F.—L.) M. E. *forfete*; whence *forfeten,* vb.—A. F. *forfeit,* O.F. *forfait,* a crime punishable by fine, a fine; also a pp. of O. F. *forfaire, forsfaire,* to trespass. — Late L. *forisfactum,* a trespass, fine; orig. pp. (neut.) of *forisfacere,* to trespass, lit. ' to do beyond.'—L. *forīs facere,* to do or act beyond or abroad; from *forīs,* out of doors; and *facere,* to do. See Foreclose.

Forfend, Forefend, to avert. (Hybrid; E. *and* F.) M. E. *forfenden.* An extraordinary compound of E. *for-,* prefix, with *fend,* a familiar abbreviation of *defend.* See For- (2) and Defend; also Fend, Fence.

Forge. (F.—L.) O. F. *forge,* a workshop. — Folk-L. **faurga,* for **favrega* (Schwan); for L. *fabrica,* a workshop. See Fabric. Der. *forge,* vb.

Forget. (E.) From For- (2) and Get. A. S. *forgetan* (E. E. T.), *forgitan.* +Du. *vergeten,* G. *vergessen.*

Forgive. (E.) From For (2) and Give. A.S. *forgefan.*+Du. *vergeven,* G. *vergében*; Goth. *fragiban,* to grant.

Forgo, Forego, to give up. (E.) Better *forgo.* A. S. *forgān,* to pass over. From For- (2) and Go.

Forjudge, to deprive of by a judgement. (F.—L.) O. F. *forjugier.*—Low L. *forisjudicāre.*—L. *forīs,* outside : and *iūdi-*

cāre, to judge. See **Forfeit** and **Judge**.

Fork. (L.) A. S. *forca.* — L. *furca*, a fork. Der. *bi-furcated.*

Forlorn, quite lost. (E.) M E. *forlorn.* A. S. *forloren*, pp. of *forlēosan*, to lose utterly; from *for-*, prefix, and *lēosan*, to lose; see **For-** (2) and **Lose.** So also Dan. *forloren*, Du. and G. *verloren*, similarly derived.

Form. (F. — L.) O. F. *forme.* — L. *forma*, shape. Brugm. ii. § 72. (√DHER.) ¶ O. F. *forme* also means ' a bench,' like E. *form.* Der. *form-ula.*

Former, more in front. (E.) Not early; XII cent.; a false formation, to suit M. E. *formest*, i. e. foremost; see **Foremost.** Formed by adding *-er* to the base *form-* of A. S. *form-a*, first, really a superl. form, where *-m-* is an Idg. superl. suffix. Cf. L. *pri-mus*, first.

Formic, pertaining to ants. (L.) For *formic-ic* ; from L. *formīca*, an ant.

Formidable, causing fear. (F. — L.) F. *formidable.* — L. *formīdābilis*, terrible. — L. *formīdāre*, to dread ; *formīdo*, fear.

Formula, a prescribed form. (L.) L. *formula*, dimin. of *forma*, a form. See **Form.**

Fornicate. (L.) From pp. of L. *fornicārī*, to commit lewdness, seek a brothel. — L. *fornic-*, base of *fornix*, a vault, arch, brothel. Hardly allied to **Furnace**; cf. rather L. *for-tis*, strong, and Skt. *dhṛ*, to bear, carry, support.

Forsake. (E.) M. E. *forsaken.* A. S. *forsacan*, to neglect, orig. to contend against, or oppose; from *for-*, prefix, and *sacan*, to contend, whence the E. sb. *sake.* See **For-** (2) and **Sake.** So also Swed. *försaka*, Dan. *forsage*, Du. *verzaken.*

Forsooth. (E.) M. E. *for sothe*, for a truth. A. S. *for sōðe* ; where *for* = for, and *sōðe* is dat. of *sōð*, truth ; see **Sooth.**

Forswear. (E.) From **For-** (2) and **Swear.** A. S. *forswerian.*

Fort. (F. — L.) O. F. *fort*, sb., a fort ; a peculiar use of F. *fort*, adj., strong. — L. acc. *fort-em*, from nom. *fortis*, strong. See **Force.**

fortalice, small fort. (F. — L.) O. F. *fortelesce* ; Late L. *fortalitia* ; see **Fortress** (below).

forte, loud. (Ital. — L.) Ital. *forte.* — L. acc. *fort-em*, strong (above).

fortify. (F. — L.) O. F. *fortifier*, to make strong. — L. *fortificāre.* — L. *forti-*,

decl. stem of *fortis*, strong ; *-ficāre*, for *facere*, to make.

fortitude. (F. — L.) F. *fortitude.* — L. *fortitūdo*, strength. — L. *forti-s*, strong ; with suffix *-tūdo.*

Forth, forward. (E.) M. E. *forth.* A. S. *forþ*; related to *fore*, before; see **Fore.** + Du. *voort*, from *voor*; G. *fort*, M. H. G. *vort*, from *vor*; cf. Goth. *faurthis*, further, from *faur-a*, before. Teut. type **fur-þo-* ; Idg. type **por-to-*. See **Further.**

Fortify, Fortitude; see **Fort.**

Fortnight, two weeks. (E.) M. E. *fourtenight*; also *fourten night.* — M. E. *fourten*, i. e. fourteen ; *night*, old pl., i. e. nights. A. S. *fēowertȳne niht.* So also *sennight* = *seven night.*

Fortress. (F. — L.) M. E. *fortresse.* — O. F. *forteresce, fortelesce.* — Late L. *fortalitia*, a small fort. — Late L. *fortis* (*domus*), a fort; L. *fortis*, strong. See **Fort, Fortalice.**

Fortune. (F. — L.) O. F. *fortune.* — L. *fortūna*, chance. — L. *fortū-*, allied to *forti-*, decl. stem of *fors*, chance ; orig. ' that which is brought,' or ' an event' ; from *ferre*, to bring; see **Fertile.**

fortuitous. (L.) L. *fortuit-us*, casual ; with suffix *-ous.* — L. *fortū-* (as above).

Forty; see **Four.**

Forward. (E.) M. E. *forward.* A. S. *foreweard*, adj. — A. S. *fore*, before ; *weard*, suffix ; see **Toward.** Der. *forward-s.* M. E. *forwardes*, where *-es* is the suffix of gen. case, used adverbially. And see **Further.**

Fosse. (F. — L.) F. *fosse.* — L. *fossa*, a ditch. — L. *fossa*, fem. of *fossus*, pp. of *fodere*, to dig. Brugm. i. § 166.

fossil, petrified remains obtained by digging. (F. — L.) M. F. *fossile*, ' that may be digged ;' Cot. — L. *fossilis*, dug up. — L. *foss-us*, pp. of *fodere* (above).

Fosset, a spigot ; see **Faucet.**

Foster, to nourish. (E.) A. S. *fōstrian*, vb. — A. S. *fōstor*, nourishment ; Teut. type **fōstrom*, for **fōd-trom*, neut.; allied to *fōda*, food. + Icel. *fōstr*, nursing, whence *fōstra*, to nurse ; Swed. *fostra*, Dan. *fostre*, to rear, bring up.

Fother, a load, heavy mass. (E.) A.S. *fōðer.* + M. Du. *voeder*, Du. *voer*; O. H. G. *fuodar*, G. *fuder.* Teut. type **fōþ-rom*, n. From **fōþ-*, strong grade of **faþ-*; see **Fathom.**

Foul. (E.) M. E. *foul*. A.S. *fūl.*+ Du. *vuil*, Icel. *fūll*, Dan. *fuul*, Swed. *ful*, Goth. *fuls*, G. *faul*. Teut. type **fū-loz*; cf. Icel. *fū-inn*, rotten. Akin to Putrid. (√PŪ.) Brugm. i. § 113.

foumart, a polecat. (E.) M. E. *fulmart, fulmard*; comp. of M. E. *ful*, foul (as above), and A. S. *mearð*, a marten. See **Marten.**

Found (1), to lay the foundation of. (F.−L.) M. E. *founden.* − O. F. *fonder.* − L. *fundāre*, to found. − L. *fundus*, a bottom, foundation. See **Fund.** Der. *found-ation.*

Found (2), to cast metals. (F.−L.) O. F. *fondre.* − L. *fundere*, to pour, cast metals. (√GHEU.) See **Fuse** (1). Der. *found-ry*, F. *fond-erie.*

Founder, to go to the bottom. (F.− L.) M. E. *foundren*, said of a horse falling. − O. F. *fondrer*, chiefly in comp. *afondrer* (obsolete), *effondrer*, to fall in (still in use); orig. to sink in. − F. *fond*, bottom. − L. *fundus*, bottom. See **Found** (1).

Foundling, a deserted child. (E.) M. E. *fundling*; formed with suffix *-l-ing* from A. S. *fund-*, weak grade of *findan*, to find.+Du. *vondeling*. See **Find.**

Fount (1), a spring. (F.−L.) Formed, by analogy with *mount*, from F. *font.* − L. *fontem*, acc. of *fons*, a fountain. Der. *fount-ain*, O. F. *fontaine*, Late L. *fontāna.*

Fount (2), **Font,** an assortment of types. (F.−L.) O. F. *fonte*, a casting of metals. − O.F. *fondre*, to cast. − L. *fundere*, to pour, cast metals. See **Found** (2).

Four. (E.) M. E. *feowur, fower, four*. A. S. *fēower.* + Icel. *fjórir*, Dan. *fire*, Swed. *fyra*, Du. *vier*, Goth. *fidwor*, G. *vier*; also W. *pedwar*, Gael. *ceithir*, O. Irish *cethir*, L. *quatuor*, Gk. τέτταρες, τέσσαρες, πίσυρες, Russ. *chetvero*, Lith. *keturi*, Pers. *chehār*, Skt. *chatvāras*. Idg. type,**qetwer-*. Der. *four-th*, A.S. *fēorþa*; *four-teen*, A.S. *fēowertēne*; *for-ty*, A.S. *fēowertig.*

Fowl. (E.) M. E. *foul*, A.S. *fugol*, a bird.+Du. *vogel*, Icel. *fugl*. Dan. *fugl*, Swed. *fogel*, Goth. *fugls*, G. *vogel*. Teut. type **fugloz*, masc.: prob. for **flugloz*, by dissimilation; the form *fluglas*, pl. occurs in Matt. xiii. 32 (Rushworth gloss), and cf. the adj. *flugol*, flying. From **flug-*, weak grade of Teut. **fleug-an-*, to fly. See **Fugleman** and **Fly.** Brugm. i. § 491.

Fox. (E.) A. S. *fox.* + Du. *vos*, G. *fuchs*. Teut. type **fuh-s-*, masc. We also find Icel. *fóa*, Goth. *fauhō*, fem. a vixen; Teut. type **fuhā*. A connexion with Skt. *puchchha-*, 'tail,' is doubtful. Der. *vix-en*. q. v.

foxglove. (E.) A. S. *foxes glōfa*, i. e. fox's glove; a fanciful name. Cf. Norw. *revbjölla*, a foxglove; lit. 'fox-bell.'

Foy, a parting entertainment, by or to a wayfarer. (Du.−F.) From Du. *fooi* (in Hexham, *foy*, 'a banquet given by one at parting from his friends'). − F. *foi*, lit. faith, from L. acc. *fidem*; cf. Late L. *fidēs*, in the sense of 'payment.' (So Franck.) But rather from F. *voie*, a way; L. *uia*. Cf. **Voyage.**

Fracas. (F.−Ital.−L.) F. *fracas*, a crash. − F. *fracasser*, to shatter. − Ital. *fracassare*, to break in pieces. − Ital. *fra*, prep., among, and *cassāre*, to break: (imitated from L. *interrumpere*). Ital. *fra* is from L. *infrā*, below. *Cassare* = L. *quassāre*, to shatter; see **Quash.**

Fraction. (F.−L.) F. *fraction.* − L. acc. *fractiōnem*, a breaking. − L. *fractus*, pp. of *frangere*, to break. Cognate with *break*; see **Break.**

fracture. (F.−L.) O. F. *fracture.* − L. *fractūra*, a breach. − L. *fractus*, pp. of *frangere*, to break.

Fractious, peevish. (E.; *and* F.−L.) A prov. E. word, as if from North. E. *fratch*, to squabble, chide; the same as M. E. *fracchen*, to creak as a cart. But it also occurs (in 1705) in the sense of *refractory*, being formed from *fraction*, in the sense of ' dissension,' a sense now obsolete ; see N. E. D. See **Fraction.**

Fragile. (F.−L.) F. *fragile.* − L. *fragilis*, easily broken. − L. *frag-*, base of *frangere*, to break. See **Fraction.** Doublet, *frail.*

fragment. (F.−L.) F. *fragment.* − L. *fragmentum*, a broken piece. − L. *frag-*, base of *frangere*; with suffix *-mentum.*

Fragrant. (F.−L.) F. *fragrant.* − L. *frāgrantem*, acc. of *frāgrans*, pres. pt. of *frāgrāre*, to emit an odour.

Frail. (F.−L.) M. E. *freel, freyl.* − O. F. *fraile*, brittle. − L. *fragilem*, acc. of *fragilis*; see **Fragile.**

Frame, to construct. (E.) M. E. *framien*; also *fremien*. A. S. *framian*, to be profitable, avail; cf. also *fremien, fremman*, to promote, effect, do, lit. to further. − A. S. *fram*, strong, good, lit.

forward; cf. *fram*, prep., from, away; see From. **+** Icel. *frama*, *fremja*, to further, from *framr*, adj., forward, *fram*, adv., forward, allied to *frā*, from. Cf. G. *fromm*, good. **Der.** *frame*, sb.

Frampold, quarrelsome. (Low G.) Obsolete. Also *frampald*, *frompall*. Allied to prov. E. *rantipole*, a romping child. Cf. E. Fries. *frante-pot*, *wrante-pot*, a peevish man; M. Du. *wranten*, to chide, Dan. *vrante*, to be peevish, *vranten*, peevish. Cf. also Dan. *vrampet*, warped; Low G. *wrampachtigh*, morose (Lübben); E. Fries. *franten*, *wranten*, to be cross. Note also Sc. *frample*, to disorder, and E. *frump*. The second element is prob. from E. *poll*, head.

Franc, a French coin. (F.–G.) M. E. *frank.* – O. F. *franc*; said to be short for *Francorum Rex* (on a coin of 1360). See Frank.

franchise. (F.–G.) M. E. *franchise.* – O. F. *franchise*, privileged liberty. – O. F. *franchis-*, stem of pres. pt. of *franchir*, to free. – O. F. *franc*, free; see Frank. **Der.** *dis-franchise*, *en-franchise*.

Frangible. (L.) Late L. *frangibilis*, breakable; a coined word. – L. *frangere*, to break. See Fraction.

Franion, a dissolute person. (F.–L.) O. F. *fraignant*, one who infringes (law); pres. pt. of *fraindre*, to break, hence to infringe. – L. *frangere*, to break. See Fragile.

Frank, free. (F.–Low L.–O. H. G.) O. F. *franc.* – Low L. *francus*, free; orig. a Frank. – O. H. G. *franko*, a Frank; perhaps named from a weapon; cf. A. S. *franca*, a javelin. The *Franks* were a Germanic people.

frankalmoign, the name of the tenure by which most church-lands are held. (F.–O. H. G. *and* L.–Gk.) Lit. 'free alms.' – F. *franc*, free; Anglo-F. *almoine* = O. F. *almosne*, alms. See Frank and Almoner.

frankincense. (F. – G. *and* L.) O. F. *franc encens*, pure incense; see Frank (above) and Incense.

franklin, a freeholder. (F. – G.) M. E. *frankelein.* – A. F. *fraunkelayn*, Langtoft, ii. 212; Low L. *francalānus*, *franchilānus.* – Low L. *francus*, free; see Frank (above). The suffix is possibly from O. H. G. *-linc* (= E. *-l-ing* as in *dar-ling*); precisely as in *chamberlain.*

Frantic. (F.–L.–Gk.) M.E. *frene-*

tik, shorter form *frentik.* – O. F. *frena-tique.* – L. *phrenēticus*, *phrenīticus*, mad. – Gk. φρενιτικός, mad, suffering from φρενῖτις, frenzy. See Frenzy.

Fraternal. (F.–L.) O. F. *fraternel.* – Late L. *frāternālis*, the same as L. *frāternus*, brotherly. – L. *frāter*, cognate with E. Brother.

fraternity. (F.–L.) O. F. *frater-nitee.* – L. acc. *frāternitātem*, brotherhood. – L. *frāternus*, brotherly. – L. *frāter*, brother. **Der.** *con-fraternity.*

fratricide (1), murderer of a brother. (F.–L.) O. F. *fratricide.* – L. *frātricīda*, a brother-slayer. – L. *frātri-*, stem of *frāter*, brother; *-cīda*, a slayer, from *cædere*, to kill; see Cæsura.

fratricide (2), murder of a brother. (F.–L.) O. F. *fratrecide* (Littré). – L. *frātricīdium*, the killing of a brother. – L. *frātri-*, stem of *frāter*, brother; *-cīdium*, a slaying, from *cædere*, to kill.

Fraud. (F.–L.) O. F. *fraude.* – L. *fraudem*, acc. of *fraus*, deceit, guile.

Fraught, to lade a ship. (Low G. *or* Friesic.) We now use *fraught* only as a pp. M. E. *frahten*, *fragten*, only in the pp. *fraught.* Cf. Swed. *frakta*, to fraught or freight, from *frakt*, a cargo; Dan. *fragta*, from *fragt*, a cargo; E. Fries. *fracht*, *fragt*, (1) a cargo, (2) charge for transport; also Du. *bevrachten*, from *vracht*; G. *frachten*, from *fracht*. See further under Freight.

Fray (1), an affray. (F.–L.) Short for *affray*, or *effray*, orig. 'terror,' as shewn by the use of *fray* in the sense of terror, Bruce, xv. 255. See Affray.

fray (2), to terrify. (F.–L.) Short for *affray*; see Affray.

Fray (3), to wear away by rubbing. (F.–L.) O. F. *freier* (also *froier*), to rub (Godefroy). – L. *fricāre*, to rub.

Freak (1), a whim, caprice. (E.) A quick movement; from M. E. *frek*, quick, vigorous. – A. S. *frec*, bold, rash; whence *frician*, to move briskly. **+** Icel. *frekr*, voracious; Swed. *fräck*, impudent, Dan. *fræk*, audacious; G. *frech*, saucy, O. H. G. *freh*, greedy; Goth. *faihu-friks*, covetous.

Freak (2), to streak. (E.) A coined word; to streak capriciously (Milton); from Freak (1).

Freckle, a small spot. (Scand.) We find both *frekell* and *freken* or *frakin.* – Icel. *freknur*, pl., freckles; Swed. *fräkne*, Dan. *fregne*, a freckle. Cf. Fleck.

Free. (E.) M. E. *frē*. A. S. *frēo*.+ Du. *vrij*; Goth. *freis*; G. *frei*. Teut. type **frijoz*; allied to Skt. *priya-*, beloved, agreeable; also to E. **Friend**. Orig. sense 'dear, beloved'; hence applied to those of the household who were children, not slaves; cf. L. *līberī*, free, also 'children.' **Der.** *freedom*. A. S. *frēodōm*; *free-stone*, transl. of F. *pierre franche*.

Free-booter, a rover, pirate. (Du.) Borrowed from Du. *vrijbuiter*, a free-booter, robber.— Du. *vrijbuiten*, to rob; *vrijbuit*, plunder, lit. 'free booty.' Du. *vrij* = E. *free*. And see **Booty**, p. 56.

Freeze. (E.) M. E. *fresen*. A. S. *frēosan*; pp. *froren*.+Icel. *frjōsa*, Swed. *frysa*, Dan. *fryse*, Du. *vriezen*, G. *frieren*. Teut. type **freusan-*. L. *prūrīre*, to itch, originally to burn (cf. *pruīna*, hoarfrost), Skt. *plōsha-*, a burning. Brugm. 1. § 562; ii. § 657. (√PREU.)

Freight, a cargo. (F.—O. H. G.) M. E. *freyte*; later *freyght*; an altered spelling of F. *fret*, the freight of a ship, the *gh* being inserted by (a true) connexion with *fraught*, q. v.— F. *fret*, 'the fraught or freight of a ship, also, the hire that's paid for a ship;' Cot.— O. H. G. *frēht*, 'earnings,' hire. This O. H. G. *frēht* is thought to be the same as G. *fracht*, a cargo; and *frēht* has been supposed to represent a Teut. type **fra-aihtiz*; from *fra-*, prefix (see **Fret**), and **aihtiz*>A. S. *ǣht*, acquisition (from *āgan*, to own). See **Own**.

Frenzy. (F.—L.—Gk.) M. E. *frenesye*. —O. F. *frenisie*.—L. *phrenēsis*. — Late Gk. φρένησις, for Gk. φρενῖτις, inflammation of the brain.—Gk. φρεν-, base of φρήν, midriff, heart, senses. See **Frantic**.

Frequent. (F.—L.) M. F. *frequent*. —L. *frequentem*, acc. of *frequens*, crowded, frequent; pres. part. of a lost verb **frequēre*, to cram, allied to *farcīre*, to cram; see **Farce**. Brugm. ii. § 713.

Fresco. (Ital.—O. H. G.) A painting on *fresh* plaster.—Ital. *fresco*, cool, fresh. —O. H. G. *frisc* (G. *frisch*). See below.

fresh. (E.; *and* F.—Teut.) M. E. *fresh*; also *fersh*, representing A. S. *fersc*. The form *fresh* is from O. F. *fres*, *freis* (fem. *fresche*): cf. mod. F. *frais*, fresh.— O. H. G. *frisc* (G. *frisch*), fresh. Teut. type **friskoz*. Allied to Lith. *prĕskas*, sweet, unsoured, i. e. unleavened (applied to bread); Russ. *priesnuii*, fresh.

Fret (1), to eat away. (E.) A. S. *fretan*, for Teut. **fra-etan*, to devour

entirely. + Goth. *fra-itan*, to devour entirely, from *fra-*, entirely, and *itan*, to eat; Du. *vreten*, G. *fressen* (= *ver-essen*). See **For-** (2) and **Eat**.

Fret (2), to ornament, variegate. (F.—L.; *and* E.) M. E. *fretten*, to adorn with interlaced work.—O. F. *freter*, to strengthen (as with iron), also to adorn; also spelt *ferter*.—O. F. *frete*, a ferrule (Cot.), also a *fret* (in heraldry); see **Fret** (3). ¶ Not influenced by M. E. *fretien*, A. S. *frǣtwan*, to adorn; from *frǣtwe*, ornament.

Fret (3), a kind of grating. (F.—L.) Common in heraldry.—O. F. *frete*, a ferrule; *frettes*, pl., an iron grating (Diez); *fretter*, to hoop; *frettĕ*, fretty (in heraldry). [Cf. Span. *fretes*, frets (in heraldry); allied to Ital. *ferriata*, an iron grating.]—F. *fer*, iron.—L. *ferrum*, iron.

fret (4), a stop on a musical instrument. (F.—L.) *Frets* are bars across the neck of the instrument; probably the same word as *fret* (3). See N. E. D.

Friable, easily crumbled. (F.—L.) M. F. *friable*.—L. *friābilis*. — L. *friāre*, to rub, crumble.

Friar. (F.—L.) M. E. *frere*.—O. F. *frere*, *freire*, lit. a brother.—L. *frātrem*, acc. of *frāter*, a brother. See **Brother**.

Fribble, to trifle. (W. Flem.—Du.) From W. Flem. *fribbelen*, *wribbelen*, to rub (as a thread) between finger and thumb.— Du. *wrijven*, to rub, rub away.

Fricassee, a dish of fowls cut up. (F.) F. *fricassée*, a fricassee; fem. of pp. of *fricasser*, to fricassee, also, to squander money. A fricassee is made of chickens, &c. cut up into small pieces. Of unknown origin. Some have suggested L *frigere*, to roast, or L. *fricāre*, to rub (Körting).

Friction. (F.—L.) F. *friction*.—L. acc. *frictiōnem*, a rubbing.—L. *frictus*, contr. pp. of *fricāre*, to rub; allied to *friāre*, to rub; see **Friable**.

Friday. (E.) A. S. *frīge-dæg*, translating L. *diēs Veneris*; where *frīge* is gen. of *Frīg*, the wife of Woden. Teut. type **frijā*, fem. of **frijoz*, dear, beloved, also 'free'; Skt. *priyā*, wife, loved one. See **Free**, **Friend**.

Friend. (E.) M. E. *frend*. A. S. *frēond*, orig. 'loving.' pres. pt. of *frēogan*, to love.+Icel. *frǣndi*, Dan. *frænde*, Swed. *frände*, only in the sense of 'kinsman'; also Du. *vriend*, G. *freund*; Goth. *frijōnds*, a friend, pres. pt. of *frijōn*, to love. Cf.

Skt. *prī*, to love. Allied to **Free**. Brugm. i. § 567. Der. *friend-ship*, A. S. *frēond-scipe*.

Frieze (1), a coarse woollen cloth. (F. — Du.?) M. F. *frize*, *frise*, ' frise ;' Cot. Perhaps due to *drap de friso*, i. e. cloth of Friesland ; with which Cotgrave identifies it. — Du. *Vriesland*, Friesland, *Vries*, a Frieslander, belonging to Friesland. So also *cheval de Frise*, a horse of Friesland ; whence *chevaux de Frise*, spikes to resist cavalry, a jesting term. ¶ Hence O. F. *friser*, to cover with a nap, to curl hair, to *frizz*. See Körting.

Frieze (2), part of the entablature of a column. (F.) M. F. *frize*, ' the broad and flat band that's next below the cornish [cornice], or between it and the architrave ;' Cot. Span. *friso*, a frieze ; allied to Ital. *fregio*, a fringe, lace, border, ornament. The Ital. *fregio* represents L. *Phrygium* (*opus*), Phrygian work.

Frigate. (F. — Ital.) M. F. *fregate*, ' a frigate ;' Cot. — Ital. *fregata*, a frigate. Origin uncertain.

Fright. (E.) M. E. *fryght*. O. Northumb. *fryhto*, A. S. *fyrhto*, *fyrhtu*, fright, allied to *forht*, timid. + O. Sax. *forhta*, Dan. *frygt*, Swed. *fruktan*, G. *furcht*, Goth. *faurhtei*, fright ; allied to O. Sax. *forht*, O. H. G. *foracht*, Goth. *faurhts*, fearful.

Frigid. (L.) L. *frīgidus*, cold, adj. — L. *frīgēre*, to be cold. — L. *frīgus*, cold, sb. + Gk. ῥῖγος, cold. Brugm. i. § 875.

Frill, a ruffle on a skirt. (Low G.) [*Frill*, vb., was a term in hawking ; a hawk that shivered, from feeling *chilly*, was said to *frill*. — O. F. *friller*, to shiver with cold. Hence some have deduced the sense of a hawk ruffling his feathers ; but for this there is no authority.] The sb. answers to W. Flem. *frul*, *frulle*, a wrinkled plait ; De Bo cites *frullen* as being round the bottom of a dress. Cf. also Swed. dial. *fröll*, a wrinkled or curled strip, as on a woman's cap, whence *fryllig*, wrinkled. De Bo also gives W. Flem. *frullen*, vb., to hang in pleats ; *hullen* en *frullen*, ribbons and trimmings. Hence perhaps a verbal form **fryllan*.

Fringe, a border of loose threads. (F. — L.) M. E. *fringe*. — O. F. *frenge* (Palsgrave), oldest form of F. *frange*, fringe ; the Wallachian form is *frimbie*, for **fimbrie* (by metathesis). — L. *fimbria*, fringe ; allied to *fibra*, a fibre ; see **Fibre**.

Frippery, worn-out clothes, trash.

(F. — L.) Stuff sold by a *fripier*. — M. F. *fripier*, ' a fripier, or broker, trimmer up of old garments, and a seller of them so mended ;' Cot. — O. F. *frepe* (also *ferpe*, *felpe*), frayed out fringe, old clothes. Prob. from L. *fibra*, fibre (Körting).

Frisk, to skip about. (F. — Teut.) From the adj. *frisk*, brisk. — M. F. *frisque*, ' friske, blithe, briske ;' Cot. ; O. F. *frique*. — O. H. G. *frisc*, G. *frisch*, fresh, brisk, lively ; see **Fresh**. Cf. Norm. dial. *frisquet*, frisky.

Frith (1), an enclosure, forest, wood. (E.) Obsolescent ; M. E *frith*, peace, also enclosure, park. Cf. W. *ffridd*, park, forest, which is borrowed from M. E. — A. S. *frið*, peace ; *friðu*, peace, security, asylum. Cf. Icel. *friðr*, Dan. Swed. *fred*, Du. *vrede*, G. *friede*, peace. Teut. type **frithuz* ; from **fri-*, base of **fri-joz*, free. See **Free**. ¶ The M. E. *frith* is also ' wooded country.' This is prob. a different word ; A. S. *gefyrhðe* (Birch, iii. 120).

Frith (2), **Firth**, an estuary. (Scand.) M. E. *firth*. — Icel. *fjörðr*, a firth, bay ; Dan. *fiord*, Swed. *fjärd*, the same. Allied to **Ford**. Brugm. ii. 108.

Fritillary, a plant. (L.) So named because the chequered markings on the corolla were in some way associated with a *fritillus*. — L. *fritillus*, a dice-box.

Fritter (1), a kind of pancake. (F. — L.) M. E. *frytowre*, *fritoure*. [Cf. F. *friteau*, ' a fritter,' Cot.] — O. F. *friture*, a frying, dish of fried fish. — O. F. *frit*, fried. — L. *frictus*, pp. of *frigēre*, to fry.

Fritter (2), a fragment ; Shak. (F. — L.) O. F. *freture*. — L. *fractūra*, a fracture. See **Fracture**.

fritter away, to diminish, waste. (F. L.) A derivative from *fritter* (2), a fragment ; whence *fritter*, vb., to cut up into fragments. See above.

Frivolous, trifling. (L.) From L. *frīuol-us*, silly ; with suffix *-ous*. The orig. sense seems to have been ' rubbed away ' ; hence *frīuola* meant broken potsherds, &c. — L. *friāre*, *fricāre*, to rub ; see **Friable**.

Friz, Frizz, to curl, render rough. (F. — Du.?) M. F. *friser*, ' to frizle, crispe, curle ;' Cot. [Cf. Span. *frisar*, to frizzle, raise the nap on frieze, from *frisa*, frieze.] Similarly the F. *friser* is from *frise*, *frize*, frieze ; see **Frieze** (1). Der. *frizz-le*, frequent. form, in commoner use ; cf. O. Fries. *frisle*, *fresle*, a lock of hair.

Fro. (Scand.) The Scand. form of *from.* — Icel. *frā*, Dan. *fra*, from. See **From**.

Frock. (F. — Low L.) M. E. *frok.* — O. F. *froc*; Low L. *froccus*, a monk's frock, also spelt *floccus* (Ducange). Prob. so called because woollen; see **Flock** (2). Cf. Port. *froco*, a snow-flake, from L. *floccus.* ¶ So Diez; but Brachet derives it from O. H. G. *hroch* (G. *rock*), a coat, in which the initial *h* is unoriginal.

Frog (1), an animal. (E.) M. E. *frogge.* A. S. *frogga, frocga.* Also A. S. *frox*, a frog. + Icel. *froskr*, Du. *vorsch*, G. *frosch.*

Frog (2), a substance in a horse's foot. (L. ?) It is shaped like a fork; perhaps a corruption of *fork*, q. v.; the F. name is *fourchette.* In any case, it has been conformed to **Frog** (1).

Frolic, adj., sportive. (Du.) XVI cent. Orig. an adj. — Du. *vrolijk*, frolic, merry. + G. *fröhlich*, merry. Formed with suffix -*lijk* (= E. *like*, -*ly*) from the O. Sax. *frō-* (as in *frō-līko*, adv.), O. Fries. *frō* (= G. *froh*), merry. Der. *frolic*, sb. and verb.

From, away, forth. (E.) A. S. *from*, *fram.* + Icel. *frā*, from; O. H. G. *fram*, forth; Goth. *fram*, from. Cf. also Icel. *fram*, adv. forward (Swed. *fram*, Dan. *frem*); Goth. *framis*, adv., further. Allied to **Frame**.

Frond, a branch. (L.) L. *frond-*, stem of *frōns*, a leafy branch.

Front. (F. — L.) M. E. *front*, forehead. — O. F. *front*, forehead, brow. — L. *frontem*, acc. of *frōns*, forehead, brow.

frontal, a band worn on the forehead. (F. — L.) O. F. *frontel.* — L. *frontāle*, an ornament for a horse's forehead. — L. *front-*, stem of *frōns*, forehead.

frontier. (F. — L.) O. F. *frontiere*, fem. — Late L. *frontēria, frontāria*, border-land. — L. *front-*, stem of *frōns*, front (hence, border).

frontispiece. (F. — L.) For *frontispice*; through the influence of *piece*. — F. *frontispice*, 'the frontispiece or fore-front of a house;' Cot. — Late L. *frontispicium*, a front view. — L. *fronti-*, decl. stem of *frōns*; *specere*, to see; see **Species**.

frontlet. (F. — L.) O. F. *frontel-et*, dimin. of O. F. *frontel*; see **frontal** (above).

Frore, frozen. (E.) A. S. *froren*, pp. of *frēosan*, to freeze. See **Freeze**.

frost. (E.) M. E. *frost, forst*; A. S. *forst* (for *frost*). + Du. *vorst*, Icel. Dan. Swed. G. *frost.* Teut. types *frustoz*, m.; *frustom*, n. From *frus-*, weak grade of *freusan-*, to freeze. See **Freeze**.

Froth. (Scand.) M. E. *frothe.* — Icel. *froða, frauð*, Dan. *fraade* [Swed. *fradga*], froth, foam on liquids. From the Teut. verb *freuthan-*, to froth up; as in A.S. *ā-frēoðan.*

Frounce, to wrinkle, curl, plait. (F. — L.) The older form of *flounce*; see **Flounce** (2).

Froward, perverse. (Scand. *and* E.) M. E. *froward*, commonly *fraward* (Northern). From Icel. *frā*, fro; and *ward.* Cf. A. S. *fromweard*, only in the sense 'about to depart'; but we still keep the orig. sense of from-ward, i. e. averse, perverse. (Cf. *wayward*, i. e. away-ward.) And see **Toward**.

Frown. (F. — Teut.) M. E. *frounen.* — O. F. *frongnier*, whence F. *refrogner*, to frown, look sullen. Cf. Ital. *infrigno*, frowning, Ital. dial. (Lombardic) *frignare*, to whimper, make a wry face. Of Teut. origin. From Teut. *frunjan-*, as in Swed. dial. *fryna*, Norw. *frøyna*, to make a wry face. (Körting, § 3324.)

Fructify. (F. — L.) F. *fructifier.* — L. *frūctificāre*, to make fruitful. — L. *frūcti-*, for *frūctus*, fruit; -*ficāre*, for *facere*, to make. See **fruit**.

frugal, thrifty. (F. — L.) F. *frugal.* — L. *frūgālis*, economical; lit. belonging to fruits. — L. *frūg-ī*, frugal; orig. dat. of *frux* (pl. *frūgēs*), fruit of the earth. Allied to **fruit**.

fruit. (F. — L.) M. E. *fruit.* — O. F. *fruit.* — L. *frūctum*, acc. of *frūctus*, fruit. — L. *frūctus*, pp. of *fruī*, to enjoy; allied to **Brook** (1). (√BHREUG.) Brugm. i. § 111; ii. § 532.

fruition. (F. — L.) O. F. *fruition*, enjoyment. — Late L. *fruitiōnem*, acc. of *fruitio*, enjoyment. — L. *fruit-us*, the same as *frūctus*, pp. of *fruī*, to enjoy.

frumenty, furmety, wheat boiled in milk. (F. — L.) O. F. *fromentee*, f.; 'furmenty, sodden wheat;' Cot. Lit. made with wheat; the suffix -*ee* = L. -*āta*, made with. — O. F. *froment*, wheat. — Late L. *frūmentum.* — L. *frūmentum*, corn; allied to L. *frūges*, fruit.

Frump, an ill-tempered person. (E.) Of doubtful origin; but cf. *frampold.* A *frump* formerly meant a 'sneer,' or expression of contempt. Cf. Low. Sc. *frample*, to disorder; *frumple*, to crease; *frump*, an unseemly fold: Dan. *vrampet*, warped.

Frustrate, to render vain. (L.) From pp. of L. *frustrāri*, to render vain. — L. *frustrā*, in vain; orig. abl. fem. of obsolete adj. *frūstros* (= **frūd-tros*), deceitful. Allied to **Fraud.**

Frustum, a piece of a cone or cylinder. (L.) L. *frūstum*, a piece cut off. Cf. Gk. θραῦσμα, a fragment, from θραύειν, to break in pieces. Prellwitz; Brugm. i. § 853.

Fry (1), to dress food. (F. — L.) M. E. *frien.* — O. F. *frire.* — L. *frīgere*, to roast. Cf. Gk. φρύγειν, to parch; Skt. *bhrajj*, to fry.

Fry (2), spawn of fishes. (F. — L.) A. F. *fry*; M. E. *fri*, also used in the sense of 'offspring.' — O. F. **fri*, variant of *froi* (F. *fray*), spawn; see Supp. to Godefroy; cf. O. F. *frier, froier*, to spawn. — L. *fricāre*, to rub.

Fuchsia, a flower. (G.) Named after *L. Fuchs*, German botanist, ab. 1542.

Fudge. (F.) Picard *fuche! feuche!* an interjection of contempt (Corblet).

Fuel. (F. — L.) M. E. *fewell* (Barbour). A. F. *fewaile*, O. F. *fouaille* (Low L. *foallia*), fuel. — Late L. *focālia*, pl. of *focale*, fuel. — L. *focus*, a hearth. See **Focus.**

Fugitive. (F. — L.) O. F. *fugitif.* — L. *fugitīuus*, fleeing away. — L. *fugit-um*, supine of *fugere*, to flee. + Gk. φεύγειν, to flee; Skt. *bhuj*, to bend, turn aside. Allied to **Bow** (1). **Der.** *centri-fugal*, q. v.; *febri-fuge, fever-few.*

Fugleman, the leader of a file. (G.) For *flugleman.* — G. *flügelmann*, the leader of a wing or file of men. — G. *flügel*, a wing, from *flug*, flight, from *fliegen*, to fly; *mann*, a man. See **Fly.**

Fugue, a musical composition. (F. — Ital. — L.) F. *fugue.* — Ital. *fuga*, a fugue, lit. a flight. — L. *fuga*, flight. See **Fugitive.**

Fulcrum, a point of support. (L.) L. *fulcrum*, a support. — L. *fulcīre*, to prop.

Fulfil. (E.) M. E. *fulfillen.* A. S. *fulfyllan*, to fill full, fulfil. — A. S. *ful*, full; *fyllan*, to fill. See **Full, Fill.**

Fulgent, shining. (L.) From stem of pres. pt. of L. *fulgēre*, to shine. + Gk. φλέγειν, to burn; Skt. *bhrāj*, to shine. **Der.** *ef-fulgent* (*ef-* = L. *ex*); *re-fulgent.*

Fuliginous, sooty. (L.) L. *fūlīginō-*

sus, sooty. — L. *fūlīgin-*, stem of *fūlīgo*, soot. Cf. Skt. *dhū-li-*, dust. Allied to **Fume.** Brugm. i. § 481.

Full (1), complete. (E.) A. S. *ful.* + Du. *vol*, Icel. *fullr*, Dan. *fuld* (for *full*), Swed. *full*, Goth. *fulls*, G. *voll.* Teut. type **fulloz*; Idg. type **polnos.* Cf. Lith. *pilnas*, full, filled; Russ. *polnuii*, full; O. Irish *lān* (< **plān*), full; W. *llawn*; Skt. *pūrna-*, Pers. *pur*; cf. Gk. πλήρης, L. *plēnus.* Idg. root **pol, *plē*, to fill. Brugm. i. §§ 393, 461. **Der.** *fill, fulfil, fulsome.*

Full (2), to full cloth, felt. (F. — L.) O. F. *fuler*, F. *fouler*, 'to full, or thicken cloath in a mill;' Cot. Also 'to trample on.' — Late L. *fullāre*, (1) to cleanse clothes, (2) to full. — L. *fullo*, a fuller.

fuller, a bleacher of cloth. (L.) A. S. *fullere*, a bleacher. — L. *fullo*, a fuller, bleacher. (See above.)

Fulminate, to thunder, hurl lightning. (L.) From pp. of L. *fulmināre*, to thunder. — L. *fulmin-*, for *fulmen*, a thunderbolt (= **fulg-men*). — L. *fulgēre*, to shine.

Fulsome, cloying. (E.) M. E. *fulsum*, from M. E. *ful*, full; with suffix *-sum* (= E. *-some* as in *winsome*). See **Full** (1).

Fulvous, Fulvid, tawny. (L.) From L. *fuluus*, tawny; Late L. *fuluidus*, somewhat tawny. Cf. **Yellow**; Brugm. i. § 363.

Fumble, to grope about. (Du.) XVI cent. — Du. *fommelen*, to fumble. + Swed. *fumla* (also *famla*); Dan. *famle.* Apparently *ml* is for *lm*; cf. Icel. *fálma*, to grope about, from the sb. appearing as A. S. *folm*, the palm of the hand, allied to L. *palma*; see **Palm.**

Fume. (F. — L.) O. F. *fum.* — L. *fūmum*, acc. of *fūmus*, smoke. + Skt. *dhūma-*, smoke; Gk. θυμός, spirit, anger. (√DHEU.) Allied to **Fuliginous.**

fumigate. (L.) From pp. of L. *fūmigāre*, to fumigate. — L. *fūm-*, for *fūmus*, vapour; *-igāre*, for *agere*, to drive about.

fumitory, a plant. (F. — L.) Formerly *fumiter.* — F. *fumeterre*, fumitory (for *fume de terre*). — Late L. *fūmus terræ*, smoke of the earth; so named from its abundance (and perhaps its curly appearance). Cf. G. *erdrauch*, fumitory, lit. 'earth-smoke'; W. *cwd y mwg*, lit. 'bag of smoke.'

Fun, merriment. (E.) XVIII cent. It orig. meant 'a trick'; from an obs. vb. *fun*, to cheat, hoax; prob. from M. E.

fon, fonne, a foolish person. See **Fond**. Cf. Irish *fonn*, delight, pleasure, song; Gael. *fonn*; prob. borrowed from E.

Funambulist, a rope-dancer. (Span. – L.) Formerly *funambulo*. – Span. *funambulo*, a funambulist. – L. *fūn-is*, a rope; *ambul-āre*, to walk: see **Amble**.

Function, performance, office. (F. – L.) M. F. *function* (F. *fonction*). – L. acc. *functiōnem*, performance. – L. *functus*, pp. of *fungī*, to perform, orig. to use. **+** Skt. *bhuñj*, to enjoy. Brugm. ii. § 628.

Fund, a store. (F. – L.) M. F. *fond*, 'a bottom, a merchant's stock;' Cot. – L *fundus*, bottom: cognate with E. Bottom.

fundament, base. (F. – L.) M. E. *fundement*. – O. F. *fondement*, foundation. – L. *fundāmentum*, foundation. – L. *fundāre*; see **Found** (1).

Funeral, relating to a burial. (F. – L.) O F. *funeral*. – Late L. *fūnerālis*, adj., from L. *fūner-* (for **fūnes-*), stem of *fūnus*, a burial. Der. *funere-al*, from L. *fūnere-us*, funereal.

Fungus, a spongy plant. (L.) L. *fungus*. **+** Gk. σπόγγος, a sponge; see Sponge.

Funnel. (Prov. – L.) M. E. *fonel*. Due to the Bourdeaux wine-trade. – Prov. *founil, enfounilh*. – Late L. *fundibulum* (Lewis and Short); L. *infundibulum*, a funnel. – L. *infundere*, to pour in. – L. *in*, in; *fundere*, to pour. Hence also Span. *fonil*, Port. *funil*, and even Bret. *founil*.

Fur. (F. – O. Low G.) M. E. *forre*. – O. F. *forre, fuerre*, a sheath, case, whence the vb. *forrer*, to line with fur; Chaucer translates *forree* by 'furred,' R. R. 408. [Cf. Span. *forro*, lining for clothes, Ital. *fodero*, lining, fur, scabbard.] – Goth. *fodr*, scabbard, orig. 'protection;' Icel. *fóðr*, lining; allied to G. *futter*, a case, lining, fur. **+** Skt. *pātra(m)*, a receptacle; cf. Gk. πῶμα, a cover. Brugm. i. § 174.

Furbelow, a flounce. (F.) Prov. F. *farbala*, a flounce, in the dialect of Hainault (Diez); the usual form is F. Span. Ital. Port. *falbala*, a flounce. Origin unknown.

Furbish, to polish, trim. (F. – O.H.G.) O. F. *forbiss-*, inceptive stem of *forbir*, to furbish, polish. – O. H. G. **furbjan*, M. H. G. *fürban*, to purify, clean, rub bright.

Furl, to roll up a sail. (F. – Arab.) Formerly spelt *furdle, farthel*, to roll up

in a bundle. From *fardel*, a bundle; see **Fardel**. Cf. F. *fardeler*, 'to truss, to make into fardles;' Cot. [F. *ferler*, to furl, is from E.]

Furlong, ⅛th of a mile. (E.) A. S. *furlang*, orig. a furrow-long, or the length of a furrow. – A. S. *furh*, a furrow; *lang*, long.

Furlough, leave of absence. (Du. – Scand.) Orig. *vorloffe*. – Du. *verlof*, leave, furlough; the same as Dan. *forlov*, Swed. *förlof*, leave. Cf. G. *urlaub*, furlough; Dan. *orlov*. β. As to the prefix, Du. *ver-*, Dan. *for-*, Swed. *för-*, are the same as E. *for-*; whilst Dan. *or-*, G. *ur-* = Goth. *us*, out. The syllable *lof*, leave, is shortened from *-lōf-*, the equivalent of G. *-laub-*, as seen in G. *er-laub-en*, to permit, and in A. S. *lēaf*, permission. See **Leave** (2); also **Believe**, **Lief**.

Furmety; see **Frumenty**.

Furnace, an oven. (F. – L.) M. E. *forneis*. – O. F. *fornaise*. – L. *fornācem*, acc. of *fornax*, an oven. – L. *fornus*, an oven; allied to *formus*, warm. Cf. Skt. *gharma-*, warmth, glow. See **Warm**. Brugm. i. § 146.

Furnish, to fit up, equip. (F. – O.H.G.) O. F. *furniss-*, inceptive stem of *fournir*, to furnish, of which an older spelling is *fornir*, the same word as Prov. *formir*, *fromir*. – O. H. G. *frumjan*, to provide, furnish; cf. O. H. G. *fruma*, utility, profit, gain; G. *fromm*, good. Allied to **Former**, **Frame**. And see **Veneer**.

Furrow. (E.) M. E. *forwe*. A. S. *furh*, a furrow. **+** Du. *voor*, Icel. *for*, Dan. *fure*, Swed. *fåre*; G. *furche*, a furrow. Teut. type **furh-*, f. Cf. W. *rhych*, a furrow; L. *porca*, a ridge between two furrows. Der. *fur-long*.

Further. (E.) Probably the comp. of *fore*, but also explained as comp. of *forth*. M. E. *furðer*. A. S. *furðra*, adj. m.; *furðor*, further, adv. **+** Du. *vorders*, adv., further; O. Fries. *fordera*, adj.; O. Sax. *forthora*, adj.; O. H. G. *fordar*, G. *vorder*, adj. Teut. type **furthero-* (i. e. **fur-ther-o-*) answering to Gk. πρό-τερ-ος, comp. of πρό. ¶ In this view the comp. suffix is *-ther* (Gk. -τερ-). Der. *further*, vb., A. S. *fyrðran*, formed from *furðor* by vowel-change of *u* to *y*.

furthest, a late form, made as the superl. of *forth*, and due to regarding *further* as the comp. of the same. The true superl. of *fore* is *first*.

Furtive. (F.—L.) M. F. *furtif*, fem. *furtive.*—L. *furtīuus*, stolen, secret.—L. *furtum*, theft.—L. *fūrāri*, to steal.—L. *fūr*, a thief.+Gk. φώρ, a thief, allied to φέρειν, to bear, carry (away). (√BHER.) Brugm. ii. § 160 (3).

Fury. (F.—L.) F. *furie.*—L. *furia*, rage.—L. *furere*, to rage.

Furze. (E.) M. E. *firse.* A. S. *fyrs*; older form *fyres.*

Fuscous, brown. (L.) L. *fusc-us*, brown; with suffix *-ous.*

Fuse (1), to melt by heat. (L.) A late word. Due to *fus-ible* (in Chaucer), *fus-ion*, in Sir T. Browne.—L. *fūsus*, pp. of *fundere*, to pour, melt. Allied to Gk. χέειν (for *χεϝ-ειν), Goth. *giutan*, to pour. (√GHEU.) Der. *fus-ible* (from O. F. *fusible*); *fus-ion.* See **Gush.**

Fuse (2); see **Fusee** (1).

Fusee (1) **Fuse.** (F.—L.; *or* Ital.— L.) '*Fuse, fusee*, a pipe filled with wild-fire, and put into the touch-hole of a bomb;' Kersey (1715). 1. *Fuse* is from Ital. *fuso*, a spindle, a shaft (of a column); also, a fuse.—L. *fūsus*, a spindle. 2. *Fusee* is from F. *fusée*, a fusee, i. e. a spindle-shaped pipe; see below.

fusee (2), a spindle in a watch. (F.— L.) O. F. *fusée*, orig. a spindleful of thread.—Late L. *fūsāta*, the same; fem. of pp. of *fūsāre*, to use a spindle.—L. *fūsus*, a spindle.

Fusil (1), a light musket. (F.—L.) Orig. not the musket itself, but the steel against which the flint struck. From F. *fusil*, 'a fire-steele for a tinder-box;' Cot. Also in mod. F., a fusil. [Cf. Span. *fusil*, a ball.]—L. *focīle*, a steel for kindling fire. —L. *focus*, a hearth; see **Focus.** Der. *fusil-eer, fusillade.*

Fusil (2), a spindle, in heraldry. (L.) A.F. *fusel* (see O. F. *fuisel* in Godefroy). Dimin. of L. *fūsus*, a spindle.

Fusil (3), easily molten. (L.) L. *fūsilis*, easily molten.—L. *fūsus*, pp. of *fundere*, to pour. See **Fuse** (1).

Fuss, haste, flurry. (E.) Probably of imitative origin, descriptive of spluttering and puffing. Cf. *fuff*, i. e. to puff, and *hiss.* ¶ It cannot be connected with M. E. *fūs*, adj., eager; A.S. *fūs*, eager, prompt.

Fust (1), to become mouldy. (F.—L.) In Hamlet, iv. 4. 39. Coined from *fusty* (A.D. 1398), answering to O. F. *fusté*, 'fusty, tasting of the cask,' Cot.—O. F.

fust, a cask; orig. a stock, trunk, log.— L. *fustem*, acc. of *fustis*, a cudgel.

fust (2), the shaft of a column. (F.— L.) In Kersey (1715).—O. F. *fust*, a trunk.—L. *fustem*, acc. of *fustis*, a cudgel, thick stick.

Fustian, a kind of coarse cloth. (F.— Ital.—Low L.—Egypt.) M. E. *fustane*; also *fustian*; A. F. *fustiane, fustain*; O. F. *fustaine.*—Ital. *fustagno*; Low L. *fustāneum.* — Arab. *fustāt*, a suburb of Cairo, in Egypt, whence the stuff first came. ¶ Introduced through Genoese commerce.

Fustigate, to cudgel. (L.) From pp. of L. *fustigāre*, to cudgel.—L. *fust-*, stem of *fustis*, a cudgel; *-igāre*, for *agere*, to drive, wield.

Fusty; see **Fust** (1).

Futile, vain. (F.—L.) F. *futile.*—L. *fūtilis, futtilis*, that which easily pours forth, also vain, empty, futile. From L. *fū-*, allied to *fundere*, to pour; cf. Gk. χέειν. See **Fuse** (1).

Futtocks, certain timbers in a ship. (E.) '*Futtocks*, the compassing timbers in a ship, that make the breadth of it;' Kersey (1715). Called *foot-stocks* in Florio, s. v. *stamine.* The first syllable is for *foot*; *futtocks* is thought to be for *foot-hooks*, and was so explained in 1644; *hook* referring to the bent shape of the timbers. Bailey gives the form *foot-hooks.*

Future, about to be. (F.—L.) O. F. *futur*, fem. *future.*—L. *futūrus*, about to be; fut. part. from *fu-ī*, I was; allied to Be. (√BHEU.)

Fuzzball, a spongy fungus. (E.) Cf. prov. E. *fuzzy, fozy*, light and spongy; Low G. *fussig*, loose, weak; Du. *voos*, spongy.

Fylfot, a peculiarly formed cross. (E.) Modern; and due to a mistake. MS.Lansd. 874, leaf 190, has *fylfot*, meaning a space in a painted window at the bottom, that *fills the foot.* Erroneously connected with the 'gammadion.'

G.

Gabardine, Gaberdine. (Span.— Teut.) Span. *gabardina*, a coarse frock. We also find M. E. *gawbardyne*; which is from O. F. *galvardine, gualvardine*, a loose frock. Perhaps a ' pilgrim's' frock; from M.H.G. *walfart* (G. *wallfahrt*), pilgrimage. — M. H. G. *wallen*, to wander; *fart*, travel, from *faran*, to go (E. *fare*).

Gabble, to prattle. (E.) Frequent. of *gab*, to prattle. Of imitative origin; cf. *jabber*. ¶ The M. E. *gabben*, to mock, is from O. F. *gaber*, to mock, which is also perhaps of imitative origin, or is allied to *gape*.

Gabion. (F. — Ital. — L.) F. *gabion*, a gabion, large basket filled with earth. — Ital. *gabbione*, a gabion; augment. of *gabbia*, a cage, also spelt *gaggia*, and allied to Span. *gavia*, a cage (for madmen). — L. *cauea*, a hollow place, cage, den, coop; see **Cage.**

Gable, a peak of a house-top. (F. — Scand.) M. E. *gable.* — O. F. *gable.* — Icel. *gafl*, Dan. *gavl*, Swed. *gafvel*, a gable. + A. S. *geafol*, a fork; Du. *gaffel*, a fork; G. *gabel*, a fork. Further allied to O. Irish *gabul*, a fork, gallows; W. *gafl*, the fork of the thighs. With a different gradation, we find Goth. *gibla*, pinnacle, G. *giebel*, Du. *gevel*, gable; O. H. G. *gebal*, head, Gk. κεφαλή, head (root-form **ghebh-*). See **Gaff.**

Gaby, a simpleton. (Scand.) M. Dan. *gabe*, a fool; Dan. dial. *gabenar*, a simpleton, allied to Dan. *gabe*, to gape (Dan. *nar* means 'fool'). Cf. Icel. *gapi*, a heedless man; *gapamuðr* (lit. gape-mouthed), the same; Icel. *gapa*, to gape; Norw. *gapa*, stupid.

Gad (1), a wedge of steel, goad. (Scand.) M. E. *gad*, a goad. — Icel. *gaddr*, a goad, spike, sting; cognate with Goth. *gazds*, a rod, Irish *gath*, L. *hasta*, a spear.

gad (2), to ramble idly. (Scand.) In Levins. The orig. sense was to run about. — Icel. *gadda*, to goad. — Icel. *gaddr* (above). Cf. *on the gad*, on the move.

Gaff, a light fishing-spear, a sort of boom. (F. — Teut.) A ship's *gaff* is named from the *forked* end against the mast; the fishing-spear is hooked. — O. F. *gaffe*, a gaff, iron hook. — Low G. *gaffel*, a two-pronged hay-fork; E. Fries. *gaffel*, a fork, a ship's gaff; Du. *gaffel*, a pitchfork; ship's gaff. Allied to G. *gabel*, a fork. See **Gable.**

Gaffer, an old man, grandfather. (F. — L.; *and* E.) From *gramfer*, West E. form of *grand-father.* See **Gammer.**

Gag. (E.) M. E. *gaggen*, to suffocate. Apparently of imitative origin; cf. *gaggle*, *guggle.* Also, W. *cegio*, to choke; *ceg*, the mouth.

Gage (1), a pledge. (F. — Teut.) M. E. *gage.* — F. *gage*, a pledge (Low L. *uadium*). — Teut. **wadjom*, n., a pledge; as in Goth. *wadi*, A. S. *wed*, a pledge. See **Wed**; and see **Wage.** From the same source are Ital. *gaggio*, Span. and Port. *gage*, a pledge.

Gage (2), to gauge; see **Gauge.**

Gaggle, to cackle as geese. (E.) A frequent. form from the imitative base *gag.* Cf. *cackle, gabble*; also Icel. *gagl*, a wild goose; *gagg*, the cry of a fox; Lith. *gagëti*, to gaggle.

Gaiety. (F. — Teut.) F. *gaieté.* — F. *gai*, gay. See **Gay.**

Gain (1), profit. (F. — Teut.) O. F. *gain*, F. *gagne*, from the verb below. [It partly displaced the M. E. *gain*, advantage, which was of Scand. origin; from Icel. *gagn*, gain, advantage; Swed. *gagn*, profit, Dan. *gavn.*]

gain (2), to win. (F. — Teut.) 'Yea, though he *gaine* and cram his purse with crunes;' and again, 'To get a *gaine* by any trade or kinde;' Gascoigne, Fruits of War, st. 69 and st. 66. — O. F. *gaigner*, F. *gagner*, to gain. This F. *gagner*, O. F. *gaagnier* (Ital. *guadagnare*), is from O. H. G. *weidenōn > weidenen*, to pasture, which was the orig. sense of the F. word; from O. H. G. *weida* (G. *weide*), pasture-ground. Cognate with G. *weide* are A. S. *wāð*, Icel. *veiðr*, hunting, the chase. Cf. L. *uē-nārī*, to hunt. **Der.** *regain.*

Gainly; see **Ungainly.**

Gainsay, to speak against. (Scand. *and* E.) The prefix is Icel. *gegn*, against; cf. A. S. *gegn, gēan*; see **Against.**

Gait, manner of walking. (Scand.) A particular use of M. E. *gate*, a way; see **Gate** (2). See also **Gantlet** (2).

Gaiter, a covering for the ankle. (F. — Teut.) F. *guêtre*, formerly *guestre* (Cot.). The spelling with *gu* shews the word to be Teutonic (*gu < G. w*). Origin doubtful; possibly allied to M. H. G. *wester*, a child's chrisom-cloth, lit. a covering; Goth. *wasti*, clothing; see **Vest.**

Gala. (F. — Ital. — M. H. G.) F. *gala*, borrowed from Ital. *gala*, festive attire; whence *di gala*, merrily; cf. *galante*, gay, lively. See **Gallant.**

Galaxy, the milky way. (F. — L. — Gk.) M. E. *galaxie.* — O. F. *galaxie.* — L. *galaxiam*, acc. of *galaxias.* — Gk. γαλαξίας, milky way. — Gk. γαλακ-, for γαλακτ-, stem of γάλα, milk. See **Lacteal.**

Gale (1), a strong wind. (Scand.) XVI cent. Of doubtful origin; but cf. Dan. *gal*, furious; Norweg. *ein galen storm*, a furious storm, *eit galet veer*, stormy weather. Cf. Icel. *galinn*, furious, from *gala*, to cry out. See **Yell**. Note F. *galerne*, a north-west wind.

Gale (2), the bog-myrtle. (E.) A.S. *gagel*.+Du. *gagel*.

Galeated, helmeted. (L.) L. *galeātus*. ─ L. *galea*, a helmet.

Galingale, the pungent root of a plant. (F.─Span.─Arab.─Pers.) M.E. *galingale*. ─ O.F. *galingal*, *garingal*. ─ Span. *galanga*, galingale. ─ Arab. *khalanjān*, galingale. ─ Pers. *khūlanjān*, galingale ; said to be of Chinese origin.

Galiot; see **Galliot**.

Gall (1), bile. (E.) M.E. *galle*. O.Merc. *galla*.+Du. *gal*, Icel. *gall*, Swed. *galla*, Dan. *galde* (for *galle*), G. *galle* ; L. *fel*, Gk. χολή. Allied to **Yellow**. Cf. Russ. *jelch*(*e*), gall (*j*=*zh*) ; *jeltuii*, yellow.

Gall (2), to rub a sore place. (F.─L.) M.F. *galler* ; M.F. *galle*, a galling, itching. Cf. Ital. *galla*, *gala*, ' a disease called a windgalle;' Florio. Also Late L. *galla*, a soft tumour; app. the same word as L. *galla*, a gall-nut; see below. ¶ But also partly E. ; cf. A.S. *gealla*, (1) gall, bile, (2) a gall on a horse. So also Du. *gal*. See above.

Gall (3), a gall-nut. (F.─L.) O.F. *galle* ─ L. *galla*, a gall-nut, oak-apple.

Gallant, gay, splendid, brave. (F.─ M.H.G.) O.F. *gallant*, better *galant*, with one *l*. Orig. pres. part. of O.F. *galer*, to rejoice. ─ O.F. *gale*, shows, mirth, festivity. (Cf. Ital. Span. Port. *gala*, festive attire.) Perhaps from M.H.G. *wallen*, O.H.G. *wallōn*, to go on pilgrimage.

Galleon, a large galley. (Span.) Span. *galeon*, a galleon. ─ Late L. *galea*, a galley. See **Galley**.

Gallery. (F.) M.F. *gallerie*, *galerie*, a gallery to walk in. ─ Late L. *galeria*, a long portico, gallery. Of unknown origin; possibly from Gk. κᾶλον, wood, timber (Körting). See below.

Galley, a low-built ship. (F.─Late L. ─Gk.?) M.E. *galeie*. ─ O.F. *galie* ; Late L. *galea*, a galley ; Late Gk. γαλέα, γαλαΐα. Orig. unknown. Körting suggests Gk. κᾶλον, wood, also sometimes a ship.

Galliard, a lively dance. (Span.─C.?) Span. *gallarda* (with *ll* as *ly*), a kind of

lively Spanish dance; perhaps through F.; cf. *galop gaillard*, 'the galliard;' Cot.─Span. *gallardo*, gay, lively. M.F. *gaillard* meant valiant or bold ; perhaps of Celtic origin ; cf. Bret. *galloud*, power, W. *gallad*, able, *gallu*, to be able; O. Irish *gal*, boldness (Thurneysen).

Gallias, a sort of galley. (F.─Ital.─ Late L.) O.F. *galeace*. ─ Ital. *galeazza*, a heavy galley. ─ Ital. and Late L. *galea* ; see **Galley**.

Galligaskins, large hose or trousers. (F. ─ Ital. ─ L.) Corruption of F. *garguesques*, *greguesques*, 'slops, gregs, gallogascoins, Venitians;' Cot. ─ Ital. *Grechesco*, Greekish. ─ Ital. *Greco*, a Greek. ─ L. *Græcus*, Greek. The name was given to a particular kind of hose worn at Venice.

Gallinaceous. (L.) L. *gallināce-us*, belonging to poultry ; with suffix *-ous*. ─ L. *gallīna*, a hen. ─ L. *gallus*, a cock.

Galliot, small galley. (F.─Late L.) O.F. *galiote*; Late L. *galeota*, small galley; dimin. of *galea*; see **Galley**.

Gallipot, a small glazed earthen pot. (F.) From *galley* and *pot*, as being brought over in *galleys*. So also *galley-tile* ; cf. *galy-halfpeny*, a galley-halfpenny, coin brought over by *galley-men*, who landed wines at a place called *Galley-key* (Thames Street).

Gallon. (F.) M.E. *galon*, *galun*. ─ O.F. *gallon*, *jalon*, a gallon ; orig. ' a large bowl;' augmentative form of the word which appears as mod. F. *jale*, a bowl. Orig. unknown.

Galloon. (F.─M.H.G.) F. *galon*, ' galoon-lace,' Cot. ; cf. O.F. *galoner*, to adorn the head (with ribbons, &c.). [Also Span. *galon*, galloon.] ─ O.F. *gale*, Span. *gala*, festivity ; see **Gallant**.

Gallop. (F.─Teut.) M.E. *galopen*; also spelt *walopen*. ─ O.F. *galoper*, vb.; *galop*, *walop* (Bartsch), sb. [Hence was borrowed O.H.G. *walopieren*, to gallop; so that it is not of O.H.G. origin.] The sb. seems to have been due to Low G. elements ; and meant 'Celtic running.'─ O. Sax. *Walh*, a Celt; and *hlōpan*, to run, to leap. See further under **Walnut** and **Leap**. ¶ The Norw. *vallhopp*, a gallop, is only a modern adaptation; as if 'field-hop.'

Gallow, to terrify. (E.) King Lear, iii. 2. 44. M.E. *galwen*. A.S. *gælwan*, to terrify; in comp. *āgælwan*.

Galloway, a nag, pony. (Scotland.) Named from *Galloway*, Scotland.

Gallowglas, Galloglas, a heavy-armed foot-soldier. (Irish.) Irish *gallo-glach*, a servant, a galloglas. — Irish *gall*, a foreigner, an Englishman; *oglach*, a youth, servant, soldier (from *ōg*, young, O. Ir. *ōac*, *ōc*, cognate with E. **Young**). It meant 'an English servitor,' as explained by Spenser, View of the State of Ireland, Globe ed. p. 640. (See N. and Q. 6 S. x. 145.)

Gallows. (E.) M. E. *galwes*. pl. A.S. *galga*, *gealga*, cross, gibbet; whence mod. E. *gallow*, the *s* being the pl. termination. + Icel. *gálgi*, Dan. Swed. *galge*, Du. *galg*, Goth. *galga*, a cross, G. *galgen*. Teut. type **galgon-*; cf. Lith. *žalga*, a pole (*ž = zh*).

Galoche, a kind of shoe. (F. — Late L. — Gk.) F. *galoche*, answering to a Romance type **galopia*, **calopia*; formed from **calopūs*, sing. of Late L. *calopodes*, wooden shoes; we also find Late L. *calopedia* (see Brachet), a clog, wooden shoe, and *calopodium*. — Gk. καλοπόδιον, dimin. of καλόπους, καλάπους, a shoemaker's last. — Gk. κᾶλο-ν, wood; πούς, a foot.

Galore, in plenty. (C.) Irish *goleor*, Gael. *gu leor*, *gu leoir*, sufficiently. Formed from Irish and Gael. *leor*, sufficient, by prefixing *go* or *gu*, lit. 'to,' but used to turn an adj. into an adverb.

Galt (1), **Gault**, clay and marl. (Scand.) Norweg. *gald*, hard ground, a place where ground is trodden hard; Icel. *gald*, hard-trodden snow.

Galt (2), a boar-pig. (Scand.) M. E. *galt*. — Icel. *göltr*, *galti*; Swed. Dan. *galt*, a hog. Cf. O. H. G. *galza*, a sow.

Galvanism. (Ital.) Named from *Galvani* of Bologna, Italy; about A. D. 1792.

Gambado, an E. substitution for F. *gambade*; see **Gambol**.

Gambit, an opening at chess. (F. — Ital. — L.) F. *gambit*. — Ital. *gambetto*, a tripping up. — Ital. *gamba*, the leg; see **Gambol**.

Gamble. (E.) A late word, put for *gamm-le* or *gam-le*, a frequent. form which has taken the place of M. E. *gamenen*, to play at games. — A. S. *gamenian*, to play at games; from *gamen*, a game. See **Game**.

Gamboge. (Asiatic.) A corruption of *Cambodia*, in the Annamese territory, whence it was brought after A. D. 1600.

Gambol, a frisk, caper. (F. — Ital. — L.) Formerly *gambold*, *gambauld*, *gambaud*. — M. F. *gambade*, 'a gamboll;' Cot. — Ital. *gambata*, a kick. — Ital. *gamba*, the leg; the same as F. *jambe*, O. F. *gambe*, Late L. *gamba*, a joint of the leg. Cf. Gael. and W. *cam*, crooked, answering to O. Celt. **kambos* (fem. **kambā*), crooked; Stokes-Fick, 78.

Game. (E.) M. E. *game*, also *gamen*. A. S. *gamen*, sport. + Icel. *gaman*, Dan. *gammen*, M. Swed. *gamman*, O. H. G. *gaman*, joy, mirth. See **Gammon** (2).

Gammer, an old lady, grandmother. (F. — L.; *and E.*) For *grammer*, West. E. form of *grand-mother*.

Gammon (1), the preserved thigh of a hog. (F. — L.) M. E. *gambon*. A. F. *gambon* (F. *jambon*), a gammon; from O. F. *gambe*, leg. See **Gambol**.

Gammon (2), nonsense; orig. a jest. (E.) M. E. *gamen*, a game; see **Game**. And see **Backgammon**.

Gamut. (F. — Gk.; *and* L.) Comp. of O. F. *game*, *gamme*, and *ut*. Here *gamme* represents the Gk. γάμμα (γ), because the musical scale was represented by *a*, *b*, *c*, *d*, *e*, *f*, *g*, the last being *g* = γ. *Ut* is the old name for *do*, the 1st note in singing, because it began an old hymn to St. John, '*Ut* queant laxis,' &c., used in learning singing. *Gamut* is the scale, from γ (*g*) to *ut* (*a*).

Gander. (E.) M. E. *gandre*. A.S. *gandra*, also spelt *ganra* (the *d* being, in fact, excrescent). + Du. *gander*. Cf. also Low G. *gante*, a gander (see *ganta* in Pliny). Teut. type **ganron-*, m. Allied to **Gannet** and **Goose**.

Gang (1), a crew of persons. (E.) A. S. *gang*, a going, progression; but the sense was affected by the related word *genge*, a gang.

gang (2), to go. (Scand.) Icel. *ganga* to go; cf. A. S. *gang*, a going, path course (whence E. *gang-way*); see **Go**.

Ganglion, a tumour on a tendon. (L. — Gk.) L. *ganglion*. — Gk. γάγγλιον.

Gangrene, a mortification of the flesh (F. — L. — Gk.) M. F. *gangrene*. — L. *gan græna*. — Gk. γάγγραινα, an eating sore Allied to γέρ-ων, an old man, from √γέρ, to grow old; cf. Skt. *jaras*, ol age. *jaraya*, to consume (see Prellwitz).

Gannet, solan goose, a sea-fowl. (E A. S. *ganot*. + Low G. *gante*, Du. *gent*, gander; M. H. G. *ganze*, O. H. G. *ganaz* a gander. From a base *gan-*; see Gander.

Gantlet (1); see Gauntlet.

Gantlet (2), **Gantlope**, a military punishment. (Swed.) Formerly *gantlope*; corrupted by confusion with *gauntlet*. Again, *gantlope* is a corruption of Swed. *gatlopp*, lit. 'a running down a lane;' to 'run the gantlope' is to run between two files of soldiers, who strike the offender as he passes. — Swed. *gata*, a lane, street (see Gate (2)); and *lopp*, a running, from *löpa*, to run, cognate with E. Leap.

Gaol, Jail, a cage, prison. (F. — L.) A. F. *gaole*, *geiole* (F. *geôle*), a prison, birdcage. — Late L. *gabiola*, *caveola*, a cage, dimin. of L. *cauea*, a den, cave, cage. — L. *cauus*, hollow; see Cage.

Gap. (Scand.) M. E. *gappe*. — Icel. and Swed. *gap*, a gap, abyss. — Icel. and Swed. *gapa*, to gape (below).

gape. (Scand.) M. E. *gapen.* — Icel. and Swed. *gapa*, Dan. *gabe.*+E. Fries. and Du. *gapen*, G. *gaffen.* Cf. Skt. *jabh*, *jambh*, to gape.

Gar (1), **Garfish,** a fish. (E.) A fish with slender body and pointed head. From A.S. *gār*, a spear; cf. Garlic. So also *pike*, *ged*.

Gar (2), to cause. (Scand.) Icel. *görua* (Noreen), Swed. *göra*, Dan. *gjöre*, to make, cause; lit. to make ready. — Icel. *görr*, *görr*, ready; see Yare.

garb (1), dress. (F. — O. H. G.) In Shak. — O. F. *garbe*, a garb, good fashion. — O. H. G. *garawī*, *garwī*, dress, preparation; cf. O. H. G. *garawen*, M. H. G. *garwen*, to get ready. — O. H. G. *garo*, ready; cognate with E. *yare*; see Gear.

Garb (2), a wheatsheaf, in heraldry (F. — O. H. G.) A. F. and Picard *garbe*. F. *gerbe*, a sheaf. — O. H. G. *garba* (G. *garbe*), a sheaf. Lit. 'what is grabbed' or caught up into a bundle by grasping. Cf. E. *grab*, Swed. *grabba*, to grasp; Skt. *grah*, Vedic *grabh*, to seize. Brugm. i. § 531.

garbage, refuse. (F. — O. H. G.) M. E. *garbage*, entrails of fowls. This agrees in form with O. F. *garbage*, *gerbage*, a tax paid in garbs or sheaves. Prob. similarly formed from O. F. *garbe*, in the sense of 'handful,' small bundle, a sense which occurs for Low L. *garba*.

Garble, to select for a purpose; hence, to corrupt an account. (F. — Span. — Arab.) Orig. to pick out, sort, sift out. — O. F. *gar-*

beller (see N. E. D.), the same as *grabeller*, to garble or sort out spices, orig. to sift. The same as Span. *garbillar*, Ital. *garbellare*, to garble or sift wares. — Span. *garbillo*, a coarse sieve. — Pers. *gharbīl*, Arab. *ghirbāl*, a sieve; Arab. *gharbalat*, sifting, searching. Rich. Dict. p. 1046.

Garboil, a commotion. (F.) M. F. *garbouil*, 'a garboil, hurliburly;' Cot. Cf. Span. *garbullo*, a crowd; Ital. *garbuglio*, a garboil, disorder. Of unknown origin. Prob. imitative. Florio has Ital. *garabullare*, to rave.

Garden. (F. — O. Frankish.) M. E. *gardin*. — A. F., O. North F. *gardin*, F. *jardin.* — O. Frank. *gardin*, (O. H. G. *gartin*), gen. and dat. of *gardo*, a yard, cognate with E. Yard, q. v. Cf. O. H. G. *gartin-āri*, a gardener.

Garfish; see Gar (1).

Gargle. (F. — Late L. — Gk.) Modified from F. *gargouiller*, 'to gargle;' Cot. — F. *gargouille*, the weasand of the throat, also a gargoyle, or mouth of a spout. So also Span. *gargola*, a gargoyle; Ital. *gargozza*, the gullet. From an imitative base *garg-*, as seen in L. *garg-arizāre*, to gargle, from Gk. γαργ-αρίζειν, to gargle; cf. Gk. γαργαρεών, the uvula. Hence also Ital. *gargagliare*, to murmur, *gargatta*, the throat. The parallel L. base is *gurg-*; see Gorge, Gurgle.

gargoyle, a spout. (F. — L.) F. *gargouille* (above).

Garish, staring, showy. (E.) Also formerly spelt *gaurish*. Allied to M. E. *gauren*, to stare (Chaucer). Cf. M. E. *gawen*, to stare; Icel. *gā*, to heed, mark.

Garland. (F. — Teut.?) M. E. *gerlond*. — O. F. *garlande*. Cf. Span. *guirnalda*, Ital. *ghirlanda* (whence Mod. F. *guirlande*), a garland. Prob. formed, with suffix *-ande*, from M. H. G. **wierelen*, frequentative of *wieren*, to adorn, from O. H. G. *wiara*, M. H. G. *wiere*, refined gold, fine ornament, crown. Cf. Wire.

Garlic, a plant. (E.) A. S. *gārlēac*, lit. 'spear-leek.' — A. S. *gār*, a spear; *lēac*, a leek, plant. See Gore (3) and Leek.

Garment. (F. — O. Low G.) M. E. *garnement.* — O. F. *garnement*, *garniment*, a robe (defence). — O. F. *garnir*, to protect; see Garnish.

Garner. (F. — L.) M. E. *garner.* — O. F. *gernier*, variant of *grenier*, a granary. — L. *grānārium*, a granary. — L. *grānum*, corn; see Grain.

garnet. (F. — L.) M. E. *garnet*, also spelt *granat*. — O. F. *granate*; M. F. *grenat*, ' a precious stone called a granat or garnet,' Cot.; Late L. *grānātus*. So called from its resemblance to the seeds of the pomegranate, or *mālum grānātum*, lit. seeded apple. — L. *grānum*, a grain, seed.

Garnish. (F. — O. Low G.) Also *warnish*. — O. F. *garnis-*, *warnis-*, stem of pres. pt. of *garnir*, *warnir*, to defend one-self, fortify, garnish. — O. Frank. **warnjan*; cf. O. H. G. *warnōn*, M. H. G. *warnen*, to guard against, provide one-self with; cf. O. H. G. *warna*, foresight, care. See **Warn**.

garniture. (F. — O. Low G.) F. *garniture*, garnishment. — Low L. *garnītūra*. — Low L. *garnītus*, orig. pp. of *garnīre*, to adorn, which is merely a Latinised form of O. F. *garnir* (above).

Garret. (F. — G.) M. E. *garite*. — O. F. *garite* (F. *guérite*), place of refuge, watch-tower. — O. F. *garir*, *warir*, to preserve. — O. H. G. *warjan*, to defend. Allied to **Weir**.

Garrison. (F. — O. Low G.) Confused with M. E. *garisoun*, *warisoun*, a reward; but the true form is M. E. *garnison*, *warnison*, defence, stores, supply. — O. F. *garnison*, store, supply. — O. F. *garnis-ant*, pres. pt. of *garnir*, to supply, garnish; see **Garnish**. And see **Warison**.

Garrote, Garrotte. (Span. — C.) Span. *garrote*, a cudgel, tying a rope tight, strangling by means of an iron collar. Formed, with dimin. suffix *-ote*, from Span. *garra*, a claw, talon, clutch, grasp. — Bret., W., and Corn. *gar*, the shank of the leg (Diez). See **Garter**.

Garrulous. (L.) L. *garrulus*, talkative. — L. *garrīre*, to chatter. Brugm. i. § 638.

Garter. (F. — C.) A. F. *garter*; O.F. *gartier* North of France, Hécart), spelt *jartier* in Cotgrave (F. *jarretière*). — O. F. and Norm. *garet* (F. *jarret*), the ham of the leg; a dimin. form. — Bret. *gar*, W. *gar*, shank of the leg; Celt. type **garris*.

Gas. (Du.) The Belgian chemist Van Helmont died A. D. 1644) invented two terms, *gas* and *blas*; the latter did not come into use. He tells us that *gas* was suggested by the Gk. χάος. See N. E. D.

Gasconade, boasting. (Gascony.) F. *gasconnade*, boasting; said to be a vice of Gascons; at any rate named from them.

Gash, to hack, cut deeply. (F. — Late L. — Gk.) Formerly *garsh*, *garse*. — O. F. *garser*, to scarify, pierce with a lancet. — Late L. *caraxāre*, short for *incaraxāre*, *incharaxāre*, to pierce, incise. Cf. Late L. *garsa*, scarification, by making incisions in the skin, called in Gk. ἐγχάραξις; whence the Late L. vb. was formed. See **Character**.

Gasp. (E.) M. E. *gaspen*, *gaispen*. The latter answers to Icel. *geispa*, Swed. *gäspa*, to yawn (cf. Dan. *gispe*). The former represents the cognate A. S. **gāspan* (not found). Icel. *geispa* is for **geipsa*; cf Du. *gijpen*, to gasp; A. S. *gipung*, a gaping.

Gastric, belonging to the belly. (Gk.) Coined from Gk. γαστρό-, from γαστήρ, the belly.

Gate (1), a door, hole, opening. (E.) M. E. *gate*, *yate*. A. S. *gæt*, *geat*, a gate, opening (whence M. E. *yate*); pl. *gatu* (whence M. E. *gate*). + Du. *gat*, a hole, opening, gap; O. Fries., O. Sax., Icel. *gat*, an opening.

Gate (2), a street. (Scand.) Common in the North; it also means ' a way.' — Icel. *gata*, Swed. *gata*, a way, path, street, lane; Dan. *gade*; cf. Goth. *gatwō*, G. *gasse*. Perhaps allied to **Gate** (1), and also to the vb. **Go**. β. *Gate* (1) answers to Teut. type **gatom*, n., but *gate* (2) to Teut. type **gatwōn-*, f. See **Gait** and **Gantlet** (2).

Gather. (E.) M. E. *gaderen*. A. S. *gaderian*, *gædrian*, to collect, get together. — A. S. *gader-*, together; also *gador-*, *geador*. + Du. *gaderen*, to collect, from (te\gader), together. Cf. A. S. *gæd*, a company, society (whence also A. S. *gædeling*, a comrade; *ge-gada*, a companion); Du. *gade*, a spouse, G. *gatte*, a husband; Goth. *gadiliggs*, a cousin. Perhaps allied to **Good**.

Gaud, a show, ornament. (L.) M. E. *gaude*. — L. *gaudium*, gladness, joy; hence, an ornament. — L. *gaudēre*, to rejoice (base *gāuid-*, as in *gāuīsus sum*, used as pt. t.). + Gk. γηθέειν, to rejoice; allied to γαίειν (= γαϝ-ίειν), to rejoice; γαῦρος, proud. Brugm. i. § 589; ii. § 694. Der. *gaud-y*, adj.

Gauge, Gage, to measure the content of a vessel. (F. — Low L.) Spelt *gage* in Shak. — O. North F. *gauger*, F. *jauger*, ' to gage,' Cot. — O. North F. *gauge*, F. *jauge*, ' a gage, instrument wherewith a cask is measured,' Cot.; Low L. *gaugia* (A. D. 1446). Of unknown origin.

Gaunt, thin, lean. (Scand.?) An East-Anglian word; perhaps Scand. Also spelt *gant* (1691). Cf. Norweg. *gand,* a thin stick, a tall and thin man, an overgrown stripling (Aasen); Swed. dial. *gank,* a lean, half-starved horse (Rietz). Doubtful.

Gauntlet. (F.—Scand.) O. F. *gantelet,* a double dimin. of *gant,* a glove.—O. Swed. *wante,* a glove; Dan. *vante,* a mitten, Icel. *vöttr* (stem *vantu-*), a glove. Cf. Du. *want,* a mitten (prob. borrowed from Scand.). Prob. from **Wind,** verb (Noreen); cf. G. *gewand,* a garment; Low G. *want,* cloth (Lübben).

Gauntlet; see **Gantlet** (2).

Gauze, a thin silken fabric. (F.—Palestine.) M. F. *gaze*; Span. *gasa.* Cf. Low L. *gazzātum,* gauze; *gazētum,* wine from Gaza. Said to be from *Gaza,* in Palestine, whence it was first brought.

Gavelkind, a sort of tenure. (E.) M. E. *gauelkynde*; answering to an A. S. form **gafol-cynd.* — A. S. *gafol,* tribute, payment; and *cynd,* kind, sort, condition. The A. S. *gaf-ol* (whence Low L. *gabulum*) is from Teut. **gab,* 2nd grade of **Give,** q. v.

Gavial, the crocodile of the Ganges. (F.—Hind.) F. *gavial* (a corrupt form). — Hind. *ghaṛiyāl,* a crocodile.

Gavotte, a dance. (F) M. F. *gavote,* orig. a dance of the *Gavots.* *Gavot* is a sobriquet, in Provence, of the mountaineers of the Alps (see Hatzfeld).

Gawk, Gawky, awkward. (F.—Scand.) From E. dial. *gawk-handed, gaulick-handed,* left-handed; *gawk,* clumsy. Here *gawk* is short for *gaul-ick,* where *ick* is a suffix. Of F. origin; cf. Burgund. *gôle,* numb with cold, said of the fingers. —Swed. Dan. *valen,* benumbed; whence Swed. dial. *val-händt,* Norw. *val-hendt,* having numbed hands. ¶ Prob. not from F. *gauche* (N. E. D.).

Gay. (F.—O. H. G.) O. F. *gai.* — O. H. G. *wāhi,* fine, beautiful.

Gaze. (Scand.) M. E. *gasen.* —Swed. dial. *gasa,* to gaze, stare at.

Gazelle, an animal. (F.—Span.—Arab.) Formerly *gazel.* — O. F. *gazel, gazelle.* —Span. *gacela.* —Arab. *ghazāl,* a wild goat, gazelle.

Gazette. (F.—Ital.) O. F. *gazette,* an abstract of news, issued at Venice. —Ital. *gazzetta,* a gazette; the orig. sense is either (1) a magpie, from Ital. *gazzetta,*

a magpie, dimin. of *gazza,* a magpie, whence it may have meant 'tittle-tattle'; or (2) a *very* small coin (perhaps paid for the privilege of reading the news), from Ital. *gazzetta,* a coin less than a farthing, probably from Gk. γάζα, a treasury.

Gear, dress, harness, tackle. (Scand.) M. E. *gere.* — Icel. *gervi, görvi,* gear, apparel. Cf. *görr, geyrr,* skilled, dressed, pp. of *göra,* to make. + A. S. *gearwe,* fem. pl., preparation, dress, ornament; A. S. *gearo,* ready; see **Yare.** And see **Gar** (2), **Garb** (1).

Geck, a dupe. (Du.) In Tw. Nt. v. 351.—Du. *gek,* formerly *geck,* a fool, sot; cf. G. *geck,* the same; Dan. *gjek,* fool; Icel. *gikkr,* a pert, rude person. ¶ Not to be confused with A. S. *gēac,* cuckoo; nor with *gowk*; nor with *gawky.*

Gecko, a nocturnal lizard. (Malay.) Also F. *gecko.* — Malay *gēkoq,* a gecko; so named from an imitation of its cry.

Ged, the fish called a pike. (Scand.) Icel. *gedda,* Swed *gädda,* Dan. *giedde,* a ged; allied to *gaddr,* a goad; see **Gad** (1). Named from the sharp, thin head; hence al-o called *pike.*

Gelatine. (F.—Ital.—L.) F. *gélatine,* kind of jelly. —Ital. *gelatina.* —L. *gelātus,* pp. of *gelāre,* to freeze. —L. *gelu,* frost; see **Gelid.**

Geld, to emasculate. (Scand.) M. F. *geld-en.* — Icel. *gelda,* Dan. *gilde,* Swed. *gälla* (for *gälda*); cf. Icel. *geldr,* Swed. *gall,* barren. Perhaps related to Goth. *giltha,* a sickle. Cf. **Galt** (2). **Der.** *geld-ing,* from Icel. *gelding,* the same.

Gelid, cool. (L.) L. *gelidus.* —L. *gelu,* frost. Allied to **Cool.** Brugm. i. § 481.

Gem. (F.—L.) M. E. *gemme.* —F. *gemme.* —L. *gemma,* a bud; also a gem, jewel. Brugm. i. § 413 (4).

Gemini. (L.) L. *geminī,* twins; pl. of *geminus,* double.

Gender (1), kind. (F.—L.) M. E. *gendre* (with excrescent *d*). —O. F. *genre,* kind. —L. *genere,* abl. case of *genus,* kind, kin. ¶ The unusual deriv. from the abl. case is due to the common phrases *genere nātus, hoc genere, omnī genere*; so also Ital. *genere,* kind.

gender (2), to produce. (F. — L.) M. E. *gendren.* — O. F. *gendrer* (Godefroy). — L. *generāre,* to beget.—L. *gener-,* for **genes,* stem of *genus* (above). And see **Engender.**

Genealogy. (F. — L. — Gk.) M. E.

genealogie. ─ O. F. *genealogie.* ─ L. *geneālogia.* ─ Gk. γενεαλογία, an account of a family, pedigree (1 Tim. i. 4). ─ Gk. γενεά, birth (allied to γένος, see genus); and λογία, an account, allied to λόγος (see Logic).

General, relating to a genus, common. (F. ─ L.) O. F. *general.* ─ L. *generālis,* belonging to a genus (stem *gener-,* for **genes*); see genus. Hence *general,* sb., a leader; *general-issimo,* from Ital. *generalissimo,* a supreme commander, with superl. suffix *-issimo.*

generate. (L.) From pp. of L. *generāre,* to produce. ─ L. *gener-,* decl. stem of *genus.*

generic, pertaining to a genus. (L.) Coined from L. *gener-,* decl. stem of *genus.*

generous. (F. ─ L.) O. F. *genereus,* later *généreux.* ─ L. *generōsus,* (properly) of noble birth. ─ L. *gener-,* as above.

Genesis, creation. (L. ─ Gk.) L. *genesis.* ─ Gk. γένεσις, origin, source; related to γένος, race; see genus.

Genet, an animal. (F. ─ Span. ─ Arab.) F. *genette,* 'a kind of weesell;' Cot. ─ Span. *gineta.* ─ Arab. *jarneit* (Dozy).

Genial. (F. ─ L.) O. F. *genial.* ─ L. *geniālis,* pleasant; adj. from *genius;* see genius.

Geniculate, jointed. (L.) In botany. From L. *geniculum,* a little knee, joint in a plant; double dimin. of *genū,* a knee. Allied to Knee.

Genie, a demon; see Jinn.

Genital. (F. ─ L.) O. F. *genital.* ─ L. *genitālis,* generative. ─ L. *genit-um,* supine of *gignere,* to beget.

genitive. (F. ─ L.) O. F. *genitif.* ─ L. *genetiuus,* belonging to birth, applied in grammar to a certain case of nouns. ─ L. *genitum* (above).

genius, inborn faculty. (L.) L. *genius,* the tutelar spirit of any one; also wit, lit. 'inborn nature.' Allied to genus.

Gennet; see Jennet.

Genteel. (F. ─ L.) XVI cent.; F. *gentil.* ─ L. *gentīlis,* belonging to the same clan, a gentile (afterwards applied to mean well-bred, &c.). ─ L. *genti-,* decl. stem of *gens,* a clan, tribe. Allied to genus.

Gentian, a plant. (F. ─ L.) O. F. *gentiane.* ─ L. *gentiāna;* named after *Gentius,* an Illyrian king, abt. B.C. 180.

Gentile. (F. ─ L.) O. F. *gentil.* ─ L. *gentīlis,* gentile; see Genteel.

gentle. (F. ─ L.) O. F. *gentil* (above).

gentry. (F. ─ L.) M. E. *gentrie,* high birth; shortened from M. E. *gentrise,* the same. ─ O. F. *genterise,* another form of *gentilise,* rank (= Late L. **gentīlitia*). ─ L. *gentīlis;* see Genteel.

Genuflection, Genuflexion, a bending of the knee. (F. ─ L.) M.F. *genuflexion.* ─ Late L. acc. *genūflexiōnem.* ─ L. *genū,* knee; *flex-us,* pp. of *flectere,* to bend.

Genuine. (L.) L. *genuīnus,* of the true *genus* or stock; allied to L. *genus* (below).

genus, kin. (L.) L. *genus* (gen. *generis,* for **geneses*), kin, race. + Gk. γένος, race; A.S. *cyn,* kin. See Kin. (√GEN.) Brugm. i. § 604.

Geography. (F. ─ L. ─ Gk.) M. F. *geographie.* ─ L. *geōgraphia.* ─ Gk. γεω- γραφία, lit. earth-description. ─ Gk. γεω- = γηο-, a combining form of γῆ, earth; -γραφία, description, from γράφειν, to write.

geometry. (F. ─ L. ─ Gk.) O. F. *geometrie.* ─ L. *geōmetria.* ─ Gk. γεωμετρία, land-measurement. ─ Gk. γεω- (as above); -μετρία, measurement, from μετρέω, I measure, μέτρον, a measure; see Metre.

georgic. (L. ─ Gk.) L. *geōrgicus,* relating to husbandry. ─ Gk. γεωργικός, the same. ─ Gk. γεωργία, tillage. ─ Gk. γεω- (as above); **ἔργειν* > ἔρδειν, to work. See Work.

Geranium, a plant. (L. ─ Gk.) L. *geranium,* Latinised from Gk. γεράνιον, a geranium or crane's bill (from the shape of the seed-pod). ─ Gk. γέρανος, a crane; allied to Crane.

Gerfalcon; see Gyrfalcon.

Germ, a seed. (F. ─ L.) F. *germe.* ─ L. *germen* (stem *germin-*), a sprout, germ. Der. *germin-ate* (from the stem).

german, germane, akin. (F. ─ L.) *Cousins-german* are cousins having the same grandfather. Formerly spelt *germain.* ─ M. F. *germain.* ─ L. *germānum,* acc. of *germānus,* closely akin. Allied to Germ.

Germander. (F. ─ L. ─ Gk.) F. *germandrée,* germander; O. F. *germandree, gemandree* (Godefroy, Supp.); cf. G. *gamander.* ─ Late L. *gamandria,* a popular alteration of Late Gk. χαμανδρυά, germander. ─ Gk. χαμαίδρυς, germander; lit. 'ground-tree,' i.e. low tree. ─ Gk. χαμαί, on the ground; δρῦς, tree.

Gerund, a part of a Latin verb. (L.)

L. *gerundium*, a gerund. **–** L. *gerundus*, that which is to be done or carried on ; a verbal adj. from *gerere* (pp. *ges-tus*), to carry on, perform, bring. (**√**GES.)

gestation, the carrying of the young in the womb. (F. – L.) M. F. *gestation*. **–** L. acc. *gestationem*, a carrying. **–** L. *gestātus*, pp. of *gestāre*, to carry, frequent. form of *gerere* (pp. *gest-us*), to bring.

gesticulate, to make gestures. (L.) From pp. of *gesticulārī*, to make mimic gestures. **–** L. *gesticulus*, a gesture, double dimin. of *gestus*, a gesture. **–** L. *gestus*, pp. of *gerere*.

gesture. (L.) Late L. *gestūra*, a mode of action. **–** L. *gestus*, pp. of *gerere*.

Get. (Scand.) M. E. *geten*, pt. t. *gat*, pp. *geten*. **–** Icel. *geta*, pt. t. *gat*, pp. *getinn*. **+**A. S. *-getan*, pt. t. *-gæt*, pp. *-geten*, to get, obtain ; Goth. *-gitan* ; cognate with L. *-hendere* (base *hed*), in *prehendere*, to seize ; Gk. χανδάνειν (base χαδ), to seize ; Russ. *gadate*, to conjecture. (**√**GHwED.) Der. *be-get*, *for-get*. Brugm. i. § 632.

Gewgaw, a plaything, specious trifle. (F.) Formerly *gugaw*, (perhaps) answering to M. E. *giuegoue*, Ancren Riwle, p. 196. The pron. of M. E. *giuegoue* is uncertain. Origin unknown ; prob. F. One sense of E. *gewgaw* is a Jew's harp ; cf. Burgundian *gawe*, a Jew's harp (Mignard). Cf. Swed. dial. *guva*, to blow ; Norw. *guva*, *gyva* (pt. t. *gauv*).

Geysir. (Icel.) Icel. *geysir*, lit. 'gusher.' **–** Icel. *geysa*, to gush ; allied to *gjōsa* (pt. t. *gaus*), to gush. See Gush.

Ghastly, terrible. (E.) M. E. *gastly*. Formed from M. E. *gasten*, A. S. *gǣstan*, to terrify ; allied to Goth. *usgaisjan*, to terrify. See Aghast. Allied words are *gasted*, terrified, K. Lear, ii. 1. 57 ; *gastness*, Oth. v. 1. 106. See Ghost.

Ghaut, a landing-place, quay, way down to a river ; mountain-pass. (Hind.) Hind. *ghāt*, Bengali *ghāṭ*. See Wilson.

Ghee, boiled or clarified butter. (Hind. – Skt.) Hind. *ghī*. **–** Skt. *ghṛta*, clarified butter ; orig. pp. of *ghṛ*, to sprinkle.

Gherkin, small cucumber. (Du. – Slav. – Low L. – Gk. – Pers.) Short for **agherkin*. **–** Du. *agurkje*, a gherkin (of which an older form was doubtless **agurken* (= *agurk-ken*), because M. Du. used the dimin. suffix *-ken* where mod. Du. uses *-je* ; in fact, the form *augurken* is preserved in E. Friesic.). Without the final *n*, we have Du. *agorke* (Sewel). **–**

Pol. *ogurek, ogorek, ogorka*, a cucumber ; Bohem. *okurka*. **–** M. Ital. *anguria*, a cucumber (Florio) ; Low L. *angūrius*, a water-melon. **–** Byzantine Gk. ἀγγούριον, a water-melon. **–** Pers. *angārah*, a melon, a cucumber ; Rich. Dict., p. 194.

Ghost, a spirit. (E.) M. E. *gost, goost*. A. S. *gāst*. **+** Du. *geest*, G. *geist*. Teut. type **gaistoz*. Of uncertain origin ; perhaps allied to Icel. *geisa*, to rage (like fire), and to Goth. *us-gais-jan*, to terrify. Brugm. i. § 816 (2).

Ghoul, a kind of demon. (Arab.) Pers. *ghōl*, an imaginary sylvan demon ; Arab. *ghuwal*, a demon of the woods ; from Arab. *ghawl*, attacking suddenly.

Giant. (F. – L. – Gk.) M. E. *giant, geant, geaunt*. **–** A. F. and O. F. *giant, geant*. **–** L. *gigantem*, acc. of *gigas*. **–** Gk. γίγας (stem γιγαντ-), a giant. Der. *gigant-ic*, from L. *gigant-*, stem of *gigas*.

Giaour, an infidel. (Pers.) *Giaour* is an Ital. spelling usual among the Franks of the Levant (Byron). Pers. *gawr*, an infidel, a fire-worshipper ; variant of Pers. *gabr*, a Gueber ; see Gueber.

Gibberish, unmeaning talk. (E.) The hard *g* separates it from the verb *gibber*, to gabble, which is the frequentative of *jibe*, and allied to *jabber*. Fuller has *Geberish*, and Camden *Gebrish* ; apparently in allusion to *Gebir*, an Arabian alchemist of the 8th century, and to the jargon of alchemy. But the word is imitative ; like *gibble-gabble*. See N. E. D.

Gibbet. (F.) M. E. *gibbet, gibet*. **–** O. F. *gibbet* (F. *gibet*), a gibbet. Prob. allied to O. F. *gibet*, a large stick, perhaps a dimin. of O. F. *gibe, gibbe*, a sort of stick shod with iron, an implement for stirring up earth. Or is *gib-et* a dimin. from M. Du. *wippe*, 'a gibbet,' in Hexham ?

Gibbon, a kind of ape. (F.) F. *gibbon*, in Buffon ; of unknown origin.

Gibbous, humped, swelling. (L.) From L. *gibbōsus*, humped (whence also *gibbose*). **–** L. *gibbus, gibba*, a hump, hunch ; cf. *gibbus*, bent.

Gibe, Jibe, to mock. (E.) Of imitative origin ; cf. E. Fries. *gībeln*, to mock, Du. *gijbelen*, to sneer. Note also Icel. *geipa*, to talk nonsense, Icel. *geip*, idle talk ; Norw. *geipa*, to make grimaces.

Giblets, the internal eatable parts of a fowl, removed before cooking. (F.) M. E. *gibelet*. **–** O. F. *gibelet*, which, according to Littré, answers to mod. F.

gibelotte, stewed rabbit. Of unknown origin; perhaps related to F. *gibier*, game.

Giddy. (E.) M. E. *gidi, gedy*, adj.; late A. S. *gidig*, insane, answering to earlier **gydig*, which would mean 'possessed by a god'; cf. A. S. *gyden*, a goddess. From A. S. *god*.

Gier-eagle, a kind of eagle. (Du. *and* F.) The first syllable is from Du. *gier*, a vulture; cf. G. *geier*, M. H. G. *gīr*, a vulture. Allied to G. *gier-ig*, greedy, and to E. **Yearn.**

Gift. (E.) M. E. *gift, yift.* – A. S. *gift*, a gift (rare); common in the pl. *gifta*, nuptials; E. Fries. *gift.* – A. S. *gifan*, to give. + Icel. *gipt*, Du. *gift*, G. *-gift* (in *mit-gift*, a dowry). ¶ The hard *g* is due to Scand. influence. See **Give.** Der. *gift-ed*.

Gig, a light carriage, light boat. (Scand.) In Shak., a *gig* is a boy's top. M. E. *gigge*, apparently a whirling thing, Ch. Ho. Fame, iii. 852 (whence E. *whirligig*). Prob. of Scand. origin; cf. Icel. *geiga*, to take a wrong direction, to rove at random. Cf. **Jig.** Prob. of imitative origin.

Gigantic; see **Giant.**

Giggle, to titter. (E.) Of imitative origin; cf. *gaggle.* Cf. E. Fries. *gīcheln*, Low G. *giggeln* (Danneil), G. *kichern*, to giggle.

Giglet, Giglot, a wanton woman. (E.?) Dimin. of *gigle*, a flirt, used by Cotgrave (s. v. *gadrouillette*); from M. E. *gigge*, the same, Plowm. Tale, 759. Perhaps allied to **Gig** or **Giggle.**

Gild, to overlay with gold. (E.) M. E. *gilden*. A. S. *gyldan*, to gild; cf. A. S. *gylden*, golden. Formed (with vowel-mutation from Teut. *u* (>A. S. *o*) to *y*) from *gold*, gold. See **Gold.**

Gill (1), organ of respiration in fishes. (Scand.) M. E. *gille.* – Dan. *giælle*, Swed. *gäl*, a gill; M. Dan. *gælle*, M. Swed. *gel*.

Gill (2), a ravine, chasm. (Scand.) Also *ghyll.* – Icel. *gil*, ravine; Norw. *gil*.

Gill (3), with *g* soft, a quarter of a pint. (F. – Late L.) M. E. *gille.* – O. F. *gelle*, a sort of wine-measure, Late L. *gella*; cf. Late L. *gillo*, a wine-vessel.

Gill (4), with *g* soft, a woman's name, a pitcher, ground-ivy. (L.) Short for *Gillian*, from L. *Iuliāna*, a fem. name due to L. *Iulius*; see **July.** Der. *flirt-gill* or *gill-flirt, jilt.*

Gillie, a boy, page. (C.) Gael. *gille, giolla*, Irish *giolla*, boy, lad; O. Irish *gilla*, a servant.

Gillyflower, a flower. (F. – L. – Gk.) Formerly *gilofer, geraflour*. Formed (by confusion with *flower*) from M. F. *giroflée*, 'a gilloflower;' Cot. From F. *clou de girofle*, the same. – Late L. *caryophyllum*, Latinised from Gk. καρυόφυλλον, a clove tree, lit. 'nut-leaf.' – Gk. κάρυο-ν, a nut; φύλλον, leaf.

Gimbals, a contrivance for suspending a ship's compass, to keep it horizontal. (F. – L.) Formerly *gimmals*; also called *gemmow* or *gemmow-ring*, a double ring, with two or more links. The forms *gem-mow* and *gimmal* correspond to M. F. *gemeau*, and O. F. *gemel*, a twin. – L. *gemel-lus*, a twin, a dimin. form of L. *geminus*, double.

Gimlet, Gimblet. (F. – Teut.) M.F. *gimbelet*, 'a gimlet or piercer;' Cot.; *guimbelet*, Godefroy (F. *gibelet*); Norman dial. *guinblet*. Of M. H. G. origin; formed from a base *wind-*, to turn or wind; cf. mod. G. *wendel-bohrer*, a wimble. Note also Icel. *vindla*, to wind up, *vindill*, a wisp. See **Wimble**, of which *gimlet* is the dimin.

Gimmal-ring; see **Gimbals.**

Gimp, a kind of trimming, made of twisted silk, cotton, or wool. (F. – O.H.G.) See Bailey's Dict. vol. ii., ed. 1731. Named from a resemblance to some kind of wimple. – M. F. *guimpe*, a nun's wimple; also *guimple* (see index to Cotgrave, s. v. *wimple*). – O. H. G. *wimpal*, a light robe, a fillet for the head; G. *wimpel*, a streamer; see **Wimple.** ¶ Prob. confused with F. *guipure*, a thread or silk lace. See **Gui-pure.**

Gin (1), to begin. (E.) Obsolete; often needlessly written *'gin*, as though *be-* were omitted. M. E. *ginnen*. A. S. *ginnan*, to begin, commonly *on-ginnan* (pt. t. *ongann*, pp. *ongunnen*). + Goth. *ginnan*, in the comp. *du-ginnan*, to begin. Brugm. i. § 376.

Gin (2), a trap, snare. (F. – L.) M. E. *gin*, short for M. E. *engin*, a contrivance. See **Engine.**

Gin (3), a kind of spirit. (F. – L.) Short for *geneva*, corruption of M. F. *genevre*, juniper. – L. acc. *iūniperum*; see **Juniper.**

Ginger, the root of a certain plant. (F. – L. – Gk. – Skt.) M. E. *ginger, gin-geuere* (= *gingevere*). – O. F. *gengibre* (F. *gingembre*). – Late L. *gingiber*; L. *zingiber.* – Gk. ζιγγίβερις. – Skt. *çṛñgavera*, ginger;

lit. 'horn-shaped,' from the horns on it. — Skt. *çṛṅga*, a horn ; *vera*, a body.

Gingerly, with soft steps. (F. — L.) From the adj. **ginger*, soft, delicate (with soft *g*). Apparently adapted from O. F. *genzor*, *gensor*, more delicate, comp. of *gent*, fine, delicate, noble ; orig. 'well-born.' — Folk-L. **gentum*, L. *genitum*, acc. of *genitus*, born (well-born), pp. of *gignere*, to beget. (N.E.D.)

Gingham, a kind of cotton cloth. (F. — Malay.) F. *guingan*. — Malay *ginggang*, striped cloth, gingham. — Malay and Javanese *ginggang*, striped (C. P. G. Scott).

Gingle; the same as **Jingle**.

Gipsy; the same as **Gypsy**.

Giraffe, a long-legged animal. (F. — Span. — Arab.) M. F. *giraffe* (F. *girafe*). — Span. *girafa*. — Arab. *zarāf*, *zarāfa(t)*.

Gird (1), to enclose, bind round. (E.) M. E. *gurden*, *girden*. A. S. *gyrdan*, to gird.+O. Sax. *gurdian*, Du. *gorden*, Icel. *gyrða*, to gird, Dan. *giorde*, G. *gürten*. Teut. type **gurdjan-* ; from **gurd-*, weak grade of Teut. **gerdan-* (pt. t. **gard*), to enclose ; cf. Goth. *bigairdan*, to begird. Allied to **Garth**, **Garden**, and **Yard**.

Gird (2), to jest at, jibe. (E.) A peculiar use of M. E. *girden*, *gurden*, to strike, cut. To *gird at*=to strike at, jest at ; a *gird* is a cut, sarcasm ; Tam. Shrew, v. 2. 58.

Girdle. (E.) A. S. *gyrdel*, that which girds.—A. S. *gyrdan*, to gird ; see **Gird**(1). +Du. *gordel*, Icel. *gyrðill*, Swed. *gördel*, G. *gürtel*.

Girl. (E.) M. E. *girle*, *gerle*, *gurle*, often used to mean 'a boy'; a child. Answering to an A.S. form **gyrel-*, Teut. **guril-*, a dimin. form from Teut. base **gur-*. Allied to N. Fries. *gör*, a girl ; Low G. *gör*, *göre*, a child. Cf. Swiss *gurre*, *gurrli*, a depreciatory term for a girl (Sanders, Ger. Dict.).

Giron, Gyron, in heraldry, the eighth part of a shield, made by drawing a diagonal line from the top corner to the centre, and from the centre horizontally towards the same side ; a right-angled triangle. (F. — O. H. G.) F. *giron*, a giron (Littré). — O. H. G. *gērun*, acc. of *gēro*, a lance, spear ; M. H. G. *gēre*, a gore or gusset in a garment, a triangular piece.—O. H. G. *gēr*, a spear, cognate with A. S. *gār*, a spear. See **Gore** (2). (Diez, Schade).

Girth. (Scand.) M. E. *gerth*.—Icel. *gjörð*, a girdle, girth ; *gerð*, girth round

the waist ; Dan. *giord*.+Goth. *gairda*, a girdle. Teut. type **gerdā*. See **Gird** (1).

Gist, the pith of a matter. (F. — L.) The *gist* is the point wherein the matter lies.—O. F. *gist* (mod. F. *gît*), it lies ; whence the proverb 'c'est là que *gît* le lièvre,' that is where the difficulty is, lit. 'that's where the hare lies.' From the F. verb *gesir* (now *gésir*), to lie.—L. *iacēre*, to lie. (O. F. *gist*=L. *iacet*.) See **Jet** (1).

Gittern; see **Cithern**.

Give. (Scand.) M. E. *giff* (Northern), *geuen*, *yeuen* (Southern) ; pt. t. *gaf* (N.), *yaf* (S.), pp. *gifen* (N.), *yiuen*, *youen* (S.). —Icel. *gefa*, Dan. *give*, Swed. *gifva*.+ A. S. *gifan*, pt. t. *geaf*, pp. *gifen* ; Du. *geven* ; Goth. *giban*, G. *geben*. Teut. type **geban-*, pt. t. **gab*. Cf. O. Irish *gab-im*, I give, I take.

Gizzard. (F. — L.) M. E. *giser* (the *d* being added). — O. F. *gezier*, *jugier*, *juisier* (F. *gésier*).—L. *gigērium*, only in pl. *gigēria* (Late L. *gizēria*), cooked entrails of poultry.

Glabrous, smooth. (L.) From L. *glaber*, smooth. Idg. stem **gladh-ro-* ; see **Glad**. Brugm. i. § 589.

Glacial, icy. (F. — L.) F. *glacial*.—L. *glaciālis*, icy.—L. *glaciēs*, ice.

glacier, a mountain ice-field. (F. — L.) F. *glacier* (a Savoy word). — F. *glace*, ice.— Folk-L. *glacia*, for L. *glaciēs*, ice.

glacis, smooth slope. (F. — L.) F. *glacis*.—M. F. *glacer*, to cover with ice.— F. *glace* (above).

Glad. (E.) A. S. *glæd*, shining, bright, cheerful, glad.+Du. *glad*, smooth, bright, Icel. *glaðr*, bright, glad, Dan. Swed. *glad*, G. *glatt*, smooth, polished. Cf. Russ. *gladkii*, even, smooth ; L. *glaber*, smooth ; see **Glabrous**.

Gladden, Gladen, a plant ; Iris *pseudacorus*. (L.) A. S. *glædene*; altered from L. *gladiolus*, a sword-lily. Dimin. of L. *gladius*, a sword ; see **Gladiator**.

Glade, an open space in a wood. (E.) The orig. sense was prob. an opening for light, passage through a wood ; from A.S. *glæd*, bright, shining. Cf. Swed. dial. *glad-yppen*, completely open, said of a lake whence the ice has all melted away.

Gladiator, a swordsman. (L.) L. *gladiātor*. — L. *gladius*, a sword.

Glair, the white of an egg. (F. — L.) M. E. *gleyre*. — O. F. *glaire*. — L. *clāra*, fem. of *clārus*, bright ; Late L. *clāra ouī*, the white of an egg.

Glaive, a sword. (F.—L.) A. F. *glaive,* a sword ; O. F. *glaive,* a sword, lance.—L. *gladium,* acc. of *gladius,* a sword.

Glamour; see **Gramarye.**

Glance, a swift dart of light, quick look ; as a verb, to glide off or from, to graze, to flash. (F.—L.) The sb. is from the verb. A nasalised form (influenced by M. E. *glenten,* to glance) of O. F. *glacer, glacier,* to glide, slip, glance.—F. *glace,* ice ; see **Glacial.** 2. M. E. *glenten* answers to the causal form of the strong verb *glinta,* to shine, still found in Swed. dialects (Rietz). See **Glint.**

Gland, a fleshy organ in the body, secreting fluid. (F.—L.) M. F. and F. *glande,* a gland ; O. F. *glandre.*—L. *glandula,* a gland ; dimin. of *glans* (stem *gland-*), an acorn.+Gk. βάλανος, an acorn. Brugm. i. § 665.

glanders, glandular swellings. (F.—L.) M. F. *glandres,* pl.—Lat. pl. acc. *glandulās,* swollen glands ; from L. *glans* (above).

Glare, to shine brightly. (E.) M. E. *glaren* ; cf. A. S. *glǣr,* amber. + Low G. *glaren,* to glow. Perhaps allied to **Glass.** Cf. Dan. *glar,* Icel. *gler,* glass (below).

Glass. (E.) A. S. *glæs.* + Du. *glas,* G. *glas* ; cf. Dan. *glar,* M. Swed. *glær,* Icel. *gler,* glass. Orig. sense prob. ' shining.' See above.

Glaucous, grayish blue. (L.—Gk.) L. *glauc-us* ; with suffix *-ous.*—Gk. γλαυκός, gleaming, bluish.

Glaze, to furnish with glass. (E.) M. E. *glasen.*—M. E. *glas,* glass ; see **Glass.**

Gleam, a beam of light. (E.) A. S. *glǣm* ; Teut. type **glaimiz.* + O. Sax. *glīmo,* brightness ; O. H. G. *glīmo, gleimo,* a glow-worm (from base **gleim-*). Allied to Gk. χλι-αρός, warm. See **Glimmer.**

Glean. (F.) M. E. *glenen.*—O. F. *glener, glaner* (F. *glaner*), to glean ; Low L. *glenāre* (A. D. 561) ; cf. Low L. *glena, gelina, gelima,* a handful. Of unknown origin. The A. S. *gilm,* a handful, whence prov. E. *yelm,* to provide handfuls of straw ready for a thatcher, will not account for the O. F. form. ¶ We also find the form to *gleame* (Levins), also spelt *gleme.*

Glebe, soil. (F.—L.) M. F. *glebe,* ' glebe, land belonging to a parsonage ; ' Cot.—L. *glēba,* soil, a clod of earth.

Glede (1), a kite, a bird so called. (E.)

M. E. *glede.* A. S. *glida,* a kite, lit. ' glider,' from its smooth flight.—A. S. *glid-,* weak grade of *glīdan,* to glide ; see **Glide.** Cf. Icel. *gleða* (the same).

Glede (2), **Gleed,** a glowing coal. (E.) A. S. *glēd* (where *ē* is from *ō,* by vowel-change).—A. S. *glōwan,* to glow ; see **Glow.** Cf. Dan. Swed. *glöd,* the same.

Glee, joy, singing. (E.) A. S. *glēo,* earlier *glīu,* joy, mirth, music. + Icel. *glȳ,* glee, gladness ; Swed. dial. *gly,* mockery. Cf. Gk. χλεύη, a jest. Brugm. i. § 633.

Gleek (1), a scoff, jest. See Nares. Prob. a particular use of **Gleek** (2).

Gleek (2), a game at cards ; in which a *gleek* meant three cards *alike* (as three kings). (F.—Du.) See Nares.—O. F. *glic,* a game at cards ; also spelt *ghelicque* (Godefroy).—M. Du. *gelijck,* alike.—M. Du. *ge-, ghe-,* Du. *ge-,* prefix (=A. S. *ge-,* Goth. *ga-*) ; M. Du. *-lijck,* Du. *-lijk,* cognate with E. *like* ; see **Like.** ¶ Hexham has *gelijk ofte ongelijk spelen,* to play at even or odds.

Glen, a narrow valley. (C.) Gael. and Irish *gleann,* O. Irish *glenn* ; W. *glyn,* a valley, glen. Celtic type **glennos.*

Glib (1), smooth, voluble. (E.) Cf. E. Fries. *glibberig,* slippery ; *glippen,* to slip.+Du. *glibberig,* slippery, *glibberen,* to slide ; Du. and Low G. *glippen,* to slip away.

Glib (2), a lock of hair. (C.) Irish and Gael. *glib,* also Ir. *clib,* a lock of hair.

Glib (3), to castrate. (E.) The same as *lib,* with prefixed *g-*=A. S. *ge-,* a common prefix. Cognate with Du. *lubben,* to castrate, M. Du. *lubben.* See **Left.**

Glide. (E.) M. E. *gliden,* pt. t. *glood.* A. S. *glīdan.* + Du. *glijden,* Dan. *glide,* Swed. *glida,* G. *gleiten.* Teut. type **gleidan-,* pt. t. **glaid,* pp. **glidanoz.*

Glimmer, verb. (E.) M. E. *glimeren.* + Low G. *glimmern,* frequent. of *glimmen,* to shine ; Dan. *glimre,* vb., cf. *glimmer,* sb., glitter ; Swed. dial. *glimmer,* vb., *glimmer,* sb., glitter. Frequent. of Dan. *glimme,* Swed. *glimma,* to shine. Cf. Swed. dial. *glim,* a glance, A. S. *gleomu* (for **glimu*), splendour ; from **glim-,* weak grade of **gleim-* ; see **Gleam.**

glimpse, a slight gleam. (E.) Formerly *glimse* ; M. E. *glimsen,* to glimpse ; formed with suffix *-s-* from **glim* (above).

Glint, to shine, glance. (Scand.) M. E. *glenten.*—Swed. dial. *glänta, glinta,* to shine ; nasalised from Icel. *glita,* to shine.

+M.H.G. *glinzen*, to glint, Swed. *glindra*. See Glitter.

Glisten, Glister, to glitter. (E.) Extended from base *glis-* of M. E. *glisien*, to shine. A. S. *glisian*; whence also *glisnian*, to shine. We also find M. E. *glisteren, glistren*, to glitter. Cf. Du. *glinsteren*, to glitter; Swed. dial. *glisa*.

Glitter. (E.) M. E. *gliteren*, to shine. A. S. *glitinian*, to shine; extended from A. S. *glitian*, to shine. **+**Icel. *glitra*, to glitter, frequent. of *glita*, to shine; Swed. *glittra*, to glitter; *glitter*, sb., a sparkle. Cf. Goth. *glit-munjan*, to glitter. From **glit-*, weak grade of **gleit-*, as in O. Sax. *glitan*, G. *gleissen*, to shine.

Gloaming, twilight. (E.) A Scot. word for even-glow, the time of becoming dusk; A. S. *æfen-glommung*, glow of eve, Hymn. Surtees, 16. 16. See Glow.

Gloat, to stare, gaze with admiration. (E.) Formerly *glote* (XVI cent.). **+** Icel. *glotta*, to grin, smile scornfully; Swed. dial. *glotta, glutta*, to peep; G. *glotzen*, to stare. Cf. Russ. *gliadiet(e)*, to look at.

Globe. (F.–L.) O. F. *globe*. – L. *globum*, acc. of *globus*, a ball; cf. *glomus*, a ball, clue.

Glomerate. (L.) From pp. of *glomerāre*, to collect into a ball. – L. *glomer-*, for **glomes*, stem of *glomus*, a ball or clew of yarn. See Globe.

Gloom. (E.) M. E. *gloumen*, to lower, as if from A. S. **glūmian*; cf. *room* from A. S. *rūm*; and prov. E. *glum*, overcast. **+**Norw. *glyma*, an overcast sky; Low G. *glum*, turbid. See Glum.

Glory. (F.–L.) M. E. *glorie*. – A. F. and O. F. *glorie* (F. *gloire*). – L. *glōria*.

Gloss (1), lustre. (Scand.) Icel. *glossi*, a blaze, *glys*, finery; Swed. dial. *glossa*, to glow; Norw. *glosa*, to glow. **+**M. H. G. *glosen*, to glow, *glos*, lustre; Du. *gloren* (Franck), E. Fries. *gloren*.

Gloss (2), a commentary, explanation. (F.–L.–Gk.) M. E. *glose*. – O. F. *glose*, 'a glosse;' Cot. – L. *glōssa*, a difficult word requiring explanation. – Gk. γλῶσσα, the tongue, a language, word needing explanation. Der. *gloss*, vb., *gloze*.

glossary. (L.–Gk.) L. *glōssārium*, a glossary; formed with suffix *-ārium* from L. *glōss-a* (above).

glossographer. (Gk.) Coined from *glōsso-*, from Gk. γλῶσσα, a hard word; γράφειν, to write.

glottis. (Gk.) Gk. γλωττίς, the mouth of the windpipe. – Gk. γλῶττα, Attic form of γλῶσσα, the tongue. Der. *epi-glottis*.

Glove. (E.) A. S. *glōf*, a glove; cf. Icel. *glōfi*, prob. borrowed from A. S. *glōf*. Possibly from *g-* (for *ge-*), prefix; and Icel. *lōfi*, Goth. *lōfa*, the palm of the hand. Der. *fox-glove*.

Glow. (E.) M. E. *glowen*. A. S. *glōwan*, to be ardent, to shine brightly. **+** Icel. *glōa*, Dan. *gloe*, to glow, stare, Swed. *glo*, to stare, Du. *gloeijen*, G. *glühen*. Brugm. i. § 156. Der. *glede* (2).

Glower, to look frowningly. (E.) E. Fries. *glüren*. Cf. Low G. *gluren*, M. Du. *gloeren*, 'to look awry, to leare,' Hexham; Du. *gluren*. **¶** M. F. *gloren*, to stare, is allied to *glare*.

Gloze, to interpret, flatter. (F.–L.– Gk.) M. E. *glosen*, to make glosses. – M. E. *glose*, a gloss; see Gloss (2).

Glue. (F.–L.) O. F. *glu*. – Late L. *glūtem*, acc. of *glūs* (gen. *glūtis*), glue; allied to L. *glūten*, glue, *glūtus*, tenacious. **+**Gk. γλοιός, mud, gum. Allied to Clay. Brugm. i. § 639.

Glum, sullen. (E.) M. E. *glommen, glomben, gloumen*, to look gloomy. E. Fries. *glumen, glümen*, to look sullen. **+** Low G. *gluum*, a sullen look, *glummen*, to make turbid; Norw. *glyme*, a sullen look, *glyma, gloma*, to look sullen. See Gloom.

Glume, a bracteal covering, in grasses. (L.) L. *glūma*, a husk, hull. – L. *glūbere*, to peel, take off the husk. See Cleave (1).

Glut, to swallow greedily. (F.–L.) M. E. *glotien*. – O. F. *glotir, gloutir*. – L. *glūtīre, gluttīre*, to swallow; cf. *gula*, the throat. Der. *glutton*.

Glutinous, gluey. (L.) L. *glūtinōsus*, sticky. – L. *glūtin-*, for *glūten*, glue.

Glutton. (F.–L.) M. E. *gloton*. – O. F. *gloton*. – L. *gluttōnem, glūtōnem*, acc., a glutton. – L. *glūtīre*, to devour.

Glycerine, a viscid fluid, of sweet taste. (F.–Gk.) F. *glycérine*; from Gk. γλυκερός, sweet; from Gk. γλυκύς, sweet.

Glyptic, relating to carving in stone. (Gk.) Gk. γλυπτικός, carving. – Gk. γλυπτός, carved. – Gk. γλύφειν, to hollow out, engrave. See Cleave (1).

Gnarl, to snarl, growl. (E.) Frequentative of *gnar*, to snarl, an imitative word. Cf. A. S. *gnyrran*, to creak; E. Fries. *gnarren*, to creak, snarl. **+**Du. *knorren*, Dan. *knurre*, to growl, Dan. *knarre*, to creak; Swed. *knorra*, G. *knurren*, to growl, G. *knarren*, to creak.

Gnarled, knotty, twisted. (E.) *Gnarled* is full of gnarls, where *gnar-l* is a dimin. of *gnar* or *knar*, M. E. *knarre*, a knot in wood. See **Knurr.**

Gnash. (E.) M. E. *gnasten*, to gnash the teeth. E. Fries. *gnastern*, *gnästern*, to gnash.+Swed. *knastra*, to crash (between the teeth); Dan. *knaske*, to gnash; Icel. *gnastan*, sb., a gnashing, *gnesta* (pt. t. *gnast*), to crack; G. *knastern*, to crackle. Imitative; so also Dan. *knase*, to crackle; Icel. *gnîsta*, to gnash, E. Fries. *gnîsen*.

Gnat. (E.) A.S. *gnætt*. Said to be named from the whirring of the wings; cf. Icel. *gnata*, to clash, *gnat*, clash of weapons.

Gnaw. (E.) M. E. *gnawen*, pt. t. *gnew*, *gnow*. A.S. *gnagan*, to gnaw, pt. t. *gnôh*, pp. *gnagen.*+Du. *knagen*, Low G. *gnauen*, O. Icel. *knaga*, mod. Icel. *naga*, Dan. *gnave*, Swed. *gnaga*. Without the *g*, we have G. *nagen*; also Dan. *nage*, to gnaw, Swed. *nagga*, whence prov. E. *nag*, to worry.

Gneiss, a rock. (G.) G. *gneiss*; from its sparkling. – O. H. G. *gneistan*, to sparkle; *gneista*, a spark. + A.S. *gnâst*, Icel. *gneisti*, a spark.

Gnome, a kind of sprite. (F. – Gk.) F. *gnome*, a gnome; a word due to Paracelsus; from the notion that gnomes could reveal secret treasures. – Gk. γνώμη, intelligence. – Gk. γνῶναι, to know. (√GEN.)

gnomon, index of a dial. (L. – Gk.) L. *gnōmōn*. – Gk. γνώμων, an interpreter (one who knows); the index of a dial. – Gk. γνῶναι, to know.

gnostic, one of a certain sect. (Gk.) Gk. γνωστικός, wise, good at knowing. – Gk. γνωστός, from γνωτός, known. – Gk. γνῶναι, to know.

Gnu, a kind of antelope. (Hottentot.) Found in S. Africa. Said to belong to the Hottentot language. See Supplement.

Go, to move about, proceed, advance. (E.) M. E. *gon*, *goon*. A.S. *gân.*+Du. *gaan*, Dan. *gaae*, Swed. *gå*; G. *gehen*; O. H. G. *gân*, *gên*. ¶ 'The Teut. *gai-* (= A.S. *gâ-*, O. H. G. *gê-*) supplanted the Idg. √I, to go, in Lat. *îre*, Gk. ἰέναι, Skt. *i*. Since Teut. *gai-* has no old primitive noun-derivatives in Teut., and takes the place of Idg. √I (the Goth. aorist *iddja* = A.S. *êode* still remains), and as it is inflected after the *-mi-* conjugation, the

supposition arises that Teut. *gaim, *gais, *gaith are contracted from the verbal particle *ga-* and the inherited *îm*, *îz*, *îth* = Skt. *êmi*, *êshi*, *êti*; cf. Gk. εἶμι.' – Kluge. But this is mere conjecture.

Goad. (E.) M. E. *gode*. A.S. *gâd*. Teut. type *gaidâ, f.+Lombardic *gaida*, a gore (Duc.); from the base **gai-*, Idg. **ghai-*, whence also A.S. *gâ-r*, Icel. *gei-rr*, O. Irish *gai*, a spear; see **Gore** (2).

Goal, the winning-post in a race. (E.) M. E. *gôl*, Shoreham, p. 145. Answering to A.S. *gâl, prob. 'an impediment;' whence A.S. *gælan*, to impede. *Goal* may have meant 'stopping-place.'

Goat. (E.) M. E. *goot*. A.S. *gât.*+Du. *geit*, Dan. *ged*, Swed. *get*, Icel. *geit*, G. *geiss*, *geisse*; Goth. *gaits*. Teut. base **gait-*; allied to L. *hædus*.

Gobbet, a mouthful, a small piece. (F. – C.) M. E. *gobet*, a small piece. – O. F. *gobet*, a morsel of food (see Littré); allied to M.F. *gob*, a gulp (in swallowing). – O. F. *gober*, to devour. – Gael. *gob*, beak, bill, mouth; Irish *gob*, mouth, beak.

gobble (1), to devour. (F. – C.) Frequentative, with suffix *-le*, from O. F. *gob-er*, to devour; see **Gobbet**.

Gobble (2), to make a gabbling noise. (E.) Imitative; a variant of *gabble*.

Gobelin, a French tapestry. (F.) Named from Giles *Gobelin*, wool-dyer of Paris, in the 16th cent.

Goblet. (F. – L.) F. *gobelet*, 'a goblet;' Cot. Dimin. of O. F. *gobel*, a cup. – Late L. *cūpellum*, acc. of *cūpellus*, a cup; dimin. of L. *cūpa*, a vat; see **Coop.** Cf. Picard *gobe*, a great cup.

Goblin. (F. – L. – G.) O.F. *gobelin*. – Low L. *gobelînus*, a goblin; properly 'a household-god'; cf. A.S. *cof-godas*, 'penates.' – M. H. G. *kobel*, a hut; dimin. of M. H. G. *kobe*, a stall, cognate with Icel. *kofi*, a hut, A.S. *cofa*, a chamber (Kluge). See **Cove.**

Goby, a fish. (L. – Gk.) For L. *gōbius*, orig. applied to the gudgeon. – Gk. κωβιός, a kind of fish, gudgeon, tench. **Der.** *gudgeon*.

God. (E.) A.S. *god.*+Du. *god*, Icel. *goð*, *guð*, Dan. *gud*, Swed. *gud*, Goth. *guth*, G. *gott*. Teut. type *guthom; Idg. type *ghutom, perhaps 'the being worshipped,' a pp. form; from Idg. root *ghu, to worship, as in Skt. *hu*, to sacrifice (to), whence *huta-*, one to whom sacrifice is offered. ¶ *Not* allied to *good*, adj.

goddess. (E.; *with* F. *suffix*.) M. E. *goddesse* (*godesse*). Made from *god* by adding the O. F. suffix *-esse* (= L. *-issa* = Gk. *-ισσα*).

godfather. (E.) M. E. *godfader*, father in baptism; from *god* and *fader*.

godhead. (E.) M. E. *godhed*, also *godhod*; the suffix answers to A. S. *hād*, office, state, dignity; see **-hood** (suffix).

Godwit, a bird. (E.) Origin unknown. Can it mean 'good creature'? A. S. *gōd wiht*, a good wight, good creature (*wiht* being often applied to animals and birds). See **Wight**.

Goffer, Gauffer, to plait or crimp lace, &c. (F. — O. Low G.) M. F. *gaufrer*, to goffer; orig. to mark like the edges of wafers. — M. F. *gauffre, goffre,* a wafer; see **Wafer**.

Goggle-eyed, having rolling and staring eyes. (E.) M. E. *gogil-eyid*. 'They *gogle* with their eyes hither and thither;' Holinshed, Descr. of Ireland, c. 1. Cf. Irish and Gael. *gogshuileach*, goggle-eyed, having wandering eyes, from *gog*, to move slightly, and *suil*, eye. But *gog* seems to be from E., and of imitative origin. Cf. prov. E. *coggle*, Bavar. *gageln*, to be unsteady.

Goitre. (F. — L.) F. *goître*, a swelled throat; from O. F. *goitron*, the same, esp. in Savoy. — Late L. acc. type **guttriōnem*, from L. *guttur*, throat.

Gold. (E.) A. S. *gold*. + Du. *goud* (for *gold*), Icel. *gull*, Swed. Dan. *guld*, G. *gold*, Goth. *gulth*. Teut. type **gul-thom*, n.; Idg. type **ghol-tom*; cf. Russ. *zoloto*, Skt. *hāṭaka-*, gold; also Pers. *zar*, gold, Zend *zaranya-*, Skt. *hiraṇya-*. Named from its colour. Allied to **Yellow**. (√GHEL.) Der. *mari-gold, gild*.

Golf, a game. (Du.) Mentioned A. D. 1457 (Jam.). The name is from that of a Du. game played with club and ball. — Du. *kolf*, a club used to strike balls with. + Low G. *kulf*, hockey-stick; Icel. *kōlfr*, clapper of a bell, *kylfa*, a club; Dan. *kolbe*, butt-end of a weapon, *kolv*, bolt, shaft, arrow, Swed. *kolf*, butt-end, G. *kolbe*, club, mace, knob.

Golosh; the same as **Galoche**.

Gondola. (Ital. — Gk. — Pers. ?) Ital. *gondola*, dimin. of *gonda*, a boat. — Gk. κόνδυ, a drinking-vessel; from the shape (Diez). Said to be of Pers. origin; cf. Pers. *kandū*, an earthen vessel.

Gonfanon, Gonfalon, a kind of banner. (F. — M. H. G.) M. E. *gonfanon*. — O. F. *gonfanon*. — M. H. G. *gundfano*, lit. 'battle-flag.' — M. H. G. *gund, gunt*, battle; *fano* (G. *fahne*), a banner, flag. Here *gunt* is cognate with A. S. *gūð* (for **gunth*), battle, war; cf. Skt. *han*, to kill. *Fano* is allied to **Vane**.

Gong. (Malay.) Malay *agōng* or *gōng*, the gong, a sonorous instrument.

Good. (E.) M. E. *good*. A. S. *gōd*. + Du. *goed*, Icel. *gōðr*, Dan. Swed. *god*, Goth. *gōds*, G. *gut*. Teut. type **gōdoz*; from **gōd-*, strong grade of **gad-*, 'fit;' see **Gather**. Allied to Russ. *godnuii*, suitable, O. Slav. *godŭ*, fit season. Der. *good-s*, sb. pl., i. e. good things, property; *good-will*, &c. Also *good-man*, i. e. master of the house, *good-wife*, mistress of the house.

Goodbye, farewell. (E.) A familiar, but meaningless, contraction of *God be with you*, the old form of farewell; very common; often written *God b'w'y*. ¶ *Not* for *God be by you*; the form *God buy you* = *God be-with-you* you (*you* repeated).

Goodman; see **Good**.

Goose, a bird. (E.) A. S. *gōs*, pl. *gēs* (lengthened *o* caused loss of *n*, and *gōs* = **gons* < **gans*). + Du. *gans*, Dan. *gaas*, Swed. *gas*. Icel. *gās*, G. *gans*. Teut. type **gans*; Idg. type **ghans-*; cf. L. *anser*, Gk. χήν; Skt. *haṃsa*, a swan; O. Irish *geis*, a swan; Lith. *żąsis*, a goose.

Gooseberry. (E.; cf. F. — M. H. G.) In Levins. From *goose* and *berry*; cf. *goose-grass*, &c. α. We also find North. E. *grosers*, gooseberries; Burns has *grozet*, a gooseberry. Apparently from O. F. **grose, *groise*, a gooseberry, not recorded, but occurring not only in the O. F. dimin. form *groisele, grosele,* a gooseberry, but also in Irish *grois-aid*, Gael. *grois-eid*, W. *grwys*, a gooseberry, all borrowed from M.E. The spelling *groisele* is as old as the 13th century (Bartsch); and answers to the form *crosela* in the dialect of Como (Monti). β. The orig. O. F. **groise* or **grose* was borrowed from M. H. G. *krūs*, curling, crisped, whence G. *krausbeere*, a cranberry, a rough gooseberry. Cf. Swed. *krusbär*, a gooseberry, from *krus*, crisp, curled, frizzled. The name was first given to the rougher kinds of the fruit, from the curling hairs on it; similarly, Levins gives the Lat. name as *uua crispa* (frizzled grape).

Gopher, a kind of wood. (Heb.) Heb. *gōpher*, a wood.

Gorbellied, having a fat belly. (E.) Compounded of E. *gore*, lit. filth, dirt (also the intestines) ; and *belly*. So also Swed. dial. *gårbälg*, a fat paunch, from *går*, dirt, contents of the intestines, and *bälg*, belly. See Gore (1).

gorcrow, carrion-crow. (E.) I. e. *gore-crow* ; see above.

Gordian. (L.–Gk.) Only in the phr. '*Gordian* knot,' i. e. intricate knot. Named from the Phrygian king *Gordius* (Γόρδιος), who tied it. An oracle declared that whoever undid it should reign over Asia. Alexander cut the knot, and applied the oracle to himself.

Gore (1), clotted blood. (E.) It formerly meant filth. A. S. *gor*, filth, dirt.+ Icel *gor*, gore; Swed. *gor*, dirt; M.Du.*goor*; O. H. G. *gor*, filth. Origin uncertain.

Gore (2), a triangular piece let into a garment, a triangular slip of land. (E.) M. E. *gore*. A. S. *gāra*, a gore, projecting piece of land ; from *gār*, a dart, a spear-point. Named from the shape. [So also Icel. *geiri*, a triangular slip of land, from *geirr*, a spear ; G. *gehre*, a wedge, gusset, gore ; Du. *geer*, a gusset, gore.] β. The A. S. *gār* (Icel. *geirr*, O. H. G. *gēr*) is from Teut. type **gaizoz*, m.; allied to Gaulish L. *gaesum*, a javelin, O. Irish *gai*, a spear.

Gore (3), to pierce. (E.) From A. S. *gār*, a spear-point (with the usual change from *ā* to long *o*).

Gorge, the throat, a narrow pass. (F. –L.) O. F. *gorge*, throat. ▬ Late L. *gorga*, variant of L. *gurgēs*, a whirlpool, hence (in Late L.) the gullet, from its voracity. Cf. L. *gurgulio*, gullet.+Skt. *gargara-*, a whirlpool.

gorgeous, showy, splendid. (F.–L.) O. F. and M. F. *gorgias*, 'gorgeous;' Cot. The O. F. *gorgias* also meant a gorget ; the sense of 'gorgeous' was orig. proud, from the swelling of the throat in pride. Cotgrave gives F. *se rengorger*, 'to hold down the head, or thrust the chin into the neck, as some do in pride, or to make their faces look the fuller ; we say, to bridle it.' Hence the derivation is from F. *gorge*, throat (above).

gorget, armour for the throat. (F.– L.) From *gorge*, i. e. throat.

Gorgon, a monster. (L.–Gk.) L. *Gorgon, Gorgō*. ▬ Gk. Γοργώ, the Gorgon.

▬ Gk. γοργός, fearful. **+** O. Ir. *garg*, fierce.

Gorilla, a kind of large ape. (O. African.) An old word revived. In the Periplus of Hanno, near the end, some creatures are described 'which the interpreters called *Gorillas*'—in Greek, γορίλλας.

Gormandise ; see Gourmand.

Gorse. (E.) Formerly *gorst*. ▬ A. S. *gorst*, gorse. Cf. Skt. *hṛsh*, to bristle.

Goshawk. (E.) Lit. 'goose-hawk.' A. S. *gōshafuc*. ▬ A. S. *gōs*, goose ; *hafuc*, hawk.

gosling. (E.) Formed from A. S. *gōs*, goose (M. E. *gos*), with double dimin. suffix *-l-ing*.

Gospel, the life of Christ. (E.) M. E. *gospel*. A. S. *godspell*. ▬ A. S. *god*, God, i. e. Christ ; *spell*, a story. Lit. 'narrative of God,' i. e. life of Christ. ¶ Orig. *gōd spell*, i. e. *good spell*, a translation of Gk. εὐαγγέλιον ; but soon altered to *godspell*; for the E. word was early introduced into Iceland in the form *guðspjall* (where *guð* =god, as distinguished from *gōð*- =good), and into Germany as O. H. G. *gotspell* (where *got* =god, as distinguished from *guot*, good).

Gossamer. (E.) M. E. *gossomer, gosesomer*, lit. '*goose-summer*.' The prov. E. name (in Craven) is *summer-goose*. Named from the time of year when it is most seen, viz. during St. Martin's summer (early November) ; geese were eaten on Nov. 11 formerly. Cf. Lowl. Sc. *go-summer* (popular variant), Martinmas. ¶ Also called *summer-colt* (Whitby) ; also *summer-gauze*. Cf. G. *sommerfäden* (lit. summer-threads), gossamer ; Du. *zomer-draden*, Swed. *sommertråd*, the same. [But in G. it is also called *mädchensommer*, lit. Maiden-summer, *der altweibersommer*, the old women's summer ; which also means St. Martin's summer.] It would appear that *summer* is here used in the sense of 'summer-film,' so that *gossamer* = goose-summer-film. (Better spelt *gossomer* or *gossummer*.)

Gossip. (E.) Now a crony ; formerly a sponsor in baptism. M. E. *gossib*, also *godsib*, lit. 'related in god.' ▬ M. E. *god*, god ; *sib*, related, from O. Northumb. *sibbo*, pl. relatives, allied to Goth. *sibja*, relationship, G. *sippe*, affinity, *sippen*, kinsmen. Cf. Skt. *sabhya-*, fit for an assembly, trusty, from *sabhā*, an assembly. Brugm. i. §§ 124 (4), 567.

Gouge, a hollow-bladed chisel. (F. — Low L.) F. *gouge.* — Low L. **gobia, *gubia,* only recorded in the form *guvia* (Span. *gubia*). Cf. Ital. *sgorbia,* gouge ; Gascon *goujo.*

Gourd. (F. — L.) F. *gourde,* formerly *gouhourde* and *cougourde* (Cot.). — L. *cucurbita,* a gourd.

Gourmand, a glutton. (F.) F. *gourmand,* 'a glutton, gormand, belly-god ;' Cot. Etym. unknown. Der. *gormandise* (for *gourmand-ise*).

Gout (1), a drop, disease. (F. — L.) M. E. *goute,* a disease supposed to be due to defluxion of humours. — O. F. *goute, goutte,* a drop. — L. *gutta,* a drop.

Gout (2), taste. (F. — L.) F. *goût,* taste. — L. *gustus,* taste ; see Gust (2).

Govern. (F. — L. — Gk.) M. E. *gouernen.* — O. F. *governer.* — L. *gubernāre,* to steer a ship, rule. — Gk. κυβερνᾶν, to steer. Cf. Lith. *kumbriti,* to steer.

Gowan, a daisy. (Scand.) North. E. *gowlan,* Sc. *yellow gowan,* corn marigold. Named from the colour. — Icel. *gulr,* Swed. *gul,* Dan. *guul,* Norw. *gul, gaul,* yellow. See Yellow.

Gowk, a simpleton. (Scand.) Icel. *gaukr,* a cuckoo, Swed. *gök.*+G. *gauch,* a cuckoo, simpleton.

Gown, a loose robe. (C.) M. E. *goune.* — W. *gwn,* a loose robe. [Irish *gunn,* Gael. and Corn. *gun,* Manx *goon,* are from E. O. F. *goune* is Gaulish.] Stokes-Fick, p. 281.

Grab, to seize. (E.) Cf. E. Fries. *grabbig,* greedy ; *grabbelen,* to grab at ; Du. *grabbel,* a scramble, *grabbelen,* to scramble for ; Low G. *grabbeln,* to grab at ; Swed. *grabba,* to grasp.+Skt. *grah,* O. Skt. *grabh,* O. Pers. and Zend *grab,* to seize. See Garb (2). Cf. Grasp.

Grace. (F. — L.) O. F. *grace.* — L. *grātia,* favour. — L. *grātus,* dear, pleasing. Brugm. i. §§ 524, 632.

Grade, a degree. (F. — L.) F. *grade,* a degree. — L. *gradum,* acc. of *gradus,* a degree, step. — L. *gradī* (pp. *gressus*), to step, walk, go. (√GHREDH.) Brugm. i. § 635 ; ii. § 707.

gradient, a gradually rising slope. (L.) L. *gradient-,* stem of pres. pt. of *gradī,* to walk, advance.

gradual, advancing by steps. (L.) Orig. *gradual,* sb., a service-book called in Lat. *graduāle,* and in E. *gradual* or *grayl.* — Late L. *graduālis,* only in neut.

graduāle, a service-book of portions sung *in gradibus,* i. e. on the steps (of the choir). — L. *gradu-s,* a step.

graduate. (L.) Late L. *graduātus,* one who has taken a degree ; pp. of Late L. *graduāre.* — L. *gradu-s,* degree.

Graft, Graff, to insert buds on a stem. (F. — L. — Gk.) *Graft* is a later form of *graff,* and due to confusion with *graffed,* pp. Shak. has pp. *graft,* Rich. III, iii. 7. 127. M. E. *graffen,* to graff, from *graffe,* sb. — O. F. *graffe,* a sort of pencil, also a slip for grafting, because it resembled a pointed pencil in shape. — L. *graphium,* a style to write with. — Gk. γραφίον, γραφεῖον, the same. — Gk. γράφειν, to write.

Grail (1), a gradual, a service-book. (F. — L.) M. E. *graile, grayle.* — O. F. *graël.* — Late L. *gradāle,* also called *graduāle ;* see **gradual.**

Grail (2), the Holy Dish at the Last Supper. (F. — L. — Gk.) The etymology was very early falsified by an easy change from *San Greal* (Holy Dish) to *Sang Real* (Royal Blood, strangely taken to mean Real Blood). — O. F. *graal, greal, grasal,* a flat dish ; with numerous other forms, both in O. F. and Late L. It would appear that the word was corrupted in various ways from Late L. type **crātalis* (cf. Late L. *grādāle,* a bowl) ; from Late L. *crāt-us,* a bowl, equivalent to L. *crāter,* a bowl ; see **Crater.** (Diez.)

Grail (3), fine sand. (F. — L.) In Spenser, F. Q. i. 7. 6 ; Vis. Bellay, st. 12. — O. F. *graisle, graile* (F. *grêle*), thin, small. — L. *gracilem,* acc. of *gracilis,* slender.

Grain. (F. — L.) M. E. *grein.* — O. F. *grain.* — L. *grānum,* a grain, corn.+Irish *grān,* W. *gronyn.* Cognate with E. **Corn.**

Grallatory. (L.) A term applied to wading birds. — L. *grallātor,* a walker on stilts. — L. *grallæ* (for **gradlæ*), stilts. — L. *gradus,* a step ; *gradī,* to walk.

Gramarye, magic. (F. — L. — Gk.) M. E. *gramery,* skill in grammar, and hence skill in magic. — O. F. *gramaire,* grammar ; see **Grammar.** Cf. O. F. *gramaire,* (1) a grammarian, (2) a magician. ¶ The word *glamour* is a mere corruption of *gramarye* or *grammar,* meaning (1) grammar, (2) magic.

Gramercy, thanks. (F. — L.) Formerly *graund mercy,* Chaucer, C. T. 8964. — F. *grand merci,* great thanks ; see **Grand** and **Mercy.**

Gramineous. (L.) From L. *grāmin-*, for *grāmen*, grass ; with suffix *-e-ous*.

Grammar. (F. — L. — Gk.) M. E. *grammere.* — O. F. *gramaire* (XIII cent.). — Late L. *grammatica*, grammar (Schwan). — Gk. γραμματική, grammar. — Gk. γραμματικός, knowing one's letters ; see below. **grammatical.** (F. — L. — Gk.) M. F. *grammatical* ; from L. *grammaticus*, grammatical. — Gk. γραμματικός, versed in one's letters. — Gk. γραμματ-, stem of γράμμα, a letter. — Gk. γράφειν, to write. See **Graphic.**

Grampus, a large fish. (F. — L.) Spelt *grampasse*, A. D. 1655. — A. F. *grampais* ; Blk. Bk. Adm. i. 152. — L. *grandem piscem*, acc. of *grandis piscis*, great fish.

Granary, store-house for grain. (L.) L. *grānāria*, pl. — L. *grānum*, corn. See **Garner.**

Grand, great. (F. — L.) O. F. *grand.* — L. *grandem*, acc. of *grandis*, great.

grandee, a Spanish nobleman. (Span. — L.) Span. *grande*, great ; also, a nobleman. — L. *grandem*, acc. of *grandis*, great.

grandeur, greatness. (F. — L.) F. *grandeur* ; formed with suffix *-eur* (L. *-ōrem*), from *grand*, great.

grandiloquent, pompous in speech. (L.) Coined from L. *grandi-*, decl. stem of *grandis*, great ; and *loquent-*, stem of pres. pt. of *loquī*, to speak ; see **Loquacious.** The true L. form is *grandiloquus.*

Grange, a farm-house. (F. — L.) O. F. *grange*, a barn, a farm-house. — Late L. *grānea*, a barn. — L. *grānum*, corn.

granite, a hard stone. (Ital. — L.) Ital. *granito*, granite, speckled stone. — Ital. *granito*, pp. of *granire*, to reduce to grains (hence, to speckle). — Ital. *grano*, a grain. — L. *grānum*, a grain ; see **Grain.**

Grant. (F. — L.) M. E. *graunten.* — O. F. *graanter*, *graunter*, later spelling of *crëanter*, *crëanter*, to caution, assure, guarantee ; whence the later senses, to promise, yield ; Late L. *crëantāre*, for **crēdentāre.* — L. *crēdent-*, stem of pres. pt. of *crēdere*, to trust. See **Creed.**

Granule, a little grain. (L.) L. *grānulum*, dimin. of *grānum*, a grain.

Grape. (F. — M. H. G.) A. F. *grape*, M. F. *grappe*, 'bunch, or cluster of grapes ;' Cot. [In E., the sense has changed, from cluster to single berry.] The orig. sense of *grappe* was 'a hook,' then clustered

fruit. — M. H. G. *krapfe*, O. H. G. *krapfo*, a hook. Allied to **Cramp.** The senses of 'hook' and 'cluster' result from that of 'clutching.'

Graphic, descriptive, pertaining to writing. (L. — Gk.) L. *graphicus*, belonging to painting or drawing. — Gk. γραφικός, the same. — Gk. γράφειν, to write. Allied to **Carve.**

Grapnel, a grappling-iron. (F. — M. H. G.) M. E. *grapenel.* Dimin. of M. F. *grappin*, a grapnel. — O. F. *grappe*, a hook. — O. H. G. *krapfo*, a hook ; see **Grape.**

grapple, to clutch. (F. — M. H. G.) Properly to seize with a grapnel. — M. F. *grappil*, sb., 'the *grapple* of a ship ;' Cot. — O. F. *grappe*, a hook (above).

Grasp. (E.) M. E. *graspen*, used in the sense 'to grope.' Also *grapsen*, in Hoccleve. Prob. for **grab-sen*, closely allied to **Grab**, q. v. Cf. E. Fries. *grapsen*, to clutch ; Low G. *grapsen* ; E. Fries. *graps*, a handful ; also Lith. *gróp-ti*, to grab (Kluge).

Grass. (E.) M. E. *gras*, *gres*, also *gers.* A. S. *gærs*, *græs.*+Du. Icel. Goth. G. *gras* ; Swed. *gräs*, Dan. *græs.* Teut. type **gra-som*, n. ; from **gra-*, the sense of which is doubtful ; cf. *grow.*

Grate (1), a framework of iron bars. (Late L. — L.) M. E. *grate.* — Late L. *grāta*, *crāta*, a grating. — L. *crātēs*, hurdles. See **Crate.**

Grate (2), to rub, scrape. (F. — Teut.) O. F. *grater* (F. *gratter*). — Swed. *kratta*, Dan. *kratte*, to scrape ; O. H. G. *chrazzōn* (< **krattōn*), to scrape.

Grateful, pleasant. (Hybrid ; F. — L. *and* E.) The first syllable is from O. F. *grat*, pleasing, from L. *grātus* ; with E. suffix *-ful.*

gratify. (F. — L.) M. F. *gratifier.* — L. *grātificāre*, *grātificārī*, to please. — L. *grāti-*, for *grātus*, pleasing ; and *-ficāre*, for *facere*, to make. **Der.** *gratific-at-ion.*

gratis, freely. (L.) L. *grātīs*, adv., freely ; for *grātiīs*, abl. pl. of *grātia*, grace ; see **Grace.**

gratitude. (F. — L.) F. *gratitude.* — Late L. *grātitūdinem*, acc. of *grātitūdo*, thankfulness. — L. *grātus*, pleasing.

gratuitous, freely given. (L.) L. *grātuīt-us*, freely given ; with suffix *-ous.* From *grātus.*

gratuity, a present. (F. — L.) O. F. *gratuité*, 'a free gift ;' Cot. — Late L.

grātuītātem, acc. of *grātuītās.*—L. *grā-tuītus* (above).

gratulate, to congratulate. (L.) From pp. of L. *grātulārī*, to wish a person joy. As if for **grāti-tulārī*; from L. *grātus*, pleasing. Brugm. i. § 986.

Grave (1), to cut, engrave. (E.) M. E. *grauen*. A. S. *grafan*, pt. t. *grōf.*+Du. *graven*, Dan. *grave*, Icel. *grafa*, M. Swed. *grafva*, Goth. *graban*, G. *graben*. Teut. type **graban-*, pt. t. **grōb*. Cf. Russ. *grob'*, a tomb, grave. Der. *grave*, sb., a thing cut or dug out; A. S. *græf*.

Grave (2), sad. (F.—L.) F. *grave.*— L. *grauem*, acc. of *grauis*, heavy.+Goth. *kaurus*; Gk. βαρύς, Skt. *guru-*, heavy. Brugm. i. § 665.

Gravel. (F. — C.) M. E. *grauel.*— O. F. *gravele*, dimin. of O. F. *grave*, gravel. Of Celtic origin; from Celt. base **gravo-*, as in Bret. *grouan*, gravel, Corn. *grow*, gravel, W. *gro*, pebbles.

Gravy. (F.—L.) M. E. *graué*, mistaken form of O. F. *grané*, a broth with powdered almonds (like grains).—L. *grānātum*, full of grains.—L. *grānum*, a grain.

Gray. (E.) M. E. *gray*, *grey*. O. Merc. *grēg*, A. S. *grǣg.*+Du. *graauw*, Icel. *grār*, Dan. *graa*, Swed. *grå*, G. *grau*, O. H. G. *grā* (gen. *grāw-es*). Teut. stems **grǣg-*, **grǣw-*, <**grǣgwoz*.

Graze (1), to scrape slightly. (E.?) Formerly *grase*. Apparently a peculiar use of *graze*, to crop grass; used of cannon-balls that rebounded from grass. So also G. *grasen*.

Graze (2), to feed as cattle. (E.) M. E. *grasen*, vb. A. S. *grasian.*—A. S. *græs*, grass; see **Grass**. Der. *graz-i-er* (cf. *bow-y-er*, *law-y-er*).

Grease. (F.—L.) M. E. *grese*, *grece*. —A. F. *greisse*, *craisse*, fatness, Ps. xvi. 10.—Late L. type **crassia.*—L. *crassus*, thick, fat. See **Crass**.

Great. (E.) M. E. *gret*, *greet*. A. S. *grēat.*+Du. *groot*, G. *gross*. Teut. type **grautoz*.

Greaves (1), **Graves,** sediment of melted tallow. (E.) E. Fries. *gräfe*; pl. *gräfen*, greaves.+M. Swed. *grefwar*, dirt; *ljus-grefwar*, lit. ' light-dirt,' refuse of tallow in candle-making; Swed. dial. *grevar*, pl., greaves; Low G. *greven*, greaves; G. *griebe*, O. H. G. *griubo*, *griupo*.

Greaves (2), leg-armour. (F.) O. F. *greves*, ' boots, also greaves;' Cot. Cf. Span. *grebas*, greaves, pl. of *greba.* — O. F.

greve, Picard *greve*, the shank, shin. Origin unknown.

Grebe, a bird. (F.) F. *grèbe*. Cot. gives *griaibe*, ' a sea-mew,' as a Savoyard word. Of unknown origin.

Greedy. (E.) A. S. *grǣdig*, *grēdig.*+ Du. *gretig*, Icel. *grādugr*, Dan. *graadig*, Goth. *grēdags*; cf. Skt. *grdhra-*, greedy, from *grdh*, to be greedy. The sb. *greed*, hunger, answers to Icel. *grāðr*, Goth. *grēdus*, hunger; Teut. type **grǣduz*.

Green. (E.) M. E. *green*. A. S. *grēne*. +Du. *groen*, Icel. *grænn*, Dan. Swed. *grön*, G. *grün*. Teut. type **grōnjoz*, earlier type **grō-niz* (Sievers). Cf. A. S. *grō-wan*, to grow. Allied to **Grow**. *Green* is the colour of *growing* herbs. Der. *greens*, pl. sb. See **Sward**.

Greengage, a green plum. Named from Sir W. *Gage*, of Hengrave Hall, near Bury, before A. D. 1725. There is also a *blue Gage*, a *yellow Gage*, and a *purple Gage*.

Greet (1), to salute. (E.) M. E. *greten*. A.S. *grētan*, to visit, address.+Du. *groeten*, G. *grüssen*; O. Sax. *grōtian*. Teut. type **grōt-jan-*; from the sb. **grōt-*, as in Du. *groet*, G. *gruss*, a salutation.

Greet (2), to cry, weep. (E.) M. E. *greten*. A. S. *grǣtan*, *grētan.*+Icel. *grāta*, Dan. *græde*, Swed. *gråta*, Goth. *grētan*.

Gregarious. (L.) L. *gregārius*, belonging to a flock. —L. *greg-*, stem of *grex*, a flock.+O. Irish *graig*, a herd of horses.

Grenade, a war-missile. (F. —Span.— L.) Formerly also *granado*, which is like the Span. form. Named from its likeness to a pomegranate, being filled with combustibles as that is with seeds. —F. *grenade*, ' a pomegranet, a ball of wild-fire ; ' Cot. —Span. *granada*, the same; *granado*, full of seeds. —L. *grānātus*, full of seeds. —L. *grānum*, a grain; see **Grain**. Der. *grenad-ier*.

Grey; the same as **Gray**.

Greyhound. (E.) M. E. *greihound*, *grehound*. A.S. *grīghund*; where *grīg-* = *grīeg-* (Icel. *grey-*), for Teut. **graujo-*. Cf. Icel. *greyhundr*, a greyhound, from Icel. *grey*, a dog, *hundr*, a hound; *grey-baka*, a bitch. ¶ Not allied to *gray*, which is represented in Icelandic by *grār*.

Griddle, a pan for baking cakes. (F. —L.) Also *girdle*. M. E. *gredil.*— O. F. *gredil* (Moisy, Dict. of Norman patois), *grëil* (Godefroy); cf. *grediller*, vb., to grill (same).—Late L. **crātīculum*, for L. *crātīcula*, a gridiron, dimin. of *crātis*, a hurdle. Der. Hence M. E. *gredire*, a griddle, afterwards turned into *gridiron*, by confusion with M. E. *ire* = E. *iron*. See Grill and Creel.

Gride, to pierce, cut through. (E.) See Spenser, F. Q. ii. 8. 36. A metathesis of *gird*, M. E. *girden*, to strike, pierce; see Gird (2).

Gridiron; see Griddle.

Grief. (F.—L.) M. E. *grief*, *gref*. — O. F. *grief*, *gref*, burdensome, sad, heavy. —L. *grauis*, heavy; see Grave (2). Der. *grieve*, vb., O. F. *grever*, L. *grauāre*, to burden; from *grauis*.

Griffin, Griffon. (F. – L. – Gk.) Better *griffon*. M. E. *griffon*. – F. *griffon*; formed from Late L. *griffus*, a griffon. – L. *gryphus*, extended form of *gryps*, a griffon. – Gk. γρύψ (stem γρυπ-), a griffon, a fabulous animal supposed to have a hooked beak. – Gk. γρυπός, curved, hook-beaked. ¶ Confused with Gk. γύψ, a vulture.

Grig, a small eel, a cricket. (E.) App. of imitative origin. Cf. *crick*, still preserved in *crick-et*; Lowl. Sc. *crick*, a tick, louse; Du. *kriek*, a cricket. ¶ In phr. 'as merry as a *grig*,' *grig* is for *Greek* (Troil. i. 2. 118); *Merygreek* is a character in Udall's Roister Doister; from L. *græcārī*, to live like Greeks; i. e. luxuriously.

Grill, to broil on a gridiron. (F.—L.) F. *griller*, to broil. – F. *gril*, 'a gridiron,' Cot.; O. F. *greïl*, *grail*. – Late L. *crātīculum*, for *crātīcula*, a small gridiron (whence F. *grille*, a grating). – L. *crātis*, a hurdle. See Crate, Creel, and Griddle.

Grilse, the young salmon on its first return from the sea to fresh water. (F.— Teut.) Orig. *grills*, pl. – O. F. *grisle. grille*, grayish. – O. F. *gris*, gray. See Grizzly.

Grim, fierce. (E.) A.S. *grim*; allied to *gram*, fierce, angry, furious. + Icel. *grimmr*, grim, *gramr*, angry; Dan. *grim*, grim, *gram*, angry; G. *grimm*, fury, *gram*, hostile. From Teut. root *grem*- (2nd grade, *gram*-). Allied to Gk. χρεμετίζειν, to neigh, χρόμη, χρόμος, noise. Brugm. i. § 572.

Grimace. (F.—Teut.) F. *grimace*, 'a crabd looke;' Cot. Of uncertain origin. Perhaps from Icel. *grimmr*, Dan. *grim*, grim, angry (above); cf. E. Fries. and Low G. *grimlachen*, to laugh maliciously. Derived by Diez from Icel. *grīma*, a mask.

Grimalkin, a cat. (E.; *partly* O.H.G.) Prob for *gray Malkin*, the latter being a cat's name. *Malkin* = *Mald-kin*, dimin. of A. F. *Mald* = *Maud*, i. e. Matilda; from O. H. G. *Mahthilt*. Here *maht* = might; *hilt* means battle. Cf. Macb. i. 1. 8.

Grime. (Scand.) Swed. dial. *grima*, a smut on the face; Dan. *grim*, *griim*, lamp-black, soot, grime. Cf. Low G. *grimmeln*, to become smutty; E. Fries. *gremen*, to begrime.

Grin, to snarl, grimace. (E.) M. E. *grennen*. A.S. *grennian*, to grin.+Icel. *grenja*, to howl. Perhaps cf. Du. *grijnen*, to weep, fret; Dan. *grine*, to grin, simper; Swed. *grina*, G. *greinen* (Noreen, § 149). See Groan.

Grind. (E.) A.S. *grindan*, pt. t. *grand*, pp. *grunden*. Allied to L. *frendere*, to gnash.

Grip, sb. (E.) M. E. *gripe*. A.S. *gripe*, a grip; from the weak grade of *grīpan* (below).

gripe. (E.) A.S. *grīpan*, pt. t. *grāp*, pp. *gripen*, to seize. + Du. *grijpen*, Icel. *grípa*, Swed. *gripa*, Dan. *gribe*, Goth. *greipan*, G. *greifen*. Teut. type *greipan-*, pt. t. *graip*, pp. *gripano*. Cf. Lith. *graibyti*, to grasp at.

Grise, Grize, a step. (F.—L.) Also spelt *greece*, *greese*, &c. The proper spelling is *grees*, and the proper sense is 'a flight of steps,' though often used as meaning a single step. *Grees* is the pl. of M. E. *gree*, *gre*, a step. – O. F. *gre*, a step (Roquefort); cf. F. *de-gré*, E. *de-gree*.– L. *gradus*, a step. Der. Prov. E. (Norf.) *grissens*, steps = *gree-s-en-s*, a treble plural.

Grisette, a gay young Frenchwoman of the lower class. (F. – M. H. G.) F. *grisette*; named from the cheap gray dress which they used to wear. – F. *gris*, gray; see Grizzly.

Griskin. (Scand.) The lit. sense is 'little pig,' now spine of a hog. Dimin. from M. E. *gris*, a pig. – Icel. *grīss*, a young pig; Dan. *griis*, Swed. *gris*, pig. ¶ Or is it for *gris-skin*, where *skin* represents Dan. *skinne*, a splint? Cf. Grizzly.

Grisled; see Grizzly.

Grisly, terrible. (E.) A. S. *grīslīc*, terrible Formed with suffix -*līc* (like) from *grīs-an* (pt. t. *grās*), to shudder. E. Fries. *grīselīk*, terrible, from *grīsen*, to shudder. + Du. *af-grijsselijk*, horrible; *af-grijzen*, horror.

Grist, a supply of corn to be ground. (E.) A. S. *grīst*. From the base of Grind.

gristle. (E.) A. S. *gristel*, cartilage; allied to *grist*, and A. S. *grīstbitiun*, to gnash the teeth. From the base of *grind*, with reference to the necessity of crunching it if eaten. So also Du. *knarsbeen*, gristle, from *knarsen*, to crunch.

Grit, coarse sand. (E.) Formerly *greet*, A. S. *grēot*, grit. + O. Fries. *grēt*, Icel. *grjōt*, G. *gries*. Allied to **Grout, Groat** (1).

Grizzly, Grizzled, grayish. (F.—M. H. G.) From M. E. *grisel*, a gray-haired man. — F. *gris*, gray. — M. H. G. *gris*, gray; cf. G. *greis*, a gray-haired man.+Du. *grijs*, O. Sax. *grīs*, gray.

Groan. (E.) M. E. *gronen.* A. S. *grānian*, to groan. Teut. type **grainōjan-*, from **grain*, 2nd grade of **greinan-*, as in O. H. G. *grīnan*, G. *greinen*, to weep, grin; Du. *grijnen*, to weep. Perhaps allied to **Grin.**

Groat (1), a particle, atom. (E.) M. E. *grot.* A. S. *grot.* From **grut-*, weak grade of **grout-* (as in A. S. *grēot*). See **Grit, Grout.**

Groat (2), a coin worth 4*d.* (Du.—Low G.) M. E. *grote.* — M. Du. *groote.* — O. Low G. *grote*, a coin of Bremen; meaning 'great,' because large in comparison with the copper coins (*Schwaren*) formerly in use there; cf. Du. *groot*, great, cognate with E. *great.*

Groats, grain of oats. (E.) M. E. *grotes*, lit. bits. — A. S. *grot*, an atom. — A. S. **grut-*; see **Groat** (1) above.

Grocer. (F.—L.) Formerly *grosser* or *engrosser*, a wholesale dealer. — O. F. *grossier*, a wholesale dealer. — O. F. *gros*, great; see **Gross. Der.** *grocer-y*, formerly *grossery.*

grog, spirits and water. (F. — L.) Short for *grogram*; it had its name from Admiral Vernon, nicknamed *Old Grog*, from his *grogram* breeches (ab. A. D. 1745); he ordered the sailors to dilute their rum with water.

grogram, a stuff. (F.—L.) Formerly *grogran*, so called from its coarse grain. — M. F. *grosgrain*, grogram. — O. F. *gros*, coarse; *grain*, grain.

Groin, the depression of the human body in front, at the junction of the thigh with the trunk. (E.) [Confused with F. Cot. gives '*groin de porc*, the head or

upper part of the shoulder-blade,' and *groin*, 'snowt of a hog.' The O. F. *groin* also means 'extremity, headland.' — Late L. type **grunnium*, from L. *grunnīre*, to grunt.] But *groin* is a variant of *grine* (in Cotg., s. v. *Aines*); fuller form *grinde* (*grynde* in Palsgrave). — A. S. *grynde*, abyss; hence, depression. Allied to **Ground. Der.** *groin-ed*, having angular curves that fork off.

Gromwell, a plant. (F.—L.) Formerly *gromelle, grumelle, gromel, grumel.* — O. F. *gremil, grenil*, 'the herb gromil, or graymil;' Cot. Prob. from L. *grānum*, a grain; from its hard seeds.

Groom. (Low G. *or* F.—Low G.) M. E. *grome.* Either from M. Du. *grom*, Icel. *gromr*, a boy, lad (Egilsson); or from O. F. **grome*, in the dimin. *gromet*, a lad, boy, servant, valet (whence F. *gourmet*), which is prob. from the same M. Du. *grom.* And see **Bridegroom. Der.** *grummet.*

Groove. (Du.) Du. *groef, groeve*, a trench, a channel, a groove. — Du. *graven* (pt. t. *groef*), to dig; see **Grave** (1).+ M. E. *grōfe*, a cave.

Grope. (E.) A. S. *grāpian*, to seize, handle; hence, to feel one's way. — A. S. *grāp*, 2nd grade of *grīpan*, to seize. See **Gripo.**

Gross. (F.—L.) O. F. *gros* (fem. *grosse*), gross, great. — L. *grossus*, fat, thick.

Grot. (F.—Ital.—L.—Gk.) F. *grotte*, a cave. — Ital. *grotta.* — L. *crypta.* — Gk. κρυπτή, a vault; see **Crypt.**

grotesque. (F.—Ital.—L.—Gk.) F. *grotesque*, ludicrous. — Ital. *grotesca*, curious painted work, such as was employed on the walls of grottoes. — Ital. *grotta* (above).

grotto. (Ital.—L.—Gk.) Better *grotta.* — Ital. *grotta* (above).

Ground. (E.) A. S. *grund.* + Du. *grond*, G. *grund*; Goth. *grundu-.* Teut. type **grunduz*; also **grunthuz*, whence Icel. *grunnr*, Dan. Swed. *grund.*

groundling, a spectator in the pit of a theatre. (E.) From *ground*, with double dimin. suffix *-l-ing*, with a contemptuous force.

grounds, dregs. (E.) So called from being at the bottom. Cf. Gael. *grunndas*, lees, from *grunnd*, bottom, ground; Irish *gruntas*, dregs, from *grunnt*, the bottom.

groundsel, a small plant. (E.) Also *groundswell* (Holland's tr. of Pliny). A.S. *grundeswelge,* as if 'ground-swallower,' but really from the older form *gundeswelge,* lit. 'swallower of pus,' from its supposed healing qualities; from A.S. *gund,* pus.

groundsill, threshold. (E.) From *ground* and *sill,* q. v. Also spelt *grunsel* (Milton).

Group. (F. – Ital. – G.) F. *groupe.* – Ital. *groppo,* a knot, heap, group. – O.H.G. *kropf,* a crop, wen on the throat, orig. a bunch; Low G. *kropp;* see Crop.

Grouse, a bird. (F. – Celtic?) *Grouse* appears to be a false form, evolved from an old pl. *grows* (1531). In 1547, the pl. was *grewes.* Of unknown origin, though the form seems to be French. Giraldus Cambrensis, Topographia Hibernica (Rolls Series, v. 47) has: 'gallinæ campestres, quas vulgariter *grutas* vocant.' ¶ Cotgrave, s. v. *griesche,* has 'the hen of the *grice* or moorgame.' This must be a mistake, as the word *grice* is otherwise unknown. Perhaps *gruta* represents a Celtic word, allied to E. *crow.*

Grout, coarse meal; **Grouts,** dregs. (E.) M. E. *grut.* – A. S. *grūt,* coarse meal. Cf. Du. *grut;* Icel. *grautr,* porridge, Dan. *gröd,* Swed. *gröt,* boiled groats; G. *grütze,* groats; allied to Lithuan. *grudas,* corn; L. *rūdus,* rubble. Cf. **Grit.**

Grove, a collection of trees. (E.) M.E. *groue* (with *u* = *v*). – A. S. *grāf,* a grove.

Grovel, to fall flat on the ground. (Scand.) Due to M. E. *groveling,* properly an adv., signifying flat on the ground; also spelt *grofling, groflinges,* where the suffixes *-ling, -linges* are adverbial; cf. *head-long, dark-ling.* – Icel. *grūfa,* in phr. *liggja ā grūfu,* to lie grovelling, *symja ā grūfu,* to swim on the belly; cf. also *grūfa, grufla,* to grovel; Swed. dial. *gruva,* flat on one's face, *ligga ā gruve,* to lie on one's face.

Grow. (E.) A.S. *grōwan,* pt. t. *grēow,* pp. *grōwen.* + Du. *groeijen,* Icel. *grōa,* Dan. *groe,* Swed. *gro.* Esp. to produce shoots, as herbs; allied to **Green.** **Der.** *grow-th;* from Icel. *grōðr,* growth.

Growl, to grumble. (F. – Low G.) Picard *grouler.* – E. Fries. *grullen;* cf. Du. *grollen,* to grumble; G. *grollen,* to rumble; Norw. *gryla,* to growl. (See *grol* in Franck.)

Grub, to grope in dirt. (E.) M.E. *grobben.* Cf. E. Fries. *grubbeln,* to grope about. + Low G. *grubbeln,* the same; G. *grübeln,* O. H. G. *grubilōn,* to rake, dig, grub. Allied to **Grave** (1).

Grudge, to grumble. (F.) M. E. *grochen, grucchen,* to murmur. – O. F. *groucier, groucher,* to murmur; Low L. *groussāre,* A.D. 1358. Probably *gru-dge, gru-nt, grow-l* are all from the same imitative base; cf. Gk. γρῦ, a grunt.

Gruel. (F. – O. Low G.) O. F. *gruel* (F. *gruau*). – Low L. **grūtellum,* dimin. of *grūtum,* meal. – O. Low G. *grūt,* Du. *gruit,* grout, coarse meal; see **Grout.**

Gruesome, horrible. (Scand.) Dan. *grusom,* cruel. – Dan. *gru,* horror; with suffix *-som,* as in *virk-som,* active. Cf. Dan. *grue,* to dread, *gruelig,* horrid. + Du. *gruwzaam,* G. *grausam;* M.H.G. *grūsam, grūwesam,* from M. H. G. *grūwe,* horror. Allied to O. Sax. *gruri,* A.S. *gryre,* horror; A.S. *be-grēosan,* to overwhelm with terror.

Gruff, rough, surly. (Du.) Du. *grof,* big, coarse, loud, blunt. + G. *grob,* coarse (whence Swed. *grof,* Dan. *grov*); O. H. G. *gerob;* E. Fries. *gruffig.*

Grumble, to murmur. (F. – G.) F. *grommeler* (Cot.). – Low and prov. G. *grummelen,* to grumble, frequent. of *grummen, grommen,* to grumble; M. Du. *grommelen,* frequent. of *grommen.* From **grumm-,* weak grade of Teut. **gremman-,* to rage, as in M. H. G. and A. S. *grimman,* to rage. Cf. G. *gram,* anger, and E. **Grim.**

Grume, a clot of blood. (F. – L.) Rare. M. F. *grume,* a cluster. – L. *grūmus,* a little heap.

Grummet, Gromet, a ship-boy, a cabin-boy. (F. – Teut.) O. F. *gromet,* a serving-boy; cf. Span. *grumete,* a ship-boy. – M. Du. *grom,* a boy; see **Groom.**

Grunsel; see Groundsill.

Grunt. (E.) M.E. *grunten.* A.S. *grunnettan,* extension of A.S. *grunian,* to grunt. + Dan. *grynte,* Swed. *grymta,* G. *grunzen;* so also L. *grunnīre,* Gk. γρύζειν. All imitative; cf. Gk. γρῦ, the noise made by a pig.

Guaiacum, a kind of resin, from lignum vitae. (Span. – Hayti.) Span. *guayaco, guayacan,* lignum vitae. From the language of Hayti.

Guanaco, a kind of Peruvian sheep. (Span. – Peruv.) Span. *guanaco* (Pineda). – Peruv. *huanacu,* a wild sheep.

Guano. (Span. – Peruv.) Span. *guano, huano.* – Peruv. *huanu,* dung.

Guarantee, sb. (F.—O. H. G.) Formerly *guaranty* or *garanty,* which are better spellings. — O. F. *garantie, garrantie,* a warranty; fem. of pp. of *garantir,* to warrant. — O. F. *garant, warant,* a warrant; see **Warrant.** Der. *guarantee,* vb.; cf. F. *garantir.*

Guard, vb. (F.—O. Low G.) O. F. *garder,* earliest form *warder,* to guard. — O. Sax. *wardōn,* to watch; cognate with A. S. *weardian,* to watch, from *weard,* sb.; see **Ward.** Der. *guard-ian;* see **Warden.**

Guava. (Span.—W. Ind.) Span. *guayaba;* borrowed from the native name in Guiana.

Gudgeon. (F.—L.—Gk.) M. E. *goione.*—F. *goujon.*—L. *gōbiōnem,* acc. of *gōbio,* a by-form of *gōbius.*—Gk. κωβιός, a gudgeon, tench.

Gueber, Gheber, a fire-worshipper. (F.—Pers.) F. *Guèbre.*—Pers. *gabr,* a priest of fire-worshippers; Rich., Dict., p. 1228.

Guelder-rose. (Du.) Here *guelder* stands for *Gueldre,* the F. spelling of the province of *Gelderland* in Holland.

Guerdon, recompense. (F.—O. H. G. and L.) O. F. *guerdon* (Ital. *guidardone*).—Low L. *widerdōnum,* a singular compound of O. H. G. *widar,* back, again, and L. *dōnum,* a gift. The word is really a half-translation of the true form O. H. G. *widarlōn,* a recompense. Here *widar =* G. *wieder,* back again; and *lōn* (G. *lohn*) is cognate with A. S. *lēan,* Du. *loon,* a reward, allied to L. *lu-crum,* gain; Brugm. i. § 490. So also A. S. *wiðer-lēan,* a recompense.

Guerilla, Guerrilla, irregular warfare. (Span.—O. H. G.) Span. *guerrilla,* a skirmish, lit. 'little war;' dimin. of *guerra,* war.—O. H. G. *werra,* war; see **War.**

Guess. (Scand.) M. E. *gessen.*—Dan. *gisse,* Swed. *gissa,* to guess.+E. Fries. and Du. *gissen,* Icel. *giska;* N. Fries. *gezze, gedse.* Allied to Dan. *gjette,* to guess; the Icel. *giska* may be for **git-ska,* a denominative vb. from a base **git-isko-,* ingenious, acute, from *geta,* to get, also, to guess. See **Get.**

Guest. (Scand.) M. E. *gest.* — Icel. *gestr,* Dan. *giest,* Swed. *gäst.*+A. S. *gæst, giest;* Du. *gast,* Goth. *gasts,* G. *gast.* Teut. type **gastiz;* Idg. type **ghostis;* cf. Russ. *gost(e),* a guest, alien; L. *hostis,*

a stranger, also an enemy. Allied to **Hostile.**

Guide. (F. — Ital. — Teut.) M. E. *gyden* (also *gyen*). — F. *guider,* to guide. — Ital. *guidare;* cf. O. F. *guier,* Span. *guiar.* The *gu* (for *w*) shows the word to be of Teut. origin. — O. Sax. *wītan* (A. S. *wītan*), to pay heed to; O. H. G. *wīzan.* Allied to **Wit.** Cf. **Guy-rope.**

Guild, Gild. (Scand.) The spelling *guild* indicates the hard *g.* M. E. *gilde.* — Icel. *gildi,* a payment, a guild; Dan. *gilde.* — Icel. *gjalda* (pres. t. *geld*), to pay; cognate with A. S. *geldan,* to pay, yield; see **Yield.**+Du. *gild;* whence G. *gilde.*

Guilder, an old Dutch coin. (Du.) Adaptation of M. Du. *gulden,* 'a gilder,' Hexham. From Teut. adj. type **gulthīnoz,* golden, from Teut. **gulth-om,* gold. See **Gold.**

Guile, a wile. (F. — O. Low G.) O. F. *guile.* From a Low G. form; see further under **Wile.** Der. *beguile,* vb., with E. prefix *be-* (= *by*).

Guillotine. (F.) Named after a French physician, *J. I. Guillotin,* died A. D. 1814. First used, 1792.

Guilt, crime. (E.) M. E. *gilt.* A. S. *gylt,* a trespass; also, a fine for a trespass. Teut. type **gultiz,* m.; perhaps related to A. S. *geldan,* to pay, yield; see **Yield.**

Guinea. (African.) First coined of African gold from the *Guinea* coast, A. D. 1663. Der. *guinea-fowl* (from *Guinea*). ¶ The *guinea-pig* is from S. America; so that it may mean *Guiana pig.*

Guipure, a lace of cords, kind of gimp. (F. — Teut.) F. *guipure.* — Teut. **wīp-an,* to wind, weave; as in Goth. *weipan,* to crown (whence *waips,* a wreath); G. *weifen,* to reel, wind.

Guise, way, wise. (F. — O. H. G.) M. E. *gise, guise.* — O. F. *guise,* way, wise, manner. — O. H. G. *wīsa* (G. *weise*), a wise; cognate with **Wise** (2).

Guitar. (F.—L.—Gk.) F. *guitare.* — L. *cithara.* — Gk. κιθάρα, a lyre; see **Cithern.**

Gules, red. (F.—L.) M. E. *goules.* — F. *gueules,* gules, red; answering to Late L. *gulæ* (pl. of *gula*), meaning (1) mouth, (2) reddened skin, (3) gules. (See *Gula* in Ducange.) — L. *gula,* the throat.

Gulf. (F. — Ital. — Gk.) Formerly *goulfe.* — F. *golfe.* — Ital. *golfo.* — Late Gk. κόλφος, a variant of Gk. κόλπος, the bosom, also, a deep hollow, bay, creek. **Der.** *en-gulf.*

Gull (1), a bird. (C.) Corn. *gullan,* a gull; W. *gwylan;* Bret. *gwelan;* O. Irish *foilenn,* 'alcedo.'

Gull (2), a dupe. (C.) The same; from the notion that a *gull* was a stupid bird. ¶ But cf. Du. *gul,* soft, good-natured; M. Du. *gulle,* 'a great wench without wit,' Hexham.

Gullet, the throat. (F. – L.) M. E. *golet.* – M.F. *goulet* (Cot.); dimin. of O. F. *gole, goule* (F. *gueule*), the throat. – L. *gula,* the throat. Brugm. i. § 499.

gully, a channel worn by water. (F. – L.) Formerly *gullet.* – M. F. *goulet,* 'a gullet, a deep gutter of water;' Cot. The same word as **Gullet** (above).

Gulp. (E.) M. E. *gulpen, gloppen, glubben.* Cf. E. Fries. and Du. *gulpen,* to swallow eagerly; Du. *gulp,* a great billow, draught, gulp. Prob. of imitative origin. Cf. Swed. *glupa,* to devour.

Gum (1), flesh of the jaws. (E.) M. E. *gōme.* A.S. *gōma,* jaws, palate. + Icel. *gōmr,* Swed. *gom;* cf. G. *gaumen,* Lith. *gomurys,* the palate. Brugm. i. § 196.

Gum (2), resin of certain trees. (F. – L. – Gk.) M. E. *gomme.* – F. *gomme.* – L. *gummi.* – Gk. κόμμι, gum. (Prob. of Egyptian origin; Coptic *komē,* gum.)

Gun. (Scand.) M. E. *gonne;* from an engine of war named *Gunilda* in 1330–1. From Icel. *Gunnhildr,* a female name.

Gunny, a coarse kind of sacking. (Hind. – Skt.) Hind. and Mahratti *goṇ, goṇī,* a sack, sacking. – Skt. *goṇī,* a sack (Yule).

Gunwale, upper edge of a ship's side. (E.) See *gunwale* or *gunnel* in Kersey (1715). A *wale* is an outer timber on a ship's side; and the *gun-wale* is a *wale* from which *guns* were pointed. A *wale* is a 'beam'; see **Wale.**

Gurgle, to purl. (Ital. – L.) In Spenser, Thestylis, 3. Imitated from Ital. *gorgogliare,* to purl, bubble, boil; *gorgoglio,* gurgling of a stream. – Ital. *gorgo,* a whirlpool. – L. *gurges,* whirlpool; cf. *gurgulio,* gullet. See **Gorge.** So also Du. *gorgel,* G. *gurgel,* throat; from L. *gurgulio.* Brugm. i. § 499.

Gurnard, Gurnet, a fish. (F. – L.; *with* Teut. *suffix.*) *Gurnard* is the better and fuller form. The word means 'a grunter,' from the sound which the fish makes when taken out of the water. –

M. F. *grongnard* (F. *grognard*), grunting, grunter, whence M. F. *gournauld, grougnaut,* gurnard (Cot.). – M. F. *grogner,* to grunt; with suffix *-ard* (= G. *hart*). –L. *grunnīre,* to grunt; see **Grunt.**

Gush. (E.) M. E. *guschen.* E. Fries. *gūsen,* to gush out. + M. Du. *guysen,* to gush out (Kilian); Icel. *gusa,* allied to *gjōsa* (pt. t. *gauss*), Norw. *gjosa,* to gush. Allied to Icel. *gjōta,* to pour, Goth. *giutan,* L. *fundere.* Cf. Du. *gudsen,* to gush. (√GHEU.) See **Gut, Geysir.**

Gusset. (F.) F. *gousset,* 'a gusset,' Cot. Also 'the piece of armour by which the arm-hole is covered,' id. Named from its supposed resemblance to a husk of a bean or pea; dimin. of F. *gousse,* husk of bean or pea; cf. Ital. *guscio,* a shell, husk; of unknown origin.

Gust (1), a sudden blast, gush of wind. (Scand.) Icel. *gustr,* a gust. – Icel. *gus-,* weak grade of *gjōsa,* to gush; see **Gush.** So also Swed. dial. *gust,* stream of air from an oven, Norw. *gust,* a gust.

Gust (2), relish, taste. (L.) L. *gustus,* a tasting; cf. *gustāre,* to taste. (√GEUS.) Allied to **Choose.** **Der.** *dis-gust.*

Gut, the intestinal canal. (E.) (The word is allied to M. E. *gote,* prov. E. *gut,* a channel.) M. E. *gutte.* A.S. *gut;* pl. *guttas;* orig. 'a channel.' Mone, Quellen, p. 333, l. 198. – A. S. *gut-,* weak grade of Teut. **geutan-,* A.S. *gēotan,* to pour. (√GHEU.) + Dan. *gyde,* a lane, M. Du. *gote,* a channel, G. *gosse,* a drain. See **Gush.**

Gutta-percha. (Malay.) The spelling *gutta* is due to confusion with L. *gutta,* a drop, with which it has nothing to do. – Malay *gatah, gutah,* gum, balsam; *percha,* the name of the tree producing it.

Gutter. (F. – L.) M. E. *gotere.* – A. F. *guttere;* O. F. *gutiere, goutiere* (Littré, s. v. *gouttière,* a gutter). Esp. used for catching drops from the eaves of a roof. – F. *goutte.* – L. *gutta,* a drop.

Guttural. (F. – L.) F. *guttural.* – L. *gutturālis,* belonging to the throat. – L. *guttur,* the throat.

Guy, a hideous creature, fright. (F. – Ital. – Teut.) Orig. used of an effigy of *Guy* Fawkes. – F. *Guy.* – Ital. *Guido;* of Teut. origin. Cf. **Guide.**

Guy-rope, Guy, a guide-rope, used to steady a weight in heaving. (F. – Teut.) O. F. *guie,* a guide. – O. F. *guier,* to guide; see **Guide.** Cf. Span. *guia,* a guy-rope.

Guzzle. (F.) Apparently suggested by O. F. *goziller*, *gosillier*, to vomit (Godefroy), understood to mean ' to swallow greedily.' The O. F. *desgosiller* had both senses (Godefroy). Cf. O. F. *gosillier*, the throat, allied to F. *gosier*, the throat. Remoter source unknown.

Gymnasium. (L.—Gk.) L. *gymnasium.* — Gk. γυμνάσιον, an athletic school, where men practised naked. — Gk. γυμνάζειν, to train naked, exercise. — Gk. γυμνός, naked. **Der.** *gymnast* = γυμναστής, a trainer of athletes; *gymnast-ic.*

Gypsum. (L.—Gk.—Arab.) L. *gypsum*, chalk. — Gk. γύψος, chalk. Prob. from Pers. *jabsīn*, lime, Arab. *jibs*, plaster, mortar; Rich. Dict., p. 494.

Gypsy. (F.—L.—Gk.—Egypt.) Spelt *gipsen*, Spenser, M. Hubbard, 86. Short for M. E. *Egypcien.* — O. F. *Egyptien.* — Late L. *Ægyptiānus*; from L. *Ægyptius*, an Egyptian. — Gk. Αἰγύπτιος. — Gk. Αἴγυπτος, Egypt. ¶ The supposition that they came from *Egypt* was false; their original home was India.

Gyre, circular course. (L.—Gk.) L. *gȳrus.* — Gk. γῦρος, ring, circle. **Der.** *gyr-ate*, from pp. of L. *gyrāre.*

Gyrfalcon, Gerfalcon, bird of prey. (F.—Teut. *and* L.) Formerly *gerfaulcon*; also *girefaucon* (used by Trevisa to translate L. *gyrofalco*). — O. F. *gerfaucon.* — M. H. G. *girvalke.* — O. H. G. *gīr-*, for *gīri*, greedy (whence also G. *geier*, a vulture); and L. *falco*, a falcon. ¶ L. *gȳrofalco* is a mistaken form.

Gyron; see Giron.

Gyves, fetters. (F.) M. E. *giues*, *gyues.* — A. F. *gives*, fetters (Godefroy). Cf. O. H. G. *be-wīfen*, to fetter.

H.

Ha, interj. (E.) An exclamatory sound. Cf. O. Fries. *haha*, to denote laughter; G. *he*; O. F. *ha!*

Haberdasher, a seller of small wares. (F.) So named from his selling a stuff called *hapertas* in A.F.; see Liber Albus. ed. Riley, pp. 225, 231. The name of this stuff is of unknown origin.

Habergeon, armour for neck and breast. (F.—O. H. G.) M. E. *habergeon*, *haubergeoun.* — O. F. *haubergeon*, *hauberjon*, a hauberk; deriv. (treated as dimin.) of O. F. *hauberc*; see Hauberk.

Habiliment, dress. (F.—L.) F. *habillement*, clothing. — F. *habiller*, to clothe, orig. ' to get ready.' — F. *habile*, ready, fit. — L. *habilis*, easy to handle, active. — L. *habēre*, to have ; see **Able.**

Habit, practice, custom, dress. (F.—L.) O. F. *habit*, a dress, a custom. — L. *habitum*, acc. of *habitus*, a condition, dress. — L. *habitus*, pp. of *habēre*, to have, keep. See Brugm. i. § 638.

habitable. (F.—L.) F. *habitable.* — L. *habitābilis*, that can be dwelt in. — L. *habitāre*, to dwell, frequent. of *habēre*, to have.

habitant. (F.—L.) F. *habitant*, pres. pt. of *habiter*, to dwell. — L. *habitāre*, frequent. of *habēre* (above).

habitat, the natural abode of a plant. (L.) L. *habitat*, it dwells (there); 3 pres. s. of *habitāre*, to dwell (above).

habitation, abode. (F.—L.) F. *habitation.* — L. acc. *habitātiōnem.* — L. *habitātus*, pp. of *habitāre*, to dwell, frequent. of *habēre*, to have.

habitude. (F.—L.) F. *habitude*, custom.—L. *habitūdo*, condition.—L. *habit-*, as in *habitus*, pp. of *habēre*, to have.

Hacienda, a farm, estate, farm-house. (Span.—L.) Span. *hacienda*, an estate, orig. employment. [The *c* is pronounced as *th* in *thin*.] O. Span. *facienda.* — L. *facienda*, things to be done; gerundive neut. pl. of *facere*, to do.

Hack (1), to cut, mangle. (E.) M. E. *hakken.* A. S. *haccian*, to cut, in the comp. *tō-haccian.* + Du. *hakken*, Dan. *hakke*, Swed. *hacka*, G. *hacken*, to chop, hack. Teut. types **hakkōn-*, **hakkōjan-*.

Hack (2); see Hackney.

Hackbut. (F.—Low G.) Also *hagbut.* — M. F. *haquebute*, ' a haquebut, a caliver' (i. e. a sort of musket); Cot. A corruption of Low G. *hakebusse* (Du. *haakbus*), an arquebus; due, apparently, to some confusion with O. F. *buter*, to thrust. Lit. ' hook-gun;' so called from the hook on the gun, by which it was hung on to a support. — Low G. *hake*, (Du. *haak*), hook; *busse* (Du. *bus*), a gun. See Arquebus; and see Hook.

Hackle (1), **Hatchel,** an instrument for dressing flax; see Heckle.

Hackle (2), long shining feathers on the neck of a cock. (E.) Probably allied to Hackle (1).

Hackney, Hack, a horse let out for hire. (E.) M. E. *hakeney.* O. F. *haquenee*, which was merely borrowed from the A. F. *hakeney* (1340), *hakenei* (130;), Low L. *hakeneius* (1292); all from M. E. *Hakeney*, i. e. Hackney in Middlesex, spelt *Hakeneia* in 1199; from A. S. *Haccanīeg*, Hacca's island. ¶ *Hack* is short for *hackney*, and quite a late form; hence *hack*, verb, i. e. to use as a hack or hackney.

Haddock, a fish. (E.) M. E. *haddok* (XIV cent.). Orig. doubtful; the Irish for 'haddock' is *codog.*

Hades, the abode of the dead. (Gk.) Gk. ᾳδης, αἴδης (Attic), ἀΐδης (Homeric), the nether world; in Homer, the god of the nether world. Of unknown origin.

Hadji, Hajji, one who has performed the pilgrimage to Mecca. (Arab.) Arab. *ḥājī*, 'a Christian who has performed the pilgrimage to Jerusalem, or a Muhammedan [who has performed] that to Mecca;' Rich. Dict., p. 549. Orig. the latter.

Hæmatite, Hæmorrhage; see Hematite, Hemorrhage.

Haft, handle. (E.) A. S. *hæft*, a handle. ▬ A. S. *haf-*, base of *hebban*, to lift; see **Heave.** ╇ Du. *heft*, Icel. *hepti* (pron. *hefti*), G. *heft*, a handle. Lit. 'that which is caught up.'

Hag. (E.) M. E. *hagge*; with same sense as A. S. *hægtis*, a fury, a witch, a hag.╇G. *hexe*, M. H. G. *hecse*, a witch, O. H. G. *hazissa*, also *hagazussa*, a fury. Perhaps connected with A. S. *haga*, a hedge, enclosure; but this is uncertain.

Haggard (1), wild, said of a hawk. (F.—G.) M. F. *hagard*, wild; esp used of a wild falcon; see Cotgrave. Perhaps the orig. sense was hedge-falcon; formed, with suffix *-ard* (<O. H. G. *hart*), from M. H. G. *hag* (G. *hag*), a hedge; see Haw.

Haggard (2), lean, meagre. (F.—G.) Really the same as the word above (Cot.). We also find *hagg-ed*, i. e. hag-like, from *hag.* 'The ghostly prudes with *hagged* face,' Gray, A Long Story, near end. ¶ Mod. G. *hager* may be from M. F. *hagard*; for G. *hagerfalk* means a haggard hawk.

Haggis, a dish of sheep's entrails, chopped up, seasoned, and boiled in the sheep's maw. (F.) M. E. *hagas, hageis.* A. F. *hagiz, hageis*; from the verb *hag*, to cut up, chop up. Of Scand. origin; cf. Swed. dial. *hagga*, to hew, Icel. *höggva.*

Haggle (1), to hack awkwardly, mangle.

(Scand.) Frequent. of North E. *hag*, to cut; as *hackle* is of *hack*, to cut. The form *hag* is from Icel. *höggva*, to hew, cognate with E. *hew*; see **Hew.** Cf. Norman dial. *haguer*, to hack.

Haggle (2), to be slow in making a bargain. (E.) In Cotgrave, s. v. *harceler.* Cf. Du. *hakkelen*, 'to hackle, mangle, faulter,' i. e. stammer (Sewel); *hakketeren*, to wrangle, cavil. It is probably the same word as **Haggle** (1). Cf. also *higgle*, to bargain.

Hagiographa, holy writings. (Gk.) Gk. ἁγιόγραφ ι (βιβλία), books written by inspiration. ▬ Gk. ἅγιο-s, holy; γράφ-ειν, to write.

Ha-ha, Haw-haw, a sunk fence. (F.) From F. *haha*, an interjection of laughter; hence a surprise in the form of an unexpected obstacle (that laughs at one). The F. word also means an old woman of surprising ugliness, a 'caution.'

Hail (1), frozen rain. (E.) M. E. *haghel, hayl.* A. S. *hægl, hagol.* ╋ Icel. *hagl*, Du. Dan. Swed. G. *hagel.* Teut. types **hag(a)loz*, m., **hag(a)lom*, n. Cf. Gk. κάχληξ, a round pebble.

Hail (2), to salute, greet. (Scand.) M. E. *heilen*; a verb coined from M. E. *heil, hail*, sb.; which is an adaptation of Icel. *heill*, prosperity, good luck, a sb. formed from the adj. *heill*, hale, sound, fortunate. Cf. A. S. *hǣl*, safety, luck. See Hale (1).

hail (3), an exclamation. (Scand.) Icel. *heill*, hale, sound; used in greeting. This word is common in greeting persons, as *far heill* = farewell, *kom heill*, welcome, hail! The Scand. verb is Icel. *heilsa*, Swed. *helsa*, Dan. *hilse*, to greet. See Hale (1).

Hair. (E.; *influenced by* F.) The true E. form was M. E. *heer.* From A. S. *hȇr, hȇr.* ╋ Du. *haar*, Icel. *hār*, Dan. *haar*, Swed. *hår*; G. *haar*, O. H. G. *hār.* Teut. type **hȇrom*, neut. Further related to Icel. *haddᵣ*, hair, Teut. type **hazdoz*; and to Lith. *kassa*, plaited hair; also to Russ. *chesat(e)*, to comb out, L. *carere*, to card wool. β. But the mod. E. form is due to confusion with A. S. *hȇre*, hair-cloth, which was replaced by M. E. *haire*, borrowed from O. F. *haire*, with the same sense; and this O. F. *haire* was from O. H. G. *hārra* (for **hārjā*), haircloth, a derivative of O. H. G. *hār*, hair.

Hake, a fish. (Scand.) Cf. Norw.

hakefisk, lit. 'hook-fish;' from the hooked underjaw. See **Hatch** (1).

Hakim, a physician, doctor. (Arab.) Arab. *ḥakīm*, wise; also, a doctor, physician. — Arab. root *ḥakama*, he exercised authority.

Halberd, Halbert, a kind of pole-axe. (F. — M. H. G.) O. F. *halebarde*. — M. H. G. *helmbarte*, mod. G. *hellebarte*; sometimes explained as an axe with a long handle; cf. M. H. G. *halm* (?), a helve (helm), or handle. But it has been better interpreted as an axe for splitting a *helm*, i. e. helmet. β. The O. H. G. *barta*, G. *barte*, a broad axe, or axe with a broad blade, is from G. *bart*, a beard. [Similarly the Icel. *skeggja*, an axe, is from *skegg*, a beard; and see **Barb** (1).] Cf. Icel. *barða*, halberd.

Halcyon, a kingfisher; as adj. serene. (L. — Gk.) *Halcyon* days = calm days; it was supposed that the weather was calm when kingfishers were breeding. — L. *halcyon, alcyon*, a kingfisher. — Gk. ἁλκυών, ἀλκυών, a kingfisher. Allied to L. *alcēdo*, the true L. name. ¶ The incorrect aspirate in Gk. was due to a fanciful etymology from ἅλ-ς, sea, and κύων, conceiving.

Hale (1), whole. (E.) M. E. *hale, hal.* O. Northumb. *hāl*, which became *hale*, while the A. S. (Wessex) *hǣl* became M. E. *hool*, now spelt *whole*. Cognate with Goth. *hails.* See **Whole**.

Hale (2), **Haul,** to drag, draw violently. (F. — O. H. G.) M. E. *halien, halen.* — F. *haler*, to haul a boat, &c. (Littré). — O. H. G. *halōn, holōn* (whence G. *holen*). + O. Sax. *halōn*, Du. *halen*, O. Fries. *halia*, E. Fries. *halen*, Low G. *halen*, to pull, haul; cf. also A. S. *geholian*, to acquire, get; L. *calāre*, to summon; Gk. καλεῖν, to summon. (√KAL). ¶ *Hale* dates from the XIV cent.; *haul* is later, appearing as *hall* in 1581.

Half, adj. (E.) M. E. *half.* O. Merc. *half*, O. Fries. *half*; A. S. *healf.* + Du. *half*, Icel. *hālfr*, Swed. *half*, Dan. *halv*, Goth. *halbs*, G. *halb.* 2. Allied to *half*, sb., from O. Merc. *half*, A. S. *healf*, sb. + Icel. *hālfa*, Goth. *halba*, G. *halb*; in all these languages the oldest sense of the sb. is 'side.' **Der.** *halve*, vb.; *be-half.*

Halibut, Holibut, a fish. (E.) So called because excellent eating for holi-days; the lit. sense is 'holy (i. e. holiday) plaice.' From M. E. *hali*, holy (see **Holy**), and *butte*, a plaice (Havelok, l.

759). So also Du. *heilbot*, halibut, from *heilig*, holy, *bot*, a plaice; Swed. *helge-flundra*, a halibut, from *helig*, holy, *flyndra*, a flounder; Dan. *helleflynder*, a halibut, from *hellig*, holy, *flynder*, flounder. See **Butt** (4).

Halidom, a holy relic. (E.) M. E. *halidom, halidam.* A. S. *hāligdōm*, holiness, a sanctuary, a holy relic. — A. S. *hālig*, holy; *-dōm*, suffix, orig. the same as *dōm*, doom. See **Holy** and **Doom**. + Du. *heiligdom*; Icel. *helgidōmr*, Dan. *helligdom*, G. *heiligthum.* ¶ *By my halidam* (with *-dam* for *-dom*) was imagined to refer to Our Lady (*dame*).

Hall. (E.) M. E. *halle.* O. Merc. *hall*; A. S. *heall, heal*, a hall, orig. a shelter. + Du. *hal*, Icel. *hall, höll*, Swed. *hall*, Dan. *hal.* Teut. type *hallā*, for *halnā*, fem.; from *hal*, 2nd grade of *helan-*, to cover (A. S. *helan*). Allied to **Helm** (2), **Hell**.

Hallelujah, Alleluia, an expression of praise. (Heb.) Heb. *halelū jāh*, praise ye Jehovah. — Heb. *halelū*, praise ye (from *hālal*, to shine, praise); *jāh*, Jah, Jehovah.

Halliard; see **Halyard**.

Halloo, Hallow, to shout. (F.) M. E. *halowen.* — O. F. *halloer*, to pursue with shouts. Of imitative origin.

Hallow, to sanctify. (E.) M. E. *hal-wen, halewen, halowen.* A. S. *hālgian*, to make holy, from *hālig*, holy; see **Holy**. So also Icel. *helga*, G. *heiligen*.

hallowmass, feast of *All Hallows*, i. e. All Saints. (Hybrid; E. *and* L.) Short for *All Hallows' Mass*, mass (or feast) of All Saints. Here *hallows'* is the gen. of *hallows*, pl. due to M. E. *halowe* or *halwe*, a saint = A. S. *hālga*, a saint, def. form of the adj. *hālig*, holy; see **Holy** and **Mass**.

Hallucination, wandering of mind. (L.) From L. *hallūcinātio*, a wandering of the mind. — L. *hallūcinārī*, better *allū-cinārī, alūcinārī*, to wander in mind, dream, rave. + Gk. ἀλύειν, ἀλύειν, to wander in mind; cf. ἠλεός, distraught.

Halm; see **Haulm**.

Halo, a luminous ring. (F. — L. — Gk.) F. *halo.* — L. acc. *halō*, from nom. *halōs.* — Gk. ἅλως, a round threshing-floor, in which the oxen trod out a circular path.

Halser; see **Hawser**.

Halt, lame. (E.) M. E. *halt.* O. Merc. *halt*; A. S. *healt.* + Icel. *haltr*, Dan. Swed. *halt*, Goth. *halts*, O. H. G. *halz.* Teut.

type *haltoz. Cf. L. claudus, lame. Der. halt, vb., A. S. healtian.

Halt! (F.—G.) F. halte.—G. halt, hold! See Hold (1).

Halter. (E.) M. E. halter (an f has been lost). A. S. hælftre, a halter.+M. Du. and G. halfter, O. H. G. halftra; O. Low G. haliftra (Schade). Teut. types *halftr, *haliftr- (Franck). From the base *halb-, app. signifying 'to hold'; see Helve. I. e. 'something to hold by;' cf. L. capistrum, a halter.

Halyard, Halliard, a rope for hoisting sails. (F.—O. H. G.) As if for hale- or haul-yard, because it hales or hauls the yards into their places; but really a perversion of M. E. halier, meaning simply 'that which hales.' See Hale (2).

Ham. (E.) M. E. hamme. A. S. hamm. +Du. ham, M. Du. hame, Icel. höm (gen. hamar); prov. G. hamme; O. H. G. hamma. Brugmann (i. § 421) connects these with Gk. κνήμη, the lower part of the leg.

Hamadryad, a wood-nymph. (L.— Gk.) L. hamadryad-, stem of hamadryas. —Gk. ἁμαδρυάς, a wood-nymph; the life of each nymph depended on that of the tree to which she was attached. —Gk. ἅμα, together with; δρῦ-s, tree.

Hame; Hames, pl., the bent sticks round a horse-collar. (E.) M. E. hame. +Du. haam. Cf. Mid. Du. hamme, 'a cratch of wood to tie beasts to, or a yoke;' Hexham. See Hem (1).

Hamlet. (F.—Teut.) M. E. hamelet, dimin. of O. F. hamel (F. hameau), a hamlet. Formed, with dimin. suffix -el, from O. Fries. hām, hēm, O. Sax. hēm, a home, dwelling; see Home.

Hammer. (E.) A. S. hamor. + Icel. hamarr, Dan. hammer, Swed. hammare, Du. hamer, G. hammer. Thought to be allied to Russ. kamen(e), a stone; as if orig. 'a stone implement;' Icel. hamarr also means 'a rock.'

Hammercloth. (Du. and E.?) Formerly hamer-cloth (1465). The cloth which covers a coach-box. Origin unknown. Perhaps orig. a cover-cloth; adapted from Du. hemel, heaven, also a cover, tester, canopy. 'Den hemel van een koetse, the seeling of a coach;' Hexham. Cf. M. Du. hemelen, 'to hide, cover, adorne;' Hexham.

Hammock, a slung net for a bed. (W. Ind.) Formerly hamaca; Span.

hamaca. A West Indian (Caribbean) word.

Hamper (1), to impede. (E.) M. E. hampren; from the same root as Icel. hamla, to stop, hinder, Norw. hamla, to strive against; cf. Swed. dial. hamla, to be awkward, to grope about. Perhaps further allied to Icel. hemja, to restrain, G. hemmen, to check. See Hem (1). 2. Or a nasalised form allied to Low G. hapern, E. Fries. haperen, to stop short; cf. Swed. dial. happla, to stammer, happa, to back a horse; Dan. happe, to stutter. See Hopple.

Hamper (2), a kind of basket. (F.— G.) Formerly spelt hanaper. — O. F. hanapier, Low L. hanapērium, orig. a vessel to keep cups in. — O. F. hanap (Low L. hanapus), a drinking-cup. — O. Frankish *hnapp-, Du. nap, O. H. G. hnapf, M. H. G. napf, a cup.+A. S. hnæp, a cup, bowl.

hanaper, old form of **Hamper** (above). Hence Hanaper office, named from the basket in which writs were deposited.

Hand. (E.) A. S. hand, hond.+Du. hand, Icel. hönd, Dan. haand, Swed. hand, Goth. handus, G. hand. Teut. type *handuz, fem. Root unknown.

handcuff. (E.) A cuff for the hand. ¶ XVIII cent.; too late for connexion with A.S. handcops, a handcuff.

handicap, a race for horses of all ages. (E.) From hand i' cap, hand in the cap, a method of drawing lots; hence, a mode of settlement by arbitration, &c.

handicraft. (E.) A. S. handcræft, a trade; the i being inserted in imitation of handiwork (below).

handiwork. (E.) M. E. handiwerc. A. S. handgeweorc. — A. S. hand, hand; geweorc, from weorc, O. Merc. werc, work. The i is due to A. S. ge.

handle, vb. (E.) A. S. handlian; formed from handle, a handle (below). Cf. Du. handelen, Icel. höndla, Dan. handle, Sw. handla, G. handeln, to handle, or to trade.

handle, sb. (E.) A. S. handle; Cp. Glos. 1904.— A. S. hand, hand.

handsel, hansel, first instalment of a bargain. (Scand.) Icel. handsal, the conclusion of a bargain by shaking hands; lit. 'handgiving,' expressed by 'hand-sale'; so also Dan. handsel, Swed. handsöl, a handsel. See Sale. ¶ The late A. S.

handselen, glossed 'mancipatio,' occurs but once; but cf. O. E. Texts, Charter 44, l. 8.

handsome. (E.) M. E. *handsum*, orig. tractable, or dexterous. — A. S. *hand*, hand; *-sum*, suffix, as in *wyn-sum*, winsome.+Du. *handzaam*, E. Fries. *handsām*, tractable, serviceable.

handy (1), dexterous. (E.) From *hand*, with suffix *-y*. ¶ The M. E. form was *hendi* (never *handi*); A. S. *hendig*, skilful; formed from *hand*, hand, with suffix *-ig* and vowel-change.+Du. *handig*, Dan. *hændig*, *behændig*, Swed. *händig*, dexterous.

handy (2), near. (E.) From *hand*, with suffix *-y*. ¶ The M. E. form was *hende*; A. S. *gehende*, near, at hand.— A. S. *hand*, hand.

Hang, to suspend, to be suspended. (E.) The history of this vb. involves that of two A. S. and one O. Norse vb.; viz. (1) the A. S. *hōn* (for **hanhan-*), pt. t. *hēng*, pp. *hangen*; (2) the A. S. weak vb., *hangian*, pt. t. *hangode*; and (3) the Icel. causal vb. *hengja*, from *hanga* (pt. t. *hēkk*, for **hēnk*, pp. *hanginn*). Cf. G. *hängen*, weak vb., from G. *hangen* (pt. t. *hing*, pp. *gehangen*). Allied to L. *cunctārī*, to delay, Skt. *çank*, to hesitate. Brugm. i. § 420.

Hanger, a short sword. (E.) So called because *hung* from the belt.

Hangnail; for *ang-nail*, a form of Agnail, q. v.

Hank, a parcel of skeins of yarn. (Scand.) Icel. *hönk*, a hank, coil; *hanki*, a hasp, clasp; Swed. *hank*, a string, Dan. *hank*, a handle, ear of a vessel. Cf. also Low G. *hank*, a handle (Lübben), G. *henkel*, a handle, ear of a vessel. Prob. allied to G. *haken*, a hook, A. S. *haca*, fastening of a door. See Hatch (1).

Hanker, to long after. (E.) Cf. prov. E. *hank*, to hanker after, of which it is a frequent form; cf. the phr. 'to *hang* about.' From the verb *to hang*. Verified by M. Du. *hengelen*, to hanker after (from *hangen*), *honkeren* (Du. *hunkeren*), to hanker after (Sewel); also Dan. *hang*, bias, inclination, E. Fries. *hang*, *hank*, bias.

Hanseatic, pertaining to the Hanse towns in Germany. (F.—O. H. G.) O. F. *hanse*, the hanse, i. e. society of merchants; with L. suffix *-āticus*.—O. H. G. *hansa* (G. *hanse*), an association; cf. Goth. *hansa*, A. S. *hōs*, a band of men. (From about A. D. 1140.)

Hansel; see Handsel.

Hansom, a kind of cab. (E.) From the name of the inventor (no doubt the same word as *handsome*). A. D. 1834.

Hap. (Scand.) M. E. *hap*.—Icel. *happ*, hap, chance, good luck; cf. A. S. *gehæp*, fit. [The W. *hap* must be borrowed from E.] Der. *happ-y*, i. e. lucky; *hap-less*, i. e. luckless; *hap-ly*, by luck (*happily* is used in the same sense); *mis-hap*; *per-haps*.

happen. (Scand.) M. E. *happenen*, *hapnen*, extended from *happen*, i. e. to hap. From the sb. above.

Hara-kiri, suicide by disembowelment. (Japanese.) From Japan. *hara*, belly; *kiri*, to cut (Yule).

Harangue. (F. — O. H. G.) O. F. *harangue*, an oration; Low L. *harenga*. The same as Span. *arenga*, Ital. *aringa*. Orig. a speech made in the midst of a *ring* of people; as shown by Ital. *aringo*, an arena, lists, also a pulpit.—O. H. G. *hrinc* (G. *ring*), a ring, ring of people, an arena, circus, lists. Cognate with A. S. *hring*, a ring. See **Ring**.

Harass. (F.) F. *harasser*, to tire out, vex, disquiet; Cot. Perhaps from O. F. *harer*, to set a dog at a beast.— O. H. G. *haren*, to call out, cry out (hence cry to a dog).

Harbinger, a forerunner. (F. — O. H. G.) M. E. *herbergeour*, one who provided lodgings for a man of rank.— O. F. *herberg-er*, to lodge, to harbour; with suffix *-our* (L. *-ātōrem*).—O. F. *herberge*, a lodging, harbour. — O. H. G. *heriberga* (below).

Harbour (1), shelter. (Scand.) M. E. *hereberᴣe*, *herberwe*. — Icel. *herbergi*, a harbour, lit. 'army-shelter.' — Icel. *herr*, an army; *barg*, 2nd grade of *bjarga*, to shelter. So likewise O. H. G. *heriberga*, a camp, lodging, from O. H. G. *heri* (G. *heer*), an army, *bergan*, to shelter (whence F. *auberge*, Ital. *albergo*). Cf. **Harry** and **Borough**. Der. *harbour*, vb.

Harbour (2), see Arbour.

Hard. (E.) A. S. *heard*; O. Fries. *herd*. + Du. *hard*; Icel. *harðr*, Dan. *haard*, Swed. *hård*, Goth. *hardus*, G. *hart*. Teut. type **harduz*, Idg. type **kartús*; cf. Gk. κρατύς, strong. Brugm. i. § 792.

Hardock, Hordock, the corn-blue-bottle; *Centaurea cyanus*. (E.) *Hardokes*, pl., is the reading in K. Lear, iv. 4. 4, ed.

1623; the quartos have *hordocks*. The same as *haudod*, used in Fitzherbert's Husbandry to mean the corn-bluebottle; see Glossary, and pref. p. xxx. Mr. Wright (note to K. Lear) shows that *hardhake* meant the *Centaurea nigra*. Both plants were called, indifferently, *knobweed, knotweed*, and *loggerheads*. Named from the *hardness* of the head of the *Centaurea nigra*; for which reason it was also called *iron-weed, iron-heads*, &c. See Plant-names, by Britten and Holland.

Hards, fibres of flax. (E.) M. E. *herdes*. A. S. *heordan*, pl.+M. Du. *heerde*, *herde*, hards (Kilian), later *hēde* (Hexham); E. Fries. *hēde*. Teut. type *hizdōn- or *hezdōn- ; cf. **Meed.** ¶ Distinct from *hard*.

Hardy, stout, brave. (F. — Teut.) M. E. *hardi*.—O. F. *hardi*, brave; orig. pp. of *hardir*, lit. to harden. — Teut. *hartjan*, as in O. H. G. *hertan*, to harden, make strong.—O. H. G. *harti* (G. *hart*), hard; see **Hard.**

Hare. (E.) A.S *hara*.+Dan. Swed. *hare*, Icel. *hēri* (formerly *here*); Du. *haas*, G. *hase*. Teut. types *hazon-, *hason-, Idg. type *kason- ; cf. O. Pruss. *sasins* (for *kasins*), W. *cein-ach*, fem. (Rhys), Skt. *çaça*, for *çasa*, a hare. The Skt. word means 'jumper,' from *çaç* (Idg. *kas-*), to jump, leap along.

harebell. (E.) From *hare* and *bell*.

Harem, set of apartments for females. (Arab.) Also *haram*. — Arab. *haram*, women's apartments, lit. 'sacred,' or 'prohibited.'—Arab. root *harama*, he prohibited (because men were prohibited from entering). The initial is the 6th letter of the Arab. alphabet. Rich. Dict., p. 563.

Haricot (1), a stew of mutton, (2) kidney bean. (F.) F. *haricot*, 'mutton sod with little turneps,' &c. ; Cot. The sense of ' bean ' is late ; that of ' minced mutton with herbs,' O. F. *hericot*, is old. Origin unknown.

Hark, Hearken. (E.) M. E. *herken*, also *herknen*. *Herknen* is from A. S. *hercnian, heorcnian*, to listen to. *Herken* corresponds to a shorter type, A.S. *heorcian* (not found), O. Fries. *herkia* ; also O. Fries. *harkia* (from the 2nd grade), E. Fries. *harken*. Teut. type *herkan-, pt. t. *hark*, pp. *hurkanoz*. The O. H. G. *hōrechen*, M. H. G. *hōrchen*, with long *ō*, must have been associated with O. H. G. *hōrjan*, G. *hōren*, to hear; cf. G. *horchen*. But the

Teut. type *herkan- can hardly be related to Hear.

Harlequin. (F.—Ital.) F. *arlequin*, *harlequin*, a harlequin. — Ital. *arlecchino*, a buffoon, jester. The Ital. word seems to correspond to the O. F. *Hellequin, Herlekin, Hierlekin*; the usual O. F. phrase was *la maisnie hierlekin* (Low L. *harlequīnī familias*), a troop of demons that haunted lonely places at night. A popular etymology connected the word with *Charles Quint* ; Max Müller, Lect. ii. 581. Prob. of Teut. origin ; cf. O. H. G. *hella cunni*, the kindred of hell ; which may have been confused with O. F. *herle, hierle*, tumult.

Harlot. (F.) Orig. used of either sex, and not always in a very bad sense ; equiv. to mod. E. 'fellow;' Ch. C. T. 649.—O. F. *herlot, arlot*, a vagabond ; Prov. *arlot*, a vagabond ; Ital. *arlotto* (Baretti), Low L. *arlotus*, a glutton. Of disputed origin. ¶ W. *herlod* is from E.

Harm, sb. (E.) M. E. *harm*. A.S. *hearm*, grief, also harm.+Icel. *harmr*, grief, Dan. *harme*, wrath, Swed. *harm*, anger, grief, G. *harm*, grief; Teut. type *harmoz*. Cf. Russ. *srame*, shame. Brug. ii. § 72. **Der.** *harm*, vb.

Harmony, concord. (F.—L.—Gk.) M. E. *harmonie*.—F. *harmonie*.—L. *harmonia*.—Gk. ἁρμονία, a joint, proportion, harmony. — Gk. ἁρμός, a joining. — Gk. *ἄρειν (ἀραρίσκειν)*, to fit. (√AR.)

Harness. (F.) The old sense was 'armour.' O. F. *harneis, harnois*, armour; whence Bret. *harnez*, old iron, armour (Thurneysen). Of unknown origin ; the G. *harnisch* is from F.

Harp. (E.) M. E. *harpe*. A. S. *hearpe*.+Du. *harp*, Icel. *harpa*, Swed. *harpa*, Dan. *harpe*, G. *harfe*. Teut. type *harpōn-, fem. ; whence F. *harpe*.

Harpoon. (F.—L.—Gk.) Formerly also *harpon*, which is the F. spelling.—F. *harpon*, a cramp-iron, a grappling-iron ; whence also Du. *harpoen*.—O. F. *harpe*, a dog's claw or paw, a clamp, cramp-iron ; cf. *se harper*, to grapple.—Late L. *harpē*, a sickle-shaped sword. — Gk. ἅρπη, a sickle. Cf. also Span. *arpon*, a harpoon, *arpar*, to claw, rend.

Harpsichord. (F.—Teut. *and* Gk.) Also *harpsechord*; with intrusive *s*.—F. *harpechorde*, 'a harpsichord;' Cot. From Teutonic and Greek ; see **Harp** and **Chord.** Cf. Ital. *arpicordo* (Florio).

Harpy. (F.—L.—Gk.) O. F. *harpie*.

‒ L. *harpȳia*, usually in pl. *harpȳiæ*.‒Gk. pl. *ἅρπυιαι*, lit. ' spoilers ' or ' snatchers.' ‒ Gk. *ἁρπ-*, base of *ἁρπάζειν*, to seize ; allied to L. *rapere.* See **Rapacious.**

Harquebus ; see **Arquebus.**

Harridan, a jade, a worn-out woman. (F.) A variant of M. F. *haridelle*, ' a poor tit, leane ill-favored jade,' Cot. ; i. e. a worn-out horse ; also used in the sense of a gaunt, ugly woman (Littré). The form remains unexplained.

Harrier (1), a hare-hound. (E.) Formerly *harier*; from *hare*. Cf. *bow-yer* from *bow*.

Harrier (2), a kind of buzzard. (E.) I. e. *harry-er*, because it destroys small birds ; see **Harry.**

Harrow, sb. (E.) M. E. *harwe*. North Fries. *harwe*. Not found in A. S. **+**Icel. *herfi*, Dan. *harv*, a harrow ; Swed. *harf*, a harrow. Apparently allied to M. Dan. *harge*, Du. *hark*, Swed. *harka*, G. *harke*, a rake. Base *har-* ? Cf. L. *car-ere*, to card wool.

Harry, to ravage. (E.) M. E. *harwen*, *herien*, *herʒien*. A. S. *hergian*, to lay waste, as is done by an army.**+**Icel. *herja*, to ravage, Dan. *hærge*, O. H. G. *harjôn*. Teut. type **harjōn-*, to harry ; from **har-joz*, an army (A. S. *here*, Icel. *herr*, Dan. *hær*, O. H. G. *hari*, G. *heer*, Goth. *harjis*). Allied to O. Pruss. *karjis*, an army ; Lith. *karas*, war.

Harsh. (Scand.) M. E. *harsh* ‒Dan. *harsk*, rancid ; Swed. *härsk*, rank, rancid, rusty. **+** G. *harsch*, harsh, rough. Cf. Lithuan. *kartùs*, harsh, bitter (of taste) ; see **Hard.**

Hart. (E.) M. E. *hert*. A. S. *heort*, *heorot*, *herut.***+**Du. *hert*, Icel. *hjörtr*, Dan. *hiort*, Swed. *hjort*, G. *hirsch*, O.H.G. *hiruz* ; Teut. stem **herut-*. Allied to L. *ceruus*, W. *carw*, a hart, horned animal ; Russ. *serna*, a chamois ; cf. Gk. *κέρας*, a horn. See **Horn.**

Harvest. (E.) A. S. *hærfest*, autumn ; orig. ' crop.' **+** Du. *herfst*, G. *herbst*, autumn ; Icel. *haust*, Dan. Swed. *höst* (contracted forms). Allied to Gk. *καρπός*, fruit ; L. *carpere*, to gather, Lith. *kerpu*, I shear. Brugm. i. § 631. And cf. Gk. *κείρειν*, to shear.

Hash, a dish of meat cut into slices, &c. (F. ‒ G.) [O. F. *hachis*, hash.] **‒** F. *hacher*, to hack. **‒** F. *hache*, an ax. **‒** O. H. G. **happja*, whence O. H. G. *heppa*, M. H. G. *hepe*, a bill, a sickle.

Hashish, Hasheesh, an intoxicating drink. (Arab.) See **Assassin.**

Haslets, Hastelets, Harslets, the inwards of a pig, &c., for roasting. (F. ‒ L.) From O. F. *hastelet*, meat roasted on a spit. ‒ O. F. *haste*, a spit. ‒ L. *hasta*, a spit ; see **Hastate.**

Hasp. (E.) A. S. *hæpse*, a fastening, clasp. catch of a door.**+**Icel. *hespa*, a hasp, a skein (of wool), Dan. Swed. G. *haspe*, hasp ; cf. M. Du. *hasp*, *haps*, a skein of wool. Cf. Low G. *happen*, *hapsen*, to snatch, clutch ; F. *happer*, to lay hold of.

Hassock. (E.) M. E. *hassok*, orig. coarse grass or sedge ; of which the old hassocks were made. A. S. *hassuc*, a tuft of coarse grass. ¶ Not from W. *hesg*, sb. pl., sedges.

Hastate, spear-shaped. (L.) L. *hastātus*, spear-like. ‒ L. *hasta*, a spear. Allied to **Gad.**

Haste, sb. (F. ‒ Teut.) M. E. *hast*, *haste*. ‒ O. F. *haste*, haste (F. *hâte*). ‒ W. Germanic **hai(f)sti-*, violence ; as in O. Fries. *haest* (Richtofen, s. v. *hast*),O. H. G. *heisti*, adj., violent ; A. S. *hǣst*, violence, Cf. Goth. *haifsts*, fem., strife. ¶ Du. *haast*, G. Dan. Swed. *hast*, haste, are all borrowed from F. **Der.** *haste*, vb. ; *hast-en*, XVI cent.

Hat. (E.) A. S. *hæt.* **+** Icel. *höttr*, a hood, later *hattr*, Swed. *hatt*, Dan. *hat*. Teut. type **hattuz*, m. If it is related to *hood*, it stands for an earlier form **hadnuz*. See **Hood.**

Hatch (1), a half-door. (E.) M. E. *hacche* ; a *hatch* also corresponds to North E. *heck*. A. S. *hæc* (gen. *hæcce*), a hurdle (?). **+** Du. *hek*, fence, rail, gate, Swed. *häck*, coop, rack. Teut. **hakjā*, f. Prob. so named as being lightly fastened with a hook. Cf. A. S. *hac-a*, a fastening of a door ; see **Hake, Hook. Der.** *hatch-es*, pl. sb., a frame of cross-bars over an opening in a ship's deck ; *hatch-way*.

Hatch (2), to produce a brood by incubation. (E.) M. E. *hacchen.* **+** Swed. *häcka*, to hatch ; Dan. *hækkebuur*, a breeding-cage. Origin unknown.

Hatch (3), to shade by minute lines, crossing each other. (F. ‒ G.) F. *hacher*, to hack, also to hatch or engrave ; see **Hash.**

Hatches ; see **Hatch** (1).

Hatchet, a small ax. (F. ‒ G.) F. *hachette*, dimin. of *hache*, an ax. See **Hash.**

Hatchment, escutcheon. (F. — L.) Shortened from *achievement*, an escutcheon; which was contracted to *átcheament* (Ferne, 1586), *hachement* (Hall, 1548); &c.

Hate, sb. (E.) M. E. *hate*. A. S. *hete*, hate; the mod. E. sb. takes the vowel from the verb *hatian*, to hate.+Du. *haat*, Icel. *hatr*, Swed. *hat*, Dan. *had*, Goth. *hatis*, G. *hass*, hate. Cf. Gk. κήδειν, to vex; W. *cawdd*, displeasure. Der. *hate*, vb.

hatred. (E.) M. E. *hatred*, *hatreden*. The suffix is A. S. *rǣden*, law, mode, condition, state, as in *hīw-rǣden*, a household; and see *kindred*.

Hauberk, a coat of ringed mail. (F. — O. H. G.) M. E. *hauberk*. — O. F. *hauberc*. — O. H. G. *halsberc*, lit. neck-defence. — O. H. G. *hals*, neck; *bergan*, to protect. See **Collar** and **Bury**.

Haughty. (F. — L.) For M. E. *hautein*, arrogant; 'Hawty, *haultain*;' Palsgrave. Cf. *booty*, from *butin*. — O. F. *hautain*, 'hauty;' Cot. — O. F. *haut*; oldest form *halt*, high. — L. *altus*, high; see **Altitude**.

Haul; see **Hale** (2).

Haulm, Halm, stalk. (E.) A. S. *healm*. + Du. *halm*, Icel. *hálmr*, Dan. Swed. *halm*; Russ. *soloma*, straw; L. *culmus*, stalk. Gk. κάλαμος, reed; W. *calaf*, stalk. Brugm. ii. § 72.

Haunch, hip, bend of the thigh. (F. — O. H. G.) F. *hanche*; O. F. *hanche*, *hanke*; Low L. *hancha* (1275). Of Teut. origin; from Frankish **hankā*, represented by M. Du. *hancke*, 'haunch or hip;' Hexham. See Körting, § 3872.

Haunt, to frequent. (F.) M. E. *hanten*, *haunten*. — O. F. *hanter*, to haunt, frequent. Origin disputed.

Hautboy, a musical instrument. (F. — L.) F. *hautbois*. — F. *haut*, high; *bois*, wood. — L. *altus*, high; Late L. *boscus*, *buscus*, L. *buxus*, box-tree; see **Box** (1). It is a wooden instrument with a high tone. Hence Ital. *oboè*, E. *oboe*, borrowed from F. *hautbois*.

Have. (E.) M. E. *hauen*, pt. t. *hadde*, pp. *had*. A. S. *habban*, pt. t. *hæfde*, pp. *gehæfd*. + Du. *hebben*, Icel. *hafa*, Swed. *hafva*, Dan. *have*, Goth. *haban*, G. *haben*. Teut. stem **habē-*. If cognate, as usually supposed, with L. *habēre*, to have, the Idg. base must be **khabh-*.

Haven, harbour. (Scand.) A. S. *hæfen*, *hæfene*. — Icel. *höfn*, Dan. *havn*,

Swed. *hamn*. + Du. *haven*, G. *hafen*, a harbour. Cf. also M. H. G. *habe*, haven; which seems to be allied to M. H. G. *hab*, Icel. Swed. *haf*, Dan. *hav*, A. S. *heaf*, sea.

Haversack, soldier's provision-bag. (F. — G.) F. *havresac*. — G. *habersack*, *hafersack*, lit. 'oat-bag.' — G. *haber*, *hafer*, oats; *sack*, a sack.

Havoc, destruction. (F.) Cf. A. F. *crier havok*; where *havok* is for O. F. *havot*. — O. F. *havot*, plunder; whence *crier havot*, E. 'cry havoc' (Godefroy). Cf. O. F. *haver*, to grapple with a hook (Cot.); and G. *haft*, seizure. Prob. from G. *heben*, to lift. ¶ The W. *hafoc*, destruction, is borrowed from E.

Haw, a hedge; also, berry of hawthorn. (E.) M. E. *hawe*, a yard. A. S. *haga*, an enclosure, yard. + Icel. *hagi*, Swed. *hage*, enclosure; Dan. *have*, garden; Du. *haag*, G. *hag*, hedge. Teut. base **hag-*; Idg. base **kagh-*, as in W. *cae*, an enclosure; see **Quay**. Der. *haw-thorn*. See **Hedge**.

Hawk (1), a bird of prey. (E.) M. E. *hauk*, *hauek* (= *havek*). A. S. *hafoc*, *heafoc*, a hawk. + Du. *havik*, Icel. *haukr*, Swed. *hök*, Dan. *hög*, G. *habicht*, O. H. G. *hapuh*. Prob. 'a seizer;' allied to E. *heave*, L. *capere*; see **Heave**. So also Low L. *capus*, a falcon, from *capere*; and L. *accipiter*, a hawk.

Hawk (2), to carry about for sale. (O. Low G.) A verb formed from the sb. *hawker*; see **Hawker**.

Hawk (3), to clear the throat. (E.) Imitative. Cf. Dan. *harke*, Swed. *harska*, to hawk; W. *hochi*, to hawk, *hoch*, the throwing up of phlegm.

Hawker, pedlar. (O. Low G.) Introduced from abroad; Du. *heuker*, a hawker, M. Du. *hoecker*, *hucker*; cf. *heukeren*, to hawk, sell by retail. So also Dan. *höker*, a chandler, huckster, *hökre*, to hawk; Swed. *hökare*, a chandler, huckster. See further under **Huckster**.

Hawse, Hawse-hole. (Scand.) *Hawse* is a round hole through which a ship's cable passes, so called because made in the 'neck' of the ship. — Icel. *háls*, *hals*, the neck; also, part of a ship's bows.+ O. Merc. *hals*, A. S. *heals*; Du. G. *hals*; allied to L. *collum*, neck.

Hawser, a tow-rope. (F. — L.) Cf. F. *haussière*, a hawser. But *hawse-r* is from M. E. *hawse*, to lift. — O. F. *halcier*, F. *hausser*, to lift, raise. — Late L. *altiāre*, to elevate. — L. *altus*, high. See **Altitude**.

Cf. M.Ital. *alzaniere*, 'a halsier [hawser] in a ship' (Florio); from *alzare*, to raise. ¶ Not allied to **Hoist**.

Hawthorn; see **Haw**.

Hay (1). (E.) M. E. *hey*. O. Merc. *hēg*; A. S. *hīg*. **+** Du. *hooi*, Icel. *hey*, Dan. Swed. *hö*, Goth. *hawi*, grass; G. *heu*. Teut. type **hau-jom*, n. Properly 'cut grass'; from the verb *to hew*; see **Hew**.

Hay (2), a hedge. (E.) A. S. *hege*, m. Teut. type **hagiz*. Allied to **Haw** and **Hedge**. **Der.** *hay-ward*, i. e. hedge-warden.

Hazard. (F. — Span. — Arab.?) F. *hasard*. **—** Span. *azar*, a hazard; orig. an unlucky throw (at dice); cf. M. Ital. *zara*, a game at dice. **—** Arab. *al zahr*, lit. the die (Devic); *al* being the Arab. def. art. But Arab. *zahr* is of doubtful authority.

Haze, a mist. (E.?) Ray has: 'it *hazes*, it misles.' Etym. unknown. We may perhaps compare the Lowl. Sc. *haar*, a sea-fog, a mist.

Hazel. (E.) M. E. *hasel*. A. S. *hæsel*. **+**Du. *hazelaar*, Icel. *hasl*, *hesli*, Dan. Swed. *hassel*, G. *hasel*; Teut. type **haselo-*; from the Idg. type **koselo-* we have L. *corulus* (for **cosulus*), W. and O. Irish *coll* (for **cosl*), a hazel.

He. (E.) A. S. *hē*; gen. *his*, dat. *him*, acc. *hine*. Fem. sing. nom. *hēo*, gen. dat. *hire*, acc. *hie*, *hī*; neut. sing. nom. *hit*, gen. *his*, dat. *him*, acc. *hit*. Pl. (all genders), nom. acc. *hie*, *hī*, gen. *hira*, *heora*, dat. *him*, *heom*. **+** Du. *hij*, O. Sax. *he*, *hi*; Goth. neut. *hita*. Allied to Lith. *szis*, this, L. *ci-trā*, on this side, Gk. *ἐ-κεῖ*, there, *κεῖνος*, that one. Brugm. i. §§ 83, 604. **Der.** *hence*, *her*, *here*, *hither*.

Head. (E.) M. E. *hed*, *heed*, *heued* (= *heved*). A. S. *hēafod*. **+** Du. *hoofd*, Goth. *haubith*, G. *haupt*, O. H. G. *houbit*; also O. Icel. *haufoð*, later *höfuð*, Dan. *hoved*, Swed. *hufvud*, M. Swed. *havud*. Teut. types **haubud-*, **haubid-*, neut.; answering to Idg. types **koupot-*, **koupet-*, which are not exactly represented. The L. *caput* (with short *a*) does not correspond in the vowel-sound, but is allied to A. S. *hafela*, *heafola*, head. (The difficulties as to this word are not yet cleared up.)

headlong, rashly, rash. (E.) M. E. *hedling*, *heuedling*, *hedlinges*. Thus the suffix is adverbial, answering to A. S. suffix *-l-ing*, really a double suffix. Cf. A. S. *bæc-ling*, backwards, *fær-inga*, suddenly.

Heal. (E.) M. E. *helen*. A. S. *hǣlan*, to make whole; formed from *hāl*, whole, with *i*- mutation of *ā* to *ǣ*; see **Whole**. So also G. *heilen*, from *heil*; Goth. *hailjan*, from *hails*.

health. (E.) A. S. *hǣlð*, health (Teut. type **hailithā*, f.), from *hāl*, whole; see **Heal** (above).

Heap, sb. (E.) M. E. *heep*. A. S. *hēap*, a heap, crowd. **+** Du. *hoop* (whence Icel. *hōpr*, Dan. *hob*, Swed. *hop*, O. H. G. *houf*); cf. also G. *haufe*, O. H. G. *hūfo*. **+** Lith. *kaupas*, O. Slav. *kupŭ*, a heap. Brugm. i. § 421 (7). **Der.** *heap*, vb.

Hear. (E.) M. E. *hēren*, pt. t. *herde*, pp. *herd*. O. Merc. *hēran*; A. S. *hȳran*, pt. t. *hȳrde*, pp. *gehȳred*. **+** Du. *hooren*, Icel. *heyra*, Dan. *höre*, Swed. *höra*, Goth. *hausjan*, G. *hören*. Cf. Gk. *ἀ-κούειν*, to hear. (Not allied to **Ear**.)

Hearken; see **Harken**.

Hearsay. (E.) From *hear* and *say*, the latter being in the infin. mood. Cf. A. S. *ic secgan hȳrde* = I heard say (Beowulf, 1346).

Hearse. (F. — L.) M. E. *herse*, hearse. The orig. sense was a triangular harrow, then a triangular frame for supporting lights at a church service, esp. at a funeral, then a bier, a carriage for a dead body. All these senses are found. **— M.** F. *herce*, a harrow, a frame with pins on it. (Mod. F. *herse*, Ital. *erpice*, a harrow.) **— L.** *hirpicem*, acc. of *hirpex*, a harrow. **Der.** *rehearse*.

Heart. (E.) M. E. *herte*. A. S. *heorte*. **+**Du. *hart*, Icel. *hjarta*, Swed. *hjerta*, Dan. *hierte*, Goth. *hairtō*, G. *herz*; Teut. type **herton-*. Further allied to Lith. *szirdis*, Irish *cridhe*, W. *craidd*, Russ. *serdtse*, L. *cor* (gen. *cordis*), Gk. *καρδία*, *κῆρ*.

Hearth. (E.) M. E. *herth*, *herthe*. A. S. *heorð*.**+**Du. *haard*; Swed. *härd*, a hearth, a forge, G. *herd*; Teut. type **herthoz*, m. Cf. Goth. *haurja*, pl., Icel. *hyrr*, embers, burning coals. Idg. base **ker-*; cf. L. *cremāre*, to burn.

Heart's-ease, a pansy. (E.) Lit. *ease of heart*, i. e. giving pleasure.

hearty. (E.) M. E. *herty*; also *hertly*; from M. E. *herte*; see **Heart**.

Heat. (E.) M. E. *hete*. A. S. *hǣtu*, *hǣto*, from **haitiu*, for **haitjō-*, f.; formed from *hāt*, hot, with the usual vowel-change. **+** Du. *hitte*, Dan. *hede*, Swed. *hetta*, Icel. *hiti*, G. *hitze*; all from the weak grade *hit-*; see **Hot**. We also find A. S. *hǣtan*, verb, to heat.

Heath. (E.) M. E. *heth.* A. S. *hǣð.* +Du. *heide*, Icel. *heiðr*, Dan. *hede*, Swed. *hed*, Goth. *haithi*, a waste ; Teut. type **haithī*, fem. Cf. W. *coed*, O. W. *coit*, a wood.

heathen, a pagan. (E.) A. S. *hǣðen*, adj. So also Icel. *heiðenn*, G. *heiden*, a heathen ; Goth. *haithnō*, a heathen woman. Lit. a dweller on a heath, orig. ' wild '; cf. Goth. *haithiwisks*, wild (Mk. i. 6); A. S. *hǣðen* a wild creature (Beow. 986). From A. S. *hǣð*, a heath (above). [Similarly L. *pagānus* meant (1) a villager, (2) a pagan.]

Heather. (E.) Usually associated with *heath* ; but the Nhumb. form *hadder* points to some different origin.

Heave. (E.) M. E. *hēuen* (=*hēven*). From A. S. *hef-*, a pres. stem of A. S. *hebban*, pt. t. *hōf*, pp. *hafen.* + Du. *heffen*, Icel. *hefja*, Swed. *häfva*, Dan. *hæve*, Goth. *hafjan*, G. *heben.* Teut. type **hafjan-*, pt. t. **hōf*; corresponding to L. *capio*, I seize ; cf. Gk. κώπη, handle. (Distinct from *have*.)

Heaven. (E.) M. E. *heuen* (=*heven*). A. S. *heofon*, *hefon.*+O. Sax. *heðan.* [Icel. *himinn*, Goth. *himins*, G. *himmel*,O.H.G. *himil*, O. Sax. *himil*, Du. *hemel*, heaven, may be from a different source.] Cf. A. S. *hūs-heofon*, a ceiling, so that the sense may have been ' canopy.'

Heavy. (E.) Hard to heave, weighty. M. E. *heui* (=*hevi*). A. S. *hefig*, heavy, hard to heave. ▪ A. S. *haf-*, stem of *hebban* (pt. t. *hōf*), to heave ; with *i*-mutation of *a.*+Icel. *höfugr*, *höfigr*, heavy, from *hefja*, to heave ; Low G. *hevig*; O.H.G. *hebīg.* See **Heave.**

Hebdomadal, weekly. (L.–Gk.) L. *hebdomadālis.* ▪ Gk. ἑβδομαδ-, stem of ἑβδομάς, a week.▪Gk. ἑπτά, seven ; see **Seven.**

Hebrew. (F.–L.–Gk.–Heb.) F. *hébreu* (*hébrieu* in Cotgr.).▪L. *Hebræus.* Gk. Ἑβραῖος.▪Heb. *'ivrī*, a Hebrew (Gen. xiv. 13), a name given to Israelites as coming from E. of the Euphrates.▪Heb. *'āvar*, he crossed over.

Hecatomb. (F.–L.–Gk.) M.F. *hecatombe.*▪L. *hecatombē.*▪Gk. ἑκατόμβη, a sacrifice of a hundred oxen.▪Gk. ἑκατόν, a hundred ; βοῦς, ox. See **Hundred** and **Cow.**

Heckle, Hackle, Hatchel, an instrument for dressing flax or hemp. (E.) M. E. *hechele*, *hekele*, E. Fries. *häkel*, *hekel.*

+Du. *hekel*, a heckle ; Dan. *hegle* ; Swed. *häckla* ; G. *hechel*, a heckle. Teut. type **hakilā*; from a base *hak-*, to pierce, bite, as in O. H. G. *hecchen*, M. H. G. *hecken* (for **hakjan*), to pierce, bite as a snake ; cf. A.S. *hacod*, a pike (fish), from its sharp teeth. Cf. **Hack** (1).

Hectic, continual, as a fever. (F.– Gk.) F. *hectique* (as if from Late L. **hecticus*).▪Gk. ἑκτικός, hectic, consumptive. ▪ Gk. ἕξις, a possession ; also, a habit of body.▪Gk. ἕξ-ω, fut. of ἔχειν, to have, hold. (√SEGH.)

Hector, a bully. (L.–Gk.) From L. *Hector.*▪Gk. Ἕκτωρ, the celebrated hero of Troy. Lit. ' holding fast ; ' from ἔχειν, to hold (above).

Hedge. (E.) A. S. *hecg*, f. (dat. *hecge*); Teut. type **hag-jā*, allied to *haga*, a haw.+Du. *hegge*, Dan. *hæg*, allied to *haag*, a haw ; G. *hecke*, f., a hedge. See **Haw.**

Heed, vb. (E.) M. E. *heden.* A.S. *hēdan*, pt. t. *hēdde.* Formed as if from sb. **hōd*, care (not found); though we find the corresponding O. Fries. sb. *hōde*, *hūde*, and the G. sb. *hut*, O. H. G. *huota*, care. +Du. *hoeden*, from *hoede*, care ; G. *hüten*, from *hut* (O. H. G. *huota*), care, guard. Brugm. i. § 754. Prob. allied to **Hood.**

Heel (1), part of the foot. (E.) A. S. and O. Fries. *hēla*, heel (whence Du. *hiel*). + Icel. *hæll*, Dan. *hæl*, Swed. *häl.* The A. S. *hēla* is prob. contracted from **hōh-ila*, dimin. of A. S. *hōh*, heel. See **Hough.**

Heel (2), to lean over, incline. (E.) Modified from M. E. *helden*, *hilden*, to incline on one side. A. S. *hieldan*, *hyldan*, to tilt, incline ; cf. *niðer-heald*, bent downwards.+Du. *hellen* (for **heldan*, O. Sax. *af-heldian*), to heel over ; Icel. *halla* (for **halða*), to heel over (as a ship), from *hallr* (<**halth-*), sloping ; Dan. *helde*, to tilt, cf. *held*, a slope ; Swed. *hälla*, to tilt. The adj. is A.S. *-heald*, O. Fries. *hald*, Icel. *hallr*, O. H. G. *hald*, inclined, bent forward ; Teut. type **halthoz.* Allied to A.S. *hold*, G. *hold*, faithful, true (to a master), Goth. *hulths*, gracious.

Heft, a heaving. (E.) In Wint. Tale, ii. 1. 45. Formed from *heave*, just as *haft* is from *have.*

Hegira. (Arab.) Arab. *hijrah* separation ; esp. used of the flight of Mohammed from Mecca ; the era of the Hegira begins on July 16, A. D. 622. Cf. Arab. *hajr*. separation.

Heifer. (E.) M. E. *hayfare*, *hekfere.*

A. S. *heahfore*, a heifer; also spelt *heahfre*, *heahfru*. The form is still unexplained.

Heigh-ho. (E.) An exclamation; *heigh*, a cry to call attention; *ho*, an exclamation.

Height. (E.) A variant of *highth* (Milton); we find M. E. *highte* as well as *he:þe* (*heghthe*). A. S. *hīehðu*, *hēahðu*, height. − A. S. *hēah*, *hēh*, high. + Du. *hoogte*, Icel. *hæð*, Swed. *höjd*, Dan. *höide*, Goth. *hauhitha*. See High.

Heinous. (F.− O. Low G.) M. E. *heinous*, *hainous*. − O. F. *haïnos*, odious; formed with suffix *-os* (L. *-ōsus*) from O. F. *haïne* (F. *haine*), hatred. − F. *haïr*, to hate. From an O. Teut. form, such as Goth. *hatjan*, O. Fries. *hatia*, to hate; see Hate.

Heir. (F.− L.) M. E. *heire*, *heir*, also *eyr.* − O. F. *heir*, *eir*. − Late L. *hērem*, for L. *hērēdem*, acc. of *hērēs*, an heir. Cf. Gk. χήρα, a widow (relict). Der. *heir-loom*, where *loom* signifies ' a piece of property,' but is the same word as E. *loom*. See Loom (1).

Heliacal, relating to the sun. (L.− Gk.) From Late L. *hēliacus.* − Gk. ἡλιακός, belonging to the sun. − Gk. ἥλιος, sun; see Solar.

heliotrope, a flower. (F.−L.−Gk.) F. *héliotrope.* − L. *hēliotropium.* − Gk. ἡλιοτρόπιον, a heliotrope, lit. ' sun-turner;' from its turning to the sun. − Gk. ἥλιο-ς, sun; τροπ-, 2nd grade of τρέπειν, to turn; see Trope.

Helix, a spiral figure. (L.− Gk.) L. *helix*, a spiral. − Gk. ἕλιξ, a spiral, a twist. − Gk. ἑλίσσειν, to turn round. Allied to Volute.

Hell. (E.) M. E. *helle*. A. S. *hel*, gen. *helle*; orig. 'that which hides.' from Teut. **helan-*, A. S. *helan*, (pt. t. *hæl*), to hide. + Du. *hel*, Icel. *hel*, G. *hölle*, Goth. *halja*. Teut. type **haljā*, fem. Allied to Cell Conceal.

Hellebore. (F.− L.− Gk.) Also *ellebore.* − O. F. *ellebore.* − L. *helleborus.* − Gk. ἑλλέβορος, the name of the plant.

Helm (1), an implement for steering a ship. (E.) Orig. the tiller or handle. A. S. *helma.* + Icel. *hjālm* (for **helm-*), a rudder; G. Fries. *helm*. The prov. E. *helm* means 'handle'; so also M. E. *halm* (Gawain, 330). Prob. allied to Helve.

Helm (2), armour for the head. (E.) M. E. *helm*. A. S. *helm*. + Du. *helm*; Icel. *hjālmr*, Dan. *hielm*, Swed. *hjelm*, G. *helm*,

Goth. *hilms*. Teut. type **hel-moz*, m.; lit. ' a covering;' from **helan-*, to cover. Allied to Skt. *çarman-*, shelter, protection. Lith. *szalmas*, a helmet, O. Slav. *shlēmŭ*, are prob. borrowed from Teut. Brugm. i. § 420. Der. *helm-et*, dimin. form. Allied to Hell.

Helminthology, history of worms. (Gk.) Coined from Gk. ἑλμινθο-, decl. stem of ἕλμινς, a worm; -λογία, a discourse, from λέγειν, to speak. The sb. ἕλμινς, also ἕλμις, means ' that which curls about'; allied to Helix.

Helot, a (Spartan) slave. (L.− Gk.) L. pl. *Hēlōtes*, from Gk. εἵλωτες, pl. of εἵλως, a helot, bondsman; fabled to have meant an inhabitant of *Helos* (a town of Laconia), enslaved by the Spartans.

Help, vb. (E.) M. E. *helpen*, pt. t. *halp*, pp. *holpen*. A. S. *helpan*, pt. t. *healp*, pp. *holpen.* + Du. *helpen*, Icel. *hjālpa*, Dan. *hielpe*, Swed. *hjelpa*, Goth. *hilpan*, G. *helfen*. Teut. type **helpan-*. Allied to Lithuan. *szelpti*, to help. Der. *help*, sb., A. S. *help helpe*; *help-mate*, suggested by *help meet* (Gen. ii. 18).

Helve, a handle. (E.) M. E. *helue* (= *helve*). A. S. *hielf*, also *helfe*, a handle. + M. Du. *helve*, handle, Low G. *helft*, M. H. G. *halp*, handle; allied to Halter and Helm (1).

Hem (1), border. (E.) A. S. *hem*. Orig. ' an enclosure;' cf. O. Fries. *ham*, *hem* (dat. *hemme*), North Fries. *ham*, an enclosure (Outzen ; prov. G. *humme*, a fence, hedge (Flügel, 1861). Der. *hem*, vb., to enclose within a border, hem in; cf. G. *hemmen*, Swed. *hämma*.

Hem (2), a slight cough to call attention. (E.) An imitative word; allied to Hum. + M. Du. *himmen*, *hemmen*, 'to call one with a hem,' Hexham.

Hematite, an ore of iron. (L.− Gk.) Named from the red colour of the powder. − L. *hæmatītēs.* − Gk. αἱματίτης, blood-like. − Gk. αἱματ-, stem of αἷμα, blood.

Hemi-, half. (Gk.) From a Lat. transcription of Gk. ἡμι-, half, cognate with L. *sēmi-*, half; see Semi-. Der. *hemi-sphere*, &c.

hemistich, a half-line, in poetry. (L.− Gk.) L. *hēmistichium.* − Gk. ἡμι-στίχιον, a half-verse. − Gk. ἡμι-, half; στίχος, a row, verse.

Hemlock. (E.) M. E. *hemlok*, *humlok*. A. S. *hemlic*, *hymlice*; also *hymblice* (Ep. Gl.). The origin of *hym*- is unknown;

the second syllable is perhaps an unstressed form of A. S. *líc*, like.

Hemorrhage, a great flow of blood. (F. – L. – Gk.) M. F. *hemorrhagie*. – L. *hæmorrhagia*. – Gk. αἱμορραγία, a violent bleeding. **–** Gk. αἷμο-, for αἷμα, blood; ραγ-, a stem of ῥήγνυμι, I burst, break; the lit. sense being a bursting out of blood.

Hemorrhoids, Emerods, painful bleeding tubercles on the anus. (F. – L. – Gk.) M. F. *hemorrhoïde*, sing., a flowing of blood. **–** L. *hæmorrhoidæ*, pl. of *hæmorrhoida*. **–** Gk. αἱμορροΐδες, pl. of αἱμορροΐς, adj., liable to a flow of blood. – Gk. αἷμο-, for αἷμα, blood ; ῥο- (as in ῥο-ος, a stream), allied to ῥέειν, to flow, cognate with Skt. *sru*, to flow ; see **Stream.**

Hemp, a plant. (L. – Gk.) M. E. *hemp* (short for *henep*). A.S. *henep, hænep.* Borrowed at a very early period from some Eastern language, whence also L. *cannabis*, Gk. κάνναβις, Pers. *kanab*, hemp, so that the word suffered consonantal letter-change. Cf. Skt. *çana*, hemp (prob. not an Idg. word). So also Du. *hennep*, Icel. *hampr*, Dan. *hamp*, Swed. *hampa*, G. *hanf* ; all of foreign origin.

Hen. (E.) A.S. *henn, hen, hæn* ; a fem. form (Teut. type **han-jā*) from A. S. *hana*, a cock, lit. 'a singer,' from his crowing ; cf. L. *canere*, to sing. **+** Du. *hen*, fem. of *haan*, a cock ; G. *henne*, f. of *hahn* ; Icel. *hæna*, f. of *hani* ; Dan. *höne*, f. of *hane* ; Swed. *höna*, f. of *hane*. (√KAN.) See **Chant.**

Hence. (E.) M. E. *hennes*, older form *henne* (whence *henne-s* by adding adv. suffix -*s*). A. S. *heonan*, for **hinan*, adv., closely allied to A. S. *hine*, masc. acc. of *hē*, he. See **He.**

Henchman, a page, servant. (E.) Formerly *hengestman, henseman, henshman* ; cf. *Hinxman* as a proper name. For *hengest-man*, i. e. groom ; from M. E. *hengest*, A.S. *hengest*, a horse. Cf. Du. and G. *hengst*, Dan. *hingst*, a horse, Icel. *hestr*, a horse.

Hendecagon, a plane figure having eleven sides. (Gk.) Named from its eleven angles. – Gk. ἕνδεκα, eleven ; γωνία, an angle ; see **Decagon.**

Henna, a paste used for dyeing the nails, &c., of an orange hue. (Arab.) Arab. *ḥinnā-a, ḥinā,* or *ḥinna-at*, the dyeing or colouring shrub (*Lawsonia inermis*) ; Rich. Dict., p. 582.

Hent, a seizure ; see **Hint.**

Hep, hip ; see **Hip** (2).

Hepatic, relating to the liver. (F. – L. – Gk.) M. F. *hepatique*. – L. *hēpaticus*. – Gk. ἡπατικός, belonging to the liver. – Gk. ἥπατ-, stem of ἧπαρ, the liver. **+** L. *iecur*; Skt. *yakṛt*, the liver. See **Liver. Der.** *hepatica*, liver-wort, a flower.

Heptagon, a plane seven-sided figure. (Gk.) Lit. 'seven-angled.' **–** Gk. ἑπτά, seven ; γωνία, an angle, allied to γόνυ, knee. See **Seven** and **Knee.**

heptahedron, a solid seven-sided figure. (Gk.) From Gk. ἑπτά, seven ; ἕδρα, a base, seat (allied to E. **Sit**).

heptarchy, a government by seven persons. (Gk.) XVII cent. **–** Gk. ἑπτ-, for ἑπτά, seven ; and -αρχία, from ἄρχ-ειν, to rule.

Her. (E.) M. E. *hire* ; from A.S. *hire*, gen. and dat. of *hēo*, she, fem. of *hē*, he ; see **He. Der.** *her-s*, M. E. *hirs, hires* (XIV cent.) ; *her-self.*

Herald. (F. – O. H. G.) M. E. *heraud.* **–** O. F. *heralt* (Low L. *heraldus*) ; O.H.G. *herolt* (G. *herold*), a herald ; note also O. H. G. *Heriold, Hariold*, as a proper name, Harold. β. The proper name is for **hari-wald*, i. e. army-rule. **–** O. H. G. *hari*, an army (G. *heer*) ; *wald, walt*, rule, power (G. *gewalt*). ¶ The precise history of the word is very uncertain.

Herb. (F. – L.) M. E. *herbe*. **–** F. *herbe*. **–** L. *herba*, grass, fodder, herb ; prob. allied to O.L. *forbea*, Gk. φορβή, pasture.

Herd (1), a flock. (E.) M. E. *herde*. A. S. *heord, hiord*, a flock. **+** Icel. *hjörð*, Dan. *hiord*, Swed. *hjord*, G. *heerde*, Goth. *hairda*. Teut. type *herdā*, f. Cf. Skt. *çardha(s)*, a herd, troop. Brugm. i. § 797.

herd (2), one who tends a herd. (E.) Usually in comp. *shep-herd, cow-herd*, &c. M. E. *herde*. A.S. *hierde, hirde*, keeper of a herd ; from A.S. *heord*, a flock. **+** Icel. *hirðir*, Dan. *hyrde*, Swed. *herde*, G. *hirte*, Goth. *hairdeis* ; all similarly derived. Cf. Lith. *kerdzus*, shepherd.

Here. (E.) M. E. *her, heer.* A.S. *hēr*, adv ; related to *hē*, he. **+** Du. *hier*, Icel. *hēr*, Dan. *her*, Swed. *här*, G. *hier*, Goth. *hēr.* Cf. L. *cis*, on this side.

Hereditary, adj. (L.) L. *hērēditārius.* **–** L. *hērēditāre*, to inherit. **–** L. *hērēdi-*, decl. stem of *hērēs*, an heir. See **Heir.**

Heresy. (F. – L. – Gk.) M. E. *heresye.* **–** O. F. *heresie.* **–** L. type **hæresia* ; for L. *hæresis.* **–** Gk. αἵρεσις, a taking,

choice, sect, heresy. — Gk. αἱρεῖν, to take.
Der. *heretic*, L. *hæreticus*, Gk. αἱρετικός,
able to choose, heretical (from the same
verb).

Heriot, a tribute paid to the lord of a
manor on the decease of a tenant. (E.)
A. S. *heregeatu*, lit. military apparel;
hence, equipments which, after the death
of a vassal, escheated to his lord; afterwards extended to include horses, &c. —
A. S. *here*, an army; *geatu*, *geatwe*,
apparel, adornment. See **Harry.**

Heritage. (F. — L.) O. F. *heritage*.
Formed, with suffix -*age* (= L. -*āticum*),
from O. F. *heriter*, to inherit. — L. *hērēditāre*, to inherit. See **Heir.**

Hermaphrodite, an animal or plant
of both sexes. (L. — Gk.) L. *hermaphro-
dītus*. — Gk. Ἑρμαφρόδιτος; coined from
Ἑρμῆς, Mercury (representing the male)
and Ἀφροδίτη, Venus (representing the
female principle).

Hermeneutic, explanatory. (Gk.)
Gk. ἑρμηνευτικός, skilled in interpreting. —
Gk. ἑρμηνευτής, an interpreter; also ἑρμη-
νεύς, the same. Allied to L. *sermo* (stem
sermōn-); see **Sermon.**

Hermetic. (Gk.) Low L. *hermēticus*,
relating to alchemy; coined from *Hermēs*,
from the notion that the great secrets of
alchemy were discovered by *Hermēs Tris-
megistus*. — Gk. Ἑρμῆς, Mercury. ¶ *Hermetically* was a term in alchemy; a glass
bottle was *hermetically* sealed when the
orifice was fused and then closed against
any admission of air.

Hermit. (F. — L. — Gk.) [M. E. *here-
mite*, directly from L. *herēmīta*.] — F.
hermite. — Late L. *herēmīta*, more commonly *erēmīta*. — Gk. ἐρημίτης, a dweller
in a desert. — Gk. ἐρημία, a desert. — Gk.
ἐρῆμος, deserted, desolate. Der. *hermit-
age*.

Hern; see **Heron.**

Hernia. (L.) L. *hernia*, a kind of
rupture.

Hero. (F. — L. — Gk.) M. F. *heroë*. —
L. *hērōēm*, acc. of *hērōs*, a hero. — Gk.
ἥρως, a hero, demi-god. Der. *hero-ic*,
M. F. *heroïque*, L. *hērōicus*.

heroine. (F. — L. — Gk.) M.F. *heroïne*.
L. *hērōīnē*. — Gk. ἡρωίνη, fem. of ἥρως, a
hero.

Heron, Hern, a bird. (F. — O. H.G.)
M. E. *heroun*, *heiron*, *hern*. — O. F. *hairon*
(F. *héron*, Span. *airon*, Ital. *aghirone*). —
O. H. G. *heigir*, M. H. G. *heiger*, a heron;

with suffixed -*on* (Ital. -*one*). + Swed.
häger, Icel. *hegri*, Dan. *heire*, a heron.
¶ Distinct from G. *häher*, a jackdaw.

heronshaw, hernshaw, a young
heron; also (by confusion) a heronry.
(F. — O. H. G.) 1. Spenser has *herneshaw*,
a heron; M. E. *heronsewe*, a young heron
(still called *heronsew* in the North). From
O. F. *herounçeau*, later form of *herounçel*,
a young heron (Liber Custumarum, p.
304), dim. of *hairon* (above); cf. *lionceau*,
lioncel, a young lion. The usual form is
F. *héronneau*, O. F. *haironneau*. 2. But
heronshaw, a heronry, is due to a (false)
popular etymology from *heron*, a heron,
and *shaw*, a wood; Cotgrave has 'hairon
niere, a heron's neast, a herneshaw, or
shaw of wood wherein herons breed.'

Herring, a fish. (E.) M. E. *heering*.
A. S. *hǣring*. [Sometimes said to be
connected with A. S. *here*, a host, army;
which seems impossible.] + Du. *haring*,
G. *häring*; O. H. G. *hâring* (Kluge).

Hesitate. (L.) From pp. of L.
hæsitāre, to stick fast; intensive form of
hærēre, to stick. + Lithuan. *gaiszti*, to
tarry. (√GHAIS.) Brugm. i. § 627.

Hest, a command. (E.) M. E. *hest*,
the final *t* being excrescent, as in *whils-t*,
amongs-t, &c. A. S. *hēs*, a command;
Teut. type *haittiz*, f. (>*haissiz*, with *ss*
for *tt*). — A. S. *hātan*, to command; Teut.
type *haitan*-. Cf. Icel. *heit*, a vow, from
heita, to call, promise; O. H. G. *heiz* (G.
geheiss), a command, from *heizan* (G.
heissen), to call, bid, command. Cf.
Goth. *haitan*, to call, name. Der. *be-hest*.
See **Hight.**

Heteroclite, irregularly inflected. (L.
— Gk.) L. *heteroclitus*. — Gk. ἑτερόκλιτος,
otherwise (i. e. irregularly) inflected. — Gk.
ἕτερο-ς, another; -κλιτος, formed from
κλίνειν, to lean (hence, to vary as a case
does); see **Lean** (1).

heterodox, of strange opinion, heretical. (Gk.) Gk. ἕτερο-ς, another; δόξ-α,
opinion, from δοκεῖν, to think.

heterogeneous, dissimilar in kind.
(Gk.) Gk. ἕτερο-ς, another; γέν-ος, kind,
kin, sort; see **Kin.**

Hetman, a captain. (Pol. — G.)
Polish *hetman* (Russ. *ataman*'), a captain of Cossacks). — G. *hauptmann*, a
captain. — G. *haupt*, head; *mann*, man.

Hew. (E.) M. E. *hewen*. A. S. *hēa-
wan*, to cut. + Du. *houwen*, Icel. *höggva*,
Swed. *hugga*, Dan. *hugge*, G. *hauen*;

Russ. *kovate*, to hammer, forge; Lith. *kauti*, to fight; cf. Lith. *kowà*, battle. Brugm. i. § 639. Allied to L. *cūdere*, to beat. Der. *hay*, q. v.

Hexagon, a plane six-sided figure. (L. – Gk.) L. *hexagōnum*. – Gk. ἑξάγωνος, six-cornered. – Gk. ἕξ, six; γωνία, an angle, from γόνυ, a knee; see **Knee**.

hexameter. (L. – Gk.) L. *hexameter*. – Gk. ἑξάμετρος, orig. an adj., i. e. having six measures or feet. – Gk. ἕξ, six; μέτρον, a measure, metre.

Hey, interj. (E.) M. E. *hei*, *hay*; a natural exclamation.+G. and Du. *hei*.

heyday (1), interj. (G. *or* Du.) Also *heyda* (Ben Jonson). Borrowed either from G. *heida*, hey there! hallo! or from Du. *hei daar*, hey there! The G. *da* and Du. *daar* both mean ' there.'

Heyday (2), frolicsome wildness. (E.) The '*heyday* of youth' means the '*high day* of youth.' The spelling *hey* is a preservation of M. E. *hey*, the usual spelling of *high* in the 14th century.

Hiatus, a gap. (L.) L. *hiātus*, a gap; from pp. of *hiāre*, to gape. Allied to **Yawn** and **Chasm**.

Hibernal, wintry. (F. – L.) F. *hibernal* – L. *hibernālis*, wintry (Vulg.). – L. *hībernus*, wintry; allied to *hiems*, winter. Also to Gk. χειμερινός, wintry, Gk χι-ών, snow, Skt. *hi-ma-*, frost. Der. *hibern-ate*.

Hiccough, Hiccup, Hicket, a spasmodic inspiration, with closing of the glottis, causing a slight sound. (E.) The spelling *hiccough* seems to be due to a popular etymology from *cough*, certainly wrong; no one ever so pronounces the word. Properly *hiccup*, or, in old books *hicket* and *hickock* which are still better forms. *Hick-et*, *hick-ock*, are diminutives of *hick* or *hik*, a catch in the voice, imitative of the sound. Cf. ' a *hacking* cough;' and see **Hitch**.+ M. Du. *huck-up*, ' the hick, or hock,' Hexham; M. Du. *hick*, ' the hick-hock,' Hexham; Du. *hik*, the hiccup, *hikken*, to hiccup; Dan. *hikke*, sb. and vb.; Swed. *hicka*, sb. and vb.; Bret. *hîk*, *hak*, a hiccough; W. *ig*, a sob, *igio*, to sob. And cf. **Chincough**.

Hickory, a N. American tree. (Americ. Indian.) Formerly *pohickery*; from the American-Indian (Virginian) name.

Hidalgo, a Span. nobleman of the lowest class. (Span. – L.) Span. *hidalgo*; O. Span. *fidalgo*, Port. *fidalgo*, a nobleman; sometimes written *hijodalgo* (Min-

sheu). Lit. ' son of something,' a son to whom a father has left an estate. – Span. *hijo*, son; *de*, of; *algo*, something. – L. *filium*, acc. of *filius*, son (whence O. Span. *figo*, later *hijo*); *dē*, of; *aliquō*, something. (So Körting. The explanation from *filius Italicus* is baseless.)

Hide (1), to cover. (E.) M. E. *hīden*, *hūden*. A. S. *hȳdan*. +Gk. κεύθειν, to hide; cf. W. *cuddio* (base **koud-*), to hide. (√KEUDH.)

Hide (2), a skin. (E.) M. E. *hide*, *hude*. A. S. *hȳd*, the skin. + Du. *huid*, Icel. *hūð*, Dan. Swed. *hud*, O. H. G. *hūt*, G. *haut*; L. *cutis*, Gk. κύτος, σκῦτος, skin, hide. (√SKEU.) ¶ The roots of *hide* (1) and *hide* (2) are prob. connected.

hide (3), to flog. (E.) Colloquial; to ' skin ' by flogging. So also Icel. *hȳða*, to flog, from *hūð*, skin.

Hide (4), a measure of land. (E.) Estimated at 120 to 100 acres, and less. (Low L. *hida*.) A.S. *hīd*, a contracted form; the full form is *hīgid*. *Hīgid* and *hīwisc* were used in the same sense, to mean enough land for one family or household. They are probably closely allied words, and therefore allied to *hind* (2); for *hīwisc* is merely the adj. formed from *hīw-a*, a domestic, one of a household; see **Hind** (2). ¶ Not connected with Hide (1).

Hideous, ugly. (F. – L. ?) M. E. *hidous*. – O. F. *hidos*, *hidus*, later *hideux*, hideous; the earliest form is *hisdos*. Supposed by some to be from L. *hispidōsus*, roughish; from *hispidus*, rough, shaggy. (See Körting, § 3363.)

Hie, to hasten. (E.) M. E. *hien*, *hyen*, *hiȝen*. A. S. *hīgian* (*higian*?), to strive after, be intent on. Cf. Du. *hijgen*, to pant; and (perhaps) Skt. *çīgh-ra-*, quick.

Hierarchy. (F. – L. – Gk.) M. F. *hierarchie*; Cot. – Late L. *hierarchia*. – Gk. ἱεραρχία, power of a ἱεράρχης, a steward or president of sacred rites. – Gk. ἱερ-, for ἱερός, sacred: and ἄρχειν, to rule. ¶ Milton has *hierarch* = Gk. ἱεράρχης.

hieroglyphic. (L. – Gk.) L. *hieroglyphicus*, symbolical. – Gk. ἱερογλυφικός, relating to sacred writings. – Gk. ἱερό-s, sacred; γλύφ-ειν, to hollow out, engrave, incise. See **Glyptic**.

hierophant, a priest. (Gk.) Gk. ἱεροφάντης, teaching the rites of worship. – Gk. ἱερό-s, sacred; φαίνειν, to shew, explain. See **Phase**.

Higgle, to bargain. (E.) Merely a weakened form of Ha gle.

High. (E.) M. E. *heigh, hey, hy.* A. S. *hēah, hēh.* **+** Du. *hoog,* Icel. *hār,* Swed. *hög.* Dan. *höi,* Goth. *hauhs,* G. *hoch.* Teut. type **hauhoz.* See How (2); and cf. G. *hügel,* a bunch, knob, hillock; also Lith. *kaukaras,* a hill; *kaukas,* a boil, swelling; Skt. *kucha-,* the female breast. (✓KEUK.)

highland. (E.) From *high* and *land*; cf *up-land, low-land.*

Hight, was or is called. (E.) The only passive vb. found in E.; *he hight =* he was named. M. E. *highte*; also *hatte, hette.* A. S. *hātte,* I am called, I was called; pr. and pt. t. passive of A. S. *hātan,* to call. So also Icel. *heiti,* I am named, from *heita,* to call; G. *ich heisse,* I am named, from *heissen,* to call, bid. β. Best illustrated by Goth. *haitan,* to call, 3 p. pres. tense (passive) *haitada*; as in 'Thomas, saei *haitada* Didymus' = Thomas, who is called Didymus, John vi. 16.

Hilarity, mirth. (F. – L. – Gk.) F. *hilarité.* – L. acc. *hilaritātem*; from *hilaris,* adj., cheerful; also *hilarus.* – Gk. ἱλαρός, cheerful. ¶ *Hilary* Term is so called from the festival of St. Hilary (L. *Hilarius*), who died Jan. 13, 367.

Hilding, a base wretch. (E.) Also *helding*; XVI cent. Prob. from M. E. *helden,* to incline, bend down. Cf M. E. *holdinge,* a bending aside; Dan. *helding,* bias; A. S. *hylding,* a bending; see Heel (2).

Hill. (E.) M. E. *hil, hul.* A. S. *hyll.* **+** M. Du. *hil*; L. *collis,* a hill; Lithuan. *kalnas,* a hill, *kelti,* to raise; Gk. κολωνός, a hill. Brugm. i. § 633. Allied to Holm and Culminate. Der. *down-hill, up-hill.*

Hilt, sword-handle. (E.) A. S. *helt, hilt.* **+** Icel. *hjalt,* Dan. *hialte,* N. Fries. *heelt,* O. H. G. *helza.* Cf O. F. *helt,* from Teut. ¶ *Not* allied to *hold*; rather, to *helve.* Cf. Low G. *helft,* ax-handle.

Him; see He.

Hin, a liquid measure. (Heb.) Heb. *hīn,* a hin; said to be Egyptian origin.

Hind (1), female of the stag. (E.) A. S. *hind.* **+** Du. *hinde*; Icel. Dan. and Swed. *hind,* M. H. G. *hinde,* O. H. G. *hinta,* a doe. Perhaps allied to Gk. κεμ-άς, young deer.

Hind (2), a peasant. (E.) The final *d* is excrescent. M. E. *hine,* a domestic.

A. S. **hīna,* a domestic, unauthenticated as a nominative, and really a gen. pl., so that *hīna* stands for *hīna man =* a man of the domestics; cf. *hīna ealdor =* chief of the domestics, a master of a household. *Hīna = hīgna,* gen. pl. of *hīwan,* domestics; cf. *hīwen,* a family, *hīwrǣden,* a household; also G. *heirath,* marriage, Goth. *heiwa-frauja,* master of a household. Cf. L. *cīuis,* a citizen. Brugm. i. § 609.

Hind (3), adj., in the rear. (E.) We now say 'hind feet'; but the older form is 'hinder feet.' We even find M. E. *hynderere* (as if hinder-er). – A. S. *hindan,* adv., at the back of, *hinder,* adv., backwards. **+** Goth. *hindar,* prep., behind; *hindana,* beyond; G. *hinter,* prep., behind, *hinten,* adv., behind; O. H. G. *hintaro,* comp. adj., hinder. We also find Goth. *hindumists,* hindmost. In O. H. G. *hintaro,* the comp. suffix is like the Gk. -τερο-; and in Goth. *hin-dum-ists,* the superl. suffix is like the L. -*tim-*(*us*) in *op-timus,* followed by -*ists =* E. -*est.* Extended from A. S. *hin-,* as in *hin-, heon-an,* hence; from *hi-,* base of *he*; see Hence.

hinder, vb. (E.) M. E. *hindren.* A. S. *hindrian,* to put behind, keep back. **–** A. S. *hinder* (above). **+** Icel. *hindra,* G. *hindern*; similarly formed. **Der.** *hindr-ance* (for *hinder-ance*).

hindmost. (E.) From *hind* and *most*; a late formation. The M. E. form was *hinderest*; cf. A. S. *hin-dema,* hindmost, a superl. form with suffix -*dema* (cf. L. *op-timus*). **+** Goth. *hindumists,* hindmost (= *hin-dum-ists,* with double superl. suffix).

Hinge. (E.) M. E. *heng,* that on which the door hangs; from M. E. *hengen,* to hang, a later variant of M. E. *hangien* (A. S *hangian*), to hang; suggested by A. S. *hengen,* a hanging, or by Icel. *hengja,* to hang. Cf. A. S. *henge-clif,* a steep cliff; and *Stone-henge*; Dan. dial. *hinge, hænge,* a hinge (Dan. *hængsel*). For the sound, cf. *singe, swinge.* See Hang. **+** M. Du. *henge, hengene,* a hinge.

Hint, a slight allusion. (E.) *Hint* is apparently 'a thing taken' or caught up; cf. Lowl. Sc. *hint,* an opportunity; *in a hint,* in a moment; *hint,* to lay hold of. From M. E. *henten,* to seize. **–** A. S *hentan,* to seize. Allied to Hunt, and to Goth. *fra-hunthan,* to seize.

Hip (1), the haunch. (E.) M. E. *hipe, hupe.* A. S. *hype.* **+** Du. *heup,* Icel. *huppr,*

Dan. *hofte*, Swed. *höft*, Goth. *hups*, G. *hüfte*, O. H. G. *huf*. Perhaps allied to Gk. *κύβος*, the hollow near the hips of cattle.

Hip (2), **Hep**, fruit of the dog-rose. (E.) M. E. *hepe*. A. S. *hēope*, a hip; *hēopbrēmel*, a hip-bramble.+O. Sax. *hiopo*, M. H. G. *hiefe*, O. H. G. *hiufo*, a bramble-bush.

Hippish. (Gk.) Equivalent to *hypochondriacal*, adj. of Hypochondria, q. v. Hence *hippish = hyp-ish*. The contraction *hipped* (= *hyp'd*) was prob. suggested by *hipped*, lamed in the hip (an older word).

Hippopotamus. (L. – Gk.) L. *hippopotamus*. – Gk. *ἱπποπόταμος*, the river-horse of Egypt. – Gk. *ἵππο-s*, horse; *ποταμό-s*, river. Gk. *ἵππος* is cognate with L. *equus*; see **Equine**.

Hire, sb. (E.) M. E. *hire*. A. S. *hȳr*, hire, wages.+Du. *huur*, Swed. *hyra*, Dan. *hyre*, prov. G. *heuer*, hire, rent; Low G. *hüren*, to hire. Teut. type *hūr-jā*, f.

Hirsute. (L.) L. *hirsūtus*, bristly, rough. Cf. L. *horrēre*, to bristle; see **Horrid**.

His ; see **He**.

Hiss. (E.) M. E. *hissen*, *hisshen*. + M. Du. *hisschen* ; Low G. *hissen*, to say *hiss !* in setting on dogs ; Gascon *hissa*, to hiss (Moncaut). An imitative word ; like G. *zischen*, to hiss.

hist, an interjection enjoining silence. (E.) Also *ist*, *'st*. Cf. Dan. *hys*, silence ! *hysse*, to hush. Milton has *hist* = summon silently, Il Pens. 55.

Histology, the science treating of the minute structure of tissues of plants, &c. (Gk.) Gk. *ἱστό-s*, a web (hence, tissue) ; -λογια, discourse, from λέγειν, to speak. Gk. *ἱστό-s* (also a mast) is allied to *ἵστημι*, to set, place. (√STA.)

History. (L. – Gk.) M. E. *historie*. – L. *historia*. – Gk. *ἱστορία*, a learning by enquiry, information. – Gk. *ἵστορ-*, stem of *ἵστωρ*, *ἵστωρ*, knowing ; for **ἴδ-τωρ*. – Gk. *ϝιδ-*, base of *εἰδέναι*, to know. (√WEID.) Allied to **Wit**. Doublet, *story*, q. v.

Histrionical, relating to the stage. (L.) From L. *histriōnicus*, relating to an actor. – L. *histriōn-*, stem of *histrio*, an actor.

Hit, to light upon, strike, attain to. (Scand.) M. E. *hitten*. – Icel. *hitta*, to hit upon ; Dan. *hitte* ; Swed. *hitta*, to find.

Hitch, to move by jerks, catch slightly. (E.) M. E. *hicchen*, to move, remove. Cf. Lowl. Sc. *hatch*, *hotch*, to move by jerks ; *hitch*, a motion by a jerk ; prov. E. *hike*, to toss, *hikey*, a swing. It describes a jerky movement ; cf. Low G. and E. Fries. *hikken*, to peck. ¶ Not allied to *hook*.

Hithe, Hythe, a small haven. (E.) M. E. *hithe*. A. S. *hȳð*, a haven.

Hither. (E.) M. E. *hider*, *hither*. A. S. *hider*. From the base of *he*, with Idg. suffix -*t(e)r*. – So also Icel. *hēðra*, O. Icel. *hiðra*, Goth. *hidrē*, L. *citrā*.

Hive, a house for bees. (E.) A. S. *hȳf*, fem. ; Teut. type **hūfiz*.+Du. *huif*, a hive (see Franck) ; Dan. dial. *hyve* ; cf. L. *cūpa*, a tub, cup. Allied to **Cupola**.

Ho, Hoa, a call to excite attention. (E.) A natural exclamation. Cf. Icel. *hō !* ho ! *hōa*, to shout out ho !

Hoar, white. (E.) M. E. *hoor*. A. S. *hār*.+Icel. *hārr*, hoar ; G. *hehr*, exalted, O. H. G. *hēr*, proud, lofty, orig. ' reverend.' Teut. type **hairoz* ; lit. ' shining,' hence, white : = **hai-roz*. The base **hai-* occurs in Goth. *hai-s*, a torch, G. *hei-ter*, orig. ' bright,' Icel. *hei-ð*, brightness ; cf. Skt. *kētu(s)*, a sign, a meteor (Kluge).

Hoard, a store. (E.) A. S. *hord*.+Icel. *hodd*, G. *hort*, Goth. *huzd*. Teut. type **huzdo-*, due to Idg. **kudh-dho-*, ' a thing hidden ;' from the weak grade of √KEUDH, as in Gk. *κεύθ-ειν*, A. S. *hȳdan* : see Hide (1). Brugm. i. § 699.

Hoarding, a kind of fence. (F. – Du. ; or Du.) Not old. Either from Du. *horde*, a hurdle, or from M. F. *hourd*, a scaffold (Cot., index), which is the same word (borrowed). See **Hurdle**.

Hoarhound, Horehound, a plant. (E.) The true *hoarhound* is the white, *Marrubium vulgare*. The final *d* is excrescent. M. E. *hor(e)houne*. A. S. *hār-hūne*, also called simply *hūne*. – A. S. *hār*, hoar ; *hūne*, hoarhound, the origin of which is unknown.

Hoarse, having a rough. harsh voice. (E.) The *r* is intrusive, but sometimes occurs in M. E. *hors*, also spelt *hoos*, hoarse. A. S. *hās*, hoarse + Dan. *hæs*, Swed. *hes*, Du. *heesch*, G. *heiser*. ¶ Icel. *hāss* seems distinct (Noreen).

Hoary ; see **Hoar**.

Hoax. (Low L.) Short for *hocus*, i. e. to juggle, cheat. See **Hocus-pocus**.

Hob (1), **Hub,** the nave of a wheel,

part of a grate. (E.) The true sense is 'projection'; the *hob* of a fire-place was orig. 'a boss or mass of clay behind the fire-place'; N. E. D. E. Fries. *hobbe*, a rough tump of grassy land rising out of water ; *hubbel*, a projection. **+** Du. *hobbel*, a knob ; G. *hübel*, O. H. G. *hubel*, a hillock. Cf. Lith. *kup-stas*, a tump of grass ; Du. *heuvel*, a hill ; A. S. *hofer*, a hump. **Der.** *hob-nail*, a nail with a projecting head.

Hob (2), a clown, rustic, a fairy. (F. — O. H. G.) 'Elves, *hobs*, and fairies;' Beaumont and Fletcher, Mons. Thomas, iv. 6. *Hob* was a common personal name, a corruption of *Robin* (like *Hodge* from *Roger*). The name *Robin* is F., and is a form of *Robert*, a name of O. H. G. origin. **Der.** *hob-goblin* ; see **Goblin.**

Hobble, to limp. (E.) M. E. *hobelen*. Equivalent to *hopp-le* ; frequentative of *hop.*+Du. *hobbelen* ; prov. G. *hoppeln*.

Hobbledehoy, a lad approaching manhood. (E.) Of unknown origin. Prob. an invention, perhaps for *hobbledy*, founded on *hobble* (above), with the addition of *hoy*, an unmeaning suffix. The Scottish *hoy* means 'shout,' both as sb. and vb.

Hobby (1), **Hobby-horse,** a toy like a horse, ambling nag, a favourite pursuit. (F.—O. H. G.) Corruption of M. E. *hobin*, a nag [whence F. *hobin*, 'a hobby;' Cot.]. *Hobin* is a variant of *Robin* ; see Hob (2). Cf. *Dobbin*, a name for a horse.

Hobby (2), a small falcon. (F. — O. Low G.) M. E. *hobi*, *hoby*. From O. F. *hobet*, a hobby; allied to F. *hobreau* (—*hob-er-el*), 'the hawke tearmed a hobby;' Cot. — F. *hober*, to stir, move about. — M. Du. *hobben*, to toss, move up and down. Cf. Hop (1).

Hobgoblin; see Hob (2).

Hobnail; see Hob (1).

Hobnob, Habnab, with free leave, at random. (E.) Compounded of *hab* and *nab*, to have, or not to have, hence applied to taking a thing or leaving it, implying free choice, and hence a familiar invitation to drink, as in 'to *hob-nob* together.' *Hab* is from A. S. *habban*, to have ; *nab* is from A. S. *nabban*, for *ne hæbban*, not to have ; see Have. Cf. *willy-nilly*.

Hock (1); see Hough.

Hock (2), a wine. (G.) From *Hochheim*, the name of a place in Germany, on the

river Main, whence the wine comes. It means 'high home.'

Hockey, a game. (E.) Also called *hawkey*; because played with a *hooked* stick so called. See N. E. D.

Hocus-pocus, a juggler's trick, a juggler. (Low L.) As far as it can be said to belong to any language, it is a sort of Latin, having the L. termination *-us*. But it is merely an invented term, used by a juggler (temp. James I) in performing tricks; see Todd's Johnson and N. E. D. Cf. L. *iocus*, a game. **Der.** *hocus*, a juggler, a trick ; *hocus*, vb., to trick, to *hoax*.

Hod, a kind of trough for carrying bricks. (F.) Modified from M. E. *hotte*, F. *hotte*, a basket, dosser; influenced by *hod*, a prov. E. form of *hold*; see Hold. In Linc. and York. *hod* means 'hold' or 'receptacle'; as in (Whitby) *powder-hod*, powder-flask; *cannle-hod*, candlestick.

Hodge-podge; see Hotchpot.

Hoe. (F. — G.) Formerly *howe*. ▬ F. *houe*, a hoe ; Norman dial. *hoe*.─O. H. G. *houwa* (G. *haue*), a hoe, lit. a hewer.─ O. H. G. *houwan*, to hew; see Hew.

Hog. (E.) M. E. *hogge*, 'maialis, est enim porcus carens testiculis;' Cathol. Anglic. p. 187. Cf. *hog-sheep*, one clipped the first year. A. S. *hogg*, Cambridge Phil. Soc., 1902, p. 13, l. 2; cf. also *Hocges-tūn*, Cod. Dipl. Moisy gives Norman dial. *hogge*, a six-months' lamb, a pig ; and *hogastre*, a two-year-old sheep ; but these are prob. from E. ¶ Not borrowed from Corn. *hoch*, W. *hwch*, a sow; for which see Sow.

Hogshead. (E.) Of E. origin; for *hog's head*; but the reason for the name is uncertain. Hence M. Du. *hockshoot*, *okshoofd*, *oxhoofd*, a hogshead; M. Dan. *hogshoved*; also Dan. *oxhoved*, Swed. *ox-hufvud*, a hogshead, but made to seem to mean 'ox-head.'

Hoiden, Hoyden, a romping girl. (M. Du.) Formerly applied to males, and meaning a rustic.─M. Du. *heyden* (Du. *heiden*), a heathen; also, a gipsy. See Heathen. ¶ The W. *hoeden* is borrowed from English.

Hoist, to heave. (M. Du.) The final *t* is due to the pp. *hoist*, used for *hoised*. The verb is really *hoise*; spelt *hyce* in Palsgrave. (Cf. *graft* for *graff*.) ─ M. Du. *hyssen*, Du. *hijsschen*, to hoise (*y* sounded as E. long *i*); cf. Dan. *heise*, *hisse*; Swed.

hissa, to hoist (cf. F. *hisser*, from Teut.). ¶ *Not* allied to F. *hausser*, to elevate.

Hold (1), to keep. (E.) O. Merc. *haldan*; A. S. *healdan* +Du. *houden*, Icel. *halda*. Swed. *hålla*, Dan. *holde*, Goth. *haldan*, G. *halten*. Teut. type **haldan-*; pt. t **he-hald*. Der. *hold*, sb.; also *be-hold*, with prefix *be-* (E. *by*); *up-hold*.

Hold (2), the cavity of a ship. (Du.) For *hole*, with excrescent *d*, due to confusion with the verb to *hold*. — Du. *hol*, a hole, cave, esp. used of the hold of a ship (Sewel). See below.

Hole. (E.) M. E. *hole*, *hol*. A. S. *hol*, a cave. + Du. *hol*, Icel. *hol*, Dan. *hul*, Swed. *hål*. Teut. type **hulom*, n.; orig. neut. of **huloz*, adj., hollow, as in A. S. *hol*, Du. *hol*, Icel. *holr*, Dan. *huul*, G. *hohl*. Cf. Goth. *us-hulōn*, to hollow out, *hul-undi*, a cave. β. Prob. A. S. *hol* is from *hol-*, weak grade of str. vb. *helan*, to cover; see **Hell**. Not allied to Gk. κοῖλος, hollow.

Holibut; see Halibut.

Holiday, a festival. (E.) For *holy day*. See Holy.

Holla, Hallo, stop! wait! (F.) Not the same word as *halloo*, to shout; but differently used in old authors. See Oth. i. 2. 56; As You Like It, iii. 2. 257. — F. *holà*, 'an interjection, hoe there;' Cot. — F. *ho*, interj.; and *là*, there (= L. *illāc*). ¶ The form *hallo* is due to a confusion with *halloo*.

Holland, Dutch linen. (Du.) From *Holland*, the name of the province. So also *hollands*, spirits from Holland.

Hollow. (E.) M. E. *holwe*, adj. A. S. *holh*, sb . a hollow place, also spelt *holg*. Cf. O. H. G. *huliwa*, a pool, puddle. Perhaps extended from A. S. *hol*, hollow; see Hole.

Holly. (E.) M. E. *holin*; so that an *n* has been dropped. A S. *holen*, *holegn*, holly. +W. *celyn*, Corn. *celin*, Bret. *kelen*, Gael. *cuilionn*, Irish *cuileann*, holly; Idg. type **kolenno-*. Cf. also Du. *hulst*, G. *hülst*, holly, O. H. G. *hulis* (whence F. *houx*).

Hollyhock, a kind of mallow. (E.) M E. *holihoc*, i. e. holy hock. Compounded of *holy*, and A. S. *hoc*, 'mallow.' [We also find W. *hocys*, mallows, *hocys bendigaid*, hollyhock. lit. 'blessed mallow,' where *bendigaid* = L. *benedictus*. W. *hocys* is from A. S. *hoccas*, pl. of *hoc*.] In A. S. the mallow is also called *hoclēaf*.

Holm, an islet in a river, flat land by a river. (Scand.) M E. *holm*. — Icel. *hōlmr*, *hōlmi*, *holmr*, an islet, flat meadow; Dan. *holm*, Swed. *holme*; whence G. *holm*, island. Cf. A. S. *holm*, billow, sea; L. *culmen*, hill-top. Allied to **Hill** and **Culminate.**

Holm-oak, the evergreen oak. (E.) Here *holm* is a corruption of M. E. *holin*, a holly. ' *Holme*, or holy [holly];' Prompt. Parv.; and see Way's note. The *Quercus ilex*, an evergreen plant; the leaves of which resemble those of holly.

Holocaust. (L. – Gk.) L. *holocaustum*, Gen. xxii. 8. — Gk. ὁλόκαυστον, a sacrifice burnt whole; neut. of ὁλόκαυστος, burnt whole. — Gk. ὅλο-s, whole; and καίειν, to burn. See **Caustic.**

Holster, a leathern case for a pistol. (Du. – O. H. G.) Du. *holster*; Low G. *holster*, a pistol-case. — G. *holfter*, a pistol-case (with change of *ft* to *st*); M. H. G. *hulfter*, a quiver; from O. H. G. *hulft*, a cover, case (Kluge). Cf. M. Dan. *holfte*, a gun-case. ¶ So Franck; who rejects the connection with Icel. *hulstr*, A. S. *heolster*.

Holt, a wood. (E.) M. E. and A. S. *holt*. + Du. *hout*, M Du. *holt*; Icel. *holt*, G. *holz*. Teut. stem **hulto-*, Idg. stem **koldo-*. Allied to O. Irish *caill*, *coill* (for **caild*), a wood; W. *celli*, a grove, Russ. *koloda*, a log, Gk. κλάδος, a twig.

Holy, sacred. (E.) [This word is equivalent to the M E. *hool*, whole, with suffix -*y*; and therefore closely allied to *whole*.] M. E. *holi*, *holy*. A. S *hālig*, holy. + Du. *heilig*, holy, Icel. *heilagr*, *helgr*, Dan. *hellig*, Swed. *helig*, G. *heilig*; Goth. *hailag*, neut. (in an inscription). Teut. type **hailagoz*, a deriv. of **hailoz* (A. S. *hāl*), whole, or of **hailoz-* or **hailiz-*, sb., good omen. Cf. Irish *cél*, W. *coel*, an omen. See **Whole.**

Homage. (F – L.) M. E. *homage*. — O. F. *homage*, the service of a vassal to his lord. — Late L. *homāticum*, *homināticum*, the service of a vassal or man. — L. *hom-o* (stem *homin-*), a man. See **Human.**

Home. (E.) M. E. *hoom*. A. S. *hām*. + Du. *heim*, *heem*; Icel. *heimr*, an abode; Dan. *hiem*, Swed. *hem*, G. *heim*; Goth. *haims*, a village. Teut. base **haimo-*, **haimi-*; cf. Lithuan. *kēmas*, a village; and perhaps Skt. *kshēma-*, safety, from *kshi*, to dwell.

Homer, a large measure. (Heb.) Heb.

khōmer, a homer, also a heap (with initial *cheth*). — Heb. root *khāmar*, to surge up.

Homicide, man-slaughter, also a man-slayer. (F. — L.) F. *homicide*, meaning (1) manslaughter, from L. *homicīdium* ; (2) a man-killer, from L. *homicūda*. — L. *hom-o*, a man ; -*cīdium*, a killing, or -*cīda*, a slayer, from *cædere*, to kill.

Homily. (L. — Gk.) L. *homīlia*. — Gk. ὁμιλία, a living together ; also converse, instruction, homily. — Gk. ὅμιλος, a throng, concourse. — Gk. ὁμ-ός, like, same, together, cognate with E. **Same** ; and (possibly) ἴλη, εἴλη, a crowd, from εἴλειν, to compress, shut in.

Hominy, maize prepared for food. (W. Indian.) W. Indian *auhúminea*, parched corn (Webster) ; Trumbull gives *appuminéonash*, with the same sense.

Hommock ; see **Hummock.**

Homœopathy. (Gk.) Englished from Gk. ὁμοιοπάθεια, likeness in feeling or condition. — Gk. ὁμοιο-ς, like ; παθ-εῖν, aorist infin. of πάσχειν, to suffer. See **Same** and **Pathos.**

Homogeneous, of the same kind throughout. (Gk.) Englished from Gk. ὁμογεν-ής, of the same race. — Gk. ὁμό-ς, same (cognate with E. **Same**), and γέν-ος, a race (cognate with E. **Kin**). So also *homo-logous*, corresponding, from λόγος, a saying, λέγειν, to say.

Homonymous, like in sound, but differing in sense. (L. — Gk.) L. *homōnym-us*; with suffix -*ous*. — Gk. ὁμώνυμος, having the same name. — Gk. ὁμό-ς, same ; ὄνυμα, ὄνομα, name. See **Same** and **Name.** Der. *homonym*, F. *homonyme*.

Hone. (E.) A.S. *hān*, a stone (with change from *ā* to long *o*, as in *bān*, bone) ; Birch, ii. 458. + Icel. *hein*, Swed. *hen*. Teut. stem **hainā*, f. Cf. Skt. *çi*, to sharpen. Brugm. i. § 200.

Honest. (F. — L.) O. F. *honeste* (F. *honnête*). — L. *honestus*, honourable ; for *hones-tus*, related to *honos*, honour See **Honour.**

Honey. (E.) M. E. *huni*. A.S. *hunig*. + Du. *honig*, Icel. *hunang*, Dan. *honning*, Swed. *honing*, G. *honig*.

honeycomb. (E.) A.S. *hunigcamb*, a honey-comb ; where *comb* is the usual E. word, though the likeness to a *comb* is rather fanciful.

honeymoon. (E.) Wedded love was compared to the full moon, that soon wanes ; Huloet, 1522. See N. E. D.

honeysuckle. (E.) Lye gives A.S. *hunigsucle*, unauthorised ; but we find A.S. *hunigsūce*, *hunigsūge*, privet, similarly named. From A.S. *sūcan*, to suck.

Honour. (F. — L.) A. F. *honur*. — L. *honōrem*, acc of *honor*, *honos* honour.

Hood, covering. (E.) A.S. *hōd*. + Du. *hoed*, G. *hut*, O. H. G. *huot*, *hōt*, a hat. Allied to **Heed** and **Hat.**

-hood, -head, suffix. (E.) A.S. *hād*, state, quality ; cognate with Goth. *haidus*, manner, way. Cf. Skt. *kētu(s)*, a sign by which a thing may be recognised ; from *kit*, to perceive. Brugm. ii. § 104.

Hoodwink. (E.) To make one *wink* or close his eyes, by covering him with a *hood*.

Hoof. (E.) M. E. *hoof*, *huf* ; pl. *hoves*. A.S. *hōf*. + Du. *hoef*, Icel. *hōfr*, Dan. *hov*, Swed. *hof*, G. *huf*. Teut. type **hōfoz*, m. Allied to Russ. *kopuito*, Skt. *çapha*, hoof.

Hook. (E.) M. E. *hok*. A.S. *hōc*. + Du. *hoek* ; also (with *a*-grade) Du. *haak*, Icel. *haki*, Dan. *hage*, Swed. *hake*, A.S. *haca*, a hook. Allied to **Hake.**

Hookah, Hooka. (Arab.) Arab. *huqqa(t)*, a vase, water-pipe for smoking.

Hoop (1), a pliant strip of wood or other material bent into a band. (E.) M. E. *hoop*, *hope*. A.S. *hōp*. + Du. *hoep* ; E. and N. Fries. and O. Fries. *hōp*.

Hoop (2), **Whoop,** to call out, shout. (F.) M. E. *houpen*, to shout. — O. F. *houper*, ' to hoop unto ;' Cot. Of imitative origin ; from *houp !* interj. ; cf. Goth. *hwōpan*, to boast.

hooping-cough, a cough accompanied by a *hoop* or convulsive noisy catch in the breath. (Formerly called *chin-cough*.)

Hoopoe, the name of a bird. (F. — L.) Formerly *houpe*, *hoope*. — F. *huppe*, apparently confused with O. F. *pupu*, another form of the same word. — L. *upupa*, a hoopoe ; the E. initial *h* is due to the F. *huppe*. + Gk. ἔποψ, a hoopoe. Of imitative origin. ¶ The F. *huppe*, a tuft of feathers, is from *huppe*, a hoopoe (from its tufted head) ; not vice versâ.

Hoot. (Scand.) M. E. *houten*. — O. Swed. *huta*, to hoot. — Swed. *hut !* interj. begone ! of onomatopoetic origin. So also Norm. dial. *houter*, to hoot ; W. *hwt !* Irish *ut !* expressions of dislike. See **Hue** (2).

Hop (1), to leap on one leg. (E.) M. E. *hoppen*, *huppen*. A.S. *hoppian*, to leap, dance. **+** Du. *hoppen*, Icel. *hoppa*, Swed. *hoppa*, Dan. *hoppe*, G. *hüpfen*. Brugm. i. § 421 (7). Der. *hopp-er* (of a mill); *hopp-le*, a fetter for horses; *hop-scotch*, a game in which children *hop* over *scotches*, i. e. lines scored on the ground. Cf. **Hobble**.

Hop (2), a plant. (Du.) Introduced from the Netherlands ; XV cent. **-** M. Du. *hoppe* (Du. *hop*), hop. **+** G. *hopfen*, hop. We also find A. S. *hymele*, Icel. *humall*, Swed. Dan. *humle*, M. Du. *hommel* (whence Late L. *humulus*); also F. *houblon*, which can hardly be allied words.

Hope (1), expectation. (E.) M. E. *hope*. A. S. *hopa*, hope ; whence *hopian*, to hope. **+** Du. *hoop*, Dan. *haab*, Swed. *hopp*, M. H. G. *hoffe*, sb. ; whence Du. *hopen*, Dan. *haabe*, Swed. *hoppas*, G. *hoffen*, to hope.

Hope (2), a troop. (Du.) Only in the phr. 'a forlorn hope,' i. e. troop. **-** Du. *verloren hoop* = lost band, where *hoop* = E. **heap**; see **Heap**. 'Een *hoop krijghs-volck*, a troupe or band of souldiers,' Hexham ; *verloren hoop* (Kilian). (Now obsolete in Dutch.)

Horde, a wandering tribe. (F. – Turk. – Tatar.) F. *horde*. **-** Turk. *ordū*, a camp. **-** Tatar *ūrdū*, a royal camp, horde of Tatars (Tartars); see Pavet de Courteille, p. 54.

Hordock; see **Hardock**.

Horehound; see **Hoarhound**.

Horizon. (F. – L. – Gk.) F. *horizon*. **-** L. *horizōn* (stem *horizont-*). **-** Gk. ὁρίζων, the bounding or limiting circle ; orig. pres. pt. of ὁρίζειν, to limit. **-** Gk. ὅρος, a boundary. Der. *horizont-al*.

Horn. (E.) A. S. *horn*.**+** Icel. Dan. Swed. G. *horn*; Du. *horen*. Goth. *haurn*; W. Gael. Irish *corn*, L. *cornu*. Allied to Gk. κέρ-ας, a horn, and to **Hart**.

Hornblende, a mineral. (G.) A *blende* named from its horn-like cleavage. G. *hornblende*. **-** G. *horn*, horn; *blende*, a 'deceitful' mineral, yielding little ore; from *blenden*, to deceive, blind, dazzle; from *blind*, blind.

Hornet, a kind of large wasp. (E.) So called from its resounding hum. A. S. *hyrnet*, a hornet. **-** A. S. *horn*, a horn, to which the word was later conformed. Cf. O. Sax. *horno-bero*, a hornet, lit. 'horn-bearer ;' A. S. *horn-bora*, a trumpeter. Hexham has M. Du. *horener*, *hornte*, a hornet, *horentoren*, a wasp, from *horen*, a

horn. **¶** It is strange that G. *hornisse*, O. H. G. *hornaz* (without vowel-change) is referred to a Teut. type **hurz-natoz* (cf. Du. *horz-elen*, to buzz), allied to L. *crābro* (for **cras-ro*), a hornet, Lith. *szirszū* (gen. *szirsz-ens*), a hornet; see Brugm. i. § 626.

Horologe, a clock. (F. – L. – Gk.) O. F. *horologe* (later *horloge*). **-** L. *hōrologium*. **-** Gk. ὡρολόγιον, a sun-dial, water-clock. **-** Gk. ὡρο-, for ὥρα, hour ; -λογιον, teller, from λέγειν, to tell.

horoscope. (F. – L. – Gk.) F. *horoscope*. **-** L. *hōroscopus*, a horoscope, from *hōroscopus*, adj., observing the hour. **-** Gk. ὡροσκόπος, observing the hour (also as sb.). **-** Gk. ὡρο-, for ὥρα, hour ; σκοπεῖν, to consider, allied to σκέπτομαι, I consider; see **Sceptic**.

Horrible. (F. – L.) O. F. *horrible*. **-** L. *horribilis*, dreadful. **-** L. *horrēre*, to dread (below).

horrid. (L.) Spenser has it in the sense of 'rough'; F. Q. i. 7. 31. **-** L. *horridus*, rough, bristly. **-** L. *horrēre* (for **hors-ēre*), to bristle ; also to dread, with reference to the bristling of the hair through terror. Cf. Skt. *hṛsh*, to bristle, esp. as a token of fear or of pleasure.

horrify. (L.) Coined, by analogy with F. words in *-fy*, from L. *horrificāre*, to cause terror. **-** L. *horri-*, for *horrēre*, to dread ; *-ficāre*, for *facere*, to make.

horror, dread. (L.) L. *horror*. **-** L. *horrēre*, to dread (above).

Horse. (E.) M. E. *hors*. **-** A. S. *hors*, pl. *hors*, it being a neut. sb.**+**Icel. *hross*, *hors*, Du. *ros*, G. *ross*, O. H. G. *hros*. Prob. 'a runner ;' cf. L. *currere* (sup. *curs-um*), to run. Brugm. i. § 516, ii. § 662.

Hortatory, full of encouragement. (L.) As if from L. **hortātōrius*, coined from *hortātor*, an encourager. **-** L. *hortārī*, to encourage; prob. allied to L. *horior*, I urge, and to E. **Yearn**.

Horticulture, gardening. (L.) Coined from L. *hortī*, gen. case of *hortus*, a garden ; *cultūra*, cultivation ; see **Culture**. L. *hortus* is allied to E. *yard* (1).

Hosanna, an expression of praise. (Gk. – Heb.) Gk. ὡσαννά. **-** Heb. *hōshī'-āh nnā*, save, we pray. **-** Heb. *hōshī'a*, save (from *yāsha'*); and *nā*, a particle signifying entreaty.

Hose. (E.) M. E. *hose*, pl. *hosen*. A.S. *hosa*, pl. *hosan*, hose, stockings. **+** Du. *hoos*, Icel. *hosa*, Dan. *hose*, G. *hose* (whence

O. F. *hose*). Der. *hos-i-er* (cf. *bow-yer*, *law-yer*).

Hospice. (F. – L.) F. *hospice.* – L. *hospitium*, a house for guests. – L. *hospiti-*, decl. stem of *hospes*, a host; see **host** (1).

hospitable. (F. – L.) M. F. *hospitable*. From Late L. *hospitāre*, to receive as a guest. – L. *hospit-*, stem of *hospes*, a host.

hospital. (F. – L.) M. E. *hospital*. – O. F. *hospital.* – Late L. *hospitāle*, a large house, a sing. formed from L. pl. *hospitālia*, apartments for strangers. – L. *hospit-*, stem of *hospes* (below).

host (1), one who entertains guests. (F. – L.) M. E. *host*, *hoste.* – O. F. *hoste*. Cf. Port. *hospede*, a host, guest. – L. *hospitem*, acc. of *hospes*, (1) a host, (2) a guest. ¶ Some make L. *hospit-* short for **hostipot-*, where *hosti-* is the decl. stem of *hostis*, a stranger, enemy, see **Host** (2); and *-pot-* means 'lord,' being allied to L. *potens*, powerful; cf. Skt. *pati-*, a master, governor, lord; see **Possible.** Thus *hospes* = **hostipotis*, guest-master, a master of a house who receives guests. Cf. Russ. *gospode*, the Lord, *gospodare*, a governor, master, from *goste*, a guest, and *-pode* (= Skt. *pati-*), lord. Brugm. i. §§ 158, 240. **Der.** *host-ess*, from M. F. *hostesse*, 'an hostesse,' Cot.; F. *hôtesse*.

Host (2), an army. (F. – L.) The orig. sense is 'enemy' or 'foreigner.' M. E. *host*, *ost.* – O. F. *host*, a host, army. – L. *hostem*, acc. of *hostis*, an enemy (orig. a stranger, a guest); hence, a hostile army, a host. + Russ. *goste*, a guest, stranger; A. S. *gæst*; see **Guest.** Doublet, *guest*.

Host (3), the consecrated bread of the eucharist. (L.) L. *hostia*, a victim in a sacrifice; O. Lat. *fostia*, lit. 'that which is slain.' – L. *hostīre*, O. Lat. **fostīre*, to strike.

Hostage. (F. – L.) O. F. *hostage*, a hostage (F. *otage*, Ital. *ostaggio*, O. Prov. *ostatje*). We also find Ital. *statico*, a hostage; and (according to Diez), both *ostaggio* and *statico* answer to a Late L. form **obsidāticus*, from Late L. *obsidātus*, the condition of a hostage. – L. *obsid-*, stem of *obses*, a hostage, one who remains behind with the enemy. – L. *obsidēre*, to stay. – L. *ob*, at, on, near; *sedēre*, to sit. ¶ Another explanation is from Late L. **hospitāticum*, a receiving as a guest; from L. *hospit-*, for *hospes*, a host; see

host (1). So Körting. The words may have been confused.

Hostel, an inn. (F. – L.) O. F. *hostel.* – Late L. *hospitāle*; see **hospital.**

hostler, ostler. (F – L.) Orig. the innkeeper himself, and so named from his *hostel* (above).

Hot. (E.) M. E. *hoot* (with long *o*). A. S. *hāt*, hot. + Du. *heet*, Icel. *heitr*, Swed. *het*, Dan. *hed*, G. *heiss*. Teut. type **haitoz*. Allied to Icel. *hiti*, G. *hitze*, heat, Goth. *heito*, fever; and cf. Goth. *hais*, a torch, Lithuan. *kaitra*, heat. **Der.** *heat.*

Hotch-pot, Hodgepodge. (F. – Du.) *Hodgepodge* is a corruption of *hotchpot*, a confused medley. – F. *hochepot*, a medley. – F. *hocher*, to shake; and *pot*, pot (see Cot.). Imitated or borrowed from M. Du. *hutspot* (lit. shake-pot), hodgepodge, beef or mutton cut into small pieces. – M. Du. *hutsen*, *hotsen*, to shake; *pot*, a pot. Cf. E. Fries. *hotjen*, to shake. See **Hustle** and **Pot.**

Hotel, an inn. (F. – L.) Mod. F. *hôtel*, the same as O. F. *hostel*; see **Hostel.**

Hottentot, a native of the Cape of Good Hope. (Du.) A name given them by the Dutch, in derision of their speech, which sounded like stammering, or a repetition of the syllables *hot* and *tot*. *En* is Dutch for 'and'; hence Du. *hot en tot* = 'hot' and 'tot.' Cf. M. Du. *hateren*, to stammer, Du. *tateren*, to stammer.

Houdah, Howdah, a seat fixed on an elephant's back. (Hind. – Arab.) Hind. *haudah.* – Arab. *hawdaj*, a litter carried by a camel, a seat placed on an elephant's back.

Hough, Hock, the joint in the hind-leg of an animal, between knee and fetlock; in man, the back part of the knee-joint. (E.) Now usually *hock*; formerly *hough*. M. E. *hough*. A. S. *hōh*, the heel; Teut. type **hanhoz*. + Icel. *hā-*, the hock, in *hā-sin*, hock-sinew. See **Heel.** *Hock* is a later form; and prob. arose from the comp. 'hough-sinew,' spelt *hōhsinu* in A.S., and *hōxene*, *hōxne* in O. Fries. (A. S. *hs* > *x*). See G. *hechse* (in Kluge); and see **Hox. Der.** *hough*, vb.; *hox*, q. v.

Hound, a dog. (E.) A. S. *hund.* + Du. *hond*, Icel. *hundr*, Dan. Swed. G. *hund*, Goth. *hunds*. Teut. type **hun-doz*, m. Allied to L. *canis*, Gk. κυών (gen. κυνός), Skt. *çvan-*, a dog; also to Irish *cu*,

W. *ci*, a dog, Russ. *suka*, a bitch, Lith. *szŭ* (stem *szun-*), a dog. Brugm. i. § 609. The final *-d* may have been suggested by confusion with Teut. **henthan-*, to catch. See **Hunt**.

Hour. (F. – L. – Gk.) O. F. *hore* (F. *heure*). – L. *hōra*. – Gk. ὥρα, a season, hour. Allied to **Year**.

Houri, a nymph of Paradise. (Pers. – Arab.) Pers. *ḥūrī*, one virgin of Paradise, *ḥūrā*, *ḥūr*, a virgin of Paradise, black-eyed nymph. From Arab. *ḥawrā*, fem. of *aḥwar*, having fine black eyes.

House. (E.) M. E. *hous*. A. S. *hūs*. + Du. *huis*, Icel. *hús*, Dan. *huus*, Swed. *hus*, Goth. *hūs*, G. *haus*. Teut. type **hūsom*, n. Possibly allied to **Hut**, **Hoard**; from √KEUDH, to hide. See **Hoard**, **Hide** (1). Brugm. i. § 796.

Housel, the eucharist. (E.) The orig. sense is 'sacrifice.' M. E. *housel*. A. S. *hūsel*. + Goth. *hunsl*, sacrifice. Allied to Lith. *szwentas*, holy, consecrated; Zend *spenta-*, holy. Brugm. i. § 377.

Housings, trappings of a horse. (F. – Teut.) The old form was *hous*; *-ings* has been added. – F. *housse*, a coverlet, 'a foot-cloth for a horse;' Cot. (Low L. *hucia*, *husia*, *hussia*, the same). Low L. type **hulstia*. – O. H. G. *hulst*, a cover. + Icel. *hulstr*, a case, sheath; A. S. *heolstor*, Goth. *hulistr*, a covering. From **hul-*, weak grade of Teut. **helan-* (A. S. *helan*), to cover, hide; cf. O. H. G. and Du. *hullen*, to cover.

Hovel, a small hut. (F. – Teut.?) M. E. *hovel*, *hovil*, a shed. Perhaps from O. F. **huvel-*, as in *huvelet*, a penthouse. – O. H. G. *hūba* (G. *haube*), a hood; M. Du. *huyve*, a tilt of a cart.

Hover. (E.) A frequentative of M. E. *hōuen* (= *hōven*), to be poised, to stay, tarry, wait. Origin uncertain; cf. *heave*. ¶ The W. *hofio*, to hover, is borrowed from M. E. *houen*.

How (1). (E.) M. E. *hou*, *hu*; A. S. *hū*. Closely related to A. S. *hwā*, who; see **Who**. + O. Fries. *hū*, O. Sax. *hwō*, Du. *hoe*. Cf. Goth. *hwaiwa*, how; Gk. πῶς.

How (2), a hill. (Scand.) M. E. *hogh*. Icel. *haugr*, a hill; Swed. *hög*, a mound; Dan. *höi*, a hill. Allied to Icel. *hār*, Swed. *hög*, Dan. *höi*, high : see **High**.

Howdah; see **Houdah**.

Howitzer, a short cannon. (G. – Bohemian.) Borrowed from G. *haubitze*, a howitzer; formerly spelt *hauffnitz*. –

Bohemian *haufnice*, orig. a sling for casting a stone; Jungmann, Bohem. Dict. i. 662. Cf. F. *obus*, from the same.

Howl. (E.) M. E. *houlen*. + M. Du. *huylen*; Dan. *hyle*; G. *heulen*, to howl. Of imitative origin; cf. L. *ululāre*, to howl, whence O. F. *huller*.

Hox, to hamstring. (E.) For *hocks*, which is from *hock-sinew*, sb., O. Fries. *hōxene*, *hōxne*, A. S. *hōh-sinu*, hough-sinew. – A. S. *hōh*, hough; *sinu*, sinew; see **Hough**. Cf. E. Fries. *haksene*, lit. 'heel-sinew,' but also the hamstring (of a horse).

Hoy (1), a kind of sloop. (Du.) M. Du. *heu*, *heude*, a flat-bottomed merchant-ship; M. Du. *hode*, *heude*; Flemish *hui*, a hoy.

Hoy (2), stop! (E.) M. E. *hoy*. Cf. Du. *hui!* hoy! come! well! Allied to **Ho**.

Hoyden; see **Hoiden**.

Hub, a projection; the same as **Hob** (1).

Hubbub. (E.) Imitative. Cf. Gael. *ub*, interj. of aversion. Formerly also *whoobub*, a confused noise. *Hubbub* was confused with *hoop-hoop*, reduplication of *hoop*; and *whoobub* with *whoop-hoop*. See **Hoop** (2), **Whoop**.

Huckaback, a sort of linen cloth. (Low G. ?) The orig. sense was prob. 'pedlar's ware;' cf. Low G. *hukkebak*, G. *huckebak*, pick-a-back. See **Huckster**.

Huckle-berry. (E.) The same as *hurtle-*, *whortle-*, *hurt-*, *hart-berry*. A. S. *heorot-berge*, i. e. hart-berry.

Huckle-bone, the hip-bone. (E.) A *huckle* is a 'small joint.' Cf. E. Fries. *hukken*, to bend, stoop, crouch; see below.

Huckster. (O. Low G.) M. E. *hukstere*, *hucster*. Formed with the fem. suffix *-ster* (for which see **Spinster**), from M. Du. *hucker*, Low G. *höker*, a hawker, also a stooper, bender, one who stoops. β. The *hawker* or *huckster* was so named from his bowed back, bent under his burden; from M. Du. *hucken*, to stoop under a burden. Cf. Icel. *hokinn*, bent, pp. of a lost strong verb (Teut. **heukan-*); also Icel. *hūka*, to sit on one's hams, Low G. *hūken*, to crouch. See Du. *heuker*, *huiken* in Franck.

Huddle. (E.) M. E. *hoderen*, *hodren*, which is an equivalent form, meaning to huddle together, as under a covert or shelter. Frequentative related to M. E. *hūden*, to hide; see **Hide** (1). ¶ But the mod. E. sense of *huddle* seems to be due to Du. *hoetelen*, 'to doe a thing unskilly,' Hexham; cf. G. *hudeln*, to bungle.

Hue (1), show, appearance, colour. (E.) M. E. *hewe*. A. S. *hiw*, *heow*, *heó*, appearance.+Swed. *hy*, skin, complexion; Goth. *hiwi*, form, show.

Hue (2), clamour, outcry. (F.—Tent.) In the phr. 'hue and cry;' A. F. *hu et cri*. M. E. *hue*, a loud cry.—O. F. *hu*, a cry; *huer*, to hoot.—M.H.G. *hū*, interj.; *hūzen*, to hoot; M. Swed. *huta*, to hoot; see **Hoot**.

Huff, to puff, bluster, bully. (E.) The old sense is to puff, blow hard; hence to bluster, vapour. An imitative word, like *puff*. Cf. Lowl. Sc. *hauch*, a forcible puff, *hech*, to breathe hard; G. *hauchen*, to breathe. ¶ To *huff*, at draughts, simply means 'to blow'; it was customary to *blow upon* the piece removed; cf. Lowl. Sc. *blaw*, to blow, also to huff at draughts; Dan. *blæse en brikke*, to huff (lit. blow) a man at draughts.

Hug, to embrace closely. (Scand.?) XVI cent. Uncertain. Perhaps of Scand. origin; cf. Icel. *hugga*, to soothe, comfort; *hugga barnið*, to soothe a child, *huga*, to mind; *hugna*, to please; M. Du. *heuge*, joy.

Huge, vast. (F.—Teut.?) M. E. *huge*, *houge*. An initial *a* has dropped.—A. F. *ahoge*; O. F. *ahuge*, *ahugue*, huge, vast (12th cent.). Of unknown origin; perhaps allied to Icel. *haugr*, a hill, whence O. F. *hoge*, *hogue*, a hill; see **How** (1).

Huguenot, a French protestant. (F. —G.) F. *huguenot*; as if from the personal name *Huguenot*. This name was in use two centuries at least before the Reformation, and is a dimin. of F. *Hugon*, acc. case from the nom. *Hugues*, Hugh. —M. H. G. *Hug*, Hugh. 2. But this form was due to popular etymology. The orig. form was G. *eidgenoss*, a confederate, appearing as Swiss Romance *eingenot*, *higueno*, a protestant (Wedgwood). From G. *eid*, an oath (see **Oath**), and *genoss* = A. S. *genéat*, a companion. ¶ 15 false etymologies of this word are noted by Scheler.

Hulk, a heavy ship. (Late L.—Gk.) M. E. *hulke*. A. S. *hulc*.—Late L. *hulka*, also *hulcum*, *holcas*, a kind of ship.—Gk. ὁλκάς, a ship which is towed, also a heavy ship, merchantman.—Gk. ἕλκειν, to draw, drag. Cf. L. *sulcus*, a furrow. Der. *hulking*, i. e. bulky, unwieldy. ¶ Distinct from M. E. *hulke*, A. S. *hulc*, a hovel.

Hull (1), husk. (E.) M. E. *hule*. A. S.

hulu, a husk, lit. 'covering;' from the same root as G. *hülse*, a husk, viz. Teut. **hul-*, weak grade of Teut. **helan-* (A. S. *helan*), to cover. See **Hell**.

Hull (2), body of a ship. (Du.) From Du. *hol*, hold. '*Het hol van een schip*, the ship's hold or hull;' Sewel. See **Hold** (2). Or the same as *hull* (1).

Hum (1), to buzz. (E.) M. E. *hummen*; an imitative word. + G. *hummen*, Du. *hommelen*, to hum. Cf. **Hem** (2).

hum (2), to trick, cajole. (E.) A particular use of *hum*, to buzz; it also meant to utter a sound expressive of contempt (Cor. v. 1. 49); also to applaud; see Richardson, and Todd's Johnson. Hence it meant to flatter, cajole, trick. So also Port. *zumbir*, to buzz, *zombar*, to jest; Span. *zumbar*, to hum, also to jest. Der. *hum*, sb., a hoax.

Human. (F.—L.) Formerly *humaine*. —F. *humain*, 'humane, manly;' Cot.—L. acc. *humānum*, human.—L. *homo*, a man; lit. 'a creature of earth,' from *humus*, ground; see **humble**. + A. S. *guma*, a man.

humane. (L.) Directly from L. *humānus*, (1) human, (2) kind (above).

humble. (F.—L.) F. *humble*.—L. *humilem*, acc. of *humilis*, humble, lowly, near the ground.—L. *humus*, the ground. Cf. Gk. χαμαί, on the ground, Russ. *zemlia*, earth, land. Brugm. i. § 604.

Humble-bee, a humming-bee. (E.) From the verb *humble*, for *hummle*, frequentative of *hum*. Cf. Du. *hommel*, a humble-bee, from *hommelen*, to hum; G. *hummel*, a humble-bee, from *hummen*, to hum; Swed. *humla*, a humble-bee.

Humbug, a hoax, piece of trickery. (E.) '*Humbug*, a false alarm, a bugbear,' Dean Milles MS. (cited in Halliwell). 'Drolleries, bonmots, and *humbugs*;' about A. D. 1740. Compounded of *hum*, hoax, and *bug*, a spectre, ghost, bugbear; the orig. sense being 'sham bugbear'; see *hum* (2) and **Bug**. Der. *humbug*, vb.

humdrum, dull, droning. (E.) Compounded of *hum*, a buzzing noise, and *drum*, a droning sound; see **Drum**.

Humeral, belonging to the shoulder. (L.) Late L. *humerālis*, belonging to the shoulder.—L. *humerus*, the shoulder; better *umerus*.+Gk. ὦμος, Goth. *amsa*, Skt. *aṁsa-*, the shoulder. Brugm. i. § 163.

Humid, moist. (F.—L.) F. *humide*. —L. *hūmidus*, better *ūmidus*, moist.—L.

hūmēre, *ūmēre*, to be moist; cf. *ūuens*, *ūuidus*, *ūdus*, moist; Gk. ὑγρός, moist.

Humiliate. (L.) From pp. of L. *humiliāre*, to humble. ‒ L. *humilis*, humble; see Humble.

humility. (F. ‒ L.) M. E. *humilitee*. ‒ O. F. *humiliteit*, humility. ‒ L. *humilitātem*, acc. of *humilitās*, humility. ‒ L. *humilis*, humble.

Hummock, Hommock, a mound, hillock, rounded mass. (E.) It appears to be a variant of *hump* or *hunch*.

Humour, orig. moisture. (F. ‒ L.) See Trench, Select Glossary, and Study of Words. The four *humours*, according to Galen, caused the four temperaments of mind, viz. choleric, melancholy, phlegmatic, and sanguine. ‒ O. F. *humor* (F. *humeur*). ‒ L. *ūmōrem*, acc. of *ūmor*, moisture. ‒ L. *ūmēre*, to be moist; see Humid.

Hump, a lump, bunch, esp. on the back. (E.) ‘*Hump*, a hunch, or lump,’ *Westmoreland*;’ Halliwell. Not found in M. E. Cf. E. Fries. *humpe*, *hump*, a bit, lump.+Du. *homp*, a lump, bunch; Low G. *hümpel*, a heap. Cf. Lithuan. *kumpas*, hunched. Parallel to *hunch*, q. v.

Hunch, a hump, round mass. (E.) A palatalised form of prov. E. *hunk*, a lump. Apparently a parallel form of *hump*; with *nk* for *mp*. Cf. W. Flem. *hunke brood*, a hunk of bread (De Bo); and perhaps Du. *honk*, a starting-post, orig. ‘a stump;’ see Franck.

Hundred. (E.) M. E. *hundred*. A.S. *hundred*; a compound word. ‒ A. S. *hund*, a hundred; and *-red*, with the sense of ‘reckoning’ or rate, to denote the rate of counting. Cf. Icel. *hund-rað*, orig. 120; G. *hund-ert*. This suffix is allied to Goth. *raþjo*, number, L. *ratio*; see Rate (1). β. The A. S. *hund* is cognate with L. *centum*, answering to an Idg. form **kəmtóm*, perhaps for **dekəmtóm*, a decad, allied to Goth. *taihunte-hund*, a hundred, which Brugmann explains as δεκάδων δεκάς. Cf. also Gk. ἑκατόν, Skt. *çatam*, Pe˙ s. *sad*, Lith. *szimtas*, Russ. *sto*, Irish *cead*, W. *cant*, a hundred. Brugm. i. § 431, ii. § 179. See Ten.

Hunger. (E.) A.S. *hungor*. + Icel. *hungr*, Swed. Dan. *hunger*, Du. *honger*, G. *hunger*; Goth. *hūhrus*, hunger. Teut. types **hungruz*, **hunhruz*, m. Allied to Lith. *kanka*, suffering. Brugm. i. § 639.

Hunt, to chase wild animals. (E.) M. E. *hunten*. A. S. *huntian*, to capture;

cf. *hunt*, sb., a hunting. Related to Teut. **hunth-*, weak grade of **henthan-*, to seize; see Hent. Cf. Brugm. i. § 701.

Hurdle. (E.) M. E. *hurdel*. A.S. *hyrdel*; a dimin. from a Teut. base **hurth-*; also early A. S. *hyrþil*. + Du. *horde*, Icel. *hurð*, G. *hürde*, M. H. G. *hurt*, a hurdle; Goth. *haurds*, a door. Allied to L. *crātēs*, a hurdle, Gk. κάρταλος, a (woven) basket. Cf. Skt. *kṛt*, to spin. The sense is a ‘plaited’ thing. Brugm. i. §§ 529, 633. (✓QERT.)

Hurdygurdy, a kind of violin, played by turning a handle. (E.) From Lowl. Sc. *hirdygirdy*, a confused noise; also *hirdum-dirdum*, the same. Cf. Lowl. Sc. *hurr*, to snarl, *gurr*, to growl. ‘Som vseþ strange wlaffyng, chytering, *harryng and garryng* ’ = some people use a strange babbling, chattering, snarling and growling; Spec. of English, ed. Morris and Skeat, p. 241, l. 163. Formed on the model of *hurlyburly*. See Hurry.

Hurl. (E.) M. E. *hurlen*, *horlen*. Not in A. S.; perhaps of Scand. origin. Cf. E. *hurleblast*, a hurricane, *hurlepool*, whirlpool, *hurlewind*, whirlwind. Also E. Fries. *hurrel*, a gust of wind; *hurreln*, to blow in gusts; *hurrel-wind*, a whirlwind. Explained by Swed. dial. *hurra*, to whir, whirl round; whence *hurrel*, a whirl, *hurrel-wind*, a whirlwind. Of imitative origin; cf. Dan. *hurre*, to buzz, Icel. *hurr*, a noise. So also M. H. G. *hurren*, to move quickly; from the sound. Cf. Hurly-burly, Hurry.

Hurlyburly, a tumult. (F. ‒ L.) A reduplicated word, the second syllable being an echo of the first. [Cf. M. F. *hurluberlu*, tumult, in Rabelais (v. prol.).] The short form *hurly* also occurs; see K. John, iii. 4. 169. ‒ O. F. *hurlee*, a howling, outcry, great noise; orig. fem. pp. of *hurler*, to howl. ‒ L. *ululāre*, to howl. Prob. confused with Hurl.

Hurrah. (G.) From G. *hurra*, M. H. G. *hurrā*. Of imitative origin; see Hurl.

Hurricane, whirlwind. (Span. ‒ Caribbean.) Span. *huracan*. ‒ Carib. *huracan* (Oviedo).

Hurry. (E.) Not allied to *harry*. Formed from an older base *hurr-*; like *scurr-y* from *skir*. M. E. *horien*, to hurry (Allit. Poems, ed. Morris, B. 883). + M. Swed. *hurra*, to swing, whirl round; Swed. dial. *hurra*, to whirl, *hurr*, sb., hurry, haste. Cf. Dan. *hurre*, to hum, whir; Icel. *hurr*, a noise; M. H. G. *hurren*, to move swiftly. See Hurl; and cf. *whir, whiz*, of similar imitative origin; whence *whurry*, to hurry (Nares).

Hurst, a wood. (E.) M. E. *hurst*; A. S. *hyrst*. + M. H. G. *hurst*, a shrub, thicket; G. *horst*; E. Fries. *hörst*.

Hurt, to dash against, to harm. (F.) M. E. *hurten, hirten*, (1) to push, dash against; (2) to injure. — O. F. *hurter* (F. *heurter*), to strike or dash against. Of unknown origin. Hardly from Celtic (Thurneysen, p. 81). The Ital. form is *urtare*, possibly from L. *urtum, unused supine of *urgēre*, to press on (Körting).

hurtle, to dash. (F.) M. E. *hurtlen*, frequent. of *hurten* (above).

Husband. (Scand.) Icel. *húsbóndi*, the master of a house, the goodman; short for *húsbúandi*. — Icel. *hús*, house; *búandi*, dwelling in, pres. pt. of *búa*, to dwell; see **Boor.** So also Swed. *hus-bonde*, Dan. *husbond*. **Der.** *husband-man, husband-ry*.

Hush. (E.) M. E. *husht*, whist, silent; prob. taken to be a pp. Cf. Swed. *hyssja*, Dan. *hysse*, to hush; Dan. *hys*, hush! A purely imitative word, allied to *hiss*.

Husk, shell. (E.) M. E. *huske*. The -*k* is a dimin. suffix; from A. S. *hús*, a house. Cf. Low G. *hüske*, a little house; E. Fries. *hüske*, a little house, core of an apple, small case; M. Du. *huysken*, a little house, a case, a husk of fruit (Kilian). See **House.**

Husky, hoarse. (E.) Apparently allied to prov. E. *husk*, dry, parched; with reference to the dryness of *husks*.

Hussar. (G. — Hungarian. — Servian. — Gk. — L.) '*Hussars, Husares*,' Coles (1684). — G. *Husar.* — Hung. *Huszar.* — Serv. *χusar*, hussar, robber, sea-robber (Popovic'). ▪ Late Gk. *κουρσάριος*, a corsair, pirate (Ducange). ▪ Late L. *cursārius*, a corsair. — L. *cursus*, a course; see **Corsair.** ¶ The word is older than the story about Mathius Corvinus (1458); see N. and Q. 8 S. ii. 156; Miklosich, p. 148.

Hussif, Hussy. (E.) Short for *huswife*, i. e. *house-wife*; cf. *hus-* in *husband*; see **Husband** and **House.** ¶ In the sense of ' case for needles, thread, &c.,' it must mean ' house-wife's companion '; it is, however, remarkable that Icel. *húsi* means ' a case.'

Hustings. (Scand.) The mod. use is incorrect; it is properly *husting*, sing., and means a council, an assembly for the choice of a candidate. M. E. *husting.* A. S. *hústing.* — Icel. *húsþing*, a council, meeting. — Icel. *hús*, a house; *þing*, a thing, also an assembly; see **House** and **Thing.** Cf. Swed. Norw. and Dan. *ting*, the same as Icel. *þing*.

Hustle, to jostle. (Du.) For *hutsle*. — Du. *hutselen*, to shake up and down, huddle together; frequent. of M. Du. *hutsen*, Du. *hotsen*, to shake. See **Hotchpot.** Cf. Du. *hotten*, to curdle; *hot*, curds; prov. G. *hotze*, a cradle, a swing; Lowl. Sc. *hott*, to move by jerks, *hotter*, to jolt.

Hut. (F. — O. H. G.) M. E. *hotte.* — F. *hutte*, a cottage; Cotgrave. — O. H. G. *hutta* (G. *hütte*), a hut. + Swed. *hydda*, a hut. Perhaps related to **Hide** (1).

Hutch, a box. (F. — Low L.) M. E. *huche, hucche.* — F. *huche*, a hutch, bin. — Late L. *hútica*, a hutch, box; of unknown origin. Perhaps Teutonic; cf. O. H. G. *huotan* (G. *hüten*), to take care of. See **Heed.**

Huzzah, Hurrah. (E.) *Huzzah* is also written *huzza.* Cf. G. *hussa*, huzzah! M. H. G. *hurrā*, hurrah! So also Swed. and Dan. *hurra*, hurrah! Cf. M. H. G. *hurren*, to move quickly; Dan. *hurre*, to hum, buzz. See **Hurry.**

Hyacinth, a flower. (F. — L. — Gk.) F. *hyacinthe.* — L. *hyacinthus.* — Gk. *ὑάκινθος*, an iris, larkspur (not our hyacinth). Doublet, *jacinth*.

Hyæna; see **Hyena.**

Hybrid, mongrel. (L.) L. *hibrida, hybrida*, a mongrel, a hybrid. Some connect it with Gk. *ὕβριδ-*, stem of *ὕβρις*, insult, wantonness, violation; but it may be Latin.

Hydra, a water-snake. (L. — Gk.) L. *hydra.* — Gk. *ὕδρα*, water-snake. — Gk. *ὕδ-ωρ*, water. Cf. Skt. *udra-s*, a water-animal, otter, A. S. *oter*. Doublet, *otter*. And see **Water.** Brugm. i. § 572.

hydrangea, a flower. (Gk.) A coined name, referring to the cup-form of the capsule, or seed-vessel. From Gk. *ὑδρ-*, for *ὕδωρ*, water; *ἀγγεῖον*, a vessel.

hydraulic, relating to water in motion. (F. — L. — Gk.) F. *hydraulique.* — L. *hydraulicus.* — Gk. *ὑδραυλικός*, belonging to a water-organ. — Gk. *ὕδραυλις*, an organ worked by water. — Gk. *ὕδρ-*, for ὕδωρ, water; αὐλός, a pipe, tube (allied to ἄημι, I blow; see **Air**).

hydrodynamics, the science relating to the force of water in motion. (Gk.) Gk. ὕδρο-, for ὕδωρ, water; and E. *dynamics*, a word of Gk. origin; see **Dynamics**.

hydrogen, a very light gas. (Gk.) The name means 'generator of water.' — Gk. ὕδρο-, for ὕδωρ, water; and the base γέν-, to produce; see **Genesis**.

hydropathy, the water-cure. (Gk.) Gk. ὕδρο-, for ὕδωρ, water; πάθ-ος, suffering, endurance of treatment; see **Pathos**.

hydrophobia, fear of water. (L. — Gk.) Late L. *hydrophobia*. Coined from Gk. ὕδρο-, for ὕδωρ, water; φόβος, fear, fright. allied to φέβομαι, I flee. (✓BHEG.)

hydropsy, dropsy. (F. — L. — Gk.) Formerly *dropsie* or *ydropsie*; the form *dropsie* being due to loss of *y*-. — M. F. *hydropisie*. — L. *hydrōpisis, hydrōpisīa*. — Late Gk. *ὑδρώπισις*, not found, from Gk. ὕδρωψ, dropsy, extended from ὕδρο-, for ὕδωρ, water. Der. *dropsi-c-al*.

hydrostatics, the science which treats of fluids at rest. (Gk.) Gk. ὕδρο-, for ὕδωρ, water; and Statics, q. v.

Hyena, Hyæna, a hog-like quadruped. (L. — Gk.) [M. E. *hyene*; from O. F. *hyene*.] L. *hyæna*. — Gk. ὕαινα, a hyena; lit. 'sow-like.' — Gk. ὗ-s. a sow, cognate with E. **Sow**; with fem. adj. suffix -αινα.

Hymen. (L. — Gk.) L. *hymen*. — Gk. ὑμήν, the god of marriage. Cf. Skt. *siv*, to connect, lit. to sew; see **Sew**.

Hymn. (F. — L. — Gk.) M. E. *ympne* (with excrescent *p*). — O. F. *ymne* (later *hymne*). — L. *hymnum*, acc. of L. *hymnus*. — Gk. ὕμνος, a song, festive song, hymn.

Hypallage, an interchange. (L. — Gk.) L. *hypallagē*. — Gk. ὑπαλλαγή, an interchange, exchange. — Gk. ὑπ-ό, under; ἀλλαγή, change, from ἀλλάσσειν, to change; from ἄλλος, another. See **Alien**.

Hyper-, prefix, denoting excess. (L. — Gk.) L. *hyper-*, for Gk. ὑπέρ, above, beyond, allied to L. *super*. Hence *hyperbaton*, a transposition of words from natural order, lit. 'a going beyond' (from βαίνειν, to go); *hyper-bole*, exaggeration, Gk. ὑπερβολή (from βάλλειν, to throw, cast); *hyper-borean*, extreme northern (from βορέας, north wind).

Hyphen, a short stroke (-) joining two parts of a compound word. (L. — Gk.)

L. *hyphen*, for Gk. ὑφέν, lit. 'under one.' — Gk. ὑφ-, for ὑπό, under; ἕν, neut. of εἷς, one (allied to L. *sim-* in *simplex*; see **Simple**).

Hypo-, prefix. (Gk.) Gk. ὑπό, under; cognate with L. *sub*.

Hypochondria, a mental disorder inducing melancholy. (L. — Gk.) Named from the spleen (which was supposed to cause it), situate under the cartilage of the breast-bone. — Late L. *hypochondria*, fem. sb.; for L. *hypochondria*, s. pl. — Gk. ὑποχόνδρια, sb. pl., the parts beneath the breast-bone. — Gk. ὑπό, under; χόνδρος, a corn, grain, gristle, cartilage of the breast-bone (cognate with G. *grand*, gravel, and allied to E. *grind*). Der. *hipp-ish*, q. v.

Hypocrisy, pretence to virtue. (F. — L. — Gk.) M. F. *hypocrisie*. — L. *hypocrisis*, I Tim. iv. 2. — Gk. ὑπόκρισις, a reply, answer, playing a part on a stage, acting of a part. — Gk. ὑποκρίνομαι, I reply, play a part. — Gk. ὑπό, under; κρίνομαι, I contend, middle voice of κρίνω, I judge. See **Critic**. Der. *hypocrite*, F. *hypocrite*, L. *hypocrita*, Gk. ὑποκριτής, a dissembler, Matt. vi. 2.

Hypogastric, belonging to the lower part of the abdomen. (F. — L. — Gk.) M. F. *hypogastrique*. — Late L. *hypogastricus*, belonging to the lower part of the belly. — Gk. ὑπογάστριον, lower part of the belly; see **Hypo-** and **Gastric**.

Hypostasis. (L. — Gk.) L. *hypostasis*. — Gk. ὑπόστασις, a standing under, groundwork, subsistence, substance, a Person of the Trinity. — Gk. ὑπό, under; στάσις, a standing, from ✓STĀ, to stand. See **Statics**.

Hypotenuse. (F. — L. — Gk.) Also *hypothenuse* (badly). — F. *hypoténuse*. — L. *hypotēnūsa*. — Gk. ὑποτείνουσα, the subtending (line); fem. of pres. part. of ὑποτείνειν, to subtend, lit. to stretch under. (✓TEN.)

Hypothec, a legal lien on property. (F. — L. — Gk.) Englished from M. F. *hypotheque*, a mortgage. — L. *hypothēca* (the same). — Gk. ὑποθήκη, lit. 'support;' a pledge. mortgage. — Gk. ὑπό, under; θη-, as in τί-θη-μι, I place. (✓DHĒ.)

hypothesis, a supposition. (L. — Gk.) L. *hypothesis*. — Gk. ὑπόθεσις, a placing under, supposition. — Gk. ὑπό, under; θέσις, a placing; from the same root as the above. See **Thesis**.

Hyson, a kind of tea. (Chinese.) In

the Amoy dialect called *chhun-tê*, lit. 'spring tea,' from *chhun*, spring, and *tê*, tea. Said to have been orig. from *hi chhun*, lit. 'blooming spring,' i. e. early crop. From Chin. *hi*, blooming; *chhun*, spring.

Hyssop, a plant. (F.–L.–Gk.–Heb.) M. E. *ysope*.–O. F. *hyssope*.–L. *hyssōpus*. –Gk. ὕσσωπος, an aromatic plant (not our hyssop).–Heb. *ēzōbh*, a plant (it is not exactly known what plant).

Hysteric, convulsive, said of fits. (F.– L.–Gk.) M.F. *hysterique*.–L *hystericus*. –Gk. ὑστερικός, suffering in the womb; hysterical.–Gk. ὑστέρα, the womb. Prob. from Gk. ὕστερος, latter, lower, comparative from the Idg. base *ud-*, out; see **Uterine** and **Out**.

I.

I, nom. case of first pers. pronoun. (E.) M. E. (Northern) *ik, i*; (Southern) *ich, uch, i*. A. S. *ic.*+Du. *ik*, Icel. *ek*, Dan. *jeg*, Swed. *jag*, Goth. *ik*, G. *ich*, Lith. *asz*, Russ. *ia*, L. *ego*, Gk. ἐγώ, ἐγών, Skt. *aham*. Idg. base, EGH- and EG-; Brugm. ii. § 434. ¶ *Me* is from a different base.

I-, neg. prefix; see **In-** (3).

Iambic, a certain metre, a short and a long syllable (◡ –). (L.–Gk.) L. *iambicus*.–Gk. ἰαμβικός.–Gk. ἴαμβος, an iambic foot, iambic verse, lampoon. (Origin doubtful.)

Ibex, a genus of goats. (L.) L. *ibex*.

Ibis, a bird. (L.–Gk.–Egypt.) L. *ibis*.–Gk. ἴβις, an Egyptian bird. Of Egypt. origin; cf. Coptic *hippen* (Peyron).

Ice. (E.) M. E. *ys, iis*. A. S. *īs.*+Du. *ijs*, Icel. *īss*, Dan. *iis*, Swed. *is*, G. *eis*. Teut. type *īsom*, neut. Der. *ice-berg*, quite a modern word; the latter element is the Du., Norw., Swed., and G. *berg*, a mountain; cf. Du. *ijsberg*, Norw. and Swed. *isbjerg*, Dan. *iisbjerg*, G. *eisberg*, an iceberg; (prob. a Norw. word). Also *ice-blink*, Dan. *iis-blink*, a field of ice, from Dan. *blinke*, to gleam.

icicle. (E.) M.E. *isikel, iseyokel*; from M. E. *ys*, ice, and *ikel*, a point of ice. –A.S. *īs-gicel*, an icicle; also written *īses gicel*, where *īses* is the gen. case. *Gicel*, O. Merc. *gecile* (Sweet, O. E. T.), means 'a small piece of ice.'+Icel. *īss-jökull*; though *jökull* is gen. used by itself in the sense of icicle; Low G. *is-*

hekel, isjäkel. 2. Icel. *jökull* is the dimin. of Icel. *jaki*, a piece of ice, cognate with Irish *aig*, W. *ia*, ice. Brugm. i. § 305.

Ichneumon. (L.–Gk.) L. *ichneumon*. – Gk. ἰχνεύμων, an ichneumon (lizard); lit. 'a tracker,' because it tracks out (and devours) crocodiles' eggs.–Gk. ἰχνεύειν, to track.–Gk. ἴχνος, a footstep.

Ichor, the juice in the veins of gods. (Gk.) Gk. ἰχώρ, juice.

Ichthyography, description of fishes. (Gk.) Gk. ἰχθυο-, from ἰχθύς, a fish; -γραφία, from γράφειν, to describe. So also *ichthyology*, from λόγος, a discourse, λέγειν, to speak.

Icicle; see **Ice**.

Iconoclast, a breaker of images. (Gk.) Coined from Gk. εἰκόνο-, from εἰκών, an image; κλάστης, a vine-pruner (but lit. a breaker), from κλάειν, to break.

Icosahedron, a solid figure with twenty equal faces. (Gk.) From Gk. εἴκοσι, twenty; ἕδρα, a base, lit. a seat, from the base ἑδ-, to sit; see **Sit**.

Idea. (L.–Gk.) L. *idea*–Gk. ἰδέα, the look or semblance of a thing, species (hence, notion).–Gk. ἰδεῖν, to see. (✓ WEID.) See **Wit**.

Identical, the very same. (L.) Formerly *identic, identick*. Formed as if from Med. (scholastic) L. *identicus*, adj. suggested by *identi-tās*; see below.

identity, sameness. (F.–Late L.– L.) F. *identité*.–Late L. acc. *identitā-tem*, sameness.–L. *identi-*, occurring in *identidem*, repeatedly; with suffix *-tas*.– L. *idem*, the same.–L. *i-*, and *-dem*; from Idg. pronominal bases I and DE.

Ides, the 15th day of March, May, July, October; 13th of other months. (F.–L.) F. *ides*.–L. *īdūs*, ides.

Idiom, peculiar mode of expression. (F.–L.–Gk.) F. *idiome*.–L. *idiōma*.– Gk. ἰδίωμα, an idiom, peculiarity of language.–Gk. ἰδιόω, I make my own.– Gk. ἴδιος, own.

idiosyncrasy, peculiarity of temperament. (Gk.) Cf. F. *idiosyncrasie*. From Gk. ἴδιο-ς, own; σύγ-κρασις, a blending together, from σύγ- (= σύν), together, κρᾶσις, a mingling. See **Crasis**.

idiot. (F.–L.–Gk.) F. *idiot*.–L. *idiōta*, an ignorant, uneducated person.– Gk. ἰδιώτης, a private person; hence, one who is inexperienced (1 Cor. xiv. 16).– Gk. ἰδιόω, I make my own.–Gk. ἴδιος, own.

Idle. (E.) M. E. *idel*. A. S. *īdel*, vain, empty, useless. + Du. *ijdel*, vain ; Dan. *idel*, Swed. *idel*, mere ; G. *eitel*, vain, trifling. Origin doubtful.

Idol. (F. – L. – Gk.) O. F. *idole*. – L. *īdōlum*. – Gk. εἴδωλον, an image, likeness. – Gk. εἴδομαι, I appear, seem ; ἰδεῖν, to see. (√WEID.) Der. *idolatry*, O. F. *idolatrie*, Late L. *īdōlatrīa*, shortened form of *īdōlōlatrīa*, from Gk. εἰδωλο-λατρεία, service to idols (where λατρεία, service, is from λατρίς, a hired servant, λάτρον, hire). Hence *idolater*, &c.

idyl, idyll, a pastoral poem. (L. – Gk.) L. *īdyllium*. – Gk. εἰδύλλιον, a short descriptive poem. – Gk. εἶδος, form, shape, figure. – Gk. εἴδομαι, I appear (see above).

If, conj. (E.) M. E. *if*, A. S. *gif* + Icel. *ef*, *if*, O. Fries. *ief*, *gef*, *ef*, O. Sax. *ef* ; Goth. *ibai*, interrog. particle, *jabai*, if ; with which cf. Du. *of*, if, whether, G. *ob*, whether ; also O. H. G. *ibu*, if, lit. ' on the condition,' dat. of *iba*, condition, doubt. Cf. also Icel. *if*, *ef*, sb., doubt. See Kluge, s. v. *ob*.

Ignition, a setting on fire. (L.) F. *ignition*. As if from L. **ignītio*. – L. *ignītus*, pp. of *ignīre*, to set on fire. – L. *ignis*, fire. + Skt. *agni-*, fire, base **egni-* ; cf. Russ. *ogone*, Lith. *ugnìs*, fire, base **ogni-*. Brugm. i. § 148. Hence also *ignis fatuus*, a vain fire ; *igne-ous*, adj.

Ignoble. (F. – L.) F. *ignoble*, not noble. – L. *i-gnōbilis*, where *i- = in*, not ; see **Noble.**

Ignominy, disgrace. (F. – L.) F. *ignominie*. – L. *ignōminia*. – L. *i-* (for *in*), not ; *gnōmin-*, for *gnōmen*, old form of *nōmen*, name, fame ; see **Noun.**

Ignore, to disregard. (F. – L.) F. *ignorer*. – L. *ignōrāre*, not to know. – L. *i-* (for *in*), not ; and base *gnō-*, as in *gnō-scere = nōscere*, to know ; see **Know.** Der. *ignor-ant, -ance* ; also *ignōrāmus*, lit. ' we ignore' that, an old law-term.

Iguana, a kind of American lizard. (Span. – W. Indian.) Span. *iguana*. Of West Indian origin. – Hayti *iuanna*, *yuana* (Eden.).

iguanodon, a fossil dinosaur, with teeth like an iguana. From *iguan-a*, and Gk. ὀδον-τ-, stem of ὀδούς, tooth.

Il- (1), for *in-*, prefix, from L. *in*, prep., when *l* follows. Exx. : *il-lapse*, *il-lusion*, &c.

Il- (2), for *in-*, negative prefix when *l* follows. Exx. *il-legal*, *il-legible*, *il-legitimate*, *il-liberal*, *il-limitable*, *il-literate*, *il-*

logical ; for which see *legal*, *legible*, &c. And see *illicit*.

Iliac, pertaining to the smaller intestines. (F. – L.) F. *iliaque*, belonging to the flanks. Formed from L. *īlia*, sb. pl., flanks, groin. See also **Jade** (2).

Iliad, an epic poem. (L. – Gk.) L. *Iliad-*, stem of *Ilias*, the Iliad. – Gk. Ἰλιάδ-, stem of Ἰλιάς, the Iliad. – Gk. Ἴλιος, Ilios, commonly known as Troy ; said to have had its name from (a mythical) *Ilus*, grandfather of Priam, and son of *Tros* (whence *Troy*).

Ill, bad. (Scand.) M. E. *ille*. – Icel. *illr* (later *illr*), ill, adj. ; Swed. *illa*, Dan. *ilde*, ill, adv. ¶ Not allied to **Evil.**

Illapse, a gliding in, a sudden entrance. (L.) L. *illapsus*, sb., a gliding in. – L. *il-* (for *in*), in ; *lapsus*, a gliding, from pp. of *lābī*, to glide. See **Lapse.**

Illation, an inference. (F. – L.) F. *illation*. – L. acc. *illātiōnem*, a bringing in, inference. – L. *il-* (for *in*), in ; *lātus* (= *tlātus*), borne, brought (= Gk. τλητός). See **Tolerate.**

Illicit, unlawful. (F. – L.) F. *illicite*, 'illicitous,' Cot. – L. *illicitus*, not allowed. – L. *il-* (for *in-*), not ; *licitus*, pp. of *licēre*, to be allowed. See **Licence.**

Illision, a striking against. (L.) From L. *illīsio*, a striking against. – L. *illīsus*, pp. of *illīdere*, to strike against. – L. *il-* (for *in*), upon ; *lædere*, to strike. See **Lesion.**

Illude, to deceive. (F. – L.) F. *illuder*, ' to illude ;' Cot. – L. *illūdere*, to mock at. – L. *il-* (for *in*), upon, at ; *lūdere*, to jest, play. See **Ludicrous.**

Illuminate, to enlighten. (L.) From pp. of L. *illūmināre* to throw light upon. – L. *il-* (for *in*), upon ; *lūmin-*, for *lumen*, light ; see **Luminary.** ¶ We also use *illumine*, *illume*, from F. *illuminer* < L. *illūmināre.*

Illusion. (F. – L.) F. *illusion*. – L. acc. *illūsiōnem*. – L. *illūsus*, pp. of *illūdere* ; see **Illude** (above).

Illustrate. (L.) From the pp. of *illustrāre*, to throw light upon. – L. *il-* (for *in*), upon ; *lustrāre*, to shine (below).

illustrious. (F. – L. ; *or* L.) A badly coined word ; either from F. *illustre*, or from the L. *illūstri-s*, bright, renowned. (Imitation of *industrious*.) β. In L. *illūstris*, the prefix *il- (= in*), upon ; *-lūstris* stands for **lou-c-stris*, from the base *lūc-*, as in **Lucid**, q. v. See Brugm. i. § 760.

Im- (1), prefix. (F.–L.) In some words, *im-* stands for *em-*, the O. F. form of L. *im-*, prefix. Or for L. *in*, in, before *b, m*, or *p*.

Im- (2), prefix. (E.) For E. *in*; as in *im-bed*, for *in-bed*.

Im- (3), prefix. (L.) L. *im-* (for *in*), in, when *b, m*, or *p* follows.

Im- (4), prefix. (F.–L.; *or* L.) Negative prefix; for L. *in-*, not. Exx.: *im-material, im-mature, im-measurable, im-memorial, im-moderate, im-modest, im-moral, im-mortal, im-movable, im-mutable, im-palpable, im-parity, im-partial, im-passable, im-passive, im-patient, im-peccable, im-penetrable, im-penitent, im-perceptible, im-perfect, im-perishable, im-personal, im-pertinent, im-perturbable, im-piety, im-pious, im-placable, im-polite, im-politic, im-ponderable, im-possible, im-potent, im-practicable, im-probable, im-proper, im-provident, im-prudent, im-pure*; for which see *material, mature*, &c.

Image, a likeness, statue. (F.–L.) F. *image.* –L. *imāginem*, acc. of *imāgo*, a likeness. Formed, with suffix *-āgo*, from the base *im* in *im-itārī*, to imitate; see **Imitate**.

imagine. (F.–L.) F. *imaginer*, to think. –L. *imāginārī*, to picture to oneself, imagine. –L. *imāgin-*, stem of *imāgo*, an image, picture; see above. **Der.** *imaginary, imagin-ation*.

Imam, Imaum, a Muhammedan priest. (Arab.) Arab. *imām*, a leader, chief, prelate, priest. –Arab. root *amma*, 'he tended towards.' Rich. Dict., p. 163.

Imbecile, feeble. (F.–L.) Formerly rare as an adj.; but the verb *imbécil*, to enfeeble, is found, and was confused with *embezzle.* –F. *imbécile*; M. F. *imbecille*, 'feeble;' Cotgrave. –L. *imbēcillum*, acc. of *imbēcillius* (also *imbēcillis*), feeble. (Root unknown.)

Imbibe, to drink in. (F.–L.; *or* L.) F. *imbiber* (16th cent.). –L. *imbibere*, to drink in. –L. *im-* (for *in-*), in; *bibere*, to drink.

Imbricated, bent and hollowed like a gutter-tile. (L.) Botanical. From pp. of L. *imbricāre*, to cover with gutter-tiles. – L. *imbric-*, stem of *imbrex*, a gutter-tile. – L. *imbri-*, decl. stem of *imber*, a shower of rain. +Gk. ἀφρός, foam; Skt. *abhra-*, a rain-cloud; Brugm. i. § 466.

Imbroglio, intrigue, perplexity. (Ital.)

Ital. *imbroglio*, perplexity. – Ital. *imbrogliare*, to entangle. – Ital. *im-* (for *in*), in; *broglio*, a broil, confusion; see **Broil** (2).

Imbrue, Embrue, to moisten, drench. (F.–L.) M. F. *embruer*; *s'embruer*, 'to imbrue or bedable himself with;' Cot. Variant of O. F. *embevrer, embreuver*, to moisten. – F. *em-* (L. *in*, in); and a causal verb *-bevrer*, to give to drink, turned into *-brever* in the 16th cent., and then into *-bruer*; see F. *abreuver* in Hatzfeld. O.F. *bevrer* answers to a L. type *biberāre*, to give to drink; from L. *bibere*, to drink. See **Beverage**.

Imbue, to cause to drink in, tinge deeply. (F.–L.) O. F. *imbuer.* – L. *imbuere*, to cause to drink in; where *-buere* is a causal form, apparently allied to *bibere*, to drink.

Imitate. (L.) From pp. of L. *imitārī*, to imitate; frequentative of *imāre*, not found; cf. L. *imā-go*. See **Image**.

Immaculate. (L.) L. *im-maculātus*, unspotted. – L. *im-* (for *in-*), not; *maculātus*, spotted. See **Maculate**.

Immediate, without intervention or means. (F. – L.) M. F. *immediat.* – L. *im-* (for *in-*), not; *mediātus*, pp. of L. *mediāre*, to be in the middle. – L. *medius*, middle. See **Medium**.

Immense. (F.–L.) F. *immense.* – L. *immensus*, immeasurable. – L. *im-* (for *in-*), not; *mensus*, pp. of *metīrī*, to measure. See **Measure**.

Immerge, to plunge into. (L.) L. *immergere* (pp. *im-mersus*), to plunge into. – L. *im-* (for *in*), in; *mergere*, to plunge. See **Merge**. **Der.** *immers-ion*.

Immigrate. (L.) From pp. of L. *immigrāre*, to migrate to. (*Im-* = *in*, in.) See **Migrate**.

Imminent, near at hand. (L.) L. *imminent-*, stem of pres. pt. of *im-minēre*, to project over. – L. *im-* (for *in*), upon; *-minēre*, to project, as in *ē-minēre*.

Immit, to inject. (L.) In Kersey (1715). L. *im-mittere*, to send into (pp. *immissus*). – L. *im-* (= *in*), in; *mittere*, to send. See **Missile**. **Der.** *immiss-ion*.

Immolate, to offer in sacrifice. (L.) From pp. of L. *immolāre*, to sacrifice, lit. to throw meal upon a victim. – L. *im-* (for *in*), upon; *mola*, meal, cognate with E. **Meal** (1).

Immunity, freedom from obligation. (F.–L.) F. *immunité*, immunity. – L. *immūnitātem*, acc. of *immūnitās*, exemption. — L. *immūnis*, exempt from public services. — L. *im-* (for *in*), not; *mūnis*, serving, obliging (whence also *commūnis*, common). See **Common**.

Immure. (F. — L.) For *emmure*. — M. F. *emmurer*, to shut up in prison, lit. to enclose with a wall. — L. *im-* (= *in*), in; *mūrus*, a wall.

Imp, a graft, offspring, demon. (Late L. — Gk.) Formerly in a good sense, meaning a scion, offspring. M. E. *imp*, a graft on a tree (A. S. *impe*); *impen*, to graft. — Late L. *impotus*, a graft (Lex Salica); [whence also Dan. *ympe*, Swed. *ympa*, G. *impfen*, O. H. G. *impitōn*, to graft]. — Gk. ἔμφυτος, engrafted; James i. 21. — Gk. ἐμφύειν, to implant. — Gk. ἐμ- (for ἐν), in; φύειν, to produce, from √BHEU, to be; see Bε.

Impact, a striking against. (L.) L. *impact-us*, pp. of *impingere*, to impinge. See **Impinge**.

Impair, to make worse, injure, weaken. (F. — L.) M. E. *empeiren*. — O. F. *empeirer*, later *empirer*, 'to impaire;' Cot. — Late L. *impēiōrāre*, to make worse. — L. *im-* (for *in*), prep., with intensive force; and *pēior*, worse, a comparative form from a lost positive. Cf. **Pessimist**.

Impale, to fix on a stake. (L.) Late L. *impālāre* (whence F. *empaler*). — L. *im-* (for *in*), on; *pālus*, a stake. See **Pale** (1).

Impart. (F. — L.) M. F. *impartir.* — L. *impartīre*, *impertīre*, to give a share to. — L. *im-* (= *in*), to, upon; *partīre*, to part, from *parti-*, decl. stem of *pars*, a part. See **Part**.

Impassive. From **Im-** (4) and **Passive**.

Impawn. From **Im-** (3) and **Pawn** (1).

Impeach, to charge with a crime. (F. — L.) The original sense was 'to hinder'; as, 'to *impeach* and stop their breath,' Holland, tr. of Pliny, b. xi. c. 3. — O. F. *empescher*, 'to hinder, stop, bar, impeach;' Cot. Older spelling *empeëscher*, where the *s* is adventitious. [Littré and Scheler connect the mod. F. *empêcher* with Prov. *empedegar*, from Late L. *impedicāre*, to fetter. — L. *im-* (for *in*), on, upon; *pedica*, a fetter, from *ped-*, stem of *pes*, a foot.] β. At the same time the usual sense of E. *impeach* and some (at least) of the senses of O. F. *empescher* above are due to O. F. *empacher*, Span. *empachar*, Ital. *impacciare*, to delay; from a Late L. frequent. form (*impacticāre*, in Körting, § 4110) of L.

impingere (pp. *impactus*), to bind, fasten; see **Pact**. See **Dispatch**.

Impede, to obstruct. (L.) From L. *impedire*, to entangle the feet, obstruct. — L. *im-* (= *in*), in; *ped-*, stem of *pes*, foot. Der. *impedi-ment*.

Impel. (L.) L. *im-pellere*, to urge on. — L. *im-* (for *in*), on; *pellere*, to drive; see **Pulsate**. Der. *impulse*, L. *impulsus*, sb., from the pp. *impulsus*.

Impend, to hang over. (L.) L. *im-pendēre*, to hang over. — L. *im-* (for *in*), on, over; *pendēre*, to hang. See **Pendant**.

Imperative. (F. — L.) F. *impératif*, imperious. — L. *imperātīuus*, due to a command. — L. *imperātum*, a command; neut. of *imperātus*, pp. of *imperāre*, to command. See **Emperor**.

imperial. (F. — L.) O. F. *emperial*, later *impérial*. — L. *imperiālis*, belonging to an empire. — L. *imperium*, an empire. See **Empire**.

Impertinent. From **Im-** (4) and **Pertinent**.

Impervious. From **Im-** (4) and **Pervious**.

Impetus. (L.) L. *impetus*, lit. 'a falling on;' a rush, attack. — L. *im-* (*in*), on; *petere*, to fall, fly, seek. See **Petition**.

Impinge, to strike against. (L.) L. *impingere*, to strike against. — L. *im-* (*in*), on, upon; *pangere*, to fasten, also to strike. See **Pact**.

Implement, a tool. (Late L. — L.) Late L. *implēmentum*, an accomplishing; hence, means for accomplishing. — L. *im-plēre*, to fill in, execute. — L. *im-* (for *in*), in; *plēre*, to fill. See **Plenary**.

Implicate. (L.) From pp. of L. *im-plicāre*, to involve. — L. *im-* (*in*), in; *plicāre*, to fold. See **Ply**.

implicit. (F. — L.) F. *implicite*. — L. *implicitus*, old pp. of *implicāre* (above).

Implore. (F. — L.) F. *implorer*. — L. *implōrāre*, to implore. — L. *im-* (= *in*), on, upon : *plōrāre*, to wail. Cf. *de-plore*.

Imply. (F. — L.) Coined from L. *im-* (*in*), and *ply*; as if from a F. **implier*; but the F. form was *impliquer*, still earlier *emploier* (whence E. *employ*). See **Ply**.

Import. (F. — L.; *or* L.) In two senses: (1) to signify. — M. F. *importer*, to signify. — L. *importāre*, to import, bring in, introduce, cause: (2) to bring in from abroad; directly from the same L. *im-*

portāre.—L. *im-* (*in*), in; *portāre*, to bring. Der. *import-ant*, i. e. importing much. See Port (1).

importable, intolerable; *obsolete.* (F. —L.) M. F. *importable.* —L. *importābilis,* that cannot be borne.—L. *im-* (*in-*), not; *portāre*, to bear.

Importune, tomolest. (F.—L.) From M. E. *importune*, adj., troublesome.—F. *importun*, 'importunate;' Cot.—L. *importūnus*, unfit, unsuitable, troublesome. Orig. 'hard of access;' from L. *im-* (*in-*), not; *portus*, access, a harbour. See Port (2). Der. *importun-ate*, from pp. of Late L. *importūnārī*, to vex, dep. vb.

Impose. (F.—L. *and* Gk.) F. *im-poser*, to lay upon.—F. *im-* (L. *in*), upon; F. *poser*, to lay. See Pose (1).

Imposition. (F.—L.) F. *imposition.* —L. acc. *impositiōnem*, a laying on.—L. *impositus*, pp. of *impōnere*, to lay on.—L. *im-* (*in*), on; *pōnere*, to lay.

impost. (F.—L.) O. F. *impost,* a tax.—L. pp. neut. *impositum* (above), a thing imposed.

Imposthume, an abscess. (F.—L.— Gk.) Better *apostume*, as in Cotgrave.— M. F. *apostume*, ' an apostume, an inward swelling full of corrupt matter.' A still better spelling is M. F. *aposteme*, also in Cotgrave.—L. *apostēma.*—Gk. ἀπόστημα, a standing away from; hence, a separation of corrupt matter.—Gk. ἀπό, away; στη-, base of ἵστημι, I set, place, stand. (√STĀ.)

Impostor. (L.) L. *impostor*, a deceiver; from L. *impōnere*, to impose, also, to impose upon, cheat. See Imposition.

Impotence. (F.—L.) F. (and O. F.) *impotence.*—L. *impotentia*, inability.—L. *impotent-*, stem of *impotens*, powerless. See Im- (4) and Potent.

Impoverish. (F.—L.) From O. F. *empovris-*, stem of pres. pt. of *empovrir*, to impoverish.—F. *em-* (= L. *in*), extremely; O. F. *povre*, poor, from Lat. *pauperem*, acc. of *pauper*, poor. See Poverty and Poor.

Imprecate. (L.) From pp. of L. *im-precārī*, to call down upon by prayer.—L. *im-* (*in*), upon; *precārī*, to pray. See Pre-carious and Pray.

Impregnable. (F.—L.) The *gn* orig. represented the sound of *n* followed by a slight glide; cf. M. E. *regne*, pron. (ren·yə), whence E. *reign.*—F. *imprenable*, 'impregnable;' Cot.—F. *im-* (=L. *in-*),

not; F. *prendre*, from L. *prehendere*, to take, seize. See Prehensile.

Impregnate, to render pregnant. (L.) From pp. of L. *imprægnāre*, to impregnate.—L. *im-* (for *in*), in; **prægnāre*, only used in the pres. pt. *prægnans*; see Pregnant.

Imprese, an heraldic device, with a motto. (F.—Ital.—L.) In Rich. II. iii. 1. 25. Also spelt *impresa* (Nares).—O. F. *imprese.*—Ital. *impresa*, ' an imprese, an embleme; also, an enterprise;' Florio. Fem. of *impreso*, undertaken (hence, adopted), pp. of *imprendere*, to undertake. —L. *im-* (*in*), in; *prehendere*, to lay hold of. Doublet, *emprise*, an enterprise, Spenser, F. Q. ii. 4. 12; from F. *emprise*, fem. pp. of *emprendre*, to undertake (Cotgrave) = Ital. *imprendere.* Der. *impresario*, an undertaker, stage-manager; from *impresa* an undertaking.

Impress. (L.) L. *impressāre*, frequent. of *imprimere*, to press upon.—L. *im-* (*in*), on; *premere*, to press. See Press.

imprint. (F.—L.) The verb, in Sir T. More, is formed as if from *im-* and *print*; but we also find M. E. *empreinten.* —O. F. *empreinte*, ' a stamp, print;' Cot. Orig. fem. of pp. of *empreindre*, ' to print, stamp;' id.—L. *imprimere*, to impress, press upon (above). See Print.

Imprison. (F.—L.) For *emprison.*— O. F. *emprisonner*, to imprison. — O. F. *em-* (for L. *in*), in; *prison*, a prison. See Prison.

Impromptu, a thing said off hand. (F.—L.) F. *impromptu.*—L. *in promptū*, in readiness; where *promptū* is abl. of *promptus*, a sb. formed from *prōmere*, to bring forward; see Prompt.

Impropriate, to appropriate to private use. (L.) Coined from L. *im-* (*in*), in; *propriāre*, to appropriate, from *proprius*, one's own. See Proper.

Improve. (F.—L.) Formerly *emprove*, for late M. E. *enprowen* (Skelton), which was itself an alteration of M. E. *approwen*, to benefit.—O. F. *aproer*, *apprower*, to benefit.—O. F. *a* (for L. *ad*, to), and *prou*, sb., profit, answering to Ital. *prode*, sb., benefit. Cf. Ital. *prode*, adj., good, valiant; see Prowess. ¶ The O. F. sb. *emprovement*, improvement, occurs in Godefroy.

Improvise. (F.—Ital.—L.) F. *im-proviser.*—Ital. *improvvisare*, to sing extemporaneous verses. — Ital. *improvviso*, sudden, unprovided for. — L. *imprōuīsus*, unforeseen. — L. *im-* (for *in-*), not; *prō*, before; *uīsus*, pp. of *uidēre*, to see. See Vision.

Impudent, shameless. (F. — L.) F. *impudent*. — L. *impudent-*, stem of *impudens*, shameless. — L. *im-* (for *in*), not; *pudens*, modest, pres. pt. of *pudēre*, to feel shame.

Impugn. (F. — L.) F. *impugner*. — L. *impugnāre*, to fight against. — L. *im-* (for *in*), against; *pugnāre*, to fight, from *pugna*, a battle; cf. *pugnus*, a fist.

Impulse; see Impel.

Impunity. (F. — L.) F. *impunité*. — L. acc. *impūnitātem*, acc. of *impūnitās*, impunity. — L. *impūni-s*, without punishment. — L. *im-* (= *in-*), not; *pœna*, punishment. See Pain.

Impute. (F. — L.) F. *imputer*. — L. *impulāre*, to ascribe. — L. *im-* (*in*), towards; *putāre*, to reckon. See Putative.

In, prep. (E.) A.S. *in*.+Du. *in*, Icel. *ī*, Swed. Dan. *i*, Goth. *in*, G. *in*, W. *yn*, O. Irish *in*, L. *in*, Gk. ἐν, ἐνί. L. *in* is for O. L. *en* (as in *en-do*)=Gk. ἐν. Der. *inn-er*, A.S. *innera*; *in-most*, A.S. *innemest* (i. e. *inne-m-est*, a double superl. form). The form *innermost* is also a corruption of A.S. *innemest*. Also *in-ward*, *there-in*, *where-in*, *with-in*, *in-as-much*, *in-so-much*, *in-ter-*, *in-tro-*. And see Inn.

In- (1), prefix. (E.) In some words, it is only the prep. *in* in composition. Exx.: *in-born*, *in-breathe*, *in-bred*, *in-land*, &c. And see Im- (1).

In- (2), prefix. (L.) In some words, it is the L. prep. *in* in composition. Exx.: *in-augurate*, *in-carcerate*, &c. Sometimes, it has passed through French; as *in-dication*, &c. ¶ It becomes *il-* before *l*, *im-* before *b*, *m*, and *p*, *ir-* before *r*.

In- (3), negative prefix. (L.; *or* F. — L.) From L. neg. prefix *in-*, cognate with E. neg. prefix *un-*; see Un- (1), An-, A- (9). ¶ It becomes *i-* before *gn*, *il-* before *l*; *im-* before *b*, *m*, and *p*; *ir-* before *r*. Der. *in-ability*, *in-accessible*, &c., &c.; for which see *able*, *access*, &c.

Inane, empty, silly, useless. (L.) L. *inānis*, void, empty. Root unknown. Der. *inan-i-ty*.

inanition, exhaustion from lack of food. (F. — L.) F. *inanition*, ' an emptying;' Cot. From the pp. of *inānīre*, to empty; from *inānis* (above).

Inaugurate. (L.) From pp. of L. *in-augurāre*, to practise augury, to consecrate, begin formally. — L. *in*, in, upon; *augur*, an augur; see Augur.

Inca, a royal title. (Peruv.) Peruv. *inca*, a title. Cf. Peruv. *çapay kapac Inca*, king of Peru (*çapay* = only; *kapac* = lord). *Inca* was orig. the chief of a tribe (Oviedo).

Incandescent, glowing hot. (L.) From stem of pres. pt. of *in-candescere*, to glow; where *candescere* is the inceptive form of *candēre*, to glow. See Candid.

Incantation. (F. — L.) F. *incantation*. — L. *incantātiōnem*, acc. of *incantātio*, an enchanting. — L. *incantāre*, to enchant. — L. *in*, on, upon; *cantāre*, to sing, frequent. of *canere*, to sing. See Enchant and Cant (1).

Incarcerate, to imprison. (L.) L. *in*, in; and *carcerātus*, pp. of *carcerāre*, to imprison, from *carcer*, a prison.

Incarnadine, to dye of a red colour. (F. — Ital. — L.) F. *incarnadin*, carnation colour (Cot.). — Ital. *incarnadino*, carnation colour (Florio); also spelt *incarnatino*. — Ital. *incarnato*, incarnate; also, of flesh colour. — L. *incarnātus*, pp. of *incarnāre*, to clothe with flesh (below).

incarnation. (F. — L.) F. *incarnation*. — L. acc. *incarnātiōnem*, embodiment in flesh. — L. *incarnātus*, pp. of *incarnāre*, to clothe with flesh. — L. *in*, on; and *carn-*, decl. base of *caro*, flesh. See Carnal.

Incendiary. (L.) L. *incendiārius*, setting on fire. — L. *incendium*, a burning. — L. *incendere*, to set on fire. — L. *in*, upon; and **candēre*, to burn (not found), allied to Skt. *chand*, to shine.

incense (1), to inflame. (L.) From L. *incensus*, pp. of *incendere*, to set on fire; see above.

incense (2), smell of burnt spices. (F. — L.) F. *encens*, incense, burnt spices. — L. *incensum*, that which is burnt; neut. of pp. of *incendere*, to set on fire (above).

Incentive. (L.) L. *incentīuus*, striking up a tune, inciting. — L. **incentus*, unused pp. of *incinere*, to sound an instrument. — L. *in*, into; and *canere*, to sound, sing. See Chant.

Inceptive. (F. — L.) O. F. *inceptif*, adj., beginning (Godefroy). — Late L. **inceptīvus* (not found). — L. *incept-us*, pp. of *incipere*, to begin; see Incipient.

Incessant, ceaseless. (F. — L.) F. *incessant*. — L. *incessant-* stem of *incessans*, unceasing. – L. *in-*, not; *cessans*, ceasing, pres. pt. of *cessāre*, to cease, frequent. of *cēdere*, to yield. See **Cease** and **Cede**.

Incest, impurity. (F.–L.) M. E. *incest.* – F. *inceste*, sb. m. – L. *incestus* (gen. *-ūs*), incest. – L. *incestus*, unchaste. – L. *in-*, not; *castus*, chaste. See **Chaste**.

Inch (1), the twelfth part of a foot. (L. – Gk.) M. E. *inche.* A. S. *ynce.* – L. *uncia*, an inch; also an ounce, one-twelfth of a pound. – Sicilian *oὐγκία*, the same. – Gk. *ὄγκος*, bulk, weight. **Doublet**, *ounce* (1). And see **Uncial**.

Inch (2), an island. (Gael.) Gael. *innis*, an island.+Irish *inis*; W. *ynys*; Bret. *enez*; Corn. *enys*.

Incident. (F.–L.) F. *incident*, ʻan incident;ʼ Cot. – L. *incident-*, stem of pres. pt. of *incidere*, to fall upon. – L. *in*, on; and *cadere*, to fall. See **Cadence**.

Incipient. (L.) L. *incipient-*, stem of pres. pt. of *incipere*, to begin. – L. *in*, upon; *capere*, to lay hold of. See **Capacious**.

Incise, to cut into. (F.–L.) F. *inciser.* – L. *incīsus*, pp. of *in-cīdere*, to cut into. – L. *in*, in; *cædere*, to cut. See **Cæsura**.

Incite. (F. – L.) F. *inciter.* – L. *incitāre*, to urge on. – L. *in*, on; *citāre*, to urge. See **Cite**.

Incline, to lean towards. (F.–L.) F. *incliner.* – L. *inclīnāre.* – L. *in*, towards; *clināre*, to lean, cognate with F. **Lean** (1), q. v. **Doublet**, *encline*.

Inclose. (F. – L.) For *enclose.* – O. F. *enclos*, pp. of *enclore*, to include. – L. *inclūdere*, to shut in. – L. *in*, in; *claudere*, to shut. See **Clause**.

include. (L.) From L. *inclūdere* (above).

Incognito, lit. unknown. (Ital. – L.) Ital. *incognito*, unknown. – L. *in-cognitus*, not known. – L. *in-*, not; *cognitus*, known. See **Cognition**.

Income, gain, revenue. (E.) Properly that which *comes in*; from *in* and *come*. So also *out-come*, i. e. result.

Incommode. (F.–L.) F. *incommoder*, to inconvenience. – L. *incommodāre*, to inconvenience. – L. *in*, not; *commodus*, fit; see **Commodious**.

Incony, fine, delicate, very dear. (E.) In Shak. For *in-conny*; where *in-* is intensive, as in M. E. *in-ly*, very; and *conny* (also *canny*) is North E., meaning skilful, gentle, pleasant, &c. From E.

can, I know (how); cf. Icel. *kunnigr*, knowing, wise.

Incorporate. (L.) L. *incorporātus*, pp. of *incorporāre*, to furnish with a body; hence to form into a body. – L. *in*, in; *corpor-*, stem of *corpus*, a body. See **Corporal** (2).

Increase. (F. – L.) M. E. *incresen*, *encresen.* – F. *en* (L. *in*); and A. F. *creiss-*, stem of pres. pt. of A. F. *creistre*, O. F. *croistre* (F. *croître*), to grow, from L. *crescere*, to grow. See **Crescent**. Der. *increase*, sb.; A. F. *encrees.*

increment. (L.) L. *incrēmentum*, an increase. L. *in*, in, used intensively; *crē-*, as in *crē-tum*, supine of *crescere*, to grow, with suffix *-mentum.* Cf. *de-cre-ment.*

Incubate. (L.) From pp. of Lat. *incubāre*, to sit on eggs to hatch them. – L. *in*, upon; *cubāre*, to lie down, to sit.

incubus. (L.) L. *incubus*, a nightmare. – L. *in-cubāre*, to lie upon (above).

Inculcate. (L.) From pp. of L. *inculcāre*, lit. to tread in, hence to enforce by admonition. – L. *in*, in; *calcāre*, to tread. See **Calk**.

Inculpate. (L.) From pp. of Late L. *inculpāre*, to bring blame upon. – L. *in*, upon; *culpāre*, to blame. See **Culpable**.

Incumbent. (L.) L. *incumbent-*, stem of pres. pt. of *incumbere*, to recline on, rest on or in (remain in); where *cumbere* is a nasalised form allied to *cubāre*, to lie down. So also *pro-cumbent*, prostrate; *re-cumbent*, lying back upon; *suc cumb*, to lie under, yield to.

Incur. (L.) L. *incurrere*, to run into, run upon. – L. *in*, upon; *currere*, to run. See **Current**.

incursion. (F. – L.) M. F. *incursion.* – L. *incursiōnem*, acc. of *incursio*, an inroad. – L. *incursus*, pp. of *incurrere*, to run into, attack (above).

Incurvate, to crook. (L.) From pp. of L. *incuruāre*, to bend into a curve. – L. *in*, in; *curuāre*, to bend. See **Curve**.

Indeed, truly. (E.) For *in deed*, i. e. in fact; see **Deed**.

Indelible. (F.–L.) For *indeleble.* – M. F. *indelebile*, ʻindelible;ʼ Cot. – L. *indēlēbilis*, indelible. – L. *in-*, not; *dēlēbilis*, destructible, from *dēlēre*, to destroy. See **Delete**.

Indemnify, to make damage good. (L.) Ill coined; from L. *indemni-s*, unharmed, free from loss; and F. -*fier*, for L. -*fic-āre*, for *facere*, to make (as in *magni-fy*). L. *indemnis* is from L. *in-*, not; and *damnum*, loss. See Damn.

indemnity. (F.−L.) F. *indemnité*. − L. acc. *indemnitātem.*−L. *in-demni-s*, unharmed, free from loss (*damnum*).

Indent (1), to cut into points like teeth. (Law L.) A law term.−Law L. *indentāre*, to notch.−L. *in*, in; *dent-*, stem of *dens*, a tooth. Der. *indenture* (F. *endenture*); so called because duplicate deeds were cut with notched edges to fit one another.

Indent (2), to make a dint in. (E.) From E. *in*, prep.; and *dent*, a dint. See Dint. Suggested by *indent* (1), but quite a distinct word.

Index. (L.) L. *index* (stem *indic-*), a discloser, something that indicates.− L. *indicāre*, to point out.−L. *in*, in, to; *dicāre*, to appoint, declare, allied to *dīcere*, to say; see Diction.

indicate. (L.) From pp. of L. *in-dicāre*, to point at, point out (above).

indict. (F.−L.) For *indite* (which is the French spelling), and so pronounced. See Indite.

indiction, a cycle of fifteen years. (L.) O. F. *indiction*, an appointment of tributes arranged for fifteen years; the lit. sense is merely 'appointment.'−L. *in-dictiōnem*, acc. of *indictio*, an appointment, esp. of a tax.−L. *indictus*, pp. of *indīcere*, to appoint, impose a tax.−L. *in*, upon; *dīcere*, to say. See Diction.

Indigenous, native. (L.) Late L. *indigen-us*, native; with suffix -*ous*.−L. *indi-* = O. Lat. *indu*, within (cf. Gk. ἔνδον); and *gen-*, as in *gen-i-tus*, born, pp. of *gignere*, to beget; see Genus.

Indigent, destitute. (F.−L.) M. F. *indigent.*−L. *indigent-*, stem of pres. part. of *indigēre*, to be in want.−L. *ind-*, for *indu*, an O. Lat. extension from *in*, in (cf. Gk. ἔνδον, within); *egēre*, to want, be in need; cf. L. *indigus*, needy. Cf. Gk. ἀχήν, poor, needy (Theocritus).

Indigo, a blue dye. (F.−Span.−L. −Gk.−Pers.−Skt.) F. *indigo.*−Span. *indico.* − L. *indicum*, indigo; neut. of *Indicus*, Indian (hence Indian dye).−Gk. ἰνδικόν, indigo; neut. of Ἰνδικός, Indian.− Pers. *Hind*, India; a name due to the river Indus. −Skt. *sindhu-*, the river Indus; a large river.−Skt. *syand*, to flow. ¶ The Persian changes initial *s* into *h*.

Indite. (F.−L.) For *endite*. M. F. *endicter*, O. F. *enditer*, to indict, accuse; also spelt *inditer.*−Late L. *indictāre*, to point out, frequent. of *indīcere*, to appoint. See Indicate. Doubtless confused with the closely related L. *indicāre*, to point out.

Indolence. (F.−L.) F. *indolence.*− L. *indolentia*, freedom from pain; hence, ease, idleness. −L. *in-*, not; *dolent-*, stem of pres. pt. of *dolēre*, to grieve. See Doleful.

Indomitable. (L.) Coined from *in-*, not; *domitāre*, to subdue, frequent. of *domāre*, to tame. See Daunt.

Indubitable. (F.−L.) M.F. *indubitable.*−L. *indubitābilis*, not to be doubted. −L. *in-*, not; *dubitābilis*, doubtful, from *dubitāre*, to doubt; see Doubt.

Induce. (L.) L. *indūcere*, to lead to. − L. *in*, in, to; *dūcere*, to lead; see Duke.

induct. (L.) From L. *induct-us*, pp. of *indūcere*, to bring in (above).

Indue (1), to invest or clothe with, supply with. (L.) In Spenser, F. Q. iii. 6. 35.−L. *induere*, to put into, put on, clothe with. The prefix is *ind-*, not *in-* (for this prefix see Indigent); cf. *ex-uuiæ*, spoils, *ind-uuiæ*, clothes. See Exuviæ.

Indue (2), a corruption of Endue, q. v.

Indulgence. (F.−L.) F. *indulgence.* − L. *indulgentia.*−L. *indulgent-*, stem of pres. pt. of *indulgēre*, to be courteous to, indulge. (Of unknown origin.)

Indurate, to harden. (L.) From pp. of L. *indūrāre*, to harden.−L. *in*, intensive; *dūrāre*, to harden, from *dūrus*, hard. See Dure.

Industry. (F.−L.) F. *industrie.*− L. *industria.* − L. *industrius*, diligent. Origin uncertain.

Inebriate. (L.) From L. *inēbriātus*, pp. of *inēbriāre*, to make drunk.−L. *in*, in, very; *ēbriāre*, to make drunk, from *ēbrius*, drunk. See Ebriety.

Ineffable. (F.−L.) F. *ineffable.*− L. *ineffābilis*, unspeakable.−L. *in-*, not; *ef-* (for *ex*), out; *fā-rī*, to speak; with suffix -*bilis*. See Fate.

Inept, foolish. (F.−L.) XVII cent. − M. F. *inepte.*−L. *ineptus*, improper, foolish.−L. *in-*, not; and *aptus*, fit. (Also *inapt*, from *in-*, not, and *apt*.) See Apt.

Inert. (L.) L. *inert-*, stem of *iners*, unskilful, inactive.−L. *in-*, not; *ars*, skill. See Art (2).

Inexorable. (F.—L.) F. *inexorable.*—L. *inexōrābilis,* that cannot be moved by intreaty.—L. *in-,* not; *exōrāre,* to gain by intreaty, from L. *ex,* out, greatly, and *ōrāre,* to pray. See **Oration.**

Infamy. (F.—L.) F. *infamie.*—L. *infāmia,* ill fame.—L. *infāmi-s,* adj., of ill fame.—L. *in-,* not, bad; *fāma,* fame. See **Fame.**

Infant. (L.) L. *infant-,* stem of *in-fans,* not speaking, hence, a very young babe.—L. *in-,* not; *fans,* pres. pt. of *fārī,* to speak.

infantry. (F.—Ital.—L.) F. *infanterie.*—Ital. *infanteria,* foot-soldiers; orig. a band of 'infants,' as young men were called. — Ital. *infante,* an infant. — L. *infantem,* acc. of *infans* (above).

Infatuate. (L.) From pp. of L. *infatuāre,* to make a fool of.—L. *in,* in, greatly; *fatuus,* foolish. See **Fatuous.**

Infect, to taint. (F.—L.) M. E. *infect,* as pp.; also *infecten,* vb. = O. F. *infect,* infected.—L. *infectus,* pp. of *in-ficere,* to put in, dye, stain.—L. *in,* in; *facere,* to put. See **Fact.**

Infer, to imply. (F.—L.) M. F. *in-ferer;* F. *inférer.*—L. *inferre,* to bring in, introduce.—L. *in,* in; *ferre,* to bring. See **Fertile.**

Inferior. (F.—L.) M. F. *inferieur.*—L. *inferiōrem,* acc. of *inferior,* lower, comp. of *inferus,* low, nether. Strictly, *inferus* is itself a compar. form, which some connect with Skt. *adhara,* lower; which is doubtful. See Brugm. i. § 589 (note).

infernal. (F.—L.) F. *infernal.*—L. *infernālis,* belonging to the lower regions. —L. *infernus,* lower; extended from *inferus* (above).

Infest, to harass. (F.—L.) F. *infester.* —L. *infestāre,* to attack.—L. *infestus,* attacking, hostile; orig. unsafe. Origin doubtful.

Infidel. (F.—L.) M.F. *infidele,* 'infidell;' Cot.—L. *infidēlis,* faithless.—L. *in-,* not; *fidēlis,* faithful, from *fidē-s,* faith. See **Faith.**

Infinite. (F.—L.) O. F. *infinit* (F. *infini*).—L. *infinītus,* unended.—L. *in-,* not; *finītus,* pp. of *finīre,* to end, from *finis,* end. See **Final.**

Infirm. (L.) L. *infirmus,* not strong, weak.—L. *in-,* not; *firmus,* firm. See **Firm.** Der. *infirm-ar-y, infirm-i-ty.*

Inflate. (L.) From pp. of L. *inflāre,* to blow into, puff up.—L. *in,* in; *flāre,* to blow. See **Flatulent.**

Inflect, to modulate the voice, &c. (L.) L. *inflectere,* lit. to bend in.—L. *in,* in; *flectere,* to bend. See **Flexible.**

Inflict. (L.) From L. *inflictus,* pp. of *infligere,* to inflict, lit. to strike upon.—L. *in,* upon; and *fligere,* to strike. See **Afflict.**

Inflorescence, mode of flowering. (F.—L.) F. *inflorescence.* From the pres. pt. of L. *inflōrescere,* to burst into blossom. — L. *in,* into; and *flōrescere,* inceptive form of *flōrēre,* to bloom. See **Flourish.**

Influence. (F.—L.) O. F. *influence,* a flowing in, esp. used of the influence of planets.—Late L. *influentia.*—L.*influent-,* stem of pres. pt. of *influere,* to flow into. — L. *in.* into; *fluere,* to flow. See **Fluent.**

influenza. (Ital.—L.) Ital. *influenza,* influence, also used of a severe catarrh. A doublet of **Influence** (above).

influx. (F.—L.) O.F. *influx.*—L. *in-fluxus,* a flowing in.—L. *in,* in; *fluxus,* pp. of *fluere,* to flow.

Inform, to impart knowledge to. (F. —L.) F. *informer.*—L. *informāre,* to put into form, mould; also, to tell, inform. —L. *in,* into; *forma,* form. See **Form.**

Infraction, violation of law. (F.—L.) F. *infraction.*—L. acc. *infractiōnem,* a weakening, breaking into.—L. *infractus,* pp. of *in-fringere* (below).

infringe. (L.) L. *infringere,* to break into, violate law. — L. *in,* into; *frangere,* to break. See **Fragile.**

Infuriate. (Ital.—L.) Ital.*infuriato,* pp. of *infuriare,* to fly into a rage.—Ital. *in furia,* 'in a fury, ragingly;' Florio.— L. *in,* in; *furia,* rage. See **Fury.** ¶ Or from Late L. pp. *infuriātus* (Ducange).

Infuse. (F.—L.) F. *infuser.*—L. *in-fūsus,* pp. of *infundere,* to pour in.—L. *in,* in; *fundere,* to pour. See **Fuse** (1).

Ingenious. (F.—L.) M.F.*ingenieux* (Cot.). — L. *ingeniōsus,* clever.—L. *ingenium,* natural capacity; see **Engine.**

ingenuous. (L.) L. *ingenu-us,* inborn, free-born, frank; with suffix *-ous.* — L. *in,* in; *gen-,* as in *gen-i-tus,* born, pp. of *gignere,* to beget. See **Genus.**

Ingle (1), fire. (C.) Lowl. Sc. *ingle,* fire. Perhaps from Gael and Irish *aingeal,* fire. Allied to Irish *ong,* Russ. *ogone,* fire. See **Ignition.**

Ingle (2), a darling, paramour. (Du. or Fries.—L.—Gk.) Also *engle* (Nares). M. Du. *ingel, engel,* an angel (hence, a term of endearment). Koolman notes E. Fries. *engel,* an angel, as being commonly used as a term of endearment and as a female name.—L. *angelus.*—Gk. ἄγγελος. See **Angel.**

Ingot, a mass of unwrought metal. (E.) M. E. *ingot,* Chaucer, C. T. 16677, &c., where it means a mould for molten metal. But the true sense is 'that which is poured in,' a mass of metal.—A.S. *in,* in; and *got-en,* poured, pp. of *gēotan,* to pour, fuse metals. Cf. Du. *ingieten,* Swed. *ingjuta,* to pour in. Also Du. *gieten,* G. *giessen,* Icel. *gjóta* (pp. *gotinn*), Dan. *gyde,* Swed. *gjuta,* Goth. *giutan,* to pour, shed, fuse; cognate with L. *fundere.* (√GHEU.) Hence F. *lingot,* for *l'ingot.* + G. *ein-guss,* a pouring in, also an ingot; Swed. *ingöte,* the neck of a mould for metals.

Ingrain, to dye of a fast colour. (F.—L.) M. E. *engreynen.* — M. F. *engrainer* (Palsg.).—F. *en graine,* in grain, with a fast colour.—F. *en,* in (L. *in*); Late L. *grāna,* cochineal dye, from *grānum,* a grain. See **Grain** and **Cochineal.**

Ingrate, ungrateful. (F.—L.) F. *ingrat.*—L. *ingrātus,* not pleasing.—L. *in-,* not; *grātus,* pleasing. See **Grateful.**

Ingratiate, to commend to the favour of. (L.) Coined from L. *in,* in; *grātia,* favour, grace. See **Grace.**

Ingredient, that which enters into a compound. (F.—L.) F. *ingrédient* (the same).—L. *ingredient-,* stem of pres. pt. of *ingredī,* to enter upon, begin (hence to enter into).—L. *in,* in; *gradī,* to go. See **Grade.**

ingress. (L.) L. *ingressus,* an entering.—L. *ingressus,* pp. of *ingredī* (above).

Inguinal, relating to the groin. (L.) L. *inguinālis* (the same).—L. *inguin-,* stem of *inguen,* the groin.

Inhabit. (F.—L.) M. F. *inhabiter.*—L. *inhabitāre,* to dwell in.—L. *in,* in; *habitāre,* to dwell. See **Habitation.**

Inhale. (L.) L. *inhālāre,* to breathe in, draw in breath.—L. *in,* in; *hālāre,* to breathe. Cf. **Exhale.**

Inherent. (L.) L. *inhærent-,* stem of pres. pt. of *in-hærēre,* to stick in. Hence *inhere,* as a verb. See **Hesitate.**

Inherit. (F.—L.) O. F. *enheriter.*—Late L. *inhērēditāre.*—L. *in,* in; *hērēd-em,* acc. of *hērēs,* an heir. See **Heir.**

Inhibit, to check. (L.) From L. *inhibitus,* pp. of *inhibēre,* to keep in, hold in.—L. *in,* in; *habēre,* to have, keep. See **Habit.**

Inimical. (L.) L. *inimīcālis,* extended from *inimīcus,* hostile.—L. *in-,* not; and *amīcus,* friendly. See **Enemy** and **Amiable.**

Iniquity, vice. (F.—L.) M. E. *iniquitee.* — F. *iniquité.* — L. *inīquitātem,* acc. of *inīquitās,* injustice.—L. *in-,* not; *æquitas,* equity. See **Equity.**

Initial, pertaining to the beginning. (F.—L.) F. *initial.*—L. *initiālis,* adj. from *initium,* a beginning.—L. *initum,* supine of *in-īre,* to go in, to enter into or upon.—L. *in,* in; *īre,* to go.

initiate, to begin. (L.) From pp. of L. *initiāre,* to begin.—L. *initium* (above).

Inject. (L.) From *iniectus,* pp. of L. *inicere,* to cast in, throw into.—L. *in,* in; *iacere,* to throw. See **Jet** (1).

Injunction, command. (L.) From L. *iniunctio,* an order.—L. *iniunctus,* pp. of *iniungere,* to bid. See **Enjoin.**

Injure. (F.—L.) F. *injurier.*—Late L. *iniūriāre;* for L. *iniūriārī,* to harm.—L. *iniūria,* harm.—L. *iniūrius,* wrong.—L. *in-,* not; *iūr-,* for *iūs,* law, right. See **Just.**

Ink. (F.—L.—Gk.) M. E. *enke.* — O. F. *enque* (F. *encre*).—Late L. *incaustum;* L. *encaustum,* the purple-red ink used by the later Roman emperors; neut. of *encaustus,* burnt in.—Gk. ἔγκαυστος, burnt in.—Gk. ἐν, in; καίω, I burn. (Cf. Ital. *inchiostro,* ink.) See **Encaustic.**

Inkle, a kind of tape. (Origin unknown.) Perhaps from M. Du. *enckel,* Du. *enkel,* single, as opposed to double; but there is no obvious connexion.

Inkling, a hint, intimation. (Scand.?) M. E. *inkling,* a whisper, murmur, low speaking. Alexander, when in disguise, feared he was discovered, because he 'herd *a nyngkiling* of his name'; Allit. romance of Alexander, 2968; where *a nyngkiling* stands for *an yngkiling.* 'To *incle* the truthe' = to hint at the truth, Alisaunder (in app. to Wm. of Palerne), 616. Origin unknown; perhaps allied to Swed. *enkel,* single; cf. *et enkelt ord,* a single word; M. Du. *enckelinge,* 'a falling or a diminishing of notes;' Hexham.

Inn, sb. (E.) M. E. *in, inn.*—A.S. *inn, in,* sb., room, dwelling.—A.S. *in,*

inn, adv., within, indoors. – A.S. *in*, prep., in. +Icel. *inni*, an inn; *inni*, adv., indoors. See **In**.

inning. (E.) Properly the securing or housing of grain, from *inn*, vb., due to *inn*, sb. (above). Also *innings*, at cricket, invariably used in the plural, because the side which is *in* consists of several players.

Innate, in-born. (L.) L. *innātus*, in-born. – L. *in*, in; *nātus*, born; see **Natal**.

Innocent. (F. – L.) F. *innocent*. – L. *innocent-*, stem of *innocens*, harmless. – L. *in-*, not; *nocens*, pres. pt. of *nocēre*, to hurt. See **Noxious**.

innocuous. (L.) L. *innocu-us*, harmless; with suffix *-ous*. – L. *in-*, not; *nocēre*, to hurt.

Innovate, to introduce something new. (L.) From pp. of L. *innouāre*, to renew, make new. – L. *in*, in; *nouus*, new. See **Novel**.

Innuendo, an indirect hint. (L.) Not to be spelt *inuendo*. From L. *innuendo*, by intimating; gerund of *innuere*, to nod towards, intimate. – L. *in*, in, at; *nuere*, to nod. See **Nutation**.

Inoculate. (L.) In old authors it means 'to engraft.' – L. *inoculātus*, pp. of *inoculāre*, to engraft, insert a graft. – L. *in*, in; *oculus*, an eye, also a bud of a plant. See **Ocular**.

Inordinate. (L.) L. *inordinātus*. – L. *in-*, not; *ordinātus*, ordered, controlled, pp. of *ordināre*; see **Ordain**. And see **Order**.

Inquest. (F. – L.) Later spelling of M. E. *enqueste*. O. F. *enqueste*. – Late L. *inquesta*, sb., from *inquesta*, fem. of Late L. *inquestus*. – L. *inquisītus*, pp. of *inquīrere*, to search into. – L. *in*, into; *quaerere*, to search. See **Query**.

inquire, late spelling of **Enquire**, q. v.

inquisition. (F. – L.) F. *inquisition*. – L. acc. *inquisītiōnem*, a search into. – L. *inquisītus*, pp. of *inquīrere*; see **Inquest** (above).

Inscribe. (L.) L. *inscrībere*, to write in or upon; pp. *inscriptus* (whence *inscription*). – L. *in*, upon; *scrībere*, to write. See **Scribe**.

Inscrutable, that cannot be scrutinised. (F. – L.) F. *inscrutable*. – L. *in-scrūtābilis*. – L. *in-*, not; *scrūtārī*, to scrutinise. See **Scrutiny**.

Insect. (F. – L.) F. *insecte*. – L. *in-sectum*, lit. 'a thing cut into,' i. e. nearly divided, from the shape. – L. *insectus*, pp. of *insecāre*, to cut into. – L. *in*, into; *secāre*, to cut. See **Secant**.

Insert. (L.) From L. *insertus*, pp. of *inserere*, to introduce, put in. – L. *in*, in; *serere*, to join, put. See **Series**.

Insidious. (F. – L.) F. *insidieux*, deceitful. – L. *insidiōsus*, treacherous. – L. *insidiæ*, pl. troops of men who lie in wait, also cunning wiles. – L. *insidēre*, to lie in wait, lit. 'to sit in.' – L. *in*, in; *sedēre*, to sit. See **Sedentary**.

Insignia. (L.) L. *insignia*, marks of office; pl. of *insigne*, which is the neuter of *insignis*, remarkable. – L. *in*, upon; *signum*, a mark. See **Sign**.

Insinuate. (L.) From pp. of L. *in-sinuāre*, to introduce by winding or bending. – L. *in*, into; *sinus* (gen. *sinūs*), a bend. See **Sinus**.

Insipid. (L.) L. *insipidus*. – L. *in-*, not; *sapidus*, savoury. See **Sapid**.

Insist. (F. – L.) F. *insister*. – L. *in-sistere*, to set foot on, persist. – L. *in*, in; *sistere*, to set, stand, from *stāre*, to stand. See **State**.

Insolent. (F. – L.) M. E. *insolent*. – F. *insolent*, saucy. – L. *insolent-*, stem of *insolens*, insolent; of doubtful origin. Perhaps 'swelling against;' from L. *in-*, against, and *sol-*, weak grade of vb. *to swell*.

Inspect. (L.) L. *inspectāre*, to observe; frequent. of *inspicere*, to look into. – L. *in*, into; *specere*, to look. See **Species**.

Inspire. (F. – L.) O. F. *enspirer*, M. F. *inspirer* (Cot.). – L. *inspīrāre*, to breathe into. – L. *in*, into; *spīrāre*, to breathe. See **Spirit**.

Inspissate, to make thick. (L.) From pp. of L. *inspissāre*, to thicken. – L. *in*, in; *spissus*, thick, dense.

Instance. (F. – L.) F. *instance*, 'instance, urgency;' Cot. – L. *instantia*, a being near, urgency. – L. *instant-*, stem of pres. pt. of *instāre*, to be at hand, to urge. – L. *in*, upon, near; *stāre*, to stand. See **State**.

Instead. (E.) For *in stead*, i. e. in the place. See **Stead**.

Instep, the upper part of the foot, where it rises to the front of the leg. (E.) Formerly *instup* and *instop* (Minsheu). These forms may be related to A. S. *stōp*, as seen in *stōp-el*, a footprint, O. Sax. *stōp-o*, a step (cf. Du. *stoep*, a set of steps,

G. *stufe*, a step, stair) ; from *stōp*, strong grade of *stapan*, to advance (whence the secondary verb *steppan*, to step). The reference seems to be to the movement of the foot in walking. See **Step**.

Instigate, to urge on. (L.) From pp. of *instīgāre*, to goad on. — L. *in*, on ; and base **stīg-*, to prick, allied to L. *stinguere*, to prick ; see **Distinguish**. See Brugm. i. § 633.

Instil. (F. — L.) F. *instiller*. — L. *instillāre*, to pour in by drops. — L. *in*, in ; *stillāre*, to drop, from *stilla*, a drop. See **Still** (2).

Instinct. (F. — L.; *or* L.) F. *instinct*, sb. — L. *instinctum*, acc. of *instinctus*, an impulse. — L. *instinctus*, pp. of *instinguere*, to goad on. — L. *in*, on ; *stinguere*, to prick. See **Distinguish**.

Institute. (L.) From L. *institūtus*, pp. of *instituere*, to set, establish. — L. *in*, in ; *statuere*, to place, from *statu-s*, verbal sb. from *stāre*, to stand. See **State**.

Instruct. (L.) From L. *instructus*, pp. of *instruere*, to build into, instruct. — L. *in*, in ; *struere*, to pile up, build. See **Structure**.

instrument. (F. — L.) F. *instrument*. — L. *instrūmentum*, an implement, tool. — L. *instruere* (above) ; with suffix *-mentum*.

Insular. (L.) L. *insulāris*, insular. — L. *insula*, an island. Cf. **Isle**.

Insult, vb. (F. — L.) F. *insulter*. — L. *insultāre*, to leap upon, scoff at, insult ; frequent. of *insilīre*, to leap upon. — L. *in*, on ; *salīre*, to leap. See **Salient**.

Insurgent. (L.) L. *insurgent-*, stem of pres. pt. of *insurgere*, to rise up or on, to rebel. — L. *in*, on ; *surgere*, to rise. See **Surge**.

insurrection. (F. — L.) F. *insurrection*. — L. acc. *insurrectiōnem*, from nom. *insurrectio*. — L. *insurrectus*, pp. of *insurgere*, to rebel (above).

Intaglio, a kind of carved work. (Ital. — L.) Ital. *intaglio*, a sculpture, carving. — Ital. *intagliare*, to cut into. — Ital. *in* (= L. *in*), in ; *tagliare* = Late L. *taliāre*, *taleāre*, to cut twigs, to cut, allied to *tālia*, *tālea*, a slip, twig.

Integer, a whole number. (L.) L. *integer*, whole, entire ; lit. untouched, i. e. unharmed. — L. *in-*, not ; **tag-*, base of *tangere*, to touch. See **Tangent**. Brugm. i. 244 (3) ; ii. § 632.

Integument. (L.) L. *integumentum*,

a covering, skin. — L. *in*, upon ; *tegere*, to cover ; see **Tegument**.

Intellect. (F. — L.) M. F. *intellect*. — L. *intellectus*, perception, discernment. — L. *intellectus*, pp. of *intelligere*, to discern. — L. *intel-*, for *inter*, between ; *legere*, to choose. See **Legend**.

intelligence. (F. — L.) F. *intelligence*. — L. *intelligentia*, perception. — L. *intelligent-*, stem of pres. pt. of *intelligere*, to discern, understand (above).

intelligible. (F. — L) F. *intelligible*. — L. *intelligibilis*, perceptible to the senses. — L. *intelligere*, to discern (above) ; with suffix *-bilis*.

Intend. (F. — L.) M. E. *entenden*. — F. *entendre*. — L. *intendere*, to stretch to, bend or apply the mind to, design. — L. *in*, to ; *tendere*, to stretch. See **Tend** (1).

intense. (F. — L.) O. F. *intense*. — L. *intens-us*, stretched out, pp. of *intendere* (above).

intent, design. (F. — L.) M. E. *entente*. — F. *entente*, intention ; participial sb. from F. *entendre*, to intend ; see **Intend**. And see below.

intent, adj. (L.) L. *intentus*, bent on ; pp. of *intendere* ; see **Intend**.

Inter. (F. — L.) M. E. *enterren*. — F. *enterrer*, to bury. — Late L. *interrāre*, to put into the ground. — L. *in*, in ; *terra*, ground. See **Terrace**. Der. *inter-ment*, F. *enterrement*.

Inter-, *prefix*, amongst. (L.) L. *inter*, among ; a comparative form, answering to Skt. *antar*, within ; closely allied to **Interior**, q. v. Also **Intel-** (before *l*).

Intercalate, to insert. (L.) From pp. of L. *intercalāre*, to proclaim that a day has been inserted in the calendar, to insert. — L. *inter*, amongst ; *calāre*, to proclaim. See **Calends**.

Intercede. (F. — L.) F. *intercéder*. — L. *intercēdere*, lit. to go between ; hence, to mediate. — L. *inter*, between ; *cēdere*, to go. See **Cede**. Der. *intercession*, from the pp. *intercess-us*.

Intercept. (F. — L.) F. *intercepter*. — L. *intercept-us*, pp. of *intercipere*, lit. to catch between. — L. *inter*, between ; *capere*, to take. See **Capacious**.

Intercourse. (F. — L.) Formerly *entercourse*. — F. *entrecours*, intercourse, commerce. — Late L. *intercursus*, commerce ; lit. a running amongst. — L. *inter*, amongst ; *cursus*, a running, course, from the pp. of *currere*, to run. See **Course**.

Interdict, sb. (L.) Law L. *inter-dictum,* a kind of excommunication; in Latin, a decree. – L. *interdictus,* pp. of *interdīcere,* to pronounce a judgment between two parties. – L. *inter,* between; *dīcere,* to say. See **Diction.**

Interest (1), profit, advantage. (F. – L.) M. F. *interest* (F. *intérêt*), an interest in a thing, interest for money (Cot.). – L. *interest,* it is profitable; 3 pers. sing. of *interesse,* to concern, lit. 'be among.' – L. *inter,* among; *esse,* to be. See **Inter-** and **Essence.**

interest (2), to engage the attention of another. (F. – L.) A curious word; formed (by partial confusion with the verb above) from the pp. *interess'd* of the obsolete verb *to interess,* used by Massinger and Ben Jonson. – M. F. *interessé,* 'interessed, or touched in;' Cot. – L. *in-teresse,* to concern (as above). **Der.** Hence *dis-interested,* from the verb *dis-interest,* orig. a pp. and spelt *disinteress'd.*

Interfere. (F. – L.) Formerly *enter-feir,* to dash one heel against the other (Blount). O. F. *s'entreferir,* to exchange blows. – F. *entre,* between; *ferir,* to strike. – L. *inter,* between; *ferire,* to strike. See **Ferule.**

Interior. (F. – L.) O. F. *interior.* – L. *interiōrem,* acc. of *interior,* comp. of *interus,* within. *In-terus* itself was orig. a comparative form, answering to Skt. *antara-,* interior. The positive is the L. *in*; in; see **In.** Brugm. i. § 466.

Interjacent. (L.) From pres. pt. of L. *interiacēre,* to lie between. – L. *inter,* between; *iacēre,* to lie. See **Jet** (1).

interjection. (F. – L.) F. *interjec-tion,* an interjection, a word *thrown in* to express emotion. – L. acc. *interiectiōnem,* a throwing between, insertion, interjection. – L. *interiectus,* pp. of L. *intericere,* to cast between; (*-icere = iacere,* to cast).

Interloper, an intruder. (Du. – F. – L. and Du.) Low G. and Du. *enterloper* (Brem. Wört.). Lit. 'a runner between;' coined from F. *entre* (< L. *inter*), between; and Du. *looper,* a runner, from *loopen,* to run, cognate with E. *leap*; see **Leap.**

Intermit, to interrupt, cease awhile. (L.) L. *intermittere,* to send apart, interrupt; pp. *intermissus.* – L. *inter,* between; *mittere,* to send. See **Missile. Der.** *in-termiss-ion,* F. *intermission,* L. acc. *in-termissiōnem*; from the pp.

Intern, to confine within limits. (F. –

L.) F. *interner.* – F. *interne,* internal, kept within. – L. *internus,* inward; from *inter,* within, and suffix *-nus.* See **Inter-.**

internal. (L.) Cf. O. F. *internel.* From L. *intern-us* (above); with suffix *-al* (L.-*ālis*).

Internecine, thoroughly destructive. (L.) L. *internecīnus,* thoroughly destructive. – L. *internecio,* utter slaughter. – L. *inter,* thoroughly (see Lewis); and *necāre,* to kill, from *nec-,* stem of *nex,* death. Cf. Gk. νέκυς, a corpse. Brugm. i. § 375.

Interpellation. (F. – L.) F. *inter-pellation.* – L. acc. *interpellātiōnem.* – L. *interpellātus,* pp. of *interpellāre,* to drive between, to hinder, interrupt. – L. *inter,* between; *pellere,* to drive. See **Pulsate.**

Interpolate. (L.) From pp. of L. *interpolāre,* to furbish up, patch, interpolate. – L. *interpolus, interpolis,* polished up. – L. *inter,* in, between; *polīre,* to polish. See **Polish.**

Interpose. (F. – L. and Gk.) F. *in-terposer,* to put between. – L. *inter,* between; F. *poser,* to put; see **Pose** (1).

Interposition. (F. – L.) F. *inter-position.* – L. acc. *interpositiōnem,* a putting between. – L. *interpositus,* pp. of *interpō-nere,* to put between. – L. *inter,* between; *pōnere,* to put. See **Position.**

Interpret, to explain. (F. – L.) M. E. *interpreten.* – M. F. *interpreter.* – L. *inter-pretārī,* to expound. – L. *interpret-,* stem of *interprēs,* an interpreter, properly an agent, broker. The latter part of the word is perhaps allied to L. *pret-ium,* price; see **Price.**

Interregnum. (L.) From L. *inter,* between; *regnum,* a reign, rule, from *regere,* to rule. See **Regent.**

Interrogate. (L.) From pp. of L. *interrogāre,* to question. – L. *inter,* thoroughly; *rogāre,* to ask. See **Roga-tion.**

Interruption. (F. – L.) F. *interrup-tion.* – L. acc. *interruptiōnem,* a breaking into. – L. *interruptus,* pp. of *interrumpere,* to break into. – L. *inter,* amongst; *rumpere,* to break. See **Rupture.**

Intersect. (L.) From L. *intersectus,* pp. of *intersecāre,* to cut between or apart. – L. *inter,* between; *secāre,* to cut. See **Secant.**

Intersperse. (L.) From L. *inter-spersus,* pp. of *interspergere,* to sprinkle amongst. – L. *inter,* among; *spargere,* to scatter. See **Sparse.**

Interstice. (F.–L.) F. *interstice.*– L. *interstitium,* an interval of space.–L. *inter,* between; *stătus,* pp. of *sistere,* to place, from *stāre,* to stand. See **State.**

Interval. (F.–L.) M.F. *intervalle,* interval.–L. *interuallum,* lit. the space between the rampart of a camp and the soldiers' tents.–L. *inter,* between; *uallum,* rampart. See **Wall.**

Intervene, to come between. (F.–L.) F. *intervenir;* Cot. – L. *interuenīre,* to come between.–L. *inter,* between; *uenīre,* to come. See **Venture.**

Intestate, without a will. (F.–L.) M.F. *intestat.*–L. *intestātus,* that has made no will.–L. *in-,* not; *testātus,* pp. of *testārī,* to make a will. See **Testament.**

Intestine. (F.–L.) F. *intestin,* adj., 'intestine, inward;' Cot.–L. *intestīnus,* inward. Formed from L. *intus,* within, cognate with Gk. ἐντός, within; extended from L. *in,* in. Cf. **Entrails.**

Intimate (1), to announce, hint. (L.) From pp. of L. *intimāre,* to bring within, to announce.–L. *intimus,* inmost, superl. corresponding to comp. *interior;* see **Interior.**

intimate (2), familiar. (L.) This form is due to confusion with the word above. It is really founded on M.F. *intime,* inward, 'secret, deer, entirely affected;' Cot.; from L. *intimus* (above).

Intimidate. (L.) From pp. of Late L. *intimidāre,* to frighten. – L. *in,* intensive prefix; *timidus,* timid. See **Timid.**

Into, prep. (E.) M.E. *into;* orig. two words. A.S. *in tō,* in to, where *in* is used adverbially, and *tō* is a preposition; see **In** and **To.**

Intone, to chant. (Late L.–L. *and* Gk.) Late L. *intonāre,* to sing according to tone.–L. *in tonum,* according to tone; where *tonum* is acc. of *tonus,* borrowed from Gk. τόνος; see **Tone.**

Intoxicate. (Late L.–L. *and* Gk.) From pp. of Late L. *intoxicāre,* to make drunk.–L. *in,* into; *toxicum,* poison, borrowed from Gk. τοξικόν, poison for arrows. Gk. τοξικόν is der. from τόξον, a bow, of which the pl. τόξα is used to mean arrows. With Gk. τόξον cf. Gk. τέχ-νη, art, or perhaps L. *taxus,* a yew-tree. See **Technical.**

Intrepid. (L.) L. *intrepidus,* fearless, not alarmed.–L. *in-,* not; *trepidus,* alarmed. See **Trepidation.**

Intricate, perplexed, obscure. (L.) From the pp. of L. *intrīcāre,* to perplex. – L. *in,* in; *trīcæ,* pl. sb., hindrances, vexations, wiles. See **Extricate.**

intrigue, to form secret plots. (F.– Ital.–L.) F. *intriguer,* (also M.F. *intriquer,* 'to intricate, perplex, insnare;' Cot.).–Ital. *intrigare* (also *intricare*), ' to intricate, entrap;' Florio.–L. *intrīcāre* (above).

Intrinsic, inherent. (F.–L.) For **intrinsec.* M.F. *intrinseque,* 'inward;' Cot.–L. *intrinsecus,* lit. 'following inwards.'– L. **intrim,* allied to *intrā,* within (cf. *interim*); *sec-us,* lit. following, from *sequī,* to follow. See **Sequence.**

Intro-, *prefix,* within. (L.) L. *intrō;* an adv. closely allied to L. *intrā;* from *interus,* inner. See **Interior.**

Introduce. (L.) L. *intrōdūcere,* to bring in.–L. *intrō,* within; *dūcere,* to bring. See **Duke.** Der. *introduct-ion* (from the pp. *introduct-us*).

Introit, an antiphon sung as the priest approaches the altar. (F.–L.) F. *introït.* –L. acc. *introitum,* from *introitus,* lit. 'entrance.'–L. *introitus,* pp. of *introīre,* to enter. – L. *intrō,* within; *īre,* to go.

Introspection. (L.) Coined from L. *introspect-us,* pp. of *introspicere,* to look into (with suffix *-ion*).–L. *intrō-,* within; *specere,* to look. See **Species.**

Intrude, to thrust oneself into. (L.) L. *intrūdere,* to thrust into.–L. *in,* in, into; *trūdere* (pp. *trūsus*), to thrust. Allied to **Threaten.** Der. *intrus-ion,* from the pp.

Intuition. (F.–L.) F. *intuition.* Formed, by analogy with *tuition,* from L. *intuitus,* pp. of *intuērī,* to look upon. –L. *in,* upon; *tuērī,* to watch. See **Tuition.**

Intumescence, a swelling. (F.–L.) F. *intumescence.* From stem of pres. pt. of L. *intumescere,* to begin to swell.– L. *in,* very; *tumescere,* inceptive form of *tumēre,* to swell. See **Tumid.**

Inundation. (F.–L.) Imitated from F. *inondation.*–L. *inundātiōnem,* acc. of *inundātio,* an overflowing.–L. *inundāre,* to overflow.–L. *in,* upon, over; *unda,* a wave. See **Undulate.**

Inure, to habituate. (F.–L.) Also spelt *enure,* i. e. *en ure;* the word arose from the phrase *in* (F. *en*) *ure,* i. e. in operation, in work, in employment, formerly common. Here *in* is the E. prep. *in*; *ure* is from O. F. *eure*, also spelt *uevre*, *ovre*, work, action; from L. *opera*, work. (Cf. *man-ure* = *man-œuvre*.) See also *manure*, *manœuvre*. See **Operate**.

Invade. (F.–L.) M. F. *invader*.– L. *inuādere* (pp. *inuāsus*), to enter, invade.–L. *in*, in; *uādere*, to go. Der. *invas-ion*, from the pp.

Invecked, Invected, in heraldry, indented with successive cusps, with the points projecting inwards. (L.) Lit. 'carried in.'–L. *inuectus*, pp. of *inuehere*, to carry inwards.–L. *in*, in; *uehere*, to carry. See **Vehicle**.

Inveigh, to attack with words, rail. (F.–L.) From F. *envahir*, O.F. *envaïr*, *enveïr*, to invade, from L. *inuādere* (see **Invade**); but popularly connected with L. *inuehere*, to carry into or to, to introduce, attack, inveigh against.–L. *in*, against; *uehere*, to bring. β. The latter etymology was suggested by the use of E. *invective*, borrowed from F. *invective*, 'an invective;' Cot.; from L. *inuectīuus*, adj., scolding, due to *inuectus*, pp. of *inuehere*. Hence Cot. has '*invectiver*, to inveigh.'

Inveigle. (F.–L.) In Spenser, F. Q. i. 12. 32. [Indirectly from F. *aveugler*, to blind; cf. E. *aveugle*, to cajole, seduce, A.D. 1547, in Froude's Hist. v. 132; and A.D. 1543, State Papers, ix. 287.] It precisely answers to Anglo-F. *enveoglir*, to blind, in Will. of Wadington's Manuel des Peches, l. 10639; spelt also *enveogler* in N. Bozon. These are mere (ignorant) variants of F. *aveugler*, to blind (like *imposthume* for *apostume*), from F. *aveugle* (A. F. *enveogles* in Bozon), blind.–Late L. **aboculum*, acc. of **aboculus*, blind (Ducange has *avoculus*, also *aboculis*, adj.). –L. *ab*, without; *oculus*, eye. ¶ Baret (1580) has: '*inveigle* ones minde, *occæcare animum*.'

Invent. (F.–L.) F. *inventer*, to devise. Formed, with suffix *-er* (L. *-āre*), from L. *inuent-us*, pp. of *inuenīre*, to come upon, find out.–L. *in*, upon; *uenire*, to come. See **Venture**. Der. *invent-ion*, &c.

Inverse, opposite. (F.–L.) M. E. *invers*.–M. F. *invers*.–L. *inuersus*, pp. of *inuertere* (below).

invert. (L.) L. *inuertere*, to turn towards or up, to invert.–L. *in*, towards; *uertere*, to turn. See **Verse**.

Invest. (F.–L.) F. *investir*.–L.

inuestīre, to clothe in or with.–L. *in*, in; *uestīre*, to clothe. See **Vest**.

Investigate. (L.) From pp. of L. *inuestīgāre*, to track out.–L. *in*, in, upon; *uestigare*, to trace, allied to *uestīgium*, a foot-track. See **Vestige**.

Inveterate. (L.) L. *inueterātus*, pp. of *inueterāre*, to retain for a long time.– L. *in*, in; *ueter-*, for **uetes-*, stem of *uetus*, old. See **Veteran**.

Invidious. (L.) From L. *inuidiōsus*, causing odium or envy.–L. *inuidia*, envy. –L. *inuidēre*, to envy, lit. to look upon (in a bad sense).–L. *in*, upon; *uidēre*, to look. See **Vision**.

Invigorate, to give vigour to. (L.) As if from pp. of Late L. **inuigorāre*, to give vigour to.–L. *in*, towards; *uigor*, vigour; see **Vigour**. Cf. Ital. *invigorire*.

Invincible. (F.–L.) F. *invincible*. –L. *inuincibilis*.–L. *in-*, not; *uincibilis*, easily overcome, from *uincere*, to conquer; see **Vanquish**.

Invite. (F.–L.) F. *inviter*. – L. *inuītāre*, to ask, request, invite. Allied to **uītus*, willing, in *in-uītus*, unwilling. Brugm. i. § 343. Doublet, *vie*, q. v.

Invocation. (F.–L.) F. *invocation*. –L. *inuocātiōnem*, acc. of *inuocātio*, a calling upon.–L. *inuocātus*, pp. of *inuocāre*, to call upon.–L. *in*, upon; *uocāre*, to call. See **Vocation**.

invoke. (F.–L.) F. *invoquer*.–L. *inuocāre*, to call upon (above).

Invoice, a particular account of goods sent out. (F.–L.) A corruption of *envois*, pl. of F. *envoi*, O. F. *envoy*, a sending; see **Envoy**. Cf. E. *voice*, from O. F. *vois*.

Involve. (F.–L.) F. *involver*, 'to involve;' Cot.–L. *inuoluere*, to roll in, roll up.–L. *in*, in; *uoluere*, to roll. See **Voluble**. Der. *involut-ion*, *involute*, from the pp. *inuolūtus*; also *involucre*, from L. *inuolūcrum*, an envelope.

Iodine, an elementary body. (Gk.) Named from the violet colour of its vapour. [Cf. F. *iode*, iodine.]–Gk. ἰώδης, contr. form of ἰοειδής, violet-like; with suffix *-ine*. – Gk. ἴο-ν, a violet; εἶδ-ος, appearance. See **Violet**.

Iota. (Gk. – Heb.) Gk. ἰῶτα, a letter of the Gk. alphabet. – Heb. *yōd*, the smallest letter of the Heb. alphabet, with the power of *y*. (Of Phœnician origin.) See **Jot**.

Ipecacuanha, a medical root. (Port. – Brazilian.) Port. *ipecacuanha* (Span.

ipecacuana). From the Brazilian name of the plant; Guarani *ipé-kaa-guaña*. *Ipé* = *peb*, small; *kaa*, plant; *guaña*, causing sickness.

Ir- (1), *prefix*. (L.; *or* F.—L.) For L. *in*, in, prep., when *r* follows.

Ir- (2), *prefix*. (L.; *or* F.—L.) For L. neg. prefix *in-*, when *r* follows.

Ire. (F.—L.) F. *ire.* — L. *īra*, anger.

irascible. (F.—L.) F. *irascible.* — L. *īrascibilis*, choleric; from *īrascī*, to become angry; with suffix *-bilis.* — L. *īra*, anger.

Iris, a rainbow. (L.—Gk.) L. *īris.* — Gk. ἶρις, a rainbow. **Der.** *irid-esc-ent*, *irid-ium*; from *īrid-*, stem of *īris*. And see **Orris.**

Irk, to weary. (E.) M. E. *irken, erken,* to tire; also *irk, erk,* adj. weary. A back formation from M. E. **irkth*, for **irgth,* later form of A. S. sb. *iergþ,* sluggishness; from *earg,* sluggish.

Iron, a metal. (E.) M. E. *iren,* also *ire.* A. S. *īren,* older forms *īsern, īsaern,* adj. and sb. + Du. *ijzer*; O. Icel. *īsarn*; O. H. G. *īsarn,* G. *eisen*; Goth. *eisarn,* sb. (whence *eisarneins,* adj.). And cf. W. *haiarn,* Corn. *hoern,* Irish *iarann,* O. Ir. *iarn,* Bret. *houarn,* iron. β. The Celtic forms answer to an O. Celt. form **īsarno-* (**eisarno-*, Stokes, in Fick, ii. 25); from which the Germanic forms may have been borrowed. At any rate, Icel. *járn* and Dan. Swed. *jern* are from O. Ir. *iarn.* Remoter origin unknown.

ironmonger, a dealer in iron goods. (E.) From *iron* and *monger*; see **Monger.**

iron-mould. (E.) See **Mould** (3).

Irony. (F. — L. — Gk.) F. *ironie* (Minsheu). — L. *īronīa.* — Gk. εἰρωνεία, dissimulation, irony. — Gk. εἴρων, a dissembler, one who says less then he thinks or means. Allied to Ionic εἴρομαι, Attic ἔρομαι, I ask, enquire, seek out (cf. ἐρωτέω, Ion. for ἐρωτάω, I ask), ἔρευνα, enquiry, search (base **reu*; Prellwitz).

Irradiate. (L.) From pp. of L. *irradiāre,* to shine upon. — L. *ir-,* for *in,* on; *radiāre,* to shine, from *radius,* a ray. See **Radius.**

Irrefragable, not to be refuted. (F. — L. — Gk.) F. *irréfragable.* — L. *irrefrāgābilis,* not to be withstood. — L. *ir-* (= *in-*, not); *refrāgārī,* to oppose, thwart, from *re-,* back, and (probably) L. *frag-,* base of *frag-or,* a noise. (For the long *a,* cf. L. *suffrāgium,* prob. from the same root.)

Irrigate, to water. (L.) From pp. of L. *irrigāre,* to flood. — L. *in,* upon; *rigāre,* to wet, moisten.

Irritate. (L.) From pp. of L. *irrītāre,* to incite, excite, provoke, tease. App. related to *irrīre, hirrīre,* to snarl as a dog; which is prob. an imitative word.

Irruption. (F.—L.) F. *irruption,* ' a forcible entry;' Cot. — L. acc. *irruptiōnem,* a breaking into. — L. *ir-* (for *in*), into; *rupt-us,* pp. of *rumpere,* to break. See **Rupture.**

Is. A. S. *is*; from √ES, to be. The general Idg. form is ES-TI, as in Skt. *as-ti,* Gk. ἐσ-τί, L. *es-t,* G. *is-t*; also O. Icel. *es,* E. *is.* See also **Be, Was.**

Isinglass, a glutinous substance made from a fish. (Du.) A corruption of M. Du. *huyzenblas* (mod. Du. *huisblad*), isinglass, lit. ' sturgeon-bladder,' whence isinglass is obtained; see Sewel. — M. Du. *huys,* sturgeon; *blaese,* bladder (Kilian). Cf. G. *hausenblase,* sturgeon-bladder, isinglass; from G. *hausen,* a sturgeon, *blase,* a bladder, from *blasen,* to blow. Cf. O. H. G. *hūso,* a sturgeon.

Islam, the religious system of Muhammed. (Arab.) Arab. *islām,* lit. ' submission.' — Arab. root *salama,* he was resigned. See **Moslem.**

Island. (E.) The *s* is inserted by confusion with F. *isle.* M. E. *iland.* A. S. *īgland.* — A. S. *īg,* an island; *land,* land; perhaps by confusion of A. S. *īg,* island, with A.S. *ēa-land,* island, lit. ' water-land.' The A. S. *īg* is also *īeg,* O. Merc. *ēg* (cf. *Angles-ey*); cognate with Icel. *ey,* Dan. Swed. *ö,* island; G. *aue,* meadow near water. The orig. Teut. form was **agwiā,* fem. of **agwioz,* belonging to water, an adj. formed from **ahwa,* water, represented by A. S. *ēa,* O. H. G. *aha,* Goth. *ahwa,* a stream, cognate with L. *aqua,* water.

Isle, an island. (F. - L.) O. F. *isle* (F. *île*). — L. *insula,* an island. See **Insular.**

Isochronous, performed in equal times. (Gk.) Gk. ἴσο-s, equal; χρόνος, time (see **Chronicle**). Brugm. i. § 345 c.

isosceles, having two equal legs or sides as a triangle. (L. — Gk.) L. *isosceles.* — Gk. ἰσοσκελής, isosceles. — Gk. ἴσο-s, equal; σκέλ-ος, a leg, side of a triangle.

Isolate, to insulate. (Ital. — L.) Suggested by Ital. *isolato,* detached, used as a term in architecture (whence also F.

isolé). — Ital. *isola*, an island. — L. *insula*, an island. See **Insular.**

Issue, progeny, result. (F. — L.) M. E. *issue*, sb. — F. *issue*, O. F. *issuë* (*eissuë*), 'the issue, end, event;' Cot. Fem. of *issu*, pp. of *issir*, to depart, go out. — L. *exīre*, to go out. — L. *ex*, out; *īre*, to go.

Isthmus, a neck of land connecting a peninsula with the mainland. (L. — Gk.) L. *isthmus*. — Gk. ἰσθμός, a narrow passage; allied to ἴθμα, a step. (√EI, to go.)

It. (E.) M. E. *hit*. A. S. *hit*, neut. of *hē*, he.+Icel. *hit*, neut. of *hinn*; Du. *het*, neut. of *hij*; Goth. *hita*. The old gen. case was *his*, afterwards *it*, and finally *its* (XVII cent.). See **He.**

Italics, a name for letters printed thus — *in sloping type*. (L.) Named from Aldo Manuzio, an *Italian*, about A. D. 1501. — L. *Italicus*. — L. *Italia*, Italy.

Itch. (E.) North E. *yuke*. M. E. *iken, icchen*, fuller form *ʒiken, ʒichen*. A. S. *giccan*, to itch, for *gyccan; cf. A. S. *gyhða*, an itching.+E. Fries. *jöken*, Du. *jeuken*, G. *jucken*, to itch; O. H. G. *jucchan*. Teut. type **jukjan-*.

Item, a separate article or particular. (L.) L. *item*, likewise; in common use for enumerating particulars; closely allied to *ita*, so. Cf. Skt. *ittham*, thus, *iti*, thus.

iterate, to repeat. (L.) From pp. of L. *iterāre*, to repeat. — L. *iterum*, again; a compar. form (with suffix *-ter*) from the pronominal base I, as in *i-tem, i-ta*. Cf. Skt. *i-tara*(*s*), another.

Itinerant, travelling. (L.) From pres. part. of O. Lat. *itinerāre*, to travel. — L. *itiner-*, stem of *iter*, a journey. — L. *it-um*, supine of *īre*, to go. (√EI, to go.)

Ivory. (F. — L.) M. E. *iuorie* (= *ivorie*). — O. F. *ivurie*, later *ivoire*. — L. *eboreus*, adj., made of ivory. — L. *ebor-*, stem of *ebur*, ivory. Perhaps allied to Skt. *ibha-*, an elephant.

Ivy, an evergreen. (E.) A. S. *ifig*; also *ifegn*. + O. H. G. *ebahewi* (G. *epheu*); Kluge. The A. S. *if-ig* seems to be a compound word. The syllable *if-* is equivalent to Du. *ei-* in *ei-loof*, ivy (where *loof* = E. *leaf*); and to *eba*(*h*)- in O. H. G. *ebah-*; but the sense is unknown.

Iwis, certainly. (E.) M. E. *ywis, iwis*. A. S. *gewis*, adj., certain (whence *gewislīce*, adv., certainly).+Du. *gewis*, adj. and adv.; G. *gewiss*, adv. Cf. Icel. *viss*, certain, sure. From Teut. type *wissoz (for *wit-toz, Idg. *wid-tos), pp. from the base *wit-*

in *wit-an*, to know; see **Wit.** (√WEID.) ¶ The M. E. prefix *i-* (A. S. *ge-*) is sometimes written apart from the rest of the word, and with a capital letter. Hence, by the mistake of editors, it has been printed *I wis*, and explained as 'I know.' This is the origin of the fictitious word *wis*, to know, given in some dictionaries.

J.

Jabber, to chatter. (F. ?) Formerly *jaber* and *jable*, of imitative origin; similar to *gabber* and *gabble*. Godefroy gives O. F. *jaber* as a variant of *gaber*, to mock. Cf. Du. *gabberen*, to jabber; Sewel. See **Gabble.**

Jacinth, a precious stone. (F. — L. — Gk.) F. *jacinthe*. — L. *hyacinthus*, a jacinth. — Gk. ὑάκινθος, a jacinth; Rev. xxi. 20. See **Hyacinth.**

Jack (1), a saucy fellow, sailor. (F. — L. — Gk. — Heb.) M. E. *Jacke, Jakke*, often used as a term of reproach, as in '*Jakke* fool,' Chaucer, C. T. 3708. Generally used formerly (as now) as a pet substitute for *John*, and perhaps due to the dimin. form *Jankin. John* is from A. F. *Johan*. — L. *Iohannes*. — Gk. Ἰωάννης. — Heb. *Yehōkhanān, Yōkhānān*, lit. 'God is gracious.' β. Apparently confused with F. *Jacques*, a common name in France. *Jaques* is from L. *Iacōbus*. — Gk. Ἰάκωβος. — Heb. *Yaʿaqōb*, Jacob; lit. one who seizes by the heel. — Heb. root ʾáqab, to seize by the heel, supplant. ¶ The name was extended to denote various implements, such as a *smoke-jack*, a *boot-jack*; so also *Jack-o'-lent, Jack-o'-lantern, Jack-pudding, Jack-an-apes* (= *Jack on apes*, with *on* — *of*).

jack (2), a coat of mail. (F. — L. — Gk. — Heb.) O. F. *Jaque*, 'James, also a Jack, or coat of maile;' Cot. Cf. Ital. *giaco*, a coat of mail, Span. *jaco*, a soldier's jacket, G. *jacke*, a jacket. Of obscure origin; but prob. due to the *Jacquerie*, or revolt of the peasantry nicknamed *Jacques Bonhommes*, A. D. 1358; and hence due to F. *Jaques*, James; see above.

Jackal, a kind of wild animal. (Turk. — Pers.) Turk. *chakāl*. — Pers. *shaghāl*. Cf. Skt. *çrgāla-*, a jackal, a fox.

Jackanapes. For *Jack on apes*, i. e. Jack of apes. See **Jack** (1).

Jacket, a short coat. (F. — L. — Gk. — Heb.) O. F. *jaquette*, a jacket; dimin. of O. F. *jaque*, a jack of mail; see **jack** (2).

jacobin. (F. – L. – Gk. – Heb.) M.E. *jacobin.* – F. *jacobin.* – Late Lat. *Jacōbīnus,* adj., formed from *Iacōbus,* and applied to a friar of the order of St. Dominick. See **Jack** (1). β. Hence one of the *Jacobin* club in the French Revolution, which first met in the hall of the *Jacobin* friars in Paris, Oct. 1789. Also the name of a hooded (friar-like) pigeon.

jacobite, an adherent of James II. (L. – Gk. – Heb.) From L. *Iacōb-us,* James (above).

Jade (1), a sorry nag, an old woman. (Scand.) M. E. *iade* (Ch.) The initial *j* is perhaps from *y*. Cf. Lowland Sc. *yaud, yawd,* a jade; Dunbar has *yald.* Of Scand. origin; borrowed from Icel. *jalda,* a mare; prov. Swed. *jäldä,* a mare (Rietz).

Jade (2), a hard dark-green stone. F. – Span. – L.) F. *jade.* The jade brought from America by the Spaniards was called *piedra de ijada,* because it was believed to cure pain in the side; for a similar reason it was called *nephritis* (from Gk. νεφρός, kidneys). – Span. *ijada,* also *ijar,* the flank; cf. Port. *ilhal, ilharga,* the flank, side. – L. *īlia,* pl., the flanks.

Jag, a notch, tooth. (Scand.) Hardly a variant of *dag.* 'Iagge, or dagge of a garment;' Palsg. 'I *iagge,* or cut a garment;' ib. From Norw. *jak,* a notch; *jaka,* to notch (Ross).

Jaggery, a coarse brown sugar. (Canarese – Skt.) A corruption of Canarese *sharkare,* unrefined sugar; H. H. Wilson. – Skt. *çarkarā;* see **Sugar.**

Jaguar, a beast of prey. (F. – Brazil.) '*Jagua* in the Guarani [Brazilian] language is the common name for tygers and dogs; the generic name for tygers is *jaquarete;*' Clavigero, Hist. of Mexico, tr. by Cullen, ii. 318. It should be written *yagoar;* for there is no *j* in Tupi-Guarani (Cavalcanti). The spelling *jaguar* is F. (in Buffon). The Dict. of Trévoux has *janouare* (error for *jauouare);* for Brazil. *yāuāra,* a dog. Spelt *jaguara,* Hist. Nat. Brasiliæ, p. 235.

Jail; see **Gaol.**

Jalap, the root of a plant. (Mexican.) Named from *Jalapa* or *Xalapa,* in Mexico. Orig. *Xalapan,* 'sand by the water.' – Mex. *xal(li),* sand; *a(tl),* water; *pan,* on, near; where *-li, -tl* are suppressed.

Jam (1), to press, squeeze. (E.) Prob. a variant of *cham,* to chew, to champ;

prov. E. *champ,* to mash, crush, also to chew; so also *champ,* hard, firm, i. e. *chammed* or pressed down. See **Champ.** ¶ But Ashe (1775) has : '*Jamb,* to confine as between two posts;' as if from **Jamb** q. v.

jam (2), a conserve of fruit. (E.) A soft substance, like that which is chewed. 'And if we have anye stronger meate, it must be *chammed* afore by the nurse, and so put into the babes mouthe;' Sir T. More, Works, p. 241 *h.* See above.

Jamb, side-post of a door. (F. – L.) F. *jambe,* a leg, also a jamb (see Cotgrave). – Folk-L. *gamba,* a leg. See **Gambol.** Der. (perhaps) *jamb,* vb. ; see **Jam** (1).

Jane, Jean, a twilled cloth. (F. – Ital.) Also '*gene* fustian,' 1580 ; cf. M. E. *Gene,* Genoa. – M. F. *Genes.* – Ital. *Genova,* Genoa.

Jangle, to sound discordantly. (F. – Scand.) M. E. *janglen.* – O. F. *jangler,* to jangle, prattle. Of Scand. origin. – Swed. dial. and Norw. *jangla,* to quarrel; cf. Du. *jangelen,* to importune, frequent. of *janken,* to howl, yelp. An imitative word; cf. L. *gannire,* to yelp.

Janizary. (F. – Ital. – Turk.) F. *Janissaires,* 'the Janizaries;' Cot. – M. Ital. *ianizzeri,* 'the Turkes gard,' Florio. Of Turk. origin; it means 'new soldiery'; from Turk. *yeñi,* new ; and *cheri,* soldiery (Devic). And *cheri* is from Pers. *charīk,* auxiliary forces (Zenker).

January. (L.) Englished from L. *Iānuārius,* a month named from the god *Iānus,* who was supposed to have doors under his protection; cf. L. *iānua,* a door.

Japan, a name given to certain kinds of lacquered work. (Japan.) Named from the country. Der. *japan,* vb., to polish.

Jape, to mock, jest, befool. (F.) Obsolete. M. E. *japen.* Apparently from O. F. *japer* (F. *japper*), to yap (as a dog). Imitative ; cf. E. *yap.*

Jar (1), to make a harsh noise. (E.) Imitative; cf. M. E. *garren,* to chide, M. E. *ʒirren,* A. S. *georran,* to creak ; Du. *gieren,* to cry ; Bavar. *garren,* to jar. Parallel to prov. E. *char,* to chide, M. E. *charken,* to creak (Prompt. Parv.) ; cf. A. S. *ceorian, cerian,* to murmur ; M. Du. *karren, kerren,* 'to crake [creak] like a cart,' Hexham ; O. H. G. *kerran,* to give a loud harsh sound. Cf. **Jargon** and **Garrulous.**

Jar (2), an earthen pot. (F. – Arab.)

M. F. *jare*, ' a jarre,' Cot.; F. *jarre*. [Cf. Span. *jarra, jarro*, Ital. *giara*.] — Arab. *jarra*, a jar (Devic).

Jargon, a confused talk. (F. — L.?) F. *jargon*, orig. the chattering of birds, jargon; O. F. *gargon, gergon*. Cf. Span. *gerigonza*, jargon; Ital. *gergone*. Prob. from an imitative base *garg* (cf. *garg-le, gurg-le*); cf. L. *garrīre*, to prate, croak. Cf. M. E. *charken*, to creak. See **Jar** (1).

Jargonelle, a kind of pear. (F. — Ital. — Pers.?) F. *jargonelle*, a kind of pear, very stony (Littré); formed (acc. to Littré) from F. *jargon*, a yellow diamond, small stone. — Ital. *giargone*, a sort of yellow diamond. Perhaps from Pers. *zargūn*, gold-coloured (Zend *zairi-gaona-*); from *zar*, gold, and *gūn*, colour (Devic).

Jasmine, Jessamine, a plant. (F. — Arab. — Pers.) F. *jasmin*. (So also Span. *jazmin*.) — Arab. *yāsemīn* (Devic). — Pers. *yāsmīn*, jasmine; *yāsamīn*, jessamine.

Jasper, a precious stone. (F. — L. — Gk. — Arab.) O. F. *jaspre* (Littré), an occasional spelling of *jaspe*, a jasper. — L. *iaspidem*, acc. of *iaspis*. — Gk. ἴασπις. — Arab. *yasb, yasf, yashb*, jasper; whence Pers. *yashp, yashf*, jasper. Cf. Heb. *yāshpheh*, a jasper.

Jaundice. (F. — L.) M. E. *iaunis*; the *d* being excrescent. — F. *jaunisse*, yellowness; hence, the jaundice. — F. *jaune* (oldest spelling *jalne*), yellow. — L. *galbinus*, greenish yellow. — L. *galbus*, yellow; (perhaps of Teut. origin; cf. G. *gelb*, yellow).

Jaunt, a ramble. (F.) From *jaunts*, pl., for *jaunce*, ' toil.' Cf. M. F. *jancer un cheval*, ' to stirre a horse in the stable till he swart [sweat] withall; or (as our) to jaunt (an old word); ' Cot.

Jaunty, Janty, fantastical. (F. — L.) Also *janty, jantee*, variants of *jantyl*, old spelling of *gentle* or *genteel*. Cf. Burgundy *jantais*, ' gentil ; ' Mignard.

Javelin. (F. — C.?) M. F. *javelin*, ' a javeling,' Cot.; allied to *javelot*, ' a gleave, dart,' id. Perhaps Celtic. Cf. O. Irish *gabul*, a fork; *gablach*, pointed, Irish *gabhla*, a spear, *gabhlan*, a fork of a tree; Gael. *gobhlan*, a prong; W. *gafl*, a fork, *gaflach*, a dart. See **Gaff**.

Jaw. (F. — L.) M. E. *iowe* (*jowe*). — O. F. (and F.) *joue*, ' the cheek, the jowle;' Cot. (Cf. Prov. *gauta*, Ital. *gota*, cheek, jaw.) — Late L. *gabata, gavata*, a bowl; from the rounding of the jaw. (Diez,

Körting.) ¶ Perhaps influenced by *chaw, chew*; Palsgrave has *chawe-bone* for *jaw-bone*.

Jay, a bird. (F.) O. F. *jay*, a jay (F. *geai*). Cf. Span. *gayo*, a jay. Of doubtful origin; perhaps from O. H. G. *wāhi*, fine, beautiful, whence F. *gai*. See **Gay**.

Jealous. (F. — L. — Gk.) M. E. *jalous, gelus*. — O. F. *jalous* (later *jaloux*). — Late L. *zēlōsus*, full of zeal. — L. *zēlus*, zeal. — Gk. ζῆλος, zeal. See **Zeal**. Der. *jealous-y*, F. *jalousie*.

Jeer. (Du.) Doubtful; perhaps from M. Du. phrase *den gek scheeren*, lit. to shear the fool, hence to jeer at one ; whence the word *gekscheeren*, or simply *scheeren*, to jeer. Now spelt *scheren*. Cf. G. *scheren*, ' to shear, fleece, cheat, plague, tease;' Flügel; E. Fries. *scheren*, the same.

Jehovah. (Heb.) Heb. *yahōvāh*, or, more correctly, *yahweh*, a proper name, rendered in the A.V. by ' the Lord.'

Jejune, hungry, meagre. (L.) L. *iēiūnus*, fasting, hungry, dry.

Jelly. (F. — L.) Formerly *gelly*. — F. *gelée*, ' gelly ; ' Cot. Orig. fem. of pp. of *geler*, to freeze. — L. *gelāre*, to freeze. See **Gelid**.

Jennet, Gennet, a small Spanish horse. (F. — Span. — Arab.) M. F. *genette*, ' a genet, or Spanish horse ;' Cot. — Span. *ginete*, a nag; but orig. ' a horse-soldier.' Of Moorish origin; traced by Dozy to Arab. *zenāta*, a tribe of Barbary celebrated for its cavalry.

Jenneting, a kind of early apple. (F. — L. — Gk. — Heb.) Prob. for *jeanneton*; a dimin. from F. *pomme de S. Jean*, an early apple, called in Italian *melo de San Giovanni*, i. e. St. John's apple. So called because, in France and Italy, it ripened about June 24, St. John's day. So also, there is an early pear, called *Amiré Joannet* or *Jeanette*, or *petit St. Jean*; G. *Johannisbirne*. F. *Jean* < Lat. acc. *Iohannem*; from Gk. Ἰωάννης, John. — Heb. *Yōkhānān*, the Lord is gracious.

Jeopardy, hazard. (F. — L.) M. E. *jupartie*, later *jopardye, jeopardie*. — O. F. *jeu parti*, lit. a divided game ; a game in which the chances were equal, hence, a risk, hazard. — Late L. *iocus partītus*, the same; also an alternative. — L. *iocus*, a game ; *partītus*, pp. of *partīrī*, to part, divide, from *parti-*, decl. stem of *pars*, a part. ¶ The diphthong *eo* = F. *eu*; cf. *people* (= F. *peuple*). See **Joke**.

Jerboa, a rodent quadruped. (Arab.) Arab. *yarbū'*, (1) the flesh of the back or loins, an oblique descending muscle; (2) the jerboa, from the use it makes of the strong muscles in its hind legs, in taking long leaps.

Jereed, a wooden javelin used in mock fights. (Arab.) Arab. *jarīd*, a palm-branch stripped of its leaves, a lance.

Jerk. (E.) We find *jerk, jert,* and *yerk* all used in much the same sense, orig. to strike with a lash, whip or rod. Of these, *jert* was regarded as equivalent to *gird* (Index to Cot.); see **Gird** (2).

Jerked beef. (Peruvian.) A singular corruption of *ccharqui,* the S. American name for 'jerked' beef, or beef dried in a particular way; see Prescott, Conquest of Peru, ch. v. From Peruv. *ccharqui,* a slice of dried beef. Also called *jerkin beef*; from Peruv. *ccharquini,* vb., to make dried beef.

Jerkin, a jacket, short coat. (Du.) Dimin. of Du. *jurk,* a frock (Sewel), by help of the once common Du. dimin. suffix *-ken,* now supplanted by *-je* or *-tje.* Cf. Westphal. *jürken,* a sort of overcoat; E. Fries. *jurken,* a child's frock. Cf. *fir-kin, kilder-kin.*

Jersey, fine wool, a woollen jacket. (Jersey.) From *Jersey,* one of the Channel Islands.

Jessamine; see **Jasmine.**

Jesses, straps round a hawk's legs. (F. – L.) Double pl.; from M. E. *ges, jesses.* – O. F. *ges, gies,* pl. of *get, giet,* a short thong, for throwing off the hawk; orig. 'a cast.' Cf. M. F. *ject,* a cast; *les jects d'un oyseau,* 'a hawkes Iesses,' Cot. – O. F. *geter,* to .cast. – L. *iactāre,* to cast; see **Jet** (1).

Jest, a joke. (F. – L.) Orig. a story, merry tale. M. E. *geste,* a story. – O. F. *geste,* an exploit, romance, tale of exploits. – L. *gesta,* for *rēs gesta,* a thing done, an exploit. – L. *gestus,* pp. of *gerere,* to carry, carry on. See **Gesture, Gerund.**

Jesuit; see below.

Jesus, the Saviour. (L. – Gk. – Heb.) L. *Iēsus.* – Gk. Ἰησοῦς. – Heb. *Yēshū'a,* Jeshua (Nehem. viii. 17); contr. form of *Yehōshu'a,* Jehoshua (Numb. xiii. 16) signifying saviour, lit. 'help of Jehovah.' – Heb. root *yāsha',* to be large, to save. Der. *jesu-it,* one of the society of Jesus.

Jet (1), to throw out, fling about, spout. (F. – L.) Formerly, to *jet* was to strut

about. M. E. *ietten,* to strut. – O. F. *jetter, geter, getter,* to throw, fling, push forth. – L. *iactāre,* to fling; frequent. of *iacere,* to throw. Der. *jet,* sb., formerly in the sense of guise or fashion, &c.

Jet (2), a black mineral. (F. – L. – Gk.) O. F. *jet, jaet,* also *jayet, gaiete,* jet (F. *jais*). – L. *gagātem,* acc. of *gagātēs,* jet. – Gk. γαγάτης, jet; so called from Γάγαι, a town in Lycia, in the S. of Asia Minor.

Jetsam. (F. – L.) Also *jettison.* An old term in Law F. for things thrown overboard from a wrecked vessel. – A. F. *getteson,* a casting; O. F. *getaison.* – L. acc. *iactātiōnem.* – L. *iactāre,* to cast; see **Jet** (1).

jetty, a kind of pier. (F. – L.) M. F. *jettée* (F. *jetée*), a cast, throw, 'also a jetty or jutty;' Cot. Orig. fem. of pp. of M. F. *jetter* (F. *jeter*), to throw; see **Jet** (1).

Jew. (F. – L. – Gk. – Heb.) M. E. *Iewe,* a Jew. – A. F. *Ieu, Geu* (F. *juif*). – L. *Iūdæus,* a Jew. – Gk. Ἰουδαῖος, an inhabitant of Ἰουδαία, Judæa. – Heb. *Yehūdāh,* Judah, son of Jacob, lit. 'illustrious.' – Heb. root *yādāh,* to throw, praise, celebrate. Der. *Jew-ry,* M. E. *Iewerie,* O. F. *Iuerie,* lit. a Jews' district; also *Jews'-harp,* a name given in derision; cf. 'the harp of David.'

Jewel, a valuable ornament. (F. – L.) M. E. *iowel, iuel.* – O. F. *joel, joiel, jouel, juel* (later *joyau*). – Late L. *iocāle,* usually in pl. *iocālia,* jewels (lit. trinkets). – L. *iocārī,* to play (O. F. *joer, jouer*). – L. *iocus,* play. See **Joke.** (Toynbee, §§ 76, 143.)

Jib (1), the foremost sail in a ship. (Dan.) So called because easily shifted from side to side; see **jib** (2) below.

jib (2), to shift a sail from side to side. (Dan.) '*Jib,* to shift the boom-sail from one side of the mast to another;' Ash (1775). Also spelt *jibe, gybe.* – Dan. *gibbe,* to jibe, jib; Swed. dial. *gippa,* to jerk up. Allied to Swed. *guppa,* to rock; see **Jump.** ¶ The form *gibe* answers to Du. *gijpen,* E. Fries. *gīpen,* to turn suddenly, said of a sail.

jib (3), to move restively, as a horse. (F. – Scand.) O. F. *giber,* to struggle with the hands and feet (Roquefort); whence O. F. *regiber* (F. *regimber*), to kick as a horse. Cf. also O. F. *giper,* to jib, as a horse (Godefroy). – Swed. dial. *gippa,* to jerk up (above).

Jibe, the same as Gibe, q. v.

Jig, a lively tune or dance. (F. – M. H. G.) O. F. *gige, gigue,* a fiddle, dance. – M. H. G. *gīge* (G. *geige*), a fiddle.

Jilt, a flirt. (L.) Formerly *jillet,* dimin. of *jill,* a flirt, orig. *Jill* or *Gillian,* a personal name. – L. *Jūliāna.* See Gill (4).

Jingle, to clink. (E.) M. E. *ginglen*; a frequentative verb from the base *jink,* allied to *chink*; see Chink (2). Also allied to Jangle.

Jinn, a demon. (Arab.) Formed from Arab. *jinna*(*t*), demons, pl.; the sing. form being *jinnīy,* Englished as *jinnee* or *genie.*

Job (1), to peck with the beak. (E. ?) Perhaps imitative. M. E. *iobben.* Cf. Gael. and Irish *gob,* mouth, beak.

Job (2), a small piece of work. (F. ?) M. E. *iob,* a piece, lump. ' *Gob,* a lump ; also, to work by the *gob*;' Halliwell. – O. F. *gob,* a mouthful ; *gobet,* a morsel. Perhaps of Celtic origin. See Job (1).

Jockey. (F. – L. – Gk. – Heb.) A North E. pron. of *Jackey,* dimin. of *Jack* as a personal name. See Jack (1).

Jocose, merry. (L.) L. *iocōsus,* sportive. – L. *iocus,* sport. See Joke.

jocular. (L.) L. *ioculāris.* – L. *ioculus,* a little jest, dimin. of *iocus,* a jest.

Jocund. (F. – L.) M. E. *joconde.* – O. F. *jocond,* pleasant, agreeable (Godefroy). – L. *iōcundus, iūcundus,* pleasant ; orig. helpful. – L. *iuuare* (supine *iū-tum*), to help ; see Adjutant.

Jog, to push slightly, jolt. (F. – Teut. ?) M. E. *ioggen.* Cf. W. *ysgogi,* to wag, stir, shake, E. *shog,* M. E. *schoggen,* to shake up and down ; Kentish *jock,* to jolt. All apparently from M. E. *schokken*; see Shock. ¶ We also find Norw. and Swed. dial. *jukka,* to jump up and down, as in riding.

John Dory, the name of a fish. (F. – L.) *John dory* is the vulgar name of the fish called the *dory. John* appears to be a mere sailor's prefix, like the *jack* in *jackass*; it can hardly be from an alleged F. *jaune dorée,* which would be tautological nonsense. *Dory* is borrowed from F. *dorée,* a dory; lit. ' gilded,' *dorée* being the fem. of the pp. of *dorer,* to gild. – L. *dēaurāre,* to gild. – L. *dē aurō,* of gold ; see Aureate.

Join. (F. – L.) O. F. and F. *joign-,* a stem of *joindre.* – L. *iungere* (pp. *iunctus*), to join. + Gk. *ζευγνύναι* ; Skt. *yuj,* to join. Allied to Yoke.

joint. (F. – L.) O. F. *joinct, joint,* a

joint, sb. – O. F. *joinct, joint,* pp. of *joindre,* to join ; see Join (above).

Joist, one of a set of timbers to support the boards of a floor. (F. – L.) Sometimes pronounced *jist* (with *i* as in *mice*). M. E. *giste.* – O. F. *giste,* a bed, couch, place to lie on, a joist ; because these timbers support the floor. – O. F. *gesir* (F. *gésir*), to lie, lie on. – L. *iacēre,* to lie. Cf. Gist.

Joke, a jest. (L.) From L. *iocus,* a jest, game. Brugm. i. § 302.

Jole ; see Jowl.

Jolly. (F. – Scand.) M. E. *ioly,* earliest form *iolif.* – O. F. *jolif,* later *joli,* ' jolly, gay, trim, fine ;' Cot. Orig. sense ' festive.' – Icel. *jōl,* a great feast in the heathen time ; cognate with A. S. *geōla,* yule. See Yule.

Jolly-boat. (Port. *and* E.) We find ' grete bote and *jolywat*' in 1495 ; but it was also spelt *gallevat* and *galleywat* (Yule). – Port. *galeota,* a galliot ; see Galliot. Perhaps the form of the word has been influenced by F. *joli.* See Jolly.

Jolt, to jerk. (E.) From *joll,* vb., to knock the *jole* or head ; cf. All's Well, i. 3. 59. Cf. *jolt-head,* a stupid fellow ; one whose head has been *joll'd* or knocked about. See Jowl.

Jonquil, a flower. (F. – Span. – L.) F. *jonquille.* – Span. *junquillo*; named from its rush-like leaves. – Span. *junco,* a rush. – L. *iuncus,* a rush. See Junk (2).

Jordan, a pot. (Unknown.) M. E. *iordan, iurdan, iordeyne*; Late L. *iurdanus* (Prompt. Parv. and Vocab.). It was orig. an alchemist's bottle (Halliwell, Way) ; perhaps once used for keeping water from the Jordan.

Joss, a Chinese idol. (Port. – L.) Not Chinese, but corrupted from Port. *Deos,* God. Cognate with Span. *Dios,* God ; O. F. *deus.* – L. *Deus,* nom., God.

Jostle, Justle, to push against. (F. – L. ; *with* E. suffix.) A frequent. form, with suffix -*le,* from M. E. *jousten,* to tilt, push against. See Joust.

Jot. (L. – Gk. – Heb.) Englished from L. *iōta,* Matt. v. 18 (Vulgate). – Gk. *ἰῶτα,* a letter of the Gk. alphabet. – Heb. *yōd,* the smallest letter of the Heb. alphabet, with the power of *y.* See Iota.

Journal. (F. – L.) Properly an adj., signifying ' daily.' – F. *journal,* daily. – L. *diurnālis,* daily ; see Diurnal.

journey. (F. – L.) M. E. *iournee.* a

day's travel. ~ F. *journée*, a day, orig. a day's work. ─ Late L. **diurnāta*, orig. the fem. pp. of Late L. *diurnāre*, to sojourn. ─ L. *diurnus*, daily. ─ L. *diēs*, a day.

Joust, Just, to tilt. (F.─L.) O. F. *jouster* (F. *jouter*), to tilt. ─ Late L. *iuxtāre*, to approach (hence, to approach with hostile intent, as in tilting). ─ L. *iuxtā*, close to, hard by (whence O. F. *jouste*, close to). β The form *iuxtā* is short for **iŭg-is-tā*, fem. abl. of the superlative form of L. *iŭg-is*, continual. From the base *iŭg-* of *iungere*, to join. (√YEUG.) Brugm. i. § 760. Der. *jostle*.

Jovial. (F.─L.) O.F.*jovial*, sanguine, lit. born under the lucky planet Jupiter. ─ L. *Iouiālis*, pertaining to Jupiter. ─ L. *Ioui-*, decl. stem. of O. Lat. *Iouis*, Jove, whence L *Iŭ-piter* (= Jove-father). *Iouis* represents *Diouis* (cf. Oscan dat. *Diuv-ei*), allied to *diēs*, day, and to *deus*, god; cf. Gk. Διός, gen. case of Ζεύς. See **Deity, Tuesday.** Brugm. i. §§ 120, 223.

Jowl, Jole, the jaw or cheek. (E.) M. E. *jolle*; all the forms are corruptions of M. E. *chol, chaul*, which is a contraction of M. E. *chauel* (*chavel*), the jowl. ─ A. S. *ceafl*, the jaw; pl. *ceaflas*, the jaws, chaps. Cf. O. Sax. *kaflōs*, pl., the jaws; Du. *kevels*, pl. the gums; G. *kiefer*, jaw, jaw-bone; also Icel. *kjaptr*, Swed. *käft*, Dan. *kiæft*, jaw. ¶ The successive spellings are A.S. *ceafl, chæfle* (Layamon), *chauel, chaul, chol, jole, jowl* (all found).

Joy. (F.─L.) M. E. *ioye.* ─ O. F. *ioye, joye*; oldest form *goye* (F. *joie*); cf. Ital. *gioja*, joy, also a gaud, jewel, Span. *joya*, a gaud. ─ L. *gaudia*, pl. of *gaudium*, joy; afterwards turned into a fem. sing. ─ L. *gaudēre*, to rejoice. See **Gaud.**

Jubilation, a shouting for joy. (L.) From L. *iūbilātio*, sb. ─ L. *iūbilātus*, pp. of *iūbilāre*, to shout for joy. ─ L. *iūbilum*, a shout of joy. ¶ Quite distinct from *jubilee*.

Jubilee, a season of great joy. (F.─L.─Heb.) M. E. *jubilee.* ─ M. F. *jubilé*, 'a jubilee;' Cot. ─ L. *iūbilæus*, the jubilee (Levit. xxv. 11); masc. of adj. *iūbilæus*, belonging to the jubilee (Levit. xxv. 28). ─ Heb. *yōbēl*, a blast of a trumpet, shout of joy. ¶ Distinct from the word above.

Judge. (F.─L.) F.*juge.* ─ L. *iūdicem*, acc. of *iūdex*, a judge, lit. 'one who points out law.' ─ L. *iū-s*, law; *dic-āre*, to point out. See **Jury** and **Diction.**

judicature. (F.─L.) F.*judicature.* ─ Late L. *iūdicātūra*, office of a judge, judgment. ─ L. *iūdicātus*, pp. of *iūdicāre*, to judge. ─ L. *iūdic-*, stem of *iūdex*, a judge.

judicial. (F.─L.) M. F. *judiciel.* ─ L. *iūdiciālis*, pertaining to courts of law. ─ L. *iūdicium*, a trial. ─ L. *iūdic-*, stem of *iūdex*, a judge (above).

judicious. (F.─L.) F. *judicieux*; as if from a L. form **iūdiciōsus.* ─ L. *iūdic-*, stem of *iūdex*, a judge.

Jug, a kind of pitcher. (Heb.) Drinking-vessels were formerly called *jacks, jills*, and *jugs*, all of which represent Christian names. *Jug* and *Judge* were usual as pet female names, and equivalent to *Jenny* or *Joan*; see *Jannette, Jehannette* in Cotgrave. Cf. *Jock* for *John*; fem. form *Jacquetta*. Of Heb. origin; see **Jenniting.**

Juggernaut, the name of an Indian idol. (Skt.) Skt. *jagannātha-*, lord of the universe, monarch of the world (Benfey, p. 465). ─ Skt. *jagat*, world; *nātha-*, protector, lord.

Juggler. (F.─L.) M. E. *iogelour.* ─ O. F.*jogleor, jougleor*; later *jongleur.* ─ L. *ioculātōrem*, acc. of *ioculātor*, a jester. ─ L. *ioculāri*, to jest. ─ L. *ioculus*, a little jest, dimin. of *iocus*, joke. See **Joke.**

Jugular, pertaining to the side of the neck. (L.) From L.*iugul-um*, or *iugul-us*, the collar-bone, which joins the neck and shoulders; dimin. of *iugum*, a yoke. See **Yoke.**

Juice. (F.─L.) M. E. *iuce, iuse.* ─ O. F. *jus*, juice, broth. ─ L. *iūs*, broth; lit. ' mixture.' +Skt. *yūsha-*, soup. (√YU.) Brugm. i. §§ 911, 922.

Jujube, a fruit. (F.─L.─Gk.─Pers.) M. F. *jujubes*, pl. (Cot.). ─ L. *zīzyphum*, a jujube; fruit of the tree called *zīzyphus.* ─ Gk. ζίζυφον, fruit of the tree ζίζυφος. ─ Pers. *zayzafūn, zīzfūn, zīzafūn*, the jujube-tree.

Julep, a drink. (F.─Span.─Pers.) F. *julep.* ─ Span. *julepe.* ─ Pers. *julāb*, julep, a sweet drink; also *gulāb*, rose-water, also julep. ─ Pers. *gul*, a rose; *āb*, water. For Pers. *gul*, see **Rose.** Pers. *āb* is cognate with Skt. *ap-*, water.

July. (F.─L.) O. F. *Julie.* ─ L. *Iūlius*, a month (formerly called *Quinctīlis*) named after Julius Cæsar, who was born in July.

Jump (1), to leap, spring, skip. (Scand.) Swed. dial. *gumpa*, to spring, jump, *gimpa*, to wag about; allied to Swed. *guppa*, to move up and down; Dan. *gumpe*, to jolt; Icel. *goppa*, to skip.+M. H. G. *gumpen*, *gampen*, to jump, *gumpeln*, to play the buffoon; prov. G. *gampen*, to jump, hop, sport (Schmeller); M. Du. *gumpen*, to dance, leap. From a Teut. str. vb. **gimpan-* (for **gempan-*); whence Dan. dial. *gimpe*, to swing, wag, Lowl. Sc. *jimp*, to jump.

jumble, to mix together confusedly. (Scand.) We also find M. E. *jombren*, Ch. Troil. ii. 1037; and *jumper*, to mix harmoniously (More). In fact, *jumb-le*, *jombren*, *jump-er* are all frequentative forms of the verb to *jump*, used transitively. Thus *jumb-le*=to make to jump, jolt together, make a discord; or, otherwise, to shake together, make to agree. See Jump (1).

jump (2), exactly, pat; also, as a verb. (Scand.) From the verb above; cf. Hamlet, i. 1. 65. Also used in the sense to agree or tally, esp. in the phr. *to jump with*. 'They *jump* not;' Oth. i. 3. 5; cf. Tam. Shrew, i. 1. 195.

Junction, a joining. (L.) From L. *iunctio*, a joining.—L. *iunctus*, pp. of *iungere*, to join. See Join.

juncture, a union, a critical moment. (L.) The sense 'critical moment' is astrological, from the 'union' of planets.—L. *iunctūra*, a joining.—L. *iunctus* (above).

June. (F.—L.) O. F. and F. *Juin.*— L. *Iūnius*, the name of the month and of a Roman *gens* or clan.

Junglo. (Hind.—Skt.) Hind. *jangal*, wasteland.—Skt. *jañgala*-, adj., dry, desert; hence *jungle*=waste land. ¶ The Hind. short *a* sounds like *u* in *mud*.

Junior, younger. (L.) L. *iūnior*, comp. of *iuuenis*, young; short for **iuuenior*. See Juvenile.

Juniper, an evergreen shrub. (L.) L. *iūniperus*, *iūnipirus*, a juniper. Of doubtful origin.

Junk (1), a Chinese vessel. (Port.— Malay.—Chin. ?) Port. (and Span.) *junco*, a junk.—Malay *jōng*; also *ajōng*. Said to be borrowed from Chinese *chw'an*, a ship, boat, bark, junk; Williams, Chinese Dict. p. 120; but this is from Malay.

Junk (2), pieces of old cordage. (Port. —L.) Port. *junco*, a rush; also junk, as a nautical term; i. e. rush-made ropes.—L. *iuncum*, acc. of *iuncus*, a rush. ¶ *Junk* also means salt meat, tough as old ropes. (But *junk*, a lump, is for *chunk*.)

junket, a kind of sweetmeat. (F.—Ital.

—L.) F. *joncade* (Cot.). Orig. a kind of cream-cheese, served up on rushes, whence its name.—Ital. *giuncata*, a kind of cream-cheese on rushes, also a junket (Florio).—Ital. *giunco*, a rush.—L. *iuncum*, acc. of *iuncus*, a rush.

Junta, a council. (Span.—L.) Span. *junta*, a congress; a fem. form of *junto* (below).

junto, a knot of men, a faction. (Span. —L.) Span. *junto*, united, conjoined.— L. *iunctus*, pp. of *iungere*, to join. See Join.

Juridical, Jurisdiction, Jurist, Juror; see Jury.

Jury, a body of sworn men. (F.—L.) O. F. *jurée*, a jury, a company of sworn men; orig. the fem. pp. of *jurer*, to swear. —L. *iūrāre*, to swear, bind by an oath.— L. *iūr-*, for *iūs*, law.+Skt. *yu*, to bind.

juridical, pertaining to courts of law or to a judge. (L.) From L. *iuridic-us*, relating to the administration of justice; with suffix *-ālis*.—L. *iūri-*, decl. stem of *iūs*, law; *dicāre*, to proclaim. See Just (1) below.

jurisdiction. (F.—L.) M. F. *jurisdiction* (F. *juridiction*).—L. *iūrisdictiōnem*, acc. of *iūrisdictio*, administration of justice.—L. *iūris*, gen. of *iūs*, law (see Just (1) below); and see Diction. ¶ So also *juris-prudence*.

jurist, a lawyer. (F.—L.) F. *juriste* (Cot.).—Late L. *iūrista*, a lawyer.—L. *iūr-*, for *iūs*, law; with suffix *-ista* (=Gk. *-ιστης*).

juror, one of a jury. (F.—L.) Imitated from F. *jureur*, a swearer, a juror.—L. *iūrātōrem*, acc. of *iūrātor*, one who swears. —L. *iūrāre*, to swear; see Jury (above).

Jury-mast, a temporary mast. (F.— L.) Short for *ajury-mast*; where *ajury*= O. F. *ajuirie*, aid, succour (Godefroy). From L. *adiūtāre*, to aid; see Aid. Cf. M. E. *iuwere*, assistance; Prompt. Parv.

Just (1), upright. (F.—L.) M. E. *iust*. —F. *juste*.—L. *iustum*, acc. of *iustus*, just, according to right; with suffix *-tus*. —L. *iūs*, right, that which is fitting; cf. Skt. *yu*, to join.

justice. (F.—L.) F. *justice*. — L. *iūstitia*, justice.—Late L. *iūstitia*, a tribunal, a judge.—L. *iūsti-*, for *iūstus*, just; see Just (1) above.

justify. (F.—L.) F. *justifier*.—L. *iūsti-*

for *iustus*, just; *-ficāre*, for *facere*, to make.

Just (2), to joust; see **Joust**.

Justle; see **Jostle**.

Jut, to project. (F.—L.) Merely a corruption of *jet*; in the same way a *jetty* or pier was formerly called a *jutty*; see **Jetty**.

jutty, a projection. (F.—L.) For *jetty*; see above. **Der.** *jutty*, vb., to project beyond.

Jute, a substance resembling hemp. (Bengali.) Bengali *jūt*, the fibres of the bark of the *Corchorus olitorius* (Wilson). From *jhōto*, vulgarly *jhuto*, the native name in Orissa (Yule).

Juvenile, young. (F.—L.) M. F. *juvenile*; F. *juvenil*.—L. *iuuenīlis*, youthful.—L. *iuuenis*, young. See **Young**.

Juxtaposition. (L. *and* F. — L.) Coined from L. *iuxtā*, near; and *position*. See **Joust** and **Position**.

K.

Kail, Kale, cabbage. (L.) Northern E. form of *cole*; see **Cole**.

Kails, ninepins. (Du.) Formerly also *keyles*; see *quille* in Cotgrave. These *kails* were cone-shaped. — Du. *kegel*, a pin, kail; *met kegels spelen*, to play at ninepins. + Dan. *kegle*, a cone, *kegler*, nine-pins; Swed. *kägla*, a pin, cone; G. *kegel* (whence F. *quille*). Apparently a dimin. of Du. *keg*, a wedge.

Kaleidoscope, an optical toy. (Gk.) From Gk. καλ-ός, beautiful; εἶδο-s, form; σκοπ-εῖν, to behold; because it enables one to behold beautiful forms.

Kalendar; see **Calends**.

Kangaroo, a quadruped. (Australian.) Said to be *not* the native Australian name, but to have arisen from some mistake; but even this is doubtful (see Morris).

Kayles; see **Kails**.

Kecksies, hemlocks. (C.) For *kecks-es*; and *kecks* is also written *kex*. See **Kex**.

Kedge (1), to warp a ship. (F.—L.?) To *kedge* is to drag a ship slowly forward, by help of a kedge-anchor, against tide. A *kedge-anchor* was formerly called a *catch-anchor* or *catch* (N. E. D.). Hence *kedge* may represent *ketch*; for *catch*.

Kedge (2), **Kidge,** brisk, lively. (E.) An East-Anglian word. M. E. *kygge*,

kydge. Cf. prov. E. *cadgy*, cheerful; and perhaps Dan. *kaad*, frolicsome; M. Dan. *kæde*, joy; Swed. *kätja*, to be wanton.

Keel (1), the bottom of a ship. (Scand.) Icel. *kjölr*, Dan. *kiöl*, Swed. *köl*, the keel of a ship (whence G. Du. *kiel*, a keel). Teut. type **kiluz*. Cf. A. S. *celae*, the beak of a ship (O. E. T.). Distinct from A. S. *cēol*, O. H. G. *kiol*, M. H. G. *kiel*, a ship.

keelhaul. (Scand. *and* E.) Also *keel-hale*, 'to punish in the seaman's way, by dragging the criminal under water on one side of the ship and up again on the other;' Johnson. From *keel* and *haul* or *hale*. Cf. Du. *kiel-halen*, G. *kielholen*.

keelson, kelson, a set of timbers next a ship's keel. (Scand.) Formerly *kelsine* (Chapman).—Swed. *kölsvin*, Dan. *kiölsviin* (Norweg. *kjölsvill*), a keelson; E. Fries. *kolswin*.+G. *kielschwein*. Lit. 'keel-swine;' but this can hardly have been the orig. sense. A better sense is given by Norw. *kjölsvill*, where *svill* answers to G. *schwelle*, E. *sill*; see **Sill**. This suffix, not being understood, may easily have been corrupted to *swine*, and afterwards, in English, to *-son*.

Keel (2), to cool. (E.) To *keel* a pot is to keep it from boiling over, lit. to cool it. — A. S. *cēlan*, to cool; for **cōljan*. — A. S. *cōl*, cool. See **Cool**.

Keelson; see **Keel** (1).

Keen, sharp. (E.) M. E. *kene*. A. S. *cēne*, where *ē* is due to an older *ō*; O. Merc. *cōene*. The orig. sense is 'skilful, experienced.' — Du. *koen*, bold, daring; Icel. *kænn* (for *kœnn*), wise, also able; G. *kühn*, bold, O. H. G. *chuoni*. Teut. type **kōnjoz*, able; from Teut. root **ken* (√GEN), to know; see **Can** (1).

Keep. (E.) M. E. *kepen*. A. S. *cēpan*, to observe, notice, attend to, keep.+M.Du. *kepen*, to keep, retain (Hexham). Teut. type **kōpjan-*; cf. A. S. *ge-cōp*, fit, suitable.

Keg, a small cask. (Scand.) Formerly also *cag*. — Icel. *kaggi*, a keg; Swed. *kagge*, Norweg. *kagge*, a keg, a round mass or heap. **Der.** *kails*.

Kelp, calcined ashes of sea-weed. Origin unknown. Also spelt *kilp*.

Ken, to know. (Scand.) M. E. *kennen*. — Icel. *kenna*, Swed. *känna*, Dan. *kiende*, to know; so also G. *kennen*; A. S. *cennan* (to declare), Goth. *kannjan*. Teut. type **kannjan-*. Causal form of *cunnan*, to

276

know, derived from Teut. base *kann (cf. can) by vowel-change of a to e. See **Can** (1).

Kennel (1), a house for dogs. (F.–L.) M. E. *kenel*. A Norman form of O. F. *chenil*, a kennel. – Late L. 'canīle, domus canis' in Wrt. Vocab. 198. 29. – L. *can-is*, a dog, with suffix -*īle*, as in *ou-īle*, a sheep-fold. Cf. Norman F. *ken*, O. F. *chen* (F. *chien*), a dog, from L. acc. *canem*, a dog.

Kennel (2), a gutter. (F.–L.) A corruption of M. E. *canel*, a channel. – A. F. *canel*, Charlemagne, ed. Michel, l. 556; O. F. *chanel*; see **Channel**.

Kerbstone. (F.–L.; and E.) Here *kerb* is for *curb*; so called because the stone was sometimes placed, as round a well, on a *curved* edge. See **Curb**.

Kerchief. (F.–L.) M. E. *curchief*, *couerchef* (*coverchef*). – O. F. *covrechef*, lit. a head-covering. – O. F. *covrir*, to cover; *chef*, the head; see **Cover** and **Chief**.

Kermes, the dried bodies of insects used in dyeing crimson. (Arab.–Skt.) See **Crimson**.

Kern (1), **Kerne**, an Irish soldier. (Irish.) Irish *ceatharnach*, a soldier. – O. Irish *cethern*, a troop. See **Cateran**.

Kern (2); see **Quern**.

Kernel. (E.) A. S. *cyrnel*, a grain : dimin. of A. S. *corn*, a grain (with the usual change from Teut. *u* (A. S. *o*) to *y*). Teut. stem *kurnilo-*. See **Corn**.

Kersey, coarse woollen cloth. (E.) Named from *Kersey* (of A. S. origin), a village three miles from Hadleigh, in Suffolk, where a woollen trade was once carried on. ¶ Not from *Jersey*, which is also used as the name of a material.

Kerseymere, a twilled cloth of fine wool. (Cashmere.) A corruption of *Cashmere* or *Cassimere*, by confusion with *kersey* above.

Kestrel, a base kind of hawk. (F.–L.) For *kesrel*; the *t* is excrescent, as in *whils-t*, &c. – M. F. *quercerelle*, 'a kastrell;' Cotgrave; F. *crécerelle*. Extended from O. F. *crecele*, *cercelle*, M. F. *quercelle*, a kestrel. Of imitative origin; cf. O. F. *cercelle*, F. *sarcelle*, a teal, from L. *querquédula*, a kind of teal.

Ketch, a small yacht or hoy. (E.) M. E. *cache*. Prob. from the verb *to catch*; see N. E. D.; s. v. **Catch.** ¶ The Du. *kits*, F. *quaiche*, a ketch, are borrowed from E. ¶ Distinct from *caïque*, q. v.

Ketchup, a sauce. (Malay.) Malay *kēchap*, *kīchap*, a sauce; soy. (In Dutch spelling, *ketjap*.)–C. P. G. Scott.

Kettle. (Scand.–L.) M. E. *ketel*. Icel. *ketill*; borrowed from L. *catillus*, a small bowl (whence also Goth. *katils*, A. S. *cetel*, Du. *ketel*, G. *kessel*, &c.). Dimin. of *catīnus*, a bowl, deep vessel for cooking food. Perhaps allied to Gk. κότυλος, a cup (Prellwitz); see **Cotyledon**.

Kex, hemlock, a hollow stem. (W.–L.) M. E. *kex*; W. *cecys*, pl., hollow stalks. Of Celtic origin; cf. W. *cegid*, hemlock Corn. *cegas*, hemlock; prob. borrowed from L. *cicūta*, hemlock. ¶ *Kex* = *kecks*, and is properly a plural form.

Key. (E.) M. E. *keye*. A.S. *cǣg*, a key; O. Fries. *kái*, *kēi*, a key.

Khan, a prince. (Pers.–Tatar.) Pers. *khān*, lord, prince; of Tatar origin. Cf. *Chingis Khan*, i. e. great lord, a Tatar title (Chaucer's *Cambuscan*).

Khedive, a prince. (F.–Pers.) F. *khédive*. – Pers. *khadīw*, *khidīw*, a great prince, sovereign; *khidēwī*, the khedive, viceroy of Egypt (Palmer). Cf. Pers. *khodā*, God.

Kibe, a chilblain. (C.?) W. *cibwst*, chilblains; explained by Pugh as standing for *cib-gwst*. – W. *cib*, a cup; *gwst*, a humour, malady, disease; hence 'a cup-like malady,' from the rounded form. The E. word has preserved only the syllable *cib*, rejecting the latter syllable. (Doubtful.)

Kick. (Scand.) M. E. *kiken* (whence W. *cicio*, to kick, colloquially). Cf. prov. E. *kink*, to kick. – Norw. *kikk*, a straining of a sinew; *kikla*, to jerk. Cf. **Kink**.

Kickshaws, a dainty dish. (F.–L.) A sing. sb.; the pl. is *kickshawses* (Shak.). A curious corruption of F. *quelque chose*, something, hence, a trifle, a delicacy. Spelt *quelquechose* by Dryden. – F. *quelque chose*. – L. *quāl-is*, of what sort, with suffix -*quam*; *caussa*, a cause, a thing. ¶ Moisy gives Norman F. *quiquechose*.

Kid, a young goat. (Scand.) M. E. *kid*. – Dan. *kid*, Swed. *kid*, Icel. *kið*, a kid. + G. *kitze*.

kidnap, to steal young children. (Scand.) *Kid*, in Tudor E. slang, means a child; *nap* is our *nab*. – Dan. *kid*, a kid; *nappe*, to nab; see **Nab**.

Kiddle, a kind of weir formed of basket-work placed in a river to catch fish. (A.F.) Anglo-F. *kidel*, pl. *kideux*; O. F. *cuidel*

(Godefroy); later form *quideau*, ' a wicker engine whereby fish is caught ; ' Cotgrave. Late L. *kidellus* ; Breton *kidel*.

Kidney. (E.) M. E. *kiden-ei*, pl. *kiden-eiren*; confused with M. E. *neris*, kidneys (Icel. *nȳra*). 1. Here *kid* answers to A. S. *cyd-, perhaps related to A. S. *codd*, a bag, pod, husk, M. E. *cod*, belly. 2. M. E. *ei*, pl. *eiren*, answers to A. S. *ǣg*, an egg, pl. *ǣgru*. See **Egg.** 3. M. E. *nere* is a Scand. word. — Icel. *nȳra*, Dan. *nyre*, Swed. *njure*, Du. *nier*, G. *niere*, a kidney.

Kilderkin. (Du.) A corruption of M. Du. *kindeken*, also *kinneken*, the eighth part of a vat. Apparently 'a little child,' because the measure is a small one as compared with a tun, vat, or barrel. But it has been ascertained to be a derivative, with the same suffix -*ken*, from a Du. spelling of O. F. *quintal*, ' a quintal or hundredweight.' See further under **Quintal.**

Kill. (E.) M. E. *killen*, more commonly *cullen*. The M. E. *cullen* prob. answers to an A. S. type *cyllan, from the weak grade *c(w)ul*- of *cwel-an*, to die. Cf. E. Fries. *küllen*, to vex, strike, beat, a parallel form ; O. H. G *chollen*, by-form of *quellan*, to vex, kill, martyr. Thus *kill* is closely related to **Quell**, q. v. For the loss of *w*, cf. *dull*, which is related to *dwell*.

Kiln. (L.) A. S. *cyln*, also *cylen* ; merely borrowed from L. *culina*, a kitchen (hence, a drying-house) ; whence also W. *cylyn*, a kiln, a furnace. See **Culinary.**

Kilt. (Scand.) The sb. is derived from the verb *kilt*, to tuck up. — Dan. *kilte*, to truss, tuck up ; Swed. dial. *kilta*, to swaddle. Cf. Icel. *kilting*, a skirt. Perhaps related to Swed. dial. *kilta*, the lap, Icel. *kjalta*, lap.

Kimbo; see **Akimbo.**

Kin, genus, race. (E.) M. E. *kin*, *kun*. A. S. *cynn*, orig. a tribe. + Icel. *kyn*, kin ; O. Sax. *kunni*, O. H. G. *chunni* ; Goth. *kuni*, tribe. Teut. type *kunjom, neut. From the weak grade of Teut. root *ken-, Idg. *gen*-. Allied to **Genus.** (√GEN.)

kind (1), sb., nature, sort. (E.) M. E. *kund*, *kind*. A. S. *cynd*, *ge-cynd*, nature ; whence the adj. below. **Der.** *kind-ly*, natural.

kind (2), adj., natural, loving. (E.) M. E. *kunde*, *kinde*. A. S. *cynde*, *ge-cynde*,

natural, in-born ; allied to Goth. -*kunds*, of such a nature. Allied to **Kin.**

kindle (1), to bring forth young. (E.) M. E. *kindlen*, *kundlen* ; from M. E. *kindel*, *kundel*, sb., a progeny ; from the A. S. *cynd*, nature, or from the adj. *cynde*, natural.

Kindle (2), to inflame. (Scand.) M. E. *kindlen*, *kundlen*, resembling **Kindle** (1); see Anc. Riwle. But it can hardly be separated from Icel. *kynda*, to inflame, kindle, Swed. dial. *kynda*, *kinda*, a sense which seems to have been suggested by Icel. *kyndill*, a torch. And Icel. *kyndill* is a mere borrowing from A. S. *candel*; from L. *candēla*, a candle. See **Candle.**

Kindred. (E.) The former *d* is excrescent. M. E. *kinrede*. — A. S. *cyn*, kin ; -*rǣden*, signifying law, state, condition (so also *hat-red* from *hate*). *Rǣden* is allied to the adj. *ready* ; cf. Goth. *ga-raideins* an ordinance.

Kine, cows ; see **Cow.**

King, a chief ruler. (E.) A. S. *cyning*, a king ; lit. 'a man of good birth ;' (cf. A. S. *cyne*-, royal, Icel. *konr*, one of gentle birth) ; — A. S. *cyn*, a tribe, kin, race ; with suffix -*ing*, as in *Ælfred Æþelwulfing* = Ælfred the son of Æthelwulf. + O. Sax. *kuning*, from *kuni*, tribe ; O. Fries. *kining* ; Icel. *konungr* ; Swed. *konung* ; Dan. *konge* ; Du. *koning* ; G. *könig*, O. H. G. *chuning* (from O. H. G. *chunni*, a kin, race). Teut. type *kuningoz, m.

kingdom. (E.) Late M. E. *kingdom* ; not really a compound of *king* and suffix -*dom*, but a substitution for early M. E. *kinedom*, A. S. *cynedōm*, a kingdom. The A. S. *cyne*- signifies 'royal,' very common in composition, and is allied to A. S. *cyn*, a tribe.

Kink, a twist in a rope. (Scand.) A Northern word. — Swed. *kink*, Norweg. *kink*, a twist in a rope. (So also Du. *kink*.) Allied to Norweg. *kika*, *kinka*, to writhe, Icel. *kikna*, to sink at the knees under a burden, Icel. *keikr*, bent back ; Norw. *keika*, to bend aside, to twist. (Teut. base *keik-, to bend.)

Kiosk, a small pavilion. (Turk. — Pers.) F. *kiosque*. — Turk. *kushk*, *köshk* (pronounced with *k* as *ki*), a kiosk. — Pers. *kūshk*, a palace, villa, portico.

Kipper, to cure salmon. (E.) This meaning is an accidental one, arising from a habit of curing *kipper-salmon*, i. e. salmon during the spawning season, which were cured because of inferior quality. A salmon, after spawning, was called a *kipper* (Pennant). A.S. *cypera*, a kipper-salmon.

Kirk, a church. (Scand.—E.—Gk.) M. E. *kirke.* — Icel. *kirkja*; borrowed from A. S. *cirice, circe,* a church. See **Church.**

Kirtle, a sort of gown or petticoat. (L.; *with* E. *suffix.*) M. E. *kirtel.* A. S. *cyrtel,* a tunic; Icel. *kyrtill,* Dan. *kiortel,* Swed. *kjortel*; evidently dimin. forms. All from L. *curtus,* short, which appears also in Du. *kort,* G. *kurz,* short. See **Curt.**

Kiss, a salute with the lips. (E.) The vowel *i* is due to the *verb,* which is formed from the *sb.* by vowel-change. M. E. *coss,* sb., a kiss; whence *kissen,* verb. A. S. *coss,* sb.; whence *cyssan,* verb.+Du. *kus,* Icel. *koss,* Dan. *kys,* Swed. *kyss,* G. *kuss,* a kiss. Teut. type **kussuz,* sb. Cf. Goth. *kukjan,* to kiss; E. Fries. *kük,* a kiss.

Kit (1), a milk-pail, tub; also, an outfit. (O. Low G.) M. E. *kit.* — M. Du. *kitte,* a wooden bowl, a tub; Du. *kit.* Cf. Norweg. *kitte,* a corn-bin.

Kit (2), a small violin. (F.—L.—Gk.) Shortened from Norman F. *quiterne* (Moisy); answering to O. F. *guiterne* (Godefroy). From L. *cithara.* — Gk. κιθάρα, a kind of lyre. See **Cithern.**

Kit (3), a brood, family, quantity. (E.) A variant of *kith.* 'The whole *kit*' = the whole kith. See **Kith.**

Kit-cat, Kit-kat, the name given to portraits of a particular size. (Personal name.) The size adopted by Sir G. Kneller for painting members of the *Kit-Kat* club, which used to meet at a house kept by *Christopher Kat* (Haydn). *Kit* is for *Christopher* (Gk. Χριστο-φόρος, lit. 'Christ-bearing').

Kitchen. (L.) M. E. *kichene.* A.S. *cycene,* f. — L. *coquīna,* a kitchen. — L. *coquere,* to cook; see **Cook.**

Kite, a bird, a toy for flying. (E.) M.E. *kite.* A. S. *cȳta,* a kite.

Kith, kindred, acquaintance. (E.) M.E. *cuððe,* kith. A. S. *cȳð,* native land, relationship. — A. S. *cūð,* known, pp. of *kunnan,* to know. See **Can** (1).

Kitten. (F.—L.) M. E. *kitoun,* from an A. F. **kitoun*; cf. O. F. (Central F.) *chitoun,* a kitten (Gower). Variant of North F. *caton,* O. F. *chatton,* a kitten. Cf. M. F. *chatton,* 'a kitling or young cat;' Cot.; augmentative of F. *chat,* a cat. — Late L.*cattum,* acc. of *cattus,* L. *cātus,* a cat. See **Cat.**

Knack, a snap, dexterity, trick. (E.)

Imitative, like **Knap.** Cf. Du. *knakken,* G. *knacken,* to crack. [The Gael. *cnac,* Irish *cnag,* a crack, W. *cnec,* a snap, are borrowed from E. *crack.*] It meant (1) a snap, (2) a snap with the finger or nail, (3) a jester's trick, piece of dexterity, (4) a joke, trifle, toy, &c. Cf. **Knock.**

Knacker, a dealer in old horses. (Scand.) It formerly meant a saddler and harness-maker (Ray). — Icel. *hnakkr,* a saddle.

Knag, a knot in wood, peg. (E.) M.E. *knagge,* a peg, a knot in wood. Not in A.S. Low G.*knagge,* a kind of peg; Swed. *knagg,* a knag, knot; Dan. *knag,* a peg, cog. We find also Irish *cnag,* a knob, peg, *cnaig,* a knot in wood, Gael. *cnag,* knob, pin, peg (all from E.).

Knap, to snap. (Du.) Du. *knappen,* to snap, crack, crush, eat (whence *knapper,* hard gingerbread, a lie). Cf. Dan. *kneppe,* to snap; Swed. *knäpp,* a snap, *knep,* a trick. A parallel word to *knack,* and of imitative origin. Cf. Gael. *cnap,* to strike, beat, thump, Irish *cnapaim,* I strike; from E. See **Knop.**

knapsack. (Du.) Du. *knapzak,* a knapsack, lit. a provision-bag. — Du. *knap,* eating, *knappen,* to crush, eat; *zak,* a sack (a word of Hebrew origin); see **Sack.**

Knapweed, Knopweed, a weed with a hard head or *knop*; see **Knop.**

Knar; see **Gnarled.**

Knave, a boy, servant, sly fellow. (E.) M. E. *knaue (knave),* a boy, servant. A.S. *cnafa,* older form *cnapa,* a boy. + So also Du. *knaap,* a lad, servant; Icel. *knapi,* servant-boy; G. *knabe,* a boy. It is probable that the initial *kn-* represents the weak grade of Teut. **ken-* (Idg. **gen-*), to produce; cf. **Knight.** But the rest of the word remains unexplained.

Knead, to mould by pressure. (E.) M. E. *kneden.* A. S. *cnedan* (pt. t. **cnæd,* pp. *cneden*), a strong verb, to knead.+ Du. *kneden,* Icel. *knoða,* Swed. *knåda,* G. *kneten*; (all from Teut. base**kneð-*). Allied to Russ. *gnetate, gnesti,* to press, squeeze; from the corresponding Idg. root **gnet.*

Knee. (E.) M. E. *kne,* pl. *knees*; also *cneo,* pl. *cneon.* A.S. *cnēo.*+Du. *knie,* Icel. *knē,* Dan. *knæ,* Swed. *knä,* G. *knie,* O. H. G. *chniu,* Goth. *kniu.* Teut. type **knewom,* n. Cf. L. *genu*; Gk. γόνυ; Skt. *jānu.* The Idg. related bases are **genu-* (as in L.), **gonu-* (as in Gk), **gneu-* (whence Teut. **kneu-*). Cf. Gk.

γνυ-πετεῖν, to fall on the knees. See Genuflection, Pentagon, &c.

kneel, to fall on the knees. (E.) M. E. *cneolien, knēlen*; A.S. *cneowlian.*✝ Du. *knielen*; Low G. *knelen* (Lübben); Dan. *knæle* (formed from *knæ*, knee).

Knell, Knoll, to sound as a bell, toll. (E.) M.E. *knillen, knollen.* A.S. *cnyllan,* to knock, beat noisily. Cf. Du. *knallen,* to give a loud report, Dan. *knalde,* to explode; Swed. *knalla,* to resound, G. *knallen,* to make a loud noise; Icel. *gnella,* to scream; M. H. G. *knüllen,* to beat. Perhaps of imitative origin, to denote a loud noise; cf. Swed. *knal,* Dan. *knald,* Swed. *knall,* G. *knall,* a loud noise. From Teut. base **knel-* (**knal-, *knul-*).

Knickerbockers, loose knee-breeches. (Du.) Named from Diedrich *Knickerbocker,* the pretended author of W. Irving's Hist. of New York; taken as the type of a New York Dutchman.

Knick-knack, a trick, trifle, toy. (E.) A reduplication of *knack,* in the sense of trifle, toy. Cf. Du. *knikken,* to snap, weakened form of *knakken,* to crack. See Knack.

Knife. (E.) M. E. *knif,* pl. *kniues* (with *u=v*). A.S. *cnīf,* a knife. ✝ Du. *knijf,* Icel. *knīfr,* Dan. *kniv,* Swed. *knif,* prov. G. *kneif*; Low G. *knīf, knīp,* a knife (Lübben). (Cf. F. *canif,* from G.) Possibly related to Nip and Nibble.

Knight, a youth, servant, man-at-arms. (E.) M. E. *knight.* A.S. *cniht,* O. Merc. *cneht,* a boy, servant. ✝ Du. *knecht,* a servant; Dan. *knegt,* man-servant, knave (at cards); Swed. *knekt,* soldier, knave (at cards); G. *knecht.* β. Perhaps *cneht=* **cn-eht,* belonging to the kin or tribe; cf. Gk. γν-ήσιος, legitimate, from γέν-ος, kin (where γν- is the weak grade of γεν-); see Kin. The suffix *-eht, -iht* is adjectival; as in *þorn-iht,* thorny, from *þorn,* a thorn.

Knit. (E.) A.S. *cnyttan,* to form into a knot, to knot; formed (by vowel-change) from Teut. **knut-,* the base of *cnotta,* a knot (Teut. type **knut-ton-*). Allied to Icel. *knȳta,* Dan. *knytte,* Swed. *knyta,* to knit; and to Icel. *knūtr,* Dan. *knude,* Swed. *knut,* a knot. See Knot.

Knob, a form of *knop.* M. E. *knobbe.* Cf. Low G. *knobbe,* Du. *knobbel,* a knob. See Knop.

Knock, to strike, rap. (E.) M. E. *knocken.* A.S. *cnucian*; Icel. *knoka.* Cf. Irish *cnagaim,* I knock; W. *cnocio,* to

knock; Corn. *cnoucye,* to knock. An imitative word, from Teut. **knuk-,* weak grade of Knack.

Knoll (1), a hillock. (E.) M. E. *knol.* A.S. *cnol.*✝Du. *knol,* a turnip, from its roundness, Dan. *knold,* a knoll, Swed. *knöl,* a bump, G. *knollen,* a knoll, clod, lump. Cf. W. *cnol,* a knoll, hillock; Swed. dial. *knall,* a knoll.

Knoll (2); see Knell.

Knop, Knob, a bump, protuberance, boss. (E.) M. E. *knop,* a rose-bud. O. Fries. *ersknop,* the rump-bone.✝Du. and Dan. *knop,* a knob, bud; Swed. *knopp,* a bud, *knop,* a knot, G. *knopf,* knob, button, knot. Apparently allied to M. E. *knap,* a knob; A. S. *cnæp,* a hill-top, Icel. *knappr,* a knob; whence Gael. *cnap,* a knob, button, boss, stud, hillock, also a slight blow; also the verb *cnap,* to thump, beat (hence, to raise a bump); W. *cnap,* a knob; Irish *cnap,* knob, bunch, hillock, *cnapaim,* I strike. See Knap.

Knot. (E.) M. E. *knotte.* A. S. *cnotta,* a knot. ✝ Du. *knot.* Cf. also O. H. G. *chnodo,* G. *knoten,* a knot (with a different dental sound). Also (with a long vowel) Icel. *knūtr,* a knot, Dan. *knude,* Swed. *knut.* And (with orig. *a*) Icel. *knöttr* (Teut. **knattuz*), a ball.

knout, a scourge. (Russ. — Scand.) Russ. *knute,* a whip, scourge. ■ Swed. *knut,* Icel. *knūtr,* a knot.

Know, to be assured of. (E.) M. E. *knowen.* A.S. *cnāwan* (pt. t. *cnēow,* pp. *cnāwen*). ✝ Icel. *knā,* O. H. G. *chnāan.* Further allied to Russ. *znate,* to know; L. *noscere* (for *gnoscere*); Gk. γι-γνώσκειν; Pers. *far-zān,* knowledge; O. Irish *gnāth,* known, accustomed, W. *gnawd,* a custom; Skt. *jnā,* to know. All from a base **gnō,* a secondary form of √GEN, to know.

knowledge. (E.) M. E. *knowlege, knauleche*; from *knowlechen,* vb., to acknowledge. Here *-lēchen* = A.S. *-lǣcan* (as in M. E. *nēhlēchen,* A.S. *nēahlǣcan,* to approach). And *-lǣcan* is from the A. S. *-lāc,* the same word as A.S. *lāc,* a game, sport, play. See Wedlock.

Knuckle, the projecting joint of the fingers. (E.) M. E. *knokil*; O. Fries. *knokele.*✝ M. Du. *knokel,* Du. *kneukel,* Dan. *knokkel,* G. *knöchel,* a knuckle. A dimin. form; the shorter form appears in M. Du. *knoke,* a bone, knuckle, G. *knochen,* a bone, Swed. *knoge,* a knuckle.

Knurr, Knur, a knot in wood,

wooden ball. (O. Low G.) M. E. *knor.*
Not in A. S. — M. Du. *knorre,* a hard
swelling, knot in wood. + Dan. *knort,*
a knot; G. *knorren,* a lump. Allied to
M. E. *knarre,* a knot. See **Gnarled.**

Koran, sacred book of the Mohamme-
dans. (Arab.) Arab. *qurān,* reading aloud,
recitation; also, the Koran. — Arab. root
qara-a, he read. (The *a* is long.)

alcoran; the same word, with the
Arab. def. art. *al* (the) prefixed.

Kraal, an enclosure, a collection of huts,
an African village. (Du. — Port. — L.) Du.
kraal, an African village. — Port. *curral,*
an enclosure; the same word as Span.
corral. See **Corral.**

Kythe, to make known. (E.) A. S.
cȳðan, to make known. — A. S. *cūð,* known,
pp. of *cunnan,* to know. See **Can** (1),
and **Uncouth.**

L.

Label, a small slip of paper, &c. (F.)
M. E. *label.* — O. F. *label, lambel,* a label
(in heraldry), a shred; mod. F. *lambeau.*
Of uncertain origin; cf. O. Lat. *lamberāre,*
to tear in pieces (Ascoli).

Labial. (L.) Late L. *labiālis,* pertaining to the lips. — L. *labium,* the lip. See
Lip.

labellum, a pendulous petal. (L.)
L. *labellum,* dimin. of *labium,* a lip.

labiate. (L.) A botanical term. — L.
labi-um, a lip; with suffix *-ate* (L. *-ātus*).

Laboratory. (L.) Formerly *elabora-
tory* (Blount). — M. F. *elaboratoire* (Cot.).
Formed from L. *ēlaborātus,* pp. of *ēlabo-
rāre,* to elaborate, work out. — L. *ē,* out;
laborāre, to work, from *labor,* labour.

laborious. (F. — L.) M. E. *laborious.* — F. *laborieux.* — L. *labōriōsus,* toil-
some. — L. *labōr-,* for *labor,* labour; with
suffix *-ōsus.*

labour, toil. (F. — L.) M. E. *labour.*
— O. F. *labour* (later *labeur*). — L. *labōrem,*
acc. of *labor, labōs,* toil.

Laburnum, a tree. (L.) L. *laburnum,*
in Pliny, xvi. 18.

Labyrinth, a maze. (F. — L. — Gk. —
Egypt.) F. *labyrinthe.* — L. *labyrinthus.*
— Gk. λαβύρινθος, a maze, a place full of
lanes or alleys. Of Egyptian origin
(Maspero).

Lac (1), a resinous substance. (Pers. —

Skt.) Pers. *lak,* gum-lac, whence crimson
lake is obtained for dyeing. — Skt. *lākshā,*
lac; also *laktaka, raktaka,* lac; *rañj,* to
dye. Der. *gum-lac, shel-lac.*

Lac (2), a hundred thousand. (Hind. —
Skt.) A *lac* of rupees = 100,000 rupees. —
Hindustani *lak* (also *lākh*), a lac. — Skt.
laksha, a hundred thousand; originally,
' a mark.'

Lace, a cord, tie. (F. — L.) M. E. *las,
laas.* — O. F. *las, laqs* (F. *lacs*), a snare,
noose. — L. *laqueus,* a noose, snare, knot.
Allied to L. *lacĕre,* to allure; cf. E. *elicit,
delight.* See **Lasso, Latchet.**

Lacerate, to tear. (L.) From pp. of
L. *lacerāre,* to tear. — L. *lacer,* mangled,
torn. +Gk. λακερός, torn; λακίς, a rent.

Lachrymal, Lacrimal, pertaining
to tears. (L.) The spelling *lachrymal* is
bad. — L. *lacryma,* better *lacruma, lacrima,*
a tear; O. L. *dacrima,* a tear. Cognate
with Gk. δάκρυ, a tear, and E. *tear;* see
Tear (1). Der. (from L. *lacrima*) *lachry-
mose,* tearful; *lachrymatory,* a tear-bottle.

Lack (1), want. (E.) The old sense is
often ' failure' or ' fault.' M. E. *lak, lac.*
Not in A. S., but cf. O. Fries. *lek,* damage,
harm, *lakia,* to attack.+Du. *lak,* blemish,
stain, *laken,* to blame; Low G. *lak,* defect,
blame; Icel. *lakr,* defective, lacking.

lack (2), to be destitute of. (E.) M. E.
lakken; weak verb; from *lak,* sb. See
above.

Lacker; see **Lacquer.**

Lackey, Lacquey, a footman, menial
attendant. (F. — Span. ? — Arab. ?) From
M. F. *laquay,* ' a lackey, footboy;' Cot.
(F. *laquais*). There was also an O. F.
form *alacay;* Littré shews that, in the
15th cent., a certain class of soldiers (esp.
crossbow-men), were called *alagues, ala-
cays,* or *lacays.* (The prefix *a-* is prob.
due to Arab. *al,* the def. article.) Prob.
from Span. *lacayo,* Port. *lacaio,* a lackey;
Port. *lacaia,* a woman-servant in dramatic
performances. — Arab. *luka',* worthless,
servile; as a sb., a slave; *lak'ā,* fem., mean,
servile. Cf. *lakā', lakī',* servile, *laka'i,*
slovenly. ¶ This is a guess; it is much
disputed; Diez connects it with Ital.
leccare, G. *lecken,* to lick.

Laconic, brief and pithy. (L. — Gk.)
L. *Lacōnicus,* Laconian. — Gk. Λακωνικός,
Laconian. — Gk. Λάκων, a Laconian, Spartan. These men were celebrated for their
brief and pithy locution.

Lacquer, Lacker, a sort of varnish.

(F. — Port. — Pers. — Skt.) M. F. *lacre*
(Cot.). — Port. *lacre*, sealing-wax. — Port.
laca, gum-lac. — Pers. *lak*, gum-lac; see
Lac (1).

Lacteal, relating to milk. (L.) From
L. *lacte-us*, milky. — L. *lact-*, stem of *lac*,
milk.+Gk. γαλακτ-, stem of γάλα, milk.
Allied to *lettuce*.

Lad, a youth. (E.) M. E. *ladde*. Prob.
the sense was 'one led,' i. e. a follower,
dependant. From M. E. *lad*, led, pp. of
lēden, to lead. See **Lead** (1). (H. Bradley, in *Athenæum*, June 1, 1894.)

Ladanum; see **Laudanum.**

Ladder. (E.) M. E. *laddre*. A. S.
hlǣder, hlǣdder, a ladder. + Du. *ladder*,
ladder, rails of a cart; O. H. G. *hleitra*,
G. *leiter*, a ladder. Cognate with Gk.
κλῖ-μαξ, a ladder; see **Climax.** Named
from sloping; see **Lean** (1). (√KLEI.)

Lade (1), to load. (E.) Formerly a
strong verb; we still use the pp. *laden*.
M. E. *laden*. A. S. *hladan* (pt. t. *hlōd*,
pp. *hladen*), meaning (1) to load, heap
up, heap together, (2) to draw out water,
lade out, drain.+Du. *laden*, Icel. *hlaða*,
Dan. *lade*, Swed. *ladda*, Goth. *-hlathan*
(in *afhlathan*), G. *laden*, to lade. Teut.
base *hlad* (not *hlath*), to lade (Kluge).
Allied to Russ. *klade*, a lading.

lade (2), to draw out water, drain.
(E.) The same word as **Lade** (1).

ladle, a large spoon. (E.) M. E.
ladel; A. S. *hlǣdel*; so named from being
used for dipping out or *lading* water from
a vessel; from M. E. *laden*, A. S. *hladan*,
to lade out; see above.

Lady. (E.) Perhaps 'loaf-kneader.'
A. S. *hlǣfdige*, a lady. — A. S. *hlāf*, a loaf;
and (perhaps) A. S. **dīge*, a kneader, from
the root seen in Goth.*deigan*,to knead; see
Dike, and see **Dairy.** ¶ *Lady* was specially used to mean the Virgin Mary;
hence *lady-bird, lady's-slipper*, &c.

Lag, late, sluggish. (C.) W. *llag*,
slack, loose, sluggish; Corn. *lac*, loose,
remiss; Gael. and Ir. *lag*, weak, feeble,
faint; O. Irish *lac*, weak.+L. *laxus*, lax;
see **Lax, Languid, Slack.**

Lagan, goods cast out in a shipwreck.
(F.) A law-term; usually explained so
as to force a false connexion with L.
ligāre, to tie. — O. F. *lagan, lagand*,
wreckage cast ashore (Godefroy). Low
L. *laganum*. Origin unknown. Perhaps
from O. Icel. *laginn*, 'positus,' old pp.
pass. of *leggja*, to lay, place (Egilsson),

also, to be driven (Vigf.). Cf. also O.F.
alagane (Godefroy).

Lagoon. (Ital. — L.) Ital. *lagone*, a
pool; also *laguna*. [Or from Span.
laguna.] The former is an augmentative
of L. *lacus*; the latter is from L. *lacūna*,
extended from *lacus*. See **Lake** (1).

Laic. (L. — Gk.) L. *laicus*, belonging
to the laity. — Gk. λαικός (the same). See
Lay (3).

Lair, den or retreat of a wild beast.
(E.) M. E. *leir*. A. S. *leger*, a lair,
couch, bed. — A. S. stem **leg-*, as in A. S.
leg-, base of *licgan*, to lie down, rest.
See **Lie** (1).+Du. *leger*, a bed, lair, from
liggen; G. *lager*, O. H. G. *legar*, a couch,
from O. H. G. *liggan*, to lie; Goth. *ligrs*,
a couch. Doublet, *leaguer.*

Laity, the lay people. (F. — L. — Gk.;
with F. *suffix*.) A coined word; from
lay, adj.; cf. *gaie-ty* from *gay*, &c. See
Lay (3).

Lake (1), a pool. (L.) A. F. *lac*. — L.
lacus, a lake. + Gk. λάκκος, a hollow,
hole, pit, pond; O. Irish *loch*, A. S. *lagu.*

Lake (2), a crimson colour. (F. — Pers.
— Skt.) F. *laque* (Cot.). — Pers. *lāk*, lake.
— Pers. *lak*, gum-lac; see **Lac** (1).

Lakh; the same as **Lac** (2).

Lama (1), a high priest. (Thibetan.)
We speak of the *grand lama* of Thibet,
i. e. chief or high priest (Webster).

Lama (2); see **Llama.**

Lamb. (E.) M. E. *lamb, lomb*. A. S.
lamb, pl. *lambru*.+Du. *lam*, Icel. *lamb*,
Dan. *lam*, Swed. and G. *lamm*, Goth.
lamb, a young sheep. Teut. type **lamboz*,
neut.

Lambent, flickering. (L.) 'A *lambent*
flame.' — L. *lambent-*, stem of pres. pt. of
lambere, to lick, sometimes applied to
flames. Allied to **Lap** (1).

Lame, disabled, esp. in the legs. (E.)
M. E. *lame*. A. S. *lama.*+Du. *lam*, Icel.
lami, Dan. *lam*, Swed. *lam*, G. *lahm*.
The orig. sense is bruised, maimed; from
a base **lam-*, to break. Cf. Russ. *lomate*,
to break; Icel. *lama*, to bruise; prov. E.
lam, to bruise.

Lament, vb. (F. — L.) F. *lamenter*. —
L. *lāmentārī*, to wail. — L. *lāmentum*, a
mournful cry; from the base *lā-*, to utter
a cry; cf. *lā-trāre*, to bark. Cf. also
Russ. *laiate*, to bark, scold.

Lamina. (L.) L. *lāmina*, a thin plate
of metal. Cf. **Omelette.**

Lammas, a name for Aug. 1. (E.)

A. S. *hlāf-mæsse*, lit. 'loaf-mass;' later spellings *hlammæsse*, *lammasse*. A loaf was on this day offered as a first-fruits of harvest. See **Mass** (2).

Lamp. (F.—L.—Gk.) O. F. *lampe.*— L. *lampas.*—Gk. λαμπάς, a torch, light.— Gk. λάμπειν, to shine. Cf. **Lantern.**

Lampoon. (F.—Teut.) F. *lampon*, orig. a drinking-song; from the exclamation *lampons!* = let us drink (Littré).—F. *lamper*, nasalised form of O. F. *lapper*, to lap up; of Teut. origin.—M. Du. *lappen*, 'to lap or licke like a dogge;' Hexham. See **Lap** (1).

Lamprey, an eel-like fish. (F.—L.) A. F. *lampreie*, O. F. *lamproie* (Ital. *lampreda*). — Late L. *lamprēda*; once spelt *lampetra*, as if 'licker of rocks,' because the fish cleaves to them, from L. *lambere*, to lick, *petra*, a rock; but this is doubtful. Cf. **Limpet.**

Lance. (F.—L.) F. *lance.*—L. *lancea.* + Gk. λόγχη, a lance. Der. *lance*, vb., to pierce; *lanc-er*.

lancegay, a kind of spear. (F.—L.; and F.—Span.—Moorish.) Obsolete. A corruption of *lance-zagaye*, compounded of *lance* (as above), and F. *zagaye*, a kind of Moorish pike. The latter word answers to Span. *azagaya* (= *al zagaya*), where *al* is the Arab. def. article, and *zagaya* is an O. Span. word for 'dart,' of Moorish origin. So Port. *azagaia*, whence E. *assegai*.

lanceolate, lance-shaped. (L.) L. *lanceolātus*, furnished with a spike.—L. *lanceola*, a spike; dimin. of *lancea* (above).

lancet. (F.—L.) M. E. *launcet.*— F. *lancette*, dimin. of *lance*, a lance (above).

lanch, another spelling of *lance*, vb., to pierce; also of *launch* (below).

launch, lanch, to hurl a spear, send (a ship) into the water. (F.—L.) M. E. *launchen, launcen*, to hurl.—O.F.*lanchier*, Picard *lancher*; F. *lancer*, to hurl, fling, dart, also to prick, pierce.—L. *lanceāre*, to wield a lance.—L. *lancea*, a lance.

Land. (E.) M. E. *land, lond.* A. S. *land.* + Du. Icel. Dan. Swed. Goth. G. *land.* Teut. type **landom*, neut. Allied to Celtic type **landā*, fem., whence Ir. *lann*, land, W. *llan*, a yard, churchyard, Corn. *lan*, Bret. *lann* (whence F. *lande*, a plain). See **Lawn.** Der. *up-land*, *out-land-ish*.

landau, a kind of coach. (G.) Said to be named from *Landau*, a town in Bavaria. *Land* is cognate with E. *land*; G. *au* is allied to *i-* in M. E. *i-land*; see **Island.**

landgrave, a count of a province. (Du.) Du. *landgraaf.*—Du. *land*, land; *graaf*, a count. Der. *landgrav-ine*, from Du. *landgravin*, fem. of *landgraaf*; see **Margrave.**

landrail, a bird; see **Rail** (3).

landscape. (Du.) Formerly *land-skip*; borrowed from Dutch painters.— Du. *landschap*, a landscape, a province.— Du. *land*, land; and *-schap*, a suffix corresponding to E. *-ship* in *friend-ship*, allied to the E. verb *shape*. ¶ The Du. *sch* sounds to us more like *sk* than *sh*; hence our spelling with *sc*.

Lane. (E.) M. E. *lane, lone.* A. S. *lane, lone*, a lane; O. Fries. *lana, lona.*+ Du. *laan*, a lane, narrow passage.

Language. (F.—L.) M. E. *langage.* —M. F. *language* (Cot.), now *langage.*—F. *langue*, the tongue.—L. *lingua*, tongue. See **Lingual.**

Languish. (F.—L.) M.E. *languishen.* —F. *languiss-*, stem of pres. part. of *languir*, to languish.—L. *languēre*, to be weak. Allied to Gk. λαγαρός, slack; Icel. *lakra*, to lag; and to **Lag.** See Brugm. ii. § 632. (√SLEG.)

languid. (L.) L. *languidus*, feeble. —L. *languēre*, to be languid or weak.

languor, dullness. (F.—L.) M. E. *languor.*—F *langueur.*—L. *languōrem*, acc. of *languor.*—L. *languēre* (above).

Laniard; see **Lanyard.**

Laniferous, wool-bearing. (L.) From L. *lāna*, wool; *ferre*, to bear. L. *lāna* is allied to **Wool.**

Lank, slender, thin. (E.) M. E. *lank.* A. S. *hlanc*, slender.

Lanner, Lanneret, a kind of falcon. (F.—L.) F. *lanier*, 'a lanner;' Cotg.— L. *laniārius*, a butcher, one that tears and rends.—L. *laniāre*, to rend. (So Diez.) Der. Hence perhaps *lanyard.*

Lansquenet, a German foot-soldier, a game at cards. (F.—G.) F. *lansquenet*, 'a lance-knight [a mistaken form] or German footman;' Cot.—G. *landsknecht*, a foot-soldier.—G. *lands*, for *landes*, gen. of *land*, country; *knecht*, a soldier (E. *knight*). Thus *lansquenet* = *land's-knight*; orig. a soldier from Germany.

Lantern. (F.—L.—Gk.) M. E. *lan-*

terne. — F. *lanterne.* — L. *lanterna, lāterna,* a lantern (not a true L. word). *Lanterna* <*lamterna*<*lampterna,* borrowed from Gk. λαμπτήρ, a light, torch. — Gk. λάμπειν, to shine. ¶ Sometimes spelt *lanthorn,* because *horn* was used for the sides of lanterns.

Lanyard, Laniard, a certain small rope in a ship. (F.—L.) Formerly spelt *lannier,* M. E. *lainere;* the final *d* being excrescent, or due to *yard.* — M. F. *laniere,* 'a long and narrow band or thong of leather;' also *lanieres,* pl. 'hawks' lunes;' Cot. Perhaps from F. *lanier,* a kind of hawk. See **Lanner.**

Lap (1), to lick up with the tongue. (E.) M. E. *lappen.* A. S. *lapian,* to lap. + M. Du. *lappen* (Hexham); Icel. *lepja,* Dan. *labe;* O. H. G. *laffan,* to lap up. + L. *lambere,* to lap with the tongue. (√LAB; Brug. ii. § 632.) Allied to *lambent.*

Lap (2), the loose part of a coat, an apron, part of the body covered by an apron, a fold. (E.) M. E. *lappe.* A. S. *læppa,* a loosely hanging portion. + Du. *lap,* Dan. *lap,* Swed. *lapp,* G. *lappen,* a patch, shred, rag. Cf. Icel. *lapa,* to hang down; Lith. *lópas,* a patch, rag. ¶ Hence *lap-el,* a flap of a coat, dimin. of E. *lap;* *lapp-et,* also dimin. of E. *lap;* also the verb *to lap over.* Cf. **Limp** (1).

Lap (3), to wrap. (E.) M. E. *lappen,* also *wlappen,* another form of *wrappen;* see **Wrap.** Quite distinct from *lap* (2).

Lapidary, one who sets precious stones. (L.) Englished from L. *lapidārius,* a stonemason. — L. *lapid-,* stem of *lapis,* a stone. Allied to Gk. λέπας, a bare rock, λεπίς, a flake, λέπειν, to peel (Prellwitz). See **Leper.**

Lapse, vb. (L.) From L. *lapsāre,* to slip, frequent. of *lābī* (pp. *lapsus*), to glide, slip, trip. Der. *col-, e-, il-, re-lapse.*

Lapwing, a bird. (E.) M. E. *lappe-winke.* A. S. *hléapewince,* as if 'one who turns about in running'; from A.S. *hléap-an,* to run; *wince,* one who turns; see **Winch.** ¶ But the older form is *laepae-uincæ* (O. E. T., p. 504); the sense of which is unknown.

Larboard. (E.?) Cotgrave has: '*Babort,* the larboard side of a ship.' Hakluyt (Voyages, i. 4) has the spelling *leereboord;* where *leere* answers to prov. E. *leer,* empty. But the M. E. form is *laddebord,* of uncertain meaning. This

form resembles Swed. *ladda,* to lade; see **Lade** (1). (The word still remains un-explained.)

Larceny, robbery. (F.—L.) The *-y* is an E. addition. — O. F. *larrecin* (F. *larcin*), larceny. — L. *latrocinium,* robbery; formed with suffix *-cinium* (as in *tīrō-cinium*) from *latro,* a robber. Allied to Gk. λάτρις, a hireling, used in a bad sense; and to λάτρον, hire.

Larch, a tree. (G.—F.) From G. *lärche,* a larch (N. E. D.). Cf. O. F. *larice* (Godefroy). — L. *laricem,* acc. of *larix,* a larch. For **darix,* and allied to E. *tree.*

Lard. (F.—L.) O.F. *lard.* — L. *lardum,* also *lārida,* lard, fat of bacon. Cf. Gk. λᾱρός, nice, λᾱρῑνός, fat. Der. *lard-er,* from O. F. *lardier,* a tub to keep bacon in (Cot.), hence a room in which to keep bacon and meat. Also *inter-lard.*

Large. (F.—L.) F. *large.* — L. *larga,* fem. of *largus,* great. Cf. O. F. *larc,* m.

largess, a liberal gift. (F.—L.) F. *largesse,* bounty. — Late L. **largītia,* not found, for L. *largītio,* a bestowing. — L. *largītus,* pp. of *largīrī,* to bestow. — L. *largus,* large, liberal.

Lark (1), a bird. (E.) Another form is *laverock* (Burns). M. E. *larke,* also *laverock.* — A.S. *lāwerce,* later *lāuerce, lāferce.* + Icel. *lævirki,* a lark; Low G. *lewerke,* O. H. G. *lērehha,* G. *lerche,* Du. *leeuwrik,* E. Fries. *lēverke,* Swed. *lärka,* Dan. *larke.* A compound word, of un-known origin.

Lark (2), a game, fun. (E.) The same word as the above; from the cheerful note of the bird. The fuller form *lavrock* (whence *larrick*) produced the form *lar-rikin'* for *larking,* now used as a slang adj., in the sense of rollicking or rowdy. See N. and Q. 7 S. vii. 345.

Larum; short for Alarum.

Larva. (E.) L. *larua,* a ghost, a mask; used as a scientific name for a cater-pillar or grub.

Larynx. (L.—Gk.) L. *larynx.* — Gk. λάρυγξ (gen. λάρυγγ-ος), throat, gullet, larynx. Der. *laryng-itis.*

Lascar, a native E. Indian soldier. (Pers.) Pers. *lashkarī,* a soldier; from *lashkar,* an army.

Lascivious. (L.) Corruptly formed from L. *lascīuus,* lustful. Cf. Skt. *lash,* to desire.

Lash (1), a thong, stripe. (F.—L.) M. E. *lasshe,* the flexible part of a whip;

cf. O. F. *lace*, a snare, a noose; O. F. *lache*, a lace (Godefroy). — Folk L.*lacium*, for L. *laqueum*, acc. of *laqueus*, a snare; see **Lace**. The relationship of this to Du. *lasschen*, to join, to scarf together, is very obscure. *Lash* in the sense of thong is from its use in lashing or binding things together. The verb *lash*, to scourge, is to use a *lash*. See below.

Lash (2), to bind firmly together. (F. — L.) O. F. *lachier*, variant of *lacer*, to lace. We also find the (perhaps unrelated) Du. *lasschen*, to join, scarf together; *lasch*, a piece, joint, seam. So also Swed. *laska*, Dan. *laske*, to scarf; Swed. Dan. *lask*, a scarf, joint. The verb is from the sb.; see above.

Lass, a girl. (Scand. ?) M. E. *lasse*, *lasce* (Mätzner). Cf. Icel. *löskr*, weak; M. Swed. *lösk*, a person having no fixed abode. Vigfusson cites O. Swed. *loska kona*, a spinster. (H. Bradley; in *Ath.* June 16, 1894.) Cf. Bavarian *lasch*, a woman (a term of contempt); Schmeller.

Lassitude, weariness. (F. — L.) F. *lassitude.* — L. *lassitūdo*, weariness. — L. *lassus*, wearied; for **lad-tus*, and allied to E. **Late**.

Lasso, a rope with a noose. (Span. — L.) From Mexican Span. *laso*; O. Span. *laso*, Minsheu. — L. *laqueus* (Folk L. *laceus*), a noose, snare, knot. See **Lace**. ¶ The mod. Span. has *lazo* (with *z* sounded as E. voiceless *th*).

Last (1), latest; see **Late**.

Last (2), a wooden mould of the foot for a shoemaker. (E.) M. E. *last*, *lest*. A. S. *lāst*, *lǣst*, a foot-track, path, trace of feet (whence the mod. sense follows). + Du. *leest*, a last, form; Icel. *leistr* the foot below the ankle; Swed. *läst*, Dan. *læst*, G. *leisten*, a shoemaker's last; Goth. *laists*, a foot-track. The Teut. base appears in Goth. *laist-*, with orig. sense 'foot-track'; from *lais-*, 2nd grade of Teut. **leisan-*; cf. Goth. *lais*, I know (find or trace out). Cf. L. *līra*, a track; see **Delirious**. Akin to **Learn**.

last (3), to endure. (E.) M. E. *lasten*, *lesten*; A. S. *lǣstan*, to observe, perform, last; orig. ' to follow in the track of;' from *lāst*, a foot-track (above). + Goth. *laistjan*, to follow after; G. *leisten*, to follow out. Cf. Goth. *laists*, G. *leisten*, sb.

Last (4), a load, large weight, ship's cargo. (E.) M. E. *last*. A. S. *hlæst*, a burden. Formed from A. S. *hladan*, to lade, load. + Dan. *last*, cargo; Swed. Du. and G. *last*, a burden. See **Lade**. ¶ A. S. *hlæst* is for **hlad-sto-* (> **hlasto-*); from *hlad-*, with suffix *-sto-*. Cf. Icel. *hlass* (< **hlad-to-*), a cart-load.

Latch (1), a catch, fastening. (E.) M. E. *lacche*, a latch, from *lacchen*, to catch. — A. S. *læccan*, to seize, catch hold of.

Latch (2), vb., to moisten. (E.) In Shak. M. N. D. iii. 2. 36. Cf. M. Du. *laken*, to flow (Oudemans); Swed. *laka*, to distil, fall by drops, *laka på*, to pour on to; from *lak*, 2nd grade of Icel. *leka*, to drip; see **Leak**. Also prov. E. *letch*, a vessel for making lye; A. S. *leccan*, to moisten; Low G. *lake*, brine.

Latchet, a little lace, thong. (F. — L.) M. E. *lachet.* — O. F. *lachet*, Norman and Picard form of O. F. *lacet*, a lace; dimin. of O. F. *laqs*, F. *lacs*; see **Lace**.

Late. (E.) M. E. *lat*; comp. *later*, *latter*, superl. *latest*, *latst* (Ormulum, 4168), *last*. A. S. *læt*, slow, late. + Du. *laat*, Icel. *latr*, Dan. *lad*, Swed. *lat*; Goth. *lats*, slothful, G. *lass*, weary. Allied to L. *lassus* (for **lad-tus*), weary. From the weak grade of the verb *to let*, i. e. let go; *late* orig. meant slothful, slow. See **Let** (1). Brugm. i. § 197.

latter, another form of *later* (above).

last (1), latest; contracted form of *latest*.

Lateen; see **Latin**.

Latent, hidden. (L.) L. *latent-*, stem of pres. pt. of *latēre*, to lie hid.

Lateral. (L.) L. *laterālis*, belonging to the side. — L. *later-*, for **lates-*, stem of *latus*, side.

Lath. (E.) North E. *lat*. M. E. *latte*. A. S. *lætt*, a lath; pl. *lætta*. + Du. *lat*; G. *latte* (whence F. *latte*); allied to G. *laden*, a board, plank, shutter. The mod. form *lath* seems to have been influenced by W. *llath*, a rod, staff, Ir. *slat*, a rod; which is cognate.

Lathe (1), a machine for turning wood, &c. (Scand.) Cf. Dan. *dreie-lad*, a turning-lathe; *væver-lad*, a loom, lit. a weaving-lathe.

Lathe (2), a division of a county. (E.) A. S. *lǣð*, M. E. *lēð*, a lathe, province; Thorpe, Ancient Laws, i. 184, 455. Perhaps allied to Icel. *láð*, land.

Lather. (E.) M. E. *lather*. A. S. *lēaðor*, lather; whence *lȳ͞ðran*, to anoint. + Icel. *lauðr*, froth, foam, soap; Swed. *löder*, lather. For the form, cf. Gk.

λουτρόν, a bath. Allied to **Lye** and **Lave**.

Latin. (F. – L.) F. *Latin.* – L. *Latīnus*, belonging to *Latium*. Der. *latim-er*, an interpreter ; for *Latiner.*

lateen, triangular, applied to sails. (F. – L.) F. *latine*, as in *voile latine*, a lateen sail ; *latine* is the fem. of *Latin*, Latin (i. e. Roman).

Latitude, breadth. (F. – L.) M. E. *latitude.* – F. *latitude.* – L. *lātitūdo* (stem *lătitūdin-*), breadth. – L. *lātus*, broad ; short for O. L. *stlātus.* Brugm. i. § 529.

Latten, a mixed metal, like pinch-beck. (F.) M. E. *latoun.* – O. F. *laton* (F. *laiton*), latten. Origin unknown. Cf. Low L. *lato*, *latōnus* ; Span. *laton* ; Port. *latão* ; Ital. *ottone*, latten.

Latter ; see **Late.**

Lattice. (F. – G.) Formerly *lattis.* M. E. *latis.* – F. *lattis*, lath-work, lattice-work. – F. *latte*, a lath. – G. *latte*, a lath ; see **Lath.**

Laud, to praise. (L.) M. E. *lauden.* – L. *laudāre*, to praise. – L. *laud-*, stem of *laus*, praise.

Laudanum. (L. – Gk. – Pers.) Now a preparation of opium, but formerly applied to a different drug. Thus Minsheu's Span. Dict. (1623) has : ' *Laudano*, the gum labdanum vsed in pomanders.' ' *Laudanum*, *Ladanum*, *Labdanum*, a sweet-smelling transparent gum gathered from the leaves of *Cistus Ledon*, a shrub, of which they make pomander, it smells like wine mingled with spices ; ' Blount, 1674. (Laudanum has a like strong smell.) – L. *lādanum*, *lēdanum*, resin from the shrub *lada* (Pliny). – Gk. λήδανον, λάδανον (same). – Gk. λῆδον, a certain shrub. – Pers. *lādan*, the gum-herb lada (Richardson).

Laugh. (E.) M. E. *laughen*, *lehghen.* O. Merc. *hlæhhan*, A.S. *hlihan* (pt. t. *hlōh*), to laugh. +Du. *lagchen*, Icel. *hlæja*, Dan. *lee*, Swed. *le*, G. *lachen*, Goth. *hlahjan* (pt. t. *hloh*). (Base **hlah* = Idg. **klak* ; cf. Lith. *kleg-ēti*, to laugh, Gk. κλώσσειν, to cluck.) Of imitative origin. Der. *laughter*, A. S. *hleahtor.*

Launch (1) ; see **Lanch.**

Launch (2), a large ship's boat. (Span.) Span. *lancha*, ' the pinnace of a ship ;' Pineda (1740). Port. *lancha*, the same. Cf. Port. *lanchara*, a kind of ship ; perhaps of Malay origin (Yule).

Laundress, a washerwoman. (F. –

L.) Formed by adding F. suffix *-ess* to M. E. *launder* or *lavander*, a washer-woman. – O. F. *lavandiere*, ' a launderesse or washing-woman ;' Cot. – Late L. *lauandāria,- dēria*, (same). – L. *lauand-*, gerundial stem of *lauāre*, to wash. See **Lave.** Der. *laundr-y* = *launder-y.*

Laurel. (F. – L.) M. E. *lorel*, *lorer*, *laurer.* – O. F. *lorier* (F. *laurier*), a laurel-tree. – O. F. *lor* (the same) ; with suffix *-ier* (L. *-ārius*). – L. *laurum*, acc. of *laurus*, a laurel-tree.

laureate. (L.) L. *laureātus*, crowned with laurel. – L. *laurea*, a laurel ; orig. fem. of *laureus*, adj. from *laurus* (above).

Lava. (Ital. – L.) Ital. *lava*, a stream (esp. of molten rock). – L. *lauāre*, to wash, lave. See **Lave.**

Lave, to wash. (F. – L.) F. *laver.* – L. *lauāre.* ✛ Gk. λούειν, to wash. Der. *lav-er*, M.F. *lavoir*, a washing-pool (Cot.); *lav-at-or-y*, F. *lavatoire*, L. *lauātōrium*, neut. of *lauātōrius*, adj., belonging to a washer. And cf. **Lather.**

Laveer, to tack. (Du. – F. – Du.) In Dryden. – Du. *laveeren*; M.Du. *laveren*, *loeveren*, ' to saile up and downe,' Hexham. – M. F. *loveër* (Littré) ; F. *louvoyer.* – F. *lof*, luff, weather-side. – Du. *loef.* See **Luff.**

Lavender, a plant. (F. – Late L.) M. E. *lavendre.* A. F. *lavendre* ; Voc. 557. 9. – Late L. *lavendula*, id. ; also *lavandula*, *livendula* ; see N. E. D. The form *livendula* points to L. *līuēre*, to be livid ; from its blueish colour. See **Livid.**

Lavish, profuse, prodigal. (E.) Formerly spelt *lavish*, *laves* ; also *lavy.* Formed with suffix *-ish* (A.S. *-isc*) from the obsolete verb *lave*, to pour out, lade out water ; M. E. *lauen*, to bale out water, whence the *metaphorical* use of *lauen*, to give bountifully. ' He *lauez* hys gyftez ' = God *lavishes* His gifts ; Allit. Poems, A. 607. It answers to A. S. *lafian*, to lave, wash, pour. Cf. Du. *laven*, G. *laben*, to refresh. ¶ The Teut. verb was perhaps early borrowed from L. *lauāre* ; see **Lave.** Cf. Norman dial. *laver*, to spend lavishly. Der. *lavish*, vb.

Law, a rule of action, edict. (Scand.) M. E. *lawe.* A. S. *lagu* (not common ; the usual A. S. word is *ǣ*) ; borrowed from Scand. Cf. O. Sax. *lag*, law. – Icel. *lög*, pl., but in sing. sense, a law, from *lag*, a stratum, order ; Swed. *lag* ; Dan. *lov.*

From Teut. *lag*, 2nd stem of **ligjan*, to lie ; see **Lie** (1). The sense is ' that which lies,' or is fixed (cf. Gk. κεῖται νόμος, the law is fixed, from κεῖμαι, I lie). **Der.** *law-y-er* (cf. *saw-y-er*). See **Lie** (1).

Lawn (1), a space of grass-covered ground, a glade. (F. – C.) M. E. *laund* (the *d* has been dropped). – O. F. *lande*, ' a land or laund, a wild, untilled, shrubby, or grassy plain;' Cot. Cf. Ital. and Span. *landa*, a heath. β. Of disputed origin; referred by Littré to G. *land* (= E. *land*), open country; but by Diez (rightly) to Bret. *lann*, a bushy shrub, of which the pl. *lannou*, like F. *landes*, means 'waste lands.' It comes to the same thing ; for E. and G. *land* are cognate with Irish *lann*, a piece of land. Cf. W. *llan*, Gael. *lann*, an enclosure, piece of land. See **Land**.

Lawn (2), fine linen. (F. place-name.) Palsgrave has *Laune lynen*, prob. for *Lan lynen*, where *Lan* is the 16th cent. spelling of *Laon*, to the N. W. of Rheims. *Lawn* was also called ' cloth of Remes,' i. e. Rheims ; see Baret's *Alvearie*.

Lax, slack. (L.) L. *laxus*, slack, loose. Allied to **Slack**. Brugm. i. § 193.

laxative, loosening. (F. – L.) F. *laxatif*. – L. *laxātīuus*, loosening. – L. *laxātus*, pp. of *laxāre*, to loosen. – L. *laxus*, lax.

Lay (1), to cause to lie down, set. (E.) M. E. *leien*, *leggen*, pt. t. *leide*, pp. *leid*. A.S. *lecgan*, pt. t. *legde*, pp. *gelegd* ; causal of *licgan*, to lie. + Du. *leggen*, Icel. *leggja*, Dan. *lægge*, Swed. *lägga*, G. *legen*, Goth. *lagjan*. Teut. type **lag-jan-*, causal verb; from **lag*, 2nd grade of **ligjan-*, to lie; see **Lie** (1). For the modern forms, see Sweet, E. Gr. § 1293.

layer, a stratum, tier, bed. (E.) The same as *lay-er*, he who lays; see N. E. D. ¶ Not M. E. *leir*, a lair, couch, place for lying down in ; hence a bed, stratum, &c.

Lay (2), a song, poem. (F. – G.) M. E. *lai*. – O. F. *lai*, said to be a Breton word. But only an O. F. name for a Breton poem ; and prob. from O. H. G. *leih*, *leich*, a game, sport, song (see Schade). Cf. A. S. *lāc*, sport.

Lay (3), pertaining to the laity. (F. – L. – Gk.) M. E. *lay*. – O. F. *lai*, secular. – L. *lāicus*. – Gk. λαικός, belonging to the people. – Gk. λαός (Attic λεώς), the people. See **Laic**, **Laity**.

Lay (4), as in **Lay-figure**. (Du.) The old word was *lay-man* (Richardson). Lit. ' joint-man,' i. e. man made with joints. – Du. *leeman*, a lay-man. Here *lee-* is for *lede-*, in compounds (Sewel) ; and Du. *leden* is the pl. of *lid*, a joint, cognate with A. S. *lið*, Goth. *lithus*, G. *g-lied*, a joint. Prob. allied to **Limb** (Kluge).

Layer ; see **Lay** (1).

Lazar, a leper. (F. – L. – Gk. – Heb.) M. E. *lazar*. – F. *lazare*. – L. *Lazarus*. – Gk. Λάζαρος, the name of the beggar in Luke, xvi. 20; contracted from Heb. name *Eleazar*. – Heb. *El'āzār*, he whom God helps. **Der.** *lazar-etto*, a plague-hospital, Ital. *lazzaretto*.

Lazy. (Low G.) *Laezie* (Spenser). – Low G. *lasich*, variant of *losich*, languid, idle (Lübben) ; *läösig*, lazy (Danneil) ; Pomeran. *läsig*, cf. *laassam*, lazy (Bremen) ; Du. *leuzig*, lazy. Allied to **Loose**.

Lea, **Lay**, **Ley**, a meadow. (E.) M. E. *lay*, *ley*, untilled land. A.S. *lēah*, *lēa* (gen. *lēage*), a lea ; cf. *Hæd-lēah*, i. e. Hadleigh. Cognate with prov. G. *loh*, a morass, low plain, Low G. *loge*, Flem. *loo* as in *Water-loo*; also with Lithuan. *laukas*, an open field, L. *lūcus*, a glade, open space in a wood. Orig. ' a clearing.' Allied to **Lucid**. Brugm. i. § 221.

Lead (1), to conduct. (E.) M. E. *leden*, pt. t. *ladde*, pp. *lad*. – A. S. *lǣdan*, to lead. + Icel. *leiða*; Swed. *leda*; G. *leiten* ; Du. *leiden*. Teut. type **laidjan-* ; from **laith* (by Verner's Law), 2nd grade of **leithan-* (A. S. *liðan*), to travel. See **Lode**.

Lead (2), a metal. (E.) M. E. *leed*. A. S. *lēad*. + Du. *lood*, Swed. *lod*, Dan. *lod*, G. *loth*, M. H. G. *lōt*. Teut. type **laudom*, neut. Cf. O. Irish *luaidhe*, lead.

Leaf. (E.) M. E. *leef*, pl. *leues* (= *leves*). A. S. *lēaf*, neut., pl. *lēaf*. + Du. *loof*, foliage; Icel. *lauf*, Swed. *löf*, Dan. *löv*, Goth. *laufs*, G. *laub*. Teut. stem **laubo-*.

League (1), a bond, alliance. (Ital. – L.) Ital. *lega*, ' a league ;' Florio. – Late L. *liga*, a league. – L. *ligāre*, to bind. See **Ligament**.

League (2), about three miles. (Prov. – L. – C.) O. F. *legue* (Roquefort) ; Prov. *legua* (Gascon *lega*). – Late L. *lēga*, *leuca* ; L. *leuga*, *leuca*, a Gallic mile ; a word of Celtic origin. Cf. Bret. *leō*, *lev*, a league ; also *leu* (in Vannes).

Leaguer, a camp. (Du.) In All's Well, iii. 6. 27. — Du. *leger*, a lair, a camp. See **Lair**, **Lie** (1). **Der.** *be-leaguer*.

Leak. (Scand.) M. E. *leken*. — Icel. *leka*, to drip, dribble, leak as a ship, str. vb. (pt. t. *lak*); cf. the causal forms seen in Swed. *läcka*, Dan. *lække*, Du. *lekken*, G. *lecken*, to leak, drop; A. S. *leccan*, to wet. ¶ The mod. E. word is Scand.; not from A. S. *leccan*. [We also find A. S. *hlec*, leaky.] **Der.** *leak*, sb., from Icel. *leki*, a leak. Prob. allied to **Lack** (Franck).

Leal, loyal, true. (F.—L.) M. E. *lēl*. — A. F. *leal*, O. F. *leial*, legal, hence just, loyal. — L. *lēgālis*, legal. **Doublets**, *legal*, *loyal*. See **Legal**.

Lean (1), to incline, stoop. (E.) M. E. *lenen*. — A. S. *hlǣnan*, to make to lean, weak verb; (cf. A. S. *hlinian*, to lean, weak verb). + Dan. *læne*, Swed. *läna*, causal forms; G. *lehnen*, intrans. Allied to L. *-clīnāre*, in *inclīnāre*, to incline; Gk. κλίνειν, to cause to lean, make to bend. (√KLEI.)

lean (2), slender, frail. (E.) M. E. *lene*. A. S. *hlǣne*, lean; orig. bending, stooping, hence thin; cf. L. *dēclīuis*, declining. Teut. type *hlainjoz*. Cf. O. Irish *clóen*, sloping, bad. Allied to A. S. *hlǣnan*, to lean (above).

Leap. (E.) M. E. *lepen*, pt. t. *leep*, pp. *lopen*. A. S. *hlēapan*, pt. t. *hlēop*, to run, jump. + Du. *loopen*, Icel. *hlaupa*, Dan. *löbe*, Swed. *lopa*, Goth. *hlaupan*, G. *laufen*, chiefly in the sense 'to run.' Teut. type *hlaupan-*.

Learn. (E.) M. E. *lernen*. A. S. *leornian*. + G. *lernen*, to learn. Teut. type *liznōn*; from *liz(a)noz*, pp. of *leisan-*, to trace out, of which the pt. t. *lais* occurs in Goth. with the sense 'I know', i. e. have found out. Hence also Teut. *laizjan-*, to teach, as in A. S. *lǣran* (G. *lehren*), to teach. Brugm. i. § 903 (c). And see **Last** (2), **Lore**.

Lease (1), to let a tenement. (F.—L.) F. *laisser*, to let go. — L. *laxāre*, to slacken, let go. — L. *laxus*, loose. See **Lax**.

Lease (2), to glean. (E.) M. E. *lesen*. A. S. *lesan*, to gather. + Du. *lezen*, to gather, to read; G. *lesen*; Goth. *lisan*, pt. t. *las*, to gather; Lith. *lèsti*, to snap up.

Leash, a thong to hold in a dog. (F. —L.) M. E. *lees*. — O. F. *lesse* (F. *laisse*), a leash. — Late L. *laxa*, a thong, a loose rope. — L. *laxus*, slack. See **Lax**. ¶ The number usually leashed together was three.

Leasing, falsehood. (E.) M. E. *lesing*. A. S. *lēasung*, falsehood; from *lēas*, false. Cf. Icel. *lausung*, falsehood; Du. *loos*, false. See **Loose**.

Least; see **Less**.

Leat, a conduit for water. (E.) A. S. *ge-lǣte*, a course, direction. From *lǣtan*, to let, permit. Cf. *in-let*, *out-let*. See **Let** (1).

Leather. (E.) M. E. *lether*. A. S. *leðer*. + Du. *leder*, Icel. *leðr*, Dan. *læder*, Swed. *läder*, G. *leder*, leather. Teut. type *lethrom*, neut.; Idg. type *letrom*, as in O. Irish *lethar*, W. *lledr*. **Der.** *leather-n*.

Leave (1), to forsake, quit. (E.) M. E. *leuen* (*leven*). A. S. *lǣfan*, to leave a heritage, leave behind one. + Icel. *leifa*, to leave. Teut. type *laibjan-*, to leave; from *laib-*, as seen in A. S. *lāf*, a remainder, Icel. *leif*, a heritage. And *laib* is the 2nd stem of Teut. *leiban-*, to remain, as in A. S. *be-līfan*, O. H. G. *bi-līban* (whence G. *bleiben*). Idg. root *leip*, as in Gk. λῖπαρής, persistent; the weak grade *lip* appears in Skt. *lip*, to smear, Gk. λίπος, grease, Russ. *lipkii*, sticky, Lith. *lipti*, to adhere to. See **Live**. Brugm. i. § 87.

Leave (2), permission, farewell. (E.) 'To take *leave*' = to take permission to go. 'By your *leave*' = by your permission. M. E. *leue* (*leve*). A. S. *lēaf*, permission. From the same root as A. S. *lēof*, dear, pleasing. The orig. sense was pleasure; hence a grant, permission. + Du. *-lof*, as in *oor-lof*, permission, *ver-lof*, leave; Icel. *leyfi*, leave, *lofan*, permission, *lob* (1) praise, (2) permission; Dan. *lov*, Swed. *lof*, praise, leave; G. *ur-laub*, *ver-laub*, leave, *er-lauben*, to permit, *lob*, praise. From Teut. base *leub-* (whence A. S. *lēof*), 2nd grade *laub-* (>A. S. *lēaf*), weak grade *lub-* (>A. S. *luf-u*, love). See **Lief**, **Love**, **Furlough**. (√LEUBH.)

Leaven, ferment. (F.—L.) M. E. *leuain* (*levain*). — F. *levain*. — L. *leuāmen*, an alleviation; here used in the orig. sense of 'that which raises.' — L. *leuāre*, to raise. — L. *leuis*, light. See **Levity**.

Lecher. (F. — G.) M. E. *lechur*, *lechour*. — O. F. *lecheor*, *lecheur*, lit. one who licks up, a man addicted to gluttony and lewdness. — O. F. *lecher* (F. *lécher*), lick. — O. H. G. *lecchōn* (G. *lecken*), to lick. See **Lick**.

Lectern, **Lecturn**, a reading-desk. (F. — Late L.) M. E. *leterone*, *lectorne*, *lectrone*, *lectrun* (Prompt. Parv.).

288

– O. F. *letrun* (Godefroy) ; *lectrun, letrin* (Littré, s. v. *lutrin*). **–** Late L. *lectrīnum*, a reading-desk, pulpit. **–** Late L. *lectrum*, a pulpit. *Not* from Gk. λέκτρον, a couch, support ; akin to Gk. λέχος, a couch, bed ; cf. L. *lectus*, a couch. For other forms, like Late L. *lectōrīnum, lectōrium,* shew that it was popularly connected with L. *lectio* (below).

Lection, a reading, portion to be read. (L.) From L. *lectio*, a reading. **–** L. *lectus*, pp. of *legere*, to read. See **Legend.**

lecture, a discourse. (F. **–** L.) F. *lecture*, a reading. **–** Late L. *lectūra*, a commentary. **–** L. *lectus*, pp. of *legere*, to read.

Ledge, a slight shelf, ridge. (E.) Palsgrave has *ledge* (i. e. support) of a shelf. Cf. Norfolk *ledge*, a bar of a gate, rail of a chair ; M. E. *legge*. [But not Swed. *lagg*, the rim of a cask, Icel. *lögg*, the ledge or rim at the bottom of a cask ; Norweg. *logg* (pl. *legger*), the lowest part of a vessel ; M. H. G. *lekke.*] Cf. also Norw. *lega*, a couch, lair, bed, support on which anything rests ; *lege*, a ledge, as of rock. All from Teut. **leg*, the base of **ligjan-*, to lie. Cf. A. S. *licgan*, Icel. *liggja*, Swed. *ligga*, Dan. *ligge*, to lie. The sense is 'support.' See **Lie** (1).

Ledger, a flat slab ; also, a book in which a summary of accounts is preserved. (E.) (We also find *leger ambassadors,* i. e. such as *remained* for some time at a foreign court.) A *ledger-book* is one that lies always ready. Similarly, in Middle-English, a large book was called a *liggar* (that which lies), because not portable. From M. E. *liggen*, A. S. *licgan*, to lie ; see **Lie** (1). Cf. Du. *legger*, one that lies down (the nether mill-stone is also so called) ; from Du. *leggen*, to lie, a common corruption of *liggen*, to lie (like *lay* for *lie* in English). ¶ Howell uses *leger-book* for 'portable book,' which is from O. F. *legier*, light. See *ledger* in Richardson.

Lee, a sheltered place ; part of a ship away from the wind. (Scand.) M. E. *lee*, shelter. **–** Icel. *hlē*, lee (of a ship) ; Dan. *læ*, Swed. *lä.*+Du. *lij* ; A. S. *hlēo, hleow*, a covering, a shelter (distinct from prov. E. *lew*, warm ; see **Lew**). ¶ The peculiar use is Scand. ; the pronunciation *lew-ard* is due to the *w* ; cf. *steward* for *sty-ward.* The Teut. type is **hlewo-* (Franck).

Leech (1), a physician. (E.) M. E. *leche.* A. S. *lǣce*, one who heals. + Goth. *lēkeis*, a leech ; cf. Icel. *læknir*, Dan. *læge*,

Swed. *läkare.* Also A. S. *lācnian*, to heal, Icel. *lækna*, Dan. *læge*, Swed. *läka*, Goth. *lēkinon*, to heal. Also O. Irish *liaig*, a leech.

leech (2), a blood-sucking worm. (E.) A. S. *lǣce*, lit. 'the healer ;' the same word as the above.

Leech (3), **Leach,** the border or edge of a sail at the sides. (E.) Cf. Icel. *līk*, a leech-line ; Swed. *lik*, Dan. *lig*, a bolt-rope.+M. Du. *lyken*, a bolt-rope (Sewel) ; Du. *lijk* (see Franck).

Leek. (E.) M. E. *leek.* O. Merc. *lēc* ; A. S. *lēac.*+ Du. *look*, Icel. *laukr*, Dan. *lög*, Swed. *lök*, G. *lauch.* Teut. type **lauko-* ; cf. A. S. *lūcan*, str. vb. (pt. t. *lēac* = Teut. **lauk*), to weed. Der. *gar-lic, char-lock, hem-lock* (latter syllable).

Leer, a sly look. (E.) The verb is a development from the sb., which is an old word. M. E. *lere*, the cheek, face, complexion, mien ; usually in a good sense, but Skelton has it in a bad sense. A. S. *hlēor*, the cheek ; hence, the face, look, mien.+Icel. *hlýr*, pl., the cheeks.

Lees, dregs of wine. (F.) Pl. of a sing. form *lee*, not used. **–** F. *lie*, 'the lees ;' Cot. (Gascon *lio*, 'lie de vin.') **–** Late L. *lia*, pl. *liæ*, lees (10th cent.). Origin unknown.

Leet, an assembly of a township. (Scand.) M. E. *lete.* A. F. *lete* ; perhaps adapted from Icel. *leið*, 'a leet ;' Vigfusson.

Left, the weaker hand. (E.) M. E. *loft, lift, luft.* A. S. *left* ; Dr. Sweet points out that 'inanis, *left*,' occurs in a gloss (Mone, Quellen, i. 443), and that the same MS. has *senne* for *synne* (sin) ; so that *left* is for *lyft*, with the sense 'worthless' or 'weak' ; cf. A. S. *lyft-ādl*, palsy. + North Fries. *leeft, leefter hond*, left hand ; M. Du. *luft, lucht*, left ; E. Fries. *lüchter*, left, *luf*, weak. β. The form of the base is **lub* ; cf. Du. *lubben* (Franck). See **Lib.**

Leg. (Scand.) M. E. *leg* (pl. *legges*). **–** Icel. *leggr*, a leg ; Dan. *læg*, the calf of the leg ; Swed. *lägg* (the same). Brugm. i. § 647(5).

Legacy. (L.) M. E. *legacie* ; a coined word (as if = L. *lēgātia*, not found) from L. *lēgātum*, a bequest, neut. of pp. of *lēgāre*, to appoint, bequeath ; allied to *lex* (stem *lēg-*), the law (below).

legal, pertaining to the law. (F. **–** L.) M.F. *legal.* **–** L. *lēgālis*, legal. **–** L. *lēg-*, stem of *lex*, law. Allied to L. *legere* ; Gk.

λέγειν, to collect. Brugm. i. § 134. (√LEG.)

legate, a commissioner. (F. — L.) M. E. *legate.* — O. F. *legat* (F. *légat*), a pope's ambassador. — L. *lēgātus,* a deputy; pp. of *lēgāre,* to appoint. — L. *lēg-,* stem of *lex,* law. See **legal.**

legatee. (L.; *with* F. *suffix.*) A law term; coined from L. *lēgāt-us,* appointed, with F. suffix *-é* (= L. *-ātus*). See above.

legend, a marvellous story. (F. — L.) M. E. *legende.* — O. F. *legende* (F. *légende*), a legend, story. — Late L. *legenda,* a legend; fem. sing. from L. *legenda,* neut. pl., things to be read. — L. *legendus,* fut. pass. part. of *legere,* to read; orig. to gather, collect. + Gk. λέγειν, to tell, speak. (√LEG.)

Legerdemain, sleight of hand. (F. — L.) O. F. *legier de main,* lit. light of hand. (Cf. Ital. *leggiere, leggiero,* light.) The O. F. *legier* answers to a Late L. type **leuiārius,* made by adding *-ārius* to L. *leui-s,* light. F. *de* = L. *dē,* of. F. *main* = L. *manum,* acc. of *manus,* a hand. See **Levity.**

leger-line, ledger-line, in music, a short line added above or below the staff. (E. *and* F.) As if for *leger-line*; where *leger* = F. *léger* (formerly *legier*), light; because these lines are small and short. But wrongly; *ledger* means 'a horizontal bar,' and is allied to *ledge* (N.E.D.). Cf. mod. F. *lignes additionnelles.*

Legible, readable. (F. — L.) O. F. *legible.* — L. *legibilis,* legible. — L. *legere,* to read. See **legend.**

legion, a large body of soldiers. (F. — L.) M. E. *legioun.* — O. F. *legion.* — L. *legiōnem,* acc. of *legio,* a Roman legion, body of from 4200 to 6000 men. — L. *legere,* to gather, select a band.

Legislator. (L.) L. *lēgislātor,* a proposer of a law. — L. *lēgis,* gen. of *lex,* a law; *lātor,* a proposer, lit. bringer, from *lātum* (for *tlātum*), to bear, bring, from √TEL; see **Tolerate.** Brugm. i. § 585 (2). Der. *legislate,* &c. See **legal.**

legist. (F. — L.) O. F. *legiste* (F. *légiste*). — Late L. *lēgista,* one skilled in the laws. — L. *lēg-,* stem of *lex,* law (with Gk. suffix *-ista* = -ιστης).

legitimate. (L.) Late L. *lēgitimātus,* pp. of *lēgitimāre,* to declare to be lawful. — L. *lēgitimus,* according to law. — L. *lēgi-,* for *lex,* law; with suffix *-ti-mus.*

Legume, a pod. (F. — L.) F. *légume,*

pulse, a pod. — L. *legūmen* (stem *legūmin-*), pulse, bean-plant. Brugm. i. § 667. Der. *legumin-ous.*

Leisure, freedom from employment. (F. — L.) M. E. *leyser.* — A. F. *leisir* (F. *loisir*), leisure; orig. an infin. mood, meaning 'to be permitted.' — L. *licēre,* to be permitted. ¶ The form is bad; it should be *leiser* or *leisir*; *pleasure* is in the same case. The suffix has been changed from *-er* or *-ir* to *-ure* (as in *measure*).

Leman, Lemman, a sweetheart. (E.) I. e. *lief man.* M. E. *lemman,* also *leofman.* — A. S. *lēof,* dear; *mann,* a man or woman. See **Lief.**

Lemma, an assumption. (L. — Gk.) L. *lēmma.* — Gk. λῆμμα, a thing taken; in logic, a premiss taken for granted; allied to Gk. εἴ-λημμαι, perf. pass. of λαμβάνειν, to take (base λαβ-). Brugm. i. § 852.

Lemming, Leming, a kind of Norwegian rat. (Norweg.) Norweg. *lemende*; also occurring as *lemming, limende, lomeldre, lomund, lomhund.* Cf. Swed. *lemel,* a lemming; Icel. *lōmundr.* Origin obscure; Aasen derives it from Norweg. *lemja,* to strike, beat, maim, lit. 'lame,' and explains it to mean 'destroying'; from the destruction committed by them; see **Lame.** But this is 'popular etymology.' The word may be Lapp; the Lapp name is *tuomek.*

Lemniscate, a curve like the figure 8. (L. — Gk.) From L. *lēmniscāt-us,* adorned with a ribbon. — L. *lēmniscus,* a pendent ribbon. — Gk. λημνίσκος, a fillet. Said to be from Gk. λῆνος, wool; which is allied to **Wool.**

Lemon. (F. — Pers.) Formerly *limon.* — F. *limon.* — Pers. *līmūn, līmūnā,* a lemon, citron. Of Malay origin.

Lemur, a nocturnal animal. (L.) L. *lemur,* a ghost; so nicknamed by naturalists from its nocturnal habits.

Lend. (E.) The final *d* is excrescent. M. E. *lenen.* A. S. *lǣnan,* to lend. — A. S. *lǣn,* a loan. + Icel. *lāna,* Dan. *laane,* Swed. *lāna,* G. *lehnen,* derivatives from the sb. See **Loan.**

Length. (E.) M. E. *lengthe.* A. S. *lengð,* fem.; for **langiðā,* with mutation of *a* to *e.* — A. S. *lang,* long. + Du. *lengte*; Dan. *længde*; Swed. *längd*; Icel. *lengd.* See **Long.** Der. *length-en.*

Lenient, mild. (L.) From pres. part. of L. *lēnīre,* to soothe. — L. *lēnis,* soft, mild.

lenity. (F.—L.) O. F. *lenité*, mildness (obsolete). **—** L. *lēnitātem*, acc. of *lēnitas*, mildness. **—** L. *lēnis* (above).

Lens, a piece of glass used in optics. (L.) So called from the resemblance of a double-convex lens to the shape of the seed of a lentil. **—** L. *lens*, a lentil.

Lent, a fast of 40 days, beginning with Ash-Wednesday. (E.) The fast is in spring-time; the old sense is simply spring. M. E. *lent, lenten*. A.S. *lencten*, the spring; supposed to be derived from *lang*, long, because in spring the days lengthen; Kluge suggests that it represents a Teut. form *langi-tīno-*, 'long day,' where *-tīno-* is allied to Skt. *dina-*, Lith. *dĕna*, a day.**+** Du. *lente*, spring; G. *lenz*, O. H. G. *lenzo*, *lenzin, lengizen*. **Der.** *lenten*, adj., from A. S. *lencten*, sb.

Lentil, a plant. (F.—L.) M. E. *lentil*. **—** O. F. (and F.) *lentille*. **—** L. *lenticula*, a little lentil; double dimin. of *lent-*, stem of *lens*, a lentil. See **Lens.**

Lentisk, the mastic-tree. (F.—L.) F. *lentisque*. **—** L. *lentiscum*, *lentiscus*, named from the clamminess of its resin. **—** L. *lentus*, sticky, pliant.

Leo, a lion. (L.—Gk.—Egypt.?) L. *leo*. **—** Gk. λέων, a lion. We also find Du. *leeuw*, G. *löwe*, Russ. *lev'*, Lithuan. *lavas*, a lion; all borrowed forms. Cf. Heb. *lāvī'*, a lion. Probably of Egyptian origin; see **Lion.**

leopard. (F.—L.—Gk.) O.F. *leopard*. **—** L. *leopardus*. **—** Gk. λεόπαρδος, a leopard; supposed to be a mongrel between a pard (panther) and a lioness. **—** Gk. λεο-, for λέων, a lion; πάρδος, a pard.

Leper. (F.—L.—Gk.) The sense has changed; *lepre* formerly meant the disease itself; and what we now call a *leper* was called *a leprous man*. 'The *lepre* of him was clensid;' Wyclif, Matt. viii. 3. **—** M. F. *lepre*, 'a leprosie;' Cot. **—** L. *lepra*. **—** Gk. λέπρα, leprosy; so called because the skin scales off. **—** Gk. λεπρός, scaly, scabby. **—** Gk. λέπος, a scale; λέπειν, to peel. Cf. Russ. *lupite*, Lithuan. *lùpti*, to peel.

lepidoptera, a term applied to insects whose wings are covered with scales. (Gk.) Gk. λεπίδο-, for λεπίς, a scale; πτερά, pl. of πτερόν, a wing (allied to E *feather*).

Leporine, belonging to a hare. (L.) L. *leporīnus*, adj., from *lepor-*, for **lepos*, stem of *lepus*, a hare.

Leprosy. (F.—L.—Gk.) A coined

word, from the adj. *leprous*; which is from M. F. *lepreux* = L. *leprōsus*, afflicted with *lepra*, i.e. leprosy. See **Leper.**

Lesion, an injury. (F.—L.) M. F. *lesion*, hurt; Cot. **—** L. *læsiōnem*, acc. of *læsio*, an injury. **—** L. *læsus*, pp. of *lædere*, to hurt. **Der.** (from *lædere*) *col-lide*, *e-lision*.

Less, smaller. (E.) Used as comp. of *little*, but from a different root. M. E. *lessè*, *lassè*, adj., *les*, adv. A. S. *lǣssa*, less, adj.; *lǣs*, adv. **+** O. Fries. *lēssa*, less. β. The form *lǣs-sa* is for **lǣs-ra*, by assimilation. The Teut. type is **lais-izon*, from a base **lais-*; cf. Lith. *lẽsas*, thin, small. The Teut. type of the adv. is **laisiz*. **Der.** *less-er*, a double comp.; *less-en*, vb.

least. (E.) M. E. *lestè*, adj., *lest*, adv. A. S. *lǣsest*, whence *lǣst* by contraction; a superlative form from the same base **lais-*.

lest, for fear that, that not. (E.) Not for *least*, but due to A. S. phrase ðȳ lǣs ðe = for the reason less that; wherein ðȳ (for the reason) was soon dropped, and lǣs ðe coalesced into *lest*. Here lǣs = less, adv.; and ðe is the indeclinable relative.

-less, suffix; see **Loose.**

Lessee. (F.—L.) O. F. *lesse* (*lessé*), pp. of *lesser*, later *laisser*, to let go (lease). See **Lease** (1).

Lesson. (F.—L.) M. E. *lesson*. **—** F. *leçon*. **—** L. *lectiōnem*, acc. of *lectio*, a reading; see **Lection.** Doublet, *lection*.

Lest; see **Less.**

Let (1), to permit. (E.) M. E. *leten*, strong verb, pt. t. *lat*, *leet*, pp. *laten*, *leten*. A. S. *lǣtan*, *lētan*, pt. t. *lēt*, *leort*, pp. *lǣten*. **+**Du. *laten* (*liet*, *gelaten*); Icel. *láta* (*lēt*, *lātinn*); Dan. *lade*, Swed. *låta*, Goth. *lētan* (*lailōt*, *lētans*); G. *lassen* (*liess*, *gelassen*). Teut. type **lǣtan*, pt. t. **lelōt*, pp. **lǣtanoz*. Idg. √LED; weak grade LAD, whence E. **Late.** Brugm. i. § 478.

Let (2), to hinder. (E.) M. E. *letten*; A. S. *lettan*, to hinder, make late. **—** A. S. *læt*, late, slow. **+** Du. *letten*, Icel. *letja*, Goth. *latjan*, to tarry; from the adj. **Late.** Teut. type **lat-jan-*; from **lat-*, slow. See **Late.**

Lethal, deadly. (F.—L.; *or* L.) M.F. *lethal*, 'deadly;' Cot. **—** L. *lēthālis*, for *lētālis*, mortal. **—** L. *lētum*, death.

Lethe, oblivion. (L.—Gk.) L. *lēthē*. **—** Gk. λήθη, a forgetting; the river of oblivion; allied to λαθ-, base of λανθάνειν, to lie hid.

lethargy, a heavy sleep. (F.—L.—Gk.) M. F. *lethargie*, a lethargy; Cot.—L. *lēthargia*.—Gk. ληθαργία, drowsiness.—Gk. λήθαργος, forgetful.—Gk. λήθη, oblivion (above).

Letter, a character. (F.—L.) M. E. *lettre*.—F. *lettre*.—L. *littera*, for older *lītera* (also *leitera*), a letter. See Brugm. i. § 930.

Lettuce, a succulent plant. (F.—L.) M. E. *letuce*.—O. F. **letuce*, only found in the form *lectus* (Palsgrave, s. v. *Lettes*); and in the Latinised form *lētūsa*, Wrt. Vocab. 787. 15.—L. **lactūcea*, fem. adj. from L. *lactūca*, a lettuce (whence F. *laitue*, Ital. *lattuga*).—L. *lact-*, stem of *lac*, milk, succulent juice. See Lacteal.

Levant, the E. of the Mediterranean Sea. (Ital.—L.) Ital. *levante*, E. wind, eastern country or part (where the sun rises).—L. *leuant-*, stem of pres. part. of *leuāre*, to raise; whence *sē leuāre*, to rise. —L. *leuis*, light.

levee, a morning assembly. (F.—L.) For F. *le lever* (Littré).—F. *lever*, to raise. —L. *leuāre* (above).

Level, an instrument for determining that a thing is horizontal. (F.—L.) M. E. *liuel, leuel* (*livel, level*).—O. F. *livel*, later spelling *liveau*; mod. F. *niveau*, a level. —L. *lībella*, a level; dimin. of *lībra*, a balance. See Librate. ¶ Hence the adj. *level*.

Lever. (F.—L.) M. E. *levour*.—F. *leveur*, a raiser, lifter.—L. *leuātōrem*, acc. of *leuātor*, a lifter.—L. *leuāre*, to lift.—L. *leuis*, light.

Leveret. (F.—L.) A. F. *leveret* (pl. *leveres*, Gaimar, Chron. l. 6239); O. F. *levrault*, 'a leveret, or young hare;' Cot.; with change of suffix. [The suffix *-ault* = Late L. *-aldus*, from O. H. G. *wald*, power, common as a suffix.] The base *lever-* is from L. *lepor-* for **lepos*, stem of *lepus*, a hare.

Leviathan. (L.—Heb.) Late L. *leviathan*, Job xl. 20 (Vulgate).—Heb. *livyāthān*, an aquatic animal, dragon, serpent; named from its twisting itself in curves.—Heb. root *lāvāh*: Arab. root *lawa'*, to bend, whence *lawā*, the twisting or coiling of a serpent.

Levigate, to make smooth. (L.) Out of use.—L. *lēuigātus*, pp. of *lēuigāre*, to make smooth.—L. *lēu-is*, smooth;

-igāre, for *agere*, to make. Cf. Gk. λεῖος, smooth.

Levin, lightning. (Scand.) M. E. *leyfnyng*, lightning; Wrt. Voc. 735.42. Prob. Scand.; not found in A. S. Cf. Icel. *leiptr* (pronounced *leiftr*), lightning.

Levite, one of the tribe of Levi. (L.—Gk.—Heb.) L. *Leuita*.—Gk. Λευίτης, Lu. x. 32.—Heb. *Levī*, one of the sons of Jacob.

Levity, lightness, frivolity. (L.) From L. *leuitas*, lightness.—L. *leuis*, light.

levy, the act of raising men for an army; the force raised. (F.—L.) F. *levée*, 'a levy, or levying of an army;' Cot. Fem. of pp. of *lever*, to raise.—L. *leuāre*, to raise.—L. *leuis* (above).

Lew, Lew-warm, tepid. (E.) M. E. *lew*, Wyclif, Rev. iii. 16. A.S. *hlēowe*, warm (found once).+Du. *lauw*, warm; Icel. *hlār, hlȳr*; G. *lau*, O. H. G. *lāo* (*lāw-*). Teut. base (perhaps) **hlēw-, hlǣw-*.

Lewd, ignorant, base. (E.—Gk.?) M. E. *lewed*, ignorant. A.S. *lǣwede*, adj., ignorant, also lay, belonging to the laity. [It may have been confused with the pp. of *lǣwan*, to betray; cf. Goth. *lēwjan*, to betray, from *lēw*, occasion, opportunity.] But it is supposed to be of Latin origin; answering to L. type **lāicātus*, belonging to the laity, parallel to Late L. *clēricātus* (whence E. *clergy*). If so, it is formed from L. *lāicus*, a word of Gk. origin. See Laic. (Sievers, § 173; Pogatscher, § 340.)

Lexicon. (Gk.) Gk. λεξικόν, a dictionary; neut. of λεξικός, adj., belonging to words.—Gk. λέξι-s, a saying.—Gk. λέγειν, to speak; see legend.

Ley, a meadow; see Lea.

Liable, responsible. (F.—L.) Formed, with suffix *-able*, from F. *li-er*, to tie.—L. *ligāre*, to tie. See Ligament.

Liane, Liana, a climbing tropical plant. (F.—L.) F. *liane* (the same); from Norman and Guernsey *lian*, a band.—L. *ligāmen*; see Lien, Limehound.

Lias, a formation of limestone. (F.) F. *lias, liais*, O. F. *liois*, a hard freestone.

Lib, to castrate. (E.) Answers to an A. S. type **lybban*; only found in the cognate Du. *lubben*, with the same sense; E. Fries. and Westphal. *lübben*. Der. *g-lib*, vb., the same (obsolete); cf. O. Du. *gelubt*. 'gelt,' Hexham. Also *lef-t*, q.v.

Libation, the pouring forth of wine in honour of a deity. (F.—L.) F. *libation*.

−L. acc. *lībātiōnem.*−L. *lībātus*, pp. of *lībāre*, to taste, sip, pour out.+Gk. λείβειν, to pour out, shed, offer a libation. Brugm. i. § 553.

Libel, a written accusation. (F.−L.) M.E. *libel*, a brief piece of writing; A. F. *libel.* − L. *libellum*, acc. of *libellus*, a little book, a notice (Matt. v. 31); dimin. of *liber*, a book. See **Library.**

Liberal. (F.−L.) M.E. *liberal.*− O. F. *liberal.*−L. *līberālis*, befitting a free man, generous.−L. *līber*, free.

liberate. (L.) From pp. of L. *līberāre*, to set free.−L. *līber*, free; Brugm. i. § 102.

libertine. (L.) Cf. Acts vi. 9.−L. *lībertīnus*, adj., belonging to a freed man, also sb., a freed man; later applied to denote the licentious liberty of a certain sect (Acts vi. 9).−L. *lībertus*, a freed man.−L. *līber*, free.

liberty. (F.−L.) M.E. *libertee.*− F. *liberté.*−L. *lībertātem*, acc. of *lībertās*, freedom.−L. *līber*, free.

Libidinous, lustful. (F. − L.) F. *libidineux.* − L. *libīdinōsus*, lustful. − L. *libīdin-*, stem of *libīdo*, *lubīdo*, lust, pleasure.−L. *libet*, *lubet*, it pleases. Cf. Skt. *lubh*, to desire. Allied to **Love.**

Library. (F.−L.) F. *librairie.*−L. *librāria*, a book-shop; fem. of *librārius*, belonging to books. − L. *libr-*, stem of *liber*, a book, orig. the bark of a tree (one of the earliest writing materials). Allied to Gk. λέπειν, to peel; Brugm. i. § 499.

Librate, to balance, be poised, move slightly when balanced. (L.) The verb is rare, and due to the sb. *libration* (Kersey). −L. acc. *lībrātiōnem*, a poising.−L. *lībrātus*, pp. of *lībrāre*, to balance.−L. *lībra*, a balance, a level; also a pound of 12 oz.+ Gk. λίτρα, a pound of 12 oz. Brugm. i. § 589.

Licence, License, leave, abuse of freedom. (F.−L.) M.E. *lycence.* − F. *licence.*−L. *licentia*, freedom to act.−L. *licent-*; from *licēre*, to be allowable. See Brugm. ii. § 587. **Der.** *licence*, more usually *license*, vb.

licentiate, one who has a grant to exercise a profession. (L.) Englished from Late L. *licentiātus*, pp. of *licentiāre*, to licence.−L. *licentia*, licence (above).

licentious. (F.−L.) F. *licencieux.* − L. *licentiōsus*, full of licence. − L. *licentia*, licence (above).

Lichen, a moss. (L.−Gk.) L. *līchēn.*

−Gk. λειχήν, lichen, tree-moss; also, an eruption on the skin. Generally connected with Gk. λείχειν, to lick up; from its encroachment. Cf. Russ. *lishai*, a lichen, a tetter.

Lichgate, a churchyard gate. (E.) So called because a corpse (in a bier) may be rested under it. The former syllable is M. E. *lich*, a corpse, but orig. the living body; from A. S. *līc*, a body; see **Like** (1).

Lick, to lap. (E.) M. E. *likken.* A. S. *liccian.* + Du. *likken*, G. *lecken.* A secondary verb allied to the primary forms seen in Goth. *bilaigon* (be-lick); Russ. *lizate*, O. Irish *ligim*, I lick, L. *lingere*, Gk. λείχειν, Pers. *lishtan*, Skt. *lih*, *rih*, to lick. (√LEIGH.) Brugm. i. § 604.

Licorice, Liquorice. (F.−L.−Gk.) M. E. *licoris.*−A. F. *lycorys*, Liber Albus, p. 224; M. F. *liquerice*, 'lickorice;' Cot. −L. *liquirītia*, liquorice; a corrupted form of *glycyrrhīza* (Pliny, Nat. Hist. xxii. 9. 11).−Gk. γλυκύρῥιζα, liquorice, lit. 'sweet root.'−Gk. γλυκύ-s, sweet; ῥίζα, root. See **Wort.**

Lictor, an officer in Rome. (L.) L. *lictor*, perhaps 'binder'; from the fasces or 'bound' rods which he bore, or from binding culprits. Allied to *ligāre*, to bind. See **Ligament.** (Doubtful.)

Lid, a cover. (E.) M. E. *lid.* A.S. *hlid*, a lid.−A.S. *hlid-*, weak grade of *hlīdan*, to cover.+Du. *lid*, a lid; Icel. *hlið*, a gate, gateway, gap, breach; M. H. G. *lit*, *lid*, a cover (obsolete).

Lie (1), to rest, abide. (E.) A strong verb. M.E. *lien*, also *liggen*, pt. t. *lay*, *ley*, pp. *leien*, *lein*. A.S. *licgan*, pt. t. *læg*, pp. *legen.*+Du. *liggen*, Icel. *liggja*, Dan. *ligge*, Swed. *ligga*, G. *liegen*, Goth. *ligan.* Related to Russ. *lejate*; Lat. base *leg-* (in *lectus*, bed); Gk. base λεχ- (in λέχος, bed). (√LEGH.) ¶ On the mod. E. form see **Sweet,** E. Gr. § 1293.

Lie (2), to tell a falsehood. (E.) M.E. *līʒen*, *lēʒen*, pt. t. *leh*, pp. *lowen*. O. Merc. *lēgan*; A.S. *lēogan*, pt. t. *lēag*, pp. *logen.* +Du. *liegen*, Icel. *ljūga*, Dan. *lyve*, Swed. *ljuga*, Goth. *liugan*, G. *lügen.* Teut. type *leugan-*, pt. t. **laug*, pp. *luganoz.* Cf. Russ. *lgate*, *luigate*, to lie; *loje*, a lie. (√LEUGH.)

Lief, dear. (E.) M.E. *leef.* A.S. *lēof.* +Du. *lief*, Icel. *ljūfr*, Swed. *ljuf*, Goth. *liubs*, G. *lieb.* Teut. type *leuboz.* Cf.

Russ. *lioboi*, agreeable, *liobite*, to love; L. *lubet*, *libet*, it pleases; Skt. *lubh*, to desire. (√LEUBH.) Allied to Love.

Liege, faithful, subject. (F. – O. H. G.) [The sense has been altered by confusion with L. *ligātus*, bound. In old use, we could speak of 'a *liege* lord' as meaning a *free* lord, in exact opposition to the imported notion.] M. E. *lige*, *lege*; *lege poustee*=free sovereignty, Bruce, v. 165. – O. F. *lige*, *liege*, liege, leal; also, free; a *liege* lord was a lord of a free band, and his *lieges* were privileged free men, faithful to him, but free from other service. – M. H. G. *ledic*, *lidic* (G. *ledig*), free, esp. from all obligations of service. Cf. Icel. *liðugr*, free, M. Du. *ledig*, free. (Disputed; see Körting, § 4736.)

Lieger, Leiger, an ambassador; see Ledger.

Lien, a legal claim, charge on property. (F. – L.) F. *lien*, a band, or tie, anything that fastens or fetters. – L. *ligāmen*, a tie. – L. *ligāre*, to tie. See **Ligament.**

Lieu, place, stead. (F. – L.) F. *lieu*. – L. *locum*, acc. of *locus*, a place. See Locus.

lieutenant, a 'locum tenens,' deputy, &c. (F. – L.) F. *lieu tenant*. – L. *locum-tenent-*, stem of *locum tenens*, one who holds another's place. – L. *locum*, acc. of *locus*, a place; *tenens*, pres. pt. of *tenēre*, to hold. See **Tenable.**

Life. (E.) M. E. *lif*, *lyf*; gen. *lyues* (*lives*), dat. *lyue* (*live*). A. S. *līf*, gen. *lifes*, dat. *līfe*. From the base of Teut. **leiban-* (pt. t. **laib*, pp. **libanoz*), to remain; as seen in Goth. *bi-leiban*, A. S. *be-līfan*, G. *bleiben*, Du. *blijven*, to remain. +Icel. *líf*, *lifi*, Dan. *liv*, Swed. *lif*, O. H. G. *līp*, life (whence G. *leib*, the body). The weak grade appears in Live, q. v. And see Leave (1). (√LEIP?)

lifeguard. (E.) From *life* and *guard*. ¶ Cf. G. *leibgarde*, a body-guard, which is a cognate word, with the orig. sense of 'life-guard,' from O. H. G. *līp*, life.

lifelong; better livelong, q. v.

Lift (1), to elevate. (Scand.) M. E. *liften.* – Icel. *lypta* (pron. *lyfta*), to lift, exalt in air, from *lopt*, air; Dan. *löfte*, Swed. *lyfta*, from *luft*, air. The Icel. *y* results, by mutation, from Teut. *u*; see Loft. Der. *up-lift.*

Lift (2), to steal. (E.) We speak of a *shop-lifter*, a thief; see Shak. Troil. i. 2. 129. To take up; hence, to take

away. The same as Lift (1). ¶ Not allied to Goth. *hliftus*, a thief.

Ligament, a band, band of tissue connecting the moveable bones. (F. – L.) F. *ligament.* – L. *ligāmentum*, a tie, band. – L. *ligā-re*, to tie; with suffix -*mentum.*

ligature, a bandage. (F. – L.) F. *ligature*, a tie, bandage. – L. *ligātūra*, a binding. – L. *ligātus*, pp. of *ligāre*, to tie.

Light (1), illumination. (E.) M. E. *light.* – O. Merc. *lēht*; A. S. *lēoht*, light. + Du. and G. *licht*; cf. Goth. *liuh-ath*, light, shewing that the *t* is a suffix. Teut. type **leuhtom*, neut. sb.; related to the adj. **leuhtoz*, as seen in E. *light*, i. e. bright, adj., G. and Du. *licht.* Co-radicate with L. *lux* (stem *lūc-*), light, Gk. λευκ-ός, white, Skt. *ruch*, to shine. (√LEUQ.) See Lucid.

lighten (1), to illuminate, flash. (E.) 1. INTRANS., to shine as lightning; 'it *lightens.*' M. E. *lightenen*, more correctly *light-n-en*, where the -*n-* is formative, and gives the sense 'to become light.' 2. TRANS. This is only the intrans. form incorrectly used with a trans. sense. The correct trans. form is simply *to light* = O. Merc. *līhtan*, from *lēoht*, sb.

lightning, an illuminating flash. (E.) Formed with suffix -*ing* from M. E. *lightnen*, to lighten (above).

Light (2), not heavy. (E.) M. E. *light.* A. S. *lēoht* (for **līht*). + Du. *licht*, *ligt*; Icel. *léttr*, Dan. *let*, Swed. *lätt*, Goth. *leihts*, G. *leicht*, O. H. G. *līht*, *līhti.* Teut. type **līhtoz*, for **linχtoz*, **lenχtoz.* Allied to Lith. *lengwas*, light; and to Lung. See Brugm. i. § 684; Sievers, § 84.

light (3), to alight, settle, descend. (E.) M. E. *lihten.* A. S. *līhtan*, vb., to alight from, lit. to make light, relieve a horse of his burden. – A. S. *lēoht* (*līht*) (above). The sense 'to descend upon' (the earth) is secondary, due to the completed action of descending from a horse.

lighten (2), to alleviate. (E.) The -*en* is merely formative, as in *strength-en.* – A. S. *līhtan*, to make light (above).

lighten (3), to alight on. (E.) Extended from light (3) above.

lighter, a boat for unlading ships. (Du.) Borrowed from Du. *ligter*, a lighter, i. e. unloader. – Du. *ligt*, light.

lights, lungs. (E.) So named from their lightness. So also Russ. *legkiia*, lights; from *legkii*, light.

Lighten (1), to flash, **Lightning**; see Light (1).

Ligneous, woody. (L.) L. *ligne-us*, wooden; with suffix *-ous.* – L. *lignum*, wood.

lign-aloes, a kind of tree. (F.–L. *and* Gk.) O. F. *lignaloes* (Godef.).–L. *lignum aloës*, lit. 'wood of aloes.' *Aloës* is gen. of *aloë*, from Gk. ἀλόη, aloe. See Aloe.

Ligule, a strap-shaped petal. (L.) In botany.–L. *ligula*, a little tongue, also spelt *lingula*, dimin. of *lingua*, tongue. See Lingual.

Ligure, a precious stone. (L.–Gk.) L. *ligūrius.* – Gk. λιγύριον, a sort of gem (amber or jacinth); Exod. xxviii. 19.

Like (1), similar. (E.) M. E. *lyk*, *lik*. A. S. *ge-līc*; as suffix, *-līc.* ✝ Du. *ge-lijk*, Icel. *līkr*, *g-līkr*, Dan. *lig*, Swed. *lik*, Goth. *ga-leiks*, G. *g-leich*, O. H. G. *ka-līh*. β. Lit. 'having the same form,' and derived from the sb. meaning 'form, shape,' viz. A. S. *līc*, form, body, Icel. *līk*, Goth. *leik*, the body, Du. *lijk*, a corpse, Dan. *lig*, Swed. *lik*, a corpse, G. *leiche*, O. H. G. *līh*. See Lichgate. Cf. Lith. *lygus*, like.

like (2), to be pleased with. (E.) The construction has altered; M. E. *liketh*, it pleases, is impersonal, as in mod. E. *if you like* = if it may please you. – A. S. *līcian*, to please, orig. to be like or suitable for. – A. S. *-līc*, *ge-līc*, like ; see Like (1).✝ Du. *lijken*, to suit ; Icel. *līka*, to like ; Goth. *leikan*, to please (similarly derived)

liken, to compare. (E.) M. E. *liknen*, to liken ; but the true sense is intransitive, viz. to be like. Cf. Swed. *likna*, (1) to resemble, (2) to liken, from *lik*, like ; Dan. *ligne*, the same, from *lig*, like.

Lilac, a shrub. (Span. – Arab. – Pers.) Span. *lilac.* – Arab. *līlak*, a lilac. – Pers. *līlaj*, *līlanj*, *līlang*, of which the proper sense is indigo-plant. The initial *l* stands for *n*, and the above forms are from *nīl*, blue, whence *nīlak* (>Arab. *līlak*), bluish. The plant is named from the 'bluish' tinge on the flowers in some varieties. (Devic.) Cf. Skt. *nīla-*, dark blue.

Lilt, to sing, dance. (Scand.) M. E. *lilting-horn*, horn to dance to ; cf. M. E. *lulten*, to resound. Formed (with added *-t*) from Norweg. *lilla*, to sing in a high tone. Cf. O. Swed. *lylla*, to lull to sleep (Rietz). Allied to Lull.

Lily, a plant. (L. – Gk.) A. S. *lilie.* – L. *līlium.* – Gk. λείριον, a lily.

Limb (1), a member, branch of a tree. (E.) M. E. *lim*. A. S. *lim.*✝Icel. *limr*, Dan. Swed. *lem.* Allied to A. S. *li-ð*, Goth. *li-thus*, G. *g-lie-d*, a joint. Cf. Lith. *lëmů*, stature, growth. See Lay (4).

Limb (2), the edge or border of a sextant, &c. (L.) L. *limbus*, a border, edging, edge.

limbo, limbus, the borders of hell. (L.) The orig. phrase is *in limbo*, where *limbo* is the abl. case of *limbus*, a border ; the *limbus patrum* was a supposed place on the border of hell, where the patriarchs abode till Christ's descent into hell.

Limbeck, the same as Alembic.

Limber (1), active, flexible. (E.) In Baret(1580). Apparently allied to Limp(1).

Limber (2), part of a gun-carriage, a frame with two wheels and a pole. (F.?) Cf. prov. E. *limmers*, thills, shafts (the *b* being excrescent). G. Douglas has *lymnaris*, shafts. Probably from O. F. *limonier*, adj., belonging to the shafts ; from *limon*, a shaft. Cf. F. *limonière*, part of a carriage including the two shafts. Etym. unknown ; perhaps allied to Icel. *lim* (pl. *limar*), branches of a tree.

Limbo, Limbus; see Limb (2).

Lime (1), bird-lime, mortar. (E.) M.E. *lym*, *liim*, viscous substance. A. S. *līm*, bitumen, cement.✝Du. *lijm*, Icel. *līm*, Dan. *liim*, Swed. *lim*, glue ; G. *leim*, glue ; L. *līmus*, slime. Idg. type *leimo-*. See Loam.

Lime (2), the linden-tree. (E.) *Lime* is a corruption of *line*, as in Shak. Temp. *v*. 10 ; and *line* is a corruption of *lind*, the lengthening of *i* having occasioned the loss of *d*. (Sweet, E. Gr. § 1607.) See Lind.

Lime (3), a kind of citron. (F.–Pers.) F. *lime.* – Pers. *līmū*, (also *līmūn*), a lemon, citron. – Malay *līmau*, a lime, a citron.

Limehound, a dog in a leash. (Hybrid ; F.–L., *and* E.) Short for *liam-hound*, used by Turberville. The M. E. *liam* or *lyam* means 'a leash.' – O. F. *liem*, now spelt *lien*, a band ; Guernsey *liam*, *lian*. – L. *ligāmen*, a tie. See Lien, Liane.

Limit. (F.–L.) F. *limite*, a limit. – L. *līmitem*, acc. of *līmes*, a boundary ; akin to *līmen*, a threshold. Cf. L. *līmus*, transverse.

Limn, to illuminate, paint. (F.–L.) M. E. *limnen*, contracted form of *luminen*, to illuminate (Prompt. Parv.). Again, *luminen* is for *enluminen.* – O. F. *enlu-*

miner, to illuminate, burnish, limn. — L. *illumināre*; see **Illuminate**.

Limp (1), flaccid, pliant. (E.) Not in early use. Apparently related, by gradation, to Bavarian *lampecht*, flaccid, down-hanging, from the verb *lampen*, to hang loosely down ; cf. Skt. *lamba*, depending, *lamb*, to hang down.

Limp (2), to walk lamely. (E.) In Shak. Mer. Ven. iii. 2. 130. We find A.S. *lemp-healt*, earlier *laempi-halt* (Ep. Gl.), adj., halting ; and a cognate form in M.H.G. *limphin*, to limp. Cf. Low G. *lumpen*, to limp.

Limpet, a small shell-fish. (L.) Formerly *lempet* (Phillips, 1706). A.S. *lempedu*, orig. a lamprey, which also sticks to rocks. — Late L. *lemprida*, for L. *lampedra*, a lamprey. See **Lamprey**. Cf. '*Lemprida*, lempedu ;' Wright's Vocab. 438. 17.

Limpid, pure, bright. (F. — L.) F. *limpide*. — L. *limpidus*, clear. Allied to **Lymph**. Brugm. i. § 102.

Linch-pin, a pin to fasten a wheel on an axle. (E.) Formerly *lins-pin*, lit. 'axle-pin.'— A.S. *lynis*, an axle-tree.+ Du. *luns*, a linch-pin, O. Low G. *lunisa*, Low G. *lunse*, G. *lünse*, a linch-pin. Teut. base **lunis-* (cf. Goth. *akw-izi*, an ax) ; from **lun-*, as in O.H.G. *lun*, a bolt, peg, pin. Perhaps from Idg. root. **leu*, (cf. Gk. λύ-ειν), to loosen.

Lind, Linden, the lime-tree. (E.) The true form of the sb. is *lind*, and *lind-en* is the adj. from it. Hence *lind-en tree* = *lind* ; the same thing. M.E. *lind*. A.S. *lind*, the tree ; also a shield, commonly of this wood.+Du. *linde*, Icel. Dan. Swed. *lind*, G. *linde*. Cf. Lith. *lenta*, a board. Doublet, *lime* (2).

Line, a thread, thin cord ; also a stroke, row, rank, verse (L. ; *or* F. — L.). In the sense 'cord,' we find A.S. *līne*, directly from L. *līnea*. In the other senses, it is from F. *ligne*, also from L. *līnea*. β. The L. *līnea* meant orig. a string made of flax, being fem. of adj. *līneus*, made of flax. — L. *līnum*, flax. Cf. Gk. λίνον, flax ; whence perhaps the L. word. Der. *out-line*.

lineage. (F. — L.) F. *lignage*, a line-age. — F. *ligne*, a line, rank. — L. *līnea*, a line (above).

lineal. (L.) L. *līneālis*, belonging to a line. — L. *līnea*, a line (above).

lineament, a feature. (F. — L.) M.F. *lineament*, Cot. — L. *līneāmentum*, a draw-ing, delineation. — L. *līneāre*, to draw a line. — L. *līnea*, a line (above).

linear. (L.) L. *līneāris*, belonging to a line. — L. *līnea*, a line (above).

linen, cloth made of flax. (L.) Used as a sb., but really an old adj., A.S. *līn-en* ; the old sb. being M.E. *lin*, A.S. *līn*, flax. — L. *līnum*, flax. (Cf. *gold-en* from *gold*.) See **linseed**.

Ling (1), a fish. (E.) M.E. *lenge* (Havelok). Named from its long slender shape. Cf. A.S. *lengu*, length. + Du. *leng*, a ling, from *lang*, long ; Icel. *langa*, Norw. *langa*, *longa*, a ling ; Swed. *långa* ; G. *länge*, a ling, also called *läng-fisch*, long fish. See **Long**.

Ling (2), heath. (Scand.) M.E. *lyng*. — Icel. *lyng*, ling, heather ; Dan. *ling*, Swed. *ljung*.

Linger, to tarry. (E.) Frequent. form of M.E. *lengen*, to tarry. — A.S. *lengan*, to prolong, put off. — A.S. *lang*, long. Cf. Icel. *lengja*, to lengthen, Du. *lengen*, to lengthen, G. *verlängern*, to prolong. See **Long**.

Lingo, a language. (Prov. — L.) Prov. *lingo* (at Marseilles), a language. — L. *lingua*, a tongue, language (below).

lingual, pertaining to the tongue. (L.) Coined from L. *lingua*, the tongue, O. Lat. *dingua*, cognate with E. *tongue*.

linguist, one skilled in languages. (L.) From L. *lingua*, a tongue, language ; with suffix *-ista* (= Gk. -ιστης).

Liniment, salve, ointment. (F. — L.) F. *liniment*. — L. *linimentum*, ointment. — L. *linere*, to smear ; cf. Skt. *lī*, to melt. Brugm. i. § 476 (5) ; ii. § 608.

Lining. (L.) Formed, with suffix *-ing*, from the verb *to line*, i.e. to cover the inside of a garment with *line*, i.e. linen ; see **linen**.

Link (1), a ring of a chain. (Scand.) O. Icel. **hlenkr*, whence Icel. *hlekkr* (by assimilation) ; Dan. *lænke*, Swed. *länk* ; G. *gelenk*, a joint, link, ring. Cf. A.S. *hlence*, or *hlenca* (which would have given *linch*). Also M.H.G. *lenken*, to bend, O.H.G. *hlanca*, hip, loin (whence perhaps **Flank**).

Link (2), a torch ; see **Linstock**.

Linnet, a bird. (F. — L.) M.E. *linet*. [A.S. *līnece*.] O.F. *linette* ; cf. F. *linotte*, 'a linnet,' Cot. Named from feeding on flax-seed and hemp-seed (cf. G. *hänfling*, a linnet, from *hanf*, hemp). — L. *līnum*, flax. We also find A.S. *līnetwige*, a linnet (whence Lowl. Sc. *lintwhite*).

linseed, flax-seed. (L. *and* E.) From M. E. *lin* = A. S. *līn*, flax, borrowed from L. *līnum*, flax; and E. *seed.*

linsey-woolsey, made of linen and woollen mixed. (L. *and* E.) Made up from M. E. *lin*, linen, and E. *wool.* See linen, under Line.

Linstock, Lintstock, a stick to hold a lighted match. (Du.) Formerly *lintstock* (Coles, 1684); but properly *luntstock,* from *lunt*, 'a match to fire guns with,' Phillips. — Du. *lontstok,* 'a lint-stock,' Sewel. — Du. *lont,* a match; *stok*; a stick (see Stock); cf. Dan. *lunte-stok*; from *lunte,* a match, *stok,* a stick. Du. *lont* seems to have been formed from M. Du. *lompe,* 'a bundle of linnen,' Hexham; lit. a lump. See Lump.

link (2), a torch. (Scand.) Prob. confused with *lint-stock* (above). But really a use of *link* (1), q. v., meaning a short length of rope.

Lint, scraped linen. (L.) Cf. Late L. *linta,* from L. *linteum,* a linen cloth; neut. of *lin-teus,* linen. — L. *līnum,* flax.

Lintel, the headpiece of a door. (F. — L.) M. E. *lintel.* — O. F. *lintel* (F. *linteau*). — Late L. *lintellus,* a lintel, for **līmitellus,* dimin. of L. *līmes* (stem *līmit-*), a boundary; see Limit.

Lion. (F. — L. — Gk. — Egypt.) F. *lion.* — L. *leōnem,* acc. of *leo,* a lion. — Gk. λέων. Cf. Heb. *lāvī',* a lion. Prob. of Egypt. origin ; from Egypt. *labai, lawai,* a lioness (whence Gk. λέαινα); see Leo.

Lip. (E.) M. E. *lippe.* A. S. *lippa, lippe,* the lip. **+** Du. *lip,* Dan. *læbe,* Swed. *läpp,* G. *lippe, lefze.* Also L. *lab-rum, lab-ium,* lip ; Pers. *lab,* lip. But the relations are not clear. Brugm. i. § 563.

Liquefy, Liquescent; see Liquid.
Liquid, moist. (F. — L.) F. *liquide.* — L. *liquidus,* liquid. — L. *liquēre,* to be clear.

liquefy, to become liquid. (F. — L.) M. F. *liquefier* (see Cot.). As if from Late L. **liquefīcāre,* to make liquid; but we only find L. *liquefierī,* to become liquid.

liquescent, melting. (L.) L. *liquescent-,* stem of pres. part. of *liquescere,* inceptive form of *liquēre,* to be wet.

liquidate, to make clear; hence, to clear off an account. (L.) From pp. of Late L. *liquidāre,* to clarify, make clear. — L. *liquidus,* liquid, clear.

liquor, moisture, strong drink. (F. — L.) M. E. *licour, licur.* — A. F. *licur*; F.

liqueur, moisture. — L. *liquōrem,* acc. of *liquor,* moisture. — L. *liquēre,* to be moist. ¶ Now accommodated to L. spelling ; we also use mod. F. *liqueur.*

Liquorice ; see Licorice.

Lisp. (E.) M. E. *lispen, lipsen.* A. S. **wlispian,* to lisp, as in *ā-wlispian,* formed from A. S. *wlisp,* also *wlips,* adj., lisping, imperfect in utterance. **+** Du. *lispen,* Dan. *laspe,* Swed. *läspa,* G. *lispeln.* (Imitative.)

Lissom ; see Lithe.

List (1), a border of cloth, selvage. (E.) M. E. *list.* A. S. *līst.* **+** Du. *lijst,* Icel. *lista,* Dan. *liste,* Swed. *list,* G. *leiste,* O. H. G. *lista.* (The *i* was orig. long.)

list (2), a catalogue. (F. — G.) F. *liste,* a list, roll ; also, a list or selvage. It meant (1) a border, strip, (2) a roll or list of names. — O. H. G. *līsta,* G. *leiste,* a border; see List (1).

List (3) ; see Lists.

List (4), to please. (E.) M. E. *lusten, listen;* 'if thee *list'* = if it please thee, Ch. C. T. 1183. A. S. *lystan,* to desire, used impersonally. — A. S. *lust,* pleasure. **+** Du. *lusten,* Icel. *lysta,* Dan. *lyste,* Swed. *lysta,* Goth. *luston,* G. *gelüsten*; all from the sb. See Lust.

List (5), to listen ; see below.

Listen. (E.) We also find *list*; also M. E. *lust-n-en* and *lust-en,* the former being deduced from the latter by a formative *n,* as in Goth. *full-n-an,* to become full. A. S. *hlystan,* to listen to. — A. S. *hlyst,* hearing; Teut. type **hlus-ti-,* from a base **hlus,* weak grade of Teut. base **hleu-s.* Cf. A. S. *hlos-nian,* to hearken; Icel. *hlusta,* to listen, from *hlust,* the ear ; W. *clust,* the ear; also L. *clu-ere,* Gk. κλύ-ειν, to hear, Skt. *çru,* to hear. (√KLEU.) See Loud.

Listless, careless. (E.) The same as *lust-less* ; Gower has *lustles,* C. A. ii. 111. From *lust,* q.v. And see List (4).

Lists, ground enclosed for a tournament. (E.) M. E. *listes,* sb. pl., the lists. Pl. of *list* (1), border, boundary. Mixed with M. F. *lisse* (F. *lice*), 'a list or tiltyard ;' Cot. Cf. Ital. *lizza,* Span. *liza,* Port. *liça,* a list for tilting ;' Late L. *liciæ,* sb. pl., barriers ; *liciæ duelli,* the lists. Origin disputed. Cf. Late L. *licia,* a stake; perhaps from Late L. *licius,* oaken < L. *īliceus* (from *īlex,* holm-oak).

Litany, a form of prayer. (F. — L. — Gk.) M. E. *letanie,* afterwards altered to *litanie.* — O. F. *letanie.* — L. *litanīa.* — Gk. λιτανεία, a prayer. — Gk. λιταίνειν, to pray. — Gk. λίτομαι, I beg, pray, λιτή, prayer, entreaty.

Literal. (F. — L.) O. F. *literal.* — L. *līterālis,* according to the letter. — L. *lītera;* see **Letter.**

literature. (F. — L.) M.F. *literature.* — L. *līterātūra,* scholarship. — L. *līterātus,* learned, skilled in letters. — L. *lītera,* a letter; see **Letter.**

Litharge, protoxide of lead. (F. — L. Gk.) M. E. *litarge.* — F. *litharge,* 'litargie, white lead;' Cot. — L. *lithargyrus.* — Gk. λιθάργυρος, lit. 'stone-silver.' — Gk. λίθ-os, a stone; ἄργυρος, silver; see **Argent.**

Lithe, pliant, flexible, active. (E.) M. E. *lithe.* A.S. *līðe, līð,* gentle, soft (for **linðe,* the lengthened *i* causing loss of *n*). **+**G. *gelinde,* O. H. G. *lindi,* soft, tender. Allied to Icel. *linr,* L. *lēnis,* soft; L. *lentus,* pliant. **Der.** *lissom,* i. e. *lithe-some.*

Lither, pestilent, stagnant, dull. (E.) In 1 Hen. VI. iv. 7. 21, '*lither* sky' means pestilent or dull lower air; cf. '*luther* eir,' pestilent air, P. Pl., C. xvi. 220. M. E. *luther, lither.* — A.S. *lýðre,* evil, base, poor (hence, sickly, dull). Not to be confused with *lithe,* pliant.

Lithography, writing on stone. (Gk.) Coined from Gk. λίθο-s, a stone; γράφειν, to write.

lithotomy, cutting for stone. (L. — Gk.) L. *lithotomia.* — Gk. λιθοτομία. — Gk. λίθο-s, stone; τομ-, 2nd grade of τεμ-, as in τέμνειν, to cut; see **Tome.**

Litigation, a contest in law. (L.) From L. *lītigātio,* a disputing. — L. *lītigātus,* pp. of *lītigāre,* to dispute. — L. *līt-,* stem of *līs,* strife; *-igāre,* for *agere,* to carry on. L. *līs* = O. Lat. *stlīs,* strife.

litigious, contentious. (F. — L.) It also once meant debateable. — F. *litigieux,* 'debatefull;' Cot. — L. *lītigiōsus,* adj.; from *lītigium,* contention. — L. *lītigāre,* to dispute (above).

Litmus, a kind of dye. (Du.) Corrupted from Du. *lakmoes,* a blue dye-stuff. — Du. *lak,* lac; *moes,* pulp; (whence G. *lackmus,* litmus). See **Lac** (1).

Litter, a portable bed. (F. — L.) M.E. *litere.* — O. F. *litiere.* — Late L. **lectīcāria,* formed from *lectīca,* a litter. — L. *lectus,* a bed; see **Lectern.** Allied to Gk. λέχ-os, a bed; and to **Lie** (1).

litter, materials for a bed, heap of

straw to lie on, confused mass of things scattered. (F. — L.) The same word applied to a straw bed for animals, &c.

litter, a brood. (F. — L.) The same word; see the various senses of M. E. *lytere* in the Prompt. Parv.; and cf. F. *accoucher,* E. 'to be in the straw.'

Little. (E.) M. E. *litel, lutel.* A.S. *lýtel* (or *lytel*), little; we also find *lýt* (or *lyt*). **+** Du. *luttel,* little, *lutje,* a little; O. Sax. *luttil;* O. H. G. *luzil, luzzil, liuzil.* Compare also A. S. *lytig,* deceitful, *lot,* deceit; Goth. *liuts,* deceitful, *luton,* to betray. All from Teut. base **leut,* orig. to stoop; see **Lout.** ¶ Not allied to *less.* The Icel. *lítill,* Swed. *liten,* Goth. *leitils,* little, seem to be from a different Teut. base **leit.* It is difficult to see how they can be related.

Littoral, belonging to the sea-shore. (L.) L. *littorālis,* adj., from *littor-* (for **littos-*), stem of *littus* or *lītus,* sea-shore.

Liturgy, public prayer. (F. — L. — Gk.) O. F. *liturgie, lyturgie.* — Late L. *liturgia.* — Gk. λειτουργία, public service. — Gk. λεῖτο-s, public; ἔργον, work, cognate with E. *work.*

Live (1), to exist. (E.) M. E. *liuien* (*livien*). O. Merc. *lifgan,* A. S. *libban,* to live, dwell; orig. to remain, be left behind.**+**Du. *leven,* to live; Icel. *lifa,* to be left, to live; Dan. *leve,* Swed. *lefva,* Goth. *liban,* to live; G. *leben,* to live, O. H. G. *lëbēn.* From Teut. **lib-,* weak grade of **leiban-,* to remain. See **Life.**

live (2), adj., alive. (E.) Short for *alive,* which is not a true orig. adj., but due to the phrase *a liue* (*a live*) = A. S. *on līfe,* in life, hence, alive. *Līfe* is the dat. case of *līf,* life; hence the *i* in *live* is long.

livelihood. (E.) Corruption of M.E. *liuelode* (*livelode*), i.e. life-leading, means of living; older spelling *liflode, liflade.* From A. S. *līf,* life; *lād,* a leading, way, provisions to live by, a course, a lode; see **Life** and **Lode.**

livelong, long-lasting. (E.) The same as *life-long,* i. e. long as life is; but *livelong* is the older spelling.

lively. (E.) M. E. *lifly,* i.e. life-like.

Liver. (E.) M. E. *liuer* (= *liver*). A.S. *lifer.* **+** Du. *lever,* Icel. *lifr,* Dan. *lever,* Swed. *lefver,* G. *leber.* Cf. Russ. *liver',* the pluck of animals (from Teut.). Allied to Armen. *leard,* liver; but not to L. *iecur.* Brugm. i. §§ 280, 557 (2).

Livery, a delivery, a thing delivered, uniform allowed to servants. (F. – L.) M. E. *liuere* (= *liverè*, three syllables). – A. F. *liveree*; F. *livrée*, 'a delivery of a thing that is given, the thing so given, a livery;' Cot. Orig. fem. of pp. of *livrer*, to deliver, give freely. – L. *līberāre*, to set free, give freely; see **Liberate**.

Livid, discoloured. (F. – L.) F. *livide*. – L. *līuidus*, bluish. – L. *līuēre*, to be bluish. Cf. W. *lliw*, O. Irish *lī*, colour, hue. Brugm. i. § 94.

Lizard, a four-footed reptile. (F. – L.) M. E. *lesarde.* – O. F. *lesarde.* – L. *lacerta*, a lizard. Cf. **Alligator.**

Llama, a quadruped. (Peruvian.) *Llama* is a Peruvian word, meaning ' flock '; Prescott. But the Peruv. Dict. gives ' *llama*, carnero de la tierra,' sheep of the country.

Llano, a level steppe or plain. (Span. – L.) Commoner in the pl. *llanos.* – Span. *llano*, pl. *llanos*, a plain; from *llano*, adj., plain, flat. – L. *plānus*, flat. See **Plain.**

Lo, behold! (E.) M. E. *lo.* A. S. *la*, an interjection.

Loach, Loche, a small fish. (F.) F. *loche*, 'the loach,' Cot.; whence also Span. *loja, locha.* Cf. Norman *loque*, a loach, a slug (Le Héricher). Origin unknown.

Load, a burden. (E.) The sense of ' burden ' seems to be due to confusion with the verb **Lade** (1); but cf. prov. E. *lead*, in the sense ' to carry.' M. E. *lāde*, a course, way, lode; also, a load. A.S. *lād*, a lode; also, carriage. See **Lode.**

Load-star, Load-stone; see **Lode.**

Loaf. (E.) M. E. *lof, loof.* A. S. *hlāf.* + Icel. *hleifr*, Goth. *hlaifs, hlaibs*, G. *laib.* Cf. Lithuan. *klĕpas*, bread (from Teut.).

Loam, clay. (E.) M. E. *lam.* A. S. *lām.* + Du. *leem*, G. *lehm*, O. H. G. *leim, leimo.* Teut. type *laimoz.* Cf. Icel. *leir* (Teut. type *laizom*), loam. Akin to **Lime** (1).

Loan, a lending, moneȳ lent. (Scand.) M. E. *lone* (= *lāne*). This corresponds to the rare A. S. *lān*, borrowed from Norse. [The true A. S. form is *lǣn*, a loan.] – Icel. *lān*, a loan; Dan. *laan,* Swed. *lån*, a loan. + A.S. *lǣn*, a loan; Du. *leen*, a grant, a fief; G. *lehn, lehen*, a fief. **β.** All from the verb seen in A. S. *lēon* (pt. t. *lāh*), to grant, Icel. *ljā*, G. *leihen*, to lend, Goth. *leihwan*; akin to L. *linquere* (pt. t. *līquī*),

Gk. λείπειν, Skt. *rich*, to leave, O. Irish *lecim*, I leave. (√LEIQ; Brugm. i. § 463.) Hence the Teut. verb *leihwan-* (as in Gothic); and the sb. *laihwniz*, *laihwnoz*, a loan, from the second grade *laihw* with suffix *-niz* or *-noz.*

Loath. (E.) M. E. *loth.* A.S. *lāð*, hateful, hostile. + Icel. *leiðr*, Dan. Swed. *led*, odious; O. H. G. *leit*, odious, orig. mournful. Teut. type *laithoz*, where *-thoz* is prob. a suffix. Allied to G. *leiden*, to suffer; but prob. *not* allied to A. S. *līðan* (pt. t. *lāð*), to travel, sail; as usually said (Kluge). Der. *loath-ly*; *-some*, suggested by M. E. *wlatsom*, detestable; also *loathe*, vb.

Lobby, a small hall, passage. (Low L. – G.) Probably from the monkish Latin *lobia, laubia*; the Ital. form is *loggia* (see **Lodge**). See Late L. *lobia, laubia, lobium*, a portico, gallery, covered way; as if from a Germ. form *laubjā.* – M. H. G. *loube*, an arbour, bower, open way along the upper story of a house (as in a Swiss *chalet*); mod. G. *laube*, a bower. Orig. made with foliage. – M.H.G. *loub* (G. *laub*), a leaf; see **Leaf.**

Lobe, flap of the ear, &c. (F. – Low L. – Gk.) F. *lobe.* – Late L. *lobus.* – Gk. λοβός, a lobe of the ear or liver. Brugm. i. § 667.

Lobster, a kind of shell-fish. (L.) A. S. *loppestre*, a corrupter form of A. S. *lopust*, a corruption of L. *locusta*, (1) a lobster, (2) a locust. It was perhaps confused with A.S. *loppe*, a flea.

Local, Locate; see **Locus.**

Loch, a lake. (Gaelic.) Gael. *loch*, a lake. + O. Irish *loch*, Corn. and Bret. *lagen*; L. *lacus*; Stokes, p. 237. See **Lake** (1).

Lock (1), a fastening. (E.) M. E. *loke.* A.S. *loc*, a fastening. + Icel. *loka*, a lock; Swed. *lock*, a lid; G. *loch*, a dungeon. From Teut. base *luk*, weak grade of Teut. root *leuk*, to fasten, whence also A. S. *lūcan*, Du. *luiken*, Icel. *lūka*, to shut, Goth. *galūkan*, to shut up.

locket, a little hinged case worn as an ornament. (F. – Scand.) Orig. a fastening (Hudibras, pt. ii. c. i. 808). – F. *loquet*, the latch of a door, dimin. of O. F. *loc*, a lock, borrowed from Icel. *loka*, a lock.

Lock (2), a tuft of hair or wool. (E.) M. E. *lok.* A. S. *locc.* + Du. *lok*, Icel. *lokkr*, Dan. *lok*, Swed. *lock*, G. *locke.* Orig. ' a curl;' cf. Icel. *lykkr*, a loop, bend, crook; also Lith. *lugnas*, pliable.

Locket; see Lock (1).

Lockram, a kind of cheap linen. (F. — Bret.) F. *locrenan,* a sort of unbleached linen; named from the place where it was made, viz. *Loc-Renan,* or *S. Renan,* near Quimper, in Brittany. — Bret. *Lok-Ronan,* cell of St. Ronan; from Bret. *lok* (L. *locus*), a cell.

Locomotion; see Locus.

Locus, a place. (L.) L. *locus,* a place. O. Lat. *stlocus,* a place.

local. (F. — L.) F. *local.* — L. *localis,* belonging to a place. — L. *locus,* a place.

locate, to place. (L.) From pp. of L. *locāre,* to place. — L. *locus,* a place.

locomotion, motion from place to place. (L.) Coined from *loco-,* for *locus,* a place; and *motion.*

Locust, a winged insect. (L.) M.E. *locuste.* — L. *locusta,* a shell-fish, also a locust.

Lode, a vein of ore, a water-course. (E.) The true sense is 'course.' A.S. *lād,* a way, course, journey; cf. A.S. *lædan,* to lead, conduct.+Icel. *leið,* lode, way, course; Swed. *led,* a course. Teut. type **laidā,* fem. From the 2nd grade of Teut. **leithan-* (A. S. *līðan*), to travel. See Lead (1). Der. *lode-star.* ¶ And see Load.

lodestar, loadstar, the polar star. (E.) Lit. 'way-star,' star that leads or guides; see Lode above.

lodestone, loadstone, a magnet. (E.) Compounded of *lode* and *stone,* in imitation of *lodestar;* it means a stone that leads or draws.

Lodge, a small house, cot, resting-place. (F. — G.) M. E. *loge, logge.* — O. F. *loge;* cf. Ital. *loggia,* Late L. *lobia,* a gallery. — O. H. G. **laubjā,* allied to *loubā,* M. H. G. *loube,* an arbour, mod. G. *laube,* a bower. — O. H. G. *loub,* G. *laub,* a leaf; see Leaf. Doublet, *lobby.*

Loft, an upper room. (Scand.) M. E. *loft,* properly 'air'; the peculiar sense is Scand. — Icel. *lopt* (pron. *loft*), (1) air, sky, (2) an upper room; Dan. Swed. *loft,* a garret. Allied to A. S. *lyft,* air, sky, Goth. *luftus,* Du. *lucht* (for *luft*), G. *luft,* the air. Der. *a-loft;* also *lofty,* i. e. 'in the air;' *lift,* vb.

Log (1), a block, piece of wood. (Scand.) The vowel has been shortened. Cf. Norw. *laag,* a fallen trunk; Icel. *lāg,* a felled tree, log; Swed. dial. *låga,* a felled tree, a tree that has been blown

down. So called from its *lying* on the ground, as distinguished from the living tree. From the 3rd (pt. pl.) grade, viz. *lāg-,* of Icel. *liggja,* to lie; see Lie (1) and Low. Der. *logg-ats, logg-ets,* a game with bits of wood; *log-wood,* so called because imported in *logs,* and also called *blockwood* (Kersey).

log (2), a piece of wood with a line, for measuring the rate of a ship. (Scand.) The same word. The Swed. *logg,* as a sea-term, whence *log-lina,* a log-line, *log-bok,* a log-book, *logga,* to heave the log, Dan. *log, log-line, log-bog, logge,* vb., seem to have been all borrowed back from E.

logger-head, a dunce, a piece of timber (in a whale-boat) over which a line is passed to make it run more slowly. (Scand. *and* E.) A similar formation to *blockhead.* Cf. Icel. *lāgar,* gen. of *lāg.*

Log (3), a liquid measure. (Heb.) In Lev. xiv. 10. — Heb. *lōg,* a liquid measure, 12th part of a *hin;* orig. 'a basin.'

Logarithm. (Gk.) Coined from Gk. λογ-, stem of λόγος, a word, a proportion, ratio; and ἀριθμός, a number; the sense being 'ratio-number.' See Arithmetic.

Loggerhead; see Log (1).

Logic, the science of reasoning correctly. (F. — L. — Gk.) O. F. *logique.* — L. *logica,* for *ars logica,* logic art. — Gk. λογική, for λογικὴ τέχνη, logic art; where λογική is fem. of λογικός, reasonable. — Gk. λόγος, a speech. — Gk. λέγειν, to say.+L. *legere,* to speak; see Legend. Hence all words in *-logy,* the chief being *astro-logy, bio-, chrono-, concho-, doxo-, entomo-, etymo-, genea-, geo-, meteoro-, minera-, mytho-, necro-, noso-, ornitho-, osteo-, patho-, philo-, phraseo-, phreno-, physio-, psycho-, tauto-, theo-, zoo-logy;* see these in their due places.

Loin. (F. — L.) M. E. *loine.* — O. F. *logne,* also *longe.* — Late L. **lumbea,* fem. of an adj. **lumbeus* (not found), from L. *lumbus,* loin. See Lumbar.

Loiter, to delay. (Du.) M. E. *loitren,* Pr. Parv. — M. Du. and Du. *leuteren,* to linger, loiter, trifle, M. Du. *loteren,* to delay, deceive, vacillate; cf. E. Fries. *löteren, lötern,* to loiter. Allied to M. Du. *lutsen,* with the same sense (Hexham). Perhaps allied to Lout.

Loll, to lounge about. (E.) M. E. *lollen, lullen.* Cf. Icel. *lolla,* 'segniter agere,' Halldórsson; M. Du. *lollen,* to sit over the fire; the orig. sense was prob. to doze; M. Du. *lolle-banck*, 'a sleeping seate,' Hexham. Allied to **Lull**.

Lollard, a name given to the followers of Wyclif. (M. Du.) It was confused with M. E. *loller*, i.e. one who lolls, a lounger, lazy fellow; see **Loll** above; but the words are prob. related. Latinised as *Lollardus* from M. Du. *lollaerd*, (1) a mumbler of prayers and hymns, (2) a Lollard, lit. 'God-praiser' or 'singer'; first applied to a sect in Brabant. Formed with suffix -*aerd* (same as E. -*ard* in *drunk-ard*) from M. Du. *lollen, lullen*, to sing; see **Lull**.

Lone, short for *alone*; see **Alone**.

Long (1), to desire, yearn. (E.) M. E. *longen*. A. S. *langian*, impers. vb. with acc., to long after, crave, desire; (distinct from *langian*, to grow long).✠ O. Sax. *langon*, impers.; Icel. *langa*, impers, and pers.; O. H. G. *langōn*, impers. Perhaps allied to G. *gelingen*, to succeed. Cf. G. *ver-langen*, to wish for. Der. *be-long*.

Long (2), extended. (E.) M. E. *long*. A. S. *lang, long*.✠Du. *lang*, Icel. *langr*, Dan. *lang*, Swed. *lång*, Goth. *laggrs* (=*langrs*), G. *lang*; L. *longus*. Brugm. i. § 642.

longevity, length of life. (L.) From L. *longæuitas*, long life. — L. *long-us*, long; *æuitas*, usually *ætas*, age; from *æui-*, a stem formed from *æuum*, life. See **Age**.

longitude. (F. — L.) F. *longitude*. — L. *longitūdō*, length; in late Lat., the longitude of a place. — L. *longi-*, stem formed from *longus*, long; with suffix -*tū-dō*. Der. *longitudin-al*, from stem *longitūdin-*.

Loo, a game at cards. (F.) Formerly called *lanterloo*. — F. *lanturelu, lanturlu*, interj., nonsense! fudge! also a game at cards. The expression was orig. the refrain of a famous vaudeville (ab. 1630), afterwards used to give an evasive answer. Being purposely nonsensical, it admits of no further etymology.

Loof; see **Luff**.

Look, to see. (E.) M. E. *loken*. A. S. *lōcian*, to look. ✠ O. Sax. *lōkōn*, to look; cf. M. H. G. *luogen*, to mark, behold, G. *lugen*, to look out. Brugm. i. § 421(7).

Loom (1), a machine for weaving cloth. (E.) M. E. *lome*, a tool, implement. A. S. *ge-lōma*, a tool, implement, instrument. Der. *heir-loom*, where *loom* meant any implement, hence a piece of furniture.

Loom (2), to appear faintly or at a distance. (E.?) Orig. sense doubtful. (Not = M. E. *lumen*, to shine, as that has a different vowel.) If it meant orig. 'to come slowly towards,' it answers exactly to E. Fries. *lōmen*, Swed. dial. *loma*, to move slowly; cf. M. H. G. *luomen*, to be weary, from the adj. *luomi*, slack. Kilian has M. Du. *lome*, slow, inactive. The Teut. base of the adj. is **lōm-*, connected by gradation with E. **Lame**. See **Loon** (2). Cf. Lowl. Sc. *loamy*, dull, slow; E. Fries. *lōmig*.

Loon (1), **Lown,** a base fellow. (O. Low G.) M. E. *lown* (spelt *lowen*, but rhyming on -*oun*), St. Cuthbert, 7957. Cf. M. Du. *loen*, 'homo stupidus,' Kilian.

Loon (2), a water-bird, diver. (Scand.) A corruption of the Shetland name *loom*. — Icel. *lōmr*, Swed. Dan. *lom*, a loon. Prob. from the *lame* or awkward motion of diving-birds on land; cf. Swed. dial. *loma*, E. Fries. *lōmen*, to move slowly; see **Loom** (2) above.

Loop, a noose. (Celtic). G. Douglas has *lowp-knot* (Æn. xii. 603); also *lowpis*, and *lowpit*, 'looped.' Apparently Northern, and borrowed from Gael. *lub*, a bend, loop, noose, winding, meander (whence Lowl. Sc. *loops*, the windings of a river). So also Irish *lub*. — Gael. and Irish *lub*, to bend; cf. O. Irish *lubtha*, bent.

Loop-hole, a small aperture in a wall. (F. — Low G.) M. E. *loupe*, P. Pl. — O. F. **loupe* (not found); Languedoc *loup*, a small window in a roof (Wedgwood). — M. Du. *lūpen*, Du. *luipen*, to lurk (see Franck); Low G. *lupen*, in the same sense as Low G. *glupen*, to peep (Lübben). Hence, the sense was 'peep-hole.' Or else from *loop* (above).

Loose, slack. (Scand.) M. E. *lous, los*; Prof. Zupitza shews (in Anglia, vii. 152) that it is due to the Scand. form. [The true M. E. form is *lees*, answering to A. S. *lēas*, (1) loose, (2) false.] — Icel. *lauss*, Swed. Dan. *lös*, loose; O. Sax. *lōs*, M. Du. *loos*, (1) loose, (2) false (where mod. Du. has *los*, loose, *loos*, false); G. *los*, loose; Goth. *laus*, empty, vain. Teut. type **lausoz*; from **laus-*, 2nd grade of Teut. **leusan-*, to lose. See **Lose**.

-less, suffix. (E.) M. E. -*lees, -les*; A. S. -*lēas*, the same as *lēas*, loose, free from (above).

loose, loosen, vb. (E.) The true form is *loose*, later *loosen* by analogy with *strengthen*, &c. A late derivative from the adj. above. Other languages derive the verb directly from the adj.; thus Du. *lossen*, Icel. *leysa*, Swed. *lösa*, Dan. *löse*, G. *lösen*, Goth. *lausjan*, to loosen, are derived (respectively) from Du. *los*, Icel. *lauss*, Swed. and Dan. *lös*, G. *los*, Goth. *laus*, loose, vain.

Loot, plunder. (Hindi.—Skt.) Hindi *lūṭ* (with cerebral *ṭ*), loot, plunder. The cerebral *t* shews that *r* is elided.—Skt. *lotra*, shorter form of *loptra*, booty, spoil. —Skt. *lup*, to break, spoil; allied to L. *rumpere*, to break. See **Rupture, Rob.** *Loot* = that which is *robbed*. (Cf. Horn, Pers. Dict. § 608.)

Loover; see **Louver.**

Lop. (M. Du.) M. Du. *luppen*, to maim, castrate, mod. Du. *lubben*. Cf. Lithuan. *lùpti*, to peel. See **Lib.**

Loquacious, talkative. (L.) Coined from L. *loquāci-*, decl. stem of *loquax*, talkative.—L. *loquī*, to speak.

Lord, a master. (E.) Lit. 'loaf-keeper.' A.S. *hláford*, a lord; early form *hláfard*, for *hláfweard*, a loaf-ward; see **Loaf** and **Ward.** ¶ For the loss of *w*, cf. A.S. *fulluht*, from *fulwiht*, baptism.

Lore, learning. (E.) M.E. *lore*; A.S. *lāre*, gen., dat., and acc. of *lār*, lore.+Du. *leer*, G. *lehre*, O.H.G. *lēra*, doctrine. Teut. type *laizā*, fem.; cf. Teut. *laizjan* (A.S. *lēran*, G. *lehren*), to teach; from *lais-*, 2nd grade of *leisan-*, to trace out; see **Learn, Last** (2).

Lorel; see **losel.**

Lorimer, a maker of horses' bits, spurs, &c. (F.—L.) Also *loriner.*—O.F. *lorinier, loreinier*, M.F. *lorimier*, later *lormier*, 'a spurrier;' Cotgrave.—O.F. *lorein, lorain*, rein, bridle, bit.—Late L. *lōrēnum, lōrānum*, a rein, bit.—L. *lōrum*, a thong.

Loriot, the golden oriole. (F.—L.) F. *loriot*, corruptly written for *l'oriot*, where *oriot* is another form of *oriol*; see **Oriole.**

Lorn, lost. (E.) M.E. *loren*, pp. of *lēsen*, to lose; see **Lose.**

Lory, a bird of the parrot kind. (Malay.) Also called *lury*; and (formerly) *nory, nury.*—Malay *lūrī, nūrī*, a lury or lory.

Lose. (E.) The form formerly in use was *lese*; M.E. *lesen*. [The mod. form *lose* has got its sound of (uu) from the influence of M.E. *lōsen*, to loose, con-

fused with M.E. *losien*, to be lost.] The M.E. *lesen* is from A.S. *-lēosan*, strong verb, to lose (pt.t. *-lēas*, pp. *-loren*). This is cognate with Du. *-liezen* (only in comp. *ver-liezen*), G. *-lieren* (only in comp. *ver-lieren*), Goth. *-liusan* (only in *fra-liusan*, to loose). Teut. type *leusan-*. Cf. L. *lu-ere*, Gk. λύ-ειν, to set free. **Der.** *lorn*, lost, A.S. pp. *-loren*; also *forlorn*, q.v.

loss, sb. (E.) M.E. *los.* A.S. *los*, destruction. Allied to **Lose**; being derived from Teut. *lus*, weak grade of *leusan-*, to lose (above).

losel, lorel, a worthless fellow, reprobate. (E.) One devoted to perdition; cf. A.S. *los*, destruction, *los-ian*, to be lost, to perish. From *lus-* (A.S. *los-*), weak grade of the strong verb *lēosan*, to lose, pp. *lor-en* (for older *los-en*). *Lor-el* is formed from the base *lor-* of the pp. in use, and *los-el* from the older form of the same. For the suffix, cf. A.S. *wac-ol*, watchful.

Lot, a portion, share. (E.) M.E. *lot.* A.S. *hlot* (<*hlutom*), lot, share.—A.S. *hlut-*, weak grade of *hlēotan* (pt.t. *hlēat*). to obtain by lot.+Du. *lot*; Icel. *hluti*, allied to str. vb. *hljōta*, to obtain by lot; Dan. *lod*, Swed. *lott*. All from the weak grade of Teut. *hleutan-*, to obtain by lot; cf. A.S. *hlīet, hlȳt*, G. *loos*, Goth. *hlauts*, a lot, from *hlaut*, 2nd grade of the same verb.

Loth; see **Loath.**

Lotion, a washing, external medicinal application. (L.) L. *lōtiōn-em*, acc. of *lōtio*, a washing.—L. *lōtus*, pp. of *lauāre*, to wash. See **Lave.** Brugm. i. § 352 (3).

Loto, Lotto, a game. (Ital.—Teut.) F. *loto*; a F. form of the Ital. *lotto*, a lottery, a word of Teut. origin; see **Lot.**

lottery. (E.; *with* F. *suffix.*) In Levins, ed. 1570. Formed by adding *-ery* to E. *lot*; cf. *brew-ery, fish-ery.* The F. *loterie* is borrowed from English or from Ital. *lotteria* (Torriano).

Lotus, the Egyptian water-lily. (L.— Gk.) L. *lōtus, lōtos.*—Gk. λωτός, (1) the Gk. lotus, (2) the Cyrenean lotus, the eaters of which were called *lōtophagi*, (3) the lily of the Nile.

Loud. (E.) M.E. *loud.* A.S. *hlūd.* +Du. *luid*, G. *laut.* Teut. type *hlūdoz*, for earlier *hlúthós* (with the accent on *o*), allied to the Idg. type *klutós* (with weak grade *klu*) as seen in L. *-clutus*, in *inclutus*, renowned, Gk. κλυτός, renowned,

Skt. *çruta-*, heard, from *çru*, to hear. (√KLEU.) Brugm. i. §§ 100, 113.

Lough, a lake. (Irish.) Ir. *loch*; see **Loch.**

Lounge, to loll about. (F.−L.) From *lungis*, an idle fellow or lounger, not an uncommon word in the 16th and 17th centuries.−F. *longis*, an idle, drowsy, and stupid fellow (Cot.). Littré supposes that this sense of *longis* was due to a pun, having reference to L. *longus*, long, hence a long and lazy man; for, strictly speaking, *Longis* is a proper name, being the O. F. form of L. *Longius* or *Longinus*, the name (in the old mysteries) of the centurion who pierced the body of Christ. This name first appears in the apocryphal gospel of Nicodemus, and was doubtless suggested by Gk. λόγχη, a lance, in John xix. 34.

Louse, an insect. (E.) M. E. *lous*, pl. *lys*. A. S. *lús*, pl. *lýs* (lice).+Du. *luis*, Dan. *luus*, Swed. *lus*, Icel. *lús*, G. *laus*. Teut. type *lūs*, fem.

Lout, a clown. (E.) The lit. sense is 'stooping,' from M. E. *louten*, to stoop, bow.−A.S. *lútan*, to stoop.+Icel. *lútr*, stooping, bent (which prob. suggested our use of the word), from *lúta*, to stoop; cf. Swed. *luta*, Dan. *lude*, to stoop, lean.

Louver, Loover, an opening in the roofs of ancient houses. (F.) M. E. *lover* (used to translate O. F. *louvert* in the Romance of Partenay, 1175), but really from O. F. *lovier*, *lover*, used as a gloss to Late L. *lodium*, a word also explained by M. E. *lover*.−Romanic type *lōdārium*, adj. form due to Late L. *lōdium*, a loover. (For the intercalated *v*, cf. F. *pouvoir*, from O. F. *pooir* = Span. *poder*.) Prob. an opening over a fireplace; from Icel. *hlǫð*, n. pl., a hearth. (Academy, Dec. '94.)

Lovage, an umbelliferous plant. (F.− L.) M. E. *louache* (Alphita).−O. F. *levesche*, *luvesche* (Wright's Voc. i. 139). Cf. Ital. *levistico*, lovage.−L. *ligusticum*, lovage, a plant of *Liguria*.−L. *Ligusticus*, belonging to *Liguria*, a country of Cisalpine Gaul.

Love, affection. (E.) M. E. *loue* (*love*). A. S. *lufu*, love. From the weak grade (*lub*) of Teut. base *leub*.+Goth. *lubo*; O. H. G. *luba*; cf. also G. *liebe*; Russ. *liobov'*; Skt. *lobha*, covetousness, *lubh*, to desire. Closely allied to **Lief.** (√LEUBH.) Der. *love*, vb.; *belove*, first appearing in M. E. *bilufien*, to love greatly.

Low (1), humble, inferior. (Scand.) M. E. *louh*, also *lah*.−Icel. *lágr*, low; N. Fries. *leeg*; Swed. *låg*, Dan. *lav*. The orig. sense is that which lies down, or lies low (as we say); from Icel. *lāg-*, stem of pt. pl. of *liggja*, to lie. See **Lie** (1). Der. *be-low* (= by low); also *lower*, vb., i. e. to let down, from *low-er*, comparative of *low*, adj.

Low (2), to bellow. (E.) M. E. *lowen*. A. S. *hlówan*, to bellow, resound.+Du. *loeijen*, O. H. G. *hlōjan*. Cf. L. *clā-māre*.

Low (3), a hill. (E.) In place-names. A. S. *hlāw*, *hlǣw*, a hill; properly a slope. +Goth. *hlaiw*, a grave; *hlains*, a hill; Lat. *clīuus*, a hill. From a Teut. base *hlai-*, 2nd grade of the Teut. root *hlei-* (Idg. √KLEI), to lean, incline. Allied to **Lean** (1).

Low (4), flame. (Scand.) Icel. *logi*, flame; cf. L. *lūx*. Allied to **Lucid.**

Lower (1), to let down. (E.) From *low-er*, comparative of adj. *low*.

Lower (2), to frown. (E.) M. E. *louren*, *luren*, to lower, frown. Cf. M. Du. *loeren*, 'to leere, to frowne,' Hexham; Low G. and E. Fries. *lūren*, to lower, frown, peer; M. H. G. *lūren*, G. *lauern*. Cf. Icel. *lūra*, to doze.

Lown; see **Loon** (1).

Loyal, faithful. (F.−L.) F. *loyal* (Cot.). − L. *lēgālis*, legal (hence, just, loyal); see **Legal.**

Lozenge, a rhombus; a small cake of flavoured sugar, &c., orig. of a diamond shape. (F.) Formerly *losenge*, esp. a shield of a diamond shape (in heraldry).− O. F. *losenge*, *lozenge* (F. *losange*), a lozenge. Origin disputed; prob. from O. F. *lauze*, borrowed from Prov. *lauza*, a square flat stone, tombstone; allied to Span. *laude*, the same.− L. *lapidem*, acc. of *lapis*, a stone. See *lausa*, *lauza*, a flat stone for buildings (Ducange).

Lubber, a dolt. (E.) M. E. *lobre*, *lobur*. Cf. M. Du. *lobben*, 'a lubbard, a clowne,' Hexham; Low G. *lobbes* (the same); Norw. *lubb*, *lubba*, one of round thick figure; *lubben*, short and thick. Also W. *llob*, a dolt, lubber, *llabi*, a stripling, looby. Cf. *lob* in Shakespeare, M. N. D. ii. 1. 16. Allied to **Lump;** cf. E. Fries. *lobbe*, *lob*, a flabby lump.

Lubricate, to make slippery. (L.) From pp. of L. *lūbricāre*, to make slippery. − L. *lūbricus*, slippery. Allied to Goth. *sliupan*, to slip. See **Slip.**

Luce, the pike; a fish. (F.—Late L. —Gk.) Lit. 'wolf-fish.'—M. F. *lucs, lus,* a pike; Cot.—Late L. *lucius,* a pike.—Gk. λύκος, a wolf; also a (ravenous) fish. Cf. 'Pyke, fysche, *dentrix, lucius, lupus;*' Prompt. Parv. 'Luce, fysche, *lucius* ;' id.

Lucid, bright. (L.) L. *lūcidus,* bright. —L. *lūcēre,* to shine; cf. *lūx,* light.+Gk. λευκός, bright; Skt. *ruch,* to shine. Allied to **Light** (1). (√LEUK.) Der. *luci-fer,* i. e. light-bringer, morning-star, from *ferre,* to bring.

Luck, fortune. (Du.—M. H. G.) M. E. *lukke* (15th c.). Not found in A.S.; and Fries. *luk* is late.—Du. *luk.* From M.H.G. *ge-lücke,* good fortune; G. *glück* (for *ge-lück*). The Fries. *luk,* Swed. *lycka,* Dan. *lykke* (like Du. *luk*) are borrowed from G. (Kluge). Perhaps akin to G. *locken,* to entice, allure.

Lucre, gain, profit. (F.—L.) F. *lucre.* —L. *lucrum,* gain. Allied to Irish *luach,* price, wages, G. *lohn,* reward, Gk. λεία (for *λαϝία), booty, Russ. *lovite,* to take as booty. Der. *lucr-at-ive,* F. *lucratif,* L. *lucrātīuus,* from pp. of *lucrārī,* to gain, from *lucrum,* gain. Brugm. i. § 490.

Lucubration, a production composed in retirement. (L.) Properly, a working by lamp-light; from L. *lūcubrātio,* the same.—L. *lūcubrātus,* pp. of *lūcubrāre,* to bring in lamps, to work by lamp-light.—L. *lūcubrum,* prob. a faint light; at any rate, obviously formed from *lūc-,* stem of *lūx,* light; cf. *lūcēre,* to shine. See **Light** (1), **Lucid.**

Ludicrous, laughable. (L.) L. *lūdic-r-us,* done in sport; with suffix *-ous.*—L. *lūdi-,* for *lūdus,* sport.—L. *lūdere,* to play.

Luff, Loof, to turn a ship towards the wind. (E.) From M. E. *lōf,* a contrivance for altering a ship's course; see Layamon, iii. 476. It seems to have been a sort of large paddle, used to assist the helm in keeping the ship right. Prob. named from the resemblance of a paddle to the palm of the hand; cf. Lowl. Sc. *loof,* Icel. *lōfi,* Goth. *lōfa,* palm of the hand. Cf. also Du. *loef,* Dan. *luv,* Swed. *lof,* weathergage; Dan. *luve,* to luff; and perhaps Bavarian *laffen,* blade of an oar, flat part of a rudder. See E. Fries. *lōf, lūf* in Koolman. Der. *laveer.*

Lug, to drag. (Scand.) Swed. *lugga,* to pull by the hair; cf. *lugg,* the forelock; Norw. *lugga,* to pull by the hair; cf. *lugg,* hair of the head. Also cf. Low G. *luken,*

to pull, pull by the hair; A. S. *lūcan,* to pull up weeds; Dan. *luge,* to weed. β. The A. S. *lūcan* is a strong verb, allied to a Teut. type *leuk-an-,* to pull (pt. t. *lauk,* pp. *lukanoz*). *Lug* is from the weak grade *luk.* Der. *lugg-age,* with F. suffix as in *bagg-age.*

Lugsail, a sort of square sail. (Scand. and E.) Prob. from the verb *to lug;* the sail is easily hoisted by a pull at the rope attached to the yard. Or named from *lugger,* its apparent derivative, as if a ship furnished with lugsails; but cf. Du. *logger,* which seems to mean 'slow ship,' from Du. *log,* slow, E. Fries. *lug.* (Doubtful.)

Lugubrious, mournful. (L.) From L. *lūgubri-s,* mournful; with suffix *-ous.*— L. *lūgēre,* to mourn. Cf. Gk. λυγρός, sad.

Lukewarm, partially warm. (E.) M. E. *luke, leuk,* tepid. (*Luke-warm* = tepidly warm.) Cf. Du. *leuk,* luke-warm; E. Fries. *lūk, luke,* tepid, weak, slack. ¶ Distinct from *lew-warm.*

Lull, to sing to rest. (E.?) M. E. *lullen.* Not in A.S.+Swed. *lulla,* Dan. *lulle,* to hum, lull; M. Du. *lullen,* to sing in a humming voice; E. Fries. *lollen,* to sing badly, howl, cry. From the repetition of *lu lu,* in lulling children to sleep. This is a drowsier form of *la! la!* used in cheerful singing; cf. *lilt;* and see **Lollard.** Cf. Gk. λαλεῖν, to speak.

Lumbar, relating to the loins. (L.) L. *lumbāris,* adj.; whence *lumbāre,* an apron (Jerem. xiii. 1).—L. *lumbus,* the loin.+A.S. *lendenu,* pl., the loins, Du. *lendenen,* pl.; Swed. *länd,* Dan. *lend,* loin; G. *lende,* haunch. Brugm. i. § 360.

lumbago, pain in the loins. (L.) L. *lumbāgo,* pain in the loins.—L. *lumbus,* loin.

Lumber (1), useless furniture. (F.— G.) Formerly *lombor* (1487); *lumbar* (Blount). Perhaps the *lumber-room* was orig. *Lombard-room,* where the Lombard broker bestowed his pledges. Cf. *Lombardeer,* a broker, *Lombard,* a bank for usury or pawns; Blount.—F. *Lombard,* a Lombard (who acted as pawnbroker in the 14th century).—L. *Longobardus,* also *Langobardus.*—G. *Langbart,* a name given to the men of this tribe. Cf. A. S. *Langbeardas,* the Lombards. (Etym. disputed.)

Lumber (2), to make a great noise. (Scand.) In Palsgrave. A frequent. verb of Scand. origin.—Swed. dial. *lomra,* to resound; cf. Swed. *ljumm*, a great noise, Icel. *hljōmr*, a sound, a tune. From Teut. base **hleu-*, to hear, whence also Goth. *hliuma*, hearing. See **Loud**.

Luminary, a bright light. (F.–L.) O. F. *luminarie*, later *luminaire*, a light, lamp.–L. *lūmināre*, a light; neut. of *lūmināris*, light-giving.–L. *lūmin-*, for *lūmen*, light. *Lūmen = *lūc-men*; from *lūcēre*, to shine. See **Lucid**.

luminous, bright. (F. – L.) F. *lumineux.* – L. *lūminōsus*, bright; from *lūmin-*, for *lūmen*, light (above).

Lump. (Scand.) M. E. *lompe, lumpe.* – Swed. dial. and Norw. *lump*, a block, stump, piece hewn off a log; Swed. *lumpor*, pl., rags; Swed. Dan. *lumpen*, paltry. Cf. Du. *lomp* (whence G. *lumpen*), a rag, lump, *lomp*, clumsy; E. Fries. *lump*, clumsy, thick, vile, lumpy.

Lunar. (L.) L. *lūnāris*, adj.; from *lūna*, moon. L. *lūna = *loucsnā*, giver of light. – L. *lūcēre*, to shine. Brugm. i. § 218. **Der.** *lun-ette, inter-lunar*; and see below.

lunatic. (F.–L.) F. *lunatique.* – L. *lūnāticus*, mad; lit. affected by the moon. – L. *lūna*, moon.

Lunch, a large piece of bread, &c. (E.?) *Lunch*, 'a gobbet, or peece;' Minsheu. Connected with *lump*, like *hunch* with *hump*, *bunch* with *bump*. See **Lump**.

luncheon, lunch, a slight meal. (E.?) *Lunch* is now used as short for *luncheon*, though *luncheon* itself is an extension from *lunch*, a lump. Cot. gives M. F. *caribot*, 'a *lunchion*, or big piece of bread,' &c.; also '*horion*, a cuff, thump, also a *luncheon* or big piece.' *Lunchion* appears to be for *lunshin*, as in 'a huge *lunshin* of bread,' Thoresby to Ray (1703), which is prob. merely short for *lunchin*(*g*). At any rate, *luncheon* is clearly from *lunch*, a large piece (above). ¶ Quite distinct from *nuncheon*.

Lung. (E.) M. E. *lunge*, pl. *lunges*, *longes*, A.S. *lungen*, pl. *lungena.*+Du. *long*, Icel. *lungu*, pl., Dan. *lunge*, Swed. *lunga*, G. *lungen*, pl. Allied to A. S. *lungre*, quickly (orig. lightly), also to Gk. ἐλαχύς, Skt. *laghu-*, light. The *lungs* are named from their lightness; cf. E. *lights*, i. e. *lungs*; Russ. *legkoe*, lung, as compared with Russ. *legkii*, light; Port. *leves*, lungs, from Port. *leve*, light; see **Light** (2). Brugm. i. § 691.

Lunge, a thrust, in fencing. (F.–L.) Formerly *longe*. The E. *a longe* is a mistaken substitute for F. *allonge* (formerly *alonge*), a lengthening; i.e. an extension of the body in delivering the thrust. – F. *allonger*, to lengthen (formerly *alonger*). – F. *a* (from L. *ad*), to; and L. **longāre*, only used in comp. *ē-longāre*, to lengthen, from *longus*, long. See **Long**.

Lupine, a kind of pulse. (F.–L.) F. *lupin.* – L. *lupīnum*, a kind of pulse; orig. neut. of *lupīnus*, wolfish, though the reason is not clear. – L. *lupus*, a wolf; see **Wolf**.

Lurch (1), to lurk, dodge, pilfer. (E.) Allied to **Lurk**. Cf. *birch*, *birk*. The senses are (1) to lie in wait, lurk, (2) to pilfer, steal. **Der.** *lurch-er*, 'one that lies upon the lurch, or upon the catch, also a kind of hunting-dog;' Phillips.

Lurch (2), the name of a game. (F.) 'To leave in the *lurch*' is due to an old game. – M. F. *lourche*, 'the game called lurche, or lurch in a game; *il demoura lourche*, he was left in the lurch;' Cot. Cot. also gives *ourche*, 'the game at tables called lurch.' – Bavarian *lurz*, beaten at draughts. Cf. Ital. *lurcio*, 'the game lurch,' Torriano. Cf. Low L. *lurculus*, 'parvus lusus;' Ducange.

Lurch (3), to devour; obsolete. (F.? – L.) 'To *lurch*, devour, or eate greedily;' Baret. – O. F. **lurcher* (?); cf. Ital. *lurcare*, 'to lurch or devour greedily,' Torriano. – Late L. *lurcārī, lurcāre*, to devour greedily.

Lurch (4), a sudden roll sideways. (E.?) '*A lee lurch*, a sudden roll (of a ship) to the leeward;' Webster. Obscure; perhaps merely *lurch* (1) in the sense to stoop or dodge; see **Lurch** (1).

Lure, a bait. (F.–G.) M. E. *lure.* – O. F. *loerre, loirre*, later *leurre*, 'a faulconer's lure;' Cot. – Teut. **lōthrom*, neut.; as seen in M. H. G. *luoder* (G. *luder*), a bait, decoy, lure. Perhaps from Teut. **lōth*, 2nd grade of **lath-*, to invite? Cf. A. S. *laðian*, Icel. *laða*, Goth. *lathōn*, G. *laden*, to invite, weak verbs.

Lurid, wan, gloomy. (L.) L. *lūridus*, pale yellow, wan.

Lurk, to lie in wait. (Scand.?) M. E. *lurken, lorken.* – Norw. *lurka*, to sneak away, go slowly; Swed. dial. *lurka*, to do anything slowly; E. Fries. *lurken*, to shuffle along. Perhaps extended from *lūr-*, as in Norw. *lura*, Dan. *lure*, to lie in wait, Dan. *lure*, (also) to listen, Swed. *lura*, to lie in wait; G. *lauern*, to lurk. See **Lower** (2).

Lury; see **Lory**.

Luscious, delicious. (F.—L.) Of doubtful origin. Still, we find in The Anturs of Arthur, ed. Robson, st. 36, 'with *lucius* drinkes;' and in Sir Amadace, st. 27, 'with *licius* drinke.' The latter form is short for *delicious*; so that *luscious* may be the same, but confused with *lusty*. Also *lushious* (Spenser); *lussyouse* (Palsgrave).

Lust. (E.) The usual old meaning is pleasure. A.S. *lust*, pleasure.+Du. *lust*, Icel. *lyst*, *losti*, Dan. *lyst*, Swed. and G. *lust*, Goth. *lustus*, pleasure. Allied to Skt. *lash*, to desire; Gk. λιλαίομαι. Brugm. i. § 518 (2). **Der.** *lust-y*, formerly 'pleasant.'

Lustration; see **Lustre** (2).

Lustre (1), splendour. (F.—Ital.—L.) F. *lustre*.—Ital. *lustro*, 'a lustre, a glasse, a shining,' Florio; cf. Late L. *lustrum*, a window.—L. *lustrāre*, to shine. Prob. from a lost adj. **lustrus* (for **lucstrus*), shining; from *lūcēre*, to shine.

Lustre (2), **Lustrum,** a period of five years. (L.) L. *lustrum*, an expiatory sacrifice; also a period of five years, because every five years a lustrum was performed. The orig. sense is 'a purification'; from *luere*, to wash, purify.

lustration, a purification by sacrifice. (L.) From L. *lustrātio*, an expiation. — L. *lustrātus*, pp. of *lustrāre*, to purify. — L. *lustrum*, an expiatory sacrifice (above).

Lute (1), a musical instrument. (F.—Arab.) M.E. *lute*.—M.F. *lut* (Cotgrave), mod. F. *luth*. We also find Prov. *laut*, Span. *laud*, Port. *alaude*, Ital. *liuto*, Du. *luit*, Dan. *lut*, G. *laute*. The Port. form shews the Arab. origin; since *al-* in *al-aude* is for *al*, the Arab. def. art. — Arab. *al*, the; *'ūd*, wood, timber, a staff, stick, wood of aloes, lute, or harp.

Lute (2), a kind of loam. (F.—L.) O.F. *lut*, clay, loam.—L. *lutum*, mud, that which is washed down. — L. *luere*, to wash. Allied to **Lave**.

Lutestring, a lustrous silk. (F.—Ital.—L.) A curious corruption of *lustring*, a sort of shining silk (Kersey).—F. *lustrine*, lutestring, lustring. — Ital. *lustrino*, lustring, tinsel; from its gloss.—L. *lustrāre*, to shine ; see **Lustre** (1).

Luxury. (F.—L.) M.E. *luxurie*.—O.F. *luxurie* (Hatzfeld), F. *luxure*. — L. *luxuria*, luxury. —L. *luxus*, pomp, excess, luxury.

-ly, a common suffix. (E.) A.S. *-līc*, adj. suffix; *-līce*, adv. suffix; from *līc*, like ; see **Like** (1).

Lye, a mixture of ashes and water, for washing. (E.) M.E. *ley*. A.S. *lēah*.+Du. *loog*, G. *lauge*, O.H.G. *louga*, lye. Perhaps allied to Icel. *laug*, a bath ; and to L. *lauāre*, to wash. Cf. **Lather**.

Lym, a lime-hound : K. Lear, iii. 6. 72. Short for **Limehound**.

Lymph, a colourless fluid. (L.) L. *lympha*, O.L. *lumpa* (Brugm. i. § 102), water, lymph, also a water-nymph. The spelling with *y* is prob. due to a supposed connexion with Gk. νύμφη, a nymph (prob. false). It is rather allied to **Limpid**.

Lynch, to punish by mob-law. (E.) From *Charles Lynch*, a Virginian planter (1736–96); Cent. Dict. The name is from A.S. *hlinc*, a ridge of land. See **Link** (1).

Lynx, a keen-sighted quadruped. L.— Gk.) M.E. *lynx*.—L. *lynx*.—Gk. λύγξ, a lynx ; allied to λευκός, bright, and named from its bright eyes. Cf. Skt. *ruch*, to shine, *loch*, to see. Cognate forms are A.S. *lox*, Swed. *lo*, G. *luchs*, Lith. *luszis*, a lynx ; and (probably) Russ. *ruise*, Pers. *rūs*, Zend *raozha* ; Student's Pastime, p. 393.

Lyre. (F.—L.—Gk.) F. *lyre*. — L. *lyra*. — Gk. λύρα, a lyre, lute. **Der.** *lyr-ic*.

M.

Macadamise, to pave a road with small broken stones. (Gael. *and* Heb.; *with* F. *suffix*.) Named after Mr. John *Macadam*, A.D. 1819. *Macadam* = son of Adam. — Gael. *mac*, son ; Heb. *ādām*, a man, from root *ādam*, to be red.

Macaroni, Maccaroni. (Ital.—L.) Ital. *maccaroni*, 'a kinde of paste meate;' Florio. Prob. from Ital. *maccare*, 'to bruise, batter, to pester,' Florio ; i.e. to reduce to pulp. — L. *māc-*, base of *mācerāre*, to macerate. See **Macerate**. **Der.** *macaronic*, i. e. in a confused or mixed state (applied to a jumble of languages).

macaroon. (F.—Ital.—L.) F. *maca-ron*, pl. *macarons*, 'macarons, little fritter-like buns, .. also the same as macaroni;' Cot. — Ital. *maccaroni* (above). ¶ Now applied to a kind of biscuit.

Macaw, a kind of parrot. (Caribbean.) Said to be the native name in the Antilles (Webster). Brazilian *macao* (Cent. Dict.).

Mace (1), a kind of club. (F.—L.) O. F. *mace* (F. *masse*).—Folk-L. **mattea*, a beetle, only preserved in dimin. *mateola*, a little beetle. See Körting. ¶ But see Franck (s. v. *metselen*).

Mace (2), a kind of spice. (F.—L.—Gk. — Skt.?) F. *macis*, mace (O. F. *maceis, macis*, Godefroy). It seems to have been confused with M. F. *macer*, which 'is not mace, as many imagine, but a reddish, aromaticall, and astringent rind of a certain Indian root'; Cot. Both prob. from L. *macer, macir*, i. e. the 'rind of a great root, which beareth the name of the tree itself,' Holland, tr. of Pliny, xii. 8. — Gk. μάκερ; doubtless of Eastern origin.

Macerate, to soften by steeping. (L.) From pp. of L. *mācerāre*, to steep; fre-quent. from a base *māc*-.

Machine. (F.—L.—Gk.) F. *machine*. — L. *māchina*. — Gk. μηχανή, a device, machine; cf. μῆχος, means. (√MĀGH.) Allied to May (1).

Mackerel, a fish. (F.—L.) O. F. *makerel* (F. *maquereau*). From Late L. *maquerellus*. Of unknown origin.

Mackintosh, a waterproof overcoat. (Gael.) Gael. *Mack-intosh*, the name of the inventor.

Macrocosm, the whole universe. (Gk.) Gk. μακρό-s, long, great; κόσμος, the world. Cf. *microcosm*.

Maculate, to defile. (L.) From pp. of L. *maculāre*, to spot.—L. *macula*, a spot, dimin. of a form **maca*, not used. **Der.** *immaculate*, orig. a pp.

Mad. (E.) [The vowel was formerly sometimes long. M. E. *maad*.] But the M. E. *măd* is from A. S. *(ge)-mēded*, mad-dened, shortened to *(ge-)mēdd* (cf. *fat*); pp. of *ge-mēdan*, to drive mad. [The M. E. *maad* answers to A. S. *mād*; cf. A. S. *ge-maad*, Corp. Gloss. 2105; hence *mād-mōd*, madness (Grein)] + O. Sax. *ge-mēd*, foolish; O. H. G. *gimeit*, vain; Icel. *meiddr*, pp. of *meiða*, to maim, hurt; Goth. *ga-maids*, maimed. The orig. sense seems to be 'severely injured'; the prefix *ge-*, *gi-*, *ga-* is unessential.

Madam, my lady. (F. — L.) F. *madame*, i. e. *ma dame*, my lady. — L. *mea domina*, my lady; see **Dame.**

Madder, a plant. (E.) M. E. *mader, madir*. A. S. *mæddre*; also *mædere*. + Icel. *maðra*, Du. *mede, mee*.

Madeira, a sort of wine. (Port.—L.) Named from the isle of *Madeira*, i.e. 'the well-wooded.'—Port. *madeira*, wood, tim-ber. — L. *māteria*, stuff, wood, timber. See **Matter** (1).

Mademoiselle, miss. (F.—L.) F. *ma*, my; *demoiselle*, damsel; see **Damsel.**

madonna, my lady. (Ital.—L.) Ital. *ma*, my; *donna*, lady, from L. *domina*; see **Dame.**

Madrepore, coral. (F. — Ital. — L. and Gk.) F. *madrépore*. — Ital. *madre-pora*. The lit. sense is 'mother-stone,' a fanciful name, due to the existence of such terms as *madre-selva*, honeysuckle (lit. mother-wood), *madre-bosco*, woodbine (lit. mother-bush), *madre-perla*, mother-of-pearl. Here *madre* is from L. *mātrem*, acc. of *māter*, mother; see **Mother.** *Pora* is from Gk. πῶρος, a light friable stone, also a stalactite. ¶ But the word has certainly been *understood* (prob. *mis-understood*) as connected with *pore*, whence numerous scientific terms such as *cateni-pora, tubi-pora, denti-pora, gemmi-pora.* 'Scientific' etymology is usually clumsy, and frequently wrong. We may conclude that F. and E. *pore* have been understood in the place of Gk. πῶρος, by confusion of ideas. See **Pore.**

Madrigal, a pastoral song. (Ital.—L.—Gk.) Ital. *madrigale*, a short song, pastoral ditty; for **mandrigale*. Florio also gives *mandriale, mandriano*, a herds-man, also a madrigal. — Ital. *mandra*, a herd, flock. — L. *mandra*, a stall, stable. — Gk. μάνδρα, a fold. + Skt. *man-durā*, stable. (The suffix *-ig-ale* = L. suffix *-ic-ālis*.)

Magazine. (F.—Ital.—Arab.) O.F. *magazin* (F. *magasin*). — Ital. *magazzino*, a storehouse. — Arab. *makhāzin*, pl. of *makhzan*, a storehouse.—Arab. *khasn*, a laying up in store.

Maggot, a grub. (E.) M. E. *magot, magat.* Cf. W. *maceiad, macai*, a maggot; *magiaid*, grubs. But *maggot* appears to be an A. F. perversion of M. E. *maddok*, the usual word for maggot. Also M. E. *maðek*, dimin. of A. S. *maþa, maþu*, a worm. + Du. *made*; G. *made*; Goth. *matha*.

Cf. also Dan. *maddik*, Norw. *makk*, Icel. *maðkr*; see **Mawkish**.

Magi, priests of the Persians. (L. — Gk. — Pers.) L. *magi*, pl. — Gk. μάγοι, pl. of μάγος, a Magian, one of a Median tribe; also an enchanter, properly a wise man who interpreted dreams. — O. Pers. *magu-*, Pers. *mugh*, *mūgh*, one of the Magi, a fire-worshipper (Horn, § 984). **Der.** *mag-ic*, short for *magic art; mag-ic-i-an.*

Magistrate. (F. — L.) F. *magistrat*, a magistrate, ruler. — L. *magistrātus*, (1) a magistracy, (2) a magistrate. — L. *magister*, a master. L. *mag-is-ter* is a double compar. form; cf. *mag-nus*, great.

Magnanimity, Magnate ; see under **Magnificent**.

Magnesia ; see **Magnet**.

Magnet, the lodestone. (F. — L. — Gk.) M. E. *magnete.* — O. F. *magnete*, also *manete* (13th cent.). — L. *magnētem*, acc. of *magnēs*, for *Magnēs lapis* = Magnesian stone, the lodestone. — Gk. Μάγνης (stem Μαγνητ-), also Μαγνήτης, Μαγνήσιος, belonging to Magnesia, in Thessaly; whence λίθος Μαγνῆτις (or Μαγνήτης), Magnesian stone, lodestone, or a metal like silver. **Der.** *magnesia*, an old name (in Chaucer, C. T. 16923, *or* G. 1455), for a mineral brought from Magnesia; now differently applied. See Schade, p. 1395.

Magnificent. (L.) L. *magnificent-*, stem of *magnificens*, lit. doing great things, hence, grand. — L. *magni-*, for *magnus*, great; *-ficens*, for *faciens*, doing, from *facere*, to do. See **magnitude**.

magnify. (F. — L.) M. E. *magnifien.* — F. *magnifier.* — L. *magnificāre*, lit. to make large. — L. *magni-*, for *magnus*, great; *-ficāre*, for *facere*, to do.

magniloquence. (L.) L. *magniloquentia*, elevated language. — L. *magni-*, for *magnus*, great; *loquent-*, stem of pres. pt. of *loquī*, to speak; see **Loquacious**.

magnitude, greatness. (L.) L. *magnitūdo*, size. — L. *magnus*, great. **+** Gk. μέγας, great; Skt. *mahant-*, great; A. S. *micel*. See **Mickle**.

magnanimity, greatness of mind. (F. — L.) F. *magnanimité.* — L. acc. *magnanimitātem.* — L. *magnus*, great; *animus*, mind.

magnanimous, high-minded. (L.) L. *magnanim-us*; with suffix *-ous* (L. *-ōsus*). — L. *magnus*, great; *animus*, mind.

magnate, a great man, noble. (F. — L.) F. *magnat.* — L. *magnātem*, acc. of

magnās, a prince (Judith v. 26). — L. *magnus*, great. ¶ *Magnate* is due to the use of L. *magnās* in Hungary and Poland.

Magnolia. (F.) A genus of plants named after Pierre *Magnol*, of Montpellier in France; died A. D. 1715.

Magpie, a bird. (F. — L. — Gk.; *and* F. — L.) Also called *magot-pie, maggotypie. Mag* is short for *Magot* = F. *Margot*, a familiar form of F. *Marguerite*, also used to denote a magpie. This is from L. *Margarīta*, Gk. μαργαρίτης, a pearl; cf. Pers. *murwārīd*, a pearl, from Skt. *mañjarī*, a pearl. *Pie* = F. *pie*, from L. *pīca*, a magpie; see **Pie** (1).

Maguey, the American aloe. (Cuba.) Of Cuban origin (Oviedo). Not Mexican, which has no *g*; the Mex. name is *metl*.

Maharajah, great king. (Hind. — Skt.) From Skt. *mahā-rāja-*, great king. Cf. L. *magnus rex*. So also *mahā-rānī*, great queen; from Hind. *rānī*, Skt. *rājñī*, queen.

Mahdi, a spiritual director. (Arab.) Arab. *mahdī*, the guided one; from *ma*, prefix, and *hady*, to guide. Cf. *hādī*, a guide. (Rich. Dict. pp. 1661, 1670.)

Mahogany, a tree. (Hayti.) From *mahagoni*, in the old Carib dialect of Hayti. (Garden and Forest, no. 438, July 15, 1896.)

Mahometan; see **Mohammedan**.

Mahout, an elephant-driver. (Hind.) Hind. *mahāwat*.

Maid, Maiden. (E.) M. E. *mayde*, merely short for earlier *maiden, meiden.* A. S. *mægden*, a maiden, cognate with O. H. G. *magatīn*, a maiden (with fem. suffix *-īn*). The form without this suffix is A. S. *mægeð*, a maiden, cognate with Goth. *magaths*, a virgin, G. *magd*. Related to A. S. *magu*, a son or kinsman, cognate with Goth. *magus*, Icel. *mögr*, and perhaps with Corn. *maw*, a boy. See Stokes (in Fick, ii. 198). Kluge compares O. Irish *macc*, W. *mab*, son. **Der.** *maiden-hood*, also spelt *maiden-head*.

Mail (1), steel network for armour. (F. — L.) O. F. *maille*, mail, also a mesh of a net. — L. *macula*, a spot, speck, hole, mesh of a net; see **Maculate**.

Mail (2), a letter-bag. (F. — O. H. G.) M. E. *male.* — O. F. *male* (F. *malle*), a bag, wallet. — O. H. G. *malaha*, a leathern wallet. Cf. Gael. and Irish *mala*, a bag (from E.). Gk. μολγός, hide, skin.

Mail (Black), a forced tribute.

(Scand.) *Mail* is a Scottish term for rent. *Blackmail* or *black rent* is the rent paid in cattle, as distinct from *white money* or silver. — Icel. *māli*, agreement, payment; cf. *māl*, speech, law-suit, agreement. Allied to A. S. *mæþel*, *mǣl*, a speech.

Maim, a bruise, hurt. (F. — G. ?) Also spelt *mahim* in Law-books (Blount). M. E. *maim*. — A. F. *mahaym*, Liber Albus, p. 281; M. F. *mehaing*, 'a maime, or abatement of strength by hurts received;' Cot. Cf. Ital. *magagna*, a defect, blemish. Orig. uncertain; cf. Bret. *machañ*, mutilation, *machaña*, to mutilate. Some derive Ital. *magagnare*, to maim, from G. *man*, man, and O. H. G. **hamjan*, to mutilate, from the O. H. G. adj. *ham*, maimed (Körting).

Main (1), sb., strength. (E.) M. E. *main*. A. S. *mægen*, strength. + Icel. *megin*, O. Sax. *megin*, strength. Allied to **May** (1) and **Might** (1).

Main (2), adj., chief, principal. (Scand.) M. E. *mayn*, adj. — Icel. *megn*, strong. ¶ Distinct from *main*, sb., which is of A. S. origin; see above.

Mainour. (F. — L.) In the phr. ' taken with the mainour' or 'taken in the manner'; i. e. caught in the act. Anglo-F. *meinoure*, *mainoure*, O. F. *maineuvre*, lit. manœuvre; hence, act. See **Manœuvre**. We find also 'to be taken *with* the manner,' i. e. with the stolen chattel in hand; A. F. *ove mainoure*.

Maintain, to keep in a fixed state, support. (F. — L.) M. E. *maintenen*. — F. *maintenir*. — L. *manū tenēre*, to hold in the hand; or more likely (in late L.) to hold by the hand, to abet. — L. *manū*, abl. of *manus*, hand; *tenēre*, to hold; see **Manual** and **Tenable**.

Maize, Indian corn. (Span. — W. Indian.) Span. *maiz*. — W. Indian *mahiz*, *mahis*, in the old Carib dialect of the isle of Hayti.

Majesty. (F. — L.) M. E. *magestee*. — O. F. *majestet* (F. *majesté*). — L. *maiestātem*, acc. of *maiestās*, dignity, honour. Here *mā-ies-* is related by gradation to *mā-ior*, comparative of *mag-nus*, great. See **Magnitude**. Brugm. ii. § 135.

major, a title of rank. (L.) L. *māior*, greater; comparative of *magnus*, great. Der. *major-domo*, imitated from Span. *mayor-domo*, a house-steward.

Make. (E.) M. E. *maken*. A. S. *ma-*

cian, pt. t. *macode*, to make. + Du. *maken*; G. *machen*. Allied to **Match** (1), q. v.

Mal-, *prefix*, bad. (F. — L.) F. *mal*. — L. *malus*, bad; see **Malice**.

Malachite, a green stone. (Gk.) Named from its colour, which resembles that of mallow-leaves. Formed with suffix *-ītēs* (Gk. *-ιτης*) from μαλάχ-η, a mallow. See **Mallow**.

Malady. (F. — L.) F. *maladie*. — F. *malade*, sick; oldest spelling *malabde*. Cf. O. Prov. *malaptes*, *malaudes*, sick. — L. *male habitus*, out of condition (hence sick, ill); cf. *male habens*, sick, Matt. iv. 24 (Vulgate). — L. *male*, badly, from *malus*, bad; *habitus*, pp. of *habēre*, to have; see **Habit**. ¶ So Schwan. Not from *male aptus* (Diez); this would mean ' foolish.'

malapert, saucy. (F. — L.) O. F. *mal appert*. — O. F. *mal*, ill; *appert*, *aspert*, expert, ready, skilful. The sense is ' badly expert,' i. e. mischievous. — L. *male*, badly; *expertus*, skilful, confused with *apertus*, pp. of *aperire*, to open; see **Expert** and **Aperient**.

malaria, noisome exhalation. (Ital. — L. *and* Gk.) Ital. *mal'aria*, for *mala aria*, bad air. — L. *mala*, fem. of *malus*, bad; and Ital. *aria*, air, which represents Late L. **āria*, for *āeria*, fem. of *āerius*, adj. from *āēr*, air. See **Air**.

Male. (F. — L.) O. F. *masle* (later *male*); F. *mâle*. — L. *masculus*, male. See **Masculine**.

Malediction, a curse. (F. — L.) M. F. *malediction*. — L. acc. *maledictiōnem*, a curse. — L. *maledictus*, pp. of *maledīcere*, to speak evil of. — L. *male*, adv., evilly; *dīcere*, to speak. So also *male-factor*, an ill-doer, from *factor*, a doer; from *facere*, to do. So also *malevolent*, lit. wishing ill; from *uolent-*, stem of *uolens*, pres. pt. of *uelle*, to will, to wish.

Malice, ill will. (F. — L.) M.E. *malice*. F. *malice*. — L. *malitia*, badness. — L. *malus*, bad.

malign, unfavourable. (F. — L.) O.F. *maling*, fem. *maligne* (F. *malin*). — L. *malignus*, ill-disposed, for **mali-genus*, ill-born (like *benignus* for **beni-genus*). — L. *mali-*, for *malus*, bad; *gen-*, base of *gignere*, to produce; see **Genus**.

malinger, to feign sickness. (F. — L. *and* G.) From F. *malingre*, adj., diseased, formerly ugly, loathsome (Cot.). — F. *mal*, badly; O. F. *haingre*, *heingre*, thin, emaciated. — L. *male*, adv., badly; G. *hager*, thin, lean (Körting).

malison, a curse. (F. — L.) A. F. *maleison*; O. F. *malison*, popular form of *malediction*; see **Malediction** above. (So also *benison* for *benediction*.)

Malkin, a kitchen-wench. (F. — O.H.G.) *Malkin* is for *Mald-kin*, the dimin. of *Mald*, *Mold*, or *Maud*, i. e. *Matilda*. See **Grimalkin**. ¶ Not the dimin. of *Mary*; cf. ' Malkyne, or Mawt, Molt,Mawde,*Matildis,Matilda*;' Prompt. Parv.

Mall (1), a large wooden hammer. (F. —L.) M.E. *malle*. — O.F. *mal*, *mail*, F. *mail*, ' a mall '; Cot. — L. *malleum*, acc. of *malleus*, a hammer.

mall (2), the name of a public walk. (F.—Ital.—G. and L.) In *Pall Mall*, and the *Mall* in St. James's Park. Named from E. *pall-mall*; M. F. *pale-maille*, because the game so called was played there; this game of *pall-mall* was like the modern *croquet*, which is imitated from it. — M. Ital. *palamaglio*, ' a stick with a mallet at one end,' for playing the game of pall-mall; Florio. Also spelt *pallamaglio*; lit. ' mallet-ball.' — Ital. *palla*, a ball; *maglio*, a mall. A hybrid word. — O. H. G. *palla*, M. H. G. *balle*, G. *ball*, a ball; L. *malleum*, acc. of *malleus*, a hammer. See **Ball**.

malleable. (F. — L.) M. F. *malleable*, ' malleable, hammerable, pliant to the hammer;' Cot. From obs. L. **malleāre*, to hammer, of which the pp. *malleātus* occurs. — L. *malleus*, a hammer.

mallet, a small mall. (F. — L.) M. E. *maillet*. — F. *maillet*, ' a mallet '; Cot. Dimin. of F. *mail*; see **Mall** (1) above.

Mallard, a wild drake. (F. — L.) M.E. *malard*. — O. F. *malard*; formed, with suffix *-ard* (of G. origin, from G. *hart*), from O. F. *male*, male. See **Male**. The suffix *-ard* was particularly applied to males, so that the idea of ' male ' appears twice.

Malleable, Mallet; see **Mall**.

Mallecho, malefaction, mischief. (Span.—L.) Hamlet, iii. 2. 147.—Span. *malhecho*, ' misdone; an euill deed;' Minsheu. — Span. *mal*, ill; *hecho*, done, pp. of *hacer*, to do. — L. *male*, ill; *factus*, pp. of *facere*, to do. See **Fact**.

Mallow, a plant. (L.) M. E. *malwe*. — A.S. *malwe*; borrowed from L. *malua*,

a mallow. + Gk. μαλάχη (= *μαλϝάχη), a mallow; named from its emollient properties; cf. Gk. μαλάσσειν, to make soft, μαλακός, soft, mild. Cf. **Malachite**.

Malmsey, a strong sweet wine. (F. — Gk.) A corruption of M. E. *malvesie*, malmsey. — A. F. *malvesy* (Ducange); F. *malvoisie*, ' malmesie '; Cot. From *Malvasia*, now called *Napoli di Malvasia* or *Monemvasia* (μον-εμβασία), a town on the E. coast of Lacedæmonia in Greece.

Malt, grain steeped in water. (E.) M. E. and O. Merc. *malt*. A.S. *mealt*, malt. — Teut. **malt-*, 2nd grade of **meltan-*, to melt, hence to steep, soften. + Du. *mout*; Icel. Dan. Swed. *malt*; O.H.G. *malz*, malt, also soft, allied to Skt. *mṛdu-*, L. *mollis*, soft. See **Melt**.

Maltreat. (F.—L.) F. *maltraiter*, to treat ill. — L. *male*, ill; *tractāre*, to handle, treat; see **Treat**.

malversation. (F.—L.) F. *malversation*, ' misdemeanor;' Cot. (Hence fraudulent behaviour.) — F. *malverser*, to behave ill. — L. *male*, ill; *uersārī*, to be engaged in, from *uersāre*, frequent. form of *uertere*, to turn; see **Verse**.

Mamaluke, Mameluke, an Egyptian light horse-soldier. (F. — Arab.) M. F. *Mamaluc*; Cot. — Arab. *mamlūk*, a purchased slave or captive, lit. ' possessed.' — Arab. root *malaka*, he possessed.

Mamma. (E.) Also *mama*; for *ma ma*, a mere repetition of *ma*, an infantine syllable. Many other languages have something like it; cf. F. *maman*, Span. Du. and G. *mama*, Ital. and L. *mamma*, a child's word for mother.

Mammalia, the class of animals that suckle their young. (L.) From L. *mammālis* (neut. pl. *mammālia*), belonging to the breasts. — L. *mamma*, the breast. Brugm. i. § 587 (3).

mammillary, pertaining to the breasts. (L.) From L. *mammillāris*, adj.; formed from L. *mamma*, the breast.

Mammon. (L. — Gk. — Syriac.) L. *mammōna*.— Gk. μαμωνᾶς, Matt. vi. 24.— Syr. *mamōnā*, which occurs in Chaldee Targums, and in the Syriac version of St. Matthew, and means ' riches.' Cf. Heb. *matmōn*, a hidden treasure, from *tāman*, to hide.

Mammoth. (Russ. — Tatar.) Russ. *mamant*', a mammoth, species of elephant. An older form is *mammot*'; see N. E. D. Said to be from Tatar *mamma*, the earth;

because the Siberian peasants thought the animal burrowed in the earth like the mole. But no such Tatar word has been found.

Man. (E.) M. E. *man*. A. S. *mann*. **+**Du. *man*, Icel. *mann-*, *maðr*, Swed. *man*, Dan. *mand*, Goth. *manna*, G. *mann* ; allied to Skt. *manu-*, a man.

manikin, manakin, a dwarf, small man. (F. − Du.) M. F. *manequin*, 'a puppet.' − M. Du. *manneken* (Hexham) ; double dimin. of Du. *man*, a man.

mankind, the race of men. (E.) A. S. *mancynn*, mankind. − A. S. *man*, man ; *cynn*, kind, race ; see **Kin.**

Manacle, a handcuff. (F.−L.) M. E. *manacle*, also *manycle*. − F. *manicle*. − L. *manicula*, dimin. of *manica*, a long sleeve, gauntlet, handcuff. − L. *manus*, the hand. See **Manual.**

manage, government of a horse, control, administration. (F. − Ital. − L.) Orig. a sb., but now superseded by *management*. See Rich. II. iii. 3. 179. − M.F. *manege*, 'the manage, or managing of a horse ;' Cot. − Ital. *maneggio*, 'a managing, a handling ;' Florio. − Ital. *mano*, the hand. − L. *manus*, the hand. Der. *manage*, vb.

Manatee, a sea-cow. (Span. − W. Indian.) Span. *manati*, a sea-cow. From its name in the language of Hayti.

Manchineel, a tree. (F. − Span. − L.) So called from its apple-like fruit. − F. *mancenille*, the fruit of the manchineel tree. − Span. *manzanilla*, the same ; also *manzanillo*, a little apple-tree, the manchineel tree ; dimin. of Span. *manzana*, an apple ; O. Span. *mazana* (Diez). − L. *Matiāna*, fem. of *Matiānus*, adj., the epithet of a kind of apple ; lit. ' Matian.' − L. *Matius*, the name of a Roman gens.

Manciple, a purveyor, esp. for a college. (F.−L.) M.E. *manciple*. − O.F. *mancipe*, *manciple*, a slave, servant ; cf. M. Ital. *mancipio*, a slave, farmer, manciple. − L. *mancipium*, a slave ; orig. ' possession.' − L. *mancip-*, for *manceps*, a taker in hand. − L. *man-us*, hand ; *cap-ere*, to take.

Mandarin, a Chinese governor of a province. (Port. − Malay. − Skt.) Not a Chinese, but Skt. word (through the Portuguese). − Port. *mandarim*, a mandarin. − Malay (and Hindu) *mantrī*, a counsellor, minister of state. − Skt. *mantrin-*, a counsellor ; *mahāmantrin-*, the prime minister. − Skt. *mantra-*, advice, counsel. − Skt. *man*, to think.

Mandate, a command. (F.−L.) M.F. *mandat*. − L. *mandātum*, a charge. − L. *mandātus*, pp. of *mandāre*, to enjoin ; lit. to put into one's hand. − L. *man-us*, hand ; *dare*, to give ; see **Manual** and **Date.** Brugm. i. § 589 (2, b).

Mandible, a jaw. (L.) L. *mandibula*, jaw. − L. *mandere*, to chew.

Mandilion, a soldier's cloak. (Ital. − Span. − Arab. − L.) See Nares. Ital. *mandiglione*, 'a mandillion, souldier's iacket ;' Florio. − Span. *mandil*, a coarse apron. − Arab. *mandīl*, a table-cloth, towel, mantle. − L. *mantīle*, a napkin.

Mandolin, a guitar. (F. − Ital. − Gk.) F. *mandoline*. − Ital. *mandolino*, dimin. of *mandola*, *mandora*, a kind of guitar. Variants of Ital. *pandora*. See further under **Banjo.**

Mandrake, a narcotic plant. (F.−L. − Gk.) M. E. *mandrake*, *mandrage* ; fuller form *mandragores* ; cf. *mandragora*, Othello, iii. 3. − O. F. *mandragore* (Ital. and Span. *mandragora*). − L. *mandragoras*. − Gk. μανδραγόρας, the mandrake.

Mandrel, the revolving axis to which turners fix their work in a lathe. (F. − Gk. ?) From F. *mandrin*, a punch, a mandrel. Perhaps from Gk. μάνδρα, an enclosed space, sheepfold, also used to mean ' the bed in which the stone of a ring is set,' much like E. *mandrel*. See **Madrigal.** But cf. Oscan *mamphur*, part of a lathe ; Brugm. i. §§ 571, 757.

Mane. (E.) A. S. *manu* ; cf. Icel. *mön* (gen. *man-ar*), a mane ; Swed. and Dan. *man*. **+**Du. *maan*, M. Du. *mane* ; G. *mähne*, O. H. G. *mana*. Cf. W. *myngen*, mane, from *mwn*, neck ; Irish *muince*, collar, from *muin*, neck ; Skt. *manyā*, the tendon forming the nape of the neck ; L. *monīle*, neck-lace. Orig. sense ' neck ' ; hence ' hair on the neck.'

Manege, the same as **Manage.**

Manganese, a metal. (F. − Ital. − Gk.) An old term, newly applied. ' *Manganese*, so called from its likeness in colour and weight to the *magnes* or loadstone, is the most universal material used in making glass ;' Blount, ed. 1674. − M.F. *manganese* (Cot.). − Ital. *manganese*, ' a stuffe or stone to make glasses with ; also, a kind of minerall stone ;' Florio. A perverted form of *magnesia*, as shewn in the Cent. Dict. ; cf. *mangnet* for *magnet* in Palsgrave ; see **Magnet.**

Mange, scab or itch in dogs. (F.−L.)

Made out of adj. *mangy*, a mistaken form, due to M. E. *maniewe*, sb. the mange.— O. F. *manjue*, mange.—O. F. *manjuer* (F. *manger*), to eat.—L. *mandūcāre*, to eat; *viandūcus*, a glutton ; *mandere*, to chew.

manger, a feeding-trough. (F.—L.) M. E. *maungeur*, Cath. Angl. — O. F. *mangeure* ; F. *mangeoire*.—F. *manger*, to eat (above).

Mangel-wurzel, (properly) a kind of beet. (G.) Corrupted from G. *man-gold-wurzel*, lit. ' beet-root.'—G. *mangold* (M. H. G. *mangolt*), beet, derived by Schade from the personal name *Manegold*; *wurzel*, root, allied to E. **Wort** (1).

Mangle (1), to mutilate. (Perhaps F.—G.) In Sir T. More, Works, p. 538. We find Anglo-F. *mangler*, to mangle (Godefroy) ; and *mahangler*, to maim, in Langtoft's Chron. i. 254. Frequent. form of O. F. *mahaigner*, to maim. — O. F. *mahaing*, a maim, hurt. See **Maim.**

Mangle (2), a roller for smoothing linen ; to smooth linen. (Du.—Late L.— Gk.) Borrowed from Du. *mangelen*, to mangle, roll with a rolling-pin ; *mangel-stok*, a rolling-pin, cylinder for smoothing linen. The corresponding Ital. word is *mangano*, ' a kind of presse to presse buckrom ;' Florio. Both Du. and Ital. words are from Late L. *manganum*, *man-gona*, a military instrument for throwing stones, worked with an axis and winch. Indeed, the Ital. *mangano* also means a mangonel.—Gk. μάγγανον, a machine for defending forts, also the axis of a pulley.

mangonel, a war-engine. (F.—Late L.—Gk.) O. F. *mangonel* (later *man-gonneau*), a mangonel.—Late L. *man-gonellus*, dimin. of *mangona* (above).

Mango, a fruit. (Port. — Malay. — Tamil.) Port. *manga*.—Malay *manggā*, formerly *mangkā*, the mango-fruit. The Malay word is of Tamil origin.—Tamil *mānkāy*, i. e. ' *mān*-fruit,' the tree being *māmarum*, i. e. *mān*-tree' (Yule).

Mangonel ; see Mangle (2).

Mangosteen, a fruit. (Malay.) Formerly *mangostan*. — Malay *manggustan* (Scott) ; *manggīsta* (Marsden).

Mangrove. (Hybrid ; Malay *and* E.) ' A sort of trees called *mangroves* ;' Eng. Garner, vii. 371 ; A. D. 1689. Meant, as I suppose, for *mang-groves*, from the peculiar growth in groves or thickets. — Malay *manggi-manggi*, the name for the tree (Crawfurd).

Mania, frenzy. (L.—Gk.) L. *mania*. —Gk. μανία, frenzy, orig. mental excitement ; cf. μένος, mind. **Der.** *mania-c*, F. *maniaque*.

Manifest, apparent. (F. — L.) F. *manifeste*.—L. *manifestus*, evident. The lit. sense is doubtful. — L. *mani-*, for *manus*, hand ; *-festus*, apparently the same as in *in-festus*, hostile. It has been doubtfully connected with *-fendere*, to strike, as in *of-fendere*.

manifesto, a written declaration. (Ital. — L.) Ital. *manifesto*, sb. — Ital. *manifesto*, adj., manifest.—L. *manifestus* (above).

Manifold ; see Many.

Manikin ; see Man.

Manioc, the cassava-plant. (Brazil.) Brazil. *manioc* ; whence Port. *mandioca*.

Maniple, a handful, small band of men, priest's scarf. (L.) L. *manipulus*, a handful, a wisp of straw used as an ensign, a band of men round such an ensign.— L. *mani-*, for *manus*, hand ; *-pulus*, lit. filling, from the weak grade (*pul*) of the root **plē*, to fill ; cf. L. *plē-nus*, full. Cf. L. *disci-pulus*, a disciple.

manipulate, to handle. (L.) A coined word, and ill coined. Cf. L. *manipulātim*, adv., by troops ; but it was rather made directly out of the sb. *mani-pulus* (above).

Manito, a spirit, fetish. (Algonkin.) Algonkin *manito*, *manitu*, a spirit, demon. (Cuoq.)

Mankind ; see Man.

Manna. (L.—Gk.—Heb.) L. *manna*. — Gk. μάννα. — Heb. *mān*, manna. β. Hardly from Heb. *mān hu*, what is this ? Exod. xvi. 15 ; but from *mān*, (it is) a gift ; cf. Arab. *mann*, favour, also manna.

Manner, way. (F.—L.) M.E. *manere*. — A. F. *manere*, M. F. *maniere*, manner, habit (Cot.) ; Late L. *manēria*. — L. *manus*, the hand.

manœuvre. (F.—L.) F. *manœuvre*, properly, handiwork.—Late L. *manuopera*, also *manopera*, a working with the hand. —L. *manū*, abl. of *manus*, hand ; *opera*, work ; see **Operate.**

Manor, (formerly) a residence for a nobleman. (F. — L.) O. F. *manoir*, a mansion.—O. F. *manoir*, *maneir*, to dwell. —L. *manēre* ; see **Mansion.**

manse, a clergyman's house, in Scotland. (L.) Late L. *mansa*, a farm, dwelling.—L. *mansus*, pp. of *manēre* (below).

mansion. (F. — L.) O. F. *mansion*, a dwelling-place. — L. *mansiōnem*, acc. of *mansio*, an abiding, abode. — L. *mansus*, pp. of *manēre*, to remain, dwell. + Gk. μένειν, to stay, remain. (√MEN.)

Mantel, a shelf over a fire-place. (F. — L.) The same word as *mantle* below ; in old fire-places, it projects like a hood, to catch the smoke. **Der.** *mantel-shelf*, *mantel-piece*.

mantilla, a long head-dress. (Span. — L.) Span. *mantilla*; dimin. of *manto*, a cloak, veil (below).

mantle, a cloak, covering. (F. — L.) M. E. *mantel.* — O. F. *mantel*, later *manteau*, 'a cloke, also the mantle-tree of a chimney ;' Cot. — L. *mantellum*, a napkin, also a cloak ; cf. L. *mantīle*, a towel. We also find Late L. *mantum*, a short cloak, whence Ital. and Span. *manto*, F. *mante*, a mantle. **Der.** *mantle*, vb., to form a covering upon, to gather a scum on a surface. Brugm. i. §§ 134 (1), 483 (7).

Mantua, a lady's gown. (Ital.) '*Mantoe* or *Mantua gown*, a loose upper garment,' &c. ; Phillips (1706). *Manto* is from Ital. *manto*, a mantle (see **mantle**) ; but *Mantua gown* must refer to *Mantua* in Italy, though this connexion arose from mere confusion. **Der.** *mantua-maker*.

Manual, done by the hand. (F. — L.) Formerly *manuel.* — L. *manuālis*, adj., from *manus*, the hand. (√ME, to measure ; Brugm. ii. § 106.)

manufacture. (F. — L.) F. *manufacture*, M. F. *manifacture*, lit. a making by the hand. — L. *manū*, abl. of *manus*, hand ; *factūra*, a making, from *facere*, to make.

manumit, to release a slave. (L.) L. *manumittere* (pp. *manumissus*), to release, lit. to send away from one's hand. — L. *manū*, abl. of *manus*, hand ; *mittere*, to send ; see **Mission. Der.** *manumission*, from the pp.

manure, vb. (F. — L.) Formerly simply ' to till,' or to work with the hand ; Othello, i. 3. 328. A contracted form of *manœuvre* ; which see.

manuscript, written by the hand. (L.) Properly an adj., but also as a sb. — Late L. *manuscriptum*, a thing written by the hand. — L. *manū*, abl. of *manus*, hand ; *scriptum*, neut. of pp. of *scrībere*, to write ; see **Scribe.**

Many. (E.) M. E. *many, moni.* A.S. *manig, monig*, many ; see Sweet, N. E. Gr.

§ 1608. + Du. *menig*; Dan. *mange*, Swed. *månge*, (perhaps) Icel. *margr* (Noreen, 359), Goth. *manags*, G. *manch*, O. H. G. *manac.* Teut. type **managoz.* Allied to Irish *minic*, Gael. *minig*, W. *mynych*, frequent, Russ. *mnogie*, pl. many. **Der.** *mani-fold* ; see **Fold.**

Map. (F. — L.) The oldest maps represented the world, and were called *mappe-mounde.* This is an O. F. form of L. *mappa mundī*, map of the world. L. *mappa* meant a napkin, hence a painted cloth. See **Mop. Der.** *apron, napery, napkin.*

Maple, a tree. (E.) M. E. *maple, mapul.* A.S. *mæpel-, mapul-* ; whence *mapul-trēo, mapulder*, a maple-tree.

Mar, to injure. (E.) M. E. *merren.* O. Merc. *-merran*, in comp. *āmerran*, to hinder ; A.S. *āmyrran*, to obstruct, waste, hinder ; cf. *gemearr*, an impediment. + M. Du. *merren*, Du. *marren*, to retard ; O. H. G. *marrjan*, to hinder, vex ; Goth. *marzjan*, to cause to stumble. Teut. base **marz-.* Brugm. i. § 903 b.

marline, a small cord used for binding ropes. (Du.) Du. *marlijn*, also *marling*, a marline. — Du. *marren*, to bind, tie ; and *lijn, -ling*, from F. *ligne*, a line. See **Moor** (2) ; and **Line. Der.** *marline-spike.*

Marabou, Marabout, a kind of African stork ; also, its downy feathers. (F. — Port. — Span. — Arab.) F. *marabout.* — Port. *marabuto.* — Span. *morabito*, a Mahommedan sage. — Arab. *murābit*, quiet, still ; a hermit, sage ; a religious sage among the Berbers (whence the bird's name came). Cf. **Maravedi.**

Maranatha, our Lord cometh. (Syriac.) Syriac *māran athā*, our Lord cometh ; cf. Arab. *mār*, lord (from Syriac).

Maraschino, a cordial. (Ital. — L.) Ital. *maraschino.* — Ital. *marasca, amarasca*, a black and sour cherry. — L. *amārus*, bitter.

Maraud, to wander in quest of plunder. (F.) M. F. *marauder*, ' to play the rogue, beg ;' Cot. — F. *maraud*, a rogue, vagabond. Etym. disputed. Bugge connects it with F. *mal*, evil ; as if for **malaud* (Late L. **malaldus*).

Maravedi, a very small coin. (Span. — Arab.) Span. *maravedi*, the smallest Spanish coin ; orig. a gold coin first struck during the dynasty of the *Almora- vides* at Cordova, A. D. 1094-1144. Cf. Port. *maravedim, marabitino*, a maravedi.

— Arab. *Murābitīn*, the Arab. name of the above-mentioned dynasty ; pl. of *murābit* ; see **Marabou.**

Marble. (F. – L.) M. E. *marbel* ; also *marbre*. **–** O. F. *marbre*. **–** L. *marmorem*, acc. of *marmor*, marble, considered as a masc. sb. ; but it is commonly neuter. **+** Gk. μάρμαρος, explained as a glistening white stone, as if from μαρμαίρειν, to sparkle ; cf. μαῖρα, dog-star, lit. ' sparkler.' See **Marmoset.**

Marcasite, a kind of iron pyrites. (F. – Span. – Pers.) F. *marcassite*. **–** Span. *marquesita*. **–** Pers. *marqashīshā* (Devic, Vüllers).

Marcescent, withering. (L.) L. *marcescent-*, stem. of pres. pt. of *marcescere*, inceptive form of *marcēre*, to wither, lit. to grow soft. Brugm. i. § 413 (8).

March (1), a border, frontier. (F. – O. H. G.) M. E. *marche*. A. F. *marche*. **–** O. H. G. *marcha*, a boundary. Cf. Goth. *marka*, a confine, coast. See **Mark** (2).

March (2), to walk with regular steps. (F. – L. ? or G. ?) F. *marcher*, to march. Of disputed origin ; perhaps from a Late L. **marcare*, to beat (hence to tramp), from *marcus*, a hammer (Scheler).

March (3), the name of a month. (F. – L.) A. F. *Marz* (pron. marts). **–** L. *Martius*, the month dedicated to *Mars.*

Marchioness. (Low L. – G.) The proper F. form is *marquise* ; the E. *marchioness* answers to Low L. *marchiōnissa*, formed with fem. suffix *-issa* (Gk. *-ισσα*) from Low L. *marchiōnem*, acc. of *marchio*, a prefect of the marches. **–** Low L. *marcha*, a boundary. **–** O.H.G. *marcha*, a boundary. See **Mark** (2).

Marchpane, a sweet cake, made with almonds and sugar. (F. – Ital.) O. F. *marcepain* ; now *massepain*. **–** Ital. *marciapane, marzapane*, a marchpane ; Florio. Origin of *marcia* unexplained, but prob. from a proper name (such as L. *Martia*) : *pane* is from Lat. acc. *pānem*, bread.

Mare. (E.) M. E. *mere*. A. S. *mere*, fem. form of *mearh*, a horse.**+**Icel. *merr*, fem. of *marr*, a steed ; Dan. *mær*, Swed. *märr*, E. Fries. *märe*, Du. *merrie* ; G. *mähre*, O. H. G. *meriha*, fem. of O. H. G. *marah*, a battle-horse. Cf. Irish and Gael. *marc*, W. and Corn. *march*, a horse, a stallion. Idg. masc. type **markos*, a horse. Cf. **Marshal.**

Margin. (L.) L. *margin-*, stem of *margo*, a border, brink ; cognate with **Mark** (2).

Margrave, a lord of the marches. (Du.) Du. *markgraaf*, a margrave. **–** Du. *mark*, a boundary, march ; *graaf*, a count. So also G. *markgraf*. (That the word is Du. appears from the fem. form *margravine*, which answers to Du. *markgravin* ; not to G. *markgräfin*.)

Marigold, a plant. (Heb. *and* E.) Compounded of *Mary* (from the Virgin Mary) and *gold* (from its colour).

Marine. (F. – L.) F. *marin*. **–** L. *marīnus*, belonging to the sea. **–** L. *mare*, sea ; cognate with **Mere** (1). Der. *marin-er.*

Marish, a marsh. (F. – L.) M. E. *maris, marais*. **–** A. F. *mareis*. **–** O. F. *mareis*, of which the oldest form was *maresc* (Hatzfeld). **–** Late L. *mariscus*, from Low G. *marsch*, a marsh. See **Marsh.**

Marital, belonging to a husband. (F. – L.) F. *marital*. **–** L. *marītālis*, adj. formed from *marītus*, a husband. This is a masc. sb. made to accompany L. *marīta*, a woman provided with a husband. **–** L. *mari-*, for *mās*, a man, husband ; see **Masculine.**

Maritime, pertaining to the sea. (F. – L.) F. *maritime*. **–** L. *maritimus*, formed with suffix *-timus* from *mari-*, for *mare*, sea.

Marjoram, a plant. (F. – L. – Gk.) M. E. *majoran* (without *r*). **–** O. F. *majorane* (Godefroy) ; F. *marjolaine*. Cf. Ital. *majorana*, Span. *mayorana*, Port. *maiorana*, marjoram, Late L. *majorāna, majoraca* ; variously corrupted from L. *amāracus*. **–** Gk. ἀμάρακος, marjoram.

Mark (1), a stroke, sign. (E.) M. E. *merke*. A.S. *mearc*, fem., mark, sign.**+** Du. *merk*, Icel. *mark*, Swed. *märke*, Dan. *mærke*, G. *marke*, M. H. G. *marc*, a mark. Cf. also Lith. *margas*, marked, variegated. Perhaps related to **Mark** (2), which seems to be an older word.

Mark (2), a march, limit, boundary. (E.) A.S. *mearc*, fem.**+**O. Sax. *marka* ; Du.*mark* ; G. *mark*, fem., O.H.G.*marcha* ; Goth. *marka*, confine, coast. So also Icel. *mörk*, f., a forest (orig. a boundary). Teut. type, **markā*, fem. Allied to L. *margo*, a margin, Zend *merezu*, Pers. *marz*, a border ; O. Irish *mruig.*

Mark (3), a coin. (E.) M. E. *mark*, A.S. *mearc, marc*, a coin ; a weight equal to half a pound; O. Fries. *merk.*+Du. *mark*; G. *mark*, a weight of silver, a coin; Icel. *mörk*. β. Orig. a particular weight. There is nothing to connect it with Mark (1).

Market. (F.–L.) Late A. S. *market*, from Picard F. *market*. [Cf. Du. G. *markt*; F. *marché*, O. Prov. *mercatz*, Ital. *mercato*, a market.] – L. *mercātus*, traffic, also a market (whence G. *markt*, &c.). – L. *mercātus*, pp. of *mercārī*, to trade; see Mercantile. (Pogatscher.)

Marl, a rich earth. (F.–L.–C.) O. F. *marle* (F. *marne*); Picard *marle*. – Late L. *margila*, dimin. of Late L. *marga*, marl; of Celtic origin (Pliny).

Marline; see Mar.

Marmalade. (F.–Port.–L.–Gk.) F. *marmelade*, Cot. – Port. *marmelada*, orig. a conserve of quinces. – Port. *marmelo*, a quince. – L. *melimēlum*, lit. honeyapple; also a quince. – Gk. μελίμηλον, a sweet apple, apple grafted on a quince. – Gk. μέλι, honey; μῆλον, an apple; see Melon.

Marmoset, a small American monkey. (F.–L.) Much older than the discovery of America; M. E. *marmosette*, a kind of ape (Maundeville, p. 210). – M. F. *marmoset*, F. *marmouset*, 'the cock of a cistern or fountain, any antick image from whose teats water trilleth, any puppet or antick;' Cot. Thus it meant a grotesque creature, orig. a grotesque ornament on a fountain. Formed, by a Parisian change of *r* to *s*, as in *chaise* for *chaire* (a chair), from Late L. *marmorētum*, a thing made in marble, applied to fountains. [Thus the *rue des marmousets* in Paris was called in Late Latin *vīcus marmorētōrum*; Littré.] – L. *marmor*, marble; see Marble. ¶ This Latin form is *incorrect*. It appears that the transference in sense from 'image' to 'ape' was certainly helped on by confusion with F. *marmot*, 'a marmoset, or little monkey;' which is a different word from E. *marmot* (see below).

Marmot, a mountain-rat. (F.–Ital. –L.) F. *marmotte*. – Ital. *marmotta*, an ape, substituted for *marmotana*, 'the mountain-rat, a marmotan' (Torriano), a marmot. From the Romansch (Grisons) name *murmont*; O. H. G. *murmuntī*, *muremunto*, a marmot. – L. *mūr-*, stem of *mūs*, mouse; and *mont-*, stem of *mons*, mountain. Thus the sense is 'mountain-mouse.' (See Diez.)

Maroon (1), brownish crimson. (F.) F. *marron*, a chestnut (hence, chestnut-colour. Cf. Ital. *marrone*, M. Ital. *marone*, a chestnut (of unknown origin).

Maroon (2), to put ashore on a desolate island. (F.–Span.) From F. *marron*, adj., fugitive, applied to a fugitive slave who takes refuge in woods. [Hence E. *maroon*, to treat as a fugitive, cause to be fugitive.] A clipped form of Span. *cimarron*, wild, unruly; hence, savage. Of unknown origin. ¶ *Negro cimarron* or *cimarron* was an everyday phrase for a fugitive slave hidden in the mountains, in Cuba, about A. D. 1846.

Marque, letters of. (F.–G.) A *letter of marque* was a permission by a ruler to make reprisals on the country of another ruler; it had particular reference to passing beyond the *march* or limit of one's own country. – O. F. *marque*, a boundary. – M. H. G. *marke*, a boundary; see Mark (2) above. See *marcha* (1) in Ducange.

marquee, a large tent. (F.–Low L. –G.) For *marquees*; the *s* being dropped because it was thought to be a plural form. An E. spelling of F. *marquise*, a large tent; orig. a tent for a marchioness or lady of rank. – F. *marquise*, a marchioness, fem. of *marquis*, a marquis; see **marquis** below.

marquess. (Span.–Low L.–G.) Span. *marques*, a marquis; see **marquis**.

marquis. (F.–Low L.–G.) M. E. *markis*. – O. F. *markis*, later *marquis*, 'a marquesse, governour of a frontire town;' Cot. – Low L. *marchensis*, a prefect of the marches. – O. H. G. *marcha*, a march or boundary. See **Mark** (2). ¶ The true O. F. form was *marchis*; altered to *markis* by the influence of Ital. *marchese*.

Marquetry, inlaid work. (F.– M. H. G.) F. *marqueterie*, inlaid work. – F. *marqueter*, to inlay, diversify, orig. to mark slightly with spots; iterative form of *marquer*, to mark. – F. *marque*, a mark. – M. H. G. *mark*, G. *marke*, a mark. See **Mark** (1).

Marrow, pith. (E.) M. E. *marow*, *mary*. O. Merc. *merg*, A. S. *mearh* (dat. *mearge*). + Du. *merg*, Icel. *mergr*, Swed. *merg*, Dan. *marv*, G. *mark*, O. H. G. *marag*; [not W. *mer*, Corn. *maru*.] Further allied to Russ. *mozg'*, Zend *mazga*, marrow; Skt. *majjan*, marrow of bones, pith of trees. Idg. type *mazgho-*; Brugm. i. § 642.

Marry. (F. — L.) M. E. *marien.* — F. *marier.* — L. *marītāre*, to marry. — L. *maritus*, a husband ; see **Marital.**

Marsh, a swamp. (E.) M. E. *mersch.* A. S. *mersc*, a marsh ; early form *merisc* < **mar-isc*, lit. mere-ish, i. e. full of meres or pools. — A. S. *mere* (for **mari*), a mere, lake. See **Mere** (1).

Marshal, master of the horse. (F. — O. H. G.) Lit. 'horse-servant,' a groom ; it rose to be a title of honour. — M. F. *mareschal* (F. *maréchal*), 'a marshall, a farrier,' Cot. — O. H. G. *marascalh*, lit. horse-servant, a groom. — O. H. G. *marah*, a horse ; *scalh*, a servant ; cf. Goth. *skalks*, a servant. See **Mare.**

Marsupial. (L. — Gk.) Applied to animals that carry their young in a sort of pouch. — L. *marsūpium*, a pouch. — Gk. μαρσύπιον, a little pouch, dimin. of μάρσυπος, a bag.

Mart, a shortened form of *market.* (F. — L.) In Hamlet, i. 1. 74. Prob. influenced by Du. *markt*, market (of Latin origin). See **Market.**

Martello tower, a watch-tower. (Ital. — L. — Gk. — Pers.) [Not so called because the watchmen gave the alarm by striking a bell with a hammer ; see Ariosto, Orlando, x. 51 ; xiv. 100. From Ital. *martello*, a hammer ; Late L. *martellus.*] But named from *Mortella* bay, Corsica (Davies). — Ital. *mortella*, a myrtle. See **Myrtle.**

Marten, a kind of weasel. (F. — Low L. — Teut.) Short for *martern* (16th cent.); M. E. *martrin* (Lydg.), adj. made of marten's fur ; from O. F. *martrin*, the same. The M. E. sb. was *marter*, *martre.* — F. *martre.* — Low L. pl. *martures.* Of Teut. origin ; cf. Du. *marter*, G. *marder*, a marten ; A. S. *mearð*, Icel. *mörðr*, Swed. *mård*, Dan. *maar* (for **maard*), a marten.

Martial, brave. (F. — L.) F. *martial.* — L. *Martiālis*, dedicated to *Mars*, god of war.

Martin, a bird. (F. — L.) F. *martin*, (1) a proper name, Martin, (2) the same name applied to various birds and animals. Thus *martin-pêcheur* is a kingfisher ; *oiseau de S. Martin* is the ring-tail, and *martinet* is a martin (Cot.). A nickname, like our *robin*, *jenny-wren*, &c. ; so that the bird is named after *Martin* as a proper name. From L. *Mart-*, stem of *Mars.*

martinet, a strict disciplinarian. (F.) So called from a F. officer named *Martinet* (temp. Louis XIV); dimin. form of *Martin.*

martinmas, martlemas, the feast of St. Martin ; Nov. 11. (F. *and* L.) *Martlemass* is a corrupt form of *Martin-mass*, suggested by *Bartle* for *Bartholomew.* See **Mass** (2).

martlet (1), a kind of bird, martin. (F. — L.) Variant of M. E. *martnet*, short for *martinet.* — F. *martinet*, 'a martlet or martin,' Cot. ; dimin. of F. *Martin.* Cf. Picard *martinet*, called *martelot* in the dep. of the Meuse (Corblet).

Martingale, a strap fastened to a horse's girth to hold his head down. (F. — Span. — Arab. ?) Also applied to a short spar, in ships, under the bowsprit ; but this is only due to a supposed resemblance to a horse's martingale. — F. *martingale*, 'a martingale for a horse;' Cot. [Referred by Littré to the wearing of breeches, called *chausses à la martingale* (Rabelais) ; but this is quite another word.] — Span. *al-martaga*, 'a kinde of headstall for a horse, trimmed, gilt, and embroidered;' Minsheu (1623) ; where *al* is merely the Arab. def. article. The sb. may be derived from Arab. *rataka*, in the sense 'to cause to go with a short step' ; see Yule. I find Arab. *rataka* given by Richardson as a verbal root, whence *ratak*, going with a short quick step.

Martinmas, Martlet (1); see **Martin.**

Martlet (2), the bird called the swift, as depicted in heraldry. (F. — L.) An E. substitution for F. *merlette*, 'a martlet, in blazon,' Cot. Lit. 'a little blackbird'; dimin. of *merle*, a blackbird ; L. *merula* ; see **Merle.** We find O. F. *merlos*, martlets ; Roll of Caerlaverock, p. 7.

Martyr. (L. — Gk.) A. S. *martyr.* — L. *martyr.* — Gk. μάρτυρ, μάρτυς, a witness, lit. one who remembers, records, or declares. Cf. Skt. *smr*, to remember.

Marvel. (F. — L.) M. E. *mervaile.* — F. *merveille.* — L. *mīrābilia*, neut. pl., wonderful things. — L. *mīrābilis*, wonderful. — L. *mīrārī*, to wonder. See **Miracle.**

Mascle, in heraldry, a perforated lozenge. (F. — L.) M. E. *mascule*, *mascle.* — O. F. *mascle*, erroneous spelling of *macle*, a mesh of a net (hence, a lozenge perforated). — L. *macula*, a mesh ; perhaps confused with O. H. G. *masca*, a mesh. Doublet, *mail* (1), q. v.

Masculine. (F. — L.) F. *masculin.* —

L. *masculīnus*, extended from *masculus*, male. **–** L. *mas-*, stem of *mās*, a male ; with double dimin. suffix *-cu-lus.*

Mash, to beat into a mixed mass. (E.) A *mash* is properly a mixture ; and to *mash* was, formerly, to mix, the M. E. form of the verb being *mēshen*, as if from A. S. **māscan*, from a sb. **māsc*. (The vowel has been shortened.) We find A. S. *māx-wyrt* (for **māsc-wyrt*), mash-wort, new beer ; so that the word is English ; but it is commoner in Scandinavian, whence Lowl. Sc. *mask*. Cf. Swed. dial. *mask*, Swed. *mäsk*, brewer's grains, whence *mäska*, to mash ; Dan. and North Fries. *māsk*, grains, mash, Dan. *mæske*, to mash, fatten pigs with grains ; Norw. *meisk*, sb., *meiska*, vb. **+** G. *meisch*, a mash, *meischen*, to mash. The sb. form appears to be the original. Cf. also Lithuan. *maisz-yti*, to stir things in a pot, from *misz-ti*, to mix. The form of the Teut. base is **maisk-*, so that it may be connected by gradation with *mix*. See **Mix.**

Mask, Masque, a disguise for the face ; masked entertainment. (F.**–**Span.**–** Arab.) The sense of 'entertainment' is the true one ; the sense of 'disguise' is secondary. 'A jolly company in maner of a *maske* ;' F. Q. iii. 12. 5. 'Some haue I sene daunce in a *maske* ;' Sir T. More, Works, p. 1039. More uses *maskers* in the sense of 'visors' (correctly, according to the Spanish use).**–** F. *masque*, a mask, visor ; a clipped form, due to F, vb. *masquer*, really short for **masquerer* ; the fuller form comes out in M. F. *masquariĕ*, masked, *masquerie, masquerade*, ' a mask or mummery ;' Cot.**–** Span. *mascara*, a masker, a masquerader ; also a mask.**–** Arab. *mask-harat*, a buffoon, jester, man in masquerade, a pleasantry, anything ridiculous.**–** Arab. root *sakhira*, he ridiculed (Dozy). Der. *masquerade*, M. F. *masquerade*, F. *masca-rade*, Span. *mascarada.*

Mason. (F.**–** O. F. ?) O. F. *masson* ; F. *maçon* ; Low L. *macio*, a mason ; we also find the forms *machio, macho, maco, mactio, mattio, matio*. From Teut. stem **mat-jon-*, i. e. cutter ; from a base **mat-*, to cut or hack, whence also E. *mattock*. Cf. O.H.G. *mezzo*, a mason, whence G. *steinmetz*, a stonemason.

Masque; see **Mask.**

Mass (1), a lump. (F.**–** L.**–** Gk.) F. *masse.***–** L. *massa.***–** Gk. μᾶζα, a barley cake ; allied to μάγμα, any kneaded mass.

– Gk. μάσσειν, to knead. Der. *mass-ive*, *mass-y* ; also *a-mass.*

Mass (2), the celebration of the Eucharist. (L.) M. E. *messe*. O. Merc. *messe*, (Matt. viii. 4) ; A. S. *mæsse*, (1) the mass, (2) a church-festival. **–** Folk-L. *messa* (Ital. *messa*) ; Late L. *missa*, (1) dismissal, (2) the mass. Usually said to be from the phr. *ite, missa est* (go, the congregation is dismissed) used at the end of the service ; in any case, the derivation is from L. *missus*, pp. of *mittere*, to send away. Cf. Du. *mis*, mass. ¶ For the change of vowel from *i* to *e*, cf. Icel. *messa*, Swed. *messa*, Dan. *messe*, O. H. G. *messa* (as well as *missa*), all in the sense of 'mass' ; also O. F. *messe*, Ital. *messa*. And see **Missal.** Der. *Candle-mas, Christ-, Hallow-, Lam-, Martin-, Michael-mas*, which see.

Massacre. (F.**–** O. Low G.?) F. *massacre*, a massacre ; *massacrer*, to massacre. Of disputed origin ; it may perhaps be referred to Low G. *matsken*, to cut, hew, Du. *matsen*, to maul, kill. Cf. G. *metzelei*, a massacre ; from *metzeln*, frequent. of *metzen*, to cut, kill. And see **Mason.**

Mast (1), a pole, to hold the sails of a ship. (E.) M. E. *mast*. A. S. *mæst*, stem of a tree, bough, mast. **+** Du. *mast*, Swed. and Dan. *mast*, G. *mast*. Probably cognate with L. *mālus* (*<*mazdos*), a mast ; Brugm. i. § 587.

Mast (2), fruit of beech-trees. (E.) The orig. sense is 'edible fruit,' used for feeding swine. A. S. *mæst*, mast. **+** G. *mast*, mast ; *mästen*, to fatten. Prob. allied to Skt. *mēda(s)*, fat ; Brugm. i. § 698.

Master. (F.**–** L.) M. E. *maister*. **–** O. F. *maistre*. **–** L. *magistrum*, acc. of *magister*, a master ; see **Magistrate.** Der. *master-y*, O. F. *maistrie*.

Mastic, Mastich, a kind of gum resin. (F.**–** L.**–** Gk.) F. *mastic*, 'mastich, a sweet gum' ; Cot.**–** L. *mastichē*.**–** Gk. μαστίχη, the gum of the tree σχῖνος, called in Latin *lentiscus*. So called because used for chewing in the East. **–** Gk. μαστ-, base of μάσταξ, mouth, μαστάζειν, to chew ; cf. Gk. μασάομαι, I chew.

masticate. (L.**–** Gk.) From pp. of L. *masticāre*, to chew, quite a late word ; properly, to chew mastic. **–** L. *mastichē*, mastic (above). ¶ The true L. word for to chew is *mandere*.

Mastiff. (F.**–** L.) The A. F. form was *mastin*, as in O. F. ; hence F. *mâtin*, a

317

mastiff. The O. F. *mastin* also meant ' a domestic'; see Godefroy. Hence the Late L. *mastīnus*, a mastiff, has been conjectured to stand for **masnātīnus*, house-dog; as if from Late L. *masnāta*, a household (see **Menagerie**). The Late L. *mastīnus* seems to have been mistaken for *mastīuus* (Ducange); and confusion set in both with M. E. *masty*, fat, large (adj. formed from *mast* (2)), and with O. F. *mestif*, mongrel, Late L. **mixtivus*, from L. *miscēre* (pp. *mixt-us*), to mix. See **Mix**.

Mastodon, an extinct elephant. (Gk.) Named from the nipple-like projections on its molar teeth. — Gk. μαστ-ός, the female breast; ὀδον-, short for ὀδοντ-, stem of ὀδούς, a tooth; see **Tooth**.

Mat. (L.) M. E. *matte*. A. S. *meatte*. — L. *matta* (Late L. *natta*), a mat; whence Du. *mat*, G. *matte*, F. *natte*, &c.

Matador, the slayer of the bull in a bull-fight. (Span. — L.) Span. *matador*, lit. slayer. — Span. *matar*, to kill. — L. *mactāre*, to kill.

Match (1), an equal, a contest, marriage. (E.) M. E. *macche*, *mache*, orig. a comrade. — A. S. *-mæcca*, whence *gemæcca*, a comrade, companion, spouse; from the more original form *-maca*, Durh. Rit. 165 (whence M. E. *make*, Ch.), *gemaca*. + Icel. *maki*, Swed. *make*, Dan. *mage*, O. Sax. *gimako*, a mate, comrade. β. All closely related to the adj. seen in Icel. *makr*, suitable, M. H. G. *gemach*, suitable; and further to A. S. *macian*, to make, or ' fit together.' ¶ *Mate*, as used by sailors, is prob. Dutch; see **Mate** (1).

Match (2), a prepared rope for firing a cannon. (F. — L. — Gk.) M. E. *macche*. — O. F. *mesche*, *meiche* (F. *mèche*), wick of a candle, match to fire a gun, ' match of a lamp;' Cot. — Late L. *myxa* (= Gk. μύξα); Late L. *myxus*, the nozzle of a lamp, through which the wick protrudes; also, a wick. — Gk. μύξα, the nozzle of a lamp; older senses being (1) mucus (2) nostril. Allied to **Mucus**. Der. *matchlock*, the lock of a gun holding a match; hence, the gun itself.

Mate (1), a companion. (O. Low G.) M. E. *mate*, a fellow (Prompt. Parv.); Low G. *mate*, mate (Lübben); *maat* (Bremen); M. Du. *maet*, ' a mate,' Hexham; Du. *maat*. + O. H. G. *gi-mazzo*, a meat-companion, mess-mate. Cf. Goth. *matjan*, to eat, *mats*, food. See **Meat**.

Mate (2), to check-mate, confound. (F.

— Pers. & Arab.) From the game of chess. *Check-mate* means ' the king is dead '; cf. M. F. *eschec et mat*, ' check-mate '; Cot. [Here *et* is not wanted.] Godefroy has ' *mat* du roi,' i. e. death of the king. — Pers. *shāh māt*, the king is dead, check-mate. — Pers. *shāh*, king (see **Check**); *māt*, he is dead, from Arab. root *māta*, he died. Cf. Heb. *mūth*, to die. ¶ Hence Turk. and Pers. *māt*, astonished, confounded, amazed, receiving check-mate; F. *mat*, ' mated, quelled, subdued,' Cot.; M. E. *mate*, confounded.

Material, substantial. (F. — L.) O. F. *materiel*. — L. *māteriālis*, adj., formed from *māteria*, matter. See **Matter**.

Maternal. (F. — L.) F. *maternel*. — Late L. *māternālis*. — L. *māternus*, belonging to a mother. — L. *māter*, mother; cognate with **Mother**.

Mathematic, pertaining to the science of number. (F. — L. — Gk.) O. F. *mathematique*. — L. *mathēmaticus*. — Gk. μαθηματικός, disposed to learn, belonging to the sciences, esp. to mathematics. — Gk. μαθηματ-, stem of μάθημα, a lesson. — Gk. μαθή-σομαι, future of μανθάνειν, to learn.

Matins, Mattins, morning prayers. (F. — L.) F. *matins*, a pl. sb. from F. *matin*, morning, orig. an adj. — L. *mātūtīnum*, acc. of *mātūtīnus*, adj., belonging to the morning. Cf. Ital. *mattino*, morning. — L. *Mātūta*, the goddess of dawn, as if from a masc. **mātūtus*, with the sense of ' early,' or ' timely.'

Matrass, a long-necked glass bottle; in chemistry. (F.) F. *matras*; also (in Cot.) *matrac*, *matraz*, *matelas*; Span. *matraz*. Perhaps Arabic; see Devic.

Matricide, murderer of a mother. (F. — L.) F. *matricide*, adj., ' mother-killing'; Cot. — L. *mātrīcīda*, a matricide. — L. *mātri-*, decl. stem of *māter*, mother; *cædere*, to slay; see **Mother**, **Cæsura**. ¶ We also use *matricide* to represent L. *mātrīcīdium*, the slaying of a mother.

matriculate, to enrol in a college. (L.) From pp. of Late L. *mātrīculāre*, to enrol; a coined word. — L. *mātrīcula*, a register; dimin. of *mātrix* (stem *mātrīc-*), meaning (1) a breeding animal, (2) womb, matrix, (3) a public register, roll, list, lit. parent-stock. See **matrix** (below).

matrimony. (F. — L.) O. F. *matrimonie*. — L. *mātrīmōnium*, marriage, lit. motherhood. — L. *mātri-*, decl. stem of *māter*, mother; with suffix *-mōn-io-*.

matrix, the womb, cavity or mould. (L.) L. *mātrix*, a breeding animal, the womb.—L. *mātri-*, for *māter*, mother.

matron, a married woman. (F.—L.) F. *matrone.*—L. *mātrōna*; extended from *mātr-*, stem of *mater*, a mother.

Matter (1), substance. (F.—L.) M. E. *matere, materie.*—O. F. *matere, matiere* (F. *matière*).—L. *māteria*, stuff, materials, useful for building, &c. Brugm. i. § 407.

matter (2), pus, a fluid in abscesses. (F.—L.) The same word as **matter** (1); see Littré, s. v. *matière*, § 8.

Mattins; see Matins.

Mattock. (E.) A.S. *mattuc.* Cf. W. *matog*, a mattock, hoe; Gael. *madag*, a pickaxe; Russ. *motuika*, Lithuan. *matikkas*, mattock (from Teutonic); see **Mason.**

Mattress. (F.—Arab.) O.F. *materas*; Picard and Walloon *matras*; F. *matelas.* Cf. Span. *al-madraque*, a mattress; where *al* is the Arab. def. art.— Arab. *matrah*, a situation, place, a place where anything is thrown; this word came to mean also anything hastily thrown down, hence, something to lie upon, a bed (Devic). —Arab. root *taraha*, he threw prostrate.

Mature, ripe. (L.) L. *mātūrus*, ripe.

Matutinal, pertaining to the morning. (L.) L. *mātūtinus*, adj., belonging to the morning. See Matins.

Maudlin, sickly sentimental. (F.— L.—Gk.—Heb.) Orig. 'shedding tears of penitence,' like Mary Magdalen. From M.E. *Maudelein*, the same as *Magdelaine.*—O.F. *Maudeleine, Magdeleine.*—L. *Magdalēnē.*— Gk. Μαγδαληνή, i.e. belonging to Magdala; Luke viii. 2.—Heb. *migdol*, a tower; whence *Magdala* as a proper name.

Maugre, in spite of. (F.—L.) The proper sense is 'ill will,' as in P. Plowman, B. vi. 242.—O. F. *malgre, maugre*, lit. ill will; but also with sense 'in spite of.'— O. F. *mal*, ill; *gre, gret*, a pleasant thing. —L. *malus*, bad; *grātum*, neut. of *grātus*, pleasing.

Maul, to beat grievously. (F.—L.) M. E. *mallen*, to strike with a mall, or mace; from M. E. *malle*, sb., a mall, mace; see **Mall** (1).

Maulstick, a stick used by painters to steady the hand. (Du.) Du. *maalstok*, lit. 'painting stick.'—Du. *malen*, to paint; and *stok*, a stick. The cognate G. *malen* signified orig. to mark, from G. *mahl*, O. H. G. *māl*, a mark, point of time; see **Meal** (2) and **Stock.**

Maund (1), a basket. (F.—Low G.) [A.S. *mand.*] Later, Picard and O.F. *mande.* —Du. *mand*; prov. G. *mand, mande, manne* (whence F. *manne*); E. Fries. *mande.*

Maund (2), a (very variable) weight. (Arab.) Arab. *mann*; Pers. *man.* Cf. Heb. *māneh*, Gk. μνᾶ. See Yule.

Maundy Thursday, the day before Good Friday. (F.—L.; *and* E.) *Maundy* is M. E. *maundee*, a command, used with esp. reference to the text '*Mandatum nouum*,' John xiii. 34. The 'new commandment' is 'that ye love one another'; but in old times it was applied to the particular form of devotion to others exemplified by Christ, when washing His disciples' feet (on the first *Maundy Thursday*). See my note to P. Plowman, B. xvi. 140. This M. E. *maundee*=O. F. *mandé*, that which is commanded; from L. *mandātum*, a mandate, command. ¶ Not connected with *maund*. Cf. O. H. G. *mandāt*, the washing of feet (Otfrid); from L. *mandātum*.

Mausoleum, a magnificent tomb. (L. —Gk.) L. *mausōlēum*, a splendid tomb, orig. the tomb of Mausōlus.—Gk. Μαυσω-λεῖον; from Μαύσωλος, Mausōlus, a king of Caria.

Mauve, mallow colour. (F.—L.) F. *mauve*, a mallow.—L. *malua*, mallow. See **Mallow.**

Mavis, the song-thrush. (F.—C.?) M. E. *mavis.*—F. *mauvis*, a throstle; cf. Span. *malvis*, a thrush. Perhaps Celtic; cf. Bret. *milfid, milvid*, a mavis, also *mil-chouid* (at Vannes); Corn. *melhues*, O. Corn. *melhuet*, a lark.

Mavourneen, my darling. (Irish.) From Irish *mo*, my; and *mhuirnin*, mutated form of *muirnin*, darling, from *muirn*, affection. (*Mh* = *v*.)

Maw, stomach. (E.) M.E. *mawe.* A.S. *maga.*+Du. *maag*, Icel. *magi*, Swed. *mage*, Dan. *mave*, G. *magen.*

Mawkish, squeamish. (Scand.; *with* E. *suffix.*) The older sense is loathsome, lit. 'maggoty.' Formed, with E. suffix -*ish*, from M. E. *mawk, mauk*, a maggot, a contracted form of M. E. *maðek*, a maggot. —Icel. *maðkr*, Dan. *maddik*, a maggot (whence Norw. *makk*=E. *mawk*). Derived from the form which appears as A. S. *maða*, Du. G. *made*, maggot. See **Moth.**

Maxillar, Maxillary, belonging to the jawbone. (L.) L. *maxillāris*, adj.; from *maxilla*, jaw-bone.

Maxim, a proverb. (F. — L.) F. *maxime.* — L. *maxima*, for *maxima sententiārum*, an opinion of the greatest importance, chief of opinions, hence a maxim (Duc.). Orig. fem. of *maximus*, greatest, superlative of *magnus*, great.

maximum. (L.) Neut. of *maximus*, greatest (above).

May (1), I am able, I am free to do. (E.) Pres. t. *may*, pt. t. *might* ; the infin. (not in use) should take the form *mow*. M. E. *mowen*, infin. ; pres. t. *may* ; pt. t. *mighte*. A. S. *mugan*, to be able ; pres. t. *mæg* ; pt. t. *mihte*. (Here *mæg* is the old perfect of a strong verb.)+O. Sax. *mugan*, pres. *mag*, pt. *mahta* ; Icel. *mega*, pres. *mā*, pt. *mátti* ; Du. *mogen*, pres. *mag*, pt. *mogt* ; Dan. pres. *maa*, pt. *maatte* ; Swed. pres. *mā̇*, pt. *mȧtte* ; G. *mögen*, pres. *mag*, pt. *mochte*; Goth. *magan*, pres. *mag*, pt. *mahta* ; Russ. *moche*, to be able, pres. *mogu* ; cf. Gk. μηχανή, means.

May (2), the fifth month. (F. — L.) O. F. *Mai.* — L. *Māius*, May.

Mayor. (F. — L.) M. E. *maire.* — F. *maire.* — L. *māior*, nom. greater ; see **Major** (above). ¶ *Mayor* is a late spelling, introduced in the middle of the 16th century ; it answers to O. F. *maior*, from L. *māiōrem*, acc. ; cf. Span. *mayor*.

Mayweed, Anthemis cotula. (E.) Formerly *mathe-weed* ; from A. S. *mægþa*.

Maze. (E.) M. E. *mase* ; we also find M. E. *masen*, to confuse. The A. S. **masian* appears in the comp. pp. *ā-masod*. Cf. Norweg. *masa-st* (where -*st* is reflexive), to lose one's senses and begin to dream, *masa*, to pore over a thing, also to prate, chatter ; Icel. *masa*, to prate, chatter; Swed. dial. *masa*, to bask in the sun, to be lazy, lounge about. Cf. E. *in a maze* = in a dreamy perplexity. The orig. sense seems to have been ' to be lost in thought,' dream or pore over a thing, whence the idea of ' perplexity ' for the sb.

Mazer, a large drinking-bowl. (F. — O. H. G.) M. E. *maser.* — A. F. *mazer* (Bozon) ; O. F. *masere*, a bowl of maple-wood, also of metal. — O. H. G. *masar*, mark in wood, also maple.+Icel. *mösurr*, a maple-tree, spotted wood ; whence *mösur-bolli*, a mazer-bowl, so called because made of maple-wood ; the maple-wood was called *mösurr* or ' spot-wood ' from its being covered with spots. But the word for spot is only preserved in

other languages, as in M. H. G. *mase*, a spot, and in E. **Measles**, q. v.

Mazurka, a dance. (Pol.) From Pol. *Mazurka*, lit. a woman of Massovia or Mazovia, a province of Poland containing Warsaw. Similarly, *polka* means 'a Polish woman' ; and secondly, a dance.

Mazzard, the head. (F. — O. H. G.) From *mazer*, a bowl ; see **Mazer.**

Me. (E.) A. S. *mē* (also *mec*, in the accusative only).+Du. *mij* ; Icel. *mēr*, dat., *mik*, acc.; Swed. Dan. *mig* ; Goth. *mis*, dat., *mik*, acc. ; G. *mir*, dat., *mich*, acc. For the stem, cf. Corn. and Bret. *me* ; Irish, Gael. W. *mi* ; L. *mihi*, dat., *mē*, acc.; Gk. μοί, ἐμοί, dat., μέ, ἐμέ, acc.; Skt. *mah-yam*, *me*, dat., *mām*, *mā*, acc.

Mead (1), a drink made from honey. (E.) M. E. *mede*. A. S. *medu*, *meodu*.+Du. *mede*, Icel. *mjǫðr*, Dan. *miöd*, Swed. *mjöd*, G. *meth* ; also Irish *mid*, W. *medd*, Lith. *middus*, Russ. *med'*, Gk. μέθυ ; Skt. *madhu*, sweet, also as sb., honey, sugar. Idg. type **medhu*, Brugm. ii. § 104. Cf. Lith. *medùs*, honey.

Mead (2), a meadow. (E.) So called because ' mown.' M. E. *mede*. A. S. *mǣd*, a mead. [Allied to prov. E. *math*, a mowing, as in *aftermath*, and A. S. *māwan*, to mow; G. *mahd*, a mowing, M. H. G. *māt*, a mowing, a mead.] Cf. M. H. G. *mate*, a meadow, Swiss *matt*, a meadow (as in *Zermatt*, *Andermatt*). Also Gk. ἄ-μητος, a harvest, ἀμάειν, to mow. See **Mow** (1).

meadow. (E.) This fuller form is due to the inflected form (dat. *mǣdwe*) of A. S. *mǣd*, a mead.

Meagre, thin. (F. — L.) M. E. *megre.* — F. *maigre.* — L. *macrum*, acc. of *macer*, thin, lean ; whence A. S. *mæger*, Icel. *magr*, Dan. Swed. G. *mager*, thin, were perhaps borrowed at an early period (unless cognate). Cf. Gk. μακρός, long.

Meal (1), ground grain. (E.) M. E. *mele*. A. S. *melu*, *meolo*.+Du. *meel*, Icel. *mjöl*, Dan. *meel*, Swed. *mjöl*, G. *mehl*. Teut. type **melwom*, neut. All from Idg. root MEL, to grind, as in O. Irish *mel-im*, Ch. Slav. *mel-jǫ*, I grind ; the 2nd grade is Teut. **mal*, to grind, as in Icel. *mala*, Goth. *malan*, O. H. G. *malan*, to grind, cognate with Lith. *malti*, L. *molere*.

Meal (2), a repast. (E.) M. E. *mele*. A. S. *mǣl*, (1) a time, portion of time, stated time ; (hence a common meal at a stated time, not a hastily snatched repast). +Du. *maal*, (1) time, (2) meal ; Icel. *māl*,

measure, time, meal; Dan. *maal*, Swed.
mål, measure, meal; Goth. *mēl*, a time;
G. *mahl*, a meal, *māl*, time. From Idg.
√ME(MĒ); cf. **Mete** and **Moon**. See
Prellwitz, s.v. μέδομαι.

Mean (1), to have in the mind, intend.
(E.) M. E. *menen*. A. S. *mǣnan*, to intend. + Du. *meenen*, Dan. *mene*, Swed.
mena, G. *meinen*. Cf. the sb. seen in
O. H. G. *meina*, thought, allied to *minni*,
memory. See **Mind**.

Mean (2), common. (E.) M. E. *mene*.
A. S. *mǣne*, usually *ge-mǣne*, common;
O. Fries. *mēne*, common. See **Common**.
¶ The peculiar sense of base, vile, may
be due to confusion with **Mean** (3), which
sometimes meant 'middling.' It does not
appear that it was confused with A. S.
mǣne, wicked, or with the Icel. *meinn*,
hurtful.

Mean (3), intermediate. (F. — L.) A. F.
meien (F. *moyen*). — L. *mediānus*, extended
form from *medius*, middle; see **Mid**.
Der. *mean*, sb., common in pl. *means*.

Mean (4), to lament. (E.) In M. N. D.
v. 1. 330 (ed. 1623). A. S. *mǣnan*, to
bemoan; see **Moan**. So also, probably,
in Merch. Ven. iii. 5. 82.

Meander, a winding course. (L. — Gk.)
L. *Mæander*. — Gk. Μαίανδρος, a winding
stream; Pliny, v. 29.

Measles, a contagious fever accompanied by small red spots on the skin.
(E.) 'Rougeolle, the *meazles*;' Cot.
M. E. *maseles* (14th cent.). From A. S.
mæsle-, a spot (Toller). Cf. Du. *mazelen*,
measles; also called *masel-sucht*, 'measell-
sicknesse,' Hexham. The lit. sense is
'small spots'; cf. M. Du. *maesche*, *masche*,
maschel, 'a spot, blot,' Hexham. The
orig. word occurs in M. H. G. *mase*,
O. H. G. *māsa*, a spot. See **Mazer**.
¶ Wholly unconnected with M. E. *mesel*,
a leper, which merely meant orig. 'a
wretch,' from O. F. *mesel*, L. *misellus*,
from L. *miser*, wretched.

Measure. (F. — L.) M. E. *mesure*. —
O. F. *mesure*. — L. *mensūra*, measure. — L.
mensus, pp. of *mētīrī*, to measure. See
Brugm. ii. § 771.

Meat. (E.) M. E. *mete*. A. S. *mete*
(for **matiz*). + Icel. *matr*, Dan. *mad*, Swed.
mat, Goth. *mats*, O. H. G. *maz*, food. Cf.
Mate (1).

Mechanic, pertaining to machines.
(F. — L. — Gk.) M. E. *mechanike*, in the
sense 'mechanic art.' — O. F. *mechanique*,

mechanical. — L. *mēchanica*. — Gk. μηχαν-
ική, science of machines. — Gk. μηχανή, a
device, machine. See **Machine**.

Medal. (F. — Ital. — L. — Gk.) O. F.
medaille. — Ital. *medaglia* (Low L. *medālia*,
medalla, a small coin). — Late L. **metāllea*,
adj. fem. — L. *metallum*, metal. See
Metal.

Meddle. (F. — L.) M. E. *medlen*,
simply in the sense 'to mix.' — A. F.
medler; O. F. *me.ler*, *mesler*, to mix
(F. *mêler*). — Late L. *misculāre*, to mix;
cf. L. *miscellus*, mixed. — L. *miscēre*, to
mix. See **Miscellaneous**.

Mediate, adj., acting by or as a means.
(L.) From L. *mediātus*, pp. of *mediāre*,
to be in the middle (Palladius). — L.
medius, middle. See **Medium**. Der.
mediat-ion, *mediat-or*.

Medic, a kind of clover. (L. — Gk.)
L. *mēdica*. — Gk. Μηδική, Median grass;
fem. of Μηδικός, belonging to *Media*.

Medicine, a remedy. (F. — L.) O. F.
medecine. — L. *medicīna*. — L. *medicus*, a
physician. — L. *medērī*, to heal. Cf.
Zend *madh*, to treat medically. Der.
medical, Late L. *medicālis*, from *medicus*
(above); *medicate*.

Medieval, relating to the Middle Ages.
(L.) Also written *mediæval*. Coined
from L. *medi-us*, middle; *æu-um*, age;
see **Medium** and **Age**.

Mediocre, middling. (F. — L.) F.
médiocre. — L. *mediocrem*, acc. of *mediocris*,
middling; formed from *medi-us*, middle.
See **Medium**.

Meditate. (L.) From pp. of L.
meditārī, to ponder. Cf. Gk. μέδομαι,
I attend to. Brugm. i. § 591.

Mediterranean, inland, said of a
sea. (L.) L. *mediterrāne-us*, situate in
the middle of the land. — L. *medi-us*,
middle; *terra*, land; see **Medium** and
Terrace.

Medium. (L.) L. *medium*, the midst,
also a means; neut. of *medius*, middle.
Allied to **Mid**.

Medlar. (F. — L. — Gk.) The name
of a tree, bearing fruit formerly called
medles. M. E. *medler*, the tree, also
called *medle-tree* (A. F. *medle* = O. F.
mesle). — O. F. *mesle*, a medlar (whence
meslier, the tree); Gascon *mesplo*. —
L. *mespilum*. — Gk. μέσπιλον, a medlar
(whence also F. *nèfle*).

Medley, confusion, mixture. (F. — L.)
M. E. *medlee*. — A. F. *medlee*; O. F. *medle*,

melle, mesle (fem. *medlee, mellee, meslee*),
pp. of the verb *medler*, to mix, confuse.
See **Meddle**. The fem. form *medlee* = F.
mêlée.

Medullar, belonging to the marrow.
(L.) L. *medullāris,* adj. − L. *medulla,*
marrow.

Meed. (E.) M. E. *mede, meed.* − A. S.
mēd, beside *meord* (with *r* for older *z*).
✛ G. *miethe,* hire; Goth. *mizdō*; Russ.
mzda, Gk. μισθός, pay, Pers. *muzd,* wages.
Idg. types **meizdhā, *mizdhā, *misdhos.*
Brugm. i. § 226.

Meek. (Scand.) M. E. *meke, meek*;
spelt *meoc,* Ormulum, 667. − Icel. *mjūkr,*
soft, agile, meek, mild ; N. Fries. *mjöck,*
Swed. *mjuk,* Dan. *myg,* soft. Cf. Du.
muik; Goth. **mūks,* in comp. *mūka-*
mōdei, gentleness. Teut. types **meukoz,*
*mūkoz.

Meerschaum, a substance used for
making pipes. (G.) G. *meerschaum,* lit.
sea-foam (because it is white and light).
− G. *meer,* lake, sea ; *schaum,* foam, lit.
scum ; see **Mere** (1) and **Scum.**

Meet (1), fit. M. E. *mete.* A. S. *mæte,*
small, orig. measured. − A. S. *mǣt-,* 3rd
grade of *metan,* to mete. Cf. G. *mässig,*
frugal, from *messen,* to mete. See **Mete.**

Meet (2), to encounter, find, assemble.
(E.) M. E. *meten.* O. Merc. *mōetan*; A. S.
mētan, to find, meet (for **mōtian*). Formed
by mutation from A. S. *mōt,* a meeting,
assembly. ✛ Icel. *mæta, mæta,* from *mōt*;
Goth. *gamōt-jan,* Swed. *möta,* Dan. *möde,*
to meet. See **Moot.**

Megatherium, a fossil quadruped,
(Gk.) Lit. 'great wild beast.' − Gk. μέγα-s.
great ; θηρίον, dimin. of θήρ, a wild beast.

megalosaurus. (Gk.) Lit. 'great
lizard.' − Gk. μεγάλο-, decl. stem allied to
μέγα-s, great ; σαῦρος, a lizard.

Megrim, a pain affecting one side of
the head. (F. − L. − Gk.) F. *migraine,*
'the megrim ;' Cot. − Late L. *hēmigrānea,*
megrim. − Gk. ἡμικράνιον, half of the
skull. − Gk. ἡμι-, half ; κρανίον, cranium.

Melancholy, sadness. (F. − L. − Gk.)
Supposed to be due to an excess of 'black
bile.' M. E. *melancolie.* − O. F. *melan-*
colie. − L. *melancholia.* − Gk. μελαγχολία,
melancholy. − Gk. μελάγχολος, jaundiced.
− Gk. μέλαν-, stem of μέλας, black ; χολή,
bile, gall, cognate with E. *gall.*

Melilot, a plant. (F. − L. − Gk.) M.F.
melilot (Cot.). − L. *melilōtos.* − Gk. μελί-
λωτος, μελίλωτον, a kind of clover, named

from the honey in it. − Gk. μέλι, honey ;
λωτός, lotus, clover.

Meliorate, to make better. (L.)
From pp. of Late L. *meliōrāre,* to make
better. − L. *melior,* better. ✛ Gk. μᾶλλον,
rather, comp. of μάλα, adv., very much.

Mellifluous, sweet. (L.) Lit. ' flowing sweetly,' ' flowing like honey.' − L.
melli-, decl. stem of *mel,* honey; *-fluus,*
flowing, from *fluere,* to flow ; see **Fluent.**
Cf. Gk. μέλι, Goth. *milith,* Irish *mil,*
W. *mêl,* honey.

Mellow, fully ripe. (E.) M. E. *melwe,*
orig. soft, pulpy. Pegge notes that, in
Derbyshire, a *mellow* apple or pear is
called a *mealy* one; and *mellow* may be
an adjectival use of *meal.* The M. E.
melwe may represent A. S. *melw-,* as in
melwe, dat. of *melu,* meal. Cf. Du.
malsch, Low G. *mals,* soft, mellow; from
Teut. **malan-,* to grind ; see **Meal** (1).
Note also Du. *molmen,* to moulder, *mul,*
soft; Goth. *gamalwiths,* crushed; Du.
mollig, soft. See Franck, s. v. *mollig.*
¶ Perhaps confused with O. Merc. *merwe,*
tender (Mat. xxiv. 32) ; A. S. *mearu,* G.
mürbe, mellow.

Melocoton, a quince, a peach grafted
on a quince. (Span. − L. − Gk.) In Nares.
Span. *melocoton* (Pineda). − Late L. *mēlum*
cotōneum (Ducange). − Gk. μῆλον Κυδώνιον, a quince. See **Quince.**

Melodrama. (F. − Gk.) Formerly
melodrame. − F. *mélodrame,* acting, with
songs. − Gk. μέλο-s, a song ; δρᾶμα, an
action, drama ; see **Drama.**

melody. (F. − L. − Gk.) M.F. *melodie.*
− L. *melōdia.* − Gk. μελῳδία, a singing. −
Gk. μελῳδός, adj., musical. − Gk. μέλ-ος, a
song ; ᾠδή, a song, ode ; see **Ode.**

Melon, a fruit. (F. − L. − Gk.) O.F.
melon. − L. *mēlōnem,* acc. of *mēlō,* an
apple-shaped melon. − Gk. μῆλον, an
apple, also applied to other fruits. Cf. L.
mālum, apple, prob. borrowed from Gk.

Melt. (E.) M. E. *melten,* pt. t. *malt,*
pp. *molten.* A. S. *meltan,* pt. t. *mealt.* ✛
Gk. μέλδειν, to melt. Allied to Skt.
mṛdu, O. Slavonic *mladu,* soft ; Brugm.
i. § 580, ii. § 690. (✓MEL.) See **Mild.**

Member. (F. − L.) F. *membre.* − L.
membrum, a member. Brugm. i. § 875.

membrane. (F. − L.) F. *membrane.*
− L. *membrāna,* a skin covering a member
of the body, a membrane. − L. *membrum.*

Memento, a memorial. (L.) L. *me-*
mentō (Luke xxiii. 42), remember me;

imperative of *meminī*, I remember; Brugm. ii. § 846. (√MEN.)

Memory. (F. – L.) M. E. *memorie.* – A.F. *memorie*; F. *mémoire.* – L. *memoria*, memory. – L. *memor*, mindful, remembering. This L. *memor* appears to be a reduplicated form; cf. Gk. μέρ-μερ-os, anxious, μέρ-ιμνα, care, thought. Allied to Skt. *smṛ*, to remember. (√SMER.)

memoir, a record. (F. – L.) Commoner in the pl. *memoirs.* – O. F. *memoires*, notes for remembrance, records; pl. of *memoire*, memory (above).

Menace. (F. – L.) O. F. *menace.* – L. pl. *mināciæ*, threats. – L. *mināc-*, stem of *minax*, full of threatenings, also, projecting forward. – L. *minæ*, things projecting forward, hanging over and ready to fall, hence threats. – L. *-minēre*, as in *ē-minēre*, to project, jut out.

Menagerie, a place for keeping wild animals. (F. – L.) F. *ménagerie*, orig. a place for keeping *household* animals (Brachet). – F. *ménager*, to keep house. – F. *ménage*, O. F. *mesnage*, a household. – O. F. *mesnee, meisnee, maisnee*, a family; the same word as Late L. *mansnada, maisnada, masnata*, Ital. *masnada*, a family (answering to a Lat. type **mansionāta*). – L. *mansiōn-*, stem of *mansio*, an abiding, abode; see **Mansion**.

Mend. (F. – L.) M. E. *menden*, short for M. E. *amenden*, to amend, by loss of *a*; see **Amend**.

Mendacity. (L.) From L. *mendācitās*, falsehood. – L. *mendāc-*, stem of *mendax*, false.

Mendicant, a beggar. (L.) L. *mendīcant-*, stem of pres. pt. of *mendīcāre*, to beg. – L. *mendīcus*, beggarly, poor.

Menial, one of a household, servile. (F. – L.) Properly an adj.; M. E. *meyneal*, as ' her *meyneal* chirche ' = the church of their household, Wyclif, Rom. xvi. 5. – O. F. *mesnee, meisnee*, a household; whence M. E. *meinee, mainee*, a household, troop, retinue, once a common word; with suffix *-al*. See **Menagerie**.

Meniver, Miniver, a kind of fur. (F. – L.) M. E. *meniuer* (*meniver*). – O. F. *menu ver, menu vair*, miniver; lit. ' little vair.' – O. F. *menu*, small, from L. *minūtus*, small; *vair*, a fur, from L. *uarius*, variegated. See **Minute** and **Vair**.

Menses. (L.) L. *mensēs*, monthly discharges; pl. of *mensis*, a month. Allied to **Month**.

menstruous. (L.) From L. *menstru-us*, monthly. – L. *mensis*, a month.

menstruum. (L.) Late L. *menstruum*, a solvent; a word in alchemy; from the notion of some solvent agency of menstrual blood.

Mensuration, measuring. (L.) From L. *mensūrātio*, a measuring. – L. *mensūrātus*, pp. of *mensūrāre*, to measure. – L. *mensūra*, measure; see **Measure**.

Mental. (F. – L.) F. *mental.* – Late L. *mentālis*, mental. – L. *ment-*, stem of *mens*, mind. Brugm. i. § 431 (2).

mention, a notice. (F. – L.) F. *mention.* – L. acc. *mentiōnem.* – L. *menti-*, decl. stem of *mens*, mind (above).

Mentor, an adviser. (Gk.) Gk. Μέντωρ, Mentor (Homer, Od. ii); explained as ' adviser '; cf. L. *monitor* (Vaniček). See **Monition**.

Mephitis, a pestilential exhalation. (L.) L. *mephītis* (Vergil).

Mercantile, commercial. (F. – L.) M. F. *mercantil*, ' merchantly;' Cot. – Late L. *mercantilis.* – L. *mercant-*, stem of pres. pt. of *mercārī*, to trade. – L. *merc-*, stem of *merx*, merchandise. Cf. Gk. μάρπτειν, to seize (Prellwitz).

mercenary. (F. – L.) F. *mercenaire.* – L. *mercēnārius*, older form *mercennārius*, a hireling. For **merced-nārius*; from *mercēd-*, stem of *mercēs*, pay. – L. *merc-*, stem of *merx*, merchandise.

mercer. (F. – L.) F. *mercier*, lit. ' a trader.' – Late L. *mercērius*, a trader. – L. *merc-*, stem of *merx*, merchandise.

merchandise. (F. – L.) M. E. *marchandise.* – F. *marchandise*, merchant's wares. – F. *marchand*, a merchant (below).

merchant. (F. – L.) M. E. *marchant.* – M. F. *marchant* (F. *marchand*). – L. *mercant-*, stem of pres. pt. of *mercārī*, to trade; see **Mercantile**.

mercury, quicksilver. (F. – L.) M. E. *mercurie*, quicksilver, named after the planet Mercury. – A. F. *Mercurie*; F. *mercure.* – L. *Mercurium*, acc. of *Mercurius*, Mercury, god of traffic. – L. *merc-*, stem of *merx*, merchandise.

mercy. (F. – L.) F. *merci*; O. F. *mercit.* – L. *mercēdem*, acc. of *mercēs*; see **mercenary**.

Mere (1), a lake. (E.) M. E. *mere*. A. S. *mere*, sea, lake, m.; orig. type **mari*, n. + Du. *meer*; Icel. *marr*, sea; G. *meer*, sea; Goth. *marei*, Russ. *more*, Lithuan.

māres, pl., W. *môr*, Gael. Irish *muir*, L. *mare*, sea.

Mere (2), pure, simple. (L.) L. *merus*, pure, unmixed (as wine).

Merelles, a game. (F.) From F. *mérelle*, a counter; Low L. *merellus*. Of unknown origin.

Meretricious, alluring by false show. (L.) L. *meretrīci-us*, pertaining to a courtesan; with suffix *-ous*. ‒ L. *meretrīc-*, stem of *meretrix*, a courtesan. ‒ L. *merēre*, to gain, receive hire.

Merge, to sink, plunge under water. (L.) L. *mergere*, to dip. + Skt. *majj*, to dip, bathe. Brugm. i. § 816.

Meridian, pertaining to mid-day. (F. ‒ L.) O. F. *meridien*. ‒ L. *merīdiānus*. ‒ L. *merīdiēs*, mid-day; formed from the old locative *merī-diē*, as if meaning 'in the clear day,' from L. *merus*, clear, *diēs*, day; but really for *medī-diē*, from *medius*, mid. Brugm. i. 587 (7).

Merino, a variety of sheep. (Span. ‒ L.) Span. *merino*, roving from pasture to pasture. ‒ Span. *merino*, an inspector of sheep-walks. ‒ Late L. *mājorīnus*, a majordomo, steward of a household; cf. Late L. *mājorālis*, a head-shepherd. From L. *māior*, greater; see **Major**.

Merit, excellence, worth. (F. ‒ L.) M. E. *merite*. ‒ O. F. *merite*. ‒ L. *meritum*, a thing deserved; orig. neut. of *meritus*, pp. of *merēre*, to deserve; orig. 'to receive as a share,' if it is allied to Gk. μέρος, a share, μείρομαι, I receive a share.

Merle, a blackbird. (F. ‒ L.) O. F. *merle*. ‒ L. *merula*, a blackbird. Cf. W. *mwyalch*, a blackbird. See **Titmouse**.

merlin, a kind of hawk. (F. ‒ L. ?) M. E. *merlion*. ‒ M. F. *esmerillon, emerillon,* 'the hawk termed a marlin;' Cot. Cf. Ital. *smerlo*, a kind of hawk. Prob. from L. *merula*, a blackbird; the initial *s* being unoriginal (Diez).

Mermaid. (E.) M. E. *mermaid*. ‒ A. S. *mere*, sea, lake; *mægden*, maiden.

Merry. (E.) M. E. *merie, mirie*. A. S. *myrge, myrige* (*mirige*), merry. Cf. O. H. G. *murg-fări*, fragile, transitory; Gk. βραχύς, short; so that A. S. *myrg-e* (for *murgjoz*) means 'lasting a short time,' and so 'making the time short.' Cf. Goth. *gamaurgjan*, to shorten. Brugm. ii. § 104. Der. *mirth*.

Mesentery. (L. ‒ Gk.) L. *mesenterium*. ‒ Gk. μεσεντέριον, a membrane in the midst of the intestines. ‒ Gk. μέσ-ος,

middle, cognate with L. *medius*; ἔντερον, entrail. See **Mid** and **Entrail**.

Mesh, the opening between the threads of a net. (E.) M. E. *maske*. A. S. *max* (=*masc*, by the common interchange of *sc* and *cs* = *x*); cf. A. S. *mæscre*, a mesh, dimin. form. + Du. *maas*, Icel. *möskvi*, Dan. *maske*, Swed. *maska*, G. *masche*, W. *masg*. Orig. sense 'a knot,' from the knots in a net; cf. Lithuan. *mazgas*, a knot, *magstas*, a knitting-needle, allied to *megsti*, verb (pres. t. *mezg-u*), to knot, weave nets. From an Idg. root *mezg*, to weave. Brugm. i. § 816 (2).

Mesmerise, to operate on the nervous system of a patient. (G.) Named from *Mesmer*, a German physician (about 1766).

Mess (1), a dish of meat, portion of food. (F. ‒ L.) M. E. *messe*. ‒ O. F. *mes*, a dish, course at table (now spelt *mets*, badly). Cf. Ital. *messo*, a course at table. ‒ O. F. *mes*, that which is sent, pp. of *mettre*, to send. ‒ L. *missum*, acc. (or neut.) of *missus*, pp. of *mittere*, to send; in late Lat., to place. See **Missile**.

Mess (2), a mixture, disorder. (F. ‒ L.) The same word as above; food badly cooked. Perhaps confused with *mash*, sb. '*Mescolare*, to mixe, to *mash*, to *mesh*;' Florio. '*Mescolanza*, a medlie, a mesh, a mixture;' id.

Message. (F. ‒ L.) F. *message*. ‒ Late L. *missāticum*, a message. ‒ L. *missus*, pp. of *mittere*, to send. Der. *messenger*, with inserted *n*, for M. E. *messager*, formed from *message* with suffix *-er*.

Messiah, the anointed one. (Heb.) Heb. *māshīakh*, anointed. ‒ Heb. *māshakh*, to anoint.

Messuage, a dwelling-house with offices. (F. ‒ L.) M. E. *mesuage*. ‒ A. F. *mesuage*, a manor-house; Low L. *messuāgium, mansuāgium*. ‒ Late L. *mansionāticum*, a mansion; prob. shortened by confusion with *mansāticum*, acc. of *mansāticus*, a mansion. ‒ L. *mansiōnem*, acc. of *mansio*, a mansion; confused with Late L. *mansa*, with a like sense and origin. See **Mansion** and **Manse**.

Meta-, prefix. (Gk.) Gk. μέτα, prep., among, with, after; as a prefix, it commonly signifies 'change.' + Goth. *mith*, A. S. *mid*, G. *mit*, with; Icel. *með*.

Metal. (F. ‒ L. ‒ Gk.) M. E. *metal*. O. F. *metal*. ‒ L. *metallum*, a mine, metal. ‒ Gk. μέταλλον, a cave, mine, mineral,

metal. Allied to μεταλλάω, I search after, explore.

metallurgy, a working in metals. (F. – L. – Gk.) O. F. *metallurgie.* – Late L. **metallurgia.* – Gk. μεταλλουργός, adj., working in metals. – Gk. μέταλλο-ν,metal; ἔργον, work; see **Work.** ¶ L. *ū* = Gk. ου < οε.

Metamorphosis, transformation. (L. – Gk.) L. *metamorphōsis.* – Gk. μεταμόρφωσις, a change of form. – Gk. μετά, here denoting 'change'; and μορφόω, I form, from μορφή, sb., shape.

Metaphor. (F. – L. – Gk.) M.F. *metaphore,* 'metaphor;' Cot. – L. *metaphora.* – Gk. μεταφορά, a transferring of a word from its literal signification. – Gk. μεταφέρειν, to transfer. – Gk. μετά, signifying 'change'; φέρειν, to bear; see **Bear** (1).

Metaphrase. (Gk.) From Gk. μετάφρασις, a paraphrasing; lit. change of phrase. – Gk. μετά, signifying 'change'; and φράσις, a phrase; see **Phrase.**

Metaphysics, the science of mind. (L. – Gk.) Formerly also *metaphysic.* – L. *metaphysica,* neut. pl. metaphysics. – Gk. μετὰ τὰ φυσικά, after physics; because the study was supposed to follow that of physics or natural science.

Metathesis. (L. – Gk.) L. *metathesis.* – Gk. μετάθεσις, transposition. – Gk. μετά, implying 'change'; θέσις, a placing; see **Thesis.**

Mete, to measure. (E.) M. E. *meten.* A. S. *metan,* to measure. + Du. *meten,* Icel. *meta* (to value), Swed. *mäta,* Goth. *mitan,* G. *messen.* Cf. L. *modus,* measure, Gk. μέδ-ομαι, I provide for. (√MED.)

Metempsychosis, transmigration of souls. (Gk.) Gk. μετεμψύχωσις. – Gk. μετεμψυχόω, I make the soul pass from one body to another. – Gk. μετ-ά, denoting 'change'; ἐμ- (for ἐν), in, into; ψυχ-ή, the soul. See **Psychical.**

Meteor. (F. – Gk.) M. F. *meteore,* 'a meteor;' Cot. – Gk. μετέωρον, a meteor; neut. of adj. μετέωρος, raised above the earth, soaring in air. – Gk. μετά, among; **ἄϝορος,* prob. from ἀείρειν, to lift (see Prellwitz).

Metheglin, mead. (W.) W. *meddyglyn,* mead, lit. healing liquor. – W. *meddyg* (from L. *medicus*), healing; *llyn,* liquor.

Methinks. (E.) Lit. 'it seems to me;' here *me* is the dat. case, and *thinks* is an impers. verb, from M. E. *þinken,* to seem. A. S. *mē þynceð,* it seems to me; from

þyncan, to seem. + O. Sax. *thunkian,* Icel. *þykkja,* Goth. *thugkjan,* i. e. **thunkjan,* G. *dünken,* to seem. Allied (by gradation) to A. S. *þanc,* a thought, and *þencan,* to think. See **Thank, Think.**

Method. (F. – L. – Gk.) M.F. *methode,* 'a method;' Cot. – L. *methodus.* – Gk. μέθοδος, an enquiry into, method, system. – Gk. μεθ-, for μετ-ά, among, after; ὁδός, a way; the lit. sense is 'a way after,' a following after. (√SED.)

Methylated, used of spirits of wine when mixed with methyl to make it undrinkable. (L. – Gk.) Formed with suffix *-ated* from *methyl,* meaning a gas procured by the destructive distillation of wood. *Methyl* is a Latinised spelling coined from Gk. μέθυ, mead, wine (see N. E. D.), and ὕλη, wood.

Metonymy, the putting of one word for another. (L. – Gk.) L. *metōnymia.* – Gk. μετωνυμία, change of name. – Gk. μετά, implying 'change'; ὄνομα, name.

Metre, Meter, rhythm, verse. (F. – L. – Gk.) M. E. *metre.* – M. F. *metre,* 'meeter;' Cot. – L. *metrum.* – Gk. μέτρον, that by which anything is measured, a rule, metre. Lit. 'measure;' cf. Skt. *mā,* to measure. See Brugm. ii. § 62. Der. *baro-meter, chrono-meter, geo-metry, hexa-meter, hydro-meter, hygro-meter, penta-meter, thermo-meter, trigono-metry, tri-meter,* &c.

Metropolis, a mother-city. (L. – Gk.) L. *mētropolis.* – Gk. μητρόπολις, a mother-state; the city of a primate. – Gk. μήτρο-, for μήτηρ, a mother; πόλις, a city. See **Mother** and **Police.**

Mettle, spirit, ardour. (F. – L. – Gk.) Another spelling of *metal;* in Shakespeare, no distinction is made between the two words in old editions, either in spelling or in use (Schmidt). With special allusion to the *metal* (or *mettle*) of a sword-blade.

Mew (1), to cry as a cat; a word of imitative origin. (E.) M. E. *mawen.* + Pers. *maw,* Arab. *mua,* mewing of a cat. Der. *mewl,* from F. *miauler,* to mew.

Mew (2), a sea-gull. (E.) M. E. *mawe.* A. S. *mǣw, mēaw, mēu,* a mew. + N. Fries. *mēwe,* E. Fries. *mēve,* Du. *meeuw,* Icel. *mār,* Dan. *maage,* Swed. *måke,* G. *möwe.* Cf. O. H. G. *mēh,* a mew.

Mew (3), a cage for hawks, &c. (F. – L.) The pl. *mews* now means a range of stabling, because the royal stables were rebuilt (A. D. 1534) in a place where the royal falcons had been kept (Stow). M. E. *mewe*, *mue*, a cage where hawks were kept when moulting.—O. F. *mue*, a moulting, also a mew for hawks; Guernsey *mue*, a mew.—F. *muer*, to change, moult. —L. *mūtāre*, to change. **Der.** *mew-s*, as above. See **Mutable**.

Mewl; see Mew (1).

Mews; see Mew (3).

Mezzotinto, a mode of engraving. (Ital.—L.) Ital. *mezzo tinto*, half tinted. —Ital. *mezzo*, mid; *tinto*, pp. of *tingere*, to tint.—L. *medius*, mid; *tingere*, to dip, dye.

Miasma, pollution, infectious matter. (Gk.) Gk. μίασμα, a stain.—Gk. μιαίνειν, to stain.

Mica, a glittering mineral. (L.) ' *Mica*, a crum, little quantity of anything that breaks off; also, a glimmer, or cat-silver, a metallick body like silver, which shines in marble,' &c.; Phillips (1706).—L. *mīca*, a crumb; cf. F. and Span. *mica*, mica. But it seems to have been applied to the mineral from the notion that this sb. is related to L. *micāre*, to shine; which is probably not the case.

Mich, to skulk, play truant. (E.) M.E. *muchen*, to pilfer. A. S. *myccan; not found, but allied to G. *meuchlings*, insidiously. **Der.** *mich-er*, *mich-ing* (Shak.).

Michaelmas, the feast of St. Michael. (F.—Heb.; *and* L.) M. E. *michelmesse*; where *Michel* = F. *Michel*, from Heb. *Mīkhāel*, lit. ' who is like unto God?' The suffix *-mas* = M. E. *messe* = A.S. *mæsse*; from L. *missa*; see **Mass** (2).

Mickle, great. (E.) M. E. *mikel*, *mukel*, *michel*, *muchel*.—A.S. *micel* (*mycel*). ╂ Icel. *mikill* (*mykill*), Goth. *mikils* ; Gk. μεγάλη, great. Cf. also Gk. μέγας, great, L. *magnus*. See **Much**.

Microcosm, a little world. (F.—L.— Gk.) F. *microcosme*.—L. *microcosmus*.— Gk. μικρόκοσμος, a little world.—Gk. μικρό-s, little, for σμικρός, little; κόσμος, world; see **Cosmetic**.

microscope, an instrument for viewing small objects. (Gk.) Gk. μικρό-s, little; σκοπ-εῖν, to see; see **Scope**.

Mid, middle. (E.) M. E. *mid*. A. S. *mid*, *midd*, adj. ╂ Du. Dan. Swed. *mid-* (in compounds); Icel. *miðr*, Goth. *midjis*, O. H. G. *mitti*, L. *medius*, Gk. μέσος, Æolic μέσσος, Skt. *madhya-*, adj., middle. Cf. Ir. *mid-*, as in *mid-nogt*, midnight. See **Medium**, **Middle**.

Midden, a dunghill. (Scand.) M. E.

midding.—Dan. *mödding* (for *mögdynge). —Dan. *mög* (Icel. *myki*), muck; Dan. *dynge*, a heap; lit. ' muck-heap '). Dan. *dynge* = Swed. *dynga*, dung; allied to E. *dung*. And see **Muck**.

Middle, adj., intervening; also as sb. (E.) M. E. *middel*, adj.; *middel*, sb. A.S. *middel*, adj. and sb.—A. S. *midd*, adj., middle.╂Du. *middel*, adj. adv. and sb.; G. *mittel*, sb., means; O. H. G. *mittil*, adj. Cf. Icel. *meðal*, prep., among. **Der.** *middl-ing* ; *middle-most*, an ill-coined superlative, on the model of *after-most*, *foremost*.

midriff, the diaphragm separating the heart from the stomach, &c. (E.) M. E. *midrif*. A. S. *midrif*, also *midhrif*.— A. S. *mid*, middle; *hrif*, the belly. ╂ O. Fries. *midref*, from *mid*, middle, *ref*, *rif*, the belly; Du. *middel-rif*. With A. S. *hrif* cf. L. *corp-us*, body.

midship, short for *amid-ship*; hence *midship-man*.

midst, the middle. (E.) *In middest*, Spenser, F. Q. vi. 3. 25; formed, with added *t*, from M. E. *in middes*, equivalent to *amiddes*; see **Amid**.

midwife. (E.) M. E. *midwif*; rarely *medewif* (Wyclif), from a false etymology which connected it with M. E. *mede* or *meed*, reward.—A. S. *mid*, prep., together with; *wīf*, a woman. Thus the lit. sense is ' a woman who is with another,' a helper. Cf. A. S. *mid-wyrcan*, to work with. So also Span. *co-madre*, lit. ' co-mother,' a midwife. Cf. Du. *medehelpen*, to assist (from *mede*, with, *helpen*, to help); G. *mit-helfer*, a helper with, assistant.

Midge. (E.) M. E. *migge*, *mygge*. A. S. *micg*, better *mycg*, a midge, gnat. ╂ Du. *mug*, Low G. *mugge*, Swed. *mygg*, Dan. *myg*, G. *mücke*. Teut. type *mugjā, f., or *mugjoz, m.; prob. ' buzzer;' cf. Gk. μύζειν, to mutter, μυῖα, a fly (Prellwitz); also Icel. *mȳ*, a midge.

Midriff, Midship, Midst, Midwife; see Mid.

Mien, look. (F.—C.) F. *mine*, ' the look;' Cot. (Whence Ital. *mina*; Hatzfeld.) Prob. from Bret. *min*, muzzle, beak (also used of men). Cf. W. *min*, lip; Ir. *men*, mouth; Corn. *mein*, *men*, lip, mouth (Thurneysen). Celtic type *maknā (**mekno-*), open mouth (Stokes).

Might (1), strength. (E.) M. E. *miȝt*. A. S. *miht*; O. Merc. *mæht*. ╂ Du. *magt*, Icel. *māttr*, Dan. Swed. *magt*, Goth.

mahts, G. *macht*. Teut. type **mah-tiz*, f.; from the verb **mag-an-*. See **May** (1).

Might (2), pt. t. of *may*. (E.) See **May** (1).

Mignonette, a plant. (F.) F. *mignonette*, dimin. of *mignon*, darling; see **Minion**.

Migrate. (L.) From pp. of L. *migrāre*, to wander. Cf. Gk. ἀμείβειν, to change.

Milch; see **Milk**.

Mild. (E.) M. E. *mild, milde*. A. S. *milde*.+Du. *mild*, Icel. *mildr*, Dan. Swed. G. *mild*; O. Sax. *mildi*, O. H. G. *milti*. Goth. *-milds*, in *un-milds*, without natural affection. Perhaps allied to Gk. μαλθακός, soft, mild, O. Irish *meld*, pleasant. Brugm. i. § 591.

Mildew. (E.) M. E. *meldew*. A. S. *meledēaw, mildēaw*, lit. honey-dew. − A. S. *mele, mil*, allied to L. *mel*, honey; *dēaw*, dew. So also Irish *milceog*, mildew; from *mil*, honey. And cf. Gk. μέλι, honey.

Mile. (L.) M. E. *mile*. A. S. *mil.* − L. pl. *mīlia*, commonly *millia*, a Roman mile. − L. *mille*, sing., a thousand; whence *mille* (pl. *millia*) *passuum*, a thousand paces, a Roman mile. Cf. Du. *mijl*, G. *meils*, Swed. *mil*, Dan. *miil*; all from L.

milfoil, yarrow. (F. − L.) Lit. ' thousand-leaf.' − F. *mille*, thousand; A. F. *foille*, F. *feuille*, leaf. − Late L. *millefolium*, milfoil. − L. *mille*, thousand; *folium*, leaf; see **Foil** (2).

Militate, to contend. (L.) From pp. of L. *mīlitāre*, to serve as a soldier. − L. *mīlit-*, stem of *miles*, a soldier.

militia, troops. (L.) L. *mīlitia*, (1) warfare, (2) troops. − L. *mīlit-*, stem of *mīles*, a soldier.

Milk. (E.) M. E. *milk*. O. Merc. *milc* (Sweet, O. E. T.); A. S. *meolc, meoluc*.+ Du. *melk*, O. Sax. *miluk*; Icel. *mjōlk*, Dan. *melk*, Swed. *mjölk*; Goth. *miluks*, G. *milch*. Teut. stem **meluk-*, fem. Allied to the old strong Teut. vb. **melk-an-*, as seen in A. S. *melcan*, Du. and G. *melken*, to stroke a cow, milk; allied to Gk. ἀμέλγειν, L. *mulgēre*, to milk, Lith. *milsz-ti*, to stroke, to milk; O. Irish *blig-im*, I milk. (✓MELG.)

milch, milk-giving. (E.) M. E. *milche, melche*, adj.; cf. A. S. *milc-en*, adj., milky. + Icel. *milkr, mjōlkr*, adj., milk-giving, from *mjōlk*, milk. So also G. *melk*, adj., milch.

milksop, an effeminate man. (E.) M. E. *milksoppe*, Ch. C. T. 13916 (B 3100).

Lit. ' bread sopped in milk;' hence, a soft fellow. − M. E. *milk*, milk; *soppe*, a sop; see **Sop**.

Mill. (L.) M. E. *miln, myln, mulne*; whence *mille, mulle*, by assimilation of *n*. A. S. *myln, mylen*. − Late L. *mulīna*, for *molīna*, a mill; extended from *mola*, a mill. See **Molar**.

Millennium, a thousand years. (L.) L. *millennium*. − L. *mille*, thousand; *annus*, year; see **Annual**.

Millet, a plant. (F. − L.) F. *millet*; dimin. of *mil*, millet. − L. *milium*, millet (whence A. S. *mil*, millet).+ Gk. μελίνη, millet.

Milliner. (Ital.) Formerly also *millaner* (Ben Jonson). Disputed; but certainly for *Milaner*, a dealer in goods brought from *Milan*, in Italy.

Million, a thousand thousand. (F. − L.) F. *million*; Late L. *millio*, lit. 'great thousand,' an augmentative form. − L. *mille*, thousand. Der. Hence *b-illion*, *tr-illion*, *quadr-illion* are formed, by a sort of analogy, in order to express shortly the ideas of *bi-million*, *tri-million*, &c.; where *bi-* means 'to the second power,' not 'twice.'

Milt (1), the spleen. (E.) M. E. *milte*. A. S. *milte*. + Du. *milt*, Icel. *milti*, Dan. *milt*, Swed. *mjälte*, the spleen; G. *milz*, O. H. G. *milzi*, milt. From the verb *to melt* in the sense to digest; cf. Icel. *melta*, (1) to malt, (2) to digest. See **Melt**.

Milt (2), soft roe. (Scand.) A corruption of *milk*, due to confusion with *milt* (1). M. E. *mylke* of *fyshe*; Vocab. 591. 16. − Swed. *mjölke*, milt, from *mjölk*, milk; Dan. *fiskemelk*, soft roe of fishes, lit. 'fish-milk;' G. *fischmilch*, milt. Cf. M. Du. *melcker van een visch*, ' the milt of a fish,' Hexham.

Mimic. (L. − Gk.) L. *mīmicus*, farcical. − Gk. μιμικός, imitative. − Gk. μῖμος, an imitator, actor, mime.

Minaret, a turret on a mosque. (Span. − Arab.) Span. *minarete*, a high slender turret. − Arab. *manārat*, a lamp, lighthouse, minaret. − Arab. *manār*, candlestick, lamp, lighthouse. Allied to Arab. *nār*, fire.+Heb. *manōrāh*, a candlestick; from *nūr*, to shine.

Mince, to cut up small. (F. − L.) M. E. *mincen*. − M. F. *mincer*, O. F. *mincier*, to mince; cf. *mince*, adj., small. − Late L. **minūtiāre*, to mince (Schwan, § 199); from Late L. *minūtia*, a small piece. − L.

minūtus, small. Cf. A.S. *minsian*, to diminish. See **Minish.** Der. *mince-pie*, formerly *minced-pie*, i.e. pie of minced meat.

Mind. (E.) M.E. *mind.* A.S. *gemynd*, memory. — A.S. *munan*, to think; *gemunan*, to remember (whence *gemynd* for **gamundi-*, by mutation). + Goth. *ga-munds*, f., remembrance. Teut. type **mundi-*, for **munthi-*, by Verner's law; Idg. type *mənti-* (cf. L. *ment-is*, gen. of *mens*, mind; Skt. *mati-*, mind). From the weak grade of √MEN, to think. Brugm. i. § 431.

Mine (1), belonging to me. (E.) M.E. *min*, pl. *mine*; often shortened to *my*. A.S. *mīn*, poss. pron. (declinable), from *min*, gen. of 1st pers. pronoun. + Goth. *meins*, poss. pron.; allied to *meina*, gen. case of 1st pers. pronoun; so in other Teut. tongues. Cf. L. *meus*. See **Me.**

my. (E.) M.E. *mi, my*; short for *min* (above), by loss of final *n*. Der. *my-self*, M.E. *mi-self*, formerly *me-self*.

Mine (2), to excavate. (F.—C.) F. *miner.* Of Celtic origin. Cf. Bret. *mengleuz*, a mine (cf. *cleuz*, hollow); W. *mwn*, ore, a mine, *mwn-glawdd*, a mine (cf. *clawdd*, a pit), O. W. *mwyn*, ore (Davies); Irish *mein*, ore; Gael. *mein*, *meinn*, ore, a mine (Thurneysen). Celtic type *meini, ore (Stokes).

mineral. (F.—C.) M.F. *mineral*, 'a minerall;' Cot. — F. *miner*, to mine (above). Cf. Span. *minera*, a mine.

Miniver; see **Meniver.**

Mingle, to mix. (E.) A frequentative form of *ming*, to mix (Surrey); M.E. *mengen*, *mingen*, to mix. A.S. *mengan*, to mix, to become mixed; a causal verb. — A.S. *mang*, a mixture, usually *gemang*, *gemong*, a mixture, crowd, assembly. + Du. *mengelen*, to mingle, from *mengen*, to mix; Icel. *menga*, G. *mengen*, to mingle. See **Among, Monger.**

Miniature, a small painting. (Ital.—L.) Ital. *miniatura*, a miniature. — Ital. *miniato*, pp. of *miniare*, to dye, paint, 'to colour or limne with vermilion or red lead;' Florio. — L. *minium*, cinnabar, red lead; said to be of Iberian origin.

Minikin, a little darling. (Du.) Used by Florio, to translate Ital. *mignone*. — Du. *minnekyn*, a cupid (Sewel); M. Du. *minneken*, my darling, dimin. of *minne*, love (Hexham). Cf. O. H. G. *minna*, love; allied to **Mind.** (√MEN.)

Minim, a note in music; ₁/₆₄th of a drachm. (F.—L.) O. F. *minime*, lit. very small. — L. *min-ima*, very small; superl. fem. allied to *min-or*, less. See **Minor.**

Minion, a favourite. (F.) F. *mignon*, sb., a favourite. — F. *mignon*, adj., minion, dainty, also pleasing, kind. Of doubtful origin. Cf. G. *minne*, love; see **Minikin.** Or from Celt. *min-*, small (Körting).

Minish, to lessen. (F. — L.) M. E. *menusen*. — F. *menuiser*, to minish (answering to Late L. *minūtiāre). — L. *minūtus*, small; see **Minute.** Doublet, *mince.*

minister. (F.—L.) M. E. *ministre.* — F. *ministre.* — L. acc. *ministrum*; nom. *minister*, a servant. L. *min-is-ter* is formed with suffix *-ter* from *min-es, allied to *min-or*, smaller; from the base *min-*, small; see **Minor.**

Miniver; see **Meniver.**

Minnow, a small fish. (E.) M. E. *menow.* A.S. *myne*, a minnow; cf. O. H. G. *muniwa*, a minnow (Kluge). ¶ We find another word, viz. M.E. *menuse*, a small fish; from O. F. *menuise*, a small fish. — Late L. type **minūtia.* — L. *minūtus*, minute, small; see **Minute.**

Minor, less. (L.) L. *min-or*, less; the positive form occurs in A. S. *min* (?), Irish *min*, small. + Icel. *minnr*, adv., less; Goth. *minniza*, less. Brugm. i. § 84.

Minster. (L.—Gk.) A.S. *mynster*; cf. O. H. G. *munistri.* From L. *monastērium*; see **Monastery.**

Minstrel. (F.—L.) M. E. *ministral*, or *menestral.* — O. F. *menestrel*, *menestral.* — Late L. *ministrālis*, a servant, retainer, hence one who played instruments or acted as jester. — L. *minister*, a servant; see **Minister.** Der. *minstrel-cy*, M. E. *minstralcie.*

Mint (1), a place where money is coined. (L.) M. E. *mint*, *mynt.* A. S. *mynet*; cf. O. H. G. *munizza* (G. *münze*). From L. *monēta*, (1) a mint, (2) money (Pogatscher). *Monēta* was a surname of Juno, in whose temple at Rome money was coined. — L. *monēre*, to warn; Brugm. ii. § 79. See **Money.**

Mint (2), a plant. (L. — Gk.) A. S. *minte.* — L. *menta*, *mentha.* — Gk. μίνθα, mint.

Minuet, a dance. (F. — L.) So called from the small steps taken in it. — M. F. *menuët*, 'smallish, little, pretty;' Cot. Dimin. of M.F. *menu*, small. — L. *minūtus*, small; see **Minute.**

minus, less. (L.) Neut. of *minor*, less; see **Minor.**

minute, sb. (L.) M. E. *minute,* sb. — L. *minūta,* a small part; orig. fem. of *minūtus,* small, pp. of *minuere,* to make small. — L. *min-,* small; base of *min-or,* less. See **Minor.**

Minx, a pert wanton woman. (Low G.) Low G. *minsk,* (1) masc. a man, (2) neut. a pert female. Cf. G. *mensch,* neut., a wench. The G. *mensch* was orig. an adj., from *mann,* a man. Cf. A. S. *mennisc,* human; from *mann,* a man. See **Man.**

Miocene, less recent. (Gk.) Gk. μείο-, for μείων, less; καιν-ός, new, recent.

Miracle. (F. — L.) F. *miracle.* — L. *mīrāculum,* a wonder. — L. *mīrārī,* to wonder at. — L. *mīrus,* wonderful. Cf. Skt. *smaya-,* wonder, from *smi,* to smile. Allied to **Smile.** Brugm. i. § 389.

mirage. (F. — L.) F. *mirage,* an optical illusion. — F. *mirer,* to look at. — L. *mīrārī* (above).

Mire, deep mud. (Scand.) M. E. *mire, myre.* — Icel. *mȳrr,* mod. *mȳri,* a bog; Swed. *myra,* Dan. *myre, myr,* a bog. + O. H. G. *mios,* M. H. G. *mies,* moss, swamp. Teut. base **meus-* > **meuz-.* Allied to **Moss.**

Mirror. (F. — L.) M. E. *mirour.* — O. F. *mireör,* later *miroir,* a looking-glass, mirror (answering to Late L. *mīrātōrium*). — Late L. *mīrāre,* to behold; L. *mīrārī.* See **Miracle.**

Mirth. (E.) M. E. *mirthe.* A. S. *myrgð, mirhð, mirigð,* mirth. — A. S. *myrge,* merry. See **Merry.**

Mis- (1), prefix. (E.) The A. S. *mis-* occurs in *mis-dǣd,* a misdeed, and in other compounds. It answers to Du. Dan. Icel. *mis-,* Swed. G. *miss-,* Goth. *missa-,* with the sense of 'wrong.' Teut. type **misso-*; Idg. type **mit-to-*; allied to O. II. G. *mīdan* (G. *meiden*), to avoid; Lat. *mittere,* to send away, pp. *missus.* Brugm. i. § 794. Der. *mis-become,* *-behave,* *-believe,* *-deed,* *-deem,* *-do,* *-give,* *-lay,* *-lead,* *-like,* *-name,* *-shape,* *-time,* *-understand.* Also prefixed to words of F. and L. origin, as in *mis-apply,* *-calculate,* *-carry,* *-conceive,* *-conduct,* *-construe,* *-date,* *-demeanour,* *-employ,* *-fortune,* *-govern,* *-guide,* *-inform,* *-interpret,* *-judge,* *-place,* *-print,* *-pronounce,* *-quote,* *-represent,* *-rule,* *-spend,* *-term,* *-use,* &c. Also to Scand. words, as in *mis-call,* *-hap,* *-take.* See **Miss** (1).

Mis- (2), prefix. (F. — L.) The proper spelling is M. E. *mes-,* as in *mes-chief,* mischief. The same as O. F. *mes-,* Span.

menos-, from L. *minus,* less; with the sense of 'bad.' Frequently confused with the prefix above. Der. *mis-adventure* (q. v.), *-alliance,* *-chance* (q. v.), *-chief* (q. v.), *-count* (q. v.), *-creant* (q. v.), *-nomer* (q. v.), *-prise* (q. v.).

Misadventure. (F. — L.) O. F. *mesaventure;* see **Mis-** (2) and **Adventure.**

Misanthrope. (Gk.) Gk. μισάνθρω-πος, adj., hating mankind. — Gk. μισ-εῖν, to hate, from μῖσ-ος, hatred; ἄνθρωπος, a man. Der. *misanthrop-ic,* *-ist,* *-y* (Gk. μισανθρωπία).

Miscellaneous, various. (L.) L. *miscellāne-us;* with suffix *-ous.* — L. *mis-cellus,* mixed. — L. *miscēre,* to mix; see **Mix.**

Mischance. (F. — L.) M. E. and O. F. *meschance;* see **Mis-** (2) and **Chance.**

Mischief. (F. — L.) M. E. *meschief.* — O. F. *meschief,* a bad result. Cf. Span. *menos-cabo,* diminution, loss. See **Mis-** (2) and **Chief.**

Miscount. (F. — L.) O. F. *mesconter;* see **Mis-** (2) and **Count.**

Miscreant, a wretch. (F. — L.) Orig. an unbeliever, infidel. — M. F. *mescreant,* 'misbelieving;' Cot. Here *mes-* < L. *minus;* see **Mis-** (2). *Creant* is from L. *crēdent-,* stem of pres. pt. of *crēdere,* to believe. Cf. Ital. *miscredente,* misbelieving; and E. *re-creant.* See **Creed.**

Miser, a niggard. (L.) Also 'a wretch'; Spenser, F. Q. ii. 1. 8. — L. *miser,* wretched. Cf. Ital. and Span. *misero* (1) wretched, (2) avaricious.

miserable. (F. — L.) M.F. *miserable.* — L. *miserābilis,* pitiable. — L. *miserārī* to pity. — L. *miser,* wretched.

Mishap. (Scand.) M. E. *mishappen,* verb, to fall out ill; see **Mis-** (1) and **Hap.**

Mishna, a digest of Jewish traditions. (Heb.) Heb. *mishnah,* a repetition, a second part. — Heb. root *shānāh,* to repeat.

Misnomer, a misnaming. (F. — L.) It answers to an O. French *mesnommer,* to misname; used as a sb. with the sense 'a misnaming.' — O. F. *mes-,* badly; *nommer,* to name. See **Mis-** (2) and **Nominal.**

Misprise, Misprize, to slight. (F. — L.) In As You Like It, i. 1. 177. — M. F. *mespriser,* 'to disesteem, contemn;' Cot. — O. F. *mes-,* badly; Late L. *pretiāre,*

to prize, esteem, from L. *pretium*, price.
See Mis- (2) and Price.

Misprision, a mistake, neglect. (F.—
L.) M. F. *mesprison*, 'misprision, error,
offence;' Cot. Cf. F. *méprise*, a mistake.
—O. F. *mes-*, badly, ill; Late L. *prensiōnem*, acc. of *prensio* (short for L. *prehensio*),
a seizing, taking, apprehending, from L.
prehendere; to take. ¶ Quite distinct
from *misprise*.

Miss (1), to fail to hit. (E.) M. E.
missen. A. S. *missan*, to miss; also, to
escape one's notice (rare). From a base
*mith-, weak grade of **meith-*, as in A. S.
and O. S. *mīðan*, to conceal, avoid, escape
notice (as well as in G. *meiden*, O. H. G.
mīdan, to avoid). See Mis- (1).+Du.
missen, Icel. *missa*, Dan. *miste* (with excrescent *t*), Swed. *missa*, O.H.G. *missan*, to
miss; also Du. *mis*, Icel. *mis*, adv., amiss;
also Du. *mis-*, Icel. *mis-*, Dan. *mis-*, Swed.
G. *miss-*, wrongly. Allied to L. *mittere*,
to send; see Missile. (√MEIT.) Der.
miss, sb., a fault, M. E. *misse*, Will. of
Palerne, 532; *miss-ing*.

Miss (2), an unmarried woman. (F.—
L.) A contraction of *mistress*; Evelyn's
Diary, Jan. 9, 1662. See Mistress.

Missal, a mass-book. (L.) Late L.
missāle, a mass-book. — Late L. *missa*,
mass; see Mass (2).

Missel-thrush; see Mistle-thrush.

Missile, a weapon that may be thrown.
(L.) Properly an adj., 'that may be
thrown.' — L. *missilis*, that may be thrown.
—L. *missus*, pp. of *mittere*, (perhaps for
*mītere), to throw, send; pt. t. *mīsi.+*
O. H. G. *mīdan*, to avoid; see Miss (1).
Brugm. i. § 930.

mission. (L.) O. F. and F. *mission.*
—L. *missiōnem*, acc. of *missio*, a sending.—L. *miss-us*, pp. of *mittere*, to send.

missive. (F.—L.) F. *missive*, 'a
letter sent;' Cot. Coined from L. *miss-us*,
pp. of *mittere*, to send.

Mist. (E.) A S. *mist*, gloom, darkness.
+Icel. *mistr*, Du. Swed. *mist*, mist. Teut.
type **mih·stoz.* Apparently formed from
the base **mig-* (>*mih-* before *st*), Idg.
*migh- (weak grade of root **meigh*); as
seen in Lithuan. *migla*, Russ. *mgla*, Gk.
ὀμίχλη, mist, Skt. *mih-ira-*, a cloud; also
Skt. *mēgh-a-*, a cloud, from the stronger
grade. (√MEIGH, to darken; perhaps
distinct from √MEIGH, as appearing in
L. *mingere*.)

Mistake, to err. (Scand.) Icel. *mis-*

taka, to take by error, make a slip.—Icel.
mis-, wrongly; *taka*, to take. See Mis-
(1) and Take.

Mister, Mr., a title of address. (F.—
L.) A corruption of *master*, due to the
influence of *mistress*, which is an older
word than *mister*; see below.

mistress, a lady of a household. (F.
—L.) O. F. *maistresse*, 'a mistress, dame;'
Cot. (F. *maîtresse*.) Fem. of O. F. *maistre*,
a master; see Master.

Mistery, Mystery, a trade, handicraft. (F.—L.) The *mystery plays* (better
spelt *mistery plays*) were so called because
acted by craftsmen; from M. E. *mistere*, a
trade, craft, Ch. C. T. 615.—O. F. *mestier*,
a trade, occupation (F. *métier*).—Late L.
misterium (also written *mysterium* by confusion with that word in the sense of
'mystery'), short form of L. *ministerium*,
employment.—L. *minister*, a servant; see
Minister.

Mistle-thrush. (E.) So called from
feeding on the berries of the mistletoe;
from A. S. *mistel*, mistletoe (below). + G.
misteldrossel, mistle-thrush.

mistletoe. (E.) A final *n* has been
lost. A. S. *misteltān.*—A. S. *mistel*, also
(like G. *mistel*) with the sense of mistletoe;
tān, a twig, cognate with Icel. *teinn*, Du.
teen, Goth. *tains*, Dan. *teen*, Swed. *ten*,
twig, spindle.+Icel. *mistelteinn*, mistletoe.
Perhaps *mistel* is related to G. *mist*, dung.
Cf. M. Du. *mistel*, bird-lime (Kilian),
' glew' (Hexham).

Mistress; see Mister.

Misty (1), adj. formed from Mist.

Misty (2), doubtful, ambiguous, as applied to language. (F.—L.—Gk.) In the
phrases ' *misty* language' and ' *mistiness*
of language,' *misty* is not from E. *mist*,
but is short for *mystic*; see Palmer, Folk-
Etymology. See Mystic.

Mite (1), an insect. (E.) M. E. *mite*,
A. S. *mīte*, a mite. + Low G. *mite*, Du.
mijt, O. H. G. *mīza*, a mite. Teut. type
*mītōn-, f. The word means ' cutter,' i. e.
biter; from Teut. base MEIT, to cut; cf.
Icel. *meita*, to cut. See Emmet.

mite (2), a very small portion. (Du.)
M. E. *mite*. —M. Du. *mijt*, *mite*, a very
small coin, mite, bit cut off. See above.

Mitigate. (L.) From pp. of L. *mīti-
gāre*, to make gentle.—L. *mīt-is*, gentle;
-igāre, for *agere*, to make.

Mitre, a head-dress, esp. for a bishop.
(F.—L.—Gk.) O. F. *mitre.*—L. *mitra*, a

cap. — Gk. μίτρα, a belt, girdle, head-band, fillet, turban.

Mitten. (F. — G. *or* C. ?) M. E. *mitaine*. — F. *mitaine*, 'a mittain, winter-glove,' Cot.; Gascon *mitano*. Origin disputed; see Hatzfeld, Körting, Scheler.

Mix, to mingle. (L.) A back formation from *mixt*, pp. — L. *mixtus*, mixed, pp. of *miscēre*, to mix. + A. S. *miscian*, to mix; G. *mischen*; also W. *mysgu*, Gael. *measg*, O. Irish *mescaim*, I mix, Russ. *mieshate*, Lithuan. *maiszyti*, L. *miscēre*, Gk. μίσγειν (for *μίγ-σκειν), to mix. Cf. Skt. *miçra*, mixed. Extended from √MEIK; cf. Gk. μίγνυμι, I mix. Brugm. i. §§ 707, 760. **Der.** *mash*, q. v.

mixture. (L.) L. *mixtūra*, a mixture. — L. *mixtus*, pp. of *miscēre*, to mix (above).

Mixen, a dunghill. (E.) M. E. *mixen*, A. S. *mixen*, *meoxen*, the same. From A. S. *mix*, *meox*, dung. — A. S. *mig-*, weak grade of *mīgan*, to urine. Cf. G. *mist*.

Mizen, Mizzen, a sail in a ship. (F. — Ital. — L.) F. *misaine*, explained by Cotgrave as 'the foresaile of a ship.' — Ital. *mezzana*, 'a saile in a ship called the poope or misen-saile;' Florio. Cf. Ital. *mezzano*, 'a meane man, between great and little;' id. The orig. sense seems to have been 'in the middle,' as a foresail between jib and mainsail. — Late L. *mediānus*, middle (whence also F. *moyen*, E. *mean*). — L. *medius*, middle. See **Medium.**

Mizzle, to rain in fine drops. (E.) Formerly *misle*, M. E. *miselen*, Cath. Angl. Cf. M. Du. *mieselen*, to drizzle, Hexham; Low G. *miseln* (Berghaus); E. Fries. *misig*, damp, gloomy. Cf. **Mist.**

Mnemonics, the science of aiding the memory. (Gk.) Gk. μνημονικά, mnemonics; neut. pl. of μνημονικός, belonging to memory. — Gk. μνήμον-, stem of μνήμων, mindful. — Gk. μνάομαι, I remember. (From *mnā*, a grade of √MEN.)

Moan, sb. (E.) M. E. *mone*, a communication, also a complaint; corresponding to A. S. **mān-* (not found), supposed to be cognate with O. Fries. *mēne*, an opinion, O. H. G. *meina*, an opinion, thought. Hence was formed A. S. *mānan*, to mean, intend, relate, also to complain, moan, lament, M. E. *mēnen*, to lament, now obsolete, its place being supplied by the form of the sb., used as a vb. See further under **Mean** (1). ¶ Cf. *means*

(some edd. *moans*) in Shak. M. N. D. v. 330. **Der.** *bemoan*, vb., substituted for M. E. *bimenen*, A. S. *bi-mǣnan*, to bemoan.

Moat. (F. — Teut.) M.E. *mote*. — O. F. *mote*, an embankment, dike; Norman dial *motte*, a moat, foss. [As in the case of *dike*, the same word means either the trench cut out or the embankment thrown up, or both together; cf. Low L. *mota*, (1) a mound, (2) a mound and moat together; also spelt *motta*.] The same word as F. *motte*, 'a clod, lump, sodd, turfe, little hill, butt to shoot at;' Cotgrave. Cf. also Ital. *motta*, a heap of earth, also a hollow, trench (like E. *moat*), Span. *mota*, a mound; Romansch *muotta*, rounded hill. Of Teut. origin; from Bavarian *mott*, peat, heap of peat (Diez). Prob. allied to **Mud**; cf. Du. *modder*, mud.

Mob (1), a disorderly crowd. (L.) A contraction of *mōbile uulgus*, i. e. fickle crowd. Both *mob* and *mobile* were in use, in the same sense, A. D. 1692–5. — L. *mōbile*, neut. of *mōbilis*, moveable, fickle. — L. *mouēre*, to move. See **Move.**

Mob (2), a kind of cap. (Du.) From Du. *mopmuts*, a woman's nightcap (where *muts* means cap); M. Du. *mop*, a woman's coif (Sewel); Low G. *mupp*, a woman's cap (Danneil).

Mobile, easily moved. (F. — L.) F. *mobile*. — L. *mōbilis*; see **Mob** (1).

Moccassin, Mocasin, a shoe of deer-skin. (N. American Indian.) From the Algonquin *makisin* (Cuoq).

Mock, to deride. (F. — L.) M. E. *mokken*. — O. F. *mocquer*, later *moquer*. According to Körting, it is the Picard form of *moucher*, to wipe the nose; and Cotgrave has *moucher*, 'to snyte, or make cleane the nose; also, to frump, mocke, scoff, deride;' for which Corblet gives the Picard form *mouker*. Cf. Ital. *moccare*, 'to blow the nose, also to mocke;' Florio. — Late L. *muccāre*, to blow the nose. — L. *muccus*, *mūcus*, mucus. See **Mucus.**

Mode. (F. — L.) F. *mode*. — L. *modum*, acc. of *modus*, measure, manner, way. Allied to **Mete.** Brugm. i. § 412.

model. (F. — Ital. — L.) M. F. *modelle* (F. *modèle*). — Ital. *modello*, 'a modell, frame, mould;' Florio. From dimin. of L. *modulus*, a standard, measure, which is again a dimin. of *modus*, measure. **Der.** *re-model*.

moderate, temperate. (L.) From pp. of L. *moderārī*, to regulate. From a stem *moder-*, for *modes-*, extended from *mod-us*, a measure. See **modest**.

modern. (F.—L.) F. *moderne.*—L. *modernus*, belonging to the present mode ; extended from a stem *moder-* (above).

modest, moderate, chaste, decent. (F. —L.) F. *modeste.*—L. *modestus*, modest, lit. ' keeping within measure.' From a neuter stem *modes-*, with suffix *-tus* ; see **moderate** (above). Brugm. ii. § 132.

modicum, a small quantity. (L.) Neut. of L. *modicus*, moderate.—L. *modus*, measure.

modify. (F.—L.) F. *modifier.*—L. *modificāre.*—L. *modi-*, for *modus*, measure, moderation ; *-ficāre*, for *facere*, to make.

modulate, to regulate. (L.) From pp. of L. *modulārī*, to measure by a standard.—L. *modulus*, dimin. of *modus*, a measure ; see **model**.

Mogul, a Mongolian. (Pers.) Pers. *Moghōl*, a Mogul ; another form of *Mongol*.

Mohair, cloth of fine hair. (Arab.) A changed spelling (by confusion with *hair*) of *mockaire* (Hakluyt, ii. 273) ; whence F. *mouaire* (1650), mod. F. *moire* ; also F. *moncayar.*—Arab. *mukhayyar*, a kind of coarse camlet or hair-cloth ; Rich. Dict., p. 1369.

Mohammedan. (Arab.) A follower of *Mohammed.*—Arab. *muhammad*, praiseworthy.—Arab. *hamada*, he praised.

Mohur, a gold coin. (Pers.) Pers. *muhr*, *muhar*, a gold coin worth 16 rupees (Wilson) ; *muhr*, *muhur*, Rich. Dict., p. 1534.

Moidore, a Portuguese gold coin. (Port.—L.) See Bailey's Dict. — Port. *moeda d'ouro*, a moidore, £1 7s. ; lit. ' money of gold.'—L. *monēta*, money ; *dē*, of ; *aurum*, gold. See **Money**.

Moiety, half. (F.—L.) F. *moitié*, a half.—L. *medietātem*, acc. of *medietās*, a middle course, a half. — L. *medius*, middle. See **Medium**.

Moil, to toil, drudge. (F.—L.) Formerly *moile*, to defile with dirt ; later *moil*, ' to dawbe with dirt, to drudge ;' Phillips. The older sense was to dirty, hence to drudge, from the dirt consequent on toil. Spenser has *moyle*, to sully, Hymn of Heav. Love, st. 32. Still earlier, we have M. E. *moillen*, to moisten, wet.—O.F. *moiller*, *moiler* (Littré), later *mouiller*, to wet, moisten ; orig. sense, to soften, which (in the case of clay) is effected by wetting it.

This verb answers to a Late L. **molliāre*, to soften ; not found. — L. *molli-s*, soft. Thus the senses were, to soften, moisten, dirty, soil oneself, drudge.

Moire, watered silk. (F.) From F. *moire*, used in two senses. In the sense *mohair*, it is borrowed from E. *mohair* (Hatzfeld). In the sense of watered silk, it may represent L. *marmoreus*, shining like marble, from *marmor*, marble (Körting) ; but this may be only a transferred sense of the former.

Moist. (F.—L.) M. E. *moiste*, often with the sense ' fresh' ; Ch. C. T. 459, 12249.—O. F. *moiste*, later *moite*. Etym. disputed ; (1) from L. *musteus*, new, from L. *mustum*, must ; (2) from L. *muccidus*, *mūcidus*, mouldy, from L. *mūcus* (Körting) ; (3) from L. *muscidus*, later form of *mūcidus* (Hatzfeld). Der. *moisture*, O. F. *moisteur*.

Molar, used for grinding. (L.) L. *molāris*, adj., from *mola*, a mill. Cf. *molere*, to grind. (√MEL.) Brugm. ii. § 690.

Molasses, syrup made from sugar. (Port. — L.) Formerly *melasses*. — Port. *melaço*, molasses ; cf. Span. *melaza* (same). — L. *mellāceus*, made with honey. — L. *mel*, honey.

Mole (1), a spot or mark on the body. (E.) M. E. *mole*. A. S. *māl*, a spot (whence *mole* by the usual change from *ā* to long *ō*). +O. H. G. *meil*, Goth. *mail*, a spot.

Mole (2), an animal. (E.) M. E. *molle*. + M. Du. and Du. *mol* ; Low G. *mull* (Berghaus). Prob. related to M. Du. *mul*, ' the dust or crumblings of turf,' Hexham ; M. E. *mul*, A. S. *myl*, dust ; which are further related to **Mould** (1). The sense may have been ' earth-grubber,' or ' crumbler,' from the weak grade of √MEL, to pound. Cf. E. Fries. *mullen*, to grub ; *mulle*, a child that grubs in the ground ; *mulle*, *mul*, a mole ; Low G.*mullworm*, a mole (Danneil). ¶ Another name was formerly *moldwarp* (1 Hen. IV. iii. 1. 149), lit. ' the animal that casts up mould.' M. E. *moldwerp* ; from *mold*, mould, *werpen*, to throw up. See **Warp**. Cf. Icel. *moldvarpa*, a mole, O. H. G. *multwurf*, G. *maulwurf*.

Mole (3), a breakwater. (F.—Ital.—L.) F. *môle.*—Ital. *molo*, *mole*, ' a great pile ;' Florio.—L. *mōlem*, acc. of *mōles*, a great heap.

molecule, an atom. (L.) Formerly *molecula* ; Bailey. Coined from L. *mōles*, a heap; the true form would have been *molicula.*

Molest, to annoy. (F.−L.) F. *molester.* − L. *molestāre.* − L. *molestus,* troublesome; formed with suffix *-tus,* from a stem *moles-,* extended from *mol-*; allied to *mōlīrī,* to strive, and to Mole (3).

Mollify, to soften. (F.−L.) M. F. *mollifier.* − L. *mollificāre.* − L. *moll-is,* soft; *-ficāre,* for *facere,* to make. Cf. Skt. *mṛdu-,* soft. Allied to **Melt**; Brugm. ii. § 690.

mollusc. (F.−L.) F. *mollusque.* − L. *mollusca,* a soft-shelled nut; which some molluscs were supposed to resemble. − L. *moll-is,* soft.

Molten, old pp. of **Melt,** q. v.

Moly, a plant. (L.−Gk.) L. *mōly.* − Gk. μῶλυ; Homer, Od. x. 305.

Moment. (F.−L.) F. *moment.* − L. *mōmentum,* a movement; hence, an instant of time; short for **mouimentum.* − L. *mouēre,* to move. See **Move.** Doublets, *momentum, movement.*

Monad, a unit, &c. (L.−Gk.) L. *monad-,* stem of *monas,* a unit. − Gk. μονάς, a unit. − Gk. μόνος, alone.

monarch, a sole ruler. (F.−L.−Gk.) F. *monarque.* − L. *monarcha.* − Gk. μονάρχης, a sovereign, sole ruler. − Gk. μον- (for μόνος), alone; and ἄρχειν, to rule.

monastery. (L.−Gk.) L. *monastērium.* − Gk. μοναστήριον, a minster. − Gk. μοναστής, dwelling alone, a monk. − Gk. μονάζειν, to be alone. − Gk. μόνος, alone. Der. *monast-ic,* from Gk. μοναστικός, living in solitude.

Monday. (E.) M. E. *monenday,* later *moneday, monday.* A. S. *mōnan dæg,* day of the moon; where *mōnan* is the gen. of *mōna,* moon. See **Moon.** A translation of L. *diēs lunæ.*

Monetary, relating to money. (L.) L. *monētārius,* lit. belonging to a mint. − L. *monēta,* (1) a mint, (2) money. See **Mint** (1).

money. (F.−L.) M.E. *moneie.* − O.F. *moneie* (F. *monnaie*). − L. *monēta,* (1) mint, (2) money; see **Mint** (1).

Monger, a dealer, trader. (L.) Hence *iron-monger, coster-monger.* M.E. *monger*; A. S. *mangere,* a dealer, merchant; A. S. *mangian,* to traffic. − L. *mango,* a dealer.

Mongoose; see **Mungoose.**

Mongrel, an animal of a mixed breed. (E.) Spelt *mungril* in Levins (1570). It stands for **mong-er-el,* i. e. a small animal

of mixed breed; cf. *cock-er-el, pick-er-el* (small pike). − A. S. *mang,* a mixture. See **Mingle.**

Monition, a warning, notice. (F.−L.) F. *monition.* − L. acc. *monitiōnem.* − L. *monitus,* pp. of *monēre,* to advise, lit. to make to think. (✓MEN.) Brugm. ii. § 794.

Monk. (L.−Gk.) M. E. *monk.* A. S. *munuc.* − L. *monachus.* − Gk. μοναχός, adj., solitary; sb., a monk. − Gk. μόν-ος, alone.

Monkey, an ape. (Low G.−F.− Ital. − L.) Borrowed from M. Low G. *Moneke,* the name of the ape's son in Reinke de Vos (where *-ke* is for *-ken,* dimin. suffix; so that the F. version has *Monnekin*; Godefroy). Formed with Low G. dimin. suffix *-ken* = G. *-chen,* from M. F. *monne,* an ape. − M. Ital. *mona, monna,* 'an ape, a munkie, a munkie-face; also a nickname for women, as we say gammer, goodie;' Florio. *Monna* is a familiar corruption of *madonna,* i. e. my lady, mistress; Scott introduces *Monna Paula* in the Fortunes of Nigel. See **Madonna.** ¶ From the same source is M. Ital. *monicchio,* 'a pugge, a munkie, an ape;' Florio. This is the Ital. equivalent of the Low G. word.

Mono-, *prefix,* sole. (Gk.) Gk. μόνο-ς, single.

monochord, a musical instrument having but *one* string; see **Chord.** So also *mono-cotyledon, mon-ocular, mon-ode, mono-logue* (from Gk. λόγος, a speech), *mono-syllable, mono-tone* ; see **Cotyledon, Ocular, Ode, Syllable, Tone.**

monopoly, exclusive sale. (L.−Gk.) L. *monopōlium.* − Gk. μονοπώλιον, right of monopoly; μονοπωλία, monopoly. − Gk. μόνο-ς, sole; πωλεῖν, to sell, barter.

Monsoon, a periodical wind. (Ital.− Malay.− Arab.) Ital. *monsone.* − Malay *mūsim,* a season, monsoon, year. − Arab. *mawsim,* a time, season. − Arab. *wasm* (root *wasama*), marking.

Monster, a prodigy. (F.−L.) F. *monstre.* − L. *monstrum,* a divine omen, portent, warning. (For **mon-es-trum.*) − L. *mon-ēre,* to warn.

Month. (E.) M. E. *moneth,* later *month.* A. S. *mōnað,* a month; from *mōna,* moon. See **Moon.** + Du. *maand*; Icel. *mānuðr,* Dan. *maaned,* Swed. *månad*; G. *monat,* Goth. *mēnōths,* a month. Teut. stem **mēnōth-.* Cf. also Lithuan. *mėnesis,* Russ. *miesiats',* L. *mensis,* Irish and W.

mis, Gael. *mios*, Gk. μήν, Skt. *mās*, a month ; all connected with **Moon**, q.v.

Monument, a memorial. (F.–L.) F. *monument*. – L. *monumentum*, a memorial. – L. *monu-*, for *moni-*, as in *moni-tus*, pp. of *monēre*, to advise, remind; with suffix *-men-tum*.

Mood (1), disposition of mind. (E.) Prob. sometimes confused with *mood* (2), but properly distinct. M. E. *mood*, mind, also temper, anger, wrath. A.S. *mōd*, mind, courage, pride.+Du.*moed*, courage ; Icel. *mōðr*, wrath, moodiness ; Dan. Swed. *mod*, G. *muth*, courage; Goth. *mōds*, wrath. Teut. type *mō-do-* (where *-do* is a suffix). Cf. Gk. μαίομαι, I strive after. Brugm. i. § 196. **Der.** *mood-y*, A.S. *mōdig*; Sweet, N.E.G. § 1608.

Mood (2), manner, grammatical form. (F.–L.) The same word as **Mode**, q.v.; but confused with *mood* (1).

Moon. (E.) M.E. *mone*. A.S. *mōna*, a masc. sb.+Du. *maan*, Icel. *māni*, Dan. *maane*, Swed. *måne*, Goth. *mēna*, G. *mond*, O.H.G. *māno*. Teut. type *mǣnon-*, masc. Cf. also Lithuan. *mĕnŭ*, Gk. μήνη; Skt. *mās*, moon, month. Perhaps it meant the 'measurer' of time. (√ME.) See Brugm. i. § 132, ii. § 132.

Moonshee, a secretary, interpreter. (Arab.) Arab. *munshī*, a secretary, a language-master or tutor.

Moor (1), a heath. (E.) M.E. *more*. A.S. *mōr*. + M. Du. *moer*, moor, mud ; *moerlandt*, peaty land ; Icel. *mōr*, Dan. *mor*, Low G. *moor*; O.H.G. *muor*, marsh, pool, sea. Teut. type *mōro-* ; perhaps related (by gradation) to Goth. *marei*, sea, lake ; or to Skt. *maru*, a desert, mountain. See **Mere**.

Moor (2), to fasten up a ship. (E.) A.S. *mār-ian*, whence *mǣrels*, a mooring-rope. Cf. Du. *meren* (Franck), usually *marren*, to tie, bind, moor a ship.

Moor (3), a native of N. Africa. (F.– L.–Gk.) F. *More*, 'a Moor;' Cot. – L. *Maurus*. – Gk. Μαῦρος, a Moor. **Der.** *black-a-moor*, corruption of *blackmoor* (Minsheu), i.e. *black Moor*.

Moose, the American elk. (W. Indian.) The native W. Indian name ; 'Knisteneaux *mouswah*, Algonquin *musu*;' cited in the Cent. Dict. Cuoq cites Algonquin *mons* (with *n*).

Moot, to discuss a point. (E.) Chiefly used in phr. 'a *moot* point.' Minsheu gives *moot* as a verb, to discuss. The

proper sense of *moot* is 'meeting,' as in *moot-hall*, hall of assembly ; hence, to *moot* is to discuss at a meeting, and 'a *moot* point' is one reserved for public discussion. M.E. *motien*, to discuss. A.S. *mōtian*, to converse, address a meeting, discuss; from A.S. *mōt*, a meeting, also *gemōt*, esp. in phr. *witena gemōt* = meeting of wise men, parliament.+Icel. *mōt*, M.H.G. *muoz*, a meeting. Teut. base *mōt-*. **Der.** *meet*.

Mop (1), an implement for washing floors. (F.–L.) In a late ed. of Florio's Ital. Dict., *pannatore* is explained by 'a maulkin, a *map* of clouts or rags to rub withal.' Halliwell gives *mop*, a napkin; *Gloucestershire*. Prob. from O.F. *mappe*, a napkin (afterwards turned into *nappe*).– L. *mappa*, a napkin (of Punic origin). See **Map**. ¶ Cf. *strop*, *strap* ; *knop*, *knap*. The Celtic forms are from E.

Mop (2), a grimace ; to grimace. (E.) The same word as *mope* (below).

mope, to be dispirited. (E.) The same word as *mop*, to grimace; cf. 'in the *mops*,' i.e. sulky (Halliwell). + Du. *moppen*, to pout, be sulky ; M. Swed. *mopa*, to mock (Ihre) ; Westphal. *möpen*, to grimace; G. *muffig*, sullen, pouting (Flügel). Bavar. *muffen*, to growl, pout. And see *mow* (3).

Moraine, a line of stones at the edges of a glacier. (F.–Teut.) F. *moraine*; cf. Ital. *mora*, a pile of rocks. – Bavarian *mur*, sand and broken stones, fallen from rocks in a valley; the lit. sense being perhaps 'crumbled material.' Cf. G. *mürbe*, soft, O.H.G. *muruwi*; Icel. *merja*, to crush.

Moral. (F.–L.) F.*moral.*–L.*mōrālis*, relating to conduct. – L. *mōr-*, from nom. *mōs*, a manner, custom.

Morass, a bog. (Du.–F.–Low G.) Du *moeras*, marsh, fen ; M. Du. *moerasch*, adj., belonging to a moor, as if from the sb *moer*, moor, mire, but really an altered form of M. Du. *marasch*, *maerasch*, a marsh (Kilian). – O.F. *maresque*, *maresche*, adj., marshy ; also, as sb., a marsh ; Low L. *mariscus*. – Low G. *marsch*, a marsh. See **Marish, Marsh**. Cf. G. *morast* (for *morask*), Swed. *moras*, Dan. *morads*, a morass ; all from Du. or Low G.

Morbid, sickly. (F.–L.) F. *morbide*. – L.*morbidus*, sickly. – L. *morbus*, disease. Allied to *mor-ī*, to die; Brugm. ii. § 701.

Mordacity, sarcasm. (F.–L.) Little used. – F. *mordacité*. – L. acc. *mordāci-*

tātem, from *mordācitās*, power to bite. — L. *mordāc-*, stem of *mordax*, biting. — L. *mordēre*, to bite. Cf. Skt. *mardaya*, to rub, break in pieces, from *mṛd*, to rub. Brugm. ii. § 794. (√MERD.)

More. (E.) This does duty for two distinct M. E. words, viz. (1) *mo*, more in number, (2) *more*, larger. **α.** The former is from A. S. *mā*, more in number, orig. an adv. form, like G. *mehr*, Goth. *mais*. **β.** The latter is from the corresponding adj. A. S. *māra*, greater; cognate with Icel. *meiri*, Goth. *maiza*, greater. See **Most.** ¶ The notion that *mo* is a positive form is quite wrong; the positive forms are *much*, *mickle*, *many*. The *r* in *more* represents an earlier *-z-*, which in the adv. (being final) was regularly lost. Brugm. i. § 200.

Morganatic. (Low L. – G.) Low L. *morganātica*, in the phrase *matrimōnium ad morganāticam*, a morganatic marriage. Coined from G. *morgen*, here short for *morgengabe*, lit. morning-gift, orig. a present made to a wife on the morning after marriage, esp. if the wife were of inferior rank. See **Morn.**

Morian, a Moor. (F. – L. – Gk.) In Pss. lxviii. 31 ; lxxxvii, 4 (P. B. version). — O.F. *Morien, Moriaine* (Godefroy). — Late L. **Maurītānus*, for L. *Maurītānicus*, a Moor. — L. *Maurītānia*, the land of the Moors. — L. *Maur-us*, a Moor. — Gk. Μαῦρος. See **Moor** (3).

Morion, an open helmet. (F. – Span.) F. *morion*. — Span. *morrion* ; cf. Port. *morrião*, Ital. *morione*, a morion. The word is Spanish, if we may accept the prob. derivation from Span. *morra*, the crown of the head ; a word of unknown origin. Cf. Span. *morro*, anything round ; *moron*, a hillock.

Mormonite. The *Mormonites* are the followers of Joseph Smith, who in 1827 said he had found the book of *Mormon*. An invented name.

Morn. (E.) M. E. *morn*, a Northern form. Short for M. E. *morwen*, Ancren Riwle, p. 22. A. S. *morgen*, whence *morwen* by the usual change of *rg* to *rw*. O. Fries. *morn*.+Du. Dan. G. *morgen* ; Icel. *morginn*, Swed. *morgon* ; Goth. *maurgins*. Teut. type **murgenoz*, m. Cf. Lithuan. *merkti*, to blink. Orig. sense prob. 'dawn.' **Doublet,** *morrow*, q. v.

morning. (E.) Short for *morwening*, Ch. C. T., A 1062 ; formed from M. E.

morwen (above) by adding the substantival (not participial) suffix *-ing* (= A. S. *-ung*). So also *even-ing*, from *even*.

Morocco, a fine kind of leather. Named from *Morocco*, in N. Africa ; which was named from the *Moors* dwelling there.

Morose. (L.) L. *mōrōsus*, self-willed ; (1) in a good sense, scrupulous ; (2) in a bad sense, peevish. — L. *mōr-*, nom. *mōs*, (1) self-will, (2) custom, use. ¶ Confused with L. *mŏra*, delay, in the 17th cent.

Morphia, Morphine, the narcotic principle of opium. (Gk.) From Gk. Μορφεύς, Morpheus, god of dreams (Ovid); lit. 'shaper,' i. e. creator of dreams. — Gk. μορφή, a shape, form. **Der.** *meta-morphosis*, *a-morph-ous* ; from μορφή.

Morris, Morris-dance. (Span. – L. – Gk.) The dance was also called a *morisco*, i. e. a Moorish dance. — Span. *Morisco*, Moorish. — Span. *Moro*, a Moor. — L. *Maurus*, a Moor. See **Moor** (3).

Morrow. (E.) M. E. *morwe*, from an older form *morwen* (from A. S. *morgen*), by loss of final *n*. See **Morn.** Thus M. E. *morwen* gave rise (1) to *morrow*, by loss of *n* ; (2) to *morn*, by loss of *w*, and contraction ; 1208. [Or else *morne*, dat., is from A. S. *morgene*, short form *morne*.] **Der.** *to-morrow* = A. S. *tō morgene*, i. e. for the morrow, where *tō* is a prep. (E. *to*), and *morgene* is dat. case of *morgen*, morn.

Morse, a walrus. (F. – Finnish.) F. *morse*. — Finnish *mursu*, a morse ; whence also Russ. *morj'*, a morse (with *j* sounded as F.*j*). The true Russ. name is *morskaia korova*, the sea-cow.

Morsel, a mouthful, small piece. (F. – L.) M. E. *morsel*. – O. F. *morsel* (F. *morceau*). Cf. Ital. *morsello*. Dimin. from L. *morsum*, a bit. — L. *morsus*, pp. of *mordēre*, to bite. See **Mordacity.**

Mortal, deadly. (F. – L.) F. *mortal*. — L. *mortālis*, adj. ; from *mort-*, stem of *mors*, death. From L. *mor-ī*, to die ; cf. Skt. *mṛ*, to die, *mṛta*, dead ; Russ. *mertvuii*, dead ; Lithuan. *mirti*, to die ; Pers. *murdan*, to die ; Gk. βροτός, mortal. Allied to **Murder.** Brugm. i. § 500.

Mortar (1), **Morter,** a vessel in which substances are pounded with a pestle. (L.) M. E. *morter*. A.S. *mortere*. — L. *mortārium*, a mortar.

mortar (2), cement. (F. – L.) M. E. *mortier*. – F. *mortier*, 'mortar ;' Cot. – L. *mortārium*, mortar ; lit. stuff pounded together; a different use of the word above.

Mortgage, a kind of security for debt. (F.—L.) O. F. *mortgage*, lit. a dead pledge; because, whatever profit it might yield, it did not thereby redeem itself, but became dead or lost to the mortgager on breach of the condition. — F. *mort*, dead; *gage*, a pledge. — L. *mortuus*, dead, pp. of *mori*, to die; *gage*, a pledge; see **Mortal** and **Gage** (1). Der. *mortgag-ee*, where *-ee* answers to the F. *-é* of the pp.

mortify. (F.—L.) M.F. *mortifier.*— L. *mortificāre*, to cause death. — L. *morti-*, decl. stem of *mors*, death; *-ficāre*, for *facere*, to make.

Mortise, a hole in a piece of timber to receive the tenon. (F.) Spelt *mortesse* in Palsgrave.— F. *mortaise*, 'a mortaise in a piece of timber;' Cot. Cf. Span. *mortaja*, a mortise. Orig. unknown; Devic suggests Arab. *murtazz*, fixed in the mark (said of an arrow), very tenacious (said of a miser).

Mortmain. (F.—L.) Property transferred to the church was said to pass into *morte main*, lit. 'dead hand,' because it could not be alienated. — L. *mortuam*, acc. fem. of *mort-uus*, dead; *manum*, acc. of *manus*, hand. See **Mortal**.

mortuary, belonging to the burial of the dead. (L.) Chiefly in the phr. 'a *mortuary* fee,' which was also called *mortuary* for short. — Late L. *mortuārium*, neut. of *mortuārius*, belonging to the dead. —L. *mortu-us*, dead; pp. of *morī*, to die.

Mosaic-work, ornamental work made with small pieces of marble, &c. (F.— Ital.—L.—Gk.) F. *mosaïque*, 'mosaicall work ;' Cot.—Ital. *mosaico*, 'a kinde of curious stone worke of diuers colours ;' Florio.—Late L. *mūsaicus*, adj., an extended form from L. *mūsæum* (*opus*), mosaic work.—Late Gk. μουσεῖον, mosaic work, lit. artistic, neut. of μουσεῖος, belonging to the muses, artistic. — Gk. μοῦσα, a muse. Cf. **Museum.**

Moslem, a Mussulman. (Arab.) Arab. *muslim*, 'a musulman, a true believer in the Mohammedan faith ;' Richardson. Cf. Arab. *musallim*, one who acquiesces. A *mussulman* is one who professes *islām*, i. e. submission to the will of God and to the orthodox faith. — Arab. *salama*, to be resigned. ¶ The E. words *moslem, mussulman, islam,* and *salaam* are all from the same Arab. root *salama.*

Mosque, a Mohammedan temple. (F. — Span. — Arab.) F. *mosquée* ; Cot. — Span. *mezquita*, a mosque. — Arab. *masjad, masjid*, a temple, place of prayer. — Arab. root *sajada*, to adore, prostrate oneself.

Mosquito, a gnat. (Span.—L.) Span. *mosquito*, a little gnat ; dimin. of *mosca*, a fly.— L. *musca*, a fly. Cf. Gk. μυῖα, Lithuan. *musè*, a fly.

Moss. (E.) M. E. *mos* ; A. S. *mos*, a swamp.+Du. *mos* ; Icel. *mosi*, moss, also a moss or moorland ; Dan. *mos*, moss, *mose*, a bog, moor ; Swed. *mossa* ; G. *moos*, moss, a swamp, O. H. G. *mos*. Teut. base **mus-* ; allied to M. H. G. *mies*, O. H. G. *mios*, A. S. *mēos*, moss (Teut. base **meus-*); and to **Mire.** Cognate with Russ. *mokh'*, moss, L. *muscus*, moss. ¶ Note E. *moss* in sense of bog, moorland ; hence *moss-trooper.* Brugm. i. § 105.

Most. (E.) M. E. *most, mēst.*—A. S. *mǣst.*+Du. *meest,* Icel. *mestr,* G. *meist,* Goth. *maists* ; the superlative form corresponding to comp. *more.* See **More.** ¶ The *o* (for early M. E. *ē*) is due to the *o* in *more.*

Mote, a particle of dust, speck. (E.) M. E. *mot.* A. S. *mot,* a mote.+Du. *mot,* sawdust ; E. Fries. *mut,* grit.

Motet, Motett, a short piece of sacred music. (F.—L.) F. *motet,* 'a verse in musick ;' Cot. [Ital. *mottetto,* 'a dittie, a wittie saying ;' Florio.] Dimin. of O. F. *mot,* a saying.—L. *muttum,* a murmur ; see **Motto.**

Moth. (E.) M. E. *mothe.* A.S. *moððe, mohðe.* + Du. *mot,* Icel. *motti,* G. *motte,* a moth ; Swed. *mått,* a mite. β. Perhaps related to A.S. *maða,* a maggot, Du. G. *made,* a maggot, Goth. *matha,* a worm. Kluge allies these forms to the verb *to mow,* i. e. to cut, as if the sense were 'cutter.' Cf. E. *after-math.*

Mother (1), a female parent. (E.) M. E. *moder.* A. S. *mōder, mōdor,* a mother ; the change from *d* to *th* is late, after A. D. 1400.+Du. *moeder,* Icel. *moðir,* Dan. Swed. *moder,* G. *mutter* ; Irish and Gael. *mathair* ; Russ. *mate,* Lithuan. *motè,* L. *māter,* Gk. μήτηρ, Pers. *mādar,* Skt. *mātā, mātṛ-.* Orig. sense uncertain.

mother (2), hysterical passion. (E.) In King Lear, ii. 4. 56. Spelt *moder* in Palsgrave ; and the same word as the above.+Du. *moeder,* a mother, womb, hysterical passion ; cf. G. *mutterbeschwerung,* mother-fit, hysterical passion.

Mother (3), lees, mouldiness. (E.) A peculiar use of **Mother** (1). Cf. Du. *moer*, lees, dregs, mother, variant of *moeder*, a mother (Franck). So also G. *mutter* (1), a mother, (2) mother, sediment. We even find Gk. γραῦς, an old woman, used in the sense of mother or dregs. ¶ Not to be connected with Low G. *mudder*, mud; or with E. *mud*.

Motion. (F. – L.) F. *motion*. – L. *mōtiōnem*, acc. of *mōtio*, movement. – L. *mōtus*, pp. of *mouēre*, to move. See **Move.**

motive. (F. – L.) M. F. *motif*, 'a moving reason;' Cot. – Late L. *mōtīvus*, moving. – L. *mōt-us*, pp. of *mouēre*, to move.

motor. (L.) L. *mōt-or*, a mover.

Motley, of different colours. (F.) M.E. *mottelee*, Ch. C. T. 271. Of uncertain origin. Perhaps from O. F. *mattelé*, 'clotted, curdled;' Cot. Cf. M. F. *mattonné*, as in *ciel mattonné*, 'a skie full of small curdled clouds;' id. [Thus the orig. sense of *motley* was merely 'spotted.'] ‒ Bavarian *matte*, curds (Schmeller). 2. Or from O. F. *motel*, M. F. *motteau*, 'a clot of congealed moisture,' Cot.; app. a deriv. of M. F. *motte*, a clod, lump; see **Moat.** Der. *mottl-ed*, for O. F. *mattelé* above, by substituting the E. pp. suffix -*ed* for the F. pp. suffix -*é*.

Motto. (Ital. – L.) Ital. *motto*, a saying, a motto. – L. *muttum*, a murmur, muttered sound; cf. L. *muttīre*, *mūtīre*, to murmur. (√MU.) Allied to **Mutter.**

Mould (1), earth. (E.) M. E. *molde*. A. S. *molde*, dust, soil, earth.+Icel. *mold*, Dan. *muld*, Swed. *mull* (for **muld*), mould; Goth. *mulda*, dust; O. H. G. *molta*, mould. Allied to the shorter forms seen in Du. *mul*, G. *mull*, A. S. *myl*, dust; cf. O. H. G. *muljan*, Icel. *mylja*, to crush. The lit. sense is 'crumbled.' From Teut. *mul*, weak grade of √MEL, to grind. See **Meal, Mill.** Der. *mould-er*, to crumble; also *mould-y* (which seems to have been confused with **Mole** (1), q. v.).

Mould (2), a model, form. (F. – L.) M. E. *molde*, with excrescent *d*. – Norman dial. *molde*, O. F. *mole*, *molle* (F. *moule*), a mould; once spelt *modle* in the 12th cent. (Littré). – L. *modulum*, acc. of *modulus*, dimin. of *modus*, a measure. See **Mode.**

Mould (3), a spot. (E.) For *mole*; *mold* in Spenser, F. Q. vi. 12. 7. 'One yron

mole defaceth the whole peece of lawne,' Lyly, Euphues, p. 39. This is now called *iron-mould* (with added *d*). We also find M. E. *moled*, spotted; hence mod. E. *mouldy* (in some senses); by confusion with *mould* (1). See **Mole** (1).

Mouldy, musty. (Scand.) Orig. distinct from *mould*, ground; also from mould as used in *iron-mould*. Formed from the sb. *mould*, mustiness, in which the final *d* is excrescent. From the M. E. verb *moulen*, *mowlen*, to grow musty; formerly very common, and much used in the pp. *mouled*. Note also the M. E. *moul*, mould, mouldiness, answering to Dan. *mul*, Swed. dial. *mul*, *muel*, *mujel*, Swed. *mögel*. Cf. also Dan. *mullen*, mouldy, *mulne*, to become mouldy; Swed. dial. *mulas*, Swed. *möglas*, to grow mouldy; Icel. *mygla*, to grow musty. From *mug-*, as in Icel. *mugga*, mugginess. See **Muggy.** Thus *mould* is 'mugginess' in this use.

Moult, to cast feathers, as birds. (L.) The *l* is intrusive. M. E. *mouten*. A. S. *mūtian* (in comp. *bi-mūtian*). – L. *mūtāre*, to change. See **Mutable.**

Mound, an earthen defence, a hillock. (F. – L.) A. F. *mund*, variant of *munt*, a hill (Vie de S. Auban). – L. *montem*, acc. of *mons*, a hill. ¶ Note also A. S. *mund*, protection, chiefly as a law-term; but also *mund-beorh*, a protecting hill, a mound.

Mount (1), a hill. (F. – L.) M. E. *mount*, *mont*. – F. *mont*. – L. *mont-*, stem of *mons*, a hill. – √MEN, to jut out; see **Mound.** Cf. A. S. *munt* (borrowed from L.).

mount (2), to ascend. (F. – L.) F. *monter*. – F. *mont*, a hill. [The verb is due to O. F. *a mont*, up-hill.] – L. *montem*, acc. of *mons* (above).

mountain. (F. – L.) O. F. *montaine* (F. *montagne*). – Late L. *montānea*, by-form of *montāna*, a mountain. – L. *montāna*, neut. pl., mountainous regions; from *montānus*, adj. from *mons* (stem *mont-*), a mountain.

mountebank, a quack doctor. (Ital. – L. *and* G.) Lit. one who *mounts a bench*, to proclaim his nostrums. – Ital. *montambanco*, a mountebank; M. Ital. *monta in banco*, the same. – Ital. *montare*, to mount; *in*, on; *banco*, a bench. Here *montare* is the same word as F. *monter*, to mount; *in* = L. *in*, on; and *banco* is from O. H. G. *banc*, a bench; see **Bank** (2).

Mourn. (E.) M. E. *murnen*. A. S

murnan, to grieve.+Icel. *morna,* Goth. *maurnan,* O. H. G. *mornēn.* Cf. A. S. *meornan,* to care, Gk. μέρ-ιμνα, sorrow. (√SMER.)

Mouse. (E.) M. E. *mous.* A. S. *mūs* (pl. *mȳs*). + Du. *muis,* Icel. *mūs,* Dan. *muus,* Swed. *mus,* G. *maus,* Russ. *muishe,* L. *mūs,* Gk. μῦς, Pers. *mūsh,* a mouse; Skt. *mūsha-,* a rat, a mouse. Perhaps from √MEUS, to steal; Skt. *mush,* to steal. See **Muscle** (1).

Moustache, Mustache. (F.—Ital. —Gk.) F. *moustache.* — Ital. *mostaccio,* 'a face, a snout, a mostacho;' Florio.— Gk. μύστακ-, stem of μύσταξ, the upper lip, a moustache, Doric form of μάσταξ, the mouth, upper lip. See **Mastic.**

Mouth. (E.) M. E. *mouth.* A. S. *mūð.*+Du. *mond,* Icel. *munnr,* Dan. *mund,* Swed. *mun,* G. *mund,* Goth. *munths.* Teut. type *munthoz,* masc.; Idg. type *mntos*; cf. L. *mentum,* the chin.

Move. (F.—L.) M. E. *mouen* (*u* = *v*). — O. F. *movoir* (F. *mouvoir*).—L. *mouēre,* to move, pp. *mōtus.* **Der.** *motion.*

Mow (1), to cut grass. (E.) M. E. *mowen,* pt. t. *mew.* A. S. *māwan,* to mow, strong vb. + Du. *maaijen,* Dan. *meie,* G. *mähen,* O. H. G. *māen.* Teut. base *mæ-.* Allied to Gk. ἀ-μά-ω, I reap, L. *me-t-ere,* to reap. Brugm. ii. § 680.

Mow (2), a heap, pile of hay or corn. (E.) M. E. *mowe,* A. S. *mūga,* a mow. + Icel. *mūgr,* a swathe, also a crowd; Norw. *muga, mua,* a heap (of hay). Cf. **Muck.**

Mow (3), a grimace; *obsolete.* (F.— M. Du.) F. *moue,* 'a moe, or mouth;' Cot.; Norman dial. *moe.* — M. Du. *mouwe,* the protruded under-lip, in making a grimace (Oudemans). Cf. **Mop** (2).

Much. (E.) M. E. *moche, muche,* adj., later forms of M. E. *mochel, muchel, michel.* For the loss of final *l,* cf. E. *wench,* from A. S. *wencel.* The change of vowel (from *michel* to *muchel*) seems to have been due to association with M. E. *lutel,* little, from A. S. *lȳtel.* The orig. A. S. form was *micel* (cf. Low Sc. *mickle*), great. + Icel. *mikill,* great; O. H. G. *mihhil*; Goth. *mikils.* Cf. Gk. μεγάλ-η, fem. of μέγας, great.

Mucilage, a slimy substance, gum. (F.—L.) F. *mucilage.*—L. *mūcilāgo* (stem *mūcilāgin-*), mouldy moisture (4th cent.). —L. *mūcēre,* to be mouldy.

Muck, filth. (Scand.) M. E. *muck.* — Icel. *myki,* dung; *møka,* to shovel dung

out of a stable; Dan. *møg,* dung; Norw. *mok-dunge,* a muck-heap, allied to *mukka,* a heap. ¶ Not allied to A. S. *meox,* dung.

Muck, Amuck, a term applied to malicious rage. (Malay.) Only in phr. 'to run amuck,' where *amuck* is all one word; yet Dryden actually has 'runs *an Indian muck,*' Hind and Panther, iii. 1188. To *run amuck* = to run about in a rage. — Malay *āmuk,* 'rushing in a state of frenzy to the commission of indiscriminate murder;' Marsden.

Mucus, slimy fluid. (L.) L. *mūcus,* slime. + Gk. μύξα, mucus; μύκης, snuff of a wick. Cf. Skt. *much,* L. *mungere,* Gk. ἀπο-μύσσειν, to cast or wipe away.

Mud, wet soft earth, mire. (E.) M. E. *mud* (not common). Not found in A. S. Cf. E. Fries. *mudde,* Low G. *mudde,* mud; M. Swed. *modd,* mud (Ihre). + Bavarian *mott,* peat; whence E. *moat,* q. v. Cf. Du. *modder,* mud.

muddle, to confuse. (E.) Lit. to dabble in mud; frequentative from *mud.* '*Muddle,* to rout with the bill, as geese and ducks do; also, to make tipsy and unfit for business;' Kersey.+Dan. *muddre,* to stir up mud, *mudder,* mud (from Du.); E. Fries. *muddelen,* to dirty; M. Du. *moddelen,* 'to mudd water,' Hexham; Pomeran. *muddeln,* to disorder.

Muezzin, a Mohammedan crier of the hour of prayer. (Arab.) Arab. *mu-azzin, mu-zin,* the public crier, who assembles people to prayers. — Arab. *azan,* the call to prayers (Palmer); *uzn,* the ear.

Muff (1), a warm, soft cover for the hands. (Walloon.—F.—Low L.) A late word. Formerly *muffe*; Minsheu. Prob. from Walloon *mouffe* (Sigart). Cf. Du. *mof*; Low G. *muff* (Berghaus); E. Fries. *muf.* The word *muffle* is found earlier, and is more widely spread; so that Wall. *mouffe* is merely a short form of F. *moufle*; see below.

muffle, to cover up warmly. (F.— Low L.) 'I *muffyll*;' Palsgrave. 'A *muffle*;' Levins (1570). — O. F. *mofle, moufle,* a kind of muff or mitten.—Low L. *muffula,* (occurring A. D. 817); also spelt *mulfola.* Cf. M. Du. *moffel,* a muff, mitten. ¶ The late appearance of Du. *mof,* and the Low L. form *mulfola,* remain unexplained. Cf.M.H.G.*mouwe,* a sleeve.

Muff (2), a simpleton. (E.) Lit. 'a mumbler,' or indistinct speaker; hence a stupid fellow. Cf. prov. E. *muff, muffle,*

to mumble; also *moffle, maffle.* **+** Du.
muffen, to dote; prov. G. *muffen,* to be
sulky. Allied to **Mumble.**

Muffle; see **Muff** (1).

Mufti, a magistrate. (Arab.) Arab.
muftī, a magistrate. Allied to Arab.
fatwā, a judgment, doom, sentence. ¶ The
phr. *in mufti* means in a civilian costume,
not in military dress.

Mug. (Low G.) In Levins (1570). Cf.
Irish *mugan,* a mug; Norw. *mugga, mug-
ge,* an open can; Swed. *mugg,* a mug. – E.
Fries. *mukke,* a cylindrical earthen vessel;
Groningen *mokke* (Molema, p. 543);
whence also Norm. dial. *moque,* a cup,
Guernsey *mogue.*

Muggy, damp and close. (Scand.)
From Icel. *mugga,* soft drizzling mist;
whence *mugguveðr,* muggy, misty weather.
Cf. Norw. *mugg,* fine rain; *muggen,* moist,
muggy; Dan. *muggen,* musty, mouldy;
mugne, to grow musty.

Mugwort, a plant. (E.) M. E. *mog-
wort.* A.S. *mucgwort.* For the latter
syllable, see **Wort** (1). The sense of
A.S. *mucg* is unknown, unless it be a by-
form of A.S. *mycg,* a midge; cf. Norw.
mugg, O. Sax. *muggia,* Du. *mug,* a midge;
O.H.G. *mucca,* a midge. [Like *flea-
bane.*]

Mulatto, one of mixed breed. (Span.
– L.)   Span. *mulato,* a mulatto. Usually
derived from Span. *mula,* a she-mule, as
being one of a mixed breed. ¶ The usual
forms for 'young mule' are *muleto,* m.,
muleta, f. Hence der. by De Sacy from
Arab. *muwallad,* lit. 'begotten'; also
used to mean 'one who has an Arabian
father and a foreign mother'; allied to
Arab. *walad,* a son. See Devic.

Mulberry. (L. *and* E.) M.E. *mool-
bery.* Here the *l* stands for an older *r,*
by dissimilation; and M. E. *oo* answers to
A. S. *ō,* as usual. Thus the M. E. *mool-
is* the same as A.S. *mōr-,* in *mōr-
bēam,* a mulberry-tree. Again, the A.S.
mōr is borrowed from L. *mōrus,* a mulberry-tree. The word *berry* is E.; see
Berry. Cf. also Gk. μῶρον, μόρον, a mulberry, μορέα, a mulberry-tree. ¶ Similarly,
G. *maulbeere,* a mulberry, is O. H. G.
mūrberi, from L. *mōrus* and O. H. G.
beri, G. *beere.*

Mulct, a fine. (L.) L. *mulcta,* a fine;
also spelt *multa.* Perhaps orig. 'damage;'
from L. *mulc-āre,* to injure. Brugm. i.
§ 756. Der. *mulct,* verb.

Mule. (F. – L.) F. *mule.* – L. *mūlus,*
a mule (whence also A. S. *mūl*).

Mulled, applied to ale or wine. (E.)
Mulled wine first appears in 1618, and is
of uncertain origin. Perhaps from M. E.
mullen, to break to powder, to crumble,
from *mull,* powder, perhaps with reference
to the powdered condiments. From A.S.
myl, powder. Blount's Gloss. has *vinum
mollitum,* as if from F. *mollir,* L. *mollīre,*
to soften.

Mullein, the verbascum. (F.) M. E.
moleyn. A. F. *moleine;* F. *molène.* The
M. E. name was *softe,* i. e. the soft. This
suggests a derivation from O. F. *mol,* soft;
from L. *mollis,* soft.

Mullet (1), a fish. (F. – L.) M. E.
molet, mulet. – F. *mulet;* Cot. Dimin.
from L. *mullus,* the red mullet.

Mullet (2), a five-pointed star. (F. –
L.) O. F. *molette,* a rowell, whence it
came to mean the 'mullet' of heraldry;
also M. F. *mollette,* 'a mullet, rowell of
a spur;' Cot. Dimin. from L. *mola,* a
mill, whence Ital. *mola,* a mill-stone, mill-
wheel, *molla,* a clock-wheel with cogs.
See **Mill.**

Mulligatawny, a hot soup. (Tamil.)
Tamil *milagu-tannir,* lit. 'pepper-water;'
Yule. Cf. Malayalam *mulaka,* pepper.

Mullion, an upright division between
lights of windows. (F.)   A corruption of
munnion, which occurs with the same
sense. The lit. sense is 'stump,' because
the *mullion* is, properly, the stump or
lower part of the division below the
tracery. – F. *moignon,* a stump. (Cf. E.
trunnion = M.F.*troignon,* dimin.of F.*tronc*
= Ital. *tronco.*) – O. F. *moing,* maimed
(Suppl. to Diez). Cf. Bret. *mouñ, moñ,*
maimed, also occurring in the forms *mank,
moñk, moñs.* Also Span. *muñon,* the stump
of an arm or leg; Ital. *mugnone,* 'a carpenter's munion or trunion,' Torriano.

Multangular, &c.; see **Multitude.**

Multitude. (F. – L.) F. *multitude.*
– L. *multitūdinem,* acc. of *multitūdo,* a
multitude. – L. *multi-,* for *multus,* many,
much; with suffix *-tūdo.* From L. *multus*
come also *mult-angular, multi-lateral,*
&c.

multifarious. (L.) L. *multifāri-us,*
manifold; with suffix *-ous.* The orig.sense
seems to be 'many-speaking,' i.e. speaking
on many subjects. – L. *multi-,* for *multus,*
many; *fārī,* to speak; see **Fate.**

multiply. (F. – L.) F. *multiplier.*

339

– L. *multiplicāre.* **– L.** *multiplic-,* from *multiplex,* many-fold; cf. *plic-āre,* to fold. See **Plait.**

Mum, a kind of beer (Low G.). In Pope. Said to have been so named after Chr. *Mumm,* a brewer of Brunswick (ab. 1487). Cf. Du. *mom* in Franck; G. *mumme.*

Mum! silence! (E.) M. E. *mom, mum,* to express the least sound made with closed lips. Cf. L. *mu,* Gk. μῦ (the same).

mumble, to speak indistinctly. (E.) For *mumm-le.* M. E. *momelen, mamelen,* to speak indistinctly; frequent. form due to M. E. *mom,* mum (above). **+** E. Fries. *mummelen;* Du. *mommelen.*

mummer, a masker, buffoon. (F. – Du.) M. F. *mommeur,* 'a mummer, one that goes a-mumming;' Cot. **–** M. Du. *mommen,* to go a-mumming; cf. *momaensicht,* a mummer's mask; Low G. *mumme,* a mask. **β.** The word is imitative, from the sound *mum* or *mom,* used by nurses to frighten or amuse children, at the same time pretending to cover their faces. Cf. G. *mummel,* a bug-bear. **Der.** *mummer-y,* M. F. *mommerie* (F. *momerie*).

Mummy. (F. – Ital. – Arab. – Pers.) F. *momie* (*mumie* in Cotgrave). **–** Ital. *mummia, mumia* (Florio). **–** Arab. *mūmiyā,* a mummy; the substance with which mummies are preserved. (Cf. Pers. *mūmāyin,* a mummy.) **–** Pers. *mūm, mōm,* wax; much used in embalming.

Mump, to mumble, sulk, beg. (Du.) A *mumper* was a cant term for a beggar. **–** Du. *mompen,* to mump, cheat (Sewel); cf. *mommelen, mompelen,* to mumble (Hexham). Thus *mump* is merely an emphatic form of *mum,* M. Du. *mommen,* to say mum, also to mask. Cf. Norw. *mumpa,* to munch. See **Mumble.**

mumps. (Du.) 'To have the *mumps*' or 'to be in the *mumps*' was to be sulky or sullen; hence it was transferred to the disease which gave one a sullen appearance. From *mump* (above).

Munch, to chew. (E.) M. E. *monchen* (Chaucer). Doubtless an imitative word, like *mump.* Kilian has M. Du. *moncken, mompelen,* 'mussitare.' Cf. E. Fries. and Low G. *munkeln,* to mumble; and see **Mump.** ¶ It cannot be from F. *manger* (< L. *mandūcāre*).

Mundane, worldly. (F. – L.) M. E. *mondain.* – F. *mondain.* – L. *mundānus,* adj. from *mundus,* the world (lit. order). –

L. *mundus,* clean, adorned. **Der.** *supramundane;* from L. *suprā,* above; *mundus,* the world.

Mungoose, a kind of ichneumon. (Telugu.) Telugu *mangīsu;* 'Jerdon gives *mangūs,* however, as a Deccani and Mahratti word;' Yule.

Municipal. (F. – L.) F. *municipal.* – L. *mūnicipālis,* relating to a township. – L. *mūnicipium,* a township which had the rights of Roman citizenship, whilst retaining its own laws. – L. *mūnicip-,* stem of *mūniceps,* a free citizen, one who undertakes duties. – L. *mūni-,* for *munus,* obligation, duty; *capere,* to take. See Brugm. i. § 208.

munificence, liberality. (F. – L.) F. *munificence.* – L. *mūnificentia;* formed from *mūnificus,* bountiful. – L. *mūni-,* for *munus,* a duty, also a present; *-fic-,* for *facere,* to make.

Muniment, a defence, title-deed. (F. – L.) M.F. *muniment.* – L. *mūnimentum,* a defence. – L. *mūnīre,* to fortify; old form *moenire.* **–** L. *moenia,* neut. pl., walls, ramparts, defences. Brugm. i. § 208.

munition. (F. – L.) F. *munition.* – L. acc. *mūnītiōnem,* a defending. – L. *mūnītus,* pp. of *mūnīre* (above). **Der.** *ammunition.*

Munnion, old form of **Mullion,** q. v.

Mural. (F. – L.) F. *mural.* **–** L. *mūrālis,* belonging to a wall. – L. *mūrus,* a wall.

Murder, Murther, sb. (E.) M.E. *mordre, morthre.* A. F. *murdre,* sb.; *murdrir,* vb. A.S. *morðor.* **+** Goth. *maurthr.* **β.** We also find A. S. *morð,* Du. *moord,* Icel. *morð,* G. *mord,* murder, death, cognate with L. *mors* (stem *mort-*); see **Mortal. Der.** *murder,* vb.

Muriatic, briny. (L.) L. *muriāticus,* lying in brine. – L. *muria,* brine, salt liquor.

Muricated, prickly. (L.) L. *mūricātus,* prickly. – L. *mūric-,* stem of *mūrex,* a prickly fish, a spike. **+** Gk. μύαξ (for *μύσαξ), a sea-muscle; from μῦς, a mouse, a sea-muscle. See **Muscle** (2).

Murky, Mirky. (Scand.) The *-y* is a modern addition. M. E. *mirke, merke.* **–** Icel. *myrkr* (for *mirkwoz,* Noreen), Dan. Swed. *mörk,* dark, mirky. **+** A.S. *mirce;* O. Sax. *mirki.* ¶ The A. S. form would have given *mirch.*

Murmur, sb. (F. – L.) F. *murmure.* **–** L. *murmur,* a murmur; *murmurāre,* to murmur.+Skt. *marmara-*, rustling sound of wind. A reduplicated form; cf. G. *murren*, Icel. *murra*, to murmur. Of imitative origin. Brugm. i. § 499.

Murrain, cattle-disease. (F. L.) M. E. *moreine*, also *morin*. — O. F. *morine*, a carcase of a beast, also a murrain; Norm. dial. *murine*. Cf. Span. *morriña*, Port. *morrinha*, murrain. = O. F. *morir* (F. *mourir*), to die. — L. *morī*, to die. See **Mortal**.

Murrey, dark red; *heraldic*. (F.—L.) In Palsgrave. — M. F. *morée*, 'a kind of murrey, or dark red colour;' Cot. [Cf. Ital. *morato*, mulberry-coloured.] — L. *mōrum*, a mulberry. See **Mulberry**.

Murrion; see Morion.

Muscadel, Muscatel, Muscadine. (F.—Ital.—L.—Pers.) M.F. *muscadel*. = M. Ital. *moscadello, moscatello, moscatino*, names of wines, from their perfume. — M. Ital. *moscato*, scented with musk. — M. Ital. *musco*, musk. — L. *muscum*, acc. of *muscus*, musk; see further under **Musk**. And see **Nutmeg**.

Muscle (1), the fleshy part of the body. (F.—L.) F. *muscle*. — L. *musculum*, acc. of *musculus*, (1) a little mouse, (2) a muscle, from its creeping appearance when moved. Dimin. of L. *mūs*, a mouse; see **Mouse**. (Cf. F. *souris*, (1) mouse, (2) muscle.)

muscle (2), **mussel**, a shell-fish. (L.) In earlier use. M. E. *muscle*, A.S. *muxle, muscle* (Wright), a muscle (fish). — L. *musculus*, a sea-muscle, also a little mouse (as above).

Muscoid, moss-like. (L. *with* Gk. suffix.) L. *musco-*, for *muscus*, moss; and Gk. suffix -ειδης, like, from ειδος, form. See **Moss**.

Muse (1), to meditate. (F.—L.) M. E. *musen*.—F. *muser*, 'to muse, dreame;' Cot. — O. F. *muse*, the mouth, muzzle (Godefroy); see **Muzzle**. The image is that of a dog sniffing the air when in doubt as to the scent; cf. Ital. *musare*, to muse, also to gape about, 'to hould ones musle or snout in the aire,' Florio, from Ital. *muso*, snout.

Muse (2), a goddess of the arts. (F.— L. — Gk.) F. *muse*. — L. *mūsa*. — Gk. μοῦσα, a muse.

museum. (L.—Gk.) L. *mūsēum*. — Gk. μουσεῖον, temple of the muses, a study, a school. — Gk. μοῦσα, a muse.

Mushroom. (F.—O. H. G.) M. E.

muscheron. — M.F. *mouscheron, mousseron*, a mushroom; extended from F. *mousse*, moss (Hatzfeld). — O. H. G. *mos* (G. *moos*), moss; see **Moss**.

Music. (F.—L.—Gk.) M. E. *musik*. — F. *musique*. — L. *mūsica*. — Gk. μουσική, musical art, fem. of μουσικός, belonging to the muses. — Gk. μοῦσα, a muse.

Musit, a small gap in a hedge. (F.— C. ?) M. F. *mussette*, 'a little hole;' Cot. Dimin. of O.F. *musse*, a secret corner. — F. *musser*, to hide. Perhaps of Celt. origin; cf. O. Irish *mūch-aim*, I hide (Thurneysen, p. 108).

Musk, a perfume. (F.—L.—Gk.—Pers.) F. *musc*. — L. *muscum*, acc. of *muscus*. — Gk. μόσχος. — Pers. *musk, misk*. Cf. Skt. *mushka*, a testicle, because musk was obtained from a bag behind the musk-deer's navel; it also means 'little mouse,' from *mush*, to steal. See **Mouse**.

Musket. (F.—Ital.—L.) M. F. *mousquet*, a musket, orig. a kind of hawk; (another sort of gun was called a *falconet*, another a *saker*, a kind of hawk). — Ital. *mosquetto*, a musket, orig. a kind of hawk, so called from its small size. Deriv. of Ital. *mosca*, a fly. — L. *musca*, a fly. **Doublet**, *mosquito*.

Muslin. (F. — Ital. — Syriac.) F. *mousseline*; O. F. *mosolin*. — Ital. *mussolino*, dimin. of *mussolo*, muslin. — Syriac *Mosul*, a city in Kurdistan, whence it first came; Arab. *Mawsil* (the same).

Musquito; see Mosquito.

Mussel; see Muscle (2).

Mussulman, a true believer in the Mohammedan faith. (Pers. — Arab.) Pers. *musulmān*, an orthodox believer. — Arab. *moslim, muslim*, a moslem; see **Moslem**.

Must (1), part of a verb implying 'obligation.' (E.) Only the pt. t. remains, which is now only used as a present. M. E. *mot, moot*, preterito-pres. t., I am able, I am free to, I ought; pt. t. *moste, muste*, I was able, I ought. A. S. *ic mōt*, preterito-pres. t.; *ic mōste*, I must, new pt. t.; infin. **mōtan.*+O. Sax. **mōtan*, pr. t. *ik mōt*, pt. t. *ik mōsta*; Du. *moeten*, to be obliged; Swed. *måste*, I must (compare the E. use); G. *müssen*, pr. t. *ich muss*, pt. t. *ich musste*; Goth. pr. t. *ik ga-mot*, pt. t. *ik ga-mosta*, lit. 'I find room.'

Must (2), new wine. (L.) M. E. *must*. A. S. *must*. — L. *mustum*, new wine; neut. of *mustus*, fresh, new.

Mustachio; see Moustache.

Mustang, a wild horse of the prairies. (Span.—L.) Span. *mesteño* (with *ñ* as *ny*), formerly *mestengo* (Pineda), in the same sense as *mostrenco*, adj., stray, having no owner. The adj. *mesteño* also means belonging to a ' mesta.'—Span. *mesta*, a body of proprietors of cattle, a company of graziers.—L. *mixta*, fem. of pp. of *miscēre*, to mingle. Cf. Span. *mestura*, a mixture.

Mustard. (F.—L.; *with* Teut. *suffix.*) M. E. *mostard.*—O. F. *mostarde* (F. *moutarde*). Cf. Ital. *mostarda*. It took its name from being mixed with *must* or vinegar (Littré).—L. *mustum*, must; with suffix -*ard* (<G. *hart*).

Muster. (F.—L.) M. E. *moustre*, a muster of men, lit. display.—O. F. *mostre*, another form of *monstre*, ' a pattern, also a muster, view, shew;' Cot. The fem. form of F. *monstre*, a monster; see Monster. Cf. O. Norm. dial. *mustrer*, Gascon *mustra*, to shew.

Musty, mouldy, damp. (L.) A doublet of *moisty*, used by Chaucer in the sense of 'new,' but by Ascham in the sense of ' moist.'—L. *musteus*, like must, new.—L. *mustum*, must. See Must (2). Perhaps influenced by F. *moisi*, ' mouldy, musty, fusty,' Cot.; from which, however, it cannot possibly be derived.

Mutable. (L.) M. E. *mutable.*—L. *mūtābilis*, changeable.—L. *mūtāre*, to change. Prob. for **moitāre*; allied to *mūtuus*, mutual, and to Gk. μοῖτος, thanks, favour (Prellwitz).

Mutchkin, a pint. (Du.) From M. Du. *mudseken* (for **mutseken*), ' the halfe pint of Paris measure,' Hexham. Lit. ' small cap;' dimin. of M. Du. *mutse* (Du. *muts*), a cap. Cf. G. *mütze*, a cap. See Amice (2).

Mute (1), dumb. (L.) From L. *mūtus*, dumb. Cf. Skt. *mūka*-, dumb. ¶ The M. E. *muet*, *mewet*, mute, is from a Romanic form **mūtettus*, formed from L. *mūt-us* (O. F. *mu*) by adding -*ettus*.

Mute (2), to dung; used of birds. (F.—M. Du.) M. F. *mutir*, ' to mute as a hawke;' Cot. Short for M. F. *es-meutir*, the same; oldest spelling *esmeltir*. —M. Du. *smelten*, *smilten*, to smelt, to liquefy; also to mute (Hexham). See Smelt.

Mutilate. (L.) From pp. of L. *mutilāre*, to maim.—L. *mutilus*, maimed. +Gk. μύτιλος, μίτυλος, curtailed, docked.

Mutiny. (F.—L.) Formed from the old verb to *mutine*; Haml. iii. 4. 83.—F. *mutiner*, ' to mutine;' Cot.—O. F. *mutin*, tumultuous. — O. F. *mute*, a sedition ; (cf. Low L. *mōta*, a pack of hounds = mod. F. *meute*). — Folk-L. **movita*, (lit. moved, hence, a movement, bustle), fem. of **movitus*, new pp. of *mouēre*, to move. Cf. mod. F. *émeute*. See Move.

Mutter, to murmur. (E.) M. E. *muttren*, *moteren*. A frequentative verb, from a base *mut-*, to express inarticulate mumbling, as in E. Fries. *motjen*, to mutter; Swed. dial. *mutla*, *muttra*, Norw. *mutra*. So also L. *muttīre*, *mūtīre*, to mutter, prov. G. *mustern*, to whisper.

Mutton. (F.—C.?) M. E. *motoun.*—O. F. *moton* (F. *mouton*), a sheep; Low L. *multo*, a sheep. Cf. Ital. *montone* (for **moltone*), a sheep. Prob. of Celtic origin, from Celt. type **moltos*, a sheep; whence Irish and Manx *molt*, Gael. *mult*, W. *mollt*, Corn. *mols*, Bret. *maout*, a wether sheep. ¶ Diez cites Prov. *mout*, Como *mot*, Grisons *mutt*, castrated, and derives all from L. *mutilus*, maimed; but this is not now accepted.

Mutual. (F. — L.) O. F. *mutuël.* Extended from L. *mūtu-us*, mutual, reciprocal, orig. ' exchanged.'—L. *mūtāre*, to change. See Mutable.

Muzzle, snout. (F.—L.) M. E. *mosel.* —O. F. *musel* (Burguy), *muzel* (A. D. 1521, Godefroy) ; later *museau*, ' muzzle,' Cot.; Norm. dial. *musel* (Du Bois). Diez shews that the orig. F. form was *morsel* (still preserved in Bret. *morzeel* or *muzel*, a muzzle, forms borrowed from O. F.). This O. F. *morsel* is a dimin. from Late L. *morsus*, a morsel, also a snout, beak.—L. *morsus*, a bite; from *morsus*, pp. of *mordēre*, to bite. See Mordacity. Cf. Ital. *muso*, snout, *morso*, a snaffle (Florio). ¶ Disputed.

My. (E.) M. E. *mi*, *my*; short for *min*, mine, by loss of final *n*. See Mine. Der. *my-self*, M. E. *mi-self*, formerly *me-self*.

Myriad. (Gk.) Gk. μυριάδ-, stem of μυριάς, the number of 10,000.—Gk. μυρίος, numberless.

Myrmidon. (L.—Gk.) Gen. in pl. *Myrmidons.*—L. *Myrmidones*, pl.—Gk. Μυρμιδόνες, pl., a warlike people of Thessaly, formerly in Ægina (Homer).

Myrrh. (F.—L.—Gk.—Arab.) M. E. *mirre.*—O. F. *mirre* (11th cent.); F. *myrrhe.*—L. *myrrha.*—Gk. μύρρα.—Arab.

murr, (1) bitter, (2) myrrh, named from its bitterness.+Heb. *mōr*, myrrh.

Myrtle. (F.−L.−Gk.−Pers.) O.F. *myrtil*, dimin. of *myrte, meurte,* the myrtle-tree.−L. *murtus, myrtus.*−Gk. μύρτος.− Pers. *mūrd*, the myrtle.

Mystery (1), a secret rite. (L.−Gk.) M. E. *mysterie.* − L. *mystērium.* − Gk. μυστήριον (Rom. xvi. 25).−Gk. μύστης, one who is initiated. − Gk. μυεῖν, to initiate.

Mystery (2), **Mistery,** a trade, handicraft ; see Mistery.

Mystic, secret, allegorical. (F.−L.− Gk.) F. *mystique.*−L. *mysticus.*−Gk. μυστικός, mystic.−Gk.μύστης,fem. μύστις, one who is initiated ; see **Mystery** (1).

mystify. (F.−Gk. *and* L.) F. *mystifier*, a modern and ill-coined word ; coined from Gk. μυστι-κός, mystic, and F. *-fier*, from L. *-ficāre*, for *facere*, to make.

Myth, a fable. (Gk.) Gk. μῦθος, a fable.

mythology. (F.−L.−Gk.) F. *mythologie.* − L. *mȳthologia.*−Gk. μυθολογία, legendary lore. − Gk. μῦθο-s, a fable ; λόγ-os, a discourse, from λέγειν, to tell.

N.

Nab, to seize. (Scand.) Prov. E. *nap* (North). From Swed. and Norw. *nappa,* Dan. *nappe,* to catch, snatch at, nab. **Der.** *kidnap.*

Nabob, an Indian prince. (Hind.− Arab.) Hind. *nawāb* or *nawwāb,* orig. a pl. sb., but used in the sing. as a title of honour. Pl. of Arab. *nāīb,* a vice-gerent, deputy, viceroy. Cf. Arab. *nawb,* supplying the place of another.

Nadir, the point of the sky opposite the zenith. (F.− Span.− Arab.) F. *nadir.* −Span. *nadir.*−Arab. *nazīr,* short for *nazīru's 'samt,* the nadir ; lit. ' corresponding to the zenith.' − Arab. *nazīr,* alike, corresponding to ; *as'samt,* the azimuth, also the zenith. See **Azimuth, Zenith.** (The *z* is here the 17th letter of the Arab. alphabet.)

Nag (1), a horse. (M. Du.) M. E. *nagge.*−M. Du. *negghe, negge,* Du. *negge, neg,* a small horse ; Du. dial. *knagge* (Molema). Cf. Low G. *nikkel,* a nag. Origin unknown.

Nag (2), to worry, tease. (Scand.) Norw. Swed. *nagga,* to nibble, peck ; cf. Dan. *nage,* Icel. *gnaga,* to gnaw ; Low G.

nagen, naggen, to gnaw, vex, nag ; *gnaggen,* to nag (Berghaus). See **Gnaw.**

Naiad, a water-nymph. (L.−Gk.) L. *naiad-,* stem of *naias.* − Gk. ναιάς, a water - nymph. − Gk. νάειν, to flow. Cf. O. Irish *snāim,* I swim. (√SNĀ.)

Nail. (E.) M. E. *nayl.* A. S. *nægel.* +Du. *nagel,* Dan. *nagle,* Swed. *nagel,* G. *nagel* ; Icel. *nagl,* the human nail, *nagli,* a nail or spike ; and cf. Goth. *ganagljan,* to nail. β. The Teut. type is *nagloz,* masc. Allied to Lithuan. *nagas,* a claw, Russ. *nogote,* a nail, Pers. *nākhun,* Skt. *nakha-,* nail of the finger or toe ; and further, to Gk. ὄνυξ, L. *unguis,* O. Irish *inga,* W. *ewin,* a nail, with a different gradation.

Naive, artless. (F.−L.) F. *naïve,* fem. of *naïf,* native, natural.−L. *nātīuus,* native.−L. *nātus,* born ; see **Natal.**

Naked. (E.) A. S. *nacod.*+Du. *naakt,* G. *nackt,* Goth. *nakwaths,* Icel. *nökviðr* ; cf. Dan. *nögen,* Swed. *naken,* mod. Icel. *nakinn.* All these are pp. forms ; cf. *nake,* to strip, in Chaucer, tr. of Boethius, bk. iv. m. 7 ; which is a back-formation. Teut. type *nakwathoz>*nakwadoz* ; Idg. type *nog(w)otós.* Allied to Skt. *nagna-,* Russ. *nagoi,* L. *nūdus,* Irish *nochd,* W. *noeth,* stripped, bare. Brugm. i. § 165. See **Nude.**

Naker, a kettle-drum. (Arab.) In Chaucer. Arab. *naqqārah,* a kettle-drum ; see Palmer's Pers. Dict., col. 659.

Name. (E.) A. S. *nama.*+Du. *naam* ; Icel. *nafn, namn,* Dan. *navn,* Swed. *namn* ; Goth. *namo,* G. *name.* Further allied to L. *nōmen,* a name ; Gk. ὄνομα, Pers. *nām,* Skt. *nāman* ; and to Ir. *ainm,* W. *enw,* name. ¶ Not allied to **Know** ; see Prellwitz. Brugm. i. §§ 399, 425.

Nankeen, Nankin, a kind of cotton cloth. (China.) So called from *Nankin,* in China.−Chin. *nan-king,* south court ; cf. *pe-king,* north court (Yule).

Nap (1), a short sleep. (E.) M. E. *nappen,* verb, to doze. A. S. *hnæppian,* verb, to doze. Cf. O. H. G. *hnaffezen,* to nap.

Nap (2), the roughish surface of cloth. (M. Du.) M. E. *noppe,* nap (Prompt. Parv.). Prob. introduced by Du. cloth-workers. [A. S. *hnoppa* is unauthorised.] − M. Du. *noppe,* ' the haire or nap of wooll or cloath ;' Hexham. Du. *nop.* Cf. M. Du. *noppen,* ' to sheare of[f] the nap ;' Hexham.+Norw. *napp,* nap ; *nappa,* to give a nap to; Dan. *noppe*, nap; *noppe*, to friz; Low G. *nobbe*, *nubbe*, nap. Allied to Norw. *nuppa*, to pluck off with the fingers; A. S. *hnoppian*, to pluck, Voc. 480. 23; Goth. *dis-hnupnan*, to be torn to pieces, *dis-hniupan*, to tear to pieces. Teut. root **hneup*.

Nape, the joint of the neck behind. (E.) M. E. *nape*; also *naupe* (Palsgrave). The same as O. Fries. *hals-knap*, nape of the neck; which links it with A. S. *cnæp*, the top of a hill; and with **Knop**.

Napery, linen for the table. (F.−L.) O. F. *naperie*. − Late L. *nāpāria*, *mappāria*, the office in a household for supplying table-linen. − Late L. *nāpa*, a cloth, for L. *mappa*, a cloth. See **Map, Napkin**.

Naphtha. (L.−Gk.−Pers.) L. *naphtha*.−Gk. νάφθα.−Pers. *naft*, *nift*, naphtha, bitumen.

Napkin, a small cloth. (F.−L.; *with* E. *suffix*.) M. E. *napekin*, also *napet*, both dimin. forms of O. F. *nape*, a cloth, from Late L. *nāpa*; see **Napery**.

Narcissus, a flower. (L.−Gk.) L. *narcissus*.−Gk. νάρκισσος; named from its *narcotic* properties. See below.

narcotic, producing stupor. (F.−Gk.) F. *narcotique*.−Gk. ναρκωτικός, benumbing.−Gk. ναρκόω, I benumb; ναρκάω, I grow numb.−Gk. νάρκη, numbness, orig. contraction; for **ἀνάρκη, i. e. contraction. Allied to **Snare** (Prellwitz).

Nard, an unguent. (F.−L.−Gk.− Pers.) F. *nard*.−L. *nardus*.−Gk. νάρδος, Mk. xiv. 3. − Pers. *nard* (whence Skt. *nalada-*), spikenard.+Skt. *naḍa-*, a reed. Horn, § 1060. Der. *spike-nard*.

Nargileh, Nargili, Nargile, a pipe or smoking-apparatus in which the smoke is passed through water. (Pers.) − Pers. *nārgīl*, a coco-nut, because these pipes were originally made with a coco-nut, which held the water. Cf. Skt. *nārikera-, nārikela-*, a coco-nut. (Devic, Yule.)

Narration. (F.−L.) F. *narration*. − L. acc. *narrātiōnem*, a tale.−L. *narrātus*, pp. of *narrāre*, to relate, lit. to make known.−L. *nārus, gnārus*, knowing, acquainted with.−√GEN, to know; see **Know**. Brugm. i. § 457 (2).

Narrow. (E.) M. E. *narowe, narewe, narwe*. A. S. *nearu*, narrow, closely drawn.+O. Sax. *naro*; Du. *naar*, dismal, sad. Perhaps allied to **Nerve** (Franck).

Narwhal, sea-unicorn. (Scand.) Dan.

Swed. *narhval*; Icel. *nāhvalr*, a narwhal. The lit. sense is 'corpse-whale'; the fish being (often) of a pallid colour; perhaps a 'popular etymology.'−Icel. *nā-r*, corpse; *hvalr*, whale.

Nasal. (F.−L.) F. *nasal*.−Late L. *nāsālis*, belonging to the nose.−L. *nāsus*, nose. See **Nose**.

Nascent, springing up. (L.) L. *nascent-*, stem of pres. pt. of *nascī*, to be born, arise, spring up, inceptive verb with pp. *nātus*. See **Natal**.

Nasturtium, a flower. (L.) Lit. 'nose-wring;' from the sharp smell.−L. *nasturtium*, cress; better spelt *nasturcium*.−L. *nās-us*, nose; *torquēre*, to twist, torment; see **Torment**.

Nasty. (Scand.) Formerly also *nasky*; see *Mau-lavé* in Cot. Cf. Swed. dial. *naskug*, nasty, dirty, also spelt *snaskig*; Swed. *snuskig*, nasty.−Swed. dial. *snaska*, to eat like a pig, be slovenly; Dan. *snaske*, to eat like a pig.+Low G. *nask*, nasty; Norw. *nask*, greedy, *naska*, to champ; E. Fries. *nasken*, G. *naschen*, O. H. G. *nascōn*, to eat dainties.

Natal, belonging to one's birth. (F.− L.) F. *natal* (O. F. *noël*).−L. *nātālis*. − L. *nātus* (for *gnātus*), born (cf. Gk. κασίγνητος, a blood relation); pp. of *nascī*, to be born. − √GEN, to beget. See **genus, Kin**. Brugm. i. § 452.

Natation, swimming. (L.) From the acc. of L. *natātio*, a swimming.−L. *natātus*, pp. of *natāre*, to swim, frequent. of *nāre*, to swim. Cf. Gk. νήχειν, to swim, O. Irish *snā-im*, I swim. See **Naiad**.

Nation. (F. − L.) F. *nation*. − L. *nātiōnem*, acc. of *nātio*, a nation. − L. *nātus*, born. See **Natal**.

native. (F.−L.) F. *natif*, 'native;' Cot. − L. *nātīuus*, natural. − L. *nātus*, born. **Doublet, naive**.

nature. (F.−L.) F. *nature*. − L. *nātūra*, nature.−L. *nātus*, born.

Natron, native carbonate of sodium. (F. − Span. − Arab. − Gk. − Heb.) A doublet of *nitre*; see **Nitre**.

Naught, Nought. (E.) M. E. *naught*. A.S. *nāwiht*, also *nāht*.−A.S. *nā*, not; *wiht*, a whit; see **No** and **Whit**. Der. *naught-y* (lit. naught-like, worthless). **Doublet, not**.

Nauseous. (L.−Gk.) L. *nauseōsus*, adj.; from *nausea*, sea-sickness.−Gk. ναυσία, sea-sickness.− Gk. ναῦς, a ship. See **Nave** (2).

Nautch, a kind of ballet-dance by women. (Hind.—Prakrit.—Skt.) Hind. (and Mahratti) *nāch,* a dance; Prakrit *nachcha.* — Skt. *nṛtya,* dancing, acting; orig. fut. pass. part. of *nṛt,* to dance, to act. Der. *nautch-girl,* a dancing-girl (Yule).

Nautical. (L.—Gk.) From L. *nautic-us,* nautical. — Gk. ναυτικός, pertaining to ships. — Gk. ναύτης, a sailor; from ναῦ-s, a ship. See **Nave** (2).

nautilus, a shell-fish. (L.—Gk.) L. *nautilus.*—Gk. ναυτίλος, a sea-man; also the nautilus (from its sailing). — Gk. ναύτης, a sailor; from ναῦ-s, a ship.

Naval. (F.—L.) F. *naval.*—L. *nāuālis,* belonging to ships.—L. *nāuis,* a ship. Cf. Gk. ναῦs. See **Nave** (2).

Nave (1), the hub of a wheel. (E.) M. E. *naue* (*u*=*v*). A.S. *nafu, nabu.* + Du. *naaf,* Icel. *nöf,* Dan. *nav,* Swed. *naf,* G. *nabe,* O. H. G. *naba.* Teut. type *nabā,* fem. Cf. Skt. *nābhi-,* the nave of a wheel, navel, centre, boss. See **Navel.** Der. *auger.*

Nave (2), the body of a church. (F.— L.) From O. F. *nave* (F. *nef*), a ship, also the body of a church; said to be named from its lengthy shape.—L. *nāuem,* acc. of *nāuis,* a ship. + Gk. ναῦs, a ship, O. Irish *nau,* Skt. *nau-.* Brugm. i. § 184.

Navel. (E.) M. E. *nauel* (*u*=*v*) ; A.S. *nafela, nabula,* navel. + Du. *navel,* Icel. *nafli,* Dan. *navle,* Swed. *nafle,* G. *nabel.* Teut. type *nabolon-* ; from the form seen in Lettish *naba,* navel ; see **Nave** (1). Cf. also Pers. *nāf,* navel ; Skt. *nābhi-,* (1) nave, (2) navel ; related (with a difference of gradation) to Gk. ὀμφαλός, navel, Lat. *umbilicus,* O. Irish *imbliu.* Similarly, *nave* (1) is allied to L. *umbō,* boss (of a shield). Brugm. ii. § 76.

Navigable, that can be traversed by ships. (F.—L.) F. *navigable.*—L. *nāuigābilis.* — L. *nāuigāre,* to navigate. — L. *nāu-,* for *nāuis,* a ship ; *-igāre,* for *agere,* to drive.

navigation. (F. — L.) F. *naviga-tion,* sailing.—L. acc. *nāuigātiōnem* ; from pp. of L. *nāuigāre* (above).

navvy, a labourer employed on rail-ways, &c. (L.) Short for *navigator,* for-merly used to mean a labourer employed on canals for *navigation*; first used, ac-cording to Haydn, about 1830.

navy, a fleet. (F.—L.) M. E. *navie.* — O. F. *navie,* orig. a single ship. — L. *nāuia,* a vessel. — L. *nāui-s,* a ship.

Nay. (Scand.) M. E. *nay.*—Icel. *nei,* Dan. *nei,* Swed. *nej,* nay. Negative of **Aye,** q. v.

Nazarite, a Jew who made vows of abstinence, &c. (Heb. ; *with* Gk. *suffix.*) Heb. *nāzar,* to separate oneself, vow, abstain ; with suffix *-ite* (=L. *-īta,* Gk. *-ιτης*).

Neap, scanty, very low ; said of a tide. (E.) M. E. *neep* ; A. S. *nēp* (or *nep*).

Near, nigh. (E.) Now used as a positive, but orig. the comparative of *nigh.* [The form *nearer* is a double compara-tive.] M. E. *nerre,* adj., *ner,* adv., nigher ; A. S. *near,* comparative adv. from *nēah,* nigh.+Icel. *nær,* adv., both positive and comparative ; orig. the latter. See **Nigh.**

Neat (1), black cattle, an ox. (E.) M. E. *neet,* both sing. and pl. A.S. *nēat,* pl. *nēat,* cattle. + Icel. *naut,* pl. *naut,* cattle ; Swed. *nöt* ; Dan. *nöd* ; M. H. G. *nōz,* cattle. Teut. type *nautom,* neut. β. Usually explained as 'domestic' or 'useful' ; from the 2nd grade (*naut*) of Teut. *neut-an,* to employ ; seen in A. S. *nēotan,* to use, employ, Icel. *njóta,* G. *geniessen,* Goth. *niutan,* to enjoy, get benefit from. Cf. Lithuan. *naudà,* use-fulness. (√NEUD.) Brugm. i. § 221. Der. *neat-herd.*

Neat (2), tidy. (F. — L.) F. *net,* masc., *nette,* fem., neat, pure.—L. *nitidus,* shining, neat.—L. *nitēre,* to shine.

Neb, beak, nose. (E.) M. E. *neb,* face. A. S. *nebb,* face.+Du. *neb,* bill, nib, mouth; Icel. *nef,* nose ; Dan. *næb* ; Swed. *näbb.* β. Further allied to Du. *sneb,* bill, beak, *snavel,* bill ; G. *schnabel,* bill, M. H. G. *snabel,* allied to M. H. G. *snaben,* to snap. And cf. Lith. *snapas,* bill.

Nebula, a misty patch of light. (L.) L. *nebula,* mist. + Gk. νεφέλη, cloud; Du. *nevel,* Icel. *nifl,* G. *nebel,* mist. Allied to Gk. νέφος, cloud, W. *nef,* O. Ir. *nem,* heaven, Russ. *nebo,* heaven ; also Skt. *nabhas,* sky, æther. Brugm. i. § 554.

Necessary. (F.—L.) O. F. *neces-saire.* — L. *necessārius,* needful. — L. *necesse,* neut. adj., necessary.

Neck. (E.) M. E. *nekke.* A.S. *hnecca,* neck, orig. nape of the neck.+Du. *nek,* G. *genick*; Teut. type *hnekkon-.* Cf. also Icel. *hnakki,* Dan. *nakke,* Swed. *nacke,* G. *nacken,* O. H. G. (*h*)*nach,* nape of the neck, back of the head ; from Teut. type *hnakkon-.* β. Orig. sense 'projection'; further allied to Irish *cnoc,* hill.

Necromancy, divination by communion with the dead. (F.–L.–Gk.) M.E. *nigromancie* (since altered).–O. F. *nigromance,* 'nigromancy, conjuring, the black art;' Cot.–Late L. *nigromantia,* corrupt form of L.*necromantīa.*–Gk.νεκρομαντεία, necromancy.–Gk. *νεκρό-s,* a corpse; *μαντεία,* prophetic power. β. Gk. *νεκρός,* is allied to *νέκυς,*a corpse; cf.L.*necāre,*to kill. (√NEK.) Gk. *μαντεία* is from *μάντις,* a seer. ¶ *Necromancy* was called ' the black art' owing to a popular etymology from L. *niger,* black; cf. the Late L. *nigromantia.*

Nectar. (L.–Gk.) L. *nectar.*–Gk. *νέκταρ,* the drink of the gods.

Need. (E.) M.E. *need.* A.S. *nīed (nȳd),* also *nēad;* O. Merc. *nēd,* necessity. + Icel. *nauðr,* necessity, *nauð,* distress; Du. *nood,* Dan. Swed. *nöd,* G. *noth, not,* Goth. *nauths.* Teut. stem *naudi-.* In late A.S. texts this word is confused in form with *nēod, nīed (nȳd),* desire ; which is related to O. Sax. *niud,* O. H.G. *niot,* desire; Teut. base **neud-.* Brugm. i. § 427 b.

Needle. (E.) Also *neeld;* M.E. *nedle,* also *nelde.* A. S. *nǣdel;* earlier form *nǣeðl.* + Du. *naald* (for **naadl*); Icel. *nál;* Dan. *naal;* Swed. *nål;* G. *nadel;* Goth. *nēthla.* β. All from a Teut. type **nê-thlā,* from root **nē,* to sew, as in G. *nähen,* to sew, L. *nēre,* Gk. *νήθειν, νέειν,* to spin. Cf. √SNĒ, as in O. Irish *snīm,* a spinning; cf. Irish *snathad,* a needle, *snathaim,*I string together, *snaidhe,*thread. See Brugm. i. § 136, ii. § 62.

Neese, Neeze, to sneeze, puff. (E.) M. E. *nesen* ; not in A.S.+Du. *niezen,* G. *niesen,* O.H.G. *niusan,* Icel. *hnjōsa,* Swed. *nysa,* Dan. *nyse.* Teut. type **hneusan-.* See **Sneeze.**

Nefarious. (L.) L. *nefāri-us,* impious ; with suffix *-ous.*–L. *nefās,* that which is unlawful.–L. *ne-,* for *nē,* not ; *fās,* law, allied to *fāri,* to speak, declare. Cf. Skt. *bhāṣ,* to speak.

Negation, denial. (F.–L.) M. F. *negation.*–L. acc. *negātiōnem,* denial. – L. *negātus,* pp. of *negāre,* to deny. Prob. from a particle (*neg-*) of negation ; cf. Lith. *negi,* also not. Brugm. ii. § 774.

Neglect. (L.) L. *neglectus,* pp. of *negligere,* to neglect.–L. *neg-,* not (see Negation) ; and *legere,* to gather, select.

negligence. (F.–L.) M.F. *negligence.* – L. *negligentia,* carelessness. – L.

negligent-, stem of pres. part. of *negligere,* to neglect (above).

Negotiate, to do business. (L.) From pp. of L. *negōtiārī,* to do business.–L. *negōtium,* business ; compounded of *neg-,* not (see **Negation**), and *ōtium,* leisure.

Negro. (Span.–L.) Span. *negro.*–L. *nigrum,* acc. of *niger,* black.

Negus. (E.) A beverage invented by Colonel *Negus* (one of a Norfolk family) in the time of Queen Anne.

Neif, Neaf, the fist. (Scand.) M. E. *neue (u=v),* dat. case.–Icel. *hnefi,* fist; Swed. *näfve,* Dan. *næve.*

Neigh. (E.) M.E.*neʒen.* A.S.*hnǣgan,* to neigh.+Low G. *neigen* (Lübben), M. Du. *neyen,* to neigh. Cf. Icel. *gneggja, hneggja,*Swed. *gnägga,* Dan.*gnegge,*Norw. *kneggja.*

Neighbour. (E.) M. E. *neighebour;* A.S. *nēahgebūr* or *nēahbūr.*–A. S. *nēah,* nigh; *būr,* or *gebūr,* a husbandman, the same word as Du. *boer,* a boor. See **Boor.** +G. *nachbar,* M.H.G. *nāchbūr*; from *nāch,* nigh, *būr,* a husbandman.

Neither. (E.) M.E. *neither* ; for *ne* (negative particle), not, and *either.* See **Either.** With A.S. *ne,* not, cf. O. Sax. *ne, ni* ; Goth. and O.H. G. *ni,* not.

Nemesis. (L.–Gk.) L.*nemesis.*–Gk. *νέμεσις,* allotment, retribution, vengeance. – Gk. *νέμειν,* to distribute. (√NEM.)

Nenuphar, a kind of water-lily. (Pers. – Skt.) Pers. *nīnūfar,* for *nīlūfar, nīlū-par, nīlūpal,* a water-lily (Devic). – Skt. *nīlōtpala,* a blue lotus. – Skt. *nīla,* blue; *utpala,* a lotus.

Neology, the introduction of new phrases. (Gk.) Gk. *νέο-s,* new ; *-λογία,* from *λόγος,* discourse, from *λέγειν,* to speak ; see **New.**

neophyte, a novice. (L.–Gk.) L. *neophytus.*–Gk. *νεόφυτος,* lit. new planted, hence, a novice.–Gk. *νέο-s,* new ; *φυτ-όν,* a plant, *φυτ-ός,* grown, from *φύειν,* to grow, cause to grow, allied to **Be.**

neoteric, novel. (L.–Gk.) L. *neōtericus.*–Gk. *νεωτερικός,* novel.–Gk. *νεώτερος,* comparative of *νέος,* new ; see **New.**

Nepenthe, Nepenthes, a drug which lulled sorrow. (Gk.) Gk. *νηπενθές,* an epithet of a soothing drug (in Homer) ; neut. of *νηπενθής,* free from sorrow.–Gk. *νη-,* neg. prefix; *πένθος,* grief, allied to *πάθος.* See **No** (1) and **Pathos.**

Nephew. (F.–L.) M. E. *neueu (=neveu).*–F. *neveu,* 'a nephew;' Cot. –

L. *nepōtem*, acc. of *nepōs*, a grandson, also a nephew.＋Skt. *napāt*, a grandson; Pers. *nawāda*, a grandson; A. S. *nefa*, a nephew; G. *neffe*, nephew; Du. *neef*. Idg. type **nepōt*; whence orig. Teut. type **nefōd*, later **nefon-*. The fem. type is Idg. **neptī-* (Skt. *naptī*, L. *neptis*), Teut. **neftī-> *niftī-* (A. S. *nift*, Du. *nicht*). **Der.** *nepotism*, favouritism to relations, from L. *nepōt-*, stem of *nepōs*. Brugm. i. § 149.

Nereid, a sea-nymph. (L.–Gk.) L. *Nēreid-*, stem of *Nēreis*. – Gk. Νηρείς, a daughter of *Nēreus* (Gk. Νηρεύς), an ancient sea-god. – Gk. νηρός, wet; cf. Gk. νάειν, to flow (Prellwitz). (√SNĀ.)

Nerve. (F.–L.) F. *nerf*; Cot.–L. *neruum*, acc. of *neruus*, a sinew. Perhaps allied to Gk. νεῦρον, a sinew, string; Skt. *snāva-*, a tendon. See Prellwitz.

Nescient, ignorant. (L.) From L. *nescient-*, stem of *nesciens*, pres. pt. of *nescīre*, not to know. – L. *ne-*, not; *scīre*, to know. See **Science**, **Nice**.

Nesh, tender, soft. (E.) M. E. *nesh*. A.S. *hnesce*, soft.＋Goth. *hnaskwus*, soft, tender.

Ness, a promontory. (E.) Seen in *Sheer-ness*, &c. A.S. *næss*, headland.＋ Icel. *nes*, Dan. *næs*, Swed. *näs*. Teut. types **nasoz* or **nassoz*, masc., **nasjom*, neut. Perhaps allied to **Nose**.

Nest. (E.) M. E. and A. S. *nest.* ＋ Du. *nest*, O. H. G. and G. *nest*; Bret. *neiz*, Irish and Gael. *nead*, O. Irish, *net*; W. *nyth*, L. *nīdus* (for **nizdus*), Skt. *nīḍa-*, a nest, a den. β. Orig. 'a place to sit in.' Explained as short for **ni-sd-os*, a place in which to sit down; cf. Skt. *ni-sad*, to sit down. Here *-sd-* is the weak grade of √SED, to sit. See **Sit**. **Der.** *nest-le*, from A.S. *nestlian*, to make a nest; *nest-l-ing*. Brugm. i. § 81.

Net (1), an implement for catching fish. (E.) A. S. *net*, *nett*.＋Du. *net*, Icel. Dan. *net*, Swed. *nät*, Goth. *nati*, G. *netz*. Teut. type **natjom*, neut. Cf. L. *nassa*, a wicker creel, Icel. *nōt*, a net.

Net (2), clear of all charges. (F.–L.) F. *net*, pure; hence, free; see **Neat** (2).

Nether, lower. (E.) M. E. *nethere*. A.S. *neoðera*, *nioðerra*, nether; a comp. adj. due to *niðer*, adv., downward, also a compar. form. To be divided as *ni-ðer*, the suffix *-ðer* being comparative, as in *o-ther*, *nei-ther* (cf. Gk.-τερος, Skt. *-tara-*). We find Skt. *ni-tarām*, adv., excessively, continually, grammatically a comp. form

from *ni*, downward, into.＋Icel. *neðri*, adj., *neðarr*, adv.; Dan. *neder-* (in comp.), whence *ned*, downward; Swed. *nedre*, G. *nieder*, nether; Du. *neder*, adv., down. Cf. Russ. *nijo* (*j* as in F.) adv., lower. **Der.** *nether-most*, corruption of A. S. *niðe-mest*, extended (by the usual superlative suffix *-est*) from an earlier **ni-ðem-a*, where *-ðe-m-* = Idg. *-to-mo* (as in L. *op-ti-mus*).

Nettle. (E.) M. E. *netle*. A.S. *netele*, *netle*.＋Du. *netel*, Dan. *nelde* (for **nedle*), Swed. *nässla* (for **nätla*), G. *nessel*. Teut. type **natilōn-*, fem. An older form appears in O. H. G. *nazza*, fem., a nettle. Cf. O. Irish *nenaid*, nettles.

Neuralgia, pain in the nerves. (Gk.) From Gk. νεῦρ-ον, a nerve, and ἄλγ-ος, pain; with suffix *-ia*. The Gk. νεῦρον may be allied to L. *neruus*; see **Nerve**.

Neuter. (L.) L. *neuter*, neither; hence, sex-less. – L. *ne*, not; *uter*, whether; see **Whether**. **Der.** *neutr-al*, &c.

Never. (E.) M. E. *neuer* (*u = v*). A.S. *næfre*. – A. S. *ne*, not; *æfre*, ever; see **Ever**.

New. (E.) M. E. *newe*; A.S. *nīwe*, *nēowe*.＋Du. *nieuw*, Icel. *nȳr*, Dan. Swed. *ny*, Goth. *niujis*, G. *neu*, L. *nouus*, W. *newydd*, Irish and Gael. *nuadh*, Lithuan. *naujas*, Russ. *novuii*, Gk. νέος (*=νέϜος*), Pers. *nau*, Skt. *nava(s)*, *navya(s)*, new. Idg. types **newios*, *newos*; Brugm. i. §§ 120, 318; ii. § 63. Allied to Skt. *nu*, now; hence new – 'that which is now,' recent. See **Now**.

newfangled, fond of novelty. (E.) The *d* has been added. M. E. *newefangel*, i. e. fond of what is new. Compounded of *newe*, new, and *fangel*, ready to catch, from the base *fang-*, as in A. S. *fangen*, pp. of *fōn*, to catch. The suffix *-el* is the same as in A. S. *sprec-ol*, fond of speaking, talkative, &c. See **Fang**.

news, tidings. (E.) Formerly *newes*, sb. pl., lit. new things; see the Kingis Quair, st. 179. It is a translation of F. *nouvelles*, news, pl. of O. F. *novel*, new. Cf. Du. *nieuws* (Sewel).

Newel, the upright column round which a circular staircase winds. (F.–L.) Formerly *nuell*. – O. F. *nuel*, *noiel*, later *noyau*, 'the stone of a plumme, the nuell or spindle of a winding staire;' Cot. – L. *nucāle*, neut. of *nucālis*, lit. belonging to a nut; hence a kernel or stone of a plum. – L. *nuc-*, stem of *nux*, a nut. ¶ Named from its *central* position. Cf. F. *nueil*, a nut (dial. of La Meuse).

Newfangled, News; see **New.**

Newt, a kind of lizard. (E.) The initial *n* is unoriginal; *a newt* stands for *an ewt*. M. E. *newte*; also *ewte*, which is a shortened form of M. E. *evete*. — A. S. *efeta*, a lizard. See **Eft.**

Next, nighest. (E.) M.E. *next*; also *nehest*, superl. of *neh*, nigh; A.S. *nēhst*, superl. of *nēh*, *nēah*, nigh. See **Nigh.**

Nias, a young hawk, a ninny. (F.—L.) M. F. *niais*, 'a neastling, ninny;' Cot. — Late L. acc. type **nīdiācem* (Ital. *nidiace*). —L. *nīdus*, a nest. See **Nest.**

Nib, point of a pen. (E.) Another form of *neb*; see **Neb.** Cf. E. Fries. *nibbe*, *nib*, Low G. *nibbe*, a neb.

Nibble. (E.) Lit. ' to nip often ;' the frequent. of *nip*, to pinch off the end of grass, &c.+Low G. *nibbeln*, *knibbeln*, to nibble, to gnaw slightly. (Cf. *dibble* from *dip*.) ¶ Or we may regard it as an attenuated form of Du. *knabbelen*, to nibble.

Nice, fastidious, delicious. (F.—L.) M. E. *nice*, foolish, simple, later fastidious, and lastly delicious. — O. F. *nice*, lazy, simple ; orig. ignorant ; Romanic **necium* (cf. Span. *necio*). — L. *nescium*, acc. of *nescius*, ignorant.—L. *ne*, not ; *scī-re*, to know. See **No** (1) and **Science.**

Niche, a recess in a wall for a statue. (F.—Ital.—L.) F. *niche*.—Ital. *nicchia*, a niche, a shell-like recess in a wall.—Ital. *nicchio*, a shell, also a nitch (Florio).—Ital. *mītulum,mȳtilum,*acc. of *mītulus,mȳtilus*, a sea-muscle. ' Derived in the same way as Ital. *secchia* from *situla*, a bucket, and *vecchio* from *uetulus*, old ; as to the change of initial, cf. Ital. *nespola* with L. *mespilum*, a medlar;' Diez. [The same change occurs in F. *natte*, a mat, and in *napkin*.] We also find L. *mūtulus*, a sea-muscle ; cf. L. *musculus*, a sea-muscle ; see **Muscle** (1). Cf. Gk. μυτίλος (Liddell).

Nick (1), a small notch. (O. Low G.) *Nick* is an attenuated form of *nock*, a notch ; see **Nock.** So also *tip* from *top*.

Nick (2), the devil. (F. — L. — Gk.) Short for *Nicolas*. [Not from A. S. *nicor*, a water-sprite, hobgoblin ; Icel. *nykr*, Dan. *nök*, *nisse*, Swed. *näck*, G. *nix*, a watergoblin. See Kluge, s. v. *Nix*.]

Nickel, a grayish white metal. (Swed. —G.) G. *kupfernickel*, nickel of copper ; shortened to Swed. *nickel*. So named by Cronstedt (a Swed. mineralogist) in 1754 (Cent. Dict.).

Nicknack; see **Knickknack.**

Nickname. (E.) M. E. *nekename*, also *ekename* ; (*a nekename = an ekename*). See Prompt. Parv. ; cf. Du. *toenaam*, G. *zuname*. From *eke* and *name*. + Icel. *auknefni*, Swed. *öknamn*, Dan. *ögenavn*, an eke-name, nickname.

Nicotian, belonging to tobacco. (F.) M. F. *Nicotiane*, ' Nicotian, tobacco, first sent into France by *Nicot* in 1560 ;' Cot. *Nicot* is a personal name.

Niece. (F.—L.) M. E. *nece*, *neyce.*— M. F. *niece* (F. *nièce*).—Late L. *neptia*, a niece.—L. *neptis*, a granddaughter, niece; used as fem. of L. *nepōs*, nephew. See **Nephew.**

Niggard, a miser. (Scand.) M. E. *nigard*; where the suffix -*ard* is of F. origin (=O. H. G. *hart*, hard). We also find M. E. *nigun*, a niggard, and *niggish*, adj., stingy; and even *nig*. — Icel. *hnöggr*, niggardly, Swed. *njugg*, niggardly, scanty ; cf. Mid. Dan. *nygger*, Swed. dial. *nugger*, stingy.+A. S. *hnēaw*, niggardly (Noreen). Cf. M. Du. *nugger*, ' nimble, carefull, or diligent,' Hexham.

Nigh. (E.) M.E. *neh, neih, ney.* A.S. *nēah, nēh*, nigh ; adv. and prep. + Du. *na*, adv., Icel. *nā-* (as in *nā-būi*, a neighbour) ; Goth. *nēhwa*, adv. and prep. ; G. *nah, nahe*, adj., *nach*, prep., nigh. Teut. type **nǣhwo-*. Root unknown.

Night. (E.) M.E. *night, niht.* A.S. *niht, neaht* ; O. Merc. *nǣht.*+Du. G. *nacht*, Icel. *nátt, nött*, Dan. *nat*, Swed. *natt*, Goth. *nahts.* Teut. type **naht-* ; Idg. type **nokt-.* + W. *nos*, Irish *nochd*, Lithuan. *naktis*, Russ. *noche*, L. *nox* (stem *noct-*), Gk. νύξ (stem νυκτ-), Skt. *nakta-.* ¶ For the old system of reckoning by *nights*, cf. *sennight, fortnight.*

nightingale. (E.) M. E. *nightingale*, earlier *nightegale* (the *n* having been inserted) ; A. S. *nihtegale.* — A. S. *nihte-*, for *niht*, night ; *gale*, a singer, from *galan*, to sing. Lit. ' singer by night.' A. S. *gal-an* is from *gal-*, 2nd stem of *giellan*, to yell. See **Yell.** So also Du. *nachtegaal*, Dan. *nattergal*, Swed. *näktergal*, G. *nachtigall*, O. H. G. *nahtagala.*

nightmare, an incubus. (E.) M. E. *nightemare.* From A. S. *niht*, night ; *mære*, a nightmare, incubus ; allied to a Teut. verb **marjan-*, to crush, Icel. *merja* (pt. t. *marði*), to crush. [*Mara* is quite distinct from A. S. *mere*, a mare, but the two have been confused in Du. *nacht-merrie*, a nightmare.]+Icel. *mara*, Swed. *mara*, Dan. *mare*, Low G. *moor*, O. H. G. *mara*, *mar*; all with the sense of incubus or crushing weight on the breast. Cf. F. *cauche-mar*, nightmare; where *cauche* is from L. *calcāre*, to tread on, press upon. Also N. Fries. *naagtmäre*, G. *nachtmahr*, nightmare.

nightshade, a plant. (E.) A. S. *nihtscada*. Cf. Du. *nachtschade*, M. Du. *nachtschaede*, G. *nachtschatten*. Also Swed. dial. *natt-skate-gräs*, as if from *natt-skata*, a bat, and *gräs*, grass (Rietz).

Nigrescent, growing black. (L.) From stem of pres. pt. of *nigrescere*, to grow black, inceptive of *nigrēre*, to be black.—L. *nigr-*, for *niger*, black.

Nihilist, a member of a revolutionary secret society, esp. in Russia. (L.) Etymologically, one who denies real existence. —L. *nihil*, nothing.

Nilgau; see Nylghau.

Nimble, active. (E.) M. E. *nimel*; the *b* is excrescent. Lit. ' ready to catch;' from A. S. *nim-an*, to catch, take, seize; with suffix *-ol*, as in *sprec-ol*, talkative. We actually find A. S. *numol* or *numul*, taking, seizing, or able to receive; from the weak grade (*num-*) of the same verb. Cf. Icel. *nema*, Goth. *niman*, G. *nehmen*, to take. Perhaps related to Gk. νέμεσθαι, to occupy, νέμειν, to distribute. (√NEM.)

Nincompoop, a simpleton. (L.) Thought to be a corruption of L. *non compos* (*mentis*), not sound in mind.

Nine. (E.) M. E. *nine*, where the final *-e* is a pl. suffix, and *nin-* is for *niȝen*, nine (Layamon). A. S. *nigon*, *nigon*, nine. +Du. *negen*, Icel. *nīu*, Dan. *ni*, Sw. *nio*, G. *neun*, Goth. *niun*; cf. also W. *naw*, Ir. *naoi*, L. *nouem*, Gk. ἐννέα, Zend *nava*, Pers. *nuh*, Skt. *nava*, nine. Idg. type *newǝn*. Brugm. ii. § 173.

Ninny, a simpleton. (E.) [Cf. Ital. *ninno*, a child (Diez). Cf. Span. *niño*, a child, one of little experience. Ital. *ninna*, a lullaby, nurse's song to lull children to sleep, also *nanna*.] Of imitative origin.

Nip. (E.) M. E. *nippen*, for *knippen*; see G. Douglas, Prol. to Æn. xii. l. 94. Not in A. S. From the weak grade (*knip-*) of a Teut. verb *kneipan-*, to pinch, as seen in Du. *knijpen*, to pinch, Dan. *knibe*, Sw. *knipa*; G. *kneifen*, *kneipen*, to pinch (from Low G.). Allied

to Lith. *gnyb-ti*, to pinch; or to Lith. *knĕb-ti*, to pinch.

Nipple, a teat. (E.) Formerly *nible* (Nares); *neble* (Palsgrave); dimin. of *nib* or *neb*; see **Neb**. Cf. O. F. *nifle*, *niffle*, a nose, Ital. *niffolo*, *niffa*, a snout, from the Teutonic (Low G. *nibbe*, a beak). Der. *nipple-wort*.

Nit, egg of a louse; a louse. (E.) M. E. *nite*, a nit, also a louse; A.S. *hnitu*, a louse's egg. + Du. *neet*; Icel. *nitr*, pl., Dan. *gnid*, Swed. *gnet*; G. *niss*; Gk. κονίς (stem κονιδ-); W. *nedd*, pl., nits; cf. also Russ. *gnida*, a nit.

Nitre. (F.—L.—Gk.—Heb.) F. *nitre*. —L. *nitrum*. — Gk. νίτρον.—Heb. *nether*, nitre. ¶ *Nitre* and *natron* are doublets, but applied to different substances. *Natron* is from F. *natron*.—Span. *natron*.—Arab. *natrūn*, *nitrūn*. — Gk. νίτρον. — Heb. *nether*. Der. *nitro-gen*, that which produces nitre, from γεν-, base of γίγνειν, to produce.

Nizam, the title of a ruler in the Deccan, in Hindustan. (Hind.—Pers.— Arab.) From the Arab. *niḍhām*, government, which the Persians pronounce as *nizām*. Though the proper sense is 'government,' in the phrase *nizām-'l-mulk* it is used as a title, meaning 'governor of the empire'; first used by Asaf Jāh in 1713 (Yule). — Arab. root *naḍhama*, he arranged or ordered. (Devic, Richardson.)

No (1), a word of refusal or denial. (E.) M. E. *no*; A. S. *nā*, *no*, adv., never, no. — A. S. *ne*, not; *ā*, ever (whence M. E. *oo*, *ō*, ever, now obsolete). See **Aye**. β. With A. S. *ne*, not, cf. Goth. *ni*, Russ. *ne*, Irish, Gael. W. *ni*, L. *ne* (in *non-ne*), Skt. *na*, not.

no (2), none. (E.) Short for *none*, q.v. Der. *no-body*, i. e. none body; it took the place of M. E. *no man*. So also *no-thing*.

Noble. (F. — L.) F. *noble*. — L. *nō-bilem*, acc. of *nōbilis*, well known. For O. L. *gnōbilis*. — L. *gnō-*, base of *nōscere* (i. e. *gnōscere*), to know; allied to E. **Know**. Der. *nobil-i·ty*, O. F. *nobilitet*, L. acc. *nōbilitātem*. Also *i-gnoble*.

Nobody; from *no* and *body*; see **No** (1).

Nock, an indentation, notch; *obs.* (M. Du.) M. E. *nokke*. — M. Du. *nocke* (Kilian), a notch in the head of an arrow; M. Swed. *nocka*, a notch; Swed. dial. *nokke*, *nokk*. The M. Swed. *nocka* also denotes the same as Icel. *hnokki*, i. e the small metal hooks holding the thread in a distaff. ¶ The M. Ital. *nocca*, a nock, is of Teut. origin. Distinct from *notch*.

Nocturn, a service of the church. (F.–L.) F. *nocturne*, a nocturn ; orig. nocturnal. – Late L. *nocturna*, a nocturn ; fem. of L. *nocturnus*, nocturnal. From *noct*-, stem of *nox*, night. See **Night**.

Nod. (E.) M. E. *nodden*. Not in A. S. ; but the orig. form began with *hn*. The orig. sense was to push, beat, shake. Cf. Icel. *hnyðja*, a rammer for beating turf ; O. H. G. *hnōtōn (hnotōn?)*, to shake ; Bavar. *notteln*, to move to and fro. Teut. base **hneud*.

Noddle, the head. (E.) M. E. *nodle*, *nodil*, the noddle, nape, back of the head. 'Occiput, a *nodyle* ;' Vocab. 673. Dimin. of **knod*, a word not found in M. E., but the same as M. Du. *knodde*, a knob (Hexham), Du. *knod*, a club ; cf. G. *knoten*, a knot, knob. This is a mere variant of *knot* (Franck). Cf. Low G. *knuddel*, a ball of yarn, a hard swelling under the skin (Berghaus).

Node, a knot. (L.) L. *nōdus*, a knot.

Noggin, a wooden cup. (Scand.) Cf. Irish *noigin*, Gael. *noigean*, a noggin ; Gael. *cnagan*, a little knob, a peg, an earthen pipkin, *cnagaire*, 'a knocker; a gill, noggin ; a quart measure;' all from E. (Macbain). Also Lowl. Sc. *noggin*, *noggie* ; spelt *knoggin* by Swift. For **knogg-en*, with *-en* as in *wood-en*, from *knog*, variant of *knag*, a knob, peg, also a keg (Jamieson), *knaggie*, a keg (id.). Of Scand. origin ; see **Knag**.

Noise. (F.–L.–Gk.) M. E. *noise*.– F. *noise*, O. F. *noise*, *nose*, a debate, quarrel, noise. Cf. Prov. *noisa*, *nausa*, *nueiza*. β. Diez holds that it can only be derived from L. *nausea*, sea-sickness, disgust, hence annoyance, &c. ; the L. word being borrowed from Gk. See **Nausea**.

Noisome, annoying, troublesome. (F. – L.; *with* E. *suffix*.) Formed from M. E. *noy*, annoyance; with E. suffix *-some*. This M. E. *noy* is short for M. E. *anoy*, *anoi*. – O. F. *anoi*, vexation; see **Annoy**.

Nole, Noll, head ; see **Noule**.

Nomad, wandering. (Gk.) Gk. νομαδ-, stem of νομάς, roaming in search of pasture. – Gk. νομός, a pasture, allotted abode. – Gk. νέμειν, to assign. (√NEM.)

Nomenclator, one who names things. (L.) L. *nōmenclātor*, lit. 'name-caller.'

– L. *nōmen*, name; *calāre*, to call; see **Calends**.

nominal. (F.–L.) F. *nominal*.– L. *nōminālis*, nominal ; belonging to a name. – L. *nōmin*-, for *nōmen*, a name; see **Noun**.

nominate. (L.) From pp. of L. *nōmināre*, to name. – L. *nōmin*-, for *nōmen* ; see **Noun**.

Non-, prefix, not. (L.) L. *nōn*, not.

nonage. (L. *and* F.–L.) I. e. *non-age*, minority. So also *non-conforming*, *non-descript*, *non-entity*, *non-juror*, *non-sense*, *non-suit*.

Nonce; see **One**.

Nonchalant, careless. (E.–L.) F. *nonchalant*, careless ; pres. pt. of O. F. *nonchaloir*, to be careless about. – O. F. *non*, not ; *chaloir*, to glow, hence to be hot over, take care for. – L. *non*, not ; *calēre*, to glow.

None. (E.) M. E. *noon*, *non*. A. S. *nān*. – A. S. *ne*, not ; *ān*, one ; see **One**. Hence *no*, as in *no-thing*, *no-body*, by loss of final *n*.

Nones, the ninth day before the ides. (L.) From L. *nōna*, ninth (i. e. ninth day), fem. of *nōnus*, ninth ; from *nouem*, nine. See **Nine**.

Nonpareil, matchless. (F.–L.) F. *non*, not ; *pareil*, equal.– L. *nōn*, not ; Late L. *pariculus*, equal, double dimin. from *par*, equal. Cf. **Apparel**.

Nonplus. (L.) 'To be at a *nonplus*,' to be in perplexity, not to be able to proceed. – L. *nōn*, not ; *plūs*, more, further.

Nook. (E.) M. E. *nōk*, a corner. Lowl. Sc. *neuk*, whence (probably) Irish and Gael. *niuc*, a corner, nook ; also Lowl. Sc. *nuik*, *nuk*, a headland. It answers to Norw. *nōk*, a nook, crook ; cf. Norw. *nakke*, a corner cut off; Dan. dial. *nogg*, a bend in a river.

Noon, mid-day. (L.) Orig. the ninth hour or 3 P.M., but afterwards the time of the church-service called *nones* was shifted to mid-day. We find A. S. *nōn-tīd* (lit. noon-tide), the ninth hour, Mk. xv. 33. – L. *nōna*, i. e. ninth hour, fem. of *nōnus*, ninth. See **Nine**.

Noose, a slip-knot. (Prov.–L.) In Beaumont and Fletcher. The word was imported from Gascony by sailors. – Gascon *nus* ; O. Prov. *notz* ; Prov. *nous*, a noose or loop. [Cf. Prov. *nous courrént*, a running noose ; pl. *nouses* ; *nous de l'araire*, a noose for mooring ships ; note Gasc. *nouset*, a knot, *nousera*, to tie a knot.] – L. *nōdus*, nom., a knot. See Knot.

Nor. (E.) M. E. *nor*, short for *nother*, neither. – A. S. *nāwðer*, contracted form of *nāhwæðer*, neither. – A. S. *nā*, not; *hwæðer*, whether.

Normal, according to rule. (L.) L. *normālis*, adj. – L. *norma*, a carpenter's square, rule, pattern.

Norman, Norse; see North.

North. (E.) A. S. *norð.*+Du. *noord*, Icel. *norðr*, Dan. Swed. G. *nord.* Root unknown; some compare Umbrian *nertru*, on the left hand (to one looking east-wards); Gk. νέρτερος, lower.

norman. (F. – Scand.) O. F. *Nor-mand.* – Dan. *Normand*; Icel. *Norðmaðr*, pl. *Norðmenn*. Lit. 'North-man.'

norse. (Scand.) From Norw. and Dan. *norsk*, Norse; Icel. *norskr*, Norse. Short for *North-isk*, i. e. *North-ish*.

northern. (E.) A. S. *norðern*; cog-nate with Icel. *norræn*, O.H.G. *nordrôni*. For the suffix, cf. L. *-āneus.* Der. *north-er-ly*, put for *north-ern-ly*.

Nose. (E.) M. E. *nose.* A. S. *nosu.* + Du. *neus.* Related, apparently by gradation, to A. S. *nasu*, nose, Icel. *nös*, Dan. *næse*, Swed. *näsa*, G. *nase*, Russ. *nos'*, Lithuan. *nosis*, L. *nāsus*, *nāres*, pl., Skt. *nāsā*, dual. Allied to Ness. Der. *nose-gay*; cf. prov. E. *gay*, a painted picture in a book, from *gay*, adj.; *nos-tril*; *nozzle*; *nuzzle*.

Nosology, science of disease. (Gk.) Gk. νόσο-s, disease; -λογία, from λόγος, discourse, from λέγειν, to speak.

Nostril. (E.) *Nostril*=*nose-thrill* or *nose-thirl.* M. E. *nosethirl* = A. S. *nosðyrl.* – A. S. *nos-u*, nose; *ðyrel*, a perforation, orifice; see Thrill.

Nostrum, a quack medicine. (L.) L. *nostrum*, lit. 'our own,' i. e. a special drug peculiar to the seller. Neut. of *noster*, ours. – L. *nōs*, we. Cf. Skt. *nas*, us.

Not (1), a word expressing denial. (E.) M. E. *not*, short form of *nought*, *naught*; see Naught.

Not (2), I know not, *or* he knows not. (E.) Obsolete. M. E. *nōt*, *noot.* A. S. *nāt.* – A. S. *ne*, not; *wāt*, I know, *or* he knows; see Wit.

Notable. (F. – L.) F. *notable.* – L. *notābilis*, remarkable. – L. *notāre*, to mark. – L. *nota*, a mark; see Note.

notary. (F. – L.) M. F. *notaire.* – L. acc. *notārium* (from *notārius*), one who

makes notes, a scrivener. – L. *nota*, a note; see Note.

Notch, an incision, a score; also, as vb., to incise, nick. (F.) For **otch*, by association with *nock*, which has a similar meaning. M. E. *ochen*, to cut, cut into, occurs in the Morte Arthure, 2565, 3676. *Notch* was often particularly used with reference to the scoring of tallies, and cricket was once scored by counting *notches.* – O. F. *oche* (F. *hoche*), 'a nick, nock, or notch, the cut of a tally;' Cot. Also *ocher*, 'to nick, nock, notch, to cut as a tally;' id. The O. F. *oche*, Gascon *osco*, is of unknown origin. ¶ There is a similar difficulty as to initial *n* in the word *nouch* or *ouch*; see Ouch.

Note, a mark. (F. – L.) F. *note.* – L. *nota*, a mark, lit. that by which a thing is known. Perhaps for **gnōta*, and allied to *nōtus*, known, pp. of *noscere*; Bréal. (For the short *o*, cf. L. *cognitus* = **cognōtus*.) Der. *not-at-ion*, from L. *notātio*, from pp. *notātus*; and see *not-able*, *not-ary* above.

Nothing. (E.) Short for *no thing*; see None.

Notice. (F. – L.) F. *notice.* – L. *nōtitia*, a being known, knowledge – L. *nōtus*, pp. of *noscere*, to know. See Know.

notify. (F. – L.) F. *notifier.* – L. *nōtificāre*, to make known. – L. *nōti-*, for *nōtus*, known; *-ficāre*, for *facere*, to make.

notion. (F. – L.) F. *notion.* – L. acc. *nōtiōnem*, an investigation, a notion. – L. *nōtus*, pp. of *noscere*, to know. See Know.

notorious. (L.) From L. *nōtōri-us*, manifest; with suffix *-ous.* – L. *nōtor*, a voucher, witness. – L. pp. *nōtus*, known. Der. *notori-e-ty*, M. F. *notorieté* (Cot.).

Not-pated, close shorn. (E.) See 1 Hen. IV. ii. 4. 78. From A. S. *hnot*, close shorn; and Pate.

Notwithstanding. (E.) M. E. *nought withstonding*, Gower. C. A. ii. 181. From *naught* and *withstand.*

Nought, the same as Naught.

Noule, Nowl, Nole, Noll, head. (E.) See Nares. Mid. Nt. Dr. iii. 2. 17. M. E. *nol.* A. S. *hnoll*, the crown of the head.+O. H. G. *hnol*, top.

Noun, a grammatical term. (F. – L.) O. F. *noun*, *non*, *nun* (F. *nom*), a name. – L *nōmen*, a name. See Name.

Nourish. (F. – L.) M. E. *norisen.* – O. F. *nouris-*, *norris-*, stem of pres. pt. of *nourir* (F. *nourrir*), to nourish. **–** L. *nūtrīre*, to nourish, suckle. Cf. **Nurse**.

Novel. (F. **–** L.) O. F. *novel* (F. *nouveau*) **–** L. *nouellus*, new, dimin. of *nouus*, new. See **New**. **Der.** *novel-ty*, from O. F. *noveliteit*, from L. acc. *nouellitātem*, newness.

novice, a beginner. (F. **–** L.) F. *novice*. **–** L. *nouīcius*, *nouītius*, new, fresh, a novice. **–** L. *nouus*, new. **Der.** *noviti-ate*, from M.F. *novitiat*, ' the estate of a novice,' Cot., from Late L. *novitiātus*, sb.

November. (L.) L. *Nouember*, the ninth month of the Roman year. **–** L. *nouem*, nine. See **Nine**.

Now. (E.) M. E. *now*, *nou*, *nu*; A.S. *nū*. **+**Du. *nu*, Icel. *nū*, Dan. Swed. O. H. G. Goth. *nu*, Skt. *nu*, *nū*. Cf. Gk. *νῦ-ν*, L. *nu-nc*. **Der.** *new*. Brugm. i. § 1042.

Noway, Noways. (E.) The older form is *noways*. **–** A. S. *nānes weges*, by no way, the gen. case used adverbially. See **None** and **Way**.

nowhere. (E.) A.S. *nāhwǣr*. **–** A. S. *nā*, not; *hwǣr*, where. See **No** (1) and **Where**.

nowise. (E.) Short for *in no wise*, M. E. *on none wise*; where *none* is dat. of M. E. *noon*, none, and *wise* is dat. of *wise*, a way, from A. S. *wīse*, a way. See **None**, and **Wise**, sb.

Noxious. (L.) L. *noxius*, hurtful. **–** L. *noxa*, hurt. **–** L. *nocēre*, to hurt ; cf. *nex*, destruction. **+** Skt. *nāça(s)*, destruction. (✓NEK.) Brugm. ii. § 794.

Nozzle, a snout. (E.) Formerly *nozle* ; dimin. of *nose*.

Nucleus, core. (L.) L. *nucleus*, small nut, kernel. **–** L. *nuc-*, stem of *nux*, a nut.

Nude, naked. (L.) L. *nūdus*, bare ; for **nogwedos*. Allied to **Naked**.

Nudge, a slight push. (E.) Lowl. Sc. *nodge*, to push, strike, strike with the knuckles ; North. E. *nog*, to jog. Perhaps of imitative origin. Cf. Norw. *nugga*, to rub, push, allied to *nyggja* (pt. t. *nogg*), to push ; Swed. dial. *nogga*, to move slightly.

Nugatory, trifling, vain. (L.) L. *nūgātōrius*, adj. from *nūgātor*, a trifler ; cf. *nūgātus*, pp. of *nūgārī*, to trifle. **–** L. pl. *nūgæ*, trifles.

Nugget, a lump of metal. (E.) Formerly *niggot* ; see Trench, Eng. Past and Present. Cf. prov. E. *nug*, a block of wood ; *nigg*, a small piece (Essex) ; *nog*, *knog*, a block of wood, knob, peg ; allied to **Knag**. See **Noggin**.

Nuisance. (F.**–**L.) F. *nuisance*, a hurt. **–** F. *nuisant*, hurtful ; pres. pt. of *nuire*, to hurt. **–** L. *nocēre*, to hurt.

Null, invalid. (F.**–**L.) F. *nul*. **–** L. *nullus*, none. **–** L. *ne*, not ; *ullus*, any, short for **ūnulus*, dimin. of *ūnus*, one.

Nullah, a water-course, bed of a torrent. (Hind.) Hind. *nāla*, a water-course (Yule).

Numb. (E.) M. E. *nome*, *nomen*, pp. seized, taken, caught with, overpowered, deprived of sensation. Pp. of M. E. *nimen* (A.S. *niman*), to take ; see **Nimble.+** Icel. *numinn*, bereft, pp. of *nema*, to take.

Number. (F.**–**L.) F. *nombre*.**–**L. *numerum*, acc. of *numerus*, a number. Cf. Gk. *νόμ-ος*, law, *νέμειν*, to distribute. (✓NEM.) **Der.** *out-number*.

numeral. (L.) From L. *numerālis*, belonging to number. **–** L. *numerus* (above).

numeration. (F.**–**L.) F. *numeration.* **–** L. acc. *numerātiōnem*, a numbering. **–** L. *numerātus*, pp. of *numerāre*, to number. **–** L. *numerus*, a number.

numerous. (F.**–**L.) M.F. *numereux* (Cot.). **–** L. *numerōsus*, adj. ; from *numerus*, sb., a number.

Numismatic, relating to coins. (L.**–** Gk.) Coined from L. *numismat-*, stem of *numisma*, current coin. **–** Gk. *νόμισμα*, a custom, also current coin. **–** Gk. *νομίζειν*, to adopt, use as coin. **–** Gk. *νόμος*, usage. **–** Gk. *νέμειν*, to distribute. (✓NEM.)

Nun. (L.) M. E. and A. S. *nunne*. **–** Late L. *nunna*, *nonna*, a nun ; orig. a title of respect ; oldest sense, 'mother.' It answers to L. *nonnus*, father, also a monk (Ducange). **+** Gk. *νάννη*, aunt ; Skt. *nanā*, mother, a familiar word used by children. Formed like *ma-ma*, *da-da* (*daddy*), and the like. **Der.** *nunn-er-y*, from O. F. *non-nerie*, which is from O. F. *nonne*, Late L. *nonna*.

Nuncheon, a luncheon. (Hybrid ; L. *and* E.) The ending is confused with that of *luncheon*. M. E. *nonechenche* (for *noneschenche*), Riley, Memorials of London, p. 265 ; lit. a 'noon-drink,' to accompany the *nonemete* or 'noon-meat.' **–** M. E. *none*, noon ; *schenche*, a pouring out of drink. **–** A.S. *nōn*, noon (of L. origin ; see **Noon**) ; *scencan*, to pour out drink. β. The A. S. *scencan* is lit. 'to pour out through a pipe ;' derived from A. S. *scanc*, a shank, hollow bone, pipe ; see **Shank**.

Nuncio, a messenger. (Ital.**–**L.) Ital.

nuncio. – L. *nuntium*, acc. of *nuntius*, a bringer of tidings. Prob. for **nouentius*, a bringer of news, from *nouus*, new.

Nuncupative, declared by word of mouth. (F.–L.) F. *nuncupatif* (Cot.). – Late L. *nuncupātīvus*,nominal. – L.*nuncupātus*, pp. of *nuncupāre*, to call by name. For **nōmi-cupāre* ; from L. *nōmen*, name, *capere*, to take. Brugm. ii. § 34.

Nuphar, a kind of water-lily. (Pers.– Skt.) Pers. *nūfar*, short for *nīlūfar* ; see Nenuphar.

Nuptial. (F.–L.) F. *nuptial.* – L. *nuptiālis*, belonging to a marriage.–L. *nuptiæ*, s. pl., a wedding.–L. *nupta*, a bride; fem. of pp. of *nūbere*, to marry, lit. 'to veil.'

Nurse. (F.–L.) Contracted from M.E. *norice, nurice.* – O.F. *norrice* (F.*nourrice*). – L. *nūtrīcia*, a nurse.–L. *nūtrīc-*, stem of *nūtrix*, a nurse.–L. *nūtrīre*,to nourish.

nurture. (F.–L.) M.E. *norture.* – O. F. *noriture* (F. *nourriture*).–L. *nūtrītūra*, nourishment ; from *nūtrītus*, pp. of *nūtrīre*, to nourish.

Nut. (E.) M.E. *note, nute* ; A.S. *hnutu.*+Du. *noot*, Icel. *hnot*, Swed. *nöt*, Dan. *nöd*, G. *nuss.* Cf. Irish *cnu*, Gael. *cno*, W. *cneuen*, a nut. **Der.** *nut-hatch*, i. e. nut-hacker ; see **Hatch** (3).

nutmeg, the musk-nut. (E. ; *and* F.– L.–Pers.–Skt.) M.E. *notemuge*, later *nutmegge.* Here -*muge* is from O. F. *mugue*, musk.–L. *muscum*, acc. of *muscus*, musk ; see **Musk.** Cf. O. F. *muguette*, a nutmeg, also called *noix muscade*, Span. *nuez moscada*, Ital. *noce moscada*, Late L. *muscāta*, nutmeg.

Nutation, a nodding. (L.) From L. *nūtātio*, a nodding.–L. *nūtare*, to nod, frequent. of *nuere*, to nod.+Gk. *νεύειν*, to nod. (√NEU.)

Nutriment, food. (L.) L.*nūtrīmentum*, food.–L. *nūtrīre*, to nourish, suckle, feed.

nutritious. (L.) L. *nūtrīti-us*, for *nūtrīcius*, adj., nourishing ; with suffix -*ous*. –L. *nūtrīc-*, stem of *nūtrix*, a nurse.–L. *nūtrīre* (above).

nutritive. (F.–L.) F. *nutritif.* Formed with F. suffix -*if* (L. -*īuus*), from *nūtrīt-us*, pp. of *nūtrīre* (above).

Nuzzle, to thrust the nose in. (E.) Formerly *nousle, nosyll* ; a frequent. verb ; from *nose*, sb. Cf. Swed. *nosa*, to smell ; also Bavar. *nuseln, nöseln*, to seek about for, also, to speak through the nose ;

E. Fries. *nüsseln*, Swed. dial. *nösla*, to nuzzle.

Nylghau, a kind of antelope. (Pers.) Pers. *nīlgāw*, a nylghau, lit. 'blue cow.' – Pers. *nīl*, blue (see **Lilac**) ; and *gāw*, a cow, allied to E. **Cow.**

Nymph. (F.–L.–Gk.) F. *nymphe.* –L. *nympha.* – Gk. *νύμφη*, a bride.

O.

O (1), **Oh,** interjection. (E.) M. E. *o* ; not in A.S.+Du. Dan. Swed. G. Goth. L. *ō* ; Gk. *ὦ*, *ὤ*. There was no distinction, formerly, between *o* and *oh*.

O (2), a circle. (E.) So called because the letter *o* is of a circular shape.

Oaf, a simpleton. (Scand.) Prov. E. *auf*, an elf.–Icel. *ālfr*, an elf. Chaucer uses *elvish* in the sense of 'simple.' A variant of *elf* ; see **Elf.**

Oak. (E.) M. E. *ook* ; A.S. *āc.* + Du. Icel. *eik* ; Dan. *eeg, eg*, Swed. *ek*, G. *eiche* ; Teut. base **aik-*.

Oakum, tow from old ropes. (E.) A. S. *ācumba*, tow. (For the sound-change, cf. E. *oak*<A. S. *āc*.) Lit. 'that which is combed out.' – A.S. *ā-*, prefix ; *cemban*, to comb, from *camb*, a comb ; see **A-** (4) and **Comb.** Cf. O. H. G. *āchambi*, tow ; of like origin.

Oar. (E.) M. E. *ore* ; A.S. *ār.*+Icel. *ār*, Dan. *aare*, Swed. *åra.* Teut. type **airā*,fem.; whence Finnish *airo* (Noreen, § 57). ¶ A connexion with Gk. *ἐρ-έτης*, oarsman, cannot be established.

Oasis. (L.–Gk.– Egypt.) L. *oǎsis.* – Gk. *ὄασις, αὔασις*, a fertile islet in the Libyan desert. Of Egypt. origin ; cf. Coptic *ouahe*, an oasis, a dwelling-place, *ouīh*, to dwell (Peyron).

Oast, Oast-house, a kiln for drying hops. (E.) M. E. *oost, ost.* A.S. *āst*, a kiln, drying-house.+Du. *eest*, M. Du. *ast* (the same). Allied to L. *æstus*, Gk. *αῖθος*, a burning heat. (√AIDH.) See **Ether.**

Oath. (E.) M. E. *ooth, oth.* A.S. *āð.* +Du. *eed*, Icel. *eiðr*, Dan. Swed. *ed*, Goth. *aiths*, G. *eid*, O. H. G. *eid.* Teut. type **aithoz* ; Idg. type **oitos*, as in O. Irish *oeth*, an oath.

Oats. (E.) M. E. *otes*, pl. A.S. *āte*, sing. ; pl. *ātan.* Perhaps allied to Icel. *eitill*, a nodule in stone, Norw. *eitel*, a gland, knot, nodule, Russ. *iadro*, a kernel, ball, Gk. οἶδος, a swelling. From the swollen shape. (√EID.)

Ob-, prefix. (L.) It changes to *oc-* before *c*, *of-* before *f*, *op-* before *p*. L. *ob*, with very variable senses ; as, towards, at, before, upon, over, about, near. Cf. Oscan *op*, near, Gk. ἔπι, upon ; Brugm. i. § 557.

Obdurate. (L.) L. *obdūrātus*, pp. of *obdūrāre*, to harden.—L. *ob* ; and *dūrus*, hard. See **Dure**.

Obedient. (F.—L.) O. F. *obedient*. —L. *obēdient-*, stem of pres. pt. of *obēdīre* (O. L. *oboedīre*), to obey.—L. *ob-*, near ; and *audīre*, to hear. See **Audience**. Brugm. i. § 250. Der. *dis-obedient*.

obeisance. (F.—L.) M. E. *obeisance*. —O. F. *obeissance*, later F. *obéissance*, service, a salute.—O. F. *obeissant*, pres. pt. of *obeir*, to obey.—L. *obēdīre* (above).

Obelisk. (F.—L.—Gk.) O. F. *obelis-que*.—L. *obeliscum*, acc. of *obeliscus*.—Gk. ὀβελίσκος, a pointed spit ; hence a thin pointed pillar ; dimin. of ὀβελός, a spit.

Obese, fat. (L.) L. *obēsus*, (1) eaten away, wasted ; (2) fat, lit. 'that which has devoured.'—L. *obēsus*, pp. of *obedere*, to eat away.—L. *ob*, near ; *edere*, to eat. See **Edible**. Der. *obes-i-ty*.

Obey. (F.—L.) M. E. *obeyen*.—O. F. *obeir*.—L. *obēdīre* to obey ; see **Obedient**. Der. *dis-obey*.

Obfuscate, to darken. (L.) From pp. of L. *ob-fuscāre*, to obscure.—L. *ob*, near ; and *fuscus*, brown. See **Fuscous**.

Obit, a funeral rite. (F.—L.) O. F. *obit*.—L. acc. *obitum*, a going to or down, downfall, death. — L. *obitum*, supine of *ob-īre*, to go near. — L. *ob*, near ; *īre*, to go.

Object, vb. (F.—L.) F. *objecter*.—L. *obiectāre*, to throw against, oppose ; frequent. of *ob-icere* (*obiicere*), to cast towards. — L. *ob*, towards ; *iacere*, to cast. See **Jet** (1).

Objurgation. (F.—L.) F. *objurga-tion*.—L. acc. *obiurgātiōnem*, a chiding.— L. *obiurgātus*, pp. of *obiurgāre*, to chide. —L. *ob*, against ; *iurgāre*, to sue, chide, which stands for **iūrigāre* ; from *iūr-*, stem of *iūs*, law, and *-igāre*, for *agere*, to drive, pursue. Cf. **Navigate**.

Oblate, widened at the sides. (L.) L. *oblātus*, spread out (at the sides).—L. *ob*, towards ; *lātus*, borne, carried out, pp. of *tollere*, to bear. See **Tolerate**.

oblation, an offering. (F.—L.) F.

oblation, an offering ; Cot.—L. acc. *oblā-tiōnem*, acc. of *oblātio*, an offering.—L. *oblātus*, used as pp. of *offerre*, to offer (but from a different root) ; see **Tolerate**.

Oblige, to constrain. (F.—L.) F. *obliger*.—L. *obligāre*, to bind together, oblige.—L. *ob*, near ; *ligāre*, to bind. See **Ligament**.

Oblique, slanting, perverse. (F.—L.) F. *oblique*.—L. *oblīquus*, *oblicus*, slanting, sideways, awry.—L. *ob* ; **līquus*, oblique (not in use).

Obliterate. (L.) From pp. of L. *oblitterare*, to efface.—L. *ob*, over ; *littera*, a letter. See **Letter**. ¶ It seems to have been associated with L. *oblinere*, to smear over ; though there is no etymological connexion.

Oblivion. (F.—L.) F. *oblivion*.—L. acc. *oblīuiōnem*, forgetfulness. — L. *oblī-uiscī*, to forget. Origin uncertain.

Oblong, long from side to side. (F.— L.) F. *oblong*.—L. *oblongus*, long across. — L. *ob*, over ; *longus*, long ; see **Long**.

Obloquy, calumny. (L.) L. *obloquium*, contradiction.—L. *obloquī*, to speak against. —L. *ob*, against ; *loquī*, to speak. See **Loquacious**.

Obnoxious, offensive. (L.) Formerly in the sense of ' liable to.'—L. *obnoxi-us*, liable to hurt or harm ; with suffix *-ous*. — L. *ob*, against ; *noxius*, hurtful. See **Noxious**.

Oboe. (Ital.—F.—L.) Ital. *oboe.* — F. *hautbois* ; see **Hautbois**.

Obolus, a small Gk. coin. (L.—Gk.) L. *obolus*.—Gk. ὀβολός, a small coin, perhaps orig. in the shape of a spike or nail ; allied to Gk. ὀβελός, a spit.

Obscene. (L.) L. *obscēnus*, *obscaenus*, *obscoenus*, repulsive, foul. Etym. unknown.

Obscure, dim. (F.—L.) F. *obscur*. —L. *obscūrus*, dark, lit. ' covered over.'— L. *ob* ; and *-scūrus*, i. e. covered ; cf. Skt. *sku*, to cover. (√SKEU.) Brugm. i. § 109 ; ii. § 74. See **Sky**.

Obsequies. (F.—L.) M.F. *obseques*, ' obsequies ;' Cot.—L. *obsequiās*, acc. of *obsequiæ*, funeral rites, lit. followings.—L. *obsequī*, to follow near, comply with.— L. *ob*, near ; *sequī*, to follow. See **Sequence**.

obsequious. (F. — L.) M.F. *obse-quieux* ; Cot.—L. *obsequiōsus*, full of compliance.—L. *obsequium*, compliance.—L. *obsequī*, to comply with (above.)

Observe. (F.—L.) O. F. *observer.*—

L. *obseruāre*, to take notice of, mark. – L. *ob*, near : *seruāre*, to keep, heed.

Obsidian, a vitreous stone. (L.) From L. *Obsidiānus lapis* (false reading for *Obsiānus lapis*), a stone found by one *Obsidius* (false reading for *Obsius*) in Æthiopia (Pliny, lib. xxxvi. c. 26, lib. xxxvii. c. 10).

Obsolescent, going out of use. (L.) From pres. pt. of L. *obsolescere*, to grow old, inceptive form of *obsolēre*, to decay. Origin doubtful; perhaps from L. *ob*, against; *solēre*, to be wont.

obsolete. (L.) L. *obsolētus*, pp. of *obsolēre* (above).

Obstacle. (F. – L.) F. *obstacle*. – L. *obstāculum*, a hindrance. – L. *ob*, against; *-stāculum*, double dimin. from *stā-re*, to stand.

obstetric, pertaining to midwifery. (L.) L. *obstetrīcius*, adj., from *obstetrīc-*, stem of *obstetrix*, a midwife; lit. an assistant, stander near. – L. *obstāre*, to stand near ; with fem. suffix *-trix* (of the agent). – L. *ob*, near; *stāre*, to stand. See **State.**

obstinate. (L.) L. *obstinātus*, resolute; pp. of *obstināre*, to set about, be resolved on ; lit. ‘to put oneself near.’ – L. *ob*, near ; and **stanāre*, to place oneself ; cf. Russ. *stanovite*, to set; from √STĀ. See **Destine.**

Obstreperous, clamorous. (L.) L. *obstreper-us*, clamorous; with suffix *-ous.* – L. *ob*, against, near ; *strepere*, to rattle.

Obstriction, obligation. (L.) Coined from L. *obstrictus*, pp. of *obstringere*, to bind, fasten. – L. *ob*, over ; *stringere*, to draw tight. See **Stringent.**

Obstruct. (L.) From L. *obstructus*, pp. of *obstruere*, to build in the way of anything, lit. build against. – L. *ob*, against; *struere*, to build. See **Structure.**

Obtain. (F. – L.) F. *obtenir*. – L. *obtinēre*, to hold, obtain. – L. *ob*, near; *tenēre*, to hold. See **Tenable.**

Obtrude. (L.) L. *obtrūdere*, to thrust against. – L. *ob*, against ; *trūdere*, to thrust. See **Thrust.**

Obtuse, blunt. (F. – L.) M. F. *obtus*, ‘dull;’ Cot. – L. *obtūsus*, blunted, pp. of *obtundere*, to beat against. – L. *ob*, against; *tundere*, to beat.

Obverse, lit. turned *towards* one, used of the face of a coin. (L.) L. *obuersus*, pp. of *obuertere*, to turn towards. – L. *ob*, towards; *uertere*, to turn. See **Verse.**

Obviate. (L.) From pp. of L. *obuiāre*,

to meet in the way, prevent. – L. *ob*, against; *uia*, way. See **Viaduct.**

obvious. (L.) L. *obui-us*, lying in the way, evident ; with suffix *-ous.* – L. *ob*, over against ; *uia*, the way.

Oca, the name of a certain edible root. (Peruvian.) Peruv. *occa*, the same.

Occasion. (F. – L.) F. *occasion*. – L. acc. *occāsiōnem*. – L. *oc-* (for *ob*), at ; and *cās-us*, pp. of *cadere*, to fall. See **Cadence.**

occident, west. (F. – L.) O. F. *occident*, west. – L. *occident-*, stem of pres. pt. of *occidere*, to fall, set (as the sun). – L. *oc-* (for *ob*), at ; *cadere*, to fall.

Occiput. (L.) L. *occiput*, back of the head. – L. *oc-* (for *ob*), over against ; *caput*, the head. See **Capital.**

Occult. (L.) F. *occulte*. – L. *occultus*, pp. of *occulere*, to cover over, conceal. – L. *oc-* (for *ob*) ; and obs. L. **celere*, to hide, allied to *cēlāre*, to hide. Cf. O. Irish *cel-im*, I hide, A. S. *hel-an*, to hide.

Occupy. (F. – L.) M. E. *occupien*. – F. *occuper.* – L. *occupāre*, to lay hold of. – L. *oc-* (for *ob*), near ; *capere*, to seize. Der. *pre-occupy*.

Occur. (F. – L.) M. F. *occurrer*. – L. *occurrere*, to run to meet, occur. – L. *oc-* (for *ob*), against ; *currere*, to run. See **Current.**

Ocean. (F. – L. – Gk.) O. F. *ocean*. – L. *ōceanum*, acc. of *ōceanus*. – Gk. ὠκεανός, the great stream supposed to encompass the earth.

Ocelot, a quadruped. (Mexican.) Mexican *ocelotl*, a tiger ; applied by Buffon to the ocelot.

Ochre, a fine clay, commonly yellow. (F. – L. – Gk.) F. *ocre*, ‘ oker ;’ Cot. – L. *ōchra.* – Gk. ὤχρα, yellow ochre ; from its pale colour. – Gk. ὠχρός, pale, wan.

Octagon, a plane 8-sided figure. (Gk.) From Gk. ὀκτα-, for ὀκτώ, eight ; γων-ία, an angle, connected by gradation with γόνυ, knee ; see **Knee.**

octahedron, a solid 8-sided figure. (Gk.) From ὀκτα-, for ὀκτώ, eight ; ἕδρα, a base, from the base ἑδ-, to sit ; see **Sit.**

octangular, having eight angles. (L.) From L. *oct-ō*, eight ; *angulus*, angle.

octant, the aspect of two planets when distant by the eighth part of a circle. (L.) L. *octant-*, stem of *octans*, an instrument for measuring the eighth of a circle. – L. *oct-ō*, eight.

octave. (F. – L.) Lit. 'eighth;' hence, eight days after a festival, eight notes in music. – F. *octave*, an octave (Cot.). – L. *octāua*, fem. of *octāuus*, eighth. – L. *octō*, eight. +Gk. ὀκτώ, eight; cognate with E. **Eight.** Doublet, *utas*.

October. (L.) L. *Octōber*, the eighth month of the Roman year. – L. *octō*, eight.

octogenarian, one who is eighty years old. (L.) From L. *octōgēnārius*, belonging to eighty. – L. *octōgēnī*, eighty each, distributive form of *octōginta*, eighty. – L. *octō*, eight; *-ginta*, probably allied to *decem*, ten. Brugm. ii. § 164.

octoroon, the offspring of a white person and a quadroon. (L.) One who is, in an eighth part, a black. Coined from L. *octō*, eight; in imitation of *quadroon*.

octosyllabic. (L. – Gk.) L. *octōsyllabicus*, having eight syllables. – Gk. ὀκτώ, eight; συλλαβή, a syllable; see **Syllable.**

Octroi, a toll. (F. – L.) F. *octroi*, O. F. *otroi*, orig. a grant; verbal sb. from O. F. *otroier*, to authorise, grant. – Late L. *auctōritāre*, by-form of *auctōrizāre*, to authorise. – L. *auctor*; see **Author.**

Ocular. (L.) L. *oculāris*, belonging to the eye. – L. *oculus*, eye; cognate with Gk. ὄμμα, eye. See **Optic.**

Odalisque, a female slave in a Turkish harem. (F. – Turk.) F. *odalisque*; better *odalique* (Devic). – Turk. *odaliq*, a chambermaid. – Turk. *oda*, a chamber.

Odd, not even, strange. (Scand.) M. E. *odde*. – Icel. *oddi*, a triangle, a point of land; metaphorically (from the triangle), an odd number (orig. *three*); hence also the phr. *standask ī odda*, to stand (or be) at odds, to quarrel; *oddamaðr*, the odd man, third man who gives a casting vote, *oddatala*, an odd number. Allied to *oddr*, a point of a weapon (for **ozdr*). +A. S. *ord*, a point of a sword, point; Dan. *od*, a point, Swed. *udda*, odd, *udde*, a point; G. *ort*, a place, M. H. G. *ort*, extreme point. Teut. type **uzdoz*.

Ode, a song. (F. – L. – Gk.) F. *ode*. – L. *ōda*, *ōdē*. – Gk. ᾠδή, a song; for ἀοιδή, a song. – Gk. ἀείδειν, to sing. Allied to O. Irish *faed*, W. *gwaedd*, a cry, shout. (✓WEID.) Der. *ep-ode*, *palin-ode*.

Odium, hatred. (L.) L. *odium*, sb. – L. *ōdī*, I hate; an old perfect tense. Cf. Armen. *at-eam*, I hate. Brugm. i. § 160.

Odour. (F. – L.) M. E. *odour*. – F. *odeur*. – L. *odōrem*, acc. of *odor*, scent.

Cf. Gk. ὄζειν (= **ὄδ-γειν*), to smell. (✓OD.) Der. *odorous*, from L. *odōr-us*, with suffix *-ous*; the accent has been thrown back.

Of, from, &c. (E.) M. E. *of*; A. S. *of*. +Du. Icel. Swed. Dan. Goth. *af*; G. *ab*. O. H. G. *aba*; L. *ab*, Gk. ἀπό, Skt. *apa* away. Brugm. i. § 560.

off, away from. (E.) An emphatic form of *of*. M. E. *of*; as in 'Smiteth *of* my hed' = smite *off* my head; Ch. C. T. 782 (Harleian MS.).

Offal, waste meat. (E.) M. E. *offal*, falling remnants, chips of wood, &c. From *off* and *fall*. +Du. *afval*, windfall, offal; Dan. *affald*, a fall off, offal; Swed. *affall*; G. *abfall*; all similarly compounded.

Offence. (F. – L.) O. F. *offence*, *offense*. – L. *offensa*, an offence; orig. fem. of pp. of *offendere*, to dash against (below).

offend. (F. – L.) M. E. *offenden*. – F. *offendre*. – L. *offendere*, to dash or strike against, injure. – L. *of-* (for *ob*), against; **fendere*, to strike. See **Defend.**

Offer. (L.) A. S. *offrian*. – L. *offerre*, to offer. – L. *of-* (for *ob*), near; *ferre* to bring, cognate with E. *bear*. Der. *offer-t-or-y*, from F. *offertoire*, L. *offertōrium*, a place to which offerings were brought.

Office, duty. (F. – L.) F. *office*. – L. *officium*, duty; lit. 'service.' Perhaps from *opi-*, for *opus*, work; and *facere*, to do (Walde). Der. *offic-er*, F. *officier*, Late L. *officiārius*; *offic-i-ous*, F. *officieux*, L. *officiōsus*.

Officinal, pertaining to or used in a shop or laboratory. (F. – L.) F. *officinal*. – L. *officīna*, a workshop, office; contracted form of *opificīna* (Plautus). – L. *opi-*, for *opus*, work; *-fic-*, for *facere*, to do.

Offing, the part of the visible sea remote from the shore. (E.) Merely formed from *off*, with the noun-suffix *-ing*. See **off.**

Offscouring. (E.) From *off* and *scour*. So also *off-set*, *off-shoot*, *off-spring*.

Oft, Often, frequently. (E.) A. S. *oft*; whence M. E. *ofte* with added *-e*, and lastly *ofte-n* with added *-n*. +Icel. *opt*, Dan. *ofte*, Swed. *ofta*, G. *oft*, Goth. *ufta*. Origin unknown.

Ogee, Ogive, a double curve. (F. – Span. – Arab.) 'An *ogiue* (*ogive*) or *ogee*, a wreath, circlet, or round band in architecture,' Minsheu. An *ogee* arch is a pointed arch, with doubly-curved sides. – M.F. *augive*, F. *ogive*, an ogive or ogee

(Cot.). **=** Span. *auge*, highest point, also meridian, apogee (cf. Port. *auge*, top) ; from the pointed top of Moorish arches, which have doubly-curved sides. **=** Arab. *āwj*, summit. **¶** Perhaps not a true Arab. word, but der. from Gk. *ἀπόγαιον*, the apogee (in which sense *āwj* is sometimes used). Der. *ogiv-al*, adj. (also written *ogee-fall !*).

Ogle, to glance at. (Du.) A frequent. form of Du. *oogen*, ' to cast sheepes eyes upon one ;' Hexham. (Cf. Low G. *oegeln*, to ogle, from *oegen*, to look at.) **=** Du. *ooge*, eye ; cognate with E. **Eye.**

Ogre, a monster. (F. **=** L.) F. *ogre.* Cf. Span. *ogro* (Diez ; but not given in most Dict., and probably from F.). Of unknown origin. The deriv. from L. acc. *augurem*, soothsayer, hence, a wizard (Körting) is not convincing. Der. *ogr-ess*, F. *ogresse.*

Oh ; see **O** (1).

Oil. (F. **=** L. **=** Gk.) M. E. *oile.* **=** A. F. *oile* (F. *huile*). **=** L. *oleum* ; from *olea*, an olive-tree. **=** Gk. *ἐλαία*, an olive-tree. See **Olive.**

Ointment. (F. **=** L.) The former *t* is due to confusion with *anoint* ; the M. E. form is *oinement.* **=** O. F. *oignement*, an anointing, also an unguent. **=** O. F. *oigne-r*, the same as *oindre*, to anoint ; with suffix *-ment.* **=** L. *ungere*, to anoint. See **Unguent.**

Old. (E.) M. E. *old.* O. Merc. *ald*, later *āld* ; (A. S. *eald*). **+** Du. *oud* (for **old*), G. *alt* ; cf. Goth. *altheis.* Teut. type **aldóz* ; Idg. type **al-tós*, formed with pp. suffix *-tós* from √AL, as seen in L. *al-ere*, Iccl. *al-a*, to nourish, bring up ; so that the sense was orig. ' brought up.' β. L. *altus*, high, is prob. the same word, with a newer sense.

Oleaginous. (L. **=** Gk.) L. *oleāgin-us*, oily, with suffix *-ous* ; adj., from *olea*, an olive-tree. See **Oil.**

Oleander, the rose-bay-tree. (F. **=** Late L.) M. F. *oleandre*, rose-bay-tree (Cot.). The same as Ital. *oleandro*, Span. *eloendro* (Minsheu), Port. *eloendro*, *loendro* ; all variously corrupted from Late L. *lōrandrum* (taken for *l'ōrandrum*). It seems to have been confused with *oleaster*. 2. Isidore gives the name as ' *arodandarum*, vulgo *lorandrum*.' This shews that the name was a corruption of *rhododendron*, due to confusion with L. *laurus*, laurel.

Oleaster, wild olive. (L. **=** Gk.) L.

oleaster, Rom. xi. 17 ; formed from *olea*, an olive-tree. **=** Gk. *ἐλαία*, an olive-tree.

Olfactory, relating to smell. (L.) L. *olfactōrius*, adj., from L. *olfactor*, one who smells, *olfactus*, a smelling. **=** L. *olfactus*, pp. of *olfacere*, *olefacere*, to scent. **=** L. *olĕ-re* (also *olēre*), to smell ; *facere*, to make, cause. This L. *olere* stands for **odere*, cf. *od-or*, scent ; and cf. L. *lacruma* for *dacruma*. Allied to Gk. *ὀδ-μή*, scent.

Oligarchy. (F. **=** L. **=** Gk.) F. *oligar-chie.* **=** Late L. *oligarchia.* **=** Gk. *ὀλιγαρχία*, government by a few men. **=** Gk. *ὀλιγ-*, for *ὀλίγος*, few, little ; and *-αρχια*, from *ἄρχειν*, to rule.

Olio, a mixture, medley. (Span. **=** L.) A mistaken form for *olia*, intended to represent Span. *olla* (pronounced *olya*), a round earthen pot, also an olio, esp. in phrase *olla podrida*, a hodge-podge. **=** L. *olla*, O. Lat. *aula*, a pot.

Olive. (F. **=** L. **=** Gk.) F. *olive.* **=** L. *olīua.* **=** Gk. *ἐλαία* (for **ἐλαίϝα*), an olive-tree. Brugm. i. § 121 (2).

Omadaun, Omadhawn, a simple-ton. (C.) Anglo-Irish ; from Irish *amadán*, a simpleton. **=** Irish *amad* (the same). **=** Irish *am-*, for *an-*, neg. prefix (cf. Gk. *ἀν-*) ; *-mad*, O. Irish *-met*, mind, cognate with L. *mens* and E. **mind.** Cf. L. *āmens*, mad.

Ombre, a game at cards. (Span. **=** L.) From Span. *juego del hombre*, lit. ' game of the man ' (whence F. *hombre*). **=** L. *hominem*, acc. of *homo*, a man. See **Human.**

Omega, the end. (Gk.) Gk. *ὠ̂*, called *ὠ μέγα*, i. e. great *o*, long *o* ; which is the *last* letter of the Gk. alphabet, as opposed to *alpha*, the *first* letter. *Μέγα* is neut. of *μέγας*, great, allied to E. **Mickle.**

Omelet, a pan-cake, chiefly of eggs. (F. **=** L.) F. *omelette, aumelette* (Cot.). These are from O. F. *amelette*, but this again was preceded by the form *alemette*, which is, through change of suffix, from *alemelle* (Scheler). The sense of *alemelle* was ' a thin plate,' still preserved in F. *alumelle*, sheathing of a ship. Godefroy gives O. F. *alemele*, blade of a knife ; thus the *omelet* was named from its shape, of a ' thin plate ' of metal. 2. Lastly *l'alemelle* is a corruption of *la lemelle*, the correct O. F. form. **=** L. *lāmella*, a thin plate, properly of metal ; dimin. of *lāmina*, a thin plate ; see **Lamina.** **¶** See this clearly traced by Scheler and Littré.

Omen, a sign of a future event. (L.) L. *ōmen*; O. Lat. *osmen*. **Der.** *ominous*.

Omit, to neglect. (L.) L. *omittere*, (pp. *omissus*), lit. 'to let go.' For **ommittere<*ob-mittere*; from *ob*, by, *mittere*, to send. See **Missile**. **Der.** *omiss-ion*, from F. *omission*, 'an omission,' from L. acc. *omissiōnem*; from the pp.

Omni-, prefix. (L.) L. *omnis*, all. **Der.** *omni-potent*, all-powerful; *omni-present*, everywhere present; *omni-scient*, all-knowing; *omni-vorous*, all-devouring; see **Potent, Present, Science, Voracious**.

omnibus, a public vehicle. (L.) So called because intended for the use of all. — L. *omnibus*, for all; dat. pl. of *omnis*. ¶ Commonly shortened to *bus*.

Omrah, a prince, lord. (Arab.) ' Aigrettes by *omrahs* worn;' Scott, Vis. of Don. Roderick, st. 31. *Omrah* is properly a plural, like **Nabob**, q. v. — Arab. *umarā*, pl. of *amīr*, a prince, emir; see **Emir**. Cf. the Arab. title *amīru'l-umarā*, prince of princes (Yule).

On. (E.) M. E. *on*; A. S. *on*. **+** Du. *aan*, Icel. *ā*, Swed. *å*, G. *an* (whence Dan. *an*), Goth. *ana*, Gk. *ἀνά*, Russ. *na*. Idg. type **ana*.

Once; see **One**.

Once, sometimes for **Ounce** (2).

One (1), single, sole. (E.) M. E. *oon*. Already written *won* in M. E. See Guy of Warwick, ed. Zupitza, note to l. 7927. A. S. *ān*, one. **+** Du. *een*, Icel. *einn*, Dan. *een*, Swed. *en*, G. *ein*, Goth. *ains*, W. *un*, Irish and Gael. *aon*, L. *ūnus*, O. L. *oinos*, Gk. **οἶνος*, one (fem. *οἴνη*, an ace on a die). Teut. type **ainoz*; Idg. type **oinos*. Cf. Lith. *vénas*; Brugm. ii. § 165. **Der.** *an*, *a*, *on-ly*, *al-one*, *at-one*.

once. (E.) M. E. *ones*; A. S. *ānes*, adv., once. Orig. gen. case (masc. and neut.) of *ān*, one; the gen. case was used adverbially, as in *need-s*, *twi-ce*, *thri-ce*.

one (2), a person, spoken of indefinitely. (E.) In the phrase ' *one* says,' *one* means ' a single person.' Merely a peculiar use of the ordinary word *one*. ¶ Not F. *on*.

Onerous, burdensome. (F. — L.) M.F. *onereux*. — L. *onerōsus*, adj. — L. *oner-*, for **ones-*, stem of *onus*, a burden.

Onion, a plant. (F. — L.) F. *oignon*. — L. *ūniōnem*, acc. of *ūnio*, a large onion; see **Union** (2).

Only. (E.) M. E. *oonli*, adj. and adv.;

A. S. *ānlīc*, adj., unique, lit. ' one-like.' — A. S. *ān*, one; *līc*, like.

Onomatopœia, name-making, the formation of a word with a resemblance in sound to the thing signified. (Gk.) Gk. *ὀνοματοποιία*, the making of a name. — Gk. *ὀνοματο-*, combining form of *ὄνομα*, a name; and *ποιεῖν*, to make; see **Name** and **Poem**. Brugm. ii. § 117.

Onset, an assault. (E.) Due to the phr. *set on!* i. e. attack! From *on* and *set*.

Onslaught, an attack. (E.) From *on* and M. E. *slaht*, A. S. *sleaht*, a stroke, blow, formed from *slēan*, to strike; see **Slay**. And cf. *slaughter*.

Onward, Onwards. (E.) From *on* and *-ward*, *-wards*; see **Toward**.

Onyx, a kind of agate. (L. — Gk.) L. *onyx*. — Gk. *ὄνυξ*, a nail; a veined gem, onyx, from its resemblance to the finger-nail. See **Nail**.

Oolite, a kind of limestone. (F. — Gk.) F. *oolithe* (with *th* sounded as *t*). — Gk. *ᾠό-ν*, egg; *λίθ-ος*, stone. Lit. ' egg-stone.' See **Oval**.

Ooze, moisture, soft mud. (E.) Formerly *wose*; M. E. *wose*. A. S. *wōs*, moisture, juice. **+** Icel. *vās*, wetness. Perhaps confused with A. S. *wāse*, soft mud; which is cognate with Icel. *veisa*, a stagnant pool. **Der.** *ooze*, vb.

Opacity; see **Opaque**.

Opal, a gem. (F. — L.) F. *opale*. — L. *opalus*, an opal. Cf. Gk. *ὀπάλλιος*, an opal; Skt. *upala-*, a stone, gem.

Opaque. (F. — L.) F. *opaque*. — L. *opācum*, acc. of *opācus*, dark, obscure. **Der.** *opac-i-ty*, from F. *opacité*, L. acc. *opācitātem*.

Open, unclosed. (E.) The verb is from the adj. *open*, which is sometimes shortened to *ope* (Coriol. i. 4. 43). A. S. *open*, adj., open, with the form of an old pp. **+** Du. *open*, adj.; Icel. *opinn*; Swed. *öppen*; G. *offen*. Teut. types **upenoz*, **upanoz*. Perhaps connected with the idea of the lifting of a tent-door; cf. A. S. *ūp*, up. See **Up**. **Der.** *open*, vb., A. S. *openian*, to make open.

Opera. (Ital. — L.) Ital. *opera*, a work, a musical play. — L. *opera*, work; see below.

operate. (L.) From pp. of L. *operārī*, to work. — L. *opera*, work; from *oper-* (for **opes-*), stem of L. *opus*, work, toil. **+** Skt. *apas*, work.

Ophidian, relating to serpents. (Gk.)

Formed with suffix -an (L. -ānus), from Gk. ὀφίδιον, ὀφείδιον, dimin. of ὄφις, a serpent. Cf. the dimin. form ζῴ-διον (see Zodiac). + Skt. ahi-, L. anguis, a snake.

ophicleide, a musical instrument. (F.—Gk.) Lit. a 'key-serpent'; because made by adding keys to an old musical instrument called a serpent (from its twisted shape). — Gk. ὄφι-s, a serpent; κλειδ-, stem of κλείς, a key.

Ophthalmia, inflammation of the eye. (Gk.) Gk. ὀφθαλμία. — Gk. ὀφθαλμός, the eye, Boeotian ὄκταλλος, for *ὀκταν-λος (cf. Skt. akshan-, eye); Doric ὀπτίλος, the eye. From Idg. base *oq-, eye; cf. Russ. oko, eye, Skt. aksha-, akshi, Lith. akìs, L. oc-ul-us. See Prellwitz. And see Ocular.

Opinion. (F.—L.) F. opinion.—L. opīniōnem, acc. of opīnio, a supposition. — L. opīnāri, to suppose, opine. — L. opīnus, thinking, expecting; only in nec-opīnus, not expecting, unexpected, in-opīnus, unexpected. Der. opine, F. opiner, L. opīnārī (above).

Opium. (L.—Gk.) L. opium. — Gk. ὄπιον, poppy-juice. — Gk. ὀπός, sap.

Opossum, a quadruped. (W. Indian.) — W. Indian opassom; in the language of the Indians of Virginia; Capt. Smith, p. 59.

Oppidan. (L.) L. oppidānus, belonging to a town. — L. oppidum, a town; O. L. oppedum. Apparently from L. op- (ob), near; *pedum (Gk. πέδον), a field, plain; Brugm. i. § 65. (Explained as 'protecting the plain'; the derivation is clearer than the sense.)

Oppilation, a stopping up. (F.—L.) M. F. oppilation, 'an obstruction;' Cot.— L. acc. oppīlātiōnem. — L. oppīlatus, pp. of oppīlāre, to stop up. — L. op (for ob), against; pīlāre, to ram, from pīlum, a pestle. And L. pīlum is for *pins-lom, from pinsere, to pound.

Opponent. (L.) L. oppōnent-, stem of pres. part. of oppōnere, to oppose. — L. ob, against; pōnere, to place. See Position.

Opportune, timely. (F.—L.) F. opportun. — L. opportūnus, convenient, seasonable, lit. 'near the harbour,' or 'easy of access.' — L. op- (ob), near; portus, access, harbour. See Port (2).

Oppose. (F.—L. and Gk.) F. opposer, to withstand. — L. op- (for ob), against; F. poser, to place, from Late L. pausāre, used to translate L. pōnere, to place. See Pose.

Opposite. (F.—L.) F. opposite.—L.

oppositus, pp. of oppōnere, to set against. — L. op- (ob), against; pōnere, to set. See Position.

Oppress. (F.—L.) F. oppresser. — Late L. oppressāre, frequent. of L. opprimere, to oppress. — L. op- (ob), near; premere (pp. pressus), to press. See Press.

Opprobrious. (L.) From L. opprobriōsus, full of reproach. — L. opprobrium, reproach. — L. op- (for ob), on, upon; probrum, disgrace.

Oppugn, to resist. (F.—L.) F. oppugner. — L. oppugnāre. — L. op- (ob), against; pugnāre, to fight, from pugnus, a fist. See Pugilism.

Optative, wishing. (F.—L.) Chiefly as the name of a mood.—F. optatif.—L. optātīuus, expressive of a wish.—L. optātus, pp. of optāre, to wish. Cf. Skt. āp, to attain.

Optic, relating to the sight. (F.—Gk.) F. optique. — Gk. ὀπτικός, belonging to the sight; cf. ὀπτήρ, a spy. From the base οπ- (for οκ-) seen in Ionic ὄπ-ωπ-α, I have seen, ὄψ-ομαι, I shall see; cf. L. oc-ulus, the eye. See Ocular.

Optimism, the doctrine that all is for the best. (L.) From L. optim-us, O. Lat. opitumus (Brugm. ii. § 73), best; with suffix -ism (Gk. -ισμος). L. op-ti-mus is a superl. form from a base op- (i.e. choice, select); cf. optāre, to wish.

option, choice. (F.—L.) F. option.— L. optiōnem, acc. of optio, choice. Allied to L. optāre, to wish; see Optative.

Opulent, wealthy. (F.—L.) F. opulent.—L. opulentus, wealthy. L. op-, base of opēs, wealth. Cf. Skt. apnas, wealth.

Or (1), conj., offering an alternative. (E.) Short for other, outher, auther, the M. E. forms, which answer to A. S. āhwœper, āwþer. But this M. E. other took the place of A. S. oððe, or.

Or (2), ere. (E.) M. E. or, unemphatic form of ēr, ere. A. S. ēr, ere; see Ere. (In the phrases or ere, or ever.)

Or (3), gold. (F.—L.) In heraldry. F. or.—L. aurum, gold.

Orach, a pot-herb. (F.—L.—Gk.) Also arrache. — F. arroche, 'orache, orage;' Cot. A Picard form corresponding to F. *arreuce (Hatzfeld). [Cf. Walloon arip, orach (Remacle); Ital. atrepice.] — L. atriplicem, acc. of atriplex, orach. — Gk. ἀτράφαξις, ἀτράφαξυς, orach.

Oracle. (F.—L.) F. oracle.—L. ōrāculum, a divine announcement; formed from *ōrā-re*, to pray, from *ōr-* (for *ōs*), the mouth (below).

oral, spoken. (L.) Coined from L. *ōr-* (for *ōs*), the mouth. **+** Skt. *āsya*, mouth ; Icel. *ōss*, mouth of a river.

Orang-outang, a large ape. (Malay.) Malay *ōrang-ūtan*, lit. 'wild man.' — Malay *ōrang*, a man ; *ūtan*, *hūtan*, woods, wilds of a country, wild.

Orange. (F. — Ital. — Arab. — Pers.) O. F. *orenge* (F. *orange*). For **narenge*, but the initial *n* was lost (in Italian), and then *arenge* became *orenge* by a popular etymology from *or*, gold. Cf. Span. *naranja*, an orange. — Ital. *arancia*, an orange ; Low Lat. *arangia*. — Arab. *nāranj*, *nārinj*. — Pers. *nārang*, an orange. Allied to Pers. *nār*, a pomegranate.

Oration. (F. — L.) F. *oration*. — L. acc. *ōrātiōnem*; cf. *ōrātus*, pp. of *ōrāre*, to pray. — L. *ōr-* (for *ōs*), the mouth. See **Oral. Doublet,** *orison*.

orator. (F. — L.) Formerly *oratour*. — F. *orateur*. — L. *ōrātōrem*, acc. of *ōrātor*, a speaker. — L. *ōrātus*, pp. of *ōrāre*, to pray, to speak (above).

Orb. (F. — L.) F. *orbe*. — L. *orbem*, acc. of *orbis*, a circle, sphere.

orbit. (L.) L. *orbita*, a track, circuit ; formed with suffix *-ta* from *orbi-*, decl. stem of *orbis*, an orb, circle.

Orc, Ork, a large marine animal ; a narwhal, or grampus. (L.) See Nares. — L. *orca*, perhaps the narwhal (Pliny).

Orchard. (L. *and* E.) M. E. *orchard*. A. S. *orceard*, older form *ortgeard*. Cognate with Goth. *aurtigards*, a garden (Gk. κῆπος). The latter element, A. S. *geard*, is the mod. E. *yard*; see **Yard.** The former element is merely borrowed from L. *hortus*, a garden, both in E. and Gothic ; see **Horticulture.** As the L. *hortus* is cognate with E. *yard*, the form *ort-geard* merely repeats the idea of ' yard.' ¶ So in Brugm. i. § 767 ; but some consider A. S. *ort-geard* as wholly Teutonic, and connect it with A. S. *wyrt-geard*, Dan. *urt-gaard*, Swed. *örte-gård*, a kitchen-garden, from A. S. *wyrt*, Dan. *urt*, Swed. *ört*, a wort. (See *Wort* in Franck.) See **Wort.**

Orchestra. (L. — Gk.) L. *orchestra*. — Gk. ὀρχήστρα, an orchestra ; which, in the Attic theatre, was a space on which the chorus danced. — Gk. ὀρχέομαι, I dance.

Orchis, a plant. (L. — Gk.) L. *orchis*. — Gk. ὄρχις, a testicle, a plant with roots

of testicular shape. **Der.** *orchid*, where the suffix *-id* was suggested by the Gk. εἶδος, shape ; cf. *cyclo-id*, *cono-id*.

Ordain, to set in order. (F. — L.) M. E. *ordeinen*. — O. F. *ordener* (later *ordonner*). — L. *ordināre*, to set in order. — L. *ordin-*, declensional stem of *ordo*, order. **Der.** *pre-ordain*.

Ordeal, a severe test, judgment by fire. &c. (E.) M. E. *ordal*. A. S. *ordēl*, *ordāl*, a dealing out, judgment, decision. O. Friesic *ordēl*. — A. S. *or-*, prefix, out ; *dēl*, *dāl*, a dealing ; see **Deal, Dole.** The prefix *or-* = Du. *oor-*, G. *ur-*, Goth. *us-*, out (hence, thorough). **+** Du. *oordeel*, O. Sax. *urdēli*, G. *urtheil*, judgment ; similarly compounded.

Order. (F. — L.) F. *ordre*, O. F. *ordine*. — L. *ordinem*, acc. of *ordo*, order. Allied to L. *ordīrī*, to begin, *orīrī*, to arise. Brugm. ii. § 128. **Der.** *dis-order*.

ordinal, shewing the order. (L.) L. *ordinālis*, adj., in order. — L. *ordin-*, declensional stem of *ordo*, order.

ordinance. (F. — L.) O. F. *ordinance*. — Late L. *ordinantia*, a command. — L. *ordinant-*, pres. pt. of *ordināre*, to ordain. See **Ordain.**

ordinary. (F. — L.) F. *ordinaire*. — L. *ordinārius*, regular (as sb., an overseer). — L. *ordin-*, decl. stem of *ordo*, order. **Der.** *ordinary*, sb.

ordination. (L.) From L. *ordinātio*, an ordinance, also ordination. — L. *ordinātus*, pp. of *ordināre*, to ordain. See **Ordain.**

ordnance, artillery. (F. — L.) Formerly, *ordinance* ; it had reference to the *bore* or *size* of the cannon, and was thence transferred to the cannon itself (Cot. ; s. v. *ordonnance*) ; see **ordinance.**

Ordure, excrement. (F. — L.) F. *ordure*. — O. F. *ord* (fem. *orde*), filthy, foul, ugly, frightful. — L. *horridus*, rough, frightful. See **Horrid.** (So Körting.)

Ore. (E.) M. E. *or*, *oor*. A. S. *ōra*, ore of metal, allied to *ōre*, a mine. E. Fries. *ūr*, ore. **+** Du. *oer*, ore. ¶ Distinct from A. S. *ār*, brass, which is cognate with Goth. *ais*, L. *aes*, brass. But the words may have been confused.

Oread, a mountain-nymph. (Gk.) From Gk. ὀρειάδ-, stem of ὀρειάς, an oread. — Gk. ὄρος, a mountain.

Organ. (F. — L. — Gk.) F. *organe*. — L. *organum*, an implement. — Gk. ὄργανον, an

360

implement; allied to ἔργον, work; see **Work.**

orgies, sacred rites, revelry. (F.–L.– Gk.) F. *orgies.* – L. *orgia,* sb. pl., a festival in honour of Bacchus, orgies. – Gk. ὄργια, sb. pl., orgies, rites, from sing. *ὄργιον,* a sacred act; allied to ἔργον, work.

Orgulous, proud. (F.–O.H.G.) Also *orgillous;* M. E. *orgeilus;* Anglo-F. *orguyllus.* – O. F. *orgoillos, orguillus,* later *orgueilleux,* proud. – O.F. *orgoil, orguil,* F. *orgueil,* pride. From an O. H. G. sb. **urguolī,* from O.H.G. *urguol,* remarkable, notable (Graff).

Oriel, a recess (with a window) in a room. (F.–L.) M.E. *oriol, oryall,* a small room, portico, esp. a room for a lady, boudoir. – O.F. *oriol,* a porch, gallery, corridor. – Late L. *oriolum,* a small room, recess, portico; prob. for *aureolum* (?), that which is ornamented with gold. – L. *aurum,* gold. ¶ See Pliny, lib. xxxiii. c. 3, for the custom of gilding apartments. Cf. **Oriole.**

Orient, eastern. (F.–L.) F. *orient.* – L. *orient-,* stem of *oriens,* rising, the east; orig. pres. pt. of *orīrī,* to rise, begin. **+** Skt. *r̥,* to rise.

Orifice. (F.–L.) F. *orifice,* a small opening. – L. *ōrificium,* an opening, lit. 'making of a mouth.' – L. *ōri-,* decl. stem of *ōs,* mouth; *facere,* to make.

Oriflamme, the old standard of France. (F.–L.) F. *oriflamme,* the sacred standard of France. – Late L. *auriflamma,* lit. 'golden flame,' because the banner was cut into flame-like strips at the outer edge, and carried on a gilt pole. – L. *auri-* (for *aurum*), gold; *flamma,* flame.

Origan, wild marjoram. (F.–L.–Gk.) F. *origan.* – L. *orīganum.* – Gk. ὀρίγανον, lit. 'mountain-pride.' – Gk. ὀρί = ὀρει-, related to ὄρος, a mountain; γάνος, beauty, ornament.

Origin. (F.–L.) F. *origine.* – Lat. *orīginem,* acc. of *orīgo,* a beginning. – L. *orīrī,* to rise.

Oriole, the golden thrush. (F.–L.) O.F. *oriol* (F. *loriot* = *l'oriot*). – L. *aureolus,* golden. – L. *aurum,* gold.

Orison, a prayer. (F.–L.) O. F. *orison, oreison* (F. *oraison*). – L. *ōrātiōnem,* acc. of *ōrātio,* a prayer; see **Oration.**

Orle, a kind of fillet, in heraldry, &c. (F.–L.) F. *orle,* m., M.F. *orle,* f., a hem, narrow border; cf. Late L. *orla,* a border, edge. – L. type **ōrula,* dimin.

of L. *ōra,* border, edge. Cf. L. *ōs,* mouth.

Orlop, a deck of a ship. (Du.) Formerly *orlope* (Phillips). Contracted from Du. *overloop,* a running over, a deck of a ship, an orlope (Sewel). So called because it traverses the ship. – Du. *over,* over; *loopen,* to run; see **Elope, Leap.**

Ormolu, a kind of brass. (F.–L.) F. *or moulu,* lit. 'pounded gold.' – F. *or,* from L. *aurum,* gold; and *moulu,* pp. of *moudre,* to grind, O. F. *moldre,* from L. *molere,* to grind.

Ornament. (F. – L.) M. E. *ornement.* – F. *ornement.* – L. *ornāmentum,* an adornment. – L. *ornāre,* to adorn.

ornate. (L.) From pp. of L. *ornāre,* to adorn.

Ornithology, the science of birds. (Gk.) Gk. ὄρνιθο-, for ὄρνις, a bird; -λογία, from λόγος, a discourse, λέγειν, to speak. Allied to A.S. *earn,* G. *aar,* W. *eryr,* an eagle, named from its soaring; cf. Gk. ὄρνυμι, I stir up, rouse.

ornithorhyncus, an Australian animal. (Gk.) Named from the resemblance of its snout to a duck's bill. – Gk. ὄρνιθο- (for ὄρνις), bird; ῥύγχος, a snout.

Orphan. (L. – Gk.) L. *orphanus.* – Gk. ὀρφανός, destitute; John xiv. 18. Allied to L. *orbus,* destitute.

Orpiment, yellow sulphuret of arsenic. (F.–L.) Lit. 'gold paint.' F. *orpiment.* – L. *auripigmentum,* gold paint. – L. *auri-* (for *aurum*), gold; and *pigmentum,* a pigment, paint, from *pingere,* to paint.

orpine, orpin, a kind of stone-crop. (F.–L.) Named from its colour. M. E. *orpin.* – F. *orpin,* 'orpin, or live-long; also orpiment;' Cot. A docked form of *orpiment* above.

Orrery, an apparatus for illustrating the motion of the planets. (Ireland.) Constructed at the expense of Charles Boyle, earl of *Orrery,* about 1715. *Orrery* is a barony in co. Cork, Ireland.

Orris, a plant. (Ital.–L.–Gk.) Formerly *orice, oris.* These are E. corruptions of M. Ital. *irios* (Ital. *ireos*). – M. Ital. *irios,* 'oris-roote,' Florio; with reference to the *Iris florentina.* Modified from L. *īris,* a rainbow, an iris.

Ort; see **Orts.**

Orthodox, of the right faith. (L.– Gk.) Late L. *orthodoxus.* – Gk. ὀρθόδοξος, of the right opinion. – Gk. ὀρθό-s, upright,

right; δόξα, an opinion, from δοκεῖν, to seem. Cf. **Arduous**. Brugm. ii. § 143.

orthoepy, correct pronunciation. (Gk.) From Gk. ὀρθοέπεια, orthoepy. — Gk. ὀρθό-s, right; ἔπ-οs, a word; see **Epic**.

orthography, correct writing. (F. — L. — Gk.) M. E. *ortographie.* — M. F. *ortographie.* — L. *orthographia.* — Gk. ὀρθο-γραφία. — Gk. ὀρθό-s, right; γράφειν, to write.

orthopterous, lit. straight-winged. (Gk.) Gk. ὀρθό-s, straight; πτερόν, a wing.

Ortolan, a bird. (F. — Ital. — L.) O. F. *hortolan.* — M. Ital. *hortolano,* a gardener, also an *ortolan,* lit. ' haunter of gardens.' — L. *hortulānus,* a gardener. — L. *hortulus,* dimin. of *hortus,* a garden; allied to **Yard**.

Orts, remnants, leavings. (E.) M. E. *ortes.* From A. S. *or-,* out (what is left); *etan,* to eat. Proved by M. Du. *orete, ooraete,* a piece left after eating, Swed. dial. *oräte, uräte,* refuse fodder. The same prefix *or-* occurs in *ordeal.* Cf. also Low G. *ort,* an ort; Dan. dial. *ored, orret,* an ort; N. Fries. *örte,* to leave remnants after eating.

Oscillate, to swing. (L.) From pp. of L. *oscillāre,* to swing. — L. *oscillum,* a swing.

Osculate, to kiss. (L.) From pp. of L. *osculārī,* to kiss. — L. *osculum,* a little mouth, pretty mouth; double dimin. of *ōs,* the mouth.

Osier, (F.) F. *osier,* ' the ozier, red withy, water-willow tree;' Cot. Cf. Late L. *ōsāria, ausāria,* a bundle of osiers or twigs of willow (9th cent.).

Osmium, a metal. (Gk.) The oxide has a disagreeable smell. — Gk. ὀσμή, ὀδμή, a smell. — Gk. ὄζειν (for *ὄδ-γειν), to smell; cf. ὀδμή, scent. See **Odour**.

Osprey, the fish-hawk. (L.) A corruption of *ossifrage,* the older name for the bird. — L. *ossifragus, ossifraga,* an osprey. — L. *ossifragus,* bone-breaking; (from its strength). — L. *ossi-,* decl. stem of *os,* bone; *frag-,* base of *frangere,* to break.

osseous, bony. (L.) L. *osse-us,* bony; with suffix *-ous.* — L. *oss-,* stem of *os,* a bone. Cf. Gk. ὀστέον, Skt. *asthi,* a bone. Brugm. i. § 703.

ossifrage. (L.) In Levit. xi. 13; see **Osprey**.

ossify, to turn to bone. (F. — L.)

From L. *ossi-,* decl. stem of *os,* bone; F. *-fier,* for L. *-ficāre,* to make, from *facere,* to make. Der. *ossific-at-ion.*

Ostensible. (L.) Coined from *ostensi-* (for *ostensus*), pp. of *ostendere,* to shew; with suffix *-bilis.* See below.

ostentation. (F. — L.) F. *ostentation.* — L. *ostentātiōnem,* acc. of *ostentātio,* display. — L. *ostentātus,* pp. of *ostentāre,* intensive form of *ostendere,* to shew, lit. stretch before. — L. *os-* (for *op-s-,* related to *ob*), near, before; *tendere,* to stretch. See **Tend** (1). For *ops-,* see Brugm. i. § 143.

Osteology, science of the bones. (Gk.) Gk. ὀστέο-ν, a bone; -λογία, from λόγος, a discourse, λέγειν, to speak. See **osseous**.

Ostler; see **Hostler**.

Ostracise, to banish by a vote written on a potsherd. (Gk.) Gk. ὀστρακίζειν, to ostracise. — Gk. ὄστρακον, a potsherd, tile, voting-tablet, orig. a shell; allied to Gk. ὄστρεον, an oyster, orig. a shell. See **Oyster**.

Ostrich, a bird. (F. — L. *and* Gk.) M. E. *ostrice, oystryche.* — O. F. *ostruce;* mod. F. *autruche.* [Cf. Span. *avestruz,* Port. *abestruz,* an ostrich.] — L. *auis strūthio,* lit. ostrich-bird. Here *strūthio* is from Gk. στρουθίων, an ostrich; extended from στρουθός, a bird.

Other, second, different. (E.) M. E. *other;* A. S. ōðer, other, second. + Du. *ander,* Icel. *annarr* (for *anthar-*), Dan. *anden,* Swed. *annan,* G. *ander,* Goth. *anthar;* Lithuan. *antras,* Skt. *antara-,* other. In Skt. *an-tara-,* the suffix is the same as the usual comparative suffix (as in Gk. σοφώ-τεροs, wiser). Cf. Skt. *an-ya-,* other, different.

Otter. (E.) M. E. *oter,* A. S. *otor.* + Du. *otter,* Icel. *otr,* Dan. *odder,* Swed. *utter,* G. *otter;* Russ. *vuidra,* Lith. *údra;* also Gk. ὕδρα, a hydra, water-snake. Teut. type *otroz,* m.; Idg. types *udros,* m., *udrā,* f. Allied to *water;* compare Gk. ὕδρα, hydra, with ὕδωρ, water. The sense is ' dweller in the water.' **Doublet,** *hydra,* q. v.

Otto, the same as **Attar**.

Ottoman, a low stuffed seat. (F. — Turk.) F. *ottomane,* an ottoman, sofa. — F. *Ottoman,* Turkish. So named from *Othman* or *Osman,* founder of the Turkish empire.

Ouch, Nouch, the socket of a precious

stone, ornament. (F.—O. H. G.) Usually *ouch*; yet *nouch* is the true form. M. E. *nouche*. — O. F. *nouche*, *nosche*, *nusche*, a buckle, clasp, bracelet (Burguy); Low L. *nusca*. — M. H. G. *nuske*, O. H. G. *nusca*, a buckle, clasp, brooch. ¶ Perhaps of Celtic origin; cf. Irish *nasc*, a tie, chain, ring, *nasgaim*, I bind (Schade, Stokes).

Ought (1), pt. t. of Owe, q. v.

Ought (2), anything; see Aught.

Ounce (1), twelfth part of a pound. (F.—L.) M. E. *unce*. — O. F. *unce* (F. *once*). — L. *uncia*, (1) an ounce, (2) an inch. Allied to Gk. ὄγκος, mass, weight. See **Inch**.

Ounce (2), **Once**, a kind of lynx. (F.—L.—Gk.) F. *once*; M.F. *lonce*, Cot. Cf. Port. *onça*, Span. *onza*, Ital. *lonza*, an ounce; also Ital. *onza*, an ounce (Florio, 1598), obtained by treating *lonza* as if = *l'onza*. — Late L. type **lyncea*, lynx-like, fem. — L. *lync-*, stem of *lynx*, a lynx. — Gk. λύγξ, a lynx; see **Lynx**. For F. *o*<Gk. *v*, cf. *grotto*, *tomb*, *torso*.

Ouphe, an elf, fairy. (Scand.) Mer. Wives, iv. 4. 49. A variant of *oaf=elf*. See **Oaf** and **Elf**.

Our, (E.) A. S. *ūre*, of us; gen. of *wē*, we. The possessive pronoun was also *ūre*, which was regularly declined. The form *ūre* stands for **ūs-er-*; cf. Goth. *unsara*, gen. pl. of Goth. *weis*, we.

Ourang-outang; see Orang-outang.

Ousel, a kind of thrush. (E.) M.E. *osel*. A. S. *ōsle*. For **omsal-*, which is for older **amsal-*.+G. *amsel*, O. H. G. *amsala*, an ousel. The L. *merula* (whence E. *merle*) can stand for **mesula*, and may be connected with G. *amsel* by gradation. See **Merle**.

Oust, to eject. (F.—L.) A. F. *ouster* (Bozon), M. F. *oster*, 'to remove;' Cot. (F. *ôter*.) Of disputed origin; some derive it from *obstāre*, to thwart, which gives the right form, but does not suit the sense; Diez suggests L. **haustāre*, a derivative of *haurīre* (pp. *haustus*), to draw water. Cf. E. *ex-haust*; and L. *exhaurīre*, in the sense 'to remove.'

Out, without, abroad. (E.) M. E. *oute*, *ute*, adv., A. S. *ūte*, *ūtan*, adv., out, without; formed (with adv. suffix *-e* or *-an*) from A. S. *ūt*, adv., out, from.+Du. *uit*, Icel. *ūt*, Dan. *ud*, Swed. *ut*, G. *aus*, Goth. *ūt* (= A. S. *ūt*), *ūta* (= A. S. *ūte*), *ūtana* (= A. S. *ūtan*); Skt. *ud*, up, out. ¶ Hence numerous compounds, such as

out-balance, *out-bid*, *out-break*, presenting no difficulty.

outer, comp. form; see Utter.

Outlaw. (Scand.) M. E. *outlawe*. — Icel. *útlagi*, an outlaw, lit. out of (beyond) the law. — Icel. *ūt*, out; *lög*, law; see Out and Law. Cf. L. *exlex*, lawless.

Outlet. (E.) M. E. *utlete*, lit. 'a letting out.' — A. S. *ūt*, out; *lǣtan*, to let.

Outmost; see Utmost.

Outrage. (F.—L.) F. *outrage*, earlier form *oltrage*, excessive violence. (Cf. Ital. *oltraggio*.) — O. F. *oltre*, F. *outre*, beyond; with suffix *-age* (<L. *-āticum*). — L. *ultrā*, beyond. See Ultra-.

Outrigger. (E. *and* Scand.) A projecting spar for extending sails, a projecting rowlock for an oar, a boat with projecting rowlocks. From Out and Rig.

Outward. (E.) A. S. *ūteweard*, outward. — A. S. *ūte*, out; *weard*, *-ward*; see Toward.

Oval, egg-shaped. (F.—L.) F. *oval*. Formed with suffix *-al* (<L. *-ālis*) from L. *ōuum*, an egg.+Gk. ᾠόν, ᾤον, an egg. The Gk. ᾤον is for **ōwiom*, related by gradation to L. *auis*, a bird (like ᾠα, a sheep-skin, from ὄις, a sheep); see Aviary. Perhaps cognate with Egg. Der. *ov-ar-y*, Late L. *ovāria*, the part of the body in which eggs are formed in birds; *ovi-form*, egg-shaped; *ovi-parous*, from L. *ōui-parus*, egg-producing (see Parent).

Ovation, a lesser Roman triumph. (F. —L.) F. *ovation*.—L. acc. *ouātiōnem*, from *ouātio*, a shouting, exultation.—L. *ouātus*, pp. of *ouāre*, to shout. + Gk. εὐάζειν, to shout, from εὐαί, εὐοῖ, interjections of rejoicing, esp. in honour of Bacchus.

Oven. (E.) M. E. *ouen* (=*oven*). A. S. *ofen*, *ofn*.+Du. *oven* Icel. *ofn*, *omn* (also *ogn*), Swed. *ugn*, G. *ofen*, Goth. *auhns*. Teut. types **uhno-*, *ufno-*; Idg. type **uqnos*. Allied to Skt. *ukhā*, a pot (cf. Gk. ἰπνός, an oven); this older sense is remarkably preserved in A. S. *ofnet*, a pot, vessel.

Over, above, across. (E.) M. E. *ouer* (=*over*). A. S. *ofer*.+Du. *over*, Icel. *yfir*, *ofr*, Dan. *over*, Swed. *öfver*, G. *über*, Goth. *ufar*; Gk. ὑπέρ, L. *s-uper*; Skt. *upari*, above. The Idg. form is **uper-*, closely related to **uperos*, upper (Skt. *upara-*, L. *s-uperus*, A. S. *yfera*). This is a comparative form from Idg. **upo-* (Skt. *upa*, near, on, under; Gk. ὑπό, L. *s-ub*, Goth.

uf, under; cf. A. S. *ufan*, E. *-ove* in *ab-ove*). Closely allied to **Up**. ¶ Hence a large number of compounds beginning with *over*, which present no difficulty.

Overt, open, public. (F.—L.) O. F. *overt* (later *ouvert*), pp. of *ovrir* (later *ouvrir*), to open. The etymology is disputed. α. Diez suggests that *ovrir* is a shortened form of O. F. *a-ovrir*, *a-uvrir* (Livre des Rois), answering to Prov. *adubrir*, to open. The latter can be resolved into L. *ad, de, operīre*, where *ad* is a mere prefix, and *de-operīre* is to uncover. β. Littré considers *ovrir* to be for *avrir*, i.e. L. *aperīre*, to open; the change being due to association with *covrir* (F. *couvrir*), to cover. Cf. Port. *avrir*, to open.

overture, a proposal, beginning. (F.—L.) O. F. *overture*, latter *ouverture*, an opening, from O. F. *overt*, open (above).

Oviform, Oviparous; see **Oval**.

Owe, to possess; hence, to possess another's property, be in debt, be obliged. (E.) M. E. *aȝen, awen, owen*, orig. 'to possess.' A. S. *āgan*, to have, possess (whence long *o* from A. S. *ā*, and *w* for *g*). ✝Icel. *eiga*, to possess, have, be bound, own; Dan. *eie*, Swed. *äga*, O.H.G. *eigan*, Goth. *aigan*, to possess. Teut. type **aigan-*. Allied to Skt. *īç*, to possess.

ought. (E.) The pres. tense of A. S. *āgan* is *ic āh*, really an old perf. tense; hence was formed the new pt. t. *āhte*, M. E. *ahte, aughte, oughte*, mod. E. *ought*.

owing, in phr. *owing to* = due to, because of. (E.) Orig. pres. pt. of *owe*, vb.

Owl, a bird. (E.) M. E. *oule*. A.S. *ūle*.✝Du. *uil*, Icel. *ugla*, Dan. *ugle*, Swed. *ugla*, G. *eule*, O. H. G. *ūwela*. Teut. types **ūwalōn-*, **uwwalōn-*, fem. Cf. also L. *ulula*, Skt. *ulūka-*, an owl. The sense is 'howler,' from an imitative root; cf. L. *ululāre*, to howl. See **Howl**.

Own (1), possessed by any one, peculiar to oneself. (E.) M. E. *aȝen, awen, owen*, contracted to *own* by loss of *e*. A. S. *āgen*, own, orig. pp. of *āgan*, to possess; see **Owe**.✝Icel. *eiginn*, Dan. Swed. *egen*, G. *eigen*, Goth. *aigans*.

own (2), to possess. (E.) M. E. *aȝnien, ahnien, ahnen, ohnen*. A.S. *āgnian*, to appropriate, claim as one's own; denom. vb., from A. S. *āgen*, own (above).✝Icel. *eigna*, to claim as one's own; from *eiginn*, one's own. **Der.** *own-er*.

own (3), to grant. (E.) A development from *own* (2), to appropriate, claim; hence, to acknowledge. See Johnson. ¶ Usually said to have been due to A. S. *unnan*, M. E. *unnen*, to grant, of which there is no clear trace.

Ox. (E.) M. E. *ox, oxe*, pl. *oxen*; A. S. *oxa*, pl. *oxan*.✝Du. *os*, Icel. *uxi, oxi*, Dan. Swed. *oxe*, G. *ochse, ochs*, Goth. *auhsa*; also W. *ych*; Skt. *ukshan-*, an ox, bull. Teut. type**ohsan-*; Idg. type **oksen-*. The Skt. *ukshan-* is usually derived from Skt. *uksh*, to sprinkle, hence, to impregnate; Brugm. ii. § 114.

Oxalis, wood-sorrel. (L.—Gk.) L. *oxalis*.—Gk. ὀξαλίς, (1) sour wine, (2) sorrel; from its sourness.—Gk. ὀξύς, acid. See **Oxygen**.

oxide, a compound of oxygen with a non-acid base. (Gk.) Coined from *ox-* (for *oxy-*, as in *oxy-gen*) and *-ide*, Gk. -ειδής, like. See **Oxygen**.

Oxlip, a flower. (E.) A.S. *oxanslyppe*, orig. an ox-slop, piece of ox-dung (a coarse name, like some other plant-names).— A. S. *oxan*, gen. case of *oxa*, ox; *slyppe*, a slop; see **Slop**. (So also *cow-slip* = *cow-slop*.)

Oxygen, a gas often found in acid compounds. (Gk.) Lit. ' acid-generator.' — Gk. ὀξύ-ς, sharp, acid; γεν-, to produce, base of γίγνομαι, I am born.

oxymel, a mixture of honey and vinegar. (L.—Gk.) L. *oxymeli*. — Gk. ὀξύμελι.—Gk. ὀξύ-ς, sharp, acid; μέλι, honey; see **Mellifluous**.

oxytone, having an acute accent on the last syllable. (Gk.) Gk. ὀξύτονος, shrill-toned.—Gk. ὀξύ-ς, sharp; τόνος, a tone; see **Tone**.

Oyer, a term in law. (F.—L.) *Oyer and terminer* means, literally, ' to hear and determine.'—A. F. *oyer* (F. *ouir*) to hear. —L. *audīre*, to hear.

oyez, oyes, hear ye! (F.—L.) Public criers begin by saying *oyes*, now corrupted into *o yes !*—A. F. *oyez*, 2 p. pl. imperative of *oyer*, to hear (above).

Oyster. (F.—L.—Gk.) M. E. *oistre*. —A. F. *oistre* (F. *huître*).—L. *ostrea*; also *ostreum*.—Gk. ὄστρεον, an oyster; named from its hard shell.—Gk. ὀστέον, a bone, shell; see **Osseous, Ostracise**.

Ozone, a substance perceived by its smell in the air after electric discharges. (Gk.) Gk. ὄζων, smelling; pres. pt. of ὄζειν, to smell. See **Odour**.

PA–PE.

Pabulum. (L.) L. *pābulum*, food ; from the base *pā-*, as seen in *pā-ui*, pt. t. of *pascere*, to feed. See **Pastor**.

Pace, a step. (F.–L.) M. E. *pas.* – F. *pas.* – L. *passum*, acc. of *passus*, a step, pace, lit. a stretch, distance between the feet in walking. – L. *passus*, pp. of *pandere*, to stretch. See **Expand**.

Pacha; see **Pasha**.

Pachydermatous, thick-skinned. (Gk.) From Gk. παχύ-ς, thick; and δερ-ματ-, stem of δέρμα, skin. Gk. παχύς is allied to Skt. *bahu-*, strong. See **Derm**.

Pacify. (F.–L.) F. *pacifier*. – L. *pācī-ficāre*, to make peace. – L. *pāci-*, decl. stem of *pax*, peace ; *-ficāre*, for *facere*, to make. See **Peace**.

Pack, a bundle. (Low G.–L.?) M. E. *pakke* (13th cent.). – M. Du. *pack* (Du. *pak*) ; cf. Icel. *pakki*, Dan. *pakke*, Swed. *packa* ; G. *pack*. [Cf. also Irish *pac*, Gael. *pac*, from E. ; Bret. *pak*, from Romanic ; Ital. *pacco*, F. *paqu-et* ; Late L. *paccus*.] Prob. of Late L. origin ; from the L. base *pangere*, as in pp. *pactus*, from *pangere*, to fasten (Körting). See **Pact**. Der. *pack-age*, with F. suffix *-age* (cf. *bagg-age*) ; *pack-et*, from F. *paquet*, a packet, bundle, dimin. form from Low G. *pakk*, M. Du. *pack*.

Pact, a contract. (L.) L. *pactum*, an agreement. – L. *pactus*, pp. of *paciscī*, to agree, inceptive form of O. L. *pacere*, to agree (Bréal). Allied to *pangere* (pp. *pactus*), to fasten, fix ; Skt. *paç*, to bind, Gk. πήγνυμι, I fasten. Brugm. i. § 200 ; ii. § 79.

Pad (1), a soft cushion. (Low G.?) Also in the sense of 'saddle' (Levins, 1570) ; also in the sense of 'bundle' (Halliwell). Of obscure origin. In the sense of cushion beneath an animal's foot, it agrees with M. Du., Low G., and Pomeranian *pad*, sole of the foot ; perhaps borrowed from Slavonic. Cf. Russ. *podoshva*, sole of the foot ; *podushka*, a cushion, pad ; also Lith. *padas*, (the same). Cf. **Pod**.

Pad (2), a thief on the high road. (Du.) We now say *foot-pad*. Formerly a *padder*, one who goes on the *pad*, i. e. foot-path. – Du. *pad*, a path ; see **Path**. (Many cant words are Dutch.) Der. *pad*, a nag, orig. *pad-nag*, a road-nag ; *pad*, vb., to tramp.

Paddle (1), to finger, dabble in water. (Low G.?) Formerly also to finger, handle ;

Haml. iii. 4. 185 ; Oth. ii. 1. 259. It is a parallel formation to *pattle*, frequent. of *pat* ; see **Pat** (1). Cf. Low G. *paddeln*, to tramp about (Danneil), frequent. of *poddon*, to tread, or *padjen*, to walk with short steps (Brem. Wört.) ; from *pad*, the sole of the foot. See **Pad** (1). Cf. also Low G. *pladdern*, to paddle in water.

Paddle (2), a little spade, esp. to clean a plough with. (E.) Formerly *spaddle* ; dimin. of *spade*. See **Spade**.

Paddock (1), a toad. (Scand.) M. E. *paddok*, dimin. of M. E. *padde*, a toad. – Icel. *padda*, Swed. *padda*, Dan. *padde*, a toad, frog. + Du. *padde*, *pad* ; E. Fries. *padde*.

Paddock (2), a small enclosure. (L.?) Not an old word ; used by Evelyn ; a corruption of M. E. *parrok*, spelt *parrocke* in Palsgrave. (So also *poddish* for *porridge*.) See **Park**.

Paddy, rice in the husk. (Malay.) Malay *pādī*, rice in the husk. It seems to have been confused with Hind. *bhāt*, cooked rice ; from Skt. *bhakta*, (properly) boiled rice, food, orig. pp. of *bhaj*, to divide, possess, &c. (See Yule.)

Padlock, a loose-hanging lock. (E.) A lock for hampers, &c. ; prob. coined by adding *lock* to prov. E. *pad*, a pannier (Norfolk). This word is also written *ped* ; see **Pedlar**.

Pæan, a hymn to Apollo. (L.–Gk.) L. *pæan.* – Gk. Παιάν, Παιών, (1) Pæan, Pæon, physician of the gods, (2) Apollo, (3) a hymn to Apollo. Der. *peon-y*.

Pædobaptism, infant baptism. (Gk.) From Gk. παιδο-, representing παῖς, a child ; and *baptism*. Cf. **Pedagogue**.

Pagan, a countryman; hence, a heathen. (L.) L. *pāgānus*, (1) a villager, (2) a pagan, because the rustic people remained longest unconverted. – L. *pāgānus*, adj., rustic. – L. *pāgus*, a village, district, canton. Some connect it with *pag-*, base of *pangere*, to fasten ; as being marked out by fixed limits ; see **Pact**.

Page (1), a boy attending a person of rank. (F.–Late L.–Gk.?) M. E. *page.* – F. *page.* – Late L. *pagium*, acc. of *pagius*, a servant. Cf. Span. *page*, Port. *pagem*, Ital. *paggio*, a page. Etym. disputed. Diez thinks that Ital. *paggio* was formed from Gk. παιδίον, a little child, dimin. of παῖς, a boy. (See Diez, Littré, Scheler.)

Page (2), one side of the leaf of a book. (F.–L.) F. *page.* – L. *pāgina*, a page, leaf. Orig. a leaf; and named from the fastening together of strips of papyrus to form a leaf. – L. *pag-*, base of *pangere*, to fasten (pp. *pac-tus* < *pag-tus*).

pageant, an exhibition, spectacle. (Late L. – L.) Orig. the moveable scaffold on which the old 'mysteries' were acted. M. E. *pagent* (Prompt. Parv.), also *pagen, pagyn*; formed, with excrescent *t* after *n*, from Late L. *pāgina*, a scaffold, stage for shows, made of wooden planks. – L. *pāgina*, a page of a book; in Late L. a plank of wood. Named from being fastened together; see **Page** (2). Der. *page-ant-r-y*.

Pagoda, an Indian idol's temple. (Port. – Pers.) From Port. *pagoda, pagode*, a pagoda. – Pers. *but-kadah*, an idol-temple. – Pers. *but*, idol, image; *kadah*, habitation. (The initial Pers. sound is sometimes rendered by *p*, as in Devic's Supp. to Littré.) Perhaps confused with Skt. *bhagavatī*, f., venerable, as the name of a goddess (Yule).

Pail. (E.) M. E. *paile*. A. S. *pægel*, a pail (Bosworth-Toller). See Anglia, viii. 450. Cf. Dan. *pægel*, half-a-pint; M. Du. *pegel*, the contents or capacity of a pot. Partly, from O. F. *paelle*, a pan, liquid measure. – L. *patella*, dimin. of *patina*, a pan.

Pain. (F. – L. – Gk.) M. E. *peine*. – F. *peine*, a pain, a penalty. – L. *pœna*, punishment, penalty, pain. – Gk. ποινή, penalty. Idg. type *$qoinā$; cf. O. Ir. *cin*, a fault (Ir. *cion*), Zend *kaēnā-*, punishment, Pers. *kīn*, revenge, Russ. *tsiena*, a price, Gk. τίνειν, to pay a price. Brugm. i. § 202. Cf. **Pine** (2).

Painim; see **Paynim**.

Paint. (F. – L.) M. E. *peinten*, vb. – F. *peint*, pp. of *peindre*, to paint. – L. *pingere*, to paint. See **Picture**.

Painter, a rope for mooring a boat. (F. – L.) Assimilated to *painter*, one who paints; but also spelt *penter* (1661); and perhaps adapted from O.F. *pentoir, pendoir* (Godefroy), a perch for hanging clothes to dry, also strong cordage. – Late L. *penditōrium*, a perch for clothes. Cotgrave has *penteur*, the name of one of the ropes which pass over the top of a mast. From Low L. **penditum*, for L. *pensum*, supine of *pendēre*, to hang.

Pair, two equal or like things. (F. – L.) M. E. *peire*. – F. *paire*, 'a pair;' Cot. – F. *pair*, 'like, equal;' id. – L. *parem*, acc. of *pār*, equal. See **Par**.

Pajamas, Pyjamas, loose drawers. (Hind. – Pers.) Hind. *p̤āejāmā, pājāmā*, drawers, lit. 'leg-clothing.' – Hind. *p̤āe*, leg; *jāma*, garment. – Pers. *pāi*, cognate with E. *foot*; *jāmah*, a garment (Horn, § 412).

Palace. (F. – L.) M. E. *palais*. – F. *palais*. – L. *palātium*, orig. a building on the *Palatine* hill at Rome; esp. a palace of Augustus on this hill. The *Palatine* hill is supposed to have been named from *Pales*, a pastoral divinity.

paladin. (F. – Ital. – L.) F. *paladin*, a knight of the round table. – Ital. *paladino*, a warrior; orig. a knight of the palace or royal household. – L. *palātīnus*; see **Palatine**.

Palæo-; see **Paleo-**.

Palanquin, Palankeen, a light litter in which travellers are borne on men's shoulders. (Port. – Hind. – Skt.) Cf. F. *palanquin*. From Port. *palanquim*, a palankeen. All from Hindustanī *palang*, a bed, bedstead (Forbes); otherwise *pālkī*, and (in the Carnatic) *pallakki* (Wilson); Pali *pallanko*, a palankeen (Yule). – Skt. *paryanka-* (Prakrit *pallanka-*), a couch-bed, bed. Apparently named from the support afforded to the body. – Skt. *pari* (= Gk. περί), round, about; *anka-*, a hook, also the flank.

Palate. (F. – L.) O. F. *palat*. – L. *palātum*, the palate, roof of the mouth.

Palatine. (F. – L.) In phr. 'count palatine;' the proper sense is 'pertaining to the palace or royal household.' – F. *palatin*. – L. *palātīnus*, (1) the name of a hill at Rome, (2) belonging to a palace; see **Palace**.

Palaver. (Port. – L. – Gk.) A parley. – Port. *palavra*, a word, parole. – L. *parabola*. – Gk. παραβολή; see **Parable**.

Pale (1), a stake, limit. (F. – L.) M. E. *paal*. – F. *pal*, 'a pale, stake;' Cot. – L. *pālum*, acc. of *pālus*, a stake. For **pac-slus*, from *pac-*, to fasten, as in *pac-iscī*, to stipulate. Brugm. ii. § 76. ¶ The heraldic *pale* is the same word; so is *pole* (1).

Pale (2), wan. (F. – L.) O. F. *pale*, later *pasle* (F. *pâle*). – L. *pallidum*, acc. of *pallidus*, pale. Allied to **Fallow**.

Paleography, the study of ancient modes of writing. (Gk.) – Gk. παλαιό-s, old, from πάλαι, adv., long ago; γράφ-ειν, to write.

paleology, archæology. (Gk.) From

Gk. παλαιό-s, old ; -λογία, discourse, from λόγος, a word, λέγειν, to speak.

paleontology, the science of fossils, &c. (Gk.) From Gk. παλαί-os, old ; ὄντο-, dccl. stem of ὤν, existing ; -λογία, discourse, from λόγος, a word, λέγειν, to speak.

Palestra, a wrestling-school. (L. — Gk.) L. *palæstra.* — Gk. παλαίστρα, a wrestling-school. — Gk. παλαίειν, to wrestle. — Gk. πάλη, wrestling.

Paletot, a loose garment. (F.) Mod. F. *paletot,* formerly spelt *palletot, palletoc,* a sort of coat ; whence M. E. *paletok,* used of a dress worn by soldiers, knights, and kings, and usually made of silk or velvet. Explained by Diez as *palle-toque,* a cloak with a hood ; from L. *palla,* a mantle, and W. *toc,* Bret. *tōk,* a cap. Littré derives O. F. *palletoc* from M. Du. *paltrok,* a mantle, but Franck says that this M. Du. word is taken (with alteration) from the O. F. word. Cf. Bret. *paltōk,* a peasant's robe ; from *pallen,* a covering (L. *palla*) ; and *tōk,* a cap. Whence also Span. *pale-toque.*

Palette, a small slab on which painters mix colours. (F. — Ital. — L.) F. *palette,* orig. a flat blade, spatula, and lastly, a palette. — Ital. *paletta,* a flat blade, spatula ; dimin. of *pala,* a spade. — L. *pāla,* a spade, shovel, flat-bladed 'peel' for putting bread into an oven. See Peel (3).

Palfrey. (F. — Low L. — C.) M. E. *palefrui, palfrei.* — O. F. *palefrei* (F. *palefroi*). — Low L. *paraverēdus,* lit. 'an extra post-horse' (White). — Low L. *para-* (Gk. παρά), beside, hence, extra ; *uerēdus,* a post-horse, courier's horse. β. Here *uerēdus* stands for **vo-redus,* from a Celtic type **vo-reido-,* a carriage-horse. — Celtic **vo* (Ir. *fo-,* W. *go-*), under, in ; and Celtic **reidā,* Gaulish L. *rēda, rhēda,* a carriage. The Celt. **vo-reido-* appears in W. *go-rwydd,* a horse. The Celt. **reidā* is from the verb seen in O. Irish *riad-aim,* I travel, ride, cognate with E. *ride* (Stokes). ¶ Cf. Du. *paard,* G. *pferd,* O. H. G. *pfer-frit,* a horse, also from *paraverēdus.*

Palimpsest, a MS. which has been twice written on, the first writing being partly erased. (Gk.) Gk. παλίμψηστον, a palimpsest, neut. of παλίμψηστος, scraped again (to renew the surface). — Gk. πάλιμ- (for πάλιν), again ; ψηστός, scraped, from ψάειν, to rub.

Palindrome, a word or sentence that

is the same whether read forwards or backwards. (Gk.) Such a word is *madam.* — Gk. παλίνδρομος, running back again. — Gk. πάλιν, again ; δρόμος, a running, from δραμεῖν, to run ; see Dromedary.

Palinode, a recantation, in song. (F. — L. — Gk.) F. *palinodie* (Cot.). — L. *palinōdia.* — Gk. παλινῳδία, a recantation, esp. of an ode. — Gk. πάλιν, back, again ; ᾠδή, an ode. See Ode.

Palisade. (F. — L.) F. *palissade,* a row of pales. — F. *paliss-er,* to enclose with pales. — F. *palis,* a pale, extended from *pal,* a pale ; see Pale (1).

Pall (1), a cloak, mantle, shroud. (L.) A.S. *pæll.* — L. *pallium,* a coverlet, cloak ; Sievers, § 80.

Pall (2), to become vapid. (F. — L.) *Pall* is a shortened form of *appal,* formerly used in the same sense. Palsgrave has *palle* and *appalle,* both in the sense of losing colour by standing as drink does ; also 'I *palle,* I fade.' See Appal.

Palladium, a safeguard of liberty. (L. — Gk.) L. *Palladium* ; Virg. Æn. ii. 166, 183. — Gk. Παλλάδιον, the statue of Pallas on which the safety of Troy depended. — Gk. Παλλάς (stem Παλλαδ-), Pallas, an epithet of Athene.

Pallet (1), a kind of mattress, properly one of straw. (F. — L.) M. E. *paillet.* — F. *paillet,* a heap of straw, given by Littré as a provincial word. Cf. *paillat,* a palliasse, in pâtois of Lyons (Puitspelu). — F. *paille,* straw. — L. *palea,* straw, chaff. +Gk. πάλη, fine meal ; Skt. *palāla,* straw ; Russ. *polova,* chaff ; Lith. *pelai,* pl., chaff.

Pallet (2), an instrument used by potters, also by gilders ; also a palette. (F. — Ital. — L.) It is a flat-bladed instrument for spreading plasters, gilding, &c. ; and is a doublet of Palette.

Palliasse, a straw mattress. (F. — L.) F. *paillasse* (with *ll* mouillés), a straw-bed ; spelt *paillace* in Cotgrave. — F. *paille,* straw ; with suffix *-ace* (<L. *-āceus*). — L. *palea,* straw. See Pallet (1).

Palliate, to cloak, excuse. (L.) From L. *palliātus,* covered as with a cloak. — L. *pallium,* a coverlet, cloak. See Pall (1).

Pallid. (L.) L. *pallidus,* pale.

pallor. (L.) L. *pallor,* paleness. — L. *pallēre,* to be pale. See Pale (2).

Pall-mall ; see Mall (2).

Palm (1), inner part of the hand. (F. — L.) M. E. *paume,* palm of the hand. — F. *paume.* — L. *palma,* the palm of the hand.+

367

Gk. παλάμη, the palm of the hand; A. S. *folm*, the same; O. Irish *lām*, W. *llaw*. Brugm. i. § 529 (2). **Der.** *palm-ist-r-y*.

Palm (2), a tree. (L.) A. S. *palm.* — L. *palma*, a palm-tree. **Der.** *palm-er*, M. E. *palmere*, one who bore a palm-branch in memory of having been to the Holy Land; hence a *palmer* or *palmer-worm*, a sort of caterpillar, supposed to be so named from its wandering about. Also *palm-ary*, deserving the palm (of victory).

Palpable, that can be felt. (F. — L.) F. *palpable* (Littré, Palsgrave). — L. *palpā-bilis*, that may be felt. — L. *palpāre, palpārī*, to feel, to handle.

Palpitate, to throb. (L.) From pp. of L. *palpitāre*, to throb.

Palsy. (F. — L. — Gk.) M. E. *palesy*, fuller form *parlesy.* — F. *paralysie.* — L. *paralysin*, acc. of *paralysis.* — Gk. παρά-λυσις; see **Paralysis**.

Palter, to dodge, shuffle, equivocate. (Scand.) Spelt *paulter* in Cotgrave, s. v. *harceler*. The orig. sense is to haggle, to haggle over such worthless stuff as is called *paltrie* in Lowland Scotch. More literally, it is ' to deal in rags, to trifle '; see further below.

paltry, worthless. (Scand.) Lowland Sc. *paltrie* is a sb., meaning trash; so also Norfolk *paltry*, 'rubbish, refuse,' Forby. But both sb. and adj. are from an old sb. *palter*, rags, which is still preserved in Danish and Swedish. — Swed. *paltor*, rags, pl. of *palta*, a rag, tatter; Dan. *pialter*, rags, pl. of *pialt*, a rag. β. We find the adj. itself in Low G. *paltrig*, ragged, from *palte*, a rag, piece torn off a cloth; and in prov. G. *palterig*, paltry, from *palter* (pl. *paltern*), a rag (Flügel). We find also M. Du. *palt*, a fragment, Friesic *palt*, a rag; E. Fries. *palterig*, *paltrig*, ragged. Possibly of Slavonic origin. Cf. Russ. *polotno, platno*, linen, *platite*, to patch.

Pampas, plains in S. America. (Peruvian.) The final *s* is the Span. pl. suffix. — Peruvian *pampa*, a plain.

Pamper, to glut. (O. Low G.) Frequent. from Low G. *pampen*, to cram. — Low G. *pampe*, broth, pap, nasalised form of *pappe*, pap. Cf. Low G. (Altmark) *pampen, pappen,* to cram oneself (Danneil). See **Pap** (1).

Pamphlet, a small book. (F.? — L.? — Gk.?) Spelt *pamflet*, Test. of Love, pt. iii. 9. 54. Etym. quite uncertain. We find F. *pamphile*, the knave of clubs, from the Gk. name *Pamphilus*; similarly, I should suppose that there was a F. form *pamfilet, or Late L. *pamphilētus, coined from L. *Pamphila* (of Gk. origin), the name of a female historian of the first century, who wrote numerous *epitomes* of history. G. Paris suggests L. *Pamphilus*, the name of a medieval Lat. comedy. We find Low Lat. *panfletus* (A. D. 1344).

Pan. (E. ?) M. E. *panne*. A. S. *panne*, a pan, broad shallow vessel; cf. Irish *panna*, W. *pan*, a pan. — Late L. *panna*, a pan (whence also Du. *pan*, G. *pfanne*, O. H. G. *pfanna*). If not of Teut. origin, it may be a corrupted form of L. *patina*, a shallow bowl, pan, bason. **Der.** *pan-cake*; *pannikin* (M. Du. *panneken*).

Pan-, prefix, all. (Gk.) Gk. πᾶν, neut. of πᾶς, all.

Panacea, a universal remedy. (L. — Gk.) L. *panacēa.* — Gk. πανάκεια, a universal remedy; allied to πανακής, all-healing. — Gk. πᾶν, all (above); ἀκέομαι, I heal, ἄκος, a remedy.

Pancreas, a fleshy gland, commonly called sweet-bread. (L. — Gk.) L. *pancreas.* — Gk. πάγκρεας, sweet-bread; lit. ' all flesh,' from its softness. — Gk. πᾶν, all; κρέας, flesh, for *κρέϝας; cf. Skt. *kravya-*, raw flesh, L. *crū-dus*, raw. See **Pan-** and **Crude**.

Pandect, a digest. (F. — L. — Gk.) Usually in pl. *pandects.* — M. F. *pandectes*, pl. (Cot.). — L. *pandectæ*, the title of a collection of laws made by order of Justinian; also (in sing.) *pandectēs.* — Gk. πανδέκται, pandects; from Gk. πανδέκτης, all-receiving, comprehensive. — Gk. πᾶν, all; δέχομαι, I receive. See **Pan-**.

Pandemonium. (Gk.) The home of all the demons. — Gk. πᾶν, all; δαίμονι-, for δαίμων, a demon; see **Pan-** and **Demon**.

Pander, Pandar, a pimp. (L. — Gk.) L. *Pandarus.* — Gk. Πάνδαρος, a personal name; the name of the man who procured for Troilus the favour of Chryseis. The *name* is from Homer (Il. ii. 827); but the *story* belongs to medieval romance.

Pane, a patch of cloth, plate of glass. (F. — L.) M. E. *pane*, a portion. — F. *pan*, ' a pane, piece, or pannell;' Cot. — L. *pannum*, acc. of *pannus*, a cloth, rag, patch. Allied to **Vane**.

Panegyric. (L. — Gk.) L. *panēgyri-cus*, a eulogy; from L. *panēgyricus*, adj.

─Gk. πανηγυρικός, fit for a full assembly, festive, solemn; hence applied to a festival oration. **─**Gk. πανήγυρις, a full assembly. **─**Gk. πᾶν, all; -ηγυρις, related to ἀγορά, a gathering, a crowd.

Panel, Pannel, a board with a surrounding frame, &c. (F.─L.) M. E. *panel,* (1) a piece of cloth, sort of saddle, (2) a schedule containing jurors' names; the general sense being 'little piece.'─ O. F. *panel,* M. F. *paneau* (later *panneau*), 'a pannel of wainscot, of a saddle,' &c.; Cot.**─**Late L. *pannellum,* dimin. of *pannus,* a cloth; see Pane. Der. *em-panel, im-panel,* to put upon a panel, enroll jurors' names.

Pang, a sharp pain. (E.?) Spelt '*prange* of love'; Court of Love, l. 1150 (ed. 1561); M. E. *pronge,* a throe, a woman's pang (Prompt. Parv.). The sense is 'a sharp stab,' a prick; see Prong. For the loss of *r,* cf. *speak* for *spreak.*

Panic, extreme fright. (Gk.) Gk. τὸ πανικόν, Panic fear, supposed to be inspired by the god Pan. **─**Gk. πανικός, adj., from Πάν, Pan, the rural god of Arcadia.

Panicle, a form of inflorescence. (L.) L. *pānicula,* a tuft; double dimin. of *pānus,* the thread wound round the bobbin of a shuttle.**+**Gk. πῆνος, the same. Allied to L. *pannus,* cloth; see Pane.

Pannage, food of swine in woods. (F. ─L.) Anglo-F. *panage;* M. F. *pasnage,* 'pawnage, mastage, monie for feeding of swine with mast;' Cotgrave.**─**Late L. *pasnāticum, pastiōnāticum,* pannage. **─** Late L. *pastiōnāre,* to feed on mast, as swine.**─**L. *pastiōn-,* stem of *pastio,* grazing, used in Late L. to mean right of pannage.**─**L. *past-us,* pp. of *pascere,* to feed.

Pannier, a bread-basket. (F.─L.) M. E. *panier.* **─**F. *panier.* **─**L. *pānārium,* a bread-basket. **─** L. *pānis,* bread. Cf. Pantry and Company.

Pannikin, a little pan. (L.; *with* E. *suffix.*) Dimin. of Pan. Cf. M. Du. *panneken,* Westphal. *pänneken,* the same.

Panoply, complete armour. (Gk.) Gk. πανοπλία, full armour. **─** Gk. πᾶν, all; ὅπλ-α, arms, armour, pl. of ὅπλον, an implement, from Gk. ἕπω, I am busy about. Brugm. ii. § 657. And see Pan-.

Panorama, a kind of large picture. (Gk.) Lit. 'a view all round.'**─**Gk. πᾶν, all; ὅραμα, a view, from ὁράω, I see. See Pan- and Wary.

Pansy, heart's-ease. (F. ─ L.) F. *pensée,* 'a thought; also, the flower paunsie;' Cot. (It is the flower of thought or *remembrance.*) Prop. fem. of pp. of F. *penser,* to think. **─**L. *pensāre,* to weigh, ponder, frequent. of *pendere,* to weigh. See Pendant. Cf. Chaucerian Pieces, xxi. 62 (note).

Pant, to breathe hard. (F.─L.?─Gk.?) M. E. *panten,* to pant (15th cent.). The O. F. *pantais* (Godefroy) meant 'shortness of breath, in hawks,' and was a term in hawking. So also F. *pantois,* shortwinded, F. *panteler,* to pant; Gascon *pantacha,* to pant; A. F. *pantoiser.* The O. F. *pantais* is a verbal sb. from O.F. *pantaisier,* to breathe with difficulty; cf. Prov. *pantaisa,* to pant, dream. Prob. from Late L. **phantasiāre,* by-form of *phantasiārī,* to imagine, dream (Ducange).**─** Gk. φαντασία, a fancy; see Fancy. (G. Paris, in Romania, vi. 628.) ¶ Not from W. *pantu,* which does not mean to press (Diez), but to sink in, indent.

Pantaloon (1), a ridiculous character, buffoon. (F.─Ital.─Gk.) F. *pantalon.*─ Ital. *pantalone,* a buffoon; from the personal name *Pantaleone,* common in Venice, St. *Pantaleone* being a well-known saint in Venice. Prob. from Gk. πανταλέων, lit. 'all-lion;' a Gk. personal name. **─** Gk. παντα-, all; λέων, lion.

pantaloons, a kind of trousers. (F.─ Ital.─Gk.) F. *pantalon,* so called because worn by Venetians.─Ital. *pantalone,* a Venetian; see above.

Pantheism, the doctrine that the universe is God. (Gk.) From Pan- and Theism; see below.

pantheon. (L.─Gk.) L. *panthēon.* **─**Gk. πάνθειον, a temple consecrated to all the gods.**─**Gk. πᾶν, all; θεῖος, divine, from θεός, god.

Panther, a quadruped. (F.─L.─ Gk.) M. E. *pantere.*─O. F. *panthere.* **─** L. *panthēra, panthēr.* **─** Gk. πάνθηρ, a panther; prob. of Skt. origin. ¶ A supposed derivation from πᾶν, all, θήρ, a beast, gave rise to numerous fables.

Pantomime, a dumb actor; later, a dumb show. (F.─L.─Gk.) F. *pantomime,* an actor of many parts in one play. **─**L. *pantomīmus.* **─** Gk. παντόμιμος, all-imitating, a pantomimic actor. **─**Gk. παντο-, for πᾶς, all; μῖμος, a mime, imitator; see Pan- and Mimic.

Pantry. (F.─L.) M. E. *pantrie.* **─**

O. F. *paneterie.* — Late L. *pānētāria, pāni-tāria*, a place where bread is made or kept. — Late L. *pāneta*, one who makes bread. — L. *pān-is*, bread, food; cf. *pascere*, to feed. (√PA.)

Pap (1), food for infants. (E.) '*Papmete* for chylder;' Prompt. Parv. (A. D. 1440). Cf. M. E. *pappe*, only in the sense of 'breast.' Of infantine origin, due to the repetition of *pa, pa*, in calling for food; cf. L. *pāpa, pappa*, the word by which infants call for food. So also Du. *pap*, E. Fries. and G. *pappe*, pap; Dan. *pap*, Swed. *papp*, paste-board. Cf. **pap** (2), **Papa**.

pap (2), a teat, breast. (E.) M. E. *pappe*. Cf. M. Swed. *papp*, the breast; changed, in mod. Swedish, to *patt*. So also Swed. dial. *pappe*, N. Fries. *pap*, *pape*, Lithuan. *pápas*, the breast. Much the same as **Pap** (1); and due to the infant's call for food.

Papa, father. (F.—L.) Not found in old books; rather, borrowed from F. *papa*. —L. *pāpa*, a father, bishop, pope. Cf. L. *pappas*, a tutor, borrowed from Gk. πάππας, papa; Homer, Od. vi. 57. Due to the repetition of *pa, pa*; see **Pap** (1), **Pope**.

papal, belonging to the pope. (F.—L.) F. *papal.* — Late L. *pāpālis*, adj., from L. *pāpa*, a bishop, spiritual father. Cf. Gk. πάπας, πάππας, papa, father (above).

Papaw, a fruit. (Span. — W. Indian.) Span. *papaya* (Pineda). — Carib *ababaï*. See Yule.

Paper. (L. — Gk. — Egyptian?) A. S. *paper*; directly from L. *papȳrus*; see **Papyrus.**

papier-maché, paper made into pulp, moulded, dried, and japanned. (F.—L.) F. *papier*, paper, from L. acc. *papȳrum*; F. *mâché*, lit. chewed, pp. of *mâcher*, L. *masticāre*, to chew. See **Masticate.**

Papilionaceous, having a winged corolla resembling a butterfly. (L.) Coined, with suffix *-āceus*, from L. *papiliōn-*, stem of *papilio*, a butterfly; see **Pavilion.**

Papillary, belonging to or resembling nipples or teats, warty. (L.) From L. *papilla*, a small pustule, nipple, teat; dimin. of *papula*, a pustule. + Lithuan. *pápas*, a teat, *pampti*, to swell out. See Prellwitz, s. v. πέμφιξ.

Papyrus. (L. — Gk. — Egyptian?) L.

papȳrus. — Gk. πάπυρος, an Egyptian rush or flag, of which a writing material was made. Prob. of Egyptian origin.

Par, equal value. (L.) L. *pār*, equal. Perhaps allied to **Pare.**

Para-, prefix. (Gk.) Gk. παρά, beside. Allied to Skt. *parā*, away, from, L. *per*, through, and to E. *for-* in *for-give.*

Parable. (F. — L. — Gk.) M. E. *parabole.* — O. F. *parabole.* — L. *parabola*, Mark iv. 2. — Gk. παραβολή, a comparison, a parable. — Gk. παραβάλλειν, to cast or put beside, to compare. — Gk. παρά, beside; βάλλειν, to cast. Brugm. ii. § 713.

parabola, a certain plane curve. (L. — Gk.) L. *parabola.* — Gk. παραβολή, the conic section made by a plane *parallel* to the surface of the cone; see **Parable.**

Parachute, an apparatus for breaking a fall from a balloon. (F.—L.) F. *parachute*, lit. that which parries or guards against a fall. — F. *para-*, as in *para-sol*; and *chute*, a fall. Here *para-* represents Port. or Ital. *parare*, to ward off; and *chute* is equivalent to Ital. *caduta*, a fall, orig. fem. of *caduto*, fallen, from L. *cadere*, to fall. See **Parasol.**

Paraclete, the Comforter. (L. — Gk.) L. *paraclētus.* — Gk. παράκλητος, called to one's aid, the Comforter (John xiv. 16). — Gk. παρακαλεῖν, to call to one's aid. — Gk. παρά, beside; καλεῖν, to call.

Parade, display. (F.—Span.—L.) F. *parade*, a show, also 'a stop on horseback,' Cot. The latter sense was the earlier in French. — Span. *parada*, a stop, halt, from *parar*, vb., to halt, also to get ready. — L. *parāre*, to get ready. See **Pare.** The sense 'display' was due to the F. verb *parer*, to deck, trim, from same L. *parāre.*

Paradigm, an example, model. (F.— L.—Gk.) F. *paradigme.* — L. *paradigma*. — Gk. παράδειγμα, a pattern, model, example of declension. — Gk. παρά, beside; δείκνυμι, I point out, show. See **Diction.**

Paradise. (L.—Gk.—Pers.) L. *paradīsus.* — Gk. παράδεισος, a park, pleasure-ground; an oriental word of Pers. origin. — Zend *pairidaēza*, an enclosure, place walled in. — Zend *pairi* (= Gk. περί), around; *diz* (Skt. *dih*), to mould, form, shape (hence to form a wall of earth). √DHEIGH; see **Dough.**

Paradox. (F.—L.—Gk.) F. *paradoxe.* — L. *paradoxum*, neut. of *paradoxus*, adj. — Gk. παράδοξος, contrary to received opinion. — Gk. παρά, beside ; δόξα, opinion, from δοκεῖν, to seem ; see **Dogma.**

Paraffine. (F. — L.) Named from its having but small affinity with an alkali. — F. *paraffine.* — L. *par-um*, little ; *affinis*, having affinity ; see **Affinity.**

Paragoge, the addition of a letter at the end of a word. (L. — Gk.) [Thus, in *tyran-t*, the final letter is *paragogic.*] — L. *paragōgē.* — Gk. παραγωγή, a leading by or past, alteration. — Gk. παράγειν, to lead past. — Gk. παρ-ά, beyond ; ἄγειν, to lead ; see **Agent.**

Paragon. (F. — Span. — Gk.) M. F. *paragon.* — M. Span. *paragon*, a model of excellence. Cf. Ital. *paragone*, 'a paragon, a match, an equal ;' Florio ; and Ital. *paragonare*, to compare. The latter answers to the Gk. παρακονάειν, to rub against a whetstone (hence, probably, to try by a touchstone, compare). — Gk. παρ-ά, beside ; ἀκόνη, a whetstone, allied to ἀκίς, a sharp point. (√AK.) See Tobler, in Zt. für roman. Philol. iv. 373.

Paragraph, a short passage of a book. (F. — L. — Gk.) Actually corrupted, in the 15th century, into *pargrafte*, *pylcrafte*, and *pilcrow* ! — F. *paragraphe.* — Late L. *paragraphum*, acc. of *paragraphus.* — Gk. παράγραφος, a line or stroke in the margin, a paragraph-mark ; hence the paragraph itself. — Gk. παρά, beside ; γράφειν, to write ; see **Graphic.** (N. B. The *pilcrow* or paragraph-mark is now printed ¶.)

Parallax, the difference between the real and apparent places of a star. (Gk.) Gk. παράλλαξις, alternation, change ; also parallax (in modern science). — Gk. παραλλάσσειν, to make things alternate. — Gk. παρά, beside ; ἀλλάσσειν, to change, alter, from ἄλλος, other ; see **Alien.**

Parallel, side by side, similar. (F. — L. — Gk.) M. F. *parallele*, Cot. — L. *parallēlus.* — Gk. παράλληλος, parallel, beside each other. — Gk. παρ-ά, beside ; *ἄλληλος, one another, only in the gen. dat. and acc. plural. β. The decl. stem ἀλληλο- stands for ἄλλο- ἄλλο-, a reduplicated form, lit. 'the other the other' or 'one another'; from Gk. ἄλλος, other ; see **Alien.**

parallelogram. (F. — L. — Gk.) M. F. *paralelograme*, Cot. — L. *parallēlogrammum.* — Gk. παραλληλόγραμμον, a figure contained by two pairs of parallel

lines. — Gk. παράλληλο-s, parallel (above); γράμμα, a line, from γράφειν, to write.

parallelopiped. (L. — Gk.) So written ; a mistake for *parallelepiped.* — L. *parallēlepipedum.* — Gk. παραλληλεπίπεδον, a body formed by parallel surfaces. — Gk. παράλληλ-ος, parallel ; ἐπίπεδον, a plane surface, neut. of ἐπίπεδος, on the ground, from ἐπί, upon, and πέδον, the ground.

Paralogism, a conclusion unwarranted by the premises. (F. — L. — Gk.) F. *paralogisme.* — L. *paralogismus.* — Gk. παραλογισμός, a false reckoning or conclusion. — Gk. παραλογίζομαι, I misreckon. — Gk. παρά, beside, amiss ; λογίζομαι, I reckon, from λόγος, reason ; see **Logic.**

Paralysis. (L. — Gk.) L. *paralysis.* — Gk. παράλυσις, a loosening aside, disabling of nerves, paralysis or palsy. — Gk. παραλύειν, to loosen aside. — Gk. παρά, beside ; λύειν, to loosen, allied to **Lose.** Der. *paralyse*, from F. *paralyser*, verb formed from F. sb. *paralysie*, paralysis. Also *paralytic*, from Gk. παραλυτικός, afflicted with palsy. Doublet, *palsy.*

Paramatta, a fabric like merino. (New S. Wales.) So named from *Paramatta*, a town near Sydney, New South Wales. Properly spelt *Parramatta* ; the lit. sense is 'place of eels'; where *parra* represents eels, and *matta*, place. *Parramatta* is also the name of the river; *Cabramatta*, ten miles off, is not a river.

Paramount, of the highest importance. (F. — L.) O. F. *par amont*, at the top, above, lit. ' by that which is upwards.' — L. *per*, by ; *ad montem*, to the hill, upwards ; where *montem* is acc. of *mons*, a hill. See **Mount.**

Paramour. (F. — L.) M. F. *par amour*, with love ; orig. an adverb. phrase. — F. *par amour*, with love ; where *par* < L. *per*, and *amour* is from L. *amōrem*, acc. of *amor*, love. See **Amatory.**

Parapet, a rampart, breast-high. (F. — Ital. — L.) F. *parapet.* — Ital. *parapetto*, a wall breast-high ; lit. 'guarding the breast.' — Ital. *parare*, to adorn, also to guard, parry ; *petto*, breast. — L. *parāre*, to prepare, adorn ; *pectus*, the breast. See **Pare.**

Paraphernalia, ornaments. (L. — Gk.) Properly the property which a bride possesses beyond her dowry. Formed by adding L. neut. pl. suffix *-ālia* to Late L. *paraphern-a*, the property of a bride over and above her dower. **—** Gk. παράφερνα, that which a bride brings beyond her dower. **—** Gk. παρά, beside; φερνή, a dower, that which is brought, from φέρειν, to bring, allied to E. **Bear** (1).

Paraphrase. (F. – L. – Gk.) M. F. *paraphrase.* **—** L. *paraphrasin*, acc. of *paraphrasis.* **—** Gk. παράφρασις, a paraphrase, free translation. **—** Gk. παρά, beside; φράσις, a phrase, from φράζειν, to speak; see **Phrase.**

Paraquito, Parakeet, a little parrot. (Span.) Span. *periquito*, a little parrot, dimin. of *perico*, a parrot. Diez supposes *perico* to be a nickname, meaning 'little Peter,' dimin. of *Pedro*, Peter. See **Parrot.**

Parasang, a measure of distance. (Gk. — Pers.) Gk. παρασάγγης, of Pers. origin. Mod. Pers. *farsang, ferseng*, a league. (Horn, § 818.)

Parasite. (F. – L. – Gk.) F. *parasite.* **—** L. *parasītus.* **—** Gk. παράσιτος, eating beside another at his table, a flatterer, toad-eater. **—** Gk. παρά, beside; σῖτος, wheat, food. Orig. in a good sense; see Gk. Lex.

Parasol, a sun-shade. (F. — Port. – L.) F. *parasol*, 'an umbrello;' Cot. — Port. *parasol* (or Ital. *parasole*), an umbrella to keep off the sun's heat. — Port. *para-r* (or Ital. *parare*), to ward off; *sol* (Ital. *sole*), sun. — L. *parāre*, to prepare; *sōlem*, acc. of *sōl*, sun. See **Parry** and **Solar.**

Parboil. (F. – L.) It now means 'to boil insufficiently,' by confusion with *part.* The old sense is 'to boil thoroughly.' — O. F. *parboillir*, to cook thoroughly, also, to boil gently (Godefroy). — Late L. *parbullīre*, L. *perbullīre*, to boil thoroughly. — L. *per*, through; and *bullīre*, to boil; see **Boil** (1).

Parcel. (F. – L.) M. E. *parcel.* — F. *parcelle*, a small piece or part. — Late L. *particella*, only preserved in Ital. *particella*, a small part. Dimin. of L. *particula*; see **Particle.**

Parch, to scorch. (F. – L.) Very difficult. M. E. *parchen*, to parch. Not the same as M. E. *perchen*, to pierce, an occasional form of *percen*, to pierce; the sense being too remote. I suggest that it meant to dry or harden like parchment; from O. F. *parche*, a shortened form of parchment which actually occurs (Bartsch, Chrestomathie, 1887, col. 309, l. 16);

whence Span. *parche*, the end of a drum. Cf. also prov. F. *pois sans parche*, for *poiš sans parchemin*; Vocab. du Haut Maine, by C. R. de M., Paris, 1859. See further below.

Parchment. (F. – L. – Gk.) M. E. *perchemin.* — O. F. *parchemin.* — L. *pergamīna, pergamēna*, parchment; fem. of L. *Pergamēnus*, belonging to Pergamos (where parchment was first invented). — Gk. περγαμηνή, parchment, from Πέργαμος, Πέργαμον, Pergamus, in Mysia of Asia Minor.

Pard, a panther, leopard. (L. – Gk.) L. *pardus.* — Gk. πάρδος. An Eastern word; cf. Pers. *pārs*, a pard; Skt. *prdāku*, a leopard. **Der.** *leo-pard, camelo-pard.*

Pardon, forgiveness. (F. – L.) M. E. *pardoun.* — F. *pardon*, sb. — F. *pardonner*, to forgive. — Late L. *perdōnare*, to remit a debt, pardon. — L. *per*, fully; *dōnāre*, to give; see **Donation.**

Pare, to shave off. (F. – L.) M. E. *paren.* — F. *parer*, to deck, trim, pare. — L. *parāre*, to get ready, prepare.

Paregoric, assuaging pain. (L. – Gk.) L. *parēgoricus*, assuaging. — Gk. παρηγορικός, addressing, encouraging, soothing. — Gk. παρηγορεῖν, to address. — Gk. παρά, beside; ἀγορά, an assembly, whence also ἀγορεύειν, to address an assembly.

Parent. (F. – L.) F. *parent*, a kinsman. — L. *parent-*, stem of *parens*, a parent, lit. one who produces. — L. *parere*, to produce. Brugm. i. § 515.

Parenthesis. (Gk.) Gk. παρένθεσις, an insertion, a putting in beside. — Gk. παρ-ά, beside; ἐν, in; θέσις, a placing; see **Thesis.**

Parget, to plaster a wall. (F. – L.) Nearly obsolete; once common. M. E. *pargeten*; as if from O. F. *pargeter*, to spread abroad, cast around, Late L. *perjactāre* (not in Ducange, but found in the 14th cent.). Cf. ' *Perjacio*, Anglice, to perjette;' Vocab. 602. 7. As if from L. *per*, fully; *iactāre*, to cast, frequent. of *iacere*, to throw. See **Jet** (1). 2. But really substituted for O. F. *porgeter*, to rough-cast a wall (Godefroy). — L. *prōiectāre*, to cast forth; from *prō* and *iactāre.* Cf. Walloon *porgeté*, to parget (Remacle). ¶ Also spelt *spargetten*, where the *s* of *spargetten* = O. F. *es-*, L. *ex* (intensive).

Parhelion, a mock sun. (L. – Gk.) L. *parhēlion.* — Gk. παρήλιον, neut. of παρήλιος, beside the sun. — Gk. παρ-ά, beside; ἥλιος, sun; see **Heliacal.**

Pariah, an outcast. (Tamil.) Tamil *paṟaiyan,* corruptly *pariah,* Malayālim *paṟayan,* a man of low caste, performing the lowest menial services; one of his duties is to beat the village drum (called *paṟai* in Tamil), whence, probably, the appellation of the caste. (H. H. Wilson.)

Parian, belonging to Paros. (Gk.) *Paros* is an island in the Ægean sea.

Parietal, forming the walls, applied to two bones in the front of the skull. (L.) L. *parietālis,* belonging to a wall. — L. *pariet-,* stem of *pariēs,* a wall.

Parish. (F. — L. — Gk.) M. E. *parische.* — F. *paroisse.* — L. *parœcia.* — Gk. παροικία, a neighbourhood; hence an ecclesiastical district. — Gk. πάροικος, neighbouring. — Gk. παρ-ά, near; οἶκος, house, allied to **Vicinage.** **Der.** *parishion-er,* formed by adding *-er* (needlessly) to M. E. *parisshen* < O. F. *paroissien,* a parishioner.

Paritory; see **Pellitory.**

Parity, equality. (F. — L.) F. *parité.* — L. *paritātem,* acc. of *paritās,* equality. — L. *pār,* equal.

Park, an enclosed ground. (E. ?) *Park* = O. F. *parc,* is a F. spelling. M. E. *parrok,* an enclosure, A. S. *pearruc, pearroc.* Cf. Irish and Gael. *pairc,* W. *park* and *parwg* (< E. *parrok*). The word is common in Teutonic tongues, as in Du. *perk,* Swed. Dan. *park,* G. *pferch,* and is prob. Teutonic: cf. M. E. *parran,* to enclose. Hence, probably, Late L. *parcus, parricus,* an enclosure; whence F. *parc,* Ital. *parco,* Span. *parque.*

Parley. (F. — L. — Gk.) F. *parler,* sb., speech, talk, a parley. — F. *parler,* vb., to speak. — Late L. *parabolāre,* to talk. — L. *parabola;* see **Parable.**

parliament. (F. — L. — Gk.; with F. suffix.) M. E. *parlement.* [We also find Late L. *parliāmentum,* corresponding to our spelling *parliament.*] — F. *parlement,* 'a speaking, parleying, a supreme court;' Cot. — F. *parler,* to speak (as above); with F. suffix *-ment* (- *mentum*).

parlour. (F. — L. — Gk.) M. E. *parlour, parlur.* — O. F. *parloir,* a parlour, lit. a room for conversation. — F. *parl-er,* to speak; with suffix *-oir* < L. *-ātōrium;* so that *parlour* answers to a Late L. form **parabolātōrium,* a place to talk in. (Cf. F. *dortoir* < L. *dormitōrium.*) See above.

Parlous. (F. — L.) Short for *perilous.*

Parochial. (L. — Gk.) L. *parōchiālis.*

— L. *parōchia,* same as *parœcia,* a parish; see **Parish.**

Parody. (F. — L. — Gk.) M. E. and F. *parodie.* — L. *parōdia.* — Gk. παρῳδία, also παρῳδή, a song sung beside (i. e. in imitation of) another. — Gk. παρ-ά, beside; ᾠδή, an ode. See **Ode.**

Parole. (F. — L. — Gk.) F. *parole,* a word, esp. a promise; the same word as Prov. *paraula,* Span. *palabra* (= **parabla*), Port. *palavra.* — Late L. *parabola,* a discourse; L. *parabola,* a parable. See **Parable, Palaver.**

Paronymous, allied in origin; alike in sound. (Gk.) Gk. παρώνυμος, formed from another word by a slight change. — Gk. παρά, beside; ὄνυμα, a name. **Der.** *paronom-as-ia,* a slight change in a word's meaning, from Gk. παρωνομασία, better παρονομασία.

Paroxysm. (F. — L. — Gk.) F. *paroxysme.* — L. *paroxysmus.* — Gk. παροξυσμός, irritation, the fit of a disease. — Gk. παροξύνειν, to irritate. — Gk. παρ-ά, beside; ὀξύνειν, to sharpen, from ὀξύς, sharp. See **Oxygen.**

Parquetry, a mosaic of wood-work for floors. (F. — Teut. ?) F. *parqueterie.* — F. *parqueter,* to inlay a wooden floor. — F. *parquet,* a wooden floor; orig. a small enclosure; dimin. of F. *parc,* a park. See **Park.**

Parricide, (1) the murderer of a father; (2) murder of a father. (F. — L.) or L.) The former is the older F. sense, and answers to F. *parricide,* L. *parricīda,* for older *pāricīdas* (Brugm. ii. § 190), a murderer of a relative. — L. *parri-,* for *pāri-,* a relative (cf. Gk. πηός, a relative, Prellwitz, s. v. πάομαι); and *cædere,* to kill (whence *-cīda,* a slayer). **2.** The second sense is directly from L. *parricīdium,* the murder of a relative, from the same sb. and vb.

Parrot. (F. — L. — Gk.) F. *Perrot,* of which the lit. sense is 'little Peter,' given to the bird as a nickname; see Cotgrave. Also written *Pierrot,* both forms being from *Pierre,* Peter. — L. *Petrum,* acc. of *Petrus,* Peter. — Gk. πέτρος, a stone, rock; also Peter. **Der.** F. *perroquet,* borrowed from Span. *perichito* or *periquito,* dimin. of *Perico,* Peter; see **Paraquito.** ¶ The F. word is prob. imitated or translated from Span. or Portuguese.

Parry, to ward off. (F. — L.) Formerly *parree,* sb., a warding off. From F. *parée,* fem. pp.; used as equivalent to Ital. *parata*, a defence, guard. ─ F. *parer*, to prepare, also to guard, ward off. ─ L. *parāre*, to prepare. See **Pare**.

Parse, to tell the parts of speech. (L.) To *parse* is to tell ' quæ *pars* orationis,' i. e. what part of speech a word is. ─ L. *pars*, a part. See **Part**.

Parsee, an adherent of the old Persian religion, in India. (Pers.) Pers. *pārsī*, a Persian. ─ Pers. *Pārs*, Persia.

Parsimony, frugality. (F. ─ L.) M. F. *parsimonie*; Cot. ─ L. *parsimōnia*, better *parcimōnia*. ─ L. *parci*-, for *parcus*, sparing; with suffix *-mōnia* (Idg. *-mōnyā*). Allied to *parcere*, to spare.

Parsley. (F. ─ L. ─ Gk.) Formerly *persely*. ─ F. *persil*; older form *peresil*. ─ L. *petroselinum*. ─ Gk. πετροσέλινον, rock parsley. ─ Gk. πέτρο-s, rock, stone; σέλινον, a kind of parsley; see **Celery**.

Parsnep, Parsnip. (F. ─ L.) Formerly *parsnep*, and still better *pasneppe*, as in Palsgrave; the *r* being intrusive. ─ O. F. *pastenaque*, a parsnip (by dropping *te*). ─ L. *pastināca*, a parsnep: perhaps orig. a root dug up. Perhaps from L. *pastināre*, to dig up. ─ L. *pastinum*, a two-pronged dibble. ¶ The ending *-nep* was assimilated to that of *turnep*.

Parson. (F. ─ L.) M. E. *persone*, which also means *person*; see Late L. *persōna*, a person of rank, a choir-master, curate, parson (Ducange). See **Person**. ¶ Blackstone gives the right etymology, but the wrong reason; the Late L. *persōna* was applied to ' rank' or dignity, and had nothing to do with a fanciful embodiment of the church in the parson's person! Der. *parson-age*.

Part. (F. ─ L.) F. *part*. ─ L. *partem*, acc. of *pars*, a part. Orig. ' a share,' that which is provided; from the same root as *portion*. Brugm. i. § 527. Der. *part*, vb.; *partake, partial*, &c.

partake. (F. ─ L.; *and* Scand.) For *part-take*, i. e. take part. Wyclif has *part-takynge*, 1 Cor. x. 16 (earlier version). See **Part** and **Take**.

Parterre. (F. ─ L.) F. *parterre*, an even piece of garden-ground. ─ F. *par terre*, along the ground. ─ L. *per terram*, along the ground. See **Terrace**.

Partial. (F. ─ L.) F. *partial*. ─ Late L. *partiālis*, referring to a part only. ─ L. *parti*-, decl. stem of *pars*, a part. See **Part**.

participate. (L.) From pp. of L. *participāre*, to take a part. ─ L. *particip*-, stem of *particeps*, sharing in. ─ L. *parti*-, decl. stem of *pars*, a part; *capere*, to take.

participle. (F. ─ L.) The *l* is an E. insertion, as in *syllable*. ─ F. *participe*. ─ L. *participium*, a participle; supposed to partake of the nature both of an adjectival sb. and a vb. ─ L. *particip*-, stem of *particeps*, sharing in; see above.

particle. (F. ─ L.) F. *particule* (16th cent.). ─ L. *particula*, double dimin. from *parti*-, decl. stem of *pars*, a part.

partisan (1), an adherent of a party. (F. ─ Ital. ─ L.) F. *partisan*. ─ Ital. *partigiano*, a partner; answering to a Late L. form **partītiānus*. ─ L. *partītus*, pp. of *partīrī*, to part, divide. ─ L. *parti*-, decl. stem of *pars*, a part. Others (see Körting), give the Late L. form as **partensiānus*, extended from *part*-, stem of *pars*, a part.

Partisan (2), **Partizan**, a halberd. (F. ─ Ital. ─ L. ?) M. F. *pertuisane*, 'a partisan, or leading-staffe,' Cot.; O. F. *pourtisaine* (15th cent., Littré); *pertesane* (Godefroy, s. v. *pertuisanier*). ─ Ital. *partegiana*, ' a partesan, iauelin;' Florio. [The M. F. *pertuisane* is an accommodated spelling, to make it look like M. F. *pertuiser*, to pierce through, due to L. *per-tundere*.] Cf. Late L. *partesāna, pertixāna*. β. Apparently connected with the word above, as if the weapon of a partisan (Diez).

Partition. (F. ─ L.) F. *partition*. ─ L. acc. *partītiōnem*, a sharing, partition. ─ L. *partītus*, pp. of *partīrī*, to divide. ─ L. *parti*-, decl. stem of *pars*, a part; see **Part**.

partner. (F. ─ L.) A curious corruption of M. E. *parcener*, frequently misread and misprinted as *partener*, by the common confusion between *c* and *t* in MSS., and through the influence of *part*. ─ O. F. *parcener*, M. F. *parsonnier*, 'a partener, or co-parcener;' Cot. ─ Late L. **partītiōnārius*, of which the shorter form *partiōnārius* occurs. ─ L. *partītiōn-em*, acc. of *partītio*, a sharing, share; see **Partition**.

Partridge, a bird. (F. ─ L. ─ Gk.) M. E. *pertriche*. ─ F. *perdrix*, where the second *r* is intrusive. ─ L. *perdīcem*, acc. of *perdix*. ─ Gk. πέρδιξ, a partridge.

Parturient, about to produce young. (L.) L. *parturient*-, stem of pres. pt. of *parturīre*, to be ready to produce young. From *part*-, as in *part-us*, pp. of *parĕre*, to produce. Brugm. ii. § 778. Der. *partur-it-ion*, F. *parturition*.

Party. (F. – L.) M. E. *partie*, usually 'a part.' – O. F. *partie*, a part, a party ; Cot. – L. *partīta*, fem. of *partītus*, pp. of *partīrī*, to divide. See **Partition**.

Parvenu, an upstart. (F. – L.) F. *parvenu*, lit. one who has arrived, hence, one who has thriven. Pp. of *parvenir*, to arrive, thrive. – L. *per-uenīre*, to arrive, come through. – L. *per*, through : *uenīre*, to come ; see **Venture**.

Parvis, a porch, room over a porch. (F. – L. – Gk. – Pers.) O. F. *parvis*, a porch, outer court before a house or church ; variant of *parevis, pareis, parais,* paradise (Low L. *paravīsus*). – L. *paradīsus*, a church-porch, outer court, paradise. See **Paradise**. The *v* was inserted in *pare-is*, to avoid hiatus.

Pasch, the Passover. (L. – Gk. – Heb.) A.S. *pascha*. – L. *pascha*. – Gk. πάσχα. – Heb. *pesakh*, a passing over ; the passover ; Exod. xii. 11. – Heb. *pāsakh*, he passed over.

Pash, to dash. (Scand.) Swed. dial. *paska*, to dabble in water, Norweg. *baska*, to dabble in water, tumble, work hard ; the same as Dan. *baske*, to slap, *baxes*, to box, Norw. *baksa*, to box ; Swed. dial. *baska, basta,* to beat ; from *bas-a*, to beat. Cp. prov. E. *bash*, of which it is a mere variant. And see **Plash, Baste** (1).

Pasha, Pacha. (Pers.) Also *bashaw*. Pers. *bāshā, bādshāh,* a governor of a province, great lord ; the same as *pādshāh,* a prince, great lord ; lit. 'a protecting king.' – Pers. *pād*, protecting ; *shāh,* king. See **Bezoar** and **Shah**.

Pasquin, Pasquinade, a lampoon. (F. – Ital.) (Formerly also *pasquil* ; M. F. *pasquille*.) – F. *pasquin* (whence *pasquinade*), a pasquin, lampoon. – Ital. *Pasquino*, 'a statue in Rome on whom all libels are fathered ; ' Florio. From the name of a cobbler at Rome, whose stall was frequented by gossips ; his name was transferred to a statue found near his stall at his death, on which the wits of the time secretly affixed lampoons ; see Haydn.

Pass, to move onward. (F. – L.) M. E. *passen*. – F. *passer*. – Late L. *passāre*, to pass. – L. *passus*, a step ; see **Pace**. β. Diez takes Late L. *passāre* to be the frequent. form of *pandere*, to stretch ; it makes but little difference.

passage. (F. – L.) F *passage*. – Late L. *passāticum*, a right of passage. – Late L. *passāre* ; see above. Der. *passenger*, for M. E. *passager*.

Passion. (F. – L.) F. *passion*. – L. *passiōnem*, acc. of *passio*, (properly) suffering. – L. *passus*, pp. of *patī*, to suffer. See **Patient**.

passive. (F. – L.) F. *passif*. – L. *passīuus*, suffering. – L. *passus* (above).

Passport. (F. – L.) F. *passeport*, written permission to travel from a port, &c. – F. *passer*, to pass ; *port*, port, from L. *portus* ; see **Pass** and **Port** (2).

Paste. (F. – L. – Gk.) O. F. *paste* ; F. *pâte*. – Late L. *pasta*, paste. – Gk. παστή, a mess of food ; orig. fem. of παστός, besprinkled, salted ; from πάσσειν, to sprinkle. The orig. sense was 'a salted mess of food.' Der. *past-y*, M. E. *pastee*, O. F. *pasté* (F. *pâté*), a pasty ; *past-r-y*, orig. a room in which pasties were kept (cf. *pantry, buttery*). And see **Patty**.

Pastel, a coloured crayon. (F. – Ital. – L.) An artist's term. – F. *pastel*, 'a pastel, crayon ; ' Hamilton. – Ital. *pastello*, a pastel. – L. *pastillum*, acc. of *pastillus*, a little loaf or roll ; the pastel being named from being shaped like a roll. Dimin. of *pastus*, food. – L. *pastus*, pp. of *pascere*, to feed. ¶ *Not* allied to *paste* ; see **pastille** below.

pastern. (F. – L.) Formerly *pastron* ; Palsgrave. – M. F. *pasturon*, 'the pastern of a horse ; ' Cot. (F. *pâturon*.) So called because a horse at *pasture* was tethered by the *pastern* ; the tether itself was called *pasture* in O. French. – O. F. *pasture*, pasture. See **pasture**.

pastille, a small cone of aromatic substances, to be burnt in a room. (F. – L.) F. *pastille*, a little lump or loaf ; see Cotgrave. – L. *pastillum*, acc. of *pastillus*, a little loaf ; dimin. of *pastus*, food ; see **Pastel**.

Pastime. (F. – L. ; *and* E.) From *pass* and *time* ; imitating F. *passe-temps*.

Pastor, a shepherd. (F. – L.) Formerly *pastour*. – O. F. *pastour*. – L. *pastōrem*, acc. of *pastor*, a shepherd, lit. ' feeder.' – L. *pastus*, pp. of *pascere*, to feed, an inceptive verb ; pp. *pā-ui*. (√PA.) Der. *pastor-al*, F. *pastoral*, L. *pastorālis*, adj.

pasture. (F. – L.) O. F. *pasture*, a feeding. – L. *pastūra*, a feeding. – L. *pastus*, pp. of *pascere*, to feed.

Pat (1), to strike lightly. (E.) In

Bacon, Nat. Hist. § 63. Most likely from a by-form of A. S. *plættan*, M. E. *platten*, *pletten* (see Stratmann), to strike; for loss of *l* cf. *patch* (1). Cf. Swed. dial. *pjätta*, to pat, *plätta*, to tap (Rietz); Bavarian *patzen*, to pat; E. Fries. *patjen*, to splash; G. *patschen*, to tap, splash; G. *platzen*, to crack; M. Du. *pletten*, 'contundere,' Kilian. Of imitative origin; cf. **Tap**, **Dab**, **Paddle**.

Pat (2), a small lump of butter. (E.) Cf. Irish *pait*, a hump, lump, *paiteog*, a small lump of butter; Gael. *pait*, *paiteag* (the same); where the form *pait* is borrowed from E. Prob. from the verb *pat* (1) above, as being *patted* into shape; just as *dab*, a small lump, is from the verb *to dab*.

Pat (3), quite to the purpose. (E.) Due to a peculiar use of *pat*, to strike, tap; see **Pat** (1). 'It will fall [happen] *pat*;' Mid. N. Dr. v. 188. Cf. *dab*, sb., an adept, from the verb *to dab*.

Patch (1), a piece sewn on a garment, a plot of ground. (E.?) M. E. *pacche*. Apparently a by-form of *platch*. '*Platch*, a large spot, a patch, a piece of cloth sewn on to a garment to repair it;' Dial. of Banffshire, by W. Gregor. Cf. Low G. *plakke*, *plakk*, (1) a spot, (2) a patch, (3) a patch or plot of ground; also M. E. *plekke*, a plot (of land), Du. *plek*, a patch of ground.

patch (2), a paltry fellow. (E.?) Temp. iii. 2. 71. *Patch* meant a fool or jester, from the parti-coloured or patch-like dress; Wolsey had two fools so named (Nares). The same word as *patch* (1). **Der.** *patch-ock*, a clown, a dimin. form, Spenser, View of Ireland, Globe ed., p. 636, col. 2; spelt *pajock*, Hamlet, iii. 2. 295.

Patchouli, a scent. (F. — Dravidian.) F. *patchouli*; of obscure origin. Apparently from E. *patcha-leaf*, i. e. 'green leaf,' imitating the vernacular *pacha-pāt*, where *pāt* is Hind. for 'leaf.' Or from Dravidian words meaning 'green leaf.' Cf. Tamil *pachchai*, green, *ilai*, leaf (Knight); Malayālim *pachchila*, green leaf (Gundert); Canarese *pachcha*, green, *yele*, leaf (Reeve).

Pate, the head. (Unknown.) M. E. *pate*. Of unknown origin; perhaps suggested by Late L. *platta*, the clerical tonsure. Cf. M. Du. *platte*, 'vertex rasus,' Kilian; G. *platte* a plate, a bald pate, in

vulgar language, the head (Flügel); M. H. G. *plate*, a plate, shaven pate. All from Gk. πλατύς, flat, broad. Cf. M. F. *pate*, a plate; Cot.

Paten. (F. — L. — Gk.) M. F. *patene* (Cot.). — L. *patina*, *patena*, a flat dish. — Gk. πατάνη, a flat (open) dish. See **Pan** and **Patent**.

Patent, open, public; as sb., an official document conferring a privilege. (F. — L.) M. E. *patente*, a patent; so called because *open* to general inspection. — O. F. *patent* (fem. *patente*), patent, wide open. — L. *patent-*, stem of pr. pt. of *patēre*, to lie open. Cf. Gk. πετάννυμι, I spread out. (√PET.) Brugm. i. § 120 (note).

Paternal. (F. — L.) F. *paternel*. — Late L. *paternālis*, fatherly. — L. *paternus*, fatherly. — L. *pater*, father. Perhaps formed with suffix *-ter* of the agent from √PA, to feed, guard. See **Father**.

Path, a way, track. (E.) A. S. *pæð*, *pað*, a path. +Du. *pad*, G. *pfad*.

Pathos. (Gk.) Gk. πάθος, suffering, emotion. — Gk. παθεῖν, used as 2 aor. infin. of πάσχειν (for *παθ-σκειν), to suffer. Allied to πένθ-ος, grief. **Der.** *path-et-ic*, from O. F. *pathetique*, L. *pathēticus*, Gk. παθητικός; extended from παθητός, subject to suffering.

Patient. (F. — L.) O. F. *patient*. — L. *patient-*, stem of pres. pt. of *patī*, to suffer. **Der.** *patience*, F. *patience*, L. *patientia*.

Patois, a vulgar dialect of French. (F. — L.) F. *patois*, country talk; which stands for an older form *patrois*, given by Godefroy (Diez, Littré). — Late L. *patriensis*, a native; hence, belonging to the natives. — L. *patria*, native country. — L. *patri-*, for *pater*, a father.

patriarch. (F. — L. — Gk.) O. F. *patriarche*. — L. *patriarcha*. — Gk. πατρι-άρχης, chief of a race or tribe. — Gk. πατρι-ά, a race; ἄρχειν, to rule. See **Arch-** (prefix).

patrician, a Roman nobleman. (L.) Formed, with suffix *-an*, from L. *patri-ci-us*, noble; a descendant of the *patrēs*, i. e. senators or fathers of the state.

patrimony. (F. — L.) M. E. *patri-monie*. — F. *patrimoine*. — L. *patrimōnium*, an inheritance. — L. *patri-*, for *pater*, father; with suffix *-mōnium* (Idg. *-mōn-yom*).

patriot. (F. — Late L. — Gk.) O. F. *patriote*. — Late L. *patriōta*. — Gk. πατριώ-της, properly, a fellow-countryman. — Gk.

πατριά, a race, from πατρι-, for πατήρ, a father. ¶ The mod. sense of *patriot* arose in *French*.

patristic, pertaining to the fathers of the church. (F.—L.) F. *patristique* (Littré). Coined from L. *patri-, pater*, a father; with the Gk. suffixes *-ist-* and *-ic*.

Patrol, a going of the rounds in a garrison. (F.) F. *patrouille*, 'a still night-watch in warre;' Cot. Lit. a tramping about; from O. F. (Picard) *patrouiller*, to paddle in water, the same word (but with inserted *r*) as *patouiller*, to paddle or dabble in with the feet; also *patrolli*, in the pâtois of Lyons (Puitspelu). Formed from O. F. *pate* (F. *patte*), the paw or foot of a beast. Of uncertain origin; perhaps imitative. Cf. Late L. *pata*, the foot of a cup, base of a tower; also G. *patsche*, an instrument for striking the hand, *patsch-fuss*, web foot of a bird; *patschen*, to strike, dabble, walk awkwardly; Low G. *pattjen*, to paddle in water with the feet (Richey); Bavarian *patzen*, to pat; see **Pat** (1). ¶ Hence also Span. *pata*, paw, *patullar*, to run through mud, *patrullar*, to patrol; and Ital. *pattuglia*, a patrol (without the inserted *r*).

Patron. (F.—L.) F. *patron*.—L. *patrōnum*, acc. of *patrōnus*, a protector; extended from *patr-*, stem of *pater*, father.

patronymic. (F.—L.—Gk.) M. F. *patronymique*. — L. *patrōnymicus*. — Gk. πατρωνυμικός, belonging to the father's name. — Gk. πατρωνυμία, a name taken from the father. — Gk. πατρ-, for πατήρ, a father; ὄνομα, a name; see **Name**.

Patten, a clog. (F.) Formerly *paten*. —F. *patin*, a patten, 'also a foot stall of a pillar;' Cot.—M. F. *pate* (F. *patte*), a paw or foot of a beast, 'also a foot-stall of a pillar;' Cot. See **Patrol**.

Patter, to strike frequently, as hail. (E.) A frequentative of *pat*; see **Pat** (1). Cf. prov. E. (Lonsdale) *pattle*, to pat gently.

Pattern, an example, model to work by. (F.—L.) M. E. *patron*; (the old spelling).—F. *patron*, 'a patron . . also a pattern, sample;' Cot. See **Patron**.

Patty, a little pie. (F.—L.—Gk.) Mod. F. *pâté*; O. F. *pasté*, a pasty.—Late L. *pastātum*, neut. of pp. of *pastāre*, to make paste.—Late L. *pasta*, paste; see **Paste**.

Paucity, fewness. (F.—L.) F. *paucité*.

—L. *paucitātem*, acc. of *paucitās*, fewness. —L. *paucus*, few; allied to **Few**.

Paunch. (F. — L.) O. F. *panche* (Picard) ; also *pance* ; F. *panse*. — L. *panticem*, acc. of *pantex*, belly, paunch.

Pauper. (L.) L. *pauper*, poor. *Pau-* is allied to *paucus*, few ; *-per*, (perhaps) to L. *parāre*, to provide. Lit. 'provided with little.'

Pause, a stop. (F. — L. — Gk.) F. *pause.*—Late L. *pausa.*—Gk. παῦσις, a pause, ceasing.—Gk. παύειν, to make to cease ; παύεσθαι, to cease. **Doublet,** *pose*, q. v.

Pave. (F.—L.) M. E. *pauen* = (*paven*). —F. *paver*, to pave.—Late L. *pavāre*, corrupt form of L. *pauīre*, to beat, strike, ram, tread down. Cf. Skt. *pavi-*, thunderbolt. **Der.** *pavement*, F. *pavement*, L. *pauīmentum*, a hard floor, from *pauīre*, to ram ; also *pav-i-or* (cf. *law-y-er*), from F. *paveur*, 'a paver,' Cot.

Pavilion. (F.—L.) M. E. *pavilon.*— F. *pavillon*, a tent ; so called because spread out like the wings of a butterfly.— L. *pāpiliōnem*, acc. of *pāpilio*, (1), a butterfly, (2) a tent.

Pavin, Pavan, a stately Spanish dance. (F.—Span.—L.—Pers.—Tamil.) F. *pavane.*—Span. *pavana*, a grave dance (see *Pavan* in Nares). Prob. from a Late L. **pāvānus*, peacock-like, from the row of stately dancers (Scheler) ; cf. Span. *pava*, a peahen, a turkey, *pavada*, a flock of turkcys, *pavo*, adj., like a peacock (whence *pavonear*, to walk with affected gravity).—Late L. *pāvus*, earlier L. *pāuo*, a peacock. See **Peacock**.

Pavise, a large shield. (F.) Also spelt *pavess, pavish, pauice, pauys, paues.* —F. *pavois*, 'a great shield ;' Late L. *pavensis*. (Span. *paves* ; Ital. *pavese*, *pavesce*, Florio.) Of uncertain origin ; perhaps from the city of *Pavia*, in Italy. Godefroy has the adj. *pavinois, paviois, pavois, pavaiz*, adj. 'de Pavie ;' as in the phr. *escus pavaiz*, shields of Pavia.

Paw. (F.) M. E. *pawe, powe*, a paw. —A. F. *powe*, O. F. *poe*, a paw ; the same as Prov. *pauta*, Catalan *pota*, a paw. Cf. Low G. *pote*, Du. *poot* (whence G. *pfote*), a paw. Perhaps from an imitative root ; cf. F. *patte*. Franck takes Du. *poot* to be of Teut. origin. Cf. E. Fries. *pote, pōt*, paw.

Pawl, a short bar, as a catch to a windlass. (F.—L.) O. F. *paul*, variant of *pal*, *pel*, a stake (whence Du. *pal*, Swed. *pall*, Norw. *pall*, a pawl; cf. W. *pawl*, a pole, stake, bar).—L. *pālum*, acc. of *pālus*, a stake. See **Pale** (1).

Pawn (1), a pledge. (F.—Teut.) F. *pan*, 'a pane, piece, panel, also a pawn, gage, skirt of a gown, pane of a hose,' &c.; Cot. In the sense of 'pane,' F. *pan* is of Latin origin; see **Pane**. In the sense of 'pawn,' F. *pan* is rather from Du. *pand*; cf. G. *pfand*, O. H. G. *phant*, a pledge. Der. *im-pawn*, to put in pledge, to pledge; *pawn*, vb.

Pawn (2), a piece at chess. (F.—L.) M. E. *paune*, *poune*, *poun*.—O. F. *paon*, a pawn (Roquefort), also *poon* (Littré); but the older form is *peon* (F. *pion*), agreeing with Span. *peon*, a foot-soldier, pawn, Ital. *pedone*, a foot-soldier, *pedona*, a pawn (Florio).—Late L. *pedōnem*, acc. of *pedo*, a foot-soldier.—L. *ped-*, stem of *pes*, foot. ¶ The O. F. *paon* is the same word; cf. F. *faon* (E. *fawn*), from Late L. *fētōnem*, shewing the same substitution of *a* for *e*; there is no need to connect it with F. *paon*, a peacock, as Littré does, ignoring the Ital. and Span. words.

Pawnee, drink. (Hind.—Skt.) Hind. *pānī*, water.—Skt. *pānīya*, allied to *pāna*, a beverage.—Skt. *pā*, to drink.

Paxwax, strong tendon in the neck of animals. (E.) M. E. *paxwax*, also *fexwax*, the latter being the right form (see Prompt. Parv.).—A. S. *feax*, *fex*, hair; *weaxan*, to grow. Thus the lit. sense is perhaps 'hair-sinew,' because it is where the hair ends; cf. G. *haarwachs*, a tendon.

Pay (1), to discharge a debt. (F.—L.) M.E. *paien*.—O. F. *paier*, *paer* (F. *payer*), to pay, to content.—L. *pācāre*, to pacify; in late Lat., to pay a debt.—L. *pāc-*, stem of *pax*, peace; see **Peace**.

Pay (2), to pitch the seams of a ship. (F.—L.) A. F. *peier* (O. F. *poier*, Godefroy), to pitch.—L. *picāre*, to pitch.—L. *pic-*, stem of *pix*, pitch; see **Pitch**. ¶ The M. E. word for 'pitch' is *peis*, from A. F. *peis* (O. F. *pois*), pitch; from L. acc. *picem*.

Paynim, Painim, a pagan. (F.—L.) 'The *paynim* bold;' F. Q. i. 4. 41. M. E. *paynim*, a pagan; but this sense is due to a singular mistake. A *paynim* is properly not a *man*, but a *country* or district, and is identical with *paganism*, formerly used to mean heathendom, or the country of pagans. Rightly used in King Horn, 803, to mean 'heathen lands.' —O. F. *paienisme*, lit. paganism; Late L. *pāgānismus*. Formed with suffix *-ismus*, from L. *pāgān-us*, a pagan. See **Pagan**.

Pea, a vegetable. (L.) Formerly *pease*, *pese*; M. E. *pese*, pl. *pesen* or *peses*. A. S. *pisa*, pl. *pisan*.—L. *pīsum*, a pea.+Gk. πίσος, a pea. (√PIS.)

Peace. (F.—L.) M. E. *pais*.—O. F. *pais* (F. *paix*).—L. *pācem*, acc. of *pax*, peace, orig. a compact; cf. *pac-*, as in *pac-tum*, a bargain; see **Pact**.

Peach (1), a fruit. (F.—L.—Pers.) M. E. *peche*.—O. F. *pesche*, a peach.—L. *persicum*, a peach; so called from growing on the *Persica arbor*, Persian tree.—Pers. *Pārs*, Persia.

Peach (2), to inform against. (F.—L.) Short for M. E. *apechen*, to impeach, a variant of *impechen*, to impeach, by the substitution of prefix *a-* (L. *ad*) for *im-* (L. *in*). See **Impeach**.

Peacock. (L.—Pers.—Tamil; *and* E.) M. E. *pecok*, *pocok*; where *cok* = E. *cock*. We also find M. E. *po*; A. S. *pēa*, *pāwa*; all from L. *pāuo* (whence Du. *paauw*, G. *pfau*, F. *paon*). The same as Gk. ταῶς, for ταϝῶς, a peacock; the change from τ to π being due to the fact that the word was foreign both to L. and Gk.—Pers. *ṭāwus*, *ṭāus*, a peacock.—O. Tamil *tōkei*, *tōgei*, a peacock; see Max Müller, Lect. on Lang. i. 190 (ed. 1891). ¶ Also *pocock*, which is still a surname.

Pea-jacket, a coarse thick jacket. (Du. *and* F.) The prefix *pea-* is borrowed from Du. *pij*, *pije*, a coat of a coarse woollen stuff; Hexham has M. Du. *pije*, 'a pie-gowne, rough gowne, such as seamen weare.' The same as Low G. *pije*, N. Fries. *pie*, *pije-jückert*.—M. Du. *pije*, or *pije-laken*, 'a rough or a hairy cloath;' Hexham. Prob. from F. *pie*, a mag-pie; cf. E. *pied*, spotted. See **Pie** (1). Also Low G. *pije*, *pigge*, *pyke* (Brem. W.), perhaps from L. *pīca*.

Peak. (F.—L.) M. E. *pec*. [Cf. Irish *peac*, a sharp-pointed thing; from E. *peak*.] A variant of *pike*, q. v. Cf. dial. of Normandy *pec*, a hob (or mark) in the game of quoits (Godefroy, s. v. *pec*); also Low G. *peek*, a pike, pointed weapon.

Peal, a loud sound, chime of bells, noise of a trumpet. (F.—L.) A shortened form of *appeal*, M. F. *apel*, *appel*; Cot. gives *appel*, pl. *appeaux*, 'chimes.' Note also

M. E. *apel*, an old term in hunting-music (Halliwell) ; this we now call a *peal*. The prefix *a-* was prob. mistaken for the E. indef. article. The O. F. *apel* is from O. F. *apeler*, vb. ; see **Appeal.**

Pean ; see **Pæan.**

Pear, a fruit. (L.)   A. S. *peru, pere.* — L. *pirum*, a pear (whence also Ital. *pera*).

Pearl. (F. – L. ?)   M.E. *perle.* – F. *perle*, 'a pearl, a berrie ;' Cot. Of unknown origin ; we find also Ital., Span., Prov. *perla*, Port. *perola, perla*. Cf. Low L. *perula*, the end of the nose (7th cent.). Perhaps for L. **pirula*, i. e. a little pear, from L. *pirum*, a pear ; cf. Span. *perilla*, (1) a little pear, (2) a pear-shaped ornament, M. Ital. *perolo*, a little button on a cap. Perhaps suggested by the various senses of L. *bacca*, (1) a berry, (2) olive-berry, (3) round fruit, (4) a pearl (Horace). See **Purl** (2).

Pearl-barley. (F.–L.; *and* E.)   F. *orge perlé*, pearl-barley (Hamilton) ; but this seems to be a corruption of *orge pelé*, ' pilled barley,' Cot. See **Peel** (1).

Peasant. (F. – L.)   O. F. *paisant*, another form of O. F. *paisan*, a peasant ; (cf. Ital. *paesano*, Span. *paisano*, a compatriot). Formed with suffix *-an* (L. *-ānus*), from O. F. *pais* (F. *pays*), a country (cf. Ital. *paese*, Span. *pais*, Port. *pais*, a country). — Late L. *pāgense*, neut. of *pāgensis*, belonging to a village. — L. *pāgus*, a village, district. See **Pagan.**

Peat, a kind of turf for fuel.   (C.) Latinised as *peta* (Ducange) ; whence *petāria*, a place for getting peat. Apparently from O. Gael. *pett*, a piece, from W. *peth*, a thing, a piece. See **Piece.**

Pebble. (E.)   A. S. *papol-stān*, a pebble-stone.

Peccable, liable to sin. (L.)   Coined as if from L. **peccābilis*, from *peccāre*, to sin.   Brugm. i. § 585.

peccadillo. (Span. – L.)   Span. *peccadillo, pecadillo*, a slight fault ; dimin. of *pecado*, a sin. – L. *peccātum*, a sin. – L. *peccātus*, pp. of *peccāre*, to sin.

peccant, sinning. (F. – L.)   First used in phr. ' *peccant* humours.' – F. *peccant*, sinning ; ' *l'humeur peccante*, corrupt humour ;' Cot. – L. *peccant-*, stem of pres. pt. of *peccāre*, to sin.

Peccary, a quadruped. (F. – Caribbean.)   F. *pécari*, a peccary (Buffon). – Carib. *pakira*, the name used in Guiana ; see N. and Q., 9 S. iv. 496. Cf. *pachira*, the name given to the peccary in Oronoko (Clavigero, Hist. Mexico) ; Span. *pacquire* (Pineda).

Peck (1), to strike with the beak, to pick up. (L.)   M. E. *pekken*, used as equivalent to *pikken*, to pick or peck up. A mere variant of *pick* ; see **Pick.**

Peck (2), a dry measure, 2 gallons. (F. – L. ?)   M. E. *pekke*, a peck. A. F. and O. F. *pek*. From the verb *pekken*, to peck or snap up ; cf. E. *peck*, to pick up (as a bird) ; prov. E. *peck*, meat, victuals. [So also F. *picotin*, a peck (measure), *picoter*, to peck as a bird.] See **Peck** (1), **Pick.**

Pectinal, lit. comb-like. (L.)   From L. *pectin-*, stem of *pecten*, a comb. – L. *pectere*, to comb. **+** Gk. πεκτεῖν, to comb, from πέκειν, to comb. (√PEK.)

Pectoral, belonging to the chest. (F. –L.)   F. *pectoral.* – L. *pectorālis*, adj., from *pector-* (for **pectos*), stem of *pectus*, the breast.   Der. *poitrel.*

Peculate, to pilfer. (L.)   From pp. of L. *peculārī*, to appropriate to one's own use. Formed as if from **peculum*, for *peculium*, private property ; see below.

peculiar, one's own, particular. (F. – L.)   M. F. *peculier.* – L. *peculiāris*, one's own. – L. *peculium*, private property ; closely allied to *pecunia*, money ; see below.

pecuniary. (F. – L.)   M.F. *pecuniaire.* – L. *pecuniārius*, relating to money or property. – L. *pecunia*, property. – O.L. *pecu*, cattle ; cf. *pecu-a*, neut. pl., cattle of all kinds, property ; *pecus*, cattle. Cf. Skt. *paçu*, cattle, cognate with Goth. *faihu*, property, A. S. *feoh*, G. *vieh*, cattle.

Pedagogue, a teacher. (F. – L. – Gk.)   M.F. *pedagogue.* – L. *pædagōgus.* – Gk. παιδαγωγός, a slave who led a boy to school ; hence, a tutor. – Gk. παιδ-, stem of παῖς, a boy ; ἀγωγός, leading, from ἄγειν, to lead. The Gk. παῖς = παϜίς, allied to L. *puer*, a boy. See **Puerile, Puberty.**

Pedal, belonging to the foot. (L.)   The *pedal* keys in an organ are acted on by the feet. – L. *pedālis*, belonging to the foot. – L. *ped-*, stem of *pēs*, foot. **+** A. S. *fōt*, foot. See **Foot.**

Pedant.   (F. – Ital. – Gk. ?)   M. F. *pedant.* – Ital. *pedante*, ' a pedante, or a schoolmaster, the same as *pedagogo* ;' Florio. The suffix *-ante* is a pres. participial form ; the stem *ped-* is prob. the same as in Ital. *pedagogo*, and therefore due to

Gk. παιδεύειν (whence a Lat. form *paedāre*), to instruct; see **Pedagogue**.

Peddle, to deal in small wares. (E.?) Coined from the sb. *pedlar*, later form of *peddar*; see **Pedlar**.

Pedestal. (Span.—Ital.—L. *and* G.) Span. *pedestal*, 'the base of a pillar,' Minsheu; borrowed from Ital. *piedestallo*, 'a footstall or treshall [threshold] of a door;' Florio. Lit. 'foot-support.' Compounded as if from L. *pedem*, acc. of *pes*, a foot; and O. H. G. *stal* (G. *stall*), a stall; see **Stall**.

pedestrian. (L.) Properly an adj.; from L. *pedestri-*, decl. stem. of *pedester*, one who goes on foot. For **pedit-tr-*; from *pedit-*, stem of *pedes*, one who goes on foot; with suffix *-ter* (Idg. *-ter*). *Ped-it-* is from *ped-*, stem of *pes*, foot; and *it-um*, supine of *īre*, to go. Brugm. ii. § 123.

pedicel, pedicle, the foot-stalk of fruit. (F.—L.) *Pedicel* is from mod. F. *pédicelle*; but *pedicle* (older and better) from M. F. *pedicule*, a leaf-stalk; Cot.—L. *pediculus*, little foot, foot-stalk, pedicle; double dimin. of *ped-*, stem of *pēs*, foot.

pedigree. (F.—L.) Old spellings *pedegree* (1627); *pedigrew* (1570); *petygrewe* (1530). Also, in Prompt. Parv. (1440) *pedegru*, *petygru*, with slight variations, explained by 'lyne of kynrede and awncetrye, *Stemma*, *in scalis*.' Also *peedegrue*, Lydgate (1426; in Polit. Poems, ii. 138). A.F. *pee de grue*, foot of a crane; from a three-line mark (like the broad arrow) used in denoting succession in pedigrees.—L. *pedem*, acc. of *pēs*, foot; *dē*, of; *gruem*, acc. of *grus*, a crane, cognate with E. **Crane**.

pediment, an ornament finishing the front of a building. (L.) The N. E. D. shows that the older form was *periment*, described as a workman's term, and corrupt English. I suggest that a *periment* was substituted for *operiment*, a covering; from L. *operīmentum*, covering (common in the Latin Vulgate version of the Bible).—L. *operīre*, to cover. A *pediment* forms a sort of cover over doors, niches, &c. For the etymology of L. *operīre*, see **Cover**. (Perhaps influenced by confusion with *impediment*.)

Pedlar, Pedler, Peddler, a dealer in small wares. (E.?) The old word was usually *peddare*, *pedder*, a man who hawked about fish in baskets called *peds*, or occasionally *pads*. See *Pedde* in Prompt.

Parv.; Norfolk *ped* (Forby); Lowl. Sc. *peddir*, a pedlar (Jamieson). The orig. sense of *ped* was 'hamper,' and the word may be related to *pad*. See **Padlock**.

Pedobaptism, infant baptism. (Gk.) From Gk. παιδο-, for παῖς, a boy; and *baptism*. Cf. **Pedagogue**.

Peel (1), to strip off skin. (F.—L.) From F. *peler*, to 'unskin'; Cot. (Cf. M. Ital. *pellare*, 'to unskin;' Florio).—O. F. *pel*, skin.—L. *pellem*, acc. of *pellis*, a skin. See **Fell** (2). ¶ Confused with F. *piller*; see below.

Peel (2), to pillage. (F.—L.) In Milton, P.R. iv. 136. Distinct from *peel*, to strip; another spelling of *pill*; see **Pill** (2).

Peel (3), a fire-shovel. (F.—L.) Once a common word.—O. F. *pele* (Littré), F. *pelle*, a fire-shovel.—L. *pāla*; see **Palette**.

Peel (4), a small castle. (F.—L.) M.E. *pēl*, a small castle, orig. a stockade or wooden fortress.—O. F. *pel* (also *pal*), a stake.—L. *pālum*, acc. of *pālus*, a stake. See **Pale** (1).

Peep (1), to chirp, cry like a chicken. (F.—L.) M. E. *pipen*.—O.F. *piper*, also *pepier*, to chirp as a bird.—L. *pīpāre*, *pīpīre*, to chirp. See **Pipe** (1) and **Peep** (2).

Peep (2), to look through a narrow aperture. (F.—L.) Palsgrave has: 'I peke or prie, *Ie pipe hors*;' i. e. I peep out. Thus *peep* is directly from F. *piper*, lit. to pipe, but also used in the sense to peep. [It arose from the exclamation *pipe!* (Du. dial. *piep!*, Molema), made by a hider in the game of *peep-bo, bo-peep*, or hide-and-seek; cf. Du. dial. *piepen*, (1) to say *piep!* (2) to peep out.] Cot. gives F. *piper*, 'to whistle, chirp like a bird, cousen, deceive, cheat, beguile;' *pipée*, 'the peeping or chirping of small birds, counterfeited by a bird-catcher, also a counterfeit shew;' *pipe*, 'a bird-call.' The F. *piper* is from L. *pīpāre*, *pīpīre*, to chirp; see **Pipe**.

Peer (1), an equal. (F.—L.) The twelve *peers* of France were of *equal* rank. M. E. *pere*, *per*.—O. F. *per*, *peer*, later *pair*, a peer; or as adj., equal.—L. *parem*, acc. of *par*, equal. See **Par**. Der. *peer-less*.

Peer (2), to look narrowly, pry. (E.?) M. E. *piren*, E. Fries. *pīren*, Westphal. *pīren*, Low G. *piren*, to look closely. Cf. also *pliren*, to peer, orig. to draw the eyelids together, so as to look closely; Swed. *plira*, Dan. *plire*, to blink.

Peer (3), to appear. (F.—L.) Short for *appear*, just as M. E. *peren* is short for *apperen*; see **Appear**.

Peevish, fretful, whimpering. (E.) M. E. *peuisch*, *peyuesshe*; also *pevych*, *pevage*, uncouth, perverse (G. Douglas). The leading idea seems to be 'whining,' 'making a plaintive cry.' Cf. Dan. dial. *piæve*, to whine; Lowl. Sc. *peu*, to make a plaintive noise. E. *pew-* in *pewet*, a bird; Low G. *pauen*, to whimper. See **Pewet**. Of imitative origin. For the suffix, cf. *thiev-ish*, *mop-ish*.

Peewit; see **Pewet**.

Peg, a wooden pin. (E.) M. E. *pegge*. Cf. Du. and Low G. *pegel*, a measure of liquid capacity, such as was marked by pegs in a 'peg-tankard.' Apparently allied to Dan. *pig*, Swed. *pigg*, a spike; W. *pig*, a peak, point; Corn. *peg*, a prick; see **Peak**.

Peise, Peize, to weigh. (F.—L.) M. E. *peisen*; A. F. *peiser*, to weigh; O.F. *poiser*; see **Poise**, which is a doublet.

Peitrel; see **Poitrel**.

Pelf, lucre, booty. (F.) M. E. *pelfyr*, *pelfrey*, 'spolium;' Prompt. Parv.—O. F. *pelfre*, booty, spoil; allied to *pelfrer*, to pilfer. See Körting, § 3221. Der. *pilfer*.

Pelican. (F.—L.—Gk.) F. *pelican*. —L. *pelicānus*, *pelecānus*.—Gk. πελεκάν, πελεκᾶς, wood-pecker, also a water-bird. Named from its large bill, as the woodpecker was named from its pecking.—Gk. πελεκάω, I hew with an ax, peck.—Gk. πέλεκυς, an ax.+Skt. *paraçu-*, an ax.

Pelisse, a silk habit. (F.—L.) Formerly a furred robe.—F. *pelisse*, *pelice*, 'a skin of fur;' Cot.—L. *pellicea*, fem. of *pelliceus*, made of skins.—L. *pellis*, a skin.

pell, a skin. (F.—L.) M. E. *pell*, *pel*.—O. F. *pel* (F. *peau*).—L. *pellem*, acc. of *pellis*, a skin. See **Fell** (2).

Pellet, a little ball. (F.—L.) M. E. *pelet*.—O. F. *pelote*, a tennis-ball. Dimin. from L. *pila*, a ball.

Pellicle, a thin film. (F.—L.) F. *pellicule*.—L. *pellicula*, a small skin; dimin. of *pellis*, a skin. See **pell**.

Pellitory (1), **Paritory**, a wild flower that grows on walls. (F.—L.) *Pellitory* is for *paritory*. M. E. *paritorie*. —M. F. *paritoire*, 'pellitory;' Cot.—L. *parietāria*, pellitory; fem. of *parietārius*,

belonging to walls.—L. *pariet-*, stem of *pariēs*, a wall.

Pellitory (2), the plant pyrethrum. (Span.—L.—Gk.) Span. *pelitre* [Ital. *pilatro*].—L. *pȳrethrum*.—Gk. πύρεθρον, a hot spicy plant.—Gk. πῦρ, fire.

Pell-mell, confusedly. (F.—L.) O.F. *pesle-mesle*, 'pell-mell, confusedly;' Cot. Spelt *pellemelle* in the XIIIth cent. (mod. F. *pêle-mêle*). [Apparently understood to mean 'stirred up with a fire-shovel.'—F. *pelle*, a fire-shovel; O. F. *mesler*, to mix up; see **Peel** (3) above, and **Medley**.] But orig. only a reduplicated form of *mesle*, as *mesle-mesle* and *melle-melle* also occur. See Körting, § 5336.

Pellucid. (F.—L.) F. *pellucide*.— L. *pellūcidus*, *perlūcidus*, transparent.—L. *per*; and *lūcidus*, lucid. See **Lucid**.

Pelt (1), to throw, cast. (L.) M. E. *pelten*, also *pilten*, *pulten*, to thrust, cast. The forms *pilten*, *pulten*, answer to an A. S. form **pyltan*.—L. *pultāre*, to beat, strike, knock. *Pultāre* (like *pulsāre*) is a derivative of *pellere*, to drive. See **Pulsate**.

Pelt (2), a skin, esp. of a sheep. (F.— L.) M. E. *pelt*, a shortened form of *peltry*, skins, *peltry-ware*, dealing in skins.—O.F. *pelleterie*, the trade of a skinner.—O. F. *pelletier*, a skinner. Formed (like *bijoutier*, with suffix *-tier* = L. *-tārius*) from O. F. *pel*, a skin.—L. *pellis*, a skin. See **Pell**. ¶ G. *pelz*, O. H. G. *pelliz*, answers to F. *pelisse*; see **Pelisse**.

Pelvis, the bony cavity in the lower part of the abdomen. (L.) L. *peluis*, a basin, hence the pelvis.

Pemmican, a preparation of dried meat. Of N. American Indian origin.

Pen (1), an instrument for writing. (F.—L.) O.F. *penne*.—L. *penna*, a feather; O. L. *pesna* (for **petna* or **petsna*). Brugm. i. § 762 (2). From √PET, to fly. See **Feather**.

Pen (2), to shut up. (L.) M.E. *pennen*. A.S. *pennian*, only in the comp. *on-pennian*, to un-pen, unfasten. *Pennian* is properly to fasten with a *pin* or peg; cf. Low G. *pennen*, to bolt a door, from *penn*, a pin or peg; see **Pin**. Note E. Fries. *penne*, *penn*, *pinne*, *pin*, a peg, a pin.

Penal. (F.—L.—Gk.) M.F. *penal*, 'penall;' Cot.—L. *pænālis*, belonging to punishment.—L. *pæna*, punishment.—Gk. ποινή, penalty. See **Pain**.

Penance. (F.—L.) M. E. and O. F.

penance, older form *penëance.* — L. *pæni-
tentia*, penitence. — L. *pænitent-*, stem of
pres. pt. of *pænitēre*, to cause to repent.
See **Penitent.**

Penchant, a strong inclination, bias
(in favour of). (F. — L.) F. *penchant*, sb.;
orig. pres. pt. of *pencher*, to lean, lean
towards. — Late L. type **pendicāre*; from
L. *pendēre*, to hang.

Pencil. (F. — L.) The old sense was
a small hair-brush for painting. — M. F.
pincel, later *pinceau*, 'a pensill, brush;'
Cot. — L. *pēnecillus*, a small tail, painter's
brush; dimin. of *pēniculus*, which is a
double dimin. of *pēnis*, a tail. For **pes-
nis*; cf. Skt. *pasa(s)*, Gk. πέος; Brugm. i.
§ 877.

Pendant, anything hanging, a hanging ornament. (F. — L.) F. *pendant*, a
pendant. — F. *pendant*, pres. pt. of *pendre*,
to hang. — L. *pendēre*, to hang; allied to
pendere, to weigh. Cf. Gk. σφενδόνη, a
sling. (√SPHEND, SPHED.) Der.
pend-ent, hanging, Latinised form of F.
pendant; *pend-ing*, Anglicised form of F.
pendant, during.

pendulous. (L.) For L. *pendulus*,
hanging. — L. *pendēre*, to hang.

pendulum. (L.) L. *pendulum*, neut.
of adj. *pendulus* (above).

Penetrate. (L.) From pp. of L.
penetrāre, to pierce into. Compounded of
pene-, base of *penes*, with, *peni-tus*, within,
with which cf. *penus*, the inner part of a
sanctuary; and *-trāre* (as in *in-trāre*), to
pass over, allied to Skt. *tara-*, a crossing.

Penguin, Pinguin, a bird. (Unknown.) In a tract printed in 1588, we
read that Sir F. Drake gave a certain
island the name of *Penguin Island* in
1587, from the penguins found there.
Selden (1613) derived it from W. *pen
gwyn*, i.e. white head. In that case, it
must first have been given to another bird,
such as the auk (the puffin is common in
Anglesey), since the penguin's head is
black.

Peninsula. (L.) L. *pēninsula*, a
piece of land nearly an island. — L. *pēne,
pæne*, almost; *insula*, an island. So also
pen-ultimate, almost the last, last but one;
pen-umbra, partial shadow.

Penitent. (F. — L.) O. F. *penitent.*
— L. *pænitent-*, stem of pres. pt. of
pænitēre, to cause to repent, better spelt
pænitēre. Cf. *pænitet*, 'it repents me.'
Allied to **Penury.**

Pennon, Pennant. (F. — L.) M.E.
penon, penoun. — M. F. *pennon*, 'a flag,
streamer; also the feather of an arrow;'
Cot. — L. *penna*, wing, feather (hence a
plume, standard). See **Pen** (1).

Penny. (E.) M.E. *peni*; pl. *penies*,
contracted form *pens* (whence mod. E.
pence). A. S. *pening, penning*, a penny;
later *penig*, whence M. E. *peni.* By-form
pending (Thorpe, Diplomatarium, p. 471);
as if formed with E. suffix *-ing* from the
base **pand.* β. This base is usually
identified with Du. *pand*, a pawn, pledge,
G. *pfand*, O. H. G. *pfant*; see **Pawn** (1)
above. In this case, the lit. sense may have
been 'little pledge,' i. e. a token, coin.+
Du. *penning*, Icel. *penningr*, Dan. Swed.
penning; G. *pfennig*, O. H. G. *phantinc,
phentinc*, dimin. of *pfant.*

Penny-royal, a herb. (F. — L.) A
popular form of the old name *pulial royal.*
Cotgrave translates M. F. *pulege* by 'penny
royall, puliall royall'; from Late L. *pūle-
gium.* The above old name is due to L.
pūlēium rēgium, a name given to the
plant from its supposed efficacy against
fleas (cf. E. *flea-bane*). From L. *pūlex*,
a flea; but this was only a 'popular'
etymology.

Pensile, suspended. (F. — L.) M. F.
pensil; Cot. — L. *pensilis*, pendent; from
*pens-us, unused pp. of *pendēre*, to hang.

pension. (F. — L.) F. *pension.* — L.
pensiōnem, acc. of *pensio*, a payment. — L.
pensus, pp. of *pendere*, to weigh, weigh
out money, pay.

pensive. (F. — L.) M. E. *pensif.* —
F. *pensif*, thoughtful. — F. *penser*, to think.
— L. *pensāre*, to weigh, ponder; frequent.
of *pendere*, to weigh.

Pent, for *penned*, pp. of **Pen** (2), q.v.

Pentagon, a plane five-sided figure.
(F. — L. — Gk.) F. *pentagone.* — L. *penta-
gōnus*, adj., pentagonal. — Gk. πεντάγωνος,
pentagonal; neut. πεντάγωνον, a pentagon.
— Gk. πεντά-, for πεντέ, five; γωνία, an
angle, from γόνυ, a knee; see **Knee.**
And see **Five.**

pentameter, a verse of five metres.
(L. — Gk.) L. *pentameter.* — Gk. πεντά-
μετρος. — Gk. πεντά-, for πεντέ, five; μέτρον, a metre.

pentateuch, the five books of Moses.
(L. — Gk.) L. *pentateuchus.* — Gk. πεντά-,
five (above); τεῦχος, a tool, also a book.

pentecost, Whitsuntide; orig. a
Jewish festival on the fiftieth day after the

Passover. (L. – Gk.) L. *pentēcostē.* – Gk. πεντηκοστή, Pentecost, Acts ii. 1 ; fem. of πεντηκοστός, fiftieth. – Gk. πεντήκοντα, fifty.

Penthouse, a shed projecting from a building. (F.–L.) Formerly *pentice*, whence it is corrupted. – M. F. *apentis, appentis*, 'a penthouse ;' Cot. – L. *appendicium*, an appendage, allied to *appendix* (the same). – L. *ap- (ad)*, to ; *pendēre*, to hang.

Pentroof, a roof with a slope on one side only. (F.–L. ; *and* E.) This has affected the sense of *penthouse*, though they mean quite different things. Here *pent* is from F. *pente*, a slope, formed from F. *pendre*, to hang. – L. *pendēre*, to hang.

Penultimate, Penumbra ; see Peninsula.

Penury, want. (F. – L.) M.F. *penurie.* – L. *pēnuria*, want, need. Cf. Gk. πεῖνα, hunger.

Peony, Pæony, a flower. (F.– L. – Gk.) Altered to suit the Lat. spelling. M. E. *pione.* – O. F. *pione* (F. *pivoine*). – L. *pæōnia*, medicinal, from its supposed virtues ; fem. of *Pæōnius*, belonging to *Pæōn*, its supposed discoverer. – Gk. παιωνία, pæony ; from Παίων, Pæon. See Pæan.

People. (F.–L.) M.E. *people, poeple.* – A. F. *people, pēple* ; O. F. *pueple* ; F. *peuple.* – L. *populum*, acc. of *populus*, people.

Pepper. (L. – Gk. – Skt.) A. S. *pipor.* – L. *piper.* – Gk. πέπερι. – Skt. *pippalī*, (1) fruit of the holy fig-tree, (2) long pepper ; from *pippala-*, the holy fig-tree.

Pepsine, one of the constituents of gastric juice. (F. – Gk.) Mod. F. *pepsine.* – Gk. πέψις, digestion ; for *πεπτις<*πεq-tis*, related to πέπτειν, to cook. (√PEQ.) See Cook.

Per-, prefix, through. (L. ; *or* F.–L.) L. *per*, through ; whence F. *per-, par-*, prefix. Allied to Gk. περί, around ; cf. also παρά, beside ; Skt. *parā*, away, forth, *param*, beyond ; E. *from.*

Perambulate, to walk about through. (L.) L. *per*, through ; and *ambulātus*, pp. of *ambulāre*, to walk about. See Amble.

Perceive. (F.–L.) O. F. *percever.* – L. *percipere*, to apprehend. – L. *per*, thoroughly ; *capere*, to seize.

perception. (F.–L.) F. *perception.*

– L. acc. *perceptiōnem.* – L. *perceptus*, pp. of *percipere* ; see above.

Perch (1), a rod for a bird to sit on ; a measure. (F.–L.) F. *perche.* – L. *pertica*, a rod, bar.

Perch (2), a fish. (F. –L. –Gk.) F. *perche.* – L. *perca.* – Gk. πέρκη, a perch ; from the dark marks. – Gk. πέρκος, περκνός, spotted, blackish ; cf. Skt. *pṛçni-*, spotted, pied, *spṛç*, to sprinkle.

Percolate. (L.) From pp. of L. *percolāre*, to filter through. – L. *per*, through ; *colāre*, to filter. See Colander.

Percussion. (L.) From L. *percussio*, a striking. – L. *percussus*, pp. of *percutere*, to strike. See Quash. Der. *re-percussion.*

Perdition. (F.–L.) F. *perdition.* – L. acc. *perditiōnem*, utter loss. – L. *perditus*, pp. of *perdere*, to lose. – L. *per*, thoroughly ; *-dere*, to put, place, representing Idg. **dhə*, weak form of √DHĒ, to place ; cf. Do.

Peregrination. (F.– L.) M.F. *peregrination.* – L. *peregrīnātiōnem*, acc. of *peregrīnātio*, a wandering. – L. *peregrīnātus*, pp. of *peregrīnārī*, to travel. – L. *peregrīnus*, foreign, adj. from *peregrī, peregrē*, adv., abroad ; cf. *pereger*, a traveller. From L. *per-*, which is either = L. *per*, through, or is related to A. S. *feor*, far ; and *ager*, land, field. See Acre and Pilgrim.

Peremptory, decisive. (F.–L.) M.F. *peremptoire.* – L. *peremptōrius*, destructive, decisive. – L. *peremptor*, a destroyer. – L. *peremptus*, pp. of *per-imere*, to take away entirely, destroy. – L. *per*, utterly ; *emere*, to take. See Exempt.

Perennial. (L.) Coined from L. *perenni-s*, everlasting ; lit. lasting throughout the year. – L. *per*, through ; *annus*, a year. See Annual.

Perfect. (F.–L.) M.E. *perfit, parfit.* – O. F. *parfit, parfeit* (F. *parfait*). – L. *perfectus*, pp. of *perficere*, to complete. – L. *per*, thoroughly ; *facere*, to make. See Fact.

Perfidious. (L.) From L. *perfidiōsus*, treacherous. – L. *perfidia*, treachery. – L. *perfidus*, treacherous. – L. *per*, away (cf. Skt. *parā*, from) ; *fidēs*, faith. See Faith.

Perfoliate. (L.) Coined from L. *per*, through ; *folium*, a leaf. See Foil (2).

Perforate. (L.) From pp. of L. *perforāre*, to bore through ; where *forāre* is cognate with E. Bore.

Perform, to achieve. (F.–O. H. G. ;

with L. *prefix.*) Corrupted from M. E. *parfournen*, later *parfourmen.* — O. F. *parfournir*, ' to perform ;' Cot. — L. *per*, thoroughly ; and O. F. *fournir*, to furnish, provide ; see **Furnish.**

Perfume, vb. (F. — L.) F. *parfumer*, to perfume, lit. to smoke thoroughly. — L. *per*, thoroughly ; *fūmāre*, to smoke, from *fūmus*, smoke ; see **Fume.**

Perfunctory. (L.) L. *perfunctōrius*, carelessly done. — L. *perfunctus*, pp. of *perfungī*, to perform fully, get through with. — L. *per*, thoroughly ; *fungī*, to perform ; see **Function.**

Perhaps. (L. *and* Scand.) A clumsy hybrid compound. — L. *per*, by (as in *perchance*, where *per* is, strictly, F. *par*); *haps*, pl. of *hap*, chance.

Peri, a fairy. (Pers.) Pers. *parī*, a winged spirit ; orig. a malevolent but beautiful female spirit ; Zend *pairikā.* Horn, § 310.

Peri-, prefix, round. (Gk.) Gk. περί, around, about.+Skt. *pari*, round about. Allied to *per-*, prefix.

Pericardium, the sac surrounding the heart. (L. — Gk.) L. *pericardium.* — Gk. περικάρδιον. — Gk. περί, around ; καρδία, the heart ; see **Heart.**

Pericarp, a seed-vessel. (Gk.) Gk. περικάρπιον, shell of fruit. — Gk. περί, around ; καρπός, fruit ; see **Harvest.**

Pericranium, the membrane that surrounds the skull. (L. — Gk.) Late L. *pericrānium.* — Gk. περικράνιον, neut. of περικράνιος, surrounding the skull. — Gk. περί, round ; κρανίον, skull.

Perigee, point of the moon's orbit nearest the earth. (Gk.) From Gk. περί, about, here ' near ' ; γῆ, earth. See **Geography.**

Perihelion, the point of a planet's orbit nearest the sun. (Gk.) Gk. περί, round, near ; ἥλιος, the sun. See **Heliacal.**

Peril, danger. (F. — L.) M. F. *peril.* — L. *perīclum*, *perīculum*, danger, lit. ' a trial.' — L. *perīrī*, to try ; an obsolete verb, of which the pp. *perītus* is common. Allied to Gk. πεῖρα, an attempt ; and ultimately to E. *fare* ; see **Fare.** Cf. E. *fear* ; G. *gefahr*, peril. (✓PER.) Der. *peril-ous.*

Perimeter, lit. ' the measure all round.' (L. — Gk.) L. *perimetros.* — Gk. περίμετρος. — Gk. περί, round ; μέτρον, a measure. See **Metre.**

Period, time of a circuit, epoch, perfect

sentence. (F. — L. — Gk.) M. F. *periode*, a perfect sentence. — L. *periodus.* — Gk. περίοδος, a going round, circuit, complete sentence. — Gk. περί, round ; ὁδός, a way ; see **Exodus.** ¶ The sense of ' circuit ' is *directly* from Gk.

Peripatetic, a walking about. (L. — Gk.) L. *peripatēticus.* — Gk. περιπατητικός, given to walking about, esp. while disputing ; a name given to followers of Aristotle. — Gk. περιπατέω, I walk about. — Gk. περί, about ; πατέω, I walk, from πάτος, a path.

Periphery, circumference. (L. — Gk.) L. *periferia*, *peripheria.* — Gk. περιφέρεια, the circumference of a circle. — Gk. περί, around ; φέρειν, to carry, cognate with E. **Bear,** vb.

Periphrasis. (L. — Gk.) L. *periphrasis.* — Gk. περίφρασις, circumlocution. Gk. περί, around ; φράζειν, to declare, express. See **Phrase.**

Perish. (F. — L.) M. E. *perischen.* — O. F. *periss-*, stem of pres. pt. of *perir*, to perish. — L. *perīre*, to come to naught, perish. — L. *per-*, used with a destructive force (like E. *for-* in *for-do*) ; and *īre*, to go.

Periwig, a peruke. (F. — Ital. — L.) Formerly *perwigge*, *perwicke* (Minsheu). This is a corrupted form, used in place of *peruke.* — F. *perruque* ; see **Perruque.**

Periwinkle (1), a plant. (L.) Formed, with suffixed *-le* and inserted *i*, from M. E. *pervenke*, a periwinkle ; A.S. *peruince.* — L. *peruinca*, a periwinkle ; also called *uinca peruinca*, a name doubtless orig. given to some twining plant. — L. *per*, through, thoroughly ; *uincīre*, to bind, allied to **Withy.**

Periwinkle (2), a small univalve mollusc. (Gk. *and* E.) A corrupt form, due to confusion with the word above. The better name is simply *winkle* ; see **Winkle.** Also found as *pennywinkle* ; Halliwell.

Perjure. (F. — L.) F. *parjurer.* — L. *periūrāre*, to forswear. — L. *per*, in the sense of ' beyond, against ' ; *iūrāre*, to swear. See **Jury.**

Perk, to make smart or trim. (F. — L.) [Cf. W. *perc*, compact, trim ; *percu*, to smarten, trim ; *percus*, smart ; all prob. from E.] M. E. *perken*, used of birds, to trim their feathers. Cf. prov. E. *perk up*, to recover from illness. All prob. from M. E. *perke*, a perch (on which a bird sits up). **–** North F. *perque, perke*, for F. *perche*; see **Perch** (1). Cf. Walloon *pierke*, a perch; and F. *être perché sur*, to be conceited of (like E. *perky*). Perhaps associated with **Pert**.

Permanent. (F.–L.) F. *permanent*. **–**L. *permanent-*, stem of pres. pt. of *permanēre*, to endure, lit. abide through. **–**L. *per*, through; *manēre*, to remain. See **Mansion**.

Permeate, to pervade, pass through small openings. (L.) From pp. of L. *permeāre*, to pass through. **–**L. *per*, through; *meāre*, to pass, go. See μοῖτος in Prellwitz.

Permit. (L.) L. *permittere* (pp. *permissus*), to let pass through, lit. send through. **–**L. *per*, through; *mittere*, to send. See **Missile**. Der. *permiss-ion*.

Permutation. (F.–L.) F. *permutation*. **–**L. acc. *permūtātiōnem*, a changing. **–**L. *permūtātus*, pp. of *permutāre*, to change thoroughly. **–**L. *per*, thoroughly; *mūtāre*, to change. See **Mutable**.

Pernicious, hurtful. (F.–L.) F. *pernicieux*. **–**L. *perniciōsus*, destructive. **–** L. *perniciēs*, destruction. **–**L. *per*, thoroughly; *nici-*, for *neci-*, decl. stem of *nex*, slaughter; see **Internecine**.

Peroration. (F.–L.) M. F. *peroration*. **–**L. *perōrātiōnem*, acc. of *perōrātio*, the close of a speech. **–**L. *perōrātus*, pp. of *perōrāre*, to complete a speech. **–**L. *per*, through; *ōrāre*, to speak. See **Oration**.

Perpendicular. (F.–L.) F. *perpendiculaire*. **–**L. *perpendiculāris*, according to the plumb-line. **–**L. *perpendiculum*, a plummet, for careful measure. **–**L. *perpendere*, to weigh or measure carefully. **–**l. *per*, thoroughly; *pendere*, to weigh.

Perpetrate. (L.) From pp. of L. *perpetrāre*, to perform thoroughly. **–**L. *per*, thoroughly; *patrāre*, to accomplish.

Perpetual. (F.–L.) M. E. *perpetuel*. **–**M. F. *perpetuel*. **–**L. *perpetuālis*, universal; in later use, permanent. **–**L. *perpetuus*, continuous, constant, perpetual. **–** L. *perpet-*, stem of *perpes*, lasting throughout, continuous. **–**L. *per*, through; *pet-*, as in *pet-ere*, to seek. See **Petition**.

Perplex. (F.–L.) *Perplexed*, pp., was first in use. **–**M. F. *perplex*, ʻ perplexed, intangled;ʼ Cot. **–**L. *perplexus*, entangled, interwoven. **–**L. *per*, thoroughly; *plexus*, entangled, pp. of *plectere*, to weave; see **Plait**.

Perquisite, a small gain. (L.) Late

L. *perquīsītum*, an extra profit above the yearly rent, arising from fines, waifs, &c.; neut. of *perquīsītus*, pp. of *perquīrere*, to seek after thoroughly. **–**L. *per*, thoroughly; *quærere*, to seek. See **Query**.

Perruque. (F.–Ital.–L.) In use in the 16th cent. **–**F. *perruque*. **–**Ital. *perrucca*, M. Ital. *perucca*, ʻ a periwig,ʼ Florio; also spelt *parucca*, id. The same as Port. *peruca*, Span. *peluca*, Sardinian *pilucca*, orig. a mass of hair, and allied to M. Ital. *piluccare*, ʻ to pick or pull out haires or feathers one by one;ʼ Florio. From Ital. *pelo*, hair. **–**L. *pilum*, acc. of *pilus*, a hair.

Perry. (F.–L.) M. E. *pereye*. ʻ Piretum, *pereye*;ʼ Vocab. 603. 11. From an A. F. form (mod. Norman *peiré*). Cf. F. *poiré*, ʻ perry, drink made of pears,ʼ Cot.; which is formed with suffix *-é* (<L. *-ātus*, made of) from F. *poire*, a pear. **–**L. *pirum*, a pear. See **Pear**.

Persecute. (F.–L.) M. F. *persecuter*, vb. **–**L. *persecūtus*, pp. of *persequī*, to pursue. **–**L. *per*, thoroughly; *sequī*, to follow. See **Sequence**.

Persevere. (F.–L.) Formerly *persever*. **–**O. F. *perseverer*. **–**L. *perseuērāre*, to persist in a thing. **–**L. *per*, thoroughly; *seuērus*, earnest. See **Severe**.

Persist. (F.–L.) F. *persister*. **–**L. *persistere*, to continue, persist. **–**L. *per*, through; *sistere*, to stand, orig. causal of *stāre*, to stand. See **State**.

Person. (F.–L.) M. E. *persone, persoune*. **–**O. F. *persone*, F. *personne*. **–**L. *persōna*, a mask used by an actor, a personage, character played by an actor, a person. **–**L. *personāre*, to sound through; the large-mouthed mask of the actor was named from the voice sounding through it. A popular etymology; for the *ō* is long. See **Sound** (3).

Perspective. (F.–L.) F. *perspective*, ʻ the optike art;ʼ Cot. **–**L. *perspectiua*, the art of inspecting; orig. fem. of *perspectīuus*, looking through. **–**L. *perspectus*, pp. of *perspicere*, to look through. **–**L. *per*, through; *specere*, to look. See **Species**.

perspicacity, keenness of sight. (F.–L.) F. *perspicacité*. **–**L. acc. *perspicācitātem*, sharp-sightedness. **–**L. *perspicāci-*, decl. stem of *perspicax*, sharp-sighted. **–**L. *per-spicere*, to see through (above).

perspicuous, clear. (L.) L. *perspicu-us*, clear; with suffix *-ous*. **–**L. *perspicere*, to see through (above).

Perspiration, a sweating. (F.–L.)

F. *perspiration.*—Late L. acc. **perspīrā-tiōnem,* lit. a breathing through.—L. *per-spīrāre,* to breathe through.—L. *per,* through; *spīrāre,* to breathe. See Spirit.

Persuade. (F.—L.) F. *persuader.*—L. *persuādēre,* to advise thoroughly, succeed in advising.—L. *per,* thoroughly; *suādēre,* to persuade. See Suasion.

Pert, saucy. (F.—L.) M.E. *pert,* shortened form of *apert,* formerly used in the same sense. See Malapert.

Pertain. (F.—L.) M.E. *partenen.*—O.F. *partenir.*—L. *pertinēre,* to extend through to, belong.—L. *per,* thoroughly; *tenēre,* to hold, hold to. See Tenable.

pertinacity. (F.—L.) F. *pertinacité* (16th cent.). Coined, with suffix *-té* < L. *-tātem,* from L. *pertināci-,* decl. stem of *pertinax,* very tenacious.—L. *per,* thorough; *tenax,* tenacious, from *tenēre,* to hold.

pertinent. (F.—L.) F. *pertinent.*—L. *pertinent-,* stem of pres. pt. of *pertinēre,* to belong to, relate to; see Pertain.

Perturb. (F.—L.) M.F. *perturber;* Cot.—L. *perturbāre,* to disturb thoroughly.—L. *per,* thoroughly; *turbāre,* to disturb. See Turbid.

Peruke; see Perruque.

Peruse. (F.—L.) The orig. sense was 'to use up,' to go through thoroughly; hence to examine thoroughly or all over, to survey; the only difficulty in the word is in its change of sense. From *per,* thoroughly; and *use,* q. v. Cf. O.F. *paruser sa vie,* to live out his life.

Pervade. (L.) L. *peruādere,* to go through.—L. *per,* through; *uādere,* to go. See Evade, Wade.

Pervert. (F.—L.) F. *pervertir.*—L. *peruertere,* to overturn, ruin, corrupt, pervert.—L. *per,* wholly; *uertere,* to turn. See Verse. Der. *perverse,* from pp. *peruersus.*

Pervicacious, wilful. (L.) Coined from L. *peruicāci-,* decl. stem of *peruicax,* wilful; allied to *peruicus,* stubborn. Perhaps from *per,* through; and *uic-,* weak grade of *uic-,* as in *uīc-ī,* pt. t. of *uincere,* to conquer. See Victor.

Pervious, penetrable. (L.) L. *perui-us,* passable; with suffix *-ous.*—L. *per,* through; *uia,* a way. See Viaduct.

Pessimist, one who complains that all is for the worst. (L.) Coined from L. *pessim-us,* worst; a superl. perhaps connected with *pēior,* worse. Brugm. ii. § 73.

Pest. (F.—L.) F. *peste.*—L. *pestem,* acc. of *pestis,* a plague.

Pester. (F.—L.) Formerly to encumber, clog; and short for *impester.*—M.F. *empestrer,* 'to pester, intangle, incumber;' Cot. (F. *empêtrer.*) Orig. 'to hobble a horse at pasture.'—Late L. *im-* (*in*), on, upon; *pastōrium,* a clog for a horse at pasture, from *pastus,* pp. of *pascere,* to feed. See Pastor.

Pestiferous. (L.) L. *pestifer-us,* or *pestifer,* plague-bringing; with suffix *-ous.*—L. *pesti-s,* plague; *ferre,* to bring. See Pest and Bear (1).

pestilent. (F.—L.) F. *pestilent.*—L. *pestilent-,* stem of *pestilens,* hurtful; formed as if from a verb **pestilēre,* from *pestilis,* pestilential.—L. *pesti-,* decl. stem of *pestis,* a plague (above).

Pestle. (F.—L.) M.E. *pestel.*—O.F. *pestel,* later *pesteil* (Cot.).—L. *pistillum,* a small pestle. See Pistil.

Pet (1), a tame animal, a child treated fondly. (Unknown.) Formerly *peat.* [Cf. Irish *peat,* sb., a pet; adj., petted; Gael. *peata,* a pet, a tame animal; borrowed from E.] The word is prob. of F. origin; but has not been traced. Perhaps from O.F. *peti,* short for *petit,* small; see Petty. And see *petiot,* dear little child, in Godefroy.

pet (2), a fit of peevishness. (Unknown.) We also find *pettish,* capricious, i.e. like a *pet* or spoilt child; see above. Hence the phr. 'to take *pet,*' or 'to take the *pet,*' i.e. to act like a spoilt child; and finally *pet,* sb., a fit of wilfulness.

Petal. (Gk.) Gk. πέταλον, a leaf (hence petal of a flower); neut. of πέταλος, spread out, flat; from the base πετ-, as in πετ-άννυμι, I spread.+L. *patulus,* spreading; from *patēre,* to spread. (√PET.)

Petard, an explosive war-engine. (F.—L.) M.F. *petard, petart,* 'a petard or petarre;' Cot. Lit. 'explosive.' Formed with suffix *-art* (= G. *hart,* hard, common as a suffix) from M.F. *peter,* to break wind. —F. *pet,* a breaking wind, slight explosion. —L. *pēditum,* neut. of *pēditus,* pp. of *pēdere* (for **pezdere*), to break wind. See Brugm. i. § 857.

Petiole, footstalk of a leaf. (F.—L.) F. *pétiole.*—L. *petiolum,* acc. of *petiolus,* little stalk.

Petition. (F.—L.) M.F. *petition;* Cot. —L. acc. *petītiōnem,* from *petītio,* a suit. —L. *petītus,* pp. of *petere,* to attack, to beseech, ask ; orig. to fall on. Allied to E. Feather. (√PET.) See Brugm. i. § 560.

Petrel, a bird. (F. – G. – L. – Gk.) Formerly *peterel*. – F. *pétrel*, *pétérel*; formed as a dimin. of *Pêtre*, i. e. Peter, and the allusion is to the action of the bird, which seems, like St. Peter, to walk on the sea. The F. form of Peter is *Pierre*; *Pêtre* is for G. *Peter*, Peter; cf. the G. name for the bird, viz. *Petersvogel* (= Peter's-fowl, Peter's-bird). – L. *Petrus*. – Gk. πέτρος, a stone, Peter (John i. 42).

petrify, to turn into stone. (F. – Gk. *and* L.) M. F. *petrifier*; as if from a L. *petrificāre, not used. – L. *petri-*, for *petra*, a rock ; *-ficāre*, for *facere*, to make. The L. *petra* is borrowed from Gk. πέτρα, a rock ; cf. πέτρος, a stone.

petroleum, rock-oil. (L. – Gk.) Coined from L. *petr-a*, rock ; *oleum*, oil. – Gk. πέτρα, rock ; ἔλαιον, oil ; see Oil.

Petronel, a horse-pistol. (F. – Span. – L.) M. F. *petrinal*, 'a petronell, or horseman's piece;' Cot. Said to have been invented in the Pyrenees ; and almost certainly derived from Span. *petrina*, a belt, a girdle (so that *petrinal* would orig. mean what was attached to the belt). Allied to Span. *petral*, a poitrel ; and named from going round the breast. – L. *pector-* (for *pectos), stem of *pectus*, the breast. See **Pectoral.**

Petty, small. (F. – C.?) M.E. *petit*. – F. *petit*, small. Cf. O. Ital. *pitetto*, small. Perhaps allied to *piece*, from a Gaulish base *pett-* (Celtic **qett-*) ; cf. Bret. *pez*, a piece ; W. *peth*, a part ; Irish *cuid*, O. Ir. *cuit*, a part, share. See Körting, § 6101 ; Stokes (s. v. *qetti*). **Der.** *petti-fogger*, where *fogger* is equivalent to M. Du. *focker*, 'a monopole or an engrosser of wares and commodities,' Hexham ; *focker* being prob. a corruption of the surname *Fugger*, Englished as *fogger* (N. E. D.).

Petulant. (L.) L. *petulant-*, stem of *petulans*, forward, pert, ready to attack. – L. *petere*, to attack. See Petition.

Pew. (F. – L. – Gk.) M. E. *pew*, *pue*. – A. F. *pui*, a platform (Liber Albus) ; O. F. *pui*, an elevated space ; *puie*, an open gallery with rails (hence applied to an enclosed space or to a raised desk to kneel at). – L. *podium*, a balcony, esp. near the arena, where distinguished persons sat. (So E. *pew* meant a place for distinguished persons in church.) – Gk. πόδιον, which came to mean a foot-stool, gallery to sit

---

in, &c. ; lit. 'little foot.' – Gk. ποδί-, for πούς, foot. See **Foot.** ¶ Cf. M. Du. *puye*, 'a pue,' Hexham ; borrowed from O. F. *puye*, *puie*.

Pewet, Peewit, the lapwing. (E.) Also *puet* (Phillips). Named from its plaintive cry ; cf. mod. Norman F. *pivit*, a pewet ; Lowl. Sc. *peu*, to make a plaintive noise ; Westphal. *pīwit*, *pīwik*, a pewet. Cf. E. *peevish.*

Pewter. (F. – Teut. ?) M. E. *pewtir*. O. F. *peutre*, *peautre*, *piautre*, a kind of metal (Roquefort). Older form *peltre*, akin to Span. *peltre*, Ital. *peltro*, pewter. Diez remarks that the Ital. *peltro* is believed to be derived from English, which he rejects, but only on the ground that *pewter* could not become *peltro*. However, *peltro* is probably (like O. F. *peautre*), an adaptation of the form found in O. F. *espeltre (*espeautre*), E. *spelter* ; see **Spelter.**

PH.

Ph. Initial *ph* is distinct from *p*, and has the sound of *f* ; it represents the Gk. φ, almost every word beginning with *ph* being of Gk. origin. The only exceptions are *pheon* (also *feon*), *philibeg*, better *fillibeg*, which is Gaelic, and *Pharisee*, really of Hebrew origin, but coming to us through Greek.

Phaeton, a kind of carriage. (F. – L. – Gk.) F. *phaéton* ; occurring A.D. 1723. – L. *Phaethon.* – Gk. Φαέθων, son of Helios, and driver of the chariot of the sun ; lit. 'shining,' being pres. part. of φαέθειν, to shine. – Gk. φάειν, to shine. See **Phantom.** See Prellwitz, s. v. φάος. (√BHĀ.)

Phalanx. (L. – Gk.) L. *phalanx.* – Gk. φάλαγξ, a battalion. See **Plank.**

Phantasm; see below.

Phantom. (F. – L. – Gk.) M. E. *fantome.* – O. F. *fantosme.* – L. *phantasma* (whence E. *phantasm*). – Gk. φάντασμα, a vision, spectre, lit. apparition. – Gk. φαντάζειν, to display. – Gk. φαν-, as in φαίνειν (= φάν-γειν), to shew, lit. to cause to shine ; whence *φάντης, one who shews (as in ἱερο-φάντης). – Gk. φά-ειν, to shine. +Skt. *bhā*, to shine. (√BHĀ.)

Pharisee, one of a religious school among the Jews. (L. – Gk. – Heb.) L. *pharisēus*, *pharisæus.* – Gk. φαρισαῖος, Matt. ix. 11, lit. ' one who separates himself.' – Heb. *pārash*, to separate.

Pharmacy. (F. – L. – Gk.) M. E. *fermacy.* – O. F. *farmacie*, later *pharmacie.* – L. *pharmacīa.* – Gk. φαρμακεία, knowledge of drugs. – Gk. φάρμακον, a drug.

Pharynx. (L. – Gk.) L. *pharynx.* – Gk. φάρυγξ, the joint opening of the gullet and wind-pipe, a cleft, a bore; allied to φάραγξ, a chasm. From the root φαρ-, to bore; see **Bore** (1). (√BHAR.)

Phase, Phasis, an appearance. (L. – Gk.) Late L. *phasis*, pl. *phases.* – Gk. φάσις, an appearance; from base φα-, to shine; cf. φά-ος, light. (√BHĀ.) β. The Gk. φάσις also means 'a saying, declaration,' in which sense it is connected with φημί, I speak, declare, from √BHĀ, to speak. **Der.** *em-phasis.*

Pheasant, a bird. (F. – L. – Gk.) Formed with excrescent *t* (after *n*) from M. E. *fesaun*, a pheasant. – O. F. *faisan.* – L. *phāsiāna*, a pheasant; for *Phāsiāna auis*, Phasian bird. – Gk. φασιανός, a pheasant, lit. Phasian, i. e. coming from the river *Phāsis* in Colchis.

Pheeze; see Feeze.

Phenix, Phœnix. (L. – Gk.) L. *phœnix.* – Gk. φοῖνιξ, a phœnix (Herod. ii. 73). Perhaps named from its bright colour, like that produced by the *Phœnician* dye; see Pliny, bk. x. c. 2.

Phenomenon, a remarkable appearance. (L. – Gk.) L. *phænomenon.* – Gk. φαινόμενον (pl. φαινόμενα), an appearance, neut. of pass. part. of φαίνειν, to shew (pass. φαίνομαι, I appear). See **Phantom, Hierophant, Sycophant.**

Pheon, a barbed arrow-head. (F. – L.) M. E. *feon*, Bk. of St. Alban's. Perhaps an error for **fleon*; since O. F. **fleon* might come from Late L. *fleto* (acc. *fletōnem*), an arrow-head.

Phial, Vial. (F. – L. – Gk.) Formerly *fyole*, *vial*, *viol*, altered to *phial* in modern editions of Shakespeare. – M. F. *phiole*, 'a violl,' Cot. (Mod. F. *fiole*.) – L. *phiala.* – Gk. φιάλη, a broad, flat, shallow cup or bowl (applied in F. to a small bottle).

Philanthropy, love of mankind. (L. – Gk.) L. *philanthrōpia.* – Gk. φιλανθρωπία, benevolence. – Gk. φιλάνθρωπος, loving mankind. – Gk. φιλ-, for φίλος, friendly, kind; ἄνθρωπος, a man.

philharmonic, loving music. (Gk.) From Gk. φίλ-ος, friendly, fond of; and L. *harmoni-a* <Gk. ἁρμονία, harmony; see **Harmony.**

philippic, a discourse full of invec-

tive. (L. – Gk.) L. *Philippicum*, pl. *Philippica*, used to denote the celebrated orations of Demosthenes against Philip. – Gk. Φίλιππος, Philip; lit. 'a lover of horses.' – Gk. φίλ-ος, fond of; ἵππος, a horse.

philology, study of languages. (L. – Gk.) L. *philologia.* – Gk. φιλολογία, love of discourse, love of literature and language. – Gk. φιλόλογος, fond of discourse; also, a student of literature and language. – Gk. φίλο-s, fond of; λόγος, discourse, from λέγειν, to speak.

philosophy, love of wisdom. (F. – L. – Gk.) M. E. *philosophie.* – F. *philosophie.* – L. *philosophia.* – Gk. φιλοσοφία, love of wisdom. – Gk. φιλόσοφος, loving knowledge. – Gk. φίλο-s, fond of; σοφός, skilful, σοφία, skill; see **Sophist. Der.** *philosoph-er*, for M. E. *philosophre*, which represents F. *philosophe*, L. *philosophus*, Gk. φιλόσοφος.

philtre, a love potion. (F. – L. – Gk.) F. *philtre.* – L. *philtrum.* – Gk. φίλτρον, a love charm, love potion, drink to make one love. – Gk. φίλ-ος, dear; -τρον (cf. Idg. *-ter-*), denoting the instrument.

Philibeg, a kilt; see **Fillibeg.**

Phlebotomy, blood-letting. (F. – L. – Gk.) M. F. *phlebotomie.* – L. *phlebotomia.* – Gk. φλεβοτομία, blood-letting, lit. cutting of a vein. – Gk. φλεβο-, for φλέψ, a vein, from φλέ-ειν, to gush; τομός, cutting, from τέμνειν, to cut; see **Tome.**

Phlegm, slimy matter in the throat, sluggishness. (F. – L. – Gk.) The use of the term was due to the supposed influence of the 'four humours'; phlegm causing a sluggish or 'phlegmatic' temperament. – M. F. *phlegme.* – L. *phlegma.* – Gk. φλέγμα (base φλεγματ-), (1) a flame, (2) inflammation, (3) viscous humour, phlegm. – Gk. φλέγειν, to burn. ✚ L. *flag-rāre*, to burn; see **Flame. Der.** *phlegmat-ic*, from base φλεγματ-.

phlox, a flower. (Gk.) It means 'flame,' from its colour. – Gk. φλόξ, flame – Gk. φλέγ-ειν, to burn (above).

Phocine, belonging to the family of seals. (L. – Gk.) From L. *phōca*, a seal – Gk. φώκη, a seal. See Prellwitz.

Phœnix; see Phenix.

Phonetic, representing sounds. (Gk.) From Gk. φωνητικός, belonging to speaking. – Gk. φωνέω, I produce a sound. – Gk. φωνή, a sound; cf. φημί, I speak (√BHĀ.) **Der.** *phono-graph*, *-logy*, &c.

Phosphorus. (L.–Gk.) L. *phos-phorus.* – G. φωσφόρος, light-bringing, i. e. producing light. – Gk. φῶς, light (=φάος, light), from base φα-, to shine; -φορος, bringing, from φέρειν, to bring. (√BHĀ and √BHER.)

photography. (Gk.) From Gk. φωτο-, for φῶς, light (above); and γράφειν, to write.

Phrase. (F.–L.–Gk.) F. *phrase.* – L. *phrasem,* acc. of *phrasis.* – Gk. φράσις, a speaking, a speech, phrase. – Gk. φράζειν (= *φράδ-γειν), to speak; cf. φραδής, shrewd. Der. *anti-phrasis, meta-phrase, peri-phrasis, para-phrase*; with prefixes *anti-, meta-, peri-, para-*.

Phrenology, science of the functions of the mind. (Gk.) From Gk. φρενό-, for φρήν, mind; -λογία, from λόγος, a discourse, from λέγειν, to speak.

Phthisis, consumption of the lungs. (L.–Gk.) L. *phthisis.* – Gk. φθίσις, consumption, decay. – Gk. φθίνειν, to decay, wane. Cf. Skt. *kshi,* to destroy, *kshiti-,* decay. Der. *phthisic,* properly an adj., from L. *phthisicus,* adj., consumptive; but used as a sb. (=L. *phthisica passio*), with the same sense as *phthisis*; often called and spelt *tisic.*

Phylactery, an amulet, amongst the Jews. (F. – L. – Gk.) M. E. *filaterie,* Wyclif. –O. F. *filaterie* (Godefroy); Mod. F. *phylactère.* – L. *phylactērium.* – Gk. φυλακτήριον, a preservative; Matt. xxiii. 5. – Gk. φυλακτήρ, a guardian. – Gk. φυλάσσειν, to guard; φύλαξ, a guard.

Physic. (F.–L.–Gk.) Orig. the healing art; hence, medicine. –O. F. *phisique,* science of medicine; also, natural philosophy. –L. *physica,* natural science. – Gk. φυσική, fem. of φυσικός, natural, physical. – Gk. φύσι-s, nature, being. – Gk. φύ-ειν, to produce. + Skt. *bhū,* to be; L. *fu-i, fo-re*; E. *be.* (√BHEU.) Der. *physic-s*; *physic-i-an*; &c.

physiognomy, visage, expression of features. (F.–L.–Gk.) M. E. *fisnomie, visnomie.* –O. F. *phisonomie,* later *phy-siognomie,* a knowledge of a man's character by his features; hence features, expression. Formed as if from L. *phy-siognōmia,* but due to the longer form *physiognōmia.* – Gk. φυσιογνωμονία, the art of reading the features; sometimes φυσιογνωμία. – Gk. φυσιογνώμων, adj., judging character. – Gk. φυσιο-, for φύσις, nature; γνώμων, an interpreter; see Gnomon.

physiology, the science of nature. (F.–L.–Gk.) F. *physiologie*; Cot. –L. *physiologia.* – Gk. φυσιολογία, an enquiry into the nature of things. – Gk. φυσιο-, for φύσις, nature; -λογία, from λόγος, a discourse, from λέγειν, to speak.

PI – PY.

Piacular, expiatory. (L.) L. *piācu-lāris,* adj., from *piāculum,* an expiation. – L. *piāre,* to propitiate. – L. *pius,* devout. See Pious.

Pianoforte, Piano. (Ital.–L.) So called from producing *soft* and *loud* effects. –Ital. *piano,* soft; *forte,* strong, loud. – L. *plānus,* level (hence smooth, soft); *fortis,* strong; see Plain and Force.

Piastre. (F. – Ital. – L. – Gk.) F. *piastre.* – Ital. *piastra,* plate of metal, also a piastre or coin; allied to Ital. *piastro,* a plaster. – L. *emplastrum,* a plaster (with loss of *em-*). See Plaster.

Piazza. (Ital.–L.–Gk.) Ital. *piazza,* a market-place, chief street. – Folk-L. *plattia*; L. *platea, platēa*; see Place.

Pibroch, a martial tune. (Gael.–L.) Gael. *piobaireachd,* a pipe-tune, tune on the bagpipe. – Gael. *piobair,* a piper. – Gael. *piob,* a pipe. – E. *pipe.* See Pipe.

Pica; see Pie (1).

Picador, a horseman with a lance, in bull-fighting. (Span.–L.) Span. *picador,* lit. a pricker. – Span. *picar,* to prick. – Late L. *pīcāre*; see Pick.

Picaninny, a negro or mulatto infant. (Span.) From *peekaneenee,* a dimin. (in Surinam) of Span. *pequeño,* small, allied to Ital. *piccolo,* small. Of uncertain origin.

Piccadill; see Pickadill.

Pice, a small copper coin. (Marathi.) Hind. and Marathi *paisā,* a copper coin; sometimes rated at four to the anna, or sixty-four to the rupee (H. H. Wilson).

Pick, to peck, pierce, also to pluck, &c. (E.) M. E. *pikken, pekken,* used as equivalent words, Ch. C. T., Group B. 4157. [Cf. Irish *pioc,* Gael. *pioc,* to pick, nibble, pluck, peck; W. *pigo,* to pick, peck, prick, choose; Corn. *piga,* to prick.] Allied to A. S. *pīcan* (written *pycan*), to peck, and the sb. *pīc,* a sharp point, Voc. 3. 13. From a Teut. base *pīc,* allied to Spike. And see Pike. From an Idg. root *spī-g*; cf. *spī-k,* as in L. *spīca.*

pickadill, piccadill, a piece set round the edge of a garment, a collar. (F.

—Span.—Teut.) Obsolete; but preserved in *Piccadilly,* a street in London, named from a certain house, which was 'a famous ordinary near St. James's'; see Blount and Nares.—M.F. *piccadille;* pl. *piccadilles,* 'the several pieces fastened together about the brimme of the collar of a doublet;' Cot. Formed, with Span. dimin. suffix *-illo,* from Span. *picado,* pp. of *picar,* to puncture; cf. Span. *picadura,* a puncture, an ornamental gusset in clothes.—Span. *picar,* to prick, from *pica,* a pike (hence a pricking instrument); a word of Teut. origin; see Pike.

pickax. (F.—L.) Not an *ax* at all, but a corruption of M. E. *pikois, pikeis,* a mattock.—O. F. *picois,* later *picquois,* a mattock.—O. F. *piquer,* to pierce, thrust into.—F. *pic,* a 'pick' or kind of mattock. —Late L. *pīca,* a pickax. Cf. A.S. *pīc,* a pike; Bret. *pic,* a pick; W. *pig,* a point, pike, Irish *piocaid,* a mattock; see Pike.

picket, a peg for fastening horses, a small outpost. (F.—L.) F. *piquet, picquet,* a little pickax, a peg thrust in the ground. Dimin. of F. *pic* (above).

Pickle, a liquid in which substances are preserved. (Teut.) M. E. *pikil, pykyl;* Prompt. Parv. Probably from *pickle,* frequent. of *pick,* in the sense to pick out or 'cleanse'; with reference to the gutting or cleansing of the fish with which the operation of pickling is begun. We find M. E. *pykelynge,* 'purgulacio,' derived from '*pykyn,*' or clensyn, or cullyn owte the onclene, *purgo, purgulo, segrego*'; Prompt. Parv. See Pick. β. We also find Du. *pekel,* pickle; which some have derived from the name of the supposed inventor of pickling, whose name is variously given as *Beukeler, Böckel,* and *Pökel;* a story unsupported by evidence.

Picnic. (F.) Found in F. as early as 1692, and in Swedish before 1788; but borrowed in those languages from Low G. Origin obscure. *Pic* is prob. from *pick* (Du. *picken*), to nibble; cf. slang E. *peck,* food; *peckish,* hungry. *Nic* is for *knick,* a trifle; another name for a picnic was *nick-nack* (Foote, Nabob, act 1).

Picture. (L.) L. *pictūra,* properly the art of painting.—L. *pictus,* pp. of *pingere,* to paint. Allied to Skt. *piñj,* to dye, colour; Gk. ποικίλος. Brugm. i. § 701.

Piddling, trifling. (Scand.?) From the verb *piddle,* to trifle (Ascham); other forms are *pittle* (Skinner), *pettle* (Halliwell).

—Swed. dial. *pittla,* to keep on picking at; frequent. of Swed. *peta,* to pick, poke.

Pie (1), a magpie; unsorted printer's type. (F.—L.) The unsorted type is called *pie,* i. e. a jumble; see pie (3); also *pi,* as if short for *pica,* from the common use of pica-type; see below. The magpie is M. E. *pie.*—F. *pie.*—L. *pīca,* a magpie. Cf. L. *pīcus,* woodpecker, Skt. *pika-,* Indian cuckoo.

pie (2), a book which ordered the manner of performing divine service. (F.— L.) Here *pie* is (as above) a F. form of L. *pīca,* which was an old name for the Ordinale; so called from the confused appearance of the black-letter type on white paper, resembling a magpie. Certain sizes of type are still called *pica.*

pie (3), a pasty. (F.—L.) M. E. *pie;* prob. the same word as *pie* (1); from the miscellaneous nature of its contents. E. *pies* seems to be Latinised as *pīcē,* Babees Book, pt. ii. 36. 51. Cf. **pie** (2). ¶ Gael. *pighe,* a pie, is from E.

piebald, of various colours, in patches. (F.—L.; *and* C.) Compounded of *pie,* a magpie, and *bald;* see Bald. The old sense of *bald,* or *ball'd,* is streaked, from W. *bal,* having a white streak on the forehead, said of a horse. Cf. *skew-bald.*

Piece. (F.—C.) M. E. *pece, piece.*— O. F. *piece;* F. *pièce.* Cf. Ital. *pezza,* Span. *pieza,* Prov. *pessa, pesa,* Port. *peça,* a piece.—Late L. *petia,* a piece; cf. Late L. *petium,* a piece of land (A. D. 757).— Celtic (Gaulish) **petti-,* a piece, portion, answering to O. Celtic **qetti-,* the same; evidenced by O. Irish *cuit* (Ir. *cuid*), a piece, share, W. *peth,* a piece, a thing, Corn. *peth,* Bret. *pez,* a piece (Thurneysen, Stokes, Körting). Esp. used of a piece of land.

piece-meal. (F.—C.; *and* E.) M. E. *pece-mele,* by pieces at a time. The M. E suffix *-mele,* lit. 'by bits,' occurs in other compounds, and is also spelt *-melum;* from A. S. *mǣlum,* dat. pl. of *mǣl,* a portion; see Meal (2).

Piepowder court, a summary court of justice formerly held at fairs. (F.—L.) The E. *piepowder* represents O. F. *pied pouldre,* i. e. dusty foot. The court was called, in Latin, *Curia pedis pulverīsātī,* the court of the dusty foot, from the dusty feet of the suitors.—F. *pied,* foot, from L. *pedem,* acc. of *pēs;* O. F. *pouldre* (= *poul-*

dré), pp. of *pouldrer*, to cover with dust, from *pouldre*, dust; see **Powder.**

Pier, a mass of stone-work. (F.—L.—Gk.) M. E. *pere.*—A. F. *pere* (F. *pierre*), a stone.—L. *petra.*—Gk. πέτρα, a rock, stone.

Pierce. (F.—L.?) M. E. *percen.*—F. *percer*; O. F. *percier* (Roland). Generally thought to be contracted from O. F. *pertuisier*, to pierce, lit. to make a hole.—O. F. *pertuis*, a hole (Ital. *pertugio*). The O. F. *pertuis* (like Ital. *pertugio*), answers to a Late L. *pertūsium, extended from L. *pertūsus*, pp. of *pertundere*, to thrust through, pierce. (Ennius has *latu' pertudit hasta*=the spear pierced his side; Lewis.) —L. *per*, through; *tundere*, to beat; see **Contuse.** ¶ Commonly accepted; some suggest Late L. *per-itiāre, to go through; cf. L. *in-itiare.* See **Initiate** and **Commence.**

Piety. (F.—L.) M. F. *pietė.*—L. *pietā-tem*, acc. of *pietās*, devoutness.—L. *pius*, devout. See **Pious. Doublet**, *pity.*

Pig. (E.) M. E. *pigge.* Prov. E. *peg* (Berks.). Cf. A. S. *pecg*; ' of swinforda *ðf pecges* ford;' Birch, Cart. Saxon. iii. 223. But the connexion is doubtful. ¶ Certain masses of molten metal are called *sows* and *pigs*; hence *pig-iron.*

Pigeon, a bird. (F.—L.) F. *pigeon*, a pigeon, a dove.—L. *pīpiōnem*, acc. of *pīpio*, lit. ' chirper.'—L. *pipire*, to chirp. See **Pipe.**

Piggin, a small wooden vessel. (E.) Cf. Gael. *pigean*, a pitcher, jar; dimin. of *pige, pigeadh*, an earthen jar; Irish *pigin*, small pail, *pighead*, earthen jar; W. *picyn*, a piggin; all borrowed from E. Prob. for *piggen, adj., from *pig*, in the sense of 'earthen vessel,' as in G. Douglas, tr. of Vergil, bk. vii. See **Pig.**

Pight, old form of *pitched*; see **Pitch** (2).

Pigment. (L.) L. *pigmentum*, colouring matter.—L. *pig-*, base of *pingere*, to paint; with suffix *-mentum.* See **Paint.**

Pigmy; see **Pygmy.**

Pike, a sharp-pointed weapon, a fish. (E.) M. E. *pike*, a peaked staff, *pic*, a spike; also M. E. *pike*, a fish, named from its sharply pointed jaws. A. S. *pīc*, a point, a pike. (Hence Irish *pice*, a pike, fork, Gael. *pìc*, W. *pîg*, Bret. *pîk*, pike, point, pickax.) Closely allied to *pick*, sb., a mattock; ultimately allied to **Spike.** See **Pick.**   **Der.** *pik-er-el*,

a young pike (fish); *pike-staff*, also found as *piked-staff*, i. e. staff armed with a pike or spike.

Pilaster, a square pillar. (F.—Ital.—L.) F. *pilastre.*—Ital. *pilastro*, ' a pilaster, a piller;' Florio.—Ital. *pila*, ' a flat-sided piller;' id.—L. *pīla*, a pillar. See **Pile** (2).

Pilch. (L.) Orig. a warm fur garment. M. E. *pilche.* A. S. *pilece, pylce.*—L. *pellicea*; see **Pelisse.**

Pilchard, a fish. (E.?) Formerly *pilcher*; cf. Irish *pilseir*, a pilchard. Of unknown origin. Cf. Dan. dial. *pilke*, to fish (in a particular manner), Swed. dial. *pilka*; from Norw. *pilk*, an artificial bait.

Pilcrow, a curious corruption of **Paragraph**, q. v.

Pile (1), a tumour, lit. a ball. (L.) Only in the pl. *piles.*—L. *pila*, a ball.

Pile (2), a pillar, heap. (L.) M. E. *pile*; F. *pile.*—L. *pīla*, a pillar, a pier of stone. ¶ In the phrase *cross and pile* (of a coin), answering to the modern 'head and tail,' the *pile* took its name from the *pile* or short pillar on which the coin rested when struck; see Cotgrave, s. v. *pile.*

Pile (3), a stake. (L.) A. S. *pīl*, a stake.—L. *pīlum*, a javelin; orig. a pestle. For **pins-lum.*—L. *pinsere*, to pound. ✛ Skt. *pish, piṁsh*, to pound. ¶ The heraldic pile (F. *pile*) is a sharp stake.

Pile (4), a hair, fibre of wool. (L.) L. *pilus*, a hair. Cf. Gk. πῖλος, felt. Brugm. ii. § 76. **Der.** *three-piled*, L. L. L. v. 2. 407.

Piles, small tumours. (L.) See **Pile** (1).

Pilfer. (F.—L.?) O. F. *pelfrer*, to rob, pilfer.—O. F. *pelfre*, plunder; see **Pelf.**

Pilgrim. (Ital.—L.) Ital. *pellegrino*, a pilgrim.—L. *peregrīnus*, a foreigner, stranger; as adj. foreign.—L. *peregrī*, adv., away from home; see **Peregrination.** Cf. O. H. G. *piligrīm*, from Ital.

Pill (1), a little ball of medicine. (F.—L.) Short for *pilule*; cf. O. F. *pile*, a pill. —F. *pilule*, ' a pill;' Cot.—L. *pilula*, a little ball, globule; dimin. of *pila*, a ball. See **Pile** (1).

Pill (2), to plunder. (F.—L.) Also spelt *peel*; and, conversely, *peel*, to strip, is spelt *pill*; the words have been confused, but are really different; see **Peel** (2). M. E. *pillen*, to plunder.—F. *piller.*—L. *pilāre*, to pull out hair, also, to plunder;

from *pilus*, hair. (Distinct from L. *com-pilāre*.) **Der.** *pill-age*, F. *pillage*.

Pillage ; see above.

Pillar. (F. – L.) M. E. *piler*. – O. F. *piler*, later *pilier*. (Span. *pilar*.) – Late L. *pīlāre*, a pillar. – L. *pīla*, pillar, pier. See **Pile** (2).

Pillau, Pilaf, a dish of meat or fowl, boiled with rice and spices. (Pers.) Pers. *pilāv, pilav*, a dish made of rice and meat ; Palmer.

Pillion. (C. – L.) Mod. Norman and Guernsey *pillon* are probably borrowed from E. Lowl. Sc. *pillyane*, in 1503 (N.E.D.) ; which was adapted from Gaelic. Pals-grave has '*pyllion* for a woman to ride on.' Cf. Irish *pilliun, pillin*, a pack-saddle ; Gael. *pillean, pillin*, a pack-saddle, cloth put under a rustic saddle ; Irish *pill*, a covering, *peall*, a skin ; Gael. *peall*, a skin, coverlet ; all from E. or from L. *pellis*, a skin.] See **Pell.**

Pillory. (F.) F. *pilori*, 'a pillory ;' Cot. Of unknown origin ; other remark-able variants occur, viz. O. F. *pilorin, pel-lorin*, Port. *pelourinho*, Prov. *espitlori*, Late L. *pilloriacum, spiliorium*. There seems to have been a loss of initial *s*.

Pillow. (L.) M. E. *pilwe* ; A.S. *pyle* ; both from L. *puluīnus*, a cushion, pillow, bolster ; whence also Du. *peuluw*, G. *pfühl*, Westphal. *pülf*.

Pilot, one who conducts ships in and out of harbour. (F. – Ital. – Gk.) M. F. *pilot*, Cot. (F. *pilote*) ; O. F. *pedot* ; cf. M. F. *piloter*, to take soundings (Palsgrave). Prob. borrowed from Ital. *pilota*, also *pedota*, a pilot (Florio) ; cf. Late L. *pedotta*, a pilot. – Late Gk. **πηδώτης*, a steersman ; formed from Gk. *πηδόν*, a rudder, blade of an oar.

Pimento, allspice. (Port. – L.) Also *pimenta*. – Port. *pimenta*, pimento. The same as O. F. *piment*, a spiced drink. – L. *pigmentum*, (1) a pigment, (2) the juice of plants ; see **Pigment.**

Pimp, a pandar. (F. – L.) Prob. a smartly dressed fellow. – M. F. *pimper*, to dress up smartly. A nasalised form of F. *piper*, to pipe, also to beguile, cheat ; cf. also Prov. *pimpar*, to render elegant, from *pimpa*, sb. (equivalent to F. *pipeau*) mean-ing (1) a pipe, (2) a bird-call, (3) a snare ; besides which, F. *piper* meant to excel in a thing. Note also F. *pimpant*, smart, spruce ; and see Littré. – L. *pīpāre*, to chirp (hence to pipe). See **Pipe.**

Pimpernel, a flower. (F. – L.?) M.F. *pimpernelle* (F. *pimprenelle*). Cf. Span. *pimpinela*, Ital. *pimpinella*. Origin un-known. ¶ Diez considers these words to be borrowed from L. **bipinella,*bipennula*, a dimin. of *bipennis*, i. e. double-winged. The pimpernel was confused with burnet (Prior) ; and the latter (*Poterium san-guisorba*) has a feather-like arrangement of its leaves. Cf. *Rosa pimpinellifolia*. If this be right (which is highly doubtful), we refer the word to L. *bi-*, double ; *penna*, a wing.

Pimple. (F.?) [Cf. A. S. *pīplian*, to be pimply. The alleged A. S. *pinpel* is Lye's misprint for *winpel* !] Prob. not an E. word, but borrowed from some O. F. or Late L. form. Cf. F. *pompette*, 'a pumple or pimple on the nose or chin,' Cot. ; and Span. *pompa*, a bubble. Also Gk. *πέμφιξ*, *πομφός*, a bubble, blister, Lith. *pampti*, to swell ; L. *papula*, a pimple.

Pin, a peg, &c. (L.) M. E. *pinne*, a peg. A. S. *pinn*, a pen, style for writing (Toller). [We find also Irish *pion*, Gael. *pinne*, a pin, peg, spigot ; W. *pin*, pin, style, pen ; Du. *pin*, pin, peg, Swed. *pinne*, a peg, Dan. *pind*, a (pointed) stick, Icel. *pinni*, a pin, Low G. *penn*, a peg.] All from L. *pinna*, a wing, fin, pen ; cognate with E. **Fin.** See Brugm. ii. § 66 (note).

Pinch. (F. – Teut.) North F. *pincher*, F. *pincer*. A nasalised form of M. Ital. *pizzare, picciare*, to nip ; cf. Ital. *pinzo*, a sting, goad, *pinzette*, pincers. The orig. sense seems to have been a slight prick with a sharp-pointed instrument, from a Teut. base *pic-*, whence E. *pike, pick* ; cf. A. S. *pīc*, a point, pike. Cf. also Du. *pinsen, pitsen*, to pinch (Hexham). **Der.** *pinchers* or *pinc-ers* ; cf. M. F. *pinces*, 'a pair of pincers ;' Cot.

Pinchbeck, a metal. (Personal name.) From the inventor, Mr. Chr. *Pinchbeck*, the elder, a London watchmaker (c. 1670-1732). From *Pinchbeck*, Lincolnshire.

Pindar, Pinner, an impounder. (E.) Formed with suffix *-er* of the agent from A. S. *pyndan*, to pen up. – A. S. *pund*, an enclosure. See **Pound** (2). ¶ Not allied to *pen* (2).

Pine (1), a tree. (L.) A.S. *pīn-trēo*, a pine-tree. – L. *pīnus*, a pine ; i. e. *pī-nus*.+Gk. *πί-τυς*, a pine ; Skt. *pītu-dāru-*, lit. 'resin-tree ;' L. *pītuīta*, phlegm, also 'resin.' See **Pip** (1). **Der.** *pine-apple*, orig. 'a fir-cone.'

Pine (2), to long for; to suffer pain, waste away. (L.—Gk.) M. E. *pinen*, to suffer, more frequently, to torment; a verb formed from M. E. *pine*, torment.—A. S. *pīn*, pain; borrowed from L. *pœna*, pain; see **Pain**.

Pinfold, a pound. (E.) For *pind-fold*; (also spelt *pund-fold*, Birch, iii. 309). —A. S. *pyndan*, to pen up (from *pund*, an enclosure); and *fold*. See **Pindar**.

Pinion, joint of a wing. (F.—L.) F. *pignon*, a gable-end; Cot. O. F. *pignon*, a feather, a pennon on a lance. Cf. Span. *piñon*, a pinion. [Again, the mod. F. *pignon* has the sense of E. *pinion*, a small wheel working with teeth into another; in which case the derivation is from L. *pinna*, the float of a water-wheel.]—L. *pinna*, a wing; see **Pin**.

Pink (1), to pierce, prick. (L. ?) M. E. *pinken*, to prick. Used as a nasalised form of *pick*. We may note E. *pink*, to cut round holes or eyes in silk cloth (Bailey), as equivalent to M. F. *piquer*, the same (Cotgrave). Cf. **Pinch**. ¶ Or from A. S. *pynca*, *pinca*, a point, which seems to have been borrowed from *punctum*; see **Puncture**.

Pink (2), half-shut, applied to the eyes. (Du.—L.) Obsolete; cf. '*pink eyne*,' Antony, ii. 7. 121.—M. Du. *pincken* (also *pinck-oogen*), to shut the eyes (Hexham). The notion is that of narrowing, bringing to a point; see **Pink** (1). Cf. Prov. E. *pink*, a very small fish, minnow.

Pink (3), the name of a flower, and of a colour. (I.) As in *violet*, *mauve*, the name of the colour is due to that of the flower. The flower is named from the delicately cut or *pinked* edges of the petals; see **Pink** (1). β. Similarly, M. F. *pince*, a pink, is from F. *pincer*, to pinch, nip; but F. *pince* and E. *pink* are not the same word; though they are related.

Pink (4), a kind of boat. (Du.) See Nares. Short for M. Du. *espincke*, also written *pincke*, 'a pinke, or a small fisher's boat,' Hexham; (whence also F. *pinque*, Span. *pingue*, a pink). The same word as Icel. *espingr*, Swed. *esping*, a long boat; named from Icel. *espi*, aspen-wood, M.Du. *espe*, an aspen-tree. See **Aspen**.

Pink-eyed, having small eyes; see **Pink** (2).

Pinnace. (F.—Ital.—L.) F. *pinace*, *pinasse*, 'the pitch-tree; also a pinnace;' Cot.—Ital. *pinaccia*, a pinnace (Florio).

So named because made of pine. —L. *pīnus*, a pine. See **Pine** (1).

Pinnacle. (F.—L.) F. *pinacle*, Cot. —L. *pinnāculum*, a pinnacle (Matt. iv. 5). Double dimin. of Late L. *pinna*, a pinnacle (Lu. iv. 9), L. *pinna*, a fin, &c. See **Pin**.

Pinnate, feather-like. (L.) L. *pinnātus*, substituted for *pennātus*, feathered. —L. *penna*, a feather. See **Pen**.

Pint, a measure for liquids. (F.—L.) F. *pinte*; cf. Span. *pinta*, a spot, mark, pint. Named from being a marked part of a larger vessel; cf. O. F. *pinter*, to measure wine.—Late L. *pincta*, a pint; for L. *picta*, fem. of *pictus*, painted, marked, pp. of *pingere*, to paint. So also Span. *pintura* = a picture.

Pioneer, a soldier who clears the way before an army. (F.—L.) Formerly *pioner*. F. *pionnier*, O. F. *peonier*, a pioneer; a mere extension of F. *pion*, O. F. *peon*, a foot-soldier, but esp. applied to sappers and miners. See further under **Pawn** (2).

Piony, the same as **Peony.**

Pious. (F.—L.) F. *pieux.*—Late L. **piōsus*, extended from L. *pius*, holy, devout. Brugm. ii. § 643.

Pip (1), a disease of fowls. (F.—L.) M. E. *pippe.*—M. F. *pepie*, 'pip;' Cot. (Mod. Norman *pipie*; Span. *pepita*, Port. *pevide*, Ital. *pipita*.)—L. *pītuīta*, phlegm, rheum, also the pip (whence **pītvīta*, **pīpīta*, Late L. *pīpido*). Hence also Du. *pip*; Swed. *pipp*, &c. β. L. *pītuīta* is from a stem *pītu-*, for which see **Pine** (1).

Pip (2), the seed of fruit. (F.—L.—Gk.) Short for *pippin* or *pepin*, the old name.— M. F. *pepin*, a pip. Allied to Span. *pepita*, a pip [quite distinct from *pepita*, pip in fowls]; and prob. to Span. *pepino*, a cucumber. β. Some have supposed that *pepin* was first applied to the remarkable seeds of the cucumber and melon; and is derived from O. F. *pepon*, L. *pepō*, a melon, borrowed from Gk. πέπων, a melon. γ. This Gk. πέπων was orig. an adj., signifying 'ripened' or 'ripe'; (cf. πέπτειν, to cook, to ripen); allied to Skt. *pach*, L. *coquere*, to cook. See **Cook**.

Pip (3), a spot on cards. (F.—L.—Gk.) Apparently a peculiar use of **Pippin**. The spots were at first called *peeps* (1604); from *peeps*, for *peepins*, i. e. apples (1600); M. E. *pepin*, a pip (Cursor Mundi).

Pipe, a musical instrument formed of a long tube; a tube, cask. (L.) M. E. *pipe*;

A.S. *pīpe*. An imitative word; but borrowed from Late L. *pīpa*, pipe ; from L. *pīpāre*, to chirp. [So also Irish and Gael. *piob*, Irish *pib*, W. *pib*; Du. *pijp*, Icel. *pīpa*, Swed. *pipa*, Dan. *pibe*, G. *pfeife*.] Cf. L. *pīpīre*, Gk. πιπίζειν, to chirp. From the cry *pi-pi* of a young bird.

Pipkin, a small earthen pot. (L., *with* E. *suffix*.) A dimin. (with suffix *-kin*) of E. *pipe*, in the sense of cask. This particular sense of *pipe* may have been imported ; it occurs both in F. and Du. ; see *pipe* in Cotgrave, *pijpe* in Hexham.

Pippin, a kind of tart apple. (F. – L. – Gk.) Named from seed-pips ; the old sense of *pippin* was a pip; see **Pip** (2). ' Perhaps an apple raised from the pip or seed ;' Wedgwood. (So Arnold's Chron.) Cf. O. F. and Norm. dial. *pepin*, an apple raised from seed.

Pique, wounded pride. (F. – L.) M. F. *picque*, *pique*, ' a pike, pike-man ; also a pike [pique], debate, quarrel ;' Cot. The same word as *pike* ; lit. ' a piercer,' that which pierces. See **Pike**. **Der.** *pique*, vb., *piqu-ant*, pres. part. of F. *piquer*, vb.

Piquet, a game at cards. (F. personal name ?) Littré says *piquet* was named from its inventor ; but see Hatzfeld.

Pirate. (F. – L. – Gk.) F. *pirate*. – L. *pīrāta*. – Gk. πειρατής, one who attempts, one who attacks, a pirate. – Gk. πειράω, I attempt. – Gk. πεῖρα (for *πέρ-ια), an attempt. See **Peril**.

Pirogue, a sort of canoe. (F. – W. Indian.) Defoe has *periagua*. – F. *pirogue* (Span. *piragua*). From the native W. Indian name ; said to be Caribbean.

Pirouette, a whirling round, quick turn. (F.) F. *pirouette*, ' a whirling about, also a whirligig ;' Cot. Dimin. of the Guernsey word *piroue*, a little wheel or whirligig (Métivier). The latter part of the word simulates F. *roue* (L. *rota*), a wheel. Allied to M. Ital. *pirolo*, a peg, a child's top. Origin unknown.

Pisces, the Fishes. (L.) L. *piscēs*, pl. of *piscis*, a fish ; cognate with E. **Fish**.

Pish ! (E.) Of imitative origin ; beginning with expulsion of breath, and ending in a hiss.

Pismire, an ant. (F. *and* E.) The old name of the ant ; from the strong urinous smell of an anthill. The first syllable is from F. *pisser* (below). β. The second is M. E. *mire*, an ant, prob. a native word. Cf. Du. *mier*, M. Du. *miere*,

E. Fries. *mīre*, an ant. Teut. type **mīron-*. β. We also find the similar (but unrelated ?) forms : Swed. *myra*, Dan. *myre*, Icel. *maurr*, an ant. Also Irish *moirbh*, W. *mōr*, pl. *myr*, Russ. *muravei*, Gk. μύρμηξ, Pers. *mūr*, *mōr*, an ant ; Corn. *murrian*, ants.

Piss. (F.) F. *pisser* ; supposed to be a Romance word, and of imitative origin.

Pistachio, Pistacho, the nut of a certain tree. (Span. – L. – Gk. – Pers.) Span. *pistacho*. – L. *pistācium*. – Gk. πιστάκιον, a nut of the tree called πιστάκη. – Pers. *pistā*, the pistachio-nut.

Pistil, in a flower. (L.) Named from the resemblance in shape to the pestle of a mortar. – L. *pistillum*, a small pestle, dimin. of an obsolete form **pistrum*, a pestle. – L. *pistum*, supine of *pinsere*, to pound. + Gk. πτίσσειν, Skt. *pish*, to pound. (√PIS.) See **Pestle**.

Pistol, a small hand-gun. (F. – Ital.) F. *pistole*. – Ital. *pistola*, ' a dag or pistoll ;' Florio. We also find M. Ital. *pistolese*, ' a great dagger,' in Florio ; and it is agreed that the name was first applied to a dagger, and thence transferred to the pistol, which even in E. was at first called a *dag* (F. *dague*, a dagger). A pistol is to a gun what a dagger is to a sword. β. The Ital. *pistolese* (= Late L. *pistolensis*) means ' belonging to Pistola ' ; so also Ital. *pistola* is from *Pistola*, now called *Pistoja*, a town in Tuscany, near Florence. The Old Lat. name of the town was *Pistōrium*. See Scheler.

pistole, a gold coin of Spain. (F. – Ital.) The name, however, is not Spanish, but French, and the coins were at first called *pistolets*. The name is of jocular origin. – F. *pistolet*, a little pistol, also a pistolet ; Cot. Diez explains that the crowns of Spain, being reduced to a smaller size than the French crowns, were called *pistolets*, and the smallest *pistolets* were called *bidets* ; cf. F. *bidet*, ' a small pistoll ;' Cot. – F. *pistole*, a pistol ; see above.

Piston. (F. – Ital. – L.) F. *piston*, ' a pestell,' Cot. ; also a piston. – Ital. *pistone*, a piston ; *pestone*, a large pestle. – Ital. *pestare*, Late L. *pistāre*, to pound. – L. *pistus*, pp. of *pinsere*, to pound. See **Pistil**.

Pit. (L.) M. E. *pit*, *put* ; A. S. *pyt*. – L. *puteus*, a well, pit (Luke xiv. 5). Perhaps a spring of pure water, from L. *putus*, pure, allied to *pūrus*; see **Pure**. Der. *pit*, vb., to set in competition, from the setting of cocks to fight in a *pit*.

Pitapat. (E.) A reduplication of *pat*, weakened from *pit* in the former instance.

Pitch (1), a black sticky substance. (L.) M. E. *pich*; older form *pik*; A. S. *pic*. ─ L. *pic-*, stem of *pix*, pitch. ╋ Gk. πίσσα (for *πίκ-ya). Cf. **Pine** (1).

Pitch (2), to throw, fall headlong, fix a camp. (L.) A palatalised form of *pick*, to throw, Cor. i. 1. 204, esp. to throw a *pike* or dart; also to plunge a sharp *peg* into the ground for fixing tents. M. E. *picchen*, pt. t. *pihte* (later *pight*). See **Pike**.

Pitcher. (F. ─ O. H. G. ─ L.) M. E. *picher*. ─ O. F. *picher*, also *pechir*; M. F. *pichier*, 'a pitcher; a Languedoc word;' Cot. ─ O. H. G. *pechāri* (G. *becher*). ─ Late L. *biccarium*, for L. *bīcārium*, a wine-vessel; prob. from Gk. βῖκος, (the same). See **Beaker**.

Pith. (E.) M. E. *pithe*. A. S. *piða*, pith. ╋ Du. *pit*, M. Du. *pitte*, Low G. *peddik*.

Pittance, a dole. (F.) M. E. *pitaunce*. ─ F. *pitance*, 'meat, food, victuall of all sorts, bread and drinke excepted;' Cot. Cf. Span. *pitanza*; Ital. *pietanza* (which is prob. corrupted by a supposed connexion with *pietà*, pity; also Span. *pitar*, to distribute or dole out allowances. β. Ducange explains Late L. *pictantia* as a pittance, orig. a dole of the value of a *picta*, which was a very small coin issued by the counts of Poitiers (Pictava). γ. But we also find Late L. *pittantia*, which Thurneysen connects with Ital. *pit-etto*, F. *pet-it*, small, allied to **Piece**.

Pity. (F. ─ L.) M. E. *pitee*. ─ O. F. *pite*, *pitet* (12th cent.). ─ L. *pietātem*, acc. of *pietās*, devoutness. ─ L. *pius*, devout. **Doublet**, *piety*. Der. *pite-ous*, for M. E. *pitous*, from O. F. *piteus* < Late L. *pietōsus*, merciful.

Pivot, a pin on which a wheel, &c. turns. (F. ─ Ital. ─ L.?) F. *pivot*. Formed, with dimin. suffix *-ot*, from Ital. *piva*, a pipe. The Ital. *piva* meant (1) a pipe, (2) a tube with fine bore; cf. *pivolo*, a peg. ─ Late L. *pīpa*, a pipe; allied to L. *pīpāre*, to chirp; see **Pipe**. ¶ So Diez; much disputed.

Pixy, a fairy. (Scand.) Also *picksy*; Cornwall *pisky*. Of Scand. origin; cf. Swed. dial. *pyske*, a dwarf, goblin (Rietz).

Placable. (L.) L. *plācābilis*, easy to be appeased. ─ L. *plācāre*, to appease.

Placard. (F. ─ Du.) F. *placard*, *plaquard*, 'a placard, inscription set up; also rough-cast on walls;' Cot. ─ F. *plaquer*, to rough-cast; also to stick or paste on; Cot. ─ Du. *plakken*, to glue or fasten up, formerly 'to plaister,' Hexham. Prob. of imitative origin (Franck).

Place. (F. ─ L. ─ Gk.) F. *place*. ─ Folk-L. *plattia*; L. *platea*, also *platēa*, a broad way, a courtyard. ─ Gk. πλατεῖα, a broad way; fem. of πλατύς, broad. ¶ A *place* was orig. a courtyard or square, a piazza. Cf. Ital. *piazza* (= F. *place*). See **Plaice**, **Plate**.

Placenta, a substance in the womb. (L.) L. *placenta*, lit. a flat cake. ╋ Gk. πλακοῦς, a flat cake; cf. πλάξ, a flat surface.

Placid. (F. ─ L.) F. *placide*, 'calm;' Cot. ─ L. *placidus*, pleasing, gentle. ─ L. *placēre*, to please. See **Please**.

Plack, a third of a (Scotch) penny. (Du.) From M. Du. *placke*, 'a French sous;' Hexham. Also, 'a spot.' ─ M. Du. *placken*, 'to plaister;' see **Placard**.

Plagiary. (F. ─ L.) F. *plagiaire*, one who kidnaps; also 'a book-theef'; Cot. ─ L. *plagiārius*, a kidnapper. ─ L. *plagium*, kidnapping; *plagiāre*, to ensnare. ─ L. *plaga*, a net.

Plague. (F. ─ L.) M. E. *plage*. ─ O. F. *plage*, *plague* (F. *plaie*). ─ L. *plāga*, a stroke, blow, injury, disaster. ╋ Gk. πληγή, a blow, plague, Rev. xvi. 21, from πλήσσειν (= *πλήκ-yειν), to strike; cf. L. *plangere*, to strike. Brugm. i. § 569.

Plaice, a fish. (F. ─ L.) O. F. *plaïse*, *plaïs*. ─ L. *platessa*, a plaice; so called from its flatness. From the base *plat-*, as seen in Gk. πλατύς, flat, broad; cf. **Place**.

Plaid. (C. ─ L.) Gael. (and Irish) *plaide*, a blanket, plaid. Allied to *peal-laid*, a sheep-skin. ─ Gael. (and Irish) *peall*, a skin. ─ L. *pellis*, a skin. See **Pell**.

Plain, flat, evident. (F. ─ L.) F. *plain*. ─ L. *plānus*, flat.

Plaint, a lament. (F. ─ L.) M. E. *pleinte*. ─ O. F. *pleinte*. ─ Late L. *plancta*, for L. *planctus*, lamentation. ─ L. *planctus*, pp. of *plangere*, to bewail. See **Plague**.

plaintiff. (F. ─ L.) M. E. *plaintif*. ─ F. *plaintif*, 'a plaintiff;' Cot. Formed with suffix *-if* (L. *-īuus*), from *planctus*, pp. of *plangere* (above).

plaintive. (F. – L.) F. *plaintive,* fem. of F. *plaintif* (above).

Plait. (F. – L.) From M. E. *plait,* sb., a fold. – O. F. *pleit, ploit, plet,* a fold. – Late L. type **plictum,* for *plic'tum,* short form of *plicitum,* by-form of L. *plicātum,* neut. of *plicātus,* pp. of *plicāre,* to fold ; see **Ply.** Cf. **Implicit** ; and see **Pleach.**

Plan. (F. – L.) F. *plan,* ' the ground-plat of a building ; ' Cot. – F. *plan,* flat ; learned form of F. *plain.* – L. *plānum,* acc. of *plānus,* flat. Properly, a drawing (for a building) on a flat surface.

plane (1), a level surface. (F. – L.) F. *plane,* fem. of *plan,* flat (above). – L. *plāna,* fem. of *plānus,* flat.

plane (2), a tool ; also to render a surface level. (F. – L.) M. E. *plane,* a tool. – F. *plane.* – Late L. *plāna,* a tool for planing. 2. We find also M. E. *planen,* to plane. – F. *planer.* – L. *plānāre,* to plane. – L. *plānus,* flat.

Plane (3), a tree. (F. – L. – Gk.) M.E. *plane.* – F. *plane.* – L. *platanum,* acc. of *platanus,* a plane. – Gk. πλάτανος, a plane ; named from its spreading leaves. – Gk. πλατύς, wide. Brugm. i. § 444.

Planet. (F. – L. – Gk.) M. E. *planete.* – O. F. *planete.* – L. *planēta.* – Gk. πλανή-της, a wanderer ; also πλανής, a wanderer ; the pl. πλάνητες means the wandering stars or planets. – Gk. πλανάομαι, I wander. – Gk. πλάνη, wandering.

Planisphere, a sphere projected on a plane. (L. *and* Gk.) From L. *plānus,* flat ; and E. *sphere,* of Gk. origin ; see **Sphere.**

Plank, a board. (F. – L.) M. E. *planke.* – N. F. (Picard) *planke* ; Norman *planque.* – L. *planca,* a flat board. Nasalised from the base *plac-,* flat ; see **Placenta.**

Plant. (L.) M. E. *plante.* A.S. *plante.* – L. *planta,* a plant ; properly, a spreading sucker or shoot ; also, the sole of the foot. From the base *plat-* ; see **Place.**

plantain. (F. – L.) F. *plantain.* – L. *plantāginem,* acc. of *plantāgo,* a plantain. Named from its spreading leaf ; allied to **Plant** (above).

plantigrade, walking on the sole of the foot. (L.) From *planti-,* for *planta,* the sole or flat part of the foot ; *grad-ī,* to walk. See **Plant, Place.**

Plash (1), a puddle, shallow pool. (E. ?) M.E. *plasche.* Cf. M. Du. *plasch,* a plash, pool ; *plasschen in 't water,* to plash or plunge in the water ; Hexham.

Cf. also G. *platschen,* Dan. *pladske* (for **platske*), Swed. *plaska* (for **platska*), to dabble ; from the Teut. base **plat,* to strike, seen in A. S. *plættan,* to strike.

Plash (2), the same as **Pleach.**

Plaster. (L. – Gk.) M. E. *plastre* ; A. S. *plaster.* [Also spelt *plaister* = O. F. *plaistre.*] – L. *emplastrum,* a plaster for wounds, the first syllable being dropped. – Gk. ἔμπλαστρον, a plaster, a form used by Galen instead of ἔμπλαστον, a plaster, neut. of ἔμπλαστος, daubed on or over. – Gk. ἐμπλάσσειν, to daub on. – Gk. ἐμ- (for ἐν), on ; πλάσσειν, to mould, form in clay or wax. Here πλάσσειν = *πλατ-γειν ; allied to E. *fold,* vb.

plastic. (L. – Gk.) L. *plasticus.* – Gk. πλαστικός, fit for moulding. – Gk. πλάσσειν, to mould (above).

Plat (1), **Plot,** a patch of ground ; see **Plot** (2).

Plat (2), to plait ; see **Plait.**

Platane, a plane-tree. (L. – Gk.) L. *platanus.* – Gk. πλάτανος ; see **Plane** (3).

Plate, a thin piece of metal, flat dish. (F. – L.) M. E. *plate.* – O. F. *plate* ; properly the fem. of *plat,* flat. – Late L. *platta,* a lamina, plate of metal, fem. of Folk-L. *plattus,* flat. Cf. Span. *plata,* plate, silver ; but the Span. word was borrowed from French ; whence also Du. Dan. *plat,* G. Swed. *platt,* flat.+Lithuan. *platus,* Gk. πλατύς, broad ; Skt. *prthus,* large. (√PLET.)

plateau, a flat space. (F. – L.) F. *plateau,* for O. F. *platel,* a small plate ; dimin. of *plat,* a plate. – F. *plat,* flat (above).

platform, a flat surface, level scaffolding ; formerly, a ground-plan, plan. (F. – L.) F. *plateforme,* ' a platform, modell ; ' Cot. – F. *plate,* fem. of *plat,* flat ; *forme,* form. See above ; and see **Form.**

platina, a metal. (Span. – F. – L.) Span. *platina* ; named from its silvery appearance. – Span. *plata,* silver. – O.F. *plate,* hammered plate, also silver plate ; see **Plate.**

platitude. (F. – L.) F. *platitude,* flatness, insipidity. Coined from F. *plat,* flat ; see **Plate.**

Platoon, a company of men. (F. – L.) Earlier form *peloton* (Stanford). – F. *peloton,* a tennis-ball, also a group of men, a platoon. Dimin. of M. F. *pelote,* a tennis-ball ; see **Pellet.**

Platter, a flat plate. (F. – L.) M.E. *plater.* – A. F. *blater* (Bozon). Formed

396

(with suffix -*er*) from O. F. *plat*, a plate; see **Plateau**.

Plaudit, applause. (L.) Formerly *plaudite* or *plaudity*. — L. *plaudite*, clap your hands; 2 pers. pl. imp. of *plaudere*, to applaud.

Play, a game. (E.) M. E. *play*. A. S. *plega*, a game, sport; also (commonly), a fight, battle. Cf. A. S. *plegian*, to play, clap; *plegian mid handum*, to clap hands. ¶ Not allied to *plight* (Franck).

Plea, an excuse. (F. — L.) M. E. *plee*, *play*. — A. F. *plee* (Bozon); O. F. *ple*, *plai*, occasional forms of O. F. *plait*, *plaid*, a plea. — Late L. *placitum*, a decree, sentence, &c. (with numerous meanings), orig. a decision, that which has seemed good. — L. *placitum*, neut. of *placitus*, pp. of *placēre*, to please. See **Plead, Please**.

Pleach, Plash, to intertwine boughs in a hedge. (F. — L.) M. E. *plechen*. — O. F. *plescier*, *plessier*, later *plesser*, 'to plash, plait young branches,' &c.; Cot. — Late L. type *plectiāre*, later *plessāre*, to pleach. — Late L. type *plectia*, later *plessa*, a thicket of woven boughs. — L. *plectere*, to weave; extended from base PLEK, to weave, whence also *plicāre*, to fold. See **Ply**.

Plead. (F. — L.) M. E. *pleden*. — O. F. *plaider*, to plead, argue. — O. F. *plaid*, a plea; see **Plea**.

Please. (F. — L.) M. E. *plesen*. — O. F. *plesir*, *plaisir*, to please (F. *plaire*). — L. *placēre*, to please. Allied to *plācāre*, to appease. Der. *pleas-ant*, from O. F. *plesir*; also *dis-please*.

pleasure. (F. — L.) An E. spelling of F. *plaisir*, pleasure (like E. *leisure* for A. F. *leisir*). This F. sb. is merely the infin. mood used substantively. — L. *placēre*; see **Please**.

Pleat, another form of **Plait**.

Plebeian, vulgar. (F. — L.) O. F. *plebeien* (F. *plébéien*); formed, with suffix -*en* (L. -*ānus*), from L. *plēbeius*, adj., from *plēbes*, more commonly *plebs*, the people. Cf. Gk. πλῆθος, a multitude.

Pledge, a security, surety. (F. — O. Low G.) M. E. *plegge*, a hostage, security. — O. F. *plege*, a surety (F. *pleige*). [Allied to O. F. *plevir*, M. F. *pleuvir*, to warrant.] — O. Sax. *plegan*, to promise, pledge one-self; cf. O. H. G. *pflegan*, to answer for (G. *pflegen*), A. S. *plēon*, to risk, *pleoh*, risk (Franck). See **Plight** (1).

Pleiocene, more recent; **Pleistocene**, most recent. (Gk.) From Gk. πλείω-ν, more, or πλεῖστο-ς, most; and καινός, recent, new. Πλείων, πλεῖστος are comp. and superl. of πολύς, much.

Plenary, full. (Late L. — L.) Late L. *plēnārius*, entire. — L. *plēnus*, full. + Gk. πληρής, πλέ-ως, full; πίμ-πλη-μι, I fill. Allied to **Full**.

plenipotentiary, having full powers. (L.) Coined from L. *plēni*-, for *plēno*-, decl. stem of *plēnus*, full; and *potenti*-, for *potens*, powerful; with suffix -*ārius*; see **Potent**.

plenitude, fullness. (F. — L.) O. F. *plenitude*. — L. *plēnitūdo*, fullness. — L. *plēni*-, for *plēnus*, full; with suffix -*tūdo*.

plenty, abundance. (F. — L.) M. E. *plentee*. — O. F. *plente*, *plentet*. — L. *plēnitātem*, acc. of *plēnitās*, fullness. — L. *plēni*-, for *plēnus*, full. Der. *plenteous*, M. E. *plenteus*, often spelt *plentivous*, from O.F. *plentivos*; from O. F. *plentif*, answering to Late L. form *plēnitīvus*.

Pleonasm. (L. — Gk.) L. *pleonasmus*. — Gk. πλεονασμός, abundance. — Gk. πλεονάζειν, to abound, lit. to be more. — Gk. πλέον, neut. of πλέων, πλείων, more, comparative of πολύς, much, allied to πλέως, full. See **Plenary**.

Plethora, excessive fullness, esp. of blood. (L. — Gk.) L. *plēthōra*. — Gk. πληθώρη, fullness. — Gk. πλῆθ-ος, a throng, crowd; allied to πλήρης, full. See **Plenary**.

Pleurisy, inflammation of the *pleura*, or membrane which covers the lungs. (F. — L. — Gk.) F. *pleurésie*. — L. *pleurisis*; also *pleurītis*. — Gk. πλευρῖτις, pleurisy. — Gk. πλευρά, a rib, side, pleura. Der. *pleuritic*, from πλευρῖτ-ις; *pleuro-pneumonia*, inflammation of pleura and lungs, from πνεύμων, a lung; see **Pneumatic**.

Pliable, flexible. See **Ply**.

pliant. (F. — L.) F. *pliant*, pres. pt. of *plier*, to bend; see **Ply**.

Plight (1), pledge; hence, as vb., to pledge. (E.) M. E. *pliht*, danger, also engagement, pledge. A. S. *pliht*, risk, danger. Formed, with suffix -*t* (Idg. -*ti*-), from the strong vb. *plēon*, (*pleh-an*), pt. t. *pleah*, to risk; cf. *pleoh*, danger. + M. Du. *plicht*, duty, debt, use; *plegen*, to be accustomed; G. *pflicht*, duty, from O. H. G. *pflegan* (G. *pflegen*), to promise or engage to do. Teut. root, *pleh*-.

Der. *plight*, vb., A. S. *plihtan*, weak vb., from *pliht*, sb.

Plight (2), to fold; as sb., a fold, also state, condition. (F.—L.) Misspelt. In all these senses, the sb. was formerly M. E. *plite*. ▬ O. F. *plite*, fem. (given as *plyte* in Godefroy, *pliste*, *plyte* in Roquefort), state, condition. ▬ L. *plicita*, fem. of *plicitus*, pp. of *plicāre*, to fold. It is the fem. of *plait*; see **Plait** and **Ply**.

Plinth, the lowest part of the base of a column. (F.—L.—Gk.; *or* L.—Gk.) F. *plinthe*.▬L. *plinthus*.▬Gk. πλίνθος, a brick, plinth. Perhaps allied to **Flint**.

Plod. (E.) Orig. to splash through water or mud; hence, to trudge on laboriously, toil onward. From M. E. *plod*, a puddle. Cf. Irish *plod*, *plodan*, a pool; *plodach*, a puddle, whence *plodanachd*, paddling in water; Gael. *plod*, *plodan*, a pool. Also E. Fries. *pludern*, to splash about in water; Dan. dial. *pludder*, Dan. *pladder*, mud. Of imitative origin; cf. **Plash** (1).

Plot (1), a conspiracy. (F.) Short for *complot*(?); for the loss of *com-*, cf. *fence* for *defence*, *sport* for *disport*.▬F. *complot*, 'a complot, conspiracy;' Cot. Of unknown origin; Körting, § 2053. β. Or, more likely, short for *plotform*, variant of *platform*, a map or plan; see **platform**. For *plotform*, see Gascoigne, Art of Venerie, 40; and cf. *plat*, a map (Mirror for Magistrates).

Plot (2), a small piece of ground. (E.) M. E. *plotte*. [Cf. *plat*, 2 Kings ix. 26.] A. S. *plot*, a plot of ground; Cockayne's Leechdoms, iii. 286. Note Dan. *plet*, as in *græsplet*, a grass-plat.

Plough. (E.) M. E. *plouh*, *plow*; also A. S. *plōh*, in the sense 'plot of land.' E. Fries. *plōg*.╋Du. *ploeg*; Icel. *plōgr*, a plough; Swed. *plog*, Dan. *plov*; also O. Fries. *ploch*, G. *pflug*. [Lithuan. *plugas*, Russ. *plug'* are borrowed from Teutonic.]

Plover, a bird. (F.—L.) M. E. *plover*. ▬O. F. *plovier*, later *pluvier*. Formed from L. **pluuārius*, equivalent to L. *pluuiālis*, rainy.▬L. *pluuia*, rain; see **Pluvial**. These birds were said to be most seen and caught in a rainy season; whence also the G. name *regenpfeifer* (rain-piper).

Pluck, to snatch. (E.) M. E. *plukken*. A.S. *pluccian*, Matt. xii. 1.╋Du. *plukken*, Icel. *plokka*, *plukka* (perhaps borrowed), Dan. *plukke*, Swed. *plocka*, G. *pflücken*. ¶ Some think it not a Teut. word; but

borrowed from Late L. *piluccāre*, whence Ital. *piluccare*, to pluck out hair; from L. *pilus*, a hair; see **Pile** (3). Der. *pluck*, sb., a butcher's term for the heart, liver, and lights of an animal, whence mod. E. *pluck*, courage, *plucky*, adj.

Plug. (Du.) M. Du. *plugge*, Du. *plug*, a peg, bung. Cf. Low G. *plugge*, Swed. *plugg*, G. *pflock*, a peg, plug.

Plum. (L.—Gk.) A.S. *plūme*, a plum; formed (by change of *r* to *l*) from L. *prūnum*, a plum. See **Prune**.

Plumage. (F.—L.) F. *plumage*, 'feathers;' Cot.▬F. *plume*.▬L. *plūma*, a feather; see **Plume**.

Plumb, a lead on a string, as a plummet. (F.—L.) Formerly *plomb*; M. E. *plom*.▬F. *plomb*, 'lead, a plummet;' Cot.▬L. *plumbum*, lead. Cf. Gk. μόλυβος, μόλυβδος, lead. Der. *plumb*, vb., to sound a depth; *plumb-er*, sb., F. *plombier*.

plumbago, blacklead. (L.) L. *plumbāgo*, a kind of leaden ore.▬L. *plumbum*, lead (above).

Plume. (F.—L.) F. *plume*. ▬ L. *plūma*, a small feather, down. Allied to E. *fly*, vb. See **Fly**. Brugm. i. § 681.

Plummet. (F.—L.) M. E. *plommet* ▬O. F. *plommet*; M. F. *plombet*; dimin. of *plomb*, lead; see **Plumb** (above).

Plump (1), full, round, fleshy. (E. or O. Low G.) M. E. *plomp*, rude, clownish also *plump*, sb., a cluster or clump. The word seems to be E., especially if the prov E. *plim*, to swell out, is an allied verb Cf. *plump*, to swell (Nares).╋M. Du *plomp*, clownish, dull (a metaphorical use from the notion of thickness); E. Fries and Low G. *plump*, bulky, thick; Swed Dan. G. *plump*, clumsy, blunt, coarse See **Plump** (3). Der. *plump-er*, a kin of vote (to *swell out* a candidate's chance against all the rest).

Plump (2), straight downward. (F. L.) Formerly *plum*, *plumb*; Milto P. L. ii. 933.▬F. *à plomb*, downright (c Ital. *cadere a piombo*, to fall plump, li like lead).▬F. *plomb*, lead.▬L. *plumbun* lead. See below, and see **Plunge**.

Plump (3), vb., to fall heavily dow (E. ?). Of imitative origin. Cf. E. Frie *plumpen*, to fall heavily, *plempen*, plunge into water; so also Du. *plompe* G. *plumpen*, Swed. *plumpa*, to fall heavil Under the influence of this word the for *plumb*, 'straight downward,' has becon *plump*. See above.

Plunder, to pillage. (G.) G. *plün-dern,* to steal trash, to pillage; from *plunder,* sb., trumpery, trash, baggage, lumber; orig. of Low G. origin; cf. M. Du. *plunderen, plonderen,* to pillage, connected with Low G. *plunnen, plunden,* E. Fries. *plünde, plünne,* rags, worthless household stuff. Hence to *plunder* is to strip a house even of its least valuable contents.

Plunge. (F.—L.) F. *plonger,* 'to plunge, dive;' Cot. Formed from a Late L. **plumbicāre,* not found, but verified by Picard *plonquer,* to plunge; see Diez, s. v. *piombare.* A frequentative form from L. *plumbum,* lead; cf. Ital. *piombare,* to throw, hurl, fall heavily like lead, from *piombo,* lead. See **Plump** (2).

Pluperfect. (L.) Englished from L. *plusquamperfectum,* by giving to *plūs* the F. pronunciation, and dropping *quam.* The lit. sense is 'more than perfect,' applied to a tense.—L. *plūs,* more; *quam,* than; *perfectum,* perfect. See **Perfect.**

Plural. (F.—L.) M. E. *plural.*—O. F. *plurel* (F. *pluriel*).—L. *plūrālis,* plural, expressive of *more* than one.—L. *plūr-,* stem of *plūs,* more. Allied to Gk. πλείων, more, πλέος, full; and to **Plenary.** Brugm. ii. § 135.

Plurisy, superabundance. (L.; *mis-formed.*) Shak. uses *plurisy* to express plethora; so also Massinger and Ford. Formed from L. *plūri-,* from *plūs,* more, by an extraordinary (prob. a jocular) confusion with *pleurisy.*

Plush. (F.—L.) F. *peluche,* 'shag, plush;' Cot. (Cf. Span. *pelusa,* nap, Ital. *peluzzo,* soft down.) From the fem. of a Late L. form **pilūceus,* hairy, not found.—L. *pilus,* hair. See **Perruque, Pile** (3).

Pluvial, rainy. (F.—L.) F. *pluvial.* —L. *pluuiālis,* rainy.—L. *pluuia,* rain.—L. *plu-it,* it rains. Cf. Skt. *plu-,* to swim. From Idg. **plu,* weak grade of √PLEU, to swim; cf. Gk. πλέειν, to swim.

Ply. (F.—L.) M. E. *plien,* to bend, to mould as wax (hence, to toil at).—F. *plier,* 'to fould, plait, ply, bend;' Cot.—L. *pli-cāre,* to fold.+Gk. πλέκειν, Russ. *pleste,* G. *flechten,* to weave, plait. (√PLEK.) Der. *pli-ant,* bending, from F. *pliant,* pres. pt. of *plier; pli-ers* or *ply-ers,* pincers for bending wire; *pli-able* (F. *pliable*).

Pneumatic. (Gk.) Gk. πνευματικός, relating to wind or air.—Gk. πνεῦμα (stem πνευματ-), wind, air.—Gk. πνέειν (for πνέϝ-ειν), to blow. Allied to **Neese.**

Pneumonia. (Gk.) Gk. πνευμονία, disease of the lungs.—Gk. πνευμον-, stem of πνεύμων, for πλεύμων, a lung, by a false connexion with πνέειν, to breathe (above). The Gk. πλεύμων is allied to L. *pulmo,* a lung; Lith. *plauczei,* pl. the lungs.

Poach (1), to dress eggs. (F.—O. Low G.?) Formerly *poch.*—F. *pocher;* Cot. gives '*œuf poché,* a potched (poached) egg.' The orig. sense was prob. 'a pouched' egg, i. e. an egg so dressed as to preserve it in the form of a pocket.—F. *poche,* a pocket; see **Pouch.** See Scheler's explanation.

Poach (2), to intrude into preserves. (F.—L.) M.F. *pocher;* Cot. explains *pocher le labeur d'autruy* by 'to poch into, or incroach upon, another man's imploiment, practise, or trade.' The old sense was 'to thrust or dig out with the fingers,' Cot. (if this be the same word); or rather, to put the thumb into. Cf. prov. E. *poach,* to tread into holes; Picard *pocher,* 'tâter un fruit avec le pouce,' *peucher,* 'presser avec le pouce;' Corblet. Perhaps from L. *pollicem,* acc. of *pollex,* the thumb; cf. O. F. *pochier, poucier,* the thumb. But partly from **Poke** (2).

Pook (1), a pustule. (E.) *Small pox* = small *pocks,* where *pocks* is pl. of *pock.* M. E. *pokke,* a pock, pl. *pokkes.* A. S. *poc,* a pustule.+E. Fries. *pok, pokke;* Du. *pok,* G. *pocke,* a pock. Cf. Gael. *pucaid,* a pimple, Irish *pucoid,* a pustule, *pucadh,* a swelling up, Gael. *poc,* to become like a bag (from E.).

Pocket, a small pouch. (F.—Scand.) M. E. *poket.*—Norman dial. **poquette,* dimin. of O. Norman *poque* (see Norman dial. *pouque,* Métivier), the same as F. *poche,* a pocket, pouch.—Icel. *poki,* a bag; cf. M. Du. *poke,* a bag (Hexham). See **Poke** (1).

Pod, a husk. (E.) Of doubtful origin. Cf. M. Du. *puden,* 'huskes,' Hexham; Westphal. *puddek,* a lump, a pudding; Low G. *puddig,* thick; prov. E. *poddy,* fat and round; *puddle,* short and fat. See **Pudding** and **Pout.**

Poem. (F.—L.—Gk.) M.F. *poëme,* Cot.—L. *poēma.*—Gk. ποίημα, a work, composition, poem.—Gk. ποιεῖν, to make.

poesy. (F.—L.—Gk.) M. E. *poesie.* —M. F. *poësie.*—L. *poēsin,* acc. of *poēsis,* poetry.—Gk. ποίησις, a composition, poem. —Gk. ποιεῖν, to make.

poet. (F.—L.—Gk.) O. F. *poëte.*—L.

poēta. — Gk. ποιητής, a maker. — Gk. ποιεῖ-ν, to make; with suffix -της of the agent.

Poignant. (F. — L.) F. *poignant*, stinging, pres. part. of *poindre*, to prick. — L. *pungere*, to prick.

point. (F. — L.) M. E. *point*. — O. F. *point*, *poinct*, a point, prick. — L. *punctum*. Sometimes from F. *pointe*, f. — L. *puncta*. Both from the pp. of *pungere* (above).

Poise, Peise, to balance, weigh. (F. — L.) M. E. *poisen*, *peisen*. — O. F. *poiser*, later *peser*, to weigh; A. F. *peiser*. — L. *pensāre*, to weigh. Allied to O. F. *pois*, A. F. *peis*, a weight (now misspelt *poids*, from a notion of its being derived from L. *pondus*, which is *not* the case). — Late L. *pensum*, *pensa*, a portion, weight; L. *pensum*, a portion weighed out to spinners, a task. — L. *pensus*, pp. of *pendere*, to weigh. See **Pendant**.

Poison. (F. — L.) F. *poison*, poison. — L. *pōtiōnem*, acc. of *pōtio*, a draught, esp. a poisonous draught; see **Potion**.

Poitrel, Peitrel, armour for a horse's breast. (F. — L.) M.F. *poitral*, Cot.; A.F. *peitral*. — L. *pectorāle*, neut. of *pectorālis*, belonging to the breast. See **Pectoral**.

Poke (1), a bag, pouch. (Scand.) M. E. *poke*. [Cf. A.S. **poca*, *pocca*, *pohha*, *pohcha*, *poha*, a bag.] — Icel. *poki*; M. Du. *poke*, a bag.

Poke (2), to thrust, push. (E.) M. E. *poken*, *pukken* (whence Irish *poc*, a blow, kick, Corn. *poc*, a shove, Gael. *puc*, to push). + Du. *poken*; E. Fries. *pokern*, frequent., to keep on poking about; Pomeran. *pök-en*; G. *pochen*. From Teut. base **puk*; of imitative origin. Der. *pok-er*.

Pole (1), a large stake. (L.) M. E. *pole*, formed (by usual change of *ā* to *ō*) from A. S. *pāl*, a pale, pole. — L. *pālus*, a stake; see **Pale** (1).

Pole (2), a pivot, end of earth's axis. (F. — L. — Gk.) O. F. *pol*. — L. *polum*, acc. of *polus*. — Gk. πόλος, a pivot, hinge. — Gk. πέλειν, to be in motion; allied to Russ. *koleso*, a wheel. (√QEL.) Brugm. i. § 652.

Pole-ax, a kind of ax. (L. and E.) From *pole* and *ax*. Cf. Westphal. *pāl-exe*, from *pāl*, a pole. But formerly *poll-ax*, from the Low G. *pollexe*, from *polle*, the poll, the head. See, accordingly, **Pole** (1) and **Poll**.

Polecat, a kind of weasel. (Hybrid.) M. E. *polcat*, where *cat* is the ordinary word; also *pulkat*. From F. *poule*, a

hen, because the *pole-cat* slays capons; see Chaucer, C. T. 12789. Cf. the pronunciation of *poul-try*, from A. F. *poletrie*; and see **Catchpoll**.

Polemical, warlike. (Gk.) From Gk. πολεμικός, warlike. — Gk. πόλεμος, war.

Police. (F. — L. — Gk.) F. *police*, orig. civil government. — L. *polītīa*. — Gk. πολιτεία, polity, government. — Gk. πολίτης, a citizen. — Gk. πόλις, a state, city. Related to πολύς, much; cf. Skt. *purī*, a town. Der. *polic-y*, O. F. *policie* < L. *polītīa*; *polit-ic*, from Gk. πολιτικός, adj. Der. *acro-polis*, *metro-polis*, *cosmo-polite*.

Policy, a warrant for money in the funds, a contract of insurance. (F. — Late L. — Gk.) Confused with *policy*, from *police*, with which it has nothing to do. — F. *police* (Hamilton; cf. M. Ital. *polisa*, a schedule, Florio). — Late L. *politicum*, *polecticum*, corruptions of *polyptychum*, a register (a common word; Ducange). — Gk. πολύπτυχον, a piece of writing in many folds, hence a long register; orig. neut. of πολύπτυχος, having many folds. — Gk. πολύ-, much; πτυχο-, crude form of πτύξ, a fold, leaf, layer, connected with πτύσσειν, to fold up. (Supp. to Diez.) β. Better thus: the Port. form *apólice*, M. Span. *póliça*, M. Ital. *póliza*, *pólisa*, prob. represent Late L. *apódissa*, *apódixa*, 'cautio de sumpta pecunia;' Duc. Cf. Port. *apodixe*, a plain proof. — Late Gk. ἀπόδειξις, a shewing forth, a proof. — Gk. ἀποδείκνυμι, I point out. — Gk. ἀπό, from, forth; δείκνυμι, I shew. (Körting, § 6258.)

Polish, to make smooth. (F. — L.) F. *poliss-*, stem of pres. pt. of *polir*. — L. *polīre*, to make smooth.

polite. (L.) L. *polītus*, polished; pp. of *polīre*, to make smooth (above).

Politic; see **Police**.

Polka, a dance. (Polish.) Said to have been first danced by a Bohemian peasant-girl in 1831, and to have been named *polka* at Prague in 1835. — Pol. *Polka*, a Polish woman. Another dance is called the *Polonaise*, with the same literal sense; another the *Cracovienne*, lit. a woman of Cracow; another the *Mazurka*, q. v.

Poll, the head, esp. the back part (O. Low G.) Hence it means also a register of heads or persons, a voting-place, &c. M. E. *pol*, a poll; *pol bi pol*, head by head, separately. — Low G. *polle*; M. Du. *polle*, *pol, bol,* 'head or pate,' Hexham ; Swed. dial. *pull,* Dan. *puld* (for *pull*). Cf. E. Fries. *pol,* round, full, fleshy. Der. *poll,* to cut off the hair of the head. Also *poll-ard,* a tree that is *polled,* leaving a large knobby head ; also, formerly, a *clipped* coin.

Pollen. (L.) L. *pollen, pollis,* fine flour. Cf. Gk. πάλη, fine meal.

Pollock, Pollack, a fish. (E.) Prob. from E. *poll*; cf. E. *pollard,* which is a name of the chub. See *pollard,* under **Poll.** Hence Irish *pullog,* a pollock; Gael. *pollag,* a whiting. (Doubtful.)

Pollute. (L.) L. *pollūtus,* pp. of *polluere,* to defile. Orig. to wash over, as a flooded river. – L. *pol-,* allied to O. Lat. *por-,* towards; *luere,* to wash ; see **Lave.**

Polo, a game. (Balti.) 'It comes from Balti ; *polo* being properly, in the language of that region, the ball used in the game;' Yule. Balti is in the high valley of the Indus.

Polony, a Bologna sausage. (Ital.) Ital. *Bologna,* where they were made (Evelyn).

Poltroon, a dastard, lazy fellow. (F. – Ital. – L.) F. *poltron,* a sluggard ; Cot. – Ital. *poltrone,* a varlet, coward, sluggard; cf. *poltrare,* to lie in bed. – Ital. *poltro,* a bed, couch ; orig. 'a colt,' also 'a varlet,' Florio. Cf. F. *poutre,* a beam, M. F. *poutre,* 'a filly,' Cot. – Late L. *pullitrum,* acc. of *pullitrus,* a colt; Duc. – L. *pullus,* a colt, foal. See **Foal.** For change of sense, cf. **Pulley, Chevron.**

Poly-, many. (L. – Gk.) L. *poly-.* – Gk. πολύ-, decl. stem of πολύς, much. + Skt. *puru-,* much. Allied to **Full.**

polyanthus, a flower. (L. – Gk.) L. *polyanthus.* – Gk. πολύανθος, many-flowered. – Gk. πολύ-, many; ἄνθος, flower.

polygamy. (F. – L. – Gk.) F. *polygamie.* – L. *polygamia.* – Gk. πολυγαμία, a marrying of many wives. – Gk. πολύ-, much; -γαμία, from γάμος, marriage.

polyglot, speaking many languages. (Gk.) Attic Gk. πολύγλωττος. – Gk. πολύ-, much, many; γλῶττα = γλῶσσα, tongue, language; see **Gloss.**

polygon, a many-sided plane figure. (L. – Gk.) L. *polygōnum.* – Gk. πολύγωνον, neut. of πολύγωνος, having many angles. – Gk. πολύ-, many; γωνία, an angle, from γόνυ, a knee.

polyhedron, a many-sided solid

figure. (Gk.) Gk. πολύ-, many; -εδρον, for ἕδρα, a base, from the base ἑδ-, to sit; see **Sit.**

polynomial. (Gk. *and* L.) Coined to go with *bi-nomial.* – Gk. πολύ-, many ; L. *nōmen,* a name, term.

Polypus, Polyp, an aquatic animal of the radiate type. (L. – Gk.) L. *polypus.* – Gk. πολύπους, many-footed. – Gk. πολύ-s, many ; πούς, a foot. ¶ Cf. F. *polype,* Ital. and Span. *polipo,* L. *polypŭs* (gen. *polypī*) ; all false forms, due to treating the Lat. ending -*pūs* as if it were -*p-ŭs.*

polysyllable. (Gk.) From *poly-* and *syllable.* Cf. Gk. πολυσύλλαβος, adj.

polytheism. (Gk.) From *poly-* and *theism.*

Pomade, Pommade. (F. – Ital. – L.) F. *pommade,* pomatum ; so called because orig. made with apples. – Ital. *pomada, pomata,* 'a pomado to supple one's lips, lip-salve,' Florio. – Ital. *pomo,* an apple. – L. *pōmum,* an apple, fruit.

Pomander, a globe-shaped box for holding ointments or perfumes. (F. – L. *and* Arab.) Spelt *pomander* (1518); *pomaunder* (Skelton). Cf. M. F. *pomendier,* 'a pom-aunder;' Palsgrave (prob. from E.) ; and note M. Span. *poma,* a pomander (Minsheu), which is a fem. form, from *pomo,* an apple. β. The suffix *-ander* is for *ambre,* amber. We find '*pomum ambre* for the pestelence'; MS. Harl. 2378, p. 324, in Medical Works of the 14th cent., ed. Henslow, p. 122. Cf. O. F. *pomme d'ambre* (Rom. Rose, 21008). – L. *pōmum,* an apple ; and see **Amber.**

Pomegranate. (F. – L.) O. F. *pome grenate* (also turned into *pome de grenate* by confusion of the sense) ; the same as Ital. *pomo granato.* – L. *pōmum,* an apple; *grānātum,* full of seeds, from *grānum,* a grain, seed ; see **Grain.**

pommel, a knob. (F. – L.) M. E. *pomel,* a boss. – O. F. *pomel* (later *pom-meau*), a pommel; lit. 'small apple.' Dimin. from L. *pōmum,* an apple.

Pomp. (F. – L. – Gk.) F. *pompe.* – L. *pompa.* – Gk. πομπή, a sending, escorting, solemn procession. – Gk. πέμπειν, to send.

Pond. (E.) M. E. *pond,* variant of *pound,* an enclosure ; it means a pool formed by damming up water; see **Pound** (2). Cf. Irish *pont,* (1) a pound, (2) a pond.

Ponder, to weigh in the mind, consider. (L.) L. *ponderāre,* to weigh. – L.

ponder-, for **pondes-*, stem of *pondus*, a weight. — L. *pendere*, to weigh. See **Pendant**.

Ponent, western. (F. — L.) M.F. *ponent*, 'the west;' Cot. — L. *pŏnent-*, stem of pres. pt. of *pŏnere*, to lay, hence to set (as the sun). See **Position**.

Poniard. (F. — L.; *with* G. *suffix*.) F. *poignard*, a dagger. — F. *poing* (O.F. *poign*), the fist; with suffix *-ard* < G. *hart* (lit. hard). [So also Ital. *pugnale*, a poniard, from *pugno*, fist; Span. *puñal*, a poniard, from *puño*, fist, handful, hilt.] — L. *pugnus*, fist. See **Pugnacious**.

Pontiff. (F. — L.) M. F. *pontif*; F. *pontife*. — L. *pontifex*, a Roman high-priest; lit. 'a path-maker' or 'road-maker,' but the reason for the name is not known. — L. *ponti-*, representing *pons*, a path, a bridge; *facere*, to make. Cf. Gk. πόντος, sea. Brugm. i. § 140.

Pontoon. (F. — L. — C.) F. *ponton*, a lighter, bridge of boats, 'a wherry,' Cot. — L. *pontōnem*, acc. of *ponto*, a boat, bridge of boats. The word is of Celt. origin; see **Punt**.

Pony. (F. — L.) Cf. Gael. *ponaidh*, a little horse, a pony; vulgar Irish *poni*, both borrowed from English. Lowl. Sc. *powney*. — O. F. *poulenet*, a little colt (Godefroy); dimin. of *poulain*, a colt, foal. — Late L. acc. *pullānum*, a young horse. — L. *pull-us*, a foal; cognate with E. **Foal**.

Poodle, a dog. (G.) G. *pudel*, a poodle; Low G. *pudel*, *pudel-hund*, allied to Low G. *pudeln*, to waddle, used of fat persons and short-legged animals. Cf. Low G. *pudel-dikk*, unsteady on the feet, *puddig*, thick. Allied to **Pudding**.

Pooh. (F.) M. F. *pouac*, 'faugh,' Cot. Cf. Icel. *pū*, pooh. Of imitative origin.

Pool (1), a small body of water. (E.) M. E. *pol*, *pool*. A. S. *pōl*; [Irish *poll*, *pull*, a hole, pit; Gael. *poll*, a hole, pit, bog, pool; W. *pwll*, Corn. *pol*, Manx *poyl*, Bret. *poull*, a pool].+Du. *poel*, G. *pfuhl*, O. H. G. *pfuol*. Teut. type *pōloz; cf. Lith. *balà*, a swamp. (The Celtic forms are borrowed.)

Pool (2), receptacle for the stakes at cards. (F. — L.) F. *poule*, (1) a hen, (2) a pool, at various games; the stakes being the eggs to be got from the hen. — Late L. *pulla*, a hen; fem. of L. *pullus*, a young animal; see **Foal**.

Poop. (F. — L.; *or* F. — Ital. — L.) F. *poupe*, *pouppe*. — L. *puppim*, acc. of *puppis*, hinder part of a ship. ¶ Or F. *poupe* is from Ital. *poppa*, poop; Hatzfeld.

Poor. (F. — L.) From M. E. *poure* (= *povre*), poor. — O. F. *povre*, poor. — L. *pauperem*, acc. of *pauper*; see **Pauper**.

Pop. (E.) 'To *poppe*, coniectare;' Levins. Of imitative origin; allied to M. E. *poupen*, to blow a horn; also to **Puff**.

Pope, the father of a church, bishop of Rome. (L. — Gk.) M. E. *pope*; A. S. *pāpa*, pope, with the usual change from *ā* to *ō*. — L. *pāpa*, pope, father; see **Papal**.

Popinjay, orig. a parrot. (F. — Bavarian *and* L.; *with modified suffix*.) M. E. *popingay*, also spelt *papeiay* (= *papejay*). The *n* is inserted as in *passe-n-ger*, *messe-n-ger*. — F. *papegai*, 'a parrot or popinjay;' Cot. Cf. Span. *papagayo*, Port. *papagaio*, a parrot; (whence Arab. *babaghā*, a parrot). β. But there is also O. F. *papegau*, a parrot (13th cent.), Ital. *papagallo*, a parrot, lit. 'a talking cock;' and this is the older form. [The change was due to the substitution of *jay* (F. *gai*, *geai*) for 'cock,' because the jay seemed to come nearer than a cock to the nature of a parrot.] Cf. Bavarian *pappel*, a parrot, from *pappeln*, to chatter (= E. *babble*). A similar name is Lowl. Sc. *bubblyjock* (i. e. babble-jack), a turkey-cock.

Poplar, a tree. (F. — L.) O. F. *poplier*; F. *peuplier*. Formed with suffix *-ier* (= L. *-ārius*) from O. F. *pople, later *peuple*, a poplar. — L. *pōpulum*, acc. of *pōpulus*, a poplar.

Poplin. (F.) F. *popeline*, a fabric; at first called *papeline*, A. D. 1667 (Littré). [Therefore not from *Poppeling* or *Popperingen*, near Ypres, in W. Flanders; as in N. and Q. 6 S. vi. 305.]

Poppy. (L.) A. S. *popig*, also *popæg*; from L. *papauer*, a poppy (with change of suffix).

Populace. (F. — Ital. — L.) F. *populace*. — Ital. *popolazzo*, *popolaccio*, 'the grosse, vile, common people;' Florio. — Ital. *popolo*, people. — L. acc. *populum*. ¶ The suffix *-accio* is depreciatory.

popular. (F. — L.) F. *populaire*. — L. *populāris*, adj., from *populus*, the people.

Porcelain. (F. — Ital. — L.) Named from the resemblance of its polished surface to that of the univalve shell with the same name. — F. *porcelaine*, *pourcelaine*, 'the purple-fish, the Venus-shell;' Cot. — Ital. *porcellana*, 'the purple-fish, a kind of fine earth, whereof they make . . *porcellan* dishes;' Florio. **β.** The shell is named from the curved shape of its upper surface, like a pig's back. **=** Ital. *porcella*, a pig, dimin. of *porco*, a hog, pig. **=** L. *porcum*, acc. of *porcus*, a pig. See **Pork**.

Porch. (F. **−** L.) F. *porche*. **=** L. *porticum*, acc. of *porticus*, a gallery, porch; formed, with suffix *-icus*, from L. *port-a*, a door; see **Port** (3).

Porcine, pig-like. (L.) L. *porc-īnus*, adj., from *porc-us*, a pig; see **Pork**.

Porcupine. (F. **−** L.) M. E. *porkepyn* (3 syllables. **=** O. F. *porc espin*, Godefroy; (now called *porc-épic*). [So also Span. *puerco espin*, Ital. *porco spinoso*.] **=** O. F. *porc*, a pig; *espin*, by-form of *espine*, a spine, prickle. **=** L. *porc-um*, acc. of *porcus*; *spīna*, a thorn; see **Spine**. **¶** But mod. F. *porc-épic* was formerly *porc espi*, derived from *spīca*, spike, not *spīna*, a thorn. We also find E. *porpin*, short for *porkepin*; whence *porpint*, altered to *porpoint*, *porkpoint*; whence *porpent-ine*; all these forms occur.

Pore (1), a minute hole in the skin. (F. **−** L. **−** Gk.) F. *pore*. **=** L. *porum*, acc. of *porus*. **=** Gk. πόρος, a passage, pore. Allied to **Fare**. (✓ PER.)

Pore (2), to look steadily, gaze long. (E.) M. E. *poren*. Cf. North Fries. *porre*, to stick, stir, provoke, E. Fries. *puren*, *purren*, to stick, thrust, bore, stir, vex; Low G. *purren*, to poke about, clean out a hole, Du. *porren*, to poke; Swed. dial. *pora*, *pura*, *påra*, to work slowly and gradually, to do anything slowly (Rietz); Norw. *pora*, to finger, poke, stir, thrust. The idea seems to be that of poking about slowly, hence to *pore over* a thing, be slow about it. We also find Gael. *purr*, to push, thrust, drive, urge, Irish *purraim*, I thrust, push; from M. E. *pouren*, *poren*; cf. Lowl. Sc. *porr*, to stab.

Pork. (F. **−** L.) F. *porc*. **=** L. *porcum*, acc. of *porcus*, a pig.**+**Lithuan. *parszas*, Irish *orc* (with usual loss of *p*), A. S. *fearh*, a pig (whence E. *farrow*). Brugm. i. § 486.

Porphyry. (F. **−** L. **−** Gk.) M. E. *porphurie*, answering to an O. F. form *porphyrie*, which Cotgrave gives only in the form *porphyre*. **=** L. *porphyrītes*. **=** Gk. πορφυρίτης, porphyry, a hard rock named from its purple colour. **=** Gk. πορφύρα, the purple-fish. See **Purple**.

Porpoise, Porpess. (F. **−** L.) M. E. *porpeys*. **=** O. F. *porpeis*, a porpoise; now obsolete (except Guernsey *pourpeis*), and replaced by *marsouin*, borrowed from G. *meer-schwein* (mere-swine). For *porc-peis. **=** L. *porc-um*, acc. of *porcus*, a pig; *piscem*, acc. of *piscis*, a fish. See **Pork** and **Fish**.

Porridge. (F.) Another form of *pottage*, which first became *poddige* (as preserved in Craven *poddish*) and afterwards *porridge*, just as the Southern E. *errish* is corrupted from *eddish* (A.S. *edisc*), stubble. Similarly, *pottanger* (Palsgrave) was an old form of *porringer*. Cotgrave has ' *potage*, pottage, porridge.'

porringer. (F.) Formed from *porrige* (= *porridge*) by inserted *n*, as in *messenger* (F. *messager*); with E. suffix *-er*. It means a small dish for porridge (above).

Port (1), demeanour. (F. **−** L.) M. E. *port*. **=** F. *port*, 'the carriage, or demeanor of a man;' Cot. A sb. due to the verb *porter*, to carry. **=** L. *portāre*, to carry. Allied to **Fare**. (✓ PER.) Der. *port*, vb., as 'to *port* arms;' and (probably) ' to *port* the hclm '; *port-ed*, P. L. iv. 980. Also *port-er*, a bearer of a burden, substituted for M. E. *portour*, from F. *porteur*. Hence *porter*, the name of a strong malt-liquor, so called from being the favourite drink of London *porters* (1730); *port-folio*, a case large enough to carry *folio* paper in (cf. F. *porte-feuille*), *port-manteau*, F. *portemanteau*, see **Mantle, Mantua**; *port-ly*, *port-li-ness*.

Port (2), a harbour. (L.) M. E. *port*. A. S. *port*. **=** L. *portus*, a harbour; cognate with E. **Ford**. Closely allied to **Port** (3). Brugm. i. § 514.

port (3), a gate, entrance. (F. **−** L.) F. *porte*. **=** L. *porta*, a gate. Allied to Gk. πόρος, a ford, way; see above. **Der.** *port-er*, F. *portier*, L. *portārius*; *port-al*, O. F. *portal*, Late L. *portāle*.

port (4), a dark wine. (Port. **−** L.) Short for *Oporto* wine. **=** Port. *o porto*, i. e. the harbour; where *o* is the def. art. (= Span. *lo* = L. *illum*), and *porto* is from L. *portum*, acc. of *portus*, a harbour.

portal; see **port** (3) above.

portcullis. (F. **−** L.) M.E. *portcolise*. **=** O. F. *porte coleïce* (13th cent.), later *porte coulisse*, or *coulisse*, a portcullis, lit. sliding door. **=** L. *porta*, a door; Late L. *cōlātīcia, (sc. *porta*), from *cōlātus*, pp. of *cōlāre*, to flow, glide, slide; see **Colander** and **Cullis**. We find the Late L. forms *cōlā-*

dissus, cōlācius, porta cōlācia, port-cullis; from the same source.

porte, the Turkish government. (F. –L.) The *Sublime Porte* is a F. translation of *Babi Ali*, the chief office of the Ottoman government, lit. 'high gate;' (Arab. *bāb*, gate, *'alīy*, high). – F. *porte*, a gate. – L. *porta*, gate; see port (3) above.

Portend. (L.) L. *portendere*, to predict; lit. to stretch out towards, point out. – L. *por-* (O. Lat. *port-*), towards; *tendere*, to stretch. **Der.** *portent*, O. F. *portent*, L. *portentum*, neut. of pp. of *portendere*.

Porter (1), a carrier; see Port (1).

Porter (2), a gate-keeper; see Port (3).

Porter (3), a kind of beer; see Port (1).

Portesse, Portous, a breviary. (F. –L.) M. E. *portous, porthors.* – O. F. *portehors*, a translation of the Latin name *portiforium.* – F. *porter*, to carry; *hors*, forth (O. F. *fors*). – L. *portāre*, to carry; *foris*, abroad.

Portico. (Ital. – L.) Ital. *portico.* – L. *porticum*, acc. of *porticus*; see Porch.

Portion. (F. – L.) F. *portion.* – L. acc. *portiōnem*, a share, from *portio*; closely allied to *part-*, stem of *pars*, a part. Brugm. i. § 527.

Portly; see Port (1).

Portrait. (F. – L.) M. F. *pourtraict*, 'a pourtrait;' Cot. – M. F. *pourtraict, pourtrait*, pp. of *pourtraire*, to portray (below).

portray, pourtray. (F. – L.) M. E. *pourtraien.* – O. F. *portraire, pourtraire*, to portray. – Late L. *prōtrahere*, to depict; L. *prōtrahere*, to draw forward, to reveal. – L. *prō*, forth; *trahere*, to draw. See Trace (1).

Pose (1), a position, attitude. (F. – L. – Gk.) Modern; but important. – F. *pose*, attitude. – F. *poser*, to place, set. – Late L. *pausāre*, to cease; also to cause to rest (substituted for L. *pōnere*, the sense of which it took up). – L. *pausa*, a pause. – Gk. παῦσις, a pause. – Gk. παύειν, to make to cease; παύεσθαι, to cease. ¶ One of the most remarkable facts in F. etymology is the extraordinary substitution whereby Late L. *pausāre*, coming to mean 'to cause to rest,' usurped the place of L. *pōnere*, to place, with which it has *no etymological connexion*. This it did so

effectually as to restrict F. *pondre* (=L. *pōnere*) to the sole sense 'to lay eggs,' whilst in all compounds it thrust it aside, so that *compausāre* (F. *composer*) usurped the place of L. *compōnere*, and so on throughout. But note that, on the other hand, the sb. *position* (with all derivatives) is veritably derived from the pp. of *pōnere*; see Position; and see Repose.

Pose (2), to puzzle by questions. (F. – L. *and* Gk.) M. E. *apposen*, to question; not really = F. *apposer*, but substituted for M. E. *opposen*, to oppose, hence, to cross-question; see Oppose. ¶ Confused with *appose*, because of *apposite*, which see. See *Appose* in N. E. D.

Pose (3), a cold in the head. (C.) In Chaucer. A. S. *gepos*, a cough (where *ge-* is a mere prefix). Borrowed from W. *peswch* or *pâs*, a cough; allied to Irish *casachdas*, Russ. *kashele*, prov. E. *hoast*, a cough, Skt. *kās*, to cough. (√QAS.)

Position. (F. – L.) F. *position.* – L. *positiōnem*, acc. of *positio*, a placing. – L. *positus*, pp. of *pōnere*, to place. **β.** *Pōnere* is for *po-sinere*, where *po-* stands for an old prep., and *sinere* is to allow; see Site. ¶ Quite distinct from *pose* (1).

positive. (F. – L.) F. *positif.* – L. *positīuus*, settled. – L. *posit-us*, pp. of *pōnere*, to set, settle.

Posse. (L.) L. *posse*, infin. to be able; used as sb., meaning 'power.' See Potent.

Possess. (L.) L. *possessus*, pp. of *possidēre*, to possess. The orig. sense was 'to remain master.' – L. *pot-*, as in *pot-is*, able, having power; *sedēre*, to sit. Cf. Potent.

Posset, a warm curdled drink. (F.) M. E. *possyt.* – M. F. *possette*, 'a posset of ale and mylke,' Palsgrave. Origin unknown; cf. L. *posca*, sour wine and water. [Irish *pusoid*, a posset, W. *posel*, curdled milk, posset, are borrowed from E.]

Possible. (F. – L.) F. *possible.* – L. *possibilis*, that may be done. Cf. L. *posse*, to be able; see Potent.

Post (1), a stake set in the ground. (L.) M. E. *post*; A. S. *post.* – L. *postis*, a post. Perhaps something firmly fixed. – L. *postus*, short for *positus*, pp. of *pōnere*, to set. See Position.

post (2), a military station, a public letter-carrier, stage on a road. (F. – Ital. –L.) Orig. a military post; then a fixed place on a line of road, a station; then a stage, also a traveller who used relays of horses, &c. — F. *poste*, masc., a carrier, messenger; fem., posting, a riding post. — Ital. *posta*. — Late L. *postus*, fem. *posta*, a post, station. — L. *positus*, pp. of *pōnere*, to place.

Post-, prefix. (L.) L. *post*, after, behind.

post-date; from *post* and *date*.

posterior, hinder. (L.) L. *posterior*, comp. of *posterus*, coming after. — L. *post*, after. **Der.** *posterior-s*, i. e. posterior parts.

posterity. (F. — L.) M. F. *posterité*. — L. *posteritātem*, acc. of *posteritās*, futurity, posterity. — L. *posteri-*, for *posterus*, coming after (above).

postern. (F. — L.) O. F. *posterle*, also spelt *posterne* (by change of suffix); later *poterne*, ' a back-door to a fort;' Cot. — L. *posterula*, a small back-door. — L. *posterus*, behind.

posthumous, postumous. (L.) L. *postumus*, the latest-born; hence, as sb., a posthumous child. Written *posthumus* owing to a popular etymology from *post humum*, forced into the impossible sense of 'after the father is in the ground or buried'; hence F. *posthume*, Port. *posthumo*; but Span. and Ital. *postumo* are right. β. L. *postumus* — **post-tu-mus*, a superl. form of *post*, behind; cf. *op-tu-mus*, best.

postil, an explanatory note or commentary on the Bible. (F. — L.) M. F. *postille*. — Late L. *postilla*, a marginal note in a Bible. Derived by Ducange from L. *post illa uerba*, i. e. after those words, because the glosses were added afterwards.

Postillion. (F. — Ital. — L.) F. *postillon*. — Ital. *postiglione*, a post-boy. — Ital. *posta*, a post; with suffix *-iglione* = L. *-iliōnem*. See post (2) above.

Post-meridian, Pomeridian, belonging to the afternoon. (L.) L. *pōmerīdiānus*, also *postmerīdiānus*, the same. — L. *post*, after; *merīdiānus*, adj., from *merīdiēs*, noon; see Meridian.

post-mortem. (L.) L. *post*, after; *mortem*, acc. of *mors*, death.

post-obit. (L.) L. *post*, after; *obitum*, acc. of *obitus*, death.

postpone, to put off. (L.) L. *post-pōnere*, to put after, delay. — L. *post*, after; *pōnere*, to put.

post-prandial, adj., after-dinner. (L.) From L. *post prandium*, i. e. after dinner. For L. *prandium*, see Brugm. ii. § 165.

postscript. (L.) L. *postscriptum*, that which is written after. — L. *post*, after; *scriptum*, neut. of pp. of *scrībere*, to write.

Postulate, a self-evident proposition. (L.) L. *postulātum*, a thing demanded (and granted); neut. of pp. of *postulāre*, to demand. Derived from *poscere*, to ask. Brugm. i. §§ 483(7), 502.

Posture. (F. — L.) F. *posture*. — L. *positūra*, arrangement. — L. *positus*, pp. of *pōnere*, to put. See Position.

Posy. (F. — L. — Gk.) In all its senses, it is short for *poesy*. It meant a short poem, esp. a short motto in verse on knives and rings, Hamlet, iii. 2. 162; hence it meant a nosegay, because the flowers chosen for it enigmatically represented a posy or motto. It even meant a collection of precious stones, forming a motto; Chambers, Book of Days, i. 221. See Poesy.

Pot. (E.) M. E. *pot*. A. S. *pott*. **+** E. Fries. Du. *pot*; Icel. *pottr*, Swed. *potta*, Dan. *potte*; Low G. *pott*. Also Irish *pota*, Gael. *poit*, W. *pot*, all from E. Also F. *pot*, Bret. *pôd*, Span. *pote*; from Low G. Teut. type **puttoz*. Hence Low L. *pottus*, also spelt *pōtus* (as if from L. *pōtāre*, to drink). Der. *to go to pot*, i. e. into the cooking-pot.

Potable, drinkable. (F. — L.) F. *potable*. — L. *pōtābilis*, drinkable. — L. *pōtāre*, to drink; *pōtus*, drunken. **+** Skt. *pā*, to drink. Allied to Gk. πόσις, drink, πῶμα, drink.

Potash. (E.) From *pot* and *ash*; ash obtained by boiling down burnt vegetable substances in a pot. Latinised as *potassa*; whence *potass-ium*.

Potation. (L.) From L. *pōtātio*, a drinking. — L. *pōtātus*, pp. of *pōtāre*, to drink. See Potable.

Potato. (Span. — Hayti.) Span. *patata*, a potato. — Hayti *batata*, a yam.

Potch, to thrust; see Poach (2).

Potent. (L.) L. *potent-*, stem of *potens*, powerful, pres. part. of *posse*, to be able, *possum*, I am able. *Possum* is short for **pot-sum* or **pote-sum*, from *potis*, powerful, orig. ' a lord;' allied to Skt. *pati-*, a master, lord, Lithuan. *-patis*, Russ. *-pode* in *gos-pode*, lord. Brugm. i. § 158. **Der.** *omnipotent*. And see Despot.

Pother, a bustle, confusion. (E.) Also *pudder*, the same; from *pudder*, vb., to stir, confuse, a variant of Potter.

Potion. (F. — L.) F. *potion*. — L.

pōtiōnem, acc. of *pōtio*, a draught. — L. *pōtus*, drunken; see **Potable, Poison**.

Pottage. (F. — Low G.) M. E. *potage*. — F. *potage*; formed with F. suffix -*age* (L. -*āticum*), from F. *pot*, a pot, of Teut. origin. See **Pot**.

Potter. (E.) To *potter* is to poke about, hence to stir, confuse, disorder, also to do a thing inefficiently; so also *pother*, to poke, disorder (Bailey, Halliwell). These are frequentative forms of *put*, to thrust; see **Put**. Cf. M. Du. *poteren*, ' to search one thoroughly,' Hexham; Du. *peuteren*, to fumble, poke about; Norw. *pota*, M. Swed. *potta*, to poke.

Pottle. (F. — Low G.) M. E. *potel*. — O. F. *potel*, a small pot, small measure; dimin. of F. *pot*, a pot. — Low G. *pott* ; see **Pot**.

potwalloper. (Hybrid.) Lit. ' one who boils a pot;' hence a voter who has a vote because he can boil a pot on his own fire. *Wallop*, to boil fast, is from M. E. *walopen*, to gallop. Golding has ' seething *a-wallop*,' boiling rapidly; tr. of Ovid, f. 82. See **Gallop**.

Pouch. (F. — M. Du.) M. E. *pouche*. — O. F. *pouche*, variant of *poche*; see **Pocket**.

Poult, a chicken. (F. — L.) M. E. *pulte*. — F. *poulet*, a chicken; dimin. of *poule*, a hen. — Late L. *pulla*, a hen; fem. of *pullus*, a young animal. See **Pool** (2). **Der.** *poult-er*, afterwards extended to *poult-er-er*; *poult-r-y* (for *poult-er-y*), A.F. *poletrie*.

Poultice. (F. — L.) Gascoigne has the pl. *pultesses* (Steel Glas, 997). — M. F. **pult-ice*, formed from M. F. *pulte*, ' a poultice;' Cot. [Cf. M. Ital. *poltiglia*, ' a pultis,' Florio.] — Late L. *pulta*, a kind of pap; from *pult*-, as in L. *pult-is*, gen. of *puls*, a thick pap, or pap-like substance. + Gk. πόλτος, porridge.

Poultry; see **Poult**.

Pounce (1), to seize with the claws. (F. — L.) Orig. a term in hawking; a hawk's claws were termed *pounces*; cf. O. F. *ponce*, a fist. A *pounce* is also a punch or stamp (Nares) ; a *pounson* was a dagger (Barbour). Cf. Gascon *pounchoun*; O. F. *poinc-on*, *punch-on* (Ital. *punz-one*, Span. *punz-on*), a punch, sharp point. Cf. Ital. *punzone*, ' a bodkin, a goldsmith's pouncer or *pounce*;' Florio. From the base seen in Ital. *punz-ellare*, to prick, goad, Span. *punz-ar*, to punch. The Span. *punzar*

answers to a Late L. **punctiāre*, not found, but regularly formed from L. *punctus*, pp. of *pungere*. See **Pungent**.

Pounce (2), fine powder. (F. — L.) F. *ponce*; ' *pierre ponce*, a pumis stone;' Cot. — L. *pumicem*, acc. of *pumex*, pumice; see **Pumice**. **Der.** *pouncet-box*.

Pound (1), a weight, a sovereign. (L.) Orig. a weight. M. E. *pund*. A. S. *pund*, pl. *pund*. — L. *pondō*, a weight, used as an indeclinable sb., though orig. meaning ' by weight ' ; allied to *pondus*, a weight. See **Ponder**.

Pound (2), an enclosure for strayed cattle. (E.) M. E. *pond*. A. S. *pund*, an enclosure. Hence *pindar*. **Doublet**, *pond*.

Pound (3), to bruise in a mortar. (E.) The *d* is excrescent. M. E. *pounen*; also *ponen*, as in comp. *to-ponen*, to pound thoroughly. — A. S. *pūnian*, to pound.

Pour. (Late L.) M. E. *pouren*, *poren*, esp. used with *out*. [The orig. sense was to purify, clarify, esp. by pressure or squeezing out; cf. O. F. *purer*, to clarify, also to pour out or drip; so also *depurer*, to clarify, to be clarified, to drip or run out.] Late L. *pūrāre*, to purify. — L. *pūrus*, pure; see **Pure**. So in Guernsey, ' J'o l'cidre qui *pure* dans l'auge,' I hear the cider pouring into the trough (Moisy).

Pourtray; see **Portray**.

Pout (1), to swell out, to sulk. (E.) See below. [W. *pwdu*, to pout, to be sullen, is from E.]

pout (2), a fish. (E.) A. S. *ǣle-pūtan*, pl., eel-pouts. The fish has the power of inflating a membrane above the eyes; hence A. S. -*pūt-a* = *pout-er*. From a Teut. base **pūt-an*-, to swell out. Cf. Du. *puit*, a frog, from its rounded shape; *puit-aal*, an eel-pout; *puist*, a pimple (from a shorter base **pū*-); Swed. *puta*, a cushion (from its shape); Swed. dial. *puta*, to be inflated). Cf. Prov. *pot*, *pout*, a full lip; *fa de pots*, to pout (Mistral). Cf. **Pudding**.

Poverty. (F. — L.) M. E. *pouertee* (= *povertee*). — O. F. *poverte*, later *povreté*, poverty (F. *pauvreté*). — L. *paupertātem*, acc. of *paupertās*, poverty. — L. *pauper*, poor. See **Pauper**.

Powder. (F. — L.) M. E. *poudre*. — F. *poudre*, O. F. *poldre*, *puldre*. Formed with excrescent *d* from L. *puluerem*, acc. of *puluis*, dust. See **Pulverise**.

Power. (F. — L.) M. E. *pöer*; later *po-w-er*, the *w* being inserted. — A. F. *poër*.

O. F. *pooir* (mod. F. *pouvoir*), to be able ; hence, as sb., power. — Late L. *potēre*, to be able ; for L. *posse*, to be able. See **Possible**, **Potent**.

Pox ; see **Pock**.

Praam, Pram, a flat-bottomed boat. (Du. — Slav.) Du. *praam* ; M. Du. *prame*. — Pol. and Bohem. *pram*.

Practice. (F. — L. — Gk.) [Formerly *practise*, from the verb *to practise*. — O. F. *practiser, pratiser*. — Late L. *practicāre*.] The M. E. form of the sb. was *praktike*. — M. F. *practique*, practice. — L. *practica*, fem. of *practicus*. — Gk. πρακτικός, fit for business ; whence ἡ πρακτική, practical science, experience. — Gk. πράσσειν (= *πράκ-γειν), to do, accomplish. **Der.** *practition-er*, formed by needlessly adding *-er* to the older term *practician*, from M.F. *practicien*, 'a practicer in law ;' Cot.

Prætor, Pretor, a Roman magistrate. (L.) L. *prætor*, lit. a goer before, leader ; for *præ-itor*. — L. *præ*, before ; *itor*, a goer, from *īre*, to go.

Pragmatic. (F. — L. — Gk.) F. *pragmatique*, belonging to business. — L. *pragmaticus*. — Gk. πραγματικός, skilled in business. — Gk. πραγματ-, stem of πρᾶγμα (= *πρακ-μα), a deed, thing done. — Gk. πράσσειν (= *πράκ-γειν), to do. See **Practice**.

Prairie, an extensive meadow. (F. — L.) F. *prairie*, a meadow. — Late L. *prātāria*, meadow-land. — L. *prātum*, a meadow.

Praise, sb. (F. — L.) O.F. *preis*, price, value, merit (hence, tribute to merit). — L. *pretium*, price, value. **Der.** *dis-praise*.

Prance. (E.) M.E. *prancen, prauncen*, used of a horse ; it means to make a show, shew off ; apparently an A. F. adaptation of M. E. *pranken*, to trim. Cf. Dan. dial. *prandse, pranse*, to go proudly, as a prancing horse ; *pransk*, proud ; Swed. dial. *prānga*, to shew off. So also M. Du. *pronken*, to make a show, to strut about ; Low G. *prunken*. See below.

Prank (1), to deck, adorn. (E.) M.E. *pranken*, to trim ; allied to obs. E. *prink*, to trim (Nares). *Prink* is a nasalised form of *prick* ; cf. Lowl. Sc. *preek*, to be spruce, *prick-me-dainty*, finical, *prink*, *primp*, to deck, to prick. *Prank* is an allied form to these ; see further under **Prick**. So also M. Du. *proncken*, to display one's dress, *pronckepinken*, *pronckeprinken*, to glitter in a fine dress ; Low G.

Dan. Swed. *prunk*, show, parade ; M. Du. *pryken*, to make a show. From a Teut. type *prenkan-*, str. vb. (pt. t. *prank*, pp. *prunkanoz*).

prank (2), a trick. (E.) An act done to shew off, a trick to make people stare ; from **Prank** (1).

Prate. (E.) M. E. *praten*. Cf. M. Swed. *prata*, Dan. *prate*, to prate, talk ; Swed. Dan. *prat*, talk ; M. Du. and Low G. *praten*, to prate ; Du. *praat*, talk. Of imitative origin ; from a base *prat*. **Der.** *pratt-le*, the frequentative form.

Prawn. (F. ? — L. ?) M. E. *prane*, Prompt. Parv. Hardly (through a lost A. F. form) from L. *perna*, a sea-mussel ; cf. M. Ital. *parnocchie*, 'a fish called shrimps or praunes ;' Florio.

Pray. (F. — L.) M. E. *preyen*. — A.F. and O.F. *preier* (F. *prier*). — L. *precārī*, to pray. See **Precarious**. **Der.** *pray-er*, M. E. *preiere*, O. F. *preiere*, from L. *precāria*, fem. of *precārius*, adj.

Pre-, beforehand. (L. ; or F. — L.) M. F. *pre-*, L. *præ-*, from L. *præ*, prep., before. For *prai*, a locative form. ¶ Hence numerous compounds, many of which, like *precaution*, are of obvious origin.

Preach. (F. — L.) M. E. *prechen*. — O. F. *precher*, *prescher* (*prêcher*). — L. *prædicāre*, to declare. See **Predicate**.

Prebend. (F. — L.) O. F. *prebende* (F. *prébende*). — L. *præbenda*, a payment, stipend from a public source ; orig. fem. of gerundive of *præbēre*, to afford, give. — L. *præ*, before, *habēre*, to have ; whence *præhibēre*, to hold forth, give, contracted to *præbēre*. **Der.** *prebend-ar-y*.

Precarious. (L.) L. *precāri-us*, obtained by prayer or as a favour, doubtful, precarious ; with suffix *-ous*. — L. *precārī*, to pray. — L. *prec-*, stem of *prex*, a prayer. +O. *fragen*, to ask ; Goth. *fraih-nan*, A. S. *frignan*, to ask ; Lith. *praszyti* ; Russ. *prosite* ; Pers. *pursīdan* ; Skt. *pracch*, to ask. (√PREK.) Brugm. i. § 607.

Precaution. (F. — L.) From **Pre-** and **Caution**.

Precede. (F. — L.) O. F. *preceder* (F. *précéder*). — L. *præcēdere*, to go before. — L. *præ*, before ; *cēdere*, to go. See **Cede**. **Der.** *preced-ent* ; *pre-cess-ion*, from the pp. *præcess-us*.

Precentor. (L.) L. *præcentor*, the leader of a choir. — L. *præ*, before ; and *cantor*, a singer, from *canere*, to sing ; see **Cant** (1).

Precept. (F.–L.) O. F. *precept.*– L. *præceptum*, a prescribed rule.– L. *præceptus*, pp. of *præcipere*, to take beforehand, give rules.– L. *præ*, before ; *capere*, to take. Der. *precept-or.*

Precinct. (L.) Late L. *præcinctum*, a boundary.– L. *præcinctus*, pp. of *præcingere*, to gird about.– L. *præ*, in front ; *cingere*, to gird. See Cincture.

Precious. (F.–L.) O. F. *precieus* (F. *précieux*).– L. *pretiōsus*, valuable.– L. *pretium*, price, value. See Price.

Precipice. (F.–L.) F. *précipice.*– L. *præcipitium*, a falling headlong down ; a precipice.– L. *præcipit-*, decl. stem of *præceps*, headlong.– L. *præ*, before ; and *capit-*, decl. stem of *caput*, head. **Der.** *precipitate*, from L. *præcipitāre*, to cast headlong.

Precise. (F.–L.) O. F. *precis*, strict. – L. *præcīsus*, cut off, concise, strict ; pp. of *præcīdere*, to cut off.– L. *præ*, in front ; *cædere*, to cut. See Cæsura.

Preclude. (L.) L. *præclūdere*, to shut off, hinder access to.– L. *præ*, in front ; *claudere* (pp. *clūsus*), to shut. **Der.** *preclus-ion*, from the pp. *præclūsus*. Cf. Conclude.

Precocious. (L.) Coined (with suffix *-ous*) from L. *præcoci-*, decl. stem of *præcox*, prematurely ripe. – L. *præ*, before ; *coquere*, to cook, to ripen. See Cook.

Precursor. (L.) L. *præcursor*, a forerunner. – L. *præ*, before ; *cursor*, a runner, from *curs-us*, pp. of *currere*, to run. See Current.

Predatory, given to plundering. (L.) L. *prædātōrius*, plundering.– L. *prædātor*, a plunderer.– L. *prædārī*, to plunder.– L. *præda*, booty. β. *Præda* = **præhed-a*, that which is seized beforehand ; from *præ*, before, and *hed-*, base of *-hendere*, to seize, get, cognate with *get* ; see Get. (So also *prendere* = *pre-hendere*.) γ. Irish *spreidh*, cattle, W. *praidd*, flock, herd, booty, prey, are from L. *præda*.

Predecessor. (L.) L. *prædēcessor.* – L. *præ*, before ; *dēcessor*, one who retires from an office, from *dēcessus*, pp. of *dēcēdere*, to depart.– L. *dē*, from ; *cēdere*, to go. See Cede.

Predicate. (L.) From pp. of *prædicāre*, to publish, proclaim, declare.– L. *præ*, before ; *dicāre*, to tell, publish, allied to *dīcere*, to say. See Diction.

predicament. (L.) L. *prædicāmentum*, a term in logic, one of the most

general classes into which things can be divided.– L. *prædicāre*, to declare (above).

Predict. (L.) L. *prædictus*, pp. of *prædīcere*, to say beforehand, foretell.– L. *præ*, before ; *dīcere*, to say. See Diction.

Predilection, a choosing beforehand. (L.) From L. *præ*, before ; *dīlectio*, choice, from *dīligere*, to choose ; see Diligent.

Preface. (F.–L.) O. F. *preface.*– L. *præfātio*, a preface. – L. *præfātus*, spoken before, pp. of *præfārī*, to speak before.– L. *præ*, before, *fārī*, to speak ; See Fate.

Prefect, a governor. (F.–L.) M. E. *prefect.* – O. F. *prefect* (F. *préfet*). – L. *præfectus*, one set over others ; pp. of *præficere*, to set before. – L. *præ-*, before ; *facere*, to make, set. See Fact.

Prefer. (F.–L.) O. F. *preferer.*– L. *præferre*, to set in front, prefer.– L. *præ*, before ; *ferre*, to bear, set. See Fertile.

Prefigure. (F.–L.) From Pre- and Figure.

Pregnant, fruitful, with child. (L.) In Milton, P. L. ii. 779. Directly from L. *prægnantem*, acc. of *prægnans*, pregnant. *Prægnans* has the form of a pres. part. of an obs. verb **prægnāre*, to be before a birth, to be about to bear.– L. *præ*, before ; **gnāre*, to bear, of which the pp. *gnātus* or *nātus* is used as the pp. of the inceptive infin. *nascī*, to be born. See Natal.

Prehensile, adapted for grasping. (L.) Coined with suffix *-ile* (L. *-ilis*) from L. *prehens-us*, pp. of *prehendere*, *prendere*, to lay hold of.– L. *præ*, before ; obsolete *-hendere*, to grasp, cognate with E. Get, q.v.

Prejudge. (F.–L.) O. F. *prejuger.* – L. *præiūdicāre*, to judge beforehand. – L. *præ*, before ; *iūdicāre*, to judge, from *iūdic-*, stem of *iūdex*, a judge. See Judge.

prejudice. (F.–L.) O.F. *prejudice.* – L. *præiūdicium*, a judicial examination, previous to a trial, also a prejudice.– L. *præ*, before ; *iūdicium*, judgment, from *iūdic-*, stem of *iūdex*, a judge.

Prelate, a church dignitary. (F.–L.) O. F. *prelat.*– L. *prælātus*, set above ; used as pp. of *præferre*, to prefer (but from a different root).– L. *præ*, before ; *lātus*, borne, set, pp. of *tollere*, to lift, bear. See Tolerate.

Preliminary, introductory. (F.–L.)

Coined from *pre-*, prefix, before; and M.F. *liminaire*, 'set before the entry of, dedicatory,' Cot. From L. *præ*, before; and *līmināris*, adj., coming at the beginning or threshold.—L. *līmin-*, stem of *līmen*, threshold. See **Limit**.

Prelude, an introduction. (F.—L.) M. F. *prelude*, 'a preludium, preface, preamble;' Cot.—Late L. *præludium.—L. *præludere*, to play beforehand, give a prelude.—L. *præ*, before; *ludere*, to play. See **Ludicrous**.

Premature. (F.—L.) From **Pre-** and **Mature**.

Premier. (F.—L.) F. *premier*, first. —L. *prīmārium*, acc. of *prīmārius*, chief. —L. *prīmus*, first. See **Prime** (1).

Premiss, Premise. (F.—L.) Better *premiss* than *premise*.—O. F. *premisse* (F. *prémisse*), in use in the 14th century (Littré).—L. *præmissa* (*sententia* being understood), a premiss, lit. that which is sent before or stated beforehand. Fem. of *præmissus*, pp. of *præmittere*, to send before.—L. *præ*, before; *mittere*, to send. See **Missile**. Der. *premis-es*, s. pl., the adjuncts of a building, first stated in full, in a lease, and afterwards referred to as the *premises*; or otherwise, due to the custom of beginning leases with *premises* setting forth the names of the grantor, grantee, and things granted. Also *premise*, vb., with accent on *i*.

Premium. (L.) L. *præmium*, profit; lit. 'a taking before;' for *præ-imium. —L. *præ*, before; *emere*, to take. Cf. **Exempt**.

Premonish, to warn beforehand. (F. —L.) Coined from *pre-*, before (for L. *præ*); and *monish*, a corrupted form of M. E. *monesten*, to warn, Wyclif, 2 Cor. vi. I. See **Admonish**. Der. *premonitor-y*, from L. *præmonitor*, one who warns beforehand, from *præmonēre*, to warn beforehand.

Prentice, short for **Apprentice**, q. v.

Prepare. (F.—L.) M. F. *preparer*; Cot.—L. *præparāre*, to make ready beforehand.—L. *præ*, before; *parāre*, to prepare. See **Pare**.

Prepense, premeditated. (F.—L.) 1. As if from M.F. *pre-*, beforehand; *penser*, to think.—L. *præ*, beforehand; *pensāre*, to weigh, ponder, frequent. form of *pendere*, to weigh; see **Pendant**. 2. But in the phr. *malice prepense*, it is an altered

form of A.F. *purpensé*, pp. of *purpenser*, to meditate on, with prefix *pur-* (F. *pour-*) from L. *prō*.

preponderate. (L.) From pp. of L. *præponderāre*, to outweigh.—L. *præ*, before; *ponderāre*, to weigh; see **Ponder**.

Preposition. (F.—L.) O. F. *preposition*.—L. acc. *præpositiōnem*, a setting before; a preposition (in grammar).—L. *præpositus*, pp. of *præpōnere*, to set before. —L. *præ*, before; *pōnere*, to place. See **Position**.

Preposterous. (L.) L. *præposter-us*, inverted, hind side before; with suffix *-ous*. —L. *præ*, before; *posterus*, later, coming after. See **Post-**.

Prerogative. (F.—L.) A. F. *prerogative*, a privilege.—L. *prærogātīva*, a previous choice, preference, privilege.— L. *præ*, before; *rogāre*, to ask. See **Rogation**.

Presage. (F.—L.) O. F. *presage*.— L. *præsāgium*, a divining beforehand.—L. *præsāgīre*, to perceive beforehand.—L. *præ*, before; *sāgīre*, to observe, perceive. See **Sagacious**.

Presbyter. (L.—Gk.) L. *presbyter*. —Gk. πρεσβύτερος, an elder; orig. elder, comparative of πρέσβυς, old. Cf. L. *priscus*, ancient.

Prescience. (F.—L.) O.F. *prescience*. —L. *præscientia*, foreknowledge.—L. *præ*, before; *scientia*, knowledge. See **Science**.

Prescribe. (L.) L. *præscrībere*, to write beforehand, prescribe; pp. *præscriptus* (whence *prescription*).—L. *præ*, before; *scrībere*, to write. See **Scribe**.

Present (1), near at hand. (F.—L.) O. F. *present*.—L. *præsent-*, stem of *præsens*, i. e. being in front or near.—L. *præ*, in front; *-sens*, for *es-ens, being, from √ES, to be. Cf. **Absent**. Der. *present-ly*; *presence*, sb., O. F. *presence*, L. *præsentia*.

present (2), to give. (F.—L.) O. F. *presenter*.—L. *præsentāre*, to place before, hold out, offer.—L. *præsent-*, stem of *præsens* (above). Der. *present*, sb., a gift.

Presentiment. (F.—L.) M. F. *presentiment*, 'a fore-feeling;' Cot.—L. *præsentī-re*, to feel beforehand.—L. *præ*, before; *sentīre*, to feel. See **Sense**.

Preserve. (F.—L.) O. F. *preserver*, to preserve.—L. *præ*, beforehand; *seruāre*, to keep. See **Serve**.

Preside. (F.—L.) O. F. *presider*, to

preside, govern. — L. *præsidēre*, to sit before, preside over. — L. *præ*, in front; *sedēre*, to sit. See Sedentary.

Press (1), to squeeze. (F. — L.) M. E. *pressen*. — F. *presser*. — L. *pressāre*, frequent. of *premere* (pp. *pressus*), to press. **Der.** *press*, sb.; *press-ure*.

Press (2), to hire men for service, make men serve as sailors, &c. (F. — L.) *Press* is a corruption of the old word *prest*, ready; whence *prest-money*, ready money advanced to a man hired for service, earnest money; also *imprest*, a verb (now *impress*), to give a man earnest money. When it became common to use *compulsion* to *force* men into service, it was confused with the verb *to press*. *Prest money* was money lent. — O.F. *prester* (F. *prêter*), to lend, advance money. — L. *præstāre*, to stand forth, come forward, furnish, offer, give. — L. *præ*, in front; *stāre*, to stand. See **State**. **Der.** *press-gang*, *im-press*, *im-press-ment*.

Prestige. (F. — L.) F. *prestige*, an illusion, fascination, influence due to fame. — L. *præstigium*, a deception, illusion, jugglery. For **præstrigium*, the 2nd *r* being lost (Brug. i. § 483). — L. *præstring-ere*, to bind fast, to dull, dim, blind. — L. *præ*, before; *stringere*, to bind. See **Stringent**.

Presume. (F. — L.) M. E. *presumen*. — O. F. *presumer*. — L. *præsūmere*, to take beforehand, presume, imagine. — L. *præ*, before; *sūmere*, to take; see **Assume**. **Der.** *presumpt-ion*, &c. (from the pp. *præsumpt-us*).

Pretend. (F. — L.) O. F. *pretendre*. — L. *prætendere*, to spread before, hold out as an excuse, allege, pretend. — L. *præ*, before; *tendere*, to stretch. See **Tend** (1). **Der.** *pretence*, misspelt for *pretense* (O. F. *pretensse*, f., Godefroy), from the fem. of Late L. *prætensus*, used for L. *prætentus*, pp. of *prætendere*.

Preter-, prefix. (L.) L. *præter*, beyond; comparative form of *præ*, before; see **Pre-**.

Preterite. (F. — L.) M. E. *preterit*. — O. F. *preterit*, m., *preterite*, fem. — L. *præteritus*, pp. of *præterīre*, to pass by. — L. *præter*, beyond; *īre*, to go.

Pretermit, to omit. (L.) L. *prætermittere*, to allow to go past. — L. *præter*, beyond; *mittere*, to send. See **Missile**. **Der.** *pretermiss-ion*, from the pp.

Preternatural. (L.) From L. *præter*,

beyond; and *natural*, adj., from *nature*. See **Nature**.

Pretext. (F. — L.) M. F. *pretexte*, a pretext. — L. *prætextum*, a pretext; orig. neut. of *prætextus*, pp. of *prætexere*, lit. to weave in front. — L. *præ*, in front; *texere*, to weave. See **Text**.

Pretty. (E.) M. E. *prati*; A. S. *prætig*, *prættig*, *pætig*, orig. deceitful, tricky; hence clever, cunning, the usual M. E. sense. Formed with suffix -*ig* from A. S. *præt*, deceit, trickery. Cf. Lowl. Sc. *pratty*, pretty, tricky, from *prat*, a trick (G. Douglas). + Icel. *prettr*, a trick; *pretta*, to cheat; E. Fries. *pret*, a trick, *prettig*, jocose, droll, pleasant; M. Du. *pratte*, *perte*, Du. *part*, a trick, deceit. Of uncertain origin.

Prevail. (F. — L.) O. F. *prevail*, 1 p. pr. of *prevaloir*, to prevail. — L. *præualēre*, to have great power. — L. *præ*, before, excessively; *ualēre*, to be strong. See **Valid**. **Der.** *prevalent*, from L. *præualent-*, stem of pres. pt. of *præualēre*, to prevail.

Prevaricate. (L.) From pp. of L. *præuāricārī*, to straddle, hence to swerve, shuffle, shift, quibble. — L. *præ*, before, excessively; *uāric-us*, straddling, from *uārus*, crooked. See **Varicose**.

Prevent. (L.) The old meaning was 'to go before'; cf. M. F. *prevenir*, 'to prevent, anticipate, forestall;' Cot. — L. *præuent-us*, pp. of *præuenīre*, to go before. — L. *præ*, before; *uenīre*, to come. See **Venture**.

Previous. (L.) L. *præui-us*, on the way before, going before; with suffix -*ous*. — L. *præ*, before; *uia*, a way.

Prey, sb. (F. — L.) A. F. *preie* (F. *proie*). — L. *præda*, prey. See **Predatory**. **Der.** *prey*, vb.

Prial, three of a sort, at cards. (F. — L.) A contraction of *pair-royal*; (see Nares).

Price. (F. — L.) M. E. *pris*. — O. F. *pris*, also spelt *preis*, price, value, merit. — L. *pretium*, price. See **Precious**.

Prick. (E.) M. E. *prikke*, *prike*, sb. A. S. *pricu*, *prica*, a point, prick, dot; *prician*, to prick. + M. Du. *prick*, Du. *prik*, a prickle; Dan. *prik*, Swed. *prick*, a dot, mark; E. Fries., Low G. *prik*. Also Du., E. Fries., Low G. *prikken*, to prick; Dan. *prikke*, Swed. *pricka*, to dot. From a Teut. base **prik*, to prick, dot. **Der.** *prick*, vb.; *prick-le*, sb., from A. S. *pricel*.

Pride. (F. — L.) M. E. *pride*, *prude*. A. S. *prȳte*, pride; regularly formed (by the usual change from *ū* to *ȳ*) from A. S. *prūt*, proud, of F. origin. See **Proud.**

Priest. (L. – Gk.) M. E. *preest*; A. S. *prēost.* Contracted (like O. F. *prestre*, O. Sax. *prēstar*, G. *priester*) from L. *presbyter.* Cf. '*Prester John.*' See **Presbyter.** ¶ Abnormal; perhaps *presbyter* was apprehended as **prebyster.*

Prig (1), to steal. (E.) Cant *prygge*, to ride, ride off with a horse which a man has to take care of; *prigger of prauncers*, a horse-stealer; see Harman's Caveat, pp. 42, 43, and p. 84, col. 3. Modification of *prick*, to spur, to ride; Spenser, F. Q. i. 1. 1. See **Prick.**

Prig (2), a pert, pragmatical fellow. (E.) From the verb *to prick*, in the sense to trim, adorn, dress up. Lowl. Sc. *prig-me-dainty*, *prick-me-dainty*, a prig. See above.

Prim, neat. (F. – L.) O.F. *prim*, masc., *prime*, fem., prime, thin, forward, also *prime*, masc. and fem., thin, slender, small, as *cheveux primes*, 'smooth or delicate hair;' Cot. The sense is first-grown, small, delicate. – L. *prīmus*, first (below). ¶ The word was perhaps confused with *prink*, to deck; see **Prank.**

prime (1), first, chief. (F. – L.) F. *prime*, properly ' prime,' the first canonical hour. – L. *prīma*, fem. of *prīmus*, first. *Prīmus* is for *prismus, and is related to *pris-cus*, ancient, *pris-tinus*, primitive, and to *prius*, adv., former. Brugm. ii. § 165. Cf. A. S. *for-ma*, first, from *fore* (see **Former**); Gk. πρῶ-τος, first, from πρό; Skt. *pra-ta-ma-*, first. **Der.** *prim-ary*; *prim-ate*, O. F. *primat*, L. acc. *prīm-ātem*, from *prīmās*, a chief man.

prime (2), to make a gun quite ready. (F. – L.) Cf. *prime*, to trim trees; *prime*, first position in fencing; and esp. the phr. ' to put into *prime* order.' A peculiar use of *prime* (1).

primero, an old game at cards. (Span. – L.) Span. *primero*, lit. ' first.' – L. *prī-mārius*, chief; see **Premier.**

primeval. (L.) Coined from L. *prīm-us*, first; *æv-um*, age; with suffix -*al*; cf. L. *prīmæuus*, primeval.

primitive. (F. – L.) F. *primitif.* – L. *prīmitīuus*, earliest of its kind. – L. *prīmit-us*, adv., for the first time. – L. *prīmus*, first.

primogeniture. (F. – L.) M. F. *primogeniture*, ' the being eldest;' Cot. – L. *prīmogenitus*, first-born. – L. *prīmo-*, for

prīmus, first; *genitus*, pp. of *gignere* (base *gen-*), to beget, produce; see **Genus.**

primordial, original. (F. – L.) F. *primordial.* – L. *prīmordiālis*, original. – L. *prīmordium*, origin. – L. *prīm-us*, first; *ordīrī*, to begin, allied to *ordo*, order.

primrose. (F. – L.) As if from F. *prime rose*, first rose; L. *prīma rosa.* Such is the popular etymology; but, historically, *primrose* is a substitution for M. E. *primerole*, a primrose. Dimin. of Late L. *prīmula*, a primrose (still preserved in Span. *primula*, the same). Again, *primula* is a derivative of *prīmus*, first. ¶ Thus the word *rose* was only associated with *primrose* by a popular blunder.

prince. (F. – L.) F. *prince.* – L. *principem*, acc. of *princeps*, a chief, lit. ' taking the first place.' – L. *prin-*, for *prīm-us*, first; *capere*, to take; see **Capital.**

principal. (F. – L.) F. *principal.* – L. *principālis*, chief. – L. *princip-*, stem of *princeps*, a chief (above).

principle. (F. – L.) The *l* is an E. addition, as in *syllable.* – F. *principe*, a principle, maxim; orig. beginning. – L. *principium*, a beginning. – L. *princip-*, stem of *princeps*, taking the first place; see **prince** (above).

Print, sb. (F. – L.) M. E. *printe*, *prente*, *preinte*; short for *empreinte*, borrowed from M. F. *empreinte*, ' a stamp, print;' Cot. See **Imprint.** Der. *print*, vb.; *re-print.*

Prior (1), former. (L.) L. *prior*, former. Used as comparative of the superl. *prīmus*; see **Prime.**

prior (2), head of a priory. (F. – L.) M. E. *priour.* – A. F. *priour*; F. *prieur.* – L. *priōrem*, acc. of *prior*, former, hence, a superior; see above.

Prise, Prize, a lever. (F. – L.) '*Prise*, a lever;' Halliwell. Hence ' to *prise* open a box,' or corruptly, ' to *pry* open.' – F. *prise*, a grasp, tight hold (hence, leverage). Orig. fem. of *pris*, pp. of *prendre*, to grasp. – L. *prehendere*, to grasp. See **Prehensile.**

Prism. (L. – Gk.) L. *prisma.* – Gk. πρίσμα (stem πρισματ-), a prism; lit. a piece sawn off. – Gk. πρίειν, for *πρίσειν, to saw. (Gk. √πρίς.) **Der.** *prismat-ic.*

Prison. (F. – L.) O. F. *prisun*, F. *prison*; cf. Ital. *prigione*, a prison. – L. acc. *prensiōnem*, acc. of *prensio*, a seizing, seizure. – L. *prensus*, for *prehensus*, pp. of *prehendere*, to seize. See **Prehensile.**

Pristine, ancient. (F. – L.) M. F. *pristine.* – L. *pristinus,* ancient; allied to L. *pris-cus,* former, and to **prime** (1).

Private. (L.) L. *prīuātus,* apart; pp. of *prīuāre,* to bereave. – L. *prīuus,* single; lit. put forward, sundered from the rest.

Privet, a shrub. (F. ? – L. ?) *Privet* is of unknown origin. *Privet* also occurs as a spelling of *private,* and one of the names of privet is *privy,* spelt *priuie* by Tusser; but there is no sure connexion. We also find, for privet, the names *prim, primprint, prime print*; perhaps *print* may have arisen from *prim't,* i. e. primed or trimmed. Prob. named from being formally cut and trimmed; cf. *prime,* to cut trees (Halliwell). See **Prim** and **Prime** (1).

Privilege. (F. – L.) O. F. *privilege.* – L. *prīuilēgium,* (1) a bill against a person, (2) an ordinance in favour of one, a privilege. – L. *prīui-,* for *prīuus,* single; *lēg-,* stem of *lex,* law.

privy, private. (F. – L.) O. F. *prive* (F. *privé*), private. – L. *prīuātus,* private; see **Private.**

Prize (1), a thing captured from the enemy or won in a lottery. (F. – L.) F. *prise,* a seizure, also, a prize; see **Prise.**

Prize (2), to value highly. (F. – L.) M. E. *prisen.* – F. *priser,* to esteem. – O. F. *pris* (F. *prix*), a price, value. – L. *pretium,* value. See **Price.**

Prize (3), the same as **Prise.**

Pro-, prefix. (L. *or* Gk. ; *or* F. – L.) L. *pro-,* prefix, before; cf. also *prō* (= *prōd*), an abl. form, used as a prep. Also Gk. πρo-, prefix; πρό, prep., before; cf. Skt. *pra,* before, away. See *pre-,* prefix; *pri-or, pri-me, pri-vate, prow, pro-vost,* &c.

Proa, Proe, Prow, Prau, a small ship. (Malay.) Malay *prāhu, prāu,* a general term for small ships.

Probable. (F. – L.) F. *probable.* – L. *probābilis,* that may be proved. – L. *probāre,* to test, prove, orig. to try the goodness. – L. *probus,* good, excellent. See **Prove.**

probation. (F. – L.) F. *probation.* – L. acc. *probātiōnem,* a trial, proof. – L. *probātus,* pp. of *probāre,* to test.

probe. (L.) A coined word; cf. Late L. *proba,* a proof. – L. *probāre,* to test; see above.

probity. (F. – L.) F. *probité,* honesty. – L. *probitātem,* acc. of *probitās,* honesty. – L. *probus,* honest, excellent.

Problem. (F. – L. – Gk.) O. F. *probleme*; F. *problème.* – L. *problēma.* – Gk. πρόβλημα, a thing thrown forward, or put forward as a question for discussion. – Gk. πρό, forward; βλῆμα, a casting, from βάλλειν, to cast.

Proboscis. (L. – Gk.) L. *proboscis.* – Gk. προβοσκίς, an elephant's trunk or 'feeder.' – Gk. πρό, in front; βόσκειν, to feed; see **Botany.**

Proceed. (F. – L.) O. F. *proceder.* – L. *prōcēdere,* to go forward. – L. *prō,* before; *cēdere,* to go. See **Cede. Der.** *process* (mod. F. *procès*); *process-ion.*

Proclaim. (F. – L.) F. *proclamer,* 'to proclame;' Cot. – L. *proclāmāre,* to call out. – L. *prō,* forth; *clāmāre,* to cry out. See **Claim.**

Proclivity. (L.) From L. *prōclīuitās,* a downward slope, tendency. – L. *prōclīuus,* sloping forward. – L. *prō,* forward; *clīuus,* a slope. (√KLEI.) Cf. **Acclivity.**

Procrastinate, to postpone. (L.) From pp. of L. *prōcrastināre,* to delay, put off till the morrow. – L. *prō,* forward, off; *crastinus,* belonging to the morrow, from *crās,* morrow.

Procreate. (L.) L. *prōcreātus,* pp. of *prōcreāre,* to generate. – L. *prō,* before, forth; *creāre,* to produce. See **Create.**

Proctor. (L.) M. E. *proketour*; short form of *procuratour.* – O. F. *procurator.* – L. acc. *prōcūrātōrem*; see **Procurator.**

Procumbent, prostrate. (L.) L. *prōcumbent-,* stem of *prōcumbens,* pres. pt. of *prōcumbere,* to sink forwards. – L. *prō,* forwards; *cumbere,* to recline, allied to *cubāre,* to lie down. See **Covey.**

Procurator. (L.) L. *prōcūrātor.* – L. *prōcūrāre*; see below.

procure. (F. – L.) F. *procurer.* – L. *prōcūrāre,* to take care of, manage. – L. *prō,* before; *cūrāre,* to take care, from *cūra,* care. See **Cure.**

Prodigal. (F. – L.) O. F. *prodigal.* – Late Lat. *prōdigālis*; due to L. *prōdigus,* lavish; for **prōd-agus.* – L. *prōd-,* forth; and *agere,* to do, act. See **Agent.**

Prodigy. (F. – L.) Englished from F. *prodige,* a prodigy, wonder. – L. *prōdigium,* a token, portent, prophetic sign. β. Perhaps for **prōdagium,* i. e. a saying beforehand, from *prōd* (*prō*), before, and **agium,* a saying, as in *ad-agium*; see **Adage.** Brugm. i. § 759.

Produce, vb. (L.) L. *prōdūcere*, to bring forward. ‒ L. *prō*, forward; *dūcere*, to lead. See **Duke. Der.** *product-ive, -ion* (from the pp. below).

product, sb. (L.) L. *prōductus*, produced; pp. of *prōdūcere* (above).

Proem. (F.‒L.‒Gk.) M. F. *proëme,* 'a proem, preface;' Cot. ‒ L. *prooemium*. ‒ Gk. *προοίμιον*, an introduction. ‒ Gk. *πρό*, before; *οἶμος*, a way, path, from √EI, to go.

Profane, impious. (F.‒L.) F. *profane.* ‒ L. *profānus*, unholy; lit. before (i. e. outside of) the temple. ‒ L. *prō*, before; *fānum*, a temple.

Profess. (F.‒L.) We find M. E. *professed*, pp., Englished from O. F. *profes,* masc., *professe*, fem., professed. ‒ L. *professus*, pp. of *profitērī*, to avow. ‒ L. *prō*, forth; *fatērī*, to speak; see **Confess.**

Proffer. (F.‒L.) From O. F. *profrir, porofrir* (Godefroy), to proffer. ‒ O. F. *por-*, prefix (L. *prō-*); and *ofrir, offrir,* from L. *offerre*, to offer. See **Offer.**

Proficient. (L.) L. *prōficient-*, stem of pres. pt. of *prōficere*, to make progress, advance. ‒ L. *prō*, forward; *facere*, to make. See **Fact.**

Profile. (Ital.‒L.) Ital. *profilo*, a sketch of a picture, outline (Florio). ‒ L. *prō*, before, in front; *fīlum*, a thread (Ital. *filo*, thread, line). ¶ The mod. F. *profil* is also from Ital. *profilo.*

Profit. (F.‒L.) M. E. *profit.* ‒ F. *profit.* ‒ L. *prōfectum*, neut. of *prōfectus*, pp. of *prōficere*, to make progress, be profitable. See **Proficient.**

Profligate. (L.) L. *prōflīgātus*, cast down, abandoned, dissolute; pp. of *prōflīgāre*, to dash down. ‒ L. *prō*, forward; *flīgere*, to strike, dash. See **Afflict.**

Profound, deep. (F.‒L.) F. *profond.* ‒ L. *profundum*, acc. of *profundus*, deep. ‒ L. *prō*, forward, hence downward; *fundus*, bottom, allied to **Bottom. Der.** *profund-ity*, M. F. *profondité.*

Profuse, lavish. (L.) L. *profūsus*, pp. of *profundere*, to pour forth. ‒ L. *prō*, forth; *fundere*, to pour. See **Fuse** (1).

Progenitor. (F.‒L.) Formerly *progenitour*. ‒ M. F. *progeniteur*. ‒ L. *prōgenitōrem*, acc. of *prōgenitor*, an ancestor. ‒ L. *prō*, before; *genitor*, a parent, from the base of *gignere*, to beget. (√GEN.) See **Genus.**

progeny. (F.‒L.) O. F. *progenie.* ‒ L. *prōgeniem*, acc. of *prōgeniēs*, lineage,

offspring. ‒ L. *prō-*, forth; *genus*, kin. See **Genus.**

Prognostic, a presage. (F.‒L.‒Gk.) M. F. *prognostique*; Cot. ‒ L. *prognōsticon.* ‒ Gk. *προγνωστικόν*, a token of the future. ‒ Gk. *πρό*, before; *γνωστικός*, good at knowing. See **Gnostic.**

Programme, Program. (F.‒L.‒Gk.) Now spelt as if from F. *programme*; formerly *programma* (1706), from L. *programma.* ‒ Gk. *πρόγραμμα*, a public notice in writing. ‒ Gk. *πρό*, beforehand; *γράμμα*, a writing, from *γράφειν*, to write.

Progress, advancement. (F.‒L.) M. F. *progrez* (F. *progrès*). ‒ L. *prōgressum*, acc. of *prōgressus*, an advance. ‒ L. *prōgressus*, pp. of *prōgredī*, to go forward. ‒ L. *prō*, forward; and *gradī*, to walk. See **Grade.**

Prohibit, to check. (L.) From L. *prohibitus*, pp. of *prohibēre*, to hold before one, put in one's way, prohibit. ‒ L. *prō*, before; *habēre*, to have, keep. See **Habit.**

Project, sb., a plan. (F.‒L.) M. F. *project* (F. *projet*), a project, purpose. ‒ L. *prōiectum*, neut. of *prōiectus*, pp. of *prōicere* (*proiicere*), to fling forth; hence (in Late L.) to purpose, plan. ‒ L. *prō*, forth; *iacere*, to cast. See **Jet** (1).

Prolate, extended in the direction of the polar axis. (L.) L. *prōlātus*, extended. ‒ L. *prō*, forward; *lātus*, carried, pp. of *tollere*, to lift, bear. See **Tolerate.**

Prolepsis, anticipation. (L.‒Gk.) L. *prolēpsis.* ‒ Gk. *πρόληψις*, lit. a taking beforehand. ‒ Gk. *πρό*, before; *λῆψις*, a seizing, from *λήψ-ομαι*, fut. of *λαμβάνειν*, to seize. See **Catalepsy.**

Proletarian, a citizen of the lowest class, useful only by producing children. (L.) From L. *prōlētārius*, one who served the state by help of his children only. ‒ L. *prōles*, offspring (below).

prolific. (F.‒L.) F. *prolifique*, fruitful. ‒ L. *prōli-*, decl. stem of *prōles*, offspring; *-ficus*, from *facere*, to make. Perhaps L. *prōles* = *prō-oles*, from *prō*, before, and **olēre*, to grow, whence *ad-olescere*, to grow up; cf. *sub-oles, ind-oles.* See **Adult.**

Prolix. (F.‒L.) F. *prolixe.* ‒ L. *prōlixus*, extended. Lit. ' that which has flowed forth ' or beyond bounds; from *prō*, forth, *liquēre, līquī*, to flow. Cf. *ē-lixus*, soaked. See **Liquid.**

Prolocutor, the chairman of a con-

ference. (L.) L. *prōlocūtor*, an advocate.
— L. *prōlocūtus*, pp. of *prōloquī*, to speak
in public. — L. *prō*, publicly ; *loquī*, to
speak. See **Loquacious.**

Prologue, a preface. (F. — L. — Gk.)
F. *prologue.* — L. *prŏlogum*, acc. of *prologus.*
— Gk. πρόλογος, a fore-speech. — Gk. πρό,
before ; λόγος, a speech. See **Logic.**

Prolong, to continue. (F. — L.) M. E.
prolongen. — F. *prolonger.* — L. *prolongāre*,
to prolong. — L. *prō-*, forward ; *longus*,
long. See **Long.** Doublet, *purloin.*

Promenade, a walk. (F. — L.) Formed
with O. F. suffix *-ade* (< L. *-āta*) from O. F.
promener, to walk. — Late L. *prōmināre*,
to drive forwards. — L. *prō*, forwards ; Late
L. *mināre*, to drive, lead ; from L. *minārī*,
to threaten. See **Menace.**

Prominent, projecting, forward. (L.)
L. *prōminent-*, stem of pres. pt. of *prōminēre*, to project forward. — L. *prō*, forward ; *-minēre*, to project. See **Menace.**

Promiscuous, mixed, confused. (L.)
For L. *prōmiscuus*, mixed. — L. *prō*, forward
(here of slight force); *miscēre*, to mix.
See **Miscellaneous.**

Promise, an agreement to do a thing.
(F. — L.) Formerly *promes.* — F. *promesse.*
'a promise;' Cot. — L. *prōmissa*, fem. of
prōmissus, pp. of *prōmittere*, to send or
put forth, to promise. — L. *prō*, forward ;
mittere, to send. See **Missile.** Der.
promiss-o-ry.

Promontory, a headland. (L.) L.
prōmonturium, a ridge, headland. Prob.
from *prōminēre*, to jut out ; see **Prominent,** and cf. **Mount.**

Promote, to advance, further. (L.)
From L. *prōmōt-us*, pp. of *prōmouēre*, to
move forward. — L. *prō*, forward ; *mouēre*,
to move. See **Move.**

Prompt. (F. — L.) F. *prompt.* — L.
promptum, acc. of *promptus, promtus*,
brought to light, at hand, ready, pp. of
prōmere, to bring forward ; for **prōd-imere.*
— L. *prōd*, forward ; *emere*, to take, bring.
Cf. **Exempt.**

Promulgate. (L.) From pp. of L.
prōmulgāre to publish. (Of unknown
origin.)

Prone. (F. — L.) M. F. *prone.* — L. *prō-
num*, acc. of *prōnus*, inclined towards.
Prōnus is prob. allied to Gk. πρηνής,
headlong ; cf. Skt. *pravaṇa*, inclined to,
prone.

Prong, spike of a fork. (E.) Spelt

prongue in Levins (1570). The M. E.
pronge, a pang, sharp pain, is the same
word. Cf. M. E. *prangelen*, to constrain
(Havelok). Also Du. *prangen*, to pinch,
oppress ; M. Du. *prangen*, to oppress,
shackle, constrain ; *prange*, a muzzle,
shackle, collar ; Low G. *prangen*, to press,
push hard ; *prange*, a stake ; G. *pranger*,
a pillory ; Goth. *ana-praggan* (= *-prangan*),
to press. All from a Teut. base **prang*,
to press, nip, push.

Pronoun. (F. — L.) Coined from L.
prō, for ; and E. *noun* ; suggested by F.
pronom, L. *prōnōmen*, a pronoun. See
Noun.

Pronounce. (F. — L.) F. *prononcer.*
— L. *prōnuntiāre*, to pronounce, lit. tell
forth. — L. *prō*, forth ; *nuntiāre*, to tell.
See **Nuncio.** Der. *pronunciat-ion*, from
L. pp. *prōnuntiāt-us*, with suffix *-iōn-.*

Proof, a test, evidence. (F. — L.) Formerly *profe* (1551) ; altered from M. E.
preef, preove. — F. *preuve*, a trial ; Cot. —
Late L. *proba*, a proof. — L. *probāre*, to test.
See **Prove, Probable.**

Prop. (E.) M. E. *proppe.* [Also Irish
propa, Gael. *prop*, a prop, support ; borrowed from E.] Cf. Du. *prop*, a stopple ;
M. Du. *prop, proppe*, 'a prop, a stopple,'
Hexham ; *proppen*, 'to prop, stay, or bear
up,' Hexham ; Low G. *propp*, a plug, G.
pfropf, a cork, also a graft. All from a
Teut. base **prup*, to stop up, to support.
¶ In the sense of 'graft,' the G. *pfropf*
is due to L. *propāgo* ; see **Propagate.**

Propagate. (L.) From the pp. of
L. *prōpāgāre* (or *pro-*), to peg down, propagate by layers ; allied to *prōpāgēs, prōpāgo*
(or *pro-*), a layer, and from the same source
as *compāgēs*, a fastening together. — L. *prō*,
forth ; *pāg-*, base of *pangere*, to fasten, set
(hence, to peg down). Der. *propagandist*,
a coined word ; from the name of the society
entitled *Congregatio de propaganda fide*,
constituted at Rome, A. D. 1622. And
see **Prune** (1).

Propel, to urge forward. (L.) L. *prō-
pellere*, to drive forward. — L. *prō*, forward ;
pellere, to drive ; see **Pulse** (1). Der.
propuls-ion, from pp. *prōpulsus.*

Propensity, an inclination. (L.)
Coined from L. *prōpensus*, hanging down,
inclining towards ; pp. of *prōpendēre*, to
hang down or forward. — L. *prō*, forward,
pendēre, to hang. See **Pendant.**

Proper, one's own, peculiar, suitable.
(F. — L.) M. E. *propre.* — F. *propre.* — L.

proprium, acc. of *proprius*, one's own.
Prob. from *prō prīuō.*

property. (F. – L.) M. E. *propertee.*
– O. F. *properté*, property (Littré), also
propriety, fitness. – L. *proprietātem*, acc. of
proprietās, property, ownership; also propriety of terms. – L. *proprius*, one's own.

Prophecy. (F. – L. – Gk.) M. E. *prophecie*, sb. – O. F. *prophecie*, variant of *pro-
phetie*, a prophecy. – L. *prophētīa.* – Gk.
προφητεία, a prediction. – Gk. προφήτης, a
prophet (below). **Der.** *prophesy*, vb.

prophet. (F. – L. – Gk.) O. F. *pro-
phete.* – L. *prophēta.* – Gk. προφήτης, one
who declares, an expounder, a prophet. –
Gk. πρό, publicly, lit. before ; φη-μί, I
speak ; with suffix -της of the agent. (√
BHĀ.) Allied to **Fame.**

Propinquity, nearness. (F. – L.)
O. F. *propinquité.* – L. *propinquitātem*,
acc. of *propinquitās*, nearness. – L. *pro-
pinquus*, near. – L. *prope*, adv., near.

Propitious, favourable. (L.) For L.
propitius, favourable. Prob. a term in
augury, with the sense ' flying forwards.' –
L. *pro-*, forward; *petere*, to seek, orig. to
fly. See **Petition.** **Der.** *propitiate*, from
pp. of L. *propitiāre*, to render propitious.

Proportion. (F. – L.) F. *proportion.*
– L. acc. *proportiōnem*, from *proportio*,
comparative relation. – L. *prō*, before, in
relation to ; *portio*, a portion ; see **Portion.**

Propose. (F. – L. *and* Gk.) F. *proposer*, lit. to place before. – L. *prō*, before ;
F. *poser*, to place, from Gk. See **Pose.**

Proposition. (F. – L.) F. *proposition.*
– L. acc. *propositiōnem*, a statement. – L.
propositus, pp. of *prōpōnere*, to put forth.
– L. *prō*, forth ; *pōnere*, to put.

propound. (L.) The *d* is excrescent ;
formerly *propoune*, *propone.* – L. *prōpōnere*
(above).

Propriety. (F. – L.) M.F. *proprieté*, a
property, also ' a comely assortment,' Cot.
– L. acc. *proprietātem*, from *proprietās*,
property ; also, propriety. – L. *proprius*,
one's own. **Doublet**, *property.*

Prorogue. (F. – L.) O. F. *proroguer.*
– L. *prōrogāre*, to propose an extension of
office, lit. to ask publicly ; hence, to defer.
– L. *prō*, publicly ; *rogāre*, to ask. See
Rogation.

Pros-, towards. (Gk.) Gk. πρός, towards ; fuller form προτί, extended from
πρό, before. ✛ Skt. *prati*, towards, from
pra, before. See **Pro-.**

Proscenium, the front part of a stage.
(L. – Gk.) L. *proscēnium.* – Gk. προ-
σκήνιον, the place before the stage (or
scene). – Gk. πρό, before ; σκηνή, a scene.
See **Scene.**

Proscribe. (L.) L. *prōscrībere*, lit.
to write publicly ; pp. *prōscriptus* (whence
proscription). – L. *prō*, publicly ; *scrībere*,
to write. See **Scribe.**

Prose. (F. – L.) F. *prose.* – L. *prōsa*,
for *prorsa orātio*, direct speech ; hence,
unimbellished speech ; fem. of *prorsus*,
forward, short for *prōuersus*, lit. turned
forward. – L. *prō*, forward ; *uersus*, pp. of
uertere, to turn. See **Verse.**

Prosecute. (L.) From L. *prōsecūtus*,
pp. of *prōsequī*, to pursue. – L. *prō*, forward ; *sequi*, to follow. See **Sequence.**
Doublet, *pursue.*

Proselyte, a convert. (F. – L. – Gk.)
O. F. *proselite.* – L. *proselytum*, acc. of
proselytus. – Gk. προσήλυτος, one who has
come to a place, a stranger, a convert
to Judaism ; Acts ii. 10. – Gk. προσέρ-
χομαι, I approach, 2 aor. προσῆλθον
(= προσήλυθον). – Gk. πρός, to ; ἔρχομαι, I
come. [Gk. ἔρχομαι and ἤλυθον are from
different roots ; the latter goes with ἐλεύ-
σομαι, I will come ; from √LEUDH.]

Prosody. (F. – L. – Gk.) F. *prosodie.*
– L. *prosōdia.* – Gk. προσῳδία, a song sung
to an instrument, a tone, accent, prosody,
(or laws of verse). – Gk. πρός, to, accompanying ; ᾠδή, an ode. See **Ode.**

Prosopopœia, personification. (L. –
Gk.) L. *prosōpopœia.* – Gk. προσωποποιία
personification. – Gk. προσωποποιεῖν, to per-
sonify. – Gk. πρόσωπο-ν, a face, a person ;
ποιεῖν, to make. Πρόσωπον is from πρός,
towards, and ὤπ-, stem of ὤψ, face, appearance. See **Pros-, Optic,** and **Poem.**

Prospect. (L.) L. *prospectus*, a view.
– L. *prospectus*, pp. of *prospicere*, to look
forward. – L. *prō*, forward ; *specere*, to look.
See **Species.** **Der.** *prospectus* = L. *prospectus*, a view.

Prosperous. (L.) L. *prosper*, adj.,
prosperous ; with suffix *-ous.* Cf. L. *pro-
sperus*, by-form of *prosper.* Lit. ' according
to one's hope.' – L. *prō*, for, according to ;
sper-, weak grade of *spēr-* for *spēs*, hope.
Der. *prosper*, vb. ; O. F. *prosperer*, L. *pro-
sperāre*, to prosper ; from *prosper*, adj.

Prosthetic, prefixed. (Gk.) Modern ;
as if for Gk. *προσθετικός*, lit. disposed to
add ; due to Gk. πρόσθετ-ος, added, put
to. – Gk. πρός, to ; θε-τός, placed, put,

verbal adj. from the base θε-, to place. See Thesis.

Prostitute. (L.) L. *prōstitūta*, f. pp. of *prōstituere*, to expose openly, prostitute. — L. *prō*, forth; *statuere*, to place, causal of *stāre*, to stand. See **State**.

Prostrate. (L.) L. *prōstrātus*, pp. of *prōsternere*, to throw forward on the ground. — L. *prō*, forward; *sternere*, to spread. See **Stratum**. **Der**. *prostrat-ion*.

Protean. (L. — Gk.) From L. *Prōteus* (misdivided as *Prōte-us*), a sea-god who often changed his form. — Gk. Πρωτεύς, a sea-god; cf. πρῶτος, first, chief.

Protect. (L.) From L. *prōtectus*, pp. of *prōtegere*, to protect; lit. cover in front. — L. *prō*, in front; *tegere*, to cover. See **Tegument**.

Protest. (F. — L.) F. *protester*. — L. *prōtestārī*, to protest, bear public witness. — L. *prō*, forth, in public; *testārī*, to witness, from *testis*, a witness. See **Testament**.

Prothalamium. (L. — Gk.) Late L. *prothalamium*. — Gk.*προθαλάμιον*, a song written before a marriage; a coined word. — Gk. πρό, before; θάλαμος, a bedroom, bride-chamber. Coined to accompany *epithalamium*, q. v.

Protocol, the first draught of a document. (F. — L. — Gk.) M. F. *protocole*, 'the first draught or copy of a deed.' — Late L. *prōtocollum*. — Late Gk. πρωτόκολλον, explained by Scheler to mean orig. a first leaf, glued on to MSS., in order to register by whom the MS. was written, &c. By a decree of Justinian, certain MSS. were to be thus accompanied by a fly-leaf. It means 'first glued on,' i. e. fastened on at the beginning. — Gk. πρῶτο-s, first; κολλᾶν, to glue, from κόλλα, glue. Πρῶτος is a superl. form from πρό, before; see **Pro-**.

protomartyr. (F. — L. — Gk.) M. F. *protomartyre*. — Late L. *prōtomartyr*. — Gk. πρωτόμαρτυρ, lit. 'first martyr.' — Gk. πρῶτο-s, first (above); μάρτυρ, a martyr; see **Martyr**.

prototype. (F. — L. — Gk.) F. *prototype*. — L. acc. *prōtotypum*. — Gk. πρωτότυπον, a prototype, neut. of πρωτότυπος, according to the first form. — Gk. πρῶτο-s, first (above); τύπος, a type; see **Type**.

Protract. (L.) From L. *prōtractus*, pp. of *prōtrahere*, to draw forward, also to extend, prolong. — L. *prō*, forth; *trahere*, to draw. See **Trace** (1), **Portray**.

Protrude. (L.) L. *prōtrūdere*, to thrust forth. — L. *prō*, forth; *trūdere* (pp. *trūsus*), to thrust. **Der**. *protrus-ion* (from the pp.). Cf. **Intrude**.

Protuberant. (L.) From stem of pres. pt. of *prōtūberāre*, to bulge out. — L. *prō*, forward; *tūber*, a swelling. See **Tuber**.

Proud. (F. — L. ?) M. E. *prud*, later *proud*; older form *prut*. A. S. *prūt*, proud; whence the Icel. *prūðr*, proud, is supposed to have been borrowed; cf. Dan. *prud*, stately. β. A late word in A. S.; and prob. merely borrowed from O. French. — O. F. *prod*, *prud*, fem. *prode*, *prude*, valiant, notable (taken in a bad sense). See further under **Prowess**. **Der**. *pride*.

Prove, to test, demonstrate. (L.) The usual old sense is to test or try. — A. S. *prōfian*. [Cf. O. F. *prover*, later *prouver*, 'to prove, try, essay, verifie;' Cot.] — L. *probāre*, to test, try the goodness of. — L. *probus*, excellent. See **Probable**.

Provender. (F. — L.) The final *r* is an O. F. addition. — O. F. *provendre* (Godefroy), usually *provende*, 'provender, also, a prebendary;' Cot. — Late L. *præbenda*, an allowance of provisions, also a prebend; see **Prebend**.

Proverb. (F. — L.) F. *proverbe*. — L. *prōuerbium*, a common saying. — L. *prō*, publicly; *uerb-um*, a word, cognate with E. **Word**.

Provide. (L.) L. *prōuidēre* (pp. *prōuīsus*), to foresee, act with foresight. — L. *prō*, before; *uidēre*, to see. See **Vision**. **Der**. *provident*, *provis-ion*.

Province. (F. — L.) F. *province*. — L. *prōuincia*, a territory brought under Roman government. (Of doubtful origin.)

Provision. (F. — L.) F. *provision*. — L. acc. *prōuīsiōnem*, foresight, forethought, purveyance. — L. *prōuīs-us*, pp. of *prōuidēre*, to provide for. See **Provide**.

Provoke. (F. — L.) F. *provoquer*; Cot. — L. *prōuocāre*, to call forth. — L. *prō*, forth; *uocāre*, to call. See **Vocal**.

Provost, a prefect. (L.) A. F. *provost*; [cf. M. F. *prevost*, 'the provost or president of a college;' Cot.] A.S. *prāfost*. — L. *præpositus*, a prefect, one set over. — L. *præpōnere*, to set over. — L. *præ*, before; *pōnere*, to put. See **Position**.

Prow, front part of a ship. (F. — L. — Gk.) O. F. *proue* (F. *proue*), prow. [Cf. Ital. *proda*.] — L. *prōra*, a prow; the 2nd *r* disappearing to avoid the double trill (as also in Prov. Span. Port. *proa*, Genoese *prua*). — Gk. πρῷρα, the prow. — Gk. πρό-, before, in front. See **Pro-**.

Prowess, bravery. (F. — L.) M. E. *prowes*, *pruesse*. — O. F. *prouesse*, prowess; formed with suffix *-esse* (< L. *-itia*) from O. F. *prou* (F. *preux*), valiant. β. Etym. disputed; we also find O. F. *prud*, *prud*, *proz*, *prous*, *pru*; Prov. *proz*, Ital. *prode*, valiant, notable (whence Ital. *prodezza*, prowess). Also O. F. *prou*, sb., advantage (whence M. E. *prow*, advantage). Although O. F. *prod* was used to translate L. *probus*, the spelling with *d* shows there is no connexion between these forms. γ. Scheler explains it from L. *prōd-*, as occurring in *prōd-esse*, to benefit; so that *prōd* was taken to mean 'for the benefit of'; and we even find F. *prou* used as an adverb, as in *prou*, 'much, greatly, enough;' Cot. *Prōd* is the old form of *prō*, before.

Prowl. (O. Low G.) M. E. *prollen*, to search after continually. 'I *prolle*, I go here and there to seke a thyng;' Palsgrave. '*Prollyn*, scrutor. *Prollynge*, or sekynge, perscrutacio;' Prompt. Parv. It also meant to rob, plunder. Like the word *plunder*, it prob. meant 'to filch trifles,' or 'to sneak after trifles'; from Low G. *prull*, *prulle*, a trifle, thing of small value (Bremen). Cf. Du. *prul*, 'a bawble' (Sewel), *prullen*, 'lumber, luggage, pelf, trumpery, toys' (id.); *prullenkooper*, a ragman (Calisch); E. Fries. *prülle*, *prül*, a trifle. Root unknown.

Proximity. (F — L.) F. *proximité*. — L. *proximitātem*, acc. of *proximitās*, nearness. — L. *proximus*, very near; a superl. form from *prope*, near. See **Propinquity**.

Proxy. (Late L. — L.) Palsgrave has *prockesy*; short for *procuracy*. — Late L. *prōcūrātia*, used for L. *prōcūrātio*, management. — L. *prōcūrāre*, to manage, to procure. See **Procure**.

Prude, a woman of affected modesty. (F. — L.) F. *prude*, M. F. *preude*, orig. in a good sense, chaste; used (but not originally) as the fem. of F. *preux*, O. F. *preu*, excellent, which at first had but *one* form for the masc. and fem. (Godefroy). Perhaps the forms *preudomme*, *preudefemme* arose from misunderstanding the O. F. phrases *preu d'omme* and *preu de femme* (Tobler). O. F. *preu* is a variant of O. F. *prod*, *prou*; see **Prowess**.

Prudent. (F. — L.) F. *prudent*. — L. *prūdentem*, acc. of *prūdens*, contr. form of

prōuidens, foreseeing, pres. pt. of *prōuidēre*, to foresee. — L. *prō*, before; *uidēre*, to see. See **Vision**.

Prune (1), to trim trees. (F. ? — L. ?) Very difficult. M. E. *proinen*, *prunen*, to dress oneself up smartly, trim; Gascoigne has *proyne*, to prune off shoots. But these are two distinct words. 1. The M. E. *proinen*, to trim, esp. used of a bird dressing its feathers, is from O. F. *poroign-*, a stem of *poroindre*, used in the same sense; from L. *prō*, prefix, and *ungere*, to anoint. 2. *Proine*, to prune trees, is from O. F. *por-roignier*, from L. *prō*, prefix, and *roignier*, to prune < L. **rotundiāre*, to make round. See **Round**.

Prune (2), a plum. (F. — L. — Gk.) F. *prune*. — L. *prūnum*. — Gk. προῦνον, shorter form of προῦμνον, a plum.

prunella, prunello, a strong woollen stuff, orig. of a *dark* colour. (F. — L. — Gk.) F. *prunelle*, a sloe (with ref. to the colour); whence *prūnella* is a Latinised form. Dimin. of F. *prune* (above).

Prurient. (L.) L. *prūrient-*, stem of pres. pt. of *prūrīre*, to itch, orig. to burn. Allied to E. **Freeze**. Brugm. i. § 562.

Pry, to peer into, search inquisitively. (F. — L.) M. E. *prien*. — O. F. *prier*, *preër*, to pillage [to search for plunder]. — Late L. *prēdāre*, to plunder, also to investigate; Duc. — L. *prœda*, prey; see **Prey**.

Psalm. (L. — Gk.) M. E. *psalm*, formerly *salm*. A. S. *sealm*. — L. *psalmus*. — Gk. ψαλμός, a touching, twitching the strings of a harp; also a song, psalm. — Gk. ψάλλειν, to touch, twitch, twang a harp. Der. *psalmod-y*, F. *psalmodie*, L. *psalmodia*, Gk. ψαλμῳδία, a singing to the harp, from ᾠδή, a song; see **Ode**.

psaltery, a stringed instrument. (F. — L. — Gk.) O. F. *psalterie* (12th cent.). — L. *psaltērium*. — Gk. ψαλτήριον, a kind of harp. — Gk. ψαλτήρ, a harper. — Gk. ψάλ-λειν, to twang a harp; with suffix *-τηρ* of the agent. Der. *psalter*, O. F. *psaltier*, a book of psalms, L. *psaltērium*, (1) a psaltery, (2) a psalter.

Pseudonym. (F. — Gk.) F. *pseudonyme* (1690). — Gk. ψευδώνυμος, adj., called by a false name. — Gk. ψεῦδ-ος, falsehood (ψευδής, false), from ψεύδειν, to lie; ὄνυμα, a name.

Pshaw, interjection. (E.) An imitative word; cf. *pish*, *pooh*.

Psychical, pertaining to the soul. (L.

—Gk.) From L. *psȳchicus.* —Gk. ψυχικός, belonging to the soul or life. — Gk. ψυχή, soul, life, orig. breath. — Gk. ψύχειν, to blow.

psychology. (Gk.) Gk. ψυχο-, for ψυχή, soul, life; -λογία, from λόγος, a discourse, from λέγειν, to speak.

Ptarmigan, a bird. (Gael.) Formerly *termigant.* — Gael. *tarmachan;* Irish *tarmochan.* ¶ The *p* was probably due to a notion of a Greek origin; but Gk. πταρμική means 'milfoil'!

Puberty. (F. – L.) F. *puberté,* youth. — L. *pūbertātem,* acc. of *pūbertās,* age of maturity. — L. *pūbes,* the signs of manhood, hair. Allied to *pū-pus, pu-er,* a boy. **Der.** *pubescence,* sb. due to *pūbescent-,* stem of pres. pt. of *pūbescere,* to arrive at puberty.

Public. (F. – L.) F. *public,* masc., *publique,* fem.; Cot. — L. *publicus,* belonging to the people; also *poublicos, poplicos* (in inscriptions). — L. *populus,* the people.

publican. (L.) M. E. *publican.* — L. *publicānus,* a tax-gatherer, Luke iii. 12; orig. an adj., belonging to the public revenue. — L. *publicus* (above).

publication. (F. – L.) F. *publication.* — L. acc. *publicātiōnem.* — L. *publicātus,* pp. of *publicāre,* to make public. — L. *publicus,* public.

publish. (F. – L.) M. E. *publishen.* An analogical formation; founded on F. *publier,* to publish. — L. *publicāre* (above).

Puce, the name of a colour. (F. – L.) Lit. 'flea-colour.' — F. *puce,* a flea; *couleur puce,* puce; O.F. *pulce.* — L. *pūlicem,* acc. of *pūlex,* a flea. ¶ Said to be the same as *puke,* which was also the name of a dark-brown colour, but the form *puke* is difficult to explain. The Picard and Walloon form of *puce* was *puche.*

Puck. (E.) M. E. *pouke.* A.S. *pūca* (Napier); whence Irish *puca,* an elf, sprite; W. *pwca, pwci.*+Icel. *pūki,* an imp.

Pucker, to gather into folds. (Scand.) Particularly used of the folds in the top of a *poke* or bag, when gathered together by drawing the string tight. So also M. Ital. *saccolare,* to pucker, from *sacco,* a sack; and E. *purse,* as 'to *purse* up the brows.' Cf. Norman F. *pouque,* for F. *poche,* a pouch, bag. See **Poke** (1).

Pudding, an intestine filled with meat, a sausage; hence, a sort of light food, made of flour, eggs, &c. (E.) M. E. *pudding, poding.* Cf. Low G. *pudding,* a pudding; *pudde-wurst,* a black-pudding;

puddig, thick, stumpy; Westphal. *puddek,* a lump, a pudding. Apparently from a Teut. base **pud,* to swell out, similar to **put;* cf. A. S. *pud-uc,* a wen (Toller); and see **Poodle** and **Pout.** β. Cf. also Irish *putog,* a pudding, Gael. *putag;* W. *poten,* a paunch, a pudding; Corn. *pot,* a bag, pudding; also W. *pwtyn,* a short round body, Gael. *put,* a buoy, inflated skin; all borrowed words. See **Pout.**

Puddle (1), a small dirty pool. (E.) M. E. *podel.* Dimin., with E. suffix *-el,* of A. S. *pudd,* a ditch, a furrow (Toller).

puddle (2), to make thick or muddy. (E.) From the sb. above.

Puerile. (F. – L.) M. F. *pueril* (15th cent.). — L. *puerīlis,* boyish. — L. *puer,* a boy.

puerperal, relating to child-birth. (L.) From L. *puerpera,* fem. adj., bearing a child. — L. *puer,* a boy; and *parere,* to bear; see **Parent.**

Puff, to blow. (E.) M. E. *puffen;* of imitative origin.+G. *puffen,* to puff, pop, Dan. *puffe,* to pop, Swed. *puffa,* to crack, push; W. *pwff,* a puff (from E.).

puffin, a bird. (E.) From its *puffed out* appearance, or from its swelling beak.

Pug, a monkey, a kind of dog. (E.) Orig. an imp, or little demon (Ben Jonson); see Nares, s. v. *puck.* A later form of *puck.* Cf. Dan. dial. *puge,* a 'puck,' sprite; and (perhaps) Dan. dial. *pugge,* a toad. 'A *pug-dog* is a dog with a short monkey-like face;' Wedgwood.

Puggry, Puggery, a scarf round the hat. (Hind.) Hind. *pagrī,* a turban; Yule.

Pugilism. (L.) From L. *pugil,* a boxer. Allied to L. *pugnus,* Gk. πυγ-μή, the fist.

pugnacious. (L.) Coined from L. *pugnāci-,* decl. stem of *pugnax,* combative. — L. *pugnāre,* to fight. — L. *pugnus,* the fist.

Puisne, Puny. (F. – L.) *Puny* is for *puisne,* a law-term, implying inferior in rank. — A. F. and M. F. *puisné,* 'puny, younger, born after;' Cot. — L. *post nātus,* born after. See **Natal.**

Puissant, mighty. (F. – L.) F. *puissant,* powerful. Cf. Ital. *possente,* powerful. From **possient-* for **possent-,* stem of a barbarous L. **possens,* substituted for L. *potens,* powerful.

Puke, to vomit. (E.?) Prob. of imitative origin, partly suggested by *spew.* Cf.

G. *spucken*, to spit; O. F. *escoupir*, to spit, *sput*, *esput*, a spitting.

Pule, to chirp, to whimper. (F. – L.) F. *piauler*, 'to cheep as a young bird, to pule or howle;' Cot. In Gascon, *pioula*. Cf. Ital. *pigolare*, to chirp, moan. Imitative words; allied to L. *pīpilāre*, *pīpāre*, to chirp; see Pipe.

Pull. (E.) M. E. *pullen*; A. S. *pullian*, to pull, pluck.✚Low G. *pulen*, to pick, pinch, pull, pluck, tear; Dan. dial. *pulle*. Cf. also Low G. *pullen*, to drink in gulps (cf. E. to take a *pull*).

Pullet. (F. – L.) M. E. *polete*. – O. F. *polete*, later *poulette*, fem. of F. *poulet*, a chicken, dimin. of F. *poule*, a hen. – Late L. *pulla*, fem. of *pullus*, a chicken. See Pool (2).

Pulley. (F. – L. – Gk.?) From F. *poulie*, 'a pully;' Cot. Cf. Ital. *puleggia*; Late L. *poledia*, a crane; Duc. Perhaps from Late L. *pōlidia*, orig. pl. of *pōlidium*<Gk. *πωλίδιον*, a little colt, dimin. of *πῶλος*, a colt. Cf. O. F. *poulier*, a pulley, answering to Late Gk. *πωλάριον*, a little colt. β. The M. E. forms are *poliue* (= *polīvè*, riming with *drīvè*), Ch.; also *poleyne*, Prompt. Parv. The latter form is from F. *poulain*, 'a fole, a colt, also the rope wherewith wine is let down into a seller [cellar], a pulley-rope;' Cot. – Late L. *pullānus*, a colt. – L. *pullus*, a young animal; see Pullet. So also F. *poulie* answers to mod. F. *poulie*. γ. The transference of sense causes no difficulty; thus M.F. *poutre*, a filly, also means a beam, and F. *chèvre*, a goat, also means a kind of crane; the names of animals are applied to contrivances for exerting force. Cf. also Late L. *polānus*, a pulley or pulley-rope, also a kind of sledge. ¶ Diez derives E. *pulley* from F. *poulie*, and then, conversely, F. *poulie* from E. *pull*. This is very unlikely. G. Paris (*Romania*, July, '98, p. 486) suggests Gk. *πολίδιον*, dimin. of *πόλος*, a pivot, axis; see Pole (2).

Pulmonary, affecting the lungs. (L.) *pulmōnārius*, affecting the lungs. – L. *pulmōn-*, stem of *pulmo*, a lung.✚Gk. *πλεύμων*, a lung. See Pneumatic.

Pulp. (F. – L.) F. *pulpe*. – L. *pulpa*, pulp of fruit, pith.

Pulpit. (F. – L.) O. F. *pulpite*. – L. *pulpitum*, a scaffold, stage for actors.

Pulsate, to throb. (L.) From pp. of L. *pulsāre*, to throb, beat; frequent. form of *pellere* (pp. *pulsus*), to drive. L. *pel-lo*

is for *pel-nō*; cf. Gk. *πίλ-ναμαι*, 'I draw near quickly;' Brugm. ii. § 612.

pulse (1), a throb. (F. – L.) F. *pouls*, 'the pulse;' Cot. – L. *pulsum*, acc. of *pulsus*, the beating of the pulse. – L. *pulsus*, pp. of *pellere* (above).

Pulse (2), grain or seed of beans, peas, &c. (L.) M. E. *puls*. – L. *puls*, a thick pap or pottage made of meal, pulse, &c. (hence applied to the pulse itself).✚Gk. *πόλτος*, porridge. **Der.** *poultice*, q. v.

Pulverise. (F. – L.) M.F. *pulverizer*; Cot. – Late L. *pulverīzāre*, to reduce to dust; L. *pulverāre*, the same. – L. *puluer-* (for *pulues-*), stem of *puluis*, dust. Allied to *pollis*, *pollen*, fine meal, *palea*, chaff; Gk. *πάλη*, meal, dust.

Puma, a quadruped. (Peruvian.) Peruv. *puma*.

Pumice. (F. – L.) [A.S. *pumic-stān*, pumice-stone.] M. E. *pomice*. – M. F. *pumice*. – L. *pūmic-*, stem of *pūmex*, pumice. From an Idg. base *poim-*, whence also A. S. *fām*, foam; from its foam-like appearance. See Foam.

Pummel, the same as Pommel.

Pump (1), a machine for raising water. (F. – Teut.) M. E. *pumpe*. – F. *pompe*. – G. *pumpe*, also *plumpe*, which is likewise an imitative form. Cf. prov. G. *plumpen*, to pump. β. The G. *plumpen* also means to plump, fall plump, move suddenly and violently, from the plunging action of the piston. It is therefore allied to E. Plump (2), of imitative origin. γ. We even find prov. E. *plump*, to pump, Corn. *plumppy*, to pump, also Du. *pomp*, Swed. *pump*, Dan. *pompa*, Russ. *pompa*, a pump, all borrowed words; and (the imitative forms) Span. and Port. *bomba*, a pump, a bomb.

Pump (2), a thin-soled shoe. (F. – L. – Gk.) So called because used for *pomp* or ornament; cf. F. *à pied de plomb et de pompe*, 'with a slow and stately gate,' i.e. gait; Cot. See Pomp.

Pumpion, Pumpkin, a kind of gourd. (F. – L. – Gk.) The old forms are *pumpion* and *pompon*. – M. F. *pompon*, 'a pumpion or melon;' Cot.; cf. Ital. *popone* (Florio); – L. *pepōnem*, acc. of *pepo*, a large melon. – Gk. *πέπων*, a kind of melon, eaten quite ripe. – Gk. *πέπων*, mellow, from *πέπτειν*, to ripen; see Cook.

Pun. (Ital. ? – L. ?) Of uncertain origin. Also used, at first, in the forms *punnet* and *pundigrion*. Perhaps the latter represents

Ital. *puntiglio*, a cavil, orig. a small point. – Ital. *punto*, a point. – L. *punctum*, a point.

Punch (1), to perforate. (F. – L.) M. E. *punchen*, to prick; which seems to have been coined from the sb. *punchion, punchon, punsoun*, a dagger, awl. See Puncheon (1).

Punch (2), to beat, bruise. (F. – L.) Short for *punish*; M. E. *punchen* and *punischen* are equivalent (Prompt. Parv.). See Punish.

Punch (3), a beverage. (Hind. – Skt.) So called from consisting of *five* ingredients, spirit, water, lemon-juice, sugar, spice; introduced from India, by way of Goa; mentioned A.D. 1669. – Hind. *panch*, five. – Skt. *pañcha*, five. See Five. ¶ The Hind. short *a* is pronounced like E. *u* in *mud*; it occurs again in *pundit*, *punkah*.

Punch (4), a short, hump-backed fellow in a puppet-show. (Ital. – L.) A contraction for *Punchinello*, which occurs A.D. 1666 (Nares). This is a corruption of Ital. *pulcinello* (by the change of *l* to *n*, the Ital. *ci* being sounded as E. *chi*). *Pulcinello* is the droll clown in Neapolitan comedy; we also find Ital. *puncinella*, 'punch, buffoon,' Meadows. A dimin. form of Ital. *pulcino*, a young chicken; cf. *pulcella*, a young girl; from L. *pullus*, the young of any animal, allied to *puer*, a boy. See Pullet. The lit. sense of *pulcinello* is little chicken; thence, a little boy, a puppet. ¶ Confused with prov. E. *punch*, short, fat, which is (perhaps) allied to Bunch. *Judy* is for *Judith*, once a common name.

Puncheon (1), a punch or awl. (F. – L.) M. E. *punchon, punsoun.* – Gascon *pounchoun*, M. F. *poinson* (F. *poinçon*); 'a bodkin, also a puncheon, a stamp,' &c.; Cot. Cf. Span. *punzon*, a punch, Ital. *punzone*, a punch, bodkin, also a winebarrel. – L. *punctiōnem*, acc. of *punctio*, a pricking, puncture. The gender of this word was changed from fem. to masc., whilst at the same time the sense was changed from 'pricking' to 'pricker.' – L. *punctus*, pp. of *pungere*, to prick; see Pungent. See also Puncheon (2).

Puncheon (2), a cask. (F. – L.?) From Gascon *pounchoun*, a punch or awl; M. F. *poinson* (F. *poinçon*), 'a bodkin. also a puncheon [steel tool], also a stamp, mark, print, or seale; also, a wine-vessell;' Cot. This is a difficult word; but I conclude that the O. F. *poinson* (F. *poinçon*) remains the same word in all its senses, and that the cask was named from the 'mark,

print, or seale' upon it, which was made with a *puncheon* or stamp. See Puncheon (1). ¶ So also M. Ital. *punzone* means both puncheon or bodkin, and puncheon or wine-vessel.

Punchinello; see Punch (4).

Punctate, dotted. (L.) Coined from L. *punct-um*, a point; with suffix -*ate* (L. -*ātus*). – L. *punctus*, pp. of *pungere*, to prick; see Pungent.

punctilio. (Span. – L.) Span. *puntillo*, a nice point of honour; dimin. of *punto*, a point. – L. *punctum*, a point; see Punctate, Point.

punctual. (F. – L.) M. F. *ponctuel*, 'punctuall;' Cot. – Late L. *punctuālis.* – *punctu-m*, a point; see Point.

punctuate. (L.) From pp. of Late L. *punctuāre*, to determine, define. – L. *punctu-m*, a point (above).

puncture. (L.) L. *punctūra*, a prick. – L. *punctus*, pp. of *pungere*, to prick.

Pundit, a learned man. (Skt.) Skt. *paṇḍita-* (with cerebral *nḍ*), adj., learned, sb., a wise man, scholar. – Skt. *paṇḍ*, to heap up or together. See note to Punch (3).

Pungent. (L.) L. *pungent-*, stem of pres. pt. of *pungere*, to prick, pt. t. *pupug-i*, pp. *punctus*. (Base PUG.)

Punish. (F. – L. – Gk.) M. E. *punischen.* – F. *puniss-*, stem of pres. pt. of *punir*, to punish. – L. *pūnīre*, to punish. – L. *pœna*, penalty. – Gk. ποινή, penalty. See Pain.

Punkah, a large fan. (Hind. – Skt.) Hind. *pankhā*, a fan; allied to *pankha*, a wing, feather, *paksha*, a wing. Allied to Skt. *paksha-*, a wing. Cf. Pers. *pankan*, a sieve, a fan. See note to Punch (3).

Punt (1), a flat-bottomed boat. (L. – C.) A.S. *punt.* – L. *ponto*, a punt (also a pontoon); a word of Gaulish origin. From Celtic type **qonto-*; cf. L. *contus* < Gk. κοντός, a punting-pole, whence prov. E. *quont, quant*, a punting-pole.

Punt (2), to play at a game at cards called basset. (F. – Span. – L.) F. *ponte*, a punt, a punter, a red ace, *ponter*, to punt. – Span. *punto*, a point, also a pip at cards. – L. *punctum*, a point. See Point. ¶ Or immediately from Spanish.

Puny; see Puisne.

Pupa, a chrysalis. (L.) L. *pūpa*, a girl, doll, puppet (hence, undeveloped insect). Fem. of *pūpus*, a boy; allied to *putus, puer*, a boy. (√ PEU.)

pupil (1), a scholar, ward. (F. – L.) O. F. *pupile*, F. *pupille* (masc.). – L. *pūpillum*, acc. of *pūpillus*, an orphan-boy, ward; dimin. of *pūpus*, a boy (above).

pupil (2), the central spot of the eye. (F. – L.) F. *pupille* (fem.). – L. *pūpilla*, a little girl, also pupil (name due to the small images seen in the pupil). Fem. of *pūpillus* (above).

puppet. (F. – L.) M. E. *popet*. – M. F. *poupette*, 'a little baby, puppet;' Cot. Dimin. of L. *pūpa*; see **Pupa** (above).

puppy, (1) a whelp; (2) a dandy. (F. – L.) 1. F. *poupée*, 'a baby, a puppet;' Cot. Here 'baby' really means 'doll,' but it is clear that, in E., the term was applied to the young of an animal, esp. of a dog. The F. *poupée* (as if < L. **pūpāta*) is a derivative of L. *pūpa*; see **Pupa** (above). 2. In the sense of 'dandy,' *puppy* represents M. F. *poupin, popin*, spruce, trim (as if < L.**pūpīnus*); from the same source. Der. *pup*, short for *puppy*.

Pur-, prefix. (F. – L.) O. F. *pur-*, F. *pour-*, *pour*, (Span. *por*), for; a curious variation of L. *prō*, for. Thus *pur-* and *pro-* are equivalent; and *pur-vey, pro-vide* are doublets.

Purblind. (F. – L. *and* E.) Orig. *pure-blind*, i.e. wholly blind, M. E. *pur blind*, Rob. of Glouc. p. 376. See **Pure** and **Blind.** It afterwards came to mean partly blind, prob. through confusion with the verb *to pore*, as Sir T. Elyot writes *pore-blind*. (Similarly *parboil*, to boil thoroughly, came to mean to boil partially.) *Pure* = wholly, Tw. Nt., v. 86.

Purchase, vb. (F. – L.) M. E. *purchasen, purchacen*. – O. F. *purchacer*, to pursue eagerly, acquire, get. – O. F. *pur* (F. *pour*), from L. *prō*; and O. F. *chacer*; see **Chase** (1).

Pure. (F. – L.) F. *pur*, masc., *pure*, fem., pure. – L. *pūrus*, pure. Cf. Skt. *pū*, to purify. (√PEU.)

purge. (F. – L.) F. *purger*. – L. *purgāre*, to purify. L. *purgare* = **pūr-igāre* (Plautus has *expūrigātio*). – L. *pūr-us*, pure; *agere*, to make.

purify. (F. – L.) F. *purifier*. – L. *pūrificāre*, to make pure. – L. *pūri-*, for *pūrus*, pure; *facere*, to make. Der. *purific-at-ion*.

Purim, an annual Jewish festival; the feast of lots. (Heb.) Heb. *pūrīm*, lots; pl. of *pūr*, a lot. See Esther ix. 26.

Puritan. (L.) A coined word, to designate one who aimed at great *purity* of life; see below.

purity. (F. – L.) M. E. *puretee*. – F. *pureté*, 'purity:' Cot. – L. acc. *pūritātem*, pureness. – L. *pūrus*, pure.

Purl (1), to flow with a murmuring sound. (E.) Cf. M. E. *prille, pirle*, a whirly-gig (toy). So also Swed. *porla*, to purl, bubble as a stream; a frequent. form from a base *pur-*, imitative of the sound. See **Purr, Purl** (4).

Purl (2), spiced beer. (F. – L.) In Phillips, ed. 1706. But it should be *pearl*. It was a term in cookery; thus *sucre perlé* is sugar boiled twice, *bouillon perlé*, jelly-broth. Cf. G. *perlen*, to pearl, rise in small bubbles like pearls. See **Pearl.**

Purl (3), to form an edging on lace, invert stitches in knitting. (F. – L.) Frequently misspelt *pearl*. Contraction of *purfle*. – M. F. *pourfiler*, to purfle, embroider on an edge. – F. *pour* (L. *prō*), confused (as often) with F. *pur* (L. *per*), throughout; *fil*, a thread, from L. *filum*, a thread. See **File** (1), **Profile.**

Purl (4), to upset. (E.) Better *pirl*; from M. E. *pirle*, a whirligig, formed by the frequent. suffix -*l* from the imitative word *pirr*, to whirl. See **Purr, Pirouette.** So also Ital. *pirlare*, 'to twirle round;' Florio. See **Purl** (1).

Purlieu, the border of a forest, &c. (F. – L.) Formerly *pourallee*, altered to *purlieu* by confusion with F. *lieu*, a place; also spelt *purley*. The O. F. *pouralee, poralee* is a sort of translation of Late L. *perambulātio*, which meant 'all that ground near any forest, which, being made forest by Henry II., Rich. I., or king John, were (*sic*) by *perambulations* granted by Henry III., severed again from the same'; Manwood's Forest Laws. The etymology is from O. F. *pur* (F. *pour*) < L. *prō*, and O. F. *alee*, a going, for which see **Alley.**

Purloin, to steal. (F. – L.) O. F. *purloignier, porloignier*, to prolong, retard, delay (hence to keep back, detain, filch). – L. *prōlongāre*, to prolong. – L. *prō*, forward; *longus*, long. See **Long. Doublet,** *prolong*.

Purple. (F. – L. – Gk.) M. E. *purpre* (with *r*). – O. F. *porpre*, later *pourpre*, purple. – L. *purpura*, the purple-fish. – Gk. πορφύρα, the purple-fish; cf. Gk. πορφύρεος, purple, orig. an epithet of the surging sea. – Gk. πορφύρειν, reduplicated form of φύρειν, to mix up, stir violently, allied to Skt. root *bhur*, to be active.

Purport, to imply. (F.—L.) O. F. *purporter, pourporter*, to declare, inform (hence, imply) ; we also find *purport*, sb., tenor (Roquefort). — O. F. *pur*, F. *pour*, from L. *prō*, according to ; *porter*, to carry, bring, from L. *portāre*. For the sense, cf. *import*. See **Port** (1).

Purpose (1), to intend. (F.—L. *and* Gk.) O. F. *purposer*, a variant of *proposer*, to propose, intend. — L. *prō*, before ; and F. *poser*, to place ; see **Pose** (1).

Purpose (2), intention. (F.—L.) M.E. *purpos*. — O. F. *purpos*, a variant of *propos*, a purpose. — L. *prōpositum*, a thing proposed, neut. of pp. of *prōpōnere*, to propose. — L. *prō*, before ; *pōnere*, to place. See **Position**.

Purr, Pur. (E.) An imitative word for various sounds, chiefly of the murmuring of a cat. Cf. Scotch *pirr*, a gentle wind ; E. *buzz* ; Irish *bururus*, a gurgling sound. See **Purl** (1), **Purl** (4), and **Pirouette**.

Purse. (L.—Gk.) M. E. *purs* ; also *pors*. A.S. *purs*, Eng. Studien, xi. 65. [Also *burs*. — O. F. *borse*, later *bourse*, a purse.] — Late L. *bursa*, a purse. — Gk. βύρση, a hide, skin ; of which purses were made. **Der.** *purse*, vb., to wrinkle up, like a purse drawn together.

Purslain, Purslane, a herb. (F.— L.) M. E. *purslane, porseleyne*. — M. F. *porcelaine, pourcelaine*, purslane ; Cot. Formed from L. *portulāca*, purslain (Pliny) ; usually spelt *portulāca*.

Pursue. (F.—L.) O. F. *porsuir, pursuir, poursuir* ; mod. Norman F. *porsuir*, mod. F. *poursuivre*, to pursue. — O. F. *por, pur* < L. *prō* ; and *suir* < Late L. *sequere*, for L. *sequī*, to follow. **Der.** *pursu-ant*, from the pres. pt. of O. F. *pursuir* ; *pursuiv-ant*, from the pres. pt. of *poursuivre* ; *pursuit*, from F. *poursuite*, fem. sb. answering to L. *prōsecūta*, fem. of the pp. of L. *prōsequī*, to pursue.

Pursy, short-winded. (F.—L.) M. E. *purcy*, also *purcyf* (Palsgrave). — M. F. *pourcif* (Palsgrave), variant of *poulsif*, 'pursie, short-winded,' Cot. — M. F. *poulser*, F. *pousser*, to push, also to pant ; see **Push**.

Purtenance. (F.—L.) Short for M. E. *apurtenance* ; see **Appurtenance**.

Purulent. (F.—L.) F. *purulent*. — L. *pūrulentus*, full of matter. — L. *pūr-*, stem of *pūs*, matter ; see **Pus**.

Purvey. (F.—L.) M. E. *purueien*, *porueien*, (*purveien, porveien*), to provide. — A. F. *purveier, purveer* (O. F. *porvoir*, F. *pourvoir*), to provide. — L. *prōuidēre*, to provide. See **Provide**.

purview, a proviso. (F.—L.) Now applied to the enacting part of a statute ; so called because it orig. began with *purveu est*, it is provided. — O. F. *porveu*, pp. of O. F. *porvoir* (F. *pourvoir*), to provide. — L. *prōuidēre*, to provide (above).

Pus, white matter from a sore. (L.) L. *pūs* (gen. *pūris*), pus. +Gk. πύον, matter ; Skt. *pūya-*, pus, from *pūy*, to stink. Allied to **Foul**. (✓PEU.) Brugm. i. § 113.

Push. (F.—L.) M. E. *possen, pussen*. — O. F. *pousser, poulser*, to push, thrust. — L. *pulsāre*, to beat, thrust, frequent. of *pellere*, to drive. See **Pulsate**.

Pusillanimous. (L.) L. *pusillanim-is*, mean-spirited ; with suffix *-ous*. — L. *pusill-us*, mean, small ; *animus*, courage. *Pusillus* is related to *pūsus*, small ; cf. *putus*, a boy. (✓PEU.)

Puss, a cat, hare. (E.) Prob. an imitative word, from the spitting of the cat. We find also Du. *poes*, Low G. *puus, puuskatte*, Swed. dial. *pus*, Norw. *puse, puus* ; Irish and Gael. *pus* (from E.). And even S. Tamil *pusei*, a cat ; *pusha* in the Cashgar dialect of Afghan. ; Lith. *puż*, a word to call a cat.

Pustule. (F.—L.) F. *pustule*. — L. *pustula*, another form of *pūsula*, a blister, pimple. Perhaps allied to Gk. φυσαλίς, a bladder, φυσάω, I blow.

Put. (E.) M.E. *putten* ; A.S. *potian*, to push, thrust ; [whence also Gael. *put*, to push, thrust ; W. *pwtio*, Corn. *poot*, to push, kick]. +Du. *poten*, to plant, set, *poot*, a twig, M. Du. *pote*, a scion, plant (see Franck) ; N. Fries. *putje*, Dan. *putte*, to put, place ; Swed. dial. *putta*, to push.

Putative, reputed. (F.—L.) F. *putatif*. — L. *putātīuus*, presumptive. — L. *putātus*, pp. of *putāre*, to think, suppose. The orig. sense was to make clean, then to make clear, to come to a clear result. — L. *putus*, clean. (✓PEU.)

Putrefy. (F.—L.) M. F. *putrefier* ; as if from L. **putrificāre* ; but the true L. forms are *putrefacere*, to make putrid, *putrefieri*, to become putrid. — L. *putri-s*, putrid (below) ; *facere*, to make.

putrid. (F.—L.) M. F. *putride*. — L. *putridus*, stinking. — L. *putri-*, decl. stem of *puter, putris*, rotten ; cf. *putrēre*, to be rotten, *pūtēre*, to stink. See **Pus**.

Puttock, a kite, hawk. (F. *and* E.) M. E. *puttok*. The surname *Puttock* was also sometimes spelt *Putthawk.* — Prov. E. *putt*, for *poult*, a chicken; and F. *hawk.* See **Poult.**

Putty. (F. — Low G.) M.F. *potée*, calcined tin, also putty; orig. a potful (of bits of broken metal); cf. M. F. *pottein*, bits of broken metal, *pottin*, solder. All from F. *pot*, a pot, of Germanic origin. See **Pot.**

Puzzle, a difficult question. (F. — L. *and* Gk.) Orig. a sb., and short for *opposal*, spelt both *opposayle* and *apposayle* in Lydgate, with the sense of question. These are from the verb *oppose*, like *deni-al* from *deny*, &c. See **Pose** (2).

Pygmy. (F. — L. — Gk.) M.F. *pygmé*, adj., dwarf-like; Cot. — L. *pygmæus*, adj., dwarf-like; from pl. *Pygmæi*, the race of Pygmies. — Gk. Πυγμαῖοι, pygmies, fabulous dwarfs of the length of a πυγμή, i.e. about 13½ in. (from the elbow to the knuckles). — Gk. πυγμή, a fist; see **Pugilist.**

Pylorus. (L. — Gk.) L. *pylōrus.* — Gk. πυλωρός, the lower orifice of the stomach, entrance to the intestines; orig. a gate-keeper. — Gk. *πυλα-ϝορός* (Prellwitz); from πύλα = πύλ-η, a gate; ϝόρος (cf. οὖρος), a keeper, watcher, allied to **Wary.**

Pyramid. (L. — Gk.) Formerly *pyramis.* — L. *pyramis* (stem *pyramid-*). — Gk. πυραμίς (stem πυραμίδ-), a pyramid. Prob. of Egyptian origin.

Pyre. (L. — Gk.) L. *pyra.* — Gk. πυρά, a funeral pile. — Gk. πῦρ, fire; allied to E. **Fire.**

pyrites. (L. — Gk.) L. *pyrītes.* — Gk. πυρίτης, a flint, pyrites; orig. an adj., belonging to fire. — Gk. πῦρ, fire.

pyrotechnic, belonging to fireworks. (Gk.) Coined from Gk. πυρο-, for πῦρ, fire; τεχνικός, artistic, from τέχνη, an art; see **Technical.**

Python, a large snake. (L. — Gk.) L. *pythōn*, a serpent slain by Apollo near Delphi. — Gk. Πύθων (the same). — Gk. Πυθώ, a former name of Delphi.

Pyx. (L. — Gk.) Shortened from L. *pyxis*, a box. — Gk. πυξίς, a box. — Gk. πύξος, box-wood. Allied to **Box** (1), **Box** (2).

Q.

Quack (1), to make a noise as a duck. (E.) M. E. *queke*, as a duck's cry; an imitative word. + Du. *kwaken, kwakken*,

G. *quaken*, Icel. *kvaka*, Dan. *qvække*, to croak, quack. Cf. L. *coaxāre*, to croak, Gk. κόαξ, a croaking.

quack (2), to cry up a nostrum. (Du.) Due to the older word *quacksalver*; hence, to act as a *quack-salver* or a *quack.* — Du. *kwakzalver*, a quacksalver. — Du. *kwakzalven*, vb., to apply salves in a trifling way. Cf. Du. *kwakken*, to croak, which came to mean 'to trifle, linger' (Franck); and Du. *zalf*, a salve; see **Salve.**

Quadragesima, forty days of Lent. (L.) L. *quadrāgēsima*, lit. fortieth; fem. of *quadrāgēsimus*; older form *quadrāgensumus*, fortieth. — L. *quadrāginlā*, forty. — L. *quadrā-*, related to *quattuor*, four; -*gintā*, allied to Gk. -κοντα (for *δεκοντα), and to L. *decem*, ten. See **quadrate.**

quadrangle. (F. — L.) F. *quadrangle.* — L. *quadrangulum*, sb., neut. of *quadrangulus*, four-cornered. — L. *quadr-*, related to *quattuor*, four; *angulus*, angle. See **Angle** (1).

quadrant. (L.) M.E. *quadrant.* — L. *quadrant-*, stem of *quadrans*, sb., a fourth part. Extended from L. *quadr-* (above).

quadrate. (L.) L. *quadrātus*, pp. of *quadrāre*, to make square. — L. *quadr-*, allied to *quattuor*, four; see **Four.** Brugm. ii. § 168.

quadrennial. (L.) For *quadriennial*, adj. — L. *quadrienni-um*, a space of four years; with suffix -*al.* — L. *quadri-*, belonging to four; *annus*, a year; see **Annals.**

quadrilateral. (L.) L. *quadrilaterus*, four-sided; with suffix -*al.* — L. *quadri-* (above); *later-*, for *lates-*, stem of *latus*, a side. See **Lateral.**

quadrille. (F. — Span. — L.) Formerly a game at cards for four. — F. *quadrille*, (1) fem., a troop of horses; (2) masc., but orig. fem., a game at cards. The former answers to Ital. *quadriglia*, M. Ital. *squadriglia*, a troop; but the latter to Span. *cuadrilla*, a meeting of four persons. — Span. *cuadra*, a square. — Late L. *quadra*, fem. of *quadrus*, square.

quadrillion, a million raised to the fourth power. (L.) Coined by prefixing L. *quadr-* i.e. four, to -*illion*, which is *m-illion* without the *m*.

quadroon. (Span. — L.) For *quartroon.* — Span. *cuarteron*, the child of a creole and a Spaniard; one who is, in a fourth part, a black; also a fourth part. — Span.

cuarto, a fourth part. – L. *quartum*, acc. of *quartus*, fourth; see **quartern.**

quadruped. (L.) L. *quadrupedus*, four-footed; *quadruped-*, stem of *quadrupēs*, *quadripēs*, four-footed. – L. *quadru-*, four times; *pēs*, a foot; see **quadrant.**

quadruple. (F. – L.) F. *quadruple.* – L. *quadruplum*, acc. of *quadruplus*, four-fold. – L. *quadru-* (above); *-plus*, signifying 'fold'; see **Double.**

Quaff, to drink in large draughts. (E.) Spelt *quaught* (Palsgrave); *quaft* (Sir T. More). A Southern form of Lowl. Sc. *waucht*, to quaff; from *waucht*, sb. a draught. – O. Northumb. **waht* = A. S. *weaht*, 'moistened'; from *weccan*, vb. to moisten. Allied to Du. *wak*, moist. See **Wake** (2).

Quagga, a quadruped. (Kaffir.) A Xosa-Kaffir word. – Kaffir *iqwara* (W. J. Davis); where the *r* is guttural. See N. and Q. 9 S. v. 3.

Quagmire. (E.) Spelt *quake-mire* in Stanihurst; i. e. quaking bog.

Quaigh, Quaich, a cup. (C. – L.) Gael. *cuach.* – L. *caucus*, a cup.

Quail (1), to cower. (F. – L.) Not from A. S. *cwelan*, to die, though perhaps sometimes confused with it. But the same word as prov. E. *quail*, to curdle, used of milk. See Prompt. Parv., and Way's note. The M. E. *quailen*, to curdle, coagulate, is from O. F. *coailler, quailier*, F. *cailler*, to coagulate, to curdle (see Supp. to Godefroy). – L. *coagulāre*; see **Coagulate.** Cf. Ital. *cagliare*, to curdle; also, to lack courage, to quail; M. Ital. *quagliare*, the same (Torriano).

Quail (2), a bird. (F. – Low L. – Low G.) M. E. *quaille.* – O. F. *quaille*, F. *caille.* – Low L. *quaquila*, a quail. – M.Du. *quackel*, Du. *kwakkel*, a quail. – M. Du. *quacken*, Du. *kwaken*, to quack. From the noise which the bird makes. See **Quack.**

Quaint, neat, odd, whimsical. (F. – L.) M. E. *queint*, also *quoint, coint*, commonly with the sense of 'famous.' – O. F. and M. F. *coint*, 'quaint, compt, neat, fine;' Cot. – L. *cognitus*, well-known, pp. of *cognoscere*, to know; see **Cognisance.** Der. *ac-quaint.*

Quake. (E.) M. E. *quaken, cwakien.* A. S. *cwacian*, to quake; cf. *cweccan*, to wag; E. Fries. *kwakkelen*, to be unsteady. Der. *Quak-er* (A. D. 1650); see Haydn.

Quality. (F. – L.) M. E. *qualitee.* – F.

qualité. – L. *quālitātem*, acc. of *quālitās*, sort, kind. – L. *quāli-s*, of what sort; Allied to E. **Which.**

qualify. (F. – L.) F. *qualifier.* – Late L. *quālificāre*, to endue with a quality. – L. *quāli-s*, of what sort; *facere*, to make.

Qualm. (E.) M. E. *qualm*, usually 'a pestilence.' A. S. *cwealm*, pestilence. **+** O. Sax. *qualm*, destruction, death; O.H.G. *qualm*, destruction. [Perhaps not the same word as Du. *kwalm*, thick vapour.] Teut. type **kwalmoz*, masc.; from **kwal*, 2nd grade of **kwel-an-*, to die. See **Quell.**

Quandary, a perplexity. (L. – Gk.) Orig. a morbid state of mind; Knt. of Burning Pestle, i. 1. It probably arose from '*condarye*, for *hypo-condarye*, a morbid state of mind. 'I, seeing him so troubled, asked him what newes . . . had put him in so great a *hypo-condarye*;' Blackhall, Brief Narration, ab. 1640 (Spalding Club), p. 175. See **Hypochondria.** (H. B.)

Quantity. (F. – L.) M. E. *quantitee.* – F. *quantité.* – L. *quantitātem*, acc. of *quantitās*, quantity. – L. *quanti-*, for *quantus*, how much. Related to *quam*; and to *quis*, who. Brugm. i. § 413.

Quarantine. (F. – L.) O. F. *quarantine* (Roquefort), usually *quarantaine*, a space of forty days. – F. *quarante*, forty. – L. *quadrāgintā*, forty; see **Quadragesima.**

Quarrel (1), a dispute. (F. – L.) M. E. *querele.* – O. F. *querele*, later *querelle.* – L. *querēla*, a complaint. – L. *querī*, to complain. See **Querulous.**

Quarrel (2), a square-headed cross-bow bolt. (F. – L.) M.E.*quarel.* – O.F.*quarrel*, M. F. *quarreau*, a diamond, square tile, cross-bow bolt. – Late L. *quadrellus*, a quarrel. – L. *quadrus*, square; see **Quadrate.**

quarry (1), a place where stones are dug. (F. – L.) Formerly *quarrer*; M. E. *quarrere*, a place where stones are squared. – O. F. *quarriere*, a quarry; F. *carrière.* – Late L. *quadrāria*, a quarry for *squared* stones. – L. *quadrāre*, to square. – L. *quadrus*, square. ¶ The sense was suggested by L. *quadrātārius*, a stone-squarer, also a stone-cutter (merely).

Quarry (2), a heap of slaughtered game. (F. – L.) M. E. *querrè.* – O. F. *curee, cuiree* (F. *curée*), intestines of a slain animal, the part given to hounds; so called because wrapped in the skin. – F.

cuir, a skin, hide. − L. *corium*, hide. See Cuirass.

Quart, the fourth of a gallon. (F. − L.) M. E. *quarte*. − F. *quarte*. − L. *quarta* (i. e. *pars*), a fourth part; fem. of *quartus*, fourth. Related to L. *quattuor*, four. Brugm. i. § 279.

quartan. (F. − L.) F. *quartaine*, recurring on the fourth day (said of a fever). − L. *quartāna* (*febris*), a quartan fever; fem. of *quartānus*, belonging to the fourth. − L. *quartus*, fourth (above).

quarter. (F. − L.) M. E. *quarter*. − O. F. *quarter*, *quartier*. − L. *quartārius*, fourth part. − L. *quartus*, fourth.

quartern, fourth of a pint. (F. − L.) Short for *quarteron*. M. E. *quarteroun*. − O. F. *quarteron*, a quartern. − Late L. *quarterōnem*, acc. of *quartero*, a fourth part. − Late L. *quarterus*, from L. *quartus*, fourth.

quartet, quartette. (Ital. − L.) Ital. *quartetto* (*quartette* is a F. spelling); dimin. of *quarto*, fourth. − L. *quartus*, fourth.

quarto, having the sheet folded into four leaves. (L.) From L. phr. *in quarto*, in a fourth part; where *quartō* is abl. of *quartus*, fourth.

Quartz, a mineral. (G.) G. *quarz*, rock-crystal; M. H. G. *quarz*.

Quash. (F. − L.) M. E. *quaschen*. − O. F. *quasser*, later *casser*, to break, quash. − L. *quassāre*, to shatter; frequent. of *quatere* (supine *quassum*), to shake.

Quassia, a South-American tree. (Personal name.) Named by Linnæus (like *dahl-ia* from *Dahl*) from *Quassi*, a negro of Surinam, who pointed out the use of the bark as a tonic in 1730. *Quassi* is a common negro name.

Quaternary, consisting of fours. (F. − L.) F. *quaternaire*. − L. *quaternārius*. − L. *quaternī*, pl., four at a time. − L. *quattuor*, four.

quaternion. (L.) L. *quaterniōn-*, stem of *quaternio*, a band of four men; Acts xii. 4. − L. *quaternī*, pl.; see above.

quatrain. (F. − L.) F. *quatrain*, a stanza of four lines. − F. *quatre*, four. − L. *quattuor*, four.

Quaver, vb. (E.) Frequent. of *quave*, M. E. *quauen* (*u* = *v*), to quake. Allied to M. E. *quappen*, to throb, palpitate. Compare **Quake**. Der. *quaver*, sb., a note in music, orig. a trill, shake. And see *quiver* (1).

Quay, a wharf. (F. − C.) Formerly *kay*, *key*; M. E. *key*, *keye*. − M. F. *quay* (F. *quai*), 'the key of a haven;' Cot. − Bret. *kaé*, an enclosure, a quay; W. *cae*, an enclosure, hedge. Celt. type **kagi-*; allied to **Haw**, **Hedge**.

Quean, a woman; used slightingly. (E.) A. S. *cwene*. + O. H. G. *quena*, a wife; Goth. *kwinō*. Teut. type **kwenōn-*. Also Irish *ben*, W. *bun*, a woman; Russ. *jena*, wife; Idg. type **g(w)enā*. Cf. Gk. γυνή, Pers. *zan*. See **Queen**. Brugm. i. § 670.

Queasy. (Scand.) M.E. *quaysy*, *queysy*, causing or feeling nausea. − Norweg. *kveis*, sickness after a debauch; Icel. *iðra-kveisa*, colic. Cf. Icel. *kveisa*, a whitlow, boil; Low G. *quese*, a blister; *quesen-kopp*, a brain-disease in sheep; E. Fries. *kwāse*, a blister, boil, worm causing giddiness in sheep.

Queen. (E.) Differing in gradation from *quean*, which spelling is restricted to the use of the word in a lower sense. A. S. *cwēn*, a woman; O. Merc. *kwōen*. + Icel. *kvān*, wife; Goth. *kwēns*, woman. Teut. type *kwēniz, fem.; Idg. type **g(w)ēni-*, cf. Skt. *-jāni-*, wife. Brugm. i. § 677. (√GwEN.)

Queer. (Low G.) A cant word. − Low G. *queer*, across; cf. *quere*, obliquity. In Awdelay's Fraternity of Vagabonds, p. 4, 'a *quire* fellow' is one who has just come out of prison; cf. Low G. *in der quere liggen*, to lie across, lie queerly. So also G. *quer*, transverse; *querkopf*, a queer fellow. G. *quer* answers to O. H. G. *twer*, transverse, Icel. *þverr* (whence E. *thwart*). See **Thwart**.

Quell, to subdue. (E.) M. E. *quellen*, to kill. A. S. *cwellan*, to kill; causal of *cwelan*, to die. + Du. *kwellen*, Icel. *kvelja*, Swed. *qvälja*, Dan. *qvæle*, to torment, choke; all causal forms. Teut. type **kwaljan-*; from *kwal, 2nd stem of **kwel-an-*, to die. See **Quail** (1).

Quench. (E.) M. E. *quenchen*. A. S. *cwencan*, to extinguish; causal of A. S. *cwincan* (pt. t. *cwanc*), to go out, be extinguished. Cf. O. Fries. *kwinka*, to be extinguished.

Querimonious, fretful. (L.) From L. *querimōnia*, a complaint. − L. *querī*, to complain; with Idg. suffixes *-mōn-jā-*.

Quern, Kern, a handmill for grinding grain. (E.) M. E. *querne*. A. S. *cweorn*, *cwyrn*; orig. 'that which grinds.' + Du.

kwvern, Icel. *kvern*, Dan. *quœrn*, Swed.
qvarn, Goth. *kwairnus*. Teut. type
*kwernuz. Cf. also Russ. *jernove*, a mill-
stone; Lith. *girna*, stone in a hand-mill.
Brugm. i. § 670.

Querulous, fretful. (L.) L. *querulus*,
full of complaints. **–** L. *querī*, to complain.
+ Skt. *çvas*, to sigh. Brugm. i. § 355.

Query, an enquiry. (L.) For *quœre*,
i. e. enquire thou. **–** L. *quœre*, imp. sing.
2 pers. of *quœrere*, to seek; for **quœs-ere*,
as in L. *quœso*, I beg. Brugm. ii. § 662.

quest, a search. (F. **–** L.) O.F.
queste; F. *quête*. **–** L. *quœsīta* (*rēs*), a thing
sought; fem. of pp. of *quœrere*, to seek.

  question. (F. **–** L.) F. *question*. **–** L.
acc. *quœstiōnem*, an enquiry. **–** L. *quœs-*,
base of *quœrere*, to seek; with suffix -*tiōn-*.

Queue, a tail. (F. **–** L.) F. *queue*,
tail. **–** L. *cauda*, a tail; see **Caudal.**

Quibble. (L.) Dimin. of *quib*, a sarcasm (Ash); which is a weakened form of
quip. See **Quip.**

Quick, living, lively. (E.) M. E. *quik*.
A. S. *cwic, cwicu*.**+**Du. *kwik*, Icel. *kvikr*,
Dan. *qvik*, Swed. *qvick*, O. H. G. *quec*.
Teut. type **kwikuz* or **kwikwoz*, allied to
the shorter Teut. type **kwiwoz*, as in Goth.
kwius, living; cf. Irish *beo*, W. *byw*, L.
uīuus, Lith. *gywas*, Russ. *jivoi*, alive; Gk.
βίος, life; Skt. *jīv*, to live. Brugm. i. §§ 85,
318, 677. **Der.** *quick-silver*; A. S. *cwic-
seolfor*.

  quicken. (E.) M. E. *quiknen*, orig.
to become alive. **–** A. S. *cwic*, alive.

Quid, a mouthful of tobacco. (E.)
Merely another form of *cud*; M. E. *quide*,
cud. See **Cud.**

Quiddity, a nicety, cavil. (L.) Late
L. *quidditās*, the nature of a thing. **–** L.
quid, what; i. e. what is it? Neut. of *quis*,
who; see **Who.**

Quiet, adj. (L.) L. *quiētus*, quiet; orig.
pp. of **quiēre*, only used in the inceptive
form *quiescere*, to be still. Cf. *quiēs*, rest.
Allied to O. Pers. *shiyāti-*, a place of
delight, home; Pers. *shād*, pleased; and
to E. **While.** Brugm. i. §§ 130, 675;
Horn, § 767. **Der.** *quiet*, sb. and vb.;
quietus, sb.; *quiescent*, from stem of pres.
pt. of *quiescere*.

Quill (1), a feather, pen. (E.?) M. E.
quille. 'Quylle, a stalk, Calamus;'
Prompt. Parv. *Quill* also meant the faucet
of a barrel, or a reed to wind yarn on.
This is a difficult and doubtful word, not
found at an early date. Apparently E.,

and of Teut. origin.**+**Low G. *kiil*, a goose-
quill (Berghaus); Westphalian *kwiəle*
(Woeste); G. *kiel*, M. H. G. *kil* or *kīl*.

Quill (2), to pleat a ruff. (F. **–** L.)
From O. F. *cuillir* (F. *cueillir*), to gather,
pluck; also used in the sense to pleat;
see Rom. Rose, 1219, and Chaucer's
translation. **–** Folk-L. **colligīre*, for L. *colligere*, to cull, collect. See **Cull.** Allied
to the Guernsey word *enquiller*, to pleat
(Métivier).

Quillet, a sly trick in argument. (L.)
Short for L. *quidlibet*, anything you choose.
– L. *quid*, anything; *libet*, it pleases (you).

Quilt, a bed-cover, &c. (F. **–** L.) M.E.
quilte. **–** A. F. and O. F. *cuilte*, a quilt
(12th cent.). **–** L. *culcita*, a cushion, mattress, pillow, quilt.

Quinary, consisting of fives. (L.) L.
quinārius, arranged by fives. **–** L. *quīnī*,
five at a time. **–** L. *quinque*, five. See
Five.

Quince. (F. **–** L. **–** Gk.) Formerly
quence, quyns. (Cf. M. F. *coignasse*, 'the
greatest kind of quince,' Cot.) Merely the
pl. form of M. E. *quyne, coine*, or *coin*,
a quince. **–** O. F. *coin*, F. *coing*, a quince.
[The same as Prov. *codoing*; cf. Ital.
cotogna, a quince.] **–** L. **cotōnium*, for
*cydōnium; (the Ital. *cotogna* being from
L. *cydōnia*, a quince). **–** Gk. κυδώνιον μῆλον,
a quince, lit. a Cydonian apple. **–** Gk.
Κυδωνία, Κυδωνίς, Cydonia, one of the chief
cities of Crete.

Quincunx, an arrangement by fives.
(L.) Applied to trees arranged like
the spots on the side of a die marked
5; L. *quincunx*. **–** L. *quinque*, five; *uncia*,
an ounce, small mark, such as a spot on
a die; see **Uncial.**

Quinine, extract of Peruvian bark. (F.
– Peruv.) F. *quinine*, formed with suffix
-*ine* (L. -*īna*), from F. *quina*, Peruvian
bark. **–** Peruvian *kina*, or *kina-kina*, said
to mean 'bark,' esp. that which we call
Peruvian bark.

Quinquagesima. (L.) L. *quinquā-
gēsima* (*dies*), fiftieth (day); fem. of *quin-
quāgēsimus*, fiftieth. **–** L. *quinquā-*, for *quinque*, five, allied to E. **Five**; -*gēsimus*, for
*-gensimus, allied to *decem*, ten; see
Quadragesima. ¶ So also *quinquan-
gular*, having five angles; *quinqui-ennial*,
lasting five years.

Quinsy. (F. **–** Gk.) Formerly also
squinancy. **–** O. F. *quinancie* (Supp. to

Godefroy, s. v. *esquinance*); also *squin-ancie* (16th cent.) ; *squinance*, 'the squin-ancy or squinzie ;' Cot. Formed (some-times with prefixed *s* = O. F. *es-*, L. *ex*, very) from Gk. κυνάγκη, lit. a dog-throttling, applied to a bad kind of sore throat. — Gk. κύν-, stem of κύων, a dog ; ἄγχ-ειν, to choke.

Quintain. (F. — L.) M. F. *quintaine*, a post with arms, for beginners to tilt at. The form of the word is such that it must be allied to L. *quintāna*, a street in the camp, which separated the *fifth* maniple from the sixth ; where was the market and business-place of the camp. Doubtless this public place was also the scene of martial exercises and trials of skill ; the Late L. *quintāna* means (1) a quintain, also (2) a part of a street (space) where carriages could pass. — L. *quintānus*, from *quintus*, fifth. For *quinc-tus*, from *quin-que*, five. See **Five.**

Quintal, a hundred-weight. (F. — Span. — Arab. — L.) F *quóntal* (Cot.). — Span. *quintal.* — Arab. *qintār*, a weight of 100 lbs. Not a true Arab. word ; but formed from L. *centum*, a hundred.

Quintessence, pure essence. (F. — L.) Lat. 'fifth essence.' — L. *quinta essentia*, fifth essence (in addition to the four elements). See below ; and **Essence.**

Quintuple, five-fold. (F. — L.) F. *quintuple.* — L. *quintuplus*, a coined word. — L. *quintu s*, fifth, for *quinctus* ; from *quinque*, five ; *-plus*, i. e. *-fold* ; see **Double.**

Quip, a taunt, cavil, (L.) Formerly *quippy ;* Drant's Horace, bk. ii. sat. 1. — L. *quippe*, forsooth (ironical). For *quid-pe* ; Brugm. i. § 585. Der. *quibble.*

Quire (1), a collection of sheets of paper. (F. — L.) Spelt *cwaer* in the Ancren Riwle. — O. F. *quaier* (13th cent.), later *quayer*, *cayer* ; mod. F. *cahier.* — Late L. *quaternum*, a collection of four leaves (we find Late L. *quaternus*, glossed by A. F. *quaer* in Wright's Voc. i. 116) ; whence also Ital. *quaderno*, a quire. Allied to L. *quattuor*, four. [The suffix *-num* is lost as in F. *enfer* from L. *infernum.*] ¶ Not from L. *quaternio*, which could not thus suffer loss of the acc. termination *-niōnem.*

Quire (2), a band of singers ; see **Choir.**

Quirk, a cavil. (M. Du. — F. — L.) M. Du. *kuerken*, 'a cunning trick,' Hex-ham. Dimin. of M. Du. *küre*, Du. *kuur*, a whim, also a cure. — F. *cure*, a cure. —

L. *cūra* ; see **Cure.** Cf. E. Fries. *küre*, *kürke*, a whim.

Quit, freed, free. (F. — L.) Orig. an adj., as in ' *quit* claim.' M. E. *quyt*, *quit*, also *quyte*, free ; adj. — O. F. *quite*, dis-charged, released, free. — Late L. *quītus*, *quittus*, altered forms of Late L. *quiētus*, at rest, hence, free. Cf. Late L. *quiēta clāmantia*, A. F. *quite claime*, E. *quit claim* ; *quiētum clāmāre*, *quītum clamāre*, to quit a claim ; *quiētāre*, *quītāre*, *quittāre*, to free from debt. See **Quiet.** Der. *quit*, vb., F. *quitter*, O. F. *quiter*, from the adj. ; hence *quitt-ance*, O. F. *quitance*, Late L. *quītantia*, *quiētantia* ; *acquit.* Cf. **Coy.**

quite. (F. — L.) M. E. *quite* ; an ad-verbial use of the M. E. adj. *quite*, free, now spelt *quit* ; see above.

Quiver (1), to shiver. (E.) Allied to obsolete adj. *quiver*, full of motion, brisk ; A. S. *cwifer*, in the comp. adv. *cwifer līce*, eagerly. Cf. M. Du. *kuyven*, *kuyveren*, to quiver (Kilian) ; E. Fries. *kwifer*, lively, *kwifern*, to be lively.

Quiver (2), a case for arrows. (F. — O. H. G.) O. F. *cuivre*, *cuevre*, *coivre*, a quiver. — O. Sax. *cokar* ; cf. O. H. G. *kohhar* (G. *köcher*), a quiver ; A. S. *cocer*, a quiver. Teut. type *kukuro-*, whence Med. L. *cucurum*, a quiver.

Quixotic. (Span.) Named from *Don Quixote* or *Quijote*, a novel by Cervantes.

Quoif ; the same as **Coif.**

Quoin, a wedge. (F. — L.) The same as F. *coin* ; see **Coin.**

Quoit, Coit, a ring of iron for throwing at a mark. (F. — L. ?) M. E. *coite*, *coyte* ; cf. Lowl. Sc. *coit*, to push about, justle. Prob. from O. F. *coitier*, *quoitier*, to press, push, hasten, incite, urge on (which prob. also had the sense ' to hurl '). Of unknown origin. Cf. Prov. *coitar*, to hasten, urge.

Quorum. (L.) It was usual to nomi-nate members of a committee, *of whom* (*quorum*) a certain number must be present to form a meeting. — L. *quōrum*, of whom ; gen. pl. of *quī*, who. Allied to **Who.**

Quota, a share. (Ital. — L.) Ital. *quota*, a share. — L. *quota* (*pars*), how great a part ; fem. of *quotus*, how great. — L. *quot*, how many ; allied to *quī*, who ; see **Who.**

quote. (F. — L.) Formerly also *cote.* — O. F. *quoter*, *coter*, to quote. — Late L. *quo-tāre*, to mark off into chapters and verses, for references ; hence, to give a reference.

‒L. *quotus*, how many, how much, with allusion to chapters, &c. ; see above.

Quoth, he said. (E.) Properly a pt. t. M. E. *quoth, quod.* ‒ A. S. *cwæð*, pt. t. of *cweðan*, to say. ✛ Icel. *kvað*, pt. t. of *kveða*, to say; Goth. *kwath*, pt. t. of *kwithan*, to say. Der. *quotha*, for *quoth he.*

Quotidian, daily. (F.‒L.) F. *quotidien.* ‒ L. *quotidiānus*, daily. ‒ L. *quoti-*, for *quotus*, how many ; *diēs*, a day. Thus *quotidiānus* = on however many a day, on any day, daily.

quotient. (F.‒L.; *or* L.) F. *quotient*, the part which falls to each man's share ; Cot. ‒ L. **quotient-*, the imaginary stem of L. *quotiens*, how many times ; which is really indeclinable. ‒ L. *quot*, how many. See **Quote.**

R.

Rabbet, to cut the edges of boards so that they overlap and can be joined. (F. ‒ L.) M. E. *rabet*, sb., Prompt. Parv. '*Rabetynge* togedyr of two bordys'; id. Apparently from O. F. *rabatre*, to abate, diminish; hence, to thin down. ‒ F. *re-* (L. *re-*), again ; and *abatre*, to abate ; see **Abate.** Confused with F. *raboter*, to plane ; from F. *rabot*, a plane ; cf. **Rebate.**

Rabbi, Rabbin, sir. (L. ‒ Gk. ‒ Heb.) L. *rabbī*, John i. 38. ‒ Gk. ῥαββί. ‒ Heb. *rabbī*, literally ' my master.' ‒ Heb. *rab*, great ; as sb., master ; and *ī*, my. ‒ Heb. root *rābab*, to be great. (The form *rabbin* is French.)

Rabbit. (Walloon ‒ M. Du.) M. E. *rabet.* ‒ Walloon *rabett* (Remacle). Dimin. of M. Du. *robbe*, dimin. *robbeken*, a rabbit (Kilian). ¶ The true E. name is *cony.*

Rabble. (M. Du.) From the noise made by a crowd. ‒ M. Du. *rabbelen*, to chatter ; Low G. *rabbeln*, to chatter, babble. The suffix *-le* gives a frequentative force; *rabble* = that which keeps on making a noise. Cf. **Rap**; and see **Rapparee.**

Rabid, mad. (L.) L. *rabidus*, mad. ‒ L. *rabere*, to rage, rave. Cf. **Rage.**

Raca. (Chaldee.) Matt. v. 22. Chaldee *rēkā*, worthless ; hence, foolish.

Raccoon, Racoon. (N. American Indian.) Spelt *rackoon* in Bailey (1735). The native W. Indian name. '*Arathkone*, a beast like a fox;' glossary of Indian Words subjoined to A Historie of Travaile into Virginia, by W. Strachey (pub. by the Hakluyt Soc. in 1849).

Race (1), a swift course. (Scand.) M. E. *ras* (North) ; [*rees* (South), from A. S. *rǣs*]. ‒ Icel. *rās*, a running, race. Teut. base **rēs-*. Hence it is not for **rans*, i. e. a running (as in Noreen).

Race (2), a family. (F.‒Ital.) F. *race.* ‒ Ital. *razza, raza*, also M. Ital. *raggia*, ' a race, broode,' Florio. Of doubtful origin ; but answering to L. type **radia*, allied to *radiāre*, to radiate. (Korting, § 6612.)

Race (3), a root. (F.‒L.) ' A *race* of ginger ;' Wint. Ta. iv. 3. 50. ‒ O. F. *rais, raiz*, a root. ‒ L. *rādīcem*, acc. of *rādix*, a root. See **Radix, Radish.**

Raceme, a cluster. (F.‒L.) F. *racème.* ‒ L. *racēmum*, acc. of *racēmus*, a cluster.

Rack (1), a grating above a manger, an instrument of torture. (E.) In some senses the word is doubtless English ; cf. M. E. *rekke*, a rack for hay. In the particular sense ' to torture,' it may have been borrowed from M. Du. *racken*, to rack, to torture. The radical sense of *rack* is to extend, stretch out ; hence, as sb., *rack* is a straight bar (cf. G. *rack*, a rail, bar) ; hence, a frame-work, such as the bars in a grating above a manger, a frame-work used for torture, a bar with teeth in which a cog-wheel can work. *On the rack* = in great anxiety ; a *rack-rent* is a rent stretched to its full value, or nearly so. Allied words are Icel. *rakkr*, straight, *rekkja*, to strain, M. Du. *racken*, to stretch, reach out, to rack ; Swed. *rak*, straight, G. *rack*, a rack, rail, *recken*, to stretch ; esp. Low G. *rakk*, a shelf, as in E. *plate-rack.* Cf. Goth. *uf-rakjan*, to stretch out. ¶ *Rack* is used in many senses ; see *rack* (2), *rack* (3), &c.

Rack (2), light vapoury clouds, mist. (Scand.) See Hamlet, ii. 2. 506 ; Antony, iv. 14. 10. M. E. *rak.* ‒ Icel. *rek*, drift, motion, a thing drifted ; cf. *skȳrek*, the rack or drifting clouds. ‒ Icel. *reka*, to drive, thrust, toss ; cognate with A. S. *wrecan*, to drive. See **Wreak.** Cf. Swed. *skeppet vräker* = the ship drifts.

Rack (3), to pour off liquor, to clear it from dregs or lees. (F.‒L.?) Minsheu (1627) speaks of ' *rackt* wines.' ‒ M. F. *raqué* ; whence *vin raqué*, ' small, or corse wine, squeezed from the dregs of the grapes, already drained of all their best moisture;' Cot. Cf. Languedoc *raqua*, to glean grapes ; *raquo*, skin of grapes (D'Hombres) ; Span. *rascon*, sour ; *rascar*, to scrape. Prob. of L. origin ; see **Rascal.**

Rack (4), the same as *wrack*; in the phr. 'to go to *rack* and *ruin*'; see **Wrack**.

Rack (5); see **Arrack**.

Rack (6), a neck of mutton. (E.) A.S. *hracca*, the back of the head (*occiput*); see Somner, and Vocab. 463. 21. ¶ We also find *rack* (7), for *reck*, to care; *rack* (8), to relate, from A. S. *racu*, an account; *rack* (9), a pace of a horse, i. e. a *rocking* pace; see **Rock** (2). Also *rack* (10), a track, cart-rut, from A. S. *racu*, a track.

Racket (1), **Raquet**, a bat with a net-work blade. (F. — Span. — Arab.) M.E. *raket*; borrowed from F.; cf. M. F. *raquette*. — Span. *raqueta*, a racket, battle-dore. — Arab. *rāhat*, the palm of the hand (hence the game of fives, which preceded rackets). To this day, tennis is called in F. *paume*, i. e. palm of the hand, though now played with bats.

Racket (2), a noise. (E.) Of imitative origin; cf. *rattle*, *rap*. So also Gael. *racaid*, a noise; Irish *racan*, noise; Gael. *rac*, to make a noise like geese or ducks.

Racoon; see **Raccoon**.

Racy, of strong flavour, spirited. (F. — Ital.; *with* E. *suffix*.) *Rac-y* = indicative of its *race*, due to its breed. See **Race** (2).

Radiant. (L.) From stem of pres pt. of L. *radiāre*, to shine. — L. *radius*, a ray.

Radical; see **Radix**.

Radish. (F. — Prov. — L.) F. *radis* (not a true F. word, but borrowed from Provençal). — Prov. *raditz*, a root. — L. *rādīcem*; see **Radix**. ¶ Or the F. *radis* is from Ital. *radice*.

Radius, a ray. (L.) L. *radius*, a ray. Doublet, *ray* (1).

Radix, a root. (L.) L. *rādix* (stem *rādīc-*), a root.+Gk. ῥάδιξ, a branch, rod; ῥάδαμνος, a twig. See **Root** and **Wort**. Der. *radic-al*, L. *rādīcālis*.

Raffle, a kind of lottery. (F. — G.) M. E. *rafle*, a game at dice. — M. F. *rafle*, *raffle*, a game at three dice; O. F. *rafle*, a gust of wind; F. *rafler*, to snatch up. — G. *raffeln*, to snatch up; frequent. of *raffen*, to snatch away, carry off hastily. See **Rap** (2).

Raft. (Scand.) M. E. *raft*, a spar, beam; orig. sense 'rafter.' — Icel. *raptr* (*raftr*), a rafter, beam (where the final *r* is merely the sign of the nom. case); Dan. *raft*, a rafter, a beam. Allied to Icel.

rāf, *rǽfr*, a roof, cognate with O.H.G. *rāfo*, a spar, rafter. Allied to Gk. ὄροφος, a roof, ἐρέφειν, to cover. (✓REBH.) ¶ Not allied to A. S. *hrōf*, a roof.

rafter, a beam to support a roof. (E.) A.S. *ræfter*. An extension of the word above.

Rag. (Scand.) M. E. *ragge*. We only find A.S. *raggie*, for **raggige*, rough, shaggy; as if formed from a sb. **ragg-*. — Norw. *ragg*, rough hair, whence *ragged*, shaggy (E. *ragged*); Swed. *ragg*, rough hair, whence *raggig*, shaggy; Icel. *rögg*, shagginess, *raggaðr*, shaggy. Orig. sense 'shagginess,' whence the notion of untidiness. ¶ The resemblance to Gk. ῥάκος, a shred of cloth, is accidental. Der. *rag-stone*, i. e. rugged stone; *rag-wort*, i. e. ragged plant.

Rage. (F. — L.) F. *rage*. — L. *rabiem*, acc. of *rabiēs*, rage. — L. *rabere*, to rage. And see **Rave**.

Ragout. (F. — L.) F. *ragoût*, a sea-soned dish. — F. *ragoûter*, to coax a sick man's appetite. — F. *re-*, again; *a*, to; *goûter*, to taste. — L. *re-*; *ad*; *gustāre*, to taste. See **Gust** (2).

Raid. (North E.) A Northern form of E. *road*. Cf. Icel. *reið*, a riding, a road. See **Road**.

Rail (1), a bar. (F. — L.) M. E. *rail*. Not found in A. S. — O. F. *reille*, a rail, bar; Norman dial. *raile*. — L. *rēgula*, a bar. See **Rule**. Cf. Low G. *regel*, a rail, cross bar; Swed. *regel*, a bar, bolt; G. *riegel*, O. H. G. *rigil*, a bar, bolt; all from L.

Rail (2), to brawl, scold. (F.) F. *railler*, to deride; O. F. *raille*, sb., mockery. Origin unknown. Der. *raill-er-y*, F. *raillerie*, banter.

Rail (3), a bird. (F. — Teut.) O. F. *raalle*; M. F. *rasle*, 'a rayle,' Cot.; F. *râle*. (From its cry.)

Rail (4), part of a woman's night-dress. (E.) See Halliwell and Palsgrave. M.E. *reȝel*. — A. S. *hrægl*, *hregl*, a dress, robe, swaddling-clothes. + O. Fries. *hreil*, *reil*; O. H. G. *hregil*, a garment. Teut. type **hragilom*, neut.

Raiment. (F. — L. *and* Scand.; *with* F. *suffix*.) Short for *arrai-ment*; see **Array**.

Rain. (E.) M. E. *rein*. A.S. *regn*, also *rēn* (by contraction).+Du. *regen*, Icel. Dan. Swed. *regn*, G. *regen*, Goth. *rign*, rain.

Raindeer; see Reindeer.

Raise. (Scand.) M. E. *reisen.* — Icel. *reisa*, to make to rise, causal of *rīsa* (pt. t. *reis*), to rise; so also Dan. *reise*, Swed. *resa*, to raise. See Rise, Rear (1).

Raisin. (F. — L.) M. E. *reisin.* — O. F. *raisin*, a grape; also a bunch. — Folk-L. *racīmum*, for L. *racēmum*, acc. of *racēmus*, a cluster.

Rajah, prince. (Skt.) Skt. *rājā*, the nom. case from the stem *rājan*, a king. Cognate with L. *rex*; see Regal.

rajpoot, a prince. (Hind. — Skt.) Hind. *rajpūt*, a prince; lit. 'son of a rajah.' — Skt. *rāj-ā*, a king; *putra*, son.

Rake (1), an implement. (E.) A.S. *raca*, a rake. + Du. *rakel*, a rake, Dan. *rage*, a poker, Swed. *raka*, an oven-rake (with base *rak-*); also Icel. *reka*, a shovel, G. *rechen*, a rake (with base *rek-*). Allied to Goth. *rikan* (Teut. type *rek-an-*, pt. t. *rak*), to collect, heap up. Cf. Icel. *raka*, vb., to rake. Der. *rake*, vb.

Rake (2), a dissolute man. (E.) *Not* M. E. *rakel*, rash, oddly corrupted to *rake-hell* (Trench, Nares), and finally shortened to *rake*. But really (see N.E.D.) from *rake* and *hell*. 'Suche a feloe as a manne should *rake helle* for'; Udall.

Rake (3), the projection of the extremities of a ship beyond the keel, the inclination of a mast from the perpendicular. (Scand.) 'In sea-language, the *rake of a ship* is so much of her hull or main body, as hangs over both the ends of her keel;' Phillips (1706). Evidently from *rake*, vb., to reach, extend (Halliwell). — Swed. dial. *raka*, to reach, *raka fram*, to reach over, project; Dan. *rage frem*, to project, jut out. Cf. Icel. *rakr*, Swed. *rak*, straight. Allied to Rack (1).

Rakehell, a vagabond; see Rake (2).

Raki, arrack. (Turk. — Arab.) Turk. *rāqī*, arrack. — Arab. *'araq*, arrack; see Arrack.

Rally (1), to re-assemble. (F. — L.) F. *rallier.* — F. *re-*, again; *allier*, to ally; see Ally. Cf. prov. F. *raller*, to rally, grow convalescent; dial. de la Meuse (Labourasse).

Rally (2), to banter. (F.) We also find the sb. *rallery*, 'pleasant drolling,' Phillips, ed. 1706. This is, of course, another spelling of *raillery*; and *rally* is merely another form of *rail* (2), from F. *railler*, to deride. See Rail (2).

Ram. (E.) A.S. *ram.* + Du. *ram*, G.

ramm. Cf. Icel. *ramr*, strong. Der. *ram*, vb., to butt, push, thrust; *ram-rod*.

Ramadan, a great Mohammedan fast. (Arab.) So called because kept in the ninth month, named *Ramadan.* — Arab. *ramaḍān*, pronounced *ramazān* in Turkish and Persian. As it is in the ninth month of the lunar year, it may take place in any season; but it is supposed to have been originally held in the hot season. The word implies 'consuming fire'; from Arab. root *rameḍ*, it was hot. (Devic, Richardson.)

Ramble. (E.) Frequentative of M. E. *ramien*(?), prov. E. *rame*, to rove, to gad about (Yks.); cf. E. Fries. *ramen*, *rāmen*, to rove, ramble. The *b* is excrescent, and *ramble* is for prov. E. *rammle*, to ramble (Whitby Glossary).

Ramify. (F. — L.) F. *ramifier*, to put forth branches (hence, to branch off). — L. *rāmi-*, for *rāmus*, a branch, bough; -*ficāre*, for *facere*, to make. With L. *rāmus*, cf. Gk. ῥάδαμνος, a twig. Brugm. i. § 529.

Ramp, Romp, to bound, leap; properly to climb, scramble, rear; also to sport boisterously. (F. — Teut.) M. E. *rampen*, to rage; cf. *ramp-ant* (F. *rampant*), rearing, said of a lion. — F. *ramper*, 'to creep, run, crawle, climb;' Cot. Orig. sense 'to clamber'; cf. M. Ital. *rampare*, to clutch, *rampo*, a hook. According to Diez, the Ital. *rampare* (Prov. *rapar*) is a nasalised form from Low G. *rappen*, to snatch hastily, Dan. *rappe*, to hasten; cf. G. *raffen*, to snatch; see Rape (1). But Körting derives Ital. *rampa*, a grip, from Low G. *ramp* (Lübben), Bavar. *rampf*, a cramp, seizure; which is allied to *rampf*, 2nd grade of O.H.G. *rimpfan*, to cramp. Cf. Ripple (2).

Rampart. (F. — L.) Also spelt *rampire*, *rampier*, *rampar.* — M. F. *rempart*, *rempar*, a rampart of a fort. — M. F. *remparer*, to put again into a state of defence. — L. *re-*, again; *im-* (*in*), in; *parāre*, to get ready. See Pare.

Ramsons, broad-leaved garlic. (E.) A double plural; for *rams-en-s.* Here *ramsen* = A. S. *hramsan*, ramsons; a pl. form, from a sing. *hramsa.* + Swed. *rams-lök* (*lök* = leek); Dan. *rams*; Lithuan. *kermusze*, wild garlic; Irish *creamh*, W. *craf*, garlic; Gk. κρόμυον, an onion (Stokes-Fick, p. 98).

Ranch, Rancho, a rude hut. (Span. — Teut.) Common in Mexico. — Span. *rancho*, a mess, set of persons who eat and drink together; formerly, 'a ranke,' Minsheu. Prob. borrowed from Prov. *renc*, a rank; O. F. *reng*; see **Rank**, **Range**.

Rancid. (L.) L. *rancidus*, rancid. Cf. L. *rancens*, stinking, as if from an infin. **rancēre*, to stink.

rancour. (F. – L.) M. E. *rancour*. – A.F. *rancour*. – L. *rancōrem*, acc. of *rancor*, spite, orig. rancidness. See above.

Random, said or done at hazard. (F. – Teut.) M. E. *randon*; esp. in phr. *in randon*, in great haste. – O. F. *randon*, the force and swiftness of a great stream; whence phr. *à randon*, in great haste, with impetuosity; from O. F. *randir*, to run swiftly. So also Span. *de rendon, de rondon*, rashly, impetuously. – G. *rand*, a brim, edge, verge, margin; whence Ital. *a randa*, with difficulty, exactly (lit. near the verge). Cf. G. *bis am rande voll*, full to the brim. The sense of O. F. *randir* has reference to the course of a *full* or *brimming* river.+ A.S. *rand*, Icel. *rönd*, Dan. *rand*, rim, verge; Swed. *rand*, a stripe. See **Rind**.

Range. (F. – O. H. G.) The sense 'to rove' arose from the trooping about of ranks of armed men. – F. *ranger* (O. F. *renger*), to range, rank, order, array, lit. 'to put into a rank.' – F. *rang* (O. F. *reng*), a rank (below).

rank (1), a row, line of soldiers, class. (F. – O. H. G.) M. E. *reng, renk*. – O. F. *reng* (F. *rang*), a rank, row, list, range. – O. H. G. *hring*, a ring, ring of men, hence a row or rank of men. See **Ring**.

Rank (2), coarse in growth, very fertile; also rancid. (E.) The sense 'rancid' is due to confusion with O.F. *rance*, 'musty,' Cot., which is from L. *rancidus*. But M.E. *rank* means strong, forward; from A.S. *ranc*, strong, proud, forward.+Du. *rank*, lank, slender (like things of quick growth); Icel. *rakkr* (for **rankr*), straight, slender, Swed. *rank*, long and thin, Dan. *rank*, erect.

Rankle, to fester. (F. – L. – Gk.) A.F. *rankler*, to fester; O.F. *draoncler, raoncler, rancler* (so that it once began with *d*; see Godefroy). – O.F. *draoncle, raoncle, rancle*, an eruption of the skin. – Late L. *dracunculus, dranculus*, (1) a little dragon; (2) a kind of ulcer (as dragons were supposed to be venomous). – Late L. *draco*, a dragon. See **Dragon**. (Phil. Soc. Trans. 1891.)

Ransack. (Scand.) Icel. *rannsaka*, to search a house, ransack; Swed. *ransaka*, Dan. *ransage*. – Icel. *rann*, a house, abode; *sak-*, related to *sækja*, to seek. The Icel. *rann* stands for **rasn*, and is the same as A.S. *ærn*, a cot, Goth. *razn*, a house; see **barn**. Cf. A. S. *ræsn*, a plank, beam; and see **Seek**. ¶ Cf. Norman dial. *ransaquer*, Gael. *rannsaich*, from Scand.

Ransom, redemption. (F. – L.) M. E. *ransoun* (with final *n*). – O. F. *raënson*, later *rançon*, a ransom. – L. *redemptiōnem*, acc. of *redemptio*, a buying back. – L. *redemptus*, pp. of *redimere*, to redeem; see **Redeem**. Doublet, *redemption*.

Rant. (Du.) M. Du. *randten*, to dote, be enraged; also spelt *randen*; see Kilian. Cf. Westphal. *rantern*, to prate.

Rantipole, a romping child. (Low G.) Cf. M. Du. *wrantigh*, E. Fries. *wranterig*, Low G. *wrantig*, peevish, quarrelsome; and **Poll**. See **Frampold**.

Ranunculus. (L.) L. *rānunculus*, a little frog; also, a plant. Double dimin. of *rāna*, a frog.

Rap (1), to strike smartly; a smart stroke. (Scand.) Dan. *rap*, a rap, tap; Swed. *rapp*, a blow; Swed. *rappa*, to beat; cf. G. *rappeln*, to rattle. Of imitative origin; allied to **Rattle**, **Racket** (2).

Rap (2), to snatch, seize hastily. (E.) M. E. *rapen*, to hasten, act hastily. Cf. M. Du. *rapen*, 'to rap up, gather,' Hexham; Du. *rap*, quick; Icel. *hrapa*, to fall, tumble, hasten, hurry; Swed. *rappa*, to seize, snatch, Dan. *rappe*, to make haste; Swed. *rapp*, Dan. *rap*, quick, brisk; G. *raffen*, to snatch. From Teut. base **hrap-*. ¶ Chiefly in the phrase to *rap and rend*. And see **Rapt**, **Rape** (1).

Rapacious. (L.) Coined from L. *rapāci-*, for *rapax*, grasping. – L. *rapere*, to grasp. Brugm. i. § 477.

Rape (1), a seizing by force. (F. – L.) A.F. and Norm. dial. *rape, rap*; cf. Late L. *rappus, rapus* (for L. *raptus*). O.F. *rapt*. – L. *raptum*, acc. of *raptus*, a rape. – L. *raptus*, pp. of *rapere*, to seize. Cf. O. F. *raper*, Gascon *rapa*, to seize. β. But, apparently, confused with M. E. *rape*, haste, hurry, a common word; see Chaucer's lines to Adam Scrivener. – Icel. *hrap*, ruin, falling down, *hrapaðr*, a hurry, *hrapa*, to hasten; Swed. *rapp*, Dan. *rap*, quick; see **Rap** (2). Der. *rape*, vb.

Rape (2), a plant. (L.) M.E. *rape*. – L. *rāpa, rāpum*, a turnip, a rape.+Gk. ῥάπυς, a turnip, ῥαφανίς, a radish; Russ. *riepa*, a turnip; G. *rübe*.

Rape (3), a division of a county, in Sussex. (E.) Of uncertain origin. It occurs in Domesday Book as *rap*, and was spelt *rope* in 1380. Prob. from A. S. *rāp*, a rope; used for measurement. See **Rope**.

Rapid. (F. – L.) F. *rapide*. – L. *rapidus*, quick, lit. snatching away. – L. *rapere*, to snatch. See **Rapacious**.

Rapier, a light narrow sword. (F. – Span. – O. H. G.) M. F. *rapiere, rappiere*, also *raspiere* (Littré); it was considered as Spanish. ' *Rapiere*, Spanische sworde;' Palsgrave, p. 908. Perhaps *raspiere* was a name given in contempt, meaning 'a rasper' or poker; hence it was called 'a *proking-spit* of Spaine'; Nares. Cf. Span. *raspadera*, a raker. – Span. *raspar*, to rasp, scratch. – O. H. G. *raspōn*, to rasp. See **Rasp**. ¶ So Diez; Littré rejects this probable solution.

Rapine. (F. – L.) F. *rapine*, ' rapine, ravine;' Cot. – L. *rapīna*, robbery, plunder. – L. *rapere*, to seize. See **Rapacious**.

Rapparee, an Irish robber. (Irish.) Irish *rapaire*, a noisy fellow, sloven, robber, thief; cf. *rapal*, noise, *rapach*, noisy. Cf. Gael. *rapair*, a noisy fellow. All perhaps from E. *rabble* (Macbain).

Rappee, a kind of snuff. (F. – O. H. G.) F. *râpé*, lit. rasped, reduced to powder; pp. of *râper*, to rasp; see **Rasp**.

Rapt, carried away. (L.) From L. *raptus*, pp. of *rapere*, to seize; see Milton, P. L. iii. 522. ¶ But in ' What thus *raps* you,' Cymb. i. 6. 51, the word may be E. See **Rap** (2).

raptorial. (L.) Used of birds of prey. – L. *raptōr-i-*, from *raptor*, one who seizes; with suffix *-al*. – L. *rapere*, to seize.

rapture. (L.) Coined, as if from L. *raptūra*, from L. *raptus*, pp. of *rapere*.

Rare. (F. – L.) F. *rare*. – L. *rārum*, acc. of *rārus*, rare.

Rascal, a knave, villain. (F. – L.) M.E. *raskaille*, the common herd. [It was a term of the chase; certain animals, not worth hunting, were so called. The hart, till he was six years old, was accounted *rascayle*.] A. F. *raskayle*, a rabble; also *rascaille*, whence mod. F. *racaille*, ' the rascality or base or rascall sort, the scumme, dregs, offals, outcasts of any company,' Cot. Due to an O. F. word cognate with Prov. Span. Port. *rascar*, to scrape; the orig. sense being ' scrapings'; cf. M. F. *rasque*, ' scurfe'; Cot. All from a Late L. *rāsicāre*, a frequent.

form from *rāsum*, supine of *rādere*, to scrape; see **Rase** (below); and **Rash** (2).

Rase, Raze, to scrape, efface. (F. – L.) M. E. *rasen*, to scrape. – F. *raser*. – Late L. *rāsāre*, to graze, to demolish. – L. *rāsum*, supine of *rādere*, to scrape. Allied to **Rodent**.

Rash (1), headstrong. (E.) M. E. *rash, rasch*, E. Fries. *rask*; cf. A. S. *ræscan*, to flash. + Du. *rasch*, G. *rasch*; Dan. Swed. *rask*, quick, rash; Icel. *röskr*, vigorous; N. Fries. *radsk*, quick. ¶ Brugm. i. § 795, connects this word with O. H. G. *rad*, a wheel; see **Rotary**.

Rash (2), a slight eruption on the body. (F. – L.) O. F. *rasche, rasque, rache*. The same as Prov. *rasca*, the itch. So called from the wish to scratch it; cf. Prov. *rascar*, to scratch, equivalent to a Late L. *rāsicāre*, to scrape. See **Rascal**.

Rash (3), to pull, tear violently. (F. – L.) ' *Rashing* off helmes;' F. Q. v. 3. 8. M.E. *aracen*, afterwards shortened to *racen*. – O. F. *esrachier* (F. *arracher*), to root up, pull away violently. – L. *exrādīcāre*, to root out. – L. *ex*, out; *rādīcāre*, to root, from *rādīc-*, stem of *rādix*, a root. See **Radix**.

Rash (4), a kind of serge. (F. – Ital.) M. F. *ras*, serge. – Ital. *rascia*, ' silk rash ;' Florio. From *Rascia*, a district in the S. of Bosnia.

Rasher, a thin slice of broiled bacon. (E.) ' *Rasher* on the coales, quasi *rashly* or hastily roasted,' Minsheu. This is right; cf. ' *Rashed*, burnt in cooking, by being too hastily dressed;' Halliwell. See **Rash** (1).

Rasorial. (L.) L. *rāsōr-i-*, from *rāsor*, one who scrapes; with suffix *-al*. – L. *rās-um*, supine of *rādere*, to scrape.

Rasp, vb. (F. – O. H. G.) M. E. *raspen*. – O. F. *rasper* (F. *râper*). – O.H.G. *raspōn*, whence G. *raspeln*, to rasp. Cf. O. H. G. *hrespan*, to pluck, to rake together. Cf. **Rap** (2).

rasp-berry, a kind of fruit. (F. – O.H.G.; *and* E.) Formerly called *raspis*, or *raspes*, but this is merely a pl. form used as a singular. Named from its uneven surface. So also M. Ital. *raspo*, a rasp, also a raspberry.

Rat. (E.) M. E. *rat*. A. S. *ræt*. + M.Du. *ratte*, Du. *rat*, Dan. *rotte*, Swed. *råtta*, G. *ratte, ratz*; Low L. *ratus, rato* (whence F. *rat*); Irish and Gael. *radan*, Bret. *raz*.

Der. *rat*, vb., to desert one's party, as rats are said to leave a falling house. And see **Ratten.**

Ratafia, a liquor. (F.—Arab. *and* Malay.) F. *ratafia*; cf. *tafia*, rum-arrack. — Malay *araq tāfīa*, the spirit called *tafia*; where *araq* is borrowed from Arab. *'araq*, arrack.

Ratch, a rack or bar with teeth. (G.) Also, a wheel with teeth; in clockwork. It answers to G. *ratsche* (N. E. D.). G. *ratsche*, a watchman's rattle (Weigand). **Der.** *ratch-et*, in watch-work, 'the small teeth at the bottom of the fusee or barrel that stop it in winding up;' Phillips.

Rate (1), a proportion, standard, tax. (F.—L.) A. F. *rate*, price, value. — L. *rata*, fem. of *ratus*, determined, fixed, settled, pp. of *reor*, I think, judge, deem. Brugm. i. § 200.

Rate (2), to scold, chide. (F.—L.) M. E. *raten*, Ch. C. T. 3463; *araten*, to reprove. Also spelt *retten*, *aretten*.—O.F. *reter*, *rateir*, *areter*, *aratter*, to accuse, to impute; Norman dial. *reter*, *retter*, to blame. — L. *ad*, to; and *reputāre*, to count. See **Repute.** ¶ Not from *rate* (1).

Rath, early; **Rather,** sooner. (E.) *Rather* is the compar. of *rath*, early, soon. A. S. *hraðe*, adv., quickly, *hræð*, adj., quick, swift; hence *hraðor*, sooner.+Icel. *hraðr*, swift; M. H. G. *rad*, *hrad*, quick; Du. *rad*, swift. Cf. O. Ir. *crothim*, I shake.

Ratify. (F.—L.) F. *ratifier*. — Late L. *ratificāre*, to confirm. — L. *rati-*, for *ratus*, settled; *-ficāre*, for *facere*, to make. See **Rate** (1).

ratio. (L.) L. *ratio*, calculation. — L. *ratus*, pp. of *reor*, I think, deem.

ration, rate or allowance of provisions. (F.—L.) F. *ration*. — L. *ratiōnem*, acc. of *ratio* (above). Doublet, *reason*.

Ratlines, Ratlins, Rattlings, the small transverse ropes crossing the shrouds of a ship. (E.; *and* F.—L.) Now turned into *rat-lines*, as if affording ladders for rats to get up by. But the old term was *raddelines*, or *raddelyng of the shrowdes*, Naval Accounts (1485–97), ed. Oppenheim, pp. 185, 207. Prob. the same as prov. E. *raddlings*, long pieces of underwood twisted between upright stakes (hence, *cross*-lines of the shrouds); cf. Du. *weeflijnen* (weave-lines), ratlines. Cf. prov. E. *raddle*, a hurdle; perhaps allied to *rod*. Palsgrave has '*radyll* of a carte.'

Rattan, a Malacca cane. (Malay.)

Also spelt *ratan* (Johnson). — Malay *rōtan*, the rattan-cane.

Ratten, to take away a workman's tools for offending the trades' union. (F. — Low L.— Teut.) *Ratten* is the Hallamshire (Sheffield) word for a rat; hence applied to working secret mischief, which is attributed to rats. 'I have been *rattened*; I had just put a new cat-gut band upon my lathe, and last night the *rats* have carried it off;' N. and Q. 3 S. xii. 192. M. E. *raton*, a rat. — F. *raton*, dimin. of F. *rat*; see **Rat.**

Rattle, to clatter. (E.) M. E. *ratelen*. A. S. **hrætelan*, only preserved in A. S. *hrætele*, *hrætelwyrt*, rattle-wort, a plant which derives its name from the rattling of the seeds in the capsules.+Du. *ratelen*, G. *rasseln*, to rattle; allied to Gk. κραδαίνειν, to shake. Cf. also Gk. κρόταλον, a rattle.

Raught, pt. t. of **Reach,** q. v.

Ravage, sb., plunder. (F.—L.) F. *ravage*, 'ravage;' Cot. — F. *ravir*, to bear away suddenly. — Folk-L. *rapīre*, L. *rapere*, to seize. See **Rapid.** **Der.** *ravage*, vb., *ravager*.

Rave. (F.—L.) M. E. *raven*. — O. F. *raver*, cited by Diez, s. v. *rêver*, as a Lorraine word; hence the derivative *ravasser*, 'to rave, talk idly;' Cot. Godefroy has O. F. *resver*, *raver*, *rever*, to stroll about, also to rave; cf. F. *râver*, dial. de la Meuse (Labourasse). Allied to Span. *rabiar*, to rave, a verb formed from the sb. *rabia*, rage, allied to L. *rabiēs*, rage. — L. *rabere*, to rage; see **Rabid.** ¶ This is the solution given by Diez; but see Körting, s. v. *rabia*.

Ravel, to untwist, unweave, entangle. (M. Du.) The orig. sense has reference to the untwisting of a string or woven texture, the ends of threads of which become afterwards entangled. To *unravel* is to disentangle; to *ravel out* is to unweave. — M. Du. *ravelen*, to ravel; mod. Du. *rafelen*, E. Fries. *rafeln*, to fray out, unweave; Low G. *reffeln*, to fray out. Cf. Du. *rafel*, E. Fries. *rafel*, *räfel*, a frayed edge. Also Norman dial. *raviler*, to ravel; Pomeran. *rabbeln*, *uprabbeln*, to ravel out. Of unknown origin; but cf. A.S. *ārafian* (or *ārāfian*?), to unravel, Gregory's Pastoral Care, ed. Sweet, p. 245, l. 22. ¶ The M. Du. *ravelen*, to dote (from O. F. *râver*, see **Rave**), is a different word. **Der.** *unravel*.

Ravelin, a detached work in fortification, with two embankments raised before the counterscarp. (F. — Ital.) F. *ravelin.* — M. Ital. *ravellino, revellino* (Ital. *rivellino*), a ravelin. Origin unknown; thought to be from L. *re-*, back, *uallum*, a rampart; which is unlikely.

Raven (1), a bird. (E.) M. E. *raven.* A. S. *hræfn, hrefn.*+Du. *raaf*, Icel. *hrafn*, Dan. *ravn*, G. *rabe.* Teut. type **hrabnoz*, m. Perhaps allied to Gk. κόρ-αξ, a raven, L. *cor-uus.*

Raven (2), to plunder, to devour. (F. — L.) Better spelt *ravin*. From M. E. *ravine*, sb., plunder. — O. F. *ravine*, rapidity, impetuosity (oldest sense ' plunder,' as in L.). — L. *rapīna*, plunder; see **Rapine.**

ravine, a hollow gorge. (F. — L.) F. *ravine*, a hollow worn by floods, also a great flood; O. F. *ravine* (above).

ravish, to seize with violence. (F. — L.) M. E. *rauischen*. — F. *raviss-*, stem of pres. pt. of *ravir*, to ravish. — Folk-L. *rapīre*, for L. *rapere*, to seize.

Raw. (E.) M. E. *raw*. A. S. *hrēaw, hrêw.*+Du. *raauw*; Icel. *hrár*, Dan. *raa*, Swed. *rå*; O. H. G. *rāo*, G. *roh.* Teut. types **hrawoz*, **hrêwoz*. Allied to L. *crūdus*, raw, Skt. *krūra-*, sore, cruel, hard; also to Gk. κρέας (for **κρεϝας*), raw flesh, Skt. *kravya-*, raw flesh; Lat. *cruor*, blood; Russ. *krove*, Lith. *kraujas*, Irish *crū*, W. *crau*, blood. Brugm. i. § 492. (√KREU.)

Ray (1). (F. — L.) O. F. *ray*; F. *rai.* — L. *radium*, acc. of *radius*, a ray. See **Radius.**

Ray (2), a fish. (F. — L.) O. F. *raye*, F. *raie.* — L. *rāia*, a ray.

Ray (3), a dance. (Du.) M. Du. *rey*, a dance; Du. *rei*, a chorus.

Rayah, a person, not a Mohammedan, who pays the capitation-tax, a word in use in Turkey. (Arab.) It may be explained as ' subject,' though the orig. sense is ' a flock,' or pastured cattle. — Arab. *raʻiyah*, *raʻiya*(*t*), a flock, subject, peasant; from *raʻy*, pasturing, tending flocks. Cf. **Ryot.**

Raze, the same as **Rase** (above).

razor. (F. — L.) F. *rasoir*, a razor, lit. a shaver.— F. *raser*, to shave; see **Rase.**

Razzia, a sudden raid. (F. — Algiers.) F. *razzia, razia*; borrowed from the Algerine *razia*, which is a peculiar pronunciation of Arab. *ghāzīa*, a raid, expedition against infidels (Devic). — Arab. *ghāzī*, a hero, a leader of an expedition.

Re-, Red-, *prefix*, again. (F. — L.; or L.) L. *re-, red-*; commonly *re-*, except in *red-eem, red-olent, red-dition, red-ound, red-undant.* ¶ Hence a large number of compounds, such as *re-address, re-arrange*, which cause no difficulty.

Reach (1), to attain. (E.) M. E. *rechen*, pt. t. *raghte, raughte*, pp. *raught.* — A. S. *rǣcan, rēcean*, pt. t. *rǣhte.*+Du. *reiken*, O. Friesic *reka*; G. *reichen.* The A. S. *rǣcan* is closely allied to the sb. *ge-rēc*, opportunity; giving as the orig. sense ' to seize an opportunity.' Teut. type **raikjan-.* (Distinct from A. S. *reccan*, to stretch.) **Der.** *reach*, sb., which also means 'a stretch in a river.'

Reach (2), to try to vomit; see **Retch.**

Read. (E.) M. E. *reden.* A. S. *rǣdan* (strong verb), to counsel, consult, interpret, read; with the remarkable pt. t. *rēord.* [Also as a weak vb., pt. t. *rǣdde*; prob. by confusion with *rǣdan*, to dispose of, to govern.] Allied to Goth. *garēdan*, to provide, Icel. *rāða* (pt. t. *reð*), to advise, G. *rathen* (pt. t. *rieth*), to advise. Teut. type **rǣdan-.* Perhaps allied to L. *rē-rī*, to think. **Der.** *riddle* (1), q. v.

Ready. (E.) M. E. *redi*; with change of suffix from A. S. *rǣde*, ready; orig. ' equipped for riding,' or ' prepared for a raid'; [*ready* =' fully dressed,' is common in Tudor E.]; usual form *ge-rǣde.* — A. S. *rād*, 2nd stem of *rīdan*, to ride. So also G. *be-reit*, ready, from *reit-en*, to ride; Goth. *garaids*, Icel. *g-reiðr*, ready; cf. Goth. *raidjan*, to order, appoint. And cf. G. *fertig*, ready, from *fahren*, to go. See **Ride.**

Real (1), actual. (F. — L.; or L.) Either from O. F. *reël* (F. *réel*), or directly from Late L. *reālis*, belonging to the thing itself. — L. *rēs*, a thing. **Der.** *real-ist.*

Real (2), a small Spanish coin. (Span. — L.) Span. *real*, lit. a ' royal ' coin. — L. *rēgālis*, royal; see **Regal.**

Realgar, red arsenic. (F. — Span. — Arab.) F. *réalgar.*— Span. *rejalgar*, red sulphuret of arsenic. — Arab. *rahj al-ghār*, powder of the mine, mineral powder. — Arab. *rahj*, powder; *al*, the; *ghār*, a cavern, mine.

Realm. (F. — L.) M. E. *roialme, realme.*— A. F. *realme* (F. *royaume*), a kingdom; answering to a Late L. **rēgālimen.*— L. *rēgālis*, royal; see **Regal.**

Ream. (F. — Span. — Arab.) M. E. *reeme.*— O. F. *raime* (F. *rame*), a ream or bundle of paper. — Span. *resma*, a ream. — Arab. *risma(t)*, pl. *rizam*, a bundle.

Reap. (E.) M. E. *repen* (pt. t. *rep*, pp. *ropen*). O. Merc. *reopan*, A. S. *repan*, pt. t. *ræp*, pt. t. pl. *rēpon*. [But a commoner form is A. S. *rīpan* (pt. t. *rāp*, pp. *ripen*); whence A. S. *rīp*, E. *ripe*; see **Ripe**. The co-existence of these two strong verbs is remarkable.] The A. S. *repan* is from a Teut. base **rep-*, whence Du. *repel*, a flax-comb (see **Ripple** (1)), and Swed. *repa*, to rip up (see **Rip**). The A. S. *rīpan* is from a Teut. base **reip-*, whence **Ripe** and **Rope**.

Rear (1), to raise. (E.) M. E. *reren*. A. S. *rēran*, to rear ; the exact equivalent of Icel. *reisa*, to raise. Teut. type **raizjan-* (cf. Goth. *ur-raisjan*, to raise up); whence A. S. *rēran*, by Verner's law. See **Raise**. Causal form of *rīsan*, to rise (pt. t. *rās* = Goth. *rais*). **Doublet**, *raise*.

Rear (2), the back part. (F. — L.) M. E. *rere*, chiefly in adv. *arere*, *arrere*, in the rear. — O. F. *riere*, backward; whence *arière* (F. *arrière*), behind, backward. — L. *retro*, backward; whence *ad retro* > F. *arrière*. See **Retro-**.

Rear (3), insufficiently cooked. (E.) M. E. *rere*. A. S. *hrēr*, half-cooked.

Rearmouse; see **Reremouse**.

Rearward, the rear-guard. (F. — L. and G.) The old spelling is *rerevuard*, M. E. *rerewarde*, i. e. guard in the rear. See **Rear** (2) and **Ward**.

Reason. (F. — L.) M. E. *resoun*, *reisun*. — A. F. and O. F. *reison* (F. *raison*). — L. *ratiōnem*, acc. of *ratio*, calculation, reason. See **Ratio**.

Reave, to rob. (E.) M. E. *reuen* (= *reven*); pt. t. *rafte*, *refte*, pp. *raft*, *reft*. A. S. *rēafian*, to despoil, lit. to strip; cf. A. S. *rēaf*, clothing, a robe, spoil, plunder. — A. S. *rēaf*, 2nd grade of strong verb *rēofan*, to break. + Icel. *raufa*, to reave, *rauf*, spoil, from *rauf*, 2nd grade of *rjūfa*, to break up, violate; G. *rauben*, to rob, *raub*, plunder. The strong verb is of the Teut. type **reuban-* (pt. t. **raub*). Cf. L. *rumpere*, to break. Brugm. i. § 701.

Rebate, to blunt a sword's edge. (F. — L.) O. F. *rebatre*, to beat back again. — F. *re-* (L. *re-*), back; O. F. *batre*, F. *battre*, to beat; see **Batter** (1).

Rebeck, a three-stringed fiddle. (F. — Arab.) O. F. *rebec*, also spelt *rebebe*; M. Ital. *ribecca*, also *ribebba*, a rebeck. — Arab. *rabāb*, *rabāba(t)*, a rebeck (Devic).

Rebel. (F. — L.) The verb is from the sb., and the sb. was orig. an adj. M. E. *rebel*, adj., rebellious. — F. *rebelle*, rebellious. — L. *rebellem*, acc. of *rebellis*, renewing war. — L. *re-*, again; *bellum*, war = O. L. *duellum*, war; see **Duel**. **Der.** *rebel*, sb. and vb.; *rebell-ion*, *-ious*.

Rebound; see **Bound** (1).

Rebuff, a repulse. (Ital.) In Milton, P. L. ii. 936. — Ital. *rebuffo*, *ribuffo*, a check. — Ital. *ribuffare*, 'to check, chide;' Florio. — Ital. *ri-* (L. *re-*), back; *buffare*, a word of imitative origin, like E. *puff*; see **Puff**.

Rebuke, to reprove. (F. — L.) M. E. *rebuken*; A. F. *rebuker*. — O. F. (Picard) *rebuker*, to defeat (a plan); O. F. *rebukier*, *rebuchier* (Godefroy). — O. F. *re-* (L. *re-*), again, back; and O. North. F. *bucquer*, *buskier*, O. F. *buschier*, to beat, orig. to cut trees, to lop. This verb is from O. F. *busche*, F. *bûche*, a log; Late L. *busca*, a log. Cf. Picard *busker*, *buker*, to strike, beat (Corblet); Walloon *busquer*, *buquer*, to strike, *buque*, a log (Sigart); Norm. dial. *bûquette*, a billet. Orig. 'to lop, to cut back.' For O. F. *rebuker*, see Chardry, Vie des Set Dormans, l. 1589.

Rebus, a representation of a word by pictures. (L.) Thus *Bolton* was represented by pictures of a *bolt* and a *tun*. — L. *rēbus*, by things, i. e. by means of things; abl. pl. of *rēs*, a thing. See **Real** (1).

Rebut. (F. — L. and M. H. G.) O. F. *rebouter*, to repulse. — L. *re-*, again; M. H. G. *bōzen*, to beat; see **Beat**.

Recall. (L. and Scand.) From L. *re-*, back; and *call*, of Scand. origin.

Recant. (L.) L. *recantāre*, to sing back, echo; also, to recant, recall. — L. *re-*, back; *cantāre*, to sing. See **Cant** (1).

Recede. (L.) L. *recēdere*, to go back. — L. *re-*, back; *cēdere*, to go; see **Cede**.

Receive. (F. — L.) A. F. *receiv-*, a stem of *receivre*, O. F. *reçoivre*. — L. *recipere*, to take back. — L. *re-*, back; *capere*, to take. See **Capacious**.

Recent. (F. — L.) M. F. *recent* (F. *récent*). — L. *recent-*, stem of *recens*, fresh, new, orig. 'beginning anew.' — L. *re-*, again; *-cent-*, a stem allied to Russ. *po-chin-ate*, to begin, O. Irish *cét-*, first; and to Gk. καινός, new (Prellwitz).

Receptacle. (F. — L.) F. *réceptacle*. — L. *receptāculum*, a place to store away. — L. *recept-us*, pp. of *recipere*; see **Receive**.

reception. (F.—L.) F. *réception*.— L. acc. *receptiōnem*, a taking back.—L. *receptus* ; as above.

Recess. (L.) L. *recessus*, a retreat.— L. *recessus*, pp. of *re-cēdere*, to recede. See **Recede**.

Recheat, a signal of recall, in hunting. (F.—L.) From A.F. *rechet*, variant of O. F. *recet*, a place of refuge, a retreat (Godefroy).—L. *receptum*, acc. of *receptus*, a retreating, retreat.—L. *receptus*, pp. of *recipere*, to receive ; see **Receive**.

recipe. (L.) L. *recipe*, take thou ; imp. of *recipere*, to receive (above).

recipient. (L.) L. *recipient-*, stem of pres. pt. of *recipere*, to receive.

Reciprocal. (L.) From L. *reciprocus*, returning, alternating. Lit. ' directed backwards and forwards ;' from L. **re-co-*, backwards (from *re-*, back) ; and **pro-co-*, forwards, whence *procul*, afar off. Brugm. ii. § 86.

Recite. (F.—L.) M. F. *reciter*.—L. *recitāre*, to recite.—L. *re-*, again ; *citāre*, to quote ; see **Cite**.

Reck, to regard. (E.) M. E. *rekken* ; often *recchen*. A.S. *reccan, reccean* (for **rak-jan*) ; but the pt. t. in use is *rōh-te*, from an infin. *rēcan* (for **rōk-jan*), from the strong grade **rōk-*. + Icel. *rækja* ; O. Sax. *rōkjan*, to reck, heed. Formed from a sb. with base *rac-*, strong grade *rōc-*, care, which exists in the cognate M. H. G. *ruoch*, O. H. G. *ruoh*, care, heed (whence the M. H. G. *ruochen*, O. H. G. *ruohhjan*, to reck). β. The Teut. stem **rōk-* is the strong grade of **rak-*, as seen in Icel. *rök*, a reason, A. S. *racu*, account, reckoning, O. Sax. *raka*, a business, affair, O. H. G. *rahha*. **Der.** *reck-less*, A.S. *rēce-lēas* ; cf. Du. *roekeloos*, G. *ruchlos*.

reckon. (E.) M. E. *rekenen*. A.S. *ge-recenian*, to explain ; allied to *ge-reccan*, *reccan*, to rule, order, direct, explain, ordain, tell.+Du. *rekenen* ; (whence Icel. *reikna*, to reckon, Dan. *regne*, Swed. *räkna*, are borrowed) ; G. *rechnen*, O. H. G. *rehhanōn*, to compute, reckon. β. All secondary verbs ; allied to the sb. seen in A. S. *racu*, an account, Icel. *rök*, neut. pl., a reason, ground, origin, O. H. G. *rahha*, a thing, subject. See **Reck**.

Reclaim ; from Re- and Claim.

Recline. (L.) L. *reclīnāre*, to lean back, lie down.—L. *re-*, back ; **clīnāre*, to lean. See **Lean** (1) and **Incline**.

Recluse. (F.—L.) M. E. *recluse*, orig. fem.—O. F. *recluse*, fem. of *reclus*, pp. of *reclorre*, to shut up.—L. *reclūdere*, to unclose ; but in late Lat. to shut up. — L. *re-*, back ; *claudere*, to shut. See **Clause**.

Recognise. (F.—L.) Formed from the sb. *recognisance* (Chaucer, C. T. 13260). —O. F. *recognisance*, an acknowledgment. —O. F. *recognis-ant*, pres. part. of *recognoistre* (F. *reconnaître*).—L. *re-cognoscere*, to know again. See **Cognisance**. **Der.** *recognit-ion* (from L. pp. *recognit-us*).

Recoil, vb. (F.—L.) M. E. *recoilen*. —A. F. *recuiller* ; F. *reculer*, ' to recoyle, retire ;' Cot. Lit. to go backwards.—F. *re-*, back ; *cul*, the hinder part. — L. *re-*, back ; *cūlum*, acc. of *cūlus*, the hinder part.

Recollect, to remember. (F.—L.) Lit. ' to gather again ;' from *re-*, again, and *collect* ; see **Collect**.

Recommend, to commend to another. (F. — L.) From Re- and Commend ; imitated from F. *recommander*, ' to recommend ;' Cot.

Recompense, to reward. (F. — L.) M. F. *recompenser*, ' to recompence ;' Cot. —L. *re-*, again ; *compensāre*, to compensate ; see **Compensate**.

Reconcile. (F.—L.) O. F. *reconcilier*.—L. *re-*, again ; *conciliāre*, to conciliate ; see **Conciliate**.

Recondite, secret. (L.) L. *reconditus*, put away, hidden, secret ; pp. of *recondere*, to put back again.—L. *re-*, back ; *condere*, to put together. β. The L. *condere* (pt. t. *condidi*) is from *con-* (*cum*), with, and the weak grade of √DHĒ, to place, put. Brugm. i. § 573.

Reconnoitre, to survey. (F.—L.) O. F. *reconoistre*, M. F. *recognoistre*, ' to recognise, to take a precise view of ;' Cot. —L. *re-cognoscere*, to know again. See **Recognise**.

Record. (F.—L.) M. E. *recorden*.— O. F. *recorder*.—L. *recordāre, recordārī*, to recall to mind.—L. *re-*, again ; *cord-*, stem of *cor*, heart. See **Heart**.

Recount. (F.—L.) F. *raconter*, to teil, relate.—F. *re-* (L. *re-*), again ; *aconter*, to account ; from *a* (L. *ad*), to, and *conter*, to count. See **Count** (2). *Recount* = *re-ac-count*.

Recoup, to diminish a loss. (F.—L. *and* Gk.) Lit. to secure a piece or shred. —F. *recoupe*, a shred.—F. *recouper*, to cut again. ‒ L. *re-*, again; and F. *couper*, to cut; see Coppice.

Recourse. (F. ‒ L.) F. *recours.* ‒ L. *recursum*, acc. of *recursus*, a running back; from pp. of *recurrere*, to run back. ‒ L. *re-*, back; *currere*, to run; see Current.

Recover. (F. ‒ L.) O. F. *recovrer*, *re-cuvrer* (F. *recouvrer*). ‒ L. *recuperāre*, to recover, also to recruit oneself. A difficult word; perhaps orig. ' to make good again,' from Sabine *cuprus*, good, of which the orig. sense may have been ' desirable,' from L. *cupere*, to desire. Brugm. ii. § 74.

Recreant. (F. ‒ L.) O. F. *recreant*, faint-hearted; pres. pt. of *recroire*, to believe again, also to give up, give back (hence, to give in). ‒ Late L. *recrēdere*, to believe again, recant, give in. ‒ L. *re-*, again; *crēdere*, to believe; see Creed.

Recreation. (F. ‒ L.) M. F. *recreation.* ‒ L. *recreātiōnem*, acc. of *recreātio*, orig. recovery from illness (hence, amusement). ‒ L. *recreātus*, pp. of *recreāre*, to revive, refresh. ‒ L. *re-*, again; *creāre*, to make. See Create.

Recriminate. (L.) From L. *re-*, again; and *crīminātus*, pp. of *crīminārī*, to accuse of crime, from *crīmin-*, for *crīmen*, a crime. See Crime.

Recruit. (F. ‒ L.) F. *recruter*, to levy troops (Littré). An ill-formed word, from *recrute*, mistaken form of *recrue*, fem. of *recrû*, pp. of *recroître*, to grow again. F. *recrue*, sb., means ' a levy of troops,' lit. ' new-grown.' ‒ L. *recrescere*, to grow again. ‒ L. *re-*, again; *crescere*, to grow; see Crescent.

Rectangle, a four-sided right-angled figure. (F. ‒ L.) F. *rectangle*, adj., right angled (Cot.). ‒ L. *rectangulus*, having a right angle. ‒ L. *rect-us*, right; *angulus*, an angle. *Rectus* was orig. the pp. of *regere*, to rule. See Regent and Angle (1).

rectify. (F. ‒ L.) F. *rectifier.* ‒ Late L. *rectificāre*, to make right. ‒ L. *recti-*, for *rectus*, right (above); *-ficāre*, for *facere*, to make.

rectilinear. (L.) From L. *rectilīne-us*, formed by straight lines. ‒ L. *recti-*, for *rectus*, right, straight; *līnea*, a line.

rectitude. (F. ‒ L.) F. *rectitude.* ‒ L. *rectitūdo*, uprightness. ‒ L. *recti-* (above); with suffix *-tūdo*.

Recumbent. (L.) L. *recumbent-*, stem of pres. pt. of *recumbere*, to recline; where *cumbere* is a nasalised form allied to *cubāre*, to lie down. See Incumbent and Covey.

Recuperative, tending to recover. (L.) L. *recuperātīuus*, (properly) recoverable. ‒ L. *recuperāre*, to recover. See Recover.

Recur. (L.) L. *recurrere*, to run back, recur. ‒ L. *re-*, back; *currere*, to run; see Current.

Recusant, opposing an opinion. (F. ‒ L.) F. *récusant*, ' rejecting,' Cot.; pres. pt. of *récuser.* ‒ L. *recūsāre*, to reject, oppose a cause or opinion. ‒ L. *re-*, back; *caussa*, a cause. See Cause.

Red. (E.) M. E. *reed* (with long vowel). A. S. *rēad.*+Du. *rood*, Icel. *rauðr*, Dan. Swed. *röd*, G. *roth*, Goth. *rauds*. Teut. type *raudoz.* Further allied to Gk. ἐρυθρός, Irish and Gael. *ruath*, W. *rhudd*, L. *ruber* (for *rudhro-*), red; cf. Russ. *ruda*, Skt. *rudhira-*, blood. Note also the Icel. strong verb *rjōða* (pt. t. *rauð*), to redden; A. S. *rēoðan*, to redden; Teut. type * *reudan-*, pt. t. * *raud.* (✓REUDH.)

Reddition, a restoring. (F. ‒ L.) F. *reddition.* ‒ L. *redditiōnem*, acc. of *redditio*, a restoring. ‒ L. *reddere*, to give back. ‒ L. *red-*, back; *dare*, to give. See Date (1).

Redeem, to atone for. (L.) Formerly *redeme.* Coined from L. *red-*, back, and *emere*, to buy. [Cf. O. M. F. *redimer*, ' to redeem;' Cot. ‒ L. *redimere*, to buy back.] Der. *redempt-ion* (from the pp. *redemptus*).

Redgum, a disease of infants. (E.) M. E. *reed gounde*, lit. ' red matter ' (of a sore); Prompt. Parv. From A. S. *rēad*, red; *gund*, matter of a sore.

Redintegration, renovation. (L.) From L. *redintegrātio*, restoration. ‒ L. *red-*, again; *integer*, whole, entire. See Integer.

Redolent, fragrant. (F. ‒ L.) M. F. *redolent.* ‒ L. *redolent-*, stem of pres. pt. of *redolēre*, to emit odour. ‒ L. *red-*, again; *olēre*, for *odēre*, to be odorous; see Odour.

Redoubt, an intrenched place of retreat. (F. ‒ Ital. ‒ L.) Ill spelt; through confusion with *redoubtable*. F. *redoute.* ‒ Ital. *ridotto*, a place of retreat. ‒ Ital. *ridotto*, *ridutto*, pp. of *ridurre*, to bring home. ‒ L. *redūcere*, to bring back. ‒ L. *re-*, back; *dūcere*, to lead. See Duke.

Redoubtable. (F. ‒ L.) M. F. *redoubtable*, terrible. ‒ O. F. *redouter*, M. F. *redoubter*, to fear. See Re- and Doubt.

Redound. (F. ‒ L.) F. *redonder.* ‒ L. *redundāre*, to overflow. ‒ L. *red-*, again, back; *unda*, a wave. See Undulate.

Redress. (F.—L.) F. *redresser*, to put straight again. —F. *re-*, again ; *dresser*, to erect, dress ; see **Dress**.

Redstart, a bird with a red tail. (E.) From **Red** ; and *start*, a tail (A. S. *steort*).

Reduce. (L.) Orig. to bring back. — L. *redūcere*, to bring back. — L. *re-*, back ; *dūcere*, to lead. See **Duke**. **Der.** *reduction* (from the pp. *reduct-us*).

Redundant. (L.) From stem of pres. pt. of L. *redundāre*, to redound. See **Redound**.

Reechy, dirty. (E.) Lit. ' smoky ; ' palatalised form of *reeky* ; cf. Low. Sc. *reekie*, smoky. See **Reek**.

Reed. (E.) M. E. *reed*. A. S. *hrēod*, a reed.+Du. *riet* ; G. *riet*, *ried*. Teut. type **hreudom*, neut.

Reef (1), a ridge of rocks. (Du.) Formerly *riff*.—Du. *rif*, a reef.+Icel. *rif*, a reef, allied to *rifa*, a fissure, rift ; Dan. *rev*, a sand-bank (*revle*, a shoal, *revne*, to split); Swed. *refva*, *ref*, a sand-bank, a cleft, gap. The Du. and Icel. *riv*, Dan. *rev*, may represent a Teut. type **rebjom*, n. ; perhaps allied to **Rib**. Cf. Norw. *ribbe*, a mountain-ridge.

Reef (2), a portion of a sail. (Du.) M. E. *riff*.—Du. *reef*, ' a riff in a sail,' Sewel ; M. Du. *rif*, *rift*, a reef.+Icel. *rif*, a reef in a sail ; Dan. *reb*, Swed. *ref*, reef; Low G. *reff*, *riff*, a small sail ; Pomeran. *räff*, a little extra sail, bonnet.

Reek, vapour. (E.) M.E. *reke*. O.Merc. *rēc*, vapour ; O. Fries. *rēk*.+Icel. *reykr*, Swed. *rök*, Dan. *rög* ; Du. *rook*, G. *rauch* ; Teut. base **rauk-*. From **rauk*, 2nd grade of Teut. **reukan-*, to smoke ; as in A. S. *rēocan*, Icel. *rjūka*, O. H. G. *riohhan*, G. *riechen*. Brugm. i. § 217.

Reel (1), a small spindle for winding yarn. (E.) M. E. *rele* ; A.S. *hrēol*, a reel. +E. Fries. *rēl* ; N. Fries. *reel*. Kluge derives A. S. *hrēol* from a form **hrōehil*, but this would give A. S. *hrēl* ; see Eng. Stud. xi. 512. **Der.** *reel*, vb., to wind, turn round, stagger.

Reel (2), a Highland dance. (Gael.) Gael. *righil*, *ruidhil*, *ruithil*, a reel.

Reest, the wood on which a plough-coulter is fixed. (E.) Also *wreest* (wrongly), *rest*. A. S. *rēost*.

Reeve (1), to pass a rope through a ring. (Du.) Du. *reven*, to reeve. — Du. *reef*, a reef in a sail ; because a reeved rope is used for reefing ; see **Reef** (2).

Reeve (2), an officer, steward. (E.)

A. S. *gerēfa*, an officer ; orig. sense perhaps ' numberer,' registrar (of soldiers); for **ge-rōfja*. From *-rōf*, a host (as in *secg-rōf*, a host of men) ; cf. O. H. G. *ruova*, a number. ¶ *Not* allied to G. *graf*. **Der.** *borough-reeve* ; *port-reeve* ; *sheriff*, q. v.

Refection, refreshment. (F. — L.) M. F. *refection*, a repast. — L. acc. *refectiōnem*, lit. a remaking. — L. *refectus*, pp. of *reficere*, to remake, restore. — L. *re-*, again; *facere*, to make. See **Fact**.

Refel. (L.) L. *refellere*, to refute, shew to be false. — L. *re-*, back ; *fallere*, to deceive ; see **Fallible**.

Refer, to assign. (F.—L.) O. F. *referer* (F. *référer*). — L. *referre*, to bear back, relate, refer. — L. *re-*, back ; *ferre*, to bear; see **Fertile**.

Refine. (F.—L.) Coined from *re-* and *fine* (1), but imitated from F. *raffiner*, to refine, comp. of L. *re-*, again, L. *af-=ad*, to, and F. *fin*, fine. **Der.** *refine-ment* ; cf. F. *raffinement*.

Reflect. (L.) L. *reflectere*, lit. to bend back, hence to return rays, &c. — L. *re-*, back ; *flectere*, to bend ; see **Flexible**.

Reform. (F.—L.) F. *reformer*, to shape anew. — L. *re-*, again ; *formāre*, to form; see **Form**.

Refract, to bend back rays of light. (L.) L. *refractus*, pp. of *refringere*, to bend back. — L. *re-*, back ; *frangere*, to break ; see **Fragile**. **Der.** *refract-or-y*, a mistaken form for *refractary*, from L. *refractārius*, stubborn, obstinate. Also *refrangible*, a mistaken form for *refringible*.

Refrain (1), to restrain, forbear. (F. — L.) M. E. *refreinen*. — O. F. *refrener*, to repress ; Cot. — L. *refrēnāre*, to bridle, hold in with a bit. — L. *re-*, back ; *frēnum*, a bit, curb. The orig. sense of *frēnum* is prob. due to a derivation from L. *frendere*, to champ ; as if for **frend-num*. If so, it is allied to **Grind**. ¶ Prob. sometimes confused with M. F. *refraindre*, ' to bridle,' Cot.; this is from L. *refringere*, to break back (below).

Refrain (2), the burden of a song. (F. — L.) F. *refrain* ; so also Prov. *refranhs*, a refrain, *refranher*, *refrenher*, to repeat. So called from frequent repetition ; the O. F. *refreindre*, to pull back, is the same word as Prov. *refrenher*, to repeat ; both are from L. *refringere*, to break back (refract, hence, to repeat). — L. *re-*, back ; *frangere*, to break ; see **Fragile**.

Refresh. (F.—L. *and* G.) M. E. *re-*

freschen. — O. F. *refreschir* ; Cot. — L. *re-*, again ; O. H. G. *frisc* (G. *frisch*), fresh. See **Fresh.**

Refrigerate. (L.) From pp. of L. *refrīgerāre*, to make cool again. — L. *re-*, again ; *frīgerāre*, to cool, from *frīgus*, cold. See **Frigid.**

Reft, pp. of *reave* ; see **Reave.**

Refuge. (F. — L.) M. E. *refuge.* — F. *refuge.* — L. *refugium*, an escape. — L. *refugere*, to flee back. — L. *re-*, back ; *fugere*, to flee ; see **Fugitive.**

refugee. (F. — L.) M. F. *refugié*, pp. of *se refugier*, to take refuge. — F. *refuge* (above).

Refulgent. (L.) From L. *refulgent-*, stem of pres. pt. of *refulgēre*, to flash back. — L. *re-*, back ; *fulgēre*, to shine. See **Fulgent.**

Refund, to repay. (L.) L. *refundere*, to pour back, also to restore, give back (see below).

refuse, to deny a request. (F. — L.) M. E. *refusen.* — O. F. *refuser* (the same as Port. *refusar*, Ital. *refusare*, to reject). answers to a Late L. type *refūsāre*, formed as a frequentative of *refundere*, to pour back, also to restore, give back (whence to reject). — L. *re-*, back ; *fundere*, to pour ; see **Fuse** (1). β. We may also note E. *refuse*, sb., O. F. *refus*, refuse ; cf. O. F. *mettre en refus, faire refus à*, to abandon, reject (Godefroy).

refute, to oppose, disprove. (F. — L.) M. F. *refuter.* — L. *refūtāre*, to repel, rebut. The orig. sense was prob. ' to beat back ; ' see **Confute.**

Regain. (F. L. *and* O. H. G.) F. *regagner.* — L. *re-*, back ; and F. *gagner*, to gain. See **Gain** (1).

Regal. (F. — L.) M. F. *regal*, royal ; Cot. — L. *rēgālis*, adj., from *rēg-*, stem of *rex*, a king. Allied to L. *regere*, to rule. Cf. Skt. *rājan-*, a king ; O. Irish *rī.* Brugm. i. §§ 135, 549 c. Der. *regal-ia*, insignia of a king ; neut. pl. of *rēgālis.*

Regale, to entertain. (F. — Ital.?) M.F. *regaler*, to entertain. Not allied to *regal*, as Cotgrave suggests ; but the same as Span. *regalar*, to make much of, pamper ; orig. to melt (Diez). 1. Diez derives it from L. *regelāre*, to melt, thaw ; from L. *re-*, back, *gelāre*, to freeze (see **Gelid**). 2. Hatzfeld derives F. *régaler* (ultimately) from Ital. *regalare*, to give presents to ; from Ital. *gala*, mirth. See **Gala.**

Regard, vb. (F. — L. *and* O. H. G.)

F. *regarder*, to look, look at, view. — L. *re-*, back ; F. *garder*, to guard, observe ; of O. H. G. origin ; see **Guard.**

Regatta. (Ital.) Orig. a strife, contention, hence a race, rowing-match. — Ital. *regatta, rigatta*, ' a strife for the maistrie ; ' Florio. — M. Ital. *rigattare*, to contend for the mastery, to wrangle, to haggle as a huckster does. So also Span. *regatear*, to haggle, retail provisions, to rival in sailing. Of unknown origin.

Regenerate. (L.) From pp. of *regenerāre*, to produce anew. — L. *re-*, again ; *generāre*, to produce, from *gener-*, for **genes-*, stem of *genus*, kindred. See **Genus.**

Regent. (F. — L.) M. F. *regent*, a regent, vice-gerent. — L. *regent-*, stem of pres. pt. of *regere*, to rule. Allied to Gk. ὀρέγειν, to stretch, Goth. *uf-rakjan*, to stretch out, Skt. *rj*, to stretch, *rāj*, to govern. (√REG.) See **Right.** Brugm. i. § 474.

regicide, slayer of a king ; slaying of a king. (F. — L.) M. F. *regicide* (Minsheu). — L. *rēgi-*, for *rex*, king, allied to *regere*, to rule ; *-cīda*, a slayer, from *cædere*, to slay. Also : from L. *rēgi-* (as before), *-cīdium*, a slaying, from *cædere.*

regimen. (L.) L. *regimen*, guidance. — L. *regere*, to rule, direct.

regiment. (F. — L.) M.F. *regiment*, ' a regiment of souldiers,' Cot. ; also, a government. — L. *regimentum*, rule, government. — L. *regere*, to rule.

region. (F. — L.) M.F. *region.* — L. *regiōnem*, acc. of *regio*, territory. — L. *regere*, to rule, govern.

Register. (F. — L.) M. F. *registre*, ' a record ; ' Cot. — Late L. *registrum*, more correctly *regestum*, a book in which things are recorded (L. *regeruntur*). — L. *regestum*, neut. of pp. of *regerere*, to bring back, record. — L. *re-*, back ; *gerere*, to carry. See **Gerund.** Cf. L. *regesta*, pl., a register.

Regnant, reigning. (L.) L. *regnant-*, stem. of pres. pt. of *regnāre*, to reign. — L. *regnum*, kingdom. — L. *regere*, to rule. See **Regent.**

Regress, return. (L.) L. *regressus*, sb. — L. *regressus*, pp. of *regredī*, to go back. — L. *re-*, back ; *gradī*, to go. See **Grade.**

Regret, sorrow. (F. — L. *and* Scand.) F. *regret*, grief ; *regretter*, to lament (Cot.). The oldest form of the verb is *regrater.* Of disputed origin ; see Scheler. The

most likely solution is that which derives
O. F. *regrater* from L. *re-*, again, and the
verb which appears in Icel. *grāta*, Swed.
gråta, Dan. *græde*, A. S. *grŵtan*, Lowl. Sc.
greit, to weep, bewail. See Greet (2).
Cf. 'I mone as a chylde dothe for the
wantyng of his nourse or mother, *je
regrete*;' Palsgrave.

Regular. (L.) L. *rēgulāris*, according
to rule. – L. *rēgula*, a rule ; *regere*, to rule.
See Regent.

Rehearse. (F. – L.) M. E. *rehersen*.
– O. F. *reherser*, *rehercer*, to harrow over
again ; hence, to go over the same ground.
– L. *re-*, again ; O. F. *hercer*, to harrow,
from *herce*, sb., a harrow. See Hearse.

Reign, sb. (F. – L.) M. E. *regne*. –
M. F. *regne*. – L. *regnum*, kingdom. – L.
regere, to rule. See Regent.

Reimburse, to refund. (F. – L. *and*
Gk.) Adapted from F. *rembourser* by
substituting L. *re-im-* for F. *rem-* (with
the same force). – L. *re-*, again ; *im-*
(for *in*), in ; F. *bourse*, a purse. See
Purse.

Rein. (F. – L.) M. E. *reine*. – O. F.
reine, rein of a bridle. (The same as Ital.
redina, Span. *rienda*, transposed form of
redina.) – Late L. **retina*, not found, but
a short form allied to L. *retināculum*, a
rein. – L. *retinēre*, to hold back. – L. *re-*,
back ; *tenēre*, to hold. See Retain.

Reindeer, Raindeer, a kind of deer.
(Scand.) M. E. *raynedere*. Formed by
adding *deer* (see Deer) to Icel. *hreinn*,
a reindeer ; cf. also O. Swed. *ren*, a reindeer, A. S. *hrān*. [We also find Dan.
rensdyr, Du. *rendier*, G. *rennthier*.] Teut.
type **hrainoz* ; a true Teut. word, as the
forms shew. β. Diez refers us to Lapp
raingo, but this is merely a bad spelling
of Swed. *renko*, i. e. rein-cow. The true
Lapp word is *påtso*, a reindeer ; nor can
the Icel. word have been suggested by
Lapp *reino*, a pasturage for rein-deer ;
Ihre, Lexicon Lapponicum, p. 374.

Reins, the lower part of the back. (F.
– L.) O. F. *reins*. – L. *rēnēs*, pl., kidneys,
reins.

Reject. (F. – L.) M. F. *rejecter* (16th
cent. ; F. *rejeter* ; oldest spelling *regeter*).
– O. F. *re-*, back ; *geter, getter*, to throw,
from L. *iactāre* ; see Jet (1).

Rejoice. (F. – L.) M. E. *reioisen*. –
O. F. *resjois-*, stem of pres. pt. of *resjoïr*
(mod. F. *réjouir*), to gladden, rejoice. – L.
re-, again ; O. F. *esjoïr*, to rejoice, from L.

ex, much, very, and *gaudēre*, to rejoice.
See Gaud.

Rejoin. (F. – L.) Lit. to join again ;
in legal language, to answer to a reply. –
F. *rejoign-*, a stem of *rejoindre*, to rejoin.
– L. *reiungere*, to join again. – L. *re-*,
again ; *iungere*, to join. See Join. Der.
rejoinder, which is the F. infin. mood used
as a sb., as in the case of *attainder*.

Relapse, to slide back into a former
state. (L.) From L. *relapsus*, pp. of *re-
lābī*, to slide back. – L. *re-*, back ; *lābī*, to
slide ; see Lapse.

Relate, to describe, tell. (F. – L.) F.
relater, 'to relate ;' Cot. – Late L. *relātāre*,
to relate. – L. *relātus*, used as pp. of *referre*,
to relate (but from a different root). – L.
re-, again ; *lātus*, for *tlātus*, borne, pp. of
tollere, to bear. See Tolerate.

Relax. (L.) L. *relaxāre*, to relax. – L.
re-, again ; *laxāre*, to slacken ; see Lax.
Doublet, *release*.

relay (1), a set of fresh dogs or horses,
a fresh supply. (F. – L.) Orig. used of
dogs and horses. – F. *relais*, a relay ;
chiens de relais, *chevaux de relais*, dogs or
horses kept in reserve ; Cot. The orig.
sense is 'a rest,' and *chiens de relais* are
dogs kept at rest ; cf. *à relais* 'at rest, that
is not used,' Cot. ; and see *relais* in
Godefroy. – O. F. *relaissier*, to relinquish.
– L. *relaxāre*, to loosen, let loose, allow
to rest ; see Lax. Cf. Italian *cani di
rilasso*, dogs kept in reserve (late edition
of Florio by Torriano, 1688).

Relay (2), to lay again. (L. *and* E.)
From *re-* and *lay*. See Lay (1).

Release. (F. – L.) M. E. *relessen*, *re-
lesen*. – O. F. *relessier* (M. F. *relaisser*), to
relax. – L. *relaxāre*, to relax ; see Relax.

Relegate, to consign to exile. (L.)
From pp. of L. *relēgāre*, to send away,
remove. – L. *re-*, again, back ; *lēgāre*, to
send, appoint ; see Legate.

Relent. (F. – L.) Altered from F. *ra-
lentir*, to slacken, to relent (cf. L. *relen-
tescere*, to slacken). – F. *ra-*, for *re-a-* (L.
re-ad) ; L. *lentus*, slack, slow, allied to
lēnis, gentle, and to E. *lithe*. See Lenient
and Lithe.

Relevant. (F. – L.) The orig. sense
is 'helpful' ; hence, of use for the matter
in hand. – F. *relevant*, pres. part. of *relever*,
to raise up, assist, help. – L. *releuāre*, to
raise again. – L. *re-*, again ; *leuāre*, to raise,
from *leuis*, light. See Levity.

Relic, a memorial. (F. – L.) Chiefly

in the pl.; M. E. *relikes.* — F. *reliques*, s. pl., 'reliques;' Cot. — L. *reliquiās*, acc. of *reliquiæ*, pl., remains. — L. *relinquere*, to leave behind. — L. *re-*, back; *linquere*, to leave. See **Relinquish, Licence.**

relict, a widow. (L.) L. *relicta*, fem. of *relictus*, pp. of *relinquere*, to leave behind (above).

Relieve. (F. — L.) M. E. *releuen* (= *releven*). — F. *relever*, to raise up, relieve. — L. *releuāre*, to raise again; see **Relevant.** Der. *relief*, M. E. *relef*, O. F. *relief* (F. *relief*), a sb. due to the verb *relever*.

Religion. (F. — L.) F. *religion*; Cot. — L. acc. *religiōnem*, from *religio*, piety; allied to *religens*, fearing the gods, pious. *Re-ligens* is the opposite of *neg-ligens*, negligent; see **Neglect.** Allied also to *di-ligent*, and to Gk. ἀλέγειν, to reverence.

Relinquish. (F. — L.) O. F. *relenquis-*, pr. pt. stem of *relenquir*, to leave (Godefroy). — L. *relinquere*, to leave behind; see **Relic.**

reliquary, a casket for relics. (F. — L.) F. *reliquaire*, ' a casket wherein reliques be kept;' Cot. — Late L. *reliquiārium* (same sense). — L. *reliquiā-*, orig. stem of *reliquiæ*, relics; see **Relic** (above).

relique; the same as **Relic.**

Relish, orig. an after-taste. (F. — L.) M. E. *reles*, an after-taste, Sir Cleges, 208. — O. F. *reles, relais*, that which is left behind; also a relay; see **Relay** (1).

Reluctant. (L.) From stem of pres. pt. of *reluctāre, reluctārī*, to struggle against. — L. *re-*, back; *luctāri*, to struggle, from *lucta*, a wrestling. Allied to Gk. λυγ-ίζειν, to bend, writhe in wrestling; Lith. *lugnas*, flexible, Skt. *ruj*, to bend, break. (√LEUG.)

Rely, to repose on trustfully. (F. — L.) We find 'to *relye* their faithe upon'; where *relye* = fasten. — F. *relier*, to bind up, or together. — L. *religāre*, to fasten. L. *re-*, back; *ligāre*, to bind; see **Ligament.** ¶ But much influenced by E. *lie*, vb., to repose, though this would have required a pp. *relain*. Der. *reli-ance*.

Remain. (F. — L.) O. F. pres. s. (*je*) *remain*; cf. M. F. impers. vb. *il remain-t*, it remains. [The infin. *remaindre* is preserved in E. *remainder*, used as a sb.] — L. *reman-eo*, I remain; *reman-et*, it remains; *remanēre*, to remain. — L. *re-*, behind; *manēre*, to stay. See **Mansion.**

Remand, to send back. (F. — L.) M.F. *remander.* — L. *remandāre*, to send back

word. — L. *re-*, back; *mandāre*, to send; see **Mandate.**

Remark, to take notice of. (F. — L. and Teut.) F. *remarquer*, to mark, note, heed. — L. *re-*, again; *marquer*, to mark, from *marque*, sb., a mark; see **Mark** (1).

Remedy. (F. — L.) M. E. *remedie.* — A. F. *remedie*, O. F. *remede*, mod. F. *remède.* — L. *remedium*, a remedy; that which heals again. — L. *re-*, again; *medērī*, to heal. See **Medicine.**

Remember. (F. — L.) O. F. *remem-brer.* — L. *rememorārī*, to remember. — L. *re-*, again; *memorāre*, to make mention of, from *memor*, mindful. See **Memory.**

Remind, to bring to mind again. (L. and E.) From **Re-** and **Mind.**

Reminiscence. (F. — L.) M. F. *re-miniscence.* — L. *reminiscentia*, remembrance. — L. *reminiscent-*, stem of pres. pt. of *reminiscī*, to remember. — L. *re-*, again; and base of *me-min-ī*, I remember. Allied to Gk. μέ-μον-α, I yearn, Skt. *man*, to think. (√MEN.)

Remit, to abate. (L.) L. *remittere* (pp. *remissus*), to send back, slacken, abate. — L. *re-*, back; *mittere*, to send; see **Missile.** Der. *remiss*, adj., from pp. *remissus*; *remiss-ion.*

Remnant. (F. — L.) M. E. *reman-aunt.* — O. F. *remanant.* — L. *remanent-*, stem of pres. pt. of *remanēre*, to remain. see **Remain.**

Remonstrate. (L.) From pp. of Late L. *remonstrāre*, to expose, to produce arguments against. — L. *re-*, again; *mon-strāre*, to show, from *monstrum*, a portent; see **Monster.**

Remorse. (F. — L.) M. F. *remors*; Cot. — Late L. *remorsus*, remorse. — L. *remorsus*, pp. of *remordēre*, to bite again, to vex. — L. *re-*, again; *mordēre*, to bite; see **Mordacity.**

Remote, distant. (L.) L. *remōtus*, pp. of *remouēre*, to remove; see **Remove.** Or from M. F. *remote*, f. 'remove, removed,' Cot.; from L. pp. f. *remōta.*

Remount, to mount again. (F. — L.) F. *remonter.* — F. *re-*, again; *monter*, to mount; see **Mount** (2).

Remove. (F. — L.) M.F. *remouvoir*, Cot. See **Re-** and **Move.**

Remunerate, to recompense. (L.) From pp. of *remūnerāre, remūnerārī*, to reward. — L. *re-*, again; *mūnerāre*, to bestow a gift, from *mūner-* (for **mūnes-*), stem of *mūnus*, a gift, also, an office. See Municipal.

Renaissance, revival of learning. (F.–L.) M. F. *renaissance*, 'a new birth,' Cot.–L. *re-*, again; *nascentia*, birth, from *nascent-*, stem of pres. pt. of *nascī*, to be born. See Natal.

Renal. (F.–L.) M. F. *renal*.–L. *rēnālis*, adj.; from *rēnēs*, s. pl., reins. See Reins.

Renard; see Reynard.

Rencounter, Rencontre. (F.–L.) F. *rencontre*, a meeting.–F. *rencontrer*, to meet.–F. *re-*, again; *encontrer*, to meet, encounter; see Encounter.

Rend. (E.) M. E. *renden*. A. S. *rendan*, to cut or tear.+O. Fries. *renda*, to tear; North Fr. *renne*, *ranne*, to tear apart. Der. *rent*, sb., from pp. *rent*.

Render. (F.–L.) M. E. *rendren*.–F. *rendre*.–L. *reddere*, to give back.–L. *red-*, back; *dare*, to give; see Date (1).

rendezvous. (F.–L.) F. *rendezvous*, 'a rendevous, place appointed for the assemblie of souldiers;' Cot.–F. *rendez vous*<L. *reddite uōs*, render yourselves; imperative pl. of *reddere* (above).

Renegade, Renegado. (Span.–L.) Span. *renegado*, an apostate, one who has denied the faith; orig. pp. of *renegar*, to forsake the faith.–L. *re-*, again; *negāre*, to deny. See Negation.

Renew. (L. *and* E.) From L. *re-*, again; and E. *new*.

Rennet (1), the prepared inner membrane of a calf's stomach, used to make milk coagulate. (E.) M. E. *renet*; from M. E. *rennen*, to run; prov. E. *run*, to congeal, coagulate. See Run. Hence *rennet* is also called *runnet* (Pegge's Kenticisms); also *erning* (Derbyshire), from A. S. *irnan*, to run. So also M. Du. *rinsel*, *runsel*, *renninge*, 'curds, or milk-runnet,' from *rinnen*, 'to presse, curdle;' Hexham. Cf. G. *rinnen*, to run, curdle, coagulate.

Rennet (2), a sweet kind of apple. (F.–L.) Formerly spelt *renate*, from an odd notion that it was derived from L. *renātus*, born again!–F. *reinette, rainette*, a rennet; the same as *rainette*, a little frog; from the speckled skin. Dimin. of F. *raine*, a frog.–L. *rāna*, a frog. Cf. Ranunculus.

Renounce. (F.–L.) F. *renoncer*.–L. *renuntiāre*, to bring back a report, also to disclaim, renounce.–L. *re-*, back; again; *nuntiāre*, to tell, bring news, from *nuntius*, a messenger. See Nuncio.

Der. *renunciat-ion*, F. *renonciation*, from L. pp. *renuntiātus*.

Renovate. (L.) From L. *renouātus*, pp. of *renouāre*, to renew.–L. *re-*, again; *nouāre*, to make new, from *nouus*, new. See Novel.

Renown, fame. (F.–L.) M. E. *renoun*.–A. F. *renoun, renun*; O. F. *renon* (12th cent.). [Cf. Port. *renome*, Span. *renombre*, renown.]–O. F. *renomer*, to make famous.–L. *re-*, again; *nōmināre*, to name, from *nōmen*, a name; see Noun.

Rent (1), a tear; see Rend.

Rent (2), annual payment. (F.–L.) M. E. *rente*.–F. *rente*. [Cf. Ital. *rendita*, rent.]–Late L. *rendita*, nasalised form of L. *reddita*, fem. of pp. of *reddere*, to render; see Render.

Renunciation. (F.–L.) M. F. *renonciation*, 'renunciation;' Cot.–L. acc. *renuntiātiōnem*, prop. an announcement. –L. *renuntiāt-us*, pp. of *renuntiāre*, orig. to announce; see Renounce.

Repair (1), to restore, amend. (F.–L.) M. F. *reparer*.–L. *reparāre*, to recover, repair, make ready anew.–L. *re-*, again; *parāre*, to get ready; see Pare. Der. *repar-able*, M. F. *reparable*, L. *reparābilis*; *repar-at-ion*, M. F. *reparation*.

Repair (2), to resort to. (F.–L.) M.F. *repairer*, to haunt; Cot. Older form *repairier* (Burguy).–L. *repatriāre*, to repair to one's own country.–L. *re-*, back; *patria*, native country, from *patri-*, for *pater*, a father.

Repartee, a witty reply. (F.–L.) F. *repartie*, 'a reply;' Cot. Orig. fem. of *reparti*, pp. of M. F. *repartir*, to re-divide, to answer thrust with thrust, to reply.–F. *re-*, again; *partir*, to part, also to rush, dart off, burst out laughing.–L. *re-*, again; *partīre*, to share, from *parti-*, for *pars*, a part. See Part.

Repast, a meal. (F.–L.) O.F. *repast*, later *repas*.–L. *re-*, again; *pastum*, acc. of *pastus*, food, from *pascere*, to feed. See Pastor.

Repay. (F.–L.) O. F. *repaier*.–O. F. *re-* (L. *re-*), back; *paier*, to pay; see Pay.

Repeal. (F.–L.) Altered from O. F. *rapeler*, F. *rappeler*, to repeal.–O. F. *re-* (L. *re-*); *apeler*, later *appeler*, to appeal. See Appeal. *Repeal*=*re-appeal*.

Repeat. (F.–L.) Formerly *repete*. M. F. *repeter*, Cot.–L. *repetere*, to attack

442

again, reseek, repeat. — L. *re-*, again ; *petere*, to attack ; see **Petition**. Der. *repet-ition*.

Repel. (L.) L. *repellere*, to drive back. — L. *re-*, back ; *pellere*, to drive ; see **Pulse**. Der. *repulse*, from pp. *repulsus*.

Repent, to rue. (F. — L.) F. *repentir*, to repent. — L. *re-*, again ; *pœnitēre*, to cause to repent ; see **Penitent**.

Repercussion. (L.) From **Re-** and **Percussion**.

Repertory, a treasury. (F. — L.) M. F. *repertoire*. — L. *repertōrium*, an inventory. — L. *repertor*, a finder, discoverer. — L. *reperīre*, to find out. — L. *re-*, again ; *parīre* (Ennius), usually *parere* to produce ; see **Parent**.

Repine. (L.) Compounded of L. *re-*, again ; and *pine*, to fret ; see **Pine** (2).

Replace. (F. — L. *and* Gk.) From *re-* (F. *re-*, L. *re-*), again ; and **Place**.

Replenish. (F. — L.) O. F. *repleniss-*, stem of pres. pt. of *replenir*, to fill up again ; now obsolete. — L. *re-*, again ; Late L. **plēnīre*, to fill, from L. *plēnus*, full.

replete, full. (F. — L.) M. F. *replet*, masc. ; *replete*, fem., full. — L. *replētus*, filled up ; pp. of *re-plēre*, to fill again. — L. *re-*, again ; *plēre*, to fill ; see **Plenary**.

Replevy, to get back detained goods on a pledge to try the right in a suit. (F. — Teut.) F. *re-* (L. *re-*), again ; O. F. *plevir*, to be surety. See **Pledge**.

Reply. (F. — L.) M. E. *replien*. — O. F. *replier*, the old form afterwards replaced by the 'learned' form *répliquer*, to reply. — L. *replicāre*, lit. to fold back ; as a law term, to reply. — L. *re-*, back ; *plicāre*, to fold. Der. *replica*, a repetition ; from Ital. *replica*, a sb. due to L. *replicāre*, to repeat, reply.

Report. (F. — L.) M. E. *reporten*. — F. *reporter*, to carry back. — L. *reportāre*, to carry back. — L. *re-*, back ; *portāre*, to carry ; see **Port** (1). The E. sense 'to relate' is due to F. *rapporter*, O. F. *raporter* ; with prefix *ra-* < L. *re-ad*.

Repose. (F. — L. *and* Gk.) F. *reposer*, to rest, pause ; Late L. *repausāre*, to pause, rest. — L. *re-*, again ; *pausāre*, to pause, from *pausa*, sb., due to Gk. παῦσις, a pause. ¶ Important ; this is the verb which seems to have given rise to *poser* and its compounds. See **Pose**.

Repository, a storehouse. (F. — L.) M. F. *repositoire*, a storehouse. — L. *repositōrium*. — L. *repositus*, pp. of *repōnere*, to

lay up, store. — L. *re-*, again ; *pōnere*, to place ; see **Position**.

Reprehend, to reprove. (L.) L. *reprehendere*, to hold back, check, blame. — L. *re-*, back ; *prehendere*, to seize, to hold. See **Prehensile**.

Represent. (F. — L.) O. F. *representer*. — L. *repræsentāre*, to bring before again, exhibit. — L. *re-*, again ; *præsentāre*, to present ; see **Present** (2).

Repress. (F. — L.) From F. *re-*, again, and *presser*, to press ; but used with sense of L. *reprimere* (pp. *repressus*) to press back, check. — L. *re-*, back ; *premere*, to press ; see **Press**.

Reprieve, vb. (F. — L.) [A doublet of *reprove*.] M. E. *repreven*, to reprove, reject, disallow ; to *reprieve* a sentence is to disallow it. — O. F. *repreuve*, 3rd pres. sing. indic. of *reprover* (F. *réprouver*), to reprove ; see **Reprove**. Cf. Schwan, § 348 (4).

Reprimand. (F. — L.) F. *réprimande*, formerly *reprimende*, 'a reproof ;' Cot. — L. *reprimenda*, a thing that ought to be repressed ; hence, a check. Fem. of the gerundive of *reprimere*, to repress ; see **Repress**.

Reprisal. (F. — Ital. — L.) M. F. *represaille*, a taking or seizing on, a reprisal. [The change of *vowel* is due to obs. verb *reprise*, to seize in return ; from F. *repris*, pp. of *reprendre* < L. *reprehendere*, (here) to seize again.] — Ital. *ripresaglia* booty. — M. Ital. *ripreso*, a taking again ; fem. of *ripreso*, pp. of *riprendere*, to reprehend, also to retake. — L. *reprehendere*, to seize again, also, to reprehend ; see **Reprehend**.

Reproach. (F. — L.) F. *reprocher*, to reproach. Cf. Span. *reprochar*, Prov. *repropchar*, to reproach ; answering to Late L. **repropiāre*, to bring near to, impute to, reproach. — L. *re-*, again ; *propi-us*, nearer, comp. of *prope*, near. See **Propinquity**. ¶ A translation of L. *obicere* (*objicere*), to bring near or cast before one, to reproach.

Reprobate. (L.) L. *reprobātus*, reproved, rejected ; pp. of *reprobāre*, to reject upon trial. — L. *re-*, back ; *probāre*, to test. See **Probable**.

reprove. (F. — L.) M. E. *reproven*, also *repreven*. — O. F. *reprover* (F. *réprouver*), to reprove, condemn. — L. *reprobāre*, to reject, reprove (above).

Reptile, crawling ; usually, as a sb. (F. — L.) F. *reptile*, 'crawling ;' Cot. — L.

reptilem, acc. of *reptilis*, creeping. – L. *reptus*, pp. of *rēpere*, to creep.+Lithuan. *reploti*, to creep.

Republic. (F. – L.) M. F. *republique*, 'the commonwealth;' Cot. – L. *rēspublica*, a republic. – L. *rēs*, a matter, state ; *publica*, fem. of *publicus*, public. See **Real.**

Repudiate. (L.) From pp. of L. *repudiāre*, to reject. – L. *repudium*, a casting off, divorce. Perhaps from L. *re-*, away ; *pud-*, base of *pudēre*, to feel shame ; cf. *pudor*, shame, *prō-pudium*, a shameful action.

Repugnant. (F. – L.) M. F. *repugnant*, pres. pt. of *repugner*, 'to repugne, thwart;' Cot. – L. *re-pugnāre*, to fight against. – L. *re-*, back ; *pugnāre*, to fight ; see **Pugilism.**

Repulse. (L.) From L. *repulsa*, sb., a refusal ; or *repulsāre*, vb. – L. *repuls-us*, pp. of *repellere* ; see **Repel.** Cf. Norman dial. *repulser*, to repulse.

Repute. (F. – L.) M. F. *reputer.* – L. *reputāre*, to repute (lit. reconsider). – L. *re-*, again ; *putāre*, to think ; see **Putative.**

Request. (F. – L.) O. F. *requeste.* – L. *requisīta*, a thing asked, fem. of pp. of *requīrere*, to ask back. – L. *re-*, back ; and *quærere*, to seek. See **Quest.**

require (F. – L.) M. E. *requeren*, but also *requiren.* – M. F. *requerir*; O. F. *requerre*, with 1 pr. s. *requier.* – L. *requīrere* (above). **Der.** *requis-ite*, from pp. *requīsītus.*

Requiem. (L.) The Mass for the Dead was called *requiem*, because it began 'Requiem æternam dona eis.' – L. *requiem*, acc. of *requiēs*, repose. – L. *re-*; *quiēs*, rest. See **Quiet.**

Requite. (F. – L.) Also spelt *requit*, Temp. iii. 3. 71. From *re-* and *quit* ; see **Quit.**

Reredos, a screen at the back of a thing, esp. of an altar. (F. – L.) From M. E. *rere*, rear ; and F. *dos*, back, from L. *dorsum*, back. See **Rear** (2) and **Dorsal.**

Reremouse, Rearmouse, a bat. (E.) A. S. *hrēremūs*, a bat; from the flapping of its wings. – A. S. *hrēran*, to agitate, allied to *hrōr*, adj., stirring, quick ; *mūs*, a mouse. Cf. prov. E. *flitter-mouse*, a flutter-mouse or bat. And cf. **Uproar.** ¶ Perhaps a popular etymology ; cf. early A. S. *hreatha-mus*, a bat ; Epinal Gl. 978.

Rereward ; see **Rearward.**

Rescind, to repeal. (F. – L.) F. *re-* *scinder*, to cancel ; Cot. – L. *rescindere*, to cut off, annul. – L. *re-*, back ; *scindere*, to cut. Allied to **Schism.** (√SKHEID.)

Rescript. (F. – L.) M. F. *rescript*, a reply in writing. – L. *rescriptum*, neut. of pp. of *rescrībere*, to write back. – L. *re-*, back ; *scrībere*, to write ; see **Scribe.**

Rescue, vb. (F. – L.) M. E. *rescouen.* – O. F. *rescourre*, to rescue, save. [The same word as Ital. *riscuotere*.] – Late L. *rescutere* (A. D. 1308); for *ex-excutere*, to drive away again. – L. *re-*, again ; *ex*, away ; *quatere*, to shake ; see **Quash.** ¶ The M. E. sb. was *rescous*, from O. F. *rescousse* < Late L. pp. fem. *rescussa*.

Research. (F. – L.) Compounded of **Re-**, again, and **Search.** Cf. Norman dial. *recerche*, research.

Resemble. (F. – L.) O. F. *resembler*. – O. F. *re-*, again ; *sembler*, to seem, be like. – L. *re-*, again ; *simulāre*, to make like ; see **Simulate.**

Resent. (F. – L.) M. F. *se resentir* (or *ressentir*), to have a deep sense of. – L. *re-*, again ; *sentīre*, to feel. See **Sense.** **Der.** *resentment.*

Reserve. (F. – L.) O. F. *reserver.* – L. *reseruāre*, to keep back. – L. *re-*, back ; *seruāre*, to keep ; see **Serve.**

reservoir. (F. – L.) F. *réservoir.* – Late L. *reseruātōrium*, a store-house, formed from *reseruāre*, to reserve. Cf. Late L. *seruatōrium*, a store-house (Lewis).

Reside. (F. – L.) M. F. *resider*, to reside, stay. – L. *residēre*, to sit or remain behind. – L. *re-*, back ; *sedēre*, to sit ; see **Sedentary.** **Der.** *resid-ence.*

residue. (F. – L.) O. F. *residu.* – L. *residuum*, a remainder, neut. of *residuus*, remaining. – L. *residēre* (above).

Resign, to yield up. (F. – L.) M. F. *resigner.* – L. *resignāre*, to unseal, annul, resign. – L. *re-*, back ; *signāre*, to sign, from *signum*, a sign, mark. See **Sign.**

Resilient. (L.) L. *resilient-*, stem of pres. part. of *resilīre*, to leap back. – L. *re-*, back ; *salīre*, to leap. See **Salient.**

Resin, Rosin. (F. – L. – Gk.) M. E. *recyn, recine.* – M. F. *resine*, ' rosin ;' Cot. Norman dial. *rosine.* – L. *rēsīna*, Jer. li. 8 (Vulgate). – Gk. ῥητίνη, resin, gum from trees. See Prellwitz.

Resist. (F. – L.) O. F. *resister.* – L. *resistere*, to stand back, withstand. – L. *re-*, back ; *sistere*, to stand, from *stāre*, to stand ; see **State.**

Resolute. (L.) L. *resolūtus*, pp. of *resoluere* (below).

resolve. (L.) L. *resoluere*, to loosen, melt; hence to separate into parts (also, to decide, resolve). — L. *re-*, back; *soluere*, to loosen; see **Solve**. Der. *resolut-ion* (from pp. *resolūtus*).

Resonant. (L.) From *resonant-*, stem of pres. pt. of L. *resonāre*, to sound back, echo, resound. — L. *re-*, back; *sonāre*, to sound, from *sonus*, sound. See **Sound** (3).

Resort, to betake oneself to. (F. — L.) M. F. *resortir, ressortir*, 'to issue, goe forth againe, resort;' Cot. Orig. a law term; to appeal. — Late L. *resortīre*, to resort to a tribunal; cf. *resortīrī*, to return to any one. — L. *re-*, again; *sortīrī*, to obtain; so that *re-sortīrī* is to re-obtain, gain by appeal. — L. *re-*, again; *sorti-*, for *sors*, a lot; see **Sort**.

Resound. (F. — L.) O. F. *resoner* (12th cent.). — L. *resonāre*; see **Resonant**.

Resource. (F. — L.) M. F. *resource*, later *ressource*, 'a new source;' Cot. — F. *re-*, again; *source*, source; see **Source**.

Respect, sb. (F. — L.) F. *respect*, 'respect, regard;' Cot. — L. *respectum*, acc. of *respectus*, a looking at. — L. *respectus*, pp. of *respicere*, to look at, look back upon. — L. *re*, back; *specere*, to see; see **Species**. Der. *respect*, vb.; *respect-able, respect-ive*; also *dis respect*.

respite, delay, reprieve. (F. — L.) O. F. *respit*, a respite. Orig. sense regard, respect had to a suit on the part of a judge. — L. acc. *respectum*, respect (above).

Respire, to breathe, take rest. (F. — L.) F. *respirer*. — L. *respīrāre*, to breathe again or back. — L. *re-*, back; *spīrāre*, to breathe; see **Spirit**.

Resplendent. (L.) From L. *re-splendent-*, stem of pres. pt. of *resplendēre*, to glitter. — L. *re-*, again; *splendēre*, to shine; see **Splendour**.

Respond. (F. — L.) O. F. *respondre*. — L. *respondēre* (pp. *responsus*), to answer. — L. *re-*, back; *spondēre*, to promise; see **Sponsor**. Der. *response*, from O. F. *respons*, an answer, from L. *responsum*, neut. of pp. *responsus*.

Rest (1), repose. (E.) A. S. *rest, ræst*, rest. Cf. Du. *rust*, Dan. Swed. *rast*, Icel. *röst* (the distance between two resting-places), Goth. *rasta* (a stage), O. H. G. *rasta*, G. *rast*, rest. The A. S. *rest*, fem., answers to Teut. type **rast-jā*, orig. 'a

halting-place,' which (like O. H. G. *rasta*) is from Teut. root **ras*, to dwell, as seen in Goth. *raz-n*, a house. See **Ransack**. Brugm. i. § 903 c.

Rest (2), to remain, be left over. (F. — L.) F. *rester*, to remain. — L. *restāre*, to stop behind, remain. — L. *re-*, back; *stāre*, to stand; see **State**. ¶ Distinct from *rest* (1), repose.

Restaurant. (F. — L.) Mod. F. *restaurant*, lit. 'restoring;' pres. pt. of *restaurer*, to restore, refresh; see **Restore**.

Restharrow, a plant. (F. *and* E.) For *arrest-harrow*, because its tough roots stop the harrow. Cf. the F. name *arrête-bœuf*, lit. 'stop-ox.'

Restitution. (F. — L.) F. *restitution*. — L. *restitūtiōnem*, acc. of *restitūtio*, a restoring. — L. *restitūtus*, pp. of *restituere* to restore. — L. *re-*, again; *statuere*, to set up, place, causal of *stāre*, to stand, see **State**.

Restive. (F. — L.) Confused with *restless*, but it really means stubborn, refusing to move. — M. F. *restif*, 'restie, stubborn, drawing backward;' Cot. — F. *rester*, to remain; see **Rest** (2). ¶ Hence E. *rusty* in the phr. *to turn rusty* = to be stubborn.

Restore. (F. — L.) O. F. *restorer*, also *restaurer*. — L. *restaurāre*, to restore. — L. *re-*, again; **staurare*, to set up; see **Store**. Brugm. i. § 198.

Restrain. (F. — L.) O. F. *restraign*, as in *restraign-ant*, pres. pt. of *restraindre* (F. *restreindre*), to restrain. — L. *restringere*, to draw back tightly, bind back. — L. *re-*, back; *stringere*, to bind; see **Stringent**. Der. *restraint*, from O. F. *restrainte*, fem. of pp. of *restraindre*.

restrict. (L.) From L. *restrictus*, pp. of *restringere*, to bind back (above).

Result, vb. (F. — L.) M. F. *resulter*, 'to rebound or leap back; also to rise of, come out of;' Cot. — L. *resultāre*, to rebound; frequent. of *resilīre*, to leap back; see **Resilient**. Der. *result-ant*.

Resume, to take up again. (F. — L.) M. F. *resumer*. — L. *resūmere*. — L. *re-*, again; *sūmere*, to take; see **Assume**. Der. *resumpt-ion* (from pp. *resumpt-us*).

Resurrection. (F. — L.) O. F. *resurrection*. — L. acc. *resurrectiōnem*. — L. *resurrectus*, pp. of *resurgere*, to rise again. — L. *re-*, again; *surgere*, to rise; see **Surge**.

Resuscitate, to revive. (L.) L. *resus-*

citātus, pp. of *resuscitāre*, to revive. – L. *re-*, again, *sus-*, up, and *citāre*, to rouse ; see **Cite**.

Ret, to steep flax. (M. Du.) M. Du. *reten, reeten*, to steep flax; Du. *reten*. Cf. Pomeran. *röten*, Swed. *röta*, Norw. *röyta*, to ret; also Du. *rete, reute*, Low G. *rate*, E. Fries. *rötte*, a retting-pit. Lit. 'to make rotten;' formed by mutation from Teut. *raut; for which see **Rotten**. Cf. Du. *rooten*, to ret.

Retail, sb. (F. – L.) *To sell by retail* is to sell by small pieces. – O. F. *retail*, a shred, paring, small piece. – O. F. *retailler*, to shred, cut small. – O. F. *re-* (= L. *re-*), again; *tailler*, to cut; see **Tailor**.

Retain. (F. – L.) F. *retenir*. – L. *re-tinēre*, to hold back; pp. *retentus*. – L. *re-*, back ; *tenēre*, to hold ; see **Tenable**. Der. *retent-ion* (from the pp.).

Retaliate, to repay. (L.) From pp. of L. *retāliāre*, to requite ; allied to *tālio*, retaliation in kind, as in *lex tāliōnis*, the law of retaliation. – L. *tāli-*, decl. stem of *tālis*, such, of such a kind. Cf. Gk. τη-λίκος, of such an age. From the Idg. base *tā-*, allied to Gk. τὸ, E. *tha-t*. See **That**.

Retard, to delay. (F. – L.) F. *retarder*, to hinder. – L. *retardāre*, to delay. – L. *re-*, again; *tardāre*, to make slow, from *tardus*, slow. See **Tardy**.

Retch, Reach, to try to vomit. (E.) A.S. *hrǣcan*, to clear the throat, hawk, spit. – A.S. *hrāca*, spittle; cf. *hrǣcgebræc*, hoarseness. ╪ Icel. *hrækja*, to spit; from *hrāki*, spittle. Prob. of imitative origin.

Retention. (F. – L.) M. F. *retention*, 'retention;' Cot. – L. acc. *retentiōnem*, a holding back. – L. *retent-us*, held back, pp. of *retinēre* ; see **Retain**.

Reticent, silent. (L.) From stem of pres. pt. of L. *reticēre*, to be very silent. – L. *re-*, back, very; and *tacēre*, to be silent. See **Tacit**.

Reticule. (F. – L.) F. *réticule*, a net for the hair, a reticule. – L. *rēticulum*, a little net; double dimin. of *rēte*, a net. ¶ Formerly also *ridicule* (both in F. and E.), by confusion with **Ridicule** (Littré). Cf. prov. F. *rédicule*, a reticule, dial. of Verdun (Fertiault).

retina, the innermost coating of the eye. (L.) Neo-Lat. *rētina* ; so called because resembling network. Coined from *rēti-*, for *rēte*, a net.

Retinue. (F. – L.) M. E. *retenue*. – O. F. *retenue*, a body of retainers ; fem. of

retenu, pp. of *retenir*, to retain ; see **Retain**.

Retire. (F. – Teut.) M. F. *retirer*, 'to retire, withdraw ;' Cot. – F. *re-*, back ; *tirer*, to pull ; see **Tier, Tirade**.

Retort, a censure returned ; tube for distilling. (F. – L.) M. F. *retort*, pp. 'twisted, violently returned,' *retorte*, 'a lymbeck,' Cot. ; lit. a thing twisted back. – M. F. *retort*, pp. of *retordre*, to twist back. – L. *retorquēre*, to twist back. – L. *re-*, back ; *torquēre*, to twist ; see **Torture**.

Retract. (F. – L.) M. F. *retracter*, 'to revoke;' Cot. – L. *retractāre*, frequent. of *retrahere*, to draw back. – L. *re-*, back ; *trahere*, to draw: see **Tract** (1).

retreat, sb. (F. – L.) M. E. *retrete*. – O. F. *retrete*, later *retraite*, a retreat, fem. of *retret*, pp. of *retraire*, to withdraw. – L. *retrahere*, to draw back (above).

Retrench. (F. – L. ?) M. F. *retrencher*, 'to curtall, diminish ;' Cot. – L. *re-*, back ; and O. F. *trencher*, to cut ; see **Trench**.

Retribution. (F. – L.) M. F. *retribution*. – L. acc. *retribūtiōnem*, requital. – L. *retribūtus*, pp. of *retribuere*, to pay back. – L. *re-*, back ; *tribuere*, to pay ; see **Tribute**.

Retrieve, to recover. (F. – L. and Gk.) Formerly *retreve*. – O. F. *retreuve*, 3rd pers. sing. indic. of *retrover*, later *retrouver*, to find again. – L. *re-*, again ; O. F. *trover*, to find ; see **Trover**.

Retro-, backwards. (L.) L. *retrō*, backwards ; a case of a comparative form from *re-* or *red-*, back. The suffix *-trō* (*-trā*), in *ci-trō, ci-trā*, answers to Goth. *-þrō* in *þa-þrō*, thence ; see Brugm. ii. § 75. See **Rear** (2).

Retrocession. (F. – L.) F. *rétro-cession*. – Late L. *retrōcessiōnem*, acc. of *retrōcessio*, a going back. – L. *retrōcess-us*, pp. of *retrōcēdere*, to go further back. – L. *retrō*, backwards ; *cēdere*, to go ; see **Cede**.

Retrograde, going backward. (F. – L.) O. F. *retrograde*. – L. *retrōgradus*, retrograde (used of a planet). – L. *retrō-gradī*, to go backwards. – L. *retrō*, back-wards ; *gradī*, to go ; see **Grade**.

retrogression. (L.) Coined from pp. of L. *retrō-gradī* (above).

Retrospect. (L.) From L. *retrō-spectus*, (unused) pp. of *retrōspicere*, to look back. – L. *retrō*, back ; *specere*, to look.

Return, vb. (F. – L.) F. *retourner* (Cot.). – F. *re-* (= L. *re-*), back; *tourner*, to turn; see Turn.

Reveal. (F. – L.) M. F. *reveler*, 'to reveale;' Cot. – L. *reuēlāre*, to draw back a veil. – L. *re-*, back; *uēlum*, veil; see Veil.

Reveille, an alarum at break of day. (F. – L.) [Cf. F. *réveil*, a reveille, M. F. *resveil*, 'a hunt's-up, or morning-song for a new married wife, the day after the marriage;' Cot.] The E. *reveillè* was a tri-syllable, and represented F. *réveillez*, wake ye, imper. plural of *réveiller*, to awaken; O. F. *resveiller*. – O. F. *re-* (L. *re-*, again); and *esveiller*, to awaken, from L. *ex*, out, and *uigilāre*, to watch (from *uigil*, awake). See Vigil. ¶ The E. word is also spelt *reveillez*; Brand, Pop. Antiq., ed. Ellis, ii. 176. The F. *réveillez* is used as a sb. (in the E. sense) in the dialect of Forez, near Lyons (Graz).

Revel, a noisy feast. (F. – L.) M. E. *reuel* (*revel*), sb. – O. F. *revel*, pride, rebellion, sport, jest, disturbance, disorder (Roquefort). – O. F. *reveler*, to rebel, hence, to riot. – L. *rebellāre*, to rebel; see Rebel. Der. *revell-er*; whence *revel-r-y.*

Revenge. (F. – L.) O. F. *revengier*, also *revencher*, to avenge oneself (F. *re-vancher*). – F. *re-* (= L. *re-*), again; O. F. *vengier*, *venger*, from L. *uindicāre*, to vindicate; see Vindicate.

Revenue, income. (F. – L.) F. *revenu*, m., and *revenüe*, f. 'revenue, rent;' Cot. From *revenu*, pp. of *revenir*, to come back. – F. *re-*, back; *venir*, to come. – L. *re-*, back; *uentre*, to come; see Venture.

Reverberate. (L.) From pp. of L. *reuerberāre*, to beat back (hence, to re-echo). – L. *re-*, back; *uerberāre*, to beat, from *uerber*, a scourge.

Revere. (F. – L.) M. F. *reverer* (F. *révérer*), to reverence. – L. *reuerērī*, to revere, stand in awe of. – L. *re-*, again; *uerērī*, to fear, feel awe, allied to E. Wary. Der. *reverence*, O. F. *reverence*, L. *reuerentia*; also *rever-end.*

Reverie, Revery. (F. – L.) F. *rêverie*, a raving, a vain fancy, a revery. – F. *rêver*, formerly *resver*, *râver*, to rave. See Rave.

Reverse. (F. – L.) M. E. *reuers* (*revers*). – O. F. *revers*. – L. *reuersus*, pp. turned backwards; pp. of *reuertere*, to turn backward. – L. *re-*, back; *uertere*, to turn; see Verse.

revert. (F. – L.) M. F. *revertir*, 'to revert, returne;' Cot. – L. *reuertere* (above).

Review. (F. – L.) From Re- and View.

Revile. (F. – L.) M. E. *reuilen* (= *revilen*); A. F. *reviler* (Gower). – F. *re-*, again; and F. *vil* (L. *uīlis*), cheap; see Vile. Lit. 'to cheapen.'

Revise. (F. – L.) O. F. *reviser*. – L. *reuīsere*, to look back upon, revisit. – L. *re-*, again; *uīsere*, to survey, from *uīsus*, pp. of *uidēre*, to see; see Vision.

Revisit. (F. – L.) From Re- and Visit.

Revive. (F. – L.) F. *revivre*. – L. *re-uīuere*, to live again, revive. – L. *re-*, again; *uīuere*, to live; see Vivid.

Revoke. (F. – L.) O. F. *revocquer* (F. *révoquer*). – L. *reuocāre*, to recall. – L. *re-*, back; *uocāre*, to call; see Vocal.

Revolt, a rebellion. (F. – Ital. – L.) M. F. *revolte*, 'a revolt;' Cot. – M. Ital. *revolta* (Ital. *rivolta*), a revolt; fem. of *revolto*, turned, overthrown, pp. of *revolvere*, to turn, roll back, overturn. – L. *re-uoluere*, to roll back (below).

revolve. (L.) L. *reuoluere*, to turn again, revolve. – L. *re-*, again; *uoluere*, to turn; see Voluble. Der. *revolut-ion*, from pp. *reuolūtus*.

Revulsion. (F. – L.) M. F. *revulsion*, 'a plucking away; also the drawing of humours from one part of the body into another;' Cot. – L. *reuulsiōnem*, acc. of *reuulsio*, a plucking back. – L. *reuulsus*, pp. of *reuellere*, to pull back. – L. *re-*, back; *uellere*, to pull, pluck. Cf. Convulse.

Reward, vb. (F. – L. *and* O. H. G.) A. F. *rewarder*; O. F. *regarder*, to look back upon, regard (with favour); see Regard. Doublet, *regard.*

Reynard, Renard, a fox. (F. – Teut.) O. F. *renard*, *regnard* (F. *renard*). – Low G. (M. Flemish) *Reinaert*, the name given to the fox in the celebrated M. Flemish epic so called. Cognate with O. H. G. *Reginhart*, lit. 'strong in counsel;' from O. H. G. *regin-*, *ragin-*, answering to Goth. *ragin*, judgment, counsel, and *hart* (E. *hard*), strong.

Rhapsody. (F. – L. – Gk.) M. F. *rapsodie*, Cot. – L. *rhapsōdia*. – Gk. ῥαψῳδία, the reciting of epic poetry, part of an epic poem, a rhapsody, tirade. – Gk. ῥαψῳδός, one who strings (lit. stitches) songs together, a reciter of epic poetry. ━ Gk. ῥαψ-, stem of fut. of ῥάπτειν, to stitch together, fasten together; ᾠδή, an ode; see **Ode.**

Rhetoric. (F.━L.━Gk.) O. F. *rhetorique*; Cot. ━ L. *rhētorica*, i. e. *rhētorica ars*, the art of rhetoric; fem. of *rhētoricus*, adj. ━ Gk. ῥητορικός, rhetorical; adj. from ῥήτωρ, an orator, speaker. For Ϝρή-τωρ, related by gradation to εἴρειν, to speak (for *Ϝέρ-yειν). Allied to **Verb.**

Rheum. (F.━L.━Gk.) M.F. *rheume.* ━L. *rheuma.* ━ Gk. ῥεῦμα (stem ῥευματ-), a flow, flux, rheum. ━ Gk. ῥεύ-σομαι, fut. of ῥέειν, to flow; (for *σρέϜ-ειν).+Skt. *sru*, to flow. Allied to **Stream.** (✔SREU.) Der. *rheumat-ic.*

Rhinoceros. (L.━Gk.) L.*rhīnocerōs.* ━ Gk. ῥινόκερως, lit. 'nose-horned.' ━ Gk. ῥινο-, for ῥίς, nose; κέρας, a horn, allied to **Horn.**

Rhizome, a rootlike stem. (F.━Gk.) F. *rhizome.* ━ Gk. ῥίζωμα, root. ━ Gk. ῥιζοῦν, to cause to take root. ━ Gk. ῥίζα, root. See **Root.**

Rhododendron. (L.━Gk.) L. *rhododendron.* ━ Gk. ῥοδόδενδρον, the rose-bay, oleander. ━ Gk. ῥόδο-, for ῥόδον, rose; δένδρον, tree. Gk. ῥόδον is of Armenian origin; see **Rose.**

Rhodomontade; see **Rodomontade.**

Rhomb, Rhombus. (L.━Gk.) L. *rhombus* (F. *rhombe*). ━ Gk. ῥόμβος, a thing twirled round, whirling spindle, a thing in the shape of a whirling spindle, a four-sided figure with equal sides but unequal angles. ━ Gk. ῥέμβειν, to revolve. Allied to **Wrinkle** (Prellwitz). See also **Rumb.**

Rhubarb. (F.━Late L.━Gk.) O. F. *reubarbe*; F. *rhubarbe.* ━ Late L. *rheubarbarum* (= *rhēum barbarum*). ━ Gk. ῥῆον βάρβαρον, rhubarb; lit. ' Rhēum from the barbarian country.' Gk. ῥῆον is an adj. from ῥά, the rha-plant, rhubarb, which was also called *Rhā Ponticum. Rhā* took its name from the river *Rha,* i. e. the Volga. And see **Barbarous.**

Rhumb; see **Rumb.**

Rhyme; see **Rime** (1).

Rhythm. (F.━L.━Gk.) M.F.*rithme,* Cot. ━ L.*rhythmus.* ━ Gk. ῥυθμός, measured motion, time, measure. ━ Gk. ῥέειν, to flow. See **Rheum.**

Rib. (E.) M. E. *ribbe.* A. S. *ribb.*+ Du. *rib,* Icel. *rif,* Swed. *ref-been* (rib-bone), Dan. *rib-been*; G. *rippe*; Russ. *rebro.*

Perhaps allied to G. *rebe,* a tendril; from the idea of clasping (Kluge).

Ribald. (F.━Teut.) M. E. *ribald, ribaud.* ━ O. F. *ribald* (F. *ribaud*). ━ LowL. *ribaldus,* a ruffian; cf. Low L. *ribalda,* a prostitute. Of Teut. origin. ━ O. H. G. *hrīpa,* M. H. G. *rībe,* a prostitute; cf. O.F. *riber,* to be wanton. The suffix *-ald* is due to O. H. G. *walt,* power. Cf. Körting, § 4019.

Riband, Ribbon. (F.) M. E. *riban, reban.* [Also Irish *ribin,* a ribbon; Gael. *ribean,* a ribbon, fillet; from E.]━O. F. *riban* (F. *ruban*), a ribbon (Littré); Gascon and Languedoc *riban*; Norman dial. *riban.* Low L. *rubānus* (A. D. 1367). Origin unknown; cf. Dan. *vride-baand,* a twisted band.

Rice. (F.━Ital.━L.━Gk.━O. Pers.) O. F. *ris,* rice; F. *riz.* ━ Ital. *riso.* ━ L. *orȳza.* ━ Gk. ὄρυζα, ὄρυζον, rice, grain. From an O. Pers. form, preserved in the Pushto (Afghan) *wrijzey, wrijey,* rice; *wrijza'h,* a grain of rice (Raverty). Hence also Arab. *uruzz, ruzz,* whence Span. *arroz,* rice. Allied forms are Pers. *birinj,* Armen. *brinj,* rice; Skt. *vrīhi-,* rice. (Horn, § 208; Yule.)

Rich. (E.) M. E. *riche.* ━A. S. *rīce,* powerful, rich. [We also find O.F. *riche,* from O. Sax. *rīki,* allied to O. H. G. *rīhhi,* M. H. G. *rīche* (G. *reich*), powerful.]+ Du. *rijk,* Icel. *rīkr,* Swed. *rik,* Dan. *rig,* Goth. *reiks.* Teut. type *rīkiz,* powerful, from the base *rīk-* as seen in Goth. *reik-s,* a ruler; cognate with the Celtic base *rīg-,* as in Gaulish *rīx,* a king (cf. O. Irish *rī,* gen. *rīg,* a king, W. *rhi,* a chief); unless the Teut. base *rīk-* is merely borrowed from the Celtic *rīg-.* Cf. L. *rēx.* gen. *rēg-is,* a king. All from ✔REG, to rule (L. *reg-ere*). See **Regent.** Brugm. i. §§ 135, 549 c.

riches. (F.━O. H.G.) M. E. *richesse,* a sing. sb.; the pl. being *richesses.* ━ F. *richesse,* wealth. ━ O. H. G. *rīhhi,* M. H. G. *rīche* (G. *reich*), rich (above). The suffix is F. *-esse,* L. *-itia.*

Rick. (E.) *Rick* is from A. S. *hrycce,* as in *corn-hrycce,* corn-rick. We also find M. E. *reck,* A. S. *hrēac,* a heap, a rick.+ Icel. *hraukr,* a rick; Du. *rook.* Cf. O. Irish *cruach,* a rick; and see **Ruck** (2).

Rickets, a disease of children, accompanied by softness of the bones and great weakness. (E.) A prov. E. word first noticed about A. D. 1620; whence the medical term *rachītis* was coined about

1650, with allusion to Gk. ῥάχις, the spine. Cf. prov. E. *rickety*, i.e. tottery, weak, unstable. Formed from M. E. *wrikken*, to twist, wrest, still in use in the phrase 'to *wrick* one's ankle.' Allied to A. S. *wringan*, to twist; see **Wring** and **Wry**. Cf. Du. *wrikken*, Swed. *ricka*, to be rickety; Swed. *rickug*, rickety.

Ricochet, the rebound of a cannon-ball. (F.) F. *ricochet*, 'the sport of skimming a thinne stone on the water, called a Duck and a Drake;' Cot. Origin unknown.

Rid (1), to free. (E.) M. E. *ridden*, *redden*. A. S. *hreddan*, to snatch away, deliver.+O. Fries. *hredda*, Du. *redden*, Dan. *redde*, Swed. *rädda*; G. *retten*. Teut. type *hradjan-. Cf. Skt. *çrath*, to untie.

Rid (2), to clear, esp. land. (Scand.) Prov. E. *rid*. M. E. *ruden* (pp. *rid*). — Icel. *ryðja* (orig. *hryðja*), to clear, clear out; Dan. *rydde*, to clear, grub up land. Teut. type *hrudjan-, from *hrud-, weak grade of *hreuthan- (Icel. *hrjōða*), to strip. ¶ Confused with *rid* (1).

Riddle (1), an enigma. (E.) Properly *riddles*; and the pl. should be *riddles-es*. M. E. *redels*. — A. S. *rǣdels*, *rǣdelse*, a riddle, ambiguity, something requiring explanation. — A. S. *rǣdan*, to discern, explain; see **Read**.+Du. *raadsel*, for *raad-is-lo-*, the A. S. *-els* being for *-isl*; G. *räthsel*, a riddle. ¶ We still say *to read* a *riddle*, i. e. to explain it.

Riddle (2), a large sieve. (E.) M. E. *ridil*. A.S. *hridder*, a vessel for winnowing corn; older form *hrider* (Sweet); the suffixed *-er* and *-il* (*-le*) being equivalent. +O. H. G. *ritera*; Irish *creathair*, Gael. *criathar*; L. *cribrum*. Lit. sense 'separater.' All from Idg. root *krei, to separate; cf. Gk. κρί-νειν. See **Critic**.

Ride. (E.) M. E. *riden*, pt. t. *rood*, pp. *riden*. A. S. *rīdan*, pt. t. *rād*, pp. *riden*. +Du. *rijden*, Icel. *rīða*, Dan. *ride*, Swed. *rida*; G. *reiten*. Also O. Irish *riad-aim*, I drive, ride. (√REIDH.) Brugm. i. § 210. Der. *road*, *read-y*.

Ridge. (E.) M.E. *rigge*, *rugge*. A.S. *hrycg*, the back of a man or beast.+Du. *rug*, back, ridge, Dan. *ryg*, Swed. *rygg*, Icel. *hryggr*; G. *rücken*, O. H. G. *hrucki*. Cf. O. Irish *croccenn*, (1) hide, (2) the back.

Ridiculous. (L.) L. *rīdicul-us*, laughable; with suffix *-ous*. — L. *rīdēre*, to laugh.

Riding, one of the three divisions of the county of York. (Scand.) For *thriding* (North-riding = North-thriding). — Icel. *þriðjungr*, the third part of a thing, third part of a shire. — Icel. *þriði*, third; cognate with A. S. *þridda*, third. See **Third, Three**. So also Norw. *tridjung*, a third part.

Rife. (Scand.) M. E. *rif*, late A. S. *rif*. — Icel. *rīfr*, munificent, abundant; M. Swed. *rif*, rife; Norw. *riv*.+M. Du. *rijf*, abundant; Low G. *rive*, abundant, munificent, extravagant. Cf. Icel. *reifr*, glad; *reifa*, to bestow.

Riff-raff, refuse. (F. — Teut.) M. E. *rif and raf*, things of small value, hence every bit. — M. F. *rif et raf*, every bit; also *rifle et rafle*. 'Il ne luy lairra *rif ny raf*, he will strip him of all;' Cot. Here *rif* or *rifle* is a thing of small value, from *rifler*, to rifle, ransack; and *rafle* is from M. F. *raffler*, to rifle, ravage. Both are words of Teut. origin, drawn together by their sound, though of different origin. F. *rifler* is from Icel. *hrífa* (see **Rifle** (1)); M. F. *raffler* is from G. *raffen*, to seize.

Rifle (1), to spoil, plunder. (F. — Teut.) M. F. *rifler*, 'to rifle, spoile;' Cot. Norm. dial. *rifler* (Duméril). Formed, with frequentative *-l-*, from Icel. *hrífa*, *rīfa*, to catch, grapple, grasp; allied to Icel. *hrífsa*, plunder.

Rifle (2), a kind of musket. (F. — Teut.) Short for *rifled gun*, from the verb *rifle*, to groove. — O. F. *rifler*, to scratch, graze (Godefroy). — Low G. *rifeln*, to furrow, chamfer; E. Fries. *riffeln* (the same), *riffel*, a groove; Dan. *rifle*, to rifle, groove, *rifle*, a groove; Swed. *reffla*, to rifle. So also G. *riefe*, a furrow; *riefen*, *riefeln*, to rifle (from Low G.). All allied to **Rivel**, and to **Rive**.

rift. (Scand.) Dan. and Norw. *rift*, rift, rent. — Norw. *riva*, Dan. *rive*, to tear. Cf. Icel. *ript*, a breach of contract. See **Rive**.

Rig (1), to fit up a ship. (Scand.) Spelt *rygge* in Palsgrave. — Norw. *rigga*, to bind up, wrap round, also to rig a ship; *rigg*, sb., rigging. Cf. Swed. dial. *rigga på*, to harness a horse. Also Westphal. *riggen*, Du. *rijgen*, G. *reihen*, to stitch together, orig. to put in a row; cf. E. Fries. *rige*, *rīge*, a row. See **Row** (1).

Rig (2), a frolic, prank. (E.?) We also find *rig*, to be wanton; *riggish*, wanton. For *wrig*, and allied to *wriggle*; see **Wriggle**. Cf. Norw. *rigga*, to rock; E. Fries. *wriggen*, to wriggle; Du. *wrikken*, to stir to and fro, *wriggelen*, to wriggle; and see **Rickets.**

Rig (3), a ridge. (E.) M. E. *rig*, Northern form of *rigge*, *rugge*, a ridge. See **Ridge.**

Right. (E.) M. E. *right*. A. S. *riht*, *ryht*; O. Merc. *reht.*+Du. *regt, recht*, Icel. *rēttr* (for **rēhtr*), Dan. *ret*, Swed. *rät*, G. *recht*, O. H. G. *reht*, Goth. *raihts*. Teut. type **rehtoz*; Idg. type **rektos*, as in L. *rectus*. Cf. W. *rhaith*, sb., right, O. Ir. *recht*; Pers. *rāst*. See **Regent.** (√REG.)

righteous. (E.) Corruption of M. E. *rightwis*; A. S. *rihtwīs*, i. e. wise as to what is right.—A. S. *riht*, right; *wīs*, wise.

Rigid. (L.) L. *rigidus*, stiff.—L. *rigēre*, to be stiff. Brugm. i. § 875.

Rigmarole. (Scand.; *and* F.—L.) Well known to be a corruption of *ragman-roll*, orig. a deed with many signatures, a long list of names; hence, a long stupid story. Lit. 'coward's roll.'—Icel. *ragmenni*, a coward, from *ragr*, a coward, and *maðr* (=*mannr*), a man; with the addition of *roll*, for which see **Roll.** The Icel. *ragr* seems to be allied to Icel. *argr*, a coward, A. S. *earg*.

Rigol, a circlet. (Ital.—O. H. G.) In Shak.—Ital. *rigolo*, a little wheel (Torriano); cf. *riga*, a line, a stripe.—O. H. G. *riga*, *rīga*, a line, the circumference of a circle (G. *reihe*). See **Row** (1).

Rile; see **Roil.**

Rill, a streamlet. (Low G.) Cf. Low G. *rille*, E. Friesic and Dan. dial. *rille*, a streamlet. Apparently for **rithele*; cf. A. S. *rīðe*, a stream; Low G. *rīde*, a stream; G. *-reide* (in place-names). See Phil. Soc. Trans. 1888, p. 166. ¶ Norm. dial. *risle*, *rille*, the name of a river, written *Ridula*, *Risila*, *Risla* in old charters (Robin, p. 432).

Rim. (E.) M. E. *rim*. A. S. *rima*, a verge, edge; cf. W. *rhim, rhimp, rhimyn*, a rim, edge.+Icel. *rimi*, a strip of land. Perhaps allied to G. *rand*, a rim, and to **Rind** (Kluge). Brugm. i. § 421.

Rime (1), verse, poetry, &c. (F.—L. —Gk.) Usually spelt *rhyme*, by confusion with *rhythm*, but not before A. D. 1550. M. E. *rime*.—F. *rime*, 'rime, or meeter;' Cot. Cf. M. F. *rithme*, 'rime, or meeter;' id. Prob. from L. *rhythmus*, rhythm; of Gk. origin; see **Rhythm.** ¶ Hence also M. H. G. *rīm*, in the sense of 'verse,'

which is a different word from M. H. G. *rīm*, O. H. G. *rīm* (A. S. *rīm*), in the sense of 'number.' From F. *rime* came also Ital. Span. Port. *rima*; also Du. *rijm*, Icel. *rīma*, G. *reim.*

Rime (2), hoarfrost. (F.) For *hrime*. A. S. *hrīm*, hoarfrost. + Du. *rijm*, Icel. *hrīm*, Dan. *riim*, Swed. *rim*. Allied to Du. *rijp*, G. *reif*, hoar-frost.

Rimer, a tool for enlarging holes in metal. (E.) From A. S. *rȳman*, to enlarge.—A. S. *rūm*, wide. See **Room.**

Rimple, to ripple, as the surface of water. (E.) To *rimple* is to shew wrinkles.—A. S. *hrympel*, a wrinkle. — A. S. *hrump-, rump-*, weak grade of *hrimpan* or *rimpan*, to wrinkle. + Du. *rimpel*, a wrinkle, *rimpelen*, to wrinkle; O. H. G. *hrimfan*, M. H. G. *rimpfen* (cf. G. *rümpfen*), to crook, bend, wrinkle. (See Franck.) See **Rumple.**

Rind. (E.) M. E. *rind*, *rinde*. A. S. *rinde*, bark of a tree, crust (of bread).+ M. Du. and G. *rinde*, bark. Allied to **Rim.**

Ring (1), a circle. (E.) M. E. *ring*. A. S. *hring.*+Du. *ring*, Low G. *ring*, *rink*, Icel. *hringr*, Swed. Dan. G. *ring*, O. H. G. *hrinc*. Teut. type **hrengoz*; Idg. type **krenghos*; also **kronghos*, as in O. Bulg. *krągŭ*, Russ. *krug(e)*, a circle. See **Rank** and **Harangue.**

Ring (2), to sound a bell. (E.) M. E. *ringen.* A. S. *hringan*, to clash, ring; a *weak* verb, as in Scand.; but English has pt. t. *rang*, by analogy with *sang* from *sing.* + Icel. *hringja*, Dan. *ringe*, Swed. *ringa.* Cf. Icel. *hrang*, a din; L. *clangere*, to clang.

Rink, a course for the game of curling, &c. (E.) A peculiar form of *ring*, in the sense of *prize-ring*, &c. Cf. Low G. *rink*, a ring.

Rinse. (F.) M. F. *rinser*, 'to reinse linnen clothes;' Cot. F. *rincer*; from O. F. *raincer* (Littré). Cf. O. F. *reincier*, to rinse (Godefroy). Of unknown origin.

Riot. (F.—O. H. G.?) O. F. *riote*, a brawling. The same as Prov. *riota*, Ital. *riotta*, dispute, strife. Of unknown origin; see Körting.

Rip. (Scand.; or F.—Scand.) M. E. *ripen*, to grope, search into; *rypen vp*, to seek out (cf. E. *rip up*). Cf. O. F. *riper*, to scratch (Godefroy). — Norweg. *ripa*, to scratch, Swed. dial. *ripa*, to scratch, pluck asunder (like E. *rip open*); Dan. *oprippe*, to rip up; Swed. *repa upp*, to rip up, *repa*, to scratch. Allied to Du. *repel*, G. *riffel*, a flax-comb; see **Ripple** (1). The Teut. base takes a double form; see **Reap**; cf. **Ripe** (below) and **Rope**.

Ripe. (E.) M. E. *ripe*. A. S. *rīpe*, fit for reaping; cf. *rīp*, harvest. ═ A. S. *rīpan*, to reap. ╋ Du. *rijp*, G. *reif*, ripe. See **Rip, Reap.**

Ripple (1), to pluck the seeds from flax-stalks. (E.) M. E. *ripplen, ripelen*, to ripple; from the sb. *ripple*, a flax-comb (Jamieson). Formed, with suffix *-le*, of the agent, from the weak grade, *rip-*, of A. S. *rīpan*, to reap, cut; see **Reap.** Cf. Swed. *repa*, to ripple flax, orig. to scratch, rip; see **Rip** (above). ╋ Du. *repelen*, to ripple, from *repel*, a ripple, from M. Du. *repen*, to beat flax; G. *riffeln*, to ripple, from *riffel*, a ripple.

Ripple (2), to cause or shew wrinkles on the surface, said of water. (Scand.) A late word; the same as **Ripple** (3) below. The older word was **Rimple**, q. v.

Ripple (3), to graze slightly. (Scand.) '*Ripple*, rescindere;' Levins (1570). Frequentative of **Rip** (above).

Rise, (E.) M. E. *risen.* A. S. *rīsan*, pt. t. *rās*, pp. *risen*.╋Du. *rijzen*, orig. to move, also in M. Du. to fall (contrary to the E. sense); Icel. *rīsa*; O. H. G. *rīsan*, to move up or down, to rise, to fall; Goth. *ur-reisan*, to arise. Teut. type *reis-an-*, to slip away. Der. *raise, rear*, vb.

Risible. (F.‒L.) F. *risible*.═L. *rīsi-bilis*, laughable.═L. *rīsus*, pp. of *rīdēre*, to laugh. See **Ridiculous.**

Risk. (F.‒Ital.‒L.) F. *risque*, peril; Cot. Orig. a maritime word.═Ital. *risco*, peril; Florio; the same word (probably) as Span. *risco*, a steep abrupt rock; whence the sense of 'peril,' as shewn by Span. *ar-riesgar*, O. Span. *arriscar*, to venture into danger (lit. to go against a rock). The orig. sense of *risco* is cut off, sheer, like a sharp rock.═L. *resecāre*, to cut back, cut off short (curiously verified by the use of the Como word *resega*, a saw, also risk; Diez); and cf. Port. *risco*, (1) rock, (2) danger.═L. *re-*, back; *secāre*, to cut: see **Section.** (See further in Diez and Körting.)

Rissole, a minced-meat fritter. (F.‒L.) F. *rissole*; O. F. *roissole, roussole.*═ Late L. type *russeola*; from L. *russeus*, reddish, or rather brownish; from the colour.═L. *russus*, red. See **Russet.**

Rite. (L.) L. *rītus*, a custom.╋Skt. *rīti-*, a going, way, usage; from *rī*, to go, flow. Cf. Brugm. ii. § 498. **Der.** *ritu-al*, from L. *rītu-*, decl. stem of *rītus*.

Rival. (F.‒L.) F. *rival*.═L. *rīuālis*, sb., one who uses the same brook as another, a near neighbour, a rival. ═ L. *rīuus*, a stream. Cf. Skt. *rī*, to go, flow.

Rive, to tear. (Scand.) M. E. *riuen* (*u=v*).═Icel. *rīfa*, pt. t. *reif*, pp. *rifinn* (>E. *riven*), to rive; Dan. *rive*, Swed. *rifva*. Cf. Gk. ἐρείπειν, to dash down; L. *rīpa*, a bank (shore). See **Reef.**

Rivel, to wrinkle. (E.) M. E. *riuelen* (*u = v*). A. S. *rifeled*, wrinkled (Eng. Stud. xi. 66); cf. *ge-riflian*, to wrinkle; a frequent. form from the weak grade of Teut. *reifan-*, as seen in Icel. *rīfa*, to rive; see **Rive** (above). Cf. A. S. *gerifod*, wrinkled; Ælf. Hom. i. 614.

River. (F.‒L.) M. E. *riuer* (*u=v*). ═ A. F. *rivere*, O. F. *riviere*. (F. *rivière*.) The same as Span. *ribera*, a shore, strand, sea-coast, Ital. *riviera*, shore, bank, also a river; Late L. *rīpāria*, (1) shore, bank, (2) river. ═ Late L. *rīpārius*, belonging to a shore. ═ L. *rīpa*, shore, bank. Allied to **Rive.**

Rivet. (F. ‒ Scand.) F. *rivet*, 'the welt of a shoe,' Cot.; also a rivet (Littré). ═ F. *river*, to rivet, clench, fasten back. ═ Icel. *rīfa*, to tack, sew loosely together; *rifa saman*, to stitch together. Cf. Shetland *riv*, to sew coarsely, Aberdeen *riv*, to rivet.

Rivulet. (L.) Dimin. from L. *rīuulus*, a small stream; dimin. of *rīuus*, a stream; lit. 'flowing.' Cf. Ital. *rivoletto* (Torriano). See **Rival.**

Rix-dollar, a coin. (Du.‒G.) Du. *rijks-daalder*, a rix-dollar.═G. *reichs-thaler*, a dollar of the empire.═G. *reichs*, gen. case of *reich*, empire, allied to G. *reich*, rich; and *thaler*, a dollar; see **Rich** and **Dollar.**

Roach, a fish. (F.‒Teut.) M. E. *roche*. ═O. North. F. and Walloon *roche*, O. F. *roce* (*rosse* in Cot.).═M. Du. *roch*, a skate; cf. Dan. *rokke*, Swed. *rocka*, a ray; Low G. *ruche*, whence G. *roche*, a roach, ray. Origin unknown. There is a remarkable confusion between roach, skate, ray, and thornback. Cf. A. S. *reohhe*, a fish.

Road. (E.) M. E. *rood, rode* (both for ships and horses).═A. S. *rād*, a road, also a raid.═A. S. *rād*, 2nd stem of *rīdan*, to ride. See **Ride. Doublet,** *raid.*

Roam. (F. – L.) M. E. *romen*. Coined from O. F. *romier*, a pilgrim to Rome; cf. O. F. *romel*, a pilgrim, *romeree*, a pilgrimage; Span. *romero*, a pilgrim; M. E. *Rome-rennere*, a runner to Rome, pilgrim; also Late L. *romeus*, Ital. *Romeo*, one who goes to Rome, a pilgrim. All from L. *Rōma*, Rome.

Roan. (F.) M. F. *rouën*; '*cheval rouën*, a roane horse;' Cot. Mod. F. *rouan*, Span. *roano*, Ital. *rovano, roano* (Florio). Origin unknown. ¶ Sometimes derived from the town of *Rouen*, with which Ital. *rovano* can have nothing to do.

Roan-tree, Rowan-tree, the mountain ash. (Scand.) Spelt *roun-tree, roan-tree, rowan-tree* in Jamieson. – Swed. *rönn*, M. Swed. *runn, rönn*, roan-tree; Dan. *rön*, Icel. *reynir*. The Icel. *reynir* is for **reyðnir<*rauðnir*, a derivative of *rauðr*, red; from the colour of the berries (Noreen). See **Red.**

Roar. (E.) M. E. *roren*. A. S. *rārian*, to bellow.+M. H. G. *rēren*; cf. Lith. *rèju*, I scold, Brugm. ii. §§ 465, 741. Perhaps of imitative origin.

Roast. (F. – G.?) M. E. *rosten*. – O. F. *rostir*, 'to rost;' Cot. (F. *rôtir*.) – O.H.G. *rostēn*, to roast. – O. H. G. *rost*, a grate, gridiron.+Du. *roosten*, to roast; *rooster*, a gridiron. Cf. also Irish *rost*, roast meat, Gael. *rost, roist*, W. *rhostio*, from E.; Bret. *rosta*, from F.

Rob (1). (F. – O. H. G.) M. E. *robben*. – O. F. *robber*, more commonly *rober*, to disrobe, spoil, strip off clothing, plunder. – F. *robe*, a robe; see **Robe.**

Rob (2), a conserve of fruit. (F. – Span. – Arab.) F. *rob*, 'the juice of black whortleberries preserved;' Cot. – Span. *rob*, thickened juice of fruit with honey. – Arab. *rubb*, 'a decoction of the juice of citrons and other fruits, inspissated juice, rob;' Richardson.

Robbins, Robins, ropes for fastening sails. (E.) Lowl. Sc. *ra-band, rai-band*. E. Fries. *rā-band*; where *rā*=yard of a ship. Cf. Icel. *rā*, Dan. *raa*, Swed. *rå*, G. *rahe*, yard; and **Band.**

Robe. (F. – O. H. G.) F. *robe*, formerly also *robbe*. – M. H. G. *roub*, O. H. G. *raup* (G. *raub*), booty, spoil; hence, a garment taken from the slain, clothing.+A. S. *rēaf*, Icel. *rauf*, sb.; see under **Reave.** Der. *dis-robe*.

Robin. (F. – O. H. G.) F. *Robin*, proper name; pet name for *Robert*. –

O. H. G. *Ruodperht* (G. *Ruprecht*, i. e. Rupert). Lit. 'fame-bright,' illustrious in fame. – O. H. G. *ruod-*, allied to Icel. *hrōðr*, fame; O. H. G. *perht*=E. *bright*. See **Hobgoblin.**

Robust. (F. – L.) F. *robuste*. – L. *rōbustus*, strong. – O. L. *rōbus* (L. *rōbur*), strength; orig. a tough tree, oak.

Roc, a huge bird. (F. – Pers.) F. *rock* (Littré). – Pers. *rukh*, the name of a huge bird; also a hero.

Rochet, a fine white linen robe, like a surplice, worn by bishops. (F. – M. H. G.) F. *rochet*, 'a frock; a prelate's rochet;' Cot. – M. H. G. *roc* (G. *rock*), a frock, coat. +Du. *rok*, O. Fries. *rokk*, A. S. *rocc*, Icel. *rokkr*, the same; Teut. type **rukkoz*.

Rock (1), a large mass of stone. (F.) O. F. *roke* (13th cent.), also *roque, rocque*; commonly *roche*, a rock. The same as Walloon *roc*, Languedoc *roquo*, f., Prov. *roca*, Span. *roca*, Port. *roca, rocha*, Ital. *rocca, roccia*, a rock. Cf. Low L. *rocca* (Ducange). We also find Ir. and Gael. *roc* (prob. from E.), and Bret. *roch* (prob. from F.). Also A. S. *stān-rocc* (11th c.). Origin unknown.

Rock (2), to shake, totter. (E.) M. E. *rokken*. A. S. *roccian* (C. Hall); N. Fries. *rocke*. + Dan. *rokke*, to rock, shake, Swed. dial. *rukka*, to wag. Allied to Dan. *rykke*, to pull, *ryk*, a pull; Icel. *rykkr*, a hasty pull; G. *ruck*, a pull, jolt; Du. *ruk*, a jerk. Teut. types **rukkōjan-, *rukkjan-*, to jolt, jerk (Franck). The base **rukk-* may be related to **renkan-*, to shake, as seen in Swed. dial. *rinka*, to shake (pt. t. *rank*, supine *runkit*); Swed. *runka*, to shake. See Rietz.

Rock (3), a distaff. (Scand.) Icel. *rokkr*, Swed. *rock*, Dan. *rok*, a distaff.+G. *rocken*; Du. *rok, rokken*.

rocket (1), a kind of fire-work. (Ital. – G.) M. Ital. *rocchetto*, 'a bobbin to winde silke upon; a squib of wilde fier;' Florio. So named from its shape, resembling that of a bobbin or a distaff. – M. H. G. *rocke*, G. *rocken*, a distaff (above).

Rocket (2), a plant. (F. – Ital. – L.) F. *roquette*. – Ital. *ruchetta*, dimin. of *ruca*, garden-rocket. – L. *ērūca*, a sort of cole-wort; whence also G. *rauke*, rocket.

Rod, a wand. (E.) See **Rood.**

Rodent, gnawing. (L.) From *rōdent-*,stem of pres. part. of *rōdere*, to gnaw. Allied to **Rase.**

Rodomontade, vain boasting. (F. –

Ital.) F. *rodomontade.* – Ital. *rodomontata,* a boast. Due to the boastful character of *Rodomonte,* in the Orlando Furioso of Ariosto, b. xiv.

Roe (1), a female deer. (E.) M. E. *ro.* A. S. *rā,* early form *rāha.*+Icel. *rā,* Dan. *raa,* Swed. *rå,* Du. *ree,* G. *reh.* Der. *roe-buck.*

Roe (2), spawn. (Scand.) For *roan*; the final *n* was dropped, being mistaken for the pl. suffix, as in *shoon* for shoes, *eyne* for eyes. M. E. *rowne.* – Icel. *hrogn,* Dan. *rogn,* Swed. *rom,* roe.+G. *rogen,* roe (whence F. *rogue,* roe).

Rogation. (F. – L.) F. *rogation.* – L. acc. *rogātiōnem,* a supplication. – L. *rogā-tus,* pp. of *rogāre,* to ask.

Rogue. (F. – C.) F. *rogue,* 'arrogant, proud, presumptuous, rude, surly;' Cot. Cf. E. *rogu-ish,* saucy. The orig. sense was a surly fellow; hence a vagabond. – Bret. *rok, rog,* arrogant, proud. Or from Low G. *rook,* a rook, a thief. (Doubtful; see Scheler.)

Roil, Rile, to vex. (F. ?) The old word *roil* meant (1) to disturb, (2) to vex. See Davies, Supp. Gloss. Of doubtful origin; prob. French. Cf. O. F. *roeillier,* to roll, to give one a beating; M. F. *rouiller,* to pummel.

Roistering, turbulent. (F. – L.) From the sb. *roister,* a bully, turbulent fellow. – F. *rustre,* 'a ruffin, royster, sawcie fellow;' Cot. By-form of O. F. *ruste,* a rustic, the *r* being epenthetic; cf. O. F. *ruistre, ruiste, ruste,* adj., strong, vigorous, rude, violent (Godefroy). – L. *rusticum,* acc. of *rusticus,* rustic. See **Rustic.**

Roll, vb. (F. – L.) M. E. *rollen.* – O. F. *roler,* F. *rouler.* – Late L. *rotulāre,* to revolve, roll. – L. *rotula,* a little wheel; dimin. of *rota,* a wheel. See **Rotary.** Der. *roll,* sb., a scroll, O. F. *role,* L. *rotulus.*

Romance. (F. – L.) O. F. *romanz, romans,* a romance. The form is due to late L. adv. *rōmānicē,* as in the phr. *rō-mānicē loquī*=O. F. *parler romanz,* to speak Romance, i. e. the vulgar Latin dialect of every-day life, as distinguished from book-Latin. *Rōmānicē,* i. e. Roman-like, is from L. *Rōmānus,* Roman. – L. *Rōma,* Rome.

romaunt. (F. – L.) O. F. *romant,* oblique case of O. F. *romanz,* a romance; see above. Der. *romant-ic.*

Romp; see **Ramp.**

Rondeau. (F. – L.) F. *rondeau,* a kind of poem, O. F. *rondel*; see **Roundel.**

Rood, the cross; a measure of land. (E.) The same word as *rod,* which is shortened from M. E. *rood* (also *rod*), a rood, a rod. Both *rood* and *rod* are used as measures, though the former is restricted to square senses, and the latter to linear; both measure, and are due to the use of a rod for measurement. A. S. *rōd,* a gallows, cross, properly a rod or pole.+O. Fries. *rōde,* gallows; O. Sax. *rōda,* cross, gallows; Du. *roede,* rod, perch, wand; G. *ruthe,* a rod of land; O. H. G. *ruota,* a rod, pole. Teut. type *rōdā,* fem., a rod, pole. ¶ The short *o* in *rod* is due to the final *d*; cf. *red, head, dead.* The A. S. *rodd* is not older than the 11th cent. Cf. **Ratlines.**

Roof. (E.) M. E. *rōf.* A. S. *hrōf.*+Du. *roef,* a cabin, Icel. *hrōf,* a shed. Cf. also Ir. *crō,* a hovel; W. *craw,* a pig-sty; Bret. *crou,* a stable. Teut. type *hrōfo-;* Idg. type *krāpo-.*

Rook (1), a kind of crow. (E.) M. E. *rook.* A. S. *hrōc.*+Icel. *hrōkr,* Dan. *raage,* Swed. *roka,* M. H. G. *ruoch,* O. H. G. *hruoh,* a jackdaw. Teut. type *hrōkoz,* masc.; cf. Gk. *κρώζειν* (for *κρώγ-yειν*), to caw. Of imitative origin; cf. Goth. *hrūkjan,* to crow.

Rook (2), a castle, at chess. (F. – Span. – Pers.) M. E. *rook.* – F. *roc.* – Span. *roque* (cf. Ital. *rocco*). – Pers. *rokh,* a rook. Said to have meant 'warrior' (Devic).

Room, space, a chamber. (E.) The old meaning is space, place. M. E. *roum.* A. S. *rūm*; 'næfdon *rūm*'=they had no room, Luke ii. 7. We also find adj. *rūm,* spacious. + Du. *ruim,* adj., spacious, *ruim,* sb., room; Icel. *rūmr,* spacious, *rūm,* space; Dan. and Swed. *rum,* adj. and sb.; Goth. *rūms,* adj. and sb., G. *raum.* Teut. type *rūmoz,* adj., whence the sb. forms are derived. Allied to L. *rūs,* open country; see **Rural.** Der. *roomy,* adj., used for M. E. *roum,* adj.

Roost, sb. (E.) M. E. *roost,* a perch for fowls. A. S. *hrōst,* the same.+M. Du. *roest,* a hen-roost; O. Sax. *hrōst,* the woodwork of a roof. Cf. Lowl. Sc. *roost,* the inside of a roof; the orig. *roost* was on the rafters inside a roof. Der. *roost,* vb.

Root (1), lowest part of a plant. (Scand.) M. E. *rote.* – Icel. *rōt,* Swed. *rot,* Dan. *rod,* a root. For *wrōt,* cognate with L. *rādix,* and allied to Goth. *waurts,* a root, A. S. *wyrt,* a wort, a root; the initial *w* being dropped, as is usual in Icelandic in the combination *wr* (later *vr*). See below. And see **Radix** and **Wort**.

Root (2), **Rout**, vb., to grub up, as a hog. (E.) A.S. *wrótan*, to grub up (strong vb.); whence prov. E. *wrout*, the same. Cf. A.S. *wrōt*, sb., a swine's snout; G. *rüssel*, a snout.+M. Du. *wroeten*, the same; Icel. *róta*, to grub up, Dan. *rode*, Low G. *wröten*, O. H. G. *ruozzan*.

Rope. (E.) M. E. *roop*. A.S. *ráp*, a cord, rope.+Du. *reep*, Icel. *reip*, Swed. *rep*, Dan. *reb*; Goth. *skauda-raip*, shoe-latchet; G. *reif*, circle, hoop, ring, sometimes a rope. All from Teut. base **raip-*, with the sense of 'strip,' hence 'string.' Perhaps from the 2nd grade of Teut. **reip-an-*, to cut; see **Reap** (Franck). And cf. **Ripe**, **Rip**. Der. *rop-y*, stringy, glutinous; *stir-rup*.

Roquelaure, a short cloak. (F.) Named after the duke of *Roquelaure* (ab. 1715).—Todd.

Rose. (E.—Gk.—Armenian.) A.S. *rose*.—L. *rosa*; borrowed from Gk. ῥόδον, a rose (whence a form **ῥοδια > rosa*); Æolic βρόδον (for **Fρόδον*). — Armen. *ward*, a rose; whence also Pers. *gūl*. See **Julep**. Der. *rhododendron* (Gk. δένδρον, a tree).

Rosemary. (F.—L.) M.E. *rosmarin*. — O. F. *rosmarin* (Cot.). — L. *rōsmarīnus*, *rōsmarīnum*, rosemary, lit. sea-dew; called *rōs maris* in Ovid. — L. *rōs*, dew; *marīnus*, marine. Named from some fancied connexion with sea-spray; altered to *rosemary* (as if for *rose of Mary*).

Rosin; see **Resin**.

Roster, a military register. (Du.) From Du. *rooster*, a grate, gridiron; hence, a list in parallel lines; lit. ' roaster.' — Du. *roosten*, to roast; see **Roast**.

Rostrum. (L.) L. *rostrum*, a beak; pl. *rostra*, a pulpit for speakers in the forum, adorned with beaks of ships taken from the Antiates. For **rōd-trum.* — L. *rōdere*, to gnaw, to peck. See **Rodent**. (Cf. *claus-trum < *claud-trum*.)

Rot, vb. (E.) A weak verb; the proper pp. is *rotted*, but *rotten* is commoner, which is a Scand. form (see below). M. E. *roten*, pp. *roted*. A.S. *rotian*, pp. *rotod.*+Du. *rotten*, to rot; O. H. G. *rozēn* (also *rōzēn*), to rot. See further under **Rotten**.

Rotary, turning like a wheel. (L.) Formed from L. *rota*, a wheel. + Gael.

and Irish *roth*, W. *rhod*, Lithuan. *ratas*; G. *rad*, a wheel. Also Skt. *ratha-*, a chariot, car. All from Idg. root RET, as in O. Irish *reth-im*, I run; Lith. *ritt-u*, I roll, turn round. Brugm. i. § 159. Der. *rotate*, from pp. of L. *rotāre*, to turn round.

Rote (1), routine, repetition. (F.—L.) M. E. *bi rote*, with repetition, by heart; lit. in a beaten track. — O.F. *rote* (F. *route*), a way, a beaten track. See **Route**.

Rote (2), an old musical instrument. (F. — G. — C.) O. F. *rote*, a kind of fiddle; answering to O. H. G. *hrota*, *rota*, a rote; Low L. *chrotta*. Of Celtic origin. — W. *crwth*, a violin; Gael. *cruit*, a harp; O. Irish *crot*, a harp. (Stokes-Fick, p. 99.) See **Crowd** (2).

Rother, an ox. (E.) M. E. *ruðer*. Late A.S. *hrūðeru*, pl.; orig. *hrȳðer*, *hrīðer*; and (in comp.) *hrīð-*. *Hrīð-<hrinð-*, cognate with G. *rind*. Cf. also Du. *rund*. See Kluge and Franck.

Rotten, putrid. (Scand.) M. E. *roten.* —Icel. *rotinn*, Swed. *rutten*, Dan. *raaden*, rotten. The Icel. *rotinn* is the pp. of a lost strong verb **rjóta*, to decay, orig. to soak, wet, allied to A. S. *rēotan*, O. H. G. *riuzan*, to weep, shed tears; cf. Lith. *raudóti*, Skt. *rud*, to weep. (√REUD.) See **Rot**. Brugm. i. § 594.

Rotundity. (F.—L.) F. *rotonditê.* — L. *rotunditātem*, acc. of *rotunditās*, roundness. — L. *rotundus*, round; see **Round**.

Rouble, **Ruble**, a Russian coin. (Russ.) Russ. *ruble*, a rouble, 100 copecks. Perhaps from Pers. *rūpīya*, a rupee (Miklosich). See **Rupee**.

Roué. (F.—L.) F. *roué*, lit. broken on the wheel; hence a profligate, supposed to merit that punishment. Pp. of *rouer*, to turn round (L. *rotāre*). — F. *roue*, a wheel. — L. *rota*, a wheel. See **Rotary**.

Rouge, red paint. (F.—L.) F. *rouge*, red. — L. acc. *rubeum*, red; (whence F. *rouge*, like F. *rage* from L. *rabiem*). Allied to L. *ruber*, red. See **Red**.

Rough. (E.) M. E. *rough*, *rugh*, *row*, *ruh*, &c. A.S. *rúh*, rough, hairy; also *rūg.*+Du. *ruig*, M. Du. *ru*, Dan. *ru*, Low G. *ruug*, O. H. G. *rūh*, G. *rauh*. Cf. Lithuan. *raukas*, a fold, *rùkti*, to wrinkle. ¶ Distinct from *raw*.

Rouleau. (F.—L.) F. *rouleau*, a roll of paper; hence, coins in a roll of paper. Dimin. of O. F. *role*, M. F. *roule*, a roll; see **Roll**.

roulette, a game of chance. (F.—L.)

F. *roulette*, a game in which a ball rolls on a turning table; dimin. of *rouelle*, a little wheel; see Rowel.

Roun, Round, to whisper. (E.) Shak. has *round*, with excrescent *d*. M. E. *rounen*. A.S. *rūnian*, to whisper. — A.S. *rūn*, a whisper. + G. *raunen*, to whisper; from O. H. G. *rūn*, a secret; see Rune.

Round. (F. — L.) O. F. *roönd*, F. *rond*. — L. *rotundus*, round. — L. *rota*, a wheel. See Rotary.

roundel, a kind of ballad. (F. — L.) O. F. *rondel*, later *rondeau*, a poem containing a line which recurs or comes *round* again. — F. *rond*, round (above).

roundelay. (F. — L.) M. F. *rondelet*, dimin. of O. F. *rondel* above. ¶ Prob. confused, in spelling, with E. *lay*, a song.

Rouse (1), to excite, to wake up. (Scand.) '*Exciter*, to stir up, *rowse*;' Cot. — Swed. *rusa*, to rush, *rusa upp*, to start up; Dan. *ruse*, to rush. Cf. A.S. *hrēosan*, to rush, to fall down quickly; from Teut. base **hreus-*.

Rouse (2), a drinking-bout. (Scand.) In Shak. means *ruus*, intoxication; Dan. *sove rusen ud* = to sleep out a rouse, to sleep oneself sober; Swed. *rus*, drunkenness. + Du. *roes*, drunkenness. Prob. allied to East Friesic *rūse*, noise, uproar, 'row;' *rūsen*, to make a noise. [G. *rausch*, a drunken fit, is borrowed from some other Tent. dialect.] ¶ Otherwise, *rouse* is short for *carouse*; *to drink carouse > to drink a rouse*; N. E. D.

Rout (1) a defeat, (2) a troop or crowd. (F. — L.) F. *route*, 'a rowt, defeature; also a rowt, heard, flock, troope; also a rutt, way, path;' Cot. — L. *rupta*, pp. of *ruptus*, broken; from *rumpere*. This L. *rupta* came to mean (1) a defeat, flying mass of broken troops; (2) a fragment of an army, a troop; (3) a way broken or cut through a forest, a way, route.

route, a way, course. (F. — L.) F. *route*, a way, route; see the word above.

routine, a beaten track. (F. — L.) F. *routine*, usual course; lit. small path. Dimin. of F. *route* (above).

Rover, a pirate. (Du.) M. E. *rover*. — Du. *roover*, a robber, pirate, thief. — Du. *rooven*, to rob. — Du. *roof*, spoil. + A. S. *rēaf*, Icel. *rauf*, G. *raub*, spoil; see Reave. Der. *rove*, vb., to wander; evolved from the sb.

Row (1), a line, rank. (E.) M. E. *rowe*. — A.S. *rāw*, *rǣw*, a row; *hegerāw*, a hedge-row. Teut. type **rai(g)wā*, fem., from a root-verb **reihwan-* (pt. t. **raihw*); whence also G. *reih-e*, a row, Du. *rij*, M. Du. *rij-e*, a row, O. H. G. *riga*, a line. Idg. root **reikh*, whence Skt. *rēkhā*, a line.

Row (2), to propel with oars. (E.) M. E. *rowen*. — A.S. *rōwan*, to row. + Du. *roeijen*, Icel. *rōa*, Swed. *ro*, Dan. *roe*, M. H. G. *rüejen*. Allied to O. Ir. *rām*, L. *rēmus*, an oar, Skt. *aritra-*, a paddle, rudder, Lithuan. *irti*, to row; Gk. ἐρετμός, a paddle, oar. Der. *rudder*.

Row (3), an uproar. (Scand.) For *rouse*; for loss of final *s*, cf. *pea*, *cherry*, *sherry*, *shay* (*chaise*). See Rouse (2).

Rowan-tree; see Roan-tree.

Rowel. (F. — L.) M. F. *rouelle*, a little wheel (on a bit or a spur). — Late L. *rotella*, dimin. of *rota*, a wheel. See Rotary.

Rowlock, Rollock, Rullock, the place of support for an oar. (E.) Spelt *orlok* in the Liber Albus, pp. 235, 237. A corruption of *oar-lock*. — A.S. *ārloc*, a rowlock. — A. S. *ār*, oar; *loc*, cognate with G. *loch*, a hole. The orig. rowlocks were actual holes, and were called also *oar-holes*.

Royal. (F. — L.) M. E. *real*, *roial*. — O. F. *real*, *roial* (F. *royal*). — L. *rēgālis*, royal; see Regal. Doublet, *regal*.

Rub. (E.) M. E. *rubben*. Not in A.S. + Dan. *rubbe*, Norw. *rubba*, E. Fries. *rubben*, to rub, scrub; Norw. *rubben*, rough, uneven; E. Fries. *rubberig*, rough; Du. *robbelig*, 'rugged,' Sewel; also (from E.) Gael. *rub*, to rub, Irish *rubadh*, a rubbing, W. *rhwbio*, to rub. Further allied to Icel. *rūfinn*, rough, Lith. *rupàs*, rough. ¶ Not allied to G. *reiben*; rather to L. *rumpere* and E. Reave.

Rubbish, broken stones, waste matter, refuse. (F. — O. H. G.) M. E. *robows*, *robeux*, Prompt. Parv.; pl. of an old form **robel*, clearly represented by mod. E. *rubble*; see below. ¶ *Rubbish* is, in fact, a corrupt form of the old plural of *rubble*.

rubble, broken stones, rubbish. (F. — O. H. G.) '*Rubble*, or *rubbish* of old houses;' Baret (1580). M. E. *robell*, Palladius, p. 13, l. 340. This answers exactly to an old form **robel*, O. F. **robel*, only found in the pl. *robeux*. 'A grete loode of *robeux*;' cited by Way in Prompt. Parv. A. F. *robous* (for **robeus*), rubbish, Liber Albus, p. 579. Obviously the dimin.

455

of F. *robe* in the sense of 'trash,' so well preserved in the cognate Ital. *roba*, 'a gowne, a robe, wealth, goods, geare, trash, pelfe,' Florio. Cf. Ital. *robaccia*, old goods, rubbish; *robiccia*, trifles, rubbish; from *roba*. See **Robe**.

Rubicund, ruddy. (F.–L.) F. *rubicond*. – L. *rubicundus*, very red. – L. *rubēre*, to be red. See **Red**.

rubric, a direction printed in red. (F. – L.) F. *rubrique*. – L. *rubrīca*, red earth; also a title written in red. – L. *ruber*, red (above).

ruby, a red gem. (F.–L.) O. F. *rubi*, *rubis*; F. *rubis* (where *s* is the old sign of the nom. case). Cf. Span. *rubi*, *rubin*, Port. *rubim*, Ital. *rubino*. – Late L. *rubīnus*, a ruby; from its colour. – L. *rubeus*, red; *rubēre*, to be red. Allied to **Red**.

Ruck (1), a fold, crease. (Scand.) Icel. *hrukka*, a wrinkle; cf. *hrokkin*, curled, pp. of *hrökkva*, to recoil, give way, curl; Norw. *rukka*, a wrinkle. Cf. Swed. *rynka*, Dan. *rynke*, a wrinkle. From Teut. base *hrenk-* (Noreen).

Ruck (2), a heap, small pile. (Scand.) Norw. and M. Swed. *ruka*, a heap; cf. Icel. *hraukr*, a rick, heap; see **Rick**.

Rudder. (E.) M. E. *roder*, *rother*. A. S. *rōðer*, a paddle. Here *rō-ðer* = rowing implement; from *rōw-an*, to row. (Paddles preceded rudders.) + Du. *roer* (for *roeder*), an oar, rudder; Swed. *roder*, *ror*; Dan. *ror*; G. *ruder*. See **Row** (2).

Ruddock, a red-breast. (E.) A. S. *rudduc*. Hence W. *rhuddog*, Corn. *ruddoc*, a red-breast. See below.

ruddy. (E.) M. E. *rody*, A. S. *rudig*, ruddy. From A. S. *rud-*, weak grade of *rēodan*, to redden, a strong verb, whence also A. S. *rēad*, red; see **Red**.

Rude. (F.–L.) F. *rude*. – L. *rudem*, acc. of *rudis*, rough, raw, rude.

rudiment. (F. – L.) F. *rudiment*. – L. *rudīmentum*, a thing in the first rough state, a first attempt. – L. *rudi-s*, rude.

Rue (1), to be sorry for. (E.) M. E. *rewen*. A. S. *hrēowan* (pt. t. *hrēaw*). + O. Sax. *hrewan*, O. H. G. *hriuwan*, G. *reuen*. Cf. Icel. *hryggr*, grieved, *hrygð*, ruth. Teut. type *hrewwan-*, to pity.

Rue (2), a plant. (F.–L.–Gk.) F. *rue*. – L. *rūta*. – Gk. ρυτή, rue; whence also G. *raute*. Cf. A. S. *rūde*, rue.

Ruff (1), a kind of frill. (E.) 'Ruffe of a shirt;' Levins (1570). So called from its uneven surface; apparently shortened

from *ruffle*, verbal sb. from *ruffle*, vb., which was in early use. See **Ruffle** (1).

Ruff (2), the name of a bird. (E. ?) Said to be named from the male having a *ruff* round its neck in the breeding season. But the female is called a *reeve*, which points to formation by vowel-change from some different source.

Ruff (3), a fish. (E. ?) M. E. *ruffe*. Origin unknown.

Ruff (4), a game at cards. (F.) A modification of O. F. *roffle*, *roufle*, *ronfle*, M. F. *ronfle*, 'hand-ruffe, at cards,' Cotgrave; *jouer à la ronfle*, 'to play at hand-ruffe, also to snore,' id. Cf. Ital. *ronfa*, ruff; *ronfare*, to snort, to trump at cards. From Tuscan *ronfiare* (F. *ronfler*), to snore, snort; supposed to be from L. *re-in-flāre*, to re-inflate (Körting). See **Inflate**. But it may be of imitative origin.

Ruffian, a bully. (F.–Ital.–Teut.) Walloon *rouffian*, M. F. *rufien*, ruffian, 'a bawd, pandar;' Cot. – Ital. *ruffiano*, *roffiano*, 'a pander, ruffian, swaggrer;' Florio. For *rufflānus*, formed with L. suffix *-ānus* from Low G. *ruffeln*, to act as pandar. See **Ruffle** (2).

Ruffle (1), to disorder a dress. (E.) M. E. *ruffelen*, to entangle, run into knots; also (apparently) to rumple, Cursor Mundi, 26391. Allied to **Ruff** (1) above. + M. Du. *ruyffelen*, to ruffle, wrinkle, *ruyffel*, a wrinkle, a crumple; E. Fries. *ruffelen*, *ruffeln*, to pleat. From *ruf*, weak grade of Teut. *reufan-*, to break, tear; see **Reave**. Cf. Lithuan. *ruple*, rough bark on old trees. Der. *ruffle*, sb.

Ruffle (2), to bluster, be turbulent. (M. Du.) Obsolete. *Rufflers* were cheating bullies, highwaymen, lawless or violent men (Nares). – M. Du. *roffelen*, *roffen*, to pandar (Oudemans); Low G. *ruffeln*, to pandar, *ruffeler*, a pimp, intriguant; Dan. *ruffer*, a pandar. A *ruffler* and a *ruffian* are much the same. See **Ruffian**.

Rug. (Scand.) Swed. *rugg*, rough entangled hair, cf. M. Swed. *ruggig*, rough, hairy; Icel. *rögg*, shagginess. Also Low G. *ruug*, rough, *rugen*, to be rough (like flocks of hair); E. Fries. *rūg*, rough, *ruge*, a roughness, a rough side of a skin; *ruger*, a rough-hided or furry animal (e. g. a cat). See **Rough**.

rugged. (Scand.) M. E. *rugged*; also *ruggy*, Ch. C. T., A 2883. The latter is from M. Swed. *ruggig*, rough, hairy. – Swed. *rugg*, rough entangled hair (above).

Rugose, full of wrinkles. (L.) L. *rū-gōsus,* adj., from *rūga,* a wringle. Cf. Lith. *raûkas,* a wrinkle, *runkù,* I grow wrinkled. Brugm. ii. § 628.

Ruin. (F. – L.) F. *ruine.* – L. *ruīna,* an overthrow. – L. *ruere,* to rush, fall down. Brugm. ii. § 529.

Rule, sb. (F. – L.) M. E. *reule, riwle.* – A. F. *reule,* O. F. *riule, reule* (F. *règle*). – L. *rēgula,* a rule. – L. *regere,* to rule. See Regent.

Rum (1), a spirituous liquor. (Prov. E.) Called *rumbo* in Smollett, Per. Pickle, c. ii and c. ix; this is short for the sailor's word *rumbowling,* grog. Orig. called *Rumbullion* in Barbadoes, A.D. 1651; from Devonsh. *rumbullion,* uproar, rumpus, which is prob. allied to Rumble.

Rum (2), strange, queer. (Hindi.) '*Rum,* gallant, a cant word;' Bailey (1737). *Rum* really means 'Gypsy'; hence 'good' from a Gypsy point of view, but 'suspicious' from an outsider's point of view. Hence *rome bouze, rum booze,* good wine. *Rom* means 'a husband, a Gypsy'; *rōmmani,* adj., Gypsy. This Gypsy word *rom* answers to Hindi *ḍom* (with initial cerebral *d,* resembling *r*), a man of low caste; Skt. *ḍōmba-,* 'a man of low caste, who gains his livelihood by singing and dancing;' Benfey.

Rumb, Rhumb, a line for directing a ship's course on a chart; a point of the compass. (F. – Span. L. – Gk.) See *Rumb* in Phillips. – F. *rumb,* 'a roomb, or point of the compasse, a line drawn directly from wind to wind in a compasse, traversboord, or sea-card;' Cot. – Span. (and Port.) *rumbo,* a ship's course (represented by spiral lines on a globe). – L. *rhombum,* acc. of *rhombus,* a magician's circle, a rhombus. – Gk. ῥόμβος, a top, a magic wheel, whirling motion; also a rhombus. See Rhomb. *Rhomb* meant revolution of the sphere, Milton, P. L. viii. 134; hence whirling or spiral lines, &c. ¶ No connexion with Du. *ruim,* which merely means room or space, or sometimes the hold of a ship, i. e. its room or capacity.

Rumble, to make a low, heavy sound. (E.) Prov. E. *rommle, rummle*; M. E. *romblen* (with excrescent *b*). Frequent. form, meaning 'to repeat the sound *rum*'; cf. L. *rūmor,* a rumour; Skt. *ru,* to hum. See Rumour. + Du. *rommelen,* Low G. and Pomeran. *rummeln,* Dan. *rumle,* to rumble, buzz.

Ruminate. (L.) From pp. of L. *rū-mināre,* to chew the cud, ruminate. – L. *rūmin-,* for *rūmen,* the throat, gullet. Allied to L. *rū-gīre,* to roar, bray, Gk. ὠ-ρυ-γή, a roaring, ὠ-ρύ-ομαι, I roar; Skt. *ru,* to hum, bray, roar. (√REU.) See Rumour.

Rummage, to search thoroughly. (Du.; *with* F. *suffix.*) Due to the sb. *rummage,* i. e. stowage. – Prov. (S. F.) *arrumage* (mod. Prov. *arrimage*), stowage. – Prov. *arrumer* (mod. Prov. *arrimer*), to stow. – L. *ad-*; and Prov. *rum,* from Du. *ruim,* a ship's hold. See Room.

Rummer, a sort of drinking-glass. (Du.) Used for Rhenish wine. 'Rhenish rummers;' Dryden. – Du. *roemer, romer,* a wine-glass; Low G. *römer,* a large wine-glass; hence G. *römer,* a rummer. Du. *roemer* is prob. from Du. *roem,* boasting, praise; as if 'a glass to drink in praise of a toast'; Franck. Cf. G. *ruhm,* praise; O. Sax. *hröm*; also Icel. *hróðr,* praise. ¶ Also M. Du. *roomer* (Hexham); which some explain as a 'Romish glass.'

Rumour. (F. – L.) M. E. *rumour.* – F. *rumeur.* – L. acc. *rūmōrem,* from *rū-mor,* a noise, murmur. Cf. L. *rūmitāre,* to spread reports. – √REU, to make a humming noise. See Rumble, Ruminate.

Rump. (E.) M. E. *rumpe.* + Icel. *rumpr,* Swed. *rumpa,* Dan. *rumpe*; M. Du. *rompe,* 'the bulke of a body or corps, or a bodie without a head,' Hexham; Du. *romp*; Low G. *rump,* trunk (of the body); G. *rumpf.*

Rumple. (E.) The M. E. form is *rimplen,* to rimple. *Rimple* and *rumple* are from the same verb, viz. A.S. *hrimpan* (pp. *gehrumpen*), to wrinkle; see Rimple. + M. Du. *rompelen, rompen,* to wrinkle; *rompel, rimpel,* a wrinkle; cf. G. *rümpfen,* to wrinkle; O. H. G. *hrimfan,* str. vb.

Run. (E.) M. E. *rinnen,* pt. t. *ran,* pp. *runnen, ronnen*; A.S. *rinnan,* pt. t. *rann,* pp. *gerunnen*; also found in the transposed form *irnan,* pt. t. *arn.* + Du. *rennen,* Icel. *renna,* Dan. *rinde,* Swed. *rinna,* Goth. *rinnan,* G. *rinner.* See Brugm. i. § 67; ii. § 654.

Runagate, a vagabond. (F. – L.) A corruption of M. E. *renegat,* an apostate, villain; Ch. C. T. 5353. [The corruption was due to a popular etymology from *runne a gate,* run on the road, hence, to be a vagabond.] – O. F. *renegat,* 'a renegadoe;' Cot. — Late L. *renegātus*, pp. of *renegāre*, to deny again, forsake the faith. — L. *re*, again; *negāre*, to deny; see **Negation**.

Rundlet, Runlet, a small barrel. (F.—L.) Formerly *roundlet*; dimin. of O. F. *rondelle*, a little barrel, named from its roundness. — F. *rond*, round. — L. *rotundus*, round. — L. *rota*, a wheel; see **Round**.

Rune, one of the old characters used for incised inscriptions. (E.) A learned term. A. S. *rūn*, a rune, mystery, secret conference, whisper. Orig. sense 'whisper' or murmur, hence a mystery, lastly an incised character, because writing was a secret known to few.+Goth. *rūna*, O. H. G. *rūna*, a secret, counsel; O. Irish *rūn*, W. *rhin*, a secret. Idg. type **rūnā*, fem. Cf. Gk. ἐρευνάω, I search out, ἔρευνα, fem., an enquiry.

Rung, a round of a ladder. (E.) M. E. *ronge*, a stake. A. S. *hrung*, a stake of a cart, beam or spar.+M. Du. *ronge*, a beam of a plough; G. *runge*, a pin, a bolt; Goth. *hrugga* (=*hrunga*), a staff. Cf. also Icel. *röng*, rib in a ship. Perhaps allied to **Ring**. The sense seems to be 'rounded stick.'

Runnel, a stream. (E.) A. S. *rynel*; cf. *ryne*, a course, allied to *runn-*, weak grade of *rinnen*, to run; see **Run**.

Runt, a bullock, heifer. (Du.) From Du. *rund* (Hexham). And see **Rother**.

Rupee, an Indian coin. (Hind. — Skt.) Hindustāni *rūpiyah*, a rupee. — Skt. *rūpya-*, handsome, also (as sb.) wrought silver. — Skt. *rūpa-*, beauty.

Rupture. (F. — L.) F. *rupture*. — L. *ruptūra*, a breakage. — L. *rupt-us*, pp. of *rumpere*, to break (pt. t. *rūpī*). Allied to **Reave**. (√REUP.) Brugm. i. § 466.

Rural, belonging to the country. F. — L.) F. *rural*. — L. *rūrālis*, adj. — L. *rūr-*, stem of *rūs*, country. See **Rustic**.

Rusa, a kind of deer. (Malay.) Malay *rūsa*, a deer. See **Babirusa**.

Ruse, a trick. (F. — L.) F. *ruse*, a trick. — F. *ruser*, to beguile; contr. from O. F. *reüser*, to refuse, recoil, escape, dodge. — L. *recūsāre*, to refuse, to oppose a cause. — L. *re-*, back; *caussa*, a cause. See **Recusant**.

Rush (1), to move swiftly forward. (E.) M. E. *ruschen*. + M. H. G. *rūschen* (G. *rauschen*), to rush, rustle, roar (as water); Du. *ruischen*, to murmur (as

water), to rustle. Cf. M. Swed. *ruska*, to rush. Perhaps the same as A. S. *hryscan*, to be strident, to rustle.

Rush (2), a plant. (E. *or* L.) M. E. *rusche*, *rische*, *resche*. A. S. *risce*, *resce*, a rush; oldest form *risc*. + Du. *rusch*, rush, reed; E. Fries. *rüske*; Low G. *rusk*; N. Fries. *rusken*, pl., rushes. Perhaps borrowed from L. *ruscum*, butcher's broom; but this does not account for A. S. *risc*. More likely allied to E. *rash*, as if of quick growth. Cf. Lowl. Sc. *rash*, a rush; also E. Fries. *risk*, quick, slender; Low G. *rusch*, quick. Der. *bul-rush* (prob. for *bole-rush*, round-stemmed rush); cf. *bull-weed*, knapweed.

Rusk. (Span.) Span. *rosca de mar*, sea-rusks, a kind of biscuit; *rosca*, a roll (twist) of bread, also a screw. Cf. Port. *rosca*, the winding of a snake. Origin unknown.

Russet. (F. — L.) M. E. *russet*. — M. F. *rousset*, 'russet, ruddy;' Cot. Dimin. of F. *roux* (fem. *rousse*), reddish. — L. *russus*, reddish. Allied to Gk. ἐ-ρυθ-ρός, red; see **Red**. Cf. Brugm. i. § 759.

rust. (E.) Prov. E. *rowst*. A. S. *rūst*, rust; orig. redness. Allied to A. S. *rudu*, ruddiness, and *rēad*, red.+Du. *roest*, Dan. *rust*, Swed. G. *rost*. Teut. type **rūsto-*, from Idg. **reudh-to-*; see **Ruddy**. Cf. Lith. *rudis*, rust; L. *rōbīgo*, *rūbīgo*; Polish *rdza*, rust. Brugm. i. § 759.

Rustic. (F. — L.) F. *rustique*. — L. *rusticus*, belonging to the country. — L. *rūs*, the country. Cf. Russ. *raviina*, a plain, Zend *ravan*, O. Irish *roe*, a plain; see **Room**.

Rustle. (E.) Cf. A. S. *ge-hruxl*, a noise, tumult. Frequent. of **Rush** (1), q. v. Cf. M. Du. *ruyselen*, 'to rustle,' Hexham; Low G. and Pomer. *russeln*; M. Swed. *ruska*, to shake, rush; G. *rauschen*, *ruschen*, to rustle, to rush.

Rut (1), a track left by a wheel. (F. — L.) F. *route*, 'a rutt, way;' Cot. See **Rout**. Doublets, *rout*, *route*.

Rut (2), to copulate, as deer. (F. — L.) M. E. *rutien*, to rut; from *rut*, sb. — M. F. *rut*, *ruit*, 'the rut of deer or boars.' — L. *rūgītum*, acc. of *rūgītus*, the roaring of lions; hence, the noise made by deer in rut-time. — L. *rūgīre*, to roar (whence M. F. *ruir*). See **Rumour**.

Ruth, pity. (E.) M.E. *reuthe*. Formed from A. S. *hrēow*, s. f., pity (cf. G. *reue*), by adding *-th*; suggested by Icel. *hryggð*, *hrygð*, ruth, sorrow. From A. S. *hréowan*, to rue; see **Rue** (1).

Rye. (E.) M. E. *reye*. A. S. *ryge*, rye. **+** Du. *rogge*, Icel. *rugr*, Dan. *rug*, Swed. *råg*, G. *roggen*; O. H. G. *rocco*. Cf. Russ. *roj(e)*, rye; Lithuan. *ruggei*, pl. sb., rye.

Ryot; the same as **Rayah**, q. v.

S.

Sabaoth, hosts. (Heb.) Heb. *tsevā'ōth*, armies; pl. of *tsāvā'*, an army. **—** Heb. *tsāvā'*, to go forth as a soldier.

Sabbath. (L. – Gk. – Heb.) M. E. *sabat*. **—** L. *sabbatum*. **—** Gk. *σάββατον*. **—** Heb. *shabbāth*, rest, sabbath, sabbath-day. **—** Heb. *shābath*, to rest.

Sable, an animal. (F. – Slavonic.) O.F. *sable*. **—** Russ. *sobole*, the sable; also a fur-tippet; Polish *sobol*. ¶ As black sable was best liked, the word *sable* (in E. and F.) also means 'black.'

Sabre, Saber. (F. – G. – Gk.?) F. *sabre*. **—** G. *säbel* (older form also *sabel*), a falchion. Said to be from Mid. Gk. *ζαβός*, crooked (Diez). We also find Russ. *sablia*, Pol. *szabla*, Hungar. *szablya*, Serv. *sablja*, Wallach. *sabie*; all supposed to be borrowed words.

Saccharine. (F. – L. – Gk. – Skt.) F. *saccharin*, adj.; from L. *saccharum*, sugar. **—** Gk. *σάκχαρον*. **—** Skt. *çarkarā*, gravel, candied sugar; see **Sugar.**

Sacerdotal. (F. – L.) F. *sacerdotal*. **—** L. *sacerdōtālis*, belonging to a priest. **—** L. *sacerdōt-*, stem of *sacerdōs*, a priest, lit. 'presenter of offerings or sacred gifts' (Corssen). **—** L. *sacer*, sacred; *dare*, to give. Cf. *dōs* (stem *dōt-*), a dowry, from *dare*.

Sack (1), a bag. (L. – Gk. – Heb. – Egyptian?) M. E. *sak*. A. S. *sacc*. **—** L. *saccus*. **—** Gk. *σάκκος*. **—** Heb. *saq*, sack-cloth, a sack of corn. Prob. of Egyptian origin; cf. Coptic *sok*, sack-cloth (Peyron). From L. *saccus* are borrowed Du. *zak*, G. *sack*, &c. Der. *sack-cloth*.

sack (2), to plunder. (F. – L., &c.) From the sb. *sack*, pillage. **—** F. *sac*, ruin, spoil. From the use of a *sack* in removing plunder; Cot. has *à sac, à sac*, 'the word whereby a commander authorizeth his souldiers to sack a place.' Cf. Late L. *saccāre*, to put into a bag; Late L. *saccus*, a garment, a purse, L. *saccus*, a sack; see above.

Sack (3), the name of an old Spanish

wine. (F. – L.) Formerly also *seck*, meaning a 'dry' wine. **—** F. *sec*, dry; *vin sec*, sack. Cf. Span. *seco*, dry. **—** L. *siccum*, acc. of *siccus*, dry. *Sherris sack* = Span. *seco de Xeres*; see **Sherry.**

Sackbut, a kind of wind-instrument. (F. – L. – Gk. – Chaldee.) F. *saquebute*, a sackbut. Substituted, by some perversion, for L. *sambūca*, Dan. iii. 5 (Vulg.), which was a kind of harp. **—** Gk. *σαμβύκη*. **—** Chald. *sabb(e)khā*, a kind of harp. ¶ Cf. Span. *sacabuche*, a tube used as a pump; also, a sackbut, trombone. Explained, by popular etymology, as 'that which exhausts the chest,' from the exertion used; as if from Span. *sacar*, to draw out, exhaust, the same as M. F. *sacquer*, to draw out hastily, lit. to draw out of a sack, from Heb. *saq*, a sack; *buche*, maw, stomach, chest.

Sacrament. (L.) L. *sacrāmentum*, an engagement, military oath, vow; in late L., a sacrament. **—** L. *sacrāre*, to render sacred. **—** L. *sacr-*, for *sacer*, sacred (below).

sacred. (F. – L.) *Sacred* is the pp. of M. E. *sacren*, to consecrate, render holy; a verb now obsolete. **—** F. *sacrer*, to consecrate. **—** L. *sacrāre*, to consecrate. **—** L. *sacr-*, for *sacer*, holy. From base *sac-* of L. *sancīre*, to make holy. Brugm. ii. § 744. (√SAK.)

sacrifice. (F. – L.) F. *sacrifice*. **—** L. *sacrificium*, lit. a rendering sacred; cf. *sacrificāre*, to sacrifice. **—** L. *sacri-*, for *sacer*, sacred; *-ficāre*, for *facere*, to make.

sacrilege. (F. – L.) M. F. *sacrilege*. **—** L. *sacrilegium*, the stealing of sacred things. **—** L. *sacri-*, for *sacer*, sacred; *legere*, to gather, steal; see **Legend.**

sacristan, sexton. (F. – L.) *Sacristan* is rare; it is commonly *sexton*, M. E. *sextein*, orig. a keeper of the sacred vestments, afterwards a grave-digger. **—** A. F. *secrestein*, M. F. *sacristain*, 'a sexton or vestry-keeper;' Cot. **—** Late L. *sacrist-a*, a sacristan; with suffix *-ānus*. **—** L. *sacr-*, for *sacer* (above); with suffix *-ista*.

Sad. (E.) The orig. sense was sated; hence tired, grieved. A. S. *sæd*, sated, satiated. **+** O. Sax. *sad*, Icel. *saðr*, Goth. *saths*, G. *satt*, sated, full. Teut. type **sa-doz*, sated; a pp. form. Allied to O. Ir. *sā-ith*, satiety, *sa-thech*, sated; L. *sa-tur*, full; Lith. *so-tùs*, full, *so-tas*, satiety; Gk. *ἀ-σαι*, *ἄ-μεναι*, to satiate. (√SA, SA.) Brugm. i. § 196. Allied to **Sate, Satiate.**

Saddle. (E.) M. E. *sadel.* A. S. *sadol.*
+Du. *zadsl,* Icel. *söðull,* Swed. Dan.
sadel, G. *sattel,* O. H. G. *satul.* Teut.
type *saduloz*; possibly borrowed from a
derivative of Idg. *sed,* to sit, in some
other Idg. language. Cf. O. Slav. *sedlo,*
Russ. *siedlo,* L. *sella* (for *sedla,* from *sedēre,*
to sit); but none of these exhibits the
grade *sad.*

Sadducee. (L. – Gk. – Heb.) L. pl.
Sadducæi. – Gk. pl. Σαδδουκαῖοι. – Heb. pl.
tsedūqīm ; pl. of *tsādōq,* just, righteous. –
Heb. *tsādaq,* to be just. Some derive it
from *Tsādōq* (*Zadok*), the founder of the
sect, whose name meant ' the just.'

Safe. (F. – L.) M. E. *sauf.* – F. *sauf,*
safe. – L. *saluum,* acc. of *saluus,* safe. See
Salvation. Cf. O. Norman dial. *saf,*
safe.

Saffron, a plant. (F. – Arab.) A. F.
saffran, F. *safran.* – Arab. *za'farān,*
saffron.

Sag, to droop. (E.) M. E. *saggen.*
Not in A. S. Low G. *sakken,* to settle (as
dregs); E. Fries. *sakken,* Du. *zakken,* to
sink ; Swed. *sacka,* to settle, sink down ;
cf. Dan. *sakke,* to have stern-way. Hardly
allied to *sink.*

Saga, a tale. (Scand.) Icel. *saga,* a
tale ; cf. Icel. *segja,* to say. See **Say** (1),
Saw (2).

Sagacious. (L.) From L. *sagāci-,*
decl. stem. of *sagax,* of quick perception ;
with suffix *-ous.* – L. *sāgīre,* to perceive by
the senses.+Goth. *sōk-jan,* A. S. *sēcan,* to
seek. See **Seek.** Brugm. i. § 187.

Sage (1), wise. (F. – L.) F. *sage.* –
Late L. *sabius,* for L. *-sapius,* whence
nesapius, unwise (Petronius) ; see Schwan.
– L. *sapere,* to be wise. See **Sapid.**

Sage (2), a plant. (F. – L.) M. E.
sauge. – O. F. *sauge.* – L. *saluia,* sage ;
from its supposed healing virtues. – L.
saluāre, to heal ; *saluus,* safe, hale, sound.
See **Salvation.**

Sagittarius. (L.) L. *sagittārius,* an
archer. – L. *sagitta,* an arrow.

Sago, a starch. (Malay.) Malay *sāgu,*
sāgū, sago, pith of a tree named *rumbiya.*

Sahib, sir, master ; a title. (Hind. –
Arab.) Hind. *sāhib.* – Arab. *sāhib,* lord,
master ; orig. ' companion.' Rich. Dict.,
p. 924.

Sail, sb. (E.) M. E. *seil.* A. S. *segel,*
segl, a sail.+Du. *zeil,* Icel. *segl,* Dan. *seil,*
Swed. G. *segel.* Teut. type *seglom,* neut.
Sense unknown ; perhaps ' driver ' ; cf. Gk.

ἔχειν νῆας, to urge on ships, Od. ix. 279.
See **Scheme.**

Saint. (F. – L.) M. E. *seint, saint.* –
A. F. *seint*; F. *saint.* – L. *sanctum,* acc.
of *sanctus,* holy. – L. *sanctus,* pp. of *sancīre,*
to render sacred ; see **Sacred.**

sainfoin. (F. – L.) F. *sainfoin,* M.F.
sainct-foin (Cot.) ; as if ' holy hay.' – L.
sanctum fænum, holy hay. ¶ But thought
to represent *sain foin,* i. e. ' wholesome
hay.' – L. *sānum fænum* ; see **Sane.**

Sake. (E.) M. E. *sake,* purpose, cause.
A. S. *sacu,* strife, dispute, crime, law-suit ;
orig. ' contention.' + Du. *zaak,* matter,
affair, business ; Icel. *sök,* a charge, crime ;
Dan. *sag,* Swed. *sak,* G. *sache.* Teut.
type *sakā,* fem., strife. From Teut.
sakan-, to contend, as in Goth. *sakan,*
A. S. *sacan,* O. H. G. *sahhan,* str. vb. See
Soke.

Saker, a kind of falcon ; a small piece
of artillery. (F. – Span. – Arab.) (The
gun was called after the falcon ; cf. *musket.*)
– M. F. *sacre,* ' a saker ; the hawk, and the
artillery so called ; ' Cot. – Span. *sacre,* a
saker (in both senses). – Arab. *saqr,* a
hawk ; Rich. Dict., p. 938. Engelmann
has shewn that the word is not of Lat.
origin, as said by Diez. (Devic ; and
Körting, § 1642.)

Salaam, Salam. (Arab.) Arab.
salām, saluting, wishing peace ; a salutation. – Arab. *salm,* saluting.+Heb. *shalōm,*
peace, from *shālam,* to be safe.

Salad. (F. – Ital. – L.) F. *salade.* –
M. Ital. *salata,* a salad of herbs ; lit.
' salted ; ' fem. of *salato,* salted, pickled,
pp. of *salare,* to salt. – Ital. *sale,* salt. –
L. *sāl,* salt. See **Salt.**

Salamander, a reptile. (F. – L. –
Gk.) F. *salamandre.* – L. *salamandra.*
– Gk. σαλαμάνδρα, a kind of lizard. Of
Eastern origin ; cf. Pers. *samandar,* a
salamander.

Salary, stipend. (F. – L.) F. *salaire.*
– L. *salārium,* orig. salt-money, given to
soldiers to buy salt. – L. *sāl,* salt. See
Salt.

Sale. (E.) M. E. *sale.* A. S. *sala.*+
Icel. *sala,* fem., *sal,* neut., a sale, bargain ;
Swed. *salu* ; O. H. G. *sala.* Orig. sense
' delivery,' or ' a handing over' ; as in
O. H. G. *sala.* Der. *sell, handsel.*

Salic, Salique. (F. – O. H. G.) F.
Salique, belonging to the Salic tribe. This
was a Frankish tribe, prob. named from
the river *Sala* (now Yssel).

σύν, together; ἕδρα, a seat, from ἕζομαι, I sit; see **Sit**.

Sans. (F.--L.) F. *sans*, without; O.F. *sens*. — L. *sine*, without. — L. *si ne*, if not, except.

Sanskrit. (Skt.) Skt. *saṁskṛta*, lit. 'symmetrically formed.' — Skt. *sam*, together; *kṛta*, made, from *kṛ*, to make; cf. L. *creāre*, to make. See **Create**.

Sap (1), juice of plants. (E.) A.S. *sæp*. **+** Du. *sap*; Low G. *sapp*; O.H.G. *saf*, cf. G. *saft*; Icel. *safi*. ¶ Not allied to Gk. ὀπός; but perhaps borrowed from L. *sapa*.

Sap (2), to undermine. (F. — Late L.) O.F. *sapper*, F. *saper*. — O.F. *sappe* (F. *sape*), a kind of hoe. (Cf. Span. *zapa*, Ital. *zappa*, mattock.) — Late L. *sappa*, *sapa*, a hoe. Origin unknown; Diez suggested Gk. σκαπάνη, a hoe; from σκάπτειν, to dig.

Sapid, savoury. (L.) Rare. L. *sapidus*, savoury. — L. *sapere*, to taste; also to be wise. Cf. O.H.G. *int-seffen*, to taste, mark. Brugm. ii. § 718. **Der. in-sipid**.

sapience. (F. — L.) F. *sapience*. — L. *sapientia*, wisdom. — L. *sapient-*, stem of pres. pt. of *sapere*, to be wise.

Saponaceous, soapy. (L. — Tent.) Coined, as if from L. **sāpōnāceus*, from L. *sāpōnem*, acc. of *sāpo*, soap (Pliny). See **Soap**.

Sapphic, a kind of metre. (L. — Gk.) L. *sapphicus*, belonging to Sappho. — Gk. Σαπφώ, Sappho of Lesbos, died about 592 B.C.

Sapphire. (F. — L. — Gk. — Heb.) F. *saphir* — L. *sapphīrus*. — Gk. σάπφειρος, a sapphire. — Heb. *sappīr* (with initial *samech*), a sapphire. Cf. Pers. *saffīr*, sapphire.

Saraband. (F. — Span. — Pers.) F. *sarabande*, a Spanish dance. — Span. *zarabanda*, a dance of Moorish origin. — Pers. *sarband*, lit. 'a fillet for fastening a lady's head-dress.' — Pers. *sar*, head ; *band*, band.

Saracen. (L. — Gk. — Arab.) L. *saracēnus*, lit. one of the Eastern people. — Late Gk. Σαρακηνός. — Arab. *sharqīn*, pl. of *sharqīy*, eastern. — Arab. *sharq*, east, rising sun. — Arab. root *sharaqa*, it rose.

Sarcasm, a sneer. (F. — L. — Gk.) F. *sarcasme*. — L. *sarcasmus*. — Gk. σαρκασμός, a sneer. — Gk. σαρκάζειν, to tear flesh, to bite the lips in rage, to sneer. — Gk. σαρκ-, stem of σάρξ, flesh. **Der. sarcastic**, Gk. σαρκαστικός, sneering.

Sarcenet, Sarsnet, a thin silk. (F. — L. — Gk. — Arab.) O.F. *sarcenet*, a stuff made by the Saracens. — Low L. *saracēnicum*, sarcenet. — L. *Saracēnus*, Saracen; see **Saracen**.

Sarcophagus. (L. — Gk.) L. *sarcophagus*, a stone tomb; made of a limestone which was supposed to consume the corpse (Pliny). — Gk. σαρκοφάγος, flesh-consuming; hence lime-stone. — Gk. σαρκο-, for σάρξ, flesh; φαγεῖν, to eat. See **Sarcasm**.

Sardine (1), a small fish. (F. — L. — Gk.) F. *sardine*. — L. *sardīna*, *sarda*. — Gk. σαρδίνη, σάρδα, a kind of fish.

Sardine (2), a gem. (L. — Gk.) L. *sardīnus*. — Gk. σαρδίνος; Rev. iv. 3. Named from *Sardis*, in Asia Minor (Pliny).

sardius, a gem. (L. — Gk.) Rev. xxi. 20. — L. *sardius* (Vulgate). — Gk. σάρδιος, σάρδιον, a gem of Sardis (above).

Sardonic, used of grim laughter. (F. — L. — Gk.) F. *sardonique*, formerly *sardonien*, in phrase *ris sardonien*, 'a forced or carelesse mirth;' Cot. — L. *Sardonicus*, usually *Sardonius*. — Gk. σαρδόνιος, also σαρδόνιος, said to be derived from σαρδόνιον, a plant of Sardinia (Σάρδω), said to screw up the face of the eater; see Vergil, Ecl. vii. 41.

Sardonyx, a gem. (L. — Gk.) L. *sardonyx*. — Gk. σαρδόνυξ, i.e. Sardian onyx. — Gk. σαρδ-, for Σάρδεις, Sardis, in Lydia; ὄνυξ, onyx. See **Onyx**.

Sarsaparilla. (Span.) Span. *zarzaparilla*, a plant. (Span.) *Zarza* means 'bramble,' perhaps from Basque *sartzia*, a bramble; *parilla* is generally referred to *Parillo*, the name of a physician who prescribed the use of sarsaparilla.

Sarsnet; see **Sarcenet**.

Sash (1), a case or frame for panes of glass. (F. — L.) Adapted from F. *châssis*, 'a frame of wood for a window,' Cot.; or from O.F. *chasse* (F. *châsse*), a case, shrine. — L. *capsa*, a case. See **Chase** (3) and **Case** (2).

Sash (2), a scarf, girdle. (Arab.) Formerly *shash*. — Arab. *shāsh*, muslin; hence, a muslin turban (Dozy). Cf. Arab. *shāshiya(t)*, a little turban (Richardson).

Sassafras, a kind of laurel. (F. — Span. — L.) F. *sassafras*. — Span. *sasafras*, from O. Span. *sassafragia*, the herb saxifrage; sassafras was so named from being supposed to possess the like virtue. — L. *saxifraga*; see **Saxifrage**.

Satan. (Heb.) Heb. *sātān*, an enemy. — Heb. root *sātan*, to persecute.

Satchel, a small bag. (F. – L., &c.) O. F. *sachel*, a little bag. – L. *saccellum*, acc. of *saccellus*, dimin. of *saccus*, a sack; see Sack.

Sate, Satiate. (L.) *Sate* is from *sated*, used as a short form of *satiate* in sense of 'satisfied.' (Suggested by L. *sat* for *satis*; *satur*, full.) – L. *satiātus*, pp. of *satiāre*, to sate, fill full. – L. *sat*, *satis*, sufficient; *satur*, full. Allied to Sad. Brugm. i. § 196. Der. *satiety*, M. F. *satieté*, from L. acc. *satietātem*, fullness.

Satellite. (F. – L.) F. *satellite*, 'a sergeant, catchpole;' Cot. – L. *satellitem*, acc. of *satelles*, an attendant.

Satin. (F. – L.) F. *satin*. (Ital. *setino*, Port. *setim*.) – Late L. *sātīnus*, *sētīnus*, satin. – Late L. *sēta*, silk; L. *sēta*, *saeta*, a bristle, a hair. Brugm. i. § 209.

Satire. (F. – L.) F. *satire*. – L. *satira*, *satura*, a species of poetry; orig. 'a medley.' Derived from *satura lanx*, a full dish, dish full of mixed ingredients; where *satura* is fem. of *satur*, full. Cf. Sate.

satisfy. (F. – L.) O. F. *satisfier* (later *satisfaire*). Formed as if from Late L. *satisficāre*, substituted for L. *satisfacere*, lit. 'to make enough.' – L. *satis*, enough; *facere*, to make. Der. *satisfaction*, from pp. *satisfactus*.

Satrap, a Persian viceroy. (F. – L. – Gk. – Pers.) F. *satrape*. – L. *satrapam*, acc. of *satrapēs*. – Gk. σατράπης. – O. Pers. *khsatra-pāvā*, guardian of a province; from *khsatra*, province, and *pā*, to protect (Spiegel). Cf. Zend *shōithra-pān*, protector of a region (Fick, i. 305), from Zend *shōithra*, a region, *pān*, protector; Skt. *kshetra-*, a field, region, from *kshi*, to dwell, and *pā*, to protect.

Saturate. (L.) From pp. of L. *saturāre*, to fill full. – L. *satur*, full. Cf. Sate.

Saturnine. (F. – L.) O. F. *saturnin* (usually *Saturnien*), under the influence of the malign planet Saturn; hence, melancholy. – L. *Sāturnus*, Saturn; said to mean 'the sower'; as if from *satum*, supine of *serere*, to sow (Festus); which is improbable.

saturday. (L. *and* E.) A. S. *Sæterdæg*, also *Sætern-dæg*, *Sæternes dæg*, i. e. Saturn's day; a translation of L. *Sāturnī diēs*; cf. Du. *Zaterdag*. – L. *Sāturnus*, Saturn; A. S. *dæg*, a day.

Satyr. (F. – L. – Gk.) F. *satyre*. – L.

satyrus. – Gk. σάτυρος, a satyr, a sylvan god.

Sauce. (F. – L.) F. *sauce*. – L. *salsa*, a thing salted; fem. of *salsus*, salted. See Salt. Der. *sauc-er*, orig. a vessel for sauce; *sauc-y*, full of sauce, pungent.

Saunders, a corrupt form of Sandalwood.

Saunter. (F. – L.) From A. F. *sauntrer*, to adventure oneself. I find mention of a man 'qe *sauntre* en ewe,' who ventures on the water, who goes to sea; Year-book of 11 Edw. III. p. 619. – A. F. *s-*, for *es-*, out (L. *ex*); and *auntrer*, for *aventurer*, to adventure or venture, from *aventure*, an adventure. See Adventure. [A mere guess.]

Saurian, one of the lizard tribe. (Gk.) From Gk. σαύρα, σαυρος, a lizard.

Sausage. (F. – L.) Formerly *sausige* (for **sausice*); cf. Guernsey *sauciche*. F. *saucisse*. – Late L. *salsicia*, fem. of *salsicius*, adj. (Georges), made of salted or seasoned meat. – L. *salsus*, salted. – L. *sāl*, salt. See Salt.

Sauterne, a wine. (F.) From *Sauterne* in France, department of Gironde.

Savage. (F. – L.) M. E. *sauage*. – A. F. *savage*; O. F. *savaige*, *salvage* (F. *sauvage*). – L. *siluāticus*, belonging to a wood, wild. – L. *silua*, a wood. See Silvan.

Savanna, a meadow-plain. (Span. – Carib.) Spelt *zauana*; R. Eden, ed. Arber, p. 148. Span. *sabana*; said to be of Caribbean origin (Oviedo). ¶ This *sabána* is different from *sábana*, a sheet for a bed; from L. *sabana*, pl. of *sabanum*, a linen cloth; used as a fem. sing. – Gk. σάβανον, a linen cloth, towel.

Save. (F. – L.) M. E. *sauuen* (= *sauven*). – A. F. *saver*, *sauver*; F. *sauver*. – L. *saluāre*, to save. – L. *saluus*, safe. See Salvation.

Saveloy, Cervelas, a kind of sausage. (F. – Ital. – L.) Formerly *cervelas* (Phillips). – F. *cervelas*, M.F. *cervelat*. – Ital. *cervellato* (Torriano), a saveloy; from its containing brains. – Ital. *cervello*, brain. – L. *cerebellum*, dimin. of *cerebrum*, brain. See Cerebral.

Savin, Savine, Sabine, a shrub. (L.) A.S. *safine*. – L. *sabīna*; orig. *Sabīna herba*, a Sabine herb. The *Sabines* were a people of central Italy.

Savory, a plant. (F. – L.) M. F. *savorée*, a popular perversion of O. F.

sarrie (whence F. *sarriette*). — L. *saturēia*, savory.

Savour. (F. — L.) O. F. *savour*, later *saveur*. — L. *sapōrem*, acc. of *sapor*, taste. — L. *sapere*, to taste. See **Sapid**.

Savoy, a kind of cabbage. (F.) Brought from *Savoy*.

Saw (1), a cutting instrument. (E.) M. E. *sawe*. A. S. *sagu*, lit. a cutter; from 2nd grade of Teut. root SEG < √SEK, to cut.+Du. *zaag*, Icel. *sög*, Dan. *sav*, Swed. *såg*, G. *säge*. See **Secant**. Der. *see-saw*, a reduplicated form; cf. *scythe*, *sedge*.

Saw (2), a saying. (E.) M. E. *sawe*. A. S. *sagu*, a saying; cf. A. S. *secgan*, to say. Allied to Lith. *pa-saka*, a saying. Doublet, *saga*. See **Say**.

Saxhorn, a kind of horn. Named after the inventor, Adolphe *Sax*, a Frenchman; ab. 1840.

Saxifrage, a plant. (F. — L.) F. *saxifrage*. — L. *saxifraga*, spleen-wort; so named because it was supposed to break stones in the bladder. — L. *saxi-*, for *saxum*, a stone; *frag-*, base of *frangere*, to break. Cf. **Sassafras**.

Saxon, a Teut. race. (L. — Teut.) Late L. *Saxonēs*, pl., Saxons. — A. S. *Seaxan*, Saxons; because armed with a short sword. — A. S. *seax*, a knife, lit. ' cutter;' Ο Frics. *sax*; cf. L. *saxum*, a stone implement. Brugm. i. § 549 c.

Say (1), to speak. (E.) M. E. *seggen*, pr. s. *sey-eth*, *sei-th*. A. S. *secgan*, North. pr. s. *seg-es*, pt. t. *sægde*, pp. *gesægd*.+Du. *zeggen*, Icel. *segja*, Dan. *sige*, Swed. *säga*, G. *sagen*, O. H. G. *sagēn*. Cf. Lithuan. *sakýti*, to say; Gk. ἔννεπε (for *ἔν-σεπ-ε), O. L. *in-sec-e*, imp. s., tell, say. See Sweet, N. E. Gr. § 1293.

Say (2), a kind of serge. (F. — L. — Gk.) O. F. *saie*, say. (Cf. Span. *saya*, *sayo*, a tunic; *sayete*, a thin stuff.) So called because used for making a kind of coat called in Latin *saga*, *sagum*, or *sagus*; Late L. *sagum*, (1) a mantle, (2) a kind of cloth. — Gk. σάγος, a soldier's mantle; allied to σαγή, harness, σάγμα, a pack-saddle; see **Sumpter**.

Say (3), to essay; short for *assay* or *essay*; see **Essay**.

Scab. (Scand.) Dan. Swed. *skab*.+ G. *schabe*; A. S. *sceab*, *scæb*, scab, itch. Lit. ' something that is scratched;' cf. L. *scabere*, to scratch, *scabiēs*, itch. See **Shave** and **Shabby**.

Scabbard. (F. — Teut.) M. E. *scaubert*,

scauberk, *scaberk*, a scabbard; answering to O. F. *escauberc*, only found in the pl. *escaubers* (Godefroy). The F. word is made up of O. F. *escale*, a scale, husk, case; and *-berc*, a protection (as in O. F. *hauberc*, *hal-berc*, a hauberk). — O. H. G. *scala*, a scale, husk, case; *bergan*, to hide, protect. Thus *scabbard* = *scauberk* = *scale-berk*, with the reduplicated sense of ' cover-cover,' or protecting case. See **Scale** (1) and **Hauberk**.

Scabious. (F. — L.) M. F. *scabieuse*, f. — L. *scabiōsa* (*herba*), a plant supposed to be good for skin-eruptions. — L. *scabiēs*, an itch. See **Scab**.

Scaffold. (F. — L. and Gk.?) M. E. *scafold*. — O. F. **escafalt*, only found as *escafaut*, *eschafaut* (also *chafaut*), mod. F. *échafaud*, a scaffold. Short for *escadafald* (Burguy), where *es-* represents L. *ex*, prep.; cf. Span. and Ital. *catafalco*, a funeral canopy, also a stage, scaffold (whence F. and E. *catafalque*). β. The former part of *catafalco* may be allied to Span. *catar*, in the sense ' to view.' The latter part is perhaps due to L. *fala*, a kind of scaffold. (Doubtful.)

Scald (1), to burn. (F. — L.) M. E. *scalden*. — O. F. **escalder*, later *eschauder*, to scald (F. *échauder*). — L. *excaldāre*, to wash in hot water. — L. *ex*, out, very; and *caldus = calidus*, hot. See **Caldron**.

Scald (2), scabby. (Scand.) For *scalled*, i. e. afflicted with the *scall*; see **Scall**.

Scald (3), a poet. (Scand.) Icel. *skald*, a poet, older form *skáld* (Noreen).

Scale (1), a shell, a flake. (F. — O. H. G.) M. E. *scale*. — O. F. *escale* (F. *écale*). — O. H. G. *scala* (G. *schale*). + A. S. *scealu*, *scalu*, a shell, husk, scale; Dan. and Swed. *skal*, a shell, pod. From Teut. base **skal*, 2nd grade of str. vb. **skel-an-*, to cleave, divide; cf. Lith. *skel-ti*, to cleave; Gk. σκάλλειν, to stir up, to hoe. (√SQEL.) See **Shale**, **Shell**, and **Skill**.

scale (2), a bowl or dish of a balance. (F. — Teut.) [Formerly also *scole*; cf. Icel. *skál*, a scale of a balance.] M. E. *scale*. — O. F. *escale*, a cup (Godefroy). — Icel. *skál*, Dan. *skaal*, Swed. *skål*, bowl; Du. *schaal*, scale, bowl. Allied to **Scale** (1); being from Teut. base *skæl-*, 3rd grade of **skelan-*.

Scale (3), a ladder, gradation. (L.) L. *scāla*, a ladder. L. *scā-la < *scan(t)-slā*, i. e. **scan(d)-slā*; from *scandere*, to climb. See **Scan**. Brugm. i. § 414.

Scalene. (L.–Gk.) L. *scalēnus*, adj. – Gk. σκαληνός, scalene, uneven.

Scall, scab on the skin. (Scand.) From Icel. *skalli*, a bald head; orig. a peeled head. Cf. Swed. *skallig*, bald, from *skala*, to peel. Allied to Swed. *skal*, a husk; see **Scale** (1). **Der.** *scald* (2)=*scalled*, afflicted with scall.

Scallion, a plant allied to garlic. (F. –L.–Gk.–Phoenician.) O. F. *escalogne*, a scallion; see further under **Shallot.**

Scallop, Scollop, a kind of shell-fish. (F.–Teut.) M. E. *skalop.*–O. F. *escalope*, a shell.– M. Du. *schelpe* (Du. *schelp*), a shell, especially a scallop-shell. Allied to **Scale** (1) and **Shell. Der.** *scallop*, vb., to cut an edge into scallop-like curves.

scalp. (Scand.) M.E. *scalp* (Northern). – Icel. *skálpr*, M. Swed. *skalp*, a sheath ; Dan. dial. *skalp*, husk, shell of a pea; also M. Ital. *scalpo*, the scalp, a word borrowed from Teutonic. Cf. M. Du. *schelpe*, a shell (hence, skull). See **Scollop.**

Scalpel, a small sharp knife. (L.) L. *scalpellum*, dimin. of *scalprum*, a knife. – L. *scalpere*, to cut.

Scammony, a cathartic gum-resin. (F. – L. – Gk.) M. F. *scammonie.* – L. *scammōnia.* – G. σκαμμωνία, σκαμωνία, scammony, a kind of bind-weed.

Scamp. (F.–L.) Formerly a vagabond, or fugitive. – O. North F. *escamper, s'escamper*, to flee ; O. F. *eschamper*, to decamp. – L. *ex*, out; and *campus*, battle-field. **Der.** *scamp-er*, to run or flee away.

Scan. (L.) Short for *scand* ; the *d* was prob. mistaken for the pp. suffix *-ed.* – L. *scandere*, to climb ; also, to scan a verse. +Skt. *skand*, to spring up. Brugm. i. § 635.

Scandal. (F.–L.–Gk.) F. *scandale.* – L. *scandalum.* – Gk. σκάνδαλον, a snare; also a scandal, offence, stumbling-block. Orig. the spring of a trap, the stick which sprang up when the trap was shut, and on which the bait was placed ; usually called σκανδάληθρον. – √SKAND, to spring up. See **Scan. Doublet,** *slander.*

Scansion. (L.) From L. *scansio*, a scanning. – L. *scansus*, pp. of *scandere*, to scan ; see **Scan.**

Scant, adj. (Scand.) M. E. *skant*, insufficient. – Icel. *skamt*, neut. of *skammr*, short, brief; whence *skamta*, to dole out (hence to scant or stint); Icel. *skamtr*, a dole. In Norwegian, *nt* appears for *mt*,

as in *skant*, a dole, *skanta*, to measure closely. Cf. O. H. G. *skam*, short. **Der.** *scant-y.*

Scantling, a cut piece of timber, a pattern. (F. – Teut. ; *with* L. *prefix*.) From O. North F. *escantillon*, for O. F. *eschantillon*, 'a small cantle, scantling, sample ;' Cot. – O. F. *es-*, prefix, from L. *ex* ; *cantel*, a cantle ; see **Cantle.**

Scapegoat. Here *scape* is short for *escape* ; see **Escape.**

Scapular, belonging to the shoulder-blades. (L.) Late L. *scapulāris*, adj., from *scapula*, pl. shoulder-blades. **Der.** *scapular-y*, a kind of scarf (worn over the shoulders), F.*scapulaire*, Late L.*scapulāre.*

Scar (1), mark of a wound. (F.–L.–Gk.) M. F. *escare.* – L. *eschara*, a scar, esp. of a burn. – Gk. ἐσχάρα, a hearth, fireplace, scar of a burn.

Scar (2), **Scaur,** a rock. (Scand.) M.E. *scarre.* – Icel. *sker*, a skerry, isolated rock; Dan. *skiær*, Swed. *skär.* So called because cut off from the main land ; see **Shear.**

Scaramouch, a buffoon. (F. – Ital.– O. H. G.) From *Scaramoche*, a famous Italian zany who acted in England in 1673 (Blount). Also called *Scaramouche*, which was the F. spelling ; but his real name was *Scaramuccia*, of which the lit. sense is ' a skirmish,' being the same word as the O. F. *escarmouche*, a skirmish. See **Skirmish.**

Scarce. (F.–L.) M. E. *scars.* – O. F. *escars, eschars*, scarce, scanty, niggard (F. *échars*). – Late L. *scarpsus*, short form of *excarpsus*, used as a substitute for L. *excerptus*, pp. of *excerpere*, to select ; see **Excerpt.** Thus the sense was ' picked out,' select, scarce.

Scare. (Scand.) M.E. *skerren*, to scare; from *skerre*, adj., timid, shy. – Icel. *skjarr*, timid, shy ; allied to *skirrask*, to shun, lit. to sheer off ; see **Sheer** (2).

Scarf (1), a light sash or band. (F.– O. Low G.) Confused, as to sound, with **Scarf** (2). The particular sense is due to O. North F. *escarpe*, O. F. and M. F. *escharpe*, a scarf; Cot. – M. Du. *scharpe*, a scrip (Oudemans) ; Low G. *schrap.* Cf. E. Fries. *scherpe*, a scarf, which, like G. *schärpe*, is prob. from F. See below.

Scarf (2), to join timber together. (Scand.) From Swed. *skarf*, a scarf, seam, joint.+Bavarian *scharben*, to cut a notch in timber, G. *scharben*, O. H. G. *scarbōn*, to cut small. From Teut. **skarb*, 2nd grade of *skerb-an-, to cut, as in A. S. sceorfan, pt. t. scearf, to scrape.

Scarify. (F. – L. – Gk.) F. scarifier. – L. scarificāre, to scarify, scratch open; from scarifāre, to scarify. – Gk. σκαριφάομαι, I scratch. – Gk. σκάριφος, a sharp pointed instrument. Allied to L. scrībere, to write, and to E. Scribe.

Scarlet. (F. – Pers.) O. F. escarlate, scarlet. (Span. escarlata, Ital. scarlatto.) – Pers. saqalāt, siqalāt, suqlāt, scarlet cloth. Orig. the name of a stuff, which was often of a scarlet colour; cf. 'scarlet reed,' Ch. Prol. 456. ¶ Hence Pers. saqlatūn, scarlet cloth, whence M. E. ciclatoun (Chaucer). The Turkish iskerlat, scarlet, is merely borrowed from Ital. scarlatto (Zenker). See Suclāt in Yule.

scarlatina, scarlet fever. (Ital. – Pers.) Ital. scarlattina. – Ital. scarlatto, scarlet cloth (above).

Scarp. (F. Ital. – Teut.) F. escarpe. – Ital. scarpa, 'a curtein of a wall;' so called because cut sharp, i. e. steep. – Du. scherp; M. H. G. scharf, scharpf, sharp; see Sharp.

Scathe, to harm. (Scand.) From Icel. skaða, Swed. skada, Dan. skade. + A. S. sceaðan (pt. t. scōd); G. Du. schaden; Goth. ga-skathjan (pt. t. ga skōth). Cf. Gk. ά-σκηθής, unharmed. **Der.** scathe, sb., Icel. skaði.

Scatter. (E.) M. E. scateren. Northern form of Shatter, q. v. + Gk. σκεδάννυμι, I sprinkle, σκέδ-ασις, a scattering; Skt. skhad, to cut. Cf. Squander.

Scavenger. (F. – Teut.) Formerly scavager; the n is intrusive. The sense has much changed; a scavager was an officer who acted as inspector of goods for sale, and subsequently had to attend to cleansing of streets. Scavage, i. e. inspection, is an A. F. word, with F. suffix -age (< L. -āticum); from O. F. escauw-er, to examine, inspect. – O. Sax. skawōn, to behold; cognate with A. S. sceáwian, to look at. See Show.

Scene. (L. – Gk.) L. scēna, scæna (whence also F. scène). – Gk. σκηνή, a sheltered place, tent, stage, scene. **Der.** pro-scenium.

Scent, vb. (F. – L.) A false spelling for sent, as in Hamlet, i. 5. 58 (ed. 1623). – F. sentir, 'to feel, sent;' Cot. – L. sentire, to feel, perceive. See Sense.

Sceptic. (F. – L. – Gk.) F. sceptique. – L. scepticus. – Gk. σκεπτικός, thoughtful,

inquiring; pl. σκεπτικοί, the Sceptics, followers of Pyrrho (3rd century, B. C.). – Gk. σκέπτομαι, I consider; see Species.

Sceptre. (F. – L. – Gk.) F. sceptre. – L. scēptrum. – Gk. σκῆπτρον, a staff to lean on, a sceptre. – Gk. σκήπτειν, to prop; also to hurl. Cf. L. scāpus, a shaft, stem.

Schedule. (F. – L. – Gk.) Formerly cedule. – M. F. schedule, cedule, 'a schedule, scrowle,' Cot.; F. cédule. – L. schedula, a small leaf of paper; dimin. of scheda (or scida), a strip of papyrus-bark. Late Gk. σχέδη, a tablet, is borrowed from L.; hence the L. word must be from the kindred Gk. σχίδη, a cleft piece of wood, from σχίζειν, to cleave. See Schism.

Scheme. (L. – Gk.) Formerly schema. – L. schēma. – Gk. σχῆμα, form, appearance, also used as a term in rhetoric. – Gk. σχη-, as in σχή-σω, fut. of ἔχ-ειν, to hold, have (base σεχ-). Cf Skt. sah, to bear. (√SEGH.)

Schism. (F. – L. – Gk.) F. schisme. – L. schisma. – Gk. σχίσμα, a rent, split, schism. – Gk. σχίζειν (base σχιδ-), to cleave. + L. scindere, Skt. chhid, to cut. Brugm. i. §§ 586, 599.

schist, slate-rock. (Gk.) Gk. σχιστος, easily cleft. – Gk, σχίζειν (above).

School (1). (F. – L. – Gk.) M. E. scole. A. F. and O. F. escole, school. – L. schola. – Gk. σχολή, rest, leisure, employment of leisure time, also a school. Orig. 'a pause;' from σχη-, a grade of the base of ἔχειν, to hold; see Scheme. (√SEGH.) **Der.** schol-ar, A. F. escoler; scholi-ast, from Gk. σχολιαστής, a commentator.

School (2), a shoal of fish. (Du.) Du. school visschen, 'a shole of fishes,' Sewel. Doublet of shoal. See Shoal (1).

Schooner. (Scand.) Properly scooner, but spelt as if derived from Dutch, which is not the case, the Du. schooner being of E. origin. First called a scooner in 1713, when the first schooner was so named in Gloucester, Massachusetts, from the remark that 'she scoons,' i. e. glides swiftly. This verb is the Clydesdale scon or scoon, to glide swiftly, applied to stones with which one makes 'ducks and drakes' in the water. – Icel. skunda, to speed. See Shun.

Schorl, black tourmaline. (Swed.) Swed. skörl (with sk as E. sh). Perhaps suggested by Swed. skör, brittle.

Sciatic, pertaining to the hip-joint. (F. – L. – Gk.) F. sciatique, adj. – L. sciaticus, corruption of L. ischiadicus, subject to gout in the hips. — Gk. ἰσχιαδικός, subject to pains in the loins. — Gk. ἰσχιαδ-, stem of ἰσχιάς, pain in the loins. — Gk. ἰσχίον, the socket in which the thigh-bone turns. **Der.** *sciatic-a*, fem. of L. adj. *sciaticus*.

Science. (F. — L.) F. *science*. — L. *scientia*, knowledge. — L. *scient-*, stem of pres. pt. of *scīre*, to know, orig. to discern. Allied to **Skill**. **Der.** *con-*, *pre-science*.

Scimetar, Cimetar. (F. *or* Ital. — Pers.?) F. *cimeterre*, 'a scymitar;' Cot. Cf. Ital. *scimitarra*, 'a simitar,' Florio. Prob. from Pers. *shimshīr*, *shamshīr*, 'a cimeter,' Rich. Dict., p. 909. Lit. lion's claw. — Pers. *sham*, nail, claw; *shēr*, lion.

Scintillation. (F. — L.) F. *scintillation*. — L. acc. *scintillātiōnem*, a sparkling. — L. *scintillāre*, to sparkle. — L. *scintilla*, a spark.

Sciolist. (L.) Formed, with suffix *-ist*, from L. *sciol-us*, a smatterer. — L. *scius*, knowing. — L. *scī-re*, to know. See **Science**.

Scion. (F. — L.) M. E. *sioun*. — O. F. *cion*, M. F. *sion*. F. *scion*, 'a scion, shoot;' Cot. Orig. 'a cutting.' — O. F. *sier*, F. *scier*, to cut. — L. *secāre*, to cut. (But the Picard form is *chion*.)

Scirrhous, pertaining to a hard swelling. (L. — Gk.) From Late L. *scirrhus*, sb., a form used for L. *scirros*, a hard swelling. — Gk. σκίρρος, σκῖρος, σκίρρωμα, a hard swelling. — Gk. σκιρός, hard.

Scissors. (F. — L.) [Ill spelt, and not from *scindere*, to cut.] M. E. *sisoures*, *cisoures*. — O. F. *cisoires*, shears; used instead of *ciseaux*, 'sizars,' Cot. The latter is the pl. of O. F. *cisel*, chisel; see **Chisel**. Both words are due to L. *cædere*, to cut; see **Cæsura**. ¶ No doubt the word was confused with L. *scissor*, which properly means 'a cutter,' hence, a tailor; from L. *scindere*, to cut.

Scoff. (Scand.) M. E. *skof*. Swed. dial. *skoff-*, as in *skoffs-ord*, n. pl., words of abuse, *skoff-sera*, to abuse; O. Fries. *schof*, a scoff; Icel. *skaup*, *skop*, mockery. Cf. M. Du. *schoppen*, *schobben*, to scoff; Icel. *skopa*, to scoff; also Dan. *skuffe*, to deceive; see **Scuffle**. The orig. sense was prob. 'a rub' or 'a shove'; cf. Swed. *skuff*, a push, G. *schupfen*, to push; see **Shove**.

Scold. (Perhaps Frisian.) M. E. *scolden*; also *skalde*, *scolde*, sb., a scold. The sb. is formed from *skald*, 2nd grade

of Teut. *skeldan-*, to scold, blame, as seen in O. Fries. *skelda*, Du. *schelden* (pt. t. *schold*), G. *schelten* (pt. t. *schalt*), to scold; cf. Dan. *skielde*, wk. vb., to scold. If the orig. sense was 'to push,' it is allied to O. Sax. *skaldan*, to push off (a boat).

Scollop; see **Scallop**.

Sconce (1), a small fort, bulwark. (F. — L.) Also applied to a helmet, and even to the head. — O. F. *esconse*, a hiding-place, sconce; orig. fem. of pp. *escons*. — L. *absconsa*, fem. of *absconsus*, used (as well as *absconditus*) as pp. of *abscondere*, to hide; see **Abscond**.

sconce (2), a candle-stick. (F. — L.) M. E. *sconce*, *scons*, a covered light, lantern. — O. F. *esconse*, a dark lantern (Roquefort). — Late L. *absconsa*, a dark lantern; from L. *absconsus*, hidden.

Scoop. (F. — Scand.) M. E. *scope*, sb. — O. F. *escope* (F. *écope*), a scoop (Hatzfeld). — Swed. *skopa*, a scoop. ✚ M. Du. *schoepe*, M. H. G. *schuofe*, a scoop; cf. G. *schöpfen*, to draw water, to scoop. From Teut. *skōp*, 2nd grade of Teut. *skap-*, as in O. Sax. *skeppian* (for *skapjan*), Du. *scheppen*, O. H. G. *schepfan* (pt. t. *scuof*), to draw up water.

Scope. (Ital. — Gk.) Ital. *scopo*, a mark to shoot at, scope; Florio. — Gk. σκοπός, a mark, a watcher; allied to Gk. σκέπτομαι, I see, spy, which is cognate with L. *specere*; see **Species**.

Scorbutic, afflicted with scurvy. (Low L.) From Low L. *scorbūtus*, scurvy; said to be Latinised from M. Du. *scheur-en*, to break, tear, and *bot*, a bone (Weigand); which is doubtful. From L. *scorbūtus* were formed Low G. *scharbock*, *schärbuuk*, scurvy; M. Du. *scheurbuyck* (Du. *scheurbuik*), scurvy. These forms are due to popular etymology, as the lit. sense of M. Du. *scheurbuyck* is 'rupture of the belly,' from *scheuren*, to tear, and *buyck* (mod. Du. *buik*), the belly. See **Scurvy**.

Scorch. (F. — L.) Orig. to flay; Knt. de la Tour, p. 6. — O. F. *escorcher*, lit. to flay (Ital. *scorticare*). — L. *ex*, off; *cortic-*, stem of *cortex*, bark, rind, husk. Confused with M. E. *scorklen*, to burn, *scorknen*, to parch; cf. Norw. *skrokkna*, to shrivel, *skrokken*, shrunken; allied to **Shrink**.

Score. (Scand.) M. E. *score*, properly a cut; hence twenty, denoted by a long cut on a cut stick. — Icel. *skor*, a score, cut; also twenty; cf. Swed. *skåra*, Dan. *skaar*, score, cut. From Teut. *skor-*, Icel. *skor-*,

weak grade of *sker-a*, to cut, shear; see
Shear.

Scoria, slag. (L.—Gk.) L. *scōria*.—
Gk. σκωρία, dross, scum.—Gk. σκῶρ, dung,
ordure.＋A. S. *scearn*, dung.

Scorn. (F.—L.) M. E. *scorn*.—O. F.
escorne, scorn; Cot.—O. F. *escorner*, to
humiliate, mock at; orig. 'to deprive of
horns;' from L. *ex*, out, *cornu*, a horn.
¶ But much influenced by M. E. *scarnen*,
to scorn, from O. F. *escarnir*, *escharnir*,
to deride; from O. H. G. *scernōn*, to
deride, a vb. due to the sb. *scern*, derision.

Scorpion. (F.—L.—Gk.) F. *scorpion*.
—L. *scorpiōnem*, acc. of *scorpio*, the same
as *scorpius*.—Gk. σκορπίος, a scorpion, also
a prickly sea-fish. (√SKERP.)

Scotch, to cut with narrow incisions.
(Scand.) To *scotch* is to cut slightly; short
for *scor-ch*, an extension of score; see **Score**.
'With knyfe *scortche* not the Boorde;'
Babees Book, p. 80. Confused with
M. E. *scorchen*, to flay, which suggested
its form.

Scot-free, free from payment. (F.—
Teut.) A. F. and O. F. *escot* (F. *écot*),
payment, esp. a contribution to a common
fund, into which it is *shot*.—Icel. *skot*, a
shot, a contribution.＋Du. *schot*, G. *schoss*,
a shot, a scot. From **skut-*, weak grade
of Teut. **skeut-an-*, to shoot. See **Shoot**.

Scoundrel. (Scand.) Lit. 'a loathsome
fellow.' Aberdeensh. *scoonrel*; for **scun-
ner-el*, where *-el* is an agential suffix.
From Lowl. Scotch *scunner*, *scooner*, to
loathe, also (formerly) to shrink through
fear, act as a coward; so that a *scoonrel*
is one who shrinks, a coward. See
Barbour, Bruce, xvii. 651. The verb *scunner* is the frequentative of the North. form
of A. S. *scun-ian*, to shun; see **Shun**.
Cf. Swed. dial. *skunna sig*, Icel. *skunda*,
to hasten.

Scour (1), to cleanse. (F.—L.) O. F.
escurer, to scour. Cf. Span. *escurar*,
M. Ital. *scurare*, to scour, rub up.—L.
excūrāre, to take great care of.—L. *ex*,
very; *cūrāre*, to take care, from *cūra*, care.
(Körting.) Or from M. Du. *schueren*.

Scour (2), to run along. (F.—L.) 'Ca-
milla *scours* the plain;' Pope.—O. F.
escorre, *escourre*, to run out (as a spy).—
L. *excurrere*.—L. *ex*, out; *currere*, to run.

Scourge. (F.—L.) A. F. *escorge*; cf.
O. F. *escorgiee* (F. *écourgée*), a scourge.
Cf. Ital. *scuriada*, M. Ital. *scoriata*, a
scourge, *scoriare*, to whip. The M. Ital.

scoriata answers to L. *excoriata*, lit. flayed
off, hence a strip of leather for a whip, a
thong; pp. of *excoriāre*, to flay off, in
Late L., to whip; see **Excoriate**.

Scout (1), a spy. (F.—L.) M. E.
scoute.—O. F. *escoute*, a spy.—O. F.
escouter, to listen.—Folk-L. **ascoltāre*,
for L. *auscultāre*, to listen; see **Auscultation**.

Scout (2), to ridicule an idea. (Scand.)
Allied to Lowl. Scotch *scout*, to pour out
a liquid forcibly, to *shoot* it out.—Icel.
skūta, *skūti*, a taunt; cf. *skot-yrði*, scoffs.
—Icel. *skūt-*, a weak grade of the base of
skjōta, to shoot. Cf. Swed. *skjuta*, (1) to
shoot, (2) to shove; *skjuta skulden på*, to
cast the blame on; Dan. *skyde*, to shoot,
cast (blame on), repel. See **Shoot**.

Scowl. (Scand.) M. E. *scoulen*. Not
in A. S.—Dan. *skule*, to scowl, cast down
the eyes; allied to E. Fries. and Low G.
schulen, Du. *schuilen*, to hide oneself, prov.
G. *schulen*, to hide the eyes, look slily,
peep. From the sb. seen in E. Fries.
schūl, Du. *schuil*, Dan. *skiul*, shelter, Icel.
skjol, shelter, cover. See **Sheal**.

Scrabble, to scrawl. (Scand.) Lit. 'to
scratch or scrape;' for prov. E. *scrapple*,
frequent. of *scrape*. Cf. Du. *schrabben*, to
scratch; F. Fries. *schrabben*, *schrappen*,
schrapen, to scratch. See **Scrape**.

Scraggy, lean, rough. (Scand.) Allied
to M. E. *scroggy*, covered with thin strag-
gling bushes. From prov. E. *scrag*,
a forked branch, lean person; cf. *scrog*, a
stunted bush.—Swed. dial. *skragga*, a weak
old man; cf. Icel. *skröggsligr*, scraggy;
North Fries. *skrog*, a lean man; Dan. *skrog*,
a carcase. See **Shrug, Shrink**.

Scramble. (Scand.) Nasalised form of
prov. E. *scrabble*, to scramble, allied to
scraffle, to scramble, *scrapple*, to grub
about; frequentatives of *scrape*, prov. E.
scrap, to scrape.

Scrannel, thin, weakly, wretched.
(Scand.) In Milton, Lycidas, 124. Prov.
E. *scranny*, thin, lean; *scrannel*, a lean
person (Lincolnshire).—Swed. dial. *skran*,
weak; Norweg. *skran*, thin, lean, dry;
Dan. *skranten*, sickly, weakly. Cf. Swed.
dial. and Norw. *skrinn*, thin, lean, weak,
dry.

Scrap. (Scand.) Icel. *skrap*, scraps,
trifles, lit. 'scrapings.'—Icel. *skrapa*, to
scrape.

scrape. (Scand.) Orig. to scratch
with something *sharp*.—Icel. *skrapa*, Swed.

skrapa, Dan. *skrabe*, to scrape. **+** Du. *schrapen*. From Teut. **skrap-*, 2nd grade of Teut. **skrepan-*, to scrape; as in A.S. *screp-an*, pt. t. *scræp*. Cf. Russ. *skrebok'*, a scraper.

Scratch. (Scand.) Due to the confusion of M. E. *skratten*, to scratch, with M. E. *cracchen*, to scratch. β. M. E. *skratten* stands for *s-kratten*, where the *s-* (due to F. *es-*, L. *ex-*) is intensive, and *kratten* is from Swed. *kratta* (below). γ. M. E. *cracchen* stands for **kratsen*. — Swed. *kratsa*, to scrape, *krats*, a scraper. — Swed. *kratta*, to rake, scrape; cf. Icel. *krota*, to engrave. From Teut. **kret-an-*, to cut (pt. t. **krat*, pp. **krot-anoz*). So also Du. *krassen* (for **kratsen*), G. *kratzen*, O.H.G. *chrazzōn*, to scratch. And see **Grate** (2).

Scrawl. (Scand.) A contraction of *scrabble*, to write carelessly. ¶ Confused with M.E. *scraulen*, to crawl, a form of *crawl* with prefix *s* (=O. F. *es-*< L. *ex*) used with an intensive force.

Scream. (Scand.) M. E. *scremen*. — Icel.*skræma*,Swed.*skräma*,Dan.*skræmme*, to scare; orig. to cry aloud. Cf. Swed. *skrän*, a scream; Dan. *skraale*, to roar.

Screech. (Scand.) Cf. M. E. *scrīken*; Lowl. Sc. *scraik*. — Icel. *skrækja*, to shriek; cf. Swed. *skrika*, to shriek, Dan. *skrige*.**+** Gael. *sgreuch*, to shriek. Cf. **Shriek.**

Screen. (F.—Teut.) M. E. *scren*. — O. F. *escren* (Littré); *escran*, 'a skreen,' Cot. (Mod. F. *écran*.) Also found as as O.F.*escranne*(Godefroy). — G.*schranne*, a railing, grate. β. In the sense of 'coarse sieve,' it is the same word; so called because it *screens* (or wards off) the coarser particles, and prevents them from coming through.

Screw (1). (F. — Teut.) Formerly *scrue*. — M. F. *escroue*, 'a scrue;' Cot.; O. F. *escroe* (Godefroy). F. *écrou*. Perhaps from Low G. *schruve*; cf. M. Du. *schroeve*, Du. *schroef*, G. *schraube*, a screw. ¶ The Icel. *skrūfa*, Swed. *skruf*, Dan. *skrue*, are from Low G. ; and it is doubtful whether the Du. and G. words are really Teutonic.

Screw (2), a vicious horse. (E.) The North E. form of *shrew*, q. v.

Scribble. (L.; *with* E. *suffix*.) Formed from *scribe* with frequent. suffix *-le*; the suffix giving it a verbal force.

scribe. (L.) L. *scrība*, a writer. — L. *scrībere*, to write, orig. to scratch or cut slightly.

Scrimmage; see **Skirmish.**

Scrip (1), a small bag. (Scand.) A. F. *escrepe*, a scarf. — Icel. *skreppa*, Swed. *skräppa*, a scrip. Orig. sense 'scrap,' because made of a scrap of stuff; cf. N. Fries. *skrap*, a scrip.

Scrip (2), a piece of writing; the same word as *script* (below).

script. (F.—L.) M. F. *escript*, 'a writing.' — L. *scriptum*, neut. of pp. of *scrībere*, to write.

scripture. (F.—L.) M. E. *scripture*, a writing. — M.F.*escripture*. — L.*scriptūra*, a writing. — L. *scriptus*, pp. of *scrībere*, to write.

scrivener. (F. — L.) Formerly a *scriven*; the suffix *-er*, of the agent, is an E. addition. M. E. *scriuein* (=*scrivein*). — O. F. *escrivain*. — Late L. *scrībānum*, acc. of *scrībānus*, a notary. — L. *scrībere*, to write.

Scrofula. (L.) L. *scrōfula*, a little pig; whence the pl. *scrōfulæ*, used in the sense of scrofulous swellings; perhaps from the swollen appearance of the glands. Dimin. of *scrōfa*, a breeding sow. So also Gk. χοιράδες, scrofulous glands; from χοῖρος, a pig.

Scroll, a roll of paper. (F. — Teut.) Dimin. (with suffix *-l*) of M. E. *scrowe*, a scroll. — M.F. *escroue*, ' a scrowle ;' Cot. — M. Du. *schroode*, a shred, strip, slip of paper; O. H. G. *scrōt* (the same). Allied to **Shred.**

Scroyles, rascals. (F.—L.) In K. John, ii. 1. 373.—O. F. *escroelles*, later *escrouelles*, lit. 'the king's evil,' i. e. scrofula; Cot. — Late L. **scrobellæ* (only found as *scroellæ*), scrofula, dimin. of **scrobula*, for *scrofula*; see **Scrofula.** Transferred, as a term of abuse, from the disease to the person said to be afflicted with it. (See Körting.)

Scrub (1), brush-wood. (Scand.) Dan. dial. *skrub*, brush-wood ; Norw. *skrubba*, the dwarf cornel-tree. See **Shrub. Der.** *scrubb-y*, mean, orig. shrubby, stunted.

Scrub (2), to rub hard. (Scand.) M. E. *scrobben*, to scrub. — Swed. *skrubba*, Dan. *skrubbe*, to scrub. **+** Low G. *schrubben*; N. Fries. *skrobbe*, E. Fries. *schrubben*. According to Franck, it is allied by gradation to Du. and E. Fries. *schrabben*, to scratch; see **Scrabble,** **Scrape.** β. It is also, perhaps, related to *shrub*. Cf. E. *broom*, from the shrub so called; Lowl. Scotch *scrubber*, ' a handful of heath tied tightly together for cleaning culinary utensils;' Jamieson.

Scruff; see Scuft.

Scruple. (F.—L.) F. *scrupule*, 'a little sharp stone .. in a mans shooe,' Cot.; hence a hindrance, perplexity, doubt, also a small weight.—L. *scrūpulum*, acc. of *scrūpulus*, a sharp stone, dimin. of *scrūpus* (the same).

Scrutiny. (L.) L. *scrūtinium*, a careful enquiry.—L. *scrūtāri*, to search into carefully, as if among broken pieces.—L. *scrūta*, s. pl., broken pieces.

Scud, to run quickly. (Scand.) Cf. Dan. *skyde*, to shoot; *skyde over stevn*, lit. 'to shoot over the stem,' to scud along; *skudsteen*, a stone quoit, called in Scotch a *scudding-stane*. Cf. Swed. dial. *skudda*, to shoot the bolt of a door. See Scuttle (3), Scout (2), and Shoot.

Scuffle. (Scand.) The frequentative of Swed. *skuffa*, to push, shove, jog. Cf. M. Du. *schuffelen*, to drive on, also to run or shuffle off, from Du. *schuiven*, to shove. See Shuffle, Shove.

Scuft, Scuff, Scruff, the nape of the neck. (Scand.) O. Icel. *skopt* (pron. *skoft*), hair of the head, mod. Icel. *skott*, a fox's tail; N. Fries. *skuft*, the nape of a horse's neck.+G. *schopf*, a tuft of hair; O. H. G. *scuft*, hair; Goth. *skuft*, hair of the head. Allied to Sheaf; cf. Icel. *skauf*, a fox's brush.

Sculk, Skulk. (Scand.) M. E. *skulken.*—Dan. *skulke*, to sculk, slink; Swed. *skolka*, to play the truant. A derivative of Dan. *skule*, to scowl; see Scowl. Allied to Icel. *skolla*, to sculk, keep aloof.

Scull (1), **Skull,** the cranium. (Scand.) M. E. *skulle, scolle*. Named from its shell-like shape.—Swed. dial. *skulle*, variant of *sköll*; Norw. *skolt*, scull. From Teut. **skol*, weak grade of **skelan-* (pt. t. **skal*), to cleave, divide. From the form **skal* we have Swed. *hufvud-skalle*, the scull (also *hufvud-skål*), and Dan. *hjerne-skal*, scull; see scale (2).

Scull (2), a small light oar. (Scand.?) Perhaps named from the slightly hollowed blades. See Scull (1). Cf. M. Swed. *skolla, skålla*, a thin plate; Swed. *hufvud-skål*, scull (of the head); *våg-skål*, scale (of a balance); *skalig*, concave. **Der.** *scull*, vb., to use sculls.

Scull (3), a shoal of fish; see School (2).

Scullery, a place for swilling dishes,

&c. (F.—L.) The suffix *-y* (= F. *-ie*) is the same as in *butter-y, pantr-y*. The orig. sense was that of 'keeping the dishes.'— O. F. *escuelerie, esculerie*, the office of keeping the dishes (Godefroy).—O. F. *escuelle* (F. *écuelle*), a dish.—L. *scutella*, a dish; dimin. of *scutra*, a flat tray.

Scullion, a kitchen menial. (F.—L.) Minsheu explains *scullion* as being named 'eo quod scutellas curat,' thus associating it with *scullery*. But there is no trace in O. F. of any such form. Palsgrave has: '*Scoulyon* of the kechyn, *souillon*;' and Cotgrave explains F. *souillon* by 'a scullion.' Perhaps this is the real source, the *c* being inserted by association with *scullery*.—F. *souiller*, to soil, to be dirty. See Soil (2) and Sully.

Sculpture. (F.—L.) F. *sculpture*.—L. *sculptūra*, sculpture, lit. a cutting.—L. *sculptus*, pp. of *sculpere*, to cut, carve; allied to *scalpere*, to cut.

Scum. (Scand.) Dan. *skum*, froth; Swed. *skum*, froth; E. Fries. *schūm*.+Du. *schuim*; G. *schaum* (as in *meer-schaum*). (√SKEU, to cover.) **Der.** *skim*.

Scupper. (F.) '*Scuppers*, the holes through which the water runs off the deck;' Coles (1684). Phillips has *scooer-holes*. For *scooer*, i. e. lader out of water; from *scoop*, vb., to lade out water. (The Du. name is *spiegat*, lit. 'spit-hole.') See Scoop.

Scurf. (Scand.) From Swed. *skorf*, Dan. *skurv*, scurf; Icel. *skurfur*, pl. + A. S. *scurf, scorf*; Du. *schurft*, G. *schorf*. From **skorf-*, weak grade of **skorfan-*, as in A. S. *sceorfan*, to scarify, gnaw. **Der.** *scurv-y*.

Scurrile, buffoon-like. (L.) L. *scurrilis*, adj., from *scurra*, a buffoon.

Scurvy, scabby, shabby. (Scand.) An adj. formed from *scurf* (above). Hence *scurvy disease*, the scurvy, much confused with F. *scorbut*, the scurvy (Littré).

Scutage, a tax on a knight's fee. (M. Lat.) From Med. L. *scūtāgium*.—L. *scūtum*, a knight's shield, orig. a shield. See Esquire.

Scutch, to beat flax. (F.—Scand.) From O. F. *escouche, escuche*, a scutch or swingle.—Norw. *skoka, skuku*, a scutch for beating flax.

Scutcheon; see Escutcheon.

Scutiform. (F.—L.) M.F. *scutiforme*, shaped like a shield.—L. *scūti-*, for *scūtum*, shield; *forma*, form.

Scuttle (1), a shallow basket or vessel. (L.) A Northern form. Icel. *skutill*; A. S. *scutel*, a vessel. — L. *scutella*, allied to *scutula*, a small tray; cf. *scutra*, a tray. See **Scullery**.

Scuttle (2), an opening in a hatchway of a ship. (F. — Span. — Teut.) O. F. *escoutille*, scuttle. — Span. *escotilla*, the hole in the hatch of a ship. — Span. *escotar*, to cut, hollow out, or slope out a garment to fit the neck or bosom. — Span. *escote*, the sloping of a jacket, &c. — Du. *schoot*, lap, bosom; Low G. *schoot*; Icel. *skaut*; see **Sheet**. ¶ So Diez; but Span. *escotilla* is rather a dimin. from Low G. *schott*, a trap-door. Cf. E. *shutter*. **Der.** *scuttle*, vb., to sink a ship by making holes in it.

Scuttle (3), to hurry along. (Scand.) Cf. Swed. dial. *skutta*, to take a long jump; also prov. E. *scuddle* (Bailey), frequent. of *scud*; see **Scud** and **Shoot**.

Scythe. (E.) M. E. *sithe*. A. S. *sīðe*, old form *sigðe*. Lit. 'cutter;' from √SEK. + Icel. *sigðr*, Low G. *seged*, *segd*; cf. O. H. G. *segansa*, G. *sense*. See **Secant**.

Se-, away, apart. (L.) L. *sē-*, prefix; full form *sed*, without.

Sea. (E.) M. E. *see*. A. S. *sǣ*, sea, lake. + Du. *zee*; Icel. *sær*; Dan. *sö*; Swed. *sjö*; G. *see*; Goth. *saiws*. Teut. type *saiwiz*.

Seal (1), a stamp. (F. — L.) M. E. *seel*. — O. F. *seel*, a signet (F. *sceau*). — L. *sigillum*, a seal, mark; dimin. form allied to *signum*, a mark. See **Sign**. **Der.** *seal*, vb.

Seal (2), a sea-calf. (E.) M. E. *sele*. A. S. *seolh*. + Icel. *selr*; Dan. *sæl*; Swed. *själ*; O. H. G. *selah*.

Seam (1). (E.) A. S. *sēam*. + Icel. *saumr*; G. *saum*; Du. *zoom*; Dan. Swed. *söm*. Teut. type *saumoz*, m. ; from root *seu-*, *siw*. (√SIW.) Cf. Skt. *sū-tra-*, a thread. See **Sew** (1).

Seam (2), a horse-load. (Late L. — Gk.) M. E. *seem*, A. S. *sēam*. Borrowed (like G. *saum*) from Late L. *sauma*, late form of *sagma*, a horse-load, pack. — Gk. σάγμα, a pack-saddle. See **Sumpter**.

Seamstress, Sempstress. (E. ; with F. *suffix*.) A. S. *sēamestre*, a seamstress; with suffix *-ess* (< F. *-esse* < Gk. *-ισσα*). — A. S. *sēam*, a seam (see **Seam**); with suffix *-estre* ; see **Spinster**.

Sear, Sere, withered. (E.) M. E. *sere*, A. S. *sēar*, dry; *sēarian*, to dry up. + M. Du. *sore*, Du. *zoor*, Low G. *soor*.

Allied to Russ. *suχoi*, dry; Lith. *sausas*, dry; Gk. αὖος (for *σαυσος*), dry; cf. Skt. *çush*, for *sush*, to dry up. Idg. type *sausos*. See **Austere**. Brugm. i. § 214.

Search, to explore. (F. — L.) M. E. *serchen, cerchen*. — O. F. *cercher* (F. *chercher*) ; prov. F. *sercher*, dial. of Verdun (Fertiault). — L. *circāre*, to go round ; hence, to explore. — L. *circus*, a ring ; see **Circus**. **Der.** *re-search*; cf. *shark*.

Season. (F. — L.) M. E. *seson*. — O. F. *seson, seison, saison*. [Cf. Span. *sazon*, O. Prov. *sadons, sasos*, Bartsch.] — Late L. *satiōnem*, acc. of *satio*, sowing-time, i. e. spring, regarded as the chief season for preparing crops. — L. *satus*, pp. of *serere*, to sow. ¶ The Span. word is *estacion*, Ital. *stagione* ; from acc. of L. *statio*, a station, hence a stage (period).

Seat, sb. (Scand.) Icel. *sæti*, a seat; Swed. *säte*; Dan. *sæde*. — Icel. *sāt-*, 3rd grade of *sitja*, to sit; see **Sit**. **Der.** *seat*, vb.

Secant, a line that cuts another, or that cuts a circle. (L.) From *secant-*, stem of pres. pt. of *secāre*, to cut. + Russ. *siech'*, to hew. Brugm. i. § 635. (√SEK.) See **Saw**, **Scythe**, **Sickle**.

Secede. (L.) L. *sēcēdere*, to go apart, withdraw. — L. *sē-*, *sed*, apart ; *cēdere*, to go. See **Cede**. **Der.** *secess-ion* (from the pp. *secess-us*).

Seclude. (L.) L. *sēclūdere*, to shut off. — L. *sē* (for *sed*), apart ; *claudere*, to shut. See **Se-** and **Clause**. **Der.** *seclus-ion*, from the pp. *sēclūs-us*.

Second. (F. — L.) O. F. *second*. — L. *secundus*, second, next following. — L. *sequī*, to follow. See **Sequence**.

Secret. (F. — L.) M. E. *secre, secree*. — O. F. *secret*, 'secret;' Cot. — L. *sēcrētus*, secret, set apart ; pp. of *sēcernere*, to separate. — L. *sē*, apart ; *cernere*, to separate. See **Se-** and **Concern**. **Der.** *secrete*, vb., from L. *sēcrētus* ; *secret-ion*.

secretary. (F. — L.) O. F. *secretaire*. — Late L. *sēcrētārium*, acc. of *sēcrētārius*, a confidential officer. — L. *sēcrēt-us*, secret (above).

Sect. (F. — L.) F. *secte*, 'a sect or faction;' Cot. — Late L. *secta*, a set of people, a suit of clothes, a suit at law. — L. *sec-* (as in *sec-undus*), base of *sequī*, to follow, sue. ¶ Not from *secāre*, to cut.

Section. (F. — L.) F. *section*. — L. *sectiōnem*, acc. of *sectio*, a cutting. — L. *sect-us*, pp. of *secāre*, to cut. See **Secant**.

Secular. (F. — L.) M. E. *seculere*. —

M. F. *seculier*, 'secular, temporall ;' Cot.
—L. *sēculāris*, secular, worldly. — L. *sēculum*, *saeculum*, a generation, an age, the world.

Secure. (L.) L. *sēcūrus*, free from anxiety. — L. *sē-*, apart from ; *cūra*, anxiety. Doublets, *sicker*, *sure*.

Sedan-chair. (F.) Named from *Sedan*, a town in France. Cf. F. *sedan*, cloth made at Sedan (Littré).

Sedate, quiet. (L.) L. *sēdātus*, pp. of *sēdāre*, to settle or make calm, causal of *sedēre*, to sit. See below.

sedentary. (F.—L.) F. *sédentaire*. — L. *sedentārius*, ever sitting. — L. *sedent-*, pres. pt. of *sedēre*, to sit. See Sit. (√SED.) Brugm. i. § 574.

Sedge. (E.) M. E. *segge*. — A. S. *secge*, g., d., and acc. of *secg*, f., sedge ; lit. 'cutter,' i. e. sword-grass ; from the shape ; cf. *secg*, m. a sword. The A. S. *secg*, f. = Teut. type **sag-jā* ; from **saχ-*, 2nd grade of Teut. root **seχ-*, to cut. + Low G. *segge*, coarse grass. Cf. Irish *seisg*, sedge. (√SEK, to cut.) See Secant.

Sediment. (F.—L.) M. F. *sediment*. — L. *sedimentum*, a settling (of dregs). — L. *sedēre*, to sit, settle. See Sit.

Sedition. (F.—L.) O. F. *sedition*. — L. acc. *seditionem*, a going apart, dissension, mutiny. — L. *sed-*, apart ; *it-um*, supine of *īre*, to go. (√EI.)

Seduce, to lead astray. (L.) L. *sēdūcere*, to lead aside. — L. *sē* (for *sed*), apart ; *dūcere*, to lead. See Se- and Duke. Der. *seduct-ion* (from the pp. *sēduct-us*).

Sedulous, diligent. (L.) L. *sēdulus*, diligent. Cf. *sēdulō*, adv. busily ; from *sē*, apart from, *dolō*, abl. of *dolus*, guile. Brugm. i. § 244.

See (1), to perceive by the eye. (E.) M. E. *seen*, *sen*. A. S. *sēon* ; pt. t. *sēah*, pp. *gesewen*. + Du. *zien* ; Icel. *sjā* ; Dan. *see* ; Swed. *se* ; G. *sehen* ; Goth. *saihwan*, pt. t. *sahw*. Teut. type **sehwan-*. Brugm. i. § 665. Der. *seer*, i. e. see-er.

See (2), seat of a bishop. (F.—L.) M. E. *se*. — O. F. *sed*, *se*, seat. — L. *sēdem*, acc. of *sēdes*, a seat. — L. *sēd-*, as in *sēd-ī*, pt. t. of *sedēre*, to sit. See Sit.

Seed. (E.) A. S. *sǣd*, seed. From A. S. *sāwan*, to sow. + Du. *zaad*, Icel. *sǣði*, *sāð*, Dan. *sæd*, Swed. *säd*, G. *saat*. Cf. Goth. *mana-sēths*, the world, lit. 'man-seed ;' Lat. *sē-men*, seed. The A. S. *sǣd* answers to Teut. type **sǣ-dom*, neut. See Sow. Brugm. i. § 132.

Seek. (E.) M. E. *seken*. A. S. *sēcan*, pt. t. *sōh-te*, to seek, strive after. + Du. *zoeken* ; Icel. *sœkja*, *sœkja* ; Dan. *söge* ; Swed. *söka* ; Goth. *sōkjan* ; G. *suchen*. Teut. type **sōk-jan-* ; from **sōk-* = Idg. **sāg-*, as in L. *sāgīre*, to perceive, Gk. *ἡγέομαι*, I consider ; cf. O. Ir. *sagim*, I seek for. Der. *be-seech*.

Seel, to close up the eyes. (F.—L.) M. F. *siller*, 'to seal up the eie-lids ;' Cot. Also spelt *ciller*. — O. F. *cil*, eye-lid. — L. *cilium*, eye-lid ; which is probably allied to Gk. *τὰ κύλα*, the parts under the eyes. See Supercilious.

Seem. (E.) M. E. *semen*. A. S. *sēman*, to satisfy, conciliate (hence, to suit, a sense due to the adj. *seemly* ; see below). For **sōm-ian*, where **sōm-* is the strong grade of *sam-*, as in E. *same*. + Icel. *sœma*, to honour, bear with, conform to, allied to *sœmr*, fit, *sōma*, to befit, and to *samr*, same. See Same.

seemly, fit. (Scand.) M. E. *semlich*. — Icel. *sœmiligr*, seemly. — Icel. *sœmr*, fit ; with suffix *-ligr*, like (-ly) ; where *sœm-* is the mutated form of **sōm-* (as in Icel. *sōm-a*, to befit), strong grade of **sam-*, as in Icel. *sama*, to beseem, cognate with Goth. *samjan*, to please, lit. 'to be the same,' agree with. — Icel. *samr*, same ; see Same.

Seer, see See.

Seesaw. (E.) A reduplicated form ; from the verb *to saw*. From the motion of a sawyer. See Saw (1).

Seethe, to boil. (E.) Pt. t. *sod* ; pp. *sodden.* M. E. *sethen*, pt. t. *seeth* (pl. *soden*), pp. *soden*. A. S. *sēoðan*, pt. t. *sēað*, pp. *soden.* + Icel. *sjōða*, pt. t. *sauð* ; Dan. *syde* ; Swed. *sjuda* ; G. *sieden*. Teut. type **seuthan-*, pt. t. **sauth*, pp. **sud-anoz*. Allied to Goth. *sauths*, a burnt-offering.

Segment. (L.) L. *segmentum*, a piece cut off ; for **sec-mentum*. — L. *secāre*, to cut. See Secant.

Segregate, to separate from others. (L.) From pp. of *sēgregāre*, to set apart from a flock. — L. *sē-*, apart ; *greg-*, stem of *grex*, a flock. See Se- and Gregarious.

Seignior. (F.—L.) O. F. *seignor*, *seigneur*, lord. — L. *seniōrem*, acc. of *senior*, older, hence, greater ; see Senior.

Seine, a large fishing-net. (F.—L.— Gk.) F. *seine*. — L. *sagēna*. — Gk. *σαγήνη*, a large fishing-net.

Seize, to grasp. (F.—Late L.) M. E.

seysen, saisen, a law term, to put one in *seisin* or possession of a thing, also, to take possession; hence, to seize, take. – O. F. *saisir, seisir,* to put in possession of, to take possession. – Late L. *sacīre,* to put, place. ¶ It is usual to refer this verb to O. H. G. **sazjan,* to set, put, place, but this is an impossible form (it was really *sezzen*); or else to Goth. *satjan,* to set, which would have given **sadir, *sair.* See **Set. Der.** *seis-in,* O. F. *seisine, saisine,* from the verb *saisir.*

Selah, a pause. (Heb.) Supposed to mean 'a pause.'

Seldom. (E.) A. S. *seldan, seldum, seldon,* seldom, lit. rarely; cf. *seld-līc,* strange, *seld-sīene,* rarely seen, strange.+ Du. *zelden,* Icel. *sjaldan,* Dan. *sielden,* Swed. *sällan,* G. *selten,* adv., seldom. Allied to Goth. *sildaleiks,* wonderful.

Select, choice. (L.) L. *sēlectus,* pp. of *sēligere,* to choose. – L. *sē-,* apart; *legere,* to pick, choose. See **Se-** and **Legend. Der.** *select,* vb.

Self. (E.) A. S. *self,* also *seolf, silf, self.*+Du. *zelf;* Icel. *sjálfr;* Dan. *selv;* Swed. *sjelf;* Goth. *silba;* G. *selb, selb-st.*

Sell (1), to deliver for money. (E.) A. S. *sellan, sillan, syllan,* to hand over, deliver; a secondary verb, from the sb. **Sale.**+Icel. *selja,* Dan. *sælge,* Swed. *sälja,* O. H. G. and Goth. *saljan,* to hand over, offer. Teut. type **saljan-.*

Sell (2), a saddle. (F. – L.) O. F. *selle,* seat, saddle. – L. *sella,* seat; for **sed-la.* – L. *sedēre,* to sit. Brugm. i. § 475. See **Saddle.**

Selvage. (Du.) Also *selvedge.* Lit. ' self-edge.' – M. Du. *selfegge,* selvage. – M. Du. *self,* self; *egge,* edge; [mod. Du. *zelfkant,* selvage; from *zelf,* self, *kant,* edge]; Low G. *sulf-egge,* self-edge, selvage.

Semblance, appearance. (F. – L.) *semblance,* appearance. – F. *sembler,* to seem. – L. *similāre, simulāre,* to make like. – L. *similis,* like. See **Simulate.**

Semi-, half. (L.) L. *sēmi-,* half.+Gk. ἡμι-, half; A. S. *sām,*half; Skt. *sāmi,* half, prob. related to Skt. *sāmya-,* equality, from *sama,* even, same (Benfey). Allied to **Same. Der.** *semi-breve,* &c.

Seminal, relating to seed. (F. – L.) M. F. *seminal.* – L. *sēminālis,* relating to seed. – L. *sēmin-,* for *sēmen,* seed. – L. *sē-* as in *sē-uī,* pt. t. of *serere,* to sow; with suffix *-men.* See **Sow** (1).

seminary. (L.) L. *sēminārium,* a seed-garden, seed-plot (hence a place of education). – L. *sēmin-* (above).

Semolina. (Ital. – L.) Ital. *semolino,* m., small seed, paste for soups; dimin. of *semola,* bran. – L. *simila,* fine wheaten flower. See **Simnel.**

Sempiternal, everlasting. (L.) F. *sempiternel.* – L. *sempitern-us,* everlasting. – L. *sempi-,* for *semper,* always; with suffix *-ter-nus.* β. L. *semper* was perhaps formerly **sem-perti,* where **sem-* probably meant ' one,' as in L. *sem-el,* once, *simplex,* one-fold. Brugm. i. § 1023 (12); ii. § 160 (1).

Sempster. (E.) Later forms **Seamstress, Sempstress;** *with* F. *suffix.* A. S. *sēamestre,* a sempster; with suffix *-ess* (= F. *-esse* < Gk. *-ισσα*). – A. S. *sēam,* a seam (see **Seam**); with suffix *-estre;* see **Spinster.**

Senary, belonging to six. (L.) L. *sēnārius,* adj., from *sēnī,* six apiece; for **sex-nī.* – L. *sex,* six; see **Six.**

Senate, a council of elders. (F. – L.) O.F. *senat.* – L. *senātum,* acc. of *senātus,* council of elders. – L. *sen-,* as in *sen-ex,* old, *sen-ium,* old age. Cf. O. Gk. ἔνος, old, Goth. *sineigs,* O. Ir. *sen,* W. *hen,* O. Skt. *sana-,* old. Brugm. i. § 117.

Send. (E.) A. S. *sendan.*+Du. *zenden;* Icel. *senda;* Dan. *sende;* Swed. *sända;* Goth. *sandjan;* G. *senden.* Teut. type **sandjan-,* for **santhjan-,* by Verner's law, from **santh,* 2nd grade of **senthan-,* to go. Hence *send* is a causal verb, meaning ' to make to go.' The Teut. **senthan-* (pt. t. **santh*) is a lost strong verb, of which the prime grade appears in Goth. *sinth-s,* A. S. *sīð* (for **sinð*), a journey, way, Teut. type **senthoz,* m., Idg. type **sentos,* as seen in O. Irish *sēt* (for **sent*), W. *hynt,* Bret. *hent* (for **sent*), a way. Cf. G. *gesinde,* followers; Goth. *gasinthja,* a travelling companion.

Sendal, Cendal, a rich thin silken stuff. (F. – Late L. – Skt.) O. F. *sendal, cendal*; Late L. *cendalum, cindādus, cindātus,* &c. So called because brought from India. – Skt. *sindhu-,* the Indus, also Scinde. – Skt. *syand,* to flow: see **Indigo.** Cf. Gk. *σινδών,* fine Indian linen.

Seneschal, a steward. (F. – Teut.) O. F. *seneschal.* Orig. sense ' old servant.' – Goth. *sin-,* old (only preserved in superl. *sin-ista,* eldest, and in *sin-eigs,* old); *skalks,* a servant. Cf. **Senate** and **Marshal.**

senile, old. (L.) L. *senīlis*, old; cf. *sen-ex,* old. See Senate.

senior. (L.) L. *senior,* older; comp. of *senex,* old.

Senna. (Ital. — Arab.) Ital. *sena* (Florio). — Arab. *sanā,* senna.

Sennet, a signal-call on a trumpet. (F. — L.) See Nares; and Wright's note to K. Lear, i. 1. 33. Also spelt *sinet.* — O. F. *sinet, senet, segnet,* presumably 'a signal'; dimin. of F. *signe,* a sign, mark, note. — L. *signum,* a signal; see Sign, Tocsin.

Sennight; short for *seven night,* a week.

Sense. (F. — L.) F. *sens,* 'sence;' Cot. — L. *sensum,* acc. of *sensus,* feeling. — L. *sensus,* pp. of *sentīre,* to feel, perceive.

sensual. (L.) Late L. *sensuālis,* endowed with feeling. — L. *sensu-s,* feeling. — L. *sensus,* pp. of *sentīre,* to feel.

sentence. (F. — L.) F. *sentence.* — L. *sententia,* a way of thinking; for **sentientia.* — L. *sentient-,* stem of pres. pt. of *sentīre,* to feel, think.

sentiment. (F. — L.) M. E. *sentement.* — O. F. *sentement;* as if from a Late L. **sentīmentum.* — L. *sentīre* (above).

Sentinel. (F. — Ital. — L. ?) M. F. *sentinelle.* — Ital. *sentinella,* 'a watch, a sentinell;' Florio. Cf. M. F. *sentinelle,* a watch-tower (Godefroy). Etym. uncertain; apparently ultimately from L. *sentīre,* to perceive. See Körting, §§ 7365, 7377.

Sentry. (F. — L.) Spelt *sentrie* in Minsheu (1627), *sentery* in Milton, P. L. ii. 412. Minsheu also has *centrie* as a short form of *sanctuary.* Cotgrave has: ' *Garite,* a place of refuge, . . a *sentry,* or little lodge for a sentinell'; also ' *Barbacane,* . . a sentrie, scout-house.' It meant a place of safety. See Sanctuary.

Sepal, a leaf or division of the calyx of a flower. (F. — L.) F. *sépale,* a sepal. Coined to pair off with F. *pétale,* a petal, by taking part of the Lat. adj. *sēp-ar,* separate, and adding the same suffix *-āle* (Littré). Thus *sep-al* is, as it were, short for *separ-al,* where *separ-* was regarded as being allied to L. *sēparāre,* to separate. See Separate.

Separate, to keep apart. (L.) L. *sēparātus,* pp. of *sēparāre,* to sever. — L. *sē,* apart; *parāre,* to get ready, set. Der. *separate,* adj., kept apart (not so old as the verb in E.). Doublet, *sever.*

Sepia, ink from the cuttlefish. (L. —

Gk.) L. *sēpia.* — Gk. σηπία, cuttle-fish, sepia.

Sepoy. (Pers.) Pers. *sipāhī* (pronounced nearly as *sepoy*), a horseman, soldier. — Pers. *sipāh, supāh,* an army (Horn, § 699).

Sept, a clan. (F. — L.) Used in the 16th cent. as synonymous with *sect,* of which it is an arbitrary variant. Ducange has Late L. *septa* for Ital. *setta* (< L. *secta*); and Wedgwood cites Prov. *cepte,* a sect. See Sect.

September. (L.) L. *September,* the seventh month of the Roman year. — L. *septem,* seven. See Seven.

septenary. (L.) L. *septēnārius,* consisting of seven. — L. *septēnī,* pl., seven apiece. — L. *septem,* seven.

septennial. (L.) From L. *septennium,* a period of seven years. — L. *septennis,* adj., of seven years. — L. *sept-em,* seven; *annus,* year.

septuagesima. (L.) Lit. 'seventieth' (day). — L. *septuāgēsima* (*diēs*) seventieth (day), fem. of *septuāgēsimus,* seventieth. — L. *septuāginta,* seventy. — L. *septem,* seven; *-ginta,* related to Gk. *-κοντα,* for **δεκοντα,* from δέκα, ten.

Sepulchre. (F. — L.) O. F. *sepulcre.* — L. *sepulcrum,* ill-spelt *sepulchrum,* a tomb. — L. *sepul-tus,* pp. of *sepelīre,* to bury. Der. *sepult-ure,* from the pp. *sepultus.*

Sequel. (F. — L.) M. F. *sequele,* 'a sequell;' Cot. — L. *sequēla,* a result. — L. *sequī,* to follow. See below.

sequence. (F. — L.) O. F. *sequence,* a sequence. — L. *sequentia,* sb., a following; from *sequent-,* stem of *sequens,* pres. pt. of *sequī,* to follow. + Lith. *sekti,* to follow; Gk. ἕπομαι, Irish *seich-im,* I follow; Skt. *sach,* to follow. (√SEQ.) Brugm. i. § 118.

sequester. (F. — L.) M. F. *sequestrer,* to sequester or lay aside. — L. *sequestrāre,* to surrender, lay aside. — L. *sequester,* a mediator, trustee, agent. Prob. orig. ' a follower.' — L. *sequī,* to follow.

Sequin, a gold coin. (F. — Ital. — Arab.) F. *sequin;* Cot. — Ital. *zecchino,* a Venetian coin. — Ital. *zecca,* a mint; Florio. — Arab. *sikka(t),* pron. *sikkah,* a die for coins.

Seraglio. (Ital. — L.) Misused in E.; the true sense is merely 'enclosure'; but it was confused with Pers. *sarāy* or *serāī,* a palace, king's court, seraglio. Really from Ital. *serraglio,* an enclosure; formed with suffix -*aglio* (< L. -*āculum*) from Late L. *serāre*, to bar, to bolt, shut in. — L. *sera*, a bar, bolt. — L. *serere*, to join together; see **Series**. And see below.

Serai, a palace. (Pers.) Pers. *serāī*, a palace (Horn, § 727).

Seraph. (Heb.) Coined from the pl. form *seraphim*. — Heb. *serāphīm*, s. pl., seraphs, lit. exalted ones (Gesenius).

Seraskier, a Turkish general. (F. — Turk. — Pers. *and* Arab.) F. *séraskier*, *sérasquier*. — Turk. *ser'asker*, chief of the army, with a light sound of *i* after the *k*. — Pers. *sar*, head (with initial *sin*); and Arab. *'askar*, an army (Devic). The Pers. *sar* is cognate with Skt. *çiras*, head; cf. Gk. *κάρα*, head. And see **Sirdar**.

Sere; see **Sear**.

Serecloth; see **Cerecloth**.

Serene. (L.) L. *serēnus*, bright, clear. Brugm. i. § 920 (4).

serenade. (F. — Ital. — L.) M. F. *serenade*. — Ital. *serenata*, music beneath a lady's window; orig. fem. of pp. of *serenare*, to make clear or to cheer, to be merry. — L. *serēnus*, bright.

Serf. (F. — L.) F. *serf*, a servant. — L. *seruum*, acc. of *seruus*, a slave. See **Serve**.

Serge. (F. — L. — Gk. — Chinese ?.) F. *serge*, a silken stuff. — L. *sērica*, fem. of *sēricus*, silken, the same as *Sēricus*, belonging to the *Sēres*. — Gk. Σῆρες, pl., Chinese; cf. *σήρ*, a silkworm. The name *Sēres* is from the Chinese *se, sei*, silk.

Sergeant, Serjeant. (F. — L.) M.E. *sergeant, sergant*. — O. F. *sergant, serjant*, an officer. — Late L. *seruientem*, acc. of *seruiens*, an officer; orig. pres. pt. of *seruīre*, to serve. See **Serve**.

Series, a row. (L.) L. *seriēs*, a row. — L. *serere*, to join or bind together (pp. *sertus*). + Gk. εἴρειν (for *σέργειν); cf. Lith. *sēris*, a thread; Icel. *sörvi*, a necklace.

Serif, the short cross-line at the end of a stroke of a letter. (Du.) Adapted (with *ser-* for Du. *schr-*) from Du. *schreef*, M.Du. *schreve*, a dash, short line. Allied to O. H. G. *screvōn*, to scratch, incise.

Serious. (F. — L.) O. F. *serieux*. — Late L. *sēriōsus*, serious. — L. *sērius*, grave, earnest. Cf. G. *schwer*, heavy; Lith. *swarùs*, heavy.

Sermon. (F. — L.) F. *sermon*. — L. *sermōnem*, acc. of *sermo*, a speech, discourse.

Serous; see **Serum**.

Serpent. (F. — L.) F. *serpent*. — L. *serpentem*, acc. of *serpens*, a serpent; orig. pres. pt. of *serpere*, to creep. + Gk. ἕρπειν, to creep; Skt. *sṛp*, to creep, *sarpa-*, a snake. Brugm. i. § 477. (√SERP.)

Serrated, notched like a saw. (L.) L. *serrātus*, notched like a saw. — L. *serra*, a saw.

Serried, crowded together. (F. — L.) F. *serrer*, to compact, press close, lock. — Folk-L. *serrāre*, for L. *serāre*, to bolt. — L. *sera*, a bolt. — L. *serere*, to join. Cf. **Seraglio**.

Serum, whey. (L.) L. *serum*, whey, serum. + Gk. ὀρός, whey; Skt. *sara(s)*, adj., flowing, sb., whey. (√ SER, to flow.) But cf. Brugm. i. § 466. Der. *ser-ous*, adj.

Serve. (F. — L.) F. *servir*. — L. *seruīre*, to serve. — L. *seruus*, a slave; cf. *seruāre*, to keep, protect. Der. *serv-ant*, from pres. pt. of F. *servir*; *serv-ice*, F. *service*, L. *seruitium*; *serv-ile*, L. *seruīlis*; *servitude*, F. *servitude*, L. acc. *seruitūdinem*; also *serf*, *sergeant*.

Service-tree, a kind of wild pear-tree. (L. *and* E.) *Service* is a corruption of *serv-ĕs* (dissyllabic), the M. E. plural of *serf* or *serve*, the name of the fruit. A. S. *syrf*, the fruit of the service-tree; *syrf-trēow*, a service-tree (correctly, sirf-tree). — L. *sorbus*, the tree; *sorbum*, its fruit.

Session. (F. — L.) F. *session*. — L. *sessiōnem*, acc. of *sessio*, a sitting. — L. *ses-sus*, pp. of *sedēre*, to sit. See **Sit**.

Set (1). (E.) A. S. *settan*, to set, make to sit; causal of *sittan*, to sit (derived from the 2nd grade *sat*). + Icel. *setja*; Dan. *sætte*; Swed. *sätta*; G. *setzen*; Du. *zetten*; Goth. *satjan*; all causal forms. Teut. type *satjan-*. See **Sit**.

Set (2). When we speak of a *set* of things, this is a variant of *sect*. The Late Latin word is *secta*, common in old wills; for which we also find *setta*.

Seton, an artificial irritation under the skin. (F. — L.) F. *séton*, in use in the 16th century; the orig. sense is 'a thread.' Formed (as if from Late L. *sēto*) from L. *sēta*, a bristle, stiff hair. See **Satin**.

Settee, a seat with a long back; apparently an arbitrary variation of *settle*, sb., which see below.

settle (1), a long bench with a high back. (E.) A. S. *setl*, a seat. + Goth. *sitls*; G. *sessel*; L. *sella* (for *sed-la*). See **Sell** (2), **Sit**.

settle (2), to fix, adjust. (E.) M. E. *setlen*. A. S. *setlan*, to fix; also, to take a seat, settle down as in a seat, from A. S. *setl*, a seat; see above. ¶ Perhaps it may have been affected by M. E. *sahtlen*, to reconcile, A. S. *sahtlian*, *sæhtlian*, to reconcile. ─ A. S. *seht*, *sæht*, reconciliation; borrowed from Icel. *sātt*, *sætt*, reconciliation, peace; which Noreen (§ 73) connects with L. *sanctus*, holy.

Seven. (E.) A. S. *seofon*, *sibun*.+Du. *zeven*; Icel. *sjau*, *sjö*; Dan. *syv*; Swed. *sju*; G. *sieben*; Goth. *sibun*; L. *septem*; Gk. ἑπτά; W. *saith*; Irish *seacht*; Russ. *seme*; Lith. *septyni*; Skt. *sapta*. Idg. type *septṃ. **Der.** *seven-teen*, A. S. *seofontŷne*; *seven-ty*, A. S. *hund-seofontig* (*hund* being dropped); *seven-th*.

Sever, to separate. (F. ─ L.) O. F. *severer*. ─ L. *sēparāre*, to separate. See **Separate. Der.** *dissever*.

several, adj. (F.─L.) O. F. *several*. ─Late L. *sēparāle*, a thing set apart.─L. *sēparāre*, to separate (above).

Severe. (F.─L.) O. F. *severe*.─L. *seuērus*, severe, serious, grave. Der. *sever-ity*, M. F. *severité*.

Sew (1), to fasten with thread. (E.) M. E. *sowen*, *sewen*. A. S. *siwian*, to sew. +Icel. *sȳja*; Dan. *sye*; Swed. *sy*; O.H.G. *siuwan*; Goth. *siujan*; L. *suere*; Lith. *suti*; Russ. *shite*; Skt. *siv*, to sew. Cf. Gk. κασ-σύειν, to sew together; and see **Hymen.** (✓SIW.)

Sew (2), to follow; the same as **Sue**; see **Sequence.**

Sewer (1), a large drain. (F.─L.) Frequently spelt *shore*. From O. F. *sewiere*, *seuwiere*, a sluice, channel for draining a pond. ─ Late L. type *exaquāria, short for Late L. *exaquātōrium*, a channel for draining.─L. *ex*, out ; *aqua*, water. (The derivation of E. *ewer* from L. *aquāria* is parallel.)

Sewer (2), the officer who formerly set and tasted dishes, &c. (F.─L.) '*Seware*, *at mete*, Depositor, dapifer, sepulator;' Prompt. Parv. [Hence M. E. *sewen*, to set meat, bring in dishes, &c.] The M. E. *seware*, *sewere* is short for *assewer*, *asseour* (N. E. D.).─O. F. *asseour*, one who sets the table.─O. F. *asseoir*, to set, place; orig. to sit beside.─L. *assidēre*, to sit by. ─L. *as-*, for *ad*, near; *sedēre*, to sit. See **Sit** and **Assess.** ¶ Perhaps confused with M. E. *sew*, pottage, from A. S. *sēaw*, juice.

Sex. (F.─L.) F. *sexe*.─L. *sexum*, acc.

of *sexus*, sex; also *secus*, n. Was it orig. 'division;' from *sec-āre*, to cut? See **Segment, Secant. Der.** *sex-u-al*, L. *sexuālis*.

Sexagenary. (L.) L. *sexāgēnārius*, belonging to sixty. ─ L. *sexāgēnī*, sixty each; distribute form of *sexāginta*, sixty. ─ L. *sex*, six; and *-ginta*, related to Gk. -κοντα, for *δέκοντα, from δέκα, ten. See **Six** and **Ten.**

sexagesima. (L.) L. *sexāgēsima* (*diēs*), i. e. sixtieth (day); fem. of *sexāgēsimus*, sixtieth, ordinal form of *sexāginta*, sixty.

sexennial. (L.) From L. *sexennium*, a period of six years. ─ L. *sex*, six; *annus*, a year.

sextant, the sixth part of a circle. (L.) L. *sextant-*, stem of *sextans*, a sixth part. ─ L. *sext-us*, sixth, from *sex*, six; with suffix *-ans*, like that of a pres. pt. of a verb in *-āre*.

Sexton; see **Sacristan.**

Sextuple, sixfold. (L.) Coined from *sextu-s*, sixth; with suffix *-ple* (as in *quadru-ple*), answering to L. *-plic-*, stem of *-plex*, as seen in *du-plex*, *con-plex*.

SH.

Shabby, mean. (E.) Also *shabbed*; *shabby* and *shabbed* are the native E. equivalents of the Scand. *scabby* and *scabbed*. See **Scab.** For the sense, cf. *scurvy* (= *scurvy*); E. Fries. *schabbig*, scabby, also miserable, mean.

Shackle. (E.) A. S. *sceacul*, bond, fetter; orig. a loose bond; from its *shaking* about.+Icel. *skökull*, pole of a carriage, from *skaka*, to shake; Swed. *skakel*, loose shaft of a carriage; Dan. *skagle*, the same. Cf. Swed. dial. *skak*, a chain. See **Shake.**

Shad, a fish. (E.) A. S. *sceadd*.+Prov. G. *schade*, a shad; cf. Irish *sgadan*, O. Irish *scatán*, a herring; W. *ysgadan*, pl., herrings.

Shaddock, a large species of orange. (E.) Named from Captain *Shaddock*, who first introduced it into the West Indies from China, late in the seventeenth century.

Shade, Shadow. (E.) M. E. *shade*, *shadwe*. A. S. *sceadu*, shadow, fem. sb. The M. E. *shade* is from the A. S. nom. *sceadu*; the M. E. *shadwe* (mod. F. *shadow*) is from the dat. case *sceadwe*. + Du. *schaduw*, Goth. *skadus*, shadow;

G. *schatten*, O. Irish *scáth*, Corn. *scod*, shade; Gk. σκότος, σκοτία, gloom.

Shaft. (E.) A. S. *sceaft*, shaft of a spear.+Icel. *skapt*, *skaft*, Dan. Sw. *skaft*; G. *schaft*, Du. *schacht* (for *schaft*). Further allied to L. *scāpus*, a shaft, stem, stalk; Gk. σκῆπτρον, Doric σκᾶπτον, a staff, sceptre. All apparently from Idg. root **skap*, to support. 2. Or else *shaf-t* = that which is *shaven* or cut smooth; from Shave, q. v.

Shag, rough hair. (E.) A. S. *sceacga*, hair. + Icel. *skegg*, Swed. *skägg*, a beard, Dan. *skiæg*, beard, awn, wattle; cf. Icel. *skaga*, to jut out. The orig. sense is 'roughness.' See Shaw. Der. *shagg-y*, adj. *Shag* tobacco is rough tobacco.

Shagreen, a rough-grained leather. (F. – Turkish.) F. *chagrin*. It was orig. made of the skin of the *back* of the horse or mule. – Turk. *sāghrī*, *saghrī*, back of a horse, shagreen.

Shah, king of Persia. (Pers.) Pers. *shāh*, a king. O. Pers. *khshāyathiya*, a king; allied to Skt. *kshatra(m)*, dominion, from *kshi*, to rule; cf. Gk. κτάομαι, I possess. Lit. sense 'ruler'; Horn, § 772; Brugm. i. § 920. See Check. Der. *pa-sha*.

Shake. (E.) A.S. *sceacan*, *scacan*, pt. t. *scōc*, pp. *scacen*.+Icel. *skaka*, Sw. *skaka*, Dan. *skage*. Teut. type **skakan-*.

Shako, a military cap. (F.—Hung.) F. *shako*. – Hungarian *csako*, a cap, shako; spelt *tsākō* in Dankovsky's Magyar Lexicon, p. 900.

Shale, a slaty rock. (G.) G. *schale*, a shell, peel, scale; whence *schal-gebirge*, a mountain formed of thin strata. Hence also O. F. *escale* and E. *scale* (1). See Scale (1).

Shall. (E.) A. S. *sceal*, I shall, I must; pt. t. *sceolde*, I should, ought. The orig. sense was 'to owe,' to be liable for; cf. Lith. *skilti*, to owe, be liable.+Icel. *skal*, pt. t. *skyldi*; Sw. *skall*; Dan. *skal*; Du. *zal*; G. *soll*; Goth. *skal*, infin. *skulan*. Cf. G. *schuld*, debt, guilt; Lith. *skelèti*, to be liable. Brugm. i. § 795.

Shalloon, a light woollen stuff. (F.) From *Chalons*, in France, E. of Paris.

Shallop, a light boat. (F. – Du.) F. *chaloupe* [whence Span. *chalupa*, 'a flat-bottomed boat,' Minsheu (1623); Port. *chalupa*]. – Du. *sloep*, a sloop. See Sloop.

Shallot, Shalot, a kind of onion. (F. –L.–Gk.–Heb.) O.F. *eschalote*, variant of *escalogne*, a shallot. – L. *ascalōnia*, a

shallot; fem. of *Ascalōnius*, belonging to Ascalon. – Gk. Ἀσκάλων, Ascalon; a chief city of the Philistines. – Heb. *Ashqelōn*.

Shallow. (E.) M. E. *schalowe*; cf. also *schold*, *schald*, Barbour, Bruce, ix. 354; for which see Shoal. An E. word; but of doubtful origin. However, M.E. *schalowe* is allied to M. E. *schal-d*, shallow, as they have a common base *schal-*. And perhaps allied to Low G. *schaal*, *schalig*, G. *schal*, insipid, stale (as liquids when little is left in the vessel); cf. Du. *verschalen*, to grow stale or flat.

Shalm; see Shawm.

Sham. (E.) A London slang term, due to Northern E. *sham*, a shame, disgrace (hence, trick). 'Wheea's *sham* is it' = whose fault is it? Whitby Glossary. See Shame.

Shamble, to walk awkwardly. (E.) Lowl. Sc. *shammel*, *shamble*, to rack the limbs with long strides; also, to distort; *shammel shanks*, crooked legs. Cf. E. Fries. *schamel*, shamefaced, modest, also poor, miserable; O. Fries. *skamel*, poor; Du. *schamel*. If this connexion be right, the adj. is formed from the sb. *shame*; see Shame.

Shambles. (L.) Orig. stalls on which butchers expose meat for sale; pl. of *shamble*, a bench, butcher's bench or stall. A.S. *scamel*, a stool.–L. *scamellum*, a stool, little bench; allied to *scamnum*, step, bench, *scabellum*, foot-stool. L. *scamnum* is for **scab-num*, **scap-num*, allied to *scāpus*, a stem. Brugm. i. § 241.

Shame. (E.) A.S. *sceamu*, *scamu*.+ Icel. *skömm*; Dan. Sw. *skam*; G. *scham*. Allied to Goth. *skanda*, shame, G. *schande*.

shamefaced, modest. (E.) Corruption of M. E. *shamefast*, modest. – A.S. *scamfæst*, lit. firm in shame, i.e. in modesty. – A.S. *scamu*, shame, modesty; *fæst*, fast, firm; see Fast.

Shammy, Shamoy, a kind of leather. (F. – G.) Orig. *chamois* leather; see Blount and Phillips. See Chamois.

Shampoo. (Hind.) Hindustani *chāmpnā*, to join, to stuff, press, thrust in, shampoo; from the kneading or pressure used in the operation. Perhaps directly from the imperative *chāmpo* of the same verb; Yule.

Shamrock. (C.) Irish *seamrog*, trefoil, dimin. of *seamar*, trefoil; Gael. *seamrag*.

Shank, lower part of the leg. (E.) A.S. *sceanca*, *scanca*, bone of the leg.

478

+Du. *schonk*, Dan. *skank*, Swed. *skank*. Further related to G. *schenkel*, shank; G. *schinken*, ham. **Der.** *skink*.

Shanty, a hut. (Irish.) Said to be from Irish *sean*, old ; *tigh*, a house.

Shape, vb. (E.) M. E. *schapen*; a new formation from the sb. *schap*, A. S. *ge-sceap*; or from the pp., on the analogy of *sceacan*, pp. *sceacen*. The A. S. vb. is *sceppan*, *scieppan*, with a weak infin.; pt. t. *scōp*, pp. *scapen*. **+** Icel. *skapa*, Swed. *skapa*, Dan. *skabe*, Goth. *ga-skapjan*, G. *schaffen*; Du. *scheppen* (weak). All from Teut. type **skapan-*, **skapjan-*, pt. t. *skōp. Cf. Lith. *skaběti*, to cut, hew. Brugm. i. § 701.

Shard, Sherd, fragment. (E.) A.S. *sceard*, a fragment; lit. ' cut thing.' From *skar, 2nd grade of **sker-an-*, to shear. See **Shear.** Cf. Icel. *skarð*, a notch. **Der.** *pot-sherd*.

share (1), a portion. (E.) A. S. *scearu*, a share, part. From *skar (above).

share (2), a plough-share. (E.) A. S. *scear*, plough-share. From the same.

Shark, a voracious fish. (F.—L.) The name of the fish is from the Tudor verb *to shark*, to prowl; *to shark* for a dinner, to try to get one; *to shark* for a living; see Cent. Dict. Prob. from North F. (Picard) *cherquier*, equivalent to O. F. *cercher* (E. *search*), later altered to mod. F. *chercher*. Cf. *cercher le braust*, ' to hunt after feasts;' Cot. Godefroy has two examples of the spelling *cherquier*. Cf. Ital. *cercare del pane*, ' to shift for how to live;' Torriano. **—** L. *circāre*, to go round. **—** L. *circus*, a ring. See **Search.** If this be right, *to shark* is a variant of *to search*, but was much used (formerly) in the sense of to prowl about for a living. Hence *shark*, sb. (1), a greedy fellow (Johnson); (2) a greedy fish.

Sharp. (E.) A. S. *scearp*.**+**Du. *scherp*, Icel. *skarpr*, Swed. Dan. *skarp*, G. *scharf*. Teut. type *skarpoz. Prob. allied to **Scrape. Der.** *scarp*, *escarpment*.

Shatter. (E.) M. E. *schateren*, to scatter, to dash as a falling stream ; hence to break in pieces. A. S. *scaterian*, to scatter, A. S. Chron. 1137. Cf. E. Fries. *schattern*, Du. *schateren*, to resound; M. Du. *schetteren*, to rattle. See **Scatter**, which is a doublet; cf. Milton, Lyc. 5.

Shave. (E.) A. S. *sceafan*, *scafan*, pt. t. *scōf*, pp. *scafen*.**+**Du. *schaven*; Icel. *skafa*; Swed. *skafva*, Dan. *skave*, Goth.

skaban, G. *schaben*; Lith. *skapoti*, to shave, cut, Russ. *skopite*, to castrate, Gk. σκάπτειν, to dig. Cf. also L. *scabere*, to scrape. (√SQAB, SQAP.) Brugm. i. §§ 569, 701.

Shaw, thicket. (E.) A. S. *scaga*.**+**Icel. *skōgr*, a shaw, wood; Swed. *skog*, Dan. *skov*, North Fries. *skōg*. Allied to Icel. *skagi*, a ness (Noreen); N. Fries. *skage*, a nook of land; cf. Icel. *skaga*, to jut out. Allied to **Shag.**

Shawl. (Pers.) Pers. *shāl* (pron. *shawl*), a shawl, mantle.

Shawm, Shalm, a musical instrument. (F.—L.—Gk.) O. F. *chalemie*, a reed pipe; allied to *chaume*, a straw; cf. M. H. G. *schalmīe*.**—**L. *calamus*, a reed. **—**Gk. κάλαμος, a reed. See **Haulm.**

She. (E.) M. E. *sche*, *scho*; also *scæ*, A. S. Chron. 1140. In the Northumbrian dialect, we find *scho* used as a dem. pronoun, though the A. S. *sēo* is the fem. of the def. article. The A. S. *sēo* would have become *see*, but this form never occurs; rather, it became *seō* (Lind. *sio*, John iv. 23); where (perhaps influenced by the Icel. m. and f. demonstr. pron. *sjā*, that), came Northumb. *scho* or *sho*; and this seems to have suggested the Midland *sche*, *she*, *sʒe* ; the true South. form being *heo*, *he* (which caused confusion with the masc. *he*). [We also find such forms as *hyo*, *hio*, *ho*, *ʒho*, *ʒo*, mod. Lanc. *hoo*; all from *heō*.] The A. S. *sēo* is the fem. of *se*, orig. ' that ;' cognate with Goth. *sa*, that.**+**Du. *zij*, G. *sie*; Icel. *sū*, fem. of *sā*, that; Goth. *sō*, fem. of *sa*, that; Gk. ἡ, fem. of ὁ; Skt. *sā*, she, fem. of *sa*, *sas*, he. For Icel. *sjā* see Noreen, § 399. See Sweet, E. Gr. § 1068.

Sheaf. (E.) M. E. *scheef*. A. S. *scēaf*, a sheaf, pile of corn shoved together.**—**A. S. *scēaf*, 2nd grade of *scūfan*, to shove. **+** Du. *schoof*, Icel. *skauf*, Bavar. *schaub*, sheaf; from Teut. *skaub, 2nd grade of **skūban-*, to shove; see **Shove.**

Sheal, a temporary summer hut. (Scand.) Also spelt *shiel*, *shielin*, *sheelin*.**—**Icel. *skjōl*, a shelter, cover, Dan. Swed. *skjul*, a shed; Icel. *skȳli*, a shed. Cf. Skt. *sku*, to cover.

Shear. (E.) A. S. *sceran*, pt. t. *scær*, pp. *scoren*.**+**Du. *scheren*, Icel. *skera*, Swed. *skära*, Dan. *skære*, G. *scheren*, to shear. Teut. type **skeran-*, pt. t. *skar, pp. *skoranoz. Allied to O. Ir. *scar-aim*, I separate, Gael. *sgar*, to sever; W. *ysgar*, to part;

Gk. κείρειν (for *(σ)κέργειν), to cut; Lith. kirwis, an axe. (√SQER.) Brugm. i. §§ 515, 631.

Sheath. (E.) A. S. sceáð, scǽð, a sheath, orig. that which separates, hence a husk, shell, pod. + Du. scheede, Dan. skede, Swed. skida, G. scheide, a sheath; Icel. skeiðir, fem. pl., a sheath (lit. things that separate or open). All from the Teut. base *skaith; for which see Shed (1). Der. sheathe, vb.

Shebeen, a liquor-shop. (Irish—E.) Apparently a dimin. (with suffix -īn) of Irish seapa, a shop.—E. shop; see Shop.

Shed (1), to part, pour, spill. (E.) Orig. 'to separate.' A. S. sceádan, scádan, pt. t. sceád, scéd, pp. sceáden, to shed; whence M. E. scheden, weak verb (with long e, but the e has been shortened, the pt. t. being shadde or shedde). + Goth. skaidan, G. scheiden, to part; O. Sax. skeðan, O. Fries. skeða, skéda. From Teut. base *skeith, varying to *skeid, to split (see Shide); or from the 2nd grade *skaith, *skaid. The Idg. root would, regularly, be *skheit, but we only find √SKHEID; cf. Gk. σχίζειν, for *σχίδγειν, to cleave; L. scindere, to cut; Lith. skédziu, I separate. All from an older √SKHEI. Brugm. i. §§ 201, 599.

Shed (2), a slight shelter, hut. (E.) O. Kentish shed (written ssed), shade; a dialectal form; Ayenbite of Inwyt. See Shade.

Sheen, fairness, splendour. (E.) M. E. schene, adj., fair. A. S. scéne, scíene, scýne, fair, 'showy;' allied to scéawian, to show, see. + O. Sax. scôni, adj.; Du. schoon, adj.; G. schön, adj.; cf. Goth. ibna-skauns, of like appearance. Teut. type *skauniz, 'showy;' see Show. ¶ Not allied to shine.

Sheep. (E.) A. S. sceáp, scép; pl. unchanged. + O. Sax. skáp; Du. schaap; G. schaf. Teut. type *skǣpom, neut.

Sheer (1), bright, pure, perpendicular. (Scand.) A sheer descent is a clear (unbroken) one. M. E. shere, bright.—Icel. skærr, Dan. skær, sheer, bright; Teut. type *skairiz. Cf. Icel. skírr, A.S. scír, bright; G. schier, Goth. skeirs (Teut. type *skeiroz); from the base (*skei-) of the verb to shine; see Shine (Noreen). ¶ The sh (for sk) is due to A. S. scír. Der. Sheer-Thursday, the day before Good Friday; cf. Icel. skíra, to cleanse, baptize.

Sheer (2), to deviate from one's course. (Du.) Du. scheren, to shear, cut, with-

draw, go away; scheerje van hier, sheer off! (Sewel). Cf. Low G. schere hen, get out! See Shear.

Sheet. (E.) M. E. schete. Anglian scéte, A. S. scíete, scýte, a sheet; also (without mutation) scéat, scéata, a corner, nook, fold of a garment, corner of a sail, hence a sheet or rope fastened to a corner of a sail, called in A. S. scéat-líne (sheet-line). Cf. A. S. scéat, 2nd grade of scéotan, to shoot, hence to jut out. The orig. sense of sheet was 'projection,' hence 'corner,' &c.+Icel. skaut, corner, sheet of a sail; Swed. sköte, the lap; Du. schoot, shoot, sprig, sheet; Goth. skauts, hem of a garment; G. schooss, flap of a coat, lap, bosom. All from Teut. *skaut, 2nd grade of *skeutan-, to shoot; see Shoot.

Sheet-anchor, an anchor to be 'shot' out in emergency. (E.) From prov. E. sheet, M.E. schéten, A.S. scéotan, to shoot. See Shoot.

Sheik, a chief. (Arab.) Arab. sheikh, an elder, chief; orig. sense 'old.'

Shekel, a Jewish weight and coin. (Heb.) Heb. sheqel, a shekel (weight).—Heb. shāqal, to weigh.

Shekinah. (Heb.) It signifies the visible presence of God; lit. 'dwelling.'—Heb. shekanāh, dwelling.—Heb. shākan, to dwell.

Sheldrake. (E.) For sheld-drake, i.e. variegated or spotted drake. Cf. Orkney sheld-fowl, a sheldrake (Cent. Dict.). 'Sheld, flecked, party-coloured;' Coles (1684). M. E. sheld is a shield; and the allusion is to the patch round the breast. Cf. A. S. scild, a shield, used also of part of a bird's plumage (Grein). So also Icel. skjöldungr, a sheldrake, skjöldóttr, dappled, from skjöldr, a shield. See Shield.

Shelf. (E.) M. E. schelfe, shelfe. A. S. scilfe, story (of a building), shelf. Orig. a thin piece, flake; allied to shell and skill.+Low G. schelf, a board, shelf; cf. schelfern, to flake off; also E. Fries. schalfer, schilfer, a chip, splinter; Du. schilfer, a scale. Extended forms, from the root of Skill and Scale.

Shell. (E.) M. E. shelle, sb. A. S. scell, scyll. + Du. schel; Icel. skel; Goth. skalja, a tile. Teut. type *skaljā, fem. The sense is 'thin flake'; cf. Swed. skala, to peel. See Scale, Skill. Der. shell, verb.

Shelter. (E.) A curious development of M. E. sheldtrume, a body of guards or troops, a squadron; frequently spelt *shel-tron*, *sheltrun*; it came to mean a guard or protection of any kind (P. Plowm., Halliwell). ━ A. S. *scildtruma*, lit. 'shield-troop,' a guard. ━ A. S. *scild*, shield; *truma*, a band of men, allied to *trum*, firm. See **Shield** and **Trim**.

Shelve, to slope down. (E.) A derivative of *shelf*, but the connexion is not clear. A *shelf* came to mean a slab of stratified rocks, also a sand-bank; and the sense of 'slope' prob. refers to the sloping edges of the latter. Torriano translates M. Ital. *stralare* by 'to shelve or go aside, aslope, awry'; a sense perhaps suggested by M. Du. *scheel*, awry, G. *schel*, *scheel*.

Shepherd. (E.) A. S. *scēaphyrde*, a keeper of sheep; see **Herd** (2). **Der.** *shepherd-ess*.

Shorbet, a drink. (Arab.) Arab. *sharbat*, a drink, draught, sherbet, syrup. ━ Arab. root *shariba*, he drank. **Der.** *shrub* (2), *syrup*.

Sherd; see **Shard**.

Shere-Thursday; see **Sheer** (1).

Sheriff. (E.) For *shire-reeve*. A. S. *scīr-gerēfa*, a shire-reeve; see **Shire** and **Reeve**. **Der.** *sheriff-al-ty*, usually spelt *shrievalty*.

Sherry. (Span.━L.) Formerly *sherris*; *sh* being an old pron. of Span. *x*. ━ Span *Xeres*, a town in Spain, near Cadiz. ━ L. *Cæsaris*, gen. case of *Cæsar*, proper name (Dozy).

Shew; see **Show**.

Shibboleth, a test-word of pronunciation. (Heb.) Heb. *shibbōleth*, an ear of corn, also a river; see Judges xii. 6.

Shide, a thin piece of board. (E.) A. S. *scīd*, a billet of wood; from the base (**skeid*) of the verb *to shed*.+Icel. *skīð*, G. *scheit*, a billet; O. Irish *scīath*, a shield. See **Shed**, **Sheath**.

Shield. (E.) A. S. *scild*, *sceld*.+Du. *schild*, Icel. *skjöldr*, Dan. *skiöld*, Swed. *sköld*, Goth. *skildus*, G. *schild*. Teut. type **skelduz*, m. Perhaps 'thin board'; cf. Lith. *skel-ti*, to split.

Shieling; see **Sheal**.

Shift. (E.) M. E. *schiften*, to divide, change, shift, remove; orig. 'to divide.' A.S. *sciftan*, to divide. + Icel. *skipta* (for *skifta*), to divide, part, shift, change; Swed. *skifta*, Dan. *skifte*, the same. Allied to Icel. *skīfa*, to cut into slices, *skīfa*, a slice, prov. E. *shive*, a slice, *sheave*, a

wheel of a pulley, Du. *schijf*, G. *scheibe*, a slice, disc. See **Shiver** (2).

Shillelagh, an oaken stick used as a cudgel. (Irish.) Named from *Shillelagh*, a barony in Wicklow famous for oaks. It means 'descendants of Elach'; from Irish *siol*, seed, descendants.

Shilling. (E.) A. S. *scilling*. + Du. *schelling*; Icel. *skillingr*; Dan. Swed. *skilling*; Goth. *skilliggs* (for **skillings*); G. *schilling*. β. The suffix *-ing* is a diminutive which occurs also in E. *farthing*, and in A.S. *pen-ing*, a penny. The base is either **skel-*, to resound, ring; or **skil-*, to divide; see **Skill**. Reason for the name uncertain; but cf. Swed. *skiljemynt*, Dan. *skillemynt*, small change, small money.

Shillyshally. (E.) Formerly *shill I, shall I*; a reduplicated form of *shall I*.

Shimmer, to glimmer. (E.) A.S. *scimrian*, frequent. form of *scīman*, *scīmian*, to shine, allied to *scīnan*, to shine; see **Shine**.+Du. *schemeren*; Swed. *skimra*; G. *schimmern*. Cf. O. H. G. *scīmo*, a bright light, Icel. *skīmi*, a gleam, Irish *sgeimh*, *sgiamh*, beauty.

Shin. (E.) A. S. *scinu*; also *scin-bān*, shin-bone. + Du. *scheen*; G. *schiene*, also a splint; Swed. *sken-ben*, Dan. *skinne-been*, shin-bone. Orig. sense perhaps 'thinly covered bone,' and allied to **Skin** (Franck; doubtful). Cf. A.S. *scia*, shin.

Shine. (E.) A. S. *scīnan*, pt. t. *scān*, pp. *scinen*. + Du. *schijnen*, Icel. *skīna*; Dan. *skinne*; Swed. *skina*; Goth. *skeinan*; G. *scheinen*. (Base SKEI.) Cf. **Sheer** (1), **Shimmer**.

Shingle (1), a wooden tile. (L.) M.E. *shingle*, corruption of *shindle* (Minsheu), as shewn by the corresponding G. *schindel*, a shingle, splint, thin piece of wood. ━ L. *scindula*, a shingle, as if from L. *scindere*, to cleave; but really for *scandula*, a shingle.

Shingle (2), coarse round gravel on the sea-shore. (Scand.) Corruption of Norweg. *singl* or *singling*, coarse gravel, shingle, named from the crunching or ringing noise made by walking on it. ━ Norweg. *singla*, to ring, tinkle, Swed. dial. *singla* (the same); frequent. form of Swed. dial. *singa*, the same word as E. *sing*; see **Sing**. Cf. Lowl. Sc. *chingle*, shingle, allied to *chink*.

Shingles. (F. ━ L.) A variant of *sengles*, pl. of the old word *sengle*, a girth; the disease encircling the body like a belt.

— O. North. F. *chengle*, O. F. *cengle*, *sangle*, 'a girth, a sengle;' Cot. **— L.** *cingula*, a belt. **— L.** *cingere*, to surround; see **Cincture.**

Ship. (E.) A. S. *scip*. **+** Du. *schip*, Icel. *skip*, Dan. *skib*, Swed. *skepp*, Goth. *skip*, G. *schiff*. Teut. type **skipom*, neut. Hence *skiff*, *skipper*, *equip*.

Shire. (E.) A.S. *scir*, a shire, province; orig.' employment, government.' Cf. A.S. *scirian*, to appoint, allot; O. H. G. *scira*, business. ¶ Not allied to **Shear.**

Shirk. (F. — L. ?) The verb *to shirk* seems to be a variant of *sherk* or *shark*, to prowl about; hence, to act in a paltry way, to keep out of danger. See **Shark.**

Shirt. (E.) M. E. *shirte*, *shurte*. A.S. *scyrte*. — A. S. *scort*, short; see **Short.+** Icel. *skyrta*, a shirt, kind of kirtle; Swed. *skjorta*, Dan. *skiorte*. So called because *short*. Doublet, *skirt*.

Shittah - tree, Shittim - wood. (Heb.) *Shittim* is a pl. form. **—** Heb. *shittāh*, pl. *shittīm*, a kind of acacia (the *t* is *teth*). Of Egypt. origin (Gesenius).

Shive, Sheave; see **Shiver** (2).

Shiver (1), to tremble. (E.) Formerly *shever*, in Baret (1580); M. E. *chiueren*, *cheueren* (*chiveren*, *cheveren*), where *ch* stands for earlier *c(k)*, as if from an A. S. **cifer*, which I suppose to be a variant of *cwifer*. See **Quiver** (1). ¶ The spelling with *sh* was due to confusion with the word below.

Shiver (2), a splinter, small piece of wood. (E.) A *shiver* is a small piece; hence *to shiver*, to break in pieces. Again, *shiver* is the dimin. of *shive*, a thin slice, the same as prov. E. *sheave*, a thin disc of wood, wheel of a pulley. E. Fries. *schife*, *schive*, *schîf*', N. Fries. *skiv*, *skeev*. **+** Du. *schijf*; Icel. *skīfa*, Dan. *skive*, Swed. *skifva*; G. *scheibe*, a slice. Teut. base **skeib*, Idg. root **skeip*; whence Gk. σκοῖπος, a potter's disc (Hesychius). See **Shift.**

Shoal (1), a multitude of fishes, a troop, crowd. (E.) Spelt *shole* in Spenser; M. E. *scole*, a troop, throng, crowd. A. S. *scolu*, a troop.+O. Sax. *skola*, a troop, band; Du. *school*, a shoal. Teut. type **skulā*, fem.; from **skul-*, weak grade of **skel-*, to separate, set apart. See **Skill.** ¶ The sailor's phrase 'a *school* of fish' exhibits the Du. form of the same word; it also appears as *scull*, Troil. v. 5. 22.

Shoal (2), a shallow, a sandbank. (E.)

Orig. an adj., meaning 'shallow,' formerly *shole*; M.E. *shold* or *shald*; see **Shallow.** A.S. *sceald*, shallow; found in place-names. Cf. Pomeran. *scholl*, shallow water; and note E. *old*, prov. E. *ole*, from O. Merc. *ald*, A. S. *eald*.

Shoar, a prop; see **Shore** (2).

Shock (1), a violent jolt. (E.) M. E. *schokken*, to shock, jolt. E. Fries. *schokken*.+Du. *schok*, sb., *schokken*, vb. ; Low G. *schokken*, *schukken*, vb. ; O. H. G. *scoc*, sb. (whence F. *choc*, sb., *choquer*, vb.). Cf. G. *schaukel*, a swing. See **Shog.**

Shock (2), a pile of sheaves of corn. (E.) M. E. *schokke*.+M. Du. *schocke*, a shock, cock, heap; so called from being tossed together; from M. Du. *schocken*, to jolt, shock, cock, heap up; see **Shock** (1) above. Cf. Swed. *skock*, a heap, flock; Dan. dial. *skok*, N. Fries. *skock*, a heap of six sheaves.

Shock (3), a rough-coated dog. (E.) *Shock-headed* is rough-headed, with shaggy hair. Perhaps from **Shock** (2), a heap.

Shoddy, a material obtained from tearing into fibres old woollen goods. (E.) Etym. uncertain ; but cf. Devon *shod*, shed, spilt, M.E. *schoden*, *scheden*, to separate; see **Shed.**

Shoe. (E.) M. E. *scho*. A.S. *sceō*, *scōh*; pl. *sceōs*, *scōs*.+ Du. *schoen*; Icel. *skōr*; Swed. and Dan. *sko*; Goth. *skōhs*; G. *schuh*. Teut. type **skōhoz*, masc.

Shog, to jog on. (E.) M.E. *schoggen*, to jog; variant of *schokken*, to jolt. See **Shock** (1); and cf. **Jog.**

Shoot. (E.) A.S. *sceōtan*, later form of *scēotan*, str. vb. [with *eō* for *ēo* as in *choose*] ; pt. t. *scēat*, pp. *scoten*, of which only the pp. *shotten* is preserved (in the phrase *shotten herring* = a herring that has lost its roe).+Du. *schieten*; Icel. *skjóta*; Dan. *skyde*; Sw. *skjuta*; G. *schiessen*. Teut. type **skeutan-*, pt. t. **skaut*, pp. **skutanoz*. Brugm. i. § 623.

Shop. (E.) A.S. *sceoppa*, a stall, booth. Allied to *scypen*, a pen for cattle. **+** Low G. *schupp*, a shed; G. *schoppen*, a shed, covert (whence O. F. *eschoppe*, a shop).

Shore (1), strand of a lake or sea. (E.) M. E. *schore*. A.S. *score* (Somner); cf. A. S. *scoren clif*, a shorn cliff, precipice. Cf. A. S. *scor-*, weak grade of *sceran*, to shear. See **Shear.**

Shore (2), **Shoar,** a prop. (E.) M. E. *schore*. Not in A. S. E. Fries. *schōr*, *schore* (also *schār*, *schare*), a prop. Cf.

482

A. S. *sceorian*, to project, jut out. **+** Du. *schoor*, a prop; M. Du. *schooren*, to under-prop; Norweg. *skora*, prop. Cf. also Icel. *skorða*, a prop, stay, esp. under a boat; *skorða*, vb., to under-prop, shore up.

Shore (3), a sewer; see Sewer.

Short. (E.) A. S. *sceort*, short. Cf. Du. *schorten*, to lack (fall short), Icel. *skortr*, shortness, O. H. G. *scurz*, short. The Teut. base would appear to be **skert-*, to cut; as if extended from **sker-*, to cut; see Shear. Cf. also Icel. *skarðr*, diminished, cut down. ¶ But as the G. *kurz* is from L. *curtus*, short, it is usual to explain all these words as borrowed from a L. type **ex-curtus*; which is improbable.

Shot. (E.) M. E. *schot*. A. S. *scot*, a shot, *ge-sceot*, implements for shooting; cf. A. S. *scot-*, weak grade of *sceotan*, to shoot. **+** Icel. *skot*, Du. *schot*, a shot, shooting; G. *schuss*, a shot. See Shoot.

Shoulder. (E.) A. S. *sculder*, *sculdor*. **+** Du. *schouder*, Swed. *skuldra*, Dan. *skulder*, G. *schulter*. Perhaps allied to O. H. G. *skerti*, the shoulder; cf. also O. H. G. *harti*, the shoulder-blade.

Shout. (E.) M. E. *shouten*; Chaucer, Troil. ii. 614. Cf. Icel. *skúta*, *skúti*, a taunt; see Scout (2).

Shove. (E.) M. E. *shouven*. A. S. *scūfan*, pt. t. *scēaf*, pp. *scofen*, to shove. **+** Icel. *skúfa*; Du. *schuiven*, G. *schieben* (pt. t. *schob*) ; Goth. *skiuban*. Teut. type **skeuban-* or **skūban-*, pt. t. **skaub*, pp. **skubanuz*. Cf. Lith. *skubùs*, quick, hasty, industrious; Skt. *ksubh*, to become agitated, *kshobha-*, agitation. Brugm. i. § 992.

shovel. (E.) A. S. *scofl*, a shovel, for lifting and shoving; cf. A. S. *scof-*, weaker grade of *scūfan* (above). **+** Du. *schoffel*; G. *schaufel*, O. H. G. *skūvala*; a form which makes a connexion with *shove* doubtful. Der. *shovel-er*, a kind of duck.

Show, Shew. (E.) M. E. *schewen*, vb. A. S. *scēawian*, to see, behold; later, to make to see, point out, show. **+** Du. *schouwen*, Dan. *skue*, G. *schauen*, to behold. Cf. Goth. *us-skaws*, cautious, wakeful. Teut. base **skaw*, Idg. root **skau*; cf. Gk. θυο-σκόος, an inspector of an offering; also L. *cau-ēre*, to heed, *cau-tus*, watchful; Gk. κοέω, I observe; Skt. *kav-i-*, wise. From the same root we have *cautious*. Brugm. i. §§ 163, 639. Der. *sheen*, *scavenger*.

Shower. (E.) M. E. *schour*. A. S. *scūr*. **+** Du. *schoer*; Icel. *skúr*; Swed.

skur; Goth. *skūra*, a storm; G. *schauer*, O. H. G. *scūr*. Brugm. i. § 627.

Shred. (E.) M. E. *shrēde*, sb. A. S. *scrēade*. **+** M. Du. *schroode*, a shred (Kilian) : Pomeran. *schrood*. From Teut. **skraud*, 2nd grade of **skreud-* ; for which see Shroud.

Shrew, a scold. (E.) M. E. *shrewe*, adj., applied to both sexes, wicked, bad. A. S. *scrēawa*, a shrew-mouse, fabled to have a very venomous bite. Der. *shrew*, to curse, talk like a shrew; *be-shrew*.

shrewd, malicious, cunning. (E.) The old sense is 'malicious.' M. E. *schrewed*, accursed, depraved, hence malicious; pp. of *schrewen*, to curse, from the adj. *schrewe*, malicious, bad (above).

shrew-mouse, an animal like a mouse. (E.) A. S. *scrēawa*; see Shrew (above).

Shriek. (E.) A native form of *screech*; from M. E. *schriken*, to shriek. See Screech. Imitative; see Shrike.

Shrievalty ; see Sheriff.

Shrift, confession. (L.) A. S. *scrift*, confession, prescribed penance. Cf. A. S. *scrif-*, weak grade of *scrīfan*, to shrive, to impose a penance; ult. of L. origin; see Shrive. **+** Icel. *skript*, Swed. *skrift*, Dan. *skrifte*; Du. and G. *schrift*, writing. See Shrive.

Shrike, the butcher-bird. (E.) Cf. Westphalian *schrīk*, a shrike; Icel. *skrīkja*, a shrike, lit. 'shrieker,' from Icel. *skrīkja*, to titter, orig. to shriek, and allied to Icel. *skrækja*, to screech. See Shriek and Screech.

Shrill. (E.) M. E. *shril*; cf. Lowl. Scotch *skirl*, a shrill cry, *skirl*, to cry aloud. Cf. E. Fries. *schrel*, Low G. *schrell*, G. *schrill*, shrill; A. S. *scralletan*, to cry aloud ; Norweg. *skryla*, *skræla*, to cry shrilly. From Teut. root **skrel* (2nd grade **skral*), to cry aloud.

Shrimp. (E.) M. E. *shrimp*; cf. Lowl. Scotch *scrimp*, to straiten, *scrimpit*, dwarf-ish. A parallel form to *shrink*; cf. A. S. *scrimman*, to shrink ; Dan. dial. *skrimpe*, a lean cow. See the traces of O. Swed. *skrimpa*, strong verb, to contract, in mod. Swed. dialects (Rietz) ; and cf. M. H. G. *schrimpfen*, to shrink, G. *schrumpfen*, Dan. *skrumpen*, shrivelled ; Du. *schrompe*, a wrinkle. See Shrink.

Shrine. (L.) A. S. *scrīn*, a box. **-** L. *scrīnium*, chest, box.

Shrink. (E.) A. S. *scrincan*, pt. t.

scranc, pp. *scruncen*, to contract, shrivel up.+M. Du. *schrinken*, to shrink, grow smaller; Swed. *skrynka*, a wrinkle. Allied to **Shrimp, Shrug.**

Shrive; see **Shrove-tide.**

Shrivel. (E.) In Shak. An E. word. +Swed. dial. *skryvla*, to shrivel up, to wrinkle; *skryvla*, a wrinkle. Perhaps allied to Swed. *skroflig*, rough, and to G. *schroff*, rugged.

Shroud. (E.) A.S. *scrūd*, garment, clothing.+Icel. *skrūð*, ornament, shrouds of a ship; Dan. and Swed. *skrud*, dress, attire. Orig. a ' shred ' of stuff, a piece cut or torn off; cf. A.S. *scrēade* (= mod. E. *shred*). The Teut. base is **skreud*, to cut; the 2nd grade **skraud* appears in **Shred,** q. v. Cf. L. *scrūta*, broken bits? Der. *scroll.*

Shrove-tide, Shrove-Tuesday. (L. *and* E.) The time for *shrift* or confession. The sb. *shrove* is formed from *shrove*, 2nd grade of *shrive* (M.E. *schriuen*, pt. t. *schroof*).—A.S. *scrīfan*, to shrive, impose a penance, pt. t. *scrāf*, pp. *scrif-en* (whence *scrif-t*, shrift).+O. Fries. *skrīva* (pt. t. *skrēf*); O. Sax. *skrīban*, to write; Du. *schrijven* (pt. t. *schreef*); Dan. *skrive* (pt. t. *skrev*); Swed. *skrifva* (pt. t. *skref*); G. *schreiben* (pt. t. *schrieb*). Teut. type **skreiban-*, pt. t. **skraib*, pp. **skribanoz.* Conjugated as a genuine Teut. verb, but probably an early borrowing from Lat. *scrībere*, to write. See **Scribe.**

Shrub (1), a low dwarf tree. (E.) M.E. *schrob*. A.S. **scrob*, a shrub; whence *scrybb*, underwood. Cf. prov. E. *shruff*, light rubbish wood, *scroff*, refuse of wood; Norw. *skrubba*, the dwarf cornel; E. dial. *scrub*, underwood; Dan. dial. *skrub*, brushwood.

Shrub (2), a drink, chiefly made with rum. (Arab.) Arab. *shirb, shurb*, a drink. — Arab. root *shariba*, he drank. See **Sherbet.**

Shrug. (E.) M.E. *shruggen*, to shiver. The old sense was to shrink, shrink up. Cf. Dan. *skrugge, skrukke*, to stoop; Swed. dial. *skrukka, skrugga*, to huddle oneself together, allied to *skrinka*, to shrink, Norw. *skrukken*, shrunken. See **Shrink.**

Shudder. (E.) M.E. *schoderen, schuderen.* Low G. *schuddern*; Dan. dial. *skuddre*, to shudder. A frequentative verb. Cf. E. Fries. *schüdden*, to shake; O. Sax. *skuddian*, to shake; M. Du. *schudden*, to shake, tremble. Also G.

schütteln, to shake, frequent. of O. H. G. *skuttan.*

Shuffle. (E.) Frequentative of *shove.* E. Fries. *schuffeln*, to shuffle along, from *schufen*, to shove, push. Cf. *scuffle*, which is the frequentative of Swed. *skuffa*, to push, shove. See **Scuffle.**

Shun. (E.) M. E. *shunien, shonien.* A.S. *scunian*, to shun, avoid; orig. sense (perhaps) to hurry away, hasten. Cf. Icel. *skunda, skynda*, Swed. *skynda sig*, Dan. *skynde*, to hasten, hurry, speed. Der. *scoundrel, schooner.*

Shunt. (E.) Prov. E. *shunt*, to turn aside; M. E. *shunten*, to start aside, avoid. Perhaps allied to **Scuttle** (3).

Shut. (E.) M. E. *shutten, shitten.* A.S. *scyttan*, to shut; to fasten a door with a bolt (called a *shuttle*). We still say 'to *shoot* a bolt.' The A.S. *scyttan* is a weak verb; cf. *scut-*, weak grade of *scēotan*, to shoot.+Du. *schutten*, G. *schützen* (from the same grade). See **Shoot.**

shuttle. (E.) So called from being *shot* across the threads in weaving. M. E. *schitel*, also a bolt of a door; A.S. *scyttel*, a bolt. Formed, with suffix *-el* of the agent, from Teut. **skut=*A. S. *scut-*, weak grade of *scēotan*, to shoot.+Dan. *skytte, skyttel*, a shuttle; cf. Du. *schiet-spoel*, a shuttle, lit. ' shoot-spool.' **Der.** *shuttle-cock*; from its being *shot* backwards and forwards like a *shuttle*, and because furnished with feathers. ¶ Not for *shuttle-cork*.

Shuttle-cock; see above.

Shy. (E.) M. E. *shey, scheouh*, said of a shy horse.—A.S. *scēoh*, timid; cf. E. Fries. *schöi.*+Dan. *sky*, shy; Swed. *skygg*, skittish, shy, coy; Du. *schuw*, shy; G. *scheu*, timid, shy, M. H. G. *schiech.* Teut. type **skeuhoz.* See **Eschew.**

Si—Sy.

Siamang, a large ape. (Malay.) Malay *siāmang.*

Sib, related. (E.) A.S. *sibb*, akin to; see **Gossip.** Cf. M. Swed. *sif*, akin to.

Sibilant, hissing. (L.) L. *sībilant-*, stem of pres. part. of *sibilāre*, to hiss.—L. *sībilus*, hissing. Imitative.

Sibyl. (L. — Gk.) L. *Sibylla.* — Gk. Σίβυλλα, a Sibyl or prophetess.

Sicca, in phr. *sicca rupee*, newly coined rupee. (Hind. — Pers. — Arab.) Hind. *sikka*, a die for coining. — Pers. *sikka(h)*, the same. — Arab. *sikka*(*h*), *sakk*, the same. Rich. Dict., pp. 839, 837. Cf. **Sequin**.

Sick. (E.) M. E. *sik*, *sēk*. A. S. *sēoc*. +Du. *ziek*; Icel. *sjúkr*; Dan. *syg*; Swed. *sjuk*; G. *siech*; Goth. *siuks*, which is related to Goth. *siukan*, to be ill (pt. t. *sauk*). Teut. type **seukoz*.

Sicker, Siker, certain, secure. (L.) M. E. *siker*. Borrowed from Late L. *sécurus*, for L. *sēcūrus*, secure; whence also O. Fries. *siker*, *sikur*, Du. *zeker*, G. *sicher*, O. H. G. *sichur*, Swed. *säker*, Dan. *sikker*, W. *sicr*. See **Secure**.

Sickle. (L.) A. S. *sicol*. — L. *secula*, a sickle, cutter. — L. *sec-āre*, to cut. See **Secant**. Cf. **Scythe, Saw** (1).

Side. (E.) M. E. *side*. A. S. *sīde*, side; allied to A. S. *sīd*, long, wide. + Du. *zijde*; Icel. *sīða* (allied to Icel. *sīðr*, long, hanging down); Dan. *side*; Swed. *sida*; G. *seite*.

Sidereal, starry. (L.) For *sideral*, from L. *sīderālis*, relating to the stars. — L. *sīder-*, for **sīdes-*, stem of *sīdus*, a star. Cf. *con-sider*.

Sidesmen. (E.) Officers chosen to assist a churchwarden; also called *sidemen*, i.e. men at one's side. Cf. L. *assessor*, one who sits beside another.

Siege. (F. — L.) The orig. sense was 'seat,' or 'a sitting down,' esp. in order to besiege a town. — O. F. *siege*, a seat, throne; F. *siège*. Not immediately from L. *sedes*, but from a verb answering to a Lat. type **sedicāre*; cf. Late L. *assedium*, a siege, for L. *obsidium*, a siege; both words being due to L. *sedēre*, to sit; see **Sedentary**. Der. *be-siege*, with E. prefix.

Sienna, a pigment. (Ital.) Made from earth of *Sienna*, a place in Tuscany.

Sierra, a chain of hills. (Span. — L.) Span. *sierra*, a saw, an outline of hills. — L. *serra*, a saw.

Siesta, orig. a noon-day nap. (Span. — L.) Span. *siesta*, the hottest part of the day, the time for a nap, gen. from one to three o'clock. But orig. the sixth hour, or noon. — L. *sexta* (*hōra*), sixth hour, noon; fem. of *sextus*, sixth. — L. *sex*, six.

Sieve. (E.) M. E. *sive*. A. S. *sife*; oldest spelling *sibi* (8th cent.). + Du. *zeef*; G. *sieb*. Teut. types **sibiz*, **siboz*, neut.; cf. Lith. *sijote*, to sift.

sift. (E.) A. S. *siftan*, to sift; allied to A. S. *sife*, a sieve. + Du. *ziften*, to sift, *zift*, a sieve; *zeef*, a sieve.

Sigh, vb. (E.) M. E. *sighen*, also *syken*.

A. S. *sīcan*, to sigh, pt. t. *sāc* (in *on-sāc*), pp. *sicen*. Cf. Swed. *sucka*, Dan. *sukke*, to sigh, groan. Of imitative origin.

Sight. (E.) M. E. *sight*. A. S. *-siht*, *gesiht*, commonly *gesihð*. Verbal sb. allied to A. S. *sēon*, to see. + Du. *gezigt*; Dan. *sigte*; Swed. *sigt*; G. *sicht*. See **See**.

Sign. (F. — L.) O. F. *signe*. — L. *signum*, a mark. Der. *sign*, vb.; *sign-at-ure*, from the pp. of the L. verb *signāre*, to sign. Brugm. i. § 762 (3). Der. *sennet*.

signal. (F. — L.) F. *signal*. — Late L. *signāle*, sb., neut. of L. *signālis*, belonging to a sign. — L. *signum*, a sign.

signet. (F. — L.) F. *signet*; dimin. of F. *signe*; see **Sign** (above).

signify. (F. — L.) F. *signifier*, to betoken. — L. *significāre*, to shew by signs. — L. *signi-*, for *signum*, a sign; *-ficāre*, for *facere*, to make.

Signor. (Ital. — L.) Ital. *signore*, sir. — L. acc. *seniōrem*; see **Seignior**.

Silence. (F. — L.) F. *silence*. — L. *silentium*, silence. — L. *silent-*, stem of pres. pt. of *silēre*, to be silent. Cf. Goth. *ana-silan*, to be silent. Der. *silent*, from L. *silent-*, stem of *silens*, pres. pt. of *silēre*.

Silex, flint. (L.) L. *silex* (stem *silic-*), flint. Der. *silic-a*. Brugm. i. § 980.

Silhouette. (F.) This meagre form of portrait, made by tracing the outline of a shadow, was named (in derision) after Étienne de *Silhouette*, French minister of finance in 1759.

Silk. (Chinese?) A. S. *seolc*, *seoluc* (cf. *milk*, A. S. *meolc*); Icel. *silki*; Ch. Slav. *shelkŭ* (Russ. *shelk'*). Perhaps from Chinese *se*, *sei*, silk; cf. L. *Sēricum*, silk, neut. of *Sēricus*, adj., belonging to the *Sēres*; from Gk. Σῆρες, pl., Chinese. See **Serge**.

Sill, base of a door. (E.) A. S. *syll*, a base, support. + Icel. *syll*, *svill*, a sill; Swed. *syll*, Swed. dial. *svill*; Dan. *syld*; G. *schwelle*, sill, threshold. Cf. Goth. *ga-suljan*, to lay a foundation. The Teut. base appears to be **swel*, to found, to form as a base; weak grade **swal*, whence G. *schwelle*; the weak grade **swul*, **sul* gives Goth. *ga-suljan* and A. S. *syll*, f. (Teut. type **sul-jā*). Der. *ground-sill*, spelt *grunsel* in Milton, P. L. i. 460.

Sillabub, a mixture of wine with milk, &c. (E.) Formerly *sillibouk*, or *merribouk*. 'Laict aigre, a sillibub or merribowke;' Cot. Apparently from E. *silly* (merry) and M. E. *bouk*, A. S. *būc*, the belly. A jocose name.

Silly. (E.) Orig. 'timely;' then happy, lucky, blessed, innocent; lastly, simple, foolish. M. E. *seli, sili*; thus *syly man* in Seven Sages, ed. Wright, 1361 = *seli man* in Seven Sages, ed. Weber, 1473. A. S. *sǣlig, gesǣlig*, timely; from *sǣl*, time, season, happiness.+Du. *zalig*, G. *selig*, blest, happy; cf. also Icel. *sæll*, Swed. *säll*, Goth. *sēls*, good.

Silo, a pit for storing grain or fodder. (Span. — L. — Gk.) Span. *silo*. — L. *sīrum*, acc. of *sīrus*. — Gk. σῑρός. Der. *en-sil-age*.

Silt. (Scand.) 1. Either formed, with participial suffix *-t*, from *sile* (M. E. *silen*), to drain. — Swed. *sila*, to drain, strain, filter; *sil*, a filter. 2. Or from M. Swed. *sylta*, mud; Dan. *sylt*, a salt-marsh. From **sult-*, weak grade of *salt-*; see **Salt.**

Silvan, Sylvan. (L.) The spelling with *y* is bad. — L. *siluānus*, belonging to a wood. — L. *silua*, a wood. Cf. Gk. ὕλη, a wood (connexion with *silua* doubtful; Brugm. i. § 102).

Silver. (E.) O. Merc. *sylfur* (Matt. x. 9); A.S. *seolfor*; earlier *siolofr*.+Du. *zilver*; Icel. *silfr*; Dan. *sölv*; Swed. *silfver*; G. *silber*; Goth. *silubr*; Russ. *serebro*; Lith. *sidábras*.

Similar. (F. — L.) F. *similaire*; as if from L. **similāris*, extended from *similis*, like. Cf. O. Ir. *samail*, Ir. *samhail*, W. *hafal*, like. Allied to *simul*, together, and to E. **Same.** Brugm. i. §§ 438, 442.

simile. (L.) L. *simile*, a comparison, a like thing; neut. of *similis*, like.

similitude. (F. — L.) F. *similitude*. — L. acc. *similitūdinem*, likeness. — L. *similis*, like.

Simious, monkey-like. (L.) From L. *sīmia*, an ape. — L. *sīmus* (Gk. σιμός), flat-nosed.

Simmer. (E.) A frequentative form, from the base *sim*, to express the sound of gentle boiling. Cf. Dan. *summe*, G. *summen*, Swed. dial. *summa*, to hum, buzz.

Simnel, a kind of rich cake. (F. — L.) O. F. *simenel*; Late L. *simenellus, siminellus*, bread of fine flour; also called *simella* in Late L. — L. *simila*, wheat-flour of the finest quality; whence *siminellus*, for **similellus*. Allied to Gk. σεμίδαλις, fine flour. Cf. **Semolina.**

Simony, traffic in ecclesiastical preferment. (F. — L. — Gk. — Heb.) F. *simonie*; Late L. *simōnia*. Named from *Simon Magus* (Acts viii. 18). — Gk. Σίμων, Simon.

— Heb. *Shim'ōn*, Simeon; lit. 'hearkening.' — Heb. root *shāma'*, to hear.

Simoom. (Arab.) Arab. *samūm*, a sultry pestilential wind; from its poisonous nature. — Arab. root *samma*, he poisoned (Devic).

Simper, to smirk. (Scand.) From Scand.; cf. Norw. *semper*, fine, smart; Dan. dial. *semper, simper*, affected, coy, prudish; M. Swed. *semper*, one who affectedly refrains from eating; cf. Bavar. *zimpern*, to be affectedly coy (from Low G.). Formed from M. Swed. *sipp, simp*, an affected woman, Swed. *sipp*, adj., finical, prim. All from the notion of *sipping*, or taking only a little at a time; hence, prudish, affected, coy, &c. Cf. Low G. *sipp*, prim, *den Mund* sipp *trekken*, to make a small mouth; and M. Du. *sippen*, to sip. See note to **Sip.**

Simple. (F. — L.) F. *simple*. — L. *simplicem*, acc. of *simplex*, lit. ' one-fold.' — L. *sim-* (appearing also in *sin-guli*, one by one, *sem-el*, once, *sim-ul*, together) and *plic-*, from *plicāre*, to fold; see **Simulate** and **Ply.** Der. *simplicity*, F. *simplicité*, from L. acc. *simplicitātem*; *simpli-fy*, to make simple.

simpleton. (F. — L.) I. e. *simple-t-on*, with double suffix; formed with F. suffix *-on* from Picard and M. F. *simplet*, a simple person, fem. *simplette*, 'a simple wench;' Cot. — F. *simple*, simple; with suffixed *-t*. (So also *musk-et-oon*.) Cf. Span. *simplon*, a simpleton.

Simulate. (L.) From pp. of L. *simulāre*, also *similāre*, to make like. — L. *similis*, like; *simul*, together, lit. ' at once.' From Idg. **sem-*, one; cf. Goth. *sama*, f. (for **sm-ía*) ; Skt. *sa-kṛt*, once; Gk. ἅ-παξ, once; Brugm. ii. § 165.

simultaneous. (L.) Late L. *simultāneus*; coined from L. *simult-im*, at the same time. — L. *simul*, together.

Sin. (E.) A. S. *synn* (*sinn, senn*).+Du. *zonde*; Icel. *synd, synð*; Dan. Swed. *synd*; G. *sünde*, O. H. G. *suntea*. Thus the A. S. *synn* represents a Teut. type **sundjā*, fem., or rather an Idg. type **sṇtjā*; where **sṇt* is the weak grade of *sent: sont*. Allied to L. *sons* (stem *sont-*), guilty, sinful, orig. ' real.' [' Language regards the *guilty* man as the man *who it was*;' Curtius.] Cf. Ion. Gk. ἐ-οντ-, stem of ἐών (for **ἐσ-ων*), being, pres. pt. of εἰμί, I am. See **Sooth.** Der. *sin*, vb.

Since. (E.) Written for *sins*, which is short for M. E. *sithens*, since. This is formed, with adverbial suffix *-s*, from M. E. *sithen*, since, a modification of A. S. *siððan*, for *sið ðan*, after that. β. The A. S. *sið* was orig. an adj., meaning 'late,' but here represents the compar. adv., later, after; cf. Goth. *seithus*, late, *seithu*, adv., late, *-seiths*, adv., later. The A. S. *ðan* is the instrumental of the definite article or demonst. pronoun. The G. *seitdem*, since, is similarly formed. See Sievers, §§ 323, 337.

Sincere. (F.—L.) O. F. *sincere.*—L. *sincērus*, pure, sincere. **Der.** *sincerity*, from M. F. *sincerité*, from L. acc. *sincēritātem*.

Sinciput. (L.) The fore part of the head; lit. 'half head.'—L. *sinciput*, half the head.—L. *sēmi-*, half; and *caput*; see Semi- and Capital. Brugm. i. § 121.

Sinder, the true spelling of **Cinder**, q. v.

Sine. (L.) From L. *sinus*, a bosom, a fold, a curve; peculiarly used. See Sinus.

Sinecure. (L.) For *sine curā*, without cure of souls; hence, an office without work.

Sinew. (E.) M. E. *sinewe*. A. S. *sinu* (dat. *sinwe*), *seonu*.+Du. *zenuw*; Dan. *sene*; Swed. *sena*; G. *sehne*; also Icel. *sin*. Perhaps allied to Skt. *snāva(s)*, a tendon.

Sing. (E.) A. S. *singan*, orig. to sing, resound; pt. t. *sang*, pp. *sungen*. **Song**; and see singe. + Du. *zingen*; Icel. *syngja*; Dan. *synge*; Swed. *sjunga*; Goth. *siggwan* (for **singwan*); G. *singen*.

singe, to scorch. (E.) For *senge*; M. E. *sengen*. A. S. *sengan*, to singe; lit. ' to make to sing,' from the hissing of a burning log, &c. Causal of *singan*, to sing (above). + Du. *zengen*, G. *sengen*, causal verbs, similarly formed.

Single. (L.) L. *singulus*, single, separate, in Plautus and in late Latin; in classical Latin, we have only *singulī*, pl., one by one. Allied to **Simple**, q. v. Brugm. i. § 441. ¶ M.E. and O. F. *sengle*.

singular. (F.—L.) M.E. *singuler.*—F. *singulier.*—L. *singulāris*, single.—L. *singulī*, pl., one by one (above).

Sinister. (L.) L. *sinister*, on the left hand, inauspicious.

Sink. (E.) Properly intransitive [the transitive form should rather end in *-ch*; cf. *drench* from *drink*]. — A. S. *sincan*,

intrans., pt. t. *sanc*, pp. *suncen.*+Du. *zinken*; Icel. *sökkva* (for *sinkva*); Dan. *synke*; Swed. *sjunka*; Goth. *sinken*; Goth. *sigkwan* (for **singkwan*). β. For the trans. form, cf. A. S. *sencan*, to cause to sink, G. *senken*. **Der.** *sink*, orig. a place into which filth *sank* or was collected; Cor. i. 1. 126. Brugm. i. §§ 421(3), 677.

Sinople, green. (F.—L.—Gk.) F. *sinople*, ' green; ' Cot. — Late L. *sinōpis*, greenish, also reddish; L. *sinōpis*, red ochre. — Gk. σινωπίς, σινωπική, a red earth found in Cappadocia, and imported from *Sinope*, on the Black Sea.

Sinus, a bend, fold, &c. (L.) L. *sinus*, a bosom, bend, bay, fold. Now only used in anatomy, and, in the form *sine*, in mathematics. **Der.** *sinuous*, L. *sinuōsus*, full of curves.

Sip, vb. (E.) M. E. *sippen*. It answers to A. S. *sypian*, to absorb moisture, a causal form allied to A. S. *sūpan*, to sup. See Sup. ¶ In the E. Fries. *sippen*, to sip, M. Du. *sippen*, to sip, Norw. *sipla*, to sip, the *i* suggests a connexion with Low G. *sipen*, to drip; but cf. E. Fries. *süpken*, to sip, Swed. dial. *syppa*, to drink. **Der.** *sip*, sb.

Siphon. (F.—L.—Gk.) F. *siphon.*—L. *siphōnem*, acc. of *siphō*, a siphon, bent pipe for drawing off liquids. — Gk. σίφων, a small pipe or reed.

Sippet, a little sop. (E.) Dimin. of *sop*, with vowel-change (from Tcut. *u* to *y* > *i*). See Sop.

Sir, Sire. (F.—L.) *Sir* is short for *sire.* — F. *sire*, sir. — L. *senior*, older, elder; (the word *seignior* being from the acc. *seniōrem*). *Sire* is a variant of O. F. *senre* < L. *senior* (see Schwan).

Sirdar, a commander. (Pers.) Pers. *sardār*, a chief. — Pers. *sar*, head (cf. Gk. κάρα) ; *-dār*, possessing, holding.

Siren. (L.—Gk.) L. *sīrēn.*—Gk. σειρήν, a nymph who enticed seamen to destruction by her magic song.

Sirloin, Surloin. (F.—L.) M.E. *surloyn*; XV cent. — O. F. *surlonge* (14th cent.), the surloin. — F. *sur*, upon, above (from L. *super*); *longe*, loin ; see Loin. ¶ The story about turning the *loin* into *sir-loin* by knighting it is mere trash.

Sirname, for **Surname**, q. v.

Sirocco, a hot wind. (Ital.—Arab.) Ital. *sirocco*, south-east wind. — Arab. *sharq*, east (Devic). See Saracen.

Sirrah. (Prov.—L.) *Sirra* (Minsheu)·

serrha (Levins). A contemptuous pronunciation of the F. *sire* by the men of Provence, who called it *sira.*—O. F. *sire*, Prov. *sira*, sir.—L. *senior*; see Sir.

Sir-reverence. (L.) Short for *save-reverence*, a translation of L. *saluâ reuerentiâ*, i. e. reverence to you being preserved, or, by your leave.—L. *saluâ*, abl. fem. of *saluus*, safe; and *reuerentiâ*, abl. of *reuerentia.*

Sirup; see Syrup.

Siskin, a song-bird. (Low G.—Slavonic.) Low G. *zieske, ziseke*, a siskin; Du. *sijsje*, where the dimin. suffix *-je* answers to an older suffix *-ken*, so that *sijsje* implies an older form *sijsken*. Cf. Dan. *sisgen*, a siskin; Swed. *siska*. Of Slavonic origin. — Polish *czyžik*, dimin. form of *czyž*, a siskin; Sloven. *chizhek*; Russ. *chij'*. See Miklosich, p. 36.

Sister. (E.) A. S. *sweostor, swuster*; M. E. *suster*; affected by Icel. *systir.*+Du. *zuster*; Icel. *systir*, Swed. *syster*, Dan. *söster*, Goth. *swistar*; G. *schwester*. Further allied to L. *soror* (for **swesor*); O. Ir. *siur*, W. *chwaer*, Lith. *sesů*; Skt. *svasar-*. Brugm. ii. § 122. Der. *cousin*, q. v.

Sit. (E.) A. S. *sittan*, pt. t. *sæt*, pp. *seten.*+Du. *zitten*; Icel. *sitja*; Dan. *sidde*; Swed. *sitta*; G. *sitzen*. Teut. type **setjan-*, pt. t. **sat*, pp. **setanoz*. Further allied to Goth. *sitan*; W. *seddu*; L. *sedêre*; Gk. ἕζομαι, I sit; Skt. *sad*. See Sedentary. (√SED.) Der. *set*.

Site. (F.—L.) F. *site*; M. F. *sit.*—L. *situm*, acc. of *situs*, a site, place.—L. *situs*, pp. of *sinere*, to let, suffer, permit; the orig. sense seems to have been to place. Hence Position, q. v. But see Brugm. i. § 920.

Sith, since. (E.) Short for M. E. *sithen*; see Since.

Situate. (L.) Late L. *situātus*, pp. of *situāre*, to place.—L. *situ-*, for *situs*, a place. See Site.

Six. (E.) A. S. *six.*+Icel., Dan., and Swed. *sex*; G. *sechs*; Goth. *saihs*; Russ. *sheste*; W. *chwech*; Gael. and Irish *se*; L. *sex*; Gk. ἕξ; Lith. *szeszi*; Pers. *shash*; Skt. *shash*. See Brugm. ii. § 170. Der. *six-th*, M. E. *sixte*, A. S. *six-ta*; *six-ty*, A. S. *sixtig*. See Sexagenarian.

Sizar, a student admitted at lower fees, at Cambridge, than a pensioner. (F.—L.) Named from *size*, formerly a farthing's-worth of bread or drink (Blount). *Size* is short for *assize*, an allowance of provisions; see Assize (1). See below.

Size (1), an allowance of food; also magnitude. (F.—L.) Short for *assize*; see Assize (1).

Size (2), weak glue. (Ital.—L.) Ital. *sisa*, 'syse or glew;' Florio. Short for *assisa*, size. So called from making colours lie flat.—M. Ital. *assisare*, 'to sute [suit] well;' Florio. —Ital. *assiso*, pp. of *assidere*, to sit; also, to situate.—L. *assidēre*, lit. to sit near.—L. *as-* (for *ad*), near; *sedēre*, to sit. See Sit.

Skain, Skene, Skean, Skein, a dagger, knife. (Irish.) Irish and Gael. *sgian*, a knife; O. Irish *scîan*; W. *ysgien*, a cutting instrument. Cf. W. *ysgi*, a cutting off; Gk. σχάειν, to slit.

Skate (1), a large flat fish. (Scand.) M. E. *scate.*—Icel. *skata*; Norw. *skata*. Cf. L. *squātus*, a skate (Pliny); also Irish *sgat*, a skate (from E.)

Skate (2), **Scate,** a frame with a steel blade, for sliding on ice. (Du.—F.—Low G.) Properly *skates*; the *s* being dropped because *skates* looked like a pl. form. [Cf. *scatches* (another form of *skateses*), pl., but usually meaning 'stilts').] —Du. *schaatsen*, skates, a pl. form, from a sing. *schaats*, whence *schaatsryder*, a skate-rider, skater (Sewel); M. Du. *skaetsen*, pl. —O. North. F. *escache*, Picard form of O.F. *eschace*, a stilt (12th cent.); whence F. *échasse*. [So also M. Du. *kaetsen*, lit. ' to catch;' from Picard *cacher*, for O. F. *chacer*.]—Low G. *schake*, a shank, leg. Thus *scatches* or *skates* are 'shanks,' contrivances for lengthening the stride; cf. F. *échasse*, a stilt, as above.

Skein, Skain, a knot (or quantity) of thread or silk. (F.—C.?) M. E. *skeyne*; a quantity of yarn.—M.F. *escaigne*, 'a skain;' Cot.; F. *écagne*. Perhaps of Celtic origin; cf. Gael. *sgeinnidh*, flax, thread (unless this is from E.). Der. (probably) *skainsmates*, companions (Shak.), as if associated in winding yarn; but cf. Skain.

Skeleton. (Gk.) Gk. σκελετόν, a dried body; neut. of σκελετός, dried. — Gk. σκέλλειν, to dry, parch.

Skellum, a cheat. (Du.) See Nares. Du. *schelm*, a rogue, villain; the Du. *sch* being rendered (as in *landscape*) by *sk*=*sc*. +G. *schelm*; O. H. G. *scelmo*, a pestilence, carrion, worthless rogue.

Skeptic; see Sceptic.

Skerry, a rock surrounded by sea. (Scand.) From Icel. *sker*, a skerry; see Scar (2).

Sketch. (Du.—Ital.—L.—Gk.) Du. *schets*, a draught, sketch.—Ital. *schizzo*, a first rough draught.—L. *schedium*, a thing made hastily; from *schedius*, adj., hastily made. — Gk. σχέδιος, sudden; allied to σχεδόν, near; from the base σχε-, to hold. Allied to **Scheme**.

Skew. (O. Low G.) M. E. *skewen*, verb, to turn aside.—M. Du. *schuwen*, *schouwen*, to avoid, shun; Low G. *schuwen*, *schouen*, to avoid. +O. H. G. *sciuhen*, G. *scheuen*, to avoid; from *scheu*, adj., shy. Thus *to skew* is to turn aside, like a shying horse, and is derived from the adj. appearing in E. *shy*. See **Shy**. **Der.** *askew*, i. e. *on the skew*.

Skewbald, piebald. (O. Low G. *and* C.) Marked in a *skew* or irregular manner; see **Bald**. Cf. *pie-bald*. ¶ We find, however, M. E. *skewed*, pie-bald; perhaps from M. E. *skewes* (blotches?), used as the pl. of *sky*, a cloud. If so, there is no connexion with **Skew** (above).

Skewer. (Doubtful.) Formerly *skuer* (A. D. 1411). Etym. unknown. ¶ Prov. E. *shiver*, a skewer, is the Scand. form answering to E. *shiver*, a small piece; cf. Dan. dial. *skivrt*, small sticks for fuel. See **Shiver** (2).

Skid. (Scand.) Orig. a thin slip of wood, to put under a wheel.—Norw. *skida*, a thin plank; cf. Icel. *skíð*, a billet of wood; see **Shide**.

Skiff. (F.—Ital.—G.) M. F. *esquif*, 'a skiffe;' Cot.—Ital. *schifo.*—M. H. G. *skif*, G. *schiff*, a ship; see **Ship**.

Skill, discernment, tact. (Scand.) M.E. *skil*, often in the sense of 'reason.'—Icel. *skil*, a distinction; cf. *skilja*, to part, separate, distinguish; Dan. *skiel*, Swed. *skäl*, reason; Dan. *skille*, Swed. *skilja*, to separate. Allied to Lith. *skelti*, to cleave; Swed. *skala*, to peel. From Teut. root **skel*; see **Scale** (1). **Der.** *skill*, vb., as in phr. 'it *skills* not,' i. e. makes no difference; from Icel. *skilja*, often used impersonally, with the sense 'it differs.'

Skillet, a small pot. (Scand.) Formerly *skellet*. A dimin., with F. suffix *-et*, of M. E. *skele* (prov. E. *skeel*), a milk-pail; Cath. Angl.—Icel. *skjóla*, a pail, bucket.

Skim, to take off scum. (Scand.) Dan. *skumme*, Swed. *skumma*, to skim; from *skum*, scum. The E. verb preserves an old vowel-change from *u* to *y*, later *i*; cf. *fill* from *full*. And cf. Dan. dial. *skimmel*,

a thin film on milk; E. Fries. *schümen*, to skim.

Skin. (Scand.) Icel. *skinn*, Swed. *skinn*, Dan. *skind*, skin. Cf. G. *schinden*, to skin, flay; also W. *cen*, skin, *ysgen*, dandriff.

Skink, to serve out wine. (Scand.) M. E. *skenken*; [also *schenken*, from A. S. *scencan*, to pour out; orig. to draw off through a pipe; from A.S. *scanc*, a shank, shank-bone, hollow bone (hence, a pipe)]. — Icel. *skenkja*, Dan. *skienke*. + Du. *schenken*, G. *schenken*, to skink. Teut. type **skankjan*-; from **skank*-, a shank, pipe of bone. See **Nunchion**.

Skip. (Scand.) M. E. *skippen*; also *skeppen* (Cursor Mundi). Cf. Swed. dial. *skopa*, to skip, leap (as animals), to dance; M. Swed. *skuppa*, *skoppa*, Rietz.; Icel. *skoppa*, to spin like a top. And cf. M. H. G. *sciuften*, to gallop. (The E. *i* is for *y*, mutation of *u*.) Cf. Mid. Dan. *skobe*, to dance, to skip.

Skipper. (Du.) Du. *schipper*, a mariner.—Du. *schip*, a ship; cognate with E. *ship*; see **Ship**.

Skirmish. (F.—O.H.G.) Also spelt *scrimmage*. M. E. *scarmishe*, sb., from *scarmishen*, vb.—O. F. *eskermiss*-, a stem of *eskermir*, to fence, fight. [Cf. M. F. *escarmouche*, 'a skirmish, bickering;' Cot.] —O. H. G. *skermen*, to defend, fight, also *scirman*. — O. H. G. *scirm* (G. *schirm*), a shield, screen, shelter, guard, defence. To *skirmish* is, properly, to fight behind cover, hence to advance, under shelter, to fight. β. Note also O. F. *eskermisor*, *escremisseor*, a fencer; *escremissement*, fencing.

Skirr, Scur, to scour a country. (F. —L.) Variants of **Scour** (2). Cf. M. E. *scurrour*, a scout.

Skirret, the water-parsnip. (Scand.) M. E. *skirwit*; older form *shirwhit*. As if 'sheer white,' from the colour of the root; from Icel. *skirr*, sheer, bright; *hvítr*, white. Prob. a popular form, and perverted from O. F. *eschervis* (M. F. *chervi*), a skirret.— Span. *chirivia*.—Arab. *karawiá*, *karwiá*; whence also **Carraway**.

Skirt. (Scand.) M. E. *skyrt*. — Icel. *skyrta*, a shirt, kind of kirtle; see **Shirt**. A doublet of *shirt*, but restricted to the lower part of a garment.

Skittish. (Scand.) From Lowl. Scotch *skit*, to flounce, caper about. This is a secondary verb, of Scand. origin, from the verb *to shoot*.—Swed. dial. *skutta*, *skötta*, to leap about; cf. *skut*, weak grade of Swed. *skjuta*, to shoot. 2. Note Swed. *skytt*, Icel. *skyti*, a marksman; whence the verb *to skit* in the sense to aim at or reflect upon a person, and the sb. *skit*, an oblique taunt. See **Shoot.**

skittles, a game. (Scand.) Formerly *skittle-pins*; so called because *shot* at by a *skittle* or projectile. — Dan. *skyttel*, a shuttle; Icel. *skutill*, a projectile, harpoon, bolt of a door. Cf. Icel. *skut-*, weak grade of *skjóta*, to shoot; see **Shoot.**

Skua, a gull, bird. (Scand.) Icel. *skúfr*, *skúmr*, the skua, or brown gull. Prob. from the colour. Cf. Icel. *skúmi*, dusk; Swed. and Norweg. *skum*, dusky, dull (of the weather), dusky (in colour); cf. **Sky.**

Skulk; see **Sculk.**

Skull; see **Scull.**

Skunk, a quadruped. (N. American Indian.) Said to be from the Abenaki *segongw*, a skunk; this is a dialect of Algonquin (Lower Canada).

Sky. (Scand.) M. E. *skye*, a cloud.— Icel. *ský*, a cloud; Dan. Swed. *sky*, a cloud. Allied to A. S. *scéo*, O. Sax. *scio*, a cloud; A. S. *scúa*, shade; Skt. *sku*, to cover. (✓SKEU.)

Slab (1), a thin slip of timber or stone. (F. — Teut.) M. E. *slab*, *slabbe*. Apparently a weakened form of prov. E. *slap*, a slab (Halliwell). — O. F. *esclape*, 'éclat; de menues *esclapes* de bois,' i. e. thin slabs of wood; Godefroy. Prob. of Teut. origin. (Wedgwood cites ' Languedoc *esclapa*, to split wood, *bos esclapa*, split logs, *esclapo*, a slab of wood or stone.') Cf. Ital. *schiappare*, to split. Perhaps from the prefix *es*- (L. *ex*), and Low G. *klappen*, to clap, make an explosive sound. (Körting, § 5453.)

Slab (2), slimy. (Scand.) The same as M. Dan. *slab*, slippery; also, mire. Prov. E. *slab*, a puddle; cf. Norw. *slabb*, filth; Irish *slab*, *slaib*, Gael. *slaib*, mire, mud. Also M. E. *slabben*, to wallow; E. Fries. *slabben*, Du. *slabben*, to lap up; Swed. dial. *slabba*, to splash, to soil. And see **Slabber** below.

Slabber, to slaver. (E.) M. E. *slaberen*, frequent. of M. E. *slabben*, to wallow (above).+E. Fries. *slabbern*, to lap, sup, or lick up; Low G. *slabbern*, *slubbern*, to slabber, lap, sip, frequent. of *slabben*, to lap; G. *schlabbern*, *schlabben*, to lap, to slabber. Cf. prov. E. *slap*, to lick up food, eat quickly; Dan. dial. *slabbe*, *slappe*, to

lap up. Of imitative origin: cf. *slobber*, *slubber*. See **Slaver.**

Slack. (E.) M. E. *slak*. A. S. *slæc*, *sleac*, slack, slow.+Icel. *slakr*; Swed. Dan. *slak*; prov. G. *schlak*, slack, loose. Teut. type **slakoz*. Orig. sense 'fluid'; see below. Allied to **Lax;** Brugm. i. § 193.

slag, dross, scoria. (Swed.) Swed. *slagg*, dross of metal; so called from flowing over when fused; Norw. *slagga*, to flow over. Cf. Icel. *slagna*, to flow over, *slag*, *slagi*, wet, damp, water penetrating walls. It is a variant of *slack*, as seen by G. *schlacke*, ' dross, slacks, sediment,' Flügel; *schlackern*, to trickle, *schlack*, slack, drossy, sloppy; Low G. *slakke*, slag.

slake, to slacken, quench, wet. (E.) A. S. *slacian*, to grow slack; cf. prov. E. *sleck*, to quench, A. S. *sleccan*, to grow slack (hence, to make slack, slacken).— A. S. *sleac*, slack; see **Slack.**+Icel. *slökva* (pp. *slokinn*), to slake; Swed. *släcka*, to quench, allay, slake, from *slak*, adj.

Slade, a valley. (E.) M. E. *slad(e)*. A. S. *slæd*. + Westphal. *slade*, a ravine; Dan. dial. *slade*, a flat piece of land.

Slag, Slake; see **Slack.**

Slam. (Scand.) Norweg. *slemba*, *slemma*, to smack, bang, slam a door; Swed. dial. *slämma*,to push hastily; Icel. *slamra*, to slam. Cf. Swed. *slammer*, a noise. Allied to **Slap.** Of imitative origin.

Slander,scandal. (F. — L. — Gk.) M. E. *sclandre*, *sclaundre*. — O. F. *esclandre*, scandal. The oldest O. F. form was *escandle*, whence *escandre*, and finally *esclandre*,with inserted *l*. It is merely another form of **Scandal,** q. v.

Slang, vulgar language. (Scand.) Norweg. *sleng*, a slinging, a device, a burthen of a song, *slengja*, to sling, *slengja kjeften*, to slang, abuse (lit. 'to sling the jaw'), *slengjenamn*, a slang-name, *slengjeord*, a slang word, insulting word. All from *slengja*, to sling, causal form from the 2nd grade of the Icel. *slyngva*, to sling. See **Sling.**

Slant, to slope. (Scand.) M. E. *slenten*, to slope, glide. — Swed. dial. *slenta*, *slänta*, causal of *slinta* (pt. t. *slant*), to slide, slip with the foot; Swed. *slinta*, to slip, glance aside. The E. adj. *slant*, sloping, answers to Swed. dial. *slant*, slippery. **Der.** *a-slant*, i. e. *on the slant*.

Slap. (E.) M. E. *slappe*, a smart blow; an imitative word; allied to **Slam.**+Low

G. *slapp*, sound of a blow, a slap ; G. *schlapp*, interj., slap ! *schlappe*, sb., a slap, *schlappen*, to slap. **Der.** *slap-bang*, violently ; *slap-dash*, off hand.

Slash. (F. — Teut.) [Lowl. Sc. *slash*, to work in wet, is from Swed. *slaska*, Dan. *slaske*, to dabble in water.] The sense 'to cut' appears in '*slish* and *slash*,' i. e. much cutting ; Tam. Shrew, iv. 3. 90. — O. F. *esclachier*, to break in pieces. — O. F. *es-* (L. *ex*), very ; and Teut. type **klakjan*, M. H. G. *klecken*, to break with a *clack* ; cf. F. *claque*, a clack, M. H. G. *klac*. (Körting, § 4541.)

Slat, a thin bar of wood. (F. — Teut.) M. E. *slat*, a slate ; see below. ¶ Hardly from Gael. and Irish *slat*, a rod, twig ; though these are related to *lath*.

Slate (1), a flake of stone. (F. — Teut.) M. E. *slat*, *sclat*. — O. F. *esclat*, a splinter, slice of wood, &c. (hence, a thin slice of slate). — O. F. *esclater*, to split, burst, shiver. This answers to a Late L. type **exclapitāre*, to break with a clap ; from L. *ex*, and Low G. *klapp*, a clap, loud noise. (Körting, § 4543.) ¶ The *a* in *slate* was orig. short.

Slate (2), to bait, ridicule, criticise sharply, abuse. (E.) M. E. *sleten* ; A.S. *slǣtan*, to bait, set dogs on (an animal) ; causal vb. from *slītan*, to slit, tear, rend ; see **Slit**.

Slattern, an untidy woman. (Scand.) From prov. E. *slutter*, to waste, to be untidy, to throw about ; frequent. of *slat*, to dash or throw about. — Icel. *sletta*, to slap, dab, dash liquids about ; Norweg. *sletta*, to fling about, jerk ; Icel. *sletta*, sb., a dab, spot of ink. Allied to which are Dan. *slat*, a slop ; *slat*, *slatten*, *slattet*, loose, flabby ; *slattes*, to become slack ; *slatte*, a slattern ; Low G. *slatje*, a slattern. ¶ *Slut* is quite distinct.

Slaughter, sb. (Scand.) M. E. *slaghter*. — Icel. *slātr*, slaughter, whence *slātra*, to slaughter cattle ; cf. Noreen, § 224. The A. S. word is -*sleaht*, whence M. E. *slaught*. ✛ Du. Swed. *slagt*, G. *schlacht* (Teut. type **slah-tā*). All from **slah*, the base of **Slay**, q. v.

Slave. (F. — L. — Gk. — Slavonic.) F. *esclave*. — Late L. *sclavus*, a Slavonian captive, a slave. — Late Gk. Ἐσκλαβηνός, the same. The origin of *Slavon-ian* is unknown ; Miklosich, p. 308.

Slaver, to slabber. (Scand.) Icel. *slafra*, to slaver ; cognate with Low G.

slabbern, to slabber. See **Slabber**. **Der.** *slaver*, sb., from Icel. *slafr*, *slefa*, slaver.

Slay (1), to kill. (E.) The form *slay* is due to the pp. *slai-n* ; else, the infin. would have been *slee*. Orig. to smite. M. E. *sleen*. — A. S. *slēan* (contracted form of **slahan*), to smite, pt. t. *slōh*, pp. *slegen* (whence M. E. *slein*, E. *slain*). ✛ Du. *slaan* ; Icel. *slā* ; Dan. *slaae* ; Swed. *slå* ; Goth. *slahan* ; G. *schlagen*. Teut. type **slahan-* ; cf. O. Irish *slig-im*, I strike.

slay (2), **sley**, a weaver's reed. (E.) A. S. *slahæ* ; see *sleahe* in A. S. Dict. ; orig. form **slæge*, gen. **slagan* ; Camb. Phil. Trans. 1899, p. 139 (231). So called from *striking* the web together. — A. S. *slēan* (<**slahan*), to strike ; see **Slay** (1).

Sleave, Sleave-silk, soft floss silk. (Low G.) 'Ravelled *sleave*,' i. e. tangled loose silk. Cf. Dan. dial. *slöve*, a knot, twist, tangle (in thread). — E. Fries. *slöve*, *slöfe*, a bow-knot, a noose ; G. dial. *schlaüfe* (G. *schleife*). From **Slip**.

Sled, a sledge. (Du.) M. E. *slede*. — M. Du. *sledde* (Du. *slede*). ✛ Icel. *sleði*, Dan. *slæde*, Swed. *släde*, a sledge ; G. *schlitten*, a sledge. From the weak grade of the verb *to slide* ; see **Slide**.

sledge. (Du.) This is a corrupt form, apparently due to *sleds*, pl. of *sled*.

Sledge-hammer. (E.) A reduplicated form ; a *sledge* means 'a hammer.' — A. S. *slecg*, dat. *slecge*, a heavy hammer, smiter. For Teut. type **slag-jā*, fem. ; from **slag*, for **slah*, base of A. S. *slēan*, to smite. ✛ Du. *slegge*, *slei*, Swed. *slägga*, Icel. *sleggja*, a sledge or heavy hammer. See **Slay** (1).

Sleek, Slick, smooth, glossy. (E.) M. E. *slike*. ✛ Icel. *slíkr*, sleek, smooth. Allied to Du. *slijk*, North Fries. *slick*, E. Fries. *slīk*, slime ; G. *schlick*, grease ; cf. the Low G. strong verb *sliken* (pt. t. *sleek*, pp. *sleken*) = G. *schleichen* (pt. t. *schlich*), to slink, crawl, move as if through mire ; see **Slink**. The Teut. type of the verb is **sleikan-*, pt. t. **slaik*, pp. **slikanoz*. Orig. sense 'greasy,' like soft mud.

Sleep, vb. (E.) A. S. *slǣpan*, *slēpan*, pt. t. *slép*. ✛ Du. *slapen* ; G. *schlafen*, to sleep. The sb. is A. S. *slǣp*, Du. *slaap*, Goth. *slēps*, G. *schlaf*, O. H. G. *slāf*, orig. 'drowsiness ;' allied to Low G. *slapp*, G. *schlaff*, lax, loose, flabby, unbent, relaxed (as in sleep). Teut. type **slēpan-*, redupl. vb. Allied to L. *lābī*, to glide ;

Russ. *slabuii*, weak, slack. Cf. E. *sleepy*,
i. e. inactive.

sleeper, a block of wood under rails;
from the vb. above. (E.) Cf. F. *dormant*, a
sleeper; from *dormir*, to sleep.

Sleet. (E.) M. E. *sleet*. From O.
Merc. *slēte, A. S. *slȳte, not found. Cf. E.
Fries. *slaite*, hail; Low G. *sloten*, pl. hailstones (Lübben); G. *schlosse*, hailstone.
From Teut. type **slauti-*; orig. sense unknown. Cf. also Dan. *slud*, sleet. ¶ Norw.
sletta, sleet, seems to be unrelated.

Sleeve. (E.) O. Merc. *slēf*, a sleeve;
A. S. *slȳf*.+M. Du. *sleve*, a sleeve; N.
Fries. *slief*; cf. M. Du. *sloove*, a veil, cover;
Du. *sloof*, an apron; Low G. *sluwe*, a husk,
shell. From Teut. root *sleub; variant form
of *sleup, whence M. H. G. *sloufe*, a cover,
allied to M. H. G. *sloufen*, to let slip, cover.
Cf. Goth. *sliupan* (pt. t. *slaup*, pp. *slupans*), to slip, creep into. It is thus allied
to *slip*, from the *slipping* of the sleeve on
and off, in dressing and undressing. See
Slip, and Slop (2).

Sleigh. (Du.) An ill-spelt word;
there is no final guttural. — Du. *slee*, short
for *slede*, a sledge; cf. Du. *sleekoets*, for
sledekoets, lit. 'a sledge-coach.' Cf. Norw.
slee, for *slede*, a sledge; see Sled.

Sleight, dexterity. (Scand.) For
sleighth; M. E. *sleighthe*. — Icel. *slægð*, sly-
ness, cunning. — Icel. *slægr*, sly. So also
Swed. *slöjd*, dexterity, from *slög*, dexterous.
See Sly, Sloid.

Slender, thin, feeble. (F. — O. Low G.)
M. E. *sclendre*, *slendre*. — O. F. *esclendre*,
'sklendre;' Palsgrave, p. 323. — M. Du.
slinder, slender, thin; as sb., a water-
snake, named from its gliding or trailing.
— M. Du. *slinderen*, also *slidderen*, to drag,
train along, trail; Low G. *slindern*, to
slide on the ice (whence Low G. *slender*,
a trailing gown). Nasalised forms from
the verb *to slide*. Cf. O. H. G. *slintan* in
Schade.

Sleuth - hound, a slot-hound; see
Slot (2).

Slice, sb. (F. — O. H. G.) M. E. *slice*,
sclice. — O. F. *esclice*, a splinter, shiver,
piece of split wood. — O. F. *esclicir*, to slit
(whence E. *slice*, vb.). — O. H. G. *slitjan,
slizzen, related to *sclīzan*, *slīzan*, to slit,
shiver (whence O. F. *esclier*, to shiver),
cognate with E. *slit*; see Slit.

Slick; see Sleek.

Slide, vb. (E.) A. S. *slīdan*, pt. t. *slād*,
pp. *sliden*. Cf. also A. S. *slidor*, slippery;

O. H. G. *slītan*, to slide, G. *schlitten*, a
sledge. Also Lith. *slidus*, slippery.

Slight, adj. (O. Low G.) M. E. *slight*,
orig. sense even or flat; then plain, smooth,
simple, trivial, &c. — M. Du. *slicht*, even,
plain, *slecht*, slight, simple, vile; cf.
slichten, 'to slight, to make even or plaine,'
Hexham; O. Low G. *slight*, even, simple,
bad.+Icel. *slēttr*, flat, smooth, trivial;
Dan. *slet*, level, bad; Swed. *slät*, smooth,
worthless, slight; Goth. *slaihts*, smooth;
G. *schlecht*, bad, *schlicht*, smooth, plain,
homely; O. H. G. *sleht*, smooth. Teut.
type *slehtoz, smooth. Root unknown.

Slim. (Du.) Orig. sense 'oblique';
thence weak, poor, thin, bad, slight; prov.
E. *slim*, crafty. — M. Du. *slim*, awry, crafty.
+ G. *schlimm*, bad, cunning; M. H. G.
slimp, oblique, slanting, awry; Dan. Swed.
slem, worthless; Icel. *slæmr*, vile.

Slime. (E.) A. S. *slīm*.+Du. *slijm*;
Icel. *slīm*; Swed. *slem*; Dan. *sliim*; G.
schleim. Cf. L. *līmus*, mud.

Sling, vb. (Scand.) From Icel. *slyngva*,
slöngva, to sling, throw, pp. *slunginn*;
Swed. *slinga*, to twist; cf. O. H. G. *schlin-
gan*, to wind, twist, sling, Du. *slingeren*,
to toss, sling. Teut. type **slengwan-*;
pt. t. *slang. ¶ A. S. *slingan* (rare), to
creep, seems to be a variant of *slincan*.
See below. Der. *sling*, sb.; *slang*, q. v.

Slink. (E.) A. S. *slincan*, to creep;
nasalised form of A. S. *slīcan (not found),
which is cognate with Low G. *slīken*, to
creep (pt. t. *sleek*, pp. *sleken*), and G.
schleichen, to creep (pt. t. *schlich*).+Swed.
dial. *slinka* (pt. t. *slank*); cf. Lith. *slinkti*, to
creep. Allied to Sleek; also to Sling.

Slip. (E.) A weak verb; due to the
weak grade of A. S. *slūpan; cf. A. S. *slip-
or*, *slipig*, slippery. + Du. *slippen*, Swed.
slippa, O. H. G. *slipfan*, to slip, weak
verbs; allied to Du. *slijpen*, G. *schleifen*,
to grind smooth, whet, polish. We also
find A. S. *slūpan*, pt. t. *slēap*, pp. *slopen*;
cf. Goth. *sliupan*, pt. t. *slaup*, pp. *slupans*,
to slip or creep into. Teut. types **sleipan-*
and **sleupan-*. The latter is allied to L.
lūbricus, slippery; see Lubricate. Cf.
Brugm. i. §§ 553, 563. Der. *slipp-er*, a
loose shoe easily slipped on; *slipper-y*,
from A. S. *slipor*, slippery, with added *-y*.
And see *sleeve*, *sloop*.

Slit. (E.) M. E. *slitten*, weak verb;
from the weak grade of *slīten*, strong verb.
— A. S. *slītan*, to slit, rend; pt. t. *slāt*, pp.
sliten.+Icel. *slīta*, Swed. *slita*, Dan. *slide*,

to rend; Du. *slijten*, to wear out; O.H.G.
slīzan, G. *schleissen*, to slit, whence *schlit-
zen*, to slice. Teut. type **sleitan-*, pt. t.
*slait. Der. *slice*.

Sliver, a splinter, twig. (E.) M.E.
sliver, dimin. of prov. E. *slive*, a slice,
chip; from M.E. *sliuen* (*sliven*), to cleave.
−A.S. *-slīfan*, to cleave, pt. t. *-slāf*; in
to-slīfan. A parallel form to A.S. *slītan*,
pt. t. *slāt*; see **Slit**.

Slobber, Slubber, to do carelessly,
to sully. (Scand.) Dan. *slubbre*, to
slabber; Swed. dial. *slubbra* to slubber,
slobber, be disorderly, frequent. of Swed.
dial. *slubba*, to mix liquids carelessly, to
be careless. Cf. also Du. *slobberen*, to
sup up; Low G. *slubbern*, to lap, sip.
Allied to **Slabber.**

Sloe. (E.) M.E. *slo.* A.S. *slā, slāh*,
pl. *slān.* ✝ Du. *slee*, M, Dn. *sloeu*; Dan.
slaaen ; Swed. *slån*; G. *schlehe*, pl. *schle-
hen*; O.H.G. *slēha.*

Slogan, war-cry. (Gael.) Gael. *sluagh-
ghairm*, the signal for battle, lit. 'cry of
the host.'−Gael. (and Irish) *sluagh*, host,
army (W. *llu*); *gairm*, outcry, *gairm*, to
cry out; cf. Irish *gairm*, W. *garm*, outcry,
O. Irish *gāir*, W. *gawr*, outcry, L. *garrīre*,
to prate. Cf. **Slughorn.**

Sloid, manual dexterity. (Swed.) Englished from Swed. *slöjd*; see **Sleight.**

Sloop, a ship. (Du.−Low G.) Du.
sloep, M. Du. *sloepe*, a sloop.−Low G.
sluup, slupe, a sloop; whence (apparently)
the O.F. *chaloupe*, a shallop; see **Shallop.**
Perhaps from Low G. *slupen*, to glide,
orig. to slip. See **Slip.**

Slop (1), a puddle. (E.) M.E. *sloppe*,
a pool.−A.S. *-sloppe, -slyppe*, the sloppy
droppings of a cow, as in *cū-sloppe* (cow-
slip); also A.S. *slyppe*, a viscid substance.
Orig. sense 'something slippery'; cf. Icel.
slöp, slimy offal of fish. See further below.

slop (2), a loose garment. (E.) M.E.
sloppe. A.S. *-slop, -slype*, in comp. *ofer-
slop, ofer-slype*, an upper garment. From
A.S. *slop-* (Teut. **slup-*), weaker grade of
slūpan, to slip; because the outer garment
is easily slipped on. So also Du. *slop*, a
gap in a hedge to slip through; prov. E.
sloppy, loose.✝Icel. *sloppr*, a slop, long
loose gown. Compare **Sleeve.**

slope, an incline. (E.) M.E. *slope*;
a-slope, on the slope, ready to slip. From
the weak grade (*slop-*) of A.S. *slūpan*,
to slip. See above.

Slot (1), a bolt of a door, bar. (Du.)

O. Fries. and Du. *slot*, a lock, fastening.−
Du. *slot-* (Teut. **slut-*), weak grade of
sluiten, to shut; so also Low G. *slot*, a
bar, from *sluten*, to shut; G. *schloss*,
a lock, a castle. We find also Swed. *sluta*,
G. *schliessen*, O.H.G. *sliozan*, to shut;
allied to O. Fries. *slūta*, also *sklūta*, to
shut; and hence to L. *claudere*, to shut;
see **Clause.** (✓SKLEUD.) ¶ *Slot*, a
narrow depression or aperture, may be
from Du. *sloot*, a trench, a furrow.

Slot (2), track of a deer. (O.F.,−
Scand.) O.F. *esclot*, track, trace.−Icel.
slōð, a track, trail (whence, immediately,
M.E. *sloth, sleuth*, a track, E. *sleuth-
hound*); Swed. dial. *slo*, a track.

Sloth. (E.) Lit. 'slowness.' For
*slow-th, directly from the adj. *slow.* See
Slow. ¶ The M.E. word was *slewth*,
from A.S. *slǣwð*, sloth; Teut. type
*slaiwiþā. Der. *sloth*, an animal (translating Span. *perezoso*, slothful, a sloth);
slothful.

Slouch, to have a clownish look or
gait. (F.) Cf. *slouch*, sb., a great lub-
berly fellow (Phillips).−O.F. *eslouscher*,
eslochier, to be loose in the joint, to waver.
−O.F. *es-* (L. *ex*), out, away; *lochier*
(F. *locher*), to shake, to be loose, prob. from
M.H.G. *lucke*, G. *locker*, loose. Perhaps
affected by Norw. *sluka*, to go slowly and
heavily, Swed. *sloka*, to droop.

Slough (1), a muddy pool, mire. (E.)
M.E. *slogh, slough.* A.S. *slōh* (stem *slōg-*),
a slough. Hardly allied to Irish *slugpholl*,
a whirlpool; *slugaim*, I swallow up; Gael.
slugan, a gulf, from *sluig*, to swallow up.
Rather, to Bavar. *schlung*, a chasm.

Slough (2), the cast skin of a snake,
&c.; the dead part which separates from
a sore. (E.) Pronounced *sluf.* M.E.
slouh, slughe, slouȝe, skin of a snake.
The corresponding word appears in Swed.
dialects as *slug* (Rietz), which is prob.
allied to G. *schlauch*, M.H.G. *slūch*, a
skin, bag.

Sloven. (Du.) M.E. *sloveyn.*−M. Du.
slof, sloef, a sloven; with M.E. suffix *-ein*
(= F. *-ain*, L. *-ānus*). Cf. Du. *slof*, careless; *slof*, sb., neglect, an old slipper;
sloffen, to neglect, to go slipshod. So also
Low G. *sluf*, slovenly; *sluffen*, to be careless. E. Fries. *sluf*, *sluffe*, a sloven;
sluffen, to be careless.

Slow. (E.) A.S. *slāw*, slow. ✝ Du.
sleeuw, Icel. *slær, sljōr*; Dan. *slöv*, Swed.
slö, blunt, dull; O. Sax. *slēu*; O.H.G. *slēo.*

Teut. type *slaiwoz*; allied to L. *laeuus*, Russ. *lievuii*, Gk. λαιός, left (of the hand).

Slow-worm. (E.) In popular etymology, it is 'a slow worm,' but the true sense is 'slay-worm,' the snake that strikes. A.S. *slā-wyrm*; where *slā* seems to be borrowed from Icel. *slā*, to strike. This is clearer from Swed. *slå* or *ormslå*, a slow-worm, where *orm* = E. *worm*, and *slå* is 'striker,' from *slå*, to strike; so also Norw. *ormslo*, a slow-worm, also called *slo*, from *slaa*, to strike.

Slubber; see **Slobber.**

Sludge, soft, greasy mud. (E.) M.E. *sluche, sliche.* North Fries. *slick*, E. Fries. *slīk*, slime.+Du. *slijk*, prov. G. *schlick*, grease; see **Sleek.** ¶ The *u* is due to confusion with E. dial. *slud*, wet mud; cf. Du. *slodder*, a sloven.

Slug, to be inactive. (Scand.) M.E. *sluggen*, vb., *slugge*, a sluggard.— Dan. *slug*, weakened form of *sluk*, appearing in *slugöret, sluköret*, having drooping ears; Swed. dial. *slogga*, to be sluggish; cf. Norw. *sloka*, to slouch, Swed. *sloka*, to droop. Note also Low G. *slukkern, slak-kern*, to be loose, *slukk*, melancholy, downcast; Du. *sluik*, slender, thin. **Der.** *slugg-ard*, with F. suffix -*ard* (= O. H. G. -*hart*, cognate with E. *hard*).

Slug-horn, a battle-cry. (C.) Ignorantly used by Chatterton and Browning to mean a sort of *horn*; but really Mid. Sc. *slogorne*, a corruption of *slogan*, a war-cry. See **Slogan.**

Sluice, a flood-gate. (F.— L.) O.F. *escluse*, 'a sluice, floudgate;' Cot.— Late L. *exclūsa*, a flood-gate; lit. shut off (water); pp. of *ex-clūdere*, to shut out.— L. *ex*, out; *claudere*, to shut.

Slum; pl. *slums*, dirty back streets. (E.) Cf. prov. E. *slump*, wet mire; Low G. *slam*, mire (Lübben); Dan. and Swed. *slam*, G. *schlamm*, mire.

Slumber, verb. (E.) The *b* is excrescent. M.E. *slumeren*, frequent. of M. E. *slūmen*; to slumber; from *slume* (also *sloumbe*), sb., slumber, A.S. *slūma*, sb., slumber. + Du. *sluimeren*; Dan. *slumre*, frequent. of *slumme*, to slumber; Swed. *slumra*, vb.; G. *schlummern*, vb. The sb. *slūma* is from Teut. root *sleu-*, to be silent; 2nd grade *slau*, whence Goth. *slawan*, to be silent (Kluge).

Slump, a sudden fall or failure. (E.) Prov. E. Cf. Swed. Dan. *slump*, a chance, accident; Low G. *slump* (Danneil); G.

schlump. Of imitative origin; cf. Norw. and Lowl. Sc. *slump*, the noise made by an object falling into water. Cf. *plump, dump.*

Slur, to contaminate, pass over lightly with slight notice. (M. Du.) The orig. sense is to trail in mud, draggle; hence, to pass over slightingly.— M. Du. *sleuren, slooren*, to drag, trail; cf. *sloorigh*, 'filthie,' Hexham, and M. E. *slor*, mud; Du. *sleuren*, to trail. Also Low G. *slüren, slören*, to draggle, Swed. dial. *slöra*, to be negligent ; Norw. *slöra*, to be negligent, sully, *slöda*, to draggle, *slöda, slöe*, a trail ; E. Fries. *sluren, slüren*, to go about carelessly and noisily.

Slut. (Scand.) M. E. *slutte.* Cf. Icel. *slöttr*, a heavy, loglike fellow ; Swed. dial. *slåta*, a slut, *slåter*, an idler ; Dan. dial. *slöter*, a slovenly person ; Norw. *slott*, an idler. Also Icel. *slota*, to droop, Norw. *sluta*, to droop; allied to Dan. *slat, slatten*, loose, flabby. Cf. *slot-*, weak grade of Norw. *sletta* (strong verb), to dangle, drift, idle about (Aasen). β. From the 2nd grade *slat(t)* we have Dan. *slatte*, a slut, and *slat*, loose; see **Slattern.** Note also Bavarian *schlotzen, schlutzen*, a slut; *schlotzen*, to be careless.

Sly, cunning. (Scand.) M. E. *sligh, sleih, slēh.* — Icel. *slægr*, sly, cunning ; Swed. *slög*, handy, dexterous ; prob. allied to **Slay.** ¶ Distinct from Swed. *slug*; Dan. *slug, slu*; Du. *sluw*; G. *schlau.* **Der.** *sleight.*

Smack (1), taste. (E.) M. E. *smak, smach.* A.S. *smæc*, taste, flavour; cf. *smæccan*, to taste. + M. Du. *smaeck*; Du. *smaak*; Dan. *smag*, Swed. *smak*; G. *geschmack*, taste. **Der.** *smack*, vb., to taste.

Smack (2), a sounding blow. (Scand.) Confused with the word above, but perhaps distinct; prob. of imitative origin. —Swed. *smacka*, to smack, Swed. dial. *smakka*, to throw down noisily ; *smäkka* to hit smartly; Dan. *smække*, to rap; E. Fries. *smakken*, to smack the lips. Cf. Dan. *smæk*, a smack, rap; Du. *smak*, a loud noise.

Smack (3), a fishing-boat. (Du.) M. Du. *smacke*, Du. *smak*, a smack, hoy; whence also Dan. *smakke.* Generally thought to stand for *snack*; cf. A.S. *snacc*, a small vessel; Icel. *snekkja*, a swift vessel, Dan. *snekke*, Swed. *snäcka.*

Small. (E.) A.S. *smæl.*+Du. Dan.

Swed. *smal*, narrow, thin; Goth. *smals*, small; G. *schmal*, narrow. Allied to Icel. *smali*, small cattle, sheep; Gk. μῆλον, a sheep; Russ. *maluii*, small. ¶ Icel. *smār*, Dan. *smaa*, Swed. *små*, small, are allied to O. H. G. *smāhi*, small.

smallage, celery. (E.; *and* F. – L.) For *small ache*; from F. *ache*, parsley < L. *apium*, parsley.

Smalt, blue enamel. (Ital. – O. H. G.) Ital. *smalto*, enamel. From the 2nd grade of O. H. G. *smelzan*, str. vb.. to become liquid, whence also O. H. G. *smelzen*, G. *schmelzen*, weak vb., to smelt; from the method of preparation; see **Smelt** (1). See also **Enamel**.

Smaragdus. (L. – Gk.) L. *smaragdus*. – Gk. σμάραγδος, an emerald. Cf. Skt. *marakata(m)*, *marakta(m)*, an emerald. See **Emerald**.

Smart, to feel pain. (E.) M. E. *smerten*. A. S. *smeortan*.+Du. *smarten*, Dan. *smerte*, Swed. *smärta*, G. *schmerzen*. Also allied to L. *mordēre*, to bite; Skt. *mṛd*, to rub, grind, crush; Gk. σμερδαλέος, terrible. (√SMERD,) **Der.** *smart*, sb. ; *smart*, adj., painful, also pungent, brisk, lively, A. S. *smeart*.

Smash. (E.) A late word. Apparently formed from E. *mash*, to mix up, by prefixing *s*- (from O. F. *es*-, L. *ex*), an intensive prefix.

Smattering, sb. (E.) M.E. *smateren*, to make a noise; hence, to prate, talk ignorantly. Cf. Swed. *smattra*, to clatter; G. *schmettern*, to smash, to resound. From a repetition of *smat*, an imitative sound; see **Smack** (2). Cf. M. H. G. *smetzen*, to prattle. [Parallel to *prat-tle*, *chat-ter*; cf. Swed. *snattra*, to chatter.]

Smear. (E.) A. S. *smirian*, to smear. – A. S. *smeru*, *smeoru*, fat, grease. So also Icel. *smyrja*, Dan. *smöre*, Swed. *smörja*, G. *schmieren*, to smear ; and Du. *smeer*, Dan. Swed. *smör*, G. *schmeer*, fat, grease, O. H. G. *smero* ; Goth. *smairthr*, fatness. Cf. O. Irish *smir*, marrow; W. *mêr*, marrow; Lith. *smarsas*, fat; Gk. μύρον, unguent. **Der.** *smir-ch*.

Smell, odour. (E.) M. E. *smel*, *smul*. Allied to Du. *smeulen*, Low G. *smelen*, E. Fries. *smälen*, to smoulder. Cf. **Smoulder. Der.** *smell*, vb.

Smelt (1), to fuse ore. (Scand.) Dan. *smelte*, to smelt; Swed. *smälta*, to smelt. (Properly a Swed. word.)+M. Du. *smilten*, *smelten*, G. *schmelzen*, to smelt. These

are causal forms; cf. Westphal. *smelten*, O. H. G. *smelzan*, str. vb., to melt. From the Teut. verb *smeltan*-, to melt, pt. t. *smalt* (whence E. *smalt*), pp. *smultanoz*. And cf. Gk. μέλδειν, to melt, render fluid. Brugm. i. § 475.

Smelt (2), a fish. (E.) A.S. *smelt*, *smylt*. +Dan. *smelt*, Norw. *smelta*. The prov. E. *smolt* means a young salmon, when it first assumes its silvery scales; and prov. E. *smolt* means 'smooth and shining.'

Smew, a small diving-bird. (E.) Also called *smee*, *smeeth*. Cognate with E. Fries. *smēnt*, Du. *smient*, smew. The Du. *smient* is explained as ' small duck'; from O. Du. *smēhi anud*, small duck; where *smēhi* is cognate with O. H. G. *smāhi*, Icel. *smā-r*, Swed. *små*, small; and *unud* (*anid*) is Du. *eend*, A.S. *ened*, G. *ente*, duck. Cf. G. *schmal-ente*, small wild duck.

Smile, vb. (Scand.) Swed. *smila*, to smile, smirk; Dan. *smile*. Allied to L. *mirārī*, to wonder at; Russ. *smiekh'*, a laugh; Gk. μειδάω, I smile; Skt. *smi*, to smile. (√SMEI.)

Smirch, to besmear. (E.) Extended from M. F. *smer-en*, to smear ; see **Smear.**

Smirk. (E.) A.S. *smercian*, *smearcian*, to smile. Cf. O. Northumb. *smeruloin*, ' deridebant,' Matt. ix. 24.

Smite. (E.) A.S. *smītan*, pt. t. *smāt*, pp. *smiten*.+Du. *smijten*; Dan. *smide*, to fling; G. *schmeissen*, to smite, fling, cast; O. H. G. *smīzan*, to throw, stroke, smear. Cf. Goth. *bismeitan*, to besmear. β. The orig. sense was to 'smear' or rub over, as in Gothic; cf. M. Swed. *smita*, to smite, *smeta*, to smear. 'To rub over' seems to have been a sarcastic expression for 'to beat'; we find *well anoynted* = well beaten, Romance of Partenay, l. 5653.

Smith. (E.) A.S. *smið*, a worker with the hammer.+Du. *smid*; Icel.*smiðr*; Dan. Swed. *smed*; G. *schmied*; Goth. *-smitha*. Cf. Icel. *smīð*, smith's work; Du. *smijdig*, G. *geschmeidig*, malleable (with *ī*). The forms *smith*, *smīth*, point to a lost strong verb *smeith-an*-, to forge, pt. t. *smaith*, pp. *smithanoz*, to forge, actually preserved in Swed. dial. *smida*, to forge, pt. t. *smed*, pp. *smiden* (Rietz). Hence, as weak verbs, Dan. *smede*, Swed. *smida*, to forge. Cf. O.H.G. *smida*, metal, Gk. σμί-λη, a graver's tool. Brugm. i. § 849. **Der.** *smith-y*, A. S. *smiððe* (Icel. *smiðja*).

Smock, a woman's shirt. (E.) M. E. *smok.* A. S. *smoc.* For *smocc*; Teut. type **smugnoz,* Idg. type **smuqnos*; Brugm. i. § 899. The Teut. **smug-* is represented by A. S. *smog-,* weaker grade of *smūgan,* to creep into. So called because 'crept into,' or put over the head. Cf. Shetland *smook,* to draw on a glove or stocking. + Icel. *smokkr,* a smock; from *smog-,* weak grade of *smjūga,* to creep through a hole, to put on a garment over the head. Cf. M. Swed. *smog,* a round hole for the head.

Smoke, sb. (E.) A. S. *smoca.* Cf. A. S. *smoc-,* weak grade of the strong verb *smēocan* (pt. t. *smēac*), to smoke, reek.+ Du. *smook,* sb.; G. *schmauch,* sb. Perhaps Irish *mūch,* smoke, W. *mwg,* smoke, are from E. Cf. Lith. *smaug-iu,* I choke; Gk. σμύχειν (2 aor. ἐσμύγην), to smoulder. Der. *smoke,* vb., from A. S. *smocian,* weak verb. Brugm. i. § 849.

Smooth, adj. (E.) M. E. *smoothe*; also *smēthe.* A. S. *smēðe,* Northumb. *smoeðe*; sometimes *smōð,* smooth. The form *smēðe* represents **smōth-joz* (with mutation of *ō* to *ē*); and further, the base **smōth-* represents a Teut. base **smanth-,* so that **smōthjoz* is for **smanth-joz,* 'creamy.' The base appears in Bohem. *smant,* cream (Russ. *smetana*); whence the G. *schmant,* cream, is borrowed. Cf. Bavar. *schmand,* cream. Der. *smoothe,* vb.

Smother, sb. (E.) Formerly *smorther*; M. E. *smorther,* a suffocating smoke, lit. 'that which stifles;' formed (with suffix *-ther* of the agent) from A. S. *smor-ian,* to stifle smother.+Du. and E. Fries. *smoren,* to stifle, smother.

Smoulder, vb. (E.) M. E. *smolderen,* vb.; from M. E. *smolder,* sb., a stifling smoke. *Smol-der* < **smol-ther.* Cf. Low G. *smelen, smölen,* to smoulder; *smöln,* to give out fumes (Danneil); Du. *smeulen.* Allied to **Smell.**

Smudge. (Scand.) M. E. *smogen* (Hall.); weakened form of *smutch.* ― Dan. *smuds,* smut, dirt; *smudse,* to soil. Cf. M. E *smod,* dirt; E. Fries. and Low G. *smudden,* to soil; Du. *smoddig,* dirty. See **Smut.**

Smug, neat, spruce. (Scand. ― G.) Formerly *smoog, smug*; weakened form of **smuk* ― Dan. *smuk,* pretty, fine, fair; (South Dan. *smugg,* N. Fries. *smock, schmuck,* Outzen); M. Swed. *smuck,* elegant, fair. ― Low G. *smuk,* neat, trim;

G. *schmuck,* trim, spruce; cf. *schmücken,* to adorn, M. H. G. *smucken,* to clothe, adorn, derived from the weak grade of the M. H. G. strong verb *smiegen,* to creep into, cognate with A. S. *smūgan,* to creep. β. Thus *smug* meant 'dressed' or 'trim'; allied to *smock,* attire. See **Smock.**

smuggle, to import or export secretly. (Scand.) Dan. *smugle,* to smuggle; cf. *i smug,* secretly, *smughandel,* contraband trade; Swed. *smuga,* a lurking-hole, Icel. *smuga,* a hole to creep through. ― Icel. *smug-,* weak grade of *smjūga,* to creep, creep through a hole, cognate with A. S. *smūgan,* to creep; see **Smock.**

Smut, a spot of dirt or soot. (E.) For the base *smut-,* cf. M. E. *smotten, bi-smoteren,* to smut; G. *schmutz,* dirt. β. We also find *smutch,* for **smuts*; from Swed. *smuts,* smut, dirt; whence Swed. *smutsa,* to soil; see **Smudge.**

Snack; see **Snatch.**

Snaffle. (Du.) For *snaffle-piece,* i.e. nose-piece. ― Du. *snavel,* a horse's muzzle; M. Du. *snavel, snabel,* bill, snout; cf. O. Fries. *snavel,* mouth; G. *schnabel,* bill. Dimin. of M. Du. *snabbe, snebbe,* Du. *sneb,* bill, lit. 'snapper;' from **snabben,* parallel form to M. Du. *snappen,* to snap up; see **Snap.** Cf. Du. *snebbig,* snappish; Lith. *snapas,* bill.

Snag, a short branch, knot on a stick, abrupt projection. (Scand.) Prob. of Scand. origin; cf. Norw. *snage,* a projecting tongue of land; Icel. *snagi,* a clothespeg. Hence, perhaps, prov. E. *snag,* to trim, cut small branches from a tree; Gael. *snaigh,* to hew, cut down, trim trees; Irish *snaigh,* a hewing, cutting.

Snail. (E.) M.E. *snayle.* A.S. *snegl, snegel,* a snail.+Icel. *snigill,* Dan. *snegl*; Swed. *snigel,* a slug. Teut. types **snagiloz, *snegiloz,* masc. Allied to A. S. *snaca,* a snake (Noreen, § 252). See below; and cf. Low G. *snigge,* G. *schnecke,* a snail.

snake. (E.) A. S. *snaca,* a snake +Icel. *snākr, snōkr*; Dan. *snog*; Swed. *snok.* From Teut. verb **snak-an-,* to creep, pt. t. **snōk,* as seen in O. H. G. *snahhan,* pt. t. *snuoh.*

Snap, vb. (Du.) Du. *snappen,* to snap, snatch. + Dan. *snappe,* Swed. *snappa,* G. *schnappen*; M. H. G. *snaben.* Base **snap,* similar to **snak.* See **Snaffle, Snatch.**

Snare, a noose. (E.) A. S. *sneare,* cord,

string, noose.+Du. *snaar*, a string; Icel. *snara*; Dan. *snare*; Swed. *snara*; O.H.G. *snarahha*, a noose. β. The O. H. G. *snarahha* shews an orig. final guttural; the sb. is from a strong verb, seen in O. H. G. *snerhan*, to twist tightly; from a base SNERH = Idg. √SNERK, whence Gk. νάρκη, cramp; see **Narcissus**. Cf. √SNER, to twist, wind; see **Nerve**. γ. All from √SNĒ, to wind, spin; whence L. *nēre*, to spin, G. *schnur*, a string.

Snarl, vb. (E.) Frequentative form of *snar*, to shew one's teeth like a dog, spelt *snarre* in Palsgrave. Not found in A. S.; but cf. M. Du. *snarren*, 'to brawl, to scould, or to snarle,' Hexham. + G. *schnarren*, to growl, snarl; M. H. G. *snar*, a growling. And see **Sneer, Snort**.

Snatch. (E.) M. E. *snacchen*, as if from **snak-*; cf. Lowland Sc. *snak*, a snap of the jaws.+Du. *snakken*, to gasp. Base **snak*, parallel to **snap*. See **Snap**. Der. *snack*, sb., a portion, lit. ' a bit snatched up,' a hasty meal, a share; *to go snacks* = to go shares. Also prov. E. *sneck*, snap or latch of a door.

Sneak. (E.) Variant of M. E. *sniken*, A.S. *snīcan*, to creep, Teut. type **sneikan*; pt. t. **snaik*, pp. **snikanoz*. The A.S. pt. t. *snāc* would give a deriv. **snācan*, representing E. *sneak*. Cf. Guernsey *snéquer*, to rob slily.+Icel. *snik-inn*, hankering after, from a lost strong verb; Swed. dial. *snika* (pt. t. *snek*), to hanker after; Dan. *sniga sig*, to sneak, slink; Gael. and Irish *snaig, snaigh*, to creep (from E.).

Sneap, to pinch, check; see **Snub**.

Sneer, to scoff. (E.) M. E. *sneren*. Cf. E. Fries. *sniren*, to frizzle, to cause a hissing noise, to sneer at; Dan. *snærre*, to grin like a dog, shew one's teeth at a person; allied to **Snarl**.

Sneeze, vb. (E.) M.E. *snesen*; Chaucer has *fnesen* (Cant. Tales, H. 62), of which *snesen*, occurring in the Camb. MS., is a modification. A.S. *fnēosan*, to sneeze. +Du. *fniezen*; Swed. *fnysa*; Dan. *fnyse*. Cf. Gk. πνέω, I breathe; see **Pneumatic**. Base **fneus-*, parallel form to **hneus-*; see **Neese**.

Sniff, to scent. (Scand.) M. E. *sneuien* (*snevien*).—Icel. **snefja*, to sniff, a lost verb, whence *snafðr*, sharp-scented, *snefill*, a slight scent; Dan. *snive*, to sniff. Similar to Icel. *snippa*, to sniff; and cf. *snoppa*, a snout.

Snip, vb. (Du.) Du. *snippen*, to snip,

clip; allied to *snappen*, to snap, intercept; see **Snap**.+E. Fries. *snippen*; Low G. *snippeln*, to cut small; G. *schnippen*, to snap, allied to *schnappen*. Cf. E. Fries. *snip*, sharp; *snip, snippe*, a small piece of land. ¶ Prob. confused with **Nip**. Der. *snip*, sb.; *snipp-et*, a small piece.

Snipe, a bird. (Scand.) M. E. *snype*.— Icel. *snipa*, a snipe; Dan. *sneppe*, a snipe; Swed. *snäppa*, a sand-piper.+Du. *snip, snep*, M. Du. *snippe, sneppe*; G. *schnepfe*. It refers to the long bill; lit. ' snipper.' See **Snip, Snap**.

Snite (1), to wipe the nose. (E.) A.S. **snȳtan*, whence *snȳting*, sb., a sneezing; E. Fries. *snüten*, to snite.+Du. *snuiten*, from *snuit*, snout, nose; Icel. *snȳta*, Swed. *snyta*, Dan. *snyde*, to snite; from Swed. *snut*, Dan. *snude*, snout; see **Snout**.

Snite (2), a snipe. (E.) M. E. *snite*. A.S. *snīte*, a snite or snipe. Cf. **Snipe**.

Snivel, to snuffle, to whimper. (E.) M. E. *snuvelen, sneuelen* (*snevelen*); as if from A.S. **snyflian*. From A.S. *snofl*, mucus. Cf. Swed. *snöfla*, Dan. *snövle*, to snuffle; Low G. *snüff, snuff*, a nose, snout. See **Snuff**.

Snob. (Scand.) Prov. E. *snob*, a vulgar person, also, a journeyman shoemaker, *snap*, a lad, servant, usually in a ludicrous sense; Lowl. Sc. *snab*, a cobbler's boy.— Dan. dial. *snopp, snupp*, bashful, silly; Icel. *snápr*, a dolt, with the notion of impostor, a boaster, used as a by-word; Swed. dial. *snöpp*, a boy, anything stumpy; cf. Swed. dial. *snöppa*, to cut off, make stumpy; and see **Snub**. Cf. Swed. *snopen*, ashamed.

Snood, a fillet, ribbon. (E.) A.S. *snōd*, a fillet; orig. ' a twist,' wreath. Cf. Icel. *snūðr*, a twist; Swed. *snodd*, a string; also W. *ysnoden*, a fillet; Irish *snāthe*, a thread. All from Idg. root **snē*, **snā*, to spin, to twist; whence G. *schnū-r*, a string; cf. Icel. *snūa*, Dan. *snoe*, Swed. *sno*, to twist, twine.

Snore, vb. (E.) M. E. *snoren*; for **fnoren*; cf. A. S. *fnora*, sb., a snoring, snore. From A. S. *fnor-* (< *fnus-*), weak grade of *fnēosan*, to sneeze; see **Sneeze**. Influenced by **Snort**.

Snort, vb. (E.) M. E. *snorten*, to snore. Low G. *snurten, snarten*, to make an explosive noise. From **snur-*; as in Low G. *snurren*, to hum, M. Du. *snorren*, to murmur. Variant forms are Dan. *snorke*, to snort; Swed. *snorka*, to threaten (orig. to fume, be angry); Du. *snorken*; G. *schnar-chen*. And see **Snarl**.

Snot, mucus from the nose. (E.) M. E. *snotte*. A. S. *ge-snot*; O. Fries. *snotte*; Du. Dan. *snot*. Allied to **Snite** (1) and *snout*.

snout. (E.) M. E. *snoute*, E. Fries. *snūte*. + Du. *snuit*; Swed. *snut*, snout, muzzle; Dan. *snude*; G. *schnauze*. Cf. Dan. *snue*, to sniff, Low G. *snau*, prov. G. *schnau*, snout, beak. From a base **sneu*; whence Teut. vb. **snūtan-*, pt. t. **snaut*, pp. **snutanoz*. From the 1st grade we have Swed. *snūt*, Du. *snuit*, E. *snout*; from the 2nd, G. *schnauze*; and from the 3rd, E. *snot*.

Snow. (E.) A. S. *snāw*.+Du. *sneeuw*, Icel. *snær*, Dan. *snee*, Swed. *snö*, Goth. *snaiws*, G. *schnee*; also Lith. *snēgas*, Russ. *snieg'*, L. *nix* (gen. *niuis*), Gk. acc. νίφα, Irish *sneachd*, W. *nyf*. (√SNEIGH.) Cf. Lith. *snigti*, to snow, L. *ningit*, Gk. νείφει, it snows. Brugm. i. § 394.

Snub, to check, reprimand. (Scand.) Also *sneb*, *snib*. M. E. *snibben*. – Dan. *snibbe*, to reprimand; Swed. *snubba*, Icel. *snubba*, N. Fries. *snubbe*, to snub, chide. Orig. to 'snip off' the end of a thing; cf. Icel. *snubbōtr*, snubbed, nipped, with the tip cut off; Swed. dial. *snubba*, to snip or clip off; E. Fries. *snubbeln*, to snap or snatch away. β. Allied to obs. E. *sneap*, to pinch, nip, answering to Icel. *sneypa*, to castrate, also to disgrace, snub; Swed. *snöpa*, to castrate. Cf. also Dan. dial. *sneve*, to dock, to snub, to nip. **Der.** *snub-nosed*, i. e. with a short or stumpy nose, as if with the end cut off.

snub-nosed; see above.

Snuff (1), to sniff, smell. (Du.) From M. Du. *snuffen*; cf. *snuyven* (Du. *snuiven*), ' to snuffe out the filth out of ones nose,' Hexham; Du. *snuf*, smelling, scent; E. Fries. *snufen*, *snuven*, to snuff up.+Swed. *snufva*, a catarrh, *snufven*, a sniff, scent; cf. G. *schnauben*, *schnaufen*, *schnieben*, to snuff, snort (from a Teut. base **sneub*); G. *schnupfen*, a catarrh, *schnupfen*, to take snuff. **Der.** *snuff*, powdered tobacco; also *snuff-le*, prov. G. *schnuffeln*, *schnüffeln*.

Snuff (2), to snip off the top of a candle-wick. (E.) M. E. *snuffen*, to snuff out a candle; cf. *snoffe*, sb., the snuff of a candle. Parallel to **snuppen*; cf. prov. E. *snop*, to eat off, as cattle do young shoots; Swed. dial. *snöppa*, to snip off, snuff a

candle; Dan. *snubbe*, to nip off. See **Snub**. **Der.** *snuff*, sb.

Snug. (Scand.) Cf. prov. E. *snug*, tidy, trimmed up; *snog*, the same. – Icel. *snöggr*, smooth, said of wool or hair; M. Swed. *snygg*, short-haired, trimmed, Swed. *snygg*, cleanly, neat, genteel; Dan. dial. *snög*, neat, smart. Cf. E. Fries. *snügge*, *snigge*, smooth, neat. Orig. 'trimmed;' hence neat, smart, tidy, comfortable. Cf. **Snag**.

So. (E.) M. E. *so*. A. S. *swā*.+Du. *zoo*, Icel. *svā*, *svo*, *so*; Dan. *saa*, Swed. *så*, G. *so*, Goth. *swa*; Teut. types **swê*, **swō*, **swa*. Cf. Gk. ὥς. β. From a case of Idg. **swos*, one's own; cf. L. *suus*, Skt. *sva*, one's own. Lit. 'in one's own way.' See Prellwitz; Brugm. i. § 362.

Soak. (E.) It also means to suck up, imbibe. M. E. *soken*, (1) to suck, (2) to soak. A. S. *socian*, to soak; from A. S. *soc-* (Teut. *suk-*), weak grade of *sūcan*, to suck. See **Suck**. Cf. W. *swga*, soaked, *sugno*, to suck.

Soap. (E.) M. E. *sope*. A. S. *sāpe*.+ Du. *zeep*; [cf. Icel. *sāpa*, Swed. *sāpa*, from A. S.]; G. *seife*. Teut. type **saipōn*, fem.; from **saip*, 2nd grade of **seipan-*, to trickle (M. H. G. *sifen*); hence also A. S. *sāp*, resin, pomade, allied to *sāpe*. ¶ L. *sāpo* (whence F. *savon*, &c.) was borrowed from Teutonic; the true L. (cognate) word seems to be *sēbum*, tallow, grease.

Soar. (F. – L.) M. E. *soren*. – F. *essorer*, to expose to air; in M. F., 'to sore up,' Cot. – Late L. **exaurāre*, to expose to air. – L. *ex*, out; *aura*, breeze, air. Perhaps L. *aura* was borrowed from Gk. αὔρα, a breeze; formed, apparently, with suffix *-ra* from √AW, variant of WE, to blow. See **Air**.

Sob, vb. (E.) M. E. *sobben*, related to A. S. *sēofian*, to lament. + G. *seufzen*, to sigh, O. H. G. *sūftōn*, to sob, O. H. G. *sūft*, a sigh, sob; all from O. H. G. *sūfan*, to sup, sup up. Allied to **Sup**. **Der.** *sob*, sb.

Sober. (F. – L.) M. E. *sobre*. – F. *sobre*. L. *sōbrium*, acc. of *sōbrius*, sober. – L. *sō-*=*sē-*, apart, hence, not; *-brius*, drunk, as in *ē-brius*. See **Ebriety**. (Doubtful.) **Der.** *sobriety*, M. F. *sobrieté*, L. acc. *sōbrietātem*.

Sobriquet, Soubriquet, a nickname. (F.) F. *sobriquet*, 'surname, nickname, a jeast broken on a man;' Cot. He also spells it *sotbriquet*, *soubriquet*.

From O. F. *soubzbriquet*, a chuck under the chin (14th cent.) ; hence, a quip, an affront, a nickname. Here O. F. *soubz*, F. *sous*, is from L. *subtus*, below ; *briquet* has been conjectured to stand for *bequet*, dimin. of *bec*, beak, mouth ; cf. Ital. *sotto-becco*, a chuck under the chin. ' Percussit super mentonem faciendo dictum *le soubriquet* ; ' A. D. 1335. See Körting, and Littré.

Soc, Socage ; see **Soke.**

Sociable. (F. – L.) F. *sociable.* – L. *sociābilis*, companionable. – L. *sociā-re*, to accompany. – L. *socius*, companion, follower ; allied to L. *sequī*, to follow. See **Sequence. Der. as-sociate, dis-sociate.**

social. (L.) L. *sociālis*, adj., from *socius* (above).

society. (F. – L.) M. F. *societé.* – L. acc. *societātem*, from nom. *societās*, fellowship – L. *socius*, a companion ; see **Sociable.**

Sock. (L.) A. S. *socc.* – L. *soccus*, a light shoe, slipper, sock, buskin of a comedian.

Socket. (F. – L. ?) Cf. F. dial. *soquette*, a stump of dead wood, patois de la Meuse (Labourasse) ; Walloon *sokett*, a stump. Godefroy has *socquet*, (apparently) a cupboard. Prob. an A. F. dimin. of O. F. *soc*, a wooden clog (A. D. 1473). Cotg. has ' *socque*, a sock or sole of durt, cleaving to the foot in a cloggy way.' Cf. Port. *socco*, wooden shoe or clog, mod. F. *socque*, a clog. β. All from L. *soccus*, sock, shoe, hence, a wooden shoe or clog. I conclude that *socket* is a dimin. of *sock*, notwithstanding the change in sense ; cf. E. *shoe*, a kind of socket, as a term in machinery (Webster). ¶ O. F. *soket*, a small ploughshare, is from a Celtic source, being allied to O. Irish *socc*, a ploughshare.

Sod. (E.) So called from the use of turf as fuel (?) ; or from its frequent wetness (?). The connexion with the verb *to seethe* appears clearly in Du. *zode*, sod, green turf, M. Du. *zode*, seething, also sod ; G. *sode*, sod, *sod*, bubbling up of boiling water ; Low G. *sood*, a well, *sode*, a turf, sod ; E. Fries. *sōd*, a well ; *sode*, a cut turf, also, boiling, cooking ; Dan. dial. *sodd*, *saadd*, a sod. (See Franck.) Cf. also A. S. *sēað*, a well, pit, *sēað*, pt. t. of *sēoðan*, to seethe ; O. Fries. *sātha*, sod, *sāth*, a well ; A. S. *ge-sod*, a cooking. See **Seethe.**

Soda. (Ital. – L.) Ital. *soda*, ' a kind of fearne ashes whereof they make glasses ; ' Florio. Fem. of Ital. *sodo*, ' solide, tough ; '

ibid. (Similarly O. F. *soulde*, glasswort, answers to L. *solida* ; prob. from the hardness of the products obtained from glasswort.) – L. *solidus*, solid, hard. See **Solid. Der. sod-ium,** a coined word.

Sodden ; see **Seethe.**

Soder, Solder, a firm cement from fusible metals. (F. – L.) Formerly *soder*, *sowder*, sometimes *soulder* ; now pronounced (sod·ɘr). – F. *soudure*, M. F. *souldure*, ' a souldering, and particularly the knot of soulder which fastens the led [lead] of a glasse window ; ' Cot. – O. F. *souder*, *soulder*, to consolidate, make firm. – L. *solidāre*, to make firm. – L. *solidus*, firm. See **Solid.**

Sodomy. (F. – L. – Gk. – Heb.) F. *sodomie*, a sin imputed to the inhabitants of Sodom. – F. *Sodome*, Sodom. – L. *Sodoma*. – Gk. Σόδομα. – Heb. *Sedōm*.

Sofa. (Arab.) Arab. *suffat*, *suffah*, ' a sopha ; ' Rich. Dict. p. 936. – Arab. root *saffa*, to draw up in line, to put a seat to a saddle ; ibid.

Soft. (E.) A. S. *sōfte*, adv. ; *sōft*, also *sēfte* adj. (with *i*-mutation). + O. Sax. *sāfto*, adv., softly ; G. *sanft*, soft ; O. H. G. *samfto*, adv., gently ; Du. *zacht*, for *zaft* (whence G. *sacht*). **Der. soft-en.**

Soil (1), ground, country. (F. L.) M. E. *soile*. – A. F. *soil* ; (cf. F. *seuil*, threshold of a door < L. *solium*). – Late L. *solea*, soil, ground. Allied to L. *solum*, ground ; whence F. *sol*, soil, ground (from which, however, the E. word cannot be directly derived). Cf. Gk. ἔδ-αφος, foundation, ground. See **Sole** (1).

Soil (2), to defile. (F. – L.) M. E. *soilen.* [Not allied to M. E. *sulen*, *sully*.] – O. F. *soillier*, F. *souiller*, to soil ; *se souiller*, to wallow as a sow. – O. F. *soil*, *souil*, ' the soile of a wild boar, the mire wherein he hath wallowed ; ' Cot. – Late L. *suillus*, a pig ; L. *suillus*, adj., belonging to swine. – L. *sūs*, a sow. See **Sow. Der. soil,** sb., a stain ; quite distinct from *soil*, ground.

Soil (3), to feed cattle with green grass, to fatten with feeding. (F. – L.) O. F. **soeler*, *saoler*, M. F. *saouler*, to glut, satiate (F. *soûler*) ; cf. O. F. *soelement*, satiety (Godefroy). – O.F. *saol*, full, cloyed. – L. acc. *satullum*, filled with food. – L. *satur*, full. See **Satiate.**

Soirée, an evening party. (F. – L.) F. *soirée*, evening ; hence, an evening party. Cf. Ital. *serata*, evening. – L. *sēr-us*, late in the day (whence Ital. *sera*, F. *soir*, evening); with suffix *-āta* (>F. *-ée*).

Sojourn, to dwell. (F.—L.) O. F. *sojorner*, *sojourner*.—L. *sub*, under; *diurnāre*, to stay, from *diurnus*, daily; which is from *diēs*, a day. See **Diary.**

Soke, Soc, a franchise, land held by socage. (E.) The A. S. *sacu* meant 'a contention,' a 'law-suit'; whence the Law term *sac*, the power of hearing suits and administering justice within a certain precinct. The A.S. *sōcn* meant 'investigation,' or 'a seeking into'; whence the Law term *soke*, the right of hearing disputes and enquiring into complaints, also, the precinct within which such right was exercised; see Blount, Spelman, Ellis, Thorpe, Schmid. β. Etymologically, *sac* (A.S. *sacu*) is the same word as **Sake**, q. v. *Soke* (A. S. *sōc-*) is the exercise of judicial power; and *soken* (A. S. *sōcn*, *sōcen*) is an enquiry; both allied to E. *seek*, and derived from A. S. *sōc*, strong grade of *sacan*, to contend; see **Seek.** Der. *soc-age*, a barbarous law term made by adding F. *-age* (L. *-āticum*) to A.S. *sōc-*. (The *o* is long.)

Solace, a relief. (F.—L.) M. E. *solas*. —O. F. *solaz* (where *z = ts*).—L. *sōlātium*, a comfort.—L. *sōlātus*, pp. of *sōlārī*, to console. Allied to L. *sollus*, Gk. ὅλος, whole (Prellwitz). Der. *solace*, vb.

Solan-goose, a bird. (Scand. *and* E.) The E. *goose* is an addition.—Icel. *sūlan*, lit. 'the gannet,' where *-n* stands for the definite article; def. form of Icel. *-sūla*, in *haf-sūla*, i. e. sea-gannet, solan goose; Norweg. *sula*, the same.

Solar, belonging to the sun. (L.) L. *sōlāris*, solar. — L. *sōl*, sun. + Icel. *sōl*, Goth. *sauil*, Lith. *saulė*, W. *haul*, Irish *sūl*, Gk. ἥλιος (see Prellwitz); Skt. *sūra-*, sun, splendour. Brugm. i. § 481.

Solder; see **Soder.**

Soldier. (F. — L.) M. E. *sodiour*, *soudiour*, *souldier*.— O F. *soldier*, *soudoier*, *souldoyer*, one who fights for pay; Late L. *soldārius*.—Late L. *soldum* pay.—Late L. *solidus*, a piece of money (whence O. F. *sol*, F. *sou*); orig. 'a solid piece.'—L. *solidus*, solid; cf. E. 'hard cash.' See **Solid.**

Sole (1), under side of foot or shoe. (L.) A. S. *sole*.—Late L. *sola*, for L. *solea*, sole of the foot, or of a shoe.—L. *solum*, the ground. See **Soil.**

Sole (2), a fish. (F.—L.) M. E. *sole*.— F. *sole*; Cot.—L. *solea*, the sole-fish.

Sole (3), alone. (F.—L.) O. F. *sol* (F. *seul*).—L. *sōlum*, acc. of *sōlus*, alone.

Solecism, impropriety in speaking or writing. (F.—L.—Gk.) M.F. *soloecisme*; Cot.—L. *solæcismus*.—Gk. σολοικισμός, a solecism.—Gk. σολοικίζειν, to speak incorrectly.—Gk. σόλοικος, speaking incorrectly, like an inhabitant of Σόλοι (*Soloi*) in Cilicia, where the Gk. dialect was corruptly spoken. Der. *solecist*, sb.

Solemn. (F.—L.) M. E *solempne*.— O. F. *solempne*.— L. *sōlemnem*, acc. of *sōlemnis*, older forms *sōlennis*, *sollennis*, annual, occurring yearly like a religious rite, religious, solemn.—L. *sollus*, entire, complete; *annus*, a year. Hence *solemn* = returning at the end of a complete year. The O. Lat. *sollus* is cognate with W. *holl*, whole, entire. Brugm. i. § 417. Der. *solemn ity*, *-ise*.

Sol-fa, to sing the notes of the gamut. (L.) It means to sing the notes by the names *si*, *la*, *sol*, *fa*, *mi*, *re*, *ut* (where, for *ut*, *do* is now used). These names are of L. origin; see **Gamut.** Der. *solfeggio*, from Ital. *solfeggio*, the singing of the gamut; cf. *sol-mi-sation*, coined from *sol* and *mi*.

Solicit. (F.—L.) M.F. *soliciter*.—L. *sollicitāre*, to agitate, arouse, urge, solicit. —L. *sollicitus*, lit. wholly agitated.—L. *solli-*, for *sollus*, whole; *citus*, aroused, pp. of *ciēre*, to shake, excite. See **Solemn** and **Cite.** Der. *solicitous*, for L. *sollicitus*; *solicit-ude*, M.F. *solicitude*, from L. *sollicitūdo*, anxiety.

Solid. F.—L.) F. *solide*.—L. *solidum*, acc. of *solidus*, firm. Der. *solidar-i-ty*, 'a word which we owe to the F. communists, and which signifies a fellowship in gain and loss, a being, so to speak, all in the same bottom;' Trench. Also *solid-i-fy*, from F. *solidifier*, to render solid.

Soliloquy. (L.) Late L. *sōliloquium*, a speaking to oneself (Augustine).—L. *sōli-*, for *sōlus*, alone; *loqui*, to speak. See **Loquacious.**

Soliped, an animal with uncloven hoof. (L.) Short for *solidiped*. — L. *solidiped-*, stem of *solidipēs*, solid-hoofed (Pliny).—L. *solidi-*, for *solidus*, solid; *pēs*, a foot; see **Foot.**

Solitary. (F.—L.) M. E. *solitarie*.— A. F. *solitarie*; cf. F. *solitaire*.—L. *sōlitārius*, solitary. Short for **sōlitātārius*, from *sōlitāt-*, stem of *sōlitās*, loneliness.— L. *sōlus*, alone.

solitude. (F.–L.) F. *solitude.*–L. *sōlitūdo.*–L. *sōli-*, for *sōlus*, alone; and suffix *-tūdo.*

solo. (Ital. – L.) From Ital. *solo*, alone.–L. *sōlus*, alone.

Solmisation : see **Sol-fa**.

Solstice. (F.–L.) F. *solstice.*–L. *solstitium*, the solstice; lit. a point (in the ecliptic) at which the sun seems to stand still. – L. *sōl*, the sun ; *-stit-um*, for *statum*, supine of *sistere*, to make to stand still, from *stāre*, to stand. See **State**.

Soluble. (F. – L.) F. *soluble.* – L. *solūbilis*, dissolvable.–L. *solu-*, base of *solū-tus*, pp. of *soluere*, to loosen ; with suffix *-bilis*. See **solve**.

solution. (F. – L.) F. *solution.*– L. *solūtiōnem*, acc. of *solūtio*, a loosing. – L. *solūt-us*, pp. of *soluere*, to loosen, solve.

solve. (L.) Late L. *solvere*; L. *soluere*, to loosen, relax, explain ; pp. *solūtus.*–L. *so-* (for *sē-*), apart; *luere*, to loosen, allied to Gk. λύ-ειν, to set free, and to E. **Lose**. Brugm. i. § 121. **Der.** *solvent*, from the stem of the pres. pt. ; and see above.

Sombre, gloomy. (F.–L.) F. *sombre*, gloomy. Cf. Port. and Span. *sombrio*, gloomy, from Port. and Span. *sombra*, shade. Diez refers these to L. *umbra*, shade, with prefix *sub*; cf. Prov. *sotz-ombrar*, to shade. (See Körting.) Littré refers them to L. *umbra*, shade, with prefix *ex* (intensive). Either solution seems possible ; the latter is the simpler. See **Umbrage**.

sombrero, a broad-brimmed hat. (Span.–L.) Span. *sombrero.*–Span. *sombra* (above).

Some. (E.) A. S. *sum*, some one, a certain one, one ; pl. *sume*, some.+Icel. *sumr*, Goth. *sums*, O. H. G. *sum*, some one; Dan. *somme*, pl.; cf. Swed. *somlige*, pl., some. Allied to **Same**. **Der.** *some-body*, *-thing*, *-time*, *-times* (where *-s* is an adverbial suffix).

-some, suffix. (E.) A. S. *-sum*, as in *wyn-sum* = E. *win-some*. Cf. G. *lang-sam*, slow. From the weak grade of Teut. **samo-*, same ; see **Same**.

Somersault, Somerset. (F. – Ital. –L.) M.F. *soubresault*, ' a sobresault or summersault, an active trick in tumbling ;' Cot. – Ital. *soprasalto.* – Ital. *sopra*, above, over; *salto*, a leap. – L. *suprā*, above, over; *saltum*, acc. of *saltus*, a leap, from pp. of L. *salīre*, to leap; see **Salient**.

Somnambulist, one who walks in his sleep. (L.) Coined (with suffix *-ist* = L. *-ista* = Gk. -ιστης, as in *bapt-ist*) from L. *somn-us*, sleep, and *ambul-āre*, to walk. See below, and see **Amble**.

somniferous, causing sleep. (L.) L. *somnifer*, sleep-bringing; with suffix *-ous.* – L. *somni-*, for *somnus*, sleep; *-fer*, bringing, from *ferre*, to bring. β. The L. *somnus* is for **swepnos*, allied to Skt. *svapna-*, Irish *súan*, W. *hun*, sleep. (√SWEP.) See **Soporiferous**.

somnolence. (F. – L.) F. *somnolence.* – L. *somnolentia*, sleepiness. – L. *somnolentus*, sleepy.–L. *somno-* (for *somnus*), sleep (above) ; with suffix *-lentus.*

Son. (E.) M. E. *sone.* A. S. *sunu.*+ Du. *zoon* ; Icel. *sunr*, Dan. *søn*, Swed. *son*, G. *sohn*, Goth. *sunus*. Teut. type **sunuz.* Cf. Lith. *sūnus*, Russ. *suin'* ; Skt. *sūnu-*, from Skt. *su*, *sū*, to beget ; Gk. υἱός, υἱύς (for **σνγνός*) ; O. Irish *suth*, birth. (√SŪ.) Brugm. i. §§ 104, 292.

Sonata. (Ital. – L.) Ital. *sonata*, a sounding, a sonata. From the fem. of pp. of Ital. *sonare*, to sound – L. *sonāre*, to sound, from *sonus*, sound. See **Sound** (3).

Song. (E.) M. E. *song.* A. S. *sang.*– A. S. *sang*, 2nd grade of *singan*, to sing.+ Du. *zang*; Icel. *söngr* ; Swed. *sång* ; Dan. and G. *sang*; Goth. *saggws* (for *sangws*) ; cf. Gk. ὀμφή, voice. See **Sing**.

songster. (E.) A. S. *sangystre*, *sangestre*, a singer. – A. S. *sang*, 2nd grade of *singan*, to sing ; with double suffix *-es-tre* of the agent. **Der.** *songstr-ess*, with F. suffix, from Gk. *-ισσα.*

Sonnet. (F. – Ital. – L.) F. *sonnet.* – Ital. *sonetto*, a sonnet, canzonet ; dimin. of *sono*, a sound, tune. – L. *sonum*, acc. of *sonus*, a sound. **Der.** *sonnet-eer*, Ital. *sonettiere*, a sonnet-writer. See **Sound** (3).

sonorous. (L.) For L. *sonōrus*, loud-sounding. – L. *sonōr-*, stem of *sonor*, sound, noise.–L. *sonāre*, to sound.–L. *sonus*, sound.

Soon. (E.) M.E. *sone.* A.S. *sōna.*+ O. Sax. *sāna*, *sāno* ; O. Fries., O. Sax. M. H. G. *sān* ; cf. Goth. *suns-aiw*, *suns*, immediately.

Soot. (E.) A. S. *sōt.*+Icel. *sōt*, Swed. *sot*; Dan. *sod* ; cf. Lith. *sódis*, soot. Perhaps from the *ō-* grade of Idg. root SED (Teut. SET), to sit, rest upon. See **Sit**. (Noreen, § 146 ; Streitberg, § 95.) Cf. also Gael. *sùith*, soot.

Sooth, true. (E.) A. S. *sōð*, true ;

whence *sōð*, neut. sb., the truth. [The A.S. *sōð* stands for *sonth-, Teut. *santh-; the loss of *n* following the lengthening of *o*.] +Icel. *sannr* (for *santhr), Swed. *sann*, Dan. *sand*; from Teut. base *santhoz, Idg. *sontos, short for *es-ont-, lit. being, that which is, from √ES, to be. Allied to L. -*sens*, being, as in *ab-sens* (stem *ab-sent*-), *præ-sens* (stem *præ-sent*-); Skt. *sat-ya*-, true. See **Suttee** and **Essence.** Der. *for-sooth*, i. e. for a truth; *sooth-say*, to say truth.

soothe. (E.) The orig. sense was to assent to as being true, hence to say yes to, humour, flatter, approve of. 'Is't good to *soothe* him in these contraries?' Com. Errors, iv. 4. 82. M. E. *soðien*, to confirm, verify. A. S. *ge-sōðian*, to confirm, prove to be true. — A. S. *sōð*, true; see **Sooth.**

soothsay. (E.) To *say sooth*, i. e. tell truth, predict.

Sop, sb. (E.) M. E. *soppe*. It answers to an A. S. *soppe, a sop (whence *soppian*, to sop up) regularly formed from *sop-* (Teut. **sup-*) weaker grade of *sūpan*, to sup. Cf. Icel. *soppa*, a sop, from the weaker grade of *sūpa*, to sup; also Du. *sop*, M. Du. *zoppe*, M. Swed. *soppa*, Low G. *soppe*, G. *suppe*. See **Sup.**

Sophist, a captious reasoner. (F. — L. — Gk.) Usually *sophister* in old authors, but the final *r* is unoriginal. — O. F. *sophiste*. — Late L. *sophista*. — Gk. σοφιστής, a skilful man, also a Sophist, teacher of arts for money (see Liddell). — Gk. σοφίζειν, to instruct. — Gk. σοφός, wise. Der. *sophist-r-y*, *sophist-ic* (Gk. σοφιστικός); *sophis-m* (Gk. σόφισμα, a device).

Sophy, a shah of Persia, A. D. 1505–1736. (Pers. — Arab.) In Shak. Merch. Ven. ii. 1. 26. Pers. *Safi*, a title. — Arab. *safīy*, pure. ¶ Distinct from *Sufi*, a Moslem mystic; from Arab. *sūfīy*, intelligent.

Soporiferous, inducing sleep. (L.) From L. *sopōrifer*, sleep - bringing; by adding -*ous*. — L. *sopōri-*, from *sopōr-*, stem of *sopor*, sleep; -*fer*, bringing, from *ferre*, to bring. The L. *sopor* is allied to Skt. *svap-na-*, sleep (from *svap*, to sleep), Gk. ὕπνος, sleep, A. S. *swefen*, a dream. (√SWEP.) Brugm. i. § 551. See **Somniferous.**

soporific, causing sleep. (L.) L. *sopōri-* (above); and -*fic-*, for *facere*, to make, cause.

Soprano. (Ital. — L.) Ital. *soprano*,

supreme; highest voice in music. — Late L. *superānus*, chief; see **Sovereign.**

Sorcery. (F. — L.) O. F. *sorcerie*, casting of lots, magic. — O. F. *sorcier*, a sorcerer. — Late L. *sortiārius*, a teller of fortunes by lots, sorcerer. — L. *sorti-*, from *sort-*, stem of *sors*, a lot.

Sordid, dirty, vile. (F. — L.) F. *sordide*. — L. *sordidus*, dirty. — L. *sordi-*, for *sordēs*, dirt. Cf. Russ. *sor'*, filth. Brugm. i. p. 1092.

Sore, adj. (E.) M. E. *sor*. A. S. *sār*, painful. + Du. *zeer*, Icel. *sārr*, Swed. *sår*, O. H. G. *sēr*, wounded, painful; cf. G. *sehr*, sorely, very, *versehren*, to wound. Teut. type *sairoz, adj. Cf. O. Irish *sáeth*, *sōeth*, tribulation; but hardly L. *sæuus*, dire. Der. *sore*, sb., A. S. *sār* (Goth. *sair*) and *sore*, adv., very; see **Sorry.**

Sorrel (1), a plant. (F. — M. H. G.) O. F. *sorel* (F. *surelle*). — M. H. G. *sūr* (G. *sauer*), sour; from its taste. So also A. S. *sūre*, sorrel, from *sūr*, sour. See **Sour.**

Sorrel (2), of a reddish-brown colour. (F. — Teut.) O. F. *sorel*; dimin. from O.F. *sor*, F. *saur*, sorrel of colour. — Low G. *soor*, sear, dried up, withered; cognate with E. *sear*. See **Sear.**

Sorrow, grief. (E.) M. E. *sorwe*, *sorȝe*. A. S. *sorge*, gen. dat. and acc. of *sorh*, *sorg*, sorrow, anxiety. + Du. *zorg*, Dan. Swed. *sorg*, G. *sorge*, Goth. *saurga*, care, grief. Teut. type *sorgā, f. Cf. O. Irish *serg*, sickness, Lith. *sirgti*, to be ill, suffer. ¶ Not allied to *sore* or *sorry*, though the present sense of *sorry* shews confusion with it. See below.

Sorry, sore in mind, aggrieved. (E.) M. E. *sory*. A. S. *sārig*, adj., sorry, sad, sore in mind; from *sār*, sore. + Du. *zeerig*, Swed. *sårig*, sore, full of sores, words which preserve the orig. sense. ¶ Spelt with two *r*'s owing to the shortening of M. E. *ō* in *sory*, due to the addition of the suffix -*y* (A. S. -*ig*); but not orig. allied to *sorrow.*

Sort, a kind. (F. — L.) F. *sorte*, fem., sort, kind; O. F. *sorte*, fem., a company; allied to F. *sort*, masc., luck, fate. — L. *sortem*, acc. of *sors*, lot. Perhaps allied to **Series.** Brugm. i. § 516 (1).

Sortie. (F. — L.) F. *sortie*, a going forth; fem. of *sorti*, pp. of *sortir*, to sally forth. Cf. Span. *surtida*, a sortie, from O. Span. *surtir*, to rise. β. F. *sortir*, Span. *surtir*, answer to a Folk-L. form *sortīre, to rise up, from *sortum, for L.

surrectum, supine of *surgere*, to rise up; see **Surge**. The contraction of *surrectum* to *sortum* is proved to be correct by Ital. *sorto*, occurring as pp. of *sorgere*, to rise ; and by Span. *surto*, pp. of *surgir*.

Sot, a stupid fellow, drunkard. (Late L.) M. E. *sot* (Ancren Riwle). A. S. *sot*, *sott*. Late L. *sottus* (Ducange) ; ab. A.D. 800. Prob. of Teut. origin ; cf. M. Du. *zot* ; M. H. G. *sote*, a sot. ¶ Distinct from Span. *zote*, a blockhead ; Ital. *zotico* (Florio has *zottico*). The Ital. *zotico* has been referred to L. *idiōticus*, idiotic, in which case Span. *zote* may represent L. *idiōtes*, of Gk. origin ; see **Idiot**. Ducange has *jotticus*, a foolish game ; cf. M. E. *jottes*, unlearned people.

Sou. (F. – L.) F. *sou*, O. F. *sol*, a coin. – Late L. *solidus*, solid, also a coin ; cf. *l. s. d.*, i. e. *librae, solidi, denarii*. See **Solid**.

Soubriquet ; see **Sobriquet**.

Souchong, a kind of tea. (Chinese.) Cantonese *siu-chung*, for *siao-chung*, ' little sort ;' Yule, p. 691.

Sough, a sighing sound. (E.) M. E. *swogh*, *swough*, from A. S. *swōgan*, to resound. Cf. Icel. *urn-sūgr*, the rushing sound of an eagle's wings ; and see **Surf**.

Soul. (E.) A. S. *sāwel*, *sāwl*. + Du. *ziel*, Icel. *sāla, sāl*, Dan. *siœl*, Swed. *själ*, G. *seele*, Goth. *saiwala*. Brugm. i. § 200.

Sound (1), adj., healthy. (E.) M. E. *sound*. A. S. *sund*. + Du. *gezond*; Swed. Dan. *sund* ; G. *gesund*. Perhaps allied to Goth. *swinths*, strong.

Sound (2), strait of the sea. (E.) M. E. *sound*. A. S. *sund*, (1) a swimming, (2) power to swim, (3) a strait of the sea, that could be swum across. + Icel. Dan. Swed. G. *sund*. Probably derived from **swum* (A. S. *swum-*), weak grade of *swimman*, to swim ; with suffix *-dœ* for Idg. pp. suffix *-tós*. Brugm. i. § 377 (2). See **Swim**. Der. *sound*, swimming-bladder of a fish, another use of the same word ; Shetland *soond*, Icel. *sund-magi*.

Sound (3), a noise. (F. – L.) The final *d* is added. M. E. *soun*. – F. *son*. – L. *sonum*, acc. of *sonus* (for **swenos*) a sound. + Skt. *svana-*, sound ; A. S. *swin*, melody. (√SWEN.) Brugm. ii. § 519.

Sound (4), to measure depth of water. (F. – L.) In Palsgrave. – F. *sonder*, to sound the depth of. Cf. Span. *sondar*, to sound ; Span. Port. *sonda*, F. *sonde*, a

sounding-lead. Diez derives F. *sonder* from a supposed L. **sub-undare*, to go under the water ; from L. *sub*, under, and *unda*, a wave ; cf. *ab-ound*, *red-ound*, and *sombre*. ¶ Yet we find A. S. *sund-gyrd*, a sounding-rod ; *sund-līne*, *sund-rāp*, a sounding-line or rope ; which point to a derivation from **Sound** (2).

Soup. (F. – Teut.) F. *soupe*. – F. *souper*, to sup. – Low G. *supen*, to drink, quaff. See **Sup**, and **Sop**.

Sour. (E.) A. S. *sūr*. + Du. *zuur*, Icel. *sūrr*, Dan. *suur*, Swed. *sur*, G. *sauer*; W. *sur*, sour, Lith. *surus*, salt ; Russ. *surovuii*, raw, coarse, harsh, rough. Brugm. i. § 114.

Source. (F. – L.) M. E. *sours*. – O. F. *sorse*, *surse* (F. *source*), a source. Here *sorse* is fem. of *sors*, old pp. of O. F. *sordre* (F. *sourdre*), to rise. – L. *surgere*, to rise ; see **Surge**.

Souse (1), pickle. (F. – G.) From O. F. *soucie*, pickle (Godefroy). – G. *sulze*, pickle ; allied to **Salt**. Hence *souse*, vb., to soak in brine.

Souse (2), **Sowse**, to swoop down upon. (F. – L.) From M. E. *sours*, the upward spring or the swoop of a bird of prey ; Ch. – O. F. *sorse*, a rise, also a source ; see **Source**. Phil. Soc. Trans 1888, p. 18.

South. (E.) A. S. *sūð*. + Du. *zuid*; Icel. *suðr*, also *sunnr*, south (cf. *suðreyjar*, lit. southern islands, Sodor, the Hebrides) ; Dan. Swed. *syd*, Swed. *sunnan*, the south ; O. H. G. *sund*, G. *süd*. β. The Teut. base is **sunth-*, south ; perhaps allied to **Sun**, q.v. Connexion with Gk. νότος, south wind (Brugmann), is doubtful ; see Prellwitz. Der. *south-ern*; cf. O. H. G. *sundrōni*, southern, Icel. *suðrœnn*.

Souvenir. (F. – L.) F. *souvenir*, sb., a remembrance ; merely the verb *souvenir*, to remember, used as a sb. – L. *subuenīre*, to occur to one's mind. – L. *sub*, under, near ; *uenīre*, to come. See **Venture**.

Sovereign. (F. – L.) M. E. *souerain* (*soverain*). – A. F. *soverein*; O. F. *souverain*. – Late L. *superānus*, chief. – L. *super*, above. See **Super-**.

Sow (1), to scatter seed. (E.) A. S. *sāwan*, pt. t. *sēow*, pp. *sāwen*. + Du. *zaaijen*, Icel. *sā*, Dan. *saae*, Swed. *sā*, O. H. G. *sāwen*, G. *säen*, Goth. *saian*. Also W. *hau*, Lith. *sēti*, Russ. *sieiate*, L. *serere* (pt. t. *sē-ui*, pp. *sa-tum*), to sow; Gk. ἵημι (for **σί-ση-μι*), I send, throw. (√SĒ, to cast.) Brugm. i. §§ 132, 310. **Der.** *seed*; cf. *season*.

Sow (2), a female pig. (E.) Also applied to oblong pieces of melted metal, whence smaller pieces branch out, called *pigs*. M. E. *sowe*. A. S. *sugu*, also *sū*.+ Du. *zog*, Icel. *sȳr*, Dan. *so*, Swed. *so*, *sugga*, G. *sau*; W. *hwch*, Irish *suig*, L. *sūs*, Gk. *ῦς*, a sow; Zend *hu*, a boar. Perhaps 'producer,' from the prolific nature of the sow. (√SŪ, to produce.) **Der.** *swine*.

Soy, a sauce. (Japanese.) Also *sooja*, 'which has been corrupted into *soy*;' Eng. Cycl. Japanese *shōyu*, soy, sauce; though the name is now given to the bean (*Dolichos soja*) whence *soy* is made. But the Jap. name for the bean is *daidzu*.

Spa, a place where is a spring of mineral water. (Belgium.) Named after *Spa*, S.W. of Liège, in Belgium.

Space. (F.—L.) F. *espace*.—L. *spatium*, a space. Allied to **Span.** Brugm. i. § 193. **Der.** *spac-i-ous*.

Spade (1). (E.) A. S. *spædu*, *spada*, a spade.+Du. *spade*, Icel. *spaði*, Dan. Swed. *spade*, G. *spaten*; Gk. *σπάθη*, broad blade, sword-blade, spathe of a flower (whence L. *spatha*, F. *épée*). From its flat surface. (√SPA, to draw out.) **Der.** *spaddle*, a paddle.

spade (2), at cards. (Span.—L.—Gk.) A substitution for the Span. *espada*, meaning (1) a sword, (2) a spade at cards. **Der.** *spad-ille*, ace of spades, F. *spadille*, Span. *espadilla*, small sword, ace of spades, dimin. of Span. *spada*, a spade (< L. *spatha* < Gk. *σπάθη*). See **Spade** (1).

Spalpeen, a mean fellow. (Irish.) Irish *spailpin*, a common labourer, a mean fellow, Gael. *spailpean*. From Ir. *spailp*, a beau; orig. pride.

Span, to measure, grasp. (E.) M. E. *spannen*. A. S. *spannan*, to bind, pt. t. *spēnn*; *gespannan*, to bind, connect.+ O. H. G. *spannan*, to extend, connect; Du. *spannen*, to span, stretch, put horses to, Dan. *spænde*, Swed. *spänna*, to stretch, span, buckle; Icel. *spenna*, to clasp. Allied to **Space** and **Spin.** (√SPA.) **Der.** *span*, sb., stretch of the hand, 9 inches in space.

Spancel. (North E.) 'A rope to tye a cows hinder legs;' Ray. From *span*, to tie, and Icel. *seil* (A. S. *sāl*), a rope. +Du. *spanzeel*; G. *spannseil*.

Spandrel. (F.—L.) The space be-

tween the outer mouldings of an arch and a horizontal line above it. As if from O. F. **espanderel*, from O. F. *espandeur*, that which spreads.—O. F. *espandre*, to spread, expand. See **Expand, Spawn.**

Spangle. (E.) M. E. *spangel*, dimin. of *spang*, a metal fastening (hence, small shining ornament). A. S. *spange*, a metal clasp.+E. Fries. and M. Du. *spange*, a thin plate of metal; Icel. *spöng*; G. *spange*, brooch, clasp, buckle.

Spaniel. (F. — Span. — L.) M. E. *spaniel*, *spaneȝeole*. — O. F. *espagneul*, a spaniel, Spanish dog. — Span. *Español*, Spanish.—Span. *España*, Spain.—L. *Hispania*, Spain.

Spank, to slap, move quickly. (E.) We also have *spanker*, a large active man or animal; *spanking*, large, lusty. An E. word.+Low G. *spakkern*, *spenkern*, to run and spring about quickly; E. Fries. *spenkelen*, *spenkern*, to burst; fly about; Dan. *spanke*, to strut about. From a base **spak*, significant of quick action; cf. E. Fries. *spaken*, to split, burst with heat. **Der.** *spank-er*, an after-sail in a barque.

Span-new, quite new. (Scand.) The *a* has been shortened by the stress upon it. M. E. *span-newe*. — Icel. *spānnȳr*, *spānȳr*, span-new, lit. 'new as a chip.' — Icel. *spānn*, a chip, shaving, spoon; *nȳr*, new. See **Spoon.**

Spar (1), a beam, bar. (E.) M. E. *sparre*. The A. S. sb. is vouched for by the derived verb *sparrian*, to fasten a door with a bar.+Du. *spar*, Icel. *sparri*, Dan. Swed. *sparre*; O. H. G. *sparro*, G. *sparren*, spar, bar. [Irish and Gael. *sparr*, beam, are from E.] **Der.** *spar*, vb., to fasten a door.

Spar (2), a mineral. (E.) A. S. *spær-stān*, a spar-stone. Cf. G. *sparkalk*, plaster. ¶ Distinct from G. *spat*, *spath*, spar.

Spar (3), to box, wrangle. (F. — Teut.) Used of fighting-cocks.—M. F. *esparer*, 'to fling or yerk out with the heels;' Cot.— Low G. *sparre*, sb., a struggling, striving; G. *sich sperren*, to struggle against, resist, oppose. Allied to Skt. *sphur*, to throb, struggle; Gk. *σπαίρειν*, *ἀσπαίρειν*, to struggle convulsively; Russ. *sporite*, to quarrel, wrangle. (√SPER.) And see **Spur, Spurn.** Brugm. i. § 509 (3).

Sparable, a small nail used for boots. (E.) Formerly *sparrow-bill*; from the shape.

Spare, frugal, lean. (E.) A. S. *spær,* spare; whence *sparian,* vb., to spare.+ Icel. *sparr,* Dan. *spar-som,* Swed. *spar-sam,* G. *spar-sam, spär-lich,* thrifty. Der. *sparing, spare-rib*; *spare,* vb., from A. S. *sparian* (above); so also Du. and G. *sparen,* Icel. and Swed. *spara,* Dan. *spare.*

Spark (1), a small particle of fire. (E.) O. Merc. *spærca* (Sweet); A.S. *spearca.*+ M. Du. *sparcke*; Low G. *sparke.* Perhaps so called from the crackling of a fire-brand, which throws out sparks; cf. Icel. *spraka,* to crackle, Lith. *spragèti,* to crackle like burning fire-wood, Gk. σφάραγος, a crackling. Brug. i. § 531.

Spark (2), a gay young fellow. (Scand.) The same as Wiltsh. *sprack,* lively. — Icel. *sparkr,* sprightly, also *sprækr*; Swed. dial. *spräker, spräk, sprüg,* talkative. Cf. **Spark** (1). Der. *sprag,* i. e. *sprack,* used by Sir Hugh, Merry Wives, iv. 1. 84.

Sparkle, vb., to throw out sparks, to glitter. (E.) Cf. Du. *sparkelen,* to sparkle. The form *spark-le* is frequentative. See **Spark** (1).

Sparrow. (E.) A. S. *spearwa.*+Icel. *spörr,* Dan. *spurv,* Swed. *sparf,* Goth. *sparwa*; O. H. G. *sparo,* G. *sper ling.* Lit. 'flutterer;' from √SPER, to quiver. See **Spar** (3). Der. *sparrow-hawk*; and see *sparable, sparoin.*

Sparse, thinly scattered. (L.) L. *sparsus,* pp. of *spargere,* to scatter, sprinkle. Allied to Gk. σπείρειν; see **Sperm.**

Spasm. (F. – L. – Gk.) F. *spasme,* the cramp. – L. *spasmum,* acc. of *spasmus.* – Gk. σπασμός, a spasm. – Gk. σπᾶν, σπάειν, to draw, pluck. (√SPA.) Der. *spasm-od-ic,* from Gk. σπασμώδης, convulsive.

Spat (1), a blow, a slap. (E.) Of imitative origin; cf. *slap, slam, pat.*

Spat (2), young of shell-fish. (E.) From *spat-,* to eject, the base of *spatter.* Cf. Du. *spat,* a speckle, spot; and see **Spatter.**

Spate, a river-flood. (F. – Teut.) Cf. Irish *speid,* a great river-flood; borrowed from E. **spate.** The same as North E. *spait,* a torrent of rain; also spelt *speat.* G. Douglas has *spait,* a torrent; cf. Verg. Aen. ii. 496. – A. F. **espeit* = O. F. *espoit,* a spouting out (Godefroy). – E. Fries. *speiten, speuten, spoiten,* W. Flem. *speeten,* Du. *spuiten,* to spout; see **Spout.**

Spats, gaiters. (E.) Short for *spatter-dashes.*

Spatter, to besprinkle. (E.) A fre-quentative of *spat-,* with the sense to throw, to splash. E. Fries. *spatten,* to burst, fly out, spirt.+Du. *spatten,* to throw, spatter, splash. Der. *spatter-dashes,* gaiters, to protect against *spatterings* and *dashes.* See **Spats.**

Spatula, a broad-bladed knife for spreading plaisters. (L. – Gk.) L. *spatula,* dimin. of *spatha.* – Gk. σπάθη, a broad blade. See **Spade** (1).

Spavin, a swelling near the joints of horses, producing lameness. (F. – Teut.) M. E. *spaveyne.* – O. F. *esparvin* (13th c., in Hatzfeld); M. F. *esparvain,* 'a spavin in the leg of a horse;' Cot. The same as Span. *esparavan,* (1) a sparrow-hawk, (2) spavin; answering to a Low L. adj. **sparvānus,* belonging to a sparrow, parallel to Late L. *sparvārius,* a sparrow-hawk, lit. belonging to sparrows; cf. G. *sperber,* a sparrow-hawk. Perhaps the lit. sense is 'sparrow like,' from the hopping or sparrow-like motion of a horse afflicted with spavin. Derived from O. H. G. *sparwe,* a sparrow, cognate with E. **Sparrow,** q. v. ¶ Generally explained as 'sparrow-hawk-like,' contrary to grammar and sense. However, the result is, in any case, doubtful.

Spaw, the same as **Spa,** q. v.

Spawn, the eggs of fish or frogs (F. – L.) From M. E. *spawnen, spanen,* to spawn, as fishes; Prompt. Parv. For *spaund,* with loss of *d.* See Wright's Voc. i. 164; N. & Q. 6 S. v. 465. – M. F. *espandre,* 'to shed, spill, pour out, scatter abroad in great abundance;' Cot. – L. *expandere,* to spread out, shed abroad; see **Expand.**

Speak. (E.) M. E. *speken,* also (before A. D. 1200) *spreken*; the word has lost an *r.* Late A. S. *specan,* A. S. *sprecan,* pt. t. *spræc,* pp. *sprecen.* + Du. *spreken*; G. *sprechen,* pt. t. *sprach.* All perhaps from Teut. base SPREK, to make a noise; cf. Icel. *spraka,* to crackle; see **Spark** (1), and Prellwitz, s. v. σφάραγος.

Spear. (E.) M. E. and A. S. *spere.*+ Du. *speer,* Icel. *spjör,* Dan. *spær,* G. *speer*; cf. L. *sparus,* a small missile-weapon, dart. Perhaps allied to *spar,* a beam, bar (hence, a pole).

Special. (F. – L.) Short for *especial*; see **Especial.**

Specie, money in gold or silver. (L.) Evolved as a sb. from the old word *species,* 'money paid by tale,' Phillips; prob. by confusion with L. abl. *speciē,* as if *paid in specie* = paid in visible coin.

species, a kind. (L.) L. *speciēs*, look, appearance, kind, sort. — L. *specere*, to look, see. +O. H. G. *spehōn*, G. *spähen*, to spy ; Skt. *paç*, *spaç*, to spy. (√SPEK, to see.) Brugm. i. § 551.

specify. (F. — L.) O. F. *specifier*, to particularise. — L. *specificāre*. — L. *specificus*, specific, particular. — L. *speci-ēs*, kind ; *-fic-*, for *facere*, to make.

specimen. (L.) L. *specimen*, an example, something shown. — L. *speci-*, for *specere*, to see ; with suffix *-men*.

specious, showy. (F. — L.) M. F. *specieux*, fair. — L. *speciōsus*, fair to see. — L. *speci-ēs*, appearance ; with suffix *-ōsus*.

Speck, a small spot. (E.) A. S. *specca*, a spot, mark. Allied to Low G. *spakig*, spotted with wet, *spaken*, to spot with wet ; M. Du. *spickelen*, to speckle, frequentative of M. Du. *spicken*, to spit ; Du. *spikkel*, a speckle, spot. Der. *speck-le*, a little speck; *speck-le*, vb.

Spectacle. (F. — L.) F. *spectacle*, a sight. — L. *spectāculum*, a show. — L. *spectāre*, to behold, frequentative of *specere*, to see.

spectator. (L.) L. *spectātor*, a beholder. — L. *spectā-re*, to see ; with suffix *-tor*. — L. *spect-um*, supine of *specere*, to see.

spectre. (F. — L.) F. *spectre*, 'an image, ghost ;' Cot. — L. *spectrum*, a vision. — L. *spec-ere*, to see.

specular. (L.) L. *speculāris*, belonging to a mirror. — L. *speculum*, a mirror. — L. *spec-ere*, to see. ¶ But Milton uses it with reference to L. *specula*, a watchtower ; also from *spec-ere* ; see below.

speculate. (L.) From pp. of L. *speculārī*, to behold. — L. *specula*, a watchtower. — L. *spec-ere*, to see. Der. *speculation*, *-ive*.

Speech. (E.) M. E. *speche*. Late A. S. *spǣce*, dat. of *spǣc*, earlier form *sprǣc*, speech. — A. S. *sprǣc-*, 3rd grade of *sprecan*, to speak. +Du. *spraak*, G. *sprache*, speech. See **Speak**.

Speed, success, velocity. (E.) A. S. *spēd*, haste, success. For *spōdiz*, with the usual change from *ō* to *ē*. — A. S. *spōw-an*, to succeed ; with suffix *-diz* (Idg. *-tis*). + Du. *spoed*, speed ; O. H. G. *spuot*, *spōt*, success, from *spuon*, to succeed. Allied to Skt. *sphīti-*, increase, prosperity, from *sphāy*, to enlarge. Brugm. i. § 156. Der. *speed*, vb., A. S. *spēdan* ; from *spēd*, sb.

Speir, to ask. (E.) Northern E. A. S. *spyrian*, to ask, track out. — A. S. *spor*, a foot-track ; allied to *spora*, a spur ; see **Spur.** + Du. *speuren*, Icel. *spyrja*, G. *spüren* ; Low G. *späören*, to track, from *spaor*, a spoor, trail (Danneil).

Spelicans, thin slips of wood. (Du.) M. Du. *spelleken*, a small pin ; dimin. of M. Du. *spelle* (Du. *speld*), a splinter. See **Spell** (4). ¶ Distinct from Du. *spalk*, A. S. *spele*, a splint.

Spell (1), an incantation. (E.) M. E. *spel*. A. S. *spel*, *spell*, a saying, story, narrative ; hence a form of words, spell. +Icel. *spjall*, a saying ; O. H. G. *spel*, narrative ; Goth. *spill*, fable. Der. *go-spel*.

spell (2), to tell the names of letters in a word. (F. — Teut.) M. E. *spellen*, of spell ; also, to tell. — O. F. *espeler*, 'to spell ;' Cot. — Du. *spellen*, to spell ; or from O. H. G. *spellōn*, to tell, relate.+ A. S. *spellian*, to tell, recount, from A. S. *spell*, a story (above) ; Goth. *spillon*, to narrate. ¶ M. E. *spellen*, in the sense 'to relate,' is from A. S. *spellian*. We also find *speldren*, to spell, in the Ormulum, from *spelder*, a splinter ; see **Spell** (4) ; but this is a different word.

Spell (3), a turn of work. (E.) Cf. A. S. *spelian*, to supply another's room, to act or be proxy for ; allied to Du. *spelen*, Icel. *spila*, G. *spielen*, to act a part, play a game ; from the sb. appearing as Du. Swed. *spel*, Icel. Dan. *spil*, G. *spiel*, a game.

Spell (4), **Spill**, a thin slip of wood, slip of paper. (E.) Formerly *speld*. M.E. *speld*, a splinter. A. S. *speld*, a torch, spill to light a candle. Orig. a splinter ; from Teut. **spaldan-* (G. *spalten*), to cleave ; a reduplicating verb, like O. H. G. *spaltan*. +Du. *speld*, a pin, splinter ; Icel. *speld*, a square tablet, orig. thin piece of board, *spilda*, a slice ; Goth. *spilda*, a tablet ; M. H. G. *spelte*, a splinter. Cf. Shetland *speld*, to split.

Spelt, a kind of corn. (L.) A. S. *spelt*, corn. Cf. Du. *spelt*, G. *spelz*. Apparently borrowed from Late L. *spelta*, spelt ; whence also Ital. *spelta*, *spelda*, F. *épeautre*, spelt.

Spelter, pewter, zinc. (Low G.) In Blount (1674). Perhaps from Low G. *spialter*, pewter ; cf. Du. *spiauter*, M. Du. *speauter*, O. F. *espeautre*. ¶ This seems to be the original of **Pewter**, q. v. The history of these words is very obscure.

Spencer, a short over-jacket. (F. — L.) Named after Earl *Spencer*, died 1845. The

name is from M.E. *spenser*, also *despenser*.
— O.F. *despencier*, a spender, a caterer,
clerk of a kitchen; Cot. — O. F. *despenser*,
to spend; frequent. of *despendre*. — L. *dispendere*, to weigh out, pay. — L. *dis-*, apart;
pendere, to weigh. See **Pendant.**

spend. (L.) A.S. *spendan*, to spend.
Shortened from L. *dispendere*, to spend,
waste, consume. We find Late L. *spendium*
for *dispendium*, *spensa* for *dispensa*; also
spendibilis monēta, money for expenses
(A.D. 922). So also Ital. *spendere*, to
spend, *spendio* (< L. *dispendium*), expense. — L. *dis-*, away, part; *pendere*, to
weigh out, pay. ¶ Or (as usually said)
from L. *expendere*, which does not suit
the F. forms; see above. It makes no
great difference.

Sperm, spawn, spermaceti. (F. — L. —
Gk.) M. E. *sperme*. — F. *sperme*, 'sperm,
seed;' Cot. — L. *sperma*. — Gk. σπέρμα. —
Gk σπείρειν (for *σπερ yειν), to sow;
orig. to scatter with a jerk of the hand.
(√SPER.) Der. *sperm-at-ic* (Gk. σπερματι-
κός); *spermaceti*, L. *sperma-cētī*, i. e. sperm
of the whale; see **Cetaceous.**

Spew, Spue. (E.) A.S. *spīwan*,
pt. t. *spāw*, pp. *spiwen*, to vomit.+Du.
spuuwen, Icel. *spýja*, Dan. *spye*, Swed. *spy*,
G. *speien*, Goth. *speiwan*; L. *spuere*, Lith.
spjauti; Gk. πτύειν (for *σπιύειν), to spit.
(√SPIW.) Allied to *puke* (1), *spit* (2).
Brugm. i. § 567.

Sphere, a globe, ball. (F. — L. — Gk.)
M. E. *spere*. — O. F. *espere*, M. F. *sphere*. —
L. *sphæra*. — Gk. σφαῖρα, a ball.

Sphinx. (L. — Gk.) L. *sphinx*. — Gk.
σφίγξ (gen. σφιγγός), lit. 'the strangler,'
because the Sphinx strangled travellers
who could not solve her riddles. — Gk.
σφίγγειν, to throttle. ¶ The story suggests
that this is a 'popular' etymology; and
that the word is foreign to Greek.

Spice. (F. — L.) M. E. *spice*, formerly
used also in the sense of *species* or kind. —
O. F. *espice*, spice. — L. *speciem*, acc. of
speciēs, a kind, which in Late L. meant
also a spice, drug. See **Species.**

Spick and Span-new, wholly new.
(Scand.) Lit. 'spike and spoon-new,'
where *spike* is a nail, and *spoon* is a
splinter. See **Spike** and **Spoon.** Cf.
Swed. dial. *spik spangande ny* in Rietz
(with many variants), and Icel. *spān-nȳr*,
lit. spoon-new, splinter-new.

Spider. (E.) M. E. *spither*, *spidre*,
A. S. *spīder* or **spīðer* (for **spinðer*),

Leechdoms, iii. 42. Formed from the verb
to spin; cf. prov. E. *spinner*, a spider. +
Du. *spin*, Dan. *spinder*, Swed. *spindel*, G.
spinne, spider or spinner. And cf. **Spindle.**

Spigot. (Prov.) M.E. *spigot*, *spikket*,
a peg for a cask. Cf. Irish and Gael.
spiocaid, spigot (from E.). — Prov. **espigot*,
(not found); but cf. Prov. *espigoun*, a
spigot, a dimin. from L. *spīca*, an ear of
corn. Cf. also Walloon *spigot*, the peak
of a shoe. Also Port. *espicho*, a spigot,
from L. *spīculum*. — L. *spīca*, a point; see
below.

Spike (1), a sharp point, a nail.
(Scand.) From Icel. *spīk*, Swed. *spik*;
cf. Dan. *spiger*, Du. *spijker*, a nail. Apparently distinct from L. *spīca*; and allied
by gradation to **Spoke.**

Spike (2), an ear of corn. (L.) L.
spīca, an ear of corn, a point.

spikenard. (F. — L. and Gk. — Pers.)
— Skt.) O. F. *spiquenard*. — L. *spīca
nardī*, spike of nard; also *nardus spīcātus*,
i. e. nard furnished with spikes, in allusion
to the mode of growth. And see **Nard.**

Spill (1), a slip of paper for lighting
candles; see **Spell** (4).

Spill (2), to destroy, shed. (Scand.)
(Not allied to *spoil*.) M. E. *spillen*, to
destroy, mar; also to perish — Icel. *spilla*,
to destroy; Swed. *spilla*, Dan. *spilde*, to
spill. + A. S. *spildan*, to destroy; O. Sax.
spildian. Teut. type **spelth-jan-*; allied
to G. *spalten*, to split.

Spin, to draw out threads. (E.) A.S.
spinnan, pt. t. *spann*, pp. *spunnen*. + Du.
spinnen, Icel. Swed. *spinna*, Dan. *spinde*,
G. *spinnen*, Goth. *spinnan*. Allied to
Lith. *pin-ti*, to weave. See **Span.**

Spinach, Spinage, a vegetable.
(F. — Span. — Arab. — Pers.) *Spinage* is a
'voiced' form of *spinach*. O. F. *espinache*,
espinage, *espinace*. — Span. *espinaca*. —
Arab. *aspanākh*, *isfānāj*; of Pers. origin
(Devic). ¶ The Ital. *spinace* and Span.
espinaca are referred, by popular etymology, to L. *spīna*, a thorn; some say the
fruit is prickly, some say the leaves are so.
See **Spine.**

Spindle. (E.) The *d* is excrescent
after *n*. M. E. *spinel*, also *spindele*. A.S.
spinl, i.e. 'spinner,' from *spinnan*, to spin.
+ M. Du. *spille* (for **spinle*); G. *spindel*,
O. H. G. *spinnila*. Der. *spindl-y*, thin
like a spindle; *spindle-tree* (Euonymus)
formerly used for spindles and skewers.

Spine, a prickle. (F. — L.) O. F. *espine*,

a thorn.—L. *spīna*, a thorn, prickle; also the back-bone. ¶ Observe that in the sense of 'back-bone' the word is Latin only, not F.

spinet, a kind of musical instrument. (F.—Ital.—L.) So called because struck by a *spine* or pointed quill. O.F. *espinette*. —Ital. *spinetta*, a spinet, also a prickle; dimin. of *spina*, a thorn.—L. *spīna*.

Spink, a finch. (Scand.) M.E. *spink*. —Swed. dial. *spink*, a sparrow; *gull-spink*, a gold-finch; Norw. *spikke* (for **spinke*), Dan. dial. *spinke*, small bird. + Gk. σπίγγος, a finch, i.e. 'chirper;' from σπί-ζειν, to chirp. Cf. σπίζα, a finch, σπίνος, a small bird. Doublet, *finch*.

Spinny, a thicket. (F. — L.) O.F. *espinei*; M.F. *espinoye*, 'a thicket, grove, a thorny plot,' Cot.; F. *épinaie*. — L. *spīnētum*, a thicket of thorns.—L. *spīna*, a thorn. See **Spine**.

Spinster, orig. a woman who spins. (E.) M.E. *spinnestere*. From A.S. *spinnan*, to spin; with A.S. suffix *-estre* (E. *-ster*). β. This suffix is a compound one (*-es-tre*). It was used in A.S. (as in Du.) solely with reference to the feminine gender, but this restricted usage was soon set aside in a great many M.E. words. Cf. Du. *spinster*, a spinster, *zangster*, a female singer; also E. *seamstress* (i.e. *seam-ster-ess*), *songstress* (i.e. *song-ster-ess*), where the F. fem. suffix *-ess* is superadded.

Spiracle. (F.—L.) F. *spiracle*, 'a breathing-hole;' Cot. — L. *spīrāculum*, air-hole. — L. *spīrāre*, to breathe.

Spire (1), a tapering stem, sprout, steeple. (E.) A.S. *spīr*, spike, stalk.+ Icel. *spíra*, spar, stilt, Dan. *spire*, germ, sprout, Swed. *spira*, a pistil, G. *spiere*, a spar. ¶ Distinct from **Spire** (2).

Spire (2), a coil, wreath. (F. — L.—Gk.) F. *spire*. — L. *spīra*, a coil, twist, wreath. —Gk. σπεῖρα (for **σπερ-ya*), a coil; allied to σπάρτον, a rope, σπυρίς, a basket. (√SPER.) Der. *spir-al*, F. *spiral*, L. *spīrālis*.

Spirit. (F.—L.) M.E. *spirit*.—A.F. *espirit*; F. *esprit*.—L. acc. *spiritum*, from *spiritus*, breath.—L. *spīrāre*, to breathe. Doublet, *sprite*.

Spirt; see **Spurt**.

Spit (1), a skewer, iron prong for roasting meat. (E.) M.E. *spite*. A.S. *spitu*, a spit.+Du. *spit*, Dan. *spid*, Swed. *spett*; M.H.G. *spiz*, G. *spiess*, a spit; cf. *spitze*, a point, top.

Spit (2), to eject from the mouth. (E.) M.E. *spitten*, A.S. *spittan*; cf. *spǽtan*, pt. t. *spǽtte*, to spit. But we also find Dan. *spytte*, Swed. *spotta*, prov. G. *spützen* (cf. G. *spucken*); from Teut. **sput-*; see **Spout**. Perhaps **spit-*, **sput-* are both from **spēw-*, the root of **Spew**. Cf. Brugm. i. §§ 279 (1), 567. Der. *spittle*, formerly also *spettle*, *spatil*, *spotil*, A.S. *spǽtl*, *spātl*.

Spite. (F. — L.) M.E. *spyt*, *spite*. Merely short for *despite*, by loss of the first syllable (as in *fence* for *de-fence*). See **Despite. Der.** *spite-ful*.

Spittle (1), saliva; see **Spit** (2).

Spittle (2), a hospital. (F.—L.) M.E. *spitel*.—O.F. *ospital*, hospital; see **Hospital.**

Splash, to dash water about. (E.) Coined by prefixing *s-* (=O.F. *es-*, L. *ex*) used for emphasis, *to plash*, used in the same sense (White Kennett). See **Plash** (1); and cf. Du. *plassen*, to plash; E. Fries. *plassen*, *plasken*, *platsken*, Dan. *pladske*, to splash, dabble.

Splay, to slope, in architecture; to dislocate a bone. (F.—L.) In both senses it can be proved to be a contraction for **Display. Der.** *splay-footed*.

Spleen. (L. — Gk.) M.E. *splen*. — L. *splēn*. — Gk. σπλήν, the spleen. Cf. Skt. *plihan-*; L. *liēn*. Brugm. i. § 549 (c). Der. *splen-etic*.

Splendour. (F.—L.) F. *splendeur*. — L. *splendōrem*, acc. of *splendor*, brightness. — L. *splendēre*, to shine. Der. *re-splendent*.

Spleuchan, a tobacco-pouch. (Gael.) Gael. *spliuchan*, Irish *spliuchan*, a pouch.

Splice. (Du.) M.Du. *splissen*, to interweave rope-ends; so named from *splitting* the rope-ends beforehand; from Du. *splitsen*, to splice (really an older form). Formed from *split-*, weak grade of Du. *splijten*, to split.+ Dan. *splidse*, to splice (for **splitse*), allied to *splitte*, to split; Swed. *splissa*; G. *splissen*, to splice. See **Split. Der.** *splice*, sb.

splint, splent, a thin piece of split wood. (Scand.) Formerly *splent*; from O.F. *esplente*, a thin steel plate. — Swed. *splint*, a kind of spike, a forelock (flat iron peg); Dan. *splint*, a splinter; cf. Low G. *splinte*, an iron pin; E. Fries. *splinte*, *splint*, the same. Cf. Swed. *splinta*, to splinter, ultimately allied to Dan. *splitte*, Swed. dial. *splitta*, to split; see **Split. Der.** *splinter*; cf. Du. and E. Fries. *splinter*.

Split. (Du.?) Apparently borrowed from M. Du. *splitten*, to split; cf. Dan. *splitte*, to split, Swed. dial. *splitta*, to disentangle or separate yarn. From the weak grade *split-* of the Teut. strong verb **spleitan-*, as seen in O. Fries. *splīta*, Du. *splijten*, E. Fries. *spliten*, Low G. *spliten*, G. *spleissen*, to split, cleave. Hence also Dan. *split*, Du. *spleet*, a split, rent, G. *spleisse*, a splinter.

Splutter, to speak hastily and confusedly. (E.) Of imitative origin; a variant of *sputter*, which is a frequentative of *spout*; see **Spout, Spurt.** It means 'to keep on *spouting* out'; *spout* being formerly used (as now) in the sense 'to talk.' 'Pray, *spout* some French;' Beaum. and Fletcher, Coxcomb, iv. 4. Cf. Low G. *sprutten*, to spout, spurt.

Spoil, to plunder. (F.–L.) M. E. *spoilen.* — O. F. *espoillier*; F. *spolier*, 'to spoile;' Cot. — L. *spoliare*, to strip off spoil. — L. *spolium*, spoil, booty; orig. skin stripped off, dress of a slain warrior. Der. *spoil,* sb.; *spoliation,* from L. pp. *spoliātus.*

Spoke, a bar of a wheel. (E.) A. S. *spāca*, a spoke. +Du. *speek*, a spoke, G. *speiche,* prov. G. *spache*, a spoke. Teut. types **spaikon-, *spaikōn-.* Allied by gradation to **Spike** (1).

Spokesman. (E.) In Shak. Two Gent. ii. 1. 151. Formed from *spoke*, pt. t. of *speak*, instead of from the infin. *speak*; for the *s*, cf. *hunt-s-man, sport-s-man.*

Spoliation; see **Spoil.**

Spondee. (L.–Gk.) The metrical foot marked (– –). — L. *spondēus.* — Gk. σπονδεῖος, a spondee, used for solemn melodies at treaties or truces. — Gk. σπονδαί, a solemn treaty, truce; pl. of σπονδή, a drink-offering, libation to the gods. — Gk. σπένδειν, to pour out. Prob. allied to **Sponsor.** Brugm. i. § 143, ii. § 802. Der. *sponda-ic.*

Sponge. (F.–L.–Gk.) O. F. *esponge* (F. *éponge*). — L. *spongia.* — Gk. σπογγιά, a sponge; also σπόγγος (Attic σφόγγος). +L. *fungus*, a fungus (from its spongy nature).

Sponsor. (L.) L. *sponsor*, a surety. — L. *sponsus*, pp. of *spondēre*, to promise. Prob. allied to Gk. σπονδαί, a truce, and to **Spondee.** Brugm. i. § 143.

Spontaneous. (L.) L. *spontāne-us*, willing; with suffix *-ous.* — L. *spont-*, as seen in abl. *sponte*, of one's own accord, from a lost nom. **spons.*

Spook, a ghost. (Du.) Du. *spook*; Low G. *spook*, Swed. *spöke*, a ghost; cf. Du. *spoken*, Low G. *spöken*, Swed. *spöka*, to haunt.

Spool, a reel for winding yarn on. (M. Du.) M. E. *spole.* — M. Du. *spoele*, a spoel, a spool, quill; Low G. *spöle.*+Swed. *spole,* Dan. *spole*, G. *spule*, spool, bobbin. Cf. Icel. *spölr* (base *spal-*), a bar.

Spoom, to run before the wind. (L.) Lit. 'to throw up *spume* or foam.'–L. *spūma*, foam.

Spoon, an instrument for supping liquids. (E.) M. E. *spon.* A. S. *spōn*, a chip, splinter of wood (which was the orig. spoon). +Du. *spaan*, Icel. *spānn, spōnn,* Dan. *spaan*, Swed. *spån*, G. *spahn*, a chip.

Spoor, a trail. (Du.) Du. *spoor*; see **Spur.** Cf. A. S. *spor*, a foot-track; see **Speir.**

Sporadic, scattered here and there. (Gk.) Gk. σποραδικός, scattered. — Gk. σποραδ-, stem of σποράς, scattered. — Gk. σπείρειν (for **σπερ-γειν*), to scatter.

spore. (Gk.) Gk. σπόρος, seed-time; also a seed. — Gk. σπείρειν, to sow.

Sporran. (Gael.–L.–Gk.) Gael. *sporan*, a purse, pouch worn with the kilt; Irish *sparan, sboran*, the same. For **s-burran* < **s-burs-an.* — L. *bursa*, a purse. — Gk. βύρσα, a hide. See **Purse.**

Sport, mirth. (F.–L.) Short for *disport, desport*; (so also *splay* for *display*). The verb is M. E. *disporten*, to amuse; see **Disport.**

Spot, a blot, mark made by wet, piece of ground. (E.) M. E. *spot.* Cf. Norw. *spott*, m., a spot, a small piece of ground (distinct from *spott*, f., mockery); Icel. *spotti, spottr*, a small piece; E. Fries. *spot*, a spot; cf. M. Du. *spotten*, to spot, stain. From Teut. **sput-*, weaker grade of **spūtan-*; see **Spout.**

Spouse. (F.–L.) From O. F. *espouse*, a spouse. — L. *sponsa*, a betrothed woman; fem. pp. of *spondēre*, to promise; see **Sponsor.**

Spout, to squirt out, rush out as a liquid out of a pipe. (E.) M. E. *spouten.* Cf. Swed. *sputa*, occasionally used for *spruta*, to squirt, spout, spurt, spatter; Du. *spuiten,* to spout, *spuit*, a squirt; Dan. *spyte*, to spit, sputter. From Teut. **spūtan-*, to spit out, with weaker grade **sput-* (Franck).

Sprack, Sprag; see **Spark** (2).

Sprain, vb. (F.–L.) Formed from O. F. *espreign-*, a stem of O. F. *espreindre,* 'to press, wring,' Cot. ; (cf. *strain* from O. F. *estreindre*). Mod. F. *épreindre*. — L. *exprimere*, to press out (whence *espreindre*, by analogy with F. forms from verbs in *-ingere*). — L. *ex*, out ; *premere*, to press. See **Press**. Der. *sprain*, sb.

Sprat, a small fish. (E.) M. E. *sprot*. A. S. *sprott*. Cf. A. S. *sprot*, a sprout. + Du. *sprot*, a sprat ; also (in M. Du.) a sprout of a tree. '*Sprat*, a small fish, considered as the fry of the herring ;' Wedgwood. From A. S. *sprot-* (Teut. **sprut-*), weaker grade of *sprūtan-*, to sprout ; with the sense of 'fry,' or young one. See **Sprout**.

Sprawl, to toss about the limbs. (E.) M. E. *spraulen*. A. S. *spreawlian*, to move convulsively, to sprawl. + Norw. *sprala*, Dan. *sprælla*, *sprælde*, Swed. dial. *sprala*, *spralla*, N. Fries. *sprawle*.

Spray (1), foam tossed with the wind. (Low G.) A late word, given in Bailey's Dict. (1735). From Low G. *sprei*, a slight drizzle (Schambach) ; in Coburg, *sprœ* ; cf. Bavar. *sprœen*, to drizzle (Schmeller) ; G. *sprühen* ; M. H. G. *sprœjen*, *sprœwen* ; Du. *sproeien* (see Franck).

Spray (2), sprig of a tree. (E.) M. E. *spray* ; answering to A. S. **sprœg*, allied to A. S. *sprœc*, a shoot, spray ; cf. Dan. *sprag*, a spray (Molbech), Swed. dial. *spragge*, a green branch, Icel. *sprek*, a stick. Cf. also Lith. *sproga*, a spray of a tree, also a rift, from *sprog-ti*, to crackle, split, sprout, bud. (Difficult and doubtful.)

Spread. (E.) A. S. *sprœdan*, to extend. + Du. *spreiden*, Low G. *spreden*, G. *spreiten* ; cf. Swed. *sprida*, Dan. *sprede*, to spread. Teut. type **spraidjan-* ; from a Teut. root **spreid*.

Spree, a frolic. (Scand.?) Cf. Irish *spre*, a spark, flash, animation, spirit ; Lowl. Sc. *spree*, a frolic, also spelt *spray* (Scott) ; cf. Swed. dial. *sprag*, lively conversation. Perhaps allied to **Spry**.

Sprig. (E.) M. E. *sprigge*. Allied to A. S. *sprœc*, a twig. + Icel. *sprek*, a stick ; Low G. *sprikk*, E. Fries. *sprikke*, *sprik*, stick, twig. Allied to **Spray** (2).

Sprightly, Spritely. (F. — L ; *with* E. *suffix*.) *Sprightly* is a false spelling ; *spritely* is from **Sprite**, q. v.

Spring, vb. (E.) A. S. *springan*, pt. t. *sprang*, pp. *sprungen*. + Du. G. *springen*, Swed. *springa*, Dan. *springe* ; Icel. *springa*, to burst, split. β. Orig. sense to 'split or crack,' as when we say

that a cricket-bat is *sprung* ; or to *spring* (i. e. burst) a mine. Teut. type **sprengan-*. Perhaps allied to Gk. σπέρχειν, to drive on (Prellwitz) ; but this is doubtful. Der. *spring*, sb., a leap, also a bursting out of water, also the budding time of year, also a crack in a mast ; *springe*, a snare made with a flexible (springing) rod, like O. H. G. *springa*.

Sprinkle. (Du. ?) Formerly *sprenkle* ; perhaps borrowed from Du. *sprenkelen*, to sprinkle. Cf. G. *sprenkeln*, to sprinkle, from M. H. G. *sprenkel*, a spot, allied to Icel. *sprekla*, Swed. *spräkla*, a little spot. See Kluge (s. v. *sprenkel*).

Sprint ; see **Spurt** (2).

Sprit, a spar extending a fore-and-aft sail. (E.) M. E. *spret*, a pole. A. S. *sprēot*, a pole ; orig. a sprout, shoot, branch of a tree. Allied to A. S. *sprūtan*, to sprout ; see **Sprout**. + E. Fries. *sprēt* ; Du. *spriet* ; M. Swed. *sprӧte*.

Sprite, a spirit. (F. — L.) The false spelling *spright* is common, and is retained in the adj. *sprightly*. M. E. *sprit*, *sprite*. — F. *esprit*, the spirit ; hence, a spirit. — L. *spīritum*, acc. of *spīritus* ; see **Spirit**.

Sprout, to germinate. (E.) M. E. *spruten*. A. S. **sprūtan* (found in the pp. *ā-sproten*) ; O. Fries. *sprūta*, strong verb, pp. *spruten*, to sprout. + Low G. *spruten*, to sprout ; Du. *spruiten*, G. *spriessen* (pt. t. *spross*) ; Swed. *spruta*, Dan. *sprude*, to squirt, spurt, spout. Teut. type **sprūtan-*, pt. t. **spraut*, pp. **sprūtanoz*. Compare **Spout**.

Spruce, fine, smart. (F. — G.) Hall's Chronicle tells us that a particular kind of fashionable dress was that in which men 'were appareyled after the manner of *Prussia* or *Spruce*' ; see Richardson's Dict. M. E. *spruce*, Prussia, P. Plowman, C. vii. 279, B. xiii. 393 ; also written (more usually) *pruce*. — O. F. *Pruce* (F. *Prusse*), Prussia. — G. *Preussen*, Prussia. See **Spruce-beer**.

Spruce-beer, a kind of beer. (G. ; *confused with* F. *and* E.) The E. name for German *sprossen-bier*, i. e. 'sprouts-beer,' obtained from the young sprouts of the black spruce fir. — G. *sprossen*, pl. of *spross*, a sprout (from *spriessen*, to sprout) ; and *bier*, cognate with E. *beer* ; see **Sprout** and **Beer**. β. Englished as *Spruce-beer*, i. e. Prussian beer, where *Spruce* meant *Prussia* ; see **Spruce** above. So also *spruce fir* (substituted for *sprossen-fichte*) meant Prussian fir; and *spruce leather* meant Prussian leather.

Spry, active. (E.?) Cf. Swed. dial. *sprygg,* very active, skittish; allied to Swed. dial. *spräg, sprak,* spirited, mettlesome. See **Spark** (2).

Spue; see **Spew.**

Spume, foam. (L.) L. *spūma,* foam; for **spoima;* Brugm. i. § 791. Cf. Skt. *phena-,* A. S. *fām,* foam.

Spunk, tinder; a match, spark, spirit, mettle. (C.—L.—Gk.) Orig. 'tinder.'— Gael. *spong,* Irish *sponc,* sponge, spongy wood, tinder.—L. *spongia,* a sponge; see **Sponge.** Cf. W. *ysbwng,* a sponge, from Latin.

Spur. (E.) M. E. *spure.* A. S. *spura, spora,* a spur.+Du. *spoor,* a spur (allied to *spoor,* a track); Icel. *spori,* Dan. *spore,* Swed. *sporre,* O. H. G. *sporo,* spur. From the weak grade of Teut. **sper-an-,* to kick. Brugm. i. § 793 (2). (√SPER.) See **Spar** (3). The orig. sense is 'kicker'; from its use on the heel; cf. Lith. *spīr-ti,* to kick. Der. *spur,* vb. See **Spoor, Spurn.**

Spurge, a plant. (F.—L.) Named from its corroding (and so cleansing away) warts.—O. F. *spurge, espurge.*—O. F. *espurger,* to purge away.—L. *expurgāre,* to cleanse away.—L. *ex,* away; *purgāre,* to cleanse. See **Purge.**

Spurious. (L.) L. *spuri-us,* false; with suffix *-ous.*

Spurn. (E.) M. E. *spurnen,* to kick against, hence to reject. A. S. *spurnan,* to kick against (pt. t. *spearn,* pp. *spornen*). Allied to **Spur.**+Icel. *sperna* (pt. t. *sparn*); Swed. *spjärna;* L. *spernere,* to despise, a cognate form. (Base **spern;* √SPER.) See **Spar** (3). Brugm. i. § 565.

Spurry, a plant. (F.—G.—Late L.) M. F. *spurrie,* 'spurry or frank, a Dutch [German] herb;' Cot. Of Teut. origin.; cf. G. *spörgel, spergel, spark,* spurry.— Late L. *spergula,* A. D. 1482 (Weigand).

Spurt (1), **Spirt,** to spout out. (E.) The older sense is to germinate. *Spurt* stands for *sprut;* M. E. *sprutten,* to sprout or shoot. A. S. *spryttan,* to produce as a sprout or shoot; causal form from A. S. *sprūtan,* to sprout. See **Sprout.**

Spurt (2), a violent exertion. (Scand.) Formerly *spirt.*—Icel. *sprettr,* a spurt, spring, bound, run. — Icel. *spretta* (pt. t. *spratt*), to start, spring; also to sprout, to

spout. Icel. *spretta* is for **sprenta, *sprinta* (Noreen). See **Sprint.**

Sputter. (E.) The frequentative of *spout.* It means 'to keep on spouting out'; hence to speak rapidly and indistinctly. Cf. Du. dial. (Groningen) *spöttern,* to sputter; Low G. *sputtern,* Norw. *sputra,* to spout. ¶ Distinct from but allied to *spatter* and *spot.*

Spy, to see. (F.—O. H. G.) Short for *espy;* see **Espy.** Der. *spy,* sb.

Squab, (1) to fall plump; (2) a sofa, a young bird. (Scand.) See *squab, squob* in Halliwell. And see *squab,* to fall plump, *squab,* with a sudden fall, in Johnson. 1. From Swed. dial. *skvapp,* a word imitative of a splash; cf. G. *schwapp,* a slap, E. *swap,* to strike. 2. From Swed. dial. *skvabb,* loose or fat flesh, *skvabba,* a fat woman, *skvabbig,* flabby; allied to Norw. *skvapa,* to tremble, shake, and cf. M. E. *quappen,* to throb, and E. *quaver,* see **Quaver.** Cf. Icel. *kvap,* jelly, jelly-like things.

squabble, to wrangle. (Scand.) Swed. dial. *skvabbel,* a dispute. — Swed. dial *skvappa,* to chide, lit. make a splashing, from the sb. *skvapp, svvapp,* a splash. Cf. Prov. E. *swabble,* to squabble, allied to *swab,* to splash over, *swap,* to strike.

Squad, a small troop. (F.—Ital.—L.) M. F. *esquadre, escadre.*—Ital. *squadra,* a squadron; see **Square.**

squadron. (F. — Ital. — L.) M. F. *esquadron.*—Ital. *squadrone;* augmentative of *squadra* (above).

Squalid. (L.) L. *squālidus,* rough, dirty.—L. *squālēre,* to be rough, parched, dirty. Der. *squal-or,* sb.

Squall, to cry out. (Scand.) Swed. *sqvala,* to gush out violently, *sqval,* a rush of water, *sqval-regn,* a violent shower of rain (E. *squall,* sb., a burst of rain); Dan. *sqvaldre,* to clamour, *sqvalder,* clamour, noisy talk; Swed. dial. *skvala,* to gush out, cry out, chatter. + Gael. *sgal,* a loud cry, sound of high wind; allied to G. *schallen,* Icel. *skjalla* (pt. t. *skall*), to resound, and W. *chwalu,* to babble.

Squander, to dissipate. (E.) Orig. to disperse, scatter abroad; Dryden, Annus Mirabilis, st. 67. Nasalised form allied to Lowl. Sc. *squatter,* to splash about, scatter, squander, prov. E. *swatter,* to throw water about; Swed. dial. *skvättra,* to squander. These are frequentatives from Dan. *sqvatte,* to splash, spurt, also to squander; Swed.

sqvätta, to squirt, Icel. *skvetta* (for
*skwenta, perhaps allied to G. σπένδειν, to
pour out; see Noreen), to squirt out water.
The *d* appears in M. Du. *swadderen*, to
dabble in water; Swed. dial. *skvadra*, to
gush out of a hole (as water). Cf. *scatter*
and Gk. σκέδ-ασις, a scattering.

Square. (F. — L.) M. E. *square*. —
O. F. *esquarré*, squared; *esquarre*, a square,
squareness. Cf. Ital. *squadrare*, to square;
squadra, a square, also a squadron of men
(orig. a square). All from Late L. **ex-
quadrāre*, intensive (with prefix *ex*) of L.
quadrāre, to square. — L. *quadrus*, four-
cornered; see **Quadrate.**

Squash, to crush. (F.—L.) **α.** The
mod. E. *squash* appears to be due to *quash*,
with the prefix *s-* = O. F. *es-* < L. *ex-*,
used as an intensive. — O. F. *esquasser*,
to break in pieces, from O. F. *es-*, and
quasser, casser, to break; see **Quash.**
β. But it commonly keeps the sense of
M. E. *squachen*, to crush. — O. F. *esqua-
chier*, to crush, also spelt *escacher*, 'to
squash;' Cot. (Mod. F. *écacher*). The
F. *cacher* answers to a Late L. type **coac-
ticāre*, due to L. *co-actāre*, to constrain,
force, press. The prefix *es-* = L. *ex*, extremely; L. *coactāre* is formed from *coact-us*,
pp. of *cōgere* (= *coigere*), to drive together.
See **Ex-** and **Cogent**; also **Con-** and
Agent. Der. *squash*, sb., an unripe
peascod (nearly flat).

squat, to cower. (F. — L.) Lit. to lie
flat, as if pressed down; the old sense is to
press down, squash. M. E. *squatten*, to
crush flat. — O. F. *esquatir*, to flatten,
crush. — O. F. *es-* (= L. *ex*), extremely;
quatir, to beat down. Diez shows that
O. F. *quatir* (Late L. type *coactīre) is
a derivative of L. *coactus*, pp. of *cōgere*,
to press, compel; see above. Cf. M. Ital.
quattare, 'to squat, lie close.'

Squaw, a female. (W. Indian.) Massachusetts *squa, eshqua*, Narragansett *squāws*,
a female (Webster); Cree *iskwew*.

Squeak, to cry out shrilly. (Scand.)
M. Swed. *skwæka*, to squeak; Swed.
sqväka, to croak; Norw. *skvaka*, to cackle;
Icel. *skvakka*, to sound like water shaken
in a bottle. Allied to **Quack.**

Squeal. (Scand.) M. Swed. *sqwæla*,
Swed. dial. *sqväla*, Norw. *skvella*, to squeal.
Used as a frequentative of *squeak*, and ap-
plied to a continuous cry. See **Squall.**

Squeamish, over-nice. (F. — Gk. ?)
Squamish, Baret (1580). M. E. *skeymous*,

sweymous, Prompt. Parv.; also *squaimous*,
skoymus, disdainful. — A. F. *escoymous*,
delicate, nice as to food (Bozon). The
form answers to L. type *schēmatōsus or
*schēmōsus; from *schēma* (Gk. σχῆμα),
scheme, form, air, mien, manner. ¶ Not
related to **Shame.**

Squeeze, to crush, press tightly. (E.)
The prefixed *s* is due to O. F. *es-* (= L. *-ex*),
very; *queeze* = late M. E. *queisen*, to
squeeze. This M. E. *queisen* probably
represents O. Merc. *cwēsan, answering to
A. S. *cwīesan, cwȳsan*, to crush, chiefly in
the comp. *tō-cwīesan.*

Squib, (1) a paper tube, with combustibles; (2) a lampoon. (Scand.) **1.**
Squibs were sometimes fastened slightly to
a rope, so as to run along it like a rocket;
whence the name. From M. E. *squippen,
swippen*, to move swiftly, fly, sweep, dash.
— Icel. *svipa*, to flash, dart, *svipr*, a swift
movement; Norw. *svipa*, to run swiftly.
2. A *squib* also means a political lampoon,
but was formerly applied, not to the *lampoon itself*, but to the *writer* of it; see
Tatler, no. 88, Nov. 1, 1709. A *squib*
thus meant a firework, a flashy fellow,
making a noise, but doing no harm. *Squib*
also means child's squirt, from its shooting
out water instead of fire. Cf. G. *schweif-
stern*, a comet.

Squill. (F. — L. — Gk.) M. F. *squille*,
'squill, sea-onion;' Cot. — L. *squilla*,
scilla. — Gk. σκίλλα, a squill.

Squinancy, old spelling of *quinsy.*

Squint, to look askew. (E.) The same
as prov. E. (Suffolk) *squink*, to wink. Of
obscure origin. Cf. M. Du. *schuyn*, 'cross,
oblique, byas-wise,' Hexham; E. Fries.
schün, oblique, awry; Du. *schuin*, oblique;
schuinen, to slant; *schuinte*, a slope, obliquity.

Squire (1), the same as **Esquire.**

Squire (2), a square, carpenter's rule.
(F. — L.) M. E. *squire.* — O. F. *esquire,
esquierre*; mod. F. *équerre.* A variant
of O. F. *esquarre*; see **Square.**

Squirrel. (F.—L.—Gk.) M.E. *squirel,
scurel.* — O. F. *escurel* (F. *écureuil*). —
Late L. *scūrellus*, a squirrel; for **sciūrel-
lus*, dimin. of *sciūrus*, a squirrel. — Gk.
σκίουρος, a squirrel; lit. 'a shadow-tail,'
from his bushy tail. — Gk. σκι-ά, shadow;
οὐρά, tail. ¶ The explanation of the Gk.
word may be due to popular etymology.

Squirt, vb. (E.) Prov. E. *swirt.* Cf.
Low G. *swirtjen*, to squirt; from *swiren*,

orig. to whir, like G. *schwirren* ; see **Swirl**. So also E. Fries. *kwirtjen*, to squirt out, to dart about, from *kwirt*, turning quickly about.

Stab, vb. (Scand.) Cf. Irish *stob-aim*, I stab; Gael. *stob*, to fix a stake in the ground, from *stob*, a stake, pointed iron or stick, stub. Apparently from Swed. dial. *stabbe*, a thick stick or stump; Icel. *stabbi*, a stub, stump, allied to *stafr*, a staff; Dan. dial. *stabb*, a short peg. Allied to **Stub, Staff,** q.v. Der. *stab*, sb.

Stable (1), a stall for horses. (F.‒L.) O. F. *estable*, a stable.‒L. *stabulum*, a stall.‒L. *stāre*, to stand still. Brugm. ii. §§ 62, 77. See **Stall**.

stable (2), firm. (F.‒L.) O.F. *estable*. ‒L. *stabilis*, firm.‒L. *stāre* (above).

stablish. (F.‒L.) Short for **Establish.**

Stack, a large pile of wood, &c. (Scand.) M. E. *stak*.‒Icel. *stakkr*, a stack of hay; *stakka*, a stump (as in our chimney-stack); Swed. *stack*, a rick, heap, stack; Dan. *stak*. Teut. type *staknoz* (Noreen). The sense is 'a pile.' Cf. Russ. *stog*', a heap, hayrick. Allied to **Stake**.

Staff. (E.) A. S. *stæf*; pl. *stafas*, staves. + Du. *staf*, Icel. *stafr*, Dan. *stab*, *stav*, Swed. *staf*, Goth. *stafs* or *stabs*, G. *stab*. Allied to O. H. G. *stabên*, to be stiff, E. Fries. *staf*, unmoved; cf. Skt. *stambh*, to make firm.

Stag, a male deer. (Scand.) Also applied (in dialects) to a male animal generally. Late A. S. *stagga* (from Norse).‒ Icel. *steggr*, *steggi*, a he-bird, drake, tomcat; Norw. *stegg*, a cock. Icel. *steggr* is said to be for *stig-joz*, lit. 'mounter ;' from *stig-*, weak grade of *stīga*, to mount; see **Stair**. (Noreen, § 140; but doubtful.)

Stage. (F. ‒ L.) A. F. and M. F. *estage*, 'a story, stage, loft, also a dwelling - house ;' Cot. [Hence it meant a stopping-place on a journey, or the distance between stopping-places.] Cf. Prov. *estatge*, a dwelling-place; answering to a Late L. form *staticum*, a dwelling-place. ‒L. *stat-um*, supine of *stāre*, to stand.

Stagger, to reel, vacillate. (Scand.) A weakened (voiced) form of *stacker*, M. E. *stakeren*.‒Icel. *stakra*, to push, to stagger; frequentative of *staka*, to punt, push, also to stagger; Norw. *stakra*, *staka*, to stagger; Swed. dial. *stagra*; Dan. dial. *stagge*, *stagle*. Allied to Icel. *stjaki*, a punt-pole; and to **Stake**.

Stagnate, to cease to flow. (L.) From L. *stagnātus*, pp. of *stagnāre*, to be still, cease to flow. ‒ L. *stagnum*, a still pool, a stank; see **Stank**. Der. *stagnant*, from stem of pres. pt. of *stagnāre*.

Staid, grave. (F. ‒M. Du.) Formerly *stay'd*, pp. of *stay*, vb., to support, make steady. See **Stay** (1).

Stain, vb. (F.‒L.) Short for **Distain**. 'I *stayne* a thynge, *Je destayns* ;' Palsgrave. The orig. sense was to dim the colour of a thing. Der. *stain*, sb.

Stair, a step up. (E.) M. E. *steir*, *steyer*. A. S. *stǣger*, a stair, step; lit. a step to climb by. Formed (with mutation to *ǣ*) from *stāg*, 2nd grade of *stīgan*, to climb. +Du. *steiger*, a stair ; cf. Icel. *stegi*, step, Swed. *stege*, ladder, Dan. *stige*, ladder, G. *steg*, a path ; respectively from Du. *stijgen*, Icel. *stīga*, Swed. *stiga*, Dan. *stige*, G. *steigen*, to mount, climb ; Teut. verb *steigan-*, pt. t. *staig*, pp. *stiganoz*. Allied to Skt. *stigh*, to ascend, Gr. στεί-χειν. (√STEIGH.)

Staithe, a landing-place. (E.) A. S. *stæð*, bank, shore. + Icel. *stöð*, harbour, roadstead; M.Du. *stade*, 'a haven.' Allied to **Stead.**

Stake, a post, strong stick. (E.) M. E. *stake*. A. S. *staca*, a stake. + Du. *staak*, Swed. *stake*, Dan. *stage*. From the Teut. base *stak*, 2nd grade of *stek-an-*, to pierce, appearing in G. *stach*, pt. t. of *stechen*, to stick, pierce; see **Stick** (1).

Stalactite, a kind of crystal hanging from the roof of some caverns. (Gk.) Formed, with suffix *-ite* (Gk. -ιτης), from σταλακτ-ός, trickling. ‒ Gk. σταλάζειν (= σταλάγ-γειν), to drip; allied to σταλᾶν, to drip.

stalagmite, a cone of carbonate of lime on the floor of some caverns. (Gk.) Gk. στάλαγμ-α, a drop ; with suffix *-ite* (Gk. -ιτης). ‒ Gk. σταλάζειν (above).

Stale (1), too long kept, vapid, trite. (E. ; *or* F. ‒ Teut.) 1. *Stale*, as a sb., means urine of cattle or horses. Cf. E. Fries. and Low G. *stallen*, Swed. *stalla*, to put into a stall, also to stale (as cattle); Dan. *stalde*, to stall-feed, *stalle*, to stale (as horses). From *stall*, sb. 2. *Stale*, adj., is that which stands too long, from M. F. *estaler*, to display wares on a stall, from *estal*, a stall. Cf. M. Du. *stel*, stale, Du. *stel*, a stall, place ; G. *stelle*, a place, *stellen*, to place, from G. *stall*, a stall. See **Stall.**

Stale (2), a decoy, bait ; Shak. (F. — Teut.) **–** A. F. *estale*, a decoy-bird (Bozon). Perhaps adapted from A. S. *stæl-*, as in *stæl-hrān*, a decoy reindeer, allied to M. E. *stale*, theft, A.S. *stalu*, theft ; allied to **Steal**.

Stale (3), **Steal**, the handle of anything. (E.) M. E. *stale*, *stele*. The latter answers to A. S. *stela*, *steola*, a stalk, stem. **+** Du. *steel*, stalk, stem, handle ; G. *stiel*, stalk, handle. Cf. Gk. στελεόν, a handle. Allied to *still* and *stall* ; the *stale* being that by which the tool is held firm and unmoved. And see **Stalk** (1).

Stalk (1), a stem. (E.) M. E. *stalke*, of which one sense is the side-piece (stem) of a ladder. A dimin. form, with suffix -*k*, from M. E. *stale*, variant of *stele* ; see **Stale** (3) above.**+**Icel. *stilkr*, Swed. *stjelk*, Dan. *stilk*, stalk ; cf. Gk. στέλεχος, stem of a tree, allied to στελεόν, a handle.

Stalk (2), to stride. (E.) M. E. *stalken*. A. S. *stealcian*, to walk warily ; allied to *stealc*, steep. **+** Dan. *stalke*, to stalk. The notion is that of walking cautiously. Cf. perhaps A. S. *stellan*, *styllan*, to leap. **Der.** *stalk-ing-horse*, a horse for stalking game : see Halliwell.

Stall, a standing-place for cattle, &c. (E.) M. E. *stal*. A. S. *steall*, station, stall.**+**Du. *stal*, Icel. *stallr*, Dan. *stald*, Swed. *stall*, G. *stall*. Teut. type **stalloz*, perhaps for **stadloz* ; cf. A. S. *standan*, to stand, E. *stead* ; Gk. σταθ-μός, a stall ; L. *stab-ulum* (for **stədh-lom*). Allied to **Stead**. Brugm. i. 593 (4). **Der.** *stalled ox*, a fatted ox ; cf. Swed. dial. *stalla*, to fatten, *stalloxe*, fatted ox (Möller).

stallion, an entire horse. (F. — O. H. G.) M. E. *stalon*. **–** O. F. *estalon* (F. *étalon*), a stallion ; so called because kept in a *stall* and not made to work.**–** O. H. G. *stal* (G. *stall*), a stall, stable ; see Stall.

Stalwart, sturdy. (E.) For *stalworth*. M. E. *stalworth*, *stelewurðe*, *stealewurðe*, *stalewurðe* ; A. S. *stælwyrðe*, pl., serviceable (said of ships) ; A. S Chron. an. 896. β. We find A. S. *gestælan* used as short for *gestaðelian*. Hence Sievers explains the form *stæl-* or *stēl-* as being contracted from *staðol*, a foundation [or from a parallel form **stæþl*]. Thus *stæl-wyrðe* is for **staðol-wyrðe*, lit. ' foundation-worthy,' i. e. firmly fixed, firm, constant ; cf. A. S. *staðol-fæst*, steadfast. The A. S. *staðel*, *staðol* is allied to **Stead**. Cf. *stead-fast*.

Stamen, male organ of a flower. (L.) Lit. ' a thread.'**–** L. *stāmen*, a thread, the warp standing up in an upright loom.**–** L. *stāre*, to stand. **Der.** *stamina*, orig. pl. of *stāmen*, lit. threads in a warp, a firm texture.

stamin, a kind of stuff. (F. — L.) M. E. *stamin*.**–**M. F. *estamine*, ' the stuffe tamine ;' Cot. **–** L. *stāmineus*, consisting of threads.**–**L. *stāmin-*, stem of *stāmen*, a thread (above). Also spelt *stammel*, *tamine*, *tammy*.

Stammer, to stutter. (E). M. E. *stameren*, vb. ; A. S. *stomrian* (Shrine, p. 42) ; from A. S. *stamer*, *stamor*, adj., stammering ; where the suffix -*er*, -*or* is adjectival. From a base **stam*, extended from √STA, to stand, remain fixed ; cf. prov. E. *stam*, to amaze, confound ; related by gradation to G. *stumm*, dumb. **+** Du. *stameren*, *stamelen*, G. *stammern*, *stammeln* ; Icel. *stamma*, Dan. *stamme*, Swed. *stamma*, to stammer ; Icel. *stamr*, O. H. G. *stam*, Goth. *stamms*, adj., stammering. See **Stem** (3).

Stamp, to tread heavily, to pound. (E.) M. E. *stampen*. A. S. *stempan* (for **stampian*).**+**Du. *stampen*, Icel. *stappa*, Swed. *stampa*, Dan. *stampe*, G. *stampfen* ; also Gk. στέμβειν, to stamp.

stampede, a panic. (Span.—Teut.) *Stampede* is a sudden panic, causing cattle to take to flight and run for many miles ; any sudden flight due to panic.**–**Span. (and Port.) *estampido*, a crash, sudden sound of anything bursting or falling. Formed as if from a verb **estampir*, akin to *estampar*, to stamp. The reference appears to be to the noise made by the blows of a pestle upon a mortar. Of Teut. origin ; see **Stamp** above.

Stanch, Staunch, to stop a flow of blood. (F. — L.) O. F. *estancher*, to stanch ; Walloon *stanchi* (Remacle). **–** Late L. *stancāre*, to stanch, a variant of Late L. type **stagnicāre*, to cause to stagnate, from L. *stagnāre*, to cease to flow ; see **Stagnate**. ¶ It is probable that the sense was influenced by G. *stange*, a pole, a bar (Körting, § 7733). **Der.** *stanch*, adj., firm, sound, not leaky ; cf. F. *étanche*, water-tight.

Stanchion, a support, beam, bar. (F. —L.) O. North F. *estanchon*, Norm. dial. *étanchon* ; M. F. *estançon*, *estanson*, 'a prop, stay ;' Cot. Not derived from the O. F. *estancher*, to prop (allied to E. *stanch*), but a diminutive of O.F. *estance*, a situation,

condition, also a stanchion (Scheler). —
Late L. *stantia*, a chamber, a house, lit.
'that which stands firm.' — L. *stant*-, stem
of pres. pt. of *stāre*, to stand. See **State**.
¶ But the word may have been confused
with O. F. *estancher*, to prop (as above),
which is the same word as *estancher*, to
staunch; for which see **Stanch**. The
ultimate root is the same either way.
(√STĀ.)

Stand. (E.) A. S. *standan*, pt. t. *stōd*,
pp. *standen*.+Icel. *standa*, Goth. *standan*;
cf. Du. *staan* (pt. t. *stond*); Swed. *stå*
(pt. t. *stod*); G. *stehen* (pt. t. *stand*).
Teut. type *standan*-, pt. t. *stōth*; base
stath,*stad*, the *n* being orig. characteristic
of the pres. tense. Allied to L. *stāre*, Gk.
ἔστην, I stood, Russ. *stoiate*, Skt. *sthā*, to
stand. (√STĀ.) See **State**, **Der**. *stand*,
sb., *standish*, short for *stand-dish*, a standing dish for pen and ink.

Standard. (F.—L.) A. F. *estandard*,
a standard or ensign, O. F. *estendard*, a
standard measure. The flag was a large
one, on a fixed (standing) pole; and hence
was modified by the influence of the verb
to stand. The O. F. *estendard*, Ital. *sten-
dardo*, are unmodified forms; from L.
extend-ĕre, to extend; with suffix -*ard*
(=O. H. G. -*hart*, suffix, orig. the same
as *hart*, hard). See **Extend**.

Stang, a pole, stake. (Scand.) M. E.
stange.—Icel. *stöng* (gen. *stangar*), a pole,
stake; Dan. *stang*, Swed. *stång*, Du. *stang*,
G. *stange*; A.S. *steng*. From the 2nd
grade of the verb *to sting*. Cf. **Stake**.

Staniel, a kind of hawk. (E.) A. S.
stāngella; lit. 'rock-yeller.' — A. S. *stān*,
rock (see **Stone**); and *gellan*, to yell (see
Yell).

Stank, a pool, tank. (F.—L.) An old
word; once common. — Walloon *stank*,
O. F. *estang*, a pond. (The same as Prov.
estanc, Span. *estanque*, Port. *tanque*, a
pond, pool.) — L. *stagnum*, a pool of stagnant or standing water. See **Stagnate**,
Stanch, **Tank**.

Stannary, relating to tin-mines. (L.)
Late L. *stannāria*, a tin-mine. — L. *stannum*, tin.

Stanza. (Ital.—L.) Ital. *stanza*, M.
Ital. *stantia*, 'a lodging, chamber, dwelling, also *stance* or staffe of verses;' Florio.
So called from the stop or pause at the
end of it. — Late L. *stantia*, an abode. —
L. *stant*-, stem of pres. pt. of *stāre*, to
stand; see **Stanchion**, **State**.

Staple (1), a loop of iron. (E.) A.S.
stapol, a post, pillar; also, a step. Orig.
sense a prop, something that holds firm.
—A. S. *stap*-, base of *stæppan*, strong
verb, to step, tread firmly; cf. *stamp*. +
Du. *stapel*, staple, stocks, a pile; Dan.
stabel, Swed. *stapel*; G. *staffel*, a step,
stapel, a staple (below).

staple (2), a chief commodity of a
place. (F.—Low G.) The sense has
changed; it formerly meant a chief market,
with reference to the place where things
were most sold. — O. F. *estaple*, M. F.
estape, 'a staple, a mart or general market,
a publique storehouse;' Cot. (F. *étape*.) —
Low G. *stapel*, a heap; hence a heap laid
in order, store, store-house; the same
word as **Staple** (1). The Du. *stapel* means
(1) a staple, (2) the stocks, (3) a pile or
heap. All from the notion of fixity or
firmness.

Star. (E.) M. F. *sterre*. A. S. *steorra*.
+ Du. *ster*; O. H. G. *sterro*. Cf. Icel.
stjarna, Dan. *stierne*, Swed. *stjerna*, Goth.
stairno, G. *stern*; also L. *stella* (for *ster-
la*), Gk. ἀστήρ, Corn. *steren*, Bret. *sterenn*,
W. *seren*, Skt. *tārā*. Orig. sense uncertain.
Cf. Brugm. i. § 473 (2).

Star-board, the right side of a ship.
(E.) M. E. *sterebourde*. A. S. *stēorbord*,
i. e. *steor bord*, the side on which the
steersman stood; in the first instance, he
used a paddle, not a helm. Cf. Icel.
ā stjörn, at the helm, or on the starboard
side. — A. S. *stēor*, a rudder or paddle to
steer with; *bord*, board, border, edge or
side; see **Steer** (2) and **Board**. The
O. H. G. *stiura* (G. *steuer*) means a prop,
staff, paddle, rudder, allied to Icel. *staurr*,
a post, stake, Gk. σταυρός, an upright pole
or stake. (√STEU, allied to √STĀ.)
+ Du. *stuurboord*, Icel. *stjörnborði*, Dan.
Swed. *styrbord*; all similarly compounded.

Starch. (E.) *Starch* is stuff that
stiffens; from the adj. **Stark**, stiff, strong.
Cf. G. *stärke*, (1) strength, (2) starch;
from *stark*, adj., strong.

Stare (1), to gaze fixedly. (E.) A.S.
starian; from a Teut. adj. *staroz*, fixed,
appearing in G. *starr*, fixed; cf. Skt. *sthira*-,
fixed, allied to *sthā*, to stand; and Gk.
στερεός, firm. (√STĀ.) + Du. *staren*;
Icel. *stara*, *stira*, to stare; Swed. *stirra*,
Dan. *stirre*, to stare; O.H.G. *starēn*.
¶ Hence '*staring* hair' is 'stiff-standing
hair.' Brugm. i. § 200.

stare (2), to glitter. (E.) M. E.

staren; whence *staring colours* = bright colours. The same word as *stare* (1); from the glittering of staring eyes.

Stark, stiff, rigid, entire. (E.) A. S. *stearc*, stiff, strong.+Du. *sterk*, Icel. *sterkr*, Dan. *stærk*, Swed. and G. *stark*. From Teut. verb **sterkan*-, to stiffen; of which the weak grade appears in Goth. *ga-staurk-nan*, to become dry, Icel. *storkinn*, pp. coagulated. Further allied to Lith. *strègti*, to become rigid, Pers. *suturg*, big, strong. Root STERG, extension of √STER; see Stare (1). **Der.** *stark*, adv., as in *stark mad.*

Stark-naked, quite naked. (E.) A substitution for M. E. *start-naked*, lit. 'tail-naked,' i. e. with the hinder parts exposed, but used in the sense of wholly naked. From A.S. *steort*, a tail; as in *red-start*, i. e. red-tail, a bird.+Du. *staart*, Icel. *stertr*, Dan. *stiert*, Swed. *stjert*, G. *sterz*, a tail; cf. Gk. στόρθη, a spike.

Starling. (E.) M. E. *sterling*, double dimin. of M. E. *stare*, a starling.—A. S. *stær*, a starling. + Icel. *starri*, *stari*, Dan. *stær*, Swed. *stare*, G. *staar*, L. *sturnus*. Cf. A. S. *stearn*, a tern.

Start, to move suddenly. (E.) M. E. *sterten*; pt. t. *stirte* (Havelok, 873), *sturte*, *storte* (Layamon, 23951). Allied to Du. *storten*, to precipitate, fall, rush, G. *stürzen*. Also, perhaps, to M. Du. *steerten*, to flee, run away. Some even connect it with A.S. *steort*, a tail. See Stark-naked. **Der.** *start-le*; A. S. *steartlian*, to stumble.

Starve. (E.) M. E. *steruen* (*sterven*), to die (without reference to the means of death). A. S. *steorfan*, pt. t. *stearf*, pp. *storfen*, to die; whence *-stierfan*, to kill (weak verb). + Du. *sterven*, G. *sterben*. Teut. type **sterban-*, pt. t. **starb*. **Der.** *starve-l-ing*, double dimin., expressive of contempt; *starv-ation*, a hybrid word, introduced from the North about 1775.

State, a standing, position, condition, &c. (F.—L.) O. F. *estat*.—L. *statum*, acc. of *status*, condition. — L. *statum*, supine of *stāre*, to stand.+Gk. ἔστην, I stood; Skt. *sthā*, to stand; cognate with E. *stand*. (√STĀ.)

Statics, the science treating of bodies at rest. (Gk.) From Gk. στατικός, at a standstill; ἡ στατική, statics.—Gk. στατ-ός, placed, standing; verbal adj. from στα-, allied to -στη- in ἵστημι, I place, stand. (√STĀ.)

Station. (F.—L.) F. *station.*—L.

statiōnem, acc. of *statio*, a standing still.—L. *statum*, supine of *stāre*. **Der.** *station-er*, orig. a bookseller who had a *station* or stall in a market-place; hence *station-er-y*, things sold by a *stationer.* Also *station-ary*, adj. See State.

statist, a statesman, politician. (F.—L.; *with* Gk. *suffix.*) Coined from *state* by adding *-ist* (L. *-ista*, Gk. -ιστης).

statue. (F.—L.) O. F. *statuë* (trisyllabic).—L. *statua*, a standing image. — L. *statu-*, for *status*, a position, standing.— L. *statum*, supine of *stāre*, to stand.

stature, height. (F.—L.) F. *stature.* — L. *statūra*, an upright posture, height. — L. *statum*, supine of *stāre*, to stand.

status, condition. (L.) L. *status*; see State.

statute. (F.—L.) F. *statut.*—L. *statūtum*, a statute; neut. of *statūtus*, pp. of *statuere*, to place, set, causal of *stāre*, to stand.

Staunch; see Stanch.

Stave, piece of a cask, part of a piece of music. (E.) Merely another form of *staff*, due to M. E. dat. sing. *staue* (*stave*) and pl. *staues* (*staves*). Cf. Icel. *stafr*, a staff, a stave; Dan. *stav*, staff, *stave*, stave. See Staff.

Stavesacre, the seeds of a larkspur; *Delphinium staphisagria.* (L. — Gk.) Lat. form of Gk. σταφὶς ἄγρια; where ἄγρια, wild, is from ἀγρός, a field (E. *acre*).

Stay (1), to prop, delay, remain. (F.— M. Du.) M. F. *estayer*, 'to prop, stay;' Cot.—M. F. *estaye*, sb. fem. 'a prop, stay;' id.—M. Du. *stade*, also *staeye*, 'a prop, stay,' Hexham; O. Flem. *staey*, a prop; allied to E. Stead. [The loss of *d* between two vowels is usual in Dutch, as in *broer*, brother, *teer* (for *teder*), tender.] See Stay (2).

Stay (2), a rope supporting a mast. (E.) A. S. *stæg*, a stay (whence F. *étai*, a ship's stay; Hatzfeld). + Du. *stag*, Icel. Dan. Swed. G. *stag.* **Der.** *stay-sail.* ¶ It is difficult to decide whether E. *stay* (2) is a survival of A. S. *stæg*, 'a rope for a mast,' or is from O. F. *estaye*, a prop, for which see Stay (1).

Stays, a bodice. (F.— M. Du.) Merely a pl. of *stay*, a support. (So also *bodice* = *bodies*.) See Stay (1).

Stead. (E.) M. E. *stede.* A. S. *stede*, a place.+Du. *stede*, *stee*, a place; cf. Du. *stad*, a town, Icel. *staðr*, *staða*, a place;

a cargo. — Span. *estivar*, to compress wool, to stow a cargo. — L. *stīpāre*, to press together. Allied to **Stiff**. Cf. Span. *estiva*, O. F. *estive*, stowage; Ital. *stiva*, ballast.

Stew, to boil slowly. (F. — Teut.) M. E. *stuwen*, orig. to bathe; formed from the old sb. *stew* in the sense of bath or hothouse (as it was called); the pl. *stews* generally meant brothels. An Anglicised form of O. F. *estuve*, a stew, stove, hothouse (F. *étuve*). — O. H. G. *stupa*, a hot room for a bath (mod. G. *stube*, a chamber). Allied to **Stove**, q. v. ¶ The history of O. F. *estuve* and of O. H. G. *stupa* is much disputed.

Steward. (E.) A.S. *stīweard*, *stīward*, a steward. Lit. 'a sty-ward;' from A.S. *stigu*, a farmyard, *weard*, a ward. The orig. sense was one who looked after the domestic animals, and gave them their food; hence, one who provides for his master's table, or who superintends household affairs. We also find *stīwita*, *stigwita*, a steward, where the former element is the same. See **Sty** (1) and **Ward**.

Stick (1), to stab, pierce, thrust in, adhere. (E.) The orig. sense was to sting, pierce, stab, fasten into a thing; hence, to be thrust into a thing, to adhere. Two verbs are confused in mod. E., viz. (1) *stick*, to pierce; (2) *stick*, to be fixed in. α. We find (1) M. E. *steken*, strong verb, to pierce, pt. t. *stak*, pp. *steken*, *stiken*; answering to an A.S. *stecan, pt. t. *stæc, pp. *stecen (not found); cognate with O. Fries. *steka*, O. Sax. *stekan* (pt. t. *stak*), E. Fries. *steken*, Low G. *steken* (pt. t. *stak*, pp. *steken*); G. *stechen* (pt. t. *stach*, pp. *gestochen*). Teut. type **stekan-* (pt. t. *stak); transferred to the *e*-series from an older type **steikan-* (weak grade *stik*); cf. Goth. *staks*, a mark, *stiks*, a point. Further allied to Gk. στίζειν (= στίγ-γειν), to prick, L. *instīgāre*, to prick, Skt. *tij*, to be sharp; and to E. **Sting**. (√STEIG.) β. We also find (2) A.S. *stician*, pt. t. *sticode*, weak verb; allied to Icel. *stika*, to drive piles, Swed. *sticka*, Dan. *stikke*, to stab, sting, G. *stecken*, to stick, set, also to stick fast, remain.

stick (2), a small branch of a tree. (E.) M. E. *stikke*. A.S. *sticca*, a stick, peg, nail. So called from its piercing or sticking into anything; the orig. sense being 'peg,' also a small bit of a tree. Allied to **Stick** (1) above. + Icel. *stika*,

a stick, E. Fries. *stikke*, *stik*; Du. *stek*; G. *stecken*.

stickleback, a small fish. (E.) So called from the *stickles* or small prickles on its back. *Stick-le* is a dimin. of *stick* (2); cf. E. Fries. *stikel*, a thorn.

Stickler, one who parts combatants, or settles disputes between two who are fighting. (E.) Now only used of one who insists on etiquette or persists in an opinion. Corruption of a sb. formed from M. E. *stightlen*, *stightlien*, to dispose, order, arrange, govern, subdue; commonly used of a steward who arranged matters, acting as a master of ceremonies. See Will. of Palerne, 1199, 2899, 3281, 3841, 5379; Destruction of Troy, 117, 1997, 2193, 13282, &c. This M. E. *stightlen* is a frequentative of A.S. *stihtan*, *stihtian*, to control. Cognate with M. Du. *stichten*, to build, impose a law; Dan. *stifte*, to institute, Swed. *stifta*, *stikta*, G. *stiften*, to found, institute. Cf. also Icel. *stētt* (for **stihti-*), a foundation, base.

Stiff. (E.) M. E. *stif*. A.S. *stīf*, stiff + Low G. *stīf* (Danneil); Du. *stijf*, Dan. *stiv*, Swed. *styf*. Allied to Lith. *stiprus*, strong, *stip-ti*, to be stiff, L. *stīpes*, a stem, *stīpāre*, to pack tight, *stipulus*, firm.

stifle. (Scand.) XVI. cent. From Icel. *stīfla*, to dam up, choke; Norweg. *stivla*, to stop, hem in, lit. to stiffen; *stivra*, to stiffen; frequentatives of Norw. *stiva*, Dan. *stive*, to stiffen. All from the adj. above. ¶ The prov. E. *stive*, to stuff, from O. F. *estiver*, to pack tight, is ult. from the same root; see **Stevedore**.

Stigmatise. (F. — Gk.) F. *stigmatiser*, to brand with a hot iron, defame. — Gk. στιγματίζειν, to mark, brand. — Gk. στιγματ-, base of στίγμα, a prick, mark, brand. — Gk. στίζειν (= *στίγ-γειν). to prick. Allied to **Stick** (1). (√STEIG.)

Stile (1), a set of steps for climbing over. (E.) M. E. *stile*. A.S. *stigel*, a stile. — A.S. *stig-*, weak grade of *stīgan*, to climb; with suffix *-el*. See **Stair.** + M. Du. and O.H.G. *stichel*.

Stile (2), the correct spelling of **Style** (1), q. v.

stiletto, a small dagger. (Ital. — L.) Ital. *stiletto*, a dagger; dimin. of M. Ital. *stilo*, a dagger. — L. *stilum*, acc. of *stilus*, an iron pin; see **Style** (1).

Still (1), motionless. (E.) M. E. *stille*. A.S. *stille*, still; cf. *stillan*, vb., to remain in a place or stall. For *steljoz;

allied to A. S. *stellan*, to place, from A. S. *stæl*, a place; cf. *steall*; see **Stall.** + Du. *stil*, still, *stillen*, to be still, *stellen*, to place, from *stal*, a stall; Dan. *stille*, Swed. *stilla*, G. *still*, still; Dan. *stille*, to still, also to place, Swed. *stilla*, to quiet; G. *stillen*, to still, *stellen*, to place; Dan. *stald*, Swed. G. *stall*, a stall. **Der.** *still*, adv., A. S. *stille*, continually, ever.

Still (2), to distil, trickle down. (L.; *or* F. – L.) In some cases, it represents L. *stillāre*, to fall in drops; more often, it is short for Distil, q. v.

still (3), sb., an apparatus for distilling. (L.) Short for M. E. *stillatorie*, a still, from *stillāt-us*, pp. of *stillāre* (above).

Stilt. (Scand.) M. E. *stilte.* – Swed. *stylta*, Dan. *stylte*, a stilt; Dan. *stylte*, to walk on stilts.+Du. *stelt*; G. *stelze*, a stilt; O. H. G. *stelza*, prop, crutch. Perhaps allied to **Stalk** (1); cf. E. Fries. *stilte*, a stem, stalk.

Stimulate. (L.) From pp. of L. *stimulāre*, to prick forward. – L. *stimulus*, a goad.

Sting. (E.) A. S. *stingan*, pt. t. *stang*, pp. *stungen.*+Icel. *stinga*, Swed. *stinga*, Dan. *stinge*. Teut. type **stengan-*. **Der.** *stang.*

stingy, mean. (E.) The same as Norfolk *stingy*, pronounced (stin-ji), nipping, unkindly, ill-humoured. Merely the adj. from *sting*, sb., which is pronounced (stinj) in Wiltshire. So also Swed. *sticken*, pettish, fretful, from *sticka*, to sting.

Stink. (E.) A. S. *stincan*, pt. t. *stanc*, pp. *stuncen.* + Du. *stinken*, Dan. *stinke*, Swed. *stinka*, G. *stinken.* Cf. Gk. ταγγός, rancid.

Stint, to limit, restrain, cut short. (E.) Orig. 'to shorten.' M. E. *stinten* (also *stentan*). A. S. *styntan*, in *for-styntan*, properly 'to make dull'; formed from A. S. *stunt*, stupid, by vowel-change from *u* to *y*. The peculiar sense is Scand.+ Icel. *stytta* (for **stynta*), to shorten, from *stuttr*, short, stunted; Swed. dial. *stynta*, to take short steps, from *stunt*, short; Dan. dial. *stynte*, to crop. See **Stunted.**

Stipend, salary. (L.) L. *stīpendium*, a tax, tribute; for **stip-pendium*, a payment in money. – L. *stip-*, stem of *stips*, small coin; *pendere*, to weigh out, pay; see **Pendant.** β. *Stips* is supposed to mean ' pile of money '; cf. *stīpāre*, to heap together.

Stipple, to engrave by means of small dots. (Du.) Du. *stippelen*, to speckle, dot over. – Du. *stippel*, a speckle; dimin. of *stip*, a point. Allied to Low G. *stippelen*, to drip as raindrops (Danneil), *stippen*, to speckle; G. *steppen*, to stitch, *stif-t*, a tack, peg, pin.

Stipulation, a contract. (F. – L.) F. *stipulation.* – L. acc. *stipulātiōnem*, a covenant. – L. *stipulātus*, pp. of *stipulārī*, to settle an agreement. – O. Lat. *stipulus*, firm, fast; allied to *stīpes*, a post. ¶ Not from *stipula*, a straw, though this is an allied word.

Stir. (E.) M. E. *stiren, sturen.* A. S. *styrian*, to move, stir. Allied to Icel. *styrr*, a stir; Du. *storen*, Swed. *störa*, G. *stören*, to disturb, O. H. G. *stōren*, to scatter, destroy, disturb. Teut. types **sturjan-, *staurjan-* (Franck). Prob. allied to **Storm.**

Stirk; see **Steer** (1).

Stirrup. (E.) For *sty-rope*, i. e. a rope to mount by; the orig. stirrup was a looped rope for mounting into the saddle. M. E. *stirop.* A. S. *stī-rāp, stig-rāp.* – A. S. *stig-*, weak grade of *stigan*, to mount; *rāp*, a rope; see **Stair** and **Rope.**+Icel. *stig-reip*, Du. *steg-reep*, G. *steg-reif.*

Stitch, a pain in the side, a passing through stuff of a needle and thread. (E.) M. E. *stiche.* A. S. *stice*, a pricking sensation. – A. S. *stician*, to prick, pierce. See **Stick** (1).

Stith, an anvil. (Scand.) M. E. *stith.* – Icel. *steði*, an anvil; allied to *staðr*, a fixed place; named from its firmness; see **Stead.** + Swed. *städ*, an anvil; M. Du. *stiet.* **Der.** *stith-y*, properly a smithy, but also an anvil, like M. E. *stethi.*

Stiver, a Dutch penny. (Du.) Du. *stuiver*, a small coin. Perhaps orig. ' bit' or small piece. Franck connects it with Low G. *stuuf*, stumpy, Icel. *stūfr*, a stump, Icel. *stȳfa*, to cut off.

Stoat, an animal. (Scand.) A late word; *stote*, Phillips, 1706; Levins, 1570. M. E. *stot*, a stoat, also a bull, stallion. See **Stot.**

Stoccado, Stoccata, a thrust in fencing. (Ital. – Teut.) *Stoccado* is an accommodated form, as if it were Spanish. – Ital. *stoccata*, ' a foyne, thrust,' Florio. – Ital. *stocco*, ' a short sword, a tuck,' Florio; with pp. suffix *-ata.* – G. *stock*, a stick, staff, trunk, stump; cognate with E. **stock.**

stock, a post, &c. (E.) The old sense

was a stump; hence a post, trunk, stem, a fixed store, fund, capital, cattle, stalk, butt-end of a gun, &c. A. S. *stocc*, stock, stump. + G. *stock*, O. H. G. *stoch*; Du. *stok*, Icel. *stokkr*, Dan. *stok*, Swed. *stock*. Allied to A. S. *stykke*, G. *stück*, a bit, fragment.

Stockade, a breastwork formed of stakes. (Span.—Teut.) Coined as if from E. *stock* (above); but adapted from Span. *estacada*, a palisade, fence. ═ Span. *estaca*, a stake, pale. ═ M. Du. *stake*, Du. *staak*, a stake; see **Stake.**

Stocking. (E.) *Stocking* is a dimin. form of *stock*, used as short for *nether-stock*. 'Un bas des chausses, *a stocking, or nether-stock*;' Cot. The clothing of the lower part of the body consisted of a single garment, called *hose*, in F. *chausses*. It was afterwards cut in two at the knees, and divided into *upper-stocks*, and *nether-stocks* or *stockings*. In this case, *stock* means a piece or stump, a piece cut off; see **Stock.**

Stoic. (L.—Gk.) L. *Stoicus*. ═ Gk. Στωϊκός, a Stoic; lit. 'belonging to a colonnade,' because Zeno taught under a colonnade at Athens. ═ Gk. στοά, στοιά (for *στοϝ-γά*), a colonnade, row of pillars; cf. στῦ-λος, a pillar. (√STEU.)

Stoker, one who tends a fire. (Du.) Orig. used to mean one who looked after a fire in a brew-house (Phillips). ═ Du. *stoker*, 'a kindler, or setter on fire,' Hexham. ═ Du. *stoken*, to kindle a fire, stir a fire. Allied to Du. *stok*, a stock, stick (hence, a poker for a fire); cognate with **Stock.** Cf. Westphal. *stoken*, to poke a fire.

Stole, long robe, scarf. (L.—Gk.) L. *stola*. ═ Gk. στολή, equipment, robe, stole. ═ Gk. στέλλειν, to equip.

Stolid, stupid. (L.) L. *stolidus*, firm, stock-like, stupid.

Stomach. (F.—L.—Gk.) M.E. *stomak*. ═ O. F. *estomac*. ═ L. acc. *stomachum*. ═ Gk. στόμαχος, mouth, gullet, stomach; dimin. of στόμα, mouth. Brugm. i. § 421.

Stone. (E.) M. E. *stoon*. A. S. *stān*. + Du. *steen*, Icel. *steinn*, Dan. Swed. *sten*, G. *stein*, Goth. *stains*. Cf. Gk. στία, a stone; O. Bulgarian *stěna*, Russ. *stiena*, a wall. **Der.** *stan-iel*.

Stook, a shock of corn. (E.) It answers to A. S. *stōc*, from *stōk-*, strong grade of *stak-*, as in E. **Stack.** + Low G. *stuke*, a stook; Swed. dial. *stuke*.

Stool. (E.) M. E. *stool*. A. S. *stōl*, seat. + Du. *stoel*, Icel. *stōll*, Dan. Swed.

stol, Goth. *stols*, seat, chair; G. *stuhl*, chair, pillar. _ Lit. 'that which stands firm.' (√STA.) Brugm. i. § 191.

Stoop (1), to lean forward. (E.) Prov. E. *stowp*; M. E. *stoupen*. A. S. *stūpian*. + M. Du. *stuypen*, O. Icel. *stūpa*, to stoop; Swed. *stupa*, to tilt, fall. Allied to **Steep** (1).

Stoop (2), a beaker; see **Stoup.**

Stop. (L.) Of L. origin. M. E. *stop-pen*, A. S. -*stoppian*, to stop up; so also Du. *stoppen*, to stop, stuff, cram, Swed. *stoppa*, Dan. *stoppe*, G. *stopfen*; Ital. *stoppare*, to stop up with tow, Late L. *stuppāre*, to stop up with tow, cram, stop. All from L. *stupa*, *stuppa*, coarse part of flax, hards, oakum, tow. Cf. Gk. στύπη, στύππη, the same. **Der.** *stopp-le*, i. e. stopper; also *estop*, A. F. *estoper*, from Late L. *stuppāre*.

Storax, a resinous gum. (L.—Gk.) L. *storax*, *styrax*. ═ Gk. στύραξ.

Store, sb. (F.—L.) M. E. *stor*, *stoor*, provisions. ═ O. F. *estor*, store, provisions (Godefroy); Late L. *staurum*, the same as *instaurum*, store. ═ L. *instaurāre*, to construct, build, restore; Late L, *instaurāre*, to provide necessaries. ═ L. *in*, in; **staurāre*, to set up, place, also found in *re-staurāre*, to restore. From an adj. **staurus* = Skt. *sthāvara-*, fixed; cf. Gk. σταυρός, an upright pole. (√STA.) **Der.** *store*, vb., O. F. *estorer*, from Late L. *staurāre = instaurāre*.

Stork, bird. (E.) A. S. *storc*. + Du. *stork*, Icel. *storkr*, Dan. and Swed. *stork*; G. *storch*. Cf. Gk. τόργος, a large bird (vulture, swan). Prob. allied to **Stark.**

Storm. (E.) A. S. *storm*, storm. + Icel. *stormr*, Du. Swed. Dan. *storm*, G. *sturm*. Teut. type **stur-moz*. From the same root as E. **Stir.**

Story (1). (F.—L.—Gk.) M. E. *storie*. ═ A. F. *storie* (Bartsch), O. F. *estoire*, a history, tale. ═ L. *historia*. ═ Gk. ἱστορία, information; see **History.**

Story (2), set of rooms on a level or flat. (F.—L.) Orig. merely 'a building' or 'thing built.' ═ O. F. *estorée*, a thing built; fem. of pp. of *estorer*, to build. ═ Late L. *staurāre*, for L. *instaurāre*, to construct, build, &c. See **Store.** **Der.** *clere-story*, i. e. *clear-story*, story lighted with windows, as distinct from *blind-story*.

Stot, stallion, bullock. (E.) M. E. *stot*. Cf. Icel. *stūtr*, a bull, Swed. *stut*, Dan. *stud*, a bull; allied to Swed. *stöta*, to push, G. *stossen*.

521   S 3

Stoup, Stoop, flagon. (M. Du.) M.E. *stope.* — M. Du. *stoop*, a large cup (Kilian); Du. *stoop*, a gallon; cf. Icel. *staup*, a knobby lump, also a stoup; Low G. *stoop*, a stoup (whence Swed. *stop*, three pints; Dan. dial. *stob*, a stoup). **+** A.S. *stēap*, a cup; G. *stauf*, a cup. Allied to A.S. *stēap*, steep; perhaps as being high and upright; see **Steep** (1), and **Stoop.**

Stout. (F. — O. Low G.) M.E. *stout.* — O.F. *estout*, stout, bold. — M. Du. *stolt*, *stout*, stout, bold; Low G. *stolt*, A.S. *stolt*, the same. **+** G. *stolz*, proud. Perhaps all from L. *stultus*, foolish, foolhardy. **Der.** *stout*, sb., a strong beer.

Stove. (E.) A.S. *stofa.* **+** M. Du. *stove*, 'a stewe, hot-house, or a baine,' Hexham; Low G. *stove*; cf. Icel. *stofa*, *stufa*, a bath-room with a stove; G. *stube*, O.H.G. *stupa*, a room (whence Ital. *stufa*, F. *étuve*). See **Stew.**

Stover, food for cattle. (F. — L.?) In Shak.; M.E. *stouer* (*stover*), necessaries. **—** O.F. *estover*, *estovoir*, necessaries; orig. the infin. mood of a verb which was used impersonally with the sense 'it is necessary.' Perhaps from L. *est opus* (Tobler).

Stow, to pack away. (E.) M.E. *stowen*, lit. to put in a place. — A.S. *stōwigan* (Sweet); from *stōw*, a place. **+** Icel. *eld-stō*, fire-place. Also Lith. *stowa*, place where a thing stands, from *stōti*, to stand. (✓STĀ.)

Straddle. (E.) Formerly *striddle* (Levins); frequentative of **Stride.**

Straggle. (E.) Formerly *stragle.* For *strackle*; cf. prov. E. *strackle-brained*, thoughtless. Apparently the frequentative of M.E. *strāken*, to roam, wander; P. Plowman's Crede, 82; with *ā* shortened before *k-l.* Cf. M. Dan. *strage*, to wander; Swed. dial. *strakla*, to stagger, totter, may be related.

Straight. (E.) M.E. *streiʒt*, orig. pp. of M.E. *strecchen*, to stretch; A.S. *streht*, pp. of *streccan*, to stretch; see **Stretch.** **Der.** *straight*, adv., M.E. *streiʒt*; *straight-way*; *straight-en.*

Strain (1), vb. (F. — L.) From *estraign-*, a stem of M.F. *estraindre*, 'to wring hard;' Cot. — L. *stringere*, to draw tight. See **Stringent.**

Strain (2), descent, lineage, birth. (E.) *Strain* in Shak.; *strene* in Spenser. M.E. *streen*, Chaucer, C.T., Cl. Tale, 157. A.S. *strēon*, gain, product, lineage, progeny; whence *strȳnan*, to beget.

Strait, adj. (F. — L.) M.E. *streit.* — A.F. *estreit* (F. *étroit*), narrow, strict. — L. *strictum*, acc. of *strictus*; see **Strict.**

Strand (1), shore. (E.) A.S. *strand.* **+** Icel. *strönd* (gen. *strandar*), margin, edge; Dan. Swed. G. *strand.*

Strand (2), thread of a rope. (Du.) The final *d* is added. — Du. *streen*, a skein, hank of thread. **+** G. *strähne*, a skein, hank, O.H.G. *streno.* Cf. Du. *striem*, a stripe.

Strange, foreign, odd. (F. — L.) O.F. *estrange.* — L. *extrāneum*, acc. of *extrāneus*, foreign, on the outside. — L. *extrā*, without. See **Extra** and **Estrange.**

Strangle, to choke. (F. — L. — Gk.) O.F. *estrangler.* — L. *strangulāre.* — Gk. στραγγαλόειν, στραγγαλίζειν, to strangle. — Gk. στραγγάλη, a halter. — Gk. στραγγός, twisted. Allied to **String** and **Strict.**

strangury. (L. — Gk.) L. *strangūria.* — Gk. στραγγουρία, retention of urine, when it falls by drops. — Gk. στραγγ-, base of στράγξ, a drop, that which oozes out (allied to στραγγός, twisted); οὖρ-ον, urine.

Strap. (L.) Prov. E. *strop*; A.S. *stropp.* — L. *struppus* (also *stroppus*), a strap, thong, fillet. (Hence F. *étrope.*)

Strappado. (Ital. — Teut.) A modified form of *strappata* (just as *stoccado* was used for *stoccata*). — Ital. *strappata*, a pulling, a wringing, the strappado. — Ital. *strappare*, to pull, wring. — H. G. (Swiss) *strapfen*, to pull tight, allied to G. *straff*, tight, borrowed from Low G. or Du. — Du. *straffen*, to punish, from *straf*, severe; cf. E. Fries. *strabben*, to be stiff.

Stratagem. (F. — L. — Gk.) M.F. *stratageme.* — L. *stratēgēma.* — Gk. στρατήγημα, the device of a general. — Gk. στρατηγός, general, leader. — Gk. στρατ-ός, army, camp; ἄγ-ειν, to lead. The Gk. στρατός is allied to στόρνυμι, I spread. See **Stratum.**

strategy. (F. — L. — Gk.) F. *stratégie.* — L. *stratēgia.* — Gk. στρατηγία, generalship. — Gk. στρατηγός (above).

Strath, a flat valley. (C.) Gael. *srath*, a valley with a river, low-lying country beside a river; Irish *srath*, *sratha*, the bottom of a valley, fields beside a river; W. *ystrad*, a flat vale. Allied to **Stratum** (below).

Stratum. (L.) L. *strātum*, a layer, that which is spread flat; neut. of *strātus*, pp. of *sternere*, to spread. **+** Gk. στόρνυμι, I spread out. (✓STER.)

Straw, sb. (E.) A.S. *strēaw* (*strēow*).

+Du. *stroo*, Icel. *strā*, Dan. *straa*, Swed. *strå*, G. *stroh*. Teut. type *strawom, n. Allied to L. *strāmen*, straw, *sternere*, to strew; see **Strew**, **Stratum**.

straw-berry. (E.) A.S. *streaw-berige*, straw-berry; perhaps from its propagation by runners; cf. *strew*.

Stray, to wander. (F. − L.) O. F. *estraier*, to wander; orig. to rove about the streets or ways. Cf. Prov. *estradier*, a wanderer in the streets, one who strays, from Prov. *estrada* (= O. F. *estree*), a street; M. Ital. *stradiotto*, a wanderer, from *strada*, street. − L. *strāta*, a street; see **Street**. Der. *stray*, *estray*, sb.

Streak, a line or long mark. (E.) M. E. *streke*, more commonly *strike*. A. S. *strica*, from **stric-*, weak grade of *strīcan*, to stroke, rub. Cf. E. Fries. *streke*, *stråke*, a stroke, streak; Du. *streek*; Swed. *streck*, a dash, streak, line; Dan. *streg*, the same. Also Goth. *striks*, a stroke with the pen; G. *strich*, from Teut. *strik, weak grade of **streikan-*; see **Strike**. Cf. also L. *striga*, a swath, furrow.

Stream. (E.) A. S. *strēam*. **+** Du. *stroom*, Icel. *straumr*, Swed. Dan. *ström*, G. *strom*. Teut. type *straumoz, m. Allied to Russ. *struia*, Irish *sruaim*, a stream. All from √SREU, to flow, which in Teut. and Russ. became STREU; cf. Skt. *sru*, Gk. ῥέειν (for *σρέϜ-ειν), to flow. Cf. **Rheum**.

Street. (L.) A. S. *strêt*; O. Merc. *strēt*; a very early loan-word; cf. Du. *straat*, G. *strasse*. − L. *strāta*, i. e. *strāta uia*, a paved way; *strāta* being fem. of pp. of *sternere*, to strew, pave.

Strength. (E.) A. S. *strengðu*; (for *strang-i-thu). − A. S. *strang*, strong. See **Strong**.

Strenuous. (L.) L. *strēnu-us*, vigorous, active; with suffix *-ous*. **+**Gk. στρηνής, strong, allied to στερεός, firm.

Stress, strain. (F. − L.) Sometimes short for *distress*; see **Distress**. Otherwise, from O. F. *estrecier*, *estressier*, to straiten, pinch, contract. This answers to a Folk-L. type *strectiāre, regularly formed from L. *strictus*, tightened; see **Strict**.

Stretch. (E.) M. E. *strecchen*. − A. S. *streccan*, pt. t. *strehte*, pp. *streht*. Formed as a causal form from A. S. *strac*, hard, rigid, violent, strong. Thus *stretch* = to make stiff or hard, as in straining a cord. **+**Du. *strekken*, to stretch, from *strak*, stretched, tight, rigid; Dan. *strække*, Swed.

sträcka; G. *strecken*, from *strack*, adj., tight. Perhaps allied to **Strong**.

Strew, Straw, vb. (E.) M. E. *strewen*. A. S. *streowian*, to strew, scatter. Closely allied to A. S. *streaw*, straw. **+**Du. *strooijen*, to strew, allied to *stroo*, straw; G. *streuen*, to strew, allied to *stroh*, straw; Goth. *straujan* (pt. t. *strawida*), to strew. From a derivative of the root STER, as in L. *ster-nere* (pt. t. *strāui*), to strew; cf. Gk. στόρνυμι, I spread; Skt. *str̥*, to spread. See **Stratum**. Brugm. i. § 570. Der. *be-strew*.

Stricken; see **Strike**.

Strict. (L.) L. *strictus*, pp. of *stringere*, to tighten, draw together, &c. See **Stringent**. Doublet, *strait*.

Stride, vb. (E.) M. E. *striden*, pt. t. *strad*. *strood*. A. S. *strīdan*, to stride, pt. t. *strād* (rare; but cf. *bestrad*, Ælf. Hom. ii. 136). So also Low G. *striden* (pt. t. *streed*), to strive, to stride; Du. *strijden*, G. *streiten*, Dan. *stride*, strong verbs, to strive, contend; Icel. *strîða*, Swed. *strida*, weak verbs, to strive. β. Teut. type **streidan-*, pt. t. *straid, pp. *strĭdanoz; whence also Icel. *strîð*, woe, strife; *strîðr*, hard, stubborn. Cf. Skt. *sridh*, to assail; also, an enemy. The orig. sense was 'to contend,' hence to take long steps (as if in contention with another). Der. *be-stride*, *strid*, *straddle*, *strife*, *strive*.

strife. (F. − Scand.) O. F. *estrif*, strife. Apparently modified from Icel. *strîð*, strife, contention. Cf. O. Sax. and O. Fries. *strîd*, strife; Du. *strijd*; G. *streit*. From the verb **Stride** (above). ¶ The connexion with G. *streben*, Du. *streven*, is obscure. Der. *strive*, vb., q. v.

Strike, to hit. (E.) M. E. *striken*, orig. to proceed, advance, to flow; hence used of smooth swift motion, to strike with a rod or sword. The verb is strong; pt. t. *strak*, pp. *striken*; the phrase ' *stricken* in years' meant ' *advanced* in years.' A. S. *strīcan*, to go, proceed, advance swiftly and smoothly; pt. t. *strāc*, pp. *stricen*.**+**Du. *strijken*, to smooth, rub, stroke, spread, strike; G. *streichen*, the same. [Cf. Icel. *strjūka*, to stroke, rub, wipe, strike; Swed. *stryka*, Dan. *stryge*, the same.] Allied to L. *stringere*, to graze, touch lightly with a swift motion; *striga*, a row of mown hay. Der. *strike*, sb., the name of a measure, orig. an instrument with a straight edge for levelling (striking off) a measure of grain. Also *streak*, *stroke*.

String. (E.) A. S. *streng*, cord ; from its being tightly twisted. – A. S. *strang*, strong, violent. Cf. Gk. στραγγάλη, a halter ; from στραγγός, tightly twisted. + Du. *streng*, string, allied to *streng*, severe ; so also Icel. *strengr*, Dan. *strœng*, Swed. *sträng*, G. *strang*, cord, string. See **Strong.**

Stringent. (L.) L. *stringent-*, stem of pres. pt. of *stringere*, to draw tight, compress, urge, also to graze, stroke ; pp. *strictus*. Perhaps allied to **Strike.**

Strip. (E.) M. E. *stripen*. A. S. *strīe-pan*, *strȳpan*, to plunder, strip ; in comp. *be-strȳpan*.+Du. *stroopen*, to plunder ; E. Fries. *stropen*, *ströpen* ; G. *streifen*, from M. H. G. *stroufen*. Teut. type **straupjan-* ; from the 2nd grade of the strong verb **streupan-*, for which cf. Norw. *strūpa*, to grip, to throttle, pt. t. *straup*. Der. *strip*, sb., a piece stripped off ; see below.

Stripe. (Du.) Orig. a streak ; M. E. *stripe* ; not an old word ; prob. a weaver's term. – M. Du. *strijpe*, a stripe in cloth, variant of *strepe* (Kilian) ; Du. *streep* ; Low G. *stripe*, a stripe. + Norw. *stripa*, Dan. *stribe*, a stripe, streak ; G. *streifen*, M. H. G. *streif*. From a Teut. base **streip*, allied to **streik* ; see **Strike.** Cf. O. Irish *srīab*, a stripe. ¶ Low G. *stripe*, a stripe, also means a strip of cloth ; although *strip* belongs strictly to the verb above.

Stripling. (E.) A double dimin. from *strip*, variant of *stripe* ; hence a lad as thin as a *strip*, a growing lad not yet filled out.

Strive. (F. – Scand.) M. E. *striuen* (*striven*), properly a weak verb. – O. F. *estriver*, to strive ; Walloon *striver*. – O. F. *estrif*, strife ; see **Strife.**

Stroke (1), a blow. (E.) M. E. *strook*. From *strāc*, 2nd grade of A. S. *strīcan*, to strike. Cf. G. *streich*, a stroke.

stroke (2), to rub gently. (E.) M. E. *stroken*. A. S. *strācian*, to stroke ; a causal verb ; from *strāc*, 2nd grade of *strīcan*, to strike. Cf. G. *streicheln*, to stroke, from *streichen*, to stroke ; see **Strike.**

Stroll, to wander. (F. – Teut.) Formerly *stroule*, *stroyle*. Formed by prefixing *s-* (O. F. *es-*, L. *ex*) to *troll*, used (in P. Pl.) with the sense 'to range' ; see **Troll.** Cf. Guernsey *étreûlaï* [= *estreulé*], adj., idle, vagabond (Métivier ; who notes that, at Valognes, dep. Manche, the equivalent term is *treulier*, i. e. 'troller') ; cf. Norm. dial. *treuler*, to rove (Moisy), dial. of Verdun *trôler*, *trauler*.

Strong. (E.) A. S. *strang*, *strong.*+ Du. *streng*, Icel. *strangr*, Dan. *streng*, Swed. *sträng* ; G. *streng*, strict. Cf. Gk. στραγγός, tightly twisted.

Strop, a piece of leather, for sharpening razors. (L.) A. S. *stropp*, a strap, from L. ; see **Strap.** Cf. Westphal. *strop*.

Strophe, part of a poem or dance. (Gk.) Gk. στροφή, a turning ; the turning of the chorus, dancing to one side of the orchestra, or the strain sung during this evolution ; the *strophe*, to which the *antistrophe* answers. – Gk. στρέφειν, to turn.

Strow; see **Strew.**

Structure. (F. – L.) F. *structure*. – L. *structūra*, a structure. – L. *structus*, pp. of *struere*, to build, orig. to heap together.

Struggle, vb. (F. – M. Du. ?) M.E. *strogelen*, *strugelen* ; apparently from A.F. *es-* (L. *ex*) prefixed to M. Du. *truggelen* (Du. *troggelen*), Low G. *truggeln*, to beg persistently, which prob. also had the same sense as E. Fries. *trüggeln*, to struggle against, as when a horse jibs or refuses to move forward, also to beg persistently. All from Teut. base **thrūg-*, as in Icel. *þrūga*, Dan. *true*, to press, ultimately related to A.S. *þryccan*, G. *drücken*, to press. (Doubtful.)

Strum, to thrum on a piano. (E.) An imitative word. Made by prefixing an intensive *s-* (=O. F. *es-*=L. *ex*), very, to the imitative word *trum* (also *thrum*), as seen in Low G. *trummen*, Du. *trommen*, to drum ; see **Drum** and **Thrum.**

Strumpet. (F. – Teut. ?) M. E. *strompet*. The form answers to O. F. **estrompette* (not found), as if from M. Du. *strompe*, a stocking. Or (if the *m* be an insertion) it is from O. F. *strupe*, Late L. *strupum*, dishonour, violation ; from L. *stuprum*. (Unexplained.)

Strut (1), to walk about pompously. (Scand.) M. E. *strouten*, to spread or swell out. – Swed. dial. *strutta*, to walk with a jolting step ; Dan. *strutte*, *strude*, to strut ; cf. Norw. *strut*, a spout that sticks out, a nozzle. The orig. sense seems to be 'to stick out stiffly' ; cf. Icel. *strūtr*, a hood sticking out like a horn ; Low G. *strutt*, rigid. + G. *strotzen*, to strut, be puffed up ; cf. *strauss*, a tuft, bunch.

strut (2), a support for a rafter. (Scand.) Orig. a stiff piece of wood ; from *strut*, to stick out or up. Cf. Icel. *strūtr*, Low G. *strutt* (above).

Strychnine. (Gk.) From Gk. στρύχ-

vos, nightshade, poison; with F. suffix *-ine*.

Stub, stump of a tree. (E.) A. S. *stybb*, a stub; E. Fries. *stubbe*.+Du. *stobbe*, Icel. *stubbi*, Dan. *stub*, Swed. *stubbe*. Allied to Icel. *stūfr*, a stump (Noreen); and see **Stab.** Also to Gk. στύπος, a stump, Skt. *stūpa-*, a heap. Allied to **Stump.**

Stubble. (F.—Late L.) M. E. *stobil*, *stoble*.—A.F. *estuble*, O. F. *estouble*.—Late L. *stupula*, *stupla*, stubble; a variant of L. *stipula*, stubble, due to the influence of Low G. *stoppel*, stubble (Lübben); Du. and E. Fries. *stoppel*, cognate with M. H. G. *stupfel*, O. H. G. *stupfila*, stubble.

Stubborn. (E.) M. E. *stoburn*, *stiborn*; also *stibornesse*, *stybornesse*, stubbornness, for which Palsgrave has *stubblenesse*. The final *n* is prob. due to misunderstanding *stibornesse* as *stiborn-nesse*; in any case, it has been added; cf. *bitter-n*, *slatter-n*. *Stubor*, *stibor* represent an A. S. form *styb-or*; *-or* being a common adj. suffix, as in *bit-or*, bitter. From A. S. *stybb*, a stub. Thus *stubborn* = stock-like, not easily moved, like an old stub or stump. See **Stub.**

Stucco. (Ital.—O. H. G.) Ital. *stucco*, hardened, encrusted; stucco.—O. H. G. *stucchi*, a crust; G. *stück*, a piece, patch; cognate with A. S. *stycce*, a piece, bit. Allied to **Stock.**

Stud (1), a collection of breeding-horses and mares. (E.) M. E. *stood*. A. S. *stōd*, a stud; orig. an establishment or herd in a stall.+Icel. *stōð*, Dan. *stod*, M. H. G. *stuot* (whence G. *gestüt*). Cf. Russ. *stado*, a herd or drove, Lith. *stodas*, a drove of horses. (√STĀ.) Der. *stud-horse*, *steed*.

Stud (2), a rivet, large-headed nail, &c. (E.) Also a stout post, prop; hence a projection, boss, support.—A. S. *studu*, *stupu*, a post.+Icel. *stoð*, Swed. *stöd*, a post; Dan. *stöd*, stub, stump; G. *stütze*, a prop. Cf. Gk. στύ-λος, a pillar. (√STEU, allied to √STĀ.)

Student. (L.) From L. *student-*, stem of pres. pt. of *studēre*, to be busy about, to study.

study, sb. (F.—L.) M. E. *studie*.—A. F. *estudie* (F. *étude*).—L. *studium*, zeal, study. Der. *studio*, Ital. *studio*, a school, from L. *studium*.

Stuff, materials. (F.—L.) O. F. *estoffe*, 'stuffe;' Cot.; Walloon *stoff* (Remacle). —L. *stupa*, *stuppa*, the coarse part of flax, hards, tow; the pronunciation of this L.

word being Germanised before it passed into French (Diez). Cf. G. *stoff*, stuff, materials. β. The sense of the L. word is better preserved in the verb *to stuff*, i. e. to cram, to stop up, M. F. *estouffer*, to stifle (Cot.), G. *stopfen*, to fill, stuff, quilt, from Late L. *stuppāre*, to stop up; whence also E. **Stop,** q. v.

stuffy, close, stifling. (F.—L.) From O. F. *estouffer*, to choke (F. *étouffer*); the same as O. F. *estoffer*, to stuff or cram up. Cf. Walloon *stoff*, stifled (Remacle).— O. F. *estoffe*, stuff (above). ¶ So Scheler, disputing the suggestion of Diez, who needlessly goes to the Gk. τύφος, smoke, mist, in order to explain *estoffe*.

Stultify. (L.) Coined, with suffix *-fy* (F. *-fier*, L. *-ficāre*), from L. *stulti-*, for *stultus*, foolish.

Stumble, vb. (E.) The *b* is excrescent. M. E. *stomblen*, *stomelen*, *stumlen*; also *stomeren*. E. Fries. *stummeln*, to go stumbling along; cf. Dan. dial. *stumle*, to stumble; Icel. *stumra*, Norw. *stumra*, to stumble; Swed. dial. *stamöla*, *stomla*, *stammra*, to stumble, falter. From the base *stum*. Practically a doublet of *stammer*, with reference to hesitation of the step instead of the speech; see **Stammer.** Cf. O. Sax. and O. H. G. *stum*, mute.

Stump. (E.) M. E. *stumpe*; E. Fries. *stump*.+Icel. *stumpr*, Swed. Dan. *stump*, stump, end, bit; Du. *stomp*; G. *stumpf*. Allied to G. *stumpf*, blunt, stumpy; Du. *stomp*, blunt, dull. Also to Lith. *stambras*, stalk of grass, &c. Brugm. i. § 424.

Stun, to make a loud din, to amaze, esp. with a blow. (E.) M. E. *stonien*. A.S. *stunian*, to make a din; *ge-stun*, a din. Cf. Icel. *stynja*, to groan, *stynr*, a groan; Du. *stenen*, G. *stöhnen*, to groan, Russ. *sten-ate*, Lith. *sten-ěti*, Gk. στέν-ειν, to groan; Skt. *stan*, to sound, to thunder. (√STEN.) Brugm. i. § 818 (2). And see **Thunder.**

Stunted, hindered in growth. (E.) From A. S. *stunt*, adj., dull, obtuse, stupid, orig. 'short;' hence, metaphorically, short of wit; also not well grown; but the peculiar sense is Scand. + Icel. *stuttr* (for *stuntr*), short, stunted (Noreen); M. Swed. *stunt*, cut short. Cf. **Stint.**

Stupefy. (F.—L.) F. *stupéfier*; cf. F. *stupéfait*, pp., directly from L. *stupefactus*, made stupid.—L. *stupē-re*, to be stupid; *facere*, to make.

stupendous. (L.) For L. *stupendus*, amazing, to be wondered at, gerundive of *stupēre*, to be amazed; with suffix *-ous*.

stupid. (F. − L.) F. *stupide*. − L. *stupidus*, senseless. − L. *stupēre*, to be amazed.

Sturdy. (F.) It formerly meant rash or reckless; hence, brave, bold. M. E. *sturdi*, *stordy*, rash. − O. F. *estourdi*, amazed, also rash, heedless; pp. of *estourdir*, 'to amaze;' Cot. (Mod. F. *étourdir*, Ital. *stordire*, to stun, amaze.) Of unknown origin; see Körting.

Sturgeon, a fish. (F. − O. H. G.) O. F. *estourgeon*, *esturgeon*; Late L. acc. *sturiōnem*, from nom. *sturio*. − O. H. G. *sturjo*, *sturo*, a sturgeon. Sometimes explained as 'a stirrer,' because it stirs up mud by floundering at the bottom of the water; cf. O. H. G. *stören*, to spread, stir (G. *stören*); see **Stir**. ✛ A. S. *styria*, *styriga*, a sturgeon, as if from *styrian*, to stir; Swed. Dan. *stör*, sturgeon, as if from Swed. *störa*, to stir; Icel. *styrja*; Du. *steur* (see Franck). Origin doubtful.

Stutter. (E.) Frequentative of *stut*, once common in the same sense. ' I *stutte*, I can nat speake my wordes redyly;' Palsgrave. M. E. *stoten*. Cf. E. Fries. *stuttern*, to stutter; Du. *stotteren* (whence G. *stottern*). From M. E. *stot-* (Teut. *stut) weak grade of Teut. root *steut, for which cf. Du. *stuiten*, to stop; 2nd grade *staut, as in Icel. *stauta*, to beat, strike, also to stutter, Swed. *stöta*, Dan. *stöde*, to strike against, G. *stossen*, Goth. *stautan*, to strike. Orig. 'to strike against,' to trip. (✓STEUD; from the weak grade come Skt. *tud*, L. *tundere*, to strike.)

Sty (1), enclosure for swine. (E.) M.E. *stie*. A. S. *stigu*, a sty, a pen for cattle. ✛ Icel. *stīa*, *stī*, sty, kennel, Swed. *stia*, pigsty, pen for geese, Swed. dial. *sti*, *steg*, pen for swine, goats, or sheep, G. *steige*, pen, chicken-coop, O. H. G. *stīa*.

Sty (2), small tumour on the eyelid. (E) The A. S. name was *stīgend*, lit. ' rising;' as if from the pres. pt. of *stīgan*, to ascend, climb, rise; but this is doubtful. M. E. *styanye*, as if it meant ' sty on eye.' ✛ Low G. *stieg*, *stieg*, sty on the eye, as if from *stigen*, to rise; E. Fries. *stiger*; Norw. *stig*, *stigje*, also *stigköyna* (from *köyna*, a pustule).

Style (1), a pointed tool for writing, a mode of writing. (F. − L.) It should be

stile, as it is not Gk. M. E. *stile*. − M. F. *stile*, *style*, ' a stile, manner of indicting;' Cot. − L. *stilus*, an iron pin for writing; a way of writing. **Der.** *stiletto*.

Style (2), the middle part of the pistil of a flower; gnomon of a dial. (Gk.) Gk. στῦλος, a pillar, long upright body like a pillar. Cf. Skt. *sthūṇā*, a pillar, post. (✓STEU, by-form of ✓STĀ.)

Styptic, astringent. (F. − L. − Gk.) F. *styptique*. − L. *stypticus*. − Gk. στυπτικός, astringent. − Gk. στύφειν, to contract, draw together, to be astringent; orig. to make firm; allied to στύπος, a stump, stem, block.

Suasion, advice. (F.−L.) M. F. *suasion*. − L. acc. *suāsiōnem*; from *suāsio*, persuasion. − L. *suāsus*, pp. of *suādēre*, to persuade, lit. 'to make sweet.' Allied to *suāuis* (=*suaduis), sweet. See **Sweet**. Brugm. i. § 187.

suave, pleasant. (F.−L.) F. *suave*; Cot. − L. *suāuis*, sweet (above).

Sub-, prefix. (L., *or* F.−L.) L. (and F.) *sub-*, prefix. Orig. form *sup; whence the comparative form *sup-er*, above, allied to Skt. *upari*, above. The prefix *s-* prob. answers to Gk. ἐξ; cf. *s-uper* with ἐξ-ύπερθε, ' from above.' *Sub* seems to have meant ' up to '; hence it also came to mean just under or below; it is allied to E. **Up**, q. v., and to Gk. ὑπό; see **Hypo-**. ¶ *Sub* becomes *suc-* before *c*, *suf-* before *f*, *sug-* before *g*, *sum-* before *m*, *sup-* before *p*, *sur-* before *r*; and see **Sus-** (below).

Subaltern, inferior to another. (F.− L.) F. *subalterne*; Cot.− L. *subalternus*, subordinate. − L. *sub*, under; *alter*, another.

Subaqueous, under water. (L.) L. *sub*, under; *aqua*, water. See **Aqueous**.

Subdivide. (L.) L. *sub*, under; and *dīuidere*, to divide. See **Divide**. **Der.** *subdivision* (from the pp.).

Subdue. (F.−L.) M. E. *soduen* (afterwards ' learnedly' altered to *subdue*). First used in the pp. *sodued*, *sodewed*.− A. F. *subdut, as in *subduz* (for *subduts*), pp. pl., subdued. − Late L. *subdutus, for L. *subditus*, subdued. − L. *subdere*, to subdue.− L. *sub*, under; *-dere*, to put, weak grade of ✓ DHĒ, to put. ¶ Not from L. *subdūcere*, with an alien sense.

Subjacent. (L.) From stem of pres. pt. of L. *sub-iacēre*, to lie under.− L. *sub*, under; *iacēre*, to lie. See **Jet** (1).

subject. (F.−L.) M.E. *suget*, *subjet*. − O. F. *suiet*, *suiect* (later *subiect*), mod. F. *sujet*, a subject.− L. *subiectus*, pp. of *sub-*

icere, to put under, subject. **–** L. *sub*, under ; *iacere*, to cast, to put.

Subjoin. (F.–L.) M. F. *subjoign-*, a stem of *subjoindre*.–L. *subiungere*, to join beneath, annex, subjoin.–L. *sub*, beneath ; *iungere*, to join. See **Join**.

subjugate, to bring under the yoke. (L.) From pp. of L. *subiugāre*, vb. **–** L. *sub iugō*, under the yoke ; where *iugō* is abl. of *iugum*, a yoke. See **Yoke**.

subjunctive. (L.) L. *subiunctīuus*, lit. joining on dependently, from the use of the subjunctive mood in dependent clauses. **–** L. *subiunctus*, pp. of *subiungere*, to subjoin ; see **Subjoin** (above).

Sublime. (F.–L.) F. *sublime*. **–** L. *sublimis*, lofty, raised on high. Perhaps from L. *sub*, and *līmen*, lintel ; ' up to the lintel ;' Brugm. ii. § 12.

Sublunar, under the moon, earthly. (L.) Coined from L. *sub*, under ; and E. *lunar*, belonging to the moon, from L. *lūna*, moon ; see **Lunar**.

Submerge, to plunge under water. (F. –L.) F. *submerger*. **–** L. *submergere*. **–** L. *sub*, under ; *mergere*, to dip ; see **Merge**.

Submit. (L.) L. *submittere*, to let down, submit, bow to (pp. *submissus*).**–** L. *sub*, under ; *mittere*, to send. See **Missile**. Der. *submiss-ion, -ive.*

Subordinate, of lower rank. (L.) From the pp. of Late L. *subordināre*, to place in a lower rank.–L. *sub*, below ; *ordināre*, to rank, from *ordin-*, stem of *ordo*, order. See **Order**.

Suborn, to procure secretly, bribe. (F. –L.) F. *suborner*. **–** L. *subornāre*. **–** L. *sub*, secretly ; *ornāre*, to furnish, properly, to adorn. See **Ornament**.

Subpœna, a writ, commanding attendance under a penalty. (L.) L. *sub* ; under ; *pœnā*, abl. of *pœna*, a penalty. See **Pain**.

Subscribe. (L.) L. *subscrībere*, to write (one's name) under ; pp. *subscriptus* (whence *subscription*). **–** L. *sub*, under ; *scrībere*, to write. See **Scribe**.

Subsequent. (L.) From stem of pres. pt. of *subsequī*, to follow close after. **–** L. *sub*, under, near ; *sequī*, to follow. See **Sequence**.

Subserve. (L.) L. *subseruīre*, to serve under another. **–** L. *sub*, under ; *seruīre*, to serve. See **Serve**.

Subside. (L.) L. *subsīdere*, to settle down. **–** L. *sub*, under, down ; *sīdere*, to

settle, allied to *sedēre*, to sit. See **Sedentary**. Brugm. i. § 882.

subsidy. (F. **–** L.) A. F. *subsidie* (Godefroy) ; F. *subside*. **–** L. *subsidium*, a body of troops in reserve, assistance ; lit. that which sits in reserve. **–** L. *sub*, under, in reserve ; *sedēre*, to sit. **Der.** *subsidi-ary*, from L. adj. *subsidiārius*.

Subsist, to live, continue. (F.–L.) F. *subsister*, ' to subsist ;' Cot. **–** L. *subsistere*, to stay, abide. **–** L. *sub*, near to ; *sistere*, to stand, also to place, from *stāre*, to stand. See **State**.

substance. (F.–L.) F. *substance*. **–** L. *substantia*, substance, essence. **–** L. *substant-*, stem of pres. pt. of *substāre*, to exist, lit. ' to stand near or beneath.' **–** L. *sub*, near ; *stāre*, to stand. **Der.** *substanti-al* ; also *substant-ive*, F. *substantif*, L. *substantīuus*, self-existent, used of the verb *esse*, and afterwards applied, as a grammatical term, to nouns substantive.

substitute, sb. (F.–L.) F. *substitut*, a substitute.–L. *substitūtus*, pp. of *substituere*, to put in stead of.–L. *sub*, near, instead of ; *statuere*, to put, place, causal of *stāre*, to stand.

Subtend. (L.) L. *subtendere*, to stretch or extend beneath.–L. *sub*, beneath ; *tendere*, to stretch. See **Tend** (1).

Subterfuge. (F.–L.) F. *subterfuge*, ' a shift ;' Cot.–Late L. *subterfugium*.–L. *subterfugere*, to escape by stealth.–L. *subter*, stealthily (from *sub*, under, with compar. suffix) ; *fugere*, to flee. See **Fugitive**.

Subterranean, Subterraneous. (L.) From L. *subterrāne-us*, underground. **–** L. *sub*, under ; *terra*, ground. See **Terrace**.

Subtle. (F.–L.) Formerly *sotil*, *sotel* ; the *b* was a pedantic insertion, and is never sounded.–O. F. *sotil*, *soutil*, later *subtil*. **–** L. *subtīlem*, acc. of *subtīlis*, fine, thin, accurate, subtle. The orig. sense of *subtīlis* was ' finely woven ;' from L. *sub*, under, closely, and *tēla*, a web, for which see **Toil** (2). **Der.** *subtle-ty*, M. E. *soteltee*, from O. F. *sotilleté*, subtlety, from L. acc. *subtīlitātem*. Brugm. i. § 134.

Subtract. (L.) From L. *subtractus*, pp. of *subtrahere*, to draw away underneath, to subtract.–L. *sub*, beneath ; *trahere*, to draw. See **Trace** (1).

Suburb. (F.–L.) A. F. *suburbe* (A. D. 1285). **–** L. *suburbium*, suburb. **–** L. *sub*, near ; *urbi-* decl. stem of

urbs, a town. Der. *suburb-an*. See
Urbane.

Subvert. (F.−L.) F. *subvertir*; Cot.
−L. *subuertere*, to turn upside down,
overthrow. −L. *sub*, beneath; *uertere*, to
turn. See Verse. Der. *subvers-ion*, from
the pp. *subuers-us*.

Succeed. (F.−L.) F. *succéder*; Cot.
−L. *succēdere* (pp. *successus*), to follow
after. −L. *suc-* (*sub*), next; *cēdere*, to go,
come. Der. *success*, O. F. *succes*, L. *successus*, result, from pp. *successus*.

Succinct, concise. (L.) L. *succinctus*,
pp. of *succingere*, to gird up, tuck up short.
−L. *suc-* (*sub*), up; *cingere*, to gird. See
Cincture.

Succory; see Chicory.

Succour. (F.−L.) M. E. *socouren.*−
O. F. *sucurre* (Burguy). Mod. F. *secourir.*
−L. *succurrere*, to run near or to, run
to help, aid.−L. *suc-* (for *sub*), near;
currere, to run. See Current.

Succulent, juicy. (F.−L.) F. *succulent.*−L. *sūculentus*, *succulentus*, full of
juice.−L. *sūcu-s*, *succu-s*, juice; with suffix
-lentus. See Suck.

Succumb. (L.) L. *succumbere*, to lie
under, to sink down.−L. *suc-* (for *sub*),
under; **cumbere*, to recline, allied to
cubāre, to lie down. See Covey.

Such, of a like kind. (E.) M. E. *swulc,
swilc. swich, such*. A. S. *swylc*.+O. Sax.
sulik, Du. *zulk*, Icel. *slīkr*, Dan. *slig*, Swed.
slik, G. *solch*, Goth. *swaleiks*. β. The Goth.
swaleiks is from *swa*, so, and *leiks*, like;
hence *such = so-like*; see So and Like.

Suck. (E.) M. E. *souken*. A. S. *sūcan*,
pt. t. *sēac*, pp. *socen*. [There is an A. S.
by-form *sūgan*; cognate with Icel. *sjūga*,
sūga, Dan. *suge*, Swed. *suga*, G. *saugen*,
Du. *zuigen*.] β. The A. S. *sūcan* is cognate with L. *sūgere*, W. *sugno*, to suck,
O. Irish *sūg-im*, I suck; cf. O. Ir. and W.
sug, Gael. *sugh*, L. *sūcus*, juice; see Succulent. Brugm. i. § 112.

suction. (F. − L.) M. F. *suction*.
Formed (as if from L. **suctio*) from L.
suct-us, pp. of *sūgere*, to suck.

Sudatory, a sweating-bath. (L.) L.
sūdātōrium, a sweating-bath; neut. of
sūdātōrius, serving for sweating. − L.
sūdātōr-, stem of *sūdātor*, a sweater.−
L. *sūdā-re*, to sweat; with suffix *-tor* (of
the agent). Cognate with E. Sweat.

Sudden. (F.−L.) M.E. *sodain*.−O.F.
sodain, *sudain* (F. *soudain*). [Cf. Ital.
subitaneo, *subitano*, sudden.] − Late L.

*subitānus, for L. *subitāneus*, sudden,
extended from *subitus*, sudden, lit. that
which has come stealthily, orig. pp. of
subīre, to come or go stealthily. −L. *sub*,
under, stealthily; *īre*, to go.

Sudorific. (F.−L.) F. *sudorifique*,
causing sweat; as if from L. **sūdōrificus*.
−L. *sūdōri-*, for *sūd-or*, sweat, allied to
sūdāre, to sweat; *-ficus*, making, from
facere, to make. See Sudatory.

Suds. (E.) The proper sense is 'things
sodden'; pl. of *sud*, which is derived from
A. S. *sud-*, weak grade of *sēoðan*, to seethe.
Cf. prov. E. *sudded*, flooded; M. Du. *zode*,
a seething, boiling; Low G. *sod*, cooked
broth, *söde*, a boiling. Cf. Sod.

Sue. (F.−L.) M. E. *suen*, *sewen.*−
A. F. *suer*; O. F. *sevre*, *suir* (F. *suivre*),
to follow.−Late L. *sequere*, to follow, used
for L. *sequī*, to follow. See Sequence.
Der. *en-sue*, *pur-sue*, *suit*, *suite*.

Suet. (F.−L.) M. E. *suet*. Formed,
with dimin. suffix *-et*, from O. F. *seu*, *suis*
(Norman *sieu*, Walloon *sew*, Littré; F.
suif), suet, fat.−L. *sēbum*, tallow, suet,
grease.

Suffer. (F.−L.) M. E. *soffren*, *suffren.*
−O. F. *soffrir* (F. *souffrir*). −Folk-L.
sufferīre, for L. *sufferre*, to undergo.−L.
suf- (*sub*), under; *ferre*, to bear. See
Fertile.

Suffice. (F.−L.) From F. *suffis-*, base
of *suffis-ant*, pres. pt. of *suffire*, to suffice.
−L. *sufficere*, to supply.−L. *suf-*, for *sub*,
under; *facere*, to make, put. See Fact.

Suffix. (L.) From L. *suffix-us*, pp. of
suffīgere, to fix beneath, fix on.−L. *suf-*
(for *sub*), beneath; *figere*, to fix. See
Fix.

Suffocate. (L.) From pp. of L.
suffōcāre, to choke; lit. to squeeze the
throat.−L. *suf-* (for *sub*), under; *fauc-*,
stem of *fauc-ēs*, sb. pl., gullet, throat.

Suffrage, a vote. (F.−L.) F. *suffrage.*
−L. *suffrāgium*, a vote, suffrage.

Suffusion. (F.−L.) F. *suffusion.*−L.
suffūsiōnem, acc. of *suffūsio*, a pouring
over.−L. *suffūsus*, pp. of *suffundere*, to
pour over.−L. *suf-* (for *sub*), under, also
over; *fundere*, to pour. See Fuse (1).

Sugar. (F. − Span. − Arab.−Pers. −
Skt.) F. *sucre*. − Span. *azucar*. − Arab.
assokkar; for *al*, the, *sokkar*, *sakkar*, sugar.
− Pers. *shakar*. − Skt. *çarkarā*, gravel, also
candied sugar. Prob. allied to Skt. *kar-
kara-*, hard.

Suggestion. (F.−L.) F. *suggestion*.

− L. acc. *suggestiōnem.* **−** L. *suggestus,* pp. of *suggerere,* to bring under, supply, suggest. **−** L. *sug-* (for *sub*), under ; *gerere,* to bring. See **Gerund.**

Suicide, self-murder ; one who dies by his own hand. (F.**−** L.) A word coined in *England* (before A.D. 1750), but on a F. model ; yet the F. *suicide* was borrowed from us. Like *homicide,* the word has a double meaning, (1) answering to L. **suīcīdium,* from L. *suī,* of himself, and *-cīdium,* a slaying, from *cædere,* to slay ; (2)=L. **suīcīda,* from L. *suī,* of himself, and *-cīda,* a slayer. See **Cæsura.**

Suit. (F.**−** L.) F. *suite,* a pursuit, suit at law, also a suite or ' following.'**−** Late L. **sequita,* variant of *secta* (L. *secūta*), a following, a sect, a suite, a suit at law, suit of clothes, set, &c. ; see **Sect.**

suite. (F.**−** L.) F. *suite* ; see above.

Sulcated, furrowed. (L.) L. *sulcātus,* pp. of *sulcāre,* to furrow.**−** L. *sulcus,* a furrow. **+** Gk. ὁλκός, a furrow ; from ἕλκειν, to draw along ; cf. A. S. *sulh,* a plough.

Sulky, obstinate, silently sullen. (E.) Not an old form, but deduced from the sb. *sulkiness,* by dropping *-ness.* However, *sulkiness* is itself a corrupt form for *sullenness,* formed by adding *-ness* to the adj. *sulken.* This appears as A. S. *solcen,* slothful, remiss ; chiefly in the comp. *ā-solcen,* also *be-solcen,* with a like sense. The sb. *āsolcennes,* sloth, disgust, sulkiness, is quite a common word. β. Further, *ā-solcen* was the pp. of a strong verb **ā-seolcan,* to be slothful or languid. Cf. Skt. *srj,* to let flow, let loose.

Sullen, morose. (F.**−** L.) Orig. solitary, hating company. M. E. *solain,* *sulain,* solitary ; also, a mess of food for one person.**−**O. F. *solain,* lonely ; given as ' a pittance for one monk ' in Roquefort, and in Ducange, s. v. *solatium* (5).**−**Late L. **sōlānus ;* equivalent in sense to O. F. *soltain,* solitary, Late L. *sōlitāneus,* rare.**−** L. *sōlus,* alone ; see **Sole** (3).

Sully, to tarnish, spot. (E.) M. E. *sulien.* A. S. *sylian,* to sully, defile, lit. to bemire. Formed (with the usual change from Teut. *u* (**>** A. S. *o*) to *y*) from A. S. *sol,* mud, mire. β. But it is doubtful if M. E. *sulien* is the same word. And if not, it must be from M. F. *souiller,* 'to soil, slurry, durty, smutch,' Cotgrave. See further under **Soil** (2), which is a doublet.

Sulphur. (L.) L. *sulphur.* Cf. also Skt. *çulvāri-,* sulphur.

Sultan. (F.**−**Arab.) F.*sultan.***−**Arab. *sultān,* victorious, also a ruler, prince ; orig. ' dominion.' Cf. Chaldee *sholtān,* dominion. Der. *sultan-a,* from Ital. *sultana,* fem. of *sultano,* sultan, from Arab. *sultān.*

Sultry, Sweltry, very hot and oppressive. (E.) *Sweltry* is the older form, and is short for *swelter-y,* from the verb to *swelter* (M. E. *swelteren, swalteren*). Again, *swelter* is a frequentative form from M. E. *swelten,* to swoon, faint, die.**−**A. S. *sweltan,* to die. **+** O. Sax. *sweltan ;* Icel. *svelta* (pt. t. *svalt*), Dan. *sulte,* Swed. *svälta ;* Goth. *swiltan,* to die. Cf. Icel. *sultr,* Dan. *sult,* hunger, famine ; from the weak grade **swult* **>****sult.* Also O.H.G. *schwelzan,* to burn, to be consumed by fire or love. The Teut. root **swelt-* seems to be an extension of **swel-,* to burn, as in A. S. *swelan,* to burn, perish with heat, Lith. *swilti,* to shine, burn, Skt. *svar,* splendour, M. Du. *zoel,* ' sultrie,' Hexham.

Sum, amount, total. (F.**−**L.) M. E. *summe.* **−** F. *somme.* **−** L. *summa,* sum, chief part, amount ; orig. fem. of *summus* (**sup-mus*), highest, superl. form from *sub* (**<****sup*), above. Brugm. i. § 762. Der. *summ-ar-y,* sb., from F. *sommaire,* ' a summary,' Cot., from L. *summārium,* a summary.

Sumach, a tree. (F.**−**Span.**−**Arab.) F. *sumac,* M. F. *sumach.***−**Span. *zumaque.* **−** Arab. *summāq,* a species of shrub, sumach.

Summer (1), hot season. (E.) M. E. *somer, sumer.* A. S. *sumer, sumor.***+**Du. *zomer,* Icel. *sumar,* Dan. *sommer,* Swed. *sommar,* G. *sommer,* O. H. G. *sumar.* Further allied to O. Irish *sam, samrad,* O. Welsh *ham,* W. *haf,* Zend *hama,* summer ; Skt. *samā,* a year. Brugm. i. § 436.

Summer (2), a beam ; see **Sumpter.**

Summerset ; see **Somersault.**

Summit, top. (F.**−**L.) F. *sommet,* top. Dimin. of O. F. *som,* top of a hill.**−** L. *summum,* highest point, neut. of *summus,* highest ; see **Sum.**

Summon. (F.**−**L.) A. F. *sommoner* (Godefroy) ; O. F. *somoner* (Roquefort), early altered to *semoner* and *semondre* (F. *semondre*), to summon. **−** L. *summonēre ;* to remind privily. **−** L. *sum-* (for *sub*) under, privily ; *monēre,* to remind.

summons, sb. (F.**−**L.) M. E. *som-*

ouns. — A. F. *somons,* earlier *somonse,* fem.; M. F. *semonce,* 'a warning, summons,' Cot.; orig. the fem. of the pp. of the verb *somoner, semondre* (above). ¶ Thus the final *s* of *summons* is not due to L. *summoneās,* as some have suggested.

Sumpter, a pack-horse. (F. — Low L. — Gk.) *Sumpter* is a derivative from M. E. *somer,* a pack-horse, which must be first considered. β. M. E. *somer* is from O. F. *somier, sommier,* a pack-horse, the same as Late L. *sagmārius,* corruptly *salmārius,* a pack-horse. — Gk. σάγμα, a pack-saddle. — Gk. σάττειν (base σακ-), to pack, fasten on a load, orig. to fasten. γ. Hence E. *sumpter,* which orig. meant (not a pack-horse, but) a pack-horse-driver, baggage-carrier. — O. F. *sommetier,* a pack-horse-driver; answering to a Late L. **sagmatarius,* for which Ducange has *summatārius, saumatērius.* — Gk. σαγματ-, stem of σάγμα (above). δ. The old word *summer,* a beam, was so called from its bearing a great weight, and is the same as M. E. *somer* (above) : cf. F. *sommier,* 'a summer,' Cot. Hence E. *bressomer,* familiar form of *breast-summer,* a beam placed breastwise, to support a superincumbent wall. ¶ I explain *sumpter* in K. Lear, ii. 4. 219, as meaning 'pack-horse-driver'; a man, not a horse.

Sumptuary, relating to expenses. (L.) L. *sumptuārius,* adj. from *sumptu-s,* expense. See below.

sumptuous, costly. (F. — L.) F. *somptuëux* (Cot.) — L. *sumptuōsus,* costly. — L. *sumptus,* expense. — L. *sumptus,* pp. of *sūmere,* to take, use, spend ; a derivative from *emere,* to take. Brugm. i. § 240.

Sun. (E.) M. E. *sonne.* A. S. *sunne,* fem. sb. + Du. *zon,* G. *sonne,* Goth. *sunnō,* all feminine ; Teut. type **sunnōn-,* fem. ¶ Cf. Icel. *sōl,* Swed. Dan. *sol,* L. *sōl,* Goth. *sauil,* Lith. *saulė,* W. *haul,* Gk. ἥέλιος (ἥλιος), Skt. *sūra-, sūrya-,* the sun. Der. *Sun-day,* A. S. *sunnan-dæg.*

Sunder, to divide. (E.) A. S. *syndrian, -sundrian,* to put asunder. — A. S. *sundor,* adv., asunder, apart. + Icel. *sundra,* Dan. *söndre,* Swed. *söndra,* G. *sondern,* to sunder ; from Icel. *sundr,* Dan. Swed. *sönder,* adv., apart, G. *sonder,* adj., separate. Cf. Gk. ἄτερ (for **sonter*), without ; allied to Gk. ἄνευ, L. *sine,* without. Brugm. i. § 500.

Sup, to imbibe, lap up. (E.) M. E. *soupen.* A. S. *sūpan* (pt. t. *sēap,* pp. *sopen*),

to sup, drink in. + Du. *zuipen,* Icel. *sūpa,* Swed. *supa,* G. *saufen,* O. H. G. *sūfan.*

Super-, prefix. (L.) L. *super,* above ; cf. L. *superus,* upper. For *s-uperus* ; where *s-* corresponds to Gk. ἐξ- ; see **Sub-.** Cf. Gk. ὑπέρ, above ; ὑπό, from under ; Skt. *upari,* above, allied to *upara-,* upper, comparative of *upa,* near, close to.

Superannuate. (L.) Formerly (and better) *superannate.* — Late L. *superannātus,* orig. that has lived beyond a year. — L. *super,* beyond ; *annus,* a year. See Annals.

Superb. (F. — L.) F. *superbe.* — L. *superbus,* proud ; one who thinks himself above others. For **super-fu-os,* one who is above (cf. L. *fu-ī,* I was) ; Brugm. ii. § 4. — L. *super,* above. See **Super-.**

Supercargo. (L. ; *and* Span. — C.) From L. *super,* above ; and Span. *cargo,* a freight. Suggested by Span. *sobrecargo,* a supercargo ; where *sobre* < L. *super.* See **Cargo.**

Supercilious, disdainful. (L.) From L. *supercili-um,* (1) an eyebrow, (2) haughtiness, as expressed by raising the eyebrows. — L. *super,* above ; *cil-ium,* eyelid, allied to Gk. τὰ κύλα, the parts under the eyes (Prellwitz).

Supererogation. (L.) From acc. of Late L. *supererogātio,* that which is done beyond what is due. — L. *supererogāre,* to pay out in excess. — L. *super,* beyond ; *ē,* out ; *rogāre,* to ask. (L. *ērogāre* = to lay out, expend.) See **Rogation.**

Superficies. (L.) L. *superficiēs,* surface, outer face. — L. *super,* above ; *faciēs,* face.

Superfine. (F. — L.) From L. *super,* above ; and *fine* (1).

Superfluous, excessive. (L.) L. *superflu-us,* overflowing ; with suffix *-ous.* — L. *super,* over ; *fluere,* to flow ; see **Fluent.** Der. *superflui-ty,* F. *superfluité,* from L. acc. *superfluitātem.*

Superinduce. (L.) L. *super,* beyond ; and *in-dūcere,* to induce. See **Induce.**

Superintendent, an overseer. (F. — L.) M. F. *superintendant* ; Cot. — L. *superintendent-,* stem of pres. pt. of *superintendere,* to superintend. — L. *super,* above ; *intendere,* to apply the mind to ; see **Intend.**

Superior. (F. — L.) Formerly *superiour.* — M. F. *superieur.* — L. *superiōrem,* acc. of *superior,* higher ; comparative from *superus*, high, which is itself an old comparative form. See **Super-**.

Superlative. (F. – L.) F. *superlatif*, Cot. – L. *superlātiuus*, as a grammatical term. – L. *superlātus*, excessive, lit. 'borne beyond.' – L. *super*, beyond; *lātus*, pp. of *tollere*, to bear. (√TEL.) See **Tolerate**.

Supernal. (F. – L.) M. F. *supernel*, 'supernall;' Cot. Answering to a Late L. *supernālis, from L. *supern-us*, upper; from *super*, above; see **Super-**.

Supernatural. (L.) From L. *super*, beyond; and *natural*, adj., from *nature*.

Supernumerary. (F. – L.) M. F. *supernumeraire* (Cot.). – L. *supernumerārius*, excessive in number. – L. *super*, beyond; *numerus*, number.

Superscription. (F. – L.) M. F. *superscription*; Cot. – L. acc. *superscriptiōnem*. – L. *superscriptus*, pp. of *superscribere*, to write above or over. – L. *super*, above; *scrībere*, to write; see **Scribe**.

Supersede. (F. – L.) O.F. *superseder*, to leave off, desist (hence to suspend or defer a matter). – L. *supersedēre*, to sit upon, to preside over, refrain, desist from. – L. *super*, upon; *sedēre*, to sit. See **Sedentary**. Der. *supersess-ion* (from pp. *supersess-us*); cf. *surcease*.

Superstition. (F. – L.) F. *superstition*. – L. acc. *superstitiōnem*, a standing near a thing, amazement, dread, religious awe, scruple. – L. *superstit-*, stem of *superstes*, one who stands near, a witness. – L. *super*, above, near; *statum*, supine of *stāre*, to stand.

Superstructure. (L.) From L. *super*, above; and **Structure**.

Supervene. (L.) L. *superuenīre*, to come upon or over, to follow, occur. – L. *super*, beyond; *uenīre*, to come. See **Venture**.

Supervise; see **Vision**.

Supine, on one's back, lazy. (L.) L. *supīnus*, lying on one's back. – L. *sup, orig. form of *sub*, up; with suffix *-īnus*.

Supper. (F. – Teut.) M. E. *soper*. – O. F. *soper* (F. *souper*), a supper. It is the infin. mood used as a sb. – O. F. *soper*, to sup (F. *souper*). – Low G. *supen*, Icel. *sūpa*, Swed. *supa*, to sup. See **Sup**.

Supplant. (F. – L.) M. E. *supplanter*. – L. *supplantāre*, to put something under the sole of the foot, trip up, overthrow. – L. *sup-* (> *sub*), under; *planta*, sole; see **Plant**.

Supple. (F. – L.) M. E. *souple*. – F.

souple, supple, pliant. – L. *supplicem*, acc. of *supplex*, with the old sense of 'bending under.' – L. *sup-* (> *sub*), under; *plic-*, as seen in *plicāre*, to fold. See **Ply**.

Supplement. (F. – L.) F. *supplément*; Cot. – L. *supplēmentum*, a filling up. – L. *supplēre*, to fill up. – L. *sup-* (*sub*), up; *plēre*, to fill. See **Plenary**.

Suppliant. (F. – L.) F. *suppliant*, pres. pt. of *supplier*, to pray humbly. – L. *supplicāre*; see below.

supplicate. (L.) From pp. of L. *supplicāre*, to beseech. – L. *supplic-*, stem of *supplex*, bending under or down, beseeching; see **Supple**.

Supply. (F. – L.) Formerly *supploy* (Levins). – O. F. *supploier*, F. *suppléer*, to supply; Cot. – L. *supplēre*, to fill up; see **Supplement**.

Support. (F. – L.) M. E. *supporten*. – F. *supporter*. – L. *supportāre*, to carry to a place; in Late L., to endure. – L. *sup-* (*sub*), near; *portāre*, to carry. See **Port** (1).

Suppose. (F. – L. *and* Gk.) F. *supposer*, to imagine. – L. *sup-* (*sub*), under, near; F. *poser*, to place, put. See **Pose**.

Supposition. (F. – L.) F. *supposition*. – L. acc. *suppositiōnem*. – L. *suppositus*, pp. of *suppōnere*, to suppose. – L. *sup-* (*sub*), near; *pōnere*, to place. See **Position**.

Suppress. (L.) From L. *suppressus*, pp. of *supprimere*, to suppress. – L. *sup-* (*sub*), under; *premere*, to press. See **Press**.

Suppurate. (L.) From pp. of L. *suppūrāre*, to gather pus underneath. – L. *sup-* (*sub*), under; *pūr-*, for *pūs*, matter. See **Pus**.

Supra-, prefix, above. (L.) L. *suprā*, above, adv. and prep.; allied to *superus*, upper; see **Super-**. Der. *supra-mundane*; see **Mundane**.

Supreme. (F. – L.) F. *suprême*. – L. *suprēmus*, highest. *Suprē-mus* is from *suprē, an adverb, with suffix *-mus*; Brug. ii. § 75. This *suprē is allied to L. *super*, above.

Sur- (1), prefix. (L.) For *sub* before *r*; only in *sur-reptitious*, *sur-rogate*.

Sur- (2), prefix. (F. – L.) F. *sur*, above. – L. *super*, above. See **Super-**.

Surcease, to cease, cause to cease. (F. – L.) Not allied to *cease* (except in popular etymology). A corruption of O. F. *sursis*, masc., *sursise*, fem., 'surceased, intermitted;' Cot. This word was also used as a sb., to signify 'delay'; hence *surcease*, vb., to delay. *Sursis* is the pp. of O. F. *surseoir*, ' to surcease, delay,' Cot. — L. *supersedēre*, to desist from, hence to delay proceedings ; see **Supersede**.

Surcharge, sb. (F.—L. *and* C.) F. *surcharge*, an over-charge.—F. *sur* (<L. *super*), above ; and **Charge**.

Surd, having no rational root (in mathematics). (L.) L. *surdus*, deaf ; hence, deaf to reason, irrational. *Surdus* also means dim ; and connexion with *sordid* is possible. Brugm. i. § 362.

Sure. (F. — L.) O. F. *seür* (F. *sûr*), earliest form *segur*.—L. *sēcūrus*; see **Secure**. Doublet, *secure*.

Surf, the foam of the waves on the shore. (E.) The *r* is intrusive; spelt *suffe*, with the sense of 'rush,' in Hakluyt's Voyages, ed. 1598, vol. ii. pt. i. 227 : ' The *suffe* of the sea [sweep or rush of the inflowing wave] setteth her [a raft's] lading dry on land.' I suppose *suffe* to be the same as ' *sough* of the sea,' also spelt *souf*, *souch* in Jamieson. M. E. *swough*, from *swoughen*, *swowen*, to make a rushing noise. Cf. ' the *swogh* of the see,' Morte Arth. 759. — A. S. *swōgan*, to make a rushing noise ; see **Sough**.

Surface. (F. — L.) F. *surface*, upper face.—F. *sur*, above ; *face*, face.—L. *super*, above ; *faciēs*, face. See **Face**.

Surfeit, sb. (F. — L.) O. F. *surfait*, *sorfait*, excess ; orig. pp. of *sorfaire*, to augment, exaggerate. — L. *super*, above ; *facere*, to make. See **Fact**.

Surge, the swell of waves. (F.—L.) ' *Surge* of the see, *uague*;' Palsgrave. Coined from O. F. stem *sourge-*, as in *sourge-ant*, pres. pt. of *sourdre*, to rise.— L. *surgere* (=*sur-rigere*, i.e. **sub-regere*), to rise. — L. *sub*, up ; *regere*, to direct. See **Regent**.

Surgeon, contracted form of *chirurgeon*; see **Chirurgeon**. So also Gascon *surgen*, a surgeon ; O. F. *surgien* (Godefroy). **Der.** *surgical*, short for *chirurgical* ; *surgery*, corruption of M. E. *surgenry*, i.e. *surgeon-ry*, or of O.F. *cirurgerie*.

Surloin; see **Sirloin**.

Surly, proud, churlish. (E.) Spelt *serly* Levins) ; *syrly*, Spenser, Shep. Kal. July, 203. Prob. from A.S. *sūr-līc, lit. ' sour-like.' We find *sowre*, meaning 'morose' (Baret) ; see **Sour**. Cf. G. *sauer*, sour, surly ; Swed. Dan. *syrlig*, sourish. Also M. E. *surdagh*, ' sour dough ;' Wrt. Vocab. 663. 22.

Surmise, an imagination, guess. (F. — L.) O. F. *surmise*, an accusation, charge ; orig. fem. of *surmis*, pp. of *surmettre*, to put upon, lay to one's charge. — F. *sur*, above ; *mettre*, to put. — L. *super*, above ; *mittere*, to send, put. See **Missile**.

Surmount. (F.—L.) F. *surmonter*.— F. *sur* (L. *super*), above ; *monter*, to mount ; see **Mount** (2).

Surname. (F. — L.; *and* E.) From F. *sur* (L. *super*), above, over ; and E. **Name**.

Surpass. (F. — L.) F. *surpasser*, to excel.— F. *sur* (L. *super*), beyond ; *passer*, to pass ; see **Pass**.

Surplice. (F.—L.) M. E. *surplis*.— F. *surplis*; Cot.—Late L. *superpelliceum*, a surplice. — L. *super*, over ; *pelliceus*, made of skins, from *pellis*, a skin ; see **Pelisse**.

Surplus. (F. — L.) F. *surplus*, ' an over-plus ;' Cot. — Late L. *superplūs*, a residuum. — L. *super*, above ; *plūs*, more. See **Plural**.

Surprise, sb. (F.—L.) O. F. *sorprise*, *surprise*, a taking unawares. Fem. of *sorpris*, pp. of *sorprendre*, *surprendre*, to surprise. — L. *super*, upon ; *prehendere*, to seize, from *præ*, before, and *-hendere*, to seize. See **Prehensile**.

Surrebutter. (F.—L. *and* O. H. G.) A legal term, meaning an answer or reply to a *rebut*. From F. *sur* (L. *super*), upon, in reply to ; and M.F. *rebouter*, to rebut, the infin. mood being used as a sb. See **Rebut**. And see **Surrejoinder**.

Surrejoinder. (F.—L.) A *rejoinder* in reply. ' The plaintiff may answer him by a *rejoinder*; upon which the defendant may *rebut*; and the plaintiff may answer him by a *surrebutter* ;' Blackstone, Comment. b. iii. c. 20. From F. *sur*, upon, in reply to ; and F. *rejoindre*, to rejoin, used as a sb. See **Rejoin**.

Surrender. (F.—L.) O. F. *surrendre*, to give up. — F. *sur* (L. *super*), above ; *rendre*, to render, from L. *reddere*, to restore. See **Render**.

Surreptitious. (L.) L. *surreptīti-us*, better *surreptīcius*, done stealthily ; with suffix *-ous*.—L. *surreptum*, supine of *surripere*, to pilfer, purloin. — L. *sur-* (*sub*), under, secretly ; *rapere*, to seize. See **Rapid**.

Surrogate, a substitute. (L.) L. *surrogātus*, pp. of *surrogāre*, to elect in place of another. ▬ L. *sur-* (for *sub*), in place of; *vvgäre*, to ask, elect. See Rogation.

Surround. (F. ▬ L.) Confused with *round.* Orig. *suround*, i.e. ' to overflow ;' as in Caxton's Statutes of Hen. VII, leaf c 7. ▬ O. F. *suronder.* ▬ L. *superundāre*, to overflow (Lewis). ▬ L. *super*, over, above ; *undāre*, to flow, from *unda*, a wave. Cf. *ab-ound, red-ound.*

Surtout. (F. ▬ L.) From F. *sur tout*, lit. ' over all.' ▬ L. *super*, over; *tōtum*, acc. of *tōtus*, all. See Total.

Surveillance, inspection. (F. ▬ L.) F. *surveillance*, superintendence. ▬ F. *surveiller*, to superintend. ▬ L. *super*, over ; *uigilāre*, to watch, from *uigil*, adj., awake. See Vigil.

Survey. (F. ▬ L.) A. F. *surveier*, *surveër* (O. F. *sourveoir*), to survey. ▬ Late L. *superuidēre*, to supervise. ▬ L. *super*, over ; *uidēre*, to see. See Vision. Doublet, *supervise.*

Survive. (F. ▬ L.) F. *survivre*, to outlive. ▬ L. *superuīuere*, to live beyond, outlive. ▬ L. *super*, beyond ; *uīuere*, to live. See Victuals.

Sus-, prefix. (L.) L. *sus-*, prefix; for **sups*, extended form of **sup*, *sub*, under.

Susceptible. (F. ▬ L.) F. *susceptible*. ▬ L. *susceptibilis*, ready to receive. ▬ L. *sus-*, for **sup-s*, under; and *capt-um*, supine of *capere*, to take. See Capacious.

Suspect. (F. ▬ L.) M. E. *suspect*, orig. a pp. with the sense suspected or suspicions. ▬ F. *suspect*, suspected. ▬ L. *suspectus*, pp. of *suspicere*, to suspect, lit. ' to look under,' mistrust. ▬ L. *su-* (for *sus-*, *sups-*), under ; *specere*, to look. See Species.

Suspend. (F. ▬ L.) F. *suspendre*. ▬ L. *suspendere* (pp. *suspensus*), to hang up. ▬ L. *sus-* (for *sups-*), extension of *sub*, under ; *pendēre*, to hang. See Pendant. Der. *suspense, suspension.*

Suspicion. (F. ▬ L.) M. E. *suspicion*. ▬ A. F. *suspiciun* ; O. F. *suspeccion*, suspicion ; later *soupeçon*, Cot. (mod. F. *soupçon*). ▬ L. *suspiciōnem*, acc. of *suspicio*, suspicion. ▬ L. *suspicere*, to suspect; see Suspect.

Sustain. (F. ▬ L.) M. E. *susteinen.* ▬ A. F. *sustein-*, a stem of O. F. *sustenir*, *sostenir* (F. *soutenir*). ▬ L. *sustinēre*, to uphold. ▬ L. *sus-* (for *sups-*), up ; *tenēre*, to hold. See Tenable. Der. *sustenance*, O. F. *sustenance*, L. *sustinentia*, sb. ; *sustentation*, from L. *sustentātio*, maintenance, from *sustentāre*, frequentative of *sustinēre*.

Sutler, one who sells provisions in a camp. (Du.) Du. *soetelaar* (Sewel) ; usually *zoetelaar* ; M. Du. *zoetelaer*, ' a scullion, a sutler, or a victualler,' Hexham. Orig. a scullion, drudge, menial who does dirty work ; formed with suffix *-aar* (= E. *-er*) from *zoetel-en*, ' to sullie,' Hexham. Cognate with Low G. *suddeln*, Dan. *sudle*, G. *sudeln*, to sully, daub. All these are frequentative forms, with suffix *el-* or *-l-* ; from Teut. **sud-*, as in Swed. *sudda*, to daub, stain, soil. Allied to Icel. *suddi*, steam from cooking, drizzling rain, *sudduligr*, wet and dank, *soð*, broth in which meat has been sodden ; all from the weak grade of Teut. **seuthan-*, Icel. *sjóða*, to seethe. Further allied to E. *suds*, and to the verb Seethe, q. v.

Suttee. (Skt.) Skt. *satī*, a true or virtuous wife, a term applied to a widow who immolates herself on the funeral pile of her husband ; hence (incorrectly) the burning of a widow. Skt. *satī* is the fem. of *sant*, being, existing, true, right, virtuous ; pres. pt. of *as*, to be. (√ES.) See Sooth.

Suture, a seam. (F. ▬ L.) F. *suture.* ▬ L. *sūtūra.* ▬ L. *sūtus*, pp. of *suere*, to sew ; see Sew.

Suzerain, a feudal lord. (F. ▬ L.) F. *suzerain*, ' sovereign, yet subaltern ;' Cot. A coined word, made from F. *sus* < L. *sūsum* or *sursum*, above ; so that F. *suzerain* answers to a Late L. **sūserānus* or **surserānus*. β. The L. *sursum* = **suuorsum*, lit. turned upwards ; from *su-*, for *sub*, up, and *uorsum* = *uersum*, neut. of pp. of *uertere*, to turn. See Verse. ¶ Prob. imitated from O. F. *soverain* (from **superānus*), which accounts for the *-er-*.

Swabber. (Du.) Older than *swab*, vb. ▬ Du. *zwabber*, ' a swabber, the drudge of a ship ;' Sewel. Cf. Du. *zwabberen*, to drudge ; Swed. *svabb*, a fire-brush, *svabla*, to swab ; Dan. *svabre*, to swab ; G. *schwabber*, a swabber. Cf. also Norw. *svabba*, Pomeran. *swabbeln*, to splash about ; E. Fries. *swabbeln*, G. *schwabbeln*, Low G. *swappen* (Danneil), to shake about (said of liquids). Of imitative origin. Compare M. E. *quappen*, to palpitate ; and E. *swap*, *swash*.

Swaddle, to swathe an infant. (E.) Formerly *swadle*, *swadell* ; for *swathel*. M. E. *swathlen*. It means to wrap in a swaddling-band, which was called a *swathel* or *swethel*. ▬ A.S. *sweðel* (once *swæðil*), a swaddling - band ; lit. 'that which swathes ;' cf. O. H. G. *swedil*, a bandage : see **Swathe**.

Swagger. (Scand.) Frequentative of *swag*, to sway from side to side. ' I *swagge*, as a fatte persons belly *swaggeth* as he goth ;' Palsgrave. — Norw. *svagga*, to swag ; cf. Icel. *sveggja*, to cause to sway. *Swag* is allied to *sway* ; see **Sway**.

Swain. (Scand.) Icel. *sveinn*, a boy, lad, servant ; Swed. *sven*, Dan. *svend*. a swain, servant.╋Low G. *sween* ; O. H. G. *swein*, a swine-herd ; A. S. *swān*, a swineherd. Teut. type **swainoz*; allied (by gradation) to **sweinom*, A. S. *swīn*, a swine, pig. Thus 'swine-herd' was the orig. sense.

Swallow (1), a bird. (E.) A. S. *swealwe*.╋Du. *zwaluw*, Icel. *svala*, Dan. *svale*, Swed. *svala*, G. *schwalbe*. Teut. type **swalwōn*, f. Cf. E. Fries. *swälke*, Low G. *swaalke*, a swallow.

Swallow (2), to absorb. (E.) M. E. *swelȝen*, *swelwen*, *swolȝhen*, *swolwen*; A.S. *swelgan*, to swallow, strong verb, pt. t. *swealh*, pp. *swolgen*. ╋ Du. *zwelgen*, Icel. *svelgja*, Dan. *svælge*, Swed. *svälja*, G. *schwelgen*. (The weak and strong forms are confused.) Der. *groundsel*, q. v.

Swamp. (Scand.) Not an old word in E. — Dan. Swed. *svamp*, a sponge, fungus ; (hence applied to swampy ground, which is the usual E. use) ; Icel. *svöppr*, a sponge. Cf. G. *sumpf*, a swamp (whence Du. *somp*) ; allied to M. H.G. *swam*, *swamp*, G. *schwamm*, a sponge, fungus ; Goth. *swamms*, sponge ; Low G. *swamm*, *swamp*, fungus ; Du. *zwam*, A. S. *swamm*, fungus. We find also prov. E. *swank*, *swang*, a swamp ; Swed. dial. *svank*.

Swan. (E.) A. S. *swan*.╋Du. *zwaan* Icel. *svanr*, Dan. *svane*, Swed. *svan*, G. *schwan*. The form resembles that of Skt. *svan*, to resound, sound, sing (L. *sonāre*).

swan-hopping, taking up swans to mark them. (E.) The usual explanation, that it stands for *swan-upping*, is right. See old tract on *upping* in Hone, Every-day Book, ii. 958. From the prep. *up*.

Swap, to strike. (E.) M. E. *swappen*, to strike ; also, to go swiftly. E. Fries. *swappen*, to strike with a noise, from *swap*, a slap, noise of a blow ; cf. Low G. *swaps*, interj. crack !, said of a slap. Imitative ; cf. *slap*, *whap* ; prov. E. *swack*, a blow.

Sward. (E.) It orig. meant skin, rind, or covering. A. S. *sweard*, the skin of

bacon, rind. *Green-sward* is the grassy covering of the land, green turf (of Scand. origin).╋Du. *zwoord*, rind of bacon ; Icel. *svörðr*, skin, sward, *grassvörðr*, greensward ; Dan. *fleskesvär*, flesh - sward. *grönsværd*, green-sward; G. *schwarte*, rind, bark, skin.

Swarm. (E.) A. S. *swearm* ; lit. ' that which hums ;' from √SWER, to hum, buzz, as in Skt. *svṛ*, to sound, *svara*-, voice, L. *susurrus*, a hum ; G. *schwirren*, to buzz. ╋Du. *zwerm*, Icel. *svarmr*, Dan. *sværm*, Swed. *svärm*, G. *schwarm*. Cf. Lith. *surma*, a pipe. Brugm. i. § 375 (8).

Swart, Swarthy. (E.) The proper form was *swart*, afterwards *swarth*, whence *swarth-y*. M. E. *swart*. A. S. *sweart*.╋ Du. *zwart*, Icel. *svartr*, Dan. *sort*, Swed. *svart*, G. *schwartz*, Goth. *swarts*. Cf. A. S. *sweorcan*, to grow dark.

Swarth, a quantity of grass cut down at one stroke of the scythe. (E.) In Tw. Nt. ii. 3. 162. An error for *swath*, as in Troil. v. 5. 25. See **Swath**.

Swash, to strike forcibly. (E.) Of imitative origin. Cf. Swed. dial. *svasska*, to make a swashing noise, as when one walks with water in the shoes. It stands for **svak-sa* ; cf. Norweg. *svakka*, to make a noise like water under the feet ; prov. E. *swack*, a blow, fall, *swacking*, crushing, huge. Der. *swash-buckler*, one who strikes or flourishes his shield.

Swath, a row of mown grass. (E.) A. S. *swæð*, a track ; *swaðu*, a track, foot-track, trace. E. Fries. *swad*, a swath.╋Du. *zwad*, *zwade*, a swath (Sewel) ; G. *schwad*. The sense of '*mown* grass' is original ; cf. Low G. *swad*, a swath, *swade*, a scythe. The earliest meaning may have been ' shred' or 'slice' ; cf. Norweg. *svada*, vb., act. and neut., to shred or slice off, to flake off. Franck suggests that *swath* answers to an Idg. pp. form **swa-to*-, from the root of the verb *to sway* ; with reference to the sweep of a scythe.

Swathe, to enwrap, bandage. (E.) M. E. *swathen*; also *swethen*. From a base *swath*- ; whence A. S. *sweðel* (*swæðil*), a swaddling-band ; *be-sweðian*, to enwrap. Cf. O. H. G. *swedil*, *swithel*, a bandage ; M. H. G. *swede*, a plaster.

Sway, to swing, incline, rule over. (E.) M. E. *sweiyen*. E. Fries. *swäien*, *swäjen*, to sway about, to swing. Cf. Swed. *svaja*, to jerk, Dan. *svaie*, Du. *zwaaijen*, to sway, swing. Allied to **Swagger**.

Swear. (E.) M. E. *sweren*. A. S. *swer-ian*, pt. t. *swōr*, pp. *sworen*, to swear.+Du. *zweren*, Icel. *sverja*, Dan. *sværge*, Swed. *svärja*, G. *schwören*. Allied to Goth. *swaran*, Icel. *svara*, to answer. Orig. 'to speak loudly;' cf. Skt. *svara-*, sound, voice. See Swarm. (√SWER.) Der. *an-swer*.

Sweat, sb. and vb. (E.) M. E. *swoot*, sweat, sb.; whence *sweten*, to sweat. A. S. *swāt*, sb.; whence *swǣtan*. vb. The A. S. *swǣtan* became M. E. *swēten*, and should be mod. E. *swet*, the vowel having been shortened; similarly A. S. *lǣtan* > M. E. *lēten* > mod. E. *let*. The spelling *sweat* is now unsuitable. The A. S. sb. *swāt* would now be *swote*, but has been superseded by the verb. + Du. *zweet*, sb.; Icel. *sveiti*, Dan. *sved*, Swed. *svett*, G. *schweiss*. Teut. stem *swaito-*. Allied to L. *sūdor*, sweat; G. ἰδίω, I sweat, ἱδρώς, sweat; W. *chwys*, sweat; Skt. *svēda-*, sweat, from *svid*, to sweat. (√SWEID.) See Suda-tory. Brugm. i. § 331 c.

Sweep, vb. (E.) M. E. *swēpen*. A weak verb, formed from the base *swǣp-*, as in *swǣpð*, 3 p. s. pres. t. of A. S. *swāpan*, to sweep. Cf. also O. Fries. *swēpa*, to sweep; E. Fries. *swēpen* (pt. t. *swēpde*), to swing, sway, vibrate. Cf. Icel. *sōpa*, to sweep, M. Swed. *swepa*, Swed. *sopa*. From Teut. base *swaip-*; seen also in O. H. G. *sweifan* (pt. t. *swief*), whence G. *schweifen*, to rove, stray, sweep along; Icel. *sveipa*, to sweep along, a weak verb, from an old verb *svīpa* (pt. t. *sveip*, pp. *svipinn*). Teut. root *sweip*. See Swoop, Swipe. Brugm. i. § 701.

Sweet. (E.) M. E. *swete*, with by-forms *swote, sote*. A. S. *swēte*, sweet (for *swōti-*); *swōte*, adv. sweetly.+ O. Sax. *swōti*, Du. *zoet*, Icel. *sœtr*, Dan. *söd*, Swed. *söt*, G. *süss*, O. H. G. *suozi*; Goth. *sūts*. β. From the Idg. √SWAD, to please; whence Skt. *svad, svād*, to taste, eat, please, *svādu-*, sweet, Gk. ἡδύς, L. *suāuis*. See Suave.

sweetheart. (E.) M. E. *swete herte*, lit. sweet heart, i.e. dear love; see Chaucer, Troil. iii. 1181, 1210, and last line.

Swell. (E.) M. E. *swellen*, pt. t. *swal*. A. S. *swellan*, pt. t. *sweall*, pp. *swollen*.+ Du. *zwellen*, Icel. *svella*, Swed. *svälla*, G. *schwellen*. Teut. type *swellan-*, pt. t. *swall*, pp. *swullanoz*. Cf. Goth. *uf-swalleins*, a swelling up. Brugm. i. § 903.

Swelter; see Sultry.

Swerve, to turn aside. (E.) M. E. *sweruen* (*swerven*). A. S. *sweorfan*, pt. t.

swearf, pp. *sworfen*, to rub, file, polish (hence to move swiftly to and fro, to turn aside in moving).+Du. *zwerven*, to swerve, wander, riot, rove; O. Sax. *swerban*, to wipe; O. Fries. *swerva*, to rove; Icel. *sverfa* (pt. t. *svarf*), to file; O. H. G. *swerban*, to run round, whirl round; Goth. *biswairban*, to wipe. Teut. type *swerban-*, pt. t. *swarb*, pp. *swurbanoz*. Cf. E. Fries. *swarven*, to wander, Swed. *svarfva*, to turn.

Swift. (E.) A. S. *swift*. From *swif-*, weak grade of A. S. *swifan*, to move quickly; with suffix *-t* (Idg. *-tos*). Cf. Icel. *svīfa*, to rove, turn, sweep; O. H. G. *sweibōn*, to move or turn quickly. Teut. base *sweib*.

Swill, to wash dishes, drink greedily. (E.) M. E. *swilien*. A. S. *swilian*, to wash. Der. *swill*, sb., hog's-wash; whence *swill*, vb., to drink like a pig, Rich. III, v. 2. 9.

Swim (1), to move about in water. (E.) A. S. *swimman*, pt. t. *swamm*.+Du. *zwemmen*, Icel. *svimma*, Dan. *svömme*, Swed. *simma*; G. *schwimmen*. Teut. type *swemman-*, pt. t. *swamm*, pp. *swummanoz*.

Swim (2), to be dizzy. (E.) From M. E. *swime*, a dizziness. A. S. *swima*, a swoon, swimming in the head. + Du. *zwijm*, a swoon; E. Fries. *swîm*; cf. Icel. *svimi*, dizziness, Dan. *svimle*, to be giddy, *besvime*, to swoon; Swed. *svimma*, to be dizzy, *swimning*, swoon; Pomeran. *swimen*, to swoon; Low G. *swimeln*, to reel (Danneil). β. A. S. *swīma* = *swī-ma*; the real base is *swī* (*swei*); whence also O. H. G. *swīnan*, to decrease, disappear, allied to Swed. *svindel*, G. *schwindel*, dizziness; Swed. *försvinna*, to disappear, Icel. *svina*, to subside (as a swelling). The orig. notion is that of failure, giving way, subsidence, &c.; see swindler.

swindler, a cheat. (G.) XVIII cent. — G. *schwindler*, an extravagant projector, a swindler. — G. *schwindeln*, to be dizzy, act thoughtlessly. — G. *schwinden*, to decay, sink, vanish, fail. + A. S. *swindan*, pt. t. *swand*, to languish; allied to O. H. G. *swīnan*, to fail. See above.

Swine, a sow, pig, pigs. (E.) M. E. *swin*, both sing. and pl. A. S. *swīn*, a pig; pl. *swīn*, swine. + Du. *zwijn*, a swine, hog; Icel. *svín*, pl. *svín*; Dan. *sviin*, pl. *sviin*; Swed. *svin*, G. *schwein*, O. H. G. *swīn*; Goth. *swein*, neut. sb.

sing.; Teut. type *swīnom, neut. So also Russ. svineya, a swine, svinka, a pig, svinoi, swinish. All diminutive or adjectival forms, like L. suīnus (Varro), related to swine, from sus, a sow. See Sow. Brugm. i. § 95.

Swing. (E.) M. E. swingen, pt. t. swang, pp. swungen. A. S. swingan, pt. t. swang, pp. swungen, to scourge, also to fly, flutter, flap with the wings. **+** Swed. svinga, Dan. svinge, to swing, whirl; G. schwingen; cf. also Goth. af-swaggwjan, to cause to doubt or despair. Teut. type *swengwan-, pt. t. *swangw, pp. *swungwanoz.

swinge, to beat, whip. (E.) M. E. swengen. A. S. swengan, to dash, strike (cf. sweng, a blow); the causal form of Swing. As if 'to flourish a whip.'

swingle, a staff for dressing flax. (M. Du.) M. E. swinglen, to beat flax; swingle, a swingle. From M. Du. swingelen, or swingen, 'to beate flax,' Hexham; see Swing. Cf. A. S. swingele, a scourging; E. Fries. swengel, G. schwengel, a pump-handle.

swingle-tree, the bar that swings at the heels of harnessed horses. (E.) M. E. swingle-tre. = M. E. swingle, a beater, but lit. 'a swinger,' or that which swings; tre, a piece of wood; see Tree. Cf. Du. zwengel, a swing; Low G. swengel (Danneil), G. schwengel, a swingle-tree.

Swink, to toil. (E.) Obsolete; once very common. A.S. swincan, pt. t. swanc, pp. swuncen, to labour, work hard. From the violent action; allied to Swing. Cf. Du. zwenk, a swing, a turn; G. schwenken, to swing, whirl about.

Swipe, to strike with a sweeping stroke. (E.) Allied to M. E. swippen; A. S. swipian, swippan, to scourge, beat, from *swip-, weak grade of Teut. *sweipan-; cf. Icel. sveipa, to sweep, swoop. Cf. A. S. swipe, a whip; Icel. svipa, to whip, svipa, a whip. In form, mod. E. swipe answers to O. Icel. svipa, to sweep, swoop. See Sweep.

Swirl, to whirl in an eddy. (Scand.) Norweg. svirla, to whirl round; frequent. of sverra (= Dan. svirre), to whirl, orig. to hum. [But not Norw. svervel, a whirlpool, svervla, to swirl.] Cf. Swed. svirra, to murmur; G. schwirren, to whir; Skt. svṛ, to sound. See Swarm.

Switch, a pliant rod. (M. Du.) For swich, palatalised form of swick. = M.

Du. swick, 'a swich, or a whip;' Hexham; cf. Low G. zwukse (Hanov. swutsche), a long thin rod. The M. Du. swick is not Low G., but borrowed from Bavar. zwick, the lash of a whip, allied to G. zwecke, a tack, wooden peg (Franck).

Swivel, a link turning on a pin or neck. (E.) Spelt swiuell in Minsheu (1627); formed, with suffix -el, from swif-, weak grade of A. S. swīfan, to move quickly (revolve). Allied to Swift. Lit. sense 'that which readily revolves.' Cf. Icel. sveifla, to spin round; from svīfa, to turn. Brugm. i. § 818 (2).

Swoon, to faint. (E.) M. E. swounen, swoghenen, swowenen, to swoon. Formed (with formative n, usually with a passive sense, as in Goth. verbs in -nan) from M. E. swowen, swoghen, to swoon, to sigh deeply, also to sough, sigh. This is a strong verb, from A. S. swōgan, to move or sweep along noisily, to sough, to sigh as the wind, a strong verb, of which the pp. geswōgen occurs with the actual sense of 'in a swoon.' 'Se læg geswōgen' = he lay in a swoon, Ælfric's Hom. ii. 336. So also A. S. geswōwung, a swooning, A. S. Leechdoms, ii. 176, l. 13. Cf. Low G. swōgen, to sigh, swugten, to swoon; Lith. swagéti, to resound. Allied to Sough, q. v.

Swoop, vb. (E.) M. E. swōpen, usually in the sense to sweep. [The ō, orig. open (< A. S. ā) became close owing to the preceding w.] A. S. swāpan, to sweep along, rush, swoop; also, to sweep (pt. t. swēop, pp. swāpen). **+** Icel. sveipa, to sweep, swoop; sōpa, to sweep; G. schweifen, to sweep. Base *swaip, allied to *swaip, 2nd grade of Teut. *sweipan-, as in O. Icel. svīpa, to move quickly. See Sweep.

Sword. (E.) M.E. swerd. A.S. sweord. **+**Du. zwaard, Icel. sverð, Dan. sværd, Swed. svärd, G. schwert. Teut. type *swerdom, neut.

Sybarite, an effeminate person. (L.—Gk.) L. Sybarīta. — Gk. Συβαρίτης, an inhabitant of Sybaris, a town named from the river Sybaris, on which it was situated; in Lucania, Lower Italy.

Sycamine, a tree. (L.—Gk.—Heb.?) L. sȳcamīnus. — Gk. συκάμινος; Luke xvii. 6. Prob. a Gk. adaptation of Heb. shiqmīm, pl. of shiqmāh, a sycamore; that it has been confused with sycamore is obvious.

Sycamore, a tree. (L.—Gk.—Heb.?)

Better *sycomore.* – L. *sycomorus.* – Gk. σῡκόμορος, as if it meant ' fig-mulberry ' ; [Gk. σῦκο-ν, fig ; μόρον, a mulberry] ; but prob. a Gk. adaptation of Heb. *shiqmāh,* a sycamore ; see above.

Sycophant. (L. – Gk.) L. *sȳcophanta,* an informer, parasite. – Gk. συκοφάντης, lit. ' fig-shewer,' also an informer, a false adviser. [Etymology certain, but the reason for the peculiar use is unknown. The usual explanation, 'informer against those who exported sacred figs from Attica,' is unauthorised.] – Gk. σῦκο-ν, a fig ; -φαντης, lit. 'shewer,' from φαίνειν, to shew. See **Hierophant.**

Syllable. (F. – L. – Gk.) The third *l* is intrusive. M. E. *sillable.* – O. F. *sillabe,* also *sillable.* – L. *syllaba.* – Gk. συλλαβή, a syllable, lit. 'holding together,' so much of a word as makes a single sound or element. – Gk. συλ-, for σύν, together ; λαβ-, base of λαμβάνειν, to take, seize.

Syllogism, a reasoning from premises. (F. – L. – Gk.) F. *syllogisme.* – L. *syllogismus.* – Gk. συλλογισμός, a reasoning. – Gk. συλλογίζομαι, I reckon together, reason. – Gk. συλ- (= σύν), together ; λογίζομαι, I reckon, from λόγος, discourse, reasoning.

Sylph, an imaginary being inhabiting the air. (F. – Gk.) F. *sylphe.* – Gk. σίλφη, a kind of worm or grub (Aristotle). On this word it would seem that Paracelsus formed the name *sylphe* ; he also used the names *gnome, salamander,* and *nymph* (all of Greek origin), to signify, respectively, a genius of earth, fire, and water. Hence the form *sylph-id,* a false form, but only explicable on the hypothesis of a Greek origin ; as if from a nom. *σιλφις (base σιλφιδ-). ¶ Littré's explanation, that *sylph* is of Gaulish origin, seems to me futile ; Paracelsus could hardly have known Gaulish.

Sylvan, misspelling of **Silvan.**

Symbol, a sign. (F. – L. – Gk.) F. *symbole.* – L. *symbolum.* – Gk. σύμβολον, a token, pledge, a sign by which one infers a thing. – Gk. συμβάλλειν, to throw together, compare, infer. – Gk. συμ- (σύν), together ; βάλλειν, to throw, put.

Symmetry. (F. – L. – Gk.) M. F. *symmetrie;* Cot. – L. *symmetria.* – Gk. συμμετρία, due proportion. – Gk. σύμμετρος, of like measure with. – Gk. συμ- (= σύν), with ; μέτρον, a measure. See **Metre.**

Sympathy. (Gk.) From Gk. συμ-

πάθεια, fellow-feeling. – Gk. συμ-, for σύν, with ; παθεῖν, to suffer. See **Pathos.**

Symphony. (F. – L. – Gk.) F. *symphonie,* Cot. – L. *symphōnia.* – Gk. συμφωνία, music (Luke xv. 25). – Gk. σύμφωνος, harmonious. – Gk. συμ-, for σύν, together ; φωνή, sound. See **Phonetic.**

Symposium, a merry feast. (L. – Gk.) L. *symposium.* – Gk. συμπόσιον, a drinking-party, banquet. – Gk. συμ- (for σύν), together ; πο-, base of πέ-πω-κα, I have drunk, πόσις, a drink. See **Potable.**

Symptom, an indication of disease. (F. – L. – Gk.) Properly a medical term. M. F. *symptome ;* Cot. – L. *symptōma.* – Gk. σύμπτωμα, a casualty, anything that befals one. – Gk. συμπίπτειν, to fall in with. – Gk. συμ- (σύν), together ; πίπτειν, to fall. (✓PET.)

Syn-, prefix. (L. – Gk. ; or F. – L. – Gk.) A Latinised spelling of Gk. σύν, together. It becomes *syl-* before *l* ; *sym-* before *b, m, p, ph* ; and *sy-* before *s* or *z.*

Synæresis, the coalescence of two vowels into a diphthong (L. – Gk.) L. *synæresis.* – Gk. συναίρεσις, a taking together. – Gk. σύν, together ; αἵρεσις, a taking, from αἱρεῖν, to take. See **Heresy.**

Synagogue. (F. – L. – Gk.) F. *synagogue.* – L. *synagōga.* – Gk. συναγωγή, a bringing together ; congregation. – Gk. σύν, together ; ἀγωγή, a bringing, from ἄγειν, to bring, drive. (✓AG.)

Synalœpha, a coalescence of two syllables into one. (L. – Gk.) L. *synalœpha.* – Gk. συναλοιφή, lit. a smearing together. – Gk. σύν, together ; ἀλείφειν, to anoint, allied to λίπος, grease. Cf. Skt. *lip,* to besmear, anoint.

Synchronism, concurrence in time. (Gk.) Gk. συγχρονισμός. – Gk. σύγχρονος, contemporaneous. – Gk. συγ-, for σύν, together ; χρόνος, time. See **Chronicle.**

Syncopate, to shorten a word by dropping a syllable. (L. – Gk.) From pp. of L. *syncopāre,* of which the usual sense is 'to swoon.' – L. *syncopē, syncopa,* a swoon ; also, syncope. – Gk. συγκοπή, a cutting short, syncope, loss of strength. – Gk. συγ- (written for σύν, together, before κ) ; κοπ-, base of κόπτειν, to cut. See **Apocope.**

Syndic. (F. – L. – Gk.) F. *syndic,* 'a syndick, censor, controller of manners ;' Cot. – L. *syndicus.* – Gk. σύνδικος, adj., helping in a court of justice ; as a sb., a syndic. **–** Gk. σύν, together ; δίκη, justice. Allied to Diction. (√DEIK.)

Synecdoche, a figure of speech whereby a part is put for the whole. (L. – Gk.) L. *synecdochē.* **–** Gk. συνεκδοχή, lit. a receiving together. **–** Gk. σύν, together ; ἐκδέχομαι, I receive, from ἐκ, out, and δέχομαι (Ion. δέκομαι), I receive. (√DEK.)

Synod. (F. – L. – Gk.) F. *synode.* **–** L. *synodum,* acc. of *synodus.* **–** Gk. σύνοδος, a coming together, a meeting. **–** Gk. σύν, together ; ὁδός, a way, a coming. See Method. (√SED.)

Synonym. (F. – L. – Gk.) F. *synonyme.* **–** L. (pl.) *synōnyma,* lit. synonyms ; from the adj. *synōnymus,* synonymous, having the same sense as another word. **–** Gk. συνώνυμος, of like meaning. **–** Gk. σύν, together ; ὄνομα, a name. **Der.** *synonymous,* from L. *synōnymus ; synonymy,* from L. *synōnymia,* Gk. συνωνυμία, likeness of name. See Onomatopœia.

Synopsis, a general view. (L. – Gk.) L. *synopsis.* **–** Gk. σύνοψις, a seeing all together. **–** Gk. σύν, together ; ὄψις, sight. **Der.** *synoptic-al,* from Gk. adj. συνοπτικός. See Optic.

Syntax. (F. – L. – Gk.) F. *syntaxe.* **–** L. *syntaxis.* **–** Gk. σύνταξις, arrangement ; hence, arrangement of words. **–** Gk. σύν, together ; τάξις, order, from τάσσειν, to arrange. See Tactics.

Synthesis. (L. – Gk.) L. *synthesis.* **–** Gk. σύνθεσις, a putting together. **–** Gk. σύν, together ; θέσις, a putting, from τιθέναι, to set, place. See Thesis. **Der.** *synthetic-al,* from Gk. συνθετικός, skilled in putting together.

Syphon, Syren ; see Siphon, Siren.

Syringe. (F. – L. – Gk.) M. F. *syringue,* 'a siringe, squirt ;' Cot. **–** L. *syringem,* acc. of *syrinx,* a reed, pipe, tube. **–** Gk. σῦριγξ, a reed, pipe, shepherd's pipe, whistle. **Der.** *syring-a,* a flowering shrub, so named because the stems were used for making Turkish pipes.

Syrup, Sirup. (F. – Span. – Arab.) M. F. *syrop ;* F. *sirop.* **–** M. Span. *xarope,* a drink ; Span. *jarope.* **–** Arab. *sharáb, shuráb,* wine, beverage, syrup. **–** Arab. root *shariba,* he drank. See Sherbet.

System, method. (L. – Gk.) XVII cent. **–** L. *systēma.* **–** Gk. σύστημα, a complex whole put together, a system. **–** Gk. σύν, together ; στῆ-ναι, to stand, pres. t. ἵστημι, I stand. See Statics.

Systole, contraction of the heart,

shortening of a syllable. (Gk.) Gk. συστολή, a drawing together. **–** Gk. συστέλλειν, to draw together. **–** Gk. σύ-ν, together ; στέλλειν, to place, put. See Diastole, Stole.

Syzygy, conjunction. (Gk.) Gk. συζυγία, conjunction. **–** Gk. σύζυγος, conjoined. **–** Gk. σύ-ν, together ; ζυγ-, weak grade of ζεύγνυμι, I join ; see Yoke, Conjugal. (√YEUG.)

T.

Tabard, a herald's coat. (F.) M. E. *tabard.* **–** O. F. *tabart, tabard,* also *tribart* (Ducange), a kind of coat. Etym. unknown. Cf. M. Ital. and L. *trabea,* a robe of state.

Tabby, a kind of waved silk. (F. – Span. – Arab.) A *tabby* cat is one marked like the silk. **–** F. *tabis* (15th cent.) ; also *atabis* (Godefroy). **–** Span. *tabi,* a silken stuff ; Low L. *attabi.* **–** Arab. *'utābī,* a rich watered silk. It was the name of a quarter in Bagdad where the silk was made ; named after prince *Attab,* great-grandson of Omeyya. (See Dozy and Devic.) **Der.** *tabi-n-et,* a variety of tabby ; from Ital. *tabin-o,* 'tabine, tabby ;' Torriano.

Tabernacle. (F. – L.) F. *tabernacle.* **–** L. *tabernāculum,* a tent ; double dimin. of *taberna,* a booth. See Tavern.

Tabid. (L.) L. *tābidus,* wasting away. **–** L. *tābēre,* to waste away, languish.

Table. (F. – L.) F. *table.* **–** L. *tabula,* a plank, flat board, table. **Der.** *tabul-ate, tabul-ar,* from L. *tabula ; tabl-eau,* from F. *tableau,* dimin. of F. *table.* Also *en-tablature, tafferel.*

Taboo, Tabu, to forbid the use of. (Polynesian.) The verb is formed from the sb. *taboo,* which is the E. pronunciation of New Zealand *tapu,* a prohibition or interdict ; pronounced *tambu* in the Solomon Islands. Kotzebue mentions the ' *Tabu,* or interdict,' in his New Voyage Round the World, London, 1830, ii. 178. ¶ Not in any way connected with the custom of *te pi,* as erroneously said in some former editions.

Tabour, Tabor, a small drum. (F. – Span. – Arab.) M. F. *tabour* (mod. F. *tambour*). **–** Span. *tambor,* M. Span. *atambor* (where *a* = *al,* the Arab. def. article). **–** Arab. *tambūr,* 'a kind of lute or guitar with a long neck, and six brass strings, also a drum.' Prob. of imitative origin ;

cf. Arab. *tabl*, a drum, *tabbāl*, a drummer. Der. *tabour-et* or *tabret*, a dimin. form ; also *tambour*.

Tabular, Tabulate ; see Table.

Tache (1), a fastening. (F.—Low G.) 'A *tache*, a buckle, a claspe ;' Baret (1580), s. v. *Claspe.* — O. F. *tache*, a nail, fastening (Godefroy). — E. Fries. *take*, a point, prick, thorn ; allied to *tak, takke*, a pointed thing, a twig ; Low G. *takk*, a point, pointed thing. See **Tack**. Cf. *attach, de-tach.*

Tache (2), a blemish. (F.) M. E. *tache*, also *tecche*, a bad habit, blemish, vice, caprice, behaviour.' — F. *tache*, 'a spot, staine, reproach ;' Cot. Also formerly spelt *taiche, teche, teque, teke*, a natural quality, esp. a vice, ill habit ; mod. F. *tache*, a stain ; Picard *take*. Cf. Ital. *tacca, taccia*, defect, stain ; Port. and Span. *tacha*, defect, flaw, crack. Root unknown ; it is difficult to connect it with **Tache** (1); yet this may be right. Ital. *tacca* also means 'notch' or 'dent'; cf. E. Fries. *takke*, a notch, *takje*, a small notch, small twig, *take* (Du. *tak*), a twig.

Tacit, silent. (L.) L. *tacitus*, silent. — L. *tacēre*, to be silent. + Goth. *thahan*, Icel. *þegja*, Swed. *tiga*, O. H. G. *dagēn*, to be silent. **Der.** *tacit-urn*, F. *taciturne*, L. *taciturnus*, silent ; *tacit-urnity*, F. *taciturnité*, L. acc. *taciturnitātem*, silence; also *re-ticent.*

Tack, a small nail, a fastening ; also to fasten. (E.) M. E. *takke, tak*, a fastening ; *takken*, to fasten together. Of E. or Low G. origin ; cf. E. Fries. Dan. *takke*, a tine, pointed thing ; Low G. *takk* (the same) ; G. *zacke*, a tooth, tine, prong, twig. Allied to E. Fries. *tak*, 'a twig, bough ;' the same as Du. *tak*, a twig. [The Irish *taca*, pin, peg, nail, fastening, Gael. *tacaid*, tack, peg, are from E.] Cf. Norman dial. *taque*, a nail. β. Hence a *tack* or rope fastening a sail ; also the verb *tack*, to sew slightly, attach. γ. The verb *to tack*, in sailing, refers to the shifting of the *tacks* in order to alter the ship's course.

Tackle, equipment, gear, tools. (Scand.) M. E. *takel.* — Swed. and M. Swed. *tackel*, tackle of a ship ; Dan. *takkel*, tackle, whence *takle*, to rig. Cf. Du. *takel*, a pulley, *takelen*, to rig. The suffix *-el* denotes the agent ; *tack-le* is that which takes or holds firmly ; cf. M. Du. *taeckel*, 'a rope to drawe a boate.' — Icel. *taka*, to grasp, seize, &c., also to take ; cf. E. Fries.

taken, to grip. ¶ The W. *tacl*, a tool, is borrowed from M. E. *takel.*

Tact. (L.) L. *tactus*, touch ; hence, delicacy. — L. *tactus*, pp. of *tangere*, to touch. See **Tangent.**

Tactics, the art of manœuvring forces. (Gk.) Gk. τακτικά, neut. pl., tactics.— Gk. τακτικός, adj., fit for arranging.—Gk. τακτός, arranged, ordered ; verbal adj. of τάσσειν (for *τάκ-γειν), to arrange, order. **Der.** *tactic-ian.*

Tadpole. (E.) Lit. a *toad* which is nearly all *poll* or head ; from its shape ; see **Poll.** Formerly called a *bullhead*, which was also the name of a small fish with a large head.

Tafferel, Taffrail, upper part of the stern of a ship. (Du.—L.) Du. *tafereel*, a panel, a picture, a tablet or board. For *tafel-eel*, dimin. of Du. *tafel*, a table ; cf. G. *täfelei*, boarded work, from G. *tafel*, a table. — L. *tabula*, a table, plank, board. Doublet, *tableau.* ¶ The spelling *taffrail* points to confusion with *rail.*

Taffeta, Taffety, a thin silk stuff. (F. — Ital.—Pers.) F. *taffetas*, 'taffata ,' Cot. — Ital. *taffetà*, 'taffeta ;' Florio. — Pers. *tāftah*, twisted, woven, taffeta. — Pers. *tāftan*, to twist, spin, curl (Horn, § 372).

Tag, a point of metal at the end of a lace, &c. (Scand.) 'An aglet or *tag* of a poynt ;' Baret (1580). — Swed. *tagg*, a prickle, point, tooth ; Norw. *tagge*, a tooth, cog. + Pomeran. *tagg*, a point, tack ; Low G. *takk*, point, tooth. See **Tack. Der.** *tag-rag*, for *tag and rag* = every appendage and shred.

Tail (1), hairy appendage, appendage. (E.) M. E. *tayl.* A. S. *tægel, tægl*, a tail.+Icel. *tagl*, Swed. *tagel*, hair of mane or tail ; Goth. *tagl*, hair ; O. H. G. *zagel*, a tail. Cf. Irish *dual*, a plait, lock of hair, Skt. *daçā*, a skirt. Brugm. i. § 783.

Tail (2), the term applied to an estate which is limited to certain heirs. (F.—L.) Better spelt *taille* ; see Todd's Johnson.— F. *taille*, a cutting, shred ; the same word as Tally (below). And see **Entail.**

tailor. (F.—L.) Properly 'a cutter,' or cutter out. M. E. *taylor.*—O. F. *tailleor*, later *tailleur*, 'a cutter ;' Cot.—F. *tailler*, to cut ; cf. F. *taille*, a slitting, an incision.—Late L. *tāliāre*, to cut ; cf. L. *tālea*, a thin rod, stick, slip ; an agricultural term for a slip or layer.

Taint, sb. (F.—L.) F. *teint*, 'a stain ;'

Cot. – F. *teint*, pp. of *teindre*, to tinge. – L. *tingere*, to dye. See **Tinge**.

Take. (Scand.) M. E. *taken*, pt. t. *tok*, pp. *taken*. – Icel. *taka*, pt. t. *tōk*, pp. *tekinn*, to lay hold of, seize, grasp, take; Swed. *taga*, O. Swed. *taka*, Dan. *tage*. + Goth. *tēkan*, to touch.

Talc, a mineral. (F. – Span. – Arab.) F. *talc*. – Span. *talco*. – Arab. *talq*, talc, mica.

Tale, a number, a narrative. (E.) M. E. *tale*. A. S. *tæl*, a number, *talu*, a narrative. + Du. *taal*, speech; Icel. *tal*, speech, *tala*, number; Dan. *tale*, speech, Swed. *tal*, number, speech, G. *zahl*, number. Der. *tal-k*, tell.

Talent. (F. – L. – Gk.) The sense of ' ability' is from the parable; Matt. xxv. F. *talent*, ' a talent in money; also will, desire;' Cot. – L. *talentum*. – Gk. τάλαντον, a balance, weight, sum of money, talent. Named from being lifted and weighed; cf. Skt. *tul*, L. *tollere*, to lift, Gk. τάλ-ας, sustaining. (✓TEL.) Allied to **Tolerate**. Der. *talent-ed*, in use before A. D. 1640.

Talisman, a spell. (Span. – Arab. – Gk.) Span. *talisman*, a magical character. – Arab. *tilsamān*, pl. of *tilsam*, *tilism*, a talisman, magical image. – Late Gk. τέλεσμα, mystery, initiation; Gk. τέλεσμα, a payment; τελεσμός, an accomplishment. – Gk. τελέειν, to accomplish, end. – Gk. τέλος, end; also initiation into a mystery.

Talk. (E.) E. Fries. *talken*, to talk; cf. *talke*, a short tale. The Low G. *taalke* means (1) a jackdaw, (2) a talkative woman. Extended (like *stalk* (1)) from A. S. *tal-*, as in *talu*, a tale, *talian*, to account, with suffix *-k-*, which seems to give a frequentative force. Cf. Icel. Swed. *tala*. Dan. *tale*, to talk. See **Tale** and **Tell**.

Tall, high in stature, lofty. (E.) [We find M. E. *tal*, which meant seemly, also obedient, obsequious, valiant; allied to A. S. *tæl*, appearing in *lēof-tæl*, friendly. So also Goth. *un-tals*, indocile, unstructed, from which we infer *tals*, docile. Note also A. S. *ge-tal*, quick, prompt; O. H. G. *gi-zal*, quick.] The mod. E. *tall* has in some cases been adopted in Celtic. Cf. W. *tal*, high, Corn. *tal*, high; Corn. *tal carn*, the high rock; W. *taldra*, tallness, loftiness.

Tallow. (E.) M. E. *talgh*. E. Fries. *talg*, *tallig*. + M. Du. *talgh*, *talch*, tallow; Du. *talk*, Low G. *talg*; Dan. Swed. *talg*; Icel. *tōlgr*. So also G. *talg*, tallow (bor-rowed from Low G.); cf. O. Merc. *tælg*, a dye.

Tally, a stick notched so as to match another stick; an exact match. (F. – L.) M. E. *taille*, a tally; for keeping accounts. – F. *taille*, a notch, cut, incision, cutting; also a tally, or score kept on a piece of stick by notches. – F. *tailler*, to cut. – Late L. *tāliāre*, to cut; cf. L. *tālea*, a slip of wood. ¶ The final *-y* in *tall-y* is due to the frequent use of F. *taillé*, pp., to signify ' notched'; cf. *lev-y*, *jur-y*, *pun-y*, where *-y* = F. *-é*.

Talmud, the body of Hebrew laws, with comments. (Chaldee.) Chaldee *talmūd*, instruction, doctrine; cf. Heb. *talmīd*, a scholar, from *lāmad*, to learn, *limmad*, to teach.

Talon. (F. – L.) Particularly used of a hawk's hind claw and toe. – F. *talon*, a heel. – Late L. *tālōnem*, acc. of *tālo*, heel. – L. *tālus*, heel.

Tamandua, an ant-eater. (Brazil.) From Guarani *tamānduá*, an ant-eater (where *à* is nasal); see Granada, Vocab. Rioplatense.

Tamarind. (F. – Span. – Arab. *and* Pers.) M.F. *tamarind*. – Span. *tamarindo*. – Arab. *tamr*, a ripe date; *Hind*, India. Lit. ' Indian date.' β. The Arab. *tamr* is allied to Heb. *tāmār*, a palm-tree. *Hind* is borrowed from Pers. (which turns *s* into *h*), and is derived from Skt. *sindhu-*, the river Indus. See **Indigo**.

Tamarisk, a tree. (L.) L. *tamariscus*, also *tamarix*, *tamarīcē*; of foreign origin. Cf. Gk. μυρίκη, a tamarisk.

Tambour, a small drum-like frame, for embroidering. (F. – Span. – Arab.) F. *tambour*, a tambour, also a drum; see **Tabour**.

tambourine. (F. – Span. – Arab.) F. *tambourin*, a tabour, dimin. of F. *tambour*, a tabour or drum: see **Tabour**.

Tame, adj. (E.) M. E. *tame*. A. S. *tam*, tame; whence *temian*, to tame. + Du. *tam*, Icel. *tamr*, Swed. Dan. *tam*, G. *zahm*. Allied to L. *domāre*, Skt. *dam*, Gk. δαμάειν, W. *dofi*, to tame. (✓DAM.) See **Daunt**.

Tammy, Tamine; the same as **Stamin**.

Tamper, to meddle, interfere with. (F. – L.) The same word as *temper*, used actively, but in a bad sense; ' to influence in a bad way.' Godefroy gives *tramper* as another form of *temprer*; and *tempreure*, *tampreure*, moderation, manner of operating, temper of a weapon. See **Temper.**

Tampion, a kind of plug. (F. — Teut.) F. *tampon*, bung, stopple; nasalised form of F. *tapon*, the same, augment. of O. F. *tampe, tape*, a bung. Cf. F. *taper, tapper*, to stop with a bung (a Picard word). — Du. *tap*, a bung, tap; Low G. *tappe*, the same. See Tap (2).

Tan. (F. — G.) From F. *tan*, 'the bark of a young oak, wherewith leather is tanned;' Cot. (Bret. *tann*, an oak, also tan.) — G. *tanne*, fir-tree. + Du. *den*, a fir-tree; M. Du. *dan*, as in '*abies*, eyn dan,' Mone, Quellen, p. 302. Der. *tan*, vb., &c.; *tan-ling*, Cymb. iv. 4. 29.

Tandem. (L.) L. *tandem*, at length; applied to two horses harnessed *at length*. A University joke.

Tang (1), a strong taste. (Du.) Cf. M. Du. *tanger*, sharp, biting to the taste; lit. pinching. — Du. *tang*, a pair of pincers; see **Tongs.** Cf. O. H. G. *zangar*, sharp to the taste; A. S. *ge-tingan*, to press hard upon (pt. t. *getang*).

Tang (2), to make a shrill sound. (E.) To *tang* is to ring out; an imitative word; allied to *tinker, tingle, twang*.

Tang (3), tongue of a buckle, the part of a knife which goes into the haft. (Scand.) Icel. *tangi*, tang of a knife, which is *nipped* by the handle; Norw. *tange*, tang of a knife, tongue of land; allied to *töng*, tongs; see **Tang** (1), Tongs.

Tang (4), seaweed; see Tangle.

Tangent. (L.) From L. *tangent-*, touching, stem of pres. pt. of *tangere* (base *tag*), to touch; pp. *tactus*. + Gk. base ταγ-, as in τεταγών, taking.

tangible. (F. — L.) F. *tangible.* — L. *tangibilis*, touchable. — L. *tangere*, to touch.

Tangle, to knot confusedly. (Scand.) Spelt *tangell* in Palsgrave. To *tangle* is ' to keep twisting together like seaweed'; a frequentative verb from North E. *tang*, sea-weed. — Dan. *tang*, Swed. *tång*, Icel. *þang*, kelp or bladder-wrack, a sea-weed (whence the idea of confused heap); cf. Icel. *þöngull*, sea-weed, Norw. *tongul*, a tangle-stalk. So also prov. E. *tangle*, sea-weed; Norman F. *tangon*, a kind of seaweed (*Fucus flagelliformis*, Métivier). Der. *en-tangle*, with F. prefix *en-* (< L. *in*).

Tanist, a presumptive heir to a prince. (Irish.) Irish *tanaiste*, apparent heir. — Irish *tanaise*, second in rank (Rhŷs).

Tank, a pool. (Port. — L.) Port. *tanque*, cognate with Span. *estanque*, O. F. *estang*, a stank, pool. — L. *stagnum*, a pool. See Stank. ¶ Anglo-Indian; see Yule.

Tankard. (F.) O. F. *tanquard*, a tankard (Rabelais); M. Du. *tanckaert*, ' a wooden [wooden] tankard,' Hexham (from F.). Prob. from Swed. *stånka*, a wooden tankard; with F. augment. suffix *-ard*. Swed. *stånka* is a dimin. of *stånna, ståndæ*, a vat (Rietz); note the *aa* in Norw. *taankar*, a tankard. Cf. Tudor E. *standard*, a tankard, standing-bowl (Greene).

Tansy, a plant. (F. — Low L. — Gk.) M. E. *tansaye, tansey*. — O. F. *tanasie, tanaisie*; earlier form *athanasie, atanasie*. (Cf. M. Ital. *atanasia*, Port. *atanasia*, tansy.) — Late L. **athanasia*, merely the Latinised form of Gk. ἀθανασία, immortality. Cf. M. Ital. *atanato* (lit. immortal), the rose-campion; Florio. Prob. from its supposed virtue, and its use in medicine. — Gk. ἀθάνατος, immortal. — Gk. ἀ-, not; θαν-εῖν, 2 aor. of θνήσκειν, to die.

Tantalise. (Gk.) Formed with F, suffix *-iser* (< L. *-izāre* < Gk. ι(ειν), from Gk. Τάνταλ ος, Tantalus, in allusion to his story. The fable was that he was placed up to his chin in water, which fled from his lips whenever he desired to drink. Allied to τανταλίζειν, ταντάλ εύειν, to oscillate, sway like a balance; intensive form from ταλ-, as in τάλαντον, a balance. See Talent.

Tantamount. (F. — L.) First used as a verb, with the sense ' to amount to as much.' — F. *tant*, so much, as much, from L. *tantum*, neut. of *tantus*, so great; and E. *amount* (of F. origin); see Amount.

Tap (1), to knock gently. (F. — Teut.) F. *taper*, M. F. *tapper*, 'to tap, hit;' Cot. — Low G. *tappen*, to grope, fumble, *tappe* a paw; E. Fries. *tappen*, to grope, *tap*, a light blow; Icel. *tapsa*, to tap. Prob. of imitative origin; cf. Russ. *topate*, to stamp with the foot, Arab. *tabl*, a drum; E. *dub-a-dub*. ¶ Perhaps a native word; M. E. *tappen* occurs rather early.

Tap (2), a short pipe to draw liquor from a cask, a plug. (E.) M. E. *tappe*. A. S. *tæppa*, (Toller); we also find A. S. *tæppere*, one who taps casks. + Du. *tap*, Icel. *tappi*, Dan. *tap*, a tap; Swed. *tapp*, a tap, handful, wisp, G. *zapfen*, a tap. β. The orig. idea was prob. a tuft or wisp of something, to stop a hole with; cf. Swed. *tapp* (above), *halm-tapp*, a wisp of straw. **Der.**

tap-root, *tap-ster*, A. S. *tæppestre*, a fem. form of *tæppere* (above); *tampion*, q. v.

Tape. (L. – Gk.) M. E. *tape*, also *tappe*. A. S. *tæppe*, a tape, a fillet; closely allied to A. S. *tæppet*, *tæpped*, a tippet, a carpet. The A. S. pl. *tæppan* probably meant strips of stuff or cloth. Borrowed from L. *tapēte*, cloth; see **Tapestry.**

Taper (1), a small wax candle. (E.) M. E. *taper*. A. S. *tapor*, *taper*. Cf. Irish *tapar*, a taper, W. *tampr*, a taper, torch.

taper (2), long and slender. (E.) *Taper* means *taper-like*, shaped like the tapers used in churches, which were sometimes thinner at the top. Holland has: '*taper-wise*, sharp-pointed in the top;' tr. of Pliny, xvi. 16. See above. ¶ The A.S. *taper-ax*, a kind of ax, is unallied; cf. Russ. *topor'*, Pers. *tabar*, an ax.

Tapestry. (F. – L. – Gk.) A corruption of the old form *tapisserie*. – F. *tapisserie*, tapestry. – F. *tapisser*, to furnish with tapestry. – F. *tapis*, tapestry, hangings; Late L. *tapēcius*. – L. *tapēte*, cloth, hangings. – Gk. ταπητ-, stem of τάπης, a carpet, woollen rug. Cf. Pers. *tabastah*, a fringed carpet; *tābīdan*, to spin, *tāftah*, taffeta; see **Taffeta.**

Tapioca. (Brazilian.) Brazilian *tapioka*, the poisonous juice which issues from the root of the cassava when pressed (Littré); hence tapioca, which is also prepared from the root of the cassava. The Tupi or Brazilian *tipi-ŏca* means 'dregs squeezed out'; from *tipi*, residue, dregs, and the verbal root *og*, *ŏk*, to take by force, pull, pluck off, hence to squeeze (Cavalcanti).

Tapir, a quadruped. (Brazilian.) Tupi or Brazilian *tapyra*, *tapīra*, a tapir.

Tar. (E.) M. E. *terre*. A. S. *teoru*, *teru*, tar; cf. also *tyrwa*. + Du. *teer*, Icel. *tjara*, Dan. *tiære*, Swed. *tjära*. β. Cf. Icel. *tyri*, *tyrvi*, resinous wood; allied to Lithuan. *darwa*, *derwa*, resinous wood, particularly the parts of the fir-tree that readily burn; also to Russ. *drevo*, a tree, *derevo*, wood, timber, W. *derw*, an oaktree, and E. *tree*. Orig. sense ' wood,' esp. resinous wood for fuel; hence resin from such wood. Allied to **Tree.**

Tar (2), a sailor; see **Tarpauling.**

Tarantella. (Ital.) A dance so called (also a tarantula); so named from Ital. *Taranto*, Tarento, a town in S. Italy.

Taraxacum, the dandelion. (Arab.) From Arab. *tarasacon*, explained as a kind of succory, Pers. *tarkhashqūn*, wild

endive; Latinised as *taraxacon*, in Avicenna. (Devic; supp. to Littré.)

Tardy. (F. – L.) F. *tardif*, tardy. (Cf. Ital. *tardivo*, tardy.) From L. *tard-us*, slow; with suffix *-īuus*.

Tare (1), a plant. (E.) M. E. *tare*, darnel (Matt. xiii. 25). Not in A. S.; but the sense is peculiar to English, as the mod. E. *tare* is short for *tare-vetch*, i. e. darnel-vetch. + M. Du. *terwe*, Du. *tarwe*, Low G. *tarve*, wheat; Lith. *dirwa*, cornfield; Skt. *dūrvā*, a kind of grass.

Tare (2), an allowance. (F. – Span. – Arab.) F. *tare*, loss, waste in merchandise. – Span. *tara*, tare, allowance in weight. Lit. ' what is thrown away.' – Arab. *tarha*, what is thrown away, detriment (Devic); *tirh*, *turrah*, thrown away. – Arab. root *taraha*, he threw prostrate, threw down.

Target, a small shield, &c. (F. – Scand.; *with* F. *suffix*.) Formerly also *tergat*; the *-et* is the F. dimin. suffix. – O. F. *targuete* (Godefroy), a small shield; dimin. of O. F. *targue* (as in Cot.), F. *targe*. – Icel. *targa*, a target, small shield; A. S. *targe*; O. H. G. *zarga*, a frame, side of a vessel, wall, G. *zarge*, frame, case, edge, border. ¶ Distinct from Arab. *darkat*, *darakat*, a shield, whence Port. and Span. *adarga*, a small square target.

Targum, a Chaldee paraphrase of the Old Testament. (Chaldee.) Chaldee *targūm*, an interpretation. – Chal. *targēm*, to interpret. Cf. Arab. *tarjumān*, an interpreter: see **Dragoman.**

Tariff. (F. – Span. – Arab.) F. *tarif*. M. F. *tariffe*, a casting of accounts. – Span. *tarifa*, a list of prices, book of rates. – Arab. *ta'rīf*, giving information, notification (because a tariff gives notice). – Arab. *'irf*, knowing, knowledge. – Arab. root *'arafa*, he knew.

Tarn, a pool. (Scand.) M. E. *terne*. – Icel. *tjörn* (gen. *tjarnar*), a tarn, pool: Swed. dial. *tjärn*, *tärn*, Norw. *tjörn*, a pool without an outlet.

Tarnish. (F. – O. H. G.) F. *terniss-*, stem of pres. pt. of *se ternir*, to become dim, lose lustre (Cot.). – M. H. G. *ternen*, O. H. G. *tarnen*, to obscure, darken; from O. H. G. *tarni*, secret (whence F. *terne*, dim). + A. S. *dernan*, *dyrnan*, to hide, from *derne*, *dyrne*, adj., secret; cf. O. Sax. *derni*, hidden, secret.

Tarpauling, a cover of tarred canvas. (E. *and* L.) It means *tarred pauling* or *tarred palling*; a *palling* is a covering, from the verb *pall*, to cover. This verb is from *pall*, sb., a cover; see **Pall**. Der. *tarpaulin*, an old name for a sailor (Smollett), now abbreviated to *tar*.

Tarragon, a plant. (Span. — Arab. — Gk.) Span. *taragona* (Diez); usually *taragontia* (cf. M. F. *targon*, *tragon*). — Arab. *tarkhūn*, dragon-wort. — Gk. δράκων, a dragon. See Devic, s. v. *estragon*; and see **Dragon**.

Tarre, to incite, set on. (E.) In Shak. Hamlet, ii. 2. 370. M. E. *terren*, *terien*, *tarien*, to irritate, provoke. — A. S. *tergan* (rare), *tirgan*, to vex, provoke; N. Fries. *tarre*, *terre*, to set on a dog. See **tarry**.

tarry. (E.) The present form is due to M. E. *tarien*, *terien*, to irritate, provoke, worry, vex; hence to hinder, delay. [This is the true source of the word, though its meaning may have been affected and fixed by the O. F. *targer*, to delay, from Late L. **tardicāre*, to delay, from L. *tardus*, slow; see **Tardy**.] — A. S. *tergan*, usually *tirgan*, to vex, provoke. ✛ Du. *tergen*, Low G. *targen*, *tarren*, to provoke; prov. G. *zergen*, to provoke.

Tart (1), acrid, sharp, severe. (E.) A S. *teart*, tart, severe. Perhaps lit. tearing, i. e. bitter. — A. S. **tar* (*tær*), 2nd grade of *teran*, to tear. See **Tear** (1).

Tart (2), a small pie. (F. — L.) M. E. *tarte*. — O. F. *tarte*, 'a tart;' Cot. It seems to be a perverted form of O. F. *torte*, F. *tourte*, a tart, Ital. *tartera*, *torta*, a pie or tart, Span. *torta*, a round cake. — L. *torta*, fem. of *tortus*, pp. of *torquēre*, to twist. Perhaps confused with L. *tracta*, a long piece of dough.

Tartan, a woollen stuff. (F. — Tatar.) 1. From F. *tiretaine*, 'linsie wolsie, or a kind therof, worn by French peasants;' Cot. — Span. *tiritaña*, a thin woollen stuff. 2. Otherwise, from M. E. *Tartarin*, orig. rich cloth of Tatary, later, coloured cloth of various hues, also spelt *tartarne*, *tartern*. See examples in N. E. D.

Tartar (1), an acid salt in casks, a concretion on the teeth. (F. — Late L. — Arab.) A term due to the alchemists; called *sal tartre*, or *tartre*, in Chaucer. — F. *tartre*, 'tartar,' Cot.; Late L. *tartarum* (by confusion with *Tartarus*). — Arab. *durd*, dregs, sediment, tartar of wine; *durdīy*, dregs. Cf. Arab. *darad*, a shedding of teeth; which Devic connects with tartar on the teeth.

Tartar (2), a native of Tartary. (Tatar.)

A perverse spelling of *Tatar*, owing to a popular etymology which regarded Tatars as let loose out of *Tartarus* or hell (see below). From *Tātar*, a Tatar or inhabitant of Tatary (as it should be spelt).

Tartar (3), Tartarus, hell. (L. — Gk.) 'The gates of *Tartar*;' Tw. Nt. ii. 5. 225. — L. *Tartarus.* — Gk. Τάρταρος, Tartarus, the infernal regions; conceived to be a place of extreme cold; cf. Gk. ταρταρίζειν, to shiver with cold.

Task, sb. (F. — L.) Lit. a tax. M.E. *taske.* — O. North F. *tasque*, Norm. dial. *tasque*, a tax, O. F. *tasche*, a task (mod. F. *tâche*). — Late L. *tasca*, another form of Late L. *taxa*, a tax. — L. *taxāre*, to tax. See **Tax**.

Tassel (1), a bunch of silk, &c., as an ornament. (F. — L.) M. E. *tassel.* — O. F. *tassel*, an ornament, fringe; also a piece of square stuff (cf. Ital. *tassello*, a square, a collar of a cloak). — L. *taxillum*, acc. of *taxillus*, a small die; dimin. of *tālus*, a knuckle-bone, a die made of knuckle-bone. *Talus = *tax-lus*, as shewn by the dimin. *taxillus*, and means a bone cut or squared; of. Skt. *taksh*, to hew, prepare, make. ¶ The application to a tassel is curious; a woodcut at p. 272 of Guillim's Display of Heraldry (1660) shews a tassel ornamented with strings and dots; these strings divide it into squares, each of which (having a dot in the middle) resembles *an ace on a die*. It was confused with L. *tessella* (see **Tesselated**); cf. '*Tessera*, tasol;' O. E. Texts.

Tassel (2); the same as **Tercel**.

Taste. (F. — L.) Orig. to handle, feel, the usual sense of M. E. *tasten*. — O. F. *taster*, to handle, feel, taste. Cf. Late L. *taxta*, O. F. *taste*, a probe for wounds; so that O. F. *taster* answers to a Late L. **taxitāre*, iterative form of *taxāre*, to feel, handle (Gellius). Again *taxāre* (<**tagsāre*) is an intensive form of L. *tangere*, to touch. See **Tangent**.

Tat, to make trimming. (Scand.) North E. *tat*, to entangle. — M. Swed. *tåtte*, Dan. dial. *tat*, Norw. *taatt*, a thread, strand of a rope, whence Norw. *tætta*, to interweave. Cf. Icel. *þáttr*, Swed. *tåt*, a strand, filament; Dan. *tot*; G. *docht*, a wick.

Tatter, a shred. (Scand.) Also spelt *totter.* — Icel. *töturr*; pl. *tötrar*, *töttrar*, rags, tatters; Norw. *totror*, *tottrur*, also *taltrar*, pl., rags, tatters. ✛ Low G. *taltern*, rags, *taltrig*, ragged; E. Fries. *talte*, a rag, *altrig*, ragged. Thus *tatter* stands for *talter*, witn loss of *l*; cf. Low G. *talt'r*, *tadder*, a rag (Danneil); perhaps also A. S. *tættec*, a rag. I suppose the orig. sense was 'that which flaps or flutters about,' and that it is closely allied to *totter*, q.v.

Tattle, vb. (E.) M. E. *tatelen, totelen, tateren*, to tattle, prattle. We also find M. E. *titeren*, to tattle, whence mod. E. *tittle*, in the phrase *tittle-tattle*. *Tattle* and *tittle* are frequentative forms, from a base TAT or TIT, expressive of the iteration of the syllables *ta, ta, ta*, or *ti, ti, ti*, to indicate constant prattling. So also Du. *tateren*, to stammer, E. *taratantara*, the sound of a trumpet, Low G. *tateln*, to tattle, *titetateln*, to tittle-tattle, *taat-goos*, a gabbling goose, a chatterer; Ital. *tatta-mella*, chat, prattle. **Der.** *tittle*, weakened form of *tattle*, as above; whence *tittletattle*.

Tattoo (1), the beat of a drum recalling soldiers to their quarters. (Du. *or* Low G.) Formerly *taptoo* (Phillips); used as early as A. D. 1663. — Du. *taptoe*, tattoo. — Du. *tap*, a tap; *toe*, to, i.e. shut, closed. Due to the phrase appearing in Low G. *tappen to slaan*, lit. 'to strike a tap to,' a proverbial phrase (like E. *shut up*) signifying to close, conclude; esp. used of closing the taps of the public-houses, at the sound of the drum. So also G. *zapfenstreich*, the tattoo, is lit. 'tap-stroke;' and Low G. *tappenslag*, the tattoo, is its equivalent. β. The Du. *tap* is cognate with E. *tap*; and Du. *toe* with E. *to*, prep. See **Tap** and **To**.

Tattoo (2), to mark the skin with figures, by pricking in colouring matter. (Tahitian.) See Cook's First Voyage, b. i. c. 17, b. iii. c. 9. — Tahitian *tatau*, tattoo-marks; derived from *ta*, a mark (Littré). The Maori *ta* means to tattoo, to mark.

Taunt, vb. (F. — L.) Hardly from O.F. *tanter* (see Littré), occasional form of *tenter*, 'to tempt, prove, essay, suggest, provoke, or move unto evill;' Cot. — L. *tentāre*, to try, prove, attack, assail, &c.; see **Tempt**. β. Rather from the M.F. phrase *tant pour tant*, 'one for another,' Cot.; cf. *tit for tat*. — O. F. *taunt, tant*, so much. — L. *tantum*, neut., so much.

Taurus. (L.) L. *taurus*, a bull. **+** Gk. *ταῦρος*. Allied to **Steer** (1).

Taut, tight, firm. (E.) M. E. *togt*. App. from *tog-* (in *tog-en*, pp. of A. S. *tēoh-an*), to pull; with added *-t*.

Tautology. (F. — Gk.) L. *tautologia*. — Gk. *ταυτολογία*, a repetition of what has been said already. — Gk. *ταυτολόγος*, repeating what has been said. — Gk. *ταυτό*, short for *τὸ αὐτό* or *τὸ αὐτόν*, the same thing; *-λογος*, speaking, from *λέγειν*, to speak.

Tavern. (F. — L.) F. *taverne*. — L. *taberna*, a hut, orig. a hut of boards; a tavern. Perhaps allied to L. *tabula*, a plank, board; see **Table**.

Taw, a game at marbles. (Gk.) Orig. the mark from which the marbles were shot, and marked (originally) with a T, to denote an exact spot. From Gk. *ταῦ*, among schoolboys; a letter-name ot Semitic origin. Cf. **Tee**.

Taw, Tew, to prepare skins, curry; also to toil. (E.) M. E. *tawen, tewan*. A. S. *tawian*, to prepare, dress, get ready; also, to scourge. Cf. A.S. *getawa*, implements. **+** Du. *touwen*, to curry leather; O. H. G. *zouwen*, to make, prepare; Goth. *taujan*, to do, cause. See **Tool**.

Tawdry, showy, gaudy. (E.) Formerly used in the phrase *tawdry lace*, which meant lace bought at *St. Awdry's* fair, held in the Isle of Ely (and elsewhere) on St. Awdry's day, Oct. 17. *Tawdry* is a familiar contraction of *St. Awdry*. β. Again, *Awdry* is a popular form of *Etheldrida*, the Latinised form of the A. S. female name *Æþelþrýð*. It means 'noble strength'; from A.S. *æðel* or *æþel*, noble, and *þrýð* or *þrýðu*, strength. Cf. Icel. *þrúðr*, the name of a goddess; and the suffix in *Ger-trude*, a name of O. H. G. origin.

Tawny. (F. — G.) For *tanny*; spelt *tenny* in heraldry. ' *Tanny* colowre, or *tawny*;' Prompt. Parv. — F. *tanné*, tawny; lit. tanned; pp. of *tanner*, to tan. — F. *tan*, sb., tan. — G. *tanne*, a fir-tree. See **Tan**.

Tax, sb. (F. — L.) M. E. *taxe*. — F. *taxe*. — F. *taxer*, to tax. — L. *taxāre*, to handle, value, appraise, tax. For **tag-sāre*; from *tag-*, base of *tangere*, to touch. **Doublet** *task*.

Taxidermy, the art of stuffing the skins of animals. (Gk.) From Gk. *τάξι-s*, order (see **Tactics**); *δέρμ-α*, a skin, from *δέρ-ειν*, to flay, cognate with **Tear** (1).

Tea. (Chinese.) Spelt *tee* in Pepys' Diary, Sept. 28, 1660; *cha* in Blount (1674). From the Amoy pronunciation (*tē*) of the Chinese name for the plant, which is (in other parts of the empire) called *ch'a* or *ts'a*; Williams, Chin. Dict.

p. 5; Douglas, Chin. Dict. of the Amoy vernacular, p. 481. Hence Ital. *cià*, tea; F. *thé*, G. *thee*, Malay *tĕh*, tea.

Teach. (E.) M.E. *techen*. A.S. *tǣcan*, to shew how to do, shew, pt. t. *tǣhte*, pp. *tǣht*. Formed (with change of *ā* to *ǣ* before *j*, as in Teut. **taikjan-*), from *tāc-* (Teut. **taik-*), base of *tāc-en*, a token. Allied to Gk. δείκ-νυμι, I shew. See **Token.**

Teak, a tree. (Malayālam.) Malayālam *tēkka*, the teak-tree; Tamil *tēkku*, the same (H. H. Wilson).

Teal, a bird. (E.) M.E. *tele* (13th cent.); not in A. S. **+** Du. *taling*, older form *taeling* (Sewel), M. Du. *teelingh*, a teal (Kilian). The A.S. form would be **tǣle*.

Team, a family, set, animals harnessed in a row. (E.) M.E. *tēm*, *teem*. A.S. *tēam*, a family, offspring.**+**Du. *toom*, a rein (from the notion of drawing or guiding); Low G. *toom*, offspring, also a rein; Icel. *taumr*, a rein; Dan. *tömme*, Swed. *töm*, a rein; G. *zaum*, a bridle. Teut. type **tau-moz*, for **taug-moz* (Noreen), from *tauh*, 2nd grade of **teuh-an-*, to draw. See **Tow** (1). (√DEUK.) Der. *teem*.

Tear (1), to rend. (E.) M.E. *teren*. A.S. *teran*, pt. t. *tær*, pp. *toren*.**+**Goth. *ga-tairan*, to break, destroy; Lith. *dir-ti*, to flay, Gk. δέρ-ειν, to flay; Russ. *dra-te*, to tear; Pers. *darīdan*, to tear; cf. W. *darn*, a fragment; Zend *dar*, to cut; Skt. *dāraya*, to tear. Teut. type **teran-*, pt. t. **tar*; pp. **turanoz*. (√DER.) Cf. also G. *zehren* (weak verb). Brugm. i. § 594.

Tear (2), a drop of fluid from the eye. (E.) M.E. *tere*. A.S. *tēar*, *tǣr*, also *teagor*; O. Northumb. *tæher*. **+** Icel. *tār*, Dan. *taar*, *taare*, Swed. *tår*, Goth. *tagr*, O. H. G. *zahar* (pl. *zaheri*, whence mod. G. *zähre*). Cf. O. Lat. *dacruma*, L. *lacrima*, Gk. δάκρυ, δάκρυμα, W. *dagr*, a tear, O. Irish *dēr*. Brugm. i. § 178. **Der.** *train-oil*.

Tease, to card wool, to vex, plague. (E.) M.E. *tēsen*. A.S. *tǣsan*, to pluck, pull.**+**M. Du. *teesen*, to pluck wool; Swed. dial. *tesa*, Dan. *tæse*, Bavarian *zaisen* (Schmeller), O. H. G. *zeisan*. All from Teut. base **teis*.

teasel, a plant. (E.) M.E. *tēsel*. A.S. *tǣsl*, *tǣsel*, lit. 'teaser,' from its use in teasing wool.**—**A.S. *tǣsan*, to tease.**+** O. H. G. *zeisala*, teasel; from *zeisan*, to tease.

Teat, nipple of the female breast. (F.

—Low G.) M. E. *tete*, *tette*. **—** O. F. *tete*, *tette*; F. *tette*.**—**Low G. *titte*, M. Du. *titte*.**+**A. S. *tit* (pl. *tittas*), whence E. *tit*, a teat; G. *zitze*. Cf. also W. *didi*, *did*, a teat. (As if from an Idg. base DI.) ¶ Distinct from Gk. τίτθη, τιτθός, a teat, which appears to be allied to Skt. *dhē*, to suck, Goth. *daddjan*, to suckle.

Teazle, i. e. teasel; see **teasel.**

Technical. (Gk.) Formed with suffix *-al* (=L. *-ālis*) from Gk. τεχνικός, belonging to the arts.**—**Gk. τέχνη, art, allied to τέκτων, a carpenter. Cf. Skt. *takshan*, a carpenter, from *taksh*, to cut wood. Allied to **Text.**

Techy, fretful; see **Tetchy.**

Ted, to spread mown grass. (Scand.) Icel. *teðja*, to spread manure, from *tað*, manure; cf. *taða*, hay grown in a well-manured field, *töðu-verk*, hay-making, lit. 'ted-work.' So also Norw. *tedja*, Swed. dial. *täda*, to spread manure; from *tad*, manure.**+**Bavarian *zetten*, O. H. G. *zettan*, to strew; cf. G. *ver-zetteln*, to scatter.

Tedious. (L.) L. *tædiōsus*, irksome.**—**L. *tædium*, irksomeness.**—**L. *tædet*, it irks one. (We also use *tēdium*, sb.)

Tee, a mark. (E.) From the use of a T to denote an exact spot. Cf. *tee-totum*; and see **Taw.**

Teem (1), to be prolific. (E.) M.E. *tēmen*, to teem; *tēm*, sb., progeny, offspring; whence mod. E. *team*. See **Team.** The M. E. *tēmen* answers to A.S. *tēman*, *tȳman*, older *tīeman*, to teem. Teut. type **taumjan-*, from **taumoz*, a team.

Teem (2), to empty. (Scand.) Icel. *tæma*, Dan. *tömme*, Swed. *tömma*, vb.; from the adj. *toom*; see **Toom.**

Teen, vexation, grief. (E.) M.E. *tene*. A.S. *tēona*, accusation, vexation.**—**A.S. *tēon*, contracted form of **tīhan*, to accuse.**+**Goth. *gateihan*, to tell, make known; G. *zeihen*, to accuse; cf. L. *dīcāre*, to make known. Allied to **Diction.** (√DEIK.) ¶ *Teen* means a making known, public accusation, reproach, injury, vexation, grief, harm.

Teetotaller, a total abstainer. (F.**—**L.; with E. *prefix and suffix.*) *Tee-total* is an emphasised form of **Total,** q.v. The word originated with R. Turner, of Preston, who, at a temperance meeting about 1833, asserted that nothing but *te-te-total* will do; see the Staunch Teetotaller, ed. by J. Livesey, of Preston, Jan. 1867. (Haydn.) See below.

Teetotum, Totum, a spinning toy. (L.) Formerly *totum* (Ash, 1775, Phillips, 1706). So called from the side formerly marked *T*, which signified *totum*, i. e. all the stake, from L. *tōtum*, neut. of *tōtus*, the whole; see **Total.** Hence the name *totum*, or *T-totum*; which may have suggested *T-total.*

Tegument, a covering. (L.) L. *tegumentum*, a covering. — L. *tegere*, to cover. +Gk. στέγειν, Skt. *sthag*, to cover. Cf. O. Irish *tech*, W. *tȳ*, a house. Allied to Thatch. (√STEG.) Brugm. i. § 632.

Teil-tree, a linden tree. (F. — L.; *and* E.) O. F. *teil*, a lime-tree; also, the inner bark of a lime-tree (mod. F. *tille*). — L. *tilia*, a lime-tree; also, the inner bark of a lime-tree. +Irish *teile.*

Telegraph. (Gk.) Modern. From Gk. τῆλε, afar; γράφειν, to write. **Der.** *telegram*, coined to express 'telegraphic message'; from γράμμα, a written character.

telescope. (Gk.) From Gk. τῆλε, afar; σκοπ-εῖν, to behold. See **Scope.**

Tell, to count, narrate. (E.) A. S. *tellan*, pt. t. *tealde*, pp. *teald*; a weak verb (for **tal-jan*). — A. S. *talu*, number, narrative; see **Tale.** +Du. *tellen*, Icel. *telja*, Dan. *tælle*, Swed. *tälja*, G. *zählen*; all from sbs. Teut. type **taljan-.*

Telluric, belonging to earth. (L.) From L. *tellūr-*, stem of *tellūs*, earth. **Der.** *telluri-um*, a rare metal.

Temerity. (F. — L.) M.F. *temerité.* — L. acc. *temeritātem*, rashness. — L. adv. *temere*, rashly. The orig. sense of *temere* was 'in the dark'; cf. Skt. *tamas*, gloom.

Temper, vb. (L.) M. E. *tempren.* A. S. *temprian*, to temper. — L. *temperāre*, to apportion, regulate, qualify. Allied to *temperī, temporī*, adv., seasonably, and to *tempus*, time; see **Temporal** (1). Brugm. ii. § 132.

tempest. (F. — L.) O. F. *tempeste* (F. *tempête*), a storm; answering to a Late L. *tempesta*, fem. of Late L. *tempestus*, adj., used instead of L. *tempestās*, season, fit time, weather, also bad weather, storm. From L. *tempus*, time (above). Brugm. ii. §§ 102, 132.

Temple (1), a fane. (L.) A.S. *templ, tempel.* — L. *templum*, a temple. + Gk. τέμενος, a sacred enclosure, piece of ground cut off; allied to τέμνειν, to cut. (√TEM.) Brugm. ii. § 76. **Der.** *templ-ar*, Late L. *templārius.*

Temple (2), flat portion of the side of the head above the cheek-bone. (F. — L.) M. E. *templis*, pl. — O. F. *temples*, pl., the temples (mod. F. *tempes*, Norm. dial. *temples*). — L. *tempora*, pl., the temples. **Der.** *tempor-al*, adj., belonging to the temples.

Temporal (1), worldly, secular. (F. — L.) M. E. *temporal.* — O. F. *temporal, temporel*, adj. — L. *temporālis*, temporal. — L. *tempor-*, for **tempos-*, stem of *tempus*, time.

Temporal (2), belonging to the temples: see **Temple** (2).

Tempt. (F. — L.) O.F. *tempter*, later *tenter*, to tempt, prove. — L. *temptāre, tentāre*, to handle, try the strength of, assail, tempt; frequentative of *tendere* (pp. *tentus*), to stretch (Bréal). See **Tend** (1).

Ten. (E.) A. S. *tȳn, tīen*, with mutation; O. Merc. *tēn.* The long vowel appears in *-teen.* + Du. *tien*; Icel. *tíu*, Dan. *ti*, Swed. *tio*; Goth. *taihun*; G. *zehn*; L. *decem*, Gk. δέκα, Lith. *deszimtis*, Russ. *desiate*, W. *deg*, Irish and Gael. *deich*, Pers. *dah*, Skt. *daça.* Teut. type **tehan*; Idg. type **dekəm.* Brugm. ii. § 174. **Der.** *ten-th*; see **Tithe.**

Tenable, that can be held. (F. — L.) F. *tenable*, 'holdable,' Cot. — F. *tenir*, to hold. — L. *tenēre*, to hold, keep; orig. to extend. +Skt. *tan*, to extend, stretch; Gk. τείνειν (for **τένγειν*), to stretch. Allied to **Thin.**

tenacious. (L.) Coined from L. *tenāc-i-*, decl. stem of *tenax*, holding fast; with suffix *-ous.* — L. *tenēre* (above).

tenacity. (F. — L.) M.F. *tenacité.* — L. *tenācitātem*, acc. of *tenācitās*, a holding firm. — L. *tenāci-* (above).

tenant. (F. — L.) F. *tenant*, holding, pres. pt. of *tenir.* — L. *tenēre*, to hold. **Der.** *lieu-tenant*, q. v.

Tench, a fish. (F. — L.) O. F. *tenche* (F. *tanche*). — L. *tinca*, a tench.

Tend (1), to aim at, move towards, incline, bend to. (F. — L.) F. *tendre.* — L. *tendere*, to stretch, extend, direct, tender. Allied to *tenēre*, to hold; see **Tenable.** (√TEN.) Brugm. ii. § 696 (3). **Der.** *tend-enc-y*, formed by adding *-y* to the obs. sb. *tendence*, coined from the stem of the pres. part. of *tendere.*

Tend (2), to take care of. (F. — L.) A docked form of **Attend.**

Tender (1), soft, delicate. (F. — L.) F. *tendre.* — L. *tenerum*, acc. of *tener*, tender, orig. thin; allied to *tenuis*, thin. (✓ TEN.) See **Thin.** Der. *tender*, vb., to regard fondly, a word more or less confused with *tender* (2); whence *tender*, sb., regard, care, K. Lear, i. 4. 230.

Tender (2), to proffer, offer, shew. (F. —L.) F. *tendre*, 'to tend, .. also to tender or offer unto ;' Cot. — L. *tendere*, to stretch out. See **Tend** (1).

tender (3), a small vessel that attends a larger, a coal-carriage attached to a locomotive engine. (F. — L.; *with* E. *suffix.*) Short for *attender*, i. e. attendant on; see **Tend** (2) and **Attend.**

tendon. (F.—L.) F. *tendon*, 'a tendon, or taile of a muscle;' Cot. From a Late L. form **tendo*, gen. *tendōnis* and *tendinis*; cf. Span. *tendon*, Ital. *tendine*, a tendon; Port. *tendão*. Lit. 'stretcher.' —L. *tendere*, to stretch.

Tendril. (F.—L.) From O. F. *tendrillons*, pl. ' tendrells ;' Cot ; or from an O. F. **tendrille*, not recorded. We also find O. F. *tendron*, 'a tender fellow, also a tendrell ;' Cot. — F. *tendre*, tender; see **Tender** (1).

Tenebrous, Tenebrious, gloomy. (F.—L.) M. F. *tenebreux.*—L. *tenebrōsus*, gloomy.—L. *tenebra*, pl., darkness. Allied to Skt. *tamisra-*, darkness, *tamas*, gloom. Brugm. i. § 413. (✓TEM.)

Tenement, a holding. (F.—L.) M. F. *tenement.*—Late L. *tenēmentum*, a fief.— L. *tenēre*, to hold.

tenet. (L.) L.*tenet*, he holds; 3rd pers. sing. pres. of *tenēre*. (Cf. *habitat, exit*.)

Tennis. (F.—L.) M.E. *tenétz* (accented on latter *e*); Gower, Balade to Henry IV, l. 295, also *tenise, teneis, teneys* ; whence Late L. *tenisia, teniludium*.—A. F. *tenetz*, F. *tenez* (< L. *tenēte*), imp. pl. of *tenēre*, to hold ; perhaps used to mean ' take this,' and ejaculated by the player in serving.

Tenny, a colour in heraldry. (F.—G.) The same as *tawny* or *tanny*; see **Tawny.**

Tenon. (F.—L.) F. *tenon*, 'a tenon, the end of a rafter put into a morteise ;' Cot. So called because it *holds fast.*—F. *tenir*, to hold fast.—L. *tenēre*, to hold.

tenor. (F. — L.) Formerly (better) *tenour*. M. E. *tenour*, import.—F. *teneur*, import, content of a matter.—L. *tenōrem*, acc. of *tenor*, a holding on; a course, tenor of a law.—L. *tenēre*, to hold. ¶ The sense of *tenor* in music (Ital. *tenore*) is due to the notion of holding or continuing the dominant note (Scheler).

Tense (1), part of a verb, indicating time of action. (F.—L.) M. E. *temps*, Chaucer, C. T. 16343. — F. *temps*, time (also O. F. *tens*). — L. *tempus*, time, also a tense.

Tense (2), tightly strained. (L.) L. *tensus*, pp. of *tendere*, to stretch ; see **Tend** (1). Der. *tense-ness*, with E. suffix.

tension, the act of straining, a strain. (F.—L.) F. *tension*, used in 16th cent. —L. *tensiōnem*, acc. of *tensio*, a stretching. —L. *tens-um*, supine of *tendere* (above). So also *tens-or*, a coined word.

tent (1), a pavilion. (F.—L.) F. *tente*. —Late L. *tenta*, a tent; fem. of L. *tentus*, pp. of *tendere*, to stretch, spread out.

Tent (2), a roll of lint used to dilate a wound. (F.—L.) M.E. *tente.*—F. *tente* ; Cot. A verbal sb. from F. *tenter* < L. *tentāre*, to try, prove, probe. Cf. Span. *tienta*, a probe. See **Tempt.**

Tent (3), a wine. (Span.—L.) From Span. *vino tinto*, a deep-coloured (lit. tinted) wine.—L. *tinctus*, pp. of *tingere*, to dye. See **Tinge.**

Tent (4), heed, attention. (F.—L.) In Lowl. Sc. *tak tent*. Short for *attent*, i. c. *attention.*

Tentacle, feeler of an insect. (L.) Coined from L. *tentā-re*, to feel; with suffix *-cu-lum* ; see **Tempt.**

tentative. (L.) L. *tentātīuus*, adj., trying, tentative.—L. *tentāre*, to try; see **Tempt.**

Tenter, a frame for stretching cloth. (F. — L.) Properly *tenture* ; but a vb. *tent* was coined, and from it a sb. *tenter*, which supplanted M.E. *tenture.*—M.F. *tenture*, a stretching.—L. *tentūra*, a stretching.— L. *tentus*, pp. of *tendere*, to stretch. See **Tend** (1). Der. *tenter-hook*.

Tenth. (E.) M. E. *tenþe*, coined (by analogy with *seven-th, nin-th*) from *ten* ; the true E. word is *tithe.*

Tenuity, thinness. (F. — L.) M. F. *tenuité.* — L. *tenuitātem*, acc. of *tenuitās*, thinness. — L. *tenui-s*, thin ; lit. ' stretched out.' Cognate with **Thin.** (✓TEN.)

Tenure. (F.—L.) F. *tenure.* — Late L. *tenūra*, a holding (of land).—L. *tenēre*, to hold. See **Tenable.**

Teocalli, a temple. (Mexican.) From *teotl*, a god ; and *calli*, a house.

Tepid. (L.) L. *tepidus*, warm. — L. *tepēre*, to be warm. ╈ Skt. *tap*, to be warm ; Russ. *topite*, to heat ; Irish *tē*, hot. (✓TEP.)

Teraphim, idols, household gods. (Heb.) Heb. *terāphīm,* s. pl., images connected with magical rites.

Terce, the same as **Tierce.**

Tercel, Tassel, the male of any hawk. (F.—L.) M. E. *tercel*; dimin. *tercel-et.* —O. F. *tercel, tiercel*; whence the dimin. *tiercelet,* 'the tassell, or male of any kind of hawke; so tearmed because he is, commonly, a third part lesse then the female;' Cot. [Another alleged reason is, that every third bird hatched was, in popular opinion, sure to be a male. So also Ital. *terzolo,* 'a tassel gentle of a hauke;' Florio.]—O. F. *tiers, tierce,* third.—L. *tertius,* third; see **Tierce.**

Terebinth, turpentine-tree. (L.—Gk.) L. *terebinthus.*—Gk. τερέβινθος, the turpentine-tree; earlier form τέρμινθος.

Tergiversation, a subterfuge, fickleness. (F.—L.) F. *tergiversation.*—L. *tergiuersātiōnem,* acc. of *tergiuersātio,* a subterfuge.—L. *tergiuersātus,* pp. of *tergiuersārī,* to turn one's back, turn right round, shuffle.—L. *tergi-,* for *tergum,* the back; *uersārī,* to turn about, pass. of *uersāre,* frequent. of *uertere,* to turn; see **Verse.**

Term. (F.—L.) M. E. *terme.*—F. *terme.*—L. *terminum,* acc. of *terminus,* boundary, limit. **+** Gk. τέρμα, limit; Skt. *tāraya,* to cause to pass over. (√TER.)

Termagant. (F.—Ital.—L.) M. E. *Termagant, Teruagant,* a (supposed) Saracen idol, hence a ranting character in old moralities [plays], and finally a scolding woman.—O. F. *Tervagant, Tervagan,* a (supposed) Saracen idol (Chanson de Roland).—Ital. *Trivigante,* the same (Ariosto, xii. 59). Explained as *Trivagante,* the moon, wandering under the three names of *Selene* (or *Luna*) in heaven, *Artemis (Diana)* in earth, *Persephone (Proserpina)* in the lower world.—L. *ter,* thrice; *uagant-,* stem of pres. pt. of *uagārī,* to wander. But perhaps Eastern.

Termination. (F.—L.) M.F. *termination.*—L. acc. *terminātiōnem,* a bounding, ending.—L. *terminātus,* pp. of *termināre,* to bound, end.—L. *terminus,* boundary. See **Term.**

terminus, end. (L.) L. *terminus* (above).

Tern, a bird. (Scand.) Dan. *terne,* *tærne,* Swed. *tärna,* Icel. *þerna,* a tern. Cf. A. S. *stearn,* a tern; and **Starling.**

Ternary. (L.) L. *ternārius,* consisting

of three.—L. *ternī,* pl., by threes.—L. *ter,* three times; *trēs,* three; see **Three.**

Terra cotta, a kind of hard pottery. (Ital.—L.) Ital. *terra cotta,* baked earth.— L. *terra,* earth (below); *cocta,* fem. of *coctus,* pp. of *coquere,* to cook; see **Cook.**

terrace. (F.—Ital.—L.) M.F. *terrace, terrasse,* a terrace, platform, plat.—M. Ital. *terraccia, terrazza,* a terrace, long mound of earth.—Ital. *terra,* earth.—L. *terra,* earth. β. *Terra*=**tersa,* i. e. dry ground; allied to O. Irish *tīr,* W. *tir,* earth; also to Gk. τέρσεσθαι, to dry up. (√TERS.) See **Torrid, Thirst.** Brugm. i. § 706 (b).

terreen, tureen, a large bowl for soup. (F.—L.) Both spellings are bad; *terrine* would be better.—F. *terrine,* an earthen pan.—L. *terr-a,* earth; with suffix *-ina,* fem. of *-inus.*

terrene, earthly. (L.) L. *terrēnus,* earthly.—L. *terra,* earth.

terrestrial. (L.) From L. *terrestri-s,* earthly; with suffix *-ālis.*—L. *terra,* earth; with suffix *-st-tr-.*

Terrible. (F.—L.) F. *terrible.*—L. *terribilis,* causing terror.—L. *terrēre,* to frighten. See **Terror.**

Terrier (1), a kind of dog. (F.—L.) M. E. *terrere,* a 'burrow-dog,' one who pursues rabbits, &c. at their holes.—F. *terrier,* as in *chien terrier,* 'a terrier;' Cot. Cf. *terrier,* 'the hole, berry, or earth of a conny [rabbit] or fox; also, a little hillock;' Cot.—Late L. *terrārius,* belonging to earth.—L. *terra,* earth. See **Terrace.**

terrier (2), a register of landed property. (F.—L.) M.F. *papier terrier,* a roll of tenants' names, &c.—Late L. *terrārius,* as in *terrārius liber,* a book wherein landed property is described.—L. *terra,* land.

Terrific. (L.) L. *terrificus,* causing terror.—L. *terri-,* for *terrēre,* to frighten; *-ficus,* causing, from *facere,* to make.

Terrine; see **terreen.**

Territory, domain. (F.—L.) F. *territoire,* a territory.—L. *territōrium,* a domain, land round a town.—L. *terra,* land. Formed as if from a sb. with decl. stem *territōri-,* i. e. possessor of land.

Terror, dread. (F.—L.) Formerly also *terrour.*—F. *terreur.*—L. *terrōrem,* acc. of *terror,* dread.—L. *terrēre,* to scare, make afraid, orig. to tremble. Cf. Gk. τρέειν (for **τρέσειν*), to tremble; Skt. *tras,* to tremble, be afraid; Lith. *triszeti,* to tremble, Russ. *triasti*, to shiver. Allied to Tremble. Brugm. ii. § 657.

Terse, concise, neat. (L.) L. *tersus*, wiped off, clean, neat, pure, nice, terse ; pp. of *tergere*, to wipe, wipe dry, polish a stone.+Gk. τρίβειν, to rub.

Tertian, recurring every third day. (F. —L.) M. F. *tertiane*, a tertian ague. — L. *tertiāna*, fem. of *tertiānus*, tertian. — L. *tertius*, third. — L. *ter*, thrice, *trēs*, three. See Tri-.

tertiary. (L.) L. *tertiārius*, containing a third part ; used to mean belonging to the third. — L. *tertius*, third (above).

Tesselated. (L.) L. *tessellātus*, checkered, furnished with small square stones (as a pavement). — L. *tessella*, a small square piece of stone, little cube ; dimin. of *tessera*, a die (to play with), small cube.

Test, a pot in which metals are tried, a trial, proof. (F. — L.) M. E. *test*, a pot or vessel used in alchemy. — O. F. *test* (F. *têt*), a test, in chemistry. — L. *testum*, an earthen vessel. Closely allied to O. F. *teste* (F. *tête*), a pot-sherd, a skull, answering to Late L. *testa*, a vessel used in alchemy. So also Ital. *testo*, a test, melting-pot, from L. *testum* ; *testa*, an earthen pot, potsherd, skull, head, burnt tile or brick, from L. *testa*, a piece of baked earthenware, potsherd, shell, skull. Perhaps *testa* = **tersta*, i. e. dried, baked ; cf. *terra*; see Terrace. But cf. Pers. *tast*, a cup ; Horn, § 389.

testaceous, having a hard shell. (L.) L. *testāce-us*, having a shell ; with suffix *-ous*. — L. *testa*, tile, shell, &c.

Testament. (F. — L.) F. *testament*, a will. — L. *testāmentum*, a will. — L. *testā-rī*, to be a witness. — L. *testis*, a witness. Der. *in-testate*, i. e. without a will ; *testa-tor*, one who makes a will, fem. *testa-trix*.

Tester, a sixpence ; flat canopy over a bed or pulpit. (F. — L.) Mod. E. (slang) *tizzie*, a sixpence ; the *tester*, *testern*, or *testoon* was named from a French coin with a head upon it (of Louis XII of France) ; in England *all* coins bore the head, so that our use of the term was borrowed. — O. F. *testre*, the head-piece of a bed ; M. F. *teston*, 'a testoon, piece of silver worth xviijᵈ. sterling ;' Cot. — O. F. *teste*, a head. — L. *testa*, tile, skull. ¶ A *tester* for a bed also appears as M. F. *testiere*, 'a headpiece,' Cot. ; from O. F. *teste* (as before).

Testicle. (F. — L.) F. *testicule*. — L.

testiculum, acc. of *testiculus*, dimin. of *testis*, a testicle.

Testify. (F. — L.) M. F. *testifier*. — L. *testificārī*, to bear witness. — L. *testi-s*, a witness ; *-ficārī*, for *facere*, to make.

testimony. (L.) L. *testimōnium*, evidence. — L. *testi-s*, a witness ; with Idg. suffixes *-mōn-io-*.

Testy, fretful. (F. — L.) M. E. *testif*, Ch. — O. F. **testif* (not found) ; M. F. *testu*, 'heady ;' Cot. — O. F. *teste*, the head ; see Tester.

Tetchy, Techy, fretful, peevish, touchy. (F. — Low G.) The sense is full of freaks, whims, or caprices ; from *tetch*, M. E. *teche*, *tecche*, *tache*, a bad habit, whim ; see Tache (2). ¶ This is the word which is now altered to *touchy*, as if sensitive to the *touch*.

Tether, a rope for fastening up. (E.) Formerly written *tedder*. M. E. *tedir*. — A. S. **tēoder* (not found) = O. Fries. *tiader*, *tieder*.+Icel. *tjōðr*, a tether, Swed. *tjuder*, Dan. *töir*, Norw. *tjōr*, *tjoder* ; Low G. *tider*, O. H. G. *zeotar*, *zieter*. Teut. type **teu-dro-*, of uncertain origin ; sometimes referred to Teut. root **teuh-*; see Team. ¶ Gael. *teadhair* is from E. Cf. Bahder, p. 147 ; Brugm. ii. § 62.

Tetragon, a figure with four angles. (F. — L. — Gk.) M. F. *tetragone*, adj., four-cornered. — L. *tetragōnus*, adj. — Gk. τετράγωνος, four-cornered. — Gk. τέτρα-, allied to τέσσαρες, four, cognate with E. **Four**; and γωνία, an angle, from γόνυ, a knee, cognate with E. Knee.

tetrahedron, a solid figure contained by four equilateral triangles. (Gk.) Gk. τέτρα- (as above) ; -έδρον, from ἔδρα, a base, which is from ἕδ-ειν, to sit ; see Sit.

tetrarch. (L. — Gk.) L. *tetrarcha*. — Gk. τετράρχης, one of four chiefs ; Luke, iii. 1. — Gk. τετρ-, allied to τέσσαρες, four ; and ἄρχειν, to rule. See Four and Arch-, prefix.

tetrasyllable, a word of four syllables. (F. — L. — Gk.) Coined from Gk. τέτρα-, four (as above) ; and συλλαβή, a syllable. Cf. M. F. *tetrasyllabe*, L. *tetrasyllabus*, Gk. τετρασύλλαβος, of four syllables. See Syllable.

Tetter, a cutaneous disease. (E.) M. E. *teter*. A. S. *teter*, a kind of itch. Cf. G. *zittermal*, a tetter ; Bavar. *zittaroch*, O. H. G. *zitaroch*. Allied to L. *derbiōsus*, scabby ; Skt. *dadru-*, a tetter.

Teutonic. (L. — Gothic.) L. *Teuto-*

nicus, adj., from *Teutones*, sb. pl., the Teutons, a people of Germany; lit. 'men of the nation,' or 'the people.' — Goth. *thiuda*, a people, nation (or from a dialectal variant of this word). See Dutch.

Text. (F. — L.) M. E. *texte*. — F. *texte*, a text, subject of a book. — L. *textum*, a thing woven, fabric, style of an author, text of a book. — L. *textus*, woven, pp. of *texere*, to weave. + Skt. *taksh*, to cut wood, to prepare; cf. Russ. *tesiate*, to hew. Further allied to **Technical**. (√TEK.) Brugm. i. § 594. **Der.** *textu-al*, from M. F. *textu-el*.

textile. (L.) L. *textīlis*, woven. — L. *textus*, pp. of *texere*, to weave.

texture. (F. — L.) F. *texture*, 'a texture, web;' Cot. — L. *textūra*, a web. — L. *textus*, pp. of *texere*, to weave.

TH.

Th. This is distinct from *t*, and should have a distinct symbol. Formerly, the A. S. þ and ð were used (but indiscriminately) to denote *both* the sounds now denoted by *th*. When þ degenerated into a symbol closely resembling *y*, *y* was at last substituted for it; hence we find *y^e* and *y^t* used, by early printers, for *the*, *that*; it is needless (I hope) to remark that *ye man* was never *pronounced* as *ye man* in the Middle Ages, as it often is *now*.

I here use ð for A. S. words, and ð or *th* for M. E. words, beginning with the sound of *th* in *that*; and þ for A. S. and M. E. words, beginning with the sound of *th* in *thin*. Observe these facts. (1) Initial *th* is always pronounced as in *thin* except (*a*) in words allied to *that*; and (*b*) in words allied to *thou*. (2) At the end of a word, it is pronounced as *th* in *thin*, except when a written *e* follows; compare *breath* with *breathe*; exceptions are *with*, *smooth*. (3) No word beginning with *th* (except *thurible*, formed on a *Greek* base) is of *Latin* origin; some (easily known) are *Greek*; *thummim* is *Hebrew*; all the rest are *English* or *Scandian*.

Than, conj. (E.) Frequently written *then*, and orig. the same word as *then*. M. E. *thanne*, *thonne*. A. S. ðonne, than. Closely allied to the def. art.; see **That**, § β. + Du. *dan*; G. *dann*, *denn*. Cf. L. *tum*.

Thane, a dignitary among the English. (E.) M. E. *þein*. A. S. *þegen*, *þegn*, *þēn*, a thane. Lit. 'child' or 'begotten.' +

Icel. *þegn*; G. *degen*, a warrior, O. H. G. *degan*. Teut. type **theznóz*, m. Allied to Gk. τέκνον, a child; from τεκ-, as in τεκ-εῖν, 2 aor. inf. of τίκτειν, to beget. (√TEK.) Brugm. ii. § 66.

Thank, Thanks. (E.) M. E *þank*, a thought, kindly remembrance, goodwill; hence *thanks*, pl., expressions of goodwill. A. S. *þanc*, *þonc*, sb., thought, favour, content, thank. + Du. *dank*, Icel. *þökk*, Dan. *tak*, Swed. *tack*, Goth. *thagks*, i.e. **thanks*, remembrance, thank. Teut. type **thankoz*, m.; from **thank*, 2nd grade of **thenkan-*, to think. See **Think**. (√TENG.) **Der.** *thank*, vb., A. S. *þancian*.

That. (E.) M. E. *that*. A. S. ðæt, orig. neuter of a demonstrative pronoun, which came to be used as the definite article. The masc. and fem. forms in use were *sē* (*se*), *sēo*, which in late A. S. were replaced by ðe, ðeo, by analogy with the neuter and other cases. The neut. ðæt is from the Teut. pronominal base THA = Idg. TO, meaning 'he' or 'that.' The suffix *-t* is merely the sign of the neut. gender, like Lat. *-d* in *i-d*, *illu-d*, *istu-d*, *qui-d*. **β.** The declension was as follows. SING. NOM. *sē*, *sēo*, ðæt [replaced in late A. S. by ðe, ðeo, ðæt]; GEN. ðæs, ðære, ðæs; DAT. ðǣm, ðām, ðǣre, ðǣm, ðām; ACC. ðone, ðā, ðæt; INSTRUMENTAL (ðȳ, ðon). PLURAL; NOM. AND ACC. ðā; GEN. ðāra, ðāra; DAT. ðām. + Du. *de*, the, *dat*, that; Icel. neut. *þat*, the; Dan. *den*, neut. *det*, the; Swed. *den*, neut. *det*, this; G. *der*, *die*, *das*, the, *dass*, that; Goth. *thata*, neut. of def. article. Cf. Lith. *tas*, *ta*, that; Russ. *tot'*, *ta*, *to*, that; Gk. τό, neut. of def. art.; Skt. *tat*, it, that; L. *-te*, *-ta*, *-tud* (in *is-te*, *is-ta*, *is-tud*).

Thatch, sb. (E.) M.E. *þak*. A. S. *þæc*, thatch; whence *þeccan*, to thatch. + Du. *dak*, sb., whence *dekken*, vb. (whence E. *deck* is borrowed); Icel. *þak*, sb., Dan. *tag*, Swed. *tak*, G. *dach*. Teut. type **thak-om*, n. From **thak*, 2nd grade of Teut. root **thek-*, to cover, cognate with L. *teg-*, as in *teg-ere*, to cover. + Gk. τέγος, στέγος, a roof; Irish *teagh*, Gael. *teach*, *tigh*, O. Irish *tech*, W. *tŷ*, a house; Lith. *stogas*, a thatch, *stegti*, to thatch; Skt. *sthag*, to cover. (√STEG, TEG.) Allied to **Tegument**.

Thaw, vb. (E.) M. E. *thōwen*; prov. E. *thow* (*ow* as in *snow*); A.S. *þawian*, to melt. + Du. *dooijen*, to thaw, from *dooi*, thaw; Icel. *þeyja*, from *þā*, sb.; Dan. *töe*, Swed. *töa*. Cf. G. *verdauen*, to digest, concoct; *thauen*, O. H. G. *douwen*, to thaw. Perhaps allied to Gk. τήκειν, to melt; W. *toddi*, to melt. ¶ *Not* allied to *dew*.

The (1), def. art. (E.) M.E. *the*. A.S. ðe, used as nom. masc. of def. art. in late MSS., but early common as an indeclinable relative; see **That**, § β.

the (2), in what (or that) degree. (E.) Only in such phrases as '*the* more, *the* merrier.' This is the *instrumental case* of the def. art. M. E. *the*; A.S. ðȳ; see **That**, § β. + Goth. *thē*, Icel. *þvī*, *þī*, inst. case of art. or dem. pronoun.

Theatre. (F. – L. – Gk.) M.F. *theatre*; Cot. – L. *theātrum*. – Gk. θέατρον, a place for seeing shows. – Gk. θεάομαι, I see. Cf. θέα, a sight; see Prellwitz.

Thee (1). (E.) A.S. ðē, dat. and acc. of ðū, thou; see **Thou**.

Thee (2), to prosper, thrive. (E.) Obsolete. M. E. *theen*. – A.S. *þēon*, *þīon* (for *þīhan*), pt. t. *þāh*, *þēah*, pp. *þigen*, *þogen*, also *gepungen*, to thrive. + Goth. *theihan*, to thrive, increase; G. *gedeihen*; Du. *gedijen*. The A.S. pp. *ge-þungen* shews that the A.S. *þīhan* is for *þinhan* (cf. O. Sax. *ge-þengian*, to fulfil). Teut. root *þinχ, *þenχ*, Idg. root *tenk*, as in Lith. *tenka*, it suffices, O.Irish *tocad*,prosperity; W. *tynged*, luck; cf. Lith. *tekti*, to suffice. Brugm. i. § 421 (3).

Theft. (E.) In place of *thefth*. M.E. *þefte*; for A.S. *þiefþ*, *þēofþ*, theft. – A.S. *þēof*, a thief. + Icel. *þȳfð*, O. Fries. *thiufthe*. See **Thief**.

Their, belonging to them. (Scand.) M. E. *thair*. – Icel. *þeirra*, of them, used as gen. pl. of *hann*, he, but really the gen. pl. of a dem. pronoun, as shewn by A.S. *þāra*; see **They**, and **That**, § β.

Theism, belief in a God. (Gk.) Coined, with suffix -*ism* (Gk. -ισμος), from Gk. θε-ός, a god. Perhaps for an older form *θεσος; cf. O. Ir. *dess*, God (Stokes-Fick, p. 151), Gk. θέσ-φατος, spoken by God (Prellwitz).

Them, objective case of *they*. (Scand.) Really an old dat. case. – Icel. *þeim*, dat. of *þeir*, they; see **They**. + A. S. *þām*, dat. pl. of def. art.; see **That**, § β.

Theme. (F. – L. – Gk.) M.E. *teme*. – O.F. *teme*, M.F. *theme*, ' a theam ;' Cot. – L. *thema*. – Gk. θέμα, that which is laid down, a theme for argument. – Gk. base θε-, to place; τί-θη-μι, I place. + Skt. *dhā*, to put; see **Do** (1). (√DHE.)

Then. (E.) Frequently written *than* in old books, and originally identical with it; see **Than**.

thence. (E.) M. E. *thennes* (dissyllabic); whence *thens*, by contraction, later written *thence*. The *s* is an adverbial suffix; earlier forms were *thenne*, *thanne*, in which a final *n* has been lost. – A. S. ðanan, thence; formed from base ða-, with the suffix -*na-n-*, or -*na-na*. The base ða- = Teut. base THA; see **That**. + G. *dannen*, O. H. G. *dannana*, thence; from base *da*-.

Theocracy. (Gk.) Lit. 'government by God.' From θεο-, for θεός, God; -κρα-τία, government, from κρατεῖν, to govern, which is from κρατύς, strong. Cf. *aristo-cracy*, *auto-cracy*, *demo-cracy*. See **Theism**.

Theodolite, an instrument used in surveying. (F. – Gk. ?) Generally said to be Greek. Formerly *theodelitus*, meaning ' a circle with a graduated border '; used A. D. 1571. Also *theodolet*, *theodelet*. Apparently imitated (it is not known why) from O. F. *theodelet*, *theodolet*, the name of a treatise, lit. ' a work by *Theodulus*,' – Gk. Θεοδοῦλος, Theodulus; llt. ' servant of God.' ' Ung *theodelet* coute viij. s. ;' Godefroy.

Theogony. (L. – Gk.) L. *theogonia*. – Gk. θεογονία, the origin of the gods. – Gk. θεό-ς, a god ; -γονία, origin, from γεν-, base of γίγνομαι, I become; see **Genus**.

theology. (F. – L. – Gk.) M. E. *theologie*. – M.F. *theologie*; Cot. – L. *theologia*. – Gk. θεολογία, a speaking about God. – Gk. θεολόγος, adj., speaking about God. – Gk. θεό-ς, a god; λέγειν, to speak.

Theorbo, a large lute. (Ital.) Formerly *theorba*. – Ital. *tiorba*; the *th* being due to the occasional F. spelling *théorbe* for *téorbe*. (*Said* to have been named after the inventor.)

Theorem. (L. – Gk.) L. *theōrēma*. – Gk. θεώρημα, a spectacle; a subject for contemplation, theorem. – Gk. θεωρεῖν, to behold. – Gk. θεωρός, a spectator. – Gk. θεάομαι, I see. See **Theatre**.

theory. (F. – L. – Gk.) M. F. *theorie*, ' theory ;' Cot. – L. *theōria*. – Gk. θεωρία, a beholding, contemplation, speculation. – Gk. θεωρός, a spectator (above).

Therapeutic, pertaining to the healing art. (F. – L. – Gk.) M. F. *therapeutique*, healing; Cot. – L. *therapeutica* (*ars*), the healing art; fem. of *therapeuticus*. – Gk. θεραπευτικός, tending. – Gk. θεραπευτής, an attendant. ─ Gk. θεραπεύειν, to wait on. ─ Gk. θεραπ-, stem of θέραψ, an assistant; cf. θεράπ-ων, a servant. From √DHER, to maintain, support; cf. Skt. *dhṛ*, to maintain, bear, *dharitrī*, a supporter.

There, in that place. (E.) M. E. *ther*, *thar*. A. S. ðǣr. The suffix -*r* seems to be due to a locatival formation like that in Skt. *upa-ri*, Gk. ὑπέ-ρ. The base is Teut. base THA; see **That.**+Du. *daar*, Icel. *þar*, Dan. Swed. *der*, Goth. *thar*, G. *da*. Compare **Here, Where.** Hence *there-*, in *there-by*, *there-in*, *there-of*, &c. Cf. G. *dar-* in *dar-in*, *dar-an*.

Thermometer, an instrument for measuring the temperature. (Gk.) From Gk. θερμό-s, warm (allied to L. *formus*, warm, Skt. *gharma-* heat); and μέτρον, a measurer; see **Metre.**

Thesaurus. (L. ─ Gk.) See **Treasure.**

These. (E.) M. E. *thise*, *these*, *theos*; a new pl. of *this*. The old pl. (A. S. *þās*) is the mod. E. *those*. See **Those.**

Thesis. (L. ─ Gk.) L. *thesis.* ─ Gk. θέσις, a thing laid down, a proposition. ─ Gk. base θε- ; cf. τίθημι, I place. **Der.** *apo-thesis, para-thesis, pros-thesis, pro-thesis*, all rare words, with prefixes ἀπό, παρά, πρός, πρό respectively; also *anti-thesis, hypo-thesis, meta-thesis, par-en-the-sis, syn-thesis*, which see.

Theurgy, supernatural agency. (L. ─ Gk.) L. *theurgia.* ─ Gk. θεουργία, divine work, magic. ─ Gk. θεό-s, a god; ἔργ-ον, a work, cognate with E. **Work.**

Thews, pl. sb., sinews; (formerly) manners. (E.) *Thews* in Shak. means sinews or strength; but M. E. *thewes* almost always means habits or manners. A. S. *þēawas*, pl. of *þēaw*, habit, custom, demeanour (orig. sense 'strength').+O. Sax. *thau*, custom; O. H. G. *dau*, *thau*, discipline. Cf. Skt. *tavas*, strong.

They. (Scand.) M. E. *thai* (gen. *thair*, dat. and acc. *thaim*, *tham*) ; chiefly in the Northern dialect. This usage is Scand., not E., as the A. S. corresponding forms were used as pl. of def. art. ─ Icel. *þeir*, nom. pl., they; *þeirra* gen. pl., their; *þeim*, dat. pl., them. So also Dan. Swed. *de*, they, *dem*, them; Dan. *deres*, Swed. *deras*, their, theirs.+A. S. *þā*, nom. pl. of def. art. ; gen. *þāra*; dat. *þām*; see **That,** § β.

Thick. (E.) M. E. *þikke*. A. S. *þicce*, thick. + O. Sax. *thikki*, Du. *dik*, Icel. *þykkr*, Dan. *tyk*, Swed. *tjok*, *tjock* ; G. *dick*.

Allied to Gael. and Irish *tiugh*, fat, thick; W. *tew*, plump, from Celtic base *tegu-*; also to **Thatch.** ¶ Not Scand.; see below.

thicket. (E.) A. S. *þiccet*, i. e. a thick set of bushes, &c.+Dan. dial. *tykke*.

Thief. (E.) Pl. *thieves*. M. E. *þeef*, pl. *þeues.* A. S. *þēof*, pl. *þēofas.* + Du. *dief*, Icel. *þjófr*, Dan. *tyv*, Swed. *tjuf*, G. *dieb*, Goth. *thiubs*. Teut. type **theuboz*, for **theufoz.* Perhaps allied to Lith. *tupėti*, to squat down (hence, to hide oneself).

Thigh. (E.) M. E. *þih*, *þeh*. O. Merc. *þēh*, A. S. *þēoh*, thigh.+Du. *dij*, Icel. *þjō*, thigh, rump, O. H. G. *dioh.* Teut. type **theuhom*, n. The orig. sense is 'thick or plump part'; allied to Lith. *tùk-ti*, to become fat, Russ. *tuch-nite*, to fatten; Russ. *tuk'*, Pol. *tuk*, sb., fat; Lith. *taukas*, sb., fat (of animals).

Thill, shaft of a cart. (E.) Also spelt *fill*; whence *fill-horse*. M. E. *þille.* A. S. *þille*, slip of wood, thin board, plank, flooring; allied to *þel*, n., a plank, as in *benc-þel*, a bench-board.+Icel. *þilja*, plank, Swed. *tilja*, a plank, floor; G. *diele*, plank, board; Du. *deel*, a plank. Teut. types **theljōn*, f., **thelom*, n. Cf. Lith. *tille*, a little plank in the floor of a boat. Cf. Skt. *tala-*, bottom, floor. (See Franck.) Doublet, *deal*, a thin board.

Thimble. (E.) M. E. *þimbil*; formed (with excrescent *b*) from A. S. *þýmel*, a thumb-stall. ─ A. S. *þūma*, thumb (with the usual change from *ū* to *ȳ*). Cf. G. *däumling*, a thumb-stall; from *daum*, thumb.

Thin. (E.) M. E. *þinne.* A. S. *þynne.* +Du. *dun*, Icel. *þunnr*, Dan. *tynd* (for **tynn*), Swed. *tunn*, G. *dünn*, O. H. G *dunni.* Cf. W. *teneu*, Gael. Irish *tana*, Russ. *tonkii*, L. *tenuis*, Gk. ταναός, Skt. *tanu-*, thin; Pers. *tunuk*, slender. Lit. 'stretched out.' (√TEN.) See **Tend** (1).

Thine, Thy. (E.) M. E. *thīn*, shortened to *thy* before a following consonant. A. S. ðīn, thy, possessive pronoun, declined as an adj. ; allied to A. S. ðū, thou.+Icel. *þinn*, Dan. Swed. *din*, G. *dein*, Goth. *theins.* **Der.** *thy-self* (=*thine self*).

Thing. (E.) A. S. *þing*, *þinc*, *þincg*, a thing, cause, orig. a discussion; cf. *þingian*, to discuss, *þingere*, a pleader.+Du. G. *ding*; Icel. *þing*, a thing, also an assembling, meeting, council (so also Dan. Swed. *ting*). Kluge compares it with Goth. *theihs*, season, time; and even with

L. *tempus*; but see *tempus* in Brugm. i.
§ 412, ii. § 132. Der. *hus-tings*, q. v.

Think. (E.) M. E. *þenken*, to think;
orig. distinct from the impers. vb. *þunchen*,
to seem, for which see **Methinks**. [But
confusion between the two was easy and
common. The pt. t. of M. E. *þenken*
should have been *thoghte*, and of M. E.
þunchen should have been *thughte*; both
were merged in the form *thoughte*, mod. E.
thought.] – A. S. *þencan*, to think, pt. t.
þôhte. A weak verb; allied to A. S. *þanc*,
a thought, also a thank. **+** Icel. *þekkja*,
Dan. *tænke*, Swed. *tänka*, G. *denken* (pt. t.
dachte); Goth. *thagkjan*, i. e. **thankjan*
(pt. t. *thâhta*). Teut. type **thankjan-*;
from **thank*, 2nd grade of root **thenk*,
Idg. **teng*; cf. O. L. *tongēre*, to think. See
Thank. Der. *be-think*, with prefix *be-* = *by*.

Third. (E.) Formerly *thrid*. M. E.
þridde, *þride*. A. S. *þridda*, third. – A. S.
þri-, for *þrēo*, three. **+** Du. *derde*, Icel. *þriði*,
Dan. *tredie*, Swed. *tredje*, G. *dritte*, Goth.
thridja, W. *trydydd*, Russ. *tretii*, Gk. τρίτος,
Skt. *tr̥tīya-*.

Thirl, to pierce; see **Thrill**.

Thirst, sb. (E.) Lit. ' dryness.' M. E.
þurst. A. S. *þurst*, *þyrst*, thirst; whence
þyrstan, vb., to thirst. **+** Du. *dorst*, Icel.
þorsti, Dan. *törst*, Swed. *törst*, G. *durst*,
Goth. *thaurstei*. β. Goth. *thaurstei* is
from the Goth. weak stem *thaurs-*, as in
-thaurs-ans, pp. of *-thairsan* (pt. t. *-thars*),
to be dry; with suffix *-tei*. The Goth.
-thairsan (Teut. **þersan-*) is cognate with
Gk. τέρσεσθαι, to become dry. Cf. Skt.
tr̥sh, to thirst; *tarsha-*, thirst. (√TERS.)
Allied to **Terrace** and **Torrid**.

Thirteen. (E.) M. E. *þrettene*. A. S.
þrēotȳne. – A. S. *þrēo*, three; *tȳn*, ten; with
pl. suffix *-e*. **+** Du. *dertien*, Icel. *þrettān*,
Dan. *tretten*, Swed. *tretton*, G. *dreizehn*.

thirty. (E.) M. E. *þritti*. A. S. *þrītig*,
þrittig. – A. S. *þrī*, also *þrēo*, three; *-tig*,
suffix denoting ' ten '; see **Ten**. **+** Du. *der-
tig*, Icel. *þrir tigir*, Dan. *tredive*, Swed.
trettio, G. *dreissig*.

This. (E.) M. E. *this*, *thes*; pl. *these*,
thuse, *thos*, &c., the forms *these* and *those*
being both used as plurals of *this*; the
plural of *that* being *tho*. Gradually *these*
became the settled pl. of *this*, whilst *those*
supplanted *tho* as pl. of *that*. – A. S. *ðes*,
ðēos, *ðis*, this; pl. *ðās*. [M. E. *tho* answers
to A. S. *ðā*, pl. of def. art.; see **That**, § β.]
β. *This* (A. S. *ðe-s*) is an emphatic form,
due to suffixing an emphatic particle to

the Teut. pronom. base THA. **+** Du. *deze*,
Icel. *þessi*, G. *dieser*.

Thistle. (E.) M. E. *þistil*. A. S. *þistel*.
+ Du. *distel*, Icel. *þistill*, Dan. *tidsel*, Swed.
tistel, G. *distel*. The *i* was once long, as
in some E. and G. dialects; cf. Somersets.
daash-l, a thistle; E. Fries. *dîssel*. Teut.
types **þistiloz*, m., **þistilā* (-).

Thither. (E.) M. E. *thider*. A. S.
ðider. Cf. Icel. *þaðra*, there; Goth.
thathrō, thence; also Skt. *tatra*, there,
thither. Formed from Teut. base THA
(Idg. TO) with a suffix which is to be
compared with L. *-tro* in *ul-tro*.

Thole (1), **Thowl**, a peg to steady an
oar. (E.) M. E. *thol*. A. S. *þol* (8th cent.).
+ Du. *dol*; Icel. *þollr*, young tree, wooden
peg, thole; Dan. *tol*; Swed. *tall*, pine-tree;
Norw. *tall*, *toll*, fir-tree, *toll*, a thole. Orig.
sense ' young tree '; hence a bit of fir-wood
for a peg. Cf. Icel. *þella*, a young pine,
þöll (gen. *þallar*), a young fir.

Thole (2), to endure. M. E. *þolien*.
A. S. *þolian*, to suffer, endure. **+** Icel. *þola*,
Dan. *taale*, Swed. *tåla*, O. H. G. *dolēn*
(whence G. *geduld*, patience), Goth. *thulan*.
Cf. L. *tollere*, *tolerare*; Gk. τλῆναι, to
suffer; Skt. *tul*, to lift. See **Tolerate**.

Thong, a strip of leather. (E.) For
thwong. M. E. *thwong*, a thong; A. S.
þwang, a thong, string, cord; also a bit.
+ Icel. *þwengr*, a thong. From **þwang*,
2nd grade of Teut. **þwengan-*, to constrain
(O. Fries. *thwinga*). See **Twinge**. Cf.
O. Fries. *thwong*, *thwang*, compulsion;
Du. *dwang*, Dan. *tvang*, Swed. *tvång*, G.
zwang, constraint.

Thorax. (L. – Gk.) L. *thōrax*. – Gk.
θώραξ, a breast-plate; also the breast, chest.
Lit. ' defender; ' cf. Skt. *dhāraka-*, a trunk
to protect clothes, from *dhr̥*, to carry,
maintain, keep. (√DHER.)

Thorn. (E.) A. S. *þorn*. **+** Du. *doorn*,
Icel. *þorn*, Dan. *tiörn*, Swed. *torn*, G.
dorn, Goth. *thaurnus*. Teut. type **þur-
nuz*, m. **+** Russ. *tern'*, the black-thorn;
Polish *tarn*, a thorn; cf. Skt. *tr̥na-*, a grass-
blade. Perhaps ' piercer '; cf. L. *terere*,
to pierce.

Thorough. (E.) Merely a by-form
of the prep. *through*, spelt *þoru* in Havelok, and *þuruh* in the Ancren Riwle. It
became an adverb, whence *thoroughly*,
adv., with added suffix. And hence, finally,
thorough, adj.

Thorp, Thorpe, a village. (E.)
A. S. *þorp*, a village. **+** Du. *dorp*, Icel. *þorp*,

Dan. Swed. *torp*, G. *dorf*; Goth. *þaurp*, a field. Teut. type **thurpo-*. Cf. Lith. *troba*, a building, house. Also Irish *treabh*, village, W. *tref*, hamlet; Idg. type **trebo-*. Brugm. i. § 553.

Those. (E.) A.S. *ðǽs*, originally the pl. of A.S. *ðes*, this. See **This**.

Thou. (E.) A.S. *ðú*, thou.+Icel. *þú*, Goth. *thu*, Dan. Swed. G. *du*; Irish and Gael. *tu*; W. *ti*; L. *tu*, Russ. *tui*; Gk. *σύ*, *τύ*; Pers. *tū*; Skt. *tvam*.

Though. (Scand.) M.E. *thogh*; [also *theigh*, A.S. *ðéah*, *ðéh*.] — Icel. *þó* (for **þauh*); cf. Dan. *dog*, Swed. *dock*.+O. Sax. *thōh*, Du. *doch*, yet, but; G. *doch*, Goth. *thauh*. Teut. type **thau-h*, in which *-h* seems to be an enclitic; cf. L. *que*, 'and.' *Thau-* is prob. from the same base as **That**. ¶ In the Du. and G. *doch*, &c., the short *o* is due to loss of emphasis.

Thought, sb. (E.) Better *thoght*. M.E. *poght*. A.S. *þôht*, *ge-þôht*, a thought, lit. thing thought of. — A.S. *þôht*, pp. of *þencan*, to think; see **Think**.+Icel. *þôtti*, *þôttr*; cf. G. *gedacht*, adj., thought of, orig. pp. of *denken*, to think.

Thousand. (E.) M.E. *þousand*. A.S. *þúsend*.+Du. *duizend*, Icel. *þúsund*, *þús-hund*, *þúshundrað*; Dan. *tusind*, Swed. *tusen*, G. *tausend*, Goth. *thusundi*. Cf. also Lith. *tukstantis*, Russ. *tuisiacha*, a thousand. ¶ Not yet explained; in Icel. *þús-hund*, the syllable *hund*=A.S. *hund*, a hundred, and is due to popular etymology, which may (however) be correct.

Thowl; see **Thole** (1).

Thrall, a slave. (Scand.) O. Northumb. *ðrǽl*, borrowed from Norse, Mk. x. 44; the *ǽ* was perhaps shortened in M.E. *þraldom*, from Icel. *þrældómr*. — Icel. *þrǽll*, a thrall, serf; Dan. *træl*, Swed. *träl*. The Icel. *þrǽll* stands for **þráhiloz*, m., and is cognate with O.H.G. *dregil*, *drigil*, a thrall, serf; lit. 'a runner,' i.e. one who runs on messages. From base of Goth. *thragjan*, A.S. *þrǽgan*, to run; allied to Gk. *τρέχειν*, to run. See **Trochee**, **Feuterer**. Der. *thral-dom*, Icel. *þrældómr*. Brugm. i. § 784.

Thrash, Thresh. (E.) *Thresh* is older; M.E. *þreshen*, for *þershen*.—A.S. *þerscan*, to thrash (strong verb). + Du. *dorschen*, Icel. *þreskja*, Dan. *tærske*, Swed. *tröska*, G. *dreschen*, Goth. *thriskan* (pt. t. *thrask*). Orig. to rattle, make a din or rattling noise; cf. Russ. *tresk-ate*, to crackle, burst, *tresk*', a crash, O. Slav. *troska*, stroke

of lightning; Lith. *treszkéti, traszkéti*, to rattle, crack. Teut. base **thresk*; Idg. root **tresk*. Prob. first used of thunder, then of the noise of the flail. Der. *thresh-old*.

Thrasonical, vain-glorious. (L. — Gk.) Coined from *Thrasōn-*, stem of *Thraso*, the name of a bragging soldier in Terence's Eunuchus. Evidently from Gk. *θρασ-ύς*, bold, spirited; allied to **Dare** (1). (√DHERS.)

Thrave, a number of sheaves of wheat. (Scand.) M.E. *þraue, þreue* (*thrave, threve*). — Icel. *þrefi*, a thrave; Dan. *trave*, a score of sheaves; Swed. *trafve*, a pile of wood; Swed. dial. *trafve*, 24 or 30 sheaves set up in shocks (F. Möller). Cf. Icel. *þref*, a loft for corn.

Thread. (E.) M.E. *þreed, þréd*. A.S. *þrǽd* (<**þrǽ-diz*), thread; lit. 'that which is twisted.'—A.S. *þráwan*, to twist.+Du. *draad*, Icel. *þráðr*, Dan. *traad*, Swed. *tråd*, thread; G. *draht*, O.H.G. *drât*, wire. Teut. type **þrǽ-diz*. See **Throw**.

Threat, sb. (E.) M.E. *þret*. A.S. *þréat*, a crowd, crush of people, also great pressure, calamity, trouble, threat. — A.S. *þréat*, 2nd grade of str. vb. *þréotan*, to afflict, vex, urge. + Goth. *us-thriutan*, to vex greatly, G. *verdriessen*, to vex; Russ. *trudite*, to make one work, urge, vex; L. *trūdere*, to push, crowd, urge. (Base TREUD.) Der. *threat-en*, vb.

Three. (E.) M.E. *þre*. A.S. *þrí* (*þrý*), *þrío* (*þréo*), three.+Du. *drie*, Icel. *þrír*, Dan. *tre*, Swed. *tre*, Goth. *threis*, G. *drei*. Cf. Irish, Gael. and W. *tri*, Russ. *tri*, L. *tres* (neut. *tri-a*), Gk. *τρεῖς* (neut. *τρί-a*), Lith. *trys*, Skt. masc. nom. pl. *trayas*; Idg. masc. nom. pl. **treyes*.

Threnody, a lament. (Gk.) Gk. *θρην-ῳδία*, a lamenting. — Gk. *θρῆν-os*, a wailing, from *θρέ-ομαι*, I cry aloud; *ῳδή*, ode; see **Drone** (1) and **Ode**.

Thresh; see **Thrash**.

Threshold, a piece of wood or stone under an entrance-door. (E.) *Thresh-old* was usually written *thresh-wold*, as if it were the piece of wood threshed or beaten by the tread of the foot; but this was due to a popular etymology (suggested by *wald*, perhaps=floor). A.S. *þerscwald*, late form of A.S. *þerscold*. — A.S. *þerscan*, to thresh; with *-old*, suffix. + Icel. *þreskölder*, threshold; from *þresk-ja*, to thresh. β. The A.S. *þerscold* is from a form **þersc-o-ðl(o)-*; cf. O.H.G. *drisc-u-*

fli. And *-ðlo-* represents Idg. *-tro-*; see Princ. of E. Etym. i. § 228 (*h*).

Thrice. (E.) For *thrīs*, contr. form of M. E. *þriës*, *þryës* (dissyllabic), where the suffix *-s* is adverbial (orig. a mark of gen. case). Earlier form *þrië.*—A. S. *þrīwa*, thrice.—A. S. *þrī*, three. See **Three.**

Thrid, a thread. (E.) Another form of *thread* (Dryden, Hind and Panther, iii. 278).

Thrift, frugality. (Scand.) M. E. *þrift*. —Icel. *þrift*, thrift; also *þrif*, the same. —Icel. weak grade *þrif-*, as in *þrif-inn*, pp. of *þrīfa*, to thrive. Cf. Dan. *trivelse*, prosperity. See **Thrive.**

Thrill, Thirl, to pierce. (E.) The old sense of *thrill* was to pierce; also spelt *thirl*, which is an older spelling. M. E. *þirlen*, *þrillen*. A. S. *þyrlian*, to pierce; shorter form of *þyrelian*, the same; lit. ' to make a hole.'—A. S. *þyrel*, *þyrel*, a hole, orig. an adj. with the sense ' pierced,' for *þyrh-il*, as shewn by the cognate M. H. G. *durchel*, pierced. Derived from A. S. *þurh*, through (with change of *u* to *y*), just as M. H. G. *durchel* is from G. *durch*, through. See **Through.**

Thrive. (Scand.) M. E. *þriuen (thriven)*, pt. t. *þrāf*, *þrof*, pp. *þriuen.*—Icel. *þrīfa* (pt. t. *þreif*, pp. *þrifinn*), to clutch, grasp, grip, seize; hence *þrīfask* (with suffixed *-sk = -sik*, self), lit. to seize for oneself, to thrive. + Dan. *trives*, Swed. *trifvas*, reflex. verb, to thrive; cf. Norw. *triva*, to seize. **Der.** *thrif-t*, q. v.

Throat, the gullet. (E.) M. E. *þrote*. A. S. *þrotu*, also *-þrote*, throat.+O. H. G. *drozza*, whence G. *drossel*, throat, throttle. Prob. allied to Du. *strot*, M Du. *stroot*, *stroote*, the throat, gullet; Ital. *strozza*, the gullet (a word of Teut. origin). We also find Swed. *strupe*, Dan. *strube*, the throat. **Der.** *throttle*, q. v.

Throb, to beat forcibly, as the heart. (E.) M. E. *þrobben*, to throb. Allied to Russ. *trepete*, palpitation, throbbing; L. *trepidus*, trembling. See **Trepidation.**

Throe, a pang. (Scand.?) M. E. *þrowe*, *thrawe*. [Cf. O. Merc. *thrauu*, ' argutiæ,' O. E. Texts; A. S. *þrēa*, a rebuke, affliction, threat, evil; which seem to have been confused with it.] Prob. from Icel. *þrā*, a throe. Cf. A. S. *þrōwian*, to suffer; O. H. G. *drōa*, burden, suffering, *druoēn*, *drōēn*, to suffer.

Throne. (F. — L. — Gk.) Formerly *trone* (Wyclif).—O. F. *trone* (F. *trône*).—

L. *thronum*, acc. of *thronus.*—Gk. θρόνος, a seat; lit. a support. (√DHER.)

Throng, a great crowd of people. (E.) M. E. *þrong*. A. S. *ge-þrang*, a throng. —A. S. *þrang*, 2nd grade of *þringan*, to crowd, press. + Du. *drang*, Icel. *þröng*, G. *drang*, a throng; cf. Dan. *trang*, Swed. *trång*, adj., narrow, close. Allied to Goth. *threihan*, to throng, Lith. *trenk-ti*, to jolt, push. **Der.** *throng*, vb.

Thropple, Thrapple, wind-pipe. (E.) *Thropple* is prob. a reduction of A. S. *þrot-bolla*, the wind-pipe; from *þrot-u*, throat, and *bolla*, prominence. See **Throttle, Throat,** and **Bowl** (2).

Throstle, the song-thrush. (E.) M. E. *þrostel.* A. S. *þrostle*, a throstle.+M.H.G. *trostel.* Teut. type **þrustlā*, fem.; Idg. type **torzdlā* ; cf. L. *turdus*, a thrush, and Icel. *þröst* (gen. *þrastar*), Swed. and Norw. *trast*, a thrush (from the 2nd grade, **þrast*, of a Teut. base **þrest*). Also, with initial *s*, Lith. *strazdas*, m., *strazda*, f., a thrush. See further under **Thrush** (1). *Throstle* has a variant *throshel* (M. E. *thrusshil*, Prompt. Parv.). Brugm. i. §§ 818 (2), 882.

Throttle, the wind-pipe. (E.) Dimin. of *throat*; cf. G. *drossel*, throat. **Der.** *throttle*, vb., to press on the wind-pipe; M. E. *throtlen.*

Through, prep. (E.) M. E. *þurh.* A. S. *þurh*, O. Northumb. *þerh*.+Du. *door*, G. *durch*, O. H. G. *duruh*; Teut. type **þurh*; allied to Goth. *thairh*, through (Teut. type **þerh*). β. The Goth. *thairh*, through, is allied to *thairkō*, a hole; from Teut. base **þerk* = Idg. base **terg*, an extension of √TER, as in L. *ter-ere*, to bore. Cf. Gk. τρώγλη, a hole. Brugm. i. § 527. **Der.** *thrill.*

Throw, to cast, hurl. (E.) M. E. *þrowen*, pt. t. *þrew*, pp. *þrowen.* A. S. *þrāwan*, to twist, hurl, whirl; pt. t. *þrēow*, pp. *þrāwen.* [The orig. sense, to twist, is preserved in *thread.*] Allied to Du. *draaijen*, to twist, whirl; O. H. G. *drāen*, G. *drehen*, to turn; all from Teut. base **þrē* = Idg. base **trē*, as in Gk. τρητός, bored through, τρῆμα, a hole. The grade **ter* appears in L. *terere*, to bore, Gk. τείρειν (for **τέργειν*), to bore. (√TER.)

Thrum (1), the tufted end of a weaver's thread. (E.) M. E. *þrum*, not found in A. S. + Icel. *þrömr* (gen. *þramar*), the edge, verge, brim of a thing (hence the edge of a web); Norw. *tröm, tram, trumm*, edge, brim; Swed. dial. *trumm, trömm*, a stump, the end of a log; M. Du. *drom*, thread on a weaver's shuttle; G. *trumm*, end of threads, thrum. Teut. base **þru*, weak grade of **þer* = Idg. **ter*. Hence it is allied to Gk. τέρμα, end, L. *terminus*; see **Term.**

Thrum (2), to play noisily. (Scand.) Icel. *þruma*, to rattle, thunder; Swed. *trumma*, to beat, drum; cf. Dan. *tromme*, a drum. See **Drum, Strum.**

Thrush (1), a bird. (E.) M. E. *þrusch.* A. S. *þrysce*, a thrush; Teut. type **thruskjōn*,f. Cf. O.H.G. *drosca* or *drōsca*, a thrush; whence G. *drossel.* Allied to **Throstle,** q. v.

Thrush (2), a disease marked by small ulcerations in the mouth. (E.) In Phillips (1706). (Not related to A. S. *þyrre*, dry.) Probably of Norse origin; from O. Norse **þruskr*; whence M. Dan. *torsk*, Dan. *trōske*, Swed. *torsk*, Norw. *trausk*, *trōsk*, the thrush on the tongue. And prob. the same as Norw. *trausk*, variant of *frosk*, a frog, also the thrush. In like manner, both Gk. βάτραχος and L. *rāna* meant (1) frog, (2) disease of the tongue.

Thrust, vb. (Scand.) M. E. *þrusten*, *þristen.* — Icel. *þrýsta*, to thrust, press, compel. Allied to **Threaten,** and to L. *trūdere*, to thrust.

Thud, a dull sound of a blow. (E.) Used by G. Douglas and Burns. A. S. *þyddan*, to strike. Cf. L. *tundere.*

Thug, an assassin. (Hindustani.) Hind. *thag, thug* (with cerebral *th*), a cheat, knave, a robber who strangles travellers; Marāthi *thak, thag*, a thug (H. H. Wilson).

Thumb. (E.) M. E. *þombe*; with excrescent *b.* A. S. *þūma*, the thumb. + Du. *duim*, Swed. *tumme*, G. *daumen*; also Icel. *þumall*, the thumb of a glove, Dan. *tommel-finger*, thumb. Lit. 'the *thick* finger;' from √TEU, to grow large. See **Tumid. Der.** *thimble.*

Thummim, perfection. (Heb.) *Urim and thummim* = light and perfection; though the forms are, strictly, plural. — Heb. *tummīm*, pl. of *tōm*, perfection, truth. — Heb. root *tāmam*, to be perfect.

Thump, vb. (E.) Allied to Icel. *dumpa*, to thump, Swed. dial. *dompa*, to thump, *dumpa*, to make a noise.

Thunder, sb. (E.) For *thuner*; the *d* is excrescent. M. E. *þoner.* A. S. *þunor.* — A. S. *þunian*, to rattle, thunder; cf. *ge-þun*, a loud noise.+Du. *donder*; Icel. *þōrr* (for *þonr*), Thor, god of thunder; G.

donner; L. *tonāre*, to thunder, Skt. *tan*, to sound. β. We further find A. S. *tonian*, to thunder, prob. from L.; but compare Skt. *stan*, to sound, thunder, sigh, *stanita-*, thunder, and E. *stun.* (√STEN.) See **Stun.**

Thurible, a censer. (L. — Gk.) English from L. *thūribulum, tūribulum*, a vessel for holding incense. — L. *thūri-, tūri-*, decl. stem of *thūs, tūs*, frankincense; with suffix *-bulum* (as in *fundi-bulum*, from *fundere*). L. *thūs* is borrowed from Gk. θύος, incense. — Gk. θύ-ειν, to burn a sacrifice. Allied to **Fume.** (√DHEU.) See **Thyme.**

Thursday. (Scand.) M. E. *þurs-day, þors-day.* A. S. *þures dæg*, Thursday. — A. S. *þures*, gen. of *þūr*, Thor; *dæg*, day. Borrowed from Icel. *þōrsdagr*, Thursday; from *þōrs*, gen. of *þōrr*, Thor, and *dagr*, a day; cf. Swed. Dan. *Torsdag.* So also A. S. *þunresdæg* (the native word); Du. *Donderdag*, G. *Donnerstag.* All translations of L. *diēs Iouis.* (See Sweet, Hist. E. Sounds, § 578.)

Thus. (E.) M. E. *thus.* A. S. *ðus.* + O. Fries. and O. Sax. *thus*; Du. *dus.* Allied to **That**; and perhaps to **This.**

Thwack, Whack, to beat. (E.) Prob. imitative. Compare Icel. *þjökka*, to thwack, thump; also *þjaka*, the same; prov. G. *wackeln*, to cudgel.

Thwaite, a clearing. (Scand.) Common in place-names. Icel. *þveit*, a paddock, orig. a clearing in woods, a cutting. — Icel. **þveit*, 2nd grade of **þvīta*, not found, but = A. S. *þwītan*, to cut. See **Thwite.** Cf. Norw. *tveit*, a cutting, also a clearing; Dan. dial. *tved.*

Thwart, transversely, transverse. (Scand.) Properly an adv.; afterwards an adj.; lastly, a verb. M. E. *thwert*, *thwart*, across. — Icel. *þvert*, neut. of *þverr*, adj., perverse, adverse. Used adverbially in phrases such as *um þvert*, across, *athwart*, *taka þvert*, to take athwart, to deny flatly. β. The Icel. *þverr*, adj., is cognate with A. S. *þweorh*, perverse, transverse, Dan. *tvær*, transverse (whence *tvært*, adv., across), Swed. *twär*, across (whence *twärt*, adv., rudely), Du. *dwar(s)*; Goth. *thwairhs*, angry; G. *zwerch*, adv., across, awry. From Teut. base **þwerh*, Idg. root **twerk*; cf. L. *torquēre*, to twist; Skt. *tarku-*, a spindle. Brugm. i. § 593 (3). Allied to **Twirl.**

Thwite, to cut. (E.) Obsolete. A. S. *þwītan*, pt. t. *þwāt*, pp. *þwiten*, to cut. **Der.** *thwaite, whittle*, q. v.

Thy; see Thine.

Thyme, a plant. (F.—L.—Gk.) The *th* is pronounced as *t*, because borrowed from French. M. E. *tyme*.—M. F. *thym*, 'the herb time;' Cot.—L. *thymum*, acc. of *thymus*.—Gk. θύμος, θύμον, thyme, from its sweet smell. Cf. Gk. θύος, incense; see Thurible. (√DHEU.)

TI-TY.

Tiara, a wreathed ornament for the head. (L.—Gk.—Pers.) L. *tiāra*.—Gk. τιάρα, τιάρας, a Persian head-dress. Doubtless of Pers. origin.

Tibert, a cat. (F.—Teut.) See Nares. O. F. *Thibaut*, Theobald.—O. Sax. *Thiodbald*; O. H. G. *Dietbald*.—O. Sax. *thiod*, O. H. G. *diet*, *diot*, people (see Dutch); *bald*, bold.

Tibia, the large bone of the leg. (L.) L. *tībia*, shin-bone.

Tic, a twitching of the muscles. (F.—Teut.) F. *tic*, a twitching; *tic douloureux*, painful twitching, a nervous disease. Formerly F. *ticq*, *tiquet*, a disease suddenly seizing a horse (Cot.). Cf. Ital. *ticchio*, a vicious habit, caprice. Most likely allied to Low G. *tukken*, to twitch; G. *zucken* (M. H. G. *zucken*, *zücken*), to twitch, shrug; with which cf. *zug*, a draught, *ziehen*, to draw (Scheler). See Touch.

Tick (1), a small insect infesting dogs, sheep, &c. (E.) M. E. *tyke*, *teke*; cf. A.S. *ticia* (Sweet, O. E. T.). [The F. *tique* is borrowed from Teutonic.] + M. Du. *teke*, Du. *teek*, Low G. *teke*, *täke*, G. *zecke* (whence Ital. *zecca*). Cf. Lith. *dygus*, sharp, *dėgti*, to sting (Franck).

Tick (2), cover of a feather bed. (L.—Gk.) M. E. *teke*, 14th cent.—L. *tēca*, *thēca*, a case (whence F. *taie*).—Gk. θήκη, a case to put a thing in.—Gk. θη-, base of τίθημι, I put, put away.

Tick (3), to beat as a watch. (E.) An imitative word, like *click*; perhaps suggested by Tick (4). Cf. G. *ticktack*, pit-a-pat; E. Fries. *tik-tak*, the ticking of a clock.

Tick (4), to touch lightly. (E.) M. E. *teck*, a light touch; whence the game called *tick* or *tig*, in which children try to touch each other. Not in A.S. E. Fries. *tikken*, to touch lightly. + Du. *tik*, a touch, pat, tick, *tikken*, to tick, pat; Low G. *tikk*, a light touch; Norw. *tikka*, to touch lightly.

Tick (5), credit. (F.—G.) Short for

ticket; Nares shews that to take things on credit was 'to take on *ticket*.' See below.

Ticket, a bill stuck up, a label. (F.—G.) M. F. *etiquet*, 'a little bill, note, or ticket, esp. such as is *stuck up* on the gate of a court;' Cot. O. F. *estiquet*, *estiquete* (Godefroy).—G. *stecken*, to stick, stick up, fix; see Stick. And see Etiquette.

Tickle. (E.) M. E. *ticklen*; frequentative form from the base *tik-*, to touch lightly; see Tick (4). It means 'to keep on touching lightly.' Hence also M. E. *tikel*, unstable, ticklish, easily moved by a touch; mod. E. *ticklish*, unstable. ¶ Not necessarily a variant of Icel. *kitla*, to tickle; but a parallel formation.

Tide. (E.) M. E. *tide*. A. S. *tīd*, time, hour, season. + Du. *tijd*, Icel. *tīð*, Dan. Swed. *tid*, G. *zeit*. Teut. type *tī-di-*. Allied to Time. Der. *tide-waiter*, an officer who *waits* for arrival of vessels with the *tide*, to secure payment of duties.

tidings. (Scand.) M. E. *tidinde*, also *tidinge*; afterwards *tidings*. Orig. 'things that happen;' cf. A. S. *tīdung*, tidings; *tīdan*, to happen. But rather from Icel. *tīðindi*, neut. pl., tidings, news, Dan. *tidende*, tidings; cf. Du. *tijding*, G. *zeitung*. All from the sb. above.

tidy, seasonable, neat. (E.) M. E. *tidy*, seasonable, from M. E. *tid* or *tide*, time; see Tide. + Du. *tijdig*, Dan. Swed. *tidig*, G. *zeitig*, timely.

Tie, vb. (E.) M. E. *tien*, *tiȝen*, *teyen*, to tie; A. S. *tīegan*, *ge-tīgan*; an unoriginal verb, from A. S. *tēag*, a bond, chain, rope.—A. S. *tēah*, Teut. type **tauh*, 2nd grade of **teuhan-*, to pull, draw; see Tow, Tug. Cf. Icel. *taug*, a tie, *tygill*, a string.

Tier, a rank, row. (F.—Late L.) Formerly *tire*, a better spelling; Florio explains Ital. *tiro* by 'a *tyre* of ordinance.'—F. *tire*, 'a draught, pull, . . also a *tire*; a stroke, hit, reach, gate, course, or continuance of course;' Cot. [Cf. Span. *tiro*, a set of mules; Ital. *tiro*, 'a shoot, shot, tire, reach, . . a stones caste, a *tyre* of ordinance;' Florio (1598).]—F. *tirer*, to draw, drag, pull, &c.—Late L. *tirāre*, to draw, pull, extend, hurl; whence also Ital. *tirare*, Span. Port. Prov. *tirar*. Of unknown origin. ¶ The A. S. *tīer*, occurring but once, is an obscure and doubtful word, and has nothing to do with it.

Tierce, Terce. (F.—L.) It meant a third hour, a third of a pipe or cask, a third card, a third thrust (in fencing).—

O. F. *tierz, tierce*, third. **–** L. *tertius*, third. **–** L. *ter*, thrice; *trēs*, three. See **Tri-, Three**.

Tiff (1), to deck, dress out. (F. – O. Low G.) M. E. *tiffen*. **–** M. F. *tiffer, tifer* (more commonly *attiffer*), 'to deck, trim, adorn;' Cotg. **–** Du. *tippen*, to cut, clip, cut off the *tip* of the hair; Low G. *tippen*, to touch lightly. See **Tip** (1).

Tiff (2), a pet, fit of ill-humour; also liquor, drink. (Scand.) Orig. ' a sniff;' hence (1) a pet, (2) a sip or draught of beer. **–** Norweg. *tev*, a drawing in of the breath, sniff, *teva*, to sniff; Swed. dial. *täv*, smell, taste; Icel. *þefa*, to sniff.

Tiffin, luncheon. (Scand.) Anglo-Indian; orig. Northern English *tiffin*, i. e. *tiffing*, sipping, eating and drinking out of due season. From *tiff*, a draught of beer. See above.

Tiger. (F. – L. – Gk. – Pers.) M. E. *tigre*. **–** F. *tigre*. **–** L. *tigrem*, acc. of *tigris*, a tiger. **–** Gk. τίγρις. **–** Zend *tighri-*, an arrow (hence perhaps a tiger, from its swiftness, also the river *Tigris*, from its swiftness); mod. Pers. *tīr*, an arrow, the river Tigris. **–** Zend *tighra*, sharp; allied to Skt. *tigma-*, sharp, from *tij*, to be sharp. Perhaps allied to **Stigma.**

Tight. (Scand.) For **thight*; but, as both Dan. and Norw. have *t* for *th*, it easily became *tight*. Orkney *thight*, water-tight; prov. E. *thite*, tight, close, compact; M. E. *tiȝt*, also *þiȝt, thyht*. **–** Icel. *þéttr*, tight, esp. water-tight; Norw. *tjett, tétt*, close, water-tight; Swed. dial. *tjett, titt*; Swed. *tät*, close, tight, solid, compact; Dan. *tæt*, tight, close, compact, water-tight. M. E. *tiȝt* shews the old guttural; the Icel. *þéttr* is for **þíhtr*, as shewn by Du. *dicht*, *digt*, G. *dicht*, tight, M. H. G. *(ge)dīhte*, adv., continually. Teut. type **þihtoz*, for **þenχtoz*. Allied to Lith. *tenku*, I have enough, *tankus*, close, tight.

Tike, a dog, low fellow. (Scand.) M. E. *tike*. **–** Icel. Norw. *tík* Swed. *tik*, a bitch; Dan. dial. *tiig*, a male dog.

Tile. (L.) M. E. *tile*, contracted form of A. S. *tigele*, a tile. **–** L. *tēgula*, a tile. **–** L. *tegere*, to cover. See **Tegument.**

Till (1), to cultivate. (E.) M. E. *tilien*. A. S. *tilian*, to labour, endeavour, strive after, to till land. **+** Du. *telen*, to breed, cultivate, till; G. *zielen*, to aim at, O. H. G. *zilōn*, to strive after, Bavar. *zelgen*, to till. From A. S. *til*, adj., beneficial, excellent; cf. O. H. G. *zil*, a goal, mark; Goth.

ga-tils, fit, convenient; A. S. *til*, sb., use. **Der.** *til-th*, A.S. *tilð*, a crop, cultivation; cf. Du. *teelt*, crop.

Till (2), to the time when. (Scand.) M. E. *til*; chiefly in the Northern dialect; O. Northumb. *til*, Matt. xxvi. 31. **–** Icel. *til*, Dan. *til*, Swed. *till*, prep., to. Also O. Fries. *til*, prep. Apparently allied to Icel. *tili, tíli*, aim, bent, cognate with O. H. G. *zil*, aim, mark; see **Till** (1).

Till (3), a drawer for money. (E.) The proper sense is 'drawer,' something that can be pulled out. Dryden has *tiller* in this sense, tr. of Juvenal, vi. 384. From M. E. *tillen*, to draw, draw out, also to allure; also spelt *tullen*. A.S. *tyllan*, only in the comp. *for-tyllan*, to draw aside, lead astray. Cf. **Toll** (2).

tiller, the handle of a rudder. (E.) Prov. E. *tiller*, a handle, lit. 'puller.' From M. E. *tillen*, to draw, pull (above).

Tilt (1), the covering of a cart. (E.) M. E. *teld*, later *telt*, the same. A. S. *teld*, a tent. The final *t* was due to the cognate E. Fries., Low G., and Dan. *telt*, Swed. *tält*, a tent. **+** M. Du. *telde*, Icel. *tjald*, G. *zelt*.

Tilt (2), to cause to heel over, to joust in a tourney. (E.) Orig. sense 'to totter'; hence to cause to totter, to upset, tilt over, upset an enemy in a tourney. M. E. *tilten, tulten*, to totter, be unsteady; answering to an A. S. **tyltan* (not found), regularly formed (by change from *ea* to *ie, y*) from A. S. *tealt*, adj., unsteady, unstable.**+** Icel. *tölta*, to amble; Norw. *tylta*, to walk on tiptoe; Swed. *tulta*, to waddle; G. *zelt*, an ambling pace. Cf. **Totter. Der.** *tilt*, sb.

Tilth; see **Till** (1).

Timber, wood for building. (E.) A.S. *timber*, material to build with; for **timro-* (the *b* being excrescent). **+** Icel. *timbr*, Dan. *tömmer*, Swed. *timmer*; G. *zimmer*. Cf. Goth. *timrjan*, to build. From Teut. base **tem-*, to build; cf. Gk. δέμ-ειν, to build; L. *dom-us*, a house. See **Dome.** Brugm. i. § 421 (8). (**√**DEM.)

Timbrel, a kind of tambourine. (F. – L. – Gk.) Dimin. of M. E. *timbre*, a small tambourine. **–** O. F. *timbre*, a timbrel. **–** L. *tympanum*, a drum. **–** Gk. τύμπανον, a drum. See **Tympanum.**

Time. (E.) A. S. *tíma*. **+** Icel. *tími*; Dan. *time*; Swed. *timme*. Teut. type **tī-man-*. Allied to **Tide.**

Timid, fearful. (F. – L.) F. *timide*. **–** L. *timidus*. **–** L. *timēre*, to fear.

timorous. (L.) Coined, with suffix -*ous*, from L. *timor*, fear. — L. *timēre*, to fear.

Tin. (E.) A.S. *tin.*+Du. *tin*, Icel. *tin*, Dan. *tin*, Swed. *tenn*, G. *zinn*. ¶ Distinct from L. *stannum* (F. *étain*).

Tincture. (L.) L. *tinctūra*, a dyeing. — L. *tinctus*, pp. of *tingere*, to dye. See **Tinge**.

Tind, to light or kindle. (E.) Also spelt *tine*; nearly obsolete. M.E. *tenden*. A. S. -*tendan*, to kindle. + Dan. *tænde*, Swed. *tända*, Goth. *tandjan*. Teut. type *tandjan-*, from the 2nd grade of a lost strong verb *tendan-*, making pp. t. *tand*, pp. *tundanoz*. See below.

tinder. (E.) M. E. *tinder*, more commonly *tunder*, *tondre*. A. S. *tyndre*, f., anything for kindling fires from a spark. Cf. O. H. G. *zuntira*, tinder. Teut. type *tund-ir-ōn*; from *tund*, weak grade of lost verb *tendan*, to kindle; see above.+ Icel. *tundr* (cf. *tandri*, fire); Dan. *tönder*, Swed. *tunder*; Du. *tonder*; G. *zunder*, tinder.

Tine (1), the tooth or spike of a fork or harrow. (E.) Formerly *tind*. M. E. *tind*. A. S. *tind*. + Icel. *tindr*, Swed. *tinne*, Dan. dial. *tind*, tooth of a rake; M. H. G. *zint*. Teut. type *tendoz*, m. ; allied to L. *dens* (gen. *dent-is*), a tooth ; cf. also Skt. *danta-*, a tooth. Noreen, § 144. See **Tooth**.

Tine (2), to kindle; see **Tind**.

Tine (3), to lose. (Scand.) Icel. *tȳna*, to lose. — Icel. *tjōn*, loss, damage; allied to A. S. *tēona*, harm; see **Teen**.

Tinge, to dye. (L.) L. *tingere*, pp. *tinctus*, to dye (see **Tint**).+Gk. τέγγειν, to wet, dye; O.H.G. *thunkōn*, G. *tunken*, to dip, steep (from the weak grade). (√TENG.)

Tingle. (E.) M. E. *tinglen*, a by-form of *tinklen*, to tinkle, which, again, is a frequentative form of M. E. *tinken*, to tink (see **tinker**), of which a weaker form is *ting*. 'To *ting*, tinnire; *tingil*, tinnire;' Levins (1570). Cf. E. Fries. *tingeln*. The orig. sense was to ring, then to vibrate, thrill, to feel a sense of vibration as when a bell is rung.

tinker. (E.) M. E. *tinkere*. So called because he makes a *tinking* sound, in the mending of metal pots, &c. From M. E. *tinken*, to ring or tinkle; Wyclif, 1 Cor. xiii. 1. Of imitative origin; cf. M. Du. *tinge-tangen*, to tingle, *tintelen*, to tinkle; E. Fries. *tinken*, *tingen*, *tengen*, to make a bell ring; L. *tinnīre*, to tinkle, ring, *tintinnum*, a tinkling. Cf. Tudor E. *tinkler*, a tinker (Levins).

tinkle, to jingle. (E.) Frequentative of M. E. *tinken*, to ring; see **tinker**.

Tinsel, gaudy ornament. (F. — L.) From M. F. *estincele*, a spark, a star-like ornament; for *escintele*. — L. *scintilla*, a spark. See **Scintillation**, **Stencil**.

Tint, a tinge of colour. (L.) Formerly *tinct*. Spenser has *tinct* = dyed. — L. *tinctus*, pp. of *tingere*, to dye; see **Tinge**. Or from Ital. *tinta*, a dye. — L. *tincta*, fem. of *tinctus*.

Tiny, very small. (F.—L.) Preceded, in Shakespeare, by the word *little*; as, 'a *little tiny* boy,' 'my *little tiny* thief,' 'pretty *little tiny* kickshaws;' spelt *tine* or *tyne* in ed. 1623. Prob. adapted, with loss of the first syllable, from O. F. and F. *tan-tinet*, very little; due to L. *tantillus*, ever so little.

Tip (1). (E.) Often associated with *top*, but not etymologically connected with it. M. E. *tip.*+Du. Swed. Dan. *tip*, Low G. *tipp*; cf. G. *zipfel*, a small tip. Allied to Du. and E. Fries. *tepel*, a nipple, teat, and to E. **Tap** (2). Cf. M. Du. *tipken*, a teat. Der. *tip*, vb., chiefly in pp. *tipped*, i. e. furnished with a silver top or iron spike; whence *tipped-staff*, later *tipstaff*, an officer with a tipped staff; cf. *tipple*.

Tip (2), to tilt. (E.) Generally in the phrase *tip up*, or *tip over*; a secondary form of *tap*. Cf. *tip and run*, i. e. tap and run (a game); *tip for tap*, blow for blow (Bullinger's Works, i. 283), now *tit for tat*. E. Fries. *tippen*, to tap lightly.+Low G. *tippen*; Swed. *tippa*, to tap, tip, strike gently, touch lightly. Cf. Icel. *tapsa*, to tap. See **Tap** (1).

Tippet. (L. — Gk.) M. E. *tipet*, *tepet*. A. S. *tæppet*, a carpet, tippet. — L. *tapēte*, cloth, hangings; see **Tapestry**.

Tipple, to drink habitually. (Scand.) Norweg. *tipla*, to tipple, frequentative of *tippa*, to drip from a point or tip; Swed. dial. *tippa*, to drip, from *tipp*, a tip; cf. Du. *tepel*, a nipple, teat; see **Tip** (1).

Tipsy. (E.) Lit. 'unsteady.' Formed from *tip* (2) with suffix -*sy*, as in *trick-sy*, &c.; see **Tip** (2) above.

Tirade, a strain of reproof. (F. — Ital. — Late L.) F. *tirade*, lit. 'a lengthening out.' — Ital. *tirata*, a drawing, a pulling. — Ital. *tirare*, to pull, draw, pluck; the same as F. *tirer*; see **Tier**.

Tire (1), to exhaust. (E.) M. E. *tirien, teorien.* A. S. *teorian,* (1) to be tired, (2) to tire; weak verb; see *Atire* in New E. Dict. '*Fatigatus,* atered;' Voc. 170. 30.

Tire (2), to deck. (F.) Both as sb. and vb. M. E. *tir, tyr,* sb.; which is merely M. E. *atir* with the initial *a* dropped. Thus *tire* is short for *attire,* like *peal* (of bells) for *appeal.* See **Attire.**

Tire (3), a hoop of iron that binds the fellies of wheels. (F.) '*Tire,* the ornament of womens heads, the iron band of a cart-wheel,' Phillips, ed. 1706. Prob. identical with *tire,* a woman's head-dress. *Tire* meant to deck, also to arrange, being short for *attire.* Palsgrave has: 'I *tyer* an egge, *Je accoustre* ; I *tyer* with garmentes,' &c. See **Tire** (2).

Tire (4), to tear a prey, as is done by predatory birds. (F. — Late L.) M. E. *tiren,* to tear a prey. — F. *tirer,* to pull, drag. See **Tirade.**

Tire (5), a train. (F. — Late L.) Only in Spenser, F. Q. i. 4. 35. From F. *tirer,* to draw; see **Tirade** and **Tier.**

Tiro, Tyro, a novice. (L.) L. *tīro,* a novice, recruit. ¶ The frequent spelling with *y* is absurd.

Tisic; see **Phthisis.**

Tissue. (F. — L.) F. *tissu,* 'a ribbon, fillet, or headband of woven stuffe;' Cot. Also *tissu,* masc., *tissue,* fem., woven; old pp. of *tistre* (mod. F. *tisser*), to weave. — L. *texere,* to weave. See **Text.**

Tit (1), a small horse or child. (Scand.) Icel. *tittr,* a tit, bird; Norw. *tita,* a little bird, small trout. Cf. prov. E. *titty,* small.

Tit (2), a teat. (E.) A. S. *tit, titt,* a teat; see **Teat.**

Titan, a giant. (L. — Gk.) L. *Tītān;* cf. *titio,* a firebrand. — Gk. Τιτάν, a giant; perhaps allied to τιτώ, day (Prellwitz).+ Skt. *titha-,* fire. (√TEITH, to burn.) Der. *titan-ic.*

Tit for tat, blow for blow. (Scand.) A corruption of *tip for tap,* where *tip* is a slight tap (Bullinger, Works, i. 283).

Tithe, a tenth part. (E.) M. E. *tithe,* also *tethe.* — A. S. *tēoða,* tenth; O. Merc. *-tegða;* fuller form *teogoða,* corresponding to Gk. δέκατος, tenth. See **Ten.**

Titillation, a tickling. (F. — L.) F. *titillation.* — L. acc. *titillātiōnem,* a tickling. — L. *tītillātus,* pp. of *tītillāre,* to tickle.

Titlark. (Scand. *and* E.) Lit. 'small lark;' from **Tit** (1) and **Lark.**

Title. (F. — L.) M. E. *title.* — O. F. *title* (F. *titre*). — L. *titulum,* acc. of *titulus,* a superscription on a tomb or altar. Der. *titul-ar,* from F. *titulaire,* titular.

Titmouse, a kind of small bird. (Scand. *and* E.) Not connected with *mouse;* the true pl. should be *titmouses,* but *titmice* is used, by confusion with *mice.* M. E. *titmose.* Compounded of *tit,* small (see **Tit** (1)); and A. S. *māse,* a name for several small birds, e. g. A. S. *frǣc-māse, col-māse, spic-māse,* all names of birds. + Du. *mees,* G. *meise,* a titmouse, small bird; Icel. *meisingr* (F. *mésange*). Teut. type*maisōn-,* f.; the sense of which was 'twittering'; cf. L. *maerēre* (for *maesēre,* cf. *maes-tus*), to lament, mourn (Franck).

Titter, to giggle. (E.) The same as M. E. *titeren,* to prattle; from a repetition of the syllable *ti,* which was also used to indicate laughter, as in the word *te-hee* (in Chaucer). See also *twitter* and *twaddle.* And see **Tattle.**

Tittle, a jot. (F. — L.) M. E. *titel.* — O. F. *title,* a title; M. F. *titre, tiltre,* 'a tittle, a small line drawn over an abridged word, also a title;' Cot. — L. *titulum,* acc. of *titulus,* a title. β. In late Latin *titulus* must have meant a mark over a word, as shewn by O. F. *title* (above). Wyclif has *titel* for the Vulgate *titulus* (Matt. v. 18).

Tittle-tattle, prattle; see **Tattle.**

To. (E.) M. E. *to.* A. S. *tō.* + Du. *toe,* G. *zu;* O. Irish *do,* Russ. *do,* to, up to. Cf. Gk. -δε, towards.

to- (2), prefix, to. (E.) Only in *to-day, to-gether, to-morrow, to-night, to-ward;* and in the obsolete M. E. *to-name,* nickname, and a few other words; see **To-day.**

To- (1), prefix, in twain, asunder, to pieces. (E.) Only retained in the phrase *all to-brake*=utterly broke asunder, Judges ix. 53. The M. E. phrase *al to-brake* meant wholly brake-asunder, the *al* being adverbial, and *to-brake* the pt. t. of *tobreken,* to break asunder. But about A. D. 1500, it was mistakenly written *all-to brake,* as if *all-to* meant 'altogether,' and *brake* was separate from *to;* and later writers much confused the matter, which is still often wrongly explained. The A. S. *tō-,* prefix, was very common, as in *tōbrecan,* to break asunder, *tōblāwan,* to blow asunder; cognate with O. Friesic *to-, te-;* and allied to O. H. G. *zar-,* G. *zer-,* signifying 'asunder.'

To- (2), prefix; see **To.**

Toad. (E.) M. E. *tode.* A. S. *tādige*, *tādie*, a toad. Der. *tad-pole.*

toad-eater. (E.) Formerly a companion or assistant to a mountebank, who pretended to eat toads, swallow fire, &c.; now represented by *toady.*

Toast (1), scorched bread. (F.—L.) O. F. *tostée,* a toast of bread; orig. pp. fem. — L. *tosta* (for **tors-ta*), pp. fem. of *torrēre,* to parch; see **Torrid.**

toast (2), a person whose health is drunk. (F.—L.) The reference is to the *toast* usually put in stirrup-cups, &c., in drinking healths; see the story in the Tatler, no. 24, June 4, 1709 (Todd).

Tobacco. (Span.—Hayti.) Span. *tabaco.* A word taken from the language of Hayti (Clavigero, Hist. of Mexico). Las Casas says that *tabaco* was the name of the pipe in which the Caribs smoked the plant.

Toboggan, a kind of snow-sledge. (Amer. Indian.) A Canadian perversion of an Amer. Indian *odabagan,* a sledge.

Tocher, a dowry. (Gael.) Gael. and Irish *tochar,* a dowry, assigned portion. — O. Irish *tochur,* a putting; *tochurim,* I put. — O. Irish *to-, do-,* to; *cuir-im,* I put, assign.

Tocsin, sound of an alarm-bell. (F.— Teut. *and* L.) M. F. *toquesing* (F. *tocsin*), an alarm-bell, or its sound; see Cot. Lit. 'striking of the signal-bell.' — O. F. *toqu-er,* to strike, touch (Picard *toker,* Norm. dial. *toquer,* to strike); O. F. *sing* (Norm. dial. *sin*), a bell, from Late L. *signum,* a bell, L. *signum,* a sign; see **Touch** and **Sign.**

Tod, a bush, a measure of wool, a fox. (Scand.) Icel. *toddi,* a tod of wool, bit, piece (the fox being named *tod* from his bushy tail).+E. Fries. *todde,* a bundle; Du. *todde,* a rag; G. *zotte, zote,* a tuft of hair, anything shaggy.

To-day, this day. (E.) Compounded of *to,* prep., and *day;* *to* being formerly used in the sense of 'for.' Thus A. S. *tō dæge =* for the day, to-day; *dæge* being the dat. of *dæg,* day. So also *to-night, to-morrow.*

Toddle, to walk unsteadily. (E.) The same as Lowl. Sc. *tottle,* to walk with short steps, and equivalent to E. *totter;* see **Totter.** Cf. *tottlish,* tottery, unsteady (Cent. Dict.); Bavarian *zotteln, zotten,* to toddle, walk feebly.

Toddy. (Hindustani — Pers.) Hind. *tārī, tādī,* 'vulgarly toddy, juice or sap of the palmyra-tree,' &c.; H. H. Wilson.— Hind. *tār,* a palm-tree, palmyra-tree.—

Pers. *tār,* a palm-tree yielding toddy; Skt. *tāla-.* ¶ The Hind. *r* has a peculiar [cerebral] sound, which has come to be represented by *d* in English.

Toe. (E.) A. S. *tā,* pl. *tān.* A contracted form; O. Merc. *tāhae.* + Du. *teen,* Icel. *tā,* Dan. *taa,* Swed. *tå,* G. *zehe;* O. H. G. *zēha,* a toe. Teut. type **taihōn.* (Further connexions unknown.)

Toft, a green knoll, open ground, homestead. (Scand.) M. E. *toft,* a knoll.— Icel. *topt* (pron. *toft*), also *tupt* (pron. *tuft*), *tofl, tomt* (the oldest spelling), a place to build on. Perhaps for **tumft-* <**tump-* (Noreen, §§ 83, 238), as if 'suitable place'; from **tum-,* weak grade of **tem-an-,* O. Sax. *teman,* to suit. Cf. G. *zunft,* a guild; O. H. G. *zumft;* and Goth. *ga-timan,* to suit.

Toga. (L.) L. *toga,* a mantle, lit. covering. — L. *tegere,* to cover. See **Teguments.**

Together. (E.) M. E. *togedere.*—A. S. *tō-gædre, tō-gædere.*—A. S. *tō,* to, *gador-, geador,* together; see **Gather.**

Toil (1), labour; to labour. (F. — L.) M.E. *toil,* disturbance, tumult; *toilen,* to pull about (the sense having somewhat altered). — O. F. *toillier,* M. F. *touiller,* to entangle, shuffle together, mix confusedly, trouble, &c.; see Cotgrave. Godefroy also gives the sb. *tooil, tooil, toil, toel,* a massacre, trouble, confusion, disorder. — L. *tudiculāre,* to stir up (Hatzfeld). — L. *tudicula,* a machine for bruising olives, dimin. of *tudes,* a mallet. — L. *tud-,* as in *tu-tud-ī,* pt. t. of *tundere,* to beat. ¶ *Toil* is often derived from M. Du. *tuylen,* to till or manure land, but it is impossible to explain it from this source; the M. E. usage is completely at variance with this view.

Toil (2), a net, snare. (F.—L.) F. *toile,* cloth; pl. *toiles,* toils, snares for wild beasts.—L. *tēla,* a web, thing woven; for **tex-la,* from *texere,* to weave. See **Text.**

toilet, toilette. (F.—L.) F. *toilette,* 'a toylet, the stuff which drapers lap about their cloths, a bag to put nightcloths in;' Cot.—F. *toile,* a cloth (above).

Toise, a measure, 6 ft. 4½ in. (F.—L.) F. *toise,* 'a fadome;' Cot. — L. *tensa,* sc. *brāchia,* neut. pl. of *tensus,* pp. of *tendere,* to stretch (reach). See **Tend.**

Tokay, a wine. (Hungary.) From *Tokay,* a town in Hungary, E. N. E. from Pesth.

Token. (E.) M. E. *token.* A. S. *tācen, tācn.* + Du. *teeken,* Icel. *teikn,* Dan.

tegn, Swed. *tecken*, G. *zeichen*, Goth. *taikns*. Teut. types *taiknom, n., *taikniz*, f. ; allied to **Teach**. Usually referred to an Idg. base **deig-*, by-form of **deik-*, as in Gk. δείκ-νυμι, I shew, cognate with Goth. *ga-teihan*, to point out; which is not wholly satisfactory.

Tolerate. (L.) From pp. of L. *toler-āre*, to put up with; allied to *tollere*, to lift, bear, take.+Skt. *tul*, to lift, Gk. τλῆναι, to suffer, A. S. *þolian*, to endure. (✓TEL.) β. From L. *tlātum*, supine of *tollere*, usually written *lātum*, are formed numerous derivatives, such as *ab-lat-ive*, *collat-ion*, *di-late*, *e-late*, *ob-late*, &c.

Toll (1), a tax. (E.; *or* L.—Gk.) M.E. *tol.* A. S. *toll*, tribute.+Du. *tol*, Icel. *tollr*, Dan. *told* (for *toll), Swed. *tull*, G. *zoll*. Teut. type *tulloz, m. ; which might be explained as < *tulnoz, from the weak grade *tul (with suffix -*noz*) of *tel, the root of **Tale**; with the sense 'that which is counted out or paid.' But the existence of by-forms, as A. S. *toln*, toll (whence *tolnere*, a toller), O. Sax. *tolna*, O. Fries. *tolne*, toll, O. H. G. *zollan-tuom*, as well as O. H. G. *zolonari*, M. Du. *tol-lenaer*, a toller, suggest that the forms are borrowed from Late L. *tolōnium*, for L. *telōnium* which is from Gk. τελώνιον, a toll-house (Matt. ix. 9); from Gk. τέλος, an end, a toll. Cf. F. *tonlieu*, a toll; from Late L. *tonleium*, *tolneum*, for L. *telōnium*.

Toll (2), to pull a bell, sound as a bell. (E.) The old use was 'to *toll* a bell,' i. e. to pull it; from M. E. *tollen*, to stir, draw, pull, allied to *tullen*, to entice, allure, and prob. to A. S. *fortyllan*, to allure ; see **Till** (3).

Tolu, a kind of resin. (S. America.) Said to be named from *Tolu*, a place on the N. W. coast of New Granada, now Colombia, in S. America.

Tom, pet name for Thomas. (L.—Gk. —Heb.) M. E. *Thomme.* — L. *Thōmās*. — Gk. Θωμᾶς, Thomas ; 'a twin.' Cf. Heb. *tōmīm*, pl., twins.

Tomahawk, a light war-hatchet. (W. Indian.) Algonkin *tomehagen*, Mohegan *tumnahegan*, Delaware *tamoihecan*, a war-hatchet. 'Explained by Lacombe from the Cree dialect : *otomahuk*, knock him down; *otāmahwaw*, he is knocked down ;' Cent. Dict.

Tomato, a love-apple. (Span.—Mexican.) Span. (and Port.) *tomate.* — Mexican *tomatl*, a tomato.

Tomb. (F.—L.—Gk.) F. *tombe.*—L. *tumba.*—Gk. τύμβα, a late form of τύμβος, a tomb. Allied to **Tumulus**.

Tomboy, a rude girl. (L.—Gk.—Heb.; *and* E.) From **Tom** and **Boy**.

Tome, a volume. (F.—L.—Gk.) F. *tome.*—L. acc. *tomum.* — Gk. τόμος, a section, a volume. — Gk. τομ-, 2nd grade of τεμ-, as in τέμ-νειν, to cut. Allied to **Tonsure**. (✓TEM.)

To-morrow; see **To-day**.

Tomtit, a small bird. (L.—Gk.—Heb.; *and* Scand.) From **Tom** and **Tit**.

Tomtom, a kind of drum. (Bengāli.) Bengāli *tantan*, vulgarly *tomtom*, a small drum. Prob. named from the sound.

Ton, Tun, a large barrel, great weight. (L.) M. E. *tonne*, a large barrel, hence a great weight. A. S. *tunne*, a barrel. So also Du. *ton*, Icel. Swed. *tunna*, Dan. *tönde*, tun, cask ; G. *tonne*, cask, weight ; Gael. and Irish *tunna*, W. *tynell*, tun, barrel. All from Late L. *tunna*, a cask (9th cent.). If the orig. sense was 'wine-skin,' perhaps from O. Irish *tonn*, skin.

Tone. (F.—L.—Gk.) F. *ton.*—L. acc. *tonum.*—Gk. τόνος, a thing stretched, a string, note, tone. — Gk. τον-, 2nd grade of τεν-, as in *τενγειν > τείνειν, to stretch. +Skt. *tan*, to stretch. (✓TEN.)

Tongs, sb. pl. (E.) M.E. *tonge, tange*, sing. sb. ; the pl. is due to the *two* arms of the instrument. A. S. *tange*, a pair of tongs, pincers; also *tang.*+Du. *tang*, Icel. *töng* (pl. *tangir*), Dan. *tang*, Swed. *tång*, G. *zange*. Orig. sense 'a biter' or 'nipper'; from a nasalised form of ✓DAK, to bite, as in Gk. δάκνειν. Brugm. i. § 420.

Tongue. (E.) M. E. *tunge, tonge*. A. S. *tunge.* + Icel. Swed. *tunga*, Dan. *tunge*, Du. *tong*, G. *zunge*, Goth. *tuggō* (=*tungō*). Teut. type *tungōn, f. + O. Lat. *dingua* (L. *lingua*), a tongue. Root uncertain. Allied to **Lingual**. Brugm. i. § 441.

Tonic. (Gk.) Lit. 'giving tone.' — Late Gk. τονικός, adj., from τόνος; see **Tone**.

To-night; see **To-day**.

Tonsil. (F.—L.) M. F. *tonsille* ; Cot. — L. *tonsilla*, formed from the pl. *tonsillæ*, the tonsils. 'There is one [Latin] sb. in -*li*, Lat. *tōlēs*, pl. m. "wen on the neck," for *tons-li-, from *tens-* "stretch" (Goth. *at-thinsan*, to draw towards one, Lith. *tẹs-ti*, to stretch by pulling) ; *tonsillæ*, "tonsils," points to an older form **tons-lo-* or *tons-lā ;' Brugm. ii. § 98.

Tonsure. (F.—L.) F. *tonsure.* — L.

tonsūra, a clipping. — L. *tonsus*, pp. of *tondere*, to shear, clip. Cf. Gk. τένδειν, to gnaw; see **Tome**.

Tontine, a kind of lottery. (F. — Ital.) F. *tontine*. Named from Laurence *Tonti*, a Neapolitan (about A.D. 1653).

Too. (E.) The emphatic form of *to*, prep.; used adverbially.

Tool. (E.) M. E. *tol, tool*. A. S. *tōl*, a tool. + Icel. *tōl*, neut. pl., tools. Lit. an implement for working with; Teut. type **tōlom*, n., for **tōu-lom*; where **tōu-* is related to **tau*, as in A S. *tuwian*, to prepare, dress, get ready. See **Taw**. Streitberg, § 85.

Toom, empty. (Scand.) M. E. *tom, toom*. — Icel. *tōmr*, Swed. Dan. *tom*, empty.

Toot (1), to peep, spy; see **Tout**.

Toot (2), to blow a horn. (O. Low G.) Spelt *tute* in Levins (1570). — M. Du. *tuyten*, 'to sound a cornet,' Hexham; cf. Du. *toethoren*, a toot-horn, bugle. Cf. Swed. *tjuta*, Dan. *tude*, to howl, to toot; Icel. *þjóta* (pt. t. *þaut*), to resound, blow a horn; E. Fries. and Low G. *tuten*, to toot; A. S. *þēotan*, to howl; cf. Goth. *thuthaurn*, a trumpet. Of imitative origin; but the M. Du. form may have been borrowed from Scandinavian.

Tooth. (E.) A. S. *tōð*, pl. *teð* and *tōðas*. Lengthened *o* produced loss of *n* (*tōð* < *tonth*).+Du. *tand*, Icel. *tönn*, Dan. *tand*, Swed. *tand*, G. *zahn*, O. H. G. *zand, zan*. Teut. stem **tanth-*; or (in Goth *tunthus*) **tmnth-*.+L. *dens* (stem *dent-*), Lith. *dantis*, W. *dant*, Skt. *danta-*, Gk. ὀδούς (stem ὀδόντ-). All participial forms are Idg. stem **(e)dónt-*; orig. sense 'eating'; from √ ED, to eat; see **Eat**.

Top (1), summit. (E.) M.E. *top*. A.S. *top*.+Du. *top*; Icel. *toppr*, tuft, top; Dan. *top*, tuft, crest, top; Swed. *topp*, summit; G. *zopf*, tuft, top. **Der**. *topp-le*, to be topheavy, tumble over.

Top (2), a child's toy. (F. — G.) M E. *top*. — A. F. **top*, only found in the dimin. form *topet*. 'Trocus, *topet*;' Glasgow MS. (Godefroy); cf. O. F. *topier*, to turn as a top; also *tupin*, a pipkin (Cot.). — M. H. G. *topf*, a top, pot, scull (apparently with reference to the large hollow humming-top).+Low G. *dop*, a shell; M.Du. *dop, doppe*, a top (also *top*, from H. G.), *dop*, a shell, *doppe*, a little pot; E. Fries. *dop, doppe*, a shell. Prob. allied to M. E. *doppen*, to dive, dip (a water-pot); and to E. **Dip**, **Deep**. Cf. M. Du. *toppen*, 'to

whipe a top;' Hexham. ¶ Or from M. Du. *top*, borrowed from M. H. G. *topf*.

Topaz, a gem. (F. — L. — Gk.) M. F. *topase*. — L. *topazus, topazion*. — Gk. τόπαζος, τοπάζιον, a topaz. ¶ Pliny derives it from an island called *Topazos*, in the Red Sea, the position of which is 'conjectural'; from Gk. τοπάζειν, to conjecture. This is 'conjectural' indeed.

Toper, a great drinker. (F. *or* Ital. — Teut.) Certainly allied to F. *tôper*, to cover a stake, a term in dice-playing; whence *tôpe*, interjection (short for *je tôpe*, I accept your offer) in the sense 'agreed!' Also used as a term in drinking; cf. M. Ital. *topa*, in dicing, agreed! throw! also (in drinking), I pledge you! Cf. Span. *topar*, to butt, strike, accept a bet. Of Teut. origin; from the *striking* of hands or of glasses together, as in Picard *toper*, to strike hands in bargaining, Ital. *intoppare*, to strike against an obstacle. Originally from the placing together of the tops of the thumbs, at the same time crying *topp!* See Ihre, Outzen, Brem. Wörterbuch.

Topiary. (L. — Gk.) *Topiary* work is a term applied to clipped trees and shrubs. L. *topiārius*, belonging to landscape gardening. — L. *topia*, fancy gardening. — Gk. τόπος, a place, district.

topic. (F. — L. — Gk.) M.F. *topiques*, 'topicks, books or places of logical invention.' — L. *topica*, sb. pl., title of a work by Aristotle. — Gk. τοπικά (the same), neut. pl. of τοπικός, local, relating to τόποι or common-places. — Gk. τόπος, a place.

topography. (F. — L. — Gk.) F. *topographie*. — L. *topographia*. — Gk. τοπογραφία, description of a place. — Gk. τόπο-s, a place; γράφ-ειν, to describe.

Topple; see under **Top** (1).

Topsyturvy. (E.) Formerly *topturvy, topsydturvy, topsy-tervy* (1528). [Not for *top-side-turvy*, where *top-side* = upper side; for *topsytervy* is the older form.] Just as *upside down* was formerly *upsodown*, so *topsytervy* prob. = *top so tervy*. *Tervy* is from M. E. *terven*, to roll, roll back (hence, overthrow); see my Gloss. to Chaucer; cf. M. E. *overtyrven*, to upset; A. S. *tearflian*, to turn, roll over; Low G. *tarven*, to roll or turn up a cuff. ¶ Explained *topside t'other way* by late writers, where *t'other way* is a false gloss.

Torch. (F. — L.) M. E. *torche*. — F.

torche, a torch, also a wreath, wreathed wisp or piece of tow (Low L. *tortia,* a torch), twist. **—** Late L. *tortica,* a torch; (cf. *porche* from *porticum*). **—** L. *tortus,* pp. of *torquēre,* to twist. See **Torture.**

torment. (F.**—**L.) O. F. *torment* (F. *tourment*). **—** L. *tormentum,* an engine for throwing stones, or for inflicting torture. Formed with suffix -*mentum* from *tor-,* for *torc-,* base of *torquēre,* to twist, hurl.

tormentil, a herb. (F.**—**L.) F. *tormentille* (Cot.) ; Late L. *tormentilla,* Voc. 713. 6. Said to be so called from its relieving tooth-ache. **—** O. F. *torment,* torment, pain (above).

Tornado, a hurricane. (Span. **—** L.) Dampier speaks of ' *tornadoes* or thundershowers.' For **tronada.* **—** Span. *tronada,* a thunder-storm. **—** Span. *tronar,* to thunder. **—** L. *tonāre,* to thunder.

Torpedo. (L.) L. *torpēdo,* numbness ; also a cramp-fish (which electrifies or numbs). **—** L. *torpēre,* to be numb (below).

torpid, sluggish. (L.) L. *torpidus,* benumbed. **—** L. *torpēre,* to be numb or stiff. Cf. Lith. *tirpti,* to grow stiff ; Russ. *terpnute,* to grow numb. Brugm. i. § 521.

Torque, a collar of twisted gold. (F. **—**L.) F. *torque,* in Littré. **—** L. *torquem,* acc. of *torques,* a twisted collar, a torque. **—** L. *torquēre,* to twist. See **Torture.** Cf. W. *torch,* a wreath, O. Irish *torc.*

Torrent. (F. **—** L.) F. *torrent.* **—** L. acc. *torrentem,* a raging stream ; from *torrens,* raging, impetuous, boiling, hot ; orig. pres. pt. of *torrēre,* to heat (below).

torrid. (F.**—**L.) F. *torride.* **—** L. *torridus,* scorched. **—** L. *torrēre,* to scorch. **+** Gk. τέρσεσθαι, to become dry. See **Terrace, Thirst.** (√TERS.)

Torsion. (F. **—** L.) F. *torsion,* ' a wresting ;' Cot. **—** L. acc. *torsiōnem,* a wringing. **—** L. *tors-,* as in *tors-ī,* pt. t. of *torquēre,* to twist.

Torso, trunk of a statue. (Ital.**—**L.**—** Gk.) Ital. *torso,* stump, trunk, stalk. **—** L. *thyrsus,* stalk, stem. **—** Gk. θύρσος, a stalk, rod, thyrsus.

Tort, a wrong. (F. **—** L.) F. *tort,* a wrong, harm ; pp. of *tordre,* to twist. **—** L. *tortus,* pp. of *torquēre,* to twist.

tortoise. (F. **—** L.) M. E. *tortuce, tortu* ; later, *tortoise,* with changed suffix ; cf. Prov. *tortesa,* a tortoise. The M. E. *tortu* answers to F. *tortue,* a tortoise ; Late L. *tortūca.* So named from the twisted

feet ; cf. O. F. *tortis,* crooked. All due to L. *tort-us,* pp. of *torquēre,* to twist.

tortuous. (F.**—**L.) M. E. *tortuos.* **—** F. *tortueux.* **—**L. *tortuōsus,* crooked.**—**L. *tortus,* pp. of *torquēre,* to twist (below).

torture. (F.**—**L.) F. *torture.* **—** L. *tortūra,* torture, wringing pain. **—** L. *tortus,* pp. of *torquēre,* to twist, wring, whirl. (√TERQ.)

Tory. (Irish.) First used about 1680 in the political sense. The Irish State Papers, Jan. 24, 1656, mention ' *tories* and other lawless persons.' **—** Irish *toiridhe, toruighe,* lit. a (hostile) pursuer, also a searcher (hence, a plunderer) ; cf. *toireacht,* pursuit, search, &c. **—** Irish *toirighim,* I fancy, I pursue, search closely. Cf. Gael. *toir,* pursuit, search ; O. Irish *toracht* (for **do-fo-racht*), pursuit ; where *do* (to) and *fo* (under) are prefixes, and *racht* is from √REG, as in L. *reg-ere,* to direct, Irish *rig-im,* I stretch out.

Toss, to jerk. (Scand. ?) Cf. W. *tosio,* to jerk, toss ; *tos,* a quick jerk, toss ; borrowed from E. Perhaps from Norw. *tossa,* to scatter, spread out ; cf. ' to *toss* hay ;' Dan. dial. *tusse,* to stir, move, shake. Allied to **Touse.**

Total. (F.**—**L.) F. *total.* **—** Late L. *tōtālis,* adj.; extended from L. *tōtus,* entire.

Totter, to be unsteady. (E.) Prov. E. *tolter,* a form occurring in Clare's Village Minstrel ; cf. Lowl. Sc. *tolter,* adj. and adv., unsteady (not a *verb,* as Jamieson says). *Tolter,* as a vb., is related to M. E. *tulten,* to tilt, be unsteady (see **Tilt** (2)); and is allied to A. S. *tealtrian,* to totter, from the adj. *tealt,* unsteady. **+** M. Du. *touteren* (<**tolteren*), to tremble, shake. Cf. prov. E. *totter,* a swing ; Bavar. *zeltern,* to hobble along.

Toucan, a bird. (F.**—**Brazil.) F. *toucan* ; a Brazilian word (Littré). **—** Guarani *tucá* ; whence Port. *tucano.* Granada gives Guarani *tùcà* (*ù* and *à* both nasal).

Touch. (F.**—** Teut.) F. *toucher.* [Also O. F. *toquer,* Walloon *toquer,* to knock or strike against ; Ital. *toccare,* to touch, strike, smite.] **—** Teut. **tukkōn,* represented by Low G. *tukken* = O. H. G. *zucchen,* G. *zucken,* to twitch, draw with a quick motion ; cf. M. Du. *tucken, tocken,* ' to knock head to head ; to touch ;' Hexham. A secondary verb, due to the weak grade (**tuh*) of Teut. **teuhan-,* as in Goth. *tiuhan,* A. S. *tēon* (<**tēohan*), to pull, draw, O. H. G. *ziohan* (G. *ziehen*), cognate with

L. *dūcere*, to draw, lead. (√DEUK.) See Tuck (1), Tow (1). Der. *toc-sin*, *tuck-et*.

Touchy, corruption of Tetchy, q. v.

Tough. (E.) M. E. *tough*. A. S. *tōh*, tough.+Du. *taai*, flexible, pliant, viscous, tough ; G. *zäh*, O. H. G. *zāhi*, tough, tenacious. Teut. type *tanχuz (>*tāhuz); allied to A. S. *ge-teng-e*, close to, oppressive, O. Sax. *bi-teng-i*, oppressive. The orig. sense is 'holding close together' or 'tenacious'; cf. Tongs.

Tour, a circuit. (F. – L.) Lit. 'a turn.' — F. *tour*, lit. a turn ; also 'a turner's wheel,' Cot. – L. *tornum*, acc. of *tornus*. – Gk. τόρνος, a lathe. See Turn.

Tourmaline, the name of a mineral. (F. – Cingalese.) F. *tourmaline*. Formed from the native name in Ceylon, where it was called *tōramalli*. Explained (vaguely) as 'a general name for the cornelian'; Clough, Singhalese Dict. (1830), ii. 246.

Tournament. (F. – L. – Gk.) M. E. *turnement*. – A. F. *tournement*, O. F. *tornoiement*, a tournament. – A. F. *tournier*, O. F. *tornoier*, to joust ; cf. A. F. *turney*, *torney*, O. F. *tornoi*, a tourney, joust, lit. a turning about. – O. F. *torner*, to turn ; see Turn.

tourney. (F. – L. – Gk.) A. F. *turney*, O. F. *tornoi* (above).

tourniquet. (F. – L. – Gk.) F. *tourniquet*, lit. 'that which turns about;' a name given to a stick turned round to tighten a bandage, to stop a flow of blood. – F. *tourner*, to turn (above). Cf. Picard *torniker*, to turn round.

Touse, to pull about, tear. (E.) M. E. *tūsen*, in comp. *tō-tūsen*, to pull about. [Cf. mod. E. *Towser*, a dog's name, lit. 'tearer.'] This answers to E. Fries. *tūsen*, to tear, pull, rend. + G. *zausen*, O. H. G. (*er*)*zūsan*, (*zir*)*zūsōn*, to tug, pull, drag about. Der. *tussle* ; cf. *toss*.

Tout, to solicit custom. (E.) A dialectal form of *toot*. M. E. *toten*, orig. to peep ; hence to be on the look-out for custom. A. S. *tōtian*, to project, stick out (hence, peep out) ; whence *Toothill*, *Tothill*, a look-out hill (W. *Twthill* at Carnarvon).

Tow (1), to tug along. (E.) M. E. *towen*, *toʒen*. O. Fries. *toga*, to pull, tow ; cf. A. S. *toh-line*, a tow-line, towing-rope. – A. S. *tog-*, as in *tog-en*, pp. of *tēohan*, *tēon*, to pull, draw. + E. Fries. *tagen*, Icel. *toga*, to pull ; O. H. G. *zogōn* ; all similarly formed from Teut. *tuh (>*tug),

weak grade of **teuhan-*, to draw, cognate with L. *dūcere*, to draw, lead. (√DEUK.)

Tow (2), coarse part of hemp. (E.) M. E. *tow*. A. S. *tow-*, occurring in *tow-līc weorc*, material for spinning, lit. 'tow-like stuff,' and in *tow-hūs*, a tow-house, house for spinning. Orig. the *operation*, not the *material*; cf. A. S. *getawa*, implements. Allied to A. S. *tawian*, to prepare, work ; see Taw and Tool. + M. Du. *touw*, tow, *touwen*, to tan leather, *touwe*, a weaver's implement ; Icel. *tō*, a tuft of wool for spinning.

Toward, Towards. (E.) M. E. *towardes*, formed by adding *-es* (genitive suffix used adverbially) to M. E. *toward*. The A. S. *tōweard* is usually an adj., with the sense 'future, about to come ;' *tōweardes* was a prep., usually put after its case. – A. S. *tō*, to ; *-weard*, in the direction of, cognate with Icel. *-verðr*, M. H. G. *-wert*, Goth. *-wairths*, and allied to L. *uersus*, towards. β. All these suffixes are derivatives of the verb appearing in E. as *worth*, to become ; see Worth (2). The same suffix appears in *afterward*, *inward*, &c. ; the lit. sense is 'that which has become' or 'that which is made to be,' or 'that which is turned'; hence *inward* = turned in, *to-ward*, turned to, &c.

Towel. (F. – O. H. G.) M. E. *towaille*. – F. *touaille*, 'a towel ;' Cot. O. F. *toaille* (Low L. *toacula*, Span. *toalla*, Ital. *tovaglia*). – O. H. G. *twahila*, *dwahila* (G. *zwehle*), a towel. – O. H. G. *twahan*, to wash.+A. S. *þwēan* (<*þwahan), O. Sax. *thwahan*, Icel. *þvā*, Swed. *två*, Dan. *toe*, Goth. *thwahan*, to wash. Cf. A. S. *þwēle*, a towel (Sweet, O. E. T.) ; *þwēal*, a bath ; from *þwēan*.

Tower. (F. – L. – Gk.) O. F. *tur*, *tour*. – L. *turrem*, acc. of *turris*, a tower. – Gk. τύρσις, τύρρις, a tower, bastion ; cf. Gael. *torr*, conical hill, tower, castle. ¶ A. S. *torr* is from L. *turris* ; and late A. S. *tur* from O. F. *tur*.

Town. (E.) M. E. *toun*, an enclosure, town. A. S. *tūn*, a fence, farm, town.+ Du. *tuin*, fence, Icel. *tūn*, enclosure, homestead, O. H. G. *zūn*, hedge ; Irish and Gael. *dūn*, a fortress, W. *dīn*, a hill-fort. Lit. 'fastness;' cf. Gk. δύ-ναμις, strength, Irish *dūr*, L. *dūrus*, firm. Brugm. i. § 112, ii. § 66.

Toxicology, the science which investigates poisons. (Gk.) From Gk. τοξικό-ν, poison for arrows (from τόξον, a bow);

-λογία, from λέγειν, to discourse. **β.** Τόξον may be from √TEKS, to hew, shape; see **Technical.** But cf. L. *taxus*, yew-tree.

Toy, sb. (Du.) Du. *tuig*, tools, utensils, implements, stuff, refuse, trash; whence *speel-tuig*, playthings, toys, lit. 'stuff to play with.' M. Du. *tuyg*, 'silver chains with a knife, cizzars, pincushion, &c. as women wear,' Sewel. **+** Icel. *tygi*, gear, Dan. *töi*, gear, *legi-töi*, a plaything, toy, Swed. *tyg*, gear, trash, G. *zeug*, stuff, trash, G. *spielzeug*, playthings. **β.** The orig. sense was stuff, material, gear; and G. *zeug* is connected with G. *zeugen*, to beget, to produce, and even to witness. So also Du. *tuig* is connected with Du.*tuigen*, to equip, to witness, E. Fries. *tügen*, to produce, prepare, equip, O. Fries. *tiuga*, *tioga*, to witness, M. H. G. *ziugen*, to produce, equip, witness; all weak verbs, due to the strong Teut. verb *teuhan-* (Goth. *tiuhan*, A. S. *téon*, O. H. G. *ziohan*, G. *ziehen*), cognate with L. *dücere*, to lead. (√ DEUK.) ¶ As to the sound, cf. *hoy*=Flemish *hui*. See **Tow** (1), **Team.**

Trace (1), a track, foot-print. (F.–L.) F. *trace*, 'trace, path, tract;' Cot. A verbal sb. from M. F.*tracer*, to trace, follow, also spelt *trasser*, to trace out, delineate. The same as Ital. *tracciare*, Span. *trazar*, to trace out, plan, sketch. These answer to a Late L. *tractiāre*, formed from *tractus*, pp. of *trahere*, to draw, drag.

trace (2), one of the straps by which a vehicle is drawn. (F.–L.) M. E. *traice*, *trace*, which Palsgrave explains by O. F. *trays*; this is a plural form = mod. F. *traits*, pl. of *trait*. – O. F. *trays*, later *traits*, *traicts*, pl. of *traict*, explained by Cotgrave as 'a teame-trace or trait.' Thus *trace* = *traits*, pl. of *trait*; see **Trait.**

Trachea, wind-pipe. (L.–Gk.) L. *trāchēa*. – Gk. τραχεία, lit. 'the rough,' from the rings of gristle round it; fem. of τραχύς, rough. Allied to τέ-τρηχ-α, pt. t. of θρίσσειν, ταράσσειν, to disturb.

Track, a course. (F.–Teut.) From F. *trac*, 'a track, beaten way;' Cot. Norm. dial. *trac*. – Du. *trek*, a draught; *trekken*, to draw, pull, tow, travel, march, &c. Allied to Low G. and E. Fries. *trekken*, O. Fries. *trekka*, and O. H. G. strong verb *trehhan*, to scrape, shove, draw; see Franck. Scheler regards F. *trac* as due to F. *tracer*, to trace; see **Trace** (1); but N. Fries. has *tracke* for Du. *trekken*.

Tract (1), a continued duration, a

region. (L.) L. *tractus*, a drawing out, course, region. – L. *tractus*, pp. of *trahere*, to draw.

tract (2), a short treatise. (L.) Short for *tractate*, now little used. – L. *tractātus*, a tractate, treatise, tract. – L. *tractātus*, pp. of *tractāre*, to handle; see **Treat.**

tractable. (L.) L. *tractābilis*, manageable. – L. *tractāre*, to handle, frequent. of *trahere* pp. *tractus*), to draw.

traction, a drawing along. (F.–L.) M. F. *traction*. – Late L. acc. *tractiōnem*, acc. of *tractio*. – L. *tract-us*, pp. of *trahere* (above).

Trade. (E.) The old sense was 'path'; hence a beaten track, regular business. Cf. M. E. *trede*, a tread, a step; from A. S. *tredan*, to tread; see **Tread.** Cf. A. S. *trod*, a track, from the weak grade of *tredan*. But the right form occurs in Low G. *trade*, Swed. dial. *trad*, a beaten path, track; from the 2nd grade of the verb. **Der.** *trade-wind*, a wind that keeps a beaten track, or blows always in the same direction.

Tradition. (L.) From acc. of L. *trāditio*, a surrender, a tradition (Col. ii. 8). – L. *trāditus*, pp. of *trādere*, to deliver. – L. *trā-*, for *trans*, across; *-dere*, for *dare*, to give. See **Trans-, Date.**

Traduce, to defame. (L.) L. *trādūcere*, to lead over, transport, also, to defame. Here *trā-* = *trans*, across; and *dūcere* is 'to lead.' See **Trans-** and **Duke.**

Traffic, vb. (F.–Ital.) F. *trafiquer*, 'to traffick;' Cot. – Ital. *trafficare*; cf. Span. *trafagar*, Port. *traficar*, *trafeguear*, to traffic. **β.** Origin unknown. It is proposed to derive the Ital. word from *traffik*, a late Hebrew form of Gk. τροπαϊκός, the Gk. rendering of L. *uictōriātus*, a silver coin bearing the image of Victory (Athen., Apr. 7, 1900).

Tragedy. (F.–L.–Gk.) O. F. *tragedie*. – L. *tragœdia*. – Gk. τραγῳδία, a tragedy; lit. 'a goat-song;' prob. because the actors were clad in goat-skins to resemble satyrs. – Gk. τραγῳδός, a tragic singer; lit. 'goat-singer.'–Gk. τράγ-ος, a he-goat; ᾠδός, a singer, contracted from ἀοιδός; see **Ode. Der.** *trag-ic*, F. *tragique*, L. *tragicus*, Gk. τραγικός, lit. 'goatish.'

Trail, vb. (F.–L.) M. E. *trailen*, to draw along, answering to A. F. *trailer*, to trail, occurring in *trailebaston* (below).

— O. F. *trailler*, to tow a boat; allied to F. *traille*, a ferry-boat with a cord. — L. *trāgula*, a drag-net, sledge, *traha*, a sledge; from *trahere*, to draw. Cf. Gascon *trailho*, a track; Port. *tralha*, a net; Span. *tralla*, a cord. ¶ M. Du. *treylen*, to draw along, is merely borrowed from F. *trailler*, 'to traile a deer, or hunt him upon a cold sent, to reel, or wind yarn,' Cot.; or else from E. *trail* (see Franck). [The A. S. *trǣglian* is a very scarce word, in a gloss, and means 'to pluck.']

trailbaston, a law term. (F.—L.) Anglo-F. *traylebastoun*, a term applied to certain lawless men. It meant 'trail-stick' or 'stick-carryer.' Fully explained in Wright's Polit. Songs, p. 383; but constantly misinterpreted. The *justices of traylbaston* were appointed by Edw. I to try them. From *trail*, vb. (above); and O. F. *baston*, a stick. See **Baton**.

train, sb. and vb. (F.—L.) M. E. *train*, sb., *trainen*, vb. — M.F. *train*, a great man's retinue; *traine*, a sledge; *trainer*, to trail along (Cot.). — Late L. *tragināre*, to drag along (Schwan). — L. *trahere*, to draw. Der. *train'd-band*, corruption of *train'd-band*.

Train-oil. (Du.; *and* F.—L.—Gk.) For *oil*, see **Oil**. Formerly *trane-oyle* or *trane*. — M. Du. *traen*, 'trayne-oyle made of the fat of whales; also a tear, liquor pressed out by the fire;' Hexham. The orig. sense is 'tear'; then drops forced out in boiling blubber, &c. Mod. Du. *traan*, a tear; cf. G. *thräne*. The G. *thräne* is really a pl. form = M. H. G. *trehene*, pl. of *trahen*, O. H. G. *trahan*, a tear; cf. O. Sax. *trahni*, pl., tears; E. Fries. *trān*, tear-drops. We also find M. H. G. *treher*, pl., tears, which may be connected with O. Northumb. *tæher*, a tear, and A. S. *tēar*, a tear. Similarly, Du. *traan* may be allied to Dan. *taar*, a tear, and to E. *tear*.

Trait, a feature. (F.—L.) F. *trait*, a line, stroke; Cot. — F. *trait*, pp. of *traire*, to draw. — L. *trahere*, to draw.

Traitor, one who betrays. (F.—L.) O. F. *traitor*, oblique case from nom. *traitre*. — L. *trāditōrem*, acc. of *trāditor*, one who betrays. — L. *trādere*, to betray; see **Tradition**.

Trajectory, the curve which a projectile describes. (F.—L.) Suggested by M.F. *trajectoire*, 'casting;' Cot. Formed as if from L. **trāiectōrius*, belonging to projection. — L. *trāiectus*, pp. of *trāicere*

(= **trā-jicere*), to throw across, fling. — L. *trā-*, for *trans*, across; *iacere*, to cast. Der. *traject* (M. F. *traject*, a ferry), the right reading for *tranect*, Merch. Ven. iii. 4. 53.

Tram, a coal-waggon, car on rails. (Scand.) We find 'sledge or *tram*' in the Complete Collier, 1708; p. 39; we even find *tram* in a will dated 1555 (Surtees Soc. Public. xxxviii. 37). The same as Lowl. Sc. *tram*, shaft of a cart, beam, bar, prov. E. *tram*, a milk-bench (orig. a log of wood). The *tram-road* was prob. at first a log-road, then a rail-road on sleepers. — Norw. *tram*, door-step (of wood); *traam*, a frame; cf. Swed. dial. *tromm*, log, stock of a tree, also a summer-sledge; M. Swed. *trām*, *trum*, piece of a cut tree. Orig. sense a beam, shaft, bar, log; then a shaft of a cart, a sledge; cf. E. Fries. *trame*, *trime*, step of a ladder, handle of a barrow; Low G. *traam*, a beam, handle of a wheel-barrow; O. H. G. *drām*, *trām*, M. Du. *drom*, a beam, O. Icel. *þram* (in *þram-valr*). ¶ The 'derivation' from *Outram* (about 1800) is ridiculous; it ignores the accent, and contradicts the history.

Trammel. (F.—L.) M. E. *tramaile*. — M. F. *tramail*, 'a tramell, or a net for partridges;' Cot. (Mod. F. *trémail*, Littré; Gascon *tramail*; Ital. *tramaglio*.) Late L. *tremac(u)lum*, a kind of net (Lex Salica). Prob. from L. *tri-*, threefold, and *macula*, a mesh, net (Diez). ¶ The Span. form *trasmallo* is corrupt.

Tramontane, foreign to Italy. (F.—Ital.—L.) M. F. *tramontain*. — Ital. *tramontano*, living beyond the mountains. — L. *trā-*, for *trans*, beyond; *mont-*, stem of *mons*, mountain.

Tramp, vb. (E.) M. E. *trampen*; not in A. S.; E. Fries. *trampen*.+Low G. and G. *trampen*, Dan. *trampe*, Swed. *trampa*, to tramp, tread; cf. Goth. *ana-trimpan* (pt. t. *ana-tramp*), to tread on. Nasalised form of base TRAP; see **Trap** (1).

trample. (E.) M. E. *trampelen*, frequent. of M. E. *trampen* (above); E. Fries. *trampeln*.+G. *trampeln*.

Tram-way; see **Tram**.

Trance. (F.—L.) F. *transe*, 'a trance, or swoon;' Cot. Lit. a passing away (from consciousness). — O. F. *transir*, to depart, die. — L. *transīre*, to pass away; see **Transit**.

Tranquil. (F.—L.) F. *tranquille*, calm. — L. *tranquillus*, at rest.

Trans-, prefix. (L.) L. *trans*, beyond, across, over. Orig. pres. pt. of a verb **trāre* (whence *in-trāre*), to pass over; cf. Skt. *tara-*, a crossing over. ¶ It occurs as *trans-*, *tran-*, and *trā-*. Brugm. ii. § 579.

Transact, to perform. (L.) From L. *transactus*, pp. of *transigere*, to complete. – L. *trans*, beyond, fully; *agere*, to do. See **Agent.**

Transalpine. (L.) From L. *transalpīnus*, beyond the Alps; see **Alp.**

Transcend. (L.) L. *transcendere*, to climb over, to surpass. – L. *tran-*, for *trans*, beyond; *scandere*, to climb.

Transcribe. (L.) L. *transcrībere*, to copy out from one book into another. – L. *tran-*, for *trans*, across, over; *scrībere*, to write. Der. *transcript*, from neut. of pp. *tran-scriptus*; also *transcript-ion*.

Transept. (L.) Lit. cross-enclosure. – L. *tran-*, for *trans*, across; *septum*, enclosure, orig. neut. of pp. of *sēpīre*, *sæpīre*, to enclose, from *sæpēs*, a hedge.

Transfer. (F. – L.) F. *transférer*. – L. *trans-ferre*, to convey across. – L. *trans*, across; *ferre*, to bear; see **Bear** (1).

Transfigure. (F. – L.) F. *transfigurer*. – L. *transfigūrāre*, to change the figure or appearance. – L. *trans*, across (implying change); *figūra*, figure.

Transfix. (L.) From L. *transfix-us*, pp. of *transfīgere*, to transfix. – L. *trans*, through; *fīgere*, to fix; see **Fix.**

Transform. (F. – L.) F. *transformer*. – L. *transformāre*, to change the shape of. – L. *trans*, across (implying change); *formāre*, to form, from *forma*, shape; see **Form.**

Transfuse. (L.) From L. *transfūsus*, pp. of *transfundere*, to pour out of one vessel into another. – L. *trans*, across; *fundere*, to pour; see **Fuse** (1).

Transgression. (F. – L.) F. *transgression*. – L. acc. *transgressiōnem*, a passage across, in late Lat. a transgression. – L. *transgressus*, pp. of *transgredī*, to go across. – L. *trans*, beyond; *gradī*, to step, go; see **Grade.**

Transient. (L.) From *transient-*, supposed stem of L. *transiens*, passing away, though the real stem is *transeunt-*; pres. pt. of *transīre*, to pass across or away. – L. *trans*, beyond; *īre*, to go.

transit. (L.) L. *transitus*, lit. a passing across. – L. *transitum*, supine of *transīre*, to pass across (above).

Translate. (F. – L.) F. *translater*, Cot. – Late L. *translātāre*, to translate (12th cent.). – L. *translātus*, transferred; used as pp. of *transferre* (but from a different root). – L. *trans*, across, beyond; *lātus*, borne, used as pp. of *ferre*, to bear. See **Tolerate.**

Translucent, allowing light to pass through. (L.) L. *translūcent-*, stem of pres. pt. of *translūcēre*, to shine through. – L. *trans*, beyond; *lūcēre*, to shine; see **Lucid.**

Transmigration. (F. – L.) F. *transmigration*. – L. acc. *transmigrātiōnem*, orig. a removing from one country to another. – L. *transmigrāre*, to migrate across. – L. *trans*, across; *migrāre*, to go; see **Migrate.**

Transmit. (L.) L. *transmittere*. – L. *trans*, across; *mittere*, to send; see **Missile.** Der. *transmiss-ion* (from pp. *transmissus*).

Transmutation. (F. – L.) F. *transmutation*. – L. acc. *transmūtātiōnem*. – L. *transmūtātus*, pp. of *transmūtāre*, to change over, shift, transmute. – L. *trans*, across; *mūtāre*, to change; see **Mutable.**

Transom, a thwart-piece across a double window, lintel, cross-beam. (L.) Shortened from *transtrom* (see Florio, under *Transtri* and *Trasti*). – L. *transtrum*, a transom (Vitruvius). – L. *trans*, going across; *-trum*, suffix (as in *arātrum*, that which ploughs, a plough).

Transparent. (F. – L.) F. *transparent*, ' clear-shining; ' Cot. – L. *trans*, through; *pārent-*, stem of pres. pt. of *pārēre*, to appear; see **Appear.**

Transpicuous, transparent. (L.) Coined, as if from L. **transpicuus*, from *transpicere*, to see through. – L. *tran-*, for *trans*, beyond; *specere*, to look. Compare *perspicuous*.

Transpire, to ooze out. (L.) From L. *tran-*, for *trans*, through; *spīrāre*, to breathe; see **Spirit.**

Transplant. (F. – L.) F. *transplanter*. – L. *transplantāre*, to plant in a new place. – L. *trans*, across; *plantāre*, to plant, from *planta*, a plant; see **Plant.**

Transport. (F. – L.) F. *transporter*, ' to carry or convey over; ' Cot. – L. *transportāre*, to carry across. – L. *trans*, across; *portāre*, to carry; see **Port** (1).

Transpose. (F. – L. *and* Gk.) F. *transposer*, to transpose, remove. – L. *trans*, across; F. *poser*, to put; see **Pose** (1).

Transposition. (F.—L.) F. *transposition.* — L. acc. *transpositiōnem.* — L. *transpositus*, pp. of *transpōnere*, to transpose.—L. *trans*, across; *pōnere*, to put; see **Position**.

Transubstantiation, the doctrine that the bread and wine in the Eucharist are changed into Christ's body and blood. (F.—L.) F. *transsubstantiation.* — Late L. acc. *transubstantiātiōnem*; see Hildebert of Tours (died 1134), sermon 93.— Late L. *transubstantiātus*, pp. of *transubstantiāre*; coined from *trans*, across (implying change) and *substantia*, substance; see **Substance**.

Transverse. (F.—L.) O. F. *transvers*, placed across. — L. *transuersus*, turned across, laid across; pp. of *transuertere*, to turn across.—L. *trans*, across; *uertere*, to turn; see **Verse**.

Trap (1), a snare, gin. (E.) M. E. *trappe.* A. S. *treppe*, a trap, for **træppe*, whence *be-træppan*, vb., to entrap (cf. F. *trappe*, of Teut. origin); E. Fries. *trappe*, *trap* (1) a step, (2) a trap.＋M. Du. *trappe*, mouse-trap; O.H.G. *trappa.* Orig. sense 'step'; a *trap* is that on which an animal steps, or puts its foot. Cf. Westphal. *trappe*, a step; Du. *trap*, a stair, step, kick; Swed. *trappa*, a stair. Allied to Du. *trappen*, to tread on, Norw. *trappa*, E. Fries. and Low G. *trappen*, to tread on, trample. Allied to **Tramp**. Cf. Span. *trampa*, a trap. **Der.** *trap*, vb.; *trap-door*, *trap-bat*.

Trap (2), to adorn, deck. (F.—Teut.) M. E. *trapped*, decked; from M.E. *trappe*, trappings of a horse, &c. Coined, with unusual change from *dr* to *tr*, by soundassociation with *trap* (1), from F. *drap*, cloth, as proved by Chaucer's use of *trappure*, trappings of a horse, from O. F. *drapure*, with the same sense (Godefroy). Cf. also Late L. *trapus*, cloth (usually *drappus*), *trappatura*, a horse's trappings, Span. and Port. *trapo*, cloth. See **Drape**. **Der.** *trapp-ings*, sb. pl.

Trap (3), a kind of igneous rock. (Swed.) Swed. *trappa*, a stair; whence *trapp*, trap-rock; cf. Dan. *trappe*, stair. So called from its appearance; its tabular masses seem to rise in steps. Cf. **Trap** (1).

trapan, trepan (2), to ensnare. (F. —O. H. G.) Formerly *trapan.* — O. F. *trappan*, *trapant*, a snare, trap - door (Roquefort); a plank (Godefroy).—Late L. *trapentum*, a plank for a trap-door.—

F. *trappe*, a trap.—O.H.G. *trappa*, a trap; see **Trap** (1).

Trapezium, an irregular four - sided figure. (L. — Gk.) L. *trapezium.* — Gk. τραπέζιον, a small table, also a trapezium. Dimin. of τράπεζα, a table, of which the orig. sense was a four-footed bench.—Gk τρα-, a reduced form of the Idg. word for 'four'; πέζα, foot, allied to πούς (stem ποδ-), a foot; see **Foot**. See Brugm. ii. § 168. **Der.** *trapeze*, F. *trapèze*, a swing in the shape of a trapezium, as thus : △. From L. *trapezium* (above).

Trappings; see **Trap** (2).

Trash, refuse. (Scand.) The orig. sense was bits of broken sticks found under trees; 'trash and short sticks,' Evelyn. Cf. Icel. *tros*, rubbish, twigs used for fuel; Norweg. *tros*, fallen twigs, half-rotten branches easily broken; Swed. *trasa*, a rag, tatter, Swed. dial. *trås*, a heap of sticks. Derived from the Swed. dial. phrase *slå i tras*, to break in pieces, the same as Swed. *slå in kras*, to break in pieces; so that *tr* stands for *kr*, just as Icel. *trani* means a crane (see **Crane**). — Swed. *krasa*, Dan. *krase*, to crash, break; see **Crash**. *Trash* means 'crashings,' i. e. bits readily *cracked* off, dry twigs that break with a *crash* or snap.

Travail, toil. (F.— L.) F. *travail*, toil, labour. The same as Ital. *travaglio*, Span. *trabajo*, Port. *trabalho*, toil, labour. According to P. Meyer (Rom. xvii. 421) it answers to Late L. *trepālium*, a kind of rack for torturing martyrs (Ducange); perhaps made of three beams (*trēs pālī*). Others make it answer to Late L. **trabāculum*, formed from L. *trab-em*, acc. of *trabs*, *trabes*, a beam. Cf. Late L. *trabāle*, an axle-tree. And see below.

Trave, a shackle. (F.—L.) A *trave* was a frame of rails for confining unruly horses. — O. F. *traf*, a beam (Supp. to Roquefort), usual form *tref* (Cot.). Cf. F. *en-traver*, to shackle, *en-traves*, shackles; (Cot.); Span. *trabar*, to clog, *traba*, a shackle.—L. *trabem*, acc. of *trabs*, a beam. **Der.** *archi-trave*, q. v.

Travel, to journey. (F.—L.) The same word as *travail*; from the toil of travelling in olden times.

Traverse, laid across. (F.—L.) M. F. *travers*, masc., *traverse*, fem. 'crosse-wise;' Cot. — L. *transuersus*, transverse. — L. *trans*, across; *uersus*, pp. of *uertere*, to turn; see **Verse**. **Der.** *traverse*, vb., F.

traverser, 'to thwart or go overthwart,' Cot.

Travertine, a kind of white limestone. (Ital.—L.) From Ital. *travertino*, formerly *tivertino* (Florio). — L. *Tīburtīnus*, adj., belonging to *Tibur*, the modern Tivoli.

Travesty. (F.—Ital.—L.) Orig. a pp., borrowed from F. *travesti*, disguised, pp. of *se travestir*, to change one's apparel. — M. Ital. *travestire*, to disguise, mask. — L. *trā-* (for *trans*), implying 'change'; *uestīre*, to clothe, which is from *uestis*, a garment; see Vest.

Trawl, to fish with a drag-net. (F.— Teut.) Walloon *trauler*, O. F. *trauler*, to go hither and thither (Roquefort); also spelt *troller*, mod. F. *trôler*; see Troll.

Tray, a shallow vessel. (E.) M. E. *trey*. A. S. **tryg*, written *trig* (A. S. Leechdoms, ii. 340). — A. S. *trog*, a trough. + Low G. *trügge* (Stratmann); deriv. of *trog*. See Trough. (Doubtful; the alleged A. S. *treg* is an error for *trog*.)

Treachery. (F.—L.) M. E. *trecherie*, *tricherie*. — O. F. *trecherie*, treachery. — O. F. *trechier*, *trichier*, to trick; cf. Ital. *treccare*, to cheat. — Late L. **triccāre*, for L. *trīcare*, to dally (Ecclus. xxxii. 15), *trīcārī*, to make difficulties. — L. *trīcae*, pl. difficulties, wiles; see Intricate.

Treacle. (F.—L.—Gk.) Formerly a medicament; the mod. *treacle* is named from resembling it in appearance. M. E. *triacle*, a sovereign remedy. — O. F. *triacle*, also spelt *theriaque* (the *l* being unoriginal, as in *syllable*). — L. *thēriaca*, an antidote against poisons, esp. venomous bites. — Gk. θηριακὰ φάρμακα, sb. pl., antidotes against the bites of wild beasts. — Gk. θηριακός, belonging to a wild beast. — Gk. θηρίον, a wild animal. — Gk. θήρ, a wild beast.

Tread, vb. (E.) M. E. *treden*. A. S. *tredan*, pt. t. *træd*, pp. *treden*. + Du. *treden*, G. *treten*. We also find Icel. *troða*, pt. t. *trað*, pp. *troðinn* (cf. E. *trodden*); Dan. *træde*, Swed. *tråda*, Goth. *trudan* (pt. t. *trath*). Der. *tread-le*, a thing to tread on (in a lathe); also *trade*.

Treason. (F.—L.) M. E. *traison*. — O. F. *traison*. — L. acc. *trāditiōnem*. — L. *trāditus*, pp. of *trādere*, to deliver over, betray. Doublet, *tradition*.

Treasure. (F.—L.—Gk.) The former *r* is intrusive. M. E. *tresor*. — O. F. *tresor* (F. *trésor*); the same as Ital. *tesoro*, Span. *tesoro*. — L. *thēsaurum*, acc. of *thēsaurus*,

a treasure. — Gk. θησαυρός, a treasure, store, hoard. — Gk. base θη-, θησ-, as in τί-θη-μι, I place, store up, fut. θήσ-ω; (the suffixes are not clear). Der. *treasur-y*, O. F. *tresorie*.

Treat, vb. (F.—L.) F. *traiter*. — L. *tractare*, to handle; frequentative of *trahere* (pp. *tractus*), to draw.

treatise. (F.—L.) M. E. *tretis*. — O. F. *tretis*, *traitis*, a thing well handled or nicely made; answering to a Late L. form *tractitius*. — F. *traiter*, to treat (above).

treaty. (F.—L.) M. E. *tretee*. — O. F. *traite* [i.e. *traité*], a treaty, pp. of *traiter*, to treat (above); Late L. *tractātus*.

Treble, threefold. (F.—L.) O. F. *treble*. — L. *triplum*, acc. of *triplus*, threefold; see Triple.

Treddle, for **Treadle**; see Tread.

Tree. (E.) M. E. *tree*, *tre* (which also means dead wood, timber). A. S. *trēo* or *trēow*, a tree, timber. + Icel. *trē*, Dan. *træ*; Swed. *trä*, timber, also *träd*, a tree (for *trä-et*, lit. the wood, with post-positive article); Goth. *triu*. Teut. type **trewom*, n. Cf. Russ. *drevo*, a tree, W. *derw*, an oak, Irish *darag*, Gk. δρῦς, oak, Skt. *dru*, wood; cf. Skt. *dāru*, a kind of pine; Gk. δόρυ, a spear-shaft. Der. *tar* (1), *trough*.

Trefoil. (F.—L.) O. F. *trefoil*. — L. *trifolium*, lit. 'three-leaf.' — L. *tri-*, allied to *trēs*, three; *folium*, a leaf. See Foliage.

Trellis, lattice-work. (F.—L.) M. E. *trelis*. — F. *treillis*, 'a trellis;' Cot. Ultimately from F. *treille*, a latticed frame. — Late L. *trichila*, *tricla*, an arbour. But the suffix *-is* is due to O. F. *treilis*, *treslis* (mod. F. *treillis*, sack-cloth), adj., applied to armour covered with a sort of lattice-work, Late L. *trislicium*, a covering of sack-cloth. — L. *trēs*, three, *licium*, a thread; cf. L. *tri-lix*.

Tremble. (F.—L.) F. *trembler*. — Late L. *tremulāre*. — L. *tremulus*, adj., trembling. — L. *tremere*, to tremble. + Lith. *trim-ti*, Gk. τρέμ-ειν, to tremble. (√ TREM.) Brugm. i. § 474. Der. *trem-or*, L. *tremor*, a trembling; *tremulous*, from L. *tremulus* (above); *tremendous*, from L. *tremendus*, lit. to be feared, gerundive of *tremere*, to fear.

Trench, vb. (F.—L. ?) M. E. *trenche*. — A. F. and O. F. *trencher*, vb., 'to cut, carve, slice, hew,' Cot. Now spelt *trancher*. β. Etym. much disputed. Cf. Prov. *trencar*, *trinquar*, Span. and Port.

trinchar, Ital. *trinciare*. Apparently from Late L. *trencāre*, to cut, substituted for L. *truncāre*, to lop, from *truncus*, the trunk of a tree. **Der.** *trench-ant*, cutting, from the pres. part. of *trencher*; also *trench-er*, a wooden plate, to cut things on, O. F. *trencheor*.

Trend, to bend away, said of direction. (E.) M. E. *trenden*, to roll, turn round. Allied to A. S. *trendel*, a circle round the sun, a ring, *ā-trendlian*, to roll; A S. *tryndel*, a ring; Du. *om-trent*, about; Dan. Swed. *trind*, round; M. H. G. *trendel*, O. H. G. *trennila*, a ball; O. H. G. *trennilōn*, to revolve. See **Trundle.**

Trental, a set of thirty masses for the dead. (F. — L.) O. F. *trentel*, *trental* (Roquefort). — F. *trente*, thirty. — L. *trigintā*, thirty. — L. *trī-*, thrice; *-ginta*, allied to Gk. *-κοντα*, short for **δεκοντα*, a decad, from δέκα, ten.

Trepan (1), a small saw for removing a piece of a broken skull. (F. — L. — Gk.) M. F. *trepan*. — Late L. *trepanum*. — Gk. τρύπανον, an auger, borer; also a trepan. — Gk. τρυπᾶν, to bore. — Gk. τρῦπα, τρύπη, a hole. From √TER, to pierce, as in L. *ter-ere*, Gk. τείρειν (= **τέρyειν*).

Trepan (2); to ensnare. See **Trapan.**

Trepang; see **Tripang.**

Trepidation. (F. — L.) M. F. *trepidation*. — L. acc. *trepidātiōnem*, a trembling. — L. *trepidātus*, pp. of *trepidāre*, to tremble. — L. *trepidus*, trembling, agitated. Cf. Brugm. ii. § 797 (note).

Trespass. (F. — L.) O. F. *trespasser*, to exceed, pass beyond (hence, in E., to sin). — O. F. *tres-*, from L. *trans*, beyond; *passer*, to pass; see **Pass.**

Tress, a plait of hair, ringlet. (F. — Gk.) M. E. *tresse*. — F. *tresse*, a tress; *tresser*, to braid hair. [The same as Ital. *treccia*, a braid, plait, Span. *trenza*.] — Late L. *tricia*, variant of *trica*, a plait. — Gk. τρίχα, in three parts, threefold; from a common way of plaiting hair (Diez, Scheler). — Gk. τρι-, thrice, allied to τρεῖς, three; see **Three.** (Doubtful.)

tressure, an heraldic border. (F. — Gk.) Formed, with F. suffix *-ure*, from F. *tresser*, to plait. — F. *tresse*, a plait (above).

Trestle, Tressel, a support for a table. (F. — L.) O. F. *trestel*, later *tresteau*, 'a tresle for a table,' Cot. (Mod. F. *trēteau*.) — Late L. **transtellum*, the same as L. *transtillum*, dimin. of *transtrum*,

a cross-beam. See **Transom.** ¶ For O. F. *tres-* < L. *trans*, cf. *tres-pass*.

Tret. (F. — L.) *Tret*, 'an allowance made for the waste, which is always 4 in every 104 pounds;' Phillips. It seems to have been an allowance made in the weighing of the goods, so as to give good weight. — O. F. *tret*, F. *trait*, lit. 'a pull;' hence, a turn of the balance. — L. *tractus*, pp. of *trahere*, to draw; see **Trace** (1) and **Tract** (1). (Phil. Soc. Trans. 1909, p. 271.)

Trey, three. (F. — L.) A. F. *treis*. — L. *trēs*, three.

Tri-, relating to three. (L.) L. *tri-*, three times; allied to *trēs* (neut. *tri-a*), three. So also Gk. τρι-, prefix; from τρεῖς (neut. τρί-a), three. See **Three.**

triad, the union of three. (F. — L. — Gk.) F. *triade*; Cot. — L. *triad-*, stem of *trias*, a triad. — Gk. τριάς, triad. — Gk. τρι-, thrice (above).

Trial; see **Try.**

Triangle. (F. — L.) F. *triangle*. — L. *triangulum*, sb.; neut. of *triangulus*, three-angled. — L. *tri-*, thrice; *angulus*, an angle; see **Tri-** and **Angle** (1).

Tribe, a race. (F. — L.) F. *tribu*, 'a tribe;' Cot. — L. *tribu-*, decl. stem of *tribus*, a tribe; cf. Umbrian *trifo*. Said to have been one of the *three* original families in Rome; as if from L. *tri-*, three. But see Brugm. ii. § 104.

Tribrach, a metrical foot containing 3 short syllables. (L. — Gk.) L. *tribrachys*. — Gk. τρίβραχυς. — Gk. τρι-, three; βραχύς, short.

Tribulation. (F. — L.) F. *tribulation*. — L. acc. *trībulātiōnem*, affliction. — L. *trībulātus*, pp. of *trībulāre*, to rub out corn; hence, to afflict. — L. *trībulum*, a sledge for rubbing out corn, consisting of a wooden frame with iron spikes beneath it. — L. *trī-*, as in *trī-tus*, pp. of *terere*, to rub; with suffix *-bulum*, denoting the agent. See **Trite.**

Tribune. (F. — L.) M. E. *tribun*. — F. *tribun*. — L. *tribūnum*, acc. of *tribūnus*, lit. the chief officer of a tribe. — L. *tribus*, a tribe; see **Tribe.**

Tribute, sb. (F. — L.) M. E. *tribut*. — F. *tribut*, tribute. — L. *tribūtum*, tribute, lit. a thing paid; neut. of pp. of *tribuere*, to assign, pay. Perhaps from L. *tribu-s*, a tribe (Bréal).

Trice (1), a short space of time. (Scand.) M. E. *at a tryse*, at a (single) pull;

Ipomydon, 392. From Trice (2), below.

β. Later, in the phr. *in a trice*, as if imitated from Span. *en un tris*, in a trice, in an instant; from *tris*, the noise made by the cracking of glass, a crack, an instant. So also Port. *triz*, cracking of glass, a crash, crack, instant; *en hum triz*, in a trice. Prob. of imitative origin; cf. Span. *tris tras*, a noise; *trisca*, a cracking, crashing; *triscar*, 'to make such a noise as of treading on glass, nut-shells, or the like;' Pineda.

Trice (2), **Trise**, to haul up, hoist. (Scand.) M. E. *trisen*, to hoist sail (orig. with a pulley). — Swed. *trissa*, a pulley, *triss*, spritsail-brace; Norw. *triss*, also *trissel*, a pulley; Dan. *tridse*, a pulley, *tridse*, vb., to trice. Cf. also Low G. *trisel*, anything that revolves, a dizziness, a top. The Brem. Wört. also cites Hamburg *drysen*, to trice; *dryse-blok*, a pulley. ¶ Orig. initial = þ.

Tricentenary. (L.) Coined from L. *tri-* and Centenary, q. v.

Trick (1), a stratagem. (Du. – F. – L.) XVI cent. — M. Du. *treke*, a trick; Du. *treek*. Prob. distinct from Du. *trek*, a pull, draught; and borrowed from O. F. *triquer*, Norman form of O. F. *tricher*, to trick. In fact, E. *trickery* is from O. F. *triquerie*, dial. form of *tricherie*, whence E. *treachery*; see Treachery; and *trick* may have been borrowed directly from Norm. dial. *trique*, a trick. ¶ But doubtless influenced by Du. *trek*, a pull, stroke, touch; from *trekken*, to pull; see below.

Trick (2), to deck out. (Du.) From the vb. *trick* below; the sb. also meant a neat contrivance, a toy, trifle, &c.

trick (3), to delineate a coat of arms. (Du.) Du. *trekken*, to draw, also (in M. Du.) to delineate, trick, or sketch out.+ O. H. G. *trehhan*, str. vb., to push.

Trickle, vb. (E.) M.E. *triklen*, short for *striklen*, *strikelen*, to trickle, frequentative of M. E. *striken*, to flow (Spec. of English, ed. Morris and Skeat, p. 48, l. 21). — A. S. *strīcan*, to flow, a particular use of *strīcan*, to strike; see Strike. Cf. *streak*, and G. *streichen*. ¶ The loss of *s* arose in the phr. *teres striklen* = tears trickle; see Ch. C. T., B. 1864, &c.

Tricolor. (F. – L.) F. *tricolore*, for *drapeau tricolore*, three-coloured flag; cf. F. *tricolor*, the three-coloured amaranth. — L. *tri-*, three; *color-*, stem of *color*, colour.

trident. (F. – L.) F. *trident*. – L. *tridentem*, acc. of *tridens*, a three-pronged spear. – L. *tri-*, three; *dens*, tooth, prong.

triennial. (L.) Coined from L. *triennium*, a period of three years. – L. *tri-*, three; *annus*, year.

Trifle. (F. – L.) M. E. *trufle*, *trefle*, rarely *trifle*. – O. F. *trufle*, mockery, raillery, a little jest, dimin. of *truffe*, a gibe, jest (Cot.). Properly a truffle, a thing of small worth; the O. F. *truffe* also means a truffle (Cot.); cf. Prov. *trufo*, a truffle, mockery. See *truffe* in Scheler. See Truffle.

Trifoliate, three-leaved. (L.) From L. *tri-*, three; *foli-um*, leaf.

triforium, a gallery above the arches of the nave and choir of a church. (L.) From L. *tri-*, for *trēs*, three; *fori-s*, a door, opening. ¶ Now usually with but *two* arches (within a third); some early examples had *three* such.

triform, having a triple form. (L.) L. *triformis*. – L. *tri-*, three; *form-a*, form.

Trigger. (Du.) Formerly *tricker*. – Du. *trekker*, a trigger; lit. 'that which draws or pulls.' – Du. *trekken*, to pull. See Track.

Triglyph, a three-grooved tablet. (L. – Gk.) L. *triglyphus*. – Gk. τρίγλυφος, a triglyph; lit. 'thrice-cloven.' – Gk. τρι-, thrice; γλύφειν, to carve, groove.

trigonometry. (Gk.) 'Measurement of triangles.' – Gk. τρίγωνο-ν, a triangle; -μετρια, measurement, from μέτρον, a measure. Gk. τρίγωνον is from τρι-, three; γων-ία, angle, allied to γόνυ, knee.

trilateral, trilingual, triliteral. (L.) From L. *tri-*, three; and *lateral*, &c.

Trill (1), to shake, quaver. (Ital.) In music. — Ital. *trillare*, to trill, shake; *trillo*, sb., a shake. An imitative word, like Span. *trinar*, to trill.

Trill (2), to turn round and round. (Scand.) Perhaps obsolete. M. E. *trillen*, Chaucer, C. T. 10630. – Swed. *trilla*, Dan. *trille*, to roll, turn round; the same as Du. *drillen*; see Drill (1).

trill (3), to trickle, roll. (Scand.) Merely a particular use of the word above. Perhaps confused with *trickle*.

Trillion. (F. – L.) A coined word; to express *tri-million*; see Billion.

Trilobite, a kind of fossil. (Gk.) It has three lobes. – Gk. τρι-, for τρεῖς, three; λοβ-ός, a lobe; -ιτ-ης, suffix.

Trim, vb. (E.) M.E. *trimen, trumen.* A.S. *trymman,* to set firm, to strengthen, set in order, prepare, array. Formed (by usual change of *u* to *y*) from A.S. *trum,* adj., firm, strong. **Der.** *trim,* sb. ; *be-trim.*

Trinity. (F.—L.) M.E. *trinitee.*— O.F. *trinite.*—L. acc. *trīnitātem,* a triad. —L. *trīnus,* pl. *trīnī,* by threes ; for **trisnus,* allied to *trēs,* three. Brugm. ii. § 66.

Trinket (1), a small ornament. (F.) M.E. *trenket,* a shoemaker's knife ; also spelt *trynket* (Palsgrave). Tusser speaks of '*trinkets* and tooles.' Hence it seems to have meant a toy-knife, such as ladies wore on chains ; and, generally, a small ornament. Prob. from O. North F. *trenquer,* to cut, by-form of *trencher,* to cut ; cf. Span. *trinchar,* Ital. *trinciare,* to cut, carve ; Span. *trinchete,* a cook's mincing-knife, a shoemaker's knife (Minsheu). See **Trench.**

Trinket (2), **Trinquet,** the highest sail of a ship. (F.—Span.—L.) M.F. *trinquet,* the highest sail ; Cot. — Span. *trinquete,* a trinket. Cf. Ital. *trinchetto,* a trinket ; Port. *traquete,* a foresail. Prob. from L. *triquetrus,* triangular (from the shape).—L. *tri-,* allied to *trēs,* three ; see **Tri-** ; -*quetrus,* of doubtful origin. The *n* may be due to Span. *trinca,* a rope.

Trio. (Ital.—L.) Ital. *trio,* music in three parts.—L. *tri-,* three ; see **Tri-.**

Trip, vb. (E.) M.E. *trippen,* to step lightly. A lighter form of the base TRAP, to tread ; see **Trap** (1) and **Tramp.** +Du. *trippen,* to skip, whence *trippelen,* to trip, dance ; Swed. *trippa,* Dan. *trippe,* to trip, tread lightly.

Tripang, an edible sea-slug. (Malay.) Malay *trīpang.*

Tripe. (F.) M.E. *tripe.* — F. *tripe* ; cf. Span. and Port. *tripa,* Ital. *trippa,* tripe. Also Irish *triopas,* sb. pl., entrails, tripes ; W. *tripa,* intestines ; Bret. *stripen,* tripe, pl. *stripou,* intestines. Of unknown origin. Perhaps from Low G. *stripe,* a stripe, also a strip.

Triple, three-fold. (F.—L.) F. *triple.* —L. *triplum,* acc. of *triplus,* threefold.— L. *tri-,* three ; -*plus,* Gk. -πλοος, -fold. See **Tri-** and **Double.**

triplicate, threefold. (L.) From pp. of L. *triplicāre,* to treble. — L. *tri-,* three ; *plicāre,* to weave, fold ; see **Ply.**

tripod. (L.—Gk.) L. *tripod-,* stem

of *tripūs.*—Gk. τρίπους (stem τριποδ-), a tripod, three-footed brass kettle, three-legged table. — Gk. τρι-, three ; πούς, foot ; see **Foot.**

tripos, an honour examination at Cambridge. (L.—Gk.) Better spelt *tripus,* as in An Eng. Garner, vii. 267 (1670). It was orig. applied to a certain M.A. chosen at a commencement to make an ingenious satirical speech ; hence the later *triposverses,* i. e. facetious Latin verses on the reverse side of which the *tripos-lists* were printed. Thus the orig. reference was (not to the *three* classes, but) to the three-legged stool used by the *Tripus,* who was also called a *Praevaricator,* or (at Oxford) a *Terræ filius ;* and the lists were named from the verses which took the place of the speech delivered by the M.A. who sat on the *tripus.* From L. *tripūs* (above).

trireme, galley with three banks of oars. (L.) L. *trirēmis,* having three banks of oars. — L. *tri-,* three ; *rēmus,* oar.

trisect. (L.) Coined from L. *tri-,* in three parts ; and *sect-um,* supine of *secāre,* to cut.

Trist ; see **Tryst.**

Trite. (L.) L. *trītus,* worn, pp. of *terere,* to rub, wear away.+Russ. *terete,* Lith. *triti,* to rub ; Gk. τείρειν (<*τέργειν), to rub. (√TER.)

Triton, a sea-god. (L.—Gk.) L.*trītōn.* —Gk. Τρίτων, a Triton. Cf. Irish *triath,* the sea ; Skt. *trita-,* the name of a deity.

Triturate. (L.) From pp. of L. *trītūrāre,* to rub down, thrash, grind.—L. *trītūra,* a rubbing. — L. *trītus,* pp. of *terere,* to rub. See **Trite.**

Triumph. (F.—L.) O.F. *triumphe,* later *triomphe.* — L. *triumphum,* acc. of *triumphus,* a public rejoicing for a victory. +Gk. θρίαμβος, a hymn to Bacchus.

Triumvir. (L.) One of three men associated in an office. L. pl. *triumuirī,* three men, evolved from the gen. pl. *trium uirōrum,* belonging to three men. — L. *trium,* gen. pl. of *trēs,* three ; *uirōrum,* gen. pl. of *uir,* a man ; see **Virile.**

Trivet, Trevet, a three-footed support. (L.) Spelt *trevid* (1493). A.S. *trefet,* Cart. Sax. iii. 367.—L. *tripedem,* acc. of *tripēs,* having three feet. — L. *tri-,* three ; *pēs,* a foot. Cf. **tripod.**

trivial, common. (F.—L.) F. *trivial.* —L. *triuiālis,* belonging to three cross-roads ; that which may be picked up anywhere, common. — L. *triuia,* a place where three roads meet.—L. *tri-*, three; *uia*, a way; see **Viaduct**.

Trochee. (L.—Gk.) L. *trochæus.*— Gk. τροχαῖος, running; also the tripping foot which consists of a long syllable followed by a short one.—Gk. τρέχειν, to run. Allied to **Thrall**.

Troglodyte, a dweller in a cave. (F. —L.—Gk.) F. *troglodyte.*—L. *trōglodyta.* —Gk. τρωγλοδύτης, one who creeps into holes, a cave-dweller.—Gk. τρωγλο-, for τρώγλη, a hole, cave; δύειν, to enter. β. Τρώγλη is from τρώγειν, to gnaw, bite, gnaw a hole. Cf. **Trout**.

Troll, to roll, sing a catch, fish for pike. (F. — Teut.) M. E. *trollen*, to roll; *to troll a catch* is to sing it irregularly (see below); *to troll a bowl* is to circulate it; *to troll* is also to draw hither and thither. —M. F. *troller*, which Cotgrave explains by 'hounds to *trowle*, raunge, or hunt out of order'; O. F. *trauler*, to run or draw hither and thither; mod. F. *trôler.* - G. *trollen*, to roll, troll.+M. Du. *drollen*, 'to troole,' Hexham; Low G. *drulen*, to roll, troll. Prob. allied to E. Fries. *drallen*, to turn, roll; and to **Drill** (1). ¶ Distinct from *trail*.

Trombone. (Ital.—G.—Slav.) Ital. *trombone*, a trombone, augmentative form of Ital *tromba*, a trumpet; see **Trump** (1).

Tron, a weighing-machine. (F. — L.) O. F. *trone*, a weighing-machine; Low L. *trona* (Ducange). — L. *trutina*, a pair of scales. Cf. Gk. τρυτάνη, tongue of a balance, pair of scales. **Der.** *tron-age*.

Troop, a crew. (F.) F. *troupe*; M. F. *trope*. Also Span. *tropa*, M. Ital. *troppa*. Origin unknown. Cf. M. Du. *trop*, Late L. *troppus*, a troop. Perhaps from Norw. *torp*, a flock, crowd, Icel. *þorp*; cf. Icel. *þyrpast*, to throng.

Trope, a figure of speech. (L.—Gk.) L. *tropus.*—Gk. τρόπος, a turn, a trope.— Gk. τρέπειν, to turn. + O. Lat. *trepere*, to turn.

trophy. (F.—L.—Gk.) F. *trophée*, 'a trophee;' Cot.—L. *tropæum*, a sign of victory. — Gk. τροπαῖον, a trophy, monument of an enemy's *defeat*. Neut. of τρο-παῖος, belonging to a defeat. — Gk. τροπή, a return, putting to flight of an enemy. — Gk. τρέπειν, to turn (above).

tropic. (F.—L.—Gk.) M. E. *tropik.* —F. *tropique*, 'a tropick;' Cot.—L. *tropicum*, acc. of *tropicus*, tropical. — Gk. τροπικός, belonging to a turn; the *tropic* is

the point where the sun appears to turn from N. to S., or from S. to N. in the zodiac. —Gk. τρόπος, a turn; see **Trope**. And see **Trepan** (1), **Trover**.

Trot, vb. (F.—L.) F. *trotter*; O. F. *troter*. We also find O. F. *trotier*, Low L. *trotārius*, a trotter. messenger, supposed to be from L. *tolūtārius*, going at a trot. —L. *tolūtim*, adv., at a trot; lit. 'liftingly,' i e. lifting the feet.—L. *tollere*, to lift; see **Tolerate**. (So Diez, Scheler, and Littré.) But cf. M. H. G. *trotten*, to run, perhaps allied to *treten*, to tread; M. Du. *tratten*, ' to goe, to pace, or to trot.'

Troth. (E.) Merely a variant of *truth*. M. E. *trowþþe*, Ormulum; see **Trow**.

Troubadour. (Prov.—L.—Gk.) A F. modification of Prov. *trobador*, also *trobaire*, a troubadour, inventor of songs or verses. Here *trobador* answers to a Late L. acc. *tropātōrem* (= Ital. *trova-tore*, Span. *trovador*); whilst F. *trouvère* answers to a Late L. nom. *tropātor*. Both from the verb *tropāre* (as seen in Ital. *trovare*, Span. *trovar*, Prov. *trobar*, F. *trouver*), to find. See **Trover**.

Trouble, vb. (F.—L.) F. *troubler*, O. F. *trubler*. It answers to a Late L. *turbulāre*, a verb made from L. *turbula*, a disorderly group, dimin. of L. *turba*, a crowd. In fact, we find O. F. *torbleur*, *tourbleur*, one who troubles. Cf. Gk. τύρβη, disorder, throng; Skt. *tvar, tur*, to hasten. See **Turbid**.

Trough. (E.) M. E. *trogh*. A.S. *troh, trog*, a hollow vessel, trough. + Du. Icel. G. *trog*, Dan. *trug*, Swed. *tråg*. Teut. type *trugóz*, Idg. type *dru-kós*; from *dru-*, as in Skt. *dru*, a tree, with adj. suffix. Thus the sense is 'wood-en'; see **Tree**.

Trounce, to beat. (F.—L.) To beat with a truncheon. — O. F. *trons*, a truncheon, m. ; *tronce*, f., variant of *tronche*, a great piece of timber, allied to *tronc*, a trunk; see **Truncheon**.

Trousers, Trowsers. (F.) The latter *r* is modern; from the old word *trowses*, or *trouses*, breeches; older forms *trowze*, *trooze*; also *trews*; esp. used of the Irish *trews* or breeches; (whence Irish *trius*, *triubhas*, trousers; M. Irish *tribus*; Gael. *triubhas*).—F. *trousses*, trunk-hose, breeches (Littré), pl. of *trousse*, O. F. *tourse*, a bundle, package, case; from O.F. *tourser*, *trousser*, to pack; see **Truss**.

trousseau, a package; bride's outfit.

(F.) F. *trousseau*, a little bundle; dimin. of *trousse*, a bundle, a pack; from O. F. *trousser*, to pack. Of doubtful origin. See **Truss**.

Trout. (L. – Gk.) A. S. *trūht*. – L. *trūcta*. – Gk. τρώκτης, a nibbler, also a fish with sharp teeth. – Gk. τρώγειν, to bite, gnaw. Lit. 'nibbler.' Cf. **Troglodyte**.

Trover, an action at law arising out of the finding of goods. (F. – L. – Gk.) O. F. *trover* (F. *trouver*), to find; orig. to devise, invent, make up poetry. The same as Prov. *trobar*, Port. Span. *trovar*, Ital. *trovare*, to versify. β. Since Ital. *v* and Prov. *b* arise from L. *p*, the corresponding Late L. form is **tropāre*, to versify. – L. *tropus*, a trope; Late L. *tropus*, a song, manner of singing. – Gk. τρόπος, a trope, also a mode in music. See **Troubadour, Trope**.

Trow, to believe, suppose. (E.) M. E. *trowen*. O. Fries. *trouwa*, E Fries. *trōen*, to believe. A. S. *trūwian*, to trow, trust, from Teut. base **trū-*; also *trēowian*, to believe, which is allied to the sb. *trēaw*, faith, trust, and to the adj. *trēowe*, true, from Teut. base **trew(w)-*. Cf. Icel. *trūa*, to trow, *trūr*, true; Dan. *troe*, to trow, *tro*, true; Swed. *tro*, to trow; Low G. *trouen*, to trow, *trou*, true; Du. *trouwen*, to marry, *trouw*, true; G. *trauen*, O. H. G. *trūwēn*, to trust, Goth. *trauan*, to believe. See **True**.

Trowel. (F. – L.) M. E. *truel*. – F. *truelle*, O. F. *truele*; Late L. *truella*, a trowel. Dimin. of L. *trua*, a stirring-spoon, skimmer, ladle (hence a trowel, from the shape); cf. L. *trulla*.

Trowsers; see **Trousers**.

Troy-weight. (F. *and* E.) Orig. a weight used at the fair of *Troyes*, a town in France, S. E. of Paris. See Arnold's Chronicle, ed. 1811, pp. 108, 191; Haydn, Dict. of Dates, &c.

Truant, an idler. (F. – C.) F. *truand*, a beggar; *truand*, adj., beggarly; Cot. [The same as Span. *truhan*. Port. *truhão*, a buffoon, jester.] – W. *truan*, wretched, a wretch; Bret. *truek*, a beggar; Gael. and Irish *truaghan*, a wretch, miserable creature. Cf. W. *tru*, wretched, Corn. *troc*. wretched, Gael. *truagh*. Irish *trogha*, miserable, O. Irish *trūag*; Celt. type **trougos*, wretched (Stokes, 138). The Late L. *trūtānus*, a wandering beggar, is from the same source.

Truce. (E.) It should rather be *trews*, i. e. pledges; it is the pl. of *trew*, a pledge of truth. (This is proved by the M. E. forms.) – A. S. *trēow*, a compact, promise, pledge, faith; cf. A. S. *trēowe*, true; see **True**.

Truck (1), to barter, exchange. (F.) M. E. *trukken*. – F. *troquer*, 'to truck, barter;' Cot. So also Span. *trocar*, to barter; whence some have thought that the F. form was borrowed. Cf. Ital. *truccare*, 'to truck, barter, to skud away;' Florio (1598). Origin disputed; the sense 'skud away' is clearly due to Gk. τρόχος, a course, from τρέχειν, to run; see **Truck** (2). β. But the Vocab. du haut Maine has *tric pour troc*, a simple exchange; and we find Norm. dial. *faire la troque*, to barter, from W. Flemish *trok*, used with respect to the (good or bad) 'sale' of goods; cf. *in trok zijn*, to be in vogue; and W. Flem. *trok* = Du. *trek*. The form *trok* is from Du. *trok-*, weak grade of *trekken*, to pull, for which W. Flemish employs *trokken*.

Truck (2), a small wheel, low-wheeled vehicle. (L. – Gk.) Modified from L. *trochus*, a wheel. – Gk. τροχός, a runner, wheel, disc. – Gk. τρέχειν, to run. **Der.** *truckle-bed*, a bed on little wheels, where *truckle* = L. *trochlea*, a pulley; Baret has: '*Pullie*, trochlea; a *truckle*, or pullie.' Cf. Span. *trocla*, a pulley.

truckle, to submit servilely to another. (L. – Gk.) From the phrase *to truckle under*, due to the old custom of putting a *truckle-bed* under a larger one; the truckle-bed being occupied by a servant, pupil, or inferior. It prob. originated in University slang, from L. *trochlea* (as above).

Truculent, barbarous. (F. – L.) F. *truculent*. – L. acc. *truculentum*, cruel. – L. *truc-*, stem of *trux*, fierce, wild.

Trudge, to march heavily. (F. – Teut. ?) Perhaps to slouch along, or go about as an idle beggar. – F. *trucher*, to beg idly; obsol. (Littré). Of Teut. origin; cf. Low G. *truggelen*, to beg fawningly, to wheedle; Du. *troggelen*, to beg, wheedle; M. Du. *truggelen*, 'to trugge up and downe a Begging,' Hexham; W. Flem. *troggelen*, to walk with difficulty; Dan. *trygle*, to importune; E. Fries. *trüggeln*, to press, push backward, also to be importunate. Allied to G. *drücken*, to press, A. S. *þryccan*, to press, afflict, prov. E. *thrutch*, to press.

True, firm, certain. (E.) M. E. *trewe.* A. S. *trēowe, trȳwe,* true. Orig. 'believed;' allied to O. Prussian *druwit,* to believe (Fick) ; Lith. *drútas,* firm. **+** Du. *trouw,* Icel. *tryggr,* Swed. *trogen,* G. *treu,* Goth. *triggws,* true. Cf. also Icel. *trúr,* true, Goth. *trauan,* to believe,trust, be persuaded. See **Trow.**

Truffle. (F. – L.) M. F. *trufle,* F. *truffe,* a round edible fungus, found underground. Span. *trufa,* a truffle. It is thought that the F. *truffe,* Span. *trufa,* answer to L. pl. *tŭbera,* truffles, whence was formed a F. fem. sb. **tufre,* easily altered to *truffe.* We also find Ital. *tartufo,* a truffle < L. *terræ tŭber,* i. e. truffle of the earth ; whence G. *kartoffel,* earlier form *tartuffel,* a potato. See **Trifle.**

Trull, a worthless woman. (G.) G. *trulle, trolle* (whence Picard *troulle*), a trull. Cognate with M. Du. *drol,* a jester, Icel. *troll,* a merry elf ; see **Droll** and **Troll.**

Trump (1), a trumpet. (F. – G. – Slav.) M. E. *trumpe, trompe.* – F. *trompe,* 'a trump;' Cot. Cf. Span. *trompa,* Ital. *tromba,* a trump. – O. H. G. *trumpa, trumba,* a trumpet. – O. Slav. type **tromba,* as in O. Slav. and Pol. *traba* (with former *a* nasal), Slovenian *tromba, trôba,* a trumpet, Russ. *truba,* a pipe, tube, trumpet.

Trump (2), one of a leading suit of cards. (F. – L.) Well known to be a corruption of *triumph* ; see Latimer's Sermons, and Nares. – F. *triomphe,* 'the card-game called ruffe, or trump ; also the ruffe or trump at it ;' Cot. : *triompher,* 'to triumph, to trump at cards;' Cot. – L. *triumphus,* triumph ; see **Triumph.**

Trumpery, nonsense. (F. – G. – Slav.) F. *tromperie,* 'a wile, fraud;' Cot. – F. *tromper,* to deceive ; orig. to sound a horn ; whence the phrase *se tromper de quelqu'un,* to play with any one, amuse oneself at their expense. See **Trump** (1).

trumpet. (F. – G. – Slav.) F. *trompette,* dimin. of *trompe,* a horn ; see **Trump** (1).

Truncate, to cut off short. (L.) From pp. of L. *truncāre,* to cut off. – L. *truncus,* a stump. See **Trunk** (1).

truncheon. (F. – L.) M. E. *tronchoun.* – O. North F. *tronchon* (Norm. dial.) ; O. F. *tronson,* a thick stick ; formed from *tronc,* a trunk ; see **Trunk** (1). Mod. F. *tronçon.*

Trundle, to roll. (F. – Low G.) Cf.

trundle-bed, a bed running on wheels; *trundle-tail,* a curly tail of a dog ; A. S. *tryndyled,* rounded ; Voc. 152. 5. – M. F. (Picard) *trondeler,* 'to trundle ;' Cot. ; Walloon *trondeler,* to roll (Sigart). Of Low G. origin ; cf. Low G. *tröndeln,* Pomeran. *tründeln,* to trundle a hoop ; O. Fries. *trund,* round ; N. Fries. *trind,* round. From Teut. **trund-,* weak grade of a lost verb **trendan-,* to roll (pt. t. **trand*) ; whence also A. S. *sin-tryndel,* a large round shield. The *i* appears in Dan. Swed. *trind,* round ; the *a,* modified to *e,* appears in M. E. *trenden,* to turn, roll, secondary verb from **trand,* 2nd grade of **trendan-.* See **Trend.**

Trunk (1), stem of a tree, &c. (F.–L.) F. *tronc,* trunk. – L. *truncum,* acc. of *truncus,* trunk, stem, bit cut off. – L. *truncus,* adj., cut off, maimed. Brugm. i. § 144. **Der.** *trunk-hose,* i. e. *trunk'd-hose,* knee-breeches, breeches cut short.

Trunk (2), of an elephant. (F. – G. – Slav.) Formerly *trump,* signifying (1) trumpet, (2) tube. – F. *trompe,* 'a trump, or trumpet, the snowt of an elephant;' Cot. Cf. O. F. *tromper,* to blow a trumpet ; see **Trump** (1).

Trunnion, one of the projecting stumps on each side of a cannon, on which it rests in the carriage. (F. – L.) F. *trognon,* a stump ; from *tronc,* a trunk ; cf. M. F. *tron,* a stump ; see **Trunk** (1).

Truss, to pack, fasten up. (F.) Ο. F. *trousser, tourser,* to pack up ; whence the sb. *trousse, tourse,* a bundle ; and the dimin. *troussel, toursel,* later *trousseau* ; see **Trousseau.** Cf. Port. *trouxa,* a pack, Span. *troja,* a soldier's knapsack. Origin doubtful ; perhaps from O. F. *tros, trous,* a small piece ; from Late L. *tursus,* L. *thyrsus,* a stalk. – Gk. θύρσος ; see **Thyrsus.** So Körting.

Trust. (Scand.) M. E. *trŭst.* – Icel. *traust,* trust, protection, firmness ; Dan. Swed. *tröst,* consolation. **+** G. *trost,* consolation, Goth. *trausti,* a covenant. Related to **Trow, True.**

truth. (E.) M. E. *trewthe, trouthe* ; A. S. *trēowð,* truth. – A. S. *trēowe,* true ; see **True. +** Icel. *tryggð,* truth. And see **Troth.**

Try, to select, test, examine, &c. (F. – L.) F. *trier,* 'to select, pick out, choose. – F. *trier,* 'to cull out;' Cot. The same as Prov. *triar,* to separate corn from the straw, also to choose. – Late L.

trītāre, to pound small ; cf. Ital. *tritare*, to pound, grind, mince, also to ponder, consider, scan.—L. *trītus*, pp. of *terere*, to rub. It meant to thresh, pulverise, separate, purify, cull, pick. (Disputed.) **Der.** *tri-al.*

Tryst, Trist, an appointment to meet. (F.—Teut.?) See Jamieson ; orig. a set station, place of meeting. M. E. *triste, tristre*, a station (in hunting), place to watch. — O. F. *triste, tristre*, station to watch (in hunting), ambush ; Low L. *trista.* Of doubtful origin ; but perhaps related to Frankish L. *trustis*, one in a place of trust (see Ducange). Allied to O. H. G. *trōst*, help, M. H. G. vb. *troesten*, to assist ; see **Trust.**

Tub, a small cask. (O. Low G.) M. E. *tubbe.*—M. Du. *tobbe*, a tub ; Low G. and E. Fries. *tubbe*, a tub.

Tube. (F.—L.) F. *tube.*—L. *tubum*, acc. of *tubus*, a tube, pipe ; akin to *tuba*, a trumpet. **Der.** *tub-ul-ar*, from L. *tubulus*, dimin. of *tubus.*

Tuber, a rounded root. (L.) L. *tūber*, a bump, tumour, also a truffle. Lit. 'swelling ;' allied to **Tumid.** Brugm. i. § 413 (8). **Der.** *tubercle*, a little swelling.

Tuck (1), to gather in a dress. (O. Low G.) M. E. *tukken.* — Low G. *tukken*, to pull up, draw up, tuck up, also to entice (= M. Du. *tocken*, to entice).+G. *zucken*, to twitch up ; O. H. G.*zucchen.* Teut. base **tukk* ; intensive form from the weak grade (*tuh) of Teut. **teuhan-*, to pull ; see **Tow** (1), **Tug, Touch.**

Tuck (2), a rapier. (F. — Ital. — G.) Short for F. *étoc*, occasional form of *estoc*, 'the stock of a tree, a rapier, a tuck ;' Cot. — Ital. *stocco*, a truncheon, rapier, tuck ; Florio.—G. *stock*, a stock, stump, &c. ; see **Stock, Stoccado.**

Tuck (3), beat of drum. (F. — Teut.) From Picard or Walloon *toquer, toker*, to touch, strike ; variant of F. *toucher*, to touch ; see **Touch, Tocsin.**

tucker, a fuller. (F.—Teut.) M. E. *touker*, lit. ' beater ;' though the cloth was worked up with the feet. — O. North F. *touker, toquer*, to beat ; variant of F. *toucher*, to touch. See **Tocsin.**

tucket, a flourish on a trumpet. (F. — Teut.) North F. *touquet*, for O. F. *touchet*, a stroke ; equivalent to Ital. *toccata*, a prelude, tolling of a bell, a tucket, a striking ; from *toccare*, to strike, touch ; see **Touch.** ¶ Or from Italian.

Tuesday. (E.) A. S. *Tiwes dæg*, the day of *Tiw*, the god of war. + Icel. *Týs-dagr*, the day of *Týr* ; Dan. *Tirsdag*, Swed. *Tisdag* ; O. H. G. *Zies tac*, the day of *Ziu*, god of war. β. The A. S. *Tiw*, Icel. *Týr*, O. H. G. *Ziu* are the same as Skt. *dēva-s*, god, and allied to L. *deus*, god, and even to L. *Iu-* in *Iu-piter*, Gk. *Zeús*, Skt. *Dyaus.* ¶ A translation of L. *diēs Martis.*

Tufa, a soft stone. (Ital.—L.) For *tufo.* — Ital. *tufo.* — L. *tōfus, tōphus.* Cf. Gk. τόφος. Origin unknown.

Tuft (1), a crest, knot. (F. — Teut.) M. E. *tuft*, but the final *t* is excrescent ; prov. E. *tuff*, a tuft.—F. *touffe*, a tuft or lock of hair.—Swed. dial. *tuppa*, a tuft, fringe ; Icel. *toppr*, a top, tuft, or lock of hair ; M. Du. *top*, a tuft ; G. *zopf.* ¶ W. *twff* is borrowed from E., and preserves the correct form.

Tuft (2), a plantation, a green knoll. (Scand.) See **Toft.**

Tug, vb. (Scand.) M. E. *toggen.* From Icel. *tog*, M. Swed. *tog*, a rope to pull by ; allied to E. Fries. *tokken*, to pull : Low G. *tukken*, to pull up, draw up ; cf. Low G. *togg*, a pull (Danneil). From the weak grade (*tuh-*) of Teut. **teuh-an-*, to pull ; see **Tow** (1), **Tuck** (1).

Tuition. (F.—L.) F. *tuition.*—L. acc. *tuitiōnem*, protection.—L. *tuit-us*, pp. of *tuērī*, to guard, protect.

Tulip, a flower. (F.—Ital.—Turk.—Pers.) M. F. *tulippe*, also *tulipan*, a tulip ; so called from its likeness to a turban. — Ital. *tulipa, tulipano*, a tulip. — Turk. *tul-bend*, a turban ; also *dulbend.*—Pers. *dul-band*, a turban ; see **Turban.**

Tulle, a kind of silk open-work or lace. (F.) Named from *Tulle*, the chief town in the department of Corrèze (France), where it was first made (Littré).

Tumble, vb. (E.) M. E. *tumblen* ; frequent. of *tomben, tumben*, to tumble. — A. S. *tumbian*, to turn heels over head, dance. + Du. *tuimelen* ; cf. G. *tummeln*, from O. H. G. *tūmōn*, to turn over and over (whence F. *tomber*) ; Dan. *tumle.* **Der.** *tumbler*, sb., (1) an acrobat, (2) a glass without a foot, which could only be set down when empty ; *tumb-r-el*, a cart that falls over, O. F. *tomberel*, from F. *tomber*, to tumble, fall over, a word of Teut. origin.

Tumefy, to cause to swell. (F. — L.) M. F. *tumefier* ; Cot. — Late L. *tumeficāre, for L. *tumefacere*, to make to swell. — L. *tumē-re*, to swell; *facere*, to make.

tumid. (L.) L. *tumidus*, swollen. — L. *tumēre*, to swell. Cf. Gk. τύλη, a swelling; Skt. *tu*, to increase. Brugm. i. § 413 (8). (√TEU.) Der. *tum-our*, F. *tumeur*, from L. acc. *tumōrem*, a swelling.

Tump, a hillock. (C.) W. *twmp*, a tump, is perhaps from E. But the word seems to be Celtic; from W. *tom*, Gael. and Irish *tom*, a hillock; cf. Gk. τύμβος, L. *tumulus*, a mound. See **Tomb.**

Tumult. (F. — L.) F. *tumulte*. — L. acc. *tumultum*, an uproar. — L. *tumēre*, to swell, surge up.

tumulus. (L.) L. *tumulus*, a mound. — L. *tumēre*, to swell. And see **Tomb.**

Tun; see **Ton.**

Tune, tone, melody. (F. — L. — Gk.) M. E. *tune*. — A. F. *tun*, F. *ton*, 'a tune, or sound;' Cot. — L. acc. *tonum*. — Gk. τόνος, a tone. See **Tone.**

Tungsten, a heavy metal. (Swed.) Swed. *tungsten*, lit. 'heavy stone.'—Swed. *tung*, heavy; *sten*, stone. Swed. *tung* = Icel. *þungr*, heavy; *sten* is cognate with E. *stone*.

Tunic. (F. — L.) O. F. *tunique*. — L. *tunica*, an under-garment; whence A. S. *tunice*. Der. *tunic-le*, *tunic-at-ed*.

Tunnel. (F. — L.) O. F. *tonnel* (later *tonneau*), a tun, great vessel; hence a tunnel (or trap) for partridges, which was an arched tunnel of wire, strengthened by *hoops* at intervals (whence the name; it was also called *tonnelle* in F.). It came to mean any kind of tunnel or shaft, e. g. the shaft or pipe of a chimney, &c. Dimin. from Late L. *tunna*, a ton; see **Ton.**

Tunny, a fish. (F. — L. — Gk.) F. *thon*; Cot. — L. *thunnum*, acc. of *thunnus*. — Gk. θύννος, θῦνος, a tunny. Lit. 'the darter.' — Gk. θύνειν, allied to θύειν, to rush along. (√DHEU.)

Tup, a ram. (Scand.) Prob. a transferred name; cf. Swed. and Norw. *tupp*, a cock, allied to Dan. *top*, a cock's crest, and to Icel. *toppr*, a top, a crest. See **Top.**

Turban. (F. — Ital. — Turk. — Pers.) Formerly *turbant*, *turribant*, *turband*; also *tolipant*, *tulipant*, *tulibant*. — M. F. *turbant*, *turban*, a turban; Cot. — Ital. *turbante*, 'a turbant;' Florio. — Turk. *tulbend*, vulgar form of *dulbend*, a turban. — Pers. *dulband*, a turban. Cf. **Tulip.**

Turbary, a right of digging turf, or a place for digging it. (F. — O. H. G.) O. F. *torberie*; Low L. *turbāria*, the same. — O. H. G. *turba*, older form of *zurba*, turf. +A. S. *turf*. See **Turf.**

Turbid. (L.) L. *turbidus*, disturbed. — L. *turbāre*, to disturb. — L. *turba*, a crowd, confused mass of people. See **Trouble.**

Turbot. (F. — L.) F. *turbot*, a fish. — Late L. *turbo*, a turbot; L. *turbo*, a spindle, reel; from its rhomboidal shape. So also L. *rhombus*, a spindle, rhombus, turbot.

Turbulent. (F. — L.) F. *turbulent*. — L. *turbulentus*, full of commotion. — L. *turbāre*, to disturb; see **Turbid.**

Tureen, the same as **Terreen,** q. v.

Turf. (E.) M. E. *turf*, pl. *turues* (*turves*). A. S. *turf.*+Du. *turf*, Icel. *torf*, sod, peat; Dan. *törv*, Swed. *torf*, O. H. G. *zurba*. Cf. Skt. *darbha-*, a matted grass, from *dṛbh*, to bind.

Turgid. (L.) L. *turgidus*, swollen. — L. *turgēre*, to swell out.

Turkey. (F. — Tatar.) Called a *Turkey* cock, or a cock of *India*, from the notion that it came from Turkey or from India; so also G. *Calecutischer hahn*, a turkey-cock, is lit. a cock of Calicut. (It really came from the New World.) From F. *Turquie*, Turkey. — F. *Turc*, a Turk. — Tatar *Turk*, a Turk; orig. an adj. meaning 'brave.' ¶ The usual Turkish word for 'Turk' is '*Osmānlī*.

Turmeric. (Arabic?) New L. *turmerica* (Minsheu). Cf. F. *terre-mérite*, turmeric (Littré; s. v. *Curcuma*); as if L. *terra merita*, apparently 'excellent earth'; but cf. *terræ meritum*, 'the produce of the earth,' in Ducange. ¶ But *terra merita*, like *turmeric*, is prob. a corruption of an Eastern word. Span. Port. *curcuma*, turmeric, are from Arab. *kurkum*, saffron; whence also L. *crocus*.

Turmoil, sb. (F. ? — L. ?) Formerly *turmöyl*; probably a corrupt form, the latter part of the word being assimilated to *moil*, q. v.; and the former part to *turn*. Prob. from M. F. *tremouille*, 'the hopper of a mill,' also called *trameul* (Cotgrave); O. F. *trameure*. β. So named from being in continual motion. — L. *tremere*, to tremble, shake. Cf. O. F. *tramoier*, to tremble.

Turn, vb. (L. — Gk.) M. E. *turnen*, *tournen*; A. S. *tyrnan*, *turnian*. [Cf. O. H. G. *turnen*, to turn.] — L. *tornāre*, to turn in a lathe. — L. *tornus*, a lathe. —

578

Gk. τόρνος, a tool to draw circles with; allied to τορός, piercing, L. *terere*, to rub, bore. (✓TER.) Der. *turn*, sb.

Turnip, Turnep, a plant. (F.—L.; *and* L.) The latter part of the word is M. E. *nepe*, a turnip, A. S. *nǣp*, borrowed from L. *nāpus*, a kind of turnip; cf. Irish and Gael. *neip*, a turnip. β. The origin of the former part is unknown; the suggestion *terræ nāpus* does not agree with the spelling, which rather resembles the F. *tour* in the sense of 'wheel,' as signifying its round shape; it looks as if it had been turned. A turner's wheel was formerly called a *turn* in English, and *tour* in French. Cf. Irish *turnapa*, a turnep, *turnoir*, a turner (from E.).

Turnpike. Formerly a name given to the old-fashioned turn-stile, which revolved on the top of a post, and resembled a frame with pikes, used for defence. From **Turn** and **Pike.**

Turpentine, exudation from the terebinth. (F.—L.—Gk.) M. F. *turbentine*; Cot.; Norman dial. *turbentine.*—L. *terebinthus.* — Gk. τερέβινθος, the terebinth-tree. See **Terebinth.**

Turpitude. (F.—L.) F. *turpitude.*—L. *turpitūdo*, baseness.—L. *turpis*, base.

Turquoise, Turkis, a gem. (F.—Ital.—Tatar.) F. *turquoise*; orig. fem. of *Turquois*, Turkish.—M. Ital. *Turchesa*, a turquoise, or Turkish stone.—Tatar *Turk*, a Turk.

Turret. (F.—L.) M. F. *tourette*; Cot. Dimin. of O. F. *tur*, F. *tour*, a tower.—L. acc. *turrem*. See **Tower.**

Turtle (1), a turtle-dove. (L.) A. S. *turtle*; formed, by change of *r* to *l*, from L. *turtur*, a turtle (whence also G. *turtel*, Ital. *tortora, tortola*). An imitative word; due to a repetition of *tur*, used to express the coo of a pigeon.

Turtle (2), the sea-tortoise. (L.) English sailors, ill understanding the Port. *tartaruga*, Span. *tortuga*, a tortoise or sea-turtle, turned these words into *turtle*; see above. The Span. and Port. words are allied to **Tortoise.**

Tush, an exclamation of impatience. (E.) Formerly *twish*, an expression of disgust. Cf. *pish* and *tut*; and cf. Low G. *tuss*, silence! Also Dan. *tysse*, to silence.

Tusk. (E.) South E. *tush* (as in Shak.). A. S. *tusc*, usually spelt *tux*; prob. originally *tūsc*. Cf. O. Fries. *tusch, tusk*; E.

Fries. *tūsk*; Icel. *toskr*. Perhaps related to **Tooth.** Brugm. i. § 795.

Tussle, to scuffle. (E.) The same as *tousle*, to disorder; frequent. of *touse*, to pull about. See **Touse.** Cf. Westphal. *tusseln*, to pull about, and E. *toss*.

Tut, an exclamation of impatience. (E.) Cf. M. F. *trut* (the same); and cf. *tush*.

Tutelage, guardianship. (L.; *with* F. *suffix*.) From L. *tūtēl-a*, protection; with F. suffix *-age* (< L. *-āticum*). — L. *tūt-us*, short for *tuitus*, pp. of *tuērī*, to guard, protect; see **Tuition.**

tutelar. (L.) L. *tūtēlāris*, protecting. — L. *tūt-us*, short for *tuitus* (above).

tutor. (L.) L. *tūtor*, a guardian, tutor. — L. *tūt-us* (above).

Tutty, a collyrium. (F.—Pers.) F. *tutie*; M. F. *tuthie*, 'tutie,' Cot. — Pers. *tūtiyā*, green vitriol. Cf. Skt. *tuttha-*, blue vitriol.

Twaddle, to tattle. (E.) Formerly *twattle*, a collateral form of *tattle.*

Twain; see **Two.**

Twang, to sound with a sharp noise. (E.) A collateral form of *tang*; see **Tang** (2). Cf. **Tingle.**

Tweak, to twitch, pinch. (E.) M. E. *twikken*; A. S. *twiccian*, pt. t. *twicc-ode*, (spelt *twiccede*, Shrine, 41); cf. A.S. *twicce*, as in A. S. *angel-twicce*, a hook-twitcher, the name of a worm used as a bait.+Low G. *twikken*, E. Fries. *twikken*, G. *zwicken*, to pinch. See **Twitch.**

Tweezers, nippers. (F.—Teut.; *with* E. *suffix*.) A surgeon's box of instruments was formerly called *a tweese*, whence small surgical instruments were called *tweezes*, a form afterwards turned into *tweezers*, and used of small nippers in particular. β. Again, the word *tweese* was really at first *twees*, the plural of *twee* or *etwee*, a surgical case; *etwee* being merely an Englished form of M. F. *estuy*, F. *étui.*—M. F. *estuy*, 'a sheath, case, a case of little instruments, now commonly termed an *ettwee*;' Cot. γ. The M. F. *estuy* is cognate with Span. *estuche*, Port. *estojo*, M. Ital. *stuccio*, *stucchio*, 'a little pocket-case with cisors, pen-knives, and such trifles in them' (*sic*); Florio.—M. H. G. *stūche* (prov. G. *stauche*), a short and narrow muff (hence a case). + Icel. *stūka*, a sleeve. ¶ Etymology quite clear; *estuy* became *etwee*, *twee*, then *twees*, then *tweeses*, and lastly *tweezers*, which might be explained as 'instruments belonging to a *tweese* or *twee*.'

Twelve. (E.) M. E. *twelf*, whence *twelf-e*, a pl. form, also written *twelue* (= *twelve*). A.S. *twelf*, *twelfe*.+O. Fries. *twilif*, Du. *twaalf*, Icel. *tōlf*, Dan. *tolv*, Swed. *tolf*, G. *zwölf*, O.H.G. *zwelif*, Goth. *twalif*. β. The Goth. *twa-lif* is composed of *twa*, two; and *-lif*, the equivalent of the Lithuan. *-lika*, occurring in *dwy-lika*, twelve. Again, the suffix *-lika* is allied to Lithuan. *lëkas*, remaining, left over, from *lik-ti*, to remain. Hence *twa-lif* = two over ten, i.e. twelve. Brugm. ii. § 175. Der. *twelf-th*, for *twelft* = A.S. *twelfta*, twelfth; *twelvemonth* = M.E. *twelfmonthe*.

twenty. (E.) A.S. *twentig.* — A.S. *twen* = *twĕn*, short for *twegen*, twain; and *-tig*, suffix allied to Goth. *-tigjus* and E. *ten*. +Goth. *twaitigjus*, Du. *twintig*, Icel. *tuttugu*, G. *zwanzig*; all similarly formed.

twibill, twybill, a two-edged bill. (E.) M. E. *twibil*. A. S. *twibill.* — A. S. *twi-*, double; *bill*, a bill; see **twice** (below).

twice. (E.) M. E. *twiës* (dissyllabic). A. S. *twiges*, a late form, for the older *twiwa*, twice. — A.S. *twi-*, double; like L. *bi-*, Gk. δι-, Skt. *dvi-*; allied to *twā*, two. See **Two**.

twig (1), a shoot of a tree. (E.) A.S. *twig* (pl. *twigu*), a twig; Northumb. *tuigge* (pl. *tuiggo*), Jo. xv. 5, 6; orig. the fork of a branch, and named from being double, the small shoot branching off from the larger one. — A.S. *twi-*, double; see above.+Du. *twijg*, Low G. *twig* (Danneil), Westphal. *twich, twick*, G. *zweig*. Cognate with Skt. *dvi-ka-*, 'consisting of two,' Gk. δισσός, double, twofold. Brugm. ii. § 166.

Twig (2), to comprehend. (C.) Irish *tuig-im*, O. Irish *tucc-im*, I understand; Gael. *tuig*, to understand.

Twilight. (E.) M.E. *twilight*. The prefix *twi-* (A.S. *twi-*) is lit. 'double' (see **twice** above); but is here used rather in the sense of doubtful or between; cf. L. *dubius*, doubtful, from *duo*, two. + G. *zwielicht*, M. Du. *tweelicht*; similarly compounded.

twill, to weave, shewing ribs. (Low G.) The word has reference to a peculiar method of doubling the warp-threads, or taking two of them together; this gives an appearance of diagonal lines, in textile fabrics. From Low G. *twillen*. [One Low G. *twillen*, to bifurcate, is allied to O.H.G. *zwinel*, twin, and to E. **Twin**.]

But *twillen* is here a Low G. spelling of M. H.G. *zwilhen*, to double; from M. H.G. *zwilch*, O. H.G. *zwilīh* adj., two-threaded, a word suggested by L. *bilix*, two-threaded (from L. *bi-*, double, *licium*, thread). Cf. G. *zwillich*, ticking.

twin. (E.) A.S. *ge-twinnas*, twins.+ Icel. *tvinnr*, in pairs; Lithuan. *dwyni*, twins; cf. L. *bīnī*, two at a time. From the A.S. *twi-*, double; the *-n* gives a collective force, as in L. *bī-n-i*, two at a time. Cf. Goth. *tweihnai*, two apiece; Bavar. *zwin-ling*, G. *zwil-ling*, a twin.

twine, vb. (E.) M. E. *twinen*, to twist together. From A. S. *twīn*, sb., a twisted or doubled thread.+Du.*twijn*, sb., a twist, twine, Icel. *tvinni*, twine; Swed. *tvinntråd*, twine-thread; also Du.*tweern*, G. *zwirn*. β. All from Teut. type *twisno->*twiz-no-*, double; the *iz* becomes *i* in A.S. *twīn*, Du. *twijn*; the *zn* becomes *nn* in Icel. and Swed.; and the *z* becomes *r* in Du. and G. The base *twis-* occurs in E. *twis-t*, Goth. *twis-*, prefix; cf. L. *bis* (for **dwis*), Gk. δίς, Skt. *dvis*, twice. Brugm. i. § 903 (c, note 2).

Twinge, to nip. (E.) M. E. *twengen*, weak vb. (*g=j*). Causal of *twingen*, str. vb., O. Fries. *twinga, thwinga* (pt. t. *twang*), to constrain, O. Sax. *bi-thwingan*, Icel. *þvinga*, Du. *dwingen*, G. *zwingen*, O.H.G. *dwingan*; Teut. type **thwengan-*, pt. t. *thwang*. Cf. also Lith. *twenkti*, to be hot, to smart; *twankas*, sultry. (√TWENK.) Der. *thong*.

Twinkle. (E.) A.S. *twinclian*, to twinkle; a frequentative form of *twink*, appearing in M.E. *twinken*, to blink, wink. Again, this is a nasalised form of M.E. *twikken*, to twitch (hence to quiver); see **Tweak.** + Bavarian *zwinkern*, frequent. of *zwinken*, to blink.

twinkling. (E.) M.E. *twinkeling*, the twitching of an eye. — M.E. *twinkelen*, to wink; the same word as E. *twinkle*.

Twinter, a beast two years old. (E.) A.S. *twi-wintre*, adj., of two years. — A.S. *twi-*, double (see **twice**), and *winter*, a winter, a year.

Twire, to peep out. (E.) In Shak. Son. 28. Only recorded in the cognate Bavarian *zwiren, zwieren*, to peep (Schmeller), M. H. G. *zwieren*, to peep out (Schade). ¶ Nares is wrong in citing *twire*=*twitter* from Chaucer; the true reading is *twitreth*.

Twirl, to turn rapidly round. (E.) It stands for *thwirl* (like *twinge* for *thwinge*).

Frequentative of A. S. *-þweran*, to turn, whence *þwiril*, the handle of a churn. Cognate with G. *querlen, quirlen*, to twirl, *querl*, a twirling-stick; from O. H. G. *tweran, dweran*, to whirl round. β. The frequent. form appears also in Du. *dwarlen*, to twirl, *dwarlwind*, a whirlwind; cf. Low G. *dweerwind*, a whirlwind. We also find Icel. *þvara*, a stirring-stick; from *thwar*, 2nd grade of Teut. **thweran-*, as seen in A. S. *-þweran*. Also E. Fries. *dwirlen, dwirlen*, to twirl, *dwarrel*, a whirl, from *dweren*, to turn; cf. Gk. τορύνη, a stirrer. (√TWER.)

Twist, vb. (E.) M. E. *twisten*, vb. formed from A. S. *twist*, sb., a rope or twisted cord. ‒ A. S. **twis-*, double (see **Twine**); with suffix *-t* (Idg. suffix *-to-*). The Du. *twist*, Dan. Swed. *tvist*, G. *zwist*, mean 'discord,' which is another sense of the same word; so also M. E. *twist*, a twig or fork of a branch; Icel. *tvistr*, the deuce, in card-playing.

Twit, to remind of a fault. (E.) Shortened from M.E. *atwiten*, to reproach. ‒ A. S. *ætwītan*, to twit, reproach. ‒ A. S. *æt*, at, upon; *wītan*, to blame, orig. to observe, hence to observe what is amiss. β. This A. S. *wītan* answers to Goth. *-weitan* in comp. *fra-weitan*, to avenge; cf. *weitjan*, to observe; allied to Goth. *witan*, to know; see **Wit** (1). Cf. Du. *wijten*, to reproach, G. *ver-weisen*, from Teut. base **weit*. (√WEID.)

Twitch, to pluck. (E.) M.E. *twicchen*, palatalised form of M. E. *twikken*, A. S. *twiccian*, to tweak. See **Tweak**. For the form, cf. A. S. *angel-twicce*. prov. E. *angletwitch*, an earthworm (N. E. D.).

Twitter, vb. (E.) Frequentative from a base *twit*; cf. *titter, tattle*, and *twaddle*; all of imitative origin.+G. *zwitschern*, to twitter, Bavar. *zwitzern*; Du. *kwetteren*, Dan. *qviddre*, Swed. *qvittra*.

Two, Twain. (E.) The A. S. forms shew that the difference between *two* and *twain* was orig. one of gender only. A. S. *twegen*, masc., two (M. E. *tweien, twein*, E. *twain*); *twā*, fem., two; neut. *twā* or *tū*, two. + Du. *twee*, Icel. *tveir*, Dan. *to*, Swed. *tvā, tu*, Goth. *twai*, G. *zwei* (also *zween*, masc.); Irish *da*, Gael. *da, do*, W. *dau*, Russ. *dva*, Lith. *dwi*, L. *duo* (whence F. *deux*, E. *deuce*), Gk. δύο, Skt. *dvāu, dvā*. Cf. also L. *bi-, bis*, twice; and the prefixes *di-, dia-, dis-*. **Der.** *a-two*, i. e. *on two* = in two.

Tybalt, the 'prince of cats.' (Low G.) In Shak. A. F. *Tebald, Tebaud*. ‒ O. Sax. *Thiod-bald*, Theobald. Cf. *Tybert*, the cat; in 'Reynard the Fox.'

Tympanum, the hollow part of the ear, &c. (L. ‒ Gk.) L. *tympanum*, a drum, tympanum. ‒ Gk. τύμπανον, a drum, roller; the same as τύπανον, a drum. ‒ Gk. τυπ-, base of τύπτειν, to strike. **Der.** *tympany*, Gk. τυμπανίας, a dropsy in which the belly is tightly stretched, as a drum.

type. (F. ‒ L. ‒ Gk.) F. *type* (Sherwood). ‒ L. *typum*, acc. of *typus*. ‒ Gk. τύπος, a blow, mark of a blow, stamp, impress, mark, mould, type, &c. ‒ Gk. τυπ-, base of τύπτειν, to strike. Cf. Skt. *tup, tump*, to hurt; allied to Gk. στυφελίζειν, to strike. (√STEU.) **Der.** *typ-ic*, Gk. τυπικός; whence *typic-al*, &c.

Typhoon, a violent whirlwind. (Arab. ‒ Gk.) [Sometimes claimed as a Chinese word meaning 'a great wind.' ‒ Chinese *ta*, great; *fäng* (in Canton *fung*), wind, whence *ta fung*, a gale, a typhoon (Williams).] But this seems to be a late mystification. In old authors the forms are *tuffon, tuffoon, tiphon*, &c. ‒ Arab. *ţūfān*, a hurricane, storm. ‒ Gk. τυφών, better τυφώς, a whirlwind. The close accidental coincidence of these words in sense and form is very remarkable, as Whitney notes. See below.

Typhus, a kind of fever. (L. ‒ Gk.) L. *typhus*. ‒ Gk. τῦφος, smoke, mist; also stupor, esp. if arising from fever; *typhus fever* = stupor-fever. ‒ Gk. τύφειν, to smoke. (√DHEU.) **Der.** *typho-id*, i. e. typhus-like, from εἶδος, resemblance.

Tyrant. (F. ‒ L. ‒ Gk.) The final *t* is added. O. F. *tiran*, also *tyrant*. ‒ L. *tyrannum*, acc. of *tyrannus*, a tyrant. ‒ Gk. τύραννος, a lord, sovereign, master; orig. in a good sense (see Prellwitz). **Der.** *tyrann-y*, F. *tyrannie*, Late L. *tyrannia*, Gk. τυραννία, sovereignty.

Tyro, misspelling of Tiro, q. v.

U.

Ubiquity, omnipresence. (F. ‒ L.) F. *ubiquité*, 'an ubiquity;' Cot. As if from L. acc. **ubiquitātem*, a being everywhere; a coined word. ‒ L. *ubīque*, everywhere. ‒ L. *ubī*, where; with suffix *-que*, allied to L. *quis*, who. **Der.** *ubiquit-ous*.

Udder. (E.) A.S. *ūder*, an udder. + M. Du. *uder*, Du. *uijer*, Icel. *jūgr* (for *jūdr), Swed. *jufver, jur*, Dan. *yver*; G. *euter*, O. H. G. *ūter*; also L. *ūber*, Gk. οὖθαρ, Skt.*ūdhar*,*ūdhan*,an udder. Brugm. i. § 113.

Ugly, frightful. (Scand.) M. E. *ugly*, *uglike.*—Icel. *uggligr*, fearful, dreadful.— Icel. *ugg-r*, fear; *-ligr*=A. S. *-līc*, like. Allied to Icel. *ugga*, to fear. **Der.** *ugliness.*

Uhlan, Ulan, a lancer. (G.—Polish.— Turkish.) G. *uhlan*, a lancer.—Pol. *ulan*, a lancer. Borrowed from Turk. *oglān*, also *ōlan*, a youth, lad. Of Tatar origin.

Ukase, an edict. (F.—Russ.) F. *ukase*. —Russ. *ukaz'*, an edict ; cf. *ukazate*, to indicate, shew, order, prescribe.—Russ. *u-*, prefix, allied to Skt. *ava*, away, off ; *kazate* to shew, Ch. Slav. *kazati*. Brugm. i. §§ 163 (note), 616.

Ulcer, a dangerous sore. (F.—L.) F. *ulcère.* — L. *ulcer-*, for **ulces-*, stem of *ulcus*, a sore.+Gk. ἕλκος, a wound, sore ; Skt. *arças*, hemorrhoids.

Ullage, the unfilled part of a cask. (Prov.—L.) '*Ullage of a cask,* that which it wants of being full ;' Phillips.—Mod. Prov. *ulhage* ; O. F. *ouillage*, *eullage*, a filling up. — Mod. Prov. *ulha* ; O. F. *ouillier, eullier,* to fill a cask up to the bung. Cotgrave spells it *oeiller*, and the sb. as *oeillage*. The Late L. type of the vb. is **oculāre*, i. e. to fill up to the *oculus*, eye, orifice. We also find O. F. *aouillier*, as if for **adoculāre*.

Ulterior, further. (L.) L. *ulterior*, further ; comp. of O. L. *ulter*, adj.

ultimate, furthest. (L.) L. *ultimātus*, pp. of *ultimāre*, to be at the last.—L. *ultimus*, last ; *ul-ti-mus* being a double superl. form from the base *ul-* ; see ultra-.

ultra-, beyond. (L.) L.*ultrā*, beyond, adv. and prep. Allied to O. Lat. *ul-s*, beyond, *ollus*, that one.

ultramarine, beyond sea ; as sb., sky-blue. (Span.—L.) Span. *ultramarino*, beyond sea ; also a blue colour.—L. *ultrā*, beyond ; *mar-e*, sea ; and suffix *-īnus* ; see **Marine.**

ultramontane, beyond the Alps. (F. — Ital. — L.) F. *ultramontain.* — Ital. *oltramontano.*—L. *ultrā*, beyond ; *montem*, acc., a mountain ; with suffix *-ānus* ; see **Tramontane** and **Mountain.**

ultramundane, beyond the world. (L.) · L. *ultrā*, beyond ; *mundānus*, worldly, from *mundus*, world ; see **Mundane.**

Umbel, an umbrella-like inflorescence. (L.) L. *umbella*, a parasol ; dimin. of *umbra*, a shade ; see **Umbrage.**

umber. (F.—Ital.—Lat.) F. *ombre*, short for *terre d'ombre*, lit. 'earth of shadow,' a brown earth used for shadowing in paintings.—Ital. *terra d'ombra*, lit. earth of shadow (Torriano).—L. *terra*, earth ; *dē*, of ; *umbra*, shadow.

Umbilical, pertaining to the navel. (F. —L.) M. F. *umbilical*, adj., from *umbilic*, navel (Cot.).—L. *umbilīcum*, acc. of *umbilīcus*, navel, middle, centre.+Gk. ὀμφαλός, navel ; cf. Skt. *nābhi-*, navel ; see **Nave** (1). Brugm. i. § 467.

Umbrage, shade of trees ; offence. (F. —L.) Properly 'shadow' ; hence, shadow or suspicion of injury. — M. F. *ombrage, umbrage*, shade, also suspicion.—F. *ombre*, shadow (with suffix *-age* < L. *-āticum*).— L. *umbra*, shadow.

umbrella. (Ital.—L.) Ital. *umbrella*, *ombrella*, a parasol ; dimin. of Ital. *ombra*, a shade.—L. *umbra*, a shade.

Umpire. (F.—L.) For *numpire*, the old form of the word ; M. E. *nompere*, *noumpere*, also *nounpere, nounpier*, P. Plowman, B. v. 337.—O. F. *nomper*, later *nompair*, peerless, odd (Cot.) ; earliest form *nonper* (Roquefort).—L. *non*, not ; *parem*, acc. of *pār*, equal. Used, like L. *impar*, in the sense of arbitrator ; the lit. sense is unequal, odd, hence a third man called in to arbitrate, a 'non-peer.' See **Non-** and **Peer.**

Un- (1), neg. prefix. (E.) Prefixed to sbs., adjs., and advs. (Distinct from *un-* (2) below.) A. S. *un-*, neg. prefix.+Du. *on-*, Icel. *ō-*, *ū-*, Dan. *u-*, Swed. *o-*, Goth. *un-*, G. *un-*, W. *an-*, L. *in-*, Gk. ἀν-, ἀ-, Zend. *an-*, *a-*, Skt. *an-*, *a-*. Readily prefixed to a large number of words ; a few of these, such as *un-couth*, of which the simple form is not used, will be found below.

Un- (2), verbal prefix, expressing the reversal of an action. (E.) Quite distinct from *un-* (1) above ; only used with verbs. Thus *to un-lock* = to reverse locking, to open that which was closed by locking. A. S. *un-*.+Du. *ont-*, G. *ent-*, O. H. G. *ant-*, Goth. *and-* (as in *and-bindan*, to unbind). Precisely the same as E. *an-* in *an-swer*, A. S. *and-*, Gk. ἀντι- ; see **Anti-**. ¶ In the case of *past participles*, the prefix is ambiguous ; thus *un-bound* may either mean 'not bound,' with prefix *un-* (1), or may mean ' undone ' or released, with prefix *un-* (2).

Un- (3), prefix. (E.) Only in *un-to*, *un-til*, which see.

Unaneled, without having received extreme unction. (E. ; *and* L. — Gk.) In Hamlet, i. 5. 77. Lit. ' un-on-oiled.' — A. S. *un-*, not; M. E. *an-eled*, from *an* (for A. S. *on*) and *eled*, pp. of M. E. *elien*, to oil, vb., from *ele*, sb., oil. The A. S. *ele*, oil, is borrowed from L. *oleum*, Gk. ἔλαιον, oil ; see **Oil**.

Unanimous, of one mind. (L.) L. *ūnanim-us*, of one mind ; with suffix *-ous*. — L. *ūn-us*, one (see **One**) ; *animus*, mind.

Uncial, large, applied to letters. (L.) L. *unciālis*, adj. from *uncia*, inch ; see **Inch**. (From the large size of the letters.)

Uncle. (F. — L.) M. E. *uncle*. — A. F. *uncle*; F. *oncle*. — L. *auunculum*, acc. of *auunculus*, a mother's brother, lit. ' little grandfather;' dimin. of *auus*, a grandfather.

Uncouth. (E.) A. S. *uncūð*, orig. unknown ; hence, strange, odd. — A. S. *un-*, not ; and *cūð*, known, pp. of *cunnan*, to know. See **Can**.

Unction. (F. — L.) F. *onction*. — L. *unctiōnem*, acc. of *unctio*, an anointing. — L. *unct-us*, pp of *ungere*, to anoint. **Dor.** *ōnctu-ous*, Late L. *unctu-ōsus*. Brugm. i. § 398. See **Unguent**.

Under, beneath. (E.) A. S. *under*. + Du. *onder*, Icel. *undir*, Dan. Swed. *under*, Goth. *undar*, G. *unter*, under. Common as a prefix. Brugm. i. § 446, ii. § 75.

Undern, a certain period of the day. (E.) The time denoted differed at different periods. The A. S. *undern* meant the third hour, about 9 a. m.; later, it meant about noon ; and, still later, the afternoon, in which sense it survives in prov. E. *aunder*, *aandorn*, *orndorns*, *doundrins*, &c. + Icel. *undorn*, O. H. G. *untorn*, Goth. *undaurni-*; the lit. sense being ' intervening or middle period.' Perhaps from A. S. *under*, with the sense ' among ' or ' between,' like G. *unter*. Cf. L. *internus*, inward ; from L. *inter*. ¶ Kluge explains it as equivalent to A. S. *un-dyrne*, ' not dark,' hence ' dawn.' (But *dyrne* usually means ' not manifest.') See Eng. Stud. xx. 334.

Understand. (E.) A. S. *understandan*, lit. to stand under or among, hence. to comprehend (like L. *intel-ligere*). — A. S. *under*, under ; *standan*, to stand.

Undertake, to take upon oneself, attempt. (E. *and* Scand.) M. E. *undertaken*, compounded of *under* and M. E. *taken*, to take. **Der.** *undertak-er*, lit. one who takes a business in hand ; Oth. iv. 1. 224.

Undulate, to wave. (L.) From pp. of L. *undulāre*, to fluctuate. — L. **undula*, dimin. of *unda*, a wave. Allied to **Water**; cf. Skt. *udan*, water, *und*, to wet, Lith. *wandŭ*, water, Russ. *voda*, water. Brugm. i. §§ 102, 594.

Uneath, scarcely, with difficulty. (E.) Obsolete. M. E. *unepe*. A. S. *unēaðe*, adv., from adj. *unēaðe*, difficult. — A. S. *un-*, not ; *ēaðe*, *ēað*, easy ; the orig. sense being waste, empty, hence easy to occupy. Cf. O. Sax. *ōði*, easy ; G. *öde*, waste, deserted, Icel. *auðr*, empty, Goth. *auths*, *authis*, desert, waste. ¶ But some dissociate A. S. *ēaðe*, O. Sax. *ōði*, from the rest.

Ungainly, awkward. (Scand. ; *with* E. *prefix and suffix*.) Formed by adding *-ly* to M. E. *ungein*, inconvenient. — A. S. *un-*, not ; Icel. *gegn*, ready, serviceable, convenient, allied to *gegna*, to meet, suit, *gegn*, against, and to F. **Again**. Cf. Icel. *ō-gegn*, ungainly.

Unguent, ointment. (L.) L. *unguentum*, ointment. — L. *unguent-*, stem of pres. pt. of *ungere*, to anoint. + Skt. *añj*, to smear. Brugm. i. § 398.

Unicorn. (F. — L.) M. F. *unicorne*, a fabulous one-horned animal. — L. *ūnicornem*, acc. of *unicornis*, one-horned. — L. *ūni-*, for *ūnus*, one (see **One**) ; *corn-ū*, a horn. See **Horn**.

uniform, adj. (F. — L.) F. *uniforme*. — L. *ūniformem*, acc. of *ūniformis*, having one form. — L. *ūni-*, for *ūnus*, one; *form-a*, form ; see **Form**.

union (1), concord. (F. — L.) F. *union*. — L. acc. *ūniōnem*, oneness. — L. *ūni-*, for *ūnus*, one.

union (2), a large pearl. (F. — L.) The same word as the above ; the L. *ūnio* means oneness, also a single pearl of a large size, also a kind of onion.

unique. (F. — L.) F. *unique*, single. — L. *ūnicum*, acc. of *ūnicus*, single. — L. *ūni-*, for *ūnus*, one.

unison, concord. (F. — L.) F. *unisson*. — L. *ūnisonum*, acc. of *ūnisonus*, having a like sound. — L. *ūni-*, for *ūnus*, one ; *sonus*, sound ; see **Sound** (3).

unit. (F. — L.) Formed by dropping the final *-y* of *unity*. ' *Unit*, *Unite*, or

Unity, in arithmetic, the first significant figure, or number 1,' &c., Phillips; see **Unity.**

unite. (L.) L. *ūnītus*, pp. of *ūnīre*, to unite. — L. *ūnus*, one.

unity, oneness. (F.—L.) M.E. *unitee*. — M.F. *unite* (*unité*). — L. *ūnitātem*, acc. of *ūnitās*, unity. — L. *ūni-*, for *ūnus*, one, cognate with **One.**

universal. (F.—L.) F. *universel* (Latinised). — L. *ūniuersālis*, belonging to the whole. — L. *ūniuersus*, turned into one, combined into a whole. — L. *ūni-* for *ūnus*, one; *uersus*, pp. of *uertere*, to turn; see **Verse.** Der. *univers-ity*, F. *université*, from L. acc. *ūniuersitātem*.

univocal, having but one meaning. (L.) From L. *ūniuoc-us*, univocal; with suffix *-ālis*. — L. *ūni-*, for *ūnus*, one; *uoc-*, allied to *uox*, voice, sense; see **Voice.**

Unkempt, i. e. uncombed; for *un-kemb'd*. From A. S. *cemban*, to comb; formed (by vowel-change of *a* to *e*) from *camb*, a comb. See **Comb.**

Unless, if not, except. (E.) Formerly *on les, on lesse*, in the phrase *on lesse that*, i.e. in less than, on a less supposition than. Thus *un-* here stands for *on*. See **On** and **Less.**

Unruly, disregarding restraint. (E.; and F.—L.) From *un-*, prefix, and *rule*; with suffix *-y*; a coined word. See **Rule.** Fabyan has *unruled*.

Until. (E.) The same word as below, with the substitution of North E. (and Scand.) *til*, to, for E. *to*. See **Till.**

unto, even to. (E.) M.E. *unto* (not in A. S.). For *und-to*; where *to* is the usual E. prep., and *und* is the O. Fries. *und, ont*, Goth. *und*, O. Sax. *und*, unto, whence O. Sax. *un-tō*, unto. A related form *oð* (< *anth*) is common in A. S.; cf. also A. S. *and-*, prefix, for which see **Un-** (2).

Up. (E.) M.E. *vp, up*; A.S. *ūp, upp*, adv. + Du. *op*, Icel. *upp*, Dan. *op*, Swed. *upp*, Goth. *iup*, G. *auf*, O.H.G. *ūf*. Allied to **Over**; cf. *ab-ove*.

Upas, the poison-tree of Java. (Malay.) Malay *ūpas*, a poisonous juice; *pūhun ūpas*, poison-tree (*pūhun=*tree).

Upbraid, to reproach. (E.) M.E. *vp-breiden*, to reproach. — A.S. *up*, up, upon, on; *bregdan*, to braid, weave, also to lay hold of, seize. The orig. sense seems to have been to lay hold of, hence to attack, accuse, &c. The A.S. *bregdan*, also =E.

braid, to weave; so that *-braid* in *up-braid* is the usual verb *braid*, used in a special sense. So also Dan. *be-breide* (lit. be-braid), to upbraid.

Upholsterer. (E.) Lengthened from *upholster*, for *uphold-ster*, another form of *upholder*, which was formerly used of a dealer in furniture; lit. one who *holds up* for sale.

Upon. (E.) A.S. *uppon*, upon. — A.S. *upp, up*, up; *on*, on. + Icel. *upp ā*, upon; Swed. *på*, Dan. *paa* (reduced forms).

Uproar, tumult. (Du.) The spelling shews confusion with E. *roar*. — Du. *oproer*, ' uprore, tumult;' Hexham. — Du. *op*, up; *roeren*, to excite, stir, move; so that *oproer* = a stirring up, commotion. + Low G. *upp-rōr* (Danneil); Swed. *uppror*, Dan. *uprör*, G. *aufruhr*. β. The verb is Du. *roeren*, Swed. *röra*, Dan. *röre*, G. *rühren*, A.S. *hrēran*, to stir; see **Reremouse.** The A.S. *hrēran* is from *hrōr*, adj., active, busy.

Upsidedown. (E.) From *up, side*, and *down*. But the M.E. form was *up-so-doun*, i. e. ' up as it were down.'

Upstart, sb. (E.) From *upstart*, vb., to start up; Spenser, F. Q. i. 1. 16; Chaucer, C. T., A. 1080. See **Start.**

Upwards; see **Up** and **-ward**, suffix.

Urbane, courteous. (L.) L. *urbānus*, belonging to a city. — L. *urb-s*, a city. Der. *urban*, doublet of *urbane*; *urban-i-ty*, F. *urbanité*, from L. acc. *urbānitātem*, courteousness.

Urchin, a hedgehog, goblin, imp, small child. (F.—L.) Orig. hedgehog; hence, goblin, imp, small child (Tempest, i. 2. 326); it being supposed that some imps took a hedgehog's shape. — Walloon *urechon*, *irchon* (Sigart); Norm. dial. *hérichon*; O. North. F. *herichon*; O.F. *ireçon, eriçon, herisson*, a hedgehog; formed with suffix *-on* (=L. *-ōnem*) from L. *ēricius*, a hedgehog, lengthened form of *ēr* (gen. *ēri-s*), a hedgehog. + Gk. χήρ, hedgehog; cf. χαράσσειν, to scratch.

Ure, practise, use. (F.—L.) Obsolete, except in *in-ure, man-ure*. (Distinct from *use*.) — O.F. *eure, uevre, ovre*, work, action. — L. *opera*, work; see **Operate.**

Urge. (L.) L. *urgēre*, to urge, drive. Allied to **Wreak.** (✔WERG.) Der. *urg-ent*, from stem of pres. part.

Urim. (Heb.) Heb. *ūrim*, lights; pl. of *ūr*, light. See **Thummim.**

Urine. (F.—L.) F. *urine*. — L. *ūrīna*. + Gk. οὖρον, urine; Skt. *vāri, vār*, water;

Icel. *ŭr*, drizzling rain; Icel. *ver*, A. S. *wær*, sea. Orig. 'water.'

Urn. (F.–L.) M. E. *urne.*–F. *urne.* –L. *urna*, urn. For **urc-na*; cf. *urc-eus*, a pitcher. Brugm. i. § 756.

Us. (E.) A. S. *ūs*, dat. pl. of *wē*, we; *ūs*, *ūsic*, acc. pl. of *wē*.+Du. *ons*, Icel. *oss*, Swed. *oss*, Dan. *os*, G. *uns*; Goth. *uns*, *unsis*, dat. and acc. pl. Teut. base **uns-*. Cf. L. *nōs*, Skt. *nas*; also Gk. *ἡμᾶς*, Skt. *asmān*, us. Brugm. i. § 437 (2); ii. § 436.

Use (1), sb. (F.–L.) M.E. *use*, *vs.* – O.F. *us*, use, usage. – L. *ūsum*, acc. of *ūsus*, use.–L. *ūsus*, pp. of *ūtī*, to use. Der. *use*, vb., F. *user*, Late L. *ūsāre*, frequent. of L. *ūtī*, to use; *us-age*, F. *usage*; *usu-al*, L. *ūsuālis*, adj., from *ūsu-*, stem of *ūsus*; use; &c.

Use (2), profit, benefit. (F.–L.) When *use* is employed, legally, in the sense of 'benefit,' it is a modernised spelling of the Anglo-F. form of the Lat. *opus*, employment, need. We find the Anglo-F. spellings *oes*, *oeps*, *uoes*; O. F. *oes*, *eus*, *ues*.

Usher, a door-keeper. (F.–L.) M.E. *uschere*, *ussher*. – A. F. *usser*; O. F. *ussier*, *uissier*, later *huissier*, 'an usher, or door keeper;' Cot. – L. *ostiārium*, acc. of *ostiārius*, a door-keeper. – L. *ostium*, a door. Extended from L. *ōs*, mouth; see **Oral**.

Usquebaugh. (Irish.) Irish *uisge beatha*, usquebaugh, whisky. – Irish *uisge*, water (see **Whisky**); *beatha*, life, O. Ir. *bethu*, allied to Gk. *βίος*, life. Brugm. i. §§ 85, 368.

Usurp, to seize to one's own use. (F.– L.) F. *usurper*. – L. *ūsurpāre*, to employ, acquire; also, to usurp. β. Clearly derived from *ūs-us*, use, but the rest of the word is obscure; Brugmann (ii. § 4) suggests *ūsu-* and *rapere*, to seize to one's own use.

usury. (F.–L.) M. E. *usurye*, *usure*. –F. *usure*, usury, the occupation of a thing. – L. *ūsūra*, use, enjoyment, interest, usury. – L. *ūs-us*, pp. of *ūtī*, to use.

Ut, the first note of the musical scale. (L.) L. *ut*. See **Gamut**.

Utas, the octave of a feast. (F.–L.) *Utas* is for *utaves*, an A. F. word corresponding to O. F. *oitauves*, pl. of *oitauve*, octave, eighth day. – L. *octāua* (*diēs*), eighth day; fem. of *octāuus*, eighth. – L. *octō*, eight. See **Octave**.

Utensil. (F.–L.) M. F. *utensile*, sb. – L. *ūtensilis*, adj., fit for use; whence *ūtensilia*, neut. pl., utensils. For **ūtent-*

tilis, from the stem of pres. pt. of *ūtī*, to use. Cf. **Use** (1).

Uterine, born of the same mother by a different father. (F.–L.) M. F. *uterin*, 'of the womb, borne of one mother;' Cot. – L. *uterīnus*, born of one mother. – L. *uterus*, womb. Cf. Gk. *ὑστέρα*, womb. Brugm. i. § 706.

Utilise. (F.–L.) F. *utiliser*, a modern word; coined from *util-e*, useful, with suffix *-iser* (Gk. *-ιζειν*). – L. *ūtilis*, useful. – L. *ūtī*, to use. Cf. **Use** (1).

utility. (F.–L.) F. *utilité.* – L. acc. *ūtilitātem*, from nom. *ūtilitās*, usefulness. – L. *ūtili-s*, useful. – L. *ūtī*, to use.

Utis, festival merriment; see **Utas**.

Utmost. (E.) M. E. *outemest.* A. S. *ūte-m-est*, double superl. form, from *ūt*, out. Doublet of *outmost*. See **Out**.

Utopian. (Gk.) An adj. due to Sir T. More's description of *Utopia*, an imaginary island, situate *nowhere*. – Gk. *οὐ*, not; *τόπος*, a place; see **Topic**.

Utter, outer. (E.) M. E. *utter*. A. S. *uttera*, which occurs as well as *ūtera*; both are comparative forms of *ūt*, out; see **Out**. Der. *utter*, vb.; cf. G. *äussern*, vb., from *äusser*, outer; also A. S. *ūt-ian*, to put out, from *ūt*, out.

utterance (1), an uttering. (E.; *with* F. *suffix*.) From the verb *to utter*, M. E. *outren*; formed from M. E. *outer*, *utter*, compar. of A. S. *ūt*, out. See **Out**.

Utterance (2), extremity. In Shak. (F.–L.) F. *outrance*, extremity. – F. *outre*, beyond. – L. *ultrā*, beyond; see **Ultra-**.

Uvula. (L.) Late L. *ūvula*, dimin. of L. *ūua*, a grape, a cluster, also the uvula. +Lith. *úga*, a berry. Brugm. i. § 223 (2).

Uxorious, excessively fond of a wife. (L.) L. *uxōri-us*, fond of a wife; with suffix *-ous*. – L. *uxōr-*, stem of *uxor*, a wife.

V.

V. In Middle-English, *v* is commonly written as *u* in the MSS.; conversely, *v* is put for *u* in a few words, chiefly *vp*, *vnder*, *vnto*, *vs*, *vse*, and the prefix *vn-*.

Vacation. (F.–L.) F. *vacation.* – L. acc. *uacātiōnem*, leisure. – L. *uacātus*, pp. of *uacāre*, to be empty or at leisure. Cf. L. *uacuus*, W. *gwag*, empty.

Vaccinate. (L.) Coined as if from pp. of **vaccināre*, to inoculate. – L. *uac-cīnus*, belonging to cows. – L. *uacca*, a cow. **+** Skt. *vaçā*, a cow. **¶** First used about 1798.

Vacillation. (F. — L.) F. *vacillation*, 'a reeling, staggering;' Cot. — L. *uacillā-tiōnem*, acc. of *uacillātio*, a reeling, wavering. — L. *uacillātus*, pp. of *uacillāre*, to reel. Cf. Skt. *vaṅk*, to go tortuously, *vakra-*, bent.

Vacuum. (L.) L. *uacuum*, an empty space; neut. of *uacuus*, empty. — L. *uacāre*, to be empty; see **Vacation.**

Vade, to fade. (Du. — F. — L.) M. Du. *vadden*, 'to fade.' Hexham. — O. F. *fader*, to fade; see **Fade.**

Vagabond. (F. — L.) F. *vagabond*, 'a vagabond;' Cot. — L. *uagābundus*, adj., strolling about. — L. *uagā-rī*, to wander; with suffix *-bundus*.

vagary. (L.) Also *vagare* (trisyllabic; Stanyhurst); orig. used as a verb; [cf. F. *vaguer*, 'to wander, vagary;' Cot.] — L. *uagārī*, to wander; see **Vague.**

Vagrant. (F. — G.) A. F. *wakerant*, a vagrant; O. F. *walcrant*, wandering, pres. pt. of *walcrer*, to wander. — M. G. *welkern*, M. H. G. *walgern*, to walk about; allied to E. **Walk.** **¶** Confused with L. *uagārī*, to wander, but not derived from it. See Phil. Soc. Trans., 1885, 1888, 1889.

Vague, unsettled. (F. — L.) F. *vague*, wandering; *vaguer*, to wander. — L. *uagus*, wandering; whence *uagārī*, to wander.

Vail (1), the same as **Veil.**

Vail (2), to lower. (F. — L.) From O. F. *avaler*, to let fall down. — F. *aval*, downward. — L. *ad uallem*, to the valley.

Vail (3), a gift to a servant. (F. — L.) A headless form of *avail*, sb., in the sense of profit, help (Palsgrave). From **Avail**, vb.

Vain. (F. — L.) F. *vain*. — L. *uānum*, acc. of *uānus*, empty, vain. Brugm. i. § 414 (3).

Vair, a kind of fur. (F. — L.) F. *vair*, 'a rich fur;' Cot. — L. *uarius*, variegated. Der. *vair-y* (in heraldry), from M. F. *vairé*, 'diversified with argent and azure;' Cot. Hence *meni-ver* (= F. *menu vair*), 'little vair.'

Valance, a fringe of drapery, now applied to a part of the bed-hangings. (F. — L.) Chaucer has 'a litel kerchief of *valence*'; Assembly of Foules, 272. Prob. named from *Valence* in France, near Lyons (still famous for silks). — L. *Valentia*, a name given to several towns, evidently from the name *Valens*, lit. 'strong.' — L. *ualent-*, stem of pres. pt. of *ualēre*, to be

strong; see **Valid.** **¶** Johnson derives it from *Valentia* in Spain, which is also famous for silks.

Vale, a valley. (F. — L.) M. E. *val*. — F. *val*. — L. *uallem*, acc. of *uallis*, valley.

Valediction, a farewell. (L.) Formed from L. *ualēdictus*, pp. of *ualēdīcere*, to say farewell. — L. *ualē*, farewell; *dīcere*, to say. **β.** L. *ualē*, lit. 'be strong,' is the 2 p. s. imp. of *ualēre*, to be strong.

Valentine. (F. — L.) Named from *St. Valentine's* day, Feb. 14. — F. *Valentin*. — L. *Valentīnus*. — L. *ualent-*, stem of pres. pt. of *ualēre*, to be strong.

valerian. (F. — L.) M. F. *valeriane*, valerian; a flower. — Late L. *ualeriāna*, valerian. Fem. of *Valeriānus*, prob. a personal name; from L. *ualēre*, to be strong.

Valet. (F. — C.) F. *valet*, 'a groom;' Cot. The same word as **Varlet**, q. v.

Valetudinary. (F. — L.) M.F. *valetu-dinaire*, sickly. — L. *ualētūdinārius*, sickly. — L. *ualētūdin-*, stem of *ualētūdo*, health (good or bad). — L. *ualē-re*, to be strong.

Valhalla, the hall of the slain. (Scand.) Icel. *valhöll* (gen. *valhallar*), lit. the hall of the slain. — Icel. *valr*, the slain, slaughter; *höll*, hall, a hall; see **Hall.**

Valiant, brave. (F. — L.) F. *vaillant*, valiant; O. F. *vailant*, pres. pt. of F. *valoir*, to profit. — L. *ualēre*, to be strong.

valid, having force. (F. — L.) F. *valide*. — L. *ualidus*, strong. — L. *ualēre*, to be strong.

Valise, a travelling-bag. (F. — Ital.) F. *valise*, 'a male [mail], wallet;' Cot. — Ital. *valigia*; corrupted in German to *felleisen*. **β.** Etym. unknown; Diez supposes it to be founded on L. *uidulus*, a leathern travelling-trunk. Devic suggests Pers. *walīchah*, a large sack, or Arab. *walīhat*, a corn-sack.

Valkyrie, Valkyria, one of the handmaidens of Odin. (Scand.) Icel. *Valkyrja*, a goddess; lit. ' chooser of the slain.' — Icel. *val*, acc. of *valr*, the slain (A.S. *wæl*); *-kyrja*, f., a chooser, from *kur-* (< **kus-*), weak grade of *kjósa*, to choose, cognate with E. *choose*.

Valley. (F. — L.) M. E. *vale*, *valeie*. — O. F. *valee* (F. *vallée*), a valley; parallel to Ital. *vallāta*, a valley, which appears to mean, literally, ' formed like a valley.' Formed with suffix *-ee* (< L. *-āta*), from F. *val*, a vale, representing L. *uallem*, acc. of *uallis*, a vale.

Valour. (F.—L.) O. F. *valor, valur, valeur,* value, worthiness. — L. *ualōrem,* acc. of *ualor,* worth. — L. *ualēre,* to be strong, to be worth.

    value. (F.—L.) M. F. *valuë,* fem. 'value;' Cot. Fem. of *valu,* pp. of *valoir,* to be worth. — L. *ualēre,* to be worth.

Valve. (F.—L.) F. *valve,* 'a foulding, or two-leafed door, or window;' Cot. — L. *ualua,* sing. of *ualuæ,* the leaves of a folding-door. Allied to L. *uoluere,* to revolve; see **Voluble.**

Vambrace, Vantbrace, armour for the fore-arm. (F.—L.) The word simply means 'fore-arm.' It is short for *avant-brace.* — M. F. *avant-bras,* 'a vambrace, armour for an arm; also, the part of the arm which extends from the elbow to the wrist;' Cotgrave. (The latter is the orig. sense.) — F. *avant,* before; *bras,* the arm. — L. *ab ante,* from before, in front; *brāchium,* arm (the pl. of which gave O. F. *brace,* arm; see Scheler). See **Van** (1) and **Vamp.** ¶ Similarly, armour for the upper part of the arm was called a *rere-brace,* i. e. rear-brace.

    Vamp, the fore-part of a shoe. (F.—L.) Short for M. E. *vampay,* also *vaumpè,* a vamp. — M. F. *avant-pied,* 'the part of the foot that's next to the toes.' — F. *avant,* before; *pied* (A. F. *pee*), foot, from L. *pedem,* acc. of *pēs,* foot.

Vampire. (F.—G.—Servian.) F. *vampire.* — G. *vampyr.* — Servian *vampir,* a blood-sucker, a supposed ghost that sucked men's blood. Prob. of Turkish origin; cf. N. Turk. *uber,* a witch (Miklosich).

    Vamplate, an iron plate protecting a lance. (F.—L.) From F. *avant,* in front, fore; and *plate.* See **Vambrace.**

Van (1), the front of an army. (F.—L.) Short for *van-guard,* which stands for M. E. *vantwarde.* — O. F. *avant-warde,* later *avant-garde,* 'the vanguard of an army;' Cot. — F. *avant,* before; O. F. *warde,* a guard; see **Advance** and **Guard** or **Ward.**

Van (2), a fan. (F.—L.) F. *van,* a fan. — L. *uannum,* acc. of *uannus,* a fan. Doublet, *fan.*

Van (3), a covered waggon for goods. (F.—Pers.) Short for *caravan,* like *bus* for *omnibus.* See **Caravan.**

Vandal, a barbarian. (L.—Teut.) One of the tribe of *Vandalī* (Pliny); answering to A.S. *Wendlas,* pl. (from *Wendil-*). Cf. Icel. *Vendill* (also *Vandill*), a proper name.

Vane, a weather-cock. (E.) A Southern form; formerly also *fane.* A. S. *fana,* a small flag.+Du. *vaan,* Icel. *fāni,* Dan. *fane,* Swed. Goth. *fana,* G. *fahne.* Teut. type **fanon-,* m. Orig. a bit of cloth; allied to L. *pannus,* a cloth; see **Pane.**

    Vanguard; see **Van** (1).

Vanilla, a plant. (Span.—L.) Span. *vainilla,* a small pod, or capsule (which is the orig. sense). Dimin. of Span. *vaina,* a scabbard, a pod. — L. *uagīna,* scabbard, sheath, pod.

Vanish. (F. — L.) M. E. *vanissen, vanisshen;* also *evanisshen.* Derived from an O. F. vb. **vanir,* with pres. pt. **vanissant.* The verb is only recorded as A. F. *evanir,* O. F. *esvanir, esvanuir;* but we find O. F. *esvanuir* and *vanuir.* Cf. Ital. *svanire,* to vanish (where *s* = L. *ex*); Late L. type **exvanīre,* for L. *ēuānescere.* — L. *ē,* out, away; *uānescere,* to vanish, lit. to become empty, from L. *uānus,* empty. See **Vain.**

    vanity. (F. — L.) F. *vanité.* — L. *uānitātem,* acc. of *uānitās,* emptiness. — L. *uānus,* vain, empty.

Vanquish. (F.—L.) M. E. *venkisen, venquisshen.* — A. F. *venquis-,* O. F. *vein-quiss-,* stem of pres. pt. of A. F. *venquir, veinquir,* occurring as a collateral form of *veincre,* to conquer (F. *vaincre*). — L. *uincere,* to conquer. Brugm. i. § 367.

Vantage. (F.—L.) Short for M. E. *avantage;* see **Advantage.**

Vapid, insipid. (L.) L. *uapidus,* stale, flat, said of wine; cf. L. *uappa,* vapid or palled wine; wine that has emitted its vapour or strength. Allied to *uapor* (below).

    vapour, mist. (F.—L.) F. *vapeur.* — L. *uapōrem,* acc. of *uapor,* vapour. + Gk. καπνός, smoke. Brugm. i. § 193.

Varicose, permanently dilated, as a vein. (L.) L. *uaricōsus.* — L. *uaric-,* stem of *uarix,* a dilated vein; of uncertain origin: cf. L. *uarus,* a blotch, pimple.

Variegate. (L.) From pp. of L. *uariegāre,* to make of various colours. — L. *uario-,* for *uarius,* of divers colours; *-igāre,* due to *agere,* to drive, to make.

    various. (L.) L. *uari-us,* variegated, diverse, manifold; with suffix *-ous.* Der. *varie-ty,* M. F. *varieté,* from L. acc. *uarie-tātem,* variety.

Varlet. (F. — C.) M. F. *varlet,* 'a groom, stripling, youth;' Cot. An older spelling was *vaslet,* dimin. of O. F. *vasal, vassal,* a vassal; see **Vassal.** The successive spellings were *vaslet, varlet, vallet, valet.*

Varnish. (F.) F. *vernis,* 'varnish;' Cot. Cognate with Ital. *vernice,* Port. *verniz,* Span. *berniz,* varnish; Late L. *vernicium, vernix, bernix.* Origin unknown. Perhaps from M. Gk. βερνίκη; see Schade, p. 1439.

Vary. (F.—L.) F. *varier.*—L. *uariāre,* to vary.—L. *uarius,* various.

Vascular. (L.) From L. *uasculum,* a small vessel; double dimin. of *uās* (below).

vase. (F.—L.) F. *vase,* a vessel.—L. *uāsum,* allied to *uās,* a vessel. Allied to Skt. *vāsana-,* a receptacle, cover.

Vassal, a dependant. (F.—C.) M. E. *vassal.*—F. *vassal,* 'a vassall, subject, tenant;' Cot. The Celtic sense is 'servant'; Low L. *uassallus;* extended from Low L. *uassus, uasus,* a servant.—O. Bret. *uuas,* Bret. *gwaz,* a servant, vassal; W., Corn. *gwas,* youth, servant; O. Irish *foss.* Celtic type **wassos.*

Vast. (F.—L.) F. *vaste.*—L. *uastus,* vast, great, of large extent.

Vat, a large vessel for liquors. (E.) M. E. *vat* (Southern); also *fat* (Northern). A.S. *fæt,* a vessel, cask. + Du. *vat,* Icel. *fat,* Dan. *fad,* Swed. *fat,* G. *fass.* Teut. ype **fatom,* n. Lit. 'that which con-.ains;' cf. E. Fries. *faten,* O. Fries. *fatia,* Du. *vatten,* to catch, contain, G. *fassen,* to seize, contain.

Vaticinate, to foretell. (L.) From L. *uāticinātus,* pp. of *uāticinārī,* to prophesy.—L. *uāticin-us,* prophetic.—L. *uāti-,* for *uātes,* a prophet, allied to Wood (2); *-cin-,* from *can-ere,* to sing, proclaim (Bréal).

Vaudeville. (F.) F. *vaudeville,* orig. a country ballad; 'so tearmed of *Vaude-vire,* a Norman town, wherein Olivier Bassel [or Basselin], the first inventer of them, lived;' Cot. Basselin was a Norman poet (died ab. 1418), whose songs were named after his native valley, the *Val de Vire; Vire* is in Normandy, S. of Bayeux.

Vault (1), an arched roof, cellar. (F.—L.) For *vaut;* the *l* was pedantically inserted. M. E. *voute, vowte, vawte, vaute.*—M. F. *voute* (also *voulte,* with inserted *l*), 'a vault, arch, a vaulted roof;' Cot. O.F. *volte,* a vault (whence the later form *voute,* mod. F. *voûte*); this is the fem. of O. F. *volt,* vaulted, lit. bent, bowed, the same as Ital. *volta.*—Late L. **voltus,* substituted

for *uolūtus,* pp. of *uoluere,* to roll, turn round. Thus a *vault* meant a 'bowed' roof, hence a chamber with bowed roof, a cellar which has an arched roof.

vault (2), to bound, leap. (F.—Ital.—L.) M. F. *volter,* 'to vault;' Cot.—M. F. *volte,* a round, turn, tumbler's gambol.—Ital. *volta,* a sudden turn; the same word as *volta,* a vault (above). See Volute.

Vaunt. (F.—L.) F. *se vanter,* to boast.—Late L. *vānitāre,* to speak vanity, flatter; (F. *se vanter* = to flatter oneself). A frequentative form from *uānus,* vain; see Vain.

Vavasour, a vassal of the second rank. (F.—C.) A. F. *vavasour.*—Low L. *vassus vassōrum,* vassal of vassals; see Vassal.

Vaward, another spelling of *vanward* or *vanguard;* see Van (1).

Veal. (F.—L.) O. F. *veël,* a calf.—L. *uitellum,* acc. of *uitellus,* dimin. of *uitulus,* a calf.+Gk. ἰταλός, a calf; cf. Skt. *vatsa-,* a calf, properly 'a yearling,' from Skt. *vatsa-,* Gk. ἔτος, a year. Allied to Wether and Veteran.

Veda, knowledge; one of the ancient sacred Skt. books. (Skt.) Skt. *veda-,* lit. knowledge.—Skt. *vid,* to know; allied to Wit.

Vedette, Vidette, a cavalry sentinel. (F.—Ital.—L.) M.F. *vedette,* a sentinel.—Ital. *vedetta,* a horse-sentry; formerly a watch-tower.—Ital. *vedere,* to see.—L. *uidēre,* to see; see Vision.

Veer. (F.—L.?) F. *virer,* to turn, veer. Said to be derived from L. *gÿrāre,* to turn round (see Gyrate), but influenced by L. *uiriola,* dimin. of *uiria* (only in pl. *uiriæ*), an armlet, large ring. Allied to Environ. Cf. also M. F. *virolet,* 'a boy's wind-mill;' Cot. (Doubtful.)

Vegetable. (F.—L.) M. F. *vegetable,* adj., 'vegetable, fit or able to live;' Cot. This is the old sense.—L. *uegetābilis,* full of life, animating.—L. *uegetāre,* to quicken, enliven.—L. *uegetus,* lively.—L. *uegēre,* to quicken, arouse. Allied to Vigour. Der. *vegetat-ion,* M. F. *vegetation* (Cot.).

Vehement, passionate. (F.—L.) M.F. *vehement* (Cot.). — L. *uehement-,* stem of *uehemens,* passionate; lit. 'out of one's mind.' β. *Uehe-* has been explained as equivalent to *ue-,* 'apart from,' as in *ue-cors,* senseless; cf. Skt. *vahis,* apart. For *mens,* mind, see Mental.

Vehicle. (L.) L. *uehiculum,* a carriage.—L. *uehere,* to carry, convey.+Skt.

vah, to carry. Allied to **Weigh** and **Wain**. (√WEGH.) Brugm. i. § 128.

Veil, sb. (F − L.) O. F. *veile*, later *voile*. − L. *uēlum*, a sail; also a cloth. For **uexlum* = **uecslum*; cf. *uexillum*, a standard. Lit. 'propeller' of a ship; from *uehere*, to carry along. Brugm. i. § 883.

Vein. (F. − L.) F. *veine*. − L. *uēna*, a vein. For **uecsna*. Lit. 'conveyer' of the blood. − L. *uehere*, to carry. Brugm. ii. § 66.

Vellum. (F. − L.) M. E. *velim*. − O. F. *velin* (F. *vélin*); cf. Late L. *vitulīnium*, or *pellis vitulīna*, vellum, calf's skin. − L. *uitulīnus*, adj., from *uitulus*, a calf. See **Veal**.

Velocity. (F. − L.) M. F. *velocité*, swiftness. − L. acc. *uēlōcitātem*. − L. *uēlōci*-, decl. stem of *uēlōx*, swift. Allied to **Volatile**. **Der.** *veloci-pede*, lit. 'swift-foot,' coined from L. *uēlōci*- (above), and L. *ped*-, stem of *pēs*, a foot.

Velvet. (F. − L.) M. E. *velouette*, *velouet*; Spenser has *vellet*. A. F. *velwet*, *veluet*; Low L. *velluētum*; answering to a Romanic type **villūtettum*. Cf. M. Ital. *veluto* (Ital. *velluto*), velvet; answering to a Late L. **villūtus*, shaggy, by-form of L. *uillōsus*, shaggy. All from L. *uillus*, shaggy hair; allied to *uellus*, fleece, and to E. **Wool**.

Venal. (F. − L.) M. F. *venal*, saleable. − L. *uēnālis*, saleable. − L. *uēnus*, *uēnum*, sale. Allied to Gk. ὦνος, a price, ὠνή, a buying; Brugm. i. § 329. **Der.** *venal-ity*.

vend, to sell. (F. − L.) F. *vendre*. − L. *uendere*; short for *uēnundare*, lit. to give or offer for sale, also written *uēnum dare*. − L. *uēnum*, sale; *dare*, to give, offer.

Veneer, to overlay with a thin slice of wood. (G. − F. − O. H. G.) Formerly *fineer*. − G. *furniren*, to furnish or provide small pieces of wood, to veneer. − F. *fournir*, to furnish; a word of G. origin; see **Furnish**.

Venerable. (F. − L.) M. F. *venerable*. − L. *uenerābilis*, to be reverenced. − L. *uenerā-rī*, to reverence. − L. *uener*-, for **uenes*, stem of *uenus*, love. **Der.** *vene-rat-ion*, from pp. of *uenerārī*.

venereal. (L.) Coined from L. *uene-re-us*, *ueneri-us*, pertaining to Venus or love. − L. *ueneri*-, decl. stem of *uenus*, love. Allied to Skt. *van*, to love, honour.

Venery, hunting. (F. − L.) M. F. *venerie*, 'hunting;' Cot. − O. F. *vener*, to hunt. − L. *uēnārī*, to hunt; see **Venison**.

Venesection, blood-letting. (L.) L. *uēnæ*, of a vein, gen. of *uēna*; and *section*. See **Vein** and **Section**.

Venew, Venue, Veney, (1) a turn or bout or thrust in fencing; (2) a locality. (F. − L.) M. F. *venuë*, 'a coming, a *venny* in fencing, turn, trick;' Cot. Lit. a coming, home-thrust; fem. of *venu*, pp. of *venir*, to come. − L. *uenīre*, to come; see **Venture**. **2.** As a law-term, *venue* is the same word, and signifies a place of arrival, locality. ¶ Apparently confused by Blackstone with O. F. *visné*, vicinity (a derivative of L. *uīcinus*, near).

Vengeance. (F. − L.) F. *vengeance*, 'vengeance;' Cot. − F. *venger*, to avenge. − L. *uindicāre*; see **Vindicate**.

Venial. (F. − L.) O. F. *venial*. − L. *ueniālis*, pardonable. − L. *uenia*, pardon; also grace, favour. Allied to *venereal*.

Venison. (F. − L.) M. E. *veneison*. − A. F. *veneisun*, M. F. *venaison*, 'venison, flesh of beasts of chase;' Cot. − L. *uēnā-tiōnem*, acc. of *uēnātio*, the chase, also game. − L. *uēnātus*, pp. of *uenārī*, to hunt. Cf. **Gain**, vb. And see **Venery**.

Venom. (F. − L.) M. E. *venim*. − A. F. *venim* (F. *venin*). − L. *uenēnum*, poison.

Venous, belonging to a vein. (L.) For L. *uēnōsus*, adj.; from *uēna*, a vein. See **Vein**.

Vent (1), an air-hole, flue. (F. − L.) '*A vent*, meatus, porus; *To vent*, aperire, enacuare;' Levins. Doubtless influenced by a popular etymology from F. *vent*, wind, as if 'air-hole'; but the true sense was 'fissure.' Formerly *fent*. '*Fent* of a gowne, *fente*;' Palsgrave. − M. F. *fente*, 'a cleft, rift;' Cot. − F. *fendre*, to cleave. − L. *findere*, to cleave. See **Fissure**. **Der.** *vent*, vb., Temp. ii. 2. 111; certainly confused with F. *vent*, wind; see **Vent** (3).

Vent (2), sale, utterance. (F. − L.) Formerly common. − F. *vente*, sale, selling. − F. *vendre*. − L. *uendere*, to sell; see **Vend**.

Vent (3), to snuff up air, breathe, expose to air. (F. − L.) See Spenser, Shep. Kal. Feb. 75; F. Q. iii. 1. 42. The word was prob. due to a misuse of *vent* (1); but the popular etymology is obvious. − F. *vent*, wind. − L. *uentum*, acc. of *uentus*, wind; cognate with **Wind** (1). **Der.** *vent-age*, air-hole, Hamlet, iii. 2. 373.

ventail, lower half of the moveable

part of a helmet. (F.–L.) M.E. *auentaile* (with prefix *a* = F. *a* < L. *ad*).– M.F. *ventaille*, 'breathing-part of a helmet;' Cot. – F. *vent-er*, to puff; with suffix *-aille* (< L. *-ācula*).– F. *vent*, wind (above).

ventilate. (L.) From pp. of L. *uentilāre*, to blow, winnow.– L. *uentulus*, a light wind. – L. *uentus*, wind.

Ventral, belonging to the belly. (L.) L. *uentrālis*, adj.; from *uenter*, the belly.

ventricle. (F.–L.) F. *ventricule*, 'the ventricle, the place wherein the meat sent from the stomack is digested;' Cot. – L. *uentriculum*, acc. of *uentriculus*, stomach, ventricle, double dimin. of *uenter*, the belly.

ventriloquist. (L.) Coined from L. *uentriloqu-us*, lit. speaking from (or in) the belly. – L. *uentri-*, decl. stem of *uenter* (above); *loquī*, to speak. See **Loquacious.**

Venture, sb. (F. – L.) A headless form of M.E. *auenture* (*aventure*), an adventure, chance.– F. *aventure*, a chance, occurrence.– L. *aduentūra*, fem. of *aduentūrus*, about to happen.– L. *ad*, to; *uentūrus*, fut. pt. of *uenīre*, to come. Cognate with E. **Come.** (√GwEM.) **Doublet,** *adventure.* Der. *venture*, vb.

Venue; see **Venew.**

Veracious, truthful. (L.) From L. *uērāci-*, decl. stem of *uērāx*, true; with suffix *-ous*.– L. *uērus*, true. See **Very.**

Veranda, Verandah, a covered balcony. (Port.– Span.– L.) Port. *varanda.*– O. Span. *varanda*, a stair-railing; in Pedro de Alcala (1505). If of native Span. origin, it may be from Span. *vara*, a rod, rail.– L. *uāra*, a forked pole. Cf. L. *uārus*, crooked. ¶ Hence also was borrowed Skt. *varaṇḍa*, a portico, which is quite a modern word; see *veranda* in Yule.

Verb, the word; the chief word in a sentence. (F.–L.) F. *verbe.*– L. *uerbum*, a word. For **uerdhum*, cognate with E. **Word.** Der. *verb-iage*, F. *verbiage*, from O. F. **verbier*, *verboier*, to talk.

Verbena. (L.) L. *uerbēna*, orig. a sacred bough; afterwards, vervain. Allied to *uerber*, a rod. See **Vervain.**

Verdant, flourishing. (F.–L.) A false form; as if from F. **verdant*, substituted for *verdissant*, pres. pt. of *verdir*, to flourish. –O. F. *verd*, green.– L. *uiridis*, green. See **Vert.** Cf. also *verdure*, F. *verdure*, lit. greenness.

Verdict. (F.–L.) M.E. *verdit* (the correct form). – A.F. and O.F. *verdit*, *veirdit.* – L. *uērē dictum*, truly said; whence Late L. *uērēdictum*, true saying, verdict.– L. *uērē*, adv., from *uērus*, true; *dictum*, neut. of *dictus*, pp. of *dīcere*, to say. ¶ Mod. F. *verdict* is from E.

Verdigris, rust of copper. (F.–L.) M.F. *verd de gris*, 'verdigrease, Spanish green;' Cot. Spelt *verte grez* in the 13th cent., and *verd de grice* in the 14th (Littré). A better form is the M.E. *verdegrece*, i.e. *verd de Grece*, lit. 'green of Greece;' so also A.F. *vert de Grece*, Vie de S. Gile, 853. Cf. '*uiride grecum*, Ang. verdegrece;' Wülker, Voc. 619. 35. M.F. *verd* (F. *vert*) is from *uiridem*, acc. of *uiridis*, green. (See Acad. 1118, Oct. 1893.)

verditer, a green pigment. (F.–L.) M. F. *verd de terre*, a green mineral; Cot. – L. acc. *uiridem*, green (above); *dē*, of; *terra*, earth.

Verge (1), a wand of office, edge, brink. (F.–L.) Distinct from *verge* (2) below. M.E. *verge*, a wand, rod, yard (in measure). – F. *verge*, 'a rod, wand, yard, hoope, ring, rood of land;' Cot. From the sense of rod it came to mean hoop, ring (hence, edge); the sense of edge also easily followed from the Law-term *verge*, i.e. limit of jurisdiction.– L. *uirga*, a rod, pliant twig. Der. *verg-er*, a rod-bearer, macebearer, F. *verger*, L. *uirgārius.*

Verge (2), to tend towards. (L.) L. *uergere*, to bend, tend, incline towards, incline. ¶ The phrase 'to be on the *verge* of' is quite distinct, and belongs to **Verge** (1).

Verify. (F.–L.) M.F. *verifier*; Cot. – Late L. *vērificāre*, to make true.– L. *uēri-*, for *uērus*, true; *-ficāre*, for *facere*, to make.

verisimilitude, likelihood. (F.– L.) M.F. *verisimilitude.*– L. *uērisimilitūdo.*– L. *uērī similis*, like the truth.– L. *uērī*, gen. of *uērum*, the truth, orig. neuter of *uērus*, true; *similis*, like.

verity, truth. (F.–L.) M.F. *verité.* – L. *uēritātem*, acc. of *uēritās*, truth.– L. *uēri-*, for *uērus*, true. See **Very.**

Verjuice. (F. – L.) F. *verjus*, verjuice; lit. 'green juice,' i.e. juice of green grapes.– O.F. *verd*, green, from L. *uiridem*, acc. of *uiridis*; *jus*, juice, from L. *iūs*; see **Juice.**

Vermicelli. (Ital.–L.) Ital. *vermicelli*, lit. 'little worms;' from the shape.

Pl. of *vermicello*, dimin. of *verme*, a worm. ▬ L. *uermem*, acc. of *uermis*, a worm. See **Worm**.

vermicular, pertaining to a worm. (L.) From L. *uermicul-us*, a little worm; dimin. of *uermis*, a worm.

vermilion. (F.▬L.) F. *vermillon*, 'a little worm, vermillion;' Cot.▬F. *vermeil*, vermilion. ▬ L. acc. *uermiculum*, dimin. of *uermis* (above). ¶ So named from the cochineal insect (see **Crimson**); but *vermilion* is now generally made from red lead.

vermin. (F.▬L.) F. *vermine*, vermin; applied to obnoxious insects, &c. As if from a Lat. adj. **uerminus*, formed from *uermi-*, decl. stem of *uermis*, a worm, cognate with E. **Worm**.

Vernacular, native. (L.) From L. *uernācul-us*, adj., native; lit. belonging to a home-born slave. ▬ L. *uerna*, a home-born slave. Lit. 'dweller;' cf. Skt. *vas*, to dwell. (√WES.) Brugm. ii. § 66.

Vernal. (L.) L. *uernālis*, extended from *uernus*, belonging to spring.▬L. *uēr*, spring.+Gk. ἔαρ (for ϝέσαρ), Russ. *vesna*, Icel. *vār*, Dan. *vaar*, Swed. *vår*, spring; the time of increasing brightness. Cf. Lith. *wasara*, summer; Skt. *vasanta-*, spring, *ush*, to burn, glow; also O. Irish *áir*, W. *gwawr*, dawn.

Vernier, a kind of scale, for fine measurement. (F.) Invented by *P. Vernier*, b. 1580, died Sept. 14, 1637.

Verse. (L.) M. E. *vers, fers* (Ormulum); A.S. *fers* (perhaps from O. Irish *fers*, also from L.). ▬ Late L. *versus*, L. *uersus*, a turning, course, row, line of poetry. ▬ L. *uersus*, pp. of *uertere*, to turn. Allied to **Worth** (1). (√WERT.) Der. *vers-ed*, imitated from L. *uersātus*, pp. of *uersāri*, pass. of frequent. of *uertere*; *vers-at-ile*, quickly turning, M. F. *versatil* (Cot.), L. *uersātilis*, versatile, likewise from L. pp. *uersātus*.

versify. (F.▬L.) F. *versifier.*▬L. *uersificāre*, to make verses.▬L. *uersi-*, for *uersus*, a verse; *-ficāre*, for *facere*, to make. Der. *versificat-ion*, from pp. *uersificātus*.

version. (F. ▬L.) F. *version.*▬Late L. *uersiōnem*, acc. of *uersio*, a version, translation.▬L. *uersus*, pp. of *uertere*, to turn.

verst, a Russian measure of length. (Russ.) Russ. *versta*, 3500 English feet;

also, age. For **vert-tā*; from √WERT (Russ. *vertiete*), to turn.

Vert, green. (F.▬L.) F. *vert*, O. F. *verd*.▬L. *uiridem*, acc. of *uiridis*, green. Cf. L. *uirēre*, to be green.+W. *gwyrdd*, green; Corn. *guirt*. Or (if these Celtic words are borrowed) allied to *vivid*; cf. Skt. *ji-ra-*, active, *ji-va*, living. Brugm. ii. § 74.

Vertebra. (L.) L. *uertebra*, a joint, vertebra.▬L. *uertere*, to turn.

vertex, top. (L.) L. *uertex*, top, pole of the sky (which is the turning-point of the stars), but afterwards the zenith.▬ L. *uertere*, to turn. Der. *vertic-al*, vertical, from L. *uerticālis*, vertical, which is from *uertic-*, for *uertec-*, stem of *uertex*, top.

vertigo, giddiness. (L.) L. *uertīgo*, giddiness.▬L. *uertere*, to turn round.

Vervain. (F.▬L.) F. *verveine*, 'vervaine;' Cot.▬L. *uerbēna*, a sacred bough; afterwards, vervain. See **Verbena**.

Very, true. (F.▬L.) M. E. *verrai.*▬ O. F. *verai* (F. *vrai*), true. Cf. Prov. *verai*, true. It answers to a Late L. type **vērācus*, allied to L. *uērāx*, true.▬L. *uērus*, true, credible (whence O. F. *voir*). +W. *gwir*, O. Irish *fīr*, true; G. *wahr*, A. S. *wēr*, true. Cf. Russ. *viera*, faith. Brugm. i. § 367.

Vesicle, a small tumour or cell. (L.) L. *uēsīcula*, dimin. of *uēsīca*, a bladder.

Vesper. (L.) M. E. *vesper*, the evening-star (Gower). ▬ L. *uesper*, evening-star, evening; cf. *uespera*, even-tide. Hence O. F. *vespre* (F. *vêpre*), evening, and *vespres* (F. *vêpres*), vespers, even-song.+Gk. ἕσπερος, adj. and sb., evening; O. Irish *fescor*, W. *ucher*, evening. Brugm. i. § 329.

Vessel. (F.▬L.) M. E. *vessel.*▬A. F. *vessel*; O. F. *vaissel*, a vessel, ship, later *vaisseau*, a vessel (of any kind). ▬ L. *uascellum*, a small vase or urn; dimin. of *uās*, a vase. See **Vase**.

Vest, a garment. (L.) L. *uestis*, a garment, clothing.+Goth. *wasti*, clothing; cf. Gk. ἕν-νυμι (= ϝέσ-νυμι), I clothe, ἑσθής, clothing, Skt. *vas*, to put on clothes. (√WES.) See **Wear**.

Vestal. (F.▬L.) F. *Vestale*, a Vestal virgin. ▬ L. *Vestālis*, belonging to a Vestal, also a priestess of Vesta. ▬ L. *Vesta*, Vesta, goddess of the flocks and household.+Gk. ἑστία, goddess of the domestic hearth.

Vestibule. (L.) L. *uestibulum*, a fore-court; lit. 'separated from the abode.'▬

L. *uē-*, separate from, *stabulum*, an abode; see **Stable** (Vaniček).

Vestige. (F.—L.) F. *vestige*, a step, foot-track.—L. *uestīgium*, foot-track.

Vestment. (F.—L.) M. E. *vestiment*. — O. F. *vestement* (F. *vêtement*). — L. *uestīmentum*, clothing.—L. *uestīre*, to clothe; from *uestis*, clothing. See **Vest**.

vestry. (F.—L.) M. E. *vestrie*; shortened from O. F. *vestiarie*; cf. M. F. *vestiaire*, 'vestry;' Cot. — L. *uestiārium*, a wardrobe; neut. of *uestiārius*, adj., from *uestis*, a robe.

vesture. (F.—L.) O. F. *vesture*, *vestëure*.—Late L. *vestītūra*, clothing.— L. *uestīre*, to clothe.—L. *uestis*, a robe.

Vetch, a plant. (F.—L.) Also *fitch*. M. E. *feche* (of which the Southern form was *veche*).—O. F. *veche*, *vece*, M. F. *vesce*, vetch (where *veche* is a Walloon and North F. form).—L. *uicia*, a vetch; whence also G. *wicke*, Du. *wikke*.

Veteran. (L.) L. *ueterānus*, experienced; as sb., a veteran.—L. *ueter-*, for **uetes*, stem of *uetus*, old, lit. 'advanced in years.' Cf. Gk. ἔτος, Skt. *vatsa-*, a year. See **Veal**.

veterinary. (L.; L *ueterīnārius*, of or belonging to beasts of burden; as sb., a cattle-doctor.—L. *ueterīnus*, belonging to beasts of burden. The L. *ueterīna* meant an animal at least a year old, one that had passed its first year; from the base **uet-*, year (above). See **Wether**.

Veto, a prohibition. (L.) L. *ueto*, I forbid; O. L. *uoto*.

Vex, to harass. (F.—L.) F. *vexer*.— L. *uexāre*, to vex; orig. intensive form of *uehere* (pt. t. *uex-ī*). See **Vehicle**.

Viaduct. (L.) L. *uia ducta*, a road conducted across (a river, &c.).—L. *uia*, a way, road; *ducta*, fem. of pp. of *dūcere*, to carry, conduct. β. L. *uia*, formerly *uea*, cannot be allied to L. *uehere* = Skt. *vah*, to carry; see **Vehicle**, **Way**.

Vial, Phial, a small bottle. (F.—L. —Gk.) M. E. *viole*, *fiole*.—O. F. and F. *fiole*.—L. *phiala*.—Gk. φιάλη, a shallow cup or bowl.

Viands, food. (F.—L.) Pl. of *viand*. —F. *viande*, food.—L. *uīuenda*, neut. pl., provisions, food; from the gerundive of *uiuere*, to live. See **Victuals**.

Vibrate. (L.) From pp. of L. *uibrāre*, to swing, shake. Cf. Skt. *vep*, to tremble. (√WEIP.) Brugm. i. § 701.

Vicar. (F.—L.) F. *vicaire*, a deputy.

— L. *uicārius*, a deputy, orig. an adj., deputed, put in place of. — L. *uic-*, base of *uicis*, gen. case, a turn, change, succession. (√WEIQ.) Brugm. i. § 701,

Vice (1), a fault. (F.—L.) F. *vice*.— L. *uitium*, blemish, fault. Der. *vic-i-ous*, F. *vicieux*, L. *uitiōsus*, faulty; *viti-ate*, from pp. of L. *uitiāre*, to injure. And see **Vituperation**.

Vice (2), an instrument for holding things firmly. (F.—L.) M. E. *vice*, orig. 'a screw,' because tightened by a screw. —F. *vis*, 'vice, a winding-staire;' Cot. O. F. *viz*.—L. *uītis*, a vine, bryony, lit. 'that which winds or twines.' (√WEI.) See **Withy**.

Vice-gerent. (F.—L.) M. F. *vicegerent*, a deputy; Cot. — L. *uice*, in place of; *gerent-*, stem of pres. pt. of *gerere*, to carry on, rule; see **Gesture**. ¶ So also *vice-admiral*; *vice-roy* (from F. *roi*, L. acc. *rēgem*, king), *vice-regal*.

Vicinage, neighbourhood. (F. — L.) Altered from F. *voisinage*, neighbourhood. — F. *voisin*, near. — L. *uīcīnus*, near, lit. 'belonging to the same street.'—L. *uīcus*, a village, street; see **Wick** (2).

vicinity, neighbourhood. (F.—L.) M. F. *vicinité*. — L. acc. *uīcīnitātem*, neighbourhood.—L. *uīcīnus*, near (above).

Vicissitude. (L.) L. *uicissitūdo*, change. Allied to *uicissim*, by turns.— L. *uic-is* (genitive), a change; see **Vicar**.

Victim. (F.—L.) F. *victime*.—L. *uictima*, a victim. Cf. Goth. *weihan*, to consecrate. Brugm. i. § 606.

Victor. (L.) L. *uictor*, a conqueror. —L. *uic-*, base of *uincere*, to conquer (pt. t. *uic-i*); with suffix *-tor*.+Goth. *weihan*, to fight; cf. A. S. *wīg*, war. (√WEIQ.) Brugm. i. § 367. Der. *victor-y*, A. F. *victorie*, L. *uictōria*.

Victuals. (F.—L.) Pl. of *victual*, a pedantic spelling of M. E. *vitaille*, provisions. — O. F. *vitaille*, usually in pl. *vitailles*, provisions.—L. neut. pl. *uictuālia*, provisions; from *uictuālis*, adj., belonging to nourishment.—L. *uictu-*, stem of *uictus*, food.—L. *uictus*, pp. of *uiuere*, to live; allied to *uīuus*, living, and to E. **Quick**. (√GwEI.) Brugm. ii. § 488.

Vicuna, a quadruped of the camel tribe. (Span.—Peruv.) Span. *vicuña*; Peruvian origin (Acosta, iv. 40).

Videlicet, viz., namely. (L.) In old MSS. and books, the abbreviation for *et* resembled *z*; hence *viet* (short for *vide-*

licet) was misread as *viz.* — L. *uidēlicet*, short for *uidēre licet*, it is possible to see, it is evident, hence, to wit, namely. — L. *uidēre*, to see ; *licet*, it is allowable ; see Vision and Licence.

Vidette ; see Vedette.

Vie, to contend for superiority. (F. — L.) M. E. *vien*, a contracted form of *envien*, to vie, contend for superiority. (Cf. *fence* for *defence*, *story* for *history*, &c.) — O. F. *envier* (*au ieu*), ' to vie ; ' Cot. The lit. sense of O. F. *envier* was to invite [quite distinct from *envier*, to envy], esp. used in gaming in the sense ' to open a game by staking a certain sum ' ; precisely as Span. *envidar*, Ital. *invitare*, to invite, to vie, or propose a stake. — L. *inuītāre*, to invite (of which *vie* is thus seen to be a doublet). See Invite. ¶ The sense was to stake a sum to draw on or invite a game, then to wager, bet against, contend, strive for the upper hand.

View, sb. (F. — L.) A. F. *view, vewe, vue* ; M. F. *veuë*, ' a view, sight ; ' Cot. Fem. of *veu*, pp. of O. F. *veoir* (F. *voir*), to see. — L. *uidēre*, to see. See Vision.

Vigil. (F. — L.) Lit. ' a watching.' F. *vigile*, ' a vigile, eve of a holy day ; ' Cot. — L. *uigilia*, a watch. — L. *uigil*, awake. — L. *uigēre*, to be lively ; cf. *uegēre*, to arouse ; allied to Wake. See Vigour. Der. *vigil-ant*, F. *vigilant*, from stem of pres. pt. of L. *uigilāre*, to watch.

Vignette, a small engraving with ornamented border. (F. — L.) First applied to borders in which vine-leaves and tendrils were introduced ; XVIIth cent. — F. *vignette*, a little vine ; pl. *vignettes*, ' branch-like flourishes ; ' Cot. Dimin. of F. *vigne*, a vine ; see Vine.

Vigour, energy. (F. — L.) O. F. *vigor* ; F. *vigueur*. — L. *uigōrem*, acc. of *uigor*, liveliness. — L. *uigēre*, to be lively ; see Vigil. Der. *vigor-ous*.

Viking, a Northern pirate. (Scand.) Icel. *víkingr*, a pirate, free-booter, rover. Lit. ' a warrior ; ' for **vígningr* (*ígn* > *ík*) ; allied to *víg*, war, Goth. *weihan*, to fight, L. *uincere*, to conquer. See Victor. (So Noreen, § 252 ; cf. Sweet, Hist. E. Sounds, § 319.) + A. S. *wícing.* ¶ Usually explained as ' creek-dweller ' ; from Icel. *vík*, a creek.

Vile. (F. — L.) F. *vil*, fem. *vile*, base. — L. *uīlis*, base, mean. + W. *gwael*, vile.

Villa. (L.) L. *uilla*, a farm-house ; O. L. *uella*. Perhaps for **uīcsla*, i. e. a

diminutive of L. *uīcus*, a village. See Wick (2).

village. (F. — L.) F. *village.* — L. *uillāticus*, adj., belonging to a farm-house. — L. *uilla* (above).

villain. (F. — L.) M. E. *vilein.* — A. F. *vilein*, servile ; as sb., a bondman, slave, villain. — Late L. *villānus*, orig. a farm-servant, hence a slave, serf, villain. — L. *uilla*, a farm-house. Der. *villain-y*, A. F. *vilanie*, servitude, baseness.

Vinculum, a link. (L.) L. *uinculum*, a bond, fetter. — L. *uincīre*, to bind.

Vindicate. (L.) From pp. of L. *uindicāre*, to arrogate, lay claim to ; cf. *uindic-*, stem of *uindex*, a claimant.

vindictive. (F. — L.) Shortened from F. *vindicatif*, ' revenging ; ' Cot. From L. *uindicāt-us*, pp. of *uindicāre*, to avenge ; with suffix *-īuus*, F. *-if*.

Vine. (F. — L.) F. *vigne*. — L. *uīnea*, a vineyard ; in Late L. (apparently) a vine. Fem. of L. *uīneus*, adj., from *uīnum*, wine ; see Wine. Der. *vine-yard*, substituted for A. S. *wīn-geard*, a vineyard, lit. ' wine-yard.' See Yard (1).

vinegar. (F. — L.) M. E. *vinegre.* — O. F. *vin egre* (F. *vinaigre*). — L. *uīnum*, wine ; *ācrem*, acc. of *ācer*, sharp. See Wine and Eager.

Vinewed, mouldy. (E.) A Southern form. Also *finewed, fenowed* (Nares). From M. E. *fenow*, mouldiness ; with suffix *-ed* ; cf. A. S. *fynegian*, to become mouldy. — A. S. *fynig*, mouldy (Joshua, ix. 5). — A. S. *fyne*, mould, moistness. Allied to Du.*vuns*, rank ; M.Du. *vunstigh*, ' mustie (as hay) ; ' Hexham.

Vintage. (F. — L.) An alteration of M. E. *vindage, vendage* ; by influence of *vint-ner.* — F. *vendange*, M. F. *vendenge*, vintage. — L. *uindēmia*, vintage. — L. *uīnum*, wine, grapes ; *-dēmia*, a taking away, from *dēmere*, to take away. *Dēmere* = **dē-imere*, from *emere*, to take.

vintner. (F. — L.) M. E. *vintener*, altered form of earlier *vineter, viniter.* — M. F. *vinetier*, ' a vintner ; ' Cot. — Late L. *uinētārius*, a wine-seller. — L. *uinētum*, a vineyard. — L. *uīnum*, grapes, wine.

Viol. (F. — Prov. — Late L.) M. F. *viole, violle*, ' a violin ; ' Cot. — Prov. *viula.* — Late L. *vīdula, vītula*, a viol ; whence also O. H. G. *fidula*, A. S. *fiþele*, a fiddle. See Fiddle.

Violate. (L.) From pp. of L. *uiolāre*, to treat with force, violate. Formed as if from an adj. *uiolus*, due to *uī-s*, force. Brugm. i. § 655.

Violent. (F. – L.) F. *violent*. – L. *uiolentus*, full of might. Formed as if from an adj. *uiolus* ; see Violate.

Violet, a flower. (F. – L.) M. F. *violet*, m., *violette*, f. (Cot.). Dimin. of M. F. *viole*, ' a gilliflower ;' Cot. – L. *uiola*, a violet. + Gk. *ἴον*, a violet. Der. *violet*, adj.

Violin. (Ital. – Late L.) Ital. *violino*, dimin. of Ital. *viola*, a viol ; see Viol.

violoncello. (Ital. – Late L.) Ital. *violoncello*, dimin. of *violone*, a bass-viol, an augmentative form of *viola*, a viol.

Viper. (F. – L.) F. *vipère*. – L. *uīpera*, a viper. Usually explained as ' that produces living young ' ; short for *uīuipara*, fem. of *uīuiparus*, producing living young ; which is hardly possible (Walde).

Virago. (L.) L. *uirāgo*, a manlike woman. – L. *uir*, a man ; see Virile.

Virgate, a measure of land. (L.) From Late L. *terra uirgāta*, land measured with a rod. – L. *uirga*, a rod ; see Verge (1).

Virgin. (F. – L.) O. F. *virgine*. – L. *uirginem*, acc. of *uirgo*, a maid. Der. *virgin-als*, the name of a musical instrument, played upon by *virgins*.

Viridity, greenness. (L.) L. *uiriditās*, greenness. – L. *uiridis*, green. See Vert.

Virile, manly. (F. – L.) F. *viril*, ' manly ;' Cot. – L. *uirīlis*, adj., from *uir*, a man. + A. S. *wer* ; O. H. G. *wer* ; Goth. *wair* ; Icel. *verr* ; O. Irish *fer*, W. *gwr*, a man ; cf. Skt. *vīra-*, a hero.

virtue. (F. – L.) M. E. *vertu*. – F. *vertu*. – L. *uirtūtem*, acc. of *uirtūs*, manly excellence. – L. *uir*, a man.

virtuoso. (Ital. – L.) Ital. *virtuoso*, one skilled in the fine arts, orig. ' virtuous.' – Ital. *virtù*, shortened form of *virtute*, virtue, also, a love of the fine arts. – L. *uirtūtem* (above).

Virulent. (F. – L.) F. *virulent*. – L. *uirulentus*, full of poison. – L. *uīrus*, poison. + Gk. *ἰός*, Skt. *visha-*, poison. Cf. Wizen.

Visage, look, face. (F. – L.) F. *visage*, face, look. – M. F. *vis*, visage ; with suffix -*age* (< L. -*āticum*). – L. *uīsum*, acc. of *uīsus*, sight, afterwards look, face. – L. *uīsus*, pp. of *uidēre*, to see.

visard, the same as visor.

Viscera, entrails. (L.) L. *uiscera*, neut. pl., entrails. Der. *e-viscer-ate*, to remove the entrails.

Viscid, sticky, clammy. (L.) L. *uis-*

cidus, sticky, clammy. – L. *uiscum*, mistletoe, birdlime. + Gk. *ἰξός*, mistletoe.

Viscount. (F. – L.) Also spelt *vicounte* (and the inserted *s* is not pronounced). A. F. *visconte*, *viconte* ; F. *vicomte*, ' a vicount, at first the deputy of an earl,' Cot. ; O. F. *viscomte* (12th cent.). – L. *uice*, in place of ; *comitem*, acc. of *comes*, a count ; see Count (1).

Visible. (F. – L.) F. *visible*. – L. *uīsibilis*, that can be seen. – L. *uīs-us*, pp. of *uidēre*, to see. + Gk. *ἰδεῖν*, to see ; Skt. *vid*, to know. Allied to Wit. (√WEID.)

vision. (F. – L.) F. *vision*. – L. *uīsiōnem*, acc. of *uīsio*, sight. – L. *uīsus*, pp. of *uidēre*, to see.

visit. (F. – L.) F. *visiter*. – L. *uīsitāre*, to visit, go to see, frequent. of *uīsere*, to behold ; from *uīsus*, pp. of *uidēre*, to see.

visor, visard, vizor. (F. – L.) The *d* is added. M. E. *visere*. – M. F. *visiere*, ' the viser, or sight of a helmet ;' Cot. Formed from M. F. *vis*, the face ; see Visage. A *visor* also meant a mask, from its covering the face ; Cotgrave has ' *faux visage*, a maske, or visard.'

vista. (Ital. – L.) Ital. *vista*, lit. a view. – Ital. *vista*, fem. of *visto*, seen, from *vedere*, to see. – L. *uidēre*, to see.

visual. (F. – L.) M. F. *visual*. – L. *uīsuālis*, belonging to the sight. – L. *uīsu-*, decl. stem of *uīsus*, sight. – L. *uīsus*, pp. of *uidēre*, to see.

Visier ; see Vizier.

Vital. (F. – L.) F. *vital*. – L. *uītālis*, belonging to life. – L. *uīta*, life ; allied to *uīuere*, to live. See Victuals.

Vitiate ; see Vice (1).

Vitreous. (L.) L. *uitre-us*, glassy ; with suffix -*ous*. – L. *uitri-*, for *uitrum*, glass. The *i* in *uitrum* is common ; some connect the word with *uidēre*, to see. ¶ L. *uitrum*, ' woad,' is cognate with E. Woad.

vitriol. (F. – L.) F. *vitriol*, ' vitrioll ;' Cot. Said to be so called from its glassy look. – L. *uitreolus*, glassy. – L. *uitreus*, glassy. – L. *uitrum*, glass (above).

Vituperation, blame. (F. – L.) M. F. *vituperation*. – L. acc. *uituperātiōnem*. – L. *uituperātus*, pp. of *uituperāre*, to blame, lit. ' to prepare (or find) a blemish.' – L. *uitu-*, for *uiti-*, base of *uitium*, a vice, fault ; *parāre*, to prepare, provide.

Vivacity. (F. – L.) F. *vivacité*, liveliness. – L. *uīuācitātem*, acc. of *uīuācitās*, liveliness. – L. *uīuāci-*, decl. stem of *uīuāx*, tenacious of life. — L. *uīuere*, to live. See **Victuals.**

vivid. (L.) L. *uīuidus*, lively. — L. *uīuere*, to live.

vivify. (F. — L.) F. *vivifier*, to quicken. — L. *uīuificāre*, to quicken. — L. *uīui-*, for *uiuus*, living; *-ficāre*, for *facere*, to make.

viviparous. (L.) From L. *uīui-parus*, producing living young. — L. *uīui-*, for *uīuus*, living; *parere*, to produce.

vivisection. (L.) Coined from L. *uīui-* (above); and *section*.

Vixen. (E.) M. E. *vixen, fixen*, a she-fox; answering to A. S. *fyx-en*, made from *fox* by vowel-change of Teut. *u* (A. S. *o*) to *y*, with fem. suffix *-en* (for *-īn-jō-*); precisely as A. S. *gyden*, a goddess, from *god*, a god. See **Fox**. Cf. G. *füchsin*, f. of *fuchs*, fox. The *v* for *f* is Southern.

Viz.; see **Videlicet.**

Vizard; see **Visor.**

Vizier, Visier, a councillor of state. (F. — Arab.) F. *vizir*. — Arab. *wazīr*, a councillor of state; orig. a porter, one who bears the burden of state affairs. — Arab. root *wazara*, to bear a burden, sustain.

Vocable, a term, word. (F. — L.) F. *vocable*. — L. *uocābulum*, an appellation, name. — L. *uocāre*, to call. — L. *uoc-*, related to *uōc-*, stem of *uōx*, voice, name (below). Der. *vocabulary*, from Late L. *uocābulārium*, a list of words.

vocal, uttering sound. (F. — L.) F. *vocal*. — L. *uōcālis*, adj., from *uōc-*, stem of *uōx*, voice, sound. + Gk. ἔπος, a word; Skt. *vacha-s*, speech, from *vach*, to speak. (✓WEQ.) Brugm. i. § 678.

vocation. (F. — L.) F. *vocation*. — L. acc. *uocātiōnem*, a calling, invitation. — L. *uocātus*, pp. of *uocāre*, to call.

vociferation. (F. — L.) M.F. *vociferation*. — L. acc. *uōciferātiōnem*, an outcry. — L. *uōciferātus*, pp. of *uōciferārī*, to lift up the voice, cry aloud. — L. *uōci-*, decl. stem of *uōx*, voice; *fer-re*, to bear, carry, cognate with E. *bear*.

Vogue, mode, fashion. (F. — Ital. — Teut.) Formerly *vogue* meant sway, authority, power. — F. *vogue*, 'vogue, sway, power; a cleere passage, as of a ship in a broad sea;' Cot. Orig. 'sway of a ship,' verbal sb. of F. *voguer*, 'to saile forth;' id. — Ital. *voga*, sb., stroke of an oar, *vogare*, to row in a galley. — M. H. G. *wāgen*, G. *wogen*, to fluctuate, be in motion on the sea. — M. H. G. *wāg*, G. *woge*,

a wave; O. H. G. *wāc*. + A. S. *wǣg*, Goth. *wēgs*, a wave; Teut. type **wǣgoz*, m.; from **wǣg-*, 3rd stem of Teut. **wegan-*, to move; see **Weigh**.

Voice. (F. — L.) M. E. *vois*. O. F. *vois* (F. *voix*). — L. *uōcem*, acc. of *uōx*, voice, sound. See **vocal**.

Void, empty. (F.) O. F. *vuide, voide* (F. *vide*); a fem. form of which the masc. is *vuit*. Origin unknown.

Volant, flying. (F. — L.) F. *volant*, pres. pt. of *voler*, to fly. — L. *uolāre*, to fly. Cf. Gk. βολή, a throw; Brugm. i. § 663.

volatile. (F. — L.) F. *volatil*, 'flying;' Cot. — L. *uolātilis*, flying. — L. *uolātus*, flight. — L. *uolāre*, to fly.

Volcano, a burning mountain. (Ital. — L.) Ital. *volcano*, a volcano. — L. *Volcā-num*, acc. of *Volcānus, Vulcānus*, Vulcan, god of fire, fire.

Vole, a field-mouse. (Scand.) Also called *vole-mouse, field-mouse, meadow-mouse, campagnol*; L. *arvicola*. A modern word; abbreviated from North E. *vole-mouse*, i. e. field-mouse. From Norw. *voll*, field; cognate with E. **Wold**. Der. *water-vole*, i. e. water field-mouse.

Volition. (F. — L.) F. *volition*. — Late L. **volitiōnem*, acc. of **volitio*, volition (prob. a term of the schools). — L. *uolo*, I wish. See **Voluntary**.

Volley. (F. — L.) F. *volée*, 'a flight;' Cot. Hence, a flight of shot. — L. *uolāta*, fem. of pp. of *uolāre*, to fly.

Volt, another spelling of **Vault** (2).

Voltaic, originated by Volta. (Ital.) From *A. Volta*, of Como, died March 5, 1826.

Voluble, fluent. (F. — L.) M.F. *voluble*, 'voluble; easily rolled, glib;' Cot. — L. *uolūbilis*, easily turned about. — L. *uolū-*, as in *uolū-tus*, pp. of *uoluere*, to roll; with suffix *-bilis*. + Goth. *walwjan*, to roll, Gk. εἰλύειν, to enfold; allied to Russ. *valite*, to roll. (✓WEL.) See **Helix**.

volume, a roll, a book. (F. — L.) F. *volume*. — L. *uolūmen*, a roll, scroll; hence, a book on a parchment roll. — L. *uolū-*, as in *uolū-tus*, pp. of *uoluere*, to roll.

Voluntary. (F. — L.) M.F. *voluntaire, volontaire*. — L. *uoluntārius*, willing. — L. *uoluntās*, free will. — L. **uolunt-*, related to *uolent-*, stem of *uolens*, willing, from *uelle*, to wish, *uolo*, I wish. + Skt. *vṛ*, to choose, select. Allied to **Will** (1). (✓WEL.) Brugm. ii. §§ 102, 493.

voluptuous. (F. – L.) F. *voluptuëux,* Cot. – L. *uoluptuōsus,* addicted to, or full of pleasure. – L. *uolupt-ās,* pleasure. – L. *uolup, uolupe,* adv., agreeably. – L. *uol-o,* I wish. Cf. Gk. ἐλπίς, hope.

Volute, a spiral scroll on a capital. (F. – L.) F. *volute* (Cot.). – L. *uolūta,* a volute; fem. of *uolūtus,* pp. of *uoluere,* to roll; see **Voluble.**

Vomit, sb. (L.) L. *uomitus,* a vomiting; whence *uomitāre,* to vomit. – L. *uomitus,* pp. of *uomere,* to vomit.+Gk. ἐμεῖν, Lith. *wemti,* Skt. *vam,* to vomit. (√WEM.)

Voracity. (F. – L.) F. *voracité.* – L. *uorācitātem,* acc. of *uorācitās,* hungriness. – L. *uorāci-,* for *uorax,* voracious, greedy to devour. – L. *uorāre,* to devour. – L. *-uorus,* devouring, as in *carni-uorus,* flesh-eating. Allied to Skt. *-gara-,* as in *aja-gara-,* goat-devouring; Gk. βορός, gluttonous. (√GwER.) Brugm. i. § 653.

Vortex, a whirlpool. (L.) L. *uortex,* also *uertex,* whirlpool. – L. *uertere,* to turn; see **Verse.**

Vote, sb. (L.) L. *uōtum,* a wish; orig. a vow. – L. *uōtum,* neut. of *uōtus,* pp. of *uouēre,* to vow. Der. *vot-ive,* L. *uōtīuus,* promised by a vow; *vot-ary,* a coined word, like *votaress, votress.*

Vouch, to warrant. (F. – L.) M. F. *voucher,* 'to vouch, cite, pray in aid in a suit;' Cot. O. F. *vochier.* – L. *uocāre,* to call, call upon, summon. See **Vocable.**

vouchsafe. (F. – L.) Formerly *vouch safe,* i. e. warrant as safe; from *vouch* and *safe.*

Vow, sb. (F. – L.) M. E. *vow, vou.* – O. F. *veu, vou* (F. *vœu*), a vow. – L. *uōtum,* a vow; see **Vote.** ¶ Hence the M. E. *avow,* sb., common in the sense of 'vow,' Chaucer, C. T. 2237, 2414; and hence the verb *avow,* to vow. Another *avow* answers to F. *avouer,* L. *aduocāre,* and is a doublet of *avouch.*

Vowel. (F. – L.) O. F. *vouel, voiel;* F. *voyelle,* 'a vowell;' Cot. – L. *uōcālem,* acc. of *uōcālis* (*littera*), a vowel, vocal letter; see **Vocal.**

Voyage. (F. – L.) M. E. *viage, veage.* – O. F. *veiage,* later *voyage.* – L. *uiāticum,* properly provisions for a journey. – L. *uiāticus,* belonging to a journey. – L. *uia,* a way. See **Viaduct.**

Vulcanise, to combine caoutchouc with sulphur by heat. (L.) Coined, with suffix *-ise,* from *Vulcan,* god of fire,

fire. See **Volcano.** Der. *vulcan-ite,* vulcanised caoutchouc.

Vulgar. (F. – L.) F. *vulgaire.* – L. *uulgāris,* belonging to the common people. – L. *uulgus, uolgus,* the common people; a throng, crowd. Der. *vulgar-ity;* also *vulgate,* the E. name for the L. version of the Bible known as the *ēditio vulgāta,* where *vulgāta* is a later form of the fem. of the pp. of *uulgāre,* to publish.

Vulnerable. (F. – L.) M. F. *vulnerable.* – L. *uulnerābilis,* liable to injury. – L. *uulnerāre,* to wound. – L. *uulner-,* for **uulnes-,* stem of *uulnus,* a wound; O. L. *uolnus.* Allied to *uellere,* to pluck, tear. Cf. Skt. *vrana-,* a wound, fracture; Gk. οὐλή, W. *gweli,* a wound. (√WEL.)

Vulpine, fox-like. (F. – L.) M. F. *vulpin;* Cot. – L. *uulpīnus,* fox-like. – L. *uulp-,* base of *uulpes,* a fox. Allied to **Wolf** (Darbishire, Reliquiæ Philologicæ, p. 92).

Vulture. (L.) L. *uultur,* a vulture; O. L. *uolturus;* lit. 'tearer.' – L. *uul-* (*uol-*), as in *uul-si,* pt. t. of *uellere,* to pluck, tear. Allied to **Vulnerable.**

W.

Wabble, Wobble, to reel, move unsteadily. (E.) Frequentative of *wap, whap,* to flutter (Halliwell); see **Wave, Whap.** Cf. E. Fries. *wabbeln,* to wabble; Low G. *wabbeln, quabbeln,* to palpitate, to wabble; Swed. dial. *vabbla,* to move food to and fro in the mouth.

Wacke, a rock derived from basalt. (G.) G. *wacke,* wacke; M.H.G. *wacke,* O.H.G. *waggo,* a kind of flint.

Wad, a small bundle of stuff, little mass of tow. (Scand.) Swed. *vadd,* wadding, M. Swed. *wad,* clothing, stuff; cf. Icel. *vaðmál,* wadmal, a plain woollen stuff.+ G. *watte,* wadding, wad (whence F. *ouate*). Der. *wadd-ing, wad-mal.* Cf. **Weed** (2).

Waddle, to walk clumsily. (E.) Frequentative of *wade* (below).

Wade, to walk slowly, esp. through water. (E.) A.S. *wadan,* pt. t. *wōd,* to wade, go.+ Du. *waden;* Icel. *vaða,* pt. t. *ōð,* to wade; (cf. Icel. *vað,* a ford;) Dan. *vade,* Swed. *vada,* G. *waten,* O. H. G. *watan,* to wade, go. Further allied to L. *uadum* (for **uadhom*), a ford, *uādere,* to go.

Wadi, a water-course, river. (Arab.) Arab. *wādī.*

Wafer. (F.—Teut.) M. E. *wafre.*— A. F. *wafre*, O. F. *waufre* (F. *gaufre*), a wafer. — M. Du. *waefel*, a wafer (Du. *wafel*); Low G. *wafel*, whence G. *waffel*, wafer. β. F. *gaufre* also means 'honey-comb'; hence Low G. *wafel* may be allied to G. *wabe*, a honey-comb, Icel. *vaf*, a weft; from Teut. *waf, 2nd grade of **weban-*, to weave; see **Weave.**

Waft. (E.) For *waff*, like *graft* for *graff*. Again, *waff* is the same as *wave*, in the sense 'to beckon by waving something'; see *waft*, pt. t. of *waff*, in Merch. Ven. v. 1. 11. See **Wave** (1).

Wag (1). (Scand.) M. E. *waggen.*— M. Swed. *wagga*, Swed. *vagga*, to wag, sway, rock. Cognate with A. S. *wagian* (>M. E. *wawen*), to wag, which is a secondary verb derived from the 2nd grade of A. S. *wegan*, to carry, move. Similarly, the Swed. *wagga* is a secondary verb, from O. Swed. *wega, Icel. *vega*, to weigh; see **Weigh.** So also Goth. *wagjan*, to shake. **Der.** *wag-tail*; *waggle*, q. v.

wag (2), a merry knave. (E.) Short for *wag-halter*, one who deserves hanging (jocosely).

Wage, a gage, pledge; pl. **Wages**, pay for service. (F.—Teut.) M. E. *wage*, pl. *wages*.—O. F. *wage*, later *gage*, a gage, pledge; hence a stipulated payment; whence O. F. *wager*, to pledge, Low L. *wadiāre.*—Low L. *wadium*; formed from Goth. *wadi*, a pledge; see **Wed.** **Der.** *wage*, vb., as in *to wage war*, orig. to declare (or pledge oneself to) war; cf. Walloon *wager*, to pledge.

wager, a bet. (F.—Teut.) M. E. *wager*, *waiour.*— O. F. *wageure*, later *gageure*, 'a wager;' Cot.—Low L. *wadiātūra*, from *wadiāre*, to pledge (above). **Der.** *wager*, vb. See also **Gage** (1).

Waggle, to wag frequently. (Scand.) Frequent. form of **Wag** (above); cf. Swed. dial. *vagla*, Swed. *vackla*, to totter; also G. *wackeln*, Pomeran. *waggeln*, to waggle; Low G. *wigelwageln*, to wiggle-waggle.

wagon, waggon. (Du.) XIVth cent. Borrowed from Du. *wagen*, a wagon; which is cognate with **Wain.**

wagtail; from **Wag** and **Tail.**

Waif, sb., a thing abandoned, a thing found astray. (F.—Scand.) M. E. *waif*, *weif*; pl. *wayues, weyues, (wayves,weyves).*—A. F. and O. F. *waif*, later *gaif*, pl. *waives, gaives*; *choses gayves*, 'weifes, things forsaken, or lost;' Cot.—O. Icel.

*weif, Icel. *veif*, anything moving or flapping about (applied, e. g. to the fin of a seal); allied to *veifa*, to vibrate, move about; see **Waive.**

Wail, to lament. (Scand.) M. E. *weilen.*—O. Icel. *wæla, Icel. *væla*, to wail; also *vála*. Lit. 'to cry wo;' from *væ*, *vei*, interj., wo! See **Wo.** Cf. Swed. dial. *väla*, to wail; Dan. dial. *vælle*, to wail, *væl*, a wail; Norw. *væla*, to bleat.

Wain, a waggon. (E.) M. E. *wain*, *wayn*; formed (by the usual change of *æg* to *ay*) from A. S. *wægn*, a wain; we also find A. S. *wǽn*, a contracted form. From the 2nd grade (*wag) of *wegan*, to carry; see **Weigh.**+ Du. *wagen* (whence E. *wagon*), Icel. *vagn*, Dan. *vogn*, Swed. *vagn*, G. *wagen.* Allied to L. *ueh-iculum*, Gk. ὄχ-ος, O. Irish *fēn*, a car. (√WEGH.)

Wainscot, panelled boards on walls of rooms. (Du.) XIVth cent.— Du. *wagenschot*, 'wainscot,' Hexham; cf. Low G. *wagenschot*, the best kind of oak-wood. As if from Du. *wagen*, a wain; but really an alteration of M. Du. *waeghe-schot*, which Kilian explains as 'oak-wood with a waving grain'; from M. Du. *waeghe* (G. *woge*, M. H. G. *wāg*), a wave, and *schot*, 'a wainscot, partition,' &c., Sewel, or 'a closure of boards,' Hexham. The Du. *schot* is cognate with E. *scot* and *shot.* ¶ Not from M. Du. *weegh*, a wall.

Waist. (E.) M. E. *wast*, waist; lit. 'the growth' of a man, or the part of the body where size and strength are developed. The same word as M. E. *wacst*, strength, answering to an A. S. form *wæxt, not found, but nearly allied to A. S. *wæstm*, growth.—A. S. *weaxan*, to grow; see **Wax** (1).+ Goth. *wahstus*, growth, increase, stature; Icel. *vöxtr*, stature, shape; Swed. *växt*, Dan. *væxt*, growth. Brugm. i. § 795 (2). **Der.** *waist-coat.*

Wait, sb. (F.—O. H. G.) Orig. a watchman, sentinel, afterwards one who is awake at night, a night-musician.—O. F. *waite*, a guard, watchman; cf. F. *guet.*— O. H. G. *wahta*, a watchman, orig. a watch, a guard, a being awake. From the Teut. base **wak-*, as in Goth. *wak-an*, to be awake; see **Wake** (1); with Teut. suffix *-ton-.* ¶ Also used in the phr. *to lie in wait*; cf. Walloon *weitier*, to spy.

wait, vb. (F.—O. H. G.) O. F. *waiter*, *waitier*, *gaiter*, later *guetter*, to watch, wait.—O. F. *waite*, a watchman, a watching (above).

Waive, to relinquish a claim. (F.—Scand.) M. E. *waiuen, weiuen (waiven, weiven),* to set aside, shun, push aside, remove.—A. F. *weiver,* M. F. *guesver,* 'to waive, refuse, abandon, give over, surrender, resigne;' Cot. (Low L. *waviāre,* to waive.)—O. Icel. **weifa,* Icel. *veifa,* to vibrate, flap, flutter, whence *veifi-skati,* a spendthrift. Cf. Norw. *veiva,* to turn (a grindstone), *veiv,* a crank, Swed. *vefva,* to wind. Allied to O. H. G. *weibōn,* to hover, move about; M. Du. *weyfelen,* to be inconstant; E. Fries. *wif,* restless. And to **Vibrate.** (√WEIP.) Cf. **Waif.** ¶ Distinct from *wave.*

Wake (1), to be brisk, cease from sleep. (E.) M. E. *waken,* pt. t. *wook*: properly intransitive; whence the weak verb *wakien,* pt. t. *waked,* to cause to wake, rouse. A.S. *wacan,* to arise, come to life, be born, pt. t. *wōc,* pp. *wacen*; whence *wacian,* weak verb, to wake, watch, pt. t. *wacode.* + Goth. *wakan* (pt. t. *wōk*), *wakjan* (pt. t. *wakida*); Du. *waken,* Icel. *vaka,* Dan. *vaage,* Swed. *vaka,* G. *wachen* (whence Du. *wekken,* Icel. *vekka,* Dan. *vække,* Swed. *väcka,* G. *wecken*). Ultimately allied to **Vigil**; see Brugm. ii. § 804. Der. *wake,* sb., a vigil, A. S. *-wacu.*

Wake (2), the track of a ship. (Scand.) In Norfolk, a *wake* means a space of unfrozen water in a frozen tarn or 'broad.' The proper sense is an opening in ice, passage through ice, hence a track of a ship through a frozen sea, or a track generally. — O. Icel. **wak-,* Icel. *vak-,* stem of *vök,* a hole, opening in ice; Swed. *vak,* Norweg. *vok* (the same). Hence Norweg. *vekkja,* Dan. *vække,* to cut a passage for ships through ice. The orig. sense was 'a wet place.' — Icel. *vökr,* wet (Lowl. Scotch *wak*); cf. Du. *wak,* moist, Gk. ὑγ-ρός, wet.

Waken, to awake. (E.) Now usually transitive, but orig. *intransitive only,* in the sense 'to become awake.' M. E. *waknen, wakenen.* A.S. *wæcnan,* to be aroused, be born; intrans. form from *wacan,* to wake; see **Wake.** ¶ The verbal suffix *-en* has now usually a *transitive* force; the M. E. suffix *-n-en* is properly *intransitive,* as in Gothic. Cf. Goth. *gawaknan,* Swed. *vakna,* Dan. *vaagne,* to become awake. Der. *a-waken,* where the prefix *a* = A. S. *ā-*; see **A-** (4).

Wale, Weal, the mark of a blow. (E.) M. E. *wale.* A. S. *walu,* a weal; also

wyrt-walu, the root of a tree (with the idea of ridge). + E. Fries. *wale,* a weal; O. Fries. *walu,* rod, wand, Icel. *völr,* a round stick, Goth. *walus,* a staff. Cf. E. Fries. *walen,* to turn round, roll; Russ. *val',* a cylinder, *valiate,* to roll. β. The sense of rod or beam is preserved in *gun-wale,* the plank along the edge of a ship protecting the guns.

Walk, vb. (E.) M. E. *walken,* pt. t. *welk,* pp. *walken.* A. S. *wealcan,* pt. t. *wēolc,* pp. *wealcen,* to roll, toss oneself about, rove about; hence, generally, to ramble, walk. Cf. M.Du. *walcken,* to press, full cloth, Swed. *valka,* to roll, full, work, Dan. *valke* (same), G. *walken,* to full. Allied to Skt. *valg,* to go by leaps. ¶ M. E. *walker,* a fuller, A. S. *wealcere.*

Wall. (L.) A. S. *weall,* borrowed from L. *uallum,* a rampart, orig. a row of stakes; Cf. L. *uallus,* a stake, palisade, lit. protection. Allied to O. Irish *fál,* a hedge.

Wallah, lit. an agent. (Hind.) H. H. Wilson explains Hind. *wālā* as one who is charged with doing any duty; Yule says it is practically an adj. suffix, like the L. *-ārius* (or E. *-er*); **as if** an agent, doer, &c. See *Competition-wallah* in Yule; we may explain this as *competition-er* = *competitor.*

Wallet, a bag, budget. (E.? or F.— O. H. G.?) M. E. *walet,* apparently equivalent to M. E. *watel,* a wattle, also a bag. In P. Plowman, C. xi. 269, where some MSS. express 'bag-full' by *watel-ful,* others have *walet-ful.* Again, Shakespeare has *wallets* for bags of flesh upon the neck (Temp. iii. 3. 46), which is the same as *wattles.* ¶ Very doubtful; the form suggests an A. F. **walet,* possibly from O. H. G. *wallōn,* to go on pilgrimage. Cf. O. F. *gauler,* to wander (Ducange).

Wall-eyed, with diseased eyes. (Scand.) '*Glauciolus,* an horse with a *waule eye*;' Cooper (1565).—Icel. *vald-eygðr,* corruption of *vagleygr,* wall-eyed, said of a horse. — Icel. *vagl,* a beam, also a beam in the eye, disease of the eye; *eygðr, eygr,* eyed, from *auga,* eye, cognate with E. *eye.* The Icel. *vagl* is the same as Swed. *vagel,* a perch, roost, sty in the eye, Norw. *vagl,* a hen-roost. Cf. Wars of Alexander, 608, 1706.

Wallop; see **Potwalloper.**

Wallow. (E.) M. E. *walwen.* A. S. *wealwian,* to roll round. Cf. Goth. *walwjan,* L. *uoluere,* to roll; see **Voluble.**

Walnut. (E.) Lit. 'foreign (Gaulish)

nut.' O. Merc. *walh-hnutu*, from O. Merc. *walh*, A. S. *wealh*, foreign; *hnutu*, a nut. + Du. *walnoot*, Icel. *valhnot*, Dan. *valnöd*, Swed. *valnöt*, G. *wallnuss*. β. The A. S. *wealh* makes the pl. *wealas*, O. Merc. *walas*, which is the mod. E. *Wales* (now applied to the country itself); cognate with O. H. G. *walah*, a foreigner, whence G. *Wälsch*, Italian. ¶ The explanation 'foreign' is inexact; the A. S. *wealh* meant a Celt, either of Wales or Gaul. In form it answers to 'one of the tribe of *Volcæ*,' who occupied Southern Gaul.

Walrus, a large seal. (Du.—Scand.) Du. *walrus*. — Swed. *vallross*, Dan. *hvalros*, a morse; lit. a 'whale-horse'; the same as A. S. *hors-hwæl*, a morse, horse-whale. — Swed. *vall*, Dan. *hval*, a whale; Icel. *hross*, a horse. Said to be named from the neighing sound made by the animal. See **Whale** and **Horse.**

Waltz, a dance. (G.) Short for G. *walzer*, a waltz (with *z* sounded as *ts*). — G. *walzen*, to roll, revolve; see **Welter.**

Wampum, small beads, used as money. (N. American Indian.) Amer. Indian *wampum*, from the Massachusetts *wômpi*, Delaware *wápi*, white (Mahn). Cf. Algonkin *wab*, white (Cuoq).

Wan, colourless. (E.) M.E. *wan*. A.S. *wann*, *wonn*, dark, black, colourless; now applied to *pale* objects deficient in colour.

Wand, a slender rod. (Scand.) M. E. *wand*. — Icel. *vöndr* (gen. *vand-ar*), a switch; M. Swed. *wand*; Dan. *vaand*. + Goth. *wandus*, a rod, orig. a pliant stick; prob. from *wand*, 2nd grade of *windan*, to wind, bind. From the use of *wands* in wicker-work.

Wander, to ramble. (E.) A.S. *wandrian*, to wander; used as frequentative of *wend*, to go; but formed from *wand*, 2nd grade of *windan*, to wind; see **Wend.** +E. Fries. *wandern*, *wandeln*; Du. *wandelen*, G. *wandeln*; Swed. *vandra*, Dan. *vandre*.

Wane, to decrease (as the moon), to fail. (E.) A.S. *wanian*, to wane, decrease. — A. S. *wan*, *won*, deficient. + Icel. *vana*, vb., from *vanr*, deficient. Cf. Goth. *wans*, lacking, Gk. εὖνις, bereft of, Skt. *ūna-*, wanting. Brugm. ii. § 67.

wanion. (E.) In the phr. *with a wanion*, i. e. with ill-luck. I believe *wanion* = North E. *waniand*, waning, pres. pt. of M. E. *wanien*, to wane; see **Wane** (above). Sir T. Moore (Works, p. 306)

writes *in the waniand*, which I explain to mean 'in the waning of the moon,' i. e. with ill-luck; see Brand, Popular Antiq. on *The Moon*. (So also Wedgwood.)

want, lack. (Scand.) M. E. *want*, first used as an adj., signifying 'deficient.'— Icel. *vant*, neut. of *vanr*, adj., lacking, which was formerly used with a gen. case following; as, *var þeim vettugis vant*, there was lacking to them of nothing, i. e. they wanted nothing. The Icel. *vanr* = A. S. *wan*; see **Wane** (above). Der. *want*, vb., Icel. *vanta*, from the neut. adj. *vant*.

wanton, unrestrained. (E.) M. E. *wantoun*, unrestrained, not educated; full form *wantowen*. — M.E. *wan-*, prefix, lacking, a neg. prefix (from A. S. *wan*, lacking); *towen* < A.S. *togen*, pp. of *teon*, to draw, to educate. See **Wane** and **Tow** (1).

Wap, to strike; see **Whap.**

Wapentake, a district. (Scand.) M. E. *wapentake*. A.S. *wæpengetæc*, not an E. word, but borrowed from Icel. *väpnatak*, lit. a weapon-touching, hence, a vote of consent so expressed; and, finally, the district governed by a man whose authority was confirmed by the touching of weapons. See Thorpe, Ancient Laws, i. 455. — Icel. *väpna*, gen. pl. of *väpn*, a weapon; and *tak*, a touching, grasping; see **Weapon** and **Take.**

Wapiti, the N. Amer. elk. (Amer. Indian.) Cree *wapitik*, 'white deer;' cf. Delaware *wápi*, white (see **Wampum**).

War. (F.—Teut.) M. E. *werre*; A. S. Chron. an. 1119. Also *war-*; we find: 'armorum oneribus, quod Angli *war-scot* dicunt,' Laws of Cnut, De Foresta, § 9. [Not common, the usual A. S. words being *wig*, *hild*, *winn*, *gūð*.]—O. F. *werre*, later *guerre* (see Low L. *werra*, *guerra*), war. — M. Du. *werre*, war, cf. *warren*, to embroil; O. H. G. *werra*, broil, confusion, strife.—O. Sax. and O. H. G. *werran*, str. vb., to confuse. Base *werr-*, for *werz-*; allied to **Worse.** Cf. G. *verwirren*, to embroil. Der. *war-fare*, i. e. war-expedition; from A. S. *faran*, to go.

Warble, to sing as a bird. (F.—O. H. G.) M. E. *werbeln*, *werbelen*. — O. F. *werbler* (Burguy). — M. H. G. *werbelen*, old form of G. *wirbeln*, to whirl, run round, warble; see **Whirl.**

Ward, a guard, watch, &c. (E.) M. E. *ward*. A.S. *weard*, masc., a guard, watchman, defender; also *weard*, fem., a guarding, protection, defence. Allied to **Wary.**

(Base *war.) **+** Icel. *vörðr*, (1) a watch-man, (2) a watching; G. *wart*, Goth. -*wards* in *daura-wards*, a door-keeper. Cf. also A. F. *warde*, sb.; see **Guard**. Der. *ward*, vb., *ward-er*, sb.; also *bear-ward*, *ste-ward*, &c.

warden, a guardian. (F. − Teut.) M. E. *wardein*. **−** A. F. *wardein*, old spelling of O. F. *gardein*, *gardain*, Low L. *gardiānus*, a guardian. **−** O. F. *warder*, later *garder*, to guard; with L. suffix -*iānus*. **−** O. Sax. *wardōn*, to watch; see **Guard**. Doublet, *guardian*.

wardrobe. (F.−G.) M. E. *warde-robe*. **−** O. F. *warderobe*, later *garderobe*, a guardrobe, i. e. place for keeping robes. See **Guard** and **Robe**.

Ware (1), merchandise. (E.) M. E. *ware*. A. S. *waru* (L. *merx*; Wright). The orig. sense was prob. 'valuables,' and the word may be allied to A. S. *waru*, protection, guard, custody.**+**Icel. *vara*, Dan. *vare*, Swed. *vara*, Du. *waar*, G. *waare*, a commodity; prob. allied to Dan. *vare*, Swed. *vara*, care; see **Weir** and **Worth** (1).

Ware (2), aware. (E.) See Acts xiv. 6. M. E. *war*; A. S. *wær*, cautious. (The true form, whence *wary* was made by adding -*y*.) See **Wary**.

Wariness; see **Wary**.

Warison, Warisoun, protection, reward. (F.−O. H. G.) M. E. *warisoun*, protection (the true sense); more common in the sense of reward or help; it also meant recovery from illness or healing. **−** O. F. *warison*, *garison*, surety, safety, provision, healing. **−** O. F. *warir*, to protect, heal. **−** O. H. G. *warjan*, *werjan*, to protect; see **Weir**.

Warlock, a wizard. (E.) M. E. *war-loghe*, a wicked one, the devil; *warlawe*, a deceiver. **−** A. S. *wǣrloga*, a traitor, perfidious man, liar, truce-breaker; (hence, a witch, wizard). Lit. 'liar against the truth.' **−** A. S. *wǣr*, truth (cognate with L. *uērum*, truth); *loga*, a liar, from *log-* (Teut. *lug-*), weak grade of *lēogan*, to lie. See **Very** and **Lie** (2).

Warm. (E.) A. S. *wearm*. **+** Du. G. *warm*, Icel. *varmr*, Dan. Swed. *varm*. Teut. type *warmoz*. Cf. Lith. *wirti*, to cook, Russ. *varite*, to boil, scorch. Brugm. i. § 680. (Doubtful; some compare *warm* with L. *formus*, Gk. θερμός, warm, Skt. *gharma-s*, heat; with labio-velar *gh*.)

Warn. (E.) A. S. *wearnian*, *warenian*, (1) to take heed, which is the usual sense, (2) to warn. But the sb. *wearn*, refusal, denial, orig. an obstacle, whence *wiernan*, to refuse, may be allied to **Weir**. **+**Icel. *varna*, to warn off, from *vörn*, a defence; Swed. *varna*, G. *warnen*. Der. *fore-warn*, *pre-warn*.

Warp, sb. (E.) M. E. *warp*. A. S. *wearp*, a warp, in weaving. **−** A. S. *wearp*, for *warp*, 2nd grade of *weorpan* (strong verb), to cast, throw, hence, to throw the shuttle. **+** Icel. *varp*, a throwing, from *varp*, 2nd grade of *verpa*, to throw; Swed. *varp*, a warp; O. H. G. *warf* (G. *werft*), from *werfen*, to throw; cf. Goth. *wairpan*, to throw. From Teut. str. vb. *werpan*-(pt. t. *warp*, pp. *wurpanoz*). Allied to Russ. *vergate*, to throw. Der. *warp*, vb., from Icel. *varpa*, to throw, cast (hence, to twist out of shape); this mod. E. *warp* is a secondary (weak) verb, not the same as A. S. *weorpan*. So also Swed. *varpa*, Dan. *varpe*, to warp a ship, from Swed. *varp*, the draught of a net.

Warrant, sb. (F.−O. H. G.) M. E. *warant*. **−** O. F. *warant*, *guarant*, later *garant*, 'a warrant;' Cot. The form *war-ant* is that of the pres. pt., with the sense 'warranting.'**−**O. H. G. *werēnt*-, stem of pres. pt. of *werēn* (G. *gewähren*), to certify, to warrant. Of obscure origin. Der. *warrant*, vb.; *warrant-y*, O.F. *warantie*, fem. sb. formed from *warantir*, to warrant; see **Guarantee**.

Warren, sb. (F.−O. H. G.) M. E. *wareine*. **−** O. F. *warenne*, *varenne*, later *garenne*, 'a warren of conies,' Cot.; Low L. *warenna*, a preserve for hares, &c.**−** O. H. G. *warjan*, to protect, preserve; see **Warison**.

Warrior. (F.−O. H. G.) M. E. *wer-riour*. **−** A. F. *werreiur*, old spelling of A. F. *guerreiur*, a warrior. **−** A. F. *wer-reier*, *guerreier*, to make war (whence E. *warray* in Spenser, F. Q. i. 5. 48, ii. 10. 21). **−** O. F. *werre*, *guerre*, war. **−** O. H. G. *werra*, strife; see **War**.

Wart. (E.) M. E. *werte*, A. S. *wearte*, a wart.**+**Du. *wrat*, Icel. *varta*, Dan. *vorte*, Swed. *vårta*, G. *warze*. Perhaps 'growth' as from a root; and allied to **Wort** (1). Some connect it with L. *uerrūca*, wart; A. S. *wearr*, a callosity.

Wary, Ware, cautious. (E.) M. E. *war*; *war-y* is a rather late form, with added -*y* (as in *murk-y*). A. S. *wær*, cautious.✝Icel. *varr*, Dan. Swed. *var*, Goth. *wars*. Cf. G. *gewahr*, aware. Allied to Gk. ὁρ-άω, I perceive, L. *uer-ērī*, to regard, dread. (✓WER.) Der. *wari-ness*.

Was, pt. t. of the verb *to be*. (E.) M. E. *was*, pl. *weren*. A.S. *wæs*, I was, he was; *wære*, thou wast; pl. *wǣron*, were; subjunctive sing. *wǣre*, pl. *wǣren*. Mod. E. substitutes *wast* for the A. S. *wǣre* in the indicative, and *wert* for the same in the subjunctive; both are late forms. β. The infin. is A.S. *wesan*, to be; cognate with Du. *wezen*, O. Icel. *vesa*, Dan. *være*, Swed. *vara*, Goth. *wisan*, to be, dwell, remain; Skt. *vas*, to dwell. (✓WES, to dwell.) γ. The form *was* answers to O. Icel. *vas*, Du. *was*, Dan. Swed. *var*, G. *war*, Goth. *was*; and the pl. *wǣre* to Icel. *vārum*, *vārut*, *vāru*, Du. G. *waren*, Swed. *voro*, Goth. *wesum*, *wesuth*, *wesun*.

Wash, vb. (E.) M. E. *waschen*, pt. t. *wessh*. A.S. *wæscan*, *waxan*, pt. t. *wōx*, pp. *wæscen*.✝Du. *wasschen*, Icel. Swed. *vaska*, Dan. *vaske*, G. *waschen* (pt. t. *wusch*). Allied to **Water**. Brugm. i. § 942.

Wasp. (E.) Prov. E. *waps*, *wops*; A.S. *wœps*, *wœfs*.✝G. *wespe*, L. *uespa*; Lith. *wapsa*, a gad-fly; Russ. *osa*, a wasp. Allied to **Weave**. Brugm. i. § 918.

Wassail. (F.) M. E. *wasseyl*, *wassayl*, orig. a drinking of a health, from the Norman *weisseil* (Wace); from O. N. *wesheill*, lit. 'be whole,' a form of wishing good health. Here *wes* (A. S. *wes*) is the old imperative of O. N. *wesa*, *vesa*, *vera*, to be; and O.N. *heill*, whole, is cognate with the A.S. *hāl*, whole. See **Hail** (2) and **Whole**.

Waste, desert, unused. (F.—O. H. G. —L.) M. E. *wast*. — O. F. *wast*, in the phrase *faire wast*, to lay waste (Roquefort); whence mod. F. *gâter* (< *gaster* < *waster*). — M. H. G. *waste*, sb., a waste, *wasten*, to lay waste. Borrowed from L. *uastus*, waste, desolate; whence *uastāre*, to lay waste. β. We also find A.S. *wēste*, O. H. G. *wuosti*, waste; these forms are not *borrowed* from Latin, but are *cognate*. So also O. Irish *fás*, empty. Idg. types *wāstos*, *wāstios*. Brugm. i. § 317.

Watch, sb. (E.) M. E. *wacche*; A.S. *wæcce*, a watch, guard. ◾ A.S. *wacan*, to wake; see **Wake** (1). Der. *watch*, vb., M. E. *wacchen*, A.S. *wæccan*, weak verb.

Water, sb. (E.) A.S. *wæter*.✝Du. *water*, G. *wasser*. Allied to Icel. *vatn*, Dan. *vand*, Swed. *vatten*, Goth. *wato*;

Russ. *voda*, Gk. ὕδωρ, L. *unda*, Lith. *wandů*, Skt. *udan-*, water. Brugm. i. § 594. Der. *water*, vb.; *otter*.

Wattle, a flexible rod, hurdle; fleshy part under the throat of a cock or turkey. (E.) The orig. sense was something twined or woven together; hence a hurdle, woven stuff, a fleshy flap on a cock's neck. M.E. *watel*, a bag; A.S. *watel*, *watul*, a hurdle. Cf. A. S. *wœtla*, a bandage.

Wave (1), to fluctuate. (E.) M. E. *wauen*. A.S. *wafian*, to wave with the hand; also, wonder at or waver in mind; cf. the adj. *wǣfre*, wavering, restless. Cf. Icel. *vafra*, *vafla*, to waver; *vafl*, hesitation; Bavar. *wabern*, to sway to and fro (Schmeller). Der. *wave*, sb., from the verb above (not the same word as M. E. *wawe*, a wave, which is allied to *wag*).

waver, vb. (E.) M. E. *waueren* (*waveren*), to wander about. ◾ A.S. *wǣfre*, restless, wandering.✝Icel. *vafra*, to waver; cf. O. H. G. *wabar-*, adj., wavering; see above.

Wax (1), to grow. (E.) M. E. *waxen*, pt. t. *wōx*, *wex*, pp. *woxen*, *waxen*. A.S. *weaxan*, pt. t. *wēox*, pp. *geweaxen*. ✝Du. *wassen*, Icel. *vaxa*, Dan. *voxe*, Swed. *växa*, G. *wachsen*, Goth. *wahsjan*, pt. t. *wohs*. Further allied to Gk. αὐξάνειν, Skt. *vaksh*, to wax, grow. Brugm. ii. § 657.

Wax (2), a substance made by bees. (E.) M. E. *wax*; A.S. *weax*. ✝ Du. *was*, Icel. Swed. *vax*, Dan. *vox*, G. *wachs*, Russ. *vosk'*, Lith. *waszkas*.

Way. (E.) M. E. *wey*, *way*. A.S. *weg*. ✝Du. *weg*, Icel. *vegr*, Dan. *vei*, Swed. *väg*, G. *weg*, Goth. *wigs*. Also Lith. *weža*, the track of a cart; perhaps Skt. *vaha-*, a way, from *vah*, to carry. See **Weigh**. (✓WEGH.) Der. *al-way*, *al-ways*, see **All**; *way-faring*, i. e. faring on the way, A. S. *weg-farende*, where *farende* is the pres. pt. of *faran*, to travel; *way-lay*, *way-worn*.

wayward, perverse. (E.) M. E. *wei-ward*, headless form of M. E. *aweiward*, adv., in a direction away from a thing; from M. E. *awei*, away, and *-ward*, suffix. See **Away**.

We, pl. of the 1st pers. pronoun. (E.) M. E. *we*. A.S. *wē*.✝Du. *wij*; Icel. *vēr*, Dan. Swed. *vi*; G. *wir*; Goth. *weis*; Skt. *vay-am*.

Weak. (E.) [The verbal form has ousted the M. E. *wook*, A.S. *wāc*, adj., weak.] A back-formation from the verb signifying to weaken; from M. E. *wēken*

(Ch.), to make weak, A. S. *wācan*; the M. E. *k* being due to association with the adj. *wook*. This verb is for **wāc-ian*, from A. S. *wāc*, weak. **+** Icel. *veikr*, adj., weak, Swed. *vek*, Dan. *veg*, pliant, Du. *week*, G. *weich*, O. H. G. *weih*. All from Teut. **waik*, 2nd grade of **wīkan-*, as in A. S. and O. Sax. *wīcan*, G. *weichen*, to yield.

Weal (1), sb. (E.) M. E. *wele*; A. S. *wela*, weal, prosperity; allied to A. S. *wel*, adv., well; see **Well** (1). **+** Dan. *vel*, Swed. *väl*, G. *wohl*, welfare.

Weal (2); see **Wale**.

Weald, a wooded region, an open country. (E.) The M. E. *wald* became *wold*; but Layamon has a by-form *wæld*; l. 21339. Caxton speaks of 'the *weeld*' of Kent, which is apparently connected with this M. E. *wæld*, but seems also to have been more or less confused with **Wild**. Shakespeare and Lyly speak of 'the *wilde*' of Kent; see **Wild** and **Wold**.

Wealth, riches. (E.) M. E. *welthe*; not in A. S. Extended from M. E. *wele*, weal; see **Weal** (1).**+**Du. *weelde*, luxury; O. H. G. *welida*, riches.

Wean, to accustom a child to bread and meat, to reconcile to a new custom. (E.) We also use the word, less properly, in the sense, 'to disaccustom,' because a child that is *weaned* to meat is also being *weaned from* the breast. M. E. *wenen*; A. S. *wenian*, to accustom; *āwenian*, to wean away or disaccustom. From an adj. base **wano-*, accustomed, found in the cognate Icel. *vanr* (Swed. *van*), accustomed (cf. *vani*, custom); from **wan*, 2nd grade of Teut. **wenan-*, to crave; see **Ween**. The weak grade appears in A. S. *gewuna*, accustomed, *wunian*, to dwell.**+**Du. *wennen*, to accustom, *afwennen*, to wean from; Icel. *venja*, Dan. *vænne*, Swed. *vänja*, G. *gewöhnen*, to accustom; Dan. *vænne fra*, Swed. *vänja af*, G. *entwöhnen*, to wean from.

Weapon. (E.) M. E. *wepen*. A. S. *wǣpen*, a weapon. **+** Du. *wapen*, Icel. *vāpn*, Dan. *vaaben*, Swed. *vapen*, G. *waffe*; Goth. *wēpna*, neut. pl., weapons. Cf. A. S. *wǣpnmann*, *wǣpmann*, a full-grown man, a male.

Wear (1), to wear clothes, to consume by use. (E.) M. E. *weren*, pt. t. *wered*. A. S. *werian* (pt. t. *werode*). **+** Icel. *verja*, O. H. G. *werian*, to wear; Goth. *wasjan*, to clothe. Allied to **Vest**. (√WES, to clothe.) See **Vest**. ¶ All the senses of

wear come from the sense of carrying clothes on the body; hence it means to consume or use up by wear, to destroy, efface. The pt. t. *wore* is modern. Not allied to A. S. *werian*, to defend, which is a different word.

Wear (2) a weir; see **Weir**.

Wear (3), to veer a ship; the same as **Veer**, q. v.

Weary, exhausted, tired. (E.) M. E. *weri*. A. S. *wērig*, tired; cf. A. S. *wōrian*, to tramp about, wander, travel. **–** A. S. *wōr-*, a moor, swampy place (tedious to tramp over) in the comp. *wōr-hana*, moorcock; O. E. Texts, p. 465.**+**O. Sax. *wōrig*, weary. (The change from *ō* to *ē* is regular.) ¶ Not allied to *wear* (1).

Weasand, Wesand, the wind-pipe. (E.) A. S. *wāsend*, the gullet; but the mod. E. *wesand* answers rather to a by-form **wēsend*. **+** O. Fries. *wāsende*, windpipe; Bavar. *waisel*, the gullet.

Weasel. (E.) M. E. *wesel*, *wesele*; A. S. *wesle*, *wesulæ*, a weasel. **+** Du. *wezel*, Icel. *-vīsla*, Dan. *væsel*, Swed. *vesla*, G. *wiesel*.

Weather. (E.) M. E. *weder*; A. S. *weder*. (The *-ther* for *-der* seems to have arisen in prov. (Northern) E.; cf. *father*.) **+**Du. *weder*, Icel. *veðr*, Dan. *veir*; Swed. *väder*, wind, weather; G. *wetter*. Allied to G. *gewitter*, a storm, Icel. *land-viðri*, a land-wind; Russ. *vietr'*, wind, breeze, Lith. *wētra*, storm. Allied to **Wind** (1); cf. Goth. *waian*, to blow, O. Irish *feth*, air.

weather - beaten, weather - bitten. (E.) Both forms seem to be correct. The former means 'beaten by the weather,' from *beat*. The latter means 'bitten by the weather,' from *bite*, and occurs in Wint. Tale, v. 2. 60; derived from Norw. *vederbiten*, Swed. *väder-biten*, lit. bitten by the weather.

Weave. (E.) M. E. *weuen* (*weven*). A. S. *wefan*, pt. t. *wæf*, pp. *wefen*. **+** Du. *weven*, Icel. *vefa*, Dan. *væve*, Swed. *vefva*, G. *weben*. Also Gk. ὑφ-αίνειν, to weave. Teut. type **weban-*. (√WEBH.) Brugm. i. § 562.

web. (E.) A. S. *webb*, a web; Teut. type **wabjom*, n.; from **wab*, 2nd grade of **weban-* (above).**+**Du. *web*, Icel. *vefr*, Dan. *væv*, Swed. *väf*, G. *gewebe*.

Wed, vb. (E.) M. E. *wedden*. A. S. *weddian*, lit. to pledge, engage; hence to betroth. **–** A. S. *wedd*, a pledge; Teut. type **wadjom*, n. **+** M. Du. *wedde*, Icel.

toil, to win, to suffer from illness (whence E. *win*). See **Win, Wound**.

Wench. (E.) M. E. *wenche*, earlier form *wenchel*, a child (male or female).— A. S. *wenclo, winclo*, sb. pl., children (of either sex). Allied to A. S. *wancol*, tottery (hence weak, infantine). From the base **wank*, seen in G. *wanken*, to totter, M. H. G. *wenken*, to render unsteady. Allied to **Wink**.

Wend, to go. (E.) Little used except in the pt. t. *went* (used as pt. t. of *to go*). M. E. *wenden*; A. S. *wendan*, to turn, also to turn oneself, proceed, go. The pt. t. *wende* became *wente*, and finally *went*. Causal of A. S. *windan*, to wind; see **Wind** (2). + Du. *wenden*, Icel. *venda*, Dan. *vende*, Swed. *vända*, Goth. *wandjan*, G. *wenden*, to turn; all causal forms.

went. (E.) See above.

Were, pl. of **Was**, q. v.

Werwolf, a man-wolf. (E.) A. S. *werewulf*, a werwolf, the devil.— A. S. *wer*, a man; *wulf*, a wolf. + G. *wührwolf*, M. H. G. *werwolf*, a man-wolf; from M H. G. *wer*, a man, and *wolf*. (Hence O. F. *garoul*, F. *garou*, now *loupgarou*, i.e. wolf-werwolf.) See **Virile**. ¶ It was supposed that fierce men could turn into wolves; cf. Gk. λυκάνθρωπος, i. e. wolfman.

West. (E.) A. S. *west*, adv., westward; *west-dǣl*, west part or quarter.+Du. *west*, Icel. *vestr*, Dan. Swed. *vest*, G. *west*. Perhaps allied to **Vesper**.

Wet, moist. (E.) M. E. *wet, weet*; A. S. *wǣt*, wet. + Icel. *vātr*, Dan. *vaad*, Swed. *vāt*, wet. Teut. type **wǣtoz*. Allied (by gradation) to **Water**. **Der.** *wet*, vb., A. S. *wǣtan*.

Wether, a castrated ram. (E.) A. S. *weðr*.+O. Sax. *wethar, withar*, Icel. *veðr*, Dan. *væder*, Swed. *vädur*, G. *widder*, Goth. *withrus*, a lamb. Lit. ' a yearling;' allied to **Veal**. Brugm. i. § 118.

Wey, a heavy weight; from two to three cwt. (E.) M. E. *wege*. A. S. *wǣge, wǣg*, a weight.—A. S. *wǣg-*, 3rd grade of *wegan*, to weigh.+Icel. *vāg*, O. H. G. *wāga*. See **Weigh**.

WH.

Wh. This is distinct from *w*. The mod. E. *wh* answers to A. S. *hw*, Icel. *hv*, L. *qu*, Gk. π, τ, κ, Idg. *kw*.

Whack, to beat; see **Thwack**. But

cf. E. Fries. and Westphal. *wackeln*, to beat, to cudgel.

Whale. (E.) M.E. *whal, qual.* A. S. *hwæl*.+Du. *walvisch* (whale-fish), G. *walfisch*, Icel. *hvalr*, Dan. Swed. *hval*. It also meant a porpoise, grampus, &c. Cf. Gk. πέλωρ, a monster. **Der.** *wal-rus*.

Whap, to beat, flutter. (E.) Also *whop, wap, wop*. M. E. *quappen*, to palpitate, throb. E. Fries. *kwabben, kwappen*, to strike violently. From a base **kwap*, to throb; see **Quaver**. Cf. also W. *chwap*, a sudden stroke, *chwapio*, to strike, slap.

Wharf (1), a place for landing goods. (E.) A. S. *hwerf*, a dam or bank to keep out water (Thorpe, Diplomatarium, pp. 341,361); *mere-hwearf*, sea-shore (Grein). — Teut. **hwarb*, A. S. *hwearf*, 2nd grade of *hweorfan*, to turn, turn about. β. This difficult word, with a great range of senses, meant a turning, reversion, turning-place, space, dam, shore, dockyard, as proved by the cognate words, viz. Du. *werf*, Icel. *hvarf*, Dan. *værft*, Swed. *varf*, M. Swed. *hwarf*, &c. The A. S. *hweorfan* answers to Goth. *hwairban*, to turn oneself about, walk, and to Icel. *hverfa*, to turn. (Base HWERB.) ¶ *Not* allied to G. *werfen*, to throw; but rather to Gk. καρπός, the wrist. **Der.** *wharf-inger*, for *wharfager*; with inserted *n* as in *messenger*, *passenger*.

wharf (2), bank of a river. (E.) In Shak. Hamlet, i. 5. 33. Cf. A. S. *merehwearf*, sea-shore (Grein); it is the same word as **Wharf** (1).

What. (E.) A. S. *hwæt*, neut. of *hwā*; see **Who**.

Wheal (1), a pimple. (E.) Distinct from *weal, wale*, a mark of a blow. Perhaps from A. S. *hwele*, a wheal (Somner); A. S. *hwelian*, to form pus; *ge-hwoled*, inflamed. Cf. also W. *chwiler*, a maggot, wheal, pimple.

Wheal (2), a mine. (C.) A Cornish word.—Corn. *hwēl*, a work, a mine. Cf. W. *chwel, chwyl*, a course, a turn.

Wheat. (E.) M. E. *whete*. A.S. *hwǣte*, wheat; Teut. type **hwaitjo-*, m.; from **hwait*, 2nd grade of **hweit-*; named from the whiteness of the meal; see **White**. + Du. *weite, weit*, Icel. *hveiti*, Dan. *hvede*, Swed. *hvete*, Goth. *hwaiteis*, G. *weizen*. **Der.** *wheat-en*, adj., A. S. *hwǣten*.

Wheedle. (E.?) Spelt *wheadle* in Blount, ed. 1674; who connects it (quite unsatisfactorily) with W. *chwedla*, to gossip, *chwedl*, a fable, tale. But perhaps from A. S. *wǣdlian*, to beg, orig. to be poor ; from *wǣdl*, poverty.

Wheel. (E.) A. S. *hwēol*, shorter form of *hweowol*, *hweogul*, a wheel ; also spelt *hweohl*.+Icel. *hjōl*, Dan. *hiul*, Swed. *hjul*, O. Swed. *hiughl* (Ihre). Teut. type *hwegwlōm, n., for *hwehwlōm, Idg. **qeqlō-*, as in Skt. *chakrá-*, a wheel, Gk. κύκλος, a wheel. Idg. **qe-qlo-* is a reduplicated form, from √QEL, to drive ; whence Gk. πόλος, an axis, Russ. *koleso*, Icel. *hvel*, a wheel. See **Cycle** and **Pole** (2). Brugm. i. § 658.

Wheeze. (E.) A. S. *hwēsan* (pt. t. *hwēos*), to wheeze. Allied to A. S. *hwōs-ta*, prov. E. *hoast*, a cough, Du. *hoest*, G. *husten*. From Teut. **hwōs-*, Idg. *qās, as in Skt. *kās*, to cough ; from √QAS, as in Irish *cas-achdach*, W. *pas*, a cough ; cf. Lith. *kosti*, to cough. See **Pose** (3).

Whelk (1), a mollusc with a spiral shell. (E.) Ill spelt ; it should be *welk* or *wilk*. M. E. *wilk* ; A. S. *wiloc*, also *weoluc*, *weluc*.+Du. *wulk*, also spelt *welk*, *wilk*, *willok*, *wullok*. Prob. named from its convoluted shell ; cf. Gk. ἕλιξ (Fέλ-ιξ), a volute ; see **Helix**. Der. *whelk'd*, i. e. convoluted, K. Lear, iv. 6. 71 ; spelt *wealk'd* in the first folio.

Whelk (2), a small pimple. (E.) M. E. *whelke*, Chaucer, C. T., A. 632. Dimin. of **Wheal** (1).

Whelm, to overturn, cover over by something that is turned over, to overwhelm, submerge. (Scand.) M.E. *whelmen*, to turn a hollow vessel upside down (Palsgrave), to turn over ; Lowl. Sc. *quhemle*, *whommle*, *whamle*, to turn upside down. Closely related to M. E. *wheluen* (*whelven*) and *ouerwheluen* (*overwhelven*), used in the same sense. β. The only difficulty is to explain the final *-m* ; this is due to the fact that *whelm*, vb., is really formed from a sb. *whelm*, standing for *hwelf-m*, the *f* being dropped because unpronounceable. This appears from M. Swed. *hvalma*, to cock hay, derived from the sb. *hwalm*, a hay-cock ; where *hwalm* is for *hwalfm, being derived from M.Swed. *hwalf*, an arch, vault ; cf. *hwälfwa*, to arch over (make into a rounded shape). Thus the suffix *-m* is substantival (as in *doo-m*, *bloo-m*, &c.), and the Teut. base is HWELB. The base convex (M. H. G. *welben*, pt. t. *walb*), the derivatives of which appear in A.S. *hwealf*, adj., convex, sb., a vault, Icel. *hválf*, *hólf*,

a vault, *hválfa*, *hólfa*, to 'whelve' or turn upside down, G. *wölben*, to arch over. γ. We thus trace the following forms, viz. base HWELB, to swell out, become convex, Icel. *hvelfa*, to vault, turn a round vessel upside down ; hence *whelm*, sb., a thing made convex, *whelm*, vb., to make convex, turn a round vessel over, capsize. Forby remarks that *whelm*, in the E. Anglian dialect, signifies ' to turn a tub or other vessel upside down, whether to cover anything with it or not.' From √QELP ; whence also Gk. κόλπος, bosom, a hollow. Der. *over-whelm*.

Whelp, a puppy. (E.) M. E. *hwelp*, sb. + Du. *welp*, Icel. *hvelpr*, Dan. *hvalp*, Swed. *valp*, M. H. G. *welf*. Root unknown.

When. (E.) M. E. *whan* ; A. S. *hwænne*, *hwonne*, when.+ M. Du. *wan*, G. *wann*, Goth. *hwan* ; W. *pan*. Allied to Goth. *hwas*, A.S. *hwā*, who. Cf. L. *quan-do*, Gk. πό-τε, when.

whence. (E.) M. E. *whennes*, older form *whanene*. – A.S. *hwanon*, whence ; closely allied to **When** (above).

where. (E.) M.E. *wher* ; A.S. *hwǣr*, where ; allied to *hwā*, who.+Du. *waar*, Icel. *hvar*, Dan. *hvor*, Swed. *hvar*, G. *war* (in *war-um*), Goth. *hwar* ; Lith. *kur*.

Wherry, a shallow, light boat. (E.) Spelt *whirry* by Latimer. Perhaps allied to **Whir** ; cf. Sc. *whirry*, to whir, to hurry. Origin unknown.

Whet. (E.) M. E. *whetten*. A. S. *hwettan*, to sharpen (<*hwat-jan.) – A. S. *hwæt*, keen, bold, brave.+Du. *wetten*, Icel. *hvetja*, Swed. *vätja*, G. *wetzen*, to sharpen, encourage ; from O. Sax. *hvat*, Icel. *hvatr*, bold, O. H. G. *hwaz*, sharp. Der. *whetstone*, A. S. *hwetstān*.

Whether, which of two. (E.) See Matt. xxvii. 21. A. S. *hwæðer*, which of two ; formed with comparative suffix *-ðer* (Idg. *-tero-*) from the base of *who*.+ Icel. *hvárr*, Goth. *hwathar* ; cf. Lith. *katras*, Gk. κότερος, πότερος, Skt. *katara-*.

Whey. (E.) M. E. *whey*. A. S. *hwǣg*, whey.+M. Du. *wey* ; Du. *hui*, *wei*. Cf. W. *chwig*, whey fermented with sour herbs.

Which. (E.) M. E. *which* ; *quhilk* (Barbour). A. S. *hwilc*, *hwelc*, which ; short for *hwi-līc*, lit. ' of what form.' – A. S. *hwi*-, allied to *hwā*, who ; *līc*, like ; see **Who** and **Like.** + O. Sax. *hwilik*, O. Fries. *hwelik*, Du. *welk*, Goth. *hwileiks*, *hwēleiks*, Icel. *hvīlīkr*, Dan. Swed. *hvilken*, G. *welcher*, O.H.G. *hwelih*. Cf. L. *quālis*, Gk. πηλίκος. Brugm. ii. § 88.

Whiff, sb., a puff. (E.) M. E. *weffe*, vapour. An imitative word, like *puff, fife.* +W. *chwiff*, a puff, *chwaff*, a gust; Dan. *vift*, a puff, gust. Cf. A.S. *hwiða*, Icel. *hviða*, a breeze.

whiffle, to blow in gusts, veer as the wind. (E.) Frequentative of *whiff*, to puff. **Der.** *whiffl-er*, a piper, fifer, hence one who goes first in a procession.

Whig. (E.?) See Todd's Johnson and Nares. *Whig* is a shortened form of *whiggamor*, applied to certain Scotchmen who came from the west to buy corn at Leith; from the word *whiggam*, employed by these men in driving their horses. A march to Edinburgh made by Argyle (in 1648) was called 'the *whiggamor's* inroad,' and afterwards those who were opposed to the court came (in 1680) to be called *whigs.* (Burnet, Own Times, b. i.) But the term had previously been applied (in 1667) to the Scotch Covenanters (Lingard). The Glossary to Sir W. Scott's novels has: '*whiggamore*, a great whig; whigging, jogging rudely, urging forward.' To *whig awa'* is to jog on briskly. Perhaps for *wig*; cf. E. Fries. *wiggen*, Norw. *vigga*, to rock; Icel. *vigg*, a horse; E. *wiggle* and *wag.*

While, a time. (E.) A.S. *hwīl*, sb., a pause, a time.+Icel. *hvīla*, a place of rest; Dan. *hvile*, rest; Swed. *hvila*, rest; G. *weile*, Goth. *hweila*, a time. Prob. allied to L. *qui-es*, rest. (√QEI.) Brugm. i. § 675. **Der.** *while*, adv.; *whiles*, M. E. *whiles*, adv. (with gen. suffix *-es*); whence *whils-t*, with added *t* (as in *amongs-t, amids-t*); also *whil-om*, formerly, from A.S. *hwīlum*, dat. pl. of *hwīl*, a time. Also *mean-while*, see **Mean** (3); also *whiling-time*, the waiting a little time before dinner (Spectator, no. 448), whence the phrase *to while away time*, probably with some thought of confusion with *wile.*

Whim, a freak. (Scand.) Skelton has *whim-wham.* – Icel. *hvima*, to wander with the eyes, as a silly person; Norw. *kvima*, to whisk about, trifle. Cf. Swed. dial. *hvimmerkantig*, giddy in the head; Norw. *kvim*, foolery (Ross). **Der.** *whimsey*, a whim, from the allied Norw. *kvimsa*, Swed. dial. *hvimsa*, Dan. *vimse*, to be giddy, skip or whisk about.

Whimper, to whine. (E.) The same

as Lowland Sc. *whimmer*, to whimper, frequentative of *whim*, another form of *whine*; see **Whine.** '[They] wil *whympe* and *whine*;' Latimer, Seven Sermons, ed. Arber, p. 77.+G. *wimmern.*

Whin, gorse. (Scand.) M. E. *whynne, quyn.* – Swed. *hven*, Norw. *hvene*, bentgrass; Norw. *hvin, hven*, purple melic grass.

Whine, vb. (E.) A.S. *hwīnan*, to whine.+Icel. *hvīna*, Swed. *hvina*, Dan. *hvine*, to whir, whiz, whine. [Cf. Icel. *kveina*, to wail, Goth. *kwainōn*, to mourn.] **Der.** *whimp-er*, q. v.

Whinyard, a kind of sword. (Scand.) Lit. *whine-yard*, where *yard* (probably) is a mere suffix (*-i-ard*). – Icel. *hvīn-a*, to whiz, whistle through the air like a weapon; the same word as E. *whine*, but used in a different way. Cf. also E. *whinny*; and Lowl. Sc. *whing-er*, a whinyard, from the verb *whinge*, an extension of *whine.*

Whip, to move quickly, to flog. (E.) M.E. *whippen*, to overlay a cord by rapidly binding the twine round it, *whippe*, a scourge. From the sense of rapid movement; M. E. *wippen*, to jump up and down suddenly, to jig.+Du. *wippen*, to skip, formerly to shake; Low G. *wippen*, to bob up and down; Dan. *vippe*, to seesaw, bob; Swed. *vippa*, to wag, jerk; G. *wippen*, to move up and down, see-saw, jerk. (I find no very early authority for the *h.*) Cf. L. *uibrāre*; see **Vibrate. Der.** *whip*, sb., M. Du. *wippe* (Hexham).

whipple-tree, a swing-bar for traces. (E.) The sense is 'piece of swingingwood,' composed of *tree* (as in *axle-tree*) and the verb *whipple*, frequent. of *whip*, to move about quickly, to see-saw (above).

Whir, to buzz. (Scand.) An imitative word, like *whiz.* – Dan. *hvirre*, to whirl, twirl; Swed. dial. *hvirra*, to whirl. Allied to **Whirl.**

Whirl. (Scand.) M. E. *whirlen*; a contraction for *whirf-len, frequent. of M. E. *wherfen*, to turn. – Icel. *hvirfla*, to whirl; frequent. of *hverfa* (pt. t. *hvarf*), to turn round; Dan. *hvirvle*, Swed. *hvirfla*, M. Du. *wervelen*, to whirl; G. *wirbeln*, to whirl, to warble. (Base HWERF.) Allied to **Wharf.** Cf. Goth. *hwairban*, to go about; Gk. καρπός, the wrist. Brugm. i. § 675. **Der.** *whirl-wind*, from Icel. *hvirfilvindr*, Dan. *hvirvelvind*, Swed. *hvirfvelvind*, a whirlwind; also *whirlpool*; *whirl-i-gig* (see **Gig**).

Whisk, to move or sweep quickly. (Scand.) The *h* is intrusive. It is properly *wisk*, orig. to wipe, brush, sweep, esp. with a quick motion, as when using a light brush; the *h* was due to confusion with *whiz, whir, whirl,* &c. ▬ Dan. *viske,* to wipe, rub, sponge, from *visk,* a wisp, rubber; Swed. *viska,* to wipe, also to wag (or whisk) the tail, from *viska,* 'whisk [*sic*], a small broom,' Widegren; Icel. *visk,* a wisp of hay, something to wipe with, a rubber.▬G. *wischen,* 'to wipe, wisk, rub,' Flügel; from the sb. *wisch,* 'whisk (*sic*), clout,' id. Cf. A.S. *weoxian* (for **wiscian*), to wipe. β. The sb. which thus appears as Icel. *visk,* Swed. *viska,* G. *wisch,* meant orig. 'a wisp.' Der. *whisker,* from the likeness to a small brush. 'Nestor *brush'd* her with his *whiskers*;' Dryden, Troilus, iv. 2. Also *whisk-y,* a light gig, easily *whisked* along.

Whisky, Whiskey, a spirit. (Gaelic.) Gaelic *uisge-beatha,* water of life, whisky; the latter element being dropped; see **Usquebaugh.**

Whisper, vb. (E.) M.E. *whisperen.* O. Northumb. *hwisprian,* to murmur, Luke xix. 7, John vii. 12.╋ M. Du. *wisperen, wispelen,* G. *wispeln.* Cf. also Icel. *hvīskra,* Swed. *hviska,* Dan. *hviske,* to whisper. (Imitative base HWIS.) Allied to **Whiz** and **Whistle.**

Whist, a game requiring silence. (E.) Orig. called *whisk,* from the sweeping up of the tricks (see **Whisk**); renamed as *whist,* from the use of the word *whist* to enjoin silence; cf. *hist* and *hush.* Chaucer has both *hush* and *whist* in the sense of 'silenced' or 'quiet'; tr. of Boethius, b. ii. met. 5, l. 1341.

Whistle, vb. (E.) A.S. *hwistlian,* to hiss; *hwistlere,* a whistler, piper. ╋ Icel. *hvīsla,* to whisper; Dan. *hvisle,* to hiss, whistle; Swed. *hvissla,* to whistle. (Base HWIS.) See **Whisper.**

Whit, a thing, particle. (E.) The *h* is misplaced; *whit* is for *wiht,* the same as *wight,* a person, also a thing, bit, whit. ▬ A.S. *wiht,* a wight, a thing, bit; see **Wight** (1). Der. *aught* = A.S. *āwiht,* one whit; whence *n-aught, n-ot.*

White. (E.) M.E. *whit.* A.S. *hwīt.* ╋Du. *wit,* Icel. *hvītr,* Dan. *hvid,* Swed. *hvit,* Goth. *hweits,* G. *weiss.* Allied to Skt. *çvēta-,* white, from *çvit,* to shine, to be white; also to Russ. *svietite,* to shine; Lith. *szwaitinti,* to illuminate. Brugm. i.

§ 319. (√KWEI.) Der. *whit-ing,* a fish with delicate white flesh, also ground chalk; also *whit-ster,* a whitener, bleacher; *whittle* (2), *wheat, Whit-sunday,* q. v.

Whither. (E.) M.E. *whider.* A.S. *hwider, hwæder,* whither.╋Goth. *hwadrē.* Cf. *hither, thither.* Allied to **Who.**

Whitlow, a painful swelling on the fingers. (Scand.) Corruption of *whick-flaw,* a whitlow (Halliwell); where *whick* is the Northern pronunciation of *quick,* i.e. the sensitive part of the finger round the nail; Icel. *kvika. Flaw* is the Swed.*flaga,* a flaw, crack, breach, flake. See **Quick** and **Flaw.** The sense is 'crack near the quick,' hence a painful sore, afterwards a painful swelling. It was corrupted first to *whitflaw* (Holland), or *whitflowe* (Palsgrave), and afterwards to *whitlow*; by confusion with *white* and *low* (4). '*Paronychia,* a *whitflaw*;' Wiseman, Surgery, b. i. c. 11.

Whit-sunday. (E.) Lit. *white Sunday,* as is perfectly certain from the A.S. name *hwīta sunnan-dæg,* Icel. *hvītasunnudagr,* Norwegian *kvitsunndag*; these are *facts,* though constantly denied by the lovers of paradoxical and far-fetched etymologies. The difficulty lies *only* in the reason for the name. 'The great festivals, Yule, Easter, and Pentecost, but esp. the two latter, were the great seasons for christening; in the Roman Catholic church especially Easter, whence in Roman usage the Sunday after Easter was called *Dominica in Albis*; but in the Northern churches, perhaps owing to the cold weather at Easter-time, Pentecost . . seems to have been esp. appointed for christening and for ordination; hence the following week was called the Holy Week, Icel. *Helga Vika*;' Icel. Dict. The case is parallel to that of *noon,* which at first meant 9th hour, or 3 P.M., but was afterwards *shifted.* So also in other cases. Cf. W. *sulgwyn,* Whitsunday; from *sul,* sun, *gwyn,* white. Der. *Whitsun-week,* short for *Whitsunday's week* (Icel. *hvītasunnudags-vika*); *Whitsun-tide,* short for *Whitsunday-tide*; cf. *Palmson* for *Palmsunday, Lowson* for *Lowsunday.*

Whittle (1), to pare or cut with a knife. From the obsolete sb. *whittle,* a knife, the same as M.E. *þwitel,* a knife, lit. 'a cutter.'▬A.S. *þwit,* weak grade of *þwītan,* to cut. See **Thwite.**

Whittle (2), to sharpen. (E.) Used as

A. S. *wīnberie, wīnberige,* a grape, lit. a wine-berry.—A. S. *wīn,* from L. *uīnum,* wine; *berige,* a berry; see **Berry.**

Wimble (1), a gimlet. (E.) M. E. *wimbil.* Cf. Dan. *vimmel,* a boring-tool; Low G. *wemel, wemmel,* a wimble (Lübben); M. Du. *weme,* ' a pearcer, or a wimble,' Hexham; M. Du. *wemelen,* 'to pearce or bore with a wimble,' Hexham. Apparently from a Teut. base **wem,* to turn; see below. Cf. Shropsh. *wim-wam,* a turnstile. **Der.** *gimlet.*

Wimble (2), active. (Scand.) In Spenser, Shep. Kal., March, 91.—Swed. dial. *vimmla,* to be giddy or skittish, frequent. of Swed. dial. *vima,* to be giddy, allied to Icel. *vim,* giddiness. Compare **Wimble** (1) and **Whim.**

Wimple, a covering for the neck. (E.) M. E. *wimpel;* A. S. *winpel,* a wimple.+ Du. *wimpel,* a streamer, pendant; Icel. *vimpill,* Dan. Swed. *vimpel,* G. *wimpel,* a pennon, O. H. G. *wimpal,* a summer robe. β. The A. S. *winpel* suggests **wind-pel;* from *wind,* the wind, and (perhaps) A. S. *pæll, pell* (L. *pallium*), a covering; cf. O. H. G. *wim-pal.* See **Wind** (1) and **Pall** (1). ¶ This would also account for the sense of 'streamer,' if *pel* can mean a strip of bright-coloured stuff. (A guess.)

Win, to gain by labour, earn. (E.) M. E. *winnen,* pt. t. *wan, won,* pp. *wonnen.* A. S. *winnan,* to fight, struggle, try to get, labour, suffer; pt. t. *wann,* pp. *wunnen.*+ Du. *winnen,* Icel. *vinna,* Dan. *vinde,* Swed. *vinna;* G. *gewinnen,* O. H. G. *winnan,* to fight, strive, earn; Goth. *winnan,* to suffer. Allied to Skt. *van,* to beg, ask for, honour; L. *uenerārī,* to honour, *uenus,* desire; W. *gwên,* a smile. (√WEN.)

Winberry; see **Wimberry.**

Wince. (F. — Teut.) M. E. *wincen.* —A. F. **wencir,* necessarily the old form of A. F. *guencir* (Toynbee), for O. F. *guenchir,* later *guincher,* to wriggle, writhe aside (Cot.).—O. Sax. *wenkian;* M. H. G. *wenken,* to wince, start aside; for Teut. **wankjan-.*—M. H. G. *wank,* 2nd grade of *winken,* to move aside, nod, beckon; see **Wink.**

winch, the crank of an axle. (E.) M. E. *winche;* prov. E. *wink;* A. S. *wince,* a winch, orig. a bent handle. Cf. A. S. *wincel,* a corner, lit. bend; from the strong verb **wincan;* see **Wink.** Note also Lithuan. *winge,* a bend or turn of a river or road.

Wind (1), air in motion. (E.) M. E. *wind;* A. S. *wind.* + Du. *wind,* Icel. *vindr,* Dan. Swed. *vind,* G. *wind,* Goth. *winds.* Teut. type **wendoz.* Further cognate with W. *gwynt,* Bret. *gwent,* L. *uentus,* wind. Orig. a pres. part., with the sense of 'blowing.' From √WĒ, to blow; whence also Skt. *vā,* to blow, *vātas,* wind, Goth. *waian,* to blow, Russ. *vieiate,* to blow, *vieter',* wind, Lithuan. *wêjas,* wind. From the same root is E. *weather,* q.v. **Der.** *wind,* to blow a horn, pt. t. and pp. *winded,* Much Ado, i. 1. 243, often oddly corrupted to *wound*! Cf. Sweet, Gr. 1367. Also *wind-fall, wind-mill,* &c.

Wind (2), to turn round, twist. (E.) M. E. *winden,* pt. t. *wand, wond,* pp. *wunden.* A. S. *windan,* pt. t. *wand,* pp. *wunden.*+Du. *winden,* Icel. *vinda,* Dan. *vinde,* Swed. *vinda* (to squint), G. *winden,* Goth. *-windan* (in *bi-windan*). Teut. type **wendan-,* pt. t. **wand,* pp. **wund-anoz.*

windlass (1), a machine with a turning axis. (Scand.) M. E. *windelas;* from Icel. *vindil-áss* (still in use), a compound of Icel. *vindill,* a winder, and *áss* (explained below). Here Icel. *vindil* = M. E. *windel,* Swed. dial. *vindel,* a winder; from the verb *to wind.* β. We also find M. E. *windas,* a windlass; Chaucer, C. T. 10498, &c. — Icel. *vindáss,* a windlass. — Icel. *vind-a,* to wind; *áss,* a pole, rounded beam, +Du. *windas,* M. Du. *windaes,* a windlass. γ. Here M. Du. *aes,* Icel. *áss,* is cognate with Goth. *ans,* a beam (distinct from Du. *as,* M. Du. *asse,* an axis, for which see **Axis**).

windlass (2), a circuit. (Scand.) Formerly *windlasse;* Hamlet, ii. 1. 65; &c. A peculiar use of **Windlass** (1), perhaps misunderstood as if used for *windlace,* a winding course; from *wind,* vb., and *lace,* a snare, twist, mod. E. *lace.*

Window. (Scand.) Orig. sense 'wind-eye,' an eye or hole for the admission of air and light. M. E. *windowe, windohe, windoge.* — Icel. *vindauga* (for **windauga*), a window; lit. 'wind-eye;' Dan. *vindue.* — Icel. *vindr,* wind; *auga,* eye; see **Eye.** ¶ Butler has *windore,* a corrupted form, as if for *wind-door.*

Wine. (L.) A. S. *wīn,* wine; borrowed from L. *uīnum,* wine (whence also G. *wein,* &c.).+Gk. οἶνος, wine; οἴνη, a vine. The Gk. οἴνη is from √WEI, to wind, twist, twine (see **Withy**); from the twining growth of the vine. Brugm. ii. § 66.

Wing. (Scand.) M. E. *winge*, *wenge*. − Icel. *vængr* (for **wængr*), a wing; Dan. Swed. *vinge*; N. Fries. *winge*.

Wink, to move the eyelids quickly. (E.) 1. M. E. *winken*, pt. t. *winkede*. − A. S. *wincian*, to wink. 2. But we also find *winken*, strong verb, pt. t. *wank*, *wonk*, shewing that there was also a strong A. S. verb **wincan*, (pt. t. **wanc*, pp. **gewuncen*), whence A. S. *wanc·ol*, wavering, and other forms. **+** M. Du. *wincken*, *wencken*, to wink; *wanck*, sb., a twinkling of an eye, an instant; Icel. *vanka*, to wink; Dan. *vinke*, Swed. *vinka*, to beckon; G. *winken*, to nod; O. H. G. *winkan*, str. vb., to move aside, stir, waver (see Schade). Cf. Lith. *wingis*, a bend of a river, *wangus*, idle, *wengti*, to shirk work, to flinch.

winkle, a kind of shell-fish. (E.) A. S. *-wincla* (in *wine-wincla*), a winkle. Named from the convoluted shell; cf. Dan. dial. *vinkel*, a snail-shell; allied to *wince*, a winch (orig. a bend, turn?). See also **Wench**.

Winnow. (E.) M. E. *windewen*, *winewen*, to winnow. A. S. *windwian*, to winnow, expose to wind. − A. S. *wind*, wind. So also O. H. G. *wintōn*, from *wint*; L. *uentilare*, from *uentus*.

Winsome, pleasant. (E.) A. S. *wynsum*, delightful; formed with suffix *-sum* from *wynn*, joy. A. S. *wynn* < Teut. **wunjā*, f., is formed (by vowel-change of *u* to *y*) from *wun-*, as in Goth. *un-wun-ands*, unrejoicing, weak grade of Idg. **wen*, to desire. See **Wont**. Cf. G. *wonne*, joy, O. Sax. *wunnia*.

Winter. (E.) A. S. *winter*, a winter, also a year. **+** Du. *winter*, Icel. *vetr*, Dan. Swed. *vinter*, G. *winter*, Goth. *wintrus*. Teut. type **wintruz*. Root unknown.

Wipe. (E.) A. S. *wīpian*, to wipe; orig. to rub with a wisp of straw. From a sb. preserved in E. Fries. *wīp*, Low G. *wiep*, a twist or wisp of straw. Allied to Goth. *waips*, a wreath; from the str. vb. *weipan*, to crown (twine).

Wire. (E.) A. S. *wīr*, a wire. **+** Icel. *vīrr*, wire; cf. Swed. *vira*, to twist; O. H. G. *wiara*, an ornament of (twisted) gold; L. *uiriæ*, armlets. Some compare Irish *fiar*, crooked (bent); from √WEI, to twine.

Wis; see **Ywis.**

Wise (1), discreet, learned. (E.) A. S.

wīs, wise. **+** Du. *wijs*, Icel. *vīss*, Dan. *viis*, Swed. *vis*, G. *weise*, wise. Teut. type **wīsoz*, for **wit-toz*, from Idg. √WEID, to know. See **Wit** (1). Thus *wise* = 'knowing'; cf. *cunning*. Brugm. i. §§ 759, 794. Der. *wis-dom*, A. S. *wīs-dōm*.

wise (2), manner, way. (E.) M. E. *wise*; A. S. *wīse*, way. Orig. sense 'wiseness' or skill; from *wīs*, adj., wise (above). **+** Du. *wijs*, Dan. *viis*, Swed. *vis*, G. *weise*, sb. Der. *like-wise* (i. e. in like wise); *other-wise*. Doublet, *guise*.

wiseacre. (Du. − G.) Borrowed from M. Du. *wijssegger*, supposed to mean a wise sayer, sooth-sayer. − G. *weissager*, supposed to mean 'wise sayer.' β. But the G. word is itself a corruption of O. H. G. *wīzago*, a prophet, seer; from O. H. G. *wīzan*, to see. The cognate A. S. word is *wītega*, a prophet, seer; from A. S. *wītan*, to observe. β. The verbs *wizan*, *wītan*, are cognate with L. *uidēre* (pt. t. *uīd-i*), to see; and closely allied to A. S. *witan*, to know: see **Wit** (1).

Wish, vb. (E.) M. E. *wischen*. A. S. *wȳscan*, to wish; for Teut. **wunskjan-*, formed from Teut. **wunsko-*, sb., a wish. Compare A. S. *wūsc-* (in comp.), which is cognate with M. Du. *wunsch*, Icel. *ōsk*, G. *wunsch*, O. H. G. *wunsc*, a wish [the derived verbs being Icel. *æskja*, G. *wünschen*, to wish]. Allied to Skt. *vānch*, to desire, wish, formed (with verbal suffix *-sko-*) from *van*, to ask. Similarly the E. word is a derivative from √WEN, to desire, whence E. *win*; see **Win**. Brugm. ii. § 90. Der. *wishful*; and see *wistful*.

Wisp, a small bundle of straw or hay. (E.) M. E. *wisp*, also *wips*. The form *wips* may be connected with the verb *to wipe*. Allied to Low G. *wiep*, Norweg. *vippa*, a wisp, Swed. dial. *vipp*, a little sheaf or bundle, Goth. *waips*, a crown (orig. a twisted wreath). Cf. Dan. *vippe*, to see-saw, go to and fro, Swed. *vippa*, G *wippen*, to go up and down, see-saw. Perhaps from the vibratory motion in rubbing; see **Whip, Vibrate.**

Wist, knew; see **Wit** (1).

Wistful, eager. (E.) The history of the word shews it to be a substitution for *wishful*, 3 Hen. VI, iii. 1. 14; which is from *wish*, sb., with suffix *-ful*. β. But it seems to have been confused with *wistly*, a word used by Shakespeare in place of M. E. *wisly*, certainly, verily, exactly, be used to; it came to be used as a sb.; and, its origin being forgotten, the pp. suffix *-ed* was again added, producing a form *wont-ed* = *won-ed-ed*! Chaucer has *woned*, i. e. *wont*, as a pp.; C. T. 8215; Troilus, i. 511. A.S. *wunod*, pp. of A.S. *wunian*, to dwell, be used to.‒A.S. *ge-wuna*, sb., custom, use, 'wont.'‒A.S. *wun-*, weak grade of √WEN, to desire, strive after; see **Win**, **Wish**. *Wont* is a habit due to acquiescence in what seems pleasant. Cf. Icel. *vanr*, adj., accustomed, *vani*, a usage, allied to *vinr*, a friend; G. *gewohnt*, wont, pp. of *wohnen*, to dwell. Der. *wont*, sb., for M. E. *wone*, usage (by confusion); hence *wont*, vb., *wont-ed*, accustomed.

Woo, to court. (E.) M. E. *wo_en*, *wowen*. A.S. *wōgian*, to woo; of obscure origin.

Wood (1), timber, forest. (E.) M. E. *wode*. A.S. *wudu*, of which the orig. form was *widu*.+Icel. *viðr*, a tree, wood; Dan. Swed. *ved*; O. H. G. *witu*. Cf. Irish *fiodh*, a wood, tree; O. Irish *fid*, a tree; W. *gwŷdd*, trees. Teut. type *widuz*. Der. *wood-en*, *-y*, *-ed*; *wood-bine*, A.S. *wudu-binde*; *-ruff*, *-wale*.

Wood (2), mad, furious. (E.) In Mids. Nt. Dr. ii. 1. 192. M. E. *wod*. A.S. *wōd*, mad, raging. + Icel. *ōðr*, Goth. *wōds*, frantic. Cf. G. *wuth*, madness. Perhaps allied to L. *uātes*, a prophet, one filled with divine frenzy; O. Irish *faith*, a prophet. Hence perhaps the name *Wōden*; see **Wednesday**.

Woodruff, a plant. (E.) M. E. *wod-ruffe*, *woderoove*. A.S. *wuderōfe*, *wudurōfe*, woodruff. The A.S. *rōfe* = O. H. G. *ruofe*, 'fragrant,' sweet-smelling. Cf. G. *waldmeister*, woodruff; L. *hastula regia*.

woodwale, a bird. (E.) Also called *witwall*, *wittal*. M. E. *wodewale*, perhaps a woodpecker. From A.S. *wudu*, a wood; the form *witwall* being due to the Low G. and M. Du. forms. The sense of *-wale* is not known.+M. Du. *weduwael*, a kind of yellow bird; Low G. *widewaal*; M.H.G. *witewal*, an oriole. (Cf. **Wittol**.)

Woof, the weft. (E.) This curious word is a corruption of M. E. *oof*, the *w* being prefixed owing to a popular etymology from *weave* (which is true, but not in the way which popular etymologists would understand). The M. E. *oof* is a contraction of A.S. *ōwef*, the woof. ‒ A.S. *ō-*, variant of *ā-* (as in *ā-wefan*), *wef*, a sb. due to *wefan*, to weave. Cf. prov. E.

abb, A.S. *āweb*, woof; from *ā-wefan*, to weave together.

Wool. (E.) M. E. *wolle*. A.S. *wull*, *wul*.+Du. *wol*, Icel. *ull*, Dan. *uld*, Swed. *ull*, G. *wolle*, Goth. *wulla*, wool. Allied to Lith. *wilna*, Russ. *volna*, Skt. *ūrṇā*, wool; L. *uellus* (for *velnus*), fleece. Also to Gk. λῆνος (for *Fλῆνος*), L. *lāna*, Irish *olann*, W. *gwlan*.

woolward, clothed in wool only, for penance. (E.) See L. L. L. v. 2. 717. M. E. *wolleward*, lit. with the skin towards (against) the wool. From *wool* and *-ward*, suffix. See **Toward**.

Woon, a governor, officer. (Burmese.) Burm. *wun*, a governor or officer of administration; lit. 'a burden,' hence presumably 'the bearer of the burden'; Yule, p. 867. See **Vizier** for the sense.

Word. (E.) A.S. *word*.+Du. *woord*, Icel. *orð*, Dan. Swed. *ord*, G. *wort*, Goth. *waurd*. Teut. type *wurdom*, n.; Idg. type *wṛdho-*. Cf. Lith. *wardas*, a name; L. *uerbum*, a word. Lit. 'a thing spoken;' from √WER, to speak; cf. Gk. εἴρειν, to speak. Doublet, *verb*.

Work, sb. (E.) M. E. *werk*. A.S. *weorc*, *werc*.+Du. *werk*, Icel. *verk*, Dan. *værk*, Swed. *verk*, G. *werk*. Teut. type *werkom*, n. Further allied to Gk. ἔργον, work, ἔοργα, I have wrought, Zend. *vareza*, a working, Pers. *warz*, gain. (√WERG.) Allied to **Organ**. Der. *work*, vb., *wright*.

World. (E.) M. E. *world*. A.S. *weoruld*, *weorold*.+Du. *wereld*, Icel. *verǫld*, Dan. *verden* (where *-en* is the article), Swed. *verld*, G. *welt*, M. H. G. *werlt*, O. H. G. *weralt*. β. The lit. sense is 'age of man' or 'course of man's life,' hence a life-time, course of life, experience of life, &c. The component parts are A. S. *wer* (Icel. *verr*, O. H. G. *wer*, Goth. *wair*), a man; and A. S. *eld*, an age (Icel. *ǫld*, Goth. *alds*, an age); see **Virile** and **Eld**.

Worm. (E.) M. E. *worm*. A.S. *wyrm*, a worm, snake.+Du. *worm*, Icel. *ormr*, Dan. Swed. *orm*, G. *wurm*, Goth. *waurms*; also L. *uermis*, a worm. Teut. type *wurmiz*, Idg. type *wṛmiz*. Brugm. i. § 371; ii. § 97. Prob. allied to Gk. ῥόμος (for *Fρόμος*), a wood-worm.

Wormwood, a bitter plant. (E.) A corrupted form, the word having no reference either to *worm* or to *wood*. M. E. *wermode*, later *wormwod*. A.S. *wermōd*. + G. *wermuth*, O. H. G. *werimuota*. Origin unknown.

Worry, to harass. (E.) M. E. *wirien,* *worowen,* orig. to strangle, and used of the worrying of sheep by dogs or wolves. A. S. *wyrgan,* to strangle, harm ; see O. E. Texts, p. 99. **+** Du. *worgen,* O. Fries. *wergia,* *wirgia,* G. *würgen,* to strangle, suffocate. β. G. *würgen* is the causal form of the M. H. G. strong verb -*wergan,* only in comp. *ir-wergan,* to strangle. Teut. base *werg,* Idg. √WERGH ; as in Lith. *wersz-ti,* to strangle, oppress. Brugm. i. § 624.

Worse, comparative adj. and adv., more bad. (E.) M. E. *wurs, wers,* adv., *wurse, werse,* adj. ; A. S. *wyrs,* adv., *wyrsa,* adj., worse. **+** O. Sax. *wirs,* adv., *wirsa,* adj. ; Icel. *verr,* adv., *verri,* adj. ; Dan. *værre,* Swed. *värre,* adj. ; M. H. G. *wirs,* adv., *wirser,* adj. ; Goth. *wairs,* adv., *wairsiza,* adj. β. The common Teut. type is *wersizon-,* adj., where -*izon-* is the comparative suffix, and the base is *wers,* to twist, entangle, confuse ; cf. O. H. G. *werran,* G. *wirren,* to twist, entangle ; see **War.** Der. *wors-en,* vb. See **Worst.**

Worship, sb. (E.) Short for *worth-ship.* A. S. *weorðscipe, wyrðscipe,* honour. – A. S. *weorð, wyrð,* adj., honourable ; with suffix -*scipe* (E. -*ship*), allied to E. *shape.* See **Worth.** Der. *worship,* vb.

Worst, superlative. (E.) A. S. *wyrst,* adv., *wyrsta,* contracted form of *wyrresta,* adj., which also occurs as *wyrresta,* Matt. xii. 45. **+** O. Sax. *wirsista,* adj. ; Icel. *verst,* adv., *verstr,* adj. ; Dan. *værst,* Swed. *värst,* O. H. G. *wirsisto.* Teut. type *wers-ist-oz,* adj. ; see **Worse.**

Worsted, twisted yarn. (E.) M. E. *worsted,* Chaucer, C. T. 264. Named from the town of *Worsted,* in Norfolk. *Worsted* stands for *Worth-stead* ; from *Worth,* an estate, and *stead,* a place.

Wort (1), a plant. (E.) M. E. *wort.* A. S. *wyrt,* a wort, plant, herb. **+** O. Sax. *wurt,* G. *wurz,* Goth. *waurts* ; cf. Dan. *urt,* Swed. *ört.* Teut. type *wurtiz,* f. ; Idg. type *wɔrdis.* Allied to Icel. *rōt,* L. *rādix,* Gk. ῥίζα, a root ; ῥάδ-αμνος, a young shoot ; W. *gwreiddyn,* O. Irish *frem,* a root. See **Radix, Root.** Brugm. i. §§ 350, 529.

Wort (2), an infusion of malt, new beer. (E.) M. E. *wort* or *worte.* A. S. -*wyrt,* in the compound *māx-wyrt,* lit. mash-wort, an infusion of worts. **+** Icel. *virtr,* Norw. *vyrt, vört,* Swed. *vört,* G. *bier-würze,* beer-wort ; M. H. G. *wirz.* β. The Icel. *virtr,* M. H. G. *wirz* are from a Teut. base *werti-* ; which differs in gradation from **Wort** (1).

Worth (1), adj., deserving of ; sb., desert, value. (E.) M. E. *wurth, worth.* A. S. *wyrðe,* adj., mutated by-form of *weorþ,* adj. valuable ; *wyrþ, weorþ,* sb., value. **+** Du. *waard,* adj., *waarde,* sb. ; Icel. *verðr,* adj., *verð,* sb. ; Dan. *værd,* adj. and sb. ; Swed. *värd,* adj., *värde,* sb ; G. *werth,* adj. and sb. ; Goth. *wairths,* adj. and sb. β. Teut. type *werðoz,* adj., valuable ; and hence Lith. *wertas,* worthy ; cf. W. *gwerth,* value ; L. *uer-ērī,* to respect. Prob. from √WER, to guard, keep. Allied to **Ware** (1) and **Wary.** Der. *worth-y,* adj., suggested by Icel. *verðugr,* worthy ; *worthless.*

Worth (2), to become, to be, to befall. (E.) In phr. *wo worth the day* = wo be to the day. M. E. *worthen,* to become. A. S. *weorðan,* to become, pt. t. *wearð,* pl. *wurdon.* **+** Du. *worden,* pt. t. *werd* ; Icel. *verða,* pt. t. *varð* ; Dan. *vorde* ; Swed. *varda* ; G. *werden* ; Goth. *wairthan,* to become, pt. t. *warth.* β. All from Teut. base WERTH, to become = √WERT, to turn ; cf. L. *uertere,* to turn, *uertī,* to turn to, become. See **Verse.**

Wot, I know, or he knows ; see **Wit** (1).

Would ; see **Will** (1).

Wound, a hurt. (E.) A. S. *wund.* **+** Du. *wond, wonde,* Icel. *und,* Dan. *vunde,* G. *wunde,* sb. We also find an older type in A. S. *wund,* G. *wund,* Goth. *wunds,* wounded, harmed ; Teut. type *wun-dóz* ; Idg. type *wɔn-tos.* Origin doubtful. Cf. **Wen, Win.**

Wourali, Ourali, Oorali, Ourari, Curari, a resinous substance, used for poisoning arrows. (Guiana.) From '*ourali,* written also *wourali, urali, urari, curare,* &c., according to the pronunciation of the various tribes' ; W. H. Brett, Indian Tribes of Guiana, 1868, p. 140.

Wrack, a kind of sea-weed ; shipwreck, ruin. (E.) Lit. 'that which is cast ashore ;' well shewn by mod. F. *varech,* (1) sea-weed cast ashore, (2) pieces of a wrecked ship cast ashore ; this F. word being borrowed from English. M. E. *wrak,* a wreck ; a peculiar use of A. S. *wræc,* 'what is driven' (Lat. *actuārius*), O. E. Texts, 37. 62. – A. S. *wræc,* for *wrac,* 2nd grade of *wrecan,* to drive, urge, wreak ; see **Wreak.** **+** Du. *wrak,* sb., a wreck, adj., broken; Icel. *rek*, anything drifted ashore; Dan. *vrag*, Swed. *vrak*, wreck, trash. Cf. Du. *wraken*, Dan. *vrage*, to reject.

Wraith, an apparition. (Scand.) Lowl. Sc. *wraith*, G. Douglas, tr. of Virgil, Æn. x. 641. The only similar word is E. *wreath*, which is sometimes used of smoke, vapour, or snow. Cf. Milton, P. L. vi. 58. ¶ Jamieson gives also an Ayrshire *warth*, with the sense of 'apparition.' Cf. Icel. *varða, varði*, a beacon, a pile of stones to warn a way-farer, Norw. *varde*, a beacon, *vardyvle* (= ward-evil?), a guardian or attendant spirit seen to follow or precede one, *vord*, an attendant spirit, Dan. dial. *vardyr, varedyr*, a ghostly creature resembling a man, who attends and preserves him. (Doubtful.)

Wrangle, vb. (E.) M. E. *wranglen*, to wrestle, also to dispute. Frequentative of *wring*, formed from the A. S. *wrang*, 2nd grade of *wring-an*; see **Wring**. Thus the sense was to keep on twisting or urging; hence to wrestle or argue vehemently. Cf. Dan. *vringle*, to twist, entangle. **Der.** *wrangle*, sb.; *wrangl-er*, a disputant in the schools (at Cambridge), once applied to a first-class man in the mathematical tripos.

Wrap, to enfold. (E.) M. E. *wrappen*; also *wlappen*, whence **Lap** (3). Cf. N. Fries. *wrappe*, to stop up. **Doublet**, *lap* (3). Cf. *en-velop*, *de-velop*.

Wrath, anger. (E.) M. E. *wraththe*, *wreththe*, A. S. *wrǣþþu*, wrath; Teut. type *wraiþiþā.*—A. S. *wrāð*, adj., wroth; Teut. type *wraiþoz*; see **Wroth**. + Icel. *reiði*, Dan. Swed. *vrede*, sb., wrath; from Icel. *reiðr*, Dan. Swed. *vred*, adj., wroth. See **Wroth**.

Wreak, to revenge. (E.) M. E. *wreken*. A. S. *wrecan*, pt. t. *wræc*, pp. *wrecen*, to wreak, revenge, punish, orig. to drive, urge, impel.+Du. *wreken*; Icel. *reka*, pt. t. *rak*, to drive, thrust, repel, wreak; G. *rächen*, to avenge; Goth. *wrikan*, to persecute. β. Allied to Lith. *wargti*, to suffer affliction; Gk. εἴργειν (for *ἐϝέργειν), to shut in; and to **Urge**. (√WERG.)

Wreath, a garland. (E.) M.E. *wrethe*. A. S. *wrǣð*, a twisted band, bandage, fillet. Formed (with vowel-change of *ā* to *ǣ*) from *wrāð*, 2nd grade of *wriðan*, to writhe, twist. See **Writhe**. **Der.** *wreathe*, vb.

Wreck, ruin, remains of what is wrecked. (E.) Formerly *wrack*; the same as **Wrack**.

Wren, a small bird. (E.) M. E. *wrenne*. A. S. *wrenna, wrænna*, a wren. Cf. Icel. *rindill*, a wren.

Wrench, a twist, sprain. (E.) M. E. *wrenche*, only in the metaphorical sense of perversion, deceit. A. S. *wrenc* (dat. *wrence*), guile, fraud, orig. crookedness or perversion, lit. 'a twist.' + G. *rank* (pl. *ränke*), a trick. Teut. type *wrankiz*, m. From *wrank-*; perhaps allied to A. S. *wringan*, to wring, twist; see **Wrinkle**. **Der.** *wrench*, vb.

Wrest, to distort. (E.) M. E. *wresten*. A. S. *wrǣstan*, to twist forcibly. From *wrǣst*, adj., firm, strong (orig. tightly strung or twisted); formed with the suffix *-t* and vowel-change of *ā* to *ǣ*, from *wrāð*, 2nd grade of *wriðan*, to twist. (For the form, see Sievers, § 232; cf. A. S. *lāst*, foot-track, from *līð-an* (pt. t. *lāð*), to travel.) Cf. Icel. *reista*, to wrest, Dan. *vriste*, to wrest.

wrestle. (E.) M. E. *wrestlen*. A.S. *wrǣstlian*, to wrestle; frequentative of *wrǣstan*, to wrest, twist about; see above. +M. Du. *wrastelen, worstelen*, to struggle, wrestle; E. Fries. *worsteln*; N. Fries. *wrassele*.

Wretch, a miserable creature. (E.) Lit. 'outcast.' M. E. *wrecche*. A. S. *wrecca, wrǣcca*, an outcast, an exile. + O. Sax. *wrekkio*, O. H. G. *racheo*, G. *recke*, a warrior (adventurer). Teut. type *wrakjon-*, m. – Teut. *wrak*, 2nd grade of *wrekan-*, to drive, urge, hence to exile; see **Wreak**. Cf. Lithuan. *wargas*, misery. **Der.** *wretch-ed*, i. e. made like a wretch.

Wretchlessness, the same as *recklessness*; see **Reck**.

Wriggle, vb. (E.) Frequentative of *wrig*, to move about, Skelton, Elinour Rumming, 176; which is a weakened form of M. E. *wrikken*, to twist; [we actually find A.S. *wrigian*, but this passed into the form *wry*.] O. Fries. *wrigia*, E. Fries. *wriggen*, Norw. *rigga* (whence *rigla*), to move about, rock. By-form of E. Fries. *wrikken*, to turn hither and thither. + Du. *wriggelen*, to wriggle, frequent. of *wrikken*, to move to and fro; Low G. *wrickeln* (Richey); Dan. *vrikke*, to wriggle, Swed. *vricka*, to turn to and fro. See **Rickets** and **Wry**.

Wright, a workman. (E.) M. E. *wrighte*. A. S. *wyrhta*, a worker. — A. S. *wyrht*, a deed, work; formed with suffix *-t* from *wyrc-an*, to work. [Teut. type

*wurhtiz; related to *werkjan-, to work.]
— A. S. weorc, work, sb. See **Work**. +
O. Sax. wurhtio, O. H. G. wurhto, a wright.
Der. cart-wright, ship-wright, wheel-
wright.

Wring, to twist. (E.) M. E. wringen,
A. S. wringan, pt. t. wrang, pp. wrungen,
to press, compress, strain, wring. + Du.
wringen; G. ringen (pt. t. rang), to
wrestle, to wring, turn. Allied to **Wry**,
and perhaps to **Worry**. **Der**. wrong.

Wrinkle (1), a small ridge or unevenness on a surface. (E.) M. E. winkel.
Perhaps allied to **Wrench**, and to A. S.
wringan, to twist. The lit. sense is 'a
little twist,' causing unevenness. + M. Du.
wrinckel, a wrinkle, allied to wringen, to
twist. ¶ Dan. rynke, Swed. rynka, Icel.
hrukka (for *hrunka), a wrinkle, forms
due to the pp. of an old strong vb.
*hrenkan, are related to **Ruck** (1). **Der**.
wrinkle, vb.

Wrinkle (2), a hint. (E.) Lit. 'a
small trick;' dimin. of A. S. wrenc, a
trick; see **Wrench**.

Wrist. (E.) M. E. wrist, wirst. A. S.
wrist, also called handwrist, i. e. that
which turns the hand about. Formed
(like wrest, q. v.) with suffix -t from
wrið-, weak grade of wriðan, to writhe,
twist about. + Low G. wrist; Icel. rist,
instep, from rið-, weak grade of riða, to
twist; Dan. Swed. vrist, instep, from vride
or vrida, to twist; G. rist, instep, wrist.

Write. (E.) The orig. sense was 'to
score,' i. e. to scratch the surface of wood
with a knife. M. E. writen, pt. t. wroot,
pp. writen (with short i). A. S. wrītan,
pt. t. wrāt, pp. writen. + O. Sax. wrītan,
to cut, write; Du. rijten, to tear; Icel.
rīta, to scratch, write; Swed. rita, to
draw; G. reissen, to cut, tear. Teut.
type *wreitan-, pt. t. *wrait, pp. *writanoz.
Der. writ, sb., A. S. gewrit, from the weak
grade writ-.

Writhe. (E.) M. E. writhen, pt. t.
wroth, pp. writhen (with short i). A. S.
wrīðan, pt. t. wrāð, pp. wriðen, to twist
about.+Icel. rīða, Dan. vride, Swed. vrida,
to wring, twist, turn; O. H. G. rīdan.
Teut.type *wreithan-. **Der**. wroth, wrath,
wreath, wrest, wrist.

Wrong, perverted, bad. (Scand.) M. E.
wrong. Late A. S. wrang, a wrong, sb.;
orig. an adj. — Icel. rangr, O. Icel.
*wrangr > vrangr, awry, wrong; Dan.
vrang, Swed. vrång, perverse. From

vrang, 2nd grade of vringa, to wring
(only preserved in the pt. t. 3 p. pl.
vrungu); cognate with E. **Wring**.+Du.
wrang, acid, sour (because acids wring
the mouth).

Wroth, angry. (E.) A. S. wrāð; from
wrāð, 2nd grade of wrīðan, to writhe. +
Du. wreed, cruel; Icel. reiðr, Swed. Dan.
vred; O. H. G. reid, reidi, twisted, curly.
See **Writhe**.

Wry, twisted, turned aside. (E.) From
the M. E. wrien, vb., to twist, bend aside;
A. S. wrigian, to turn, incline towards.
See **Wriggle**. **Der**. a-wry, for on wry,
Barbour, Bruce, 4. 705.

Wych-elm; see Witch-elm.

Wyvern, Wivern, a two-legged
dragon, in heraldry. (F.—L.) The final
n is added, as in bitter-n. M. E. wiuere
(wivere), a serpent. — A. F. wyvre, O.F.
wivre (F. givre), a viper. — L. uīpera, a
viper; see **Viper**. ¶ The w is due to G.
influence; as if from O. H. G. *wīpera,
borrowed from L.

X.

Xebec, a small three-masted vessel.
(Span. — Turk.) Span. xabeque. — Turk.
sumbakī, a kind of ship. Cf. Pers. sum-
buk, Arab. sumbūk, a small boat, a pinnace. (Devic; Rich., p. 852.)

Y.

Y-, prefix. (E.) In y-clept, y-wis. M.E.
y-, i-; A.S. ge-, a common prefix. This
prefix appears as e- in e-nough, and as a-
in a-ware.+Du. G. ge-, prefix; Goth. ga-,
prefix.

Yacht. (Du.) Du. jagt, M. Du. jacht,
a swift boat, a hunting. — Du. jagen, to
hunt, chase. + G. jagen, to hunt. See
Yaw.

Yak, a wild ox. (Thibet.) Thibetan
gyag, a male yak, where the symbol g is
used to denote a peculiar Thibetan sound;
H. A. Jäschke, Dict. p. 668.

Yam, a large esculent tuber. (Port. —
W. African.) Port. inhame, a yam
(Littré). Formerly called inamia in
Benin; Hakluyt, ii. 2. 129.

Yankee, a citizen of New England, or
of the United States. (North. E.) In use
in Boston, 1765. Dr. Wm. Gordon, in his
Hist. of the American War, ed. 1789, vol. i.
pp. 324, 325, says it was a favourite cant

word in Cambridge, Mass., as early as 1713, and that it meant 'excellent,' as 'a *yankee* good horse.' The word may have spread from the students through New England, and have thence obtained a wider currency. It appears to be the same as Lowl. Sc. *yankie*, a sharp, clever, forward woman; cf. Lowl. Sc. *yanker*, an agile girl, an incessant talker, a smart stroke, *yank*, a jerk, smart blow, *yanking*, active (Jamieson). We also find *yank*, to jerk. But many now accept the conclusion that *Yankee* was a Dutch nick-name, formed (like *Chinee* from *Chinese*) from Du. *Jan Kees*, a familiar form of the common Du. name *Jan* (John) *Cornelius*. (Proposed by Dr. H. Logeman.)

Yap, to yelp. (E.) Of imitative origin; cf. E. Fries. and Low G. *jappen*, to gasp; F. *japper*, to yap. Note also Lowl. Sc. *yaup*, to yelp, from Icel. *gjálpa*. See **Yelp.**

Yard (1), an enclosed space. (E.) M.E. *yerd*. A.S. *geard*, an enclosure, court. + Icel. *garðr* (whence E. *garth*), Dan. Du. *gaard*, Swed. *gård*; Goth. *gards*, a house; O.H.G. *gart*, a circle; allied to O.H.G. *garto*, a garden, Goth. *garda*, a fold. Teut. type **gardoz*, m.; Idg. type **ghortos*, as in O. Irish *gort*, a field, *lub-gort*, a garden; L. *hortus*, a garden; Gk. χόρτος, a courtyard. But the connexion with Gk. χόρτος is not certain. **Doublets**, *garden*, *garth*. **Der.** *court-yard*, *orchard*.

Yard (2), a rod, 36 inches, cross-bar on a mast. (E.) M.E. *yerde*, *yerde*, a stick, rod. A.S. *gyrd*, *gerd*, a rod.+Du. *garde*, a twig, rod, G. *gerte*, a switch; O.H.G. *gerta*; Teut. type *gardjā*, f. Allied to O. Bulg. *žrŭdĭ* (Russ. *jerde*), a rod. But not to Icel. *gaddr*, Goth. *gazds*, a goad. Streitberg, § 125 (4).

Yare, ready. (E.) M.E. *yare*, *yare*, ready. A.S. *gearu*, *gearo*, ready, quick, prompt. + Du. *gaar*, done, dressed (as meat); Icel. *görr*, ready; O.H.G. *garo*, ready; cf. G. *gar*, adv., wholly. Teut. type **garwoz*. Allied to **Gear.**

Yarn. (E.) M.E. *yarn*. A.S. *gearn*, thread. + Du. *garen*, Icel. Dan. Swed. G. *garn*. Allied to Gk. χορδή, a cord, orig. a string of gut; cf. Lith. *žarnos*, Icel. *garnir*, guts. See **Cord, Chord.**

Yarrow, the plant milfoil. (E.) M.E. *yarowe*, *yarwe*. A.S. *gæruwe*, *gearuwe*, *gearwe*, yarrow. + Du. *gerw*, G. *garbe*, O.H.G. *garawa*. If allied to **Yare**, perhaps it meant 'that which dresses,' or puts

in order; from the old belief in its curative properties as a healer of wounds.

Yataghan, Ataghan, a dagger-like sabre, with doubly curved blade. (Turk.) Turk. *yātāghān*, the same; Zenker's Dict. pp. 917, 958.

Yaw, to go unsteadily, as a ship. (Scand.—Du.) Icel. *jaga*, to move to and fro; also, to hunt.—Du. *jagen*, to hunt. See **Yacht.**

Yawl (1), a small boat. (Du.) Du. *jol*, a yawl, a Jutland boat; M. Du. *jolle-ken*, 'a small barke.'+Dan. *jolle*, Swed. *julle*, a yawl; E. Fries. *jül*, *jülle*; Low G. *jolle* (Lübben). Root unknown.

Yawl (2), to howl. (E.) Also *yole*, *yowl* (Halliwell). M.E. *ʒaulen*. Also M.E. *goulen*. Cf. E. Fries. *jaueln*, Low G. *jaueln*, to yawl. + Icel. *gaula*, Norw. *gaula*, to low, bellow, roar; cf. Du. *jolen*, to groan. Imitative. Cf. **Yell.**

Yawn, to gape. (E.) M.E. *geonien*, *yonien*; whence E. *yawn*, by lengthening of *ŏ* to open long *o*; cf. E. *frost*, *broth*.—A.S. *geonian*, to yawn. Also *ginian*; from *gin-*, weak grade of *-gīnan*, strong verb, to gape widely.+O.H.G. *ginēn*, to yawn; cf. Icel. *gína*, to gape, pt. t. *gein*. Allied to L. *hiare*, to gape; see **Hiatus.** (✓GHEI.)

Ye. (E.) M.E. *ye*, *ʒe*, nom.; *your*, *ʒour*, gen.; *you*, *ʒou*, *yow*, dat. and acc. pl. A.S. *gē*, nom. ye; *ēower*, gen. of you; *ēow*, to you, you, dat. and acc. + Du. *gij*, ye, *u*, you; Icel. *ēr*, *ier*, ye, *yðar*, your, *yðr*, you; Dan. Swed. *i*, ye, you; G. *ihr*; Goth. *jūs*, ye, *izwara*, your, *izwis*, you. β. The common Idg. base is YU; whence Lith. *jus*, ye; Gk. ὑ-μεῖς, ye, Skt. *yū-yam*, ye. Brugm. ii. § 436.

Yea, verily. (E.) This is the simple affirmative; *yes* is a strengthened form, often accompanied by an oath in our early writers. M.E. *ye*. A.S. *gēa*, *geā*, yea.+ Du. Dan. Swed. G. *ja*, Icel. *jā*; Goth. *ja*, *jai*; W. *ie*; Gk. ἦ, truly. **Der.** *yes*.

Yean, Ean, to bring forth young. (E.) Here the prefixed *y-* answers to an A.S. prefix *ge-*. A.S. *ēanian*, to ean; *ge-ēanian*, to yean. We find *ge-ēane eowa* = the ewes great with young, Gen. xxxiii. 13; cf. Swed. dial. *öna*, to yean, *vara i ön*, to be with lamb (Rietz, p. 114). Teut. type **aunōjan*, to yean. From Teut. type **auno-* (for **agwno-*), corresponding to L. *agnus*, a lamb (Kluge). Cf. Irish *ūan*, W. *oen*, Corn. *oin*, Bret. *oan*, Manx *eayn*, a lamb. Hence Manx *eayney,* to yean. ¶ Sievers derives *ean* from A. S. *eowu,* a ewe; see **Ewe.** Brugm. i. § 671. **Der.** *yean-ling,* a new-born lamb.

Year. (E.) M. E. *ȝeer, yeer,* often unaltered in the plural (hence 'a *two-year* old colt'). A. S. *gēar, gēr,* a year; pl. same.+Du. *jaar,* Icel. *ār,* Dan. *aar,* Swed. *år,* G. *jahr,* Goth. *jēr.* Teut. type *yêrom, n.* Cf. Zend *yār(e),* a year. Perhaps allied to Gk. *ὥρος,* a season, year, *ὥρα,* season, hour; Skt. *yātu-,* time. Lit. ' that which passes.' (√YĒ, to pass; from √EI, to go.) Brugm. i. § 308, ii. § 587.

Yearn (1), to long for. (E.) M. E. *yernen.* A. S. *giernan,* to yearn, be desirous.— A. S. *georn,* adj., desirous. + Icel. *girna,* to desire, from *gjarn,* eager; Goth. *gairnjan,* to long for, from *-gairns,* desirous (Teut. type *gernoz*). β. Again, the adj. is from the verb appearing in O. H. G. *gerōn,* G. *be-gehren,* to long for; allied to Gk. *χαίρειν,* to rejoice, *χαρά,* joy, Skt. *hary,* to desire. (√GHER.)

Yearn (2), to grieve. (E.) Also spelt *earn, ern;* Hen. V. ii. 3. 3, ii. 3. 6; Jul. Cæs. ii. 2. 129; Merry Wives, iii. 5. 45; Rich. II. v. 5. 76; Hen. V. iv. 3. 26; the prefixed *y-* being due to A.S. prefix *ge-,* as in the case of *yean.* From A. S. *eorn-;* as in *eorn-igende,* murmuring; *eorn-ful,* anxious; *eorn-lic,* diligent; perhaps allied to **Earnest.**

Yeast. (E.) M. E. *yeest, yest.* A. S. *gist,* yeast. + Du. *gest, gist,* N. Fries. *jēst,* Icel. *jast, jastr,* Swed. *jäst,* Dan. *giær,* G. *gäscht, gischt.* Teut. base *yest-.* All from √YES, to ferment, appearing in O. H. G. *jesan,* G. *gähren,* to ferment, Gk. *ζέειν,* to boil, whence also E. *eczema,* q. v. **Der.** *yeast-y* or *yest-y,* frothy, Hamlet, v. 2. 199.

Yede, went. (E.) M. E. *yede, ȝede;* also *eode.* A. S. *ge-ēode,* also *ēode,* went, only in the pt. t. Cf. A. S. *ēodon,* pt. t. pl., with Goth. *iddjēdun,* pt. t. pl. Perhaps A. S. *ēo-=*ī-o,* from √EI, to go. Cf. Skt. *ayāt, iyāt,* he went. Brugm. i. § 309 (2); ii. § 478.

Yelk; see **Yolk.**

Yell. (E.) M. E. *yellen.* A. S. *gellan, giellan,* to cry out, resound. + Du. *gillen,* Icel. *gella,* also *gjalla* (pt. t. *gall*), Dan. *giælle, gialde,* Swed. *gälla,* G. *gellen,* to sound loud and shrill. Teut. type *gellan-,* pt. t. *gall.* Allied to Icel. *gala,* pt. t. *gōl,* to sing, O. H. G. *galan;* A. S. *galan,*

pt. t. *gōl,* whence E. *nightin-gate.* **Der.** *stan-iel.*

Yellow. (E.) M. E. *yelwe, yelu.* A.S. *geolo, geolu,* yellow. + Du. *geel,* G. *gelb.* Teut. type *gelwoz,* Idg. type *ghelwos.* Allied to L. *heluus,* light yellow, Gk. *χλόη,* young verdure of trees, Russ. *zelenuii,* green, Skt. *hari,* green, yellow. Further allied to **Gall** (1). **Der.** *yolk.*

yellow - hammer, yellow - ammer, a song-bird. (E.) The *h* is an ignorant insertion; *ammer* answers to A.S. *amore,* a small bird.+M. Du. *emmerick,* a yellow-ammer, G. *gelbammer, goldammer,* yellow-ammer or gold-ammer, *emmerling,* the same; O. H. G. *amero.*

Yelp, to bark shrilly. (E.) M. E. *yelpen,* also to boast. A. S. *gielpan,* pt. t. *gealp,* pp. *golpen,* to boast, exult, talk noisily. + Icel. *gjālpa,* to yelp; M. H. G. *gelfen.* Allied to **Yell.** Cf. **Yap.**

Yeoman. (E.) M. E. *yoman,* also *yeman.* It appears to answer to an A. S. *gēaman* (not found), which might become *gēaman;* these would give *yeman, yoman* in M. E. The word is cleared up by the existence of O. Fries. *gāman,* a villager, from *gā,* also *gō,* a village, and *man,* a man; so also M. Du. *goymannen,* arbitrators appointed to decide disputes, from M. Du. *gouwe,* a hamlet (Hexham). Cf. also G. *gau,* a province, Goth. *gawi,* a district; O. H. G. *gawi* (without mutation), and O. H. G. *gewi* (with mutation), like Bavarian *gäu,* whence *gäumann,* 'landmann.' Observe *yore,* as compared with *year.* Many solutions have been proposed of this difficult word.

Yerk, the same as **Jerk.**

Yes. (E.) A strengthened form of *yea.* M. E. *yis, yus.* A. S. *gise, gese,* yes. Prob. short for *gēa swā,* i. e. yea, so; see **Yea.**

Yesterday. (E.) M. E. *yisterdai;* from A.S. *geostra, gystra* (yester-), and *dæg,* a day.+Du. *gisteren, dag van gister,* G. *gestern;* Goth. *gistradagis,* tomorrow. β. Cf. Lat. *hester-* in *hes-ter-nus,* adj., belonging to yesterday; where again the syllable *hes-* is cognate with Icel. *gær,* Dan. *gaar,* Swed. *går,* Lat. *her-i,* Gk. *χθές,* Skt. *hyas,* yesterday. The suffix *-ter* is of a comparative form, as in *in-ter-ior,* &c. Brugm. i. §§ 624, 923.

Yet. (E.) M. E. *yet, yit.* A. S. *git, get, giet,* moreover. + O. Fries. *ieta, ita,* M. H. G. *iezuo, ieze,* yet; cf. G. *jetz-t,* now. Origin obscure.

Yew, a tree. (E.) M. E. *ew.* A. S. *īw.* + Icel. *ȳr,* G. *eibe,* O. H. G. *īwa,* yew. We also find Irish *eo,* W. *yw, ywen,* Corn. *hivin,* Bret. *ivin,* a yew. ¶ *Not* allied to *ivy.*

Yex, to hiccough. (E.) M. E. *yexen, yesken.* A. S. *giscian,* to sob, sigh. Prob. allied to L. *hiscere,* to yawn, *hiāre,* to yawn; see **Yawn.** (√GHEI.)

Yield. (E.) M. E. *gelden, yelden,* pt. t. *yald,* pp. *yolden,* to pay; hence, to yield up. A. S. *gieldan, gildan,* pt. t. *geald,* pp. *golden,* to pay, give up. + Du. *gelden,* Icel. *gjalda,* Dan. *gielde,* to pay; Swed. *gälla,* to be worth; G. *gelten,* pt. t. *galt,* to be worth; Goth. *fra-gildan,* to pay back. (Teut. base GELD.) **Der.** *guild.*

Yoke, sb. (E.) M. E. *yok.* A. S. *geoc, gioc, ioc,* a yoke for oxen. + Du. *juk,* Icel. *ok,* Dan. *aag,* Swed. *ok,* Goth. *juk,* G. *joch.* Teut. type **yukom,* n.; Idg. type **jugom*; cf. W. *iau,* L. *iugum,* Russ. *igo,* Lith. *jungas,* Gk. ζυγόν, Skt. *yuga-,* a yoke, a couple. Lit. ' that which joins;' all from the weak grade of √YEUG, to join. See **Join.** **Der.** *yoke,* vb.

Yolk, Yelk, yellow part of an egg. (E.) M. E. *yolke, yelke.* A. S. *geoleca, geolca,* the yolk, lit. ' yellow part.' ─ A. S. *geolu,* yellow; see **Yellow.**

Yon, adj., at a distance. (E.) M. E. *yon, ʒon.* A. S. *geon,* yon; Ælfred, tr. of Gregory's Past. Care, ed. Sweet, p. 443. + Icel. *enn,* the, orig. that, confused with *hinn*; Goth. *jains,* G. *jener,* yon, that. β. Allied to Skt. *ya-s,* who, orig. that ; Gk. ὅς (for *yos*). From the same base are *ye-a, ye-s, ye-t.* **Der.** *yond-er,* M. E. *yonder,* adv.; cf. Goth. *jaindre,* adv., yonder, thither.

Yore, formerly. (E.) M. E. *yore.* A. S. *geāra,* adv., formerly; lit. ' of years, during years,' orig. gen. pl. of *geār*; see **Year.**

You. (E.) Properly the dat. and acc. of *ye*; see **Ye.**

your. (E.) M. E. *your.* A. S. *eōwer,* your; orig. gen. pl. of *gē,* ye; see **Ye.** **Der.** *your-s,* M. E. *youres,* from A. S. *ēowres,* gen. sing. masc. and neut. of *ēower,* your, possessive pronoun.

Young. (E.) M. E. *yong, yung.* A. S. *geong, giung, iung,* young. + Du. *jong,* Icel. *ungr,* Dan. Swed. *ung,* G. *jung,* Goth. *juggs* (for **jungs*). Teut. **yun-goz,* short for **yuwungoz.* β. These forms answer to Lat. *iuuencus,* a young animal, heifer; cf. Skt. *yuvaça-,* W. *ieuanc,*

young. Other forms (without the final guttural) are L. *iuuenis,* Lith. *jaunas,* Skt. *yuvan,* Russ. *iunuii,* young; from Idg. base **yuwen-.* **Der.** *young-ling, young-ster*; also *youn-ker,* borrowed from Du. *jonker, jonkheer,* i. e. young sir, compounded of *jong,* young, and *heer,* sir, a lord.

youth. (E.) M. E. *youthe*; earlier *ʒuweðe, ʒuʒeðe,* youth. A. S. *geogoð, geoguð, iuguð.* [The middle *g* became *w,* and then disappeared.] + O. Sax. *juguð,* Du. *jeugd,* G. *jugend,* O. H. G. *jugund*; Teut. type **yugunthiz,* f. (where *-unth-* > A. S. *-ūð* > *-uð*); from Idg. base **yuwṇt-,* which is from **yuwen-* (above). Cf. L. *iuuenta*; also L. *iuuentās,* Skt. *yuvatā,* youth.

Yowl; see **Yawl** (2).

Yucca, a genus of American liliaceous plants. (Span. ─ Caribbean.) Span. *yuca,* said to be a word of Caribbean origin.

Yule, Christmas. (E.) M. E. *ʒole, yole.* A. S. *gēol, geohol,* the feast; also *iula, gēola,* the name of a month. December was called *se ǣrra gēola,* the former yule; and January *se æftera gēola,* the latter yule. We also find Icel. *jól,* a feast in December, *ȳlir,* December, and Goth. *jiuleis,* November. Of disputed origin. ¶ The attempt to connect this word with *wheel* is futile.

Ywis, certainly. (E.) M. E. *ywis, iwis*; often written *Iwis, I-wis,* in MSS., whence, by a singular error, the fictitious verb *wis,* to know, has been evolved by lexicographers, though unknown to our old MSS. A. S. *gewis,* adj., certain, which came to be used as an adverb. β. Here the *ge-* is a mere prefix; see **Y-** (above); the adj., *wis,* certain, answers to Teut. type **wissoz,* Idg. type **wid-tos,* an old pp. signifying ' known,' hence ' sure'; from √WEID, to know. (*dt* > *ss.*) See **Wit,** vb. + Du. *gewis,* adj. and adv., certain, certainly; G. *gewiss,* certainly; Icel. *viss,* certain, Dan. *vis,* Swed. *viss,* certain; Dan. *vist,* Swed. *visst,* certainly.

Z.

Zamindar, Zemindar, a landholder. (Hind. ─ Pers.) Hind. *zamīndār,* a land-holder. ─ Pers. *zamīn,* earth, land (allied to L. *humus*); *dār,* holding, possessing.

Zanana, Zenana, the female apartments. (Hind. ─ Pers.) Hind. *zanāna,* the women's apartments. — Pers. *zanān*, women; pl. of *zan*, a woman, which is cognate with E. **Quean**.

Zany, a buffoon. (Ital. — Gk. — Heb.) O. Ital. *Zane*, Ital. *Zanni*, a familiar form of *Giovanni*, John; used to mean 'a sillie John, a gull, a noddie, clowne, foole, simple fellowe in a plaie,' Florio. — Gk. Ἰωάννης, John. — Heb. *Yōkhānān*, i. e. the Lord graciously gave. — Heb. *Yŏ*, the Lord; *khānan*, to shew mercy.

Zariba, Zareeba, an enclosure, slight defence. (Arab.) Used in newspapers with reference to the war in the Soudan. — Arab. *zarībat*, 'a fold, a pen, an enclosure for cattle; den or haunt of wild beasts; lurking-place of a hunter;' Rich. Dict. p. 775.

Zeal. (F. — L. — Gk.) Formerly *zele*. — M. F. *zele*, 'zeale;' Cot. (Mod. F. *zèle*.) — L. *zēlum*, acc. of *zēlus*, zeal. — Gk. ζῆλος, ardour. Doric ζᾶλος, Idg. type *yā-los*; perhaps from *yā*, to drive; as in Skt. *yātṛ*, a driver (Prellwitz). Der. *zeal-ot*, M. F. *zelote*, 'zealous,' Cot.; from L. *zēlōtes*, Gk. ζηλωτής, a zealot.

Zebra. (Port. — W. African.) Port. *zebra* (Span. *cebra, zebra*). According to Littré, the word is of Ethiopian origin, but this is due to some mistake, as the name originated in Congo. (N. and Q., 9 S. v. 480.)

Zedoary, an E. Indian root resembling ginger. (F. — Low L. — Pers.) M. F. *zedoaire*, Cot. — Low L. *zedoāria*. — Pers. *zadwār, zidwār*, zedoary; also spelt *jadwār*. ¶ The O. F. forms were *citouart, citoual, citoal*; whence M. E. *cetewale*, Chaucer, C. T. 13691.

Zend, an ancient Persian dialect. (Zend.) Properly the translation into the Pehlevi language of the *Avesta*, or Zoroastrian scriptures; but commonly used to denote the language, an ancient Persian dialect, in which the *Avesta* is written. It is supposed that *Avesta* means the 'text,' and *Zend* the 'commentary' or 'explanation.' The word *zend* is mod. Persian (Palmer); also written *zand* (Richardson); and corresponds to Zend *zaiñti*, knowledge, information, appearing in the compounds *ā-zaiñti, paiti-zaiñti*, knowledge, and answering to an Idg. form *ganti*, from the Idg. root GEN, to know (Fick, i. 67, 321). See **Can** (1). β. *Avesta* has been explained as meaning 'the settled' text (Skt. *ava-*

sthita, from *ava-sthā*, to be firm: root STĀ); or, otherwise, as meaning 'that which is proclaimed or made known' (cf. Skt. *ā-vid*, to report: root WEID). See Max Müller, Lectures, 8th ed. i. 237.

Zenith. (F. — Span. — Arab.) M. E. *senyth*. — O. F. *cenith*; F. *zénith*. — Span. *zenit*, O. Span. *zenith*. — Arab. *samt*, a way, road, path, tract, quarter; whence *samt-ur-ras*, the zenith, vertical point of the heavens; also *as-samt*, an azimuth. β. *Samt* was pronounced *semt*, of which Span. *zenit* is a corruption; again, *samt* is here short for *samt-ur-ras* or *semt-er-ras* (as above), lit. the way overhead, from *ras*, the head. See **Azimuth**.

Zephyr. (F. — L. — Gk.) M. F. *zephyre*, the west wind. — L. *zephyrum*, acc. of *zephyrus*, the west wind. — Gk. ζέφυρος, the west wind.

Zero. (Ital. — Low L. — Arab.) Ital. *zero*, short for *zefiro*. — Low L. *zephyrum* (Devic). — Arab. *sifr*, a cipher; see **Cipher**.

Zest. (F. — L. — Gk.) Formerly a chip of orange or lemon-peel, used for flavouring drinks; hence, something that gives a relish, or simply a relish. — M. F. *zest*, 'the thick skin whereby the kernell of a wallnut is divided,' Cot.; hence, a slice of lemon-peel. — L. *schistus, schistos*, lit. cleft, divided. — Gk. σχιστός, divided. — Gk. σχίζειν, to cleave; see **Schist**.

Zigzag, having sharp, quick turns. (F. — G.) F. *zigzag*. — G. *zickzack*, a zigzag; [whence *zickzack segeln*, to tack, in sailing.] Reduplicated from *zacke*, a tooth; with reference to *zacken-werk*, notched work; hence *zickzack* is 'in an indented manner.' Cf. E. Fries. *takken*, to notch (whence E. *tack*, in sailing). See **Tack**.

Zinc, a metal. (F. — G.) F. *zinc*. — G. *zink*, zinc; of uncertain origin. Perhaps allied to *zinn*, tin; and meaning 'tin-like.' But see Schade.

Zodiac, an imaginary belt in the heavens, containing the twelve *signs*. (F. — L. — Gk.) F. *zodiaque*. — L. *zōdiacus*. — Gk. ζῳδιακός, sb., the zodiacal circle; so called from containing the twelve constellations chiefly represented by animals. — Gk. ζῳδιακός, adj., belonging to animals. — Gk. ζῴδιον, a small animal; dimin. of ζῷον, a living creature. See **Zoology**.

Zone, a belt. (F. — L. — Gk.) F. *zone*. — L. *zōna*. — Gk. ζώνη, a girdle; for *ζώσνη. — Gk. ζώννυμι (= *ζωσ-νυμι), I gird.

Cf. Lith. *jōsta*, a girdle, from *jōsti*, to gird. (✓YŌS.)

Zoology. (Gk.) From Gk. ζῶο-ν, a living creature, animal; and -λογία, allied to λόγος, discourse, from λέγειν, to speak. **β.** Gk. ζῷον is neut. of ζῶος, living; allied to ζωή, life, ζάειν, ζῆν, to live. Allied to Zend *ji*, to live; see **Vivid.** (✓GwEI.) Brugm. ii. § 488.

zoophyte. (F. – Gk.) F. *zoophyte.* – Gk. ζωόφυτον, a living being; an animal-plant. – Gk. ζωό-s, living; φυτόν, a plant, that which has grown, from φύειν, to pro-duce, grow, from ✓BHEU, to exist. See Be.

Zouave, one of a body of soldiers in the French service, orig. Arabs. (F. – N. African.) F. *Zouave.* – N. African *Zouaoua,* a tribe of Kabyles living among the Jurjura mountains in Algeria.

Zymotic, a term applied to diseases, in which a poison works through the body like a ferment. (Gk.) Gk. ζυμωτικός, causing to ferment. – Gk. ζυμόω, I cause to ferment. – Gk. ζύμη, leaven. Allied to L. *iŭs*, broth; see **Juice.**

APPENDIX

I. LIST OF PREFIXES

THE following is a list of the principal prefixes in English, shewing their origin. It is, perhaps, not quite exhaustive, but contains nearly all of any consequence. For further information, see the etymologies of the words *a-down*, &c., in the Dictionary.

A- (1), in a-down. (E.) See **Of-** (below).

A- (2), in a-foot. (E.) See **On-** (below).

A- (3), in a-long. (E.) See **An-** (5).

A- (4), in a-rise. (E.) A.S. *ā-*, intensive prefix to verbs.

A- (5), in a-chieve. (F. — L.) See **Ad-**.

A- (6), in a-vert. (L.) See **Ab-**.

A- (7), in a-mend. (F. — L.) See **Ex-** (1).

A- (8), in a-las. (F. — L.) O.F. *a-*; from L. *ah!* interj.

A- (9), in a-byss. (Gk.) See **An-** (2).

A- (10), in a-do. (E.) For *at do*.

A- (11), in a-ware. (E.) M. E. *i-*; *y-*; A. S. *ge-*, prefix. See **Y-**.

A- (12), in a-pace. (E.) For *a pace*; *a* for *an*, indef. art.

A- (13), in a-vast. (Du.) Du. *hou vast*, hold fast. (Doubtful.)

A- (14), in a-pricot. (Arab.) Arab. *al*, def. art. See **Al-** (4).

Ab- (1); ab-dicate, ab-undance. (L.; *or* F. — L.) L. *ab*, from. Lengthened to *abs-* in *abs-cond*; cf. Gk. *ἄψ.* **+** E. *of*; Gk. *ἀπό*; Skt. *apa*, away from. See **Apo-**, **Of-**. This prefix also appears as *a-*, *adv-*, *av-*, *v-*; ex. a-vert, adv-ance, av-aunt, v-anguard.

Ab- (2); ab-breviate. (L.) Used for L. *ad*; see **Ad-**.

Abs-; abs-cond, abs-ent, abs-tract. (L.; *or* F. — L.) L. *abs-*, extended form of *ab*; see **Ab-** (1).

Ac-; see **Ad-**. Also for **A-** (4) in ac-cursed; and for **A-** (2) in ac-knowledge.

Ad-; ad-apt, ad-dress. (L.; *or* F. — L.) L. *ad*, to, at, for. **+** Goth. *at*, A. S. *æt*, E. *at*. This prefix appears as *a-*, *ab-*, *ac-*, *ad-*, *af-*, *ag-*, *al-*, *an-*, *ap-*, *ar-*, *as-*, *at-*; ex.: a-chieve, ab-breviate, ac-cede, ad-mire, af-

fix, ag-gress, al-lude, an-nex, ap-pend, ar-rogate, as-sign, at-tract.

Adv-; see **Ab-** (1).

Af-; see **Ad-**. Also for **A-** (11) in af-ford; for **A-** (4) in af-fright; and for **Ex-** (1) in af-fray.

After-. (E.) E. *after*, prep.; A.S. *æfter*.

Ag-; see **Ad-**.

Al- (1), all; al-most. See **All**, p. 12.

Al- (2); see **Ad-**.

Al- (3); al-ligator. (Span. — L.) Span. *el*, def. art. **—** L. *ille*, he.

Al- (4); al-cohol. (Arab.) Arab. *al*, def. art. This also appears as *a-*, *ar-*, *as-*, *el-*, *l-*. Ex.: a-pricot, ar-tichoke, as-sagai, el-ixir, l-ute. See **L-** (2).

Am- (1); am-bush. (F. — L.) F. *em-.* **—** L. *im-*, for *in*, prep.; see **In-** (2).

Am- (2); am-brosia. (Gk.) See **An-** (2).

Am- (3); am-bassador; see **Ambi-**.

Am- (4); am-putate. (L.) Short for *amb-*, *ambi-*; see below.

Ambi-, Amb-; ambi-dextrous; amb-ition. (L.; *or* F. — L.; *or* C.) L. *ambi-*, on both sides, around. **+** Gk. *ἀμφί*; O. Irish *imm-*; see **Ambassador**, p. 14. See below.

Amphi-. (Gk.) Gk. *ἀμφί*, on both sides, around; L. *ambi-*; see **Ambi-**.

An- (1); see **Ad-**.

An- (2), **A-** (9), negative prefix. (Gk.) Gk. *ἀν-*, *ἀ-*, neg. prefix. Hence *am-* in am-brosia; *a-* in a-byss. **+** L. *in-*, E. *un-*; see **In-** (3), **Un-** (1).

An- (3); see **Ana-**.

An- (4); an-oint. (F. — L.) For F. *en-*. **—** L. *in*, prep.; see **In-** (2).

An- (5); an-swer. (E.) A.S. *and-*, in reply to, opposite to. **+** Goth. *and-*; Du. *ent-*; G. *ent-*; Gk. ἀντί. Shortened to *a-* in a-long; and allied to *un-* in verbs. See **Anti-** (1), **Un-** (2).

An- (6); an-cestor. (F—L.) See **Ante-**.

Ana-, **An-** (3); ana-gram, an-eurism. (Gk.) Gk. ἀνά, upon, on, up. **+** A.S. *on*, Goth. *ana*. See **On-**.

Anci-; anci-ent. (F.—L.) See **Ante-**.

Ann-; ann-eal. (E.) See **Anneal** in the Dictionary, p. 18.

Ant-; ant-agonist. (Gk.) See **Anti-**.

Ante-. (L.) L. *ante*, before. Also *anti-*, *anci-*, *ant-*, *an-*; as in anti-cipate, anci-ent, ant-ique, an-cestor.

Anth-; anth-em. (Gk.) See below.

Anti- (1), **Ant-**. (Gk.) Gk. ἀντί, against, opposite to. Also *ant-*, *anth-*, as in ant-agonist, anth-em. See **An-** (5), **Un-** (2).

Anti- (2); see **Ante-**.

Ap-; ap-pend; see **Ad-**.

Aph-; aph-æresis; see below.

Apo-. (Gk.) Hence *aph-* in aph-æresis. Gk. ἀπό, from, off. **+** L. *ab*; A.S. *of*; see **Ab-** (1), **Of-**.

Ar- (1); see **Ad-**.

Ar- (2); ar-tichoke; see **Al-** (4).

Arch-, **Archi-**, **Arche-**; arch-bishop, arch-angel, archi-tect, arche-type. (Gk.) Gk. ἀρχί-, chief. **—** Gk. ἄρχειν, to be first.

As- (1); as-sign; see **Ad-**.

As- (2); as tonish; see **Ex-** (1).

As- (3); as-sagai; see **Al-** (4).

At-; see **Ad-**.

Auto-, **Auth-**, self. (Gk.) Gk. αὐτό-s, self. Hence *auth-* in auth-entic; *eff-* in eff-endi.

Av-; av-aunt. (F. – L.) F. *av-*; from L. *ab*; see **Ab-** (1).

Ba-; ba-lance; see **Bi-**.

Be-. (E.) A.S. *be-*, *bi-*, the same as *bī*, by, prep.; E. *by*.

Bi-, double. (L.) L. *bi-*, double, from an earlier form *dui-*, related to *duo*, two. **+** Gk. δι-, double, allied to δύω, two; Skt. *dvi-*, allied to *dva*, two; E. *twi-* in twi-bill. Hence F. *bi-* in bi-gamy, F. *ba-* in ba-lance; and see below.

Bin-; bin-ocular. (L.) L. *bīn-ī*, distributive form allied to *bi-* (above).

Bis-; bis-cuit. (F.—L.) F. *bis*, L. *bis*, twice; extended from *bi-* (above). Cf. E. *twice*; see **Dis-**.

By-; by-path. A.S. *bī*; see **By**, p. 70.

Cat-; cat-echism; see **Cata-**.

Cata-, down. (Gk.) Gk. κατά, down, downwards. Hence *cat-*, *cath-*, in cat-echism, cath-olic.

Cath-; cath-olic; see below.

Circum-, round. (L.) L. *circum*, around, prep. Hence *circu-* in circu-it.

Co-, **Coi-**; see **Com-**.

Col-; see **Com-**.

Com-. (L. *or* F.—L.) L. *com-*, together, used in composition for *cum*, prep. together. **+** Gk. σύν, together; see **Syn-**. It appears as *co-*, *col-*, *com-*, *con-*, *cor-*, *coun-*; ex.: co-agulate, col-lect, commute, con-nect, cor-rode, coun-cil. Also as *coi-* in coi-l; *cou-* in cou-ch, cou-sin; *co-* in co-stive, co-st; *cu-* in cu-ll, cu-stom; *cur-* in cur-ry (1). ¶ *Combustion* is perhaps for comb-ustion.

Con-; con-nect; see **Com-**.

Contra-, against. (L.) L. *contrā*, against. Allied to *contrō-* in contro-vert, contro-versy; loses final *a* in Ital. contr-alto. Hence F. *contre*, against, as in contr-ol; but the F. form is usually written *counter-* in English. Hence also *countr-y*.

Cor-; cor-rode; see **Com-**.

Cou-; cou-ch, cou-sin; see **Com-**.

Coun-; coun-cil; see **Com-**.

Counter-. (F.—L.) See **Contra-**.

Cu-; cu-ll, cu-stom; see **Com-**.

Cur-; cur-ry (1); see **Com-**.

D-; d-affodil; see **Do-** (1).

De- (1); de-scend, de-bate. (L.; *or* F.—L.) L. *dē*, down, downward. Used with an oppositive sense in de-form; with an intensive sense in de-clare, &c. Changed to *di-* in di-stil. Distinct from the prefix below.

De- (2); de-face, de-fame, de-feat, de-fray. (F.—L.) F. *dé-*, O.F. *des-*, from L. *dis-*, apart; see **Dis-**. Distinct from the prefix above.

De- (3); de-vil; see **Dia-**.

Dea-; dea-con; see **Dia-**.

Demi-, half. (F.—L.) F. *demi*. **–** L. *dīmidius*, half; see **Demi-** in Dict., p. 135.

Des-; des-cant; see **Dis-**.

Di- (1); double. (Gk.) Gk. δι-, double, allied to δίs, twice, and δύο, two; see **Bi-**. Ex. di-lemma, di-syllable (*often written* dissyllable).

Di- (2); apart, away. (L.) See **Dis-**.

Di- (3); di-stil; see **De-** (1).

Dia-. (Gk.) Gk. διά, through, between.

apart; allied to **Di-** (1). Shortened to *di-* in di-æresis; appearing as *de-*, *dea-*, in de-vil, dea-con.

Dif-; see Dis-.

Dis-, apart, away. (L.; *or* F.—L.) L. *dis-*, apart, in two, another form of *bis-*, double; *dis-* and *bis-* are variants from an older form *duis-*, double, also used in the sense in two, apart; see Bis-. *Dis-* becomes *des-* in O. French, also *dé-* in later F.; but the O. F. *des-* is sometimes altered to *dis-*, as in dis-cover. The various forms are *di-*, *dif-*, *dis-*, *des-*, *de-*, and even *s-*; as in di-verge, dif-fuse, dis-pel, des-cant, de-feat, de-luge, s-pend.

Dou-; dou-ble; see Duo-.

Duo-, Du-, two, double. (L.) L. *duo*, two; cognate with E. *two*. Only in duo-decimo, duo-denum; shortened to *du-* in du-al, du-plicate, &c. Appearing as *dou-* in dou-ble, dou-bt; as *do-* in do-zen.

Dys-, badly. (Gk.) Gk. δύς, badly, with difficulty. Some connect it with To- (2).

E- (1); e-normous; see Ex- (1).

E- (2); e-nough; see Y-.

E- (3); e-lope. A. F. *a-*, perhaps for O. F. *es-*, L. *ex*; see Ex- (1).

E- (4); e-squire. (F.) This *e-* is a F. addition, of purely phonetic value, due to the difficulty which was experienced in pronouncing initial *sq-*, *sc-*, *st-*, *sp-*. So also in e-scutcheon, e-state, e-special; to which add e-schew.

Ec-; ec-logue. (Gk.) Gk. ἐκ, also ἐξ, out. + L. *ex*, Lithuan. *isz*, Russ. *iz'*, out; see Ex- (1). Also *el-*, *ex-*, as in el-lipse, ex-odus.

Ef-; see Ex- (1).

Eff-; eff-endi; see Auto-.

El- (1); el-lipse; see Ec-.

El- (2); el-ixir; see Al- (4).

Em- (1); em-brace. (F.—L.) F. *em-*; L. *im-*, for *in*; see In- (2).

Em- (2); em-piric; see En- (2).

Em- (3); em-bassy; see Am- (3).

En- (1); en-close. (F.—L.) F. *en-*; L. *in-*; see In- (2).

En- (2); en-ergy. (Gk.) Gk. ἐν, in. + L. *in*; A.S. *in*. Becomes *em-* before *p*, in em-piric. See Em- (2), In- (1), In- (2).

En- (3); en-emy. (F.—L.) Negative prefix; see In- (3).

Endo-, within. (Gk.) Gk. ἔνδο-ν, within; extended from ἐν, in; see En- (2), and Indi-.

Enter-; enter-tain. (F.—L.) F. *entre*.

—L. *inter*, among; see Inter-. Shortened to *entr-* in entr-ails.

Ep-, Eph-; see below.

Epi-, upon. (Gk.) Gk. ἐπί, upon. + Skt. *api*; allied to L. *ob-*. See Ob-. It appears as *ep-*, *eph-*, in ep-och, eph-emeral.

Es-; es-cape; see Ex- (1).

Eso-, within. (Gk.) Gk. ἔσω, within; from ἐς, εἰς, into.

Eu-, well. (Gk.) Gk. εὖ, well; neut. of εὖς, good. + Skt. *vasu-s*, good; cf. Goth. *ius-iza*, better. Hence *ev-* in ev-angelist.

Ev-; ev-angelist; see above.

Ex- (1), out of, very. (L.; *or* F.—L.) L. *ex*, also *ē*, out of; also used intensively. + Gk. ἐξ, ἐκ, out. See Ec-, and see below. It appears as *a-*, *as-*, *e-*, *ef-*, *es-*, *ex-*, *iss-*, *s-*, in a-mend, as-tonish, e-normous, ef-fect, es-cape, ex-tend, iss-ue, s-ample; also as *af-*, *a-*, in af-fray, a-fraid.

Ex- (2), out of, away. (Gk.) Gk. ἐξ, out; as in ex-odus. See above.

Exo-, without. (Gk.) Gk. ἔξω, outside, without; adv. from ἐξ, out (above).

Extra-, beyond. (L.) A comparative abl. form, from L. *ex*, out; see Ex- (1). Cf. *exter-* in exter-ior, exter-nal. It appears also as *stra-* in stra-nge; *cf.* estra-nge.

For- (1), in place of. (E.) E. *for*, prep.; in *for-as-much*, *for-ever*, which might just as well be written as separate words instead of compounds. Allied to Per-, Pro-.

For- (2); for-give. (E.) A.S. *for-*, intensive prefix. + Icel. *for-*, Dan. *for-*, Swed. *för-*, Du. G. *ver-*, Goth. *fra-*, Skt. *parā-*.

For- (3); for-feit. (F.—L.) F. *for-*, prefix. = L. *forīs*, outside, out of doors. Also in *for-close*, sometimes spelt *fore-close*; and in *for-judge*.

For- (4); for-ward; see Forth-.

Fore- (1), before. (E.) A.S. *fore*, for, before, prep.; *fore*, adv. Allied to For- (1). See Fore, p. 194.

Fore- (2); fore-go. (E.) A bad spelling of *for-go*; see For- (2).

Forth-. (E.) In *forth-coming*, *forthwith*. A.S. *forð*, forth; see p. 195.

Fro-; fro-ward. (Scand.) Icel. *frā*; see Fro, p. 200.

Gain-, against. (Scand.) Icel. *gegn*, against. Ex. gain-say.

Hemi-, half. (Gk.) Gk. ἡμι-, half. + L. *sēmi-*, half; see Semi-. Shortened to *me-* in me-grim.

I. LIST OF PREFIXES

Hetero-, other. (Gk.) Gk. ἕτερο-s, other.

Holo-, entire. (Gk.) Gk. ὅλο-s, entire.

Homo-, same. (Gk.) Gk. ὁμό-s, same; cognate with E. *same*. Lengthened to *homœo-*, like, in homœo-pathy.

Hyper-, above, beyond. (Gk.) Gk. ὑπέρ, above; see **Over-**.

Hypo-, Hyph-, Hyp-. (Gk.) Gk. ὑπό, under. +L. *sub*, under; see **Sub-**. Hence *hyph-* in hyph-en; *hyp-* in hyp-allage.

I- (1); i-gnoble; see **Il-** (3).

I- (2); i-wis; A.S. *ge-*; see **Y-**.

Il- (1); il-lude; see **In-** (2).

Il- (2); il-legal; see **In-** (3).

Im- (1); im-bed; see **In-** (1).

Im- (2); im-mure, im-merge; see **In-** (2).

Im- (3); im-mortal; see **In-** (3).

In- (1); in-born. (E.) A.S. *in*, prep. It also becomes *im-* before *b* and *p*; as in im-bed, im-park. See below.

In- (2); in-clude. (L.; *or* F.—L.) L. *in*, in. +Gk. ἐν, in; A.S. *in*. See **In-** (1), **En-** (2). It appears as *am-, an-, em-, en-, il-, im-, in-, ir-*, in am-bush, an-oint, em-brace, en-close, il-lude, im-mure, in-clude, ir-ritate.

In- (3), negative prefix. (L.) L. *in-*, neg. prefix. +Gk. ἀν-, ἀ-, neg. prefix; E. *un-*, before nouns. See **An-** (2), **A-** (9), **Un-** (1). It appears as *en-, i-, il-, im-, in-, ir-*, in en-emy, i-gnoble, il-legal, im-mortal, in-firm, ir-regular.

Indi-, Ind-; indi-genous, ind-igent. (L.) O. Lat. *indu*, within. +Gk. ἔνδον, within; see **Endo-**.

Intel-; see below.

Inter-, between. (L.) L. *inter*, between. A comparative form, allied to L. *inter-ior*, within; cf. L. *inter-nus*, internal. It appears as *intel-* in intel-lect, *enter-* in enter-tain; and cf. entr-ails; see **Enter-**. Closely allied are L. *intro-*, within, *intrā-*, within.

Intra-, within; see **Inter-**.

Intro-, within; see **Inter-**.

Ir- (1); ir-ritate; see **In-** (2).

Ir- (2); ir-regular; see **In-** (3).

Iss-; iss-ue. (F.—L.) F. *iss-*, from L. *ex*; see **Ex-** (1).

Juxta-, near. (L.) L. *iuxtā*, near.

L- (1); l-one. (E.) Short for *all*; l-one = al-one. See **Al-** (1).

L- (2); l-ute. (Arab.) Short for Arab. *al*, the, def. art. See **Al-** (4).

Male-, Mal-, Mau-, badly. (L.; *or* F.—L.) L. *male*, badly, ill; whence F. *mal*, which becomes *mau-* in mau-gre.

Me-; me-grim; see **Hemi-**.

Meta-, Meth-, Met-, among, with, after; also used to imply change. (Gk.) Gk. μετά, among, with, after. +A.S. *mid*, G. *mit*, Goth. *mith*, with. It appears also as *meth-* in meth-od, *met-* in met-eor.

Min-; min-ster; see **Mono-**.

Mis- (1); mis-deed; mis-take. (E. *and* Scand.) A.S. *mis-*, wrongly, amiss. +Icel. Dan. Du. *mis-*; Swed. *miss-*; Goth. *missa*, wrongly. Allied to *miss*, vb.

Mis- (2), badly, ill. (F.—L.) O.F. *mes-*, from L. *minus*, less; used in a depreciatory sense. Appearing in mis-adventure, mis-alliance, mis-chance, mis-chief, mis-count, mis-creant, mis-nomer, mis-prise, mis-prision. Quite distinct from **Mis-** (1).

Mono-, Mon-, single. (Gk.) Gk. μόνο-s, single, sole, alone. Hence *mon-k*, *min-ster*.

Multi-, Mult-, many. (L.; *or* F.—L.) From L. *multus*, much, many.

N- (1); n-ewt, n-ickname, n-uncle. (E.) *A newt = an ewt*, where the prefixed *n* is due to the indef. article. *A nickname = an eke-name*. *My nuncle = mine uncle*, where the *n* is due to the possessive pronoun. In *n-once*, the prefixed *n* is due to the dat. case of the def. article, as seen in M. E. *for then anes*, lit. 'for the once.'

N- (2), negative prefix. (E. *or* L.) In *n-one*, the prefixed *n* is due to A.S. *ne*, not. In *n-ull*, it is due to the cognate L. *ne*, not. See **Ne-**.

Ne-, Neg-. (L.) L. *ne*, not; *nec* (whence *neg-* in *neg-ligere*), not, short for *ne-que*, nor, not. In ne-farious, neg-ation, neg-lect, neg-otiate, ne-uter. See **N-** (2).

Non-, not. (L.; *or* F.—L.) L. *nōn*, not; O. Lat. *noenum*, for *ne oinom, i.e. *ne ūnum*, not one; see above. It appears as *um-* in um-pire, for *numpire*.

O-; o-mit; see **Ob-**.

Ob-. (L.; *or* F.—L.) L. *ob*, near; allied to Gk. ἐπί, upon, near; Skt. *api*, moreover, Lith. *apë*, near. See **Epi-**. The

627

force of *ob-* is very variable ; it appears as *o-*, *ob-*, *oc-*, *of-*, *op-*, also as extended to *os-* (for *ops*?) in o-mit, ob-long, oc-cur, of-fer, op-press, os-tensible.

Oc- ; oc-cur ; see **Ob-**.

Of- (1) ; of-fal. (E.) A.S. *of*, of, off, away. This word is invariably written *off* in composition, except in the case of *offal*, where its use would have brought three *f*'s together.+L. *ab*, Gk. ἀπό ; see **Ab-** (1), **Apo-**. It appears as *a-* in *a-down*.

Of- (2) ; of-fer ; see **Ob-**.

Off- ; see **Of-** (1).

On-, on, upon. (E.) A.S. *on*, on.+Gk. ἀνά. See **Ana-** (above). It often appears as *a-*, as in a-foot, a-sleep, &c.

Op- ; op-press ; see **Ob-**.

Or- (1) ; or-deal, or-ts. (E.) A.S. *or-* ; cognate with Du. *oor-*, O. Sax. and G. *ur-*, Goth. *us*, away, out of.

Or- (2) ; or-lop. (Du.) Short for Du. *over*, cognate with E. *over* ; see **Over-**.

Os- ; os-tensible ; see **Ob-**.

Out-. (E.) A.S. *ūt*, adv., E. *out*.+ Goth. *ut*, G. *aus*, Skt. *ud*, out. Shortened to *ut-* in utt-er ; and to *ut-* in ut-most.

Outr- ; outr-age. (F.—L.) F. *outre*.— L. *ultrā*, beyond ; see **Ultra-**.

Over-. (E.) A.S. *ofer*, E. *over*, prep.+ Goth. *ufar*, L. *s-uper*, Gk. ὑπέρ, Skt. *upari*, above. A comparative form allied to **Up**, q. v. See **Hyper-**, **Super-**, **Or-** (2).

Pa- ; pa-lsy ; see **Para-**.

Palin-, **Palim-**, again. (Gk.) Gk. πάλιν, back, again. It becomes *palim-* in palim-psest.

Pan-, **Panto-**, all. (Gk.) Gk. πᾶν, neut. of πᾶς, all ; παντο-, decl. form of the same, occurring in panto-mime.

Par- (1) ; par-son ; see **Per-**.

Par- (2) ; par-ody ; see **Para-** (1)

Para- (1), beside. (Gk.) Gk. παρά, be- side. Allied to E. *for*, L. *per*, also to Gk. περί. See **Per-**, **Peri-**, and **For-** (1). It becomes *pa-* in pa-lsy, *par-* in par-ody. ¶ Quite distinct from *para-* in para-chute, para-pet, para-sol, from L. *parāre*.

Para- (2) ; para-dise. Zend *pairi*= Gk. περί ; see **Peri-**.

Pel- ; pel-lucid ; see **Per-**.

Pen- ; pen-insula. (L.) L. *pæn-e*, almost.

Per-, through. (L. ; *or* F.—L.) L. *per*, through. Allied to **Para-** and **For-** (1). It appears also as *par-* in par-son, par- don ; as *pel-* in pel-lucid ; and as *pil-* in pil-grim.

Peri-, around. (Gk.) Gk. περί, around. +Skt. *pari*, Zend *pairi*, round about. Allied to **Para-**, &c.

Pil- ; pil-grim ; see **Per-**.

Po- ; po-sition ; see **Por-** (1).

Pol- ; pol-lute ; see **Por-** (1).

Poly-, many. (Gk.) Written for Gk. πολύ-, decl. form of πολύ-*s*, much, many. Allied to E. *full*.

Por- (1) ; por-tend. (L.) L. *por-*, to be compared with Gk. παρά, beside (Brug- mann, ii. § 35). See **Para-** (1). It appears as *pol-*, *por-*, in pol-lute, por- tend ; and is allied to *po-* in po-sition.

Por- (2) ; por-trait ; see **Pro-**.

Post-, after. (L.) L. *post*, after, behind. Hence F. *puis*, appearing as *pu-* in pu-ny.

Pour- ; pour-tray ; see **Pro-**.

Pr- (1) ; pr-ison ; see **Pre-**.

Pr- (2) ; pr-udent ; see **Pro-** (1).

Pre-, **Præ-**, before. (L.) L. *pre-*, for *præ*, prep., before ; for older, **prai*. Allied to **Pro-**. This prefix occurs also in pr-ison ; and is curiously changed to *pro-* in pro-vost ; and appears as *prea-* in prea-ch.

Preter-, beyond. (L.) L. *præter*, beyond ; comparative form of *præ*, before.

Pro- (1), before, instead of. (L. ; *or* F.—L.) L. *prŏ-*, before, in front, used as a prefix ; also *prō*, short for *prod*, abl. case used as a preposition, which appears in *prod-igal*. Allied to Gk. πρό, before, Skt. *pra*, before, away ; also to E. *for*. See below ; and see **For-** (1). It appears also as *prof-*, *pour-*, *por-*, *pur-*, *pr-*, in prof-fer, pour-tray, por-trait, pur-vey, pr-udent ; where *pour-*, *por-*, *pur-* are due to the F. form *pour*.

Pro- (2), before. (Gk.) Gk. πρό, before ; cognate with **Pro-** (1). In pro-logue, pro-phet, pro-scenium, pro-thalamium.

Pro- (3) ; pro-vost ; see **Pre-**.

Prod- ; prod-igal ; see **Pro-** (1).

Prof- ; prof-fer ; see **Pro-** (1).

Pros-, in addition, towards. (Gk.) Gk. πρός, towards. Allied to **Forth-** and **Por-** (1).

Proto-, **Prot-**, first. (Gk.) From Gk. πρῶτο-*s*, first ; superl. form of πρό, before ; see **Pro-** (2). Shortened to *prot-* in prot- oxide.

Pu- ; pu-ny ; see **Post-**.

Pur- ; pur-vey. (F.—L.) See **Pro-** (1).

R- ; r-ally ; see **Re-**.

Ra- ; ra-bbet ; see **Re-**.

Re-, Red-, again. (L.) L. *re-, red-* (only in composition), again, back. *Red-* occurs in red-eem, red-integration, red-olent, red-ound, red-undant, red-dition; and is changed to *ren-* in ren-der, ren-t. In re-ly, re-mind, re-new, it is prefixed to purely E. words; and in re-call, re-cast, to words of Scand. origin. It appears as *r-* in r-ally (1), r-ansom; and as *ru-* in ru-nagate. 2. *Re-* is frequently prefixed to other prefixes, which sometimes coalesce with it, so that such words require care. For example, rabbet = re-a-but; ragout = re-a-gout; rampart = re-em-part; cf. also re-ad-apt, re-col-lect, re-con-cile, re-sur-rection, &c.

Rear-; see Retro-.

Red-, Ren-; see Re- (above).

Rere-; rere-ward; see Retro-.

Retro-, backwards, behind. (L.) L. *retrō-*, backwards, back again; a comparative form from *re-*, back; see Re-. The prefixes *rear-, rere-*, in rear-guard, rere-ward, are due to L. *retrō*, and are of F. origin.

S- (1); s-ober, s-ure; see So-.

S- (2); s-pend; see Dis-.

S- (3); s-ample; see Ex- (1).

S- (4); s-ombre; see p. 501.

Sans-, without. (F.−L.) F. *sans*, without. − L. *sine*, without; see Sine-.

Se-, Sed-, away, apart. (L.) L. *sē-*, apart; O. Lat. *sed-*, apart, which is probably retained in sed-ition. The orig. sense was probably 'by oneself.' It appears as *s-* in s-ure; cf. sober.

Semi-, half. (L.) L. *sēmi*, half. + Gk. ἡμί-, half; see Hemi-. It appears as *sin-* in sin-ciput.

Sine-, without. (L.) L. *sine*, without; lit. if not. − L. *si*, if; *ne*, not. Hence F. *sans*, without.

So-; so-journ; see Sub-.

Sover-, Sopr-; see Super-.

Stra-; stra-nge; see Extra-.

Su-; su-spect; see Sub-.

Sub-, under. (L.) L. *sub*, under, (sometimes) up. Allied to Gk. ὑπό, under; Skt. *upa*, near, under; also to E. *up* and *of*. See Hypo-, Of-, Up-. *Sub* also appears as *s-, so-, su-, suc-, suf-, sug-, sum-, sup-, sur-*, in s-ombre (?), so-journ, su-spect, suc-ceed, suf-fuse, sug-gest, sum-mon, sup-press, sur-rogate. It is also extended to *sus-* (for *sups-*); as in sus-pend.

Subter-, beneath. (L.) L. *subter*, beneath; comparative form from *sub*, under; see Sub-.

Suc-, Suf-, Sug-, Sum-, Sup-; see Sub-.

Super-, above, over. (L.) L. *super*, above. + Gk. ὑπέρ, over, beyond; A. S. *ofer*, E. *over*. See Hyper-, Over-; also Sub-. Hence *supra-*, beyond, L. *suprā*. Also *sover-* in sover-eign, which is a F. form; and *sopr-* in sopr-ano, which is an Ital. form. Also F. *sur-* = L. *super*.

Supra-, beyond; see above.

Sur- (1); sur-rogate; see Sub-.

Sur- (2); sur-face; see Super-.

Sus-; sus-pend; see Sub-.

Sy-, Syl-, Sym-; see Syn-.

Syn-, with, together with. (Gk.) Gk. σύν, with. It appears as *sy-, syl-, sym-*, and *syn-*, in sy-stem, syl-logism, sym-metry, syn-tax.

T- (1); t-wit. (E.) *Twit* is from A. S. *æt-wītan*, to twit, reproach; thus *t-* is here used for E. *at*.

T- (2); t-awdry. (F.−L.) *Tawdry* is for *Saint Awdry*; thus *t-* is here the final letter of *sain-t*.

T- (3); t-autology. (Gk.) Here *t-* represents Gk. τό, neuter of def. article.

Thorough-, through. (E.) Merely another form of E. *through*.

To- (1), to-day. (E.) A.S. *tō*, to.

To- (2), intensive prefix. (E.) Obsolete, except in *to-brake*. A.S. *tō-*, apart, asunder; prob. cognate with L. *dis-*, apart. See Dis-. ¶ Some connect it with Gk. δύς-; see Dys-.

Tra-, Tran-; see below.

Trans-, beyond. (L.) L. *trans*, beyond. Shortened to *tran-* in tran-scend; and to *tra-* in tra-duce, tra-verse, &c. Hence F. *tres-*, occurring in tres-pass; and *tre-* in tre-ason.

Tre- (1), **Tres-.** (F.−L.) See above.

Tre- (2); tre-ble. (F.−L.) See below.

Tri- (1), thrice. (L.) L. *tri-*, thrice; allied to *trēs*, three. Hence tri-ple, tre-ble, &c.; and *tra-* in tra-mmel.

Tri- (2), thrice. (Gk.) Gk. τρι-, thrice; allied to τρία, neut. of τρεῖς, three. Hence tri-gonometry, &c.

Twi-, double, doubtful. (E.) A.S. *twī-*, double; allied to *twā*, two. Hence twi-bill, twi-light.

Ultra-, beyond. (L.) L. *ultrā*, beyond; allied to O. Lat. *ulter*, adj., appearing in *ulter-ior*, which see in Dict. Hence F. *outre*, beyond, appearing in outr-age; also in E. utter-ance (2), corruption of F. *outr-ance*.

Um-; um-pire; see **Non-**.

Un- (1), negative prefix to nouns, &c. (E.) A.S. *un-*, not; cognate with L. *in-*, not, Gk. *ἀν-*, not. See **An-** (2), **In-** (3).

Un- (2), verbal prefix, signifying the reversal of an action. (E.) A.S. *un-*, verbal prefix; cognate with Du. *ont-*, *ent-*, G. *ent-*, O.H.G. *ant-*, Goth. *and-*. The same as E. *an-* in *an-swer*; see **An-** (5), **Anti-**.

Un- (3); un-til, un-to. (O. Low G.) See *un-to* in Dict., p. 584.

Un- (4), **Uni-**, one. (L.) L. *ūn-us*, one; whence uni-vocal, with one voice; un-animous, of one mind; &c. Cognate with L. *one*.

Under-. (E.) A.S. *under*, E. *under*, prep.

Up-. (E.) A.S. *up*, E. *up*, prep. Allied to **Of**, **Sub-**, **Hypo-**.

Ut-, Utt-. (E.) See **Out**.

Utter-. (F.—L.) Only in *utter-ance* (2). F. *outre*, L. *ultrā*; see **Ultra-**.

V-; v-an (1). (F.—L.) See **Ab-** (1).

Ve-, apart from. (L.) L. *uē-*, apart from. Only in ve-stibule, and (possibly) in ve-stige.

Vice-, Vis-, in place of. (L.; *or* F.—L.) L. *uice*, in place of, whence O.F. *vis*, the same. The latter appears only in vis-count.

Wan-, negative prefix; see **Wanton** in its due place; p. 599.

With-, against. (E.) A.S. *wið*, against; the sense is preserved in with-stand. In with-hold, with-draw, it signifies ' back.'

Y-; y-wis, y-clept. (E.) A.S. *ge-* prefix; M.E. *i-*, *y-*. This prefix appears as *a-* in a-ware, as *i-* in i-wis (*for* y-wis) and as *e-* in e-nough. See **A-** (11), **E-** (2).

II. SUFFIXES

THE number of suffixes in modern English is so great, and the forms of several, especially in words derived through the French from Latin, are so variable, that an attempt to exhibit them all would tend to confusion. The best account of their origin is to be found in Brugmann, Grundriss der Vergleichenden Grammatik der Indogermanischen Sprachen. An account of Anglo-Saxon suffixes is given at p. 119 of March, Comparative Grammar of the Anglo-Saxon Language. Lists of Anglo-Saxon words, arranged according to their suffixes, are given in Loth, Etymologische angelsæchsisch-englische Grammatik, Elberfeld, 1870. Simple accounts of English suffixes in general are given in Morris, Historical Outlines of English Accidence, pp. 212–221, 229–242, in Nesfield, Historical English and Derivation, pp. 185–252, and in the two Series of my Principles of English Etymology, to which the reader is referred. See also Koch, Historische Grammatik der Englischen Sprache, vol. iii. pt. 1, pp. 29–76. It is clearly established that the Indo-germanic languages abound in suffixes, each of which was originally intended slightly to modify the meaning of the root to which it was added, so as to express the radical idea in a new relation. The force of many of these must, even at an early period, have been slight, and in many instances it is difficult to trace it; but in some instances it is still clear, and the form of the suffix is then of great service. The difference between *lov-er*, *lov-ed*, and *lov-ing* is well marked, and readily understood. One of the most remarkable points is that most Indo-germanic languages delighted in adding suffix to suffix, so that words are not uncommon in which two or more suffixes occur, each repeating, it may be, the sense of that which preceded it. Double diminutives such as *parti-c-le*, i.e. a little little part, are sufficiently common. The Lat. superl. suffix *-is-si-mus* is a simple example of the use of a treble suffix, which really expresses no more than is expressed by *-mus* alone in the word *prī-mus*. The principal Indo-germanic suffixes, as given by Brugmann, are these : *-o, -i, -u, -yo, -wo, -mo, -mi, -men (-mon), -meno (-menā), -no, -tno, -ni, -nu, -en (-on), ent (ont), -lo, -li, -ro, -ri, -ru, -er (-or), -es (-os), -to, -mento, -ti, -ti-on, -tā-ti, -tu, -tū-ti, -ter (-tor, -tr), -tūro, -id, -d, -d-en, -d-on, -tū-den, -do, -go, -ko, -k, -sqo, -sqā, -bho.* But these can be readily compounded, so as to form new suffixes ; so that from *-men-to* was formed *-mento* (as in E. *argu-ment*).

One common error with regard to suffixes should be guarded against, namely, that of mis-dividing a word so as to give the suffix a false shape. This is extremely common in such words as *logi-c, civi-c, belli-c-ose,* where the suffix is commonly spoken of as being *-ic* or *-ic-ose.* This error occurs, for instance, in the elaborate book on English Affixes by S. S. Haldemann, published at Philadelphia in 1865 ; a work which is of considerable use as containing a very full account, with numerous examples, of suffixes and prefixes. The truth is that *civi-c* (Lat. *cīuicus*) is derived from Lat. *cīui-*, declensional stem of *cīui-s*, a citizen, with the suffix *-cus* (Idg. *-ko*); and *logi-c* is from Gk. λογι-κός, from λογι-, for λόγο-, declensional stem of λόγος, a discourse, with the suffix *-κος*, as before. Compare Lat. *cīui-tās*, Gk. λογο-μαχία. Of course, words in *-i-c* are so numerous that *-ic* has come to be regarded as a suffix at the present day, so that we do not hesitate to form *Volta-ic* as an adjective of *Volta*; but this is English misuse, not Latin etymology. Moreover, since both *-i-* and *-ko* are Idg. suffixes, such a suffix as *-i-κos, -i-cus*, is possible both in Greek and Latin ; but in the particular words above cited it is clearer to consider the *-i-* as due to the original stem.

One more word of warning may perhaps suffice. If we wish to understand a suffix, we must employ comparative philology, and not consider English as an absolutely isolated language, with laws different from those of other languages of the Aryan family. Thus the *-th* in *tru-th* is the -ð of A. S. *trēow-ð*, gen. case *trēow-ðe*, fem. sb. This suffix answers to that seen in Goth. *gabaur-ths*, birth, gen. case *gabaur-thais*, fem. sb., belonging to the *-i*-stem declension of Gothic strong substantives. The true suffix is therefore to be expressed as Teut. *-thi*, cognate with Idg. *-ti*, so extremely common in Latin ; cf. *dō-ti-*, dowry, *men-ti-*, mind, *mor-ti-*, death, *mes-si-* (<*met-ti-*), harvest, that which is mown. Hence, when Horne Tooke gave his famous etymology of *truth* as being ' that which a man *troweth*,' he did in reality suggest that the *-ti-* in Lat. *mors* is identical with the *-i* in *mori-i-ur* or in *ama-t*; in other words, it was a mere whim.

III. SELECT LIST OF LATIN AND GREEK WORDS

IN the former edition of this work a list of Indo-germanic roots was given, as determined, for the most part, by Fick. The later researches of Brugmann and others have much modified the former results, chiefly because the vowel-sounds have been more exactly appreciated. As a list of roots is not usually much required in practice, it has been here replaced by a useful and practical list of some of the more important words in Latin and Greek which are, mostly, of rather frequent occurrence in English compounds and derivatives. In some cases, the form of the root is given, chiefly when the derivatives from it are rather numerous. Both of these lists might be largely increased, but it has not been deemed worth while to include such words as present no difficulty. For example, the Greek word κόσμος, order, is purposely omitted, because its derivatives (viz. *cosm-ic, cosm-etic,* and words beginning with *cosmo-*) can readily be found at p. 114. On the other hand, the Greek ἄλλος is inserted, for the sake of such derivatives as *par-all-ax, par-all-el.*

SELECT LIST OF LATIN WORDS

THE following list contains the principal Latin words which are (mostly) productive of rather numerous derivatives in English, and readily admit prefixes. Words that have produced but few derivatives, or that are of no especial interest, are excluded.

ac-, as in *āc-er, ac-idus, ac-ūtus*, sharp — acerbity, acid, acrid, acrimony, acumen, acute, aglet, ague, eager, eglantine, exacerbate. (✓AK, to be sharp.)

ædē-s, a temple — edify, edile; *cf.* estuary, ether, oasthouse. (✓AIDH, to burn.)

æqu-us, equal — adequate, equal, equanimity, equation, equilibrium, equinox, equipollent, equity, equivalent, equivocal, iniquity.

ag-ere, to drive — act, agent, agile, agitate, agriculture, ambiguous, coagulate, cogent, cogitate, counteract, enact, essay, exact, examine, exigent, peregrination, pilgrim, prodigal, transact. Cf. Gk. ἄγειν ; p. 644. (✓AG to drive.)

alb-us, white — alb, album, albumen, auburn.

al-ere, to nourish, grow up — adolescent, adult, aliment, alimony, altar, altitude, alto, coalesce, contralto, exalt, haughty, hautboy, proletarian. (✓AL, to nourish.)

al-ius, other — alias, alien, alibi, aliquot, alter, altercation, alternate, subaltern. Cf. Gk. ἄλλος ; p. 645.

am-āre, to love — amatory, amenity, amiable, amicable, amity, amorous, amour, enamour, enemy, enmity, inimical, paramour.

ambul-āre, to walk — amble, ambulance, ambulation, circumambulate, perambulate.

ang-ere, to choke — angina, anguish, anxious; *cf.* ail, anger, awe, ugly. (✓AGH, to choke.)

anim-a, breath, *anim-us*, mind — animal, animadvert, animate, animosity ; equanimity, magnanimous, pusillanimous, unanimous. (✓AN, to breathe.)

ann-us, a year — annals, anniversary, annual, biennial, triennial, &c. ; perennial, superannuate.

apt-us, fit — adapt, adept, apt, aptitude, attitude, inept. (✓AP, to bind.)

aqu-a, water — aqua-fortis, aquatic, aquarium, aquarius, aqueduct, aqueous, ewer, sewer (1), subaqueous; *cf.* ait, eyot, island.

arm-a, arms — alarm, alarum, ambry (aumbry), arm (2), arms, armada, armadillo, armament, armistice, armour, army.

art-em, acc., skill — art, artifice, artillery, artisan, inert.

asper, rough — asperity, exasperate.

audī-re, to hear — audible, audience, audit, obedient, obeisance, obey, oyer, oyez.

aug-ēre, to increase — auction, augment, august, author, auxiliary ; *cf.* eke (1). (✓AUG, to increase.)

aur-is, the ear — auricula, auricular, auscultation, scout (1); *cf.* ear (1).

aur-um, gold — aureate, dory, loriot, or (3), oriel, oriflamme, oriole, ormulu, orpiment, orpine.

aui-s, a bird — auspice, aviary, bustard, ostrich.

barb-a, beard — barb (1), barbel, barber; *cf.* beard.

barr-a (Late L.) — bar, barracks, barrel, barricade, barrier, barrister, debar, embargo, embarrass.

bass-us, low — abase, base (2), basement, bass (1), bass-relief, bassoon, debase.

bat-ere (popular L.), to beat — abate, battalion, batter (1), batter (2), battery, battle, battledoor, combat, debate, rebate.

bell-us, beautiful — beau, beauty, beldam, belladonna, belle, embellish.

bib-ere, to drink — beaver (3), beverage, bevy, bib, imbibe, imbrue (embrew).

bon-us, good — bonny, boon, *adj.*, bounty.

brāchi-a, arms — brace, bracelet, brassart, embrace, vambrace.

breu-is, short — abbreviate, abridge, breve, brevet, breviary, brevity, brief (1), brief (2).

brocc-a (Late L.), a pointed stick — broach, brocade, broccoli, brochure, brocket, broker, brooch.

bucc-a, mouth — debouch, disembogue, embouchure.

bull-a, a bubble, boss — bill (3), billet (1), boil (1), budge (1), bull (2), bullet, bulletin, bullion, ebullition, parboil.

busc-us (popular L.), a bush — ambuscade, ambush, bush (1), bouquet, emboss (2).

bux-us, a box-tree — box (1), box (2), bush (2) ; *cf.* bushel, pyx.

caball-us (popular L.), a horse — cavalier, cavalcade, cavalry, chevalier, chivalry.

cad-ere, to fall — accident, cadaverous, cadence, caducous, cascade, case (1), casual, chance, cheat, coincide, decadence, decay, deciduous, escheat, incident, occasion, occident.

cæd-ere, to cut — cæsura, circumcise, concise, decide, excision, incise, precise; *also* homi-cide, sui-cide, &c.; *also* chisel, scissors.

cæl-um, heaven — ceil, ceiling, celestial.

cal-āre, to summon — calends, calendar, conciliate, council, intercalate, reconcile; cf. *clāmāre* (below).

calc-āre, to tread — caulk, causeway, cockatrice.

calc-em, acc., lime — calcareous, calcine, calculate, calx, chalk.

cal-ēre, to be hot — caldron, calenture, caloric, calorific, caudle, chafe, chaldron, nonchalant, scald (1).

camer-a, a chamber — camera, chamber, chamberlain, comrade. (✓KAM, to bend, cover, vault over.)

camp-us, a plain — camp, campaign, campestral, champagne, champaign, champion, decamp, encamp, scamp.

canāl-is, a canal — canal, channel, kennel (2).

cancrī, lattice-work — cancel, chancel, chancellor, chancery.

cand-ēre, to shine — candelabrum, candid, candidate, candle, candour, cannel-coal, censer, chandelier, chandler, incandescent, incendiary, incense (1), incense (2), kindle (2). (✓QEND, to shine.)

can-is, a dog — canine, kennel (1); cf. cynic, hound.

cant-āre, to sing — accent, canorous, cant (1), canticle, canto, canzonet, chant, descant, enchant, incantation, incentive, precentor, recant; cf. hen.

cāp-a (popular L.), a cape — cap, caparison, cape (1), capuchin, chapel, chaperon, chaplet, cope (1), escape, scape.

cap-er, a goat — cab, cabriolet, caper, capricorn, capriole, cheveril, chevron.

cap-ere, to seize, lay hold of, contain — accept, anticipate, cable, caitiff, capable, capacious, capsule, captious, captive, captor, capture, case (2), casement, cash, casket, catch, cater, chase (1), chase (2), chase (3), conceit, conceive, conception, deceive, deception, encase, enchase, except, imperceptible, inceptive, incipient, intercept, occupy, perceive, perception, precept,

purchase, receive, receptacle, reception, recipe, recipient, sash (1), susceptible; cf. haft, heave, heft. (✓QAP, to seize, take hold of.

cap-ut, the head — achieve, cabbage (1), cad, cadet, cape (2), capital (1), capital (2), capital (3), capitation, capitol, capitular, capitulate, captain, cattle, chapiter, chapter, chattels, chief, chieftain, corporal (1), decapitate, hatchment, occiput, precipice, sinciput.

carn-, stem of *caro*, flesh — carnage, carnal, carnation, carnival, carnivorous, carrion (from *caro*), charnel, incarnadine, incarnation.

carp-ere, to cull — excerpt, scarce; cf. harvest. (✓QERP, to cut.)

cār-us, dear — caress, charity, cherish; cf. whore.

cas-a, a cottage — casino, cassock (?), chasuble.

cast-us, chaste — caste, castigate, chaste, chasten, chastise, incest.

catēn-a, a chain — catenary, chain, chignon, concatenation.

caud-a, the tail — caudal, coward, cue, queue.

causs-a, a cause — accuse, because, cause, excuse, recusant, ruse.

cau-us, hollow — cage, cajole, cave, concave, excavation, gabion, gaol, jail.

cēd-ere, to come, yield — abscess, accede, access, ancestor, antecedent, cease, cede, cess, cessation, cession, cess-pool, concede, decease, exceed, excess, incessant, intercede, precede, predecessor, proceed, recede, recess, retrocession, secede, succeed.

cēl-āre, to hide — cell, cellar, conceal, occult; cf. hall, hell, hole. (✓KEL, to hide.)

cent-um, a hundred — cent, centenary, centennial, centesimal, centigrade, centipede, centuple, centurion, century, quintal.

cēr-a, wax — cerecloth, cerement, ceruse.

cerebr-um, brain — cerebral, cervelas (saveloy).

cern-ere, to separate — concern, decree, decretal, discern, discreet, discriminate, excrement, excretion, secret, secretary. *See* Gk. κρίνειν; p. 645.

cert-us, sure — ascertain, certain, certify.

cing-ere, to gird — cincture, enceinte, precinct, shingles, succinct.

circ-us, a ring — circle, circus, research, search, shark.

cist-a, a chest — chest, cist, cistern, cistvaen.

cit-āre, to incite — cite, excite, incite, recite, resuscitate, solicit.

cīu-is, a citizen — cit, citadel, citizen, city, civil.

clām-āre, to call out — acclaim, acclamation, claim, clamour, declaim, declamation, exclaim, exclamation, proclaim, proclamation, reclaim, reclamation.

clār-us, clear — claret, clarify, clarion, clear, declare, glair.

claud-ere, to shut — clause, cloister, close (1), close (2), closet, conclude, exclude, include, preclude, recluse, seclusion, sluice; *cf.* slot (1). (✓SKLEUD, to shut.)

clāu-is, a key — clavicle, clef, conclave.

clī-uus, a slope — acclivity, declivity, proclivity; *cf.* decline, encline, incline, recline; *also* lean (1), low (3). Cf. Gk. κλίνειν; p. 645. (✓KLEI, to lean.)

cohort-em, acc., an enclosure — cohort, cortege, court (1), court (2), courteous, courtesan, courtesy, courtier, curtain, curtsey; *cf.* garden, garth, yard (1). (✓GHER, to contain.)

cōl-āre, to trickle — colander, culvert (?), cullis, percolate, portcullis.

col-ere, to till — colony, cultivate, culture; agriculture; *cf.* bucolic. (✓QEL, to turn round, to till.)

coll-um, the neck — collar, collet, colporteur, decollation.

cond-ere, to hide — abscond, sconce (1), sconce (2).

contrā, against — counter, encounter, rencontre, rencounter.

coöper-īre, to cover — cover, coverlet, covert, curfew, discover, kerchief.

cōpula, a bond — copulate, couple.

coqu-ere, to cook — biscuit, concoct, cook, decoct, kitchen, precocious; *also* apricot, terra-cotta. (✓PEQ, to cook.)

cord-, from *cor*, the heart — accord, concord, cordial, courage, discord, quarry (2), record; *cf.* heart.

cor-ium, leather — cuirass, excoriate, scourge.

corn-u, a horn — core (?), corn (2), cornea, cornel, cornelian, corner, cornet, cornucopia, unicorn; *cf.* horn, hart.

corōn-a, a wreath — corolla, corollary, coronal, coronation, coroner, coronet, crown.

corp-us, body — corporal (2), corps, corpse, corpulent, corpuscle, corse, corset, corslet, incorporate.

cost-a, a rib — accost, coast, costal, cutlet.

crass-us, thick, dense — crass, cresset, grease.

crāt-es, a hurdle — crate, creel, grate (1), griddle, gridiron, grill; *cf.* hurdle.

creāre, to create, make — create, creole, procreate, recreation.

crēd-ere, to believe — credible, credit, credulous, creed, grant, miscreant, recreant.

crep-āre, to crackle, burst — crevice, decrepit, discrepant.

cresc-ere, to grow — accretion, accrue, concrete, crescent, crew, decrease, decrement, excrescence, increase, increment, recruit.

crēt-a, chalk — cretaceous, crayon.

crocc-us (popular L.), a hook — crochet, crosier, crotchet, crouch.

cruc-em, acc., a cross — cross, crucial, crucify, cruise, crusade, excruciate.

cub-āre, to lie down — concubine, covey, incubate, incubus; *cf.* incumbent, procumbent, recumbent, succumb.

culp-a, blame — culpable, culprit, exculpate, inculpate.

culter, a coulter — coulter, curtleaxe, cutlass, cutler.

cumul-us, a heap — accumulate, cumulate.

cune-us, a wedge — coign, coin, cuneate, quoin.

cūp-a, a vat — coop, cowl (2), cupola, goblet; *cf.* cup.

cup-ere, to desire — concupiscence, covet, cupid, cupidity.

cūr-a, care — accurate, assure, curate, cure, curious, ensure, proctor, procurator, procure, proxy, scour, secure, sicker, sinecure, sure.

curr-ere (*curs-*), to run — coarse, concourse, concur, corridor, corsair, courier, course, current, curricle, cursive, cursory, discourse, discursive, excursion, incur, incursion, intercourse, occur, precursor, recourse, recur, succour. *Also* hussar, kraal; *cf.* horse.

curu-us, bent — curb, curve, curvet, incurvate, kerbstone.

damn-um, loss — condemn, damage, damn, indemnify, indemnity.

da-re, to give — condone, dado, date (1), die (2), donation, dowager, dower, pardon, reddition, render, rendezvous, rent (2), surrender, tradition, traitor, treason. (✓DO, to give.)

decem, ten — dean, decanal, decemvir, decennial, decimal, decimate, decussate, denary, dime; *cf.* decade, ten, tithe.

dec-ēre, to become — decent, decorate, decorum.

dent-em, acc., tooth—dandelion, dental, denticle, dentifrice, dentist, dentition, indent, indenture; *cf.* tine, tooth.

deus, god—adieu, deify, deity, deist; *cf.* jovial; and see *diēs* (below).

dīc-ere, to say, *dic-āre*, to tell—abdicate, addict, condition, contradict, dedicate, dictate, diction, dictionary, dight, ditto, ditty, edict, index, indicate, indict, interdict, preach, predicament, predicate, predict; *cf.* avenge, benediction, benison, judge (adjudge, adjudicate, judicature, judicial, judicious, prejudge, prejudice), malediction, malison, valediction, verdict, vindicate. (√DEIK, to show.)

diē-s, a day—adjourn, dial, diary, dismal, diurnal, journal, journey, sojourn.

dign-us, worthy—condign, dainty, deign, dignify, dignity, disdain.

dol-ēre, to grieve—condole, doleful, dolour, indolence.

dom-āre, to tame—daunt, indomitable; *cf.* tame. (√DAM, to tame.)

domin-us, a lord—dam (2), dame, damsel, danger, demesne, domain, dominate, domineer, dominical, dominion, domino, don (2), donna, duenna, dungeon; *cf.* monkey.

dūc-ere, to lead—abduction, adduce, conduce, conduct, conduit, deduce, deduct, doge, douche, ducal, ducat, duchess, duchy, duct, ductile, duke, educe, induce, induct, introduce, produce, product, redoubt, reduce, seduce, superinduce, traduce; *cf.* educate. (√DEUK, to lead.)

duo, two—belligerent, deuce (1), deuce (2), double, doublet, doubloon, doubt, dozen, dual, dubious, duel, duet, duodecimal, duodenum, duplicate, duplicity, indubitable, rebel, redoubtable; *cf.* two.

dūr-us, hard—durance, duration, dure, duress, endure, indurate, obdurate.

ed-ere, to eat—edible, esculent, obese; *cf.* eat. (√ED, to eat.)

em-ere, to take—assume, consume, ensample, example, exemplar, exemplify, exempt, impromptu, peremptory, premium, presume, prompt, ransom, redeem, resume, sample, sampler, sumptuary, sumptuous.

err-āre, to stray—aberration, err, erratum, erroneous, error.

es-se, to exist, be—absent, entity, essence, present, quintessence. Cf. are, sin, sooth; *also* suttee. (√ES, to dwell, exist.)

exter-, as in *exter-ior*, outer—estrange, exterior, external, extra, extraneous, extreme, extrinsic, strange.

fac-ere (pt. t. *fē-ci*), to do—affair, affect, comfit, confect, counterfeit, defeasance, defeat, defect, deficient, difficulty, discomfit, effect, efficacy, efficient, facile, facsimile, fact, faction, factitious, factotum, faculty, fashion, feasible, fetish, feat, feature, fiat, forfeit, hacienda, infect, mallecho, perfect, prefect, proficient, profit, refection, suffice, sufficient, surfeit. (√DHĒ, to put, place.)

faci-ēs, face—deface, efface, façade, face, superficies, surface.

fall-ere, to deceive—default, fail, fallacy, fallible, false, faucet, fault, refel.

fā-rī, to speak—affable, confabulate, confess, defame, fable, fairy, fay, ineffable, infamy, infant, infantry, nefarious, preface, profess; *cf.* ban. (√BHA, BHĀ, to speak.)

-fend-ere, to strike—defend, fence, fend, offend.

fer-re, to bear—circumference, confer, defer (1), defer (2), differ, fertile, infer, offer, prefer, proffer, refer, suffer, transfer; *cf.* bear (1), barrow (2), bier. (√BHER, to bear.)

feru-ēre, to boil—effervesce, fervent, fervid, ferment.

fest-um, a feast—feast, festal, festival, festive, fête.

fid-em, acc., faith—affiance, affidavit, confide, defy, diffident, faith, fealty, fidelity, fiducial, infidel, perfidious; *cf.* bide. (√BHEIDH, to trust.)

fīg-ere (*fix-*), to fix—affix, fix, prefix, suffix, transfix.

fīl-um, a thread—defile (2), enfilade, filament, file (1), filigree, fillet, profile, purl (3).

fing-ere (*fig-*), to fashion—configuration, effigy, faint, feign, fiction, figment, figure, transfigure; *cf.* dairy, dike, ditch, dough. (√DHEIGH, to knead, mould.)

fīn-is, end—affinity, confine, define, final, finance, fine (1), fine (2), finial, finical, finish, finite, refine, superfine; *cf.* paraffine.

firm-us, firm—affirm, confirm, farm, firm, firmament, infirm. (√DHER, to support.)

flāgrā-re, to burn—conflagration, flagrant; *cf.* flambeau, flame, flamen (?), flamingo. (√BHLEG, to burn.)

flect-ere, to bend—circumflex, deflect, flection, flexible, inflect, reflect.

flīg-ere (*flict-*), to strike—afflict, conflict, inflict, profligate.

flōr-em, acc., a flower—deflower, efflorescence, ferret (2), fleur-de-lis, floral, florid, florin, floscule, flour, flourish, flower, inflorescence; *cf.* blow (2), bloom, blossom.

flu-ere, to flow — affluence, confluence, defluction, effluence, floss, fluctuate, fluent, fluid, fluor-spar, flux, influence, influenza, influx, superfluous.

foc-us, a hearth — focus, fuel, fusil (1).

fŏd-ere (*foss-*), to dig — foss, fossil.

foli-um, leaf — exfoliate, foil (2), foliage, folio, perfoliate, trefoil.

form-a, form — conform, deform, form, formula, inform, reform, transform. (√DHER, to support.)

fort-em, acc., strong — comfort, deforce, effort, force (1), fort, forte, fortify, fortitude, fortress ; *cf.* borough. (√BHERGH, to protect.)

frang-ere (*frag-*), to break — fraction, fracture, fragile, fragment, frail, frangible, infraction, infringe, irrefragable, refract, refrain (2) ; *cf.* break. (√BHREG, to break.)

fric-āre, to rub — fray (3), friction.

front-em, acc., forehead — affront, confront, effrontery, front, frontal, frontier, frontispiece, frontlet ; *cf.* flounce (2).

fru-ī (*fruct-*), to enjoy — fructify, fruit, fruition, frumenty ; *cf.* frugal, brook (1). (√BHREUG, to enjoy.)

fug-ere, to flee — fugitive, fugue, refuge, refugee, subterfuge ; *cf.* bow (1). (√BHEUG, to bend.)

fund-ere (*fūs-*), to pour — confound, confuse, confute, diffuse, effuse, foison, fuse (1), fusil (3), futile, infuse, profuse, refund, refuse, refute, suffuse, transfuse ; *cf.* gut, chyle, chemist. (√GHEU, to pour.)

fund-us, bottom — found (1), founder, fund, fundament, profound ; *cf.* bottom.

fung-ī (*funct-*), to perform — defunct, function, perfunctory.

gaudi-um, joy — enjoy, gaud, joy, rejoice.

gel-u, frost — congeal, gelatine, gelid, jelly ; *cf.* chill, cool.

gen-us, kin — congenial, congenital, degenerate, engender, engine, gender (1), gender (2), general, generate, generic, generous, genial, genital, genitive, genius, genteel, gentile, gentle, gentry, genuine, genus, gin (2), indigenous, ingenious, ingenuous, progenitor, progeny, regenerate ; *cf.* kin. (√GEN, to produce.)

ger-ere (*gest-*), to bear — congeries, congestion, digest, exaggerate, gerund, gestation, gesticulate, gesture, jest, register, suggestion.

glūtin-, for *glūten*, glue — agglutinate, conglutinate, glue, glutinous.

grad-ī (*gress-*), to step — aggress, con-gress, degrade, degree, digress, egress, grade, gradient, gradual, graduate, grail (1), grallatory, grise, ingredient, ingress, progress, regress, retrograde, retrogression, transgression. (√GHREDH, to go.)

grand-is, great — aggrandise, gaffer, gammer, gramercy, grand, grandee, grandeur, grandiloquent ; *cf.* grampus.

grān-um, grain — engrain, garner, garnet, grain, granary, grange, granite, granule, grenade, pomegranate ; *cf.* corn. (√GER, to grind.)

grāt-us, pleasing — agree, congratulate, grace, grateful, gratify, gratis, gratitude, gratuitous, gratuity, gratulate, ingratiate, ingrate.

grau-is, heavy — aggravate, aggrieve, grave (2), grief, grieve.

greg-em, acc., a flock — aggregate, congregate, egregious, gregarious, segregate.

gross-us, thick — engross, grocer, grog, grogram, gross.

gust-us, a tasting — disgust, gust (2), ragout ; *cf.* choose, choice. (√GEUS, to taste.)

hab-ēre, to have — able, avoirdupois, binnacle, cohabit, debenture, debt, deshabille, devoir, due, duty, endeavour, exhibit, habiliment, habit, habitable, habitant, habitat, habitation, habitude, inhabit, inhibit, prebend, prohibit, provender.

hær-ēre (*hæs-*), to stick — adhere, cohere, hesitate, inherent.

hēr-ēs, an heir — heir, hereditary, heritage, inherit.

hom-o, a man — homage, homicide, human, humane, ombre.

horr-ēre, to bristle — abhor, horrible, horrid, horrify, horror, ordure ; *cf.* hirsute.

hum-us, the ground — exhume, humble, humiliate, humility.

int-us, within — denizen, intestine ; *cf.* entrails, interior, internal.

ī-re, to go — adit, ambient, ambition, arrant, circuit, commence, concomitant, constable, count (1), county, exit, eyre, initial, initiate, issue, itinerant, obit, perish, prætor, preterite, sedition, sudden, trance, transient, transit ; *cf.* isthmus. (√EI, to go.)

(*i=y.*) *iac-ere*, to throw — abject, adjacent, adjective, agistment, amice (1), circumjacent, conjecture, deject, ejaculate, eject, gist, inject, interjacent, interjection, jesses, jet (1), jetsam, jetty, joist, jut, jutty, object, project, reject, subjacent, subject, trajectory.

ioc-us, a jest—jeopardy, jewel, jocose, jocular, joke, juggler.

iūdex, a judge; see *dīcere*; p. 635.

iung-ere (*iug-*), to join—adjoin, conjoin, conjugal, conjugate, enjoin, injunction, join, joint, jugular, junction, juncture, junta, junto, rejoin, subjoin, subjugate, subjunctive; *cf.* yoke, syzygy. (√YEUG, to join.)

iūr-āre (*iūs-*), to swear—abjure, adjure, conjure, injure, juridical, jurisdiction, jurist, juror, jury, just (1), justice, justify, objurgation, perjure.

iuu-āre, to help—adjutant, aid, coadjutor.

lāb-ī (*laps-*), to glide, slip—collapse, elapse, illapse, lapse, relapse; *cf.* sleep.

labōr-em, acc., labour—belabour, elaborate, laboratory, laborious, labour.

lac-ere, to entice — delectable, delicate, delicious, delight, dilettante, elicit.

lǣd-ere (*lǣs-*), to hurt—collide, collision, elide, elision, illision, lesion.

lau-āre, *lu-ere*, to wash—ablution, alluvial, antediluvian, deluge, dilute, laundress, lava, lave, lavender, lotion; *cf.* lather, lye. (√LOU, to wash.)

lax-us, slack—lax, laxative, lease (1), leash, lessee, relax, relay (1), release, relish; *cf.* slack.

lēg-āre, to appoint — allege, colleague, college, delegate, legacy, legate, legatee, relegate; *cf. legere* (below).

leg-ere, to collect, read—coil (1), collect, cull, diligent, elect, elegant, eligible, intellect, intelligence, intelligible, lection, lecture, legend, legible, legion, lesson, neglect, negligence, predilection, recollect, select; *cf.* leal, legal, legislator, legitimate, loyal; also *lēg-āre* (above). (√LEG, to collect.)

leu-is, light—alleviate, elevate, leaven, legerdemain, leger-line, levant, levee, lever, levity, levy, relevant, relieve.

līber, free — deliver, liberal, liberate, libertine, liberty, livery.

lībra, a balance — deliberate, level, librate.

lic-ēre, to be allowable—illicit, leisure, licence, licentiate, licentious.

lig-āre, to bind—alligation, alloy, ally, league (1), liable, lictor, lien, lime-hound, ligament, ligature, oblige, rally (1).

līmen, a threshold — eliminate, lintel, preliminary.

linqu-ere, to leave — delinquent, dereliction, relic, relict, relinquish, reliquary; *cf.* eclipse, ellipse. (√LEIQ, to leave.)

līn-um, flax, *līn-ea*, a line—align (aline), delineate, line, lineage, lineal, lineament, linear, linen, lint; *cf.* lining, linnet, linseed, linsey-woolsey.

liqu ēro, to be fluid—deliquesce, liquefy, liquescent, liquid, liquidate, liquor.

lītera, a letter—alliteration, letter, literal, literature, obliterate.

loc-us, a place—allocate, allow (1), collocate, couch, dislocate, lieu, lieutenant, local, locate, locomotion, locus.

long-us, long—eloign, elongate, longevity, longitude, lunge, oblong, prolong, purloin; *cf.* long.

loqu-ī, to speak—allocution, circumlocution, colloquy, elocution, eloquent, loquacious, obloquy, prolocutor, soliloquy, ventriloquist.

lūc-ēre, to shine — elucidate, illuminate, illustrate, limn, lucid, lucubration, luminary, luminous, lunar, lunatic, lustre (?), pellucid, sublunar, translucent; *cf.* light (1). (√LEUQ, to shine.)

lūd-ere, to play—allude, collude, delude, elude, illude, illusion, ludicrous, prelude.

mag-n-us, great — magistrate, magnanimous, magnate, magnificent, magnify, magniloquence, magnitude, main (2), majesty, major, master, maxim, maximum, mayor, merino, miss (2), mister, mistress.

mal-us, bad—malady, malapert, malaria, malediction, malice, malign, malinger, malison, maltreat, malversation, maugre.

mand-āre (of. *manus*), to put into the hands of, enjoin — command, commend, commodore, countermand, demand, mandate, maundy Thursday, recommend, remand. See *manus*.

man-ēre, to remain — manor, manse, mansion, mastiff (?), menagerie, menial, messuage, permanent, remain, remnant. (√MEN, to remain.)

man-us, hand — amanuensis, maintain, manacle, manage, manciple, manege, manifest, maniple, manipulate, manner, manœuvre, manual, manufacture, manumit, manure, manuscript.

mās (*māri-*), a male—emasculate, male, mallard, marital, marry, masculine.

meā-re, to go — congé, permeate.

med-ērī, to be a remedy — medicine, remedy.

medi-us, middle — demi-, immediate, mean (3), mediate, medieval, mediocre, mediterranean, medium, meridian, mezzotinto, mizen, moiety.

mel, honey—marmalade, melilot, mellifluous, molasses ; *cf.* mildew.

memor, remembering — commemorate, memoir, memory, remember. (✓SMER, to remember.)

mend-um, a fault — amend, amends, emendation, mend.

ment-em, acc., mind, *mon-ēre*, to advise—comment, demented, memento, mental, mention; admonish, demonstrate, mint (1), moidore, monetary, money, monition, monster, monument, muster, premonish, remonstrate, summon, summons; *cf.* mind, mean (1); *also* amnesty, automaton, mnemonics. (✓MEN, to think.)

mer-ēre, to earn—demerit, meretricious, merit.

merx (merc-), traffic — amerce, commerce, market, mart, mercantile, mercenary, mercer, merchandise, merchant, mercury, mercy.

mēt-īrī (mens-), to measure—commensurate, dimension, immense, measure, mensuration.

migrā-re, to wander—emigrate, immigrate, migrate, transmigrate.

min-ārī, to threaten—amenable, commination, demean (1), demeanour, menace, promenade.

min-ēre, to project—eminent, imminent, prominent. (✓MEN, to project.)

minu-ere, to diminish, *min-or*, less—administer, comminute, diminish, diminution, minim, minish, minister, minor, minstrel, minuet, minus, minute, mistery.

mīr-us, wonderful—admire, marvel, miracle, mirage, mirror ; *cf.* smile. (✓SMEI, to wonder at.)

misc-ēre, to mix—meddle, medley, miscellaneous, promiscuous; *cf.* mix.

mitt-ere (miss-), to send—admit, commissary, commit, compromise, demise, dimissory, dismiss, emit, immit, intermit, mass (2), mess (1), message, missal, missile, mission, missive, omit, permit, premiss, premises, pretermit, promise, remit, submit, surmise, transmit.

mod-us, manner—accommodate, commodious, incommode, mode, model, moderate, modern, modest, modicum, modify, modulate, mood (2), mould (2) ; *cf.* meditate, mete. (✓MED, to measure.)

mol-ere, to grind—mill, molar, mullet (2); *cf.* molest ; *also* meal (1). (✓MEL, to grind.)

mōl-es, a heap—demolish, emolument, mole (3), molecule.

moll-is, soft—emollient, moil, mollify, mollusc; *cf.* melt, smelt (1). (✓MELD, Teut. SMELT, to melt.)

mon-ēre ; see *ment-em*.

mont-em, acc., a hill—amount, mount (1), mount (2), mountain, mountebank, paramount, remount, surmount, tantamount, tramontane; *cf.* mound. See *minēre*. (✓MEN, to project.)

mord-ēre (mors-), to bite — mordacity, morsel, remorse ; *cf.* muse (1), muzzle. (✓MERD, to rub, bite.)

mor-ī, to die—morbid, mortal, mortgage, mortify, mortmain, mortuary, murrain ; *cf.* murder; *also* amaranth, ambrosia. (✓MER, to die.)

mou-ēre (mōt-), to move — commotion, emotion, mob (1), mobile, moment, motion, motive, motor, move, mutiny, promote, remote, remove.

mūn-us, a duty—municipal, munificence, remunerate.

mūt-āre, to change—commute, mew (3), moult, mutable, mutual, permutation, transmutation.

nascī, to be born, *nāt-us (gnāt-us)*, born —agnate, cognate, impregnate, innate, naive, nascent, natal, nation, native, nature, pregnant, preternatural, supernatural. (✓GEN, to beget.)

nect-ere (nex-), to bind—annex, connect, connexion.

negā-re, to deny—abnegate, deny, negation, renegade, runagate.

noc-ēre, to hurt — innocent, innocuous, noxious, nuisance, obnoxious. (✓NEK, to destroy.)

nōmen, a name—cognomen, denominate, ignominy, nomenclator, nominal, nominate, noun, pronoun, renown; *cf.* nuncupative; *also* name, onomatopœia, synonym, &c.

noscere (gnoscere, *gnōt-), to get to know — acquaint, cognisance, cognition, connoisseur, ignoble, ignore, incognito, noble, notice, notify, notion, notorious, quaint, recognise, reconnoitre. Cf. Gk. γνῶναι ; E. kin, &c. (✓GEN, GNŌ, to know, get to know.)

not-a, a mark—annotate, denote, notable, notary, note.

nou-us, new — innovate, novel, novice, renovate ; *cf.* neology, neophyte, neoteric ; *also* new.

nūb-ere (nupt-), to marry — connubial, nuptial.

numer-us, a number—enumerate, number,

numeral, numeration, numerous, super-numerary. (√NEM, to apportion.)

nunti-us, a messenger—announce, an-nunciation, denounce, enunciate, nuncio, pronounce, renounce.

nūtrī-re, to nourish — nourish, nurse, nurture, nutriment, nutritious, nutritive.

ocul-us, eye — binocular, inoculate, in-veigle, monocular, ocular; *cf.* ophth-almia, optics, canopy; eye. (√OQ, to see.) See Gk. ὀπτικός; p. 646.

odi-um, hatred—annoy, ennui, noisome, odium.

od-or, scent — olfactory, odour, redo-lent; *cf.* osmium, ozone. (√OD, to smell.)

opt-āre, to wish—adopt, optative, op-timism, option; *cf.* copious, copy, office, opulent.

opus (*oper-*), work — co-operate, inure, opera, operate, ure, use (2).

orb-is, a circle—exorbitant, orb, orbit.

ord-o (*ordin-*), order—co-ordinate, extra-ordinary, inordinate, ordain, order, ordinal, ordinance, ordinary, ordination, ordnance, primordial, subordinate.

orī-rī, to rise — aborigines, abortion, orient, origin.

orn-āre, to adorn — adorn, ornament, ornate, suborn.

ōs (*ōr-*), the mouth—adore, inexorable, oracle, oral, oration, orator, orifice, orison, osculate, peroration.

pac-ere, pac-iscī (*pact-*), to agree; *pangere* (*pact-*), to fasten—appease, compact (1), compact (2), dispatch, impact, impinge, pacify, page (2), pageant, pale (1), palette, palisade, pallet (2), pay (1), peace, peel (3), pole (1), propagate, repay. (√PAG, PAK, to fasten.)

pann-us, a cloth — counterpane, pane, panel, pannel, panicle.

pār, equal—apparel, compeer, disparage, disparity, pair, par, parity, peer (1), prial, umpire.

par-āre, to prepare—apparatus, compare, emperor, empire, imperative, imperial, para-chute, parade, parapet, parasol, pare, parry, prepare, rampart, repair (1), separate, sever, several; *cf.* sepal.

par-ere, to produce, *pār-ēre*, to come to sight—apparitor, appear, parent, parturient, repertory, transparent.

part-em, acc., part—apart, apartment, apportion, compartment, depart, impart, parcel, parse, part, partake, participate, participle, particle, partisan (1), partition,

partner, party, portion, proportion, re-partee.

pasc-ere (*pā-, past-*), to feed—pabulum, pannage, pastel, pastern, pastille, pastor, pasture, pester, repast; *cf.* feed, fodder, food, foster. (√PĀ, to feed.)

pater (*patr-i-*), father—expatriate, pater-nal, patois, patrician, patrimony, patristic, patron, pattern, repair (2); *cf.* patriarch, patriot, patronymic (*from* Gk.); *also* father.

pat-ēre, to lie open, *pand-ere*, to spread—compass, expand, pace, pass, passage, pass-port, pastime, patent, surpass, trespass; *cf.* paten. (√PET, to spread out.)

pat-ī (*pass-*), to suffer—compassion, com-patible, passion, passive, patient.

pauper, poor—impoverish, pauper, poor, poverty; *cf.* few.

pectus (*pector-*), the breast—expectorate, pectoral, peitrel (poitrel).

ped-em, acc., foot—biped, expedite, im-pede, pawn (2), pedal, pedestal, pedes-trian, pedicel, pedigree, pediment, pie-powder, pioneer, quadruped; *cf.* im-peach; *also* tripod, tripos (Gk.); *also* foot, fetter.

pell-ere (*puls-*), to drive—appeal, appel-lant, compel, dispel, expel, impel, inter-pellation, peal, pelt (1), propel, pulsate, pulse (1), pursy, push, repeal, repel.

pell-is, skin—peel (1), pelisse, pell, pel-licle, pelt (2), pilch, pillion (?), plaid (?), surplice; *cf.* fell (2).

pend-ere (*pens-*), to weigh, *pend-ēre*, to hang—append, compendious, compensate, counterpoise, depend, dispense, expend, impend, pansy, pendant, pending, pendu-lous, pendulum, pensile, pension, pensive, penthouse, pentroof, perpendicular, poise, ponder, pound (1), prepense, preponderate, propensity, recompence, spencer, spend, suspend.

-perī-rī, to try—experience, expert, par-lous, peril; *cf.* pirate, pore (1); *also* fare, ford. (√PER, to fare.)

pet-ere, to fly, attack—appetite, compe-tent, competitor, impetus, petition, petulant, repeat; *also* pen, pennon; *cf.* feather. (√PET, to fly.)

pil-a, a ball—pellet, pile (1), piles, pill (1), platoon; *cf.* bullace (in Supple-ment, p. 662).

pil-us, a hair—depilatory, periwig, perru-que, peruke, pile (3), plush, wig.

ping-ere (*pict-*), to paint—depict, paint, picture, pigment, pimento, pint.

pi-us, holy – expiate, piacular, piety, pious, pity.

plac-ēre, to please – complacent, complaisant, placable, placid, plea, plead, please, pleasure.

plang-ere, to lament – complain, plaint, plaintiff, plaintive.

plant-a, a plant – plant, plantain, plantigrade, supplant, transplant.

plān-us, flat – esplanade, explain, pianoforte, plain, plan, plane (1), plane (2), planisphere ; *cf.* placenta, plank.

plaud-ere, to applaud – applaud, explode, plaudit, plausible.

plē-nus, full, *(com)plē-re*, to fill – accomplish, complement, complete, compliance, compliment, compline, comply, depletion, expletive, implement, plenary, plenitude, plenty, replenish, replete, supplement, supply ; *cf.* polygon ; full. (✓PLE, to fill.)

plic-āre, to fold, *plect-ere* (*plex-*), to plait – accomplice, apply, complex, complexion, complicate, complicity, deploy, display, employ, explicate, explicit, exploit, implicate, imply, perplex, plait, pleach (plash), pleat, pliant, plight, ply, reply, splay, supple, suppliant, supplicate ; *hence also* -ple *in* sim-ple, tri-ple, quadruple, -ble *in* dou-ble ; *cf.* simplicity, duplicate, treble, triplicity, &c.

plōr-āre, to weep – deplore, explore, implore.

pōn-ere (*posit-*), to place – apposite, component, composite, composition, compost, compound, deponent, deposit, deposition, disposition, depot, exponent, exposition, expound, imposition, impost, impostor, interposition, juxtaposition, opponent, opposite, ponent, positive, post (1), post (2), postillion, postpone, posture, preposition, proposition, propound, provost, purpose (2), repository, supposition, transposition.

popul-us, people – depopulate, populace, popular, public, publican, publication, publish.

port-āre, to carry – comport, deport, disport, export, import, importable, port (1), porter (1), porter (3), portesse (portous), portfolio, portly, portmanteau, purport, report, sport, support, transport.

port-us, a harbour, *port-a*, a gate – importune, opportune, porch, port (2), port (3), port (4), portcullis, porte, porter (2), portico.

pos-se (*pot-ent-*) – posse, possible, potent, power, puissant. (✓ES, to exist.)

pōtā-re, to drink – poison, potable, potation ; *cf.* potion.

prec-ārī, to pray – deprecate, imprecate, precarious, pray. (✓PREK, to ask.)

præd-a, prey – depredation, predatory, prey (see below).

prehend-ere, to seize – apprehend, apprentice, apprise, comprehend, comprise, emprise, enterprise, impregnable, imprese, imprison, prehensile, prentice, prise (prize), prison, prize (1), prize (3), reprehend, reprisal, surprise ; *cf.* get. (✓GHwED, to seize.)

prem-ere (*press-*), to press – compress, depress, express, impress, imprint, oppress, print, repress, reprimand, sprain, suppress.

preti-um, price – appraise, appreciate, depreciate, praise, precious, price, prize (2).

prīm-us, first – premier, prim, prime (1), prime (2), primero, primeval, primitive, primogeniture, primrose, prince, principal, principle ; *cf.* prior (1), prior (2), pristine ; *also* first, fore, former.

prīv-us, single – deprive, private, privilege, privy.

prob-us, good – approbation, approve, disprove, improve, probable, probation, probe, probity, proof, prove, reprieve, reprobate, reprove.

prop-e, near – approach, approximate, propinquity, proximity, reproach.

propri-us, one's own – appropriate, impropriate, proper, property, propriety.

pugn-us, fist – impugn, oppugn, poniard, pugnacious, repugnant ; *cf.* pugilism ; pygmy (Gk.).

pull-a (late L.), a hen – pool (2), poult, poultry, pullet ; *cf.* foal, filly.

pung-ere (*punct-*), to prick – appoint, compunction, counterpoint, expunge, poignant, point, pounce (1), punch (1), puncheon, punctate, punctilio, punctual, punctuate, puncture, pungent, punt (2) ; *cf.* embonpoint.

pūr-us, pure – expurgate, pour, pure, purge, purify, puritan, purity, spurge. (✓PEU, to purify.) See *put-us*.

pūs (*pūr-*), matter – purulent, pus, suppurate ; *cf.* putrid ; foul. (✓PŪ, to stink.)

put-us, clear – account, amputate, compute, count (2), depute, discount, dispute, impute, putative, recount, repute.

quær-ere (*quæst-*), to seek – acquire, conquer, conquest, disquisition, enquire, exquisite, inquest, inquire, inquisition, per-

ten-ēre, to hold — abstain, appertain, appurtenance, attempt, contain, content, continent, continue, continuous, countenance, countertenor, detain, entertain, impertinent, obtain, pertain, pertinacity, pertinent, purtenance, rein, retain, retinue, sustain, tempt, tenable, tenacious, tenacity, tenant, tenement, tenet, tenon, tenor, tent (2), tentacle, tentative, tenure; *cf.* tend, lieutenant, maintain.

tenu-is, thin — attenuate, extenuate, tenuity; *cf.* thin. (√TEN, to stretch.)

ter-ere (trīt-), to rub — attrition, contrite, detriment, tribulation, trite, triturate; *cf.* try. (√TER, to bore.)

termin-us, end — determine, exterminate, term, termination, terminus.

terr-a, earth — inter, parterre, subterranean, terrace, terreen (tureen), terrene, terrestrial, terrier (1), terrier (2), territory; *cf.* torrid, thirst. See *torr-ēre.*

terr-ēre, to scare — deter, terrible, terrific, terror.

test-is, a witness — attest, contest, detest, intestate, protest, testament, testify, testimony.

tex-ere, to weave — context, pretext, subtle, text, textile, texture, tissue, toil (2), toilet. (√TEK-S, from TEK, to cut out.)

tim-ēre, to fear — intimidate, timid, timorous.

ting-ere (tinct-), to dye — distain, stain, taint, tent (3), tincture, tinge, tint.

toll-ere (lāt-), to lift — ablative, collation, correlate, delay, dilate, elate, extol, oblate, oblation, prelate, prolate, relate, superlative, translate; *cf.* emblements, legislator, tolerate; *also* atlas, talent, tantalise; thole. (√TEL, to endure.)

torn-us, a lathe — attorney, contour, detour, return, tour, tournament, tourney, tourniquet, turn, turnpike. (*Borrowed from* Gk. τόρνος; *from* √TER, to bore.)

torqu-ēre (tort-), to twist — contort, distort, extort, retort, torch, torment, tormentil, torque, torsion, tortoise, tortuous, torture; *cf.* tart (?).

torr-ēre (tost-), to dry up — toast, torrent, torrid; *cf.* thirst. (√TERS, to be dry.)

trah-ere (tract-), to draw — abstract, attract, contract, detract, distract, entreat, estreat, extract, portrait, pourtray, protract, retract, retreat, subtract, trace, tract, tractable, trail (?), train, trait, treat, treatise, treaty.

trēs (tri-, ter-), three — tercel, ternary,

tertian, tierce, treble, trental, trey, triangle, tricentenary, tricolor, &c., trillion, trinity, trio, triple, triplicate, trireme, triumvir, trivet, trivial; *cf.* triad, tribrach, triglyph, trigonometry, trihedron, tripod, tripos (Gk.); *perhaps* tress, tressure; *cf.* three.

tribu-s, a tribe — attribute, contribute, distribute, retribution, tribe, tribune, tribute.

trūd-ere, to thrust — abstruse, detrude, extrude, intrude, obtrude, protrude; *cf.* thrust. (√TREUD, to thrust.)

tu-ērī (tuit-, tūt-), to protect — intuition, tuition, tutelage, tutelar, tutor.

tum-ēre, to swell — intumescence, tumefy, tumid, tumult, tumulus; *cf.* tuber, thumb. (√TEU, to swell.)

tund-ere (tūs-), to beat — contuse, obtuse, pierce (?). (√TEUD, Teut. STEUT, to beat.)

turb-a, a crowd — disturb, perturb, turbid, turbulent.

ultrā, beyond — antepenultima, outrage, penultima, ulterior, ultimate, ultramarine, ultramontane, ultramundane, utterance (2).

umbr-a, shade — adumbrate, umbel, umber, umbrage, umbrella.

und-a, a wave — abound, abundance, inundation, redound, redundance, superabound, surround, undulate; *cf.* hydrogen, hydra; water, wet, otter. (√WED, to be wet.)

ung-ere (unct-), to anoint — anoint, ointment, unction, unctuous, unguent.

ūn-us, one — annul, null, onion, unanimous, unicorn, uniform, union (1), union (2), unique, unison, unit, unite, unity, universal, univocal.

ūt-ī (ūs-), to use — abuse, peruse, use, usurp, usury, utensil, utilise, utility.

(u = w.) uād-ere (uās-), to go — evade, evasion, invade, pervade; *cf.* wade. (√WADH, to go.)

uag-ārī, to wander — extravagant, vagabond, vagary, vague.

ual-ēre, to be strong — avail, convalesce, countervail, prevail, vail (3), valediction, valentine, valerian, valetudinary, valiant, valid, valour, value.

uall-is, a valley — avalanche, vail (2), vale, valley.

uān-us, vain — evanescent, vain, vanish, vanity, vaunt.

uap-or, vapour — evaporate, vapour: *cf.* vapid.

uari-us, various — meniver, vair, variegate, variety, various, vary.

uār-us, crooked (whence *uārīc-*) — divaricate, prevaricate, varicose.

uās, a vessel — extravasate, vascular, vase, vessel.

ueh-ere (*uect-*), to carry — convex, inveigh, vehement, vehicle, vex ; *cf.* reveal, veil, vein, venesection ; *also* wag, waggon, wain, way, weigh, wey. (✓WEGH, to carry.)

uell-ere (*uuls-*), to pluck — convulse, revulsion.

uend-ere, to sell — vend, vent (2) ; *cf.* venal. (✓DO, to give.)

uen-īre (*uent-*), to come — advent, adventure, avenue, contravene, convene, convenient, convent, convention, covenant, covin, event, intervene, invent, parvenu, prevent, revenue, saunter, souvenir, supervene, venture, venew ; *cf.* come ; *see* Gk. βαίνειν ; p. 645. (✓GwEM, to go, come.)

uerb-um, a word — adverb, proverb, verb, verbal, verbiage ; *cf.* word.

uerg-ere, to incline — converge, diverge, verge.

uert-ere (*uers-*), to turn — adverse, advert, advertise, avert, controversy, converse, convert, divers, diverse, divert, divorce, inverse, invert, obverse, pervert, prose, reverse, revert, subvert, transverse, traverse, verse, versify, version, vertebra, vertex, vertigo, vortex ; *cf.* verst, worth (2), weird. (✓WERT, to become.)

uēr-us, true — aver, veracious, verdict, verify, verisimilitude, verity, very.

uest-is, clothing — divest, invest, travesty, vest, vestment, vestry, vesture ; *cf.* wear (1). (✓WES, to clothe.)

uet-us (*ueter-*), old — inveterate, veteran, veterinary ; *cf.* wether.

uia, a way — convey, convoy, deviate, devious, envoy, impervious, invoice, obviate, obvious, pervious, previous, viaduct, voyage. See *uehere*. (✓WEGH, to carry.)

uid-ēre (*uīs-*), to see — advice, advise, envy, evident, improvise, invidious, provide, proviso, prudent, purvey, purview, review, revise, revisit, supervise, survey, videlicet, view, visage, visard, visible, vision, visit, visor, vista, visual ; *cf.* wise, wiseacre, wit (2), wot ; *and* Gk. ἰδεῖν ; p. 645. (✓WEID, to see.)

uig-il, wakeful (*uig-or*), — invigorate, reveille, surveillance, vigil, vigour ; *cf.* wake. (✓WEG, to wake.)

uinc-ere (*uict-*), to conquer — convince, evict, evince, invincible, vanquish, victor.

uīu-ere (*uict-*), to live — convivial, revive, survive, viands, victuals, vital, vivacity, vivid, vivify, viviparous, vivisection ; *cf.* viper, _wyvern ; *also* quick, biology. (✓GwIW, to live.)

uol-o, I wish, *uel-le*, to will — volition, voluntary, voluptuous.

uolu-ere (*uolūt-*), to roll — circumvolve, convolve, devolve, evolve, involve, revolt, revolve, vault (1), vault (2), voluble, volume, volute ; *cf.* helix. (✓WEL, to wind, turn, roll.)

uou-ēre (*uōt-*), to vow — devote, devout, vote, vow.

uox (*uōc-*), voice, *uoc-āre*, to call — advocate, advowson, avocation, avouch, convoke, evoke, invocation, invoke, provoke, revoke, vocable, vocal, vocation, vociferation, voice, vouch, vouchsafe, vowel ; *cf.* epic. (✓WEQ, to speak.)

SELECT LIST OF GREEK WORDS

The following list contains the principal Greek words that appear in compounds or in several derivatives. Such as have produced but few derivatives, or are of but little interest, are excluded.

ἄγ-ειν, to drive — agony, antagonist, axiom ; epact, paragoge, stratagem, strategy ; dem-, ped-, syn-agogue. Cf. L. *agere* ; p. 632. (✓AG, to drive.)

αἱρ-εῖν, to take — aphæresis, diæresis, heresy, heretic, synæresis.

αἰσθάν-ομαι, I perceive — æsthetic, anæsthetic.

ἀκ-, as in ἀκ-μή, a point, ἄκ-ρος, pointed — acacia, acme, aconite, acrobat, acropolis, acrostic. *See* L. *ac-* ; p. 632. (✓AK, to pierce.)

ἄλλ-ος, other — allopathy, parallax, parallel, parallelogram. Cf. L. *alius*; p. 632.

ἀρχ-ή, a beginning — anarchy, arch-, arch, archæology, archaic, archetype, archipelago, architect, architrave, archives, heptarchy, hierarchy, monarch, oligarchy, patriarch, tetrarch.

ἀστήρ, a star — aster, asterisk, asteroid, astrology, astronomy; *cf.* disaster.

βαίν-ειν (βα-), to go, come — base (2), basis, diabetes. Cf. L. *uenīre*, E. *come.* (✓GwEM, to come.)

βάλλ-ειν, to cast (βελ-, βολ-) — belemnite, devil, diabolic, emblem, embolism, hyperbole, palaver, parable, parabola, parley, parliament, parlour, parole, problem, symbol.

βίο-s, life — amphibious, biography, biology. (✓GwIW, to live.)

βόμβ-ος, a humming — bomb, bombard, bound (1), bumper; *cf.* boom (1).

βύρσ-η, a hide — bursar, disburse, purse, reimburse; *cf.* sporran.

γάμ-ος, marriage — bigamy, cryptogamia, monogamy, polygamy.

γέν-, as in γέν-ος, race — endogen, exogen, genealogy, genesis; *cf.* cosmogony. (✓GEN, to beget.)

γῆ, earth — apogee, geography, geometry, georgic, perigee; *cf.* ogee.

γλῶσσ-α (γλωττ-), the tongue — epiglottis, gloss (2), glossary, glossographer, glottis, gloze; *also* bugloss, polyglot.

γνῶ-ναι, to know — diagnosis, gnome, gnomon, gnostic, prognostic. Cf. L. *noscere*; p. 638. (✓GEN, GNO, to know.)

γράφ-ειν, to write, γράμ-μα, a letter — autograph, digraph, lithograph, paragraph, photograph; -graphy (*as in* biography, &c.); graphic, graft; anagram, diagram, epigram, glamour, gramarye, grammar, grammatical, programme, telegram. Cf. E. *carve.* (✓GREBH, to carve.)

δέρμ-α, skin — derm, epidermis, pachydermatous. Cf. E. *tear* (1). (✓DER, to flay.)

δο-, cf. δί-δω-μι, I give — anecdote, antidote, dose. Cf. L. *do*, I give. (✓DO, to give.)

ἕδρα, a seat — cathedral, chair, chaise; octahedron, polyhedron, tetrahedron. Cf. L. *sedēre*, E. *sit.* (✓SED, to sit.)

ἔργ-ον (ὀργ-), work — energy, exergue, organ, orgies; lit — metall-, the-urgy; *cf.* work. (✓WERG, to work.)

ἔχ-ειν (ὀχ-, σχη-), to hold — epoch, hectic, Hector, scheme. (✓SEGH, to endure, hold in.)

ἥλι-ος, sun — aphelion, heliacal, heliotrope, parhelion, perihelion.

θεάο-μαι, I see — amphitheatre, theatre, theorem, theory.

θέ-μα, a theme, θέσ-ις, a thesis, τί-θη-μι, I place — anathema, antithesis, apothecary, epithet, hypothec, hypothesis, metathesis, parenthesis, synthesis, theme, thesaurus, thesis, treasure. Cf. E. *do*. (✓DHĒ, to put, place.)

θε-ός, a god — apotheosis, atheism, enthusiasm, pantheon, polytheism, theism, theocracy, theogony, theology, theurgy.

ἰδ-εῖν (εἰδ-), to see — idea, idol, idyll; *cf.* wit. (✓WEID, to see.)

ἴδιο-s, own — idiom, idiosyncrasy, idiot.

ἵστη-μι (στα-), I stand — apostasy, apostate, ecstasy, hypostasis, imposthume, statics, system; *cf.* stand. (✓STA, to stand.)

καί-ειν (καύ-σω), to burn — caustic, cauterise, encaustic, holocaust, ink.

κάλυξ, a cup — calyx. See L. *cēlāre*; p. 633.

κεῖμαι, I lie down — cemetery, coma. (✓KEI, to lie.)

κέλλειν, to drive — bucolic, pole (2), cylinder; *cf.* accelerate, celerity. (✓QEL, to drive.)

κέντρ-ον, a spike, goad — centre. centrifugal, centripetal, concentric, eccentric.

κλί-νειν, to lean, slope — anticlimax, climacter, climate, climax, clime, clinical, enclitic; *cf.* lean (1), low (3). See L. *clīuus*; p. 634. (✓KLEI, to lean.)

κόλαφος, a blow — cope (2), coppice, copse, coupon, recoup.

κρατ-ύς, strong — aristo-cracy, auto-, demo-, theo-cracy; *cf.* hard.

κρί-νειν, to judge — crisis, criterion, critic, diacritic, hypocrisy. See L. *cernere*; p. 633.

κρύπτ-ειν, to hide — apocrypha, crypt, cryptogamia, cryptogram, grot, grotesque, grotto.

λαμβάν-ειν (λαβ-, ληψ-), to seize — catalepsy, epilepsy, syllable; dilemma, lemma.

λόγ-ος, a saying, λέγ-ειν, to speak — analogy, apologue, apology, catalogue, decalogue, dialect, dialogue, eclectic, eclogue, epilogue, eulogy, lexicon, logarithm, logic, monologue, prologue, syllogism; *also* -logy, *as in* astro-logy, &c. (✓LEG, to collect.) See L. *legere*; p. 637.

μέτρ-ον, a measure — diameter, metre, perimeter, symmetry; *cf.* baro-meter, chrono-meter, &c. (✓MĒ, ME, to measure.)

μόν-ος, single — minster, monad, monarch, monastery, monk, monochord, monopoly, mono-.

νέμ-ειν, to assign—nemesis, nomad, numismatic; astro-nomy, eco-nomy, &c. (✓NEM, to apportion, take.)

ὁδ-ός, a way—episode, method, period, synod.

ὄζ-ειν (ὀδ-), to smell—osmium, ozone; cf. odour. (✓OD, to smell.)

ὄνομα, a name — anonymous, homonymous, metonymy, onomatopœia, paronymous, patronymic, pseudonym, synonym; cf. noun, name. See L. nōmen; p. 638.

ὀξ-ύ-s, sharp — oxalis, oxide, oxygen, oxymel, oxytone, paroxysm.

ὀπτικ-ός, visual—catoptric, dioptric, optic; cf. autopsy, ophthalmia, synopsis; also ocular. See L. oculus; p. 639. (✓OQ, to see.)

πάθ-ος, suffering—antipathy, apathy, pathos, sympathy; allo-, homœo-pathy.

παῦσ-ιs, a pause—pause, pose (1); whence appose, compose, decompose, depose, dispose, expose, impose, interpose, oppose, pose (2), propose, purpose (1), repose, suppose, transpose; also puzzle.

πέτρ-os, stone, πέτρ-α, rock—petrel, petrify, petroleum, pier, samphire.

ποιν-ή, a penalty—impunity, pain, penal, penance, penitent, pine (2), punch (2), punish, repent, repine, subpœna. (✓QEI, to appraise, fine, pay.)

πυξίς, a box—pyx, bush (2), bushel. See L. buxus; p. 632.

πῦρ, fire—bolt (2), bureau, empyrean, pelleter, pellitory (2), pyre, pyrites, pyrotechnic; cf. fire.

ῥέ-ειν (ῥευ-), to flow—catarrh, diarrhœa, rheum, rheumatism, rhythm, rime (1) or rhyme; cf. stream. (✓SREU, to flow; Teut. root STREU.)

σκέπτο-μαι (σκοπ-), I consider — bishop, episcopal, sceptic, scope, stereoscope, telescope, &c.

σπείρ-ειν (σπερ-, σπορ-), to sow—sperm, spore, sporadic. (✓SPER, to scatter.)

στέλλ-ειν (στολ-), to send—apostle, diastole, epistle, stole, systole.

στρέφ-ειν (στροφ-), to turn—antistrophe, apostrophe, catastrophe, strophe.

τάσσ-ειν (τακτ-, ταξ-), to arrange—syntax, tactics taxidermy.

τλῆ-ναι, to suffer, endure—atlas, tantalise, talent; cf. L. tollere; p. 643. (✓TEL, TLĒ, to endure.)

τόμ-os, a section—anatomy, atom, entomology, epitome, tome; cf. litho-tomy, phlebo-tomy; also contemplate, temple. (✓TEM, to cut.)

τόν-os, a tone—attune, barytone, diatonic, intone, monotonous, oxytone, tone, tonic, tune; cf. hypo-tenuse. (✓TEN, to stretch.) See L. tendere; p. 643.

τόρν-os, a tool to draw circles with; see tornus in the list of Latin primitives; p. 643. (✓TER, to bore.)

τρόπ-os, a turn—trope, trophy, tropic; also contrive, retrieve, troubadour, trover.

τύπ-os, a blow—antitype, archetype, stereotype, timbrel, tympanum, type.

ὕδ-ωρ, water—dropsy, hydra, hydrangea, hydraulic, hydro-, hydropsy; cf. water, otter. (✓WED, to wet.)

φαίν-ειν (φαν-), to shew — diaphanous, epiphany, fancy, fantastic, fantasy, phantom, phenomenon; cf. hiero-phant, sycophant.

φέρ-ειν (φορ-), to bear—diaphoretic, metaphor, periphery, phosphorus. (✓BHER, to bear.)

φλέγ-ειν, to burn—phlegm, phlox; cf. flagrant. (✓BHLEG, to burn.)

φύ-ειν, to produce—physic, physiology, physiognomy; neo-phyte, zoo-phyte; imp. (✓BHEU, to become.)

φων-ή, sound—anthem, antiphon, euphony, phonetic, symphony, telephone; cf. blame, blaspheme, euphemism, prophet. (✓BHĀ, to speak.) Cf. L. fārī; p. 635.

χάρτ-η, a leaf of paper — card, carte, cartel, cartoon, cartouche, cartridge, cartulary, chart, charter, écarté.

χέ-ειν, to pour—chyle, chyme; cf. alchemy. (✓GHEU, to pour.) Cf. L. fundere; p. 636.

χρόν-os, time — anachronism, chronicle, chronology, chronometer, isochronous, synchronism.

ᾠδ-ή, a song—epode, monody, ode, palinode, parody, prosody. (✓WEID, to cry out.)

IV. HOMONYMS

HOMONYMS are words which, though spelt alike, differ considerably in meaning. They may be divided into two classes : (*a*) homonyms from entirely different roots, or at any rate by no means closely connected ; (*b*) homonyms from the same root, not differing very widely in origin. Those which belong to the latter class are distinguished by being printed in italics. For further information, see the Dictionary.

abide, *air*, allow, *along*, amice, an, ancient, angle, arch, arm, art, ay.

baggage, bail, bale, *balk*, ball, band, bang, *bank*, barb, bark, barm, barnacle, barrow, base, basil, bass, baste, bat, *bate*, batten, *batter*, bay, beam, bear, beaver, beck, beetle, *bend*, bid, bile, bill, billet, *bit*, blanch, blaze, blazon, *bleak*, blot, blow, *board*, boil, bolt, boom, boon, boot, bore, botch, bottle, bound, bourn, bow, bowl, box, *braid*, brake, brat, brawl, bray, *braze*, breeze, *brief*, broil, brook, buck, budge, buff, *buffer*, buffet, bug, bugle, bulk, bull, bump, bunting, burden, burn, *bury*, bush, busk, but, butt.

cab, cabbage, calender, *calf*, can, *canon*, cannon, cant, cape, caper, *capital*, card, carousal, carp, case, celt, chap, char, chase, chink, chit, chop, chuck, cleave, *close*, clove, *club*, clutter, cob, cobble, cock, cockle, cocoa, cod, codling, *cog*, coil, colon, *compact*, con, *contract*, cope, corn, *corporal*, *cotton*, count, counterpane, *court*, cow, cowl, crab, *crank*, crease, cricket, croup, crowd, cuff, *cunning*, curry, cypress.

dab, dam, dare, date, deal, *defer*, defile, demean, desert, *deuce*, die, *diet*, *distemper*, dock, don, down, *dowse*, drab, dredge, drill, drone, duck, dudgeon, *dump*, dun.

ear, earnest, egg, *eke*, elder, emboss, endue, entrance [1. *from* enter ; 2. *from* trance], even, *exact*, excise.

fair, fallow, *fast*, fat, fawn, fell, ferret, feud, file, *fine*, *firm*, fit, flag, *fleet*, *flip*, flock, flounce, flounder, flue, fluke, flush, foil, fold, font, *fool*, for (for-), forbear, force, fore-arm, found, fount, *fratricide*, fray, *freak*, fret, frieze, frith, frog, fry, full, fuse, *fusee*, fusil, *fust*.

gad, gage, *gain*, gall, gammon, *gang*, gantlet, gar, garb, gate, *gender*, gill, gin, gird, glede, *gleek*, glib, gloss, gore, gout, grail, grate, grave, graze, greaves, greet, groat, *gull*, gum, gust.

hack, *hackle*, *haggard*, *haggle*, hail, hale,

hamper, *handy*, harbour, harrier, hatch, hawk, hay, heel, helm, hem, *herd*, hey-day, hide, hind, hip, hob, hobby, hock, hold, *homicide*, hoop, hop, hope, host, how, hoy, hue, hull, *hum*.

il-, im-, in- (*prefixes*), *incense*, indent, indue, ingle, *interest*, *intimate*, ir- (*prefix*).

jack, jade, *jam*, jar, jet, *jib*, *job*, *jump*, junk, just.

kedge, keel, kennel, kern, *kind*, kindle, kit, knoll.

lac, *lack*, *lade*, lake, lama, lap, *lark*, *lash*, last, latch, lathe, lawn, lay, lead, league, *lean*, lease, leave, leech, let, lie, *lift*, light, lighten, *like*, limb, limber, lime, limp, ling, link, list, *litter*, *live*, lock, log, *long*, loom, loon, low, lower, lumber, lurch, lustre, lute.

mace, mail, main, *mall*, mangle, march, mark, maroon, martlet, mass, mast, match, mate, *matter*, maund, may, mead, meal, mean, meet, mere, mess, mew, *might*, milt, mine, mint, mis-, miss, *mite*, mob, mole, mood, moor, mop, *mortar*, mother, mould, *mount*, mow, muff, mullet, *muscle*, muse, must, mute, mystery.

nag, nap, nave, neat, net, nick, *no*, not.

O, *one*, or, ought, ounce, *own*.

pad, paddle, paddock, page, pale, pall, pallet, *pap*, partisan, pat, *patch*, pawn, pay, peach, *peck*, peel, *peep*, peer, pellitory, pelt, pen, perch, periwinkle, *pet*, *pie*, pile, pill, pine, pink, pip, pitch, plane, plash, plat, plight, plot, plump, poach, poke, pole, pool, pore, *port*, *porter*, pose, *post*, pounce, pound, *pout*, *prank*, *present*, press, *prig*, *prime*, *prior*, prize, pure, *puddle*, pulse, pump, punch, *puncheon*, punt, *pupil*, *puppy*, purl, purpose.

quack, quail, quarrel, quarry, quill, quire, quiver.

race, rack, racket, rail, rake, rally, rank, rap, rape, rash, rate, raven, ray, reach, real, rear, reef, reel, reeve, refrain, relay, rennet, rent, repair, rest, rid, riddle, rifle, rig, rime, ring, ripple, rob, rock, rocket, roe, rook, *root*, rote, rouse, row, ruck, rue, ruff, ruffle, rum, rush, rut.

sack, sage, sallow, sap, sardine, sash, saw, say, scald, scale, scar, scarf, *sconce*, scour, scout, screw, scrip, scrub, scull, scuttle, seal, seam, see, sell, set, *settle*, sew, sewer, *share*, shed, sheer, shingle, shiver, shoal, shock, shore, shrub, *size*, skate, slab, *slay*, *slop*, slot, slough, smack, smelt, snite, snuff, soil, sole, sorrel, sound, souse, sow, spade, spar, spark, spat, spell, spill, spire, spit, spittle, spray, spurt, squire, stale, stalk, *staple*, *stare*, stay, *steep*, steer, stem, stern, *stick*, stile, still, stoop, story, strain, strand, *stroke*, *strut*, stud, sty, style, summer, swallow, swim.

tache, tail, tang, tap, *taper*, *tar*, tare, tart, tartar, tassel, tattoo, tear, teem, temple, temporal, *tend*, *tender*, tense, tent, *terrier*, *the*, thee, thole, thrum, thrush, tick, tiff, till, tilt, tine, tip, tire, tit, to-, *toast*, toil, toll, toot, top, tow, *trace*, *tract*, trap, trepan, trice, trick, trill, trinket, truck, trump, trunk, tuck, tuft, turtle, twig.

un-, *union*, use, *utter*, utterance.

vail, van, *vault*, vent, verge, vice.

wag, wake, ware, wax, weal, weed, weld, well, *wharf*, wheal, whelk, whittle, wick, wight, *will*, wimble, wind, *windlass*, *wise*, *wit*, wood, *wort*, worth, *wrinkle*.

yard, yawl, yearn.

V. LIST OF DOUBLETS

Doublets are words which, though apparently differing in form, are nevertheless, from an etymological point of view, one and the same, or only differ in some unimportant suffix. Thus *aggrieve* is from L. *aggrauāre*; whilst *aggravate*, though really from the pp. *aggrauātus*, is nevertheless used as a verb, precisely as *aggrieve* is used, though the senses of the words have been differentiated. In the following list, each pair of doublets is entered only *once*, to save space.

abbreviate—abridge.
absolve—assoil.
adamant—diamond.
aggrieve—aggravate.
ait—eyot.
alarm—alarum.
allocate—allow (1).
ameer—emir (omrah).
amiable—amicable.
an—one.
ancient (2)—ensign.
announce—annunciate.
ant—emmet.
anthem—antiphon.
antic—antique.
appeal, *sb.*—peal.
appear—peer (3).
appraise—appreciate.
apprentice—prentice.
aptitude—attitude.
arc—arch (1).
army—armada.
arrack—rack (5), raki.
assay—essay.
assemble—assimilate.
assess—assize, *vb.*
attach—attack.

balm—balsam.
banjo—mandolin.
barb (1)—beard.
base—basis.
bashaw—pasha.
baton—batten (2).
beadle—bedell.
beaker—pitcher (?).
beef—cow.
beldam—belladonna.
bench—bank (1), bank (2).
benison—benediction.
blame—blaspheme.
boss—botch (2).
bound (2)—bourn (1).
bower—byre.
box (2)—pyx, bush (2).
breve—brief.
brother—friar.
brown—bruin.

cadence—chance.
caitiff—captive.
caldron, cauldron — chaldron.
calumny—challenge.
camera—chamber.

cancer—canker.
card (1)—chart, carte.
case (2)—chase (3), cash.
cask—casque.
castigate—chasten.
catch—chase (1).
cattle—chattels, capital (2).
cavalier—chevalier.
cavalry—chivalry.
cell—hall.
chaise—chair.
chalk—calx.
champaign—campaign.
channel—canal, kennel (2).
chant—cant (1).
chapiter—capital (3).
chateau—castle.
check, *sb.*—shah.
chicory—succory.
chief—cape (2).
chieftain—captain.
chirurgeon—surgeon.
choir—chorus, quire (2).
choler—cholera.
chord—cord.
chuck (1)—shock (1).
church—kirk.

cipher—zero.
cithern—guitar, kit (2).
clause—close, *sb.*
climate—clime.
coffer—coffin.
coin—coign, quoin.
cole—kail.
collect—coil, cull.
collocate—couch.
comfit—confect.
commend—command.
complacent—complaisant.
complete, *vb.*—comply.
compost—composite.
comprehend—comprise.
compute—count (2).
conduct, *sb.*—conduit.
confound—confuse.
construe—construct.
convey—convoy.
cool—gelid.
corn (1)—grain.
corn (2)—horn.
corral—kraal.
costume—custom.
cot, cote—coat.
couple, *vb.*—copulate.
coy—quiet, quit, quite.
crape—crisp.
crate—hurdle.
crease (1)—crest.
crcel—griddle, grill.
crevice—crevasse.
crimson—carmine.
crop—croup (2).
crypt—grot.
cud—quid.
cue—queue.
curari—wourali.
curricle—curriculum.

dace—dart, dare (2).
dainty—dignity.
dame—dam, donna, duenna.
date (2)—dactyl.
dauphin—dolphin.
daywoman—dairywoman.
deck—thatch.
defence—fence.
defend—fend.
delay—dilate.
dell—dale.
dent—dint.
deploy—display, splay.
depot—deposit, *sb.*
descry—describe.
desiderate—desire, *vb.*

despite—spite.
deuce (1)—two.
devilish—diabolic.
die (2)—dado.
dike—ditch.
direct—dress.
dish—disc, desk, dais.
disport—sport.
distain—stain.
ditto—dictum.
diurnal—journal.
doge—duke.
dole—deal, *sb.*
doom— -dom (*suffix*).
drill—thrill, thirl.
dropsy—hydropsy.
due—debt.
dune—down (2).

eatable—edible.
éclat—slate (1.)
elf—oaf, ouphe.
emerald—smaragdus.
emerods—hemorrhoids.
employ—imply, implicate.
emprise—imprese.
endow—endue (1).
endue (2)—indue (1).
engine—gin (2).
entire—integer.
envious—invidious.
enwrap—envelop.
escape—scape.
escutcheon—scutcheon.
especial—special.
espy—spy.
esquire—squire (1).
establish—stablish.
estate—state, status.
estop—stop.
estreat—extract.
etiquette—ticket.
example—ensample, sample.
exemplar—sampler.
extraneous—strange.

fabric—forge, *sb.*
fact—feat.
faculty—facility.
fan—van (1).
fancy—fantasy, phantasy.
fashion—faction.
fat (2)—vat.
feeble—foible.
fell (2)—pell.
feud (2)—fief.
feverfew—febrifuge.

fiddle—viol.
fife—pipe, peep (1).
finch—spink (?).
finite—fine (1).
fitch—vetch.
flag (4)—flake.
flame—phlegm.
flower—flour.
flush (1)—flux.
foam—spume.
font (1)—fount.
foremost—prime.
fragile—frail.
fray (1)—affray.
fro—from.
fungus—sponge.
furl—fardel.
fuse (1)—found (2).

gabble—jabber.
gaffer—grandfather.
gage (1)—wage, wed.
gambado—gambol.
game—gammon (2).
gaol—jail.
gaud—joy.
gear—garb (1).
genteel—gentle, gentile.
genus—kin.
germ—germen.
gig—jig.
gird (2)—gride.
girdle—girth.
gramarye—grammar, glamour.
granary—garner.
grise—grade.
guarantee, *sb.*—warranty.
guard—ward.
guardian—warden.
guest—host (2).
guile—wile.
guise—wise (2).
gullet—gully.
gust (2)—gusto.
guy (2)—guide, *sb.*
gypsy—Egyptian.

hale (1)—whole.
hamper (2)—hanaper.
harangue—ring, rank (1).
hash—hatch (3).
hautboy—oboe.
heap—hope (2).
helix—volute.
hemi- —semi-.
history (1)—story.

hoop (2)—whoop.
hospital — hostel, hotel, spital.
human—humane.
hyacinth—jacinth.
hydra—otter.
hyper- —super-.
hypo- —sub-.

illumine—limn.
inapt—inept.
inch—ounce (1).
indite—indict.
influence—influenza.
innocuous—innoxious.
invite—vie.
invoke—invocate.
iota—jot.
isolate—insulate.

jaggery—sugar.
jealous—zealous.
joint—junta, junto.
jointure—juncture.
jut—jet (1).
jutty—jetty.

kith—kit (3).
knot—node.

lac (1)—lake (2).
lace—lasso.
lair—leaguer; *also* layer (?).
lake (1)—loch, lough.
lap (3)—wrap.
launch, lanch—lance, *vb.*
leal—loyal, legal.
lection—lesson.
levy—levee.
lieu—locus.
limb (2)—limbo.
lineal—linear.
liquor—liqueur.
lobby—lodge.
locust—lobster.
lone—alone.
lurk—lurch (1).

madam—madonna.
major—mayor.
male—masculine.
malediction—malison.
mangle (2)—mangonel.
manœuvre—manure, mainour.
mar—moor (2).

march (1)—mark (2), marque.
margin—margent, marge.
marish—marsh.
mash, *sb* —mess (2).
mauve—mallow.
maxim—maximum.
mean (3)—mizen.
memory—memoir.
mentor—monitor.
metal—mettle.
milt (2)—milk.
minim—minimum.
minster—monastery.
mint (1)—money.
mister—master.
mob (1)—mobile, moveable.
mode—mood (2).
mohair—moire.
moment—momentum, movement.
monster—muster.
morrow—morn.
moslem—mussulman.
mould (1)—mulled.
musket—mosquito.

naive—native.
naked—nude.
name—noun.
natron—nitre.
naught, nought—not.
neither—nor.
nucleus—newel.

obedience—obeisance.
octave—utas, utis.
of—off.
onion—union (2).
ordinance—ordnance.
orpiment—orpine.
osprey—ossifrage.
otto—attar.
outer—utter (1).
overplus—surplus.

paddle (2)—spatula.
paddock (2)—park.
pain, *vb.*—pine (2).
paladin—palatine.
pale (2)—pallid.
palette—pallet (2).
paper—papyrus.
paradise—parvis.
paralysis—palsy.
parole—parable, parle, palaver.

parson—person.
pass—pace.
pastel—pastille.
pate—plate (?).
paten—pan (?).
patron—pattern.
pause—pose (1).
paynim—paganism.
pelisse—pilch.
pellitory (1)—parity.
penance—penitence.
peregrine—pilgrim.
peruke—periwig, wig.
phantasm—phantom.
piazza—place.
pick—peck (1), pitch (2).
picket—piquet.
piety—pity.
pigment—pimento.
pistil—pestle.
pistol—pistole.
plaintiff—plaintive.
plait—pleat, plight (2).
plan—plain, llano.
plateau—platter.
plum—prune (2).
poignant—pungent.
point—punt (2).
poison—potion.
poke (1)—pouch.
pole (1)—pale (1), pawl.
pomade, pommade—pomatum.
pomp—pump (2).
poor—pauper.
pope—papa.
porch—portico
porridge—pottage.
posy—poesy.
potent—puissant.
poult—pullet.
pounce (1)—punch (1).
pounce (2)—pumice.
pound (2)—pond.
pound (3)—pun, *vb.*
power—posse.
praise—price.
preach—predicate.
premier—primero.
priest—presbyter.
private—privy.
probe, *sb.*—proof.
proctor—procurator.
prolong—purloin.
prosecute—pursue.
provide—purvey.
provident—prudent.

puny—puisne.
purl (3)—profile.
purpose (1)—propose.
purview—proviso.

quartern—quadroon.

raceme—raisin.
rack (1)—ratch.
radix—radish, race (3), root (1), wort (1).
raid—road.
rail (2)—rally (2).
raise—rear (1).
rake (3)—reach.
ramp—romp.
ransom—redemption.
rapine—ravine, raven (2).
rase—raze.
ratio—ration, reason
ray (1)—radius.
rayah—ryot.
rear-ward—rear-guard.
reave—rob.
reconnaissance—recognisance.
regal—royal.
relic—relique.
relish—relay (1).
renegade—runagate.
renew—renovate.
reprieve—reprove.
residue—residuum.
respect—respite.
revenge—revindicate.
reward—regard.
rhomb, rhombus—rumb.
ridge—rig (3).
rod—rood.
rondeau—rondel.
rote (1)—route, rout, rut.
round—rotund.
rouse (2)—row (3).
rover—robber.

sack (1)—sac.
sacristan—sexton.
saw (2)—saga.
saxifrage—sassafras.
scabby—shabby.
scale (1)—shale.
scandal—slander.

scarf (1)—scrip (1), scrap.
scatter—shatter.
school (2)—shoal, scull (3).
scot(free)—shot.
screech—shriek.
screw (2)—shrew.
scuttle (1)—skillet.
sect, sept, set (2)—suite, suit.
sennet—signet.
separate—sever.
sergeant, serjeant—servant.
settle (1)—sell (2), saddle.
shawm, shalm—haulm.
shed (2)—shade.
shirt—skirt.
shred—screed.
shrub (2)—syrup, sherbet.
shuffle—scuffle.
sicker, siker—secure, sure.
sine—sinus.
sir, sire—senior, seignior, señor, signor.
skewer—shiver (2).
skiff—ship.
skirmish—scrimmage, scaramouch.
slabber—slaver.
sleuth—slot (2).
sloop—shallop.
snivel—snuffle.
snub—snuff (2).
soil (1)—sole (1), sole (2).
soprano sovereign.
sough—surf.
souse—sauce.
species—spice.
spell (4)—spill (1).
spend—dispend.
spirit—sprite, spright.
spoor—spur.
sprit—sprout, sb.
sprout, vb.—spout.
squall—squeal.
squire (2)—square.
stank—tank.
stave—staff.
stock—tuck (2).
stove—stew, sb.
strait—strict.
strap—strop.
superficies—surface.
supersede—surcease.

suppliant—supplicant.
sweep—swoop.

tabor—tambour.
tache (1)—tack.
taint—tent (3), tint.
tamper—temper.
task—tax.
tawny—tenny.
tend (1)—tender (2).
tense (2)—toise.
tercel—tassel (2).
thread—thrid.
tithe—tenth.
to—too.
ton—tun.
tone—tune.
tour—turn.
tract (1)—trait.
tradition—treason.
treachery—trickery.
trifle—truffle.
tripod—trivet.
triumph—trump (2).
troth—truth.
tuck (1)—touch.
tulip—turban.

umbel—umbrella.
unity—unit.
ure—opera.

vade—fade.
valet varlet.
vast—waste.
veal—wether.
veneer—furnish.
venew, veney—venue.
verb—word.
vertex—vortex.
viaticum—voyage.
viper—wyvern, wivern.
visor—vizard.
vizier, visier—alguazil.
vocal—vowel.

wain—wagon, waggon.
wattle—wallet (?).
weet—wit (1).
whirl—warble.
wight (1)—whit.
wrack—wreck, rack (4).

VI. DISTRIBUTION OF WORDS ACCORDING TO THE LANGUAGES FROM WHICH THEY ARE DERIVED

THE Dictionary shews from what language each word is derived, as far as its etymology is at present ascertained. The largest classes of words are the following.

1. Words of purely ENGLISH origin, most of which are found in Anglo-Saxon, or in Old Friesian, or are words of imitative origin.

2. Words of SCANDINAVIAN or OLD DANISH origin, due to the frequent incursions of the Danes, many of whom permanently settled in England. Their speech was closely allied to the oldest English as represented by Anglo-Saxon.

3. Words of CELTIC origin, few of which can be due to the ancient Britons. Most of the words in this class have been borrowed from Welsh, Gaelic, or Irish in comparatively modern times.

4. Words of LATIN origin; borrowed (1) from Latin directly; (2) through the medium of French. Both these classes of words are very large. Here also may be included words of Late Latin origin, chiefly borrowed from the debased or rustic Latin, which employed words not to be found in the best classical authors.

5. Words of GREEK origin; borrowed (1) from Greek directly; (2) through the medium of Latin; (3) through the medium of Latin, and afterwards of French; (4) through the medium of French (the word not being used in Latin).

6. HYBRID WORDS, made up from two different languages. Such a word is *bankrupt*, *bank* being of Teutonic, but *-rupt* of Latin origin. Words of this character are rather numerous, but their component parts are, in most cases, easily accounted for.

Words *strictly* belonging to the above classes are numerous, and will not be further noticed here. But there are also other smaller classes of words which are here brought particularly under the reader's notice.

Before proceeding to enumerate these at p. 655, a few remarks upon some of the classes already mentioned may be useful.

1. ENGLISH. Among these we must include :

Place-names : canter, carronade, dunce, galloway, jersey, kersey. *Personal names* : kit-cat, negus, pinchbeck, shaddock, shrapnel.

Also a word that seems to have been originally English, and to have been re-borrowed.
Portuguese from English : dodo (?).

2. Among SCANDINAVIAN WORDS we must also include the following :

Icelandic : geysir.
Swedish : dahlia, gantlet (gantlope), slag. sloid, trap (3), tungsten, weld (1).
German from Swedish : nickel.
Danish : floe, jib (1), jib (2).
Norwegian : lemming (leming).
French from Scandinavian : abet, baggage, barbed, bet, bondage, brandish,

brasier (brazier), breeze (3), equip, flounder (2), gable, gallop, gauntlet, gawky, jib (3), jolly, locket, Norman, pocket, rivet, slot (2), strife, strive, waif, waive, wicket.
Dutch from Scandinavian : doit, furlough, walrus.
Russian from Swedish : knout.

3. Among CELTIC WORDS we may also include the following :

Welsh : bragget, coracle, cromlech, crowd (2), eisteddfod, flannel, flummery, maggot, metheglin (*of L. origin*; p. 663).

Gaelic : airt, capercailzie, cateran, clachan, clan, claymore, coronach, corrie, duniwassal, fillibeg (philibeg), gillie, inch

(2), loch, mackintosh, ptarmigan, reel (2), slogan, spleuchan, whisky.

Irish : colleen, culdee, gallow-glass, kern (1) *or* kerne, lough, mavourneen, orrery, rapparee, skain (skene), shanty, shillelagh, spalpeen, tanist, Tory, usquebaugh.

Cornish : wheal (2).

Breton : dowlas.

Latin from Celtic : punt (1).

French from Celtic (or Breton) : beak, bijou, bilge, bound (2), bourn (1), bracket, brail, bray (2), budget, bulge, car, cark, career, carpenter, carry, carriage, charge, chariot, cloak (cloke), dolmen, garter, gobbet, gobble (*with* E. *suffix*), gravel, javelin, lay (2), lockram, mavis, mien, mine (2), mutton, petty, piece, quay, truant, valet, varlet, vassal.

Spanish from Celtic : cargo, galliard, garrote (garrotte).

Italian from Celtic : caricature.

French from Italian from Celtic : caroche.

French from Latin from Celtic : ambassador, barge, bark (1), embassy, feuterer, league (2), marl, palfrey, pontoon.

French from German from Celtic : rote (2).

4. Among LATIN WORDS we may also include the following :

Late Latin from French from Latin : crenellate.

Italian from French from Latin : oboe.

Spanish from French from Latin : platina.

Dutch from French from Latin : buoy, cashier, commodore, domineer, excise, foy, quirk.

Provençal from Latin : battledoor.

French from Provençal from Latin : badinage, fad, fig, radish. *Also, from Southern French* : cabin, cabinet, funnel, noose, puncheon (1), puncheon (2), tulle.

Spanish from Provençal from Latin : flamingo.

Italian from Latin : accordion, allegro, alto, antic, askance, attitude, belladonna, brave, broccoli, canto, canzonet, caper (1), casino, catacomb, cicerone, comply, contralto, cupola, curvet, dado, dilettante, ditto, doge, donna, duel, duet, ferret (2), forte, granite, gurgle, incognito, influenza, infuriate, intaglio, isolate, lagoon (lagune), lava, league (1), levant, macaroni (maccaroni), madonna, manifesto, maraschino, Martello tower, mezzotinto, miniature, motto, nuncio, opera, pediment, pianoforte, piano, pilgrim, portico, profile, punch (4), punchinello, quartet (quartette), quota, semolina, seraglio, signor (signior), size (2), soda, solo, sonata, soprano, stanza, stiletto, travertine, trio, tufa, umbrella, velvet, vermicelli, virtuoso, vista, volcano.

French from Italian from Latin : accolade, alarm (alarum), alert, apartment, arcade, artisan, battalion, bulletin, burlesque, cab (1), cabbage (2), cabriolet, cadence, camp, campaign, cape (2), caprice, capriole, caress, carnival, cascade, cavalcade, cavalier, cavalry, citadel, colonel, colonnade, compartment, compliment, concert, contour, corridor, corsair, cortege, costume, countertenor, courier, courtesan, cuirass, custard, disgrace, dome, douche, ducat, escort, esplanade, façade, faggot (?), falchion, favourite, festoon, filigree, florin, fracas, fugue, gabion, galligaskins, gambit, gambol, gelatine, imprese, improvise, incarnadine, infantry, junket, lavender, lutestring, macaroon, manage, manege, marmot, mizen (mizzen), model, mole (3), motet, musket, niche, ortolan, paladin, palette, pallet (2), parapet, partisan (1), pastel, peruke, pilaster, pinnace, piston, pivot, poltroon, pomade (pommade), populace, porcelain, post (2), postillion, redoubt, reprisal, revolt, rocket (2), salad, sallet, salmagundi, savcloy (cervelas), sentinel ?, sentry ?, serenade, somersault (somerset), sonnet, spinet, squad, squadron, termagant, terrace, tramontane, ultramontane, umber, vault (2), vedette (vidette).

Dutch or Low German from French from Italian from Latin : monkey.

German from Italian from Latin : barouche.

Spanish from Latin : alligator, ambuscade, armada, armadillo, booby, brocade, capsize, carbonado, cask, casket, chinchilla, cork, corral, corregidor, cortes, desperado, disembogue, dispatch, don (2), duenna, firm (2), funambulist, grandee, hacienda, hidalgo, junta, junto, lasso, llano, mallecho, matador, merino, mosquito (musquito), mustang, negro, olio, ombre, peccadillo, picador, primero, punctilio, quadroon, real (2), renegade (renegado), salver, sherry, sierra, siesta, sombrero, stevedore, tent (3), tornado, vanilla.

Portuguese from Spanish from Latin: verandah.

French from Spanish from Latin: calenture, capstan, casque, comrade, creole, doubloon, dulcimer, escalade, farthingale (fardingale), grenade, jade (2), jonquil, manchineel, parade, petronel, punt (2), quadrille, risk, sassafras, spaniel.

Portuguese from Latin: auto-da-fe, ayah, binnacle, caste, cobra, joss, junk (2), lingo, madeira, moidore, molasses, pimento, port (4), tank.

French from Portuguese from Latin: corvette, fetich (fetish), parasol.

Dutch from Portuguese from Latin: kraal.

Dutch from Latin: anker, bung, cant (2), cornel, cruise, easel, pink (2), tafferel (taffrail).

Scandinavian from English from Latin: kindle.

German from Latin: drilling.

French from High German from Latin: baldric, coif, fife, pitcher, spurrey, waste.

Scandinavian from Latin: bush (1).

Russian from Teutonic from Latin: czar.

French from Portuguese from Arabic from Greek from Latin: apricot.

French from Spanish from Arabic from Latin: quintal.

Late Latin: baboon, barrister, campanula, cap, capital (3), cope (1), edible, elongate, elucidate, fine (2), flask, grate (1), hoax, hocus-pocus, implement, indent (1). intimidate, pageant, plenary, proxy; *and perhaps others.*

French from Late Latin: ambush, ballet, bar, barbican, bargain, base (1), bassoon, bittern, burden (2), burl, cape (1), dominion, felon?, ferret (1), festival, flagon, flavour, frock, funeral, gauge (gage), gouge, hutch, oleander.

French from Provençal from Late Latin: ballad.

French from Italian from Late Latin: basement, canton, capuchin.

French from Spanish from Late Latin: caparison.

German from Hungarian from Servian from Late Greek from Latin: hussar.

5. Among GREEK WORDS we must also include the following:

Latin from Greek: abyss, acacia, allegory, alms, amaranth, amethyst, &c., &c.

Late Latin from Greek: bursar, cartulary, catapult, chamomile (camomile), hulk, imp, intoxicate, magnesia, pericranium, &c.

Italian from Latin from Greek: biretta, grotto, madrigal, orris, piazza, torso.

French from Italian from Latin from Greek: agate, air (2), baluster, balustrade, cannon, canopy, espalier, grotesque, medal, mosaic, piastre.

Dutch from Italian from Latin from Greek: sketch.

Spanish from Latin from Greek: melocotone, morris, pellitory (2), sambo, savanna (savannah), silo, spade (2).

French from Spanish from Latin from Greek: castanets, cochineal, rumb (rhumb).

Portuguese from Latin from Greek: buffalo, palaver.

French from Portuguese from Latin from Greek: marmalade.

Provençal from Latin from Greek: troubadour.

Scandinavian from Latin from Greek: beaker.

Dutch from Latin from Greek: bush (2).

French from German from Latin from Greek: chamberlain, petrel (peterel).

Celtic from Latin from Greek: sporran, spunk.

French from Late Latin from Greek: acolyte, anchoret (anchorite), apoplexy, apostasy, apothecary, bombast, bottle (1), butler, buttery, bushel, calender (1), calm, card (1), carte, cauterise, celandine, chronicle, clergy, climacter, climate, clinical, dredge (2), embrocation, fleam, galoche, gash, germander, liturgy, lobe, mangonel, patriot, policy.

Dutch from Late Latin from Greek: mangle (2).

Italian from Greek: archipelago, banjo, barytone, gondola, scope.

French from Italian from Greek: cartel, cartridge (cartouche), emery, gulf, mandolin, manganese, moustache (mustache), pantaloon (1), pantaloons, pedant?, pilot.

French from Spanish from Greek: paragon.

French from Greek: acrobat, catalogue, mandrel (?), ophicleide, stearine, steatite, stigmatise.

French from German from Greek: sabre?

Scandinavian from English from Greek: kirk.

Arabic from Greek: elixir, typhoon.

Spanish from Arabic from Greek: talisman, tarragon.

Portuguese from Spanish from Arabic from Greek: albatross.

French from Spanish from Arabic from Greek: alembic, limbeck.

French from Arabic from Greek: alchemy.

French from Italian from Arabic from Greek: carat.

Hebrew from Greek: sanhedrim.

Turkish from Greek: effendi.

6. Words of HYBRID origin cannot very well be classed, from the nature of the case. To the above six classes we may add these following.

7. Words of LOW GERMAN origin. The following words I call 'Old Low German' for want of a better name. Many of them may be truly English, but are not to be found in Anglo-Saxon. Some may be Friesic. Others may yet be found in Anglo-Saxon. Others were probably borrowed from the Netherlands at an early period, but it is difficult to assign the date. The list will require future revision, when the history of some at least may be more definitely settled.

askew, bought, bout, brake (1), bully, cranberry, cringle, fib, fob, frampold, fraught, hawk (2), hawker, huckaback, huckster, kit (1), knurr (knur), lazy, loon (1) (lown), mate (1), minx, mum, nick (1), nock, pamper, plump ?, poll, prowl, queer, rabbit, rabble, rantipole, rill, skew, slight, toot (2), tuck (1), twill.

French from Old Low German: border, butty, chuck (1), dace, dare (2), dart, filter, fur, garment, garnish, garrison, goffer, growl, gruel, guard, guile, hackbut, hamlet, heinous, lampoon, loop-hole?, massacre ?, mute (2), pledge, poach (1)?, pottage, pottle, putty, staple (2), stout, supper, wafer. *Perhaps* paw.

Late Latin from Old Low German: allodial.

Dutch from Low German: groat (2), sloop.

French from Low Latin from Low German: quail (2).

Dutch from French from Low German: morass, skate (2).

8. Words borrowed from DUTCH.

aloof, avast, beleaguer, bluff, boom (2), boor, bouse (boose), brackish, brandy, bruin, bulk (2), bumpkin, burgher, buskin, caboose, cam, catkin, cave in, clamp, clank, clinker, dapper, deal (3), delf, derrick, dirk?, dock (3), drawl, drill (1), duck (4), duffel, foist, freebooter, frolic, fumble, gas, geck, golf, groove, gruff, guelder-rose, guilder, heyday (1), hold (2), holland, hop (2), hope (2), hottentot, hoy (1), hoy (2), hull (2), hustle, isinglass, jerkin, kails, kilderkin, knap, knapsack, knickerbockers, landgrave, landscape, lay (4), leaguer, lighter, link (2), linstock (lintstock), litmus, loiter, margrave, marline, mob (2), moor (2), mump, mumps, mutchkin, ogle, orlop, pad (2), pink (4), plack, plug, quacksalver, rant, ray (3), reef (1), reef (2), reeve (1), roster, rover, ruffle, rummer, runt, school (2), selvage (selvedge), serif, sheer (2), skellum, skipper, sled (sledge, sleigh), slim, sloven, slot (1), slur, smack (3), snaffle, snap, snip, snuff (1), spelicans, splice, spook, spoor, steenbok, stipple, stiver, stoker, strand (2), stripe, sutler, swab, switch, tang (1), tattoo (1), toy, trick (2), trick (3), trigger, uproar, wagon (waggon), wainscot, yacht.

Middle Dutch: deck, doxy, firkin, hoiden (hoyden), hoist, lollard, lop, mite (2), mother (2), nag (1), nap (2), ravel, ret, split, spool, stoup, swingle, tub.

Named from towns in Flanders or Belgium: cambric, dornick, spa.

French from Dutch (or Middle Dutch): arquebus, brick, clinquant, clique, cracknel, dig, droll, fitchet, frieze (1), friz (frizz), gleek (1), gleek (2), hackbut, hoarding, hotch-pot (hodge-podge), manikin (manakin), mow (3), mummer, mute (2), placard, pouch, shallop, staid, stay (1), stays.

Spanish from Dutch: filibuster.

9. Words borrowed from GERMAN. The number of words borrowed *directly* from German is very small; but many came in indirectly through the medium of French. See 10 below.

bantling, bismuth, cobalt, Dutch, elk, feldspar, fuchsia, fugleman, gneiss, hock (2), huzzah, landau, mangelwurzel, maulstick, meerschaum, mesmerise (*with* F. *suffix*), plunder, poodle, quartz, shale, spruce-beer, swindler, trull, wacke, waltz, zinc.

German (Moravian) personal name: camellia.

Dutch from German: crants, dollar, etch, holster, luck, rix-dollar, wiseacre.

Polish from German: hetman.

10. Other words of TEUTONIC origin. *Teutonic* is here used as a general term, to shew that the following words (derived through French, Spanish, &c.) certainly or probably belonged originally to the Teutonic family, though they cannot in all cases be referred to a definite Teutonic language.

French from Teutonic: abandon, agraffe, allegiance, allure, attach, attire, bacon, ball (1), bale (3), balloon, band (2), bandy, banish, bank (2), banner, banneret, baste (3), bawd, bawdy, beadle, belfry, bend (2), bistre, bivouac, blanch (1), blank, blanket, blister, block, blue, board (2), booty, border, boss, botch (2), bottle (2), brach, brawl (2), brawn, bray (1), bream, brewis, browse, brunette, brush, burgeon, burgess, burin, burnet, burnish, butcher, butt (1), button, buttress, carcanet, carousal (1), carouse, chamois, chine, choice, chuck (1), coat, coif, coterie, cotillon, cramp, cratch, crayfish, cricket (1), croup (2), cruet, crupper, crush, dally, dance, éclat, egret, enamel, equerry, ermine, eschew, escrow, espy, etiquette, fauteuil, fee (fief), feuter, filbert, flange, flank, flatter, flawn, flinch, flunky, forage, foray, franc, franchise, frank, franklin, freight, frisk, frown, furbish, furnish, gaff, gage (1), gaiety, gain (2), gaiter, gallant, galloon, garb (1), garb (2), garden, garland, garret, gay, gimlet, gimp, giron, goblin, gonfanon (gonfalon), grape, grapnel, grapple, grate (2), grimace, grisette, grizzled, grizzly, guarantee, guipure, guise, grumble, habergeon, haggard (1), haggard (2), halbert (halberd), hale (haul), halyard, halt (2), hamlet, hamper (2), hanseatic, harangue, harbinger, hardy, hash, haste, hatch (3), hatchet, hauberk, haunch, haversack, herald, heron, hob (2), hobby, hoe, hoop (2), housings, hovel, hubbub, hue (2), huge, Huguenot, hut, jay, jig, jog, lampoon, lansquenet, lattice, lecher, liege, list (2), lodge, lumber (1), lure, mail (2), maim, malkin, marque (letters of), marquee, marquetry, marquis, marshal, marten, mason (?), mazer, moat, moraine, motley, mushroom, orgulous, ouch (nouch), pawn (1), perform (*with* L. *prefix*), pewter, pump (1), quiver (2), quoif, raffle, rail (3), ramp, random, range, rank (1), rappee, rasp, raspberry (*partly* E.), ratten, rebut (*with* L. *prefix*), retire (*with* L. *prefix*), reynard (renard), ribald, riffraff, rifle (1), riches, roast, rob, robe, robin, rochet, romp, rubbish, rubble, Salic (Salique), saloon, scabbard, scale (1), scale (2), scallop (scollop), scarf (1), scavenger, scot(free), screen, screw (1), scroll, seneschal, shammy (shamoy), skiff, skirmish, slab (1), slash, slat, slate (1), slender, slice, sorrel (1), sorrel (2), soup, spar (3), spate, spavin, spell (2), spruce, spy, stale (1), stallion, stew, stroll, strumpet?, sturgeon, supper, tache (1), tampion, tan, tap (1), tarnish, tawny, teat, tenny, tetchy, Tibert, tic, tick (5), ticket, tiff (1), top (2), touch, towel, track, trap (2), trapan, trawl, trepan (2), trist, troll, trudge, tuck (3), tucker, tuft (1), tweezers, vagrant, wafer, wage, wager, wait, war, warble, warden, wardrobe, warison, warrant, warren, warrior, whoop, wince, wizard, zigzag.

German from French from Old High German: veneer.

Low Latin from French from Teutonic: feud (2), feudal.

Low Latin from Teutonic: allodial, bedell, bison, corrody, faldstool, marchioness, morganatic, Vandal.

Italian from Teutonic: balcony, ballot, bandit, bunion, fresco, lobby, loto (lotto), rocket (1), smalt, stoccado (stoccata), strappado, stucco, tucket.

French from Italian from Teutonic:

attack, bagatelle, banquet, escarpment, gala, group, guide, guy, ruffian, scaramouch, scarp, tuck (2), vogue.

Spanish from Teutonic : demarcation,

flotilla, gabardine, guerilla (guerrilla), marquess, ranch, stampede, stockade.

French from Spanish from Teutonic : amice (2), rapier, scuttle (2).

11. Words of indeterminate ROMANCE origin. The *Romance* languages, which include French, Italian, Spanish, and Portuguese, are, strictly speaking, unoriginal, but we cannot always trace them. A large number of terms belonging to these languages are derived from *Latin, Greek, Celtic,* &c. Those in this section are words of which the origin is local, obscure, or unknown.

French : abash, agog, antler, arras, artesian, average, awning, baboon, barnacles, barren, barter, basket, bastard, bastile, baton (batoon), batten (2), battlement, bauble, bavin, bayonet, beaver (2), beg, beggar, beguine, bevel, bezonian, bice, biggen, bigot, billet (2), billiards, blazon (2), blemish, blond, blouse, bobbin, boisterous, bonnet, boot (2), boudoir, bourd, bran, brattice, breeze (2), brisket, broider, broil (1), broil (2), budge (2), buff (2), buffer (1), buffer (2), buffet (1), buffet (2), buffoon, bugle (3), burbot, burganet (burgonet), busk (2), cabbage (2), caddis, cajole, caliber (calibre), calipers, caliver, carp (1), caul, chablis, chagrin, champagne, chaudron, cheval-de-frise, chiffonier, cockade, crare, curlew, dagger, debonair, disease, drab (2), drape, dupe, ease, embattle, emblazon, embrasure, embroider, embroil, flout, flute, fricassee, frieze (2), frill, frippery, furbelow, gallery, galley, galliot, gallon, garboil, gasconade, gavotte, gewgaw, gibbet, gibbon, giblets, gill (3), glean, gobelin, gormandize, gourmand, greaves, (2), grebe, grouse, grudge, guillotine, gusset, guzzle, haberdasher, hackney, haha, halloo, harass, haricot, harlot, harridan, haunt, havoc, hod, holla, lawn (2), lees, lias, lists, loach, loo, lozenge, lurch (2), magnolia, maraud, maroon (1), merelles, mignonette, minion, mortise, musit, Nicotian, notch, paletot,

pamphlet?, patrol, patten, pavise, paw, pillory, pirouette, piss, pittance, poplin, rail (2), ricochet, rinse, riot, roan, roquelaure, sauterne, savoy, sedan (chair), shalloon, silhouette, sobriquet, sturdy, tabard, tire (2), tire (3), tripe, troop, trousers, trousseau, truck (1), truss, tulle, valise, varnish, vaudeville, vernier, void.

French from Provençal : charade, flageolet.

Italian : andante, bergamot (1), bravo, cameo, caviare, fiasco, galvanism, imbroglio, mantua, milliner, ninny, polony, rebuff, regatta, sienna, trill, voltaic.

French from Italian : bastion, brigade, brigand, brigantine, brig, brisk, brusque, buckram, bust, canteen, canton, carcase, carousal (2), casemate, cassock, catafalque, charlatan, cornice, frigate, gallias, gazette, jane, pasquin, pasquinade, pistol, pistole, rash (4), ravelin, rodomontade, theorbo, tontine.

Spanish : anchovy, banana, bastinado, bilbo, bilboes, bravado, cachucha, cigar, cinchona (chinchona), cockroach, embargo, fandango, galleon, launch (2), paraquito, quixotic, rusk, sarsaparilla ; *cf.* trice (1).

French from Spanish : barricade, bizarre, cannon (2), caracole, chopine, cordwainer, embarrass, fanfare, maroon (2), morion (murrion).

Portuguese : cocoa (1), dodo, emu.

Dalmatian : argosy, dalmatic.

12. Words of SLAVONIC origin. This is a general term, including Russian, Polish, Bohemian, Servian, &c.

French from Slavonic : cravat, sable.

French from German from Slavonic : calash, trump (1), trumpery, trumpet.

Italian from German from Slavonic : trombone.

Low German from Slavonic : siskin.

Dutch from Slavonic : praam.

Polish : mazurka, polka.

German from Bohemian : howitzer.

French from German from Servian : vampire.

French from Latin from Greek from Slavonic : slave.

Russian : copeck, drosky, rouble (ruble), samovar, steppe, verst.

French from Russian : ukase.

13. A word of LITHUANIAN origin.

Dutch from German from Lithuanian : eland.

14. Words of PERSIAN origin.

Persian: bakshish, bashaw, bazaar, bulbul, caravansary, carboy, dervis (dervish), divan, durbar, firman, giaour, houri, Lascar, mogul, mohur, nargileh, nylghau, Parsee, pasha (pacha, pashaw, bashaw), peri, roc, sash (2), sepoy, serai, shah, shawl, sirdar.

Hindustani from Persian: pajamas, toddy, zamindar, zanana.

Greek from Persian: parasang.

Latin from Greek from Persian: asparagus, cinnabar, laudanum, Magi, paradise, tiara?.

French from Latin from Greek from Persian: jujube, magic, musk, myrtle, nard, parvis, sandal, satrap, tiger.

French from Italian from Latin from Greek from Persian: rice.

Spanish from Latin from Greek from Persian: pistachio (pistacho).

Italian from Greek from Persian: gondola.

Dutch from Slavonic from Low Latin from Greek from Persian: gherkin.

French from Latin (or Late Latin) from Persian: peach (1), zedoary.

French from Italian from Latin from Persian: muscadel (muscatel), muscadine.

Italian from Persian: scimetar (cimeter)?.

French from Italian from Persian: jargonelle, taffeta (taffety).

French from Spanish from Persian: julep, marcasite, rook (2), saraband.

Portuguese from Persian: pagoda.

French from Persian: bezique, calender (2), caravan, check, checker (chequer), checkers (chequers), chess, chicanery, exchequer, gueber, khedive, lemon, lime (3), scarlet, tutty, van (3).

Latin from Greek from Arabic from Persian: arsenic.

Low Latin from Arabic from Persian: borax.

French from Latin from Arabic from Persian: balas (ruby).

French from Arabic from Persian: azure, jasmine.

French from Italian from Arabic from Persian: mummy, orange.

Spanish from Arabic from Persian: lilac.

French from Spanish from Arabic from Persian: bezoar, calabash, galingale, spinach.

Turkish from Persian: jackal, kiosk.

French from Italian from Turkish from Persian: tulip, turban.

15. Words of SANSKRIT origin.

Sanskrit: avatar, brahmin (brahman), champak, juggernaut, pundit, rajah, Sanskrit, suttee, Veda.

Latin from Greek from Sanskrit: pepper.

French from Latin from Greek from Sanskrit: beryl, brilliant, ginger, mace (2), saccharine.

French from Low Latin from Sanskrit: sendal (cendal).

Persian from Sanskrit: bang (2), lac (1), nenuphar, nuphar.

French from Latin from Greek from Persian from Sanskrit: sandal(wood).

French from Spanish from Latin from Greek from Persian from Sanskrit: indigo.

French from Portuguese from Persian from Sanskrit: lacquer (lacker).

French from Persian from Sanskrit: lake (2).

French from Spanish from Arabic from Persian from Sanskrit: aniline, sugar.

Arabic from Sanskrit: kermes.

Spanish from Arabic from Sanskrit: carmine.

French from Arabic from Sanskrit: crimson.

French from Italian from Arabic from Sanskrit: candy.

Hebrew from Sanskrit: algum.

Hindustani from Sanskrit: cheetah, chintz, ghee, gunny, jungle, lac (2), loot, maharajah, nautch, pawnee, punch (3), punkah, rajpoot, rupee.

Portuguese from Hindustani from Sanskrit: palanquin.

Canarese from Sanskrit: jaggery.

Portuguese from Malay from Sanskrit: mandarin.

Portuguese from Sanskrit: banyan.

16. Words of MAGYAR or HUNGARIAN, or of FINNISH origin. (These languages do not belong to the Indo-germanic family.)

Hungarian: tokay.

French from Hungarian: coach, shako.

French from Finnish: morse.

17. Words of TURKISH origin. (This language does not belong to the Indo-germanic family.)

Turkish: agha (aga), bey, caftan, chibouk, chouse, horde, turkey.

Persian from Turkish: begum.

French from Turkish: caïque, dey, odalisque, ottoman, shagreen.

French from Italian from Turkish:

bergamot (2), janizary, turquoise.

Spanish from Turkish: xebec.

German from Polish from Turkish: uhlan.

French from German from Hungarian from Turkish: dolman.

18. Words of SEMITIC origin. The principal Semitic languages are Hebrew, Arabic, Chaldee, Syriac, &c.; the borrowed words in English being somewhat numerous.

Hebrew: alleluia (allelujah), bedlam, cab (2), cherub, corban, ephod, gopher, hallelujah, hin, homer, Jehovah, jug, log (3), Messiah, mishna, Nazarite (*with* Gk. *suffix*), purim, Sabaoth, Satan, Selah, seraph, shekel, Shekinah (Shechinah), shibboleth, shittah (tree), shittim (wood), teraphim, thummim, urim. *Cf.* davit.

Greek from Hebrew: hosannah; *from Phoenician*: alphabet, delta, iota.

Latin from Greek from Hebrew: amen, bdellium, cassia, cinnamon, cumin (cummin), Jacobite, Jesus, jesuit, jot, Levite, manna, Pasch, Pharisee, rabbi (rabbin), sabbath, Sadducee, sycamine?, sycamore?, Tom. *Also* balsam?, jordan?.

French from Latin from Greek from Hebrew: cade, camel, cider, earnest (2), ebony, elephant, Hebrew, hyssop, jack (1), Jacobin, Jew, jockey, lazar, maudlin, nitre, sapphire, shallot, simony, sodomy.

French from Spanish from Arabic from Greek from Hebrew: natron.

Italian from Greek from Hebrew: zany.

Latin from Hebrew: damson, leviathan.

French from Latin from Hebrew: jubilee.

French from Hebrew: cabal.

French from a place in Palestine: gauze.

Syriac: Maranatha.

Latin from Greek from Syriac: abbot, damask, mammon.

French from Latin from Greek from Syriac: abbess, abbey.

French from Italian from Syriac: muslin.

Chaldee: raca, talmud, targum.

French from Latin from Greek from Chaldee: sackbut.

Arabic: alkali, alkoran, arrack, attar (of roses), azimuth, cadi, drub (2), emir, fellah, hadji, hakim, harem, hashish,

hegira, henna, hookah (hooka), imam, islam, jerboa, jinn, koran, mahdi, Mahometan (Mohammedan), mohair, moonshee, moslem, muezzin, mufti, omrah, otto, rack (5), ramadan, rayah, ryot, salaam (salam), sheik, sherbet, shrub (2), simoom, sofa, taraxacum.

Latin from Greek from Arabic: gypsum, naphtha, saracen, sarsnet.

French from Greek from Arabic: civet.

French from Latin from Greek from Arabic: jasper, myrrh.

Low Latin from Arabic: alcohol, algebra.

French from Low Latin from Arabic: tartar (1).

Italian from Arabic: artichoke, botargo, felucca, senna, sirocco, zero.

French from Italian from Arabic: arabesque, baldachin, benzoin, magazine, sequin.

Spanish from Arabic: alguazil, arsenal, atabal, bonito, caraway (carraway), cid, dragoman, maravedi, minaret, mulatto.

French from Spanish from Arabic: alcove, amber, basil (2), borage, carafe, cipher, cotton (1), cubeb, garble, gazelle, genet, giraffe, hazard?, jennet (gennet), lackey (lacquey), martingale, mask (masque), masquerade, mosque, nadir, ogee (ogive), racket (1) (raquet), realgar, ream, rob (2), saker, sumach, syrup (sirup), tabby, talc, tabor, tambour, tambourine, tare (2), tariff, zenith.

French from Portuguese from Spanish from Arabic: marabout.

Portuguese from Arabic: albacore, assagai (*Moorish*).

French from Arabic: admiral, assassin, bedouin, burnouse, calif (caliph), camlet, carob, fardel?, faquir, furl?, jar (2), lute (1), Mamaluke (Mameluke), mate (2), mattress, moire, rebeck, saffron, sultan, vizier.

French from Algerine: razzia.
Persian from Arabic: ghoul, houri, mussulman, sophy.
Hindustani from Arabic: houdah, nabob, sahib.

Hindustani from Persian from Arabic: nizam, sicca.
Turkish from Arabic: coffee, raki.
Italian from Malay from Arabic: monsoon.

19. Words of ASIATIC origin, but NEITHER ARYAN NOR SEMITIC.

Hindustani: anna, bandanna, bangle, bungalow, chutny, cowry, dacoit, ghaut, mahout, nullah, shampoo, thug, wallah.
French from Hindustani: gavial.
E. Indian place-names: calico, cashmere (kerseymere).
Hindi: dawk, rum (2).
Bengali: dingy, jute, tomtom.
Balti: polo.
Marathi: pice.
Portuguese from Canarese: areca.
Malay from Canarese: bamboo.
Malayalim: teak.
Portuguese from Malayalim: betel.
Tamil: catamaran, cheroot, coolie, mulligatawny, pariah; *cf.* pavin (pavan), peacock.
Portuguese from Malay from Tamil: mango.
Telugu: bandicoot, mungoose.
French from Dravidian: patchouli.
Cingalese: anaconda.
French from Cingalese: tourmaline.
Malay: babirusa, bamboo [from *Canarese*], caddy, cajuput (cajeput), cassowary, cockatoo, crease (2) *or* creese, dugong, durian, gecko, gong, gutta-percha, junk, ketchup, lory (lury), mangosteen, muck (amuck), orang-outang, paddy, proa, rattan, rusa, sago, siamang, tripang, upas.
French from Malay: gingham, ratafia.
French from Arabic from Malay: camphor.
Chinese: bohea, china, Chinese, congou, hyson, nankeen, souchong, tea; *cf.* silk.
Malay from Chinese: sampan.
French from Latin from Greek from Chinese: serge.
Japanese: harakiri, japan, soy.
Portuguese from Japanese: bonze.
Java: bantam.
Annamese: gamboge.
Tatar: tartar (2).
Russian from Tatar: cossack.
Persian from Tatar: khan.
French from Turkish from Tatar: horde.
French from Italian from Tatar: turquoise.
French from Tatar: turkey.
Mongolian (through Persian): mogul.
Thibetan: lama (1).
Australian: boomerang, dingo, kangaroo, parramatta, wombat.
Tahitian: tattoo (2).
Polynesian: taboo.
Maldive: atoll.

20. Words derived from various AFRICAN languages.

Hebrew from Egyptian: behemoth, ephah.
Latin from Greek from Hebrew from Egyptian: sack (1).
French from Latin from Greek from Hebrew from Egyptian: sack (2), satchel.
Latin from Greek from Egyptian: ammonia, ibis, leo, oasis, paper?, papyrus?.
French from Latin from Greek from Egyptian: gum (2), gypsy, labyrinth?, lion.
French from Italian from Low Latin from Egyptian: fustian.
French from Barbary: barb (2).
Morocco: fez, morocco.
West African: baobab, canary, chimpanzee, guinea; *also* gorilla (Old African), yam. *From a negro name*: quassia.
Congo: zebra; *cf.* banana.
Kaffir: gnu, quagga.
French from Malagasy: aye-aye.

21. Words derived from various AMERICAN languages.

North-American Indian: caucus?, hickory, hominy, manito, moccasin (mocassin), moose, opossum, pemmican, racoon (raccoon), skunk, squaw, toboggan, tomahawk, wampum, wigwam.
Mexican: coyote, jalap, ocelot.

Spanish from Mexican: cacao, chocolate, copal, tomato?.

Cuba: maguey.

Hayti: mahogany.

Spanish from Hayti: cassava, guaiacum, maize, manatee, potato, tobacco.

Caribbean (or other West Indian languages): cayman, hammock, macaw.

Spanish from West Indian: cacique, cannibal, canoe. guava, hurricane, iguana, papaw, savannah.

French from West Indian: buccaneer, caoutchouc, peccary, pirogue.

Peruvian: inca, jerked (beef), llama, oca, pampas, puma.

Spanish from Peruvian: alpaca, coca, condor, guanaco, guano.

French from Peruvian: quinine.

Brazilian: ai, manioc, tapioca, tapir.

Portuguese from Brazilian: ipecacuanha.

Spanish from Brazilian: ananas.

French from Spanish from Brazilian: agouti.

French from Brazilian: cashew-nut, jaguar, toucan.

South American (Colombia): tolu.

SUPPLEMENT

[THE words marked * have already been considered; I here give some new suggestions concerning them. The rest are additional.]

Assagai, Assegai. (Port. — Berber.) Introduced into Africa by the Portuguese. — Port. *azagaia*, a dart, javelin, slender lance. For *az-zaghāya*; from *az-*, for *al*, Arab. def. article, and Berber *zaghāya*, the native name of a Berber weapon adopted by the Moors (whence F. *zagaie*). See Devic. Cf. **Lancegay** (p. 283).

*Baste (1), to beat. (Scand.) Of Scand. origin; Rietz gives Swed. dial. *basta*, vb., to beat, *basta*, sb., a stroke; under the heading *basa*, p. 25, col. 2.

*Baste (2), to pour fat over meat. (Scand.) Prob. of Scand. origin; Kalkar gives M. Dan. *baste*, to broil, fry, grill, bake; whence the E. word may have been borrowed.

*Blot, a spot. (F. — L.) The verb *to blot* corresponds to M. F. *blotter*, ' to blot, stain, blemish, defile; ' Cot. From M.F. *blotte*, O. F. *blote* (also *bloste*), a clod or clot of earth; also a tumour, swelling, or blotch (see Godefroy); cf. *plotte*, *pelote*, *pelotte*, a ball (Cotgrave). — Late L. **pilotta* (*pelōta*, *pilōta*), a little ball; dimin. of L. *pila*, a ball. See below.

*Blotch, a pustule, boil, tumour. (F. — L.) From O. F. *bloche*, a clod of earth; allied to *bloustre*, a tumour, boil; both given by Godefroy s. v. *bloste*; cf. *blosse*, a tumour (Roquefort). — Late L. **pilottea*, lit. ' ball-like ; ' from **pilotta*, *pilōta*, *pelōta*, a little ball; dimin. of *pila*, a ball. See Blot, Bullace.

*Bud. (E.) Certainly of native E. origin. M. E. *budde*, *bodde*. The A. S. form was prob. **budda*, with the sense of knob or round head; cf. Swed. dial. *bodda opp*, to become leafy, *boddoter*, full of leaves; *flen-budder*, bald-headed, *bådd*, a head. The cognate M. H. G. word is *butte*, mod. prov. G. (Strassburg) *butt*, G. *hage-butte*, the fruit of the dog-rose; whence the Du. (borrowed word) *bot*, M. Du. *botte*, a bud, O. F. *boter*, F. *bouter*, to put forth buds, and F. *bouton*, a bud (whence E. *button*).

Clipper, a quick horse; a fast-sailing ship. (Du.) M. Du. *klepper*, a steed, courser; so named from the clapping sound made by its hoofs (Franck). — Du. *kleppen*, to clap, by-form of *klappen*, to clap. Cf. **Clap.** So also Pomeran. *klöpper*, a clipper, from *kloppen*, to beat.

Clock (of a stocking). When stockings were made of cloth, it was necessary to let in a piece of the shape of a gore or gusset above the ankle; cf. prov. E. *gusset*, the clock of a stocking (E. D. D.); *clocks*, ' the gores of a ruff,' Randle Holme, qu. by Fairholt; G. *zwikkel*, clock of a stocking, gore or gusset of a shirt. This wedge-shaped insertion bore a rough resemblance to the old shape of a bell; and hence the name. See **Clock.** Cf. Du. *klink*, clock of a stocking; *klinken*, to resound.

*Cockney. In addition to the origin given at p. 97, it is probable that the use of the word was influenced by the O. F. pp. *acoquiné*, M. F. *accoquiné*, ' made tame, inward, familiar; also, grown as lazy, sloathfull, idle as a beggar '; Cot. Such loss of the unstressed initial *a* is common.

Compound, the enclosure in which an Anglo-Indian house or factory stands. (Malay.) From Malay *kampong*, an enclosure.

Cozier, a cobbler. (F. — L.) From O. F. *cousere*, a cobbler (Godefroy, s. v. *couseor*). — O. F. *cous-*, as in *cous-ant*, pres. pt. of *cousdre* (F. *coudre*), to sew. — Lat. *con-*, together; *suere*, to sew.

Dawdle, to loiter. (E.) Variant of prov. E. *doddle*, to go slowly. Allied to E. Fries. *dudden* (whence the frequentative *duddern*), to be stupid, mazed, drowsy; Du. *dutten*, to doze; cf. O. Fries. *dud-slek*, a stupefying stroke. Prob. allied to Icel. *doði*, deadness; and hence to *dauðr*, death. Berghaus gives Low G. *dödeln*, to dawdle, loiter; *döden*, to kill. Rietz gives Swed. dial. *dödolger*, a lazy fellow, dawdler. See **Dude.**